D0081640

CONDUCTORS ON RECORD

CONDUCTORS ON RECORD

by

JOHN L. HOLMES

GREENWOOD PRESS
Westport, Connecticut

Published in the United States by Greenwood Press,
a division of Congressional Information Service, Inc.

English language edition, except the United States,
published by Victor Gollancz Ltd., London

First published 1982

Library of Congress Cataloging in Publication Data:

Holmes, J L
Conductors on record.

Includes discographies.
1. Conductors (Music)—Bio-bibliography. 2. Conductors (Music)—Discography. I. Title. II. Series.
ML105.H65 785'.092'2 [B] 80-28578
ISBN 0-313-22990-2 (lib. bdg.)

Library of Congress Catalog Card Number: 80-28578
ISBN: 0-313-22990-2
Printed in the United States of America

for Élise

PREFACE

THIS BOOK WAS conceived in Los Angeles in 1971, and work commenced on it in 1972 when I was in Canberra, before departing for a posting in Bangkok that year. My life in the Australian Trade Commissioner Service has taken me to a number of cities which are a music-lover's delight: London, Los Angeles, Tel-Aviv and Berlin in particular, and the book itself was written in those places as well as in Bangkok, Saigon, Jerusalem, Istanbul, Ankara, Brussels, Canberra and in Switzerland and Austria.

I acknowledge the help of many who have assisted me. First must be my wife, Elise, who encouraged me from the first word until the last, read, discussed and criticised everything I have written, as well as editing it. My Californian friends Eric Welsh and Don Ray stimulated me to start work on the book, and numerous others have helped me, in one way or another, on the long journey. My publisher, Livia Gollancz, I also thank, since she recognised the purpose of the book as soon as I showed her the first pages of the manuscript, and patiently waited for the final typescript to arrive, well beyond the expected deadline. My employers, the Department of Trade and Resources in Canberra, unwittingly made my task easier by sending me to live in some of the most musical cities in the world, and there is of course a panel of distinguished music critics, in Britain, the United States and in Europe, who have constantly advised and informed me, also without their knowledge. To all I offer my grateful thanks.

BERLIN
JUNE 1979

J.L.H.

INTRODUCTION

I STARTED TO write this book with an objective that I eventually found impossible to realise: to include in it all conductors, orchestral and choral, who have made gramophone records, since the beginning of recording in the first years of this century. Every conductor was to have a biography, a discography, and, where appropriate, a discussion of his style, importance and place in the history of the art. Experience soon showed that, for many reasons, biographical information about many artists, past and present, is very difficult to find, and that complete discographies are also difficult to compile from available sources. Perhaps as many as 25 per cent of the conductors who have made records have therefore been omitted from this book, simply for lack of information.

Unquestionably, many of the conductors about whom I could discover nothing never existed at all; their names were the inventions of the record companies, who had to conceal their real identities, and sometimes that of the orchestras, because of copyright. Others have vanished into obscurity after brief visits to the recording studios. It has come as a surprise to realise that some major record companies know and care little about the identity of artists whom they have recorded, and that many musicians and musical organisations do not bother to answer letters. Another adverse factor has been the destruction of the archives of some German record companies during World War II. Some countries, such as Hungary and Czechoslovakia, possess very helpful and effective national organisations able to provide biographical information about their artists; in others it is a major achievement to find any information at all about their conductors. Many readers will therefore find errors and omissions in this book, for which I can only apologise, and the record collector may be disappointed not to be able to locate a reference to conductors or recordings that he personally knows, has heard, or maybe owns. There will be a supplementary volume of the book published, I hope, in a few years' time, and I will be happy to receive any advice from readers, and perhaps from the artists themselves, with additional information or corrections to include in the supplement.

In compiling this book, containing many names of people, places and works in foreign languages, one is immediately faced with the problem of translation, spelling and transliteration. For Russian names, for example, several options occur in transcribing from the Cyrillic script, even in such a familiar name as Tchaikovsky. Generally the attempt has been made to give the correct spelling, in the original language, except for languages in other scripts. For names of places, the spellings used in *The Times Concise Atlas of the World* (1972 edition) have been mostly given. Some titles of foreign works have been kept in the English version, such as *William Tell* and *The Merry Wives of Windsor*, which is traditional for English readers, as is also the traditional spelling of Handel.

It has not been my purpose to enter complete details of recordings, including the dates and places of recording and the names of all the record companies who have issued each disc. Nor has the composer's name always been shown for each recorded work; I have assumed that most readers would be familiar with a great number of compositions and their respective composers, and to include both in every mention of the work would lengthen the book appreciably and unjustifiably. I have had to develop certain rules, such as giving only the Köchel numbers for Mozart piano concertos, and omitting popular titles, such as *Pastoral* for Beethoven's Symphony No. 6, *Unfinished* for Schubert's Symphony No. 8, and *Classical* for Prokofiev's Symphony No. 1.

What constitutes a record? There can be no problem, of course, regarding regular commercial issues, both 78 r.p.m. and long-playing; in more recent years, many performances have also appeared on tape and/or cassette, but to be consistent, I have discussed only recordings proper. In published discographies of many conductors, tapes and recordings in private collections, taken from broadcasts and actual performances, are also included; these have been excluded from this book. However, some societies have issued records for their members of performances of great conductors otherwise unavailable, from broadcast performances or re-issues of earlier recordings, and these are included. One such organisation was the Arturo Toscanini Society in the United States, which issued many performances not only by Toscanini, but by Cantelli also; the demise of this society has meant that the records are now difficult to find. Interest in the great conductors of the past has certainly grown in recent years, and the number of re-issues on LP, taken from earlier recordings of Beecham, Walter, Furtwängler, Weingartner, Mengelberg and others is increasing. I hope that this book will help younger record collectors to place these artists in historical perspective; in fact, I can say that my original motive for writing it is my affection for the old pre-war 78 r.p.m. discs of the distinguished artists of those days, and my dismay that they may vanish into obscurity.

Although I myself am an incurable collector of gramophone records, and pursue them as a cat chases mice, I have an ever growing conviction of the limitations of the plastic disc as a medium for listening to music. Another objective of this book is to direct attention away from the conventional view of gramophone records, as an end in themselves, which can lead the unwary into believing that when he (or she) listens to this or that wonderful recording of this or that symphony or opera, he is participating in an authentic musical experience. At a certain level, I suppose he is, as much as one does in glancing at certain pages of *Playboy* magazine, or watching a football final on television. Records have their uses, and we would be lost without them; they are also misused, and the reader might find a note of churlishness in my treatment of some conductors who allow themselves to assume more importance than the music they conduct, in their recordings as in the concert hall. I recall a conversation with Carlo Maria Giulini, who said that we are very small people who are trying to perform the music of great geniuses; I am perverse enough to believe that a musician who is not the servant of his art degrades himself, as well as the music he performs. There seems indeed to be a high correlation between great conductors and their humility before the music they love to perform. It is inevitable that, to some, great music is above all a saleable commodity, and not necessarily a priceless cultural heritage, but at the same time I have to admit that if music, in the form of gramophone records, were not saleable at all, there would be no record companies.

Let me take this a stage further. Music exists because of the contribution of three essential parties: the composer, the interpreter, and the listener. The composer somehow conceives the music in his imagination, and transfers the sounds to paper as a number of markings. Sometimes these markings are the most meagre, and give only the roughest indication of his intentions; in Monteverdi, for example, the score has actually to be re-constructed, and the debate appears to be endless as to what he had in mind, or how the initial performance of the work was executed. In other cases, especially of composers in more recent times, the instructions on the score are very explicit; but even so, in the case of Mahler for example, it is surprising how interpretations by different conductors of the same score can vary, despite the proliferation of instructions. So the performer must draw his own conclusions regarding the composer's intentions in the score, first as to the actual notes to be played, the dynamics, phrasing, tempi, balance between the instrumental groups, and so on; then, certainly as important as the rest, he must make up his mind about the *meaning* of the music – the composer's emotional, dramatic and maybe intellectual purpose. Of course, some conductors in the past have gone way beyond this, and have introduced their own alterations to the score, believing that they thus served better the composer's intentions, or rendered the music more appealing to the public. Whoever thinks that all the conductor does is beat the time cannot have looked at a score, or have heard two performances of the one symphony. Compare the recorded performances of Beethoven's Symphony No. 5 by Carlos Kleiber and by Pierre Boulez: both perform all the notes correctly, but one sees a *meaning* behind the notes that apparently does not occur to the other. It may be true of certain composers, such as Stravinsky, that only a precise performance of the notes is required, but with almost all 19th-century music, it cannot be the case. One of the conductors in this book – Kurt Sanderling – put the point succinctly, when he said that a precise performance of the *adagio* of Beethoven's Symphony No. 9 can be dull, but an imprecise performance can be marvellous.

Having made all his decisions, the conductor appears before his orchestra, to realise his conception of the music. The orchestra is an instrument, in fact the most complicated of instruments, on which the performer cannot practise; the conductor must come to the rehearsal fully prepared, and has to persuade, charm, convince, coerce, or inspire (according to temperament) every one of the 50 to 100 players to perform each note of the piece, exactly as he has conceived it. Some can do it immediately, without hesitation, no matter with which orchestra they are working, and these conductors usually are the ones that produce the distinctive sound, and the interpretations completely unique in themselves, and who, I might add, receive the highest fees. It is arguable, however, that the great orchestras have musical personalities so strong that only the finest conductors are able to produce their own interpretations with them. No one, often least of all the conductor, can really explain how the magical act occurs, when he makes the musicians in his orchestra play exactly how he wants, beyond statements that he does it with his eyes or with his upbeat, or whatever; some dance like ballerinas, others have impassive, small movements, some have seraphic countenances, and others show acute anguish, some have the most graceful gestures, and others disturbing awkwardness. Yet even though the conductor's demeanour, behaviour and his actions create the scene, build the atmosphere and the tension of a concert, which influence the audience as much as the players, in the final analysis it is all irrelevant, and it is only the *sound* that counts.

We turn to the third party in the triumvirate: the listener. He brings many variables to his listening experience. He may be relaxed, composed, and full of joyful anticipation, after a leisurely journey to the concert hall. Or he may be tired after a day's work, cross with coping with the traffic and finding a parking space, in a supreme effort to get himself to his seat before the concert is due to start. The location of the seat itself tempers his experience: the people around him, the special acoustics of the position, and his view of the performers. His understanding of the music on the programme is important too; he may be familiar with one piece, from records, previous concerts, his own playing of the work from a piano score, or possibly from studying the score. A vast number of concert-goers have, I am amazed to find, an extraordinary ignorance of music, even of the common facts of musical history, and are puzzled why Bartók should sound so different from Haydn. They are the ones who 'know what they like, and like what they know', and their influence has much to do with the narrow limitations of concert programming. Others are less opinionated and attend concerts without any idea of what to expect, and perhaps are more responsive to music with which they are not familiar. Still others have in mind memorable performances, maybe which they have heard in the past and which have stirred them emotionally, although not always strictly for musical reasons, and they may be disappointed if that experience is not repeated. Most important, at a concert the listener is in a state of expectancy, and in a certain frame of mind: he has been, possibly, thinking about it for days, or at least hours, or perhaps he has had to queue or save for the ticket; or maybe the programme, the conductor or soloist, or the orchestra, have aroused his special interest. His expectations and his reaction to the performance are also bound to be affected by those of the audience around him.

Putting together these factors in the equation – the conception of the conductor, his ability to inspire his musicians, the skill of the musicians themselves, the preconceptions and expectations of the listener, and the peculiarities of the concert hall – each concert performance of a given work is unique, a special, unrepeatable event. There is another factor, too: scarcely any artist is able to give exactly the same performance of the same work twice; not only does their subjective feeling for the work vary according to the mood of the moment, but often they have consciously to vary their interpretations to suit the acoustics of the auditorium, the abilities of the players, and maybe the audience. Remember that Mahler would alter the orchestration of his symphonies according to the auditoriums in which he conducted them, and I was told by someone close to Toscanini in his NBC days that he performed many pieces with fast tempi because he was fearful of boring the vast radio audience he knew was listening. So at a concert, the listener hears a new act of musical creation, to which he contributes, as much as the conductor and the players.

With the listener to gramophone records we have another situation altogether. If we accept that music was written to be performed by an interpreter before an audience, which is certainly true of most of the standard repertoire, our magical triumvirate is shattered. First of all, the music is performed in a recording studio, and the attempt is made, often successfully, to have it note perfect, which is aided by all kinds of technical tricks not necessarily the responsibility of the conductor. A recording engineer (or producer) is in charge, and he may of course be a very sensitive and knowledgeable musician himself. But nowadays the technical aspect of the recording has a very high priority, so much so that some conductors believe that what appears on the disc finally released to the public is more the producer's interpretation of the piece, rather than the conductor's. Some conductors, such as Stokowski and Karajan, involve themselves in every aspect of the recording process, and one can expect that the final product (even the cover, in the case of Karajan) is as they want it: at the other extreme, others take no interest at all. The producer is responsible, after the actual recording is completed, for the dynamics, the balance of the instrumental groups, the joining together of the best pieces of many performances of the work, and so on; rarely is the recording one of an actual continuous performance.

When the listener places the record on the turntable in his home, he experiments at correcting the conductor, with his own variations of the volume, the bass and treble balance, and so on; thus, what he hears can be quite different from what the conductor intended him to hear, which presumably is fairly close to what the composer wrote. The record reviewers, who earn their living from informing the public of their evaluations of new records, and who thus perform a valuable task, usually compare the new disc with others of the same work, both for performance and recording quality, frequently announcing their decision which is the *best* performance to buy. In these circumstances, individuality in performances in any form is suspicious, and the trend started by Muck and Toscanini for literal, absolutely straightforward readings devoid of any subjective element at all, has now become re-inforced by the critics' preference for precision in execution. No wonder then that many recorded performances are 'safe', and lack spontaneity, and their purely musical value or otherwise can go unnoticed in the listener's preoccupation with the quality of the recording as a technical exercise *per se*. Many readers will miss in this book any mention of the technical aspects of recordings: they are not my concern. This book is about conductors, not recording engineers, and their records are documents of their performances, whatever their technical limitations. It must be clear to any musician that a fine performance not so well recorded is preferable to a mediocre performance well recorded: musical values must have precedence. The grave danger with the LP record is that music can become a kind of high-brow Muzak; the ultimate corruption of great music is committed by the person who walks to his hi-fi stereo amplifier, places on the turntable Mozart's Symphony No. 40, Beethoven's Symphony No. 9, or whatever, and then continues to chat with his guests, as though he had introduced some acceptable background noise, as the managements of airports imagine they are doing. Of course, there is much 'classical' music that is meant for just that purpose, even by Mozart. Equally objectionable, to my ears at least, are the jazz and pop arrangements of great music; the argument that these records introduce people to music they would not normally hear is invalid on any grounds but commercial ones.

From what I have just written, the reader will understand that I am not convinced that there can possibly be any one recording of a given piece of music that is the *best*. Certainly, it could be demonstrated that one may be *better* than some others, because there are fewer mistakes in the execution, or one conductor's conception may have a validity which is somehow demonstrably better than another. But a performance can be nothing more than that, even though it may be an excellent recording by a great artist, with a great orchestra. It is a unique performance, without doubt, but unique like all others. It is inconceivable that one performance can be the ultimate, either live or recorded. Anyone who has listened to recordings of the Beethoven symphonies will know how different are the readings of Weingartner, Toscanini, Furtwängler, Böhm, Klemperer, Cluytens, Schuricht, Walter, Ansermet, Schmidt-Isserstedt, Mengelberg, Karajan, Bernstein, Jochum, Davis, Abbado, Kubelik, Solti, Haitink, Ormandy, Leinsdorf, and indeed everybody else in the field. All of these artists bring to their interpretations an integrity and a unique conception, and every performance is different. Some may strike us as dull, some as unperceptive, some as profound, some as superficial, and so on, but it is our preconceptions that add to this judgement as much as the objective performance. Each conductor has studied the same notes, probably for many years, and has performed each many times; his recording, whatever its shortcomings, is a document of his interpretation, and should have something to tell us about both him and the music. The more experienced listener will probably come to each recording with his own preconceptions as to how *he* thinks the work should go, or how he thinks it compares with the ideal performance he knows, but if he has some understanding of the musical tradition from which the conductor has come, he will be more ready to listen to a performance obviously different from his ideal. In the case of the inexperienced listener, the record is often the *only* performance he knows, and he is in danger of accepting it as the way the music must always sound; it is wise, therefore, for the beginner to buy two or three recordings of the one work so that he does not come to believe that any one performance is definitive. With the number of cheap label re-issues now on the market, I would suggest that two cheaper recordings of the one work are better than one top-price one, for this reason. Bearing in mind what I have written about modern recordings, it is also instructive (and to some amusing, if not alarming) to listen to performances of conductors of earlier generations, who lived in times of different performing conventions, and were proud of their individuality.

For me, then, recordings have immense value, but they must not be considered as substitutes for the real thing, the real *sound*: the concert. Records are fascinating documents of conductors' interpretations, even with the limitations I have indicated. For most people their first inestimable and obvious worth is that they can hear music at all, in their own time and in their own homes. The invention of the LP record vastly increased the availability of music to the general public, of which many have taken advantage. Yet, except for the great interest in baroque music, the orchestral repertoire has been slow to expand beyond the conventional works performed before 1950, and to extend to the range of music available on record.

From time to time I have been asked the question: 'What do you think have been the best gramophone recordings made?' There have been many magazine articles and books published on this subject; committees of illustrious record critics meet from time to time to decide it; academies and other institutions issue Grands Prix du Disque for their own selections; and I am sure that anyone with any experience of collecting and listening to records will have his own list of favourites. In any event, I am going to chance my arm and will finish with my own selection; it is naturally a highly personal one and inevitably restricted to the records I have heard; all have been examples I have turned to endlessly of marvellous music-making.

First of all, a couple of very old 78s, both among the first electrical recordings: Dawn and Siegfried's Rhine Journey from *Götterdämmerung* (with the Symphony Orchestra under Coates), and Bach's *Toccata and Fugue in D minor* in Stokowski's arrangement, with the Philadelphia Orchestra. I suppose I should be ashamed to admit that I came to Bach through Stokowski.

Beecham's 78s with the London Philharmonic included numerous treasures, but for me the greatest were Haydn's Symphonies Nos 93, 99 and 104, Mozart's Symphonies Nos 35, 36, 39 and 40, Schubert's Symphony No. 5, and Brahms' Symphony No. 2, and most of all his Handel arrangement *The Faithful Shepherd*. After the war came *Don Quixote* and *Ein Heldenleben*, and of his great LP series with the Royal Philharmonic I would put at the top the final *Ein Heldenleben*. His Berlin *Die Zauberflöte* is indisputably one of the most enduring operatic recordings. Of other British conductors, I include Beethoven's Piano Concerto No. 3 of Boult, with Solomon and the BBC Symphony Orchestra.

All of Toscanini's records with the New York Philharmonic-Symphony Orchestra and the BBC Symphony Orchestra are numbered on my list, especially Beethoven's Symphonies Nos 1, 4 and 7, Haydn's Symphony No. 101, the Rossini overtures and the *Tragic Overture* of Brahms. His later NBC Symphony discs, with some notable exceptions, were, for whatever reason, simply not on this level. Mengelberg and the Concertgebouw Orchestra made many sizzling records, such as *Les Préludes* and the *Romeo and Juliet* fantasy-overture; Stokowski and the Philadelphia Orchestra produced a dazzling array in the great romantic repertoire, for example Brahms' Symphony No. 1 and *Scheherazade*. So also did Koussevitzky and the Boston Symphony, whose *Harold in Italy*, Brahms Symphony No. 3 and Sibelius Symphony No. 5 and *Tapiola* were especially remarkable.

Still in the era of 78s, in Vienna HMV and Columbia produced two great series with Weingartner and Walter, and with the Vienna Philharmonic. Weingartner's Beethoven Symphonies Nos 1, 3, 7, 8 and 9 were the performances that set the standard for my generation. Walter's Beethoven Symphony No. 6 and *Leonore No. 3* overture, Mozart Symphonies Nos 38 and 41, Haydn Symphonies Nos 96 and 100, Schubert Symphony No. 8, Brahms Symphonies Nos 1 and 3, the *Siegfried Idyll* and *Die Walküre* Act I, Mahler Symphony No. 9 and *Das Lied von der Erde* were particularly beautiful, with a characteristic silky string tone, which he later re-produced for the great Mahler Symphony No. 4 with the New York Philharmonic-Symphony Orchestra. Furtwängler's Tchaikovsky Symphony No. 6 and the pieces from *Tristan und Isolde* and *Parsifal* complete the list.

After the war, many great 78s were also issued, especially with Furtwängler and Karajan with the Vienna Philharmonic, van Beinum and the Concertgebouw Orchestra and others, but then, if we knew it, we were holding our breath for the avalanche of LP records that was to come. It would be difficult to list all the *great* ones, from the Krauss discs of Richard and Johann Strauss (for Decca) and Kletzki's Berlioz overtures (with the Philharmonia Orchestra for Columbia), to the present day, but I will mention a few that I treasure. These are Furtwängler's *Tristan und Isolde* (with Flagstad *et al.* and the Philharmonia Orchestra), Karajan's *Così fan tutte* and Bruckner Symphony No. 8 (the first, with the Berlin Philharmonic for EMI), Jochum's Mozart Symphony No. 40 (with the Bavarian Radio Symphony Orchestra), Stokowski's Shostakovich Symphony No. 11 (with the Houston Symphony Orchestra), Szell's Dvořák Symphony No. 8 (with the Concertgebouw Orchestra), van Beinum's *Symphonie fantastique* (with the Concertgebouw Orchestra), Solti's Suppé overtures (with the London Philharmonic Orchestra), Abbado's Mahler Symphony No. 2 (with the Chicago Symphony Orchestra), Giulini's Mahler Symphony No. 1 (with the Chicago Symphony Orchestra), Boulez's *Le Sacre du printemps* (with the Cleveland Orchestra), Klemperer's Beethoven Symphony No. 6 (with the Philharmonia Orchestra), Erich Kleiber's *Le Nozze di Figaro* (with the Vienna Philharmonic *et al.*), Carlos Kleiber's Beethoven Symphony No. 5 (with the Vienna Philharmonic), Sanderling's Rachmaninov Symphony No. 2 (with the Leningrad Philharmonic), de Sabata's *Tosca* (with the La Scala Orchestra *et al.*), Chalabala's *The Golden Spinning Wheel* (with the Czech Philharmonic Orchestra), Dorati's Haydn Symphonies Nos 100 and 101 (with the London Symphony Orchestra for Mercury), Ormandy's Shostakovich Symphony No. 1 (with the Philadelphia Orchestra) and Reiner's Beethoven Symphony No. 6 (with the Chicago Symphony Orchestra).

The closing year for the discographies for the conductors included in this book is 1977.

A

Abbado, Claudio (b. 1933). Born in Milan into a most musical family, his father a violinist and teacher at the Giuseppe Verdi Conservatory in Milan and his mother a pianist, Abbado studied the piano and composition before entering the Verdi Conservatory. In 1956 he came to the Vienna Academy of Music to study conducting under Swarowsky; there one of his fellow pupils was Zubin Mehta, and the two of them later went to the United States together. As a child Abbado had heard Toscanini, Walter, de Sabata and Kubelik, and he has said that his decision to become a conductor came when he was eight years old and heard Guarnieri conducting Debussy's *Nocturnes*. He was a conductor from the beginning, and did not graduate from the position of an orchestral player. His first opportunity came in 1958 in Trieste, and in that year he also won the Koussevitzky Prize at the Berkshire Music Center in Massachusetts. His career nonetheless started slowly; after some freelance engagements he took part in the Dmitri Mitropoulos International Conductors' Competition in New York in 1963, and emerged as co-winner with Calderón and Kosler. One of the awards following the competition was service for a year as assistant conductor of the New York Philharmonic Orchestra, where he closely observed Bernstein and Szell, but an unexpected result of this experience was his poor opinion of the New York Philharmonic, who, in his own words, 'play well but don't love music' (*New York Times*, 4 February 1973).

After hearing Abbado conduct in Berlin, Karajan invited him to conduct at the 1965 Salzburg Festival, where he led Mahler's Symphony No. 2, and for the performance was awarded the Philips Prize. The next year he appeared at the Edinburgh Festival with the New Philharmonia Orchestra in Mahler's Symphony No. 6, and made a marked impression. He first conducted at La Scala, Milan, in 1965, and in the following year conducted Bellini's *I Capuleti e i Montecchi* there, a performance which was taken on tour to Expo '67 at Montreal. In 1968 he was appointed permanent conductor at La Scala, graduating to artistic director in 1971; during that time the La Scala company and orchestra developed into a considerable ensemble, and with the company he gave performances at the Munich Olympic Games (1972), toured on exchange to the Bolshoi Theatre, Moscow (1974) and to Covent Garden (1975), and went to Washington for the US bicentennial celebrations (1976). He was awarded the Mozart Medal in Vienna in 1971, became principal conductor of the Vienna Philharmonic Orchestra (1971), principal guest conductor of the London Symphony Orchestra (1972) and will become conductor of that orchestra in 1979, to succeed Previn, and became musical director of the European Community Youth Orchestra (1977). He appears in the United States as a guest conductor, and has the highest praise for the Chicago, Cleveland and Philadelphia Orchestras.

Abbado is one of the handful of distinguished young conductors who have emerged to take the place of the disappearing older generation who dominated European and American opera houses and orchestras in the decades after World War II. Many believe that he has assumed the mantle of Toscanini, and he has many characteristics similar to those of the great maestro: intense musicality, tension, concentration and vigour in his conducting, a phenomenal memory, a distaste for publicity, a scrupulous regard for the composer's intentions, and a repugnance of Fascism, which was perhaps intensified by his mother's imprisonment by the Nazis during the war for sheltering a Jewish child. He is a man of wide cultural and social interests, with a modest and reticent personality; he has a marked disdain for acclamation, and never seeks to promote himself or to lobby for appointments. He dislikes the conventional acclamation at the end of performances. Although he has a large repertoire, extending from Bach to Nono, he is not in a hurry to present major works for which he does not think himself completely prepared. His musical sympathies are the broadest, and he has worked unobtrusively to widen the repertoires at La Scala and Vienna. At La Scala he doubled the length of the season, introduced cheaper-priced performances for students and people with lower incomes, and introduced works novel to the audience. For instance, *Wozzeck* was presented, although it required 40 rehearsals. Because he feels it brings him into closer contact with his players and singers, he usually conducts without a score. Despite their immense vitality and drive, his performances on record and in the concert hall can sometimes be disconcertingly impersonal, calculated and hard-driven, and fail to come to life. His utter fidelity to the score and his refusal to introduce subjective exaggerations of expression perhaps add to this occasional impression of coldness and over-attention to detail. On the other hand in works such as Beethoven's Symphony No. 3 and Tchaikovsky's Symphony No. 6, his interpretations can be overpowering in the brilliance of their execution and the intensity of their dramatic expression; William Mann wrote after a performance of the Tchaikovsky work at Edinburgh that Abbado was 'conducting the symphony that Tchaikovsky composed, not a subjective revision of it'.

Abbado is a major recording artist for Decca and DGG, and has made many brilliant records. His first disc was produced in 1967, an outstanding performance of Beethoven's Symphony No. 7 and *Prometheus* overture (with the Vienna Philharmonic Orchestra). His subsequent records have included the four Brahms symphonies (No. 1 with the Vienna Philharmonic, No. 2 with the Berlin Philharmonic, No. 3 and the *Variations on the St Antony Chorale* with the Dresden Staatskapelle, and No. 4 with the London Symphony, all for DGG), Mendelssohn's Symphonies Nos 3 and 4, Tchaikovsky's Symphony No. 5, Prokofiev's Symphonies Nos 1 and 3, *Chout* and a suite from *Romeo and Juliet*, Rossini's overtures *Il barbiere di Siviglia*, *La Cenerentola*, *La gazza ladra*, *L'Italiana in Algeri*, *Il Signor Bruschino* and *L'Assedio di Corinto*, Liszt's Piano Concerto No. 1 and Chopin's Piano Concerto No. 1 (with Argerich), Rachmaninov's Piano Concerto No. 3 (with Berman), Hindemith's *Symphonic Metamorphoses on a Theme of Weber*, Janáček's *Sinfonietta*, Stravinsky's *Pulcinella*, *Jeu de cartes*, *L'Oiseau de feu* and *Le Sacre du printemps*, Berg's *Lyric Suite*, *Three Pieces for Orchestra* and *Altenberg Lieder* (with Price, and the London Symphony Orchestra), Mozart's Mass K. 139, Beethoven's Symphony No. 8, Schubert's Symphony No. 8, the Mendelssohn and Tchaikovsky Violin Concertos (with Milstein), Brahms' Piano Concerto No. 2 (with Pollini), Bruckner's Symphony No. 1 and Tchaikovsky's Symphonies Nos 4 and 6 (with the Vienna Philharmonic Orchestra *et al.*), Mozart's Piano Concertos K. 466, K. 467, K. 503 and K. 595 (with Gulda and the Vienna Philharmonic Orchestra), the Mendelssohn and Tchaikovsky Violin Concertos (with Milstein and the Vienna Philharmonic Orchestra), Mahler's Symphony No. 2 (with the Chicago Symphony Orchestra *et al.*), Nono's *Como una ola* (with the Bavarian Radio Symphony Orchestra *et al.*), Debussy's *Nocturnes*, the *Daphnis et Chloé* Suite No. 2 and *Pavane pour une infante défunte*, the *Romeo and Juliet* fantasy-overture and Scriabin's *Poème d'extase* (with the Boston Symphony Orchestra), Brahms' *Rinaldo* and *Schicksalslied* and Tchaikovsky's Symphony No. 2 (with the New Philharmonia Orchestra), Brahms' Serenade No. 2 and *Academic Festival Overture*, Ravel's *Piano Concerto in G* and Prokofiev's Piano Concerto No. 3 (with Argerich, and the Berlin Philharmonic Orchestra), the operas *La Cenerentola*, *Il barbiere di Siviglia* and *Carmen* (with the London Symphony Orchestra *et al.*), *Simon Boccanegra* and *Macbeth* (with the La Scala Orchestra *et al.*), a disc of opera choruses and a recital by Ghiaurov, and the six *Brandenburg Concertos* (with the La Scala Orchestra for CBS).

Abbado, Michelangelo (b. 1900). Born in Alba, and the father of Claudio, the conductor, and Marcello, a pianist and composer, Abbado studied at the Giuseppe Verdi Conservatory in Milan, became professor of violin there (1925), and then director (1965), and has also been conductor of the Milan String Orchestra (since 1941). He has recorded Tartini's *Concerto Grosso in A* and *Violin Concerto in E* (with Gulli and the Angelicum Orchestra for Angelicum, and issued in the United States by Music Guild), Vivaldi's Cello Concerto P. 434 (with Caruana), *Violin and Cello Concerto in A* (with himself and Caruana), Three-Violin Concerto P. 278 and Four-Violin Concerto P. 367, Cambini's Piano Concerto Op. 15 No. 3 (with Claudio Abbado), Pergolesi's *Violin Concerto in B flat major*, Albinoni's *Violin Concerto in A*, Bonporti's Concerto Op. 4 No. 8, Corelli's Sonata Op. 5 No. 12, and Tartini's *Violin Concerto in D* (with himself and the Milan String Orchestra for EMI), and Ghedini's *Concerto spirituale* (with the Angelicum Orchestra for Angelicum).

Abendroth, Hermann (1883–1956). Born and educated at Frankfurt am Main, Abendroth studied in Munich with Thuille (composition), Wirzel-Langenham (piano) and Mottl (conducting). He became a bookseller, but soon abandoned this career to be a conductor. His initial appointments were with the Munich Orchestral Society (1903–4) and with the Music Lovers' Society at Lübeck (1905–11), at the same time being with the Lübeck City Theatre (from 1907), and then was music director at Essen (1911–14). His first important post came in 1914 as director of the Gürzenich Concerts at Cologne, in succession to Steinbach; Cologne was the centre of his activities until 1934, and he became general music director there in 1918, leader of the Lower Rhine Music Festival (1922) and a professor at the conservatory. He also conducted in many other European cities, recorded with the London Symphony Orchestra, conducted opera and concerts in Berlin, and was at this time recognised as one of the most distinguished German conductors and interpreters of Bach, Mozart, Beethoven, Schubert, Brahms and Bruckner. In 1933 the Nazis removed him from his posts in Cologne, but the next year he was permitted to assume the music directorship of the Leipzig Gewandhaus Orchestra, following the dismissal of Walter, and at the same time he became a professor at the Leipzig Conservatory. In 1943 and 1944 he led *Die Meistersinger* at Bayreuth, became music director of the German National Theatre at Weimar (1945), chief conductor of the Leipzig Radio Symphony Orchestra (1949) and then of the Berlin Radio Symphony Orchestra (1953). The first German conductor to be invited to the USSR after the war, he was later, in 1950, debarred from conducting at Düsseldorf because of his Communist sympathies. He died of a stroke at Weimar in 1956 and was given a state funeral; his memory is widely respected in DR Germany today, where he is remembered for the great spiritual strength of his Beethoven performances.

Abendroth's recording activities started in the 1920s. His major 78 r.p.m. sets were a Vivaldi concerto and Mozart's *Serenata notturna* (with the Cologne Chamber Orchestra for Odeon), the Beethoven Symphony No. 5 and the overture to *Der fliegende Holländer* (with the Berlin Philharmonic Orchestra for Odeon), a Handel concerto grosso (with the Cologne Chamber Orchestra for Parlophone), Brahms' Symphony No. 1, *Finlandia* and Dohnányi's ballet *The Veil of Pierrette* (with the Berlin Philharmonic Orchestra for Parlophone), Brahms' Symphonies Nos 1 and 4 (with the London Symphony Orchestra for HMV) and Reger's *Variations on a Theme of Hiller* (with the Paris Conservatoire Orchestra for HMV). After World War II he appeared on the Urania label in the West, conducting the Leipzig Gewandhaus, the Leipzig Radio Symphony and the Leipzig Philharmonic Orchestras, in performances originating with Eterna. The major works in this series were Haydn's Symphonies Nos 88 and 97, Mozart's Symphonies Nos 38 and 41, Beethoven's Symphonies Nos 1, 4 and 9, Schubert's Symphony No. 9, Schumann's Symphony No. 4, *Manfred* overture, Cello Concerto (with Tortelier) and Piano Concerto (with Wührer), Brahms' four Symphonies and Violin Concerto (with Manke), Tchaikovsky's Symphonies Nos 4 and 6, and Violin Concerto (with Schulz), Sibelius' Symphony No. 2, Dvořák's Cello Concerto (with Hoelscher), *Pictures at an Exhibition*, Pfitzner's *Kleine Sinfonie*, Eisler's *Rhapsodie*, Popov's Symphony No. 2, Amirov's *Caucasian Dances*, Arensky's *Silhouettes* and Liadov's *Baba Yaga*. Supraphon released Brahms' Symphony No. 3 (with the Prague Radio Orchestra), and Saga (in Britain) have re-issued Tchaikovsky's Symphony No. 4. Eterna (in DR Germany) have recently also re-released some of these discs.

Abravanel, Maurice de (b. 1903). Born in Salonika, Greece, of Portuguese Jewish parents, of whom an ancestor was chancellor to Ferdinand and Isabella of Spain, Abravanel moved with his family to Switzerland when he was six. He lived in the same building as Ansermet in Lausanne, and at Ansermet's home met Stravinsky, Poulenc, Milhaud and Honegger. While studying medicine at Lausanne University he organised an orchestra of students, abandoned medicine for music and took lessons with Kurt Weill in Berlin, where he made his debut as a conductor. In 1924 he conducted his first *Die Zauberflöte*, was a friend of Walter and Hindemith, and conducted at Zwickau, Altenberg, Kassel and in other German cities. He left Berlin for Paris in 1933, and became music director of Balanchine's ballet company which performed in Paris and London. The next year he toured Australia with the British National Opera Company, returning to Australia in 1935–6 and again in 1946, the last time to conduct a series of concerts in Sydney with an *ad hoc* orchestra sponsored by a local newspaper. In the years 1936 to 1938 he was at the New York Metropolitan Opera conducting French, German and Italian operas, and in 1940–41 he appeared at the Chicago Opera. Between 1941 and 1949 he directed musical comedy on Broadway, conducting most of Weill's plays, and also conducted the New York Philharmonic Orchestra.

Abravanel entered the most rewarding phase of his career in 1947, when he was appointed music director of the Utah Symphony Orchestra; his tenure there has been the longest of any conductor with an orchestra in the United States, except for Ormandy with the Philadelphia Orchestra. He created the orchestra from scratch: 'When I got there I could barely get the musicians through the first movement of the *Eroica*. I auditioned anyone who wanted to try playing. The best players became teachers for the others' (*New York Times*, 17 July 1977).

Most of the musicians in the orchestra are now from Utah and about 70 per cent are Mormons, although Abravanel is not concerned about their religion when engaging them. Until 1978 the orchestra played in the Mormon Tabernacle, but then moved to its new auditorium. Since 1955 he has spent his summers as director of the Music Academy of the West at Santa Barbara.

After some early 78s with the Carnegie Pops Orchestra, of the *Flight of the Bumble Bee*, the *Tritsch Tratsch Polka* and the Dance of the Camorristi from *I gioielli della Madonna* (for Columbia), Weill's *Street Scene* (with soloists and an orchestra for Columbia), and accompaniments for Pons and Singher (for Columbia), and LPs of *Coppélia*, excerpts from *Swan Lake*, *Capriccio italien*, *Capriccio espagnol*, the *Russian Easter Festival* overture, Rachmaninov's Piano Concerto No. 2 and *Rhapsody on a Theme of Paganini* (with Lewenthal) and Haydn's Symphonies Nos 93, 94, 103 and 104 (with the Vienna State Opera Orchestra for Westminster), Abravanel has enjoyed a remarkable recording career with the Utah Symphony Orchestra, joined on occasion by the Mormon Tabernacle Choir of Salt Lake City. Their first recording was *Judas Maccabaeus*, for Concert Hall; then came a contract with Westminster, for which he recorded *Israel in Egypt*, Franck's *Symphony in D minor*, Saint-Saëns' Symphony No. 3 (with Schreiner), excerpts from *Swan Lake*, Copland's *El Salón México*, *Billy the Kid* suite, the waltz from *Billy the Kid* and four dance episodes from *Rodeo*, the Grieg Piano Concerto (with Nibley) and the two *Peer Gynt* suites, *Les Sylphides* and excerpts from *Giselle*, Grofé's *Grand Canyon Suite*, Gershwin's *Rhapsody in Blue* and *Piano Concerto* (with Nibley), *An American in Paris* and *Porgy and Bess* suite. His subsequent alliance with Vanguard and more recently with Vox, has resulted in a remarkable range of recorded music for a conductor and orchestra never seriously considered to be in the very top rank of American combinations. Vanguard's sponsorship of the Utah Symphony and Abravanel has been one of the more enlightened aspects of the recent recording scene in the United States; altogether Abravanel has made over 80 records with the orchestra for various labels, and more than a million of these records have been sold. Lately, he has ventured into recording some of the standard classical repertoire, such as the Tchaikovsky and Brahms symphonies, where he has come into direct competition with the great international conductors and orchestras who have recorded them; although he may be a little detached and cool-headed in his readings, the interpretations are straightforward, clearly executed and absolutely honest, even if they may not be memorably distinctive. Spread over some years, he has also recorded the nine Mahler symphonies, the first American conductor to do so.

With the Utah Symphony Orchestra *et al.* Abravanel has recorded Bach's *Ricercare*, two chorale preludes (arranged by Schoenberg) and *Choral Variations on 'Vom Himmel hoch'* (orchestrated by Stravinsky), Handel's *Samson* (for Bach Guild), Scarlatti's *Messa di Santa Cecilia* (for Bach Guild), Beethoven's *Die Geschöpfe des Prometheus*, Berlioz's *Grande Messe des Morts*, Brahms' four symphonies, *Tragic* and *Academic Festival Overtures* and *Variations on the St Antony Chorale* (for Vox), Tchaikovsky's six symphonies, *Manfred*, *Francesca da Rimini*, *Romeo and Juliet* fantasy-overture, *Hamlet*, *Marche slave* and *1812* overture (for Vox), complete *Swan Lake* and *Nutcracker*, the nine Mahler symphonies, Rimsky-Korsakov's *Antar*, Ippolitov-Ivanov's *Caucasian Sketches*, the Russian Sailors' Dance from Glière's *The Red Poppy*, Grieg's *Four Norwegian Dances*, *Wedding Day at Troldhaugen*, Piano Concerto (with Johannesen), the two *Peer Gynt* suites, *Sigurd Jorsalfar* and *Symphonic Dances* (for Vox), Schubert's *Rosamunde* music (with Davrath), Goldmark's *Rustic Wedding Symphony*, Rachmaninov's Symphony No. 3 and *Chanson géorgienne* (with Davrath), Prokofiev's Symphony No. 2 and *Le Pas d'acier*, Bloch's *Israel Symphony* and *Schelomo* (with Nelsova), Gershwin's Piano Concerto and *Rhapsody in Blue* (with Lewenthal) and symphonic picture (arr. Bennett) from *Porgy and Bess*, Honegger's *Le Roi David*, *Judith* and *Pacific 231*, Milhaud's *La Création du monde*, *Pacem in Terris* and *L'Homme et son désir*, Vaughan Williams' Symphony No. 6, *Flos Campi* (with Lenz), *The Lark Ascending* (with Chausow), *Dona Nobis Pacem*, *Fantasia on a Theme of Thomas Tallis*, *Fantasia on Greensleeves* and *Five Variants of Dives and Lazarus*, Gottschalk's Symphony No. 1, *Gran Tarantella* (with Nibley) and *Nuit des tropiques*, Satie's *Parade*, *Les Aventures de Mercure*, *La Belle excentrique*, *Un Songe d'une nuit d'été*, *Relâche*, *En habit de cheval*, *Gymnopédies*, *Trois Morceaux en forme de poire*, *Deux Préludes posthumes et une gnossienne*, *Les Fils des étoiles* and *Jack in the Box*, Varèse's *Amériques*, *Nocturnal* and *Ecuatorial*, Walton's *Belshazzar's Feast* (with Peterson), Lazarof's *Structures sonores*, Harris' *Folksong Symphony* (for EMI), Copland's *Lincoln Portrait* (with Heston), *Our Town*,

Quiet City and *Outdoor Overture*, a scenario from Kern's *Showboat*, Gould's *Latin American Symphonette* and *American Salute*, music by Leroy Anderson, Stravinsky's Violin Concerto (with Spivakovsky), Robertson's *Punch and Judy* overture, *The Book of Mormon* and Violin Concerto (with Spivakovsky), Rorem's Symphony No. 3 and Schuman's Symphony No. 7 (for Turnabout), Bernstein's *Candide* overture, Siegmeister's *Western Suite* and Nelhybel's *Étude symphonique*. Of these, Varèse's *Amériques*, Milhaud's *Pacem in Terris*, and all the orchestral music of Satie had not previously been recorded.

Ackermann, Otto (1909–60). Born in Bucharest, Ackermann studied at the Royal Academy there and in Berlin. At the age of fifteen he conducted the Royal Romanian Opera on tour; he was conductor at the Düsseldorf Opera (1927–32), at Brno (1932–5), was principal conductor at the Berne Municipal Theatre, was chief conductor at the Zürich Opera (1948–53) and finally general music director at the Cologne Opera (1953–60). While in Berne he assumed Swiss nationality. He made guest appearances at other European opera houses and was particularly noted for his interpretations of the Wagner operas.

In Britain and the United States Ackermann's reputation as a recording artist was primarily for his idiomatic leadership in EMI's recordings of operettas of Johann Strauss and Lehár, viz. *Die Fledermaus*, *Wiener Blut*, *Der Zigeunerbaron*, *Eine Nacht in Venedig*, *Das Land des Lächelns* and *Die lustige Witwe*, which were made in the first years of LP with the Philharmonia Orchestra and with Elisabeth Schwarzkopf heading the casts; Walter Legge, the EMI impresario (and Schwarzkopf's husband), was the producer. All of these, except *Die Fledermaus*, were re-issued by EMI in 1978. Ackermann also conducted the Vienna State Opera Orchestra *et al.* for Decca in *Der Freischütz*, issued in 1951. His other recordings for EMI included *Moldau* and *From Bohemia's Meadows and Forests* from *Má Vlast*, Strauss's *Vier letzte Lieder* and excerpts from *Capriccio* (with Schwarzkopf), the Grieg and Schumann Piano Concertos (with Moiseiwitsch), two Bach violin concertos (with Kogan and E. Gilels), Mozart's Piano Concerto K. 450 (with Solomon), and Liszt's Piano Concerto No. 1 and *Hungarian Fantasia* (with Anda). All were with the Philharmonia Orchestra; with the Paris Opéra Orchestra he accompanied an aria recital by Crespin.

La Guilde Internationale du Disque recorded him in another, more representative series of performances. Included were Mozart's Symphonies Nos 22, 24, 27 and 31, and *Peter and the Wolf* (with the Amsterdam Philharmonic Orchestra); a two-trumpet concerto (with Hausdörfer and Sevenstern) and viola d'amore concerto (with van Helden) of Vivaldi, Mozart's Symphonies Nos 4, 10, 11, 14, 17, 26, 30 and 31, Piano Concerto K. 491 (with Johannesen) and Horn Concerto K. 495 (with Zwagerman), a Weber Clarinet Concerto (with d'Hondt), Beethoven's Piano Concerto No. 5 (with Kann), the Mendelssohn Violin Concerto (with Kaufman) and *Erste Walpurgisnacht*, and Britten's *Simple Symphony* (with the Netherlands Philharmonic Orchestra *et al.*); Mozart's Piano Concerto K. 537 (with Pelleg) and overtures to *Don Giovanni* and *Die Entführung aus dem Serail*, Beethoven's Symphonies Nos 5 and 7, Schubert's Symphony No. 8, the overture to *Tannhäuser* and preludes to Acts I and III of *Die Meistersinger*, Brahms' Symphony No. 3, and Dvořák's Symphony No. 9 and Cello Concerto (with Tortelier, and the Zürich Tonhalle Orchestra); Schumann's Symphony No. 4 and *Genoveva* overture, *Don Juan* and *Till Eulenspiegel* (with the Frankfurt Radio Symphony Orchestra); Mozart's Symphony No. 41 and Piano Concertos K. 40, K. 41 and K. 107 No. 3 (with Balsam, and the Winterthur Symphony Orchestra); *An der schönen blauen Donau* and *Kaiserwalzer* (with the Berne Symphony Orchestra); and *Die Entführung aus dem Serail* (with the Gürzenich Orchestra, Cologne, *et al.*).

In 1976 the United States company Discophilia began to issue a series of six discs in which Ackermann conducts the South-west German Radio Symphony Orchestra. These performances originated from broadcasts in 1951–4, as well as some of the Mozart symphonies recorded with the Netherlands Philharmonic Orchestra mentioned above. The third disc of the series contained, among other pieces, rarely recorded excerpts from Strauss's *Die schweigsame Frau* and *Guntram*.

Addison, John (b. 1920). Born in West Cobham, Surrey, Addison studied at the Royal College of Music, was for six years on active service in World War II, and was professor of composition at the RCM (1951–7). He is a successful composer whose music is accomplished and has popular appeal, and includes scores for films, the theatre and television. Pye recorded him in 1958 conducting the Pro Arte Orchestra in the music for his ballet *Carte blanche*; the performance was re-issued in 1966.

Adler, F. Charles (1889–1959). Adler is a relatively little known conductor but he has made a remarkable contribution to the repertoire of the gramophone, directing the first LP recordings of a number of major works including Mahler's Symphonies Nos 3 and 6 and Ives' Symphony No. 2. His career was very cosmopolitan. Born in London, the son of an American father and a Bavarian mother, he studied in Munich where one of his teachers was Mahler. He was a choirmaster at the first performance of Mahler's Symphony No. 8. He started his career as a conductor assisting Mottl at the Royal Opera at Munich (1908–11), was chief conductor at the Düsseldorf Opera (1913), and from 1923 to 1933 was with the German State Opera at Berlin, where he also owned a publishing house, Edition Adler. With the advent of the Nazis in 1933 he went to the United States and in 1937 founded the Saratoga Springs Music Festivals in New York State. As a guest conductor he performed Bruckner and Mahler at a time when these composers were little known in the US; subsequently he was awarded the Schoenberg and Bruckner Medal of the US Bruckner Society.

After World War II and in the early days of LP Adler recorded in Vienna a number of important works, some entirely new to the catalogues, for two companies, Composers Recordings and Alpha. The orchestra was an *ad hoc* group, and was variously named on the record labels the Vienna Orchestral Society, the Vienna Philharmonia Orchestra, the Vienna Festival Orchestra and the Vienna Orchestra. His recordings for Alpha included Bruckner's Symphonies Nos 1, 3, 6 and 9, the *Overture in G minor* and the Mass No. 1, Mahler's Symphonies Nos 3 and 6, Reger's *Variations on a Theme of Hiller*, Liszt's *Dante Symphony*, Ives' Symphony No. 2, d'Albert's *Tiefland*, James' Symphony 1, Cowell's *Saturday Night at the Fire House*, Antheil's *McKonkey's Ferry Overture*, Jacobi's *Music Hall Overture*, North's *Holiday Set* and Siegmeister's *Sunday in Brooklyn*, as well as Beethoven's arrangement for piano of his Violin Concerto and Artur Schnabel's Piano Concerto (both played by Helen Schnabel, the daughter-in-law of Schnabel). For Composers Recordings he recorded Ballou's *Prelude and Allegro*, Bauer's *Suite for Strings* and *Prelude and Fugue*, Claflin's *Fishhouse Punch*, Gerschefski's *Saugatuck Suite*, Kohs' Symphony No. 1, Lora's Piano Concerto (with Wollmann), Luening's *Symphonic Fantasia* and *Kentucky Rondo*, McBride's *Punch and the Judy*, Scott's *Binorie Variations* and *Hornpipe and Chantey*, Weiss's *Variations for Orchestra* and Wigglesworth's Symphony No. 1. He also recorded Weill's *Die Dreigroschenoper*, with soloists, chorus and chamber orchestra of the Vienna State Opera, for Vanguard. Adler's performances were marked by their diligence and conscientiousness (to quote Kolodin); they were pioneering, and served a useful purpose. But his capacities as a conductor were too limited to make the survival of these records imperative.

Adler, Peter Hermann (b. 1899). Born at Jablonec, Czechoslovakia, Adler studied in Prague, conducted in Brno (1923), Bremen (1928–31), Kiev (1932–37) and Prague (1938), came to the United States in 1940, and appeared as a guest conductor with various orchestras. In 1949 he was co-founder of NBC television opera, and was its music director until 1960. From 1957 to 1967 he was conductor of the Baltimore Symphony Orchestra, and since 1967 has been artistic and music director of NET TV Opera Theatre. The New York Metropolitan Opera engaged him for the 1972–73 season. His recordings include Weill's folk-opera *Down in the Valley* (with the RCA Victor Chorus and Orchestra for RCA), a recital of Mozart arias (with Price and the New Philharmonia Orchestra for RCA) and a recital with Pavarotti (with the New Philharmonia Orchestra *et al.* for Decca).

Adler, Kurt (1907–77). Born in Neuhaus, Czechoslovakia, Adler was educated in Vienna, conducted at the Berlin State Opera (1927–9) and at the German Opera at Prague (1929–32), then went to Russia where he was at the Kiev Opera (1933–5) and at Stalingrad (1935–7). He migrated to the United States in 1938, first appeared as a concert pianist, conducted in Canada and Mexico, and in 1943 joined the Metropolitan Opera, New York, as chorus-master and assistant conductor, and remained with the company until 1973. He is not to be confused with Kurt Herbert Adler, the artistic director of the San Francisco Opera. He recorded Weill's *Die Dreigroschenoper* (with the Vienna State Opera Orchestra *et al.* for Vanguard), *Samson et Dalila* (with the Romanian Radio Symphony Orchestra *et al.* for Electrecord) and a recital of sacred music (with Pavarotti and the National Philharmonic Orchestra for Decca).

Adler, Samuel (b. 1928). Born in Mannheim, Germany, Adler came to the United States in 1939, studied at Boston University and then at Harvard with Piston, Randall Thompson and Hindemith, and with Copland, Fromm,

Geiringer, Koussevitzky *et al.* He served in the US army in 1950 and was conductor of the Seventh Army Symphony Orchestra in Germany, toured Germany and Austria with the orchestra and also conducted other orchestras and opera companies and at the Royal Dutch Ballet (1952). He has been professor of composition at North Texas State University (1958–66), professor of composition at the Eastman School of Music, Rochester, NY (since 1966) and chairman of the composition department (since 1973). When in Texas he conducted the Dallas Chorale (1954–6), the Dallas Lyric Theater (1955–7), was director of music at the Temple Emanu-El, Dallas (1953–66) and eastern regional director of the Contemporary Music Project. He has composed numerous works including five symphonies, four operas, chamber and choral pieces, has received many awards and commissions and has written many articles in musical journals as well as an *Anthology for the Teaching of Choral Conducting.* His recordings include Gershwin's *Rhapsody in Blue* and *Concerto in F*, and music by Gottschalk (with List and the Berlin Symphony Orchestra, for Turnabout).

Aeschbacher, Niklaus (b. 1917). Born in Trogen, Switzerland, Aeschbacher was educated at the Zürich Conservatory and at the Hochschule für Musik in Berlin. He was a repetiteur at Zittau, Saxony, and at Braunschweig, was conductor then music director at the Berne City Theatre (1942–54 and 1958–9) and conductor of the NHK Symphony Orchestra, Tokyo (1954–6). He returned to Berne in 1956, was music director at Kiel (1959–63), general music director at Detmold (1964–72) and since 1972 has been a professor at the North-West Music Academy at Detmold. He has composed operas, orchestral and chamber music, and has given performances of the music of many Swiss composers. His recordings include Sutermeister's *Max und Moritz* (for DGG) and *Die Schwarze Spinne* (for CT, Switzerland) and Mieg's Two-Piano Concerto (for Elite), and he was the pianist in Borodin's Piano Quintet (with the Mottier Quartet, for Columbia).

Ahlendorf, Herbert (b. 1915). Ahlendorf is descended from an old family of musicians with genealogical ties with the Bach family. He studied at the Hochschule für Musik, Berlin, in Leipzig, Salzburg and Vienna under Mengelberg, Krauss and Furtwängler and was assistant conductor to Furtwängler until 1939. For several years he was director of the conservatory in West Berlin, has collaborated with Karajan and has been secretary to the Karajan conducting competitions. For Supraphon he conducted the Prague Symphony Orchestra *et al.* in Mahler's *Das klagende Lied.*

Ahronovich, Yuri (b. 1932). Born in Leningrad, Ahronovich studied as a child at the Central School of Music, which was attached to the Leningrad Conservatory, and after an interruption to his studies during the war, resumed at the Conservatory and was a pupil of Sanderling and Rakhlin. He became conductor of the Saratov Philharmonic Orchestra (1956), principal conductor of the Moscow Radio Symphony Orchestra (1964–72) and then was appointed chief conductor of the Gürzenich Orchestra at Cologne (1975). He has regularly conducted major orchestras and at opera houses in Europe and the United States. Ahronovich has expressed high admiration for his teacher, the conductor Rakhlin, whose exaggeratedly expressive style has apparently influenced his own interpretative outlook. This is evident from his recordings of Tchaikovsky's *Manfred* symphony and the four Rachmaninov piano concertos and the *Rhapsody on a Theme of Paganini* (with Vasary and the London Symphony Orchestra, for DGG). He has also recorded the two Prokofiev Violin Concertos (with Wally and the French National Orchestra for Decca and Aristocrate), Mussorgsky's *Sorochintsy Fair* (with the Moscow Radio Symphony Orchestra *et al.* for Melodiya), Shostakovich's Symphony No. 1 and the two Beethoven Romances (with Kogan and the USSR State Symphony Orchestra for Melodiya).

Akiyama, Kazuyoshi (b. 1941). Born in Tokyo where he studied at the Toho School of Music, graduating in 1963, Akiyama made his debut as a conductor with the Tokyo Symphony Orchestra the next year, and then became its permanent conductor and music director. He also was appointed principal guest conductor of the Osaka Philharmonic Orchestra (1965), assistant conductor of the Toronto Symphony Orchestra (1968–9), resident conductor and music director of the Vancouver Symphony Orchestra (since 1972) and music director of the American Symphony Orchestra, although the latter orchestra has been inactive since Stokowski's departure in 1972. He was awarded the Torii Prize in 1974 for his 'outstanding contribution to the development and advancement of classical music in Japan'. He recorded Khachaturian's Violin Concerto (with Tokunaga and the Tokyo Symphony Orchestra), Prokofiev's Violin Concerto No. 1 and excerpts from *Romeo and Juliet* (with Staryk and the Vancouver Symphony Orchestra, for CBC), Respighi's *Fontane di Roma* (with the Toronto Symphony Orchestra for CBC) and Lees' Violin Concerto (with Ricci and the American Symphony Orchestra for Turnabout).

Akos, Francis (b. 1922). Born in Budapest and educated at the Budapest Academy, Akos won prizes as a violinist and was a concertmaster in Budapest, Göteborg and at the Berlin Opera (1950–53). He emigrated to the United States in 1954, and became concertmaster of the Chicago Symphony Orchestra. He recorded as a solo violinist and as a conductor with the Chicago String Orchestra (for Pirouette), the works including Telemann's *Don Quixote*, Corelli's Concerto Grosso Op. 6 No. 8, Mozart's Divertimento K. 136, Dvořák's *Serenade in E*, Wolf's *Italian Serenade* and Barber's *Adagio for Strings*.

Akulov, Yevgeni (b. 1905). Akulov was educated at the Gnessin Music Institute and the Moscow Conservatory, where he studied conducting with Golovanov and Sardjaev, and from 1930 was assistant conductor, then conductor, at the Bolshoi Theatre, Moscow. He became chief conductor of the Moscow Stanislavsky and Nemirovich-Danchenko Musical Theatre (1938), and a professor at the Lunacharsky Institute of Theatrical Art. His recordings include Arensky's *The Fountain of Bakhchisarai*, the incidental music to Tchaikovsky's *Dmitri the Impostor*, Tchaikovsky's opera *Undine*, *Le Coq d'or* (together with the conductor Kovalyov), *La Fille de Madame Angot* and *La Belle Hélène* and excerpts from Dargomizhsky's *Rogdana* and *Mazeppa* (with the Moscow Radio Symphony Orchestra *et al.*) for Melodiya.

Akutagawa, Yasushu (b. 1925). A son of the author Ryonosuke Akutagawa, Akutagawa was born in Tokyo, where he studied at the Academy of Music under Iguchi (1943–9). He has been director of the Yamaha Foundation for Music Education, and composed the ballets *The Dream of the Lake* and *Paradise Lost*, the music for the film *Gate of Hell*, and many other works. He conducted the Tokyo Symphony Orchestra in recordings of his own *Symphonic Triptych* and *Prima Sinfonia* (for Toshiba).

Albert, Herbert (b. 1903). Born at Lausick, Albert studied at Hamburg and Leipzig, and after starting his career as a pianist, was conductor at Rudolstadt, Kaiserslautern and Wiesbaden (1926–34), general music director at Baden-Baden (1934–7), conductor at the Stuttgart Opera (1937–44), at Breslau (1944–6), music director at the Leipzig Gewandhaus (1946–8), at Graz (1950), and in 1952 became general music director at Mannheim. Period in the United States issued an LP in which he conducted the Mannheim National Symphony Orchestra in Haydn's Symphony No. 94, and in 1957 Saga in Britain released a performance of Lalo's *Symphonie espagnole* with him conducting the Pasdeloup Orchestra, and with Accardo the soloist.

Albert, Rudolf (b. 1918). Albert studied at the city of his birth, Frankfurt am Main, conducted for radio stations at Frankfurt and Baden-Baden and at the Munich Opera, and was also chief conductor of the Niedersachs Symphony Orchestra at Hannover. He had a reputation as an interpreter especially of Mozart and of contemporary composers. His recordings were, on 78 r.p.m. discs, Beethoven's Symphony No. 3 (with the Turin Radio Orchestra for Polydor) and the *Fidelio* overture (with the Berlin Philharmonic Orchestra for Odeon), and on LP, the Mozart Piano Concertos K. 456 and K. 491 (with Schilhawsky and the Bavarian Radio Orchestra, for Nonesuch), Schumann's Symphony No. 3 (with the Munich Philharmonic Orchestra for Mercury), Tchaikovsky's Symphony No. 4 (with the Paris Philharmonic Orchestra for Counterpoint), Stravinsky's *Symphony in C*, *Petrushka* and *L'Oiseau de feu* (with the Cento Soli for Club français du Disque), some orchestral excerpts from Wagner operas (with the Munich Philharmonic Orchestra for Counterpoint), Klebe's *Romantic Elegy* (for DGG), Prokofiev's Cello Concerto (with Albin and the Cento Soli, for Club français du Disque), and the Mendelssohn Violin Concerto, Bruch's Violin Concerto No. 1, Mozart's Violin Concerto K. 219 and Spohr's Violin Concerto No. 6 (with Field and the Berlin Symphony Orchestra for Telefunken).

Albert, Werner Andreas (b. 1935). Born in Weinheim, Albert studied at the Hochschule für Musik at Mannheim and at Heidelberg, and at Heidelberg University, was a conducting pupil of Karajan and Rosbaud, and became conductor of the Heidelberg Chamber Orchestra (1961–3). He was then principal conductor of the North West German Philharmonic Orchestra at Herford (1963–71), the Gulbenkian Orchestra in Lisbon (1971–4), the Nuremberg Symphony Orchestra and the Bavarian Youth Orchestra (since 1974), and lecturer at the

Nuremberg Academy of Music (since 1977). His recordings include Handel's Concerto Grosso Op. 6 No. 5, Leclair's *Oboe Concerto in C major* (with Weinz) and Telemann's *Viola Concerto in G major* (with Koch, and the Heidelberg Chamber Orchestra for da Camera); the Mozart Clarinet Concerto (with Fadle), Horn Concerto No. 3 (with Mansfeld) and Beethoven's Symphony No. 9 (with the North-West German Philharmonic Orchestra *et al.* for da Camera); Puccini's *Messa di Gloria* (with the North-West German Philharmonic Orchestra *et al.* for Schwann); Dvořák's Symphony No. 9 and Tchaikovsky's Symphony No. 6 (with the Philharmonia Hungarica for da Camera); Sutermeister's Cello Concertos Nos 1 and 2 (with Nyffenegger), Corette's *Harpsichord Concerto in A major* (with Heuler), Debussy's *La Mer* and *Nocturnes*, and Wolf-Ferrari's Cor Anglais Concerto (with Lencses) and *Idillio* (with the Nuremberg Symphony Orchestra for Colosseum); oboe concertos by Haydn and Dittersdorf (with Lencses and the Collegium Classicum for Fono); Rossini's *Petite Messe solennelle* (with the North-West German Philharmonic Orchestra *et al.* for Fono), and Pillney's *Eskapaden eines Gassenhauers* and Ochs' *Humoristische Variationen über 's kommt ein Vogel geflogen* (with the North-West German Philharmonic Orchestra for Electrola-EMI). Oryx issued Beethoven's Symphony No. 9 in 1968 in Britain, but critical reception was somewhat cool.

Albin, Roger (b. 1920). Born in Beausoleil, France, Albin studied at the Paris Conservatoire and was first cellist at the Paris Opéra (1938) and later with the Monte Carlo National Orchestra. Later he recorded, as a cellist, the Prokofiev Cello Concerto and the Ravel Trio (for Musidisc). He returned to the Paris Conservatoire to study composition with Messiaen and Milhaud (1945–8), became musical director at Nancy (1960–61) and at Toulouse (1961–6), and in 1966 was appointed musical director of the ORTF Orchestra at Strasbourg. With that orchestra he recorded the *Fantaisie pour piano et orchestre* of Debussy and of Fauré (with Barbizet), Ibert's *Diane de Poitiers* and Barbaud's *French Gagaku*, and with Capecchi and the ORTF Instrumental Ensemble Komives' oratorio *La vera istoria della cantoria di Luca della Robbia* (for Barclay).

Albrecht, George (b. 1935). Born in Bremen, Albrecht studied with Grevesmuhl, van Kempen, Eichhorn and Landes-Hindemith, and was first violinist of the Hermann Grevesmuhl Chamber Orchestra (1948–56). He made his debut as a conductor in 1949, won the Prix d'Excellence at the Accademia Chigiana at Siena (1954), was conductor at Bremen (1958–61), at Hannover (1961–5), and has been general music director at Hannover (since 1965). For Intercord he recorded Wagner's *Symphony in C major* and the overture to Marschner's *Hans Heiling* (with the Lower Saxony State Orchestra, Hannover).

Albrecht, Gerd (b. 1935). Born in Essen, Albrecht studied conducting at the Hochschule für Musik at Hamburg, and musicology at the Kiel and Hamburg Universities. He was a repetiteur and conductor at the Württemberg State Opera, Stuttgart (1958–61), first conductor at Mainz (1961–3), general music director at Lübeck (1963–6) and Kassel (1966–72), chief conductor at the Deutsche Oper, West Berlin (from 1972) and conductor at the Zürich Tonhalle (from 1975). For DGG he recorded Haydn's Organ Concertos (with Tramnitz and the Bamberg Symphony Orchestra).

Alessandrescu, Alfred (1893–1959). Born in Bucharest, Alessandrescu studied at the Schola Cantorum in Paris under d'Indy, from 1926 to 1940 was director of the Bucharest Philharmonic Orchestra, and from 1933 to 1947 music director of the Bucharest Radio. His compositions include symphonic pieces, chamber music and songs. For Electrecord he recorded works by the Romanian composers Dumitrescu and Rogalski, with the Romanian Radio Symphony Orchestra.

Alessandro, Victor (1915–76). Alessandro was born in Waco, Texas; his father was director of music and school bands at Houston. He studied under Hanson and Rogers at the Eastman School of Music at Rochester, NY, at the Salzburg Mozarteum and at the Accademia di Santa Cecilia, Rome, where he was a pupil of Pizzetti. Returning to the United States, he was appointed music director of the Oklahoma City Symphony Orchestra (1938–51), then became music director of the San Antonio Symphony Orchestra (1951–76), the Mastersingers choral group, the San Antonio Grand Opera Festival and the Rio Grande Valley Music Festival. He has been given the Alice Ditson Award, has been honoured by the Italian government, and has conducted in Hungary, Norway and Finland as well as with US orchestras and at the San Francisco and New York City Operas.

Alessandro recorded Mozart's Piano Concertos K. 453 and K. 459 (with Hambro and the Oklahoma City Symphony Orchestra for

Royale), Brahms' *Hungarian Dances* and Debussy's *Le Martyre de Saint-Sébastien* (with the Oklahoma City Symphony Orchestra for Brunswick), Rodrigo's *Concierto Andaluz* and *Concierto de Aranjuez*, and Vivaldi's *Mandolin Concertos* in *A* and *C*, and Four-Violin Concerto (with guitarists Celedonio, Celin, Pepe and Angel Romero and the San Antonio Symphony Orchestra for Mercury, and re-issued by Philips in Europe), and Corigliano's Piano Concerto and Strauss's *Parergon zur Symphonia Domestica* (with Somer and the San Antonio Orchestra for Mercury).

Alexandrov, Boris (b. 1905). After studying at the Moscow State Conservatory, Alexandrov was conductor of the Central Theatre of the Soviet Army (1929–37), deputy chief of the Soviet Army Song and Dance Company (1937–46), becoming the Company's chief in 1946, and has been an assistant professor at the Moscow State Conservatory from 1933. His compositions include operettas, a ballet, an oratorio, songs and vocal pieces. He has made a number of recordings with the Soviet Army Chorus, and also conducted Prokofiev's *Alexander Nevsky* (with the Pro Musica Symphony Orchestra *et al.* for Turnabout).

Alfvén, Hugo (1872–1960). A composer known beyond his native Sweden for his attractive orchestral piece *A Midsummer Vigil*, Alfvén wrote a considerable volume of music including five symphonies, ballets, orchestral suites and songs. He was a fine conductor, particularly of his own works. He recorded his Symphony No. 3 for HMV in the 1930s with the Stockholm Concert Society Orchestra. Westminster released an LP with him conducting *A Midsummer Vigil* and his ballet pantomime *The Mountain King*; later in 1976 there appeared a disc in England issued by the Swedish Society in which he conducted the Royal Opera Orchestra in his suite *The Prodigal Son* and *The Mountain King*, again.

Alldis, John (b. 1929). Alldis was a choral scholar at Cambridge University where he studied under Boris Ord and was a teacher of vocal technique at drama schools. In 1962 he founded and conducted the John Alldis Choir, his purpose being to create a choir of about sixteen voices in which each member was potentially a soloist, particularly to perform rarely heard romantic works and contemporary music. It performed, *inter alia*, the European première of Stravinsky's *Requiem Canticles* and the British première of Stockhausen's *Mikrophonie II*, toured Germany, Scandinavia and other European countries and Australia, and through its ranks passed singers such as John Shirley-Quirk, Robert Tear, Philip Langridge and Felicity Palmer. Its recording commitments grew, as when the choir was expanded up to about 80 members, it provided the chorus for over 100 operatic and other recordings. More recently Alldis has revived the original small choir to regenerate the performance of new choral music in Britain. He has also been conductor of the London Symphony and London Philharmonic Choirs and the Danish Radio Choir. In his own right he has recorded for Argo with the choir (called then the Alldis Singers) music by Bruckner, Schoenberg, Debussy and Messiaen, and for Tower music by Williamson.

Allers, Franz (b. 1905). Born in Carlsbad (now Karlovy Vary), Czechoslovakia, and educated at the Prague Conservatory and the Hochschule für Musik and University in Berlin, Allers was an assistant conductor at Bayreuth and at the Paris Wagner Festival, and was general music director at Aussig, Czechoslovakia. He has conducted many of the major orchestras in Europe and the United States, conducted ballet in London, South America and Canada, and from 1963 has appeared at the New York Metropolitan Opera. After settling in the US he conducted operettas and musicals on Broadway, and in 1960 toured the USSR with *My Fair Lady*. From 1973 he has been general music director at the Komische Staatsoper at Munich. For RCA, Philips, EMI, Ariola and Colosseum he has recorded numerous comedies and operettas with German orchestras, including *La Vie parisienne*, *Der Zigeunerbaron*, *Eine Nacht in Venedig*, *Die lustige Witwe*, *Der Graf von Luxemburg*, *Der Bettelstudent* and *Porgy and Bess*, in addition to the *Nutcracker* suite (with the Budapest Philharmonic Orchestra for Hungaroton) and an aria recital with Jan Peerce (with the Vienna Festival Orchestra for Vanguard).

Almeida, Antonio de (b. 1929). Almeida was born in Paris, the son of a Portuguese father and an American mother, who migrated to Argentina when he was a boy. He studied under Ginastera at Buenos Aires, under Hindemith at Yale University and later under Szell, Koussevitzky and Bernstein. In the United States he played horn, bassoon, oboe, clarinet and cello in various student orchestras. He was conductor of the Portuguese Radio Orchestra and at the Lisbon Opera (1957–60), was director of the Stuttgart Philharmonic Orchestra (1960–64), was then engaged as a guest conductor with major orchestras in Europe and the US, conducted the five orchestras then playing in Paris as well as at the Paris Opéra, and in 1969 was appointed principal guest conductor of the Houston Symphony Orchestra, dividing his time between the US and Europe. His repertoire is catholic, extending from the baroque and classical eras to Mahler and Shostakovich.

As a recording artist, Almeida's major enterprises have been with Haydn, and with lesser known French romantic composers. He has recorded (for Iramac) 23 unfamiliar symphonies of Haydn, including Nos 62, 66, 67, 69, 70, 71, 74, 75, 76, 77, 78 and 79, with the orchestra of the Haydn Foundation, which was established by H. C. Robbins Landon, and includes as soloists Wallez, Pierlot, Barboteu and Delmotte. Robbins Landon's editions of the Haydn symphonies are followed in the recordings. Almeida also directed a recording of Haydn's opera *L'infedeltà delusa,* which was made in Rome and was issued in France by Le Chant du Monde, and in the US by Musical Heritage Society. His style in these Haydn discs is idiomatic and crisp. The French music he has pioneered on disc has been Schmitt's *La Tragédie de Salomé*, Duparc's *Lénore* and Chausson's *Vivienne* (with the New Philharmonia Orchestra for RCA), Fauré's *Pavane*, *Madrigal*, *Caligula* and *Shylock* (with the ORTF Chamber Orchestra *et al.* for Barclay), Dukas' *La Péri*, *L'Apprenti sorcier* and *Polyeucte* (with the Czech Philharmonic Orchestra for Supraphon), Bizet's early student opera *Le Docteur Miracle* (with L'Orchestre Lyrique de l'ORTF *et al.* for Barclay), excerpts from Halévy's *La Juive* (with the New Philharmonia Orchestra *et al.* for RCA), Lalo's *Symphony in G minor*, *Rapsodie norvégienne* and the overture to *Le Roi d'Ys* (with the Monte Carlo National Opera Orchestra for Philips). His other recordings include Mahler's Symphony No. 5 (with the Monte Carlo National Opera Orchestra for La Guilde Internationale du Disque), ballet music from the Verdi operas (with the Monte Carlo National Opera Orchestra for Philips), Feld's Symphony No. 1 (with the Czech Philharmonic Orchestra for Supraphon), Gluck's *Iphigénie en Tauride* (with the Lisbon Opera for Penzance Records), Donizetti's *L'elisir d'amore* (with the Philadelphia Lyric Opera for Celebrity), ballet music from the Rossini operas (with the Monte Carlo National Opera Orchestra for Philips), harp concertos by Boieldieu, Rodrigo, Villa-Lobos and Castelnuovo-Tedesco and Rodrigo's *Sones en la Giralda* (with Michel) and Rodrigo's *Concierto de Aranjuez* and *Fantasia para un gentilhombre* (with Lagoya, and the Monte Carlo National Opera Orchestra for Philips), and a series of eight LPs of excerpts from major symphonic works for RCA's educational programme, *Adventures in Music*.

Alonso, Odon (b. 1925). Born in Leon, Spain, Alonso was a choral director for the Spanish Radio (until 1952), conductor of the Spanish National Orchestra (1952–6), of the Madrid Philharmonic Orchestra (1956–8) and of the Spanish Radio and Television Orchestra (from 1968). His recordings include Vivaldi's *Guitar Concerto in D* with Yepès, E. Halffter's *Rapsodia portuguesa* and Turina's *Rapsodia sinfonica* (with Soriano and the Spanish National Orchestra for Alhambra, and issued in Britain by Decca), Palau's *Concierto levantino*, and Rodrigo's *Musica para un Codice Salmantino*, *Concierto de Aranjuez* and *Fantasia para un gentilhombre* (with Yepès and the Spanish Radio Orchestra for Alhambra and Decca), and Bacarisse's Guitar Concerto (with Yepès and the Spanish Radio Orchestra for DGG), and Concertino (with Yepès and the Spanish Radio Orchestra for Philips).

Alpaerts, Jef (b. 1904). The son of the Belgian composer Flor Alpaerts, Jef Alpaerts was born in Antwerp and studied at the Antwerp Conservatoire and the École Normale in Paris with Cortot and d'Indy. In 1936 he was appointed professor at the Antwerp Conservatoire, and in that year established the Collegium Musicum Antverpiense to give performances of old music. He also founded and directed the Association des Concerts Mozart et Classiques de Belgique. He recorded Beethoven's Symphony No. 8 and Piano Concerto No. 3, and Alfidi's Piano Concerto No. 2 (with Alfidi, and the Antwerp Philharmonic Orchestra, for Jubilee).

Alwin, Karl (1891–1945). A native of East Prussia, Alwin studied in Berlin with Humperdinck and became Muck's assistant at Berlin and Bayreuth. After conducting appointments at Halle, Posen, Düsseldorf and Hamburg, he was from 1920 to 1938 at the Vienna State Opera. In 1938 he left Austria and conducted at the Mexican National Opera until his death. He married the soprano Elisabeth Schumann with whom he made some superb records, as a pianist, of Strauss and Schubert lieder. They were divorced in 1936. In the 1930s Alwin recorded with the Vienna Philharmonic Orchestra for HMV some orchestral excerpts from the operas of Wagner and Strauss; the Strauss in particular was noted for its feeling and strength. In 1951 the Schwann catalogue announced a recording of Mahler's Symphony No. 8, with the Vienna Philharmonic Orchestra and Vienna State Opera Chorus, conducted by Alwin. The record was not actually released; rumour had it that it was in fact a performance by Stokowski in New York the year before.

Alwyn, Kenneth (b. 1928). Born in London and a graduate and later Associate of the Royal Academy of Music, Alwyn gained initial experience in New Zealand as musical director of the Royal Choral Union there, and then was a conductor at the Sadler's Wells Theatre Ballet (1952–6) and the Royal Ballet, Covent Garden (1956–9). He was associated with the British Broadcasting Corporation, conducted extensively for both radio and television, and more recently has been conductor of the BBC Northern Ireland Orchestra. He also has appeared with major orchestras in Britain, Europe, North America and Japan. Of his recordings one has been particularly successful: a Tchaikovsky collection of the *1812* overture, *Capriccio italien* and *Marche slave* (with the London Symphony Orchestra for Decca), which was first released in 1958 and is still on issue in Britain and the United States. Other discs include a Gershwin collection (with Binns and the Sinfonia of London for EMI), a collection of Rossini overtures (with the New Symphony Orchestra for Richmond, USA), and of Sullivan overtures (with the Royal Philharmonic Orchestra for EMI), suites from *Swan Lake* and *Peer Gynt* (with the London Philharmonic Orchestra for Richmond), the Israeli composer Ben Haim's Symphonies Nos 1 and 2 (with the Royal Philharmonic and London Philharmonic Orchestras, respectively, for EMI), Hammerstein's arrangement of Bizet's *Carmen*, *Carmen Jones* (for Helidor) and Clarke's *Trumpet Voluntary* and Wood's arrangement of *God Save the Queen* (with the London Symphony Orchestra for Decca).

Alwyn, William (b. 1905). The British composer Alwyn studied at the Royal Academy of Music and was professor of composition there from 1926 to 1955. His best known music was that which he wrote for a number of films in the 1940s, including *Odd Man Out*, *Desert Victory*, *The Way Ahead*, *The Fallen Idol* and *The Magic Box*, but his output includes five symphonies and much other music, some of which was written to commissions from the Arts Council, the British Broadcasting Corporation and for other patrons. His compositions are written in an immediately attractive, well-orchestrated and accessible idiom which is unmistakably English in its ancestry. He has also published an anthology of 20th-century French poetry, translated into English. In recent years Lyrita have issued fine recordings of Alwyn conducting the London Philharmonic Orchestra in all of his five symphonies, his *Sinfonietta*, symphonic prelude *The Magic Island* and four of his *Elizabethan Dances*.

Amaducci, Bruno (b. 1925). Born in Lugano, Switzerland, Amaducci studied at the Giuseppe Verdi Conservatory in Milan and at the École Normale in Paris, and first appeared as a conductor in 1950 with the Swiss Italian Radio Station. He has conducted a number of European orchestras and at various opera houses; for Austrian Television he conducted a series of operas by Haydn, and for the French Radio operas by Lully. On the 50th anniversary of the death of Puccini in 1974 he conducted programmes of music by the Puccini family, stemming from the first Giacomo Puccini in 1712, whose music he found in parts of Tuscany. He has written musical studies, has taught conducting at the École Normale, was president of the committee for the recording of neglected works of the International Association of Music Libraries, and was founder and president of the Ricerche musicali nella Svizzera italiana. His recordings include Cimarosa's *Il maestro di capella* (with Corena and the Pomeriggi Musicale Orchestra for Decca), Vivaldi's *The Four Seasons* (Discophiles Français *et al.*), Mozart's Symphony No. 41, Tchaikovsky's Piano Concerto No. 1 (with Tacchino), overtures by Mozart, Rossini and Suppé, and other pieces by Lully, Vivaldi and Boccherini (for Match Records, Paris), Handel's Organ Concerto Op. 4 No. 2 and a Haydn Organ Concerto (with Sebestyén for Disci Angelicum, Milan), and Flury's Violin Concerto (with Urs Flury and the Swiss Italian Radio Orchestra for Fono).

Amfitheatrov, Daniele (b. 1901). Born in St Petersburg, Amfitheatrov is the son of the writer of the same name and the grandson of Sokolov, the composer. He studied at the St Petersburg Conservatory, left Russia in 1921, and continued his studies in Prague and with Respighi at the Accademia di Santa Cecilia in Rome. He became an Italian citizen, was assistant to Molinari in Rome (1924–9) and chief conductor of the orchestra of Radio Turin. At this time he recorded the overture to *Prince Igor* (with the EIAR Orchestra for Cetra). In 1937 he moved to the United States, first becoming assistant conductor with the Minneapolis Symphony Orchestra, then going to

Texas and finally to Hollywood, where he turned his considerable skill as a composer to writing music for films. He was responsible for the music for *The Virginian*, *Lassie Come Home* and other screen classics. His more serious compositions include a piano concerto and several symphonic poems, one being *American Panorama* into which he introduced jazz.

Amy, Gilbert (b. 1936). Amy was born in Paris, studied with Messiaen and Milhaud, attended the summer course at Darmstadt and in 1950 studied conducting with Boulez, succeeding him as director of the Concerts du Domaine Musical. Amy's career has been divided between conducting and composing, and in 1975 he performed some of his works in London with the London Sinfonietta. In 1976 he was appointed conductor of one of the orchestras of the ORTF. In 1978 the Nouvel Orchestre Philharmonique de Radio-France was formed; it is directed by Amy and is to undertake the performance of a wide repertoire, ranging from chamber music to lyrical and orchestral works. Erato recorded him directing the ORTF National Orchestra with Jarry (violin) in two of his compositions, *Chant* and *Trajectoires*; to quote the record jacket: 'Amy's orchestra is unsparing in its reined-in brutality, a bedlam of noise . . .' Everest has also released a disc of him conducting the Domaine Musical Ensemble in music of himself and Webern.

Ančerl, Karel (1908–73). Bohemian by birth, Ančerl studied composition with Křička and Hába, and conducting with Talich at the Prague Conservatory. From 1929 to 1931 he was an assistant to Scherchen in Germany, and his career as a conductor started in 1930 at the Liberated Theatre in Prague. In 1933 he was appointed conductor of the Prague Radio Orchestra and remained there until 1939; he spent most of the war in Nazi concentration camps, was sentenced to death for attempting to escape, but was saved by the end of the war. His entire family perished during the war. Ančerl was able to resume his career in 1945 when he returned to the Prague Radio Orchestra, succeeding Jeremiáš, and also became chief conductor of the newly-established Prague Opera (1946–9). In 1950 he took Talich's place as artistic director and chief conductor of the Czech Philharmonic Orchestra, and until his departure from Czechoslovakia with the Russian occupation in 1968 was professor of conducting at the Academy of Musical Arts in Prague. He toured as a guest conductor in Europe, the United States, Asia and Australia, and received many distinguished honours in his homeland. In 1969 he was appointed chief conductor of the Toronto Symphony Orchestra, and appeared with other orchestras in North America.

Ančerl was at his best in the romantic and modern repertoire, where he gave firm, authoritative and unaffected readings. He recorded extensively with the Czech Philharmonic Orchestra for Supraphon, and produced a number of exceptionally fine discs. The works recorded included Mozart's Piano Concerto K. 271 (with Steurer), Bassoon Concerto (with Bidlo), Violin Concerto K. 215 (with D. Oistrakh), Horn Concerto No. 3 (with Štefek) and overture to *Die Zauberflöte*, Beethoven's Symphony No. 5 and Romance No. 2 (with D. Oistrakh), the Schumann Cello Concerto (with Navarra), the Mendelssohn Violin Concerto and Bruch's Violin Concerto No. 1 (with Suk), Brahms' Symphonies Nos 1 and 2, *Tragic Overture* and Double Concerto (with Suk and Navarra), *Invitation to the Dance*, *Till Eulenspiegel*, *Má Vlast* and the overture to *The Bartered Bride*, Dvořák's Symphonies Nos 6 and 9, Violin Concerto and *Romance* (with Suk), the overtures *Husitska*, *Othello*, *My Home*, *Amid Nature* and *Carnaval*, some *Slavonic Dances* and the *Requiem* (also issued by DGG), Tchaikovsky's Piano Concerto No. 1 (with Richter), *Capriccio italien*, *1812* overture, and suites from *Nutcracker* and *Swan Lake*, *Pictures at an Exhibition* and *A Night on the Bare Mountain*, *In the Steppes of Central Asia*, *Capriccio espagnol*, *Les Préludes*, the overtures *Le Carnaval romain*, *William Tell*, *Oberon*, *Prince Igor*, *Russlan and Ludmilla*, *Leonore No. 3* and the prelude to *Lohengrin*, Stravinsky's *Mass* and *Cantata*, *Petrushka*, *Le Sacre du printemps*, *Les Noces*, *Symphony of Psalms* and *Oedipus Rex*, Mahler's Symphonies Nos 1 and 9, Bloch's *Schelomo* (with Navarra), Lalo's *Symphonie espagnole* (with Haendel), Respighi's *Adagio con variazione* (with Navarra), Bartók's *Concerto for Orchestra*, Violin Concerto No. 2 (with Gertler), Viola Concerto (with Karlovsky) and Piano Concerto No. 3 (with Bernathova), Prokofiev's Piano Concertos Nos 1 (with Richter) and 2 (with Baloghová), Symphony No. 1, Symphonie Concertante (with Navarra), *Alexander Nevsky*, excerpts from *Romeo and Juliet* and *Peter and the Wolf*, Shostakovich's Symphonies Nos 1, 5, 7 and 10, Cello Concerto No. 1 (with Sádlo) and *Festival Overture*, Hindemith's Cello Concerto (with Tortelier) and Violin Concerto (with Gertler), Britten's *Young Person's Guide to the Orchestra*, Janáček's *Sinfonietta*, *Taras Bulba* and *Glagolitic Mass*, Ravel's *Tzigane* (with

Haendel), Berg's Violin Concerto (with Suk), Hartmann's *Concerto funèbre* (with Gertler), Martinů's Symphony No. 6, Piano Concerto No. 3 (with Páleníček), *Three Frescoes*, *Memorial to Lidice*, *Parables*, *Bouquet of Flowers* and *The Prophecy of Isaiah*, Novák's *Slovak suite* and *In the Tatras*, Dobiáš' Symphony No. 2 and *Czechoslovak Polka*, Hanuš' *Sinfonia Concertante*, Kabeláč's *The Mystery of Time*, Kapr's *In Soviet Land*, Slavický's *Rhapsodic variations* and *Three Moravian Dance Fantasies*, Hurník's *Ondras*, Kalabis' Violin Concerto (with Snítil), Suk's *Fantasy* (with Suk), Krejčí's Symphony No. 2 and Mácha's *Variations*.

In addition, Ančerl also recorded the Stravinsky Violin Concerto (with Schneiderhan and the Berlin Philharmonic Orchestra for DGG), Dvořák's Symphony No. 9 and the *Slavonic Dances* Nos 1 to 8, *Moldau*, the *Romeo and Juliet* fantasy-overture, the *Nutcracker* suite, excerpts from *Swan Lake*, and the waltz from *The Sleeping Beauty* (with the Vienna Symphony Orchestra for Philips), Mozart's Symphony No. 36 (with the Dresden Staatskapelle for Ariola), the Brahms Double Concerto (with Oistrakh and Sádlo and the Prague Symphony Orchestra for Supraphon), and Beethoven's Symphony No. 5, Martinů's Symphony No. 5 and Willan's Symphony No. 2 (with the Toronto Symphony Orchestra for CBC).

Anda, Géza (1921–76). Anda studied with Dohnányi at the Franz Liszt Academy at his birthplace, Budapest, and made his first appearance in that city as a pianist in 1938. In 1939 he performed Brahms' Piano Concerto No. 2 with Mengelberg, in the next year won the Liszt Prize, and in 1941 played in Berlin with the Berlin Philharmonic Orchestra under Furtwängler. He escaped from Hungary in 1942, settled in Zürich, and in 1955 became a Swiss citizen. After World War II he won international renown as one of the foremost pianists of his generation, particularly as a performer of the Mozart and Bartók concertos, recording the latter with Fricsay. He developed as a conductor and in Britain became associated with the English Chamber Orchestra and the Northern Sinfonia.

Anda recorded the complete Mozart piano concertos for DGG in the 1960s, directing them from the keyboard, with a group entitled the Camerata Academica of the Salzburg Mozarteum. Although in some of the concertos his highly individual readings have attracted some adverse criticism, his comprehensive musicianship and his fine sense of style are unquestioned. Rather unpredictably his recording of the Piano Concerto No. 21 in C major K. 467 topped record sales in the United States for an entire year (1969) after it had been used in the soundtrack of the Swedish film *Elvira Madigan*. In fact in the public mind the piece itself has become known as the 'Elvira Madigan Concerto.' Anda himself disclaimed any complicity in promoting his record in this fashion, as it was selected without his prior knowledge for the film's background music by the director, Bo Widerberg. So Anda had the distinction of being the one conductor of classical music who reached the 'top of the charts'.

Directing Mozart concertos from the keyboard was in every way sound practice to Anda. 'Why shouldn't a pianist do this?' he asked. 'I distrust the late nineteenth-century tradition that specialises these activities. In Mozart's time a competent musician was expected to do both. Even much later – in Liszt's time, for example – this was still true. Liszt obviously felt obliged to do *everything*' (*Stereo Review*, September 1969, p. 81).

Andersén, Harald (b. 1919). Born in Helsinki, Andersén is a choir leader, organist and teacher whose work has transformed choral singing in Finland. He has founded and led a number of outstanding choirs, including the men's choir Svenska Sångare (1949–59), the Helsinki Cathedral boys' choir Cantores Minores (1959–60), the chamber choir Chorus Sanctae Ceciliae (1953–65), the Klemetti Institute and Wegelius Institute Choirs (1957 onwards), the Sibelius Academy Choir (1959 onwards) and the Radio Chamber Choir (1961 onwards). From 1958 he has been director of church music at the Sibelius Academy, from 1966 a professor at the Academy, and has edited and published many books of sacred music. His records include a disc for Philips of choral music of Bergman, Johansson, Kokkonen and Rautavaara, with soloists and the Akademiska Sangforeningen and the Finnish Radio Chamber Orchestra.

Andersen, Kartsen (b. 1920). Born in Oslo, and educated in Norway and Italy, Andersen was musical director at Stavanger (1954–64), Bergen (from 1964) and chief conductor of the Iceland Symphony Orchestra (from 1973). He has recorded Svendsen's violin and cello concertos and four *Norwegian Rhapsodies* (with the Harmonien's Orchestra *et al.* for Norskkulturrads Klassikerserie), a trombone concerto by Ross and Egge's Symphony No. 1 (with the Bergen Symphony Orchestra *et al.* for Composers Recordings) and Bibalo's *Sinfonia* and *Notturna* (with the Bergen Symphony Orchestra for Philips).

Andor, Ilona (1904–77). Andor studied at the Academy of Music at Budapest, graduated as a choral conductor, and founded the Kodály Choir of Budapest in 1950, and conducted the Choir until her death. She recorded discs of the choral music of Kodály, and Brahms' works for female chorus, with the Zoltán Kodály Children's Chorus, for Hungaroton.

André, Franz (1893–1975). Born in Brussels, André first studied with his mother who was an excellent pianist, then at the Brussels Conservatoire where he came into contact with Collaer and Ysaÿe; he was noticed by César Thompson, through whom he became assistant professor of the violin class. In 1912 he went to Berlin, played the violin in the Blüthner Orchestra, and then studied conducting and composition with Weingartner. Returning to Brussels in 1913 he taught the violin at the Conservatoire and fought for four years in the Belgian Army in World War I. He joined the Belgian Radio Orchestra as a violinist when it was formed in 1923 and soon after became its conductor, and successively led the Orchestre de Radio-Belgique, the Orchestre-Radio de l'Institut National de Radiodiffusion and finally the Grand Orchestre Symphonique de l'INR, which he founded and conducted until 1958, and led a final performance for his 80th birthday in 1973. From 1940 to 1945 he was also conductor of the Brussels Conservatoire Orchestra. His interpretations of the music of the early 20th century, of impressionist and *avant-garde* composers were particularly noteworthy, and his performances of modern works were well known at concerts and festivals throughout Europe; he gave first performances of a number of works including some by Milhaud, Bartók, Florent Schmitt and Hindemith, and adapted for orchestra works by Bach, Leclair, Rameau, Lully, Grétry and Sacchini. From the first time it was held in 1951 he was intimately associated with the Queen Elisabeth International Competition in Brussels, accompanying the finalists with the orchestra, and at the end of his career he was director of the Queen Elisabeth Young Musicians Orchestra. In 1952 he was awarded the Schoenberg prize by the Austrian minister for education for his activities promoting contemporary music and that of Schoenberg in particular. His own compositions included music for radio plays. Although he was an influential figure and a household name in Belgium and conducted in Belgium throughout World War II, his impact outside his own country was limited.

From 1948 André recorded extensively with the Brussels Radio Orchestra for Telefunken, first on 78s, and then during the first years of LP. These discs made a deep impression at the time, especially in the repertoire for which he was most suited by temperament: Franck, Ravel, Debussy, Dukas, Berlioz, Chabrier and Poot. His recordings included an arrangement of Bach's *Italian Concerto*, Handel's Organ Concerto No. 10 (with Tellier), Beethoven's Symphonies Nos 1, 4 and 7, Liszt's *Hungarian Rhapsodies Nos 1*, *2*, *3*, *6* and *14* and *Les Préludes*, the *Menuet des follets* from *La Damnation de Faust*, Tchaikovsky's Symphony No. 4, *Serenade in C major*, *1812* overture, *Nutcracker* suite and *Romeo and Juliet* fantasy-overture, *Pictures at an Exhibition* and *A Night on the Bare Mountain*, *Scheherazade*, Liadov's *The Enchanted Lake*, *In the Steppes of Central Asia* and the Polovtsian Dances from *Prince Igor*, Glazunov's *Valse de Concert No. 1*, Enesco's *Romanian Rhapsody No. 1*, the Marches from *A Midsummer Night's Dream* and *Le Prophète*, the waltzes from *Der Rosenkavalier*, *Valse triste*, the Dance of the Hours from *La Gioconda*, Mottl's suite arranged from Grétry's *Céphale et Procris*, the Franck *Symphony in D minor* and *Psyché*, the *L'Arlésienne* Suites Nos 1 and 2, Debussy's *Danse* (arr. Ravel), *La Mer* and *Iberia*, *Boléro*, the *Daphnis et Chloé* Suites Nos 1 and 2, *Rapsodie espagnole* and *Valses nobles et sentimentales*, *L'Apprenti sorcier*, *Danse macabre* and *Le Carnaval des animaux*, the waltz from *Faust*, suites from *Coppélia* and *Sylvia* and the waltz from *La Source*, *Nights in the Gardens of Spain* (with Gousseau), Hartmann's Symphony No. 4, *Pini di Roma* and *Fontane di Roma*, the intermezzo from *Notre Dame*, Chabrier's *España* and *Marche joyeuse*, the overtures to *Il barbiere di Siviglia*, *Tancredi*, *William Tell*, *Zampa*, *Si j'étais Roi*, *La Muette de Portici*, *Fra Diavolo*, *Mignon*, *Dichter und Bauer*, *Leichte Cavallerie*, *Die schöne Galatea*, *Orphée aux enfers* and *Le Carnaval romain*, Alpaerts' *Pallister*, Poot's *Allegro symphonique* and *Ouverture joyeuse*, Jongen's *Walloon Dance No. 2* and de Boeck's *Rapsodie dahomienne*. Decca also recorded him, on 78s, conducting the London Philharmonic Orchestra in Franck's *Le Chasseur maudit*. When the major conductors of international status came to record the standard repertoire on LP, André's discs were generally eclipsed, despite their vitality and precision. His outstanding recording was perhaps the Hartmann Symphony No. 4, which was highly praised when it was released in 1952.

Andreae, Marc (b. 1939). Born in Zürich, the grandson of the conductor Volkmar Andreae and the son of two pianists, Andreae studied at the Zürich Conservatory, assisted his grandfather at rehearsals and concerts of the Tonhalle Orchestra, and formed and directed his own orchestra of music students. He studied further with Nadia Boulanger in Paris and with Ferrara at the Accademia di Santa Cecilia in Rome, was assistant to Peter Maag (1967–8) and from 1969 has been chief conductor of the Orchestra della Radio Svizzera Italiana at Lugano. He has conducted many major orchestras in Europe and at festivals in Lucerne, Paris, Ascona, Leipzig, Saint Moritz, Bergamo and Brescia. His repertoire extends from baroque to contemporary music, and he has discovered and performed many previously unknown works of Schumann, Weber, Schubert, Rossini, Donizetti, Tchaikovsky *et al.* In 1978 he was made an honorary member of the Italian Anton Bruckner Society.

Andreae has recorded in recent years some out-of-the-way music for BASF with the Munich Philharmonic Orchestra, including the Joachim orchestration of the Schubert *Grand Duo*, D. 812, which has been held to be the lost *Gastein Symphony*, two sinfonias of Friedrich Witt, one of which is the *Jena Symphony* once supposed to have been by Beethoven, the *Symphony in G minor* and *Overture, Scherzo and Finale* of Schumann. The symphony was composed by Schumann in 1832, had never been published and was revised and edited by Andreae for this recording. Other unusual recordings are the Schumann *Piano Concerto in A minor*, the first movement being the composer's first version, together with the *Introduction and Allegro* Op. 92 for piano and orchestra (with Frager and the Hamburg State Philharmonic Orchestra for BASF), and Schubert's opera *Die Verschworenen* (with the French Radio Orchestra *et al.*). He has also recorded *Pictures at an Exhibition* with the instrumentation by Touschmaloff and Rimsky-Korsakov, and other orchestral pieces by Mussorgsky, trumpet concertos by Haydn, Hummel and Leopold Mozart (with Reinhardt) and pieces by Winter, Frölich and Witt (all with the Munich Philharmonic Orchestra for BASF), Weber's two piano concertos (with Frager), *Grand Potpourri for Cello and Orchestra* (with Bylsma) and the overtures *Oberon*, *Euryanthe*, *Abu Hassan*, *Beherrscher der Geister*, *Turandot* and *Preciosa* (with the North West German Radio Symphony Orchestra for RCA) and Lefèvre's Clarinet Concerto (with Brunner and the Orchestra della Radio Svizzera Italiana for CT, Switzerland).

Andreae, Volkmar (1879–1962). Born in Berne, Andreae studied in Berne and Cologne and in 1900 was appointed assistant conductor at the Munich Court Opera. He returned to Switzerland in 1902 and became the conductor of the Zürich Tonhalle Orchestra, leading the orchestra for 43 years (1906–49), the Male Voice Choir (1904–20), the Winterthur Stadtsangerverein, and director of the Zürich Conservatory (1914–39). He enjoyed a reputation as a fine conductor and appeared at concerts in Germany, Spain and Italy, where in 1911 he gave the first performance in Milan of the *St Matthew Passion*. His many compositions include symphonies, and an opera about some of the adventures of Casanova. Bruckner was regarded as his speciality, and he recorded the first three numbered Bruckner symphonies on LP with the Vienna Symphony Orchestra for Amadeo and Philips. The editions used were the Haas for Symphony No. 1, the Schalk for No. 2 and a combination of both for No. 3. Earlier recordings included a Vivaldi concerto grosso, the overture to *Die Entführung aus dem Serail*, the gavotte from *Idomeneo* and Mozart's Andante K. 315 (with Nada, flute, and with the Zürich Tonhalle Orchestra for Columbia). Much later, on LP, appeared the Schumann Piano Concerto (with Gulda and the Vienna Philharmonic Orchestra for Decca).

Andrewes, John (b. 1915). Born in Canterbury and educated at Cambridge University and at the Royal College of Music, Andrewes was the music director of the Continental Ballet (1947), was with the editorial and promotional staff of Boosey and Hawkes (from 1954), and has been musical director of the Finchley Children's Music Group (from 1959). In 1967 Argo released a recording of Williamson's children's opera *Julius Caesar Jones*, with Andrewes conducting his Finchley Group.

Angelov, Stoyan (b. 1931). Born in Sofia, Angelov attended the Sofia Music School, graduated in 1950, then studied conducting at the Sofia State Conservatory under A. and G. Dimitrov, Hadjiev and Goleminov, and later studied with Vladigerov. He formed and conducted a youth symphony orchestra (1949), conducted the orchestra at the children's theatre at the Palace of Pioneers in Sofia (1956–60), and since 1960 has worked with the Bulgarian Radio. He lectures at the State Conservatory and the Institute for Musicians and Choreographers at Sofia, has written theoretical works and articles and reviews for journals, and has composed orchestral, vocal and other music, and scores for radio and the theatre. His records, with the Bulgarian Radio Orchestra, include *Russlan and Ludmilla*,

Sorochintsy Fair, *Mozart and Salieri*, excerpts from *Sadko*, *The Snow Maiden* and *May Night*, Hadjiev's *The Silver Slippers*, Bazer's *The Fair of a Doll*, Stoyanov's Symphony No. 4 and *Farewell*, Yossiffov's *Snow Maiden and the Seven Dwarfs* and Tekeliev's *The Roads of Anxiety*.

Angerer, Paul (b. 1927). Born in Vienna, Angerer studied at the Vienna Academy and was organist and choirmaster at St Thekla in Vienna (1940–48). He then was a violist in the Vienna Symphony Orchestra (1947–8), the Zürich Tonhalle Orchestra (1948–9) and the Suisse Romande Orchestra (1949–52), and returned as first violist to the Vienna Symphony (1952–7). He was leader of the Vienna Chamber Orchestra and a member of the Vienna Baroque Trio (1956–63), became first conductor in Bonn (1964), and was musical director at Ulm (1966–7), at the Salzburg Opera (1967–72) and of the South-West German Chamber Orchestra at Pforzheim (from 1971). A prolific composer, he has written oratorios, operas, orchestral pieces, concertos, chamber music and works for solo instruments.

Angerer's recordings include Geminiani's Concerti Grossi Opp. 2, 3 and 4, and Handel's Concerti Grossi Op. 6 (with the South-West German Chamber Orchestra for Vox), Werner's *The Curious Musical Instrument Calendar* and a collection of Viennese dances by Mozart, Beethoven and Schubert (with the Vienna State Opera Orchestra for Nonesuch), Haydn's *Harpsichord Concerto in D* (with Brendel and the Vienna Chamber Orchestra for Turnabout) and three *German Dances* (with the Vienna Volksoper Orchestra for Turnabout), Mozart's Piano Concertos K. 453 (with Gulda and an orchestra for Vanguard), K. 449 and K. 451 (with Klien and the Vienna Pro Musica Orchestra for Turnabout), K. 453, K. 459, K. 503 and K. 595 (with Brendel and the Vienna Volksoper Orchestra for Turnabout), the Two-Piano Concerto (with Brendel and Klien, and the Vienna Volksoper Orchestra for Turnabout) and the Rondos K. 382 (with Brendel and the Vienna Pro Musica Orchestra for Turnabout), Beethoven's Piano Concerto No. 2 (with Gulda and an orchestra for Vanguard), Dussik's Two-Piano Concerto and Schumann's *Andante and Variations* Op. 46 (with T. and R. Grünschlag and the Vienna Volksoper Orchestra for Turnabout), guitar concertos by Fasch, Krebs and Vivaldi (with Ragossnig and the South-West German Chamber Orchestra for Vox), Porpora's Cello Concerto (with Blees), Sammartini's *Viola Pomposa Concerto in C* and Vivaldi's Viola d'Amore Concerto (with Koch, and the South-West German Chamber Orchestra for Vox), Dvořák's *Serenade in E major* and Janáček's *Idyll* (with the South-West German Chamber Orchestra for Turnabout), Grieg's *Holberg Suite* and Sibelius' *Suite Champêtre* (with the South-West German Chamber Orchestra for Claves), a collection of dances by Mozart, Schubert, Beethoven and Lanner (with the Vienna Volksoper Orchestra for Christophorus) and Borodin's *Nocturne* and *Scherzo in D*, Grieg's *Two Elegiac Melodies*, Saint-Saëns' *Sarabande* and Volkmann's Serenade No. 2 (with the South-West German Chamber Orchestra for Christophorus).

Annovazzi, Napoleone (b. 1907). Born in Florence, and a graduate of the Conservatorio Benedetto Marcello at Venice, Annovazzi conducted opera at Riga (1934), Barcelona (1942–52), Valencia (1953–5) and has since been active in Dublin, Barcelona and Madrid. In 1963 Saga (UK) issued discs of excerpts from *Madama Butterfly* and *La traviata* in which he directed the Hamburg Radio Orchestra with Italian casts.

Anon. Many records have appeared in which the conductor has remained anonymous. Most of these were operatic arias, made in the pre-war days. A celebrated performance of Chopin's Piano Concerto No. 1, played by Dinu Lipatti and issued by Seraphim, has both orchestra and conductor unidentified; the recording originated from a radio transcription, apparently in Switzerland. Also, a recording of Beethoven's Piano Concerto No. 1, issued by EMI on 78s with Gieseking and the Philharmonia Orchestra, failed to name the conductor. A curious attempt to conceal the name of both orchestra and conductor was made for a pre-war disc issued in the United States by Victor of excerpts from Gluck's *Don Juan* ballet; the orchestra was called the Victor Chamber Orchestra, and was conductorless, but it was actually the Berlin Chamber Orchestra under Hans von Benda, and the names were suppressed apparently because of anti-Nazi feeling at the time.

The identity of orchestras on many records is much more puzzling, particularly some in London and Vienna. In many of Boult's records with the London Philharmonic Orchestra, contractual restraints caused it to appear on some labels as the London Philharmonic Promenade Orchestra; the same thing happened to records by Leinsdorf, Scherchen and Rodzinski with the same orchestra. Also,

Henry Krips recorded collections of waltzes with the Philharmonia Orchestra, which EMI chose to rename the Philharmonia Promenade Orchestra for the occasion. In the United States, Charles O'Connell recorded with the RCA Victor Symphony Orchestra, which was apparently the Philadelphia Orchestra. In fact, both the names Columbia Symphony Orchestra and RCA Victor Symphony Orchestra occasionally conceal the identity of a famous orchestra. The Vienna Philharmonic for a long period was under contract to Decca, and it undoubtedly appeared, in whole or in part, with other companies under other names; the Vienna State Opera Orchestra, for instance, is essentially made up of the same members, minus the first desk players. This is also the difference between the Boston Symphony and the Boston Pops Orchestras.

The identity of conductors of many performances recorded (ostensibly) in Eastern Europe after the war is difficult to determine. It is clear that names, and maybe orchestras, were inventions; certainly on-the-spot investigations with orchestral managements and musical authorities in Berlin and Leipzig have revealed that many conductors alleged to have recorded there are quite unknown.

Anosov, Nikolai (1900–62). Born in Borisoglebsk, in Russia, Anosov received a wide education, was a fine pianist and spoke about ten languages. He composed, wrote a book concerning reading orchestral scores, was a conductor of distinction in both the opera house and concert hall, and was a professor of conducting at the Moscow Conservatory, where one of his pupils was his son, Gennadi Rozhdestvensky. He recorded with the USSR State Symphony Orchestra and the Moscow Radio Symphony Orchestra; the performances were released on various labels in the West, such as DGG, Artia, Parliament, Monarch and Le Chant du Monde. Included were the two *L'Arlésienne* suites, Tchaikovsky's Piano Concerto No. 2 (with Nikolayeva), the *Romeo and Juliet* fantasy-overture, *Souvenir de Florence* and a complete *Queen of Spades*, Balakirev's *Overture on Russian Themes*, Dvořák's three *Legends*, Prokofiev's Piano Concertos Nos 1 (with Richter) and 3 (with Nikolayeva), and suites from *Romeo and Juliet* and *Lieutenant Kijé*, Kabalevsky's Symphony No. 2, Rimsky-Korsakov's *Tsar Saltan* suite, Galynin's *Suite for String Orchestra*, and Shchedrin's Symphony No. 1. The Romanian record organisation also issued the Kabalevsky overture *Colas Breugnon*, Tchaikovsky's *Francesca da Rimini* and Prokofiev's Piano Concerto No. 3 (with Serbescu), in which he conducted the USSR State Symphony Orchestra, and Supraphon Prokofiev's Symphony No. 7 and the Sibelius Violin Concerto (with Sitkovsky, and the Czech Philharmonic Orchestra).

Ansermet, Ernest (1883–1969). Born in Vevey in the French-speaking region of Switzerland (Suisse Romande) where both his mother and grandfather were musicians, the young Ansermet was himself a musician from childhood. As it was not possible for him to follow a career as a musician, he studied mathematics at Lausanne University and the Sorbonne, and while he taught mathematics at the high school at Geneva (1903–9) he studied music with several eminent teachers, including Ernest Bloch. At first his ambition was to become a composer, but after coming into contact with Nikisch, Weingartner and Mottl he decided in 1910 to be a conductor. His first concert was at Montreux, when he substituted for someone else at a performance of Beethoven's Symphony No. 5, and this led to his appointment to direct the Kursaal concerts at Montreux. There he remained until 1913, when he directed concerts at Geneva; Stravinsky recommended him to Diaghilev and in 1915 he became conductor with the Ballets Russes of Diaghilev. He conducted at their season in London in 1919 and was active with the company on and off until 1923, touring with them in Europe, North and South America, and leading the world premières of Ravel's *La Valse*, Falla's *The Three-cornered Hat* and some ballets of Stravinsky. In 1920 he presented a concert of Stravinsky's music in London, giving a lecture beforehand about the composer, and conducted the first performance in Germany of *Le Sacre du printemps* in 1922. Later, in 1928, he was conductor, with Fourestier, of l'Orchestre Symphonique de Paris.

Ansermet's career culminated in 1918 with the foundation of l'Orchestre de la Suisse Romande. His name was inseparable from the orchestra for 50 years, until he handed over its direction to Paul Kletzki. At the end of World War I, Suisse Romande was devoid of a professional symphony orchestra, except for a small one at the Geneva Theatre, but with the help of some influential enthusiasts in Geneva and other towns of the region, Ansermet assembled a number of musicians, mostly foreigners, to form the orchestra – French windplayers, Viennese brass, and string players from Belgium, Italy and from Switzerland itself. His aim to develop local talent finally led to four out of five of the orchestra's membership in 1946 being Swiss. In 1935, when the Swiss

Radio formed its orchestra in Lausanne, the Suisse Romande Orchestra was reformed in Geneva, with support from the city and state authorities and from private subscribers. Ansermet worked towards widening the repertoire so that it was more representative than the other two major Swiss orchestras, the Zürich Tonhalle and the Winterthur. Under him the Suisse Romande Orchestra presented regular concerts in Geneva, Montreux and Vevey, as well as a limited opera season, mainly of French operas. With guest appearances in England, Germany, France, Poland, Scandinavia, Belgium, Holland, the United States and South America, he acquired an international reputation during the years between the two world wars for the intelligence and brilliance of his interpretations. After 1945 he was invited to Paris, Brussels, the Hague and London, and in 1948 and 1949 successfully toured the US, conducting the NBC Symphony Orchestra and those at Chicago, Dallas, Cleveland, Philadelphia, and in some other cities. Many first performances for the US were included in his programmes.

Reserved in his gestures, Ansermet was nonetheless precise in his directions to the orchestra. He recognised that many orchestral players need no advice about how to play; the conductor is superior to them because of his broader outlook and his understanding of the music, historically and culturally: 'he has more fantasies, references and background' (*New York Star*, 26 December 1948, p. 14). While he believed it necessary for the conductor to know the score by heart, he always conducted with the score, as in conducting from memory he saw the danger of following the main melodic line and neglecting the secondary voices. Because of his association with the ballet and its composers, he concentrated for most of his life in performing the music of Stravinsky, Prokofiev, Ravel, Debussy and also Hindemith, Bartók and others, but in his last decades he turned more to the classical repertoire. Disagreeing with Boulez, who said that music must be interpreted in the spirit of the time, Ansermet believed that it must be interpreted in the spirit of the composer. He quoted Rimsky-Korsakov's remark that there are two kinds of music: one when you just play the notes, and you have everything, and the other when you must play the notes in a certain manner, with a certain feeling for the right sound. Ravel, Ansermet said, can be performed exactly as written, but Debussy requires an understanding of the music, and the performer then has to realise the musical idea. An orchestra's style is not simply perfection in playing, but the method in which it plays, which corresponds to a way of feeling, and it is the conductor's task to bring the musicians to participate in this feeling. The orchestra's regular conductor can form the orchestra's style, which is scarcely altered by a guest conductor; Ansermet himself had difficulty performing Debussy and Stravinsky with the Vienna Philharmonic because he found that their special style had not the equality of sound and the exact rhythm required by the music. Some conductors, such as Toscanini, impose their own personal style on all the music they conduct, but Ansermet himself tried in his own style to illustrate as much as possible the composer's style. He emphasised that the indications in the score are relative, and performances require much more than just observing the text: 'Making music cannot be reduced to performing what is written, because music is not an acoustic phenomenon: it is something which is inside the acoustic phenomenon and as truth cannot be formulated' (*New York Star*, 26 December 1948, p. 14). As each performer sees the same piece from a different point of view and has his own vision of this truth, there can be more than one satisfactory performance of the same piece.

Despite the catholicity of his musical sympathies, Ansermet was only a truly convincing interpreter in a restricted range of music, notably Stravinsky, Debussy, Ravel, Bartók and some other modern composers. He championed Stravinsky, whose technique, writing and conception he admired, but he fell out with him on aesthetics. Contemporary atonal music roused his hostility; to him it had no meaning, and could only be of interest to a coterie. To enunciate his position he published in 1916 *The Foundations of Music in the Human Consciousness*, in which he deprecated the tonal disintegration of the music of Schoenberg, arguing that structural complexity did nothing to replace traditional forms based on the intervals of the third, fourth and fifth. He also recorded a lecture, with musical illustrations, making much the same point.

Ansermet's recording career commenced in 1919, and his last session in the studios was with the New Philharmonia Orchestra directing *L'Oiseau de feu*, which was released by Decca after his death in 1969, together with excerpts of the rehearsal. He recorded a set of the Handel Concerti Grossi with the Decca String Orchestra first, and before 1939 had assisted Stravinsky in preparing recordings of some of his music; Ansermet rehearsed and gave public performances of *Les Noces* in London and the *Symphony of Psalms* in Brussels, and some other pieces, but Stravinsky then conducted the actual recordings with the same forces. Prior to 1931 he had conducted the Royal Philharmonic Orchestra for Columbia in the Schumann Piano Concerto with soloist Fanny Davies; on 78s he also recorded excerpts from Honegger's *Le Roi David* (for Columbia) and Stravinsky's *Capriccio* (with Stravinsky and the Straram Orchestra for Columbia), Mozart's Symphonies Nos 40 and 41, Honegger's *Pastorale d'été* and Falla's *Nights in the Gardens of Spain* (with Blancard, and the Suisse Romande Orchestra, for Odeon). Fame as a recording artist came in 1946 when he signed an exclusive contract with Decca and recorded *Petrushka* and *L'Oiseau de feu* in the new full-frequency-range-recording sound. He was then in Britain to conduct the première of Britten's *The Rape of Lucretia* at Glyndebourne. At first, he recorded on 78s with the London Philharmonic, London Symphony and Paris Conservatoire Orchestras, but all his later discs for Decca, except his very last, were with his own Suisse Romande Orchestra. He felt that he had established with them a more personal style, despite the reservations many critics had about the orchestra's virtuosity. He recorded a prolific amount of music; many of his successful discs he re-recorded for stereo, but sometimes he could not quite repeat the same magic. He knew this, and felt that the reason was that the recording technicians were tending to supplant the musicians, and that musical values were often lost. A good example was the second (1965) recording of Debussy's *Pelléas et Mélisande*, although without having heard the earlier version of 1952, it would be judged fine enough.

Ansermet's discography for Decca included *Pictures at an Exhibition*, *Scheherazade*, *La Valse* and Ravel's *Shéhérazade* (with Danco, and the Paris Conservatoire Orchestra on 78s), *Petrushka*, *L'Oiseau de feu*, *Symphony of Psalms* and *Pictures at an Exhibition* (with the London Philharmonic Orchestra on 78s), *La Boutique fantasque* and Chopin's Piano Concerto No. 2 (with Ballon, and the London Symphony Orchestra, on 78s), and on LP with the Suisse Romande Orchestra (some also issued first on 78s, others on mono, and others on stereo), Bach's Suites Nos 2 and 3, and Cantatas Nos 45, 67, 101, 105 and 130, Handel's Organ Concertos Nos 1 and 2 (with Demessieux), Marcello's *Oboe Concerto in C minor* (with Reversy), Vivaldi's *Bassoon Concerto in D minor* (with Helaerts), Haydn's Symphonies Nos 29, 81 to 87 and 90, and Trumpet Concerto (with Longinetti), trumpet concertos by Hummel and Leopold Mozart (with Cuvit), Mozart's Symphonies Nos 34 and 38, the Serenade K. 361 and Flute Concerto No. 2 (with Pepin), the nine Beethoven symphonies and the overtures *Coriolan*, *Egmont*, *Prometheus*, *Fidelio* and *Leonore No. 2* and the *Grosse Fuge*; Schumann's Symphonies Nos 1 and 2, *Manfred* overture, Cello Concerto (with Gendron) and *Adagio and Allegro for Horn* (with Leoir), Weber's overtures *Abu Hassan*, *Oberon*, *Der Freischütz*, *Preciosa*, *Jubel*, *Euryanthe* and *Rübezahl*, Mendelssohn's Symphony No. 4, incidental music for *A Midsummer Night's Dream*, and the overtures *The Hebrides*, *Ruy Blas* and *Die schöne Melusine*, Liszt's *Faust Symphony*, *Two Episodes from Lenau's Faust* and *Hunnenschlacht*, the four Brahms symphonies, *Variations on the St Antony Chorale*, *Academic Festival Overture*, *Tragic Overture* and *Alto Rhapsody* (with Watts), the preludes to *Die Meistersinger* and *Lohengrin*, the Prelude and Good Friday Music from *Parsifal* and the Funeral Music from *Götterdämmerung*, Tchaikovsky's Symphony No. 6, the complete ballets *Nutcracker*, *Swan Lake* and *The Sleeping Beauty*, the Suites Nos 3 and 4, and the *Rococo Variations* (with Gendron), *Capriccio espagnol*, a suite from *Le Coq d'or*, *May Night* overture, the *Russian Easter Festival* overture, *Antar*, *Scheherazade*, *Christmas Eve*, *Dubinushka*, the Sea Episode from *Sadko* and The Flight of the Bumble Bee from *Tsar Saltan*, Borodin's Symphonies Nos 2 and 3, the overture and Polovtsian Dances from *Prince Igor* and *In the Steppes of Central Asia*, *Pictures at an Exhibition*, *A Night on the Bare Mountain*, the gopak from *Sorochintsy Fair* and excerpts from *Khovanshchina*, Glinka's *Kamarinskaya*, *Jota aragonesa*, *Waltz-fantasy* and the overture to *Russlan and Ludmilla*, Glazunov's two *Concert Waltzes*, *The Seasons* and *Stenka Razin*, Liadov's *Baba Yaga*, *Eight Russian Folksongs* and *Kikimora*, Balakirev's *Tamar*, Rachmaninov's *The Isle of the Dead*, Stravinsky's *Petrushka*, *L'Oiseau de feu*, *Le Sacre du printemps*, *Pulcinella*, *Le Chant du rossignol*, *Renard*, *Apollon Musagète*, *Le Baiser de la fée*, *Circus polka*, *Les Noces*, *Oedipus Rex*, *Symphonies of Wind Instruments*, *Symphony of Psalms*, *Symphony in C major*, *Symphony in Three Movements*, *Concerto for Piano and Wind* and *Capriccio* (with Magaloff), Prokofiev's Symphonies Nos 1, 5 and 6, Piano Concerto No. 3 (with Katchen), two Violin Concertos (with Ricci), excerpts from *Romeo and Juliet* and *Cinderella*, a suite from *The Love of Three Oranges*, *L'Enfant prodigue* and *Scythian Suite*, Sibelius' Symphonies Nos 2 and 4 and *Tapiola*, the Berlioz overtures *Le Corsaire*, *Benvenuto Cellini* and *Béatrice et Bénédict*, *Symphonie fantastique*,

Nuits d'été (with Crespin) and excerpts from *La Damnation de Faust*, Franck's *Symphony in D minor*, *Les Éolides* and *Le Chasseur maudit*, Debussy's *La Mer*, *Images*, *Nocturnes*, *Prélude à l'après-midi d'un faune, Jeux, Boîte à joujoux*, *Pelléas et Mélisande*, *Printemps*, *Six Épigraphes antiques*, *Petite Suite*, *Clair de lune* (arr. Caplet), *Marche écossaise*, *Khamma*, *Le Martyre de Saint-Sébastien*, and *Première Rapsodie* (with Gugholz), Ravel's *Boléro*, *La Valse*, *Valses nobles et sentimentales*, *Rapsodie espagnole*, *Ma Mère l'Oye*, and the two Piano Concertos (with Blancard), *Daphnis et Chloé*, *Le Tombeau de Couperin*, *Pavane pour une infante défunte*, *Shéhérazade* (with Danco and Crespin), *Deux mélodies hébraïques* (with Danco), *Alborada del gracioso*, *L'Heure espagnole* and *L'Enfant et les sortilèges*, *L'Apprenti sorcier* and *La Péri*, Bizet's *Symphony in C major*, *Jeux d'enfants*, suite from *La Jolie Fille de Perth*, *Patrie* overture, the two *L'Arlésienne* suites and a *Carmen* suite, Honegger's Symphonies Nos 2, 3 and 4, *Pacific 231*, *Cantate de Noël* and *Le Roi David*, Roussel's Symphonies Nos 3 and 4, *Petite Suite* and *Le Festin de l'araignée*, Fauré's *Pelléas et Mélisande*, *Masques et bergamasques*, prelude to *Pénélope*, and *Requiem*, Saint-Saëns' Symphony No. 3, *Danse macabre* and *Le Rouet d'Omphale*, Chabrier's *Suite pastorale*, *España*, *Marche joyeuse*, *Habanera*, and Danse slave and Fête polonaise from *Le Roi malgré lui*, Lalo's *Symphonie espagnole* (with Ricci), *Namouna*, *Rapsodie norvégienne*, Scherzo and andantino from *Divertissement*, Magnard's Symphony No. 3, Chausson's *Symphony in B flat*, Albéniz's *Iberia* (arr. Arbós) and *Navarra*, Bartók's Piano Concerto No. 3 (with Katchen), *Concerto for Orchestra*, *Music for Strings, Percussion and Celesta*, *Dance Suite*, *Romanian Folk Dances* and *Two Portraits*, Villa-Lobos' Piano Concerto No. 1 (with Ballon), Martin's *Petite Symphonie concertante*, *Concerto for seven wind instruments, strings and percussion*, *Études for String Orchestra*, Violin Concerto (with Schneiderhan), and *In Terra Pax*, Falla's *Three-cornered Hat* (twice, with Danco and Berganza), *El amor brujo* (with de Gabarian) and interlude and dance from *La vida breve*, Weber's Bassoon Concerto (with Helaerts), Turina's *Danzas fantásticas*, suite from *Sylvia* and the complete *Coppélia*, Geiser's *Symphony in D minor*, Oboussier's *Antigone* – recitative, air and elegy, Brasileiro's Piano Concerto (with Ballon), *Pini di Roma* and *Fontane di Roma*, and the overtures to *Orphée aux enfers, La Belle Hélène*, *Zampa*, *Le Roi d'Ys*, *Rosamunde*, *Le Domino noir*, *Si j'étais Roi*, and *La Dame blanche*. In the United States there also was issued a disc of pieces by Kelly and Philips, in which he conducted the University of Illinois Orchestra.

A number of Ansermet's mono LPs continued in the catalogues on cheaper labels and stood their ground for many years. Later, when his repertoire widened, he recorded the *Paris* symphonies of Haydn, the complete Beethoven and Brahms symphonies, and others by Mendelssohn, Schumann and Sibelius, and some other works by these composers, as well as overtures and other music by Weber, Berlioz, Wagner, *et al.* His characteristic style, his elegance and clear texture, were always present, but too often his cool musical temperament and intellectual objectivity were in the way of the necessary emotional involvement to make his readings absolutely convincing, as if his wish to present the style of the composer had caused him to neglect his own feelings for the music. Even so, many of Ansermet's recorded performances came off well, such as Schumann's Symphony No. 2, the Franck symphony, the Mendelssohn Symphony No. 4 and the Prokofiev symphonies, but the Berlioz overtures, Wagner preludes and Sibelius symphonies were generally uninspired. Beethoven and Brahms symphonies need more than the clarity and competence that he brought to them, and most critics regarded his performances of them as lightweight. To be fair to him, he should be judged in the music for which he had a special affinity, which was French and Russian rather than German, which requires a heroic style neither he nor his orchestra possessed. Other conductors have since recorded alternative readings of the French repertoire, superb in their own right, but Ansermet's will always command admiration.

Antill, John (b. 1904). Antill studied at the New South Wales Conservatorium at his native Sydney, conducted opera in Australia in 1932–3, and in 1934 joined the staff of the Australian Broadcasting Commission. He became a musical editor in 1950 and remained with the Commission until his retirement in 1968. His compositions include ballets, operas, overtures, song cycles, a harmonica concerto, instrumental pieces, choral music and music for plays and films. By far his best known work is the ballet suite *Corroboree*, which was derived from the rhythmic patterns in Australian aboriginal music. It was premièred in Sydney in 1946 by Eugene Goossens, who later recorded the work with the Sydney Symphony Orchestra for EMI and with the London Symphony Orchestra for Everest. Antill himself has recorded *Corroboree* with the Sydney Symphony Orchestra for EMI, as well as his Harmonica Concerto (with soloist Easton, for RCA) and *Overture for a Momentous Occasion* (for Festival), with the same orchestra.

Antonicelli, Giuseppe (b. 1897). Born in Castrovillari, Cosenza, Antonicelli first graduated as a lawyer and practised law, and at the same time studied music in Turin. His father was a general in the Italian army, and his mother an opera singer. He started his career as a repetiteur at the Teatro Regio in Turin, made his debut as a conductor in Novara, conducted at La Scala, Milan (1934–7), was artistic director and conductor at Trieste (1937–43 and 1950–56), and joined the Metropolitan Opera, New York (1947–50), where he conducted Italian opera. In 1947 he recorded *La Bohème*, with the Metropolitan Opera Orchestra and the major soloists Bidu Sayao and Richard Tucker; it was issued in the Metropolitan Opera Association's series, and was re-issued by CBS and later in Britain in 1974. He also conducted a recording of *Un ballo in maschera* with the Metropolitan company; it was released by Classic Editions, but was immediately withdrawn.

Antonini, Alfredo. Born in Alessandria, Italy, Antonini studied at the Milan Conservatory and during his last year there played as organist and pianist in the La Scala Orchestra under Toscanini. He migrated to the United States, joined the Columbia Broadcasting System in 1941, arranged and directed the music for many television and radio presentations and has been a guest conductor with orchestras in North and South America, Norway and Germany, where he has been acclaimed for his fine musicianship. He recorded Antheil's *Serenade No. 1*, Creston's *Dance Overture*, Dello Joio's *Meditations on Ecclesiastes*, Koussevitzky's Double Bass Concerto (with Karr) and Moore's *Cotillon* suite and *Farm Journal* (with the Oslo Philharmonic Orchestra for Composers Recordings), Hovhaness's *Ave Maria*, *Christmas Ode* and *Easter Cantata* (with the Bamberg Symphony Orchestra *et al.* for Composers Recordings), and Bergsma's *Fortunate Islands*, Claflin's *Teen Scenes*, Hively's *Summer Holiday*, Haufrecht's *Square Set*, Sanjuán's *La Macumba* and Riegger's *Dance Rhythms*, *Romanza*, and *Music for Orchestra* (with the Santa Cecilia Orchestra, Rome, for Composers Recordings).

Apelt, Arthur (b. 1908). Born in Eibau, Germany, Apelt studied at the Orchestral School of the Dresden Staatskapelle, was then a choral assistant at Dresden (1934–5), conducted at Göttingen (1936–40), Aussig (1940–43), Wuppertal (1945–54), Wiesbaden (1954–8), and since 1958 has been a resident conductor at the Berlin State Opera in East Berlin. He has been a guest conductor in Western Europe and in Hungary. For Eterna he recorded excerpts from Dvořák's *Rusalka*, and Beethoven's Italian arias and scenes, and arias with orchestra (with the Berlin Staatskapelle *et al.*).

Appia, Edmond (1894–1961). Born in Turin, Appia studied the violin at the Geneva Conservatoire, with Capet in Paris and at the Brussels Conservatoire. He toured Europe, taught in Switzerland and in 1935 was appointed conductor of Radiodiffusion Suisse at Lausanne. He recorded Handel's *Music for the Royal Fireworks* (with the Vienna State Opera Orchestra for Vanguard), a number of canzoni of Gabrieli (with the Gabrieli Festival Orchestra for Vanguard), Reichel's Piano Concertino (with Montandon and the Suisse Romande Orchestra for Decca) and Menasce's Divertimento, *Petite Suite* and Piano Concerto No. 2 (with the composer and the Vienna State Opera Orchestra for Vanguard).

Applewhite, Frederick (b. 1935). Born at Coleby, Lincolnshire, Applewhite was educated at the Royal College of Music, London, and first conducted in 1972 with the London Youth String Ensemble. He has been a violinist with the London Philharmonic and Sadler's Wells Opera Orchestras and teaches for the Inner London Education Authority. Cameo Classics issued a disc in which he conducts the London Youth Strings in works by Holst and Wirén.

Arámbarri y Garate, Jésus (1906–60). Born in Bilbao, Arámbarri studied at the Conservatorio Vizcaino de Musica (until 1928), with Dukas, Flem and Golschmann in Paris, and with Weingartner in Basel (1932). Returning to Bilbao (1933), he took over the Municipal Orchestra, which in 1939 he expanded to a permanent symphony orchestra. He was the conductor of the Madrid Concert Orchestra (from 1953), was president of the Spanish Association of Conductors, and a professor at the Madrid Conservatory. He recorded Arriaga's *Symphony in D*, *Nonetto*, overture *Los Esclavos Felices* and cantata *Agar*, and Moreno Torroba's *Concierto de Castilla* (with the Madrid Concert Orchestra, and with Tarragó the soloist in the latter, which was issued in the United States by Odyssey).

Arbós, Enrique Fernández (1863–1939). Arbós studied the violin with Monasterio at the conservatory at his birthplace, Madrid, with Vieuxtemps in Brussels and with Joachim in Berlin, and for a time was concertmaster of the Berlin Philharmonic Orchestra. He toured Europe, taught at the Hamburg Conservatory and returned to Madrid at the invitation of the Queen of Spain to be professor of violin at the Madrid Conservatory. In 1889 he came to Britain to be concertmaster of the orchestra at Glasgow, gave solo recitals in London (1890) and was appointed professor of violin at the Royal College of Music (1894–1916). He then became known as an orchestral conductor, appeared with great success in London, Liverpool, St Petersburg and Moscow, and in Madrid where from 1902 to the outbreak of the Civil War he spent three months of every year leading concerts with the Madrid Symphony Orchestra. He worked arduously and with great devotion to cultivate a knowledge and love of symphonic music among his native people and introduced much new music, such as *Le Sacre du printemps*, of which he led the Spanish première in 1932. He visited the United States and conducted the major orchestras, toured in Europe, was made an honorary professor at the Franz Liszt Academy in Budapest and was president of the Spanish section of the International Society for Contemporary Music and took a major part in the Society's congress in Barcelona in 1936. With the outbreak of the Spanish Civil War he retired from public life. He also won a reputation as a composer of light music and for his arrangements of numbers from Albéniz's *Iberia*. Columbia recorded him directing the Madrid Symphony Orchestra in *Iberia*, a suite from *The Three-cornered Hat*, Turina's *La Procesión del Rocío*, the *Danza Española* No. 6 of Granados, a Sarabande of Corelli and his own *Noche de Arabia*. These performances were completely idiomatic and, although they were recorded in the late 1920s and early 1930s, their authenticity ensured their retention in the Columbia catalogue for some years.

Arends, Henri (b. 1921). Born at Maastricht, Holland, Arends was educated at the conservatory there, and studied conducting with Zecchi at Salzburg and with van Kempen at Siena. He was a violinist with the Limburg Symphony Orchestra, was a conductor with Philips at Eindhoven (1951–3), became assistant conductor of the Amsterdam Concertgebouw Orchestra (1953) and then conductor of the North Holland Philharmonic Orchestra (1957). With the Concertgebouw Orchestra he gave first performances of works by Hemel and Dresden, *inter alios*. His only recording appears to be Franco's Symphony No. 5 (with the North Holland Philharmonic Orchestra for Composers Recordings).

Argenta, Ataulfo (1913–58). Born in Santander, Argenta entered the Madrid Conservatory at the age of thirteen, and after being awarded the Premio Extraordinario award for piano and the Kristina Nilsson prize, studied in Belgium and Germany. He taught the piano at Kassel, then returned to Spain at the end of the Civil War. In 1944 he was appointed conductor of the Madrid Chamber Orchestra, and two years later was principal conductor of the Spanish National Orchestra in Madrid. He toured most successfully as a conductor in Europe and South America, in 1952 conducted at a festival in Granada which became an annual event, but his career was tragically cut short by his sudden death in 1958. He was a fine interpreter of Spanish, French and Russian music, in which he could exhibit his feeling for orchestral colour, but for the German and Austrian classics he was far less suited by temperament.

At the time of his death, Argenta was making a series of brilliant recordings for Decca, and many were issued posthumously. His reading of *Symphonie fantastique* (with the Paris Conservatoire Orchestra) and Debussy's *Images* (with the Suisse Romande Orchestra) had a clarity and vitality which placed them in the front rank, and his Tchaikovsky Symphony No. 4 (with the London Symphony Orchestra) was one of the best performances of this score on record at its release in 1956. For Decca he also recorded the Albéniz/Arbós *Iberia*, Liszt's *Faust Symphony*, *El amor brujo* and Turina's *Danzas fantásticas* (with the Paris Conservatoire Orchestra), *Les Préludes* (with the Suisse Romande Orchestra), *España*, *Capriccio espagnol*, Moszkowski's *Spanish Dances* and the Tchaikovsky Violin Concerto (with Campoli, and the London Symphony Orchestra), the two Liszt piano concertos (with Katchen and the London Philharmonic Orchestra), Falla's Harpsichord Concerto (with Veyron-Lacroix), *Il retablo de Maese Pedro* and *The Three-cornered Hat*, Guridi's *Ten Basque Dances*, Halffter's Sinfonietta, Rodrigo's *Concierto de Aranjuez* (with Yepès) and Turina's *Oración del Torero*, *Procesión del Rocío* and *Sinfonia Sevillana* (with the Spanish National Orchestra), Falla's *Nights in the Gardens of Spain* (with Soriano), and *The Three-cornered Hat*, the intermezzo from Granados' *Goyescas*, Rodrigo's *Concierto de*

Aranjuez (with Yepès) and Turina's *Sinfonia Sevillana* (with the Madrid Chamber Orchestra), Usandizaga's *Las Golodrinas* (with the Grand Symphony Orchestra *et al.*), and pieces by Breton (with the Grand Symphony Orchestra). He also recorded the intermezzo from Luna's *La picara molinera*, (with the Madrid Chamber Orchestra for Montilla), *The Three-cornered Hat* (with the Madrid Symphony Orchestra for Montilla), Schubert's Symphony No. 9, Ravel's *Pavane pour une infante défunte*, *Rapsodie espagnole*, *Ma Mère l'Oye* and *Alborada del gracioso*, and Ohana's *Lament for the Death of a Bullfighter* and an arrangement for harpsichord of the sarabande from his Guitar Concerto (with Gouarne and the Centi Soli Orchestra for Omega). Earlier, he had directed over 20 records of zarzuelas, by Breton, Chapi, Chueca, Jiménez, Serrano and Vives, which were issued by Decca in England in the early days of LP. The zarzuela is a relatively short operetta which satirises contemporary events and people, with vivid Spanish colour and atmosphere. Argenta's recordings have all but disappeared from the British catalogue, although Decca have re-issued some of his most successful discs in the United States on their London label, including *Symphonie fantastique*, *Images* and *Retablo de Maese Pedro*.

Argento, Pietro (b. 1909). Born in Giogo del Colle, Bari, Italy, Argento studied at the Naples Conservatory and at the Accademia di Santa Cecilia under Molinari. His debut as a conductor was at Foggia, and he was conductor with the Italian Radio at Milan and with the Chamber Orchestra of the Quartet Society in Rome. He also lectured at the Accademia di Santa Cecilia in Rome. His recordings include Mozart's Horn Concerto No. 4 (with Ceccarossi and the Rome Radio Orchestra for Cetra), de Nardis's *Scene Abruzzesi*, suites Nos 1 and 2, *Le Carnaval des animaux*, the prelude to Act III of Catalini's *La Wally*, Debussy's *La Boîte à joujoux* (with the Naples Scarlatti Orchestra for Coliseum) and orchestral arrangements of *Tosca* and *Madama Butterfly* (with the Rome Symphony Orchestra for Kingsway).

Armand, Georges (b. 1918). Born in Toulouse, Armand studied at the Toulouse Conservatoire and at the Paris Conservatoire, and became first violin soloist (concertmaster) with Radiodiffusion française. In 1955 he was appointed violin soloist of the Toulouse Chamber Orchestra, and succeeded Auriacombe as its conductor. With the orchestra he has performed in Japan, the United States, the USSR, West Germany, Spain, South America, Romania, Yugoslavia, the Middle and the Far East, and has participated in many international festivals. As conductor he has recorded with the orchestra the complete Organ Concertos of Handel (with Rogg) and four Viola d'Amore Concertos of Vivaldi (with Pons), for EMI.

Arndt, Günther (b. 1907). Arndt studied at his birthplace, Berlin, where he taught at a secondary school (1934), and after World War II was associated with the Radio-in-American-Sector there. In 1949 he formed the Berlin Motet Choir, and in 1955 the RIAS Chamber Choir, and won a reputation as a distinguished choral conductor. He made records with the Berlin Motet Choir for Electrola, Telefunken and DGG; when the conductor Fritz Lehmann suffered a fatal illness during the recording of Bach's *Christmas Oratorio*, with the Berlin Philharmonic Orchestra, the Berlin Motet Choir *et al.*, in 1957, Arndt stepped in to complete the work. He also recorded Bach's motets *Jesu, mein Freude* and *Lobet den Herrn* (with the Berlin Motet Choir for Ducretet-Thomson), Schubert's *Die Nacht*, *Ständchen*, *Nachtgesang im Walde*, *Gesang der Geister über den Wassern* and *Der Morgenstern* (with the RIAS Chamber Choir *et al.* for EMI), motets by Schütz (with the RIAS Chamber Choir for Telefunken), choral pieces by Gabrieli, Hassler, Ferrabosco, Dowland, Schütz, Praetorius, Schein, Pezel, Krieger, Lasso, Pachelbel *et al.* (in Electrola's series of music in German and Austrian towns, with the RIAS Chamber Choir), Beethoven's *Die Himmel rühmen des Ewigen Ehre* and Bruckner's *Ave Maria* (with the Berlin Radio Symphony Orchestra *et al.* for Philips).

Arnell, Richard (b. 1917). The British composer studied at the Royal College of Music, was active as a conductor in New York (1939–47), and returned to live in London in 1948. He was much encouraged by Beecham, who recorded his ballet *Punch and the Child* (re-issued by CBS in 1974) and who commissioned some orchestral pieces by him. Arnell conducted the Pro Arte Orchestra in 1958 in several 45 r.p.m. discs of extracts from his ballets *The Great Detective* and *The Angels*.

Arnold, Malcolm (b. 1921). One of the most successful British composers of the present day, Arnold was born at Northampton and studied at the Royal College of Music, where he was a pupil of Gordon Jacob. He won the Cobbett Competition Prize and joined the London Philharmonic Orchestra in 1942 as third trumpet player, becoming principal trumpet a year later. He divided his time for the next six years between the London Philharmonic Orchestra, the BBC Symphony Orchestra and short spells in the army, then became a full-time composer. His many compositions, usually written to commissions, include overtures, symphonies and concertos, ballet scores (including the ballet for the coronation of Queen Elizabeth II, *Homage to the Queen*), piano and chamber works, and dozens of film scores, the most famous being for *The Bridge on the River Kwai* for which he received an Oscar. His music is popular in style and vividly orchestrated; it sometimes exhibits a bizarre sense of humour, such as in the *Grand Grand Overture*, written for one of the Hoffnung concerts, with parts for floor polisher, vacuum cleaner and rifles, and a *Grand Concerto Gastronomique* for eater, waiter, food and orchestra. In recent years he has conducted frequently, although his technique is described as unorthodox. Five companies (EMI, RCA, Philips, Everest and Desto) have issued records of him conducting various British orchestras in his own music; included are his *English Dances*, *Tam O'Shanter*, *Grand Grand Overture* and *Rhapsody* from the film *Sound Barrier* (with the Royal Philharmonic Orchestra for EMI), the Symphony No. 2 and overture *Beckus the Dandipratt* (with the same orchestra for Philips), the Symphony No. 3 and *Scottish Dances* (with the London Philharmonic Orchestra for Everest and Desto), his Guitar Concerto (with Bream and the Melos Ensemble, for RCA), and his Symphony No. 5, *Four Cornish Dances* and *Peterloo* (with the City of Birmingham Orchestra for EMI).

Ashkenazy, Vladimir (b. 1937). Born in Gorky, in the USSR, Ashkenazy studied the piano with Oborin at the Moscow Conservatory, made his debut as a soloist when he was 17, and won the first prize at the Chopin International Competition in Warsaw (1955), the Brussels International Competition under the auspices of Queen Elisabeth of Belgium (1956) and the Tchaikovsky Competition in Moscow (1962). He left the USSR and came to live in London in 1963, and became celebrated for his superb performances particularly of Mozart, Beethoven, Schumann, Chopin and of Russian composers. He now lives in Iceland, his wife's homeland. In recent years he has appeared as a conductor, showing a special interest in the orchestral music of Mozart, Brahms, Tchaikovsky, Sibelius and Rachmaninov. His records, as a conductor, have been of Prokofiev's Symphony No. 1 and symphonic tableau *Autumn* (with the London Symphony Orchestra for Decca), the Tchaikovsky Violin Concerto and *Valse-Scherzo* (with Belkin and the New Philharmonia Orchestra for Decca), and Villa-Lobos' *Bachianas brasileiras No. 3* and *Mome precoce* (with Ortiz and the New Philharmonia Orchestra for EMI).

Atherton, David (b. 1944). Born in Blackpool, Atherton grew up in a musical family, learned the piano, recorder and clarinet as a child, and played in the National Youth Orchestra during his school holidays. He graduated with a BA in music at Cambridge, where he came under the influence of Willcocks and Leppard, and organised concerts including Berlioz's *Béatrice et Bénédict*. Lord Harewood, who heard the performance, drew him to the attention of Solti, then the musical director of the Royal Opera House, Covent Garden, who in 1967 invited Atherton to join the staff at Covent Garden. He was promoted to conductor there in the next year, and was the youngest conductor in the House's history. In 1967 he also founded the London Sinfonietta and as its musical director (until 1973) gave the first performances of many important works of contemporary British composers. He has since conducted the major orchestras in Britain and has appeared in North America, Israel and the Far East. At Covent Garden he has led a number of repertory operas, as well as Tippett's *King Priam*, has conducted with the Welsh National Opera, and in 1968 became the youngest conductor in the history of the Henry Wood Promenade Concerts.

Atherton's most important achievement as a recording artist so far has been a five-disc set of the entire music for chamber ensembles of Schoenberg, which was issued by Decca in the year of the composer's centenary. The orchestra was the London Sinfonietta; with them he also recorded, on three LP discs, Weill's *Kleine Dreigroschenmusik*, Violin Concerto (with Liddell), *Berliner Requiem*, *Happy End*, *Mahagonny Singspiel* and *Pantomime* (for DGG). He also recorded music by Welsh composers: Walters' *Divertimento*, Mathias' *Divertimento* and *Prelude, Aria and Finale*, and Williams' *Sea Sketches* (with the English Chamber Orchestra for Decca), Milner's *Roman Spring* and *Salutatio Angelica* (with the London Sinfonietta for Decca), Hoddinott's Harp Concerto (with Ellis), Clarinet Concerto (with de Peyer) and Mathias' Piano Concerto No. 3 (with Katin, and the London Symphony Orchestra for Decca), Mathias' *Dance Overture*, *Invocation and Dance*, Harp Concerto (with Ellis) and *Ave Rex* (with the London

Symphony Orchestra *et al.* for Decca), and Hoddinott's *Music for Orchestra – The Sun, the Great Luminary of the Universe*, Sinfonietta No. 3 and Symphony No. 3 (with the London Symphony Orchestra for Decca), and *Night Music*, Sinfonietta No. 1, Concertino, and *Dives and Lazarus* (with the New Philharmonia Orchestra *et al.* for Argo). His other recordings have been Bennett's Guitar Concerto (with Bream and the Melos Ensemble for RCA), Ligeti's *Melodien*, Double Concerto and Chamber Concerto (with Nicolet, Holliger and the London Sinfonietta for Decca), Birtwistle's *Verses for Ensembles*, *Fields of Sorrow* and *Nenia – The Death of Orpheus* (with the London Sinfonietta for Decca), Tippett's *Songs for Dov* (with Tear and the London Sinfonietta for Argo), Hamilton's *Voyage* and *Epitaph for This World and Time*, and Dick's *Symphony for Strings* (with the London Sinfonietta for Composers Recordings), and Tavener's *Celtic Requiem*, *Copias* and *The Whale* (with the London Sinfonietta *et al.* for Apple); the last-named is a dramatic cantata which made a considerable impact when it was premièred at the London Sinfonietta's first concert in 1968, and was recorded in 1970.

Atterberg, Kurt (1887–1974). The Swedish composer Atterberg was born in Göteborg, was self-taught, conducted at the Dramatic Theatre at Stockholm (1915–21), was music critic with the *Stockholm-Tidningen* (1919–57) and secretary of the Royal Swedish Academy of Music (1940–53). He conducted orchestras in Sweden and many European countries, did much work to make the music of his native Sweden widely known, and composed, *inter alia*, nine symphonies, five operas and five concertos.

Atterberg recorded his *Suite pastorale* and *Ballade and Passacaglia* on 78 r.p.m. discs for HMV, his orchestral score *The Foolish Virgins* for Telefunken and his Symphony No. 6 for Polydor. The Symphony No. 6 brought him some international notoriety; it was awarded by a jury of composers the first prize in a competition held by the Columbia Phonograph Company in connection with the Schubert Centenary in 1928. The Philadelphia Orchestra under Stokowski recorded it, and Beecham with the Royal Philharmonic Orchestra (in 1928). The critic Ernest Newman questioned the work's originality, and Atterberg admitted it was a hoax and that he had deliberately imitated the styles of some of the composers on the jury, which included Glazunov, Alfano and Nielsen; he even wrote a pamphlet about the adventure entitled *How I Fooled the World*. He himself recorded the symphony with the Berlin Philharmonic Orchestra. It did not pass into complete oblivion; Toscanini, for one, conducted it with the NBC Symphony Orchestra in 1943. The Columbia Phonograph Company first conceived the competition in order to complete the *Unfinished* Symphony. It aroused such opposition amongst musicians and composers that its terms were altered to offer the prize for the best symphony *per se*. More recently, Discofil (Sweden) issued LPs of Atterberg conducting the Stockholm Radio Symphony Orchestra in his *Suite barocco* and *Suite pastorale*.

Atzmon, Moshe (b. 1931). Born in Hungary where he learned the cello as a child, Atzmon migrated with his family to Palestine in 1944. He studied the piano at Tel-Aviv Conservatory, served for two years in the army where he studied the horn, and became a professional horn player in symphony and opera orchestras in Israel. He studied further at the Tel-Aviv Academy of Music (1958–62), conducted the Tel-Aviv Municipal Orchestra and in 1962 came to London where he was encouraged by Dorati to enter various international conducting competitions. During the next two years he won the Guildhall School Conducting Prize, the Kapsalis Cup, the Leonard Bernstein Prize for Conducting, and second prize in the Dmitri Mitropoulos International Competition for Conductors in New York. Then after taking first prize in the Liverpool International Conductors' Competition, he received engagements with major British orchestras, was appointed chief conductor of the Sydney Symphony Orchestra (1969–71), musical director of the Basel Symphony Orchestra, and chief conductor of the North German Radio Orchestra in Hamburg in succession to Schmidt-Isserstedt (from 1971). He conducted at the Salzburg Festival in 1967, and for the first time conducted opera in Berlin in 1969.

Atzmon's records to date have included Tchaikovsky's Symphony No. 3 (with the Vienna Symphony Orchestra for DGG); all the Mozart overtures (with the Basel Symphony Orchestra for Ariola); the Mendelssohn overtures *The Hebrides*, *Meeresstille und glückliche Fahrt*, *Athalie*, *Die Heimkehr aus der Fremde* and *Ruy Blas*, the two Liszt Piano Concertos (with Ohlsson) and Rachmaninov's Piano Concerto No. 2 and *Rhapsody on a Theme of Paganini* (with Anievas, and the New Philharmonic Orchestra, for EMI); Bach's Violin Concertos Nos 1 and 2 (with Schneiderhan and the Vienna Baroque Orchestra), Beethoven's Piano Concerto No. 1 and *Rondo in B flat* (with Pressler) and two Romances (with Ozim), the Brahms Double Concerto (with

Ozim and Palm) and Serenade No. 1 (with the Vienna State Opera Orchestra, for La Guilde Internationale du Disque); and Butterley's *Explorations* and Douglas's *Three Frescoes* (with the Sydney Symphony Orchestra for Festival).

Auberson, Jean-Marie (b. 1920). Born in Chavornay, Switzerland, Auberson studied at the Lausanne Conservatory and was a string player with the Lausanne Chamber Orchestra (1943–6) and with the Suisse Romande Orchestra (1946–9). He then studied conducting with van Kempen at the Accademia Chigiana at Siena, with von der Nahmer at Vienna and with Wand at Cologne (1950–51), returned to the Lausanne Chamber Orchestra for five years, and since has been a conductor with Radio Beromünster at Zürich, the Suisse Romande Orchestra at Geneva and with the Basel Radio Symphony Orchestra, as well as conductor of symphony concerts, opera and ballet in Switzerland and abroad. His programmes include many works of modern Swiss composers. He has made records for La Guilde Internationale du Disque of Bach's *Magnificat* and Cantata No. 57, and Mozart's Mass K. 427 (with the Vienna State Opera Orchestra *et al.*); Bach's Violin and Oboe Concerto (with Fenyves and Holliger) and oboe concertos by C. P. E. Bach, Marcello and Bellini (with Holliger); Handel's Organ Concertos Op. 4 Nos 1, 2, 4 and 6 (with Rogg, and the Geneva Baroque Orchestra); a disc of arrangements for cello and orchestra including Handel's *Largo*, Gounod's *Ave Maria*, Boccherini's *Minuet* and Saint-Saëns' *Le Cygne* (with Fournier and the Paris Concerts Orchestra); the Grieg Piano Concerto (with Pressler), Bruch's Violin Concerto No. 1 and the Tchaikovsky Violin Concerto (with Varga, and the Vienna Festival Orchestra) and the Chopin *Andante spianato et grande polonaise* (with Pressler and the Vienna State Opera Orchestra). He has also recorded Alessandro's *Theme and Variations* and Vibert's *Chanson de la nuit* (with the Geneva Studio Orchestra for CT), Schibler's Double Flute Concerto (with Buxtorf and Eisenhoffer and the Suisse Romande Orchestra for Da Camera Magna), Staempfli's *Ornamente* (with an ensemble for CT), Vuataz's *Quatre rondeaux de Charles d'Orléans* (with Rogner and the Beromünster Radio Orchestra for CT) and Zbinden's *Jazzific 59–16* (with Zbinden and the Suisse Romande Orchestra for CT).

Aubert, Louis (1877–1968). Born in Paramé, France, Aubert studied at the Paris Conservatoire with Fauré and d'Indy, and later taught there. He composed an opera, ballets, orchestral, instrumental and vocal music, and arranged some pieces of Chopin into a potpourri entitled *La Nuit ensorcelée*, which he recorded on 78 r.p.m. discs before World War II with an anonymous orchestra for Columbia.

Auriacombe, Louis (b. 1917). Born at Pau, a town in the Pyrénées, Auriacombe first attended the local conservatory, then studied the violin at Toulouse Conservatoire where he later took first prize for piano and attended singing classes. In 1940 he sang Rudolfo opposite the Mimi of Ninon Vallin in *La Bohème*, but later that year was taken prisoner of war, and was not released until 1945. Resuming his career, he was a violinist in the Toulouse Symphony Orchestra, gave up singing, and was invited by Markevitch to study conducting at his course at Salzburg. After his debut there as a conductor in 1953 he returned to Toulouse and formed a chamber orchestra from the members of the symphony orchestra. Markevitch again invited him to Salzburg and to Mexico, and he achieved a success touring France in 1956–7 with a company performing Fauré's *Pénélope*. He continued to conduct his orchestra at Toulouse and toured with them in Europe, the USSR and the United States, and appeared at many European festivals.

Auriacombe's recordings with the Toulouse Chamber Orchestra have included some of the *Brandenburg Concertos* and orchestral suites, and a concerto for two pianos of Bach and Stravinsky's *L'Histoire du soldat* (for Vega), concerti grossi, concertos and sonatas by Rameau, Albinoni, Corelli, Couperin, Bach, Handel, Vivaldi and Telemann (for EMI and Musidisc), piano and violin concertos of Haydn (for EMI) *Eine kleine Nachtmusik*, the Two-Piano Concerto K. 365, the Sinfonia Concertante K. 364 and the Flute and Harp Concerto K. 299 of Mozart (for EMI), three of Rossini's string sonatas, Vivaldi's *The Four Seasons* and flute concertos, motets and other concertos, Guézec's *Successif-Simultané* and Roussel's *Pour une fête de printemps*, Piano Concerto (with Zaval) and Cello Concerto (with Tétard, for EMI), and with the Paris Conservatoire Orchestra Satie's *Parade*, *Relâche* and *Gymnopédies* Nos 1 and 3 (for EMI). Some of these performances have been released in the United States on Nonesuch and Seraphim.

Austin, Frederick (1872–1952). Born in London into a musical family, Austin was first an organist, taught at the Liverpool College of Music, and made his debut as a baritone in London in 1902. He sang in oratorio and opera, performed the solo part in the first English performances of Delius' *Sea Drift*, was Gunther in the Richter *The Ring* at Covent Garden, and was a prominent member of the Beecham opera companies; Beecham has described him as 'one of the most versatile and accomplished musicians of the day' (*A Mingled Chime*, London, 1944, p. 42). Austin arranged Gay's *The Beggar's Opera* for its revival at Hammersmith in 1920, also singing and acting the part of Peachum, and in 1924 became the artistic director of the British National Opera Company. His orchestral compositions and incidental music were also performed in their day. HMV recorded him in 1920 and again in 1923 conducting excerpts from his arrangement of *The Beggar's Opera*.

Austin, Richard (b. 1903). Son of Frederick Austin (above), Richard Austin was born at Birkenhead, Lancashire, and studied at the Royal College of Music in London, and in Munich. After appointments with the Bristol Symphony Orchestra, the Carl Rosa Opera Company and with theatres in London, he succeeded Sir Dan Godfrey as musical director of the Bournemouth Orchestra in 1934, remaining until 1940. During World War II he was musical adviser, Northern Command (1941–5), became a professor at the Royal College of Music in 1946 and director of its opera department in 1953. In 1947 he founded the New Era Concert Society, whose programmes included new music and little-known symphonic masterpieces. Austin's recordings have included *The Beggar's Opera*, in his father's arrangement (for Argo), the *Hungarian Dances* of Brahms (with the Sinfonia of London for Liberty), pieces by Balfour Gardiner (with the London Symphony Orchestra for Argo) and some concerto accompaniments.

Autori, Franco. Born in Naples, Autori came to the United States in 1928 and became a US citizen eight years later. He has been musical director of the Buffalo Philharmonic Orchestra (1936–45), associate conductor of the New York Philharmonic Orchestra (1949–59), conductor of the Chautauqua Symphony Orchestra (1944–52), musical director of the Tulsa Philharmonic Orchestra (1961–71), a member of the international jury for the Festival de Musica da Guanabara in Brazil (1968–70), and has conducted at the Chicago Civic Opera and Ravinia Opera Companies. He is married to the Polish pianist Lygia Berezynska. He recorded for the Bartók label the *Dance Suite*, *Rhapsody No. 2* and *Two Portraits* of Bartók, and a transcription by Serly of Mozart's *Fantasia in F minor* K. 608, all with the New Symphony Orchestra of London.

Avison, John (b. 1915). Born in Vancouver, Avison studied at the Toronto Conservatory, the Universities of British Columbia, Washington and Yale and at the Juilliard School. At Yale he was a pupil of Hindemith. He played with orchestras in Vancouver, toured as an accompanist to major soloists, was co-founder of the Vancouver Chamber Orchestra (1938) and was its conductor (1939 and from 1945). After service in the Canadian army in World War II (1939–45), he was associate music director of the Aspen Festival, Colorado (1952–6), the Canadian representative at the Commonwealth Conference of Arts, London (1965), on the faculty at the University of Victoria, BC (since 1967), is a member of the Canada Council Arts Advisory Committee, is conductor of the Vancouver Radio Orchestra, has conducted the major orchestras in Canada and several in the United States, and has written music and conducted for radio and television. He has also made a number of records, including Haydn's Symphony No. 99 (with the Edmonton Symphony Orchestra for CBC), Mozart's Serenade K. 320 and two Marches K. 408, a Purcell suite (arr. Barbirolli), Schubert's Symphony No. 3, Arriaga's *Symphony in D*, Dvořák's *Legends* and *Czech Suite*, Schumann's *Overture, Scherzo and Finale*, a Mendelssohn overture, a suite from *The Three-cornered Hat*, Respighi's *Trittico botticelliano*, the Nielsen Flute Concerto (with Aitkin), Chabrier's *Souvenir de Munich* (arr. Françaix), *Le Tombeau de Couperin*, Milhaud's *Suite française*, Roussel's *Le Festin de l'araignée*, Moeran's *Sinfonietta*, Revueltas' *Rides*, Delius' *Song Before Sunrise*, and pieces by the Canadian composers Willan, Champagne, Turner, Healey, Ridout, Arnold, Felton, Adaskin, Mather, Archer (with the Vancouver Chamber Orchestra for CBC) and Beecroft (with the Toronto Symphony Orchestra for RCA), symphonies by J. C. and C. P. E. Bach, and Turner's *Symphony for Strings* (with the Vancouver Chamber Orchestra for Decca).

Avshalomov, Aaron (1894–1965). Born in Siberia, the composer Avshalomov studied at the Zürich Conservatory and in 1914 went to Shanghai in China. There he made a study of Chinese music and wrote a number of works based on Chinese subjects and using Chinese melodies. Included were the operas *Kuan Yin* and *The Great Wall* and his *Piano Concerto in G major on Chinese Themes and Rhythms*, which Columbia (US) recorded in 1937 with the pianist Gregory Singer and Avshalomov conducting the Shanghai Municipal Orchestra. In 1947 Avshalomov migrated to the United States, settled in New York, and continued composing symphonies and other music.

Avshalomov, Jacob (b. 1919). Son of Aaron Avshalomov, Jacob Avshalomov was born in China, studied music in Peking, and in 1937 came to the United States where he carried on his studies with Toch in Los Angeles and Bernard Rogers in New York. After World War II he taught at Columbia University (1946–56), was appointed conductor of the Portland Junior Symphony Orchestra in 1954, and recorded with them for Composers Recordings his own cantata *How Long, O Lord* and *Phases of the Great Land*, his father's *Peiping Huntings* and *Piano Concerto in G major on Chinese Themes and Rhythms*, Bloch's *Suite symphonique* and *Symphony for Trombone and Orchestra*, and compositions by Bergsma, Diamond, Harris, Lees and Ward.

Azmalparashvili, Shalva (b. 1903). Born in Tiflis (modern Tbilisi), Georgia, Azmalparashvili studied at the conservatory there and was a conductor with the Tbilisi Opera (1938–54). Monarch issued a disc in the United States in which he conducted the Georgian State Symphony Orchestra in Lagidze's *Sachidao*.

B

Babušek, František (1905–54). Born in Bratislava and educated at the Academy of Music there, Babušek played the double-bass and tuba in the Bratislava Radio Orchestra (1929–30) and in the Prague Radio Orchestra (1931–8), and also studied composition with Suk, Novák and Křička and conducting with Dědeček. From 1939 he was conductor of the Bratislava Radio Orchestra, and became its chief conductor (1942–52). He was a popular conductor of the Beethoven symphonies and the romantic repertoire; his own compositions included a piano concerto, fantasy for organ and orchestra and a nonet. He recorded with the Bratislava orchestra some dances by Schneider-Trnavský.

Baci, Ludovic. After studying at the conservatories at Cluj-Napoca and Moscow, where he was a pupil of Anosov, the Romanian conductor Baci became conductor of the Romanian Radio-Television Symphony Orchestra, and there led first performances in Romania of many compositions by Schoenberg, Webern, Stravinsky *et al.* as well as of Romanian composers. He established an orchestra in Bucharest to perform early music and has been a guest conductor in West and East European countries. For Electrecord and with the Romanian Radio-Television Orchestra he has recorded music by the Transylvanian composers Bacfarc, Reilich, Speer, Caianu and Junior, as well as Bentoiu's *The Sacrifice of Iphigenia*, Petra-Basacopol's *Concertino* (with Hamza), Vieru's Flute Concerto (with Pop) and oratorio, *Clepsidra II*, a Mozart aria recital (with Pantea), and pieces by Lazar, Constantinescu, Sartorius and Lerescu.

Baciu, Ion (b. 1931). The Romanian conductor Baciu studied at the Ciprian Porumbescu Conservatory, Bucharest, and first conducted with the Bucharest University Choir. He was appointed conductor of the Ploieşti Philharmonic Orchestra (1955–62), conductor of the Moldova Philharmonic Orchestra at Jassy (1962), undertook post-graduate studies at the Vienna Academy of Music, and toured the United States (1967) and FR Germany with the Moldova orchestra (1971 and 1974). He has been rector and professor of conducting at the George Enesco Conservatory at Jassy (or Iasi) where he founded and conducts the students' symphony orchestra, and also conducts at the Jassy Opera. For Electrecord with the Moldova Philharmonic Orchestra he recorded Constantinescu's *Rhapsody No. 2*, Caudella's Violin Concerto, *Three Symphonic Pieces* and prelude to the opera *Petru Rares*, and pieces by Palade and Bughici.

Bader, Roland (b. 1938). Born in Wangen, south Germany, Bader studied church music in Stuttgart with Nowakowski, David and Grischkat, the piano with Lautner, and conducting with Hörner. He then became a kantor in churches near Stuttgart, in 1965 formed and conducted the Stuttgart Philharmonic Vocal Ensemble, and conducted orchestral concerts with the Stuttgart Philharmonic Orchestra. He was music director at Oberhausen (1970–73) where he conducted concerts and opera, conducted the Bach Choir in Bonn, and taught at the Folkwang Hochschule in Essen. Since 1974 he has been conductor of the St Hedwig's Choir in West Berlin, which he led on a tour of the United States in 1977; in Berlin he conducts his own concerts with the Choir and also prepares them for performances with the Berlin Philharmonic and Berlin Radio Symphony Orchestras. He has also toured in France, Italy, and Switzerland, and has been a guest conductor at Hamburg, Cologne, Coblenz and with the Philharmonia Hungarica.

The St Hedwig's Choir originated at the St Hedwig's Catholic Cathedral in Berlin, but since the cathedral is situated in what was the Soviet sector of the city, the Choir moved to West Berlin after the division of the city. It has not performed as such in East Berlin since 1975; St Hedwig's Cathedral now has another choir participating in its masses and church activities, and the St Hedwig's Choir performs regularly at the St Johannes Basilica in West Berlin, under Bader's direction.

Bader has recorded the Mozart Requiem, the Brahms *Ein deutsches Requiem*, and *Elijah* (with the Stuttgart Philharmonic Orchestra and Choir *et al.* for Vox), Mozart's Divertimento K. 136, *Eine kleine Nachtmusik* and a sinfonia by Michael Haydn (with the Camerata Academica Salzburg for Calig Verlag), masses by Schumann, Weber and Kreutzer, and Michael Haydn's *Tenebrae factae sunt* (with the Stuttgart Philharmonic Orchestra and Choir *et al.* for Schwann), Donizetti's *Messa di Gloria e*

Credo (with the St Hedwig's Choir, the Berlin Radio Symphony Orchestra *et al.* for Schwann), the Mozart Masses K. 49 and K. 65 (with the Berlin Radio Symphony Orchestra *et al.* for Schwann), and some discs of *a capella* music (with the Stuttgart Philharmonic Choir for Schwann).

Badger, Harold (b. 1930). Born in Melbourne, Badger studied in Australia and at the Royal College of Music, London, and was a conducting pupil of Buesst, Austin and Tzipine. He first conducted in York (1950), was on the staff of the Australian Broadcasting Commission, and was appointed director of the Melba Memorial Conservatorium in Melbourne (1963). His compositions include orchestral, chamber and instrumental works, and a ballet, *Melbourne Cup*. He conducted a recording of Le Gallienne's *Voyageur* (with the Australian Ballet Guild Orchestra for W & G).

Badura-Skoda, Paul (b. 1924). The eminent Austrian pianist Badura-Skoda first studied with Edwin Fischer, graduated from the Vienna Academy of Music in 1948, and has since achieved an international reputation as an interpreter, particularly of the Viennese classics. In the early years of LP he recorded many chamber works, concertos and solo recitals for Westminster, and also Mozart's Piano Concertos K. 449 and K. 482, directing the Vienna Konzerthaus Orchestra from the keyboard. In 1973 Supraphon issued several fine discs in which he both played and conducted Mozart's Piano Concertos K. 467, K. 482 and K. 491, and Rondos K. 382 and K. 386, with the Prague Chamber Orchestra.

Bagin, Pavol (b. 1933). Born in Košice, Czechoslovakia, Bagin studied with Suchoň, with Očenáš, Jurovský and Schimpel at the Bratislava Conservatory, and with Rajter at the Faculty of Liberal Arts at Bratislava. He became chief conductor with the Czech Army Artistic Ensemble (1957), with which he toured in Eastern European countries, worked with the Ministry of Culture, and then became director of the Slovak National Theatre at Bratislava. He toured with the Theatre in Yugoslavia (1973), conducted Shchedrin's ballet *Anna Karenina* in East Berlin (1978), and has filled many important posts in the musical life of Czechoslovakia, including chairman of the Slovak Musical Fund, and membership of the Slovak Music Council, the Slovak Union for the Protection of Copyright, the Federal Union of Czechoslovak Composers and of the editorial committee of the magazine *Musical Life*. He has recorded more than 200 Slovak folk songs in various arrangements, and Cikker's *She Dug a Well* (for Opus).

Bahner, Gert (b. 1930). Born in Neuwiese, Germany, Bahner studied at the Hochschule für Musik at Leipzig, was a repetiteur at the Berlin Komische Oper (1954–8), and was conductor at Potsdam (1958–62), general music director at Karl-Marx-Stadt (1962–5), conductor at the Berlin Komische Oper (1965–73) and then at the Leipzig Opera where he first led performances of *The Ring*. He has also been a guest conductor in the USSR, Czechoslovakia, Yugoslavia, Austria, and the Netherlands. He has recorded Manfred Schubert's Clarinet Concerto (with Michallik and the Leipzig Radio Symphony Orchestra), Matthus' Violin Concerto (with Scherzer) and *Der letzte Schuss* (excerpts) and Cilenšek's Piano Concerto (with Zechlin, and the Berlin Radio Symphony Orchestra), all for Eterna.

Bailly, Louis (b. 1882). Born in Valenciennes, Bailly studied at the Paris Conservatoire, was violist in the Flonzaley Quartet (1917–24) and in the Capet, Geloso, Elman and Curtis Quartets, was head of the viola and chamber music departments of the Curtis Institute of Music at Philadelphia, and appeared as a soloist in recitals and with major orchestras in the United States. For Victor he recorded, on 78 r.p.m. discs, with the Curtis Chamber Music Ensemble, Bloch's Concerto Grosso No. 1, Sibelius' *Canzonetta* and Tansman's '*Triptyque*' *for String Orchestra*.

Baines, Francis (b. 1917). Born in Oxford, Baines studied at the Royal College of Music, London, where he became a professor. He has lectured on ancient instruments, and is leader of the Jaye Consort of Viols. His compositions include two symphonies, a violin concerto and chamber music, and he has recorded with the Jaye Consort of Viols for Pye, Argo Vox, EMI and Harmonia Mundi. Among these recordings is a two-disc set for Bach Guild entitled *The Art of Ornamentation and Embellishment in the Renaissance and Baroque*.

Bainton, Edgar (1880–1956). Born in London, Bainton studied at the Royal College of Music under Davies, Stanford and Charles Wood, became conductor of the Newcastle-on-Tyne Philharmonic Orchestra (1900) and director of the Newcastle Conservatory (1912). During World War I he was interned in Germany; after his release he conducted concerts with the Concertgebouw Orchestra at Amsterdam. In 1934 he went to Sydney, Australia, to be director of the State Conservatorium of Music there (1934–48). He was a composer of some distinction of the English school, and his Symphony No. 3 was issued on the Australian Brolga label, conducted by Heinze. As a conductor his only recording was Hutchens' *Phantasy Concerto*, in which he conducted the Sydney Symphony Orchestra with duo-pianists Hutchens and Evans.

Bairstow, Sir Edward (1874–1946). Born in Huddersfield, Bairstow was assistant to Bridge at Westminster Abbey, was organist and choirmaster in London, Wigan, Leeds and at York Minster (1913–46), was awarded a D. Mus. at Durham University (1901) and conducted a number of choral societies, including the Leeds Philharmonic Society and the Bradford Festival Choral Society. He became professor of music at Durham (1929), president of the Royal College of Organists (1929–30), composed anthems and other church music including the *Introit* for the coronation of King George VI (1937), and wrote the textbooks *Counterpoint and Harmony* (1937) and *The Evolution of Musical Form* (1943). In 1926 HMV issued discs of him conducting the Royal Choral Society and the Royal Albert Hall Orchestra in the *Sanctus* and *Gloria* from Bach's *Mass in B minor*.

Bakala, Břetislav (1897–1958). Born at Frystak, Czechoslovakia, Bakala studied under Neumann at the Brno Conservatory and under Janáček at Prague. Except for two years in the United States in 1925–6 when he was accompanist to the cellist Hans Kindler, he worked almost entirely with the Brno Radio Orchestra, and after 1940 with the Brno Philharmonic Orchestra. He was a considerable specialist in the music of Janáček and edited his last opera *From the House of the Dead*, and recorded the work, together with excerpts from *Káta Kabanová*, the overture to *The Makropoulos Case*, *Lachian Dances*, *Taras Bulba*, the *Glagolitic Mass* and the finale to *The Cunning Little Vixen* (with the Brno Radio Orchestra *et al.*), *The Ballad of Blaník Hill* and *The Fiddler's Child* (with the Brno Philharmonic Orchestra) and the *Sinfonietta* (with the Czech Philharmonic Orchestra). His other recordings were of Dvořák's Symphony No. 9 (with the Brno Philharmonic Orchestra), Michna's Mass No. 1 and Slavický's *Moravian Dances* (with the Brno Radio Orchestra); all were recorded for Czech record companies, except the Dvořák symphony, which appeared on the Polish label.

Balaban, Emanuel (1895–1973). Born in New York, Balaban studied at the Institute of Musical Art, New York, and in Europe with Fritz Busch. He accompanied the violinists Zimbalist, Elman and Morini, and appeared as a conductor at the Dresden Opera and with orchestras in Berlin, Leipzig, Dresden, New York and Washington DC. From 1929 to 1944 he was director of the opera department at the Eastman School of Music at Rochester, NY, and in 1947 joined the Juilliard School. He conducted modern opera and stage presentations in New York, and recorded for Columbia the two Menotti operas *The Medium* and *The Telephone*, both of which were issued on 78 r.p.m. discs and LP. He also recorded Mayer's *Essay for Brass and Wind* with the New York Brass and Woodwind Ensemble for Composers Recordings.

Balazs, Frederic (b. 1920). Educated at the Music Academy at his birthplace, Budapest, Balazs won a prize for violin playing in 1936, conducted in Budapest and came to the United States during World War II. After war service he became musical director of the Wichita Falls Symphony Orchestra (1948–52) and of the Tucson Symphony Orchestra (1952–66), where he also organised an American Contemporary Music Center, and directed the summer festival at Woodstock. He was chairman of the Youth Orchestras Project of the National Federation of Music Clubs and regional chairman of the Metropolitan Opera Auditions, was musical director of the Cincinnati Conservatory Philharmonic Orchestra (1966–70) and artist and composer-in-residence at Windham College, Vermont. His compositions include chamber and vocal music, and *Two Dances for Flute and Orchestra*, which he recorded with the Philharmonia Hungarica for Composers Recordings. For the same company he also recorded a piece by Mourant and Tremblay's Symphony with the Hamburg Symphony Orchestra.

Bales, Richard (b. 1915). Born in Alexandria, Virginia, Bales studied at the Eastman School of Music (1932–6), the Juilliard School (1939–41) and under Koussevitzky at Tanglewood (1940). From 1936 to 1939 he was conductor of the Virginia–North Carolina Symphony Orchestra, and in 1943 became the conductor and music director of the National Gallery Orchestra at Washington DC. In addition, he was music director of the National Symphony Orchestra (1947), conductor of the Eastman Chamber Orchestra (1965–7) and a guest conductor with many orchestras in the United States. He has many compositions to his credit, and three of these he recorded with the Cantata Singers and the National Gallery Orchestra for the WCFM label: *The Confederacy*, *The American Revolution*, and *The Union*, each being a choral arrangement of traditional American songs. His other discs for the same label and with the National Gallery Orchestra include Handel's *Dettingen Te Deum* and *Water Music*, some Mozart pieces including the Piano Concerto K. 451 (with Haien) and the Horn Concerto No. 3 (with Mason Jones), a disc of overtures by Handel and another of overtures to early operas of Mozart, the Ives Symphony No. 3, and Hopkinson's *Beneath a Weeping Willow's Shade*.

Balkwill, Bryan (b. 1922). Born in London, Balkwill graduated at the Royal Academy of Music; his first appointment was as repetiteur then assistant conductor of the New London Opera Company (1947–8). He then was associate conductor of the International Ballet Company (1948–9) and musical director and principal conductor of the London Festival Ballet (1950–52). In 1950 he worked with Busch at Glyndebourne, continuing there as an associate conductor to Gui until 1958. He was musical director of the Arts Council's Opera for All (1953–63), first conducted at the Royal Opera House, Covent Garden in 1953, was conductor there from 1959 to 1965, became musical director of the Welsh National Opera (1963–7) and conductor of the Sadler's Wells Opera Company, later called the English National Opera (1957–69), and its musical director from 1966 to 1969. Since 1969 he has toured in Europe and North America, conducting both opera and symphony concerts. In 1960 EMI released a disc of excerpts, in English, of *Madama Butterfly* with Balkwill conducting the Sadler's Wells Opera Company. His only other recording has been an accompaniment with the Suisse Romande Orchestra for a recital by Sir Geraint Evans for Decca.

Balzer, Hugo (b. 1894). Born in Duisburg, Balzer studied at the Duisburg and Cologne Conservatories, at the latter under Steinbach. He conducted at Koblenz and Essen and in 1929 was appointed general music director at Freiburg; in 1934 he moved to Düsseldorf where he conducted opera and concerts and in 1940 was appointed professor at the conservatory there. From 1940 he also conducted at Detmold. In the early years of LP he made many records for the American company Royale, embracing a number of major musical masterworks. Almost all were with the Berlin Symphony Orchestra. Included were some *Brandenburg Concertos* and orchestral suites of Bach, *Ein musikalisches Opfer*, the *Mass in B minor* and the *St Matthew Passion*, Haydn's Symphonies Nos 7 and 101, Mozart's Symphonies Nos 35, 36, 39 and 41, Beethoven's Symphonies Nos 1 and 7, the spurious *Jena Symphony*, Piano Concertos Nos 1 (with Everett) and 2 (with Stein) and the *Missa Solemnis*, Schubert's Symphonies Nos 2 and 6, *Symphonie fantastique*, Mendelssohn's Symphonies Nos 3 and 4, four Weber overtures, Liszt's *Faust Symphony*, *Festklange*, *Mazeppa*, *Tasso*, *Mephisto Waltz* and Piano Concertos Nos 1 and 2 (with Hüttner), the Verdi *Requiem*, Tchaikovsky's Symphonies Nos 3 and 4, *Serenade in C major*, a suite from *The Sleeping Beauty*, Piano Concerto No. 1 (with Hüttner) and the Violin Concerto (with Malachowsky), *Scheherazade*, Brahms' Symphony No. 1, the Dvořák Cello Concerto (with Seidler), the Franck symphony, *From Bohemia's Meadows and Forests*, *In the Steppes of Central Asia*, suites from *The Three-cornered Hat* and *El amor brujo*, and *Nights in the Gardens of Spain* (with Hüttner), *Peer Gynt* Suites Nos 1 and 2, Mahler's Symphony No. 4 (with Campenhausen), Sibelius' Symphony No. 2, *Don Juan*, *El Salón México* and *Gianni Schicchi*. Also, with the Prague Opera Chorus and Orchestra he recorded *Judas Maccabaeus*. Appraisals of these records are difficult to locate in the usual references, as Royale discs were of variable technical quality, and most reviewers overlooked them.

Bamberger, Carl (b. 1902). Born in Vienna, Bamberger studied at the Vienna University and in 1924 received his first conducting appointment at the Danzig Opera. He joined the conducting staff at the Darmstadt Opera where Böhm was musical director, made extensive concert tours in Egypt, North and South America, and from 1931 to 1935 conducted in Russia. He migrated to the United States in 1937 and became resident conductor at the Mannes College in New York. He has been a frequent guest conductor in the US, and has conducted radio concerts in Stuttgart, Vienna and other European cities. He has edited and introduced a useful book, *The Conductor's Art* (McGraw Hill, 1965). Bamberger first appeared as a recording artist on an HMV 78 r.p.m. set of Bach's *Triple Concerto in A minor*. He has recorded an extensive repertoire for La Guilde Internationale du Disque, and many of these performances have been released internationally on a number of labels. The works recorded included Handel's *Water Music*, Mozart's Symphony No. 32, Schumann's Symphony No. 1 and Franck's *Symphonic Variations* (with Entremont, and the Netherlands Philharmonic Orchestra); Tchaikovsky's Piano Concerto No. 1 (with Bianca and the Paris Concerts Orchestra); Schubert's Symphony No. 8 and *Rosamunde* incidental music (with the Pasdeloup Orchestra); *Fidelio*, Schubert's *Mass in A flat*, Liszt's *Les Préludes* and *Hungarian Fantasy* (with Bianca), and Brahms' *Tragic Overture*, *Ein deutsches Requiem* and *Alto Rhapsody* (with Hoffmann and the North German Radio Symphony Orchestra *et al.*); Haydn's Trumpet Concerto (with Bräunig), Beethoven's Symphony No. 2, *Leonore No. 3* overture and Piano Concertos Nos 1 and 2 (with Goldsand), abridged versions of *Die Meistersinger* and *Lohengrin*, the prelude and Liebestod from *Tristan und Isolde*, Forest Murmurs from *Siegfried*, Dawn, the Rhine Journey and Siegfried's Funeral Music from *Götterdämmerung*, the overture, Venusberg Music and the Entry of the Guests from *Tannhäuser*, the prelude and Sailors' Chorus from *Der fliegende Holländer* and the Good Friday Music from *Parsifal*, Brahms' Symphonies Nos 1, 2 and 4, Piano Concerto No. 2 (with Goldsand) and Violin Concerto (with Odnoposoff) and excerpts from *Aida* (with the Frankfurt Opera Orchestra *et al.*); *La Bohème*, and abridged versions of Lehár's *Das Land des Lächelns* and Kálmán's *Gräfin Maritza* (with the Opera Society Orchestra *et al.*). Very few of these discs have been issued commercially in Britain or the US; one was *Fidelio*, which included Julius Patzak in the cast and was released by Nonesuch. It was described by George Movshon, the *High Fidelity* critic, as a 'neat, professional and well-integrated performance'.

Bamboschek, Giuseppe (1890–1969). Bamboschek studied at the conservatory in his native Trieste and made his debut as a conductor at the opera there at the age of eighteen. In 1916 he was appointed conductor at the New York Metropolitan Opera, remaining there until 1929, when he conducted for films and radio and continued as a guest conductor with opera companies in the United States. At the Met. he conducted performances with artists such as Galli-Curci and Chaliapin, and at that time also appeared with major US symphony orchestras. In the early 1940s Victor issued an abridged version, on eight 78 r.p.m. discs, of *Il barbiere di Siviglia*, which Bamboschek conducted with distinction.

Baranovich, Kreshimir (b. 1894). The Croatian composer and conductor Baranovich studied in Vienna and toured as a conductor with Anna Pavlova's ballet company (1927–8), became a professor at the Belgrade Academy of Music (1945), conductor with the Belgrade National Opera (1946–62) and director of the Serbian State Symphony Orchestra (1951–61). He composed symphonic music, operas and ballets, employing Yugoslav folk melodies and rhythms; his ballet *The Gingerbread Heart* was presented with some success at the Edinburgh Festival in 1951, and the music was recorded in 1955 by Decca with the Belgrade Philharmonic Orchestra under Baranovich. Between 1955 and 1957 Decca also issued recordings of four operas by Russian composers, performed by artists, the chorus and orchestra of the Belgrade National Opera with Baranovich conducting: *Boris Godunov*, *Khovanshchina*, *The Snow Maiden* and *The Queen of Spades*. These were warmly welcomed at the time, especially *Khovanshchina* and *The Snow Maiden*, both of which were later re-issued and remained in the British catalogue in 1978.

Barati, George (b. 1913). Born in Györ, Hungary, Barati studied under Weiner and Kodály at the Franz Liszt Conservatory and was first cellist in the Budapest Symphony and Budapest Opera Orchestras (1935–8). He migrated to the United States, studied composition with Sessions at Princeton University (1939–43), was a band-leader in the US army (1943–6), and played in the San Francisco Symphony Orchestra (1946–50) and the California String Quartet (1947–50). He founded and conducted the Princeton Chamber Ensemble (1939–43) and conducted the Barati Chamber Orchestra in San Francisco (1948–52) and the Honolulu Symphony Orchestra (1950–67). Since then he has been conductor of the Santa Cruz County Symphony Orchestra and executive director of the Montalbo Center for the Arts in Saratoga. He has composed orchestral and instrumental music, chamber and choral pieces and an opera based on a Polynesian subject. He has recorded Bach's *St Luke Passion*, Haydn's Masses Nos 4 and 12 and Schubert's Masses Nos 1 and 4 (with the Vienna State Opera Orchestra and Academy Choir, for Lyricord), Saint-Saëns' *Suite algérienne* and Tcherepnin's *Georgiana Suite* (with the Frankenland State Symphony Orchestra for Lyricord), Binkerd's Symphony No. 2 and a symphony by Ulysses Kay (with the Oslo Philharmonic Orchestra for Composers Recordings), Stevens' *Symphonic Dances* (with the London Philharmonic Orchestra for Composers Recordings), Dai Kong Lee's *Polynesian Suite* and Symphony No. 1 (with the

Nuremberg Symphony Orchestra for Composers Recordings) and his own Cello Concerto (with Michelin and the London Philharmonic Orchestra for Composers Recordings).

Barbe, Helmut (b. 1927). Born in Halle, Germany, Barbe studied with Pepping, Schulze and Grote at the Church Music School in Berlin (1946–52) and conducting with Jakobi (1953–4). He was appointed organist and choirmaster at St Nicholas Church at Spandau (1950) and has taught at the Church Music School at Berlin since 1955. He was director of the Berlin Student Kantorei (1965–8) and of the Student Kammerchor (since 1968), and has written a number of choral works, one of which, *Canticum Simeonis*, has been recorded with the South-West German Chamber Orchestra *et al.* under Martin. As a conductor he has recorded Bach's Cantatas Nos 13 and 166 (with the St Nicholas Choir *et al.*, for Johannes Stauda and released in the United States by Vanguard) and a collection of chorales and arias from Bach cantatas (for Cantate).

Barber, Samuel (b. 1910). Born in West Chester, Pennsylvania, Barber studied at the Curtis Institute, with Vengerova for piano and Reiner for conducting. His aunt was the contralto, Louise Homer, and Barber himself sang in a recording of his *Dover Beach* for baritone and string quartet (for RCA). He has achieved eminence as one of the major American composers of his generation, but has enjoyed a limited reputation as a conductor. During a visit to England in 1951 he recorded three of his major compositions for Decca with the New Symphony Orchestra: the *Medea* ballet suite, Symphony No. 2 and the Cello Concerto (with Nelsova). A coupling of the first two of these performances was re-issued by Everest.

Barbier, Guy (b. 1924). Born in Namur, Belgium, Barbier studied at the Royal Music Conservatory, Brussels and under Swarowsky at the Academy of Music in Vienna. He first conducted in 1957, appeared with major orchestras in East and West Europe, Japan, Israel and Canada, was appointed permanent conductor of the Lyon Opera (1967) and the Belgian National Opera (1968), and toured with the Béjart Ballet. He recorded for Classics for Pleasure the overtures to *The Bartered Bride* and *Die Meistersinger*, *Le Carnaval romain* and *Finlandia* (with the London Philharmonic Orchestra) and Rodrigo's *Concierto de Aranjuez* (with Zaradin and the Philomusica Orchestra).

Barbini, Ernesto. Born in Venice, Barbini studied at the conservatory there and at Padua, gave organ and piano recitals and conducted concerts and opera throughout Italy. Just before World War II he migrated to the United States, served in the US army, became a conductor with the Metropolitan Opera, New York (1945–52), conductor and musical adviser to the Canadian Opera Company, director of the opera school at the University of Toronto and of the Collegium Musicum (1953) and music director and conductor of the Manitoba Opera Association (1974). He also regularly conducts in Italy, France and Belgium. For La Guilde Internationale du Disque he conducted a recording of *Aida* (with the Rome Opera Orchestra *et al.*).

Barbirolli, Sir John (1899–1970). Born in London of Italian and French parents, Barbirolli studied at Trinity College of Music (1911–12) and the Royal Academy of Music (1912–17) and began his career at the age of ten, playing the cello with the Queen's Hall Orchestra under Sir Henry Wood. In 1915 he joined the orchestra as a cellist, its youngest player, and at the same time was a member of several string quartets. He made his debut as a conductor in 1925 with his own Barbirolli String Orchestra and in the following year gave the first London performance of Berg's *Chamber Concerto*. He joined the British National Opera Company in 1926 and became an assistant conductor at Covent Garden two years later, conducting mainly Wagner and Italian opera. He was also principal conductor of the Covent Garden touring company until 1933.

Barbirolli's career as an orchestral conductor proper started with his appointment to the BBC Scottish Orchestra at Glasgow in 1933. At this time he also led the Northern Philharmonic Orchestra centred at Leeds, conducted at the Leeds Festival and occasionally appeared with the London Philharmonic, London Symphony and BBC Symphony Orchestras. In 1936 he was a guest conductor with the New York Philharmonic-Symphony Orchestra for six weeks, and his subsequent engagement to succeed Toscanini as the orchestra's principal conductor caused a sensation. His great skill as an accompanist was partly responsible for his appointment; he had conducted the London Philharmonic in concerto recordings with Fritz Kreisler and Jascha Heifetz and the London Symphony with Artur Rubinstein, and these artists had reported about him favourably to the management of the New York orchestra. He was also reported to be Toscanini's choice, but the contrast between him and Toscanini was something of a shock. Many New York critics held that the orchestra deteriorated under Barbirolli's leadership, yet attendances improved during his tenure. His years in New York were marred by the intrigues of conductors, critics and others who created difficulties for him. One of the most damaging remarks was about his ability as an accompanist, which led him later to be adamant in refusing to accompany anyone on record.

He returned to England in 1943, in the middle of the war, answering a call from the Hallé Orchestra in Manchester, which had declined to a mere 23 musicians. Previously under Richter and Harty the orchestra had been one of the finest in England. Barbirolli was permanent conductor of the Hallé Orchestra until 1958 when he stepped down to become principal conductor; his leadership transformed the orchestra so that it could take its place again alongside its rivals in London. In 1946 he refused to accept the appointment as conductor of the BBC Symphony Orchestra, although he would have received twice the salary he was paid with the Hallé. The offer was repeated in 1950, and again refused. In 1951 he was a guest conductor for a season at Covent Garden, and his performances of Italian repertoire, as well as *Tristan und Isolde*, were acclaimed. He succeeded Stokowski as conductor-in-chief of the Houston Symphony Orchestra in 1961, relinquishing the position in 1964 to become conductor emeritus. He appeared at the first post-war Salzburg Festival, at the Edinburgh Festival, and led many successful concerts with overseas orchestras, particularly with the Berlin Philharmonic. He married (by a second marriage) the oboist Evelyn Rothwell in 1939, was knighted in 1949, was appointed laureate conductor for life of the Hallé Orchestra in 1968, and received the Gold Medal of the Royal Philharmonic Society and the Bruckner and Mahler Medals of the Mahler/Bruckner Society of America. He died during a rehearsal of the Philharmonia Orchestra in London in preparation for a tour to Japan.

Barbirolli was an outstanding interpreter of the later classics and romantics, particularly Brahms, Sibelius, Bruckner and Mahler. His interest in Mahler was aroused as late as 1960 by the critic Neville Cardus. British composers enjoyed his warmest advocacy and he was one of the finest performers of Elgar, Delius and Vaughan Williams. Although his later career has marked him as a symphonic conductor almost exclusively, much of his earlier experience was in the opera house; he could claim to have opera in his blood, as both his father and grandfather played in the orchestra at the première of Verdi's *Otello* in 1887. He led the first performances in England of *Turandot* and *Der Rosenkavalier*; his *Madama Butterfly* and *La Bohème* at Covent Garden in 1928 were well regarded. In the early 1950s he occasionally conducted at Covent Garden and in his last years made outstanding recordings of *Madama Butterfly* and *Otello*. His scores were prepared meticulously and he would never consider undertaking a performance or recording unless he was completely ready. In his early years his performances were clean and with marked rhythms, although some critics noted a certain restlessness. Later his very intensity of feeling and his highly personal interpretations caused some to find them lacking in vitality and almost sentimental. His Beethoven, Brahms, Strauss and Mahler became expansive and grand, with an inclination to linger over melody and detail. Good examples of his later style are his recordings of Beethoven's Symphony No. 3, the four Brahms symphonies and *Ein Heldenleben*. In the Elgar symphonies his tempi were markedly slower than those of Elgar and Boult. Small in stature, Barbirolli was amicable towards orchestral players, although he retained their respect and could enforce discipline. While he wore spectacles to read scores, he would not conduct with them, as they hindered his communication with his musicians.

In a recording career that commenced in 1911 and finished in the year of his death in 1970, Barbirolli recorded an enormous range of music, from Purcell to Schoenberg. His earliest discs were for Edison Bell, when he played the cello with his sister at the piano. The next series were made with the Kutcher and Music Society String Quartets for the National Gramophone Society in 1925–6, and with the introduction of electrical recording in 1927 he directed the National Gramophone Society Chamber Orchestra in Corelli's Concerto Grosso Op. 6 No. 8, Haydn's Symphony No. 104, Debussy's *Danse sacrée et danse profane* (with Bartlett, piano), a Purcell Suite for Strings (his own arrangement), the andante from Mozart's Cassation No. 2, Elgar's *Introduction and Allegro*, Delius' *Summer Night on the River* and Warlock's *Serenade for Delius' 60th Birthday*. In the same year he recorded for Electron the overtures to *Der fliegende Holländer* and *Hänsel und Gretel*, the prelude to Act III of *Die Meistersinger*, and some operatic arias. In 1928 he commenced recording for HMV, his first discs being the Haydn Symphony No. 104, *Eine kleine Nachtmusik*, the overture to *Die Entführung aus dem Serail*, the hornpipe from Purcell's *The Married Beau*, Elgar's *Introduc-*

tion and Allegro and Rosse's *The Merchant of Venice* suite (with the John Barbirolli Chamber Orchestra), Casals' *Sardana* and an arrangement of *Possenti numi* from *Die Zauberflöte* (with the London School of Cellos), and Haydn's *Cello Concerto in D* (with Suggia and an orchestra). His subsequent recordings for HMV, until 1938, were Delius' *A Song before Sunrise* and Schubert's *Rosamunde* Ballet No. 2 and *Marche militaire* (with the New Symphony Orchestra), selections from *Carmen* and *Faust*, the overture to *Maritana*, Grieg's Symphonic Dance No. 4, Luigini's *Ballet Russe* and excerpts from Glazunov's *The Seasons* and *Les Ruses d'amour* (with the Royal Opera House, Covent Garden, Orchestra), a selection from *Tannhäuser*, the intermezzo from *Cavalleria rusticana*, the Tchaikovsky Violin Concerto (with Elman), and the Dance of the Hours from *La Gioconda* (with the London Symphony Orchestra), separate movements from harpsichord concertos of Bach and Haydn, Saint-Saëns' *Valse caprice* and Raff's *Fileuse* (with Arnaud, and an orchestra), a suite from *Swan Lake*, Quilter's *Children's Overture* and the overture to *Fra Diavolo* (with the London Philharmonic Orchestra), Järnefelt's *Berceuse* and *Praeludium*, the overture to *The Bohemian Girl*, the Peer Gynt Suite No. 1, d'Erlanger's *Midnight Rose*, the homage march from Grieg's *Sigurd Jorsalfar* and a suite from *Sylvia* (with a symphony orchestra), and accompaniments for the singers Zanelli, Olczewska, Nellie Walker, Dawson, Giannini, Hislop, Widdop, Inghilleri, Gigli, Crooks, Chaliapin, Melchior, Pons, Austral, Schorr, Leider, *et al.*, of which the most famous record was the quintet from Act III of *Die Meistersinger*. In these years he established a reputation as an accompanist, recording, in addition to the concertos mentioned above, Bach's *Concerto for Two Pianos in C* (with Bartlett and Robertson), Violin Concerto No. 2 (with Elman and an orchestra), the Beethoven and Brahms Violin Concertos (with Kreisler and the London Philharmonic Orchestra), Beethoven's Piano Concerto No. 4 (with Backhaus and the London Symphony Orchestra), the Grieg Piano Concerto (with Backhaus and the New Symphony Orchestra), Mozart's Violin Concerto K. 219, the Glazunov Violin Concerto, Vieuxtemps' Violin Concerto No. 4, the Tchaikovsky Violin Concerto and Wieniawski's Violin Concerto No. 2 (with Heifetz and the London Philharmonic Orchestra), Sarasate's *Zigeunerweisen*, and Saint-Saëns' *Havanaise* and *Introduction et rondo capriccioso* (with Heifetz and the London Symphony Orchestra), the Schumann Cello Concerto (with Piatigorsky and the London Philharmonic Orchestra), Mozart's Piano Concertos K. 482 (with Fischer and an orchestra) and K. 488, Chopin's Piano Concerto No. 1 and Tchaikovsky's Piano Concerto No. 1 (with Rubinstein and the London Symphony Orchestra), Mozart's Piano Concerto K. 595 (with Schnabel and the London Symphony Orchestra) and Chopin's Piano Concerto No. 2 (with Cortot and an orchestra).

In his years with the New York Philharmonic-Symphony Orchestra he recorded with them his arrangement of a suite of Purcell's music, the Schumann Violin Concerto (with Menuhin), Schubert's *Five German Dances* D. 90 and Symphony No. 4, Debussy's *Iberia*, Tchaikovsky's *Francesca da Rimini*, Respighi's *Fontane di Roma* and an excerpt from his *Ancient Airs and Dances* Suite No. 3 (for Victor), the Bruch Violin Concerto (with Milstein), the Brahms Symphony No. 2 and *Academic Festival Overture*, the overtures *Le Carnaval romain* and *The Bartered Bride*, *La Valse*, *Capriccio espagnol*, Debussy's *Petite Suite* (arranged by Büsser) and First Clarinet Rhapsody (with Goodman), the Sibelius Symphonies Nos 1 and 2, and the Theme and Variations from Tchaikovsky's Suite No. 3. Back in England, he was soon recording with the Hallé Orchestra for HMV, and the first set to be released was the Bax Symphony No. 3, in 1943; in the next year followed the newly-composed Symphony No. 5 of Vaughan Williams. His other 78 r.p.m. discs with the Hallé Orchestra for HMV were oboe concertos arranged by him from Pergolesi and Corelli (with Evelyn Rothwell), the overture to *Le nozze di Figaro*, Mozart's Oboe Concerto (with Rothwell) and the andante from the Cassation K. 63, Beethoven's Symphony No. 5 and *Egmont* overture, suite from *Die Meistersinger*, the *Rienzi* overture and the preludes to Acts I and III of *Lohengrin*, the overtures to *Euryanthe*, *Der Freischütz*, *Hänsel und Gretel*, *Rosamunde*, *Die schöne Galatea* and *Don Pasquale*, Haydn's Symphony No. 83, *Symphonie fantastique*, Mendelssohn's Symphony No. 4, *The Hebrides* overture and the scherzos from the Octet and *A Midsummer Night's Dream*, Grieg's *Peer Gynt* Suite No. 1 and his orchestration of one of the *Lyric Pieces*, a suite from *Swan Lake*, Fauré's *Shylock* suite, Sibelius' Symphony No. 7, excerpts from *Sylvia*, Turina's *Danzas fantásticas*, Delius's Walk to the Paradise Garden from *A Village Romeo and Juliet*, *Two Aquarelles* and *A Song of Summer*, Elgar's *Enigma Variations*, *Cockaigne*, *Serenade in E minor*, *Elegy*, *Dream Children*, *Bavarian Dance No. 2* and *Introduction and Allegro*, Rubbra's Symphony No. 5

and Rubbra's arrangement of Farnaby's *Improvisation on Virginal Pieces*, Vaughan Williams' overture *The Wasps*, *Fantasia on a Theme of Thomas Tallis* and *Fantasia on Greensleeves*, Michael Heming's *Threnody for a Soldier Killed in Action*, Chabrier's *España*, a suite from *Der Rosenkavalier*, the two *l'Arlésienne* suites, Stravinsky's *Concerto in D*, Lehár's *Gold und Silber* waltz, Ireland's *The Forgotten Rite*, *Mai-Dun* and *These Things Shall Be*, Grainger's *Londonderry Air*, and the Strauss *Radetzky March* and *Rosen aus den Süden*. His other 78s were the overture to *La gazza ladra* and his own arrangement of a Concerto Grosso from music by Corelli (with the Augusteo Symphony Orchestra, Rome, for HMV).

Some of these were later issued on LP; in addition EMI recorded, on LP, a further number of discs with the Hallé Orchestra: Haydn's Symphony No. 96, Schubert's Symphony No. 9, *Capriccio espagnol*, Brahms' Symphony No. 3, symphonic fragments from Strauss's *Die Liebe der Danae*, *Prélude à l'après-midi d'un faune*, *Le Carnaval des animaux* (with Rawicz and Landauer), *The Enchanted Lake*, Sibelius' Symphony No. 2 and *The Swan of Tuonela*, Fauré's *Pelléas et Mélisande* suite, Ibert's *Divertissement*, Villa-Lobos' *Bachianas Brasileiras No. 4*, the preludes to Acts I and III of *La traviata*, Vaughan Williams' *Sinfonia antarctica*, *Five Variants of Dives and Lazarus*, Tuba Concerto (with Catelinet) and Oboe Concerto (with Rothwell), the waltzes from *Der Rosenkavalier*, and the Strausses' *An der schönen blauen Donau*, *Kaiserwalzer*, and *Unter Donner und Blitz*.

Barbirolli then recorded for Pye from 1955 to 1961, with the Hallé Orchestra, and some of these discs were released variously in the US by Mercury and Vanguard. Included were Handel's Organ Concerto Op. 7 No. 1 (with Chadwick), Oboe Concerto No. 1 (with Rothwell) and suites from *Rodrigo* and *Serse*, Oboe Concertos of Albinoni, Marcello, Cimarosa (arranged by Benjamin), Corelli, Pergolesi and Haydn (with Rothwell), his Purcell suite, Mozart's Symphonies Nos 29 and 41, Beethoven's Symphonies Nos 1 and 8, and Piano Concerto No. 5 (with Katz), *Symphonie fantastique* and excerpts from *La Damnation de Faust*, Brahms' Symphony No. 4, *Academic Festival Overture* and Double Concerto (with Campoli and Navarra), a suite from *Die Meistersinger*, the overture to *Der fliegende Holländer*, the prelude and Liebestod from *Tristan und Isolde*, and the prelude to Act I of *Lohengrin*, Dvořák's Symphonies Nos 7, 8 and 9, *Scherzo capriccioso*, the *Legends* Nos 4, 6 and 7, and *Serenade in D minor*, the Grieg *Symphonic Dances*, *Peer Gynt* Suite No. 1 and *Two Elegiac Melodies*, Mahler's Symphony No. 1, Nielsen's Symphony No. 4, Gounod's *Petite symphonie*, Sibelius' Symphonies Nos 1 and 5, *Pohjola's Daughter*, *Valse triste*, and *Pelléas et Mélisande*, *Ma Mère l'Oye*, *La Valse*, *Daphnis et Chloé* Suite No. 2, *La Mer*, Tchaikovsky's Symphonies Nos 4, 5 and 6, *Romeo and Juliet* fantasy-overture and *Marche slave*, Elgar's *Introduction and Allegro*, *Enigma Variations*, Symphony No. 1, *Elegy* and Cello Concerto (with Navarra), Vaughan Williams' Symphony No. 8, *London Symphony* and *Fantasia on Greensleeves*, Bax's *The Garden of Fand*, Butterworth's *A Shropshire Lad*, Delius' *Idyll*, prelude to *Irmelin*, Walk to the Paradise Garden from *A Village Romeo and Juliet*, *Once I pass'd through a Populous City*, *On Hearing the first Cuckoo in Spring*, and the intermezzo from *Fennimore and Gerda*, the overtures *Die Zauberflöte*, *Leonore No. 3*, *Oberon*, *William Tell*, *Semiramide*, *Hebrides*, *La forza del destino*, *The Merry Wives of Windsor*, *Die Fledermaus*, *Der Zigeunerbaron*, *Hänsel und Gretel*, *Morgen, Mittag und Abend in Wien*, *Die schöne Galatea*, *Pique Dame*, *Leichte Cavallerie* and *Banditstreiche*, the ballet music from *William Tell*, intermezzi from *Cavalleria rusticana* and *Manon Lescaut*, Chabrier's *Marche joyeuse*, dances from German's *Nell Gwynn*, Waldteufel's *Skaters' Waltz*, Sousa's *The Stars and Stripes Forever*, the Dance of the Hours from *La Gioconda*, Clarke's *Trumpet Voluntary*, the Andante Cantabile from Tchaikovsky's Quartet No. 1, an excerpt from Massenet's *Scènes alsaciennes*, the Strausses' *Pizzicato Polka*, *Annen Polka*, *Perpetuum mobile*, *An der schönen blauen Donau* and *G'schichten aus dem wiener Wald*, Grainger's *Mock Morris*, *Londonderry Air*, *Molly on the Shore* and *Shepherd's Hey*, and an operatic recital with Lafayette and Lewis.

When he returned to EMI in 1962, Barbirolli re-recorded some of his familiar repertoire, but added many remarkable recordings, especially Mahler's Symphonies Nos 5 and 6 and *Rückert Lieder* (with Baker, and the New Philharmonia Orchestra) and Symphony No. 9 (with the Berlin Philharmonic Orchestra), *Ein Heldenleben* (with the London Symphony Orchestra), the four Brahms symphonies, the *Academic Festival* and *Tragic Overtures* and *Variations on the St Antony Chorale* (with the Vienna Philharmonic Orchestra), Elgar's Symphony No. 2, *Falstaff* and *The Dream of Gerontius*, and the seven Sibelius symphonies (with the Hallé Orchestra), Schoenberg's *Pelléas et Mélisande* (with the New Philharmonia Orchestra), the Verdi

Requiem and *Otello* (with the New Philharmonia Orchestra *et al.*) and *Madama Butterfly* (with the Rome Opera Orchestra *et al.*). His other discs were Purcell's *Dido and Aeneas* (with the English Chamber Orchestra *et al.*), his arrangement of *Sheep May Safely Graze* from Bach's Cantata No. 208, an *Elizabethan Suite* (arranged from pieces by Byrd, Farnaby, Bull and Anon.), cello concertos of Haydn, Monn and Elgar (with du Pré and the London Symphony Orchestra), a Corelli Oboe Concerto (with Rothwell and the New Philharmonia Orchestra), Beethoven's Symphony No. 3 and his own *Elizabethan Suite* (with the BBC Symphony Orchestra), the Grieg *Peer Gynt* incidental music and the *Norwegian Dances* (with the Hallé Orchestra), Brahms' Piano Concertos Nos 1 and 2 (with Barenboim and the London Symphony Orchestra), the prelude to *Die Meistersinger*, Tchaikovsky's *Serenade in C major*, Arensky's *Variations on a Theme of Tchaikovsky*, Bax's *Tintagel*, Delius' *A Song of Summer*, *Walk to the Paradise Garden* and the prelude to *Irmelin* and Ireland's *London Overture* (with the London Symphony Orchestra), *In a Summer Garden*, La Calinda from *Koanga*, the entr'acte and serenade from *Hassan* (with Tear), *Late Swallows*, *Summer Night on the River*, *A Song before Sunrise*, *On Hearing the First Cuckoo in Spring* and *Appalachia* (with the Hallé Orchestra *et al.*), *Finlandia*, *Pohjola's Daughter*, *Karelia*, *Valse triste*, *Pelléas et Mélisande*, *The Swan of Tuonela*, *The Return of Lemminkäinen*, *Rakastava* and the *Romance in C* (with the Hallé Orchestra), Elgar's *Introduction and Allegro*, *Serenade in E minor*, Vaughan Williams' *Fantasia on a Theme of Thomas Tallis* and *Fantasia on Greensleeves* (with the Sinfonia of London), Mahler's *Lieder eines fahrenden Gesellen*, *Kindertotenlieder* and No. 4 of the *Rückert Lieder* (with Baker and the Hallé Orchestra), Berlioz's *Nuits d'été* and Ravel's *Shéhérazade* (with Baker and the New Philharmonia Orchestra), Debussy's *La Mer* and *Nocturnes* (with l'Orchestre de Paris), *Francesca da Rimini*, Strauss' *Metamorphosen*, Elgar's *Froissart*, *Elegy*, *Sospiri* and *Pomp and Circumstance* Marches Nos 2, 3 and 5 (with the New Philharmonia Orchestra), *Sea Pictures* (with Baker and the London Symphony Orchestra), Symphony No. 1, *Enigma Variations*, *Cockaigne* and *Pomp and Circumstance* Marches Nos 1 and 4, and Vaughan Williams' Symphony No. 5 (with the Philharmonia Orchestra), and the Strausses' *Radetzky March*, *Perpetuum mobile*, *An der schönen blauen Donau*, *Champagne Polka*, *Unter Donner und Blitz*, the overture to *Der Zigeunerbaron*, waltzes from *Der Rosenkavalier* and Lehár's *Gold und Silber* waltz (with the Hallé Orchestra).

Barbirolli also recorded Albinoni's Oboe Concertos Op. 7 Nos 3 and 6, the Cimarosa/Benjamin Oboe Concerto and Marcello's Oboe Concerto (with Rothwell and the Pro Arte Orchestra for Pye), Beethoven's Piano Concerto No. 4 and Chopin's Piano Concerto No. 1 (with Josef Hoffman and the New York Philharmonic-Symphony Orchestra for the International Piano Library), Franck's *Symphony in D minor* (with the Czech Philharmonic Orchestra for Supraphon), Mendelssohn's Symphony No. 4 and *Capriccio espagnol* (with the George Enesco State Symphony Orchestra for Electrecord), and Sibelius' Symphony No. 2 (with the Royal Philharmonic Orchestra for Reader's Digest). Some commercial records have also been issued of him rehearsing Delius' *Appalachia*, recalling his memories of Cheltenham, introducing recordings by Yvonne Arnaud, and in conversation with Ronald Kinloch Anderson and Eamonn Andrews.

Mahler's Symphony No. 9 with the Berlin Philharmonic Orchestra was one of the finest recordings ever made of a Mahler symphony when it was released in 1964. Barbirolli had established a special rapport with the orchestra, and it was the orchestra themselves who had requested that they should record the symphony with him after an overwhelming concert performance. He had conducted the Berlin Philharmonic for ten years and regarded it as the world's finest; the orchestra and the Berlin audiences, too, had a high regard for him. Many of his other recordings were extremely fine, and some could be numbered among the greatest: Sibelius' Symphony No. 2, with the Royal Philharmonic Orchestra and re-issued by RCA in 1976 after it first appeared for Reader's Digest, is an excellent example of his warmth and dramatic power; if one had to choose another, perhaps the *Madama Butterfly* would qualify.

Bardgett, Herbert (1894–1962). Born in Glasgow and educated at St Mary's Cathedral there, Bardgett was chorus master of the Nottingham Harmonic Society, choral director of the Leeds Musical Festival (from 1934), chorus master of the Huddersfield Choral Society (from 1936), associate conductor of the Leeds Philharmonic Society (from 1956), conductor of the Bradfield Old Choral Society (from 1958), and conductor of the children's concerts of the Hallé and the Royal Liverpool Philharmonic Orchestras. EMI issued 45 r.p.m. discs of him conducting the Leeds Philharmonic Choir in excerpts from Stainer's *The Crucifixion*.

Barenboim, Daniel (b. 1942). Born in Buenos Aires, son of a professor of music and a music teacher, both of Russian descent, Barenboim learnt the piano from his father and gave his first recital at Buenos Aires at the age of seven. Two years later the family moved to Europe and he gave concerts at Salzburg, playing Bach's *Concerto in D minor* at the Salzburg Festival in 1952, at the age of ten. There he studied chamber music with Mainardi and joined Markevitch's conducting class, applying the knowledge he had gained previously from his father. He also met Furtwängler. The family moved to Vienna and then to Israel in 1952, which was to become their home. He was awarded a scholarship by the American–Israel Cultural Foundation, which took him to Paris to study composition with Nadia Boulanger, and in 1956 he became the youngest person to receive the diploma of the Accademia di Santa Cecilia in Rome. Even at this point his repertoire as a pianist included 15 piano concertos and all the Beethoven sonatas. He was also then speaking five languages.

Although Barenboim wished to conduct from an early age, he became known first as a young but greatly gifted pianist. In 1956 he played a Mozart concerto in London under Krips, and the next year appeared in New York with Stokowski and the Symphony of the Air. While he was receiving a normal schooling in Israel he was a regular soloist with the Israel Philharmonic Orchestra, and toured the United States, South America and Australia. In 1961 he made his first professional appearance as a conductor with the Haifa Symphony Orchestra, and conducted with the Sydney and Melbourne Symphony Orchestras the next year; in 1964 he was a soloist with the English Chamber Orchestra in London and a year later conducted them from the keyboard in a Mozart concerto. He became a regular conductor of this orchestra and ever since has spent two months of each year with them, as well as touring abroad and recording with them. At this time Barenboim was appearing with the Berlin Philharmonic and New York Philharmonic Orchestras as a pianist, and in 1965 toured the USSR. He also performed in that year at the Edinburgh Festival and in 1967 played the entire Beethoven sonatas in a series of recitals in London, Tel-Aviv and Vienna. Later, in 1975, he was to perform and direct the complete Mozart piano concertos in London, New York and Paris with the English Chamber Orchestra and in Tel-Aviv with the Israel Philharmonic Orchestra.

Barenboim's career as a conductor became firmly established in 1968 with his debut in New York with the London Symphony Orchestra, substituting for its regular conductor, Kertész. Orchestras which he has regularly conducted are the Israel Philharmonic, Chicago Symphony, New York Philharmonic, Cleveland, Berlin Philharmonic and the London Philharmonic. He has also appeared at La Scala, Milan, and has directed Mozart operas at successive Edinburgh Festivals. In 1975 he was appointed musical director of the Orchestre de Paris, conducting his first concert with them in April of that year. Simultaneously he has pursued his career as an outstanding piano recitalist and concerto performer, chamber player and accompanist to singers who include Fischer-Dieskau and Janet Baker. In fact he is one of the finest accompanists appearing before the public today. In 1967 he married the British cellist Jacqueline du Pré, and now centres his activities in London where he is closely associated with those other highly accomplished musicians, Vladimir Ashkenazy, Itzhak Perlman and Pinchas Zukerman.

Through playing piano duets and studying the scores with his father, Barenboim became familiar with the symphonic repertoire as a child. Both Fischer and Furtwängler have had a deep influence on him as an interpretative artist: 'Furtwängler astonished me by his all-round vision. He really understood the inner logic of music and through inter-relating themes and subtle changes of tempo he was able to make a movement seem like a single organic growth. I can truly say that there is not a day passes when I don't think "I wonder what Furtwängler would think about this".' He is quick to add that a superficial imitation of Furtwängler's interpretations is pointless, and in any case impossible. He played Furtwängler's piano concerto in Berlin in 1964 on the tenth anniversary of the great conductor's death; his performance with Mehta and the Los Angeles Philharmonic Orchestra has been available on a private label. Fischer gave him the idea of conducting from the keyboard; he told him however that to direct Mozart concertos from the keyboard effectively it was first necessary to become a conductor and learn a thorough understanding of the orchestra. Other musicians who have influenced him are Nadia Boulanger and Barbirolli, who revealed to him the art of accompanying with the orchestra. His symphonic repertoire is broadly catholic, ranging through Bach, Haydn, Mozart, Beethoven, Schubert, Schumann, Brahms, Bruckner, Tchaikovsky and Elgar to the Second Viennese School. He gave the first performance ever of Bruckner's Symphony No. 9 in Paris in 1971 and has recorded several other Bruckner symphonies. He is an enthusiastic advocate of Elgar and has conducted the symphonies with orchestras in the US and Europe who had never performed the music before. In 1974 and 1975 were issued his recordings with the London Philharmonic Orchestra of the two Elgar symphonies, and in addition the Violin Concerto (with Zukerman), *Enigma Variations*, *Falstaff*, *In the South*, *Cockaigne*, *Sea Pictures* (with Minton), *Imperial March*, the *Pomp and Circumstance Marches* and *The Crown of India* suite, and with the English Chamber Orchestra *Chanson de nuit*, *Chanson de matin*, *Elegy*, *Serenade*, *Salut d'amour*, *Romance*, *Rosemary*, *Carissimi* and *Sospiri* (for CBS), and the Cello Concerto (with the London Philharmonic Orchestra and du Pré, for EMI). These were sensitive and imaginative readings.

Philips recorded Barenboim when he was aged 13 in some remarkable LPs of piano pieces by Shostakovich, Pergolesi, Kabalevsky, Mendelssohn, Brahms and J. C. Bach. Discs of the Beethoven *Diabelli Variations* and some sonatas followed, issued by Westminster. Then for EMI he recorded the complete Beethoven sonatas, between 1967 and 1970, at the same time as he was performing the cycle in public. The Mozart piano concertos were also recorded, the final disc appearing in 1975, and for this series he conducted the English Chamber Orchestra from the keyboard. His first orchestral records were also with the English Chamber Orchestra and were of the mature Mozart symphonies, from No. 29 to No. 41. Issued between 1967 and 1970, these performances confirmed him to be an outstanding Mozart interpreter, but some critics expressed reservations about some of the symphonies, particularly the last three. In his other orchestral and choral recordings his unusually subjective temperament leads to intensely romantic readings, immediately reminiscent of Furtwängler; his emphasis on the dramatic aspects of the work, and the choice sometimes of unconventional tempi are also evident.

In the 1970s, Barenboim has made a prodigious number of recordings, for EMI, CBS, DGG, and RCA. Included have been Bach's *Magnificat*, the Bruckner *Te Deum* and Mass No. 3, and the Schumann Cello Concerto and the Saint-Saëns Cello Concerto No. 1 (with du Pré, and the New Philharmonia Orchestra for EMI), the five Beethoven Piano Concertos (with Rubinstein and the London Philharmonic Orchestra for RCA), the Beethoven Romances and the Sibelius Violin Concerto (with Zukerman) and Brahms' *Ein deutsches Requiem* (with the London Philharmonic Orchestra *et al.* for DGG), the Dvořák Violin Concerto and Romance (with Perlman and the London Philharmonic Orchestra for EMI), the Dvořák Cello Concerto (with du Pré and the Chicago Symphony Orchestra for EMI), the Beethoven Violin Concerto (with Zukerman), Schumann's four symphonies, *Manfred* overture and Konzertstück Op. 92, Bruckner's Symphonies Nos 4 and 9, Saint-Saëns' Symphony No. 3, *A Night on the Bare Mountain*, *Capriccio espagnol*, *Russian Easter Festival* overture and the Polovstian Dances from *Prince Igor* (with the Chicago Symphony Orchestra for DGG), the Beethoven Violin Concerto (with Stern) and Tchaikovsky's Symphony No. 4 (with the New York Philharmonic Orchestra for CBS), the Mozart Divertimento K. 205, *Eine kleine Nachtmusik*, Serenade K. 361, Sinfonia Concertante K. 297b, Concertone (with Stern and Zukerman), the Violin Concertos K. 211, K. 218 and K. 219, and Rondo K. 373, Rondo Concertante K. 261a and Adagio K. 261 (with Zukerman), *Requiem*, *Le nozze di Figaro* and *Don Giovanni*, Haydn's Symphonies Nos 44, 49, and 82 to 87, and Sinfonia Concertante, Pleyel's Sinfonia Concertante (with Stern and Zukerman), Bach's *Violin Concertos in E major* and *A minor* (with Zukerman), the Double Violin Concerto (with Perlman and Zukerman), arrangements for violin of the Harpsichord Concerto No. 1 (with Perlman) and No. 5 (with Zukerman) and the Violin and Oboe Concerto (with Perlman and Black), Beethoven's Violin Concerto arranged for piano (with himself the pianist), the Haydn *Cello Concerto in C* and the Boccherini *Cello Concerto in B flat* (with du Pré), the Dvořák and Tchaikovsky String Serenades, Schoenberg's *Verklärte Nacht*, Hindemith's *Trauermusik*, the *Siegfried Idyll*, Bartók's *Divertimento* and *Music for Strings, Percussion and Celesta*, (with the English Chamber Orchestra *et al.* for EMI), Cimarosa's *Il Matrimonio segreto*, Vaughan Williams' *The Lark Ascending* (with Zukerman) and *Fantasia on Greensleeves*, excerpts from Walton's music for *Henry V*, Delius' *On Hearing the First Cuckoo in Spring*, *Summer Night on the River*, *Two Aquarelles* and excerpts from *Fennimore and Gerda* (with the English Chamber Orchestra for DGG), Rodrigo's *Concierto de Aranjuez* and Villa-Lobos' Guitar Concerto (with Williams and the English Chamber Orchestra for CBS), Vaughan Williams' Oboe Concerto (with Black) and Tuba Concerto (with Jacobs, and the Chicago Symphony Orchestra for DGG), Mozart's Flute Concerto K. 313 and Andante K. 315 (with Debost) and Oboe Concerto (with Bourgue), Bizet's

Symphony in C major and suite from *La jolie Fille de Perth* and the Fauré *Requiem* (with the Orchestre de Paris *et al.* for EMI), Berlioz's *Harold in Italy* (with Zukerman), *Te Deum*, excerpts from the *Romeo et Juliette* symphony and the Royal Hunt and Storm from *Les Troyens*, Chausson's *Poème*, Fauré's *Berceuse* and the Saint-Saëns' Violin Concerto No. 3 (with Stern), *España*, *Prélude à l'après-midi d'un faune*, Ibert's *Escales*, and the *Daphnis et Chloé* Suite No. 2 (with the Orchestre de Paris *et al.* for CBS), Franck's *Symphony in D minor*, *Rédemption*, *Le Chasseur maudit* and Guy-Ropartz's arrangement of *Nocturne* (with Ludwig, and the Orchestre de Paris for DGG), and the Mozart Two-Piano Concerto K. 365 and Three-Piano Concerto K. 242 (with Ashkenazy, Fou Ts'ong and himself, and the English Chamber Orchestra for Decca).

With this achievement behind him, Barenboim is still a young man, and some observers believe that he has tried to do too much too quickly, and that he cannot follow the two careers of conductor and pianist at the same time. This he disregards, feeling that the one complements the other. It is tempting, but misleading, to contrast his crowded career with that of Toscanini, who did not conduct a full performance of Beethoven's Symphony No. 9 until he was 33, or Walter who was 40 before he thought himself ready to conduct Mozart's Symphony No. 40. The jet aircraft, the LP record, the number and quality of orchestras and the huge expansion of the audience make these comparisons pointless. Also, the comprehensiveness of his early training, his great gifts and his supreme self-confidence have made it possible for him to do so much in music so well. Gramophone records provide valuable documents of his artistic development as his career progresses.

Barlow, Howard (1892–1972). A native of Plain City, Ohio, Barlow showed musical gifts as a child, and at high school at Denver was taught by W. J. Whiteman, from whom he received his only lesson in directing music. He studied at the University of Colorado, Reid College in Oregon and at Columbia University. After service with the US infantry in France in World War I, he made his debut as a conductor in 1919 at Peterboro, New Hampshire, with the National Federation of Music Clubs, and in 1923 formed and conducted the American National Orchestra in New York. This group was disbanded in 1925, and after directing musical activities at the Neighbourhood Playhouse he was appointed musical director for the Columbia Broadcasting System when it was organised in 1927. Until 1943, when he was engaged as musical director for the Voice of Firestone by the National Broadcasting Company, Barlow conducted the CBS Symphony Orchestra in weekly broadcast concerts. He endeavoured to develop the musical taste of his audience by introducing less well-known music to his programmes, and regularly included the music of American composers. Works were commissioned for the programmes from Copland, Harris, Hanson, Thompson and others. Also, he gave the first performance of Schoenberg's *Pierrot Lunaire* in the US. His concerts for the NBC Firestone programmes, however, tended to revert to familiar music from opera and operetta; Barlow explained that any variation from this pattern brought protests from listeners. He was permanent conductor of the Baltimore Symphony Orchestra (1940–43) and on occasion conducted the New York Philharmonic-Symphony Orchestra (1943–5).

Barlow was a careful, painstaking musician who memorised all his programmes. His performances were competent, but he had the disadvantage of directing orchestras that were only moderately good and which he rarely managed to raise above their normal standard. Nonetheless during the 1930s he made over 200 recordings with the CBS Symphony Orchestra in an enterprising repertoire ranging from symphonies of Haydn to Ravel's *Ma Mère l'Oye*, and including Griffes' *The White Peacock*, Macdowell's *Indian Suite* and Deems Taylor's *Peter Ibbetson* and *Through the Looking Glass*. The major works recorded included Goldmark's *Rustic Wedding symphony*, Liszt's *Orpheus*, Schubert's Symphony No. 2, Mendelssohn's Symphony No. 5, Franck's *Les Éolides* and Haydn's Symphonies Nos 94, 98 and 101. It is possible to dismiss these recordings as stop-gaps in the Columbia catalogue, but it would be fairer to give Barlow his due as a musician who did something to expand musical horizons through the media of both radio and records.

Barnett, John (b. 1917). Born in New York where he attended the Manhattan School of Music (1930–36), Barnett studied conducting with Barzin, Walter, Weingartner, Enesco and Malko. He was conductor of the Stamford City Symphony Orchestra (1939–42), the New York City Symphony Orchestra (1940–42), was a bandmaster in the US army (1942–6), associate music director of the Los Angeles Philharmonic Orchestra, music director of the Hollywood Bowl and of the Pacific Coast Music Festival, conductor of the Phoenix and San Diego

Symphony Orchestras, and under a special grant from the US State Department founder and conductor of the bi-national Japan–America Philharmonic Orchestra, which he took on a concert tour of Japan. He was musical director of the National Orchestral Association (1958–70) and has conducted the Westchester Philharmonic Symphony Orchestra and the Guild Opera Company of Los Angeles. He recorded popular pieces such as The Dance of the Hours from *La Gioconda* and *Marche slave* (with the Hollywood Bowl Orchestra for Capitol), Chopin's Piano Concerto No. 1 (with Lhevinne and the National Orchestral Association Orchestra for Vanguard), Etler's *Concerto for Brass Quintet, Strings and Percussion* and two pieces by Riegger (with the Alumni of the National Orchestral Association and the American Brass Quintet, for Composers Recordings).

Baron, Samuel (b. 1925). A native of New York and a graduate of the Juilliard School, Baron is a distinguished flautist, and professor at the State University of New York. He was director of the New York Woodwind Quintet (1949–69) and is a member of the Bach Aria Group (since 1965). He has conducted recordings of Gabrieli's *Sacrae Symphoniae* (with the New York Brass Ensemble for Period), the Beethoven Septet (with the New York Woodwind Ensemble for Counterpoint), a harpsichord concerto by Rieti (with Marlowe and the Baron Chamber Orchestra for Composers Recordings), Hovhaness' *Sharagan and Fugue*, Jones' *Four Movements* and McGrath's *Six Brevities* (with the New York Brass Quintet for Desto), Franchetti's *Three Italian Masques* and Laderman's *Theme, Variations and Finale* (with the New York Woodwind Quintet and the Saidenberg Chamber Players, for Composers Recordings).

Barshai, Rudolf (b. 1924). Born in Labinskaya, in the Krasnador district of the USSR, Barshai studied with Zeitlin, at the Moscow Conservatory and Academy of Music, and with Musin at the Leningrad Conservatory. He performed as a violist and in chamber groups with Shostakovich, Richter, Oistrakh and Rostropovich. In 1955 he formed the Moscow Chamber Orchestra, which was the first in the USSR, and led its initial concert after six months' training. The orchestra soon became internationally famous for its superb tone, ensemble and style. Barshai orchestrated and arranged baroque and contemporary music for it. With the orchestra he performed and recorded the symphonies of Beethoven (except No. 9), believing that the chamber orchestra of 45 players of today is indistinguishable from that of a full symphony orchestra of the classical and early romantic periods. In fact, he and his orchestra were most at home with the music of Bach, Haydn, Mozart, Beethoven and Schubert. He has conducted other major symphony orchestras in the USSR, and frequently appears in Europe to conduct and record. A Soviet Jew, but claiming no interest in political dissent, Barshai left the USSR in 1977 and emigrated to Israel, where he became the conductor of the Israel Chamber Orchestra. Western orchestras have found him an exhausting and meticulous rehearser.

Many of the first records of the Moscow Chamber Orchestra under Barshai were released on Western labels under their agreements with Melodiya, and included some *Brandenburg Concertos*, and symphonies and concertos of Haydn and Mozart with great Russian instrumentalists such as Gilels, Oistrakh and Kogan as soloists. One fine example is the Mozart Sinfonia Concertante K. 364, when Barshai teamed with Oistrakh. EMI recorded the orchestra together with the Bath Festival Orchestra, under Barshai, during a visit to England in 1963, playing Tippett's *Concerto for Double String Orchestra*; this disc also included Barshai's arrangement of Prokofiev's *Visions fugitives*. Decca and Philips released records of the orchestra; in the mid 1960s EMI issued a coupling of subtle and beautiful readings of Mozart's Symphony No. 40 and Schubert's Symphony No. 5, in addition to Bach's Harpsichord Concertos Nos 1, 4 and 5, Haydn's *Piano Concerto in D* and Mozart's Piano Concerto K. 414 (with Devetzi), Vivaldi's Concerti Op. 3 Nos 10 and 11, Telemann's *Suite in C*, *Concerto in B flat*, and *Three-Oboe Concerto in F minor* and the Bartók *Divertimento*, and in 1971 Shostakovich's Symphony No. 14, shortly after the work's première. Almost all of these discs have now been deleted.

In the USSR, Barshai's recordings with the orchestra have included Bach's *Two-Harpsichord Concerto in C* (with Vedernikov and Richter), the Violin Concertos No. 1 (with D. Oistrakh), No. 2 (with Kogan) and the Double Concerto (with Kogan and E. Gilels, and also with D. and I. Oistrakh and the National Philharmonic Orchestra; these concertos were released in the US by MK and Bruno); *Die Kunst der Fuge*, some concertos of Haydn and Mozart, Mozart's Symphonies Nos 29 to 41 and Serenade K. 250, Vivaldi's *The Four Seasons*, the *Water Music*, some concertos of Telemann, Pergolesi's *Stabat Mater*, Ravel's *Introduction et allegro*, the Beethoven symphonies mentioned above and Piano Concerto No. 2 (with Lill), Britten's *Simple Symphony* and Lokshin's *Shakespeare Sonnets* (with baritone Kratov).

Barth, Fred (b. 1929). Born in Zürich and educated at the conservatory there, Barth has been musical director of the Zürich Kammersprechchor since 1953. In 1959 he founded a series of concerts devoted to contemporary works for chamber orchestra, and has toured in FR Germany, Italy, Holland and Scandinavia. For CT (Switzerland) he recorded Vogel's *Arpiade* (with the Zürich Kammersprechchor *et al.*).

Bartholomée, Pierre (b. 1937). Born in Brussels where he studied at the Conservatoire Royal (1952–7), Bartholomée was later a pupil of Pousseur and Boulez, and founded and directed the ensemble Musiques Nouvelles (1962–77), which was active in performing contemporary music in Belgium and other European countries. He also was co-founder of the Musical Research Centre in Wallonia, lectured at the Conservatoire Royal, has been a music producer for the Belgian Radio, has been a guest conductor with orchestras in Belgium, and was appointed conductor of the Liège Philharmonic Orchestra (1977). His compositions include orchestral, vocal and other pieces for various instrumental groups. He has recorded Franck's *Messe solennelle* (for Musique de Wallonie), and Pousseur's *Les Ephémérides* (with Musiques Nouvelles for BASF).

Bartl, Josef (b. 1903). Born in Brno, Bartl studied with Jirák and Ostrčil at the Prague Conservatory (1922–7), was a repetiteur at the Ostrava Theatre (1931–5), conductor at the South Bohemian Theatre at České Budějovíce (1939–45), director of the Karlovy Vary Symphony Orchestra (1945–7), conductor of the Ustí Opera (1947–52) and at the Košický Theatre (1952–6) and finally at the Prague National Opera. His compositions include a symphony, and he has written a study of the life and works of Smetana. For Supraphon he recorded scenes from Fibich's *The Tempest*.

Bartoletti, Bruno (b. 1926). Born near Florence, and a student of the flute at the conservatory there, Bartoletti became a flautist in the Maggio Musicale Fiorentino. He once acted as a substitute conductor at one of these festivals, achieved an immediate success, and after World War II was a repetiteur at the Teatro Comunale at Florence, working with Rodzinski, Mitropoulos, Serafin and Gui. His debut as an operatic conductor was in 1954 with *Rigoletto*, and two years later he was appointed conductor at the Lyric Opera in Chicago. Continuing his activities in Italy, Europe and in Buenos Aires, he became chief conductor at the Teatro Comunale at Florence (1962), then permanent conductor at the Rome Opera House (1964). In addition to Italian opera his repertoire includes Berg, Prokofiev and Shostakovich. In the 1970s he has recorded *Il barbiere di Siviglia* (with the Bavarian Radio Symphony Orchestra *et al.* for DGG), *Manon Lescaut* (with the New Philharmonia Orchestra *et al.* for EMI), *Un ballo in maschera* (with the Santa Cecilia Orchestra *et al.* for Decca) and Vivaldi's *Gloria* and *Credo* (with the Maggio Musicale Fiorentino *et al.* for DGG). The Rossini opera was re-issued in 1975 by DGG on a cheaper label, and was welcomed for the sparkle and charm of Bartoletti's direction. Earlier he had recorded a disc of operatic arias with di Stefano (and the Maggio Musicale Fiorentino for DGG).

Barzin, Léon (b. 1900). Barzin was born in Brussels and came to the United States as a boy of two, eventually becoming a US citizen in 1924. His father was a member of the orchestra of the New York Metropolitan Opera and his mother a ballerina. He studied the violin with his father and later with Ysaÿe, and joined the New York Philharmonic Orchestra as first viola (1925), playing solo with Mengelberg, Furtwängler and Toscanini. He was appointed assistant conductor of the American Orchestral Society (1929), which became the National Orchestral Association, with Barzin as its artistic director and principal conductor. He was musical director of the Hartford Symphony Orchestra in Connecticut (1939–40), director of a music radio station in New York (from 1944), musical director of the Ballet Society (1947–8), musical director of the New York City Ballet Company (1948), artistic director of the Symphony of the Air (1956) and at the same time continued as musical director of the National Orchestral Association. For Vox he recorded with the New York City Ballet Orchestra Prokofiev's *The Prodigal Son*, Hershey Kay's *Western Symphony*, Bizet's *Roma*, Chabrier's *Bourrée fantasque*, *Marche joyeuse*, *Fête polonaise* and the interlude from *Gwendoline*, and Thomson's *Filling Station*, in addition to Bruch's Violin Concerto No. 1 and the Mendelssohn Violin Concerto (with Milstein and the Philharmonia Orchestra for EMI); he also conducted the orchestra in the recording of Klemsenger's *Tubby the Tuba*.

Basarab, Mircea (b. 1921). Born in Bucharest, Basarab studied at the Bucharest Academy of Music and at the Institute of Economics and Juridical Science, and first conducted with the Romanian Radio-Television Symphony Orchestra (1947). He became permanent conductor of the George Enesco Philharmonic Orchestra in Bucharest (1954) and general music director of the Istanbul State Symphony Orchestra in Turkey (1974), and has toured in the USSR, Europe and the Far East. He impresses audiences with his authority and forceful personality, and occasionally a melancholic streak in his nature emerges, which adds depth to his interpretations. For the Romanian company Electrecord he has recorded Beethoven's Symphonies Nos 4, 5 and 6, Tchaikovsky's Symphonies Nos 4 and 6, Strauss's *Burleske* and Horn Concerto No. 1, the Cello Concerto and Guitar Concerto of Boccherini, two cello concertos of Haydn, Constantinescu's *La Nativité* and his own *Rhapsodie* (with the George Enesco Philharmonic Orchestra *et al.*) and the Tchaikovsky Violin Concerto (with the Romanian Radio-Television Orchestra *et al.*)

Bašić, Mladen. Born in Zagreb where he studied at the conservatory, Bašić later continued his studies at the Paris Conservatoire (1951–2) and after a short time as a concert pianist became conductor and artistic director of the Croatian National Theatre Opera House at Zagreb (1945–59). He was chief conductor at the Mozarteum and at the opera house at Salzburg (1959–68), toured throughout Europe, was principal conductor at the Frankfurt Opera (1969), musical director of the Split Festival and artistic director of the Split Opera (1969–70). Since 1970 he has been conductor of the Zagreb Philharmonic Orchestra, and has a wide repertoire from baroque to *avant-garde* music. He recorded Mozart's Serenades K. 203 and K. 320, and Marches K. 237 and K. 408 (with the Salzburg Mozarteum Orchestra for Oriole), and Lisinski's *Porin* (with the Zagreb Opera Orchestra *et al.* for Jugoton).

Basile, Arturo (1914–68). Born in Canicattini Bagni, Sicily, Basile studied at the Turin Conservatory, and in 1946 was awarded first place in the competition for young conductors at the Accademia di Santa Cecilia in Rome. He was one of the permanent directors of the Italian Radio and Television symphony orchestras (1943–53), was artistic adviser to the Cetra record company (from 1949), and was very active as an operatic conductor both in Italy and abroad. He died in 1968 in a car accident. For Cetra he recorded a number of operas: *Le Villi*, *L'Arlesiana*, *Tosca*, *Andrea Chénier*, *Cavalleria rusticana*, *Bastien und Bastienne*, *La fanciulla del West*, Paisiello's *Semiramide in villa*, Montemezzi's *L'amore dei tre re* and Pizzini's *Al Piemonte*, in addition to Monteverdi's *Il combattimento di Tancredi e Clorinda* and the overture to Paisiello's *La molinara*; these were with the Milan Radio Orchestra or the Turin Symphony Orchestra. His other recordings included *Il trovatore* (with the Rome Opera Orchestra *et al.* for RCA), *Cavalleria rusticana*, *Tosca* and an abridged *Andrea Chénier* (with the Societa Italiana dell'Opera for La Guilde Internationale du Disque), a collection of Verdi arias (with Leontyne Price and the Rome Opera Orchestra for RCA), the *William Tell* ballet music, the Dance of the Hours from *La Gioconda*, and a collection of Verdi opera choruses (with the Teatro Comunale Bologna Chorus and Orchestra for RCA), the *Brandenburg Concerto No. 1* and a suite from Handel's *Water Music* (with the Santa Cecilia Orchestra for Reader's Digest), and *Till Eulenspiegel*, the *Russian Easter Festival* overture, the overture *Le Carnaval romain*, the prelude and Liebestod from *Tristan und Isolde*, a Strauss waltz, and the overtures to *La forza del destino*, *Il barbiere di Siviglia*, *Carmen* and *Die Fledermaus* (with the Teatro Comunale Bologna Orchestra for Reader's Digest).

Bastin, Maurice (b. 1884). Born in Brussels, Bastin studied at the Schola Cantorum, Paris, was a repetiteur and conductor at the Paris Opéra-Comique (1907–20), conductor of the Théâtre Royal de la Monnaie, Brussels (1920–46), musical director of the Marseille Opera (1947–9) and chief conductor at the Théâtre Royal de la Monnaie (from 1949). For Columbia he conducted the Théâtre's orchestra *et al.* in two dances from *La vida breve* and in excerpts from Thomas' *Mignon*.

Bátiz, Enrique (b. 1944). The Mexican conductor Bátiz studied as a pianist at the Juilliard School and as a conductor in Poland. In 1971 he was appointed general music director of the Mexico State Symphony Orchestra which was created by Carlos González, the governor of the State of Mexico, and has its home at Toluca, a small city west of Mexico City. Most of the players, who come from Europe, the United States and Mexico, are under the age of 30. With the orchestra Bátiz toured Guatemala and Venezuela (1974) and the US (1975), and he has been a guest conductor in North America, West and East Europe. His recordings with the orchestra have been of Tchaikovsky's Symphony No. 5, a suite from *Carmen*, the overture to *Dichter und Bauer*, Revueltas' *Sensemayá*, Galindo's *Sones de Mariachi*, a Dvořák *Slavonic Dance* and Bruch's Violin Concerto No. 1 (with Novelo). All have been issued by CBS.

Battisti, Frank (b. 1931). Born in Ithaca, New York, Battisti was educated at Ithaca College, was chairman of the music department of Ithaca Public Schools (1961–7), conductor of the Baldwin-Wallace College Symphonic Wind Ensemble (1967–9), the New England Conservatory Wind Ensemble (1969–74) and the Mass Youth Wind Ensemble (1970–74), and was visiting conductor of the Harvard Concert Band and chairman of the musical education department of the New England Conservatory (1970–74). He has also conducted wind ensembles in the United States and abroad, and founded the National Wind Ensemble Conference and the Mass Youth Wind Ensemble. He recorded Benson's *Star-Edge* (with Sinta, saxophone), and *Helix* (with Phillips, tuba), Huggler's *Celebration* and a piece by Persichetti (with the Ithaca High School Band for Golden Crest), and Hindemith's *Symphony in B flat for Wind Band* and Persichetti's Symphony No. 6 for Wind Band (with the New England Conservatory Wind Ensemble for Golden Crest/New England Conservatory).

Baud-Bovy, Samuel (b. 1906). Born in Geneva, Baud-Bovy studied folk music in Greece about which he later wrote a book, then studied under Nilius and Adler at the Geneva Conservatoire and at the Institut Jacques-Dalcroze, with Dukas in Paris and was a conducting pupil of Weingartner and Scherchen. In 1936 he was awarded a Ph.D at Geneva University, where he lectured in Greek; since 1933 he has been teacher of the orchestral class and from 1957 director of the conducting class. He was president of the Association des Musiciens Suisses (1955–60) and of the International Society for Music Education (1961–3). His recordings have been Binet's *Six Chansons* (with Cuénod and the Lausanne Chamber Orchestra), Gagnebin's *Suite sur les psaumes huguenots* and Jean-Jacques Rousseau's *Salve Regina* (with the Geneva Studio Orchestra *et al.* for CT, Switzerland).

Baudo, Serge (b. 1927). Baudo was born at Marseille; his father was professor of oboe at the Paris Conservatoire and his uncle the cellist Paul Tortelier. He studied at the Paris Conservatoire under Fourestier and won first prizes for percussion, chamber music and conducting, played the timpani with the Lamoureux, Paris Opéra and Paris Conservatoire Orchestras under Walter, Munch, Knappertsbusch *et al.* (1949–57), and in 1950 first conducted in Paris. His initial appointment came with the Radio Orchestra at Nice (1959–62); he conducted regularly at the Aix-en-Provence Festivals (from 1959); at Karajan's invitation took over from him the conducting of Debussy's *Pelléas et Mélisande* at La Scala, Milan, and was appointed by Munch permanent conductor of the Orchestre de Paris (1967). He then became artistic director of the Rhône-Alpes regional orchestra. Like Fournet, he believes in the importance of regional orchestras in French musical life and the need to support the musicians and musical public involved in them. He has appeared at the Paris Opéra-Comique, the Berlin Deutsche Oper, La Scala, the Vienna State Opera and the New York Metropolitan Opera and with major orchestras and festivals in Europe, in addition to visiting Israel, Canada, Japan and other European countries. Among contemporary conductors he has a special regard for Böhm and Karajan. His compositions include symphonic works, theatre and film music. He has a reputation as an interpreter of French music, and has given many first performances of contemporary works by Krapp, Mihalovici, Turner, Constant, Milhaud and Messiaen, whose *Et expecto resurrectionem mortuorum* he premièred at Chartres in 1965.

Baudo has recorded Honegger's five symphonies, best-known orchestral pieces and *Jeanne d'Arc au Bûcher*, the *Prélude à l'après-midi d'un faune*, *Jeux* and *Clarinet Rhapsody* (with Boutard) of Debussy, *La Valse*, *Boléro*, *Daphnis et Chloé* Suite No. 2 and *Alborada del gracioso* (with the Czech Philharmonic Orchestra for Supraphon), Fauré's *Ballade* (with Devtzi) and *Pelléas et Mélisande* and Milhaud's *Suite provençale* (with the Paris Conservatoire Orchestra for Chant du Monde, and the first two issued in the United States by Nonesuch), Fauré's *Dolly*, *Masques et bergamasques*, and *Pelléas et Mélisande*, *Pictures at an Exhibition*, *Ma Mère l'Oye*, Roussel's *Bacchus et Ariane* and *Psalm 80*, Dutilleux's Cello Concerto (with Rostropovich), the five piano concertos of Saint-Saëns and d'Indy's *Symphonie sur un chant montagnard français* (with Ciccolini, and with the Orchestre de Paris for EMI), Poulenc's *Aubade* (with Février and the Lamoureux Orchestra for Chant du Monde), some Mozart dances and the Haydn Trumpet Concerto (with the Paris Collegium Musicum *et al.* for Vogue), the Khachaturian Violin Concerto (with Erlih), Roussel's *Le Festin de l'araignée* and

Tchaikovsky's Suite No. 4, *Marche slave* and *Nutcracker* Suites Nos 1 and 2 (with the Centi Soli for Musidisc), Honegger's *Le Roi David* (with the Paris Opéra Orchestra *et al.*), and Liszt's two Piano Concertos (with Magaloff and the Zürich Radio Orchestra, for La Guilde Internationale du Disque), Kosma's *Baptiste* and *Ballade de celui qui chante dans les supplices* (with the Paris Opéra Orchestra for Vega), a suite from *Carmen* (with the Yomuiri Nippon Symphony Orchestra), Honegger's *Christmas Cantata* (with the Prague Symphony Orchestra *et al.* for Supraphon), and Chaynes' Piano Concerto (with Loriod) and Organ Concerto (with Alain and the ORTF Philharmonic and Chamber Orchestras for Erato, and issued in the United States by Musical Heritage Society).

Bauer, Gerhard Rolf (b. 1932). Born in Munich where he studied at the Hochschule für Musik under Lehmann and Eichhorn, Bauer was a repetiteur and conductor at Meiningen (1955), Rostock (1959) and Gotha (1961), and first conductor of the Dresden Philharmonic Orchestra (1962). He then became music director at the State Theatre at Karl-Marx-Stadt (1965), where he led distinguished performances of *Mathis der Maler*, Dessau's *Puntila*, von Einem's *Besuch der alten Dame*, *Porgy and Bess* and Moltschanov's *The Unknown Soldier*, was artistic director and chief conductor at Gotha (1975), has been a guest conductor in the USSR, Czechoslovakia and Poland, with the Dresden Staatskapelle and Dresden Philharmonic Orchestra, and with other orchestras in DR Germany. He has recorded Mozart's *Litaniae Lauretanae* (with the Dresden Cathedral Choir, Orchestra *et al.*, issued in the United States by Everest), and Rosenfeld's Piano Concerto (with Rösel) and Cello Concerto (with Schwab, and the Dresden Staatskapelle for Eterna).

Bauer, Hans (b. 1939). Born in Vienna where he studied at the Academy of Music under Opnoposoff, Bauer was concertmaster of the Scandinavian Youth Orchestra, the International Mozart Youth Orchestra and the International Orchestra of the Jeunesses Musicales at the Brussels World Fair (1958). He came to North America, studied at the Juilliard School and at Tanglewood under Leinsdorf, was conductor of the Guelph Symphony Orchestra, of the Etobicoke Philharmonic Orchestra and the York Concert Society, all in Canada, and music director at the University of Waterloo in the United States. In Canada he gave the first local performances of Mahler's Symphony No. 6 and Bruckner's Symphony No. 5. He has also been a guest conductor with major orchestras in Britain, the US, FR Germany, Austria and with the Peking Symphony Orchestra. In 1977 EMI issued a disc in which he conducted the New Philharmonia Orchestra in Arriaga's *Symphony in D major* and Franz Schmidt's *Variations on a Hussar's Song*.

Bauer-Theussl, Franz (b. 1928). Born in Zillingdorf, Lower Austria, Bauer-Theussl studied at the Vienna Academy of Music under Krauss and Seidlhofer and won awards in London and Geneva as a pianist. He was with the municipal theatre at Baden, near Vienna (1950–52), made his debut as a conductor at the Salzburg Landestheater (1953), was assistant conductor at the Salzburg Festival (1953–7), resident conductor at the Vienna Volksoper (1957), musical director of the Netherlands Opera, Amsterdam (1960–64) and was appointed general music director at the Vienna Volksoper. He has also conducted opera in France, FR Germany, Monte Carlo, Norway and Sweden. For Bellaphon and Intercord, Bauer-Theussl has recorded discs of excerpts from the operettas *Die lustige Witwe*, *Ein Walzertraum*, *Paganini*, *Die Gräfin Maritza*, *Der Graf von Luxemburg* and *Csardasfürstin* (with the Vienna State Opera Orchestra *et al.*), for Ariola excerpts from *Tosca*, *La Bohème*, *Les Contes d'Hoffmann* and *Il trovatore* (with the Vienna Volksoper Orchestra *et al.*) and for Vox the four Mozart horn concertos (with Mühlbacher and the Vienna Volksoper Orchestra).

Baumgartner, Rudolf (b. 1917). After attending school, the university and the conservatory in his native Zürich, Baumgartner finished his violin studies in Paris and Vienna, where his teachers were Stefi Geyer, Carl Flesch and Wolfgang Schneiderhan. He performed as a soloist and in chamber ensembles in many European countries and in 1956, together with Schneiderhan, founded the Festival Strings Lucerne, which gave its first concert at the International Festival of Music at Lucerne in the same year. He has been the permanent director of the orchestra until now, and with them has toured Europe, North and South America, South Africa, Japan and Israel, as well as participating in all the important European festivals. He has also been director of the Lucerne Conservatory since 1960 and in 1968 became the director of the International Festival at Lucerne. The repertoire of the Festival Strings Lucerne covers the string-orchestra literature from the baroque to the present day; more than 30 contemporary works have been premièred by the ensemble, including compositions by Françaix, Xenakis, *et al.* The orchestra draws its membership from the Lucerne Conservatory, so that it is always being regenerated and has an average age of 25; but being under Baumgartner's permanent direction it retains its style and sound.

The Festival Strings Lucerne under Baumgartner were recorded by DGG, mainly on the Archiv label, from 1959 to the mid 1960s, in music including the Bach *Brandenburg Concertos*, *Ein musikalisches Opfer*, Harpsichord Concertos Nos 1, 2, 4 and 5 (with Kirkpatrick), the Flute, Violin and Harpsichord Concerto (with Nicolet, himself and Kirkpatrick), the Violin Concertos (with Schneiderhan and himself, in the Double Concerto), and Cantatas Nos 56 and 202 (with Seefried), Purcell's *Married Beau* suite, *Pavane* and *Chaconne*, Schütz's *St Matthew Passion*, Telemann's Viola Concerto (with Koch) and *Ouverture Quixote*, Festing's *Concerto in D*, Baston's Concerto No. 2, Roman's Sinfonia No. 20, Tartini's Cello Concerto (with Mainardi), Flute Concerto (with Nicolet) and Concerto Concertante (with Schneiderhan), a flute concerto by Blavet (with Nicolet), Geminiani's Concerto Grosso Op. 3 No. 2, Vivaldi's *The Four Seasons* (with Schneiderhan), Op. 3 No. 11 *et al.*, pieces by Gibbons, Stölzel, Pergolesi and Woodcock, Haydn's *Divertimento in E flat*, Mozart's Divertimentos K. 136, K. 137 and K. 138, *Serenata notturna*, Piano Concertos K. 414 (with Weber), K. 415 (with Haskil) and K. 449 (with Horszowski) and Flute Concertos (with Linde), and, the only modern work, Respighi's *Il tramonto* (with Seefried). These were distinguished performances and were admired for their purity of style; in particular the Brandenburg Concertos were recognised as one of the finest sets ever recorded. Baumgartner and his orchestra left the record scene until recently, when Eurodisc issued records of them performing *L'estro armonico* and a number of concertos of Vivaldi, the four Mozart Horn Concertos (with Bujanovsky) and the two Flute Concertos (with Galway).

Bazelon, Irwin (b. 1922). Born in Chicago, Bazelon graduated from De Paul University and later studied with Milhaud and Bloch, and composed soundtracks for documentary and industrial films and television dramas. He has conducted various symphony orchestras in the United States with his own compositions. Composers Recordings have released records of him conducting his *Chamber Concerto* (with the CRI Chamber Ensemble) and *Propulsions* (with a percussion group). His Symphony No. 5 (*Churchill Downs*) has also been recorded by the Indianapolis Symphony Orchestra under Solomon.

Beaucamp, Albert (1921–67). Born in Rouen, the son of Henri Beaucamp (1885–1937) who was organist at Rouen Cathedral, Beaucamp was, from 1945, director of the Rouen Conservatoire, and also conductor of the Rouen Chamber Orchestra. With this ensemble he recorded for Philips suites from Purcell's *The Virtuous Wife*, *The Old Bachelor*, *Abdelazar* and *The History of Dioclesian*, Telemann's *Don Quichotte*, *L'Impérial*, *La Bouffone* and *L'Espiègle*, Corelli's *Oboe Concerto in F minor* (with André), a dance suite of Corelli, Leclair's Violin Concerto Op. 7 No. 1 and Gaviniès' Concerto Grosso Op. 4 No. 2 (with Claire Bernard), Molter's *Clarinet Concerto in A*, Pokorny's *Clarinet Concerto in B flat* and J. Stamitz's Clarinet Concerto No. 3 (with Lancelot), and Albinoni's *Trumpet Concerto in D minor*, Leopold Mozart's *Trumpet Concerto in D*, Telemann's *Trumpet Concerto in F minor*, Vivaldi's Trumpet Concerto P. 406, and Clarke's *Trumpet Voluntary* (with André).

Beaudet, Jean-Marie (b. 1908). Born in Thetford Mines, Quebec, Beaudet studied at the Séminaire de Quebec and the Université Laval (1924–9) and with Dupré and Nat in Paris (1929–32). He was organist at St Dominique, Quebec (1928–9 and 1932–7), and in 1937 joined Radio Canada where he held a number of positions connected with programming and production. He taught at the Quebec Conservatoire and at the École Vincent d'Indy (1948–52), was executive secretary of the Canadian Music Centre (1955–61) and director of music at the National Arts Centre, Ottawa (from 1967). He has conducted orchestras in Canada, France and Czechoslovakia and regularly conducted a concert series for Canadian Television. The Canadian Broadcasting Corporation issued a disc on which he conducted Champagne's *Symphonie gaspésienne* (with the CBC Montreal Orchestra).

Beaudry, Jacques. Born in Canada, Beaudry studied with van Kempen and with van Otterloo at the Brussels Conservatoire, and was the first North American conductor to tour the USSR (1957), returning there in 1959 and 1962 with the Montreal Symphony Orchestra. He has also conducted in France, Switzerland, Czechoslovakia and Poland, joined the Paris Opéra (1967) and toured the United States with the Stuttgart Ballet Company (1973 and 1975). He has recorded a symphony by Hétu, Joachim's *Concertante* and Papineau-Couture's *Pièce concertante No. 3* (with the CBC String Orchestra, for Canadian Broadcasting Corporation).

Beck, Haydn (b. 1899). Born in Wanganui, New Zealand, Beck gave violin recitals in Australia and New Zealand as a child, studied the violin in England and with Ysaÿe at the Brussels Conservatoire, played in orchestras in London, and in 1920 became leader of the symphony orchestra in Sydney under Verbrugghen. He conducted theatre orchestras, led the orchestra of the Ballet Russe de Monte-Carlo under Dorati during its tour of Australia (1937), appeared as a violin soloist, and was concertmaster of the Melbourne Symphony Orchestra and of the orchestras conducted by Ormandy during his tour of Australia (1944). He was leader of the Adelaide Symphony Orchestra and professor of violin at Adelaide Conservatory and then at the New South Wales Conservatorium in Sydney (1943–53), and at that time formed and conducted the Civic Symphony Orchestra at Marrickville in Sydney. In 1953 he went to London, played with the Philharmonia Orchestra, moved to Portugal to lead the Oporto Symphony Orchestra, and became professor of violin at the conservatory there. A Sydney company, Diaphon, recorded him conducting the Civic Symphony Orchestra in several LPs, which included Handel's Oboe Concerto No. 3 (with Tancibudek), *Eine kleine Nachtmusik*, Tchaikovsky's *Serenade in C major*, Purcell's *Suite for Strings* (arranged by Coates), and Elgar's *Introduction and Allegro*. These were the first LP records made in Australia.

Bedford, David (b. 1937). The English composer Bedford was born in London and studied at the Royal Academy of Music with Berkeley, at Venice with Nono, and gained experience at the electronic studios in Milan. His composition *Tentacles of the Dark Nebula* (1964) was recorded by Decca with him directing the London Sinfonietta and with Pears the soloist. Also on this disc are pieces by Berkeley and Lutosławski, conducted by their respective composers. Bedford's work is a distinguished piece with, according to one critic, an 'almost magical and enchanted atmosphere'.

Bedford, Steuart (b. 1939). A Londoner, Bedford studied at the Royal Academy of Music where he subsequently became a professor, and was an organ scholar at Worcester College, Oxford. He joined the staff of the Glyndebourne Festival Opera Company and was artistic director of the English Opera Group from 1971. He made his debut at the Royal Opera, Covent Garden in 1973, leading the stage première of Britten's television opera *Owen Wingrave*, and returned in 1974 to conduct Britten's *Death in Venice*, which he had previously led at the première at the Aldeburgh Festival. He also conducted the work at the New York Metropolitan Opera and the recorded performance of it for Decca (1974). Bedford has also conducted numerous operas in England, Wales, Denmark and the United States, is a considerable pianist and since 1974 has been artistic director of the Aldeburgh Festival, which was originally founded by Britten. With Colin Graham he formed the English Music Theatre Company, inspired by the ideals of the East German theatrical producer Walter Felsenstein, deriving the company from the English Opera group. His recordings have been *Death in Venice* (mentioned above, with the English Opera Group and the English Chamber Orchestra, for Decca), Holst's *The Wandering Scholar* (with the same forces, for EMI), and the Mozart Clarinet Concerto and Haydn Trumpet Concerto (with Puddy and Howarth, respectively, and the St James Orchestra for Classics for Pleasure). His direction of the Holst opera earned the warmest appreciation of Imogen Holst, the composer's daughter, who commented on Bedford's keen understanding of Holst's music.

Beecham, Sir Thomas (1879–1961). Beecham was born in St Helens in Lancashire, into a wealthy family which had derived its fortune from manufacturing patent medicines, more especially the famous Beecham's Pills. He showed early precocity in music, and after attending his first concert at the age of six, started piano lessons. Although he received no formal training in music, he studied composition thoroughly and mastered several instruments; later in life he was scathing about the value of musical academies and conservatories, but had to suffer the jibes of some of his great contemporaries that he was an amateur. After 18 months at Wadham College, Oxford, he returned to St Helens to join the family business; he formed the St Helens Orchestral Society, an orchestra with some professional players, and gave his first public concert with them in 1899. In that year, his father, Joseph Beecham, became mayor of St Helens, and engaged the Hallé Orchestra under Hans Richter for an inaugural concert at the town hall. Richter was unavailable at the last moment, the young

Thomas Beecham substituted for him, and conducted without score or rehearsal Beethoven's Symphony No. 5, Tchaikovsky's Symphony No. 6, and the overture to *Tannhäuser* and the prelude to *Die Meistersinger*.

Joseph Beecham was a noted patron of music, and eventually was the landlord of the Royal Opera House at Covent Garden. But in 1900 Thomas quarrelled with his father and left home; he travelled in Europe, came to London in 1902 to take a post conducting a touring opera company, collaborated with Charles Kennedy Scott in founding the Oriana Madrigal Choir, and in 1905 conducted his first London concert with an ensemble drawn from the members of the Queen's Hall Orchestra. He established and conducted the New Symphony Orchestra (1906), formed another, the Beecham Symphony Orchestra (1908), and after a reconciliation with his father in 1910 gave the first of his Covent Garden opera seasons with his father's financial backing, inviting Strauss and Walter as guest conductors. He brought Diaghilev's Russian Ballet to London (1911), took his orchestra to Berlin, and during the next years conducted concerts and directed the Beecham Opera Company at Covent Garden and in other London theatres, where he introduced many new and unfamiliar operas. At the end of his life he estimated that he had conducted nearly 90 different operas, covering the Italian, French, German and Russian repertoire, and English operas when he could find them. During World War I he was indefatigable in keeping music alive in Britain, touring with his opera company, and conducting the Hallé and London Symphony Orchestras. Financial difficulties brought a hiatus in 1920; his opera company became the British National Opera Company, and when he conducted again it was in 1923 with the London Symphony Orchestra. He performed in Britain, Europe and the United States, became director of the Leeds Triennial Festival and the Norwich Festival, and in 1929 led the great Delius Festival in London, where he conducted the entire programmes from memory.

Anxious to establish and lead a full-time orchestra in London which would be comparable to the best in Europe and the US, Beecham first negotiated unsuccessfully with the British Broadcasting Corporation and the London Symphony Orchestra; the BBC founded its own BBC Symphony Orchestra in 1930 which, under Boult, became itself a most distinguished ensemble. Beecham recruited many of the best available British instrumentalists and founded the London Philharmonic Orchestra; the leader was Paul Beard, the first oboist Leon Goossens, and the first clarinettist Reginald Kell. The first concert was in the Queen's Hall in October 1933 and the programme was a typical Beecham choice: the overture *Le Carnaval romain*, Mozart's Symphony No. 38, *Brigg Fair* and *Ein Heldenleben*. From then until he left it in 1940 it took its place amongst the finest in Europe; Beecham thought it reached its peak in performance during its German tour in 1937. During those years he also conducted memorable seasons at Covent Garden, invited Reiner, Kleiber, Walter and Furtwängler to share the direction, organised and conducted a Sibelius Festival of six concerts in London (1938), and conducted in Brussels and Paris. He left England at the beginning of World War II, toured Australia, Canada and the US, and finally ended up with the Seattle Symphony Orchestra, which he conducted from 1941 to 1943. When he returned to Britain in 1945, the connection with the London Philharmonic could not be re-established, and so in 1947 he founded his last great orchestra, the Royal Philharmonic, which he directed until his death in 1961. In 1960 he invited Rudolf Kempe to become the orchestra's associate conductor. He led his second Delius Festival in 1946, appeared at the Glyndebourne and Edinburgh Festivals, organised a festival of the music of Strauss (1947), toured extensively, particularly in the US (1951), returned to Covent Garden for memorable performances of *Die Meistersinger*, was made a Companion of Honour (1957), and published an autobiography *A Mingled Chime* (1944) and a biography of Delius (1959).

Wood and Boult would also have to be considered if one were to name the greatest British conductor, but for the international public, Beecham has pride of place. He is indisputably of the first rank of conductors, and with both the London Philharmonic in the 1930s and the Royal Philharmonic later he led orchestras of the greatest eminence. His impact on British musical life was enormous: he founded five orchestras, kept opera alive in England for almost a decade, although he lost a fortune doing it, and was a major influence in the revival of the music of Mozart, of whom he was one of the finest interpreters. He did as much as anyone to establish Sibelius in the repertoire, and through his complete dedication to the task he almost convinced his countrymen that Delius was a great composer. He said that he was first attracted to Delius' music because he was a composer he had never seen or heard before, whose music was not like any other, and nobody seemed to know what to make of it: 'I found it as alluring as a wayward woman and determined to tame it . . . and it wasn't done in a day.' At the same time, he avoided giving first performances of Delius' music: 'I always let somebody else make a damned fool of himself with the music, and then I came along later and showed how it's got to be done.' His Delius performances are legendary; Eric Fenby, Delius' amanuensis and also at one time Beecham's secretary-assistant, regards Beecham's recordings of 1929 as his best, especially *In a Summer Garden*, *On Hearing the First Cuckoo in Spring* and *The Walk to the Paradise Garden*. With Delius he exaggerated the composer's own nuances for greater expression, and took care that the melodic strands passed from voice to voice.

Although Beecham's musicianship was fundamentally intuitive, it was based on careful scholarship and preparation, an extraordinary memory, and a unique ability to inspire his players. When he first conducted *Der Rosenkavalier* in London he led the rehearsals from memory; he usually conducted without a score, but he experienced several disastrous lapses in the concert hall and opera house. During his career he created miracles with many orchestras of the second, or even third rank, inspiring them to play much better than they imagined they could, and so demonstrated Mahler's adage that there are no bad orchestras, only bad conductors. For his own orchestras he recruited the best players, trusted them to play as well as they could, and allowed them freedom in phrasing the solo passages. He fervently believed that music has to be enjoyed, and that most important is the lyrical line: 'The grand tune is the only thing in music that the great public really understands, and flexibility is what makes it alive.' He also said: 'If I cannot sing a work, I cannot conduct it.' (H. Atkins and A. Newman, *Beecham Stories*, London, 1978). Musicological scholarship concerned him not at all: he performed Haydn from corrupt editions, and the researches of Robbins Landon passed him by. In his recording of Handel's *Solomon* he used his own edition, which omitted some numbers, and re-orchestrated and re-arranged the order of the rest. For his third recording of *Messiah* in 1960, he commissioned Eugene Goossens to re-arrange the work for modern symphony orchestra, and then made his own embellishments to Goossens' score, justifying the result by saying that Handel would have scored the work this way if he were alive today. The recording remains one of the most extraordinary aberrations in the history of the gramophone record. He arranged ballet scores from Handel's works, and even assembled a piano concerto from his music.

As a conductor, Beecham had little interest in the scores of Elgar and Mahler, which have explicit directions throughout; these appeared to restrain his scope in interpreting the music. He called Elgar's Symphony No. 1 'the musical equivalent of St Pancras Station', and after conducting the Vaughan Williams *Pastoral Symphony* was heard to say 'A city life for me!'. He gave exemplary performances of Strauss and Wagner, but generally had little sympathy for the great German composers; he once remarked: 'I would give the whole of Bach's *Brandenburg Concertos* for Massenet's *Manon* and would think I had vastly profited by the exchange.' Bruckner was beyond his horizon, and although he is reputed to have been ill-at-ease with Beethoven and only interested in Brahms' Symphony No. 2, the composers he most often performed during his years with the London Philharmonic were Beethoven and Brahms, as well as Mozart, whom he revered most of all. He had no time for most of the music of the 20th century: 'No composer has written as much as a hundred bars of worthwhile music since 1925. *Wozzeck* is ingenious, but uncivilised and uncharming.' Also: 'For me much of Schoenberg is unintelligible, and remains unintelligible, much as I study his scores', and of Stravinsky: 'There is behind his façade of ingenious notes and patterns no continuous personality.'

At rehearsals Beecham talked little, despite all the quips and banter heard in the LP rehearsal record that was issued in the 1950s. Details did not concern him, except maybe in Mozart and Delius, and he was always relaxed, with the score in front of him, as if refreshing his memory. His usual procedure was to run through a complete movement of a work, comment at the end about points of interpretation, then play the piece again. He said to the orchestra: 'Forget about bars. Look at the phrase, please. Remember that bars are only the boxes in which the music is packed.' Sometimes he showed remarkable patience in achieving his objective, and once took a full three-hours' rehearsal session perfecting the first four minutes of the overture to *William Tell*. But like Nikisch and Furtwängler, his concert performances were true improvisations, and what occurred at rehearsal was no guide to the final performance. His scores of Handel, Mozart, Schubert, Rossini, Berlioz and Delius were marked in the greatest detail, and aspiring conductors could well study his recording of *Scheherazade* to learn how carefully he phrased and balanced the music. Between the final rehearsal and the concert he would sometimes re-mark the orchestral parts, and the players would have to be quite sure that they followed his instructions. His scores, incidentally, are being collected at the Central Library at St Helens. Occasionally he would arrive at the concert hall and would assemble the principals and give them final directions about certain points in the score, for them to pass on to their sections. So every concert was a new performance and a separate act of interpretation. He was rarely satisfied with any performance, and set out to make each better than the last one of the work. During the performance itself he always looked directly at the players in solo passages; all the members of his orchestras spontaneously gave of their best. Noticeably, at the beginning of a concert, he bowed first to the orchestra, and then to the audience. His touch with his players is illustrated by Stephen Trier, a bass clarinettist in the Royal Philharmonic. In a performance of *Irmelin* at Oxford one evening Trier missed an important cue. Next evening, as the same passage came around, he was suddenly aware of Beecham making an expansive and exaggerated gesture in his direction as if to say: 'All yours, my boy', accompanied by an enormous wink. During a speech at a luncheon to celebrate his 80th birthday he said: 'I just get the best players and let them play. . . . At rehearsal they play the piece through; any mistakes they know about as well as I do, so we play it through again; then they know it. And *I* know what they are going to do. . . . *They don't know what I am going to do* . . . so that at the performance everyone is on his toes, and we get a fine performance.'

From the earliest days of the gramophone record until the era of stereophonic sound, Beecham was one of the most active and successful contributors to the record catalogues. His first recording was made in 1910, and was an orchestral arrangement of selections from d'Albert's *Tiefland*, and his last *Ein Heldenleben*, made in 1959. With his two great orchestras, the London Philharmonic and the Royal Philharmonic, he was as much concerned with producing recorded performances as concerts. A complete list of his recordings is impossible to include here, but can be found in a double number of *Le Grand Baton*, the quarterly of the American branch of the Sir Thomas Beecham Society, issued in August–November 1969 and compiled by Ward Botsford. His Handel recordings have been referred to; he made three *Messiahs* – in 1928, 1950 and 1960, the first of which was a revelation because of its faster tempi and its contrast with the prevailing tradition. His Handel arrangements included his first recording with the London Philharmonic: *The Origin of Design*. Others were *The Gods Go a'Begging*, *The Faithful Shepherd* and *Love in Bath. The Faithful Shepherd*, recorded twice, with the London Philharmonic and the Royal Philharmonic, was, at its first appearance, one of the most beautiful and evocative recordings he ever made; perhaps a little of the magic had disappeared in the LP version, but its recent re-issue in the US is a wonderful reminder of his art. *Love in Bath* was an arrangement of arias, choruses and dances from various Handel operas and originated as a ballet called *The Great Elopement*, of which the subject was the playwright Sheridan's romance with Elizabeth Linley. It is a rousing performance, but the music is probably more Beecham than Handel.

His recordings of Mozart and Haydn symphonies were possibly Beecham's finest. The Mozart symphonies with the London Philharmonic were re-issued on LP transfers in 1973, but he had repeated nearly all of them on LP with the Royal Philharmonic. Yet, as with *The Faithful Shepherd*, whether they are equal to the earlier performances is debatable. Many detect an excessive degree of expression in the later performances, and miss the poise and balance evident in the earlier ones. In 1958 EMI issued the complete *London* symphonies of Haydn (Nos 93 to 104), and these were re-issued in 1973. Previously, with the London Philharmonic, he had recorded Symphonies Nos 93, 97, 99 and 104, and with the Royal Philharmonic No. 40; No. 104 in particular was a performance of profound penetration. Although his Haydn has been criticised by scholars because of the unauthentic editions and inappropriate style, few lovers of the composer would be without them. He also recorded on LP *The Seasons* in an English-language version. The only Mozart operas recorded were *Die Zauberflöte* and *Die Entführung aus dem Serail*; the former, performed by the Berlin Philharmonic and an excellent cast from the Berlin State Opera, was first issued in HMV's Mozart Opera Society in 1937, and has been re-issued several times on LP transfers, lately by Turnabout and World Record Club. Again, it is an indispensable performance. *Die Entführung* came later, with the Royal Philharmonic.

Although Beecham performed the Beethoven and Brahms symphonies in concerts, he attempted no complete recordings of either series. On 78s his Beethoven Symphonies Nos 2 and 4 and Brahms' Symphony No. 2 were highly regarded, as were the LPs of Beethoven's and Brahms' Symphonies No. 2 (for EMI). Columbia (US) issued Beethoven's Symphonies Nos 3, 6 and 8, EMI No. 7 and the

Beecham Society Nos 4 and 9, the latter from the opening concert of the 1956 Edinburgh Festival, as well as Brahms' Symphony No. 3, which he led in New York, and the *Variations on the St Antony Chorale*. The Brahms symphony is an extraordinary performance and, together with Sibelius' Symphony No. 2 with the BBC Symphony Orchestra and recorded at a concert, is an excellent example of the excitement and cumulative tension of a live Beecham performance. His Beethoven is incisive and well shaped, but contrasts with the heavier textures and dramatic weight of most Northern European conductors. It is as if he were looking back to Haydn, rather than forward to Bruckner. Schubert was a Beecham favourite and he recorded all the symphonies except No. 9; the *Unfinished* and the No. 5 were among his best 78s with the London Philharmonic. He was another of the British conductors who performed Berlioz so well, although his recordings of *Symphonie fantastique* and *Harold in Italy* had to wait for LP. The 19th and early 20th century composers of whom he made superb recordings included Mendelssohn, Rossini, Tchaikovsky, Wagner, Strauss, Liszt, Bizet, Franck, Grieg, Borodin, Balakirev, Goldmark, Rimsky-Korsakov, Dvořák and Weber, as well as Sibelius, Debussy, Elgar, and of course, Delius. Only a few examples of recordings which have been scarcely approached by other conductors are *Francesca da Rimini* (with the London Philharmonic), *Don Quixote* and *Ein Heldenleben*, the *Faust Symphony* of Liszt, Balakirev's Symphony No. 1, Goldmark's *Rustic Wedding Symphony*, *Scheherazade*, the *L'Arlésienne* suites and the Franck Symphony. He also had the rare ability of taking a minor piece of music and making it sound a masterpiece; good examples are his recordings of *España*, excerpts from Grétry's *Zémire et Azor* and the *Arrival of the Queen of Sheba* from Handel's *Solomon*.

Even though he devoted so much of his career to opera, there were disappointingly few recordings. On 78s he recorded *Faust* twice (in 1928 and 1948), and Delius' *A Village Romeo and Juliet*, but the second *Faust* and the Delius were weakened by inadequate singing and poor balance. In 1935 he recorded the last act of *La Bohème*; later in 1957 came the mono LP of a well-nigh perfect recording of the opera, in which the artistry of Los Angeles and Björling as well as Beecham's magical conducting of the RCA Victor Orchestra made the set one of the finest operatic performances on disc. Earlier in 1947 he recorded a complete *Elektra*, but because of the unsatisfactory contribution of one of the major singers only the Recognition Scene was released by EMI on four 78s; the whole opera in this performance, together with *Ariadne auf Naxos*, was later issued by the Beecham Society. Two other Beecham opera performances preserved on disc are a superb *Carmen* and *Les Contes d'Hoffmann*. Putting together the *Carmen* took over two years; *Les Contes d'Hoffmann* originated as a film track and is, incidentally, the only record of Beecham issued by Decca. Columbia recorded him with the London Philharmonic and both EMI and CBS recorded him with the Royal Philharmonic; he also made discs for RCA, and with the Columbia Symphony and Philadelphia Orchestras, in one instance, for CBS.

The Sibelius recordings of Beecham deserve special mention. Of course, Sibelius would have made his way if Beecham had not played his music at all, as the composer had other powerful advocates such as Ormandy, Kajanus and Koussevitzky, apart from the British conductors Wood, Cameron, Sargent, Barbirolli and more recently Davis. Beecham recorded five of the seven symphonies and much of the other orchestral music; especially notable was Symphony No. 6, in an early post-war Royal Philharmonic 78 set, and Symphony No. 4 with the London Philharmonic, which has been reissued on an LP transfer by World Record Club; he also made a considerable contribution to the sets of the Sibelius Society, issued in the 1930s by HMV. Re-issues of the Beecham recorded legacy continue, as they should. CBS released in recent years some of the great performances he made for them, including some Berlioz, Delius, Haydn and *The Faithful Shepherd*, and EMI in 1976 issued LP transfers of his pre-war Delius performances, in a five-disc set. The Sir Thomas Beecham Society (address: 1298 Los Olivos Avenue, Los Osos, California 93401) has issued much new material including in addition to the works referred to above, the Berlioz *Grande messe des morts*, *Harold in Italy*, *Don Quixote* and a complete *Les Troyens*, Godard's Violin Concerto No. 2 (with Campoli), Bloch's Violin Concerto (with Szigeti) and the overture and Venusberg Music from *Tannhäuser*.

To the man in the street, Beecham was more widely known for his wit than as a musician; Neville Cardus said that he was the best English wit since Oscar Wilde, and his sallies frequently aroused attention if not indignation. Maybe his public image was a cloak to hide his true self, which, as several close to him have pointed out, was of a rather uncertain and timid personality, with possibly a sense of inferiority stemming from his provincial upbringing. Sometimes his witticisms had a touch of malice which offended some; there were enough to be brought together by Harold Atkins and Archie Newman in their *Beecham Stories* (London, 1978). As an example, he once engaged for a performance of *Messiah* a soprano who was unfamiliar with the work. When he met her later he asked her how she was progressing in learning the part. 'I've been working hard on it', she replied, 'the score goes with me everywhere – to work, to meals, up to bed at night . . .' 'Then', he replied, 'I trust we may look forward to an immaculate conception?'

Beer, Sidney (1899–1971). Born in Liverpool, Beer was educated at Oxford and studied at the Royal College of Music, the Salzburg Mozarteum and at the Vienna Academy of Music. He first conducted at Salzburg in 1932 and later with the Vienna, Czech, Berlin and London Philharmonic Orchestras; he led a performance of *Rigoletto* at Covent Garden Opera House in 1938. He married the Baroness Adeheid von Massberg in 1939 and gave considerable financial support to musical activities in London in the following years. The National Symphony Orchestra was formed by him in 1942, and with them he toured France and Switzerland in 1946. Despite his reputation as a social dandy and musical dilettante, Beer was a sound conductor and made some successful recordings on 78s for Decca with the National Symphony Orchestra during and after World War II. The most notable were the Debussy *Nocturnes* and Ravel's *Ma Mère l'Oye*; others included *Don Juan*, Tchaikovsky's Symphony No. 5, a suite from *Swan Lake*, the overture *Le Carnaval romain*, the Grieg Piano Concerto (with Lympany), Siegfried's Rhine Journey and Funeral Music from *Götterdämmerung*, the *L'Arlésienne* Suite No. 1, *Prélude à l'après-midi d'un faune* and the intermezzo from *Manon Lescaut*.

Beinum, Eduard van (1901–59). The successor to Mengelberg as musical director of the Amsterdam Concertgebouw Orchestra, van Beinum was born at Arnhem into a musical family and became a violist in the Arnhem orchestra at the age of 16. He studied at the Amsterdam Conservatory, was conductor of the Toonkunst Choir at Schiedam (1921–30), of the Toonkunst Choir and Orchestral Society at Zutphen (1923–31), and conductor of the Haarlem Symphony Orchestra (1927–31). He was then appointed assistant conductor in succession to Dopper with the Concertgebouw Orchestra (1931), became principal conductor with Mengelberg (1938), and, after Mengelberg was banished from musical life in Holland in 1945, was chief conductor of the orchestra, and remained so until his death in 1959. He was obliged to retire for a year in 1950 because of bad health, and in 1954 toured with the Concertgebouw Orchestra in the United States. He was also principal conductor of the London Philharmonic Orchestra for the 1948–9 season, and from 1956 spent two months of each year with the Los Angeles Philharmonic Orchestra. He suffered a fatal heart attack while rehearsing Brahms' Symphony No. 1 with the Concertgebouw Orchestra.

Both as a musician and as a personality van Beinum was at the opposite pole to Mengelberg, and Amsterdam audiences found his modest, reserved and undemonstrative style a startling contrast to the flamboyant and autocratic virtuoso conductor who had ruled the orchestra for almost 50 years. Mengelberg imposed his personality on all the music he conducted; van Beinum's creed was always to let the music speak for itself. He believed that the emotional content of the music manifested itself more effectively this way, rather than seeking to exaggerate almost every nuance. This was true, but only up to a point; his Beethoven and Brahms, especially after Mengelberg's, was found to be somewhat sober and understated, and performances of the romantics sometimes unexciting. In all his performances the most striking aspects were the discipline, balance and precision of the orchestra, a sustained tension and an acute alertness to the pulse of the music. He saw himself as on the same level as the players in the orchestra and his relations with them were based on mutual respect. Even when the work was a Beethoven symphony, he always had the score open in front of him.

Van Beinum's repertoire was firmly based on the Viennese classics, Haydn, Mozart, Beethoven and Schubert, all of whom he found closest to him. He also gave memorable performances of Bach, especially the *St Matthew Passion*. He frequently performed Debussy, Ravel and Bruckner, and gave the original versions of some of the symphonies in London. The modern composers he conducted were Bartók, Kodály, Stravinsky, Janáček, Roussel, Szymanowski, Shostakovich and Britten, Russians such as Tchaikovsky and Rimsky-Korsakov, and also Strauss and Wagner, although for the latter two he had no particular commitment. His Berlioz was exceptionally successful. Mahler entered his repertoire only after 1945, as Mahler's music was proscribed in Nazi-occupied Europe. His temperament was at first ill at ease with Mahler's music, but his readings soon showed his growing sympathy for it. He seldom conducted opera; he served contemporary Dutch composers well, but to him the second Viennese school was *terra incognita*.

His early death at the age of 58 limited van Beinum's recording career to a dozen years, but he made many significant records, mostly for Decca and Philips, and for a short while with Polydor and Telefunken. In Britain he first came to the notice of the record collector with some Decca 78 r.p.m. discs with the London Philharmonic Orchestra, the first being a superb *Leonore No. 2* overture. His other discs in this series with the London Philharmonic, many of which were among the first LPs, included the Handel/Harty *Water Music*, Haydn's Symphony No. 100, Mozart's Symphony No. 35, overtures and *Die Geschöpfe des Prometheus* of Beethoven, the Mendelssohn Violin Concerto (with Campoli) and *The Hebrides* overture, Brahms' Symphony No. 3 and *Variations on the St Antony Chorale*, the *L'Arlésienne* suites Nos 1 and 2, Polovtsian Dances from *Prince Igor*, the *Romeo and Juliet* fantasy-overture, Elgar's *Wand of Youth* Suite No. 1, *Elegy* and *Cockaigne* overture, *Lieder eines fahrenden Gesellen* (with Zareska), the Sibelius Violin Concerto (with Damen) and Arnold's overture *Beckus the Dandipratt*.

All his other recordings were with the Amsterdam Concertgebouw Orchestra, and encompassed a wide range of music. The major works were: a suite from *Carmen*, Franck's *Symphonic Variations* (with Anda) and Reger's *Variations on a Theme of Mozart* and *Ballet Suite* (for Polydor), *The Swan of Tuonela* (for Telefunken), the Bach orchestral suites, some symphonies of J. C. Bach, Mozart's Symphony No. 29, Clarinet Concerto (with de Wilde), the Flute and Harp Concerto (with Barwahser and Berghout) and the Serenade K. 320, Beethoven's Symphony No. 2, Piano Concertos Nos 2 and 4 (with Casadesus) and Violin Concerto (with Grumiaux), Schubert's Symphony No. 3, Mendelssohn's Symphony No. 4, the four Brahms symphonies, *Academic Festival Overture*, *Variations on the St Antony Chorale* and Violin Concerto (with Grumiaux), Bruckner's Symphonies Nos 8 and 9, *Scheherazade*, *Nutcracker* suite, *Moldau*, *Boléro*, *La Valse*, *Images* and *Nocturnes* of Debussy, *L'Oiseau de feu* and *Le Chant du rossignol*, the *Háry János* suite, *Das Lied von der Erde* (with Merriman and Haefliger) and *Lieder eines fahrenden Gesellen* (with Merriman), and Badings' Concerto for Two Violins (with Krebbers and Olof, for Philips); and Haydn's Symphonies Nos 94, 96 and 97, Mozart's Symphony No. 33 and Piano Concerto K. 491 (with K. Long), Schubert's Symphonies Nos 4 and 5, and *Rosamunde* overture and excerpts, incidental music from *A Midsummer Night's Dream*, the Handel/Harty *Music for the Royal Fireworks*, Brahms' Symphony No. 1, two overtures, *Variations on the St Antony Chorale* and Piano Concerto No. 1 (with Curzon), *Symphonie fantastique*, a collection of Rossini overtures, Franck's *Psyché*, Bruckner's Symphony No. 7, Lalo's *Symphonie espagnole* (with Campoli), *En Saga* and *Tapiola*, Ravel's *Introduction et allegro* and *Rapsodie espagnole*, *Le Sacre du printemps*, Bartók's *Concerto for Orchestra*, Debussy's *Danse sacrée et danse profane*, Britten's *Young Person's Guide to the Orchestra* and four interludes and passacaglia from *Peter Grimes*, Reger's *Variations on a Theme of Mozart*, Pijper's Symphony No. 3 and Diepenbrock's incidental music to *Marsyas*. Very few of these records have survived, although a number enjoyed a prolonged life in the catalogues on cheaper labels. Many of them were memorable, but especially noteworthy were the Bartók *Concerto for Orchestra*, *Symphonie fantastique*, Brahms' Symphony No. 1, *Le Sacre du printemps*, Mahler's Symphony No. 4 and the three Bruckner symphonies.

Van Beinum also recorded music by Dutch composers for Donemus: H. Andriessen's *Miroir de peine* (with Kolassi), Escher's *Musique pour l'esprit en deuil*, Flothuis' *Symphonic Music* and Lier's *Divertimento facile*.

Beissel, Heribert (b. 1933). Born in Wesel, Germany, Beissel studied at the Hochschule für Musik at Cologne, and was first a repetiteur at the Bonn Opera. He was founder and conductor of the Chur Cölnische Orchestra at Bonn (1959–65), won first prize at a young conductors' competition at Hannover (1962), toured Japan and France (1967), became chief conductor of the Hamburg Symphony Orchestra (1970) and a professor at the Hochschule für Musik at Hamburg (1974), was a guest conductor with the Duisburg Philharmonic Orchestra (1974) and the North German Radio Orchestra at Hamburg (1977), and toured in Spain, Austria and throughout FR Germany. His recordings have included Wagner's *Symphony in C major*, Rubinstein's Symphony No. 6 and ballet music from *The Demon*, Chopin's Piano Concertos Nos 1 and 2, *Krakowiak*, *Andante spianato et Grande Polonaise*, *Grand Fantasy on Polish Airs* and *Variations on Mozart's La ci darem la mano* (with Simon), Hummel's Piano Concerto *Grand Concerto Les Adieux* and Kalkbrenner's Piano Concerto No. 1 (with Kann, and the Hamburg Symphony Orchestra for Vox and Turnabout), and Haydn's Mass No. 9 (with the Rhineland Academy Instrumental Ensemble *et al.* for Intercord).

Bell, John (b. 1926). Born in London, Bell studied at Cambridge, the Guildhall School of Music and Drama, and at the Hochschule für Musik at Munich, and made his debut as a conductor with the Carl Rosa Opera Company in England. His conducting appointments have been with the Carl Rosa Company, the Pfalztheater at Kaiserslautern, and at the city theatres at Münster-Westfalen and Krefeld/Mönchengladbach. He has a wide repertoire of operas of all periods and regularly conducts symphony and youth concerts. He has recorded Wagner's early operas *Die Feen* and *Das Liebesverbot* (with the International Youth Orchestra *et al.* for Colosseum), Siegfried Wagner's symphonic poem *Gluck*, scherzo *Und wenn die Welt voll Teufel wär*, and the prelude to the opera *Die heilige Linde* (with the Berlin Symphony Orchestra for Mixtur), and Respighi's *Suite for Organ and Strings* (with Schwarz and the Berlin Symphony Orchestra for Mixtur).

Bellezza, Vincenzo (1888–1964). A major Italian conductor of opera, Bellezza studied at the Naples Conservatory and made his debut at the San Carlo Opera at Naples in 1908 in *Aida*. After conducting in many Italian opera houses he was principal conductor at the Teatro Colón in Buenos Aires from 1920. He was with the Metropolitan Opera, New York (1926–35), first appeared at Covent Garden in 1926, a year later led the first *Turandot* there, and conducted at Melba's farewell performance of *La Bohème* (1926). He made a deep impression at Covent Garden with his profound knowledge of Italian operas, his devotion to detail at rehearsal and his strange English: he always referred to the brass instruments as the 'Metal Club'. However, his popularity waned and in 1930 he left London, to return again in 1935. At this time he was active principally at the Rome Opera. In 1957 he visited London again to direct an Italian season at the Stoll Theatre. His recordings included an accompaniment for Chaliapin (issued in 1926), some operatic overtures and choruses (with the Covent Garden Orchestra and Chorus), intermezzi from *I gioielli della madonna* (with the London Symphony Orchestra), all on pre-war 78 r.p.m. discs for HMV, *La traviata* (78s, post-war), and *Il tabarro* (mono LP, with the Rome Opera Company for EMI).

Bellugi, Piero (b. 1924). Born in Florence and educated at the conservatory there, the Accademia Chigiana at Siena and the Mozarteum at Salzburg, Bellugi went to the United States and studied conducting under Kubelik and Bernstein. He conducted orchestras at Oakland, California, and Portland, Oregon, from 1956 to 1960, returned to Europe, conducted at La Scala, Milan, has been permanent conductor of the Turin Radio Symphony Orchestra and teaches conducting at the Turin Conservatory. He has recorded Paganini's Violin Concertos Nos 1 and 4 (with Grumiaux and the Monte Carlo National Orchestra for Philips), Bottesini's Grand Duo for Violin and Double Bass (with Ricci and Petrucchi) and Paganini's Violin Concerto No. 4 (with Ricci, and the Royal Philharmonic Orchestra for Unicorn and CBS (US)).

Bělohlávek, Jiří (b. 1946). Born in Prague, Bělohlávek first studied the cello with Jaroš and attended the Conservatory and Academy of Music at Prague (1960–72), where he studied conducting with Liška, Veselka, Brock and Klíma. At that time he was leader and conductor of the Orchestra Puellarum Pragensis, won first prize in a young conductors' competition in Czechoslovakia (1970) and was a finalist in the International Competition Herbert von Karajan in West Berlin (1973). He was appointed assistant conductor of the Czech Philharmonic Orchestra (1970–72), conductor of the Brno State Philharmonic Orchestra (1972–8) and chief conductor of the Prague Symphony Orchestra (from 1977), and has been a guest conductor with major orchestras in his own country, Hungary, DR Germany, Austria, Belgium *et al.* Bělohlávek's recordings include Khachaturian's *Gayaneh* and *Masquerade* (with the Brno State Philharmonic Orchestra for Supraphon), Martinů's *Gilgamesh* (with the FOK Orchestra *et al.* for Supraphon), the two Liszt piano concertos (with Kameníková and the Brno State Philharmonic Orchestra for Supraphon), Kalabis' Symphony No. 3 (with the Czech Radio Symphony Orchestra for Panton), the Sibelius Violin Concerto and Prokofiev's Violin Concerto No. 2 (with Hudeček and the Prague Radio Symphony Orchestra for Panton), the Bartók *Divertimento*, Ravel's *Ma Mère l'Oye* and *Pavane pour une infante défunte*, *Elégies* by Jirko and Boháč, Lucký's *Octet*, Hanuš' *Prague Nocturnes*, Podest's *Partita* and Tausinger's *Sinfonica bohemica* (with the Czech Philharmonic Orchestra for Panton).

Benda, Hans von (1888–1972). Born in Strasbourg and a descendant of the violinist Franz Benda (1709–86), von Benda studied at the

Stern Conservatory and university in Berlin, and with Sandberger in Munich. He was musical director of the Berlin Radio (1926–34), artistic director of the Berlin Philharmonic Orchestra (1935–9), and conductor of the Berlin Chamber Orchestra (from 1932 until the 1950s), touring throughout Europe, Latin and South America, Australia and the Far East with the orchestra. He was active as a conductor in Spain (1948–52) and was director of music for Free Berlin (1954–8). He recorded the *Brandenburg Concertos Nos 2* and *5*, and the Suites Nos 1 and 3, Mozart's Symphony No. 36, Serenade K. 250 and *Les Petits Riens*, Leopold Mozart's *Toy Symphony* and Pergolesi's Concertino No. 2 (with the Berlin Chamber Orchestra for Telefunken); Mozart's Divertimento K. 251 (with the Berlin Chamber Orchestra for Polydor), Frederick the Great's overture *Il re pastore*, the allegro and minuet from Haydn's Symphony No. 28, and the last movement from Symphony No. 73, the third movement from Mozart's Serenade K. 320 and the March K. 249, and selections from Gluck's *Don Juan* (with a chamber orchestra for HMV); Handel's *Concerto in F major* and *Music for the Royal Fireworks*, Mozart's Symphony No. 32, Schubert's Symphony No. 5, Dvořák's *Serenade in E major* and Respighi's *Ancient Airs and Dances* Suite No. 3 (with the Berlin Philharmonic Orchestra for Telefunken), Frederick the Great's *Sinfonia in D*, Quantz's *Flute Concerto in E* and a flute concerto of Hasse (with Zöller), C. P. E. Bach's *Harpsichord Concertato Concerto in D* (with Smigelski and Hartig), Vivaldi's *Violin Concerto in G* (with Gieseler), and an aria from Graun's *Montezuma* (with Lorengar, and the Berlin Philharmonic Orchestra for EMI); and an overture of Muffat (with a chamber orchestra for Classic). The Respighi was a particularly good record for its time.

Bengtsson, Ingmar (b. 1920). Born in Stockholm and educated at the Royal High School of Music in Stockholm (1937–40), the Schola Cantorum Basiliensis (1947), Basel University and Uppsala University (1955), Bengtsson appeared at Stockholm as a pianist (1942), was co-founder of the Lilla Chamber Orchestra (1943–8), music critic for the *Svenska Dagbladet* (1943–59), taught at Uppsala University (from 1948), and made broadcasts on the Swedish Radio (1954–8). He recorded Koch's Piano Concerto No. 3 (with Solyon and the Militaermusik of Stockholm) and a composition by Deak (with the Musikkören si Skellifka), both for Caprice.

Benjamin, Arthur (1893–1960). Born in Sydney, Australia, Benjamin studied at the Royal College of Music, London, served in the Royal Flying Corps in World War I and became a prisoner of war, was professor of piano at the Sydney Conservatorium of Music (1919–22), taught at the Royal College of Music (1923–35), where his pupils included Britten, Mathieson and Weldon, and appeared as a piano soloist in London. He conducted the Vancouver Radio Symphony Orchestra (1939–46), returned to England to devote his time to composition, and toured Australia as a pianist in 1950. His compositions include the operas *A Tale of Two Cities* and *Prima Donna*, orchestral, vocal and instrumental music, the popular *Jamaican Rumba*, and a *Concertino for Piano and Orchestra* and *Concerto quasi una fantasia*. For Everest he conducted the London Symphony Orchestra in the last two named works, with Crowson the soloist.

Bennett, Robert Russell (b. 1894). A native of Kansas City and the son of two musicians, Bennett started his career as a theatre organist and orchestral string player, and worked for a musical publisher in New York. In World War I he organised and conducted army bands; afterwards he became a musical arranger, studied for four years with Nadia Boulanger in Paris (1926–30), and then won fame as an arranger for the musical theatre, working with Kern, Porter, Friml, Gershwin, Berlin, Rodgers and Loewe. Despite his enormous success in this field, he had no wish to write a show score; instead, his own compositions include six symphonies, three concertos, an organ sonata, orchestral suites and three operas. His Violin Concerto was recorded by Kaufmann and the London Symphony Orchestra under Herrmann for Citadel. Bennett arranged Bizet's *Carmen* for the all-Negro production *Carmen Jones*, which enjoyed a great success both on Broadway and as a film; this was a brave act, for Mahler once said that *Carmen* was one of the most perfectly scored of operas, and that in it 'not a superfluous note could be found' (Louis La Grange, *Mahler*, London, 1974, p. 382). Bennett played the piano in a 78 r.p.m. disc for Columbia of his piano-and-violin work entitled *Hexapoda – Five Studies in Jitteroptera*. More recently he conducted the RCA Victor Symphony Orchestra in some LPs, including arrangements from *West Side Story* and *Porgy and Bess*, and of music by Richard Rodgers and orchestrated by himself for the television documentary, *Victory at Sea*.

Benson, Warren (b. 1924). Born in Detroit, and educated at the University of Michigan, Benson was professor of music and composer-in-residence at Ithaca College, New York (1953–7), and from 1967 has been professor of composition at the Eastman School of Music at Rochester University. Of his many compositions he recorded *Three Pieces for Percussion Quartet*, *Variations*, and other pieces (with the Ithaca Percussion Ensemble for Golden Crest).

Benzi, Roberto (b. 1937). Born in Marseille of Italian parents, Benzi was taken to Italy as a child and started piano lessons with his father. He became a child prodigy, continued his studies with Cluytens in Paris, and gave a public recital as a pianist at Bayonne at the age of ten. The next year he conducted an orchestra in Paris and appeared in two films as a child actor and musician. After completing his musical and academic education, he embarked on his vocation as a conductor in his early 20s and took part in tours and festivals in North and South America and North Africa. His first major engagement was in 1959 when he conducted *Carmen* at the Paris Opéra; in the cast was the French soprano Jane Rhodes, whom he later married. In 1961 he took the same production to Japan. Appearances as a guest conductor in France, throughout Europe, the Americas and Japan followed; in 1962 he toured Holland with the Hague Philharmonic Orchestra and in 1964 commenced his long association with the Amsterdam Concertgebouw Orchestra, which culminated in the orchestra's tour of the United States and South America in 1970–71, when he joined the chief conductor, Haitink. He substituted dramatically and successfully for Karajan with the Berlin Philharmonic Orchestra in 1968, has been a guest conductor with the Philadelphia, Cleveland, Pittsburgh and Montreal orchestras, and in 1972–3 conducted *Faust* at the New York Metropolitan Opera.

Benzi has made many records for Philips; these include Haydn's Symphonies Nos 55 and 85, Leopold Mozart's *Toy Symphony*, the overtures *Coriolan*, *Egmont*, *Leonore No. 3*, *William Tell*, *Il barbiere di Siviglia*, *La scala di seta*, *Il Turco in Italia*, *L'Italiana in Algeri* and *La gazza ladra*, the ballet music to *William Tell*, Liszt's *Hungarian Rhapsody No. 2* and *Les Préludes*, Chopin's Piano Concerto No. 1 and Liszt's *Fantasy on Hungarian Folk Tunes* (with Magaloff), *Danse macabre* and other orchestral pieces of Saint-Saëns, and excerpts from *Carmen* (with the Lamoureux Orchestra *et al.*), Bizet's *Symphony in C major*, *Jeux d'enfants* and a suite from *La jolie fille de Perth* (with the London Symphony Orchestra), Liszt's *Faust Symphony* and *Mephisto Waltz*, and Rabaud's *La Procession nocturne* (with the Hungarian State Symphony Orchestra *et al.*), suites from *Coppélia* and *Sylvia*, *The Three-cornered Hat* and *El amor brujo* and excerpts from *Faust* (with the Paris Opéra Orchestra), Borodin's Symphony No. 2, a suite from *Tsar Saltan*, Lalo's Cello Concerto, Saint-Saëns' Cello Concerto No. 1 and Fauré's *Élégie* (with Gendron and the Monte Carlo National Orchestra), and an aria recital by Carreras (with the Royal Philharmonic Orchestra). For Cassiopée he also recorded Fauré's *Ballade* and *Fantaisie* (with Heidsieck and the Orchestre du Festival du Grand Rué).

Béreau, Jean-Sébastien. After studying at the Paris Conservatoire under Fourestier, Milhaud, Rivier, Martenot *et al.*, Béreau graduated in 1957 with first prize for conducting. He also holds the composition prize of the W. and N. Copley Foundation, in the US. In 1963 he was appointed director of the Metz Conservatoire and Symphony Orchestra, in 1967 director of the Rouen Conservatoire and Chamber Orchestra, and in 1973 director of the Strasbourg Conservatoire, where he teaches conducting. In addition he has had for four years a summer school for conductors at St Céré and Sarlat, and has himself conducted orchestras throughout France. For Arion he conducted the Rouen Chamber Orchestra in a disc of music by Destouches, Forqueray and de Mondonville, which was also released in the US by Musical Heritage Society.

Berezowsky, Nicolai (1900–53). Schooled as a violinist at the Imperial Capella in his native St Petersburg (1908–17), Berezowsky was a member of the Bolshoi Theatre Orchestra and musical director of the School of Modern Art in Moscow. In 1922 he migrated to the United States, attended the Juilliard School, was a violinist in the New York Philharmonic Orchestra (1923–9) and later was a member of the Coolidge and Kroll String Quartets. He was assistant conductor for CBS (1932–6 and 1941–*c.* 1946), conducted in Germany and composed much music, some pieces of which he conducted with leading American orchestras. His Quartet No. 1 was recorded (with the Coolidge Quartet for Victor, on 78 r.p.m. discs), and also his *Brass Suite* (with the Voisin Brass Ensemble for Kapp) and his *Christmas Festival* overture (with the Oslo Philharmonic Orchestra under Lipkin for Composers Recordings). As a conductor he directed a 78 r.p.m. set of an abridged *Boris Godunov* (with Kipnis *et al.* and the Victor Symphony Orchestra for Victor), which was at one time re-issued by RCA on an LP transfer.

Berg, Natanael (1879–1957). Born in Stockholm, Berg studied veterinary science, and also attended the Stockholm Conservatory, studying under Lindegren and Günther (1897–1901). He studied music further in Paris (1907) and Vienna (1919). He was a veterinary surgeon in the Swedish army (1908–39), but at the same time composed operas, symphonies and other orchestral works, concertos, chamber music and vocal pieces. EMI recorded him on a 78 r.p.m. disc conducting the Stockholm Radio Orchestra in his *Pezzo sinfonico – scherzo*.

Berglund, Paavo (b. 1929). Born in Helsinki, Berglund learned the violin as a boy with an instrument made by his grandfather, and studied at the Sibelius Academy in Helsinki and in Vienna and Salzburg. His first professional appointment was as violinist with the Finnish Radio Symphony Orchestra (1949); he helped form the Helsinki Chamber Orchestra and became its conductor (1952), was appointed assistant conductor of the Finnish Radio Symphony Orchestra (1956), four years later became its chief conductor, and was appointed conductor of the Finnish Radio Chamber Orchestra (1965). He toured Europe, Japan and Australia, and directed the Finnish Radio Symphony Orchestra's first English tour in 1967. In 1972 he was appointed principal conductor of the Bournemouth Symphony Orchestra, in succession to Silvestri, who had developed it into one that could be compared without loss to the major London orchestras, and under Berglund the orchestra has maintained, perhaps enhanced, this standard. He is now also principal conductor of the Helsinki Philharmonic Orchestra.

As a Finn, Berglund has an intense interest in presenting the music of Sibelius, and his idiomatic and convincing recordings of Sibelius' music have done much to fire the recent revival of interest in the composer. Apart from the Symphony No. 4 and *Tapiola*, which was made with the Finnish Radio Symphony Orchestra and released by Decca, he has recorded so far a number of Sibelius works with the Bournemouth Symphony Orchestra (for EMI) in vivid, energetic performances that capture the composer's unique qualities and which set forth the grandeur of the music as well as its instrumental colour. He has also been concerned to ensure that the editions of the scores are correct. This series commenced with the *Kullervo* symphony, an early work which Sibelius did not publish and in which Berglund edited certain passages which he thought needed amendment. Also recorded are Symphonies Nos 1, 4, 5, 6 and 7, the Violin Concerto (with Haendel), *The Bard*, *En Saga*, *Scènes historiques*, *The Océanides*, *Tapiola*, *Pohjola's Daughter*, *Luonnotar* (with Valjakka), *Finlandia*, the intermezzo from the *Karelia* suite, *Valse triste*, *King Christian II* suite, *Swanwhite* and *The Swan of Tuonela* and *Return of Lemminkäinen*. Shostakovich is another composer whom he has recorded extensively, covering Symphonies Nos 5, 6, 7 and 10, the Cello Concerto No. 1 (with Tortelier) and the two piano concertos (with Ortiz). Of these the Symphony No. 7 (the *Leningrad*) is a superb performance of a work that has been due for revival after many years of critical disparagement.

Berglund's other recordings with the Bournemouth orchestra for EMI include the Franck Symphony and *Symphonic Variations* (with Kersenbaum), Bliss's Cello Concerto (with Noras) and *Miracle in the Gorbals*, Nielsen's Symphony No. 5, Glazunov's Piano Concerto No. 1 (with Ogdon), Prokofiev's *Summer Night*, the two *Peer Gynt* suites, Järnefelt's *Praeludium*, Alfvén's *Midsummer Vigil* and elegy from *King Gustav II* suite, a suite from *Le Coq d'or*, Prokofiev's *Summer Night* suite, Vaughan Williams' Symphony No. 6 and Oboe Concerto (with Williams), Walton's Cello Concerto (with Tortelier) and Yardumian's *Passacaglia, Recitative and Fugue* (with Ogdon). For EMI he also accompanied Ogdon in the Grieg and Schumann Piano Concertos (with the New Philharmonia Orchestra). For Finnlevy he recorded Englund's *Epinikia* (with the Helsinki Philharmonic Orchestra), and for Decca Sibelius' Symphony No. 4 and *Tapiola*, Kokkonen's Symphony No. 3 and Sallinen's *Mauermusik* (with the Finnish Radio Orchestra).

Berio, Luciano (b. 1925). Born in Oneglia, Italy, Berio received a traditional musical education from his father and grandfather, who were musicians, and studied with Ghedini in Milan and with Dallapiccola in the United States, and was a pupil of Giulini in Milan for conducting. Because of Italy's isolation during the war, he first encountered contemporary music in 1945 when he heard Milhaud's *La Mort d'un tyran*; his musical outlook changed rapidly as he absorbed many new ideas. His compositions use a variety of combinations of instruments and *avant-garde* techniques and devices, including electronic sounds. Possibly his most widely known work, but at the same time the least representative, is the *Sinfonia*, which is a commentary on contemporary times which in its second movement incorporates fragments of many composers such as Beethoven, Ravel and Mahler, in an evocative pastiche. It was first performed in the US in 1968 and then in London in 1969, and was recorded with Berio conducting the New York Philharmonic Orchestra and the Swingle Singers by CBS. Other recordings in which he conducts his own music are *Chemins II* and *III* (with Trampler and the Juilliard Quartet for RCA), *Laborintus II* (with Musique Vivante for BASF), *Concerto for Two Pianos and Orchestra* (with Ballista and Canino and the London Symphony Orchestra for RCA), *Nones* and *Allelujah II* (with the London Symphony Orchestra, and with Boulez also conducting in the latter piece, for RCA), *A-Ronne* and *Cries of London* (with Swingle II for Decca), *Epifanie* and *Folksong Suite* (with Berberian and the Juilliard Ensemble, for RCA), *Agnus*, *Air*, *O King*, *El Mar la Mar*, *Melodrama*, *Evó*, *Points on the Curve to Find*, *Concertino* and *Chemins IV* (with the London Sinfonietta for RCA), *Différences* (with the Juilliard Ensemble for Philips, and with the Domaine Musical for Mainstream), *Chamber Music* (with Berberian and the Juilliard Ensemble for Philips) and *Recital I (for Cathy)* (with Berberian and the London Sinfonietta for RCA); Cathy Berberian, the soprano, was for a time the composer's wife.

Berkeley, Sir Lennox (b. 1903). The English composer Berkeley was born in Oxford, studied at Merton College, Oxford, and in Paris with Nadia Boulanger. He has conducted recordings of his music only in recent years, principally for Lyrita, who first issued in 1971 *Mont Juic – Four Catalan Dances*, written in 1937 in collaboration with Britten. Then followed the Symphony No. 3, *Divertimento in B flat*, *Partita for Chamber Orchestra*, *Serenade for Strings* and Canzonetta from the *Sinfonietta Concertante*. All were with the London Philharmonic Orchestra. Berkeley also conducted the London Sinfonietta in his *Four Ronsard Sonnets* (with Pears, for Decca).

Bernard, Anthony (1891–1963). A Londoner, Bernard studied with Holbrooke, Granville Bantock and Ireland, and received his first appointments as an organist and choirmaster at several churches in London, and became widely known as an accompanist. In 1921 he founded the London Chamber Orchestra which he conducted for many years in an annual series of concerts. Its repertoire covered music from the early masters of the baroque to 20th-century composers such as Falla and Delius; the latter permitted him to record one of his pieces before it was heard in public. Bernard was a professor at the Royal College of Music (1922–5), conducted with the British National Opera Company (1926), directed the Dutch Chamber Orchestra at the Hague (1922–6), organised and directed a festival of Italian music from the 11th to the 20th centuries in London (1930), became director of the New English Music Society (1928), was musical director at the Shakespeare Memorial Theatre at Stratford-upon-Avon (1932–42), where he composed the incidental music for some of the plays, and conducted at festivals at Canterbury and Cambridge. He also conducted concerts with the London Symphony Orchestra, and with orchestras in Copenhagen, the Hague, Madrid, Athens and in other European cities.

Bernard made many records on 78s with his London Chamber Orchestra, and was the first to record Falla's *El amor brujo*. His 78 r.p.m. sets included the *Brandenburg Concertos*, Corelli's Concerto Grosso Op. 6 No. 8, Respighi's *Trittico botticelliano* and *El amor brujo* (for Brunswick); *Eine kleine Nachtmusik*, some pieces by Purcell, Berkeley's *Divertimento in B flat*, Walton's overture *Portsmouth Point* and Warlock's *Capriol Suite* (for Decca); Bach's Cantata No. 82 (with Hotter); and, with the Philharmonia Orchestra, the sinfonia from Cantata No. 42, the Harpsichord Concerto No. 7 (with Malcolm), Violin Concertos No. 1 (with Varga), No. 2 (with de Vito) and the Double Violin Concerto (with Menuhin and de Vito), Beethoven's Romance No. 2 (with Varga), the Arrival of the Queen of Sheba from *Solomon*, and Fauré's *Pavane* and *Masques et bergamasques* (for EMI). His LP recordings included Marenzio's *Scendi dal paradiso*, *Venere* (with the London Chamber Singers, in EMI's *History of Music in Sound*), Handel's Concerti Grossi Op. 3 and Oboe Concertos (with Casier and the Centi Soli, issued by Nonesuch), *Water Music* and *Music for the Royal Fireworks* (with the London Symphony Orchestra for Counterpoint), Organ Concertos Op. 4 Nos 1, 2 and 4 and Op. 7 No. 1 (with Downes for Mercury) and the *Ode for St Cecilia's Day* (for Music Guild), Purcell's *The Indian Queen* (for Music Guild), two concertos for viola d'amore by Vivaldi (with Sabatini for Decca), Warlock's *Capriol Suite*, Dvořák's *Notturno* and motets by A. Scarlatti (for EMI).

Bernard, Marcel. An enigmatic conductor for whom no biographical details can be found, but who conducts the Westminster Symphony Orchestra (*sic*) in the nine Beethoven symphonies, issued by Ricordi in Italy. Classics for

Pleasure in Australia have also released discs in which he conducts the London Symphony Orchestra in various symphonies by Mozart, Beethoven, Schubert, Schumann and Brahms, and other works such as the ballet *Petrushka*. The performances themselves are competent and forthright.

Bernardi, Mario (b. 1930). Born in Kirkland Lake, Ontario, Canada, of Italian migrant parents, Bernardi was sent to Italy as a boy to receive his education, studied at the Conservatorio Benedetto Marcello in Venice and graduated at the age of 17. At the end of World War II he returned to Canada, attended the Royal Conservatory of Music at Toronto, began a career as a concert pianist but soon turned to conducting. He became a coach then conductor with the Canadian Opera Company, Toronto (1953–8), then in 1963 came to England and was engaged by the Sadler's Wells Opera Company. Within three years he was chief conductor and musical director of the company (1966–9). He made his United States debut at the San Francisco Opera (1967) and returned to Canada to become director of music and resident conductor at the new National Arts Center at Ottawa (1969). He has conducted with the New York City Opera, at the Aspen Music Festival, and was invited to conduct the Chicago and Pittsburgh Symphony Orchestras. In 1972 he was made a Companion of the Order of Canada.

As a pianist, Bernardi recorded for Decca the two Prokofiev violin sonatas with Steven Staryk. His recordings as a conductor include *Hänsel und Gretel* (with the Sadler's Wells Company for EMI), Mozart's Symphony No. 41, *Serenata notturna*, Violin Concerto K. 219 (with Staryk) and aria *Ombra felice*, K. 255 (with Forrester), arias by Haydn (with Alarie and Simoneau), Prokofiev's Symphony No. 1, Beecroft's *Improvvisazioni Concertanti No. 2*, Somers' *Five Songs for dark voice* (with Forrester) and Prévost's *Évanescence* (with the National Arts Center Orchestra for RCA), Haydn's Symphony No. 83, Dittersdorf's four *Ovid Symphonies*, Schubert's Symphony No. 6, Brahms' Serenade No. 1, the *Siegfried Idyll*, arrangements of Mozart quartets and some Mozart concerto accompaniments (with the National Arts Center Orchestra, for Canadian Broadcasting Corporation).

Bernède, Jean-Claude (b. 1935). Born in Angers, into a musical family, Bernède studied at the Paris Conservatoire, where he was awarded first prize for the violin (1957); he was a pupil of Calvet. With his Bernède String Quartet he won a major prize at the International Competition in Munich (1965), toured Europe and the United States, studied with Dervaux and Markevitch, and in 1973 was appointed conductor of the Rouen Chamber Orchestra. With his Quartet he has performed all the Beethoven quartets in Paris in 1975, and more recently conducted with the Lamoureux Orchestra the nine Beethoven symphonies, and with the Pasdeloup Orchestra a festival of Russian music. With the Rouen Chamber Orchestra he has toured West Germany, Spain, Japan and Latin America, and has recorded the *Brandenburg Concertos*. He has also made records with the Bernède String Quartet, for Pathé-Marconi and Chant du Monde.

Bernet, Dietfried (b. 1940). Born in Vienna, Bernet studied at the Academy of Music there, with Swarowsky and Mitropoulos, first conducted in Vienna in 1958, won first prize at the Liverpool International Conductors' Competition (1962), and became assistant conductor with the Vienna Volksoper (1963–4). He was appointed resident conductor with the Volksoper, general music director at Mainz, and has conducted at opera houses in FR Germany, and at the Spoleto Festival in Italy. His recordings include Lully's *Grand divertissement royal* and music for plays by Molière, Telemann's *Two-Horn Suite in F* (with Freund and Sungler) and *Tafelmusik*, Morin's *La Chasse au cerf* and *Suite de Fanfares in C*, Leopold I's *Balletti*, *Il lutto dell'universo* and two Sonatas, an aria from Ferdinand III's *Drama Musicum*, Joseph I's *Aria for Lute* and *Sepolcro*, Barsanti's Concerto Grosso Op. 3 No. 10, J. Stamitz's *Flute Concertos in D*, *D* and *G* (with Schaub) and Orchestral Trios Nos 1, 2 and 3, Haydn's Symphony No. 31 and *Cassation in B*, and Mozart's *Galimathias Musicum*, K. 32 (with Langfort and the Austrian Tonkünstler Orchestra for Musical Heritage Society); Schumann's *Konzertstück*, Weber's Concertino and Schoek's Horn Concerto (with Baumann), Spohr's Violin Concerto No. 8 and Vieuxtemps' Violin Concerto No. 5 (with Christian and the Vienna Symphony Orchestra for BASF), and aria recitals with McCracken (with the Vienna State Opera Orchestra for Decca), and Ingeborg Hallstein (with the Vienna Hofburg Orchestra for BASF).

Bernstein, Leonard (b. 1918). Born in Lawrence, Massachusetts, of a family of Jewish migrants who had come from Rovno, Russia, Bernstein showed exceptional musical talent as a child, composed a piano concerto at the age of thirteen, and a year later took piano lessons from Helen Coates, who was later to become his personal secretary. He attended his first concert at the age of sixteen, hearing the Boston Symphony Orchestra under Koussevitzky, and as a schoolboy produced and directed comedies, operettas and operas with the Boston Public School Orchestra. At Harvard (1935–9) he studied with Merritt, Piston and Edward Burlingame Hill, and met Copland and Mitropoulos who were to become lasting influences. From 1939 to 1941 he was at the Curtis Institute in Philadelphia, studying conducting with Reiner, piano with Vengerova and orchestration with Randall Thompson, and was a conducting pupil of Koussevitzky at the Berkshire Music Center at Tanglewood (1940–41). Rejected for military service, he worked as an arranger and transcriber in New York, then was engaged by Rodzinski as assistant conductor with the New York Philharmonic-Symphony Orchestra (1943–4). When Bruno Walter fell ill before a concert in November 1943 Bernstein substituted and made a sensational debut with a programme that included *Don Quixote*, the *Manfred* overture and the prelude to *Die Meistersinger*.

Engagements as a guest conductor followed, but at that time he began making his mark as a composer, with his *Jeremiah Symphony* (Symphony No. 1), the ballet *Fancy Free* and the musical *On the Town*. Now financially independent, he was able to accept an honorary appointment as conductor of the New York City Symphony Orchestra (1945–8), which was an important period in his development. His programmes included much 20th-century music; writing in 1946, Virgil Thomson said that 'Bernstein conducts like a master when he knows and really likes a score' (*Music Reviewed, 1940–1954*, p. 187). At this time he conducted many orchestras throughout the United States and Europe, and as far afield as Prague and Tel-Aviv. He was music adviser to the Israel Philharmonic Orchestra (1948–9), head of the orchestra and conducting department at the Berkshire Music Center (1951–5) and professor of music at Brandeis University (1951–6). He launched a series of television lectures on music (1955) with an estimated audience of 11 million, achieved success with his musical *Wonderful Town* (1953), wrote scores for *Candide* (1956), *West Side Story* (1957) and the film *On the Waterfront*, made his operatic debut with *Medea* at La Scala, Milan (1953) and conducted the opening concert at the Frederic H. Mann Auditorium at Tel-Aviv (1957). After appearing frequently as a guest conductor with the New York Philharmonic Orchestra, he was appointed co-principal conductor of the orchestra with Mitropoulos (1957–8), then sole musical director (1959–69). This gave him the distinction of being the first native-born American to lead a major US orchestra, and on his resignation in 1969 he was honoured with the title 'laureate conductor'.

Bernstein's retirement after twelve years with the New York Philharmonic was partly the result of his desire to give more time to composition, but afterwards he has increasingly turned his attention to opera and has appeared with great success in Vienna, New York and London. He sees that the symphony orchestra is now undergoing a crisis because it is not being fed a living stream of music as it was in the period of its evolution, from Mozart to Mahler. He believes that as a composer he can do something to contribute to the orchestra's repertoire of contemporary music. At the same time he feels that the lifestream of music in the present day is not to be found in the concert hall, and that the orchestra is basically now a vehicle for performing the great works of the classical and romantic eras and has little contact with modern composition. He is not, of course, alone in this assumption; for instance his successor with the New York Philharmonic, Boulez, took active steps to remedy the situation.

His array of talents has made Bernstein one of the most widely known, publicised and popular musicians of the day. As well as being a conductor he is an accomplished pianist and has recorded piano concertos by Mozart, Ravel and Shostakovich; his television talks, for which he has prepared over 100 scripts ranging from a discussion of the *St Matthew Passion* to explanations of jazz, were published in part in two books, *The Joy of Music* and *The Infinite Variety of Music*, and his Charles Eliot Norton lectures at Harvard (1973) entitled *The Unanswered Question* have received wide circulation. He has in these ways attempted to bridge the gap between the world of pop and the musically naïve, and the world of the symphony orchestra and its great repertoire. In 1974 he led the New York Philharmonic in a concert at Central Park, New York, which was attended by 130,000 people. He by nature needs to communicate, to explain, to educate and to share his own private joy with all.

Some of Bernstein's musical comedy and ballet scores were immediately successful; *West Side Story* is a significant work in that it brought the Broadway musical into the concert hall. His serious music has been less durable. Some of the compositions have religious implications, and while he is a man of wide religious sympathies the emotional outlook of these pieces is essentially Jewish, and deliberately so. He premièred his Symphony No. 1 with the Pittsburgh Symphony Orchestra in 1944; his Symphony No. 2 (1949, entitled *The Age of Anxiety*) has an important piano part, and in the scherzo harp, celeste and percussion join the piano in a jazz passage. The Symphony No. 3 the *Kaddish* (1963), has a spoken part which is a somewhat familiar colloquy with God, and although Bernstein has pointed out with justification that the questioning of God is a time-honoured Jewish tradition, to many the composition's overstatement is an embarrassment. His last major work was the *Mass* written for the opening of the Kennedy Center for the Performing Arts at Washington, DC (1971). It goes further than the *Kaddish Symphony*; some hold it to be blasphemous. Bernstein himself gives this 'theatre piece for singers, players and dancers' great personal significance, saying that it is a composition he has been writing all his life. Critical assessment of the work has been contradictory, from the verdict that it is a 'sincere expression of a crisis of faith', to Martin Bernheimer's judgement that it is a 'pretentious exercise in well-crafted banality', which is not far removed from Olin Downes' comments written after the first concert performance of *The Age of Anxiety*, in 1950: 'Wholly exterior in style, ingeniously constructed, effectively orchestrated, and a triumph of superficiality.' Probably the *Mass* should be seen live on the stage if it is to find any justification as music, drama, or religious experience, for its combination of incongruous musical styles in the form of a Broadway spectacle can be completely unconvincing, if not repellent, on record. Bernstein, however, has written one piece with religious inspiration which does not descend to bathos: the *Chichester Psalms*. His one orchestral work which is a popular concert piece, at least in the US, is the overture to his less-than-successful musical comedy, *Candide*. Composition appears to be no problem to him, and he says that the musical ideas come freely, but that he throws away at least ten times as much as he saves.

As a conductor, Bernstein's repertoire extends from the baroque of Bach and Vivaldi to modern European composers such as Bartók, Vaughan Williams, Stravinsky, Prokofiev and Shostakovich, and includes the Americans Ives, Copland and Harris. He has had little time for twelve-tone music, and in his hundreds of records there is no Berg or Schoenberg. He is essentially a romantic interpreter, attracted by the emotional surge and dramatic impact of the music. The self-discipline of the classical style is possible, but difficult for him, despite his superb recordings of Haydn symphonies. The lack of reserve in his interpretations is matched by his extravagant gestures on the podium, evident from his very first years as a conductor, and more than one critic has found it intolerable to watch his choreographic feats and facial expressions. Bernstein himself is not conscious of these movements, and orchestral players report that he is exactly the same at rehearsals when there is no audience. No music in his hands is allowed to speak for itself; it is projected with such intensity and expressiveness that the composer's intention can sometimes be lost, and it is only too evident that Bernstein must, above all, arrest and rivet the attention of the listener. He is in no sense a stylist, but of much of the repertoire he gives passionately committed performances.

Prior to his association with the New York Philharmonic, Bernstein made a number of records with various orchestras. Included were his *Facsimile* (for RCA), and Symphony No. 1 (with the St Louis Symphony Orchestra, for RCA) and Blitzstein's *Airborne Symphony* (with the New York City Symphony Orchestra for RCA); these appeared first on 78 r.p.m. discs. Following were Beethoven's Symphony No. 3, Brahms' Symphony No. 4, Schumann's Symphony No. 2 and Tchaikovsky's Symphony No. 6 (with the New York Stadium Concerts Symphony Orchestra for Brunswick), his *Fancy Free* (with the Ballet Theatre Orchestra for Decca), and *On the Town*, Copland's *Billy the Kid*, Gershwin's *An American in Paris* and Ravel's *Piano Concerto in G* (with the Victor Symphony Orchestra for RCA), Stravinsky's *L'Histoire du soldat* and *Octet* (with members of the Boston Symphony Orchestra for RCA), Ravel's *Shéhérazade* (with Tourel and the CBS Symphony Orchestra for Columbia), Hill's *Prelude for Orchestra*, Foss's *Time Cycle*, Dallapiccola's *Tartiniana*, Shapero's Symphony, Lopatnickoff's Concertino, Milhaud's *La Création du monde*, Copland's *El Salón México* and his own *Fancy Free* (with the Columbia Symphony Orchestra for Columbia). He also recorded, as a pianist, the Copland Sonata, some of his own music, and Mussorgsky's *Songs and Dances of Death* (with Tourel, for Columbia).

His years with the New York Philharmonic and his contract with Columbia have made Bernstein one of the most recorded conductors ever, and of all conductors his art is one of the most exhaustively represented on disc. In 1978 records of him with the New York Philharmonic were still being issued. In addition he made records with the Columbia Symphony, London Symphony (Mahler's Symphony No. 8), the Israel Philharmonic, the Vienna

Philharmonic, the Danish Royal Orchestra and the New York Metropolitan Opera, and more recently with the English Bach Festival Orchestra, the Orchestre de Paris and the French National Orchestra. From Bach's *St Matthew Passion* to Bloch's *Sacred Service*, his discography encompasses the complete symphonies of Beethoven, Schumann, Brahms, Sibelius and Mahler, as well as innumerable records of the music of Haydn, Mozart, Bartók, Berlioz, Copland, Debussy, Ravel, Dvořák, Ives, Mendelssohn, Nielsen, Prokofiev, Strauss, Shostakovich, Stravinsky, Tchaikovsky, Vaughan Williams, Wagner, Messiaen, Roussel and of course himself. Probably the most outstanding have been the six *Paris* symphonies of Haydn and the nine Mahler symphonies. The Haydn symphonies won the most enthusiastic praise from the eminent Haydn scholar, H. C. Robbins Landon, who called Bernstein 'one of the greatest, if not the greatest, interpreter of Haydn's music we have today, either [in the US] or in Europe'. The Mahler symphonies have a searing intensity: the music finds a ready mirror in Bernstein's own temperament. In Mozart, Beethoven, Schumann, Schubert and Brahms, Bernstein encounters problems of style which his innately romantic musical nature does not help him to solve. Paul Henry Lang conceded his conscientiousness in his recordings of the Beethoven symphonies, but summed them up as having 'more talent than taste'. Nonetheless, his Beethoven Symphony No. 3 must be listed among his best records. The others? Probably *Harold in Italy* and *Symphonie fantastique* (with the New York Philharmonic, and recently with the French National Orchestra), Bach's *Magnificat*, Bartók's *Concerto for Orchestra*, Brahms' Piano Concerto No. 2 (with Watts), the discs of pieces of Copland and Gershwin, the Franck symphony, Mendelssohn's Symphony No. 3, *Pictures at an Exhibition*, Shostakovich's Symphony No. 5, Sibelius' Symphony No. 5, *Till Eulenspiegel* and *Don Juan*, and *Le Sacre du printemps*.

In addition to American composers such as Ives, Harris, Copland, Foss and Schuller, and the Soviet composer Denisov, Bernstein has championed the cause of Europeans less well known in the US, particularly Nielsen and Vaughan Williams. He recorded Nielsen's Symphonies Nos 4 and 5 with the New York Philharmonic and No. 3 with the Danish Royal Orchestra, and for his recording of the Symphony No. 5 he received the Sonning Prize in Denmark. However, these performances of the Nielsen symphonies were criticised for being too exaggerated and romanticised. An interesting if ultimately unsuccessful experiment was a disc of the Dave Brubeck Quintet (a jazz ensemble) joining the New York Philharmonic, which only served to illustrate the difficulty of combining these two remote musical elements. Three choral works which Bernstein recorded with success have been the Bloch *Sacred Service*, Janáček's *Glagolitic Mass* and the Vaughan Williams *Serenade to Music*, which was performed by him at the opening concert at the Philharmonic Hall at Lincoln Center. His fine recordings of the Beethoven *Missa Solemnis*, Debussy's *Le Martyre de Saint-Sébastien*, Haydn's *The Creation* and the Verdi *Requiem* must also not be overlooked.

Bernstein in addition made a major mark as a conductor of opera. He directed the US première of *Peter Grimes* at Tanglewood in 1946, and in 1953 was the first American-born musician to conduct at La Scala, Milan, where his *Medea* aroused some controversy; a recording of the performance has been issued by Cetra. He returned to La Scala many times, but his first real triumph was with *Falstaff* at the New York Metropolitan in 1964, which he had earlier conducted at Covent Garden, London, and later recorded in 1967 with the Vienna Philharmonic and Fischer-Dieskau leading the cast. His performance of *Der Rosenkavalier* in Vienna in 1967 was also sensational, and this production was eventually recorded and released in 1972. In 1973 his *Carmen* with the New York Metropolitan was issued by DGG. In *Der Rosenkavalier* and *Carmen* he takes more leisurely tempi than usual, as if to dwell on the sentiment in the first and on the orchestral colour in the second. In 1977 he signed a contract with DGG under which he would record his three symphonies, the *Serenade for Violin, Strings and Percussion* and the *Meditations* from his *Mass*, with the Israel Philharmonic Orchestra, as well as the complete Beethoven symphonies with the Vienna Philharmonic.

Bernstein is the most significant and accomplished American conductor to have appeared so far. His vast talent and musicianship must be given high praise, but even so his final place among the great conductors is a problem. He represents, to the rest of the world, so many familiar aspects of American culture: charisma, brilliance given to overstatement, and a certain lack of emotional restraint that makes it difficult for him to distinguish between sentiment and sentimentality. But he is just over 60, not old for a conductor, and when one considers Walter, Toscanini, Beecham and Klemperer beyond that age, there may well be wonders yet to be revealed.

Bertini, Gary (b. 1927). Born in Bessarabia, Bertini received his musical education under Seter and Singer at the Academy of Music in Israel, at the Giuseppe Verdi Conservatory in Milan, at the Paris Conservatoire and at the Paris Musicological Institute, where he studied composition with Honegger. On returning to Israel he founded Rinat, the Israel Chamber Choir (1955), and the Israel Chamber Orchestra (1965). He first conducted the Israel Philharmonic Orchestra in 1958 and in 1960 was associate conductor of the orchestra during a world tour. In 1959 he appeared with the New York Philharmonic Orchestra and with other orchestras in the United States, Europe and Japan, in 1962 conducted for the Martha Graham Dance Company during its tour of Israel and has been musical director of the Batsheva Dance Company. In recent years he has appeared frequently in Britain, particularly with the BBC Symphony Orchestra, and since 1971 has been chief conductor of the Scottish National Orchestra. In 1975 he led a revival of Dukas' *Ariane et Barbe-bleue* in Paris, in 1976 conducted the Paris Opéra on its American tour for the US Bicentennial, in that year made his debut with the Berlin Deutsche Oper, and in 1977 conducted at La Scala, Milan. Since 1975 he has been a professor at Tel-Aviv University and in 1976 he was appointed artistic adviser to the Israel Festival.

Bertini's many recordings include two flute concertos of Vivaldi (with Nicolet and the Israel Chamber Orchestra for RCA), Mendelssohn's Symphonies Nos 1, 3 and 4 and *The Hebrides* overture (with the Hamburg State Philharmonic Orchestra for BASF), Beethoven's Piano Concertos Nos 3 and 5 (with Frager and the same orchestra for BASF), Debussy's *Printemps*, *Petite suite* (orch. Busser) and *Danse* and *Sarabande* (orch. Ravel) (with the Swedish Radio Symphony Orchestra for BASF), Shostakovich's Violin Concerto No. 1 (with Tellefsen and the same orchestra for BASF), Weill's Symphonies Nos 1 and 2 (with the BBC Symphony Orchestra for EMI), Webern's *Five Pieces for Orchestra* Op. 10 and Cantata No. 1 (with Harper and the English Chamber Orchestra for EMI), Dallapiccola's *Sicut Umbra* (with Michelow and the London Sinfonietta for Argo), Rossini's *L'Italiana in Algeri* (with the Dresden Staatskapelle *et al.* for BASF), Mahler's arrangement of Weber's opera *Die drei Pintos* (with the Munich Philharmonic Orchestra *et al.* for RCA) and songs of Schubert orchestrated by Brahms, Liszt, Reger, Berlioz *et al.* (with Prey and the Munich Philharmonic Orchestra for RCA). He has also made recordings of Israeli composers, including Orgad's *Mizmorim*, Tal's Cello Concerto, Avni's *Meditations on a Drama*, Seter's *Midnight Vigil*, and *Yemenite Suite*, Natra's *Song of Deborah* and *Sabbath Cantata*, Sheriff's *Music* and Ehrlich's *Be ye not as your fathers* (for CBS), Partos' *Visions*, *Yizkor* and *Shiluvim* (for RCA). With the Rinat Israel Chamber Choir he recorded Israeli songs, and chansons of the 16th century (for Aima and CBS).

Bertola, Giulio (b. 1921). Born in Murano, Italy, Bertola studied at the Marcello Conservatory at Venice and with Malipiero, and made his debut as a conductor in Venice in 1948, where he became assistant conductor at the Teatro la Fenice. He was musical director and resident conductor of the Italian Radio and Television Orchestra in Milan, and was awarded the Medaglia d'Oro in 1972. His recordings include Pergolesi's *In coelestibus regnis*, *Salve Regina*, *Domine ad adjuvandum me festina* and *Confitebor tibi*, and Monteverdi's *Gloria*, *Venite, videte*, *Exulta filia Sion*, *Salve Regina* and *Crucifixus* (with the Angelicum Orchestra and Chorus *et al.* for Angelicum, and issued also by Musical Heritage Society), Rossini's *Petite Messe solennelle* (with the Milan Polyphonic Choir *et al.*, issued by Everest), Marcello's *Psalms 2*, *3*, *8* and *10* (with the Milan Polyphonic Choir for Schwann), and Nono's *La fabbrica illuminata* (with the RCA Italiana Choir for Wergo).

Besvodni, Igor (b. 1930). Born in Tbilisi, Besvodni first studied the violin with his father, won first prize at the Kubelik Competition at Prague (1949) and the Bach Competition at Leipzig (1950), and continued his studies at the Moscow Conservatory with Yampolsky (1953–5). He has taught at the Moscow Conservatory (since 1957), becoming a professor (1972), and in 1970 made his debut as a conductor in Moscow. He has recorded, as conductor, Beethoven's Triple Concerto (with Malinin, Gratsch and Shakovskaya, and the Moscow Philharmonic Orchestra).

Bettarini, Luciano (b. 1914). Born in Prato, the Italian conductor, pianist and composer Bettarini studied at the Florence Conservatory and was conductor at the Florence Lyric Theatre (1939–49), worked with Radio Italiana, and in 1969 formed the Prato Concerts Society and an ensemble to perform 17th-century music. His compositions include liturgical and choral works, pieces for solo instruments and music for films and the theatre. For

RCA Italiana he recorded Franchetti's *Cristoforo Colombo.*

Bialoguski, Michael (b. 1917). Born in Kiev of Polish parents, Bialoguski studied medicine at Vilna University and the violin at Vilna Conservatory; after escaping from Lithuania at the outbreak of World War II he arrived in Sydney, Australia, graduated in medicine at Sydney University, was a violinist in the Sydney Symphony Orchestra, and as an intelligence agent was involved in the Petrov spy affair. He emigrated to London in 1964, studied conducting at the Accademia Chigiana in Siena (1967), made his debut as a conductor with the New Philharmonia Orchestra (1969), conducted other British orchestras, and was appointed principal conductor of the Commonwealth Philharmonic Orchestra (1974). In 1971 Unicorn issued a disc on which he conducted the New Philharmonia Orchestra in Voříšek's *Symphony in D* and Martinů's Symphony No. 6.

Bierdiajew, Walerian (1885–1956). Born in Grodno, then in Poland, Bierdiajew studied at Leipzig with Reger for composition and with Nikisch for conducting. He first conducted at Dresden in 1906, returned to Poland and there held major positions as conductor of symphony orchestras and opera companies. His records include Tchaikovsky's Symphony No. 6 (with the Polish National Symphony Orchestra, issued by DGG) and two operas by Moniuszko, *The Haunted Manor* and *Halka*, both with the Poznań Opera Company.

Biffoli, Renato (b. 1932). Born in Turin, Biffoli was engaged in 1944 by Radio Italiana as first violinist in a chamber orchestra, where he stayed uninterrupted until 1955. In 1946, with a string quartet which he founded, he won a prize at an international competition in Geneva, and later gave concerts in Italy, Switzerland and Austria, both as a soloist and member of the quartet. In 1960 Vox issued a disc in which he led the Accademici di Milano in Vivaldi's *The Four Seasons.*

Bigot, Eugène (b. 1888). Born in Rennes, France, Bigot studied at the Paris Conservatoire and started his career conducting at the Théâtre des Champs-Élysées (1912–14). During World War I he fought in the French army and was awarded the Croix de Guerre. He became assistant conductor of the Concerts Pasdeloup (1919), conductor of the Ballets Suédois (1920), conductor of the Société des Concerts du Conservatoire (1923), director of music at the Théâtre des Champs-Élysées (1925), first conductor with Radio Française (1928), president and conductor of the Concerts Lamoureux (1935–50), principal conductor of the Théâtres Lyriques Nationaux, chief conductor of the Paris Opéra-Comique (1936–47) and principal conductor of Radio-Télévision Française (from 1947). He also conducted French seasons at many opera houses in Europe, and his compositions include ballets and suites for orchestra. Bigot made many records before and after World War II on 78 r.p.m. discs; the major set was Charpentier's *Louise*, in an abridged version with the great French singers Ninon Vallin and Georges Thill. This was for Columbia, and is still available in France in an LP transfer. His other records include Mozart's Piano Concerto K. 450 and Bartók's Piano Concerto No. 2 (with Foldès and the Lamoureux Orchestra for Polydor), Mozart's Piano Concertos K. 453 and K. 503 (with Gaby Casadesus) and Paganini's Violin Concerto No. 1 (with Ricci and the Lamoureux Orchestra for Polydor), Saint-Saëns' Violin Concerto No. 3 and Ravel's *Tzigane* (with Ricci and the Lamoureux Orchestra for Vox), the overtures to *Mignon* and *Gwendoline*, Mozart's Piano Concerto K. 491 and Weber's *Konzertstück* (with Robert Casadesus) and the Schumann Piano Concerto (with Nat, and the Paris Symphony Orchestra for Columbia), Lalo's *Namouna* (with the Paris Conservatoire Orchestra for Columbia), *Symphonie espagnole* (with Bobesco), Ibert's Flute Concerto (with Moyse) and Hubeau's Violin Concerto (with Merckel, and the Lamoureux Orchestra for Columbia), the overture *Le Carnaval romain*, Lalo's *Rapsodie norvégienne* (abridged), harpsichord concertos by Handel and Haydn (with Landowska), Mozart's Flute Concerto K. 313 (with Moyse) and Falla's *Nights in the Gardens of Spain* (with Descaves, and the Paris Conservatoire Orchestra for HMV), Tchaikovsky's *Variations on a Rococo Theme* (with Fournier and the Lamoureux Orchestra for HMV), the overture *Benvenuto Cellini*, the Schumann Cello Concerto (with Navarra), Brahms' Piano Concerto No. 2 (with Zaan) and Paganini's Violin Concerto No. 1 (with Benedetti, and the Lamoureux Orchestra for Pathé). He also accompanied singers such as Martinelli, Thill and Micheau in operatic arias.

Binge, Ronald (b. 1910). Born in Derby, Binge has been a freelance composer and conductor, and has composed light orchestral pieces, film music, and music for brass and military bands. He recorded for Decca his Saxophone Concerto (with Voss) and *Saturday Symphony* (with the South German Radio Orchestra), and a collection of waltzes by Joseph Gungl (with the London Promenade Orchestra).

Bjerregaard, Carl (b. 1928). Born in Detroit, Michigan, Bjerregaard studied the flute and other woodwind instruments at the Western Michigan and Michigan State Universities, and was director of bands at Western Michigan and Florida State Universities. He has been a guest conductor of bands and wind ensembles throughout the United States, and has also commissioned many new wind compositions. Composers Recordings issued a disc in which he conducts the Western Michigan University Wind Ensemble in Penn's *Ultra Mensuram*.

Björlin, Ulf (b. 1933). Born in Stockholm, Björlin studied conducting with Markevitch in Salzburg, and later was a student with Nadia Boulanger and Eugène Bigot in Paris. When he returned to Sweden he became an assistant conductor at the Stockholm Royal Opera, was a producer for the Swedish Radio, a music director at the Royal Dramatic Theatre, and a teacher at the Stockholm Opera School. He has conducted orchestras and opera companies in Scandinavia, and as an arranger and conductor has become a popular personality on television, radio and records in Sweden. He has recorded a four-disc set of the orchestral music of Berwald, including the four symphonies, the Piano Concerto (with Migdal), the Violin Concerto (with Tellefsen), *Elfenspiel*, *Festival of the Bayadères*, *Serious and Light Follies*, *Memories of the Norwegian Mountains*, *Wettlauf*, and the overtures to *Estrella di Soria* and *Drottningen av Golconda* (with the Royal Philharmonic Orchestra for EMI), Larsson's *Lyrical Fantasy* and *Pastoral Suite*, and Blomdahl's *Prelude and Allegro* and *Games for Eight* (with the Stockholm Philharmonic Orchestra for EMI), Almquist's songs from *Fria Fantasier* (with an instrumental ensemble *et al.* for EMI), Roman's *Oboe Concerto in B* (with Gillblad) and Uttini's ballet *Les Chinois* (with the Stockholm Baroque Ensemble for EMI), his own *Epitaph for Lars Gorling*, Ravel's *Piano Concerto in G* (with Ribbing) and Werle's *Sinfonia da camera* (with the Norrköping Symphony Orchestra for EMI), and dances from Naumann's opera *Gustav Wasa*, selections from Roman's *Drottningholm Music* and the overture to Uttini's *Il re pastore* (with the Drottningholm Chamber Orchestra for EMI).

Black, Frank (1894–1968). Born in Philadelphia, Black first studied music, then chemistry, graduated from Haverford College and finally resumed the study of the piano with Joseffy in New York. He wrote songs for vaudeville and was conductor of the Fox Theater in Philadelphia (1923–34). He was appointed music director of the National Broadcasting Company in New York (1928), conducted the NBC String Orchestra and, on occasion, the NBC Symphony Orchestra, and filled guest engagements with other major American orchestras. A capable and discerning conductor, he was interested in less familiar repertoire especially of modern composers, and pioneered the creation of special music for dramatic productions for radio. He scored Edna St Vincent Millay's *The Murder of Lidice* and Alice Duer Miller's *The White Cliffs of Dover*. Victor issued 78 r.p.m. discs of him conducting the NBC String Orchestra in a symphony by C. P. E. Bach, Brahms' *Liebeslieder Waltzes*, Roussel's *Sinfonietta*, Arensky's *Variations on a Theme of Tchaikovsky*, Miaskovsky's *Sinfonietta* and the canzonetta from *Rakastava* of Sibelius.

Black, Stanley (b. 1913). The British danceband leader, conductor, pianist, composer and arranger Black was born in London and was educated at the Matthay School of Music. He started to compose at the age of twelve, and one of his juvenile compositions was broadcast by the BBC Symphony Orchestra conducted by Dr Joseph Lewis. Black grew interested in jazz and became a leading jazz pianist and arranger. In 1944 he came under contract to the Decca Record Company as house conductor, and sales of LP albums of Black and his dance band have totalled over three million copies. He was conductor of the BBC Dance Orchestra (1944–52), and music director of the Associated British Pictures Corporation (1958–64). Black has written many popular ballads and dance tunes and has arranged and composed numerous film scores, one of which, for *Summer Holiday*, won him an award. In recent years he has developed as a conductor of serious music, conducting orchestras in Britain, Europe, Japan and New Zealand; he conducted the Royal Philharmonic Orchestra in a concert series (1967), was principal conductor of the BBC Northern Ireland Orchestra (1968–9), toured Japan in 1965, 1967 and 1969, conducted the major orchestras there and was appointed assistant conductor of the Osaka Philharmonic Orchestra (1971). He has no difficulty in encompassing these various styles of music, saying, 'It's all music, music to be studied and enjoyed and made available for others to enjoy; the only unforgivable music is that which is boring, badly written or badly performed.' His highly effective skill as a conductor of light classical music has been demonstrated in LP albums he has made for Decca with the London Philharmonic, London Symphony, London Festival, Royal Philharmonic and Netherlands Radio Orchestras, in programmes including the ballet music of Tchaikovsky, Delibes and Khachaturian, excerpts from Massenet's *Le Cid* and Meyerbeer's *Les Patineurs*, some *Slavonic Dances* of Dvořák, Liszt's *Hungarian Rhapsody No. 2*, *Moldau, Capriccio espagnol, Capriccio italien, Marche slave*, Borodin's *Notturno*, the Polovtsian Dances from *Prince Igor*, Enesco's *Romanian Rhapsody No. 1*, *A Night on the Bare Mountain*, *In the Steppes of Central Asia*, Prokofiev's Symphony No. 1 and the march and scherzo from *The Love of Three Oranges*, Ravel's *Rapsodie espagnole* and *Boléro*, Grofé's *Grand Canyon Suite*, and the Tchaikovsky *Serenade in C major*.

Blareau, Richard (b. 1910). Born in Lille, Blareau was a pupil of Gaubert and pursued a career as a conductor in the fields of both light and classical music. In 1947 he first conducted at the Paris Opéra. In the mid 1950s he made records for Decca of excerpts from *Giselle* (with the Paris National Opéra Orchestra), Messager's *Les deux pigeons*, and *Fête polonaise* and *Danse slave* from Chabrier's *Le Roi malgré lui* (with the Paris Opéra-Comique Orchestra), a suite from Khachaturian's *Masquerade* (with the Paris Conservatoire Orchestra) and excerpts from Gounod's *Mireille* (with the Paris Conservatoire Orchestra *et al.*) Later he also recorded for Decca Lecocq's *La Fille de Madame Angot*, Offenbach's *La Fille du tambour-major* and Strauss' *Three Waltzes*.

Blazhkov, Igor (b. 1936). Born in Kiev where he studied under Klimov at the Conservatory, Blazhkov became assistant conductor of the Ukrainian State Symphony Orchestra at Kiev while still a student (1958–60), then was the orchestra's conductor (1960–62). In 1963 he was appointed a conductor of the Leningrad Philharmonic Orchestra, took the advanced conducting course directed by Mravinsky at the Leningrad Conservatory (1965–7), and became the artistic director and conductor of the Kiev Chamber Orchestra (1969–76). He is now chief conductor of the Ukraine State Symphony Orchestra. He edited a selection of Stravinsky's letters which was published in the USSR in 1977, has written articles for *Ruch Muzyczny* (Warsaw), and was made Artist of the Ukrainian SSR in 1973. His repertoire includes much modern music, including that by American composers. His records for Melodiya have been Stravinsky's *Le Chant du rossignol* (with the Moscow Radio Symphony Orchestra), Shostakovich's Symphonies Nos 2, 3 and 14 (with the Leningrad Philharmonic Orchestra *et al.*), cello concertos by Sauget and Tishchenko (with Rostropovich and the Leningrad Philharmonic Orchestra), Gubarenko's Symphony No. 1 (with the Moscow Radio Symphony Orchestra), as well as Schoenberg's *Serenade* Op. 24, and Piano Concerto, Ives' *Tone Roads No. 3*, Hindemith's *Kammermusik No. 1*, Stravinsky's *Movements*, Britten's *Variations on a Theme of Frank Bridge*, Shostakovich's *Two Pieces* Op. 11, the Adagio from Mahler's Symphony No. 10, Telemann's *Schulmeister*, Scarlatti's Sinfonias Nos 4 and 5, Dittersdorf's *Sinfonia concertante*, Cimarosa's *Il maestro di capella*, Haydn's Sinfonia Concertante, Tishchenko's Symphony No. 3 and Piano Concerto, Stankovich's *Frescoes*, Klibanov's *Suite for Strings No. 1*, and Znosko-Borovsky's Concertino and Flute and Oboe Concertos.

Blech, Harry (b. 1910). Born of Polish parents in London, Blech studied the violin with Sarah Fennings at the Trinity College of Music and appeared in public as a soloist at a very early age. After leaving school at sixteen he studied with Sevcik in Czechoslovakia and later with Catterall at the Manchester College of Music, was first violinist with the Hallé Orchestra (1929–30) and with the BBC Symphony Orchestra (1930–36), and formed the Blech String Quartet in 1936 which eventually disbanded in 1950. He started conducting for Dame Myra Hess at the National Gallery Concerts in London during World War II, and in 1942 formed the London Wind Players, which grew into the London Mozart Players in 1949. In that year he also founded the Haydn–Mozart Society of which Sir William Walton became the president. The London Mozart Players gave concerts of the popular works of Mozart and his contemporaries, as well as of many lesser known pieces of the period, and were selected to take part in the inaugural concerts to mark the opening of the Royal Festival Hall in London in 1952. The orchestra played up to 100 concerts each year, and Blech, with characteristically stylish and sympathetic performances, cultivated an audience who appreciated a part of the repertoire largely neglected by the major symphony orchestras. The orchestra, and Blech, have remained active to the present day.

After World War II Blech recorded on 78 r.p.m. discs the Haydn Symphony No. 94, some Mozart contradances and the overtures to *Fra Diavolo*, *Hänsel und Gretel*, *The Merry Wives of Windsor* and *Iphigénie en Aulide* (with the Suisse Romande Orchestra for Decca), Mozart's Divertimento K. 186 (with the London Wind Players for Decca), the overtures to *Armida* and *Lucio Silla* (with the London Mozart Players for EMI) and Mozart's String Quartet K. 421 and Chausson's *Chanson perpétuelle* (with the Blech String Quartet, and with Teyte and Moore in the Chausson, for Decca and EMI respectively). Then on LP he embarked on an impressive series with the London Mozart Players, which included (for Decca) Haydn's Symphony No. 49 and Mozart's Divertimento K. 131, and (for EMI) Haydn's Symphonies Nos 86, 103 and 104, and the *Salve Regina in G minor*, Mozart's Symphonies Nos 28, 31, 32, 33, 34, 35, 36, 38, 39, 40 and 41, the Serenade K. 320, the Sinfonia Concertante K. 364 (with Brainin and Schidlof), the Twelve Minuets K. 568 and three Dances K. 605, the Piano Concertos K. 453 and K. 503 (with Matthews), for Two Pianos K. 365 and Three Pianos K. 242 (with Vronsky and Babin *et al.*), the Bassoon Concerto (with Camden), the Mass K. 317, and some concert arias (with Seefried), K. Stamitz's Bassoon Concerto (with Camden), a symphony by Arriaga, and Schubert's Symphonies Nos 3, 4, 5 and 6 and five German Dances. Capitol (US) released discs of Bach's Violin Concerto No. 1, Mozart's Violin Concerto K. 219 and the Goldmark Violin Concerto, in which he conducted the Philharmonia Orchestra (called the 'Festival Orchestra' in some re-issues) with Milstein the soloist, and of Mozart's Piano Concerto K. 491 (with Kentner and the Philharmonia Orchestra), and Classics Club the Mozart Flute and Harp Concerto (with Adeney and Ellis and the London Mozart Players). After many years away from the recording studios, Blech reappeared with the London Mozart Players in 1972 on a Unicorn disc, in Haydn's Concerto for Violin and Piano (with the Weiss Duo), and in 1974 in a new series for Abbey, with Haydn's Symphonies Nos 90 and 91, Mozart's Symphonies Nos 35, 36 and 41, the Piano Concerto K. 488 (with Roll) and Divertimento K. 251, and Schubert's Symphony No. 5.

Blech, Leo (1871–1958). Born in Aachen, Blech abandoned a business career to enrol at the Hochschule für Musik in Berlin, and returned to Aachen as conductor at the Municipal Theatre (1893–9), also studying composition with Humperdinck in the summers in Munich. Appointments followed at the German Opera at Prague (1899–1906), as principal conductor at the Berlin State Opera (1906–23) where he succeeded Muck, as general music director at the Charlottenburg Opera, Berlin (1923–5), and again at the Berlin State Opera (1926–37). He was reputedly tolerated by the Nazis although he was Jewish because of his immense popularity with the public and because he was originally appointed to the post by Kaiser Wilhelm II. But while he was in Riga on an engagement in 1937 he was informed that it would not be safe for him to return to Germany, and he remained as conductor of the Riga Opera until 1941, then moved to Sweden where he was appointed to the Royal Opera at Stockholm. He returned to Berlin in 1949, resumed his position at the State Opera, and retired in 1954. He composed a number of symphonies, choral music, orchestral works, piano music, many songs, four operas and two operettas; some of the operas met with considerable success in their day, *Versiegelt* (1908) being produced in Hamburg and New York. Although certainly not as brilliant a conductor as his most famous contemporaries, he was recognised as one of the most conscientious, knowledgeable and discerning interpreters of German opera, particularly of Mozart, Wagner and Strauss, who requested that he direct the Berlin première of *Elektra* in 1909. His reputation stood high with singers; Lauritz Melchior was once asked who was the best conductor with whom he had sung, and answered 'Leo Blech. He knew his singers' strengths and weaknesses. When one was singing in the worst part of one's register, the orchestra played loudly, but when one was at one's best, the orchestra was soft.'

Blech's first records were made with the Berlin State Opera Orchestra in the early 1920s for HMV, when he accompanied Fritz Kreisler in the Beethoven, Mendelssohn and Brahms Violin Concertos. He went on to record with the same orchestra Haydn's Symphony No. 94, Mozart's Symphony No. 34, three movements from the Serenade K. 361, the Divertimento K. 240, *Eine kleine Nachtmusik*, the *Masonic Funeral Music*, the *Adagio and Fugue in C minor*, the ballet music from *Idomeneo*, the overtures to *Die Entführung aus dem Serail*, *Così fan tutte*, *Le nozze di Figaro* and *Die Zauberflöte*, and the Andante for Flute and Orchestra K. 315, Mottl's arrangement of Gluck ballet music, Schubert's Symphonies Nos 5 and 8, the overtures to *Il barbiere di Siviglia*, *Der Freischütz*, *Oberon*, *Preciosa*, *Jubel*, *Donna Diana*, *Mignon*, *Tannhäuser* and *Der fliegende Holländer*, the preludes to *Die Meistersinger* and *Lohengrin*, and to Acts I and III of *Carmen*, a *Slavonic Dance* of Dvořák, the

Liszt *Hungarian Rhapsody No. 1*, *Tod und Verklärung* and the waltzes from *Der Rosenkavalier*, *Moldau*, the Brahms *Alto Rhapsody* (with Onegin), Johann Strauss's *Radetzky March*, *Perpetuum mobile*, intermezzo from *Indigo* and waltz from *Der Zigeunerbaron*, Tchaikovsky's *Serenade in C major*, the polka and furiant from *Schwanda*, an aria from *Samson et Dalila* (with Onegin), Wagner's *Homage March*, the Entrance of the Gods into Valhalla from *Das Rheingold* (with Schorr), excerpts from *Die Walküre* (with Leider and Schorr), excerpts from *Siegfried* and *Götterdämmerung*, the Entry of the Guests and Pilgrims' Chorus from *Tannhäuser*, arias from *Tannhäuser* and *Der fliegende Holländer* (with Berglund), and excerpts from Act III of *Tristan und Isolde*. With the Berlin Philharmonic Orchestra he also recorded the overtures *Le Carnaval romain* and *Der Barbier von Bagdad* and the March of the Priests from *Die Zauberflöte*, and with the London Symphony Orchestra Mozart's *Les petits riens*, the minuet from the Divertimento K. 334 and three *Country Dances*, Schubert's Symphony No. 9, the Mendelssohn overture *Meeresstille und gluckliche Fahrt* and the last movement from the Symphony No. 4, excerpts from Brahms's Serenade No. 1, Grieg's *Norwegian Dances* and the overtures *Anacréon*, *Oberon* and *Orphée aux enfers*. All were for HMV; for Polydor he also recorded the *Leonore No. 3* overture and *Les Préludes*, with the Berlin State Opera Orchestra. The Brahms Violin Concerto (with Kreisler and the Berlin State Opera Orchestra) has been re-issued on an LP transfer by EMI in FR Germany and Japan.

Bliss, Sir Arthur (1891–1975). One of the leading British composers of the 20th century, Bliss was educated at Pembroke College, Cambridge, and at the Royal College of Music under Stanford, Vaughan Williams and Holst. He served with distinction as an officer in the Grenadier Guards in France in World War I, was wounded in 1916 and gassed in 1918. After two years in California (1923–5) he became professor of composition at the Royal College of Music, and musical director of the British Broadcasting Corporation (1941–5). He was knighted in 1950, succeeded Bax as Master of the Queen's Musick (1953), was president of the Performing Rights Society, President of the Composers Guild of Great Britain, was made KCVO in 1969 and a Companion of Honour in 1971. The music he composed in his early years was original to the point of eccentricity, but later he became more conservative and traditional in form and style.

Bliss was active as a conductor as early as 1919, and made recordings of some of his first compositions, *Conversations* and *Madam Noy* in 1923, for Columbia. Other 78s were a suite from his famous film score *Things to Come* (with the London Symphony Orchestra for Decca, in 1936) and *Welcome to the Queen* (with the Philharmonia Orchestra for EMI in 1954). He made a number of LPs of his own music: the *Colour Symphony*, *Introduction and Allegro* and Violin Concerto (with Campoli and the London Symphony Orchestra for Decca), the *Theme and Cadenza for Violin and Orchestra* (with Campoli and the London Philharmonic Orchestra for Decca), *Music for Strings* and *Miracle in the Gorbals* (with the Philharmonia Orchestra for EMI), *Checkmate* and a suite arranged from Purcell's music (with the Sinfonia of London for World Record Club), *Welcome to the Queen*, *Things to Come* and Elgar's five *Pomp and Circumstance* Marches (with the London Symphony Orchestra for RCA), the *Introduction and Allegro* (with the Leicestershire Schools Orchestra for Argo), *Hymn to Apollo*, *Mêlée fantasque*, three numbers from the ballet *Adam Zero*, *Rout*, the *Serenade for Baritone and Orchestra* and *The World is Charged with the Grandeur of God* (with the London Symphony Orchestra *et al.* for Lyrita), and his arrangement of the National Anthem (with the London Symphony Orchestra and Chorus for Classics for Pleasure). Music by other composers which he recorded comprised a suite arranged by Baines from Handel's *Water Music* (with the Sinfonia of London for World Record Club), Arne's *Rule Britannia*, the march from *Things to Come*, Borodin's *Notturno*, Arrival of the Queen of Sheba from Handel's *Solomon*, Parry's *Jerusalem*, Holst's *Marching Song*, Vaughan Williams' *Fantasia on Greensleeves*, the Rossini overture *Il viaggio a Reims* (with the Philharmonia Orchestra *et al.* for Reader's Digest) and Elgar's *Cockaigne* (with the New Philharmonia Orchestra for Reader's Digest).

Blitzstein, Marc (1905–64). Blitzstein studied at the university at his native Philadelphia, at the Curtis Institute, with Nadia Boulanger in Paris and with Schoenberg in Berlin. He returned to the United States, composed for films and the theatre, and while in England during World War II with the US air force wrote a symphonic cantata *The Airborne* which was later recorded by Bernstein. He developed a form of musical play for the stage which combined social commentary, wit, satire and effective characterisation, and two of these 'plays in music' were recorded under his direction: *The*

Cradle will Rock (Musicraft) and *No for an Answer* (Keynote), both on 78 r.p.m. discs. Both sets have become collectors' items. *The Cradle will Rock* was produced in New York in 1937, and, as with *No for an Answer* (1941), took left-wing political themes for its plot. *The Cradle will Rock* was later recorded on LP for Composers Recordings, but otherwise Blitzstein's music is not represented in the present-day catalogue.

Bloch, Ernest (1880–1959). The Swiss-born composer Bloch was active as a conductor early in his career and conducted orchestral concerts at Lausanne and Neuchâtel during the seasons 1909 and 1910. In 1916 he visited the United States, where he led a concert of his own compositions with the Boston Symphony Orchestra. Later he became an American citizen and was frequently engaged to conduct his own music with American orchestras. During a visit to London in 1949 he recorded his *Sacred Service* and *Schelomo* for Decca, and these were amongst the first LPs issued by that company. The orchestra was the London Philharmonic, and in the *Sacred Service* the Cantor was Marko Rothmüller; the choir was also the London Philharmonic. Zara Nelsova was the cellist in *Schelomo*. Instead of Hebrew, the *Sacred Service* was sung in English; tempi were far faster than indicated in the score, apparently because Bloch was anxious to present the work in the best possible light and to have it gain general recognition. This proved to be a tragic mistake; it was not until Bernstein recorded it in Hebrew with the spacious tempi correctly shown that the piece became widely known and respected.

Blomstedt, Herbert (b. 1927). Born in Springfield, Massachusetts, the Swedish conductor Blomstedt studied at the Royal School of Music at Stockholm, at the University of Uppsala, then with Tor Mann in Stockholm, with Markevitch at Salzburg, and with Bernstein at the Berkshire Music Center in Massachusetts. He also took part in courses in contemporary music at Darmstadt, and in the performance of old music at the Schola Cantorum in Basel. After making his debut as a conductor with the Stockholm Philharmonic Orchestra in 1954, he became conductor of the Norrköping Radio Orchestra (1954), won first prize in the International Conductors' Competition at Salzburg (1957), was chief conductor of the Danish Radio Symphony Orchestra (1967–77) and of the Stockholm Radio Symphony Orchestra (since 1977). He has conducted the Dresden Staatskapelle since 1969, in 1972 became the orchestra's permanent guest conductor, in 1975 its chief conductor, and in 1978 took up the position of general music director; he has conducted the orchestra in tours of Japan (twice), Austria, the USSR, Czechoslovakia, Hungary, Sweden and West Berlin, and in festivals at Salzburg, Vienna, Holland, Edinburgh, and others in West Germany and Switzerland. Since 1961 he has taught conducting at the Stockholm Conservatory, and became a professor there in 1965; he has also been a guest professor at summer courses at Santiago de Compostella, Monte Carlo, and Aspen and Loma Linda in the United States. In Sweden he has been awarded the Knighthood of the Northern Star and is a member of the Royal Music Academy, and in Denmark he received the Knighthood of the Dannebrogen Order.

Blomstedt made his first recording in 1956, Bäck's *Sinfonia da camera* (with the Stockholm Radio Symphony Orchestra for Discofil). Since then, in chronological order, he has recorded Lidholm's *Poesis* and Rosenberg's Symphony No. 2 (with the Stockholm Philharmonic Orchestra for Discofil), *Le Sacre du printemps* (with the Stockholm Philharmonic Orchestra for Expo Norr), Rosenberg's Symphonies Nos 3 and 4 (with the Stockholm Philharmonic and the Stockholm Radio Symphony Orchestras respectively, for EMI), Lidholm's *Toccata e Canto* and *Drei Gesänge mit Streichorchester* (with Rödin), and Stenhammar's *Mellanspel ur Sången* and *Suite aus Chitra* (with the Stockholm Philharmonic Orchestra for EMI), Nordheim's *Canzona* and *Epitaffio*, Arnestad's *Aria appassionata* and Kvandal's *Symfonisk Epos* (with the Oslo Philharmonic Orchestra for Philips), Nordal's *Adagio*, Rydman's *Symphony of the Modern World* and Nordheim's *Eco* (with the Stockholm Radio Symphony Orchestra for EMI), and Nørgård's *Luna* (with the Danish Radio Symphony Orchestra for Dansk Musikantologi), Høffding's *Det er ganske vist*, and Gudmundsen-Holmgren's *Chronos* (with the Danish Radio Symphony Orchestra for EMI), Nørgård's *Iris* (with the same orchestra for Caprice), Mozart's two Flute Concertos and *Adagio* K. 315 (with Walther), Oboe Concerto (with Mahn), and four Horn Concertos and *Rondo* K. 371 (with Damm, and the Dresden Staatskapelle for Eterna), the seven Nielsen symphonies, *Symphonic Rhapsody*, *Rhapsody* overture, *Saga-Drøm*, *Pan and Syrinx*, *Andante lamentoso*, *Bøhmisk-Dansk Folketone*, *Helios* overture, Violin Concerto (with Tellefsen), Flute Concerto (with Lemsser) and Clarinet Concerto (with Stevenson, and the Danish Radio Symphony Orchestra for EMI), Dvořák's Symphony No. 8 (with the Dresden Staatskapelle for Eterna), Matthus' Piano Concerto (with Schmidt and the Dresden Staatskapelle for Nova), Beethoven's Symphonies Nos 3 and 7, and *Leonore* (with the Dresden Staatskapelle *et al.* for Eterna), Nørholm's Violin Concerto (with Hansen and the Danish Radio Symphony Orchestra for Bis), Mozart's Divertimenti K. 136, K. 137 and K. 138, the *Adagio and Fugue in C minor*, Horn Concertos Nos 1 and 2 (with Damm) and Flute Concertos (with Walter, and the Dresden Staatskapelle for Eterna).

The Nielsen discs were issued in 1975 and were then welcomed as a fine achievement, although Blomstedt took a rather sober view of the composer's major symphonic works. The two Beethoven symphonies, with the Dresden Staatskapelle, appear to be the first in a complete cycle, but, as in *Leonore* (the first version of *Fidelio*), Blomstedt does not impress as having any special insight as a Beethoven interpreter.

Bloomfield, Theodore (b. 1923). A native of Cleveland, Ohio, Bloomfield graduated from the Oberlin Conservatory (1944), studied conducting at the Juilliard School and at the same time played the French horn in the National Symphony Orchestra. He was a pupil of Monteux and of Arrau, and first conducted publicly with the New York Little Symphony (1945). His transcription of the Bach *Toccata and Fugue in C major* was given its first performance by Monteux with the San Francisco Symphony Orchestra in 1946. He won a nationwide competition to be appointed apprentice conductor and pianist with the Cleveland Orchestra under Szell (1947), and he founded and conducted the Cleveland Little Symphony and the Civic Opera Workshop (1947–52). He was music director of the Portland (Oregon) Symphony Orchestra (1955–9), of the Rochester Philharmonic Orchestra (1959–63), conductor at the Hamburg State Opera (1964–6), general music director of the Frankfurt Opera and artistic director of the Frankfurt Museum Concerts (1966–8) and chief conductor of the Berlin Symphony Orchestra (1975–9). In Europe he has been a guest conductor with many orchestras and opera companies. Everest recorded him conducting the Rochester Philharmonic Orchestra in Ravel's *Rapsodie espagnole* and *La Valse*, and Sibelius' Symphony No. 5 and *Finlandia*. For MGM he had previously directed the MGM Symphony Orchestra in Villa-Lobos' *Bachianas brasileiras* Nos 1 and 4, Shostakovich's Piano Concerto No. 1 and Lambert's *Concerto for Piano and Nine Instruments* (with Pressler), and for Composers Recordings the Rochester Philharmonic in Rogers' *Variations on a Song by Mussorgsky*. He has so far made no records in Europe.

Blot, Robert (b. 1907). Son of the painter Eugène Blot, Blot studied the violin at the conservatoires of Dijon and Reims, and then studied at the Paris Conservatoire. He was the first horn player at the Concerts Colonne (1935–46) and conductor at the Paris Opéra (1948–63), taught conducting at the Paris Conservatoire and has conducted the Paris Youth Orchestra (since 1944). He conducted the major orchestras in Paris and toured with the Paris Opéra in North and South America, the USSR and in other European countries. For EMI he has recorded excerpts from *Coppélia* with the Paris Opéra Orchestra.

Blum, David (b. 1935). A native of Los Angeles, Blum trained at the Aspen Institute of Music (1954) and at the Juilliard School (1955) and was greatly influenced by Richard Lert, the German conductor resident in Los Angeles, and by Lotte Lehmann and Pablo Casals. His career as a conductor commenced with the Young Artists' Chamber Orchestra in Los Angeles (1952); he appeared with the Debut Orchestra, Los Angeles (1953–5), the David Blum Chamber Orchestra, Los Angeles (1958–9), and then as a guest conductor with orchestras in Berlin, Munich, Frankfurt, Mannheim, London and Israel (1959–61). In 1961 he settled in New York and founded the Esterházy Orchestra, modelled on the orchestra of Haydn at Eisenstadt when he was in the service of the Esterházy princes. The orchestra specialises in 18th-century music in addition to the neglected symphonies of Haydn, tours the United States and has recorded for Vanguard. Blum's interest in the music of the 18th century was aroused by the work of H. C. Robbins Landon, and he aims to present Haydn's music as experimental, enterprising and revolutionary. Certainly the Haydn symphonies he has recorded with the Esterházy Orchestra for Vanguard – Nos 39, 52, 59, 60, 70, 73, 75, 81, 90 and 91 – have all these qualities, and are stylish contributions to the recent vast increase in recordings of Haydn's works. Other music recorded by Blum and his orchestra are Mozart's Divertimento K. 334 and March K. 445 (for Vanguard) and a suite and some concertos of Telemann (for Bach Guild). Blum's own compositions include a tone poem, *Cyrano de Bergerac* (1959).

Blum, Tamás (b. 1927). Born in Budapest, Blum was a piano pupil of Pál Kadosa, and studied conducting with Ferencsik in Budapest and with Kletzki in Lausanne. He was a repetiteur and assistant conductor at the Budapest Opera (1945–9), made his debut there as a conductor (1950), was director of the Csokonai Theatre in Debrecen (1953–8) and then became resident conductor at the Zürich Opera. He won the Liszt Award (1956 and 1963) and translated the librettos of a number of operas into Hungarian, including *Rigoletto*, *Otello*, *Eugene Onegin*, *Tristan und Isolde*, *Pelléas et Mélisande* and *Wozzeck*. For Hungaroton he recorded Petrovics' opera *C'est la Guerre*, with the Hungarian State Opera Orchestra *et al.*

Boatwright, Howard (b. 1918). Born in Newport News, Virginia, Boatwright studied at Yale University with Hindemith, was a teacher there (1938–64), and became dean of the music school at Syracuse University (1964). He wrote chamber music, sacred and other vocal music, and gave recitals as a violinist. For Overtone he conducted A. Scarlatti's *St John Passion* (with the Yale Orchestra *et al.*).

Bobesco, Lola (b. 1929). Born in Craiova, Romania, Bobesco studied the violin with her father, then at the Paris Conservatoire with Chailley and Bouchert. She made her debut in Bucharest in 1935, played concertos at the age of eleven in Paris with Paray and Munch, and subsequently appeared throughout Europe as a soloist. Taking up residence in Belgium, she became the leader of the Wallonia Chamber Orchestra, also called the Eugène Ysaÿe Ensemble, and director of the violin class at the Conservatoire Royal in Brussels. As soloist she directed Mozart's Violin Concertos K. 218 and K. 219 (with the Eugène Ysaÿe Ensemble for Omega/Vega), and also recorded as conductor van Malderen's *Symphony in D major*, de Croes' Violin Concerto (with herself), Bernier's *Trois liturgies* (with Defraiteur), and Devreese's *Mouvement* (with the Solistes de Bruxelles for Alpha), pieces by G. B. Sammartini, Corelli, Riccioti and Vivaldi, Bach's Violin and Oboe Concerto (with herself and Gilis), and Quinet's *Sérénade* (with the Solistes de Bruxelles, for a Belgian company).

Bobescu, Jean (b. 1890). Born in Romania into a family of musicians, Bobescu graduated from the Jassy Conservatory (1911) and was appointed head of the violin class at the Craiova Conservatory. He made his debut as a conductor in Bucharest (1918), became first conductor at the Cluj Opera (1920) and at the Bucharest Opera (1940) and was at the same time head of the opera class at the Bucharest Conservatory. He toured in France before World War II and later in Belgium, Poland, Turkey and Czechoslovakia. His records, for Electrecord, include discs of excerpts from *La traviata* and *Rigoletto* (with the Bucharest State Opera Orchestra *et al.*), ballet music from the operas *Aida*, *Lakmé*, *Eugene Onegin*, *Faust*, *Le Cid* and *Carmen* (with the Bucharest State Opera Orchestra), two overtures by Rossini (with the Romanian Film Orchestra), Buicliu's Violin Concerto (with Ruha), Constantinescu's Symphony, and an aria recital (with Herlea, and the Romanian Radio Symphony Orchestra).

Boboc, Nicolae (b. 1920). Born in Ilia, Romania, Boboc studied at the Bucharest Conservatory (1940–47), taught music in Bucharest (1945–53), was director of the conservatory at Arad (1948–59), conductor of the Timişoara Philharmonic Orchestra (1959) and first conductor of the Timişoara State Opera (1963–74). He has toured as a guest conductor in Czechoslovakia, Bulgaria, Hungary, DR Germany, France, Austria, Egypt, Holland, Poland, FR Germany and Switzerland, and has composed symphonic, chamber and choral music and music for the theatre. He was awarded the title of Artist Emeritus of the Romanian Socialist Republic in 1964. Electrecord has issued a disc with him conducting the Timişoara Philharmonic Orchestra *et al.* in the Mozart *Requiem*.

Bodanzky, Artur (1877–1939). Bodanzky studied at the conservatory in his native Vienna and after several years as a violinist in the Vienna Opera Orchestra was Mahler's assistant at the Vienna Opera (1902–4). He conducted at the Prague Opera (1906–9), the Mannheim Opera (1909–12) and in 1914 led the first performance of *Parsifal* at Covent Garden, London. This made the way for his appointment to the New York Metropolitan Opera to succeed Hertz as the chief conductor of the German repertoire. He was active in New York from 1916 to 1931, also conducting the New Symphony Orchestra and directing the Society of Friends of Music. He remained in New York until his death. Bodanzky's conducting showed some of the characteristics of his first mentor, Mahler; meticulous and thorough, his readings were nonetheless highly dramatic. However, in direct opposition to Mahler's practice, he had no hesitation in abridging and trimming the Wagner operas, and said on his arrival in New York that if the length of a Wagnerian music drama bored the public, it should be cut. Bodanzky gave shortened versions of *Siegfried*, *Götterdämmerung* and *Parsifal*, as well as an abbreviated *Der Rosenkavalier*. But at this time even Toscanini pruned Wagner, omitting either the Norn Scene or Waltraute's Narration from *Götterdämmerung*. Yet, when Bodanzky led *Lohengrin* in 1921 he included a customarily unheard ensemble in Act II. He also presented Gluck's *Iphigénie en Tauride* in 1921 in the Strauss edition which shortened the earlier acts, and added two excerpts from *Orfeo* for a ballet, and composed recitatives for *Der Freischütz* and *Fidelio*. Irving Kolodin writes that Bodanzky once conducted *Tannhäuser* in 1925 with Melchior without the benefit of either a rehearsal or conversation with him. Bodanzky recorded in Europe for Odeon the overtures to *Die Zauberflöte*, *Benvenuto Cellini*, *The Merry Wives of Windsor*, *Die Fledermaus*, *Mignon*, *Die Meistersinger*, *Si j'étais Roi*, *Morgen, Mittag und Abend in Wien* and *Die schöne Galatea*, the preludes to Acts I and III of *Lohengrin*, and the scherzo from *A Midsummer Night's Dream* (with the Berlin State Opera Orchestra), the Strauss waltz *Wein, Weib und Gesang* and the overture *The Hebrides* (with the Berlin Philharmonic Orchestra). Some of these records were issued in Britain by Parlophone.

Boepple, Paul (1896–1970). Born in Basel, Switzerland, Boepple studied at the Basel University and Conservatory, at the Royal Music Academy in Munich and then with Jacques-Dalcroze in Geneva, and was a teacher at the Dalcroze Academy there (1919–27). He was conductor at the Théâtre du Jorat at Mézières (1923–5) where he conducted the world premières of Honegger's *Le Roi David* and *Judith*. In 1926 he went to the United States as director of the Dalcroze School of Music in New York (1926–32), taught at the Chicago Music College (1932–4), at the Westminster Choir School at Princeton University (1935–8) and at Bennington College, Vermont (from 1944). In 1936 he was appointed conductor of the Dessoff Choir, which had been founded originally by Margarete Dessoff, and of the Motet Singers of New York. Musicraft issued 78 r.p.m. discs of him conducting the Motet Singers in Mozart's Mass K. 192, a Buxtehude *Missa brevis* and a motet by Schein; later, on LP, he recorded *Israel in Egypt* (with the Dessoff Choir *et al.* and the Symphony of the Air for Vox), Palestrina's *Magnificat* No. 33, *Missa Assumpta est Maria* and *Stabat Mater* (with the Dessoff Choir for Concert Hall), pieces by Pérotin-le-Grand (with the Dessoff Choir for Capitol), Josquin des Prés' *Missa de beata Virgine* and some motets (with the Dessoff Choir for Turnabout), and a recital of baroque choral music (with the Dessoff Choir and the New York Brass Ensemble for Concert Hall).

Boettcher, Wilfried (b. 1929). Born in Bremen, Boettcher studied the cello at the Hochschule für Musik at Hamburg and with Casals, Tortelier and Fournier, and was for several years first cellist with the Bremen Radio Orchestra and the Hannover Opera Orchestra. In 1958 he became lecturer in cello and chamber music at the Vienna Academy of Music and the next year founded the Vienna Soloists, which soon became an accomplished ensemble, performing in European festivals and touring in the United States and Japan. He was appointed professor of orchestral training, cello and chamber music at the Hochschule für Musik at Hamburg (1965), chief conductor of the Hamburg Symphony Orchestra (1967–72), permanent guest conductor of the Hamburg State Opera, and principal conductor of the Turin Radio Orchestra (1974), in addition to joining the German Opera in West Berlin.

Boettcher's recordings have included Bach's Cantata No. 151 (with the Vienna State Opera Orchestra *et al.* for Nonesuch), a Telemann cantata (with the Vienna Chamber Orchestra *et al.* for La Guilde Internationale du Disque), harpsichord concertos by C. P. E. Bach and J. C. Bach (with Neumeyer), Telemann's *Spring Cantata* and Concerto Grosso (with the Hamburg Telemann Society Orchestra for Philips), Oboe Concerto (with Koch) and *Sonata a 4 in G* (with the Hamburg Telemann Society Orchestra for DGG), oboe concertos by Albinoni, Fischer, Leclair and Vivaldi (with Lardrot and the Vienna Soloists for Vanguard), guitar concertos by Giuliani, Torelli and Carulli (with Scheit and the Vienna Festival Orchestra for Turnabout), Lebrun's Oboe Concerto (with Koch and the Hamburg Telemann Society Orchestra for Philips), recorder concertos by Naudot, Sammartini, Scarlatti and Telemann (with Conrad and the Vienna Soloists for Bach Guild), Haydn's Symphonies Nos 6, 7, 8, 15, 16 and 17 (with the Vienna Festival Orchestra for Turnabout), Mozart's Piano Concertos K. 459 and K. 460 (with Brendel and the Vienna Volksoper Orchestra for Turnabout), K. 453 and K. 491 (with Pressler and the Vienna Chamber Orchestra for GID), Clarinet Concerto (with Eichler and the Vienna Symphony Orchestra for GID), Horn Concertos Nos 1 and 3 (with Freund and the Vienna Symphony Orchestra for GID), arias (with Hollweg and the English Chamber Orchestra for Philips, and Janowitz and the Vienna Symphony Orchestra for DGG), and Serenades K. 239 and K. 320 (with the Vienna Festival Orchestra for Turnabout), and Serenade K. 203 (with the Vienna Chamber Orchestra for Musical Heritage Society), Beethoven's Piano Concerto No. 1 and Choral Fantasia (with Brendel and the Stuttgart Philharmonic Orchestra for Turnabout), the Cherubini symphony and Weber's Symphony No. 1 (with the New Philharmonia Orchestra for Philips). At their best these performances were graceful and admirable, and attracted attention to Boettcher's fine sense of style with these composers.

Boezi, Ernesto (1856–1946). Born in Rome, Boezi studied with Ballabene and was organist at San Luigi dei Francesi (1880), conductor of the Società musicale Romana (1879–86) and of the Cappella Giulia (1905), and was until 1918 technical director of the Pontificia Scuola Superiore di musica sacra, founded by Pope Pius X. He composed an opera *Don Paez* and many sacred choral works, of which he recorded his *Missa Solemnis* for HMV with the choir of the Cappella Giulia.

Bohlke, Erich (b. 1895). Born in Stettin (modern Szczecin) and educated at the Hochschule für Musik in Berlin and in Vienna, and at the Friedrich Wilhelm University in Berlin, Bohlke was music director at Rudolstadt (1924) and Koblenz (1926–7), chief conductor of Wiesbaden (1929) and with the Berlin Radio (1931), music director at Magdeburg (1932) and Oldenburg (1947), became a freelance composer and conductor and an honorary member of the Rheinische Philharmonia. He recorded Schumann's Symphony No. 3 (with the Rhineland Philharmonic Orchestra for Intercord).

Böhm, Karl (b. 1894). Born in Graz, Austria, Böhm studied law at the University of Graz, at the same time taking lessons in piano and theory at the Graz Conservatory. His father, an amateur musician and lawyer, and friend of Richter, believed that he should have a profession to fall back on if he was unsuccessful as a musician. Böhm continued his musical studies at the Vienna Conservatory under Mandyczewski, and after being injured in an accident while serving in the Austrian army in World War I he returned to civilian life, received the degree of Doctor of Laws at Graz (1919) and became a prompter at the Graz Opera. He never studied conducting formally, but accepted Richter's advice that he would know immediately if he would make a conductor by standing in front of an orchestra. He finally abandoned law for music and was appointed first conductor at Graz (1920). While he was conducting a performance of *Lohengrin*, Karl Muck was present in the audience, was impressed and offered to assist him in the study of Wagner's operas. Muck also recommended him to Walter, then at the Munich Opera, who engaged Böhm (1921); Böhm was deeply influenced by Walter's great performances of the Mozart operas at Munich, although he has come to believe that Walter's readings of Mozart were too sentimental: 'You will find every emotion in Mozart's music,' he has said, 'but he is never sentimental' (*The Guardian*, 1 December 1977). On the other hand, he thought Strauss's tempi too fast in Mozart. After Walter's departure, he worked with Knappertsbusch, and then left for Darmstadt where he became first conductor (1927–31), was for the next two years in Hamburg, then succeeded Busch as music director at Dresden (1934–43), finally moving to the Vienna State Opera. At Dresden he enjoyed ideal conditions, working continuously with the same singers and orchestral players, and was not disturbed by travel and other conducting engagements.

At Darmstadt Böhm conducted one of the first performances of Berg's *Wozzeck* (1928); Berg himself was present for the last days of the rehearsals. Since then Böhm has been a leading interpreter of the two Berg operas, *Wozzeck* and *Lulu*, and has recorded both for DGG. He also enjoyed a close association with Richard Strauss, which began in 1933 when Strauss visited him in Hamburg during his preparation of *Arabella*. Later, at Dresden, Böhm gave the first performance of *Die schweigsame Frau* and *Daphne*, which Strauss had dedicated to him. Böhm conducted most of Strauss's major orchestral works and operas in the presence of the composer, and has said that Strauss always insisted that, above all, the words of the libretto be clearly audible. When *Die schweigsame Frau* was being rehearsed for its première, Böhm complained that the thickness of the woodwind passages made it impossible to hear the words, and Strauss rewrote and lightened the wind parts. In addition, Böhm heard Strauss conduct many of his symphonic poems and operas, and these experiences have given him such a profound insight into their interpretation that his own performances have an unmistakable authority. In 1936, after Böhm brought the Dresden State Opera to Covent Garden to present *Der Rosenkavalier* and *Tristan und Isolde*, he was invited back to conduct *Elektra* and *Salome* on the same programme, but refused on artistic grounds.

After World War II Böhm was permitted to appear again as a conductor in 1947, and was director of the Vienna State Opera (1950–53). His first appearance at Vienna had been much earlier in 1933, with *Tristan und Isolde.* He was engaged for a five-year contract in 1954 and conducted *Fidelio* at the first performance of the reconstructed opera house on the Ringstrasse the next year, but drew strong local criticism through his absences from Vienna, particularly in South America where he was director of the German repertoire at the Teatro Colón in Buenos Aires (1950–54). He resigned after his contract had run only fifteen months, and was succeeded by von Karajan, although he was to continue to conduct in Vienna. He first appeared in the United States in 1956 when he was a guest conductor with the Chicago Symphony Orchestra; Bing, who had known Böhm previously when he was on the staff at Darmstadt, engaged him for the New York Metropolitan Opera, where he made a triumphant first appearance with *Don Giovanni* (1957). Later he was to lead notable performances at the Met. of *Die Meistersinger* (1959), *Wozzeck* (1959), *Parsifal* (1961), *Fidelio* (1963), *Daphne* (1964), *Der fliegende Holländer* (1965), *Salome* (1965), *Die Frau ohne Schatten* (1966) and *Lohengrin* (1966). Despite his concentration on the German repertoire at the Met. and at the Teatro Colón, Böhm has conducted much Italian opera, both in Italy and Germany; once he prepared *Falstaff* at Dresden and had 25 ensemble rehearsals and fifteen stage rehearsals. Altogether, he has conducted 150 different operas in his career. In 1962 he led *Tristan und Isolde* at Bayreuth, toured with the Berlin Philharmonic Orchestra to Japan, and first conducted *The Ring* at Bayreuth in 1963, and in 1967 he conducted the Vienna Philharmonic Orchestra when they toured the US and Canada. In 1970 he received the Great Gold Medal for distinguished service to Viennese music, and was also named General Music Director of Austria. In 1973 he conducted the London Symphony Orchestra at Salzburg, and in 1977 was named the orchestra's president, in succession to Sir Arthur Bliss.

Böhm has come to occupy a position of eminence among European conductors, and more particularly he is one of the very finest interpreters of Austro-German music. He seems to have grown in self-assurance after the departure of so many of his contemporaries. As a personality he is authoritarian, talks quietly, but quickly gains the respect of his orchestra. His gestures are economical and he commands an immense dynamic range with little effort. Like so many great conductors it is his eyes that communicate most to his players. His interpretations are poised, unaffected by mannerisms and quite devoid of eccentricity. He makes no special effort to point up details or to exaggerate a dramatic point or to heighten a climax, but he is perfectly precise in matters of tempi, dynamics and phrasing. In Mozart, Beethoven, Schubert, Brahms and Bruckner, all of whose symphonies he has recorded, his performances are unfailingly spacious and beautiful, as exemplified by the recordings of the Beethoven Symphony No. 6 and the Bruckner Symphony No. 4 with the Vienna Philharmonic. But in music that calls for a touch of demon or virtuosity, such as Beethoven's Symphony No. 7, the smoothness of his conducting lacks tension and the final incandescence is missing. His Mozart is urbane, supremely well judged and balanced; the sound is big, perhaps too big to be truly authentic in style, and sometimes there is the hint that while the music is left to speak for itself, craftsmanship may have imperceptibly replaced inspiration. We are in another world from the pointed elegance of Beecham, the intense lyricism of Walter and the crisp accuracy of Szell.

As a recording artist Böhm has had a long and illustrious career which has reached a climax of considerable glory. It started in the 1930s with a series of 78 r.p.m. recordings for HMV with the Saxon State Orchestra when he was in Dresden. Included were the Mozart Horn Concerto K. 447 (with Zimalong), Violin Concerto K. 219 (with Dahmen), *Eine kleine Nachtmusik*, and the overtures to *Le nozze di Figaro* and *Die Entführung aus dem Serail*, Beethoven's Symphony No. 9, overtures *Egmont* and *Leonore No. 3*, the Violin Concerto (with Strub), and Piano Concertos Nos 3 (with Kolessa), 4 (with Gieseking) and 5 (with Fischer), Weber's overtures *Oberon* and *Der Freischütz*, the Brahms Violin Concerto (with Schneiderhan) and Piano Concerto No. 2 (with Backhaus), the Bruckner Symphonies Nos 4 and 5, the Pfitzner *Symphony in C major*, Reger's *Variations and Fugue on a Theme of Mozart*, the complete Act III of *Die Meistersinger*, the overtures to *Die Meistersinger, Der fliegende Holländer* and *Tannhäuser*, the prelude to Act III and Bridal Chorus from *Lohengrin*, *Till Eulenspiegel*, *Don Juan*, the dance from *Salome*, the waltzes from *Der Rosenkavalier* and scenes from *Daphne*, overtures *Hänsel und Gretel*, *The Bartered Bride*, *Die Fledermaus* and *Donna Diana*, and Tchaikovsky's *Capriccio italien*. There also appeared the overture to *The Merry Wives of Windsor* (with the Berlin Philharmonic Orchestra for HMV) and the Schumann Piano Concerto (with Gieseking and the Prussian State

Orchestra for Columbia). After World War II he recorded, again for HMV on 78 r.p.m. discs, Mozart's Symphonies Nos 35 and 41, the overture to *Der Schauspieldirektor* and the rondo from the Serenade K. 250, Beethoven's Piano Concerto No. 3 (with Backhaus), Schubert's Symphony No. 8, Brahms' Symphony No. 1, a Strauss waltz and polka and the czardas and intermezzo from Schmidt's *Notre Dame* (with the Vienna Philharmonic Orchestra), the ballet music from Lortzing's *Undine* and the dance from *Salome* and waltzes from *Der Rosenkavalier* (with the Danish State Orchestra), and Act II Scene II from *Die Walküre* and the love duet from Act II of *Tristan und Isolde* (both with Flagstad and Svanholm and the Philharmonia Orchestra).

On LP, Böhm recorded for Decca, Vox, Philips, Urania and finally for DGG, with whom he came under contract in 1960. His records on LP include Mozart's Symphonies Nos 34, 36, 38 and 41, *Così fan tutte*, *Die Zauberflöte*, and the Piano Concerto K. 595 (with Backhaus), Beethoven's Symphony No. 8, Piano Concertos Nos 1, 2 and 3 (with Backhaus) and No. 1 (with Gulda), Schubert's Symphonies Nos 5 and 8, Weber's overtures *Preciosa*, *Oberon*, *Euryanthe* and *Peter Schmoll und seine Nachbarn*, Brahms' Symphony No. 3 and Piano Concerto No. 1 (with Backhaus), Strauss's *Vier letzte Lieder* (with della Casa) and *Die Frau ohne Schatten* (with the Vienna Philharmonic Orchestra *et al.* for Decca); Mozart's Symphony No. 40, Beethoven's *Leonore No. 3* overture and *Egmont* incidental music, Bruckner's Symphony No. 7 and the Grieg Piano Concerto (with Wührer, and with the Vienna Philharmonic Orchestra for Vox); Mozart's Symphonies Nos 39, 40 and 41 (with the Amsterdam Concertgebouw Orchestra for Philips), the Mozart *Requiem* and *Le nozze di Figaro*, and the Beethoven Choral Fantasia (with Richter-Haaser, and with the Vienna Symphony Orchestra for Philips); Beethoven's Piano Concerto No. 5 (with Ney and the Vienna Philharmonic Orchestra for Urania) and Schumann's Symphony No. 1 and Pfitzner's *Symphony in C major* (with the Saxon State Orchestra for Urania).

For DGG Böhm's recorded repertoire has been comprehensive: the entire symphonies of Mozart and Schubert (with the Berlin Philharmonic) and of Beethoven and Brahms (with the Vienna Philharmonic); he has also completed Bruckner's Symphonies Nos 3, 4, 7 and 8 (with the Vienna Philharmonic). He had earlier recorded some of these symphonies with the Berlin Philharmonic, but the complete sets were issued in recent years. His other discs include *The Seasons* of Haydn (with the Vienna Symphony Orchestra *et al.*), Mozart's Serenades K. 239, K. 250 and K. 320 and *Eine kleine Nachtmusik*, the Clarinet Concerto (with Prinz), Bassoon Concerto (with Zeman), Flute Concerto No. 1 (with Tripp), Oboe Concerto (with Turetschek) and Flute and Harp Concerto (with Schulz and Zabaleta, and with the Vienna Philharmonic), the Piano Concertos K. 459 and K. 488 (with Pollini and the Vienna Philharmonic), K. 595 and the Two-Piano Concerto K. 365 (with Gilels and E. Gilels, and the Vienna Philharmonic), the two Sinfonie Concertante, *Le nozze di Figaro* (with the Berlin Opera *et al.*), *Don Giovanni* (with the Prague National Theatre *et al.*), *Die Zauberflöte* (with the Berlin Philharmonic *et al.*), *Così fan tutte* (with the Vienna Philharmonic *et al.*), *Die Entführung aus dem Serail* and *Der Schauspieldirektor* (with the Dresden Staatskapelle *et al.*), Haydn's Symphonies Nos 88 to 92 and the Sinfonia Concertante (with the Vienna Philharmonic), the Beethoven *Missa Solemnis* and *Fidelio* and the overtures *Egmont*, *Prometheus* and *Coriolan* (with the Vienna Philharmonic *et al.*), excerpts from Handel's *Giulio Cesare*, Reger's *Variations and Fugue on a Theme of Mozart*, *Tristan und Isolde* and *Der fliegende Holländer* (with the Bayreuth Festival Orchestra *et al.*), *Don Juan*, *Till Eulenspiegel*, *Also sprach Zarathustra*, the dance from *Salome* and the *Festival Prelude* (with the Berlin Philharmonic), *Ein Heldenleben* (with the Saxon State Orchestra and the Vienna Philharmonic), *Der Rosenkavalier* (with the Dresden Staatskapelle *et al.*), *Daphne* (with the Vienna Symphony Orchestra *et al.*), and *Ariadne auf Naxos* (with the Bavarian Radio Symphony Orchestra *et al.*), *Capriccio* (with the Bavarian Radio Symphony Orchestra *et al.*), *Elektra* (with the Dresden Opera Orchestra *et al.*), and *Salome* (with the Hamburg Opera Orchestra *et al.*), Mahler's *Kindertotenlieder* and *Rückert Lieder* (with Fischer-Dieskau and the Berlin Philharmonic), *Wozzeck* and *Lulu* (with the Berlin Opera *et al.*), *Die Fledermaus* (with the Vienna Philharmonic *et al.*), and a disc of the music of Johann Strauss, *Peter and the Wolf* and *Le Carnaval des animaux* (with the Vienna Philharmonic). At the same time earlier performances of some of the Mozart operas remain in the catalogue: *Die Zauberflöte* (with the Vienna Philharmonic *et al.* for Decca), and *Così fan tutte* (with the Vienna Philharmonic *et al.* for Decca, and with the Philharmonia *et al.*, for EMI).

Along with Karajan and Jochum, Böhm is the foremost living exponent of the great

Austro-German tradition of conducting. His art is extremely well documented on gramophone records, and he has been, for almost five decades, one of the major recording artists. With the astonishing number of records he has made it is inevitable that in some he may not scale the heights as he has undoubtedly in others, but the unfailing taste and integrity of his profound musicianship is never called into question.

Bokstedt, Bertil (b. 1919). Born in Malmö, Sweden, Bokstedt studied at the Royal Academy of Music at Stockholm and began his career as a repetiteur at the Royal Swedish Opera. He was appointed conductor (1954), directing both opera and ballet, and two years later became conductor of the Drottningholm Court Theatre. He has been artistic manager of the theatre since 1969 and in 1971 succeeded Gentele as general manager of the Royal Swedish Opera. Decca recorded him accompanying Nilsson with the Vienna State Opera Orchestra in a recital of songs by Sibelius, Grieg and Rangström, and for EMI he accompanied Jussi Björling with the Royal Swedish Opera Orchestra.

Bolberitz, Tamás (b. 1940). Born in Budapest, Bolberitz played the violin in a chamber orchestra at the age of twelve, and in his teens conducted several orchestras. He studied composition with Sugár at the Béla Bartók Music School (1958–61) and conducting with Koródy at the Franz Liszt Academy (1961–6), and then became a repetiteur at the Budapest State Opera, commencing to conduct there a year later. Since then he has also conducted concerts with the major Hungarian symphony orchestras, as well as others in East Europe. In 1972 Hungaroton issued a disc in which he conducted the Budapest Symphony Orchestra in Brahms' Symphony No. 1.

Bomhard, Moritz (b. 1908). Born in Berlin and educated at the Leipzig University and Conservatory, Bomhard migrated to the United States in 1936 and studied conducting at the Juilliard School. He was conductor of the Princeton University Orchestra and Glee Club, served in the US army in the Far East (1942–5), organised and was music director of a travelling opera company based in New York (1946–51), conducted in Europe (1951), then organised, managed and has been artistic director of the Kentucky Opera Association at Louisville. He was also professor of music at Louisville University and collaborated with the Louisville Orchestra in promoting and recording new works by contemporary composers. In 1963 he represented the Ford Foundation in Berlin, and conducted at the Hamburg State Opera and in other German cities. He recorded Mohaupt's *Double Trouble* and a suite from Liebermann's *School for Wives* (with the Louisville Orchestra *et al.* for Louisville).

Bon, Willem (b. 1940). The Dutch conductor Bon studied at the Royal Conservatory at the Hague, and with Stotijn, van Otterloo, Horvat, Fournet and Dixon. He was appointed assistant conductor of the Amsterdam Concertgebouw Orchestra (1973) and is permanent conductor of the Amsterdam Sinfonietta, which was founded in 1966. He also is a prolific composer. With the Amsterdam Sinfonietta he recorded Tchaikovsky's *Serenade in C major*, Stravinsky's *Concerto for Strings in D major* and pieces by Grieg and Vivaldi (for EMI) and with the Netherlands Radio Philharmonic Orchestra his own Symphony No. 2 *Les Prédictions* (for Donemus).

Bondon, Jacques (b. 1927). Born at Boulbon, Bouches-du-Rhône, Bondon studied the violin at Marseille and then composition in Paris with Koechlin, Milhaud and Rivier. He has composed music for films and radio, orchestral and instrumental music and several operas. He has conducted some of his own compositions on record: the Guitar Concerto (with Ragossnig and the Lamoureux Orchestra, issued in the United States by Victrola), *Kaleidoscope* (with a chamber ensemble *et al.*) and *Suite for the Tenth Winter Olympics* (with the Lamoureux Orchestra *et al.*, the last two issued in the US by Musical Heritage Society), and his Quartet No. 1 and *Giocoso*, for violin and string orchestra, have also been recorded. He also conducted a recording of Landowski's Concerto for Ondes Martenot, Strings and Percussion (with Jeanne Loriod and the Contemporary Music Chamber Orchestra, issued by Musical Heritage Society).

Bongartz, Heinz (1894–1978). Born in Krefeld, Germany, Bongartz was educated at the conservatories at Krefeld and Cologne, under Ney, Neitzel and Steinbach. He became a choral conductor (1919), conductor at the Mönchengladbach Opera (1923), of the Berlin Symphony Orchestra (1924–6), at the Landeskapelle at Meiningen (1926–30), at Gotha (1930–33), of the Blüthner Orchestra in Berlin (1933), at Kassel (1933–7), was general music director at Saarbrücken (1939–44), chief conductor of the Pfalz Orchestra at Ludwigshafen (1945), professor at the

Hochschule für Musik at Leipzig (1946–7), and conductor of the Dresden Philharmonic Orchestra (1947–64). He was also a guest conductor in East and West Europe, the USSR, China, Cuba and the Middle East, was awarded the Gustav Mahler Gold Medal by the Gustav Mahler Society in Vienna (1966), and received awards in DR Germany.

Bongartz made a number of distinguished recordings with orchestras in DR Germany, some of which have been issued in the West by Philips, Urania, DGG and Electrola. Included were the *Brandenburg Concertos Nos 3* and *5*, Beethoven's two *Romances* (with Suske), Piano Concerto No. 1 and *Rondo in B major* (with Rösel) and *Wellington's Victory*, and Bruckner's Symphony No. 6 (with the Leipzig Gewandhaus Orchestra); Brahms' Serenades Nos 1 and 2, Dvořák's Symphony No. 7, Hindemith's *Nobilissima Visione*, Haydn's Symphony No. 94, Reger's *Sinfonietta*, Rachmaninov's Symphony No. 1, the *Oberon* overture, Paganini's Violin Concerto No. 1 and Sarasate's *Zigeunerweisen* (with Voicu) and Kodály's *Concerto for Orchestra* (with the Dresden Philharmonic Orchestra); Beethoven's incidental music for *Egmont* (with the Berlin Staatskapelle *et al.*); Prokofiev's Piano Concerto No. 2 (with Rösel and the Leipzig Radio Symphony Orchestra); Reger's *Variations and Fugue on a Theme of Mozart* (with the Dresden Staatskapelle); and also *Finlandia*, *Valse triste*, Tchaikovsky's Piano Concerto No. 2, Mahler's *Rückert Lieder*, Prokofiev's Violin Concerto No. 2, Rachmaninov's *Variations on a Theme of Paganini*, Reger's *Vier Tondichtungen nach Arnold Böcklin* and *An die Hoffnung*, Hindemith's *Mathis der Maler* symphony, Thilman's Symphony No. 4 and *Partita piccola*, Cilenšek's Symphony No. 1, Finke's *Suite for Orchestra*, Hohensee's *Konzertante Ouvertüre*, Kurz's Trumpet Concerto and Lohse's *Divertimento* (with orchestras and soloists unidentified).

Some of these performances are still available on Eterna. Garnet, in FR Germany, has also issued Reger's *Sinfonietta* in which Bongartz conducts the West German Radio Orchestra (*sic*). Bongartz's style is essentially German – broad tempi, unaffected phrasing, legato smoothness of strings and woodwinds, controlled yet powerful expression; these qualities are well illustrated in the performances of the Bruckner symphony and Reger *Variations*, in particular.

Bonneau, Paul (b. 1918). Born at Moret-sur-Loing, France, Bonneau studied at the Paris Conservatoire, and since 1944 has been director of light music for Radio France, for which he has conducted over 1,500 concerts. He has also composed film scores and has adapted operettas and musical comedies, especially for performance at the Théâtre du Châtelet in Paris. He has recorded Chabrier's *España*, *Bourrée fantasque*, *Marche joyeuse* and *Suite pastorale*, and Grieg's *Norwegian Dances*, *Two Norwegian Melodies* and *Wedding Day at Troldhaugen* (with the Orchestre du Théâtre des Champs-Élysées, for Charlin), Dutilleux's ballet *Le Loup* and Messager's *Les deux Pigeons* and *Isoline* (with the same orchestra, *et al.*), Lopez's *La Toison d'or* (with the Orchestre du Théâtre du Châtelet *et al.*), Youmans' *No No Nanette* and Straus' *Walzertraum* (with the Colonne Orchestra *et al.* for EMI), excerpts from Benatzky's *White Horse Inn* and Friml's *Rose Marie* (with an orchestra, *et al.*, for Philips and Pathé, respectively), Mareuil and Tirmont's *Rendez-vous à Paris*, and arias and duets from operettas (with Raynal, Millet, *et al.*, and the Monte Carlo National Orchestra).

Bonynge, Richard (b. 1930). Bonynge was playing the piano at the age of four, then studied the bassoon and piano at the New South Wales State Conservatorium of Music at his birthplace, Sydney; there he came under the influence of its director, Sir Eugene Goossens. After appearances in Australia as a concert pianist he travelled to England and attended the Royal College of Music, where his attention turned to opera and ballet. He had met his fellow Australian, the soprano Joan Sutherland, whom he coached in the *bel canto* style of singing; the two were married in 1954 and since then their two careers have been inseparable. He started as a conductor in 1962 when he took over at short notice at an orchestral concert at which Joan Sutherland was appearing in Rome. His first opera was *Faust*, in Vancouver in 1963, and thereafter he has conducted opera extensively in the United States, most particularly in Philadelphia and San Francisco. More recently he has become musical director of the Australian Opera. He has made an intense study of the operas of Bellini and his period, and has introduced into Sutherland's performances of this repertoire embellishments and ornaments from many sources. His sympathy for the singers makes him an effective and distinguished opera conductor, although his musical interests range beyond the opera house. As he customarily conducts for all of Sutherland's operatic and concert appearances around the world he has exceptional opportunities to excel in this medium. He gives little attention to modern operas, saying that present-day composers do not write for singers: 'This is why I think if we are to enjoy singing we have to go back and do the composers who wrote for singers, who knew what singing was all about.'

Bonynge's first records were made in 1962, when he directed Handel's *Alcina* for Decca with Sutherland leading the cast. Virtually all his subsequent records have been made for Decca, and he has conducted almost every recording in which Sutherland has appeared. He has been most successful, indeed outstanding, in the repertoire in which he is most expert – the operas of Bellini and Donizetti, and has recorded *La Fille du régiment* and *Lucia di Lammermoor* (with the Covent Garden Orchestra), *Maria Stuarda* (with the Bologna Theatre Orchestra), *L'elisir d'amore* (with the English Chamber Orchestra), *Norma*, *I Puritani* and *Beatrice di Tenda* (with the London Symphony Orchestra), and *La sonnambula* (with the Maggio Musicale Fiorentino). His other operatic recordings have been *Don Giovanni* (with the English Chamber Orchestra), *Les Contes d'Hoffmann* (with the Suisse Romande Orchestra), Graun's *Montezuma* (excerpts, with the London Philharmonic Orchestra), Handel's *Giulio Cesare* (excerpts, with the New Symphony Orchestra), *Faust*, *Semiramide* and *Rigoletto* (with the London Symphony Orchestra), *Lakmé* (with the Monte Carlo National Opera Orchestra), *Il trovatore* and Leoni's *L'Oracolo* (with the National Philharmonic Orchestra), Massenet's *Thérèse* and Meyerbeer's *Les Huguenots* (with the New Philharmonia Orchestra), Bononcini's *Griselda* (excerpts, with the London Philharmonic Orchestra) and Shield's *Rosina* (with the London Symphony Orchestra). Other discs with Sutherland included Glière's Concerto for Coloratura and Orchestra and Harp Concerto (with Ellis), and *Messiah* (with the English Chamber Orchestra). While many did, some of these recordings did not receive universal acclaim. *Les Huguenots* was eagerly awaited but when it arrived critical enthusiasm was cool to Bonynge's direction, and criticism was again heaped on his head for ornamentation in *Messiah* which was taken to unusual lengths and caused one writer to note that he seemed 'determined to make the straight crooked and the plain places rough.'

Discs of overtures and sinfonias from Handel operas and oratorios and sinfonias of J. C. Bach and Salieri (with the English Chamber Orchestra) again were praised with faint damns, but Bonynge's many records of 19th-century ballet music and operatic overtures have been uniformly successful and show him at his best in purely orchestral music. Included have been *Coppélia* (with the Suisse Romande Orchestra), *Sylvia* (with the New Philharmonia Orchestra), *Giselle* (with the Monte Carlo National Opera Orchestra), *Nutcracker* and *Swan Lake* (with the National Philharmonic Orchestra), Burgmüller's *La Péri* and Offenbach's *Le Papillon* (with the London Symphony Orchestra), discs of excerpts and pieces of ballets by Minkus, Rossini, Drigo, Løvenskjold, Tchaikovsky, Donizetti, Auber, Helsted, Luigini, Saint-Saëns, Massenet, Rubinstein, Czibulka, Kreisler, Assafieff, Lincke, Delibes, Catalini and Krupinski (with the London Symphony Orchestra), and overtures and excerpts from operas by Donizetti, Rossini, Maillart, Offenbach, Verdi, Hérold, Wallace, Meyerbeer, Massenet, Cherubini, Gounod, Boieldieu, Bizet, Saint-Saëns, Delibes and Auber (with the London Symphony Orchestra). Two other discs have been a collection of overtures by the 18th-century composers Kraus, Gassmann, Boieldieu, Paër, Grétry, Sacchini, Haydn and Salieri (with the English Chamber Orchestra) and Massenet's *Scènes alsaciennes*, *Scènes dramatiques* and the march from *Cendrillon* (with the National Philharmonic Orchestra).

Bopp, Joseph (b. 1908). Born in Mulhouse, Bopp studied at the Strasbourg Conservatory, in Paris with Le Roy, and in Basel with Weingartner (1932–3) and Münch (1936–8). He was a flautist in the Mulhouse City Orchestra and with the Basel Orchestral Society; in 1943 he joined the Schola Cantorum Basiliensis, and has toured and recorded as a flautist. He conducted the Schola Cantorum Basiliensis in a recording of the Boccherini Cello Concerto (with Wenzinger, for DGG).

Borbély, Gyula (b. 1930). Born in Budapest, Borbély was a pupil of Kodály, Somogyi and Szervánsky at the Franz Liszt Music Academy at Budapest, and graduated as a conductor with distinction in 1954. He conducted the Hungarian State Symphony Orchestra and the Hungarian Radio and Television Orchestra (1952), and has been a regular conductor of the Budapest State Opera. He toured in Austria and in East European countries, including the USSR; his repertoire extends from the baroque era to Bartók, Kodály and Prokofiev, and critics have commented on his dramatic sense, his control of orchestral balance and his sensitivity. For Hungaroton he has recorded flute concertos by Boccherini, Vivaldi and Szervánsky (with Jeney and the Hungarian Radio and Television Orchestra), the Mozart Clarinet Concerto (with Meizl) and Szervánsky's *Concerto in memoriam József Attila* (with the Hungarian State Orchestra).

Borchard, Leo (1899–1945). Born in Moscow, Borchard was active as a conductor in Germany, where he was an assistant to Walter and Klemperer. After the German collapse at the end of World War II he assembled the members of the Berlin Philharmonic Orchestra and directed their first concert, but was unfortunately killed by a soldier of the occupying forces. With the Berlin Philharmonic Orchestra he recorded a suite from *Nutcracker* (for Ultraphone), the overture to Suppé's *Banditenstreiche*, Wotan's Farewell from Act III of *Die Walküre* (with Reinmar the soloist) and Françaix's Concertino (with the composer at the piano, for Telefunken).

Boskovsky, Willi (b. 1909). A Viennese, Boskovsky enrolled at the Vienna Academy at the age of nine, studied the violin with Mayrecker and Moravec, and graduated at seventeen having won the Fritz Kreisler Prize. He soon made a name as a solo violinist and continued making solo appearances until 1939. He joined the Vienna Philharmonic Orchestra in 1932, and in 1939 Knappertsbusch made him one of the orchestra's four leaders. In 1937 he founded the Boskovsky Trio, and in 1947 the Boskovsky Quartet. At an initial concert in 1947 when he led a group performing the Schubert Octet and the Beethoven Septet, the Vienna Octet came into being; Boskovsky remained its leader until 1958, and his brother Alfred Boskovsky was the Octet's clarinet player. His career as a conductor started in 1954 when he was asked to direct for the first time the Vienna New Year's Concert, which he has continued to do ever since.

Boskovsky is renowned for his superb recordings for Decca of the music of Johann Strauss and others of the Strauss family, and of the dance music of Mozart. He has explained that, when Johann Strauss was alive, his music was used generally for balls, entertainment and dancing. 'Then it fell into the hands of second-rate players, and people got tired of it. Now we have rescued these wonderful pieces and they are really listened to for their own sake. People realise how subtle the music is, as well as how friendly and gay. Even players who often begin by thinking of it as second-class come to change their minds, once they can play it really well.' Repeating the earlier success for Decca of Clemens Krauss with the Vienna Philharmonic Orchestra, Boskovsky has led the same orchestra on a number of magnificent Strauss discs, the first being issued in 1958, and continuing almost to the present day. A selection of ten of the most popular items from these discs, issued on a Decca cheap label in 1969, made the Top Twenty. In the entire Strauss discography Boskovsky's records lead the field. Other records, made for Philips and Vanguard, have been issued of the Viennese dance music of Strauss, Lanner and their contemporaries. To cap them all, in 1973 Decca issued *Die Fledermaus*, with a cast including Gedda, Rothenberger and Fischer-Dieskau, and Boskovsky conducting the Vienna Symphony Orchestra. For EMI he has since recorded Zeller's *Der Vogelhändler* and Suppé's *Boccaccio* (with the Vienna Symphony Orchestra *et al.*) Strauss' *Wiener Blut* (with the Cologne Opera Orchestra *et al.*), Lehár's *Paganini* (with the Bavarian State Opera Orchestra *et al.*), a collection of waltzes by Strauss (with the Johann Strauss Orchestra of Vienna), a collection of waltzes and polkas of Waldteufel (with the Monte Carlo National Opera Orchestra) and the Liszt *Hungarian Rhapsodies Nos 1, 4* and *6*, the *Rákóczy March* and the *Hungarian Battle March* (with the Philharmonia Hungarica); for Decca a selection of Brahms *Hungarian Dances* and Dvořák *Slavonic Dances* (with the London Symphony Orchestra) and for Eterna the *Rosamunde* music of Schubert (with the Dresden Staatskapelle *et al.*).

Perhaps even more impressive has been the complete dances, marches and minuets of Mozart, issued on nine discs by Decca between 1964 and 1967, with Boskovsky leading the Vienna Mozart Ensemble; more recently the group has been recording all the Mozart cassations, serenades and divertimentos, except those for woodwind. The musicians' unerring sense of style and impeccable playing in the two series defy analysis; Boskovsky has said that he learned the real understanding of Mozart's music from performing the violin concertos with Bruno Walter in the 1930s. His ensemble is made up of fine and diligent young artists from the Vienna Philharmonic, who, he has pointed out, do not keep looking at their watches during recording sessions. Their devotion to their task is evident in every note they play, as well as in the absolute authority of their leader.

Bosse, Gerhard (b. 1922). Born in Wurzen, Bosse studied in Weimar, and became the concertmaster of the Leipzig Gewandhaus Orchestra, leader of the Leipzig Bach Orchestra, and professor of violin at the Felix Mendelssohn

Bartholdy Hochschule für Musik at Leipzig. He has toured many foreign countries, and has participated in Bach festivals in several countries. His recordings include Bach's Cantatas Nos 199 and 209 (released by Eurodisc) and the Flute, Violin and Harpsichord Concerto (with Hörtsch, himself and Kästner), and the Three-Harpsichord Concerto (with himself, Glass and Nietner, released by Philips); all were with the Leipzig Bach Orchestra, which is an ensemble from the Gewandhaus Orchestra.

Boulanger, Nadia (1887–1979). The distinguished French composer, teacher and conductor Nadia Boulanger was born in Paris and was educated at the Paris Conservatoire; she won the Prix de Rome (1908), taught at the Conservatoire from where she retired in 1957, at the École Normale de Musique in Paris, and from 1949 was director of the American Conservatory at Fontainebleau. Her influence on some generations of musicians, especially Americans, was immense; in Copland's estimation it was incalculable. Among her pupils were Copland himself, Piston, Harris, Barenboim and Berkeley, and she had a close association with Markevitch. She lived in the United States from 1939 to 1943; she had first visited the country in 1925 and conducted major symphony orchestras. In 1937 she was the first woman to conduct an entire programme at the Royal Philharmonic Society in London, gave the first performance in England of the Fauré *Requiem*, and afterwards conducted the work scores of times. Her uniqueness as a teacher lay in her ability to develop the individuality of all her students, each of whom had a different experience with her. She taught all styles of music, including the twelve-tone system, but gave it little attention, for she believed that music written in this manner is too tense. In her estimation few masterpieces have yet appeared in twelve-tone music; she accepted *Wozzeck* as one, but not *Lulu*. Electronic and aleatoric music had no appeal to her. She asked: 'But who makes the music?' Although she was credited with being one of the first to perform Monteverdi in modern times, she pointed out that d'Indy was the first to do so in France, but he made the mistake of performing it in French.

In 1937 HMV issued three sets of discs, Françaix's *Piano Concerto in D* (with the composer at the piano, and Boulanger conducting the Paris Philharmonic Orchestra), the Brahms *Liebeslieder* waltzes (with a vocal group and with Boulanger and Lipatti the duo-pianists) and a five-disc set of the first music of Monteverdi ever to be recorded (with Boulanger directing a French vocal and instrumental ensemble). The selection of the Monteverdi pieces was made by her, and the recording was a revelation, and was described by Sackville-West and Shawe-Taylor in *The Record Guide* (1951) as 'one of the purest treasures the gramophone has given us'. The music was transferred to LP, and has been reissued on many labels. Her other recordings have included excerpts from Charpentier's *Médée*, Claude's *Chansons*, excerpts from the operas of Rameau, and a disc of French Renaissance vocal music, including pieces by Josquin, Jannequin, Le Jeune, Lassus, Costeley, Sermisy, Mauduit and Bonnet (for Brunswick).

Boulez, Pierre (b. 1925). Born in Montbrison, France, Boulez learned the piano as a boy; he was encouraged by the soprano Ninon Vallin to take formal teaching, but after several unsuccessful attempts to enter the conservatoires at Lyon and Paris as a piano student, he eventually came to Paris and studied composition with Messiaen, Leibowitz and with Honegger's wife, Andrée Vaurabourg, at the Paris Conservatoire. From there he graduated with honours in 1945, and immediately became known as an *enfant terrible* and as an outspoken opponent of conservative elements in music by leading a demonstration at a concert of some of Stravinsky's neo-classical pieces in Paris. In 1945 he also heard for the first time Schoenberg's Quintet for Wind Op. 26, which struck him as the most radical revolution in music since Monteverdi, and as the only possible musical language for our time. His first appointment was in 1946 as musical director of the Compagnie Renaud-Barrault, and in his first appearance at the theatre played the Ondes Martenot, an electronic instrument, in some incidental music to *Hamlet* by Honegger. With Barrault's company he toured Europe, North and South America and the Far East. At this time and with the help of Barrault and his actress wife, Madeleine Renaud, he founded and organised the Domaine Musical concerts in Paris, which were devoted to performances of contemporary music and to rarely heard masterpieces of the past. The Domaine Musical concerts scored a triumph in 1957 when Stravinsky directed the first performance of *Agon*. Boulez conducted in public for the first time in 1956 when he substituted for Rosbaud at the première of his *Le Marteau sans maître*, and in 1957 Scherchen entrusted him with conducting his own *Visage nuptial* in Cologne, and so started his distinguished international career.

In 1960 Boulez left Paris and joined the South-West German Radio at Baden-Baden, where he made his home; the Radio had offered him a small income for the right to the first performances of his works. Under the influence of Rosbaud, then the musical director of the Radio Orchestra, he developed as a conductor, at first of his own music. In 1963 he returned to Paris to lead a remarkable first performance there of *Wozzeck*, and after making his London debut in 1964 with the BBC Symphony Orchestra he progressed rapidly as an international celebrity. He made his debut in the United States with the Cleveland Orchestra (1965), appeared at the Edinburgh Festival (1965), conducted *Parsifal* at Bayreuth (1966), conducted *Tristan und Isolde* with the Bayreuth Company on a tour to Japan, led performances of *Pelléas et Mélisande* at Covent Garden (1969) and finally was appointed chief conductor of the BBC Symphony Orchestra (1971–5), musical director of the New York Philharmonic Orchestra (1971–7) and principal guest conductor of the Cleveland Orchestra. In 1975 he became director of the Institut de Recherche et de Co-ordination Acoustique/Musique at Beaubourg in Paris (the result of an initiative by the late President Pompidou, financed by the French government), with the aim of bringing together performers, composers and scientists to find new approaches to composing and performing modern music. The Institut provides the best possible environment and equipment for composers, and plans to bring new works into the repertoire. In 1976 Boulez returned to Bayreuth to conduct the controversial *Ring* produced by Chéreau.

Although his commitments as a conductor have in the past brought a diminution to his output as a composer, Boulez remains one of the foremost composers to emerge since World War II; he attempts to apply serial techniques to all the elements of music, in addition to melody, as it originated with Schoenberg. His early piano sonatas created an immediate impression, which was later confirmed by *Le Soleil des eaux* (1948), *Structures* (1952), *Le Marteau sans maître* (1955), *Pli selon pli* (1960), *Doubles* (1958), *Domaines* (1968) and a work in memory of Stravinsky, *Explosante-fixe* (1973). However, his leadership of the *avant-garde* in Paris was uncompromising and abrasive; differences about aleatoric music (that is, where elements in a composition are left in an indeterminate state) have divided him from most of his contemporaries, and despite his high regard for Stockhausen he has given little attention to electronic music. He once contemplated collaborating in a stage work but has no ambition to write an opera. He regards his former teacher Messiaen as the only great French composer to appear between the two world wars; to him Debussy is the only French composer of the last two centuries who is universal, and among British composers he is interested in Goehr, Davies, Bennett and more particularly Birtwistle. As a conductor he is not concerned with much of the music of the 19th-century classics, such as Brahms, Tchaikovsky and Strauss, since they were not innovators compared to Beethoven, Berlioz, Debussy and Wagner, who have accordingly earned his admiration. He prefers to perform rarely heard classical and modern pieces and to develop new ways of including them in his programmes.

Conducting started for Boulez as a hobby, to give him the chance to hear his own music and to learn what was practical when writing for the orchestra. When he accepted the appointments in London and New York he aimed to bring about a vast and radical change in orchestral programmes and in the organisation of concert life. For him musical life must be revitalised so that it is part of a genuine living culture and part of the musical creative activity of our time, not a 'kind of second-rate enjoyment'. At present, he says, 'audiences try to rediscover at concerts the first emotions they felt on hearing classical music', but he feels no obligation to provide them with that opportunity. Audiences have to be brought into contact, readily and willingly, with music written today, but this implies being familiar with the music from which it springs, that is the Second Viennese School of Schoenberg, Berg and Webern, who provided the indispensable link between Strauss, Mahler, Debussy and the other late romantic and impressionist composers, and the composers of today. His mission then has been to have the music of Schoenberg, Berg and Webern accepted as part of the regular orchestral repertoire, and in London and New York he had ample opportunity to work towards these ends. He re-arranged concert programmes, found new ways and places to have concerts to bridge the gap between audiences and performers. His influence was certainly marked, if not profound; in New York the result was that the audience for the New York Philharmonic concerts became decidedly younger as the more elderly and conservative members drifted away (perhaps to return with the advent of Zubin Mehta); in London the BBC Symphony Orchestra is only one of a number of orchestras giving regular concerts, but it became highly proficient at performing contemporary music.

Despite the self-imposed limitations of his

repertoire, Boulez is undoubtedly one of the finest conductors of the day. Klemperer called him 'the only man of his generation who is an outstanding conductor and musician'. (P. Heyworth, *Conversations with Klemperer*, London, 1973, p. 93). Technically he is exemplary: he uses no baton, and his left hand is employed merely to measure a crescendo. His ear is extremely acute and his ability to single out one player in the orchestra for correction has brought many players to despair. His sound is unique; no matter how much he insists that his orchestra is simply playing the notes accurately, the lean, clear Boulez sound emerges. When he conducted the Philadelphia Orchestra their characteristic tonal bloom vanished and the cool sound of the Boulez orchestra took its place. His profound understanding of musical structure gives continuity and coherence to the music, and it never becomes a series of brilliant episodes. He reacts strongly against the traditional readings of the great musical masterpieces and casts an iconoclastic eye at the interpretations of the great conductors of the past. His generation, he feels, has no use for the traditions of the past; 'for me, the right tradition is to give a new face to each generation. Generally, the danger of maintaining a style or tradition is that, on the contrary, you maintain mannerisms.' He believes his generation sees the music of the past through a different perspective from earlier performers: 'my generation wants to combine a high degree of precision with a great deal of interpretative freedom'. Scores, he says, 'must be interpreted in the spirit of the time. How Bach was played in 1920 is not how we like to hear him today. The superficial elegance that people appreciated in Mozart is not what we admire in him [now].' His conducting of *Pelléas et Mélisande* illustrated this point; to him it is cruel and mysterious, not sweet and gentle, as it is in the usual French tradition. Even so, it has been noted that the cold precision of his earlier recordings has given way more recently to something more warm and humane.

Rehearsals with Boulez are calm and even-tempered. He gives more time to the music that interests him, sometimes to the detriment of other music on the programme. Usually he goes through a piece completely, then bit by bit, repeating passages and sometimes separate groups of instruments until he is satisfied. His manner at concerts is completely without any trace of flamboyance, and his facial expression rarely betrays emotion. 'I do get excited,' he explains, 'but I am not obliged to look excited.' In the words of Winthrop Sargent, 'his attitude seems to be that of a strict physician who is going to see that you take your medicine whether you like it or not.'

In his early years as a conductor Boulez made a number of recordings with the Domaine Musical ensemble, which were released by Everest, and included Schoenberg's *Verklärte Nacht*, *Pierrot Lunaire*, *Serenade* Op. 24, *Three Pieces for Chamber Orchestra*, and the Chamber Symphony No. 1, as well as Messiaen's *Sept Haï-Kaï*, Pousseur's *Madrigal III*, Éloy's *Équivalences*, Webern's Symphony and two Cantatas, and Stravinsky's *Renard*, *Concertino* and *Symphonies of Wind Instruments*. For La Guilde Internationale du Disque he conducted the Hague Philharmonic Orchestra in Handel's *Water Music*, which was released by Nonesuch; for this score he has a predilection and recorded it again in 1975 with the New York Philharmonic. The first of his recordings of *Le Sacre du printemps* was also made for GID and released by Nonesuch, with the Orchestre National de RTF; it brought the comment from Stravinsky that 'apart from sloppiness . . . there are some very bad tempi. [The performance] is [not] good enough to be preserved.' Boulez made handsome amends in the 1970 disc of the work with the Cleveland Orchestra. His other recordings in Europe at this time were Stravinsky's *Les Noces* (with the Paris Opéra Orchestra *et al.* for GID), a Flute Concerto and Cello Concerto of C. P. E. Bach (with Rampal and Bex respectively, for Vox), his own *Le Marteau sans maître* (for Harmonia Mundi), Milhaud's *Christophe Colomb* (the Barrault production complete, for Telefunken) and Messiaen's *Et exspecto resurrectionem mortuorum* and *Couleurs de la cité céleste* (for Erato).

Except for the Berg Violin Concerto and the Bartók Rhapsodies Nos 1 and 2 (with Menuhin and the BBC Symphony for EMI), the Bartók Piano Concertos Nos 1 and 3 (with Barenboim and the New Philharmonia for EMI), Birtwistle's *The Triumph of Time* and his own *Le Soleil des eaux* (with the BBC Symphony *et al.* for Argo), and *Le Sacre du printemps* and *Études pour orchestre* of Stravinsky (with the Orchestre NRTF for Festival), all his subsequent records have been produced for CBS. They are a spectacular series, and many have become contemporary classics of the gramophone. Of his own music he recorded *Pli selon pli* (with the BBC Symphony), *Le Marteau sans maître* (with Minton and Ensemble Musique Vivante) and *Livre pour cordes* (with the New Philharmonia); of the Second Viennese School there is Schoenberg's *Five Pieces for Orchestra*, *Music to Accompany a Film Score*, *A Survivor from Warsaw*, *Variations* Op. 31, *Moses und Aron* and *Gurrelieder* (with the BBC Symphony *et al.*), *Verklärte Nacht* (with the New York Philharmonic), Berg's Violin Concerto (mentioned above), *Altenberg Lieder*, Chamber Concerto and *Three Pieces* Op. 6 (with the BBC Symphony *et al.*), *Lyric Suite* (with the New York Philharmonic) and *Wozzeck* (with the Paris Opéra). His other recordings include Bartók's *Music for Strings, Percussion and Celesta*, *Two Rhapsodies* and *Bluebeard's Castle* (with the BBC Symphony), *Dance Suite*, *Concerto for Orchestra*, *The Miraculous Mandarin* and *The Wooden Prince* (with the New York Philharmonic) and the Piano Concertos Nos 1 and 3 (mentioned above), Messiaen's *Poèmes pour Mi* (with Palmer and the BBC Symphony), Stravinsky's *Le Sacre du printemps* (mentioned above), *L'Oiseau de feu* and *Petrushka* (with the New York Philharmonic), Debussy's *Images*, *Danse sacrée et danse profane* (with the Cleveland Orchestra), *La Mer*, *Prélude à l'après-midi d'un faune*, *Jeux*, *Nocturnes*, *Printemps* and *Rhapsodie No. 1 for Clarinet* (with the New Philharmonia) and *Pelléas et Mélisande* (with the Royal Opera, Covent Garden), Ravel's *Une Barque sur l'océan*, *Daphnis et Chloé*, *Valses nobles et sentimentales*, *Le Tombeau de Couperin*, *La Valse*, *Menuet antique* and *Ma Mère l'Oye* (with the New York Philharmonic) and *Concerto in D for Left Hand* (with Entremont and the Cleveland Orchestra).

Other music Boulez has recorded is Dukas' *La Péri*, Roussel's Symphony No. 3, Falla's Harpsichord Concerto and a suite from *The Three-cornered Hat*; also there are discs of overtures by Berlioz and Wagner (with the New York Philharmonic), Mahler's *Das klagende Lied* and Adagio from the Symphony No. 10, and Berlioz's *Symphonie fantastique* and *Lélio* (with the London Symphony), Beethoven's Symphony No. 5 and *Meeresstille und glückliche Fahrt* (with the New Philharmonia *et al.*) and *Parsifal* (with the Bayreuth Festival Orchestra *et al.*). Of these latter discs, the *Symphonie fantastique* was an outstanding example of his musicianship, but the Beethoven symphony was almost a curiosity with its slow tempi and uncommitted air. For Donemus he recorded the Dutch composers Schat's *Entelechy No. 2* and Vlijmen's *Gruppi* (with the Amsterdam Concertgebouw Orchestra); also his own *Le Marteau sans maître* (with an ensemble for BASF).

The opera sets – *Parsifal*, *Pelléas et Mélisande* and *Wozzeck* – were recorded after performances in opera houses, and exemplify his highly personal approach to these scores. *Wozzeck* was criticised for certain inaccuracies; *Pelléas et Mélisande* demonstrated his untraditional approach to this music, and *Parsifal* was too much for those who had been affected by Knappertsbusch's devoted reading. Desmond Shawe-Taylor wrote of its 'chilly effect, as though of a deconsecrated cathedral through which we are shepherded in pretty smart time.' Yet, with *Gurrelieder* (issued in 1975), Boulez appeared to relax his former severity in managing this huge, sensuous score, as if he were coming closer to the aesthetic of the late romantics, which he had earlier despised.

Boult, Sir Adrian (b. 1889). The son of a Liverpool merchant, Boult was born at Chester, Lancashire, and studied at Christ Church, Oxford, where he was awarded a D.Phil. in Music. At Oxford he came into contact with Sir Hugh Allen, who was then professor of music. Afterwards he went to the Leipzig Conservatory, where he observed Nikisch and studied with Reger (1912–13). He returned to England, gave some orchestral concerts in Liverpool, conducted opera at Covent Garden where he assisted with the Bodanzky performance of *Parsifal* (1914), and came into prominence when he directed several concerts of the Royal Philharmonic Society (1918). He was with the War Office and the Commission Internationale de Ravitaillement in World War I, and has told the story that at one point he helped to organise the supply of footwear to the British army; in his office, surrounded by boots, Vaughan Williams made the first revision of his *London Symphony*. From 1919 to 1930 he was a member of the teaching staff of the Royal College of Music; among his students were Leslie Heward and Constant Lambert. His subject was conducting; in 1921 he published *A Handbook on Conducting* and 42 years later produced another volume, *Thoughts on Conducting*. In the early 1920s he conducted the British Symphony Orchestra, which had been formed by ex-service musicians, the London Symphony Orchestra, the Diaghilev Ballet Company and the British National Opera Company, leading *Die Walküre*, *Parsifal* and *Otello*.

Boult's first major appointment was with the City of Birmingham Orchestra (1924–30). In 1930 he was named director of music at the British Broadcasting Corporation and permanent chief conductor of the newly formed BBC Symphony Orchestra. His work with the orchestra in its formative years was possibly his greatest contribution to British music. When it was assembled most of the best players in Britain were recruited for the front desks, and as it was a permanent radio orchestra there was ample rehearsal time and its standards were higher than those then prevailing in the country. In its first concert in October 1930 was included Brahms' Symphony No. 4, for which Boult had 12–15 rehearsals. The orchestra became one of the leading ensembles in Europe until World War II; the London Philharmonic, formed by Sir Thomas Beecham in 1932 because he had been precluded from conducting the BBC Symphony, was a rival. Toscanini had the highest regard for the BBC Symphony and conducted it on visits to England in 1935, 1937, 1938 and 1939, and the exceptional results he achieved with it in his recordings in England were not accidental.

Boult remained with the BBC until 1950 when he was obliged to resign, having reached the retiring age for a civil servant. In his 20 years with the orchestra he led 1,536 concerts, an average of 77 a year. In the 1920s and 1930s he toured frequently in Germany, Austria, Spain, Czechoslovakia and in the United States, where he was one of the very few guest conductors with the Boston Symphony Orchestra. To these overseas audiences he introduced much British music; at the Salzburg Festival in 1935 he presented a programme entirely of British music. All his life he has been a consistent champion of British music both on record and in concert; Vaughan Williams, Holst, Elgar, Bliss, Moeran, Ireland and others have received his dedicated patronage, and he believes that Parry, Stanford and Rubbra are the most underrated British composers in this century. Curiously, Boult never recorded Delius and gave him virtually no attention. He was knighted for services to music in 1937 and was awarded the Gold Medal of the Royal Philharmonic Society in 1944. After retiring from the BBC he became principal conductor of the London Philharmonic Orchestra (1950), but resigned from the position after leading them on a tour to the USSR in 1956. He nonetheless retained a close connection with the London Philharmonic, and in 1959–60 spent the season with the City of Birmingham Symphony Orchestra. Also, from 1962 to 1966 he returned to the staff of the Royal College of Music.

Boult is a modest, patient and undemonstrative musician with catholic musical tastes. Despite his success with *Wozzeck*, which he presented after intensive preparation with the BBC Symphony and soloists in the 1933–4 season, he professes little comprehension of twelve-tone music; in 1931 he performed, with apparent distinction, the Schoenberg *Variations for Orchestra*, but said that when he came to do the piece again three years later in Vienna, performing it, incredibly, for the first time there, he found nothing in the score to remind him of the previous performance. He then remarked to himself that if someone had said to him that it was an entirely new set of variations on a different theme he would have believed them. He dislikes showmanship of any kind, once saying that a conductor should appeal to the eyes of the orchestra and to the ears of the audience. On the podium his stance is exceptionally still; he never uses his feet and his left hand comes into play only sparingly. In rehearsal he is economical, and in a symphony he will play to the end of the exposition before replaying unsatisfactory passages. He endeavours to have the composer present when rehearsing a new work, although he once found one British composer so exasperating at a rehearsal that he greeted her: 'Good morning, Dame Ethel, and what are your tempi for today?' From his public performances it would be difficult to detect his personal preferences, but he has remarked that he considers it his duty to make the best of whatever score he is given: 'As an executant I am not, and have no right to be, a critic of any kind, even to the extent of having preferences or favourites.'

Boult has said that the greatest influences on him as a young man were Richter, because of the solidity and architectural power of his conducting, and Wood, whose performances had affection and beauty. In later years he much admired Weingartner, Furtwängler and Walter. Casals, too, was a profound teacher; Boult once spent a month at Barcelona observing him rehearsing his orchestra. From Nikisch Boult learned to talk with the point of his baton and not with his voice at rehearsals. In his autobiography, *My Own Trumpet* (1973) he named those who were the greatest conductors in his experience: for Bach – Steinbach and Hugh Allen; for Haydn and Mozart – Strauss and Walter; for Beethoven – Richter, Safanoff, Furtwängler and Weingartner; for Brahms – Steinbach; for Wagner – Richter, Walter (for *The Ring* and *Die Meistersinger*) and Nikisch (for *Tristan und Isolde*); for Tchaikovsky – Wood and Safanoff. Boult's own strength as a conductor is best revealed in music in large forms and breadth of structure; his emotional reserve makes him less impressive, some may say dull, in highly coloured but less significant music. His acute ear gives him an unusual capacity for achieving a fine balance among the instrumental groups, and he appeals to the musicians to listen to one another. He rarely edits a score, but in Beethoven follows Weingartner's alterations. Normally he obeys scrupulously the composer's instructions, particularly with Elgar. He conducts familiar repertoire from memory, otherwise he uses a score.

Boult has now recorded longer than any living artist, from 1920 to the present day. His first discs were with the British Symphony Orchestra: *La Boutique fantasque*, *The Good-humoured Ladies* (the Scarlatti/Tommasini ballet score), Butterworth's *A Shropshire Lad*, Bliss's *Rout*, and the overture, Witch's Ride and Dream Pantomime from *Hänsel und Gretel* (for HMV). Other early discs were Ethel Smyth's *Two Interlocked French Folk Melodies* and the minuet from *Fête galante* (with the Light Symphony Orchestra for HMV), Schubert's Symphony No. 8, the Franck *Symphonic Variations* and Liszt's Piano Concerto No. 1 (with Anderson Tyler and the British Symphony Orchestra for Edison Bell Velvet Face), the overture to *Der Freischütz* and the procession from Act III of *Die Meistersinger* (with the Festival Symphony Orchestra for Vocalion). His next records did not appear until 1931, when he began a famous series for HMV with the new BBC Symphony Orchestra, and continued until his departure from the BBC in 1950. The first was the Good Friday Music from *Parsifal*; major works were Bach's Suite No. 3, Mozart's Symphonies Nos 32 and 41, Beethoven's Symphony No. 8 and Piano Concerto No. 3 (with Solomon), Schubert's Symphony No. 9, the Brahms *Tragic Overture* and Piano Concertos Nos 1 (with Backhaus) and 2 (with Schnabel), Tchaikovsky's *Serenade in C major*, and *Capriccio italien*, Holst's *The Planets*, Bliss's *Music for Strings*, Elgar's Symphony No. 2, Cello Concerto (with Casals), *Enigma Variations* and *Introduction and Allegro*, Vaughan Williams' *Fantasia on a Theme of Thomas Tallis* and Sibelius' *The Océanides* and *Night Ride and Sunrise*, which were included in the Sibelius Society albums. Also included were a number of overtures and preludes, including *Così fan tutte*, *Alceste*, *Coriolan*, *Masaniello*, *Les Francs-juges*, *Le Roi Lear*, *Leichte Cavallerie*, *Die Meistersinger*, *Tristan und Isolde*, *Euryanthe*, *Der Freischütz*, *The Merry Wives of Windsor*, *Manfred*, *Hänsel und Gretel*, *The Hebrides*, *Ruy Blas* and *Portsmouth Point*, and other pieces. He also recorded on 78s *A Shropshire Lad* and *Kikimora* (with the Hallé Orchestra), the *Music for the Royal Fireworks* and the *Academic Festival Overture* (with the London Philharmonic Orchestra), the Bliss Piano Concerto (with Solomon and the Liverpool Philharmonic Orchestra), Vaughan Williams' Symphony No. 6 and Parry's *Blest Pair of Sirens* (with the London Symphony Orchestra *et al.*).

With the advent of LP, Boult recorded with a number of companies in addition to EMI, and his name appeared on a variety of labels around the world. Most of these performances were with the London Philharmonic Orchestra, but contractual problems caused it to be called the Philharmonic Promenade Orchestra on some labels (Nixa, Pye, Westminster, Marble Arch and Vanguard, for example). The range of music recorded was extensive, and included the Schumann and Brahms symphonies, four of the Beethoven symphonies, as well as the nine Vaughan Williams symphonies – the latter he recorded twice (except No. 9). His recordings for EMI from the beginning of LPs until the present have been of C. P. E. Bach's *Symphony in F*, J. C. Bach's *Piano Concerto in A* (with Collet), Haydn's *German Dances*, Monn's Cello Concerto (with Pleeth) and two movements from Stamitz's *Symphony in E flat* (with the London Philharmonic Orchestra, in the series 'History of Music in Sound'), *Music for the Royal Fireworks*, the Mendelssohn Violin Concerto and Ravel's *Tzigane* (with Rabin), the four Brahms symphonies, *Tragic Overture* and *Alto Rhapsody* (with Baker), the overture to *The Merry Wives of Windsor*, the Mendelssohn and Sibelius Violin Concertos (with Menuhin), Elgar's Symphony No. 1, *Enigma Variations*, *Dream Children*, *Nursery Suite*, five *Pomp and Circumstance* Marches, *Froissart*, *Cockaigne*, *In the South*, arrangement of Handel's *Overture in D minor*, *Three Bavarian Dances*, *Chanson de matin*, *Chanson de nuit*, two *Wand of Youth* suites, *The Kingdom* and *The Music Makers*, Parry's *Blest Pair of Sirens*, Vaughan Williams' Symphonies Nos 1, 2, 5, 7, 8 and 9, Two-Piano Concerto (with Vronsky and Babin), *Fantasia on the Old 104th*, *The Lark Ascending* and *Song of Thanksgiving* (with Pougnet), *The Wasps*, *Serenade to Music* and *The Pilgrim's Progress*, Simpson's Symphony No. 1 and Williamson's Violin Concerto (with Menuhin, and with the London Philharmonic Orchestra *et al.*), the overture and Turkish March from *Die Ruinen von Athen* of Beethoven, Mozart's Piano Concertos K. 466 and K. 482 (with Annie Fischer), Bruch's *Scottish Fantasia* and Wieniawski's Violin Concerto No. 1 (with Rabin), Wolf's *Italian Serenade* and Mahler's *Kindertotenlieder* (with Ludwig, and the Philharmonia Orchestra), the Beethoven Violin Concerto (with Suk) and *Coriolan* overture, the preludes to Acts I and III of *Lohengrin* and *Die Meistersinger*, the *Tannhäuser* overture and the prelude to Act I of *Tristan und Isolde*, the Elgar Violin Concerto (with Menuhin), Holst's *The Planets*, and Vaughan Williams' Symphonies Nos 3, 4 and 6, *In the Fen Country*, *The Lark Ascending* (with Bean) and *Norfolk Rhapsody No. 1* (with the New Philharmonia Orchestra *et al.*),

Dohnányi's Piano Concerto No. 2 and *Variations on a Nursery Song* (with Dohnányi the soloist) and the Dvořák Cello Concerto (with Rostropovich, and the Royal Philharmonic Orchestra), Vaughan Williams' Symphony No. 6, *English Folk Song Suite*, *Job* and *Greensleeves* fantasia (with the London Symphony Orchestra), Berkeley's Violin Concerto (with Menuhin and the Menuhin Festival Orchestra), and Holst's *Hymn of Jesus* (with the BBC Symphony Orchestra and Chorus).

Between 1950 and 1966 Boult also recorded for Decca. The series included *Sheep may safely graze* and the Air from the Suite No. 3 of Bach (with the Covent Garden Orchestra), *Messiah* (twice, with the London Philharmonic Orchestra *et al.* in 1954 and with the London Symphony Orchestra *et al.* in 1961), a recital of Handel arias (with McKellar and the Covent Garden Orchestra), separate recitals of arias of Bach and Handel (with Ferrier and Flagstad, and the London Philharmonic Orchestra), and a recital of popular sacred songs (with Flagstad and the London Philharmonic Orchestra), the Beethoven Violin Concerto (with Ricci), the Mendelssohn Violin Concerto, the Bruch *Scottish Fantasia* and the Elgar Violin Concerto (with Campoli), Bruch's Violin Concerto No. 1 and Wieniawski's Violin Concerto No. 2 (with Elman), Chopin's Piano Concerto No. 2 (with Gulda), the Franck *Symphonic Variations* and the scherzo from Litolff's *Concerto symphonique* (with Curzon), the Tchaikovsky Violin Concerto (with Elman), *Concerto fantasia* (with Katin), *1812* overture and *Hamlet*, Lalo's Cello Concerto and Saint-Saëns' Cello Concerto No. 1 (with Nelsova), Rachmaninov's Piano Concerto No. 1 (with Katin), Piano Concerto No. 2 (with Curzon), and the *Rhapsody on a Theme of Paganini* and Dohnányi's *Variations on a Nursery Song* (with Katchen, twice, in 1954 and 1960), Elgar's *Three Bavarian Dances*, *Chanson de matin* and *Chanson de nuit*, a suite from Prokofiev's *The Love of Three Oranges*, Bax's *Tintagel*, Butterworth's *A Shropshire Lad* and *The Banks of Green Willow*, Holst's *The Perfect Fool* ballet music and *Egdon Heath*, Vaughan Williams' Symphonies Nos 1 to 8, *Job*, *Old King Cole*, *Partita* and *The Wasps*, Walton's *Scapino* overture, *Siesta* and Bach arrangement *The Wise Virgins*, and Searle's Symphony No. 1 (with the London Philharmonic Orchestra), Holst's *Hymn of Jesus* (with the BBC Symphony Orchestra and Chorus), Mahler's *Kindertotenlieder* and *Lieder eines fahrenden Gesellen* (with Flagstad and the Vienna Philharmonic Orchestra), Tchaikovsky's Symphony No. 3, Variations from the Suite No. 3, and Prokofiev's *Lieutenant Kijé* suite (with the Paris Conservatoire Orchestra).

In these years, Boult made records for Pye and Nixa, and some were released also by Vanguard (in the US) and Marble Arch (in Britain). Included were the *Water Music*, Beethoven's Symphonies Nos 3, 5, 6 and 7, *Coriolan*, *Leonore No. 3*, *Fidelio* and *Egmont* overtures, Mendelssohn's Symphonies Nos 3 and 4 and music from *A Midsummer Night's Dream*, Schubert's Symphony No. 9, the four Schumann symphonies, Berlioz' overtures *Béatrice et Bénédict*, *Benvenuto Cellini*, *Le Carnaval romain*, *Le Corsaire*, *Les Francs-juges*, *Rob Roy*, *Le Roi Lear* and *Waverley*, the four Brahms symphonies, *Tragic* and *Academic Festival Overtures* and *Alto Rhapsody* (with Sinclair), Tchaikovsky's Symphonies Nos 5 and 6, and the *Romeo and Juliet* fantasy-overture, suites from *Coppélia* and *Sylvia*, and the *Naila* waltz of Delibes, the Suppé overtures *Die schöne Galatea*, *Boccaccio*, *Fatinitza*, *Leichte Cavallerie*, *Morgen, Mittag und Abend in Wien* and *Dichter und Bauer*, the Bartók *Divertimento* and *Music for Strings, Percussion and Celesta*, Sibelius' *En Saga*, *Finlandia*, *The Swan of Tuonela*, *Lemminkäinen's Return*, *The Bard*, *Night Ride and Sunrise*, *The Océanides*, *Tapiola*, and the prelude to *The Tempest*, the Prokofiev Piano Concerto No. 1 and the Khachaturian Piano Concerto (with Katz), Elgar's Symphony No. 2 and *Falstaff*, Vaughan Williams' *Fantasia on a Theme of Thomas Tallis*, *Norfolk Rhapsody No. 1* and *Fantasia on Greensleeves*, Holst's *The Planets*, Walton's Symphony No. 1 and *Belshazzar's Feast*, and Britten's *Matinées musicales*, *Soirées musicales*, *Young Person's Guide to the Orchestra* and the interludes and passacaglia from *Peter Grimes* (with the London Philharmonic Orchestra and its *nom-de-disque*, Philharmonic Promenade Orchestra, and the London Philharmonic Choir *et al.*).

For Westminster, Boult recorded Mozart's Symphony No. 40 and *Eine kleine Nachtmusik*, the Chopin Piano Concertos Nos 1 and 2 (with Hesse-Bukowska), Liszt's Piano Concertos Nos 1 and 2, *Hungarian Fantasia*, *Totentanz*, and *Wanderer Fantasia* (arranged after Schubert; with Farnadi), *The Planets*, and Vaughan Williams' *English Folksongs Suite*, *Fantasia on a Theme of Thomas Tallis* and *Fantasia on Greensleeves* (with the Vienna State Opera Orchestra *et al.*), Elgar's *Cockaigne*, the Mendelssohn overtures *Meeresstille und glückliche Fahrt*, *Die schöne Melusine*, *Ruy Blas* and *The Hebrides*, Respighi's *Feste romane* and *Rossiniana*, and Vaughan Williams' *Old King Cole* and music for *The Wasps* (with the

London Philharmonic and Philharmonic Promenade Orchestras), and for World Record Club, Beethoven's Romance No. 2 (with Bress), Mendelssohn's Symphony No. 4 and Violin Concerto (with M. Smith), Clarke's *Trumpet Voluntary*, the Schumann and Grieg Piano Concertos, and the scherzo from Litolff's *Concerto symphonique* (with Cherkassky), the overture and dances from *The Bartered Bride*, Bruch's *Kol Nidrei* (with Bunting), Tchaikovsky's Piano Concerto No. 1 (with Cherkassky), Violin Concerto (with Bress), *Romeo and Juliet* fantasy-overture, *1812* overture and *Marche slave*, Elgar's *Introduction and Allegro* and *Enigma Variations*, the Dance of the Hours from *La Gioconda*, the Dance of the Tumblers from *The Snow Maiden*, Saint-Saëns' *Wedding Cake* (with Pryor) and *Danse macabre*, Strauss's *Radetzky March*, Stravinsky's *Circus Polka*, the intermezzo from *I gioielli della Madonna*, and the overtures *Academic Festival* of Brahms, *Ruslan and Ludmilla*, *Die Zauberflöte*, *Dichter und Bauer*, Walton's *Portsmouth Point* and Gershwin's *Cuban Overture* (with the London Philharmonic Orchestra).

His recordings for other companies comprised Vivaldi's Violin Concerto Op. 8 No. 6 (with Menuhin and the Philharmonia Orchestra for Victor, US), Mahler's *Lieder eines fahrenden Gesellen* (with Thebom), Rachmaninov's Symphonies Nos 2 and 3, and Rimsky-Korsakov's *Russian Easter Festival Overture* (with the London Philharmonic Orchestra for Victor), *The Planets* (with the BBC Symphony Orchestra *et al.* for Victor), the Handel Organ Concertos (with E. Power Biggs and the London Philharmonic Orchestra for Columbia, US), Tchaikovsky's *Romeo and Juliet* fantasy-overture and *Hamlet* (with the London Philharmonic Orchestra for Stereo Fidelity), Handel's *Acis and Galatea* (with the Philomusica Orchestra *et al.* for L'Oiseau Lyre), Haydn's Symphony No. 104, Mozart's Symphony No. 35, Schubert's Symphony No. 4, and *Capriccio italien* (with the London Philharmonic Orchestra for La Guilde Internationale du Disque and issued by Perfect, US), Barsukov's Piano Concerto No. 2 (with Barsukov), Hindemith's *Symphony in E flat*, Mahler's Symphony No. 1, Vaughan Williams' *Job* and Symphony No. 9 (the latter with a speech by Boult) and Shostakovich's Symphony No. 6 (with the London Philharmonic Orchestra for Everest, some also issued by World Record Club), Elgar's Symphony No. 2 (with the Scottish National Orchestra for Classics for Pleasure) and a demonstration of the instruments of the orchestra (with the London Philharmonic Orchestra for Classics for Pleasure), *Les Préludes*, *A Night on the Bare Mountain*, Elgar's *Pomp and Circumstance* March No. 1, *The Hebrides* overture, and Sullivan's *Overture di ballo* (with the New Symphony Orchestra for Reader's Digest), and finally a series of music by British composers for Lyrita: Parry's *English Suite*, *Lady Radnor's Suite*, *Overture to an Unwritten Tragedy* and *Symphonic Variations* (with the London Symphony Orchestra), Elgar's two symphonies, Bax's *November Woods*, Rubbra's Symphony No. 7, Vaughan Williams' *Fantasia on a Theme of Thomas Tallis*, Holst's *Beni Mora*, *Hammersmith: Prelude and Scherzo*, *Somerset Rhapsody*, *Fugal Overture* and *Japanese Suite*, Ireland's *Mai Dun*, *The Forgotten Rite*, *Legend*, *Satyricon* overture, *London* overture, *Epic March*, *The Holy Boy*, *Concertino pastorale*, *Minuet*, *Elegy*, *The Overlanders*, *Scherzo and Cortège*, *Tritons*, Piano Concerto (with Parkin) and *These Things Shall Be* (with Case and the London Philharmonic Choir), and Moeran's Cello Concerto (with Coetmore), *Overture for a Masque*, *Rhapsody No. 2* and *Sinfonietta* (with the London Philharmonic Orchestra).

Of his 78 r.p.m. sets, Boult considered Elgar's Symphony No. 2 and *The Planets* as his most satisfying; Beethoven's Symphony No. 8 and Schubert's Symphony No. 9, also with the BBC Symphony, were other superb recordings, as was Beethoven's Piano Concerto No. 3, with Solomon, which could be selected as the most representative of Boult's style and for its marvellous orchestral playing. His close *rapport* with his soloists was partly the result of his custom of returning to the opening ritornello of the concerto after he, the soloist and the orchestra had been through the first movement, and he had heard how the soloist treated it. He conducted the first public performance of five movements of *The Planets* in 1919 and subsequently recorded the complete work four times, and he also recorded the two Elgar symphonies three times each. A unique technical feat was achieved in the recording studio with the disc of Bach and Handel arias with the great British contralto, Kathleen Ferrier. Boult recorded the recital with her and the London Philharmonic on a mono LP in 1953; in 1960, after her tragic death, he and the same orchestra assembled again and recorded exactly the same programme for stereo, accompanying Ferrier's voice which was dubbed from the older disc. The recordings of *Messiah* were successively regarded as the finest available of the work, until the recent 'authentic' performances of Davis, Mackerras *et al.*

Critics have rated the four Brahms symphonies recently recorded very highly, although their recording was originally something of an afterthought. After completing the schedule of recordings of Elgar and Vaughan Williams in a series of sessions in 1970, it was found that there were two spare, and the recording producer suggested a Brahms symphony. The ensuing record of Brahms' No. 3 was so successful commercially that the set of four was completed later. The *Brandenburg Concertos*, recorded in 1974, were played with full orchestras; Boult felt that the current spate of recordings with smaller ensembles was insufficiently full blooded. In all his recordings it is obvious that there is nothing enigmatic about Boult's musical personality: he is thoroughly honest, self-effacing, conscientious and perceptive. History appears to have cast him as the supremely authoritative interpreter of British music, a role he undoubtedly covets and deserves, but this can obscure the wide cast of his musical sympathies. The early LPs of the Rachmaninov and Shostakovich symphonies made this point, but his more recent records have also helped to redress the matter.

Bour, Ernest (b. 1913). Born in Thionville, France, Bour studied at home with his father, at the conservatoire and university at Strasbourg, at the Paris Conservatoire and with Scherchen (1933–4). His appointments have included musical director of Strasbourg Radio (1935–9), teacher at Strasbourg Conservatoire (1940–41), conductor of the Strasbourg City Orchestra (1941–7) and conductor of the South-West German Radio Orchestra at Baden-Baden (1964), where he succeeded Rosbaud. He has been a regular guest conductor in many European cities, at festivals and with the French Radio, and has introduced many new and unknown compositions, including the French première of Hindemith's *Mathis der Maler*. In the late 1940s EMI (Columbia) issued a superb, perhaps unsurpassed, performance of Ravel's *L'Enfant et les sortilèges*, in which he conducted the French National Radio Orchestra *et al.*; but the arrival of LP soon after caused the recording to be superseded. Since then he has recorded the Stravinsky Violin Concerto (with Grumiaux and the Amsterdam Concertgebouw Orchestra for Philips), Jolivet's *Andante Concertino* (with Delmotte and Baudo) and Piano Concerto (with Descaves), *The Hebrides* overture and the overture and nocturne from *A Midsummer Night's Dream* (with the Champs-Élysées Theatre Orchestra for Ducretet-Thomson), Saint-Saëns' Symphony No. 3 (with the Champs-Élysées Theatre Orchestra for Telefunken), Halffter's *Anillos*, *Lineas y puntos* and *Secuencias*, the Cello Concertos of Hindemith and Zimmermann (with Palm), Ligeti's *Continuum*, *Atmosphères*, *Lontano* and *Ramifications*, Yun's *Réak*, Pablo's *Initiatives*, Haubenstock-Ramati's *Tableau 1 (1967)* and *Vermutungen*, Wittinger's *Irreversibilitazione*, Hartmann's Symphony No. 1, Lutosławski's Symphony No. 2 and Fortner's *Prismen* (with the South-West German Radio Orchestra for Wergo, and re-issued in some cases on other labels), Kunst's *Trajectoire* (with the Netherlands Radio Chamber Orchestra *et al.* for Donemus) and Leeuw's *Symphonies of Winds* and Kunst and Vriend's *Elements of Logic* (with the Hague Philharmonic Orchestra for Donemus).

Boutry, Roger (b. 1932). Born in Paris, Boutry studied at the Paris Conservatoire, won prizes as a pianist and conductor there, and was awarded the Prix de Rome (1954) and the Grand Prix Musical of the City of Paris (1963). He toured Europe, the USSR and Australia as a pianist, has appeared in France and in Monte Carlo as a conductor, and has published a number of compositions including orchestral works, concertos, chamber and instrumental music. He has recorded *Pictures at an Exhibition*, *A Night on the Bare Mountain*, the *Romeo and Juliet* fantasy-overture, the Flight of the Bumble Bee from *Tsar Saltan* and excerpts from *L'Arlésienne* (with the Musique de la Garde Républicaine, Paris, for Déesse), and, as a pianist, Schumann's *Konzertstück for Piano and Orchestra* (with Ristenpart and the Saar Chamber Orchestra for Musidisc).

Bowers, Robert Hood (1877–1941). Born at Chambersburg, Pennsylvania, Bowers studied (*inter alia*) at the Chicago Auditorium Conservatory and was a conductor of theatre and radio orchestras. He was recording director of the Columbia (US) Phonograph Company, and also at one time the musical director of the Aeolian Phonograph Company, and taught at the School of Radio Technique, New York. He recorded Grieg's *Norwegian Bridal Procession* (with an unnamed orchestra for Columbia).

Bozza, Eugène (b. 1905). Born in Nice, Bozza studied at the Paris Conservatoire, won the Prix de Rome in 1934, was conductor at the Paris Opéra-Comique (from 1939) and director of the Valenciennes Conservatoire. In a colourful and accessible style he wrote symphonies, concertos, an opera, an oratorio (*La Tentation de Saint Antoine*) and chamber music for wind instruments, of which his *Suite française* has been recorded by the Munich Wind Soloists for Colosseum. On 78 r.p.m. discs he conducted his *Concertino for Saxophone and Orchestra* (with Mule) and *Rapsodie niçoise for Violin and Orchestra* (with Merckel), both for Florilège.

Bragg, George (b. 1925). Born in Meridian, Mississippi, and educated at the North Texas State University, Bragg founded and directed the Texas Boys' Choir at Fort Worth and the Texas Boys' Choir School, now called the Trinity Valley School. He has toured extensively with the choir, and recorded, *inter alia*, Britten's *A Ceremony of Carols* and other carols (for Decca) and motets by G. Gabrieli (also with the Gregg Smith Singers for CBS).

Braithwaite, Nicholas (b. 1939). Born in London, the son of Warwick Braithwaite, Braithwaite studied conducting under Miles at the Royal Academy of Music and in 1970 became an Associate of the Academy. He studied further at Bayreuth and with Swarowsky in Vienna (1961) and on his return to Britain (1963) founded the Salomon Orchestra and Salterello Choir. His first appointment was as assistant conductor to Silvestri with the Bournemouth Symphony Orchestra (1967–70) and since then he has been active with a number of British orchestras, the Glyndebourne Festival Opera Company, the Sadler's Wells (English National) Opera Company, the Royal Opera, Covent Garden, and the Hamburg State Opera, and has also conducted in France and Finland. At the English National Opera he led a highly praised production of Penderecki's *The Devils of Loudun*. Since 1975 he has made records for Lyrita, including Arnold Cooke's Symphony No. 3 and suite *Jabez and the Devil*, Bridge's *Phantasm* for piano and orchestra (with Wallfisch) and Berkeley's Symphony No. 2 (with the London Philharmonic Orchestra), Moeran's Rhapsody No. 3 (with McCabe) and Berkeley's Piano Concerto (with Wilde, and with the New Philharmonia Orchestra). Europa (in FR Germany) have also issued a disc containing *Finlandia* and *Valse triste* (with the London Philharmonic Orchestra).

Braithwaite, Warwick (1898–1971). A New Zealander, Braithwaite studied at the Royal College of Music in London and in 1919 became a conductor with the O'Mara Opera Company. Two years later he joined the British National Opera Company as a repetiteur, and was appointed music director of the BBC's radio station at Cardiff (1921). He was conductor of the National Orchestra of Wales (1928–31) and conductor of the Cardiff Musical Society (1924–32); he returned to London and joined the Sadler's Wells Opera Company with Collingwood, and until his departure in 1940 conducted many important productions of the company. He then turned his attention to symphonic music, was conductor of the Scottish Orchestra (1940–46) and on occasion conducted the London Philharmonic and other major orchestras in Britain. He was appointed principal conductor of the Sadler's Wells Ballet Company (1948) and conducted at the Royal Opera, Covent Garden (1949–53), where his most successful performances were *Madama Butterfly*, *Tosca* and *Manon*. He was with the National Orchestra of New Zealand (1953–4), artistic director of the Australian National Opera Company (1954–5) and musical director of the Welsh National Opera Company (1956–60), and then in 1960 returned to the Sadler's Wells Company. He wrote about his ideas on conducting in *The Conductor's Art*.

Braithwaite made a number of recordings, primarily of ballet music. On 78 r.p.m. discs he made *Finlandia* and the overture to *Oberon* (with the National Symphony Orchestra for Decca), four *Pomp and Circumstance* Marches (with the London Symphony Orchestra for Decca), Prokofiev's *Cinderella* (with the Covent Garden Orchestra for Columbia), Grainger's *Molly on the Shore*, *Mock Morris*, *Handel in the Strand* and *Londonderry Air* (with the Philharmonia Orchestra for Columbia), various excerpts from *Messiah* (with the Sadler's Wells Orchestra *et al.* for HMV), and on LP a series with the Covent Garden Orchestra for Parlophone, many of which were released in the United States by Mercury and MGM. Included were the ballet music from *Lakmé*, *William Tell*, *Faust*, *Le Cid* and *Aida*, Massenet's *Scènes alsaciennes*, Mozart's *Les petits riens*, the Dance of the Hours from *La Gioconda*, a suite from *Nutcracker*, excerpts from *Swan Lake* and *Sleeping Beauty*, *La Boutique fantasque*, the overture and excerpts from *Rosamunde*, Britten's *Matinées musicales* and *Soirées musicales*, *Les Sylphides*, Bizet's *Jeux d'enfants*, suite from *La jolie fille de Perth* and excerpts from *L'Arlésienne*, Chabrier's *Suite pastorale*, excerpts from *Coppélia* and *Sylvia*, overtures to *William Tell*, *Il Signor Bruschino* and *Il matrimonio segreto*, Respighi's *Rossiniana*, the Scarlatti/Tommasini *Good-humoured Ladies*, and Malipiero's *Cimarosiana*. He also recorded Rodrigo's *Madrigales amatorios* (with del Pozo and the Philharmonia Orchestra for EMI) and Järnefelt's *Berceuse* and *Praeludium* (with the Covent Garden Orchestra for EMI).

Brant, Henry (b. 1913). Born in Montreal, Brant studied at the Institute of Musical Art and the Juilliard School, both in New York, and with Riegger, Copland and Antheil. He taught at Columbia University, the Juilliard School and at Bennington College; his compositions have been remarkable for their novelty and innovations, including effects achieved through placing instruments in various parts of the hall. He recorded his *Signs and Alarms* and *Galaxy 2* (with the Columbia Chamber Ensemble, for Columbia Special Products), *Angels and Devils* (with Wilkins and a flute ensemble for Composers Recordings), and *Millennium II* (with the Lehigh University Instrumental Ensemble for Lehigh).

Bream, Julian (b. 1933). Born in London, Bream first studied the guitar with his father, then at the Royal College of Music and later with Segovia, and is one of the leading performers on guitar and lute, particularly of music of the Renaissance and pre-classical period. He has made numerous recordings as an instrumentalist; as a conductor and soloist with the Julian Bream Consort he has recorded Vivaldi's *Guitar Concerto in D* (arranged for lute), Rodrigo's *Concierto de Aranjuez*, the Courtly Dances from Britten's *Gloriana*, and a collection entitled *An Evening of Elizabethan Music* (for RCA).

Brecher, Gustav (1879–1940). Born in Eichwald in Bohemia, Brecher studied at Leipzig and made his debut as a conductor there (1897). He was given assistance by Mahler and Strauss, conducted opera at Vienna and Olmütz (1899–1902), at Hamburg (1903–10), was first conductor at the Cologne Opera (1911–15) and at Frankfurt am Main (1916–23) and was general music director at Leipzig (1924–33), where he led performances of Křenek's *Jonny spielt auf* (1927) and Weill's *Aufstieg und Fall der Stadt Mahagonny* (1930). He wrote musical criticism, edited operas, and one of his compositions, the symphonic poem *Rosmersholm*, was performed by Strauss in Leipzig in 1896. Although Jewish he hesitated too long in leaving Germany and he and his wife perished in the English Channel while fleeing from the Nazis. Brecher was a friend of Klemperer, who considered him an excellent operatic conductor; Klemperer said that he himself learned much from Brecher, especially the importance of the upbeat, which makes the orchestra attentive. For Parlophone Brecher conducted the Leipzig Gewandhaus Orchestra in the overture to *Der Freischütz*.

Brediceanu, Mihai (b. 1920). Born in Brasov, Romania, where his father was a composer and musicologist, Brediceanu showed prodigious musical talent as a child, studied at the Bucharest Conservatory under Muzicescu, Lindenberg and Perlea, and won the George Enesco Prize for composition, and the prize for conducting at the International Youth Festival in Bucharest in 1953. He became a conductor with the Bucharest State Opera, permanent conductor with the Bucharest Philharmonic Orchestra (1958) and then musical director of the Bucharest State Opera (1959), conducted at festivals and opera houses in Greece, Czechoslovakia, Poland, the USSR, France and Monaco, has been visiting professor at Syracuse University, New York since 1971, and was awarded the title Artist Emeritus by the Romanian government. He has developed a new theory about the structure of musical language, and in 1970 invented a pluri-metronome to control poly-temporal structures in music and choreography. His recordings include Enesco's opera *Oedipus* (with the Bucharest Opera Orchestra *et al.* for Déesse) and Symphony No. 1 (with the George Enesco Symphony Orchestra for Electrecord), *Il barbiere di Siviglia* (with the Bucharest Symphony Orchestra *et al.* for Electrecord), Mahler's *Lieder eines fahrenden Gesellen* (with Iordăchescu) and Britten's *Serenade for Tenor, Horn and Strings* (with Bădănoiu, Teodorian, and the George Enesco Symphony Orchestra), and several discs of operatic arias (for Electrecord).

Breisach, Paul (1896–1952). Born in Vienna, Breisach studied at the Academy of Music there, was an assistant to Strauss at the Vienna State Opera, was a conductor at Mannheim (1921–4), and from 1924 conducted at the Berlin State Opera. He first conducted in the United States at the Metropolitan Opera in New York (1941) and conducted there in the 1945–6 season, and was principal conductor at the San Francisco Opera from 1946 until his death in 1952. He recorded extracts from the Wagner operas with Janssen and Melton, and from Grétry's *Richard Coeur de Lion* with Singher, with the Metropolitan Opera Orchestra for Columbia and Victor.

Breitner, Tamás (b. 1929). The Hungarian conductor Breitner studied at the Franz Liszt Academy at Budapest under Farkas, Kókai, Szabolosi, Kodály, Milhály and Somogyi, graduated in 1956, and has since conducted the major Hungarian symphony orchestras as well as being the principal conductor of the Budapest Operetta Theatre for ten years. Since 1960 he has been the conductor of the Pécs Philharmonic Orchestra and musical director of the Pécs Opera House in Southern Hungary. He was awarded the Liszt Prize in 1974. His recordings have been of Mozart's Piano Concertos K. 415 and K. 488 (with Sirokay and the Hungarian State Orchestra), Schumann's Symphony No. 4 and *Genoveva* overture (with the Pécs Philharmonic Orchestra), David's Symphony No. 4 and Sinfonietta (with the Budapest Symphony Orchestra), two suites by Weiner (with the Hungarian Radio Orchestra), Kadosa's Symphonies Nos 6 and 7 (with the Hungarian State Symphony Orchestra) and discs of excerpts from *Der Zigeunerbaron* and *Zigeunerliebe* (with the Hungarian Radio Orchestra *et al.*), all for Hungaroton.

Bress, Hyman (b. 1931). Born in Cape Town, Bress first appeared in public as a violinist at the age of seven, studied at the Curtis School of Music, Philadelphia (1946–51), was concertmaster of the Montreal Symphony Orchestra (1956–60), leader of the Montreal String Quartet (1958–60) and toured internationally and recorded as a violin virtuoso. For Baroque he played and conducted concertos of Vivaldi, with the Sinfonia of Montreal.

Bret, Gustave (1875–1969). Born in Brignoles, France, Bret studied at the Paris Conservatoire under Lavignac, Widor, d'Indy and Guilmant, was the first to perform all the organ works of Franck in Paris (1903–4) and formed and conducted the Société J. S. Bach, performing with them the major choral works of Bach. He conducted the major orchestras in Paris, toured in Germany and Czechoslovakia, was a newspaper critic and composed choral music including an oratorio *Les Pèlerins d'Emmaüs*. For HMV he recorded, with his Bach Choir *et al.*, Bach's Cantata No. 212, parts of the *Magnificat* and the Concertos in C major and A minor, Vivaldi's Concerto Grosso Op. 3 No. 10 and the Fauré *Requiem*.

Brico, Antonia (b. 1902). Born in Holland and brought to the United States as a child, Brico studied at the University of California, Berkeley, and at the Berlin State Academy of Music under Muck. She first appeared as a pianist in 1919, was a coach at the Bayreuth Festival (1928) and made her debut as a conductor with the Berlin Philharmonic Orchestra (1920). After returning to the US she conducted at the Hollywood Bowl, and was a guest conductor with many major orchestras in the US and Europe. As it was then almost impossible for a woman conductor to receive a regular appointment, she organised and conducted the New York Women's Symphony Orchestra (1935) which became the Brico Symphony Orchestra and included male players (1939). Moving to Denver, Colorado, she was a guest conductor with the Denver Symphony Orchestra and the regular conductor of the Denver Businessmen's Orchestra (1946–76), which was renamed the Brico Symphony Orchestra in her honour. She met Sibelius in Finland and won his praise after conducting a concert of his music in his presence. In 1975 she returned to New York for the first time since 1939 to take part in the Mostly Mozart Festival at the Lincoln Center; subsequently Columbia issued a disc in which she conducted the Festival orchestra in Mozart's Symphony No. 35 and the overtures to *Le nozze di Figaro*, *Don Giovanni* and *Die Zauberflöte*. The symphony gave evidence of her musicianship, even if the overtures were just less convincing.

Bridge, Frank (1879–1941). In recent years there has been a renewed interest in Frank Bridge, mostly owing to the efforts of his former pupil, Benjamin Britten. Of Bridge's output it is his chamber music and his songs that have in particular attracted affection and attention. Nonetheless he was a prominent chamber player and conductor in his day, both in the concert hall and opera house, frequently appeared with orchestras in London, was a dependable substitute for Sir Henry Wood at the London Promenade Concerts and toured the United States in 1933 conducting his own compositions with some of the major orchestras. Of his orchestral works one that achieved popularity was his suite *The Sea*, which he recorded in 1926 with the London Symphony Orchestra for Columbia. He also recorded his own *Christmas Dance* and *Poem No. 2*, the overtures to *Mireille* and *Hänsel und Gretel* and Ravel's *Pavane pour une infante défunte* (with the New Queen's Hall Orchestra for Columbia). He also made some records as a pianist, including a Bach Double Concerto (with Catterall, and Harty conducting, for Columbia).

Bridge, Sir Frederick (1844–1924). Born in Oldbury, near Birmingham, Bridge was a choirboy at Rochester Cathedral, became an organist at Windsor and at Manchester Cathedral, graduated B.Mus. at Oxford (1868), and was professor at Owens College, Manchester (1872–5). He was then organist at Westminster Abbey for 36 years, conductor of the Royal Choral Society, the first King Edward Professor of Music at the University of

London, and was knighted on the occasion of Queen Victoria's Diamond Jubilee (1897). He wrote many choral and sacred works, and published a number of books on musical subjects. In 1923 Columbia issued a record of him conducting an ensemble in an arrangement by him entitled *Old London Cryes of Will Shakespeare's Time*.

Bridgewater, Leslie (1893–1975). Born in Halesowen, Worcestershire, Bridgewater studied under Bowen and Gerard at the Birmingham School of Music, was with the light music section of the British Broadcasting Corporation (1935–42) and became musical adviser for the Shakespeare Memorial Theatre (1948–59), for which he wrote songs and incidental music for the Shakespeare plays. He also wrote incidental music for productions in London of Restoration, Victorian and modern plays, and a piano concerto. For Westminster he conducted the Westminster Light Orchestra in his own songs from Shakespeare plays (with Dickie the singer), dances by Purcell, Lawes and Jones, his arrangement of Corrette's *Le Malade imaginaire*, waltzes of Gungl, the *Hungarian Dances* of Brahms, the *Nutcracker* suite and excerpts from *Rosamunde* as well as Schubert's *Marche militaire* No. 1.

Brieff, Frank (b. 1912). Born in New Haven, Connecticut, Brieff studied the violin at the Manhattan School of Music, at the New York University, at the Juilliard School and with Nadia Boulanger in Paris. He was violist with the Guilet String Quartet (1942–8), violist with the NBC Symphony Orchestra under Toscanini (1948–52), then became the conductor of the Bach Aria Group (1952–64), and of the New Haven Symphony Orchestra (since 1952). He was a member of the Guilet Quartet when it recorded for Concert Hall and Vox. As a conductor, he recorded Bach's Cantatas Nos 60, 127 and 155, and excerpts from some others (with the Bach Aria Group for RCA), Cantata No. 58 and some arias (with the Bach Aria Group for Decca, US), Bach's Two-Harpsichord Concertos Nos 1 and 2 (with Appleton and Field, and the Castle Hill Festival Orchestra for Lyrichord), and Mahler's Symphony No. 1 (with the New Haven Symphony Orchestra, for CBS, issued on the Odyssey label). The latter was the first recording of the symphony (later followed by Ormandy's) to include the *Blumine* movement as originally conceived by Mahler, but subsequently deleted from the published score. Brieff has received the award of the Mahler-Bruckner Society.

Britten, Benjamin (1913–76). The eminent British composer Britten was born at Lowestoft in East Anglia, studied the piano with Harold Samuel and composition with Frank Bridge while still at school, and then the piano with Arthur Benjamin and composition with John Ireland at the Royal College of Music in London. After spending the early years of World War II in the United States he settled in Aldeburgh, Suffolk, and in 1948 Britten, Peter Pears and Eric Crozier organised the first Aldeburgh Festival of Music and the Arts. It opened with his cantata *Saint Nicolas*; the festivals have continued in June and July of each year and are now based at The Maltings at Snape, Saxmundham, Suffolk. Many of Britten's compositions have received their first performance at the festivals, but other modern British music is also performed. Celebrated local and international artists, such as Richter, Rostropovich and Pears have also taken part. He was highly honoured, receiving the Companion of Honour (1953) and Order of Merit (1965), and was made a Life Peer in the last year of his life.

Like Elgar before him and more latterly Stravinsky, Britten had the good fortune to have a major record company (Decca) interested in recording his music under his own direction. Not only has this helped to familiarise the musical public with his work almost as it has appeared, but there now exists superbly performed and recorded documents of how Britten believed his music should sound. At the same time, it must be admitted that any recorded performance of a work such as the *War Requiem*, excellent though it may be in its own right, can give only a partial impression of the aural perspectives and scope of the music. Luckily Britten was a competent conductor; in his younger years he was obliged to conduct the first performances of his own works, and from the time of *Albert Herring* until *Death in Venice*, when he was too ill, he led the premières of his works himself. In Imogen Holst's words, 'in 20 years' experience – some of it painful – he has discovered how to make his beat so clear that it can convey the music itself and can draw superlative playing from the orchestra he is working with. Any rehearsal he takes is a lesson on how to avoid wasting time. Every detail has been thought out beforehand: the family motto of "Never Unprepared" is still very much to the point.' His success as a conductor led to many more requests to conduct than he was ready to accept, as he refused to surrender more time than he had to from composition. He was an exacting musician and demanded the utmost in technique and concentration from the musicians he directed.

Britten recorded all his major compositions for Decca, including all his published operas except *Gloriana* and *Death in Venice*, which was recorded in 1974 with Steuart Bedford conducting. Only excerpts from *Gloriana* have been recorded, but not by Britten. Britten appeared first on record as a conductor on some post-war Decca 78 r.p.m. discs of the *Serenade for Tenor, Horn and Strings* (with Pears, Brain and the Boyd Neel String Orchestra) and *A Ceremony of Carols* (with the Morriston Boys' Choir and harpist Korchinska); in 1954 the *Sinfonia da Requiem* (with the Danish State Radio Orchestra) and *Diversions on a Theme* (with Katchen and the London Symphony Orchestra) were issued. From then until 1971 the series continued, with the operas *The Little Sweep* and *The Turn of the Screw* (with the English Opera Group Orchestra *et al.*), *Peter Grimes* (with the Covent Garden Orchestra *et al.*), *Albert Herring*, *Owen Wingrave* and *The Rape of Lucretia* (with the English Chamber Orchestra *et al.*), *A Midsummer Night's Dream* and *Billy Budd* (with the London Symphony Orchestra *et al.*), *The Prince of the Pagodas* and the *Spring Symphony* (with the Covent Garden Orchestra *et al.*), *Nocturne*, *Cantata Misericordium*, *The Young Person's Guide to the Orchestra*, the *Serenade for Tenor, Horn and Strings* (with Pears and Tuckwell) and the *War Requiem* (with the London Symphony Orchestra *et al.*), *A Boy Was Born* (with the English Opera Group Chorus *et al.*), *Sinfonia da Requiem* (with the New Philharmonia Orchestra), the *Cello Symphony* (with Rostropovich), *Simple Symphony*, *Variations on a Theme of Frank Bridge*, the Piano Concerto (with Richter), Violin Concerto (with Lubotsky) and *Les Illuminations* (with Pears, and with the English Chamber Orchestra), *Curlew River*, *The Burning Fiery Furnace* and *The Prodigal Son* (with an instrumental ensemble *et al.*) and *Children's Crusade* and *The Golden Vanity* (with the Wandsworth School Boys' Choir), *Rejoice in the Lamb* and *A Boy is Born* (with the Purcell Singers), his arrangement of the National Anthem (with the London Symphony Orchestra and Chorus), *Psalm 150*, *Gemini Variations on a Theme of Kodály* and *Friday Afternoons* (with the Downside School Choir) and *Saint Nicolas* (with the Aldeburgh Festival Orchestra *et al.*). This list does not include the works in which he accompanies on the piano, nor does it do justice to the contribution of Peter Pears to many of the recordings.

At the 1956 Aldeburgh Festival Britten both played and conducted Mozart's Piano Concerto K. 414, and Decca subsequently released the performance on disc. Previously Decca had issued some other recordings made at the festivals, including Arne's *Rule Britannia* and *Now All the Air shall Ring*, with Britten conducting. In 1968 he turned his attention to recording music of other composers, sometimes with remarkable success. His performances of the *Brandenburg Concertos* and the *St John Passion* of Bach are everywhere deeply committed, but reservations have been made about stylistic miscalculations in the first and the editing of the music in the second. Similarly Purcell's *Fairy Queen* was re-arranged extensively by Imogen Holst and Britten in collaboration; granted their licence to do this, the result was one of his finest performances on disc. The two Mozart symphonies, Nos 38 and 40, are conducted with imagination, although some mannerisms intrude; Symphony No. 40 is remarkable because all the repeats, even in the slow movement, are observed. He also recorded the *Serenata notturna*, Schubert's Symphony No. 8, Schumann's *Scenes from Goethe's Faust*, a collection of pieces by Percy Grainger, and *The Dream of Gerontius*, the latter an exceptional performance – a 'haunting, emotional and searing account', revealing Britten's devotion to the score. All the recordings since 1968 were made in The Maltings at Snape, which has an extraordinary acoustic quality. Britten was also a fine pianist, and many consider him to be one of the greatest accompanists of his time; his recordings of Schubert's song cycles *Die schöne Müllerin* and *Winterreise* with Pears are transfigured by the artistry and insight of both artists.

The Aspen Institute at Colorado established the Aspen Award for Services to the Humanities in 1963, and Britten was selected as the first recipient. During his address at the presentation he remarked, *inter alia*, that any piece of music is written by the composer with certain conditions of performance in mind, and that a musical experience is much more intense and rewarding if the circumstances correspond to what the composer intended, 'if the *St Matthew Passion* is performed on Good Friday in a church, to a congregation of Christians; if the *Winterreise* is performed in a room, or in a small hall of truly intimate character to a circle of friends; if *Don Giovanni* is played to an audience which understands the text and appreciates the allusions. The further one departs from these circumstances, the less true and more diluted the experience is likely to be.' He went on: 'If I say the loudspeaker is the principal enemy of music, I don't mean that I am not grateful to it as a means of education and study, or as an evoker of memories. But it is not a part of a true musical *experience*. Regarded as such it is simply a substitute, and dangerous because deluding. Music demands more from the listener than simply the possession of a tape machine or a transistor radio. It demands some preparation, some effort, a journey to a special place, saving up for a ticket, some homework on the programme perhaps, some clarification of the ears and some sharpening of the instincts. It demands as much effort on the listener's part as the other two corners of the holy triangle of composer, performer and listener.' He qualified this position later, pointing out that a record is wonderful to have provided we realise that it is a substitute, not the real thing. 'Like reproductions of paintings, records can serve an essential educational purpose, but a record *can* give a wrong impression of a piece of music.'

Bródy, Tamás (b. 1913). Born at Kolozsvar/Cluj in Romania, Bródy studied at the Budapest Academy, and has composed numerous film scores, operettas, instrumental and vocal works. He has recorded for Hungaroton Liszt's *Malédiction* (with Wehner), and discs of excerpts from the operettas *Der Vogelhändler*, *Gräfin Dubarry*, *Les Bayadères* and *Czardasfürstin* (with the Hungarian Radio Symphony Orchestra *et al.*), and excerpts from Jacobi's *Sybil* (with the Budapest Philharmonic Orchestra).

Broekman, David (1902–58). Born in Leyden, Broekman studied at the Hague Conservatory and conducted opera in Holland and Germany. In 1924 he migrated to the United States, was a musical editor for a firm of publishers, wrote film scores including *All Quiet on the Western Front* and *The Phantom at the Opera*, and a book *The Shoestring Symphony*, about his experiences in Hollywood. He went to live in New York, where he was active as a conductor and wrote several symphonies. For Decca (US) he recorded the *Brandenburg Concerto No. 3* with the New York Concertmasters Ensemble.

Broman, Sten (b. 1902). Born in Uppsala, Sweden, Broman studied at the German Music Academy, Prague, and with Sachs in Berlin. He was a violist in string quartets in Sweden, and became conductor of the Malmō Philharmonic Orchestra (1946). His compositions include symphonies, a ballet and chamber music; Ehrling recorded his Symphony No. 7. As a conductor he recorded Berwald's *Memories of the Norwegian Alps* and *Serious and Light Follies* (with the Stockholm Radio Orchestra for Caprice).

Bron, Onissim (b. 1895). Born in Novomoskovsk, Russia, Bron studied at the Kiev Conservatory under Puchalsky and Glière, and was a conductor at Tbilisi (1922–4), Baku (1924–5), Kharkov (1925–6), the Nemirovich-Danchenko Theatre in Moscow (1926–30), Kiev (1930–32), and the Kirov Theatre in Leningrad (1937–44), was artistic director and chief conductor at the Belorussian Opera (1944–8), and chief conductor at the modern opera ensemble of the All Russian Theatre Company (1948–52). He recorded *Les Pêcheurs de perles* (with the Bolshoi Theatre Orchestra *et al.*), and *La Cenerentola* and *Madama Butterfly* (with the Moscow Radio Symphony Orchestra, *et al.*), each in Russian.

Brott, Alexander (b. 1915). The Canadian composer and conductor Alexander Brott was educated at the Quebec Academy of Music (1931–2), McGill University (1930–35), the Juilliard School (1935–7) and at the Chicago University. He was first concertmaster of the Montreal Symphony Orchestra, then assistant conductor of the orchestra, in 1939 founded and has since been musical director of the McGill Chamber Orchestra, which he led on a tour of the USSR in 1966, and more recently toured Switzerland with the orchestra. He has conducted the Montreal Pops Concerts and has been musical director of the Kingston Symphony Orchestra (since 1965) as well as being professor of music and conductor-in-residence at McGill University and conducting orchestras in Canada and Europe. His many compositions include symphonic music, a violin concerto, instrumental, vocal and chamber music, and he has orchestrated Ravel's *Gaspard de la nuit*, three Brahms intermezzi and Schumann's *Kinderszenen*. Some of his works have been performed by Beecham, Stokowski and Klemperer, including his symphonic pieces *War and Peace*, *From Sea to Sea* and *Royal Tribute*.

Brott has recorded with the McGill Chamber Orchestra his own *Circle, Triangle, Four Squares* (for Canadian Broadcasting Corporation and RCA), *From Sea to Sea* and *Arabesque* (for RCA), *Spheres in Orbit* (for Baroque), and *The Young Prometheus* and *Profundum Praedictum* (for RCA and Select), in addition to two Telemann suites, concertos by Haydn and Benda and Roussel's *Sinfonietta* (for Pirouette), Schubert's Symphony No. 5, some dances by Mozart, Beethoven and Schubert, a symphony and a concerto by Boyce, a symphonie concertante of Saint-Georges and Rameau's *La Poule* (for CBC), two Haydn symphonies (for Decca), Vallerand's *Strings in*

Motion, Gluck's *Sinfonia concertante* and Pépin's *Monade* (for RCA). He also recorded Jones' *Miramachi Ballad*, Papineau-Couture's Piano Concerto (with Manny) and his own *Paraphrase in Polyphony* (with the CBC Radio Orchestra for RCA).

Brott, Boris (b. 1944). Born in Montreal, Brott is the son of Alexander Brott; he appeared as a violin soloist with the Montreal Symphony Orchestra when he was five, at fourteen won a scholarship from the Mexican Government to study conducting with Markevitch and soon after won the Pan American Conductors Competition. He made his debut as a conductor in Mexico City (1958), returned to Canada, studied at the Montreal Conservatoire and McGill University, founded the Philharmonic Youth Orchestra of Montreal (1959), studied conducting with Monteux and was assistant conductor with the Toronto Symphony Orchestra (1963–5). He became principal conductor of the Northern Sinfonia, England (1964–8), music director of the Lakehead Symphony Orchestra (1968–72), won the Gold Medal at the Dmitri Mitropoulos International Conductors' Competition in New York (1968), was assistant conductor with Bernstein at the New York Philharmonic Orchestra (1968–9), music director of the Regina Symphony Orchestra (1971–3), of the Hamilton Philharmonic Orchestra (since 1969), chief conductor of the BBC Symphony Orchestra of Wales (since 1972), and principal conductor of the CBC Winnipeg Orchestra (from 1976). Brott also has guest engagements with orchestras in Canada, the United States, Mexico and in Europe. As a young man he won warm acclaim in Britain and Canada, particularly for the authority and sensitivity of his conducting, for the intensity of feeling and the command of style in a wide range of music, from Bach to Shostakovich.

When he was with the Northern Sinfonia (1964–8) Brott made a series of recordings which were released in the US by Mace, although they did not appear in Britain. Included were Rawsthorne's *Divertimento*, Arnold's *Sinfonietta*, Britten's *Simple Symphony*, suites from four operas of Handel, the Dvořák wind serenade and Gounod's *Petite Symphonie*, the German Dances of Mozart, Schubert and Beethoven, symphonies by Cannabich, Holzbauer and Richter and early orchestral works by Mozart, Rossini and Mendelssohn. For the Canadian Broadcasting Corporation he also recorded Poulenc's *Sinfonietta*, a concerto grosso of McCauley, Sibelius' *Pelléas et Mélisande*, Ravel's *Le Tombeau de Couperin* and excerpts from *Pulcinella* (with the Hamilton Philharmonic Orchestra), Fiala's *Montreal* and Kelsey Jones' *Miramichi Ballad* (with the Montreal Symphony Orchestra) and Debussy's *En bateau* and Wirén's *March* (with the Edmonton Symphony Orchestra).

Brown, Earle (b. 1926). Born at Lunenburg, Vermont, Brown studied mathematics and engineering at Northeastern University, Mass. (1944–5), then studied the Schillinger techniques of composition and orchestration and taught these techniques at Denver, Colorado (1950–52). He assisted Cage and Tudor (1952–5), was a recording engineer and editor for Capitol Records (1955–60), and is artistic director of the Contemporary Sound Series for Time-Manhattan Records (since 1960). He has been composer-in-residence at the Peabody Institute, Maryland (1968–72), at West Berlin (1970–71), at conservatories at Rotterdam (1974) and Basel (1975), and at the Tanglewood and Aspen festivals (1975), and has been a guest lecturer at the California Institute of Arts and at the University of California, Berkeley. Brown has written many compositions for orchestra, chamber ensembles, keyboard instruments and magnetic tapes, and some of these have been recorded in the United States and Europe. For Composers Recordings he directed, with a chamber ensemble *et al.*, his *Times Five* and *Novara*.

Brown, Harold (b. 1909). Born in New York, and educated at Columbia University, and the National Orchestral Association, Brown studied conducting with Bernstein, Lipkin and Barzin, and composition with Nadia Boulanger, Copland, Wagenaar and Goldmark, and was also at the Pius X School of Liturgical Music. He was a violist with various orchestras, and associate professor of music at Mansfield State College, Pennsylvania. He founded and has conducted the Renaissance Chorus, New York (1954), and with the ensemble recorded Isaac's motets from *Choralis Constantinus No. 3*, Josquin's *Missa una masque de Biscaia*, a mass of Ockeghem, Martini's *Magnificat* and Finck's *Missa de Beata Virgine* (for Counterpoint/Esoteric).

Brown, Howard (b. 1930). Born in Los Angeles, Brown studied at Harvard University, taught at Wellesley College, Massachusetts (1958–60), was an associate professor at the University of Chicago (1960–72), King Edward Professor of Music at King's College, University of London (1972–4), and finally has been professor of music at the University of Chicago (from 1974). Among his numerous publications are studies of aspects of the music of pre-Renaissance times. With the Chicago University Collegium Musicum he recorded vocal music of the early and late 15th century (for Pleiades).

Bruck, Charles (b. 1911). Born in Timişoara, Romania, Bruck studied in Paris at the École Normale, with Nadia Boulanger, Perlemuter and Monteux, and at the Vienna Conservatory. He was Monteux's assistant with the Paris Symphony Orchestra, became musical director at Cannes-Deauville (1949–50), at the Netherlands Opera (1950–54), conductor of the Strasbourg Radio Symphony Orchestra (1955–65) and conductor of l'Orchestre Philharmonique de l'ORTF (1965–70). His recordings include the Brahms Violin Concerto and Paganini's Violin Concerto No. 1 (with Kogan and the Paris Conservatoire Orchestra for EMI), Prokofiev's opera *L'Ange de feu* (with the Paris National Opera Orchestra *et al.* for Westminster, and later released in Britain by Decca), Constant's *24 Preludes for Orchestra* and Nigg's Violin Concerto (with the ORTF Orchestra and with Ferras in the latter, for DGG), Vivaldi's Concertos P. 127 and P. 279, and P. 88 and P. 405 (with Magaziner and the Paris Symphony Orchestra for Polymusic), Chabrier's opera *Une Éducation manquée* (for Chant du Monde), Landowski's Symphonies Nos 1 and 3 (with the ORTF Orchestra for Philips), Xenakis' *Nomos Gamma* and *Terretektorh*, Malec's *Oral* and Ohana's *Synaxis* (with the ORTF Orchestra for Erato) and Gluck's *Orfeo ed Euridice* (with the Netherlands Opera Orchestra *et al.* for EMI). The latter recording was issued in 1978 and originated at a performance at the 1951 Holland Festival, with a cast headed by the great British contralto Kathleen Ferrier, who performed the work just before her death.

Brückner-Rüggeberg, Wilhelm (b. 1906). Born in Stuttgart, Brückner-Rüggeberg studied at the Munich Academy where one of his teachers was Hausegger. In 1928 he received his first appointment as chorusmaster at the Munich State Opera, and after engagements as conductor at Essen, Oberhausen, Dortmund, Gera/Rudolstadt, Ulm and Kiel, he was a guest conductor with the Berlin Philharmonic Orchestra, at the Berlin State Opera and at Munich, and finally became conductor with the Hamburg Opera (1938–71). He also has appeared in Vienna, South America *et al.*; in 1976 he was professor at the Hochschule für Musik in Hamburg. For Philips he recorded in the late 1950s and early 1960s four major works of Kurt Weill: *Die Dreigroschenoper*, *Aufstieg und Fall der Stadt Mahagonny*, *Die sieben Todsünden der Kleinbürger* and *Happy End*, all with the singer/actress Lotte Lenya, Weill's widow, who had taken part in the original performances and now supervised the recordings. In the past few years they have been re-issued by CBS in Britain. Brückner-Rüggeberg's other recordings include pieces by Handel, Telemann, Mattheson, Keiser *et al.* for the series *Cities and Residences* issued by Electrola, with a disc each devoted to music in Hamburg, Dresden, Düsseldorf, *et al.*, excerpts from *Don Giovanni* (with soloists and the Hamburg Radio Symphony Orchestra, issued by Saga), the two *Peer Gynt* suites (with the Hamburg State Opera Orchestra, issued by Stereo-Fidelity and Musical Heritage Society), Svendsen's *Romance in G major* (with Garde and the Hamburg Philharmonic Orchestra for Polydor), the *Brandenburg Concerto No. 3* and *Eine kleine Nachtmusik* (with the North-West German Philharmonic Orchestra) and Mozart's Piano Concerto K. 488 (with Eschenbach and the Hamburg State Philharmonic Orchestra for Somerset/Miller International).

Brüggen, Frans (b. 1934). Born in Amsterdam, Brüggen studied the flute at the Amsterdam Conservatory and musicology at Amsterdam University. He became a virtuoso with the recorder, won many prizes, toured extensively and is the leader of the Dutch ensemble Quadro Amsterdam, as well as soloist with early music groups. He is also professor of recorder at high schools for music in Amsterdam and The Hague. For Telefunken he has made many records as a recorder soloist, and has conducted Telemann's complete *Tafelmusik*, *Suite in F* (with Schröder) and *Viola Concerto in G major* (with Doktor, and the Concerto Amsterdam), a collection entitled *English music for recorder and consort of gambas from the 16th and 17th centuries* (with the Brüggen Consort of Old Instruments), and for Philips Mozart's Violin Concertos K. 207 and K. 211 (with Schröder and the Amsterdam Mozart Ensemble).

Brün, Herbert (b. 1918). Born in Berlin, Brün studied at the Jerusalem Conservatory in Israel, and with Wolpe and Pelleg. He conducted research into electronic music at Paris, Cologne and Munich, and joined the School of Music at the University of Illinois to study computer systems in relation to composition. Composers Recordings issued a disc in which he directs the University of Illinois Chamber Players in his *Gestures for Eleven*.

Brusilow, Anshel (b. 1928). Born in Philadelphia, Brusilow graduated from the Curtis Institute of Music (1943) and the Philadelphia Music Academy (1947), and was concertmaster and assistant conductor of the New Orleans Symphony Orchestra (1954–5) and concertmaster of the Philadelphia Orchestra (1959–66). In 1961 he founded the Philadelphia Chamber Orchestra and conducted it until 1965, and the following year became the conductor of the Philadelphia Chamber Symphony Orchestra. In 1970 he was appointed executive director and conductor of the Dallas Symphony Orchestra. For RCA he recorded with the Philadelphia Chamber Symphony a fine series including Haydn's Symphony No. 60, Cherubini's *Symphony in D*, Brahms' Serenade No. 1, Tchaikovsky's Suite No. 4, Arensky's *Variations on a Theme of Tchaikovsky*, Françaix's *Serenade for Small Orchestra*, Ibert's *Capriccio* and *Suite symphonique*, Ravel's *Le Tombeau de Couperin*, Strauss's *Le Bourgeois gentilhomme*, Wolf's *Italian Serenade* and Yardumian's *Come, Creator Spirit*; for EMI he recorded with the Bournemouth Symphony Orchestra Balakirev's *Russia*, Borodin's Symphony No. 2, Rimsky-Korsakov's *Sarka* and Yardumian's Symphony No. 1, *Armenian Suite* and *Cantus animae et cordis*.

Brussen, Jan (b. 1918). Born in Amersfoort, Netherlands, Brussen studied conducting with van Kempen at Siena (1950–52), was a violinist and guest conductor with the Netherlands Radio Philharmonic Orchestra (1945–57), assistant conductor of the Amsterdam Concertgebouw Orchestra (1957–60), musical director of the Overÿssel Philharmonic Orchestra (from 1960), conductor and director of the Netherlands Students' Orchestra (1954–73), and has been a guest conductor in Czechoslovakia, FR Germany and Britain. He recorded Telemann's *Flute Concerto in D major* (with Barwahser and the Amsterdam Chamber Orchestra for Telefunken).

Brymer, Jack (b. 1915). Born in South Shields, Brymer became a schoolmaster and studied music at London University before serving in the Royal Air Force in World War II. After the war he was engaged as principal clarinet by Beecham for the Royal Philharmonic Orchestra in 1947, and left in 1963 to join the BBC Symphony Orchestra. He was on the staff of the Royal Academy of Music (1951–8), has been a professor at the Royal Military School of Music, was a member of the London Baroque Ensemble and director of the London Wind Soloists. Decca recorded the London Wind Soloists under his direction in five superb discs of Mozart's wind music, released originally in 1963–4, as well as other records of wind music by Haydn, J. C. Bach and Beethoven. This ensemble was brought together from the remarkable wind players whom Beecham had collected in his orchestra. Brymer has also appeared as the clarinet soloist in two recordings of Mozart's clarinet concerto, one with Beecham and the other with Davis, and in other concertos and chamber works.

Buckley, Emerson (b. 1916). Born in New York, Buckley was educated at Columbia College and the University of Denver, and has followed a successful career as a conductor of opera, ballet, symphony concerts and in radio and television, and has appeared in major cities in North America. Since 1950 he has been musical director and conductor of the Opera Guild of Great Miami, in 1955 he made his debut with the New York City Opera, and since 1963 he has been conductor of the Fort Lauderdale Symphony Orchestra. His other appointments as a conductor include the Mendelssohn Glee Club (1954–63), Puerto Rico Opera Festival (1954–8), Central City Opera Festival (1956–69), Seattle Opera (1964–74), and Baltimore Opera (1972–5). At the New York City Opera, where he was from 1955 to 1967, he conducted a number of world premières of American operas. He recorded two of the most popular contemporary American operas, Douglas Moore's *The Ballad of Baby Doe* (with the New York City Opera Chorus and Orchestra *et al.* for MGM, and later re-issued by Helidor), and Robert Ward's *The Crucible* (with the City Center Orchestra *et al.* for Composers Recordings).

Buesst, Aylmer (b. 1883). The Australian conductor Buesst was born and educated in Melbourne, and studied at Brussels and the Leipzig Conservatory under Nikisch. He conducted opera at Breslau, Aussig and Görlitz (1910–14) and then came to England where he conducted with the Moody-Manners Opera Company (1914–16), the Beecham Opera Company (1918–20), was chorusmaster at Covent Garden (1920) where he conducted *Die Meistersinger* (1921), was one of the founders and conductor of the British National Opera Company (1922–8), conducted the Carl Rosa Opera Company (1928–30) and the Old Vic and Sadler's Wells Company (1930–33), was assistant music director of the BBC (1933–6), conductor of the Scottish Orchestra (1939–40) and professor of conducting at the Guildhall

School of Music (1946). He wrote a fine guide to *Der Ring des Nibelungen*. In 1928 Columbia issued a complete recording of *Cavalleria rusticana*, in English, in which he conducted the British National Opera Company.

Bugeano, Constantin. The Romanian conductor Bugeano entered the Bucharest Conservatory at the age of 11, studied there with Perlea and at Salzburg with Krauss. Before World War II he was conductor at the Bucharest Opera, and after the war he became conductor of the Bucharest Philharmonic Orchestra. He was director of the Cluj Opera (1948–52), of the Bucharest Opera (1955–7), conductor of the Bucharest Philharmonic Orchestra (again after 1957) and of the Romanian Film Orchestra (1962–3). His recordings for Electrecord reflect the breadth of his repertoire and include the Bach orchestral Suites Nos 1 to 4 (with the Romanian Film Orchestra, except No. 2, with the Cluj Philharmonic Orchestra), three Mozart overtures, Beethoven's Piano Concerto No. 3 (with Lupu) and the two violin Romances (with Constantinescu), Enesco's Symphony No. 2, pieces by Jora, Rogalski, Stroe and Niculescu (with the Romanian Film Orchestra), Pergolesi's *La serva padrona* (with the Bucharest Philharmonic Chamber Orchestra *et al.*) and Prokofiev's two Violin Concertos (with Bernard and the Bucharest Philharmonic Orchestra).

Buketoff, Igor (b. 1915). A native of Hartford, Connecticut, Buketoff studied at the University of Kansas, the Juilliard School and the Los Angeles Conservatory of Music and Art, and taught at the Juilliard School (1935–45), the Chautauqua School of Music (1941–7) and at Columbia University (1943–7). He was the first winner of the Alice Ditson Award for young conductors (1942), toured the United States and Europe with a Broadway company presenting Menotti's operas *The Medium* and *The Telephone*, and conducted the Fort Wayne Philharmonic Orchestra (1948–66), the Young People's Concerts of the New York Philharmonic Orchestra (1948–53), the Iceland State Symphony Orchestra (1964–5) and the St Paul Opera Association (since 1968). He has been a guest conductor in Europe and South America and has conducted at festivals at Camden, Cheltenham, Harrogate, Prague and in Holland. In 1967 he was again honoured by the Ditson Committee for his promotion of contemporary American music, and is now a faculty member at the University of Houston.

In 1957 Buketoff founded a World Music Bank for the international exchange and promotion of contemporary music. Juries in each country subscribing to the bank select the music; a master list of recommendations is compiled and circulated to all the contributing nations, thus bringing to their attention the works considered to be most worthy of performance. Buketoff has been chairman of the organisation, which has benefited from grants from the Rockefeller Foundation. He was also director of the contemporary composers' project of the Institute of International Education (1967–70), which collaborated with RCA Victor to record major 20th-century music under his baton. In this series there appeared Bax's *Overture to a Picaresque Comedy*, Bennett's Symphony No. 1, Berkeley's Divertimento, Lees' Concerto for String Quartet and Orchestra, and Sessions' Symphony No. 3 (with the Royal Philharmonic Orchestra), Sommer's *Vocal Symphony*, Klusák's *First Inventions* and Fišer's *Fifteen Prints* (with the London Symphony Orchestra), and piano concertos by Mennin and Yardumian (with Ogdon and the Royal Philharmonic Orchestra). His other recordings have been Gottschalk's Symphonies Nos 1 and 2 and *Escenas campestres* (with the Vienna State Opera Orchestra for Turnabout), Ward's Symphony No. 3 and *Sacred Songs for Pantheists* (with the Iceland Symphony Orchestra for Composers Recordings), Jacob Avshalomov's *The Taking of T'ung Kuan* and Cazden's *Three Ballads from the Catskills* (with the Oslo Philharmonic Orchestra for Composers Recordings) and Tchaikovsky's *1812* overture, *Spring Cantata* and three Russian folk-songs arranged by Rachmaninov (with the New Philharmonia Orchestra *et al.* for RCA); this latter record was a best-seller for over 70 consecutive weeks.

Bunney, Herrick (b. 1915). Born in London and educated at the Royal College of Music, Bunney was organist and master of music at St Giles' Cathedral, Edinburgh (from 1946), and was conductor of the Edinburgh Royal Choral Union, the Edinburgh University Singers and the Elizabethan Singers, London. He has recorded as an organist, and led the Elizabethan Singers in records of carols and folk songs (for Argo).

Bünte, C. A. (b. 1925). Born in Berlin and the son of a professor of piano and a teacher of singing, Bünte studied at the Berlin Conservatory (1945–6) and at the Berlin International Institute of Music (1946–9), where he was a pupil of Celibidache. For 25 years he was chief conductor of the Berlin Symphony Orchestra (1949–73) in West Berlin, and has also been a guest conductor with major orchestras in Western Europe. In 1962 the Association of German Critics awarded him their prize for his performances with the Berlin Symphony Orchestra, particularly of music by Beethoven and Bruckner, and he has been acclaimed for his well-prepared, virile and straightforward interpretations and for his firm but unfussy manner before the orchestra.

He has recorded Danzī's Cello Concerto and Weber's *Grand potpourri* (with Blees), Dusík's Piano Concerto and Field's Piano Concerto No. 2 (with Kyriakou), Viotti's Violin Concerto No. 22 (with Lautenbacher) and Double Concerto (with Galling and Lautenbacher), Hummel's Piano Concerto and *La Galante* (with Galling), Beethoven's *Piano Concerto in E flat major* (written when the composer was 14) and Rössler's *Piano Concerto in D major*, wrongly ascribed to Beethoven (with Galling), and Busoni's *Konzertstück* (with Glazer), Divertimento for Flute (with Klemeyer), *Rondo Arlecchinesco* (with Moser) and Concertino for Clarinet (with Triebskorn, and the Berlin Symphony Orchestra, for Vox, and its associate labels, Turnabout and Candide); a collection of German Dances by Haydn, Mozart *et al.* (with the Berlin Symphony Orchestra for Columbia); the overtures and preludes to *Aida*, *Un ballo in maschera*, *I vespri siciliani*, *Nabucco* and *La traviata*, Smetana's *Šárka*, overture to *Libuše*, and the Dance of the Comedians from *The Bartered Bride* (with the Berlin Symphony Orchestra for Intercord); Casella's *Scarlattiana*, Pizzetti's *Concerto dell'estate*, Walton's *Façade* suite, Vaughan Williams' *English Folksongs Suite* and three movements from Holst's *The Planets* (with the Berlin Symphony Orchestra for La Musica Moderna); and *Boléro*, *Rhapsody in Blue* (with Bianca), *An American in Paris* and a suite from *Swan Lake* (with the Hamburg Symphony Orchestra for Vega).

Burgess, Grayston (b. 1932). Born in Cheriton, Kent, Burgess was educated at the Canterbury Cathedral Choir School, and at King's College, Cambridge. He was a countertenor in Westminster Abbey Choir (1955–69), and performed at Covent Garden as Oberon in Britten's *A Midsummer Night's Dream*; as a solo countertenor he has given recitals and made records. In 1963 he founded and directed the Purcell Consort of Voices, and made his debut as a conductor at the Aldeburgh Festival in that year. As director of the Purcell Consort he has made many records for Argo and Candide/Turnabout, including Josquin's *Petite Camusette* and *Déploration sur la morte de Johan*, Dunstable's *Laudi* and Motets, Ockeghem's *Vive le Roy*, *El Grillo*, *La Bernadina* and *Ave Maria*, Machaut's *La Messe de Notre Dame*, ballades and other pieces, church music of Byrd, Davy's *St Matthew Passion*, madrigals by East and Monteverdi, and a collection by Tomkins, Weelkes, Young *et al.*, sacred and secular music of Dunstable, music of Albert, the Prince Consort, music by Scheidt, Schein and Schütz, and discs of collections entitled *Doulce Mémoire: 16th-Century French Chansons*; *English Madrigals from the Reign of Queen Elizabeth*; *English Secular Music of the Late Renaissance*; *The Eton Choir Book*; *High Renaissance Music in England*; *Lo, Country Sports*; *Music all Powerful – to Entertain Queen Victoria*; *The Triumphs of Oriana*; *To Entertain a King*; and *Victorian Ballads and Pieces*. In these performances the Purcell Consort was joined, on occasion, by the Elizabeth Consort of Viols, the Jaye Consort of Viols, the Purcell Instrumental Ensemble, Musica Reservata, the London Sackbut Ensemble and the Philip Jones Brass Ensemble. These records have been widely praised for their superb musicianship and style.

Burghauser, Jarmil (b. 1921). Born at Písek, in southern Bohemia, Burghauser studied at the Prague Conservatory (1940–44) and at the Charles University (1945–8) and commenced his career as a choirmaster at the Prague National Theatre (1946–53). He has composed music for films, the theatre and television, operas, orchestral and chamber works, published a thematic catalogue of Dvořák, and edited the complete critical editions of Dvořák, Fibich and Janáček. Supraphon issued a disc on which he conducted the *Shakespeare Festival March* of Smetana, with the Czech Philharmonic Orchestra.

Burgin, Richard (b. 1892). Born in Warsaw, Burgin studied the violin at the St Petersburg Conservatory with Auer and made his debut in 1903 with the Warsaw Philharmonic Orchestra. He was concertmaster of the Helsinki Symphony Orchestra (1912–15), the Oslo Symphony Orchestra (1916–19) and the Boston Symphony Orchestra (1920–65), and was appointed assistant conductor of the Boston Symphony by Koussevitzky in 1927. Koussevitzky did not like guest conductors to appear with the orchestra and preferred to call on Burgin, who could maintain his method and discipline with the players. Later, in 1953, Burgin was also appointed conductor of the New England Conservatory Orchestra and of the Harvard University Orchestra. His records as a conductor have been limited: excerpts from Bach cantatas and organ concertos by Poulenc and Hindemith (with E. Power Biggs and the Columbia Chamber Orchestra for Columbia, US), pieces by Gabrieli and Frescobaldi (with E. Power Biggs and the New England Brass Ensemble for Columbia, US), concertos by J. C., C. P. E. and W. F. Bach (with the Zimbler Sinfonietta for Boston) and a distinctive performance of Britten's *Serenade for Tenor, Horn and Strings* (with Lloyd, Stagliano and the Boston Symphony Strings for Boston).

Burkhard, Paul (1911–77). Born in Zürich where he studied at the Conservatory, Burkhard was with the Berne City Theatre (1932–4), and then was resident composer at the Zürich Theatre (1939–44) and conductor of the Zürich Radio Orchestra (1944–57). He was a guest conductor in Baden-Baden, Munich, Vienna, Berlin, Hamburg and London, where, besides being noted for conducting Offenbach, he directed his own compositions, which included operettas, musicals, musical comedies, songs and arrangements. He recorded his overture to *Der Schuss von der Kanzel* (with the Beromünster Radio Orchestra, for Communauté de travail pour la diffusion de la musique suisse), *D'Zäller Glichnis*, *D'Zäller Wienacht*, *D'Zäller Josef* and *D'Zäller Ooschtere* (with a Youth ensemble from Zell im Tösstal, for EMI), *Jugend-Messe* (with the Ergebenen Orchestra *et al.* for EMI), *Noah* (with the Engelburg School Orchestra *et al.* for EMI), the musical *Feuerwerk* (with the Graunke Symphony Orchestra *et al.* for Ariola) and *Freu dich mit uns, Jona* (with the Collegium Johanneum Ostbevern for FSM), and Liebermann's *Suite on Swiss Folk Songs* (with the Beromünster Radio Orchestra for Decca).

Busch, Adolf (1891–1952). Born in Siegen, Westphalia, Busch was brought up in an intensely musical environment; among his brothers were the conductor Fritz and the cellist Hermann. He had his first violin lessons at the age of two and gave his first violin recital at the age of five. A wealthy industrialist undertook to finance his musical studies; he attended the conservatories at Cologne (under Hess and Steinbach) and Bonn (under Grüters). He performed under Steinbach's baton in Vienna and London and in Berlin played the Busoni Violin Concerto with the composer conducting. Busch was then appointed concertmaster of the Vienna Konzertverein and in 1919 he founded the Busch Quartet and Busch Trio. Hermann Busch was also a member of the quartet, and the two brothers combined with Rudolf Serkin, Adolf's son-in-law, in the Busch Trio. Recitals of these ensembles, as well as of Busch and Serkin together, were a celebrated feature of pre-war musical life in Europe; some of their recordings have been re-issued, treasured for their insight and profundity. In 1922 Busch was appointed director of the Hochschule für Musik in Berlin, and at that time he was recognised as Germany's finest violinist. When the Nazis forbade him to perform with Serkin, a Jew, Busch renounced his German citizenship in 1933 and made his home in Switzerland; in 1939 he moved to the United States where he formed a chamber orchestra and in 1950 founded his School of Music at Marlboro, Vermont, where he died two years later. He composed much music, mainly for orchestra and chamber ensembles.

In 1935 Busch formed the Adolf Busch Chamber Players to perform the *Brandenburg Concertos* at the Florence May Festival, and afterwards he recorded the Concertos and the Bach orchestral Suites for HMV, later adding the Handel *Concerti Grossi* Op. 6 (on 25 78 r.p.m. records), the Bach *Violin Concerto in E major*, the Bach Double Violin Concerto (also with Francis Magnes), the Mozart Violin Concerto K. 219, the Mozart Piano Concerto K. 449 (with Serkin), the *Serenata notturna* and *Adagio and Fugue in C minor*, a prelude from a Corelli sonata, and his arrangement of the *Grosse Fuge* of Beethoven. The Bach records were one of the glories of the pre-LP catalogue; deeply felt, flexible and tonally vibrant, they were more romantic in style than is usual today in performances of Bach's music. The *Serenata notturna* was an exquisite example of Mozart style, with a magical balance of the vitality and sentiment. The *Brandenburg Concertos* and the Bach Suites were once re-issued by EMI on LP; the *Brandenburg Concerto No. 5* has been available in the Seraphim (US) album *The Age of the Great Instrumentalists: Six Concertos*, and Turnabout more recently issued a disc containing the *Serenata notturna*, the *Adagio and Fugue in C minor* and the Piano Concerto K. 449 (with Serkin). In the United States, Busch recorded the Bach Clavier Concerto No. 1 (with Istomin and the Busch Chamber Players). Busch's dedication and integrity are summed up in his remark that 'an artist should never draw attention to the beauty of his playing, but only to the beauty of the work being played'.

In 1978 CBS issued in the US on the Odyssey label Bach's Violin Concerto in E major and the Double Violin Concerto, as well as the Bach Sonata No. 3 and some piano and violin sonatas of Beethoven and Schumann, played by Busch and Serkin together.

Busch, Fritz (1890–1951). Adolf was the violinist in the Busch family and Fritz was the pianist; like his brother, Fritz was a child prodigy. At the age of seven he was giving piano recitals in his native Siegen in Westphalia, and at twelve he had lessons on almost every orchestral instrument. He studied at the Cologne Conservatory under Steinbach, and after conducting some concerts at Bad Pyrmont in 1909 he was appointed conductor at the municipal opera at Riga. Afterwards he was music director at Gotha (1911–12) and at Aachen; in 1914 he was called up for the German army, was wounded and discharged and returned to Aachen. In 1918 he had a brilliant success leading the Berlin Philharmonic Orchestra at a Max Reger festival at Jena, succeeded von Schillings as general music director at the Stuttgart National Theatre, and in 1922 followed Reiner as music director at the Dresden Opera. He left Dresden and Gemany abruptly in 1933 after an ugly brush with Nazi stormtroopers. He had strong anti-Nazi sympathies; he had refused an invitation to conduct at Bayreuth, and his promotion of modern music earned him the disfavour of the regime. He first went to Buenos Aires, where he conducted at the Teatro Colón for a season, and in 1934 settled in Denmark, trained and conducted the Danish State Radio Symphony Orchestra which he took, years later in 1950, to the Edinburgh Festival. From 1934 he also conducted the summer seasons of the Glyndebourne Opera in Sussex. He continued at Glyndebourne until World War II, returned in 1950 and 1951, when in his last appearance he conducted the entire season of four Mozart operas. From 1941 to 1945 he was active again in Buenos Aires and conducted in New York both opera and symphony concerts from 1945 to 1950; he made his debut at the Metropolitan Opera with *Lohengrin* at the opening night of the 1945–6 season.

When he was at Dresden Busch had the reputation of being one of the finest German conductors, and under his leadership the Dresden Opera enjoyed an era of great brilliance, particularly in its presentations of the operas of Mozart and Wagner. At this time the premières of many operas took place: Strauss's *Intermezzo* and *Die Ägyptische Helena*, Hindemith's *Kokoschka* and *Cardillac*, Weill's *Der Protagonist* and Busoni's *Doktor Faust*. When Toscanini resigned from the New York Philharmonic-Symphony Orchestra in 1936 he suggested that Busch should take his place, but Busch declined. When he conducted in New York his complete lack of eccentricity as a personality and as a musician, and his straightforward interpretations devoid of any excess, caused him to suffer in comparison with many of the other great conductors then current, such as Stokowski, Koussevitzky, Toscanini and Rodzinski. Yet, his musicianship is recognised in Europe to this day, and those who worked with him at Glyndebourne admired his strong personality, his unostentatious command and his sense of humour. There are many stories of him at this time. When he was rehearsing the overture to *Don Pasquale*, which has a difficult beginning, the entry was not together; he quietly put down his baton, waited for silence and said: 'Everyone in this wonderful orchestra is invited to play', after which there was no trouble. The great baritone Baccaloni was once lax in his observance of Mozart's rhythms; Busch sent him a telegram of good-humoured protestation, signed 'Wolfgang Amadeus Mozart'. When rehearsing he would play the piano part exuberantly, but adding many touches not in the score, to distract the singer's attention, as if he were trying to put him off, which assured him that the singer would be unperturbed on the stage no matter what might happen. He did not allow the singers to wear glasses at ensemble rehearsals as he wanted to know who would not see his beat.

At Glyndebourne Busch was responsible for Mozart productions of a standard as superb as those of Walter at Munich. A wealthy English businessman, John Christie, had built an opera house in his country estate near Lewes in Sussex in 1934, so as to produce operas in which his wife, Audrey Mildmay, could sing. Christie secured Busch, Carl Ebert and Rudolf Bing, all refugees from Nazi Germany; Busch and Ebert had worked together at Dresden. Christie was first interested in Wagner, but Busch and Ebert persuaded him to have Mozart instead. Later the repertoire was widened beyond Mozart; the company closed during World War II, resumed and flourished again after the war and today is one of the most delightful attractions of the English musical year. The exceptional polish of the productions resulted from the great care Busch took in casting, preparation and conducting, his insistence on adequate rehearsals and the production of each opera as a complete and unified conception. HMV recorded three of these Glyndebourne operas with Busch: *Le nozze di Figaro* (1936) and *Don Giovanni* and *Così fan tutte* (1937), and together with Beecham's *Die Zauberflöte*, issued them as their Mozart Opera Society series. *Le nozze di Figaro* was released first in three volumes; curiously, the first volume contained only the ensembles, the second the overture and arias and duets from Acts I and II, and the third the arias and duets from the remaining two acts. Later sanity returned and all the numbers were sorted out into their correct sequence. LP transfers of the four Mozart Opera Society sets have been available from time to time on various labels, including World Record Club, Turnabout and Classics for Pleasure, and despite their age they will always claim the admiration of Mozart enthusiasts. They were a revelation in their day and document a splendid phase in opera performance in the pre-war years.

Before 1933 Busch had recorded for Polydor the overture to *La forza del destino* (with the Dresden Philharmonic Orchestra) and Helen's awakening, and death, from *Die Ägyptische Helena* (with the Berlin State Opera Orchestra). His other pre-war recordings included the waltzes from *Der Rosenkavalier* and excerpts from *Daphne* (with the Saxon State Orchestra for HMV), *Don Juan* (with the London Philharmonic Orchestra for HMV), *Till Eulenspiegel* and Mozart's Symphony No. 36 (with the BBC Symphony Orchestra for HMV). After the war there were excerpts from *Idomeneo* and *Così fan tutte* (with the Glyndebourne Company for HMV), Haydn's Symphony No. 88 and Sinfonia Concertante, Mozart's Symphony No. 36 and some Contradances, the overture to *Der Freischütz* and Brahms' Symphony No. 2 (with the Danish State Radio Orchestra, for HMV), *Eine kleine Nachtmusik* and the *Leonore No. 3* overture (with the Danish State Radio Orchestra for Telefunken), some arias from the Wagner operas (with Ralf, Traubel *et al.* and the New York Metropolitan Orchestra for Columbia), Haydn's Symphony No. 101 and Beethoven's Symphony No. 8 (with the Vienna Symphony Orchestra for Philips). His few LP recordings are more difficult to identify. Some performances originating from live radio broadcasts in 1950 and 1951 were issued by Polydor, including Beethoven's Symphony No. 9 and *Leonore No. 2* overture, the *Tragic Overture* of Brahms and Mendelssohn's Symphony No. 4; La Guilde Internationale du Disque released Schubert's Symphony No. 5 and Mendelssohn's overture *Die schöne Melusine* (with the Winterthur Symphony Orchestra); Masterseal and some other labels issued Beethoven's Symphonies Nos 3 and 8 and Haydn's Symphony No. 101 (with the Austrian Symphony Orchestra [*sic*]), and a series issued by the Friends of Fritz Busch, in the US, issued the prelude and Liebestod from *Tristan und Isolde*, and presumably other performances. If one were to select a shining example of Busch's art as a symphonic conductor, Brahms' Symphony No. 2 with the Danish State Radio Orchestra would do admirably; in its day, before LP, it was hailed as one of the finest readings to appear of the work on record.

Bushkötter, Wilhelm (1887–1967). Born in Höxter, Westphalia, Bushkötter studied the cello, graduated at Halle (1912), was a conductor at Davos (1912), Hamburg (1920), Altona (1923), Berlin Radio (1924–6), Cologne Radio (1926–36), Stuttgart Radio (1936–8) and Dortmund (1938), taught in Berlin (1945–9) and returned to conduct with the Cologne Radio (1950–53). For Polydor he led the Berlin Symphony Orchestra in the overture to Suppé's *Die Banditenstreiche*.

Büsser, Henri-Paul (1872–1973). The French composer and conductor Büsser was a pupil of Franck and Guiraud, a disciple of Gounod and a teacher of Debussy. At the age of seven he was a member of the Toulouse Symphony Orchestra, and at the age of twelve he composed a mass. After studying the organ and composition at the Paris Conservatoire he was appointed with Gounod's intervention organist at Saint-Cloud, where he remained from 1892 to 1922. He won the Prix de Rome (1893), became a conductor at the Paris Opéra-Comique (1902), then at the Paris Opéra (1905–39) and was director of the Opéra-Comique (1939–41). In 1947 he was named president of the Académie des Beaux Arts. He composed much music including five operas and orchestrated Debussy's two-piano *Petite Suite* and reconstructed the score of the same composer's *Printemps*, the original of which had been lost in a fire. His compositions *Pièce de concert*, for harp and orchestra, and *Marche de fête* have been recorded. In 1931 he recorded a complete *Faust* for Columbia with soloists, chorus and orchestra of the Opéra-Comique; his direction was effective and idiomatic, and the performance appeared on an LP transfer in 1976, released by Club 99 in New York.

Butterley, Nigel (b. 1935). Born in Sydney, the Australian composer Butterley studied at the New South Wales Conservatorium of Music, has been on the music staff of the Australian Broadcasting Commission, and studied in England with Priaulx Rainier. Among his compositions, *In the Head the Fire* was awarded the Italia Prize in 1966. For World Record Club he conducted an instrumental group in his *Laudes*.

Byrns, Harold (b. 1903). Born Hans Bernstein in Hannover, Byrns studied at the Stern Conservatory in Berlin, was choirmaster under Kleiber and Blech at the Berlin State Opera, and in 1933 was a conductor at Lübeck. He was a champion of the music of Mahler, Berg, Bartók, Schoenberg, Stravinsky and Hindemith, left Germany in 1933, went first to Italy then to the United States, where he became an American citizen. From 1948 to 1950 he led the Los Angeles Chamber Orchestra, which also performed as the Byrns Chamber Orchestra. Returning to Germany he conducted at the Komische Oper in East Berlin (1958–61) and is now active in FR Germany. He prepared piano arrangements of Mahler's symphonies and in 1967 was awarded the medal of the Mahler Society of America, the same year that Leonard Bernstein received the same honour. He recorded his arrangement of Smetana's *Bohemian Dances*, Suk's *Serenade for Strings*, Arensky's *Variations on a Theme of Tchaikovsky*, Grieg's *Holberg Suite*, Bartók's *Music for Strings, Percussion and Celesta*, Honegger's *Concerto da camera* and Strauss's *Duet Concertino* (with the Los Angeles Chamber Orchestra or the Byrns Chamber Orchestra for Capitol), Rachmaninov's Piano Concerto No. 2 and *Rhapsody on a Theme of Paganini* (with Frugoni and the Vienna Pro Musica Orchestra for Vox), the Stravinsky Violin Concerto (with Gitlis and the Colonne Orchestra for Vox) and *Capriccio* (with Zelka and the South-West German Radio Orchestra for Vox), and Berg's *Chamber Concerto* (with Gitlis, Zelka and the Vienna Wind Ensemble for Vox).

C

Cage, John (b. 1912). Born in Los Angeles and educated at Pomona College, Cage studied with Buhlig, Weiss, Schoenberg and Cowell, was awarded a Guggenheim Fellowship (1949), taught composition at the New School for Social Research, New York (1955–60), was musical director of the Merce Cunningham Dance Company (1944–68), visiting professor at the school of music at Illinois University (1967–8), and artist-in-residence at the University of California, Davis (1969). His compositions are numerous, and many have been recorded; he led the Manhattan Percussion Ensemble in Russell's *Three Dance Movements*, and *Double Music for Percussion and Orchestra*, which he wrote with Lou Harrison (for Mainstream).

Caillat, Stéphane (b. 1928). Born in Irigny, France, Caillat studied in Lyon and Paris, was director and founder of the Stéphane Caillat Vocal Ensemble, of the 'Per cantar e sonar' Ensemble for the performance of Renaissance music, is a conductor with Radio-France, technical counsellor for choral work with the Ministry of Youth, Sport and Leisure, and director of the Centre d'études polyphoniques et chorales de Paris. He has conducted throughout Western Europe, and in Czechoslovakia, DR Germany, Algeria and Canada, and since 1968 has led many performances of contemporary music. His recordings include Delalande's *De profundis*, *Sacris Solemnis* and *Regina coeli*, and Vivaldi's *Gloria*, *Kyrie* and *Lauda Jerusalem* (with the Stéphane Caillat Vocal Ensemble and the Jean-François Paillard Chamber Orchestra for Erato, the Delalande also being issued in the US by Musical Heritage Society).

Calabro, Louis (b. 1926). Born in Brooklyn, New York, Calabro studied at the Juilliard School and has taught at Bennington College since 1955. He has won awards and commissions for his compositions, including two Guggenheim Fellowships and two Elizabeth Coolidge Chamber Music Awards. For Composers Recordings he led the Eastman Brass Ensemble in his own *Environments*.

Cameron, Basil (1884–1975). Born in Reading, Berkshire, the son of a church organist, Cameron learned the violin as a boy and performed a concerto in public at the age of eight. At 14 he was leading an orchestra at Scarborough, then went to Berlin to study with Joachim and Bruch. Returning to England in 1908 he played five seasons with the Queen's Hall Orchestra, and in 1912 he assumed the name of Basil Hindenberg, was appointed conductor of the Torquay Municipal Orchestra and established a reputation for festivals of the music of Wagner and Strauss which he organised. With World War I he changed his name back to Cameron and served with the British army in France. From 1923 to 1930 he was conductor of municipal orchestras at Hastings and Harrogate, then became prominent in London leading the Royal Philharmonic Orchestra and in the north the Scottish Orchestra. After a visit to the United States in 1932 to conduct the San Francisco Symphony Orchestra he was appointed co-conductor of that orchestra with Dobrowen, but after two years he accepted the appointment of permanent conductor of the Seattle Symphony Orchestra. Its progress under his direction was considerable. At this time, during a European tour, he became known to Sibelius, who promised him the first performance of his Symphony No. 8, which, of course, never came into being. In the US he premièred symphonies of Bax and Malipiero and directed a series of radio broadcasts for the Columbia Broadcasting System. Returning to London in 1938 Cameron was active with orchestras there and in the provinces, and in 1939 conducted *Tristan und Isolde* at Covent Garden, remarkable because he substituted for a sick Beecham without a rehearsal. He also assisted Wood with the direction of the Promenade Concerts and helped to keep music alive in Britain during the war. Afterwards he continued as a guest conductor of major orchestras in Britain and Europe. A genial personality, his reserved nature shunned showmanship. He was always interested in seeking out new music and in encouraging young composers.

Cameron's first recordings were for Decca, on 78s, with the Hastings Philharmonic Orchestra: *Peer Gynt* Suite No. 1, the overtures to *Oberon*, *Semiramide*, *Raymond*, *Dichter und Bauer* and *Morgen, Mittag und Abend in Wien*, and German's *Welsh Rhapsody* and *Henry VIII* dances. In the 1940s he recorded, for Decca, the *Peer Gynt* Suites Nos 1 and 2, the overtures to *Zampa* and *Les Diamants de la couronne*, the ballet music from *William Tell*, the Handel/Harty *Water Music* and Sibelius' Symphony No. 2 and *Tapiola* (with the London Philharmonic Orchestra), *Capriccio espagnol*, Dvořák's Symphony No. 8 and the Tchaikovsky Violin Concerto (with Haendel, and with the National Symphony Orchestra) and Franck's *Symphonic Variations* (with Hess and the City of Birmingham Orchestra); for EMI he also directed Mozart's Piano Concerto K. 449 (with Horsley), Brahms' Piano Concerto No. 1 (with Arrau) and Saint-Saëns' Piano Concerto No. 2 (with Moiseiwitsch and the Philharmonia Orchestra), Rachmaninov's *Rhapsody on a Theme of Paganini* (with Moiseiwitsch), Kodály's *Dances from Galánta* and *Valse triste* and pieces from the *Karelia* and *King Christian II* suites of Sibelius (with the London Philharmonic Orchestra), Grieg's *Lyric Suite*, the overture to *Béatrice et Bénédict* and Handel's Oboe Concerto No. 3 (with Goossens, and with the Liverpool Philharmonic Orchestra), Prokofiev's Violin Concerto No. 2 (with Kogan) and Benjamin's Harmonica Concerto (with Adler, and with the London Symphony Orchestra). At best, his recordings were competent and at worst, dull. The shorter works gave him the best results but in the Dvořák and Sibelius symphonies his straightforwardness and avoidance of any trace of sentiment or exaggeration conveyed little impression of a positive musical personality at work.

Campbell, Sidney (b. 1909). Born in London and educated at Dunelm, and a Fellow of the Royal College of Organists and the Royal School of Church Music, an associate of the Royal College of Music and a licentiate of the Royal Academy of Music, Campbell has been organist and choirmaster at the Queen's Free Chapel of St George at Windsor Castle (since 1961). He has recorded both as organist and conductor; in the latter capacity he led Vaughan Williams' *Mass in G minor* (with the Renaissance Singers) and Britten's *A Ceremony of Carols* (with Korchinska and the Canterbury Cathedral Choir, for Decca).

Cantelli, Guido (1920–56). Born in Novara, Italy, Cantelli played as a boy in his father's military band, was organist at the local church at the age of ten, conducted the town's choral society and gave piano recitals at the age of fourteen. After studies at the Milan Conservatory, he returned to Novara in 1941 to become conductor and artistic director of the Teatro Coccia, which had been founded in 1899 by Toscanini. In 1943 he was forced to join the Italian army, but refused to support Fascism, and was sent to a Nazi labour camp in Stettin for two years; his health deteriorated but after transfer to Bolzano he escaped to Milan. He was caught by the Fascists, but was saved from a death sentence by the liberation of Italy. With the end of the war he resumed his musical career, conducted the La Scala Orchestra in a programme which included Tchaikovsky's Symphony No. 6, and appeared with orchestras in Italy, Belgium, Austria and Hungary. Toscanini heard him rehearsing the La Scala Orchestra in Milan in May 1948 and immediately invited him to be a guest conductor with the NBC Symphony Orchestra; Cantelli's first radio concert in New York was in January 1949 and he visited the United States each year to conduct the NBC Symphony, the New York Philharmonic, the Boston Symphony and other major orchestras. In 1950, together with de Sabata, he led the La Scala Orchestra at the Edinburgh Festival and in the following years conducted at the Lucerne, Salzburg and Venice Festivals. His life was tragically cut short by an air crash in Paris; he had just been appointed principal conductor at the La Scala Opera but had yet to conduct his first opera there.

From the first time he heard him conduct, Toscanini held the highest regard and affection for Cantelli, believing that he himself conducted in the same way at Cantelli's age, and he attended many of Cantelli's rehearsals and concerts in New York. No doubt his musical influence on Cantelli was profound, but it would be wrong to conclude that Cantelli tried to copy Toscanini. He was in his own right an extraordinarily gifted musician, whatever his relationship with the older man. He differed from the elderly Toscanini in his musical interpretations, but Toscanini probably saw in him the lyricism and fluency of his own early style. Cantelli possessed a remarkable memory and conducted without scores at both rehearsals and concerts. His passionate demands for perfection and his complete involvement in every note produced a high degree of tension at rehearsals and recording sessions, when he would repeat a passage almost endlessly to achieve what he wanted. Frequently he surprised himself at the very high standard of the performance that resulted, although on occasion he could be reduced to tears when he could not produce the desired result. He was characterised well by C. J. Luten: 'The precision and refinement of the orchestral playing, the clearly fastidious care for attack, chording and sonority, these technical achievements were guided by exquisite musical taste. All expression occurred within the framework of the composer's instructions regarding tempo, dynamics, rhythm and phrasing, and . . . Cantelli had the power to achieve rubato inside the bar, so that the barlines themselves were always equidistant.' (*The Cantelli Legacy*, brochure of the Arturo Toscanini Society).

Cantelli's first records, made for RCA Victor with the NBC Symphony Orchestra, were of Haydn's Symphony No. 93, Rossini's overture *Le Siège de Corinthe*, the *Mathis der Maler* symphony, *Pictures at an Exhibition* and Franck's *Symphony in D minor*. For Columbia (US) he recorded Vivaldi's *The Four Seasons* with the New York Philharmonic Orchestra. In 1948 he signed a contract with EMI and his first discs were made in Italy with the Santa Cecilia Orchestra: the overture to *Le Siège de Corinthe*, Casella's *Paganiniana* and Busoni's *Berceuse élégiaque*. When he visited Britain in 1950 with the La Scala Orchestra he recorded Tchaikovsky's Symphony No. 5 in London in just one day, and this disc became one of EMI's best-selling LPs. His subsequent recordings were with the Philharmonia Orchestra and were of Mozart's Symphony No. 29 and *Ein musikalischer Spass*, Beethoven's Symphony No. 7, Brahms' Symphonies Nos 1 and 3, Mendelssohn's Symphony No. 4, Schubert's Symphony No. 8, Schumann's Symphony No. 4, Tchaikovsky's Symphony No. 6 and *Romeo and Juliet* fantasy-overture, Debussy's *La Mer*, *Prélude à l'après midi d'un faune*, *Nuages* and *Fêtes* and a suite from *Le Martyre de Saint-Sébastien*, Ravel's *Daphnis et Chloé* Suite No. 2 and *Pavane pour une infante défunte*, *L'Apprenti sorcier*, dances from *The Three-cornered Hat* and the *Siegfried Idyll*. His death prevented the completion of a disc of Beethoven's Symphony No. 5, of which the first three movements were recorded.

The advent of stereo has spelt the virtual elimination of all Cantelli's recordings, although some have been re-issued, such as Beethoven's Symphony No. 7, the Mendelssohn and Schubert symphonies and a Debussy collection. However the Arturo Toscanini Society in the US released a series of performances of Cantelli with the NBC Symphony Orchestra, prepared from radio tapes, which expand his discography considerably. The works included were the largo from Handel's *Xerxes*, an andante of Geminiani, Gabrieli's *Aria della Battaglia* and *Canzon for Eight Brass Voices*, Vivaldi's *Concerto for Two Violins in A* and *Concerto Grosso in A major*, Haydn's Symphony No. 88, Mozart's Divertimento K. 334 and Piano Concerto K. 467 (with Gieseking), Beethoven's Symphonies Nos 1 and 5 and Piano Concerto No. 4 (with Backhaus), Schubert's Symphonies Nos 2 and 9, Schumann's Symphony No. 4, Cherubini's *Symphony in D*, the Corelli Concerto Grosso Op. 6 No. 8, the Rossini overtures *La Cenerentola*, *Semiramide*, *Il Signor Bruschino* and *Le Siège de Corinthe*, Verdi's overtures *La forza del destino* and *I vespri siciliani*, Tchaikovsky's Symphonies Nos 4, 5 and 6, the overtures to *Rienzi* and *Euryanthe*, the Dvořák Piano Concerto (with Firkusny), *La Valse*, *Boléro*, Stravinsky's *Le Chant du rossignol*, *Feux d'artifice* and *Jeu de cartes*, Bartók's *Concerto for Orchestra* and *Music for Strings, Percussion and Celesta*, dances from *The Three-cornered Hat*, the overture *School for Scandal* of Barber, Britten's *Sinfonia da Requiem*, Busoni's *Tanzwalzer*, and Hindemith's *Concert Music for Strings and Brass Instruments*. Rococo (US) have also released Beethoven's Symphony No. 5, Pizzetti's *Preludio a un altro giorno* and Busoni's *Berceuse élégiaque* (with the New York Philharmonic Orchestra), and Discocorp *Così fan tutte* (recorded live at La Scala in 1956).

Cao, Pierre (b. 1937). Born in Luxembourg, Cao studied at the Metz and Brussels Conservatoires, in 1968 won second place at the Malko Conductors' Competition in Copenhagen, and in 1969 became conductor of the Radio Luxembourg Orchestra. He is now a professor at the Luxembourg Conservatoire, and retains his connection with the orchestra, with which he has made a number of recordings for Vox and its associate labels, Candide and Turnabout. Included have been Liszt's *Dante Symphony*, Schumann's Violin Concerto (with Lautenbacher), Paganini's *Sonata for Viola and Orchestra* (with Koch), Massenet's *Scènes hongroises*, Lalo's *Rapsodie norvégienne*, Chabrier's *Fête polonaise*, Saint-Saëns' three Violin Concertos, *Havanaise* and *Introduction et rondo capriccioso* (with Ricci), Medtner's Piano Concerto No. 3, Goetz's *Piano Concerto in B flat*, d'Albert's Piano Concerto No. 2 and Reinecke's Piano Concerto No. 1 (with Ponti), Bartók's *Scherzo* (with Sándor), Mosonyi's Piano Concerto and Hiller's Piano Concerto (with Rose), and Volkmann's Cello Concerto (with Blees).

Capdevielle, Pierre (1906–69). Born in Paris, Capdevielle studied with Gédalge, Vidal, d'Indy, Emmanuel and Philippe, won the Prix Blumental in 1938, was director of chamber music broadcasts for the French Radio and founded the ORTF Chamber Orchestra (1952). He composed an opera, a cantata and many other works, and recorded Lully's *Te Deum* (with the Paris Chamber Music Society Orchestra *et al.* for Telefunken), Charpentier's *Tenebrae factae sunt* and the prelude to Act IV of *David et Jonathas* (with the Paris Chamber Orchestra for Ducretet-Thomson) and Debussy's *Danse sacrée et danse profane* (with Jamet and an ensemble for Ducretet-Thomson).

Cape, Safford (b. 1906). After studying at his native Denver, Colorado, Cape migrated to Europe, took up residence in Brussels, married the daughter of Professor Charles van den Borren and became engrossed in the study of medieval and Renaissance music. He became convinced that many works of great beauty of these periods were unknown, and founded the Brussels Pro Musica Antiqua ensemble, which performed pre-classical music in an authentic manner. The Pro Musica Antiqua under Cape contributed extensively to the monumental 78 r.p.m. collection issued by HMV in the 1950s, *The History of Music in Sound*. Later DGG released a series of mono LPs of the group all of which reflected Cape's scholarship and authoritative direction, and the ensemble also recorded for other companies such as the Bach Society and Dover. To those interested in early music these records were indispensable, and he was the forerunner of a number of musicians who have since specialised in this repertoire, to Rooley, Munrow and Otten of recent times. Most of Cape's records were in the form of anthologies of particular styles or phases, such as music at the Burgundian Court or French chansons, while others surveyed the music of individual composers including Binchois, Josquin, Dunstable and Ockeghem.

Capolongo, Paul (b. 1940). Born in Algeria and educated at the conservatory at the Algerian University, the Paris Conservatoire and the Berkshire Music Center in Massachusetts, Capolongo competed successfully for the Koussevitzky Prize and in the Dmitri Mitropoulos International Conductors' Competition, and was assistant conductor to Bernstein with the New York Philharmonic Orchestra in 1967–8. Previously he had been conductor of the French Army Symphony Orchestra (1961–3), musical director of the Quito National Orchestra, Ecuador (1963–6), music director and permanent conductor of the Cyrne Art Festival, Corsica (1966). His recordings include a fine disc of the *Bachianas brasileiras* Nos 2, 5, 6 and 9 (with Mady Mesplé and the Paris Orchestra for EMI) and d'Indy's *Symphonie sur un chant montagnard français*, Franck's *Symphonic Variations*, Fauré's *Ballade* (with Bucquet and the Monte Carlo Opera Orchestra for Philips) and Schumann's Violin Concerto and Fantasy for Violin and Orchestra (with Fontanarosa and the French Radio Philharmonic Orchestra for IPG).

Capuana, Franco (1894–1969). Capuana was born in Fano and studied at the Conservatorio San Pietro a Majella in Naples. He made his debut as a conductor in Brescia in 1919 and for the next ten years was active in opera houses in Italy and in Cairo. He conducted at the San Carlo Opera at Naples (1930–37), where he also directed the Orchestra Stabile Sinfonica, was at La Scala, Milan (1937–40 and 1946–52) and also appeared in South America. In 1946 he conducted the first post-war performance at Covent Garden, London (*La traviata*) with the San Carlo Company; he returned to Covent Garden with the La Scala Company in 1950 and again in the next year as a guest conductor. Although in Italy he was regarded as an expert in the German repertoire, notably Wagner and Strauss, and had presented operas and other pieces by Janáček, Hindemith and Honegger, elsewhere he was known only for his performances and recordings of Italian opera. On the strength of his appearances at Covent Garden, Rosenthal described him as 'a first-class routinier of the Italian school, who respected the Toscanini–Verdi tradition'. As a composer Capuana wrote, *inter alia*, an operetta *La piccola irredenta* and a symphonic poem *La Resurrezione di Lazzaro*. He recorded opera for Decca, Cetra, Urania and Remington in the 1950s and early 1960s; his most distinguished set was *La sonnambula* for Cetra, with Pagluighi, Tagliavini and Siepi, and has been rated as one of the very finest recordings ever made of Italian opera. Other operas he recorded were *Adriana Lecouvreur* and *La fanciulla del West* (for Decca), *Otello* (for Cetra), *Aida* and *Turandot* (for Remington) and *Lucia di Lammermoor* and *Mefistofele* (for Urania). *La sonnambula* and *Otello* have been re-issued by Everest, and *Mefistofele* by Nixa and BASF.

Caracciolo, Franco (b. 1920). Born at Bari, Italy, Caracciolo studied at the Conservatorio San Pietro a Majella in Naples, and took Molinari's course in conducting at the Accademia di Santa Cecilia in Rome. He started conducting as a young man, appeared extensively in Italy and abroad, conducted at festivals in Salzburg, Berlin, Granada, Strasbourg, Venice and Florence, and conducted regularly at La Scala, Milan, and with the Scarlatti Orchestra of Naples, of which he was the leading conductor (1949–64). He has since been permanent conductor of the Milan Symphony Orchestra of the Italian Radio and Television.

In the 1950s, Columbia (EMI) issued a number of discs in which he conducted the Naples Scarlatti Orchestra, for the most part of Italian baroque music. Included were Boccherini's *Symphonies in A major* and *C minor*, Cimarosa's Two-Flute Concerto (with Tassinari and Esposito) and Oboe Concerto (arranged by Benjamin, with Gallesi), Paisiello's *La Scuffiara* overture, A. Scarlatti's Symphony No. 5 and Concerto Grosso No. 3, Leo's *Cello Concerto in D major* (with Caramia), Vivaldi's Concertos P. 235 and P. 311, Sacchini's *Edipo a Colono* overture, Tartini's Concerto Grosso No. 58, Haydn's Symphonies Nos 86 and 92, the Lully/Mottl Ballet Suite, Respighi's *Gli uccelli* and *Trittico Botticelliano*, Petrassi's *Ritratto di don Chisciotte* and Malipiero's Symphony No. 6. Colosseum also released Traetta's *Minuetto cantato*, Schütz's *Weihnachtshistorie*, Napoli's *Symphony in D minor* (adagio and scherzo), the overture and an aria from Piccinni's *Atys*, a dance from Pizzetti's *La Pisanella*, Britten's *Variations on a Theme of Frank Bridge*, Busoni's Clarinet Concertino (with Sisillo), Casella's *Scarlattiana*, Halffter's Sinfonietta and Hindemith's ballet *Der Dämon*. He also recorded Boccherini's *Symphony in C major*, Viotti's Violin Concerto No. 3 (with Principe) and Pergolesi's *Stabat Mater* (with the Naples Rossini Orchestra *et al.* for Decca), Mozart's Piano Concerto K. 415 (with Michelangeli and an orchestra for SID), Beethoven's Piano Concerto No. 5 (with Michelangeli and the Bergamo Festival Orchestra for IGI), and A. Scarlatti's *San Filippo* (with the Angelicum Orchestra *et al.* for Angelicum). The Pergolesi *Stabat Mater* was a particularly successful disc; first recorded in 1965, it was re-issued by Decca in 1974.

Carewe, John (b. 1933). A native of Derby, Carewe studied at the Guildhall School of Music, with Walter Goehr, Deutsch and Boulez, and at the Paris Conservatoire with Messiaen. He founded the New Music Ensemble in London and was assistant to Pritchard and Gibson in the Musica Viva series, was on the staff of Morley College (1958–66), conductor of the BBC Welsh Orchestra (1966–71) and musical director and principal conductor of the Brighton Philharmonic Society (since 1974). He has recorded a suite from Stravinsky's *L'Histoire du soldat* and Milhaud's *La Création du monde* (with the London Symphony Orchestra Chamber Group for Everest), Bedford's *Music for Albion Moonlight* (with the BBC Symphony Orchestra for Argo), Maxwell Davies' *Leopardi Fragments* and Bennett's *Calendar* (with the Melos Ensemble for Argo), and Williamson's *Symphony for Voices* (with the Alldis Choir, Melos Ensemble *et al.* for Argo).

Caridis, Miltiades (b. 1923). A Greek born in Danzig (Gdansk), Caridis studied at the Academy of Music in Vienna, and conducted at Graz, Cologne and Vienna. He has been the conductor of the Danish Radio Symphony Orchestra, the Philharmonia Hungarica, the Oslo Philharmonic Orchestra and the Duisburg Symphony Orchestra. His records include Beethoven's Piano Concertos Nos 3 and 5, and Liszt's Piano Concerto No. 1 (with Hoffman and the Philharmonia Hungarica, for Marble Arch and Musical Heritage Society), excerpts from *Hänsel und Gretel* (with the Vienna Volksoper Orchestra *et al.* for Ariola), Saeverud's two suites for *Peer Gynt* (with the Oslo Philharmonic Orchestra for NFK, Norway), and Bach's Harpsichord Concertos Nos 1, 4 and 5 (with Heiller and the Vienna State Opera Orchestra, issued by Bach Guild and Pye).

Carner, Mosco (b. 1904). Born in Vienna, Carner studied at the New Vienna Conservatory and under Adler at the Vienna University from where he graduated Doctor of Music. He conducted opera in Vienna, Troppau and Danzig, migrated to England in 1933 where he has worked as a critic, conducted the major London orchestras on occasion, published *A Study of Twentieth-Century Harmony*, *Of Men and Music* and *Puccini: a Critical Biography*, and has contributed to *Grove's Dictionary of Music and Musicians* and other histories and studies of music. Decca recorded him on 78 r.p.m. discs, after World War II, conducting a chamber ensemble *et al.* in Phyllis Tate's *Nocturne*.

Carste, Hans (b. 1909). Born in Frankenthal (Pfalz), Carste studied at the Academy of Music and the University of Vienna, became director of the Berlin Radio (1948), and composed film music and an operetta *Lump mit Herz*. He recorded Gershwin's *Rhapsody in Blue* and Piano Concerto (with Mitchell and the RIAS Orchestra for Ariola), and a collection entitled *Introduction to German Lieder* (with Felicia Weathers and a chamber orchestra for Decca).

Cartigny, Gérard (b. 1921). Born in Paris, Cartigny studied at the Paris Conservatoire with Touche and Roger-Ducasse, and, owing to his association with a Benedictine Father who was an organist and pupil of César Franck, became interested in research into little known music of the past, travelled throughout Europe and collected a vast library of these pieces. At the end of World War II he founded and conducted a string orchestra with which he gave concerts in France, Switzerland and FR Germany; in 1950 he performed with Edwin Fischer all the Bach keyboard concertos and also presented a series of broadcasts for French Radio entitled 'Unknown treasures from European libraries'.

Cartigny's recordings have included Bach's Concerto Grosso BWV 1055, Harpsichord and Oboe Concerto BWV 1059 (with Grémy-Chauliac and Chambon), Oboe and Violin Concerto BWV 1060 (with Chambon and Jarry), Organ Concerto BWV 1052 (with Schoonbroodt), Concerto BWV 1055, Harpsichord Concerto No. 1 (with Schoonbroodt) and Sinfonia BWV 1071, Corette's *Ballet des âges*, *Concerto de Noël*, *Le Phénix* and *Carillon des morts*, and Tapray's Symphony Op. 12, Concertante symphonie and Organ Concerto Op. 1 No. 1 (with Schoonbroodt and Gendre, and the Gérard Cartigny Chamber Orchestra for Charlin), Vivaldi's Bassoon Concerto P. 386 (with Faisandier), Flute Concerto P. 77 (with Castagnier), Oboe and Bassoon Concerto P. 129 (with Casier and Faisandier), Two Cello Concerto (with Tournus and Fleury) and Two-Oboe and Two-Clarinet Concerto (with the same orchestra for Ducretet-Thomson), Boismortier's Sonata Op. 34, Dauvergne's Symphony Op. 3 No. 1 and Mouret's *Chamber Concerto in E* (with the same orchestra for Music Guild), and Léonard's Violin Concerto No. 4 and Vieuxtemps' *Fantasia appassionata* (with Jongen and the Liège Symphony Orchestra for Charlin).

Carvalho, Eleazar de (b. 1912). Born in Iguatu, Brazil, of Dutch and Indian descent, Carvalho joined the Brazilian national navy corps where he served until 1936; at the same time he was studying at the National School of Music and graduated as a conductor in 1940. He played the tuba in the orchestra at the Rio de Janeiro Opera and in the Brazilian Symphony Orchestra, in 1941 had his first opportunity to conduct the orchestra and became its associate conductor. He also conducted opera at Rio de Janeiro (1942–4) and in 1945 led the first Beethoven cycle performed in Brazil. In 1946 he came to the United States, studied with Koussevitzky (who made him his assistant at the Berkshire Music Center) and was guest conductor with the Boston Symphony Orchestra. He conducted other American orchestras, remained the principal conductor of the Brazilian Symphony Orchestra, and first appeared in England in 1953. He became conductor of the St Louis Symphony Orchestra (1963–9), of the Hofstra University Orchestra in Hempstead, New York, and in 1971 returned to Brazil to conduct. He has composed the operas *The Discovery of Brazil* (1939) and *Tiradentes* (1941), and also *The White Symphony*. As a conductor he is reserved in his gestures, does not use a score, and has taken pains to perform modern and contemporary music. His only record has been for CBS with the London Symphony Orchestra and Lewenthal in Rubinstein's Piano Concerto No. 4 and the last movement of Scharwenka's Piano Concerto No. 2.

Casadesus, Jean-Claude (b. 1935). Born in Paris and nephew of the pianists Robert and Gaby Casadesus, Casadesus graduated from the Paris Conservatoire as a percussionist and as such took part as a soloist in contemporary music concerts. He studied conducting with Dervaux at the École Normale, was a pupil of Boulez at Basel, then became resident conductor of the Paris Opéra and Opéra-Comique in 1969, director of the Nantes Section of the Orchestre Philharmonique des Pays de la Loire in 1971, and also director of the Orchestre Philharmonique de Lille. He has made guest appearances with major orchestras in Belgium, Britain, Canada, Czechoslovakia, Switzerland, the USSR *et al.*, as well as the international festivals in France, where his authority, technique and musicianship have won praise. His records include Beethoven's Symphony No. 9 (with the Orchestre Symphonique Sessions Internationales de Sainte-Céré *et al.* for Mondiodis), the two Haydn Violin Concertos (with Manzone), Wieniawski's Violin Concertos Nos 1 and 2 (with Gitlis and the Monte Carlo National Orchestra for Philips), Poulenc's cantata *Le Bal masqué* (with Souzay and the ensemble for EMI) and Dutilleux's Symphony No. 1 (with the Orchestre Philharmonique de Lille, for Calliope).

Casals, Enrique (b. 1892). A younger brother of Pablo Casals, Enrique Casals studied the violin as a child, then in Barcelona, Brussels and Prague, and at the age of 20 was concertmaster of the Imperial Symphony Orchestra at St Petersburg. For a time he was in Argentina, returned to Spain in 1927, opened a music academy at Barcelona, helped Pablo form his orchestra and became its assistant conductor and concertmaster. He remained in Barcelona during the Civil War and after, again assisted Pablo to organise the Prades Festivals and led the second violins in the festival orchestra. Pablo recorded two of Enrique's compositions at the 1955 Festival, *Lluny* and *Tarragona*. EMI recorded Enrique conducting the Profesional da Camera, Barcelona in a concert of Nardini.

Casals, Pablo (1876–1973). Casals has been acclaimed as one of the greatest and most complete musicians in Europe of the past 100 years. This reputation could have been won almost solely by his great artistry as a cellist, but he was also a conductor, pianist, composer, teacher and founder of orchestras and festivals. His stature was further enhanced by his uncompromising stand against political oppression and his untiring efforts to aid refugees from war-torn Spain. He was born in Tarragona, and preferred to call himself a Catalan rather than a Spaniard. He was a musical prodigy in the Mozartian tradition and said that he learned to express himself in music before he could talk, could sing in time before he could form words, and by the age of five had mastered the piano. At eight he had composed his first musical piece and had played the solo violin at a local concert. At nine his father gave him a cello, and he was taken to Barcelona for serious study at the age of eleven. At 12 he could play, to some degree, almost every orchestral instrument. As a boy of 14 he was supporting himself playing the cello in a string trio in a café; the composer Albéniz happened to visit the café, recognised Casals' genius and arranged to introduce him to the Queen Regent in Madrid, who granted him a stipend to continue his studies at the Royal Conservatory in Madrid. In 1895 he went to Paris, played as a cellist at the Opéra and taught at the Conservatoire. In 1905 he formed a trio with Alfred Cortot and Jacques Thibaud which became world famous, and by 1910 he was touring Europe and the United States as a cello virtuoso.

Casals' desire to conduct seemed to be inborn. When he was sixteen the composer Granados asked him to conduct the rehearsals of his first opera, *María del Carmen*, and later Casals conducted the Lamoureux, London Symphony, New York Symphony, Vienna Philharmonic and BBC Symphony Orchestras. He has said that he felt as much at home playing the cello or the piano, or holding the conductor's baton, but he preferred the orchestra as the supreme medium for interpretation. Casals was a good pianist and once even considered abandoning his career as a cellist to accompany his wife, Susan Metcalfe, an American singer. Every morning until his last days he would play several Bach preludes and fugues on the piano, for he regarded Bach as the supreme genius of music, and held this daily exercise to be essential for his psychological well-being. In 1920 he established his own orchestra at Barcelona, the Orquesta Pau Casals. He engaged 88 musicians, paid them their salaries out of his own pocket and in the first eight years of the orchestra's existence personally subsidised it until it paid its own way. He aimed to bring the music of the great classics to his native Catalonians, and directed the orchestra until all musical life in Spain was stopped by the Civil War in 1936.

Then Casals left Spain and never returned. He lived in retreat at Prades in the Pyrénées, but in 1950 after twelve years of self-imposed exile he consented to play in public again on the bicentenary of Bach's death. He decided to hold a Bach festival at Prades, and musicians such as Szigeti, Stern and Serkin hastened to offer their services. The festival was such a success that the next year Casals moved it to the nearest town, Perpignan, where it became an annual event. He appeared as both cellist and conductor, and a group of the world's leading artists performed with him the music of Bach, Mozart and Beethoven. Later in 1956 he settled in Puerto Rico and the festivals were transferred there; finally he conducted at Serkin's summer Marlboro Musical Festival at Vermont, U.S.A. He refused to set foot in Spain after the Civil War and was adamant in his conviction that Franco overthrew a legitimately elected democratic government. After playing in some countries after World War II, to triumphant acclaim, he withdrew to Prades again, since he disapproved of the general recognition of the Franco regime. Apart from teaching and his annual festivals, he never resumed his former international career either as soloist or conductor, and refused many offers to play and conduct in Europe and the United States, with the exception of conducting the Marlboro Festival Orchestra (until 1973).

Casals has described how he trained his orchestra at Barcelona. His first aim was to create an atmosphere of artistic endeavour, to achieve perfect intonation and to concentrate on the accent and expression suitable for the work in hand. Only precise rhythm and tempo satisfied him, and he would repeat his directions until the players were convinced, preferring persuasion to the imposition of his will. The first work he rehearsed was the Ride of the Valkyries, which was taken note by note. When he conducted other orchestras he insisted on three long rehearsals, no matter how familiar the music was to the players; this sometimes caused a furore, particularly once when he directed a Beethoven symphony with the Vienna Philharmonic. He never conducted from memory, calling it a useless accomplishment. Among his contemporaries he had the highest regard for Toscanini, Furtwängler and Stokowski. He had little time for music written later than Richard Strauss, and most modern music he thought was 'anti-natural, like trying to walk with one's feet upside down'.

Some recordings were made in 1928–9 of Casals directing his orchestra at Barcelona, of Beethoven's Symphonies Nos 1 and 4, and with the London Symphony Orchestra in the overture *Coriolan* and Brahms' *Variations on the St Antony Chorale*; these have been re-issued on LP transfers by Electrola. In 1929 three concerts were organised in Paris to commemorate the 100th anniversary of the birth of Brahms; one of them was an orchestral concert at which Thibaud played the Violin Concerto with Cortot conducting, Cortot then played the Piano Concerto No. 2 conducted by Casals, and finally the Double Concerto was played with Casals and Thibaud the soloists and Cortot the conductor. This last performance was repeated in Barcelona with Casals' orchestra and it was then recorded by HMV; it was the last time that Cortot, Thibaud and Casals played together. At the festivals at Prades, Perpignan and later at Puerto Rico recordings were made by Philips and CBS; included were Mozart's Symphony No. 28, *Eine kleine Nachtmusik*, Sinfonia Concertante K. 364, the Piano Concertos K. 271 (with Hess), K. 449 (with Istomin), K. 482 (with Serkin) and K. 595 (with Horszowski), the Violin Concerto K. 219 (with Morini) and Flute Concerto K. 313 (with Wummer, and with the Perpignan Festival Orchestra), Bach's *Brandenburg Concertos*, the Suites Nos 1 and 2, *Ein musikalisches Opfer*, Harpsichord Concerto No. 5 (with Haskil, piano), Violin Concerto No. 1 (with Stern), Violin Concerto in D minor (with Szigeti), Double Violin Concerto (with Stern and Schneider), Concerto for Violin and Oboe (with Stern and Tabuteau) and Triple Concerto in A minor (with Horszowski, Wummer and Schneider; all with the Prades Festival Orchestra); Haydn's Symphony No. 45, Mozart's Symphony No. 36, Schubert's Symphony No. 8 (with a rehearsal of the first movement) and Casals' own *El Pessebre* (with the Puerto Rico Festival Orchestra). *El Pessebre* ('The Manger') was an oratorio telling of the mysterious birth night of Jesus Christ, which was written by Casals as a move to promote world peace. At the Marlboro Festivals he recorded the *Brandenburg Concertos* and suites of Bach, Mozart's Symphonies Nos 35, 38, 40 and 41, Beethoven's Symphonies Nos 7 and 8, Schubert's Symphony No. 8 and Mendelssohn's Symphony No. 4; these records were made when Casals was near or at his 90th birthday, and are distinguished by the same profound musicality, expressiveness, concentration and utter conviction that marked his recordings as a cellist and chamber player. As with every great musician who discards conventional interpretations and seeks again the musical meaning of the score, his readings do not please everyone, but in his Bach and Mozart in particular, which have been amply documented on record, his forceful musical personality can only be admired.

It is probable that Casals' recordings as a cellist will be remembered longer than those he made as a conductor. The most famous are the Dvořák Cello Concerto, made in 1937 with Szell and the Vienna Philharmonic Orchestra, and the six cello suites of Bach. The latter were recorded between 1936 and 1939 and have been scarcely out of the catalogue since. It is salutary to recognise the depth of the preparation that Casals gave to these suites; when he was studying the cello at Barcelona as a youth he came across an edition of them when casually rummaging through a music shop. 'I forgot entirely the reason for my visit to the shop and could only stare at this music which nobody had told me about . . . I took the suites home and read and re-read them. For twelve years after that I studied and worked every day with them. I was nearly 25 before I had the courage to play one of them in public' (*The Tablet*, 3 November 1973). In addition to *El Pessebre* some of his other compositions have been recorded: eight choral pieces sung by the choir of the Monastery of Montserrat have been released by Everest, and two pieces for cello ensemble, *Les Rois mages* and *Sardana*, with Casals himself directing, were issued by Philips. Philips also recorded him conducting the Lamoureux Orchestra with Gendron playing Boccherini's Cello Concerto and Haydn's *Cello Concerto in D major*.

Casella, Leopoldo (1902–72). Born in Montevideo, Casella studied at the conservatories at Parma and Frankfurt am Main, graduated from the latter in 1920, and became pianist for Berne Radio (1928). He was appointed conductor of the Italian Radio Orchestra of Switzerland (1932), was a member of the Committee of the Association of Swiss Musicians (1937–54), conducted orchestras in Switzerland and abroad, and was a member of a number of juries for international music prizes. He recorded Raff's

Sinfonietta, Flury's *Festival Overture*, and Wartensee's Two-Clarinet Concerto (with the Italian Radio Orchestra *et al.* for CTS).

Cassuto, Alvaro (b. 1938). Born in Oporto, Portugal, Cassuto studied with Santos and Graça, at Darmstadt (1960–61), with Ligeti, Messiaen and Stockhausen, and for conducting with Karajan, de Freitas, Branco and Ferrara. He has been assistant conductor of the Gulbenkian Orchestra in Lisbon (1965–8), with the Little Orchestra in New York (1968–70), conductor then music director of the National Radio Orchestra in Lisbon (from 1970), and lecturer and conductor of the orchestra at the University of California, Irvine (from 1974). He was awarded the Koussevitzky Prize (1969), and has toured and conducted in South America and Europe, as well as in the United States. He recorded Ginastera's Piano Concerto (with Somer and the University of California, Irvine, Symphony Orchestra for Orion).

Caston, Saul (b. 1901). Born in New York, Caston studied at the Curtis Institute in Philadelphia and played the trumpet with the Philadelphia Orchestra (1918–45). He was associate conductor of the Philadelphia Orchestra (1936–45), conductor of the Reading Symphony Orchestra (1941–5) and in 1945 was conductor of the Denver Symphony Orchestra. He conducted the Philadelphia Orchestra on a Columbia 78 r.p.m. disc containing the Sailors' Dance from Glière's *The Red Poppy* and Batuque from Fernândez's opera *Malazarte*.

Castro, Juan José (1895–1968). Born in Buenos Aires, one of four brothers each of whom became an outstanding musician, Castro studied in Paris with d'Indy and Risler, returned to Argentina and played in chamber music ensembles. He then devoted himself to composition and conducting, founded and conducted the Renaissance Orchestra in Buenos Aires (1929), conducted at the Teatro Colón (1930–43), became director at the Buenos Aires Philharmonic Orchestra (1931), toured extensively in South America, visited New York as a Guggenheim Fellow (1934), succeeded Kleiber as conductor of the Havana Philharmonic Orchestra (1947–8), was conductor of the Victorian Symphony Orchestra in Melbourne, Australia (1951–3), of the National Symphony Orchestra in Buenos Aires (1955–60) and director of the Puerto Rico Conservatory (1959). His outspoken political views brought him into conflict with authority and in 1944 he was forced to leave the Teatro Colón for denouncing the Axis powers, and in 1951 to leave the country for disagreements with President Perón. He was a thoroughly musical and severely disciplined conductor who took painstaking and exhaustive care in preparing works; during his career he conducted 642 concerts with orchestras in nineteen countries, with a repertoire of 589 works. A prolific composer, his opera *Proserpina y el extranjero* won the Verdi Prize at La Scala, Milan (1951), and was produced there in 1952. His *Sonatina española*, published in 1953, has been recorded by Desto. Castro's only recording appears to be a coupling of Villa Lobos' *Caixinha de Bôas Festas* and Falla's *Homenajes* with the Rome Symphony Orchestra for RCA.

Cattini, Umberto (b. 1922). From a family of musicians, Cattini was born in Verona, studied at the conservatories at Parma and Milan, where he was a pupil for conducting of Votto, and at the Accademia di Santa Cecilia at Siena with Guarniero. He made his debut as a conductor at Verona (1943), and has been professor of conducting at Bologna Conservatory and artistic director of the Verona Philharmonic Society. His recordings include Cavalli's *Messa concertata*, Sammartini's *Magnificat*, Carissimi's *Diluvium universale*, concertos of J. C. Bach, Boccherini's Sinfonia concertante and Sinfonia Op. 12 No. 4 and Hindemith's Organ Concerto Op. 46 No. 2 (with Esposito and the Angelicum Orchestra, Milan, for Angelicum and Schwann), and Donizetti's *Rita, ou le Mari battu* (with the Turin Radio Orchestra *et al.* for Cetra).

Cauchie, Maurice (b. 1882). Born in Paris, Cauchie was a distinguished musicologist and a specialist in French music of the 16th and 17th centuries. He edited the works of Jannequin and Couperin, wrote a fine study entitled *L'Opéra-comique en France* and a history of Renaissance music. He was also a conductor of some consequence and directed two albums of 78 r.p.m. discs, issued on the Columbia (US) label, of arias and orchestral excerpts from the operas of Lully. These discs were much prized in their day and Cauchie showed himself in them to be a sensitive and eloquent musician.

Čavdarski, Vanča (b. 1930). Born in Vladimirovo in Yugoslavia, Čavdarski studied conducting at the Academy of Music in Belgrade and with Schmidt-Isserstedt at Hamburg. He was a viola player with the Belgrade Philharmonic Orchestra (1953–7), conductor then musical director of the Macedonian Philharmonic Orchestra at Skopje (1965–70), associate conductor with the Australian Opera at

Sydney (1970–72), conductor of the Christchurch Symphony Orchestra, New Zealand and of the Tasmanian Symphony Orchestra in Australia (from 1973), and has been a guest conductor in Britain, the USSR, Romania and Australia. For Jugoton he recorded Prošev's *Sonce na Prastarata Zemja* (with the Macedonian Philharmonic Orchestra *et al.*).

Ceccato, Aldo (b. 1934). Born in Milan into a musical family, Ceccato learned the piano as a boy and developed an enthusiasm and talent for jazz. He graduated with honours from the Verdi Conservatory at Milan and for many years was a professional jazz pianist, giving numerous concerts and broadcasts. At the same time he also was a concert pianist and devoted time to composition. In 1958 he studied with Wolff and van Otterloo in Holland, and in the next year abandoned jazz and went to Berlin to study at the Hochschule für Musik on a conducting course. In 1960 he was an assistant to Celididache at the Accademia Chigiani at Siena, and in 1962 made his last appearance as a concert pianist with the Tchaikovsky Piano Concerto No. 1. His debut as a conductor of opera took place in Milan with *Don Giovanni* in 1964, and in that year he undertook his first orchestral concerts with the Angelicum Chamber Orchestra in three concerts of the music of Vivaldi. In 1964 he also won first prize in the International Competition of the Italian Radio for young conductors; engagements followed to conduct opera and concerts throughout Europe. In 1969 he made his operatic debut in the United States at the Chicago Lyric Theatre, and the following year saw his debut in the concert hall with the New York Philharmonic Orchestra. Appearances with other US orchestras followed and in 1971 he was appointed principal conductor of the Detroit Symphony Orchestra, and became the orchestra's music director in 1973. In 1975 he became general music director of the Hamburg Philharmonic Orchestra and music director of the Meadow Brook Festival. He married the daughter of the great Italian conductor Victor de Sabata in 1966; they met when she thanked him for a fine performance of a symphonic poem by her father. He conducts from memory, but his conducting manner is somewhat reserved compared to many of his contemporaries; his technique is focused at the end of his baton and facial expressions and eye-to-eye contact with his musicians are re-assuring rather than instructive.

Ceccato has recorded *La traviata* (with the Royal Philharmonic Orchestra *et al.* for EMI) and *Maria Stuarda* (with the London Philharmonic Orchestra *et al.* for ABC), Vivaldi's *The Four Seasons* (with the Angelicum Orchestra for Angelicum and issued by Audio Fidelity), Saint-Saëns' Piano Concerto No. 4, Liszt's *Totentanz* and *Fantasia on Hungarian Folk Tunes* (with Campanella and the Monte Carlo National Orchestra for Philips), Ravel's *Rapsodie espagnole*, *Valses nobles et sentimentales*, *Menuet antique* and *Pavane pour une infante défunte* (with the Slovak Philharmonic Orchestra for Supraphon), Mendelssohn's Piano Concertos 1 and 2 and *Rondo brilliant* (with Ogdon and the London Symphony Orchestra for EMI), and a recital by Grace Bumbry (with the Bavarian State Opera Orchestra for EMI).

Celibidache, Sergiu (b. 1912). Born in Roman, Romania, Celibidache spent his early life in Jassy (modern Iasi), the capital of Moldavia, where his father was prefect. He studied in Paris and in wartime Berlin at the Hochschule für Musik and the university, studying philosophy to avoid military conscription, and wrote a thesis on the music of Josquin des Prés. He won a conducting competition with Berlin Radio, made his debut with the Berlin Philharmonic Orchestra in 1945 and in 1948 became the orchestra's chief conductor and artistic adviser, touring the United States with it and sharing the podium with Furtwängler. He left the Berlin Philharmonic in 1952, appeared as a guest conductor in Europe, Israel, Japan, Latin and South America, has been permanent conductor of the Stockholm Radio Symphony Orchestra, the French National Orchestra and, from 1972, the South-West German Radio Orchestra at Stuttgart and the Bamberg Symphony Orchestra. His compositions include four symphonies and a piano concerto.

Celibidache is a legend in his own time, as much for his elusiveness as for his commanding musicianship. What is remarkable about him is the extraordinary lengths to which he goes to prepare a performance. With the Berlin Philharmonic he expected ten or twelve rehearsals for each concert, and today refuses engagements if he cannot be guaranteed five or six rehearsals. He has said that the number of rehearsals he requires for a concert depends on the quality of the orchestra and that the better the orchestra the more he rehearses it, because the possibilities are greater. He rehearses the orchestra almost to the point of exhaustion, allows absolutely nothing to pass and expects the maximum concentration and effort from the players. He appeals first to the musicians' intelligence and musical sensitivity before seeking technical perfection in the performance. He prefers to work with radio orchestras, where the time for rehearsals is more generous, but nonetheless dislikes radio concerts as such. He sets a limit to the concerts he will conduct, demands very high fees, and avoids confronting new orchestras too often, as well as touring with his own orchestra. His memory is phenomenal and he rehearses without a score without making a mistake, although he says that his memory is purely functional and he has no memory for numbers in the score. His sound is unique and is partly achieved by having the bass instruments play extremely quietly. Of other conductors he admires Ferrara, Weingartner and Furtwängler, but dismisses Toscanini with: 'If music were just notes he would have been superb.' 'There is no miracle in music', he has remarked, 'only work. Music is neither beautiful nor ugly; it either exists or it does not exist. To realise its existence in sound one has to work over it for a long period with profound concentration. I would prefer to do nothing than be content with an approximation or with mediocrity' (*Réalités*, August 1973, p. 90). Many orchestral players regard him as a genius, some as a misguided talent.

Although Celibidache made some records early in his career, recording is now anathema to him, and the entire concept is unacceptable: 'Like peas, music cannot be canned. It loses its flavour, its scent, its life. The tape which makes the recordings possible consists of lots of little bits stuck together from different versions. This means the end of the continuous and basic pulse necessary to bring the work to life in sound. Also the acoustic conditions of a recording are never the same as those of a live performance, and so a recording is a treason to music because the listener never hears what the artist wants him to hear.' On another occasion he compared a record to going to bed with a picture of Brigitte Bardot. He made recordings between 1945 and 1950 for several companies, but these were not considered remarkable in themselves. They were Prokofiev's Symphony No. 1, Mendelssohn's Symphony No. 3 and Violin Concerto (with Borries, and the Berlin Philharmonic Orchestra for EMI), Brahms' Violin Concerto (with Haendel and the London Symphony Orchestra for EMI), Mozart's Symphony No. 25, Tchaikovsky's Symphony No. 5 and a suite from *The Nutcracker* (with the London Philharmonic Orchestra for Decca), Shostakovich's Symphony No. 7 (with the Berlin Philharmonic Orchestra for Urania), the overture *Les Francs-juges*, the Debussy (arr. Busser) *Petite Suite*, and Roussel's *Petite Suite* (with the Berlin Radio Orchestra for Urania) and the *Egmont* overture (with the Berlin Philharmonic Orchestra for Period). More recently transcripts of some radio performances have been issued by Rococo, including Beethoven's Piano Concerto No. 5 (with Michelangeli and the Swedish Radio Orchestra), Tchaikovsky's No. 6 (with an unnamed orchestra) and Sibelius' Symphony No. 2 (with the Swiss Festival Orchestra).

Cellini, Renato (1912–67). Born in Turin into a theatrical family, Cellini studied the cello, piano and organ as a boy, and gave concerts as a cellist at the age of ten. He continued his musical studies under Alfano and Ghedini and graduated from the Turin Conservatory (1930). He then began to conduct, and after World War II prepared the Italian operas programmed for performance at the Glyndebourne Festival. In 1947 he conducted *Le nozze di Figaro* at the Edinburgh Festival. He joined the staff of the Metropolitan Opera, New York (1948–54), where he was responsible for preparing operas in the Italian and French repertoire, but only conducted performances of six of them. He was principal conductor at the Opera Nacional at Mexico City (1948–50), conducted at the Cincinatti Summer Opera, was artistic director of the New Orleans Opera (1954–64), founded the Experimental Opera Theatre of America, and was a guest conductor at Caracas, Mexico City and La Scala, Milan. When he was with the Metropolitan Opera he made a number of recordings for RCA, including *Pagliacci*, *Cavalleria rusticana*, *Il trovatore* and *Rigoletto*; the casts were most distinguished and included Milanov, Björling, Barbieri, Warren and Moscana, and the orchestra the RCA Victor Symphony. He also recorded albums of arias and duets with these artists; recently Cetra issued performances of *La favorita* and *Werther* in which he conducts the Mexico City Opera. His conducting was efficient and professional, if not always very imaginative.

Cerha, Friedrich (b. 1926). Born in Vienna where he studied at the Academy of Music and the university, Cerha was active as a violinist and teacher, founded, with Schwertsik in Vienna, an ensemble to perform new music, and since 1960 has been artistic director of the electronic studio at the Academy of Music. He has composed a number of works especially for chamber ensembles. For Turnabout and Candide he recorded Schoenberg's *Pierrot Lunaire*, Debussy's *Chansons de Bilitis*, Satie's *Socrate* and other pieces, Ravel's *Trois Poèmes de Stéphane Mallarmé* (with Escribano), Ligeti's *Aventures* and *Nouvelles aventures*, and Varèse's *Offrandes*, *Hyperprism*, *Intégrales*,

Ionisation and *Octandre* (with the Die Reihe Ensemble).

Chabrun, Daniel (b. 1925). Born in Mayenne, the French conductor Chabrun divides his time between the concert hall and theatre, has conducted the major Parisian and provincial orchestras, is noted for his interest in contemporary music, and has given many first performances of present-day compositions. At the Paris Conservatoire he has held classes in the technical aspects of recording and audio-visual transmission. His recordings have been Loucheur's Violin Concerto (with Erlih and the ORTF National Orchestra for Barclay), Nigg's *Visages d'Axel* (with the ORTF Philharmonic Orchestra for Barclay), Ohana's *Trois graphiques* (with Ponce and the Prado Philharmonic Orchestra for Arion) and *Silenciaire* (with the Percussions de Strasbourg *et al.* for Barclay).

Chailley, Jacques (b. 1910). Born in Paris and educated at the Paris Conservatoire and at the Sorbonne, Chailley studied conducting with Mengelberg and Monteux, and made his debut as a conductor in 1929 with the ballet *Ma Mère l'Oye* in the presence of Ravel. He was conductor with the Comédie Française (1942), since 1945 has conducted principally choirs, and was conductor of the vocal ensemble of the Paris Conservatoire (1947–52). In addition he has on occasion conducted the Paris Conservatoire Orchestra and the Société des Concerts Oubradous, and has a special interest in French music from the Middle Ages to the 18th century. Since 1960 he has been more concerned with composition and musicology than with conducting. He has recorded his own *Missa Solemnis a capella* (with the Notre Dame Choir for Telefunken), Marc-Antoine Charpentier's *Messe pour plusieurs instruments au lieu des orgues* and pieces by Louis XIII (with the Paris Ancient Instruments Ensemble, released by Nonesuch), excerpts from Schütz's *St Mark Passion* (with the Alaudo Choir *et al.* for Studio SM), and Michael Haydn's *Organ Concerto in C major* (with Alain and the Jean-François Paillard Chamber Orchestra for Erato).

Chalabala, Zdeněk (1899–1962). Born at Uherské Hradiště, Moravia, Chalabala studied the violin as a boy, and during army service founded a women's choir with the help of his mother, a pianist. After demobilisation he studied with Hoffman and Novák in Prague, then graduated in violin, conducting and composition at the Brno Conservatory. He founded and conducted the Slovak Philharmonic Orchestra (1924–5), became Neumann's assistant at the Brno National Theatre (1925) and became its principal conductor after Neumann's death (1929). With Talich he was conductor at the Prague National Theatre (1936–45), then conductor at the Ostrava Opera (1945–7), the Brno Opera and the Slovak National Theatre at Bratislava (1948–52), then director of the Prague National Theatre (1953 to his death in 1962). He was permanent guest conductor at the Bolshoi Theatre at Moscow and at Leningrad (1956–9), and in 1958 he presented *Jenufa* for the first time at the Bolshoi Theatre. His compositions include orchestral and vocal music and an orchestration of Mussorgsky's *Nursery Songs*.

Chalabala was a distinguished conductor with a romantic temperament, inclined towards Czech opera and especially to the epic Russian operas. He made a considerable contribution to the gramophone, particularly in Czech opera, and recorded Dvořák's *Rusalka* and *The Devil and Kate*, Smetana's *The Bartered Bride*, *The Devil's Wall* and *The Kiss*, Fibich's *Sarka*, Suchoň's *The Whirlpool* and *Svatopluk*, and Foerster's *Eva*, with either the Prague National Opera or the Bratislava Opera Companies. These performances were completely idiomatic, but since they were all mono recordings they have not generally survived in the Supraphon catalogue; one, *The Kiss*, was re-issued in 1977. Two other notable discs which enjoyed some currency in the West were of superb performances of the Dvořák symphonic poems *The Wild Dove*, *The Golden Spinning Wheel*, *The Noon-day Witch* and *The Water Goblin*, all with the Czech Philharmonic Orchestra. He also recorded, with the Czech Philharmonic, spirited versions of *Scheherazade*, *Gayaneh* and a collection of operatic preludes and overtures.

Chapple, Stanley (b. 1900). Born in London, Chapple studied at the Royal Academy of Music, was a repetiteur with the British National Opera Company (1918–21), musical director of the Vocalion Gramophone Company (1924–9), conductor of opera at the Guildhall School of Music (1935–9), conducted for the British Broadcasting Corporation (1937–9), was assistant conductor at the Berkshire Music Center, Massachusetts (1939–47), conductor of the St Louis Civic Chorus (1946–8) and director of the music school at the University of Washington, Seattle (from 1948). He recorded Mendelssohn's Symphony No. 4, Beethoven's Piano Concerto No. 4 (with York Bowen) and Howells' *Puck's Minuet* (with the Aeolian Orchestra), the *Siegfried Idyll*, Malipiero's *La Cimarosiana*, Holst's

Country Song No. 1, a *Spanish Dance* of Granados, and two interludes from Elgar's *Falstaff* (with the Modern Chamber Orchestra), all for Vocalion, and recorded when he was with the company.

Charlet, André (b. 1927). Born in Lausanne, Charlet studied at the Conservatoire there, at the Geneva Conservatoire, with Swarowsky at the Academy of Music in Vienna, and with Messiaen and Fourestier at the Paris Conservatoire. He founded and conducted the Choeur des Jeunes, the Chorale du Brassis and the Choeur de la Radio Romande (1957), which performs regularly with the Suisse Romande Orchestra and the Lausanne Chamber Orchestra. The Choeur also took part in Ansermet's recordings for Decca of, amongst other works, Beethoven's Symphony No. 9, *Le Roi David* and Stravinsky's *Symphony of Psalms*. Charlet has recorded, variously with the three choirs, for Swiss record companies, choral works by Apothéloz, Barblan, Binet, Boller, Bourgeois, Bovet, Broquet, Doret, Gindron, Jaques-Dalcroze, Mermoud, Reichel, Sutermeister and Wiblé.

Charpentier, Gustave (1860–1956). The French composer Charpentier's fame rests solely on his opera *Louise*, which owed its popularity to its realism and social outlook (radical for its time), as much as to its musical originality. In 1887 he won the Prix de Rome and while in Rome wrote *Impressions d'Italie* and a four-act symphonic drama *La Vie du poète*. The first work was popular in European concert halls, and the latter was incorporated in a later but unsuccessful opera, *Julien*. He recorded, as a conductor, none of *Louise*, but a 78 r.p.m. set of *Impressions d'Italie* with an unidentified orchestra, and another of *La Vie du poète*, with soloists, chorus and the Pasdeloup Orchestra, was released by HMV in the early 1930s, both conducted by the composer. There was also a disc of an excerpt from the incidental music to Molière's *Le Bourgeois gentilhomme* in the HMV catalogue, in which Charpentier conducted the chorus and orchestra of the Comédie Française, with d'Ives as soloist.

Charpentier, Jacques (b. 1933). Born in Paris, Charpentier studied the piano and composition with Messiaen and Aubin, travelled to India and studied the country's music which has influenced some of his compositions. He has conducted recordings of his *Pour le Kama Sutra* (with the Paris Percussion Ensemble for La Guilde Internationale du Disque), and *Récitatif*, for violin and orchestra (with Erlih) and Symphony No. 3 (with the ORTF Philharmonic Orchestra for Barclay). The symphony is intended to give a musical portrait of Shiva, the king of the dance.

Chávez, Carlos (1899–1978). Born near Mexico City, Chávez was a piano pupil of Ponce, Ogazón and Fuentes, but claimed that he was largely self-taught. He started composing at the age of nine. After studying in Paris, Berlin and New York, he formed the Symphony Orchestra of Mexico in 1928 and conducted it until 1949, when he retired to devote himself to composition; his achievement in training the musicians of the orchestra, with the help of Silvestri, Revueltas and Ansermet, and in educating the musical public, was quite extraordinary. He made many guest appearances with major orchestras in the United States, and in visits to New York in 1937 and 1938 created a remarkable impression when he conducted the New York Philharmonic in a performance of Beethoven's Symphony No. 9. While he was director of the National Conservatory in Mexico City (1928–34), his reforms encountered opposition, but his strong personality, immense culture and organising talent brought great developments, and the Conservatory had many outstanding pupils. He was also head of the Fine Arts Department of the Mexican Government (1933–4) and director-general of the National Institute of Fine Arts (1946–52), received numerous honours, and in 1958–9 lectured at Harvard University. His first composition to attract attention was the ballet *The New Fire* (1921); later his *Horse Power Symphony* was presented by Stokowski at Philadelphia (1932). His output included six symphonies, ballet scores, orchestral pieces, concertos, songs and choral works, and a *Toccata for Percussion*; his music is highly colourful and distinctive, and although it draws on Mexican folk melodies and the sound of native instruments, he could not be called a folklorist composer.

Chávez recorded much of his own music: *Sinfonía India*, *Sinfonía de Antígona*, and *Chacona en Mi menor* (with the Mexico Symphony Orchestra for RCA), *Xochipilli-Macuilxochitl*, *La paloma azul* and *Danza a Centeol* (with the Orquesta de musicos nortamericanos y mexicanos *et al.* for Columbia), all on 78 r.p.m. discs; on LP there was *La hija de Cólquide*, *Sinfonía India*, *Corrido de El Sol* and *Republican Overture* (with the Mexican Symphony Orchestra for Decca, US, and Brunswick), *Sinfonía India*, *Sinfonía de*

Antigona and *Sinfonía romantica* (with the New York Stadium Orchestra for Everest), the Violin Concerto (with Szeryng and the Mexican National Symphony Orchestra for Columbia), Piano Concerto (with List and the Vienna State Opera Orchestra for Westminster), the six symphonies (with the Mexican National Symphony Orchestra for Columbia), *Moncayo Huapango* (with the Mexican National Symphony Orchestra for Brunswick) and an arrangement of Yaqui Indian music by Sandi (for Columbia). In 1973 he visited London and recorded his ballet *Four Suns* and two movements from another ballet *Piramide* (with the London Symphony Orchestra for CBS). On 78s he also recorded Galindo's *Sones Mariachi* (with an unnamed orchestra for Columbia) and on LP MacDowell's Piano Concertos Nos 1 and 2 (with List and the Vienna State Opera Orchestra for EMI).

Chaynes, Charles (b. 1925). Born in Toulouse where he graduated from the conservatory, Chaynes studied with Milhaud, Rivier, Jean and Noël Gallon at the Paris Conservatoire, was awarded the Prix de Rome (1951) and became programme director of Radio France (1964). He conducted a record of his *Concordances* (with Ivaldi, piano, and the Paris Percussion Ensemble for La Guilde Internationale du Disque).

Chiarelli, Gaspare (b. 1932). Born in Hamilton, Ontario, where he attended the local conservatory, Chiarelli was a member of the Hamilton Philharmonic Orchestra (1949–50), graduated from the Toronto University and studied further at the Accademia di Santa Cecilia in Rome (1955–7) and at the Royal College of Music, London (1957–9). He studied conducting with Goossens (1958–62), Ferrara, Zecchi and Barbirolli, and played the viola in London orchestras. Returning to North America he played in the Cincinnati Symphony Orchestra (1968–9), was music director and conductor of the Hamilton Symphony Orchestra, Ohio, taught at universities at Cincinnati and Portland, was conductor of the Junior Symphony Society of Vancouver (1973–4), and was appointed music director of the Northwest Symphony Society of Canada, at Vancouver, although the orchestra was not actually formed. For Unicorn he recorded Goossens' *Divertissement* with the National Philharmonic Orchestra, which was released in 1977.

Chistyakov, Boris (b. 1914). After graduating from the Kiev Music School (1937) Chistyakov became conductor at the Schevchenko Theatre Orchestra at Kiev, where he is still active. In 1960 he received the title of People's Artist of the Ukrainian SSR. He has recorded Scorulsky's *Song of the Woods* and Lysenko's opera *Natalka Poltavka* (both with the Kiev Schevchenko Theatre Orchestra *et al.*).

Chmura, Gabriel (b. 1946). Born in Wrocław, Poland, Chmura grew up in Israel, studied at the Tel-Aviv Academy of Music and then with Dervaux, Swarowsky and Ferrara in Paris, Vienna and Italy respectively. He won the Gold Medal at the Cantelli Competition in Milan (1971), first prize at the Karajan Competition in Berlin (1971) and was appointed general music director at Aachen (1974). He has also conducted orchestras in FR Germany, Scandinavia, Austria, Italy and Israel. For DGG, with the London Symphony Orchestra, he recorded the Mendelssohn overtures *The Hebrides*, *A Midsummer Night's Dream*, *Ruy Blas*, *Die schöne Melusine* and *Meeresstille und glückliche Fahrt*.

Chwedczuk, Zbigniew (b. 1921). Born in Warsaw, Chwedczuk was educated at the Higher Musical School at Łódź, was conductor of the Łódź State Philharmonic Orchestra (1950–54), the Kraków State Philharmonic Orchestra (1954–8), the Kraków City Opera (1955–8), artistic director and first conductor of the Pomeranian State Philharmonic Orchestra at Bydgoszcz (1958–72) and of the Gdańsk Opera and Philharmonic Orchestra (from 1972). He has conducted elsewhere in Poland and abroad, and has gained awards for his work in promoting contemporary Polish music. He has recorded Zeidler's *Vespers* and Zwierzchowski's *Requiem* (with the Pomeranian Philharmonic Orchestra *et al.*, released in the United States by Musical Heritage Society), and also Kurpinski's Clarinet and Oboe Concerto, Lessel's Variations for Flute and Orchestra, and Milwid's Sinfonia concertante.

Cikker, Jan (b. 1911). Born in Banská Bystrica, Czechoslovakia, Cikker was educated at the Conservatory there and at the Master School of Composition, Prague. He taught at the Bratislava Conservatory (1939–51) and at the School of Musical Arts (from 1951), and composed orchestral and concerted works and operas. For Ultraphone he conducted the Bratislava Radio

Orchestra in his own Concertino (with pianist Macudyinski).

Cillario, Carlo Felice (b. 1915). Born at San Rafael, Argentina, Cillario studied in Buenos Aires and later at the Bologna Conservatory. His musical career started as a violinist with solo recitals in Italy and other countries; he won the Paganini Prize and was a professor at the Accademia di Santa Cecilia in Rome. In 1942 he studied conducting under Cerniatinsky and Enesco and made his debut at the Odessa Opera, conducted the Bucharest Philharmonic Orchestra and in 1947 was appointed conductor of the orchestra at the University of Tucumán in Argentina. After returning to Italy he conducted the orchestra at the Angelicum in Milan for five years and then pursued an active and successful career conducting opera and symphony concerts in London, Rome, Naples, Venice, Paris, Buenos Aires, Chicago, San Francisco, and with the Australian Opera Company. He is joint musical director at the Royal Opera in Stockholm and made his debut at the New York Metropolitan Opera in the 1972–3 season.

Cillario has made a number of records in Italy with the Angelicum Orchestra for the Angelicum label, and many of these have been released elsewhere by RCA, Schwann, Audio-Fidelity and Musical Heritage Society, although none appear to have been issued in Britain. They include Vivaldi's *Psalm 126* (*Nisi Dominus*), Perosi's *Il Natale del Redentore*, *Transitus animae* and *La Risurrezione di Cristo*, Carissimi's *Felicitas beatorum*, *Judicium extremum* and *Lamentatio damnatorum*, Monteverdi's *La favola d'Orfeo*, Handel's *Salve Regina*, *Donna che in celi*, *Aci, Galatea e Polifemo* and Concerto Grosso Op. 6 No. 10, Stradella's *S. Giovanni Battista*, Leo's *La Morte di Abele*, Rossi's *Giuseppe, figlio di Giacobbe*, Mozart's Symphony No. 40, overture to *Le nozze di Figaro*, *Eine kleine Nachtmusik*, *Adagio and Fugue in C minor*, *Ascanio in Alba*, *Lucio Silla* and *La Betulia liberata*, and Rossini's *Stabat Mater*. The three last-named works of Mozart's youth were of particular interest. His other recordings include Dinu Lipatti's *Romanian Dances* and Concertino for Piano and Orchestra (with Blumental and the Milan Philharmonic Orchestra for Everest), *Boléro* and *Feste Romane* (with the Romanian Radio Symphony Orchestra for Electrecord), excerpts from *Lucia di Lammermoor* (with the Rome Symphony Orchestra *et al.* for Ariola), aria recitals with Hagegard (and the Royal Chapel Orchestra for Caprice) and Caballé (with the RCA Italiana Orchestra for RCA) and *Norma* (with the London Philharmonic Orchestra *et al.* for RCA).

Cimara, Pietro (1887–1967). Born in Rome and a graduate of the Accademia di Santa Cecilia where he studied under Respighi, Cimara conducted there until 1927, when he was appointed conductor at the New York Metropolitan Opera, where he remained for 30 years. He wrote many songs which were published in Italy and the United States. His only record appears to have been an accompaniment to Bidú Sayáo in a recital of Puccini arias with the Metropolitan Opera Orchestra.

Ciolan, Antonin (1883–1970). Born in Jassy (modern Iasi), Romania, Ciolan studied first with Musicescu and Caudella and then in Berlin, Dresden and Leipzig with Nikisch, Draeseke and Nicodé. He became director of the Jassy Conservatory, founded the Jassy Musical Society, was director and chief conductor of the George Enesco Symphonic Society and was chief conductor of the Bucharest Philharmonic Orchestra (1947). He also conducted the Romanian Symphony Orchestra and Chorus, was a professor at the art institute of Cluj-Napoca, chief conductor of the Magyar Opera (1949), professor of conducting at the G. Dima Conservatory (1950), and founder, artistic director and chief conductor of the Cluj-Napoca State Philharmonic Orchestra (1955–70). He was responsible for developing this latter orchestra to a high level, and also for training Romanian conductors such as Elenescu, Chisadji, Simon, Popescu and Sbârcea. For his service to music in Romania he was awarded the distinctions of Honoured Professor and People's Artist of the SRR. For Electrecord he recorded Brahms' Symphony No. 1 and Tchaikovsky's Symphony No. 5, with the Cluj-Napoca State Philharmonic Orchestra.

Civil, Alan (b. 1929). Born in Northampton, and educated at the Northampton College of Art and the Guildhall School of Music, Civil was a pupil of Aubrey Brain and van Stemm; he was principal horn player with the Royal Philharmonic Orchestra (1952–5), co-principal then principal horn player with the Philharmonia Orchestra (1955–66) and then with the BBC Symphony Orchestra (from 1966), and professor of horn at the Royal College of Music, London. He has made many solo appearances, recorded the Mozart Horn Concertos twice (with Klemperer and Kempe), has played in chamber ensembles including the London Wind Soloists, and has composed a symphony for brass and percussion, songs and chamber music for brass. In 1976 Decca issued a disc of orchestral excerpts from *Carmen*, arranged by Howarth, in which Civil conducted the Kingsway Symphony Orchestra.

Clemencic, René (b. 1928). Born in Vienna, Clemencic was educated at the Vienna University and studied further in France, Holland and Germany. He is director of the Capella Musica Antiqua and of the Drama Musicum in Vienna, a teacher at the Vienna Academy of Music, musical adviser to the Institute of European Studies, lecturer at the Accademia Internazionale di Musica da Camera at Rome and lecturer at the Fundación Bariloche in Argentina. He has transcribed and produced preclassical music dramas, has written a study concerning old musical instruments, and has given concerts in Austria and abroad. His records include Palestrina's *Five Ricercare* and a collection entitled *Festive Baroque Music for Winds* (for DGG-Archiv), three madrigals of Monte, the collections *Carols and Motets for the Nativity of Medieval and Tudor England* and *Christmas Carols and Motets of Medieval Europe* (with the Deller Consort, for Bach Guild), Josquin's *Missa Hercules Dux Ferriae*, *Musica Sacra, Salzburger Renaissance*, Monteverdi's *Missa da capella*, Andrea Gabrieli's *Ricercar*, Giovanni Gabrieli's 2 Motets and pieces by Telemann, Handel, Zanetti and Vivaldi (for CBS), four discs of the *Carmina Burana*, three of the *Cantigas de Santa Maria*, three of the troubadours Bernard de Ventadorn, Peire Vidal, Comtessa de Dia, Folquet de Marselha, Marcabrun and Raimon de Miraval, Dufay's *Missa Ave Regina Coelorum*, *Missa sine Nomine*, *Missa Caput* and *Missa Ecce Ancilla*, Monteverdi's *Il Combattimento di Tancredi e Clorinda* and *Messa a 4 voce*, Obrecht's *Missa Fortuna Desperata*, Ockeghem's *Requiem*, Marcello's *XII Suonate a flauto solo*, and separate collections *Dances of the Renaissance*; *Recorder, lute and guitar*; *Music at the Court of Marguerite of Austria*; *Plaisirs de la Renaissance*; *Le Roman de Fauvel*; *René Clemencic and his Recorders* and *René Clemencic and his Flutes* (for Harmonia Mundi).

Cleva, Fausto (1902–71). Born in Trieste, Cleva studied at the Trieste and Milan Conservatories and first conducted at Milan at the age of seventeen. He was brought to the United States the next year by Gatti-Casazza, the director of the New York Metropolitan Opera, to be the company's assistant chorus master. He became an assistant conductor, but then was appointed musical director of the Cincinnati Opera in 1941 and general manager of the Chicago Civic Opera (1944–6). After appearing also with the Philadelphia and San Francisco Operas, he returned to the New York Met. in 1950 to conduct opera in the Italian repertoire. Cleva died in Athens while conducting a performance of *Orfeo ed Euridice* at the Herodes Atticus theatre, just after he had celebrated his 50 years with the New York Met. During those years he had conducted 657 performances of 27 different operas. Critical opinions of his conducting were not invariably laudatory; Eaton, the chronicler of the Met., wrote that he 'became the inevitable routinier, always dependable, increasingly uninspired'. In the early years of LP, Columbia (US) issued a series of operas in association with the New York Met., and of these Cleva conducted *Lucia di Lammermoor*, *Faust*, *Pagliacci* and *Cavalleria rusticana*; the *Lucia di Lammermoor* and *Pagliacci* were re-issued in the 1970s. There were also discs of excerpts from *Norma*, *Don Carlos*, *Samson et Dalila*, *Otello* and *La Bohème*, orchestral excerpts from *Aida*, the overture to *La forza del destino* and the preludes to Acts I and III of *La traviata* (with the Metropolitan Opera Orchestra *et al.* for Columbia), aria recitals with Pinza, Tucker, Tebaldi and others, *Luisa Miller* (with the RCA Italian Opera Ensemble for RCA), Catalani's *La Wally* (with the Monte Carlo National Opera Orchestra *et al.* for Decca), *Tosca* (with the Metropolitan Opera Orchestra *et al.* issued by L'Estro Armonico) and orchestral excerpts from *La traviata*, *Le Coq d'or*, *Faust* and *Mefistofele* and part of *Capriccio espagnol* (with the Cincinnati Symphony Orchestra for Brunswick).

Cloëz, Gustave (1890–1970). Born in Quincy, France, Cloëz was a pupil of Lévy and de Bériot, was conductor at the Paris Opéra-Comique (1922–46), with the Grand Ballet du Marquis de Cuevas, conductor with the Bordeaux Opera (1955–7) and was associated with the dancer Ida Rubinstein. He recorded extensively on 78 r.p.m. discs, including pieces by Blaumont, Couperin, Destouches, Gluck, Lully, Schobert and Mouret (with the Versailles Chamber Orchestra for Anthologie Sonore), Mozart's Flute and Harp Concerto K. 299 (with Crunella, Jamet and Symphony Orchestra) and *Bastien und Bastienne* (with the Paris Conservatoire Orchestra *et al.* for Anthologie Sonore), an abridged *Cavalleria rusticana* (issued by Decca US), *Prélude à l'après-midi d'un faune* and excerpts from *L'Enfant prodigue* (with the Paris Opéra-Comique

Orchestra for Odeon), Debussy's *La boîte à joujoux*, excerpts from Delibes' *La Source*, Gounod's *Funeral March of a Marionette*, the *Peer Gynt* Suite No. 2, Liszt's Piano Concerto No. 2 (with Trouard), the overture to *Phèdre*, Mozart's Piano Concerto K. 459 (with Boskoff) and *A Night on the Bare Mountain* (with the Paris Philharmonic Orchestra for Odeon), *El amor brujo*, the overture to *Le Roi d'Ys*, Massenet's *Scènes alsaciennes* and part of *Scènes pittoresques*, *Scheherazade*, Saint-Saëns' *Suite algérienne*, the overture to *Die Zauberflöte*, orchestral excerpts from *Siegfried*, the Rhine Journey and Funeral Music from *Götterdämmerung*, the overture and Venusberg Music from *Tannhäuser*, the prelude to Act III of *Tristan und Isolde*, and *A Faust Overture* (with a Symphony Orchestra for Odeon), the introduction to Mussorgsky's *Sorochintsy Fair* (with a symphony orchestra, issued by Parlophone), Liszt's *Hungarian Fantasia* (with Trouard and the French Radio Orchestra for Odeon), the ballet music from *Faust* (with the Lamoureux Orchestra for Odeon), the ballet music from *Orfeo ed Euridice* (with the Paris Conservatoire Orchestra for Odeon), the *L'Arlésienne* Suites Nos 1 and 2, the waltzes from *Nutcracker* and *The Sleeping Beauty* and two *Hungarian Dances* of Brahms (with the Paris Opéra Orchestra for Odeon), Serra's ballet *Doña Iñes de Castro* (with the Aievas Ballet Orchestra for Telefunken), and a recital of arias by artists of the Paris Opéra and Opéra-Comique (for CBS).

Cluytens, André (1905–67). Born in Antwerp where he studied the piano at the Royal Flemish Conservatory, Cluytens became at the age of sixteen assistant to his father who was conductor at the Royal Theatre at Antwerp, and in 1927 he became the first conductor at the theatre. He moved to France (1932), conducted at opera houses at Toulouse, Lyon, Bordeaux and Vichy, settled in Paris and became a French citizen. He was appointed principal conductor and then musical director at the Paris Opéra (1944), director of the Paris Opéra-Comique (1947) and then, at the same time, chief conductor in succession to Munch of the Paris Conservatoire Orchestra (1949), principal conductor of the Belgian National Orchestra and, later on, chief conductor of the French National Radio Orchestra. He conducted at the Vienna State Opera and in 1956 toured the United States with the Vienna Philharmonic Orchestra, sharing the podium with Schuricht. A request to substitute for Jochum in 1955 made him the first French conductor to appear at the Bayreuth Festival, where he conducted until 1958, leading *Tannhäuser*, *Die Meistersinger* and *Lohengrin*. He was a superb conductor of the French repertoire, and his readings of the Beethoven symphonies were widely respected, but they were inclined to a certain straightforwardness and stolidity. Of the nine symphonies which he recorded with the Berlin Philharmonic Orchestra, the *Pastoral* was a performance of the utmost distinction.

During World War II Cluytens recorded Bizet's overture *Patrie* (with the Paris Conservatoire Orchestra for Columbia), and later made a number of 78 r.p.m. discs, including C. P. E. Bach's Cello Concerto No. 3 (with Navarra), the overture to *Don Giovanni*, *Ma Mère l'Oye*, *An American in Paris* and Fauré's *Ballade* (with Marguerite Long, and the Paris Conservatoire Orchestra for Columbia); Strauss' *Burleske* (with Meyer) and the overture *La Princesse jaune* (with the Paris Conservatoire Orchestra for HMV); *Carmen* and *Les Contes d'Hoffmann* (with the Paris Opéra-Comique Orchestra *et al.* for Columbia); Lalo's *Symphonie espagnole* (with Francescatti and an orchestra for Columbia); the overtures to Hérold's *Le Pré aux clercs* and Gounod's *Mireille* (with the Paris Opéra-Comique Orchestra for HMV); Haydn's Symphonies Nos 94 and 104, the *Prometheus* overture, *L'Enfance du Christ*, Chopin's *Andante spianato et Grande Polonaise* (with Darré), *In the Steppes of Central Asia* and three dances from *The Three-cornered Hat* (with the Paris Conservatoire Orchestra for Pathé); the two *L'Arlésienne* suites (with the French National Radio Orchestra for Pathé); and Delage's *Poèmes hindous* (with Angelici and an instrumental ensemble for HMV).

With the advent of LP and until his death Cluytens was very active in the recording studios. Paramount were the nine Beethoven symphonies, and the *Egmont* and *Leonore No. 3* overtures, mentioned above (with the Berlin Philharmonic Orchestra for EMI), and the complete orchestral music of Ravel and *Pelléas et Mélisande* (with the French National Radio Orchestra *et al.* for EMI), and *L'Heure espagnole* (with the Paris Opéra-Comique Orchestra *et al.* for EMI). These constituted a distinguished series, and included many other superlative performances; included were Schumann's Symphony No. 3 and *Manfred* overture, and Tchaikovsky's Symphony No. 2 and *A Night on the Bare Mountain* (with the Berlin Philharmonic Orchestra for EMI); Beethoven's Piano Concerto No. 3 (with Gilels), Chopin's Piano Concerto No. 2 (with Marguerite Long), Tchaikovsky's Piano Concerto No. 1 (with Ciccolini), Saint-Saëns'

Symphony No. 3 (with Roget) and Piano Concerto No. 3 (with Gilels), *Boris Godunov*, Rachmaninov's Piano Concerto No. 3 (with Gilels), the two Ravel Piano Concertos (with François), *Mireille* (in the Busser-Carré revision), Roussel's Symphonies Nos 3 and 4, Stravinsky's *Perséphone* and Menotti's Piano Concerto (with Boukoff, and the Paris Conservatoire Orchestra for EMI); the first movement of *Eine kleine Nachtmusik*, the first movement of Beethoven's Symphony No. 5, the second movement of Beethoven's Symphony No. 8, the fourth movement of Mendelssohn's Symphony No. 4, the second movement of Dvořák's Symphony No. 9, the third movement of Tchaikovsky's Symphony No. 4, the third movement of Tchaikovsky's Symphony No. 6, Moldau and From Bohemia's Meadows and Forests, from *Má Vlast*, *Don Juan* and the love scene from *Feuersnot*, and *Hänsel und Gretel* (with the Vienna Philharmonic Orchestra *et al.* for EMI); Delage's *Chants de la jungle* (with Angelici and an orchestra for EMI); the Beethoven Violin Concerto (with Oistrakh), *Symphonie fantastique*, Schumann's Symphony No. 4, the Franck *Symphony in D minor*, *Le Chasseur maudit*, *Psyché* and *Rédemption*, Bizet's *Symphony in C major*, *Patrie* overture, two *L'Arlésienne* suites and *La Jolie Fille de Perth* suite, *Le Rossignol*, *Le Martyre de Saint-Sébastien*, *La Boîte à joujoux* (orchestrated by Caplet) and *Children's Corner* (orchestrated by Caplet), Shostakovich's Symphony No. 11 and two Piano Concertos (with Shostakovich), and Bondeville's *Gaultier-Garguille* (with the French National Radio Orchestra *et al.* for EMI); *Faust*, suites from *Coppélia* and *Sylvia*, excerpts from *La Damnation de Faust* and Berlioz's *Roméo et Juliette* symphony, and the overtures *Le Carnaval romain*, *Benvenuto Cellini*, *Le Roi Lear*, *Le Corsaire* and *Béatrice et Bénédict* (with the Paris National Opera Orchestra for EMI); the Fauré *Requiem* (with Les Chanteurs St Eustache *et al.* for EMI); *Le Roi d'Ys* (for EMI); *Carmen*, *Les Contes d'Hoffmann*, *Les Pêcheurs de perles*, Poulenc's *Les Mamelles de Tirésias*, and the Death of Emma from Bondeville's *Madame Bovary* (with the Paris Opéra-Comique Orchestra *et al.* for EMI); *L'Enfance du Christ* (with the French National Radio Orchestra *et al.* for Pathé and Vox); the *Oberon* overture (with the Paris Opéra-Comique Orchestra for Pathé); *Prometheus* overture, *Capriccio espagnol*, *A Night on the Bare Mountain*, *Pavane pour une infante défunte*, the *Russian Easter Festival* overture and *In the Steppes of Central Asia* (with the Paris Conservatoire Orchestra for Pathé); *Scheherazade* (with the French National Radio Orchestra for Pathé); and *Symphonie fantastique*, *Capriccio espagnol*, *La Valse*, *In the Steppes of Central Asia* and *A Night on the Bare Mountain* (with the Philharmonia Orchestra for EMI).

Coates, Albert (1882–1953). Coates was born in St Petersburg of a Yorkshire businessman and a Russian mother, and as a boy studied the violin, cello and organ, and had some lessons in composition from Rimsky-Korsakov. At twelve he was sent to England for his education, eventually studying science for four years at Liverpool University. He returned to Russia to work in the office of his father's woollen mill, but soon abandoned business for music, entered the Leipzig Conservatory to study the piano, cello and composition, and as a fledgling cellist in the Gewandhaus Orchestra came under the influence of Nikisch, from whom he took conducting lessons. He became Nikisch's assistant at the Leipzig Opera (1904), where he made his debut as a conductor when he substituted for him in *Les Contes d'Hoffmann*. Nikisch recommended him for the post of chief conductor at Elberfeld Opera (1905); two years later he was at the Dresden Opera with von Schuch, and became first conductor with Bodanzky at Mannheim (1909). After the success of an initial guest engagement to conduct *Siegfried*, in 1910 he was appointed director of the Imperial Opera at St Petersburg, where he remained until 1918. At this time he added many Russian operas and orchestral works to his repertoire, and was familiar with many leading Russian musicians, particularly Scriabin. He visited London to conduct the London Symphony Orchestra and to present Wagner at Covent Garden, alternated with Bodanzky in *Parsifal*, and shared a season with Nikisch. When the tsar's director of opera resigned in the 1917 revolution, Coates was appointed president of the Petrograd Opera House by the management committee, a post later confirmed by the Bolsheviks; but the worsening famine caused him to leave Russia through Finland in 1919.

He returned to England and took charge of the London Symphony Orchestra for several years, greatly assisting its re-establishment after a period of difficulty. Beecham engaged him as an artistic co-director and senior conductor at the first post-war season of the English Opera Company; in 1922 he conducted *The Ring* at Covent Garden, where he also led *Boris Godunov* in 1928, *Siegfried* in 1935 and *Tristan und Isolde* in 1937 and 1938. From 1922 to 1925 he was chief conductor of the Leeds Festival, and his other European appearances included the Berlin State Opera (1931), the Vienna Philharmonic Orchestra (1935), as well as at Rotterdam, Stockholm and in the USSR, where he returned three times. From 1927 to 1929 he conducted extensively in opera houses in Italy, in the 1920s and 30s he was also active in the United States, and in 1923 was the first British conductor to perform at the Paris Opéra. Walter Damrosch invited him to New York in 1920, and he returned there in succeeding years for conducting engagements. One result was that from 1923 to 1925 he spent part of each year at the Eastman School of Music at Rochester, NY, teaching conducting and directing the Rochester Symphony Orchestra. The years during World War II were passed in the United States; he returned to Britain in 1945, but in 1947 retired to live in South Africa, where he occasionally conducted the local orchestras and taught conducting at Cape Town University. He died in South Africa. His prolific compositions included operas, symphonic music and songs; the operas numbered amongst them *Samuel Pepys* and *Pickwick*, and in 1936 he formed the British Drama Opera Company, apparently to present *Pickwick*, which had a cast of more than 40 characters. Ernest Newman remarked that the music was more Russian in flavour than English, and opinion varied as to its success. In his later years in the US, Coates wrote music for films, including *Song of Russia*, and conducted for a film of *Pagliacci*.

Coates was one of the greatest British conductors in the first half of this century, both in the opera house and concert hall, with a wider range of musical sympathies than almost any other. In addition he was a superb choral conductor, especially of the major choral masterpieces. He was not only a spectacular interpreter of the Russian repertoire, but was also sound in the German classics. In the words of Burnett James (in *The Gramophone*, March 1954) he 'was a vast whirlwind of a man – vast alike in physical proportions and in the capacity for living and working. As a conductor he hurled himself voraciously on the orchestra, and the impact was invariably explosive and enormously exciting. A pernickety or devitalised performance from Coates was unthinkable. He loved colour and warmth and high drama, and it was only natural that he should have a special affinity for Russian music. He was a leading interpreter of Scriabin, and he introduced to London audiences many of Scriabin's orchestral works at a time when that composer was much in the fashion. As a Wagner conductor he held the firm belief that the pulse and balance of Wagner's music were often destroyed by hurried and insensitive tempi. Under his baton the Wagnerian music-dramas grew and expanded with massive dignity and an irresistible impulse. He was incapable of half measures: his *crescendi* were overwhelming, and his *fortissimi* volcanic in eruption. But he was also capable of wonderful tenderness – the whole gamut of orchestral colour came within his scope so long as it was warm and glowing and lovely. . . . He was a great-hearted and often disconcerting man, who lived on this earth with visible as well as audible relish.' He regarded his orchestral players as friends, and frequently called them by their Christian names.

Coates' recording career started in 1919, on his return to England from Russia; for the Columbia Gramophone Company he recorded with the London Symphony Orchestra the *Romeo and Juliet* fantasy-overture, and a two-disc version of *Scheherazade*. His other early records were Scriabin's *Poème d'extase*, the *Siegfried Idyll*, a suite from Purcell's music arranged by himself, and the third movements of Beethoven's Symphony No. 7 and Tchaikovsky's Symphony No. 6. In 1921 he switched to the Gramophone Company (HMV), and made many famous discs with a group entitled 'The Symphony Orchestra', whose members were predominantly from the London Symphony Orchestra, and then later with the London Symphony Orchestra itself, and also with the Royal Albert Hall Orchestra. His records, between 1921 and the introduction of electrical recording in 1925, were of Mozart's Symphony No. 41 and the overture to *Der Schauspieldirektor*, Beethoven's Symphonies Nos 7 and 9, Brahms' Symphony No. 1, Tchaikovsky's Symphony No. 5 and *Francesca da Rimini*, *L'Oiseau de feu*, *Don Juan*, *Till Eulenspiegel*, *Tod und Verklärung*, *Kikimora*, *Ma Mère l'Oye*, Debussy's *Golliwog's Cake Walk*, the overtures to *Oberon* and *Der Freischütz*, a suite from *Le Coq d'or*, the Dance of the Tumblers from *The Snow Maiden*, the Polovtsian Dances from *Prince Igor*, *Siegfried Idyll*, a number of excerpts from the Wagner operas, as well as *Salome*, *Boris Godunov*, and Boito's *Nerone* and *Mefistofele*.

Coates' first electrical recordings were the choral pieces *God is a Spirit* of Sterndale Bennett, and O Gladsome Night, from Sullivan's *The Golden Legend*. Then followed a vast range of records, including Bach's *Mass in B minor*, and long extracts again from the Wagner operas, which until the 1930s were almost all that existed of these works in the catalogues, apart from the overtures and preludes. The series continued until the early

1930s, and included Bach's *Toccata in F* (arranged by Esser), Fantasia from the *Fantasia and Fugue in C minor* (arranged by Elgar), and *Fugue in G* (arranged by Holst), Mozart's Symphony No. 41, the overture to *Der Schauspieldirektor* and excerpts from the *Requiem*, Beethoven's Symphonies Nos 3 and 7 and *Prometheus* overture, the overture to Handel's Chandos Anthem No. 2 (arranged by Elgar), Soul of the World from Purcell's *Ode on St Cecilia's Day*, and Bax's *Mater Ora Filium* (with the Leeds Festival Chorus), two choruses from Mendelssohn's *Elijah* (with the Royal Choral Society), Brahms' Piano Concerto No. 2 (with Rubinstein), the overtures to *Oberon*, *Russlan and Ludmilla*, *May Night* and *Die Feen*, and *Carnival* and *Hamlet*, Tchaikovsky's Symphonies Nos 1, 3 and 6, *Romeo and Juliet* fantasy-overture, *Francesca da Rimini*, *Marche slave*, *La Valse*, Borodin's Symphony No. 2, *In the Steppes of Central Asia*, the overture, dances and march from *Prince Igor*, *Capriccio espagnol*, the Procession of the Nobles from *Mlada*, the Introduction and Bridal Cortège from *Le Coq d'or*, excerpts from *Tsar Saltan* and *The Legend of the Invisible City of Kitezh*, *Dubinushka*, the Dance of the Tumblers from *The Snow Maiden*, *Les Préludes*, *Mephisto Waltz*, Liszt's *Hungarian Rhapsody No. 1* and *Hungarian Storm March*, the Prelude and Dream Pantomime from *Hänsel und Gretel*, *Don Juan*, *Till Eulenspiegel*, *Fontane di Roma*, *Petrushka*, the march from *Le Chant du Rossignol*, Liadov's *Eight Russian Folksongs*, *Music Box* and *Kikimora*, the Dance of the Persian Slaves from *Khovanshchina*, *Kamarinskaya*, *A Night on the Bare Mountain*, Rachmaninov's Piano Concerto No. 3 (with Horowitz), *Le Pas d'acier*, excerpts from *The Love of Three Oranges*, Jupiter, Uranus, Mercury and Mars from *The Planets*, the Dance of the Spirits of the Earth from *The Perfect Fool*, and excerpts from *Carmen*, *Faust* and *Boris Godunov*. Among the artists in the Wagner and other operatic records were Chaliapin, Schorr, Leider, Melchior and Widdop.

When Coates returned to London after World War II in 1945, he made some records for Decca with the London Symphony and National Symphony Orchestras: Tchaikovsky's Symphony No. 6 and the *Romeo and Juliet* fantasy-overture, the Introduction and Bridal Cortège from *Le Coq d'or*, the Dance of the Tumblers from *The Snow Maiden*, *A Night on the Bare Mountain*, and the Gopak from *Sorochintsy Fair*. His name, as a recording conductor, has almost vanished from sight, and only appears on occasional re-issues of Wagner excerpts featuring the great singers with whom he recorded, and with the Seraphim release of Rachmaninov's Piano Concerto No. 3, with Horowitz. More than most, he is a conductor who would have thrived in the LP high-fidelity era, but he is also one whose recordings at the time when the gramophone was becoming established, pointed the way to the glories that were to follow in the 1930s and later.

Coates, Eric (1886–1957). Born at Hucknall, Nottinghamshire, Coates studied the viola and composition at the Royal Academy of Music in London, played in the Hamburg, Cathie and Walenn Quartets and was leading viola in Wood's Queen's Hall Orchestra (1912–18). He composed light, melodic orchestral works which were so successful that he was able to leave orchestral playing in 1918 and devote himself entirely to composition. Some of his music, such as the *Knightsbridge March* from his *London Suite* (1932) and *By the Sleepy Lagoon* became immensely popular. He was particularly skilful at drawing musical illustrations of London life and scenes. Coates conducted some of his own music on early 78 r.p.m. recordings, including the *Summer Days* suite and *Wood Nymphs* (with the New Queen's Hall Orchestra for Columbia); later he recorded *London* and *London Again* (with the Philharmonic Promenade Orchestra for Parlophone) and the *Three Elizabeths* and *Four Centuries* suites (with the New Symphony Orchestra for Decca).

Coffin, Berton (b. 1910). Born in Fairmont, Virginia, Coffin studied at the Chicago Musical College (1935), the Eastman School of Music (1938) and Columbia University (1946–50), performed as a baritone in oratorio, opera and recitals, and has taught singing at the College of Music at Colorado University. He has published as author or co-author *The Singer's Repertoire* (in five volumes, 1956–60), *Word-by-Word Translations of Songs and Arias* (1966), *Phonetic Readings of Songs and Arias* (1964) and *The Singer's Technique* (1975). With the Colorado University Orchestra and Festival Choir he recorded Cherubini's *Requiem in C*, for Owl 3.

Cohen, Elie. Cohen was a member of the conducting staff of the Paris Opéra-Comique from 1922 until shortly before World War II, and led there the first Paris performances of a number of operas and ballets. With the Opéra-Comique Orchestra *et al.* he conducted, for Columbia, celebrated recordings of *Carmen*, *Manon* and *Werther*; these were issued in the early 1930s;

Werther, with a cast including Ninon Vallin and Georges Thill, was especially admired. His other discs, all pre-war 78s, included excerpts from Thomas' *Mignon* (with the Orchestre du Théâtre Royal de la Monnaie *et al.*), Massenet's incidental music to *Les Érinnyes*, the overture to *A Midsummer Night's Dream* (with an unnamed orchestra for Columbia), Cantaloube's *Songs of the Auvergne* (with Madeleine Grey and an orchestra for Columbia) and the ballet music from Gluck's *Orfeo ed Euridice* (with the Paris Symphony Orchestra for Columbia).

Collingwood, Lawrance (b. 1887). Born in London, Collingwood was a chorister at Westminster Abbey (1897–1902), organist at St Thomas' Hospital (1905), All Hallows', Gospel Oak (1906) and St Swithin's, London Stone (1919–30), and an organ scholar at Exeter College, Oxford (1907–11). After visiting St Petersburg during two long vacations he went to live in Russia (1912), was a pupil at the St Petersburg Conservatory (1913–17) and assisted Albert Coates at the St Petersburg Opera. After the Russian revolution he returned to England, then was interpreter to Churchill's expedition to northern Russia. He won a Carnegie award for a symphonic poem which he conducted at Queen's Hall (1921), joined the Old Vic as chorusmaster, replaced Charles Corri as chief conductor at the Old Vic and later at Sadler's Wells (1931–47), where he did much fine work in developing the company's repertoire. In 1934 his own *Macbeth* became the first full-length English opera to be presented at the theatre. He later wrote a second opera, *The Death of Tintagiles*, as well as a piano concerto, a piano quintet, piano music and a number of songs. After becoming associated with HMV, he worked with Coates, Blech, Walter, Seidler-Winckler *et al.* as coach, organist, chorusmaster, orchestrator and recording supervisor, and followed Landon Ronald as adviser to EMI. Until he retired from EMI in 1972 and especially after World War II he was responsible for almost all the recording sessions at EMI with Cantelli, Beecham, Sargent, Kletzki, Kempe and Furtwängler, and was at Toscanini's last recording session in London. During World War II he took the Sadler's Wells Opera Company on tour to over 50 towns in the British Isles, and for his work received the CBE in 1948; he conducted over 30 different operas, including first performances in Britain of *Tsar Saltan*, *The Snow Maiden*, the original edition of *Boris Godunov*, and first performances in English of *Der Rosenkavalier* and *The Bartered Bride*. He conducted *Le nozze di Figaro* at Sadler's Wells on the day of his diamond wedding in 1974.

Collingwood made his first records in 1927, after he had joined HMV, and these were excerpts from *Die Walküre*, *Götterdämmerung* and *Tristan und Isolde*, with the great Wagnerian singers of the time, Leider, Austral, Ljungberg, Schorr, Widdop, Fry, Andrésen *et al.* and the London Symphony Orchestra. In the pre-war years he also conducted Dohnányi's *Variations on a Nursery Tune* (with the composer and the London Symphony), Mozart's Piano Concerto K. 491 (with Fischer and the London Philharmonic), a Vivaldi violin concerto (with Elman and the New Symphony Orchestra), Beethoven's Romance No. 1 (with Elman and the London Philharmonic), Gounod's *Judex* (with the New Symphony Orchestra), the triumphal march from Elgar's *Caractacus*, Delibes' *Naila Waltz* and excerpts from *Sylvia*, Mozart's Symphony No. 40, Grainger's *Shepherd's Hey*, Balfour-Gardiner's *Shepherd Fennel's Dance*, and the panorama from *The Sleeping Beauty* (with the Royal Opera House Orchestra, Covent Garden), the overture to *The Bartered Bride* (with the Sadler's Wells Orchestra), Mussorgsky's *Trepak* (with Chaliapin), the incidental music from *Le Roi s'amuse* and Elgar's *Dream Children* (with the London Symphony Orchestra). Later, he recorded 78 r.p.m. discs of the Prologue and Dance of the Tumblers from *The Snow Maiden*, Elgar's *Chanson de matin* and *Chanson de nuit*, the Polka and Fugue from *Schwanda the Bagpipe Player*, *Carnival* overture and *In the Steppes of Central Asia* (with the Philharmonia Orchestra), and the *Egmont* and *Manfred* overtures (with the London Symphony Orchestra). On LP, there was issued Elgar's *Nursery Suite*, *Bavarian Dances* and *Serenade*, Brahms' *Tragic* and *Academic Festival Overtures*, Schumann's *Overture, Scherzo and Finale*, and Saint-Saëns' *Wedding Cake* (with Johannesen, and the London Symphony Orchestra), the prelude to *Die Meistersinger*, the Waltz and Polonaise from *Eugene Onegin*, and *Prélude à l'après-midi d'un faune* (with the Westminster Symphony Orchestra). The collection of Elgar pieces with the London Symphony Orchestra was later re-issued with great success by Music for Pleasure.

Collins, Anthony (1893–1964). Born in Hastings, Collins served for four years in the British army in World War I and then studied at the Royal College of Music, London. He joined the London Symphony Orchestra where he led the violas, and after filling a similar position in the Covent Garden Opera House Orchestra, resigned in 1936 to devote himself to conducting and composition. His first experience as a conductor was with the Carl Rosa and Sadler's Wells Opera Companies and with provincial orchestras in England. He led the London Symphony Orchestra conducting an Elgar symphony, and in 1939 founded and directed the London Mozart Orchestra which performed during the London Music Festival in that year. Collins departed for the United States in 1939, appeared as a conductor in New York and Los Angeles and composed film scores for RKO. He returned to England in 1945, conducted and wrote more film music, but moved back to the US in 1953 and eventually died in Los Angeles. Apart from music for films his compositions included two symphonies, two violin concertos, some short operas, chamber music and much light music. He also orchestrated Schubert's *Grand Duo*, D. 812.

Collins won a lasting reputation as a recording artist for his cycle of Sibelius symphonies, which he recorded on mono LP with the London Symphony Orchestra for Decca. 'Collins never made a dull record,' wrote Robert Layton (*The Great Records*, London, 1967, p. 22). 'He was the ideal recording conductor for he could combine a sense of style with a natural gift for spontaneity, peculiarly suited to the conditions of the recording studio. He had a masterly touch with the music of Sibelius and, for the present writer, who learned his early Sibelius (Symphonies 1 and 2) with Kajanus, there is no other conductor who is as convincing in this music.' Previously, on 78 r.p.m. discs, Collins had recorded a number of pieces by Granville Bantock for Paxton, including the *Celtic Symphony*, *Two Heroic Ballads*, *Four Chinese Landscapes*, *Two Hebridean Sea Poems*, the Processional from *King Solomon* and the overture to *The Frogs* (with the London Promenade Orchestra). Also on 78s were Mozart's Symphony No. 33 (with the London Mozart Orchestra) and a suite from *Carmen* (with the London Philharmonic Orchestra). On early mono LPs there followed the Mozart Bassoon Concerto (with Helaerts) and Clarinet Concerto (with de Peyer), Delius' *Brigg Fair*, *On Hearing the First Cuckoo in Spring*, *The Walk to the Paradise Garden*, *A Song of Summer*, *Paris*, *Summer Night on the River* and *In a Summer Garden*, Mozart's Piano Concerto K. 449 and Strauss's *Burleske* (with Gulda), Mendelssohn's Piano Concertos Nos 1 and 2 (with Katin), Paganini's Violin Concertos Nos 1 and 2 (with Ricci), the Sibelius symphonies mentioned above and *Pohjola's Daughter*, *Night Ride and Sunrise*, *Pelléas et Mélisande*, and the *Karelia* overture, Elgar's *Falstaff* and Tchaikovsky's *Capriccio italien* and *Francesca da Rimini* (with the London Symphony Orchestra), the waltzes from *Der Rosenkavalier*, the Dream Pantomime from *Hänsel und Gretel* and *El amor brujo* (with the London Philharmonic Orchestra), Mozart's Piano Concertos K. 503 and K. 537 (with Gulda), Elgar's *Introduction and Allegro* and *Serenade*, Vaughan Williams' *Fantasia on a Theme of Thomas Tallis* and *Fantasia on Greensleeves*, Sullivan's overture *di Ballo*, Gardiner's *Shepherd Fennel's Dance*, Grainger's *Shepherd's Hey* and Britten's *Soirées musicales* and *Matinées musicales* (with the New Symphony Orchestra) and Walton's *Façade* (with Sitwell, Pears and the English Opera Ensemble). All of these were for Decca; for EMI he recorded *Invitation to the Dance*, *A Night on the Bare Mountain*, *Danse macabre*, *España* and Sibelius' *Romance in C*, *Karelia* suite, *En Saga*, *The Swan of Tuonela* and *Finlandia* (with the Royal Philharmonic Orchestra) and for World Record Club Mozart's Symphonies Nos 40 and 41 (with the Sinfonia of London). The Tchaikovsky coupling of *Francesca da Rimini* and *Capriccio italien* were fine performances and are still listed in the catalogues, as are Mozart's Symphonies Nos 40 and 41 which were re-issued by Classics for Pleasure, and *Façade*, on Decca's Eclipse label.

Colombo, Pierre (b. 1914). Born at Vevey, Colombo studied science at Lausanne University, then attended the Basel Conservatory and was a pupil for conducting with Scherchen and Krauss. In 1953 he was appointed conductor of the symphony orchestra at Johannesburg, where he also conducted ballet and opera. During his subsequent international career he has conducted opera and symphony orchestras in Western and Eastern Europe and has taken part in festivals at Montreux, Sofia, *et al.* In Switzerland he founded the Geneva Chamber Orchestra, which is made up of musicians from the Suisse Romande Orchestra, which he has also conducted frequently. In addition to being president of La Tribune Internationale des Compositeurs and a member of the International Music Council of UNESCO, he has been a member of the juries for various international competitions such as the Herbert von Karajan Conductors' Competition, Concours international de Genève and the Concours Long-Thibaud.

Colombo first made 78 r.p.m. and mono LP records for L'Oiseau Lyre with the Lamoureux Chamber Orchestra and the L'Oiseau Lyre Ensemble; included were Bach's Harpsichord

Concertos BWV 1054 and BWV 1056, C. P. E. Bach's Harpsichord *Concerto in D minor*, and Haydn's Harpsichord *Concerto in D major* (with Nef), J. C. Bach's Symphonies Op. 9 No. 2 and Op. 18 No. 4, Barsanti's Concerti Grossi Op. 3 Nos 4 and 10, Cimarosa's *Two-Flute Concerto in G* (with Rampal and Hériché), Delalande's *Symphonies pour les soupers du Roy* No. 1, Rameau's *Les Paladins* Suites Nos 1 and 2 (arranged by Desormière), Ricciotti's Concertinos Nos 2, 3, 5 and 6 (attributed to Pergolesi), Bond's Trumpet Concerto No. 1 (with André), Clarke's *Suite in D*, Mudge's Concerto for Strings, and Mozart's Symphonies Nos 1 and 6, and 8 to 11. He also recorded Bach's *Magnificat* (with the Kalmar Orchestra *et al.* for L'Oiseau Lyre), Mozart's *Requiem* (with the Vienna State Opera Orchestra *et al.* for La Guilde Internationale du Disque), Beethoven's *Die Geschöpfe des Prometheus*, *Così fan tutte* and the two Ravel Piano Concertos (with Milà and the Monte Carlo National Orchestra *et al.* for La Guilde Internationale du Disque), Haydn's *Violin Concerto in G* (with Gawriloff and the Geneva Radio Chamber Orchestra for La Guilde Internationale du Disque), Honegger's dramatic legend *Nicolas de Flue* (for Nestlé) and two interludes from Bloch's opera *Macbeth* (with the Geneva Studio Orchestra for CT).

Comissiona, Sergiu (b. 1928). The Romanian conductor Comissiona was born in Bucharest; he studied the violin at the Bucharest Music Academy, and conducting with Silvestri and Lindenberg. After a brief period as a violinist with the Romanian State Ensemble he conducted at the Romanian State Opera and with the Bucharest Philharmonic Orchestra. In 1959 he moved to Israel, where he organised the Israel Chamber Orchestra and toured with them to the United States in 1963. He also became conductor of the Haifa Symphony Orchestra (1959), music director of the Göteborg Symphony Orchestra in Sweden (1967) and appeared as a guest conductor with the Stockholm Philharmonic, London Philharmonic and Berlin Radio Symphony Orchestras, as well as at the Covent Garden and Stockholm Opera Houses. In 1969 he was appointed music director and chief conductor of the Baltimore Symphony Orchestra, Maryland, where he has achieved a considerable measure of success, and is also now conductor of the Chautauqua Symphony Orchestra, New York. His first records were with the Haifa Symphony Orchestra for Pye in 1965, and were of Bach's Clavier Concertos Nos 1 and 5 and two Harpsichord Concertos of Haydn (with Pelleg), Mozart's Piano Concertos K. 365 (with Eden and Tamir) and K. 456 (with Salzman), Clementi's *Symphony in D major*, Boccherini's *Serenade in D major*, Schubert's Symphonies Nos 3 and 6 and a collection of Jewish prayers. Critical reception of these discs was somewhat muted. With the Stockholm Philharmonic Orchestra he recorded Pergament's *Fyra dikter av Edith Södergran* and music by Kokkonen, Langgaard, Rydman and Lewkovitch, Britten's *Les Illuminations* and Kodály's *Dances from Galánta*, and with the Swedish Radio Symphony Orchestra Blomdahl's *Forma Ferritonans* (for Caprice and EMI); for Phono Club (Geneva) he directed the Israel Chamber Orchestra in Roussel's *Sinfonietta* and Stravinsky's *Apollon Musagète*, and for Decca the Suisse Romande Orchestra in Chopin's Piano Concerto No. 2 and Falla's *Nights in the Gardens of Spain* (with de Larrocha) and Poulenc's Two-Piano Concerto (with Eden and Tamir). More recently with the Baltimore Symphony Orchestra he has recorded Laderman's *Concerto for Orchestra* and Britten's *Diversions on a Theme* (with Fleischer, for Desto) and Mendelssohn's Symphony No. 3 and *Hebrides* overture, for Vox.

Confalonieri, Giulio (1896–1972). Born in Milan, where he studied at the University, and also at the Bologna Conservatory, Confalonieri lived in London, and then returned to Milan to become a teacher and music critic. He edited music by Cherubini and Cimarosa, *et al.*, and published a biography of Cherubini. As a conductor, he recorded his own *Gala* (*Dali in Venice*) and his arrangement of Alessandro Scarlatti's *La Dama spagnola e il cavaliere*.

Constant, Marius (b. 1925). After winning the Enesco Prize in 1943 at the conservatory in his native Bucharest, Constant went to Paris and studied at the Paris Conservatoire and the École Normale (1946–9), where his teachers were Boulanger, Honegger, Messiaen and Fournet. From 1947 to 1952 he was a member of the *musique concrète* laboratory, Club d'Essai, and from 1963 to 1971 president and music director of Ars Nova, an orchestra in Paris formed to perform modern music and to practise collective improvisation. The Ars Nova group performed over 100 new works and was especially valuable to *avant-garde* composers because of the flexibility afforded by the technical skills of its individual members. Constant has been particularly interested in the most advanced aspects of 20th-century music: he has commented, 'Our era is one of upheaval. In my opinion, it will produce few works of art. But this upheaval will produce new horizons.' In 1967 he lectured at Stanford University; in 1970, at the International Conductors' Course of the Netherlands Radio at Hilversum, he taught *avant-garde* repertory. He came into prominence as a composer in 1958 when Bernstein performed his *Twenty-four Preludes* for orchestra, and several of his later compositions, *Turner* (1961), *Les Chants de Maldoror* (1962) and *Chaconne et marche militaire* (1968) were widely played. He collaborated for some time with the choreographer Roland Petit; the ballet *In Praise of Folly* was first performed in Paris in 1966 and at La Scala, Milan, in 1967. Another ballet, *Paradise Lost*, was premièred at Covent Garden by Nureyev in 1967, and a mime-drama *Candide* received its first performance by Marceau in 1970 at the Hamburg Opera. Constant has won many awards including the Italia Prize and the Koussevitzky Prize, has been a guest conductor with many orchestras in Europe and North America and was appointed director of the dance at the Paris Opéra, where his first productions were *Hommages à Varèse* (1973) and *Un Jour ou deux* with music by Cage.

Constant's recordings include Debussy's *Le Martyre de Saint-Sébastien* and the Rhapsodies for Clarinet and Saxophone (with Deplus and Deffrayet respectively), Messiaen's *Hymnes*, *L'Ascension* and *Offrandes oubliées*, Varèse's *Amériques* and *Arcana*, and his own *Candide*, *Chaconne et marche militaire* and *Turner* (with the Orchestre National de l'ORTF for Erato), Bancquart's *Concerto* and Nikiprowetzky's *Hommage à Antonio Gaudi* (with the same orchestra for Barclay), Messiaen's *Sept Haï-Kaï*, Xenakis' *Medea*, *Oresteia*, *Polytope* and *Syrmos*, Mihalovici's *Study in Two Parts*, Ohana's *Signs* and *Syllabaire pour Phèdre*, and his own *Septentrion*, *Le Paradis perdu*, *In Praise of Folly* and *Fourteen Stations* (with the Ars Nova Ensemble for Erato) and trumpet concertos by Hummel, Telemann, Tomasi and Jolivet (with Thibaud and the English Chamber Orchestra for DGG).

Conta, Iosif (b. 1924). Born at Birzova, the Romanian conductor Conta studied the violin at an early age, graduated from the Timişoara Academy of Music (1948) and from the Ciprian Porumbescu Conservatory in Bucharest, where his conducting teachers were Silvestri and Georgescu. After experience in England, France and FR Germany, he was appointed artistic director and chief conductor of the Romanian Radio-Television Symphony Orchestra in Bucharest, and has appeared as a guest conductor in Eastern and Western Europe, the USSR, the United States and South America. With the Romanian Radio-Television Orchestra he has recorded for Electrecord Beethoven's Symphony No. 9, Violin Concerto (with Szeryng) and Piano Concertos No. 1 (with Gheorgiu) and No. 5 (with Lupu), Mozart's Piano Concerto K. 488 (with Fotino), Weber's Konzertstück (with Gheorgiu), Bach's *Violin Concerto in E major* (with Szeryng), *Symphonie fantastique*, *Les Préludes*, Wieniawski's Violin Concerto No. 2 (with Voicu), the overture *Leichte Cavallerie*, Brahms' Hungarian Dances Nos 5 and 6 and other popular pieces, accompaniments to recitals of operatic arias, and music by Romanian composers, including Porumbescu's *Ballad* (with Voicu), Varga's *Concerto for Orchestra* and *Liberation Spark*, Jora's *When the Grapes are Ripening*, *Return from the Bottom* and Symphony No. 17, Constantinescu's Triple Concerto, Piano Concerto, Concerto for String Orchestra and Seven Songs (with Graftos), Dumitrescu's Sinfonietta, Concerto for Orchestra and Suite No. 3, Vancea's Concerto for Orchestra, Olah's *The Endless Column*, Tăranu's *Symetries*, Mendelssohn's Symphonie Concertante, Bentoiu's Violin Concerto (with Gheorgiu) and Piano Concerto No. 2 (with Cosma), Enesco's Sinfonia Concertante, *Romanian Poem*, two *Romanian Rhapsodies*, Suite and *Vox Maris*, Ciortea's Concerto for Orchestra and Octet, Bughici's Symphonies Nos 1 and 3 and Dramatic Dialogue for Flute and Orchestra, Capoianu's *Film Variations*, Berger's Violin Concerto (with Constantinescu) and Cello Concerto (with Ilea), Brediceanu's *La seceris*, Andricu's Symphony No. 11, and Gábor's *Sinfonietta* (with the Cluj Philharmonic Orchestra).

Cooper, Emil (1877–1960). Born at Kherson, Russia, Cooper studied at the Odessa Conservatory, was a violin pupil with Hellmesberger in Vienna, and then studied in Moscow under Taneyev and Nikisch. His first appointment was at the Kiev Opera (1900), and later in Moscow he led the first performance there of *Die Meistersinger* and the world première of *Le Coq d'or* (1904). A year later he conducted the Russian première, at the Imperial Opera, of *The Ring*, became conductor of the Zimin opera company in Moscow (1907), conducted Diaghilev's Russian ballet and opera company in Paris (1909) and conducted *Boris Godunov* at Covent Garden, which, according to Rosenthal (*Two Centuries of Opera at Covent Garden*), 'made an impact in London such as had not been experienced since the first performances of *The Ring* and *Tristan und Isolde* in the 1880s.' He also conducted at the Maryinsky Theatre and the Philharmonic Society in Leningrad, but left Russia in 1923 for Paris. He toured South America in 1924, was musical director of the Riga Opera (1925–8), conducted with the Chicago Civic Opera (1929–32), visited Paris, Bordeaux and Milan (1932–6), lived in Monte Carlo (1936–9), returned to the Chicago Civic Opera (1939), conducted at the New York Metropolitan Opera (1944–50), including first performances there of *Khovanshchina* and *Peter Grimes*, and finally was musical director of the Montreal Opera Guild. When in Riga Cooper led some excerpts from *Boris Godunov* on Columbia 78s; later he recorded an abridged version of the same opera, with Ezio Pinza and the Metropolitan Opera Company.

Copland, Aaron (b. 1900). Born in Brooklyn, New York, Copland studied the piano with Victor Wittgenstein and Clarence Adler and composition with Robin Goldmark. He spent three years in Paris where he was a student of Nadia Boulanger, and after his return to New York received a Guggenheim Memorial Fellowship which gave him the opportunity to have another two years in Europe (1925–7). He took up teaching and lecturing at the School for Social Research in New York (1927–37) and collaborated with Sessions in a series of concerts to promote the music of contemporary composers (1928–31). The RCA Victor Company gave him an award in 1930 for his *Dance Symphony*; he performed his Piano Concerto with major US orchestras, toured Latin America as lecturer and pianist, lectured at Harvard University (1951–2) and wrote books and articles about music. Copland's influence on younger American composers, such as Bernstein, was at first considerable, but when they turned to the twelve-tone system it soon diminished. His own compositions include symphonies, concertos, film scores, ballets, theatre pieces, songs and other music, much of which is widely performed in the US and to a limited extent overseas. After attempting unsuccessfully to write in the twelve-tone system himself, he abandoned composition and turned to conducting. In his own words (*High Fidelity*, November 1970, p. 63): 'An elderly and wise woman once gave me some excellent advice. "Aaron," she said, "it is very important as you get older to engage in activity that you didn't engage in when you were young, so that you are not continually competing with yourself as a young man.' The conductor's baton was my answer to the problem. Conducting, as everyone knows, is a bug, and once you are bitten, it is the very devil to get rid of. What makes it worse is the fact that you get better at it all the time – more expert in rehearsing, more adept at gesture, more relaxed in performance. By now [1970] I have worked with more than 50 symphony organisations in countries around the world.'

Copland has recorded as conductor a considerable part of his own music. Included have been the *Short Symphony*, the *Dance Symphony*, *Statements*, *Two Pieces for String Orchestra*, *Billy the Kid*, *An Outdoor Overture*, *Quiet City*, *Our Town*, *Rodeo*, *Music for a Great City*, *Fanfare for the Common Man*, *Appalachian Spring*, *Lincoln Portrait*, *John Henry*, *Letter from Home*, *Down a Country Lane*, *Danzón Cubano* and *Dance Panels* (with the London Symphony Orchestra, for CBS), the Piano Concerto (with Smit and the Rome Symphony Orchestra for Concert Hall, with Wild and the Symphony of the Air for Vanguard and also with himself as soloist and with Bernstein and the New York Philharmonic Orchestra for CBS), the Symphony No. 3, *Statements* and *Billy the Kid* (with the London Symphony Orchestra for Everest), *Lark*, *Las Agachadas* and *In the Beginning* (with the New England Conservatory Chorus for CBS), *Appalachian Spring* and a suite from *The Tender Land* (with the Boston Symphony Orchestra for RCA), an abridged version of *The Tender Land* (with the New York Philharmonic Orchestra *et al.* for CBS), the Clarinet Concerto (with Goodman and the Columbia String Orchestra, and later with the Columbia Symphony Strings for CBS), *Old American Songs* Sets I and II (with Warfield and the Columbia Symphony Orchestra for CBS), *Latin American Sketches*, *El Salón México*, *The Red Pony* and some other film music (with the New Philharmonia Orchestra for CBS). He has also recorded some of his own music as a pianist, in addition to the Piano Concerto, mentioned above.

Coppola, Anton (b. 1917). Born in New York, Coppola studied with Papi, Guerrieri, Breisach and Giannini, made his debut as a conductor at Brooklyn in 1941, was an oboist at the Radio City Music Hall, New York, has been active as a conductor of opera with many companies in the United States, and is guest conductor of the Manhattan School of Music Orchestra. For Desto he has recorded Beeson's *Lizzie Borden*, with the New York City Opera Company.

Coppola, Piero (1888–1971). Born in Milan to parents who were well-known singers, Coppola gave piano recitals at the age of eleven, studied piano and composition at the Milan Conservatory and commenced his career as chorus-master at the Teatro Regio in Turin in 1912. He soon won a reputation as a conductor of both opera and symphonic music and was active in Milan, Brussels, Paris, London and Oslo. In 1912 he attracted attention in Brussels by leading Puccini's *La fanciulla del West*, repeating the performance in Florence. Coming to London in 1914 he became artistic director of HMV, but settled in Paris in 1920, where he was prominent as a conductor and as a protagonist of French composers and modern music in general. He was amongst the first to recognise Poulenc and Prokofiev, and brought Prokofiev to London to record his Piano Concerto No. 3, conducting the accompaniment himself. A prolific composer in his early years, he wrote (*inter alia*) operas, symphonies and concertos, reputedly of great length. HMV engaged him after World War I as its house conductor for their Paris studios, a position he retained until 1940. He recorded profusely during this period, mostly with the Paris Conservatoire Orchestra, and although an Italian his speciality was French music, in which he had a considerable talent for capturing the idiom. He was meticulous in obeying the composer's directions and in establishing the feeling and atmosphere of a piece. In an appreciation of him written just after his death, Robert Layton wrote (The Gramophone, May 1971, p. 1773) that with Coppola 'there was no attempt to project his personality on to the composer he conducted; like many of the great conductors of the period, he trusted the composer to speak for himself and his readings are thus free from affectation. His account of Debussy's *Iberia* still strikes me as having more atmosphere, delicacy and flair than most of the readings at present in the catalogue. He has just the right degree of rubato in the middle movement, just the right feeling for texture and colour, and a genuine warmth and spontaneity.'

Before World II, all Coppola's recordings were made for HMV, and included Handel's Organ Concerto Op. 4 No. 6, an arrangement of the Suite No. 11 in D minor, and Haydn's Harpischord Concertos in D and F (with Roesgen-Champion), Mozart's Flute Concerto K. 314 (with Moyse) and Flute and Harp Concerto (with Moyse and Laskine), Schumann's Symphony No. 3, Franck's *Psyché* and *Rédemption*, an incomplete *La Damnation de Faust* (with the Pasdeloup Orchestra *et al.*), *Carmen* (with the Opéra-Comique Orchestra *et al.*), Saint-Saëns' Symphony No. 3, *Phaéton*, and two movements from the *Suite algérienne*, Debussy's *La Mer*, *Nocturnes*, *Iberia*, *Printemps*, *Children's Corner*, excerpts from *Le Martyre de Saint-Sébastien* and *Pelléas et Mélisande*, *La Damoiselle élue* (with soloists and the Pasdeloup Orchestra), Rhapsody for Clarinet and Orchestra (with Hamelin), Rhapsody for Saxophone and Orchestra (with Viard), *Petite Suite* (arr. Busser), and arrangements by Molinari of *L'Isle joyeuse* and *Cloches à travers les feuilles*, Ravel's *Boléro*, *Rapsodie espagnole*, *Daphnis et Chloé* Suite No. 1, Fox-trot from *L'Enfant et les sortilèges*, *Ma Mère l'Oye*, *Pavane pour une infante défunte*, *Le Tombeau de Couperin*, *Valses nobles et sentimentales* and *Don Quixote* (with Singher), Dukas' *La Péri*, Massenet's *Scènes alsaciennes* (with the London Symphony Orchestra), d'Indy's *Istar Variations*, Chausson's *Symphony in B flat*, Roussel's *Suite in F*, and Danse des Nymphes from *La Naissance de la lyre*, Honegger's *Rugby* and *Pacific 231*, Lalo's *Namouna* Suite No. 1 and overture to *Le Roi d'Ys* (with the London Symphony Orchestra), Prokofiev's Piano Concerto No. 3 (with the composer and the London Symphony Orchestra), Falla's *Nights in the Gardens of Spain* (with van Barentzen), Balakirev's *Tamar*, the Final Scene (with Marjorie Lawrence) and excerpts from Strauss's *Salome*, Respighi's *Pini di Roma*, Rimsky-Korsakov's *Antar Symphony* and the overture and an aria from Reyer's *Sigurd* (with Marjorie Lawrence). Except where indicated, these recordings were with the Paris Conservatoire Orchestra or other, unidentified, orchestras. After World War II, Decca recorded Coppola in Schumann's Symphony No. 1 (with the National Symphony Orchestra) and Grieg's *Symphonic Dances* (with the London Symphony Orchestra). He also played the piano in a four-piano concerto of Vivaldi, conducted by Bret.

Corboz, Michel (b. 1934). Born in Fribourg, Corboz was a member of the local church choir, and first came into contact with Monteverdi through Nadia Boulanger's 78 r.p.m. records. He studied at the Fribourg Conservatory, and in 1953 became choirmaster at Notre Dame at Lausanne, where he also led the French choral group A Coeur Joie. He teaches at the Conservatoire at La Chaux-de-Fonds, and in 1968 founded and conducted the Lausanne Vocal Ensemble, which is made up of fifteen professional singers, and soon became famous for the standard of its performances. Other choral groups he conducts are the choir at Lausanne University and the Gulbenkian Foundation Choir at Lisbon. His first records with the Lausanne Vocal Ensemble, for Erato, were of masses of Monteverdi and Scarlatti and some pieces by Ingegneri; then in 1966 appeared Monteverdi's *Vespro della beata Vergine* and *La favola d'Orfeo*, followed by a six-disc collection of the church music of Monteverdi, *Selva morale e spirituale*, and a selection of Monteverdi's madrigals, Delalande's *De Profundis*, Bach's *Magnificat*, *Mass in B minor*, and short masses, G. Gabrieli's *Sacrae Symphoniae* (Volume II), Goudimel's Mass and Psalms, Bassano's Seven Psalms and Chansons and Madrigals of the Renaissance, and Vivaldi's *Gloria*, *Kyrie* and *Credo*. More recently the Ensemble has recorded Delalande's *Regina Coeli*, Bach's *St John Passion*, more sacred music of Vivaldi, Haydn's Mass No. 10, motets by Scarlatti, and Bach's Cantatas Nos 11, 58, 78 and 198.

With the Choir and Orchestra of the Gulbenkian Foundation at Lisbon, Corboz has recorded, also for Erato, the Bach's Harpischord Concertos BWV 1052, 1055 and 1056 (with Maria-José Pires), Carissimi's *Jephte*, *Ezechias*, *Abraham and Isaac*, and *Tolle Sponsa*, Charpentier's *Messe pour les trépassés* and *Miserere des Jésuites*, Gabrieli's *Sacrae Symphoniae* (Volume I), Mozart's *Requiem* and Fauré's *Requiem*. The Monteverdi *Vespro* was awarded Le Grand Prix du Disque International, and later *Orfeo* gained Corboz an Académie du Disque Français Grand Prix, the Schallplattenpreis, the Dutch Edison Award, the Grand Prix des Discophiles, and a Japanese Golden Disc Prize. His recordings, particularly the Monteverdi works, are examples of Corboz's profound understanding of the composer's music, as well as the high standard of the Lausanne Vocal Ensemble. Many of the records have been released in the United States by Musical Heritage Society.

Cornut, Guy (b. 1937). Born in Lyon, France, Cornut first studied medicine and in 1952 made his debut as a conductor with a choir at the Lyon University. He founded L'Ensemble Vocal de Lyon (1962) and has since conducted it in a repertoire of Renaissance and baroque music, and French music of the 17th and 18th centuries. Between 1967 and 1971 the Ensemble collaborated with Auriacombe and the Toulouse Chamber Orchestra in performing the major works of Bach, and since 1973 the Ensemble has performed with the Lyon Orchestra under Baudo. With the Ensemble and the Ensemble de Musique Ancienne de Lyon, Cornut has recorded for Erato Gastoldi's *Balleti*, Delalande's *De Profundis*, Campra's *Messe*, Corrette's *Laudate Dominum*, Desmaret's *Mystères de notre Seigneur Jésus Christ*, Foggia's *La Passion de notre Seigneur Jésus Christ* and Giay's *Troisième Leçon du Vendredi Saint*.

Cortot, Alfred (1877–1962). Born in Nyon, Switzerland, of French parents, Cortot came to France as a child, studied at the Paris Conservatoire, gained a brilliant reputation in Paris for his performances of the Beethoven concertos, then toured Europe as a piano virtuoso. In 1898 he went to Bayreuth where he became a repetiteur at the festivals, assisting Mottl and Richter, returned to Paris in 1901 and founded the Association des Concerts Alfred Cortot, and enthusiastically promoted the music of Wagner. In 1902 he made his debut as a conductor, gave the first performances in France of *Parsifal*, *Götterdämmerung*, Brahms' *Ein deutsches Requiem*, Beethoven's *Missa Solemnis* and Liszt's *The Legend of Saint Elizabeth*, and conducted many new and unpublished works of the French composers of the day. He was conductor of the Concerts Populaires at Lille (1904–08), in 1905 formed the internationally famous trio with Casals and Thibaud, was professor of piano at the Paris Conservatoire (1907–18) and during World War I was chief of the Ministry of Public Instruction and Fine Arts. In those years he devoted himself to the intensive study of the piano, to emerge as the foremost French pianist of his time; he eventually gave up conducting altogether in favour of a career as a concert virtuoso. Celebrated as one of the greatest interpreters of Chopin and the romantic piano literature, he toured Europe and the United States. During World War II he was appointed to an official music position under the Nazi occupation, and after the war was forbidden to play in France for a period, but continued to play in Germany. His piano recordings, both as soloist and as a member of the Cortot-Thibaud-Casals trio have been constantly revived; some, such as the Schubert *Trio in B flat*, are among the greatest chamber music recordings ever made. But as a conductor his records were limited to a set of the *Brandenburg Concertos* which he completed with the École Normale Orchestra in the early 1930s, and Brahms' Double Concerto, in which he conducted the Casals Orchestra of Barcelona, with Casals and Thibaud the soloists (see Casals).

Corwin, George (b. 1929). Born in Goshen, New York, Corwin graduated as a Doctor in Musical Arts; he has been a teacher and professor at the Eastman School of Music, Rochester, at Ball State University in Indiana, and at the University of Victoria, British Columbia. With the Ball State Instrumental

Ensemble and Chorus he recorded Hood's *Pange Lingua* and *Puer nobis nascitur*, Knight's *Miracles* and Logan's *Songs of Our Time* (for Golden Crest).

Costa, Othmar (b. 1928). Born in St Jakob, Defereggen, Austria, Costa studied at Innsbruck and at the Hochschule für Musik in Vienna, where his teachers included Swarowsky for conducting. He was first a school teachèr, and has been conductor of the Walther von der Vogelweide Chamber Choir at Innsbruck (since 1961) and conductor of the Innsbruck Chamber Orchestra (since 1969). He has recorded Vaňhal's Bassoon Concerto (with Streicher) and songs by Wolkenstein (with soloists, and the Innsbruck Chamber Orchestra for Telefunken), and Lechner's Mass No. 3 and *St John Passion* (with the Walther von der Vogelweide Chamber Choir and the Collegium Pro Musica, for Telefunken).

Cossetto, Emil (b. 1918). Born in Trieste, Cossetto studied conducting at the Academy of Music in Zagreb and was conductor of the Radio Choir and Lado Ensemble in Zagreb, the Yugoslav National Army Symphony Orchestra in Belgrade, and of the Moša Pijade Cultural and Folkloric Association in Zagreb. For Jugoton he recorded motets by Lukačić, Tajčević's *Četiri Duhovna Stiha* and Bersa's *Sunčana Polja*, with the Cultural and Folkloric Association Chorus, and the Slovenian Philharmonic Orchestra.

Cotte, Roger (b. 1921). Born at Clamart near Paris, Cotte studied at the Paris Conservatoire under Martenot and Chailley, was musical director of a student theatrical ensemble and also studied at the Uppsala University, Sweden. He became director of the Laon Academy for Ancient Music and the producer for ancient music for Radio-Télévision Française. He has directed music for radio and records, especially of the composers Rousseau, Blavet, Corrette, Campra, Beaujoyeul and Dumont, and made a series of records with the title *Musiciens Francs-Maçons*. His published works include a general discography of J. S. Bach (1951), and the studies *Louis XIII Musician* (1952), *Musicians in the History of Freemasonry* (1951) and *Music in the Encyclopedia* (1951). In addition to being leader of the Paris Ancient Instruments Ensemble, he is a recorder virtuoso, an expert on French composers who emigrated to Sweden, and organist at the Swedish Church in Paris (since 1960). Arion (France) recorded him directing the Paris Ancient Instruments Ensemble *et al.* in a collection of French dances of the Renaissance (which was also issued in the United Stated by Nonesuch), a disc of concertos by Handel, Hasse and Schröter, and Rousseau's opera *Le Devin du village*.

Couraud, Marcel (b. 1912). Born in Limoges, France, Couraud studied at the École Normale, came under the influence of Nadia Boulanger, and was an organ student with Marchal. The outbreak of World War II interrupted his studies, and after the fall of France he was a prisoner-of-war for several months. In 1941 he returned to Limoges, and in 1945 formed the Marcel Couraud Vocal Ensemble, which soon became celebrated for its artistry and musicianship. His repertoire with his Ensemble ranged from Bach to Jolivet and Messiaen, but his sympathies are such that he is equally at home with the operettas of Offenbach. In 1954 he undertook the direction of the Stuttgart Choral and Symphonic Ensemble, has toured extensively in Europe, and has taken part in festivals in Bordeaux, Strasbourg, Vienna and Edinburgh. He became the director of the Choir of the French Radio (1967), and has directed for the French Radio a series of 'forgotten operas'.

Couraud's recordings divide themselves into several parts. Of baroque and pre-baroque music, he recorded vocal music of Josquin and Monteverdi in 78s for Discophiles Français, and, on LP, Monteverdi's Madrigals, Books 1, 4 and parts of 5 and 6 (with the Marcel Couraud Vocal Ensemble for Haydn Society), Bach's *Brandenburg Concertos*, *Magnificat*, *Easter Oratorio*, and Cantatas Nos 11, 31 and 65 (with the Stuttgart Baroque Ensemble *et al.* for Philips), Bach's Motets (with the Stuttgart Vocal Ensemble *et al.* for Decca, US), Vivaldi's *The Four Seasons* (with the Stuttgart Soloists for Philips, and the Stuttgart Chamber Orchestra for Mercury), Vivaldi's *Gloria*, *O qui coeli terraeque* and *Stabat Mater* (with the Stuttgart Pro Musica Orchestra *et al.* for Vox), excerpts from Catel's *L'Auberge de Bagnères* (with the Jean-François Paillard Chamber Orchestra for Erato), Couperin's *Les Nations* (with the Stuttgart Baroque Ensemble for Mercury), Rameau's *Concerts en sextuor* (with the Stuttgart Soloists for Philips), *Pygmalion* and excerpts from *Les Indes galantes* (with the Lamoureux Orchestra *et al.* for DGG-Archiv), Delalande's *De Profundis* (with the Stuttgart Pro Musica *et al.* for Vox), K. Stamitz's Sinfonia concertante (with the Stuttgart Soloists for Vox), Lully's *Dies Irae* and *Psalm 50* (with the Lamoureux Orchestra *et al.* for DGG-Archiv), Mozart's *Exsultate jubilate* and *Benedictus sit Deus* (with Sailer and the Stuttgart Pro Musica for Vox), and J. C. Bach's Harp concerto (with Challen and the Antiqua Musica Orchestra for Philips).

He also recorded discs of highlights from operas with the Karlsruhe Opera Company for Philips; there were *William Tell*, *Carmen*, *Werther*, *Faust* and *La Juive*. For Erato there were also the Offenbach operettas *Ba-ta-clan* (with the Jean-François Paillard Orchestra *et al.*), and *Les Bavards* (with the ORTF Orchestra *et al.*), and for Turnabout Boieldieu's *La Tante Aurore* (with the ORTF Orchestra *et al.*). He recorded, in addition, a suite from *Carmen* and the two *L'Arlésienne* suites (with the Bamberg Symphony Orchestra for Vox), and the overture to Méhul's *Les deux aveugles de Tolède* (with the Jean-François Paillard Orchestra for Erato).

Of 20th-century music, Couraud recorded Messiaen's *Cinq Rechants* and *Trois petites liturgies de la présence divine*, Xenakis' *Nuits* and Penderecki's *Stabat Mater* (with the ORTF Chorus *et al.* for Erato), Amy's *Récitatif, Air et Variation*, Jolas' *Sonate à douze*, Mâche's *Danaé*, and Malec's *Dodécaméron* (with the ORTF Chorus *et al.* for ORTF). Earlier, on 78s, he had recorded Debussy's *Chansons de Charles d'Orléans*, Ravel's *Trois Chansons*, and Milhaud's *Cantate des deux cités* and *Cantate de la guerre* (with Joachim and a chorus, for Discophiles Français).

Cowen, Sir Frederic (1852–1935). Born in Kingston, Jamaica, Cowen was brought to England as a child to study with Benedict and Goss, and later studied at Leipzig (1865–6) and Berlin (1867–8). He was conductor of the London Philharmonic Society (1888–92 and 1900–07), of the Liverpool Philharmonic Society (1896–1913), succeeded Hallé at Manchester (1896–99), conducted the Handel Triennial Festivals at the Crystal Palace (1903–12) and the Cardiff Festival (1902–10), and was knighted in 1911. His many compositions included operas, symphonies, orchestral, choral, chamber music and songs, and his publications included a glossary of musical terms with the title *Music as She is Wrote* (London, 1915), and biographies of Haydn, Mozart, Mendelssohn and Rossini. On several early HMV discs, issued in 1915, he conducted an orchestra in dances from his suites *Old English Dances* and *The Language of Flowers*.

Cox, Ainslee (b. 1936) A native of Texas, Cox studied composition and conducting at the University of Texas, performed professionally as a singer, timpanist and accompanist, and made his debut as a conductor at Carnegie Hall in New York with Stokowski's American Symphony Orchestra in 1967. He was assistant to Stokowski (1968–72), to Boulez and Bernstein with the New York Philharmonic Orchestra, and since 1973 has been musical director of the Oklahoma Symphony Orchestra. At Oklahoma he has received the award of the American Society of Composers, Authors and Publishers for his work in presenting contemporary music by both American and European composers. He is also well known as a band conductor and is co-conductor of the Goldman Band in New York City. His recordings include Elgar's *Serenade in E minor* (with the Royal Philharmonic Orchestra for Decca) which was coupled with Stokowski's performance of the *Enigma Variations* with the Czech Philharmonic Orchestra, Prokofiev's Piano concertos Nos 2 and 3 and Sgambati's Piano Concerto (with Bolet and the Nuremberg Symphony Orchestra for Colosseum).

Craft, Robert (b. 1923). Born at Kingston, New York, and educated at the Juilliard School, Craft had at the age of sixteen heard Stravinsky conduct *Le Sacre du printemps* and soon afterwards Schoenberg direct *Pierrot Lunaire*. These he regards as the most important experiences in his life, an opinion later borne out by his association with Stravinsky from 1949 until the latter's death in 1971, and by his series of recordings of Schoenberg, Berg and Webern. In 1949 Craft and others founded the Chamber Art Society to present concerts in New York Town Hall, and contacted Stravinsky concerning the orchestral parts of the *Symphonies of Wind Instruments*. Stravinsky replied that he was preparing a new version and would like to conduct it himself, without a fee. This he did, and then asked Craft to assist him prepare a performance of *Orpheus* at the New York City Ballet. So commenced Craft's long and productive collaboration with Stravinsky, which (among other things) brought Stravinsky to a more sympathetic appreciation of twelve-tone music. Craft toured the world with Stravinsky, shared the podium, rehearsed the orchestras which Stravinsky then conducted at the concerts themselves, prepared the orchestras and other musical forces for CBS's definitive Stravinsky edition, in which the composer appears on the label as conductor, and produced six volumes of dialogues and observations with and by Stravinsky, culminating in his *Stravinsky: Chronicle of a Friendship* (1972).

This intimate involvement with the great composer has evoked much criticism and speculation as to where Craft ends and Stravinsky begins, in the records as well as the books. Craft himself has made it clear that from two-thirds to three-quarters of the work in preparing a Stravinsky performance was his own: he was responsible for every detail, while Stravinsky would intervene for some of the final decisions about tempi or phrasing. Lillian Libman, Stravinsky's personal secretary, is more specific, saying (in *And Music at the Close; Stravinsky's Last Years* (1972)) that parts of the final performances on the records were frequently taken from Craft's rehearsal tapes, and, in any event, Stravinsky conducted an orchestra at the official takes rehearsed according to Craft's tempi and interpretation, often different from the composer's. According to Libman, Stravinsky did not listen to playbacks and was not involved in editing the final recorded performance, but he never allowed the release of a record containing none of his takes. He forbade the release of some of the records on these grounds, and in the case of the *Mass*, whose release he stopped, he was not even in the studio when most of the final performance was taped. Similar points have been made about the books of the conservations and records of travels, where factual errors have been detected; Craft has stated, somewhat ambiguously, 'Don't think that what Stravinsky says in print isn't really what he wants to say.' (*High Fidelity*, July 1964, p. 25.)

There are two Crafts other than the one the public identifies with Stravinsky. The first is the pioneer recorder for CBS of the music of Weber, Berg and Schoenberg. The Webern set was the first to appear and was then indispensable for anyone interested in 20th-century music; Webern's acceptance is now sufficiently universal for even von Karajan and the Berlin Philharmonic Orchestra to perform and record some of his music. With Schoenberg, Craft had much more music to cover; the project was only partly achieved, and even then it was only possible because of the commercial success of the Stravinsky series. The performances were variable in quality and some have been superseded by more recent recordings by conductors such as Boulez and Atherton, but this reflects no discredit on Craft, whose efforts have been as responsible for the current interest in the Second Viennese School as some more influential advocates. In addition, he has recorded other 20th-century music: Boulez's *Le Marteau sans maître*, Stockhausen's *Zeitmesse No. 5*, Antheil's *Ballet mécanique*, Debussy's *Chansons de Bilitis*, Hindemith's *Hérodiade*, and Varèse's *Offrandes*, *Arcana*, *Déserts*, *Octandre*, *Ionisation*, *Intégrales*, *Hyperprisme* and *Densité 21.5* (with various orchestras and groups, for CBS). There are also some discs of Stravinsky unequivocally attributable to him: *Renard* and the *Suite No. 1* (with the New York Chamber Orchestra), *Capriccio* (with Entremont and the Columbia Symphony Orchestra) and *Les Noces* (with the Gregg Smith Singers and Columbia Ensemble). One curiosity among the Schoenberg recordings is Schoenberg's orchestration of Brahms' Piano Quartet No. 1 Op. 25 (with the Chicago Symphony Orchestra); this version has not been otherwise recorded, and was regarded by Klemperer as much more beautiful than the original.

The other Craft is the regular orchestral conductor with an interest in performing music in the everyday repertoire and with a range of enthusiasms from composers of the late Renaissance through the 19th-century romantics and on to the moderns with whom he is readily associated. Craft is fundamentally intellectual in his approach to music; he is widely read, highly articulate and absorbed in artistic and aesthetic problems. His rehearsal technique reflects these attitudes in its emphasis on precision and balance rather than on spontaneity and lyrical expressiveness. His remaining records include Bach's Cantatas Nos 131 and 198, Mozart's Serenade K. 361, and discs of the music of Schütz and Gesualdo. Although a controversial figure, he has made an immense contribution to recorded music.

Cree, Edgar (b. 1914). Born in Sheffield, Cree was appointed assistant organist at Peterborough Cathedral at the age of seventeen, won an organ scholarship to King's College, Cambridge, and studied with Vaughan Williams at the Royal College of Music. He became a junior conductor with the BBC, served as a navigator and pilot with the RAF in World War II, then was appointed conductor of the symphony orchestra of the South African Broadcasting Corporation where he remained for 28 years. In South Africa he has been a member of the Performing Arts Board, a guest conductor with local orchestras, and received the first honorary degree of Doctor of Music from the University of Natal, and has toured extensively in Europe. Cree recorded Britten's *Soirées musicales* and *Matinées musicales* (with the New Symphony Orchestra for Decca; first issued in 1964 and still in the catalogue), operatic recitals by Joyce Barker and Bruce Martin (with the Pro Arte orchestra for EMI) and Mimi Goertse (with the SABC National Orchestra for Bell).

Cristescu, Mircea (b. 1928). Born in Brasov, Romania, Cristescu studied the violin as a child, and graduated at the Ciprian Porumbescu Conservatory at Bucharest (1954) where he was a pupil of Silvestri. He was appointed conductor of the Bucharest Symphony Orchestra (1957) and of the George Enesco Philharmonic Orchestra (1962), was one of the founders and is conductor of the Cluj-Napoca Chamber Orchestra, and has toured in Britain, France, FR Germany and other European countries, the USSR and the United States. His repertoire extends from the baroque to Boulez; he has impressed with his musicianship, undemonstrative technique and his kinship with Silvestri in matters of style. His recordings for Electrecord include Haydn's Symphonies Nos 94 and 101, Mozart's Serenade K. 250, Vivaldi's *The Four Seasons*, Bartók's *Divertimento* and Britten's *Variations on a Theme of Frank Bridge* (with the Cluj-Napoca Chamber Orchestra), *Eine kleine Nachtmusik*, the Mozart Violin Concerto K. 268 (with Constantinescu), Tchaikovsky's *Serenade in C major*, Respighi's *Gli uccelli*, Dragoi's *Peasant Divertissement* and Constantinescu's *Concerto for String Orchestra* (with the Budapest Chamber Orchestra), Vieru's Cello Concerto (with Orlov) and Capoianu's *Divertimento* (with the Romanian Philharmonic Orchestra), the Mozart Clarinet Concerto (with Popa) and Flute and Harp Concerto (with Alexandru and Corjus, and the George Enesco Philharmonic Orchestra), *El amor brujo*, *Capriccio espagnol*, *España*, Rachmaninov's *Rhapsody on a Theme of Paganini* (with Li-Min-Tchan), Negrea's *Izbuc*, and *Through the Romanian Western Mountains*, Vieru's *Concerto for Orchestra*, Dimitrescu's Suite No. 3 and Feldman's Flute Concerto (with Alexandru, and with the Romanian Film Symphony Orchestra), Mozart's Piano Concerto K. 537 (with Halmos), a Mozart aria recital (with Petrescu), Brahms' Symphony No. 3, Stroe's *Burlesque* overture, Tarami's *Sequences*, Popovici's *Concerto for Orchestra*, Constantinescu's Violin Concerto (with Ruha), Silvestri's *Three Pieces for String Orchestra*, concertos by Dittersdorf, Absil's *Romanian Rhapsody* and Makos' Concertante Symphony (with the Cluj Philharmonic Orchestra), Absil's *Les Chants du mort* (with the Romanian Radio Orchestra *et al.*), Weber's Clarinet Concertos Nos 1 and 2 and Concertino (with Popa), Bruch's Violin Concerto No. 1 and Glazunov's Violin Concerto (with Marcovici) and Berger's Symphony No. 6 (with the Bucharest Philharmonic Orchestra).

Cruchon, Pierre (b. 1908). Born in Brioux, France, Cruchon was music director of the Lyon Opera (1935–67), chief conductor at Marseille (from 1951), conductor at the Paris Opéra-Comique, also appeared with major French orchestras and is the author of a book about the oboe. He recorded excerpts from *La Damnation de Faust* (with the Pasdeloup Orchestra *et al.* for Pléiade) and excerpts from Massé's *Les Noces de Jeanette* (with the Paris Opéra-comique Orchestra *et al.* for EMI).

Crumb, George (b. 1929). Born at Charleston, West Virginia, Crumb was educated at the Mason College of Music, at the Universities of Illinois and Michigan and at the Hochschule für Musik, Berlin, and has been professor of composition at the University of Pennsylvania. He was awarded the Pulitzer prize in 1968 for his *Echoes of Time and the River* and the Koussevitzky International Recording Award in 1971. He has directed recordings of his compositions *Night Music I* (for Composers Recordings), and *The Voice of the Whale* and *The Night of the Four Moons* (for Columbia US).

Csányi, László (b. 1925). The Hungarian Csányi studied with Vásárhelyi at the Franz Liszt Academy at Budapest, graduated as a choral conductor in 1950, and has been leader of the famous Children's Chorus of the Hungarian Radio. With the chorus and the Hungarian Radio and Television Orchestra he recorded Süssmayr's *Das Namensfest*, for Hungaroton.

Cundell, Edric (1893–1961). Born in London and educated at Trinity College of Music, Cundell was a horn player at Covent Garden under Nikisch, taught at Trinity College (1920–37), conducted the Westminster Choral Society (1920) and the London Stock Exchange Orchestra (1924) and founded the Edric Cundell Chamber Orchestra (1935). He succeeded Ronald as principal of the Guildhall School of Music (1938–59), was chairman of the music panel of the Arts Council, and received the CBE (1938). He composed symphonic, concerted, choral and chamber music, won the Hammond Prize for chamber music (1933), and was a guest conductor with the Sadler's Wells Opera Company and with the major London orchestras. For Decca he directed the New Symphony Orchestra with Katin in Tchaikovsky's Piano Concerto No. 1, in an early mono LP recording.

Currie, John (b. 1934). Born in Prestwick, Currie was educated at the Royal Scottish Academy of Music and at the Glasgow University. He has been a lecturer in the Department of music, Glasgow University (1964–71), director of music at Leicester University (since 1971) and chorus-master of the Scottish National Orchestra Chorus (since 1965), and music critic for *The Scotsman* (since 1962). His compositions include a song cycle, film and incidental music and *Inventions for Audience and Orchestra*. La Guilde Internationale du Disque recorded him conducting Handel's *Israel in Egypt* (with the Israel Symphony Orchestra *et al.*, also issued by Concert Hall), and Mozart's *Litaniae Lauretanae* (with the John Currie Singers).

Czajkowski, Renard (b. 1934). After graduating from the State High School of Music in Katowice in 1963, Czajkowski won first prize at a conducting competition at Katowice (1964) and took second place at the International Conducting Competition at Brussels (1967). He has conducted the leading Polish orchestras, participated in festivals at Poznań and Warsaw, conducted in Brussels and Paris, and is now artistic director and conductor of the Poznań Philharmonic Orchestra. For the Polish Record Company he recorded Baird's music-drama *Tomorrow* (with the Poznań Philharmonic Orchestra *et al.*).

Cziffra, György, Jr. (b. 1943). Born in Budapest, the son of the piano virtuoso of the same name, Cziffra entered the Budapest Conservatory at the age of twelve, but in 1956 left Hungary for France with his parents. He continued his piano studies with Cortot at the École Normale and studied conducting at the Paris Conservatoire. He then conducted the Radio Luxembourg Orchestra in programmes of contemporary music, conducted other orchestras in France, Italy, Switzerland, Spain, Belgium, Japan and FR Germany, and in 1966 established an annual festival at the Chaise-Dieu Abbey. Composers prominent in his repertoire are Debussy, Ravel, Roussel, Bartók and Hindemith. Cziffra made records accompanying his father in Franck's *Symphonic Variations* Grieg's Piano Concerto (with the Budapest Philharmonic Orchestra), Chopin's Piano Concerto No. 1 (with the Monte Carlo National Opera Orchestra), and the two Liszt Piano Concertos, the *Hungarian Fantasia* and *Totentanz*, and Rachmaninov's Piano Concerto No. 2 (with the Orchestre de Paris), with several short pieces by Mendelssohn and Bizet as make-weights for the disc with the Rachmaninov concerto. In Europe these records have been issued by EMI and in the United States by Connoisseur Society.

Czyż, Henryk (b. 1923). Born at Grudziadz, Poland, Czyż studied law and philosophy at the Copernicus University at Torun, and then at the State Academy of Music at Poznań he studied conducting with Bierdiajew and composition with Szeligowski. He started his career as a conductor at Poznań Opera House, became second conductor to Fitelberg with the Polish Radio National Symphony Orchestra at Katowice (until 1957), chief conductor of the Łódź Philharmonic Orchestra (1957–62), taught conducting at the State Academy of Music at Kraków (1962–6), was artistic director and first conductor of the Kraków Philharmonic Orchestra (1962–8), general music director at Düsseldorf (1968–71) and artistic director of the Łódź Philharmonic Orchestra (since 1968). He has toured in Europe, North and South America and has been a frequent conductor of the Berlin and Leningrad Philharmonic Orchestras. His compositions include symphonic, chamber and film music, as well as several operas.

Czyż has recorded with the Polish Record Company Szymanowski's Symphony No. 2, Fitelberg's arrangement of the *Prelude in B flat minor* and excerpts from *King Roger*, Beethoven's Symphony No. 5 and Penderecki's *Passion According to St Luke*, *Dies Irae*, *Polymorphia* and *De natura sonoris*. These latter performances were with the Kraków Philharmonic Orchestra and were released in Western Europe and the United States by Philips; in the US, RCA issued another performance of the *Passion According to St Luke* in which Czyż directs the Cologne Radio Symphony Orchestra, with the same four soloists as on the Philips disc. Other recordings by Czyż include *An American in Paris* for Helidor (DGG), and Schumann's oratorio *Das Paradies und die Peri* (with the Düsseldorf Chorus and Symphony Orchestra *et al.* for EMI).

D

Daetwyler, Jean (b. 1907). Born in Basel, Daetwyler studied in Paris at the Schola Cantorum and the École César Franck (1927–38), was a student of d'Indy, de Lioncourt, Bertelin and de Valois, returned to Switzerland, became a professor at the Sion Conservatoire and composed numerous works, many of which he has directed himself. Of his compositions he has recorded the *Ski Symphony* (with the Lausanne Chamber Orchestra *et al.* for Philips), *Alpine Symphony* (with the Lucerne German Music Society Orchestra for Philips), Concerto for Alpine Horn (with Molnar and the Lucerne City Orchestra for Évasion), *Messe valaisanne* (with Varone and a choral and instrumental ensemble for Évasion), and *Requiem for the Atomic Era*, Violin Concerto, Concerto for Strings and Percussion and Three Motets (with the Lausanne Chamber Orchestra *et al.* for Évasion).

Dahinden, Clemens (b. 1912). Born in Altdorf, Switzerland, Dahinden studied at the Zürich University and Conservatory, then was a violin pupil with Carl Flesch in Germany and in London. He became second concertmaster of the Winterthur Symphony Orchestra (1934), studied conducting with Scherchen, was second violin in the Winterthur String Quartet (1939), lectured at the Winterthur Conservatory, and was appointed conductor of the Winterthur Symphony Orchestra (1950). He recorded for La Guilde Internationale du Disque with, but for some exceptions, the Winterthur Symphony Orchestra, and these records were released on various labels such as Westminster, Concert Hall and Musical Masterpieces. Included were Bach's Suites Nos 1 and 2 (with Graf, flute), Harpischord Concertos Nos 1 and 5 (with Johannesen), *Two-Harpsichord Concerto in C major* (with Andreae and Sack) and Oboe and Violin Concerto (with Parolari and Rybar), Handel's Concerti Grossi Op. 6 Nos 6 and 12 and *Oboe Concerto in B flat* (with Maisonneuve, and the Paris Chamber Orchestra), Vivaldi's *L'estro armonico* Op. 3 Nos 6, 7, 9 and 11 (with Kaufman and the Musical Masterpieces Society Orchestra), Op. 8 Nos 5 to 12 (with Kaufman), Op. 9 and Two-Mandolin Concerto (with Parolari), *Two-Violin Concerto in D* (with Kaufman and Rybar) and *Oboe Concerto in D minor* (with Parolari), Torelli's Violin Concerto Op. 8 No. 3 (with Kaufman) and *in D minor* (with Rybar), Bach's Two-Harpsichord Concerto BWV 1060 (with Andreae and Stock), Violin Concerto BWV 1056 (with Rybar), and Violin and Oboe Concerto (with Rybar and Parolari), Nardini's *Violin Concerto in E minor* (with Rybar), Haydn's *Flute Concerto in D major* and Divertimento for Flute and Strings (with Urfer), K. Stamitz's *Harpsichord Concerto in D major* (with Pelleg), Boccherini's *Symphony in A major*, Dittersdorf's Symphonies Nos 76 and 96, Beethoven's arrangement of his Violin Concerto as a Piano Concerto (with Balsam), Mendelssohn's Symphony No. 4, Schubert's *Adagio and Rondo concertante in F* (with Pelleg) and Vaughan Williams' *Concerto accademico* (with Kaufman). For CTS (Switzerland) he also recorded music of Swiss composers, viz. Schibler's Symphony Op. 44, Schoeck's Serenades Op. 1 and Op.27, and Mieg's *Toccata, Arioso and Gigue* (with the Winterthur Symphony Orchestra).

Dähler, Jörg (b. 1933). Born in Berne, where he studied at the Berne Conservatory, Dähler then studied the harpsichord with Neumeyer at Freiburg, taught at the Basel Academy of Music (1962–7) and at the Berne Conservatory (since 1962) and became conductor of the Berne Chamber Choir (1974). He has conducted famous chamber orchestras in Switzerland and abroad, and performs as a soloist and accompanist. For Claves (Switzerland) he has recorded Keiser's *St Mark Passion* and concertos by Albinoni, J. S. and W. F. Bach and Vivaldi (with the Camerata Berne), Galuppi's *Magnificat* and Vivaldi's *Gloria* (with the South-West German Chamber Orchestra *et al.*).

Dalgat, Dzhemal (b. 1920). Born in Dagestan, USSR, Dalgat graduated from the Leningrad Conservatory in 1947 and studied conducting under Khaikin. He became a conductor at the Kirov Theatre, Leningrad, where he has a reputation for his temperament, originality and discipline. As well as the customary operatic repertoire he has a special interest in Prokofiev and Britten. His recordings have been of Prokofiev's *Love of Three Oranges* (with the Moscow Radio Symphony Orchestra *et al.* for Melodiya, also issued by EMI), Franck's *Psyché* and Prokofiev's *Sinfonietta* (with the same orchestra, issued by Westminster), Kazhlayev's ballet *Girl of the Caucasian Mountains* (with the Leningrad Kirov Ballet Orchestra for Melodiya), and Debussy's *Fantasia for Piano and Orchestra* (with Jocheles and the USSR State Symphony Orchestra, issued by Ariola).

Damrosch, Walter (1862–1950). Walter Damrosch's mother was a soprano who sang Ortrud in the first performance of *Lohengrin*; his father, Leopold Damrosch, was a famous violinist and conductor who had been concertmaster of Liszt's orchestra at Weimar and conductor of the Breslau Philharmonic Orchestra, and who had migrated to the United States with his family in 1871, founding the New York Oratorio Society in 1873 and the New York Symphony Society in 1878. Walter was born in Breslau. His early ambition to be a pianist was frustrated when he injured one of his fingers. He assisted his father in preparing for a performance of the Berlioz *Grande Messe des morts* and consequently was elected permanent conductor of the Newark Harmonic Society. After a visit to Germany, where he attended the première of *Parsifal* at Bayreuth, he became assistant conductor to his father at the New York Metropolitan Opera in 1884, substituting for him in performances of *Tannhäuser* and *Die Walküre*. When Leopold died a year later Walter stepped into his shoes as conductor of the Oratorio Society (1885–98) and the Symphony Society (1885–91), and became second conductor at the Metropolitan Opera. In 1887 he studied conducting in Germany with von Bülow; he returned to the Met. but left them in 1894 to found his own company so that he could present the Wagner operas which had fallen from the Met.'s repertoire. Later in 1900 he returned to the Met. to lead the Wagner presentations that had been resumed there. With the New York Symphony Society he gave many first performances for the United States, notably of *Parsifal*, in a concert version, the Brahms Symphonies Nos 3 and 4 and Tchaikovsky's Symphonies Nos 4 and 5. In fact throughout his life he was a devoted advocate of new composers and new music; he included for instance Sibelius in his programmes and commissioned *Tapiola*.

Damrosch travelled widely in the US with the New York Symphony Orchestra, stimulating interest in music in many provincial centres. During World War I he went to France to advise General Pershing about the organisation of US army bands, and in later years he toured with the New York Symphony in England, France, Belgium, Italy and Cuba. In 1925 he pioneered broadcast symphonic music and through his weekly radio broadcasts, which continued until 1942, did much to cultivate musical taste among young people in the US. He composed some operas and other music which enjoyed a mild success in their day; of the operas *The Man without a Country* was presented at the Met. in 1937 and *The Opera Clock* by the New York Opera Company in 1942. To celebrate the 50th anniversary of his arrival in the US a concert in Carnegie Hall brought together the New York Philharmonic, the New York Symphony and the Philadelphia Orchestras, with separate items conducted by Stransky, Bodanzky, Coates, Mengelberg and Stokowski. Contemporary critics and fellow musicians tended to take Damrosch rather lightheartedly. When he visited the US in 1918 Prokofiev commented that he was advised to show Damrosch his *Scythian Suite*, as he would not be likely to understand it. 'Even when I played for him my first concerto, he turned the pages in the wrong places. And after he had heard my *Classical Symphony* he remarked: "It is charming, just like Kalinnikov." Indignant, I left him, but later discovered that he meant it as a sincere compliment' (V. Seroff, *Sergei Prokofiev*, London, 1968, p. 126). Nevertheless, Virgil Thomson, writing in 1942 (*Music Reviewed*, p. 67), said that Damrosch got the loveliest sound out of the New York Philharmonic (the eventual successor to the New York Symphony), although his readings were variable. Be that as it may, Damrosch was a much venerated figure in American musical life and has been described in his lifetime as the 'dean of American music'.

Compared to his famous contemporaries, Damrosch's recordings were few. They were of Brahms' Symphony No. 2, *Ma Mère l'Oye* and the *Entrance of the Little Fauns* from Pierné's *Cydalise et le chèvre-pied* (with the New York Symphony Orchestra for Columbia), Fauré's *Pavane*, the *Perpetuum mobile* from Moszowski's Suite No. 1, Saint-Saëns' *Henry VIII* dances and a ballet suite arranged from Gluck's music by Gevaert (with the New Symphony Orchestra for Victor).

Danon, Oskar (b. 1913). Born in Sarajevo, Yugoslavia, Danon studied at the Prague Conservatory (1933–8) and at the Charles University at Prague, and made his debut as a conductor there in 1938. Until 1941 he was conductor at the Sarajevo Opera and with the Sarajevo Philharmonic Orchestra, as well as being artistic manager of the Avant-Garde Theatre there. During World War II he was a partisan soldier in Tito's forces, and in 1945 became director of the Belgrade Opera and the Belgrade Philharmonic Orchestra. He has been a guest conductor with orchestras and operas in France, Britain, Austria, Italy, Holland, DR Germany, the USSR and Japan. In 1962 he visited the United States to conduct at the Chicago Lyric Opera and in that year also appeared at the Edinburgh Festival with the Belgrade National Opera. He has composed orchestral and instrumental music, songs and choral pieces, including a patriotic work, *Kozara*.

In 1955–6 Decca recorded three operas with Danon conducting the Belgrade National Opera: *Prince Igor*, *A Life for the Tsar* and *Eugene Onegin*; all were successful recordings, and the latter two are still available. Danon's direction of these operas was precise and spontaneous. The operas were sung in their original Russian. (Normally the Belgrade National Opera performs Russian operas in Serbo-Croat.) His other recordings include Massenet's *Don Quichotte* (with the Belgrade National Opera for Cetra and re-issued by Everest), *Die Fledermaus* (with a fine cast and the Vienna State Opera Chorus and Orchestra for RCA), *Scheherazade*, *L'Apprenti sorcier*, *Pulcinella* and *Orpheus* (with the Czech Philharmonic Orchestra for Supraphon), *Petrushka*, the overture to *The Bartered Bride*, a suite from *The Love of Three Oranges*, *Capriccio espagnol*, *The Golden Spinning Wheel*, Enesco's *Romanian Rhapsody No. 1* (with the Royal Philharmonic Orchestra for Reader's Digest), and Gershwin's *Piano Concerto in F* and *Rhapsody in Blue* (with Lewenthal and the Metropolitan Symphony Orchestra for Reader's Digest).

Dantel, Jean-Pierre (b. 1917). Born in Ancenis, France, and educated at the Paris Conservatoire, Dantel won the Prix de Rome in 1946 and made his debut as a conductor in 1951. He is the founder and director of the Caen Chamber Orchestra, and has edited and performed French composers of the 17th and 18th centuries, including especially Rameau, Leclair, Campra, Jacques Aubert, and Mondonville. In addition to classical composers such as Haydn and Mozart, Stravinsky, Honegger and Britten are also in his repertoire. Vox issued a disc, on the Turnabout label, in which he conducts the Caen Chamber Orchestra in Rameau's *Marche* and *Danses d'Acanthe et Céphise*, Berton's *Chaconne*, Charpentier's overture to *Le Malade imaginaire* and dance from *Médée*, and Couperin's *Sultane*.

Darlow, Denys (b. 1921). Born in London and educated at the Royal College of Music and the Royal College of Organists, Darlow was conductor of the Tilford Bach Festival Choir and Orchestra, and organist and choirmaster at St George's Church, Hanover Square, London. He has been a guest conductor in Europe and the United States, and has written a book, *Musical Instruments for Children* (1963). With the Tilford Bach Festival Choir *et al.* he recorded Portuguese baroque music by Pedro da Esperanca and Cardoso (for Oryx).

Dart, Thurston (1921–71). Born in London, Dart was a chorister at the Chapel Royal, Hampton Court, studied at the Royal College of Music (1938–9) and then at London University, where he took a degree in mathematics in 1942. He served with distinction on operational research with the Royal Air Force; after the war he studied with van den Borren in Brussels and in 1947 became an assistant lecturer in music at Cambridge, subsequently being appointed lecturer in 1962. From 1964 until his death in 1971 he was professor at King's College, London University. An eminent musicologist, Dart made a special study of Renaissance and baroque music, edited many works for the recorder, and published a significant study, *The Interpretation of Music* (1954). As a conductor he was artistic director of the Philomusica of London (1955–9), a chamber orchestra drawn from the players of the old Boyd Neel Orchestra. He was also an accomplished organist and harpsichordist, and his first records were made in 1950 as harpsichordist with the Jacobean Ensemble, for Argo. His major recordings as conductor were of the Bach *Brandenburg Concertos* and Suites, the Double Violin Concerto, Concerto for Flute, Violin and Harpischord and Harpischord Concerto No. 4, Dowland's *Lachrymae*, Handel's *Water Music* and two Epistle Sonatas of Mozart, and *Eine kleine Nachtmusik* and *Serenata notturna* (with the Philomusica, for Argo); other discs were a collection of dances from Shakespeare's time, an organ concerto, songs and canzonettas of J. C. Bach, some Concerti Grossi of Scarlatti, Corelli and Geminiani (with the Boyd Neel Orchestra *et al.* for Argo), music by Couperin and a collection of Jacobean consort music (with the Jacobean Ensemble for Argo) and a sinfonia from *Jephtha*, a suite from *Rodrigo* and excerpts from *Alcina*, of Handel (with the Philomusica *et al.* for Argo).

David, Johann Nepomuk (b. 1895). Born at Eferding, Upper Austria, David studied at the Vienna Academy of Music, was an organist and teacher, then professor and finally director at the Hochschule für Musik at Leipzig, director of the Mozarteum at Salzburg (1945–8) and professor at the Hochschule für Musik at Stuttgart (1948–63). His compositions include eight symphonies, organ, choral and chamber works, and in the vast scale of his symphonies he has been recognised by some as the natural successor to Bruckner, although his music has a discouraging asperity. He has published editions of Bach's *Das wohltemperierte Klavier* and Mozart's Symphony No. 41, and has been awarded the Austrian State Prize, the Franz Liszt Prize, the Mozart Prize, the Bach Prize (Hamburg) and the Mendelssohn Prize (Leipzig). Some of his music has been recorded, including a *Deutsche Messe*, organ works and his Violin Concerto, in which he conducted the Munich Philharmonic Orchestra with Lukas David, for DGG.

Davies, Dennis Russell (b. 1944). Born at Toledo, Ohio, and educated at the Juilliard School, New York, Davies studied the piano with Epstein and Gordnitzki and conducting with Mester and Morel. He was a finalist in the Busoni Piano competition in 1966, taught at Juilliard (1968–71), with Berio founded and led The Ensemble in New York, in 1972 was appointed music director of the St Paul Chamber Orchestra at Minnesota, and with the orchestra toured Eastern Europe and the USSR (1974–5). He has been music director of the Cabrillo Music Festival (since 1974), of the White Mountain Festival of the Arts (since 1975), of the Norwalk Symphony Orchestra (1968–72), and of the Juilliard Ensemble (1968–74). He first conducted opera in Europe with *Pelléas et Mélisande* at the Netherlands Opera (1974), and has since appeared in London, Milan, Rome, Spoleto *et al.*, and has been a regular guest conductor at the Stuttgart Opera where, in 1975, he started a series of all the stage works of Henze. He is a dedicated performer of new music, both as pianist and conductor, and has given premières of compositions by Berio, Cage, Henze, Maderna, Persichetti *et al.* At the 1978 Bayreuth Festival he conducted *Der fliegende Holländer*.

Davies' recordings include Thorne's Piano Concerto, both as pianist and conductor (with the St Paul Chamber Orchestra for Serenus), Overton's *Pulsations* and Trimble's *Panels 1* (with the CRI Chamber Orchestra for Composers Recordings), Phillips' *Canzona III* (with the Juilliard Ensemble for Composers Recordings), Bolcom's *Open House* and *Commedia* (with Sperry and the St Paul Chamber Orchestra for Nonesuch), Michael Haydn's *Symphony in G*, Mozart's Cassation K. 62a and J. C. Bach's Sinfonia Op. 6 No. 6 (with the St Paul Chamber Orchestra for Nonesuch).

Davies, Meredith (b. 1922). A native of Birkenhead, Davies showed exceptional musical talent as a child, studied at the Royal College of Music, London, and was an organ scholar at Keble College, Oxford. After serving for five years as an officer in the Royal Artillery in World War II, he was appointed organist at St Alban's Cathedral in 1947, and two years later moved to a similar position at Hereford, also being the musical director of the Three Choirs Festivals at Hereford in 1952 and 1955. He studied conducting with Previtali at the Accademia di Santa Cecilia at Rome, and became assistant conductor of the City of Birmingham Orchestra (1957–9) as well as organist and lecturer at New College, Oxford. In 1960 he gave up the post at Oxford to devote himself to a career as a conductor, has been a guest conductor at the Aldeburgh Festival, chief guest conductor with the BBC Welsh Orchestra (1960–62), musical director of the English Opera Group (1962–4), appeared at Sadler's Wells and Covent Garden and fulfilled guest engagements in Europe and South America. In 1962 he conducted the world première of Britten's *War Requiem* at the newly-completed Coventry Cathedral; from 1964 to 1971 he was musical director of the Vancouver Symphony Orchestra, and has been chief conductor of the BBC Training Orchestra (since 1969) and musical director of the Royal Choral Society (since 1971). Davies has participated as conductor in a number of significant records of English music, including Delius' operas *A Village Romeo and Juliet* (with the Royal Philharmonic Orchestra *et al.*) and *Fennimore and Gerda* (with the Danish Radio Symphony Orchestra *et al.*), couplings of the Violin Concerto (with Menuhin) and Double Concerto (with Menuhin and Tortelier) and of the *Idyll*, a setting of Whitman's *Once I Passed through a Populous City*, and the *Requiem*, which had remained in obscurity for almost half a century because of its unconventional and humanistic view of life. These were with the Royal Philharmonic Orchestra; he also recorded Vaughan Williams' *Magnificat* and *Riders to the Sea* (with the London Orchestra Nova *et al.*) and *Sir John in Love* (with the New Philharmonia Orchestra *et al.*). All were for EMI.

Davis, Andrew (b. 1944). Born at Ashridge, Hertfordshire, Davis received his early musical education at the Royal Academy of Music, was an organ scholar at King's College, Cambridge

(1963–7) and studied with Ferrari at the Accademia di Santa Cecilia in Rome on a scholarship awarded by the Italian Government (1968). He was chosen by Groves with three others to take part in the Royal Liverpool Orchestra Society seminar for young British conductors, which led to his appointment as principal guest conductor of the orchestra (1974). He was associate conductor of the BBC Scottish Orchestra (1970–71), and came into prominence dramatically in London in 1970 when he first substituted for Inbal and later for Rozhdestvensky in concerts with the BBC Symphony Orchestra. He was appointed associate conductor of the New Philharmonia Orchestra (1973), made his North American debut with the Detroit Symphony Orchestra (1974), conducted concerts with the New York Philharmonic Orchestra, and became music director of the Toronto Symphony Orchestra (1975), and led the orchestra on a tour to China (1978). He has conducted major orchestras in Britain, Europe, Israel and the United States, and is a regular conductor at the Proms and the Glyndebourne Festival.

In a short time Davis has come to the fore as a major British conducting talent, and has won the widest respect for his keen rhythmic sense, his understanding of style, the clean execution he achieves and the strong dramatic tension of his interpretations. His musical sympathies are wide, and his repertoire ranges from Bach to Shostakovich; he professes a special preference for Elgar, Schumann, Berg, Stravinsky, Mahler and Beethoven. His first appearance on record was as the organist in the Concerti Grossi Op. 6 of Handel with the St Martin-in-the Fields Orchestra (1964); since then he has recorded Rachmaninov's Piano Concerto No. 2 (with Vered and the New Philharmonia for Decca), Britten's *Young Person's Guide to the Orchestra* and excerpts from Prokofiev's *Cinderella* (with the London Symphony for CBS), Hoddinott's Symphony No. 5, Piano Concerto No. 2 and Horn Concerto (with Jones and Tuckwell, respectively, and the Royal Philharmonic for Decca), Duruflé's *Requiem* and *Danse lente*, the Franck Symphony and Fauré's *Pelléas et Mélisande*, the two suites from *Peer Gynt* and recital of Grieg's songs (with Söderström, and the New Philharmonia for CBS), a disc of British patriotic music including the *Pomp and Circumstance* March No. 1, *Rule, Britannia* and Walton's *Crown Imperial* (with the London Philharmonic for Classics for Pleasure), Shostakovich's Symphony No. 10 (with the London Philharmonic for Classics for Pleasure), Elgar's *Falstaff* and *Enigma Variations* (with the New Philharmonia for Lyrita) and Borodin's Symphonies Nos 1, 2 and 3, and excerpts from *Prince Igor* (with the Toronto Symphony Orchestra and Toronto Mendelssohn Choir for CBS).

Davis, Colin (b. 1927). Born at Weybridge, Surrey, Davis studied the clarinet, first at Christ's Hospital and then at the Royal College of Music with Thurston, and was for two years a musician with the Household Cavalry. Self-taught as a conductor, he gained his initial experience with the Kalmar Orchestra (1949) and with the Chelsea Opera Group (1950), where his first appearance as a conductor was with *Don Giovanni*. In 1952 he was one of the conductors of the Festival Ballet at the Royal Festival Hall, London, and in 1957 was appointed assistant conductor of the BBC Scottish Orchestra. In 1958 he made a brilliant debut at Sadler's Wells Opera with *Die Entführung aus dem Serail*, attracting attention as a fine conductor of Mozart, which was confirmed the next year when he substituted for Klemperer in concert performances in London of *Don Giovanni* with the Philharmonia Orchestra and a cast that included Sutherland and Schwarzkopf. He made his first appearances in the United States and Canada in 1959, and in the following year conducted at Glyndebourne where he substituted for Beecham in *Die Zauberflöte*, and also conducted ballet at Covent Garden. In 1962–3 he toured Japan with the London Symphony Orchestra, whom he also conducted on a worldwide tour in 1964. He was musical director of Sadler's Wells Opera (1965–70) and of the English Chamber Orchestra, conducted first at Covent Garden in opera with *Le nozze di Figaro*, was chief conductor of the BBC Symphony Orchestra (1967–71) and in 1971 was appointed chief conductor and artistic adviser at Covent Garden; at the same time he remained with the BBC Symphony Orchestra as joint-principal guest conductor and was appointed principal guest conductor of the London Symphony, the Boston Symphony and the Amsterdam Concertgebouw Orchestras. He had previously declined the appointment of musical director of the Boston Symphony. He also appears as guest conductor with the New York Philharmonic Orchestra and the New York Metropolitan Opera, and conducted *Tannhäuser* at the Bayreuth Festivals in 1977 and 1978.

Davis is probably the major British conductor to emerge since Beecham, and the musicians who perform with him are frequently impressed with his great love of music and his sense of conviction in the works he conducts. Like Beecham, a good part of his reputation is as an interpreter of Mozart and Berlioz, and he is often claimed to be the finest living exponent of Berlioz. A modest and unassuming personality, although perfectly sure of himself, his relations with orchestral players are unlike the autocratic manner of many of his Continental colleagues. British orchestras react rather uncertainly to him, and his first years at Covent Garden were somewhat difficult, but his touch with American orchestras is more sure. His skill in responding to the latters' susceptibilities has been expressed in the words of one of the Boston Symphony: 'He has a way of telling us what we need to know without insulting our intelligence.' His rehearsal methods are unauthoritarian; the work is run through first and then detailed attention is given to unsatisfactory passages. It has been suggested that he is apt to give too much attention to detail to the detriment of the music's broad line, but for composers with whom he is most sympathetic this is scarcely evident. He once expressed his attitude to conducting as 'taking care of something that has a life of its own. It's like holding the bird of life in your hand. Hold it too tight and it dies. Hold it too lightly and it flies away' (*The Gramophone*, December 1967, p. 311). Beyond Mozart and Berlioz, he has a name as an interpreter of Handel, Stravinsky and Tippett, and has also been acclaimed in composers such as Berg, Britten, Sibelius and Debussy. At Covent Garden his repertoire has expanded to include Wagner; his leadership of *The Ring* has been acclaimed for its penetration and persuasiveness, and is quite distinctively his own. At the New York Met. he led brilliant performances of *Wozzeck*, *Peter Grimes* and *Pelléas et Mélisande*, although in the last-named his interpretation was a little too far from the traditional for many tastes. More recently at Covent Garden his *Idomeneo* has impressed, and this opera he regards as Mozart's greatest: 'In no other opera, I think, does he so closely identify with his characters. . . . Mozart was an even greater master of this kind of *opera seria* than he is of *drama giocosa* or *opera buffa*. I don't believe that Mozart ever equalled the passion that he poured into music that expresses all the predicaments, nor did he ever again use the chorus as one of the principal characters'. Davis eschews the literalness, intensity and fast tempi of Toscanini, feeling that this style is 'unspacious'. He does not acknowledge the particular influence of any other great conductor, and in this sense he is an original. The idea of complete faithfulness to the score he scorns: 'The score is like a two-dimensional map of Everest, not like Everest itself. We must make the score into a real experience. Music is the events that take place between key relationships, the weight, size and feel of a chord as compared with what has gone on before'. Naturally this view is antipathetic to much modern music, in which Davis cannot find any emotional meaning, although his admiration extends to Tavener, Birtwistle, Maxwell Davies and Henze, but certainly not to Stockhausen. Until the recent past the late romantics, with the notable exception of Elgar, had no immediate attraction to him. Yet he did not hesitate to conduct Wagner at Covent Garden, and lately has expressed interest in Bruckner and Mahler. Sibelius too has become associated with him, particularly after his spectacular recordings of the symphonies with the Boston Symphony Orchestra.

As in the opera house, Davis first made his mark as a recording artist as an interpreter of Mozart. His very first records were of the Mozart Symphonies Nos 29, 34 and 39 (with the Sinfonia of London) and of the Oboe Concerto (with Leon Goossens and the Sinfonia of London). The two discs were issued originally by World Record Club in 1958 and have since been released on other labels. A year later came a disc including *Eine kleine Nachtmusik* and *Serenata notturna* (with the Philharmonia Orchestra for EMI) and two years afterwards a collection of Mozart overtures (with the Royal Philharmonic Orchestra for EMI). From 1960 he recorded a number of Mozart symphonies and two divertimenti (variously with the English Chamber Orchestra for L'Oiseau Lyre, and with the London Symphony Orchestra for Philips), the Violin Concertos and Sinfonia Concertante K. 364 (with Grumiaux, Pelliccia and the London Symphony for Philips), the *Concertone* (with the English Chamber Orchestra *et al.* for L'Oiseau Lyre), the Flute Concertos and Andante K. 315 (with Barwahser and the London Symphony Orchestra for Philips), the Clarinet Concerto (with Brymer) and the Flute and Harp Concerto (with Barwahser and Ellis and the London Symphony Orchestra for Philips) and a number of the Piano Concertos (with Haebler and the London Symphony for Philips). In 1967 he recorded the *Requiem*, (with the BBC Symphony Orchestra *et al.* for Philips) and in 1973 the Mass K. 317 and K. 427, the *Kyrie* K. 341, *Ave verum corpus*, *Exsultate jubilate* (with Kanawa) and *Vesperae solennes de confessore* K. 339 (with the London Symphony *et al.* for Philips). His series of Mozart operas commenced in 1969 with *Idomeneo* (with the BBC Symphony Orchestra *et al.*), *Le nozze di Figaro* (in 1971 with the BBC Symphony Orchestra *et al.*), *Don Giovanni* (in 1973 with the Covent

Garden Orchestra *et al.*), *Così fan tutte* (in 1975 with the Covent Garden Orchestra *et al.*), *La clemenza di Tito* (in 1977 with the Covent Garden Orchestra *et al.*), *Der Schauspieldirektor* and *Lo sposo deluso* (in 1977 with the London Symphony Orchestra *et al.*). It is arguable whether Davis is yet fully equipped to record all the Mozart operas; in *Le nozze di Figaro* he approaches the standards of the great Kleiber set of 1959 in his authority and sensitivity, but in *Don Giovanni* and *Così fan tutte* a certain brusqueness is evident, and *Idomeneo* is gravely weakened by some inadequate soloists.

The Berlioz series recorded by Davis has been an unqualified success. His first Berlioz recordings were for L'Oiseau Lyre: *L'Enfance du Christ* (in 1960, with the Goldsbrough Orchestra *et al.*), *Béatrice et Bénédict* (in 1963, with the London Symphony *et al.*) and a disc including *La Mort de Cléopâtre*, *Méditation religieuse*, *La Mort d'Ophélie* and *Sara la baigneuse* (with Pashley, the English Chamber Orchestra *et al.*). After signing the exclusive contract with Philips, the series continued with *Harold in Italy* (with Menuhin), *Symphonie fantastique* (in 1964 with the London Symphony and in 1975 with the Amsterdam Concertgebouw), a disc of overtures, the *Roméo et Juliette* symphony, the *Te Deum*, *Symphonie funèbre et triomphale*, *Marche funèbre pour la dernière scène de Hamlet*, *Les Nuits d'été* and some songs, *Les Troyens*, *Grande Messe des morts*, *Benvenuto Cellini*, *La Damnation de Faust*, and a second *L'Enfance du Christ*. In most cases the orchestra employed was the London Symphony, and for *Les Troyens* and *Benvenuto Cellini* he led the Royal Opera Orchestra as the recordings were made when the operas were being performed at Covent Garden. *Les Troyens* alone is an immense achievement, and the Davis/Berlioz/Philips enterprise is one of the complete and unblemished successes in the recent history of the gramophone.

Two other composers who have had a special significance for Davis are Tippett and Stravinsky. Since recording the Piano Concerto of Tippett with Ogdon in 1963, he has gone on to make the Symphonies Nos 1, 2 and 3, the *Concerto for Orchestra* and the *Suite for the Birthday of Prince Charles* (with the London Symphony), the operas *The Midsummer Marriage* and *The Knot Garden* (with the Covent Garden Orchestra *et al.*) and the oratorio *A Child of Our Time* (with the BBC Symphony *et al.*); all were for Philips. His Stravinsky discs were made mostly early in his recording career, and included *Oedipus Rex* (with the Royal Philharmonic *et al.* for EMI), *Danses concertantes*, *Dumbarton Oaks*, *Concerto for Strings*, *Cantata* and *Mass* (with the English Chamber Orchestra *et al.* for L'Oiseau Lyre), the Piano Concerto (with Bishop-Kovacevich and the London Symphony for Philips), and *Le Sacre du printemps* (in 1963 with the London Symphony and in 1978 with the Amsterdam Concertgebouw, for Philips). As already mentioned, he recorded the seven Sibelius symphonies, with *Finlandia* and *Tapiola* (with the Boston Symphony) and has now completed seven of the Beethoven symphonies. The first to appear was the Symphony No. 7 (with the Royal Philharmonic in 1962, a superlative performance); later were issued the Symphonies Nos 2, 3, 4, 5 and 8 (with the BBC Symphony) and Nos 6 and 7 (with the London Symphony), as well as the overtures *Fidelio* (with the Sinfonia of London, for World Record Club), *Egmont* and *Leonore No. 3* (with the BBC Symphony) and *Prometheus* and Leonore No. 2 (with the London Symphony), the five Piano Concertos (with Bishop-Kovacevich and the BBC Symphony and London Symphony) and Violin Concerto (with Grumiaux and the Amsterdam Concertgebouw). His other recordings include Purcell's *Dido and Aeneas* (with the Academy of St Martin-in-the-Fields *et al.*), *Messiah* (with the London Symphony *et al.*), three sinfonias of J. C. Bach and the overture to *La clemenza di Tito* (with the English Chamber Orchestra for L'Oiseau Lyre), Haydn's Symphonies No. 84 (with the English Chamber Orchestra for L'Oiseau Lyre) and Nos 88 and 99 (with the Amsterdam Concertgebouw), a collection of Rossini overtures (with the Royal Philharmonic for EMI), the Brahms *Variations on the St Antony Chorale* (with the Sinfonia of London for World Record Club) and Violin Concerto (with Grumiaux and the New Philharmonia), Mendelssohn's Symphony No. 4 and excerpts from the incidental music to *A Midsummer Night's Dream* (with the Boston Symphony) and *The Hebrides* overture (with the Sinfonia of London for World Record Club), the Dvořák Symphony No. 7 (with the Amsterdam Concertgebouw), *Serenade in E major* and *Symphonic Variations* (with the London Symphony), Spohr's Clarinet Concerto No. 1 and Weber's Clarinet Concerto No. 2 (with de Peyer and the London Symphony), Wagner's *Siegfried Idyll* (with the Sinfonia of London for World Record Club), *Wesendonck Lieder* and some arias (with Nilsson and the London Symphony), the Schumann and Grieg Piano Concertos (with Bishop-Kovacevich and the BBC Symphony), the overtures *Coriolan*, *Die Meistersinger*, *The Merry Wives of Windsor*, *Die Zauberflöte*, *Hebrides* and *Der Freischütz* (with the BBC

Symphony), excerpts from *Carmen* (in English, with the Sadler's Wells Company, for EMI), the Grieg Piano Concerto and Scherzo from the *Concerto symphonique* of Litolff (with Katin and the London Philharmonic for Decca), Rachmaninov's Piano Concerto No. 2 (with Katin and the New Symphony for Decca), Tchaikovsky's Piano Concerto No. 2 (with Magaloff and the London Symphony), Bartók's Piano Concertos Nos 1 and 3 (with Bishop-Kovacevich and the London Symphony) and No. 2 (with Bishop-Kovacevich and the BBC Symphony), Rodrigo's *Concierto de Aranjuez* (with Bream and the Melos Ensemble for RCA), Elgar's *Cockaigne* overture and *Enigma Variations* (with the London Symphony), Gerhard's Symphony No. 4 and Violin Concerto (with Neaman and the BBC Symphony for Argo), Puccini's *Tosca* (with the Covent Garden Orchestra *et al.*) and *The Last Night at the Proms*, (with the BBC Symphony, recorded at the Final Proms concert in 1969).

These recordings of Davis have not always attracted universal admiration, particularly with the Beethoven and Sibelius symphonies. Unusual tempi have occasionally drawn the critics' fire, and a certain straightforwardness has given some readings a perfunctory air. Davis's performances are quite distinct from Karajan's grand smooth line, Bernstein's dramatic intensity and Maazel's preoccupation with expressive detail. At the age of 50 he is still, by conductors' standards, a young man and will no doubt go on to contribute much more to the gramophone. After the acclaim that greeted his recent *Tosca*, his Wagner productions at Covent Garden and Bayreuth, and his confessed interest in Mahler and Bruckner, it will be very interesting to see what insights he will bring to future recordings.

Davison, Arthur (b. 1923). Born in Montreal, Davison is the grandson of one of Canada's most distinguished playwrights. He began playing the violin at the age of three and when he was twelve he was giving regular broadcast recitals. After studies at the Conservatoire de Musique at Montreal, with the conductor Wilfred Pelletier and at McGill University, he came to England in 1948 with a scholarship to the Royal Academy of Music, studied there with Sammons and Beard, and played in the Philharmonia Orchestra. In 1956 he founded the London Little Symphony Orchestra and became artistic director of the Virtuosi of England, a group of superb instrumentalists. His other activities have included conducting the Royal Amateur Orchestral Society, the Croydon Symphony Orchestra and the National Youth Orchestra of Wales. During frequent tours of Canada and the United States he has conducted the New York City Ballet and for CBS Radio and Television, and has been active with the Danish Royal Orchestra and the Royal Danish Ballet. In 1974 he was awarded the CBE.

Under contract to Classics for Pleasure in Britain, Davison has enjoyed an immense success as a recording artist. Because the CFP label is widely distributed and cheap, many of his records have become best sellers, although there are probably more polished performances of some of the works among fully priced discs. In 1974 he received an award to mark the sale of 500,000 records and in 1977 EMI/CFP presented him with a Gold Disc for the sale of over a million records and cassettes conducted by him. His performances of baroque music, in particular *The Four Seasons*, excerpts from *Messiah*, organ concertos of Handel (with Kynaston), *Water Music*, *Music for the Royal Fireworks*, pieces by Purcell, the *Brandenburg Concertos* and Violin Concertos of Bach (with Bean and Sillito) with the Virtuosi of England, have an undeniable vigour, but many problems of style have remained unsolved. On the other hand his recordings of Dvořák's Symphony No. 7 (with the London Philharmonic Orchestra), some Mozart dances, Leopold Mozart's *Toy Symphony* and *Peter and the Wolf* (with the London Little Symphony Orchestra) and *Pictures at an Exhibition* and Shostakovich's *Festival Overture* (with the National Youth Orchestra of Wales) are admirable. His other discs include *Eine kleine Nachtmusik*, Mozart's Piano Concerto K. 467 and the four Horn Concertos (with Lympany and Brown respectively and the Virtuosi of England), marches by Tchaikovsky, Verdi, Berlioz and Strauss (with the London Philharmonic Orchestra, all for CFP) and Hoddinott's *Welsh Dances*, *Investiture Dances* and *Concerto Grosso No. 2* and Mathias' *Sinfonietta* and *Welsh Dances* (with the National Youth Orchestra of Wales for Polydor/BBC, a disc sponsored by the Arts Council of Wales). Classics for Pleasure's enterprise demonstrates the value of marketing good music effectively and also has projected Davison as a recording conductor who would otherwise be little known outside the concert hall. His own response has, on balance, justified the venture.

Davisson, Walther (b. 1885). Born at Frankfurt am Main, Davisson trained as a violinist, played in the Rebner Quartet (1906–13), taught the violin at the Leipzig Conservatory (from 1918), and was director at the Conservatory (1932–42). He became a professor at the Hochschule für Musik at Halle (1947–8) and director of the Hochschule für Musik at Frankfurt am Main (1950), and also conductor of the orchestra. In the 1950s Vox issued performances of him conducting Bach's Violin Concertos Nos 1 and 2 and Double Concerto (with Barchet and Beh), and Beethoven's Piano Concertos Nos 2 and 3 (with Wührer, and the Stuttgart Pro Musica Orchestra), and in 1961 the Beethoven Triple Concerto (with Wührer, Gimpel and Schuster) and the Brahms Double Concerto (with Gimpel and Schuster, and the Württemberg State Orchestra).

Deáky, Zsolt. The Hungarian conductor Deáky studied at the Franz Liszt Academy at Budapest, at the Giuseppe Verdi Conservatory in Milan and with Swarowsky in Vienna, and has conducted in Vienna, London and Los Angeles. His recordings include Haydn's Symphony No. 104 (with the South-German Philharmonic Orchestra for BASF), Beethoven's overtures *Egmont* and *Coriolan* (with the Nuremberg Symphony Orchestra for Intercord), Beethoven's Piano Concerto No. 5 (with Nakajima), Schubert's Symphonies Nos 1 and 3, Blacher's Variations for Orchestra, Rubinstein's Piano Concerto No. 5 (with Ruiz), Brüll's *Macbeth* overture and Piano Concerto (with Cooper), Rheinberger's Piano Concerto (with Ruiz), Raff's Piano Concerto and Dreyschock's *Konzertstück* (with Cooper, and with the Nuremberg Symphony Orchestra, for Colosseum and issued in the United States by Genesis).

Dearnley, Christopher (b. 1930). Born in Wolverhampton and educated at Worcester College, Oxford, Dearnley was assistant organist at Salisbury Cathedral (1954–7), then organist and choirmaster there (1957–68), and organist at St Paul's Cathedral (1968). He has recorded as an organist, and with the Salisbury Cathedral Choir recorded a disc of anthems by Purcell, Blow, Wise, Boyce, Greene, Battishill and Croft (for Argo), and other collections (for Oryx and Abbey).

Decker, Franz-Paul (b. 1923). Born in Cologne and a graduate of the University and State Institute for Musical Education at Cologne, Decker was appointed assistant conductor at the Giessen Municipal Theatre (1944–6), was musical director at Krefeld (1946–50), conductor at Wiesbaden Theatre (1950–53) and conductor of the Wiesbaden Symphony Orchestra in succession to Schuricht (1953), and general music director at Bochum (1956), being then the youngest to hold such a position in FR Germany. He conducted the opening concert at EXPO Brussels (1958), was permanent conductor and artistic director of the Rotterdam Philharmonic Orchestra (1962–8), of the Montreal Symphony Orchestra (1967–75), and artistic adviser and principal guest conductor of the Calgary Philharmonic Orchestra (1976). He has toured in South America, Australia and New Zealand, is a regular guest conductor in Britain, Europe, the USSR and the United States, and was made professor-in-residence at the Sir George Williams University, Montreal (1973). His recordings include Mozart's Piano Concerto K. 482 and a Haydn Piano Concerto (with Demus and the Berlin Radio Symphony Orchestra for DGG), Beethoven's Symphony No. 3 (with the Rotterdam Philharmonic Orchestra for DGG), Brahms' Piano Concerto No. 1 (with Gelber and the Munich Philharmonic Orchestra for EMI), Schafer's *Son of Heldenleben* and Pepin's Symphony No. 3 (with the Montreal Symphony Orchestra for Canadian Broadcasting Corporation).

De Fabritiis, Oliviero (b. 1902). Born in Rome, De Fabritiis studied composition and conducting with Setaccioli and Refice, and made his debut at the Adriano Theatre in Rome. For many years he was active as a conductor in major opera houses in Italy and abroad and until 1943 was artistic secretary of the Rome Opera House. In 1971 he was appointed artistic adviser to the Vienna Festival. In the record catalogues he is distinguished by three operatic recordings which he made in Italy for HMV in the years just before and in the early part of World War II, all of which were marked by the high standard of singing and orchestral playing. These were *Tosca* (with Gigli, Caniglia, Borgioli *et al.* and the Rome Opera Chorus and Orchestra), *Madama Butterfly* (with Gigli, Toti dal Monte *et al.* and the same orchestra and chorus) and *Andrea Chénier* (with Gigli, Caniglia *et al.* and the La Scala Orchestra and Chorus). These recordings have been re-issued at various times in LP transfers in Britain and the United States. After World War II he recorded *La Cenerentola* (with the Maggio Musicale Fiorentino *et al.* for Decca), aria recitals with Tebaldi and Suliotis (for Decca), and *Aida*, from a performance in Mexico City in 1951 (issued by L'Estro Armonico).

Defauw, Désiré (1885–1960). The distinguished Belgian violinist and conductor Defauw was born in Ghent. At the age of 14 he impressed a visiting impresario, who offered to take him on a concert tour of the United States. His parents refused, but a year later Defauw became concertmaster of the winter concerts at Ghent. He made his London debut in 1910, toured until 1914 with great success as a violin virtuoso and formed his own string quartet (1913). During World War I he was in England, conducted for the first time in London, formed the Allied String Quartet and with it toured the country. After the war he taught at the Antwerp Conservatory, conducted the Brussels Conservatory Orchestra (from 1920), conducted at the Théâtre de la Monnaie in Brussels (until 1925), became director of the Conservatoire Royal, founded the Concerts Defauw, and established and conducted the Belgian National Orchestra (1937). He was a guest conductor with the NBC Symphony Orchestra in New York (1938); in 1940 he left Belgium for North America, conducted at Montreal, was director of the Quebec Conservatory, and in 1943 succeeded Stock as conductor of the Chicago Symphony Orchestra. He remained in Chicago until 1949, a time marred by the hostility of the local critics who disparaged both his talents and his programmes. After a short return to Belgium, he took up another appointment in the US, with the Gary Symphony Orchestra (1950–58).

In Belgium, Defauw recorded excerpts from Bach's *St John Passion* (with the Brussels Conservatoire Royal Choir and Orchestra for Columbia), Mozart's Violin Concerto K. 268 (with Dubois), Bach's Suite No. 3, Haydn's Symphony No. 41, Grétry's ballet suite *Céphale et Procris*, Part 4 of Franck's *Psyché*, Respighi's *Gli uccelli*, *Till Eulenspiegel*, the prelude to d'Indy's *Fervaal*, *Mephisto Waltz*, Glazunov's *Stenka Razin* and *Interludium in modo antico*, and the Rhine Journey from *Götterdämmerung* (with the Brussels Conservatoire Orchestra, variously for Columbia and HMV). His recordings with the Chicago Symphony Orchestra included the Handel/Harty *Water Music* and Handel's Concerto Grosso Op. 6 No. 10, the overture to *The Bartered Bride*, Strauss's *Burleske* and Weber's *Konzertstück* (with Arrau), the Mendelssohn Violin Concerto (with Elman), the Tchaikovsky Violin Concerto (with Morini), Prokofiev's *Scythian Suite*, Stravinsky's *Feux d'artifice*, *Le Chasseur maudit* and the interlude from Franck's *Rédemption*, Borodin's Symphony No. 2 and (again) *Gli uccelli*. Apart from Franck, Defauw was not regarded as a specialist in music of the French school, and his recordings reflect his preference and skill for colourful music. Some of these performances, such as *Gli uccelli*, were superb, showing temperament even if they were not greatly refined.

Defossez, René (b. 1905). Born at Spa, Belgium, Defossez studied first with his father, and then at the Liège Conservatory, won the first Belgian Prix de Rome (1935), taught at the Brussels and Liège Conservatories, and conducted at the Théâtre de la Monnaie in Brussels. His compositions include operas, ballets, oratorios, symphonies, a piano concerto and chamber music. He recorded Rasse's Violin Concerto (with Hasselet and the Belgian National Orchestra for Telefunken), Haydn's *Cello Concerto in C major* (with Aldulescu and the Bucharest Philharmonic Orchestra for Electrecord), Rachmaninov's Piano Concerto No. 3 (with Alfidi and the Belgian National Orchestra for DGG), the Sibelius Violin Concerto and Chausson's *Poème* (with Fried) and the Brahms Violin Concerto (with Korsakov, and the Belgian Radio Orchestra for DGG), Jongen's *Symphonie concertante* (with the Orchestre de Liège for Musique de Wallonie), Leduc's *Divertissement* (with Isselée and the Solistes de Liège) and his own ballet-cantata *Le Pêcheur et son âme* (with the Orchestre Symphonique de Liège *et al.*) The Brahms concerto was performed during the Concours International Reine Élisabeth in Brussels in 1971.

Delage, Roger (b. 1922). Born at Vierzon, France, Delage studied at the Paris Conservatoire, made his debut as a conductor in 1950, and in 1959 founded the Collegium Musicum of Strasbourg. He is professor of chamber music at the Strasbourg Conservatoire, has conducted chamber orchestras throughout France, and has a special interest in Chabrier, whose operetta *Fisch-ton-Kan* he orchestrated. With the Collegium Musicum he recorded, among other works, Pleyel's *Symphonie périodique No. 6* (issued in the United States by Musical Heritage Society), Campra's *Oratorio de Noël* and motets *In convertendo Dominus* and *Exurge Domine* (issued by Charlin and Schwann).

Deller, Alfred (1912–79). Born in Margate, the British counter-tenor Deller was a member of the choirs of Canterbury (1940–47) and St Paul's Cathedrals (1947–61), and gave his first solo recital at a concert conducted by Tippett at Morley College in 1944. In 1950 he formed his own vocal and instrumental ensemble, the Deller Consort, to give authentic performances of English and other vocal consort music of the Renaissance and baroque eras. The artists in the Consort are established soloists, and the ensemble has travelled widely, performing at festivals in Edinburgh, Vienna, Salzburg, Amsterdam, Copenhagen *et al.*, and has toured

Australia and New Zealand, Japan, Israel, the United States, Scandinavia and other countries. In 1963 Deller also founded and became artistic director of the Stour Music Festival, and as a result of the response in France to his early 78 r.p.m. records as a counter-tenor he established a music festival and summer school, the Academy of English Music, at the Abbaye de Sénanque in Provence, and set up his own record company in France. The outstanding counter-tenor of his time, he has done more than any other to revive the music written for this voice. He has explained that he became a conductor because he found that not all conductors have a natural sympathy for singers, or understand the natural fall of the phrase and the need for a slight hiatus for breath.

Deller has recorded as a conductor with the Deller Consort, and with instrumental groups such as the Clemencic Consort, Collegium Aureum, Vienna Musica Antiqua, Vienna Concentus Musicus, Renaissance Chamber Ensemble, Stour Music Festival Orchestra, Morley Consort, King's Music, Oriana Orchestra, Baroque String Ensemble, Consort of Viols of the Schola Cantorum, Basel, and the Jaye Consort of Viols, and with various vocal soloists. Most of the records were originally made for Harmonia Mundi, and many have been issued in the United States by RCA (Victrola) and Vanguard. Included have been Monteverdi's *Messa a quattro voci*, *Lagrime d'amante*, *Lamento d'Arianna*, *Tirsi e Clori*, and a number of madrigals, Gesualdo's *Benedictus miserere*, *Nine Responses for Maundy Thursday*, *Nine Responses for Good Friday*, *Nine Responses for Holy Saturday*, Nocturnes Nos 1 and 2, and a number of madrigals and motets, Pérotin's *Sederunt Principes*, *Dic Christi Veritas*, *Pater Noster*, *Viderunt omnes*, *Alleluja Navitas* and *Notre Dame Organa*, de Machaut's *Messe Nostre Dame*, Vecchi's *L'amfiparnasso*, Byrd's *Mass for Three Voices*, *Mass for Four Voices*, *Mass for Five Voices* and motets, Purcell's *Dido and Aeneas*, *King Arthur*, *The Fairy Queen*, *Ode on St Cecilia's Day*, *The Earth Trembled*, *O How Happy's he*, *Love's Goddess Sure was Blind*, *Welcome to All the Pleasures*, *Raise Raise the Voice*, *Hear ye Sullen Powers Below*, *Music for a while*, *Come Away Do not Stay*, *Man that is Born of Woman*, *In Guilty Night*, *Olinda*, Pavane and trio, *Funeral Sentences*, *Te Deum* and *Jubilate Deo in D*, and collections entitled *Songs and Catches*, *Songs*, *Ayres* and *Anthems*, Handel's *Alexander's Feast* and *Acis and Galatea*, Le Jeune's *Mass in D*, Morley's *Laboravi*, madrigals and canzonets, Palestrina's *Ave verum*, Bassano's Ricercare V, Frescobaldi's Canzoni I, Grandi's *O quam pulchra es* and *Cantabile Domine*, Parsons' *Ave Maria*, Tallis's *Lamentations of Jeremiah the Prophet*, *Salvator mundi* and other sacred music, Tomkins' madrigals and sacred pieces, Gibbons' sacred pieces, Wilbye's madrigals, Blow's *Amphion Angelicus* and Jannequin's chansons, and collections entitled *Christmas Carols and Motets of Medieval Europe*; *From Heaven Above*; *Album of Beloved Songs*; *Carols and Motets for the Nativity of Medieval and Tudor England*; *Cruel Mother*; *English, French and Italian Madrigals and Songs*; *Madrigal Masterpieces*; *Music of Medieval France*; *English Madrigals and Folksongs*, *Shakespearian Songs and Consort Music*; *Tavern Songs, Catches and Glees*; *Elizabethan and Jacobean Music*; *The Flowering of French Chanson*; *English Cathedral Music*; *Notre Dame, c.1200*; *Three Ravens* and *Hymns to the Virgin*; some pieces by anonymous composers were also recorded, as well as a contribution to the two-disc set *The Art of Ornamentation and Embellishment in the Renaissance and Baroque*.

Del Mar, Norman (b. 1919). Born in Hampstead, Del Mar studied with Vaughan Williams and Lambert at the Royal College of Music, and during World War II served with the Royal Air Force as a horn player in its Central Band. After the war he founded and conducted the Chelsea Symphony Orchestra in a series of concerts noted for their adventurous programmes. In 1946 he joined the Royal Philharmonic Orchestra as a horn player and in the following year Beecham engaged him as musical assistant and associate conductor for the orchestra. He then conducted part of the Strauss Festival presented by Beecham at Drury Lane. Del Mar later said: 'I owe everything to Beecham.' In 1947 he also led the Croydon Symphony Orchestra, a semi-professional group similar to the Chelsea Symphony. He became an assistant conductor at Sadler's Wells Opera (1948), principal conductor of The English Opera Group (1949), professor of conducting at the Guildhall School of Music (1955), conductor of the Yorkshire Symphony Orchestra (1954) and conductor of the BBC Scottish Orchestra (1960). In these years he developed a reputation as an interpreter of Mahler and Bruckner, 20th-century music, and in particular British composers. Since 1966 he has conducted the New BBC Orchestra, later renamed the Academy of the BBC, a training orchestra with the purpose of bridging the gap for young players between the music academies and membership of the symphony orchestras. In recent years he has also been a freelance conductor of opera and in the concert hall, has been particularly active in Scandinavia, and was awarded the CBE in 1975. He has written an important three-volume study of the music of Richard Strauss.

Del Mar's first recording was a 78 r.p.m. set of Tchaikovsky's *Variations on a Rococo Theme* (with Tortelier and an orchestra for HMV). Since then, on LP, his recordings have been almost entirely of 20th-century British music. Included have been Elgar's *Enigma Variations* and *Pomp and Circumstance Marches* (with the Royal Philharmonic Orchestra for DGG), Vaughan Williams' *Concerto Grosso*, Delius' *Air and Dance*, Warlock's *Serenade to Frederick Delius* and Elgar's *Serenade* (with the Bournemouth Symphony Orchestra for EMI), Britten's *Noye's fludde* (with the English Chamber Orchestra *et al.* for Argo), Gerhard's *Concerto for Orchestra* and Rawsthorne's Symphony No. 3 (with the BBC Symphony Orchestra for Argo); Lutyens' *Quincunx* and Maw's *Scenes and Aria* (with the BBC Symphony Orchestra for Argo), Berkeley's Symphony No. 1 and Double Piano Concerto (with Beckett and McDonald and the London Philharmonic Orchestra for Lyrita), Bax's Symphony No. 6 (with the New Philharmonia Orchestra for Lyrita), Musgrave's Clarinet Concerto (with de Peyer), Banks' Horn Concerto (with Tuckwell) and Searle's *Aubade* (with Tuckwell, and with the New Philharmonia Orchestra for Argo), Delius' Violin and Cello Concerto (with Cohen and Warburg and the Royal Philharmonic Orchestra for Pye), Violin Concertos of Fricker and Goehr (with Neaman and the Royal Philharmonic Orchestra for Argo), Britten's *Prelude and Fugue*, Lutyens' *Ô saisons, Ô châteaux* and Schoenberg's *Suite for Strings* (with the Royal Philharmonic Orchestra for EMI), Goehr's *Little Symphony* and Tippett's *Concerto for Orchestra*, (with the London Symphony Orchestra for Philips), Hoddinott's Symphony No. 2 and *Variants for Orchestra* (with the London Symphony Orchestra for Pye), Maw's *Sinfonia* and *Sonata for Strings* (with the English Chamber Orchestra *et al.* for Argo), Crosse's *Changes* (with the London Symphony Orchestra *et al.* for Argo), Elgar's *Chanson de matin*, *Chanson de nuit*, *Sérénade lyrique*, *Dream Children*, *Contrasts*, *Soliloquy* (with L. Goossens), *Woodland Interlude* from *Caractacus*, two Interludes from *Falstaff* and three *Bavarian Dances* (with the Bournemouth Sinfonietta for Lyrita), Tchaikovsky's *Romeo and Juliet* fantasy-overture, *1812* overture and *Marche slave* (with the New Philharmonia Orchestra for Contour), Beethoven's Symphony No. 5 and the overtures to *Tannhäuser* and *Die Meistersinger* (with the London Symphony Orchestra for Musical Appreciation).

Delogu, Gaetano (b. 1934). Born in Messina, Sicily, Delogu started playing the violin as a child, studied both law and music at university, then was a conducting pupil with Ferrara in Rome and Venice. After winning first prize at the Young Conductors' Competition in Florence, he conducted in Italy for four years and in 1968 won first prize at the Dmitri Mitropoulos International Conductors' Competition in New York, which brought him a year as assistant to Bernstein and Szell. Since then he has based his activities in Italy but has conducted many of the major symphony orchestras in Europe, appeared at Covent Garden to conduct operas by Puccini, and made his United States debut with the Cleveland Orchestra. His first record was a lively, originally conceived and well-played coupling of Haydn's Symphonies Nos 83 and 101 (with the London Philharmonic Orchestra, issued by Classics for Pleasure in 1975), which was followed by Mahler's Symphony No. 1 (with the same orchestra for Classics for Pleasure, in 1977). He also recorded Hindemith's *Symphonic Metamorphoses on Themes of Weber* and *Nobilissima Visione* (with the Czech Philharmonic Orchestra for Supraphon).

Del Tredici, David (b. 1937). Born in Cloverdale, California, Del Tredici studied at the University of California, Berkeley, and at Princeton University with Sessions, and taught at Harvard University. Of his compositions he has recorded *Night Conjure – Verse* (with the Marlboro Festival Players *et al.* for Composers Recordings).

De Main, John (b. 1944). Born in Youngstown, Ohio, De Main studied at the Juilliard School, graduating in 1968, and at Aspen and Tanglewood. He began conducting at the age of fourteen in his home town, was associate conductor of the National Educational Television Opera Project, won the Julius Rudel Award at New York City Opera, was associate conductor at the San Francisco Opera, with the St Paul Chamber Orchestra and Norwalk Symphony Orchestra, was music director of the Texas Opera Theater and Kenley Players, then principal conductor and artistic director of the Houston Grand Opera. With the latter company he conducted a production of *Porgy and Bess* as part of the American Bicentennial celebrations in 1976, which was so successful that it was transferred to New York for a 16-week run.

A recording of this excellent performance was released by RCA in 1977.

De Preist, James (b. 1936). Born in Philadelphia and educated at the University of Pennsylvania, De Preist studied with Persichetti at the Philadelphia Conservatory and then toured the Middle and Far East in 1962 conducting and lecturing on American music. After being stricken with poliomyelitis he resumed conducting in 1963, won first prize at the Dmitri Mitropoulos International Conductors' Competition in New York (1965), was associate conductor to Bernstein with the New York Philharmonic Orchestra (1965–6) and has since conducted many orchestras in the US and abroad. He was appointed associate conductor of the National Symphony Orchestra in Washington DC (1971) and has been musical director of the Quebec Symphony Orchestra (since 1974). For the Swedish label Caprice he recorded Pergament's *The Jewish Song* (with the Stockholm Philharmonic Orchestra *et al.*), and for Delos Hindemith's *Nobilissima Visione* and *The Four Temperaments* (with Rosenberger and the Royal Philharmonic Orchestra).

Dennington, Arthur (b. 1904). Born in London and educated at the Guildhall School of Music, Dennington was conductor of the Modern Symphony Orchestra (from 1931) and of the University of London Musical Society, the Newbury Amateur Orchestral Union and the Tottenham Municipal Orchestra, and was musical director of the Northern Polytechnic. For Rare Recorded Editions he conducted the Modern Symphony Orchestra in discs of overtures by Auber and ballet music and overtures by Cherubini. He also conducted the London Classical Orchestra in *Peter and the Wolf* (with Gilbert Harding as narrator) for Concert Artist, but the record does not appear to have been issued.

Denzler, Robert (b. 1892). The Swiss conductor and composer Denzler was born into a distinguished and long-established family at Zürich, where he was a pupil of Volkmar Andreae at the Conservatory. After further studies at Cologne and a period as a musical assistant at Bayreuth, he was appointed municipal music director at Lucerne (1912–15), music director at the Zürich Opera (1915–27) and the first conductor at the Charlottenburg Opera in Berlin (1927–32). In 1925 he organised a Wagner festival in Geneva which was repeated annually until 1931; on occasion between 1920 and 1931 he toured with the Suisse Romande Orchestra. Denzler returned to the Zürich Opera in 1932, and until 1946 was its musical director and chief conductor. The world premières of Berg's *Lulu* (1937) and Hindemith's *Mathis der Maler* (1938) were his responsibility, both operas having been banned in Nazi Germany. After 1947 he divided his time between conducting opera and concerts in Europe, and composition; his output of choral, symphonic and other music is said to show the influence of Richard Strauss. Decca recorded him in the days of mono LP, in Chausson's *Symphony in B flat*, and Honegger's Symphony No. 3 and *Chant de joie* (with the Paris Conservatoire Orchestra) and Tchaikovsky's Symphony No. 4 and the Berlioz overtures *Benvenuto Cellini* and *Béatrice et Bénédict* (with the Suisse Romande Orchestra).

Dervaux, Pierre (b. 1917). Dervaux was born in Paris where his father was a trombone player in the Colonne Orchestra. At the age of 9 he entered the Paris Conservatoire, and at 17 he became the timpanist in the Pasdeloup Orchestra, conducting his first concert in 1945 with that orchestra. He was appointed chief conductor at the Paris Opéra-Comique (1948), conductor of the Pasdeloup Concerts (1948), chief conductor (1954) and then musical director (1971) of the Paris Opéra, president of the Colonne Concerts (1952), conductor of the Quebec Symphony Orchestra (1968–9), director of the Orchestre des Pays de la Loire (1971) and conductor at the Chicago Lyric Opera, and has taught at the Montreal Conservatoire and at the École Normale in Paris. A widely acclaimed conductor, he has a reputation especially for his interpretations of French music.

Dervaux recorded on 78s Schoenberg's Chamber Symphony No. 1 (with the Pasdeloup Orchestra for Dial). Then on LP he recorded *La Mer*, *Iberia*, *Fêtes*, *La Valse*, *Rapsodie espagnole* and the *Daphnis et Chloé* Suite No. 2 (with the Colonne Orchestra for La Guilde Internationale du Disque); the *Russian Easter Festival* overture, *1812* overture, *Marche slave*, Enesco's *Romanian Rhapsody No. 1*, the waltz from *Eugene Onegin*, the overtures to *Russlan and Ludmilla* and *A Life for the Tsar*, *In the Steppes of Central Asia* and the gopak from *Sorochintsy Fair* (with the Amsterdam Philharmonic Orchestra for La Guilde Internationale du Disque); Ravel's two Piano concertos (with Robert Casadesus) and Chabrier's *España*, *Bourrée fantasque*, overture to *Gwendoline*, *Habanera*, *Marche joyeuse* and *Fête polonaise* (with the Paris Conservatoire Orchestra for EMI); *Danse macabre*, *La Jeunesse d'Hercule*, *Phaéton* and *Le Rouet d'Omphale*, and Satie's *Mercure*, *Socrate*, *Geneviève de Brabant*, *La*

Messe des pauvres and *La Diva de l'Empire* (with l'Orchestre de Paris for EMI); *Les Dialogues des Carmélites* and excerpts from *Thaïs* (with the Paris Opéra Orchestra *et al.* for EMI); excerpts from *Faust* (with the Cologne Radio Orchestra *et al.* for EMI); Tchaikovsky's Piano Concerto No. 1 (with Cziffra and the French National Radio Orchestra for EMI); *Les Pêcheurs de perles*, Charpentier's *Impressions d'Italie* and Massenet's *Scènes pittoresques* (with the Paris Opéra-Comique Orchestra *et al.* for EMI); d'Indy's *Istar* and *Wallenstein* (with l'Orchestre des Pays de la Loire for EMI); the Bach *Three-Keyboard Concerto in D minor* (played on pianos) and Casadesus' Three-Piano Concerto (with Robert, Gaby and Jean Casadesus and the Colonne Orchestra for EMI); *Le Carnaval des animaux* and Poulenc's Two-Piano Concerto (with Whittemore and Lowe, and the Philharmonia Orchestra for EMI); Saint-Saëns' three Violin Concertos, *Morceau de concert*, *Havanaise*, *Introduction et rondo capriccioso*, *Marche héroïque* and two *Romances*, and Ysaÿe's *Caprice d'après l'étude en forme de valse de Saint-Saëns* (with Hoelscher and the New Philharmonia Orchestra for EMI); excerpts, in French, from *Rigoletto* and *La traviata* (with the Paris Opéra Orchestra *et al.* for Pathé); Dutilleux's Symphony No. 1 (with the Paris Opéra Orchestra for CIDM); Hossein's *Persepolis* (with the Paris Opéra Orchestra *et al.* for Edici); excerpts from *Lakmé* (with the Lamoureux Orchestra *et al.* for Philips); Bizet's *Jeux d'enfants* (with the Colonne Orchestra for Trianon); excerpts from *Carmen* (with the Pasdeloup Orchestra *et al.* for Vox); Poulenc's Piano concerto (with Haas-Hamburger and the Pasdeloup Orchestra for Period); Hossein's Symphony and Piano Concertos Nos 2 and 3 (with Boukoff and the Monte Carlo Opera Orchestra for Edici); *Boléro*, *Pavane pour une infante défunte*, *Prélude à l'après-midi d'un faune* and a suite from *The Love of Three Oranges* (with the Hamburg State Philharmonic Orchestra, issued by Marble Arch); and Planquette's *Les Cloches de Corneville*, Ganne's *Les Saltimbanques*, Lehár's *Paganini* and Messager's *Véronique* (for Telefunken).

Desarzens, Victor (b. 1908). Born at Château-d'Oex in Switzerland, Desarzens learned the violin as a boy, and studied at the Lausanne Conservatoire with Porta for the violin and von Hoesslin for conducting. After continuing his studies with Enesco, he became a first violin with the Suisse Romande Orchestra, but left to form a string quartet with which he gave many concerts. He also appeared as a solo violinist. In 1941 he formed a chamber ensemble primarily to present performances on Radio Lausanne; this group was later called the Lausanne Chamber Orchestra and achieved considerable distinction, taking part in festivals and giving concerts throughout Europe. He has also conducted the Winterthur Symphony Orchestra since 1948, and after Scherchen left the orchestra in 1950 he was made its chief conductor. He is also head of the Romande Radio Foundation and in this capacity has performed many contemporary works.

Desarzens recorded for L'Oiseau Lyre on 78 r.p.m. discs the *Brandenburg Concerto No. 5*, the *Harpsichord Concerto in A major* (with Nef) and the *Concerto for Harpischord, Flute and Violin in A minor* (with the Lausanne Chamber Orchestra). Then in the early years of LP he made a number of discs, including two suites from Rameau's ballet *Platée* (with the Lausanne Chamber Orchestra for La Guilde Internationale du Disque), Mozart's Piano Concertos K. 271 (with Kraus and the Vienna State Opera Orchestra for GID), K. 451 (with Balsam and the Winterthur Symphony Orchestra for GID), and K. 503 and K. 595 (with Fou Ts'ong and the Vienna State Opera Orchestra for Westminster), the Sinfonia Concertante K. 271b and K. 365 and the Serenades K. 239 and K. 320 (with the Lausanne Chamber Orchestra for Westminster), *Eine kleine Nachtmusik*, the *Academic Festival* and other popular overtures and Liszt's *Hungarian Rhapsody No. 9* (with the Vienna State Opera Orchestra for Reader's Digest), Beethoven's Piano Concerto No. 3 (with Kraus and the Amsterdam Philharmonic Orchestra for GID), Piano Concerto No. 4 and Rondo in B Flat, Weber's *Konzertstück* and the Schumann Piano Concerto (with Kraus and the Vienna State Opera Orchestra for GID), Weber's two symphonies (with the Lausanne Chamber Orchestra for Westminster), the Schumann Violin Concerto (with Rybar and the Lausanne Symphony Orchestra for GID), the Mendelssohn and Tchaikovsky Violin Concertos (with Rybar and the Vienna Festival Orchestra for GID), Liszt's *Tasso* (with the Winterthur Symphony Orchestra for GID) and *Hungarian Rhapsody No. 2* (with the Vienna Festival Orchestra for GID), Tchaikovsky's Symphony No. 5 and *1812* overture (with the Vienna Festival Orchestra for GID), a Gounod symphony, the overtures to *Euryanthe* and *Abu Hassan*, *Capriccio espagnol*, introduction and march from *Le Coq d'or*, and the prelude to *Khovanshchina* (with the Winterthur Symphony Orchestra for GID), Saint-Saëns' Piano Concerto No. 3 (with Pozzi and the Winterthur

Symphony Orchestra for GID), Ibert's Flute Concerto (with Graf and the Winterthur Symphony Orchestra for GID), Sibelius' *Pelléas et Mélisande* and Martin's *Concerto for Seven Wind Instruments, Timpani Percussion and Strings* (with the Winterthur Symphony Orchestra for GID), Martin's *Le Vin herbé* (with the Winterthur Symphony Orchestra *et al.* for Westminster), Strauss's *Le Bourgeois gentilhomme* and *Metamorphosen*, Elgar's *Introduction and Allegro*, Britten's *Variations on a Theme of Frank Bridge* and *Prelude and Fugue* and Schoenberg's *Verklärte Nacht* (with the Lausanne Chamber Orchestra for Westminster), Shostakovich's Piano Concerto No. 2 (with List and the Vienna State Opera Orchestra for Westminster), Zbinden's *Concerto da Camera* (with Engel and the Lausanne Chamber Orchestra for Amadeo) and *Fantasy for Flute* (with Nicolet and the Lausanne Chamber Orchestra for CTS), Schibler's *Lyric Concerto for Flute* (with Nicolet and the Lausanne Chamber Orchestra for da Camera Magna), Burkhard's Violin Concerto (with Schneeberger and the Lausanne Chamber Orchestra for CTS), Perrin's *Landschaft der Seele* (with Devallier and the Lausanne Chamber Orchestra for CTS) and Regamey's *Five Studies* (with Retchitzka and the Lausanne Chamber Orchestra for CTS). A number of the discs for La Guilde Internationale du Disque were issued on other labels, such as Nixa, Vanguard, Concert Hall and Musical Masterpieces.

Desormière, Roger (1893–1963). The French conductor Desormière was born at Vichy, studied at the Paris Conservatoire with Koechlin, and in 1924 received his first position as a conductor with the Swedish Ballet. A year later he started a five-year term with Diaghilev's Ballets Russes, touring throughout Europe with the company. Before his appointment as musical director at the Paris Opéra-Comique in 1937 he had become widely known as a operatic and symphonic conductor, most particularly for his direction of Debussy's *Pelléas et Mélisande*. He was with the Opéra-Comique until 1945, after which he joined the Paris Opéra and was active for several years in London with the BBC. In 1949 he led the Paris Radio Orchestra at the Edinburgh Festival, and brought the Opéra comique to London to present *Pelléas et Mélisande* at Covent Garden. The following year he was stricken with aphasia and was forced to retire; his concert appearances also became much less frequent. In his earlier days Desormière was a follower of Satie, and was always a fine and enthusiastic interpreter of modern French music. He took part in most of the annual festivals of the International Society for Contemporary Music, but at the same time was much interested in Renaissance and pre-classical music, and as the director of La Société de la Musique d'Autrefois from 1930 he carried out research, edited and performed neglected music of those eras. Peter Heyworth has described him as the finest French conductor of his generation; Boulez admired the sobriety and functionalism of his gestures; Desormière had conducted the première of Boulez's *Le Soleil des eaux* in 1948.

Desormière made numerous recordings, mainly on 78 r.p.m. discs, and they reflect the wide range of his musical interests. Most notable was the complete recording of *Pelléas et Mélisande* which was accomplished in France during World War II, and released on 20 records by HMV. This set was a sensation; some critics have preferred the performance to the later LPs by Ansermet. David Hall wrote in 1948 that 'one has the feeling throughout the performance that all concerned are working together as a perfectly integrated team intent only on bringing Debussy's score to the most complete and vivid possible realisation'. The set is still available on an LP transfer in France. His other records of modern French music include the incidental music to Lesur's *L'Étoile de Séville* (for Florilège), Sauget's cantata *La Voyante* (for L'Oiseau Lyre), Milhaud's *Suite provençale* and *L'Homme et son désir* (for Champrosay), Jolivet's *Petits ballets* (for EMI), Messiaen's *Trois petites liturgies* and *Les Offrandes oubliées* (for Pathé), Koechlin's Septet and *Sonata for Clarinet and Orchestra* (with Lefèbre, for L'Oiseau Lyre), Sauguet's Piano Concerto (with Gontaut-Baron and the Paris Conservatoire Orchestra for Columbia), Rivier's Symphony No. 3 (with the French National Radio Orchestra for EMI), excerpts from Chabrier's opera *L'Étoile* (with the Paris Opéra-Comique for Pathé), some marionette plays of Delannoy (for Florilège), *Boléro*, *La Mer*, and Nuages and Fêtes from Debussy's *Nocturnes* (with the Czech Philharmonic Orchestra for Supraphon). On 78s for L'Oiseau Lyre he had recorded French baroque music, including Gervaise's *Danceries de la Renaissance*, Rameau's *Les Paladins* and selections from *Hippolyte et Aricie*, Couperin's *L'Apothéose de Lully*, *L'Apothéose de Corelli*, *Les Concerts Royaux* Nos 4, 9 and 13, *Le Parnasse* and other pieces, Campra's *L'Europe galante*, Montéclair's *Jephté* suite, Boismortier's Bassoon Concerto (with Oubradous) and Delalande's *Symphonies pour les soupers du Roy*. After World War II he recorded, for Decca, Bizet's *Patrie* and *Jeux d'enfants*,

Chabrier's *Habanera* and Debussy's *Marche écossaise* (with the National Symphony Orchestra, on 78s), and later went on to record on LP for the same company excerpts from *Coppélia* and *Sylvia*, *The Sleeping Beauty* and *Swan Lake*, Ibert's *Divertissement*, Poulenc's *Les Biches*, Ippolitov-Ivanov's *Caucasian Sketches*, the Chopin/Douglas *Les Sylphides* and the Scarlatti/Tommasini *The Good-humoured Ladies* (all with the Paris Conservatoire Orchestra).

His other records included Grétry's *La Rosière républicaine* (arranged by Meyrowitz, with the Paris Philharmonic Orchestra for Le Chant du Monde), Weber's *Andante e rondo ongarese* (with Oubradous and the Paris Conservatoire Orchestra for L'Oiseau Lyre), Franck's *Symphony in D minor* (with the Paris Philharmonic Orchestra for Supraphon), the *Nutcracker* Suite (with an orchestra for Capitol) and excerpts from *Swan Lake* (with the French Symphony Orchestra for Capitol), Glazunov's *The Seasons* (with the French National Symphony Orchestra for EMI) and Violin Concerto (with Candala and the Pierné Orchestra for Columbia), *L'Arlésienne* Suites Nos 1 and 2 and a suite from *Carmen* (with the Czech Philharmonic Orchestra for Supraphon), Massenet's ballet from *Le Cid* (with the Paris Philharmonic Orchestra for Le Chant du Monde), Prokofiev's *Lieutenant Kijé* suite and suite from *The Love of Three Oranges*, a suite from *Le Coq d'or*, and *Capriccio espagnol* (with the French National Symphony Orchestra for EMI), Bartók's Rhapsody No. 1 (with Foldès and the Lamoureux Orchestra for Vox), and Hindemith's Violin Concerto (with Merckel and the Lamoureux Orchestra for EMI).

Dessau, Paul (b. 1894). Born in Hamburg, Dessau studied at the Klindworth-Scharwenka Conservatorium in Berlin (from 1910) as a pupil of Zojic and Behm. He was a repetiteur at the Hamburg Opera (1913), served in the German army in World War I, conducted at the Cologne Opera (1919–23), at Mainz (1923–4) and in Berlin (1925–33). He left Germany in 1933 and lived in France and the United States, returned to Berlin in 1948, was vice-president of the German Academy of Arts in East Berlin (1957–62) and a member of the Academy of Arts in West Berlin (1965–8). His compositions include film music and other orchestral works, in addition to two operas for children and another to a libretto of Brecht, *The Trial of Lucullus*, which includes a part for a piano with metal-covered hammers. Another opera, *Puntila*, was first performed in Berlin in 1966 and is based on Brecht's play *Mr Puntila and his Valet Matti*; in 1971 DGG issued a complete recording of it with Dessau conducting soloists, the chorus and orchestra of the German State Opera, Berlin, and the Berlin Staatskapelle. He also recorded his *In Memoriam Bertold Brecht* and *Symphonic Variations on Themes of J. S. Bach and C. P. E. Bach* (with the Leipzig Gewandhaus Orchestra for Eterna, and issued by Philips), *Lilo Herrman* and *Lenin*: *Orchestral Music No. 3* (with the Berlin Radio symphony Orchestra). Dessau has been highly honored in DR Germany, although his music has been received with less enthusiasm in the West.

Devátý, Antonín (b. 1903). Born at Skuteč, Czechoslovakia, Devátý studied at Žerotin's Music School at Olomouc and then at the Prague Conservatory under Wiedermann, Křička, Ostrčil and Talich, graduating in 1926. He also studied conducting privately with Dědeček (1935–8) and Novák (1943–9), worked as a violinist (1926–35), conducted for the Czech Radio in Ostrava and Brno (1938–51) and then became chief conductor of the Pilsen Radio Orchestra (1952). He has also toured the USSR and Eastern Europe, and has composed concertos, chamber music and vocal works of some distinction. For Supraphon he recorded the Krommer-Kramář Oboe Concerto (with Hanták and the Brno Radio Orchestra).

Devos, Gérard (b. 1927). Born at Lille, Devos studied at the Paris Conservatoire, graduated as a harpist, studied composition with Aubin and Messiaen, and won first prize for the harp at the Prague International Festival (1947) and at the International Competition for Young Conductors at Besançon (1956). He succeeded Wolff as president and permanent conductor of the Concerts Pasdeloup Association (1970) and conducts the symphonic repertoire in France and abroad, as well as contemporary music especially of French composers. He has recorded a Handel's *Terpsichore* ballet suite and *Harp Concerto in B flat* (with Mildonian and the Pasdeloup Orchestra for Musidisc and released in the United States by Nonesuch), Paganini's Violin Concerto No. 1 and Prokofiev's Violin Concerto No. 2 (with Hassan and the New Philharmonia Orchestra for Classics for Pleasure).

Diener, Hermann (1897–1955). Born in Rostock, Diener studied in Berlin with Adolf Busch and from 1924 to 1928 directed his own chamber orchestra in Heidelberg. In 1928 he became conductor of the Berlin Collegium

Musicum at the Berlin Academy for School and Church Music, and in 1934 was appointed professor there. He recorded with the Collegium Musicum his own arrangement of Bach's *Die Kunst der Fuge*, Handel's Concerti Grossi Op. 6 Nos 1 and 5, Corelli's Concerto Grosso Op. 6 No. 8, Schiassi's *Christmas Symphony*, Pachelbel's Canon, a concertino and a concerto by Torelli and the Bach Double Violin Concerto, (with himself and Hampe the soloists), all for HMV, and on 78 r.p.m. discs.

Dilkes, Neville (b. 1930). Born in Derby into a family of musicians, Dilkes studied at the Trinity College of Music, became a teacher, and conducted the Kettering Symphony Orchestra in the Midlands (1958–63) and the Opera da Camera (1961–7). He studied conducting first with Boult and then with Dixon at the international conductors' course in Holland in 1963. Previously in 1961 he had formed the Midland Sinfonia, based in Nottingham, an orchestra which subsequently changed its name to the English Sinfonia. With the orchestra he has made three discs for EMI, containing fine performances of Harty's *John Field Suite*, Bridge's *There is a Willow*, Butterworth's *A Shropshire Lad*, *English Idyll*, and *The Banks of Green Willow*, Bax's *Dance in the Sun*, Leigh's *Concertino*, Ireland's *The Holy Boy*, Warlock's *Capriol Suite* and several pieces and the *Symphony in G minor* of E. J. Moeran. This latter work leans somewhat heavily on Sibelius and Bax, but its mood and character give it a secure if minor place in British symphonic literature.

Dimitriadi, Odissei (b. 1908). Born at Batumi, Georgia, Dimitriadi studied at the Tbilisi Conservatory (1926–30) and in Leningrad (1930–36). He was director of the music high school at Sukhumi (1936–7), teacher of conducting at Tbilisi Conservatory (1937–41), conductor at the Georgian Opera (1937–65), chief conductor of the Georgian State Symphony Orchestra (1947–52), conductor at the Bolshoi Theatre, Moscow (from 1965), and professor of conducting at the Moscow Conservatory (from 1968). He has recorded Taktakishvili's Symphony No. 1 and Arakishvili's overture *The Tale of Shota Rustaveli* (with the Moscow Radio Symphony Orchestra).

D'Indy, Vincent (1851–1931). Although the French composer d'Indy never held an official position as a conductor, several writers have commented that he had great gifts in this capacity and that he was particularly successful conducting his own music. He toured Spain, Russia and the United States, where he appeared in 1905 with the Boston Symphony Orchestra. In 1931, the year of his death, he recorded his *Le Camp de Wallenstein*, which he had written 50 years earlier. This performance was re-issued on an LP transfer by Perennial, coupled with Roussel and Schmitt also conducting their own compositions, *Le Festin de l'araignée* and *La Tragédie de Salomé*, respectively. This LP transfer includes the short address by the composer that was issued with the original recording.

Dixon, Dean (1915–76). Born in New York of West Indian parents, Dixon studied the violin at the Institute of Musical Arts in New York and conducting with Stoessel at the Juilliard School, and took a degree at Columbia University. He formed his own orchestra in New York in 1932 and a year later made his debut as a violinist. His first public appearance as a conductor was in 1937 leading the chamber orchestra of the League of Music Lovers in New York, and in the next year he founded the New York Chamber Orchestra. In 1941 he became the first Negro conductor to lead the New York Philharmonic Orchestra, and in the following three years he was a guest conductor with the Philadelphia and Boston Symphony Orchestras. In 1944 he founded the American Youth Orchestra which he led until 1949 when he left the United States; he was with the Israel Philharmonic Orchestra (1950–51), was conductor of the Göteborg Symphony Orchestra in Sweden (1953–60), principal conductor of the Hesse Radio Symphony Orchestra at Frankfurt am Main (1961–70) and principal conductor of the Sydney Symphony Orchestra (1964–7). He first appeared in London in 1963 with the BBC Symphony Orchestra, returned to Sydney in 1973 to conduct some of the opening concerts at the Sydney Opera House, toured extensively in Italy, Switzerland, Czechoslovakia and in the Scandinavian countries, and returned with great success to the US in 1970. He was an accomplished interpreter with a style that had more in common with conductors of northern Europe than with the more extrovert and polished directors of the great American symphony orchestras; his repertoire was rooted in the European classics which he performed with the utmost attention to clarity and balance, although sometimes his readings could be somewhat straightforward and solemn.

Of Dixon's recordings the most notable were Tchaikovsky's Symphony No. 6 (with the Cologne Radio Symphony Orchestra, issued by CBS-Realm, Marble Arch and Everest), and Brahms' Piano Concerto No. 2 (with Jenner and the Vienna Volksoper Orchestra, issued by World Record Club and Marble Arch). His others included Mozart's Piano Concertos K. 413 and K. 482, and MacDowell's Piano Concertos Nos 1 and 2 (with Rivkin and the Vienna State Opera Orchestra), the Dvořák Cello Concerto (with Janigro and the Vienna State Opera Orchestra), the incidental music to *Rosamunde* (with the Vienna State Opera Orchestra *et al.*), Schubert's Symphonies Nos 4 and 5 (with the London Philharmonic Symphony Orchestra), Schumann's Symphonies Nos 3 and 4 (with the Vienna State Opera Orchestra), and Liszt's *Orpheus*, *Mazeppa*, *Les Préludes* and *Hunnenschlacht* (with the London Philharmonic Symphony Orchestra); these discs were issued on mono LP by Westminster and Nixa. Also there was excerpts from *The Bartered Bride*, and *Moldau* (with the Cologne Radio Symphony Orchestra for CBS-Realm). He recorded music by a number of American composers for the American Recording Society, some of these discs being re-issued later by Desto; the orchestra was originally called the ARS Orchestra, but in Desto's revival of the performances it was called the Vienna Symphony Orchestra. The works were Luening's *Prelude on a Hymn Tune by Billings* and *Two Symphonic Interludes*, Cowell's Symphony No. 5, MacDowell's *Indian Suite*, Mason's overture *Chanticleer*, Moore's Symphony No. 2, Powell's *Rapsodie nègre*, Sowerby's *From the Northern Prairie*, Ward's Symphony No. 2, Swanson's Symphony No. 2, Thompson's Symphony No. 2, Creston's *Partita*, Piston's Symphony No. 2 and Hanson's Symphony No. 4. Of American music he also recorded Gershwin's *An American in Paris* and *Rhapsody in Blue* (with Rivkin and the Vienna Symphony Orchestra for Pathé-Vox). Towards the end of his life he made a series of discs for Barenreiter and many of these were issued by Nonesuch, Supraphon and Oryx; included were Haydn's Symphonies Nos 48 and 92, Mozart's Symphonies Nos 33 and 34, Weber's Symphonies Nos 1 and 2 and a selection of Brahms' *Hungarian Dances* (with the Prague Chamber Orchestra), Mendelssohn's Symphony No. 3, Beethoven's Symphony No. 7, Brahms' Symphony No. 1 and the overtures *Tragic*, *Manfred*, *Faust* (Wagner) and *Die Schöne Melusine* (with the Prague Symphony Orchestra).

Dixon often said that as his career progressed he was first referred to as the American Negro conductor, Dean Dixon, then as the American conductor, Dean Dixon, and then as the conductor, Dean Dixon. But he would not feel that he had reached his peak until he was referred to simply as Dean Dixon.

Dixon, James (b. 1928). Educated in Iowa where he first conducted in 1951, Dixon was conductor of the Seventh Army Symphony Orchestra in Germany (1953–4), of the University of Iowa Symphony Orchestra (1954–9), and won the Elizabeth Sprague Coolidge International Conducting Award in 1955. He then was conductor of the New England Conservatory Orchestra, Boston (1959–61), associate conductor of the Minneapolis Symphony Orchestra (1961–2), again of the University of Iowa Symphony Orchestra (since 1962), and of the Tri-City Symphony Orchestra, Davenport, Iowa (since 1965). He was made an honorary member of the Bruckner Society in 1961 and received the Gustav Mahler Medal in 1963. For Composers Recordings he conducted the Royal Philharmonic Orchestra in Anderson's *Chamber Symphony*, Brozen's *In Memoriam*, Thorne's *Liebesrock* and Wuorinén's Piano Concerto (with the composer as soloist).

Dmitriev, Aleksander (b. 1935). Born in Leningrad, Dmitriev studied at the Leningrad Conservatory under Kudriavtseva, Tiulin and Rabinovich, and became conductor of the Karelian Radio and Television Symphony Orchestra (1961), and principal conductor of the same orchestra the next year. He was a prize-winner at the Second USSR Competition for Conductors (1966), was appointed principal conductor of the Maly Opera and Ballet Theatre in Leningrad (1973) and then principal conductor of the Leningrad Philharmonic Orchestra (1977). For Melodiya he has recorded Miaskovsky's Violin Concerto (with Feigin and the Moscow Radio Symphony Orchestra), and Balakirev's Piano Concerto and Medtner's Piano Concerto No. 1 (with Zhukov and the USSR Radio and Television Orchestra).

Dobrowen, Issay (1891–1953). Born at Nizhniy-Novgorod, Russia, Dobrowen played the piano in public at the age of five, and later studied composition at the Moscow Conservatory with Taneyev and the piano at the Vienna Academy of Music with Godowsky. In 1917 he became a professor at the Moscow Conservatory and two years later made his debut as a conductor at the Bolshoi Theatre. In 1922 he went to Dresden to direct the first performance in Germany of *Boris Godunov*; he became the principal conductor at the Dresden Opera with Fritz Busch and appeared in opera houses and concert halls in Berlin, Halle, Stockholm, Helsinki and Leningrad. After conducting at the Vienna

Volksoper (1924–7) and directing the Dresden Philharmonic Concerts, he was general music director at the Royal Opera at Sofia (1927–8) and conductor of the Oslo Philharmonic Orchestra (1927–31). In 1931 he departed for the United States, became an associate conductor of the New York Philharmonic-Symphony Orchestra and for two seasons was principal conductor of the San Francisco Symphony Orchestra (1933–4), and also appeared with the San Francisco Opera. At this time he was also active with the Oslo Philharmonic Orchestra and remained there until the Nazi occupation of Norway. When Huberman organised the Palestine Symphony Orchestra in 1937 Dobrowen was chosen as the conductor; he was also a regular conductor at the Budapest Opera (1936–9) and during World War II he led the Stockholm Opera and the Göteborg Philharmonic Orchestra. After 1945 he conducted throughout Europe, in 1948 directed Russian operas at La Scala, Milan, and led *Boris Godunov* at Covent Garden in 1952. In many of his opera engagements he was his own producer and stage director as well as conductor. He was also a prolific composer and his output included two piano concertos and an opera *A Thousand and One Nights*. Although best known for his brilliant performances of Russian music, he gave poised, sensitive and well-disciplined readings of the standard repertoire, from Haydn, Mozart and Beethoven to the great romantic works of the 19th century. He was particularly successful with music calling for grand effects from a great mass of performers, but was also able to produce performances of the finest sensibility; his conducting of *Le nozze di Figaro* at Covent Garden in 1952 was, according to Rosenthal, the finest heard since the war, even better than Krips' or Kleiber's. Dobrowen died in Oslo after a long illness; his last appearance was at a performance of Beethoven's Symphony No. 9.

Dobrowen first recorded in the 1930s; he made discs of four *Slavonic Dances* of Dvořák, the Polovtsian Dances from *Prince Igor*, the *Rustle of Spring* of Sinding and Grieg's *Symphonic Dances* (with the Berlin State Opera Orchestra for Odeon), and he conducted the Vienna Philharmonic Orchestra in accompaniments to Huberman in violin concertos of Bach and Mozart, for Columbia. After 1945 he was under contract for HMV, for whom he made many recordings, mostly on 78 r.p.m. discs, and some LPs; many of them were inevitably of Russian music, being *Scheherazade*, the *Russian Easter Festival* overture, Tchaikovsky's Symphony No. 4, and Piano Concerto No. 1 (with Solomon), the waltz and polonaise from *Eugene Onegin*, Liadov's *Berceuse*, the Dance of the Persian Slaves from *Khovanshchina*, the overture and Polovtsian Dances from *Prince Igor* and suites from *Le Coq d'or* and *Tsar Saltan* (with the Philharmonia Orchestra), Tchaikovsky's *Serenade in C major* and *Francesca da Rimini* and the overture to *Russlan and Ludmilla* (with the Danish State Radio Symphony Orchestra), Liadov's *Kikimora*, Borodin's Symphony No. 2, and *Boris Godunov* (with the French National Radio Orchestra *et al.*). Undoubtedly the *Boris Godunov* was the most significant, and showed how fine an interpreter he was of this opera; it was the Rimsky-Korsakov version of 1908, with some minor cuts, and with Boris Christoff, with whom he also recorded arias from other Russian operas. In addition, Dobrowen conducted performances of the Piano Concertos Nos 2 and 3 of Nikolai Medtner, with the composer as pianist, and these discs were in three 78 r.p.m. albums of Medtner's music issued under the auspices and financial support of the Maharajah of Mysore, who was an enthusiast for the composer. The Medtner concertos were not transferred to LP, and, except for a recent Russian recording, have not appeared in the catalogue since.

Dobrowen's other recordings included Haydn's Symphony No. 104, Beethoven's Piano Concertos Nos 2 and 4 (with Schnabel), Brahms' Piano Concert No. 2 (with Solomon) and Violin Concerto (with Neveu), Grieg's Symphonic Dance No. 1, Chausson's *Poème* (with Neveu), the Bacchanale from *Samson et Dalila*, the overtures *Le Carnaval romain* and *Die Meistersinger*, the Entry of the Guests from *Tannhäuser*, the Prelude and Good Friday Music from *Parsifal* and Isolde's Narrative and Curse from *Tristan und Isolde* (with Flagstad *et al.*, and with the Philharmonia Orchestra) and Liszt's Piano Concerto No. 1 (with Schiøler and the Danish Radio Symphony Orchestra). The Tchaikovsky and Brahms Piano Concertos with Solomon were re-issued in 1977, along with other Solomon concerto recordings; on its original release the American critic David Hall had described the recording of the Brahms concerto as virtually definitive.

Dobrodinský, Jan (b. 1925). Born at Kunzak, Czechoslovakia, into a musical family where his father and brother were both members of the Czech Philharmonic Orchestra, Dobrodinský studied the French horn at the Prague Conservatory, graduated in 1948, then studied conducting at Bratislava with Talich and Rajter. He played the French horn in the Czech Chamber Orchestra, the Prague National Theatre

Orchestra and the Slovak Philharmonic Orchestra, was conductor of the Slovak Philharmonic Choir and of the Slovak Philharmonic Orchestra (from 1954). He has composed a number of choral works. For Supraphon he recorded Krumpholz's Harp Concerto No. 5 (with Bedrich Dobrodinský, his father, and the Prague Symphony Orchestra).

Dobrzański, Tadeusz (b. 1918). Born in Sambor, USSR, Dobrzański studied both law and music, and was leader and conductor of the Polish Radio and Television Choir at Kraków (from 1948). He has conducted at festivals in Eastern and Western Europe, has composed numerous popular pieces for radio, theatre etc., has received various prizes for his music, and was awarded the Order of Merit, Kraków (1969). With the Musicae Antiquae Collegium Varsoviense he recorded Żebrowski's *Magnificat*, Kobierkiewicz's *Ego Mater* and Szarzyński's *Jesu Spes me*, and with the Warsaw Chamber Orchestra *et al.* Martini's *Coeli Chori resonante*, Elsner's *Wiśliczanki* and Kamieński's *Tradycja zalatwiona*.

Dobson, Michael (b. 1923). Born in Wavendon, Buckinghamshire, Dobson was a chorister at New College, Oxford, studied at the Royal Academy of Music in London and also in Paris, and later became an Associate and Fellow of the Royal Academy of Music. He was principal oboist with the London Philharmonic Orchestra (1944–54), became a soloist and a chamber music player, principal oboist with the London Mozart Players and with the Bath and Menuhin Festival Orchestras, and after conducting the London Mozart Players in a series of concerts at Kingston-upon-Thames in 1961, formed his own orchestra, the Thames Chamber Orchestra, the following year. He has since appeared with the orchestra in London and elsewhere, and has been a guest conductor in Britain, Europe, Australia and the United States. He has recorded, as a conductor, a disc of Concerti Grossi of Boyce and wind concertos of Woodcock (with Black and Bennett and the Thames Chamber Orchestra for Continental Record Distributors) and Martin's *Ballade* for Viola, Wind and Percussion (with Menuhin and the Menuhin Festival Orchestra for EMI).

Dods, Marcus (b. 1918). Born in Edinburgh and a graduate of Cambridge University and the Royal Academy of Music, Dods was assistant music director to the Rank Organisation, where he arranged, composed and conducted music for films (1947–51), conductor and chorus-master with Sadler's Wells Opera Company (1952–6), principal conductor of the BBC Concert Orchestra (1966–9) and musical director of the London Concert Orchestra (from 1972). He has conducted live and on records many West End musicals such as *Oliver* and *Maggie May*, and his other records have included excerpts from Gilbert and Sullivan operettas and ballet music, and Williamson's opera *The Happy Prince* (with the Academy of St Martin-in-the-Fields *et al.* for Argo).

Dohnányi, Christoph von (b. 1929). Grandson of the composer Ernst von Dohnányi, Dohnányi was born in Berlin, studied there at the Hochschule für Musik and at Munich where he won the Strauss Prize for conducting in 1951. He went to the United States, was a fellow at Tanglewood under Bernstein and studied with his grandfather at the Florida State University. He was first a pianist, but in 1952 Solti brought him to the Frankfurt Opera as a coach. From there he moved on to conduct orchestras at Lübeck (1957–63) and Kassel (1963–4), was conductor of the West German Radio Orchestra at Cologne (1964–8), became chief conductor at the Frankfurt Opera (1968–77) and in 1977 was appointed musical director of the Hamburg Opera. He has appeared in both opera houses and concert halls in London, Vienna, Rome and in many other cities, and was chosen by Henze in 1956 to lead the first performances of his operas *Der junge Lord* in Berlin and *The Bassarids* at Salzburg in the following year. In 1967 he led *Tannhäuser* at Bayreuth and later made his debut in the US with *Der fliegende Holländer* in Chicago, and conducted at Covent Garden with *Salome*. He is a serious personality but shows wit and charm readily; he is not an autocratic conductor and believes that the intense work of the opera house is the best training for his profession. He takes as his models Walter, Busch, Beecham and de Sabata, all of whom he greatly admires. His modesty is shown in his conviction that he should thoroughly understand and perform the symphonies of Haydn and Mozart before proceeding to those of Beethoven and Brahms, and in his disapproval of display. He does not wish to become known as a specialist in any composer or era and has a strong commitment towards performing modern operas. (He holds that it is more difficult to conduct an opera of Mozart than one of Berg, since Berg's wishes are more evident.) However he regrets that few contemporary composers have the inclination or the ability to write in operatic forms, or to write a continuous piece of an hour's length.

Dohnányi's major recordings have been a fine performance of *Der junge Lord* (with the

Berlin German Opera Orchestra *et al.* for DGG), a suite from *Lulu* and the finale from *Salome* (with Silja and the Vienna Philharmonic Orchestra for DGG), Mendelssohn's Symphonies Nos 1 and 5 (with the Vienna Philharmonic Orchestra for Decca), Mendelssohn's Symphony No. 1 and *Die erste Walpurgisnacht* (with the Frankfurt Museum Orchestra *et al.* for Turnabout), the *Egmont* overture (with the Vienna Symphony Orchestra for Philips), *Orpheus*, *Mazeppa* and *Mephisto Waltz* (with the Munich Philharmonic Orchestra for DGG), *Moldau* and the overture and polka from *The Bartered Bride* (with the Philharmonia Hungarica for Ariola) Fortner's *Triplium* (with the Cologne Radio Symphony Orchestra for Wergo), Kelemen's *Changeant* (with the same orchestra for Philips), the Grieg and Schumann Piano Concertos (with Arrau and the Amsterdam Concertgebouw Orchestra for Philips), the Schumann Cello Concerto and Tchaikovsky's *Variations on a Rococo Theme* (with Gendron and the Vienna Symphony Orchestra for Philips).

Dohnányi, Ernst von (1877–1960). The famous Hungarian musician and composer Dohnányi first became celebrated as a piano virtuoso, and toured Europe and the United States extensively before World War I. In 1919 he was appointed conductor of the Budapest Philharmonic Orchestra and appeared as a guest conductor with many other European and US orchestras. After 1948 he lived permanently in the US. His ability as a pianist was very highly rated; in Grove's *Dictionary of Music and Musicians* Blom wrote that 'the breadth of his phrasing, his command of tone-gradation and the exquisite beauty of his tone are such as to satisfy the most exacting hearer'. He recorded, as a pianist, his own *Variations on a Nursery Theme* (with the London Symphony Orchestra under Collingwood for HMV in 1929) and the *Piano Concerto in G* (with himself also conducting and the Budapest Philharmonic Orchestra); his only recording as a conductor was a movement from his *Ruralia Hungarica* (with the London Symphony Orchestra, which was a fill-up to the *Variations* above).

Dolmetsch, Carl (b. 1911). Born in Fontenay-sous-Bois, Paris, Dolmetsch studied with his father, Arnold Dolmetsch, the Swiss instrument maker and musician who became expert in the restoration, manufacture and performance of old instruments, and established the firm Arnold Dolmetsch Ltd., of which Carl is now the managing director. Carl first performed as a recorder player at the first Haslemere Festival in England in 1925, which Arnold had promoted in order to perform chamber music on reproductions of old instruments. Carl subsequently performed in many countries throughout the world, and made many records; as conductor of the Dolmetsch Consort he has recorded discs of Elizabethan and Jacobean music (for Nonesuch).

Dommett, Leonard (b. 1929). Born in Toowoomba, Australia, Dommett was educated at the Melbourne Conservatorium, joined the BBC Symphony Orchestra as a violinist (1949), was leader and deputy conductor for the Ballet Rambert, and then played with major London orchestras. After returning to Australia in 1953 he played in the Brisbane and Sydney Symphony Orchestras, became leader and deputy conductor of the South Australian Symphony Orchestra (1961) and then of the Melbourne Symphony Orchestra (1965), and was assistant conductor of the latter orchestra during its tour of the United States in 1970. He has recorded Williamson's Piano Concerto No. 3 (with the composer and the London Philharmonic Orchestra for Lyrita), Lovelock's Flute Concerto (with Hill and the Melbourne Symphony Orchestra for Festival), *Eine kleine Nachtmusik*, Elgar's *Serenade*, Wirén's *Serenade* and Barber's *Adagio for Strings* (with the Melbourne Symphony Orchestra for RCA).

Doneux, Edgar (b. 1920). Born in Liège, Doneux was appointed conductor at the Théâtre Royal there (1940) and was conductor-in-chief at the Théâtre Royal de la Monnaie, Brussels (1945–9). He then became conductor-in-chief of the symphony and chamber orchestras of the Belgian Radio (1949), and with the Belgian Radio Chamber Orchestra gave concerts in many countries, as well as appearing as a guest conductor with major orchestras and at festivals in Europe. Since 1967 he has been the musical director of the Ballet de Wallonie, conducted amateur choirs in Frameries-Borinage, was promoter and adviser of the Festival of Chimay (1959–62) and co-founder of the Festival of Nerja in Malaga (1971).

Doneux has recorded Grétry's *Les fausses Confidences ou l'amant jaloux*, *Richard Coeur de Lion* and Act I of *Panurge dans l'isle des lanternes* (with the Belgian Radio Chamber Orchestra *et al.* for Musique en Wallonie), *Zémire et Azore*, a disc of music by Grétry, Gossec and Grisar, a four-disc series entitled *The Belgian Violin School* which includes concertos and pieces by Ysaÿe, Vieuxtemps, Léonard, Croes, Prume and Bériot (with violinists Raskin, Van Neste, Debot and Werthen), Shostakovich's

Piano Concerto No. 1 (with Slusjny), Bourguignon's Piano Concerto, *Berceuse* and two dances, Brenta's ballet *Florilège de valses*, songs by Lekeu (with Poliart), flute concertos by Grétry and Loeillet (with Magnée), Saint-Saëns' Cello Concerto No. 1 (with Bartse) and pieces by Poot (with the Belgian Radio Chamber Orchestra *et al.* for EMI), excerpts from *Lakmé*, *Coppélia* and *La Source*, the Grétry/ Mottl ballet suite, Lalo's *Scherzo* and pieces by Gluck and Saint-Saëns (with the Belgian National Radio Orchestra for Maestro), the Haydn Symphony No. 63, a sinfonia of J. C. Bach and some dances of Grétry (with the European Chamber Orchestra for EMI), and suites from *Nutcracker* and *The Sleeping Beauty* (with an unnamed orchestra for Allegro).

Dorati, Antal (b. 1906). Born in Budapest where his father was a violinist at the Budapest Opera and in the Budapest Philharmonic Orchestra and his mother a music teacher, Dorati studied at the Franz Liszt Academy under Weiner, Bartók and Kodály, who were frequent visitors to the Dorati household. At 18 he was then the youngest person to graduate from the Academy. Immediately afterwards, in 1924, he joined the Budapest Opera as a repetiteur and made his professional debut there as a conductor, and at the same time studied philosophy at the University of Vienna. In 1928 Busch engaged him as his assistant at the Dresden Opera, but in the next year he became musical director and principal conductor at the Münster Opera (1930–32). In his years at Münster he also appeared with other orchestras and in opera houses in Germany, Hungary and Czechoslovakia; he moved to Paris in 1932, conducted orchestras in Great Britain and France, and after an engagement with the French National Radio he was appointed principal conductor of the Ballet Russe de Monte Carlo (1933–40) with which he toured Europe and the United States, and also conducted concerts in Australia (1938–40). He first conducted in the US in 1937, appearing with the National Symphony Orchestra at Washington DC; in 1941 he took up residence in the US and eventually became a US citizen in 1947. His first appointment was as musical director of the American Ballet Theatre (1941–5), and he was also director of the New Opera Company in New York (1941–2). When the Dallas Symphony Orchestra was re-organised in 1945 Dorati was engaged as its musical director; in 1949 he moved to Minnesota to succeed Mitropoulos as conductor of the Minneapolis Symphony Orchestra, and was named its musical director in 1954. He left Minneapolis in 1960, believing he had achieved as much as he could with the budget allowed for the orchestra. Returning to Europe he received a Ford Foundation grant to enable him to study Italian baroque and pre-baroque music, and conducted both concerts and opera in London, Vienna, Rome, Hamburg and other centres. In 1963 he was appointed chief conductor of the BBC Symphony Orchestra; his term was completed in 1966, he toured with the Israel Philharmonic Orchestra, became principal conductor of the Stockholm Philharmonic Orchestra (1967–74), musical director of the National Symphony Orchestra at Washington DC (1970–75), remaining afterwards as its principal guest conductor, was senior conductor of the Royal Philharmonic Orchestra in London (1975 onwards), and has been appointed musical director of the Detroit Symphony Orchestra. He toured the US with the Stockholm Philharmonic in 1968 and 1970, has appeared as a guest conductor with almost all the major symphony orchestras and opera houses in the world, and has been instrumental in maintaining the Philharmonia Hungarica, first in Vienna and now in FR Germany, and is honorary president of the orchestra, which is made up of musicians who left Hungary in 1956. He was a composer before he became conductor and his compositions include a symphony, a cello concerto, three serenades for orchestra, a *Missa Brevis* for mixed choir and percussion, a ballet *Magdelena*, a cantata *The Way of the Cross* and some chamber music. Of his ballet arrangements there is the familiar *Graduation Ball*, from the music of Johann Strauss.

Because he could claim to be the leading ballet conductor of his generation, he has tended to be typed, unfairly, as a ballet conductor, despite his wide experience in conducting the symphonic and operatic repertoire. But his years as a ballet conductor taught him that conductors cannot remain long doing this, since, in his view, the dancer's discipline is fundamentally non-musical, as opposed to that of the singer. He has a formidable reputation as an effective trainer of orchestras and can point to the Dallas Symphony, the London Symphony, the BBC Symphony and more recently the National Symphony Orchestra, where his work was eminently successful. The London Symphony's level of excellence in the mid 1960s was due in some measure to Dorati's work with them in the previous years, both in recording and in the concert hall. Orchestral players once found him somewhat irascible, but now he claims to be more easy going. Even the most difficult scores he conducts from memory.

Mercury Records contracted Dorati to make

100 recordings with the Minneapolis Symphony Orchestra and a further 50 with the London Symphony. If we add to these his 48 discs in the series of complete Haydn symphonies for Decca, the three Haydn operas so far recorded and numerous other discs he has made for other companies, he counts as one of the most prolific conductors on record. Despite the excellence of many of these recorded performances, especially of the Haydn symphonies, he has never really stood among the greatest interpreters of the central repertoire of the German and Viennese classics. His style is too intense, clipped and hard-driven to result in performances that are stamped with the apparent intellectual profundity of the German school of conductors. Dorati is at the opposite pole to, say, Klemperer or Böhm, but his orchestral texture is characteristically lighter than that of Szell or Toscanini. It is not unreasonable to make these comparisons, as Dorati is capable of thrilling readings in the concert hall of scores like the *Missa Solemnis*, and his Beethoven and Brahms symphonies on record are dramatic and exciting. He defends himself, saying that he sees no necessity to establish a standard interpretation of a musical work: 'To me, a criterion of a great piece is its endurance to be played in many different ways. If it can be played in only one way, it's not a great work.' He has remarked, perhaps too modestly, that he makes 'not bad music with a strong conviction and 100 per cent honesty'. A contributing factor to his reputation as a superficially brilliant interpreter of the standard repertoire was the tonal quality of his records for Mercury with the Minneapolis orchestra, which had a characteristically thin string sound and light bass.

Dorati recorded ballet music with the London Philharmonic Orchestra before World War II: a suite from *Swan Lake*, Boccherini's *Scuola di ballo* (arranged by Françaix), Strauss's *Le Beau Danube* (arranged by Desormière), Erlanger's *Les cent Baisers*, Bizet's *Jeux d'enfants*, Chabrier's *Cotillon*, the ballet music from Dargomizhky's *Russalka*, the pas de deux from Stravinsky's *Le Baiser de la fée*, as well as *Scheherazade* and Tchaikovsky's *Hamlet* (for HMV and Columbia). In his early years in the US he recorded *El amor brujo* (with the Ballet Theatre Orchestra for Decca, US), Glazunov's *The Seasons*, Copland's *Rodeo*, Liszt's Piano Concerto No. 1 and Tchaikovsky's Piano Concerto No. 1 (with Rubinstein), Prokofiev's Piano Concerto No. 3 (with Kapell), and Bartók's Violin Concerto No. 2 (with Menuhin, and with the Dallas Symphony Orchestra for RCA) and Grieg's Piano Concerto (with Rubinstein and the Victor Symphony Orchestra for RCA). The Bartók Violin Concerto was the first recording of the work, and the first of three for both Dorati and Menuhin.

At Minneapolis, Dorati's series with the Minneapolis Symphony Orchestra for Mercury was very extensive. Many were released by Philips in Europe, and by Musical Masterpieces, and some are still being re-issued in the US and Britain. Included were Mozart's Symphony No. 40, Beethoven's Symphonies Nos. 3, 4, 5 and 8, and the overtures *Coriolan*, *Egmont*, and *Leonore No. 3*. Brahms' Symphonies Nos 2 and 3, Dvořák's *Slavonic Dances* and Violin Concerto (with Milstein), *Scheherazade*, *Pictures at an Exhibition*, the prelude from *Khovanshchina*, Borodin's Symphony No. 2 and the overture to *Prince Igor*, *Ein Heldenleben*, *Don Juan*, *Till Eulenspiegel*, *Tod und Verklärung*, the waltzes from *Der Rosenkavalier*, *Symphonie fantastique*, dances from *The Bartered Bride*, the overture *Le Carnaval romain*, collections of overtures by Rossini and Verdi, the complete ballets *Coppélia*, *Nutcracker*, *Swan Lake* and *The Sleeping Beauty*, *Capriccio italien*, *Marche slave*, the *1812* overture, *Francesca da Rimini*, Tchaikovsky's Symphony No. 5, Mendelssohn's Symphony No. 4, *La Mer*, *Nocturnes*, *Daphnis et Chloé*, *Alborada del gracioso*, *Pavane pour une infante défunte*, Albéniz's *Iberia*, interlude and dance from *La vida breve*, Bartók's Violin Concerto No. 2 (with Menuhin), *Concerto for Orchestra*, *Divertimento*, Suite No. 2, *The Miraculous Mandarin*, *Hungarian Sketches* and *Romanian Dances*, *Háry János*, Prokofiev's Symphony No. 5, *L'Oiseau de feu*, *Petrushka*, *Le Sacre du printemps*, *Fontane di Roma*, *Pini di Roma*, *Feste romane*, *Vetrate di chiesa*, *Young Person's Guide to the Orchestra*, Ginastera's *Variaciones concertantes*, Copland's Symphony No. 3, *Rodeo*, *El Salón México*, Schuller's *Seven Studies on a Theme of Paul Klee*, *Graduation Ball* (Dorati's arrangement) and waltzes of Strauss, Offenbach's *Gaîté parisienne* (arranged by Rosenthal) and *Helen of Troy* (Dorati's arrangement), Rachmaninov's Piano Concerto No. 2 (with Janis), a symphonic picture from *Porgy and Bess* (arranged by Bennett), *An American in Paris*, Gould's *Spirituals*, Bloch's *Sinfonia breve* and his own *Symphony (1957)*.

With the London Symphony Orchestra, for Mercury, the series continued, with some duplications, and included suites from *Water Music* and *Music for the Royal Fireworks*, Haydn's Symphonies Nos 45, 100 and 101, Mozart's Symphonies Nos 36 and 40, *Eine kleine Nachtmusik*, Beethoven's Symphonies

Nos 5 and 6, *Wellington's Victory*, and the overtures *Die Weihe des Hauses*, *Egmont*, *Prometheus* and *Leonore No. 3*, Mendelssohn's Symphonies Nos 3 and 4, the Violin Concertos of Mendelssohn, Schumann, Brahms, Tchaikovsky and Khachaturian (with Szeryng), Liszt's *Hungarian Rhapsodies Nos 1* to *6*, *Les Préludes*, Dvořák's Cello Concerto, Bruch's *Kol Nidrei*, Saint-Saëns' Cello Concerto No. 1 and Tchaikovsky's *Variations on a Rococo Theme* (with Starker), Brahms' Symphonies Nos 1 and 4, *Academic Festival Overture* and *Hungarian Dances*, Chopin's Piano Concerto No. 1 (with Bachauer), Tchaikovsky's Symphonies Nos 1, 4 and 5, the *Romeo and Juliet* fantasy-overture, Dvořák's Symphony No. 8, *A Night on the Bare Mountain*, *Moldau*, *Capriccio espagnol*, a suite from *Le Coq d'or*, *Russian Easter Festival* overture, the overtures to *Mignon*, *Nabucco*, *La forza del destino*, and *Tannhäuser*, the preludes to Act III of *Tannhäuser*, Acts I and III of *Die Meistersinger* and of *La traviata*, the *Carnival* and *The Hebrides* overtures, the Good Friday Music from *Parsifal*, the prelude and Liebestod from *Tristan und Isolde*, Berg's *Lulu* suite, excerpts from *Wozzeck* (with Pilarcycz), *Three Pieces for Orchestra* and *Five Pieces for Orchestra*, Schoenberg's *Five Pieces*, Bartók's *Concerto for Orchestra*, *Bluebeard's Castle* (with Szönyi and Szekely), *The Wooden Prince*, *Two Portraits*, *Hungarian Sketches* and *Romanian Dances*, Copland's *Billy the Kid*, *Appalachian Spring* and *Danzón Cubano*, a suite from *Gayaneh*, Respighi's *Brazilian Impressions* and *Gli uccelli*, *Valse triste*, Rachmaninov's Piano Concerto No. 3 (with Janis), suite from *Lieutenant Kijé*, *Scythian Suite*, the Polovtsian Dances from *Prince Igor*, *L'Oiseau de feu*, *Le Chant du rossignol*, *Scherzo à la russe*, *Feux d'artifice*, *Tango* and other pieces by Stravinsky, and Enesco's *Romanian Rhapsodies Nos 1* and *2*.

In the early years of LP, Dorati made other records, including Bartók's *Divertimento* and Mozart's Symphony No. 31 (with the Minneapolis Symphony Orchestra for RCA); Dvořák's Symphony No. 9 and *Slavonic Rhapsodies*, excerpts from *La Damnation de Faust* and the love scene from Berlioz's *Roméo et Juliette* symphony, the complete *Má Vlast*, the overture and dances from *The Bartered Bride*, *Pictures at an Exhibition*, *Nutcracker*, Schubert's overture *In the Italian Style*, and the overtures *The Hebrides*, *Meeresstille und glückliche Fahrt*, *Der Freischütz*, *Preciosa*, *Euryanthe*, and *Oberon* (with the Amsterdam Concertgebouw Orchestra for Philips); Schubert's Symphony No. 8, the *Romeo and Juliet* fantasy-overture, *The Miraculous Mandarin*, and Kodály's *Peacock Variations* (with the Chicago Symphony Orchestra for Mercury); Beethoven's Symphony No. 6, the incidental music for *A Midsummer Night's Dream*, two suites from *Carmen* and the two *L'Arlésienne* suites (with the Vienna Symphony Orchestra for Philips).

Later, there appeared Arensky's *Variations on a Theme of Tchaikovsky*, Tchaikovsky's *Serenade in C major*, Bartók's *Dance Suite*, *Mikrokosmos Suite* and *Two Portraits*, Kodály's *Háry János*, *Dances of Galánta*, *Dances of Marosszék*, *Ballet Music*, *Concerto for Orchestra*, *Minuetto serio*, *Peacock Variations*, *Summer Evening*, *Symphony in C major* and *Theatre Overture*, and Resphigi's three suites of *Ancient Airs and Dances* (with the Philharmonia Hungarica for Mercury and Decca); *Der fliegende Holländer* (with the Covent Garden Orchestra *et al.* for Decca); Bartók's *Concerto for Orchestra* and *Divertimento*, and Kodály's *Peacock Variations* and *Psalmus Hungaricus* (with the Hungarian Symphony Orchestra *et al.* for Qualiton); *Divertimento* and *The Miraculous Mandarin* (with the BBC Symphony Orchestra for Philips); Messiaen's *Chronochromie*, Gerhard's Symphony No. 1 and dances from *Don Quixote*, Koechlin's *Les Bandar-log* and Boulez's *Le soleil des eaux* (with the BBC Symphony Orchestra for Argo), *Romeo and Juliet* fantasy-overture, excerpts from Berlioz's *Roméo et Juliette* symphony, and the dance from *Salome* (with the Royal Philharmonic Orchestra for Reader's Digest); Haydn's Symphonies Nos 59 and 81 (with the Festival Chamber Orchestra for Philips); Androoy's *Piet Hein Rhapsody* (with the Hague Philharmonic Orchestra for Philips); Dvořák's *Slavonic Dances* (with the Bamberg Symphony Orchestra for Vox); Sibelius' Symphony No. 2, Rosenberg's *Voyage to America*, Blomdahl's *Sisyfos* suite and Berwald's Symphony No. 2 (with the Stockholm Philharmonic Orchestra, released in the US by RCA); Blomdahl's Symphony No. 3 and Pettersson's Symphony No. 10 (with the Stockholm Philharmonic and Swedish Radio Orchestras, respectively, for EMI); Pettersson's Symphony No. 7 (with the Stockholm Philharmonic Orchestra for Discofil); Sibelius' *The Oceanides*, *Night Ride and Sunrise* and *Luonnotar* (with Jones and the London Symphony Orchestra for EMI); Bartók's Viola Concerto and Violin Concertos Nos 1 and 2 (with Menuhin and the New Philharmonia Orchestra for EMI); Dvořák's Symphony No. 9 (with the New Philharmonia Orchestra for Decca); a collection of Strauss waltzes (with the London Philharmonic Orchestra for Decca); Milhaud's *Le Boeuf sur le toit*, Françaix's *Concertino*, Satie's *Parade* and Auric's *Ouverture* (with the London Symphony Orchestra for Philips); *Scythian Suite* and a suite from *The Love of Three Oranges* (with the BBC Symphony Orchestra for Philips); Gerhard's *The Plague*, Messiaen's *La Transfiguration de Notre Seigneur Jésus-Christ*, Dallapiccola's *Il prigioniero*, Debussy's *Iberia* and *Nocturnes*, Tchaikovsky's Symphony No. 4, *Romeo and Juliet* fantasy-overture, *Fate*, *The Storm*, *Francesca da Rimini*, *Hamlet* and *Voyevoda*, and the Entry of the Gods into Valhalla from *Rheingold*, Ride of the Valkyries, Wotan's Farewell and Magic Fire Music from *Die Walküre*, and Dawn, Funeral Music and Finale from *Götterdämmerung* (with the National Symphony Orchestra, Washington, *et al.* for Decca); *Háry János* suite and *Lieutenant Kijé* suite (with the Netherlands Radio Orchestra for Decca); his own Piano Concerto (with his wife, Ilse von Alpenheim, and the National Symphony Orchestra for Turnabout); Haydn's *The Creation*, *Carmina Burana*, *Young Person's Guide to the Orchestra*, *Peter and the Wolf*, *La Boutique fantasque* and *Rossiniana* (with the Royal Philharmonic Orchestra *et al.* for Decca); Beethoven's Symphonies Nos 4, 5, 6, 8 and 9 (with the Royal Philharmonic Orchestra *et al.* for DGG); and *L'Oiseau de feu* (with the Royal Philharmonic Orchestra for Enigma Classics).

Despite this vast achievement, at the head of Dorati's immense discography are the complete 104 symphonies of Haydn, which he recorded for Decca with the Philharmonia Hungarica Orchestra between 1971 and 1974. To them he has added two more symphonies in B flat major, the second version of the Symphony No. 22, the first version of the Symphony No. 63, the three alternative endings to the Symphony No. 53, and the alternative ending of the Symphony No. 103, the *Sinfonia concertante* and 24 Minuets. They are spirited, stylish and thoroughly convincing performances, powerful and charming where they need to be. It would be impossible to call the series definitive, but the uniform excellence of the performances must rate the series as one of the finest monuments in the history of the gramophone. As if this were not enough, Dorati embarked on recording the Haydn operas, in collaboration with the European Broadcasting Union and the Radio Suisse Romande. The orchestra is the Lausanne Chamber Orchestra, with the Suisse Romande Radio Chorus, and the editions for the recordings have been prepared by H. C. Robbins Landon from the original manuscripts. There are 15 Haydn operas, plus some fragments; the first to be recorded in 1976 was *La fedeltà premiata*, followed by *La vera costanza* and *Orlando Paladino*. Most of the operas are being broadcast in Europe before being issued on record. To complete the Haydn cycle, Doráti has also recorded the two Cello Concertos (with Varga and the Bamberg Symphony Orchestra for Vox) and six Piano Concertos (with Ilse von Alpenheim and the Bamberg Symphony Orchestra for Turnabout).

Dostal, Nico (b. 1895). Born at Korneuburg, near Vienna, and educated at the Vienna Academy of Music, Dostal was a conductor at Innsbruck (1918) and at the Reinhardt Theatre, Berlin, and composed numerous operettas. Of these, he has recorded discs of excerpts from *Clivia*, *Manina*, *Monika* and *Die ungarische Hochzeit* (with the Berlin Symphony Orchestra *et al.* for Ariola), and a complete *Die ungarische Hochzeit* (with the Philharmonia Hungarica *et al.* for EMI).

Douatte, Roland (b. 1921). Born in Paris, Douatte became a violinist and studied conducting with Fournet. He founded the Collegium Musicum de Paris (1950) and the record company Critère (1960), was musical director of the Festival du Marais in Paris (1964–8), founded Nuits Musicales de Paris (1970), was music director of the Festival de Provins (1971), founded the Festival Musique au Grand Palais à Paris (1972), conducted the Orchestre de Chambre Ard Artem of Metz (1975) and the Santiago Chamber Orchestra in Chile (1976), and also conducted orchestras in Argentina and Brazil. He was one of the first in France to perform the baroque repertoire, and to rediscover especially the music of Vivaldi and Telemann.

Douatte has made a number of records which have been issued in France by Philips, Musidisc, Éditions phonographiques parisiennes, Ducretet-Thomson, Critère, Centrepoint, Eko and Les Quatre Saisons, some in the United States by Lyrichord, Nonesuch, London International and Music Guild, and in Britain by Monarch. Included in his discography are, with the Collegium Musicum de Paris, Bach's *Brandenburg Concerto No. 1*, the seven Harpsichord Concertos (with Gerlin, Dreyfus, Verlet, Hénon and Tedeschi), Flute, Violin and Harpsichord Concerto (with Larrieu, Pasquier and Gerlin), Oboe and Violin Concerto (with Chambon and Wallez), an excerpt from Cantata No. 147 and the sinfonia from the Cantata No. 174, Albinoni's *Adagio*, Telemann's *Overture in D major*, *Overture in C major – Hamburger Ebb und Fluth*, *Le Tintamarre* suite, *Suite in G minor*, *Concerto in D major*, *Tafelmusik No. 2*, Three-Violin Concerto (with Gendre, Wallez and Laroque), Flute, Violin and Cello Concerto (with Rampal, Gendre and Neilz), Concerto for Trumpet, Oboe, Violin, Viola, Cello and Harpsichord, and Motet BWV 226a (arranged for orchestra), Vivaldi's Concerto Op. 3 No. 10, Concertos Op. 10, *Il pastor fido* suite, Concertos P. 143, P. 363, P. 427, P. 438, *Sinfonia in C major*, Violin Concertos P. 325 and P. 373 (with Alès), *The Four Seasons*, Two-Horn Concerto (with Barboteu and Coursier), Two-Trumpet Concertos (with André and Lagorce, Delmotte and Adriano, and Delmotte and André), six Flute Concertos (with Eustache and Beckensteiner), Four-Violin Concerto (with Wallez, Jacquillat, Lepinte and Carracilly), and *Guitar Concerto in D* and *Mandolin Concerto in C* (with Aubin), Handel's Concerti Grossi Op. 3, *Alexander's Feast*, overtures to *Hercules* and *Rodelinda*, and *Oboe Concerto in B flat* (with Maisonneuve), Charpentier's *Marche de triomphe*, Delalande's *Symphonies pour les soupers du Roy* – Suite No. 4, Marin's *La Chasse du Cerf*, Lully's *Fanfares pour le Carrousel de Monseigneur*, Mouret's *Suites de Symphonies* Nos 1 and 2, Pachelbel's Canon, Couperin's *Steinkerque*, Philidor's marches, Music for Four Timbales and *Le Mariage de la Grosse Cathos* suite, Corelli's Concerti Grossi Op. 6 Nos 1 and 8, and Sonata Op. 5 No. 1, Geminiani's Concerto Grosso (unidentified), Locatelli's Concerto Op. 1 No. 8, Manfredini's Concerto Grosso Op. 3 No. 12 and *Sinfonia da chiesa* Op. 2 No. 12, Torelli's Concerto Grosso Op. 8 No. 6, Ricciotti's Concertinos Nos 1 and 2, Corrette's pieces from *Le Malade imaginaire*, A. Scarlatti's Concerti Grossi Nos 1, 2 and 4, and Sinfonia No. 4, Haydn's Two-Lyra Concertos Nos 1 to 5, arranged for flute and oboe (with Rampal and Pierlot), and Mozart's Symphonies Nos 24, 26, 28 and 41, overture to *Der Schauspieldirektor*, *Eine kleine Nachtmusik*, Divertimentos K. 136 and K. 138, four Horn Concertos (with Barboteu) and Piano Concerto K. 107 (with Veyron-Lacroix).

Douatte's other records include Mozart's Symphonies Nos 20 and 33 (with the Prague Chamber Orchestra), Bizet's *Symphony in C Major*, Sibelius' *Finlandia*, *Valse triste*, *Lemminkäinen in Tuonela* and *Rakastava*, a suite from Prokofiev's *Romeo and Juliet*, and Satie's *Geneviève de Brabant*, *Parade* and *Relâche* (with the Luxembourg Radio and Television Orchestra), Debussy's *Petite Suite* and *Danse sacrée et danse profane*, and Satie's *Gymnopédies* (with the Orchestre Radio-Suisse Italienne), and Schoenberg's Quintet Op. 26 (with the Paris Wind Ensemble), all for Musidisc.

Douglas, Clive (1903–77). Born in Rushworth, Victoria, Australia, Douglas studied at the Melbourne Conservatorium of Music, and from 1936 to 1966 was a staff conductor with the Australian Broadcasting Commission. He conducted the Brisbane Symphony Orchestra (1941–7), was assistant conductor of the Sydney Symphony Orchestra (1947–53) and of the Victorian Symphony Orchestra (1953–66), and taught composition at the Melbourne Conservatorium (1959–63). He composed much music, including three symphonies and a number of orchestral suites, tone poems and other pieces, usually on Australian themes, and has received many awards for his compositions. Of these, the Australian Broadcasting Commission recorded, with Douglas conducting various Australian orchestras, Symphonies Nos 1 and 2, *Carwoola*, *Five Pastels*, *Wangadilla*, *Festival in Natal*, *Opals*, *Coolawidgee*, *Terra Australis*, *Sinfonietta*, *Variations symphoniques* and *Divertimento*, and in 1952 EMI issued an LP disc in which he conducted the Victorian Symphony Orchestra in his symphonic poem *Sturt 1829*. Other compositions of Douglas that have been recorded are *Essay for Strings* (with the Melbourne Symphony Orchestra under Paul for ABC), *Olympic Overture* (with the Sydney Symphony Orchestra under Heinze for EMI) and *Three Frescoes* (with the Sydney Symphony Orchestra under Atzmon for Festival).

Downes, Edward (b. 1924). Downes graduated from university at his native Birmingham (1944) then studied at the Royal College of Music (1944–6) and became a lecturer at Aberdeen University. In 1948 he was awarded a Carnegie Scholarship enabling him to study conducting for two years with Scherchen, after which he was engaged as a conductor with the Carl Rosa Opera Company (1950–51) and in 1952 he became a staff conductor at the Covent Garden Opera. Until he left in 1969 he conducted almost every opera in the repertoire, including a complete *Ring*; since then he has devoted himself more to symphonic music, although on occasion he has returned to the opera house. In 1970 he premièred Brian's Symphonies Nos 14 and 21, and Bennett's opera *Victory*, and in the same year toured Japan with the New Philharmonia Orchestra. He was appointed musical director and chief conductor of the Australian Opera (1972–4) and led the first performance of an opera (*War and Peace*) at the Sydney Opera House after its opening in 1973. Previously in 1963 he had led the Western première of Shostakovich's *Katerina Ismailova* at Covent Garden. His recordings have included Bax's Symphony No. 3 and *The Happy Forest* (with the New Philharmonia Orchestra for RCA, first issued in 1969 and re-issued in 1977), the overtures to *Le nozze di Figaro*, *William Tell*, *Russlan and Ludmilla*, *Der Freischütz*, and *Die Meistersinger* (with the London Philharmonic Orchestra issued by Marble Arch and Stereo Fidelity), excerpts from Verdi's *Falstaff* and an aria recital by Merrill (with the New Symphony Orchestra *et al.* for Decca), Hindemith's *Der Schwanendreher* and the Walton Viola Concerto (with Doktor and the London Philharmonic Orchestra, issued on Odyssey), Gershwin's *Piano Concerto in F* and MacDowell's Piano concerto No. 2 (with Szidon and the London Philharmonic Orchestra for DGG), the two Liszt Piano Concertos (with Davis and the Royal Philharmonic Orchestra for Decca), aria recitals by Price (with the New Philharmonia Orchestra for RCA), Crespin, Nilsson, Prevedi, McCracken and Resnik (with the Covent Garden Orchestra for Decca) and Ghiaurov (with the London Symphony Orchestra for Decca) and a series of eight LPs of orchestral accompaniments to operatic arias for various voices (with the London Philharmonic Orchestras for Audio Spectrum).

Dragon, Carmen (b. 1914). Born in Antioch, California, Dragon was educated at Santa Fe College in his native state and has made his musical career as a conductor, composer and arranger for films, radio and recordings. In 1944 he received an Oscar for the score of the film *Cover Girl*, and has composed many other film scores for Hollywood studios, songs and musicals, as well as a *Santa Fe Suite*. On record he is identified as a brilliant conductor of light and popular classical items in a series of LPs with the Hollywood Bowl Orchestra (alias the Los Angeles Philharmonic), collected under titles such as *Echoes of Spain*, *Starlight Concert*, *La Danza*, *Fiesta*, *Chopin by Starlight* and *Russkaya*. He also recorded with the Capitol Symphony Orchestra separate LP collections of music by Beethoven, Grieg, Tchaikovsky and Stephen Foster, and for Columbia excerpts from *Hänsel und Gretel*. He has said that when he discussed the contract to make these records with Capitol, he was told: 'Now don't come back to us next year and tell us you want to do Beethoven's Fifth.' Dragon lives in Los Angeles where he has directed the regular concerts of the Glendale Symphony Orchestra since 1963.

Dressel, Heinz (b. 1902). Born in Mainz, Dressel studied at the Cologne Conservatory under Abendroth and in 1927 became a theatre conductor at Plauen. Later he was conductor at Lübeck, Münster and Freiburg, and in 1956 was appointed director of the Folkwang School at Essen. He has recorded Handel's *Lotario* overture, a Dittersdorf Clavier Concerto and a suite by Telemann (with Salling and the Folkwang Chamber Orchestra for Philips), Bialas' *Sinfonia piccola* and *Serenata*, and Hindemith's *Five Pieces for String Orchestra* (with the Essen Chamber Orchestra for Barenreiter) and Beethoven's Piano Concerto WoO 4 (with Grychtolowna and the Folkwang Chamber Orchestra for Philips).

Drewanz, Hans (b. 1929) Born in Dresden, Drewanz studied at the Hochschule für Musik at Frankfurt am Main, was a choral conductor (1950), assistant to Solti at the Frankfurt Opera (1953–9), first conductor at Wuppertal Opera (1959–62) and general music director at Darmstadt (since 1963). He has recorded Scriabin's *Piano Concerto in F sharp minor*, with Ponti and the Hamburg Symphony Orchestra for FSM (Germany).

Dreyfus, George (b. 1928). Born in Wuppertal, Dreyfus and his family migrated to Australia in 1939, where he studied at the Melbourne University Conservatorium and was a bassoon player in the Victorian Symphony Orchestra, Melbourne. He returned to Germany to study the bassoon with Oehlberger, then played the instrument in various Australian orchestras and chamber groups. His first composition was published in 1965; his later works include vocal, instrumental, orchestral and film music, and several operas. He conducted his *From Within Looking Out*, with an ensemble, for World Record Club.

Dubrovsky, Viktor (b. 1927). After studying the violin and conducting at the Moscow Conservatory, Dubrovsky was principal conductor of the Byelorussian Philharmonic Orchestra at Minsk (1956–62), and then artistic director of the N. P. Osipov State Russian Folk Orchestra (since 1962). He has recorded for Melodiya Scriabin's *Piano Concerto in F sharp minor* (with Neuhaus and the USSR State Symphony Orchestra) and Martinů's Cello Concerto (with Chomizer and the Moscow Philharmonic Orchestra).

Ducloux, Walter (b. 1913). Born in Switzerland, Ducloux studied at the University of Munich and at the Vienna Academy of Music, and assisted Toscanini at the Lucerne Festival in 1938 and 1939. He went to the United States, conducted opera in New York (1940–42) and was a band leader in the US army (1943–6). He returned to Europe, conducted opera in Prague and Brno (1946–8) and came back to New York in 1949 to become music director of 'Voice of America' broadcasts. In 1953 he joined the University of Southern California to head the opera department of the school of music. He recorded for MGM a disc of excerpts from *Tristan und Isolde*, with Farrell and Blankenberg and the MGM Studio Symphony Orchestra.

Dudarova, Veronika (b. 1916). Born in Baku, the Soviet conductor Dudarova was a pupil of Anosov and Ginzburg, and has been the chief conductor and artistic director of the Moscow State Symphony Orchestra. In 1960 she was awarded the title of People's Artist of the Russian Republic. With the Moscow State Symphony Orchestra (called the 'Moscow Region Orchestra') she recorded Chaikin's Accordion Concerto (with Kazakov) and Tchaikovsky's *The Storm*, *Fate*, *The Voyevode* and *Overture in F major*.

Dufallo, Richard (b. 1933). The American clarinettist and conductor Dufallo conducted the Dallas Symphony, the Chicago Symphony, the Pittsburgh Symphony and the New York Philharmonic Orchestras in performances of contemporary music, and was associate conductor of the Buffalo Philharmonic Orchestra during the tenure of Lukas Foss (1962–70). He has recorded Orbón's *Partita 2* (with the Columbia University Contemporary Music Group) and Simon's *The Pied Piper of Hamelin* (for Composers Recordings), Schwartz's *Concert Piece for Ten Players* and *Texture* (with the New Cantata Orchestra of London for Opus One), Takemitsu's *The Dorian Horizon*, Del Tredici's *Syzygy*, Xenakis' *Akrata*, Nono's *Canciones a Guiomar* (with the Festival Chamber Orchestra for Columbia), and Escher's Symphony No. 2 (with the Rotterdam Philharmonic Orchestra for Donemus).

Dunand, Robert (b. 1928). Born at Carouge, Switzerland, Dunand studied at Geneva University and Conservatoire, at the Salzburg Mozarteum and in Venice. He was musical editor of the *Courrier de Genève* and a musical writer (1946–61), a percussion player in the Suisse Romande Orchestra (1951–8) and on occasion with foreign orchestras. On the staff of the Geneva Radio he was in charge of broadcasts of contemporary music and of the Centre of Sound Research, and is now responsible for musical and dramatic presentations at Radio Suisse Romande. He has conducted the Suisse Romande Orchestra, and in 1951 founded the orchestra of the Jeunesses Musicales de Suisse, which also serves as the Collegium Academicum de Genève, and has given many first performances of both ancient and contemporary music, doing much to promote the work of Swiss composers, both at home and abroad. In 1960 he became a professor at the Geneva Conservatoire. He has made a number of recordings for La Guilde Internationale du Disque with the Collegium Academicum, including Rameau's *Les Indes galantes*, Vivaldi's *Juditha triumphans* and *Guitar Concertos in D* and *A* (with Quevedo), Handel's Organ Concertos (with Rogg, on four discs), Haydn's *Trumpet Concertos in E flat* and *D major*, Clarke's *Trumpet Voluntary*, Purcell's *Sonata in D major* and trumpet overture to *The Indian Queen* and Leopold Mozart's Trumpet Concerto (with Delmotte), Franceschini's *Sonata for Two Trumpets in D major*, D. Gabrieli's Trumpet Sonata No. 2, Barsanti's Concerto Grosso Op. 3 No. 10, Torelli's *Trumpet Concerto in D major*, Corelli's *Trumpet Sonata in D major* and Vivaldi's Two-Trumpet Concerto Op. 46 No. 1 (with Cuvit and Debonneville), excerpts from Rousseau's *Le Devin du village*, Mozart's Organ Sonatas (with Delor), Two-Piano Concerto K. 365 (with Slatkine and Duport) and Three-Piano Concerto K. 242 (with Slatkine, Duport and Russel), both Cimarosa's and Paer's *Il maestro di capella* (with Corena and Retchitzka), Beethoven's *Mass in C major*, Rossini's *Il Signor Bruschino*, Mendelssohn's Concerto for Violin, Piano and Strings (with Soh and Naboré) and Rodrigo's *Concierto de Aranjuez* (with Quevedo). None of these discs has been released commercially in Britain or the United States, although some may have been distributed by the Concert Hall Record Club. For CTS (Switzerland) he also recorded Apothéloz's Concertino and Schibler's Cello Concerto (with Filippini and the Orchestre des Jeunesses Musicales).

Dunn, Richard (b. 1929). Born in Birmingham, Alabama, Dunn studied at the University of California, Berkeley, the Vienna Academy of Music, the Music Academy of the West, and at the Juilliard School. He was a horn soloist, and first appeared as a conductor in Vienna in 1956; he was then associate conductor for Walt Disney Productions, lectured at the University of California, Santa Barbara, and conducted the Santa Barbara Summer Symphony. He recorded Telemann's *Suite in F for Three Horns, Two Violins and Continuo* and Three-Horn Concerto, Barsanti's Two-Horn Concerto and Handel's Two-Horn Concerto (with Stagliano and Berv, and the Kapp Sinfonietta for Amadeo, Kapp, and Decca in Britain), and Bach's Suite No. 1 and Cantata No. 51 (with the Festival Orchestra of New York *et al.* for Decca, US).

Dunn, Sir Vivian (b. 1908). Dunn's father was the director of music with the Royal Marines, in London, and Dunn studied at Cologne Conservatory and at the Royal Academy of Music in London. He was a violinist in the Queen's Hall Orchestra under Wood and was a foundation member of the BBC Symphony Orchestra in 1930. In 1931 he was appointed director of music, Royal Marines, and retired as principal director in 1968. He has made many records with the Royal Marines Band, and over a million copies of them have been sold; one included Vaughan Williams' *English Folksongs Suite*, Jacob's *Music for a Festival*, and Milhaud's *Suite française*. He also recorded in the 1970s Sullivan's overture *In Memoriam*, suite from *The Merchant of Venice* and incidental music for *The Tempest* (with the City of Birmingham Symphony Orchestra for EMI), a collection of pieces by Grainger, Quilter, Toye, Gibbs and Gardiner (with the Light Music Society Orchestra for EMI), Clark's *Trumpet Voluntary*, Purcell's *When I am Laid in Earth*, the minuet from Handel's *Berenice*, the overture to *The Yeomen of the Guard*, Nimrod from *Enigma Variations*, the March from Bliss's *Things to Come*, Walton's *Crown Imperial*, Vaughan Williams' *Fantasia on Greensleeves*, and Rosamund from Quilter's *Where the Rainbow Ends* (with the Bournemouth Symphony Orchestra for Polydor).

Dünnwald, Josef (b. 1909). Born in Düsseldorf, Dünnwald began the piano at the age of five and gave his first concert at nine. He studied at the Cologne University and Academy of Music, but a visit to the Bayreuth Festival made him decide to become a conductor. He studied with Abendroth, was a repetiteur at Wiesbaden (1934) where he also conducted operas and operettas, was conductor at Saarbrücken (1938) and Stuttgart Staatstheater (1939), and after World War II became first conductor there; he took part in the rebuilding of the opera house, and reconstructed the Stuttgart Radio Symphony Orchestra with the co-operation of the American military government. He was appointed chief conductor at Stuttgart in 1951; his repertoire extends from Gluck and Mozart to Berg and Dallapiccola, and includes 90 operas. In addition he has been a guest conductor with the Stuttgart Ensemble in London, Edinburgh, Athens, New York and Rio de Janeiro. In 1974 he was awarded the Bundesverdienstkreuz, and in 1977 he acted as general music director at Lübeck. His compositions include symphonies, ballets, a piano concerto and songs; his ballet *Metamorphosen* won a prize and was performed by Ansermet and the Suisse Romande Orchestra, and Leitner also conducted the work and a symphony at Stuttgart. Nixa and Classics Club released in the early years of LP a recording of *Così fan tutte*, in which Dünnwald conducted the Stuttgart Ton-Studio Orchestra *et al.*; he also recorded an aria recital (with Herlea and the Wurttemberg State Opera Orchestra for Intercord).

Durian, Ohan (b. 1922). An Armenian born in Jerusalem, Durian studied at the Conservatory there, and with Desormière and Martinon in Paris. He took part in the Sixth World Youth Festival in Moscow in 1957, returned to Soviet Armenia, became chief conductor of the Armenian Philharmonic Orchestra (1960–65) and conductor of the Armenian Opera (from 1971), founded and conducted the Armenian Radio and Television Symphony Orchestra (1967), and conducted at the Leipzig Opera (1965–9). He has toured in East and West Europe, and has composed symphonic and choral music. For Philips he recorded Shostakovich's Symphony No. 12 (with the Leipzig Gewandhaus Orchestra).

Duruflé, Maurice (b. 1902). The French composer and organist Duruflé has been one of the foremost virtuosi of the instrument in Europe. He studied the organ with Tournemire and Vierne, and at the Paris Conservatoire, where his composition teacher was Dukas. In 1944 he became professor of harmony at the Conservatoire. His high degree of self-criticism has limited the number of compositions he has published, but of these the most widely acclaimed is the *Requiem*, first performed in 1947 under Desormière. Erato has recorded Duruflé himself conducting the work with the Lamoureux Orchestra, the Caillard and Caillat Choirs and soloists. Other of his compositions he has recorded, with the ORTF Orchestra, are the *Danses pour orchestre* and his four *Motets*; on the same disc is his Mass, *Cum Jubilo*, conducted by Soyer.

Dutoit, Charles (b. 1936). Born in Lausanne, Dutoit studied the violin, viola, piano, percussion, composition and conducting at the Lausanne Conservatory, the Geneva Music Academy and then in Italy and in the United States. He was a member of the Lausanne Chamber Orchestra and made his debut as a conductor in 1959, played as an orchestral viola player and a member of a string quartet, and in 1964 conducted the Berne Symphony Orchestra in *La Sacre du printemps*, which led to his appointment as permanent conductor of the orchestra (1967–77) and to von Karajan inviting him to conduct at the Vienna Festival the following year. He conducted the Zürich Radio Symphony Orchestra (1964–7), the Zürich Tonhalle Orchestra (1966–71), has been music director of the National Orchestra of Mexico for two years, principal conductor of the Göteborg Symphony Orchestra in Sweden (since 1975) and music director of the Montreal Symphony Orchestra (since 1977). He has also appeared in many countries as a guest conductor, toured South America, Japan and South Africa, and made his debut in London in 1966 and in the US at Los Angeles in 1972. His repertoire extends from Monteverdi to Messiaen, and includes opera, ballet, chamber music, oratorio and symphonic music. He has specialised in the music of Stravinsky and his first recording for Erato, *L'Histoire du soldat*, received a Grand Prix du Disque of the Académie Charles Cros. Other Stravinsky works recorded were *Pulcinella* and *Apollon Musagète* (with the English Chamber Orchestra for Erato), *Petrushka* (with the London Symphony Orchestra for DGG), *Les Noces*, *Renard* and *Ragtime* (with the Lausanne University Choir *et al.* for Erato). In the 1970s he also made records of Honegger's *Le Roi David* (for Erato), Falla's *Master Peter's Puppet Show* and Harpsichord Concerto (with Veyron-Lacroix, *et al.*, for Erato), Tchaikovsky's Piano Concerto No. 1 (with Argerich and the Royal Philharmonic Orchestra for DGG), Mendelssohn's Violin Concertos in D minor and E minor (with Accardo and the London Philharmonic Orchestra for Philips), the six Paganini Violin Concertos (with Accardo and the London Philharmonic Orchestra for DGG), Wildberger's *Music for Twenty-two Solo Strings* (with the Orchestra della Radio Svizzera Italiana for CTS), Stenhammar's Piano Concerto No. 1 (with Mannheimer and the Göteborg Symphony Orchestra for Sterling), and Kelterborn's *Five Madrigals* (with Speiser and the Lucerne Festival Orchestra for CTS).

Duvauchelle, Pierre (b. 1906). Born in Le Mesnil-Esnard, France, Duvauchelle studied with Marguerite Long, Capet and Gaubert, and founded the Paris Chamber Orchestra in 1934. With the orchestra he recorded on 78 r.p.m. discs several concertos from Vivaldi's *L'estro armonico* (for Lumen) and Haydn's Symphony No. 49 (for Columbia).

Dykes Bower, John (b. 1905). Born in Gloucester, Dykes Bower was educated at Corpus Christi College, Cambridge, where he was an organ scholar, was John Stewart of Rannoch Scholar in Sacred Music (1922–8), organist and choirmaster at Truro Cathedral (1926–9), organist at New College, Oxford (1929–33), Durham Cathedral (1933–6) and St Paul's Cathedral (from 1936). He has been a professor at the Royal College of Music, president of the Incorporated Association of Organists (1949–50), associate director of the Royal School of Church Music (1945–52) and served in the RAF volunteer reserve in World War II. Columbia recorded him, on 78 r.p.m. discs, with the St Paul's Cathedral Choir performing hymns, anthems and motets of Bach, Sweelinck, Fairfax, Tallis, Morley, Boyce, Wesley, Child, Blow, Ouseley, Taverner, Humphrey, Greene, Walford Davies, Parry and Howells, and with the Royal School of Church Music Choir in a work of Stanford; with the St Paul's Choir he also recorded for Columbia an LP of sacred music for Christmas and Easter.

E

Eckerberg, Axel Sixten (b. 1909). Born in Hjältevad, Sweden, Eckerberg studied at the Stockholm Conservatory (1927–32), then studied the piano with Sauer in Vienna and Phillipp in Paris, and conducting with Weingartner at Basel and Kabasta in Vienna. In 1937 he became conductor of the Göteborg Radio Orchestra, and in 1939 of the Göteborg Orchestral Society, at the same time appearing internationally as a pianist. In 1947 he was admitted to the Royal Musical Academy in Stockholm and after 1947 he was a guest conductor in numerous cities in and out of Europe. He has written a number of compositions including two symphonies and two piano concertos. With the Göteborg Radio Orchestra he has recorded for Regent (US) and with the Göteborg Symphony Orchestra for Telefunken, all on 78 r.p.m. discs; the works recorded were of the Swedish composers Söderman (Piano Concerto, with Leygraf the soloist), Stenhammar (Symphony No. 2), Wirén (*Serenade*) and Larsson (*Pastoral Suite*) as well as *Finlandia* of Sibelius.

Eckertsen, Dean (b. 1928). Both in Utah, Eckertsen was educated at the Chicago Musical College, the University of Denver, Berkshire Music Center and the University of Utah. He conducted in many cities in the United States, premièred music by contemporary composers, and in 1951 made his New York debut at Carnegie Hall. Eckertsen recorded, for Vox in the 1950s, the complete Corelli Concerti Grossi Op. 6 with a group called the Corelli Tri-Centenary String Orchestra (Corelli was born in 1653), also some Concerti Grossi by Geminiani and Locatelli. For Dover he recorded the Geminiani Concerti Grossi Op. 2 and the Locatelli Concerti Grossi complete (with the Musici Virtuosi di Milano). The Corelli set of three LP records was a particularly successful issue and the stereo version is still available in the US, but Eckertsen does not appear to have made any further discs in recent years.

Egk, Werner (b. 1901). Born in Auchsesheim, Bavaria, Egk studied the piano with Herzel-Langenheim and composition with Orff, although as a composer he was largely self-taught. From 1929 he was active as a conductor in Bavaria, and from 1934 to 1940 conducted at the Berlin State Opera. He was appointed head of composition at the Reichsmusikkammer, a body set up by the Nazis in 1933 to administer musical life in the Third Reich. Although Egk was acceptable to Nazi officialdom, they initially disapproved of his opera *Peer Gynt*, but they soon changed their minds when Hitler himself expressed enthusiasm for the work. After World War II Egk's ballet *Abraxas* was suppressed on moral grounds by the Bavarian Ministry of Education after its première in Munich in 1948. Egk returned to Berlin to become the director of the Berlin Hochschule für Musik in 1950, but three years later took up residence in Munich and has since been the president of the Association of German Composers. He is known today as one of the most distinguished composers in Germany and is best known for his operas, particularly *Die Zaubergeige* (1935), *Peer Gynt* (1938), *Columbus* (1941), *Circe* (1948), *Irische Legende* (1955) and *Der Revisor* (1957). His musical style is somewhat eclectic and skirts around Hindemith's polyphony and the twelve-tone school; it is melodic, ingenuous and theatrically effective. Egk has recorded some of his music; on 78 r.p.m. discs for HMV he recorded his ballet *Joan von Zarissa* (with the Paris Opéra Orchestra) and for Telefunken a coupling of *Waffentage* and *Totenklage* (with Berlin State Opera Orchestra), written for the Olympic Games in Berlin in 1936. More recently DGG have issued LPs of him conducting the Bavarian Radio Symphony Orchestra in his *Quattro canzoni* (with the soprano, Seefried), *Geigenmusik* (with the violinist Wilkomirska) and *Die chinesische Nachtigall*, in addition to excerpts from his opera *Die Zaubergeige* (with the Bavarian State Opera). His conducting on these discs is accomplished and lively. Urania also issued an early LP in which he conducted Mozart's Symphony No. 25 (with the Berlin Radio Orchestra).

Egmond, Piet van (b. 1912). Born in Amsterdam and educated at the Amsterdam Academy of Music, Egmond was organist with the Netherlands Broadcasting Company and the BBC, and conductor of the Amsterdam Oratorio Choir, with whom he has performed in France, Britain, FR Germany and Belgium. For La Guilde Internationale du Disque he recorded as conductor the Bach *St Matthew Pas-*

sion (with the Rotterdam Chamber Orchestra *et al.*).

Ehmann, Wilhelm (b. 1904). Born in Freistadt, Ehmann completed his training as a teacher, studied music, literature and philosophy at the universities at Freiburg and Leipzig, and was professor of music, director of the Musicological Institute and director of musical education at Innsbruck (1940). After service in the German navy in World War II, he became director of church music for the Westphalian Church (1948), lectured at Münster University, and founded the Westphalian School for Church Music and the Westphalian Kantorei in Herford. He directs an annual international school for choral conductors, and is artistic director of the Cantate record company at Damstadt. An authority on Lutheran church music, particularly on performance practice during the Reformation, and in the music of Bach and Schütz, he has written a number of musical studies, and has edited early German music for publication.

Ehmann has made many recordings with the Westphalian Kantorei for Cantate and Barenreiter, a number having been released in the United States by Nonesuch, Vanguard and Musical Heritage Society. Included are the Bach Motets and Cantatas Nos 4, 36, 37, 49, 64, 76, 84 and 182, Praetorius' *Polyhymnia caduceatrix et panegyrica* and Christmas music, Schütz's *Die Geburt useres Herren Jesu Christi*, *St John Passion*, *Magnificat*, Psalms 24, 30, 33, 41 and 45, *Geistliche Konzerte*, *Kleine geistliche Konzert* (Nos 1 to 44) and *Musikalische Exequien*, cantatas by Buxtehude, Distler's Motets and *Der Jahrkreis*, Melchior's *Acht Gleichnisse aus den Evangelien des Matthäus und Lukas*, the Psalms of David, songs of Paul Gerhardt, excerpts from *Messiah*, chorales and arias from the Bach cantatas, a collection entitled *Music of the Reformation*, Haydn's Mass No. 2, Mendelssohn's Motets, and collections entitled *The Golden Age of Wind Music* (with the Detmold College of Music Oboe Ensemble and the Hannover College of Music Recorder Ensemble), and *Early Brass Music of the 17th Century* (with the Ehmann Ensemble, issued by CMS-Oryx).

Ehrlich, Julius (b. 1894). Born at Frankfurt am Main and educated at the Hochschule für Musik there, Ehrlich was director of the radio orchestra at Hannover (1923–8), conductor at Bückeburg (1923–8), conductor at the Leningrad Opera and professor at the Leningrad Conservatory (1930–33), conductor at the Royal Flemish Opera and of the chamber orchestra at Antwerp (1934–6), director of the Milwaukee Symphony Orchestra (1939–47) and director of the Annual Brotherhood Week concerts, Milwaukee (1955–63). He recorded, for Columbia before World War II on 78s, with the Paris Symphony Orchestra Mossolov's *Steel Foundry*, another Russian piece of the same period, *The Dnieper Water Power Station* by Meytuss, and Shostakovich's *Age of Gold* ballet, and accompanied Chaliapin in some songs by Maximilian Steinberg, the son-in-law of Rimsky-Korsakov.

Ehrling, Sixten (b. 1918). Born in Malmö, Sweden, Ehrling studied the piano, organ and conducting at the Stockholm Conservatory, became a repetiteur at the Stockholm Royal Opera (1936–40), conductor at Göteborg (1942–4), conductor at the Royal Opera (1944–53) and then principal conductor there (1953–60). He studied also at Dresden (1941), London and Paris (1946), led the conductors' course at the Salzburg Mozarteum (1954) and became a member of the Royal Music Academy in Sweden (1956). In 1960 he left Sweden to make a career abroad and since then has become the first internationally known Swedish conductor. In 1963 he was appointed musical director of the Detroit Symphony Orchestra; he has conducted often at the New York Metropolitan Opera and has appeared as a guest conductor in the United States, Europe, Japan and Australia. He is also a fine pianist and accompanist, and is a professor at the Juilliard School in New York.

Ehrling recorded, on 78s, as a pianist, Wiklund's Piano Concerto No. 1 (with the Stockholm Concert Association Orchestra under Frykberg for HMV) and Frumerie's Sonata No. 2 (with Temko, viola, for HMV) and as a conductor, Pergament's *Entrance* and *Dance of the Robots* (with the Swedish Radio Orchestra for HMV) and Wirén's Cello Concerto (with Gröndahl and the Swedish Radio Orchestra for HMV). He made LP records in the 1950s with the Stockholm Radio Orchestra of the seven symphonies of Sibelius, as well as the *Four Legends* and the Violin Concerto (with Camilla Wicks). These were released in Britain and the United States variously by Capitol and Mercury, and the series was one of the first complete sets of Sibelius symphonies to appear. It was a distinguished achievement, although the performances were later eclipsed. For EMI he accompanied David Oistrakh with the Stockholm Festival Orchestra in the Beethoven and Sibelius Violin Concertos, which were the first recordings made by the great Russian violinist in the West. His other records include

Tchaikovsky's Piano Concerto No. 1 (with Gilels and the Stockholm Philharmonic Orchestra for Regent), some overtures of J. Strauss (with the same orchestra for Regent), Blomdahl's *Chamber Concerto* (with the London Symphony Orchestra for Decca), Symphony No. 3 (with the Stockholm Philharmonic Orchestra, issued by Turnabout), and his oratorio *In the Hall of Mirrors* (with the Stockholm Philharmonic *et al.* for Caprice), a disc of overtures and orchestral pieces by Berwald (with the Stockholm Philharmonic, issued by Turnabout), two symphonies by Berwald (with the London Symphony Orchestra for Decca), Lidholm's *Rites* and Rosenberg's *Uvertyr till Marionettes* (with the London Symphony for Decca), Larsson's *Variations for Orchestra* (with the Stockholm Radio Orchestra for Discophil), songs by Frumerie and Karkoff (with Meyer and the Stockholm Philharmonic Orchestra, released by RCA), Holmboe's Symphony Op. 105 and Nystroem's *Sinfonia breve* (with the Göteborg Symphony Orchestra for Caprice) and Bäck's *Game Around a Game*, Larsson's *Concertino for Clarinet and Strings* (with Janson) and Nystroem's *Concerto Ricercante* (with Laretei, and the Stockholm Philharmonic Orchestra for Philips).

Eibenschütz, José (1872–1952). Born in Sulzhayn, Hartz, Eibenschütz studied at the Hoch Conservatory at Frankfurt am Main, was conductor at Turku, Finland (1894–1905), at Görlitz (1905–08), with the Hamburg Philharmonic Orchestra (1908–21), with the Olso Philharmonic Orchestra (1921–7), was general music director at Nauheim (1926–7), was head of the North German Broadcasting Company at Hamburg (1928) and conducted in Scandinavia and the USSR (1938–46) and in Germany (after 1946). Urania issued a recording of him conducting the Leipzig Radio Orchestra in Tchaikovsky's *Romeo and Juliet* fantasy-overture.

Eichhorn, Kurt (b. 1908). Born in Munich, Eichhorn studied at the Würzburg Conservatory and at the Munich Hochschule für Musik, and made his debut as a conductor at Bielefeld in 1937. He was a conductor at the Dresden Opera (1941–5), at the Munich State Opera and with the Munich Philharmonic Orchestra (1945–56), at the Gärtnerplatz State Theatre in Munich (1956–66) and with the Bavarian Radio Symphony Orchestra (1967–75). He also was a professor at the Munich Academy of Music (1948–72), and his particular interests have been the operas of Verdi, Puccini, Wagner and Orff. In the early 1950s he recorded Strauss's ballet *Josephslegende* (with the Munich State Opera Orchestra for Urania), which was a fill-up to Kempe's *Der Rosenkavalier.* His later records include Orff's *Die Kluge*, *Der Mond*, *Carmina Burana*, *Ludus de nato infante mirificus* and *Comoedia de Christi Resurrectione* (with the Bavarian Radio Symphony Orchestra *et al.* for Ariola/Eurosdisc, and recorded under the composer's supervision), and *Lamenti* (with the same orchestra for BASF), excerpts from *Zar und Zimmerman*, (with the Munich Philharmonic Orchestra for DGG), *Hänsel und Gretel*, *Die schöne Galatea* and the Wagner edition of Gluck's *Iphigénie en Aulide* (with the Bavarian Radio Orchestra *et al.* for Ariola/Eurodisc). RCA have released *Hänsel und Gretel* and *Iphigénie en Aulide* in Britain and the US.

Eisler, Hanns (1898–1962). Born in Leipzig, Eisler studied at the Vienna Academy of Music, was a pupil of Schoenberg, won the Music Prize of the City of Vienna (1924), and taught in Berlin (1925–32). His first composition to attract attention was *Newspaper Cuttings*, for voices and piano; he wrote other pieces, or 'musical cartoons', based on current events. When the Nazis came into power his published compositions were destroyed; he left Germany for the USSR and then the United States, where he was a resident from 1933 to 1948. He taught in New York, worked in Hollywood where he was musical assistant to Charlie Chaplin (1942–7), and wrote a book, *Composing for the Films* (New York, 1947). In 1947 the Unamerican Activities Committee of the Senate sought to have him deported, but after widespread protests he was allowed to leave the country peacefully the following year. He returned to Vienna, then went to live in DR Germany, where in 1950 he was awarded the National Prize for composing the country's national anthem, together with Becher. His early compositions utilised the twelve-tone method, but later he wrote simplified tonal melodies; he wished to write music that would appeal to proletarian tastes. Today little of his music is known outside Germany, but in the GDR he is a revered figure, and the Hochschule für Musik in East Berlin is named after him. Decca (US) released *Mr Pickwick's Christmas*, narrated by Charles Laughton, with music written and conducted by Eisler, composed in his years in the US. Later, for DGG, he directed his Septets Nos 1 and 2, and Nonet No. 1 (with the Berlin State Opera String Quartet *et al.*), and for Eterna the intermezzo and final chorus from his cantata *Mitte des Jahrhunderts* and his *Klingende Dokumente III* (with the Berlin Staatskapelle *et al.*).

Elenescu, Emanuel (b. 1911). Born in Piatra Neamt, the Romanian composer and conductor Elenescu studied at the Iasi Conservatory under Ciolan, became the permanent conductor of the Bucharest Radio-Television Symphony Orchestra (1933), and has also conducted in the USSR, Bulgaria, Hungary, Poland, Yugoslavia, FR and DR Germany, Belgium, Italy, France and Cuba. His compositions include orchestral works and concertos, and his repertoire as a conductor is centred on the music of the 19th and early 20th centuries. For Electrecord he has conducted the Bucharest Radio-Television Orchestra (also known as the Romanian Radio-Television Symphony Orchestra) in Berlioz's *Roméo et Juliette* symphony, and in a number of works by Romanian composers, including Berger's Symphony No. 5, Jora's *Demoiselle Mariutza*, Chiriac's *Bucharest of Old Times*, Enesco's Symphony No. 3, Dumitrescu's Symphony No. 1, Capoianu's Violin Concerto (with Hamza), Cuclin's Symphony No. 11, Profeta's *Prince and Beggar*, Suite No. 1, Mendelssohn's Violin Concerto No. 2 (with Hamza), Istrate's *Stereophonic Music for Two String Orchestras*, Grigoriu's *Symphonic Variations*, Cuclin's Symphony No. 16, Niculescu's *Scenes*, Grigoriu's *Cosmic Dream*, Negrea's *Stories from Grui*, Constantinescu's *Symphony in D major*, Andricu's Symphony No. 6, Popovici's Symphony No. 4, Vancea's *Priculiciul* ballet and *Sinfonietta*, and Grigoriu's *Homage to George Enesco*.

Elgar, Sir Edward (1857–1934). The great English composer Elgar was an experienced conductor, although he did not pursue a professional career as such. For several years from the age of 22 he coached a band made up of attendants at the Worcester County Asylum, and later, in 1911–12, he was the conductor of the London Symphony Orchestra; of its thirteen concerts in that season he led six, Nikisch took three, and Mengelberg, Steinbach and Doret one each. Although Richter conducted the first performances of the *Enigma Variations*, the Symphony No. 1 and *The Dream of Gerontius*, it was Elgar himself who premièred *Falstaff* and the Symphony No. 2. Reed, the leader of the London Symphony Orchestra and an intimate of Elgar, said that he always remained a little diffident and undecided in his interpretations of other men's music; London critics who wrote about his concerts with the London Symphony commented about an intensely dramatic account of Beethoven's Symphony No. 7, despite a near breakdown in the last movement, and a much less inspired performance of the Franck symphony. He conducted his own music from the beginning, and in his lifetime very few would have disagreed that some of the finest performances of his works were given under his direction. He was stiff in his movements and his beat was rigid, unimaginative and not always clear, but the inspiration to the players came from the expression on his face and certain gestures of his left hand. Orchestras revered him and there is no doubt that they gave him the performances he wanted. He was generally easy to work with, although small errors by the players could affect his concentration.

Elgar recorded nearly all his own orchestral music for HMV, mostly with the London Symphony Orchestra. Virtually all of these records have been re-issued at one time or another on LP transfers by EMI, World Record Club and Pearl. What we hear in these records is startlingly different from the 'Elgar tradition' represented in conductors such as Barbirolli, Boult and Sargent. Elgar is much less self-indulgent and expressive than these, and in fact he himself said that other people made his music sound 'too assertive'. An example would be the Nimrod variation in the *Enigma Variations*, which is in no way sad or solemn in Elgar's recording, compared to the almost overpowering eloquence of many present day performances. David Cairns has written about Elgar's conducting of his own works on record: 'Flexibility of pulse is combined with bold, firmly shaped phrasing, a strong incisive bass line and an attack positively ferocious in its energy. . . . The Barbirolli purple passage is conspicuously absent. Elgar evidently felt his scoring linearly, and the result is an orchestral texture that is almost abrasive and a clarity of detail which reaches its height in the masterly performance of *Falstaff*. . . . Yet so sure is Elgar's touch, so sensitive as well as dynamic, that, after the first shock, we never feel that the music's character is being sacrificed to mere energy. It emerges at least as strongly as [with other conductors], and in a way that must significantly alter our idea of it' (*Sunday Times*, 17 August, 1975).

Elgar's first records as a conductor were made in 1914, and were a set of eight 78s of the incidental music to Algernon Blackwood's play *The Starlight Express*. Then followed *Carissima*, the *Pomp and Circumstance Marches Nos 1* and *4*, *Salut d'amour*, *Sea Pictures* (with Megane), an abridged *Cockaigne*, Cello Concerto (with Beatrice Harrison), an abridged Violin Concerto (with Hall), *Carillon* (with Ainley), *Bavarian Dances Nos 1, 2* and *3*, the Prelude and Angel's Farewell from *The Dream of Gerontius*, excerpts from the two *Wand of*

Youth suites, *Chanson de nuit*, *Polonia*, *The Sanguine Fan* and *Enigma Variations* (with the Symphony Orchestra, 1914–21), *Cockaigne*, *In the South*, the Symphony No. 2, *Enigma Variations*, *Pomp and Circumstance Marches Nos 1* and *2*, an extract from *The Saga of King Olaf*, *Chanson de nuit* and Meditation from *The Light of Life* (with the Royal Albert Hall Orchestra, 1921–6), the *Bavarian Dances Nos 1*, *2* and *3*, the Symphonies Nos 1 and 2, the *Pomp and Circumstance Marches Nos 3*, *4* and *5*, the *Wand of Youth* Suite No. 1, *Severn Suite*, Violin Concerto (with Menuhin), *In the South*, *The Crown of India*, *Chanson de matin*, *Civic Fanfare*, an extract from *The Banner of St George*, an extract from *The Music Makers*, the minuet from the *Beau Brummel* suite, *Falstaff* and the *Nursery Suite* (with the London Symphony Orchestra, 1926–32), *Carissima*, Cello Concerto (with Harrison), two interludes from *Falstaff*, *May Song*, the minuet from the *Beau Brummel* suite, *Rosemary*, *Salut d'amour*, *Sérénade lyrique* and *Mazurka* (with the New Symphony Orchestra, 1928–9), *Elegy*, *Froissart*, *Serenade* and *Gavotte* (with the London Philharmonic Orchestra, 1933–4), *Cockaigne*, the *Pomp and Circumstance Marches Nos 1* and *4* and the prelude to *The Kingdom* (with the BBC Symphony Orchestra, 1932–3). He also recorded his transcription of the Bach *Fantasia and Fugue in C minor* and the Handel *Overture in D minor* (with the Royal Albert Hall Orchestra), the Fugue only from the Bach work (later, with the Royal Albert Hall Orchestra) and the National Anthem (with the London Symphony Orchestra and Philharmonic Chorus), and the World Record Club issued, as a fill-up for one of its releases of Elgar performances, part of a rehearsal of the third movement of the Symphony No. 2.

In 1971 EMI issued a five-disc set of transfers of these Elgar recordings which included the symphonies, *Falstaff* and the *Enigma Variations*. Later in 1975 another six-disc album appeared which included the two overtures *In the South* and *Froissart* and a number of the smaller works, and at the same time there was published Jerrold Northrop Moore's *Elgar on Record* which gave technical information about the recordings and much of the correspondence between the composer and the Gramophone Company during their long association. The documentation of Elgar as an interpreter of his own music by these records has only been approached in recent years by that accorded to Britten, Copland, Stravinsky and Henze. Several reservations should be added: it was often remarked by his contemporaries that no two performances of Elgar were identical; in addition he did not always obey his own instructions and he sometimes altered tempi without any indication. So these recorded performances cannot be regarded as definitive, and perhaps serve to demonstrate that no performance can be definitive. Also, all Elgar's records were made towards the end of his life.

Eliasberg, Karl (b. 1907). After graduating from the violin class at the Leningrad Conservatory (1928), Eliasberg was artistic director and principal conductor of the Leningrad Radio Symphony Orchestra (1931–53), and was named Honoured Artist of the RSFSR (1944). He has been active with orchestras in Leningrad and there premièred Shostakovich's Symphony No. 7 when the city was under siege. He recorded the Brahms Double Concerto (with D. Oistrakh, Kushnevitzky and the Leningrad Radio Symphony Orchestra), Schumann's *Manfred* overture (with the Leningrad Philharmonic Orchestra), the Grieg Piano Concerto, *Le Carnaval des animaux* and Liapunov's *Solemn Overture on Russian Themes* (with the USSR State Symphony Orchestra, and with Murailev in the Grieg).

Elkus, Jonathan (b. 1931). Born in San Francisco and educated at the University of California, Berkeley, and at Stanford University, Elkus has been professor of music at Lehigh University. He has composed operas, chamber music, songs and music for brass bands, and has written a book entitled *Charles Ives and the American Band Tradition*. Lehigh University recorded its own concert band and instrumental ensemble, conducted by Elkus, in music by Riegger, Ruggles and Ives.

Ellenberg, David (b. 1917). Born in London and educated at the Royal College of Music and the Accademia di Santa Cecilia, Rome, Ellenberg was conductor and musical director of the Ballet Rambert and conducted opera, ballet and concerts in Britain, Europe, the United States, China, Israel and South Africa, and also appeared at the Royal Opera House, Covent Garden and at Sadler's Wells. He recorded for Decca the overture to *La favorita* with the London Symphony Orchestra.

Elmendorff, Karl (1891–1962). Born in Düsseldorf, Elmendorff first studied philology but in 1913 became a pupil of Steinbach and Abendroth at the Cologne Conservatory. His first appointments as a conductor were at Düsseldorf and Mainz, and his subsequent career took him to Hagen, Aachen, Munich (1925–32), Wiesbaden, Kassel, the Berlin

State Opera (1938–41), Mannheim, Dresden (1941–5), Kassel (1948–51) and finally to Wiesbaden. He appeared regularly at the Bayreuth Festivals (1927–42) and also directed Wagner operas at the Florence May Festival.

At Bayreuth in 1928 he led *Tristan und Isolde*, and this performance was recorded by Columbia, on 38 discs. Acts I and II were complete, but for some reason Act III was abridged. One record in this set was devoted to a discussion about the structure of the opera by Ernest Newman. Although the principal singers in this recording – Gaarad and Larsen-Todsen – were not the best available exponents of their roles at the time, when Melchior and Leider were at their prime, the orchestral playing was superb and the set was altogether a distinguished one. Then in 1930 Toscanini conducted both *Tristan und Isolde* and *Tannhäuser* at Bayreuth, while Elmendorff was responsible for the *Ring*. Toscanini's *Tannhäuser* was a very remarkable performance, but while Columbia were prepared to record it, Toscanini's contract with Victor prevented him from conducting on the recording. Elmendorff was substituted, although Toscanini's influence on the recorded performance was very evident. The outcome was one of the finest early recordings of a Wagner opera, even allowing for some patches of inferior singing and for the opera being slightly cut. An LP transfer of the *Tannhäuser* has been available in Germany.

On 78s Elmendorff also recorded von Einem's *Concerto for Orchestra* (with the Saxon State Orchestra for DGG). Later, in the 1950s, Urania and Preiser released LPs of him leading the Dresden State Opera Orchestra *et al.*, believed to be recorded from radio broadcasts. These were *Don Giovanni*, *Luisa Miller*, *Fra Diavolo, Der Corregidor* (Wolf), and *The Taming of the Shrew* (Goetz). He also recorded a disc of excerpts from *Otello* (with the Berlin State Opera Orchestra *et al.*, issued by BASF), excerpts from *Don Giovanni* (in German, with the Saxon State Orchestra *et al.* for DGG), the Entry of the Gods into Valhalla from *Das Rheingold* (with the Berlin State Opera Orchestra for DGG) and the Prelude to Act III and Pilgrims' Chorus from *Tannhäuser* (with the Wurttemberg State Opera Orchestra *et al.* for Vox).

Enesco, Georges (1881–1955). The great Romanian violinist, composer, conductor and teacher Enesco was born at Dorohoi; he started playing the violin at four, at seven entered the Vienna Conservatory, and made his debut as a violinist at Slănic-Moldova just before his eighth birthday. He completed his studies with Fauré and Massenet at the Paris Conservatoire; in 1897–8 his works were being performed in Paris, and he then appeared as a violinist, pianist and conductor, giving many first performances of contemporary works. He divided his time between Paris and Bucharest, and among his pupils were Menuhin, Grumiaux, Gitlis and Totenberg. He wrote a number of major compositions, including the opera *Oedipe* and three symphonies, but his international reputation as a composer appears to rest now on his popular Romanian Rhapsodies for orchestra, and his third Violin Sonata. His musicianship was prodigious. Casals considered him, with Tovey, the greatest musician he ever knew. Menuhin, who was his devoted pupil, has recounted that, in Paris, Ravel appeared in Enesco's studio, asking him to play with him his new piano and violin sonata for the publishers, who at that time heard everything before committing themselves. Enesco and Ravel played through the sonata once and Enesco then asked Ravel to repeat it 'just to be on the safe side'. Ravel agreed and to his amazement Enesco put the score down and at the second time through played every note from memory. (See Y. Menuhin, *Unfinished Journey*, London, 1977, p. 101). In Paris Enesco conducted the Lamoureux Orchestra and was engaged as a guest conductor by other European Orchestras. After World War I, which he spent in Romania, he organised concerts in Bucharest and in 1923 he went to the United States and performed both as conductor and violinist; later in the 1930s he appeared for several seasons as a guest conductor with the New York Philharmonic-Symphony Orchestra, and returned to the US after World War II to tour again as a conductor and violinist. Barbirolli has written that Enesco really had no pretensions at being a conductor, but his performances have been characterised as 'direct, vigorous and authoritative'. David Hall commented in 1948 that one of the finest performances he remembered of the Beethoven Symphony No. 3 was with the New York Philharmonic-Symphony under Enesco's baton (*The Record Book*, New York, 1948, p. 552).

Enesco recorded in Paris for HMV in the 1930s the accompaniments for a number of concertos with the young Menuhin, as well as the *Prélude à l'après-midi d'un faune* and *Pavane pour une infante défunte* (the two latter with unidentified orchestras). After World War II, there appeared the *Brandenburg Concerto No. 5* and Bach's Harpsichord, Flute and Violin Concerto (with Chailley-Richez, Rampal and Ferras), and Harpsichord and

Two-Flute Concerto (with Chailley-Richez, Crunelle and Rampal, with the Paris Chamber Orchestra for Decca), Rodrigo's *Concierto de estio* (with Ferras and the Paris Conservatoire Orchestra for Decca), Schumann's Symphony No. 2 (with the London Philharmonic Orchestra for Decca), his own Suite No. 1 (with the Budapest Philharmonic Orchestra for Electrecord), his *Romanian Rhapsodies Nos 1* and *2* (with the Colonne Orchestra for Remington) and *Romanian Rhapsody No. 1* (with the USSR State Symphony Orchestra for Supraphon), as well as some others for Electrecord when he joined Dinu Lipatti in his first and second Violin Sonatas.

Engel, Lehman (b. 1910). Born in Jackson, Mississippi, Engel attended the Cincinnati Conservatory and College of Music and the Juilliard School, and studied composition with Goldmark and Sessions. He was musical director of the State Fair Musicals at Dallas (1949–52), director of the musical and dramatic theatre at the Academy of America (1962–5), founded and directed the BIM Musical Theater Workshop (1961), directed the Madrigal Singers and other choirs, and conducted musicals on Broadway. His compositions include five operas, symphonies, a viola concerto, chamber and instrumental music, and he has written, *inter alia*, *Planning and Producing Music for Classical Tragedy*, *Musical Shows*, *Renaissance to Baroque* and an autobiography *The Bright Day* (1956). For Columbia and Gamut he recorded a number of 78 r.p.m. discs with the Madrigal Singers, including a *Missa brevis* of Palestrina, the Bach motet *Jesu meine Freude* and pieces by Dowland, Farmer, Janequin, Victoria, Brahms, Holst, Hindemith and William Schuman, as well as Handel's *Il pastor fido* (abridged, with the Columbia Chamber Orchestra *et al.*). After he became a conductor of successful musicals on Broadway, he recorded, all for Columbia, an abridged version of Menotti's *The Consul*, Weill's *Lady in the Dark*, and *Porgy and Bess*, with the original casts and productions. *Porgy and Bess* was later re-issued on Odyssey.

Entremont, Philippe (b. 1934). Born in Reims into a musical family, Entremont studied at the Paris Conservatoire, and in 1953 won the Marguerite Long–Jacques Thibaud Piano Competition, and in that year made his debut in the United States. After an outstanding career as a concert pianist, making many records for CBS, he first appeared as a conductor in London in 1970. He has recorded, conducting from the keyboard, Mozart's Piano Concertos K. 415 and K. 453 (with the Paris Collegium Musicum), and as conductor, Satie's *Parade*, *Relâche*, and *Gymnopédies Nos 1* and *3*, in Debussy's arrangements (with the Royal Philharmonic Orchestra), Mozart's Symphonies Nos 28 and 29, *Les petits riens* and the ballet music from *Idomeneo* (with the Vienna Chamber Orchestra), all for CBS. La Guilde Internationale du Disque issued a disc of him playing the Mozart Piano Concertos K. 466 and K. 488, with the Frankfurt Symphony Orchestra conducted by Jean Entremont, his father.

Ephrikian, Angelo. Italian by birth and of Armenian descent, Ephrikian completed his studies with a degree in violin and composition, and then attended the school of Malipiero in Venice. He made an extensive study of the music of 18th-century Venice, and played an important part in the re-discovery of Vivaldi, whose *The Four Seasons* he first came into contact with in Venice in 1945. After studying the Vivaldi manuscripts in the library at Turin, he decided to supervise the transcription and publication of Vivaldi's vocal and instrumental music, founded the Institutio Italiano Antonio Vivaldi with Malipiero the artistic director, and during the next 25 years saw the publication of 530 volumes of the composer's music. In addition he re-discovered many works of Marcello, Galuppi, A. and D. Scarlatti, Boccherini, Monteverdi, da Venosta *et al.*, and with the Orchestra della Scuola Veneziana played all the Vivaldi works, including premières of *Beatus Vir*, *Dixit Dominus*, *La sena festegiante* and the first version of *Juditha*. With the orchestra he made numerous tours, but after it was disbanded in 1950 he became director of the Orchestra Italiana da Camera, resident conductor of the symphony orchestra of the AIDEM in Florence, and with this group represented Italy at the Brussels World Fair in 1968 with the first performance of Vivaldi's opera *La fida ninfa*. He was artistic director of the recording company Arcophon (1959–73), which recorded Peri's *Euridice*, produced originally in 1600 for the wedding of Henry IV of France and Marie de Medici and the first opera for which the music has survived complete. Ephrikian's recording with the Solisti di Milano was released in 1974 and is claimed to be the first successful attempt to bring the work back to musical life with absolute fidelity to the text; it was released in the United States by Musical Heritage Society. Ephrikian is now president of the Collegium Musicum Europae in Brussels, resident conductor of the Solisti di Milano and also conducts the Bologna Philharmonic Orchestra, which took part in one of the Leipzig Bach Festivals.

Ephrikian's other recordings include Monteverdi's *Vespro della beata Vergine*, *Magnificat*, *Beatus Vir*, *Il ballo*, *Mentre vaga angioletta* and *Il combattimento di Tancredi e Clorinda* (with the Scuola Veneziana Orchestra *et al.*, issued by Period), and excerpts from the *Vespro della beata Vergine* (with the same artists for Contrepoint), Vivaldi's concertos P. 87, P. 165, P. 273, P. 407 and P. 435 (with the Vienna Chamber Orchestra for Musidisc), Violin Concertos Op. 6 Nos 1 to 6 (with Ferraris, Fantini, Pocaterra, de Carli and the Solisti di Milano for Harmonia Mundi), *The Four Seasons* (with the Scuola Veneziana Orchestra for Erato, and the Solisti di Milano for Harmonia Mundi), Violin Concerto Op. 10 No. 2 (with Novello), Two-Horn Concerto, and Concertos P. 87 and P. 385 (with the Scuola Veneziana Orchestra for Stradivari), Violin Concerto P. 164 (with Fantini), Violin Concerto P. 368 (with Bobesco), Concerto P. 14 and Concerto for Diverse Instruments P. 226 (with the Solistes de Bruxelles and the Solisti di Milano, issued by Seraphim), Bassoon Concerto P. 401 (with Montanari and the La Scala Orchestra for Colosseum), Sinfonia *Al Santo Sepolcro* (with the Solisti di Milano for Bach Guild and for Telefunken), *Dixit Dominus* (with the Vienna State Opera Orchestra *et al.* for Period), *Salve Regina* (with Borelli and the Vienna Chamber Orchestra for Renaissance), *Stabat Mater* (with Heynis and the Solisti di Milano for Telefunken), *Sonata a quattro in E flat* (with the Solisti di Milano for Telefunken), and *Juditha triumphans* (with the Scuola Veneziana Orchestra *et al.* for Period), Boccherini's Symphonies Op. 35 Nos 1 to 6 (with the Bologna Philharmonic Orchestra for Telefunken), A. Scarlatti's *Stabat Mater* (with the Scuola Veneziana Orchestra *et al.* for Lyrichord and Vox) and Symphonies Nos 1 to 12 (with the Solisti di Milano for Harmonia Mundi), Pergolesi's *Concertinos Nos 1* to *4* (with the Winterthur Symphony Orchestra for Westminster), *Viola Concerto in B flat*, *Sinfonia in F major* and *Mass in F major* (with the Solisti di Milano *et al.* for Harmonia Mundi), Marcello's concertos Op. 1 Nos 1 to 12 (with the Solisti di Milano for Harmonia Mundi), Gesualdo's complete Madrigals (with the Italian Vocal Quintet for Harmonia Mundi and Telefunken), and Stradella's Symphony for Trumpet and Eight Violas (with Tarr) and Symphony for Two Cornets (with the Bologna Philharmonic Orchestra for Harmonia Mundi).

With Ephrikian's records, it is difficult to determine from the catalogue listings for which company each was originally made, and which other companies have released the same recordings. In some cases, different instrumental groups are named for the same works, maybe for the same recorded performances.

Epstein, David (b. 1930). Born in New York and educated at Princeton and Brandeis Universities and the New England Conservatory of Music, Epstein studied composition with Sessions, Babbitt, Milhaud and Fine, and conducting with Szell, Rudolf and Solomon, and taught at Antioch College, Ohio (1957–62). He conducted opera at the Antioch Shakespeare Festival (1957), was music director at the Antioch Music Festival (1960), founded and was music director of the Youth Symphony Orchestra for New York (1963–6), has been professor of music and conductor of the orchestra at the Massachusetts Institute of Technology (since 1965), conductor and music director of the Harrisburg Symphony Orchestra (since 1974) and music director of the Worcester Orchestra, Massachusetts (since 1976). He has also been a guest conductor with orchestras in London, Munich, Vienna, Israel, Prague, Portugal, and Berlin as well as in the United States. His compositions include chamber music, cantatas and vocal music, incidental and film music and a symphony, and he has written articles for various musical publications and a book entitled *Beyond Orpheus: Studies in Musical Structure* (MIT Press). Desto have recorded some of his chamber music, but as a conductor Epstein himself has recorded Bloch's Concerto Grosso No. 1 (with the Czech Radio Orchestra for Everest), Perle's *Three Movements for Orchestra* (with the Royal Philharmonic Orchestra for Composers Recordings), Lerdhal's *Wake* (with soprano Beardslee and the Boston Symphony Chamber Players for DGG), Dugger's *Music for Synthesizer and Six Instruments* (for DGG), Copland's *Dance Symphony*, Piston's *The Incredible Flutist*, and the Piano Concertos of Barber and Copland (with Ruskin and the MIT Symphony Orchestra for Turnabout).

Erb, Donald (b. 1927). Born in Youngstown, Ohio, and educated at Kent State University, the Cleveland Institute of Music and Indiana University, Erb has composed orchestral, instrumental and other music, and recorded his *Reconnaissance* (with an ensemble for Nonesuch). Others of his compositions which have been recorded, by other artists, are *Bass Piece*, *Diversion for Two*, *Trio*, *Phantasma*, *Harold's Trip to the Sky*, *Sonneries*, *Symphony of Over-*

tures, *Endgame*, *Seventh Trumpet*, *Concerto for Solo Percussion* and *Three Pieces for Brass Quintet and Piano*.

Erdélyi, Miklós (b. 1928). Born in Budapest, Erdélyi studied the organ, composition and conducting at the Franz Liszt Academy, and at the age of nineteen attracted notice with his conducting at the Budapest Chamber Opera. He was appointed conductor of the Hungarian Radio Choir (1950–52) and then conductor at the Budapest Opera (1951), conducted orchestras in Hungary, toured in the USSR, Europe and the United States, led the Hungarian State Symphony Orchestra during a tour in Britain and in January 1974 was a successful last-minute substitute at a concert with the Berlin Philharmonic Orchestra. He was awarded the Kossuth Prize, the Liszt Prize (1960) and the title 'Outstanding Artist of the Hungarian People's Republic' (1967). His musical interests extend from Bach and Handel to Bartók and Prokofiev, and he has attracted warm praise both in Hungary and abroad for his sure sense of style, sensitive musicianship and his control of orchestral balance and dynamics. He has recorded extensively for Qualiton with various Hungarian orchestras, the works including the Bach Suite No. 2, suites from Handel's *Rodrigo* and *Ariodante*, Michael Haydn's *Mythologische Operette*, *Konzertstück* for Organ and Orchestra of Werner, the Schumann Piano Concerto (with Hernádi), the Brahms Violin Concerto (with Kovács), Boismortier's Oboe Concerto (with Pongrácz), excerpts from *Die Zauberflöte*, *La Bohème*, *Manon Lescaut*, *Aida*, *Tosca* and Weill's *Aufstieg und Fall der Stadt Mahagonny*, Hindemith's *Der Schwanendreher* (with Bársony), Bartók's *Four Pieces*, *Two Pictures*, *Two Portraits*, *Hungarian Sketches*, *Romanian Folk Dances*, Suite No. 2 and *Transylvanian Dances*, Kodály's *Songs of Örzse* (with Házy), Kadosa's Symphonies Nos 4, 6 and 7 and Piano Concerto No. 4 (with Kiss), Petrovics' *The Book of Jonah*, songs by Horusitzky (with László), Sárközy's *Sinfonia concertante*, Tardos' *Upon the City Outskirts*, *In Memoriam Martyrum*, *The New God* and *Evocatio*, Soproni's *Ovidii Metamorphoses*, Ránki's *Three Historical Tableaux*, Sárai's *Diagnosis 69*, Papp's *Dialogue for Piano and Orchestra* (with Szücs) and *Meditations in Memory of Milán Füst*, Kósa's *Orpheus*, *Eurydice*, *Hermes*, and accompaniments to recitals by the singers Simándy, Ilosfalvy and Házy.

Erede, Alberto (b. 1908). Born in Genoa, Erede graduated at the Milan Conservatory and studied conducting with Weingartner at Basel and with Busch at Dresden. He first conducted at Turin in 1935, leading the entire *Ring* cycle. Busch engaged him for the Glyndebourne Festival Opera where he was active from 1934 to 1939. He also conducted the Salzburg Opera Guild (1935–8), and first visited the United States with the company in 1937, when he conducted the NBC Symphony Orchestra in New York. After World War II he was appointed principal conductor of the Italian Radio Orchestra in Turin (1945), returned to Glyndebourne (1946), was musical director of the New London Opera Company, and a guest conductor at many leading European opera houses (1946–50); Rudolf Bing, who had worked with him at Glyndebourne, then engaged him for the Italian repertoire at the New York Metropolitan Opera (1950–55). He was musical director at the Deutsche Oper am Rhein at Düsseldorf (1958–62), conducted *Lohengrin* at Bayreuth (1968) and has been a guest conductor with major orchestras and opera houses in West and East Europe. His repertoire embraces scores of operas, ranging from *L'Incoronazione di Poppea* to *The Rake's Progress*; he has a reputation as a company conductor and for training young singers. In her history of the New York Met., Quaintance Eaton wrote that his time there was 'too short a period considering his fire and verve and his ability to hold a performance, plus the fact that the singers like him' (*Opera Caravan*, New York, 1957). On the other hand, Bing hinted in his autobiography (*5000 Nights at the Opera*, London 1972, p. 130) that Erede did not make a sufficiently strong mark at the Met. to remain there longer than 1955. In 1952 Erede conducted *Cavalleria rusticana* and *Pagliacci* at the Met. and Virgil Thomson wrote that he 'did not play up much their Italianate vividness, their urgency. He seemed rather to be seeking in them grace and transparency, for all the world as if they were oratorios by Saint-Saëns' (*Music Reviewed, 1940–1954*, p. 326).

Be that as it may, Erede has made a highly significant and successful contribution to recorded opera. In the early years of LP in Britain, Decca issued a remarkable number of operas and in the years 1950–55 Erede conducted a high proportion of them. These were *La Bohème*, *Tosca*, *Madama Butterfly*, *Turandot*, *Aida*, *Rigoletto*, *Otello*, *Il trovatore*, *Il barbiere di Siviglia*, *La favorita*, *Cavalleria rusticana*, *Pagliacci* and *Roméo et Juliette*. The orchestras and opera companies were the Santa Cecilia, Rome, the Maggio Musicale Fiorentino, and for *Roméo et Juliette* the Paris Opéra. The first of the series were *La Bohème*, *Tosca*,

Madama Butterfly and *Aida*, and these all included the great soprano Renata Tebaldi, then at the height of her powers; these LP records were an almost unbelievable revelation to opera lovers until then accustomed to changing the records and the needles in their vast 78 r.p.m. opera sets every four minutes. Erede's contribution in all these sets was invariably competent, incisive and musical. The *Otello* was re-issued by Decca as late as 1975 and *Il barbiere di Siviglia* in 1977, and the performances can reasonably be compared with later recordings. Earlier, Erede made some 78 r.p.m. discs, Ravel's *Valses nobles et sentimentales* and the *Leonore No. 3* overture (with the Turin Symphony Orchestra for Decca), *Ma Mère l'Oye* and an excerpt from Zandonai's *Roméo et Juliette* (with the Italian Radio Orchestra for Parlophone), the Beethoven Romance No. 2 and Vitali's Chaconne (with de Vito and the Philharmonia Orchestra for EMI), and excerpts from *Falstaff* (with Stabile *et al.* and the La Scala Orchestra for Capitol); on LP he also recorded Verdi arias (with Fischer-Dieskau and the Berlin Philharmonic Orchestra for EMI), *Exsultate jubilate* and an aria from *Il re pastore* of Mozart (with Gueden and the Santa Cecilia Orchestra for Decca), an aria recital with Corena (with the Santa Cecilia Orchestra for Decca), the overtures to *Don Pasquale*, *Nabucco*, *I vespri siciliani* and *L'Italiana in Algeri*, the prelude to Act III of *La Wally* and intermezzo to *Manon Lescaut* (with the New Symphony Orchestra for Decca), Paganini's Violin Concertos Nos 1 and 2 (with Menuhin and the Royal Philharmonic Orchestra for EMI), *Fontane di Roma* (with the Suisse Romande Orchestra for Decca), *La Bohème* (in German, Berlin State Opera Orchestra *et al.* for DGG), excerpts from *Les Pêcheurs de perles* (with the Paris Conservatoire Orchestra *et al.* for Decca) and *Il barbiere di Siviglia* (from a performance in 1950 at the New York Met., issued by Cetra).

Eriksson, Gunnar (b. 1936). Born in Bengtsfors, Sweden, Eriksson was educated at the Kungliga Musikhögskolau, Stockholm, made his debut as a choral conductor in 1956 with Enskede Domskör in 1956, conducted the Enskede Kammarkör (1956–62) and is now conductor of the Göteborg Kammarkör (since 1962). He has also been a guest conductor with the Danish Radio Choir and the Swedish Radio Chamber Choir. For EMI he has conducted the Göteborg Kammarkör and an instrumental ensemble in Back's *Cat Journey* and Johanson's *Vad Sager*, and with the choir excerpts from *Peer Gynt* and *Four Psalms* of Grieg, and songs by Sandell, Ahnfeldt and others (for Sirius and Proprius).

Ermler, Mark (b. 1932). The son of an eminent Soviet film director, Ermler was born in Leningrad and was educated at the Leningrad Conservatory, where he studied conducting under Khaikin and Rabinovitch. He graduated in 1956, and straightaway joined the conducting staff of the Bolshoi Theatre in Moscow. His first production on his own was the première of Prokofiev's *The Story of a Real Man*; his repertoire of more than 50 operas includes works by Mozart, Beethoven, Berlioz, Verdi, Bizet and Puccini, in addition to Mussorgsky, Glinka, Borodin, Rimsky-Korsakov, Tchaikovsky and Prokofiev. He also directs ballet and symphony concerts, and has conducted orchestras in the USSR and abroad, and has toured in Europe, North America and Japan; reputed to have an extraordinary memory, he has an immaculate technique, and his records are examples of the fine sense of style and subtlety of his conducting.

Ermler's recordings include *Tosca*, *Madama Butterfly*, *Prince Igor*, Tchaikovsky's *Yolanta* and *The Queen of Spades*, Rachmaninov's *Francesca da Rimini*, Prokofiev's *The Story of a Real Man*, many discs of opera choruses (with the Bolshoi Theatre Chorus) and accompaniments to recitals of operatic arias, as well as the Waltz and Krakowiak from Glinka's *A Life for the Tsar*, the Polovtsian Dances from *Prince Igor* and excerpts from Rimsky-Korsakov's *Pan Voyevoda* and *Snow Maiden*, and Procession of the Nobles from *Mlada* (with the Bolshoi Theatre Orchestra). Few of these have so far been released in the West; in Britain EMI have issued a disc of choruses from Russian operas, in France and FR Germany there has been *Prince Igor* and in FR Germany alone *Tosca*; in the US (on Melodiya/Angel) *Prince Igor*, *The Queen of Spades* and a disc of excerpts from *Cavalleria rusticana* and *Il trovatore* (with Arkhipova and Pyravko). The recording of *Prince Igor* is claimed to be the only integral version with the polonaise in Act II completed by Glazunov; a version of the opera as Borodin wrote it was produced in East Berlin in 1978, omitting the overture (compiled by Glazunov) and other additions.

Eros, Peter (b. 1932). Born in Budapest and educated at the Franz Liszt Academy there, Eros was associate conductor of the Amsterdam Concertgebouw Orchestra (1960–65), chief conductor of the Malmö Symphony Orchestra (1967–9) and musical director of the San Diego Symphony Orchestra, California (since 1972). He has toured Australia and South Africa three times, and has been a guest conductor with major orchestras in the United States, Britain, Austria, the Netherlands, FR Germany, Spain, Israel and in Latin and South America. For Donemus he recorded the Dutch composer Ruyneman's *Hieroglyphs*, with an instrumental ensemble.

Esser, Heribert (b. 1929). Born at Rheinhausen, Germany, and educated at the Hochschule für Musik and the university at Cologne, Esser was assistant conductor to Sawallisch at Wiesbaden (1956), conductor at Cologne (1961) and general music director at Braunschweig (1962). For a DGG disc issued in 1969 he conducted the Vienna Symphony Orchestra in Paganini's Violin Concertos Nos 1 and 2, for which Ashkenasi was the soloist.

Etcheverry, Jésus (b. 1915). Born in Bordeaux of Basque parents, Etcheverry was an infant prodigy on the violin and at the age of 21 became a professor at the Casablanca Conservatoire, where he remained for ten years. He started conducting when, as leader of the Casablanca Opera Orchestra, he was called on to take charge of a performance of *Rigoletto* at the last moment. This led to his immediate appointment as director of music. He has conducted opera at Casablanca (1944–5), Nancy (1947–57), Tunis (1949–53), and Luxembourg (1948–57), and in 1957 became conductor at the Paris Opéra-Comique. He also has led opera and concerts at other French, Belgian and Swiss cities. An unassuming personality, he nonetheless maintains a firm control over his singers and musicians through his undisputed authority and competence. Philips, Vega, IPG and Decca have recorded him conducting a number of operas and operettas, some complete and some as highlights. Included are *Thaïs*, *Manon*, *Rigoletto*, *Pagliacci*, Reyer's *Sigurd*, Rabaud's *Marouf*, *Il barbiere di Siviglia*, *Les Cloches de Corneville*, *La Fille de Madame Angot*, *Les Mousquetaires au couvent*, *Das Land des Lächelns*, *Ein Walzertraum*, *Im weissen Rössl*, and *Chanson d'amour* (on themes of Schubert). *Thaïs* was originally recorded by Vega in 1961 but was re-issued by Decca in Britain in 1974 when Etcheverry's direction was warmly praised. His other recordings have included *Peter and the Wolf*, *Le Carnaval des animaux*, *Les Sylphides*, *Les Patineurs*, Luigini's *Ballet égyptien*, the ballet music from *Faust* and *Le Prophète*, and suites from *Coppélia and Sylvia* (with the Lamoureux Orchestra for Philips).

Etti, Karl (b. 1912). Born in Vienna and educated at the Vienna Academy of Music under Kabasta, Weingartner, Krips and Marx, Etti conducted the Vienna Boys' Choir (1937–8), at the German Theatre (1938–45), the Vienna Symphony Orchestra (1945–7) and for the Vienna Radio and the Vienna Männergesangverein (since 1947). In 1962 he became a teacher at the Vienna Academy. He has composed an opera, *Dagmar*, and an oratorio. His recordings include Kreutzer's *Das Nachtlager von Granada* (with the Vienna Academy Orchestra *et al.* for Preiser), a collection entitled *Christmas in Germany* (with the Vienna Woods Boys' Choir for La Guilde Internationale du Disque), and several other collections (with the Vienna Woods Boys' Choir for Everest).

Evrard, Jane (b. 1898). Born at Neuilly-Plaisance, Jane Evrard was an accomplished violinist at the age of 14, and at 19 married the conductor Gaston Poulet. In 1930 she formed the first women's orchestra in Paris which she conducted regularly in concerts and radio broadcasts until World War II. The orchestra consisted of 22 female string players, and she was the first permanent woman conductor in France. Her repertoire included baroque, classical and many unknown works, and contemporary French composers wrote for her, such as Roussel (*Sinfonietta*, 1934), Florent Schmitt (*Symphony for Strings 'Janiana'*, 1941) and Rivier (Symphony, 1938). The orchestra was nicknamed the 'fairies' Orchestra' and enjoyed success in France, Spain, Portugal and Holland. After World War II Jane Evrard conducted ballet; she reformed the orchestra in 1961 but then decided not to continue with it. Why are there so few women conductors? She writes: 'The reason probably is that a woman, on her own, would have to exercise her authority over a group which often lacks discipline and resents receiving orders from anyone not of its own kind. I do not think that a form of dress seeking to play down feminine grace would help to break down this resistance. On the contrary, masculine-type clothes would only increase the mocking hostility of these representatives of the stronger sex' (personal communication, September 1975).

With her orchestra Jane Evrard made several recordings for HMV in the 1930s, the Roussel *Sinfonietta*, Couperin's third *Leçons de ténèbres* and some other pre-classical music.

Ewerhart, Rudolf (b. 1928). Ewerhart was born in Germany, studied at the conservatories at Cologne and Freiburg, and in 1950 made his first radio recordings as a conductor, organist and harpsichordist. He is the founder and conductor of the Trier Motet Choir, and has been active teaching, conducting and as an organist at Münster in Westphalia. He was under contract to Vox in the early years of LP recording and was responsible for some highly significant enterprises: Monteverdi's *Il Ritorno d'Ulisse in patria* and *L'Incoronazione di Poppea*, and Handel's *Resurrezione*. The Monteverdi operas were excellently performed, but were released too early to receive much attention. Handel's *Resurrezione*, which has been compared with *Messiah* in the level of its musical inspiration, has been recorded only by Ewerhart. In these sets he conducted the Münster Santini Orchestra. In other discs for Vox/Turnabout he conducted Bach's Cantatas Nos 202, 203, 204, 209, 211 and 212, and Cantatas by Caldara (with the Wurttemberg Chamber Orchestra *et al.* for Turnabout), a collection of festival music of the 18th century (with a brass ensemble for Turnabout), Carissimi's *Balthazar* and two oratorios by Anerio (with the Münster Church Music School *et al.* for Turnabout), organ sonatas by Albertini and Müller, J. C. Bach's *Salve Regina* and Galuppi's *Rapida cerva* (with the German Bach soloists *et al*, for FSM, Münster).

F

Faerber, Jörg (b. 1929). Born in Stuttgart, Faerber was educated there at the Hochschule für Musik and majored in conducting. His career started in Stuttgart and at the Heilbronn Theatre, and in 1966 he became conductor of the Württemberg Chamber Orchestra at Heilbronn, which has since become one of the leading chamber ensembles in Europe. Vox have recorded him and his orchestra in a number of outstanding LP discs of baroque music, which have been released on the Turnabout label, the most remarkable being the *Brandenburg Concertos*, which led the field for some years as one of the best sets available. His other discs, with the Württemberg Chamber Orchestra, include the eight symphonies of Boyce, Vivaldi's *The Four Seasons*, Concerti P. 133, P. 134, P. 209 and P. 266, *Trio Sonata in G*, *Flute Concerto in D minor* (with Pohlers), Mandolin Concerto and Two-Mandolin Concerto (with Grund and Rumetsch), *Piccolo Concertos in A* and *C* (with Linde) and Viola d'Amore Concerto (with Lemmen), bassoon concertos by J. C. Bach, Mozart, Weber, Graun, Boismortier, and K. Stamitz, and Weber's Andante and *Hungarian Rondo* (with Zukerman), Handel's Organ Concerto No. 13 (with Rilling), Albinoni's Adagio (arr. Haas), Michael Haydn's Viola and Harpsichord Concerto (with E. and L. Wallfisch), Hummel's Viola Fantasia (with E. Wallfisch), Krommer's Clarinet Concerto (with Glazer), K. Stamitz's Cello Concerto (with Blees), Viola Concerto (with E. Wallfisch), Clarinet Concerto (with Glazer) and Flute Concerto (with Wanausek), Dittersdorf's Double-bass Concerto (with Hörtnagel), Sinfonia concertante (with Hörtnagel and Lemmen) and Harp Concerto (with Storck), Telemann's *Suite in D*, Two-Viola Concerto and *Viola Concerto in G* (with E. Wallfisch and Koch), and Three-Violin Concerto (with Lautenbacher, Schaefer and Egger), trumpet concertos by Manfredini, Torelli, Albinoni, Biber and Stölzel (with Schneidewind, Pasch, Tarr *et al.*), Cimarosa's Two-Flute Concerto (with Dohn and Steinkraus), Corette's Organ Concerto (with Rilling), Leopold Mozart's *Toy Symphony* and *Eine musikalische Schlittenfahrt*, Mozart's Organ Sonata No. 4 (with Rilling), Piano Concertos K. 413 and K. 450 (with Frankl), Violin Concertos K. 218 and K. 219 (with Pauk), Flute Concertos No. 1 (with Schwegler) and No. 2 (with Linde), Flute and Harp Concerto (with Patéro and Storck), Sinfonia Concertante K. 297b, *Ein musikalischer Spass* and the overtures to *Apollo et Hyacinthus*, *Il sogno di Scipione*, *Bastien und Bastienne*, *Il re pastore*, *Mitridate*, *Ascanio in Alba*, *Idomeneo*, *Der Schauspieldirektor* and *La clemenza di Tito*, Salieri's Flute and Oboe Concerto (with Dohn and Sous), Benda's *Harpsichord Concerto in F* (with L. Wallfisch), Vaňhal's Viola Concerto (with E. Wallfisch), piano concertos by Paisiello and K. Stamitz (with Blumenthal), Rössler/Rosetti's *Horn Concerto in D* (with Penzel), Weber's Clarinet Concerto No. 1 (with Glazer), Haydn's Sinfonia Concertante, and Mendelssohn's Violin and Piano Concerto (with Lautenbacher and Dosse) and *Violin Concerto in D minor* (with Lautenbacher). Of more recent music, he has also recorded *Le Carnaval des animaux*, Tcherepnin's *Ten Bagatelles*, Mouravieff's *Nativité*, Shostakovich's *Chamber Symphony*, Krol's *Variations on Bach's Magnificat* (for Erato) and Arensky's Piano Concerto No. 2 (with Littauer and the Berlin Symphony Orchestra for Fono).

Failoni, Sergio (1890–1948). Born at Verona, Failoni studied the cello in Verona and Milan, made his debut as a conductor at Como and was an assistant to Toscanini at La Scala (1921–2). He then conducted in other Italian opera houses, in London, Madrid and Santiago, and was a resident conductor at the Budapest Opera from 1928 to his death. He returned to La Scala in 1946–7 and to Parma in 1947. His recordings include Respighi's *Ancient Airs and Dances* Suite No. 1 (with the EIAR Orchestra for Soria) and the overture to *Nabucco*, the prelude to Act III of *Lohengrin*, *Finlandia* and the dance from *Salome* (with the EIAR Orchestra for Cetra).

Falla, Manuel de (1876–1946). The great Spanish composer Falla was a fine pianist and an experienced conductor; he appeared as a guest conductor with the Orquesta Pau Casals at Barcelona and frequently toured Europe to lead his own works. However, Barbirolli, who played the cello in the orchestra in the London season for the Diaghilev Ballets Russes in 1919, has told the story that, on Diaghilev's insistence, Falla conducted *The Three-cornered Hat*, but the performance soon came to a halt when some cross-rhythms were reached which Falla was at a loss to conduct. An early Columbia 78 r.p.m. set was issued of him directing his own Harpsichord Concerto.

Faller, Robert (b. 1924). Born at Le Locle, Switzerland, Faller studied at the conservatory at La Chaux-de-Fonds under Appia, graduated with the diploma for violin in 1943, and continued his studies at the Berne Conservatory and in Paris with Enesco, Hewitt and Moyse. He joined the Lausanne Chamber Orchestra, became director of the La Chaux-de-Fonds Conservatory (1956) and conducted many concerts, notably of the great choral works, with the Lausanne Chamber Orchestra and the Suisse Romande Orchestra, studied conducting with Kubelik and Markevitch, and now has a considerable repertoire ranging from Renaissance music to work by contemporary composers. For Erato he conducted Martin's oratorio *Golgotha* (with the Lausanne University Orchestra and Chorus *et al.*, issued in the United States by Musical Heritage Society), and for Disques VDE Reichel's *Gloria* (with the Bienne Orchestral Society *et al.*) and *Suite for Chamber Orchestra* (with the La Chaux-de-Fonds Conservatory Orchestra).

Fantapié, Henri-Claude (b. 1938). Born in Nice, Fantapié studied at the Nice Conservatoire and the Monaco Academy of Music, where he took first prize for conducting; in Paris he was a pupil of Bigot, Chorafas and Toldra for conducting and of Dutilleux for composition, and also studied musicology at the Sorbonne. He was a prizewinner at the international competition for young conductors at Besançon in 1959. With the Orchestre de Chambre de Monaco he gave more than 100 concerts (1958–62), toured Europe, Africa and the US, and then was conductor of the Ensemble instrumental de musique contemporaine Henri-Claude Fantapié (1962–4), which in 1964 became Les Solistes de Paris. With the orchestra he has given many first performances of contemporary works and has revived early music; he has been a guest conductor with major orchestras, teaches conducting for the French Ministry of Culture, has conducted European youth orchestras, and with Les Solistes de Paris has appeared at many international festivals. His compositions include orchestral and instrumental works, a clarinet quintet and a horn concerto; he has written studies of jazz music and the music of Finland, and was from 1966 to 1972 secretary-general of the National Syndicate of Orchestral Conductors, and is director of the Noisy-le-Sec Conservatoire.

Fantapié's recordings with Les Solistes de Paris have been Domenico Scarlatti's 17 symphonies for orchestra (for Adès), Haydn's *Stabat Mater* and *Libera* (for Ars/Studio France), concertos by Vivaldi, Jacchini, Aldrovandini, Franceschini, A. Scarlatti, Telemann and Tartini (with Soustrot and Koch), four concertos of Vivaldi (with Ito and Dorigny), three motets of Vivaldi (with Bondi), a flute concerto of Telemann (with Koch), motets of Couperin, Haydn's Symphony No. 44 and *Violin Concerto in F major* and works by Villa-Lobos for voice and instruments (with Bondi, for Société Française de Productions Phonographiques).

Farberman, Harold (b. 1929). A native of New York, Farberman was educated at the Juilliard School of Music and the New England Conservatory (1951–6), and was a percussionist and timpanist with the Boston Symphony Orchestra (1951–63) and with radio, television and theatre orchestras in New York. He was music director and conductor of the New Arts Orchestra at Boston (1957–63), of the Colorado Springs Symphony Orchestra (1966–71) and of the Oakland Symphony Orchestra (1971 onwards), and has been a guest conductor with major orchestras in the United States, Britain, Denmark, Belgium, FR Germany, Israel and Central America. His compositions are many and a number have been recorded, such as his Alto Saxophone Concerto, *Elegy, Fanfare and March*, *Three States of Mind*, *New York Times – August 30, 1964*, *Five Images*, *Quintessence*, *Greek Scene* and *Alia* (all by Serenus), and *Evolution* and *Music Inn* Suite (with the Boston Percussion Ensemble for Mercury). Distribution of these records, however, has been confined to the United States.

Farberman has made his name as a protagonist for the music of Charles Ives. In 1965–6 he conceived and prepared two one-hour presentations for the National Education Television Network in the US about Ives and his music, and later he recorded the Ives four symphonies and *Hallowe'en* (with the New Philharmonia Orchestra for Vanguard), the *Browning Overture*, *Circus Band March*, *In the Cage*, *In the Inn*, *In the Night*, and *The Unanswered Question* (with the Royal Philharmonic Orchestra for Vanguard). Other Ives discs were *The Indians*, *Hallowe'en* and *Over the Pavements* (with the Boston Chamber Ensemble for Cambridge) and *The Celestial Country* (with the London Symphony Orchestra *et al.* for Composers Recordings). These were all authoritative and sympathetic performances and he remains the only conductor to have recorded all four Ives symphonies. Other American music he has recorded is Kupferman's *Chamber Symphony* and *Divertimento* (with the Copenhagen Prisma Players and the Stuttgart Philharmonia respectively for Cambridge), Imbrie's Symphony No. 3 (with the London Symphony Orchestra for Composers Recordings), Balada's *Geometrias No. 1* and Custer's *Cycle for Nine Instruments* (with the Francis Chagrin Ensemble for Serenus), Lessard's *Sinfonietta concertante* and Kupferman's *Libretto for Orchestra* (with the New Philharmonia Orchestra for Serenus), Nelhybel's *Three Modes for Orchestra* (with the Stuttgart Philharmonia for Serenus) and his own Alto Saxophone Concerto and *Elegy, Fanfare and March* (with Estrin and the Stuttgart Philharmonia for Serenus). From the standard repertoire, he has recorded Mozart's Symphonies Nos 25 and 40 (with the Munich Chamber Orchestra for Musical Heritage Society), Beethoven's Symphony No. 8 and Schumann's Symphony No. 4 (with the Royal Philharmonic Orchestra, also for MHS), Bartók's *Divertimento* and *Sonata for Two Pianos and Percussion* (with the Boston Chamber Ensemble for Cambridge), Schoenberg's arrangement of Handel's Concerto Grosso Op. 6 No. 7 (with the Lenox Quartet and London Symphony Orchestra for Desto), bassoon concertos by Weber and Hummel (with Miller and the Copenhagen Chamber Orchestra for Cambridge), trumpet concertos by Albrechtsberger and Molter (with Ghitalla and the Boston Chamber Ensemble for Cambridge) and several discs for Columbia (US) combining jazz and symphony orchestras.

Faris, Alexander (b. 1921). Born in Caledon in Northern Ireland, Faris studied music at Oxford and after service in Europe with the Irish Guards in World War II resumed his studies at the Royal College of Music where he won prizes for conducting and music criticism. He joined the Carl Rosa Opera Company (1947), first as choirmaster and later became a conductor (1949). He became a conductor with the Sadler's Wells Opera Company (1960–69) where his repertoire included for the most part Offenbach, Rossini and Gilbert and Sullivan. In 1955 he wrote the score for the award-winning documentary film *Rowlandson's England*, which led to his being granted a fellowship to study composition at the Juilliard School in New York. On returning to Britain he conducted stage shows including Bernstein's *Candide*, and ballet at Covent Garden (1960–61). He has written music criticism for *The Times* and articles for *Chambers Encyclopedia*. His recordings have included abridged performances for the World Record Club of some Offenbach and Gilbert and Sullivan operas (with the Westminster Symphony Orchestra *et al.*), Haydn's Symphonies Nos 92 and 104, Grieg's *Holberg Suite* and Dvořák's *Serenade in E* and *Nocturne* (with the Sinfonia of London).

Farncombe, Charles (b. 1919). Born in London, Farncombe graduated in engineering from London University (1940), was an officer in the British army (1942–7), then studied at the Royal School of Church Music (1947–8) and the Royal Academy of Music (1948–51), where he won the Mann Prize. Since the inception of the Handel Opera Society in 1955 he has been its musical director, and in 1970 became chief conductor of the Drottningholm Court Theatre in Sweden. He was awarded the CBE (1977), became a Fellow of the Royal Academy of Music (1963), received the Gold Medal of the Friends of Drottningholm (1971) and was made Honorary Fellow of the Royal Swedish Academy of Music (1972). With Mackworth Young he wrote *What Happens in Singing*. He has recorded a selection of Handel pieces (with Brannigan, the Handel Opera Society Chorus and the Philomusica of London for EMI), a disc of choruses from the music of Handel (with the Handel Opera Society Chorus and Orchestra for Decca) and a disc of the music of Roman (for DGG).

Farnon, Robert (b. 1917). Born in Toronto, Canada, Farnon studied the piano, violin and trumpet, was a trumpeter in the Canadian Broadcasting Corporation Symphony Orchestra (1936–42) and conductor of the Canadian Army orchestra (1943–6). He went to London, and became famous for his many compositions, arrangements, film scores, performances with his own orchestra, and for his many records of light and popular music. A Robert Farnon Appreciation Society (37 Copes Close, Oadby, Leicester LE2 4DF) has been formed and has available a discography of his records; among them is a 'symphonic picture' of *Porgy and Bess*, which Farnon arranged and conducted with the London Festival Orchestra for Decca.

Fasano, Renato (b. 1902). The Italian conductor, pianist and composer Fasano founded the Collegium Italicum in 1947, which was a chamber orchestra of exceptionally fine quality made up of the best available Italian instrumentalists. It undertook concert tours with a repertoire consisting of music of the Italian composers of the 18th century; almost every programme included a work of Vivaldi, and the only non-Italian composer performed was Bach. The orchestra eventually changed its name to the Virtuosi di Roma, and it also appeared on record labels as the Rome Collegium Musicum and the Rome Polyphonic Ensemble.

With this orchestra, Fasano recorded for a number of companies, and his first disc, in fact his only 78 r.p.m. record, was of Vivaldi. The Virtuosi di Roma have not been, of course, the only European chamber ensemble to specialise in and to record this repertoire, but their style and finesse were exemplary, and Fasano played an important role in the great interest in baroque music that came with the LP record. The works he recorded included Bach's Four-Harpsichord Concerto BWV 1054, and Vivaldi's Cello Concerto P. 434 (with Mazzacurati, for Parlophone); Vivaldi's Concertos P. 132, P. 133, P. 134, P. 235, P. 238, P. 280, P. 427, P. 438 and Op. 8 No. 5, Two-Oboe Concerto P. 85 (with Zanfini and Visai), *L'estro armonico* Op. 3 (edited by Fasano), *Il cimento dell'armonia e dell' inventione*, Op. 8 (including *The Four Seasons)*, Two-Horn Concertos P. 320 and P. 321, and Concerto Op. 10 No. 3, Valentini's Concerto No. 3, A. Scarlatti's Concerto No. 6 and *Pastorale*, Leo's Cello Concerto (with Mazzacurati), Albinoni's Concertos Op. 2 No. 3 (edited by Giazotto), Op. 7 No. 6 (edited by Paumgartner), and No. 9 (edited by Giazotto), Pergolesi's *Concertino in G* (edited by Fasano), Marcheselli's *Concerto in D*, Bassani's *Canzoni amorose* (edited by Malipiero), Galuppi's *Il filosofo di campagna* (edited by Wolf-Ferrari), Corelli's Concerti Grossi Op. 6 Nos 2, 4, 6, 7 and 8, Boccherini's *Pastorale*, Torelli's Concerto a quattro, Marcello's *Oboe Concerto in C minor* (with Zanfini), Clementi's Symphony Op. 18 No. 2, Rossini's *Petite Messe solennelle*, and Respighi's *Ancient Airs and Dances* Suite No. 3 (for EMI); Vivaldi's Concertos P. 410, P. 419, and Op. 3 Nos 2, 8 and 12, Concerto Grosso Op. 8 No. 1 (allegro), Viola d'amore Concertos P. 287 and P. 288 (with Sabatini) and Violin and Two-Cello Concerto P. 58, Pergolesi's Concertino No. 5, Torelli's Concerto a quattro, Rossini's *Sonata in C*, Cambini's *Piano Concerto in G* (with Santoliquido), Bonporti's Violin recitative (with Mozzato) and Marcello's *Oboe Concerto in C minor* (with Zanfini, for Brunswick); Vivaldi's Concertos P. 143, P. 231 and P. 407 (for Fonit); Vivaldi's Concerto P. 235, Viola d'amore Concerto P. 166 (with Sabatini), and Two-Violin Concerto P. 28 (with Malanotte and Scaglia, for Cetra-Soria, France); Vivaldi's *Beatus Vir*, *Credo* and *Stabat Mater*, and Gluck's *Orfeo ed Euridice* (for RCA); Vivaldi's Concertos P. 143, P. 231, P. 406, P. 407 and P. 410, *Violin Concertos in C minor* (with Pellicia), *in E major* (with Ferro) and P. 419 (with Pellicia), Viola d'amore Concerto P. 288 (with Sabatini), Oboe Concerto P. 259 (with Zanfani), *Cello Concerto in G* (with Amfiteatrof), Violin and Cello Concerto P. 388 (with Pellicia and Amfiteatrof), Two-Cello Concerto P. 411 (with Amfiteatrof and Mazzacurati), Violin and Two-Cello Concerto P. 58 (with Pellicia, Amfiteatrof and Mazzacurati), Flute Concerto P. 342, Oboe and Violin Concerto P. 406, Two-Violin Concertos P. 2 and Op. 3 No. 8 (with Mozzato and Malanotte), and Two-Violin and Cello Concerto P. 326 (with Ferro, Mozzato and Mazzacurati), Albinoni's *Sonata in G minor* and Violin Concerto Op. 9 No. 7 (with Pellicia), A. Scarlatti's Concerto for Six Strings, Tartini's *Violin Concerto in E major* (with Ferro), Cirri's Cello and Flute Concerto, Marcello's *Aria in A minor*, and Pergolesi's Four-Violin and Cello Concerto (for Decca, US); Paisiello's *Piano Concerto in C major* (with Santoliquido for Polydor); Pergolesi's *La serva padrona*, Paisiello's *Il barbiere di Siviglia* and Rossini's *La cambiale di matrimonio* (for Cetra, issued in the United States by Everest).

Fauré, José Rodriguez (b. 1912). Born in Avellaneda, Argentina, Fauré studied at the Auber Conservatory and with Panizza and Pizzetti, and made his debut as a conductor at Buenos Aires. He subsequently conducted in Italy with the Italian Radio and Rome Philharmonic Orchestra, has been a guest conductor in the USSR and Europe, and received the Order of Merit from the Italian government. His compositions include orchestral, chamber and film music. For the Argentinian Odeon company he recorded the overture to Gluck's *Alceste*, Gomes' *Il Guaranj* overture and Williams' *El Rancho abandonado* (with the Avellaneda Municipal Orchestra), and Ugarte's *De mi tierra* Suite No. 1 and part of Rubinstein's *Bal costumé* (arr. Erdmansdorfer, with the Teatro Colón Orchestra) and Ugarte's *Prelude in G minor* (with the Avellaneda College Symphony Orchestra).

Fayer, Yuri (1890–1971). Born in Kiev, Fayer graduated from Kiev Conservatory and went on to study the violin and composition at the Moscow Conservatory. After playing as a violinist in a symphony orchestra (1916–19) he became assistant conductor at the Bolshoi Theatre (1919–23) and then chief conductor there (1923). He retired in 1963 and in that time conducted over 50 ballets, including over 400 performances of *Swan Lake*. He received many Soviet decorations and medals, including the Order of Lenin and the Stalin Prize (four times). In 1956 he conducted the Bolshoi Ballet on its visit to London, and he also appeared in Belgium, France and the United States; in 1958 EMI released a fine mono recording of the complete *Giselle* ballet music, in which he conducted the Covent Garden Orchestra. Conducting the Bolshoi Theatre Orchestra he recorded *The Sleeping Beauty*, *Nutcracker* and *Swan Lake*, *Coppélia*, Glière's *The Red Poppy*, a suite from Prokofiev's *Romeo and Juliet*, Glazunov's *Raymonda*, and *Les Ruses d'amour*, Rubinstein's *Bal costumé* and *Trepak*, and the *William Tell* overture; some of these performances appeared on various labels in the West, including Fidelity, Saga, Colosseum and Camden.

Fedoseyev, Vladimir (b. 1932). Born in Leningrad, Fedoseyev studied at the Mussorgsky Music School there, at the Moscow Music Institute and at the Moscow Conservatory. He was appointed conductor and artistic director of the USSR Radio-Television Orchestra of Russian folk instruments (1959–74), and also conducted concerts and opera in Moscow and Leningrad. He became principal conductor and artistic director of the USSR Radio-Television Symphony Orchestra in 1975, and has toured as a guest conductor in Eastern and Western Europe, the United States and Japan. His recordings, made in the USSR, include Tchaikovsky's opera *Tcherevichky*, Rimsky-Korsakov's *May Night* and *The Snow Maiden*, Glazunov's Symphonies Nos 5, 6 and 7, Taneyev's Symphony No. 2, Shostakovich's Symphony No. 5, Sviridov's *Spring Cantata*, *Snow Storm* and *Time, Forward*. Most were with the Moscow Radio Symphony Orchestra.

Fekete, Zóltan (b. 1909). A native of Budapest and a graduate of the Franz Liszt Academy there, Fekete went to the United States in 1937 and was associated with the New York Midtown Orchestra. After World War II he returned to Europe, and in the first years of LP made a number of records with the Salzburg Mozarteum Orchestra and the Vienna State Opera Orchestra; these performances were good, if not remarkably so, and were issued on various labels in Europe and the United States: Columbia, Eurochord, MGM, Lyricord, Saturn, Mercury, Remington, Fidelity, Concert Artist, Delta, *et al.* Possibly the most significant was *Das klagende Lied* of Mahler; Fekete's was the first recording of the revised version in two movements. His other recorded performances were *Kindertotenlieder* (with Rosza) and the *Rückert Lieder* (with Steingruber), Mozart's *Exsultate jubilate* and Schubert's *Salve Regina* (with Lorand), Schubert's *Grand Duo* (in Oeser's orchestration) and *Schneewittchen* ballet (in his own arrangement), the Haydn Symphonies Nos 86 and 88, Bruckner's Symphony No. 3, the Bartók Suite No. 1, his edition of Haydn's *Symphony in C major*, his own *Caucasus* ballet suite, Spelman's *Pervigilium Veneris*, Mozart's Divertimento K. 334, Tchaikovsky's *The Tempest* and a suite from *The Sleeping Beauty*. He compiled from the music of Gluck and Handel some orchestral suites, and conducted on record three of the latter: *The Triumph of Time and Truth*, *Alceste* and *Jephtha*. Despite its title the *Jephtha* suite includes as well as the overture to that opera pieces from *Solomon*, *Judas Maccabaeus* and *Athalia*. Supraphon also issued a disc on which he conducted the Prague Symphony Orchestra in Berlioz' overtures *Le Corsaire* and *Benvenuto Cellini*, and d'Indy's *Istar* and *La Mort de Wallenstein*.

Feldbrill, Victor (b. 1924). Born in Toronto, Canada, Feldbrill studied there at the Royal Conservatory of Music, at the Royal College of Music and the Royal Academy of Music in London, and was later a pupil of Monteux in Maine (1949–50) and of van Otterloo in Hilversum (1956). He first conducted with the Toronto University Symphony Orchestra (1942), was a bandsman in the Royal Canadian Navy (1942–5), conducted the Royal Conservatory Summer School Orchestra (1946–50), was a violinist and occasional conductor with the Toronto Symphony Orchestra (1949–56), and became the orchestra's associate conductor in 1956. He founded and conducted the Toronto Chamber Players (1952–3), was conductor and musical director of the Winnipeg Symphony Orchestra (1958–68) and of the National Youth Orchestra of Canada (1960–63), resident conductor of the Toronto Symphony Orchestra, in succession to Ančerl (1973–7), music director of the Toronto Youth Symphony Orchestra (1969–78) and conductor of the University of Toronto Orchestra. He has been a guest conductor with the Brussels Radio (1961), in the USSR (1963 and 1967), in Italy and Britain and with many orchestras in Canada. His records include Adaskin's *Rondino* and Turner's *Variations and Toccata* (with the Winnipeg Symphony Orchestra for RCA), a symphony by Pentland (with the Winnipeg Chamber Ensemble for RCA), Somers' *The Fool* (with an instrumental ensemble *et al.* for CBC), Morawetz's Symphony No. 2, Weinzweig's Piano Concerto (with Helmer) and Symonds' *The Nameless Hour* (with the Toronto Symphony Orchestra for CBC), a symphony by Somers (with the CBC Wind Symphony Orchestra for CBC), Jones' *The Jones Boys*, Chotem's *North Country*, Weinzweig's *Barn Dance*, MacMillan's *À Saint Malo*, Cable's *Newfoundland Rhapsody*, Adaskin's *Algonquin Symphony* and Champagne's *Danse villageoise* (with the Toronto Philharmonia Orchestra for Dominion).

Fellowes, Edmund (1870–1951). Born in London and educated at Oriel College, Oxford, Fellowes was ordained a priest in 1895 and became Minor Canon of St George's Chapel, Windsor, where he was also choirmaster. He was active in the Oxford Musical Club and in the madrigal societies at Bristol and Windsor, edited and published the distinguished and comprehensive compilations *English Madrigal School* (1913–24, in 36 volumes), *The English School of Lutenist Song-Writers* and *English Cathedral Music from Edward VI to Edward VII* (1941), was a member of the editorial committee for the Carnegie Trust's *Tudor Church Music*, edited the complete edition of Byrd's music, lectured in the United States, published studies of Byrd, Gibbons, English madrigal verse and the English madrigal composers, and was made a Companion of Honour in 1944. Fellowes also edited the series of records of English church music which was sponsored by the British Council and was issued in 1950; he himself recorded for HMV with the St George's Chapel Choir the Church of England service, psalms and other sacred pieces by Garett, Walmisley, Wesley, Turle, Purcell and Battishill.

Felumb, Svend Christian (b. 1898). Born in Copenhagen, Felumb studied with Nielsen and Bruce, and in Paris with Blenzel and Vidal, and from 1924 to 1947 was oboist with the Danish Royal Orchestra. He then conducted the Tivoli Concert Symphony Orchestra at Copenhagen until 1962, and was founder of the New Music Society, to promote modern Danish music. He made 78 r.p.m. records for HMV of music from Nielsen's *Aladdin* and some waltzes of Lumbye (with the Tivoli Orchestra), Tarp's Piano Concerto (with Harder and the Copenhagen Philharmonic Orchestra), and songs by Nielsen (with Schiøtz and Islandi and the Copenhagen Philharmonic Orchestra) and for Odeon a song from Nielsen's *Maskarade* (with Byrding and the Tivoli Orchestra). Later on LP he recorded Svendsen's *Polonaise*, Shostakovich's *The Age of Gold* suite, the overture to *La Belle Hélène*, a polka from Riisager's ballet *Slaraffenland*, and the waltz from *Faust* (with the Tivoli Orchestra, for Sonora and Mercury).

Fenby, Eric (b. 1906). Born in Scarborough, Fenby was a self-taught musician, and from 1928 to 1934 lived with Delius at Grez-sur-Loing in France, acting as his amanuensis; following this experience he wrote *Delius as I knew him* (1936). He became professor of composition at the Royal Academy of Music, and apart from arrangements of Delius' music his compositions include a symphony and chamber music. He recorded as a pianist the Delius violin sonatas (with Holmes), and as a conductor Delius' *Caprice and Elegy for Cello and Orchestra* (with Harrison, and an unnamed orchestra, in 1930, and re-issued by World Record Club in 1975).

Fendler, Eduard (b. 1902). Born in Leipzig, Fendler studied at the Stern Conservatory in Berlin, with Brecher for conducting, and also privately with Leichentritt for composition. He conducted from 1927 to 1941 in Germany, France and Holland after making his debut in Cologne; from 1930 to 1933 he was director of the Symphony Chamber Orchestra in Berlin. He left Europe and became conductor of the symphony orchestra at Ciudad Trujillo in the Dominican Republic (1942–4), then of the orchestra at San José, Costa Rica (1948–9) and was in the United States in 1945–7 and later from 1949. In 1952 he was appointed conductor of the Mobile Symphony Orchestra in Alabama. He was interested in promoting broadcast music and in recording less familiar music, and revived a number of neglected works of Haydn, Mozart, Boccherini, Benda and other composers of that era. He made a number of 78 r.p.m. records of music by Haydn, Mozart, Lully, Clérambault, Vivaldi and Purcell, for HMV, Vox, L'Oiseau Lyre and Boîte à Musique, with the Paris Conservatoire Orchestra and various chamber orchestras, and some of these works such as Haydn's Symphony No. 53 and the *Cassation of F major* he rediscovered and recorded for the first time. His recordings included Purcell's *Abdelazar* (for Vox), Haydn's Symphony No. 53, and *Overture in D major*, and two movements from the Notturno No. 6, Mozart's Marches K. 335 and K. 408, *Serenata notturna*, and *Overture in B flat* K. 311a, (with the Paris Conservatoire Orchestra for HMV), Clérambault's Sinfonia and the overture to Lully's *L'Amour médecin* (with the Paris Conservatoire Orchestra for

Boîte à Musique), Haydn's *Cassation in F major*, Mozart's Minuets K. 195 and Bassoon Concerto (with Oubradous and an orchestra for L'Oiseau Lyre), Symphony No. 20 and a movement from the Serenade K. 320 (for Vox), the Andante for Flute and Orchestra K. 315 and Vivaldi's Flute Concerto Op. 10 No. 3 (with Lavaillette and the Paris Conservatoire Orchestra for Pathé), Haydn's Notturno No. 4 (with the NBC Orchestra for Elaine Music Shop) and Poulenc's *Le Bal masqué* (for Esoteric).

Fennell, Frederick (b. 1914). A native of Cleveland, Ohio, Fennell studied at the National Music Camp at Interlochen, the Eastman School of Music and at the Mozarteum in Salzburg (1938). In 1939 he joined the Eastman School to teach conducting and remained there for 23 years. He studied with Koussevitzky and was his personal assistant at Tanglewood in 1948; in 1945 he had become associate conductor of the Eastman School Orchestra and also conductor of the Eastman Pops Orchestra. In 1952 he founded the Eastman Wind Ensemble and in that year made the first of his 25 discs for Mercury with the Ensemble. This group consisted of the wind section of the standard symphony orchestra with saxophones added. In recent years Fennell has been conductor-in-residence at the University of Miami Music School; for the 1974–5 season he was resident conductor of the Miami Philharmonic Orchestra.

Fennell recorded with the Eastman Wind Ensemble and the Eastman Pops Orchestra. His discs with the Wind Ensemble covered an extraordinary range from legitimate concert band music by Sousa, Barber, Hanson, Piston, Persichetti, Gould and other American composers, and British composers including Holst and Vaughan Williams, to canzoni and sonatas of Gabrieli, to the Strauss *Serenade in E flat for Thirteen Winds*, Mozart's Serenade K. 361, the Stravinsky *Symphonies of Wind Instruments*, Holst's *Suites in E flat* and *A major* and Hindemith's *Symphony in B flat for Concert Band*. Included also were a number of arrangements for wind band of music such as the Sullivan/Mackerras *Pineapple Poll*, *Finlandia*, *Marche militaire No. 1* of Schubert, and the Good Friday Music from *Parsifal*. In these discs Fennell demonstrated his acute ear for balance and style in each of these very different pieces, and for the degree of vibrato sound suitable for each work. In wind-band music his discs have been among the finest issued. He also recorded a disc of the music of Leroy Anderson (with the Eastman-Rochester Pops Orchestra for Mercury) and music for concert band by Joseph Wagner (with the Miami Symphonic Wind Ensemble for Orion).

Ferencsik, János (b. 1907). Ferencsik was educated at the conservatory at his native Budapest, was engaged as a coach at the Budapest State Opera in 1927, and became a conductor there in 1930. He was musical assistant at the Bayreuth Festival (1930–31) and conducted at the Vienna State Opera (1948–50). Since 1952 he has been the musical director of the Hungarian State Symphony Orchestra, and with this ensemble toured the United States (1972) and Japan and Australia (1974). From 1957 to 1974 he was musical director and chief conductor at the Budapest State Opera, and from 1966 to 1968 musical director of the Danish Radio Symphony Orchestra. In addition he has conducted major orchestras and in opera houses in many European countries, the United States, USSR and South America, and has appeared at the Vienna, Salzburg and Munich festivals. One of the most distinguished Hungarian musicians, he has his home in Budapest and his honours include the Kossuth Prize, the highest state decoration in Hungary, and on his 70th birthday he was awarded the Order of the Flag and was appointed an honorary professor of the Franz Liszt Academy.

Ferencsik has recorded extensively, usually with the Hungarian State Symphony, Budapest Philharmonic, Hungarian National Opera and Budapest Symphony Orchestras, and these discs have been released variously by Qualiton, DGG, Westminster, Music Guild, Artia, Parliament, Bruno and EMI. Of Hungarian composers he recorded Liszt's *Tasso*, *Hungarica*, *Mephisto Waltz*, *Orpheus*, *Les Préludes*, the *Faust* and *Dante* symphonies, *Requiem*, *Coronation Mass*, *Missa Solemnis* and *The Legend of St Elizabeth*, Bartók's *Concerto for Orchestra*, *The Wooden Prince*, *Kossuth*, Suite No. 1, *The Miraculous Mandarin*, Piano Concertos Nos 1 and 2 (with Zempleni and Wehner, respectively) Viola Concerto (with Lukács), *Hungarian Peasant Songs*, *Cantata Profana* and two Violin Rhapsodies (with Kovács), Kodály's *Symphony in Memoriam Arturo Toscanini*, *Dances from Galánta*, *Dances from Marosszék*, *Ballet Music*, *Háry János*, *The Spinning Room*, *Missa Brevis*, *Te Deum* and some choral works (with the Hungarian Radio and Television Chorus and the Kodály Girls Chorus), Erkel's *Bánk Bán*, Farkas' *Waiting for the Spring* and *Planctus et Consolationes*, Ránki's *The Tragedy of Man* and *Song of the City*, Dávid's *Overture*, Viola Concerto (with Lukács) and Horn Concerto (with Tarjáni), Lajtha's Symphonies Nos 4 and 9, and Bozay's *Pezzo Concertanto* and *Pezzo Sinfonico*. Everest also issued Kodály's *Psalmus Hungaricus* and the Bartók *Dance Suite* (with the London Philharmonic Orchestra), and Supraphon the Bartók Violin Concerto No. 1 and two Violin Rhapsodies (with Gertler) and Kodály's *Peacock Variations* (with the Brno State Philharmonic Orchestra).

In the non-Hungarian repertoire, Ferencsik made a 78 r.p.m. recording of Schubert's Symphony No. 8 (with the Budapest Philharmonic Orchestra for Patria), and LPs of the *Water Music* (with the Brno State Philharmonic Orchestra for Supraphon), Haydn's Symphonies Nos 82 and 94, and Mass No. 9, Mozart's Symphonies Nos 39 and 41 and the Two- and Three-Piano Concertos (with Kocsis, Ránkin and Schiff), the nine Beethoven symphonies, *Egmont* overture and Violin Concerto (with Kovács, and the Hungarian State Symphony Orchestra for Qualiton), the Piano Concerto No. 3 (with de la Bruchollerie and the Budapest Philharmonic Orchestra for Qualiton), Symphonies Nos 2 and 4 and overtures *König Stefan* and *Die Weihe des Hauses* (with the Czech Philharmonic Orchestra for Supraphon), Brahms' Piano Concerto No. 2 (with Katchen and the London Symphony Orchestra for Decca), Schoenberg's *Gurrelieder* (with the Danish Radio Symphony Orchestra *et al.* for EMI) and excerpts from *Carmen* (with the Hungarian State Opera for Qualiton).

Many of these discs have been widely acclaimed, more particularly Liszt's Requiem, Haydn's Mass No. 9 and Brahms' Piano Concerto No. 2. The Beethoven symphonies encountered a varied reception: Paul Henry Lang (in *The Recordings of Beethoven*, Wyeth Press, 1971, pp. 16–17) was somewhat caustic of Symphony No. 4, but called No. 2 capable. However, the series with the Hungarian State Symphony Orchestra was distinguished by Ferencsik's exemplary musicianship and sense of style.

Ferrara, Franco (b. 1911). Born at Palermo, Ferrara studied at the conservatories at Palermo and Bologna, toured Italy as a pianist and violinist, was concertmaster of the Florence orchestra and became a conductor in 1938. He had a very small repertoire, but was a remarkable conductor. Ill-health forced him to abandon his career; he taught conducting at Perugia (1958) and Hilversum (1959), lectured at the Accademia di Santa Cecilia at Rome and has composed orchestral, concerted and instrumental music. His recordings include Beethoven's Symphony No. 8 (with the Santa Cecilia Orchestra for HMV, on 78s), the overture to *La forza del destino* (with the La Scala Orchestra for HMV), Respighi's three suites of *Ancient Airs and Dances* (with the Rome Symphony Orchestra for Everest) and the one-act operas *La serva padrona* and *La scala di seta* (with the Rome Philharmonic Orchestra *et al.* for RCA).

Ferraris, Franco (b. 1922). Born in Alessandria, Italy, and educated at the Giuseppe Verdi Conservatory in Milan, Ferraris started his career as an assistant conductor at La Scala, Milan (1947–54), then conducted in many opera houses throughout Europe. He has composed songs and has transcribed music by Bellini, Rossini and Grieg. He recorded accompaniments for songs by the tenor Corelli, for EMI.

Ferrero, Willy (1906–54). The son of an Italian clown, Ferrero was born in Portland, Maine, was taken to Italy as a child, and at the age of six conducted a concert at the Teatro Constanzi in Rome. Two years later, he toured Europe as a conductor, and won admiration for his intuitive musicianship. After World War I, he conducted opera and concerts in Italy, and graduated at the Vienna Academy of Music in 1924. Hailed as a child prodigy, his later career was somewhat of an anticlimax. Nonetheless, he made a number of 78 r.p.m. recordings for Cetra with EIAR Symphony Orchestra, including *Boléro*, *Scheherazade*, *Kikimora*, *Gli uccelli*, the Dance of the Persian Slaves from *Khovanshchina*, Turina's *La Oración del Torero*, a concerto grosso of Vivaldi, and Debussy's *Fêtes*. Also, he recorded *A Night on the Bare Mountain* (with the La Scala Orchestra for HMV), Vivaldi's Two-Violin Concerto P. 222 (with the Italian Radio Orchestra for Tempo), and *Till Eulenspiegel* (with the Milan Symphony Orchestra for Homochord).

Fiedler, Arthur (1894–1979). Fiedler was born in Boston, where his father was an Austrian migrant who played in the first violin section of the Boston Symphony Orchestra and was a member of a famous string quartet. The Fiedler family returned to Vienna in 1910, and Arthur Fiedler became a student at the Royal Academy of Music in Berlin, studying the violin, piano and conducting. He first conducted an orchestra at the age of seventeen. In 1914 he returned to the United States and joined the second violin section of the Boston Symphony under Muck, later changing to viola, and played in the orchestra when Muck recorded with it in 1917. After serving in the US army in

1918, he returned to the orchestra and was also active as an accompanist and coach. In 1924 he formed and conducted the Boston Sinfonietta, a chamber orchestra made up of members of the Boston Symphony, which also became known on records as the Arthur Fiedler Sinfonietta. In 1929 he organised public open-air 'Esplanade' concerts in Boston, and in 1930 he was appointed conductor of the Boston Pops (short for Popular) Concerts, and continued to conduct until his death, thus making him the longest reigning conductor of a major American symphony orchestra. The Boston Pops in reality is the Boston Symphony Orchestra without its principal players, and was formed originally in 1887 to provide a season of lighter music for Boston audiences. The orchestra plays every evening from May to mid-July, and then moves to the Esplanade for its summer free open-air series. Fiedler's programmes with the Boston Pops were a subtle mixture of popular classics, current pop melodies, arrangements and excerpts from American musicals, Viennese waltzes and polkas, ballet music, marches and familiar overtures and orchestral pieces. Apart from the Boston Pops, Fiedler had a strenuous programme of bookings as a guest conductor leading similar programmes with other American orchestras and, on occasion, overseas tours. On the other, more serious, side of his musical personality he was also conductor of the Cecilia Society, the Boston University Glee Club, the MacDowell Club of the Boston University and the Boston Male Choir.

Despite his avuncular appearance and his world-wide reputation as an extroverted conductor of popular music as diverse as a Bach transcription to a Beatles melody, Fiedler's real self was that of a serious businesslike, highly professional musician who knew exactly what he was doing and was completely devoted to preparing and performing the music in his chosen field, as expertly as he could. Being identified with the Boston Pops type of programme, he accepted the fact that he was only engaged for this, and so, like some other American practitioners in this field, he had to forgo any opportunity of conducting more serious music. He had to face hostility and derogation from fellow conductors, musicians and critics who dismissed him as a vulgar populariser, but he himself saw a serious purpose behind his music-making, believing that his records and concerts led people to better music ('better' is his own word). Fiedler was careful to avoid personal contact with his audience, claimed that he was unaware of the audience behind him when he conducted, but at the same time he was careful to note their reaction to each of the pieces he presented. In his attitude to both his audience and his music he was quite unsentimental. His unique achievement was that he had done more than anyone to bridge the gap between *Oklahoma!* and the *Unfinished* Symphony.

Fiedler rated as one of the most successful artists ever to record. His LP records for RCA Victor have sold over 50 million copies, but despite this he was recorded by DGG. His first recordings with the Boston Pops were made in July 1935 in Symphony Hall, Boston. The auditorium was not air-conditioned at the time and he has described how the entire orchestra was undressed to the limits of decency in the stifling heat. Their first best-selling hit was Gade's *Jealousy*, which was the first record of a symphony orchestra to sell over a million copies. It is scarcely possible to list even his most popular discs because his complete discography runs to scores of pages. In addition to arrangements of popular hits, folk tunes, marches and so on, there are many of the more familiar pieces of composers such as Grieg, Tchaikovsky, Rimsky-Korsakov, Brahms and Schubert, as well as overtures, ballet music, waltzes, polkas etc. of Strauss, Offenbach, Suppé and many others, even extending to Beethoven's overture *Die Weihe des Hauses*. Understandably not all of these pieces flourish under Fiedler's no-nonsense briskness and the Boston Pops' forthright style, but the general standard was high, and Fiedler and his orchestra were anything but sloppy. It would be quite wrong to dismiss the Boston Pops records as musically inferior to performances of the same pieces by other great orchestras and conductors; some, such as the *Russian Easter Festival* overture of Rimsky-Korsakov can stand comparison with any. One would not choose Fiedler for the *Siegfried Idyll*, but for the overture *Dichter und Bauer* or for *Gaîté parisienne* it is another matter. The audience to which the records are aimed can be estimated by the titles of some of the LP albums: *Great Music for Great Lovers*, *Hearts in 3/4 Time*, *Music for a Summer Night*, and *Fiedler Ole!*

RCA took the plunge in 1971 with one major symphonic disc under Fiedler's direction, Dvořák's Symphony No. 9, with the Boston Symphony Orchestra, which was a considerable performance. The serious side of Fiedler had previously been demonstrated by his 78 r.p.m. records with the Fiedler Sinfonietta, including Corelli's Concerto Grosso Op. 6 No. 11, some Handel organ concertos (with E. Power Biggs), Mozart's Divertimento K. 287 and Serenade K. 388, and Hindemith's *Der*

Schwanendreher, in which the composer was the viola soloist.

Fiedler, Max (1859–1939). The German conductor and composer Max Fiedler was born at Zittau, attended the Leipzig Conservatory (1877–80) and joined the staff of the Hamburg Conservatory, eventually becoming its director in 1904. He gave up a career as a concert pianist to become conductor of the Hamburg Philharmonic Orchestra in 1882, and in his 26 years with the orchestra he established himself as a major figure in the German musical world. He visited the United States in 1905, conducting the New York Philharmonic Orchestra, and London in 1907, appearing with the London Symphony Orchestra, and then from 1908 to 1912 was conductor of the Boston Symphony Orchestra. He found it difficult to secure an appointment at a major musical centre when he returned to Germany, but became musical director of the Essen Symphony Orchestra in 1916, remaining with this ensemble until 1933. He then lived in Berlin and occasionally conducted the Berlin Philharmonic Orchestra. Fiedler did not attract superlatives when he lived in the US; one New York critic wrote that he was a well-equipped musician in the technical details of his art and entirely at home on the conductor's stand, but he did not convey the impression that he was a deeply poetical or musically stimulating nature. He recorded two Brahms symphonies, the overtures *Abu Hassan* and *Der Freischütz* and accompanied Elly Ney in Brahms' Piano Concerto No. 2, all with the Berlin Philharmonic Orchestra for Polydor, and made in the early 1930s. The performance of Brahms' Symphony No. 2 was included in the DGG album *The Early Days* (issued in 1974), and is significant in that Fiedler was famous as an interpreter of Brahms, whose contemporary he was in Hamburg.

Field-Hyde, Margaret (b. 1905). Born in Cambridge, Field-Hyde studied with her father and in Germany, especially the performance of 12th- to 15th-century vocal music. She appeared as a soprano in concerts, opera and oratorios in Britain, and formed the vocal quintet the Golden Age Singers, with which she toured Europe and North America, and made many recordings. Included have been Dowland's *Ayres for Voices* (with Bream, for Argo), madrigals of Monteverdi, Monteverdi's *Il pastor fido* and a collection from Marenzio's *Il pastor fido*, canzonets, ballets and madrigals of Morley, and madrigals of Tomkins (for Westminster).

Finck, Hermann. The first major orchestral recording was made by the English branch of the Odeon Company in 1909; it was a suite from *Nutcracker*, with the London Palace Orchestra conducted by Hermann Finck. He has remained just a name in the history of the gramophone record; his biographical details do not appear to have been published, and this was his sole recorded performance.

Fine, Irving (1914–62). Born in Boston, Fine was educated at Harvard University, studied composition with Nadia Boulanger, conducting with Koussevitzky and choral conducting with Davison. He was associate professor of music at Harvard (1945–50), faculty member of the Berkshire Music Center (from 1946) and professor of music at Brandeis University, Massachusetts (from 1950). His compositions included orchestral, vocal, chamber and instrumental music; Desto released a disc on which he conducted the Boston Symphony Orchestra in his Symphony (1962), and also with Leinsdorf leading the Boston Symphony in his *Toccata concertante*, *Serious Song* and *Lament*.

Finzi, Christopher. Son of the English composer Gerald Finzi (1901–56), Finzi conducted the English Chamber Orchestra with Janet Baker in his father's *Dies Natalis*. The recording was originally issued by the World Record Club in 1964, and has since been reissued by Everest and EMI.

Fischer, Ádám (b. 1949). Born in Budapest, where he attended the Béla Bartók Conservatory, Fischer studied conducting with Swarowsky in Vienna and with Ferrara in Venice and Siena (1970–71), was a repetiteur at the Graz Opera (1971–2), conductor of the St Pölten Theatre (1972–3), was a prize-winner at the Guido Cantelli Conductors' Competition in Milan (1973), and a repetiteur at the Vienna State Opera (1973–4). He was then principal conductor of the Helsinki National Opera (1974–7) and also assistant conductor of the Helsinki Philharmonic Orchestra (from 1975), first conductor at the Karlsruhe Opera (1977–8), has conducted major orchestras in Hungary, and has been a guest conductor in FR and DR Germany, Finland, Italy and Sweden. For Hungaroton he recorded Haydn's Symphonies Nos 88 and 100 (with the Hungarian State Symphony Orchestra).

Fischer, Eduard (b. 1930). Born in Prague, Fischer first studied music privately and then at the Prague Conservatory under Sádlo, Micka and Brože, and was a conducting student with Smetáček, Klíma and Doležil. He graduated with distinction in 1954. He was conductor of choirs at the conservatory and at high schools, became conductor of the orchestra and choir of the Ministry of the Interior (1955), and principal conductor of the Philharmonic Orchestra at Gottwaldov (1957). He toured with success in Cuba in 1962. His recordings include Handel's Concerti Grossi Op. 6, Hurník's *Musica da camera*, Válek's Symphony No. 9 and Řezáč's *Torso of a Schumann Statue* (with the Prague Chamber Soloists for Supraphon), Bárta's *Ludi*, Feld's *Three Frescoes* and Mácha's *Rychlík Variations* (with the Prague Chamber Orchestra for Supraphon), Tischenko's Symphony No. 3 and Slonimsky's *Concerto buffo* (with Musici de Praga for Supraphon), Martinů's Piano Concerto No. 2, Ježek's *Fantasy for Piano and Orchestra* (with Novotný) and ballet suite, and Válek's Symphony No. 11 (with the Prague Symphony Orchestra for Panton), and Šesták's Symphony No. 3, Pauer's *Canto festivo* and overtures by Pauer, Jirásek, Horký, Doubravský and Kohoutek (with the Czech Radio Symphony Orchestra for Panton).

Fischer, Edwin (1886–1960). Born in Basel, Fischer studied with Huber at the Basel Conservatory and later with Krause in Berlin, where he became a teacher at the Stern Conservatory (1905–14). Although probably more famous as a pianist, particularly in the music of Bach, Mozart, Beethoven, Schubert and Brahms, he was also a distinctive conductor. From 1926 to 1928 he conducted the Musikverein at Lübeck, and for the three following years directed the Bachverein in Munich. Later he formed his own chamber orchestra in Berlin and made many successful tours of Europe, but after 1942 lived in his native Switzerland and was stricken with paralysis from 1954 until his death. Throughout his life he believed that music, particularly that of the great classical masters, was a divine emanation from eternity, and that the true musician's greatest joy is to be its humble interpreter. He was not concerned about perfection of technique; 'we must search for the inner experience of art, and in this the player's own personality is a kind of creator. And to achieve this we must sacrifice any lurking feelings of self-importance, all vanity, all preconceived ideas. One must in fact attain to a kind of childlike innocence' (Quoted in B. Haggin, *Music on Records*, New York, 1941, pp. 157–8).

Fischer made many records as a pianist, of which the most celebrated were the complete *Das wohltemperierte Klavier* of Bach. With his chamber orchestra he recorded a number of performances for HMV in Berlin in the 1930s. Included were Haydn's Symphony No. 104, Mozart's Symphony No. 33, five movements from Mozart's Serenade K. 361 and the *Brandenburg Concertos*. Also, conducting from the keyboard, he recorded a group of Bach and Mozart concertos (K. 453 and K. 466), with his orchestra, and Haydn's *Piano Concerto in D* (with the Vienna Philharmonic Orchestra for HMV). Later, with the Philharmonia Orchestra on LP, he both played and directed Beethoven's Piano Concertos Nos 3 and 4 and conducted the *Brandenburg Concertos* Nos 2 and 5. In London in the early 1950s he played all the Beethoven concertos, conducting from the keyboard, except the *Emperor*, when he called in a conductor. His recordings made the same impression as his concert appearances; Bernard Haggin, the critic quoted above, wrote of the Haydn Symphony No. 104 that it was 'not only superb in musical outline, warmth, spirit and force, but enchanting in the way an ensemble performance by a small group of fine musicians can be – in the sensitiveness and fluidity of the perfectly co-ordinated progression, the balance of instrumental lines, the matching and blending of the colours and sonorities' (*ibid.*). Fischer's Bach would be considered too romantic today, but as Denis Matthews has said, 'after playing Bach with Fischer one might remain an agnostic, but could never be an atheist'. Recently, IGI in the US issued discs of Fischer playing Mozart's Concertos K. 482 and K. 491 and Symphony No. 35 (also conducting the Danish Chamber Orchestra).

Fischer-Dieskau, Dietrich (b. 1925). Born in Berlin, Fischer-Dieskau studied with Georg Walter and Weissenborn in Berlin, served with the German army in World War II and was a prisoner of war in Italy, and in 1948 was able to resume his career as a baritone. He made his debut as a concert and opera artist in that year, and has since become recognised as one of the greatest singers of our time. His recordings of lieder are so comprehensive that they include the entire output, at least for male voice, of the songs of Schubert, Schumann, Brahms and Strauss, and have encompassed composers such as Haydn, Mendelssohn, Wolf, Fauré, Schoeck, Britten and Meyerbeer; sales of his lieder records have totalled more than ten million, and of them all *Winterreise* has been a best-seller. His repertoire in oratorio and of operatic roles is almost as impressive and authoritative, ranging from Gluck and Mozart to Busoni and Berg, and, after much study and observation of other artists singing the role, he recently added Hans Sachs (*Die Meistersinger*), which he regards as the most taxing role. After achieving this pre-eminent position as the most versatile and prolific singer to make records, Fischer-Dieskau turned his attention to conducting and made his debut in London in 1973 with the English Chamber Orchestra. He had in fact studied conducting before he became a singer, and so it came naturally to him. Conducting occupies about a quarter of his time: 'I would like to do still more, but there is always the question of time. Eating scores is not like eating potatoes. I hope my singing experience helps me here. After all, breathing is one of the main elements in every kind of music-making, but there are many technical aspects of conducting that have nothing to do with the voice.' He has the wish to conduct Wagner some day: 'I think I might find him easier than Mozart or Verdi because he is very close to how I feel.' Among conductors of Wagner, he has the greatest respect for Furtwängler; 'he had the most natural way of giving the most expression to the music.' His repertoire as a conductor is restricted to the romantic composers, but he is interested also in Stravinsky, Berg and Schoenberg. Orchestral musicians who have played under him feel that experience will teach him to convey what is in his head through his hands.

In 1973 EMI issued Fischer-Dieskau's first record as a conductor, when he led the New Philharmonia Orchestra in Schubert's Symphonies Nos 5 and 8, which were warm and lyrical performances as distinguished as those he made of Schubert as a lieder singer. His later discs have been of Brahms' Symphony No. 4, and *Harold in Italy* (with the Czech Philharmonic Orchestra, the latter with Suk, for Eurodisc/Ariola), the Schumann Piano Concerto and *Allegro appassionato* (with Barenboim and the London Philharmonic Orchestra for EMI), Symphonies Nos 2 and 3 and the *Manfred Overture* (with the Bamberg Symphony Orchestra for BASF).

Fischer-Dieskau, Klaus (b. 1921). Brother of Dietrich, Fischer-Dieskau was born in Berlin and educated at the Hochschule für Musik there. He was leader of the Hugo Distler Chorus, teacher of interpretation in Berlin, on the staff of DGG at Hamburg, organist and conductor at the Dreifaltigkeitskirche in Berlin (1963) and guest professor at the University of Illinois (1969). For DGG he recorded Schütz's *St Matthew Passion*, with (amongst others) Dietrich and Lore Fischer-Dieskau.

Fistoulari, Anatole (b. 1907). Born in Kiev, Fistoulari studied as a child with his father, Grigory Fistoulari, who was a prominent musician in St Petersburg. He came first before the public as a child prodigy when he conducted Tchaikovsky's Symphony No. 6 at the age of seven at Kiev, and when he was twelve he conducted an opera at Bucharest and orchestras in Germany and Holland. During World War I he lived in Paris, and later, in 1931, he conducted the Grand Opéra Russe there with the Colonne Orchestra and Chaliapin, with whom he toured France and Spain. In 1933 he was with the Ballet Russe de Monte Carlo in Paris and London and toured with the company in France and Italy, and in the United States in 1937. In 1939 he joined the French army, but after the capitulation of France managed to reach England and to resume his career. He conducted opera and symphony concerts in Britain, especially with the London Symphony and London Philharmonic Orchestras, conducted opera in New York, toured France and the USSR with the London Philharmonic Orchestra in 1956, and was a guest conductor in many other countries. In 1942 he married Mahler's daughter Anna, but the marriage was dissolved in 1956. In 1948 he became a British citizen.

Fistoulari's recording career started in the 1940s with Decca, when he made a number of 78 r.p.m. discs with the London Symphony, National Symphony and New Symphony Orchestras; this series included Beethoven's Symphony No. 7 and Schubert's Symphony No. 8, the overtures *Fra Diavolo*, *Norma*, *The Queen of Spades*, *Mignon*, *Rosamunde*, *L'Italiana in Algeri* and *The Guardsman* of Tchaikovsky, Tchaikovsky's Piano Concerto No. 1 (with Orloff), Mendelssohn's Piano Concerto No. 1 (with Joyce), the Khachaturian Piano Concerto (with Lympany), the Dance of the Hours from *La Gioconda*, *Invitation to the Dance*, *Marche slave*, the Sailors' Dance from *The Red Poppy*, the Hungarian March from *La Damnation de Faust*, the ballet music from *Faust*, a suite from *Carmen*, and pieces from *Rosamunde*. On 78s he also recorded Tchaikovsky's *Variations on a Rococo Theme* (with Markevitch and the Lamoureux Orchestra for Polydor). Of these records, the Beethoven Symphony No. 7 in particular was a completely competent performance.

On LP, Fistoulari's recordings have been many. They include the overtures *Donna Diana*, *The Merry Wives of Windsor* and *Il segreto di Susanna*, Liszt's *Les Préludes*, *Mazeppa* and *Totentanz* (with Jacquinot), Grieg's *Four Norwegian Dances*, *Peer Gynt* Suite No. 1, *Holberg Suite*, *Two Elegiac*

Melodies and *Symphonic Dance No. 4*, Strauss's *Burleske*, Honegger's *Concertino*, Milhaud's Piano Concerto No. 1, Debussy's *Fantaisie* and d'Indy's *Symphonie sur un chant montagnard français* (with Jacquinot), Ravel's *Tzigane* (with Lockhart), Poulenc's *Les Biches* and *Aubade* (with Jacquinot), Fauré's *Dolly*, Tchaikovsky's Suite No. 4, *The Tempest*, *Hamlet*, *The Slippers* and *Romeo and Juliet* fantasy-overture, Rimsky-Korsakov's Piano Concerto (with Jacquinot), *May Night* overture, *Skazka* and suites from *The Snow Maiden* and *The Maid of Pskov*, Glazunov's *Valse de concert* No. 1 and *Stenka Razin*, Borodin's *Nocturne* and Prokofiev's *Lieutenant Kijé* suite (with the Philharmonic Orchestra for Parlophone, and some issued in the US by MGM), suites from *Russlan and Ludmilla* and *Ivan the Terrible* (with the London Symphony Orchestra for EMI), Dukas' *La Péri*, d'Indy's *Istar* and introduction to *Fervaal*, and Saint-Saëns' Piano Concerto No. 5 (with Jacquinot and the Westminster Symphony Orchestra for Parlophone), excerpts from Tchaikovsky's Suite No. 1, Rimsky-Korsakov's *Mlada*, Glinka's *Valse-Fantaisie* and Luigini's *Ballet égyptien* (with the Royal Philharmonic Orchestra for Parlophone), Liszt's Piano Concerto No. 1 (with Cherkassky and the Philharmonia Orchestra for EMI), the Brahms Violin Concerto, Saint-Saëns' Violin Concerto No. 3 and Chausson's *Poème* (with Milstein and the Philharmonia Orchestra for EMI), Turina's *Canto a Sevilla* (with Los Angeles and the London Symphony Orchestra for EMI), Liszt's Piano Concertos Nos 1 and 2 (with Kempff), the Grieg Piano Concerto (with Curzon), Tavares' Piano Concerto (with Blumenthal), Rachmaninov's Piano Concerto No. 3 (with Ashkenazy), excerpts from *Werther* and *La Damnation de Faust*, Saint-Saëns' *Havanaise* and *Introduction et rondo capriccioso* (with Campoli) and *Swan Lake* (with the London Symphony Orchestra for Decca), *The Sleeping Beauty*, the *Nutcracker* Suites Nos 1 and 2, *Aurora's Wedding*, the ballet music from *Faust*, the Dance of the Hours from *La Gioconda* and the overture to *Mignon* (with the Paris Conservatoire Orchestra for Decca), Rachmaninov's Piano Concerto No. 2 (with Katchen), the *pas de deux* from Minkus' *Don Quixote* and the Strauss arrangement by Dorati, *Graduation Ball* (with the New Symphony Orchestra for Decca), the Khachaturian Violin Concerto (with Ricci and the London Philharmonic Orchestra for Decca), Liszt's *Hungarian Rhapsodies Nos 1* to *6* (with the Vienna State Opera Orchestra for Vanguard), *Finlandia*, *Valse triste*, *The Swan of Tuonela* and *Festivo* (with the London Symphony Orchestra for Mercury), the Beethoven Violin Concerto (with Milstein and the Philharmonia Orchestra for World Record Club), excerpts from *Swan Lake* (with the Amsterdam Concertgebouw Orchestra for Decca), *Giselle*, *Coppélia*, *Sylvia* and *The Sleeping Beauty* (with the London Symphony Orchestra for Mercury), *Gayane* (with the London Symphony Orchestra for Everest), Tchaikovsky's Piano Concerto No. 1 (with Wild and the Royal Philharmonic Orchestra for Reader's Digest), suites from *Coppélia* and *Sylvia* (with the Royal Philharmonic Orchestra for Reader's Digest and the RIAS Orchestra for Everest), Glière's *The Red Poppy* and Ippolitov-Ivanov's *Caucasian Sketches* (with the London Philharmonic Orchestra for RCA), and Schumann's *Carnaval*, and suites from *Nutcracker*, *Coppélia* and *Giselle* (with the Covent Garden Orchestra for RCA).

These LP records were made in the 1950s and early 1960s; in 1972 Decca issued a Tchaikovsky Symphony No. 4 with Fistoulari conducting the Royal Philharmonic Orchestra. Something had happened in the meantime, for the performance was unsteady in tempi, phrasing and dynamics, a disappointing contrast to the style and brio of his earlier recordings.

Fitelberg, Gregor (1879–1953). Born in Dvinsk, Latvia, and Polish by adoption, Fitelberg studied at the Warsaw Conservatory and in 1896 won international prizes for a violin sonata and a trio which he composed. In 1905 in association with his friend Szymanowski and some others he founded the Society of Young Polish Composers, and throughout his life he championed the music of his compatriots, particularly Szymanowski. After playing the violin in the Warsaw Philharmonic Orchestra he was appointed the orchestra's principal conductor in 1908. From 1911 to 1914 he was in Vienna, conducted at the Court Opera, but during World War I he went to Russia where he conducted opera, ballet and symphony concerts at St Petersburg and Moscow. In 1921 he moved to Paris to conduct for Diaghilev's Ballets Russes, and two years later returned to Poland to take up again his position with the Warsaw Philharmonic Orchestra. Leaving Poland and Europe in 1940, he travelled first to Buenos Aires and then to the United States, staying there from 1942 to 1945. In 1945–6 he conducted a series of concerts in London with the London Philharmonic Orchestra, introducing the music of young Polish composers, and in 1947 he returned to Poland and resumed his activities. His own compositions included two symphonies, a symphonic poem and some chamber music.

Fitelberg made some records when he was in England after World War II, with the London Philharmonic Orchestra for Decca; these are of Tchaikovsky's Symphony No. 3 and Piano Concerto No. 2 (with Eileen Joyce), the *Tsar Saltan* suite, the Polovtsian Dances from *Prince Igor* and the prelude to *Die Meistersinger*. Another set made at this time for Parlophone was the then unfamiliar Violin Concerto No. 1 of Szymanowski (with soloist Eugenia Uninska and the Philharmonia Orchestra). This latter recording was nothing less than sensational; in England *The Record Guide* (by E. Sackville-West and D. Shawe-Taylor, London, 1951, p. 592) summed it up as 'wonderful', and David Hall in the United States commented on the 'astounding mastery' of the performance of both soloist and orchestra (*Records, 1950*, New York, p. 467). It enjoyed a short currency on LP in the United States. Fitelberg also directed some other 78 r.p.m. discs of orchestral music of the 19th-century Polish composer Moniuszko, with Polish orchestras.

Fjeldstad, Øivin (b. 1903). The Norwegian conductor Fjeldstad studied at the Oslo Conservatory under Lange, at the Leipzig Conservatory under Davisson, and at the Berlin Conservatory under Krauss. He made his debut as a violinist in 1921, and played in the Oslo Philharmonic Orchestra (1924–45). His first appearance as a conductor was with that orchestra in 1931; he was appointed chief conductor of the Norwegian State Broadcasting Orchestra (1945–62), the Norwegian State Opera (1958–9), and of the Oslo Philharmonic Orchestra (1962–9). He has been a guest conductor with many orchestras in Europe, North America, Israel and the USSR, and has received many awards in his native Norway. His recordings demonstrate his range and versatility as a conductor; almost all have been with the Oslo Philharmonic, and have been released on a number of labels. The works recorded include Beethoven's Symphony No. 3 and Schubert's Symphony No. 8 (for Reader's Digest); Mozart's Symphony No. 40, Mendelssohn's Symphony No. 4, a collection of Strauss waltzes, and Grofé's *Grand Canyon Suite* (for RCA); the *Peer Gynt* music of Grieg (with the London Symphony Orchestra *et al.* for Decca), which has held a pre-eminent place in the catalogues since it was first issued in 1958, Tchaikovsky's Symphony No. 4 (with the National Youth Orchestra of Britain, for Classics for Pleasure); and *Götterdämmerung*. The Wagner opera has been his major recording venture; it was complete except for minor cuts, and was broadcast by the Norwegian State Radio System on three separate nights of 1956, with Flagstad and a Norwegian cast, except for Svanholm, a Swede. This performance was later issued by Decca in Britain in 1956. Fjeldstad conducted the combined Oslo Philharmonic and Norwegian State Radio Orchestras; the occasion was to provide Flagstad with her final opportunity to sing Brünnhilde, and despite the deficiencies of the recording *per se*, Fjeldstad proved in the event to be a more than adequate Wagnerian conductor.

Fjeldstad has also recorded much Scandinavian music for Nerax and Phonogram Norsk with the Oslo Philharmonic Orchestra *et al.*, and some of these performances have been reissued on labels such as Mercury and Composers Recordings. The works recorded include Bezanson's *Rondo Prelude*, Braein's *Serenade*, Brustad's Symphony No. 2, Bull's Trumpet Concerto (with Koebeck), Saeverud's Symphony No. 2, *Sinfonia dolorosa* and *Galdreslåtten*, Nystedt's *The Seven Seals*, Svendsen's Symphony No. 2, *Carnival in Paris*, *Festival Polonaise*, *Norwegian Rhapsodies Nos 2* and *3* and *Norwegian Artists' Carnival*, Sinding's *Symphony in D minor* and Piano Concerto (with Knardahl), Valen's *Le Cimetière Marin*, *La Isla de las Calmas*, *Sonetto di Michelangelo* and Piano Concerto (with Riefling), Halvorsen's *Entry of the Boyars*, *Fossegrimen* and *Norwegian Rhapsodies Nos 1* and *2*, Groven's *Hjalarljod*, *The Bridegroom* and *Margit Hjukse*, Monrad-Johansen's *Symphonic Fantasy* and *Voluspaa*, Goodenough's *Elegy*, Jensen's *Symphony in D* and *Japanese Spring*, and Hovland's *Lamenti*.

Flagello, Nicolas (b. 1928). Born in New York of parents of Italian origin, Flagello studied at the Manhattan School of Music and then in Italy with Pizzetti at the Accademia di Santa Cecilia. Returning to the United States, he taught at the Manhattan School of Music, toured as an accompanist with various singers, played the violin, viola and oboe in orchestras, and was assistant conductor in the Chicago Lyric Opera (1960–61). He has written many compositions, including orchestral works, concertos and operas, and recorded a number of them with the Orchestra Sinfonica di Roma for Serenus, including the suite *Lautrec*, *Concerto for Strings*, *Contemplazioni di Michelangelo*, *Island in the Moon* (with Tatum), *Lyra* and some concerted works. His other recordings include eleven compositions by Nelhýbel, two pieces by Lessard, Rieti's Cello Concerto (with Amfitheatrof), Piano Concerto No. 3 (with

Santoliquido) and suite *La Fontaine* (also with the Orchestra Sinfonica di Roma for Serenus), Abramson's *Piano Dance* and Reif's *Philidor's Defense* (with the Orchestra Camerata Romana for Serenus), a disc of popular pieces including *España*, *Marche slave* and *Prélude à l'après-midi d'un faune* (with the Rome Royal Orchestra for 20th-Century Fox), and a disc of songs with tenor Richard Tucker (and the Columbia Symphony Orchestra for CBS).

Flämig, Martin (b. 1913). Born in Aue, Saxony, Flämig studied sacred music in Dresden and at the Academy of Sacred Music at Leipzig under Högner, Straube and David. He was cantor and organist at Leisnig (1936), a teacher at the Hochschule für Musik at Dresden (from 1946), becoming a professor and conductor of the choir. In 1948 he was appointed cantor at the Church of Reconciliation at Dresden, director of sacred music for the Evangelical (Lutheran) Church in Saxony and director of the School for Sacred Music in 1949. He then moved to Switzerland and was conductor of the Zürich Radio Choir (1960–71); returning to DR Germany in 1971 he succeeded Mauersberger as conductor of the Dresden Kreuzchor and in 1973 was appointed the choir's general music director. In Switzerland he recorded with the Zürich Radio Choir *et al.* Burkhard's *Das Gesicht des Jesaja* and *Christi Leidensverkündigung* (for Musicaphon), *Die Sintflut* and *Psalm 148* (for Laudinella) and Mass Op. 85 (for CT), Brunner's *Die Versuchung Jesu* (for Fono), Diener's *Psalm 69*, Kuhn's *Der Mensch lebt und besteht nur eine kurze Zeit*, Matthes' *Ist Gott für uns* (for CT), Studer's *Lasset eure Lenden umgürtet sein* (with the Evangelische Singgemeinde for CT), Mareschall's *Psalms 33* and *47* and Wolleb's *Psalm 150* (with the Basel Münster Choir for Fono), and collections entitled *Musik aus dem Berner Münster* and *Musik aus dem Basler Münster* (for Fono), *Morgenlieder* and *Abendlieder* (for Laudinella-Reihe). With the Dresden Kreuzchor *et al.* he has recorded the Bach *Christmas Oratorio* and the Masses BWV 233, BWV 234, BWV 235 and BWV 236, Schütz's *Auferstehunghistorie*, *St Matthew Passion*, *St John Passion* and *Psalms of David*, parts 2 and 3, and Pepping's *Te Deum* (with the Kreuzchor and the Dresden Philharmonic Orchestra *et al.*, for Eterna and released in Western Europe by DGG – Archiv and Eurodisc).

Fletcher, Percy (1879–1932). Born in Derby, Fletcher conducted at theatres in London and composed a number of pieces of smaller, melodious orchestral pieces. He recorded for the Vocalian Company when the latter existed in the 1920s, the works including a suite from *Carmen*, excerpts from *Sylvia*, *Coppélia* and *La Source*, Luigini's *Ballet égyptien* and *Suite russe*, the overtures to *Die Zauberflöte* and *Le nozze di Figaro*, the Hungarian March from *La Damnation de Faust*, a *Slavonic Dance* of Dvořák, Järnefelt's *Praeludium* and *Berceuse* (with the Aeolian Orchestra) and MacDowell's *Woodland Sketches* and several waltzes of Tchaikovsky (with the Regent Symphony Orchestra).

Fletcher, Peter (b. 1936). Born in Grimsby, Fletcher was an organ scholar at Jesus College, Cambridge, and organist at Beverley Minster (1962–6). He became music adviser to the East Riding of Yorkshire, founded the East Yorkshire Youth Orchestra, was music inspector for the Inner London Education Authority (1966), conductor of the London Schools Symphony Orchestra, was appointed professor of music at Dalhousie University, Canada (1973) and has on occasion conducted the Atlantic Symphony Orchestra. In 1973 he recorded, for Pye, with the London Schools Symphony Orchestra and soloist Daggers, Bloch's *Viola Suite* and *Suite hébraïque*.

Flipse, Eduard (1896–1973). Born in Wissekerke in Zeeland, Flipse was at the Rotterdam Conservatory, and studied conducting with Cornelius at Utrecht. He was principal conductor of the Rotterdam Philharmonic Orchestra (1930–65) which developed under him to become one of the leading orchestras in Holland, alongside the Amsterdam Concertgebouw and Hague Philharmonic Orchestras. He was also appointed chief conductor of the Antwerp Philharmonic Society in 1962, and was professor of piano at the Rotterdam Conservatory. His compositions include operettas, orchestral and choral pieces.

On 78 r.p.m. discs for Odeon Flipse recorded *Moldau* and *Don Juan* with the Rotterdam Philharmonic, and accompanied de Groot in Strauss' *Burleske* with the Brussels Radio Orchestra. Later, for Philips on LP, he undertook two major recordings: in 1954 Mahler's Symphony No. 8, and in 1955 Mahler's Symphony No. 6. Both were made at concerts with the Rotterdam Philharmonic Orchestra *et al.* The Symphony No. 8 recording was the first of that work, but the performance was characterised by Deryck Cooke as 'earthbound'. Flipse also recorded Pijper's Piano Concerto (with Henkemans and the Rotterdam Philharmonic for Philips) and *Six Adagios* (with the Hague

Residentie Orchestra for Philips), two works of the Dutch-American composer Johan Franco, the *Fantasy for Cello and Orchestra* (with Brill) and *The Virgin Queen's Dream Monologue* (with Lenchner and the Rotterdam Philharmonic Orchestra for Composers Recordings).

Flury, Richard (1896–1967). Born in Biberist, Switzerland, Flury studied at the Universities of Basel, Berne and Geneva, and in Vienna, and was conductor of the Zürich Academy Orchestra (1923–6), the Harmonie Choir in Berne and the Solothurn Symphony Orchestra (1919–49), and taught music at the Solothurn Conservatory and Cantonal School (from 1930). In 1929 a festival was held in Solothurn of his compositions, which he also conducted with radio orchestras in Zürich and Lugano and in Vienna. He recorded his own *Waldsinfonie* (with the Swiss-Italian Radio Orchestra) and *Fasnachtssinfonie* (with the Beromünster Studio Orchestra), both for Fono.

Folprecht, Zdeněk (1900–61). Born in Turnov, Folprecht studied at the Prague Conservatory under Foerster, Novák and Talich, conducted at the Bratislava Opera (1923–9), with the Amateur Slovak Philharmonic Orchestra (1925–39) and at the Prague National Theatre (1939–61). He collaborated with the composer Nedbal to perform his stage works, conducted for the Czech Radio and toured East and West Europe. His compositions included arrangements of folk songs, an orchestral fantasy *In the Forlorn Valley* and a cantata *Czech Spring*. He recorded with the Prague National Theatre Orchestra *et al.* excerpts from Kovařovic's *The Dogheads* (for Supraphon), the prelude to Act III and the Devil's Dance from Dvořák's *The Devil and Kate*, (for Supraphon), and a collection of Italian opera overtures (issued in the United States by Parliament).

Forbes, Eliot (b. 1917). Born in Cambridge, Massachusetts, and educated at Harvard University, Forbes has been assistant professor of music at Princeton University (1947–54), associate professor (1954–8) and then professor of music at Harvard (1958–61), and Fanny Peabody Professor of Music (from 1961). He was conductor of the Harvard Glee Club and Radcliffe Choral Society (1958–71), with which he recorded Josquin's *Missa Mater Patris et Filia* and motets, a two-disc set from the first International University Choral Festival (for RCA), and Bach's Motets and Cantata No. 118 (with the Aeolian Singers for Decca). Forbes also edited Thayer's *Life of Beethoven* (1964), compiled and edited *The Harvard Song Book* (1966), and prepared an edition of Beethoven's Symphony No. 5 (1971).

Forest, Jean Kurt (1909–75). Born in Darmstadt and educated at Wiesbaden, Forest was concertmaster of orchestras in Berlin and Wiesbaden, was with the radio orchestra at Frankfurt am Main (1930–33), at Hamburg (1934–6), and then was conductor at Braunschweig (1939). He was director of choral music for the Berlin Radio (1948) and chief conductor there (1949–51), then with the GDR Television (1952–5), and from 1955 lived in Berlin. He composed music in many forms, including operas, operettas and musicals, and recorded excerpts from his opera *Die Blumen von Hiroshima* with the Berlin Radio Symphony Orchestra, for Eterna.

Forrai, Miklós (b. 1913). Born in Magyarszék, Baranya, Hungary, Forrai studied at the Franz Liszt Academy in Budapest (1931–7) and was chorusmaster of the Forrai Chamber Choir (1936). He conducted a series of children's concerts (1936–44), has been chorusmaster of the Budapest Choir (from 1948) and professor at the Franz Liszt Academy (since 1941). In 1955 he received the Liszt Award and in 1963 the Artist of Merit award; he has often performed in Vienna and Prague and has published many collections of vocal music. His recordings include Liszt's *Missa Choralis*, the oratorio *Christus*, the cantata *Prometheus* and Psalms Nos 13, 18, 23, 69, 125 and 129, Schumann's Requiem and *Requiem for Mignon*, and Sugár's *Hunyadi* (with the Budapest Choir and the Hungarian State Symphony Orchestra *et al.* for Hungaroton).

Forster, Karl (1904–63). Born in Grossklenau, Germany, Forster studied philosophy and theology at Regensburg, and church music and musicology at Munich University. In 1934 he was appointed choirmaster at the Protestant Cathedral in Berlin, and at the same time built up and conducted the choir at the Catholic Cathedral at St Hedwig, which had been founded originally in the 19th century. Under his leadership, the St Hedwig's Choir became one of the most distinguished in Germany, but after the division of the city, when St Hedwig's became situated in East Berlin, the choir moved to West Berlin where it performs in concerts with the Berlin Philharmonic and Berlin Radio Symphony Orchestras. In 1952 Forster became music director at the Free University and at the Technical University in West Berlin also. He wrote several masses and motets. With the St Hedwig's Choir and the

Berlin Philharmonic and Berlin Symphony Orchestras and various soloists he recorded a number of major choral compositions for Electrola/EMI, all superbly performed. Included were Bach's *St Matthew Passion* and *St John Passion*, *Messiah*, *The Creation* and Haydn's *Te Deum* and Mass No. 3, Bach's Cantatas Nos 208, 211 and 212, Mozart's Mass K. 427, Schubert's *German Mass*, Rossini's *Stabat Mater* and Bruckner's Masses Nos 2 and 3. Schwann have also issued Mozart's *Benedictus sit Deus*, *Exsultate jubilate* (with Berger) and *Vesperae solennes de confessore*. Some of these performances were released in Britain by EMI; the *St John Passion* and Cantata No. 211 (the *Coffee Cantata)* and Cantata No. 212 (the *Peasant Cantata*) were re-issued in the United States on the Seraphim label.

Forster, Paul (b. 1915). Born in Romanshorn, Switzerland, Forster studied at the Zürich Music Academy (1936–40 and 1944–5), has been music director in Herisau, choral director at Thurgau and St Gallen, and conductor at Appenzell am Rhein. He has given first performances of works by many Swiss composers and has been an adjudicator at many choral festivals in Switzerland. He has written many choral works and some chamber music. His recordings include Baumgartner's *An das Vaterland* (with the Liederkranz am Ottenberg for CTS, Switzerland) and Huber's *Entschluss* (with the St Gallen State Orchestra *et al.* for Ex Libris).

Fortner, Wolfgang (b. 1907). Born in Leipzig where he studied at the conservatory and university, Fortner was professor of composition at the Institute for Protestant Church Music at Heidelberg (1931–53) and also taught at the Hochschule für Musik at Freiburg (1935–41) and the North-West German Academy of Music at Detmold (1954–7). He was founder and director of Musica Viva at Heidelberg (1946), Freiburg (1958) and Munich (1964). Although he is a significant composer of operas, orchestral, choral and instrumental works, his music is not often heard outside Germany; both Fischer-Dieskau and Prey have recorded some of his songs. DGG issued a mono LP in which he conducted the Tibor Varga Chamber Orchestra of the North-West German Academy of Music in his own *Sechs Madrigale für Violinen und Violoncelli* and *Vorübungen zu den Madrigalen*, and more recently Wergo released a disc in which he conducts the Cologne Radio Symphony Orchestra *et al.* in his *Die Pfingstgeschichte nach Lukas*.

Foss, Lukas (b.1922). The American composer, teacher, pianist and conductor Foss was born in Berlin and received his early tuition as a pianist from Julius Goldstein, and then attended the Paris Conservatoire (1935–7). After coming to the United States with his parents in 1937 he studied composition with Thompson, piano with Vengerova and conducting with Reiner at the Curtis Institute at Philadelphia (1937–40), and then from 1939 to 1943 was with Koussevitzky at Tanglewood, at that time also studying composition with Hindemith at Yale University and also with Julius Herford. At the age of seventeen he appeared as a guest conductor with the Pittsburgh Symphony Orchestra, in 1944 was engaged as pianist with the Boston Symphony Orchestra, and appeared as a solo pianist with many orchestras in the US and Europe. From 1950 to 1952 he was in Rome on a Fulbright scholarship, and from 1953 to 1963 was professor of advanced composition at UCLA. He became music director of the Buffalo Philharmonic Orchestra (1963–70) and there founded the Buffalo Center for the Creative and Performing Arts to encourage experimental composition. Previously, in 1955–7, he had directed the Ojai Festival in California, visited the USSR with Aaron Copland for the US State Department in 1960, and in 1965–6 directed the New York Philharmonic's summer festival at Lincoln Center. He has been conductor of the Brooklyn Philharmonia in New York and of the Jerusalem Symphony Orchestra in Israel, resigning from the latter position in 1977.

Since his ten years at UCLA, Foss has given much time to lecturing, demonstrating and encouraging young musicians at universities in the US. His purpose has been to involve these people in creative activity. At Buffalo he attracted the younger generation to his concerts by presenting novel and extraordinary programmes such as introducing Indian and rock groups to play with the orchestra. He agrees with Boulez and others that symphony orchestras are inevitably museums playing the music of past eras, which ended with Mahler; he says that the music written today is essentially for smaller ensembles, and the perfection of modern records makes it difficult to attract young people to concerts to hear the standard repertoire, at least in the US.

As well as being a remarkable pianist, Foss has been a prolific composer almost since childhood. He developed from a purely classical style to one influenced by Copland, Stravinsky and Hindemith, and his more notable early compositions include an opera *The Jumping Frog of Calaveras County*, an oratorio *Parable of Death*, two piano concertos, a string quartet, and *The Song of Songs*. Then he adopted the improvisatory techniques associated with composers such as Cage, Stockhausen and Brown. In *GOED*, which Foss recorded with the Buffalo Philharmonic for Vox in 1972, the players are divided into four groups which play different material in random combinations; his stated purpose is to write music with a high degree of inspiration in which the detail changes every time the piece is played. This, of course, rules out the permanence of a record *a priori*, and listeners considering the music in its context with other symphonic music are bound to comment that Foss, the composer, has abrogated his artistic responsibility in avoiding the conscious direction of the music, or a commitment to its content, either emotional or musical. The impression on one critic (Max Harrison of *The Gramophone*) was that the music sounded like orchestral doodling, less purposeful than when the orchestra is tuning before a concert. Foss has recorded more of his own music: *Baroque Variations* (with the Buffalo Philharmonic for Nonesuch), *Elytres*, *Paradigm* and *Ni Bruit ni Vitesse* (for DGG), *The Prairie* (with the Brooklyn Philharmonia *et al*. for Turnabout), *Paradigm 'for my friends'* (for DGG) and *Studies in Improvisation* (for RCA). Bernstein has also recorded Foss' *The Song of Songs* (with Jennie Tourel and the New York Philharmonic Orchestra for Composers Recordings).

Foss originally recorded, as a pianist, the *Three-Part Inventions* of Bach, and with the Zimbler Sinfonietta the Bach Clavier Concertos Nos 1 and 5 and Hindemith's *The Four Temperaments*. Then with the Zimbler Sinfonietta he recorded, as conductor, Bartók's *Divertimento*, Ives' *The Unanswered Question*, Milhaud's Symphony No. 4, Skalkottas' *Little Suite for Strings*, Tansman's *Triptych for Orchestra*, Telemann's Suite for Flute and Strings (with Pappoutsakis), Vaughan Williams' *Concerto accademico* (with Fuchs), and Mozart's Serenade No. 1, *Serenata notturna* and Sinfonia concertante K. 365 (with Joseph and Lillian Fuchs). More recently he has recorded for Nonesuch with the Buffalo Philharmonic Cage's *Concerto for Prepared Piano* (with Takahashi), Penderecki's *Capriccio for Violin* (with Zukofsky) and *De natura sonoris*, Xenakis' *Akrata* and *Pithoprakta*, and the *Four Legends* of Sibelius, and for Turnabout Copland's *Quiet City*, Ives' *From the Steeples and Mountains*, Ruggles' *Angels* and *Men and Mountains*, and Subotnick's *Lamentations*.

Foster, Lawrence (b. 1941). Born in Los Angeles of Romanian parents, Foster studied conducting and opera with Fritz Zweig and piano with Joanne Grauden in that city, and came under the influence of Walter and Böhm when in his teens. For two seasons he studied in Europe as a member of the Bayreuth Festival master classes, then made his debut as a conductor in 1960 with the Young Musicians' Foundation Debut Orchestra in California. He also became associate conductor of the San Francisco Ballet, holding this post until 1965 and undertaking three national tours, and was appointed assistant conductor to Mehta with the Los Angeles Philharmonic Orchestra (1963–5). The next year he won the Koussevitzky Memorial Conducting Prize and other awards at the Berkshire Festival at Tanglewood, and worked with Schuller, Leinsdorf and Boult. On Alexander Goehr's invitation he made his debut in Britain with the English Chamber Orchestra in 1965, conducted the Royal Philharmonic Orchestra in 1968 and then was appointed chief guest conductor of the Royal Philharmonic (1969–73), touring the United States with the orchestra in 1969 and 1972. After guest appearances with the Houston Symphony Orchestra in the 1970–71 season he was appointed conductor-in-chief of the orchestra in 1971, and was elevated to music director in 1972. Since then he has conducted in Israel, FR and DR Germany, Sweden, Denmark, Switzerland, Romania, Spain and France, has continued to conduct the Los Angeles Philharmonic and Chicago Symphony Orchestras at Ravinia, has appeared with many of the major US orchestras, and conducts and teaches at the Aspen Festival, Colorado. He has also conducted opera in Edinburgh, Stuttgart and Milan, and in 1976 led Walton's *Troilus and Cressida* at Covent Garden. He is one of the few American conductors to pursue a double career in the US and Europe.

A man of quiet demeanour, Foster is at the other pole to the charismatic, flamboyant stereotype of the American conductor. He is a highly accomplished artist, whose performances of music ranging from Mozart to Mahler, Stravinsky and Birtwistle display taste, judgement and style. Less inclined to give many guest appearances on the world concert scene, he believes it necessary to give more time to the Houston Symphony, so that a firm rapport can be established with the players, and so that he can create the sound he wants from the orchestra. Although he has been an advocate of contemporary music, he now finds that much music written today is beyond the reach of the public. He holds that record-making today leads to standardised interpretations, with the result that conductors are disinclined to present anything but a conventional reading of a standard work. Having conducted all the London orchestras, he says that 'they are like summer and winter, night and day, each with their own individual qualities'; he reserves special praise for the Dresden Staatskapelle, acknowledging the orchestra's remarkable sound, phenomenal discipline and ensemble – 'It's like digging into pure gold'. (*The Gramophone*, April 1977, p. 1530).

In 1977 Foster recorded *Troilus and Cressida* (with the Covent Garden Orchestra *et al.* for EMI); his other recordings have been Shifrin's *The Rise and Fall of the Third Reich* (with the MGM Orchestra *et al.* for MGM), Mozart's Symphony No. 40, the overture to *Le nozze di Figaro*, Piano Concerto K. 467 (with Vered) and Horn Concerto No. 4 (with Civil, and the Royal Philharmonic Orchestra for Decca), Beethoven's Piano Concerto No. 3 (with Lupu and the London Symphony Orchestra for Decca), Paganini's Violin Concerto No. 1 and Sarasate's *Carmen Fantasy* (with Perlman), Shostakovich's Piano Concerto No. 2 and Ogdon's Piano Concerto No. 1 (with Ogdon, and the Royal Philharmonic Orchestra for Decca), Saint-Saëns' Violin Concerto No. 3 and Vieuxtemps' Violin Concerto No. 5 (with Kyung-Wha Chung, and the London Symphony Orchestra for Decca), and the two Ravel piano concertos (with de Larrocha and the London Philharmonic Orchestra for Decca).

Fougstedt, Nils-Erik (1910–61). Born in Turku, Finland, Fougstedt studied at the Helsinki Conservatory (until 1934), at Salzburg and in Italy (1934), Berlin (1936 and 1938) and France. He taught at the Sibelius Academy in Helsinki (1933–8), was conductor of the Finnish Radio Orchestra (1944–61) and became the orchestra's chief conductor in 1951. He also conducted many Finnish choirs, composed two symphonies, several concertos, orchestral, vocal, chamber and film music, conducted concerts in most European countries and visited the United States in 1951. For a Finnish record company he recorded Sibelius' *Kuolema* and *Scene with Cranes*, with the Finnish Radio Orchestra.

Fourestier, Louis (1892–1976). Born in Montpellier, Fourestier studied under d'Indy at the Paris Conservatoire and was a follower of Dukas. In 1924 he won the Rossini Prize and the next year the Grand Prix de Rome for composition. He later wrote orchestral works, chamber music and cantatas, which met with some success. After conducting at Marseille, Bordeaux, Angers, Cannes and Vichy, he was with the Paris Opéra-Comique from 1927 to 1932, and in 1938 became conductor at the Paris Opéra. From 1945 to 1963 he taught conducting at the Paris Conservatoire, and appeared as a guest conductor at the New York Metropolitan Opera in 1946–7 and 1947–8. Kolodin in his history of the Met. commented that Fourestier's competence when he was in New York was nothing more than good routine, but he had the grace to add that he was best known in Paris as a symphonic conductor, particularly of Beethoven and Wagner. Almost all his recordings were of French music, of which he gave strong, clear, idiomatic performances. On 78 r.p.m. discs he recorded a complete *Samson et Dalila* (with the Paris Opéra for Pathé), Lalo's *Namouna* Suites Nos 1 and 2 and Delibes' *Sylvia* (with the Paris Opéra Orchestra for HMV), Chabrier's *España* (with the Paris Opéra for Pathé), Lalo's *Norwegian Rhapsody* (with the Colonne Orchestra for Pathé), Roussel's *Le Festin de l'araignée* (with the Paris Opéra-Comique Orchestra for Pathé) and the prelude to *Faust* (with the Paris Opéra Orchestra for Bluebird). His LPs included the five piano concertos of Saint-Saëns (with Darré and the ORTF Orchestra for Pathé), Chabrier's *Bourrée fantasque*, *España*, *Habanera*, overture to *Gwendoline*, *Marche joyeuse* and *Ode à la musique* (with the Colonne Orchestra for Pathé), Messager's *Les Deux Pigeons* and *Isoline* suite, prelude to Act I to *Lohengrin* and Forest Murmurs from *Siegfried* (with the Paris Opéra Orchestra for Pathé), Saint-Saëns' *La Jeunesse d'Hercule*, *Phaéton*, *Le Rouet d'Omphale* and *Danse macabre* (with the Colonne Orchestra for EMI), *Symphonie fantastique*, *La Mer* and *Nocturnes* (with the Cento Soli Orchestra for Musidisc), Aubert's *Habanera* and Charpentier's *Impressions d'Italie* (with the Paris Opéra Orchestra for EMI), Lalo's *Le Roi d'Ys* overture and *Scherzo*, and Saint-Saëns' *Suite algérienne* (with the FNRO Orchestra for Pathé).

Fournet, Jean (b. 1913). Born in Rouen, Fournet studied the flute and conducting with Gaubert at the Paris Conservatoire and soon after started his career as conductor of the Orchestra de la Radiodiffusion française and later at the Paris Opéra. His appointments have included President of the Association des Concerts Pasdeloup and until 1957 musical director of the Paris Opéra-Comique. Since then he has been guest conductor at opera houses and with orchestras in the principal countries of Europe, has appeared regularly with the Amsterdam Concertgebouw Orchestra (since 1950), was appointed conductor of the Netherlands Radio

Orchestra (1961), principal conductor and artistic director of the Rotterdam Philharmonic Orchestra (1969–73) and then director of the newly-formed Orchestre de l'Ile-de-France, one of the French regional orchestras which have done much to develop orchestral playing and musical audiences and to bring about a minor musical renaissance in France. This latter development owes much to Marcel Landowski. Fournier's overseas activities have taken him to the Lyric Opera in Chicago, the Teatro Colón in Buenos Aires, and to Israel, Canada and Japan where he conducted the first local performance of *Pelléas et Mélisande* in 1959. He was also professor of conducting at the École Normale de Musique in Paris (1944–62) and since 1966 has taught conducting at the master classes arranged by the Netherlands Radio at Hilversum.

Since the first records he made in France on 78 r.p.m. discs, Fournet has been one of the most distinguished interpreters of French music on disc. In wartime Paris he made two very remarkable recordings, both for French Columbia, of the Berlioz *Grande Messe des morts* and *La Damnation de Faust*, both with the French National Radio Orchestra *et al*. The performance of the *Grande Messe des morts* employed the complete instrumental and vocal forces specified by the composer and the set was described by David Hall in his *Record Book* (1948) as the most significant recording made anywhere in the world during the war years, and was truly superb in every respect. Fournet's other 78 r.p.m. discs included Ravel's *Piano Concerto in G major* (with Passini), the overtures to *Der Freischütz*, *Phaéton*, the overtures to *Phèdre* and *Les Deux Pigeons* and Rabaud's arrangement of Fauré's *Dolly* (with the Colonne Orchestra for Pathé), *Symphonie espagnole* (with Menuhin), Haydn's *Cello Concerto in D major* (with Tortelier) and the overture to *Zampa* (with the Colonne Orchestra for HMV), Saint-Saëns' Cello Concerto No. 1 (with Navarra and an orchestra for HMV), Lalo's Cello Concerto (with Navarra and the Colonne Orchestra for Polydor), *Le Tombeau de Couperin* and Pierné's *Divertissement sur un thème pastoral* (with the Colonne Orchestra for Columbia).

In the LP era Fournet has made many records, almost entirely of French music. Included have been four operas: *Louise* (with the Paris Opéra-Comique for Philips), *Pelléas et Mélisande* and *Les Pêcheurs de perles* (with the Lamoureux Orchestra *et al.* for Philips) and *Mignon* (with the Lamoureux Orchestra *et al.* for DGG). In the early 1950s he made some fine discs for Decca of unusual works, including Chabrier's *Ode à la musique* and excerpts from *Le Roi malgré lui*, and Debussy's *La Damoiselle élue* (all with the soprano Micheau and the Paris Conservatoire Orchestra *et al.*) and Fauré's *Requiem* (for Philips). He recorded with the Lamoureux Orchestra for Philips a series of discs, including the two Ravel Piano Concertos, d'Indy's *Symphonie sur un chant montagnard français*, Fauré's *Ballade*, Franck's *Symphonic Variations* and the Saint-Saëns Piano Concerto No. 2 (with Doyen), Lalo's *Namouna* Suite No. 1, *Norwegian Rhapsody* and *Symphonie espagnole* (with Grumiaux), Massenet's *Scènes alsaciennes* and *Scènes pittoresques*, the overture to *Phèdre* and excerpts from *Le Jongleur de Notre Dame*, overtures by Auber, Boieldieu and Thomas, *L'Arlésienne* Suites Nos 1 and 2, a suite from *Carmen* and *Patrie*, Chabrier's *España*, *Gwendoline* overture, *Marche joyeuse*, *Fête polonaise* and *Suite pastorale*, Chausson's *Poème* (with Grumiaux), Saint-Saëns' Piano Concerto No. 5 (with Tagliaferro), *Suite algérienne*, *La Princesse jaune* overture and bacchanale from *Samson et Dalila*, the ballet music from Rabaud's *Marouf*, the Fauré *Requiem*, Franck's *Rédemption* and *Le Chasseur maudit*, the prelude to *Faust*, suites from *Sylvia* and *Coppélia*, excerpts from *Il trovatore*, *In the Steppes of Central Asia*, *A Night on the Bare Mountain*, *Capriccio espagnol*, the *Russian Easter Festival* overture and Glinka's *Kamarinskaya*. In the second half of the 1960s he undertook for Supraphon some recordings of French music with the Czech Philharmonic Orchestra: they are *La Mer*, *Printemps*, *Iberia* and *Nocturnes* of Debussy, and Franck's *Psyché*, *Le Chasseur maudit*, *Les Éolides*, *Les Djinns* and *Rédemption*, as well as a suite from *The Three-cornered Hat*.

Fournier's other recordings have included Inghelbrecht's *Requiem* and *Vézelay* (with the ORTF Orchestra for Charlin), a suite from *Sylvia*, the overture to *La Dame blanche* and the ballet music from *Faust* (with the Paris Opéra Orchestra for Philips), the Chausson symphony (with the Pasdeloup Orchestra for Philips), Debussy's *Nocturnes*, Ravel's *Rapsodie espagnole* and *Menuet antique* (with the Paris Conservatoire Orchestra for Philips), the *Peer Gynt* Suite No. 1 of Grieg, which is a digest of the play of Ibsen, with music, (with the Lamoureux Orchestra for Pathé), the Lalo *Symphonie espagnole* (with Menuhin and the Colonne Orchestra for EMI), *L'Apprenti sorcier*, *Peer Gynt* Suites Nos 1 and 2, *A Night on the Bare Mountain*, *Les Éolides*, the *Prélude à l'après-midi d'un faune* and excerpts from *La Damnation de Faust* (with the Amsterdam

Concertgebouw Orchestra for Philips), Rachmaninov's Piano Concerto No. 2 and Tchaikovsky's Piano Concerto No. 1 (with Boukoff) and *Scheherazade* (with the Vienna Symphony Orchestra for Philips), Fauré's *Requiem* and *Pavane* (with the Rotterdam Philharmonic Orchestra *et al.* for Philips), the Mendelssohn and Tchaikovsky Violin Concertos (with Ricci) and Debussy's *Iberia*, *Nocturnes* and *Prélude à l'après-midi d'un faune* (with the Netherlands Radio Orchestra for Decca), H. Andriessen's Symphony No. 3, Badings' Piano Concerto (with de Groot), Hemel's Symphony No. 4, Henkemans' *Villonnerie* (with Kruysen) and Leeuw's *Music for Strings* (with the Rotterdam Philharmonic Orchestra for Donemus).

Fox, Frank (b. 1909). Born in Bistrita, Romania, Fox studied in Vienna, Berlin and London, and has composed more than 250 film scores, as well as radio and television incidental music, and musicals including *Kuriositäten* and *Es fing so harmlos an*. Eurodisc issued discs of him conducting excerpts from the operettas *Boccaccio*, *Die Czardasfürstin*, *Gräfin Mariza*, *Schön ist die Welt* and *Der Graf von Luxemburg*; the last-named was issued in 1960 by EMI in Britain.

Françaix, Jean (b. 1912). The French composer Françaix was born in Le Mans, was educated at the Paris Conservatoire and studied privately with Nadia Boulanger. His first composition to be published was a piano suite when he was nine years of age; his music has been aptly described as 'invariably elegant, if for the most part emotionally detached.' (E. Sackville-West and D. Shawe-Taylor, *The Record Book*, London, 1955, p. 284). Turnabout issued a disc on which he conducted the Luxembourg Radio Orchestra in his Piano Concerto (with Pailliard-Françaix), Viola Rhapsody (with Koch) and Violin Suite (with Lautenbacher).

Franci, Carlo (b. 1927). Born in Buenos Aires, Franci studied at the Accademia di Santa Cecilia in Rome, and first conducted opera at Spoleto in 1959. He has been active in opera houses in Europe and South America, has conducted major orchestras in London, Berlin, Vienna, Monaco, Madrid and Budapest, first conducted at the New York Metropolitan Opera in 1968, and has since conducted the company in New York and on tour in the United States. For Decca he recorded a collection of choruses from Verdi operas (with the Santa Cecilia Orchestra *et al.*), an aria recital with Del Monaco (with the Santa Cecilia Orchestra), and for Philips another aria recital with Deutekom (with the Rome Radio-Television Symphony Orchestra) and a recital of arias from *La traviata*, *I Lombardi*, *et al.* (with Deutekom, *et al.*, and the Monte Carlo National Orchestra).

Francis, Alun (b. 1943). Born in Kidderminster, Francis was educated at the Royal Manchester College of Music (1960–63) and was a horn player in the Bournemouth Symphony Orchestra. He became conductor and later music director of the Ulster Orchestra at Belfast (1966–7), then was artistic director of the Northern Ireland Opera Trust (from 1974), music director of the Tehrān Opera (1976–7) and from 1974 has been a guest conductor with orchestras in Britain, FR Germany, Italy, Israel, Norway, Hong Kong, Mexico, Iceland, Austria *et al.* His compositions have been widely performed. For Opera Rara (London) he conducted Donizetti's *Ugo, Conte di Parigi* (with the Philharmonia Orchestra *et al.*) and Offenbach's *Christopher Columbus* (with the London Mozart Players *et al.*).

Frandsen, John (b. 1918). Born in Copenhagen, Frandsen studied at the Royal Danish Conservatory and from 1945 to 1953 was an organist at Copenhagen. Just before World War II he became a choral conductor with the Danish Radio and in 1946 made his debut as an opera conductor with *Peter Grimes* at the Royal Theatre in Copenhagen. In 1956 he was appointed a conductor with the Royal Danish Opera Company, in 1958 he led the Danish Radio Symphony Orchestra during its second tour of the United States, and is conductor at the Royal Chapel, Copenhagen, and artistic manager of the Helsingborg Symphony Orchestra, Sweden. He is regarded as perhaps the great romantic among present-day Danish conductors. His earliest recording was the Nielsen Clarinet Concerto in 1947 (with Cahuzac and the Royal Danish Orchestra for EMI), and in the mid 1950s there appeared a fine Nielsen Symphony No. 3 with him conducting the Danish Radio Symphony Orchestra (for Philips), the overtures *A Midsummer Night's Dream*, *Le nozze di Figaro*, *Carnival* and *Russlan and Ludmilla*, Brahms' Symphony No. 4 and *Tragic Overture*, and the Grieg Piano Concerto (with Joyce, and the Royal Danish Orchestra for Saga). The Brahms symphony was described in Greenfield, March and Stevens' *Guide to the Bargain Classics* (1964) as 'an excellent, straightforward reading, always alive and with plenty of warmth'. Frandsen's other recordings include the overture to *Der*

Freischütz, and Riisager's *Monument for Kingo* and *Torgutik Dance* (with the Royal Danish Royal Orchestra for EMI), Bentzon's *Symphonic Trio*, Langgaard's Symphony No. 4 and Høffding's *Fantasies Nos 1* and *2* (with the Danish Radio Symphony Orchestra for EMI), Hartmann's *Haakon Jarl*, Gade's *Echoes of Ossian* overture and Kuhlau's overture and ballet music to *The Elves' Hill* (with the Danish Radio Symphony Orchestra for Philips).

Franks, Dobbs (b. 1933). Born in Arkansas, Franks studied at the Juilliard School, served for two years in the US navy, and became assistant to the conductor Robert Shaw. He toured New Zealand as a conductor (1965), was appointed conductor of the orchestra at Canterbury, New Zealand, became a conductor with the Australian Elizabethan Opera Company (1969) and the Australian Ballet Company (1971–2), and has been a guest conductor with symphony orchestras in Australia. He recorded Hollier's *Musick's Empire* (with Meyers and the Sydney Symphony Orchestra for Festival).

Freccia, Massimo (b. 1906). Freccia studied at the conservatory in his native Florence and then in Vienna with Schalk, and made his debut as a conductor with the Santa Cecilia Orchestra in Rome in 1928. He appeared in many Italian and European cities, from 1933 to 1935 conducted the Budapest Symphony Orchestra, was a guest conductor at the Lewisohn Stadium in New York (1938–40), at Toscanini's invitation conducted the NBC Symphony Orchestra (1947–54), was conductor of the Havana Philharmonic Orchestra (1939–43), the New Orleans Symphony Orchestra (1944–52), the Baltimore Symphony Orchestra (1952–9) and chief conductor of the Italian Radio Television Symphony Orchestra in Rome (1959–65). He has taken part in many European musical festivals and has been a guest conductor with major orchestras in Europe, Australia, Japan and South Africa. His compositions include two symphonic poems and an arrangement of the Bach *Passacaglia and Fugue in C minor*. Freccia's first recording was of the *Rosamunde* overture, on a 78 r.p.m. disc (with the Havana Philharmonic Orchestra). Then for Reader's Digest he made a number of LP recordings, including Haydn's Symphony No. 94, Mozart's Symphony No. 40 and Mendelssohn's Symphony No. 4 (with the Santa Cecilia Orchestra), Tchaikovsky's Symphony No. 4, a suite from *L'Oiseau de feu*, *Pini di Roma*, *La Mer*, the overture to *Rienzi* and a number of smaller pieces (with the Rome Philharmonic Orchestra), and *Romeo and Juliet* fantasy-overture, a suite from *Swan Lake*, the *1812* overture and *Marche slave* (with the London Philharmonic Orchestra), *Symphonie fantastique* (with the Royal Philharmonic Orchestra), the waltzes from *Faust*, *Der Rosenkavalier* and the Tchaikovsky *Serenade in C major* (with the Vienna State Opera Orchestra) and *Fontane di Roma* and *Feste Romane* (with the New Philharmonia Orchestra). He has also recorded Shostakovich's Symphony No. 5 (with the Royal Philharmonic Orchestra for Classics for Pleasure), flute concertos by Stamitz, C. P. E. Bach and Hoffmeister (with Larrieu), and horn pieces by Saint-Saëns, Dukas, Chabrier, d'Indy and Corrette (with Bourgue and the Monte Carlo National Orchestra for Decca (France)).

Frederick IX (1899–1972). Apart from his interests in rowing, sailing, cycling, motoring and railroading, King Frederick IX of Denmark was an accomplished musician. He studied with Hohlenberg and Høeberg, and frequently conducted the Royal Opera Orchestra; his preference was for the symphonies of Beethoven, Schubert, Brahms and Tchaikovsky and the preludes of Wagner. He also conducted Kuhlau's *The Elves' Hill*, the first Danish lyrical work, on occasion *Cavalleria rusticana*, and accompanied Fischer in Beethoven's Piano Concerto No. 5. For Tono he recorded Schubert's Symphony No. 8 (with the Copenhagen Orchestra) and the overture to *The Elves' Hill* (with the Royal Opera Orchestra).

Fredman, Myer (b. 1932). Born in Plymouth, Fredman studied at Dartington Hall and the National School of Opera with Tausky and Gelhorn. In 1959 he joined the Glyndebourne Festival Opera music staff, where from 1968 to 1973 he was first conductor. He has also appeared as a guest conductor for the British Broadcasting Corporation, in Belgium, Ulster, FR Germany, France, Poland, Romania and Australia, as well as at the Sadler's Wells Opera in London and with the New Opera Company in South Australia, becoming the latter's musical director in 1976. His operatic repertoire extends from Cavalli to modern composers such as Maw, Musgrave and von Einem, and in symphonic music from the baroque composers to Berg and Messiaen. Nonetheless on record he has been cast as a specialist in 20th-century British music; he has recorded Rubbra's *Inscape* and Still's *Concerto for Strings* and *Elegy* (with the Jacques String Orchestra *et al.* for Decca), Bax's Symphonies Nos 1 and 2 and Havergal Brian's Symphonies Nos 6 and 16 (with the London Philharmonic Orchestra for Lyrita), Robert Still's Symphony No. 4,

Benjamin's *Overture to an Italian Comedy*, and the Walk to the Paradise Garden from *A Village Romeo and Juliet* (with the Royal Philharmonic Orchestra for Lyrita). In all these performances Fredman's direction has been exceptionally convincing.

Freeman, Paul (b. 1936). Born in Richmond, Virginia, Freeman graduated from the Eastman School of Music, Rochester, in 1963 and then studied at the Hochschule für Musik in Berlin, and with Lindemann, Monteux and Lert. He has been conductor of the San Francisco Conservatory Orchestra (1966–7), director of the San Francisco Community Music Center (1966–8), music director of the San Francisco Little Symphony (1967–8) and associate conductor of the Dallas Symphony Orchestra (1968–70). His present appointments are conductor-in-residence of the Detroit Symphony Orchestra and principal guest conductor of the Helsinki Philharmonic Orchestra. In 1967 he was a winner of the Dmitri Mitropoulos International Conductors Competition, and in the following year of the special award to conduct *Tristan und Isolde* at the 1968 Festival of the Two Worlds at Spoleto, Italy. He has made many guest appearances with major orchestras in the United States and with others in Britain, FR Germany, Poland and in other European countries. One of the first Negroes to lead a senior US orchestra, Freeman has emerged as one of the foremost younger US conductors.

For the 'Black Composer' series of Columbia (US), Freeman has been appointed artistic director, and this 20-disc anthology will cover the music of black symphonic composers from Joseph, Chevalier de Saint-Georges (1739–99) to those of the present day. So far, to 1978, there has been released Cordero's Violin Concerto (with Allen) and *Eight Miniatures* (with the Detroit Symphony Orchestra), Wilson's *Akwan*, Anderson's *Squares* and Hakim's *Visions of Ishwara* (with the Baltimore Symphony Orchestra), Nunes-Garcia's *Requiem* (with the Helsinki Philharmonic Orchestra *et al.*), Walker's Piano Concerto (with Hinderas), Smith's *Ritual and Incantations*, and Hailstock's *Celebration!* (with the Detroit Symphony Orchestra), an excerpt from Coleridge-Taylor's *Hiawatha's Wedding Feast*, Brown's *Danse nègre*, Still's *Afro-American Symphony*, *Highway I, U.S.A.* and arias (with Brown), Saint-Georges' Symphony No. 1, *Symphonie concertante for Two Violins and Orchestra* (with Fried and Laredo), and Scena from *Ernestine* (with Robinson), Still's *Sadhji* ballet, Sowande's *African Suite*, White's Violin Concerto (with Rosand), Walker's Trombone Concerto (with Wick) and *Lyric for Strings* and Kay's *Markings* (with the London Symphony Orchestra). His other recordings have been of Kay's *Six Dances* (with the Westphalian Symphony Orchestra for Turnabout), Haubiel's *Gothic Variations* (with Granat), d'Indy's *Symphonie sur un chant montagnard français* and Poulenc's *Aubade* (with Jones), Kabalevsky's Piano Concerto No. 3 (with Preston), Rubinstein's Piano Concerto No. 3 (with Preston) and Zádor's *Studies* (with the Westphalian Symphony Orchestra for Orion), C. P. E. Bach's *Piano Concerto in A* and Prokofiev's Piano Concerto No. 1 (with White and Syme resp. and the Philharmonia Orchestra for Orion), Chaminade's Konzertstück (with Johnson) and Milhaud's Concerto for Two Pianos (with Yarbrough and Cowan, and the Royal Philharmonic Orchestra for Orion), a cello concerto by Kokkonen (with the Helsinki Philharmonic Orchestra *et al.* for Finnlevy), and a collection entitled *The Glory of Christmas* (with the Royal Philharmonic Orchestra *et al.* for Musical Heritage Society). *Time* magazine listed the first four volumes of the Black Composers Series among the top classical recordings for 1975, and the fourth disc of the series, the Violin Concerto and *Eight Miniatures* of Cordero, received the 1974 Koussevitzky International Recording Award.

Freitas Branco, Pedro (b. 1896). The brother of the Portuguese composer Luís Freitas Branco, Pedro studied in Lisbon and in 1926 founded a Portuguese opera company. His career as a symphonic conductor commenced in 1928, and in 1934 he became conductor of the Portuguese State Symphony Orchestra, showing a special aptitude for the large orchestral works of composers such as Strauss, Stravinsky and Ravel. Ravel invited him to conduct a festival of his music in Paris in 1932. He conducted in many European countries and appeared in Britain in World War II. Freitas Branco's major contribution to the gramophone, before the advent of LP, was a six-disc 78 r.p.m. set of the Arbós arrangement of five of the twelve pieces of Albéniz's piano pieces entitled *Iberia*, a brilliant performance in which he conducted the Lamoureux Orchestra for HMV. Other recordings were the *Pavane pour une infante défunte* (with an unidentified orchestra for Columbia) and Lalo's Cello Concerto (with Suggia and the London Symphony Orchestra for Decca). On LP he recorded a suite from *The Three-cornered Hat* and *Master Peter's Puppet Show* of Falla (with the Madrid Concerts Orchestra for Erato), Turina's *Danzas fantásticas*, *La*

Oración del Torero and *La Procesión del Rocío* (with the Madrid Symphony Orchestra for Telefunken), *Boléro*, *La Valse*, *Valses nobles et sentimentales*, *Alborada del gracioso* and *Pavane pour une infante défunte* (with the Champs-Élysées Theatre Orchestra for Telefunken), the Bacchanale from *Samson et Dalila* and *Danse macabre* (with the Champs-Élysées Theatre Orchestra for Ducretet-Thomson) and *El amor brujo* (with the Madrid Symphony Orchestra for Ducretet-Thomson).

Frémaux, Louis (b. 1921). Born in Aire-sur-Lys in the Pas-de-Calais, Frémaux's musical studies started at the Valenciennes Conservatoire. In 1940 he was sent to a labour camp by the Nazis; he escaped to join the resistance movement, and in 1945–6 served as a captain in the French Foreign Legion in Vietnam, where he was awarded the Croix de Guerre and the Légion d'Honneur. He entered the Paris Conservatoire in 1947, studied with Fourestier and Chailley and took first prize for conducting in 1952. Erato signed him for a recording contract after a concert with a student orchestra for his conducting diploma; he had prepared a programme of French baroque music, but with the death of the principal of the Conservatoire, Delvaincourt, in a car accident, the concert became a memorial for Delvaincourt and was attended by major figures in the French musical world. In 1956 he became permanent conductor of the Monte Carlo Opera Orchestra for ten years, and was a guest conductor in Europe, Japan and Brazil; in 1968 he first came to Birmingham as a guest conductor and made such an impression that in the following year he was appointed principal conductor of the City of Birmingham Symphony Orchestra, although he was simultaneously contracted to the Lyon orchestra. His tenure at Birmingham has been markedly successful and has been largely responsible for a dramatic change in the standard of the orchestra and its stature in the city and in the country at large. He toured south-eastern Europe with the orchestra in 1972, has appeared with other major British orchestras and with others in Europe, and in 1976 toured Australia; in 1977 his appointment as conductor of the Sydney Symphony Orchestra was announced. He has been described as a 'charming, popular, capable, often brilliant, hard-working and understanding conductor, not set on self-glorification nor one particularly interested in his own advancement'.

Most of Frémaux's early records for Erato were of French baroque music: Delalande's *Beatus vir*, *Usquequo Domine*, *Exaltabo te*, *Nisi Dominus* and some motets, Gilles' *Requiem*, Rameau's *In convertendo*, Campra's *Requiem*, *Te Deum* and some motets, other pieces by Mouret, Gautier, Marchand, Charpentier, Dumont and Monteclair (with the Chorale Caillard and the Jean-François Paillard Chamber Orchestra) and Blanchard's *Te Deum* (with the Chorus and Orchestra of Radio-Télévision Française). One of these performances, Gilles' *Requiem*, was particularly fine and won the Grand Prix du Disque in 1956; he recorded it a second time for stereo. His other discs were Poulenc's *Stabat Mater* (with the Colonne Orchestra *et al.* for Vega), du Mont's *Benedictus*, *Magnificat* and *Nisi Dominus* (with the Jean-François Paillard Chamber Orchestra *et al.* for Musique en Wallonie), Favre's *Cantate du jardin vert* (with the Paris Opéra Orchestra *et al.* for Petit Ménestrel), Poulenc's *Le Bal masqué* (for Vega), a collection of organ, brass and timpani music called *Dans la gloire des Invalides*, Schumann's Piano Concerto, *Konzertstück in G*, and *Introduction and Allegro in D* (with Sebök and the Pasdeloup Orchestra for Erato), *Symphonie fantastique*, *Pictures at an Exhibition*, Tchaikovsky's Piano Concerto No. 1 (with Sebök), *Peter and the Wolf*, *Le Carnaval des animaux*, and Fauré's *Requiem* (with the Monte Carlo Opera Orchestra *et al.* for Erato); *La Péri*, *L'Apprenti sorcier*, *Parade*, *The Young Person's Guide to the Orchestra*, Turina's *Danzas fantásticas*, Milhaud's *Le Carnaval d'Aix*, Prokofiev's *Overture on Hebrew Themes* and *Russian Overture*, the mazurka from *A Life for the Tsar*, the Dance of the Birds from *The Snow Maiden*, Glinka's *Kamarinskaya* and *Fantasy on Two Russian Folksongs*, the Polovtsian Dances from *Prince Igor*, an aria recital (with Scotto), and the overtures to *La forza del destino*, *I vespri siciliani*, *La scala di seta*, *Il barbiere di Siviglia*, *L'Italiana in Algeri*, *Norma*, *Carmen*, *Mignon*, *Si j'étais Roi*, *Le Calife de Bagdad* and *Fra Diavolo* (with the Monte Carlo Opera Orchestra for DGG), Barsukov's Piano Concerto No. 2 (with Tessier), and the two Chopin Piano Concertos (with François and the Monte Carlo Opera Orchestra for Pathé).

After his arrival in Birmingham, Frémaux recorded for EMI with the City of Birmingham Symphony Orchestra (*et al.*), and scored some notable successes. In this series were Walton's Bach arrangement *The Wise Virgins*, Berlioz's *Grande Messe des morts*, overtures *Le Carnaval romain* and *Benvenuto Cellini*, *Marche funèbre* and excerpts from *La Damnation de Faust* and *Les Troyens*, Bizet's *Symphony in C major* and *Roma*, Saint-Saëns' Symphony No. 3, Cello Concerto No. 1 and *Allegro appassionato* (with

Paul Tortelier), *Wedding Cake* (with de la Pau), *Caprice* (with Yan Pascal Tortelier) and *Le Carnaval des animaux*, *Prélude à l'après-midi d'un faune*, *España*, *L'Apprenti sorcier*, *Boléro*, *Danse macabre*, *Pacific 231*, the overtures to *Barbe-bleue*, *La Belle Hélène*, *La Grande-Duchesse de Gérolstein*, *Orphée aux enfers* and *La Vie parisienne*, Massenet's *Scènes pittoresques*, *Dernier sommeil de la Vierge* and ballet music from *Le Cid*, Ibert's *Divertissement*, Poulenc's *Le Biches*, Piano Concerto (with Ortiz) and *Gloria*, Fauré's *Ballade* and the Scherzo from Litolff's *Concerto symphonique* (with Ogdon), Satie's *Gymnopédies*, Walton's *Façade* suite, *Gloria*, *Orb and Sceptre*, *Crown Imperial* and *Te Deum*, McCabe's Symphony No. 2 and *Notturni ed Alba* (with Gomez), and an aria recital (with Hughes).

Frešo, Tibor (b. 1918). Born in Spišský Štiavník, Slovakia, where his father was an organ teacher, Frešo graduated from the Bratislava Academy of Music in 1939, and soon became known as a composer, music critic and pianist, and was a producer for the Slovak Radio (1937–9). He studied composition with Pizzetti and conducting with Molinari at the Accademia di Santa Cecilia in Rome (1939–42), made his debut as a conductor with the Bratislava Radio Orchestra (1942), was conductor at the Slovak National Theatre at Bratislava (1942–9), at the Košice Opera (1949–52), was principal conductor of the Slovak Philharmonic Orchestra at Bratislava (1952–3), returned to the Slovak National Theatre as chief conductor (1953), and has appeared as a guest conductor in the USSR, and in Eastern and Western Europe. His compositions include a *Stabat Mater* and orchestral, chamber and vocal works. He recorded Suchoň's opera *The Whirlpool* (with the Bratislava Radio Symphony Orchestra *et al.*) and accompaniments for a number of operatic arias, for Supraphon.

Fricke, Heinz (b. 1927). Born in Halberstadt, Germany, Fricke studied there (1946–8) and with Abendroth in Weimar (1948–50), was conductor at the Leipzig City Theatre (1950–60), general music director at Schwerin (1960–61) and then at the Berlin State Opera in East Berlin (from 1961). He also teaches at the Hochschule für Musik in East Berlin, and has conducted both opera and concerts in East and West Europe, South America and Cuba. He has recorded excerpts from *Don Carlos*, *Der Waffenschmied*, Meyer's *Reiter der Nacht*, and recitals of operatic arias with Süss and Büchner, and of operatic duets with Lear and Stewart (with the Berlin Staatskapelle for Eterna), and a recital with Bolkestein (with the Berlin Staatskapelle for BASF).

Fricsay, Ferenc (1914–63). Born in Budapest, Fricsay studied at the Budapest Academy of Music under Kodály and Bartók, and conducted his first concert, with the Hungarian Radio Orchestra, at the age of 15. His father had been a conductor before him, and he was able to play every instrument of the orchestra except the harp. In 1935 he was appointed conductor of the orchestra at Szeged, where he remained during World War II. In 1945 he conducted the first symphony concert in liberated Budapest, and also appeared for the first time at the Budapest Opera. In 1949 he became general music director of the Berlin State Opera and chief conductor of the Radio-in-American-Sector (RIAS) Orchestra in Berlin, which was the first of the six radio orchestras to be established in FR Germany and West Berlin after World War II, and was unique in that it was made up entirely of new players, many of whom had migrated from DR Germany. Fricsay remained with the orchestra until 1954, and a year later it changed its status and name to Berlin Radio Symphony Orchestra. He was also music director of the Bavarian State Opera at Munich (1949–52), but resigned following disagreements with the management. Previously, in 1947, he had achieved a measure of international fame when he took over from Klemperer the preparation and direction of von Einem's opera *Dantons Tod* at the Salzburg Festival. He also conducted in Vienna, London, Holland, Israel and South America, and made his debut in the United States with the Boston Symphony Orchestra in 1953. After leaving Berlin in 1954, he was engaged as conductor of the Houston Symphony Orchestra in Texas, in succession to Kurtz, but a dispute with the orchestra's management caused him to resign after conducting only a few concerts. He returned to the Bavarian State Opera for three years (1956–8), returned to Berlin (1959) to conduct the Berlin Radio Symphony Orchestra, and became musical adviser to the new Deutsche Oper in West Berlin. He died in Basel at the age of 48. Undoubtedly his great achievement was in developing the RIAS Symphony Orchestra to be one of the finest in FR Germany, and the many records he made with it are eloquent evidence of the fine standard it attained. Part of this was due to the exceptionally good players it recruited, part to Fricsay's strict discipline with the string players, and the meticulous preparation that preceded every performance. His manner of unfolding each work to the players at rehearsal commanded their absolute attention.

Fricsay signed his first recording contract with DGG in 1948, and in the first decade of the LP record became one of DGG's most important artists. His series of records with the RIAS, Vienna Symphony and Berlin Philharmonic Orchestras, and in the case of *Fidelio* with the Bavarian State Opera Orchestra, was a significant part of the DGG catalogue. His repertoire on records included Haydn's Symphonies Nos 44, 48, 95, 98, 100 and 101, *Te Deum* and *The Seasons*, Mozart's Symphonies Nos 29, 35, 39, 40 and 41, the *Adagio and Fugue in C minor*, *Masonic Funeral Music*, Piano Concertos K. 466, K. 459 and K. 595 (with Haskil), Rondos K. 382 and K. 386 (with Annie Fischer), Clarinet Concerto (with Geuser), *Eine kleine Nachtmusik*, *Exsultate jubilate* and *Laudate Dominum* (with Stader), Mass K. 427, *Requiem*, *Die Entführung aus dem Serail*, *Don Giovanni*, *Le nozze di Figaro* and *Die Zauberflöte*, Beethoven's Symphonies Nos 1, 3, 5, 7, 8 and 9, the overtures *Egmont* and *Leonore No. 3*, the Piano Concerto No. 3 (with Annie Fischer), Triple Concerto (with Schneiderhan, Fournier and Anda) and *Fidelio*, Schubert's Symphony No. 8, Schumann's Symphony No. 1, *Orfeo ed Euridice*, Weber's *Konzertstück* and Franck's *Symphonic Variations* (with Weber), Weber's Clarinet Concerto No. 1 (with Geuser), *Invitation to the Dance*, Rossini's *Stabat Mater*, ballet music from *Otello*, *La Boutique fantasque* and the overtures to *Il barbiere di Siviglia*, *La scala di seta*, *Tancredi*, *Semiramide*, *Il Signor Bruschino*, *Il viaggio a Reims*, *L'Italiana in Algeri* and *La gazza ladra*, Smetana's *Moldau* and *From Bohemia's Meadows and Forests*, Brahms' Piano Concerto No. 2 (with Anda), Double Concerto (with Schneiderhan and Starker) and *Variations on the St Antony Chorale*, the Mendelssohn Violin Concerto (with Schneiderhan), incidental music to *A Midsummer Night's Dream*, *Les Préludes* and the *Hungarian Rhapsodies Nos 1* and *2* of Liszt, the overture *Le Carnaval romain* and excerpts from *La Damnation de Faust*, preludes and highlighs from *Carmen*, Dvořák's Symphony No. 9 (twice, with the RIAS and Berlin Philharmonic Orchestras) and Violin Concerto (with Martzy), music of Johann Strauss, the ballet music from *Faust*, *Der fliegender Holländer*, Tchaikovsky's Symphonies Nos 4, 5 and 6, *Serenade in C major*, *1812* overture, the waltz and polonaise from *Eugene Onegin*, the waltz from *The Sleeping Beauty*, and excerpts from *Swan Lake*, *Don Juan*, *Till Eulenspiegel* and *Burleske* (with Weber), Tcherepnin's *Bagatelles*, Concertinos by Françaix and Honegger (with Weber), Ravel's *Introduction et allegro*, *Prélude à l'aprés-midi d'un faune* and *Danse sacrée et danse profane*, *Scheherazade*, Prokofiev's Symphony No. 1, Glière's Symphony No. 3 (abridged), *Le Sacre du printemps*, *Petrushka*, *Le Baiser de la fée*, *Symphony of Psalms*, *Oedipus Rex* and *Capriccio* (with Haas), the Verdi *Requiem*, dances from *Otello* and the preludes to *Aida*, *Nabucco*, *La traviata*, *La forza del destino* and *I vespri siciliani*, Mahler's *Rückert Songs* (with Forrester), Bartók's Violin Concerto No. 2 (with Várga), *Duke Bluebeard's Castle*, *Concerto for Orchestra*, *Divertimento*, *Dance Suite*, *Music for Strings, Percussion and Celesta*, *Two Portraits* (with Schulz), Piano Concertos 1, 2 and 3 and *Rhapsody* (with Anda) and the Piano Concerto No. 2 (with Haas), *Nights in the Gardens of Spain* and *Rhapsody on a Theme of Paganini* (with Weber), *In the Steppes of Central Asia*, the Polovtsian Dances from *Prince Igor*, *A Night on the Bare Mountain*, *L'Apprenti sorcier*, *Boléro*, *La Valse*, the Dance of the Hours from *La Gioconda*, Kodály's *Psalmus Hungaricus*, *Galánta Dances*, *Marosszék Dances* and *Háry Janós* suite, Sarasate's *Zigeunerweisen* (with Zacharias), Liebermann's *Furioso* and *Volkslieder Suite*, Hubay's *Hungarian Csardas Scenes*, von Einem's *Ballade*, *Capriccio* and Piano Concerto (with Herzog), Martin's *Petite Symphonie concertante*, Blacher's *Variations on a Theme of Paganini*, Egk's *Abraxas* and *Französische Suite*, the finale from Fortner's Symphony, Hartmann's Symphonies Nos 4 and 6, Hindemith's *Symphonic Dances*, and the Bruch and Glazunov Violin Concertos (with Morini).

Although Fricsay had a special love for Mozart and conducted at his concerts all the classical composers in the regular symphonic repertoire, his particular intensity and style did not favour these works. He was much more convincing in the later romantics, particularly Verdi and Tchaikovsky, in addition to modern composers such as Bartók and Stravinsky. He championed many contemporary composers, and premièred Martin's *Le Vin herbé* and Orff's *Antigonae* at Salzburg. His recordings of Haydn and Mozart were finely executed, but they were never truly distinctive in style or feeling. Similarly, the Beethoven symphonies had their grand moments, but an occasional rhythmic slackness robbed the performances of their full stature. Nevertheless, some of his recordings were sensational in their day, and the frequent re-issue of Tchaikovsky's Symphony No. 6, with its great excitement and superb phrasing, is justified even after 20 years. Other outstanding recordings were the Verdi *Requiem*, the Bartók and Kodály discs, and *Le Sacre du printemps*, which was a performance making apparent the musical rather than the barbaric qualities of the work. The operas that he recorded were amongst the earliest operatic essays on LP; *Don Giovanni* and *Le nozze di Figaro* were maybe less than perfect, but Fricsay's performances were as successful as most of the others that succeeded them. *Orpheo ed Euridice*, *Fidelio* and *Der fliegende Holländer* were also impressive, although in *Fidelio* one misses the gravity and concentration found in some of the best later recordings. In 1974 the Ferenc Fricsay Gesellschaft was founded in FR Germany, to promote the memory of his achievements through publications, sponsoring the re-issue of his recordings, promoting young conductors, and commissioning new compositions.

Fried, Oscar (1871–1941). Born in Berlin, Fried was a pupil first of Humperdinck in Frankfurt am Main and then of Scharwenka in Berlin. He played the horn in orchestras in Germany and studied musical theory, at the same time supporting himself by breeding dogs. He composed prolifically, was influenced mostly by Wagner and not at all by Brahms; one of his works was a setting for solo voices and orchestra of *Verklärte Nacht*, Dehmel's poem later made familiar by Schoenberg. In 1904 he scored a success with his choral composition *Das trunkene Lied* and his career as a conductor started in 1905 when he was appointed to lead the Stern Choral Society in Berlin. At the very first concert he presented Liszt's *The Legend of St Elizabeth*. Two years later he became the first director of the Gesellschaft der Musikfreunde in Berlin, and shortly after took over as conductor the Blüthner Orchestra, presenting concerts made up entirely of music by modern composers such as Sibelius, Delius, Borodin, Busoni and Schoenberg. He founded and directed the Berlin Symphony Orchestra, actually the same as the Blüthner Orchestra, and after two years with them (1925–6) he toured Europe, the USSR and the United States. After leaving Nazi Germany in 1934 he directed the Tiflis Opera in the USSR and later the All-Union Radio Orchestra in Moscow. He became a Soviet citizen in 1940.

Fried was a friend and confidant of Mahler. He conducted Mahler's Symphony No. 2 in the composer's presence and was assisted at the rehearsals by the young Klemperer. In Berlin he also led Mahler's Symphony No. 6 with Mahler again in the audience and Klemperer playing the celesta. In 1906 he conducted the first Russian performance of the Symphony No. 2 in St Petersburg and in 1920 directed all the Mahler symphonies in a cycle in Vienna. Along with Walter and Mengelberg, Fried was one of the very few conductors given authority by Mahler to alter the orchestration of his symphonies when demanded by the acoustics of the halls or by the qualities of the orchestras performing them. It is fascinating but ultimately inconclusive to conjecture how close to Mahler's was Fried's recorded performance of the Symphony No. 2; the records were made in 1924, some years after Mahler's death, and Fried's interpretations were notoriously changeable. Other conductors close to Mahler – Walter, Klemperer and Mengelberg in particular – have recorded their own idiosyncratic performances of Mahler symphonies, and all are remarkably unlike one another. In the first movement of the Symphony No. 2 Fried is uninhibited with his tempi variations, there are extraordinary violin glissandi, rubati and flexible tempi in the second movement, and it is noticeable that, like Walter, he does not observe the *caesura* in one of the first movement's greatest climaxes.

As a conductor Fried was an extraordinary and controversial personality. Despite the violence of his gestures, his irascibility and his limitless demands, Klemperer considered him a brilliant conductor and Mahler embraced him after a performance of his Symphony No. 2. In Germany he was better known as an interpreter of modern music than of classical and early romantic music; he had the reputation of being an uneven performer as his interpretations of the same work differed from performance to performance, although this was not unusual at the time, when conductors and other interpretive musicians were inclined to regard each performance as an improvisation. He fascinated some orchestral players, but others thought him mad. Strangely the American critic David Ewen wrote in 1936 that Fried's performances were too academic to stir very great enthusiasm, and that in the United States he gave the 'often formalistic and stilted readings of the traditional German Kapellmeister who knows his score thoroughly but who has very little either in personality or in insight to contribute to it'. (*The Man with the Baton*, New York, 1936, p. 257.) Something must have happened on the trip across the Atlantic.

As a recording artist, Fried also had a remarkable career. Before World War I he appeared in a film, conducting the complete *Symphonie fantastique*, which was made by the Messter Film Company in Berlin. In 1924 he conducted the Berlin State Opera Orchestra *et al.* for Polydor in sets of Bruckner's Symphony No. 7 and Mahler's Symphony No. 2, the latter on 22 sides, as well as Beethoven's Symphonies Nos 2 and 3 and Brahms' Symphony No. 1. Later he recorded for Polydor Beethoven's Symphony No. 9, *Eine kleine Nachtmusik*, Wagner's *Faust Overture*, the two *Peer Gynt* suites and an aria from *Der Freischütz* (with the Berlin State Opera Orchestra), *Les Préludes* and *Mazeppa*, *Scheherazade* and *L'Oiseau de feu* (with the Berlin Philharmonic Orchestra), and for Columbia Tchaikovsky's Symphony No. 6 and suites from *Nutcracker* and *Sylvia* (with the Royal Philharmonic Orchestra for Columbia). Writing in 1969, in *The Gramophone*, Roger Wimbush said that the performance of *Les Préludes* had never been surpassed. The Bruckner and Mahler symphonies have been re-issued on LP transfers by the Bruno Walter Society in the United States, and *L'Oiseau de feu* was included in the album *The Early Days* of DGG. In 1971 Melodiya released a two-disc commemorative album on the centenary of Fried's birth and it included a live concert recording of him conducting the USSR State Symphony Orchestra in *Symphonie fantastique*.

Friisholm, Lavard (b. 1912). The Danish conductor Friisholm started his career as a violinist in the Erling Bloch Quartet, and in 1914 was a co-founder of the Collegium Musicum in Copenhagen. He has also been chairman and conductor of the Society of Young Musicians, and is artistic director of the Randers City Orchestra. His recordings include Bach's Two-Harpsichord Concertos BWV 1060, BWV 1061 and BWV 1062 (with Viderø and Sørensen), and Three-Harpsichord Concerto BWV 1063 (with Viderø, Sørensen and Møller, and the Collegium Musicum for Haydn Society), Handel's *Concertos for Orchestra in B flat* and *F major* (with the Collegium Musicum for Parliament), Scheibe's *Passion Cantata*, Borup-Jørgensen's *Nordic Summer Pastoral*, Holm's *Pezzo concertante*, Olsen's Sinfonia and *Schicksalslieder von Hölderlin*, and Bentzon's *Symphonic Trio* (with the Collegium Musicum for EMI).

Froment, Louis de (b. 1921). De Froment studied at the School of Music at his birthplace, Toulouse, then attended the Paris Conservatoire where his teachers were Fourestier, Bigot and Cluytens, and in 1948 was awarded first prize for conducting. He founded his own chamber orchestra with the flautist Jean-Pierre Rampal the first soloist, and together they toured Europe. He became musical director at the Vichy Opera, of the Nice-Côte d'Azur Symphony Orchestra, and of the Orchestre Lyrique in Paris, then was appointed permanent conductor of the Luxembourg Radio Orchestra (1958). He has toured in Western and Eastern Europe, North and Central America, and has been a prodigious recording artist, having made more than 120 LP records for many companies.

In the early years of LP, de Froment recorded for L'Oiseau Lyre with an orchestra called the L'Oiseau Lyre Orchestral Ensemble. The works recorded included Muffat's *Florilegie* II, Suite I, Lully's ballet *Le Temple de la paix*, Delalande's *Symphonies pour les soupers du Roy* (2nd series), *Caprice-Fantaisie No. 2* and *Concert de trompettes pour les festes sur le canal de Versailles*, Rameau's *Les Indes galantes*, excerpts from *Dardanus*, *Platée* suite, two gavottes from *Zaïs* and a sarabande from *Zéphyre*, Durante's *Harpsichord Concerto in B flat* (with Gerlin), Albinoni's Oboe Concerto Op. 9 No. 2 (with Pierlot), Paisiello's *Harpsichord Concerto in C* (with Gerlin), Fischer's *Le Journal de printemps*, Auletta's *Concerto in G* (with Gerlin, Rampal, Alès, and Doukan), Mancini's *Concerto a quattro in E minor*, Vivaldi's Violin Concerto P. 407 (with Alès), Cello Concerto P. 434 (with Albin), Violin and Cello Concerto P. 388 (with Alès and Albin), Oboe Concertos Op. 8 No. 9 and P. 306 (with Maisonneuve) and Concertos P. 135, P. 235, P. 292 and P. 406, Marcello's *Oboe Concerto in C minor*, A. Scarlatti's *Oboe Concerto in F* and Vivaldi's Oboe Concerto Op. 8 No. 12 (with Pierlot), C. P. E. Bach's *Flute Concertos in A minor* and *G major* (with Rampal), J. S. Bach's Violin and Oboe Concerto (with Alès and Pierlot), J. C. Bach's Sinfonia No. 4 and Sinfonia concertante, Mozart's Symphonies Nos 2 to 11, Sinfonia Concertante K. 297b and Clarinet Concerto (with Lancelot), Pleyel's Sinfonia Concertante No. 5, Gossec's *Symphony in E flat*, Weber's Clarinet Concerto No. 1 (with Lancelot) and Bassoon Concerto (with Hongne), Françaix's *Invocation* and Martin's Harpsichord Concerto (with Nef). He also recorded Vivaldi's Flute Concertos Op. 10 (with Rampal and a chamber orchestra for Felsted). Many of these records, such as those of dance music from the operas of Rameau, were especially successful.

After his appointment with the Luxembourg Radio Orchestra, de Froment made numerous records with them, principally for Vox, many of which were released on Turnabout and Candide. Included were the complete orchestral works of Debussy, on six LPs, as well as the Piano Fantasia (with Dosse), Clarinet Rhapsody (with Dangain) and Saxophone Rhapsody (with Londeix), Ravel's two Piano Concertos (with Simon), *Valses nobles et sentimentales*, *Nights in the Gardens of Spain* (with Sandor), Fauré's *Ballade* and *Fantaisie* (with Johannesen) and *Pelléas et Mélisande*, Mendelssohn's Piano Concerto No. 1 and Schumann's Piano Concerto (with Firkusny), Mendelssohn's and Tchaikovsky's Violin Concertos (with Rosand), Grieg's Piano Concerto (with Soon-Kin Wong), Tchaikovsky's Piano Concerto No. 3 and Hiller's *Piano Concerto in F sharp* (with Ponti), Saint-Saëns' Symphonies Nos 1, 2 and 3, five Piano Concertos, *Africa*, *Rapsodie d'Auvergne* and *Wedding Cake* (with Tacchino), *Danse macabre*, *La Jeunesse d'Hercule*, *Phaéton*, *Le Rouet d'Omphale*, the *Henry VIII* ballet music, Cello Concerto No. 1 and *Allegro appassionato* (with Varga), and *Morceau de concert* and Harp Fantasy (with Michel), Satie's *Parade* and *Relâche*, Schumann's *Introduction and Allegro in G* (with Ponti, Chabrier's *España*, *Gwendoline* overture, *Fête polonaise*, *Danse slave*, *Habanera*, *Marche joyeuse* and *Suite pastorale*, Prokofiev's Symphony No. 1, five Piano Concertos (with Tacchino), two Violin Concertos (with Ricci), Sinfonia concertante (with Varga) and suites from *Romeo and Juliet* and *The Love of Three Oranges*, Violin Concertos of Ernst, Hubay and Joachim, Ysaÿe's *Chant d'hiver*, Hubay's *Heire Kati* and Godard's *Concerto romantique* (with Rosand), Ravel's *Tzigane*, Rimsky-Korsakov's *Fantasia*, Sarasate's *Airs bohémiens*, Wieniawski's *Fantaisie*, *Légende* and *Souvenir de Moscou*, Chausson's *Poème*, Berlioz's *Rêverie et caprice*, and the prelude to Saint-Saëns' *Le Déluge* (with Fantanarosa), Chopin's Piano Concerto No. 2 and *Andante spianato and Grande Polonaise* (with Rigutto), and Kemmer's *The Lions' Concerto* and *Concerto rotarienne* (with Kemmer).

De Froment's other recordings include Tomasi's Trumpet Concerto (with André), Chaynes' Trumpet Concerto (with André) and *Four Illustrations for the Jade Flute* (with Rampal, and the Luxembourg Radio Orchestra for Musical Heritage Society); Cimarosa's *Il maestro di capella* (with Cortis) and Oboe Concerto (with Maisonneuve and the Paris Instrumental Ensemble for CBS); *Symphonie fantastique*, Dvořák's Symphony No. 9, and the preludes to *Die Meistersinger* and Acts I and III of *Lohengrin*, the overture to *Der fliegende Holländer*, and the prelude and Liebestod from *Tristan und Isolde* (with the Luxembourg Radio Orchestra for CBS); Rousseau's opera *Le Devin du village* (with the Froment Orchestra *et al.* for EMI); Gluck's *Orphée* (with the Aix-en-Provence Festival Choir and Concert Society Orchestra *et al.* for EMI); *Die Zauberflöte* (in French, with the Colonne Orchestra *et al.* for EMI); Straus's *Ein Walzertraum* (for EMI); Strauss's two Horn Concertos (with Bourgue) and Rodrigo's *Concierto de Aranjuez* (with Dentroh and the Luxembourg Radio Orchestra for Decca); Haydn's Horn Concerto No. 2 and Michael Haydn's Horn Concerto (with Bourgue, and the Luxembourg Radio Orchestra for IPG); Rameau's *Six Concertos en sextuor* and Semenoff's *Le Compagnon de Voyage* (with the Luxembourg Radio Orchestra for Philips); concertos by Pergolesi, Telemann, Vivaldi, Handel, Corelli and Haydn, the Shostakovich Piano Concerto No. 1 (with Joye), Despard's Symphony and Roussel's Sinfonietta and *Le Marchand de sable qui passe* (with the Paris Instrumental Ensemble *et al.* for Allegro); Guénin's Symphony No. 2 (with the Luxembourg Radio Orchestra for Oiselet); Bartók's Viola Concerto (with Lemoire) and *Divertimento* (with the Paris Instrumental Ensemble for Club National du Disque); flute concertos by Ibert and Rivier (with Rampal and the Lamoureux Orchestra for Music Guild); and Landowski's *Les Adieux* (with the Luxembourg Radio Orchestra for La Guilde Internationale du Disque).

Of all de Froment's records, the Debussy collection, which is claimed to be all the composer's orchestral music, is by far his most ambitious project; the music has some of the greatest masterpieces of the 20th century, which have been recorded by many of the leading conductors and orchestras. De Froment and his orchestra can scarcely compare with these. The Vox set comprises six discs, but the problem has not been satisfactorily solved as to what should be included and what omitted of the orchestrations of the piano pieces by other hands; *La Boîte à joujoux* was recorded, but the *Children's Corner* and *Petite Suite*, orchestrated by Caplet and Busser respectively when Debussy was alive, are excluded. As in all de Froment's recorded performances with the Luxembourg orchestra, the Debussy works vary in competence; at best they are stylish and good, but at worst the orchestra's standard of execution is no better than provincial. In many of these pieces, de Froment has difficulty keeping the music flowing and maintaining atmosphere in slow tempi, but in *Jeux*, with its strong rhythms, these problems disappear.

Froschauer, Helmuth (b. 1933). Born at Wiener Neustadt, Austria, Froschauer was a member of the Vienna Boys' Choir, studied at the Vienna Academy of Music, and made his debut as a conductor in 1957 at Buenos Aires. He has since conducted at the Vienna State Opera, with the Vienna Singverein der Gesellschaft der Musikfreunde, and at festivals at Salzburg, Berlin and Bregenz. In the 1970s he recorded Field's Piano Concerto No. 1 and Hummel's *Rondo brilliant on a Russian Folk Theme* (with Blumental and the Prague Chamber Orchestra for RCA), Field's Piano Concerto No. 3 and Czerny's *Piano Concerto in A minor* (with Blumental and the Vienna Chamber Orchestra for Turnabout), Liszt's *Rhapsodie espagnole* (with Blumental and the Prague Chamber Orchestra for Turnabout), Paderewski's Piano Concerto and Rubinstein's *Konzertstück* (with Blumental and the Vienna Pro Musica Orchestra for Turnabout), K. Stamitz's three Orchestral Quartets Op. 4 Nos 1, 4 and 6, Albinoni's *Sinfonias in D*, *G* and *G* and Sonata Op. 2 No. 3, Haydn's *Symphony B in B flat* and overtures *La fedeltà premiata*, *Orlando Paladino*, *Lo speziale*, *Acide* and *Overture in D*, and Mozart's Piano Concertos K. 238 and K. 459 (with Kann), K. 246 and K. 537 (with Foster), K. 271 and K. 491 (with Battista), K. 451 and K. 595 (with Abram), and K. 453, K. 467, K. 488 and K. 503 (with List, and the Vienna Chamber Orchestra, for Musical Heritage Society).

Frotzheim, Herbert (b. 1912). Born in Kevelaer am Niederrhein, where his father was an artist and singer and his mother a pianist, Frotzheim studied at Frankfurt am Main, and in Berlin with Rother and Thomas. He returned to Berlin after World War II, conducted the Berlin Radio Chorus (1947–8), formed the RIAS Chamber Chorus and worked with Fricsay, then chief conductor of the RIAS Symphony Orchestra, in choral and operatic performances. He was a professor at the Hochschule für Musik in Freiburg (from 1955) and was deputy director and member of the Selection Commission for Musicians at the German Academic Exchange Service at Bonn (1974–7). In addition to collaborating with Fricsay in the latter's recordings of *Der fliegende Holländer*, the Verdi *Requiem*, *A Midsummer Night's Dream*, *Die Entführung aus dem Serail* and the *Symphony of Psalms*, he recorded himself, between 1960 and 1964, Mozart's *Missa Brevis* K. 275 and Schubert's *Mass in G major* (with the Freiburg School of Music Chorus and Orchestra *et al.* for Christophorus, issued in the United States by Decca), and Stravinsky's *Mass*, *Credo*, *Pater Noster* and *Ave Maria* (with members of the South West German Radio Orchestra *et al.* for Christophorus).

Frühbeck de Burgos, Rafael (b. 1933). Son of a Spanish mother and a German father, who settled in Burgos, Frühbeck added the 'de Burgos' to his name to identify himself as a Spaniard. He first took violin lessons at the age of seven, performed in public at twelve, as a youth played in a local orchestra and conducted student ensembles. After attending the conservatories at Bilbao and Madrid, he studied law at Madrid University and conducted zarzuelas at small Madrid theatres. He was in the Spanish army for three years when he was a bandmaster at Santander (1953–6). From 1956 to 1958 he was at the Hochschule für Musik at Munich studying with Lessing and Eichhorn, and on his return to Spain became conductor of the Bilbao Municipal Symphony Orchestra (1959–62). In 1962 he succeeded Argenta as conductor of the Spanish National Orchestra at Madrid and became widely known in Europe and later in North and South America as a guest conductor. His other appointments, in addition to the Spanish National Orchestra, have been general music director of the Düsseldorf Symphony Orchestra (1966–71) and music director of the Montreal Symphony Orchestra in Canada (1975–6).

After Argenta's death in 1958 Frühbeck de Burgos emerged as the leading Spanish conductor, and has won a worldwide reputation not only as an interpreter of Spanish music but for his performances of the repertoire from Bach to Stravinsky. He was the first to perform the complete *St Matthew Passion* in Spain, and in his regular concerts in Madrid he includes *avant-garde* music of Spanish and other composers. The one conductor who has impressed him most was Knappertsbusch, whom he heard often at Munich; Knappertsbusch, says Frühbeck, conducted concerts without rehearsals, and the result could be either disastrous or a sublime experience. Frühbeck de Burgos himself conducts mostly from memory, but does not memorise contemporary pieces which he expects to perform only once. He has found that recording is the surest way to become familiar with a work, although his successful recording of *Elijah* and the many performances of the oratorio which he was later called on to give, somewhat jaded his enthusiasm for it. He feels at home with orchestras on both sides of the Atlantic, and of all he considers the Berlin Philharmonic and the Philadelphia Orchestras the most exciting to conduct. The problem of attracting young people to concerts of classical music he finds to be only true in the United

States, and says this probably is due to the way in which orchestras are organised and financed there. With his orchestra in Madrid a third of each series is open to the public and not to subscribers, and the average age of the audience would be in the early twenties. This is, he says, a common experience in Europe. (Personal interview, December 1975.)

Counting the 40 or so zarzuelas he has recorded for Spanish Columbia, Frühbeck de Burgos has made over 80 records, for EMI, Decca, DGG and Alhambra. Since his first one in the mid 1960s his recorded performances have been of a consistently high standard. Foremost are his discs of Spanish music: *El amor brujo* (with Mistral and the New Philharmonia Orchestra for EMI), *La vida breve* (with Los Angeles *et al.* and the Spanish National Orchestra for EMI), Halffter's *Rapsodia española* (with Soriano) Esplá's *Don Quixote*, Ohana's Guitar Concerto and Rodrigo's *Fantasía para un gentilhombre* (with Yepès and the Spanish Orchestra for Decca), *Nights in the Gardens of Spain* (with Soriano) and Turina's *Danzas fantásticas* (with the Paris Conservatoire Orchestra for EMI), guitar concertos by Rodrigo and Giuliani (with Diaz and the Spanish National Orchestra for EMI), Parish-Alvars' Harp Concerto (with Zabaleta and the Spanish National Orchestra for EMI), Ohana's *Trois graphiques* and Ruiz-Pipo's *Peintures* (with Yepès and the London Symphony Orchestra for DGG), Falla's *Atlantida* (with the Spanish National Orchestra *et al.* for EMI), Arriaga's Sinfonia and overture, *Los Esclavos felices*, Torróba's *Homenaje a la Seguedilla* and *Luisa Fernanda*, Bacarisse's Guitar Concerto (with Yepès), Vives' *Bohemios*, Halffter's Violin Concerto (with Martin) and Rodrigo's Cello Concerto (with Corostola, and with the Spanish National Orchestra for Alhambra), and a *Suite española* (with the New Philharmonia Orchestra for Decca) which is his own arrangement of pieces by Albéniz. One may add, perhaps, *Carmen* (with the Paris Opéra Orchestra *et al.* for EMI).

Of his other records many have been outstanding, such as the Mozart *Requiem* (with the New Philharmonia Orchestra *et al.* for Decca), Schumann's Symphony No. 3 (with the London Symphony Orchestra for Decca) and *Le Pélerinage de la rose* (with the Düsseldorf Symphony Orchestra *et al.* for EMI), *Elijah* (with the New Philharmonia Orchestra *et al.* for EMI) and *St Paul* (with the Düsseldorf Symphony Orchestra *et al.* for EMI) and *Carmina Burana* (with the New Philharmonia Orchestra *et al.* for EMI). His approach to each piece is entirely fresh and where he feels so he does not hesitate to discard tradition. Before his recording of *Elijah* he studied the score carefully with Wilhelm Pitz, the then chorusmaster of the New Philharmonia Chorus, and established a reading in which tempi were faster than usually accepted in England. He insisted on a true flamenco singer for *El amor brujo*, certain that the music was written for that particular voice. In *Carmen* he went back to the original spoken dialogue, and in *Carmina Burana* he sought to avoid a romantic approach to the music, emphasising more the poetry of the words.

The remainder of Frühbeck de Burgos' records include Beethoven's Piano Concerto No. 4 (with Bishop-Kovacevich and the New Philharmonia Orchestra for World Record Club), the overture to *A Midsummer Night's Dream* (with the London Symphony Orchestra for Decca), *Le Sacre du printemps*, Prokofiev's Symphony No. 1, the intermezzo to *Goyescas*, *Pavane pour une infante défunte*, *Alborada del gracioso*, *Pini di Roma* and *Fontane di Roma*, Stravinsky's *Feux d'artifice* and *Circus Polka*, Rossini's Clarinet Variations, Weber's Clarinet Concertino and Clarinet Concerto No. 1 (with de Peyer), the Dvořák and Glazunov Violin Concertos and Prokofiev's Violin Concertos Nos 1 and 2 (with Milstein) and *Daphnis et Chloé* (with the New Philharmonia Orchestra *et al.* for EMI), a song recital with de los Angeles (with the Sinfonia of London for EMI), Bruch's *Violin Concerto in G minor* and Mendelssohn's in E minor (with Voccou and the London Symphony Orchestra for Decca), Franck's *Symphonic Variations* and Khachaturian's Piano Concerto (with Larrocha and the London Philharmonic Orchestra for Decca), *España* and *Boléro* (with the New Philharmonia Orchestra for Decca), Falla's Harpsichord Concerto (with Soriano *et al.* for World Record Club), and Mendelssohn's *Violin Concertos in E minor* and *D minor* (with Menuhin and the London Symphony Orchestra for EMI).

Frykberg, Sten (b. 1910). Born in Göteborg, Frykberg studied at the Sonderhausen Conservatory and in England and in the United States. After conducting at Göteborg, Gävle and Hälsingborg, he became a conductor with the Stockholm Radio Orchestra (1945–60), of the Göteborg Symphony Orchestra (1960–67), and again of the Stockholm Radio Orchestra (after 1967). He recorded the overture to Berwald's *Estrella de Soria* (with the Stockholm Opera Orchestra for Decca, on a 78 r.p.m. disc), Wiklund's Piano Concerto No. 1 (with Ehrling and the Stockholm Concert Association Orchestra for HMV, on 78s), Larsson's

Violin Concerto (with Gertler), Blomdahl's *Pastoral Suite*, Fernström's *Concertino*, Morales' *Gamacho's Wedding* and overture *Abu Casems tofflor* (with the Swedish Radio Orchestra for Decca), Stenhammar's *Sentimental Romance* (with Kyndel and the Stockholm Radio Orchestra for Radio Ganst), Atterberg's Symphony No. 4, Agrell's *Sinfonia*, Larsson's *Four Vignettes*, and an overture by Henneberg (with the Norrköping Orchestra).

Fuchs, Johannes (b. 1903). Born in Schwende, Switzerland, Fuchs graduated from the Zürich Conservatory (1925–8), and then studied singing. He became a choral conductor, assisted Schuricht in preparing Beethoven's *Missa Solemnis*, conducted choirs in Zürich and Baden, and in 1929 founded the Zürich Chamber Choir. He was conductor and organist at Baden (1937–45), conductor at the cathedral at St Gallen (1945); with the Zürich Chamber Choir he performed the great choral masterpieces as well as contemporary Swiss works, and toured internationally. His recordings include Barberini's *Iste est qui ante Deum* (with the St Gallen Cathedral Choir, for Fono) and Jenny's *Lauda anima mea* (with the Zürich Chamber Choir for CT, Switzerland).

Fuente, Luis Herrara de la (b. 1916). Born in Mexico, Fuente studied at the University of Mexico and with Scherchen in Switzerland, and started his career as a pianist and artistic director of the university radio in Mexico City. He founded and conducted the University Radio Chamber Orchestra (1946), was assistant conductor of the National Symphony Orchestra of Mexico (1949–50) and founder and conductor of the chamber orchestra of the National Institute of Fine Arts (1951). He was resident conductor of the National Symphony Orchestra of Mexico (1954–72), toured with the orchestra in the United States (1956) and Europe (1958), was resident conductor of the Symphony Orchestra of Chile (1959), the Patronage Chamber Orchestra in Mexico City (1961), resident conductor of the National Symphony Orchestra of Peru (1965–71), conducted at the first Casals Festival held in El Salvador (1968), and was conductor of the first cycle of Wagner operas at the Mexican Opera (1971). He has been a guest conductor with orchestras and at festivals in Canada, the US, Latin America, Europe and New Zealand, and has received many awards and distinctions in Mexico and elsewhere. He recorded Revueltas' *Homenaje a Federico García Lorca*, Moncayo's *Huapango*, Ayala's *Tribú* and Galindo's *Sones mariachi* (with the Mexican National Symphony Orchestra for EMI).

Furst, János (b. 1935). Born in Budapest, Furst studied at the Franz Liszt Academy, the Paris Conservatoire and the Brussels Academy, then settled in Ireland where he became a violin soloist and orchestral leader. In 1963 he formed the Irish Chamber Orchestra, in 1971 made his debut in London with the London Mozart Players, and toured Portugal with the Royal Philharmonic Orchestra. In 1972 he substituted for Kempe in a performance of Beethoven's Symphony No. 9 with the Royal Philharmonic in London and his success on that occasion led to many British and overseas engagements. In 1974 he was appointed chief conductor of the Malmö Orchestra and was invited to become the chief conductor of the Cape Town Symphony Orchestra. Furst has recorded a disc of orchestral music from the Tchaikovsky operas *The Voyevode*, *The Oprichnik* and *Mazeppa* (with the Bamberg Symphony Orchestra for Turnabout), Schumann's Piano Concerto, *Introduction and Allegro appassionato* and *Introduction and Allegro* (with Frankl and the Bamberg Symphony Orchestra for Turnabout), and Tchaikovsky's *Nutcracker* suite and Rosenberg's *Sinfonia concertante* (with the Malmö Symphony Orchestra for Lyssna).

Furtwängler, Wilhelm (1886–1954). Son of Adolf Furtwängler, a distinguished professor of archaeology, Furtwängler was born in Berlin, spent his childhood in Munich, and was given a private education. He studied music under Rheinberger, von Schillings and Beer-Walbrunn, and conducting with Mottl; at his very first concert with the Kaim Orchestra in Munich, at the age of 20, he conducted his own first symphony and Bruckner's Symphony No. 9, which was then not well known. He continued to compose throughout his life, but realised that conducting would be his destiny when he found out that people did not understand or appreciate his music. After experience at Breslau, with Mottl in Zürich and Pfitzner in Strasbourg, he succeeded Abendroth at Lübeck (1911–15), Bodanzky at Mannheim (1915–19), where he directed both opera and symphony concerts, and Mengelberg at the Frankfurt Museum Concerts, was engaged by the Vienna Tonkünstlerverein for a series of concerts (1919–21), was conductor of the Berlin Staatskapelle (1920–22), and followed Strauss as music director of the Berlin State Opera (1919). Then, in 1922, at the age of 36, he replaced Nikisch as music director of the Berlin Philharmonic and Leipzig Gewandhaus

Orchestras, remaining with the latter until 1928. He appeared in England in 1924–5, in the United States in 1925–7, conducted the New York Philharmonic Orchestra (1927–9), toured in Buenos Aires, Cairo, Paris, Brussels and Lucerne. He was offered the directorship of the New York Philharmonic, but declined it; in 1928 he was appointed musical director of the Vienna Philharmonic Orchestra in succession to Weingartner; he brought the Berlin Philharmonic to London, conducted at the Salzburg and Bayreuth Fesitvals (1931–2), was awarded the Goethe Gold Medal (1932), became musical director of the Berlin State Opera (1933), and conducted *The Ring* at Covent Garden (1937).

When the Nazis came to power in 1933, Furtwängler soon found himself in conflict with them. He resigned from his positions with the Berlin Philharmonic Orchestra, the Berlin State Opera and the Reichsmusikkammer, of which he had, for a short time, been deputy president. The Nazi condemnation of Hindemith, and later Rheinhardt, Schnabel, Klemperer and Walter aroused his opposition, and he succeeded in protecting many musicians or their wives who were being persecuted by the Nazis. During the entire period of the Nazi regime he remained in Germany, except for tours, and took up again the directorship of the Berlin Philharmonic Orchestra (1935). He was offered the post of permanent conductor of the New York Philharmonic Orchestra in 1936, but hostility to him in the US because of his association with the Nazis caused him to decline; later, in 1949, a similar attempt to appoint him conductor of the Chicago Symphony Orchestra came to nothing. During the war he would not leave Germany, as the Nazis would not have allowed him to return; he was opposed to the regime, but proud of being a German. At the very end of the war, Speer, the Nazi minister for armaments and war production, who frequently attended Furtwängler's concerts in Berlin, advised him to go to Switzerland when he was leaving for an engagement in Vienna, as Speer had reason to fear for his safety. After the war, Furtwängler was absolved by the Allied Kommandatur of any Nazi sympathies; in the last decade of his life he conducted the Berlin Philharmonic and Vienna Philharmonic Orchestras, was a guest conductor in London, Copenhagen, Paris and Buenos Aires, conducted at the Lucerne, Salzburg and Edinburgh Festivals, and led Beethoven's Symphony No. 9 at the Bayreuth Festival in 1951; but he never returned to the United States. Switzerland was his final home. His widow has said that he died a tortured man, ashamed of what Germany had done, and depressed because of a worsening impairment of his hearing.

Even during his lifetime, Furtwängler was a legend. He saw himself as the embodiment of the German romantic tradition, particularly as it is expressed in Beethoven, Brahms and Bruckner. He possessed an almost mystical belief that music is the revelation of the human soul. Early in his career he became famous for his performances of Beethoven; he perceived in the sonata-form structure of Beethoven and Brahms the tragic element of all great music which results from the clash of the heroic and lyrical elements from which it is constructed. He once remarked that Bruckner was not primarily a musician at all, but a descendant of the great German mystics, and in the words of Walter Abendroth, 'he performed the Bruckner symphonies as if they were the ritual of a non-denominational religion which had found its expression in the music of the 19th century'. In his concert programmes between 1911 and 1940 he conducted Beethoven 1,045 times, of which the Symphony No. 5 appeared most frequently. Brahms was included in his programmes 519 times, and far behind came Haydn (200) and Mozart (173).

Furtwängler's style was essentially improvisatory and was at the opposite pole to Toscanini's, with whom he is traditionally contrasted. Perhaps Toscanini's influence, in the long run, has been greater, because his precision and objectivity can be more easily followed than Furtwängler's subjectivity, which must come from the artist's own perception and sensitivity. Toscanini himself could not tolerate Furtwängler as a man or musician, and he is held by some to be mainly responsible for barring Furtwängler from performing in New York after World War II. Furtwängler thought more about the works he interpreted than most musicians and his knowledge of the scores he conducted was exhaustive. Two idiosyncracies marked him off: his indecisive beat, and his varying tempi within movements. His baton technique has been described as insecure and uncertain, perhaps reflecting his indecision in personal, artistic and political affairs. But this lack of clarity was, in some measure, deliberate, for it produced the diffused and full string sound and the expressive intensity on the part of the players that he was seeking. There is a story of a concertmaster who watched his wavering baton preparing for the upbeat, and said 'Courage, maestro'. He did not determine his tempo modifications before a performance: Barenboim, who was greatly influenced by Furtwängler, has said that 'he was one of the few musicians who managed an equilibrium between intellectual understanding and a spontaneous feeling at the actual performance. He managed to rehearse in such a way that gave him the freedom to do things in the evening that were quite different from the preparations; but the basic principles of his interpretation were always well established. He was able to perceive structure without limiting his emotional response' (*The Gramophone*, May 1976). Nevertheless, as convincing as these tempi modifications may have been in performance, they are inevitably disconcerting in a record or a broadcast, where the essential element of communication between the interpreter and his audience is missing. Furtwängler realised this; he believed that the mechanical processes involved in recording were unsympathetic to inspired musical performance, and had little interest in recording techniques. He knew that his performances were inseparable from the mood of the occasion, and that more often than not they would sound eccentric or even perverse on a permanent record; many of the broadcast performances issued on record since his death could be regarded as too idiosyncratic to survive in this form. It was not until he recorded *Tristan und Isolde* with Flagstad and Suthaus and the Philharmonia Orchestra, a year before his death, that he acknowledged the value of the gramophone. He also had a reputation for slow tempi, but this was not always justified, for although he slowed down for moments of great poignancy, he hurried through passages he found less interesting, particularly in opera. His *Ring*, altogether, is faster than Solti's, and his *Parsifal* was the fastest ever. Even so, his readings did become slower as he grew older. For him orchestral tone was based on the lower instruments, especially the bassoon.

Some of Furtwängler's compositions have appeared on gramophone records. His Symphony No. 2 in which he conducted the Berlin Philharmonic Orchestra was issued on mono LP by DGG and was re-issued in 1977. It is a curious work of great length and is almost a summation of romantic music, with overtones of Brahms, Bruckner and Tchaikovsky. His piano concerto has been revived by Barenboim, whose performance with the Los Angeles Philharmonic Orchestra under Mehta has been available on a private label. Barenboim himself said that 'you must listen to it with your hat on, so that you can doff it as you meet César Franck, Bruckner, Tchaikovsky, Wagner and Strauss in it, but then you suddenly realise that most of these composers didn't write a piano concerto, and this work fills some kind of gap' (*The Gramophone*, May 1976). It is sombre, doom-laden music, and the second movement, which Edwin Fischer had previously recorded with Furtwängler, is almost a paraphrase of Bruckner. Musical Heritage Society have also released Furtwängler's *Violin Sonata in D major*, a 47-minute work in two movements, performed by Müller-Nishio and Dennemarck.

Furtwängler's records before World War II were relatively few, compared to many of his famous contemporaries. His first were the *Der Freischütz* overture and Beethoven's Symphony No. 5, with the Berlin Philharmonic Orchestra for Polydor, in 1926. For the same company with the Berlin Philharmonic he went on to record the *Brandenburg Concerto No. 3*, *Eine kleine Nachtmusik*, the Hungarian March from *La Damnation de Faust*, *Invitation to the Dance*, the Cavatina from Beethoven's String Quartet Op. 130, the prelude to Act I of *Lohengrin*, Brahms' *Hungarian Dances Nos 1* and *10*, *Till Eulenspiegel* and the overtures *Die Entführung aus dem Serail*, *Le nozze di Figaro*, *Il barbiere di Siviglia*, *A Midsummer Night's Dream*, *La gazza ladra*, *Hebrides* and *Die Fledermaus*. But his most highly praised prewar discs were those that he made for HMV when the Berlin Philharmonic visited London in 1938: Beethoven's Symphony No. 5, Tchaikovsky's Symphony No. 6, the prelude and Good Friday Music from *Parsifal*, and the prelude and Liebestod from *Tristan und Isolde*. In fact, many critics regarded this *Pathétique* as one of the finest 78 r.p.m. sets ever, and it has often been re-issued on LP transfers. He made many exceptional LP records, which are now treasured memories of his art. First is the *Tristan und Isolde* mentioned above, a performance of intense and lyrical beauty, and unquestionably one of the very greatest operatic realisations on disc. His Beethoven Symphony No. 9 was recorded at the first Bayreuth Festival after World War II in 1951, and is a titanic, monumental performance. Furtwängler however was not satisfied with this recording. But he was, for once, pleased with one of the Symphony No. 9 which he made with the Philharmonia Orchestra in London in 1954 and which for some unexplained reason has not been released. After this performance he told his wife: 'This time, I had one foot in the other world' (*Los Angeles Times*, 17 December 1972). In 1954 he also began to record a complete *Ring* for EMI with the Vienna Philharmonic Orchestra *et al.* but *Die Walküre* was all that resulted from this project and was, indeed, his last studio recording. There exist, however, three other recordings of the complete *Ring* cycle conducted by him, the 1937–8 Covent Garden production, the 1950 performance at

La Scala, and the recordings made in the RAI studios in Rome in late 1953 for radio transmission. For this latter enterprise the finest musicians were culled from all the Italian orchestras and the best German singers were assembled; each act, and *Das Rheingold* complete, were broadcast without interruption after it had been rehearsed and performed. After protracted and difficult negotiations these performances were released by EMI in 1972, and while the quality of the recording itself and the orchestral playing in no way compete with the stereo recordings of *The Ring* by Solti, Böhm and Karajan, Furtwängler conducts with the greatest insight and understanding of this vast score. The reviving of the set resulted in an unexpected commercial success, and even taking into account the earlier *Tristan und Isolde*, it is the best example of his genius as a conductor. Deryck Cooke's comment about the performance is illuminating; he said that Furtwängler saw *The Ring* as a 'stark, heavy, brooding work, a profound tragedy set in a primitive world of ancient gods and heroes. He brings out the meaning of every detail in the score, and has the ability to make the music surge, or seethe, or melt – a great spiritual experience' (*The Gramophone*, October 1976). The La Scala *Ring* was taken from tapes of a performance in 1950. Other operas that have been released on record have also, in the main, been derived from tapes of performances at post-war Salzburg Festivals, and are *Fidelio*, *Der Freischütz*, *Don Giovanni*, *Le nozze di Figaro* and *Otello*, and a *Die Meistersinger* from the 1943 Bayreuth Festival.

After World War II, Furtwängler recorded for EMI, DGG and Decca, first on 78 r.p.m. discs and later on mono LP; almost all of these discs have been re-issued since and many are still available. In addition to the operas noted above, there were included (with the Vienna Philharmonic Orchestra for EMI) Haydn's Symphony No. 94, Mozart's Symphony No. 40 *Eine kleine Nachtmusik* and the Serenade K. 361, Beethoven's Symphonies Nos 1, 3, 4, 5, 6 and 7, *Fidelio*, the overtures *Coriolan*, *Leonore Nos 2* and *3*, Brahms' Symphony No. 1, the *Variations on the St Antony Chorale* and the *Hungarian Dances Nos 1*, *3* and *10*, Schubert's Symphony No. 8 and the overture, Ballet Music No. 2 and Entr'acte No. 3 from *Rosamunde*, *Don Juan*, *Till Eulenspiegel* and *Tod und Verklärung*, *Les Préludes*, Tchaikovsky's Symphony No. 4 and the waltz and finale from the *Serenade in C major*, *Moldau*, Johann Strauss's *Pizzicato Polka* and *Kaiserwalzer*, the *Siegfried Idyll*, Dawn, Siegfried's Rhine Journey and Funeral Music from *Götterdämmerung*, the Ride of the Valkyries from *Die Walküre*, the preludes to Acts I and III and the Dance of the Apprentices from *Die Meistersinger* and the overture to *Der fliegende Holländer*, and the overtures to *Alceste*, *Iphigénie en Aulide*, *Anacreon*, *Oberon*, *The Merry Wives of Windsor*, *Manfred* and *Hebrides*. He also recorded Beethoven's Piano Concerto No. 5 (with Edwin Fischer), the Violin Concerto and two Romances (with Menuhin), Mahler's *Lieder eines fahrenden Gesellen* (with Fischer-Dieskau), the closing scene from *Götterdämmerung* (with Flagstad) and Bartók's Violin Concerto No. 2 (with Menuhin, and the Philharmonia Orchestra for EMI), Brahms' Symphonies Nos 2, 3 and 4, Bruckner's Symphonies Nos 7 and 8, the Mendelssohn Violin Concerto (with Menuhin), Beethoven's Symphony No. 8 and Leonore No. 3 overture and the *Symphonic Dialogue* from his own Piano Concerto (with Edwin Fischer, and with the Berlin Philharmonic Orchestra for EMI), Brahms' Symphony No. 2 (with the London Philharmonic Orchestra for Decca), the Franck *Symphony in D minor* (with the Vienna Philharmonic Orchestra for Decca), Bach's Suite No. 3, Handel's Concerti Grossi Op. 6 Nos 5 and 6, Haydn's Symphony No. 88, Mozart's Symphony No. 39, *Eine kleine Nachtmusik*, the overtures to *Le nozze di Figaro* and *Die Entführung aus dem Serail*, Schubert's Symphonies Nos 8 and 9, Schumann's Symphony No. 4, the overtures *Alceste*, *Egmont*, *Leonore No. 2*, *Rosamunde* and *Euryanthe*, Beethoven's Symphonies Nos 4 and 5, the Violin Concerto (with Schneiderhan), Piano Concerto No. 4 (with Hansen) and *Grosse Fuge*, Brahms' Symphony No. 3 and *Variations on the St Antony Chorale*, Bruckner's Symphonies Nos 7 and 9, Hindemith's *Symphonic Metamorphosis on Themes by Weber*, Strauss's *Metamorphosen* and *Don Juan*, and his own Symphony No. 2 (with the Berlin Philharmonic Orchestra for DGG), the Beethoven and Brahms Violin Concertos (with Menuhin and the Lucerne Festival Orchestra for EMI), Beethoven's Symphony No. 9 (with the Bayreuth Festival Orchestra *et al.* for EMI) and the second movement of Bruckner's Symphony No. 7 (with the Berlin Philharmonic Orchestra for Telefunken).

To anyone interested in Furtwängler virtually every performance on these records will be absorbing. Some of them are disconcertingly idiosyncratic, such as Brahms' Symphony No. 2 (with the London Philharmonic Orchestra) with its extraordinary tempi changes, the Franck Symphony (with the Vienna Philharmonic Orchestra) which seems to be interminable, and Beethoven's Symphony No. 4 (with the Vienna Philharmonic Orchestra), where tempi and phrasing devitalise the music. But there are also a multitude of marvels, such as the opening of Bruckner's Symphony No. 7 (with the Berlin Philharmonic Orchestra), which can almost make the sceptic accept Furtwängler's mystical view of the composer's music, the magical transition between the third and fourth movements of Schumann's Symphony No. 4 (with the Berlin Philharmonic), and the accompaniment to the Brahms Violin Concerto (with Menuhin and the Lucerne Festival Orchestra), which is a good illustration of Menuhin's own words that Furtwängler could make the music 'flow'. (Personal interview, April 1973.) Interestingly, Furtwängler's Haydn and Mozart had a firmness and decisiveness which was frequently absent from performances of later composers, and it has been suggested that he saw both Haydn and Mozart as anticipating Beethoven.

Since the time of his death, many records have appeared on various labels of Furtwängler performances, taken from 78 r.p.m. and LP records, and from tapes of live concerts and broadcasts, but sometimes with very unsatisfactory results, which do the memory of the conductor no good. These discs, the good and the not so good, include Beethoven's Symphony No. 8, the *Leonore No. 3* overture and Brahms' *Ein deutsches Requiem* (with the Stockholm Philharmonic Orchestra *et al.* by EMI), Beethoven's Piano Concerto No. 4 (with Scarpini and the RAI Orchestra for Discocorp), Beethoven's Symphony No. 9, a *Leonore* overture, and *Don Juan* (with the Vienna Philharmonic, 1953, for Discocorp), Beethoven's Symphony No. 9, Brahms' *Variations on the St Antony Chorale* and *Till Eulenspiegel* (with the Berlin Philharmonic *et al.* by Everest), Beethoven's Symphonies Nos 3, 5, 6 and 9, Schubert's Symphony No. 8 and Brahms' Symphony No. 4 (with the Berlin Philharmonic by Turnabout), Brahms' Piano Concerto No. 2 (with Fischer and the Berlin Philharmonic for Turnabout), Beethoven's Symphony No. 6, Bruckner's Symphony No. 8, and the three preludes from Pfitzner's *Palestrina* (with the Berlin Philharmonic by Rococo), the Sibelius Violin Concerto (with Kulenkampff and the Berlin Philharmonic for Unicorn), the Mendelssohn and Brahms Violin Concertos (with de Vito and the Radio Italian Orchestra by Rococo), Bruckner's Symphonies Nos 5 (with the Vienna Philharmonic by Rococo), No. 7 (1951) and No. 8, with the *Tannhäuser* and *Euryanthe* overtures (by Discocorp), Brahms' Symphony No. 1 (with the Radio Italiana Orchestra by the Bruno Walter Society), Tchaikovsky's Symphony No. 5, two of Debussy's *Nocturnes* and *Rapsodie espagnole* (with the Radio Italiana Orchestra by Discocorp), Stravinsky's *Le Baiser de la fée* (with the Berlin Philharmonic by Discocorp), the complete Brahms symphonies (with the Vienna and Berlin Philharmonic by Discocorp), Haydn's Symphonies Nos 88 (with the RAI Orchestra) and 94 (with the Vienna Philharmonic, by Discocorp), Schubert's Symphony No. 9, Franck's *Symphony in D minor* and Sibelius' *En Saga* (with the Vienna Philharmonic by Discocorp), the *Rosamunde* overture (with the RAI Orchestra for Discocorp), the complete *Ring* (with the La Scala Orchestra, mentioned above), the *Coriolan* overture, the Schumann Symphony No. 1 and Bruckner's Symphony No. 4 (with the Vienna Philharmonic by Decca, from a concert in Munich in 1951), the Tchaikovsky Symphony No. 6 (with the Berlin Philharmonic for DGG), the Mozart Piano Concerto K. 466 (with Lefèbre) Beethoven's Symphony No. 5, Piano Concerto No. 4 (with Hansen) and *Leonore No. 2* overture, and Brahms' Symphonies Nos 3 and 4 (with the Berlin Philharmonic for Unicorn) excerpts from *Die Meistersinger*, *Der fliegende Holländer*, *Die Walküre*, *Tristan und Isolde*, *Parsifal*, and the *Siegfried Idyll* (with the Vienna and Berlin Philharmonic for Unicorn), and the operas *Le nozze di Figaro* (Salzburg, 1953), *Don Giovanni* (Salzburg 1953), *Die Zauberflöte* (Salzburg, 1949), *Der Freischütz* (Salzburg, 1954), *Otello* (Salzburg, 1951), *Orfeo ed Euridice* (La Scala, 1951) and *Die Meistersinger* (Bayreuth, 1943, for Discocorp *et al.*). Some performances with the Berlin Philharmonic have also been issued by Melodiya in the USSR, apparently taken from tapes of concerts; these include Beethoven's Symphony No. 7, Strauss's *Symphonia domestica*, and a collection of overtures and shorter pieces.

G

Gabrilowitsch, Ossip (1878–1936). Born in St Petersburg, Gabrilowitsch studied at the Conservatory under Rubinstein, Liadov and Glazunov, and graduated in 1894 as the winner of the Rubinstein Prize. He was a pupil of Leschetizky in Vienna and made his debut as a pianist in Berlin in 1896. He toured Europe and the United States with enormous success, and in a series of six concerts presented in a number of European and American cities he performed a total of eighteen piano concertos showing the development of the concerto from Bach to Rachmaninov. He conducted concerts in New York in 1907 and led the Kaim Orchestra at Munich from 1910 to 1914; at the outbreak of World War I he was arrested as a spy but was released the next day. Going to Zürich and then to the United States, he was appointed the first conductor of the newly formed Detroit Symphony Orchestra in 1918, although he also continued as a pianist. His wife was Clara Clemens, a soprano and the daughter of Mark Twain, and they frequently gave joint recitals. His leadership of the Detroit orchestra was very successful, and from 1928 he was a guest conductor with the Philadelphia Orchestra. Bruno Walter, a close friend of Gabrilowitsch, has written of his poetic personality and its wonderful effect on his musicians, as well as his fine and interesting programmes. He made some discs for Victor with the Detroit Symphony Orchestra, the *Academic Festival Overture*, *España*, the minuet from Brahms' Serenade No. 1 and the Dance of the Blessed Spirits from *Orfeo ed Euridice*. On record he impressed as a restrained and sensitive conductor but sometimes lacking in dramatic power.

Gaburo, Kenneth (b. 1926). Gaburo was educated at the Eastman School of Music, Rochester, the Accademia di Santa Cecilia, Rome, and at the University of Illinois. He has held a number of academic posts, most recently at the University of California, San Diego (from 1968), and has composed orchestral, chamber, vocal and instrumental pieces. Nonesuch issued a disc on which he conducted the University of Illinois Contemporary Chamber Players in his *Antiphony III* and *IV*, *Exit Music I* and *II*, *The Wasting of Lucrecetzia* and *Fat Millie's Lament*.

Gaillard, Paul-André (b. 1922). Born in Veytaux-Montreux, Switzerland, Gaillard studied the violin with Feustel and theory at the Institut de Ribaupierre at Montreux. He continued his studies at the Lausanne Conservatory (1936–8), the Winterthur School of Music (1938–42), the Geneva Conservatory, privately with von Hoesslin and at the Zürich Conservatory. He joined the St Gall Municipal Orchestra, conducted choirs in Suisse Romande and also toured in Britain, Luxembourg, FR Germany, Belgium, Italy and Poland, became director of the Seminar for International Studies at the Bayreuth Festival (1951), conductor of the international choir (1957) and musical assistant there (1961), and was appointed professor of musical history at the Lausanne Conservatory (1956) and president of the Swiss Society of Professional Music Directors (1962). His many compositions include choral, vocal, piano and chamber music, and he has written numerous musical monographs and articles. For La Guilde Internationale du Disque he recorded Handel's *Belshazzar* (with the Collegium Academicum de Genève).

Gaillard, Marius-François (b. 1900). Born in Paris and educated at the Paris Conservatoire, Gaillard began his career as a pianist, and then founded a series of symphony concerts in Paris, which he conducted from 1928 to 1949. He composed orchestral, dramatic, vocal and chamber music, and travelled extensively collecting primitive music. For Columbia, HMV, Pathé and Odéon, he recorded 78 r.p.m. discs with various French orchestras of the Bach Harpsichord Concerto in A major and the Mozart Piano Concerto K. 37 (with Roesgen-Champion), the Mozart Symphony No. 36, *Eine kleine Nachtmusik*, Minuets K. 463, *German Dances* K. 573 and the overture to *Der Schauspieldirektor*, a Haydn Harpsichord Concerto (again with Roesgen-Champion), and Schubert's Symphonies Nos 3 and 4.

Galliera, Alceo (b. 1910). Born in Milan, Galliera studied at the Milan Conservatory, where his father was a teacher, and in 1923 was himself appointed a professor of composition and organ at the conservatory. He first attracted attention as a conductor in 1941 when he led the Santa Cecilia Orchestra in Rome, and after World War II he appeared with great success at the Lucerne Festival, in England, Israel, South America, South Africa and Australia, where he was appointed resident conductor of the Melbourne Symphony Orchestra (1950–51). From 1957 to 1960 he was conductor of the Genoa Opera, but since then he has become much less prominent on the international scene. His compositions include orchestral works, chamber music, cantatas and a ballet *The Wise and Foolish Virgins*, which was produced at La Scala, Milan. Galliera's reputation is somewhat similar to that of many other Italian conductors as a fiery, brusque and authoritarian personality; his repertoire has been relatively small and orthodox but within these limitations he has produced dramatic performances. In London in the post-war years he distinguished himself with his direction of a cycle of the Beethoven symphonies.

When EMI was establishing its catalogue after the war, Galliera conducted the Philharmonia Orchestra in a number of recordings, both on 78 r.p.m. and LP, some of which were particularly fine, such as Beethoven's Symphony No. 7, Dvořák's Symphony No. 9 and Franck's *Symphony in D minor*. Among his other records, then still on 78 r.p.m. discs, were dances from *The Three-cornered Hat*, *Don Juan*, *Les Éolides*, a suite from *L'Oiseau de feu*, *La Mer*, *Nocturnes*, *Prélude à l'après-midi d'un faune*, the *Egmont* overture, some Rossini overtures and some concerto accompaniments, most notably with Schnabel in Beethoven's Piano Concerto No. 5, Lipatti in the Grieg Piano Concerto and Grumiaux in the Mendelssohn Violin Concerto. Many of these performances were re-issued on LP, and his new recordings were again of music in the popular repertoire, such as collections of Rossini and Verdi overtures, *Capriccio italien*, the *Romeo and Juliet* fantasy-overture, *La Boutique fantasque*, *Tod und Verklärung*, *Fontane di Roma*, *Brazilian Impressions*, *Capriccio espagnol*, Borodin's Symphony No. 1 and a *Carmen* in which Callas headed the cast. Some outstanding concerto recordings were also included, the most prominent being Beethoven's Piano Concertos Nos 1, 3, 4 and 5 (with Arrau), Tchaikovsky's Piano Concerto No. 1, Beethoven's Piano Concerto No. 1 and Rachmaninov's Piano Concerto No. 2 (with Anda), and the Brahms Double Concerto (with Oistrakh and Fournier), which, coupled with the *Tragic Overture*, is still in the catalogues.

Galliera's other recordings include Monteverdi's *La favola d'Orfeo* (for EMI), Mozart's Symphonies Nos 29 and 35, and Sinfonia Concertante K. 364 (with Gulli and Giuranna) and Sinfonia Concertante K. 297b (with the Angelicum Orchestra for Angelicum), Clarinet Concerto (with Amodio and the Berlin Civic Orchestra for DGG), Piano Concertos K. 175, K. 242, K. 246, and K. 466 and the Rondos K. 382 and K. 386 (with Haebler and the London Symphony Orchestra for Philips), Two- and Three-Piano Concertos (with Haebler, Hoffman and Bunge and the London Symphony Orchestra for Philips) and arias from the operas (with Hollweg and the Vienna Symphony Orchestra for Philips), the Grieg Piano Concerto (with Michelangeli and the La Scala Orchestra for Telefunken), the two Ravel Piano Concertos (with Haas and the Monte Carlo National Opera Orchestra for Philips) and *Rigoletto* (with the Bavarian State Opera Orchestra *et al.* for Electrola). Most of these records have been issued only in Europe. Certainly with his English discs for EMI, Galliera had the great advantage of recording with the Philharmonia Orchestra which was then a very remarkable ensemble. While many of his recordings provided ample evidence of his fine musicianship, sometimes there were lapses, as in the Strauss Oboe Concerto (with Leon Goossens), which was curiously insensitive.

Gallini, Franco (b. 1924). Gallini studied conducting with Votto and Giulini at the conservatory at his native Milan, conducted concerts in Italy, Belgium, Sweden *et al.*, was librarian and teacher at the Bologna Conservatory (1960–62), and founded and conducted the Piccolo Scala Opera in Milan (1957). He edited operas of Pergolesi, Hasse and others, and recorded Pergolesi's *Livietta a Tracollo* (with the Arzignano Orchestral Society *et al.* for Cetra) and *La serva padrona* (with the Piccolo Scala Orchestra *et al.* for EMI), and Paganini's Violin Concerto No. 4 (with Grumiaux and the Lamoureux Orchestra for Philips).

Gamba, Piero (b. 1936). Born the son of a violinist in Rome, Gamba started his musical education at the age of eight, and within six months conducted his first concert at the Rome Opera House. By the age of 14 he had finished his musical training, and soon afterwards composed three symphonic poems. A remarkable career as a conductor followed, in which he has conducted 120 major symphonic orchestras in 300 cities of 40 countries. He founded the Symphonicum Europae (1964), under the patronage of the late Queen Elisabeth of Belgium and others, and has been music director and conductor of the Winnipeg Symphony Orchestra in Canada (since 1972). His repertoire is large, ranging from the baroque to Henze, and in addition to giving piano recitals, he on occasion conducts concertos from the keyboard. Although a mild man in everyday life, on the podium he is exceptionally demonstrative; he has the utmost respect for the written score, and regards himself as his most severe critic. In 1962 he was awarded the Arnold Bax Memorial Medal in Britain.

Gamba has made a number of recordings for Decca with the London Symphony Orchestra; the most distinguished were the five Beethoven concertos and Choral Fantasia (with Katchen), and in this series he revealed himself to be a Beethoven interpreter of considerable stature. The other discs included the overtures to *William Tell*, *Tancredi*, *Le Siège de Corinthe*, *Il Signor Bruschino*, *La gazza ladra*, *La scala di seta*, *Il barbiere di Siviglia*, *Semiramide*, *La Cenerentola*, *I vespri siciliani*, and Mancinelli's *Cleopatra*, Black's *Overture to a Costume Comedy*, the Dance of the Hours from *La Gioconda*, the intermezzo from *Cavalleria rusticana*, the preludes to Acts I and III of *La traviata*, Martucci's *Notturno in G flat*, Paganini's Violin Concerto No. 1, Saint-Saëns' Violin Concerto No. 3, Sarasate's *Zigeunerweisen* and Wieniaski's *Légende* (with Campoli), Bruch's and Mendelssohn's Violin Concertos, Saint-Saëns' *Introduction et rondo capriccioso* and Sarasate's *Carmen Fantasy* and *Zigeunerweisen* (with Ricci). For EMI, he recorded the *Romeo and Juliet* fantasy-overture, *Danse macabre* and *Capriccio espagnol* (with the Philharmonia Orchestra) and for Tono (Denmark) the *Egmont* overture and *L'Apprenti sorcier*.

Gamley, Douglas (b. 1924). Born in Melbourne, Australia, and educated at the Melbourne Conservatorium, Gamley was a repetiteur with the Melbourne Opera in 1947, emigrated to London and studied with Reizenstein, Blacher and Goehr. He became assistant to the film music director Hollingsworth, conducted for radio and television, and later, encouraged by Robert Farnon, was an arranger of songs. He has recorded the overtures *Pique Dame*, *Leichte Kavallerie*, *La Muette de Portici*, *Le Cheval de bronze*, *Orphée aux Enfers* and *Zampa* (with the Royal Philharmonic Orchestra for EMI), waltzes of Waldteufel (with the National Philharmonic Orchestra for Decca), and with the National Philharmonic Orchestra for Reader's Digest a number of pieces, including the overtures *Egmont*, *Le nozze di Figaro*, *Le Cheval de Bronze*, *Russlan and Ludmilla*, *Pique Dame*, *I vespri siciliani* and *Yeoman of the Guard*, excerpts from *The Sleeping Beauty*, Balakirev's *Islamey*, some *Slavonic Dances* of Dvořák, the dances from *The Bartered Bride*, excerpts from Bizet's *Jeux d'enfants* and some pieces by Grieg and Sibelius.

Gamson, Arnold (b. 1926). The American conductor Gamson studied at the Juilliard School of Music and at the Paris Conservatoire, then with Allen Sven Oxenburg established the American Opera Society, to present rarely performed operas in concert versions in New York. The first opera, *L'Incoronazione di Poppea*, in Gamson's own edition, was presented in 1952, and the Society continued until 1971, in that time performing five operas in each season. Some of the productions were Gluck's *Le Cadi dupé* and *Paride ed Elena*, Purcell's *Witch of Endor*, Handel's *Giulio Cesare* (in which Schwarzkopf and Forrester appeared together), Cherubini's *Medea*, and Rossini's *Moïse* and *La gazza ladra*. Gamson conducted the Society until 1961; he was obliged to do much editing of many of the scores; *Paride ed Elena*, for instance, was so full of errors that it almost had to be rewritten. In 1956 he was assistant conductor with the New York City Opera, in 1960 appeared with the New York Philharmonic Orchestra, and is conductor of the Westchester Summer Symphony Orchestra. Columbia (US) issued, *c.* 1960, a disc on which he conducted the Columbia Symphony Orchestra in excerpts from *Medea* (with Farrell in the title role).

Ganz, Rudolph (1877–1972). Born in Zürich, Ganz studied there and at Lausanne, Strasbourg and in Berlin with Busoni. He first appeared in public as a cellist at the age of twelve; later, in 1899 he again gave concerts as a pianist in Berlin, and his Symphony No. 1 was premièred a year later. He migrated to the United States, joined the staff at the Chicago Musical College (1900–05), toured the US, Canada and Europe as a pianist, was conductor of the St Louis Symphony Orchestra (1921–7) and finally was director of the Chicago Musical College (1929–54). He conducted for the first time many new compositions of Ravel, Debussy, Busoni, Bartók *et al.* He made some recordings as a pianist, as well as a handful with the St Louis Symphony Orchestra for Victor: the dances from German's *Henry VIII*, the overture *The Hebrides*, the first *Pomp and Circumstance* march and the waltz *Ein Künstlerleben*. He also recorded on 78 r.p.m. discs the *Holberg Suite* of Grieg with an ensemble called the Metropolitan Symphony Orchestra, for Pilotone.

Garaguly, Carl von (b. 1900). Born in Budapest, Garaguly learnt the violin with his father, performed in public at the age of six, and when he was eleven and twelve toured as a violinist. After studying at the Hungarian State Academy at Budapest (1907–08) and at the Hochschule für Musik in Berlin (1914–16), he was a member of the Berlin Philharmonic Orchestra (1917–18) and professor at the Arad State Academy in Hungary (1918–20). From 1920 to 1923 he toured Austria, Germany, Switzerland and Scandinavia giving violin recitals, settled in Göteborg to become leader of the Göteborg Symphony Orchestra (1923–30) and of the Stockholm Philharmonic Orchestra (1930–40). In 1930 he became a Swedish subject; in 1940 he founded the Garaguly Quartet, and in 1941 started his career as a conductor with the Stockholm Philharmonic Orchestra of which he was permanent conductor from 1941 to 1953. For the following five years he conducted the Bergen Philharmonic Orchestra, was a guest conductor in Denmark, Holland and other European countries, was made a member of the Swedish Royal Academy, and is now conductor of the South Jutland Symphony Orchestra.

Garaguly's records include several fine concertos for Tono on 78s with the Danish Radio Symphony Orchestra and pianist Schiøler, of Tchaikovsky's Piano Concerto No. 1 and Beethoven's Piano Concerto No. 5. For HMV in Sweden he recorded, also on 78s, Larsson's *Music for Orchestra* and Rosenberg's *Concerto for String Orchestra*, with the Swedish Radio Orchestra and the Stockholm Concert Society Orchestra respectively. In 1965 Turnabout issued an excellent performance of Nielsen's Symphony No. 2 coupled with the same composer's *Little Suite*, in which Garaguly conducted the Tivoli Concert Hall Symphony Orchestra. The Garaguly Quartet also recorded, on 78s, Rosenberg's Quartet No. 4.

García-Asensio, Enrique (b. 1937). Born in Valencia, García-Asensio studied at the Royal Academy of Music in Madrid, the Hochschule für Musik in Munich, and later with Celibidache at the Accademia Chigiana in Siena. In 1962 he won the Italian Radio and Television Prize for conducting, and was conductor of the Las Palmas Philharmonic Orchestra (1962–4), the Valencia Municipal Orchestra (1964–6) and since 1966 permanent conductor of the Spanish Radio and Television Symphony Orchestra in Madrid, and professor of conducting at the Royal Academy of Music there from 1970. In 1967 he won first prize at the Dmitri Mitropoulos International Conductors' Competition in New York, was assistant conductor of the National Symphony Orchestra in Washington DC (1967–8) and in 1971 toured the United States with the Spanish Radio and Television Symphony Orchestra. He has recorded in Spain for a number of local labels, including music by Albéniz, Benguerel, Montsalvatge, Rodrigo, Halffter, Bernaola, de Pablo and Quadreny, as well as some zarzuelas and a disc of Catalan flute music (with Rampal). With the English Chamber Orchestra for Ensayo (Spain) he also recorded Rossini overtures including *Il barbiere di Siviglia*, *La gazza ladra*, *La Cenerentola*, *L'Italiana in Algeri*, Tchaikovsky's *Serenade in C major*, Dvořák's *Serenade in E major*, Britten's *Simple Symphony*, Hindemith's *Five Pieces*, Respighi's third suite of *Ancient Airs and Dances* and the double guitar concertos of Castelnuovo-Tedesco and Santorsola, for Zambra (Spain) *Un Concierto de Genero Chico* (with Berganza), which received the Charles Cross Prize for the best record of 1976, and for Argo a collection of pieces by Purcell. Pye released the Dvořák and Tchaikovsky serenades in 1974 in Britain, and CBS the disc of double guitar concertos in Britain and the United States in the same year. Musical Heritage Society in the US has also issued Rodrigo's *Fantasia para un gentilhombre* (with Betetti), Albéniz's *Rumores de la Caleta* and Villa-Lobos' *Preludio No. 4* and *Choros No. 1* (with the Madrid Concert Orchestra).

Gardelli, Lamberto (b. 1915). Born in Venice, Gardelli made his first public appearance at the age of eight as a pianist. When studying at the Liceo Musicale Rossini at Pesaro he formed a student orchestra which played together for two years. He also studied singing and composition, the latter with Petrassi, and some of his compositions have been widely performed. After accompanying singers such as Gigli, Schipa and Cigna, and coaching at the Rome Opera House, he was for eight years assistant to Serafin, beginning as a prompter. He made his debut at the Rome Opera in 1941 with *La traviata* and after World War II left Italy to take up an appointment with the Royal Swedish Orchestra (1946–55), eventually becoming court conductor and taking Swedish citizenship. From 1955 to 1961 he was permanent conductor of the Danish Radio Symphony Orchestra and then succeeded Klemperer at the Budapest Opera, and also conducted the Budapest Philharmonic Orchestra. In recent years he was also appointed music director of the Berne Theatre and a conductor of the Royal Opera at Copenhagen. His other international engagements have included Glyndebourne, Covent

Garden and the New York Metropolitan Opera, as well as many of the major European orchestras. His compositions include four operas, symphonic music, a concerto for trombone, cornet and bassoon, songs and a requiem mass.

Gardelli has the widest range of musical sympathies, in the concert hall and in the opera house. In his early years in Italy he worked closely with the composers Mascagni, Giordano, Zandonai, Pizzetti and Petrassi, and when he was in Sweden he studied and performed the music of Nielsen, Sibelius and other Scandinavian composers. In Hungary he has been an acclaimed interpreter of baroque music which he performed with his own ensemble, and recorded *The Four Seasons* for Hungaroton with the Hungarian Radio Orchestra. He introduced Bruckner's symphonies to the musical public in Budapest, overcoming the initial resistance of the orchestra. However, like so many other Italian conductors, his international reputation, at least to record-buyers, is confined to his association with Italian opera, and more particularly in his case with the early operas of Verdi, which he has played an important role in reviving. In Italian opera he has repeatedly shown himself, through his records, as a fine interpreter, giving much vitality and expression to the scores, proving the musical strength of operas previously neglected or dismissed by other conductors.

Decca, EMI and Philips have recorded a number of Italian operas in which Gardelli conducts a variety of orchestras and companies, including the Maggio Musicale Fiorentino, the Monte Carlo and Vienna State Operas, and the Royal Philharmonic and Santa Cecilia Orchestras. The early Verdi series started in 1968 with *Nabucco* (for Decca) and continued with *Macbeth* (for Decca), *I Lombardi*, *Attila*, *Un giorno di regno*, *Il corsaro* and *I masnadieri* (for Philips) and also included *La forza del destino* (for EMI). His other operatic recordings are the three operas in Puccini's *Il trittico* which was made in 1962, *Fedora*, *Pagliacci*, *Il segreto di Susanna*, *La Gioconda* (for Decca) and *Guillaume Tell* (for EMI). *Guillaume Tell* was issued in 1973 and was a notable success; the entire opera was recorded on five LP discs, the cast (which included Caballé, Gedda, Bacquier and Hendrikx) was ideal and Gardelli's direction admirable. Recording the opera was made possible by the financial backing of Robert Slotover.

In Hungary, Gardelli recorded for Qualiton *La traviata* and *Rigoletto* (in Hungarian, with the Hungarian State Opera Orchestra *et al.*), excerpts from *Il barbiere di Siviglia* and *Un ballo in maschera* (with the Hungarian Radio Orchestra *et al.*), the *Romeo and Juliet* fantasy-overture, *A Night on the Bare Mountain* and *The Hebrides* overture (with the Budapest Philharmonic Orchestra), and *Pini di Roma* (with the Hungarian Radio Orchestra). His other discs include *Pini di Roma*, *Fontane di Roma* and the *Belfagor* overture of Respighi (with the London Symphony Orchestra for EMI), the Rossini overtures *Guillaume Tell*, *La gazza ladra*, *Il Signor Bruschino*, *Le Siège de Corinthe*, *Il barbiere di Siviglia* and *La scala de seta* (with the New Philharmonia Orchestra for Decca), Pizzetti's *La Pisanella* and *Concerti dell'Estate* (with the Suisse Romande Orchestra for Decca), Vives' *Doña Francisquita* (with the Spanish Philharmonic Orchestra for Alhambra), and *La traviata* (with the Berlin Staatskapelle *et al.* for BASF).

Gardiner, John Eliot (b. 1943). Great-nephew of the composer Balfour Gardiner, Gardiner first heard Monteverdi in a performance by Nadia Boulanger at a Dartington Summer Music School when he was six; he studied at Cambridge, with Dart in London, with Boulanger in Paris, attended conducting courses, and was an apprentice conductor with the BBC Northern Symphony Orchestra. At Cambridge he formed the Monteverdi Choir, came to prominence with a performance of his own edition of the Monteverdi *Vespro della Beata Vergine* at a Promenade Concert in London (1968), then specialised with the Monteverdi Choir and Orchestra in performances of pre-baroque and 18th-century French music, as well as 20th-century music, and in 1971 discovered Rameau's last opera *Les Boréades*. He became convinced that it is necessary to use old instruments in performing music up to 1750, but believes that one must choose the type and size of the ensemble to suit the hall and acoustic conditions when presenting pre-baroque music. With his Monteverdi Orchestra he has aimed to have an orchestra that can perform on both old and modern instruments. With the Choir and Orchestra *et al.* he has recorded the Monteverdi *Vespro della Beata Vergine* (for Decca in 1975), Purcell's *Come Ye Sons of Art* and *Funeral Music for Queen Mary* (for Erato), motets of Monteverdi and Gesualdo (for Argo), laments by Monteverdi, Wilbye, Gibbons and Morley (for Abbey), music by G. Gabrieli, Bassano and Monteverdi (for Decca), lute concertos by Handel, Kohout and Vivaldi (with Bream for RCA) and Berkeley's Guitar Concerto and Rodrigo's *Concierto de Aranjuez* (with Bream for RCA).

Gatz, Felix (1892–1942). Born in Berlin, Gatz studied at the Universities of Berlin, Heidelberg and Erlanger, and was a pupil of Nikisch and Scheinpflug. He conducted at the Lübeck Opera (1923–33), was professor of aesthetics at the Vienna Academy of Music (1925–34), migrated to the United States and was a professor at Duquesne University, Pittsburgh (1934–6), New York University (1936–7), and at the University of Scranton, Pennsylvania (from 1937), where he founded the Scranton Philharmonic Orchestra in 1939. From 1923 to 1933 he was conductor for the Bruckner Society and gave concerts with the Berlin Philharmonic Orchestra; at that time he recorded part of the Bruckner *Te Deum* with the Bruckner Choir, orchestra and soloists, for a German label which was released in England by Parlophone and in the United States by Decca.

Gaubert, Philippe (1879–1941). The French flautist, composer and conductor Gaubert was born at Cahors and studied at the Paris Conservatoire. In 1905 he won the Prix de Rome for composition, and on returning to France became a leading flute player and professor of the instrument at the Conservatoire. After serving with distinction in the French army in World War I he was appointed principal conductor of the Paris Conservatoire Orchestra in succession to Messager, a post he held until 1938. In 1920 he also became first conductor at the Paris Opéra and remained there until his death. At the Opéra he was chiefly concerned with producing new works by French composers and with presenting Wagner operas. He composed several operas, ballets, symphonic and other music; his opera *Nailla* was performed in Paris in 1927. He made records for Columbia with the Paris Conservatoire Orchestra and with the Straram Orchestra in the late 1920s and early 1930s. Included were *In the Steppes of Central Asia*, *Nuages* and *Fêtes* from Debussy's *Nocturnes*, Duparc's *Aux Étoiles*, *Le Rouet d'Omphale*, *L'Apprenti sorcier*, Franck's *Symphony in D minor*, *Scheherazade*, the overture to *Le nozze di Figaro*, Chopin's Piano Concerto No. 2 (with Marguerite Long), Tchaikovsky's Symphony No. 6, *La Valse* and the *Daphnis et Chloé* Suite No. 2. Pathé also issued a disc in which he conducted an unidentified orchestra in Auric's *La plus belle histoire*. Both Hall and Kolodin in their surveys of recorded music in the 1930s wrote that Gaubert's *Pathétique* was a reticent, conservative reading, but that his performance of *L'Apprenti sorcier* demonstrated the wit and fantasy of the score.

Gauk, Alexander (1893–1963). Born in Odessa, Gauk graduated at the Petrograd Conservatory in 1917, where he had been a pupil of Tcherepnin and Glazunov. He conducted ballet at the Leningrad Opera and Ballet Theatre (now the Kirov Theatre) (1920–27), taught at the Leningrad Conservatory, where his students included Mravinsky and Melik-Pashayev (1927–34), was artistic director and chief conductor of the USSR State Symphony Orchestra, the All-Union Radio Orchestra and Grand Symphony Orchestra (also known as the Moscow Radio Symphony Orchestra) from 1934, and was professor of conducting at the Moscow Conservatory from 1948. He was responsible for restoring and performing the score of Rachmaninov's Symphony No. 1, which had been suppressed by the composer after its disastrous première in 1897.

Gauk made numerous records in the USSR with the USSR State Symphony Orchestra, the Moscow Radio Symphony Orchestra, the Moscow Philharmonic Orchestra and the Bolshoi Theatre Orchestra. Many of these found their way to the West and were issued either on the Russian label or on British or American labels such as Parlophone, Mercury, Decca, HMV, Classic, Bruno, Artia, Perfect, Liberty, Vanguard, Urania, Saga, Monarch, Compass and Ariola. On pre-electric 78 r.p.m. discs there was Beethoven's Symphony No. 5; later recordings, some of which were on 78s, included Mozart's Piano Concertos K. 488 (with Yudina) and K. 491 (with Bashkirov), Beethoven's Piano Concerto No. 5 (with Oborin), Violin Concerto (with Oistrakh) and *Coriolan* overture, Mendelssohn's Symphony No. 4 and Violin Concerto (with Oistrakh), the Schumann Piano Concerto (with Richter) and *Konzertstück in F major*, Chopin's Piano Concerto No. 1 (with Neuhaus), *L'Apprenti sorcier*, some Brahms *Hungarian Dances* and Strauss waltzes, *Jeux d'enfants*, *Symphonie espagnole*, and Bruch's Violin Concerto No. 1 (with Oistrakh), Saint-Saëns' *Introduction et rondo capriccioso* (with Kogan) and Piano Concerto No. 2 (with Gilels), the overtures *Hebrides*, *La gazza ladra* and *Der fliegende Holländer*, Balakirev's *Islamey*, *Russia*, *Overture on Russian Themes* and Piano Concerto (with Shirinsky), Tchaikovsky's Symphonies Nos 3 and 6, *Manfred*, Suites Nos 1 to 4, *Marche solenelle*, incidental music to *The Snow Maiden*, Violin Concerto (with Oistrakh), *Variations on a Rococo Theme* (with Knushevitzky) and *Valse-Scherzo* (with Kogan), Rimsky-Korsakov's Symphony No. 3 and suite from *The Snow Maiden*, Liadov's *Baba Yaga*, Cui's Suite No. 3, Glinka's Overture to *Prince*

Kholmsky, *Valse fantaisie*, *Festival Polonaise* and Polka No. 1, Scriabin's *Piano Concerto in F sharp minor* (with Feinberg), Taneyev's Symphony No. 1, Arensky's *A Dream on the Volga*, Serov's *Cossack Dance*, Glazunov's *Wedding Procession*, *Les Ruses d'amour*, *Scènes de ballet*, *Ballade*, *Valses de concert* Nos 1 and 2, Glière's Harp Concerto (with Dulova), the Dance of the Kashmir Brides from Rubinstein's *Feramors*, Shostakovich's Symphonies Nos 6 and 9, Ballet Suites Nos 1, 2 and 3, *Festival Overture*, *Memorable Year 1919*, Piano Concerto No. 2 (with Shostakovich) and music for the film *The Fall of Berlin*, Dargomizhsky's *Baba-Yaga* and *Kaza Chok*, Miakovsky's Symphonies Nos 11, 17, 18, 22 and 27, *Scherzo in B flat* and Violin Concerto (with Oistrakh), Prokofiev's Violin Concerto No. 1 (with Oistrakh), *Overture on Russian Themes*, and *Romeo and Juliet* Suite No. 2, Rachmaninov's Symphony No. 2, Piano Concerto No. 2 (with Oborin) and *Caprice bohémien*, Rakov's Violin Concerto (with Oistrakh), Khachaturian's Symphonies Nos 1 and 2, Violin Concerto (with Oistrakh), Cello Concerto (with Knushevitzky) and *Spartacus* ballet, an aria from Shaporin's *On the Field of Kalikov* (with Pirogov), Kareyew's Symphony No. 3 and *Don Quixote*, Boris Tchaikovsky's Sinfonietta, Vassilenko's *Suite on Chinese Themes*, Vlassov's *Rhapsody on Romanian Themes*, Veprik's *Song of Triumph* and Knipper's *Youth Overture*. In Britain, Saga have issued a disc including the overtures *Coriolan*, *The Hebrides*, *Der fliegende Holländer* and *La gazza ladra*, conducted by Gauk; the performances have vitality and conviction, and are a good example of his artistry.

Gavazzeni, Gianandrea (b. 1909). The Italian conductor, composer, critic and author Gavazzeni was born in Bergamo, studied as a boy at the Liceo Musicale di Santa Cecilia in Rome, and then at the Milan Conservatory where he graduated as a pianist in 1929, and after further studies with Pizzetti and Pilati he was awarded his diploma in composition two years later. He became known first as a composer, and many of his works written when he was in his twenties were widely performed in Italy, including the *Concerto bergamasco*, the one-act opera *Paolo e Virginia* and the ballet *Il furioso nell'isola di San Domingo*. Through conducting his own compositions and then other music, he emerged as one of the most successful conductors in the country, and was active in Milan, Bologna, Florence, Rome and other Italian cities, as well as in other European opera houses. From 1966 to 1968 he was the artistic director at La Scala. In addition to these achievements Gavazzeni has written studies about Donizetti, Pizzetti, Mussorgsky, and about Wagner's *Siegfried*, and a number of other essays on musical subjects. He is an authority on Bellini, and revived the Verdi operas *I masnadieri*, *I vespri siciliani* and *Jérusalem*, which was the second version of *I Lombardi*, in French, for which the town council of Busseto, which was closely associated with Verdi, gave him the freedom of the city in 1970, an honour which had previously been awarded only to Boito, Pizzetti and Toscanini. He has also led revivals of Donizetti's *Anna Bolena*, Pizzetti's *Assassinio nella cattedrale* (after T. S. Eliot) and Mascagni's *L'amico Fritz*.

Gavazzeni's recordings have been exclusively of Italian opera and were made in the first decade or so of LP, for EMI, Decca, DGG, RCA, Mercury and Cetra. Included were *Madama Butterfly* (for EMI), an early success in 1955 with Los Angeles and di Stephano, *Andrea Chénier* (for Decca), *Il Turco in Italia* (for EMI), *Un ballo in maschera* (for Decca and for DGG), *Rigoletto* (for Mercury), *L'elisir d'amore* (for Cetra), *L'amico Fritz* (for EMI), *La Gioconda* (for Decca) and *Simon Boccanegra* (for RCA). The orchestras and opera companies employed were the Radio Italiana, Rome Opera, La Scala, Covent Garden and Maggio Musicale Fiorentino. Generally they were a distinguished series, and Gavazzeni showed himself to be a dramatic conductor with a firm control of proceedings. In addition, L'Estro Armonico have issued a performance of *Anna Bolena*, recorded at La Scala in 1957.

Geissler, Fredrick (b. 1946). Born in Bethesda, Maryland, Geissler was educated at the University of Virginia and Cornell University, and played the bassoon in army bands when on military service in Vietnam. He became assistant professor at the George Peabody College for Teachers (1974–7) and at the University of Virginia (from 1977). He conducted a recording of his *Variations on a Modern American Trumpet Tune*, with the Cornell University Wind Ensemble, for Cornell.

Gelbrun, Artur (b. 1913). Born in Warsaw where he attended the State Conservatory of Music, Gelbrun studied conducting at the Accademia di Santa Cecilia in Rome and the Accademia Chigiana in Siena. He has conducted in a number of European countries, and has composed symphonies, concertos, ballet music, oratorios and chamber music. He now lives in Israel. Everest issued a disc with him conducting the Kol-Israel Broadcasting Orchestra in his *Lament for the Victims of the Warsaw Ghetto* (with Harpanas), and *Songs of the Jordan River.*

Gellhorn, Peter (b. 1912). Born in Breslau and educated at the University and State Academy of Music in Berlin, Gellhorn came to England in 1935 and was director of music at Toynbee Hall (1935–9), assistant conductor with Sadler's Wells Opera (1941–3), conductor with the Carl Rosa Opera Company (1945–6), conductor and head of the music staff at Covent Garden (1946–53), conductor and chorus-master at the Glyndebourne Festival Opera (1954–61), director of the BBC Chorus (1961–72) and co-founder and musical director of the Opera Barga, Italy (1967–9). He has broadcast as both conductor and pianist, and lectures on music. His records as a conductor are a mono LP for EMI, later released in the United States on Seraphim, of Bach's Cantata No. 51 and Mozart's *Exsultate jubilate* (with Schwarzkopf and the Philharmonia Orchestra), and the Pastoral Symphony and Hallelujah Chorus from *Messiah* (with the Turin Polyphonic Choir and Orchestra for Angelicum, Italy). He has also recorded as a piano accompanist.

Gelmini, Hortense von (b. 1947). Born in Bosen, Gelmini was educated at the Hochschule für Musik at Freiburg, studied the piano with Seeman and conducting with Travers, as well as the cello, clarinet and trumpet. She founded her own orchestra, the Orchestra Gelmini, and toured Munich, Frankfurt am Main, Cologne and Stuttgart. She has recorded Shostakovich's Piano Concerto No. 1 (with Solter and Schackenberg), Genzmer's *Sinfonietta* and Roussel's *Sinfonietta* (with the Orchestra Gelmini for RBM), and Bruckner's Symphony No. 9 (with the Nuremberg Symphony Orchestra for Colosseum).

Georgescu, George (1887–1964). Georgescu was born in Sulena, Romania, and began to play the violin at the age of five. In 1910 he went to Berlin, studied the cello and attended the Hochschule für Musik. After a hand injury had prevented him from continuing as a cellist in a string quartet, he turned to conducting, and was taught by Nikisch and Strauss; later he became a notable interpreter of the Strauss tone poems. His debut as a conductor was with the Berlin Philharmonic Orchestra in 1918, and his success led to other engagements in Berlin and Dresden. In 1920 he returned to Bucharest to become director-general of the Romanian Philharmonic Orchestra and director of the Bucharest Opera. During a long and distinguished career he was a guest conductor with many major orchestras in Europe, the USSR and the United States. His symphonic repertoire was comprehensive, and his demeanour on the podium was modest and unaffected. His readings were noted for their adherence to the composers' intentions, their elegance and smooth flowing style, and their clear detail.

On 78 r.p.m. discs Georgescu recorded his compatriot Enesco's *Romanian Rhapsody No. 1* (with the Bucharest Philharmonic Orchestra), and in the post-war years Supraphon and Electrecord (the Romanian record company) issued a number of records with him directing the Czech Philharmonic, the Romanian Philharmonic and the George Enesco Philharmonic Orchestras. The works recorded included Haydn's Symphony No. 104 and *Cello Concerto in D major* (with Aldulescu), Mozart's Sinfonia Concertante K. 297b and the overture to *Le nozze di Figaro*, the nine Beethoven symphonies and the overtures *Egmont*, *Coriolan* and *Leonore No. 3*, Schubert's Symphony No. 8, the Mendelssohn Violin Concerto (with Voicu), Brahms' *Variations on the St Antony Chorale*, Tchaikovsky's Symphony No. 6, *Don Juan*, *Till Eulenspiegel* and *Tod und Verklärung*, Liszt's Piano Concerto No. 1 (with Gheorghiu) and *Totentanz* (with Mihaly), Khachaturian's Symphony No. 2, Enesco's Symphony No. 1, Lalo's *Symphonie espagnole* (with Voicu), Rachmaninov's *Rhapsody on a Theme of Paganini* (with Gheorghiu), Constantinescu's *Three Symphonic Dances*, Dumitrescu's oratorio *Tudor Vladimirescu* and Popa's *Rhapsody* (with the Timisoara State Philharmonic Orchestra). For Qualiton he also recorded Liszt's Totentanz again, with Bacher and the Hungarian State Symphony Orchestra.

Gerdes, Otto (b. 1920). Born in Cologne where he was educated at the Hochschule für Musik, Gerdes studied conducting with Abendroth and was first engaged as a conductor at various small provincial theatres. He later conducted at opera houses in Dresden, Berlin, Munich, Koblenz, Leipzig and Milan, with radio orchestras at Cologne and Baden-Baden, and led concerts with the Dresden Staatskapelle. In 1956 he was appointed the artistic recording supervisor with DGG, later becoming artistic director. He has since resumed his career as a conductor, appearing at Parma, Milan and Turin.

Gerdes recorded initially for Eterna the prelude to *Die Meistersinger*, overture to *La forza del destino*, intermezzi from *Notre Dame*, *Pagliacci* and *Cavalleria rusticana* and a *Carmen* suite (with the Leipzig Radio Orchestra), and the overtures to *Die Zauberflöte* and *Der Freischütz*, and the ballet music from *Aida* (with the Berlin Radio Orchestra). His first record for DGG was made when he substituted for a conductor who had fallen ill when he was recording excerpts from *Eugene Onegin*; this was followed by another disc of excerpts from *Otello*. His subsequent recordings were of Dvořák's Symphony No. 9, Brahms' Symphony No. 4 and the prelude to *Die Meistersinger* (all with the Berlin Philharmonic Orchestra for DGG), a complete *Tannhäuser* (with the Berlin Opera Orchestra *et al.* for DGG, in 1970), and a set of two discs containing Wolf's *Italian Serenade*, symphonic poem *Penthesilia* and some choral pieces and lieder (with the Vienna Symphony Orchestra *et al.* and the singers Lear and Stewart). This set was made at a live performance in Vienna in 1968, and is significant for making available *Penthesilia* on record. In all these recordings Gerdes shows himself to be a sound, if not dramatically exciting, conductor.

Gerecz, Arpad (b. 1924). Born at Dunakeszi, Hungary, Gerecz studied at the Franz Liszt Academy in Budapest and at the Geneva Conservatoire. He also studied conducting with van Kempen at Hilversum and with G. L. Jochum at Duisberg, became a Swiss citizen (1962), toured as a violinist and conductor in Europe, the US and Canada, taught at the Lausanne Conservatoire, and became assistant conductor of the Lausanne Chamber Orchestra (1958). He founded and was violinist with the Hungarian Trio, conducted at the Théâtre Royal de la Monnaie in Brussels, and has also been active with the Suisse Romande Radio Orchestra. He has recorded Looser's *Cello Rhapsody* (with Looser and the Lausanne Chamber Orchestra for CT), and Isoz's Alphorn Concerto (with Molnar and the Lausanne Chamber Orchestra for Sonopresse).

Gerelli, Ennio (b. 1907). Born in Cremona, Gerelli studied at the Bologna Conservatory, and was an assistant conductor at La Scala, Milan (1935–40). He founded the Angelicum Society in Milan, which he directed until 1953, is professor of conducting at the Parma Conservatory, has appeared as a conductor in many European cities, and has composed orchestral and chamber music. His recordings include Pergolesi's Concertino No. 2, Vivaldi's *Concerto in G major*, Cavalieri's *Rappresentazione di anima e di corpo*, and Carissimi's *Jonas* (with the Angelicum Orchestra *et al.* for Compania Generale Disco); Perosi's *La passione di Cristo*, Pergolesi's Concertino No. 1, *Contrasti crudeli*, *Luce digli occhi miei* and *Salve Regina No. 4*, Chiarini's *Il geloso schernito*, Manfredini's Sinfonia da chiesa Op. 2 No. 12, and Vivaldi's Bassoon Concerto P. 69 (with Montanari), Concerto Op. 10 No. 2 (with Tassinari) and *Stabat Mater* (with the Angelicum Orchestra *et al.* for Angelicum); Galuppi's Concerto for String Orchestra (with the Milan Chamber Orchestra for Telefunken); Monteverdi's *Il ballo della ingrate*, Cimarosa's *Il maestro di cappella* (with Muageri), and excerpts from *Il matrimonio segreto* (with the Milan Chamber Orchestra *et al.* for Vox); Handel's *Il pastor fido* and Paisiello's *Nina* (with the Milan Chamber Orchestra *et al.* for Cetra); Carissimi's *Jepthe* (with the Angelicum Orchestra *et al.* for Vox, originally on 78 r.p.m. discs); Grieg's *Holberg Suite* (with the Angelicum Orchestra for Classic); Rossini's *Il signor Bruschino* (with the Milan Philharmonic Orchestra *et al.* for Vox); and Pergolesi's *Il geloso schernito* (with the Teatro Olmo Villa Orchestra *et al.* for Cetra). *Il signor Bruschino* was originally released in 1954, remained in the catalogues for 20 years, and was a lively and affectionate performance.

Gerhardt, Charles (b. 1927). Born in Detroit, Gerhardt started to learn the piano at five, to compose at nine, and studied both music and science at the College of William and Mary and the Universities of Illinois and Southern California. He became a recording engineer with RCA and then was a producer, conductor and orchestrator. He produced records with Stokowski and other RCA artists and was associated with Toscanini during the last seven years of his life. Toscanini encouraged him to become a conductor; Gerhardt has said that he learned from Toscanini more about music in one day than from an entire college education. Other conductors who influenced him in his musical life were Kempe and Horenstein. He was also a recording producer for Westminster, returned to RCA and for Reader's Digest produced some 600 LPs in twelve years. He first recorded as a conductor when he substituted for a sick conductor with the Royal Philharmonic Orchestra in 1961 in a Reader's Digest project, and in 1964 formed the RCA Victor Symphony Orchestra which was essentially a recording ensemble and which eventually became, in 1971, the National Philharmonic Orchestra.

Gerhardt himself has conducted in approximately 50 LP records of music, including

Haydn's Symphony No. 100 (with the Royal Philharmonic Orchestra), *Moldau*, the *Mephisto Waltz*, incidental music for *A Midsummer Night's Dream*, overtures by Mozart, Weber, Lalo and Offenbach, the Polovtsian Dances from *Prince Igor*, Ravel's *Introduction et allegro*, *Boléro*, *Le Tombeau de Couperin* and *Pavane pour une infante défunte*, Fauré's *Pavane*, Satie's *Gymnopédies Nos 1* and *2*, *Romeo and Juliet* fantasy-overture and *1812* overture, Korngold's Cello Concerto (with Gabarra), Hanson's Symphony No. 2, Griffes' *The White Peacock* and *The Pleasure Dome of Kubla Khan*, arrangements of popular pieces for flute and orchestra (with Galway), and a number of dances and other short pieces (with the RCA Victor Symphony Orchestra and the National Philharmonic Orchestra). He also made a series of twelve LP records entitled *Classic Film Scores*, which is a collection of original film scores by Tiomkin, Korngold, Steiner, Newman, Waxman, Hermann and Rosza, all of which were issued by Reader's Digest in a subscription series, and later by RCA.

Gerlin, Ruggero (b. 1899). Born in Venice, Gerlin studied at Milan Conservatory, and from 1920 to 1940 was pupil and collaborator with Landowska in Paris. In 1941 he joined the staff of the Naples Conservatory and since 1947 has lectured at the Accademia Chigiana at Siena. He has made a number of records as a harpsichord player, including the concertos of Bach with the Collegium Musicum under Douatte, which were issued in France by Musidisc and in the United States and Britain by Nonesuch; previously he had recorded on 78s as a harpsichordist for Cetra, MIA (Italy) and Anthologie Sonore. As a conductor he recorded, again on 78 r.p.m. discs for Anthologie Sonore, music by Rameau, and for Cetra two Mozart Organ Sonatas.

German, Sir Edward (1862–1936). Born in Whitechurch, Shropshire, where he organised a band and taught himself the violin, German studied at the Royal Academy of Music in London, played the violin in orchestras for a short time, then became the musical director of the Globe Theatre, London (1888), and wrote, with great success, incidental music for the theatre's productions. He also completed Sullivan's last opera *The Emerald Isle*, composed two symphonies and other orchestral music, and light operas including his best known work, *Merrie England*. He recorded the latter in 1918, with the Light Opera Orchestra *et al.* for G & S; he also recorded, between 1915 and 1925, for HMV, pieces from his incidental music for *As You Like It*, *Much Ado about Nothing*, *Henry VIII* and *Nell Gwynn* and his *Gypsy Suite*, the overture *The Tempter*, *Theme and Variations*, *Valse gracieuse* from the *Leeds Suite*, dances from *Tom Jones* and Davis' *Harvest Dance* (with the Royal Albert Hall Orchestra *et al.*)

Gershwin, George (1898–1937). After studying the piano, harmony and counterpoint with Hambitzer, Hutcheson, Kilenyi and Goldmark in New York, Gershwin worked as a pianist and rehearsal conductor for Victor Herbert and Jerome Kern, and at that time also started composing popular songs. He appeared many times in the United States as a pianist and conductor, and performances of him as a pianist have been preserved on piano rolls and on record, including the 1924 acoustic recording with the Paul Whiteman Orchestra of *Rhapsody in Blue*. As a conductor he recorded *An American in Paris*, in a cut version, with an unidentified orchestra for Victor in 1930. Mark 56 Records (US) have issued a rehearsal of part of *Porgy and Bess* and of the *Second Rhapsody*, and the Smithsonian's American Musical Theater Series music from *Lady, Be Good!*. The *Rhapsody in Blue*, *An American in Paris* and the *Piano Concerto in F* have since been recorded innumerable times; in 1976–7 *Porgy and Bess* appeared in two excellent recordings, one by the Cleveland Orchestra *et al.* under Maazel, and the other with the Houston Grand Opera Company conducted by De Main, for Decca and RCA respectively.

Ghedini, Giorgio (b. 1892). Born in Cuneo, Piedmont, Ghedini studied in Turin and Bologna, was a conductor at the Teatro Regio in Turin, but turned to composition and teaching at the conservatories in Turin, Parma and Milan. Colosseum (US) released performances of him conducting his *Two-Cello Concerto* (with the Naples Scarlatti Orchestra *et al.*) and *Litanie della Vergine* (with an orchestra *et al.*) and Bach's *Ein musikalisches Opfer* (with the Naples Scarlatti Orchestra).

Ghione, Franco (1889–1964). Born in Acqui, Italy, Ghione studied the violin with his father, and after graduating from the Parma Conservatory was assistant conductor to Toscanini at La Scala (1922–3), and later became principal conductor there. He appeared as a guest conductor in European opera houses, and in 1937 went to the United States to conduct with the Detroit Civic Opera Company. He was associate conductor of the Detroit Symphony Orchestra

(1937–40) and after World War II was the chief conductor of an Italian opera company which toured Australia. Before the war he recorded two famous opera sets for HMV: *Pagliacci* (with Gigli, Pacetti, Basiola *et al.* and the La Scala Orchestra and Chorus) and *Turandot* (with Cigna, Merlin, Poli *et al.* and the Radio Italiana Orchestra and Chorus). The latter was the first complete recording of *Turandot*, and in 1975 was still listed in the Cetra-Everest catalogue. Both of these sets were most expertly led. In 1956 he conducted a *Cavalleria rusticana* (with the Milan Orchestra *et al.* for Decca), but this time his direction was much less incisive. He also recorded on 78 r.p.m. discs the overture to *Il viaggio a Reims* and the intermezzo from *Fedora* (with the La Scala Orchestra).

Giardino, Jean (b. 1906). Born in Paris, Giardino learned the violin as a child, studied at the Paris Conservatoire where he won first prize as a violinist, and studied composition under Emmanuel and Lehnert. At the age of sixteen he joined the Lamoureux Orchestra as a violinist and played under Chevillard, Paray, Toscanini, Monteux, Walter and Strauss. In 1931 he was appointed artistic director of Radio Morocco, started conducting, and in 1935 substituted for the conductor of the Paris National Orchestra, which led to his appointment as a conductor of Radiodiffusion Française in 1937. After World War II he toured Europe, South and Central America and North Africa, and later in 1966 he toured Japan and in 1968 Israel. He made 78 r.p.m. recordings for Pathé-Marconi with the Paris Conservatoire Orchestra, including *Boléro*, *Till Eulenspiegel*, the overture and some numbers from Schumann's *Manfred* music, Fauré's *Pelléas et Mélisande*, Glazunov's *Stenka Razin*, *Pictures at an Exhibition* and the gopak from *Sorochintsy Fair*, the Fête polonaise from *Le Roi malgré lui* and Rachmaninov's Piano Concerto No. 2 (with Blumenthal). *Pictures at an Exhibition* won a Grand Prix du Disque in 1947. Although acclaimed in his native France, Giardino is virtually unknown as a conductor in Britain and the United States, either as a concert or a recording artist.

Gibson, Sir Alexander (b. 1926). Born in Motherwell, Scotland, Gibson studied the piano at the Academy of Music in Glasgow, and attended Glasgow University, served for four years in the Royal Corps of Signals (1944–8), then studied at the Royal College of Music in London under Austin. He was a conducting pupil of Markevitch at the Salzburg Mozarteum, and of van Kempen at the Accademia Chigiana at Siena, and won second place at the first competition for young conductors at Besançon. He became a repetiteur at the Sadler's Wells Opera Company (1951–2), was assistant conductor of the BBC Scottish Orchestra (1952–4), was a staff conductor at Sadler's Wells (1954–7), made his debut at Covent Garden in 1956 with *Tosca*, and was appointed musical director of Sadler's Wells (1957–9). In 1959 he was engaged as musical director of the Scottish National Orchestra, the first long-term resident conductor this orchestra had enjoyed in its 60 years in existence, and he is now the longest serving director of any orchestra in Britain. With financial aid from the Arts Council, Scottish Television and friends, he founded the Scottish Opera in 1962, and its scope and reputation grew to culminate in productions of *Les Troyens* and the first complete *Ring* to be staged in Scotland, under Gibson. He has been a guest conductor with many of the major symphony orchestras in Britain, Europe, the United States and Australia; in 1967 he was awarded the CBE and in 1977 he was knighted. His contribution to the cause of opera and symphonic music in Scotland has been inestimable, and his fine and exacting musicianship has been amply demonstrated in his many records with the Scottish National Orchestra. Very little has been recorded of the Scottish Opera, except for a disc of excerpts from *Der Rosenkavalier*, under Gibson's direction issued in 1975. Nonetheless his work with the company has won high praise; writing in *The Musical Times* (February 1972), Andrew Porter commented on Gibson's reading of the complete *Ring* as 'colourful, constructed on a large scale, and urgent. By *Götterdämmerung* it had achieved greatness: the house was afire with that kind of collective ecstasy, rapture in the Wagnerian experience, associated with conductors like Furtwängler, Knappertsbusch and Goodall'.

As a symphonic conductor Gibson first appeared on record in 1960, conducting the London Symphony Orchestra for RCA in Sibelius' Symphony No. 5 and *Karelia* suite. In 1966 Saga issued a coupling of Sibelius' Symphonies Nos 3 and 7 with the Scottish National Orchestra, and other Sibelius discs have followed: Symphonies Nos 1, 2 and 5, and *En Saga* (for Classics for Pleasure), *Karelia*, *The Bard*, *Festivo* and the *King Christian II* suite (for EMI), and *Scènes historiques*, *Rakastava* and *Valse lyrique* (for RCA). The series for Classics for Pleasure has also included Dvořák's Symphony No. 9 and *Carnival* overture (with the London Philharmonic Orchestra), Tchaikovsky's Symphonies Nos 4 and 5, Beethoven's Piano Concertos Nos 1, 3 and 5, and the Choral

Fantasy (with Lill), Mendelssohn's Symphony No. 3 and *The Hebrides* overture, Mahler's *Das Lied von der Erde* (with Hodgson and Mitchinson), excerpts from *Un ballo in maschera*, Bruch's Violin Concerto No. 1 and *Scottish Fantasy* (with Hassan), excerpts from *Der Rosenkavalier*, mentioned above, *Ma Mère l'Oye*, *Jeux d'enfants*, *Le Carnaval des animaux*, *L'Apprenti sorcier*, *Danse macabre* and *La Boutique fantasque* (with the Scottish National Orchestra *et al.*). Gibson's other recordings include the complete music for violin and orchestra of Mozart (with Szeryng and the New Philharmonia Orchestra for Philips), a suite from *Carmen* (with the Covent Garden Orchestra for Decca), pieces from the *L'Arlésienne* suites and Bizet's *Symphony in C major* (with the Suisse Romande Orchestra for Decca), Berlioz's *La Mort de Cléopâtre* and excerpts from *Les Troyens* (with Baker and the London Symphony Orchestra for EMI), the overtures *Le Carnaval romain*, *Benvenuto Cellini*, *Béatrice et Bénédict*, *Le Corsaire* and *Le Roi Lear* (with the London Symphony Orchestra for EMI), a recital of 18th-century arias (with Berganza and the Covent Garden Orchestra for Decca), Elgar's Symphonies Nos 1 and 2, *Coronation Ode* and *The Spirit of England* (with the Scottish National Orchestra *et al.* for RCA) and *The Dream of Gerontius* (with the Scottish National Orchestra *et al.* for CRD), Walton's *Belshazzar's Feast* (with the Scottish National Orchestra *et al.* for RCA), some Mozart dances, Arnold's *Four Scottish Dances* and Prokofiev's Symphony No. 5 (with the Scottish National Orchestra for Waverley), Strauss's *Rosen aus dem Süden*, *Annen-polka*, *Kaiserwalzer*, *Tritsch-tratsch*, *Wiener Blut* and *Wein, Weib und Gesang* (with the Scottish National Orchestra for EMI), the *Peer Gynt* incidental music (with the Royal Philharmonic Orchestra *et al.* for World Record Club), Rachmaninov's Piano Concerto No. 1 and Saint-Saëns' Piano Concerto No. 2 (with Binns and the London Philharmonic Orchestra for World Record Club), Paganini's Violin Concertos Nos 1 and 4 (with Szeryng and the London Symphony Orchestra for Philips), the Delius Piano Concerto and Debussy's Fantasy (with Kars and the London Symphony Orchestra for Decca), a collection of Rossini overtures (with the London Festival Orchestra for Crossroads), Tchaikovsky's Symphony No. 6, *Les Sylphides*, *Finlandia*, *The Swan of Tuonela*, the *Peer Gynt* Suite No. 1 and Dvořák's *Carnival* overture (with the London Festival Orchestra for Reader's Digest), *Capriccio italien* (with the New Symphony Orchestra for Reader's Digest), the overture to Ethel Smyth's *The Wreckers*, Harty's *With the Wild Geese*, McCunn's overture *The Land of the Mountain and Flood* and German's *Welsh Rhapsody* (with the Scottish National Orchestra for EMI), Thea Musgrave's *Concerto for Orchestra* (with the Scottish National Orchestra for Decca), Hamilton's Violin Concerto and Goehr's Violin Concerto (with Parikian and the Scottish National Orchestra for EMI) and Bennett's Piano Concerto (with Bishop and the London Symphony Orchestra for Philips). In these recordings Gibson shows himself to be an extremely sound but somewhat cautious musical personality, inclined to be reserved in music calling for the expansive romantic gesture. But this may be, to some listeners, erring on the right side.

Gielen, Michael (b. 1927). Gielen was born in Dresden where his father was a distinguished opera producer, and emigrated to Argentina with his family. He studied the piano with Leuchter in Buenos Aires (1942–9), and in 1947 became a repetiteur at the Teatro Colón, and in 1949 gave a recital of the complete piano music of Schoenberg. In 1950 he returned to Europe, studied in Vienna with Polnauer, became a coach and conductor at the Vienna State Opera (1952–60) and began to win a reputation as a conductor of both the Viennese classics and of contemporary music. He was first conductor at the Royal Opera, Stockholm (1960–65), conducted at Cologne (1965–8), was musical director of the Belgian National Orchestra at Brussels (1969–73) and chief conductor at the Netherlands Opera (1973–5). In 1977 he took up the appointment of general music director and chief conductor at the Opera at Frankfurt am Main, and replaced Boulez as chief guest conductor of the BBC Symphony Orchestra. He has conducted widely in Europe and the United States, toured Australia and has been closely associated with the radio orchestras at Cologne and Frankfurt am Main. He is now an Austrian citizen. A composer of some distinction, he sets time aside from his conducting commitments for a period each summer for composition. His principal works include *Variations* for a string quartet (1949), *Four poems of Stefan George* (1955–8), *Variations* for 40 instruments (1959), *Ein Tag tritt hervor* (1960–63) and *Die Glocken sind auf falscher Spur*, a melodrama and interludes for six musicians (1967–9).

When he was in Vienna, Gielen recorded some Bach cantatas for Bach Guild, and made a number of recordings for Vox, including a Gluck flute concerto (with Wanausek), the two Chopin Piano Concertos and the Lalo Piano

Concerto (with Frugoni), the two Liszt Piano Concertos, *Malédiction* and *Totentanz*, and the Schubert–Liszt *Wanderer Fantasy* (with Brendel), Bartók's Piano Concertos Nos 2 and 3 (with Sandor), Franck's *Symphony in D minor* and *Symphonic Variations* (with Frugoni), Prokofiev's Piano Concertos Nos 2 and 3 (with Wührer), Bartók's *Sonata for Two Pianos and Percussion* (with Sandor and Reinhardt), and Rachmaninov's Piano Concerto No. 2 and Tchaikovsky's Piano Concerto No. 1 (with Blumenthal). Various Viennese orchestras were employed. A more unusual disc was a coupling of the violin and piano concertos of Schoenberg, performed by Marschner and Brendel respectively, with the South West German Radio Symphony Orchestra, and issued in 1958 by Turnabout; this recording was immensely important in introducing the music of Schoenberg's later period to a great number of people. Gielen further established himself as one of the major living interpreters of Schoenberg, with a recording for Philips of *Moses und Aron*, in which he conducted, *inter alios*, the Austrian Radio Chorus and Symphony Orchestra; the discs were released in 1975, and that year were awarded first prize by the Eighth Annual High Fidelity/Montreux International Record Awards, being selected by a jury of record critics from seven countries. Other recordings of contemporary music include Zimmermann's opera *Die Soldaten* (with the Gürzenich Orchestra *et al.*), de Pablo's *Tombeau* (with the North German Radio Orchestra), Kagel's *Heterophonie* and Ligeti's *Requiem* and Cello Concerto (with Palm and the Frankfurt Radio Symphony Orchestra), Nono's *Canti di vita e d'amore* (with the Saar Symphony Orchestra *et al.*) and *Per Bastiana* (with the Berlin Radio Symphony Orchestra) and Ruzicka's *Metastrofe* (with the Berlin Radio Symphony Orchestra), and Halffter's *Symposion* (with the Cologne Radio Symphony Orchestra). All of these were for Wergo. Also recorded have been Stockhausen's *Carré*, in which he conducted one of the four orchestras, for Philips, Hambraeus' *Transfiguration* (with the Swedish Radio Orchestra for Discophil), Werle's *The Dream of Thérèse* (with the Royal Court Orchestra *et al.* for Discophil), Mozart's Symphony No. 41 (with an orchestra for Music Treasures of the World, US), *Scheherazade* (with the Vienna State Opera Orchestra for Grand Award, US), and Beethoven's Symphonies Nos 2, 3, 7 and 8 (with the Vienna State Opera Orchestra, and issued by Audio Fidelity and Orion). Critical reception of the Beethoven symphonies was not exactly encouraging, suggesting that Gielen's readings were neither convincing nor well played.

Gierster, Hans (b. 1925). Born in Germany and educated at the Hochschule für Musik at Munich and at the Salzburg Mozarteum, Gierster became Krauss' assistant at the Munich Opera (1942). He was then conductor at Düsseldorf Opera (1945–52), at the Munich Opera (1952–6), general music director at Freiburg (1956–65) and at Nuremberg (1965–71), and became conductor of the music theatres as well as general music director at Nuremberg (from 1971). He has appeared at festivals at Munich, Edinburgh, Glyndebourne, Zürich, Vienna, Berlin and Florence, and has been a guest conductor with many of the major European orchestras. He has recorded excerpts from Lortzing's *Zar und Zimmerman* and Kienzl's *Der Evangelimann* (with the Bavarian State Opera Orchestra *et al.* for DGG), and Huber's *Inwendig voller Figur* (with the Nuremberg Symphony Orchestra for Wergo).

Gillesberger, Hans (b. 1909). Born in Ebensee in Upper Austria, Gillesberger was a chorister at Salzburg Cathedral, graduated in law at Vienna University and studied sacred music at the Vienna Academy of Music. He was conductor of the Vienna Boys' Choir (1942–5), was second director of the chorus of the Vienna State Opera (1943–53), and has been conductor of the Vienna Chamber Choir. With the Choir in particular, he has made a number of recordings, including motets and instrumental pieces of Josquin and Lassus (with Musica Antiqua for Bach Guild), masses by Dufay and Obrecht (with Musica Antiqua for Vanguard), Gabrieli's *Sacrae Symphoniae* and other pieces (with the Gabrieli Festival Choir and brass ensemble for Bach Guild), Haydn's *Stabat Mater* (for Lyrichord), Masses Nos 1, 5 and 6 (with the Vienna Symphony Orchestra for Lyrichord), and Nos, 5, 7 and 11 (with the Vienna Volksoper and Symphony Orchestras for Turnabout), Organ Concertos Nos 1 and 2 (with Heiller and the Vienna State Opera Orchestra for Haydn Society) and *12 German Dances* (with the Vienna State Opera Orchestra for Haydn Society), Mozart's Mass K. 259 (with the Vienna Volksoper Orchestra for Turnabout), Schubert's *Deutsche Messe* and *Mass in B flat* (with the Vienna Volksoper Orchestra for Turnabout), Bruckner's Mass No. 2 (with the Vienna State Opera Orchestra for Lyrichord) and Liszt's *Missa Choralis* (for Turnabout).

His most significant recording, however, has been of the *St John Passion* of Bach, made in

1967 by Telefunken. This performance attempts to be completely faithful to the composer's instrumental and vocal forces; boys' voices, in the persons of the Vienna Boys' Choir, replace sopranos and contraltos in both choruses and solos, and the Concentus Musicus performs, as it customarily does, on original instruments. His brisk tempi expunge all trace of romantic sentiment. The conditions of the performance generally approximate Bach's own at the St Thomas Church at Leipzig, and for that reason it is a most valuable recording; yet while it may be possible to be scrupulously accurate in duplicating outward circumstances, the *style* in which the work was performed is much less certain.

Gillis, Don (b. 1912). Born in Cameron, Missouri, and educated at the Texas Christian University where he became assistant conductor of the orchestra, Gillis worked for the Fort Worth radio station as a trombone player and arranger, and joined the National Broadcasting Company in New York in 1943. There he was in charge of programme planning, re-organised the NBC Symphony of the Air and wrote a number of broadcast programmes. He was composer-in-residence at the National Music Camp and director of the American Opera Workshop. He has composed much music with patriotic subjects, such as *The Alamo*, *An American Symphony*, *A Symphony of Free Men* and *To an Unknown Soldier*, religious music, including a cantata *The Crucifixion*, and *Symphony of Faith*, and music written with tongue-in-cheek. Among the latter is a symphonic suite entitled *Thoughts Provoked on Becoming a Prospective Papa*, and Symphony No. 5½, composed he has explained 'for fun' between his Fifth and Sixth Symphonies, and first performed by Toscanini in 1947. Among the first LPs issued by Decca in 1950 were two in which Gillis conducted the New Symphony Orchestra in *Portrait of a Frontier Town*, *The Man who Invented Music*, *The Alamo* and Symphony No. 5½.

Gimpel, Bronislaw (b. 1911). Born in Poland and a violin pupil of Flesch and Huberman, Gimpel held positions in Königsberg and Göteborg, came to the United States in 1937 and became concertmaster of the Los Angeles Philharmonic Orchestra. He has been the soloist in recordings of the Brahms' Violin Concerto *et al.* and in chamber music ensembles, and appeared as a conductor in a Nixa disc in 1952, with a symphony orchestra accompanying the pianist Balsam in Mendelssohn's Piano Concerto No. 2 and in Mozart's Piano Concerto K. 175.

Ginzburg, Leo (1901–1966). Born in Warsaw, Ginzburg was a pupil of Sarajev and Scherchen, conducted in Baku and Moscow, and was a professor at the Moscow Conservatory where one of his pupils was the conductor Stassevich. In 1966 he was made First Artist of the Russian Republic. His recordings include the incidental music to *King Lear* of Balakirev, Massenet's *Scènes napolitaines* and the Tchaikovsky *Symphony in E flat major*, arranged by Bogatyrev (with the USSR State Symphony Orchestra), Rubinstein's *Trot de cavalerie* and *Valse caprice* (with the Bolshoi Theatre Orchestra), excerpts from Bizet's *L'Arlésienne* suites (with the Moscow Philharmonic Orchestra) and Prokofiev's Piano Concerto No. 4 (with Verdernikov and the USSR State Symphony Orchestra).

Giordano, Umberto (1867–1948). The composer of *Andrea Chénier* and *Fedora* had no particular reputation as a conductor, and there appears to exist only one record of him in that role. Cetra recorded him on a 78 r.p.m. disc conducting the intermezzo from his opera *Il Re*, with the EIAR Orchestra.

Giovaninetti, Reynald (b. 1932). Born in Sétif in Algeria, Giovaninetti studied at the Sorbonne and the Paris Conservatoire, and won awards at the international conductors' competition at Besançon, and for composition at Divonne les Bains. His first engagement was with Radio-Télévision Française; since then he has appeared with French orchestras and opera companies, has conducted at the theatres of Besançon, then Mulhouse, was appointed director of the Marseille Opera (1968) where he was made artistic director (1972) and was dismissed unexpectedly (1977), and has conducted at international festivals and in England, Japan and the United States. He has recorded for La Guilde Internationale du Disque, making discs of excerpts from Rossini's operas *La Cenerentola*, *Il Signor Bruschino*, *Le Comte Ory*, *L'Italiana in Algeri* and *Otello*, from Offenbach's *Orfée aux enfers*, *Les Contes d'Hoffmann*, *La Fille du tambour-major*, *La Grande-Duchesse de Gérolstein*, *La Périchole* and *La Belle Hélène*, and the overtures to *Norma* and *Don Pasquale* (with the Monte Carlo National Opera Company), and for Disque Mondiophonie *Cavalleria rusticana* (in French). A pirate recording has also been available of him conducting Goldmark's *Die Königin von Saba*, in New York.

Girard, André (b. 1913). Born in Paris, Girard was director of Les Ballets des Champs-Élysées, musical director of Le Grand Ballet du Marquis de Cuevas, was with La Compagnie Renaud-Barrault, where he did orchestrations and directed productions, and at the same time formed and conducted his own chamber orchestra. He was director of chamber music for the French Radio and Television (ORTF, 1964–74) and during this time 300 scores were performed, two thirds by French composers, many of contemporary music. He also conducted the major French orchestras and at the Opéra-Comique. His recordings, with the ORTF Chamber Orchestra, include Barraud's *Three Studies for Orchestra*, *Rhapsodie dionysienne* and Flute Concerto (with Rampal, for Erato), *Une Saison en enfer* and Rivier's Piano Concerto and Trumpet and Saxophone Concerto (with Motard, Delmotte and Deffrayet, for ORTF), and Martinet's *Mouvement symphonique No. 1* and *Prométhée* (with the ORTF Chamber and Philharmonic Orchestras respectively, for Barenreiter).

Giulini, Carlo Maria (b. 1914). Born in Barletta in southern Italy, Giulini learned the violin as a boy, studied in Rome, first privately, at the Conservatorio di Musica di Santa Cecilia and then at the Accademia di Santa Cecilia under Molinari. As a student he played the viola in a string quartet, and for five years in the Augusteo Orchestra under many of the great conductors of the 1930s, including Strauss, Furtwängler and Walter. During the early part of World War II he was an officer in the Italian army, but with the arrival of the Nazis in Italy he went into hiding because of his anti-Fascist sympathies. He emerged in 1944 to conduct at the Augusteo the first concert to celebrate the liberation of Rome; the programme included Brahms' Symphony No. 4. In the same year he was appointed deputy to Previtali with the Radio Italiana Orchestra in Rome, and became the musical director of the orchestra in 1946. He conducted many radio performances of opera, the first being *Hänsel und Gretel*. In 1949 he conducted at festivals at Strasbourg, Prague and Venice, and in 1950 was conductor of the Milan Radio Orchestra; in Milan he became a close friend of Toscanini, after the latter had heard him conduct a radio performance of the Haydn opera, *Il mondo della luna*.

Giulini's operatic debut was at Bergamo in 1951; the next year he conducted at La Scala for the first time, with Falla's *La vida breve*, and was appointed as assistant to de Sabata, whom he succeeded as principal conductor in 1954. At La Scala he worked closely with Maria Callas. In 1955 he appeared first in Britain, conducting *Falstaff* at the Edinburgh Festival, and in the United States with the Chicago Symphony Orchestra. In 1958 came his famous collaboration with Visconti in *Don Carlos* at Covent Garden, and in these years he became widely celebrated as a conductor of opera, symphonic and choral music. He first conducted the Verdi *Requiem* in London in 1962, and recorded it several years later; his interpretation of this work was described by Alec Robertson as 'the most musical and the most spiritual one ever remembers hearing'. In 1969 he became permanent guest conductor of the Chicago Symphony Orchestra, afterwards music director of the Vienna Symphony Orchestra, and in 1978 conductor of the Los Angeles Philharmonic Orchestra.

In 1969 Giulini decided that he would cease to conduct opera and would devote his attention to symphonic music. He had become dissatisfied with the restricted time given to preparing roles, to the inadequacy of the casts he had to work with, and with the frequent need to compromise and make do with conditions as they were. He now rigidly limits the number of engagements he accepts and avoids social occasions; his contract with the Los Angeles Philharmonic expressly excludes social activities. He has, also, no interest in orchestral administration. Routine is absolutely anathema to him: he conducts for three weeks, then devotes the next four weeks to meditation and study: 'We have to deal with genius, and we are small men. We must understand what is behind the notes. We must not forget that Beethoven, Mozart and Bach wrote those things, and we must try all our lives to understand what they say. Reading the score is not enough – how many changes did the great composers make in their scores?' (Personal interview, July 1977). For him every rehearsal and performance takes the proportions of an important event. Although he is now the leading living Italian conductor, he is quite different in temperament from other Italians such as Toscanini and de Sabata. He is known to musicians as a gentle, gracious man, of impressive suavity and elegance, who beguiles and inspires his players rather than terrifying or bullying them. He keeps to a limited repertoire and feels no necessity to be a missionary for new composers, as his interest is in music that has entered the bloodstream of the people. His sense of perfection and inability to compromise with conditions less than his own demands, which caused him to give up conducting opera, also bring him to seek the highest standards in his work with symphony orchestras. Before he led the Israel

Philharmonic Orchestra on a world tour in 1960 he gave them 20 purely technical rehearsals, as well as the programme rehearsals for the tour. In Los Angeles in 1975 he asked for and was given fifteen hours of rehearsals for Mahler's Symphony No. 9. He said: 'One cannot play Mahler the way one plays Brahms. One cannot even play the Ninth as one plays the First. It is a matter of getting the notes and fingers in the right place first, and then trying to understand the conception. Mahler demands a special sound, a special reception of mood and structure. The orchestra must understand this so it becomes second nature by performance time, so it becomes part of the body. Mahler demands special attention.' In fact, all music to him demands special attention.

Giulini takes recording very seriously; to him a record is a document in the development of interpretation, and brings the best performances to people who never have the chance of hearing a great orchestra. But, to its disadvantage, a recording fixes just one moment of performance, and it is impossible to do twice the same performance. There can be no perfect performance; he learned, as a player in the Augusteo Orchestra, that great conductors interpreted the same piece very differently, but all were right, in their own ways. All great music has new life with changes in interpretation. The problem in recording is to bring life to the performances; to him, life is more important than perfection. His first recording for EMI was the Cherubini *Requiem Mass*; he and his musicians worked very hard, but when he heard the first complete recording he saw that it was good, but 'a most beautiful cadaver'. He said to the players: 'Take the next day off, then the next day we will do a live performance.' When the time came, he said: 'Do forget that there is a microphone. We play this piece and we try to make music.' Life then flowed into the music. He is also concerned to produce the same sound on record as one hears in the hall, and to try as much as possible to play long takes. He prefers to rehearse the piece, perform it at concerts four times, then to record it; he believes it wrong to rehearse in the recording studios because the approach to the music is false.

Giulini's first records were for Cetra, on 78s, when he was with Radio Italiana at Rome. He then recorded Milhaud's *L'Apothéose de Molière*, Malipiero's *Monde Céleste* and Alessandro Scarlatti's *Il trionfo dell'onore*. Walter Legge of EMI heard him rehearsing the La Scala Orchestra in *La vida breve*, and straightaway asked him to sign a contract with the company, and his first recording for them was the Cherubini *Requiem Mass in C minor* (mentioned above) with the Santa Cecilia Academy Chorus and Orchestra in 1953. Until his recent contract with DGG and except for his operatic recordings, Mozart's Symphonies Nos 40 and 41 (with the New Philharmonia Orchestra for Decca), the Schumann Piano Concerto (with Rubinstein and the Chicago Symphony Orchestra for RCA) *Iphigénie en Tauride* (with the Paris Conservatoire Orchestra *et al.*, issued by Vox), *La traviata* (issued by Cetra from a 1955 La Scala performance) and *Il barbiere di Siviglia* (issued by L'Estro Armonico from a 1956 La Scala performance), all his subsequent performances were made for EMI, first with the Philharmonia and New Philharmonia Orchestras and later with the Chicago and London Symphony Orchestras. His first mono records made in the 1950s were a distinguished series, and included *The Four Seasons*, Haydn's Symphony No. 94, the Franck *Symphony in D minor*, Tchaikovsky's Symphony No. 2, dances from *The Three-cornered Hat*, *Daphnis et Chloé* Suite No. 2, and Boccherini's *Symphony in C minor*. One of the finest was a disc bringing together a suite from *L'Oiseau de feu*, *Jeux d'enfants* and *Ma Mère l'Oye*, made in 1958, and still available in the US on the Seraphim label. Two operas were also issued on mono LP: *L'Italiana in Algeri* and *La serva padrona*, both with the La Scala Company.

In the 1960s and later he recorded many more standard works, such as Beethoven's Symphonies Nos 6, 7, 8 and 9, Brahms' Symphonies Nos 1, 3 and 4, Schubert's Symphony No. 8, Tchaikovsky's Symphony No. 6, Dvořák's Symphonies Nos 8 and 9, collections of overtures by Rossini and Verdi, *La Mer* and *Nocturnes*, *El amor brujo*, *Rapsodie espagnole*, the orchestral movements from Berlioz's *Roméo et Juliette* symphony, a coupling of *L'Oiseau de feu* and *Petrushka*, and Mahler's Symphony No. 1. Less familiar was the Beethoven *Mass in C major*. A number of concerto accompaniments were also recorded, including the two Brahms Piano Concertos (with Arrau), and the Piano Concerto No. 1 (with Weissenberg). Probably the greatest of his recordings were his famous readings of the Verdi *Requiem* (with the Philharmonia Chorus and Orchestra, et *al.*, issued in 1964), and *Don Carlos* (with the Covent Garden Orchestra *et al.*, made in 1971); the latter is often claimed to be one of the greatest operatic recordings made in the last three decades. He also directed two other outstanding operatic sets, both made in 1961: *Don Giovanni* and *Le nozze di Figaro* (with the Philharmonia Orchestra and outstanding casts). There has also appeared

Donizetti's *Don Sebastian*, taken from a performance in Florence in 1955.

In 1977 he commenced recording for DGG with the Chicago Symphony Orchestra, his first sets being Mahler's Symphony No. 9, *Pictures at an Exhibition* and Prokofiev's Symphony No. 1. He regards the Chicago Symphony as the finest possible in technique, sensitivity, intelligence and in their capacity to concentrate. He has a special feeling for Mahler's Symphony No. 9, has played it with all the greatest orchestras, and has waited many years to record it. Although he thinks it the most difficult score to record, because of its dynamics, counterpoint, its deep intensity and directness, he found the Chicago orchestra's capacity to concentrate astonishing. It was a great surprise to the DGG engineers that the recording had to stop only once to correct a playing mistake.

In the symphonies and concertos of Beethoven and Brahms, critics have found Giulini's interpretations somewhat uneven. Sometimes his depth of expression, lyrical intensity and refinement of nuance could result in slow and unsteady tempi, which give an impression of waywardness and lack of dramatic urgency. To this degree he has been likened to Furtwängler, although he himself is not conscious of being Furtwängler's heir. These performances of Giulini contrast with the rhythmically steady and utterly straightforward readings of northern European conductors such as Karajan, Böhm, Kleiber, Klemperer and Schmidt-Isserstedt, and even more so with the crispness and tension of Toscanini. It is evident in the concert hall that he conceives the music with greater intensity and feeling than most other conductors; for instance, the *Scherzo* of the Beethoven Symphony No. 9 takes a more *musical* shape than heard with almost any other conductor. Some critics mistakenly remarked that his Mahler Symphony No. 1 was an Italianate view of the music, and *ipso facto* unidiomatic, a view which surprised Giulini. His interpretation, he said, was quite intentional; moreover, he pointed out, he grew up in the southern Tyrol, not far from the places that gave Mahler so much inspiration. 'I heard the same sounds, saw the same beauties.'

Glazunov, Alexander (1865–1936). The Russian composer Glazunov was active as a conductor, first appearing at the Paris Exhibition of 1889 when he led his Symphony No. 2. Later he shared the leadership of the Russian Symphony Concerts at St Petersburg with Liadov and Rimsky-Korsakov, and in 1928 toured a number of European countries and the United States, conducting usually his own music. He was reported to be an indifferent conductor, but he enjoyed conducting so much that he accepted every invitation offered him. Students and the professors at the St Petersburg Conservatory so liked him that when he directed the student orchestra the players tried hard to give a satisfactory performance in spite of him. He made one recording of his own music, the ballet *The Seasons*, with an unidentified orchestra, for Columbia. It was so poorly conducted that it is scarcely an authoritative document.

Glière, Reinhold (1875–1956). The Russian composer Glière was born in Kiev, studied at the Moscow Conservatory, was a conducting pupil of Fried in Berlin (1905–07), and made his debut as a conductor in Russia in 1908. His subsequent career was more in the direction of composition, pedagogy and the collection of folk music. Some records have come from Russia with him conducting his own music: the ballets *The Red Poppy* and *The Bronze Horseman* (with the Bolshoi Theatre Orchestra), the Horn Concerto (with Polekh and the Bolshoi Theatre Orchestra), and the Symphonies Nos 1 (with the Moscow Radio Orchestra) and 3 (with the Moscow Philharmonic Orchestra). The Symphony No. 3, *Ilya Murometz*, has also been given stunning recordings by conductors such as Stokowski, Ormandy, Scherchen, Rachmilovich, Fricsay and Rakhlin.

Glindemann, Ib (b. 1934). Born in Copenhagen, Glindemann was educated at the Royal Danish Academy of Music, led his own jazz orchestra (1952–60), conducted the Jutland symphony orchestra (1960–64), conducted a jazz orchestra for Radio Denmark (1964–8), and since then has been a freelance conductor, composer and arranger. He has written many film, radio and television scores, conducted the Royal Danish Ballet on tour in 1964, and has recorded light music and jazz. RCA Italiana released a disc in which he conducted the Scandinavian Philharmonic Orchestra in his own and Haydn's trumpet concertos (with Hovalt).

Gmeindl, Walter (b. 1890). Born in Hainburg, Austria, Gmeindl studied with Schreker in Vienna, was a theatre conductor at Munich, taught composition at the Berlin Academy of Music (1922–45), and was then at the Vienna Academy of Music. He has composed orchestral, choral and chamber music. Polydor issued a number of 78 r.p.m. discs of him conducting Haydn's Symphony No. 92 (with the Berlin Philharmonic Orchestra), Torelli's Sinfonia

No. 6 (with the Berlin Radio Wind Ensemble), J. C. Bach's Clavier Concerto No. 1 (with Stadelman) and *Sinfonia in B flat* and Cannabich's *Symphony in B major* (with the Berlin State Opera Orchestra), and the Stamitz *Symphony in E flat*, Leopold Mozart's *Symphony in D major* and Wagenseil's *Symphony in D major* (with the Berlin Municipal Orchestra).

Gmür, Hanspeter (b. 1936). Born in St Gall, Switzerland, Gmür studied at the Lucerne Conservatory (1954–8), founded and was musical director of the Collegium Musicum of Lucerne (1955–8), and studied conducting in Munich (1959–61) and at Hilversum with van Otterloo and Ferrara (1959). He was conductor at St Gall (1961–4), at Klagenfurt, Austria (1964–8), won an award for the promotion of culture in St Gall (1967), and since 1968 has been a guest conductor in FR Germany, Italy, Yugoslavia, Romania and Czechoslovakia. He has recorded Bach's Violin Concertos Nos 1 and 2 (with Büchner and the Munich Bach Soloists and the Bamberg Symphony Orchestra for BASF), Bach's Suite No. 3 and trumpet concertos by Hummel, Richter, Telemann, and Torelli (with Quinque, and the Bamberg Chamber Orchestra for Intercord), Handel's *Music for the Royal Fireworks* and Haydn's Symphony No. 100 (with the South German Philharmonic Orchestra for BASF), Haydn's Symphony No. 97 and overtures *L'incontro improviso*, *L'isola disabitata* and *L'anima del filosofo* (with the Nuremberg Symphony Orchestra for Colosseum), J. C. Bach's Sinfonia Op. 6 No. 1 (with the Frankisches Kammer Orchester for Colosseum), Beethoven's Symphonies Nos 1 and 8, and Piano Concerto No. 5 (with Rosengarten), *Symphonie fantastique* and Dvořák's Symphony No. 9 (with the South German Philharmonic Orchestra for Sonopresse), the Brahms' Violin Concerto (with Schneider) and Piano Concerto No. 2 (with Goldman, and the Munich Symphony Orchestra for Sonopresse) and excerpts from *Aida* (with the Nuremberg Symphony Orchestra *et al.* for Sonopresse).

Goberman, Max (1911–62). Born in Philadelphia, Goberman studied the violin with Auer and conducting with Reiner at the Curtis Institute, was a violinist with the Philadelphia Orchestra (1928) and soon after founded the New York Sinfonietta with which he presented a wide ranging repertoire. He conducted the Ballet Russe de Monte Carlo on its Australian tour in 1940, organised and conducted the National Youth Administration Symphony of New Jersey, and was musical director of the Ballet Theatre and the New York City Opera. His career then took two separate directions: on the one hand he became the highly-paid conductor of Broadway musicals, and on the other he founded a record company in 1959, the Library of Recorded Masterpieces. His purpose with this company was to record quite simply the entire orchestral works of Vivaldi and Haydn, and before his death three years later he had gone a good way towards his goal, completing 75 of Vivaldi's concertos, on 17 LP records, and about 45 of the Haydn symphonies. In addition he managed to record the Concerti Grossi Op. 6 of Corelli, Bach's *Brandenburg Concertos*, the Suite No. 3, the sinfonia from Cantata No. 174, the *Two-Harpsichord Concerto in C minor* and three chorales, Mozart's Symphony No. 38, *Eine kleine Nachtmusik*, and *Eine kleine deutsche Kantate*, Beethoven's Symphony No. 8 and overtures *Fidelio* and *Leonore No. 1*, Mendelssohn's *Meeresstille und glückliche Fahrt* overture, Schubert's Symphony No. 8, *Magnificat* and *Rosamunde* overture, Brahms' *Liebeslieder Waltzes* and *New Liebeslieder Waltzes*, *Academic Festival* and *Tragic Overtures* and *Variations on the St Antony Chorale*, the *Tannhäuser* Overture and Bacchanale, the preludes to Acts I and III, Dance of the Apprentices and Finale from *Die Meistersinger*, Tchaikovsky's *Romeo and Juliet* fantasy-overture, 4th movement from Suite No. 3 and *Andante cantabile*, *Jeux*, *Prélude à l'après-midi d'un faune* and *Nocturnes*, the Prokofiev Symphony No. 1, *Overture on Hebrew Themes*, *Lieutenant Kijé* suite, and scherzo and march from *The Love of Three Oranges*. In the Vivaldi he conducted the New York Sinfonietta, in the Corelli and Haydn the Vienna State Opera Orchestra, and in the other works the Vienna State Opera Orchestra and the Vienna Symphony Orchestra.

The albums of the Library of Recorded Masterpieces were released on a monthly subscription basis and in the Haydn symphonies scores and excellent programme notes were included with each album. Their presentation surpassed any other records issued, before or since; the Haydn symphonies were performed according to the new edition of H. C. Robbins Landon, and the series was the first attempt at a complete recorded edition of the Haydn symphonies, which finally came to fruition with the separate sets of Märzendorfer and Dorati. Other conductors, notably Jones and Almeida, have recorded many of the Haydn symphonies, but it was tragic that Goberman's untimely death cut short his heroic effort to complete them. Goberman's Haydn is strong, driving and intensely dramatic, in many ways close to the Dorati readings in feeling. Following Robbins Landon's contention that the horn parts in the Haydn symphonies, at least up to the *London* symphonies, were for *alto* horns (*The Symphonies of Joseph Haydn*, pp. 125f), the horn parts were played an octave higher than usual, sometimes with an electrifying effect. The Vivaldi series was re-issued by Musical Heritage Society in the US, and the Corelli Concerti Grossi and the Haydn Symphonies, up to No. 22, on the Odyssey label. Goberman did not record the symphonies in numerical order and of the ones re-issued, the Symphony No. 18 had to be interpolated with a performance by Mackerras and the London Symphony Orchestra. Odyssey also released the Schubert Symphony No. 8, *Magnificat* and *Rosamunde* overture. Also, some early discs, on 78 r.p.m., of the New York Sinfonietta were issued on the Timely label and included pieces by Boyce, Pergolesi, and Locatelli; on Columbia there was a Mozart Divertimento K. 287 in which Szigeti joined Goberman's orchestra, and for Young People's Records some country dances by Mozart and Leopold Mozart's *Toy Symphony*.

Godfrey, Sir Dan (1868–1939). Born in London into a family of distinguished regimental bandmasters, Godfrey was educated in Germany and at the Royal College of Music, and in 1890 became conductor of the London Military Band and Corps of Commissionaires Band. After conducting opera in South Africa (1891–2) he was appointed conductor of the Winter Gardens Orchestra in Bournemouth (1893), and in the next year became resident musical adviser and director of music at Bournemouth; in 1896 the Bournemouth Municipality took over his orchestra and established the Bournemouth Municipal Orchestra, the first of its kind in England. In 1895 he started an annual 28-week season of symphony concerts in Bournemouth, directing them until his retirement in 1934. The repertoire of the orchestra covered classical and romantic symphonies, overtures and concertos, as well as the modern music of the day. He gave a great number of first performances of the music of British composers, and brought many of these composers to Bournemouth to conduct their own works. He achieved a considerable standard with his orchestra, was recognised for his services to British music when he was knighted in 1922, and published his memoirs *Memories and Music* in 1924. He made a number of arrangements for military band and also composed dances and marches.

Godfrey was one of the pioneers of recording in England. In the years 1925–6 Columbia issued a set of him conducting the London Symphony Orchestra in Vaughan Williams' *London Symphony*, as well as Debussy's *Petite Suite* and some *Slavonic Dances* of Dvořák. With either his Bournemouth Municipal Orchestra or others not identified he also recorded for Columbia Mozart's Symphony No. 41, various popular orchestral pieces such as the *Pique Dame*, *Zampa* and *Orfée aux enfers* overtures, the homage march from *Sigurd Jorsalfar*, the coronation march from *Le Prophète*, German's *Henry VIII* dances, Coleridge-Taylor's *Petite Suite de concert* and Wagner's *Kaisermarsch*, and for Regal-Zonophone a 'selection' from *Don Giovanni*.

Godfrey, Isidore (1900–77). Educated at the Guildhall School of Music, Godfrey joined the D'Oyly Carte Opera Company in 1925, which, until the copyright of the Gilbert and Sullivan operas ran out in the 1950s, had a theatrical and recording monopoly of them. He was first chorus master and assistant conductor, and became musical director in 1929, a post he retained until his retirement in 1968. He conducted the company and performed the Gilbert and Sullivan operas during eleven tours of Canada and the United States. His first recording of one of the operas was made in 1933, of an abridged version of *The Sorcerer*, and *The Mikado*. These were for HMV; in 1949 he started for Decca a series on LP with the D'Oyly Carte Opera Company with *Trial by Jury*, going on to record ten others of the operas, and repeating them all again after 1958 on stereo recordings. The last to be recorded was the second stereo remake of *The Pirates of Penzance* in 1968; *HMS Pinafore*, *Iolanthe*, *The Gondoliers*, *Cox and Box* and *Patience* were complete with the spoken dialogue. A rarely heard opera, *Utopia Ltd.*, was represented by excerpts. Despite weaknesses here and there, these recordings gave an excellent impression of the style and spirit of the Gilbert and Sullivan operas in the unique way in which they were preserved for the 60 or 70 years during which the performances were scarcely varied at all.

Goehr, Walter (1903–60). The son of a merchant (and father of Alexander Goehr), Goehr was born in Berlin, showed prodigious musical talent as a child, and at the age of seventeen was the assistant conductor at a theatre. He studied at the Prussian Academy of Arts, at the Stern Academy and with Schoenberg in Berlin, was musical director of the Reinhardt Theatre and conductor for the German Radio (1925–31), when he composed the music for *Malpopita*, one of the first radio operas. In 1933 he emigrated to England, was musical director for the HMV and Columbia record companies, conducted the BBC Theatre Orchestra (1946–9) and the Morley College Orchestra and Choir, was active as a guest conductor throughout Europe and South America, and conducted the first performances of Tippett's *A Child of Our Time* and Britten's *Serenade for Tenor, Horn and Strings*. His compositions include symphonic, chamber and film music; amongst the latter is the score of Lean's *Great Expectations*. Goehr was an early pioneer of the music of Schoenberg; he edited music by Purcell, Mussorgsky and Monteverdi, and his arrangement of the latter's *Vespro della Beata Vergine* has been widely performed.

Before World War II Goehr made records for HMV and Columbia, two of his finest sets being Bizet's *Symphony in C major* (with the London Philharmonic Orchestra) and Grieg's *Holberg Suite* (with the London Chamber Orchestra). Others made at this time included *Les Sylphides*, *La Boutique fantasque*, the gopak from *Sorochintsy Fair*, the intermezzo and march from Sibelius' *Karelia* suite, *Invitation to the Dance* (in the Weingartner orchestration), some Strauss waltzes and Bizet's *Danse bohémienne* (with the London Philharmonic Orchestra), Leopold Mozart's *Toy Symphony* and the waltz from Toye's *The Haunted Ballroom* (with the Orchestra Raymond), Elgar's *Sospiri*, the serenade from Milhaud's Symphony No. 3 and *Boléro* (with unidentified orchestras), Bach's *Two-Violin Concerto in D minor* (with Szigeti and Flesch), a Handel Viola Concerto (with Primrose), the Haydn Trumpet Concerto (with Eskdale), Mozart's Adagio K. 261 and Kreisler's *Violin Concerto in C major* (with Pougnet), Weber's Clarinet Concertino (with Kell), Mendelssohn's Piano Concerto No. 1 (with Dorfman and the London Symphony Orchestra), Tchaikovsky's Piano Concerto No. 1 (with Petri and the London Philharmonic Orchestra), Saint-Saëns' *Introduction et rondo capriccioso* and Bruch's Violin Concerto No. 1 (with Campoli), Mozart's Piano Concertos K. 456 (with Kraus and the London Philharmonic Orchestra for Parlophone) and K. 537 (with Landowska), the Schumann Piano Concerto (with Hess and the London Philharmonic Orchestra), Rachmaninov's Piano Concerto No. 2 (with Moiseiwitsch and the London Philharmonic Orchestra) and the third movement from Varèse's *Octandre*. When Decca was expanding its 78 r.p.m. catalogue, he recorded for that company Mozart's Symphony No. 39, Liszt's *Hungarian Rhapsody No. 2*, and *On Hearing the First Cuckoo in Spring* (with the National Symphony Orchestra), the *Peer Gynt* Suite No. 1 (with the London Symphony Orchestra) and *Moldau* and dances from *The Bartered Bride* (with the BBC Theatre Orchestra). For Schott he also recorded Tippett's Concerto for Double String Orchestra.

In the decade before his death, Goehr was extremely active as a recording artist, and made LP records with a vast repertoire ranging from Monteverdi to Shostakovich, with a bewildering variety of orchestras, for La Guilde Internationale du Disque. These performances were issued in different countries on a number of labels such as Concert Hall, Musical Masterpieces, Audio Fidelity, Nixa, Vanguard, Nonesuch and Perfect. Some works were recorded twice, presumably on mono and stereo, and in some cases different orchestras were named for the same performance. Included were Corelli's Concerti Grossi Nos 1 to 4, Mozart's Divertimentos K. 136, K. 137 and K. 138, and Dvořák's *Serenade in E minor* (with the Boyd Neel Orchestra); Mozart's Piano Concerto K. 466 (with Pelleg), Violin Concerto K. 219 (with Olof) and Clarinet Concerto (with d'Hondt), Schubert's *Rosamunde* overture and *Overture in the Italian Style*, Tchaikovsky's Piano Concerto No. 1 (with Mewton-Wood) and Barber's Violin Concerto (with Kaufman, and the Musical Masterpieces Symphony Orchestra); *Messiah*, *Giulio Cesare* and *Acis and Galatea* (with the Handel Society, London, Chorus and Orchestra *et al.*); Mozart's Mass K. 317, *Requiem*, *Ave verum corpus* and *Masonic Funeral Music*, Haydn's *The Seasons* and Beethoven's *Missa Solemnis* (with the North German Symphony Orchestra and Chorus *et al.*); Vivaldi's *The Four Seasons* and *L'estro armonico* (with Gawriloff *et al.*) and Tchaikovsky's *Serenade in C major* (with the Frankfurt Chamber Orchestra); Telemann's *Oboe d'amore Concerto in E minor* (with van Slochteren and the Concert Hall Chamber Orchestra); Monteverdi's *Sonata sopra Sancta Maria* and *Il combattimento di Tancredi e Clorinda*, Handel's Organ Concertos Nos 13, 14 and 15 (with Pelleg) and *Apollo e Daphne*, Wondratschek's Harpsichord Concerto (with Pelleg), the two Liszt Piano Concertos (with Entremont), Chopin's Piano Concerto No. 2 (with Mewton-Wood) and excerpts from *Die Fledermaus* and *Der Zigeunerbaron* (with the Zürich Radio Orchestra *et al.*); the *Brandenburg Concerto No. 3*, the Lully (arr. Mottl) Ballet Suite, *Messiah*, Haydn's Symphonies Nos 46 and 96, Mozart's Symphony No. 39, *Eine kleine Nachtmusik* and excerpts from *Don*

Giovanni and *Le nozze di Figaro*, Beethoven's Symphonies Nos 6 and 9, *Coriolan*, *Egmont* and *Prometheus* overtures, Piano Concerto No. 3 (with Johannesen) and the incidental music for *Die Ruinen von Athen*, Witt's *Jena Symphony* (once attributed to Beethoven), Schubert's *Wanderer Fantasy* (arr. Liszt, with Johannesen), the Schumann Piano Concerto (with Mewton-Wood), Mendelssohn's Symphony No. 3 and incidental music to *A Midsummer Night's Dream*, the overture *Le Carnaval romain*, Chopin's Piano Concerto No. 1 (with Mewton-Wood), Tchaikovsky's Symphony No. 4, *Romeo and Juliet* fantasy-overture, *Elegy*, *Fate*, *The Voyevoda*, and Violin Concerto (with Odnoposoff), Bruch's Violin Concerto No. 1 (with Odnoposoff), Bruckner's Symphony No. 3, Dvořák's Symphonies Nos 3 and 5, *Pictures at an Exhibition* and *A Night on the Bare Mountain*, the Grieg Piano Concerto (with Johannesen), *Scheherazade*, the Verdi *Requiem* and excerpts from *Rigoletto*, *Il trovatore* and *La traviata*, Franck's *Symphony in D minor*, *Les Éolides*, *Psyché*, *Le Chasseur maudit* and *Symphonic Variations* (with Entremont), *Boléro*, Rachmaninov's Piano Concerto No. 2 (with Entremont), Debussy's First Clarinet Rhapsody (with d'Hondt) and *Fantaisie* (with Pelleg), *El amor brujo* (with Delorie), *L'Oiseau de feu*, Saint-Saëns' Symphony No. 3 and *Le Carnaval des animaux*, Moszkowski's Piano Concerto (with Kann), and excerpts from *Carmen*, *Faust*, *Die Fledermaus* and *Der Zigeunerbaron* (with the Netherlands Philharmonic Orchestra *et al.*); Bach's *Mass in B minor*, Mozart's Violin Concertos K. 207 and K. 219 (with Parikian) and a recital of arias from the Mozart operas (with Simoneau), Beethoven's *Ritterballet*, the overture *Le Carnaval romain*, Brahms' Piano Concerto No. 1 (with Yankoff), Dvořák's *Czech Suite*, *Peer Gynt* Suite No. 1, *Le Carnaval des animaux*, a suite from *Carmen*, and Fauré's *Ballade* (with Johannesen) and *Masques et bergamasques* (with the Amsterdam Philharmonic Orchestra *et al.*), Beethoven's Symphony No. 5, *Egmont* overture, and *Moldau* (with the London Symphony Orchestra); Beethoven's Symphonies Nos 8 and 9 and *Twelve German Dances*, and *The Bartered Bride* (with the Frankfurt Radio Symphony Orchestra *et al.*); Beethoven's Triple Concerto (with Santiliquido, Parikian and Amfitheatrof) and Tchaikovsky's Symphony No. 5 (with the Rome Philharmonic Orchestra); a fantasia by Purcell, Haydn's *Violin Concerto in G major* (with Skipka), Schubert's Symphony No. 1, overtures *In the Italian Style*, *Alfonso und Estrella* and *Die Zauberharfe* and 16 *German Dances*, Elgar's *Serenade* and *Enigma Variations*, Honegger's *Pastorale d'été*, Shostakovich's Piano Concerto No. 1 (with Mewton-Wood), and Gershwin's *Piano Concerto in F*, *Variations on 'I got Rhythm'* (with Bianca) and *Rhapsody in Blue* (with Entremont, and the Concert Hall Symphony Orchestra); Haydn's *The Creation* and the Suppé overtures *Die schöne Galatea*, *Dichter und Bauer*, *Leichte Cavallerie*, *Banditenstreiche*, *Boccaccio* and *Morgen, Mittag und Abend in Wien* (with the Vienna State Opera Orchestra); *L'Incoronazione di Poppea*, *The Hebrides* overture and Saint-Saëns' Cello Concerto No. 1 (with Tortelier, and the Zürich Tonhalle Orchestra); Bach's Flute, Violin and Harpsichord Concerto (with Otto, Gawriloff and Wührer), Two-Violin Concerto (with Gawriloff and Lechner) and *Die Kunst der Fuge*, Mozart's *Serenata notturna*, Piano Concertos K. 37, K. 39, K. 107, K. 238 and K. 246 (with Balsam), and K. 466 (with Pelleg), Violin Concertos K. 216 and K. 218 (with Parikian) and K. 219 (with Olof), and Clarinet Concerto (with d'Hondt, and the Hamburg Chamber Orchestra); *L'Arlésienne* Suite No. 1 and suites from *Coppélia*, *Sylvia* and *La Source* (with the Pasdeloup Orchestra); the Glazunov and Dvořák Violin Concertos (with Odnoposoff) and the ballet music from *Faust* (with the Paris Concerts Orchestra); the *Brandenburg Concertos Nos 4* and *5*, Vivaldi's Concerto Op. 3 No. 6, arranged for harmonica (with Larry Adler), a Tartini violin concerto (with Rostal), Haydn's Symphony No. 96 and *L'isola disabitata* overture, Mozart's Symphony No. 36 and *German Dances* K. 600, Beethoven's Symphony No. 8, two *German Dances*, Piano Concerto No. 2 (with Balsam), two Romances (with Rostal), and *Die Geschöpfe des Prometheus*, Mendelssohn's Piano Concerto No. 1 (with Pelleg), Tchaikovsky's Piano Concertos Nos 2 and 3 and *Concert Fantasy* (with Mewton-Wood), and Suites Nos 1, 2 and 3 (with the Winterthur Symphony Orchestra); Beethoven's Symphonies Nos 1 and 4, excerpts from *The Bartered Bride*, and *Nutcracker* Suite (with the Frankfurt Opera Orchestra *et al.*), excerpts from *Swan Lake* and *The Sleeping Beauty* (with the Rome Opera Orchestra); excerpts from *Rigoletto* and *Il trovatore* (with the New York Opera Society Orchestra *et al.*); Beethoven's Piano Concerto No. 4 (with Mewton-Wood), Lalo's *Symphonie espagnole* (with Odnoposoff) and the Bliss Piano Concerto (with Mewton-Wood and the Utrecht Symphony Orchestra); the Stravinsky Piano Concerto (with Mewton-Wood and the Hague Philharmonic Orchestra); and excerpts from *Die lustige*

Witwe (with the Opera Society Orchestra *et al.*).

Other recordings made by Goehr included Tippett's Concerto for Double String Orchestra (with the Philharmonia Orchestra for EMI), the Brahms' Violin Concerto (with Wolf and the London Symphony Orchestra for Musical Appreciation), the Tchaikovsky Violin Concerto (with Spivakovsky and the London Symphony Orchestra for Everest), the *Peer Gynt* Suite No. 1, Solveig's Song, the march from *Die Ruinen von Athen* and the intermezzo from *Cavalleria rusticana* (with the Israel Radio Orchestra for Arzi), Schoenberg's Chamber Symphony No. 1 (with the Berlin Chamber Orchestra for Eterna), and Eisler's *Deutsche Sinfonie* (with the Berlin Staatskapelle *et al.* for Eterna).

In the concert hall, Goehr was never considered among the top flight of European conductors, but he was always an accomplished and completely dependable musician. His interpretations of the standard repertoire, so well represented in the above discography, were straightforward, unmannered and well executed. His recordings were widely distributed in the early years of LP, and he did much to expand the repertoire by recording music such as the *Prometheus* ballet of Beethoven and the Tchaikovsky suites, as well as many of the major orchestral works. These records have all but disappeared from the British catalogues.

Gohl, Willi (b. 1925). Born in Zürich, Gohl studied at Küsnacht and at the Zürich Conservatory, and since 1959 has been the director of the conservatory. He has conducted the Zürich Association for Singing Teachers, and in 1954 formed the Zürich Singkreis with which he has toured Switzerland and abroad. He is also the harpsichordist in Die Kammermusiker and in the Winterthur Baroque Quintet. Turnabout has released discs in which he has conducted the Zürich Chamber Orchestra *et al.* in the Haydn Mass No. 1, and *Non nobis te*.

Gold, Ernest (b. 1921). Born in Vienna, where his father was a lawyer and amateur violinist and his maternal grandfather a pupil of Bruckner and at one time president of the Gesellschaft der Musikfreunde, Gold was educated at the Conservatory and Academy of Music there; in 1938 the family migrated to the United States. He studied in New York with the National Orchestral Association, but after the success of his compositions *Pan American Symphony*, and Piano Concerto No. 1, he moved to Los Angeles and devoted himself to writing film music for Hollywood studios. Altogether he has written scores for about 75 films, including *The Secret of Santa Vittoria*, *On the Beach*, *It's a Mad, Mad, Mad, Mad World* and *Exodus*, for which he won an Academy Award (1960). In 1958 he became musical director of the Santa Barbara Symphony Orchestra (1958–60), founded the Senior Citizens Orchestra, Los Angeles, was president of the West Coast Branch of the National Association of American Composers, Authors and Conductors, and now composes, conducts, lectures, writes educational music and works with the musical theatre. His recordings include eight of his film scores of which *Exodus* (RCA) was especially successful, his *Songs of Love and Parting* (with Marni Nixon) and Castelnuovo-Tedesco's *Coplas* (with the Vienna Volksoper Orchestra for Crystal), and Hovhaness's *Avak, the Healer*, *Tzaikerk*, *Prayer of St Gregory* and *Armenian Rhapsody No. 1* (with the Crystal Chamber Orchestra for Crystal).

Goldberg, Szymon (b. 1909). Born in Włocławek, Poland, Goldberg studied the violin as a child with Flesch in Berlin and at sixteen was the concertmaster of the Dresden Philharmonic Orchestra. Four years later Furtwängler appointed him concertmaster of the Berlin Philharmonic Orchestra, where he remained until 1934 when he was forced to leave Germany. In those years he played in a trio with Hindemith and Feuermann, and later in a duo with Lili Kraus. During a tour of the Dutch East Indies in 1942 he was taken prisoner by the Japanese, and during his imprisonment he made many contacts with Dutch people which came to fruition when he was asked in 1955 to take over the leadership of the Netherlands Chamber Orchestra. He has conducted other chamber orchestras throughout the world, and has also conducted major symphony orchestras in Europe and the United States. After World War II he toured as a violinist in Australia and New Zealand, the United States and Europe.

In 1960 and in the following years Philips recorded the Netherlands Chamber Orchestra under Goldberg in a series of fine performances, including the Bach *Brandenburg Concertos* and Cantata No. 170, Haydn's Symphonies Nos 39, 44, 57 and 83, the *Horn Concerto in D major* (with Woudenberg) and *Piano Concerto in D major* (with Haebler), Mozart's Symphony No. 29, Sinfonia Concertante K. 297b and K. 364 and *Eine kleine Nachtmusik*, and Hindemith's *The Four Temperaments*, *Five Pieces for String Orchestra* and *Trauermusik*. For Donemus he also recorded Frid's *Rhythmic Studies* and Ponce's *Concierto da camera* (with Pollard, and the Netherlands Chamber Orchestra). In these discs the style, finesse and precision of Goldberg and the orchestra were admirably exhibited. He also recorded as a violinist for Parlophone, first on 78 r.p.m. discs with Lili Kraus, all the Beethoven Violin and Piano Sonatas, and on LP concertos by Bach and Mozart, the Brahms Violin and Piano Sonatas and the Schumann Sonata No. 1 (with Balsam, for Decca US), and Milhaud's *The Four Seasons* (with the composer conducting, for Philips).

Goldsbrough, Arnold (1892–1964). Born in Gomersal, Yorkshire, Goldsbrough studied music privately and at the Manchester College of Music, and at the Royal College of Music under Holst and Boult. He was music master at Westminster School (1921–4), assistant organist at Westminster Abbey and organist at St Martin-in-the-Fields, director of music at Morley College (1924–9), and professor of organ at the Royal College of Music from 1923. He had a reputation as a choral trainer, accompanist, organist, adjudicator and conductor. He was promoter of the Arnold Goldsbrough Concerts and the Arnold Goldsbrough Orchestra, which subsequently became the English Chamber Orchestra. Colin Davis' first recording of *L'Enfance du Christ* in 1961 was made with the Goldsbrough Orchestra. Goldsbrough recorded as a choral conductor, orchestral conductor with his own Goldsbrough Orchestra and as a harpsichordist, in Purcell's *Sonata in G minor for Violin and figured bass* (with Grinke for Decca), *Holy Musik* (for Schwann) and a collection of anthems and church music (with Lewis, Morison, the Ambrosian Singers and the Goldsbrough Orchestra for EMI), and Vaughan Williams' *Five Variants of Dives and Lazarus* (for Decca). Then, in EMI's *History of Music in Sound*, he made a considerable contribution, recording performances of Vivaldi's Concerto P. 406 (with Brain and Roberts), Schütz's *Saul, Saul, was verfolgst du mich?*, G. Gabrielli's *In ecclesiis benedicte Domino*, Buxtehude's *Ich halte es dafür*, the Trumpet Overture to Purcell's *Indian Queen*, the Air from Telemann's *Suite in E minor*, an excerpt from Cavalli's *Egisto*, excerpts from Handel's *Susanna* and *Giulio Cesare*, the final chorus from Bach's Cantata No. 50, and the Kyrie from Bach's *Mass in F major* (with the Goldsbrough Orchestra *et al.*).

Goldschmidt, Arthur. No biographical details have been found for Arthur Goldschmidt, who made a number of recordings on 78 r.p.m. discs and on LP with various French and other orchestras. His records included Vivaldi's Concerto Op. 8 No. 10 (with the Pro Musica Orchestra for Polydor), C. P. E. Bach's *Piano Concerto in C major* and Haydn's *Harpsichord Concerto in F major* (with Roesgen-Champion and the Paris Conservatoire Orchestra for Lyrichord), Haydn's Symphonies Nos 45, 85 and 102 (with the Paris Conservatoire Orchestra for Pathé), Mozart's *Les Petits Riens* (with the Paris Conservatoire Orchestra for AS), Divertimento K. 131 (with a chamber orchestra for AS), Divertimento K. 251 (with a chamber orchestra for Pathé), German Dances K. 600 (with the Paris Conservatoire Orchestra for Pathé), Divertimento K. 247, Serenade K. 320, Flute Concerto K. 314 (with Rampal), Flute Concerto K. 313 (with Marseau), Oboe Concerto (with Pierlot), Violin Concertos K. 207 and K. 211 (with Erlih), the overture to *Così fan tutte* and the Piano Concertos K. 467 and K. 503 (with Roesgen-Champion, and with the Lamoureux Orchestra, for Pathé, Ducretet-Thomson and other labels), the *Adagio and Fugue in C minor*, *Les petits riens*, and the overtures to *Le nozze di Figaro*, *Idomeneo* and *Die Entführung aus dem Serail* (with the Champs-Élysées Theatre Orchestra, for Ducretet-Thomson), the Mozart Piano Concerto K. 595 (with Foldès and the Vienna Pro Musica Orchestra for Vox) and Roesgen-Champion's *Concertino* (with the composer and an orchestra for Florilège).

Goleminov, Kamen (b. 1940). Son of the composer and conductor Marin Goleminov, Goleminov was born in Sofia, studied at the Bulgarian State Conservatory and performed as a pianist. He studied further under Ferrara at the Accademia di Santa Cecilia in Rome and in Vienna and Hilversum (1962–4), and took part successfully in the Guido Cantelli Conducting Competition in Stresa in 1965. He became conductor of the Rousse State Philharmonic Orchestra (1965), the Varna State Philharmonic Orchestra (1966), the Pleven Philharmonic Orchestra (1967–9), the Rousse State Philharmonic Orchestra (1969–73) and of the Bulgarian Radio Symphony Orchestra and at the Sofia State Opera (from 1973). He has toured Italy with the Opera, the Rousse Philharmonic and the Bulgarian Chamber Orchestra, was conductor-in-residence at Michigan State University (1972) and also conducted at the Bayreuth Youth Festival. His repertoire ranges from the baroque to the Second Viennese School and includes contemporary Bulgarian composers. For the Bulgarian record organisation he has recorded with the Bulgarian Radio Symphony Orchestra his father Marin Goleminov's Symphony No. 2, *Variations on a*

Theme of D. Hristov, Violin Concerto (with Letchev), *Symphonic Poem* and ballet suite *The Daughter of Kaloyan*, as well as Respighi's *Ancient Airs and Dances*, Suite No. 2.

Goleminov, Marin (b. 1908). Born in Kyustendil, Bulgaria, Goleminov studied the violin at the Sofia Conservatory (1927–31), composition with Dukas and d'Indy and conducting with Labaye at the Schola Cantorum in Paris (1931–4) and composition with Haas and conducting with Knappe at the Munich Academy (1938–9), and was a member of the Avramov Quartet (1935–8). He has been a teacher at the Bulgarian State Conservatory since 1947, was director of the Sofia National Opera and toured Eastern Europe as a conductor. His compositions include operas, symphonic and chamber music, and he has published a book about orchestration. For the Bulgarian recording organisation he recorded his own Symphony No. 3 and ballet *Nestinarka* (with the Sofia State Philharmonic Orchestra and the Bulgarian Radio and Television Orchestra, respectively).

Golovanov, Nikolai (1891–1953). Born in Moscow, the Russian pianist, composer and conductor Golovanov studied under Ippolitov-Ivanov and Vasilenko at the Moscow Conservatory and became first choirmaster (1918–28) and then conductor (1930–36) at the Bolshoi Theatre. In 1919 he was co-founder of the Bolshoi Theatre Opera Studio, which later became the Stanislavsky Opera Theatre, in 1922–3 toured Europe as accompanist for his wife, the leading soprano A. V. Nezhdanova, and was professor of opera and orchestration at the Moscow Conservatory (1925–9). He was chief conductor of the Bolshoi Symphony Orchestra and of the Great Symphony Orchestra of the State Radio, i.e. the Moscow Radio Symphony Orchestra (1948–53). The Stalin Prize was awarded to him in 1946, 1949, 1950 and 1951. He was specially noted for his performances of Russian composers such as Borodin, Mussorgsky, Rimsky-Korsakov and Scriabin; in the years 1926–8 he objected to the move to change the repertoire of the Bolshoi Theatre to operas and ballets with political themes, but finally was obliged to give way. He was a prolific composer; his output included the operas *Princess Yurata* and *The Hero's Tomb*, symphonies, the symphonic poems *Salome* and *From Verhaeren*, orchestral suites, songs and choral music.

Golovanov made an extraordinary number of gramophone records. On 78 r.p.m. discs he recorded with the USSR State Symphony Orchestra *Scheherazade*, the Kalinnikov Symphony No. 1, excerpts from Khachaturian's *Gayaneh* and the prelude to *Khovanshchina*. On LP he conducted the Moscow Radio Symphony Orchestra, the Bolshoi Theatre Orchestra and the USSR State Symphony Orchestra in Mozart's Violin Concerto K. 219 (with Oistrakh), Beethoven's Symphony No. 1, the *Egmont* overture, and the Triple Concerto (with Oistrakh, Knushevitzky and Oborin), excerpts from the incidental music to *A Midsummer Night's Dream*, the *Peer Gynt* Suites Nos 1 and 2, *Sigurd Jorsalfar* and *Lyric Suite* of Grieg, Liszt's *Mazeppa*, *Orpheus*, *Prometheus*, *Tasso*, *Hungaria* and *Hunnenschlacht*, Svendsen's *Norwegian Folksong Suite* and *Zorahayde* and the prelude and Liebestod from *Tristan und Isolde*, the overtures and preludes to *Rienzi*, *Tannhäuser*, *Die Meistersinger* and *Parsifal*, and the *Siegfried Idyll*.

Of Russian composers his recordings included, in addition to the 78s mentioned above, Tchaikovsky's Symphony No. 1, *The Tempest*, *1812* overture and *Marche slave*, complete *Boris Godunov* and *Sadko* and excerpts from *Prince Igor*, Rimsky-Korsakov's *Christmas Eve*, suites from *Tsar Saltan* and *Le Coq d'or*, the mazurka from *Pan-Voyevoda* and overture to *The Tsar's Bride*, *Pictures at an Exhibition*, *A Night on the Bare Mountain* and the prelude to *Khovanshchina*, Liadov's *Song of Grief*, Ippolitov-Ivanov's *Song of Ossian*, Balakirev's *Tamara*, Glazunov's Symphonies Nos 5, 6 and 7, *March on a Russian Theme*, *Serenade in A major*, *From the Middle Ages*, *Stenka Razin* and *Valse de concert No. 1*, Glière's *Concerto for Coloratura and Orchestra* (with Kazantseva), *Peter and the Wolf* and the march and scherzo from *The Love of Three Oranges*, Scriabin's Symphonies Nos 1, 2 and 3, *Poème d'extase* and *Rêverie*, and Rachmaninov's Symphony No. 3, *The Rock* and *Aleko*.

Golschmann, Vladimir (1893–1972). A native of Paris and born of Russian parents, Golschmann studied the violin at the Schola Cantorum and played in three of the major symphony orchestras in Paris. His career as a conductor started with a small ensemble which included Iturbi and Thibaud, and then in 1919 with the patronage of Albert Verley he established the Concerts Golschmann where he performed the music of *Les Six* (the contemporary French composers Milhaud, Poulenc, Auric, Honegger, Tailleferre and Durey) as well as the customary repertoire. This led to engagements with the leading Parisian and provincial orchestras, and in 1920 Diaghilev selected him to conduct his revival of *Le Sacre du printemps.* During the following years he conducted ballet, at contemporary music festivals, was for five years conductor of the Bilbao Symphony Orchestra, and from 1928 to 1930 conductor of the Scottish Orchestra. His first appearances in the United States were with the New York Symphony Orchestra in 1924; in 1931 he was invited to conduct the St Louis Symphony Orchestra and, on the recommendation of Damrosch and Koussevitzky, was straightaway appointed conductor of the orchestra. He remained at St Louis until 1958, continued as a guest conductor in the US, Latin America and Europe, and was conductor of the Denver Symphony Orchestra (1964–70). A most accomplished musician and conductor, he had a reputation for brilliance rather than profundity, but altogether fell short of greatness as an interpreter. Nonetheless the St Louis Symphony Orchestra under him developed into a fine ensemble, even if it did not challenge the leading US orchestras.

Golschmann enjoyed an active recording career, and avoided being tagged as a specialist in any school or composer. Victor recorded him on 78 r.p.m. discs with the St Louis Symphony Orchestra in a wide repertoire, including the Entrée and Rondeau du sommeil from Rameau's *Dardanus*, Mozart's Symphony No. 38, the Haydn Symphony No. 103, excerpts from *Swan Lake*, a dance from *La vida breve*, Sibelius' Symphony No. 7, *Nights in the Gardens of Spain* (with Rubinstein), Tansman's *Triptyque for String Orchestra*, *Verklärte Nacht*, Milhaud's *Suite provençale*, Prokofiev's *Symphony No. 1* and Shostakovich's *Age of Gold* suite. With the NBC Symphony Orchestra he also recorded Beethoven's Piano Concerto No. 2 (with Kapell) and Rachmaninov's Piano Concerto No. 2 (with Rubinstein). Of these early discs, he achieved real distinction with Sibelius' Symphony No. 7, in which he made a lasting impression with his firm grasp of a difficult score.

On LP, Golschmann made many more recordings with the St Louis Symphony Orchestra for RCA, Capitol, and Columbia, and some of these were re-issued in recent years by Pickwick. Included were Mozart's Symphony No. 38 and Piano Concerto K. 488 (with Rubinstein), *Francesca da Rimini*, the *Romeo and Juliet* fantasy-overture and excerpts from *Swan Lake*, the Franck *Symphony in D minor*, a *Carmen* suite, *Invitation to the Dance*, *La Mer*, *Symphonie espagnole* (with Milstein), excerpts from *Coppélia* and *Sylvia*, Easdale's ballet *The Red Shoes*, *La Valse* and *Valses nobles et sentimentales*, the ballet music from *Faust*, dances from *The Three-cornered Hat*, Bartók's Piano Concerto No. 3 and Prokofiev's Piano Concerto No. 3 (with Pennario), Satie's *Trois Gymnopédies*, Prokofiev's *Chout*, Milhaud's *Le Boeuf sur le toit*, Rachmaninov's *Piano Concerto No. 2* (with Pennario) and Shostakovich's Symphony No. 5. Capitol also recorded him with the Concert Arts Symphony Orchestra in Liszt's Piano Concerto No. 1 and Chopin's Piano Concerto No. 2 (with Pennario), Copland's *Quiet City*, Ravel's *Le Tombeau de Couperin*, Creston's *Two Choric Dances*, Diamond's *Rounds*, Honegger's *Pastorale d'été*, and Barber's *Adagio for Strings*, Columbia with the Columbia Symphony Orchestra accompanying Gould in the Bach harpsichord concertos and Beethoven's Piano Concerto No. 1, and RCA in Vaughan Williams' Two-Piano Concerto (with Whittemore and Lowe and the Robin Hood Dell Orchestra) and Mozart's Adagio K. 261 and Rondo K. 373 (with Milstein and the Victor Symphony Orchestra). Finally, for Vanguard he embarked on another series with the Vienna State Opera Orchestra, which included Bach's Violin Concerto No. 2, Nardini's *Violin Concerto in E* and Vivaldi's Violin Concerto P. 343 (with Elman), Vivaldi's *La Cetra* Nos 4, 8, 9 and 12 (with Makanowitzky and Boskovsky), Mendelssohn's Symphony No. 4 and excerpts from the incidental music for *A Midsummer Night's Dream, Symphonie fantastique*, Brahms' Symphony No. 4, Dvořák's Symphony No. 9, Tchaikovsky's Symphony No. 6, *Pictures at an Exhibition* and *A Night on the Bare Mountain*, suites from Kabalevsky's *The Comedians* and Khachaturian's *Gayaneh*, Enesco's two *Romanian Rhapsodies*, the Khachaturian Violin Concerto and Saint-Saëns' *Introduction et rondo capriccioso* (with Milstein), Bloch's Violin Concerto and Bartók's Rhapsody No. 1 (with Totenberg), Bloch's *Concerto symphonique* and the Scherzo from Litolff's *Concerto symphonique* (with Mitchell). For Vanguard he also recorded Harris's *Folksong Symphony* (with the American Festival Chorus and Orchestra), and Barber's *Stopwatch and Ordnance Map*, *Music for a scene from Shelley*, *Essay No. 2* and *Serenade* (with the Symphony of the Air).

Gomez, Julio (b. 1886). Born in Madrid and educated at the conservatory and university there, Gomez was director of the archaeological museum in Toledo (1911), head of the music division of the National Library at Madrid, and librarian at the Madrid Conservatory. He was also a music critic and editor and composed symphonies, comic operas and other pieces. Montillo released a disc on which he conducted the Madrid Symphony Orchestra in his *Suite in A major*.

Gönnenwein, Wolfgang (b. 1933). Born in Schwäbisch Hall, Gönnenwein studied at the Stuttgart Academy of Music and at Heidelberg and Tübingen Universities. Since 1959 he has been conductor of the South German Madrigal Choir at Stuttgart, which consists of 30 to 35 singers, and has toured with him in FR Germany and Europe. He has recorded extensively with the Choir; included have been Bach's Cantatas Nos 32, 39, 78, 79, 80, 106, 126, 140, 148 and 149 (for EMI), and the Cantatas Nos 29, 127, 135 and 171 (for Cantata), the *St Matthew Passion* and Mozart *Requiem* (with the Consortium Musicum *et al.*), *Easter Oratorio*, Handel's *Dettingen Te Deum* and Mozart's Mass K. 427 (with the South West German Chamber Orchestra *et al.*) and the Beethoven *Country Dances* and *German Dances* (with the Consortium Musicum, for EMI), *The Creation* and *The Seasons* of Haydn (with the Ludwigsburg Festival Orchestra *et al.* for Vox), the Bruckner Mass No. 2 (with the South West German Chamber Orchestra *et al.* for Odeon), *The Seasons* (with the Bavarian State Opera Orchestra *et al.* for Electrola), the *St Mark Passion* (reconstructed from Bach's works, with the Pforzheim Chamber Orchestra *et al.* for Epic), Bach's *Magnificat* and Cantatas Nos 29 and 135, *Violin and Oboe Concerto* (with Hendel and Winschermann) and Harpsichord Concerto No. 7 (with Malcolm, and the German Bach Soloists for Cantate, with some issued by Oryx in Britain), Beethoven's *Missa Solemnis* (with the Collegium Aureum *et al.*) and the Brahms *Ein deutsches Requiem* (with the Ludwigsburg Festival Orchestra *et al.*, for BASF).

Goodall, Reginald (b. 1905). Born in Lincoln where he was a chorister at the Cathedral, Goodall learned the piano from his father, studied the violin and piano at the Royal College of Music under Sargent, Benjamin and Reid, and then went to Munich and Vienna for further studies. He was assistant to Coates at Covent Garden (1936–9) and to Sargent with the Royal Choral Society, and his career as a conductor started at Sadler's Wells (1944) where he conducted the première of *Peter Grimes* (1945) and shared the first performances of *The Rape of Lucretia* at Glyndebourne (1946). He was then invited by Rankl to join the music staff at Covent Garden; he visited Germany and was assistant to Furtwängler, Krauss, Klemperer and Knappertsbusch, and studied *Wozzeck* with Kleiber in Berlin and later conducted the opera at Covent Garden. There he led numerous performances of Italian and German operas and conducted several Wagner operas on tour, but during Solti's directorship at Covent Garden (1961–71) he was not called on to conduct at all. In recent years he has conducted *Die Meistersinger* and the complete *Ring* at the English National Opera Company, formerly Sadler's Wells Opera, at the Coliseum, London. In the past decade Goodall has emerged as one of the greatest living Wagnerian conductors, and has frequently been compared to Furtwängler and Knappertsbusch for the style and brilliance of his performances. Working with them he learned the art of keeping up the pace but slowing down for the significant passages; yet his interpretations have a broad, unhurried majesty and a conviction that go far beyond imitation. He insists on allowing the music to unfold naturally: 'Wagner was the last great German classical composer and every note must sound'. (Interview, *Daily Telegraph*, 13 December 1975). He stubbornly demands meticulous preparation before performance, coaches the singers and instrumentalists individually and has countless group rehearsals; both singers and players respect his knowledge and are inspired by his love of the music. He feels no bitterness about his neglect at Covent Garden before Solti's departure, and thinks that he may have matured in that time. In fact he is untypically modest for a great conductor. He is a firm believer in presenting Wagner in English translation, as the text is as important as the music. He accepts concert engagements rarely, since he only conducts music he knows: 'otherwise it is just traffic directions'.

Goodall's appearances with the English National Opera conducting *The Ring* are now one of the major events of the London musical scene. As the result of a collaboration between EMI and Peter Moores, he has recorded with the company in Andrew Porter's translation *Das Rheingold* (1975), *Die Walküre* (1976) and *Siegfried* (1974), and *Götterdämmerung* is in preparation. In addition the second and third scenes from Act III of *Götterdämmerung* were released by Unicorn in 1973. In these performances Rita Hunter is the Brünnhilde, Norman Bailey the Wotan and Alberto Remedios the Siegfried. Earlier, Goodall made some 78 r.p.m. discs for Decca with the National Symphony Orchestra of the *Leonore No. 1* and *1812* overtures. He also directed a performance for HMV on six 78 r.p.m. discs of *The Rape of Lucretia*, with the original Glyndebourne cast which included Pears and Cross and which was recorded under Britten's supervision.

Goodman, Bernard (b. 1914). Born in Cleveland, Ohio, and educated at the Western Reserve University and the Cleveland Institute of Music, Goodman studied privately with Carlton Cooley and Szell, and was a member of the Cleveland Orchestra (1936–46). He was professor of music at Cornell University (1946–7) and at the University of Illinois (from 1947), conducted the University of Illinois Symphony Orchestra (from 1950), the Champaign-Urbana Symphony Orchestra (from 1960) and the Bloomington-Normal Symphony Orchestra (from 1970). He has also been a member of the Walden String Quartet with whom he has recorded for Desto, Columbia *et al.* music by Bergsma, Carter, Imbrie, Ives, Palmer, Kodály and Szymanowski. For Composers Recordings he led the University of Illinois Symphony Orchestra in Riegger's Symphony No. 4, and for the University's own label Weigel's *Prairie Symphony*.

Goossens, Eugène, II (1867–1958). Son of Eugène Goossens I, the Belgian conductor who came to live in England and conducted with the Carl Rosa Opera Company, and father of Sir Eugene Goossens, Goossens was born in Bordeaux and was educated at the Brussels Conservatoire and the Royal Academy of Music in London. He became a conductor with the Carl Rosa Opera Company (1899–1915), conducted other British opera companies, with Beecham at His Majesty's Theatre in 1917 and with the British National Opera Company in 1926. Sir Eugene said of his father that his knowledge of opera was such that he had forgotten as much as he, Sir Eugene, knew. Goossens II recorded for HMV *Pagliacci*, in English, with an English cast and the British National Opera Company Chorus and Orchestra.

Goossens, Sir Eugene (1893–1962). Born in London into a family of Belgian musicians, Goossens' father and grandfather were conductors before him. At the time of his birth his father was a violinist at the Royal Opera House and his mother was a singer; his brother was Leon, the oboist, and his two sisters became professional harp-players. Goossens entered the Bruges Conservatoire at the age of ten, and in 1896 enrolled at the Liverpool College of Music, proceeding to the Royal College of Music in London in 1907, where he conducted the orchestra in his first major composition, *Chinese Variations*. From 1912 to 1915 he was a violinist in the Queen's Hall Orchestra and in the Philharmonic String Quartet, and in 1913 Wood invited him to conduct the *Chinese Variations* at a Promenade Concert. His conducting activities started in earnest in 1915 when he became assistant to Beecham; he made his mark with the première of Stanford's *The Critic* in 1916. He conducted provincial orchestras, was conductor of the Leeds Orchestral Concerts, and in 1921 founded his own orchestra of carefully selected players, and presented a series of subscription concerts; the first programme included the first concert performances of *Le Sacre du printemps* in London. This led to engagements with Diaghilev's Ballets Russes, with the main London orchestras, the Carl Rosa and British National Opera Companies and with European orchestras.

In 1923 Goossens was invited by George Eastman of the Kodak company to direct the orchestra he was forming at Rochester, New York, and he remained in Rochester as conductor of the Philharmonic Orchestra for eight years. He succeeded Reiner as music director of the Cincinnati Symphony Orchestra in 1931, became a United States citizen in 1943, and in 1947 was appointed conductor of the Sydney Symphony Orchestra and director of the New South Wales State Conservatorium of Music in Sydney. In Australia he achieved much in developing musical taste and performing standards, and under him the Sydney Symphony Orchestra became an ensemble of some distinction. When in the US he conducted most of the major orchestras, but surprisingly was never invited to conduct at the Metropolitan Opera. He was knighted in 1955, but resigned from his positions in Sydney after legal convictions on a customs charge. Goossens spent the last years of his life in London.

Early in his career Goossens was considered one of the most significant of the young generation of British composers. His first opera, *Judith*, was premièred by him at Covent Garden in 1929 and his second, *Don Juan de Mañara*, in 1937. Both were to libretti by Arnold Bennett; Harold Rosenthal sums them up saying: 'In them his operatic experience is evident in the dramatic presentation of libretti whose merits are primarily literary, though his own highly chromatic yet chaste style is itself not essentially operatic.' (*Concise Dictionary of Opera*, London, 1964, p. 158). By the time of the publication of his Symphony No. 1 in 1939 many thought Goossens had compromised his individuality, and that involvement in interpreting other men's music had engendered an almost anonymous eclecticism. The Symphony No. 2 was completed in 1944, and a large-scale oratorio, *The Apocalypse*, received its première in Sydney in 1954. Perhaps his most characteristic music is found in his early quartets, *By the*

Tarn and *Jack o'Lantern*, and the Oboe Concerto he wrote in 1927 for his brother Leon, who later recorded it. Like many musicians of his generation, Goossens had no reservations about arranging other people's music; he recorded his orchestration of six dance movements from Bach's *French Suites*, performed the Brahms *Sextet in G major* with full string orchestra, and prepared the bizarre orchestration of *Messiah* which was recorded by Beecham.

Although a kind and generous man, Goossens hid his shyness under a cloak of arrogance. He had a remarkable reputation for his facility in assimilating and conducting difficult scores at short notice; one day in 1931 in London Beecham asked him to take over a performance of *Sadko* that evening, an opera he had never heard, in a language quite unfamiliar to him, with only a piano rehearsal with the principals. He wrote in his memoirs that 'the ovation which followed the opera counted less in my ears than the sweeter music of thanks from the singers for a completely – to them – routine and uneventful evening'. (E. Goossens, *Overture and Beginners*, London, 1951.) He was by no means a flamboyant or overtly colourful figure, but he had a sure touch for attracting public attention, and never missed an opportunity. When the soprano Marjorie Lawrence visited Sydney in 1951 he programmed concert versions of both *Salome* and *Elektra* within a week of each other; when Menuhin came he arranged a special concert for him to perform the Beethoven and Brahms Violin Concertos. He was completely at home with the great romantic and impressionist scores of the late 19th and early 20th centuries, and his musical world was that of France of the 1920s. Wagner, Mahler, Strauss, Elgar, and the Russians were his *métier*, where his clarity, precision and comprehensive command of large forces combined to produce exhilarating performances. But his Haydn, Mozart and Beethoven were much less convincing, although the performances were tidy enough. Nonetheless his programmes surveyed the repertoire from Bach to Stravinsky, but avoided atonal music and the Second Viennese School. There was an impression in his conducting that he was, as also in his works, emotionally uncommitted, and in the final analysis cold, which prevented him from aspiring to true greatness as a musician. Perhaps he revealed his emotional nature in his memoirs when he wrote (in 1951) that the most moving thing he ever heard in the concert hall was a presentation of Pierné's cantata *The Children's Crusade*, with 600 children and a small adult choir.

In 1923 Goossens made the first recording of an orchestral piece by Bach – the *Brandenburg Concerto No. 3* – with the Royal Albert Hall Orchestra for HMV. With the same orchestra and for HMV he also recorded the *Air* from the Bach Suite No. 3, the overtures to *The Bartered Bride* and *May Night*, *Petrushka*, Liadov's *Kikimora*, Debussy's *Golliwog's Cakewalk*, orchestral arrangements of music from *Tosca* and *Madama Butterfly*, *La Boutique fantasque*, Grainger's *Molly on the Shore*, an abbreviated *Saga of King Olaf* of Elgar (with Davies), *Brigg Fair*, *On Hearing the First Cuckoo in Spring*, Beethoven's Piano Concerto No. 5 (with Lamond), and his own *Tam o'Shanter*. Velvet Face issued *Danse macabre*, with an unnamed orchestra. His other 78 r.p.m. discs, made before World War II, were of Schubert's Symphony No. 8 and *Marche militaire No. 1*, the *Hungarian March* from *La Damnation de Faust*, the *1812* overture and the waltz from *Eugene Onegin*, *Scheherazade* (abridged on two discs), the *Peer Gynt* Suite No. 1, Grieg's *Lyric Suite*, *L'Arlésienne* Suite No. 1, and Franck's *Le Chasseur maudit* (with the Royal Opera House Orchestra, Covent Garden, for HMV), Granados' *Spanish Dances* Nos 2, 5 and 6 (with the New Light Symphony Orchestra for HMV), Turina's *Danzas fantásticas*, Sibelius' *En Saga* and *Valse triste*, the ballet music from *Le Cid*, Glazunov's *Scènes de ballet*, the *Peer Gynt* Suite No. 2, Bax's *Tintagel* and *Mediterranean*, and the ballet music from his own *Judith* (with the New Symphony Orchestra for HMV), *Pagliacci* and *Madama Butterfly* (with the British National Opera Company, in English, for Columbia), Dvořák's *Carnival* overture and a suite from *The Sleeping Beauty* (with the Hollywood Bowl Orchestra for Victor), a suite from *Le Coq d'or*, the polonaise from *Eugene Onegin*, excerpts from *Coppélia* and a suite of six of the dances from Bach's *French Suites*, arranged by himself (with the London Symphony Orchestra for HMV), *La Boutique fantasque*, Schumann's *Carnaval*, *Peer Gynt* Suite No. 1, the Polovtsian Dances from *Prince Igor*, the *Nutcracker* suite, a Handel Oboe Concerto (with Leon Goossens), the Scarlatti/Tommasini ballet *The Good-humoured Ladies*, and Grieg's *Two Elegiac Melodies* (with the London Philharmonic Orchestra).

With the Cincinnati Symphony Orchestra he recorded an interesting and substantial repertoire for Victor on 78s: *Le Chant du rossignol*, *The Walk to the Paradise Garden*, Dorati's arrangement of music from *Der Rosenkavalier*, the Walton Viola Concerto (with Primrose) and Violin Concerto (with Heifetz), Chabrier's *Marche joyeuse*, Tchaikovsky's Symphony

No. 2, *Pini di Roma*, Schumann's Symphony No. 4 and Vaughan Williams' Symphony No. 2. With one exception, the Schumann symphony, these discs were warmly received. Another series was recorded by EMI with the Sydney Symphony Orchestra: his own Symphony No. 2, Beethoven's Symphony No. 2, Mendelssohn's Symphony No. 3, Turina's *Sinfonia sevilliana*, *Danse macabre*, the polka and fugue from *Schwanda*, Massenet's *Scènes pittoresques*, Butterworth's *A Shropshire Lad*, Grainger's *Londonderry Air*, Alfred Hill's *Green Water*, and John Antill's ballet *Corroboree*, which Goossens had discovered and performed in Sydney and London. This series contained some good performances, and demonstrated the fine quality of the Sydney orchestra; the Beethoven and Mendelssohn symphonies received straightforward and well-executed readings.

After World War II, Goossens also made many records in England for EMI, on mono and stereo LPs, mostly of music for which he had a special aptitude. Included amongst these discs were *Pictures at an Exhibition*, the Khachaturian Violin Concerto (with Igor Oistrakh), *L'Apprenti sorcier*, *La Boutique fantasque*, *Boléro*, *Alborada del gracioso*, *Rapsodie espagnole* and Debussy's *Iberia* (with the Royal Philharmonic Orchestra), Fauré's *Fantaisie* and d'Indy's *Symphonie sur un chant montagnard français* (with Johannesen and the London Symphony Orchestra), Lalo's *Symphonie espagnole* and Saint-Saëns' *Habanera* and *Introduction et rondo capriccioso* (with Menuhin), Wieniawski's Violin Concerto No. 2 and Paganini's Violin Concerto No. 1 (with Rabin), *Fontane di Roma*, Scriabin's *Rêverie* and *Poème d'extase*, the Albéniz/Arbós *Iberia*, the *Russian Easter Festival* overture and suite from *Le Coq d'or*, Balakirev's *Islamey*, the polka and fugue from *Schwanda* and excerpts from *The Bartered Bride* (with the Philharmonia Orchestra). After he left Sydney, he was engaged by Everest to record a number of discs with the London Symphony Orchestra, and these were probably his most representative series. They were Stravinsky's *Ebony Concerto*, *Le Sacre du printemps*, *Petrushka* and *Symphony in Three Movements*, Tchaikovsky's *Manfred* symphony, *Scheherazade*, *Symphonie fantastique*, *Feste Romane*, the *Symphonic Dances* of Rachmaninov, Antill's Corroboree, Villa-Lobos' *The Little Train of the Calpira*, Ginastera's ballets *Panambi* and *Estancia*, Antheil's Symphony No. 4, the Schumann Piano Concerto and the Franck *Symphonic Variations* (with Katin), Mozart's Violin Concerto K. 216 and the Hindemith Violin Concerto (with Fuchs). His remaining recordings were Britten's *Simple Symphony*, *Les Illuminations* and *Serenade for Tenor, Horn and Strings* (with Pears, Brain, and the New Symphony Orchestra for Decca), Robert Still's Symphony No. 3 (with the London Symphony Orchestra for Saga, and later re-issued by Lyrita), Mendelssohn's Symphonies Nos 4 and 5 (with the London Symphony Orchestra for Saga), the Khachaturian Cello Concerto (with Orlov and the Romanian Philharmonic Orchestra for Electrecord), *Peter and the Wolf*, a suite from Khachaturian's *Masquerade*, Rachmaninov's Piano Concerto No. 3 and Chopin's Piano Concerto No. 2 (with Schein, and the Vienna State Opera Orchestra, for Kapp), and the two Beethoven *Romances* and the Double Violin Concertos of Bach and Vivaldi (with David and Igor Oistrakh and the Royal Philharmonic Orchestra for DGG).

Gorvin, Carl (b. 1912). Born in Siebenburgen, Hermannstadt, Germany, Gorvin studied musicology at Bucharest University and in 1934 conducted at the German State Theatre in Bucharest. He studied conducting with Krauss, was a repetiteur at Kiel, was a conductor at Eger, Wuppertal and Göttingen, permanent conductor at the Berlin State Opera (1951–3) and general music director of Kaiserslautern (1959–69). He was a distinguished specialist in pre-romantic music, and recorded Bach's Cantata No. 158 (with the Hannover Academy Choir and Orchestra for DGG), Buxtehude's *Laudate Dominum* and *Schaffe in mir, Gott* (with Schwarzweller and an ensemble for DGG), Frederick the Great's *Sinfonia in D* and Quantz's Flute Concerto (with the Seiler Chamber Orchestra *et al.* for DGG), Leopold Mozart's *Toy Symphony*, *Eine musikalische Schlittenfahrt*, and *Cassation in G*, Handel's Concerto Grosso Op. 3 No. 3 and Oboe Concertos Nos 1 and 3 (with Töttcher), a concerto by J. C. F. Bach (with the Berlin Bach Orchestra *et al.* for DGG), Stamitz's *Trio for Orchestra*, *Oboe Concerto in C* (with Töttcher), *Clarinet Concert in B flat* (with Michaels) and a sinfonia, Haydn's *Cello Concerto in D* and Wagenseil's Cello Concerto (with Mainardi, and the Munich Chamber Orchestra for DGG), concertos by Telemann (with the German Bach Soloists *et al.* for Barenreiter) and excerpts from Monteverdi's *Vespro della Beata Vergine* and other works (with the Berlin Chamber Ensemble *et al.* for DGG).

Górzyński, Zdzislaw (b. 1885). The Polish conductor Górzyński studied at the Kraków Conservatory and in Vienna with Schalk, was a conductor of light music for the Polish Radio (until 1939), and after World War II conducted in Warsaw and Poznań, as well as in opera houses in Switzerland, Czechoslovakia and Hungary. His recordings include Moniuszko's *Halka*, excerpts from Różycki's ballet *Pan Twardowski* (with the Warsaw Opera House Orchestra *et al.*), Moniuszko's *Flis* (with the National Philharmonic Orchestra *et al.*) and an aria recital (with Ochman), for the Polish record company.

Gosman, Lazar (b. 1926). Born in Kiev, Gosman studied at the Moscow Conservatory, graduated with honours in 1949, and was appointed deputy concertmaster of the Leningrad Philharmonic Orchestra. He founded and led the Leningrad Philharmonic Quartet (1951), was instructor of the quartet class at the Leningrad Conservatory (1961–75), and was appointed leader of the Leningrad Chamber Orchestra, which consisted of musicians from the Philharmonic Orchestra (1962). The repertoire of the orchestra was very extensive; at a concert in April 1971 they performed a programme of the music of Britten in the presence of the composer. Gosman left the USSR for the West in 1977.

With Gosman as leader, the Leningrad Chamber Orchestra has recorded the *Brandenburg Concertos*, *Water Music*, works by Telemann, Corelli, Vivaldi and Marcello, Haydn's Symphonies Nos 45 and 73 and two Horn Concertos (with Buyanowsky), Mozart's Piano Concertos K. 456 and K. 488 (with Wirssaladse), Horn Concertos (with Buyanowsky) and a divertimento, pieces by Hindemith, Britten and Villa-Lobos, *Le Carnaval des animaux*, Shostakovich's Symphony No. 14, and works by Salmanov, Levitin, Mysliveček and Nergamenshchikov. Some of these recordings have been released by Eurodisc and by Victor, Japan. Gosman also conducted in recordings of Prokofiev's Symphony No. 1 and the Franck *Symphonic Variations* (the latter with Grinberg, both with the Moscow Radio Symphony Orchestra, released by Eurodisc).

Gotovac, Jakov (b. 1895). Born in Split, Yugoslavia, Gotovac studied with Dobronić, Hrazdire and Hatze, and with Marx at the Vienna Academy of Music, and was a conductor of the Zagreb Opera. For Jugoton he recorded his own *Ero s onoga svijeta* (with the Zagreb HNK Chorus and Orchestra, *et al.*).

Gotti, Tito (b. 1927). Born in Bologna, where he studied at the University and Conservatory, Gotti was a conducting pupil of Swarowsky at the Vienna Academy of Music. He has taught at the Bologna Conservatory since 1961, is director of the Teatro Comunale at Bologna, and has conducted throughout Italy and in Austria, FR Germany, Poland, France, Switzerland and Czechoslovakia. His special interest is the music of the baroque period, particularly of the Venice and Bologna schools, and he has edited and performed masses, operas and other works by Colonna, Perti, D. and G. Gabrieli, Cazzati, Vitali, Torelli, Vivaldi and Caldara. He has also published a guide to polyphonic analysis and other musical articles and monographs. His recordings include Colonna's *Mass for Five Voices*, *Dixit Dominus* and *Beatus Vir* (with the Lausanne Chamber Orchestra and Lausanne University Choir *et al.*, for Erato and issued in the United States by Musical Heritage Society), Mayr's *Grand Prelude*, Paer's Organ Concerto and four Organ Sonatas of Valeri (with Tagliavini and the Milan Chamber Orchestra for Erato and Ricordi), Vitali's Sinfonia, Torelli's *Concerto a quattro in G minor*, a motet and aria of Perti (with Grist), G. Gabrieli's *Sonata a quattro e a cinque* and Gazzati's *Sonata a cinque* (with André and the Teatro Comunale Orchestra, Bologna, for Erato and issued in the United States by Musical Heritage Society), and several discs of collections of pieces by Italian baroque composers, in Erato's series, *Castles and Cathedrals*.

Gould, Morton (b. 1913). A native of New York and son of a Viennese migrant, Gould was composing as a child, and at the age of eight was given a scholarship by Walter Damrosch to the New York Institute of Musical Art. He went on to the New York University School of Music and had completed the two-year curriculum by the time he was fifteen. His career as a musician started soon after; at seventeen he was touring colleges giving lecture-demonstrations, playing the piano in dance bands and theatres. He joined the staff of the National Broadcasting Company as one of a duo-piano team, and in 1934 was conductor, composer and arranger of his own radio show. In 1943 he became musical director of another radio show, the Chrysler Hour, for which he wrote some of his most successful compositions, such as the *Latin American Symphonette* and the *American Symphonette*, which was later used for the ballet *Interplay*. His versatility as pianist, composer, conductor and arranger, particularly of music for light entertainment, is extraordinary. In 1934 Stokowski performed his *Chorale and Fugue for Jazz* with the Philadelphia Orchestra, and his later works include *Spirituals for Or-*

chestra, *Lincoln Legend*, four symphonies, a *Concerto for Orchestra*, the ballet *Fall River Legend*, the *Jekyll and Hyde Variations for Orchestra*, some concertos including one for tapdancer and orchestra, music for school bands, film scores, ballet scores, musical comedies and the music for television documentaries. The ease with which he moves from one medium and idiom to another, from the world of pop and jazz, to musical comedy, to patriotic marches, to symphonic music, is bewildering, but in this facility he is not different from many other gifted American musicians, such as Bernstein, Previn and Fiedler. In their native background they fit easily and naturally, but transferred, say, to the other side of the Atlantic their show-biz associations cast suspicion on their credentials to perform the great symphonic works, a suspicion that is often unjustified. Gould himself has a more serious side to his musical personality: he was responsible for unearthing Ives' Symphony No. 1, which had long been considered lost, and he was one of the first to perform the suppressed Symphonies Nos 2 and 3 of Shostakovich.

Gould's recording career has reflected his many musical facets. From the days of 78 r.p.m. records he has recorded his own music, starting with a series with the Robin Hood Dell Orchestra for Columbia, and including the *American Concertette* (in which he plays the piano), *American Salute*, *Cowboy Rhapsody*, *New China March*, and the *Red Cavalry March*. Others of his own compositions he has recorded are *Mediterranean*, the *Tapdance Concerto* (with dancer Daniels) and *Family Album* (with the Rochester Pops Orchestra for Columbia), *American Symphonette No. 2*, *Cowboy Rhapsody*, *New China March*, *Interplay*, *Fall River Legend* and *Latin American Symphonette* (with his own orchestra for Columbia), *Derivations for Clarinet and Band* (with Goodman and the Columbia Jazz Ensemble for Columbia), a collection of marches (with the Knightsbridge Symphonic Band for Everest), the Quickstep from the Symphony No. 3 (with the New York Philharmonic-Symphony Orchestra for Columbia), *Fourth of July*, *Home for Christmas* and *Yankee Doodle* (with the Morton Gould Symphonic Band for Columbia).

Music other than his own which he has recorded includes, on 78s, excerpts from Grieg's *Lyric Suite*, *Solveig's Song* and some *Norwegian Dances* (with the Robin Hood Dell Orchestra for Columbia), and on LP the *Grand Canyon Suite*, *Scheherazade*, Beethoven's *Wellington's Victory*, Copland's *Billy the Kid* and *Rodeo*, the *1812* overture, *Boléro*, Tchaikovsky's *The Seasons* (an arrangement for piano and orchestra by Gould of the piano suite), Sibelius' *Pohjola's Daughter*, *Lemminkäinen's Return*, *Finlandia*, *The Swan of Tuonela*, and *Valse triste*, a disc of arrangements of music by Weill, an orchestral arrangement of music from *Carmen*, Vaughan Williams' *Fantasia on a Theme of Thomas Tallis*, *English Folksong Suite* and *Fantasia on Greensleeves* and Eric Coates' *London Every Day*, music for harmonica and orchestra by Vaughan Williams, Arnold, Benjamin and Milhaud (with Adler, and with his own orchestra for RCA), Gershwin's Rhapsody No. 2 and *Variations on I Got Rhythm* (with Levant and an orchestra for Columbia) and Prokofiev's March Op. 99 (with the Morton Gould Symphonic Band for Columbia). Another series with the Chicago Symphony Orchestra, for RCA, included the Ives Symphony No. 1, *Three Places in New England*, *Orchestral Set No. 2*, and *Robert Browning Overture*, Copland's *Dance Symphony*, Miaskovsky's Symphony No. 21, Rimsky-Korsakov's *Antar Symphony*, a collection of Tchaikovsky waltzes, Nielsen's Symphony No. 2 and Clarinet Concerto (with Goodman) and his own *Spirituals*. Shostakovich's Symphonies Nos 2 and 3 were recorded in London with the Royal Philharmonic Orchestra *et al.*, for RCA. Admittedly some of these performances have a trace of slickness about them, but at his best, as in the Shostakovich and Sibelius discs, Gould shows himself to be a completely sympathetic interpreter.

Gracis, Ettore (b. 1915). Born in La Speria, Italy, Gracis studied at the Conservatorio Benedetto Marcello in Venice, was permanent conductor at the Maggio Musicale Fiorentino (1948–50), at I Pomeriggi Musicali di Milano (1950–59) and at the Teatro La Fenice in Venice (1959–71), and has taken part every year since 1947 in the Festival of Contemporary Music in Venice. His recordings include some Rossini overtures and a coupling of the Ravel *Piano Concerto in G major* and Rachmaninov's Piano Concerto No. 4 (with the Philharmonia Orchestra for EMI); the latter disc was first issued in 1958 with Michelangeli the soloist, was released again in Britain in 1974, and has always been a greatly admired recording. Also with Michelangeli he recorded Mozart's Piano Concerto K. 450 (with the Milan Afternoon Chamber Concerts Orchestra). Other recordings have been *Don Pasquale* (with the Maggio Musicale Fiorentino *et al.* for DGG), *Il campanello di notte* (with the Teatro La Fenice company for DGG), Verdi's *Quattro pezzi sacri*, Alessandro Scarlatti's *Stabat Mater* and

Concerti Grossi Nos 1 to 6, and four of the Concerti Grossi Op. 6 of Corelli (with the Naples Scarlatti Orchestra *et al.* for DGG), the Mendelssohn Symphonies Nos 3 and 4 and Violin Concerto (with the Teatro La Fenice Orchestra *et al.* for Le Club français du Disque), Pergolesi's *Stabat Mater* and *La serva padrona*, Cimarosa's *Il maestro di cappella* and several overtures and some Concerti Grossi (with the I Pomeriggi Musicali di Milano *et al.* for Le Club français du Disque; *La serva padrona* was re-issued in the United States by Nonesuch), and Falla's *Master Peter's Puppet Show* (with the Milan Afternoon Chamber Concerts Orchestra *et al.* for Fonit).

Graf, Peter-Lukas (b. 1929). Born in Zürich, Graf studied the flute with Moyse and conducting with Bigot at the Paris Conservatoire, and in 1953 won first prize in flute at the International Music Competition at Munich. He was first flautist with the Winterthur Symphony Orchestra (1951–7), conductor at the Lucerne State Theatre (1961–6) and since 1973 has taught at the Basel Conservatory. As both soloist and conductor he has toured in Europe, South America, Israel, Australia and Japan. He has recorded as a conductor Spohr's *Concertante No. 1 for Violin, Harp and Orchestra*, Bach's Suite No. 2 and Concerto for harpsichord, Flute and Violin, and Saint-Saëns' Cello Concerto No. 1 (with Strack and the English Chamber Orchestra *et al.* for Claves), the Mozart Flute Concertos and Harp and Flute Concerto (with the Lausanne Chamber Orchestra *et al.* for Claves), von Schauensee's *Musikalische Eurensteit* and von Wartensee's Symphony No. 3 (with the Orchestra della Radio Svizzera *et al.* and the Zürich Tonhalle Orchestra respectively, for CT, Switzerland). Musical Heritage Society in the United States has issued some of these discs.

Grainger, Percy (1882–1961). The Australian composer, folk-song collector, teacher, virtuoso pianist and conductor Grainger conducted his own music from time to time, but because he was antipathetic to the music of Haydn, Mozart and Beethoven, he would not accept a permanent appointment as a conductor of a symphony orchestra. He made his first recordings as a pianist in 1908 (for The Gramophone Company), and his last in 1950 (for RCA); he made many recordings for Columbia (US) between 1917 and 1931, including a celebrated one of the Chopin Piano Sonata No. 2. As a conductor he recorded his *Colonial Song* (with an orchestra *et al.*), *Irish Tune from County Derry* (with the Kasschau Solo Choir) and *Shepherd's Hey* (with the Columbia Symphony Orchestra *et al.*), for Columbia (US).

Gras, Léonce (b. 1908). Born at Borgerhout, near Antwerp, Gras studied at the Conservatoire Royal in Brussels, where he was a conducting pupil of Defauw and André, and was a piano pupil in Paris with Nat and Askenase. He was pianist with Diaghilev's Ballets Russes, accompanied Kipnis, Feuermann *et al.*, and conducted at the Flemish Royal Opera at Antwerp. He became director of music with the Belgian Radio and Television (1953) and professor at the Brussels Conservatoire Royal (1959), lectured and performed Belgian music at universities in the United States, and as a conductor was prominent in performing music by Belgian composers. His recordings include Flor Alpaert's *Flemish Idyll*, Benoit's *De Pacificatie van Gent*, Blockx's *Kermisdag* and *Rapsodie dahomienne* (with the Belgian National Orchestra for Omega/Vega), and Eycken's *Poema* and Vogel's *Wagadus Untergang durch die Eitelkeit* (with an ensemble for Exhibis).

Graulich, Gunther (b. 1926). Born in Stuttgart, Graulich studied at the Hochschule für Musik there and at the Universities of Stuttgart and Tübingen, and became conductor of the Stuttgart Motet Choir and Matthäuskantorei. He has recorded Vivaldi's *Gloria*, *Magnificat*, and *Dixit Domine*, excerpts from *Messiah*, and the Bach *St John Passion* (with the Stuttgart Motet Choir and Bach Orchestra for FSM), Bach's Cantatas Nos 25 and 103 (with the Stuttgart Motet Choir and Heidelberg Chamber Orchestra *et al.*, released in Britain and the United States by Oryx), and Dvořák's Mass Op. 86 (with the Stuttgart Motet Choir for Cerus-Verlag).

Graunke, Kurt (b. 1915). Born in Stettin (modern Szczeczin), Graunke studied there, in Berlin and in Vienna with Havemann, Schneiderhan and Grabner; from 1936 to 1944 he was a solo violinist and he conducted in Vienna in 1941–2. In 1945 he founded and conducted the Graunke Symphony Orchestra in Munich with which he gave concerts and radio performances, and recorded film music. He was also a guest conductor in Berlin, Bamberg, Vienna, Frankfurt am Main and Munich. His compositions include symphonies and a violin concerto; he recorded his Symphony No. 2 and the concerto (with David the soloist and the Graunke Symphony Orchestra for EMI). His other recordings include the Haydn Symphony No. 94, Leopold Mozart's *Toy Symphony*, a suite from *The Nutcracker* (with the Graunke Symphony Orchestra for Musical Treasures of the World), Liszt's *Mazeppa*, Dohnányi's *Symphonic Minuets* and *Wedding Waltz*, Borodin's Symphony No. 1, R. Strauss's *Festmarsch* and a suite from Rimsky-Korsakov's *The Invisible City of Kitezh* (with the Bavarian Radio Symphony Orchestra for Urania), overtures by Suppé, short pieces by Grieg and Tchaikovsky and The Dance of the Hours from *La Gioconda* (with the Bavarian Radio Symphony Orchestra for DGG), *Till Eulenspiegel* and *The Young Person's Guide to the Orchestra* (with the Graunke Symphony Orchestra for Buena), Delos' film music for *Friedhofer* and Godard's *Berceuse* (with the Graunke Symphony Orchestra). Some other conductors, such as Camarata, Heger, Mattis, Reger and Starke, have also recorded with the Graunke Symphony Orchestra.

Gravina, Gilbert, Count. Gravina's mother was Blandine, the daughter of Cosima Wagner and her first husband, Hans von Bülow, and his father was the Italian Count Gravina. He studied mathematics and astronomy and then music, under Nicodé and Schoenberg for composition, and Richter, Muck and Strauss for conducting. He also conducted opera and concerts in Germany, Italy, Switzerland, Austria and Hungary. He recorded the prelude to *Die Meistersinger* and the *Siegfried Idyll*, and Siegfried Wagner's Violin Concerto (with Abel), the prelude to the opera *An allem ist Hütchen schuld* and an excerpt from *Heidenkönig*, both also by Siegfried Wagner (with the Nuremberg Symphony Orchestra for Colosseum).

Greenbaum, Hyam (1901–42). Born in Brighton, Greenbaum studied at the Brighton School of Music (1909–12) and at the Royal College of Music, London (1913–15), and was a violinist in the Queen's Hall Orchestra and in the Brosa String Quartet (1925–9). He became a recording manager for the Decca Record Company (1929), musical director for the impresario C. B. Cochrane (1930–34), television music director for the BBC (1936–9), director of the BBC Revue Orchestra (1939–41), and on occasion conducted the BBC Symphony Orchestra. He was an associate of Schoenberg, Lambert and other contemporary composers, and performed their works; he was highly regarded by those who knew him as an interpretative musician. He composed a *Sea Poem* for orchestra, and a piece for oboe and orchestra. Vocalian recorded him conducting the Aeolian Orchestra in Haydn's Symphony No. 92, Mozart's Symphony No. 40, Rameau's *Rigodon de Dardanus*, and a suite and the waltzes from *Der Rosenkavalier*.

Greenberg, Noah (1919–66). Born in New York, Greenberg studied music privately, and for five years (1944–9) served as a seaman in the US merchant marine. In 1952 with Bernard Krainis he founded the New York Pro Musica, a choral and instrumental group specialising in performing music from the Renaissance and earlier periods. Among the group's most successful revivals were the medieval liturgical music dramas *The Play of Daniel* (1958), and *The Play of Herod* (1963). The New York Pro Musica toured Europe in 1960 and 1963, and the USSR in 1964; after Greenberg's death in 1966 the group continued under various conductors until it was finally disbanded in 1973. Its influence in encouraging the performance of early music in colleges and in the concert hall in the United States was significant.

With the Pro Musica, Greenberg made a series of superb recordings for Columbia (US), Esoteric and Decca (US). Two of its most successful discs were *The Play of Daniel* and *The Play of Herod*, mentioned above, but in addition there was vocal and instrumental music of the medieval and Renaissance periods from many European countries and of the composers Monteverdi, Josquin, Isaac, Rossi, Franck, Praetorius, Obrecht, Schütz, Tallis, Banchieri, Blow, Morley, Purcell, Handel *et al*. The most representative sample of the group's fine work is a seven-disc memorial edition issued by Everest, taken from the original Esoteric recordings; included in the anthology are Banchieri's *Festino*, Blow's *Ode on the Death of Purcell*, Handel's Cantata No. 13 and three Trio Sonatas, Elizabethan madrigals of Morley, and pieces by Purcell. Greenberg was not the first to revive this repertoire; in Europe his countryman Safford Cape played and recorded this music with his Pro Musica Antiqua in Belgium in the 1930s, as did August Wenzinger in Switzerland, but Greenberg must be given the credit for introducing a wide range of great and unknown music to American audiences.

Gregor, Bohumil (b. 1926). The Czech conductor Gregor was a pupil at the Prague Conservatory and started his career as a double-bass player in the Prague National Theatre Orchestra. He studied conducting with Ančerl and Chalabala, first conducted in 1947 at the National Theatre at a performance of *Madama Butterfly*, and in 1948 conducted at the Brno Opera, with the Army Artistic Ensemble in

Prague and at the Prague National Theatre, and was conductor at the Ostrava National Theatre (1958–62). Since then he has conducted at the Stockholm Opera for five years and also at Hamburg, San Francisco, in Holland and elsewhere. His international reputation has been as an interpreter of the operas of Janáček, for which he shared the responsibility of performing them in the original Czech and in foreign translations. Despite this, he feels himself best suited to Italian opera which he conducts dramatically and with emotional fire. For Supraphon he has conducted in recordings with the Prague National Opera of Janáček's *The Makropoulos Case*, *The Cunning Little Vixen*, *From the House of the Dead* and *Jenůfa*. The latter was issued in Britain for a short period by EMI and for longer in the United States by Angel, and in this set Gregor's performance is effective and idiomatic. He also recorded the overtures to *Der Schauspieldirektor*, *Semiramide* and *Il barbiere di Siviglia* (with the Czech Philharmonic Orchestra), the chorus from Act IV Scene III of *Boris Godunov*, and aria recitals with Adam, Kniplová, Soukupová and Švorc.

Grevillius, Nils (1893–1970). The Swedish conductor Grevillius studied at the Academy of Music in his native Stockholm, was concertmaster of the Royal Opera Orchestra in Stockholm (1911–24), studied conducting at Sondershausen and London, was assistant conductor of the Stockholm Concert Society (1914–20), and coached at the Royal Opera. He conducted for the Swedish Ballet in Paris (1922–3), was a guest conductor at the Tonkünstlerverein in Vienna (1922–3), conductor at the Théâtre des Champs-Élysées in Paris (1924), and conductor of the Stockholm Radio Orchestra (1927–39). In 1930 he was appointed court conductor and became administrative director of the Royal Opera in 1932. In his appearances abroad he did much to make Swedish music more widely known, and was associated with the tenor Jussi Björling, with whom he made many records as accompanist. On 78 r.p.m. discs for HMV he recorded Alfvén's *A Midsummer Vigil* and the elegy from the *Gustav Adolf II Suite* (with the Stockholm Concert Society Orchestra), excerpts from *Die Fledermaus* (with the Stockholm Opera), and the intermezzo and Apache Dance from *I gioielli della Madonna*. More recently, Discophil (Sweden) have issued records of his conducting the Stockholm Philharmonic Orchestra *et al.* in Alfvén's Symphonies Nos 3 and 4, and *Fran Havsbandet*, Atterberg's *De favitska jungfrurna*, and Lindberg's *Leksands svit*.

Grikurov, Eduard (b. 1907). Born in Tiflis (modern Tbilisi), Grikurov studied under Gauk at the Leningrad Conservatory, was conductor of the Andreiev Folklorist Instruments Orchestra (1935–6), conductor (1937–56) and principal conductor (1964–9) at the Maly Opera House, and teacher at the Leningrad Conservatory (1934–5, 1946–53 and from 1960). He has recorded Tchaikovsky's *Yolanta* (with the Maly Theatre Orchestra *et al.*), and Glière's Concerto for Coloratura Voice (with Maksimova and the Leningrad Philharmonic Orchestra). The latter performance was released in the United States by Monarch.

Grischkat, Hans (b. 1903). A native of Hamburg, Grischkat first studied science at the Tübingen University, then attended the Hochschule für Musik at Stuttgart where he studied the organ. In 1924 he founded the Reutlinger Choral Society, in 1931 the Swabian Singers and in 1936 the Grischkat Choral Society in Stuttgart. In 1946 he joined the Hochschule für Musik at Stuttgart as a lecturer and in 1950 became professor of choral conducting. This was his *forte* and in the first decades of the LP he recorded extensively as a choral conductor for a number of United States companies: Vox, Dover, Period, Lyrichord and Renaissance. The major works he encompassed were Bach's *Mass in B minor*, the four Lutheran Masses, excerpts from the *Christmas Oratorio*, four *Sanctus*, and Cantatas Nos 5, 6, 11, 19, 28, 37, 43, 50, 64, 104, 112, 149, 153, 154, 161, 172, 185, 189, 201 and 205, three Passions and the *Christmas Oratorio* of Schütz, Monteverdi's *Vespro della Beata Vergine*, Vivaldi's *Beatus Vir*, Handel's *Belshazzar*, and choral music by Lassus, Lübeck, Pergolesi and Buxtehude. The choirs and orchestras performing the music were from Stuttgart, and were variously known as the Swabian Singers, the Stuttgart Chorus, the Stuttgart Choral Society, the Stuttgart Academy Choir, the Stuttgart Tonstudio Choir, the Stuttgart Orchestra, the Stuttgart Pro Musica Orchestra, the Bach Orchestra, the Bach Ensemble, the Bach Festival Orchestra and the Stuttgart Tonstudio Orchestra. Maybe they were all, or nearly all, the same musicians; their performances, under Grischkat, were consistently competent. By the mid 1970s all that remained of these discs in the British catalogue were Schütz's *Christmas* and *Easter Oratorios*, on the Turnabout label.

Grofé, Ferde (1892–1972). Born in New York, Grofé was educated in Los Angeles and Germany, and was for a time a violist in the Los Angeles Philharmonic Orchestra. He played the violin and piano in theatre and dance bands including Paul Whiteman's Orchestra, and in 1924 scored Gershwin's *Rhapsody in Blue*. As a conductor he appeared at the Hollywood Bowl, at the Robin Hood Dell and at Carnegie Hall, conducting his own music including the highly successful *Grand Canyon Suite*, which has been recorded by at least fifteen conductors, with Toscanini at the top of the list. Grofé conducted some records of his own compositions: two *Grand Canyon Suites*, one with the Capitol Symphony Orchestra coupled with the *Death Valley Suite* (for a Capitol LP), and the other for Everest coupled with his *Piano Concerto in D major* (with Sanroma and the Rochester Philharmonic Orchestra), *Atlantic Crossing* (a work for narrators, choir and orchestra, with the New Symphony Orchestra *et al.* for Everest) and *Aviation Suite* (with the Hollywood Studio Orchestra for Remington).

Grøndahl, Launy (b. 1886). Born in Ordrup near Copenhagen, Grøndahl learned the violin as a boy and was a member of the Casino Theatre orchestra at Copenhagen when he was only thirteen. He went abroad to study, in Paris, Italy and Vienna, returned to become president of the Society of Young Musicians in Copenhagen, and in 1925 conducted the first concert of the orchestra that was to become the Danish State Radio Orchestra. He was permanent conductor of the orchestra in its early years and toured with it in a number of European countries. In 1950 he appeared at the Edinburgh Festival and the next year at the Royal Festival Hall, London, with the orchestra, giving performances (*inter alia*) of the Nielsen symphonies. Among EMI's first LP releases in 1952 was Nielsen's Symphony No. 4 (the *Inextinguishable*), in which Grøndahl led his orchestra in a powerful performance. This disc, with others of Nielsen symphonies under his compatriots Jensen and Tuxen, were the first to arouse public interest in the composer in Britain. Grøndahl's other records included Hartmann's *Funeral March for B. Thorvaldsen* (on 78s, with the Danish Radio Wind Ensemble), Nielsen's *Andante lamentoso* (with the Danish National Orchestra for Odeon), overture and Dance of the Cockerels from Nielsen's *Maskarade*, In the Blue Grotto from Gade's *Napoli* ballet (with the Danish State Radio Orchestra for EMI) and Schierbeck's *Fête galante* overture (with the same orchestra for Mercury).

Grossman, Ferdinand (1887–1970). Born in Tulln, the Austrian conductor Grossman studied in Linz and with Weingartner in Vienna, founded a Volkskonservatorium in Vienna in 1923, and was appointed choirmaster of the Vienna Singverein by Furtwängler. He became choral director of the Vienna State Opera (1930), and was director of the Vienna Boys' Choir (1939–45 and from 1956). He founded the Vienna Chamber Choir at the Vienna Academy of Music (1946), and with the choir toured Europe and the United States. His compositions include some chamber music and an a capella *German Mass*.

Grossman recorded in the 1950s and later for Lyrichord, Vox, Westminster and Philips, directing various Viennese choirs and orchestras in many major choral works, chief among which were some Palestrina masses, motets of Schütz, Vivaldi's *Gloria*, Bach's *St Matthew Passion*, *St John Passion*, *Christmas Oratorio*, *Easter Oratorio* and motets *Komm, Jesu, komm* and *Jesu, mein Freude*, Mozart's Masses K. 167, K. 220, K. 317 and *Requiem*, *Exsultate, jubilate* and *Benedictus* K. 117, Haydn's Masses Nos 2, 10 and 11, Schubert's Masses Nos 2 and 3, Bruckner's Mass No. 3 and Mendelssohn's *St Paul*. In another vein altogether, Whitehall issued records in which he conducted *Scheherazade*, suites from *Swan Lake* and *Nutcracker*, Tchaikovsky's Piano Concerto No. 1 and Rachmaninov's Piano Concerto No. 2 (with Rivkin and the Vienna Festival Orchestra), and Philips a disc of Strauss waltzes and polkas (with the Vienna Concert Orchestra).

Grossman, Herbert. The American conductor Grossman conducted opera and concerts in Europe and the United States, was conductor of the NBC Opera Company and associate conductor of the Baltimore and Pittsburgh Symphony Orchestras. He led the premières of Menotti's operas *Maria Golovin* and *Labyrinth*, and regularly conducted NBC's Christmas presentation of *Amahl and the Night Visitors*, which he recorded for RCA with the NBC Opera Company. For Composers Recordings he also recorded, with the Vienna State Opera Orchestra *et al.*, Weisgall's opera *The Tenor*.

Grote, Gottfried (b. 1903). Born in Oberfrohna, near Chemnitz (now Karl-Marx-Stadt), Grote was educated at the Berlin Academy of Music (1924–5) and the Hochschule für Musik at Cologne (1926–7), and became organist at Mönchen-Gladbach and Wüppertal under von Hoesslin. He was conductor of the School for Religious Music in Berlin (1935) and conductor of the State and Cathedral Choirs in Berlin (1955) and professor at the Academy of Music there. He has published editions of the *Cantiones sacrae* of Schütz and choral pieces of Bach, and other sacred music. For Cantate he recorded Pepping's *Deutsche Messe* and a *St Matthew Passion*, both with the Berlin State and Cathedral Choirs.

Groves, Sir Charles (b. 1915). A Londoner, Groves was enrolled at the Choir School of St Paul's Cathedral at the age of eight, and later studied at the Royal College of Music in London. He began his career as a free-lance accompanist then joined the British Broadcasting Corporation in 1938 as a chorus master, became conductor of the BBC Theatre Orchestra (1942), the BBC Revue Orchestra (1943) and the BBC Northern Symphony Orchestra (1944–51). From 1951 to 1961 he was conductor of the Bournemouth Symphony Orchestra; it was, in 1951, the Bournemouth Municipal Orchestra, and was about to cease its existence, but Groves fought for its survival and it was reformed as the Bournemouth Symphony Orchestra, under the aegis of the Western Orchestral Society Ltd., and Groves was its first musical director. From 1961 to 1963 he was the first full-time director of the Welsh National Opera, and from 1963 to 1977 music director and conductor of the Royal Liverpool Philharmonic Orchestra. At Liverpool he instituted the post of associate conductor, and in 1967 he himself was appointed associate conductor of the Royal Philharmonic Orchestra, although he continued to spend most of the year in Liverpool. In 1973 he was knighted, and in 1978 began as music director with the English National Opera. He has toured in Australia, South Africa, South America and throughout Europe; with the Royal Philharmonic Orchestra he has visited FR Germany, Switzerland, Poland and the United States. He conducts the Munich Philharmonic Orchestra regularly, and there leads the annual New Year's Eve performance of Beethoven's Symphony No. 9.

Early in his career Groves was greatly influenced by Toscanini, Beecham, Furtwängler and Wood. At the BBC he prepared the choir for Toscanini's London performances of Brahms' *Ein deutsches Requiem*, Verdi's *Requiem* and Beethoven's *Missa Solemnis*. In Liverpool he became the first British conductor to perform the complete cycle of Mahler symphonies with his own orchestra. He has a special fondness for large-scale choral works such as Mahler's Symphony No. 8 and Berlioz' *Grande Messe des morts*, but also encourages and performs new music. Anxious to avoid being recognised as a specialist, he has nonetheless become known as a fine interpreter of British music in particular, as his records demonstrate. In fact he believes that the insistence on conducting from memory on the part of many conductors is one of the causes of specialisation. He enjoys recording, and has said that he would record anything, although he sees clearly the artistic snares involved: 'The medium itself has created all sorts of problems, wonderful as it is – the idea of putting a bar in here, a bar there. I like to try and get a thing through with as few takes as possible, not to "sole and heel" so much. . . . One wonders whether the slavish accuracy that the recording masters have imposed on us is an end in itself – I doubt it. You can have a thing accurate in itself and as dull as ditchwater' (*Hi Fi News and Record Review*, June 1974, p. 90). On another occasion, when he was appointed successor to Lord Britten as president of the National Youth Orchestra, he said that the perfect recording techniques of modern gramophone records had spread the misapprehension that there was one true and only authentic version of each musical work. 'On the contrary, each experience of a piece of music should be a fresh one, to which one brings an independent judgement without preconceptions.'

Groves' first records were LPs for Fidelity and Saga with the Bournemouth Symphony Orchestra, of Beethoven's Symphony No. 4 and Brahms' *Academic Festival Overture*, Delius' *On Hearing the First Cuckoo in Spring*, Holst's *Somerset Rhapsody* and Elgar's *Introduction and Allegro*; the performances were straightforward and vigorous, an apt description for virtually all his records. All of Groves' records, for EMI, have been of British composers, apart from discs of Dvořák's Symphony No. 6 (with the Royal Philharmonic Orchestra), Mendelssohn's Piano Concerto No. 1 and Saint-Saëns' Piano Concerto No. 2 (with Adni and the Royal Liverpool Philharmonic Orchestra), several discs of less familiar orchestral music of Sibelius, such as *In Memoriam*, *Legends*, incidental music to *The Tempest*, *Suite champêtre* and *Suite mignonne*, a collection of overtures by Suppé, Verdi, Hérold, Rezniček, Thomas and Mendelssohn, excerpts from Handel's operas and oratorios (with organist E. Power Biggs), some medleys of short popular orchestral pieces, and guitar concertos of Rodrigo and Dodgson (with Williams and the English Chamber Orchestra). Pride of place goes to the Delius series: *Sea Drift*, *Song of the High Hills*, *Songs of Sunset* (with Janet Baker), *Cynara*, *An Arabesque*, *Paris*, *Eventyr*, *Dance Rhapsody No. 1*, (with the Royal Liverpool Philharmonic Orchestra, *et al.*), the *Mass of Life* (with the London Philharmonic Orchestra *et al.*), *Koanga* (with the London Symphony Orchestra *et al.*) and *North Country Sketches*, *Life's Dance* and *A Song of Summer* (with the Royal Philharmonic Orchestra). These performances inevitably invite comparison with the famous original recordings of Beecham of much of the same music, but it is scarcely a valid criticism of Groves to suggest that, fine though they are, they do not efface the finesse and utter conviction of Beecham's own performances. Groves himself is a devout admirer of Beecham and especially of his Delius recordings, and his association with him goes back to his days at the Royal College of Music when he played in the orchestra conducted by Beecham in *A Village Romeo and Juliet*. Groves has pointed out that Beecham invariably gave intense preparation to all his scores, above all to Delius, whom he edited considerably, not only in questions of balance but in inserting expression marks. Beecham's interpretations cannot be imitated by others; they are essentially his own conception of Delius' intention. Groves is sure that he must try to find for himself what lay behind the composer's mind and to make his own estimate. 'It's bad enough to try and satisfy the memory of the composer, let alone the memory of another conductor's idea. Which still does not detract from my worshipping of Beecham's conducting.'

Elgar has also fared sympathetically in Groves' hands. With the Liverpool orchestra he has recorded *Caractacus*, two discs of lesser-known orchestral music, such as the *Nursery Suite*, the *Severn Suite* and a suite from *The Crown of India*, and the Violin Concerto, in which Hugh Bean, the soloist gives a distinctively individual reading. Other British music recorded is Sullivan's *Symphony in E flat*, the overture *Di Ballo*, and a selection of overtures and popular pieces (with the Royal Liverpool Philharmonic Orchestra), Arnold's Symphony No. 2 and *English Dances* (with the Bournemouth Symphony Orchestra), Grace Williams' *Fantasia on Welsh Nursery Tunes*, *Trumpet Concerto* (with Snell), *Carillons* (with Camden) and *Fairest of Stars* (with Price and the London Symphony Orchestra), Bliss's *Morning Heroes*, a symphony for orator, chorus and orchestra written as a tribute to the composer's young brother and other fellow comrades-in-arms who fell in World War I (with the Royal Liverpool Philharmonic Orchestra *et al.*), *Colour Symphony* and music for *Things to Come* (with the Royal Philharmonic Orchestra), Maxwell Davies' *Second Fantasia on John Taverner's 'In Nomine'* (with the New Philharmonia Orchestra), Walton's *Spitfire Prelude and Fugue*, *Crown Imperial*, *Orb and Sceptre*, *Capriccio Burlesco* and *Johannesburg Festival Overture*, Eric Coates' *London Suite*, *London Again*, *Summer Days*, *The Three Elizabeths*, *The Three Bears*, *Cinderella*, etc., (with the Royal Liverpool Philharmonic Orchestra). All these discs were for EMI; for Argo, he conducted the Argo Chamber Ensemble in Lambert's Piano Concerto (with Watson).

Grüber, Arthur (b. 1910). Born in Essen, Grüber gave piano recitals in Sweden as a boy of fourteen, and his opera *The Black Galley* was then performed in public at Stockholm. He was awarded scholarships by Queen Alexandrine of Denmark and the Prussian Ministry of Culture (1925–7), wrote orchestral suites for plays by Shakespeare and Goethe (1928–30), studied at the Hochschule für Musik at Cologne under Braunfels and Abendroth (1930–32), and became assistant to Steinberg at the Frankfurt Opera (1932). In 1934 he was unexpectedly called on to conduct *The Ring*, which led to his appointment as music director at Frankfurt (1934–8). His subsequent appointments were director of the Wüppertal Opera (1938), first conductor at the Deutsche Oper, Berlin (1939–44), guest conductor at the Paris Opéra (1942) and general music director at Halle (1944). After military service and a period as a prisoner-of-war (1944–7), he became music director at the Hamburg Opera (1947–51), at the Berlin Komische Oper (1951–5), chief conductor of the Radio Eireann Symphony Orchestra, Dublin (1951–5), general music director at Braunschweig (1954–62) and at the Baden State Theatre, Karlsruhe (from 1962), and teacher of conducting at the Baden Academy of Music (from 1963). His compositions include an opera *Trotz wider Trotz* (1948) and a cantata *Ode to Peace* (1953).

Grüber recorded for Odeon with the Berlin Philharmonic Orchestra in the years 1940–44, overtures by Auber, Lortzing, Mozart, Busoni and Pfitzner, some *Hungarian Rhapsodies* of Liszt, preludes and orchestral excerpts from the Wagnerian operas, Grieg's *Symphonic Dances* and the Polovtsian March and Dances from *Prince Igor*, as well as accompaniments to song and operatic recitals for Telefunken and Electrola. In 1955 he recorded the Brahms and Bruch Violin Concertos (with Gimpel and the Berlin Symphony Orchestra) and the two *Peer Gynt* suites, also with the Berlin Symphony Orchestra (for Europäischer Phonoklub, of which the Brahms concerto was released by Ariola). In 1968 he recorded for Vox the Henze Violin Concerto (with Lauterbacher and the Radio Luxembourg Orchestra), Ghedini's *Concerto dell'albatro* (with the Philharmonia

Hungarica *et al.*), a group of pieces by Lutosławski (with the Berlin Symphony and Hamburg Symphony Orchestras) and Hindemith's one-act opera *Hin und zurück*, *Der Dämon* suite, and dances from a marionette play, *Nusch-Nuschi* (with the Berlin Symphony Orchestra and the Stuttgart Soloists *et al.*).

Grüner-Hegge, Odd (1899–1973). Born in Oslo, Grüner-Hegge studied the piano and composition at the Oslo Conservatory and was a student of conducting with Weingartner. He came into prominence first in 1917 as a composer, the next year as a pianist, and from 1925 to 1930 was music critic for an Oslo newspaper. His debut as a conductor was in 1927, and in 1931 he was appointed conductor of the Oslo Philharmonic Orchestra, becoming the orchestra's music director in 1945. He was permanent conductor of the Oslo National Theatre from 1932 to 1937 and then director of the Norwegian Opera from 1960. Many major European orchestras engaged him as a guest conductor, and his compositions included chamber music and orchestral works. With the Oslo Philharmonic, Grüner-Hegge made a number of recordings which were released in about 1960 by RCA (on the Camden label), Rondo, Mercury, Readers Digest and on a Norwegian label. Included were Brahms' Symphonies Nos 1 and 3, Mendelssohn's Symphony No. 4, Tchaikovsky's Symphonies Nos 5 and 6, the *Peer Gynt* suites, Beethoven's Piano Concerto No. 5 (with Riefling) and the Grieg Piano Concerto (with Baekkelund and Riefling), *Finlandia*, a *Carmen* suite, *Marche slave*, the *Nutcracker* suite, and the overtures *1812*, *William Tell* and *Die Fledermaus*. Mercury also issued a performance of *Peer Gynt* in which Grieg's music was presented in its stage sequence. Of Norwegian composers other than Grieg, he recorded Svendsen's Symphonies Nos 1 and 2 and *Zorahayde* overture, Jensen's *Partita sinfonica* and incidental music to *The Drover*, Eggen's *Bøgulv the Fiddler*, the Rustic Dance from *Liti Kjersti* and Dance Scene from *Olav Liljenkrans*, Braein's *Concert Overture* and his own *Elegiac Melody*. He also recorded the Grieg Piano Concerto (with Jenner and the Bayreuth Radio Orchestra, issued by CBS-Realm). All these performances were lively, sympathetic and well played, perhaps with more enthusiasm than subtlety.

Guadagno, Anton (b. 1925). Born in Castellamare del Golfo, Sicily, Guadagno studied at the Conservatorio Vicenzo Bellini at Palermo, at the Accademia di Santa Cecilia at Rome, and at the Mozarteum at Salzburg. He conducted the Radio Italiana orchestras at Rome and Turin, migrated to the United States where he became a US citizen, was principal conductor of the Philadelphia Lyric and Cincinnati Summer Operas and appeared at opera houses in Vienna, London, Hamburg, Paris, Madrid, San Francisco and New Orleans, and is now conductor at the Vienna Volksoper. His recordings have been of Puccini's early operas *Le Villi* and Act II of *Edgar* (with the Vienna Volksoper Orchestra *et al.* for RCA) and aria recitals with Caballé, Verrett, Domingo, Tebaldi, Milnes and Corelli (with various orchestras for RCA, EMI and Decca).

Guarino, Piero (b. 1919). Born in Alexandria, Egypt, Guarino studied at the Athens Conservatory and in Italy with Casella. In 1950 he founded the Alexandria Conservatory and in 1960 became director of the Chamber Orchestra of the Accademia Musicale Napolitana. He has composed orchestral music, concertos *et al.* For Golden Crest he recorded with the orchestra Bucchi's *Concerto lirico* and a Sinfonia for cello attributed to Pergolesi (with Magendany in the latter).

Guarnieri, Antonio (1883–1952). Born in Venice, Guarnieri played the cello in the Martucci Quartet, made his debut as a conductor in Siena (1904), and was engaged to conduct in Vienna (1912). He soon resigned because of disagreements about working conditions, and eventually became principal conductor at La Scala, Milan, in succession to Toscanini (1929), and was conducting there almost until his death. Giulini, who knew him well, has expressed the highest opinion of his talent as a conductor. Guarnieri recorded the Vivaldi Concerto Op. 3 No. 2, the *Semiramide* overture, *Jeux d'enfants*, Martucci's Symphony No. 2, the prelude to Act III of *La Wally*, and the Dance of the Water Nymphs from *Loreley* (with the La Scala Orchestra for HMV), excerpts from *Tosca* (with the Milan Symphony Orchestra for Philips), some movements from Respighi's *Ancient Airs and Dances* Suite No. 1 (with the Milan Symphony Orchestra for Parlophone), Zandonai's *Francesca da Rimini* (with the Italian Radio Orchestra *et al.* for Cetra), and *Manon* (with the La Scala Orchestra *et al.* for Cetra).

Guenther, Felix (b. 1886). Born in Trautenau, Austria, Guenther studied at the Vienna Conservatory and at the Berlin University, and from 1903 toured as an accompanist with many soloists. He was a professor at the Humboldt Hochschule, Berlin (1924–6) and at the

Popular University of the City of Berlin (1926–33), then migrated to the United States, taught at Queen's College, and conducted the Interscholastic Glee Club, both in New York. He wrote books about Weingartner (Berlin, 1918), and Schubert's songs (Stuttgart, 1928). Nixa issued a mono LP in which he conducted the Vienna Symphony Orchestra in C. P. E. Bach's Symphonies Nos 1 and 3, and J. C. Bach's *Sinfonia concertante*.

Guest, George (b. 1924). Born in Bangor, North Wales, Guest was, as a boy, a chorister at Bangor Cathedral (1933–5) and at Chester Cathedral (1935–9). His father was an organist, and as a schoolboy he studied the organ with Boyle at Chester Cathedral. After service with the Royal Air Force in India and Europe (1942–6) he was awarded an organ scholarship to St John's College, Cambridge (1947–51), where he succeeded Orr as organist and choirmaster (1951). He became a lecturer in music (1953), then professor of harmony and counterpoint at the Royal College of Music (1960–61), and is now organist to Cambridge University, a member of the Council of the Royal College of Organists, and director of studies in music at St John's, Downing and Queens' Colleges in Cambridge. He was also director of the Berkshire Boys Choir in the United States (1967–70), a group assembled from boys and men from the leading American choirs.

The choir of St John's College, Cambridge, with whom Guest has made over 50 LP records, has an experience and tradition going back 450 years. Its membership is composed of choristers on scholarships who board at the college school, and the tenor and bass parts are taken by university students who enter the college as choral scholars. The choir's typical sound is somewhat more astringent than is usual with British cathedral choirs; Guest has cultivated this tone as he believes it more suited to the music of composers like Monteverdi and Palestrina. Guest himself has long been interested in plainsong and French choral music, and his other preferences are for the music of Elgar and for Welsh hymn tunes. *The Dream of Gerontius* is to him a finer work than the *Mass in B minor* of Bach, as it is a perfect fusion of Cardinal Newman's poetic vision with Elgar's deeply mystical music.

Guest has recorded extensively for Argo, the Decca subsidiary, with the St John's College Choir; many pieces have been of a capella music, and in other music he has recorded with the Academy of St Martin-in-the-Fields. Included are five of the great Masses of Haydn: the Nos 7, 8, 10, 11 and 12, and even taking into account previous recordings of some of these masses, this series has fully revealed the glory of some of Haydn's most magnificent music. These five Masses, together with the Mass No. 9 (*Nelson*) which had been recorded earlier by Argo with the King's College Choir, the London Symphony Orchestra *et al.* under Willcocks, have been re-issued as a boxed set by Decca. Also recorded are Victoria's *Litaniae de beata Virgine*, Mass, Requiem and motets, Praetorius' Psalms 24, 47 and 108, *The Lord ascendeth* and *The Head that once was crowned with thorns*, Monteverdi's *Laudate pueri*, *Et queant laxis* and two masses, Palestrina's *Magnificat*, *Exsultate Deo*, *Antiphon: Assumpta est Maria*, *Missa brevis*, *Missa assumpta est Maria et al.*, Gesualdo's *O vos omnes*, Gabrieli's *Missa brevis*, Byrd's *Psallite Domino et al.*, Purcell's *Funeral Music*, *Symphoniae sacrae*, verse anthems, *Te Deum*, *Jubilate Deo*, and other pieces, Michael Haydn's *Salve Regina*, Mozart's *Ave verum corpus*, music by Tallis and Weelkes, Liszt's *Missa Choralis*, Beethoven's *Mass in C*, Bruckner's motets, Schubert's *Masses in A flat* and *E flat*, sacred music by Blow, Humphrey, Locke, Walmsley, Nares, Goss, S. Wesley, S. S. Wesley, Greene, Harris, Marbeck, Mundy, Walker, Campbell, Farrant, Gibbons, Bainton, Batten, Bairstow, Howells, Vaughan Williams, Ireland, Orr and Tippett, Duruflé's *Requiem* and motets, Fauré's *Requiem*, *Messe basse* and *Cantique*, Howell's *Magnificat* and *Nunc dimittis*, Banchieri's *Omnes genti*, Langlais' *Messe solenelle*, Messiaen's *O sacrum convivium*, Poulenc's *Litanies à la Vierge Noire*, Britten's *A Ceremony of Carols*, *Rejoice in the Lamb*, *Hymn to the Virgin*, *Festival Te Deum*, *Hymn to St Peter*, *Hymn to St Columba*, *Jubilate Deo* and *Missa brevis*, and Stainer's *Crucifixion*. When the last-named was released in 1962, many considered it unworthy of the attention that Guest had given it, because of the unsophisticated nature of the music, its simplicity of utterance, absence of counterpoint and straightforward melodies and harmonies. Guest defended Stainer, calling him an all-round scholar and musician who brought a dramatic power into his writing, rarely matched by his successors.

Guhl, Adolf Fritz (1919–77). Born in Wittenberge/Prignitz, Guhl studied at the Berlin Academy of Music with Gmeindl, Heitmann, Fischer, Martienssen and Hindemith, was with the Berlin State Opera (1945) and was artistic director of the Klindworth-Scharwenka Conservatory in Berlin (1948–51). He was conductor for the broadcasting company of DR Germany, with the Berlin Radio Symphony Orchestra in East Berlin, and with the Leipzig Radio Symphony Orchestra, of which he became chief conductor in 1963. He was also music director of the Berliner Ensemble (1950–53), chief conductor of the GDR film orchestra (1945–57) and a lecturer at the Hochschule für Musik in East Berlin, and toured in Czechoslovakia, Poland, Romania and Bulgaria. His recordings included Handel's *Oboe Concerto in G minor* (with Watzig) and some Concerti Grossi from Op. 3 and Op. 6 (with the Berlin Radio Chamber Orchestra), a complete *The Sleeping Beauty*, Kabalevsky's *The Comedians*, Shostakovich's *Ballet Suite No. 1* and Svendsen's *Romance* (with the Berlin Symphony Orchestra), Miaskovsky's *Lyric Concertino*, Glière's *The Bronze Horseman*, Wagner's *Polonia* overture and songs with Ernst Busch (with the Berlin Radio Symphony Orchestra), Neef's Piano Concerto (with Gary) and Violin and Piano Concerto (with Arens and Garay), Eisler's *Lenin Requiem*, *Die Teppichweber von Kujan-Bulak*, *Ernste Gesänge*, *Winterschlacht-Suite*, *Deutsche Sinfonie*, *Ballade von der Judenhure Marie Sanders* and *Lied der Werktätigen*, Raupp's *Metamorphosen*, *Essay for Violin and Orchestra* and *Concerto animato* (with Vermes) and Zimmermann's *L'Homme* (with the Leipzig Radio Symphony Orchestra), Suites Nos 5 and 6 (with the Collegium Musicum, Leipzig) and *Die Mutter*. Some of these performances were issued in the West by Urania.

Gui, Vittorio (1885–1975). Born in Rome where he studied at the Accademia di Santa Cecilia, Gui made his debut as a conductor at the Teatro Adriano in Rome in 1907. Three years later he became conductor at the San Carlo Opera at Naples, conducted symphony concerts at the Augusteo and elsewhere and was engaged by Toscanini for La Scala for the 1923–4 and 1924–5 seasons. In 1925 in collaboration with Guido Gatti he founded and was musical director of the Teatro di Torino, where he introduced many new and unfamiliar operas and symphonic works, developing a standard that was amongst the highest in Italy. In 1928 he created the Stabile Orchestrale Fiorentino and from this orchestra grew the Maggio Musicale Fiorentino, of which Gui was the director from 1933 to 1936. This orchestra also was the origin of the Teatro Comunale, where he conducted until 1943. In 1936 Beecham invited him to Covent Garden to conduct the Italian repertoire, which he did with great distinction. In 1948 he began his association with the Glyndebourne Festival Opera Company, conducted them at the Edinburgh Festival and continued until his last appearance at Glyndebourne in 1965. In that period he conducted fifteen separate operas and introduced three Rossini operas then very little known. In 1960 he was appointed an artistic counsellor to the Glyndebourne company. After 1965 he conducted both opera and concerts in Italy, and gave his last concert just two weeks before his death in Florence at the age of 90. His compositions include songs, chamber music, symphonic works, orchestral transcriptions and an opera for children *La fata Malerba*; he was also the author of musical essays and criticisms.

Gui was recognised early in his career as a brilliant conductor, and later when he appeared in London in the 1930s, he was hailed as the finest Italian conductor since Serafin. From his first years he conducted an extensive symphonic and operatic repertoire from memory. His style was quite free of mannerisms and his conducting has been described (D. Hall, ed., *The Opera Book*, London, 1948, p. 654) as 'at all times elegantly reserved'. As happens to so many Italian conductors, he was known internationally as an interpreter of Italian opera, but his distinction in the fields of oratorio and symphonic music, at least in his own country, was overlooked. At La Scala he conducted *Lohengrin* and *Salome*, and gave the first performances in Italy of *Ariadne auf Naxos* and *L'Heure espagnole*. Many of his earlier records were of symphonic music; before World War II he made a number of 78 r.p.m. sets for Cetra which included the *Leonore No. 3* overture, Brahms' Symphonies Nos 2 and 3, *Till Eulenspiegel*, the Rhine Journey from *Götterdämmerung*, and his arrangements of Bach's *Kommst du nun, Jesu, vom Himmel* and Franck's *Prélude, aria et finale* (with the Maggio Musicale Fiorentino), *Norma*, the introduction to Pergolesi's *Orfeo*, Haydn's *The Seasons*, the *Coriolan* overture, Franck's *Psyché et Eros*, Scriabin's *Rêverie* and Liadov's *Eight Russian Folksongs* (with the EIAR Orchestra *et al.*). Some of these recordings were also issued by Polydor, Parlophone and Decca. Later, some American companies such as Remington issued LP discs of him conducting Mendelssohn's Symphony No. 5 and the overtures *Die schöne Melusine*, *The Hebrides*, *Iphigénie en Aulide*, *Namensfeier*, *Tancredi*, *L'inganno felice*, *L'Italiana in Algeri*, *Le Siège de Corinthe*, *Anacréon*, *Les Deux Journées*, *Oberon* and *Il segreto di Susanna* (with the Austrian Symphony Orchestra), Schubert's Symphony No. 8, *Peer Gynt* Suite No. 1, *Finlandia*, excerpts from *Werther*, the overtures to *Tannhäuser* and *Der fliegende Holländer*, *A Night on the Bare Mountain*, the Polovtsian Dances from *Prince Igor*, *Prélude à l'après-midi d'un faune*, *L'Apprenti sorcier* and *Kamarinskaya* (with the Maggio Musicale Fiorentino Orchestra), and Cetra released *Aida* (with the Italian Radio Symphony Orchestra *et al.*), Mozart's Symphony No. 40 and Brahms' Symphony No. 4 (with the Maggio Musicale Fiorentino Orchestra).

When Gui was with the Glyndebourne Company, he recorded for EMI with the Glyndebourne Festival Orchestra, which was substantially the Royal Philharmonic Orchestra of Beecham. These releases included Haydn's Symphonies Nos 39, 60, 83 and 95, Mozart's Symphonies Nos 38 and 39, the overtures *Tancredi*, *Semiramide*, *La Cenerentola* and *Alceste*, and *Jeux d'enfants*. The operas he recorded at this time were the summit of his achievement on records: *La Cenerentola*, *Le Comte Ory*, *Il barbiere di Siviglia* and *Le nozze di Figaro*, which were taken from Glyndebourne productions in the 1950s. They had a vintage quality about them, but unfortunately were made before the age of stereo, and despite their superlative quality and occasional reissue, they have now disappeared from the catalogues. L'Estro Armonico have also released another performance of *Norma* which Gui conducted at Covent Garden in 1952, *Parsifal* from an Italian Radio broadcast in 1950, and Nabucco from the San Carlo Opera at Naples in 1950; EMI also recorded *Mefistofele* (with the Rome Opera Orchestra *et al.*), and there has also appeared Spontini's *Agnes von Hohenstaufen*, taken from a live performance.

Gülke, Peter (b. 1934). Born in Weimar, Gülke studied at the Franz Liszt Hochschule there, at the Friedrich Schiller University at Jena, and at the Karl Marx University at Leipzig, and was awarded a Ph.D. in musicology in 1958. He was a repetiteur at the Rudolfstadt Theatre (1959), music director at Stendal (1964) and at Potsdam (1966), was a free-lance conductor and musicologist (1969–72), music director at Stralsund (1972) and since 1976 conductor at the Dresden State Opera and lecturer at the Hochschule für Musik in Dresden. For Eterna he has recorded the Beethoven *Piano Concerto in E flat major* WoO 4 and Zimmermann's *Der Schuhu und die fliegende Prinzessin*.

Gulyás, György (b. 1916). Born at Köröstarsa, Hungary, Gulyás studied at the Franz Liszt Academy in Budapest, organised and was director of the Music School at Békéstarhos, founded and conducted the Choir there (1946–54), and was director of the Zoltán Kodály Music School at Debrecen. Many new Hungarian and foreign choral works have been premièred by the Zoltán Kodály Choir and the Debrecen Philharmonic Orchestra under his direction; he has been an adjudicator at international choral festivals, has conducted orchestras in Eastern and Western Europe, and was awarded the Franz Liszt Prize in 1959 and the title Merited Artist of the Hungarian People's Republic in 1970. For Hungaroton he has recorded discs of the choral music of Kodály, with the Zoltán Kodály Choir of Debrecen.

Gurlitt, Manfred (1890–1972). Born in Berlin where his father was a well-known landscape painter, Gurlitt studied with Breihaupt, Kaun, Humperdinck and Muck, was an operatic coach at the Berlin State Opera (1908–10), at the Bayreuth Festival (1911) and conductor at Essen (1911–12), Augsburg (1912–14), and Bremen (1914–27). After conducting at Berlin, Hamburg, Vienna and elsewhere he came under attack from the Nazis, who banned his compositions and forced him to leave Germany. He went to Japan where he was a teacher and conductor (1939), organised opera and concerts there, and returned to FR Germany in 1953 to perform some of his works. He composed, *inter alia*, nine operas, one of which was a setting of Büchner's play *Wozzeck*, written at the same time as Berg's. In 1929 he recorded for Polydor the Beethoven Violin Concerto, with soloist Josef Wolfsthal and the Berlin Philharmonic Orchestra, and this performance was included in the DGG album *The Early Days*, which was issued in 1973. His other recordings included Bach's Cantata No. 56 (with the Victor Chamber Orchestra *et al.*, for Victor, Japan), an excerpt from Krenek's *Jonny spielt auf* and the overture to *La gazza ladra* (with the Berlin State Opera Orchestra), the overtures to *Le Calife de Bagdad* (with the Grand Symphony Orchestra for Odeon) and *Die Meistersinger* (with the Berlin Philharmonic Orchestra, for Polydor).

Guschlbauer, Theodor (b. 1939). After attending the Academy of Music in his native Vienna, Guschlbauer studied conducting with Swarowsky in Vienna, and with Matačic and Karajan in Salzburg. He was conductor of the Vienna Baroque Ensemble (1961–9), a repetiteur and assistant conductor at the Vienna Volksoper (1964–6), conductor at the Landestheater, Salzburg (1966–8), music director at the Lyon Opéra, France (1968–75), general music director at Linz (since 1975), and has conducted at many European cities and festivals. He has emerged as a stylish interpreter of the Austrian classics; if his performances of Haydn, Mozart, Schubert and Beethoven are not especially individual, they are sensitive, unmannered and highly musical.

For Erato he has recorded Haydn's Symphonies Nos 53, 61 and 77, the overture and an air from *Acis and Galatea*, and *Aria di Corridino* (with Stämpfli), Mozart's Divertimento K. 287, Cassation No. 1, Oboe Concerto (with Pierlot), Masses K. 194 and K. 220, *Exsultate, jubilate* (with Hansmann), *Ave verum corpus*, *Vesperae solennes de confessore* and *Misericordias Domine*, Hoffmeister's *Flute Concerto in G* and Holzbauer's *Flute Concerto in D* (with Rampal), Monn's *Symphony in E flat*, excerpts from Cesti's *Il pomo d'oro*, Wagenseil's *Symphony in D*, Dittersdorf's *Sinfonia concertante in D* and Double-Bass Concerto (with Streicher), Fux's *Overture in C major*, Reutter's *Servizio di Tavola*, Schmelzer's *Serenata con altre* and *Arie*, and Muffat's Concerto No. 4 (with the Vienna Baroque Ensemble *et al.*); Haydn's Scherzando No. 6, Sinfonia Concertante, overture to *L'Incontro improviso* and Trumpet Concerto (with André), Mozart's Symphonies Nos 31, 36, 38, 39, 40 and 41, Sinfonia Concertante K. 297b, Bassoon Concerto (with Hongne) and Rondo K. 371 (with Barboteu), the Weber overtures *Der Freischütz*, *Oberon*, *Euryanthe*, *Abu Hassan*, *Jubel* and *Peter Schmoll und seine Nachbarn*, Clarinet Concerto No. 1 (with Lancelot), Bassoon Concerto (with Hongne) and Horn Concertino (with Barboteu), and Mendelssohn's Violin Concerto (with Amoyal) and overtures *Die schöne Melusine* and *The Hebrides*, Reinecke's *Harp Concerto in E minor* (with Laskine) and *Flute Concerto in D* (with Rampal), and Strauss's *Burleske* (with Hubeau), Horn Concerto No. 2 (with Barboteu), Oboe Concerto (with Pierlot) and a suite from *Der Rosenkavalier* (with the Bamberg Symphony Orchestra); Bach's Harpsichord Concerto BWV 947 (with Langfort), Marcello's *Oboe Concerto in D minor* (with Hertel), Muffat's Sonata No. 1 and Mozart's Piano Concerto K. 107 No. 1 (with Langfort, and the Austrian Tonkünstler Orchestra); the two Mozart Flute Concertos, Andante K. 315 and Rondo K. Anh. 184 (with Rampal and the Vienna Symphony Orchestra); Beethoven's Symphony No. 6 and Schubert's Symphony No. 9 (with the New Philharmonia Orchestra); Kodály's *Concerto for Orchestra* and *Háry János* suite (with the ORTF Orchestra); Mozart's Symphonies Nos 23 and 29, *Eine kleine Nachtmusik* and Violin Concertos K. 216 and K. 218 (with Kantarow) and Haydn's Organ Concertos (with Alain) and *Cello Concertos in C major* and *D major* (with Lodéon and the Bournemouth Sinfonietta); Dvořák's Symphony No. 8 (with the Yomiuri Nippon Symphony Orchestra); and Mozart's Piano Concertos K. 271, K. 453 and K. 467, and Rondos K. 382 and K. 386 (with Pires and the Gulbenkian Foundation Orchestra).

For other companies apart from Erato, Guschlbauer has recorded Ries' Piano Concerto No. 3 (with Blumental and the Salzburg Chamber Orchestra for Unicorn); Kuhlau's Piano Concerto and Platti's Piano Concerto No. 1 (with Blumental and the Salzburg Symphony Orchestra for Turnabout), and the Strauss waltzes *An der schönen blauen Donau*, *Kaiserwalzer*, *Künstlerleben* and *Wein, Weib und Gesang* (with the London Philharmonic Orchestra for Classics for Pleasure).

Gutter, Robert (b. 1938). Born in New York, Gutter studied at the school of music at Yale University, and at the Accademia Chigiana at Siena where he graduated with a diploma for conducting. He has been music director and conductor of the Des Moines Symphony and Springfield Symphony Orchestras, Ohio, is now music director and conductor of the Springfield Symphony Orchestra, Massachusetts, and has been a guest conductor in Italy, Sweden and El Salvador. For Opus One he recorded with the Springfield Symphony Orchestra Fussell's *Three Processionals*, Schubel's *Fracture*, Stranberg's *Sea of Tranquillity*, Spratlan's *Two Pieces*, Stern's *Carom* and Thome's *Fanfare, Fugue and Funk*.

Gyulay Gaál, Ferenc (b. 1915). Born in Budapest, where he studied at the Academy of Music, Gyulay Gaál was first a repetiteur at the Budapest Opera (1939), and later at the Royal Revue Theatre, and became a conductor at the Operetta Theatre (1943). He is also a conductor for television and films, has conducted in cities in Eastern and Western Europe, and has composed operettas, songs and music for films. As a conductor he has made numerous recordings, including a disc of excerpts of Kálmán's *Countess Maritza*, with the Hungarian Radio Orchestra *et al.* for Hungaroton.

H

Haas, Karl (1900–69). Born in Karlsruhe, Haas studied at the Universities of Munich and Heidelberg, but in 1939 was forced by the Nazis to leave his position with the Stuttgart Radio. He went to England, bringing with him a valuable library on microfilm of old music which he had personally photographed in libraries in Europe. In 1941 he founded the London Baroque Ensemble, an *ad hoc* group which gave scope for his enthusiasm for instruments such as the viola d'amore, the viola pomposa and the basset-horn. He gave many public and broadcast recitals with the Ensemble, and was also director of music for the Bristol Old Vic, and wrote incidental music for performances there. Many of the pieces he recorded with the London Baroque Ensemble have an exceptional interest, such as a delightful and beautifully played *Overture in C major* of Handel, scored for two clarinets and corno di caccia. Haas himself was a specialist in old music for military and other wind bands, and some of his records were of music in this category.

Haas recorded for Parlophone (EMI), at first on 78 r.p.m. discs, and later on LP, and also on LP for Westminster (some issued in Britain by Nixa) and Pye (issued in the United States by Vanguard). These recordings included Bach's Suite No. 1, *Brandenburg Concertos*, Harpsichord Concerto No. 6 (with Malcolm, C. and S. Taylor), *Two-Harpsichord Concerto in C minor* (with Salter and Spinks), Flute, Violin and Harpsichord Concerto (with Morris, Pougnet and Malcolm), Violin Concerto BWV 1045 (with Goren), *Sinfonia in F* BWV 1071 and Cantatas Nos 152 and 202, C. P. E. Bach's Harpsichord and Fortepiano Concerto (with Malcolm and Salter) and Wind Sonatas, Telemann's *Suite in D major*, Boyce's eight Symphonies, Tartini's *Sinfonia in A major*, Handel's Two Arias for Two Horns, Oboes and Bassoons, Harp Concerto Op. 4 No. 6 (with Korchinska), Gavotte, March and *Overture in C major*, Lully's *Marche pour le régiment du Roi*, Philidor's *La Marche royale*, *La Marche pour le Roi de la Chine* and *La Marche du Prince d'Orange*, Boccherini's *Flute Quintet in E flat* (with Adeney), String Sextet Op. 24 No. 1, *Sinfonia concertante in G* and Sextet Op. 41, Pergolesi's *Flute Concerto in G* (with Adeney), A. Scarlatti's *Concertato in D for Flute and Trumpet*, Vivaldi's Concerto for Two Oboes and Two Clarinet's, Tartini's *Symphony in A*, Albinoni's *Concerto à cinq* and Concerto for Two Oboes d'amore, Bassoon and Horn, Fux's *Sonata in F major*, Haydn's Symphony No. 22, *Notturno in C major*, *Divertimenti in C, G, F, A minor* and *E flat*, *March for the Prince of Wales*, Quartet Op. 2 No. 3 (in the original version with two horns), Scherzando No. 1, Minuets Nos 9 and 11, *Feldpartita*, *Fortepiano Concerto in D major* (with Scherzer) and Harpsichord and Violin Concerto (with Salter and Pougnet), Michael Haydn's Mass, Dittersdorf's *Violin Concerto in G major* (with Pougnet), *Partita in D minor* and Sinfonia Concertante, Mozart's *Serenata notturna*, Serenades K. 375 and K. 388, Notturni K. 437 and K. 439, Canzonetta K. 549 (with Scheepers, Sinclair and Evans) and Piano Concerto K. 499 (with Scherzer), Beethoven's Six Minuets (Grove's No. 139) and *Musik für die grosse Wacht-Parade*, Cherubini's *Pater Noster* (with Pougnet) and *Marches pour la Garde nationale*, Schubert's *Konzertstück* (with Eitler), Dvořák's *Serenade in D minor* and *Gavotte in G minor*, Strauss's *Suite in B flat*, Wind Symphony No. 1 and Sonatina No. 1, Gounod's *Petite symphonie*, Arnell's *Serenade* and Kay's *Miniature Quartet*.

Haas, Robert (1886–1960). Born in Prague, Haas studied at the universities in Prague, Berlin and Vienna, and taught at the Institute for Music History in Vienna (1908–09). He conducted in theatres in Germany (1910–14), and after service in the Austrian army in World War I became the chief of the music department of the National State Library in Vienna, and from 1923 taught at the Vienna University. Lyrichord issued two LP discs of the music of the Middle Ages and Renaissance respectively, in which he conducted the Collegium Musicum.

Haenchen, Hartmut (b. 1943). Born in Dresden, Haenchen was a member of the Dresden Kreuzchor as a boy, and studied at the Hochschule für Musik at Dresden (1960–66). He was conductor of the Robert Franz Singakademie and State Symphony Orchestra at Halle (1966), won first prize in the Carl Maria von Weber Competition for Conductors at Dresden (1971), was first conductor at Zwickau (1972), conductor of the Dresden Philharmonic Orchestra (1973) and chief conductor of the Mecklenburg Staatskapelle at Schwerin (1976).

He has also toured in East and West Europe, the USSR and Japan. For Eterna he has recorded trumpet concertos by Vivaldi, Neruda, Hertel and Michael Haydn (with Güttler and the Berlin Chamber Orchestra).

Hagen, Hans (b. 1902). Born in Dresden and originally a cellist, Hagen has been active as a conductor in Munich, Leipzig, Chemnitz and Berlin. He has recorded Tchaikovsky's *Serenade in C major* and *1812* overture (with the Bavarian Symphony Orchestra, issued by Everest), Dvořák's *Slavonic Dances*, Op. 46, *Moldau*, and some *Hungarian Dances* of Brahms (with the Austrian Symphony Orchestra, by Everest), Liszt's *Hungarian Rhapsody No. 2* (with the Vienna Symphony Orchestra, by Everest), two discs of waltzes by Strauss and Lanner (with the Vienna Philharmusica Orchestra for Pacific, and issued by Vogue, and partly by Saga and Urania), *Die schöne Galatea* and *Der Opernball* (with the Vienna Operetta Orchestra *et al.*, for La Guilde Internationale du Disque, the first issued by Vox), *Die lustige Witwe* and *Czardasfürstin* (with the Vienna Volksoper Orchestra *et al.*, issued by Saga), and a collection of the national anthems of the world (with the Vienna State Opera Orchestra, issued by Everest).

Hager, Leopold (b. 1935). Educated at the Mozarteum in his native Salzburg, Hager was an assistant to Paumgartner and was in charge of student opera productions. He made his debut as a conductor at Mainz in 1958, where he was a repetiteur and assistant conductor (1957–62), became conductor at Linz (1962–4) first conductor at Cologne (1964–6), general music director at Freiburg (1965–9) and then finally in 1969 chief conductor and music director of the Mozarteum Orchestra and at the Landestheater in Salzburg, also being a resident conductor at the Vienna State Opera. He is a guest conductor at the Bavarian State Opera and at the Teatro Colón in Buenos Aires, in 1976 made his debut at the New York Metropolitan, and with the Mozarteum Orchestra he toured in Japan and in the United States. Mozart, Bruckner and Strauss have a special place in his repertoire. His recordings, with the Mozarteum Orchestra, have included Mozart's Symphonies Nos 10, 32, 35 and 38 (for BASF), and 40 and 41 (for Turnabout), Piano Concertos K. 37, K. 39, K. 175, K. 271, K. 449, K. 453, K. 456, K. 466, K. 488, K. 491, K. 503 and K. 595 (with Engel, part of a complete series using the new Mozart edition based on the original text, and issued in FR Germany and Britain by Telefunken, in France by Valois and in the US by Everest), the Flute Concertos (with Schulz) and the Violin Concerto K. 211 (with Diedrichsen), *Bastien und Bastienne*, *Lucio Silla*, *Il re pastore* and *Ascanio in Alba* (with the Mozarteum Orchestra *et al.* for BASF), *Mitridate, Re di Ponto* (with the Mozarteum Orchestra *et al.* for DGG), Strauss's *Metamorphosen* (with the Nuremberg Symphony Orchestra for Colosseum). Beethoven's Symphonies Nos 5 and 7, the *lento assai* from String Quartet Op. 130 and the *lento* from String Quartet Op. 135, and Gluck's overtures *Alceste* and *Iphigénie en Aulide* (with the Salzburg Mozarteum Orchestra for Pye).

Hahn, Reynaldo (1875–1947). Born in Caracas, Venezuela, Hahn came to Paris at the age of three, was a pupil of Massenet, Dubois and Lavignac at the Paris Conservatoire, and became prominent as a pianist, composer, conductor and critic. His operettas and songs in particular enjoyed some popularity outside France, but his instrumental works have been described as 'warmed-over Massenet', despite their refinement and skill. He conducted performances in recordings by HMV of his suite *Le Bal de Béatrice d'Este*, and Piano Concerto No. 1 (with Magda Tagliafero; re-issued in 1976 by World Record Club), and for Decca Mozart's Piano Concerto K. 537 (with Tagliafero and the Pasdeloup Orchestra).

Haitink, Bernard (b. 1929). Although born in Amsterdam into an unmusical background, Haitink's first interest in music was awakened when he was taken to a concert where Mengelberg conducted the Concertgebouw Orchestra, and he started to learn the violin at the age of nine. After studying at the Amsterdam Academy of Music under Hupka, he joined the Netherlands Radio Philharmonic Orchestra as a violinist; then he attended the Netherlands Radio course for conductors at Hilversum where he was a pupil of Leitner, became assistant conductor to the Radio Orchestra in 1955, and then principal conductor in 1957. In the meantime in 1956, he was asked to substitute for Giulini in a performance of Cherubini's *Requiem* with the Concertgebouw Orchestra, was invited to conduct them occasionally, toured Britain with them in 1959, and made his first records with the orchestra in that year. After van Beinum's death in 1959 he was, in 1961, appointed joint permanent conductor of the orchestra together with Jochum, and in 1964 became sole permanent conductor and artistic director. In 1967 the London Philharmonic Orchestra appointed him their principal conductor and artistic adviser, and two years later he became the orchestra's artistic director. In addition to appearances as a guest conductor with the major European and American orchestras, he has conducted, in his early years, at the Netherlands Opera, and in 1972 led his first performance at the Glyndebourne Festival Opera, which he will take over as musical director in 1979. Each year he now gives 25 concerts in London and 50 in Amsterdam. His debut in the United States occurred in Los Angeles in 1957, and in Britain in Liverpool in 1961; he has often toured overseas with the Concertgebouw Orchestra, and in 1957 visited the USSR with the London Philharmonic. In 1971 he was awarded the Gold Medal of the Vienna Mahler Society.

Compared to so many of the charismatic conductors of his and earlier generations, Haitink is a startling contrast. He is unassuming but completely self-confident, shy but approachable; his manner on the podium is sober, incisive and such that he communicates immediately and directly with his players. He dislikes histrionics directed towards the audience, certain that this creates the wrong atmosphere. 'There is no mystique about conducting,' he said, 'but it is a job, a profession of its own. The technique is not so difficult, but you must have the gift to communicate, to *listen* to the orchestra, a certain gift to inspire the players. There are moments when you feel unhappy, when you can't get what you want, but you must work it out inside yourself. Conducting should not be made to look difficult: when I go to the theatre I don't want to be confronted with the problems of the actors. . . . I think conducting is a down-to-earth profession. The things that are not down-to-earth I keep to myself' (interview, *Daily Telegraph*, February 1977). He settles on an interpretation after reading and re-reading the score, but does not attempt to mark the score: 'Interpretation is something that cannot be written down. It must be in one's blood, or nowhere.' Rehearsals are neither exhaustive nor exhausting; he talks as little as possible, does not wish to impose his will on the orchestra at any cost, and rarely uses the full three hours allotted to him, believing that the standard of performance can easily be impaired, and that the extra finish must come at the concert itself. In fact, after the final rehearsal, his players wonder what the standard of the concert will be. When he is a guest conductor he never attempts to change the orchestra to fit his own ideals: 'I want to get the best out of an ensemble, but to keep its own character.' His apparent calm has its limits; more than once he has left the concert hall, taking his orchestra with him, annoyed by inattentive audiences.

Growing up in Holland in the shadow of Mengelberg and van Beinum, Haitink shares their eclecticism and their devotion to Mahler and Bruckner. After van Beïnum's death he was asked to conduct a Mahler symphony for the Concertgebouw Orchestra's 75th anniversary; he had had no experience with Mahler, conducted the Symphony No. 1, became fascinated with the composer, and then learned a new symphony each year. His performances of the Mahler and Bruckner symphonies have become famous, both on record and in the concert hall; they are at another pole of expression, but not of intensity, compared to more subjective and overtly dramatic conductors such as Bernstein and Solti. Haitink dislikes performing the Mahler symphonies too often, feeling that while Mahler's world may be absorbing, it is not healthy. Under his baton, the romantic composers receive powerful, finely judged, unmannered and unexaggerated readings. Some may regard his interpretations as unremarkable and too literal to have definite character, but like his great predecessor with the Concertgebouw Orchestra, van Beinum, he is temperamentally averse to highly personal interpretations. His awe for the great composers he conducts obliges him to perform their music as faithfully and as clearly as he can. Beethoven was introduced rather late into his concerts, for despite his great love for the composer, he was at first frightened to perform his works, and even now has refused to record the *Missa Solemnis*, saying that he is not ready for it. He studied the Beethoven scores closely, read many books about him, and went to Vienna to see the first edition of the *Eroica*, where the careful dynamic markings of Beethoven convinced him that performances must be absolutely faithful to the scores, even to not doubling the woodwind. He once named as his favourite music the late Beethoven piano sonatas and string quartets, and the Bartók quartets. He knows his limitations; he is wary of Bach, because of the stylistic problems involved, and is content to leave the latest modern music to others. Another composer, Sibelius, he finds difficult to present effectively in the concert hall. The upshot of it all is that the Concertgebouw Orchestra has remained in the very top flight of European orchestras under his leadership, and the London Philharmonic has advanced, since he took charge, to a pre-eminent position among British orchestras, as measured by the box office and by critical appraisal. He has been reluctant to accept opportunities to take over American orchestras, for despite his admiration for them, the status of the conductor and the inflexibility of rehearsal times, in particular, are not to his taste.

Philips made their first records with Haitink and the Concertgebouw Orchestra in 1959, and except for a disc with the Lamoureux Orchestra and a number more recently with the London Philharmonic Orchestra, he has recorded with them ever since. The first LP was a coupling of Beethoven's Symphony No. 8 and Mendelssohn's Symphony No. 4, and separate discs of the complete incidental music for *Rosamunde* and *A Midsummer Night's Dream*. Since then he has recorded music ranging from the Beethoven symphonies to Shostakovich; a surprising omission has been Mozart and Haydn, except for the latter's Symphonies Nos 96 and 99. Pride of place in his discography are the complete symphonies of Brahms, Mahler and Bruckner, with the Concertgebouw Orchestra, and of Beethoven and the tone poems of Liszt, with the London Philharmonic Orchestra. His other discs, all superb performances and many outstanding, are, with the Concertgebouw Orchestra, Haydn's Symphonies Nos 96 and 99, the Beethoven Piano Concertos (with Arrau), Violin Concerto (with Krebbers, the concertmaster of the Concertgebouw Orchestra, and Szeryng) and the two Romances (with Szeryng), Brahms' Piano Concertos Nos 1 (with Arrau) and 2 (with Arrau and Brendel), Violin Concerto (with Szeryng), Double Concerto (with Szeryng and Starker), *Academic Festival* and *Tragic Overtures*, *Variations on the St Antony Chorale*, and *Alto Rhapsody* (with Heynis), the Mendelssohn and Bruch Violin Concertos (with Grumiaux), Dvořák's Symphonies Nos 7 and 8, the *Scherzo capriccioso* and some *Slavonic Dances*, Schubert's Symphonies Nos 5, 8 and 9, the overtures *Le Carnaval romain*, *Russlan and Ludmilla* and *La forza del destino*, the Bruckner *Te Deum*, Mahler's *Kindertotenlieder* and *Lieder eines fahrenden Gesellen* (with Prey), *Das klagende Lied* (with Harper, Procter, Hollweg *et al.*) and *Das Lied von der Erde* (with Baker and King), Tchaikovsky's Symphonies Nos 4 and 6, the Violin Concerto (with Grumiaux), *Romeo and Juliet* fantasy-overture, *1812* overture, *Francesca da Rimini*, *Capriccio italien* and *Marche slave*, *Pictures at an Exhibition*, *Danse macabre*, the Polovtsian Dances from *Prince Igor*, *Don Juan*, *Till Eulenspiegel*, *Also sprach Zarathustra*, *Ein Heldenleben* and the waltzes from *Der Rosenkavalier*, *The Young Person's Guide to the Orchestra*, *Peter and the Wolf*, *L'Oiseau de feu*, preludes to *Die Meistersinger*, *Parsifal* and *Lohengrin* and the prelude and Liebestod to *Tristan und Isolde*, the *Háry János* suite, the two suites from *Daphnis et Chloé*, *La Valse*, *Le Tombeau de Couperin*, *Pavane pour une infante défunte*, *Valses nobles et sentimentales*, *Alborada del gracioso*, *Ma Mère l'Oye*, *Rapsodie espagnole*, *Menuet antique*, *La Mer*, *Marche écossaise*, *Prélude à l'après-midi d'un faune*, Debussy's Clarinet Rhapsody No. 1 (with Pieterson), Bartók's *Concerto for Orchestra*, *Dance Suite*, *Music for Strings, Percussion and Celesta*, the Violin Concerto No. 2 and Two Rhapsodies (with Szeryng), Escher's *Le Tombeau de Ravel* and Andriessen's *Symphonic Study*. His other discs with the London Philharmonic Orchestra have been the Beethoven five Piano Concertos and *Choral Fantasy* (with Brendel) and *Coriolan* overture, the Dvořák Cello Concerto and *Silent Woods* (with Gendron), *Enigma Variations*, *The Planets*, *Scheherazade*, Shostakovich's Symphony No. 10, *Petrushka*, *L'Oiseau de feu* and *Le Sacre du printemps*. The disc with the Lamoureux Orchestra was of the Stravinsky Violin Concerto and the Mozart Violin Concerto K. 207 (with Oistrakh).

Haitink has also recorded a number of compositions by Dutch composers for Donemus: L. Andriessen's *Nocturnes* (with Lugt), Barren's *Musica per orchestra*, Diepenbrock's *Elektra* Suite, excerpts from *Marsyas* and *Die Nacht* (with Baker), Dresden's Violin Concerto No. 2 (with Juda), Flothuis' *Canti e giuochi*, *Hymnus* (with Spoorenberg) and *Per sonare ed ascoltare*, Gilse's *Three Songs from Gitanjali* (with Lugt), Hemel's Violin Concerto (with Krebbers), Henkemans' *Tre aspetti d'amore* and *Partita*, Horst's *Réflections sonores*, Landre's *Variazioni senza tema*, Leeuw's *Ombres*, Lier's *Holy Song* (with Ameling, Maran and Hoekman), Pijper's Symphony No. 2 and Vermeulen's Symphony No. 7 (with the Concertgebouw Orchestra), and Diepenbrock's overture *The Birds* (with the Netherlands Radio Philharmonic Orchestra).

In all these performances, clarity, thoughtfulness and moderation distinguish the interpretation. In many great conductors one is aware that the music is the vehicle for the demonstration of magnificent orchestral tone; with Haitink it is the opposite, although one is nonetheless struck by the brilliance of the orchestral execution. He does not aim to overwhelm with volume or expressive gestures. In Bruckner, for instance, he keeps the pianissimi very low and does not exaggerate the fortissimo climaxes, and with this the music gains breadth. About the Bruckner series, Deryck Cooke wrote in *The Gramophone*: 'I can pay Haitink no greater tribute than to say that, whatever reservations I may have about his performance of this or that movement, the overall effect of each symphony is such that I can think of none better, and few as good.' The recordings of the Mahler symphonies attracted scarcely less praise from Cooke; for example, of the Symphony No. 9, he wrote: 'This great Mahler record, which in spite of the illustrious competition (from Walter, Klemperer, Solti and Bernstein), I can only hail as the ideal Ninth, beyond any criticism.' For a conductor, Haitink is still a young man, and there are many records he has yet to make, to be anticipated with tingling pleasure by record lovers.

Halffter, Cristobal (b. 1930). Born in Madrid, Halffter studied at the Conservatory there with Conrado del Campo, and privately with Tansman. He conducted the Orchestra Manuel de Falla (1955–63), toured Europe, the United States and Latin America as a conductor, taught composition at the Madrid Conservatory (1962–6) and became the Conservatory's director (1964), and was music director of the Madrid Radio Symphony Orchestra (1962–6). He resigned the directorship of the Conservatory in 1966 to devote himself to conducting, composing and lecturing, travelled widely, was in Berlin in 1967 on a scholarship from the Deutscher Akademischer Austauschdienst, and from 1968 to 1970 lived in Spain with a grant from the Ford Foundation. His compositions include *Yes, Speak Out, Yes*, written for the 20th anniversary of the Declaration of Human Rights, *Symphony for Three Instrumental Groups*, *Sequences*, *Symposium*, *Lines and Dots*, *Rings*, *Fibonaciana* and other pieces commissioned by various foundations and authorities. His recordings as a conductor include his own *Missa Ducal*, *Antifona*, and *Dos Movimientos para timbal y cuerda* (with the Spanish National Orchestra for Hispavox) and Rodrigo's *Concierto de Aranjuez* and *Fantasia para un gentilhombre* (with de la Maza and the Manuel de Falla Orchestra, for RCA).

Halffter, Ernesto (b. 1905). Born in Madrid and the uncle of Cristobal Halffter, Halffter studied at the Colegio Aleman in Madrid and privately with Falla and Ravel. In 1931 he founded the Seville Conservatory which he directed until 1936 and there established the Orquesta Betica da Camera, but after the Spanish Civil War he made his home in Portugal. From 1966 he was musical adviser for the Spanish television network, and has been active as a conductor in Europe and South America, also being honorary conductor of the Madrid Symphony Orchestra. He was considered to be one of the leading younger Spanish composers, and among his compositions is the four-act opera, *The Death of Carmen*. For Columbia he made several recordings of Falla's *Nights in the Gardens of Spain*, the first on 78s with Navarro and the Orquesta Betica da Camera, and the other on LP with Ciccolini and the French National Radio Orchestra. His other recordings are Falla's *Homenajes* (with the French National Radio Orchestra for Columbia), *La vida breve* (with the Barcelona Opera Orchestra and Los Angeles *et al.*, for EMI) and *Master Peter's Puppet Show* (with the Champs-Élysées Theatre Orchestra *et al.* for Ducretet-Thomson).

Halsey, Louis (b. 1929). Born in London, Halsey was a Choral Scholar at King's College, Cambridge, and studied with Ord, Dart, Stevens and Deller. He has been a musical producer with the BBC (from 1963), artistic director of the Thames Concerts Society (from 1969), and founder and conductor of the Elizabethan Singers (1953–66), the Thames Chamber Choir (from 1964), the Louis Halsey Singers (from 1967), and the Louis Halsey Baroque Orchestra (from 1977). He has conducted many orchestras and at many festivals in Britain, has toured Canada (in 1973) and the US (in 1977), and has lectured, broadcast and contributed to musical journals and publications. His repertoire, both as a choral and orchestral conductor, extends from Monteverdi to the present day, and he has commissioned new music from a number of contemporary composers; the Louis Halsey Baroque Orchestra performs major works of the baroque period authentically, playing instruments of the period.

Halsey's recordings include part-songs by Schubert and Britten, and other choral collections (with the Elizabethan Singers for Argo), motets by Gabrieli, Monteverdi and Schütz, the complete motets of Bach, Carissimi's *Historia di Jonas*, Cavalli's *Missa pro defunctis* and part-songs of Delius, Elgar and Warlock (with the Louis Halsey Singers for L'Oiseau Lyre), Parry's *Songs of Farewell* and Stanford's part-songs (with the Louis Halsey Singers for Argo), and Joubert's *Pro Pace Motets* and *Hymns to St Oswald* (with the Louis Halsey Singers and Neary, organ, for Pearl).

Halvorsen, Leif (1887–1959). Born in Oslo, Halvorsen studied there and in Paris, and with Auer in St Petersburg, was a music critic in Oslo (1917), conducted at the Oslo Comic Opera (1918–21) and then directed choral societies in Oslo. EMI issued a 78 r.p.m. disc in which he conducted the Handelsstandens Chorus and orchestra in Grieg's *Land Sighting*, with Neergaard, baritone.

Hammelboe, Arne (b. 1916). Born in Copenhagen, Hammelboe studied with Videro, Hansen, Andersen and Mayer-Radon, conducted a theatre orchestra (1935–6) and made his debut at the Tivoli Concert Hall in Copenhagen in 1936. He was conductor with the Gaubier Ballet (1936–8), of the Unterhaltung Orchestra at the Danish Radio (1943–4), at the Det Kongelege Theatre (1945–6) and at the Odense Theatre (1948–9), and then taught conducting (1957) and became a professor (1964) at the Copenhagen Conservatory. He recorded several discs of the dance music of Lumbye ('the Danish Strauss') with the Royal Danish Orchestra (for Philips and Mercury).

Hammond, Arthur (b. 1904). A native of Sheffield, Hammond was onetime conductor and musical director with the Carl Rosa Opera Company. He recorded music by the British composer Joseph Holbrooke, namely the Piano Concerto (*The Song of Gwyn ap Nudd*; with Lynden and the London Promenade Orchestra for Paxton) and the overture to *The Children of the Don* (with an unnamed orchestra for Decca).

Handley, Vernon (b. 1930). Born at Enfield, North London, and educated at Balliol College, Oxford and the Guildhall School of Music and Drama, Handley has been musical director and conductor of the Guildford Philharmonic Orchestra and Choir since 1962, and in 1966 became professor for orchestra and conducting at the Royal College of Music. In addition he has appeared as a guest conductor with many of the major British orchestras, and toured FR Germany in 1966. He broadcasts frequently and his repertoire as a conductor includes a high proportion of British, and unfamiliar, music of the 20th century. His conducting style has been largely influenced by Boult, whose economical gestures and placement of the orchestra he has adopted. In his recordings he has shown himself to be a thoughtful, original and accomplished musician. His first records were with the Guildford Philharmonic Orchestra, in 1965, of Bax's Symphony No. 4 and symphonic poem *The Tale the Pine Trees Knew* (for Concert Artist); the performances had severe limitations but the orchestra's remarkable progress was evident in his next record, Bax's *Symphonic Variations* (with pianist Joyce Hatto), when reservations about its technique were no longer necessary. Since 1974 he has recorded *Prélude à l'après-midi d'un faune*, *La Mer* and Fauré's *Masques et bergamasques*, Tchaikovsky's *Hamlet* and *Francesca da Rimini*, Tippett's *Concerto for Double String Orchestra* and Vaughan Williams' *Fantasia on a Theme by Thomas Tallis* (with the London Philharmonic Orchestra for Classics for Pleasure), *Capriccio italien* (with the London Philharmonic Orchestra for Europa, FR Germany), Dvořák's Symphony No. 9 (with the New Philharmonia Orchestra for Enigma), Elgar's music for *The Starlight Express* (on two LPs, with Hammond-Stroud and the London Philharmonic Orchestra for EMI), Maconchy's *Proud Thames* and Geoffrey Bush's *Music 1967* (with the London Philharmonic Orchestra for Lyrita), and David Bedford's *Star's End* (with Oldfield, Cutler and the Royal Philharmonic Orchestra for Virgin). Handley had previously premièred Bedford's work, and this recording achieved some commercial success.

Hanell, Robert (b. 1925). Born in Czechoslovakia, the East German conductor Hanell was the director of a chorus at Teplice at the age of eighteen, was a conductor at Zwickau, Meiningen, Gera and Gorlitz, then was with the Berlin Komische Oper (from 1955). He conducted the Berolina concerts and at the Berlin Staatsoper, and is now chief conductor of the Radio Symphony Orchestra in East Berlin. He has a special reputation as a conductor of light operas, operettas and musicals, and has himself composed twelve operas. For Eterna he has recorded selections from Offenbach's *Salon Pitzelberger* (with the Berlin Staatskapelle *et al.*), a collection of marches from operettas (with the Berlin Radio Symphony Orchestra), a collection of smaller pieces including Boccherini's Minuet from Op. 13 No. 5, Braga's *Serenade* and Bohm's *Calm as the Night* (with the Leipzig Radio Symphony Orchestra, issued by Philips), excerpts from Masanetz's *In Frisco ist der Teufel los* and Thurm's Trumpet Concerto (with Meinl, the Berlin Radio Symphony Orchestra *et al.*), and his own *Esther* (with the Berlin Staatskapelle *et al.* for Eterna).

Hannikainen, Tauno (1896–1968). Born in Jyväskylä, Finland, into a musical family, Hannikainen studied at the Helsinki University and at the Sibelius Academy. After taking part in the military struggle against Russia that resulted in Finland's independence, he studied the cello under Casals, was a cellist in the Helsinki City Symphony Orchestra, and toured in a trio with his two brothers, Ilmari and Arvo. In 1922 he became conductor of the Finnish Opera Association, in 1927 conductor of the Turku Symphony Orchestra, and appeared as a guest conductor in Vienna, Paris, Milan and other European cities. His first appearance in the United States was in 1938 with the Boston Symphony Orchestra; he remained until 1951, conducting the Duluth Symphony Orchestra (1942–7), and the Chicago Civic Orchestra (1947–50), and was assistant conductor with the Chicago Symphony Orchestra (1948–50). At the expressed wish of Sibelius he left Chicago to return to Finland to become musical director and conductor of the Helsinki City Symphony Orchestra (1950–63), restoring the orchestra to one of the first rank, and also was head of the Institute of Music in Helsinki. His mark as a conductor has been as an interpreter of Sibelius, and in Helsinki he directed many concerts and festivals of his music. His records have been of Sibelius' music: the Symphonies Nos 2 and 5 and the *Karelia* suite (with the Sinfonia of London for World Record Club), *Four Legends* and the Symphony No. 4 (with the USSR State Symphony Orchestra for Melodiya) and *Tapiola* and the Violin Concerto (with Spivakovsky and the London Symphony Orchestra for Everest). These performances were poised, sensitive and completely idiomatic, but Hannikainen's natural restraint robbed the music of some of its inner tension and true excitement.

Hanousek, Vladimir (b. 1907). Born in Przemyśl, Poland, Hanousek studied at the Prague Conservatory (1924–8) and with Suk and Hoffman, and performed as a solo violinist and chamber player. He was a member of the Prague Radio Symphony Orchestra (1946–60), and then artistic leader of the Prague Chamber Orchestra (1960–66). He has composed sacred, symphonic, vocal and instrumental music, and as a conductor recorded Janáček's *Concertino* (with Kvapil and the Prague Chamber Harmony for Panton).

Hanson, Howard (b. 1896). The American conductor, composer, teacher, administrator and indefatigable protagonist for American music, Hanson, was born at Wahoo, Nebraska. His parents were Swedish migrants and he began to study music as a boy of seven years of age. He studied first at the University of Nebraska, the Institute of Musical Art in New York (which later became the Juilliard School) and finally at Northwestern University, from where he graduated in 1916. For three years (1918–21) he was a professor of theory and composition at the College of the Pacific at San Jose, California; in 1921 he won the first national competition for the American Prix de Rome, and spent three years in Rome. There he wrote one of his most popular compositions, the Symphony No. 1 (*Nordic*), which was first performed by the Augusteo Orchestra in 1922. When he returned to the United States in 1924 he conducted the Rochester Symphony Orchestra, and was then appointed director of the Eastman School of Music at Rochester, New York, which had been endowed by George Eastman, the founder of the Kodak company. Hanson remained in this position for 40 years, finally resigning in 1964 to become the director of the Institute of American Music at the University of Rochester. After his appointment at the Eastman School he conducted some of his compositions with US orchestras, but was struck by the slender opportunities that American composers had for hearing their music performed. He resolved to remedy this situation and in 1925 started with Eastman's support a series of American music festivals at Rochester at which he conducted new music by native composers. In his 40 years with the School he performed more than 1,000 compositions of 600 different US composers. To do this, he established from among faculty members and students the Eastman-Rochester Symphony Orchestra, and in 1961–2 toured Europe, the USSR and North Africa with the Orchestra. In addition to many guest engagements with US orchestras, he was invited in 1933 to conduct a programme of American works with the Berlin Philharmonic Orchestra. He now deplores the continued neglect of the American musical heritage, blaming the indifference of many brilliant young American conductors for their own country's composers, and the regulations of the American Federation of Music who have priced themselves out of the recording market. Hanson has been active in many musical organisations and has been honoured with numerous doctorates and awards, such as the Pulitzer Prize, which he was awarded in 1944. He is the author of an important text, *Harmonic Materials of Modern Music*, published in 1960.

While Hanson has the widest sympathy for all new ideas and developments in music, his own compositions are firmly cast in the traditional romantic mould. His best known works are the Symphonies Nos 1 (*Nordic*) and 2 (*Romantic*), *The Lament for Beowulf*, the symphonic poems *Lux Aeterna* and *Pan and the Priest* and the opera *Merry Mount*. The latter was performed in 1934 at the New York Metropolitan and was given a mixed reception. In fact, critical appraisal of Hanson's music has been somewhat cool; in 1948 David Hall wrote in *The Record Book* that it was a blend of Tchaikovsky, Sibelius and Wagner, although many have written that the influence of Sibelius is uppermost. The emergence of a truly individual musical personality does not occur. Nonetheless Koussevitzky recorded Hanson's Symphony No. 3 with the Boston Symphony Orchestra.

Hanson's first recordings were on 78 r.p.m. discs for RCA, of Copland's *Music for the Theater*, Kennan's *Night Soliloquy*, Griffes' *The White Peacock*, Skilton's *Two Indian Dances*, Still's *Afro-American Symphony*, Vardell's *Joe Clark Steps Out*, Sowerby's *Corries Autumn Time*, Loeffler's *Pagan Poem* and his own Symphonies Nos 1 and 2, *The Lament for Beowulf*, and *Merry Mount* suite. Columbia then issued mono LPs with him conducting Grieg's *Holberg Suite*, Riegger's Symphony No. 3, Mennin's Symphony No. 3 and his own Symphony No. 2 and Piano Concerto (with Firkusny). The Grieg was one of the very few works he was to record of a composer other than an American. He and the Eastman-Rochester Symphony Orchestra were then engaged under contract by Mercury, and there followed a remarkable series of LP discs which surveyed American music, past and present, and earned him the accolade of being the greatest advocate of American music on record, a title he must share with Robert Whitney. The compositions he recorded were many and included Barber's Symphony No. 1, Essay No. 1, *Adagio for Strings*, overture to *The School for Scandal*, *Capricorn Concerto* and *Medea*, Barlow's *The Winter's Past*, *Night Song* and *Oboe Rhapsody*, Bergsma's *Gold and the Señor Commandante*, Copland's *Quiet City*, Cowell's Symphony No. 4, Canning's *Fantasy on a Hymn Tune of Justin Morgan*, Carpenter's *Adventures in a Perambulator*, Carter's *The Minotaur*, Chadwick's *Symphonic Sketches*, Donovan's *New England Chronicle*, Foote's *Suite in F major*, Griffes' *Roman Sketches*, *Fabled Dome of Kubla Khan*, *Bacchanale*, *The White Peacock* and *Clouds*, Grofé's *Grand Canyon* and *Mississippi Suites*, Gershwin's *Rhapsody in Blue*, and *Piano Concerto* (with List) and *Cuban Overture*, Gould's *Latin American Symphonette*, *Fall River Legend* and *Spirituals*, Guarnieri's *Dansa brasileira*, Harris' Symphonies Nos 3 and 4, Hively's *Three Hymns*, Hovhaness' *Concerto No. 1 for Orchestra*, and *Prelude and Quadruple Fugue*, Herbert's Cello Concerto No. 2 (with Miquelle), Ives' Symphony No. 3 and *Three Places in New England*, Keller's *Serenade*, Kennan's *Three Pieces for Orchestra* and *Night Soliloquy*, Loeffler's *Memories of My Childhood*, *La Bonne Chanson*, and *Poem for Orchestra*, Lane's *Four Songs*, Lo Presti's *The Masks*, Mennin's *Arioso*, McBride's *Mexican Rhapsody*, MacDowell's *Indian Suite* and Piano Concerto No. 2 (with Sanroma), McCauley's *Five Miniatures*, McPhee's *Tabuh and Tabuhan* and *Toccata*, Mitchell's *Kentucky Mountain Portraits*, Moore's *The Pageant of P. T. Barnum*, Nelson's *Savannah River Holiday*, Peter's *Sinfonia in G major*, Porter's *Poem and Dance*, Phillips' *Selections from McGuffey's Readers* and *American Dance*, Paine's *Oedipus Tyrannus overture*, Piston's Symphony No. 3 and *The Incredible Flutist*, Randall Thompson's *The Testament of Freedom*, Riegger's Symphony No. 3 and *New Dance*, Rogers' *Soliloquy*, *Leaves from the Tale of Pinocchio*, *Once Upon a Time* and *Five Fairy Tales*, Reed's *La fiesta Mexicana*, Still's *Sahdji*, Sessions' *The Black Maskers*, Taylor's *Through the Looking Glass*, Triggs' *The Bright Land*, Vardell's *Joe Clark Steps Out*, and his own Symphonies Nos 1, 2, 4 and 5, *Elegy*, *Song of Democracy*, *Fantasy Variations on a Theme of Youth*, *The Lament for Beowulf*, *Merry Mount* suite, *Mosaics*, *Songs from Drum Taps*, *Cherubic Hymn*, *Pastoral* and *Serenade*. Composers other than American that were recorded by Mercury in this series were Liadov's *The Enchanted Lake*, *Baba Yaga* and *Kikimora*, Bloch's *Schelomo* and *Concerto Grosso No. 1* and Ginastera's *Overture to the Creole 'Faust'*; Columbia also released the Riegger Symphony No. 3. Each of these pieces was accorded a competent performance, but Hanson's music and his records of American music have, however, gained very limited currency in Britain or in Europe.

Another fascinating set of LP records made by Hanson was a number of lectures illustrated by musical examples by the Eastman-Rochester Orchestra, entitled *The Composer and his Orchestra*, which discussed first individual instruments and the instrumental families, and then the technique of applying instrumental colour, singly and in groups, in the process of composition. He used as examples some of his best-known compositions, reconstructing them stage by stage as the work is scored from the original musical sketch.

In 1975 the Institute of American Music at the Eastman School, of which Hanson is the director, began to re-issue his more important recordings with the Eastman-Rochester Orchestra. The first ten records included *The Composer and His Orchestra*, some of his own music and pieces listed above by Kennan, Rogers, Bergsma, Thompson, Taylor, Carpenter, Phillips and Lane. In addition to being a memorial of Hanson's achievement as conductor and expositor of American music, the discs are a valuable and representative collection of music of a particular generation of American composers, whose music has failed to enter the international concert repertoire.

Harbison, John (b. 1938). Born in Orange, New Jersey, Harbison studied at Harvard University (1956–60), the Hochschule für Musik in Berlin (1960–61) and at Princeton University (1961–3), was composer-in-residence at Reid College, Oregon (1968–9), and has been associate professor of music at the Massachusetts Institute of Technology since 1969. He was musical director of the Cantata Singers and Ensemble (1969–73), leading them in his own composition *Five Songs of Experience*, which was recorded by Composers Recordings.

Harnoncourt, Nikolaus (b. 1929). Born in Berlin, Harnoncourt studied the cello with Grümmer, attended the Vienna Academy of Music, and from 1952 to 1969 was a cellist in the Vienna Symphony Orchestra. When still a student he became interested in early music and old instruments, and gave many concerts playing the viola da gamba. In 1953 he founded the Concentus Musicus Wien to perform music written between 1200 and 1800, and closely studied problems of performance and the technique of playing old instruments. His wife, Alice, is leader of the ensemble. Through tours in Europe and the United States and its series of recordings, the Concentus Musicus has become one of the foremost groups presenting early and baroque music played in an authentic manner. Harnoncourt has edited new editions of Bach's *Mass in B minor*, *St Matthew Passion* and *St John Passion*, and has prepared new scores of the Monteverdi operas *Il ritorno d' Ulisse in patria* and *L'Incoronazione di Poppea*, was appointed a professor at the Mozarteum and Institute of Musicology at Salzburg in 1972, and has given lectures and courses in many countries.

Harnoncourt has explained that in his young years he could not believe that the 18th-century sonatas for stringed instruments were as dull as they then sounded when performed. But he found that playing them on the instruments of the time was not the full answer; 'Our first step was to discover an adequate performance and this included a lot of things which are more important than the instruments. I think one can effect a very good performance of baroque music with modern instruments up to a threshold beyond which it is impossible to proceed. After this point certain conditions occur which the modern instruments cannot fulfil' (*The Gramophone*, August 1977, p. 283). In his study of the old instruments in Vienna, he found that they could adequately bring to life once more the timbres of the baroque era. Generally the instruments can be played well, since Bach would not have allowed his musicians to play his music badly. 'If they had been unable to play his scores then he would have written simpler music for them and I think, therefore, that Bach's works are in a sense portraits of his performers.' In the Concentus Musicus, each musician is a very good player on the equivalent modern instrument. Harnoncourt cannot conceive of an alternative modern method of performing baroque music; to him the modern method is 'an unsorted blend of geniality, 19th-century tradition, and ignorance'. A genuine modern interpretation he has yet to hear.

Since the *Brandenburg Concertos* were issued by Telefunken in 1966, the Concentus Musicus under Harnoncourt has made a number of recordings of baroque and pre-baroque masterpieces which have brought international awards, such as the Grand Prix du Disque, Deutsche Schallplattenpreis, and the Prix Mondial du Disque de Montreux. Then followed the Bach Suites, the *St Matthew Passion* and the *Mass in B minor*, and Monteverdi's *La favola d'Orfeo*, and Harnoncourt signed an exclusive contract with Telefunken in 1971 for a duration of ten years. The subsequent recordings include sonatas by Biber, Fux's *Concentus musico instrumentalis*, Handel's *Belshazzar*, Organ Concertos Opp. 4 and 7 (with Tachezi) and some other concertos, Monteverdi's *Il ritorno d'Ulisse in Patria*, *L'Incoronazione di Poppea*, *Lettera amorosa* and *Lamento d'Ariana*, Mozart's four Horn Concertos (with Baumann), Rameau's *Castor et Pollux*, Bach's *Christmas Oratorio*, *Missa 1733*, *Ein musikalisches Opfer*, the Cembalo Concertos (with Leonhardt), the Violin Concertos (with Alice Harnoncourt and Pfeiffer) and sinfonias from the cantatas, Telemann's *Der Tag des Gerichts*, *Suites in A minor* and *F minor* and Double Concertos, concertos and other pieces by Vivaldi, Schmelzer, Fux, Farina, Biber, Marais, C. P. E. Bach, J. C. Bach and W. F. Bach, Stamitz, Richter, Holzbauer, Haydn, Monn, Wagenseil, and Gassman, a collection of pre-classical music in Mannheim and Vienna, collections of recorder concertos (with Brüggen), and arias of Handel, Telemann and Bach (with van Egmond, Esswood and Berberian). Together with Gustav Leonhardt, he has undertaken the recording of all Bach's cantatas, which must rank as one of the most ambitious projects in the history of the gramophone record. By the end of 1977, Cantata No. 68 had been released, together with Nos 211 and 213.

Critical reception of the recorded performances of the Bach *Mass in B minor* and the cantatas has, however, not always been sympathetic, and the view of some critics has been that the attempt to produce authentic performances has disposed of the baby with the bath water. In the cantatas, for instance, the players tend to eschew all the colour, sentiment and feeling for atmosphere, indeed the expressiveness that Bach intended. The Monteverdi operas have brought similar reservations; writing in *The Gramophone*, Denis Arnold remarked on the participation of oboes, violins, trumpets etc. in the vocal music, and on the use of constant ornamentation by these instruments in *L'Incoronazione di Poppea*, which could be regarded as anachronistic. Yet it must be admitted that the preparation of a performing score from the original manuscripts, which differ among themselves in many respects, presents problems whose solutions will never satisfy everyone, certainly scholars with their own very definite ideas. Again, Harnoncourt's new scoring of *Il ritorno d'Ulisse in Patria*, in which there are many anachronistic intrusions, could scarcely be claimed to be a reconstruction of mid-17th century performing practice. Perhaps these matters may only concern experts and not the general musical public, who recall the controversy regarding Leppard's production of *L'Incoronazione di Poppea* at Glyndebourne some years earlier. However, the recording of *Castor et Pollux*, issued in 1972, roused none of these reservations and received wide praise, and *Il ritorno d'Ulisse in Patria* was listed as the record of the year in 1972 by *Stereo Review*, and the Bach Mass and Passions attracted many similar awards.

Harris, Sir William (b. 1883). Born in London, Harris studied at New College, Oxford, and at the Royal College of Music, was organist and choirmaster at New College (1919–28), at Christ Church Cathedral, Oxford (1928–33), conductor of the Oxford Bach Choir (1926–33), at St George's Chapel, Windsor Castle (1933–61) and of the Windsor and Eton Choral Society (1944–9). He composed organ and choral works, including *The Hound of Heaven* and *Michelangelo's Confession of Faith*. Columbia issued 78 r.p.m. discs of him conducting the St George's Chapel Choir in anthems and other sacred music by Vaughan Williams, Alcock, Elgar, Howells, Mundy, Farrant, Armstrong, Harwood, Wood, Moeran and himself.

Harrison, Guy Fraser (b. 1894). Born in England, Harrison came to the United States by way of an organist and choirmaster's post in Manila, and joined the staff of the newly founded Eastman School of Music. He was conductor of the Eastman Theater Orchestra (1924–9), the Rochester Civic Orchestra (1929–51), was associate conductor of the Rochester Philharmonic Orchestra (1930–51) and conductor of the Oklahoma City Symphony Orchestra (1951–73). With the Oklahoma orchestra he recorded (for Composers Recordings) Haines' *Concertino for Seven Solo Instruments*, La Montaine's Piano Concerto (with Keyes), Norton's *Partita* and Pozdro's Symphony No. 3.

Harrison, Julius (1885–1963). Born in Stourport, Worcester, Harrison studied at the Birmingham and Midland School of Music under Granville Bantock, conducted with the Beecham Opera Company and the British National Opera Company, and was associated with Bodanzky, Richter, Nikisch and Weingartner in productions of the Wagner operas. He succeeded Goossens as conductor of the Handel Society in London (1925), and was permanent conductor of the Hastings Philharmonic Orchestra (1930–40). He was forced to retire from public life as a conductor because of deafness, and then he devoted himself to composition. He recorded with the Hastings Philharmonic Orchestra the overture to *Fra Diavalo*, Holst's *Marching Song*, the waltz from *Eugene Onegin* and Tchaikovsky's *Andante cantabile* (for HMV, issued by Decca in the United States), and with the London Philharmonic Orchestra Elgar's *Imperial March*, the Coronation March from Meyerbeer's *Le Prophète*, the marche militaire française from Saint-Saëns' *Suite algérienne* and Halvorsen's *Entry of the Boyars* (for Decca).

Harsanyi, Nicholas (b. 1913). A graduate of the Franz Liszt Academy (1934) and the University (1936) at his birthplace, Budapest, Harsanyi emigrated to the United States and during World War II was conductor of a US army orchestra. He was head of the instrumental department, Westminster Choir College, Princeton, New Jersey (1948–67), lecturer in music at Princeton University (1954–64) and made his debut as a conductor in New York in 1956. He was music director and conductor of the Princeton Chamber Orchestra (1965–70), of the Interlochen Arts Academy Orchestra (1967–70), and dean of the School of Music at the University of North Carolina and music director and conductor of the North Carolina School of Arts Orchestra and the Piedmont Chamber Orchestra (since 1970). He has also been a guest conductor in the US and in Europe, and has toured with the Princeton and Piedmont Chamber Orchestras. He has recorded Mayer's *Brief Candle* (with the Princeton Chamber Orchestra for Desto), Martirano's *O, O, O, O, That Shakespeherian Rag* (with the Princeton Chamber Orchestra and Singers for Composers Recordings), Bach's Violin Concerto No. 1 and Mozart's Violin Concerto K. 218 (with Morini), Britten's *Les Illuminations* (with Janice Harsanyi), Dello Joio's *Meditations on Ecclesiastes*, Dvořák's *Serenade in E major* and Mozart's Divertimento K. 136 (with the Princeton Chamber Orchestra for Decca (US)), Barber's *Knoxville: Summer of 1915* and La Montaine's *Songs of the Rose of Sharon* (with Steber and the Greater Trenton Symphony Orchestra for Standard).

Hartemann, Jean-Claude (b. 1929). Born in Vezet, France, and educated at the École Normale and the Paris Conservatoire, Hartemann was a prize-winner at the Besançon International Competition for Young Conductors, and in 1948 founded the Clermont-Ferrand Young People's Music movement. He was conductor at the Dijon Theatre (1957–60), music director at the Metz City Theatre (1960–63), conductor (1963–8) and then director (1968) of the Paris Opéra-Comique, founder and president of the Ensemble Instrumental de France (1966–70), co-director of the Solistes de Paris orchestra (since 1975), professor of conducting and of chamber music at the Schola Cantorum in Paris (since 1972), and has been a guest conductor of orchestras in France, Spain, Holland, Belgium, Luxembourg *et al.* His recordings include *Scheherazade* (with the Paris Opéra Orchestra for Edici), Gounod's *Messe solennelle à Sainte Cécile* (with the Paris Conservatoire Orchestra *et al.* for EMI), Chabrier's *Une Éducation manquée* (for EMI), Offenbach's *La Grande-Duchesse de Gérolstein* (for RCA), *Die Fledermaus* (for Polydor), excerpts from *Mignon* and Messager's *Véronique* (for EMI), Hossein's Piano Concerto No. 1 (with Ringeissen) and song cycle (with Guillot, and the Monte Carlo National Orchestra for La Guilde Internationale du Disque), and excerpts from an operetta *Chanson d'amour*, on themes of Schubert (with the Paris Conservatoire Orchestra *et al.* for Pathé).

Harty, Sir Hamilton (1879–1941). Born in Hillsborough, County Down, Ireland, Harty received his musical education from his father and at twelve was a church organist and choirmaster in County Antrim. In 1900 he went to London and achieved distinction as a pianist, chamber music player and composer, but most of all as an accompanist. His first appearances with orchestras in London were as conductor of his own compositions, including the tone poem *With the Wild Geese*, which marked him as one of the foremost younger composers in Britain. In 1913 he conducted *Tristan und Isolde* at Covent Garden. After four years with the Royal Navy in World War I he was appointed conductor of the Hallé Orchestra at Manchester in 1920 on the recommendation of Beecham, and he remained with the orchestra until 1933; in that time he trained and led an orchestra superior to any other in England. Its later rivals, the BBC Symphony and London Philharmonic Orchestras, were not formed until the early 1930s. After his resignation from the Hallé Orchestra he was conductor-in-chief of the London Symphony Orchestra for a season. He conducted the Hallé Orchestra occasionally later, toured the United States first in 1931 and then returned annually, and in 1934 visited Australia. He was knighted in 1925 for his services to music; in his last years his activities were interrupted by ill-health.

Harty's fame as a conductor rests chiefly on his years with the Hallé Orchestra. Bernard Shore, who was familiar with his work in Manchester, described him in *The Orchestra Speaks*: 'An exquisite musician, full of imagination and spontaneity, and with the wayward spirit of the true virtuoso.' As a man, Harty chose to impose his will on his players through his great personal charm and gentle manner; he had a ready wit, and when he reproached a section of the orchestra for playing a passage too loudly, the leader said: 'But, sir, the passage is marked forte,' to which he replied, 'Well, make it twenty'. His choice of programmes was conservative; he had little interest in Haydn, Brahms, Franck or Wagner, although he gave imaginative performances of the Brahms symphonies. He was unattracted by modern music and performed few novelties, but gave sympathetic readings of the Sibelius symphonies and conducted the first performance in England of Mahler's Symphony No. 9. His Mozart and Beethoven were idiosyncratic, and to Mozart he applied unusual tempi and rubato, although he employed a small orchestra and reduced dynamics. In the Beethoven symphonies he preceded the second subject with an exaggerated ritenuto. Today, Harty's name is remembered for two things: his arrangements of Handel's *Music for the Royal Fireworks* and *Water Music* into concert suites for modern symphony orchestra, and his readings of Berlioz. He was an indefatigable advocate of Berlioz, and as much as anyone was responsible for the quip that Berlioz is Britain's national composer. His performances of *Symphonie fantastique* were remarkable, but unfortunately he never recorded the work. He did record the overture *Le Roi Lear*, the march from *Les Troyens*, the Queen Mab Scherzo from the *Roméo et Juliette* symphony (with the Hallé Orchestra for Columbia), the overture to *Béatrice et Bénédict*, *Le Corsaire*, *Marche funèbre pour la dernière scène de Hamlet*, and Roméo seul and Grande fête chez Capulet from the *Roméo et Juliette* symphony (with the London Philharmonic Orchestra for Columbia); most of these were collected on an LP transfer and were issued by World Record Club in Britain in 1971. The performances are vigorous, incisive, poised and poetic, and despite the age of the original recordings, there is a glimpse of the characteristically silky string tone he evoked from the Hallé and London Philharmonic Orchestras, partly because he did not insist on uniform bowing. He also recorded the Hungarian March from *La Damnation de Faust*, which was unique because he observed Berlioz's diminuendo at the conclusion.

Harty made many other recordings for Columbia. Included were Bach's Suite No. 2, Haydn's Symphony No. 101, Mozart's Symphony No. 35, Bassoon Concerto (with Camden) and Violin Concerto K. 219 (with Catterall), Clarke's *Trumpet Voluntary*, Beethoven's Symphony No. 4, Schubert's Symphony No. 9, the overture *Alfonso und Estrella* and the overture and numbers from *Rosamunde*, Mendelssohn's Symphony No. 4, the Brahms Violin Concerto (with Szigeti), Saint-Saëns' Cello Concerto No. 1 (with Squire), an arrangement of the Schubert Arpeggione Sonata (with Cassado), the overtures to *The Bartered Bride*, *Abu Hassan* and Stanford's *Shamus O'Brien*, Tchaikovsky's Piano Concerto No. 1 (with Solomon) and the Cossack Dance from *Mazeppa*, Dvořák's Symphony No. 9, the Liszt *Hungarian Rhapsody No. 2*, the prelude to *Khovanshchina*, *Capriccio espagnol*, The Flight of the Bumble Bee from *Tsar Saltan*, Senaillé's *Allegro spiritoso* (with Camden), Elgar's *Enigma Variations* and *Dream Children*, Davies' *Solemn Melody*, his arrangement of the traditional *Londonderry Air* and the scherzo from his own *Irish Symphony* (with the Hallé Orchestra); the *Water Music* and *Music for the Royal Fireworks*, Mozart's Divertimento K. 334 and Sinfonia Concertante K. 364 (with Sammons and Tertis), Balakirev's *Russia*, *Valse triste*, the overture to *The Bartered Bride*, Schubert's *Marche militaire* No. 1, and the polka and fugue from *Schwanda the Bagpipe Player* (with the London Philharmonic Orchestra); Bruch's Violin Concerto No. 1 (with Sammons and an orchestra), Handel's Organ Concerto in D major (with the London Symphony Orchestra *et al.*), By the Wayside from Elgar's *The Apostles* (with Labette, Williams, Eisdell and Noble, and the Hallé Chorus and an orchestra), and two excerpts from *Lohengrin* (with Licette, Brunskill, Mullings and Lark, and chorus and orchestra). Although he disliked contemporary music, he premièred Walton's Symphony No. 1 in 1934, and recorded the work with the London Symphony Orchestra for Decca; with the same orchestra he also recorded a Handel suite and Haydn's Symphony No. 95. His own recordings of the *Water Music* and *Music for the Royal Fireworks* were popular for many years; a best seller, too, for three decades, was a single 78 r.p.m. disc coupling *Nymphs and Shepherds* of Purcell and the Dance Duet from *Hänsel und Gretel*, with the Manchester Children's Choir and the Hallé Orchestra under Harty. He also made records as a pianist, and was the solo pianist in Lambert's recording of *The Rio Grande*. In today's catalogue, there are recordings of Harty's *John Field Suite* (with Dilkes and the English Sinfonia for EMI) and *With the Wild Geese* (with Gibson and the Scottish National Orchestra for EMI).

Harvey, Trevor (b. 1911). Born in Freshwater, Isle of Wight, Harvey was Heberden Organ Scholar at Brasenose College, Oxford, was with the BBC (1935–42) and director of music for the British Forces network in Germany (1945–6), when he conducted many German orchestras. Since then he has been a freelance conductor and critic for both *The Gramophone* and the BBC. For Decca he recorded in 1952 Sowande's *African Suite* (with the New Symphony String Orchestra).

Haslam, David (b. 1940). Born in Loughborough, Haslam studied at the Royal Academy of Music in London and was first flautist in the Scottish National Orchestra (1959–61) and the Northern Sinfonia at Newcastle-upon-Tyne (since 1961), and has also been associate artistic director of the Northern Sinfonia. He was flautist in a set of the *Brandenburg Concertos* issued by Enigma; he has recorded, as a conductor, *Peter and the Wolf* and his own *Juanita the Spanish Lobster* (with the Northern Sinfonia *et al.* for Continental Record Distributors).

Haug, Hans (1900–67). Born in Basel, Haug studied at the Basel Conservatory and Munich Academy of Music, conducted at the Basel

Theatre (1928–34), with the Suisse Romande Orchestra (1935–8), with the Beromünster Radio Orchestra (1938–43) and with the Zürich Radio Orchestra. He founded La Chanson Romande, conducted the Choeur de Lausanne and taught at Lausanne and La Chaux de Fonds. He frequently toured abroad as a conductor, was a member of the jury at many international musical competitions and composed a wide variety of music. For HMV he recorded on 78 r.p.m. discs Liebeskind's Symphony No. 1 (with the Zürich Radio Orchestra), and on LP his own *Élégie* (with Meylan, oboe, and the Lausanne Chamber Orchestra for CTS), and Roy's *Ballade* (with the Geneva Studio Orchestra for CTS).

Hausegger, Siegmund von (1872–1948). Born in Graz, Hausegger received his first musical instruction from his father, Friedrich von Hausegger, who was a professor of music and musical commentator, particularly of Wagner. The young Hausegger later studied with Carl Pohlig, a pupil of Liszt, and at the Styrian Musikverein. He started a notable career as a conductor in Graz in 1895, and in 1897 was an assistant at Bayreuth. His subsequent appointments were with Weingartner at the Kaim Orchestra in Munich (1899–1902), the Museum Concerts at Frankfurt am Main (1903–06), the Hamburg Philharmonic Orchestra (1910–20) and the Munich Philharmonic Orchestra (1920–36). At Munich, until 1934 he was also president of the Academy of Music, and in 1936 was awarded the Beethoven Prize of the Prussian Academy of Arts. He was also active as a conductor in Berlin, and appeared elsewhere in Europe. In his day he enjoyed a reputation as a composer, writing in the late German romantic idiom. His output included choral and orchestral works and songs, and the best known of his orchestral music were two symphonic poems, *Dionysische Phantasie* and *Barbarossa*. He was a conductor of considerable force and feeling, with an exemplary respect for the composer's intentions, particularly in the symphonies of Bruckner, which he preferred to perform in the original versions. An unusual characteristic during his tenure at Hamburg was the short introductory talks he gave before each work he conducted.

Hausegger's one recording was a significant one in the pre-war era, the Bruckner Symphony No. 9, with the Munich Philharmonic Orchestra in the original version. At a concert in 1932 with the orchestra, he performed the Symphony No. 9 in the only known version, which had been recomposed by Löwe after Bruckner's death, and then followed it with the original version. In 1935 in Munich, he also gave the first performance of the original version of Bruckner's Symphony No. 5. Writing of the concert in 1932, the first president of the International Bruckner Society, Max Auer, said: 'A huge painting being freed from the dust of centuries, so that outlines which formerly had been only dimly discernible suddenly became clearly visible, and all colours acquired a luminosity comparable to an old church window.'

Hawthorne, Joseph (b. 1908). Born in Princeton, Massachusetts, Hawthorne was educated at Princeton University, the American Conservatory at Fontainebleau and the Juilliard School. He was first violist with the Dallas Symphony Orchestra (1945–9), conductor of the Chattanooga Symphony Orchestra, Tennessee (1949–55), the Toledo Symphony Orchestra, Ohio (1955–64), the Provincetown Symphony Orchestra, Massachusetts (1955–69) and the Duluth Symphony Orchestra, Minnesota (1967 onwards). He received the Medal of the Bruckner-Mahler Society in 1954. He recorded a concerto grosso of Geminiani, a violin concerto of Vivaldi and Haydn's Symphony No. 22, with the Provincetown Symphony Orchestra (for Listening).

Heald-Smith, Geoffrey (b. 1930). Born in Mexborough, Yorkshire, Heald-Smith was educated at the Royal College of Music, London, has been a recital pianist and teacher, and is music adviser to the City of Hull and conductor of the City of Hull Youth Orchestra. He has appeared as a conductor on radio and television, inaugurated promenade concerts in Hull, and has a special interest in presenting programmes incorporating both light and symphonic music. In 1977 a record was released by Gough and Davy, Hull, in which he conducted the City of Hull Youth Orchestra in German's Symphony No. 2 and Jacob's comedy overture *The Barber of Seville goes to the Devil*; their second record has been of Granville Bantock's *Hebridean Symphony* and *Macbeth* overture.

Heath, Edward (b. 1916). The former British Prime Minister had formal training in music, was an organ scholar at Oxford, and has experience in amateur music making and choral conducting. He has been a member of the council of the Royal College of Music, vice-president of the Bach Choir, and chairman of the London Symphony Orchestra Trust. In 1971 he conducted the London Symphony at a concert in London, in 1975 toured West Germany with the orchestra, and in 1976 during a visit to the United States conducted the Chicago Symphony and Philadelphia Orchestras. The *Cockaigne* overture of Elgar appears to be his *pièce de résistance*; his performance with the London Symphony was released on an LP disc by EMI, coupled with some other pieces conducted by Previn. Heath gave a surprisingly warm and expansive reading. He has also recorded Christmas carols (with the BBC Singers), Dankworth's *Tom Sawyer's Saturday* (with Richard Baker, narrator), the overture to *La Cenerentola*, the third movement of the Handel Organ Concerto Op. 4 No. 4 (with Birch) and the Entry of the Queen of Sheba from *Solomon* (with the BBC Academy Orchestra), also for EMI, and recorded live at a Robert Mayer Concert in December 1973 in the Royal Festival Hall, London.

Hedwall, Lennart (b. 1932). Born in Göteborg, Sweden, Hedwall studied conducting with Mann and composition with Blomdahl, and after further studies in Vienna, Paris, Darmstadt and Hilversum, first conducted as an amateur and then as a professional in 1958. Since then he has conducted at the Göteborg Lyric Theatre, the Drottningholm Court Theatre and the Royal Opera at Stockholm, and with the Swedish Broadcasting Corporation, and has appeared in Finland, Holland, Norway and Czechoslovakia. He was artistic director of the Örebro Orchestral Association (1968–74) and conductor of the Swedish Chamber Orchestra (1969–74). Later he became a free-lance conductor and a teacher at the Swedish Opera School. He also performs as a pianist, harpsichordist and organist, broadcasts and writes about music, and made his debut as a composer when his String Quartet was broadcast in 1950. His compositions include organ, choral, chamber and orchestral music; he has received a number of state scholarships for composition and since 1973 has been vice-president of the Society for Swedish Composers. As a conductor he has recorded for Discofil with the Örebro Chamber Orchestra Grieg's *Heartwounds*, Järnefelt's *Berceuse*, Sibelius' *Suite mignone*, the intermezzo from Nielsen's *Little Suite*, Larrson's *Concertino* and *Evening Folk Songs*, von Koch's *Musica malinconica*, his own *Canzona*, and other pieces by Wirén, Björkander, Bull, and Peterson-Berger.

Heger, Robert (1886–1978). Born in Strasbourg, where his father was a member of the municipal orchestra, Heger studied at the Strasbourg Conservatory, at Zürich under Kempter and at Munich under von Schillings. His first appointment as a conductor was at Strasbourg (1907), then followed Ulm/Donau (1908), Barmen (1911), and the Vienna Volksoper (1911). He was principal conductor at the Nuremberg Opera (1913–21), assistant to Walter at Munich (1921) where he also conducted orchestral concerts, conductor at the Vienna State Opera and director of the concerts of the Gesellschaft der Musikfreunde (1925–33), then conductor at Kassel and at the Berlin State Opera (1933–45). After World War II he was again active in Berlin and Munich, where he was president of the Hochschule für Musik (1950–54). He came to London with Walter in the 1920s, in 1928 conducted *The Ring* and *Parsifal* at Covent Garden, and returned in the 1930s to conduct Wagner and some other operas. He has himself composed operas including *Lady Hamilton*, *Der verlorene Sohn*, *Ein Fest zu Haderslev* and *Der Bettler Namenlos*, orchestral works, chamber music and songs, some to words by Lotte Lehmann, and has arranged some Mahler songs for orchestra. He was a highly respected conductor, particularly of German opera. He was acknowledged to be conscientious and technically most competent, but limited in his interpretative imagination. This was illustrated by his ability to take over another conductor's performances and continue the latter's interpretation, as he did in the German season at Covent Garden in the middle 1920s, when Walter directed the first performances and Heger the later ones. He last visited London in 1953 with the Bavarian State Opera.

Before World War II Heger recorded for a number of companies, and his discography included the final scene from *Salome* (with Enik and the Berlin State Opera Orchestra for Telefunken), excerpts from *Siegfried* (with the London Symphony Orchestra), *Peer Gynt* Suite No. 1, *Moldau*, the overture to *Il segreto di Susanna*, and the Dance of the Hours from *La Gioconda* (with the Berlin State Opera Orchestra, for Odeon), arias from Wagner operas with Melchior and Schorr, Goldmark's *Rustic Wedding* symphony, Mozart's Serenade K. 320, the overtures *Abu Hassan*, *Pique Dame*, *Morgen, Mittag und Abend in Wien* and *Idomeneo*, and an abridged *Der Rosenkavalier* (with the Vienna Philharmonic Orchestra *et al.* for HMV), the overtures *Abu Hassan*, *Der Freischütz*, *Donna Diana* and *Alessandro Stradella*, the *Rosamunde* Ballet Music Nos 1 and 2, *Capriccio italien*, the waltzes from *Der Rosenkavalier*, choruses from *Tannhäuser* and *Der fliegende Holländer*, the prelude and Liebestod from *Tristan und Isolde*, dances from *The Three-cornered Hat*, Reger's *Eine vaterländische*

Ouvertüre, the Strauss waltzes *Morgenblätter* and *Künstlerleben*, and Svendsen's *Carnival in Paris* (with the Berlin Philharmonic and Berlin State Opera Orchestras for Polydor). The most famous of these was the records of *Der Rosenkavalier*, which Heger made in Vienna in 1933. Walter had conducted the opera in unforgettable performances in Vienna and London, and as he was not available for the recordings, Heger took over. The opera was abridged and recorded on thirteen 78 r.p.m. discs, and the cast included Lotte Lehmann, Elisabeth Schumann, Maria Olczewska and Richard Mayr, who made up Walter's original cast. It was a sublime and unique artistic achievement and was without doubt among the finest operatic recordings made between the wars; it has been re-issued on an LP transfer many times, and is even now available in Britain.

After World War II Heger again came into prominence as an operatic conductor on records, and the sets he made confirmed his mastery in this capacity. The operas issued were *Tannhäuser*, *Undine*, *Der Wildschütz*, *Zar und Zimmerman*, *The Merry Wives of Windsor*, *Der Evangelimann* of Kienzl, *Rigoletto*, *Der Freischütz* and *Martha*. Most were with the Bavarian State Opera company, an exception being *The Merry Wives of Windsor* (with the Dresden Staatskapelle *et al.*), and were issued by Electrola, EMI, DGG, Urania, Eterna, Vox and Nixa. In 1971 Preiser released *Lohengrin*, in which Heger led the Berlin Staatskapelle, and BASF also have issued discs of excerpts from *Die Entführung aus dem Serail*, *Andrea Chénier*, *Lohengrin* and *Tristan und Isolde* (with the Berlin State Opera). His other LP discs include Haydn's Symphony No. 103 (with the Bamberg Symphony Orchestra, issued by Mercury), Schumann's Symphony No. 3 and *Manfred* overture (with the Bamberg Symphony Orchestra for Ariola), Strauss's *Josephslegende* ballet (with the Bavarian Radio Symphony Orchestra for BASF), Schubert's *Rosamunde* music (with the Bavarian Radio Symphony Orchestra *et al.* for EMI), Rheinberger's *The Star of Bethlehem* (with the Graunke Symphony Orchestra *et al.* for EMI), Respighi's *Concerto gregoriano* (with Richartz and the Berlin Municipal Orchestra for DGG), a song recital by Schlusnus (with the Bavarian Radio Symphony Orchestra for DGG), von Schillings' *Glockenlieder* (with Anders and the Berlin State Opera Orchestra for DGG), the Mozart Symphony No. 35 (with the Prussian State Orchestra for Urania), Britten's *Les Illuminations* (with Anders and the Prussian State Orchestra), Spohr's Violin Concerto No. 8 (with Schulz and the Berlin Radio Orchestra for Urania), Mozart's Symphony No. 33 and the overture to *Le nozze di Figaro* (with the Austrian Symphony Orchestra for Remington) and the Schumann Piano Concerto (with Chailly-Richez and the Austrian Symphony Orchestra for Remington).

Heider, Werner (b. 1930). Born in Fürth, Bavaria, Heider studied in Nuremberg and at the Hochschule für Musik in Munich, and has been the artistic director of the 'Colloquium Musicale', 'Kammermusik+Jazz', and the 'Ars Nova Ensemble Nuremberg'. He has given many concerts in and outside FR Germany, and his compositions have won prizes at Stuttgart (1965), Nuremberg (1967), Erlangen (1968) and Fürth (1970). For Colosseum he recorded with the Nuremberg Symphony Orchestra his own works *Bezirk* (with Gröschel), *Da sein, Einander* (with Rosin), *Konturen* (with Gawriloff), *Kunst-Stoff* (with Deinzer) and *Strophen* (with Deinzer), and Hashagen's *Mobile Szenen* (with Fink), *Percussion VI* (with Fink) and *Trip in the Air*.

Heidger, Gerd (b. 1926). Born in Düsseldorf, Heidger studied at the Hochschule für Musik and at the University at Cologne, and made his debut as a conductor in 1951. He was a repetiteur and conductor at the Cologne Opera (1951–8), conductor at the Frankfurt am Main Opera under Solti (1958–60), general music director at Krefeld-Mönchengladbach (1960–65), and at Giessen (since 1965). In addition, he has been a guest conductor with orchestras at Cologne, Stuttgart, Frankfurt am Main and Berlin, and in France, Holland and Spain. His recordings have been of Mozart's Symphony No. 29 and some concert arias (with the Hessian Radio Symphony Orchestra *et al.* for Amadeo), Handel's *Music for the Royal Fireworks* and Oboe Concertos Nos 1 and 3 (with Plath and the Frankfurt Chamber Orchestra for La Guilde Internationale du Disque) and discs of waltzes and polkas by the Strausses and Lanner (with the Vienna Festival Orchestra, also for GID).

Heiller, Anton (b. 1923). The Austrian organist, harpsichordist, conductor and composer Heiller was born in Vienna; after showing prodigious talent as a child, he attended the Vienna Academy of Music (1941–2), and in 1945 was appointed professor of organ in the sacred music department of the Academy, the youngest man to hold this post. He made his debut as a conductor in 1948 with the Vienna Symphony Orchestra. His best-known compositions are a Toccata for two pianos, organ sonatas and sacred vocal music; Amadeo recorded and issued some of his motets. His international reputation, however, is primarily as an organist; in this capacity he has toured extensively, won first prize at the International Organ Contest at Haarlem (1952) and the Golden Tulip in the Netherlands for improvisations which included double-fugues and passages in retrograde. In the 1950s he recorded for Philips the complete organ music of Bach. In 1969 he received the Austrian Grand Prize for Music.

As a conductor, Heiller has recorded Bach's Three-Harpsichord Concerto BWV 1064 and Four-Harpsichord Concerto BWV 1065 (for Haydn Society), flute concertos of Stamitz, Telemann and Michael Haydn (with Wanausek and the Vienna Pro Musica Orchestra for Vox), Bach's Cantatas Nos 51 and 209 (with the Vienna State Opera Orchestra *et al.* for Bach Guild), Haydn's Symphonies Nos 26 and 36 (with the Vienna Chamber Orchestra for Parlophone), and Nos 83 and 84 (with the Collegium Musicum for Period), *Piano Concerto in G major* (with E. Heiller and the Collegium Musicum for Haydn Society), Horn Concerto No. 1 (with Koch and the Vienna Symphony Orchestra for Erato), Trumpet Concerto (with Wobisch and the Vienna State Opera Orchestra for Erato), and Violin Concerto No. 2 (with Bertschinger and the Collegium Musicum for Haydn Society), and Corelli's Concerto Grosso Op. 6 No. 8 (with the Vienna Chamber Orchestra for Renaissance).

Heinrich, Siegfried (b. 1935). Born in Dresden and educated at the Hochschule für Musik at Frankfurt am Main, Heinrich was assistant conductor with the Dresden Kreuzchor, the Frankfurt Student Choir (1954), with the Hessian Chamber Orchestra at Frankfurt (1957), conducted with radio orchestras and at opera houses in Europe, and has been artistic director of the Hersfeld Festival Concerts. His repertoire extends from the music of the Renaissance to the *avant-garde* of Penderecki and Ligeti. He recorded Telemann's *St Luke Passion* (with the Hessian Chamber Orchestra, Hersfeld Festival Choir *et al.*, for Cantate).

Heintze, Hans (b. 1911). Born near Goslar, Germany, Heintze studied the organ with Ramin, was kantor and organist at Bad Oldesloe (1932–4), St Sophie's, Dresden (1934–40), St Thomas, Leipzig (1940) and St John's, Lüneburg (1949–57), taught the organ at the Hochschule für Musik in Berlin (1955) and from 1958 was in charge of music at the Evangelical Church, organist at St Peter's and professor at the Conservatory, all in Bremen. He has made a number of records as an organist; as a conductor he recorded for Cantate with the Bremen Bach Orchestra and the Cathedral Choir Bach's Cantatas Nos 33, 95, 99 and 199. The first two were issued in the US by Vanguard and Musical Heritage Society.

Heinze, Sir Bernard (b. 1894). Born in Shepparton, Australia, Heinze was educated at Melbourne University and attended the Royal College of Music, London (1912) on a scholarship. After five years' service in the Royal Artillery in World War I he studied in Paris under d'Indy and Lejeune and in Berlin under Hess, and toured Europe as a violinist with the Lejeune Quartet. He returned to Australia (1924), joined the staff of the University Conservatorium in Melbourne, and became Ormond Professor of Music there (1925–56). He was conductor of the Melbourne University Symphony Orchestra (1924–32) and the Melbourne Symphony Orchestra (1933–56), was director of the New South Wales State Conservatorium of Music in Sydney (1956–66), and toured Europe in the 1930s and Canada in 1947. He has been one of the vital forces in developing musical performance in Australia and in promoting music among younger audiences, and for his services he was knighted in 1949 and appointed a Companion of the Order of Australia in 1975. His strength as a conductor lies more in romantic music than that of earlier periods. His records include Beethoven's Symphony No. 5 (with the Australian Youth Orchestra for EMI), the prelude to *Die Meistersinger* (with the Sydney Symphony Orchestra for EMI), Jacob's arrangement of Byrd's *The Bells* and *The Earl of Oxford's March* and the *Fantasia on Greensleeves* of Vaughan Williams (with the Sydney Symphony Orchestra for Radiola), and a two-disc collection of music by Ravel, Sibelius, Vaughan Williams, Stravinsky, Massenet, Butterworth, Elgar, Rimsky-Korsakov, Adam, Holst and Kabalevsky (with various Australian orchestras for World Record Club). In addition he has recorded works by Australian composers: Alfred Hill's *Linthorpe* (with the Sydney Symphony Orchestra for WRC), and Viola Concerto (with Pikler and the Sydney Symphony Orchestra for RCA), Hanson's *Fern Hill* and Dreyfus' *Jingles* (with the West Australian Symphony Orchestra for Festival), Bainton's Symphony No. 3 (with the Sydney Symphony Orchestra for Brolga), Sculthorpe's *Sun Music III* (with the Sydney Symphony Orchestra for EMI), Lovelock's *Divertimento* (with the Sydney Symphony Orchestra for WRC), and James' *Australian*

Christmas Carols (with the Sydney Symphony Orchestra *et al.* for WRC).

Helliwell, Clifton (b. 1907). Born at Farnworth and educated at the Royal Manchester College of Music, Helliwell was an accompanist with the British Broadcasting Corporation (1929–34), assistant conductor of the BBC Empire Orchestra (1935–9), served in the British army (1942–6) and then returned to the BBC as assistant conductor of the BBC Theatre Orchestra. He published a translation of Martin's *Le Vin herbé*, and recorded on an early LP for Nixa Stainer's *The Crucifixion* (with the Whitehall Choir *et al.*).

Hellmann, Diethard (b. 1928). Born in Grimma, Saxony, Hellmann studied at the Leipzig Academy of Music (1944–8), where he was a lecturer and cantor (1948–55), then he was cantor at the Mainz Christuskirche (from 1955), director of the Mainz Bach Choir and Orchestra, and professor at the Munich Academy of Music (since 1962). He has toured Europe as a conductor, organist and harpsichordist, and has published editions of baroque music and reconstructions of the *St Mark Passion* and some cantatas of Bach. He has recorded with the Mainz Bach Choir and Orchestra *et al.*, Bach's Cantatas Nos 34, 157, 169 and 189 (for Cantate), No. 200 and Psalm 51 (issued by Oryx) and Nos 119 and 129 (issued by Musical Heritage Society).

Heltay, László. Born in Budapest where he studied under Kodály and Bárdos at the Franz Liszt Academy of Music, Heltay came to England in 1956, studied at Merton College, Oxford, and in 1964 was appointed assistant conductor of the New Zealand Broadcasting Corporation Symphony Orchestra; a year later he became director of the New Zealand Opera Company. He returned to London in 1967 to be conductor of the Phoenix Opera Company and assistant to Klemperer, and has since been a freelance conductor, performing with many major orchestras in Britain and abroad. He is now musical director of the Collegium Musicum in London, the Brighton Festival Chorus, and the Chorus of the Academy of St Martin-in-the-Fields, with which he has toured in Europe. His recordings have been of Brian's Symphony No. 22 and *Psalm 23* (with the Brighton Festival Chorus and the Leicestershire Schools Symphony Orchestra for CBS), and Kodály's *Missa Brevis* and *Pange lingua* (with the Brighton Festival Chorus for Decca).

Hemberg, Eskil (b. 1938). Born in Stockholm and educated at the Royal College of Music there (1957–64), Hemberg first conducted at Llangollen, Wales (1961). He was executive producer and head of the choral department of the Swedish Broadcasting Corporation (1963–70), planning manager at the Institute for National Concerts (since 1970), president of the Swedish Composers' Association (1971) and conductor of the Stockholm University Chorus (since 1959), with which he toured the United States three times and has made many recordings. Included among them is a performance of extracts from Pettersson's *Barfotasånger*, which was issued in Britain by CRD/ Caprice.

Henderson, Roy (b. 1899). Born in Edinburgh, Henderson served in World War I and afterwards studied at the Royal Academy of Music, London. He made his debut as a baritone at short notice in Delius' *Mass of Life* in London in 1925, and after a distinguished career, including performances with the Glyndebourne Festival Opera and at Covent Garden, retired from the concert platform in 1952 to devote his time to teaching. He conducted a number of choirs as a hobby, including the Nottingham Oriana Choir, the Huddersfield Glee and Madrigal Society and the Bournemouth Municipal Choir, adjudicated in international competitions, and conducted master classes in singing in Canada and Holland. One of his pupils was the illustrious contralto, Kathleen Ferrier, with whom he recorded for Decca in 1947 Pergolesi's *Stabat Mater*, with the Boyd Neel Orchestra, the Nottingham Oriana Choir and the soprano Joan Taylor. He also made other records with this choir, as a baritone soloist and took part in the celebrated Glyndebourne Mozart opera recordings in the 1930s.

Henderson, Skitch (b. 1918). Lyle Russell Cedric ('Skitch') Henderson was born in Birmingham, England, and came to the United States as a boy. In his early teens he worked as an organist and pianist for a radio station in North Dakota, played the piano in dance bands, was accompanist to Judy Garland and Mickey Rooney, and became a staff pianist for Metro-Goldwyn-Mayer. During World War II he was a fighter pilot with the RAF and the USAF, and became a US citizen. After the war he returned to Hollywood, conducted for radio shows and wrote film music, and studied with Schoenberg, Toch and Albert Coates, who introduced him to symphonic music. He joined the music department of NBC in 1949, eventually becoming its musical director (1956–9), conducted some concerts with the NBC Symphony Orchestra, and took lessons in conducting from Reiner. In 1953 he founded and conducted the New York Pops Orchestra; he was music director of the Scranton Philharmonic Orchestra (1959–62) and in 1971 became music director of the Tulsa Philharmonic Orchestra. He has conducted major orchestras in the US, Canada, Britain, FR Germany, France and Australia. In 1960 he recorded *Peter and the Wolf* and *Le Carnaval des animaux* (with Beatrice Lillie, Katchen and Graffman, and the London Symphony Orchestra for Decca), and he has also recorded a disc of selections from *Porgy and Bess* (with Warfield and Price for RCA).

Hendl, Walter (b. 1917). Born in West New York, New Jersey, Hendl studied the piano with Clarence Adler, at the Curtis Institute under Saperton and Reiner, and with Koussevitzky at the Berkshire Center at Tanglewood (1941–2). After service with the US air force (1942–5) he composed the music for the Broadway hit *Dark of the Moon*, and conducted it for the first year of its two-year run (1945–6). He appeared as a guest pianist with the CBS Symphony Orchestra, was engaged as a guest conductor with the Pittsburgh Symphony and Boston Symphony Orchestras, and was assistant conductor and pianist with the New York Philharmonic Orchestra (1946–9). He taught at the Juilliard School (1947–50), was music director of the Dallas Symphony Orchestra (1949–59), associate conductor to Reiner with the Chicago Symphony Orchestra (1959–64), directed music festivals at Ravinia, Caramoor and Chautauqua, was music director of the Chautauqua Symphony Orchestra (1953–72), and director of the Eastman School of Music (1964–73). He has conducted widely in the United States, toured the Far East with the Symphony of the Air (1955), as well as appearing in South America, Europe and the USSR. Since 1972 he has been a guest conductor and teacher of conducting at the Juilliard School and is conductor of the Erie Philharmonic Orchestra.

Hendl first appeared on record as a pianist in the Beethoven Triple Concerto, together with Corigliano and Rose and the New York Philharmonic Orchestra under Walter. In 1951 he made a number of records in Europe for the American Recording Society, which was sponsored by the Alice M. Ditson Fund of Columbia University; this was a substantial series and included music by a number of American composers, and was the forerunner of the later work of Hanson with Mercury, Whitney with Louisville, and Composers Recordings, in recording music by US composers. The American Recording Society first issued the discs on its own label, which named Hendl as conducting the Society's orchestra, but many of the recordings were later re-issued by Desto with the orchestra identified as the Vienna Symphony Orchestra. The music which Hendl recorded in this series was Schuman's *American Festival* overture, Sessions' *The Black Maskers*, Thomson's film music *The River*, Harris' Symphony No. 3, Haieff's Piano Concerto (with Smit), McBride's Violin Concerto (with Wilk), Taylor's *Portrait of a Lady*, Barber's *Music for a Scene from Shelley* and overture to *The School for Scandal*, Copeland's *Appalachian Spring* and *Music for the Theater*, Moross' *The Scandalous Life of Franky and Johnny*, Bloch's *Three Jewish Poems*, Griffes' *Poem* (with Wanausek), Creston's *Partita*, Ives' *Three Places in New England* and Rogers' *Leaves from the Tale of Pinocchio*. Hendl also recorded concerto accompaniments for RCA, including MacDowell's Piano Concerto No. 3 and Prokofiev's Piano Concerto No. 3 (with Cliburn and the Chicago Symphony Orchestra), Beethoven's Piano Concerto No. 3 (with Graffman and the Chicago Symphony), Rózsa's Violin Concerto No. 2 (with Heifetz and the Dallas Symphony Orchestra), Lalo's *Symphonie espagnole* (with Szeryng and the Chicago Symphony), Paganini's Violin Concerto No. 1 and Saint-Saëns' *Introduction et rondo capriccioso* (with Friedman and the Chicago Symphony), the Sibelius Violin Concerto (with Heifetz and the Chicago Symphony), the Glazunov Violin Concerto (with Heifetz and the RCA Victor Symphony Orchestra) and Prokofiev's *Ugly Duckling* and four numbers from *Music for Children* (with an orchestra for Young People's Records).

Henking, Bernhard (b. 1897). Born in Schaffhausen, Switzerland, Henking studied at the Zürich Conservatory and at the Hochschule für Musik in Berlin (1917–21). He was a conductor at Baden (Aargau) and of the Magdeburg Cathedral Choir (1925), and became director of the Aschersleben Evangelical Church Music School (1936). He returned to Zürich (1939) and became kantor of the Reformed Church community of Winterthur and St Gall, conductor of the Swiss Heinrich Schütz Choir (1942), and conductor of the Zürich Bach Choir (1951). He recorded J. S. Bach's *Unser Leben ist Schatten* and J. C. Bach's motet *Ich lasse dich nicht* (with the Heinrich Schütz Choir for Cantate), and Bach's Cantata No. 118 and the sinfonia from Cantata No. 42 (with the Winterthur Symphony Orchestra *et al.* for Concert Hall).

Henschel, Sir George (1850–1934). Pianist, friend of Brahms, orchestral conductor, composer, teacher and one of the most important lieder singers of his time, Henschel was born in Breslau, studied at Breslau, Leipzig and Berlin, and made his debut as a pianist in Berlin in 1866. In the same year as the first performance of *Die Meistersinger* in Munich (1866), he sang the part of Hans Sachs at a concert performance of the opera. After further study in Berlin he gave recitals as a singer and in 1875 sang in the *St Matthew Passion* of Bach, conducted by Brahms. He appeared in London, again as a singer, but was then appointed first conductor of the Boston Symphony Orchestra in 1881. His inexperience as a conductor did not, however, please the concert-goers of Boston, who replaced him three years later. Settling in London in 1884 he became a British citizen and took a very active part in local musical life, both as singer and conductor. He founded the London Symphony Concerts (*not* the London Symphony Orchestra) in 1886, and conducted them until 1897. During the years 1893 to 1895 he also led the Scottish Symphony Orchestra and conducted Wagner at Covent Garden. Oratorios and operas from his own pen were presented in England, the United States and Germany; at a performance of his opera *Nubia* in Dresden he substituted at the last moment for one of the singers who had become ill. Fuller-Maitland, in *Grove's Dictionary of Music and Musicians*, described Henschel's *Mass for Eight Voices* as a work of great beauty, and some of his songs became very popular. In 1931 he conducted a commemorative concert with the Boston Symphony Orchestra with a programme almost identical to his first with them in 1881. He accompanied himself at the piano in lieder recitals, and in his 79th year became a popular radio vocalist. Just before his death he held an exhibition of paintings in London. He was knighted in 1914. He was a genial, dignified musician, who, according to Goossens, won the hearts of the orchestra by his unaffected approach to conducting. Towards the end of his life HMV and Columbia issued a handful of records of him in his dual role of singer and accompanist; these included *Ich grolle nicht* from Schumann's *Dichterliebe*, in which he was reputed to be incomparable. The only recording in which he appeared as a conductor was Beethoven's Symphony No. 1, made in 1927 with the Royal Philharmonic Orchestra; it was part of a series of the nine Beethoven symphonies recorded at the time by Columbia, and the other conductors were Beecham, Wood, Harty and Weingartner.

Henze, Hans Werner (b. 1926). Born in Gütersloh, Germany, Henze was playing the piano as a child, and studied at the State Music School at Braunschweig from 1942 until he was drafted into the German army in 1944. He was captured by the British, and was a prisoner-of-war in England; after the war he became a repetiteur at the theatre at Bielefeld, and in 1947 resumed his studies under Fortner at the Church Music School at Heidelberg (1946–8), then with Leibowitz in Paris (1948), who introduced him to the twelve-tone music of Schoenberg and Webern. He also took part in the Darmstadt summer new-music sessions. He had started to compose as a teenager, began his professional career as a pianist, and in 1948 became musical director at the German Theatre at Constance. In 1950 he was artistic director of the ballet of the Hessian State Theatre at Wiesbaden, where he composed ballets and incidental music. His publishers granted him a monthly allowance, and, being unhappy with the musical atmosphere in his native land, he moved to Italy in 1953 and has lived there ever since, working with the communist government in Tuscany in cultural development programmes.

Henze's music has been as controversial as his political outlook, both of which have been closely interrelated. In his early years he composed in a more or less rigid serial style, but later his music developed a more eclectic idiom which separated him from the *avant-garde* and marked him off as one of the leading conservatives among composers of his generation, writing for conventional instruments played by conventional methods in traditional forms. In recent years he has identified himself with revolutionary political attitudes and his music has been deeply influenced by political factors, which he says have brought him to write 'more critically, more slowly, and with less self-pity, less concern with individual problems, or more identification of these with the world's problems' (*The Gramophone*, April 1972, p. 1691). This, he believes, has improved his work and made it stronger and more humble at the same time. His many compositions include symphonies, concertos, cantatas and operas; many critics recognise him as one of the most significant composers of the day. Demonstrations and outbursts have occurred at many of the first performances of his works; at the intended première of *Das Floss der Medusa* a political uproar prevented the start of the performance.

Henze finds that conductors are frequently disinclined to prepare and present modern scores, so has taken up conducting to perform and promote his own music, but would prefer to devote all his time to composition. His experiences as a conductor have varied according to the orchestras, some of which he finds too inattentive. Since 1967 DGG have recorded many discs with him directing his compositions: Symphonies Nos 1 to 5 (with the Berlin Philharmonic Orchestra), Symphony No. 6 (with the London Symphony Orchestra), the Violin Concerto (with Schneiderhan and the Bavarian Radio Symphony Orchestra), the Piano Concerto No. 2 (with Eschenbach and the London Philharmonic Orchestra), the Double-bass Concerto (with Karr and the English Chamber Orchestra), *Essay on Pigs* (with the Philip Jones Brass Ensemble), *Tristan – Preludes for Piano, Orchestra and Tapes* (with Francesch and the Cologne Radio Orchestra), *Elegy for Young Lovers* (with the Berlin Radio Symphony Orchestra, Berlin Opera Orchestra *et al.*), *Cantata della Flaba Estrema*, *Whispers from Heavenly Death* and *Being Beauteous* (Moser, Berlin Philharmonic Chamber Orchestra *et al.*), *Muses de Sicile* (with the Dresden Staatskapelle *et al.*), *Moralitäten* (with the Leipzig Gewandhaus Orchestra *et al.*), *Ode to the West Wind* (Palm, Schneiderhan and the Bavarian Radio Symphony Orchestra), and *Das Floss der Medusa* (with the Hamburg Radio Symphony Orchestra *et al.*). He has also recorded for Decca and L'Oiseau Lyre his Violin Concerto No. 2 and *Concerto for Violin, Tape, Voice and 13 Instrumentalists* (with Langbein), *Compases para Preguntas ensimismadas* (with Fukai), *Kammermusik*, *Labyrinth*, *Apollo und Hyazinthus*, *L'Usignolo dell'Imperatore*, *In Memoriam – die Weisse Rose* and *Wiegenlied der Mutter Gottes*, all with the London Sinfonietta *et al.*

Herbig, Günther (b. 1931). Born at Ustí nad Labem in Czechoslovakia, Herbig studied with Abendroth at the Franz Liszt Hochschule at Weimar and made his debut as a conductor at the Weimar Opera in 1957. He remained at Weimar until 1962, at the same time teaching conducting at the Hochschule, and studied further with Scherchen, Jansons and Karajan. He became music director at Potsdam (1962–6), assistant conductor and then general music director of the Berlin Symphony Orchestra in East Berlin (1966–72), and was appointed chief conductor and artistic director of the Dresden Philharmonic Orchestra (1972), in succession to Masur. He has been a guest conductor in many East European countries, in Britain and South America, and has toured with the Berlin Symphony, Leipzig Gewandhaus and Dresden Philharmonic Orchestras; in 1974–6 he visited FR Germany, Britain, Poland, Spain, Czechoslovakia, Italy, Austria, Japan and the USSR with the Dresden Philharmonic. He has made a number of records for Eterna, which have been released in West Europe by Eurodisc, Philips, Polydor and other companies. The works he has recorded have included Haydn's Symphonies Nos 95 to 104, Kunad's Organ Concerto, a number of divertimenti, cassations, marches and serenades of Mozart, the Reger Piano Concerto (with Webersinke) and Prokofiev's Symphony No. 1 (with the Dresden Philharmonic Orchestra), Beethoven's *Ritterballet* and *Die Geschöpfe des Prometheus*, Haydn's Symphonies Nos 3 and 10, the incidental music to *A Midsummer Night's Dream*, the four Brahms symphonies, Nielsen's Symphony No. 5, Eisler's *Symphonic Studies*, *Ernste Gesänge* (with Leib), *Glückliche Farht*, *Es lächelnt der See*, *Das Vorbild* and *Goethe Rhapsodie*, Matthus' *Little Concerto for Orchestra*, Tittel's *Music for String Orchestra*, Herrmann's Chamber Symphony, Medek's *Die betrunkene Sonne*, Thurm's *Drei Tierfabeln* and Werzlau's *Symphonic Studies* (with the Berlin Symphony Orchestra), Dessau's *Orchestral Music No. 4* (with the Berlin Staatskapelle) and Kunad's Organ Concerto (with Collum and the Dresden Philharmonic Orchestra). The performances of the Haydn *London* symphonies were brisk and energetic, if not especially distinctive.

Herrmann, Bernard (1911–75). Herrmann was born in New York and was the son of a migrant Russian doctor. He showed a precocious interest in composing, studied with Percy Grainger at New York University, at Columbia University and the Juilliard School, and also with Reuben Goldmark. He first conducted musicals on Broadway and in 1931 founded and conducted the New Chamber Orchestra in New York, which continued until 1934 and gave the first performances in the United States of works by composers such as Milhaud, Varèse, Ives and Gershwin. He joined the Columbia Broadcasting System as director of educational programmes in 1932, became a staff conductor in 1938 and eventually was the chief conductor of the CBS Symphony Orchestra from 1942 to 1959. In this capacity he gave much rarely performed music, including a series of programmes of the music of Ives, and in particular he introduced to American listeners music by British composers including Rubbra, Rawsthorne, Lambert, Berners and Delius. In 1956 he gave the first broadcast performance in Britain of Ives' Symphony No. 2. He composed a considerable range of music, symphonies, other orchestral and concerted music, an opera *Wuthering Heights* and a large-scale cantata *Moby Dick*, and numerous film scores, among them for the films *Citizen Kane*, *The Magnificent Ambersons*, *Anna and the King of Siam*, *Psycho*, *Marnie*, *North by Northwest* and *Vertigo*. His compositions are in the neo-romantic idiom, and the scores of *Moby Dick* and *Wuthering Heights* never really lose their kinship with film music. He said, in an interview just before his death, 'I don't see any use to write a language no one understands. I don't understand Boulez – last month in London, when he said: "I will never conduct Tchaikovsky, Strauss or Puccini". I suppose the crap he's doing is better, I mean, he's a talented man, but he doesn't have any feeling' (*High Fidelity*, September 1976, p. 67). He was a conductor of great skill and experience, but, except for his film scores, his recording activities were confined to England where he lived for the last ten years of his life.

In 1967 Herrmann recorded, for Pye, *Wuthering Heights* (with the Pro Arte Orchestra *et al.*), before it had ever been produced in a theatre; the four-disc set was later re-issued in 1972 by Unicorn, who also released *Moby Dick* (with the London Philharmonic Orchestra *et al.*). Unicorn also issued suites, with Herrmann conducting from his film scores *The Devil and Daniel Webster*, *Psycho*, and *Citizen Kane* (called *Welles Raises Kane*); Decca also issued discs of parts of his film scores such as *Jane Eyre*, *The Snows of Kilimanjaro*, *Journey to the Centre of the Earth*, *The Day the Earth Stood Still* and *The Battle of Neretva*. Of other compositions, he recorded his Symphony, *For the Fallen* and *The Fantasticks* (with the National Philharmonic Orchestra for Unicorn); of other composers there were Raff's Symphony No. 5 (with the London Philharmonic Orchestra for Unicorn), *The Planets*, *Finlandia*, *L'Apprenti sorcier*, *Les Préludes*, Honegger's *Pastorale d'été*, Fauré's *Pavane*, Satie's *Gymnopédies*, Debussy's *Clair de lune* and *La plus que lente*, and Ravel's *Five-o'clock Foxtrot* (with the London Philharmonic Orchestra for Decca), Cyril Scott's Piano Concerto Nos 1 and 2 and *Early One Morning* (with Ogdon and the London Philharmonic Orchestra for Lyrita), Ives' Symphony No. 2 (with the London Symphony Orchestra for Decca), a suite from Weill's *Die Dreigroschenoper*, Gershwin's *Variations on 'I got Rhythm'* (with Parkhouse), Stravinsky's *Ragtime*, Milhaud's *La Création du monde* and *Saudades do Brasil*, and Satie's *Les Aventures de Mercure*, *Le Belle excentrique* and *Jack in the box* (with the London Festival Ensemble for Decca), and film music by Shostakovich, Walton, Rózsa, Lambert, Bliss, Vaughan Williams and Bax (with the National Philharmonic Orchestra for Decca).

Hertz, Alfred (1872–1942). One of the many emigré conductors who dominated musical life in the United States in the first half of this century, Hertz was born in Frankfurt am Oder, and his first composition, as a child, was a funeral march written after he had received a spanking. He was educated at the Raff Conservatory and in 1891 embarked on his first appointment at the Halle State Theatre. He then conducted at Altenburg (1892–5), Elbefeld (1895–9) and Breslau (1899–1902), and in 1902 was engaged by the New York Metropolitan Opera to take charge of the German repertoire. In his thirteen years at the Met. he led 27 different operas, many being new works by American composers. He was responsible for two *Ring* cycles in 1904, and shared the season in 1908 with Mahler and Toscanini. He led the first performances in the United States of *Salome* and *Der Rosenkavalier*, and the world première of Humperdinck's *Der Königskinder*, and also conducted successful performances of *Götterdämmerung*, *Tannhäuser* and *Tristan und Isolde* at Covent Garden in 1910. Wearying of the opera house, he left New York in 1915 and was appointed conductor of the San Francisco Symphony Orchestra, where he remained until 1930; he inaugurated symphony concerts at the Hollywood Bowl in Los Angeles in 1922, was a guest conductor at the San Francisco Opera, and from time to time conducted a radio programme, the Standard Symphony Hour (1927–37).

In 1903 Hertz conducted *Parsifal* at the New York Met., in the first stage production outside Bayreuth, and this invited the wrath of Cosima Wagner and other Wagnerites who had sought to prevent stage productions outside Bayreuth. As a consequence he was barred from appearing at Bayreuth or at any other major German opera house. (Although there had been other unauthorised performances of *Parsifal* in Europe, the United States and South America before the copyright expired in 1913, Bodanzky conducted the first extra-Bayreuth stage production at Covent Garden in 1914.) Hertz was a temperamental personality and was often the centre of controversies with singers, fellow conductors and opera-house managers. His abilities as a conductor have been described variously as 'brilliant', 'respectable' and 'heavy-handed', which probably tells us more about the describers than about Hertz. When he was at the New York Met. his Wagner performances were noted for the dominance of the orchestra at the expense of the singers. His musical sympathies were wide, ranging from Beethoven to Schoenberg, for whom he had a rare respect. He made records for Victor with the San Francisco Symphony Orchestra in the late 1920s, including the overtures *Leonore No. 3*, *Der Freischütz*, *Phèdre* and *A Midsummer Night's Dream* and the march from the latter, *Les Préludes*, *Capriccio espagnol*, the ballet music from *Le Cid*, Glazunov's *Valse de concert No. 1*, Gounod's *Funeral March of a Marionette*, the Brahms' *Hungarian Dances Nos 5* and *6*, the Liebestod from *Tristan und Isolde*, Schubert's *Marche militaire No. 1* and an entr'acte from *Rosamunde*, Kreisler's *Liebeslieder* and *Caprice viennois*, an extract from *Coppélia*, and Moszkowski's *Serenade* and Auber's *Aubade*. Previously he had recorded some excerpts from *Parsifal* with the Berlin Philharmonic Orchestra.

Hétu, Pierre (b. 1936). Born in Montreal, Hétu studied at the Quebec Conservatoire and Montreal University, with Lindenberg and Fourestier in Paris, and with Galliera and Celibidache at the Accademia Chigiana in Siena, and in 1961 won the first prize at the International Competition for Young Conductors at Besançon. He also studied at Tanglewood, Massachusetts, became assistant conductor with the Montreal Symphony Orchestra (1964–8), conducted for the Canadian Opera Company at Toronto (1966), was music director for the Kalamazoo Symphony Orchestra (1968–73) and conductor of the Edmonton Symphony Orchestra (since 1973). He has recorded Quesnel's *Colas et Colinette* (with the Montreal Radio Orchestra *et al.* for CBC), and Prévost's *Fantasmes* and Somers' *Fantasia* (with the Montreal Symphony Orchestra for RCA).

Heward, Leslie (1897–1943). Born in Littleton, Yorkshire, Heward was one of the brightest stars in the English musical firmament before his early death in 1943. Bernard Shore, who played under him as well as under many other great conductors, described him as a brilliant, gifted musician, and one of the finest conductors anywhere; immediately after his death Boult said that his staggering technical skill and sensitive musicianship and steady development marked him out for the very highest world honours. As a boy Heward was a chorister at Manchester Cathedral, and first trained as an organist. He studied at the Royal College of Music under Stanford and Vaughan Williams and was at the same time assistant music master at Eton College. His early musical experience included playing a cinema organ, and at the Royal College of Music he played the timpani in the orchestra. His first appointment was as a conductor with the British National Opera Company; he became music director of the South African Broadcasting Corporation and conductor of the Cape Town Symphony Orchestra (1924), which brought him to London in 1925 to play at the Wembley Exhibition. After leaving South Africa in 1927 he succeeded Boult as conductor of the City of Birmingham Orchestra (1930), but eventually ill health restricted his activities and he died in Birmingham at the age of 46. He was an excellent orchestral trainer and won for the Birmingham orchestra a national reputation. For his day, he had a wide repertoire, but his deepest sympathies were towards Dvořák and Sibelius; however, when he chose to perform music to which he was not particularly attracted, he gave it his closest attention. His readings were straightforward and devoid of exaggeration, always searching for the meaning behind the notes. Orchestral players were invariably responsive to him, and his conducting reflected the humility of his personality, which avoided any form of exhibitionism. He composed orchestral, chamber and other music, but destroyed a good part of it.

Heward's records were made for Columbia, mostly with the Hallé Orchestra, although he was never its permanent conductor. His major recordings were of Haydn's Symphony No. 103, the *Prince Igor* overture and the *Symphony in G minor* by Moeran. The latter was his finest recording achievement and was warmly acclaimed; writing in 1948, long after it was first issued, the American critic David Hall said (in *The Record Book*, p. 846) 'one of the most thrilling listening experiences in the entire disc literature', although he had reservations about the originality of the music. Heward's command of expressive string playing was beautifully caught in his discs of the Borodin *Notturno*, the Mozart *Adagio and Fugue in C minor*, both with the Hallé Orchestra, and *Eine kleine Nachtmusik*, Tchaikovsky's *Andante Cantabile* and *Rakastava* of Sibelius, these being with the Heward String Orchestra. He also recorded Liszt's Piano Concerto No. 2 (with Petri and the London Philharmonic Orchestra), Grieg's Piano Concerto (with Moiseiwitsch and the Hallé Orchestra), Ireland's Piano Concerto (with Joyce and the Hallé Orchestra) Shostakovich's Piano Concerto No. 1 (with Joyce, Lockwood and the

Hallé Orchestra) and an aria recital (with Hammond and the Hallé Orchestra) as well as Svendsen's *Carnival in Paris* (with an unnamed orchestra for Decca), and Duparc's *Phidylé* (with Teyte and the London Philharmonic Orchestra for HMV).

Hewitt, Maurice (1884–1971). Born at Asnières, France, Hewitt was a member of the Capet Quartet (1908–28), founded and was first violin of the Hewitt Quartet (1928–39), was director of violin and chamber music at the Cleveland Institute of Music (1931–4), professor at the American Conservatory at Fontainebleau (1920–37) and professor at the Paris Conservatoire (1942–54). He founded the Hewitt Chamber Orchestra in 1939 with which he recorded for Discophiles Français; many of these records were released in the United States by Vox and Haydn Society. They were generally favourably reviewed, but none is now available in France or the US. The music recorded included the four orchestral suites of Bach, excerpts from Rameau's *Les Indes galantes*, *Six Concerts en sextuor* and other pieces, Handel's *Water Music*, a dance suite by Delannoy, Mozart's Symphonies Nos 32, 33, 34, 40 and 41, the Divertimento K. 281, the Serenades K. 361, K. 375 and K. 388, *Eine kleine Nachtmusik*, *Masonic Funeral Music*, the Overture K. 311a, the Twelve Minuets K. 585, the Clarinet Concerto (with Étienne), Piano Concertos K. 466 and K. 488 (with Meyer), Beethoven's Symphony No. 7 and the *Coriolan* and *Egmont* overtures, Schubert's Symphonies Nos 4 and 8, and the overtures *Die Zauberharfe* and *In the Italian Style*. Philips also issued a series of five discs under the general title of *Fastes et divertissements de Versailles*, which included music by Leclair, Francoeur, Blavet, Couperin, Delalande, Bernier, Boesset, Thiers du Mont, Marchand, Lefèvre and Clérambault.

Hickox, Richard (b. 1948). Born at Stokenchurch, Buckinghamshire, Hickox was educated at the Royal Academy of Music (1966–7) and was an organ scholar at Queens' College, Cambridge (1967–70), where he conducted for the Purcell Society. His professional debut as a conductor was at a Bach concert at St John's, Smith Square, London; he formed and is musical director of the Richard Hickox Singers and Orchestra with which he performs music from the 14th to the 20th centuries, aiming at being 'stylistically satisfying as well as enjoyable to performers and audiences alike' (*The Gramophone*, January 1978). He is organist at St Margaret's Church, Westminster, music director of the Woburn Festival, and has taken part in the Henry Wood Promenade Concerts, various festivals, radio performances *et al.* With his Singers and Orchestra he has recorded a collection of English medieval carols, the two Bach *Lutheran Masses in G minor* and *G major*, pieces by Albinoni, Pachelbel, Bononcini and Purcell (for Argo), part-songs and other vocal pieces by Parry and Stanford (for Prelude), Byrd's *Mass for 4 Voices* and *Mass for 5 Voices*, and Rubbra's *Missa Cantuariensis, Missa in Honorem Sancti Dominici*, *Dormi Jesu* and *That Virgin's Child Most Meek* (for RCA).

Hidas, Frigyes (b. 1928). Born in Budapest and educated at the Franz Liszt Academy there, Hidas was conductor and musical director of the Budapest National Theatre (1952–66), and was awarded the Erkel Prize (1959). He has composed a symphony, several concertos, an opera, ballets, incidental, vocal and chamber music, and recorded oboe concertos by himself and Haydn (with Pongracz and the Hungarian Radio Orchestra for Hungaroton).

Hilbish, Thomas. After graduating from the University of Miami (1941), Hilbish studied further at the Westminster Choir College and at the Columbia, Rutgers and Indiana Universities, and then privately with Herford in New York (1955–64). He was music supervisor in the Princeton Public Schools, visiting lecturer at various universities, and is now director of choirs at the University of Michigan School of Music and chairman of the conducting department. He has trained choirs to perform with the New York Philharmonic Orchestra under Bernstein and Schippers, and was twice director of the US Universities Chorus; at the Festival of Two Worlds in Spoleto, Italy, in 1969, the University of Michigan Chamber Choir under his direction was choir-in-residence. His recordings include Martirano's *O, O, O, O, That Shakespeherian Rag* (with the Princeton Chamber Singers for Composers Recordings) and Thompson's *Americana*, Carter's *To Music* and Shifrin's *The Odes of Spring* (with the University of Michigan Chamber Choir for New World).

Hill, William (b. 1925). Born in Jackson, Mississippi, Hill was educated at the University of Southern Mississippi and the New England Conservatory of Music, served in the US navy (1941–5), was with the Atlanta Symphony Orchestra (1951–4) and became an associate professor at Georgia State University (1955). In 1963 he founded the Symposium of Contemporary Music for Brass at Georgia State University, and in 1967 toured the Middle East,

Pakistan and Ceylon with a brass ensemble. For Golden Crest he recorded the *Three Equale for Four Trombones* by Beethoven, some dances of Bach and other pieces, with the Georgia State College Brass Ensemble.

Hillis, Margaret (b. 1921). Born in Kokomo, Indiana, Hillis studied at the Indiana University and the Juilliard School (1947–9), and taught conducting at the Union Theological Seminary in New York (1950–60). She founded and was musical director of the American Choral Foundation (1954), was musical director and conductor of the American Concert Choir and Orchestra, New York (from 1950), was choral conductor of the American Opera Society, New York (1952–68), conductor and director of the Chicago Symphony Chorus (from 1957), musical director of the Kenosha Symphony Orchestra, Wisconsin (1961–8), resident conductor of the Chicago Civic Orchestra (from 1967), musical director of the Choral Institute (1968–70), chairman of the department of choral activities, school of music, Northwestern University (from 1970), and musical director of the Elgin Symphony Orchestra, Illinois (from 1971). She has often conducted the Chicago Symphony Choir and Orchestra in choral works, and in October 1977 substituted for Solti to lead a performance of Mahler's Symphony No. 8. Vox issued an early LP of her conducting the New York Concert Choir and instrumental ensemble in Stravinsky's *Les Noces*, *Ave Maria* and *Pater Noster*, and Bartók a collection of Bartók's choral music, with the Concert Choir.

Hilsberg, Alexander (1900–61). Born in Lódź, Poland, Hilsberg was a child prodigy as a violinist and gave a public recital in Warsaw when he was nine years old. After touring through Russia and Poland, he entered the St Petersburg Conservatory in 1910 where one of his fellow students under Leopold Auer was Jascha Heifetz. In 1917 he was engaged as a teacher of violin first at Tomsk Conservatory in western Siberia, and then at Harbin in Manchuria. He founded and played in a string quartet, but in 1923 went to the United States and joined the Philadelphia Orchestra in 1926. Five years later he was appointed concertmaster of the orchestra, and in 1936 made his debut as conductor of the orchestra at its summer concerts at Robin Hood Dell. In 1945 he became associate conductor of the orchestra, successfully substituting for Ormandy on occasion, and in 1947 was made head of the orchestra department at the Curtis Institute. After many engagements as a guest conductor in the US he succeeded Freccia in 1952 as musical director and conductor of the New Orleans Philharmonic-Symphony Orchestra. He made a few recordings: Bernstein's *Fancy Free* coupled with Walton's *Façade* suite (with the Philadelphia Pops Orchestra for Columbia); the Tchaikovsky Violin Concerto (with Stern and the Philadelphia Orchestra for Columbia); and Wieniawski's Violin Concerto No. 2 (with Elman and the Robin Hood Dell Orchestra for Victor).

Hindemith, Paul (1895–1963). Born in Hanau in Germany, Hindemith learned the violin and the viola as a child, played as a youth in cinemas, cafés and theatres to earn his living, and studied at the Hoch Conservatory at Frankfurt am Main; he became leader of the orchestra at the Frankfurt Opera and in 1923 its chief conductor. At this time he was also violist in the Amar String Quartet and was active particularly in the chamber music festivals at Donaueschingen. These festivals gave birth to *gebrauchsmusik*, 'utility music', which was a reaction against the extravagances of late romantic expressiveness, and was intended for specific use and not as a means of personal expression. Although he was recognised as one of the leaders of the *avant-garde* in the 1920s, he rejected dodecaphony; in 1927 he became professor of music at the Berlin State Conservatory and his fame as a composer became widespread. His antipathy to the Nazis' artistic schemes inevitably brought him into conflict with the regime, and finally all performances of his music were banned. Furtwängler was involved in a celebrated controversy with the Nazis in 1934 when he attempted to perform a symphony drawn from Hindemith's opera *Mathis der Maler*, which had as its background the Peasants' War of 1524 and an uprising against authority. Hindemith left Germany for Turkey in 1935, then went to the United States in 1937, was active as a soloist and conductor, mainly of his own compositions, in 1939 became professor of music at Yale University, and in 1946 was granted US citizenship. After World War II he conducted in Europe, settled in Switzerland in 1953, took up an appointment at Zürich University and continued to conduct and compose until his death.

As a conductor Hindemith recorded many of his major compositions. Telefunken issued a 78 r.p.m. set of him conducting the *Mathis der Maler* symphony with the Berlin Philharmonic Orchestra, and later for DGG with the same orchestra he made LP records of the *Mathis der Maler* symphony again, as well as the *Die Harmonie der Welt* symphony, *Symphonic Dances*, *Symphonic Metamorphosis on Themes by Weber, Theme and Variations for String Orchestra and Piano* (with Otte), *Concert Music for Piano, Brass and Harps* (with Haas), *Concerto for Orchestra*, and the overture *Cupid and Psyche*. Telefunken also issued the *Philharmonic Concerto* (with the Berlin Philharmonic Orchestra), and the choral work *Apparebit repentina dies*; Contemporary Records released the *Kammermusik* Op. 24 No. 1 and Op. 36 No. 2 (in which he conducted the Philharmonic Chamber Ensemble), Decca the Violin Concerto (with Oistrakh and the London Symphony Orchestra) and Everest the *Requiem for Those We Love* (with the Vienna Symphony Orchestra *et al.*) and the symphony *Die Harmonie der Welt* (with the Vienna Festival Orchestra), Columbia (US) *When Lilacs Last in the Dooryard Bloom'd* (with the New York Philharmonic Orchestra and the Schola Cantorum), and he also recorded with the Yale University Music School Choir pieces by Dufay, Lassus, Monteverdi, Gabrieli and Gesualdo, and the Bach Motet *Singet dem Herrn*. EMI, on their Columbia label, recorded him conducting the Philharmonic Orchestra in the *Concert Music for Strings and Brass*, the *Symphony in B flat for Concert Band*, *Nobilissima Visione*, Clarinet Concerto (with Cahuzac), Horn Concerto (with Brain) and the *Sinfonia Serena*. Frequently an impressive performer of his own music, Hindemith was more limited as a conductor of other composers. He also recorded, as a violist, his *Trauermusik* and *Der Schwanendrehrer* (with an orchestra conducted by Reibold, for Victor, on 78 r.p.m. discs).

Hinreiner, Ernst (b. 1920). Born in Salzburg and educated at the Mozarteum there (1928–38), Hinreiner saw military service and was a prisoner-of-war (1938–45), and afterwards studied conducting at the Mozarteum (1945–7). He became a repetiteur at the Mozarteum opera school (1947) and since 1947 has been a conductor and producer for Radio Salzburg. In 1951 he founded and conducted the Salzburg Radio and Mozarteum Choir, was appointed professor of music at the Mozarteum (1956), and founded the Konzertvereinigung Salzburger Mozart-Chor (1966). His repertoire is primarily concerned with the sacred music of Bach, Mozart, Haydn, Beethoven and Bruckner, and in 1956 he was awarded the Mozart Medal, in 1964 the title of professor by the Austrian Federal President, and in 1970 the 'Ring der Stadt Salzburg'. His recordings, all with the Mozarteum Orchestra *et al.*, include Schütz' *Resurrection* (for Music Guild), Michael Haydn's *Requiem*, Joseph Haydn's Mass No. 11, Mozart's Masses K. 139, K. 140 and K. 337, *Davidde penitente* K. 469, *Vesperae de Dominica* K. 321, *Exsultate jubilate* (with Rizzoli), *Benedictus sit Deus* K. 117 and *Kyries* K. 322 and K. 341 (for Schwann), and *Lucio Silla* (for BASF), and with the Vienna Capella Academica organ concertos by Werner, Vaňhal, Salieri and Graun (with Haselböck for Schwann).

Hirsch, Hans Ludwig (b. 1924). Born in Memmingen and a graduate of the Academy of Music and University at Munich, Hirsch attended the master classes of Petrassi at the Accademia Chigiana at Siena, and was assistant to Sanzogno, Lehel and Sawallisch. He was founder and conductor of the Munich Vocal Soloists and of the chamber orchestra Florilegium Musicum, and conducted at the Hamburg Opera, the La Fenice Theatre, Venice, and at the Bavarian State Opera, Munich; he has given concerts with the Munich Chamber Orchestra and the Philharmonia Hungarica. Since 1975 he has been artistic director of the International Association Claudio Monteverdi in Venice, and in February 1976 began as conductor and harpsichord player to direct Monteverdi's complete works at La Scala, Milan.

Hirsch has recorded Lassus' *Morescas* and *Prophetiae Sibyllarum* (with the Munich Vocal Soloists for Telefunken); Cavalli's *Messa concertata* (with the Munich Vocal Soloists and the Bavarian State Opera Orchestra for Telefunken); minuets, German dances and country dances by Beethoven (with the Philharmonia Hungarica for Telefunken); Telemann's *Pimpinone* (with the Florilegium Musicum *et al.* for EMI); excerpts from Cavalli's *Egisto*, Pergolesi's *Orfeo*, Mozart's *Exsultate jubilate* (with Donath), and his own Concerto for Oboe, Bassoon and Strings (with the Bavarian State Opera Orchestra *et al.* for Eurodisc); Albinoni's Concertos Op. 7 Nos 1, 2 and 4, Op. 9 No. 3 and Op. 10 No. 1, and Vivaldi's Horn Concerto No. 1 (with Klamand), Trumpet Concerto F. 9 (with Zapf) and Symphonies Nos 4, 7, 10 and 11 (with the Accademia Instrumentalis Claudio Monteverdi for Claves); Scarlatti's *La contessa della stagioni*, Monteverdi's *I grandi lamenti* and cantatas by Scarlatti (for Tudor); and Rossini's *Petite Messe solennelle* (with the Solisti Monaco *et al.* for RCA).

Hlaváček, Libor (b. 1926). Born in Znojmo, in Moravia, Czechoslovakia, Hlaváček learned the violin as a child and studied at the Brno Conservatory and at Janáček's Academy of Musical Arts. As a violinist he was concertmaster at the Brno Opera, the Smetana Theatre at Prague, and of the Prague Radio

Symphony Orchestra, played in the Novák Quartet and the Czech Nonet, and appeared as a soloist in many countries. After studying conducting with Talich and Chalabala, he conducted symphony and chamber orchestras in Czechoslovakia; for some years he taught violin, chamber music and conducting at the Prague Conservatory, formed and conducted the chamber orchestra Musici Pragenses (1962), toured as conductor of the Prague Chamber Orchestra, and in 1972 was awarded first prize at the International Chamber Orchestra Contest sponsored by the Herbert von Karajan Foundation. He is chief conductor of the Middle Bohemian Symphony Orchestra at Poděbrady.

Hlaváček has recorded for Supraphon both as violinist and conductor; he accompanied Josef Suk with the Prague Chamber Orchestra in a highly praised recording of the Mozart Violin Concertos, and also recorded Wieniawski's Violin Concerto No. 1 and Ernst's Violin Concerto (with David and the Prague Symphony Orchestra), Haydn's Piano Concertos (with Kameníková and the Virtuosi Pragenses) and Violin Concertos and Concerto for Piano and Violin (with Matoušek and Adamec and the Prague Chamber Orchestra), Vivaldi's *The Four Seasons* (with Suk and the Prague Chamber Orchestra), viola concertos by Telemann, Handel and J. C. Bach (with Malý and the Prague Chamber Orchestra), Bach's Cantata No. 60, Benda's *Symphonies in F, G, C, E flat* and *G*, Mysliveček's Notturnos, Rosetti's *Notturno in D*, Michna's *Magnificat* and *Missa Sancti Venceslai*, Hindemith's *Five Pieces for String Orchestra*, Roussel's Sinfonietta, Britten's *Simple Symphony* and Honegger's *Prelude, Arioso and Fughetta on BACH* (with the Musici Pragenses).

Hochstrasser, Alois (b. 1941). Born in Waidhofen an der Ybbs in Lower Austria, Hochstrasser studied at the Hochschule für Musik in Vienna under Gillesberger and Uhl, graduated as a conductor and choirmaster in 1965, and continued his studies with Swarowsky, Frank Martin, Gardelli and Celibidache. He was choral director at the Graz Cathedral (1966–71) and director of the choral and orchestral concerts of the Graz Choir, and in 1972 founded the Capella Classica Orchestra, with which he led an annual series of concerts called 'Contact Musical'. He has been a guest conductor with the Graz Philharmonic Orchestra and Lower Austrian Tonkünstler Orchestra, and with others in Austria, FR Germany, Hungary and DR Germany, and is also conductor of the Ensemble Wiener Secession. His recordings have been of the complete *Epistle Sonatas* of Mozart (with Haselböck and the Graz Capella Classica, for Vox), Haydn's *The Creation* (for Preiser), Keiser's *St Mark Passion* (for Calig, Munich), Rimsky-Korsakov's *Mozart and Salieri* (for Preiser), Schmidt's oratorio *The Book with Seven Seals* (for Preiser-Electrola) and Brahms' *Nänie* and *Schicksalslied* (for Preiser).

Hodkinson, Sydney (b. 1934). Born in Winnipeg, Manitoba, Hodkinson studied at the Eastman School of Music, Rochester, at Princeton University with Carter, Sessions and Babbitt, and at the University of Michigan. He taught at Rochester and in New York (1955–8), at the University of Virginia (1958–68), Ohio University (1963–6), the University of Michigan (1968–73) and at the Eastman School of Music (since 1973). He has received numerous awards, commissions, grants and fellowships for his compositions, and his orchestral works have been performed in North America and France. As a conductor he has been active in North America, and has recorded his *Valence* and Harris' *Ludus* (with the St Paul Chamber Orchestra for Composers Recordings).

Høeberg, Georg (1872–1950). Born in Copenhagen, Høeberg studied at the Conservatory there and in Berlin, was a member of the Copenhagen Royal Orchestra, professor of violin at the Conservatory (1910–14), director of the Danish Konzertvereins, and conductor of the Royal Opera (1914–30). He also appeared as a guest conductor at Hamburg and Stockholm. His compositions included an opera, symphonic works, chamber music and songs. He recorded Lumbye's *Indian War Dance* and *Railway* (with the Copenhagen Royal Orchestra for Polydor) and Børresen's *Olympic Hymn* (with the Danish Radio Symphony Orchestra for EMI).

Hoesslin, Franz von (1885–1946). Educated at the university of his birthplace, Munich, Hoesslin studied with Mottl and Reger, whose influence is uppermost in his later compositions. He first conducted at the St Gall Municipal Theatre in Switzerland (1908–11), and then was at Riga (1912–14). After serving in the German army in World War I he resumed his career, conducting at Lübeck (1919–20), Mannheim (1920–22), the Berlin Volksoper (1922–3), Dessau (1923–6), Barmen-Elberfeld (1926), Bayreuth, where he was the Festival director (1927–8), and at Breslau (1932–5). He left Germany to live in Switzerland with his wife, the singer Erna Liebenthal, who had been expelled by the Nazis. He made guest appearances in other European countries throughout his career, and at Bayreuth he led *The Ring* in 1927 and 1928, and *Parsifal* in 1934. In 1927 Columbia recorded him with the Bayreuth Festival Orchestra in the Entry of the Gods into Valhalla from *Das Rheingold*, the Ride of the Valkyries from *Die Walküre* and Forest Murmurs, the Prelude to Act III and Fire Music from *Siegfried*.

Hoffmann, Wolfgang. Born in Karlsruhe, Hoffmann studied with Stiehler, Kempe and Oppel, first conducted with the Leipzig Gewandhaus Orchestra (1940), and has been musical director of the Palatinate Chamber Orchestra at Mannheim-Ludwigshafen. His compositions include a *Christmas Oratorio* and *Requiem*, and he has recorded J. C. Bach's *Sinfonietta in C major*, Fasch's *Symphony in G major* and the sinfonia from Haydn's *La vera constanza* (with the Mannheim Soloists, issued by Nonesuch); Vivaldi's *Cello Concerto in D minor* (with Storck), *Flute Concerto in D major* (with Linde) and *Concerto in D minor* (with the Seiler Chamber Orchestra for DGG-Archiv); Haydn's Piano Concerto No. 3 (with Zartner and the Nuremberg Symphony Orchestra for Colosseum); Richter's *Sinfonia con fuga*, Cannabich's *Sinfonia pastorale*, K. Stamitz's Orchestra Quartet and Holzbauer's Symphony (with a chamber orchestra for DGG-Archiv); Bach's *Die Kunst der Fuge*, Cannabich's Sinfonia concertante, Vogler's *Comic Ballets* and Rosetti's *Symphony in G minor* (with the Palatinate Chamber Orchestra for da Camera, issued in Britain by Oryx); K. Stamitz's *Symphony in E major*, J. Stamitz's Symphony No. 1, Beethoven's *Ritterballet*, Witt's *Symphony in C major*, the overture to Kraus's *Olympia*, Toeschi's Entr'actes Nos 2 and 3, Telemann's *Trumpet Concerto in D major*, Torelli's Trumpet Concerto No. 1, Korn's *Morgenmusik* and his own *Concerto gregorianico* (with Quinque and the Palatinate Chamber Orchestra for RBM).

Hogwood, Christopher (b. 1941). Born in Nottingham, Hogwood studied under Leppard and Dart at Cambridge University, with Puyana in Spain, under Leonhardt and Mary Potts, and at the Charles University at Prague. As performer, musicologist, scholar, writer and broadcaster he has made a major contribution to the revival of interest in medieval and Renaissance music in Britain, was a founder-member of the Early Music Consort in London, and is the regular harpsichordist with the Academy of St Martin-in-the-Fields. He edited for publication music by Croft, J. C. Bach and Purcell, and arranged J. C. Bach's harpsichord concertos for performance on what might well have been the original instruments. In 1973 he founded the Academy of Ancient Music, a complete early classical orchestra playing on authentic instruments of the period; he sees the use of period instruments in performing pre-classical music as important, especially for restoring the balance in favour of wind and brass. In 1975 he was appointed artistic director of the King's Lynn Festival. With the Academy of Ancient Music, Hogwood has recorded for L'Oiseau Lyre overtures of Arne, Purcell's *Elegy on the Death of John Playford*, *Elegy on the Death of Thomas Farmer* and *Elegy on the Death of Matthew Locke*, and a collection of pieces from Purcell's stage works, Geminiani's Concerti Grossi Op. 3, Locke's incidental music for *The Tempest*, Vivaldi's *Stabat Mater*, *Nisi Dominus*, *Concerto in G minor* and Concerti Op. 10 Nos 1 to 6, K. Stamitz's Clarinet Concerto (with Hacker), J. Stamitz's *Symphonies in G* and *D* and *Sinfonia pastorale*, and *Messiah*, in which the attempt is made to reproduce, as closely as possible, an actual performance of Handel's day.

Hollenbach, Theodore (b. 1916). Born in Brooklyn, New York, Hollenbach studied at the Eastman School of Music and with Monteux, and made his debut as a conductor in 1945 with the Rochester Philharmonic Orchestra. He is a teacher at the University of Rochester and Nazareth College, Rochester, and is conductor of the Rochester Bach Festival, the Rochester Oratorio Society, and the Corning Philharmonic Orchestra. He has a special interest in major works for chorus and orchestra, received the Mahler-Bruckner Medal for performances of Mahler's Symphony No. 8, and in 1956 recorded for Columbia (US) Berlioz' *Grande Messe des morts*, with the Rochester Oratorio Society Chorus and Orchestra, which was also released by Philips.

Holliger, Heinz (b. 1939). The eminent oboist Holliger was born in Langenthal, Switzerland, studied the oboe at Berne and Paris, and composition with Veress and Boulez at Berne and Basel. He has been a soloist at many festivals and in many countries, and many composers such as Huber, Wildberger, Veress, Beck, Kelterborn and Wyttenbach have been inspired to write compositions for him to perform. He himself has written incidental, and instrumental music. Acknowledged as perhaps the finest oboist of the day, he has recorded extensively for the instrument, and as a conductor recorded his *Glühende Rätsel* (with Deroubaix and an instrumental ensemble, for CTS, Switzerland).

Hollingsworth, John (1916–63). Born in Enfield, Hollingsworth studied at the Guildhall School of Music, and first conducted the London Symphony Orchestra in 1937. During World War II he was associate conductor of the Royal Air Force Symphony Orchestra, and after the war he conducted various orchestras in Britain, becoming associate conductor to the J. Arthur Rank film organisation (1946–9), musical director of the films division of the Central Office of Information (1947–52), and conductor of the Sadler's Wells Ballet (1950–54). He also was director of the Tunbridge Wells Symphony Concerts, conducted opera at Covent Garden and toured in North America and in some European countries, as well as taking part in festivals. For ten years he was an associate conductor with the Henry Wood Promenade Concerts.

Hollingsworth's records included the *Nutcracker* suite (with the London Symphony Orchestra for Everest), Mackerras's Sullivan arrangement *Pineapple Poll* (with the Pro Arte Orchestra for Pye), *Les Patineurs* of Meyerbeer, a suite from *Hänsel und Gretel*, Sibelius' *Romance in C major*, Svendsen's *Carnival in Paris*, the Dance of the Cockerels from Nielsen's *Maskarade*, the Elegy from Alfvén's *Gustav Adolf II Suite* and *Swedish Rhapsody*, and Grieg's *Elegiac Melodies* and *Sigurd Jorsalfar* (with the Covent Garden Orchestra for EMI), Arnold's *Tam O'Shanter* overture and Ibert's *Le Cirque* (with the Royal Philharmonic Orchestra for Mercury), and suites from *Swan Lake* and *The Sleeping Beauty* (with the Sinfonia of London for World Record Club).

Hollreiser, Heinrich (b. 1913). Born in Munich where he attended the Academy of Music, Hollreiser studied conducting privately with Elmendorff and started his career as a conductor at Wiesbaden (1932). From there he progressed to the opera houses at Darmstadt, Mannheim and Duisburg, was conductor with Krauss at the Bavarian State Opera in Munich (1942–5), general music director at Düsseldorf (1945–52), conductor at the Vienna State Opera and with the Vienna Symphony and Bamberg Symphony Orchestras (1952–61), chief conductor at the Berlin German Opera (1961–4), guest conductor with the Berlin Philharmonic, Vienna Philharmonic, Vienna Symphony, Berlin Radio Symphony, North German Radio and Suisse Romande Orchestras, and with opera companies at Munich, Moscow, Berlin, Tokyo, Montreal, London and New York. He has conducted at the Munich Festivals since 1964, at the Bayreuth Festivals he has led *Tannhäuser* (1973 and 1974) and *Die Meistersinger* (1975), and at the Vienna State Opera conducted *The Ring* (1976). Previously in Vienna he had led the first performance there of *The Rake's Progress* and a revival of *Wozzeck*, and more recently he has been active again at the Berlin German Opera.

Hollreiser's first records appear to have been the overtures to *Tannhäuser* and *Euryanthe* (with the Bavarian State Opera and Bavarian Radio Orchestras respectively, for Mercury). When Vox produced its extensive catalogue with European conductors and orchestras in the first decades of LP, Hollreiser was one of the artists with whom they recorded. His performances were invariably competent and tasteful, in the firm tradition of his German background, if not, ultimately, inspired. His many discs for Vox included the Mozart Piano Concertos K. 238, K. 246, K. 414, K. 450, K. 453, K. 456, K. 466, K. 488, K. 537 and K. 595 (with Haebler) and K. 466 and K. 488 (with de la Bruchollerie), Beethoven's Piano Concerto No. 5, the Grieg Piano Concerto and Tchaikovsky's Piano Concertos Nos 1 and 2 (with Wührer), the Tchaikovsky and Mendelssohn Violin Concertos (with Gitlis) and Concertinos by Stravinsky, Honegger and Janáček (with Klein, and the Vienna Pro Musica Orchestra); Orff's *Catulli Carmina*, (with a Viennese ensemble); *A Night on the Bare Mountain*, the Polovtsian Dances from *Prince Igor*, the *Russian Easter Festival* overture and Bartók's *Cantata Profana* (with the Vienna Symphony Orchestra *et al.*); Stravinsky's *Apollon Musagète* and *Pulcinella* (with the Vienna Chamber Orchestra); the Beethoven Violin Concerto and two Romances (with Gimpel), Schubert's Symphonies Nos 4 and 8, Brahms' Symphony No. 1 and *Academic Festival Overture*, Dvořák's Symphony No. 9, Tchaikovsky's Symphonies Nos 4 and 5, *Invitation to the Dance*, Bruckner's Symphony No. 4, the Bartók *Concerto for Orchestra*, *1812* overture, *Les Préludes*, *Finlandia*, waltzes from *Der Rosenkavalier*, the preludes to *Die Meistersinger* and Acts I and III of *Lohengrin*, the prelude and Liebestod to *Tristan und Isolde*, Strauss's *Metamorphosen* and Stravinsky's *Jeu de cartes* (with the Bamberg Symphony Orchestra); and Tchaikovsky's Symphony No. 6 (with the Trieste Philharmonic Orchestra).

His other records include *Der Barbier von Bagdad* (with the Bavarian Radio Orchestra *et al.* for Eurodisc), excerpts from *Madama Butterfly* (in German, with the Munich Philharmonic Orchestra *et al.*) and from *Eugene Onegin* (with the Bamberg Symphony Orchestra *et al.*), for DGG, *Der Zigeunerbaron* and excerpts from *Die Fledermaus* (with the Vienna Philharmonic Orchestra *et al.*) and *Rienzi* (with the Dresden Staatskapelle *et al.*), for EMI; excerpts from Handel's *Giulio Cesare* and the intermezzo from Strauss' *Capriccio* (with della Casa and the Vienna Philharmonic Orchestra, for Decca), Prokofiev's Violin Concerto No. 1 (with Odnoposoff and the Zürich Radio Orchestra, for Concert Hall); Brahms' Symphony No. 1 (with the Hamburg Symphony Orchestra, for Everest); excerpts from *Der Freischütz*, Chopin's Piano Concertos Nos 1 and 2 (with Harasiewicz), a collection of opera choruses, Wagner's *Wesendonk Lieder* (with Zadek and the Vienna Symphony Orchestra *et al.*), and Křenek's *Jonny spielt auf* (with the Vienna Volksoper Orchestra *et al.*), for Philips.

Holst, Gustav (1874–1934). *The Planets* of Holst is one of the most popular British orchestral works, if the number of recordings made of it is any guide. Holst himself made two recordings: the first was an acoustic one made in 1923, and the second was in 1926, after the introduction of electrical recording. Their separate identification is confused because Columbia replaced the acoustic records with electrical ones with the same disc numbers, with a 'R' after the number to indicate that it was the later recording. The new electrical process at first required that the grooves on the disc should be farther apart with less playing time for each side, so that Holst tended to hurry the later performance, and a certain tension is often apparent. Both performances were with the London Symphony Orchestra, and the second was re-issued by EMI, in surprisingly good sound, in an LP transfer in 1972. Holst was scarcely an experienced professional conductor, and frequently admitted his limitations. Yet he had played the trombone for many years in the Carl Rosa Opera Company and the Scottish Orchestra, and so understood conducting from the players' point of view. According to his daughter, Imogen, 'he knew that many instrumentalists ask no more than a clear beat and gave it to them', a secret shared by some more eminent conductors. Orchestras enjoyed working with him when he conducted his own music, as he had the ability to communicate his enthusiasm to them. His other orchestral works which he recorded were *Beni Mora* suite, *Two Songs Without Words* and the *St Paul's Suite*, all in brisk performances, with the London Symphony Orchestra for Columbia; they were reissued on an LP transfer by Pearl in 1975, together with four songs for voice and violin.

Holst, Imogen (b. 1907). The daughter of Gustav Holst, Imogen was born at Richmond, Surrey, studied with her father at the Royal College of Music, became a music mistress at several schools, and was active with the English Folk Dance Society. Her own compositions include mainly piano pieces and folk song arrangements, and she was associated with Britten and the Aldeburgh Festival. In addition she has written books about her father, Purcell and Britten, and has the distinction of being one of the few women conductors to make records, directing some exceptionally good LP discs of her father's music. The first, of the *Choral Fantasia* and a setting of *Psalm 86* (with the Purcell Singers, the English Chamber Orchestra, Baker and Partridge) was originally for the World Record Club and was one of the first signs of the present revival in interest in Holst's music. Others have included the *Brook Green Suite*, *Fugal Concerto*, *St Paul's Suite*, *Lyric Movement* and the Nocturne from the *Moorside Suite* (with the English Chamber Orchestra *et al.* for Lyrita), the short opera *Savitri* (with the English Chamber Orchestra *et al.* for Argo), *The Golden Goose*, *Capriccio* and *Concerto for Two Violins and Orchestra* (with Hurwitz and Sillito, and the English Chamber Orchestra for Lyrita), and the *Six Choruses*, *Seven Partsongs* and other choral works (with the Purcell Singers *et al.* for Argo). Earlier, among Decca's first LP releases, she conducted the Aldeburgh Festival Orchestra *et al.* in Arne's *Rule Britannia* and an excerpt from *The Faery Prince*.

Honegger, Arthur (1892–1955). Born in Le Havre of Swiss parents, the composer Honegger studied at the Zürich Conservatory and then at the Paris Conservatoire where his teachers included d'Indy for conducting. Throughout his life, composition absorbed him and he had no special reputation as a conductor; as such Scheckel described him as performing 'imaginary tasks of sinewy prowess that rivalled the achievements of Herculean fable . . . he was literally breathless and panting by the time he reached the end of his exertions'. He conducted some of his own music on record, both as pianist and conductor. For HMV with French orchestras on 78s there were his Symphony No. 3 and the prelude to *The Tempest*, for Columbia the Cello Concerto (with Maréchal) and for Odeon *Pastorale d'été*, *Rugby* and *Pacific 231*. It was the last-named work for which he became best known in the

1930s, despite his essential seriousness as a composer. Telefunken and Westminster later issued an LP set in which he conducted the French National Radio Orchestra, soloists *et al.*, in his *Le Roi David*, which has in more recent years become accepted as representative of him as a composer, and has been successfully recorded by Ansermet, Abravanel, Dutoit and others.

Honegger, Marc (b. 1926). Born in Paris and educated at the Sorbonne, Honegger taught at the Universities of Paris (1954–8) and Strasbourg (from 1958), published *La Musique française de 1830 à 1914* (1962) and edited the *Dictionnaire de la musique* (1970–77). Westminster issued an LP disc of Canteloube's *Noëls populaires français*, in which he conducted the Paris Traditional Choir and the Champs Élysées Orchestra.

Hoogstraten, Willem van (1884–1965). Born in Utrecht, van Hoogstraten studied the violin with Alexander Schmuller, then at the conservatories of Cologne and Prague. As a violinist he gave recitals with the pianist Elly Ney, to whom he was married from 1911 to 1927. He started conducting at Hamburg, was conductor at Krefeld (1914–18), conductor of the New York Philharmonic summer concerts (1922–38), associate conductor of the New York Philharmonic Orchestra (1923–5), conductor of the Portland Symphony Orchestra, Oregon (1925–37), director of the Salzburg Mozarteum (1939–45) and from 1949 conductor of the Stuttgart Philharmonic Orchestra. He was a fine conductor with a particular reputation for his readings of Brahms. With Elly Ney he recorded, on 78s for HMV, in the early 1930s, Mozart's Piano Concerto K. 450 (with a chamber orchestra), and Strauss's *Burleske* (with the Berlin State Opera Orchestra). Later, on LP, he conducted the Stuttgart Philharmonic Orchestra in Schubert's Symphonies Nos 2 and 3 (for Period) and Mendelssohn's Symphony No. 1 (for Remington), and with Elly Ney and the Nuremberg Symphony Orchestra Beethoven's Piano Concertos Nos 3, 4 and 5 (for Colosseum, FR Germany).

Hopkins, Antony (b. 1921). Born in London, Hopkins studied at the Royal College of Music with Cyril Smith (1940–44), joined the staff of Morley College where he worked with Tippett and soon was writing incidental music for stage, screen and radio, including music for fifteen productions of Shakespeare's plays at the Stratford-upon-Avon theatre. He became director of the Intimate Opera Company (1952) for which he wrote a number of one-act operas, of which *Ten O'Clock Call*, *Hands Across the Sky* and *Three's Company* were the most successful. Other compositions include ballet scores, piano and vocal music, and the scores for the films *Pickwick Papers*, *Decameron Nights*, *Cast a Dark Shadow*, and others. He has been awarded the Radio Italia Prize several times for incidental music for broadcasts, and has attracted wide attention as a broadcaster and lecturer about music who is particularly effective in analysing and explaining familiar musical masterpieces. He recorded twelve 45 r.p.m. talks on music for Jupiter Records, of which four were subsequently reproduced on a single LP by Classics for Pleasure. His publications include the books *Talking about Symphonies*, *Talking about Concertos* and *Talking about Sonatas*, which cover much the same ground. As a conductor he has long been associated with the Norwich Philharmonic Society, and recorded Delalande's *Te Deum* and *Confitemini*, with the Boyd Neel Orchestra *et al.* for L'Oiseau Lyre, Arne's *The Cooper*, for Saga, and his own opera *Three's Company*. With the Avalon Singers he also recorded his *Riding to Canonbie* and Williamson's *The Brilliant and the Dark* (for Rediffusion).

Hopkins, John (b. 1927). A native of Preston, Yorkshire, Hopkins studied at the Royal Manchester College of Music, the Guildhall School of Music and Drama and at the Salzburg Mozarteum under Zecchi. He conducted student orchestras and from 1946 to 1948 played the horn and cello in the Royal Air Force Central Band and Orchestra. He became first apprentice conductor with the Yorkshire Symphony Orchestra and conductor of the Halifax Orchestral Society (1948–9), assistant conductor of the BBC Scottish Orchestra and conductor of the BBC Scottish Singers (1949–52), conductor of the BBC Northern Orchestra (1952–7), conductor of the National Orchestra of the New Zealand Broadcasting Corporation and music director of the New Zealand Opera Company (1957–63), director of music for the Australian Broadcasting Commission (1963–73) and dean of the school of music at the Victorian College of the Arts at Melbourne (1973). He toured Britain and the Far East with the Sydney Symphony Orchestra in 1965 and 1974 respectively, has been a guest conductor in many countries, and in New Zealand and Australia has done much to expand musical performance and to bring music to wider audiences. His various appointments have given him a proficiency in an exceptional range of musical styles and periods, and he has introduced many new compositions into his programmes.

In New Zealand Hopkins recorded for EMI and Kiwi a disc of overtures by Berlioz, Brahms *et al.* (with the New Zealand Radio Orchestra), two discs of music by Glinka, Schubert, Mahler, Bizet, Rachmaninov and Kodály (with the National Youth Orchestra of New Zealand) and Farquhar's Symphony (with the New Zealand Radio Orchestra, issued in Britain by Oryx). In Australia he has recorded Dvořák's Symphony No. 8 and the Hungarian March from *La Damnation de Faust* (with the Australian Youth Orchestra for Music for Pleasure), Britten's *Young Person's Guide to the Orchestra*, Vaughan Williams' *Fantasia on Greensleeves* and Järnefelt's *Berceuse* (with the same orchestra for EMI), Tchaikovsky's Symphony No. 5 (with the Sydney Symphony Orchestra for EMI), Scriabin's Symphony No. 3 and Goossens' *Sinfonietta* (with the Sydney Symphony Orchestra for World Record Club), Saint-Saëns' Cello Concerto No. 1 (with Homitzer and the Moscow Philharmonic Orchestra for Melodiya and WRC), and two discs of music by Percy Grainger (with the Sydney Symphony Orchestra for WRC). He has also recorded a number of works by contemporary Australian composers: Sculthorpe's *Sun Music I* and *Irkanda IV* (with the Melbourne Symphony Orchestra for WRC), *Music for Japan* (with the Australian Youth Orchestra for EMI) and *Rites of Passage* (with the Victorian College of Arts Orchestra *et al.* for WRC), Le Gallienne's *Sinfonietta* (with the Melbourne Symphony Orchestra for WRC), Butterley's *In the Head the Fire* and Ahern's *After Mallarmé* (with the Sydney Symphony Orchestra for WRC), Conyngham's *Water . . Footsteps . . Time* and Sutherland's *Haunted Hills* (with the Melbourne Symphony Orchestra for Festival), Fowler's *Chimes, fractured* (with the Sydney Symphony Orchestra for Festival), Meale's *Clouds, Now and Then* and *Homage to Garcia Lorca* (with the West Australian Symphony Orchestra for Festival), and *Nocturnes* (with the Sydney Symphony Orchestra for WRC), and *The Display* (with the Sydney Symphony Orchestra for WRC), and Butterley's *Barry Humphries at Carnegie Hall* (with the Sydney Symphony Orchestra for Philips).

Horenstein, Jascha (1898–1973). The son of a Russian industrialist and an Austrian mother, Horenstein was born in Kiev, and at the age of six was taken with his family first to Königsberg and then to Vienna. His mother taught him the piano, and at Vienna he learned the violin with Adolf Busch, studied Indian philosophy at the university and was a pupil of Marx and Schreker at the Academy of Music. In Vienna he conducted a student group, and by the time he was 20 he had determined to be a conductor. When Schreker went to Berlin to the Hochschule für Musik there, Horenstein followed him, and in Berlin he conducted the Schubert Choir. He became Furtwängler's assistant, rehearsed Bach's *Mass in B minor* for him at Frankfurt am Main in 1923, and the next year made his debut with the Vienna Symphony Orchestra with a programme that included the then little-known Symphony No. 1 of Mahler. In Berlin he conducted the Blüthner Concerts in 1924, the Berlin Symphony Orchestra (1925–8), and was a guest conductor for concerts with the Berlin Philharmonic Orchestra in 1926. He gave the première of Berg's *Lyric Suite* in Berlin in 1929 and made records for Polydor with the Berlin Philharmonic. As a young man he came into contact and worked with Schoenberg, Berg, Webern, Stravinsky, Rachmaninov, Strauss, Nielsen, Busoni and Janáček, and performed their music all his life.

In 1929 Horenstein was appointed director of the Düsseldorf Opera on Furtwängler's recommendation. He remained there until the Nazis forced him to leave Germany as he was a Jew, and Düsseldorf was the only permanent appointment he held throughout his life. A second-rate position was never acceptable to him, and he later said that he had never been offered a first-rate one on satisfactory conditions. He went to Paris, and in the 1930s travelled extensively, conducting in Brussels, Vienna, Warsaw and in the USSR, toured Australia and New Zealand, was one of the four conductors, including Toscanini, to conduct the new Palestine Symphony Orchestra, and visited Scandinavia with the Ballet Russe de Monte Carlo. Settling in the United States in 1941, his debut in 1942 was with an orchestra called the Works Project Administration Symphony. He became a US citizen and went on to conduct many of the major orchestras in the US and South America. After World War II he returned to Europe, took up residence in Lausanne, and was in constant demand. In 1950 he introduced *Wozzeck* to Paris, in 1958 conducted a memorable Beethoven *Missa Solemnis* at the Leeds Festival when he substituted for Klemperer, and in 1959 he conducted Mahler's Symphony No. 8 for the BBC, setting off the revival and enthusiasm for Mahler in Britain; in 1961 he led *Fidelio* at Covent Garden, where he last appeared with *Parsifal* just before his death, and in 1964 he presented *Doktor Faust* of Busoni in New York. In London he gave many concerts and was particularly associated with the London Symphony Orchestra, as well as the BBC Northern Symphony Orchestra in Manchester.

Although Russian by birth, Horenstein was a conductor completely nurtured in the German tradition at a critical epoch. In Vienna he was just too late to witness Mahler conducting, but as a youngster he was at concerts conducted by Nikisch, Walter and Weingartner, whose influence remained with him throughout his life. Later he remarked that he could not conduct Brahms' Symphony No. 4, Mahler's Symphony No. 9 or the *Leonore No. 3* overture without recalling the Nikisch performances he heard as a boy. His mentor, Furtwängler, was also a decisive influence; from him he said he learned 'to search for the meaning of the music rather than being concerned with the music itself, to emphasise the metaphysical side of the work rather than its empirical one' (*High Fidelity*, October 1973). A lifelong interest in Indian philosophy with its stress on the spiritual life, and how it should dominate our actions, brought him to the same conclusion. Another conductor he admired was Stokowski, for the width of his repertoire, the sense of occasion he brought to every performance, the number of important works he premièred, and for his profound impact on a vast audience. Even though he was a short and seemingly frail man, he was very energetic and meticulous in preparing works for performance; routine performances would not be tolerated, even from the greatest orchestras, and with less distinguished ensembles he was quick to assess their capabilities and expected nothing less. The result was that he was always able to elicit the highest standard with every orchestra he conducted.

In rehearsal Horenstein played long stretches of the work, to establish continuity, and then proceeded to the details. In the words of Joel Lazar, his assistant in the last three years of his life: 'The exceptional unity and continuity that characterised his performances arose from the way he controlled rhythm, harmony, dynamics and tempo so that each individual moment might receive the most vivid characterisation, but the overall line and cumulative effect would not be lost' (*ibid.*). Horenstein disregarded minor ensemble mistakes to maintain the overall flow of the music. The technique of conducting, and indeed of recording, was not important to him; it was the result that was significant. Seeking ever for the meaning behind the notes he would first start with the literal performance of them, then give careful attention to the particular style of the music and the period and influences at the time when it was written. The imposition of his own self on the music was scarcely possible. His first loves were Mahler and Bruckner and his conception of them was derived from the Vienna of Nikisch, Walter and Furtwängler; in his recording of the *Brandenburg Concertos* he used authentic instruments, including a viola da gamba played by Nikolaus Harnoncourt. In Mozart he was elegant, precise and subdued; with, for example, the trio of the Symphony No. 40 of Mozart he produced an exquisite and profound effect. In his valedictory *Parsifal* at Covent Garden, the orchestra played with a flexibility and delicacy that resembled chamber music.

Before he was 30 Horenstein had recorded Bruckner's Symphony No. 7 and *Kindertotenlieder* (with Rehkemper and the Berlin Philharmonic Orchestra for Polydor); although he fought against it, he ran the risk from the beginning of being categorised as a Bruckner and Mahler specialist. His other 78 r.p.m. recordings of this period included some Mozart overtures, Schubert's Symphony No. 5, Haydn's Symphony No. 94 and two chorale preludes of Bach orchestrated by Schoenberg (also with the Berlin Philharmonic for Polydor). He first achieved international recognition with the records he made for Vox in the first years of LP and later; many were much admired in their day and were the standard against which recordings of the works were judged afterwards. Especially notable were Mahler's Symphonies Nos 1 and 9, *Kindertotenlieder* and *Lieder eines fahrenden Gesellen* (with Foster), and Bruckner's Symphonies Nos 8 and 9. The others, for Vox, were the *Brandenburg Concertos* (mentioned above), Haydn's Symphonies Nos 101 and 104 and *The Creation*, Mozart's Symphonies Nos 38, 39 and 41, the *Requiem* and *Vesperae solennes de confessore* K. 339, Beethoven's Symphonies Nos 3, 5, 6 and 9 (the latter being the first time when the entire symphony was accommodated on one disc) and the overtures *Coriolan*, *Egmont*, *Prometheus* and *Leonore No. 3*, Brahms' Symphony No. 3 and *Variations on the St Antony Chorale*, Dvořák's Symphony No. 9, Bruch's Violin Concerto No. 1, the Sibelius Violin Concerto and Bartók's Violin Concerto No. 2 (with Gitlis), Janáček's *Sinfonietta* and *Taras Bulba*, Liszt's *Faust Symphony* and *Mephisto Waltz*, Prokofiev's Symphonies Nos 1 and 5, the *Chout* Suite No. 1 and *Lieutenant Kijé* suite, the two Ravel Piano Concertos (with Perlemuter), Shostakovich's Symphony No. 5, *Don Juan*, *Till Eulenspiegel* and *Tod und Verklärung*, *Le Sacre du printemps* and a suite from *L'Oiseau de feu*, the preludes to *Lohengrin* and *Die Meistersinger*, the overture to *Tannhäuser*, the prelude and Liebestod to *Tristan und Isolde* and *Ein Faust Ouvertüre*, and Schoenberg's *Chamber Symphony No. 1* and *Verklärte Nacht*. The orchestras in these records were a Viennese ensemble variously called the Vienna Pro Musica Orchestra, the Vienna State Philharmonia and the Vienna Symphony Orchestra, in addition to the South-west German Radio Orchestra, the Bamberg Symphony Orchestra and some Paris orchestras.

Other records made by Horenstein were a mono LP of *Metamorphosen* of Strauss and Stravinsky's *Symphony of Psalms* (with the French National Radio Orchestra *et al.* for Pathé, and issued in Britain by EMI), Tchaikovsky's Symphony No. 6 (with the London Symphony Orchestra for EMI), and Bruch's *Scottish Fantasy* (with Oistrakh and the London Symphony Orchestra for Decca); the Reader's Digest association issued a remarkable group of performances, in their subscription albums, some of which have been issued separately in recent years by RCA. Included were the Beethoven Violin Concerto (with Gruenberg), Dvořák's Symphony No. 9, excerpts from Korngold's *Violanta*, Rachmaninov's four Piano Concertos and *Rhapsody on a Theme of Paganini* (with Wild) and *The Isle of the Dead*, the Schumann Piano Concerto (with Frager), *Siegfried Idyll*, the overture to *Der fliegende Holländer* and the Venusberg Music from *Tannhäuser* (with the Royal Philharmonic Orchestra), Brahms' Symphony No. 1 (with the London Symphony Orchestra), Tchaikovsky's Symphony No. 5 (with the New Philharmonia Orchestra), and overtures, waltzes and polkas of J. Strauss (with the Vienna Symphony and Vienna State Opera Orchestras).

As if in response to an urgent imperative to document Horenstein for posterity, before it was too late, the British company Unicorn made a series of superb discs in 1969–71 with him conducting the London Symphony and New Philharmonia Orchestras, some of which have been released in the United States by Nonesuch. The works recorded were Mahler's Symphonies Nos 1, 3 and 4, the *Mathis der Maler* symphony, *Tod und Verklärung*, Nielsen's Symphony No. 5 and *Saga-Drøm*, some orchestral pieces by Panufnik, and Robert Simpson's Symphony No. 3. Another recording, Mahler's Symphony No. 6, which was recorded at two live concerts in Sweden with the Stockholm Philharmonic Orchestra in 1966, has also been issued by Unicorn, and Mahler's Symphony No. 4 (with the London Symphony Orchestra and Margaret Price) was re-issued by Classics for Pleasure. Other tapes of concert and radio performances by Horenstein exist; one in particular is *Das Lied von der Erde*, in a performance he made for broadcast by the BBC with the BBC Northern Orchestra, with John Mitchinson and Alfreda Hodgson in 1972. It would be a poignant reminder of what are said to be some of Horenstein's last words: 'One of the greatest regrets in dying is that I shall never again be able to hear *Das Lied von der Erde*.'

Horst, Anthon van der (1899–1965). Born in Amsterdam, Horst was educated at the Toonkunst Conservatory, where he was appointed professor of the organ after graduation. He was organist at the English Reformed (Presbyterian) Church at Amsterdam (1918–41), and afterwards was organist at the Netherlands Protestant Association at Hilversum. From 1931 he was conductor of the Royal Oratorio Society and Netherlands Bach Society in Amsterdam and the Royal Choral Society 'Excelsior' at the Hague. His performances with the Bach Society of the *Mass in B minor*, the *St Matthew Passion* and other choral masterpieces brought consolation to large audiences during the Nazi occupation of the Netherlands. His recordings include Bach's Cantata No. 169, Handel's *Dettingen Te Deum* (with the Netherlands Bach Society, for Philips), Arne's Organ Concerto No. 5, Handel's Organ Concertos Nos 4, 8, 14, 15 and 16 and Concerto Grosso Op. 6 No. 6, a Haydn organ concerto, three Vivaldi concertos, the Albinoni *Adagio* and the Corelli Concerto Grosso Op. 6 No. 8 (with organist Klerk and the Amsterdam Chamber Orchestra for Telefunken). All have been on LP.

Horvat, Milan (b. 1919). Born in Pakrac, Yugoslavia, Horvat studied at the Zagreb Academy of Music, and made his first public appearance as a pianist. He also graduated in law. He was first a conductor with the Zagreb Radio Choir (1945), then conductor of the State Philharmonic Orchestra and professor of conducting at the Zagreb Academy of Music (1946–53), conductor of the Radio Eireann Symphony Orchestra in Dublin (1953–8), the Zagreb Philharmonic Orchestra (1958–69), the Austrian Radio Orchestra in Vienna (1969–75), and of the Zagreb Symphony Orchestra (since 1975). Since 1976 he has also been a professor at the Hochschule für Musik at Graz in Austria.

Horvat's first records were Haydn's *Harpsichord Concertos in D major*, *F major*, *G major* and *C major* (with Veyron-La Croix), Mozart's

Violin Concertos K. 216 and K. 219 (with Fournier) and Piano Concertos K. 467 and K. 537 (with Demus) and Mendelssohn's two Piano Concertos (with Gianoli, and the Vienna State Opera Orchestra for Westminster); more recently he has recorded Hindemith's *Mathis der Maler* symphony and Shostakovich's Symphonies Nos 1 and 9 (with the Zagreb Philharmonic Orchestra for Turnabout), the Beethoven Violin Concerto and two *Romances* (with Ozim and the Zagreb Philharmonic Orchestra for Philips), Shostakovich's Piano Concerto No. 1 (with Radic and the Zagreb Philharmonic Orchestra for Philips), music by Kuljerić and Sakač (with the Zagreb Radio Symphony Orchestra for Jugoton), and by Devük (with the Zagreb Philharmonic Orchestra for Jugoton), and music by the Irish composers Bodley, Baydell, Duff, Kelly, Larchet, May and Potter (with the Radio Eireann Symphony Orchestra for Decca, US).

Houdret, Charles (b. 1905). Born in Verviers, Belgium, and educated at the Liège Conservatoire, Houdret became in 1927 the director of the Queen Elisabeth Musical Foundation and in 1937 the director of the orchestra of the Chapelle Musicale Reine Elisabeth, with whom he conducted a number of concerts. He also organised the Concours International Eugène Ysaÿe in 1937–8, and composed orchestral and chamber music. With the Chapelle Musicale Reine Elisabeth Orchestra he recorded for HMV, *c.* 1939, Schubert's Symphony No. 5, and *Don Juan*.

Houtmann, Jacques. Born at Mirecourt, France, Houtmann studied at the Nancy Conservatoire and at the École Normale de Musique in Paris under Fournet and Dutilleux, and won first prize at the Competition for Young Conductors at Besançon (1961). He appeared as a conductor under Munch's sponsorship (1962), studied under Ferrara in Rome (1962), won first prize at the Dmitri Mitropoulos International Conductors Competition (1964) and was then assistant to Bernstein with the New York Philharmonic Orchestra. Since then he has conducted orchestras in France, Italy, Czechoslovakia, Switzerland, Spain, the United States, Canada and South America, was for four years permanent conductor of the Rhône-Alpes Philharmonic Orchestra and is the music director of the Richmond Symphony Orchestra, Virginia. He has recorded three symphonies and the *Grande Messe des morts* of Gossec, with the Liège Symphony Orchestra *et al.* for Charlin and Musique en Wallonie.

Hovhaness, Alan (b. 1911). The son of a professor of chemistry, and of Armenian descent, Hovhaness was born in Somerville, Massachusetts, and studied at the New England Conservatory with Converse and at Tanglewood with Martinů. He taught composition at the Boston Conservatory (1948–51), where he conducted the student orchestra, then moved to New York where he devotes most of his time to composition, receiving commissions and honours from the Guggenheim Foundation, the Louisville Orchestra, and many other institutions. He has been successfully conducting his own music with major orchestras in the United States, and conductors such as Stokowski, Monteux and Reiner have performed his orchestral works. Reiner recorded his *The Mysterious Mountain* with the Chicago Symphony Orchestra. Critics have detected many strong influences in his music, among them Bruckner, Tchaikovsky, Rimsky-Korsakov, Respighi, Sibelius, Messiaen, Vaughan Williams and even Grofé. He conducted his Piano Concerto No. 1 (with Mario Ajemian) and *Tzaikerk* (with Anahid Ajemian, violin, and Kaplan, flute, and an orchestra for Dial), and later conducted recordings of eight of his 25 symphonies: Nos 6 and 25 (with the Polyphonia Orchestra of London, for Poseidon), Nos 9 and 24 (with the National Philharmonic Orchestra for Poseidon), Nos 11 and 21 (with the Royal Philharmonic Orchestra for Poseidon), No. 19 (with the Sevan Philharmonic Orchestra for Poseidon) and No. 23 (with the Highline and Shoreline College Bands for Poseidon), as well as *Fra Angelico*, *Lady of Light* and *Requiem and Resurrection* (with the Royal Philharmonic Orchestra for Poseidon), *Koke no niwa* (for Composers Recordings), *Prayer of St Gregory* (with the Polyphonia Orchestra for Poseidon), *Armenian Rhapsody No. 3* and *Mountains and Rivers Without End* (with the Royal Philharmonic Orchestra for Poseidon), Piano Concerto No. 1 (with Ajemian), *Is There Survival*, *The Flowering Peach*, *Orbit No. 1* and *Lousadzak* (with the Manhattan Chamber Orchestra for MGM, some also issued by Folkways).

Howarth, Elgar (b. 1935). Born at Cannock, Staffordshire, the son of a brass-band conductor, Howarth won a scholarship because of his cornet playing in his teens, attended Manchester University, and after graduating studied at the Royal Manchester College of Music. He played the trumpet in the orchestra at the Royal Opera House, Covent Garden (1958–63), was principal trumpet with the Royal Philharmonic Orchestra (1964–72), first trumpet with the

Philip Jones Brass Ensemble (1966), the London Sinfonietta, the London Brass Soloists and the Vesuvius Ensemble. He first conducted with the London Sinfonietta in Venice, conducted the ensemble in its London concerts, and soon developed a reputation as a conductor especially of contemporary music. He is also conductor of the Percussion Ensemble of London and the Grimethorpe Colliery Band. His compositions include concertos for trombone and trumpet. His recordings include a finely executed Stravinsky programme of the *Octet*, *Dumbarton Oaks* and a suite from *L'Histoire du soldat* (with the Nash Ensemble for Classics for Pleasure), Hsien's *Yellow River Concerto* (with Vered and the National Philharmonic Orchestra for Decca), Xenakis' *Synaphai*, *Aroura* and *Antikhton* (with the National Philharmonic Orchestra for Decca), Rodby's Saxophone Concerto (with Pittel), *Festival overture* and *Variations for Orchestra* (with the London Sinfonietta for Crystal), Ligeti's Flute and Oboe Concerto, and *San Francisco* (with the Swedish Radio Symphony Orchestra *et al.* for Crystal), and music by Birtwistle, Takemitsu, Henze, Elgar, Bliss, Holst, Ireland and himself (with the Grimethorpe Colliery Band for Decca).

Hrnčíř, Joseph (b. 1921). Born in Prague where he studied conducting with Dědeček at the Prague Conservatory, Hrnčíř was a pupil of Talich (1949–50) and of Abendroth in Berlin and Leipzig, and also attended courses on philosophy at the Charles University in Prague (1945–9). He was appointed conductor of the Teplice Symphony Orchestra (1948), the Plzeň Radio Orchestra (1949–51), the Prague Radio Orchestra where he became chief conductor (1957), and was also professor of conducting at the Prague Conservatory (1959–60). He has made many recordings for broadcast, especially of Czech contemporary music, and has conducted abroad. For Panton he has recorded Janáček's *Lenin*, Horký's *Dimitrov*, Šesták's Concerto for String Orchestra, Juchelka's Clarinet Concerto, Kubik's *February*, Kostal's oratorio *Nikola Suhay* and Vacek's *May* symphony (with the Czech Radio Symphony Orchestra *et al.*).

Hubad, Samo (b. 1917). Born in Ljubljana, Yugoslavia, Hubad studied composition and conducting at the music academy there, graduated in 1941, and was appointed conductor at the Ljubljana Opera House a year later. He was its director from 1948 to 1952, was conductor of the Slovenia Philharmonic Orchestra (from 1949), of the Zagreb Philharmonic Orchestra (from 1955) and has also conducted in Vienna, Munich, Zürich and Paris. In 1957 Philips issued a recording of Mussorgsky's *Sorochintsy Fair*, in which he conducted the Slovenian National Opera; for Jugoton he also recorded Bersa's *Sunčana polja*, Skerjanc's Piano Concertino (with Tomšič-Srebotnjak), and operatic aria recitals with Gerlovič and Pospiš (with the Slovenia Philharmonic Orchestra).

Hug, Theo (b. 1906). Born in Berne, Hug studied the violin at the Berne Conservatory and in Paris with Hewitt, Enesco and Studer. He was appointed in 1927 second leader for the Berne Music Society Orchestra, was a member of the Berne String Quartet, a teacher at the Berne Conservatory and conductor of the Berne Radio Chamber Ensemble. With the latter group he recorded Hess's *Salmo* (with Graf) and Sturzenegger's *Fresko* (for CTS, Switzerland), and Schoeck's *Elegie* (with Loosli for Disco).

Hughes, Robert (b. 1933). Born in Buffalo, New York, Hughes studied composition with Chávez and Kirchner at the University of Buffalo (1952–6), with Dallapiccola in Florence (1959–60) and at Darmstadt, studied conducting at the Mozarteum in Salzburg, and composition with Harrison at Aptos, California (1961). He conducted at the University of Buffalo (1956–9), was co-founder and assistant director of the Cabrillo Music Festival (1963–8), bassoonist and assistant conductor with the Oakland Symphony Orchestra (1963–72 and 1976–8), conductor of the Oakland Symphony Youth Orchestra (1964–70), assistant conductor of the San Francisco Ballet (1966–9), conductor of the Western Opera Theatre (1972) and conductor of the Arch Ensemble (1977). He has taught at the University of Buffalo and in universities and colleges in California, has composed a number of film scores, ballets, orchestral, chamber and vocal compositions, and in 1977 was composer-in-residence with the San Francisco Symphony Orchestra. He has recorded Rorem's *Water Music* (with the Oakland Symphony Youth Orchestra for Desto), Pound's *Le Testament* (with the Western Opera Theatre for Fantasy), his own *Cadences* and *Sonitudes* (with the Oakland Symphony Youth Orchestra for Arch) and the soundtrack of the film *One Flew over the Cuckoo's Nest* (for Fantasy).

Hughes, Owain Arwel (b. 1942). Born in Cardiff and educated at the University College, Cardiff, and at the Royal College of Music,

London, Hughes studied conducting with Haitink, Kempe and Boult, and first appeared as a conductor in London in 1968. He has since performed with many orchestras and choirs in Britain, and has recorded Fanshawe's *African Sanctus* (with the Ambrosian Singers for Philips).

Humble, Keith (b. 1927). The Australian-born musician Humble studied first in Australia and then in Paris, where he was assistant to Leibowitz at the Centre de Musique. He performed as pianist and conductor in Europe and the United States, directing contemporary music ensembles, has been a lecturer at the University of California, San Diego, and was appointed there professor and co-chairman of the Centre for Experimental Music and Related Research, and at the same time became in 1974 foundation professor of music at Latrobe University in Australia. He has appeared as a composer and conductor in festivals at Las Vegas and Los Angeles, as a pianist won the National Critics' Award in 1976 and 1977, and at Latrobe University is also musical director of the Australian Contemporary Music Ensemble. With the Ensemble he has recorded for Cherry Pie Stravinksy's *Octet*, Davidovsky's *Synchronism No. 2* and Gerhard's *Libra*, and with the Australian Percussion Ensemble, the Melbourne Symphony Orchestra *et al.* Bonighton's *Sequenza* and other pieces.

Humphris, Ian (b. 1927). Born in Clacton-on-Sea and an Associate of the Royal College of Music and the Royal Academy of Music, Humphris has been musical director of the Linden Singers (from 1950) and the National Westminster Choir (from 1965), and has presented many music programmes for radio and television. He has recorded with the Linden Singers (for World Record Club), and also recorded a fine disc of the choral music of Holst (with the Baccholian Singers of London, the Philip Jones Brass Ensemble and the English Chamber Orchestra, for EMI).

Hunsberger, Donald (b. 1932). Born in Souderton, Pennsylvania, Hunsberger studied the trombone with Stoll of the Philadelphia Orchestra, and played in bands and in a local orchestra. He completed the Doctor of Musical Arts degree at the Eastman School at Rochester, where he was appointed a graduate assistant to Frederick Fennell; he was appointed conductor of the Eastman Symphony Band (1962) and the Eastman Wind Ensemble (1965). He has published wind orchestrations of music from the Renaissance to the present day, contributed articles about the development of wind instruments, and founded the National Center for Symphonic Wind Ensemble at the Eastman School (1973). His recordings, all with the Eastman Wind Ensemble, have been of pieces by Penderecki, Mayuzumi and Williams (for DGG), by Sousa, Reed, Surinach, Nixon, Persichetti, Hartley and Dahl (two discs for Decca, US), by Epstein (for Desto) and a three-record set entitled *Homespun America* (for Vox).

Hunt, Donald (b. 1930). Born in Gloucester, Hunt was articled to the organist Sumsion and became assistant organist at Gloucester Cathedral (1948–54). He was founder and conductor of the Saint Cecilia Singers (1949–54), organist at Saint John's, Torquay and conductor of the Torquay Philharmonic Society, conductor of the Lansdowne Singers (1955–7), organist and choirmaster of the Leeds Parish Church and conductor of the Halifax Choral Society (from 1957). He has also been choral director for the Leeds Festival and conductor of the Leeds Philharmonic Society (since 1962) and the Yorkshire Sinfonia, and a lecturer at the Leeds College of Music. In addition to organ recitals, playing the Leeds town hall organ, Hunt has recorded Parry's *Blest Pair of Sirens*, his own *Te Deum*, the Brahms *Academic Festival Overture* and an Albinoni concerto grosso (with the Leeds Phiharmonic Society for Abbey), and Handel's *The King shall Rejoice*, *Zadok the Priest* and excerpts from *Samson*, *Israel in Egypt* and *Judas Maccabaeus* (with Honor Sheppard, the Halifax Choral Society and the Yorkshire Sinfonia, for Oryx).

Hupperts, Paul (b. 1919). Born in Gulpen, Holland, and educated at Utrecht, Hupperts' debut as a conductor was with the Royal Netherlands Choral Society in Maastricht in 1945. He was conductor of the Limburg Symphony Orchestra (1947), the Utrecht Symphony Orchestra (1949), and permanent guest conductor of the Netherlands Radio Orchestra (since 1973), and has also conducted the Amsterdam Concertgebouw and Rotterdam Philharmonic Orchestras. He is a specialist in contemporary music, has led numerous first performances, and has made many recordings for broadcast of the music of Dutch composers. His recordings include Schubert's Symphony No. 3 and excerpts from the *Rosamunde* music, Brahms' *Academic Festival Overture* and *Variations on the St Antony Chorale*, Bizet's *Symphony in C major*, *L'Apprenti sorcier*, *Les Préludes*, *In the Steppes of Central Asia*, *Finlandia*, *Moldau*, the Polovtsian Dances from *Prince Igor*, Paganini's Violin Concerto No. 2

(with Odnoposoff) and the Schumann Cello Concerto (with Navarra, and with the Utrecht Symphony Orchestra for La Guilde Internationale du Disque), Fauré's *Élégie* (with Michelin and the Haarlem Symphony Orchestra for Concert Hall), Huber's Violin Concerto (with Schneeberger and the Netherlands Radio Orchestra for Wergo) and a series for Donemus of Dutch composers: Andriessen's Symphony No. 1 (with the Netherlands Radio Orchestra), Barren's *Variazioni per orchestra*, Badings' Symphony No. 8, Gilse's *Thijl*, Hellendaal's Concerto Grosso Op. 3 No. 1, Kox's Violin Concerto (with Olof) and *Cyclophony No. 5*, Kunst's *Arboreal*, Landre's *Symphonic Permutations*, Leeuw's *Mouvements rétrogrades*, Mul's *Sinfonietta*, Pijper's Symphony No. 2 and Vlijmen's Sonata (with the Utrecht Symphony Orchestra), Brons' *Prisms*, Fesch's Violin Concerto (with Noske), Kruyf's *Einst dem Grau* (with Melita) and Rosier's Trumpet Sonata (with Marinus, and the Netherlands Chamber Orchestra), Eisma's *Little Lane* (with Coppens), Fesch's Concerto Grosso, Heppener's *Cantico delle creature de S. Francesco d'Assisi* (with Ameling), Kox's *Cyclophony No. 2* (with Werner) and Leeuw's *Spatial Music* (with the Netherlands Radio Chamber Orchestra).

Hurst, George (b. 1926). Born in Edinburgh, his father a Romanian and his mother Russian, Hurst studied the piano with Isserlis, and in his early teens went to Canada and entered the Royal Conservatory of Music at Toronto. He won a prize for composition, and then studied conducting with Monteux. He taught and conducted at the Peabody Conservatory, Baltimore (1947–53), and in 1953 made his debut in London with the London Philharmonic Orchestra. He has lived permanently in Britain since 1955. In 1957 he was appointed assistant conductor of the London Philharmonic, conducted extensively in Britain, visited South Africa to conduct the Cape Town Orchestra, and in 1958 became the principal conductor of the BBC Northern Symphony Orchestra. He has since appeared with orchestras in Canada, FR Germany, France, Switzerland, Denmark and Israel, and in 1968 was appointed artistic adviser to the Western Orchestral Society, which incorporates the Bournemouth Symphony Orchestra and the Bournemouth Sinfonietta. His platform manner is modest and without mannerisms, and he generally conducts without a score; his gestures are precise and evocative. His repertoire ranges from Mozart to Shostakovich, and he shows particular affinity with romantic composers such as Tchaikovsky, Dvořák, Berlioz and Shostakovich.

Hurst made a number of records for the Saga label in the 1960s with the Hamburg Pro Musica and Royal Danish Orchestras; these were of Beethoven's Symphonies Nos 3 and 6, Schubert's Symphony No. 8 and excerpts from the *Rosamunde* music, Tchaikovsky's Symphony No. 5, Bach's Violin Concerto No. 2 and the Beethoven Violin Concerto (with Loveday), Beethoven's Piano Concerto No. 5, Tchaikovsky's Piano Concerto No. 1 and Rachmaninov's Piano Concerto No. 2 (with Fiorentino) and the Schumann Piano Concerto (with Hatto). According to Edward Greenfield in *A Guide to the Bargain Classics*, Hurst's tendency towards fast tempi resulted in exciting moments in these performances, but was disastrous in the Schubert *Unfinished*. An inclination to hurry the music was also evident in a disc of Wagner orchestral excerpts which Hurst recorded for Decca with the New Philharmonia Orchestra in 1971. He also recorded with the Bournemouth Symphony Orchestra a fine *The Planets* (for Contour), and Elgar's *Cockaigne*, *Imperial March*, *Pomp and Circumstance Marches Nos 1* and *4*, *Chanson de matin*, *Chanson de nuit* and *Salut d'amour* (for Polydor), and with the Bournemouth Sinfonietta Elgar's *The Starlight Express*, suite from *King Arthur*, *Sursum Corda*, *Sospiri*, Minuet from *Beau Brummel*, Burlesco from *The Spanish Lady*, and *Adieu*, and Vaughan Williams' *The Poisoned Kiss* (overture), Two Hymn Tune Preludes, *The Running Set* and *Sea Songs* (for Polydor), Holst's *St Paul's Suite*, Elgar's *Serenade*, Ireland's *Concertino pastorale* and Warlock's *Capriol Suite* (for RCA).

Hurwitz, Emanuel (b. 1919). Born in London and educated at the Royal Academy of Music, Hurwitz has been the leader of some distinguished chamber ensembles, including the Melos Ensemble, the Hurwitz Chamber Orchestra, the English Chamber Orchestra, the London Piano Quartet, and the Aeolian String Quartet, who have recently recorded all Haydn's Quartets. He conducted the English Chamber Orchestra in an excellently played disc of pieces by J. C. Bach, Arne, Avison, Boyce, Locke and Purcell (for Decca, released in 1966); later he recorded with the Hurwitz Chamber Orchestra separate discs of concertos by the English baroque composers Stanley and Avison, contributed to a record of sinfonias by J. C. Bach (together with Colin Davis and the English Chamber Orchestra), and conducted the Mozart Violin Concerto K. 216, arranged for bassoon (with Brooke and the Serenata of London for Blenheim).

Husa, Karel (b. 1921). Educated first at the Conservatory (1941–4) and the Academy of Music (1945–7) at his native Prague, Husa received a scholarship from the French Government and studied at the École Normale in Paris, and was a pupil of Nadia Boulanger and Honegger, and for conducting with Fournet, Bigot and Cluytens. One of his early compositions, Sinfonietta, had been performed and received an award in Prague, and further compositions brought the Lili Boulanger Prize (1950) and the Bilthoven Contemporary Festival Prize (1951). He conducted the Prague Radio Orchestra (1945–6), then was conductor of the Belgian Radio and Television Symphony Orchestra (1951–2), the Lausanne Chamber Orchestra (1952–3), and recorded in Paris with the Orchestre des Cento Soli and the Orchestre des Solistes de Paris (1952–3). In 1954 he went to the United States where he has taught at Cornell University, conducted the University orchestra and also the Ithaca Chamber Orchestra. He has been a guest conductor with many orchestras in the US and Europe; his compositions have been frequently performed in many European musical festivals, as well as in the US. His *Music for Prague 1968* has been given more than 4,000 times, and in 1969 his String Quartet No. 3 was awarded the Pulitzer Prize. On his 50th birthday, in one week at the University of Wisconsin, he directed performances of eleven of his important compositions, from every period of his career. He has recorded for Le Club Français du Disque with the Cento Soli Orchestra Brahms' Symphony No. 1, and Bartók's *Two Rhapsodies* (with Erlih) and *The Miraculous Mandarin*, which was the work's first European recording. His other recordings include his own *Mosaïques* (with the Stockholm Radio Orchestra for Composers Recordings), *Nocturne* (with the Orchestre des Solistes de Paris for Composers Recordings), Symphony No. 1 and *Serenade for Woodwinds with Strings, Harp and Xylophone* (with the Prague Symphony Orchestra for Composers Recordings), his own *Fantasies for Orchestra* and Palmer's *Memorial Music* (with the Orchestre des Solistes de Paris for Cornell University), Bach's *St John Passion*, Beethoven's *Mass in C major* and *Missa Solemnis*, Berlioz's *Grande Messe des morts*, Brahms' *Nänie*, Orff's *Carmina Burana* and Honegger's *Le Roi David* (with the Cornell Symphony Orchestra *et al.* for Cornell University), and his own *Music for Prague 1968* and *Apotheosis of this Earth* (with the University of Michigan Symphony Band for Golden Crest).

Huybrechts, François (b. 1946). Born in Antwerp, Huybrechts studied in Brussels, Antwerp and Paris, and with Maderna, and assisted Bernstein in New York. He has been conductor of the Wichita Symphony Orchestra in Kansas. Decca recorded him in 1971 conducting Janáček's *Taras Bulba* and *Lachian Dances* (with the London Philharmonic Orchestra), and later Nielsen's Symphony No. 3 (with the London Symphony Orchestra).

Hye-Knudsen, Johan (b. 1896). Born at Nyborg in Denmark and the son of a conductor, Hye-Knudsen was trained as a cellist, and after four years as a member of the Royal Orchestra at Copenhagen he conducted the orchestra in 1926. Since then he has conducted every form of musical production at the Royal Theatre, and has been with the orchestra for a generation. In addition he has conducted popular open-air concerts in a Copenhagen park, the University Students' Choral Society, has on occasion conducted the Danish Radio Symphony Orchestra, and has also appeared in other Scandinavian countries and in the United States. His most successful composition is his opera *Kirke og Orgel* (Church and Organ), first produced in 1947. Decca recorded him as a cellist in a trio by Riisager; as a conductor he recorded, on 78 r.p.m. discs, Nielsen's *Saga-Drøm*, the overture and excerpts from *Maskarade*, excerpts from *Aladdin* and *Little Suite for Strings*, Grieg's *Elegiac Melodies*, Kuhlau's *The Elves' Hill* overture, Lange-Müller's *Renaissance* overture and incidental music to *Once Upon a Time*, Svendsen's *Festival Polonaise*, Enna's *The Little Matchseller* overture, Lumbye's *Dream Pictures*, Riisager's *Quarrtsiluni*, the polonaise and waltz from Gade's ballet *Et Folkesagn*, excerpts from Nielsen's *The Mother*, and accompaniments for Melchior, Schiøtz *et al.* (with the Copenhagen Royal Opera Orchestra for HMV), the prelude to Børresen's *The Royal Guest* and a suite from Henriques' *The Little Mermaid* (with the same orchestra for Polydor), and Bellman's *Blasen nu Alla* and a capella music by Riisager (with the Copenhagen Student Singing Society for HMV); Vox later issued on the Turnabout label LP discs of him conducting the same orchestra, called this time the Danish Royal Opera Orchestra, in Gade's Symphony No. 1, *Nachlage von Ossian* overture and selections from *The Fairy Spell*, incidental music to *Once Upon a Time* of Lange-Müller, and excerpts from Kuhlau's *The Elves' Hill*.

I

Ibert, Jacques (1890–1962). The French composer Ibert never enjoyed a particular reputation as a conductor, although he was from 1937 to 1955 director of the French Academy in Rome, and assistant director of the Paris Opéra from 1955 to 1957. Nonetheless he made several records of his own music, for HMV on 78 r.p.m. discs: the *Divertissement*, and accompaniments to Chaliapin in songs included in his music for the film *Don Quichotte*. In both sets the orchestras are unidentified.

Iimori, Taijiro (b. 1940). Born in Manchuria, Iimori studied at the Toho Gakuen School of Music and at the Manhattan School of Music under Perlea. He was an assistant conductor at the Fujiwara Opera, Tokyo (1961–4), at Bremen (1967–70), Mannheim (1970–73), at the Bayreuth Festivals (1971–2) and is resident conductor of the Hamburg State Opera and of the Yomiuri Nippon Symphony Orchestra, Tokyo, with whom he made his symphonic debut in 1965. At the Dmitri Mitropoulos Competition for Conductors in 1966 he won fourth prize, took the same award at the Herbert von Karajan Competition in 1969 and was named musician of the year by the Japanese Cultural Ministry in 1973. Da Camera recorded him conducting the Capella Classica at Graz in the Beethoven Violin Concerto, with Camirelli the soloist.

Inbal, Eliahu (b. 1936). A graduate of the Conservatory and Academy of Music at his birthplace, Jerusalem, Inbal made his first appearance as a conductor with the Israel Youth Orchestra in 1956. During his military service he was leader of the Army Symphony Orchestra, and afterwards he continued his studies at the Paris Conservatoire (1960–63) and at conductors' courses at Hilversum and Siena, where he was a pupil of Celibidache. Following the award of first prize in the Guido Cantelli International Competition for Conducting in Novara in 1963, he received many international engagements, and took part in festivals, tours and concerts in Europe, Israel, Japan, the United States and Australia. He has conducted opera in Italy and FR Germany, and in 1974 was appointed chief conductor of the Frankfurt Radio Symphony Orchestra.

Inbal first recorded, with the Ramat Gan Chamber Orchestra for La Guilde Internationale du Disque, Mozart's Divertimentos K. 136, K. 137 and K. 138, and the *Adagio and Fugue in C minor* and Grieg's *Holberg Suite*. In 1969 he signed an exclusive contract with Philips and since then has made a number of records for the company. He has recorded Schumann's four symphonies and his *Overture, Scherzo and Finale* (with the New Philharmonia Orchestra), *La Mer* and *Nocturnes* of Debussy (with the Concertgebouw Orchestra), overtures of Weber (with the London Philharmonic Orchestra), Saint-Saëns' Symphonies Nos 1 and 2, Tchaikovsky's *Fate*, *The Voyevode*, *The Storm* and *The Tempest*, Bartók's *Four Orchestral Pieces*, *Two Images* and *Two Portraits* (with the Frankfurt Radio Orchestra), Puccini's *Messa di Gloria* (with the Frankfurt Radio Orchestra *et al.*), the Beethoven Triple Concerto (with Arrau, Szeryng and Starker and the New Philharmonia Orchestra), works for oboe and orchestra by Bellini, Molique, Rietz and Moscheles (with Holliger and the Frankfurt Radio Orchestra), the complete works for piano and orchestra of Chopin (with Arrau and the London Philharmonic Orchestra) and of Tchaikovsky, and Gershwin's Rhapsody No. 2 (with Werner Haas and the Monte Carlo National Orchestra), and Saint-Saëns' Cello Concertos Nos 1 and 2, Suite and *Allegro appassionato*, cello concertos by Schumann, Khachaturian and Prokofiev, Bloch's *Schelomo* and Bruch's *Kol Nidrei* (with Walewska, and the Monte Carlo National Orchestra). His first recordings, of the Schumann symphonies and the Debussy coupling, invited comparison with performances of the great conductors, and so were a brave venture; although he created an impression, at least in these works, of tending to drive the music too hard, his exceptional talent was generally recognised.

Inghelbrecht, Désiré-Émile (1880–1965). Born in Paris and educated at the Paris Conservatoire, Inghelbrecht first came to public notice as a composer. He directed the Théâtre des Champs-Élysées when it was founded in 1913, and toured with the Swedish Ballet (1919–22), for whom he wrote the ballet *El Greco*. In 1924 he joined the Opéra-Comique, becoming its conductor in 1932. Two years later he founded and was chief conductor of the Orchestre National de la Radiodiffusion française (also known on record as the French National Radiodiffusion Orchestra and the French National Orchestra), which is now one of the two symphony orchestras of the state-owned French Radio. He insisted that the members of the new orchestra should be permanent, should be selected by open competition, that rehearsal time should be generous and that no more than two concerts should be given each week, preferably before an audience. The orchestra quickly became one of the leading ones in France, and was selected by Toscanini for his series of concerts at the Paris Opéra in 1935. Inghelbrecht was appointed conductor of the Paris Opéra in 1945, and Rosenthal then became the orchestra's chief conductor. In 1953 Inghelbrecht accompanied the orchestra on a tour to England and conducted three concerts.

Inghelbrecht was a friend of Debussy late in the composer's life, and gave many performances of Debussy's music when it was not widely known. He recorded, on 78 r.p.m. records for Columbia, the *Nocturnes* (with the Debussy Festival Orchestra), and on LP *La Mer*, *Iberia*, *La Damoiselle élue*, *L'Enfant prodigue* and *Le Martyre de Saint-Sébastien* (with the Champs-Élysées Orchestra *et al.* for Telefunken), *Prélude à l'après-midi d'un faune*, *Nocturnes* and *Marche écossaise* (with the French National Radio Orchestra for EMI), and *Pelléas et Mélisande* (with the French National Radio Orchestra *et al.*, for ORTF). In these performances his precision and special feeling for the composer are well in evidence. On 78s he also recorded *L'Apprenti sorcier* and Chabrier's *Marche joyeuse* (with the Pasdeloup Orchestra for Pathé) and the *Peer Gynt* Suite No. 1 (with an unidentified orchestra, also for Pathé). On LP there was also Fauré's *Requiem*, *Pelléas et Mélisande* and *Shylock* suite, excerpts from *Faust*, the *Peer Gynt* Suites Nos 1 and 2, Dutilleux's *Le Loup*, *Ma Mère l'Oye*, *Rapsodie espagnole* and the complete *Daphnis et Chloé* (with the Champs-Élysées Orchestra, for Ducretet-Thompson, with the *Daphnis et Chloé* also being issued by EMI).

Inghelbrecht was a composer of some distinction; his output included ballets, orchestral pieces, operas, choral music, a *Requiem*, chamber and piano music. In the current French catalogue there are recordings of his *Requiem* and *Vézelay*, a symphonic '*évocation*' for soloists, choir and orchestra, both conducted by Fournet for Chant du Monde. Inghelbrecht himself recorded his charming suite, *Dernières Nurseries*, for Pathé on 78s, and later for Ducretet-Thompson with the Champs-Élysées Orchestra on LP. He also wrote several books and pamphlets about conducting.

Inoue, Michi (b. 1946). Born in Tokyo, Inoue started piano studies at six, attended the Toho Gakuen School of Music and won a conductors' competition in Tokyo. He was artistic director of the Toho Gakuen Symphony Orchestra and associate conductor of the Tokyo Metropolitan Symphony Orchestra, in 1971 won first prize in the Guido Cantelli Competition, conducted the La Scala Orchestra and then many other Italian orchestras, studied with Celibidache, and in the next season conducted in Paris, Cologne, Vienna, Geneva and elsewhere. His debuts in London and the United States followed, and he has appeared throughout Europe, Brazil, South Africa and New Zealand. For Trio Electrics, Tokyo, he has recorded Mozart's Symphony No. 29 and Schubert's Symphony No. 8, *inter alia*, with the Salzburg Mozarteum Orchestra.

Irving, Ernest (1878–1953). Born in Godalming, Surrey, Irving conducted in theatres in London (1900–40), appeared as a conductor in Paris and Madrid, was a member of the management committee of the Royal Philharmonic Society, and in 1935 became musical director for Ealing Film Studios, arranging, composing and conducting music for films. He also wrote incidental music for the theatre. He recorded some of the music by Lord Berners for the film *Nicholas Nickleby*, with the Philharmonia Orchestra, on 78s, for Columbia.

Irving, Robert (b. 1913). Born in Winchester, Irving took piano lessons as a boy and was educated at Winchester College and New College, Oxford, reading Classical Greats. During his last year at Oxford he began studying at the Royal College of Music in London under Sargent and Lambert. He became a repetiteur at Covent Garden, but returned to Winchester as music master in 1936. In 1939 he enlisted in the Royal Air Force and was awarded the DFC twice during World War II. After the war he was conductor of the BBC's orchestra at Glasgow (1945–8), and in 1949, on the recommendation of Lambert, became a conductor with the Sadler's Wells Ballet; shortly afterwards he was appointed the company's music director. In 1958 he was appointed conductor of the New York City Ballet, and has also conducted for the Martha Graham Dance Company, as well as appearing as a guest conductor with symphony orchestras in Europe and the United States. He has a considerable reputation as a conductor of ballet, and is one of the few conductors who have remained a ballet conductor throughout their career. Jack Barnes, a *New York Times* critic, once wrote: 'If you want a reliable concert, just go to the New York City Ballet and shut your eyes.'

Irving recorded after the war on 78 r.p.m. discs, and continued making records for 20 years. Most of his records have naturally been of ballet music, but he has made some in the symphonic repertoire. He recorded for EMI on 78s *Giselle* (with the Covent Garden Orchestra), the *Peer Gynt* Suite No. 2 (with the London Symphony Orchestra), Berners' *Les Sirènes*, the ballet music from *Faust* and Vaughan Williams' music for the films *The Loves of Joanna Godden* and *Scott of the Antarctic* (with the Philharmonia Orchestra); the last-named was metamorphosed into the composer's Symphony No. 7. With the arrival of LP, he went on to record ballet suites from Gluck's music arranged by Mottl and from Grétry's arranged by Lambert (with the New Symphony Orchestra for Decca), Walton's *Façade* Suites Nos 1 and 2, Lambert's *Horoscope*, the ballet music from *Le Cid*, *Les Patineurs* of Meyerbeer (with the London Symphony Orchestra for Decca), the ballet *The Lady and the Fool*, arranged from Verdi's music by Mackerras (with the New Symphony Orchestra for Decca), Debussy's *Printemps* and *Danse* (arr. Ravel), Turina's *Danzas fantásticas* and *La procesión del Rocío*, excerpts from Prokofiev's *Cinderella*, Lecocq's *Mam'zelle Angot* and Glazunov's *Birthday Offering* and a collection entitled *Immortal Pas de Deux* (with the Royal Philharmonic Orchestra for EMI), *Carnaval*, excerpts from *Sylvia*, *Coppélia* and *Swan Lake*, Dohnányi's *Suite in F sharp minor*, Tchaikovsky's *Hamlet* overture, Arnold's *English* and *Scottish Dances* and *Homage to the Queen*, Britten's *Matinées musicales* and *Soirées musicales*, *La Boutique fantasque*, the Dance of the Hours from *La Gioconda*, *Invitation to the Dance*, the *Nutcracker* suite, Shostakovich's *The Age of Gold* and Bartók's *The Miraculous Mandarin* (with the Philharmonia Orchestra for EMI), *Les Sylphides*, excerpts from *Coppélia* and a complete *Sleeping Beauty* (with the Covent Garden Orchestra for EMI), Tchaikovsky's *Valse-Scherzo* and *Souvenir d'un lieu cher* (with Milstein and an orchestra for EMI), a collection of popular orchestral pieces (with the Sinfonia of London for World Record Club), Glazunov's *The Seasons*, Tommasini's Scarlatti arrangement *The Good-humoured Ladies*, and Walton's Bach arrangement *The Wise Virgins* (with the Concert Arts Orchestra for Capitol, USA), the Liszt Piano Concerto No. 1 and *Hungarian Fantasy* (with Bolet and the Symphony of the Air for Everest), Gounod's Symphony No. 1, Bizet's *Symphony in C major*, Stravinsky's *Agon* and *L'Oiseau de feu*, a complete *Nutcracker*, Kay's *Western Symphony* and *Stars and Stripes*, and Tchaikovsky's Piano Concerto No. 3 (with Sadoff, and the New York City Ballet Orchestra for Kapp). Irving's last records were for Capitol in 1964–6, and were Bernstein's *Fancy Free* and *Facsimile*, Copland's *Appalachian Spring* and *Rodeo* (with the Concert Arts Orchestra).

Iturbi, José (b. 1895). Born in Valencia, Spain, Iturbi learned the piano as a child, and by the age of seven was virtually a professional pianist, playing in cinemas and dance halls. At eight he entered the Valencia Conservatory, went to Barcelona to study with Joaquin Malats, and then, with financial assistance from well-wishers in Valencia, studied at the Paris Conservatoire. After graduating he moved to Switzerland, played in a fashionable café, and became a teacher in the Geneva Conservatoire. His reputation as a concert pianist grew throughout Europe, and by 1930 he had toured the United States several times, performing with great success, especially the music of Mozart and of Spanish composers. His first appearance as a conductor was in Mexico City in 1933, and after guest engagements in New York and Philadelphia he was appointed permanent conductor of the Rochester Philharmonic Orchestra in 1936, where he remained until 1944. In those years he conducted the major US orchestras, toured with Ormandy and the Philadelphia Orchestra, and made his conducting debut in London. Occasionally he conducted the orchestra from the keyboard in concerts by Mozart, Grieg and Liszt, although not always with complete success. His volatile temperament made him the centre of many controversies; once he stopped a broadcast concert because he objected to the sentimental popular songs he found he had to accompany, and on another occasion he refused to appear on the same programme with the Benny Goodman Sextet on the grounds that jazz and symphonic music did not mix. Hollywood starred him in a film when he was cast as himself, and he afterwards made several films. As a conductor, he was at first highly praised, but later he attracted criticism since his performances seemed too concerned with striving for exaggerated effects.

Apart from his solo piano recordings, Iturbi made 78 r.p.m. records of Mendelssohn's Symphony No. 3, Dvořák's Symphony No. 9 and Gould's *American Symphonette No. 4* (with the

Rochester Philharmonic Orchestra for Victor); these were acclaimed as fine performances. Conducting from the keyboard he recorded Mozart's Piano Concertos K. 466 and K. 365 (with his sister Amparo in the latter), and the Beethoven Piano Concerto No. 3 (with the Rochester Philharmonic Orchestra for Victor), the Mendelssohn Piano Concerto No. 1 and the Liszt Piano Concerto No. 1 (with the Victor Symphony Orchestra for Victor) and Liszt's *Hungarian Fantasia* (with the Valencia Symphony Orchestra for HMV). With the Valencia Symphony Orchestra, for HMV, he also recorded dances from *The Three-cornered Hat*, Palau-Boix's *Marcha burlesca* and *Seguidillas*, and Rodrigo's *Homenaje a la Tempranica*.

Ivanov, Konstantin (b. 1907). The Russian conductor Ivanov was born at Yefremov in the Tula district, studied at the Moscow Conservatory under Ginzburg, and graduated in 1937. He was conductor of the Red Army Theatre (1935–7), won third prize at the State Conductors' Competition in Moscow (1938), was conductor of the USSR State Symphony Orchestra (1938–9), of the Stanislavski Opera House (1939–41), the Moscow Radio Symphony Orchestra (1941–6), then was principal conductor of the USSR State Symphony Orchestra (1946–65), touring Czechoslovakia with the latter orchestra in 1949–50. He was awarded the Stalin Prize in 1949 and in 1958 the title People's Artist of the USSR. In the years 1960–62 he conducted in the United States, Canada, Austria, France and again in Czechoslovakia.

With the exception of Beethoven's Symphony No. 1, which he recorded in Romania, Ivanov has made 78 r.p.m. and LP records with the USSR State Symphony and the USSR Radio Symphony Orchestras for Melodiya. Included have been Beethoven's Symphonies Nos 3, 7 and 8 and the *Leonore No. 3* overture, Rimsky-Korsakov's *Antar*, Tchaikovsky's Symphonies Nos 1, 2, 3, 4 and 5, the Piano Concerto No. 1 (with Gilels), the *Romeo and Juliet* fantasy-overture, and *The Voyevoda*, Borodin's Symphonies Nos 1 and 2, Balakirev's *Russia* and *Tamar*, Glazunov's Symphonies Nos 1, 5 and 6, Rachmaninov's Piano Concerto No. 2 (separately with Nikolayeva and Krainev), and Piano Concerto No. 3 (with Nikolayeva and Oborin), Scriabin's Symphony No. 3, Miaskovsky's Symphonies Nos 5, 16 and 21, the overture to *Russlan and Ludmilla*, Liadov's two *Polonaises*, *Kikimora*, *The Enchanted Lake* and *Baba Yaga*, Eschpai's Symphony No. 2 and his own Symphony No. 9. Tchaikovsky's Symphony No. 4 and the Glinka overture were released on mono LP by DGG; Supraphon issued Glazunov's Symphony No. 5 in which he conducted the Czech Philharmonic Orchestra, and on 78s Columbia released some discs of him conducting a dance suite by Rakov, with the Moscow State Philharmonic Orchestra. Critical assessment of these performances is difficult to find; he is known to be averse to recording, believing that an audience is necessary to inspire the orchestra and conductor.

In the USSR and Eastern Europe there is also a disc available in which Ivanov conducts the USSR State Symphony Orchestra in the Tchaikovsky *1812* overture and *Marche slave*. Western listeners would be surprised to hear these versions of these familiar scores; the Soviet composer Schebalin arranged them so that the Tsar's hymn is replaced by a chorus from Glinka's *A Life for the Tsar*.

Iwaki, Hiroyuki (b. 1932). Born in Tokyo, Iwaki was a percussion student at the Tokyo Music Academy and also a graduate of the Tokyo Art University. He was assistant conductor of the NHK Symphony Orchestra (1956), studied with Karajan, and conducted in Vienna and Berlin. He became conductor of the NHK Symphony Orchestra and toured with it in the United States, and has been a guest conductor with many of the major orchestras in Europe. In 1974 he was appointed chief conductor of the Melbourne Symphony Orchestra in Australia. His records include Beethoven's Symphony No. 9 (with the NHK Symphony Orchestra *et al.* for Vox), pieces by the Japanese composers Mayuzumi, Miyoshi and Takemitsu (with the same orchestra for Odyssey), Liszt's *Hungarian Rhapsodies Nos 2*, *5*, *6*, *12* and *15* (with the Vienna State Opera Orchestra for La Guilde Internationale du Disque), Messiaen's *Couleurs de la cité céleste*, *Oiseaux exotiques*, *Réveil des oiseaux* and *Sept Haï-Kaï* (with Kimura and the Tokyo Concerts Orchestra for Decca), Bartók's *Concerto for Orchestra* and the prelude and Liebestod from *Tristan und Isolde* (with the Melbourne Symphony Orchestra for RCA), and music by the Dutch composers Ruyneman (*Hieroglyphs*) and Vermeulen (Symphony No. 2), with the Hague Philharmonic Orchestra for Donemus.

J

Jackson, Frederick (1905–72). After studying at the Royal Academy of Music, London, Jackson joined the staff of the Academy and became noted as an outstanding piano teacher and choral conductor. From 1947 he was the conductor of the London Philharmonic Choir, and in 1961 Saga issued an LP set of him conducting the Choir and the London Philharmonic Orchestra with soloists Harper, Watts, Robertson and Stalman in *Messiah*; at the end of 1977 this recording was still in the catalogue. The performance was a traditional one, in that a large choir was employed. Jackson's enthusiasm and unconventional repertoire were famous. He died while conducting the Verdi *Requiem* at the Royal Academy of Music.

Jackson, Francis (b. 1917). Born in Malton, Yorkshire, Jackson studied with Bairstow, was organist at Malton Park Parish Church (1933–40) and became organist and master of the music at York Minster in 1946, and conductor of the York Musical Society and of the York Symphony Orchestra. He has given organ recitals throughout Britain, in Europe and in Canada, and has written a symphony, choral and organ music. He has made many records as an organist, and Columbia issued 78 r.p.m. discs of him conducting the York Minster Choir in anthems and sacred music by Byrd, Tallis, Stanford, Bairstow, Child, Ouseley, Walford-Davies, C. H. Wood, Gray and Goss, which were included in the *Anthology of English Church Music*.

Jacob, Bernard (b. 1918). Born in Calcutta, Jacob attended the Calcutta School of Music, then studied at Balliol College, Oxford, and made his debut as a conductor with the Oxford University Orchestra in 1938. He conducted orchestras in Calcutta (1953–69) and from 1952 has conducted concerts in London, more recently with the London Mozart Players. His programmes include works of all periods not frequently heard, and he has also conducted in Holland, Scandinavia, Greece, Japan and Israel. Unicorn recorded him in 1973 conducting the London Mozart Players in clarinet concertos by Copland and Crusell, with de Peyer the soloist.

Jacobi, Frederick (1891–1952). Born in San Francisco, Jacobi studied in New York and Berlin, and in the United States with Bloch. He was an assistant conductor at the New York Metropolitan Opera (1913–17), taught at the Juilliard School of Music, and received awards from the Society for the Publication of American Music for his compositions. SPA (Society of Participating Artists) issued recordings of his Violin Concerto (with Gertler) and *Concertino* (with Irene Jacobi), which he conducted.

Jacques, Reginald (1894–1969). Born in Ashby-de-la-Zouch, the English conductor, organist, and musical scholar Jacques studied at Queen's College, Oxford. He was severely wounded during World War I. On his return to Oxford, he came under the influence of Hugh Allen, and took his degree of Doctor of Music. In 1926 he became organist at Queen's College, conductor of the Oxford Harmonic Society (1923–30), and director of the Oxford Orchestral Society (1930–36). From 1932 to 1960 he was music director of the Bach Choir, which had been founded in London in 1875, and numbered among its previous conductors Otto Goldschmidt, Stanford, Allen, Vaughan Williams and Boult. Jacques left Oxford in 1936, and then founded the Jacques String Orchestra, which became a much-appreciated institution in British musical life. He was also director of music for the Council for the Encouragement of Music and the Arts (1940–45), which later became the Arts Council of Great Britain, and taught at the Royal College of Music. His compositions included songs and choral arrangements, and he wrote a perceptive text-book, *Voice Training in Schools*.

Jacques was known for his devoted performances of the great Bach and Handel choral works. His major, and undoubtedly his best, recording was for Decca, an almost complete *St Matthew Passion*, in English and on 21 78 r.p.m. discs. Sackville-West and Shawe-Taylor in *The Record Guide* (1951) described this performance as 'typical of the English style which has been developed over many years; its great merit is the rich and vigorous choral singing and the straightforward, unromantic conception of the music'. By present-day conventions of Bach performance, Jacques' reading would be considered as anachronistic. He also recorded with his orchestra for Columbia on 78s the minuet from Handel's *Berenice*, three dances from

Purcell's *The Fairy Queen* and his *Rejoice in the Lord Alway*, Holst's *St Paul's Suite*, Vaughan Williams' *Fantasia on Greensleeves*, Foulds' *Celtic Lament* and Howells' *Elegy* (for viola, string quartet and string orchestra); for Decca there was the opening chorus from Bach's Cantata No. 140 and *Jesu Joy of Man's Desiring* from Cantata No. 147 (with the Cantata Singers and the Jacques Orchestra). Among the early LPs issued by Decca in 1950 were several of Jacques conducting Bach's Cantatas Nos 11 and 67 and the Motets *Komm, Jesu, komm* and *Der Geist hilft unserer Schwachheit auf* (with the Cantata Singers and the Jacques Orchestra). Kathleen Ferrier's participation in the cantatas has assured their frequent reissue.

Jacquillat, Jean-Pierre (b. 1935). Born in Versailles and educated at the Paris Conservatoire, Jacquillat studied conducting with Dervaux, Cluytens and Munch, and was first percussion player in the Paris Opéra Orchestra. After he took over the leadership of a small orchestra in Paris, his success attracted attention and led to engagements with some of the major French orchestras. He first conducted opera at Lyon in 1967; in that year he was appointed assistant conductor to Munch with the newly formed Orchestre de Paris, and with the orchestra toured the USSR and North America. He has since been a frequent guest conductor in Western and Eastern Europe, North and South America, and in France has conducted at the Paris and Lyon Opéras, and with major Parisian and provincial orchestras. He has now succeeded Markevitch as conductor of the Lamoureux Orchestra.

Jacquillat made some fine records for Pathé Marconi in 1969–70 with the Paris Orchestra, some of which were released in Britain by EMI. They included *L'Apprenti sorcier*, *Danse macabre*, *Pavane pour une infante défunte*, *España*, *Prélude à l'après-midi d'un faune*, a scherzo by Lalo, Berlioz's arrangement of *La Marseillaise*, Roussel's *Suite in F*, *Pour une fête de printemps*, Concertino for cello (with Tétard) and Piano Concerto (with Laval), Hahn's *Le Bal de Béatrice d'Este*, Messager's *Les Deux Pigeons* and excerpts from *Isoline*. In these performances he revealed himself as a sensitive and accomplished artist, not obsessed by effect for its own sake. In 1973 EMI also issued a disc in which he accompanied de Los Angeles with the Lamoureux Orchestra in Chausson's *Poème de l'amour et de la mer* and Canteloube's arrangements of *Chants d'Auvergne*; a second disc of Canteloube's songs was later released.

Jaeggi, Oswald (1913–63). Born in Basel, Jaeggi studied at the Papal Academy of Music in Rome (1937–40), conducted at Einsiedeln (1947–9), at St Augustin's Church at Bozen-Gries (1950) and with the Leonhard Lechner Chamber Chorus (1952), touring with these choirs in many countries. He premièred contemporary compositions, including Křenek's *Missa duodecim tonorum*, conducted at Innsbruck and in other cities, taught children singing and was responsible for sacred music on the German programme of Radio Italiana. He has recorded his own *Proprium 'Dum Clamarem'* (with the Innsbruck Symphony Orchestra *et al.* for Fono).

Jahoda, Fritz (b. 1909). Born in Vienna where he studied at the University (1928–30), Jahoda conducted opera at Düsseldorf (1930–33) and Graz (1934–8), and then migrated to the United States in 1939, becoming a US citizen in 1945. He was a professor at the New York City University (1946–74), was a member of the New York Trio (1951–61), and returned to Vienna to conduct in 1947 and 1958. For Composers Recordings he conducted the CRI Chamber Ensemble in Brunswick's *Septet in Seven Movements*.

Jakus, Jean (b. 1918). A Belgian, born in Calais, Jakus studied at the University of Louvain, the Royal Conservatory of Music in Brussels and at the Hochschule für Musik at Heidelberg, studied conducting under Kleiber and van Kempen, and was assistant to Markevitch at the Salzburg Mozarteum. He has conducted many orchestras in Europe, particularly radio symphony orchestras in Berlin, Luxembourg, Dublin and Saarbrücken. In 1958 he founded the Choir of the European Communities, and in 1974 also founded the European Philharmonic Orchestra which was made up from young prize-winners from academies of music in the member states of the European Economic Community. His records include four symphonies by the 18th-century composer Pierre van Maldere (with the Liège Soloists, for Polydor), the two Mozart Flute Concertos (with Magnin), Bach's Suite No. 3 and Handel's *Water Music* and *Music for the Royal Fireworks* (with the Heidelberg Chamber Orchestra for Da Camera).

Jalas, Jussi (b. 1908). Born in Jyväskylä in Finland, Jalas was educated at the Sibelius Conservatory and Helsinki University, and studied in Paris with Monteux and Rhené-Baton. He was a member of the Sibelius Conservatory, teaching composition and conducting, and has conducted the Finnish National Opera (1945), the Helsinki City Symphony Orchestra and the Finnish Radio Orchestra, as well as appearing as a guest conductor in Europe, the United States, Japan and South Africa. He is a son-in-law of Sibelius, and was responsible for the first performance of the *Kullervo* symphony, written by Sibelius in his youth and forbidden performance in his lifetime. In the opera house, Jalas' repertoire ranges from Puccini to Berg and Shostakovich. He has recorded Sibelius' *Four Legends*, *In Memoriam*, incidental music for *The Tempest*, *Scaramouche*, *Finlandia*, *Kuolema*, *Scènes historiques* Sets 1 and 2, *King Christian II* Suite, *Swanwhite* Suite and *Andante festivo* (with the Hungarian State Symphony Orchestra for Decca), *Suite champêtre* (with the Finnish Radio Orchestra for Symfonie, Finland), and excerpts from *Pelléas et Mélisande* and *The Tempest* music (with the Finnish Radio Orchestra for Rytmi, Finland), Leif's *Saga Heroes Symphony* (with the Iceland Symphony Orchestra for ITM), and recitals of operatic arias (with Sills and Treigle, and the Vienna Radio Orchestra for Westminster).

James, Philip (b. 1890). Born in Jersey City, James was a bandmaster in the American Expeditionary Force in World War I, was a conductor with the Victor Herbert Opera Company (1919–22), the New Jersey Symphony Orchestra (1922–9), the Brooklyn Orchestral Society (1927–30), the Bamberger Little Symphony (1926–36), and taught music at Columbia and New York Universities. He has composed symphonic and other music, and before 1941 he recorded, for Victor, Hadley's *October Twilight* and *Concertino* (with Howard and the Victor Symphony Orchestra).

Jancsovics, Antal (b. 1937). Born at Orosháza, Hungary, Jancsovics was, as a schoolboy, a member of the Györ Philharmonic Orchestra, and then studied conducting with Kórody at the Franz Liszt Academy in Budapest, where he found an interest in performing rare and old music. He graduated in 1963, joined the Budapest State Opera, was chief conductor of the Franz Liszt Symphony Orchestra and director of the conservatory at Sopron in West Hungary (1967), took third place in the international competition at the Accademia di Santa Cecilia in Rome (1968), won praise at the Dmitri Mitropoulos Competition in New York (1969), was director of the Györ Conservatory (1970–72) and was appointed principal conductor of the Györ Philharmonic Orchestra (1975). In addition, he has toured in the USSR, Eastern and Western Europe, North and South America. For Hungaroton he has recorded a recital of Mozart arias (with Réti), the Grieg Piano Concerto and the Ravel *Piano Concerto in G* (with Jando, and the Budapest Philharmonic Orchestra), the Schumann and Lalo Cello Concertos (with Onczay), the preludes to *Die Meistersinger* and *Parsifal*, the overture to *Tannhäuser* and *Ein Faust Ouvertüre* (with the Budapest Symphony Orchestra) and Brahms' Piano Concerto No. 1 (with Falvai and the Hungarian State Symphony Orchestra).

Janigro, Antonio (b. 1918). Born in Milan and a graduate of the Conservatory there, Janigro studied further with Alexanian in Paris, and became internationally celebrated as a solo cellist. His recording of *Don Quixote* with Reiner and the Chicago Symphony Orchestra, originally released in 1961, still holds its place in the catalogue. He also teamed with Paul Badura-Skoda and Jean Fournier in a trio that made many superb discs for Westminster in the 1950s. He joined the Zagreb Conservatory in Yugoslavia in 1939, where he was in charge of the advanced cello class until 1953. He was the conductor of the Zagreb Radio-Television Orchestra (1954–64), founder and conductor of the orchestra I Solisti di Zagreb (1954–67), conductor of the Angelicum Orchestra in Milan (1965–7), and then conductor of the Saar Chamber Orchestra after the death of Ristenpart in 1968. From 1965 he was also in charge of the advanced cello class at the Robert Schumann Conservatory at Düsseldorf. He has appeared as a guest conductor with orchestras in many countries and has taken part in numerous international festivals.

Janigro's records as a conductor, with I Solisti di Zagreb and the Milan Angelicum Orchestra, were significant, and paramount amongst them were the six Haydn symphonies, Nos 44 to 49, which were issued by Philips in Britain; at their time in 1965 they were an important addition to Haydn's recorded symphonies. They were performed with exemplary finesse and style. His other records with the Zagreb orchestra included some concerti grossi by Torelli and Corelli, Purcell's *Sonata in D for Trumpet and Strings* and trumpet overture to *The Indian Queen*, pieces by Couperin, Pergolesi and Telemann, many concertos of Vivaldi including *The Four Seasons* (with Tomasow), the eight symphonies of Boyce, Bach's Suite No. 2, *Brandenburg Concerto No. 5*, some chorales, the Flute, Violin and Harpsichord Concerto (with Tripp, Pinkava and Heiller) and the Violin and Oboe Concerto (with Klima and Lardrot), oboe concertos by Bellini, Donizetti, Salieri and Boccherini (with

Lardrot), Leopold Mozart's *Toy Symphony*, Haydn's *Die sieben letzten Worte des Erlösers am Kreuz*, Mozart's Divertimentos K. 136, K. 137 and K. 138, *Eine kleine Nachtmusik*, *Serenata notturna* and Piano Concertos K. 271 and K. 449 (with Brendel), Rossini's String Sonatas, Britten's *Simple Symphony*, Respighi's *Ancient Airs and Dances* Suite No. 3, Barber's *Adagio for Strings*, Shostakovich's *Scherzo*, Webern's *Five Movements for Strings*, Roussel's Sinfonietta and an aria recital by Forrester. These performances were issued on many labels, such as Bach Guild, Mercury, Philips, Vanguard and RCA; Vanguard also released a three-disc set entitled *The Virtuoso Trumpet*, in which Helmut Wobisch and several others played trumpet concertos by baroque composers, and another set of two discs for the Bach Guild demonstrated the art of ornamentation and embellishment in the Renaissance and baroque periods. His other records include Bach's Cantatas Nos 51 and 199, Schubert's *Mass in A flat*, and the Bruckner *Te Deum* and five Motets (with the Angelicum Orchestra and the Italian Polyphonic Chorus for Angelicum, and issued in the US by Musical Heritage Society), Bach's Cantatas Nos 53, 54 and 169 (with the Vienna Chamber Orchestra *et al.* for Bach Guild), Haydn's Symphonies Nos 22 and 26, and the overtures to *L'Isola disabitata* and *Orlando Paladino*, *La Boutique fantasque* and *Rossiniana* (with the Vienna Festival Orchestra for Vanguard), and Ligeti's *Ramifications* (with the Saar Radio Chamber Orchestra for Wergo).

Janowski, Marek (b. 1941). Janowski was born in Warsaw and was raised in Wuppertal in Germany. He studied mathematics and later music at Cologne University, for a short time studied in Vienna and then attended the Accademia Chigiana in Siena. He conducted concerts in Italy, at the age of 20 was a repetiteur at Aachen, and a year later was a conductor at the Cologne Opera. His first important appointment was in 1964 as first conductor at the Deutsche Oper am Rhein in Düsseldorf; two years later he moved to Hamburg and became first conductor there (1969–74), also making guest appearances at Stuttgart, Cologne and Munich. In 1970 he visited London with the Cologne Opera and led the British première of Henze's *Der junge Lord*, and later conducted at the Paris Opéra and with the Dresden Staatskapelle. In 1973 he was appointed general music director at Dortmund. His operatic repertoire ranges from Mozart to Strauss and Wagner, but he believes strongly that young conductors should conduct modern music. His few recordings have been unusual and of special interest; in the early 1970s he recorded for Philips Penderecki's *The Devils of Loudun* (with the Hamburg State Opera), and for EMI the overtures to *Die Feen* and *Liebesverbot* and some marches of Wagner (with the London Symphony Orchestra). In 1976, 150 years after the death of Weber, EMI issued the first recording of *Euryanthe*, in which Janowski directed a superbly realised performance with the Dresden Staatskapelle, the Leipzig Radio Chorus and a strong Western cast.

Jansons, Arvid (b. 1914). Born in Liepāja, Latvia, Jansons studied at the conservatories at Liepāja and Leipzig, and was a violinist in opera and ballet orchestras in Latvia. He conducted the Riga Opera and Philharmonic Orchestra (1944–52), and then became a conductor with the Leningrad Philharmonic Orchestra (1952). He was a guest conductor in other cities, toured abroad with the Leningrad Philharmonic Orchestra, and was awarded the State Prize of the USSR (1951). He has recorded Tchaikovsky's Symphony No. 3 and Suite No. 1 (with the Moscow Radio Symphony Orchestra), and Boccherini's Cello Concerto (with Shafran and the Leningrad Philharmonic Orchestra).

Janssen, Werner (1899–1965). Born in New York, Janssen was educated at Dartmouth College, New Hampshire, and studied with Converse, Friedheim and Chadwick at Boston. He soon was to receive success as a composer of popular music, and later wrote the scores for the revues *Ziegfeld Follies* of 1925 and 1926. He studied conducting with Weingartner at Basel (1920–21) and with Scherchen at Strasbourg (1921–5), and in 1930 won a fellowship with the American Academy at Rome, where he studied with Respighi at the Accademia di Santa Cecilia. His debut as a conductor took place in Rome in 1930 with the Royal Orchestra, and following this success he toured Italy and conducted in Berlin, Budapest, Riga and Helsinki, where in 1934 he led a concert of the music of Sibelius, who was present and gave his warm approval. Also in 1934 he became the first New Yorker to conduct the New York Philharmonic-Symphony Orchestra in a programme of music by Haydn, Carpenter, d'Indy and Sowerby. In 1935–7 he conducted major US orchestras, including the Chicago Symphony, visited Europe again in 1937, conducting in London and Helsinki. When he returned to the US he was appointed conductor of the Baltimore Symphony Orchestra (1937–9), and went to Hollywood as musical director of Walter

Wagner Productions at Paramount (1939–42), writing many film scores, such as *Blockade* and *The General Died at Dawn*. In Los Angeles he organised and conducted the Janssen Symphony Orchestra (1940–52), which specialised in performing unusual and contemporary music. In 1941 he toured South America, was conductor of the Utah Symphony Orchestra at Salt Lake City (1946–7), of the Portland Symphony Orchestra in Oregon (1947–9) and of the San Diego Philharmonic Orchestra in California (1952–4). Later he conducted again in Europe. His best-known compositions are *New Year's Eve in New York*, for orchestra and jazz band, *Louisiana Symphony* and some chamber music.

Janssen made a series of records for Victor with the Janssen Symphony Orchestra on 78 r.p.m. discs. The music he chose was very adventurous for the time; it included the *Jena Symphony* of Witt, (first attributed to Beethoven), Villa-Lobos' *Chorus No. 10*, excerpts from Shostakovich's *Lady Macbeth of Mtsensk* (later revised and called *Katerina Ismailova*), Beethoven's *König Stephan* overture and *Wellington's Victory*, Ives' *The Housatonic at Stockbridge* (No. 3 of *Three Places in New England*), Liadov's *The Enchanted Lake*, the prelude to Schoenberg's *Genesis* and a 'scenario for orchestra' from Kern's *Show Boat*. On two 78s for Artist Records he was the first to record some excerpts from *Wozzeck*, with the soprano Charlotte Boerner, and for the same company he also recorded on LP Gilbert's ballet *Dance in Place Congo*, Copland's *Quiet City*, Sibelius' *The Swan of Tuonela*, Cowell's *Ancient Desert Drone*, Ives' *Housatonic at Stockbridge* and an arrangement of Debussy's *La Cathédrale engloutie*. Some of these pieces were re-issued later by Everest, along with *Wellington's Victory* and the *König Stephan* overture, with the orchestra re-named the Los Angeles Symphony Orchestra. His later records included Virgil Thomson's Cello Concerto (with Silva) and a suite from *The Mother of Us All*, Schoenberg's arrangement of the Handel Concerto Grosso Op. 6 No. 7, Borodin's *Tati Tati, Polka, Requiem and Mazurka*, Hindemith's *Symphony in E flat*, two Bach fugues and pieces by Mozart (with the Janssen Symphony Orchestra for Columbia, US), Handel's Oboe Concerto No. 1 (with Gassman), Haydn's Horn Concerto No. 2 (with Alfred Brain), Villa-Lobos' *Bachianas brasileiras Nos 1* and *2*, Chorus Nos 4, 7 and 10 and aria, *On a Song of Our Country*, Berg's *Der Wein* (with Boerner) and three orchestral excerpts from Shostakovich's *Lady Macbeth of Mtsensk* (with the Janssen Symphony Orchestra *et al.* for Capitol), Blomdahl's *Aniara* (with the Vienna Volksoper Orchestra and Chorus for Columbia, US), and Prokofiev's *War and Peace* (with the Vienna State Opera Orchestra *et al.* for Helidor). Altogether, Janssen was a significant pioneer of new music for the gramophone.

Järnefelt, Armas (1869–1958). Born in Viborg, Finland, Järnefelt studied at the Helsinki Conservatory, in Berlin with Busoni and in Paris with Massenet, and gained his first experience as a conductor at Magdeburg and Düsseldorf. He returned to Finland and conducted the orchestra at Viborg (1898–1903), was director of the Helsinki Opera (1903–07), where he introduced the operas of Wagner, and moved to Sweden to become conductor of the Royal Opera at Stockholm (1907–32). Sibelius married his sister; he became a naturalised Swede in 1910. He was again director and conductor of the Helsinki Opera (from 1932), and also conductor of the Helsinki Municipal Orchestra (1942–3). In Scandinavia he was noted for his performances of Mozart, Beethoven and Wagner. His compositions included film, orchestral, choral and chamber music, but he is best known for his *Berceuse* and *Praeludium* for small orchestra. He recorded the latter on 78 r.p.m., as well as his *Prélude funèbre*, and *Finlandia*, *Valse triste*, Glazunov's *The Seasons*, Sinding's *The Rustle of Spring*, and *From Foreign Parts* (composer unidentified), with the Berlin State Opera Orchestra for Odeon and Parlophone, his film score *The Song of the Flame-Red Flower* (for Odeon). Other music he recorded, for Odeon and Siemens, included the Sibelius Violin Concerto (with Ignatius and the Berlin Philharmonic Orchestra), *Berceuse*, four movements from the *King Christian II* suite, Halvorsen's *Entry of the Boyars*, the *Peer Gynt* Suite No. 1, Liadov's *Kikimora* and *The Enchanted Lake*, the waltz from *Eugene Onegin*, and the march and waltz from Suppé's *Boccaccio*.

Jaroff, Serge (b. 1896). Born in Moscow, Jaroff studied at the Synodal-Academy for Church Singing, was an officer in the Cossack army, and founded the world-famous Don Cossack Choir and the Jaroff Women's Chorus. With the Choir he recorded many discs of Russian folk and sacred music (for Decca, US, and DGG).

Järvi, Neheme. The Estonian conductor Järvi's first teacher was his brother Vallo; he then studied at the Tallinn School of Music and at the Leningrad Conservatory under Rabinovich, and at the same time played in the Estonian Radio Orchestra as a percussionist. After graduating he took lessons from Mravinsky, and in 1963 became director of the Tallinn Opera and conductor of the Estonian Radio Orchestra. He appeared in many cities of the USSR and abroad, and won first prize in 1971 at the international competition for conductors at the Accademia di Santa Cecilia, Rome, and in that year was awarded the title People's Artist of the Estonian SSR. He has recorded Tchaikovsky's Piano Concerto No. 1 and Saint-Saëns' Piano Concerto No. 2 (with Sokolov and the USSR Radio and Television Orchestra), *Don Juan* and *Till Eulenspiegel* (with the USSR Radio and Television Orchestra), and Stravinsky's *Scherzo à la russe*, *Four Norwegian Moods* and *Circus Polka* (with the Moscow Philharmonic Orchestra), for Melodiya.

Jaubert, Maurice (1900–40). Born in Nizza, Italy, Jaubert studied at the conservatory there, came to Paris in 1920 and was musical director for Pathé Films. He composed film music, an opera, a ballet, orchestral, chamber and vocal music, and recorded for HMV Delannoy's *Jeunesse valse*, with the Yvonne Gouverné Chorus and Orchestra.

Jenkins, Newell (b. 1915). The American musicologist and conductor Jenkins was born in New Haven, Connecticut, and received his initial musical education at the Yale School of Music. He studied at the orchestral school of the Saxon State Orchestra at Dresden, the Freiburg Music Seminar, the National Orchestral Association, the Accademia Chigiana at Siena, and was also a pupil of Carl Orff. In 1940 he founded the Yale Opera Group and became conductor of the William Byrd Society of New York; during World War II, from 1942 to 1945, he was with the American Field Service in Africa and Europe, and afterwards was conductor of the Bologna Chamber Orchestra (1948–53), founded and was musical director of the Piccolo Accademia Musicale at Florence (1953–7), founded and was musical director of the Clarion Concerts in New York (1957 to the present), and was conductor of the Westchester Symphony Orchestra (1959–62). In 1963 he toured with the Clarion Concerts Orchestra in the USSR and Romania, this being the first overseas concert tour by a United States chamber orchestra. He has also been a guest conductor in Norway, Sweden and more especially Italy, and has filled academic appointments at the universities of New York (1964–71), and California (1971–4). He has carried out extensive research on Giovanni Sammartini (1700–1775), who was one of the first symphonists, and in conjunction with Dr Bathia Churgin has published a thematic catalogue of Sammartini's works.

Jenkins is a foremost authority on baroque and early classical music, and has made many records of the composers of those periods. The works recorded include Vivaldi's *Two-Oboe Concerto in C major* (with Caroldi and Alvarosi), Two-Oboe and Two-Clarinet Concerto (with Caroldi, Alvarosi, Gonizzi and Tassis), and Concerto for Violin and Two Orchestras P. 368 (with Redditi, and the Milan Chamber Orchestra for Washington); Pugnani's Symphony No. 5, Paisiello's Harpsichord Concerto (with Bussotti), Rössler's Horn Concerto (with Rossi), Sarti's Concertone, Giovanni Sammartini's Cantata *Giuna sei pur*, *Symphony in G major* and Violin Concerto No. 2 (with Abussi), Giuseppe Sammartini's *Oboe Concerto in F major* (with Gallesi), Viotti's Violin Concerto No. 4 (with Abussi) and *Piano and Violin Concerto in E flat* (with Bussotti and Abussi), Albinoni's Oboe Concerto Op. 9 No. 2 (with Gallesi), Boccherini's *Symphony in F major*, Brunetti's Symphonies Nos 1, 22, 31 and 33, Cambini's Cantata *Andromaque* (with Tyler), Clementi's *Piano Concerto in C major* (with Bussotti), Corelli's Sonata Op. 5 No. 2, Durant's Concerto No. 4, Galuppi's Overture No. 2, Giordani's Piano Concerto Op. 20 No. 2 (with Bussotti), and Valentini's *Oboe Concerto in C major* (with Prestini, and the Italian Chamber Orchestra for Haydn Society); Mayr's *Medea in Corinto* and Cherubini's *Missa Solemnis* (with the Clarion Concerts Orchestra *et al.* for Vanguard); Zelenka's *Suite in F* and *Simphonie à 8 Concer* (with the Clarion Concerts Orchestra for Decca, US); Bach's Two-Harpsichord Concerto BWV 1061 (with Puyana, Galves and the Clarion Concerts Orchestra for Philips); J. C. Bach's Symphony Op. 18 No. 2 (with the Bologna Orchestra for Contrepoint); Vivaldi's Two-Mandolin Concertos P. 78, P. 79 and P. 83 (with the Orchestra Accademia dell'Orso for Musidisc); symphonies by Sammartini (with the Orchestra Accademia dell'Orso, issued by Saga); Mozart's Serenades K. 375 and K. 388 (with the Everest Woodwind Octet for Everest); Biber's *Fidicinium Sacroprofanum – Battalia*, Dandrieu's *Caractères de la guerre*, Neubaur's Symphony Op. 11, Brunetti's Symphony No. 23, Kraus's *Symphony in C minor*, Locatelli's Concerto Grosso Op. 7 No. 6 (with Biffoli) and *Il pianto d'Arianna*, Geminiani's *The Enchanted Forest*, Giovanni Sammartini's *Symphonies in A*, *C*, *D*,

E flat and *G*, Lampugnani's *Two-Flute Concerto in D major* (with Tassinari and Martinotti), and Mozart's Country Dance K. 587 (with the Angelicum Orchestra for Angelicum, and issued in the United States by Nonesuch); Giovanni Sammartini's *Symphony in F*, *Violin Concerto in F* (with Salvi) and *Tre angeli che cantano*, and Giulini's *Symphony in F major* (with the Angelicum Orchestra for Angelicum, issued in the United States by Musical Heritage Society); and the 20th-century American Flanagan's *Another August* (with Barton, Lee and the Royal Philharmonic Orchestra for Composers Recordings). Few of Jenkins' records have been released in Britain, but those that have, including Geminiani's *The Enchanted Forest*, Locatelli's *Il pianto d'Arianna*, and symphonies by Brunetti and Kraus (both contemporaries of Haydn) were received with warm critical approval.

Jenny, Albert (b. 1912). Born in Solothurn, Switzerland, Jenny studied at the Berne Conservatory, the Hoch Conservatory at Frankfurt am Main, and at the Hochschule für Musik at Cologne, taught music at Stans (1936–44), and then was conductor and teacher at the Swiss Catholic Sacred Music School in Lucerne, conducted the choir of St Karl and of the Hofkirche St Leodegar, the Lucerne Concert Association, the Cäcilienverein at Solothurn and of the Frohsinn Men's Chorus at Lucerne. He led the chorus at the Lucerne Festivals (1946–52) and has been an inspector of music at schools in Solothurn. For Fono with the Lucerne Chamber Orchestra *et al.* he has recorded his own *Tollite portas*, *Jubilate Deo*, *Beata – Magnificat*, *Justorum animae* and *Et introibo ad altarem Dei*.

Jensen, Thomas (1898–1963). Educated at the conservatory at his native Copenhagen, and later in Germany, Jensen was first a cellist and organist. From 1936 to 1948 he was conductor of the Tivoli Concert Hall Orchestra in Copenhagen, together with Felumb; with Tuxen he conducted the Danish Radio Symphony Orchestra (hereafter DRSO) during its first tour of the United States in 1952, and was its conductor from 1953 to the end of his life in 1963. He played a very significant role in introducing the music of his great compatriot Nielsen to European and American audiences; in 1947 Decca issued, on 78 r.p.m. discs, one of the first Nielsen symphonies to be recorded, at least by an English company, No. 2 (*The Four Temperaments*), in which Jensen conducted the DRSO; this was followed in 1952 with an LP of the Symphony No. 1 and in 1954 of No. 5. Tono, the Danish company, also recorded the Symphony No. 6 (*Sinfonia semplice*), and this performance was released on other labels in Britain and the US. All of these were with the DRSO, and were outstanding for the vigour and complete conviction of the performances. Decca re-issued the Symphonies Nos 1 and 5 several times and, coupled together, they still hold a place in the catalogue. His other records of Nielsen's music were of the *Helios* overture and *Moderen* march (with the Copenhagen Philharmonic Orchestra for Decca), the Flute Concerto (with Jespersen) and suite from *Maskarade* (with the DRSO for Decca), and prelude to Act II of *Saul and David* (with the Tivoli Concert Orchestra for Tono).

On 78s Jensen also recorded Kuhlau's *The Elves' Hill* overture, Hartmann's *Triumphant March of the Gods* and Gade's *Echoes of Ossian* overture (with the Copenhagen Philharmonic Orchestra for Odeon), the *Leonore No. 3* overture, *Pomp and Circumstance March No. 1*, Coates' *Knightsbridge March* and Lange-Müller's *Renaissance* overture (with the Tivoli Symphony Orchestra for Tono), the Beethoven Romance No. 2 (with Telmanyi and the Tivoli Concert Orchestra for Tono), the Mendelssohn Violin Concerto (with Telmanyi and an orchestra for Tono), Riisager's *Marche tartare* and other pieces (with the Copenhagen Philharmonic Orchestra for Columbia), *Slaraffenland*, *Two Danish Disciple-Songs* and *On the Occasion of. . . .* (with the Copenhagen Philharmonic Orchestra for HMV), Concertino for Trumpet (with Eskdale and the DRSO for Tono), *Little Overture* (with the DRSO for Tono) and ballet *Twelve with the Mail* (with the Copenhagen Royal Opera Orchestra for Tono), Svendsen's Romance (with Anderson and the Copenhagen Philharmonic Orchestra for HMV), *Moldau*, the *1812* overture and the Tchaikovsky Violin Concerto (with Wolf, and the DRSO for Tono); his LPs included Sibelius' *Four Legends*, *Karelia* suite and *Finlandia* (with the DRSO for Decca), Riisager's *Concertino for Trumpet and String Orchestra* (with Eskdale) and *Little Overture* (with the DRSO for Mercury) and *Primavera* overture (with the DRSO for EMI), Grieg's *Four Symphonic Dances*, the Sibelius Violin Concerto and Sarasate's *Zigeunerweisen* (with Telmanyi, and the DRSO for Tono), *Prélude à l'après-midi d'un faune*, the ballet music from *Le Cid*, *Marche slave*, a dance from *The Bartered Bride* and pieces by Johann Strauss (with the Århus Municipal Orchestra for Tono). Of these, the *Four Legends* of Sibelius was highly regarded when it was originally issued in 1953, and was still available in 1977.

Jeremiáš, Otakar (1892–1962). Born in Pisek, Czechoslovakia, into a family of distinguished musicians, Jeremiáš studied at the Prague Conservatory and with Novák. He played the cello in the Czech Philharmonic Orchestra, was a teacher at the music school at Ceské Budějovice, eventually becoming its director (1918–28). He was conductor of the Prague Radio Orchestra (1929–45), the director of the Prague National Opera (1945–7 and 1948–51). His compositions include the operas *The Brothers Karamazov* and *Till Eulenspiegel*, in addition to symphonic, choral, film, vocal and chamber music, and he also wrote studies on Janáček, on conducting and orchestration, and many articles and other commentaries about music. His recordings for Supraphon and Ultraphone were with the Prague Radio Orchestra (also known as the Czech Radio Orchestra) and included a complete *Má Vlast*, *Wallenstein's Camp*, the introduction and polonaise to *Prague Carnival*, the scherzo from the *Symphony in E major* and *The Czech Song*, all by Smetana, the complete *Slavonic Dances*, the Symphony No. 9, the overtures *My Home* and *Hussite*, and an orchestration by Siedel of Dvořák's Waltzes Op. 54, and Fibich's symphonic poem *Spring*; the Dvořák waltzes were with the Czech Philharmonic Orchestra.

Jerger, Wilhelm (b. 1902). Born in Vienna, Jerger has since childhood been very much a part of Viennese musical life. He was a member of the Vienna Boys' Choir, studied at the Vienna Academy of Music (1916–22) and University (1925–7), and was a double-bass player in the Vienna Philharmonic and Vienna Symphony Orchestras. During World War II he was manager of the Vienna Philharmonic Orchestra, and after the war studied musicology at Freiburg University, published editions of Mozart's letters, and of letters written to the Vienna Philharmonic Orchestra, and was director of the Bruckner Conservatory at Linz (1958–74). His compositions include a *Partita for Orchestra* and *Salzburg Court and Baroque Music*; he recorded the latter for Eurodisc with the Bamberg Symphony Orchestra, together with Leopold Mozart's *Bauerhochzeit*. This disc was released in the United States by Mace. During the war HMV recorded, in Austria, Jerger conducting the Vienna Philharmonic in Tchaikovsky's *Serenade in C major*, and three of Mozart's *German Dances* K. 605.

Jílek, František (b. 1913). Born in Brno, Jílek studied at the Brno Conservatory with Kvapil, Chalabala and Balatka, and then at the Prague Conservatory with Novák. He was a repetiteur at the Brno Opera and pianist with the Brno Radio Chamber Orchestra (1937–9), was assistant conductor with Vogel at the Ostrava Opera (1939–48), professor at the Janáček Academy at Brno, conductor at the Brno Opera (1948) and then music director there (since 1952), as well as conducting the Brno State Philharmonic Orchestra and the Brno Radio Orchestra, and has been a guest conductor in DR Germany, Yugoslavia and Finland. At Brno he led the first performance of the complete operatic works of Janáček in 1956, and of a complete cycle of Smetana's operas in 1959. For Supraphon he recorded Smetana's *The Two Widows*, excerpts from *The Devil's Wall* (with the Prague National Theatre Orchestra *et al.*), organ concertos by Brixi, Linek and Stamitz (with Veselá and the Martinů Chamber Orchestra), Czech polkas and dances of Smetana, Lídl's *Hic homo sum* and Kohoutek's *Teatro del Mondo* (with the Brno State Philharmonic Orchestra *et al.*).

Jiráček, Václav (b. 1920). Born at Hradec Králové in Czechoslovakia, Jiráček studied at the Prague Conservatory (1939–44) and was a pupil at Talich's master class (1944–6). He was a repetiteur at the Prague German Theatre (1944–5) and at the Prague National Theatre (1945–8), conductor at the Ostrava Opera (1948–51), with the Prague Radio Symphony Orchestra (1951–61), director of the Brno Radio Symphony Orchestra (1961) and of the Ostrava State Philharmonic Orchestra (1962). For Supraphon he recorded Shostakovich's Piano Concerto No. 2 (with Voskresensky and the Prague Radio Symphony Orchestra), *Harold in Italy* (with Cerny and the Czech Philharmonic Orchestra), Suchoń's *Balladic Suite* (with the Czech Philharmonic), Feld's Flute Concerto (with Rampal and the Czech Philharmonic), the overture to *Benvenuto Cellini* (with the Czech Philharmonic) and the finale to *Die Meistersinger* (with the Prague Radio Symphony Orchestra *et al.*). Olympic have also issued *Das Lied von der Erde* (with Makos and Dorag, and the Prague Radio Symphony Orchestra).

Jirák, Karel (b. 1891). Born in Prague, Jirák studied at the Prague University and privately with Novák and Foerster, and became conductor at the Hamburg City Opera in 1915. He then conducted at the Brno National Theatre (1918–19), taught at the Prague Conservatory (1920–30), and was music director and principal conductor of the Czechoslovakian Radio (1930–45). In 1947 he went to the United States and was professor of music at the Roosevelt

College in Chicago. His many compositions include an opera, four symphonies, orchestral, chamber, piano and vocal music. He also wrote a text book on musical forms, as well as musical commentaries and monographs. With the Czech Radio Orchestra he made a series of 78 r.p.m. discs for Supraphon and Esta, which included Smetana's *Má Vlast* and *Fishermen*, Dvořák's complete *Slavonic Dances* and *Slavonic Rhapsodies Nos 1, 2 and 3*, Novák's *Slovak Suite* and *Moravian Dances*, Janáček's *Lachian Dances* and scherzo from the *Suite for String Orchestra*, and Suk's *Meditation on an old Bohemian Chorale*.

Jirouš, Jiří (b. 1923). Born in Prague, where he studied at the Charles University and at the Conservatory under Hába and Talich, Jirouš was an assistant conductor at the Prague National Theatre (1942–5), made his concert debut at Amsterdam in 1946, became a resident conductor at the Prague National Theatre, and also conducted in Belgium, France, Holland, Italy and Switzerland. He has composed a violin concerto, film scores, *et al.* For Supraphon he conducted the recording of Hába's opera *The Mother* (with the Prague National Theatre Orchestra *et al.*).

Joachim, Otto (b. 1910). Born in Düsseldorf, Joachim studied at the Buths-Neitzel Conservatory there (1916–28) and at the Rheinische Musikschule at Cologne (1928–31), and performed as a violinist, violist and viola da gamba player. He migrated to Canada, was co-founder and violist in the Montreal String Quartet, founded the Montreal Consort of Ancient Instruments (1958), and was principal violist in the Montreal Symphony Orchestra. With the Consort of Viols and the Montreal Bach Chorus he recorded, as conductor, a disc of the music of the Renaissance (for Turnabout).

Jochum, Eugen (b. 1902). Born at Babenhausen in southern Germany into a musical family and the brother of Otto (composer) and Georg Ludwig (conductor), Jochum was playing the piano at the age of four and the organ at seven. After attending the Augsburg Conservatory he studied at the Munich Academy of Music (1922–4), and his first appointment was as a repetiteur at Mönchengladbach. His debut as a conductor was with the Munich Philharmonic Orchestra in 1926 at a concert with a programme including the *Leonore No. 3* overture and Bruckner's Symphony No. 7. Its success led to an appointment with the Kiel Opera (1926–9), where he conducted seventeen operas in his first season, as well as leading the Lübeck symphony concerts at the same time. Furtwängler's recommendation was responsible for his engagement by the Mannheim Opera (1929); he was principal conductor at Duisburg (1930) and with the Berlin Radio Symphony Orchestra (1931–3), also giving concerts each season with the Berlin Philharmonic Orchestra and conducting at the Berlin State Opera. With the advent of the Nazis he left Berlin to become music director of the Hamburg Opera and the Hamburg Philharmonic Orchestra, succeeding Muck and Böhm. He remained there until 1949 and was also active in other German cities; during the Hitler era he avoided joining the Nazi Party.

In 1949 Jochum founded and was principal conductor of the Bavarian Radio Symphony Orchestra, and was with the orchestra for 25 years, raising it to become one of the most distinguished in Germany. In 1953 he conducted for the first time at Bayreuth, leading *Tristan und Isolde*, and returned in 1971, 1972 and 1973. He led the Bavarian Radio Symphony Orchestra at the Edinburgh Festival in 1957, first visited the United States in 1958, and since 1962 has regularly conducted at the Berlin German Opera and in other German opera houses. On the death of van Beinum in 1961 he was appointed, with Haitink, co-conductor of the Amsterdam Concertgebouw Orchestra; Haitink became principal conductor in 1964, but Jochum remained a frequent guest conductor with the orchestra. He toured the US and Japan with the orchestra in 1961, and was again in Japan in 1968. In 1975 the London Symphony Orchestra appointed him 'conductor laureate'. His many honours include election as president of the German section of the International Bruckner Society in 1950, the Würzburg Kulturpreis in 1967, and the Brahms and Bruckner Medals.

A tall, erect and unfailingly courteous man, Jochum has, since childhood, found his musical background in the great Austro-German classics. His preferences have always been for Bach, Haydn, Mozart, Beethoven, Schubert, Brahms, Wagner and Strauss, of whom he has now come to be recognised as one of the greatest living interpreters. As a conductor he can be identified with the romantic tradition represented most of all by Furtwängler, as opposed to the objective tradition whose greatest exponent was Toscanini. Jochum feels no compulsion to maintain exactly steady tempi, particularly in Brahms and Bruckner; in fact it is against his musical nature to do so. The search for the inner character, drama and spirituality of the music takes precedence over a concern for literal accuracy in matters of tempo or historical authenticity. His own deep religious convictions are reflected in his interpretations of Bach and Bruckner in particular, which have a powerful intensity and emotional elevation equalled by very few other musicians. Bach and Wagner were his first decisive influences when he was a young man. Although he recorded no Bach until comparatively recently, he has now made sets for Philips of the *Mass in B minor* and the *Christmas Oratorio* (with the Bavarian Radio Symphony Orchestra *et al.*), and the *St Matthew Passion* and the *St John Passion* (with the Concertgebouw Orchestra *et al.*). In performing Bach he gives virtually no attention to historical accuracy with regard to ornamentation in either the vocal or the instrumental writing, so that his interpretations could never appeal to purists. But, for example, in the *St John Passion*, the Netherlands Radio Chorus under Jochum sings with such great feeling, conviction and drama that the performance has a very powerful impact, fully consistent with the text; it is an interesting contrast to Gillesberger's (on Telefunken), which seeks to reproduce the performing practices of Bach's time, but is completely without sentiment.

Jochum made his first records for Telefunken in 1932, when he accompanied Edwin Fischer in a Mozart concerto. His subsequent Mozart recordings have revealed him as one of the very finest interpreters of this composer. In the 1930s he recorded Symphony No. 41 with the Hamburg Philharmonic Orchestra for Telefunken, and then after World War II DGG issued on mono LPs Symphonies Nos 33, 36, 39 and 40 with the Bavarian Radio Symphony Orchestra, and Telefunken Symphony No. 40 with the Concertgebouw Orchestra. DGG added the *Requiem*, in a performance with the Vienna Symphony Orchestra *et al.*, on the Archiv label, in which the music was incorporated into the complete liturgy, and the Serenade K. 361 with the members of the Bavarian Radio Symphony Orchestra. In the 1960s Philips released performances with the Concertgebouw Orchestra of Symphonies Nos 35, 36, 38 and 41; Nos 39 and 40 were either not recorded or not released. In all these, Jochum demonstrated the most perceptive Mozart style; Symphony No. 40, for instance, is a superbly refined and intensely moving reading with orchestral playing of great beauty. The stereo discs with the Concertgebouw Orchestra are arguably the finest performances of these works to have been recorded, despite the magnitude of the competition. One of the Mozart operas which Jochum recorded is *Così fan tutte*, with the Berlin Philharmonic Orchestra *et al.*, released by DGG in 1963; it, too, stands among the finest recordings of Mozart operas.

Jochum himself has confessed that Haydn came to him much later in life than Mozart, and his recorded performances of Haydn were not made until after World War II. DGG released Symphonies Nos 88, 91, 98 and 103, and the Mass No. 3, with the Bavarian Radio Symphony and the Berlin Philharmonic Orchestras, in fine performances, but later, in 1973, with the London Philharmonic Orchestra, he recorded again for DGG the complete Symphonies Nos 95 to 104, a set that was acclaimed for its superlative musicality, imagination and spontaneity. In 1967 Philips also issued *The Creation*, with the Bavarian Radio Symphony Orchestra *et al.* His first Beethoven recordings were made in the 1930s and early 1940s for Telefunken with the Berlin Philharmonic and Hamburg Philharmonic Orchestras; Symphonies Nos 3, 7 and 9. DGG recorded, after World War II, Jochum with the Berlin Philharmonic in Symphonies Nos 3, 6 and 7 and with the Hamburg Philharmonic Symphony No. 8; later for stereo he repeated Symphony No. 3 and added Symphonies Nos 1, 2, 4 and 8, all with the Berlin Philharmonic, with some overtures to complete the discs. The Violin Concerto, with Schneiderhan, and the Berlin Philharmonic also appeared. Philips issued Symphony No. 5 with the Berlin Philharmonic and a disc of overtures with the Concertgebouw Orchestra, and then in 1969 Jochum recorded the complete nine symphonies and some overtures with the Concertgebouw Orchestra. At least several of these performances of the symphonies were criticised for tempo changes which were considered by some to be disastrous to the music; yet Paul Henry Lang, in *High Fidelity*, described the series in the highest terms, in his review of all recordings of the nine symphonies released up to 1971. At best, Jochum's Beethoven is deeply felt and superbly poised, but at less than best, his idiosyncracies have been described as mannered wilfulness. The coupling of Symphonies Nos 1 and 8 with the Berlin Philharmonic was re-issued on a cheap label in Britain in 1976 and is an excellent example of the conductor's style. Another notable Beethoven recording by Jochum is the *Missa Solemnis*, also released by Philips *c.* 1970, with the Concertgebouw Orchestra, Netherlands Radio Chorus *et al.*

Jochum's Brahms performances have always encountered criticism for the variations of tempi within movements. On 78s for Telefunken he had recorded Symphonies No. 1 (with the Berlin Philharmonic), 2 and 3 (with the Hamburg Philharmonic), and later from 1955 to 1960 he completed the four symphonies with the Berlin Philharmonic for DGG; Symphony No. 3 also appeared with the Hamburg Philharmonic for Telefunken. Similar reservations have always been made about his Bruckner; while it is readily conceded that his performances profoundly penetrate the music's unique spiritual world, it does this at the expense of its architectural structure. Jochum has said that from his earliest years he saw no problems with performing Bruckner, compared to Mozart and Beethoven, and the music came to him naturally. His changes of tempo within movements, which to others are so destructive of the music's continuity, are an integral part of his conception of the music and contribute to the intensity of the performances. He always conducts from the Novak editions, and he believes that, as it is very difficult to discover Bruckner's final wishes in the various revisions of the symphonies, every conductor has to make his own decisions. He refuses to conduct the Symphony No. 0, respecting Bruckner's wish that it be not heard. Telefunken recorded on 78s Symphonies Nos 4 and 5 with the Hamburg Philharmonic, and No. 7 with the Vienna Philharmonic. Later in 1951 DGG issued Symphony No. 8 with the Hamburg Philharmonic, and then followed Symphonies Nos 7 and 4, with the Berlin Philharmonic and Bavarian Radio Symphony Orchestras respectively. Then a complete Bruckner cycle (excluding No. 0) was prepared in the mid 1960s by Jochum with the Berlin Philharmonic and Bavarian Radio Symphony Orchestras, and in 1965 Philips also released another Symphony No. 5, with the Concertgebouw Orchestra, taken from a live concert. Other Bruckner works recorded by Jochum are the *Te Deum* (twice, in 1951 and 1965), the Masses Nos 1, 2 and 3, and the *Psalm 150*; these four works and the Motets were re-issued as a set by DGG in 1973. Other records which Jochum made for Telefunken on 78s, mainly with the Berlin Philharmonic, included some Wagner preludes and the *Tristan und Isolde* prelude and Liebestod, several Weber overtures and the Dvořák Violin Concerto (with Kulenkampff). For Philips he recorded the *Magnificat* of Kurt Mengelberg, the cousin of the conductor, the Reger *Serenade* (both with the Concertgebouw Orchestra), although Urania issued another performance of the Reger *Serenade*, and the Mozart Symphony No. 33, with the Berlin Philharmonic. Coupled with Mozart's Symphony No. 40 issued in 1959 by DGG was a fine Schubert Symphony No. 5; Jochum also recorded Symphonies Nos 4 and 8 of Schubert with the Concertgebouw Orchestra (for Philips), and Symphony No. 9 with the Bavarian Radio Symphony Orchestra (for DGG). Schumann's Symphony No. 4 (with the Concertgebouw Orchestra) was also issued by Philips, as well as a Strauss disc containing *Don Juan*, *Till Eulenspiegel* and a suite from *Der Rosenkavalier*. His complete opera recordings have been, in addition to *Così fan tutte* mentioned earlier, *Der Freischütz* (1960), *Lohengrin* (1961) and *Die Entführung aus dem Serail* (1966), with the Bavarian Radio Symphony Orchestra *et al.* (for DGG). Another LP of orchestral excerpts from Wagner operas was issued by Philips, and DGG included the *Parsifal* prelude and Good Friday Music with Bruckner's Symphony No. 5. Jochum's only Mahler recording has been *Das Lied von der Erde*, issued in 1963 by DGG (with Merriman, Haefliger and the Concertgebouw Orchestra).

Despite his identification with the Austro--German classics, Jochum is attracted to and performs recent composers, such as Orff, Egk and Hartmann, who dedicated his Symphony No. 6 to him. In the late 1950s Jochum recorded the three cantatas of his friend, Carl Orff: *Carmina Burana*, *Catulli Carmina* and *Trionfi d'Aphrodite* (with the Bavarian Radio Symphony Orchestra *et al.*); in 1968 he re-recorded *Carmina Burana* (with the Berlin Opera Orchestra and Chorus *et al.*). A Sibelius collection, including *The Oceanides*, *Night Ride and Sunrise* and music from *The Tempest* was recorded (with the Bavarian Radio Symphony Orchestra on a mono LP for DGG); for Donemus he recorded music by Dutch composers: Heppener's *Eglogues* and Landre's Symphony No. 3 (with the Concertgebouw Orchestra). Some concerto accompaniments include the two Brahms Piano Concertos in quintessential performances by Gilels and the Berlin Philharmonic (for DGG). In 1975 he signed an exclusive contract with EMI to make records in London, Dresden and Munich; so far have been released Haydn's Symphonies Nos 93, 94, 95 and 98 (with the Dresden Staatskapelle), the four Brahms symphonies and the *Tragic* and *Academic Festival Overtures* (with the London Philharmonic Orchestra), the *Enigma Variations* and *Variations on the St Antony Chorale* (with the London Symphony Orchestra), and Bruckner's Symphony No. 3 (with the Dresden Staatskapelle: the first of the complete nine with this orchestra).

Jochum, Georg Ludwig (1909–71). Brother of Eugen, Jochum was born at Babenhausen in southern Germany, and studied at the Munich Academy of Music with Hausegger and Haas.

He was music director at Münster (1932–4), conductor of concerts and opera at Frankfurt am Main (1934–7), general music director at Linz (1940–45), general music director and head of the conservatory at Duisburg (1946–58) and conductor of the Bamberg Symphony Orchestra (1948–50). He toured as a guest conductor in Europe, Japan and South America. His recordings include C. P. E. Bach's Sinfonias Nos 15, 16 and 17 (with the Hamburg Chamber Orchestra for Pathé), Haydn's Symphony No. 85 and *Cello Concerto in D* (with Hoelscher and the North-West German Philharmonic Orchestra, for Monarch), Mozart's Symphonies Nos 27 and 30 (with the Bamberg Symphony Orchestra for L'Oiseau Lyre), Schubert's Symphonies Nos 3 and 5 (with the Hamburg Chamber Orchestra for Pathé) and Nos 1 and 3 (with the North-West German Philharmonic Orchestra for Monarch), Bruckner's Symphonies Nos 2 and 6, Dvořák's *Carnival* overture and Spohr's Clarinet Concerto (with Hammerle) and String Quartet Concerto (with the Linz Bruckner Symphony Orchestra for Urania; Bruckner's Symphony No. 2 was issued in Britain by Saga), Spohr's Violin Concerto No. 8 and Beethoven's Romance No. 2 (with Borres and the North-West German Philharmonic Orchestra for Mace), Glazunov's Violin Concerto (with Gabriel and the RIAS Orchestra for Remington), Tchaikovsky's Piano Concerto No. 2 (with Böttner and the Berlin Symphony Orchestra for Electrola), Kodály's *Dances from Galánta* (with the Berlin Philharmonic Orchestra for Urania) and Shostakovich's Piano Concerto No. 1 (with List and the Vienna State Opera Orchestra for Westminster).

Johanos, Donald (b. 1928). One of the few American conductors to be in charge of a major symphony orchestra in the United States, Johanos was born at Cedar Rapids, Ohio, and studied the violin and conducting at the Eastman School of Music. At the same time he was a violinist in the Rochester Philharmonic Orchestra, then under Leinsdorf. After conducting community orchestras at Altoona and Johnstown, Pennsylvania, he was awarded a three-year grant to study conducting from the American Symphony Orchestra League and the Rockefeller Foundation. During this time he worked under Ormandy, Szell, Beecham, van Beinum and Klemperer. He was appointed associate conductor of the Dallas Symphony Orchestra (1957), resident conductor (1961) and musical director (1962), at the same time appearing as guest conductor with other major symphony orchestras in the US. In 1970 he became associate conductor to the Pittsburgh Symphony Orchestra under Steinberg, and is conductor of the Pittsburgh Symphony Chamber Orchestra. He has made records for Vox and its other label, Turnabout, with the Dallas Symphony Orchestra, of Ives' *Holidays Symphony*, Scriabin's Symphonies Nos 4 and 5, Rachmaninov's *Symphonic Dances* and *Vocalise*, Copland's *Rodeo*, *Billy the Kid*, and *Fanfare for the Common Man*, Schuller's Symphony, Erb's *Symphony of Overtures*, *Seventh Trumpet* and *Concerto for Percussion* (with Dahlgren) and Eaton's *Concert Piece for Synkret and Orchestra*.

Johnson, Thor (1913–1975). Born in Grand Rapids, Wisconsin, Johnson was organising and leading an orchestra when he was thirteen. After graduating from the universities of North Carolina and Michigan, he studied conducting in Europe with Weingartner, Walter, Malko and Abendroth, and on his return to the United States in 1937 conducted orchestras at Ann Arbor, Asheville, Grand Rapids and the University of Michigan, where he became an assistant professor. In 1940–41 he studied with Koussevitzky at the Berkshire Music Center, served with the US army (1942–6), and came into prominence as a conductor of army symphony orchestras. In 1946–7 he was professor of conducting at the Juilliard School, and in 1947 he succeeded Goossens as musical director of the Cincinnati Symphony Orchestra, being one of the first native-born Americans to conduct a major US symphony orchestra. Remaining there until 1967, he introduced many new works and commissioned a number of new pieces from American composers. He was professor and head of orchestral activities at Northwestern University (1958–64), director of the Interlochen Arts Academy (1964–7) and musical director of the Nashville Symphony Orchestra (1967–75).

Johnson made a number of records with the Cincinnati Symphony Orchestra. Among Decca's first LP releases in Britain in 1951 were his Schubert Symphony No. 3, *Nuits d'été* of Berlioz (with Suzanne Danco), J. C. Bach's *Sinfonia in E flat major*, Alfvén's *Midsummer Vigil* and Grieg's music for *Sigurd Jorsalfar*. For Remington there were Dvořák's Symphony No. 8, Tchaikovsky's Symphony No. 2, Sibelius' *Pohjola's Daughter* and *The Origin of Fire* (with the Helsinki University Choir *et al.*), Brant's Saxophone Concerto (with Rascher), Ward's Symphony No. 3, Prokofiev's Piano Concerto No. 2 and Gershwin's *Piano Concerto in F* (with Bolet) and

Stein's *Three Hassidic Dances*. Composers Recordings also issued Chou Wen-Chung's *Landscapes*, Fischer's *Hungarian Set*, Lessard's *Concerto for Winds and Strings* and Nagel's Trumpet Concerto (with the Fish Creek Symphony Orchestra *et al.*) and Westminster a collection of orchestral arrangements of music by Chopin (with the Vienna State Opera Orchestra); for Columbia (US) he also recorded some discs of American Moravian music with the Moravian Festival Orchestra and Chorus; Johnson's father was a Moravian clergyman.

Jolivet, André (1905–74). Born in Paris, Jolivet experimented in literature, drama, and painting before taking up the serious study of music, becoming a pupil of Le Flem and Varèse. In 1935 he founded, together with Messiaen and Lesur, a group which became known as 'La Jeune France', to promote new music and international contacts. In 1945 he was appointed musical director of the Comédie-Française, from 1960 was adviser of music at the French Ministry of Culture, president of the Concerts Lamoureux (1963–8) and professor of composition at the Paris Conservatoire (1965–70). His compositions include five symphonies, twelve concertos, a string quartet, seven large works for solo instruments, choral and solo vocal pieces and stage works; his music employs many elements and displays many influences. He has recorded many of these compositions, including the *Danses rituelles* (with Rostropovich and the French National Orchestra for EMI), *Suite delphique* and *Epithalame* (with the ORTF Madrigal Ensemble *et al.* for EMI), *Suite française* (with the Colonne Orchestra for EMI), Trumpet Concertino and Trumpet Concerto (with André) and Cello Concerto No. 1 (with Navarra and the Lamoureux Orchestra for EMI), the Cello Concerto No. 2 (with Rostropovich and the French National Orchestra for EMI), the Concerto for Ondes Martenot (with Jeanne Loriod and the French National Orchestra for Vega), the Concertino for Cello and Orchestra (with d'Arco and the Lamoureux Orchestra for Westminster), the Flute Concerto and Suite for Flute and Percussion (with Rampal and the Lamoureux Orchestra for Erato), Harp Concerto (with Laskine and the French National Orchestra for Erato), and Concerto for Bassoon, Strings, Harp and Piano (with the Paillard Orchestra *et al.* for Erato). Some of these discs, for Erato, have been released in the United States by Musical Heritage Society.

Jones, Geraint (b. 1917). Born in Porth, Glamorganshire, Jones studied at the Royal Academy of Music (1935–9), and during World War II became widely known for his concerts at the National Gallery in London. In 1946 he presented a series of sixteen recitals in which he performed the complete organ works of Bach; he toured the United States, Canada and Europe in the years 1948 to 1950, specialising in the music of Bach. He was, from 1948, musical director of the Lakes District Festival, and from 1951 to 1953 musical director of Bernard Miles' Mermaid Theatre in London, directing remarkable performances of Purcell's *Dido and Aeneas*, with Flagstad in the cast. The great soprano contracted with Miles to sing the part of Dido twice nightly in return for a pint of stout for each performance, after she had heard Miles' monologue *The Truth about Tristan*. Also in 1951, Jones formed the Geraint Jones Chorus and Orchestra, and with them gave many concerts and broadcasts; in 1969–70 he led a series of concerts in the Royal Festival Hall, performing all the Mozart piano concertos.

EMI issued in 1953 the Mermaid Theatre performance of *Dido and Aeneas*, with Flagstad and Schwarzkopf *et al.*, conducted by Jones, and World Record Club re-issued the disc in 1969. In 1957 Decca recorded Gluck's *Alceste*, again with Jones and his choir and orchestra and Flagstad, and this too was re-issued in 1969. His other records have been Purcell's *Music for the Funeral of Queen Mary*, the *Magnificats* of J. S. and C. P. E. Bach, Bach's Cantata No. 147 and motet *Jesu meine Freude* (for EMI), Cantatas Nos 56 and 82 (with Souzay for Pathé-Marconi), and Handel's *Utrecht Te Deum*, *Jubilate* and *Zadok the Priest* (for DGG-Archiv).

Jones, Granville (b. 1922). Born in Cymmer, Glamorganshire, and educated at the Royal Academy of Music, London, Jones was leader of the Boyd Neel Orchestra (1952), was a violinist in the London Symphony Orchestra and with the London String Quartet (1957–9) and musical director and leader of the Philomusica Orchestra. In 1960 L'Oiseau Lyre issued a disc of him conducting the Philomusica Orchestra in performances of Handel's *Alexander's Feast* (Concerto Grosso in C), *Harp Concerto in F* (with Ellis and Dart) and Harp and Lute Concerto (with Ellis and Dupré).

Jones, Kenneth (b. 1924). Born in Bletchley, Buckinghamshire, Jones studied at Queen's College, Oxford and at the Royal College of Music, where he became a professor in 1958. He served in the RAF (1942–7), was assistant conductor of the London Symphonic Players

(1952), and of the Redhill and Reigate Choral Society (1956–64), and was conductor of the Wimbledon Symphony Orchestra (1961–70) and of the Sinfonia of London. His compositions include choral, symphonic, chamber and instrumental music, and scores for films, television and the theatre. Lilac Records issued Balfe's opera *The Daughter of St Mark*, in which he conducted the Gala Opera Group.

Jones, Leslie (b. 1905). Born at Hanley, Stoke-on-Trent, Jones was playing the saxhorn and piano at the age of six, and the organ in his teens. He qualified as a solicitor while conducting the local Stoke orchestra and operatic society in his spare time. Before World War II he formed the Newcastle-under-Lyme String Orchestra, and after the war the Stoke-on-Trent Symphony Orchestra. In 1953 he founded his own professional chamber orchestra in Manchester, and when he moved to London two years later, abandoned the law to devote his full time to music. He formed the Little Orchestra of London, which is an *ad hoc* ensemble including many principals and ex-principals of the permanent London orchestras who have been playing together in this and other similar chamber orchestras for many years. In 1964 Pye initiated the famous series of Haydn symphonies, performed by the Little Orchestra of London conducted by Jones, with a disc containing Symphonies Nos 19, 31 and 45. Jones went on to record for Pye and later for Nonesuch about 70 of the Haydn symphonies, and *The Seven Last Words of Christ*; many had not been recorded before, and the series came to a conclusion in 1967 with the *Paris* symphonies (Nos 82 to 87) and in 1969 with the *London* symphonies (Nos 93 to 104). Later, he re-recorded Symphonies Nos 101 and 104 for Oryx, believing that he could improve on the performances in the earlier set. All these recordings of Haydn symphonies were fine and idiomatic performances, and immediately gained Jones a lasting place in the history of the gramophone; together with Goberman, he pioneered the way for Dorati and Märzendorfer, who both were to record all the Haydn symphonies. Perhaps with the *London* set Jones was less successful than with the rest, as he naturally encountered comparison with the many other performances by eminent conductors. Furthermore, a harpsichord continuo is used throughout, which pleased some critics but annoyed others.

Jones' other recordings with the Little Orchestra of London have been Michael Haydn's Symphonies Nos 16 and 33 and *Violin Concerto in A* (with Armon), the string serenades of Dvořák and Tchaikovsky, Rawsthorne's *Concerto for String Orchestra*, Berkeley's *Serenade for Strings* and Fricker's *Prelude, Elegy and Finale* (for Pye), J. C. Bach's Symphonies Op. 18 Nos 3 and 5 and *Sinfonia concertante*, the four *Leipzig Symphonies* of C. P. E. Bach (for Nonesuch), Bach's Harpsichord Concertos Nos 1 and 5 (with Lester) and *Violin Concerto in E* (with Armon), Handel's *Music for the Royal Fireworks*, *Water Music* and *Concerto a due cori in F*, Stanley's Concerti Op. 2, Haydn's six Divertimenti, and Mozart's Clarinet Concerto (with King), Oboe Concerto (with Wickens), *Serenata notturna* and Sinfonia Concertante K. 364, a *Notturno* of Spohr and the Dvořák *Serenades in E* and *D minor* (for Oryx), and Grieg's *Holberg Suite* and *Two Elegiac Melodies*, Nielsen's *Little Suite* and Sibelius' *Rakastava*, and Beethoven's Symphonies Nos 1 and 8 (for Unicorn). In the latter coupling, Jones employed an orchestra of only 30 strings, with winds befitting the composer's intentions, tempi adhering to the 'fast' metronome markings, and with no alterations to the scoring, so giving a closer impression of the music as Beethoven probably heard it, and maybe conceived it.

Jones, Philip (b. 1928). Born at Bath into a family of brass players, Jones studied at the Royal College of Music, London, began his career playing the trumpet in the Royal Opera House Orchestra, Covent Garden, and played in all the major orchestras in London. In 1951 he founded the Philip Jones Brass Ensemble, which was made up of leading London brass instrumentalists, and pioneered the concert performance of brass chamber music in Britain, with a repertoire drawn from the last five centuries and including music especially written for them. Jones was also head of the school of wind and percussion at the Royal Northern College of Music in Manchester (1975–7). With the Ensemble he has recorded, for Argo and Decca, Renaissance music by Lappi, Banchieri, Gabrieli, Massaino, Scheidt, Locke, Brade, Dering, Holborne, Tomkins, Franchos, Agricola, Lassus, Becchi, Byrd and Gibbons, and more recent music including Strauss's *Stadt Wien*, Grieg's *Funeral March*, Bozza's *Sonatine*, fanfares from Dukas' *La Péri* and Jolivet's *Narcisse*, Poulenc's Sonata, Schuller's Symphony, Bliss's *Antiphonal Fanfare*, Simpson's *Canzona*, Britten's *Fanfare for St Edmundsbury*, fanfares by Haan, Bullock, Bax, Bennett, Tippett, Copland, and Jolivet's *Fanfares pour Britannicus*, Altenberg's Concerto, Beethoven's Three Equali, Mozart's Divertimento No. 5, Arnold's Brass Quintet, Dodgson's

Suite, and Sonata, Salzedo's Divertimento, Ewald's Symphony, Addison's Divertimento, Gardner's Theme and Variations, Bennett's *Commedia IV*, Maurer's Four Pieces, the Waltz from *The Sleeping Beauty*, Simon's Quartet, Arban's *Étude charactéristique* (arr. Howarth), Arnold's Fantasy for Trombone, Dufay's *Pasce tuos* (arr. Howarth), Previn's *Four Outings*, Howarth's *Two Processional Fanfares*, Brian's fanfare from *The Cenci*, Walton's *Spitfire Prelude and Fugue* (arr. Howarth), Byrd's *Earl of Salisbury's Pavane* (arr. Wiggins), Gervaise's Six Renaissance Dances (arr. Attaignant), Purcell's Trumpet Tune, the *Agincourt Song* and *Greensleeves* (arr. Howarth), *et al.*

Jones, Samuel (b. 1935). Born in Inverness in the United States, Jones was educated at Millsaps College, Jackson, Mississippi, studied composition with Hanson, Rogers and Barlow at the Eastman School of Music, and conducting with Lert at Orkney Springs. He conducted the Alma Symphony Orchestra (1961), the Saginaw Symphony Orchestra (1962–5), was composer-in-residence at Delta College, Michigan (1964–5), conducted the Rochester Philharmonic Orchestra (1965–73) and since 1973 has been dean of the Shepherd School of Music, Rice University, Houston, Texas. Of his many compositions he has recorded his *Let Us Now Praise Famous Men* and *Elegy*, with the Houston Symphony Orchestra, for Composers Recordings.

Jongen, Léon (b. 1885). Born at Liège, the Belgian composer Jongen studied at the Conservatory there, and in 1913 won the Grand Prix de Rome. He taught at the Brussels Conservatory (from 1934), and took his brother Joseph's place as director (1939–49). His compositions included an orchestral work *Malaisie*, which he recorded with the Belgian National Orchestra for Decca.

Jordá, Enrique (b. 1911). Born in San Sebastian, Spain, Jordá studied at the Madrid University, went to the Sorbonne at Paris, and at the same time studied composition with Le Flem, conducting with Ruhlmann and organ with Dupré. After graduating in philosophy and letters, he decided to devote himself entirely to music. He was conductor of the Basque Ballet (1937–9), conducted in France and Belgium, was principal conductor of the Madrid Symphony Orchestra (1942–5), toured Europe, and was appointed principal conductor of the Cape Town Symphony Orchestra in South Africa (1948–54). His debut in the United States took place in 1952 at San Francisco, and from 1954 to 1964 he was conductor of the San Francisco Symphony Orchestra, in succession to Monteux. His term at San Francisco was marred by controversies between critics about him, and an attack on him and his orchestra by Georg Szell. Since 1964 he has been musical director of the Antwerp Philharmonic Orchestra, and has made many tours as a guest conductor in Europe, Israel, South and North America. His compositions include ballets and choral music.

As a conductor Jordá is most effective in the music of his native Spain and in colourful romantic scores, and he has attracted acclaim for his temperament and musical sensitivity. He has had a relatively restricted recording career; in the late 1940s he was under contract for Decca and made 78s and mono LPs for that company with the Paris Conservatoire Orchestra and several London orchestras. Most successful among these were dances from *The Three-cornered Hat*, *El amor brujo*, *Nights in the Gardens of Spain* (with Curzon), *Russian Easter Festival* overture, and the prelude to *Khovanshchina*. Other recordings included Haydn's Symphony No. 88, Mozart's Symphony No. 36, Dvořák's Symphony No. 9, *Les Préludes*, *Francesca da Rimini*, *Symphonie espagnole* (with Haendel), *L'Apprenti sorcier*, Brahms' Piano Concerto No. 1 (with Curzon), the overture to *Russlan and Ludmilla*, the Danse slave from *Le Roi malgré lui*, the prelude to *La Damoiselle élue*, Turina's *Danzas fantásticas*, *La procesión del Rocío*, Albéniz' *El puerto* and *Triana*, a dance from *La vida breve* and Granados' *Spanish Dances* Nos 2, 5 and 6. Later for RCA he recorded *Nights in the Gardens of Spain* (with Rubinstein and the San Francisco Symphony Orchestra) and Rachmaninov's Piano Concerto No. 2 (with Brailowsky and the same orchestra); for Composers Recordings Imbrie's *Legend for Orchestra* and Cushing's *Cereus* (with the San Francisco Orchestra), for Everest a complete *The Three-cornered Hat* (with Howitt and the London Symphony Orchestra), and for DGG guitar concertos with Segovia and the Symphony of the Air. Very few of his early records in particular remain in the catalogue; probably his most successful disc was a Decca LP, issued in 1951, where he conducted the Paris Conservatoire Orchestra in a collection of pieces by Falla, Granados, Turina and Albéniz, which was still available 20 years later.

Jordan, Armin (b. 1932). Born in Lucerne, Jordan studied law and literature at the University of Freiburg, and music at the conservatories at Freiburg, Lausanne and Geneva. He had conducted a student orchestra in 1949 at Freiburg, and started his professional career as a repetiteur and then conductor at the theatre at Biel. He has regularly conducted orchestras in Switzerland, notably the Suisse Romande Orchestra, has also been first conductor at the Zürich Opera, chief conductor at the Basel Opera, and a guest conductor in Brussels, Aix-en-Provence, Lyon, Hamburg and Vienna. In 1961 he founded and conducted the Orchestre de Chambre Armin Jordan, and in 1973 was appointed artistic director of the Lausanne Chamber Orchestra, with which he toured FR Germany, with a repertoire from the classical period to the 20th century. His recordings include Mozart's Piano Concertos K. 414 and K. 459 (with Pires and the Lausanne Chamber Orchestra for Erato), Violin Concertos K. 211, K. 218, K. 271a and K. 294a (with Gulli and the Collegium Academicum de Genève for La Guilde Internationale du Disque) and K. 216 and K. 219 (with Gulli and the Lausanne Chamber Orchestra for GID), Cimarosa's *Il maestro di capella* and other pieces (with the Lausanne Chamber Orchestra *et al.* for Erato), Du Puy's Overture *Ungdom og Galskab* and Stalder's *Sinfonia in E minor* (with the Orchestra della Radio Svizzera Italiana for CTS) and Mieg's Piano Concerto No. 2 (with Weisbrod and the Basel Symphony Orchestra for Ex Libris) and *Mit Nacht und Nacht* (with Haefliger and the Basel Symphony Orchestra for Ex Libris).

Jordans, Hein (b. 1914). Born in Venlo, where his father was a well-known Dutch musician, Jordans studied at the Amsterdam Conservatory, at Salzburg with Krauss and at Maastricht with Herman. His career started as second conductor with the Arnhem Orchestra, then he was first conductor at Maastricht, second conductor with the Amsterdam Concertgebouw Orchestra (1945), conductor of the Netherlands Youth Orchestra, and then in 1950 principal conductor with the Brabant Philharmonic Orchestra at 's Hertogenbosch. He has also conducted all the Dutch symphony orchestras as well as many others in Europe, was for many years conductor of the Toonkunst Choirs in The Hague and Amsterdam, and is now permanent conductor of the Philips Philharmonic Choir at Eindhoven. He has recorded a sinfonia by J. C. Bach, Beethoven's Symphony No. 3, Dvořák's Symphony No. 9, the Brahms and Bruch Violin Concertos (with Krebbers) and Tchaikovsky's Piano Concerto No. 1, Rachmaninov's Piano Concerto No. 2 and Chopin's Piano Concerto No. 1 (with Jacques Klein, and with the Brabant Philharmonic Orchestra for Philips), and Orthel's *Scherzo No. 2* (with the Concertgebouw Orchestra for Donemus).

Jöris, Hans-Herbert (b. 1925). Born in Viersen, Germany, Jöris studied at the Hochschule für Musik at Cologne with Wand and Jarnach, was assistant conductor at Dortmund and Cologne (1951–9), first conductor at the Dortmund Opera (1959–66) and first conductor at Hannover and resident conductor of the Youth Symphony Orchestra of Lower Saxony (since 1966). With the Hannover Chamber Orchestra he recorded flute concertos of J. C. Bach, Boccherini, Grétry and Quantz (with Martin), the Mendelssohn Violin Concerto (with Heutling), dances by Mozart, Beethoven and Schubert, and Skalkottas' *Greek Dances* (for Leuenhagen & Paris).

Josefowitz, David (b. 1918). Born in Kharkov, Russia, Josefowitz studied the violin at the age of seven at the Klindworth-Scharwenka Conservatory in Berlin, and later in Switzerland. He went to the United States, studied chemistry and chemical engineering at the Massachusetts Institute of Technology and at the Brooklyn Polytechnic Institute, where he received a Ph.D in science, and at the same time continued his musical studies at the New England Conservatory at Boston. In 1946 with his brother Sam, he created the original Concert Hall Society record club and the Musical Masterpieces Society, and has since established similar record clubs in many European countries, Japan, Australia and New Zealand. He has taken great interest in the musical and technical production of recordings; records made under his supervision have won many prizes. During this time he worked closely with Monteux, Busch, Schuricht, Munch, Goehr and other artists, and from them acquired his professional experience as a conductor. Although he has conducted in many records for Concert Hall and its associates, he has appeared only occasionally on the concert platform, and his activities as a conductor for records were in a way a natural outcome of his experience as a record producer.

Josefowitz's recordings as a conductor include Vivaldi's Concertos Op. 8 Nos 1 to 4 (*The Four Seasons*) and Nos 5 to 12 (with Ozim, violin and Rosso, oboe), and Mozart's *Vesperae de Dominica* and *Laudate Dominum* (with the Collegium Academicum de Genève *et al.*); Telemann's overtures *Hamburger Ebb und Fluht* and *Les Nations anciennes et modernes* and Trumpet Concerto in D, and Pergolesi's Concertinos Nos 1, 2, 3 and 5 (with the Paris Baroque Orchestra); Corelli's Concerto Grosso Op. 6 No. 8 (with the Concert Hall Chamber Orchestra); Handel's *Israel in Egypt* (with the Jerusalem Chamber Orchestra *et al.*) and *Johannespassion* (with the Israel Symphony Orchestra *et al.*); Haydn's Symphonies Nos 94, 96, 100 and 102, Mozart's Symphony No. 41, Beethoven's *Ritterballet*, *Christus am Ölberge* and a collection of his dances, and Chopin's Piano Concerto No. 1 (with Pressler, and the Vienna State Opera Orchestra); the Boccherini Cello Concerto and Haydn's *Cello Concerto in D* (with Greenhouse and the Vienna Chamber Orchestra); Schubert's Symphonies Nos 2, 3 and 9 (with the Vienna State Symphony Orchestra); *Eine kleine Nachtmusik* and the Brahms *Hungarian Dances* (with the Vienna Festival Orchestra); Beethoven's Symphony No. 5 and Dvořák's Symphony No. 9 (with the Hamburg Symphony Orchestra); Schubert's Symphonies Nos 1 and 5 (with the Frankfurt Radio Symphony Orchestra); the Mendelssohn Violin Concerto (with Gawriloff and the Hamburg Radio Orchestra); *Die Zauberflöte* (with the South-West German Philharmonic Orchestra *et al.*); Mendelssohn's Symphony No. 1 and Mozart's Sinfonia Concertante K. 297b (with the Paris Opéra Orchestra); and Schumann's Symphony No. 1 and overture *Genoveva*, the Brahms Violin Concerto (with Soh), Tchaikovsky's Piano Concerto No. 2 (with Szidon), excerpts from *Otello* of Verdi, *Pictures at an Exhibition*, the overtures to *Russlan and Ludmilla* and *A Life for the Tsar*, *El amor brujo* and *Nights in the Gardens of Spain* (with Barbizet), Prokofiev's Symphony No. 1 and *The Love of Three Oranges* and *Lieutenant Kijé* suites (with the Monte Carlo National Orchestra); and excerpts from Künnecke's *Der Vetter aus Dingsda* (with the Zürich Operetta Ensemble). Some of these ensembles are obviously *noms d'enregistrement*. In the US, Audio Fidelity have issued the performance of Beethoven's Symphony No. 5.

Joseph, Irving (b. 1925). Born in New York, Joseph studied at Columbia University and worked as an arranger, conductor and accompanist with major dance bands and popular singers. He arranged and conducted a number of record albums and a television series *Our American Musical Heritage*, and was musical director of a production of Weill's *Die Dreigroschenoper* and of a concert version of *Jesus Christ Superstar*. Among his discs is one in which he accompanies his wife Felicia Sanders in songs of Weill, with his own orchestra (for Mainstream).

Jouve, André (b. 1929). Born in Marseille and educated at the Paris Conservatoire, Jouve was president of the French Concerts Orchestra (1955). He recorded Charpentier's *Messe de minuit* (with the Paris Chamber Orchestra *et al.* for Telefunken), Vivaldi's Violin Concerto P. 383, Concertos Op. 8 No. 8 (with Casier), and Op. 10 No. 5 (with Castagnier), Bassoon Concerto P. 72 (with Faisandier) and *Gloria*, Mozart's *Exsultate jubilate* (with Alarie), some Mozart arias (with Stich-Randall) and Prokofiev's *The Ugly Duckling* (with the Paris Chamber Orchestra and the Champs-Élysées Theatre Orchestra *et al.* for Ducretet-Thomson), excerpts from *Lakmé* (with the Lamoureux Orchestra *et al.* for Philips), and Rebel's *Les Éléments* (with the Orchestre Lyrique d'ORTF for ORTF).

Jürgens, Jürgen (b. 1925). Born in Frankfurt am Main, Jürgens studied there with Thomas and at the Hochschule für Musik at Freiburg with Lechner. His interest was awakened in Italian choral music, and in particular in Monteverdi; he founded an Italian Choir at Freiburg University with whom he won fourth prize in 1953 at an international competition in Rome. Since 1955 he has conducted the Hamburg Monteverdi Choir, which he founded with the assistance of the Italian Cultural Institute, and since 1960 has lectured in musical theory at the Hamburg University; he was made musical director at the University in 1966 and professor in 1977. He has also led an oratorio choir and symphony orchestra, and the Camerata Accademica of Hamburg, which is an instrumental ensemble specialising in early baroque music. With the Monteverdi Choir he has given concerts in Rome and abroad, and has directed the Choir in a number of distinguished recordings, including motets by Josquin (for DGG), madrigals by Monteverdi (separate discs for DGG and Telefunken, the latter with the Leonhardt Consort), Monteverdi's *La favola d'Orfeo* (with the Hamburg Camerata Accademica *et al.* for DGG) and *Vespro della beata Vergine* (for Telefunken), Schütz's *St Luke Passion* and *Seven Words from the Cross*, and the Bach Cantatas Nos 106 and 182 (with the Leonhardt Consort for Telefunken), and No. 198 (with the Amsterdam Concerto for Telefunken), Dallapiccola's *Canti di prigionia*, Peragallo's *De Profundis* and Petrassi's *Nonsense* (for Telefunken), Gagliano's *La Dafne* (for DGG), and cantatas by Telemann (for Philips).

K

Kabalevsky, Dmitri (b. 1904). The Soviet composer Kabalevsky was born at St Petersburg and was educated at the Scriabin Music School and the Moscow Conservatory, where he later became professor of composition. He is also a pianist, conductor and critic, and has been in the midst of the controversies that have taken place in the USSR about the place and content of music, through which he and his music appear to have emerged relatively unscathed. His music is vigorous and cheerful and so is more suited for short forms. As a conductor he has recorded some of his own music; on 78s he conducted his Violin Concerto (with Oistrakh and the USSR State Symphony Orchestra); later on LP there have been the Symphony No. 4 and Cello Concerto (with Shafran, and the Leningrad Philharmonic Orchestra), *The Comedians*, *Spring*, *Overture Pathétique* and *Requiem* (with the Moscow Philharmonic Orchestra *et al.*), musical sketches for *Romeo and Juliet* (with the Moscow Radio Symphony Orchestra), Piano Concertos No. 2 (with Ginsberg) and No. 3 (with Gilels) and Cello Concerto (with Shafran, and the USSR State Symphony Orchestra) and the overture *Colas Breugnon* (twice, with the Bolshoi Theatre Orchestra and the Czech Philharmonic Orchestra). He also recorded excerpts from *Boris Godunov* (with the Maryinsky Theatre Orchestra, Leningrad, *et al.*).

Kabasta, Oswald (1896–1946). Born in Mistelbach in Lower Austria, Kabasta studied at the Vienna Academy of Music and at Klosterneuburg, and taught singing in high schools in Austria. His first appointment as a conductor was with the theatre at Baden near Vienna in 1924. He conducted opera and concerts at Graz (1926–31), was a guest conductor with the Gesellschaft der Musikfreunde in Vienna, was director of Music and first conductor for the Vienna Radio (1931–7), toured Europe with the Vienna Radio Orchestra (1936 and 1938), taught conducting at the Academy of Music, and conducted at the Linz Bruckner Festivals (1936 and 1937). In 1938 he was appointed conductor of the Munich Philharmonic Orchestra, succeeding von Hausegger, but after World War II he committed suicide because of his association with the Austrian Nazis. He enjoyed a reputation as an interpreter of the Austrian romantic composers, particularly Bruckner and Franz Schmidt, whose Symphony No. 4 he premièred in 1934. He made a number of records with the Munich Philharmonic Orchestra for EMI, including Mozart's Symphony No. 41, Beethoven's Symphonies Nos 7 and 8 and *Coriolan* overture, Schubert's Symphony No. 3, Bruckner's Symphony No. 7, Dohnányi's *Symphonic Minutes*, Respighi's *Brazilian Impressions*, the prelude to *La forza del destino*, and *The Legend of Prince Eugen* by the Austrian composer Theodor Berger. The last-named piece, and the Bruckner Symphony No. 7, were recorded by Electrola in Germany during World War II. *Brazilian Impressions* was available in Britain after the war, and was a quite brilliant performance.

Kagel, Mauricio (b. 1931). Born in Buenos Aires, Kagel studied there, conducted a chamber orchestra and at the Teatro Colón, and came to FR Germany in 1957, where he has worked at the studio for electronic music at Cologne. Most of his compositions use *avant-garde* techniques and employ a complex serial method, electronic music and aleatoric elements; they include *Acustica*, *Heterophonie*, *Exotica*, *Staatstheater* and *Ludwig Van*, which has thematic fragments of Beethoven's music. He has recorded *Staatstheater* (with the Hamburg State Philharmonic Orchestra *et al.* for EMI), and *1898* (with an instrumental ensemble and choir of children from Steilshoop School, Hamburg, for DGG). The latter was commissioned by DGG for the 75th anniversary of the establishment of the company, and employs 'Stroh' violins, which have a horn on an aluminium plate instead of a sound box, and has a specially selected group of schoolchildren. In the work he attempted to provide a 'musical X-ray of the end ot the 19th century and at the same time to reconstruct the typical sounds of the first, acoustically unstable gramophone records' (Polydor information sheet, September 1973). Describing the work, the critic Dominic Gill said in the *Financial Times* that 'it contains a kind of grave beauty, and progresses like a priestly ritual – lit with all manner of colours, subtle shades and sparks'.

Kahlhöfer, Helmut (b. 1914). Born in Elberfeld, Germany, Kahlhöfer studied at Cologne and Salzburg, was a church musician at

Cologne (1937) and at Wuppertal (1945) where he became director of church music (1954), and since 1965 has taught choral conducting at the Folkwang Academy at Essen and has been conductor of the Kantorei Barmen-Gemarke. He has recorded the Bach motets (with the Barmen-Gemarke Schola Cantorum and Collegium Aureum, for BASF), and Cantatas Nos 46, 61, 65, 132, 207a and 214 (with the Kantorei Barmen-Gemarke and the German Bach Soloists for Cantate), cantatas by Buxtehude (with the Berlin Bach Orchestra *et al.*), Monteverdi's *Magnificat*, psalms and the *Magnificat* of Schütz (with the Kantorei Barmen-Gemarke for Bärenreiter). Some of these performances were issued in the United States by RCA, Vanguard and Musical Heritage Society.

Kajanus, Robert (1856–1933). After studying at the Conservatory at his birthplace, Helsinki, with Faltin, at Leipzig under Richter and Reinecke, and at Paris with Svendsen (1879–80), Kajanus spent several years in Dresden and returned to Helsinki in 1882. He founded the Helsinki Philharmonic Society, the first permanent symphony orchestra in Finland, and developed the orchestra so that he could give concerts of the standard classics; he remained its conductor for 50 years. In 1888 he led the orchestra in the first local performance of Beethoven's Symphony No. 9, and in 1900 visited, with the orchestra, the major European cities, including Paris, where both he and Sibelius led the orchestra at the World Exhibition. This was the first opportunity the outside world had to hear Sibelius' music. In 1897 he became director of music at the Helsinki University, a post he retained until his retirement in 1926, and continued to conduct his Helsinki orchestra, which changed its name several times over the years. In 1919 he founded the Nordic Music Festival, which became a three-yearly event. Before Sibelius, he was the foremost Finnish composer of his day, and wrote symphonic and choral music; his symphonic poem, *Aino*, inspired Sibelius to write his *Kullervo* symphony, and after the successful première of *Kullervo* Kajanus commissioned Sibelius to write a piece for his orchestra, which resulted in *En Saga*. Personal relations between the two great Finns became clouded once or twice, but nonetheless Kajanus was the first to champion and perform Sibelius' music. Despite the excellence of later performances of Sibelius' works by a number of conductors, Kajanus' interpretations must be considered to have come as close as possible to the composer's intentions. Kajanus was also a fine interpreter of the entire classical repertoire.

In 1930 the Finnish government wished to see recorded the two first symphonies of Sibelius, so that Finnish music would be introduced to a wider international public. It was arranged to record them with the Columbia Gramophone Company of England, with a subsidy from the Finnish government. For these recordings Sibelius nominated Kajanus to conduct, saying: 'Very many are the men who have conducted these symphonies during the last 30 years, but there is none who have gone deeper and given them more feeling and beauty than Robert Kajanus' (Robert Layton, on the record sleeve). Kajanus came to England, and recorded the two symphonies with an unnamed English orchestra that same year, at the same time conducting several Sibelius concerts in London. Later, in 1932, just before his death, he recorded sets of Symphonies Nos 3 and 5, *Tapiola*, the *Karelia* suite and *Pohjola's Daughter*, which were issued as part of the Sibelius Society albums of HMV; he also recorded *Belshazzar's Feast* (with the London Symphony Orchestra, as were the other 1932 recordings) and Sibelius' *March of the Finnish Infantry* (with the Helsinki Orchestra).

In the subsequent decade many conductors – Koussevitzky, Beecham, Boult, Ormandy, Barbirolli, Rodzinski, Stokowski, Schneevoigt *et al.* – recorded Sibelius' music, but Kajanus was the first to do so on this scale. His unique qualities as an interpreter of Sibelius have been admirably described by Layton: 'A marvellous sense of continuity (and) a supremely classical sense of balance. Momentary beauty of incident is not allowed to detract attention from the sheer flow of the argument. There is no self-indulgence or excessive interest in colouristic detail.' Layton also remarks that 'no conductor, apart from the composer himself, could lay claim to more intimate knowledge of the scores, and performances (on the records) offer a valuable link with the kind of reading they would have received at the beginning of the century'. All of these performances, except the *March*, were re-issued by World Record Club on excellent LP transfers in 1973; they are indispensable for those with an enquiring interest in Sibelius, and are a fascinating study for others familiar with the interpretations of later generations of conductors.

Kajdasz, Edmund (b. 1924). Born in Poznań, Kajdasz was a member of the Poznań Cathedral Choir, and with the Choir took part in the World Congress of Church Music in Frankfurt am Main in 1936, and at the Festival of Fine Arts in Paris in 1937. He studied in Berlin (1940–44), then at Wrocław (1946), with

Ramin at Leipzig, Mauersberger in Dresden, Koch in Berlin, and Abendroth at Weimar. He taught at the National Music School and at Wrocław and Katowice, was choral conductor with the Polish Radio (from 1948), conductor of the Choir at Wrocław Cathedral (1952–8), and conductor of the Śląsk Philharmonic Choir in Katowice (from 1958). He has recorded, for Polskie Nagrania, Moniuszko's Mass and *Ostrobramska Litany* Mass, Mielczewski's *Vesperae Dominicales*, Gorczycki's *Missa Paschalis*, Zieleński's *Magnificat* and eight Motets, Pekiel's *Missa Pulcherrima*, Leopolita's *Missa Paschalis* and pieces by Maxylewicz, Lilius, Staromiejski and Szarzyński (with the Wrocław Radio Choir *et al.*), and a collection of Renaissance madrigals and chansons (with the Cantores Minores Wratislaviensis). Some of these performances have also been released in the United States by Musical Heritage Society.

Kakhidze, Djansug (b. 1936). Born in Tbilisi, Georgia, where he studied under Dimitriadi at the Conservatory, Kakhidze studied further with Markevitch, was conductor of the State Capella Chorus (1955–62), principal conductor of Tbilisi Opera and Ballet Theatre (1965–8), conducted at the Łódź Opera (1971–3), conducted orchestras in Poland, and in 1973 was appointed music director and principal conductor of the Georgian State Symphony Orchestra. He has conducted the Leningrad Philharmonic Orchestra, the USSR State Symphony Orchestra and others in the Ukraine, Latvia, Lithuania and Estonia, as well as in East European countries. In 1977 he was invited to conduct in Holland and was contracted to return to conduct the Amsterdam Philharmonic Orchestra. His awards include the Rustaveli State Prize (1976) and the title People's Artist of the Georgian SSR. For Melodiya he has recorded, *inter alia*, the Schubert symphonies, Khachaturian's *Gayaneh*, Kancheli's Symphonies Nos 1 and 2, Machavariani's Symphony No. 2 and Kvernadze's ballet *Berikaoba*.

Kamu, Okko (b. 1946). Kamu's father was a double-bass player in the Helsinki City Orchestra; Kamu was born in Helsinki and began to learn the violin in his third year. He first attended the Sibelius Academy at the age of six, and in 1964 founded and led a string quartet named after Suhonen, his violin teacher at the Academy. In 1965 he joined the Helsinki Philharmonic Orchestra as leader of the second violins, and then became concertmaster of the Finnish National Opera Orchestra (1966–8). He first conducted at the Lucerne Festival in 1966 and then with the Helsinki Philharmonic Orchestra in 1968, was third conductor with the Finnish National Opera (1968–9), conductor at the Royal Opera, Stockholm (1969–70), first conductor of the Helsinki Radio Symphony Orchestra (1970–71) and then became the orchestra's chief conductor and music director (1971–7). He is also principal conductor and music director of the Oslo Philharmonic Orchestra (since 1975), and principal guest conductor of the Norrköping Symphony Orchestra in Sweden (since 1973). In 1969 he won first place at the first International Herbert von Karajan Conductors' Competition, which led to many guest appearances in Europe and the United States, and he has also conducted in Eastern Europe, Israel, Japan and Australia, and has led the Finlandia String Quartet. In addition to the central repertoire, he specialises in contemporary Scandinavian music.

Kamu's recordings have included Sibelius' Symphonies Nos 1 and 3, *The Bard*, *En Saga*, the *Karelia* suite and *Four Legends* (with the Helsinki Radio Symphony Orchestra for DGG) and Symphony No. 2 (with the Berlin Philharmonic Orchestra for DGG), Pettersson's Symphony No. 6 and Bucht's Symphony No. 7 (with the Norrköping Symphony Orchestra for Bis), Sallinen's Symphonies Nos 1 and 3 (with the Helsinki Radio Symphony Orchestra for Bis) and Symphony No. 2 (with the same orchestra for Caprice), Bruch's Violin Concerto No. 1 and the Mendelssohn Violin Concerto (with Yong Uck Kim and the Bamberg Symphony Orchestra for DGG), and concertos by Mozart, Grieg, Tchaikovsky *et al.*, and excerpts from Peterson-Berger's opera *Arnljot* (with the Stockholm Philharmonic Orchestra *et al.* for EMI). The Sibelius recordings in particular have been highly praised, even if occasionally marked by a certain impetuosity.

Kapp, Richard (b. 1936). Born in Chicago, Kapp studied in FR Germany (1957–8), was a conductor and accompanist at Tanglewood, Massachusetts (1962), and graduated in law (1966). He has been permanent musical director of Young Audiences Inc., associate conductor under Perlea of the orchestra and opera theatre at the Manhattan School of Music in New York, and conductor of the Philharmonia Virtuosi of New York. The Ford Foundation engaged him as a consultant to investigate the numbers of black musicians and the problems confronting them in orchestras in the United States. His recording career with Vox has concentrated on reviving music popular half a century ago or longer, and which is now virtually unknown.

Kapp has recorded for Vox and its associated labels, Rameau's *Le Temple de la gloire* (with the Philharmonia Virtuosi of New York), Raff's Symphony No. 2, Schumann's *Overture, Scherzo and Finale*, Bronsart's Piano Concerto, and Thalberg's Piano Concerto and *Concert Fantasy on Les Huguenots* (with Ponti, and the Westphalian Symphony Orchestra), Tchaikovsky's Piano Concertos Nos 1 and 2 (with Ponti and the Prague Symphony Orchestra), Raff's Piano Concerto and *Ode to Spring*, and Tchaikovsky's Piano Concerto No. 3 (with Ponti and the Hamburg Philharmonic Orchestra), Scharwenka's Piano Concerto No. 2 (with Ponti and the Hamburg Symphony Orchestra), Rameau's *Zoroastre* (with the Hamburg Chamber Orchestra), and excerpts from *Les Troyens* and *La Damnation de Faust*, and the *King Lear* overture (with the Philharmonia Hungarica). Columbia (US) issued a collection of pieces by Bach, Pachelbel, Albinoni *et al.* called *Greatest Hits of the 1720s* (with the Philharmonia Virtuosi of New York).

Karajan, Herbert von (b. 1908). Karajan's family came to Austria from Macedonia; his great-grandfather was the director of the court library in Vienna, his grandfather a physician, and his father a doctor who was a clarinettist in the Mozarteum Orchestra in Salzburg, where Herbert was born. The 'von' in his name is inherited from his Viennese forebears and indicates their aristocratic status. When he was three, he started playing the piano, gave his first recital at four, and toured as a pianist when he was fourteen. He studied at the Mozarteum under Paumgartner, who encouraged him to become a conductor; the final decision was taken when he heard Toscanini conduct in Vienna, where he was studying musicology at the University under Schalk. To give him the opportunity to conduct, his father hired the Salzburg Symphony Orchestra; afterwards Karajan substituted for another conductor at a concert in Ulm in 1927, and was engaged as conductor there in 1928. He remained at Ulm for seven years, where his experience was comprehensive – coach and chorusmaster, as well as conductor. He held summer courses for conductors at Salzbuig (1930–34), and in 1935 succeeded Busch as first conductor at Aachen, where he was later appointed music director, the youngest in Germany. In 1937, on Walter's invitation, he came to the Vienna State Opera to conduct *Tristan und Isolde*, but refused a permanent appointment there because of the unsatisfactory rehearsal conditions. In the following year he conducted the Berlin Philharmonic Orchestra in a concert, and astounded the orchestra by demanding string rehearsals for a programme made up of Mozart's Symphony No. 35, *Daphnis et Chloé* Suite No. 2, and Brahms' Symphony No. 4. After leading *Fidelio* at the Berlin State Opera in 1938, he was engaged as conductor (1938–42), and also reorganised the symphony concerts of the opera orchestra. Before World War II he made guest appearances in Belgium, the Netherlands, Sweden, Denmark and Italy; he left Aachen finally in 1941 to become musical director of the Berlin State Opera, and to conduct the Berlin Staatskapelle.

Karajan was a member of the Nazi Party from 1933 to 1942; he later said that he was obliged to join the party to win the appointment at Aachen. He was ıhe holder of an 'SD' card, which gave him many privileges, but fell into disfavour with the party because of his first marriage to a woman of Jewish extraction. In Berlin, the Nazi leaders played him off against Furtwängler, an ironic situation for, along with Toscanini, Furtwängler was the conductor he admired most. At the end of World War II he was forbidden to conduct, and retired to Italy; in 1947 he was denazified and conducted the Vienna Philharmonic Orchestra, but Furtwängler's position in Vienna prevented him from taking a permanent appointment with the orchestra. So he became conductor of the Vienna Symphony Orchestra, and elevated it to a standard rivalling the Vienna Philharmonic; he was also the conductor of the Singverein of the Gesellschaft der Musikfreunde, and was appointed their artistic director for life in 1948; he presented an annual series of concerts and toured with the Society in Europe. His Nazi associations have lived on with him; in 1954 when he toured the United States with the Berlin Philharmonic Orchestra there were protests, but these were answered by declarations about his apolitical and exclusively musical outlook. Even now he is not welcome to conduct in Israel, and some major Jewish musicians still refuse to play with him.

Karajan's emergence after the war was largely the responsibility of Walter Legge of EMI, who had heard him conduct at Aachen, and engaged him for a series of recordings with the Vienna Philharmonic Orchestra. In 1950 Legge appointed him the principal conductor of the Philharmonia Orchestra, which he had established primarily for recording purposes; Karajan remained with the orchestra until 1962, and with them made numerous recordings and toured the US in 1956. In 1948–9 he conducted a season of German opera at La Scala, Milan, and in 1950 became the first German to be appointed a conductor and director there. In 1948 he first conducted at the Salzburg Festival, and was its artistic director from 1956 to 1960. In 1951 he led *The Ring* and *Die Meistersinger* at Bayreuth, and in 1952 *Die Meistersinger* again; in 1954 he replaced Furtwängler, who had just died, as conductor of the Berlin Philharmonic Orchestra for its tour of the US, and returned to the US with the Vienna Philharmonic the next year. In 1954 he also toured Japan. His career reached its zenith when the Berlin Philharmonic named him its principal conductor in 1955; he accepted the position on condition that it would be a lifetime appointment. He has declined all other invitations to be principal conductor or music director of other orchestras, but from 1956 to 1960 he was artistic director of the Vienna State Opera, in 1967 established his own Salzburg Easter Festival, and in 1968 set up the Herbert von Karajan Musical Foundation. This organisation has amongst its projects examining ways of aiding sick people with music, a music school in Berlin where the section leaders of the orchestra are the professors, a biennial conductors' contest alternating with a youth orchestras' contest, and research (in conjunction with the University of Salzburg) into the physical and psychological stress attendant on the profession of music. For a short period in 1969 he was artistic supervisor of the new Orchestre de Paris, and in 1977 he returned to conduct the Vienna State Opera for a festival of nine performances, and became artistic director of the Vienna Festival. He has been awarded the Grand Cross with Star and Epaulette of the Federal Republic of Germany.

Public attention in Europe has been attracted to Karajan almost as much for his glamorous life as for his conducting. His enthusiasm for skiing, sports cars, aeroplanes and yachts has brought him as much notice as is normally associated with film stars, and disputes and controversies have marked his career. He has become the most commanding – and highest paid – conductor in Europe, and in 1977 received over $3,600 for each of the nine opera performances in Vienna. His egomania has eclipsed that of all other conductors; Walter Legge has said, 'Previously he seemed anxious to absorb information from the people around him. Now he seems only to want praise' (*Sunday Times*, 1 August 1976). However one reacts to him as a personality, there can be no doubt at all that he is a completely dedicated, utterly professional and exhaustively painstaking musician. Some would qualify this by adding that his progress to pre-eminence has been the result of a deliberate and ruthless opportunism, as much as of his own musical genius. While Beecham and Stokowski may have understood the value of gramophone records to promote themselves and their orchestras, Karajan's exploitation of recordings is so sophisticated that their attempts now appear infantile. At present he has contracts with the three major recording companies – DGG, EMI and Decca – and he decides himself what works he will record, how they will be recorded, and selects the dates, the soloists, the tapes and even the designs of the record covers. He is so successful that a third of the DGG discs sold in Britain are those of Karajan.

Early in his career Karajan's entry into the auditorium was awe-inspiring. He would walk to the podium with an expression of acute, trancelike concentration; before the orchestra he would pause, motionless, almost interminably, before the first downbeat, and when conducting his eyes would close and his body would sway. These mannerisms have been much modified in later years. He has always conducted from memory; when the tenor Jon Vickers asked him how he beat a particularly difficult passage in Act III of *Tristan und Isolde*, he immediately demonstrated his method, although he had not a score at hand or had conducted the opera for eleven years. When he conducts he does not cue entries, and his beat does not indicate bar lines; while this presents no problem for the Berlin Philharmonic, players in other orchestras have narrowly avoided disaster. At rehearsals he uses few words (despite the constant chatter in the rehearsal record issued by DGG of the last movement of Beethoven's Symphony No. 9), he is never rude, works quickly, is completely prepared and gives scrupulous attention to all details. His patience is endless; when he first took over the Singverein of the Gesellschaft der Musikfreunde, he took the greatest pains to train the choir to sing with the tone required. For a new opera production at Salzburg he allows 240 hours of rehearsals, and for the preparation of Beethoven's Symphony No. 9 for a tour of the Berlin Philharmonic in 1970 he called for over 100 hours of rehearsals.

At first, Karajan's reputation was made with performances of Bach, Mozart, Beethoven, Brahms, Wagner, Tchaikovsky and Bruckner, but after World War II he added Verdi, Puccini, Bartók, Sibelius and others. More recently the second Viennese school and Mahler have been included in his repertoire. In 1975 a set of records in which he conducted music by Schoenberg, Berg and Webern was issued by DGG, whose advertisements for it included a statement by him that he had delayed recording the music until his orchestra was completely at one with the idiom. Even so, it would be difficult for anyone to claim that Karajan is a champion of unfamiliar composers or new music, and Henze is the only contemporary composer he performs. His repertoire is conservative and was for a long period forced to be so by the artistic strictures of the Nazi period. Generally he has followed musical taste rather than attempted to create or influence it, and has shown nothing of the enterprise of say Stokowski, Beecham or Koussevitzky. This is probably a reflection of the musical culture of which he is such a prominent ornament, and it is perhaps unreasonable to expect a conductor of his age to pioneer new music. His discovery of Mahler, at least in the concert hall, was an event, although he has pointed out that he was brought up on Mahler's music when he was studying in Vienna.

Much has been written about the Karajan 'sound', and his smooth, tensionless orchestral style. There can be no doubt that the Berlin Philharmonic had elements of this sound before he became its principal conductor; the magnificent and supple strings, the superb woodwinds, singly or blended as a group, the marvellous horns and brass, and the sumptuous basses – all these inspired just the same praise under Furtwängler as they do now under Karajan. He inherited a tradition, and enhanced it, but within five years of his coming to Berlin the orchestra was largely renewed because of retirements. His production of this sound is an inexplicable alchemy, like every great conductor's special sound, but we can derive some clues from his own statements about his approach to music. He has discovered, he says, the importance of his pulse rate in relation to tempo: 'Different conductors have different pulse rates and their tempi are often mathematical proportions of this. Bach's music is nearly always the pulse of the heartbeat. Again, I know this from my long experience of yoga. I know what my heartbeat is: I feel it in every part of me. And if I fall into the pulse at the start of a piece of music it is a physical joy. In this way your whole body makes music' (*The Gramophone*, April 1978, pp. 1681ff.). Also, he has explained that every musical masterpiece has one climax, and 'the end must feel as though it is the end'. Experience has taught him where to apply his concentration in the piece, at the decisive moment, at the climax; and it has also brought him to understand how to maintain one pulse through an entire work. With the heroic and tragic composers his performances are marvellous, but with others, the style does not suit. Performances can appear calculated, preordained and devoid of spontaneity. The very perfection of his orchestral sound brings about its interpretative weakness, for his special concern for the architecture of the piece, building it up towards its climax, gives the music its smooth surface, but mutes the sforzandos and minimises the dramatic effect of unexpected modulations or sharp changes in dynamics, suggesting an external view rather than an intense expression of the drama within, from behind the notes. Stravinsky made this point clear in his comments about Karajan's recording of *Le Sacre du printemps*, when he objected to his 'sostenuto style' and declared: 'I doubt if *The Rite* can be performed satisfactorily in terms of Herr von Karajan's traditions. . . . There are simply no regions for soul-searching in *The Rite of Spring*.' At the other end of the musical spectrum, Karajan has equal difficulty in performing Haydn and Mozart, despite the excellence of some of the Mozart opera recordings; we hear superb orchestral performances but readings that are fundamentally superficial. Haydn's wit and muscle, Mozart's elegance and poignancy are often absent. It is not surprising that he has said that the most difficult movement for him in all Beethoven is the first of the Symphony No. 1; it is the closest to Haydn. Even so, it is absurd for some critics to refuse to review Karajan's records, because his performances are contrived, apparently beyond tolerance. Karajan himself has taken this up, saying: 'So much nonsense is talked, particularly by some critics about "manipulating" the music. The verb is used detrimentally, and why should it be? The composer manipulates from the moment he picks up his pen. The concert hall manipulates because each seat is different. . . . And my manipulation as a conductor is that I try to bring out the sound that I want. That is my handwriting' (*The Times*, 12 October 1977).

Karajan has made many magnificent recordings of opera, yet they do not give an adequate impression of his great impact on opera performance, particularly at La Scala and Vienna. He first conducted Wagner at La Scala, but soon developed into a superb conductor of Italian opera, and in Vienna he produced as well as conducted Verdi and Puccini. Some contend that, for him, production is mainly a matter of lighting or darkening. He takes immense care in preparing operas; for *Die Walküre* in Vienna in 1957 there were 25 lighting rehearsals alone. When he was working with Vienna and La Scala simultaneously he developed a close liaison between the two houses, bringing the leading singers from La Scala to join his productions at Vienna, but this made him unpopular in Vienna, since the ensemble principle was always important there. He has, however, said that he left the Vienna Opera because of the lack of rehearsal time, and the deteriorating conditions there. More recently, he has declared that unless the great opera houses combine their resources and bring together the best available casts for particular shared productions, opera could be eclipsed, but his warning, and his offer, were not taken up. In 1965 he founded a company Cosmotel to produce opera films for television, starting with *La Bohème*, directed by Zeffirelli, and later including *Carmen* and *Otello*, which he directed himself. By assembling the finest casts for these films and conducting the Berlin Philharmonic, he believed that the public would not tolerate ensemble opera with its inevitably lower standards. But the enormous costs of producing filmed opera, particularly the last, *Otello*, brought the project to an end. Karajan also believes in the superiority of records over concert performances, as the sound is so much clearer, although, ironically, some commentators consider that his concert performances are much more exciting than his recordings of the same works.

Karajan's first record was the overture to *Die Zauberflöte*, made in 1938 with the Berlin State Opera Orchestra for Polydor. Then from 1939 to 1943 he recorded, for Polydor, Beethoven's Symphony No. 7, the overtures to *Anacreon* and *La forza del destino* and the preludes to Acts I and III of *Die Meistersinger* (with the Berlin State Opera Orchestra), Tchaikovsky's Symphony No. 6, Dvořák's Symphony No. 9, *Moldau*, and Johann Strauss's *Künstlerleben* and *Kaiserwalzer*, and the overtures to *Zigeunerbaron* and *Die Fledermaus* (with the Berlin Philharmonic Orchestra), Mozart's Symphonies Nos 35, 40 and 41, the overture to *Semiramide* and the preludes to Acts I and III of *La traviata* (with the EIAR Symphony Orchestra), the overtures *Leonore No. 3*, and *Der Freischütz*, Brahms' Symphony No. 1, *Don Juan* and the dance from *Salome* (with the Amsterdam Concertgebouw Orchestra). While he was debarred from conducting in public before denazification, Legge recorded him with the Vienna Philharmonic Orchestra, from 1946 to 1950; these records were issued by Columbia on 78s, and some of the later ones on LP. Included in this series were, first Schubert's Symphony No. 9 and Beethoven's Symphony No. 8, followed by Mozart's Symphonies Nos 33 and 39, the Clarinet Concerto (with Wlach), two German Dances, the *Masonic Funeral Music*, the *Adagio and Fugue in C minor*, *Eine kleine Nachtmusik*, *Le nozze di Figaro*, and *Die Zauberflöte*, Beethoven's Symphonies Nos 5 and 9, Brahms' Symphony No. 2 and *Ein deutsches Requiem*, Tchaikovsky's Symphony No. 6 and *Romeo and Juliet* fantasy-overture, the first recording of Strauss's *Metamorphosen*, choral excerpts from *Tannhäuser*, *Der fliegende Holländer*, *Lohengrin* and *Die Meistersinger*, a number of waltzes and overtures of Johann and Josef Strauss, the overture *Donna Diana*, intermezzi from *Manon Lescaut* and *Cavalleria rusticana*, two Puccini arias (with Schwarzkopf) and the Presentation of the Silver Rose from Act II of *Der Rosenkavalier* (with Seefried and Schwarzkopf). In this period he also recorded the Schumann Piano Concerto (with Lipatti and the Philharmonia Orchestra) and Mozart's Piano Concerto K. 467 (also with Lipatti, and the Lucerne Festival Orchestra). Some of these Vienna Philharmonic recordings, such as of Brahms' Symphony No. 2, were not issued in Britain. These records made an immediate impact; the two Beethoven symphonies marked Karajan as the successor to Weingartner, and the *Deutsches Requiem*, and the Schubert and Tchaikovsky symphonies, were also remarkable.

After he joined the Philharmonia Orchestra, Karajan's association with EMI continued until the mid 1950s, and resulted in a magnificent series of orchestral, choral and operatic discs, with a repertoire spanning from Bach to Bartók. Paramount were the nine Beethoven and four Brahms symphonies, and the operas *Ariadne auf Naxos*, *Così fan tutte*, *Die Fledermaus*, *Falstaff*, *Hänsel und Gretel*, *Il trovatore* and *Der Rosenkavalier*; also included were the Bach *Mass in B minor*, the Handel/Harty *Water Music* suite, Mozart's Symphonies Nos 35, 38 and 39, four Horn Concertos (with Brain), Clarinet Concerto (with Walton), *Eine kleine Nachtmusik*, the Divertimento K. 287 and Sinfonia Concertante K. 297b, Leopold Mozart's *Toy Symphony*, Beethoven's *Missa Solemnis*, *Egmont*, *Leonore No. 3* and *Coriolan* overtures and *Ah! perfido* (with Schwarzkopf), Mozart's Piano Concertos K. 488 and K. 491, Beethoven's Piano Concertos Nos 4 and 5, the Franck *Symphonic Variations* and the Grieg Piano Concerto (with Gieseking), *Symphonie fantastique*, the overture *Le Carnaval romain* and March from *La Damnation de Faust*, Schubert's Symphony No. 8, Liszt's *Hungarian Rhapsody No. 2* and *Les Préludes*, the Rossini overtures *Il barbiere di Siviglia*, *La gazza ladra*, *William Tell*, *L'Italiana in Algeri*, *La scala di seta* and *Semiramide*, Brahms' *Variations on the St Antony Chorale*, Tchaikovsky's Symphonies Nos 4, 5 and 6, and suites from *Nutcracker*, *Swan Lake* and *The Sleeping Beauty*, *Pictures at an Exhibition*, *Peter and the Wolf*, the two

L'Arlésienne suites and a suite from *Carmen*, *Don Juan* and *Till Eulenspiegel*, Sibelius' Symphonies Nos 2, 4, 5, 6 and 7, *Tapiola*, *Finlandia* and *Valse triste*, the Bartók *Concerto for Orchestra*, *La Mer*, *Rapsodie espagnole*, *Pini di Roma*, the Offenbach/Rosenthal *Gaîté parisienne*, *Invitation to the Dance*, Britten's *Variations on a Theme of Frank Bridge*, Vaughan Williams' *Fantasia on a Theme of Thomas Tallis*, Leimer's *Piano Concerto in C* (with the composer as soloist; issued only in FR Germany), and Strauss waltzes, operatic intermezzi and ballet music. For EMI he also recorded with the Berlin Philharmonic Mozart's Symphony No. 29, *Eine kleine Nachtmusik*, and some German Dances, the Handel/Harty *Water Music* suite, Dvořák's Symphony No. 9, *Moldau*, Tchaikovsky's Symphony No. 4, Schumann's Symphony No. 4, Brahms' Piano Concerto No. 2 (with Richter-Haaser), Bruckner's Symphony No. 8, the prelude to *Die Meistersinger*, the overture to *Tannhäuser* and the prelude and Liebestod from *Tristan und Isolde*, Bartók's *Music for Strings, Percussion and Celesta* and Hindemith's *Mathis der Maler* symphony, and, with the La Scala Orchestra *et al.*, *Madama Butterfly*.

In 1959 Karajan recorded for Decca, with the Vienna Philharmonic Orchestra, Haydn's Symphonies Nos 103 and 104, Mozart's Symphonies Nos 40 and 41, Beethoven's Symphony No. 7, Brahms' Symphonies Nos 1 and 3 and the *Tragic Overture*, Dvořák's Symphony No. 8, a suite from *Giselle*, the *Peer Gynt* suites, *Also sprach Zarathustra*, *Till Eulenspiegel*, *Don Juan*, *Tod und Verklärung* and the dance from *Salome*, the *Romeo and Juliet* fantasy-overture and *Nutcracker* suite, *The Planets*, the operas *Aida*, *Die Fledermaus* and *Otello*, and a disc of Christmas music with soprano Leontyne Price; also, for RCA, he recorded *Carmen* with the Vienna Philharmonic *et al.*, and later, *Boris Godunov* and *Madama Butterfly* with the Vienna Philharmonic *et al.* for Decca. The series he has recorded for DGG with the Berlin Philharmonic Orchestra commenced in 1959 with *Ein Heldenleben*; he recorded the work again in 1974, and was to repeat a number of works a second time with the Berlin Philharmonic, such as the nine Beethoven symphonies and the four Brahms symphonies, so that he has recorded them three times over. The DGG records have included Bach's *Brandenburg Concertos*, Suites, *Mass in B minor* and *St Matthew Passion*, Handel's Concerti Grossi Op. 6, Vivaldi's *Four Seasons* and other concertos, pieces by Albinoni and Boccherini, concertos by Torelli, Corelli, Manfredini and Locatelli, and trumpet concertos by Hummel, Leopold Mozart, Telemann and Vivaldi (with André), Haydn's *The Creation* and *The Seasons*, Mozart's Symphonies Nos 29, 32, 33, 35, 36, 37, 38, 39, 40 and 41, *Eine kleine Nachtmusik*, *Serenata notturna*, the Divertimenti K. 136, K. 137, K. 138, K. 247, K. 251, K. 287 and K. 334, the four Horn Concertos (with Seifert), Violin Concertos K. 216 and K. 219 (with Mutter), the *Adagio and Fugue in C minor*, the Mass K. 317 and the *Requiem*, Schubert's Symphonies Nos 8 and 9, the four Schumann symphonies and the *Overture, Scherzo and Finale*, the Beethoven symphonies (twice), the overtures *Leonore Nos 1*, *2* and *3*, *Egmont*, *Coriolan*, *Die Weihe des Hauses*, *Fidelio*, *Prometheus*, *König Stephan*, *Die Ruinen von Athen*, *Prometheus* and *Namensfeier*, *Wellington's Victory*, the *Egmont* music, Violin Concerto (with Ferras), Piano Concerto No. 1 (with Eschenbach), *Fidelio* and the *Missa Solemnis* (twice), *Symphonie fantastique* (twice) and excerpts from *La Damnation de Faust*, *Les Préludes*, *Tasso*, *Mephisto Waltz* and the *Hungarian Rhapsodies Nos 2*, *4* and *5* of Liszt, the four Brahms symphonies (twice), *Tragic Overture*, *Variations on the St Antony Chorale*, some Hungarian Dances, Piano Concerto No. 2 (with Anda), Violin Concerto (with Ferras) and *Ein deutsches Requiem*, Dvořák's Symphony No. 9, *Scherzo capriccioso*, Cello Concerto (with Rostropovich) and some *Slavonic Dances*, the Rossini String Sonatas Nos 1, 2, 3 and 6 and overtures *La gazza ladra*, *La scala di seta*, *Semiramide*, *Il barbiere di Siviglia* and *L'Italiana in Algeri*, Weber's overtures *Der Freischütz*, *Oberon*, *Peter Schmoll und seine Nachbarn*, *Beherrscher der Geister*, *Euryanthe* and *Abu Hassan*, the five Mendelssohn symphonies and *The Hebrides* overture, the two *L'Arlésienne* suites and a *Carmen* suite, Bruckner's Symphonies Nos 4, 5, 7, 8 and 9 (the last twice) and *Te Deum*, *Das Rheingold*, *Die Walküre*, *Siegfried*, *Götterdämmerung* and the *Siegfried Idyll*, Tchaikovsky's Symphonies Nos 4, 5 and 6 (twice), Violin Concerto (with Ferras), *Romeo and Juliet* fantasy-overture, *Rococo Variations* (with Rostropovich), *Capriccio italien*, *Marche slave*, *1812* overture, *Serenade in C major*, Piano Concerto No. 1 (with Berman), and suites from *Swan Lake*, *Nutcracker* and *The Sleeping Beauty*, *Les Sylphides* (Chopin, arr. Douglas), a suite from *Coppélia*, La Mer and *Prélude à l'après-midi d'un faune*, *Boléro*, and *Daphnis et Chloé* Suite No. 2, *Symphonia domestica*, *Also sprach Zarathustra*, *Don Juan*, *Till Eulenspiegel*, *Tod und Verklärung*, *Don Quixote* (twice, with Fournier and Rostropovich), *Metamorphosen*, the dance from *Salome*, *Vier letzte Lieder* (with

Janowitz), the Horn Concerto No. 2 (with Hauptmann) and the Oboe Concerto (with Koch), *Scheherazade*, *Pictures at an Exhibition*, Sibelius' Symphonies Nos 4, 5, 6 and 7, *En Saga*, *Finlandia* (twice), *Tapiola* (twice), *Valse triste* and the Violin Concerto (with Ferras), *Le Sacre du printemps* (twice), *Apollon Musagète*, *Concerto in D*, *Symphony in C* and *Circus Polka* of Stravinsky, Bartók's *Concerto for Orchestra* (twice) and *Music for Strings, Percussion and Celesta*, *Moldau*, *Vyšehrad* and dances from *The Bartered Bride*, Shostakovich's Symphony No. 10, Prokofiev's Symphony No. 5, Honegger's Symphonies Nos 2 and 3, Respighi's *Ancient Airs and Dances* Suite No. 3, *Pini di Roma* and *Fontane di Roma*, the Suppé overtures *Banditenstreiche*, *Dichter und Bauer*, *Leichte Cavallerie*, *Morgen, Mittag und Abend in Wien*, *Pique Dame* and *Die schöne Galatea*, the Offenbach/Rosenthal *Gaîté parisienne*, the *Peer Gynt* Suites Nos 1 and 2 and *Sigurd Jorsalfar*, the Verdi *Requiem*, *Il trovatore* and the overtures, preludes and sinfonias from the Verdi operas, Lehár's *Die lustige Witwe*, *La Bohème*, Mahler's Symphonies Nos 5 and 6, *Das Lied von der Erde* (with Ludwig and Kollo), *Kindertotenlieder* and *Rückert Lieder* (with Ludwig), Schoenberg's *Verklärte Nacht*, *Pelléas et Mélisande* and *Variations for Orchestra* Op. 31, Berg's *Three Orchestral Pieces* Op. 6 and three movements from the *Lyric Suite*, and Webern's *Passacaglia* Op. 1, *Five Movements* Op. 5, *Six Movements for Orchestra* Op. 6 and *Symphony*, a collection of Prussian and Austrian marches, the 17 national anthems of the nations belonging to the Council of Europe, with his own arrangement of the European Anthem, and collections of Strauss waltzes and other pieces, intermezzi and ballet music from operas, and other short pieces. For DGG he also recorded the Mozart *Requiem* and Strauss's *Salome* (with the Vienna Philharmonic *et al.*), Tchaikovsky's Piano Concerto No. 1 (with Richter and the Vienna Symphony), and Orff's *De temporum fine comoedia* (with the Cologne Radio Chorus and Orchestra *et al.*). Cetra has also issued his *Tristan und Isolde* from the 1952 Bayreuth Festival.

Karajan's second series of records for EMI commenced in 1970, and has included Mozart's Symphonies Nos 35, 36, 38, 39, 40 and 41, Flute Concerto No. 1 (with Blau), Flute and Harp Concerto (with Galway and Helmis), Bassoon Concerto (with Piesk), Clarinet Concerto (with Leister), Oboe Concerto (with Koch) and Sinfonia Concertante K. 297b, Haydn's Symphonies Nos 83, 101 and 104, the five Beethoven Piano Concertos (with Weissenberg), *Fidelio* and *Missa Solemnis*, Brahms' Violin Concerto (with Kremer), *Variations on the St Antony Chorale*, *Tragic Overture* and *Ein deutsches Requiem*, Bruckner's Symphonies Nos 4 and 7, Tchaikovsky's Symphonies Nos 4, 5 and 6, *Tristan und Isolde*, the overture and Venusberg Music from *Tannhäuser*, the preludes to Acts I and III of *Lohengrin* and *Parsifal*, the prelude and Liebestod from *Tristan und Isolde*, the prelude to *Die Meistersinger* and the overture to *Der fliegende Holländer*, Sibelius' Symphonies Nos 4 and 5, *Finlandia*, *En Saga*, *Tapiola*, and *The Swan of Tuonela*, Dvořák's Symphony No. 9 and *Moldau*, *La Mer*, *Prélude à l'après-midi d'un faune*, *Boléro*, *Otello*, the eight Schubert symphonies and the *Rosamunde* music, Rachmaninov's Piano Concerto No. 1 and Franck's *Symphonic Variations* (with Weissenberg) (all with the Berlin Philharmonic *et al.*), *Die Meistersinger* (with the Dresden Staatskapelle *et al.*), Franck's *Symphony in D minor*, the Tchaikovsky Piano Concerto No. 1 (with Weissenberg), and Ravel's *La Valse*, *Rapsodie espagnole*, *Alborada del gracioso* and *Le Tombeau de Couperin* (with l'Orchestre de Paris).

No conductor in the history of the gramophone record can approach Karajan in the scope and standard of his recorded output. There are certainly parts of the repertoire where he is not heard at his best, as I have indicated, but the Bruckner symphonies, for example, are incomparable, as are the recent Mahler symphonies, almost all the opera sets, the Prokofiev, Shostakovich and French impressionist records, and, of course, the Beethoven and Brahms sets. Many of his earlier records have been re-issued at cheaper prices, including the magical *Così fan tutte* from his early EMI days, and transfers of his 78s with the Vienna Philharmonic have appeared; no doubt many more re-issues will continue to delight the record collector. One can ponder wistfully at the music he has *not* recorded: Reger, Nielsen, and the remaining Wagner operas, for instance, but the harvest in the Karajan granary has been bountiful, almost beyond measure.

Karajan, Wolfgang von (b. 1906). Born in Salzburg and the brother of Herbert, Karajan studied at the Mozarteum, and also took a diploma in engineering at the Technical High School in Vienna (1932). He married the concert pianist Hedy Budischowsky, and in Vienna had his own physics laboratory. After World War II he became a resident of Salzburg, and developed an interest in small organs and in the presentation of concerts with an ensemble of these instruments. For this purpose, he founded the Wolfgang von Karajan Ensemble, and has been given the title of Professor by the Austrian President. He produced an edition of Bach's *Die Kunst der Fuge*, for performance by a group in which the organ is the main instrument, and this he recorded for Schwann. He also recorded as a conductor the Haydn *Organ Concerto in C* (with Hedy von Karajan), Michael Haydn's Viola and Organ Concerto (with Pitamic and Hedy von Karajan), and Mozart's Piano Concertos K. 459 and K. 537 (with Andreae, and the Camerata Accademica, Salzburg, issued in the United States by Musical Heritage Society).

Karasik, Simon (b. 1910). Born in Altona, Pennsylvania, and educated at the Eastman School of Music, Karasik was a trombone player (1938–53) in various radio and theatre orchestras in New York, and also taught the trombone and conducted wind and brass ensembles. He has taught at the Mannes College of Music (since 1953), the State University of New York at Stony Brook (since 1966), and the Queen's College of the City University of New York (since 1972). His recordings have been Haufrecht's *Symphony for Brass and Timpani* (for Composers Recordings), the *Ricercare* from Bach's *Ein musikalisches Opfer* and the fourth movement of Tomasi's *Fanfares liturgiques* (for Hi-Fi Stereo Records), all with the New York Brass Society.

Karr-Bertoli, Julius (b. 1920). Born in Munich and educated at the academy of music there, Karr-Bertoli was a conductor at Dortmund (1943–5), was pianist and conductor for the Bavarian Radio (1945–60), and since 1955 has made guest appearances, mainly abroad. For Electrecord (Romania) he conducted the Bucharest Philharmonic Orchestra in Pergolesi's Concertinos Nos 2 and 6, and the Romanian Film Orchestra in Vancea's *Symphonic Trilogy*.

Kašlík, Václav (b. 1917). Born in Poličná, Czechoslovakia, Kašlík studied at the Charles University, the Prague Conservatory and the Prague Academy of Music, where he was a conducting student with Talich. He was conductor at the Brno Opera (1942–5), artistic director of the Opera '5 May' in Prague (1945–8), and director of the Prague National Theatre (1948 onwards). His compositions include operas, ballets and symphonic music, and he recorded the *Nutcracker* Suite of Tchaikovsky for Supraphon with the Prague Radio Symphony Orchestra.

Katims, Milton (b. 1909). Born in New York of Russian and Hungarian parentage, Katims was educated at Columbia University and began his career as a violist. He was first-desk violist in the NBC Symphony Orchestra under Toscanini (1943–53), a teacher at the Juilliard School (1946–54), and a member of some distinguished chamber-music ensembles. He conducted the NBC Symphony and the Buffalo Philharmonic Orchestras (1947–54), was musical director of the Seattle Symphony Orchestra (1954–76), and then became head of the music school at the University of Houston. In his years at Seattle he did much to raise the standard of the orchestra and to widen its repertoire, and he has been a guest conductor with other orchestras in the United States, Israel, Japan and other countries. Katims' close association with Toscanini and with Casals has influenced his conducting, which is noted for its vitality and dramatic intensity. He is reported to provide his audience with cough lozenges and to illustrate performances with slides. Katims made many records as a violist with chamber groups such as the Budapest String Quartet, in string quintets by Mozart, Beethoven and Dvořák, the New York Piano Quartet and in the Casals Festival ensembles. As a conductor he accompanied Stern in a disc of popular pieces (with the Columbia Concerto Orchestra for Columbia), recorded Gould's *Venice* and *Vivaldi Gallery* (with the Seattle Symphony Orchestra for RCA), Campos-Parsi's *Divertimento del Sun* (with the Casals Festival Orchestra for Cook), Berwald's Symphony No. 3 and Hindemith's *Symphonic Metamorphoses on a Theme by Weber* (with the Seattle Symphony Orchestra on the orchestra's own label), Dohnányi's *Suite in F sharp minor* and *Variations on a Nursery Theme* (with Siki) and suites from Glière's *The Red Poppy*, Shostakovich's *The Age of Gold* and Rimsky-Korsakov's *Sadko* (with the Seattle Symphony Orchestra for Vox).

Katlewicz, Jerzy (b. 1927). Born in Bochnia, Poland, Katlewicz studied at the High School of Music at Kraków and in Austria and Italy. He was appointed artistic director and first conductor at the Kraków Opera and second conductor of the Kraków Philharmonic Orchestra (1952–7), won first prize at the International Competition for Young Conductors at Besançon (1955), was artistic director and first conductor of the Baltic Philharmonic Orchestra and Opera at Gdańsk (1961), toured the USSR, the Far East and Australasia with the Polish National Radio Orchestra (1963), and was appointed artistic director and first conductor of the National Kraków Philharmonia of Karol Szymanowski (1968). He teaches conducting at Kraków Academy of Music and conducts extensively in Eastern and Western Europe, with a repertoire that includes the works of Lutosławski and Penderecki. He himself has composed music for the theatre and has received many distinguished awards in Poland. His recordings with the National Philharmonic Symphony Orchestra for the Polish recording company include a disc of Mozart overtures, and the Piano Concertos K. 466 and K. 488 (with Czerny-Stefańska), the Mendelssohn and Glazunov Violin Concertos (with Kulka) and Penderecki's *Canticum Canticorum Salomonis*, *Cantate* and *Strophe*.

Kaufman, Louis (b. 1905). Born in Portland, Oregon, Kaufman studied the violin with Kneisel, won the Loeb Prize (1927) and the Naumberg Award (1928), and since 1950 was active in Europe as a soloist. He made a number of records as a violinist in the early years of LP, for Capitol and Nixa, and both played and conducted Torelli's Concertos Op. 8 (with the L'Oiseau Lyre Ensemble, for L'Oiseau Lyre), and Vivaldi's Concertos Op. 9 (with the French National Radio String Orchestra for Classic).

Kazandžiev, Vasil (b. 1934). The Romanian conductor and composer Kazandžiev studied composition with Iliev and Vladigerov, and became conductor at the Sofia National Theatre (1957). He has composed orchestral, chamber, instrumental and choral music, and music for films. For Balkaton he conducted the Bulgarian Chamber Orchestra in Raichev's Symphony No. 4 and Kyurkchusky's *Adagio*, and the Sofia Soloists Chamber Ensemble *et al.* in Schubert's Masses Nos 2 and 3, a selection of Gabrieli's *Sacrae Sinfoniae*, his own *Images de Bulgarie* and *Icones vivantes*, and pieces by Pipkov and Nikolov.

Kegel, Herbert (b. 1920). Born in Dresden, Kegel studied at the school of the Saxon State Orchestra at Dresden under Blacher, Böhm, Heintze, Stier, Lederer and von Schönberg (1935–40). He saw military service in World War II; an injury to his hand forced him to abandon thoughts of a career as a concert pianist. He was a theatre conductor in Pirna and Rostock (1946–9), conductor (1953–8) and general music director (1958–60) of the Leipzig Radio Choir and conductor (1953–60) and chief conductor (from 1960) of the Leipzig Radio Symphony Orchestra. In 1977 he became chief conductor of the Dresden Philharmonic Orchestra. From 1975 he has also been a professor at the Hochschule für Musik at Dresden. He is now one of the major conductors in DR Germany, and has been awarded the Artists' Prize (1959), the National Prize of the GDR (1961) and the Artur Nikisch Prize of Leipzig (1974). His repertoire includes the major composers of the 19th century, as well as music by Martinů, Hartmann, Dallapiccola, Nono, Lutosławski, Stravinsky, Bartók, Hindemith, Schoenberg, Webern, Janáček, Kodály, Orff, Shostakovich, Dessau, Penderecki, Henze and Britten, whose *War Requiem* he led at the International Bach Festival in Leipzig in 1966. He has performed in many countries in Eastern and Western Europe, Latin and South America; in the GDR he has led premières of works by Dessau, Meyer, Alan Bush, Wagner-Régeny, Schenker, Goldman *et al.*, and first local performances of music by Stravinsky, Orff, Schoenberg, Prokofiev, and Penderecki. In Leipzig, some of his major achievements were performances of Mahler's Symphony No. 6, Berlioz *Grande Messe des morts*, Schoenberg's *Moses und Aron*, Berg's *Wozzeck* and Wagner's *Parsifal*; his recordings of the last three, with the Leipzig Radio Symphony Orchestra *et al.* for Eterna, have been especially impressive, although they have not been released in the West.

Kegel has made a number of recordings for Eterna, in addition to the three mentioned above; many have been issued in Europe and the United States on various labels, such as DGG, Urania, Philips, Telefunken, Wergo and Vanguard. Included have been Handel's *Messiah* and *Utrecht Te Deum* and Weber's *Kampf und Sieg* (with the Berlin Symphony Orchestra *et al.*), Bériot's *Scène de ballet* (with the Leipzig Philharmonic Orchestra), Beethoven's *Mass in C major* (with the Leipzig Gewandhaus Orchestra *et al.*), excerpts from *Boris Godunov*, Addinsell's *Warsaw Concerto* (with the Dresden Philharmonic Orchestra *et al.*), Haydn's *The Seasons*, Mozart's Masses K. 139, K. 192 and K. 259, *Litaniae de venerabili altaris sacramento*, *Misericordias* and *Venite populi*, Mendelssohn's Piano Concertos Nos 1 and 2 (with Gheorgiu), Weber's *Abu Hassan* overture, Stravinsky's *Jeu de cartes*, Suites Nos 1 and 2 and *Dumbarton Oaks*, *Carmen* (in German), excerpts from Prokofiev's *Betrothal in a Monastery*, Shostakovich's *The Execution of Stepan Razin* (with Vogel), Casella's *Serenade for Small Orchestra*, Orff's *Der Mond*, *Carmina Burana*, *Catulli Carmina* and *Trionfo di Afrodite*, the Polovtsian Dances from *Prince Igor*, a collection of Strauss waltzes, Bartók's Violin Concerto No. 2 (with Garay), a viola concerto by Stamitz and Hindemith's *Der Schwanen-*

dreber (with Lipka), Weill's *The Seven Deadly Sins*, Britten's *War Requiem*, *Les Illuminations* and *Serenade for Tenor, Horn and Strings* (with Schreier), Nono's *Como una ola de fuerza y luz*, Dessau's Sinfonia No. 2, *Die Verurteilung des Lukullus* and *Appell der Arbeiterklasse*, the *Jüdische Chronik* with sections by Blacher, Wagner-Régeny, Hartmann, Henze and Dessau, Kochan's Piano Concerto (with Zechlin) and *Concerto for Orchestra*, Meyer's *Sinfonia concertante* and *Poem for Viola and Orchestra* (with Bender), Cilenšek's *Konzertstück*, Lohse's Symphony No. 2, and an aria recital (with Schreier, and with the Leipzig Radio Symphony Orchestra).

Kehr, Günter (b. 1920). Born in Darmstadt, the violinist and conductor Kehr studied at the universities of Cologne and Berlin, as well as at the conservatories at these two cities and at Frankfurt am Main, and from 1945 was a violin soloist and chamber musician, giving the first performances in Germany of the Hindemith and Bartók Violin Concertos. He was the violinist of the Kehr Trio, which was founded in 1949, was director of the Peter Cornelius Conservatory in Mainz (1953–60), and in 1959 was appointed professor of chamber music at the Cologne Conservatory. He has been musical director and conductor of the Mainz Chamber Orchestra since its foundation in 1955, choosing its instrumentalists from all parts of FR Germany. Through its concert tours, broadcasts and recordings it has acquired an international reputation, being one of the first-class German chamber orchestras that excel in the music of the baroque and classical periods.

Kehr recorded for Vox and Dover with his Trio and other chamber ensembles, and as a violinist recorded the Bach Violin Concertos with the Mainz Chamber Orchestra. But his reputation as a recording artist rests primarily as conductor of the Mainz Chamber Orchestra, with which he has recorded extensively for Vox, released for the most part on the Turnabout label and in Vox-Box sets of three or so records. His discography includes the Bach *Brandenburg Concertos*, Suites, Violin Concertos, Harpsichord Concertos (with Galling *et al.*), the Handel Concerti Grossi Op. 3 and a collection of overtures from operas and oratorios, Monteverdi's *Il Combattimento di Tancredi e Clorinda* and three madrigals, Lully's *Le Bourgeois gentilhomme*, Rameau's *Les Indes galantes*, Pergolesi's *Stabat Mater*, Telemann's *Suite in F, et al.*, Locatelli's *The Art of The Violin* (with Lautenbacher), Biber's *Serenade* (with Malaguti), Reutter's *Servizio di tabula* (with Zickler), a concerto grosso of Muffat, Purcell's *Behold, I bring you glad tidings*, A. Scarlatti's *Oh, di Betlemme* (with Stoklassa), trumpet concertos by Fasch, Handel, Hertel, Purcell, Telemann, Torelli and Vivaldi (with Zickler and Thal), Corrette's Concerto for Harpsichord and Flute, and two flute concertos (with Pohlers), Dittersdorf's Symphony *Die Rettung der Andromeda durch Perseus*, Pezel's *Deliciae musicales*, Rosenmüller's *Studentenmusik*, concertos by C. P. E., J. C. F., J. C. and W. F. Bach, di Capua's *La Zingara*, Haydn's *Cantilena pro adventu 'Ein' Magd, ein' Dienerin'* (with Stoklassa and the Purcell Singers), Mozart's Symphonies Nos 1 to 34, Piano Concertos K. 449, K. 456 and K. 467 (with Klien), Serenade K. 204 and March K. 215. For DGG/Archiv he has also recorded concertos by Torelli, Corelli, Manfredini and Locatelli. These performances were all played in exemplary style, but with modern instruments. Fine examples of Kehr's musicianship and of the excellence of the Mainz orchestra are the Turnabout discs containing Mozart's Symphonies Nos 18, 19 and 24 on the one, and the Nos 20, 23 and 25 on the other.

Keilberth, Joseph (1908–68). Born in Karlsruhe into a musical family, Keilberth was a coach at the Karlsruhe Opera at the age of seventeen, and within ten years was the theatre's chief conductor (1935–40). He was conductor of the German Philharmonic Orchestra at Prague (1940–45), was a guest conductor at that time at Hamburg and with the Berlin State Opera, was conductor of the Dresden Staatskapelle (1945–51), of the Hamburg Philharmonic Orchestra and of the Bavarian State Opera at Munich (1951), became musical director of the Opera in 1959 and held this post until his death. From 1949 he was also conductor of the Bamberg Symphony Orchestra (formerly the German Philharmonic Orchestra at Prague), and with them toured a number of European countries (1951) and the United States and Latin America (1954). He first appeared at the Bayreuth Festival in 1952, conducted *The Ring* from 1952 to 1956, *Lohengrin* in 1953 and *Der fliegende Holländer* in 1955 and 1956, appeared with the Hamburg State Opera at the Edinburgh Festival in 1952, and took part in the Lucerne and Salzburg Festivals. He died while conducting a performance of *Tristan und Isolde* at Munich.

Keilberth's reputation and activities were mostly centred in Germany, and in many ways he represented German musicianship at its most typical. He was an authoritative interpreter of the Austrian and German classical and romantic repertoire, and while he preferred above all Mozart, Bruckner and Wagner, he also gave sympathetic performances of Smetana and Dvořák, and of such 20th-century composers as Stravinsky, Prokofiev, Milhaud, Britten and Orff. His recording career started during World War II with Telefunken when he was in Prague, recording with the German Philharmonic Orchestra Haydn's Symphony No. 101, Mozart's Symphonies Nos 38 and 39, Schumann's Symphony No. 4, Wolf's *Italian Serenade*, the overture to Egk's *Die Zaubergeige* and the three preludes from Pfitzner's *Palestrina*. Ducretet-Thomson also issued on 78s Reger's *Böcklin* suite (with the German Philharmonic Orchestra), and HMV the Schumann Cello Concerto (with Hoelscher and the Berlin State Opera Orchestra). Some of these performances were later released by Capitol in the United States on mono LPs. His post-war records were released by Telefunken, DGG, Decca, Electrola and Urania. In 1955 Decca recorded him conducting *The Ring* at Bayreuth, but difficulties with conflicting contracts of the artists concerned prevented the records from being issued. Nonetheless, they were later released on a pirate label, identified as the Dresden State Opera conducted by Fritz Schreiber, but were withdrawn after legal action.

Urania's discs with Keilberth as conductor were *Lohengrin* (with the Munich State Opera Orchestra *et al.*) and Dvořák's *Rusalka* (with the Saxon State Orchestra *et al.*), the Gluck/Mottl ballet suite and the overture to *Alceste* (with the German Philharmonic Orchestra). The series for Telefunken continued on LP with the Hamburg Philharmonic, the Berlin Philharmonic, the Bavarian Radio Symphony and the Bamberg Symphony Orchestras, and included were Beethoven's Symphonies Nos 1 to 8 (but not, apparently, No. 9); these performances were fresh, vital, and with some expansive tempi. With the Bamberg Symphony Orchestra he recorded Haydn's Symphonies Nos 85 and 101, Mozart's Symphonies Nos 28, 29, 30, 35, 36, 38, 39, 40 and 41, Divertimento K. 113, Serenades K. 239, K. 250 and *Eine kleine Nachtmusik*, Notturno K. 286, two Minuets K. 403, German Dances K. 509 and K. 571, and the overtures to *Die Zauberflöte* and *Der Schauspieldirektor*; his Haydn and Mozart were not especially distinctive. Also with the Bamberg Symphony Orchestra were Schubert's Symphonies Nos 6 and 8, Schumann's Symphony No. 1, the overtures *Coriolan*, *Euryanthe*, *Der Freischütz* and Pfitzner's *Das Käthchen von Heilbronn*, the prelude to *Die Meistersinger*, Brahms' Symphonies Nos 3 and 4, *Academic Festival Overture* and some *Hungarian Dances*, Dvořák's Symphony No. 9, *Carnival* overture and some *Slavonic Dances*, *Don Juan*, *Till Eulenspiegel*, waltzes and polkas of Johann Strauss, *Moldau* and *From Bohemia's Meadows and Forests*, Reger's *Ballet Suite* and *Variations and Fugue on a Theme of Mozart*, and Gotovac's *Sinfonischer Kolo*. With the Berlin Philharmonic Orchestra he recorded overtures *Leonore No. 3*, *Coriolan* and *Egmont*, Brahms' Symphonies Nos 1 and 2 and Bruckner's Symphony No. 6, and with the Bavarian Radio Symphony Orchestra orchestral excerpts from *Der Rosenkavalier*, *Salome*, *Intermezzo* and *Die schweigsame Frau*, and with the Hamburg Philharmonic Orchestra Brahms' Symphonies Nos 3 and 4, Dvořák's Cello Concerto (with Hoelscher), Bruckner's Symphony No. 9, Reger's *Variations and Fugue on a Theme of Hiller*, and Hindemith's *Nobilissima Visione* and *Symphonic Metamorphosis on Themes by Weber*.

Keilberth's operatic recordings were significant, and were fine examples of his great strengths as a conductor. They were, in addition to the *Rusalka* and *Lohengrin* for Urania mentioned earlier, *Der fliegende Holländer* (the Bayreuth Festival performance of 1955, for Decca), *Lohengrin* (also Bayreuth, 1955, for Decca), *Der Freischütz* (with the Berlin Philharmonic Orchestra *et al.*, issued in 1960 by EMI, and recently re-released on Seraphim in the US), *Arabella* and *Die Frau ohne Schatten* (with the Bavarian State Opera Orchestra *et al.* for DGG), *Salome* (with the Dresden State Opera, issued by Musical Treasures of the World, US), *Die Meistersinger* (with the Bavarian State Opera Orchestra *et al.* for Ariola/Eurodisc), Hindemith's *Cardillac* (with the Cologne Radio Symphony Orchestra *et al.* for DGG) and *Aida* (with the Stuttgart Radio Orchestra *et al.* for Bellaphon). An interesting and little-known work is Pfitzner's cantata, *Von deutscher Seele* ('The German Soul'), issued by DGG in 1967, in which Keilberth conducted the Bavarian State Radio Orchestra *et al.*; it is a setting of extracts from poems by Eichendorff, in which the composer recognised the true spirit of German artistic aspiration. Keilberth was associated with Pfitzner in his early years, and the fine performance reveals the intermittent beauty of the work.

Kelterborn, Rudolf (b. 1931). Born in Basel, Kelterborn studied at the Basel Conservatory and at Zürich, Salzburg and Detmold, and was a pupil at Blacher, Fortner, Markevitch and Krannhals. He taught at the Basel Academy of Music (1955–60), joined the staff of the West German Music Academy at Detmold

(1960–68), was a professor at the Hochschule für Musik at Zürich (1968–75), head of the music department at Swiss Radio (1975) and editor of the *Swiss Music Review* (1968–75). His compositions have been widely performed and he occasionally conducts his own works. For Bärenreiter he recorded his *Octet* with the Zürich Chamber Music Ensemble.

Kemény, Endre (b. 1925). The Hungarian conductor Kemény studied the violin with Waldbauer, composition with Lajtha and conducting with Somogyi at the Franz Liszt Academy of Music in Budapest, was a violinist with the Hungarian National Philharmonic Orchestra and conductor of the Kecskemét Symphony Orchestra. He recorded Kósa's Symphony No. 8 with the Hungarian State Symphony Orchestra for Hungaroton.

Kempe, Rudolf (1910–76). Born at Niederpoyritz, near Dresden, Kempe studied the piano as a child and later took lessons on the violin and oboe. He was educated at the Orchestra School of the Saxon State Orchestra at Dresden, and in 1929 joined the Dortmund Opera orchestra as first oboist, and very soon after was appointed first oboist with the Leipzig Gewandhaus Orchestra. A fellow member of the orchestra was Charles Munch, and in the orchestra he played under Furtwängler, Strauss, Beecham, Walter, Klemperer and Kleiber. In 1933 he became a repetiteur with the Leipzig Opera, and made his debut as a conductor there with *Der Wildschütz* of Lortzing in 1935. He joined the German army in 1942, but within a year had returned to conducting, enjoying an unofficial permanent leave. From then until 1948 he was first conductor and then music director at the opera at Chemnitz (now Karl-Marx-Stadt), and also conducted at the Berlin State Opera and at orchestral concerts in Berlin, Leipzig and Dresden. After a year at the Weimar National Theatre (1948–9), he was engaged as the general music director at the Saxon State Theatre at Dresden, where he also conducted the Staatskapelle concerts (1949–52), and then was music director at the Bavarian State Opera at Munich (1952–4), also appearing as a guest conductor at other major opera houses in Europe and South America. At the Vienna State Opera he conducted Mozart, Verdi and Strauss in 1951–2, and came to London in 1953 to conduct Strauss operas with the visiting Bavarian State Opera Company. He was invited to Covent Garden to lead *Salome*, conducted *The Ring* there in 1954 and 1956, and from then on appeared in London frequently, but declined the offer to be music director at Covent Garden in 1956. His debut in the United States occurred in 1955 when he conducted *Arabella*, *Tannhäuser* and *Tristan und Isolde* at the New York Metropolitan, and in that year he directed Pfitzner's *Palestrina* at the Salzburg Festival. Serious illness curtailed his activities in 1956 and later in 1963–4. Beecham invited him to become associate conductor of his Royal Philharmonic Orchestra in 1960, and after Beecham's death in 1961 Kempe was first appointed chief conductor of the orchestra, then artistic director in 1964, and finally 'conductor for life' in 1970. Nonetheless he departed from the orchestra in 1975 when he was engaged as chief conductor of the BBC Symphony Orchestra, in succession to Boulez. Previously, in 1965, he had become chief conductor of the Zürich Tonhalle Orchestra, and in 1966 general music director of the Munich Philharmonic Orchestra. His first appearance at the Bayreuth Festivals was in 1960, when he led *The Ring*; he also conducted there in 1962, 1963, 1964 and 1967. He was married to the operatic soprano Elisabeth Lindermeier.

Many orchestral musicians who played under Kempe regard him as one of the greatest conductors of his generation, and to them his premature death was an irreparable loss. In the earlier stages of his career opera occupied most of his attention, but in the last phase of his life his appearances in the concert hall were more numerous. His experience as a conductor of opera was vast; ironically the musical public tended to regard him as a Wagner and Strauss specialist, but at Vienna he conducted the Italian repertoire almost exclusively, and the opera he conducted the most times in his life was *Carmen*. He first conducted *The Ring* in Barcelona in 1954, prior to his great success with the tetralogy in London; he went to Barcelona to learn the score by rehearsing a less-than-perfect orchestra. In opera his sympathies extended from Mozart to Strauss, and included unfamiliar German composers as well as Verdi, Puccini, Bizet, Offenbach and Orff. In the concert hall he excelled in Mozart, Haydn, Beethoven, Brahms, Bruckner, Tchaikovsky, Mahler and Strauss; he conducted Schoenberg, Webern and Berg but had little interest in *avant-garde* music. After he had performed a very modern score he was asked what school it was, and he replied with a chuckle, 'No school at all.' He had a remarkable understanding of the music of Delius, which he conducted with great insight at the Delius Festival at Bradford in 1962.

Kempe conducted most of his repertoire from memory; his technique was exemplary and his gestures and beat were models of clarity, with which he could convey to the orchestra how he wished to portray the music. At rehearsals he was relaxed, and his verbal comments were few and quietly spoken, although musicians found that he created a unique atmosphere which made them quite nervous. In performance, he was fiery and impassioned, but only for the music, and his players then were inspired to perform better than their best. He placed the second violins on the right. The music of Beethoven, Brahms, Bruckner, Strauss and Wagner was given a warm sonority, the interpretations were unmannered, unhurried, and the climaxes were paced carefully so that tension was built gradually. The music was articulated beautifully, and the drama revealed cumulatively. In the Wagner operas the music was in a continuous lyrical flow, far removed from the feverish excitement generated by fast, accurate playing. Critics were sometimes tempted to complain that he smoothed out the dramatic peaks; Harold Rosenthal, for instance, wrote about his 'chamber music' approach to *The Ring* (*Concise Oxford Dictionary of Opera*, p. 200). His warmth and sense of balance made his Brahms memorable, but just before he died he led an impetuous and fiery performance of the Symphony No. 4 with the BBC Symphony Orchestra in London. The scrupulous attention he gave to each instrumental line, as well as to the dramatic structure of the piece, made him one of the finest conductors of Richard Strauss, but in the highly charged music of Berlioz, Tchaikovsky and Rimsky-Korsakov, for instance, his restraint took away the last ounce of bravura.

For someone who was not keen on recording, Kempe has an exceptional list of records to his credit, of music ranging from Bach to Britten. His first were opera sets made for Urania, and issued in Britain by Nixa and in the US by Vox – *Der Rosenkavalier*, *Die Meistersinger* and *Der Freischütz* (with the Dresden Staatskapelle *et al.*), and *Lohengrin* (with the Bavarian State Opera Orchestra *et al.*); these were recorded in 1950–52. For Urania he also recorded the Khachaturian Cello Concerto (with Posegga and the Leipzig Radio Symphony Orchestra) and the Glière Harp Concerto (with Joff and the Leipzig Philharmonic Orchestra); he also recorded in Eastern Europe in these years Mendelssohn's Symphony No. 3 (with the Dresden Staatskapelle for Supraphon), and later the *L'Oiseau de feu* suite, Britten's *Sinfonia da Requiem* and the Moonlight Music from *Capriccio* (with the Dresden Staatskapelle for Eterna), the overtures *Die Fledermaus* and *Morgen, Mittag und Abend in Wien*, the Strauss waltzes *Sphärenklänge* and *G'schichten aus dem Wiener Wald* and polka *Leichtes Blut*, and Lehár's *Gold und Silber* waltz (with the Dresden Staatskapelle for Ariola/Eurodisc) and *Ariadne auf Naxos* (with the Dresden Staatskapelle *et al.* for EMI). Then for EMI he made a number of extremely fine LPs, in London, Vienna and Berlin; these included Haydn's Symphony No. 104, Mozart's Symphony No. 34, *Eine kleine Nachtmusik* and the overtures to *Così fan tutte*, *Idomeneo*, *Die Zauberflöte* and *Le nozze di Figaro*, and Tchaikovsky's Symphony No. 6 (with the Philharmonia Orchestra), the Gluck/Mottl ballet suite, the incidental music for *Rosamunde*, the preludes to Acts I and III of *Lohengrin*, the prelude and Good Friday Music from *Parsifal* and the prelude and Liebestod from *Tristan und Isolde*, Tchaikovsky's Suite No. 3, the overture and dances from *The Bartered Bride*, the overtures *Le Carnaval romain*, *Der Opernball*, *The Hebrides*, *The Merry Wives of Windsor*, *Orphée aux enfers*, *Donna Diana*, *Die Fledermaus*, *Morgen, Mittag und Abend in Wien* and *Oberon*, the ballet music from Bayer's *Die Puppenfee*, a dance from Gotovac's *Ero der Schelm*, the waltz from *Faust*, the *Háry János* suite, Lehár's *Gold und Silber* waltz, the intermezzo from *L'amico Fritz*, the Dance of the Hours from *La Gioconda*, the intermezzo from *Notre Dame*, the Strausses' *Radetzky March*, *Im Krapfenwald'l*, *Leichtes Blut* polka, *G'schichten aus dem Wiener Wald*, the intermezzo from *Tausend und eine Nacht*, *Dynamiden*, *Sphärenklänge* and *Kaiserwalzer* (with the Vienna Philharmonic Orchestra), the Bach Suite No. 3, the Mozart *Requiem*, Beethoven's Symphony No. 3, overtures *Coriolan*, *Egmont*, *Fidelio*, *Leonore No. 3* and *Prometheus*, and Piano Concerto No. 5 (with Gimpel), *Symphonie fantastique*, Schumann's Symphony No. 1 and *Manfred* overture, *Die Meistersinger*, the overture to *Der fliegende Holländer*, the *Tannhäuser* overture and Venusberg music and Dawn and Siegfried's Rhine Journey from *Götterdämmerung*, the four Brahms symphonies, *Tragic Overture*, *Variations on the St Antony Chorale*, Piano Concerto No. 1 (with Gimpel), Violin Concerto (with Menuhin) and *Ein deutsches Requiem*, Tchaikovsky's Symphony No. 5 and the waltz and polonaise from *Eugene Onegin*, arias from *The Bartered Bride*, *Eugene Onegin* and *Rusalka* (with Lindermeier), Dvořák's Symphony No. 9 and *Scherzo capriccioso*, Mahler's *Kindertotenlieder* (with Fischer-Dieskau), and Strauss's *Don Quixote* (with Tortelier) and *Till Eulenspiegel* (with the Berlin Philharmonic Orchestra).

Kempe also made other records for EMI, including the nine Beethoven symphonies and overtures *Egmont*, *Leonore No. 3* and *Prometheus* (in 1971–3, with the Munich Philharmonic Orchestra, *et al.*), Brahms' Symphony No. 4 and Piano Concerto No. 2 (with Leonardo-Gelber), Dvořák's *Scherzo capriccioso*, the overture and dances from *The Bartered Bride*, the overture, nocturne, scherzo and wedding march from *A Midsummer Night's Dream*, a suite (arranged by himself) from *Hänsel und Gretel* and the polka and fugue from *Schwanda the Bagpiper* (with the Royal Philharmonic Orchestra), *Scheherazade* (with the Royal Philharmonic Orchestra, issued by World Record Club and Classics for Pleasure), Handel's *Music for the Royal Fireworks* and *The Bartered Bride* (with the Bamberg Symphony Orchestra *et al.*), *Lohengrin* (with the Vienna Philharmonic Orchestra *et al.*), excerpts from *Das Rheingold* (with the Berlin German Opera Orchestra *et al.*), and the great series of Strauss's orchestral music, with the Dresden Staatskapelle, including *Eine Alpensinfonie, Also sprach Zarathustra*, *Le Bourgeois gentilhomme*, *Don Juan*, *Don Quixote* (with Tortelier), *Ein Heldenleben*, *Till Eulenspiegel*, *Tod und Verklärung*, *Metamorphosen*, *Macbeth*, *Aus Italien*, *Symphonia domestica*, *Josephslegende*, the *Suite from Harpsichord pieces by Couperin*, the dance from *Salome*, the waltz from *Schlagobers*, the waltzes from *Der Rosenkavalier*, the *Duet Concertino*, *Burleske* (with Frager), the two Horn Concertos (with Damm), the Oboe Concerto (with Clement), the Violin Concerto (with Hoelscher), and *Panathenäenzug* and *Parergon zu Symphonia domestica* (with Rösel).

His recordings for other companies were of Haydn's Symphony No. 93 (with the Munich Philharmonic Orchestra for Da Camera), Korngold's *Symphony in F sharp* (with the Munich Philharmonic Orchestra for RCA), Janáček's *Glagolitic Mass* (with the Royal Philharmonic Orchestra, Brighton Festival Chorus, *et al.* for Decca), Bruch's Violin Concerto No. 1 and *Scottish Fantasy* (with Kyung Wha-Chung and the Royal Philharmonic Orchestra for Decca), Schubert's Symphony No. 9, Strauss's *Metamorphosen*, Dvořák's *Serenade in E major* and Liszt's *Totentanz*, the Schumann Piano Concerto, the Grieg Piano Concerto and Tchaikovsky's Piano Concerto No. 1 (with Freire, and the Munich Philharmonic Orchestra for CBS), the four Mozart Horn Concertos and Rondo K. 371 (with Civil, also issued by World Record Club), Beethoven's Piano Concerto No. 5 (with Firkusny) and Strauss's *Ein Alpensinfonie* (with the Royal Philharmonic Orchestra for RCA), Chopin's Piano Concerto No. 2 (with Cherkassky), Dvořák's Symphony No. 9, Strauss's Horn Concerto No. 1 (with Civil), *Don Juan*, and *Pini di Roma* (with the Royal Philharmonic Orchestra for Reader's Digest), Beethoven's Symphony No. 5, Dvořák's Symphony No. 9 and Bruckner's Symphony No. 8 (with the Zürich Tonhalle Orchestra for Tudor, Switzerland), *Eine kleine Nachtmusik*, Schubert's Symphony No. 8, *Moldau*, the *Euryanthe* overture, Brahms' Symphony No. 2 and *Variations on the St Antony Chorale* and the two *L'Arlésienne* suites (with the Bamberg Symphony Orchestra for Ariola/Eurodisc), Mozart's Piano Concerto K. 595 (with Gulda), the four Brahms Symphonies and *Tragic Overture*, Dvořák's Symphony No. 8, the prelude to *Die Meistersinger*, the Bruckner Symphonies Nos 4 and 5, and Schoeck's cantata *Vom Fischer un syner Fru* (with the Munich Philharmonic Orchestra *et al.* for BASF/Acanta).

Kempe's death at the age of 66, just after he had been appointed chief conductor of the BBC Symphony Orchestra, robbed the world of a great musician who was reaching the most productive period of his career. He was the natural successor to the great German conductors of a generation before him, and with whom he had come into contact at Leipzig early in his life. Fortunately he has left as his legacy many exceptionally fine records, through which his musicianship can be evaluated and appreciated: the Beethoven and Brahms symphonies, the Strauss tone poems, and the later opera sets, will be prized for many years to come.

Kempen, Paul van (1893–1955). Born in Leiden, Holland, Kempen studied the violin at the Amsterdam Conservatory and played in the Concertgebouw Orchestra under Mengelberg, who influenced him later when he became a conductor. His first appointment was at Dortmund (1916), then he was at Oberhausen (1932–4), and became conductor at Dresden (1934–42) and then at Aachen (1942), where he succeeded Karajan. He conducted the Netherlands Radio Orchestra at Hilversum, taught at the conductors' course at the Accademia Chigiana at Siena, and finally was music director at Bremen (1953). A committed performer of Mahler and Bruckner, as well as the Austrian and German classical repertoire, he was the first conductor in Germany to perform the original versions of the Bruckner symphonies, and was awarded the Bruckner Medal in Vienna. He was a man of energy and vitality, a fine organiser and a sober personality; he strove for precision and delicacy of tone in his direction of the orchestra. Although he was a Dutchman, he remained and conducted in Germany throughout the Nazi era, but he resisted political interference with the direction of the Dresden Philharmonic Orchestra.

Kempen made a considerable number of recordings. His first was of the Mozart Organ Sonatas (with Bunk and the Dortmund Conservatory Orchestra for Polydor), then, on 78s, followed a series with the Dresden Philharmonic Orchestra for Polydor, including the overtures *Le nozze di Figaro*, *Egmont*, *Coriolan*, *Die Weihe des Hauses*, *Jubel*, *Euryanthe*, *Der Freischütz*, *Preziosa*, *Die Zauberharfe*, *Le Carnaval romain*, *I vespri siciliani*, *Der fliegende Holländer*, Pfitzner's *Die Käthchen von Heilbronn*, *Mignon*, *Martha*, *La Dame blanche*, *Faust*, *Zampa*, *Zar und Zimmermann*, *Der Wildschütz*, *Der Barbier von Bagdad*, *Don Pasquale* and Kreutzer's *Nachtlager in Granada*, Mozart's Piano Concerto K. 466 and Rondo K. 382 (with Kempff), and Violin Concerto K. 218 (with Stanke), Beethoven's Symphonies Nos 2 and 5 and Piano Concerto No. 3 (with Kempff), *Invitation to the Dance*, Schubert's Symphony No. 8, Schumann's Symphony No. 4, two *Hungarian Dances* of Brahms, Dvořák's Cello Concerto (with Mainardi), dances from Gluck's *Orfeo ed Euridice*, Grieg's *Symphonic Dances* and the *Peer Gynt* Suites Nos 1 and 2, Liszt's *Mazeppa*, the *Siegfried Idyll*, *Marche slave* and *Nutcracker* suite. For Polydor he also recorded on 78s the Schumann Cello Concerto (with Mainardi and the Berlin State Opera Orchestra), Tchaikovsky's *Serenade in C major* (with the Reichswander Orchestra), Beethoven's Symphony No. 8, *Die Weihe des Hauses* overture, the five Piano Concertos (with Kempff) and Violin Concerto (with Schneiderhan), Brahms' Symphony No. 4, *Academic Festival Overture*, nine *Hungarian Dances* and Violin Concerto (with Schneiderhan), the *William Tell* and *Benvenuto Cellini* overtures, *Capriccio italien* and Reger's *Variations and Fugue on a Theme of Hiller* (with the Berlin Philharmonic Orchestra), the Brahms Violin Concerto (with de Vito and the German Opera House Orchestra), the Piano Concerto No. 2 (with Aeschbacher and the Berlin Philharmonic Orchestra), Haydn's Symphony No. 104, Schubert's Symphony No. 9 and Sibelius' Symphony No. 5 (with the Amsterdam Concertgebouw Orchestra), *Les Préludes* (with the Berlin Philharmonic Orchestra) and *Tasso* (with the Berlin State Opera Orchestra), Dvořák's Violin Concerto (with Prihoda and the Berlin State Opera Orchestra), the overtures to *I vespri siciliani*, *Der fliegende Holländer* and *Tannhäuser* (with the La Scala Orchestra) and to *Der Freischütz*, *The Merry Wives of Windsor* and *Il barbiere di Siviglia* (with the Berlin State Opera Orchestra). For Telefunken, on 78s, he also conducted the Netherlands Radio Orchestra in Mahler's Symphony No. 4 (with Bijster) and Bruckner's Symphony No. 4.

Kempen's LP recordings were, for Telefunken Bruckner's Symphony No. 7 and Sibelius' Symphony No. 7 (with the Concertgebouw Orchestra), and for Philips Beethoven's Symphonies Nos 1, 3, 7 and 8, and *The Hebrides* overture (with the Berlin Philharmonic Orchestra), Tchaikovsky's Symphonies Nos 5 and 6, the *Romeo and Juliet* fantasy-overture, the *1812* overture and *Marche slave* (with the Concertgebouw Orchestra), *Serenade in C major* and Suite No. 4, the overtures *La Fille du régiment*, *William Tell*, *A Midsummer Night's Dream* and *Il barbiere di Siviglia* (with the Lamoureux Orchestra), Bruckner's Symphony No. 4, intermezzi from *Cavalleria rusticana* and *Pagliacci*, choruses from *Aida* and *Nabucco*, the overture to *La forza del destino*, and the preludes to Acts I and III and the Wedding Chorus from *Lohengrin* (with the Netherlands Radio Orchestra *et al.*) and the Verdi *Requiem* (with the Santa Cecilia Orchestra *et al.*).

Kerby, Paul. Born in South Africa, Kerby studied at the Royal College of Music, London, and started as a conductor at the Capitol Theatre, New York. He was foreign adviser to the Salzburg Festival (1926), was resident in Vienna (1926–33) where he conducted the Vienna Symphony and Vienna Philharmonic Orchestras, as well as other orchestras at Frankfurt am Main, Wiesbaden and Budapest, and was musical director in Vienna for the Columbia Phonograph Company. He led the Chicago Symphony Orchestra in a Viennese concert as official representative of the Austrian government, conducted at the Chicago Opera (1933–4) in his own English translation of *Le Coq d'or*, and conducted part of the summer season of the New York Philharmonic-Symphony Orchestra at Lewisohn Stadium (1936). For Columbia (US) before World War II he recorded with the Vienna Symphony Orchestra the overtures to *Le Calife de Bagdad*, *Mireille* and *Eine Nacht in Venedig*, Waldteufel's *Skaters' Waltz*, Moszkowski's *Spanish Dances* Nos 1 to 4, and Grieg's *Peer Gynt* music, and with the Vienna State Opera Chorus and Orchestra the Pilgrims' Chorus from *Tannhäuser*, and the Bridal Chorus from *Lohengrin*.

Kersjes, Anton (b. 1923). Born at Arnhem, Holland, Kersjes studied conducting with Hupka in Amsterdam and with Bigot in Paris, and made his debut as a conductor in 1949, leading the *St Matthew Passion*. In 1953 he joined the Art-Month Chamber Orchestra, which became the Amsterdam Philharmonic Orchestra, and of which he is now the first conductor. He has toured Belgium, France, FR Germany, Austria, Italy and the USSR with the orchestra, and conducted numerous concerts for Netherlands Television. He also is a guest conductor with the Netherlands Opera and teaches conducting at the Sweelinck Academy of Music in Amsterdam. His repertoire ranges from Gabrieli to modern Dutch composers, and encompasses Mozart, Beethoven, Shostakovich, Bruckner, Mahler, Nielsen and Sibelius. His recordings all with the Amsterdam Philharmonic Orchestra include the Dvořák Violin Concerto and Tchaikovsky's *Souvenirs* (with Krebbers for EMI), oboe concertos and concerted pieces by Bellini, Hummel, Kalliwoda, Rietz, Molique and Rimsky-Korsakov (with de Vries for EMI), flute concertos of C. P. E. Bach and Quantz (with de Quant for EMI), Bach's *Double Concerto in D minor* and the two Beethoven *Romances* (with Verhey and Bor for Philips), Beethoven's Symphony No. 1, Schubert's Symphony No. 8 and Bizet's *L'Arlésienne* Suites Nos 1 and 2 (for PMC) and Gluck's *Orfeo ed Euridice* (with Heynis, the Toonkunst Choir and the Amsterdam Philharmonic for EMI).

Kertész, István (1929–73). Born in Budapest, Kertész studied the violin, composition and conducting at the Franz Liszt Academy, and graduated as a conductor. He was principal conductor of the Györ Philharmonic Orchestra (1953–5) and conductor at the Budapest Opera (1955–6), left Hungary after the uprising in 1956, studied conducting with Previtali at the Accademia di Santa Cecilia in Rome, and made appearances at the opera houses in Hamburg, Frankfurt am Main and West Berlin. He became general music director at Augsburg Opera (1958–63), conductor at the Salzburg Festival (1961–4), music director at the Cologne Opera (1964–73), principal conductor of the London Symphony Orchestra (1965–8) and conductor of the Gürzenich Orchestra at Cologne (1971–3). He was a frequent guest conductor with major symphony orchestras and in opera houses in Europe, North and South America, particularly with the Cleveland, Vienna Philharmonic and Israel Philharmonic Orchestras. His United States debut had taken place with the Detroit Symphony Orchestra 1961; he took part in many festivals in Europe, and led the London Symphony Orchestra on several international tours.

When Kertész was drowned while swimming in the Mediterranean at Tel-Aviv, at the age of 44, the world lost a most distinguished musician who was already reputed to be one of the finest conductors of his generation. His naturally warm personality was reflected in his music-making, which seemed spontaneously lyrical and heartfelt. His readings of Mozart, Schubert, Dvořák and Bruckner had this special distinction. His association with the London Symphony Orchestra was, at the end, marred by a conflict concerning the extent of his control over the orchestra's artistic policy, which is inevitably an uneasy matter for a conductor contracted to a self-governing orchestra. Nonetheless his London concerts, his tours with the orchestra and his records with the Vienna Philharmonic as well as the London Symphony, in addition to his guest appearances elsewhere, won him wide recognition. At rehearsals he was subdued and even offhanded, but at concerts before the public he was transformed and the orchestra responded readily to his own delight in performing the music. He was not typically Hungarian, if one accepts that precision and dramatic tension are the qualities most characteristic of Hungarian conductors perhaps better known than Kertész; his performances were usually relaxed, sensitive and direct, and drew beautiful playing from his orchestras.

In the last decade or so of his life, Kertész recorded for Decca and made a number of fine discs. With the Vienna Philharmonic Orchestra he recorded Mozart's Symphonies Nos 25, 29, 33, 35, 36, 39 and 40, *Eine kleine Nachtmusik*, March K. 408 and the *Requiem*, the Schubert symphonies and overtures, Dvořák's Symphony No. 9 and the Brahms symphonies and *Variations on the St Antony Chorale*; with the London Symphony Orchestra there were Mozart's Piano Concertos K. 488 and K. 491 (with Curzon), K. 246 and K. 271 and Rondo K. 386 (with Ashkenazy), and the Masonic music, including the cantatas and *Masonic Funeral Music*, the two Brahms Serenades, the nine Dvořák symphonies, *Serenade in D minor*, *Symphonic Variations*, *Scherzo capriccioso*, *The Golden Spinning Wheel*, *Water Goblin*, *Noonday Witch*, the overtures *Carnival*, *In Nature's Realm*, *Othello*, *My Home* and *Husitská* and the *Requiem*, Rossini's *Stabat Mater*, Bruckner's Symphony No. 4, Bartók's Piano Concerto No. 3 (with Katchen) and *Bluebeard's Castle*, Kodály's *Háry János*, *Psalmus Hungaricus*, *Galánta Dances* and

Peacock Variations, the two Ravel Piano Concertos (with Katchen), the two Strauss Horn Concertos and Franz Strauss's Horn Concerto (with Tuckwell), and the *Pini di Roma*, *Fontane di Roma* and *Gli uccelli*. His only opera recording, for Decca, was *La clemenza di Tito* (with the Vienna State Opera Orchestra *et al*); he also recorded with the Israel Philharmonic Orchestra for Decca the Grieg and Schumann Piano Concertos (with Katchen) and some *Slavonic Dances* of Dvořák, *Moldau* and the overture and dances from *The Bartered Bride*. For EMI he conducted with the Philharmonic Orchestra Beethoven's Piano Concerto No. 5 and Mozart's Piano Concertos K. 453 and K. 537 (with Richter-Haaser), and with the Philharmonia Hungarica the two Liszt Piano Concertos (with Karolyi); he also recorded Beethoven's Symphony No. 4 and *Coriolan* overture, the Mozart Clarinet Concerto (with Dorr) and Sinfonia Concertante K. 364 (with Lautenbacher and Koch) and the Haydn Sinfonia Concertante, with the Bamberg Symphony Orchestra, and issued in Britain, minus the Clarinet Concerto, by Oriole, and the Clarinet Concerto and Sinfonia Concertante K. 364 by Nonesuch.

Many of Kertész's records remain in the catalogue. In the United States Vox has issued, in Vox Boxes, the four Brahms symphonies and the last three Dvořák Symphonies, and the *Scherzo capriccioso* and *Othello* overture. They are superb souvenirs of a fine conductor, whose musical culture was in a direct line from Nikisch.

Kessler, Jerome (b. 1942). Born in Ithaca, New York, Kessler studied law at Columbia College and at the law school at the University of California, Los Angeles, the cello with Goodman, Varga, Rose and Schuster, and conducting with Karp and Monteux. He played in film and television orchestras, was founder and a member of the Beverly Hills Trio, and founder and conductor of the Cello Octet. He has recorded as a cellist, and as a conductor with I Cellisti, pieces by Casals, Linn and Erlich, and Vivaldi's Concerto Op. 3 No. 11 (for Orion and Pye).

Ketting, Otto (b. 1935). Born in Amsterdam, Ketting studied at The Hague Conservatory, and in Munich with Hartmann, and was for some years a trumpeter in the Hague Philharmonic Orchestra. He then turned to composition, was a lecturer in composition at the Rotterdam Conservatory (1967–71) and at the Hague Conservatory (1971–4). As a conductor, he has performed with various orchestras, and recorded for Donemus his *For Moonlight Nights* (with Quant, flute) and *Time Machine* (with the Rotterdam Philharmonic Orchestra).

Khachaturian, Aram (1903–78). An Armenian, born in Tiflis, and a graduate of the Gnessin Music School and the Moscow Conservatory, Khachaturian composed music impregnated with the idiom of folk melodies. His straightforward, florid and fundamentally superficial style did not save him from being condemned in 1948, together with Shostakovich and others, by the Central Committee of the Communist Party for modernist tendencies; nonetheless, he was (at various times) secretary and deputy chairman of the USSR Union of Composers, a deputy to the Supreme Soviet, a member of the presidium of the USSR Societies of Friendship and Cultural Relations with Foreign Countries, and received the Order of Lenin and the Stalin Prize a number of times. In addition to his ever-popular ballet suites, concertos and symphonies, he wrote patriotic pieces with titles such as *The Song of Stalin*, *Ode in Memory of Lenin* and *Ballad of the Motherland*. Some think his Symphony No. 3 the noisiest piece of music ever written, even noisier than *Feste Romane* of Respighi. He toured Europe and the United States, the latter in 1968, as a conductor of his own music.

Khachaturian recorded a number of his own compositions. In the USSR he made discs of his Symphony No. 2, Piano Concerto (with Oborin) and Violin Concerto (with David Oistrakh, and the so-called National Philharmonic Orchestra), Piano Concerto (with Petrov), the suite *The Battle for Stalingrad* and Violin Concerto (with Kogan, and the USSR State Symphony Orchestra), the Concert Rhapsody for Cello and Orchestra (with Shakhovskaya, and also with Georgian) and the Concert Rhapsody for Piano and Orchestra (with Petrov, and the Moscow Radio Symphony Orchestra), and a suite from *Masquerade* (with the Bolshoi Theatre Orchestra). In 1955 he visited London and recorded for EMI with the Philharmonia Orchestra the Violin Concerto (with David Oistrakh), *In Memoriam* and suites from *Gayane* and *Masquerade*; later, in 1977, EMI recorded him again with the London Symphony Orchestra in suites from *Gayane* and *Spartacus*. His other recordings include another disc of suites from *Gayane* and *Spartacus*, and the Symphony No. 2 (with the Vienna Philharmonic Orchestra for Decca), *In Memoriam* and a suite from *Masquerade* (with the Prague Radio Symphony Orchestra for Supraphon) and the Violin Concerto (with Claire Bernard and the Bucharest Symphony Orchestra for Philips).

Khaikin, Boris (1904–78). A native of Minsk, Khaikin studied at the Moscow Conservatory under Malko and Sarojev. He was chief conductor and music director at the Stanislavsky Opera Theatre, Moscow (1933–6), chief conductor and artistic director of the Leningrad Maly Theatre (1936–44), chief conductor at the Leningrad Kirov Theatre (1944–53), a professor at the Leningrad Conservatory (1935–53), conductor of the Bolshoi Theatre, Moscow (from 1954) and professor at the Moscow Conservatory. He has received many Soviet awards, including the Stalin Prize in 1946 and 1951. His records, all made in the USSR, have been released in the West on various labels, but more recently under Melodiya's agreement with EMI; they reveal him to be an artist noted more for his straightforward vigour than for his subtlety. He has recorded the operas *A Life for the Tsar*, *Mazeppa*, *Eugene Onegin*, *The Queen of Spades* (with the Bolshoi company), *Khovanshchina*, and Tchaikovsky's *The Maid of Orleans* (with the Kirov Opera company) and Dargomyzhsky's *The Stone Guest* (with the Moscow Radio Orchestra *et al.*); in 1975 EMI released a second performance of *Khovanshchina* under him, with the Bolshoi company. His other recordings included the *Gayaneh* ballet (with the Leningrad Kirov Theatre Orchestra), Tchaikovsky's Symphony No. 2 (with the USSR State Symphony Orchestra), *The Seasons* of Glazunov and the Dvořák Cello Concerto (with Rostropovich and the Moscow Radio Symphony Orchestra), Glazunov's Symphony No. 2 and Chopin's Piano Concerto No. 1 (with Feltzmann, and the Moscow Philharmonic Orchestra), Dvořák's *Notturno*, Liadov's *From the Olden Days* and the finale from *Mlada* by Borodin (with the Leningrad Philharmonic Orchestra), Liszt's *Dante Symphony*, the Weber Bassoon Concerto (with Bogorad), two Mozart Horn Concertos (with Polekh), the Dvořák Cello Concerto (with Rostropovich), excerpts from *The Sleeping Beauty*, Rimsky-Korsakov's Symphony No. 1 and *Song of Oleg the Wise*, Glière's Coloratura Concerto (with Mirochnitchenka) and Harp Concerto (with Erdele), and an operatic recital (with Bieschu).

Kiel, Piet (b. 1937). Born at Ouder Amstel, Holland, and educated at the Amsterdam Conservatory, Kiel is a choral conductor, organist and music school director, has arranged unpublished music of Buxtehude and has composed choral pieces. For CBS he has recorded a disc of chorales and choruses from the *St Matthew Passion* of Bach, with the St Bavo's Cathedral Boys' Choir and the Haarlem Oratorio Choir and Baroque Ensemble.

Kielland, Olav (b. 1901). Born in Trondheim, Norway, Kielland studied at the Leipzig Conservatory and with Weingartner in Basel. In addition to guest appearances abroad he was conductor at Göteborg (1925–31), Oslo (1931–45), Trondheim (1946–8) and Bergen (from 1948). His compositions include three symphonies, a violin concerto, piano pieces and a *Concerto Grosso Norvegense*, which he recorded with the Oslo Philharmonic Orchestra for Composers Recordings.

Kilbey, Reginald (b. 1907). Born in London, Kilbey won an All-England Scholarship to the Trinity College of Music at the age of ten, performed the Elgar Cello Concerto and conducted in public at the age of 13. He was a cellist in the London Symphony Orchestra, a member of the de Groot Trio, played with the BBC London Studio Players, and has become well known for his many radio and television appearances. He has recorded, *inter alia*, Coates' *The Three Elizabeths* suite, *The Merrymakers* overture, *The Jester at the Wedding*, *Miniature Suite* and the march from *Calling all Workers* (with the City of Birmingham Orchestra, for EMI).

Kindler, Hans (1892–1949). Born in Rotterdam into a musical family, Kindler studied the piano and cello at the Rotterdam Conservatory, and was also a pupil of Casals. His first public appearance was at the age of ten, as a cellist; at seventeen he was a soloist with the Berlin Philharmonic Orchestra. He joined the Charlottenburg Opera at Berlin as first cellist at nineteen, at the same time being the principal teacher of the instrument at the Klindworth-Scharwenka Conservatory there. During a visit to the United States in 1914 he was obliged to remain because of the outbreak of World War I, and became first cellist with the Philadelphia Orchestra under Stokowski. He relinquished this position in 1919 to resume his career as a soloist, toured the US and Europe and acquired a formidable reputation for his solo, concerto and chamber performances. He first conducted in 1927 when he led the Philadelphia Orchestra, and soon established a name as an interpreter of modern music. He premièred Stravinsky's *Apollon Musagète* at Washington DC in 1928. In 1931 he abandoned completely his career as a cellist, fearful of having to play repeatedly the same pieces all his life, and then established the National Symphony Orchestra in Washington DC. His success as permanent conductor of the orchestra was immediate, and despite the economic depression the orchestra was able to expand its concert season, to tour the country, to broadcast and to make records. In 1948 he resigned as the orchestra's conductor. During his career he was a diligent advocate for new music and gave many first performances; of the orchestra's repertoire of 700 works a high proportion were modern compositions. He had an extraordinary memory and always conducted without a score. Although Kindler was never comparable as a conductor to his illustrious colleagues who led the top US orchestras, he was widely respected for his musicianship. Writing in 1943, David Ewen described the National Symphony Orchestra under Kindler as an excellent ensemble, among the country's greatest, having spirit and vitality in performance, a rich tone and a facile technique.

Victor made a series of records of Kindler and the National Symphony Orchestra, the major works being Brahms' Symphony No. 3, the Tchaikovsky Symphony No. 3 and *Don Juan*. Other recorded pieces were Handel's *Overture in D minor* and suite from *Il pastor fido*, a Suite for Strings by Corelli, some 16th-century Dutch tunes, a Toccata by Frescobaldi (arranged by Kindler), *Moldau*, Weinberger's *Czech Rhapsody*, Enesco's *Romanian Rhapsody No. 2*, Järnefelt's *Berceuse* and *Praeludium*, Liszt's *Hungarian Rhapsody No. 6*, Saint-Saëns' *Le Rouet d'Omphale*, the Dream Pantomime from *Hänsel und Gretel*, and music by American composers, Schuman's *American Festival* overture, Mary Howe's *Stars*, Dai-Kong Lee's *Prelude and Hula*, and the Brazilian Fernandez's *Batuque*. Many of the shorter works were given fine performances by Kindler, but the Brahms and Tchaikovsky symphonies attracted adverse comment; the Tchaikovsky Symphony No. 3 was labelled prosaic and heavy-handed by more than one contemporary reviewer.

Kingsley, Gershon (b. 1928). Born in Bochum, Westphalia, Kingsley was educated at the Jerusalem Conservatory, the Juilliard School and Columbia University, founded the First Moog Quartet and conducted the Robert Joffrey Ballet *et al.* His compositions include *What is Man*, *God and Abraham*, *Concerto Moogo* and *Sabbath for Today*. He directed the Theatre Four Production in 1964 of Blitzstein's *The Cradle Will Rock*, which was recorded by Composers Recordings, and accompanied some discs for Vanguard by the tenor Jan Peerce, as well as Cantaloube's *Anthologie des chants populaires* with soprano Netania Davrath.

Kirchner, Leon (b. 1919). A native of New York but educated at the University of California, Berkeley, Kirchner also studied with Stravinsky, Toch, Schoenberg, Klemperer, Bloch and Sessions. He served in the US army (1943–6), taught at universities in California and at Harvard (since 1961), has appeared as a conductor and a pianist with the New York Philharmonic and other orchestras, and is principal conductor at the Boston Philharmonic Orchestra. His String Quartets Nos 1 and 2 were awarded the New York Music Critics' Circle Prize in 1950, and the Quartet No. 3 the Pulitzer Prize in 1967. He has recorded, as a conductor, some of his own compositions, the *Concerto for Violin, Cello and Ten Wind Instruments and Percussion* (with Spivakovsky, Parisot and a chamber ensemble, for Philips), and *Lily* (with Hoagland and the Columbia Chamber Soloists, for CBS).

Kis, István (b. 1920). The Hungarian choral conductor Kis received his diploma as a vocal and music teacher in 1949, worked as a music teacher and was conductor and artistic director of the Hungarian Army Chorus. With the Chorus he recorded Liszt's *Missa Choralis* and four sacred male choruses, for Hungaroton.

Kisch, Royalton (b. 1919). A Londoner, Kisch was educated at Cambridge University, and conducted many London, provincial and European orchestras in the 1940s. Eventually his interest in art proved stronger and he became the director of an art gallery in London specialising in English and French paintings of the present century. After World War II and in the early days of LP records he was the conductor in some successful records for Decca, with the London Symphony, New Symphony and National Symphony Orchestras. Included were Haydn's Symphonies Nos 92 and 99, Mozart's Symphony No. 32, the overtures to *The Bartered Bride*, Gluck's *Alceste* and *Iphigénie en Aulide*, Cimarosa's *Il matrimonio segreto* and *Gli orazi ed curiazi* and Sinigaglia's *Le baruffe chiozzotte*, Bruch's Violin Concerto No. 1 (with Campoli), Liszt's Piano Concerto No. 1 and the Schumann Piano Concerto (with Lympany). His direction was musical, crisp and stylish.

Kittel, Bruno (1870–1948). Born in Posen, Kittel studied in Berlin, played in orchestras as a violinist, then was conductor of the Royal Theatre Orchestra at Brandenburg (1901–09). He founded and directed the Brandenburg Conservatory (1901–14), and in 1902 established his own choral society, the Kittel Choir, in Berlin, which became famous as one of the foremost choirs in Europe. In 1935 he was appointed director of the Stern Conservatory in

Berlin. He made some distinguished recordings for Polydor: Beethoven's *Missa Solemnis*, Mozart's *Requiem* and Bach's *St Matthew Passion*, the latter being an abridged version which was produced during World War II. All were with the Berlin Philharmonic Orchestra and the Kittel Choir *et al.* He also recorded the *Olympic Hymn* written by Strauss for the 1936 Olympic Games in Berlin.

Klee, Bernhard (b. 1936). Born in Schleiz in Thüringen, Klee was a member of the St Thomas Church Choir at Leipzig (1948–55), studied at the Hochschule für Musik at Cologne, was a repetiteur at the Cologne Opera (1957), and at the Berne State Theatre (1958). He was musical assistant to Sawallisch and conductor at the Cologne Opera, conductor at Salzburg (1962–3), Oberhausen (1963–5) and Hannover (1965–6), then was general music director at Lübeck (1966–77), conductor of the Düsseldorf Symphony Orchestra (1977) and music director of the North German Radio Orchestra at Hannover. Since his tenure at Lübeck, Klee has not accepted a permanent appointment at an opera house, as he feels unable to make the necessary compromises to work in a repertory theatre. He first conducted the Berlin Philharmonic Orchestra in 1968, regularly conducts the London Symphony Orchestra, has toured in Japan, and has conducted at Covent Garden and at the Edinburgh Festival. Recently he has had a special interest in Mahler, and conducted his Symphony No. 8 at the opening of Düsseldorf's new concert hall; he is also interested in introducing British music to German audiences. His recordings have been of the Mozart Flute Concertos (with Zöller and the English Chamber Orchestra for DGG), Haydn's Symphonies Nos 6, 7 and 8, and 22, 23 and 24 (with the Prague Chamber Orchestra for DGG), Mozart's Symphony No. 26 and the incidental music for *Thamos, König in Ägypten* (with the Berlin Staatskapelle *et al.* for Philips), Beethoven's incidental music for *Die Ruinen von Athen* (with the Berlin Philharmonic Orchestra for DGG) and *Christus am Ölberge* (with the Vienna Symphony Orchestra *et al.* for DGG), bassoon concertos by Vañhal, Stamitz and Müthel (with Turkovic and an ensemble for DGG) and *The Merry Wives of Windsor* (with the Berlin Staatskapelle *et al.* for DGG); he also accompanied as pianist recitals of Mozart songs with Prey and his wife, the soprano Edith Mathis, for DGG).

Kleiber, Carlos (b. 1930). The son of Erich Kleiber, Carlos Kleiber was born in Berlin and left Germany with his father and mother in 1935 to live in South America. He began his musical studies in Buenos Aires in 1950, but briefly studied chemistry in Zürich. His first experience was at the Gärtnerplatz Theatre in Munich, and in 1954 he made his debut conducting an operetta at Potsdam. His subsequent appointments have been at Düsseldorf (1956), Zürich (1964), Stuttgart (1966) and Munich (1968), although he has now no wish to accept a permanent musical post. Like his father, Kleiber is a most scrupulous and fastidious conductor; he is however unpredictable in temperament. His early successes were with outstanding performances of operas such as *Wozzeck*, *Elektra*, *Der Rosenkavalier* and *Tristan und Isolde*, which he also conducted at Bayreuth in 1976. In recent years he rarely conducts outside of Germany and even then stipulates a high fee and an exceptional number of rehearsals; he has become one of the most sought-after conductors in Europe. So far he has made few recordings. The first was *Der Freischütz* (with the Dresden Staatskapelle *et al.* for DGG) in 1973, and the second, which was released in 1976, was of Beethoven's Symphony No. 5 (with the Vienna Philharmonic Orchestra, for DGG). It was immediately acclaimed as a most remarkable achievement, even when compared to his father's outstanding recording of the work with the Amsterdam Concertgebouw Orchestra, issued by Decca in 1957; its combination of unflagging urgency, spontaneity and concentration is almost unparalleled among present-day recordings. In 1977 he followed this recording with one of Beethoven's Symphony No. 7, with the same orchestra. He has also recorded *Die Fledermaus* and *La traviata* (with the Bavarian State Opera Orchestra *et al.* for DGG), and the Dvořák Piano Concerto (with Richter and the Bavarian State Opera Orchestra for EMI).

Kleiber, Erich (1890–1956). Born in Vienna, Kleiber studied at the Prague Conservatory, and decided to be a conductor when he heard Mahler conducting his Symphony No. 6. He became a chorus-master at the German Theatre at Prague, and made his debut as a conductor in 1911 directing the stage music for a comedy. He was also then known as a fine accompanist, and started composing in his student years; his compositions later included violin and piano concertos, orchestral and chamber works. He was appointed third conductor at Darmstadt (1912–19), where the first opera he conducted was *La Belle Hélène*. His following appointments were first conductor at Barmen-Elberfeld (1919–21), at Düsseldorf

(1921–2) and Mannheim (1922–3), and then in 1923 he became general music director at the Berlin State Opera. At Düsseldorf he had established a reputation with performances of *Pierrot Lunaire*, *Das Lied von der Erde* and the Verdi *Requiem*, at Mannheim for his première of Bittner's *Das Rosengärtlein*, and then in Berlin, prior to his appointment, with a remarkable *Fidelio*. His years in Berlin (1923–34) constituted one of the most memorable epochs in German musical performance. He led great productions of *Jenůfa* (1924), *Wozzeck* (1925) and Milhaud's *Christophe Colomb* (1930), and also performed much modern music with the Berlin Philharmonic Orchestra – Busoni, Schoenberg, Strauss, Berg and Bartók – as well as Berlioz, Liszt and Reger, and a cycle of concerts of the unfamiliar music of Mozart. In 1925 he toured with the Vienna Philharmonic Orchestra, leading Mahler's Symphony No. 3 in Budapest, in 1926 visited Buenos Aires for the first time, and in 1927 conducted in the USSR. A close friend of Berg, he was determined to perform the Five Symphonic Pieces from *Lulu* in 1934, although he knew the Nazi regime's hostility to atonal music; like Fritz Busch, Kleiber was not a Jew, but would never tolerate interference by the Nazis with his selection of programmes. He resigned from his Berlin post in December 1934 and left Germany the next year.

Kleiber then conducted concerts and some opera in London, Prague, Brussels, Buenos Aires, Amsterdam, Salzburg and in Switzerland, and in 1939 took up residence in Buenos Aires and became an Argentinian citizen. He conducted opera at the Teatro Colón, and trained and led the symphony orchestra in Buenos Aires, also touring other countries in South America and conducting all manner of orchestras. From 1943 to 1948 he was with the Havana Philharmonic Orchestra, and in 1948 returned to Europe. In 1951 he accepted the position of conductor at the Berlin State Opera in East Berlin, but his dissatisfaction with conditions imposed on him brought his resignation in 1955. In his last years he was a guest conductor in London, Vienna and in other European musical centres, and was particularly active in Cologne and Stuttgart.

Kleiber was unquestionably a great conductor, especially with Mozart and Beethoven. He apparently had little interest in Bach or Brahms, and his enthusiasm for Mahler and Bruckner waned as he grew older. He was a warm exponent of the music of many modern composers, and loved the dances and waltzes of Mozart and Johann Strauss. An unremitting perfectionist, he sought to recreate music exactly as written by the composer; even the most familiar score was re-studied before rehearsal, and he demanded that his performers play or sing the notes exactly as they appeared. In his words, 'there are two enemies to good performance: one is routine and the other is improvisation' (John Russell, *Erich Kleiber*, London, 1957). His musicianship was however not simply a technical perfection of execution; this was only the beginning. He said: 'When I conduct, I leave it to my heart, and my feelings, and my respect for what the composer wrote, to tell me what to do. Everything else comes second to me – if it comes at all!' (ibid.). He brought to his interpretations a humanity, a vigour and a passion that made them all unique.

In rehearsal Kleiber was careful to ensure that his musicians understood the meaning of what they were playing, and his explanations and directions were short, witty and to the point. Once when rehearsing the choir for Beethoven's Symphony No. 9, he asked the singers to avoid sentimentality, saying it 'is like eating honey with your fingers' (Information from the author's wife, a member of the choir). When preparing an opera, he saw to it that the orchestral players each had a libretto. After intense rehearsal for a concert, when he was satisfied that his musicians had mastered the score, his direction of the orchestra changed, and at the concert itself his movements were small and his demeanour quiet. He never rehearsed more than necessary, but when he was in Berlin he enjoyed five rehearsals for every concert. Finally, on the day of the concert, no music was played; instead he would read a long catalogue of errors committed at the general rehearsal the previous day, adding that the composer had drawn his attention to them. Before every rehearsal he memorised the score as well as the numbered indications, and he even took the trouble to learn the names and seating of the orchestral players. At the concert itself he avoided signalling the coming points of excitement or climax beforehand to the audience, and impressed on his players not to do this in preparing their instruments.

Kleiber started recording for Polydor, Telefunken, Odeon, Ultraphone and HMV in the 1930s. With the Berlin Philharmonic Orchestra for Telefunken he recorded Schoenberg's arrangement of Bach's *St Anne Fugue*, the In ballo from Handel's *Alcina*, Haydn's *German Dances Nos 2*, *4* and *12*, and the Serenade from the String Quartet Op. 3 No. 5, *Eine kleine Nachtmusik*, Beethoven's Symphony No. 2, second movement of Symphony No. 8 and the overtures *Egmont* and *Coriolan*, Schubert's Symphony No. 8, the second movement of the

Symphonie fantastique, the overture to *Benvenuto Cellini* and the Hungarian March from *La Damnation de Faust*, Liszt's Tarantella from *Venezia e Napoli*, *Invitation to the Dance* and the *Preciosa* overture, the Funeral Music from *Götterdämmerung*, *Capriccio italien*, Dvořák's *Scherzo capriccioso* and the Wedding Dance from *The Little Dove*, the overture to *Iphigénie en Aulide*, *Der Opernball*, *The Merry Wives of Windsor*, *Der Zigeunerbaron*, *Die Fledermaus*, *Donna Diana*, *The Bartered Bride*, *Leichte Cavallerie* and Meyerbeer's *Ein Feldlager in Schlesien*, Lanner's *Die Schönbrunner* waltz, the Strauss waltzes *Accelerationen*, *An der schönen blauen Donau*, *Kaiserwalzer*, *Tausend und eine Nacht*, *Wein, Weib and Gesang* and *Dorfschwalben aus Österreich*, *Till Eulenspiegel* and the waltzes from *Der Rosenkavalier*, Janáček's *Lachian Dance No. 1* and Stravinsky's *Feux d'artifice*. His other 78 r.p.m. discs were *Danse macabre* (with the Berlin State Opera Orchestra for Telefunken), a number of Mozart's *German Dances* from K. 509, K. 571, K. 600 and K. 605, the overture to *Idomeneo*, Schubert's Symphony No. 8, the Scherzo, Nocturne and March from *A Midsummer Night's Dream* and Dvořák's Symphony No. 9 (with the Berlin Philharmonic Orchestra for Polydor), four of Mozart's *German Dances* from K. 600, K. 602 and K. 605, Beethoven's Symphony No. 2, *Moldau*, the overtures *Le Carnaval romain* and *The Merry Wives of Windsor*, two numbers from the *Rosamunde* music and *L'Oiseau de feu* (with the Berlin State Opera Orchestra for Polydor), Beethoven's Symphony No. 2 (with the Brussels Philharmonic Orchestra for Capitol), *Les Préludes* and the preludes to Acts I and IV of *Carmen* (with the Czech Philharmonic Orchestra for Ultraphone), Dvořák's *Slavonic Dance No. 6* (with the Berlin State Opera Orchestra for Odeon), Mozart's Symphony No. 38 (with the Vienna Philharmonic Orchestra for HMV), Mozart's Symphony No. 39 and the overture and andante from *Rosamunde* (with the Berlin State Opera Orchestra from HMV), the Strauss waltzes *Du und Du*, *Künstlerleben* and *Dorfschwalben aus Österreich* (with the Vienna Philharmonic Orchestra for RCA) and the overture to *Der fliegende Holländer* and the prelude to *Die Meistersinger* (with the Berlin State Opera Orchestra for Vox).

However, Kleiber's finest work for the gramophone came in the last decade of his life when he was under contract to Decca. Then his major undertakings were Mozart's Symphony No. 40 (with the London Philharmonic Orchestra), Beethoven's Symphonies Nos 3, 5, 6 and 7 (with the Amsterdam Concertgebouw Orchestra) and the No. 9 (with the Vienna Philharmonic Orchestra *et al.*), Tchaikovsky's Symphonies Nos 4 and 6 (with the Paris Conservatoire Orchestra), and *Der Rosenkavalier* and *Le nozze di Figaro* (with the Vienna Philharmonic Orchestra and soloists from the Vienna State Opera). To complete the picture were the overtures to Handel's *Berenice*, *Le Carnaval romain* and *Der Zigeunerbaron*, and the Joseph Strauss waltz *Sphärenklänge* (with the London Philharmonic Orchestra). After his death, Decca released another Beethoven Symphony No. 3 (with the Vienna Philharmonic Orchestra), Mozart's Symphony No. 39 and some *German Dances*, Weber's Symphony No. 1 and Schubert's Symphony No. 9 (with the Cologne Radio Symphony Orchestra), and DGG included LP transfers of *Moldau* and the Nocturne from *A Midsummer Night's Dream*, originally recorded in 1928, in its album *The Early Days*. 'Pirate' operatic recordings of Kleiber have included *I vespri siciliani* (by L'Estro Armonico, from a performance in Florence in 1951) and *Fidelio* (by Rococo).

Kleiber's recordings of the Beethoven symphonies were one of the features of Decca's early LP catalogue. With the possible exception of the *Pastoral* and the *Choral*, these performances reached great heights, and demonstrated his direct link with Weingartner in Beethoven interpretation. Many have argued that his Symphony No. 5 was the greatest recording ever made of that much-recorded work, maybe until that of his son, Carlos Kleiber, was issued in 1975. Kleiber did the *Eroica* for the second time for Decca with the Vienna Philharmonic, but would not allow its release; the reason is not clear, but it has been suggested that an imperfect balance of the horns was responsible, although John Russell in his biography of Kleiber pointed out that he was never satisfied with his performances of the work, and that the music, particularly the *marcia funebre*, affected him profoundly. On one occasion he was found weeping in his room after conducting it. This Vienna Philharmonic performance is a marvellous one, and if comparisons have to be made, it stands with the Weingartner/Vienna Philharmonic, Klemperer/Philharmonia, and the 1953 Toscanini/NBC Symphony performances as the greatest recordings of the symphony. Kleiber's meticulousness is illustrated in his recording of Beethoven's Symphony No. 7; in the last bar of the *allegretto* the strings continue to play pizzicato, whereas it is customarily played arco (i.e. with the bow, abandoning the previous marking pizzicato). When queried, Kleiber argued that from his examination of the manuscript of the score, it was his conviction that Beethoven meant this to be. Strauss and Klemperer also adopted the pizzicato ending. The *Rosenkavalier*, recorded in 1954, is a profoundly perceptive reading; in it Kleiber was concerned to maintain a balance between the singers and the orchestra, so that the conversational sections of the work would not be lost. *Le nozze di Figaro* – one of Kleiber's precious 'three Fs': *Fidelio*, *Figaro* and *Freischütz* – is a miracle of style and ensemble, and with Beecham's *Die Zauberflöte* and Karajan's *Così fan tutte* is one of the indispensable classics of recorded Mozart opera.

Kleinert, Rolf (b. 1911). Born in Dresden, Kleinert studied at the Saxon State Orchestral School there, and after many engagements as a choral, orchestral and operatic conductor, became conductor of the Leipzig Radio Symphony Orchestra (1947) and first conductor of the Berlin Radio Symphony Orchestra, in East Berlin (1951); he was appointed general music director of the orchestra after Abendroth's death in 1959. He has, since 1953, been a guest conductor in Czechoslovakia, Poland, Bulgaria, Italy and Britain. Urania and other Western companies have issued a number of recordings of him, made in DR Germany, in which he conducted the Shostakovich Symphony No. 10 (with the Leipzig Gewandhaus Orchestra), Witt's *Jena Symphony*, Grieg's *Holberg Suite*, *Capriccio espagnol*, Malipiero's Violin Concerto (with Kirmse) and the complete *The Merry Wives of Windsor* (with the Leipzig Radio Symphony Orchestra *et al.*), Haydn's Symphony No. 101, Méhul's Symphony No. 1, Liszt's *Hungaria* and *Festklänge*, Bruch's Violin Concerto No. 2 (with Moris), Saint-Saëns' Symphony No. 2 and Violin Concerto No. 1 (with Denyi), Mahler's *Kindertotenlieder* (with Lail), Casella's *Italia* and *Serenade*, Prokofiev's *Scythian Suite* and *Semyon Kotko* suite, Shostakovich's Symphony No. 6, Britten's *Soirées musicales*, Alfred Mendelsohn's *The Downfall of Doftana* (with the Berlin Radio Symphony Orchestra) and Kunad's *Sinfonietta* (with the Berlin Radio Symphony Orchestra).

Klemens, Mario (b. 1936). Born in Chlumec, Czechoslovakia, and educated at the Prague Conservatory and Academy of Music, Klemens first conducted with the Prague Symphony Orchestra (1959), won first prize at the International Competition for Young Conductors at Besançon (1966), was conductor at the Plzeň Opera (1966), the State Ballet Ensemble (1970) and the Košice State Philharmonic Orchestra (1972). He has recorded cello concertos by Rejcha and Vranický (with Sádlo and Musici de Praga, for Panton).

Klemetti, Heikki (1876–1953). Born in Kuortane, Finland, Klemetti studied at the Stern Conservatory, Berlin, and founded and conducted the Suomen Laulu (1900), a Finnish choir with which he toured Europe and the United States. He published a history of music and a book on voice production, composed and arranged choral music, and collected and published the hymnal of the State Church of Finland (1924). He recorded the Sanctus from Bach's *Mass in B minor* (with the Helsinki Chorus and Orchestra for Odeon).

Klemperer, Otto (1885–1973). Born in Breslau which was then in Germany, with a father who was a businessman and a mother a professional piano teacher, Klemperer was taken with his family at the age of four to Hamburg, and after attending the Realgymnasium des Johanneum there, he studied at the Hoch Conservatory at Frankfurt am Main. In 1902 he went to Berlin and was a student of piano and violin at the Klindworth-Scharwenka and Stern Conservatories. When he was studying composition and conducting with Pfitzner he decided to become a conductor, and made his debut in 1905 in Berlin with Max Reinhardt's production of *Orphée aux enfers*, which at that time he conducted 50 times. He nonetheless admired Offenbach for the rest of his life. Later that year he conducted the off-stage choir in Mahler's Symphony No. 2 at a performance under Fried and attended by Mahler. When he was on tour in Vienna accompanying a cellist, he visited Mahler and played the scherzo from the symphony from memory, having previously made a piano reduction of the entire score. Mahler gave him his visiting card with his recommendation written on it, which enabled him to obtain an appointment as choirmaster and conductor at the German Opera in Prague in 1907. During his three years at Prague he visited Munich and Vienna from time to time to assist at the rehearsals of Mahler's later symphonies.

Again with Mahler's help, Klemperer became a conductor at the Hamburg Opera (1910); there then followed a succession of appointments, at Barmen (1913), Strasbourg (1914–16), Cologne (1916–24) and Wiesbaden (1924–7), and in those years he was a guest conductor at Barcelona (1920), Rome (1923), Moscow (1924), Leningrad (1925) and New York (1926). He continued to visit the USSR until 1936. In 1927 he was engaged as the director of the Kroll Opera in Berlin, which had just been established to present new operas and experimental productions of traditional operas. The Kroll was the third opera house in Berlin, where Kleiber was at the State Opera, Walter at the Charlottenburg Opera and Furtwängler with the Berlin Philharmonic Orchestra. Klemperer was at the Kroll until 1931 when political pressures and financial difficulties forced its closure. At the end of his life he said that this was the most satisfying period of his career, as conditions were ideal and the limitations of repertory opera were avoided. In the four years he staged *Oedipus Rex*, Schoenberg's *Die glückliche Hand* and *Erwartung*, Hindemith's *Cardillac* and *Neues vom Tage*, and Janáček's *From the House of the Dead*, some for the first time, as well as the operas of Mozart, Beethoven, Wagner, Puccini *et al.* in some experimental productions. He also conducted concerts with the Kroll orchestra, performing all Stravinsky's music. In fact Klemperer was then famous for his interest in performing contemporary music, and it was only in the last two decades of his life that he restricted himself to the repertoire from Bach to Bruckner, and became recognised as one of the foremost interpreters of Beethoven, Brahms and Bruckner. It has been suggested that this was because he could then only conduct works which he could direct only with the simplest gestures.

In 1928 he visited London, returning the next year, to conduct at the Courtauld-Sargent concerts, where he gave what is thought to be the first performance in Britain of Bruckner's Symphony No. 8. After 1931 he conducted at the Berlin State Opera, but as he was a Jew, the Nazis dismissed him in 1933. (Actually, he had converted from Judaism to the Roman Catholic faith in 1919, but left the Church in 1967.) Ironically Hitler attended one of his last performances in Berlin, and Hindenburg had just presented him with the Goethe Medal for his 'outstanding contribution to German culture', when, soon after, a Berlin newspaper declared that 'his whole outlook ran counter to German thought and feeling'. He fled with his family to Austria and then to Switzerland, where he was offered the conductorship of the Los Angeles Philharmonic Orchestra. He remained in California from 1935 to 1939, conducted the New York Philharmonic-Symphony and Philadelphia Orchestras, and in 1937 organised the Pittsburgh Symphony Orchestra, although he refused to be its permanent conductor. At Los Angeles he knew Schoenberg, and performed the latter's transcription of Brahms' *Piano Quartet in G minor* with the orchestra there. The manager of the orchestra said to him: 'I don't know why people say that Schoenberg has no melodies. That was very melodic.'

Grave physical and financial troubles followed. In 1939 he had an operation for a brain tumor, which left him partly paralysed, and from then on he could not conduct with a baton. Engagements became scarcer. In 1940 he led the chamber orchestra of the New School of Social Research in New York in some Bach concerts, and for a short time he was conductor of the New York City Symphony Orchestra. He suffered from cyclothymia, and experienced an uncontrollable succession of euphoric and depressive states of mind; after an incident in a New York sanatorium, the publicity it was given prejudiced his career further. To prove his complete sanity and competence, he hired an orchestra for a concert at Carnegie Hall, with a programme of his own transcription of a Bach trio sonata, *Eine kleine Nachtmusik*, Hindemith's *Nobilissima Visione* and Beethoven's Symphony No. 3. He made the violinists and violists stand throughout to maintain a proper tension. This concert was a success, and engagements with orchestras throughout the US resulted. He had become a US citizen in 1940, but altogether he was not satisfied with his experience in the US, and later a controversy about his passport with the immigration authorities because of his prolonged periods overseas made him more unhappy. While he acknowledged the superb skill of the great American orchestras, he missed the warmth of the playing of those in Europe, and thought none could compare with the Vienna Philharmonic, for one.

Klemperer returned to Europe after World War II, conducted in Italy, Sweden, Switzerland and France, and made his first appearance in London in 1947. This was with the Philharmonia Orchestra, who were then puzzled by his beat. The Budapest Opera engaged him as music director (1947–50), but when he was prevented from performing a work of Schoenberg there, he did not return to Budapest after completing a successful tour of Australia, during which he conducted Mahler's Symphony No. 2 four times in Sydney, to full houses. An accident at the Montreal airport in 1951 forced him to conduct from a chair for several years. In 1954 he settled in Zürich, but most of his activities from then on were in London. Another accident, in 1958, when his hotel bedroom caught fire, stopped him from conducting *Tristan und Isolde* at the New York Met. His career came to a triumphant conclusion when he was appointed principal conductor of the Philharmonia Orchestra in 1959; in 1964 the orchestra's founder, Walter Legge, attempted to disband it, but the members re-constituted themselves as the New Philharmonia Orchestra. Klemperer was appointed president, and led them at their inaugural concert with Beethoven's Symphony No. 9 at the Royal Albert Hall. At Covent Garden he conducted *Fidelio* in 1961, *Die Zauberflöte* in 1962, and *Lohengrin* in 1963, and his Beethoven cycles in London were major events. He composed several symphonies, a violin concerto, five operas, choral and chamber music, and wrote several books of recollections; as a pianist he performed in chamber music ensembles in Berlin.

In contrast to the tribulations he experienced after his expulsion from Germany, Klemperer's final years saw him acclaimed as one of the greatest conductors of the century; in his own ironical words, 'I am the last of the classical school – when Bruno Walter died, I put my fees up.' Despite the immense success of his concerts in London and elsewhere, it was through the gramophone record that he became universally known; Legge, who contracted him for EMI and who supervised his records with the Philharmonia Orchestra, must take the credit for ensuring Klemperer's full recognition as a great artist. Klemperer's extraordinary misfortunes gave him a heroic aura; in his early life he was a tall, overpowering figure, but to watch him in his last years being assisted to the chair at the podium, to lead a powerful performance of a Beethoven symphony with the most meagre gestures, was a moving sight. Wieland Wagner summed him up this way: 'Classical Greece, Jewish tradition, medieval Christendom, German romanticism and the realism of our time make Klemperer the conductor a unique artistic phenomenon.' As an interpreter of Beethoven, Brahms and Bruckner his performances had a rock-like inevitability that placed him in the same class as Toscanini, although their musical styles were poles apart. In one respect they were similar: both saw the score as their only authority, and the intense study of the score was the essential preparation for the performance of any music, no matter how familiar. But in contrast to Toscanini, whose tempi were faster in his later life, Klemperer's grew perceptibly slower. Traditional approaches and extra-musical meanings meant nothing to him. Complete faithfulness was the beginning of any revelation about the meaning of the music. He came to every rehearsal with his mind completely made up about his interpretation, and how to resolve the music's problems, and with his commanding presence he never needed to raise his voice to the players. His gestures were severely economical, especially after his worsening impairment, but he conveyed his intentions very adequately with his eyes. With some orchestras unaccustomed to him, his sparse gestures were confusing, which led the players to follow the section leaders closely; some claim that this was the main reason for the high standard of playing he achieved. His natural irascibility was sometimes exacerbated by his fluctuating psychological condition, and he was quite intolerant of musicians not prepared to accept unreservedly his direction or to devote themselves entirely to the cause of art.

Klemperer's performances of the repertoire from Bach to Strauss were characterised by deliberate tempi and a particular orchestral sound. He was at a loss to explain how he created this sound; like so many conductors it was so much a part of his musical personality that he probably could not recognise it himself. His only comment when Peter Heyworth queried him about it was that he considered the upbeat very important, and that the conductor's hand should give the musicians the opportunity to play as though they were quite free. But the observer might notice other factors. Klemperer was most concerned about clarity and balance. He sought a big sound, and gave special prominence to the woodwinds. Beauty of tone, for its own sake, never interested him. Tempi were steady, each note and pause given its exactly value, and every phrase its precise measure. Second violins were placed on the right, as they seldom are in unison with the first violins, and so must be heard independently. Clear articulation by the strings was assisted by careful bowing and dynamic markings. Frequently his readings impressed with their enormous power and profundity, but this was certainly not always the case, as his slow tempi could render the music ponderous and devitalised. His performance of Beethoven's Symphony No. 9 for instance, impressed some as incredibly powerful, but to others it was simply laboured. His tempi in the Mozart operas certainly gave him the opportunity to reveal much detail, but the music was often devoid of charm or drama. His Haydn and Brahms were grave, but without sentiment; in Mahler he excused his disregard for lyrical beauty and feeling on the grounds that he was not a moralist. When he conducted in Vienna in the early 1930s, the members of the Vienna Philharmonic believed that he, not Furtwängler or Walter, was the greatest and most impressive conductor of Bruckner's symphonies. The greatness of his style is well illustrated in the recorded performance of Beethoven's Symphony No. 6 with the Philharmonia Orchestra: in the first movement, the tempo is absolutely firm and its unhurried steadiness gives the music breadth and calm. In the crescendi the clarity of the woodwinds and his careful dynamic control create an overwhelming impression. Yet, later, the scherzo is taken so slowly that the notes are separated and all vitality is lost. When he was questioned about his slow tempi, his answer was: 'You will get used to it'.

Klemperer's association with Mahler and Strauss in his early years did not make him an automatic advocate of all their music. He would not conduct Mahler's Symphonies Nos 1 and 6, but considered Symphonies Nos 8 and 9 the composer's greatest. He disliked all of Strauss after *Salome*, except *Metamorphosen*, even describing *Die Frau ohne Schatten* as an ugly and incomprehensible opera. He felt it necessary to make slight alterations to the scoring of the Beethoven and Schumann symphonies, but believed that these retouchings were only right for himself and should not be imitated by others. Of present-day conductors he especially admired Boulez, whose rehearsals and concerts he attended, approving of his Haydn and Mozart as much as his Debussy and modern repertoire.

Klemperer's first recordings were made for Polydor in 1924–5 by the acoustic process, and were of Beethoven's Symphonies Nos 1 and 8 and the adagio of Bruckner's Symphony No. 8, (with the Berlin State Opera Orchestra). Between 1926 and 1931 he also recorded for Polydor Beethoven's Symphony No. 8, the *Egmont*, *Coriolan* and *Leonore No. 3* overtures, Schubert's Symphony No. 8, the overtures *A Midsummer Night's Dream* and *Euryanthe*, the *Siegfried Idyll*, Nuages and Fêtes from Debussy's *Nocturnes*, *Alborada del gracioso* and Weill's *Dreigroschenmusik* (also with the Berlin State Opera Orchestra). For HMV/Electrola he recorded the *Academic Festival Overture*, the Dance of the Seven Veils and the prelude to *Tristan und Isolde*, and for Odeon/Parlophone Brahms' Symphony No. 1, *Don Juan* and *Till Eulenspiegel* and the overtures to *La Belle Hélène* and *Fra Diavolo*. Some of these discs were issued on other labels in the US. After World War II he recorded with the Paris Pro Musica Orchestra for French Polydor the *Brandenburg Concertos*, which were later released on LP, arrangements of Bach's *Nun komm, der Heiden Heiland* and *Bist du bei mir*, Mozart's Symphonies Nos 25 and 36 and *Eine kleine Nachtmusik*.

His next period of recording was for Vox with the Vienna Symphony and Pro Musica Orchestras, between 1947 and 1952. The works recorded were Beethoven's Symphonies Nos 5 and 6, the *Missa Solemnis* and the Piano Concerto No. 4 (with Novaes), Mendelssohn's Symphonies Nos 3 and 4 and *The Hebrides* overture, the Schumann Piano Concerto and Chopin's Piano Concerto No. 2 (with Novaes), Bruckner's Symphony No. 4, Mahler's Symphony No. 2 and *Das Lied von der Erde*. There was also Schubert's Symphony No. 4 with the Lamoureux Orchestra. These discs drew dramatic attention to Klemperer's status as an interpreter, particularly of Beethoven, Bruckner and Mahler, and were the prelude to his great acclaim in the last two decades of his life. The characteristic slow tempi were evident in places, but some of the performances, the two Beethoven symphonies and the *Missa Solemnis*, were arresting for their commitment and utter sense of command. The authors of *The Record Guide* (Sackville-West and Shawe-Taylor) wrote about the Symphony No. 5 that Klemperer 'treats the work as if he had just discovered its greatness, illuminating every page with a ceaseless care for detail'.

In 1952 Klemperer signed a contract with EMI but was forced to cancel it because his American citizenship and membership of the American Musicians' Union prevented him from recording in Europe. He therefore gave up his US passport, signed the contract again, took up residence in Zürich, and commenced a vast recording programme which only concluded with his death. Until 1964 he conducted the Philharmonia Orchestra, and thereafter the New Philharmonia; he also made one disc with the French National Radio Orchestra. Klemperer is one conductor who is adequately, if not exhaustively, represented by his records, and this series for EMI is largely responsible for his pre-eminent reputation. The first discs he made for EMI were a coupling of *Nobilissima Visione* and Brahms' *Variations on the St Antony Chorale*; his discography encompasses the complete symphonies of Beethoven, Brahms and Schumann, Bruckner's Symphonies Nos 4, 5, 6, 7, 8 and 9, Beethoven's Piano Concertos (with Barenboim), the three Mozart operas *Die Zauberflöte*, *Le nozze di Figaro*, and *Così fan tutte*, Mozart's Symphonies Nos 29, 31, 35, 36, 38, 39, 40 and 41, Haydn's Symphonies Nos 88, 92, 95, 98, 100, 101, 102 and 104, Mendelssohn's Symphonies Nos 3 and 4, Schubert's Symphonies Nos 5, 8 and 9, Tchaikovsky's Symphonies Nos 4, 5 and 6, Mahler's Symphonies Nos 2, 4, 7 and 9 and *Das Lied von der Erde*, the operas *Fidelio* and *Der fliegende Holländer* and Act I of *Die Walküre*, the Bach *Brandenburg Concertos*, the orchestral suites and *St Matthew Passion*, the *Missa Solemnis*, *Messiah*, *Ein deutsches Requiem*, and *Alto Rhapsody* of Brahms, *Tod und Verklärung*,

Don Juan, *Till Eulenspiegel* and *Metamorphosen* of Strauss, discs of orchestral excerpts from the Wagner operas, overtures by Mozart, Beethoven, Brahms, Schumann, Weber *et al.*, Dvořák's Symphony No. 9, the Franck *Symphony in D minor*, *Symphonie fantastique*, Mozart's *Eine kleine Nachtmusik*, *Serenata notturna* and Serenade K. 361, the incidental music to *A Midsummer Night's Dream*, the Beethoven and Brahms Violin Concertos (with Menuhin and Oistrakh respectively), the Schumann Piano Concerto and Liszt's Piano Concerto No. 1 (with Annie Fischer), and his own Symphony No. 2 and *Merry Waltz*, and other pieces by other composers. The only relatively modern music he recorded for EMI was Stravinsky's *Pulcinella* and *Symphony in Three Movements*, and Weill's *Die kleine Dreigroschenmusik*.

To name the greatest of all Klemperer's recordings would be virtually impossible, as his interpretations, like Furtwängler's and Toscanini's, do not command universal admiration. For instance, many would claim that his Beethoven *Eroica* (the first on mono, with the old Philharmonia Orchestra, rather than the stereo re-make) may be his greatest record, but others (e.g. Paul Henry Lang, in *High Fidelity*) have deprecated it. His *Fidelio* was described by Harold Rosenthal as 'one of the greatest operatic recordings of the post war period'; probably there are few dissenters from that judgement. His other recordings with claims to greatness are the *St Matthew Passion*, the *Missa Solemnis* and Mahler's Symphony No. 2, but it may not be going too far to say that in almost all his performances there are elements of greatness which transcend the confines of his style.

Klemperer had a sardonic sense of humour. In 1954, after Krauss and Furtwängler had died, he commented 'Ah, it has been a good year for conductors'. He once refused to conduct the *Enigma Variations* in the Royal Festival Hall, declaring that the acoustics of the building did not suit that kind of music. When he was recording *Der fliegende Holländer*, one of the singers was dissatisfied with his performance and asked: 'Please may I sing again?' Klemperer growled: 'Why? It might get worse.' The singer answered: 'Ah, but it might go better,' to be crushed with 'We can't wait that long!' After recording the Beethoven concertos with Barenboim, with whom he had formed a rapport, he summoned him to his hotel one morning, where the young musician found a singer, a piano and a pile of Klemperer's own songs. After running through many of them, Klemperer asked: 'Do you like my compositions, Mr Barenboim?' Barenboim hesitated and replied: 'No, Dr Klemperer'. After he had left, Klemperer said to his daughter, Lotte, 'I like that boy, he is honest . . . but he is no judge of music!'

Klenau, Paul von (1883–1946). Born in Copenhagen, Klenau studied there, in Berlin, Munich and Stuttgart. Among his teachers were Bruch and von Schillings. He started conducting at Freiburg in 1907, was later conductor at the Stuttgart Court Opera (1908–14) and of the Copenhagen Philharmonic Society (1922–30), and in 1920 founded the Vienna Singakademie and Konzerthaus Gesellschaft. He performed Delius in Europe, conducted a concert of his music at Frankfurt am Main to commemorate the composer's 60th birthday, and led the *Mass of Life* in Vienna and London in 1925; he also gave the first performance of the revised version of Schoenberg's *Gurrelieder* in Vienna. Klenau's compositions include three symphonies, ballets and seven operas, of which *Michael Kohlhaas* and *Gudrun auf Island* and the ballet *Klein Idas Blumen* were the most successful. In the mid 1920s he recorded for Columbia with the Royal Philharmonic Orchestra *Prélude à l'après-midi d'un faune*, *Ibéria* and the Cortège et air de danse from *L'Enfant prodigue*.

Kletzki, Paul (1900–73). Born in Łódź, Poland, Kletzki studied the violin in Warsaw with Mlynarski, and in Berlin, and returned to Łódź to play in the orchestra there (1914–19). He lived in Berlin (1921–33) where he studied, composed, and began to conduct; in 1934 he moved to Milan and taught at the Scuola Superiora di Musica. At the outbreak of World War II he took up residence in Switzerland, and eventually became a Swiss citizen; after the war he travelled widely and conducted in Europe, North and South America, Australia and Israel, where he became closely associated with the Israel Philharmonic Orchestra. On Toscanini's invitation he took part at the opening of La Scala in 1949. In 1954 he was appointed co-conductor of the Liverpool Philharmonic Orchestra with Pritchard, but relinquished that position when he was not permitted to conduct at the Edinburgh Festival. He was conductor of the Dallas Symphony Orchestra (1958–61), the Berne Symphony Orchestra (1964) and succeeded Ansermet as conductor of the Suisse Romande Orchestra (1967–70). He collapsed and died in Liverpool while rehearsing the orchestra there. During his years in Berlin, he came under the influence of Furtwängler, and later said that all the knowledge of musical reproduction (*sic*) that he absorbed until 1935 he owed to Furtwängler. His preferences were the romantic composers of Germany and Central Europe: Beethoven, Schubert, Brahms and Mahler, although he was also a masterly interpreter of Berlioz, Tchaikovsky, Sibelius and Schoenberg.

After World War II Kletzki became a major recording artist for EMI. Among his first releases was a fine and unmannered Symphony No. 4 of Brahms (with the Lucerne Festival Orchestra); his other 78s included the *Leonore No. 3* overture, Schubert's Symphony No. 8 and three entr'actes from *Rosamunde*, Berlioz' overtures *Le Carnaval romain*, *Benvenuto Cellini* and *Béatrice et Bénédict*, the *Siegfried Idyll*, the overture to *Der fliegende Holländer* and the preludes to Acts I and III of *Lohengrin*, Chopin's Piano Concerto No. 2, Liszt's Piano Concerto No. 2 and Rachmaninov's Piano Concerto No. 3 (with Małcużyński), the scherzo and intermezzo from *A Midsummer Night's Dream*, Brahms' *Tragic Overture* and *Hungarian Dances Nos 2, 3* and *5*, Tchaikovsky's Symphony No. 5, *Capriccio italien*, *A Night on the Bare Mountain*, the overture to *Russlan and Ludmilla*, *Valse triste* and *En Saga*, Barber's *Adagio for Strings* and Artur Schnabel's *Rhapsody for Orchestra* (with the Philharmonia Orchestra); and *Pictures at an Exhibition*, *Boléro* and *Daphnis et Chloé* Suite No. 2 (with the French National Radio Orchestra).

Among EMI's first LP releases was a collection of the four Berlioz overtures *Le Corsaire*, *Benvenuto Cellini*, *Béatrice et Bénédict* and *Les Francs-juges*, which were magnificently played by the Philharmonia Orchestra under Kletzki, and caused regret that he never went on to record more of this composer. His LP records for EMI included the incidental music for *A Midsummer Night's Dream* and the overtures *Ruy Blas* and *Die Heimkehr aus der Fremde*, the overture and Venusberg Music from *Tannhäuser*, the prelude and Liebestod from *Tristan und Isolde*, Brahms' Double Concerto (with Ferras and Tortelier) and *Variations on the St Antony Chorale*, *Scheherazade*, the *Tsar Saltan* suite, Tchaikovsky's Symphony No. 6, *Manfred*, *Serenade in C major* and *Capriccio italien*, Borodin's Symphony No. 2, Ippolitov-Ivanov's *Caucasian Sketches*, the Dance of the Persian Slaves from *Khovanshchina*, Glinka's *Jota aragonesa*, Chopin's Piano Concerto No. 1 (with Pollini), Sibelius' Symphonies Nos 1 and 2, the overtures to *The Bartered Bride*, *Zampa*, *The Merry Wives of Windsor*, *Leichte Cavallerie*, *Pique Dame* and *Die schöne Galatea*, *Boléro*, Prokofiev's Symphony No. 5, Mahler's Symphony No. 4 (with Loose), the Adagietto from the Symphony No. 5, and *Das Lied von der Erde* (with Fischer-Dieskau and Dickie); the Berg Violin Concerto (with Gertler) and Bloch's Violin Concerto No. 1 (with Menuhin, and the Philharmonia Orchestra); the Handel/Harty *Music for the Royal Fireworks*, the overture *Iphigénie en Aulide*, Clarke's *Trumpet Voluntary*, Schubert's Symphony No. 8 and incidental music for *Rosamunde*, Brahms' Symphony No. 1, the *1812* overture, *Marche slave* and *Francesca da Rimini* (with the Royal Philharmonic Orchestra); Mahler's Symphony No. 1 (with the Vienna Philharmonic Orchestra); the four Schumann symphonies, *Manfred* overture and *Introduction, Scherzo and Finale*, Mendelssohn's Symphony No. 3 and overture *Meeresstille und glückliche Fahrt*, Mahler's Symphonies Nos 1 and 9, Schoenberg's *Verklärte Nacht* and Ben Haim's *Fanfare for Israel* (with the Israel Philharmonic Orchestra).

His remaining recordings included Beethoven's Romance No. 2 (with Kulenkampff and the Berlin Philharmonic Orchestra for Telefunken); the nine Beethoven symphonies (with the Czech Philharmonic Orchestra for Supraphon, and released on other labels including Musical Heritage Society, Ariola and Valois) and *Egmont* overture (with the Czech Philharmonic Orchestra for Ariola); Schoeck's *Sommernacht* (with the Geneva Studio Orchestra for CT and Genesis), Rachmaninov's Symphonies Nos 2 and 3, *A Night on the Bare Mountain*, Nielsen's Symphony No. 2, Hindemith's *Mathis der Maler* symphony and Lutosławski's *Concerto for Orchestra* (with the Suisse Romande Orchestra for Decca); Beethoven's Symphonies Nos 1, 3 and 5 (with the South-West German Radio Orchestra for La Guilde Internationale du Disque); and Beethoven's Symphony No. 6, Tchaikovsky's Symphony No. 4, and Dvořák's *Slavonic Dances* Op. 46 Nos 1, 2, 3, 6, 7 and 8, and Op. 72 Nos 2, 7 and 8 (with the Paris National Orchestra for GID).

All of these recordings gave Kletzki full rein to demonstrate his great flair for romantic music, and some magnificent and lasting performances were counted among them. *Scheherazade* and Tchaikovsky's Symphony No. 6, which were originally released in 1961, held their places among the finest recordings of these works ever made; the Berg Violin Concerto made a powerful impression when it was first issued in 1954, Bloch's Violin Concerto No. 1 was re-issued in 1975, and Chopin's Piano Concerto No. 1 has become a gramophone classic. The Mahler symphonies were marred by cuts in the finale of No. 1 and in the second movement of No. 9; in *Das Lied von der Erde* a baritone replaces the customary contralto, and after 17 years this recording is still available in Britain. The Beethoven symphonies, with the Czech Philharmonic Orchestra, were soundly conceived, as one might expect, but the readings lacked the authority to mark them out from others familiar to record collectors. A curious flaw occurred in the *Leonore No. 3* overture, on 78s with the Philharmonia Orchestra, when an apparent slip occurred and was recorded in a flute passage. Of the discs he made with the Suisse Romande Orchestra, the two Rachmaninov symphonies were especially beautiful performances.

Klíma, Alois (b. 1905). Born at Klatovy, Czechoslovakia, Klíma learned to play many instruments as a boy, and conducted his local school band. He studied mathematics and physics at Prague University, but after a while turned to music, entered the Prague Conservatory where he studied composition with Křička and Rídky, and conducting with Doležil and Dědeček. He graduated in 1935, was conductor of the Košice Radio Orchestra (1936) and of the Ostrava Radio Orchestra (1936–8), then became chief conductor of the Prague Opera Studio (1939–46). He was chief conductor of the Prague Radio Symphony Orchestra (1951–71), has toured abroad with this orchestra and as a guest conductor, and has taught orchestral playing and conducting at the Prague Conservatory and Academy of Music. Among his recordings, for Supraphon, are Reicha's *Overture in C major* (with the Prague Chamber Orchestra), Cello Concertos of Haydn and Boccherini (with Sádlo and the Prague Radio Symphony Orchestra), Mozart's Piano Concerto K. 482 (with Boschi and the Czech Philharmonic Orchestra), the *Prometheus* overture of Beethoven, polkas of Hilmar, Raichl's Symphony No. 2, Prokofiev's Piano Concerto No. 3 (with Maxian), Kabalevsky's Piano Concerto No. 3 (with Štěpán), Novák's *In the Tatras*, Dvořák's *Czech Suite*, Jaroch's *The Old Man and the Sea*, and Mussorgsky's *Songs and Dances of Death* (with Borg, and the Prague Radio Symphony Orchestra), Fibich's *Spring* (with the Czech Philharmonic Orchestra), Suk's *War Triptych* (with the Brno State Philharmonic Orchestra), Prokofiev's *Summer Day* and *Winter Camp Fire* (with the Prague Chamber Orchestra), the *Norwegian Dances* Nos 1 and 2 and other pieces of Grieg, Khachaturian's Piano Concerto (with Jemelík and the Czech Philharmonic Orchestra), Saint-Saëns' Cello Concerto No. 1 and Tchaikovsky's *Variations on a Rococo Theme* (with Chuchro and the Czech Philharmonic Orchestra). He also recorded Dobiáš' *Sonata for Piano, Strings, Wind and Percussion* (with the Czech Radio Symphony Orchestra for Panton).

Klink, Waldemar (b. 1894). Born in Heidenheim and educated at the Hochschule für Musik, Berlin, and at the Augsburg Choral School, Klink was a teacher, and became a conductor of the Nuremberg Men's Choir and Nuremberg Chamber Choir (1924) and director of the Nuremberg Singing School (1935). He created his own Choral Society (1945) and with its choir toured in Germany and abroad. For Colosseum he recorded Thomas' *Christmas Night Oratorio*, with the Nuremberg Choral Society.

Klobucar, Berislav (b. 1924). Born and educated at Zagreb, Klobucar studied at the Salzburg Mozarteum, and conducted at the Zagreb Opera (1941–51), at the Vienna State Opera (1951–61), was a permanent guest conductor at the German Opera in West Berlin, and was appointed general music director at Graz (1961). He conducted *Die Meistersinger* and *Lohengrin* at the Bayreuth Festival in 1968, and *Die Meistersinger* in 1969. For Electrola he recorded single discs of highlights from *Tosca*, *Madama Butterfly*, *Le nozze di Figaro*, *Martha* and *Zar und Zimmermann* (with distinguished soloists and the Berlin Symphony Orchestra).

Klopfenstein, René (b. 1927). Born at Lausanne, Klopfenstein studied at the University of Basel, at the Salzburg Mozarteum and the Paris Conservatoire. In his career he has been a music critic, secretary-general of the Schola Cantorum in Paris, for ten years the artistic director of an international record company, and the director of the Montreux music festival. He has been active as a conductor in France, FR Germany, the USSR, Japan, Latin America, Australia *et al.*, and is especially known as a performer of the Viennese repertoire of Mozart, Schubert, and Bruckner. For La Guilde Internationale du Disque he recorded Mozart's Symphonies Nos 5, 11 and 17 and the *Lambach* symphony (with the Camerata Academica at Salzburg), Lalo's *Symphonie espagnole* (with Ferras) and excerpts from *Namouna* (with the Monte Carlo National Orchestra); for Philips, organ concertos by C. P. E. Bach, Arne and Haydn (with Guillou and the Berlin Brandenburg Orchestra, and for the Haydn, the Winterthur Collegium Musicum).

Kloss, Erich (1898–1967). Born in Schleiz, Germany, Koss studied in Leipzig, Stuttgart and Munich, started his career as a pianist, but then became a conductor. He first conducted in Berchtesgaden and in Switzerland, was appointed conductor and pianist with the Munich Radio (1930), deputy director of the Reichs Symphony Orchestra (1936), and chief conductor of the Nuremberg Symphony Orchestra (1949), also making guest appearances with the Munich and Dresden Philharmonic Orchestras. He recorded Frederick II's Flute Concerto No. 3 (with Schneider), Prince Louis Ferdinand's Rondo for Piano and Orchestra (with Graif), Dittersdorf's *Symphony in A minor*, Wilhelmine's Harpsichord Concerto (with Spilling), Debussy's *Fantasia* (with Schultes) and Saxophone Rhapsody (with de Vries), and Strauss's *Dance Suite after Couperin* and *Schlagobers* ballet (with the Frankenland Symphony Orchestra for Lyrichord); Rózsa's *Concert Overture*, *Three Hungarian Sketches*, *Theme, Variations and Finale*, *Background to Violence* and *Lust for Life* suite (with the Frankenland Symphony Orchestra for Decca, US), *Hungarian Serenade*, *North Hungarian Peasant Songs and Dances* (with Colbentson, violin), and *The Vintner's Daughter* (with the Frankenland Symphony Orchestra for MGM), and music for the films *Quo Vadis* and *Spellbound* (with the Frankenland Symphony Orchestra for Capitol); Strauss's Horn Concerto No. 1 (with Huth and the Frankenland Symphony Orchestra for Urania); Zádor's Divertimento and *Variations on a Hungarian Folk Song* (with the Frankenland Symphony Orchestra for Orion); Mozart's Piano Concerto K. 466 (with Zartner), C. P. E. Bach's Double Concerto Wq 47 (with Gröschel and Zartner), Liszt's *Tasso*, Brahms' Piano Concerto No. 2 (with Leimer), the overture to *I vespri siciliani*, Grieg's *Lyric Suite* and *Symphonic Dance No. 4*, Strauss's *Burleske* (with Nakajima), Reger's Suite Op. 128, Violin Concerto (with Shiokawa) and *Variations and Fugue* Op. 88, and Siegfried Wagner's *Konzertstück* (with Wiesner, flute) and overture to *Der Bärenhäuter* (with the Nuremberg Symphony Orchestra for Colosseum).

Knappertsbusch, Hans (1888–1965). Born in Elberfeld, Germany, Knappertsbusch conducted school orchestras as a boy, proceeded to Bonn University to study philosophy, then to the Cologne Conservatory to study under Steinbach and Lohse (1909–12). His debut as a conductor was at Mühlheim in 1911, and in 1912 he conducted at a Wagner festival in Holland. His first appointment was at Bochum, from where he went to Elberfeld (1913–18), Leipzig (1918), Dessau (1919–22), and finally was engaged with a life-long contract at the Bavarian State Opera at Munich in 1922, succeeding Walter. Here he became renowned for his performances of the operas of Wagner, Strauss and Mozart. His unhesitating hostility to the Nazis, and his refusal to join the Nazi party, finally led to his enforced retirement in 1936, on Hitler's personal direction. He moved to Vienna where he conducted at the Vienna State Opera, and at the concerts of the Vienna Philharmonic Orchestra, but was obliged to abandon these activities when the Nazis annexed Austria. He gave guest appearances in some non-Fascist countries in Europe; previously in 1936 he had been invited by Beecham to conduct at Covent Garden but his permit to leave Germany was withheld. He did however appear in London in 1937 to conduct *Salome*. After the war he re-emerged and soon established himself with his interpretations of Beethoven, Brahms, Wagner, Bruckner and Strauss. His *Parsifal* at Bayreuth in 1951 has become legendary; he continued at Bayreuth although he held the post-war productions in disdain. In 1954 he resumed his directorship at the Munich Opera, but absented himself for an entire year in protest at the delay in rebuilding the National Theatre there; he also made guest appearances to conduct Wagner at Milan and Paris.

Knappertsbusch was a superb conductor whose true genius was revealed in the theatre. His very presence in the pit was sufficient for the atmosphere to become electric with expectation. He was revered by audiences and players alike. Zubin Mehta, who observed him in his student years in Vienna, once remarked that Knappertsbusch put a great amount of tension in music: 'He could play the Brahms *Third Symphony* at half the tempo and you'd still not be bored, because it would make musical sense. He was a great technician and a phenomenal conductor of Wagner opera.' He disliked rehearsing and could never appreciate the need for accuracy when making a record. Culshaw (in *Ring Resounding*) tells the story that when Knappertsbusch was recording a Strauss waltz, as usual without rehearsal, at one of the many repeats half the orchestra went on while the other half went back. The resulting choas lasted only four bars, after which the piece was back on the rails. At the end he called out to Culshaw, 'Can you use that? We don't need to do it again, do we?' Culshaw told him what had happened. He said: '*Scheisse* – do you think anyone else will know?' It is easy to understand that he could not adapt himself to the discipline of the recording studio, where the spontaneity of his interpretations could not flourish. Not many of his studio recordings were wholly successful, but his finest recording was his 1951 Bayreuth performance of *Parsifal*, taped by Decca engineers during rehearsals and the actual performances. On Rosenthal's authority the performance was generally considered the finest of this century, and this great recording is a superb testimony; it captures his magical performance, and has remained one of the best recordings of Wagner opera ever made. The later *Parsifal*, issued by Philips from Knappertsbusch's 1962 Bayreuth performance, has much better sound but did not quite equal the earlier one. There is another recording of him that might do him true justice, should it ever be released. It is the 1951 Bayreuth performance of *Götterdämmerung*, recorded during performance by Decca, but withheld from public release apparently because of conflicting contractual agreement of one of the singers. According to Culshaw, who supervised the recording, Knappertsbusch was magnificent. Because of Knappertsbusch's incompatibility with the recording process, he was passed over in favour of Solti for the Decca *Tristan und Isolde* of 1961, and it is ironical that the rival *Tristan und Isolde* of Böhm, issued by DGG in 1967, was recorded in performance at Bayreuth. However, Discocorp have released a *Tristan und Isolde* conducted by Knappertsbusch, taken from a performance with the Bavarian Radio Symphony Orchestra *et al.* in 1950. Bellaphon have also issued excerpts from a *Parsifal* with the German Opera Orchestra, Berlin, *et al.*

Before World War II Knappertsbusch made a number of recordings, including the prelude to Act III of *Die Meistersinger*, the overture and march from *Tannhäuser*, the Transformation Scene from *Parsifal*, and the Ride of the Valkyries from *Die Walküre* (with the Berlin Philharmonic Orchestra for Polydor), *Mazeppa* (with an unnamed orchestra for Polydor), the overture to *Russlan and Ludmilla*, the waltz scene from *Intermezzo*, the dance from *Salome* and J. Strauss's *Kusswalzer* (with the Berlin State Opera Orchestra for Parlophone), the *Rienzi* overture and the Rhine Journey from *Götterdämmerung* (with the Vienna Philharmonic Orchestra for HMV), Beethoven's Symphony No. 3, *Les Préludes*, *Invitation to the Dance* and the prelude to Act I of *Palestrina* (with the Berlin Philharmonic Orchestra for HMV), Haydn's Symphonies Nos 94 and 100, Mozart's Symphony No. 39 and *German Dances* K. 509 and K. 600, Beethoven's Symphony No. 7 and *Till Eulenspiegel* (with the Berlin State Opera Orchestra for Odeon) and the overture to *Undine* (with the Berlin Symphony Orchestra for Parlophone). Haydn's Symphony No. 94 was also issued by Parlophone.

Decca placed Knappertsbusch under contract after the war, and his first discs (78 r.p.m.) were of Brahms' Symphony No. 2 (with the Suisse Romande Orchestra), the overtures to *Tannhäuser* and *Rienzi*, the prelude to Act III of *Lohengrin* and a suite from *Die Meistersinger* (with the London Philharmonic Orchestra) and the prelude to Act I of *Lohengrin* (with the Zürich Tonhalle Orchestra). Then among the first LPs issued in 1951 by Decca was a complete Act II of *Die Meistersinger*, to be followed by Acts I and III, with the same cast and the Vienna State Opera Orchestra and Chorus. The complete opera is a fine reading, with Knappertsbusch's typically sedate tempi. Other Wagner excerpts recorded at this time were the overtures to *Tannhäuser*, and *Der fliegende Holländer*, the preludes to Acts I and III of *Die Meistersinger*, Siegfried's Rhine Journey and Funeral Music from *Götterdämmerung*, the Ride of the Valkyries from *Die Walküre*, the *Siegfried Idyll*, and the *Wesendonck Lieder* (with Flagstad, and with the Vienna Philharmonic Orchestra). In preparation for their eventual recording of the entire *Ring*, Decca produced Act I of *Die Walküre*, with him again conducting the Vienna Philharmonic, with Flagstad, Svanholm and Van Mill. Despite superb singing, the total effect of the performance was curiously slow-moving and detached. There is, however, a complete *Ring*, with Knappertsbusch conducting, available on disc: it has been issued by L'Estro Armonico, and is taken from his 1957 Bayreuth performances.

Apart from Wagner, Knappertsbusch accompanied Curzon in magisterial performances of Beethoven's Piano Concertos Nos 4 and 5 and Brahms' Piano Concerto No. 2 (with the Vienna Philharmonic), and led *Don Juan*, *Tod und Verklärung* (with the Paris Conservatoire Orchestra), the Bruckner Symphonies Nos 3, 4, 5 and 7, the Brahms *Academic Festival* and *Tragic Overtures*, *Variations on the St Antony Chorale* and *Alto Rhapsody* (with West), the *Nutcracker* Suite, Schubert's *Marches Militaires*, some Strauss waltzes and other music, the overture to *The Merry Wives of Windsor* and *Invitation to the Dance* (with the Vienna Philharmonic Orchestra). Westminster also issued, with the Munich Philharmonic Orchestra, Bruckner's Symphony No. 8, the overtures to *Der fliegende Holländer* and *Tannhäuser*, the preludes to *Lohengrin*, *Die Meistersinger* and *Parsifal*, the prelude and Liebestod to *Tristan und Isolde* and the *Siegfried Idyll*. The Bruckner symphonies are scarcely convincing, and one can only guess that the magic of the concert performance could not be captured in the recording studio. The disc of the Brahms overtures and *Variations on the St Antony Chorale* was re-issued by Decca on a cheap label in the United States; it is an interesting example of Knappertsbusch's deliberate style and of the particular tonal quality he produced with his orchestra, but it would be unlikely to excite listeners accustomed to the brilliance and precision of American orchestras.

Knight, Gerald (b. 1908). Born in Par, Cornwall, Knight was educated at the School of English Church Music and the Royal College of Music, was organist and choirmaster at St Augustine's Church, Queen's Gate (1931–7) and at Canterbury Cathedral (1937–52), and has been director of the Royal School of Church Music from 1952. He was joint musical editor of *Hymns Ancient and Modern, Revised*. Columbia recorded him conducting the Canterbury Cathedral Choir in sacred pieces by Tallis, Wesley, Crotch, Merbecke, Tye, Hilton, Greene, Stanford, Philips, Farrant and Battishill, which were included in the *Anthology of English Church Music*.

Knothe, Dietrich (b. 1929). Born in Dresden, Knothe was a member of the St Thomas Choir in Leipzig under Ramin, studied at the Hochschule für Musik there under Heinrich and Bölsche and at Berlin-Charlottenburg with Peter and Lederer. He was a choral conductor at Magdeburg (1952–3), leader of the Leipzig Radio Choir (1953–62), founded the Capella Lipsiensis (1955) for the performance of music of the 15th, 16th and 17th centuries, and has since conducted the Berlin Singakademie, in East Berlin. His recordings include masses by Obrecht and Ockeghem, and a collection of German songs and dances from the 15th and 16th centuries (with the Capella Lipsiensis, issued by DGG), Handel's *Belshazzar*, *Utrecht Te Deum* and *Ode for the Birthday of Queen Anne* (with the Berlin Singakademie and Chamber Orchestra), Beethoven's Canons (with the Berlin Singakademie), *Elegiac Song*, Chamber Cantatas and Italian Songs (with the Berlin Double Quartet *et al.*), Schubert's *Lazarus* (with the Berlin Staatskapelle *et al.*), and Eisler's *New German Folksongs* and *National Hymn of the German Democratic Republic* (with the Berlin Radio Choir *et al.* for Eterna), and *Tempo der Zeit* (with the Berlin Singakademie for Nova), Dessau's *An die Mütter und an die Lehrer* and Eisler's *Werke des Übergangs* (with the Berlin Singakademie *et al.* for Nova) and Schwaen's *Der neue Kolumbus* (with the Leipzig Radio Symphony Orchestra *et al.* for Nova).

Kobayashi, Ken-Ichiro (b. 1940). Born in Fukushima, Japan, Kobayashi was educated at the Tokyo University of Fine Arts and Music (1960–64), and then studied conducting with Yamada and Watanabe and composition with Ishiketa. In 1970 he was a winner of the Min-On International Conductors Competition, in 1972 made his debut with the Tokyo Symphony Orchestra, and in 1974 won first prize in the Budapest International Conductors Competition. He is permanent conductor of the Tokyo Metropolitan Symphony Orchestra, special guest conductor of the Tokyo Symphony Orchestra, guest conductor of the Amsterdam Philharmonic, Hungarian State Symphony and Hungarian Radio Symphony Orchestras, and professor at the Tokyo College of Music, and has conducted numerous orchestras in West and East Europe, and at festivals in Athens, Bratislava, Marton Vasán (Hungary), Rimini, Prague and Lucerne. His repertoire ranges from Bach to Webern, and he has recorded *Don Juan*, *Till Eulenspiegel* and *Le Sacre du printemps*, with the Budapest Symphony Orchestra for Hungaroton.

Kober, Dieter (b. 1920). Born in Germany, Kober received his initial musical training there, migrated to the United States and was naturalised as a US citizen in 1942. He studied at the Universities of Nebraska and Chicago, the Chicago Musical College, with Ganz in Chicago and with Markevitch at the Salzburg Mozarteum. He taught at the Chicago Musical College (1949), and the Chicago City College (1950), founded and conducted the Collegiate Sinfonietta of Chicago (1950) and the Chicago Chamber Orchestra (1952), becoming its musical director (1962), was director of music at the Chicago Art Institute (1951–6), organised the Lakeside Promenade Concerts sponsored by the Chicago Park District (1963), and has appeared as a guest conductor in Canada and Europe. For Turnabout he recorded Handel's *Water Music* with the Chicago Chamber Orchestra.

Koch, Helmut (1908–75). Born at Barmen, Wuppertal, Koch studied in Cologne, Essen and Düsseldorf, and in Winterthur with Fiedler, Lehmann and Scherchen. He became the leader of the Schubert Choir of the Berlin Radio (1931–8), taught music privately, was a member of the Reichs Radio, artistic director of the Kristall and Odeon record companies

(1938–45), conductor of the German Soloists Society (1945), and founder and conductor of the Berlin Radio Chamber Orchestra (1945) and Choir (1948), in East Berlin. He was appointed chairman of the Choral Committee of the German Democratic Republic (1960), professor at the Hochschule für Musik in East Berlin (1951), and general music director of the Berlin Singakademie (1963), conducted at the Berlin State Opera, and became a member of the German Academy of Arts in DR Germany (1965).

Koch made records after World War II, mostly with the Berlin Radio Choir, and a number of these discs were released in the West on various labels. They were distinguished performances, although he was in no sense a pioneer of the use of original instruments or performing practices. Included were Schütz's *St Matthew Passion*, Bach's four orchestral suites, *Brandenburg Concertos* and Cantatas Nos 205 and 206, four symphonies of C. P. E. Bach, Telemann's *Tafelmusik*, *Tageszeiten* and *Pimpinone*, Handel's *Arminio* and choruses from the oratorios, Carissimi's *Jephte*, A. Scarlatti's *La rosaura*, Pergolesi's *Concerti Armonici* and two Flute Concertos (with Walter), Mozart's *Bastien und Bastienne* and *Der Schauspieldirektor*, Leopold Mozart's *Toy Symphony*, *Die Bauernhochzeit* and *Eine musikalische Schlittenfahrt*, violin concertos of Vivaldi, Nardini and Viotti (with Scherzer), trumpet concertos of Torelli, Telemann, Haydn and Leopold Mozart (with Krug), Beethoven's *12 Country Dances*, *11 Viennese Dances*, *6 Country Dances* and *12 German Dances*, Mendelssohn's *Violin Concerto in D minor* (with Schmahl), Pillney's *Eskapaden eines Gassenhauers*, Geissler's Symphony No. 5 and *Schöpfer Mensch*, and Zechlin's Chamber Symphony (with the Berlin Chamber Orchestra *et al.*), Bach's Cantatas Nos 201 and 211, Monteverdi's *La favola d'Orfeo* and *Vespro della beata Vergine*, Handel's *Dettingen Te Deum*, *Water Music* and *Music for the Royal Fireworks*, Haydn's *The Creation*, *The Seasons* and Mass No. 9, Mozart's Mass K. 427 and *Requiem*, Beethoven's *Ritterballet*, *Cantata on the Death of Emperor Joseph II*, *Christus am Ölberge*, *Meeresstille und glückliche Fahrt*, *Bundeslied*, *Opferlied*, *Chor zum Festpiel* and *Die Weihe des Hauses* (with the Berlin Radio Symphony Orchestra *et al.*); Handel's *Saul*, *Judas Maccabaeus*, *Belshazzar* and *Messiah* (with the Berlin Symphony Orchestra *et al.*); *La serva padrona* (with the Berlin State Opera Orchestra *et al.*); a collection of German choral music of the 16th and 20th centuries, Gluck's *The Marriage of Hercules and Hebe*, Brahms' *Ein deutsches Requiem* and *Neue Liebeslieder*, Hindemith's *Als Flieder jüngst mir in Garten blüht*, Schoenberg's *Friede auf Erden*, Krause-Graumnitz's *An die Nachgeborenen*, Meyer's Harp Concerto and *Mansfelder Oratorium*, and Zechlin's *Wenn der Wacholder blüht*.

Kodály, Zoltán (1882–1967). The eminent Hungarian composer Kodály was active as a conductor during his lifetime, particularly as an interpreter of his own music. In 1928 he led his *Psalmus Hungaricus* at the Leeds Festival and was inspired to introduce the idea of choral festivals to his native Hungary. His work and influence was one of the most important factors in developing a widespread and sophisticated approach to music in Hungary, and the emergence of so many distinguished conductors and musicians in that country, has been, in some measure, a result of his efforts. Solti, who was a student of Kodály, has said of him (in an interview in the German magazine *Audio*, August 1977, pp. 72–4) that he was a fine man but not a good teacher; 'When he didn't like anybody, this person was dead for him. Sometimes he didn't speak for days. He disliked people in general, and was very curt. But he was very intelligent, and in few words said a lot of good things. If you were ready to get them into your mind, you could learn.' In 1962 DGG issued a disc of him conducting the Budapest Philharmonic Orchestra in his own *Concerto for Orchestra* and *Summer Evening*; EMI had previously released a mono LP with him leading the Hungarian State Symphony Orchestra and the Budapest Choir in his *Missa brevis*, and Artia issued in the United States a coupling of him conducting the Hungarian Concert Orchestra and the Budapest Chorus in his *Te Deum* and *Psalmus Hungaricus*. These latter performances were later released by Turnabout as one of their historical series.

Koekelkoren, Martin (b. 1921). Born in Valkenburg, Holland, Koekelkoren played the clarinet in the Maastricht Municipal Symphony Orchestra, studied at the Amsterdam Conservatory, and first conducted the Royal Male Choir 'Mastreechter Staar' in 1947. With this choir he has toured in many European countries and has made a number of records of a wide variety of music, from Mozart's *Ave verum corpus* to songs from American musical comedy, sometimes accompanied by the Limburg Symphony Orchestra. He has also taught at the Maastricht Conservatory since 1950.

Koetsier, Jan (b. 1911). After completing his studies in Berlin, the Dutch conductor Koetsier was assistant conductor of the Amsterdam Concertgebouw Orchestra, became assistant conductor of the Bavarian Radio Symphony Orchestra (1950), was appointed the orchestra's principal conductor (1957), and also regularly conducted the Munich Philharmonic and Bamberg Symphony Orchestras. He recorded Suder's *Chamber Symphony*, with the Munich Philharmonic Orchestra, for Da Camera.

Köhler, Siegfried (b. 1923). Born in Freiburg im Breisgau, Köhler studied at the Hochschule für Musik there, was a harpist and conductor with the Heilbronn City Theatre (1941–2), conductor at Freiburg (1946), at the Düsseldorf Opera (1954–7), then at Cologne, where he was the substitute general music director and leader of the opera school at the Hochschule für Musik. Since 1964 he has been general music director at Saarbrücken, teaches at the Hochschule für Musik there, and has composed musicals and film scores. His recordings include Weill's *Der Ja-Sager* (with the Düsseldorf Children's Choir and Orchestra, for DGG), piano concertos by Mayr, Ries and Weber, as well as Weber's *Konzertstück* and *Polacca brillante* (with Littauer and the Hamburg Symphony Orchestra for Turnabout), and the violin concertos of Joachim and Zimmermann (with Rosand and Lautenbacher respectively, with the Luxembourg Radio Orchestra for Candide).

Koizumi, Kazuhiro (b. 1949). Born in Kyoto, Koizumi studied conducting and composition from the age of fourteen; in 1970 he won first prize at the second Min-On International Conductors' Competition in Japan, and in the same year was appointed assistant conductor to Ozawa with the Japan Philharmonic Orchestra. In 1973 he won first prize in the third Karajan International Conductors' Competition in Berlin; since then he has toured in Austria, Italy, Poland, France, FR Germany and Britain, and in 1975 became musical director of the New Japan Philharmonic Orchestra. He has recorded the Lalo Violin Concerto (with Wallez and the Philharmonic Orchestra of Radio France for Bellaphon), and Dohnányi's *Variations on a Nursery Theme* and Rachmaninov's *Variations on a Theme of Paganini* (with Ortiz and the New Philharmonia Orchestra for EMI).

Kolar, Victor (1888–1957). Born of Bohemian parents in Budapest, Kolar studied at the Prague Conservatory under Ševčik and Dvořák, and in 1900 migrated to the United States. He was a violinist in the Pittsburgh Symphony and the New York Symphony Orchestras (1905–20), and in 1914 became Damrosch's assistant in New York. In 1920 he was associate conductor of the Detroit Symphony Orchestra and when Gabrilowitsch died in 1935 he succeeded him as conductor of the orchestra. He resigned in 1941. His compositions included symphonic and vocal music. For Decca (US) he recorded, on 78s with the Detroit Symphony Orchestra, Enesco's *Romanian Rhapsody No. 1*, the two *Peer Gynt* suites, and *Scheherazade*, which was an estimable performance.

Komor, Vilmos (b. 1895). Born in Budapest where he studied at the Budapest Academy of Music, Komor was secretary of the Budapest Philharmonic Association (1921–8), and organised a chamber orchestra from among the members of the Budapest State Opera Orchestra (1928). He was conductor at the Városi State Theatre (1928–32), then artistic director of the State Opera, artistic director and conductor of the Omike Society (1939–44), again at the State Opera (1945), and guest conductor with the Berlin State Opera, and Leipzig Gewandhaus and Dresden Staatskapelle Orchestras. He received the Kossuth Award in 1963, and was responsible for many first performances of operas and symphonies of Hungarian composers. His records, for Qualiton, include *Pagliacci* and *Cavalleria rusticana* (in Hungarian) and Erkel's *Bank Ban* and *László Hunyadi* (with the Budapest Philharmonic Orchestra *et al.*), accompaniments to opera recitals by Melis and Agay, and orchestral excerpts from *Faust* and *La traviata* (with the Hungarian State Opera Orchestra).

Kondrashin, Kyril (b. 1914). Born in Moscow where both his parents were string players in Koussevitzky's orchestra, and later in the Bolshoi Theatre orchestra, Kondrashin learned the piano as a boy, and studied at the Moscow Conservatory under Khaikin (1931–6). His first experience as a conductor was as an assistant at the Nemirovich-Danchenko Musical Theatre (1934–7), where the first opera he conducted was *Madama Butterfly*. He became conductor at the Maly Theatre in Leningrad (1938–42), and permanent conductor at the Bolshoi Theatre in Moscow (1943–55); he last conducted opera in Chicago in 1958, and then turned his attention to symphonic music. He was conductor of the USSR State Symphony Orchestra (1956–60), and then musical director and principal conductor of the Moscow Philharmonic Orchestra (1960–75). He toured Europe and the United States, and it was his appearances with Van Cliburn after the latter had won the Tchaikovsky Prize in 1958 that made him an international celebrity. He was awarded two Stalin Prizes (1948 and 1949), and in 1956 was named People's Artist of the Russian Republic. He unexpectedly sought political asylum in Amsterdam while visiting the Netherlands to conduct the Concertgebouw Orchestra.

Kondrashin sees himself in the same tradition as the great conductors of the past, who strove to produce their own unique sound and style with their orchestras. He has written several books on conducting, which have yet to be translated into English. His records include the Shostakovich symphonies, which are brilliantly performed, with immense panache and commitment; his other records of Russian music have been equally interesting, but his discs of the symphonies of Beethoven, Brahms and Mahler give a fascinating impression of how the masterpieces of Western musical literature are heard by Russian audiences. Some tempi, the balance of texture of the orchestral sound, the phrasing of many passages, and an acute dynamic control, amounting almost to a mannerism, are the most distinctive characteristics of his interpretations.

Records of Kondrashin as a conductor first appeared in the West on a number of labels, including Bruno, Monitor, Saga, MK, Colosseum, Period, Parlophone, Vanguard, Everest, Turnabout, La Guilde Internationale du Disque, and Concert Hall. Following the agreement with EMI and Melodiya, many of his recordings have been issued in Britain and the United States. His earliest recordings were mostly concerto accompaniments: Bach's *Harpsichord Concerto in A minor*, Tchaikovsky's *Concert Fantasy* and Nikolayeva's Piano Concerto (with Nikolayeva), Beethoven's Triple Concerto (with Oistrakh, Knushevitzky and Oborin), Mozart's Two-Piano Concerto (with Gilels and Zak), Mozart's Violin Concertos K. 216, K. 218 and K. 271a, Rondos K. 269 and K. 373 and Adagio K. 261, Lalo's *Symphonie espagnole*, Taneyev's *Suite de concert*, Chausson's *Poème*, Saint-Saëns *Introduction et rondo capriccioso*, Glière's *Romance*, Prokofiev's Violin Concerto No. 1, and Violin Concertos of Beethoven, Mendelssohn, Brahms, Dvořák, Tchaikovsky, Glazunov and Sibelius (with David Oistrakh), Prokofiev's Piano Concertos Nos 1 and 5, and Glazunov's Piano Concerto (with Richter), Prokofiev's Piano Concerto No. 3, Saint-Saëns' Piano Concerto No. 2, Chopin's Piano Concerto No. 1, Liszt's Piano Concerto No. 1 and Mendelssohn's Piano Concerto No. 1 (with Gilels), a Vivaldi Concerto, Vieuxtemps' Violin Concerto No. 5 and Khrennikov's Violin Concerto (with Kogan), and Scriabin's Piano Concerto (with Bashkirov). The orchestras were variously described as the National Philharmonic and the USSR State Symphony, and in some instances the Moscow Philharmonic. Other recordings made at this time were *Capriccio espagnol*, Liadov's *Eight Russian Folksongs*, Saint-Saëns' Piano Concerto No. 5, Prokofiev's Piano Concerto No. 1, Rimsky-Korsakov's Piano Concerto and Glazunov's Piano Concerto (with Richter), Wieniawski's *Souvenir de Moscou* (with Barinova), Tchaikovsky's *Pezzo capriccioso* and Glazunov's *Chant du ménestrel* (with Rostropovich), and Rachmaninov's Piano Concerto No. 4 (with Zak, and the Moscow Youth Symphony Orchestra); *Brandenburg Concerto No. 5* (with the USSR State Symphony Orchestra); *The Bartered Bride*, *Russlan and Ludmilla*, and Moniuszko's *Halka* (with the Bolshoi Theatre Orchestra *et al.*); Shostakovich's Symphonies Nos 1 and 8, Khachaturian's Symphony No. 3, Rachmaninov's *The Bells*, and Hindemith's *Symphonic Metamorphoses on a Theme by Weber* (with the Moscow Philharmonic Orchestra *et al.*).

In the early 1960s, Kondrashin also made records for Western companies; these included Brahms' Violin Concerto, Lalo's *Symphonie espagnole* and Tchaikovsky's *Sérénade melancolique* (with Kogan and the Philharmonia Orchestra for EMI); the two Liszt Piano Concertos (with Richter and the London Symphony Orchestra for Philips, still available on both sides of the Atlantic, and generally conceded to be among the best recordings of both works); Rachmaninov's Piano Concerto No. 1, Liszt's Piano Concerto No. 2, and Prokofiev's Piano Concerto No. 3 (with Janis and the Moscow Philharmonic Orchestra for Mercury); Mozart's Sinfonia Concertante K. 364 (with David and Igor Oistrakh and the Moscow Philharmonic Orchestra for Decca); Rachmaninov's Piano Concerto No. 2 (with Ashkenazy and the Moscow Philharmonic Orchestra for Decca); *Capriccio espagnol*, *Capriccio italien* and suites from Kabalevsky's *Masquerade* and *The Comedians* (with the RCA Victor Symphony Orchestra for RCA); and Tchaikovsky's Piano Concerto No. 1 (with Cliburn and the Symphony of the Air for RCA). The last-named disc repeated Cliburn's success at the Tchaikovsky Competition in Moscow, and was the first classical LP record to reach sales of a million copies. Everest released in 1967 a Moscow performance led by Kondrashin of Shostakovich's Symphony No. 13, which contains the setting of Yevtushenko's poem about the massacre of Jews at Kiev by the Nazis, *Babi*

Yar, and a warning about anti-semitism, and which was the subject of controversy in the USSR.

The EMI Melodiya series included Beethoven's Symphony No. 4 and *Prometheus* overture, the *Romeo and Juliet* fantasy-overture, Mahler's Symphonies Nos 1 and 9, Kalinnikov's Symphony No. 1, Prokofiev's *Scythian Suite* and *Cantata for the 20th Anniversary of the October Revolution*, Shostakovich's Symphonies Nos 1 to 15 (although all have not been released in Britain or the US), *The Execution of Stepan Razin* (with Gromadsky), and the cantata *The Sun Shines over our Motherland*, Rachmaninov's *The Bells*, Piano Concerto No. 3 (with Zak) and *Symphonic Dances*, Sviridov's *Kursk Songs* and Shchedrin's *Mischievous Melodies* and *Not Love Alone* (with the Moscow Philharmonic Orchestra *et al.*). More recently in the USSR have been released recordings of Kondrashin conducting the four Brahms symphonies, Mahler's Symphonies Nos 5 and 7, Rachmaninov's Piano Concerto No. 3 (with Mogilevski), Khachaturian's Symphony No. 3 and Piano Concerto (with Flier), Shchedrin's *Orchestral Scherzo* and Boris Tchaikovsky's Violin Concerto (with Pikaisen); all are with the Moscow Philharmonic Orchestra.

König, Gustav (b. 1910). Born in Schwabach, König studied at the Munich Academy of Music and University, was conductor at Osnabrück (1932–4), Stettin (1934–6), the Berlin People's Opera (1938–41), Aachen (1941–3) and then Essen (1943). For DGG he recorded Bialas' *Indian Cantata*, songs by Liszt and sacred pieces by Mozart (with Waechter, Stader and the Berlin Radio Symphony Orchestra) and Genzmer's Flute Concerto (with Scheck and the Berlin Philharmonic Orchestra); these recordings were made in the first years of LP.

Konoye, Hidemaro (1898–1973). Born in Tokyo, Konoye was the younger half-brother of Prince Konoye, the Japanese statesman with whom he was frequently confused. He was head of the Imperial Music Academy in Tokyo, founded and conducted the Japanese New Symphony Orchestra which is now the NHK Symphony Orchestra, and was a guest conductor before World War II in many cities in Europe and the United States. His son, Hidetake Konoye, is also a conductor in Japan. He composed symphonic and choral music, and arranged for modern orchestra ancient Japanese court music; *Etenraku*, an 8th-century Japanese ceremonial prelude, arranged by him, was recorded on a 78 r.p.m. disc by Stokowski and the Philadelphia Orchestra. He made some fine discs on 78s with the Berlin Philharmonic Orchestra of Haydn's Symphony No. 91 (for Polydor), Mozart's Sinfonia Concertante K. 297b (for Columbia) and *A Night on the Bare Mountain* (for Polydor), and with the New Symphony Orchestra in Japan a recording issued in 1930 of Mahler's Symphony No. 4 (for Japanese Parlophone), Leopold Mozart's *Toy Symphony* and Entry of the Little Fauns from Pierné's *Cydalise et le chèvre-pied* (for Polydor).

Kontarsky, Bernard (b. 1937). Born in Iserlohn, Westphalia, the brother of the pianists Alfons and Alois, Kontarsky studied at the Hochschule für Musik and the University at Cologne, became a pianist and conductor, and was appointed to the Württemberg State Opera at Stuttgart. Turnabout issued a disc in 1976 on which he conducts the Luxembourg Radio Orchestra in Milhaud's *La Muse ménagère*, Piano Concerto No. 2 (with Johannesen) and *Suite Cisalpine* (with cellist Blees), and Saint-Saëns' Piano Concerto No. 4 (also with Johannesen).

Konvalinka, Miloš (b. 1919). Born in Nové Město in Moravia, Konvalinka studied at the Brno Conservatory (1939–43), conducted at Göttingen (1943), at Ústí (1947–8), at the Košice National Theatre (1948–9), and at Olomouc (1951–4), and is now director of the Prague National Opera. His compositions include orchestral, vocal and instrumental works. He has recorded for Panton Železný's Symphony No. 2 and *Concertante Music*, Flosman's *Concertante Music*, Drejsl's *Symphony for String Orchestra* (with the Musici de Praga), Matěj's Cello Concerto, Bárta's Symphony No. 3, Jirko's *An Evening with Rimbaud* (with the Ostrava Janáček Philharmonic Orchestra), Flosman's *Sonata for Soprano and Strings* (with the Prague Chamber Orchestra), Flosman's overture *Fire in the Mountains*, Kubín's *Sinfonietta*, Petrov's *Poem* and Kancheli's Symphony No. 4 (with the Prague Radio Symphony Orchestra), and for Supraphon Flosman's Violin Concerto No. 2 (with the Prague Radio Symphony Orchestra *et al.*).

As his recordings suggest, Konvalinka has a strong commitment to performing the music of contemporary Czech composers, and has conducted at least 200 of their works in concerts, about half being premières. He has said: 'The principle that an unperformed work is a dead work, no matter how good it is, is unequivocally valid. This gives the conductor a very weighty task: carefully to select and systematically to include in programmes the works of contemporary composers in such a way that the widest range of listeners comes into contact with them and the composers have the opportunity to test from the performance of their work the success of the problems of realisation of the creative concept. I have defended this principle from the start of my artistic activity.'

Konwitschny, Franz (1902–62). Konwitschny was born at Fulnek in northern Moravia, and was the son of a conductor. He studied at the German Music Society School at Brno and at the Leipzig Conservatory, and became a violist in the Leipzig Gewandhaus Orchestra under Furtwängler. He then moved to Vienna, was a violinist in the Fitzner String Quartet and a teacher at the Volkskonservatorium. His career as a conductor started in 1927, when he was appointed a repetiteur at the Stuttgart Opera, and he quickly rose to become second, then principal conductor (1930). He was general music director at Freiburg im Breisgau (1933–8), general music director and conductor of the Opera and Museum Concerts at Frankfurt am Main (1938–44), music director at the Hannover Opera and guest conductor at the Hamburg State Opera (1946–9), conductor of the Leipzig Gewandhaus Orchestra (1949–62), chief conductor at the Dresden State Opera (1953–5), and general music director at the Berlin State Opera (from 1955), replacing Kleiber, in the rebuilt State Opera House in East Berlin. He toured extensively, led a fine *Ring* at Covent Garden (1959), conducted both the London Philharmonic and Leipzig Gewandhaus Orchestras in London (1961), and toured Japan with the Gewandhaus Orchestra (1961). He died while conducting in a television broadcast in Belgrade.

Konwitschny was a distinguished conductor, who gave spacious and convincing performances of the standard repertoire, particularly of Beethoven, Brahms, Bruckner and Wagner, but by temperament he was more at home in the opera house than in the concert hall. He disliked rehearsing, was utterly relaxed in performance, and gave his musicians free rein; he was able to resume control at once if ensemble became slack. He was extremely popular in Leipzig; after his death, the state funeral there passed along streets lined with people for a distance of ten kilometres. Musicians called him 'Konwhisky', and before performances of *Tristan und Isolde* he was said to drink six bottles of champagne. There are still many anecdotes told about him in Leipzig; in the finale of *Fidelio* once, he ceased conducting, went to the desk of a viola player, and marked the score with fingerings, and in the course of a Wagner opera he would take out his handkerchief, wipe his brow, and wave with it to friends in the audience. He accommodated himself as comfortably to the Communists as he did to the Nazis, yet he was, secretly, a devout Catholic, who had masses said regularly for his soul, and at his funeral the Communist hierarchy in the German Democratic Republic were obliged to sit through a Requiem Mass.

Most of Konwitschny's recordings were made in East Europe, and were issued there on local labels, but a number were released in the West by Philips, DGG, EMI, Ariola, Eurodisc and Urania, and by other companies in the United States. His records included Beethoven's nine Symphonies and overtures, Schumann's four Symphonies, *Overture, Scherzo and Finale*, *Manfred* and *Genoveva* overtures and *Konzertstück* for four horns, Bruckner's Symphonies Nos 4, 5 and 7, Reger's *Variations and Fugue on a Theme of Hiller*, Shostakovich's Symphony No. 10, Bach's Violin Concerto No. 2 and the two Beethoven *Romances* (with David Oistrakh), Mendelssohn's Violin Concerto and Wieniawski's Violin Concerto No. 2 (with Igor Oistrakh), and Gerster's Symphony No. 2, *Festival Overture* and *Oberhessischer Bauerntanz* (with the Leipzig Gewandhaus Orchestra); *Leonore No. 3* overture, Tchaikovsky's Symphony No. 5, Bruckner's Symphony No. 2, and Prokofiev's Violin Concerto No. 1 (with Stanske, and the Berlin Radio Symphony Orchestra); Beethoven's Symphony No. 5 (with the Leipzig Radio Symphony Orchestra); Beethoven's Symphony No. 3, Witt's *Jena Symphony*, Mozart's Symphony No. 41 and Violin Concerto K. 219 (with David Oistrakh), Brahms' Piano Concerto No. 1 (with Kempff), Brahms' and Tchaikovsky's Violin Concertos (with David Oistrakh), and Strauss's *Symphonia domestica* (with the Saxon State Orchestra); Beethoven's Violin Concerto (with Suk), Schubert's Symphony No. 9, Bruckner's Symphony No. 4, *Till Eulenspiegel*, the overtures to *Tannhäuser* and *Der fliegende Holländer*, and the preludes to *Tristan und Isolde* and *Die Meistersinger* (with the Czech Philharmonic Orchestra); *Leonore No. 2* overture and Dvořák's Symphony No. 9 (with the Bamberg Symphony Orchestra for Ariola); Bruckner's Symphony No. 4, *Don Juan*, *Till Eulenspiegel*, a suite from *Der Rosenkavalier* and the dance from *Salome* (with the Vienna Symphony Orchestra); *Siegfried Idyll*, the overtures to *Der fliegende Holländer*, *Rienzi*, *Die Feen* and *Das Liebesverbot*, the preludes to *Parsifal* and *Lohengrin*, Ride of the Valkyries and Magic Fire Music from *Die Walküre*, Entry of the

Gods into Valhalla from *Das Rheingold*, prologue, Rhine Journey, Funeral Music and Finale from *Götterdämmerung*, Good Friday Music from *Parsifal* and Strauss's *Eine Alpensinfonie* (with the Munich State Opera Orchestra for Urania); *Der fliegende Holländer*, *Tannhäuser*, and excerpts from *Götterdämmerung* (with the Berlin Deutsche Oper Orchestra *et al.* for EMI) *Das Liebesverbot* (with the Munich State Opera Orchestra *et al.*, issued by Nixa); and Shostakovich's Symphony No. 11 and Butting's Symphony No. 9.

Konwitschny's recordings of the Beethoven symphonies were imaginative, if not greatly inspired. He usually adopted broad tempi, yet his readings had vitality, and in one or two instances, such as the Symphony No. 7, the performances were magnificently fiery. When the symphonies were first issued separately in 1960 or thereabouts, the repeats were included, and this was clearly Konwitschny's intention. Later, Philips re-issued the symphonies as a set after Konwitschny's death, but eliminated the repeats; this mutilation can scarcely be justified. The Schumann and Bruckner symphonies were also performed with great assurance, although the readings were not distinctive enough to set them apart from others. His records with the Leipzig Gewandhaus Orchestra were notable for the dark, firm tone of the orchestra, although in some respects the orchestra had not the polish of the leading European and American orchestras. The two Wagner operas were superbly directed, and the Beethoven Violin Concerto (with Suk and the Czech Philharmonic Orchestra) was one of the most sublime performances of the work ever recorded.

Koppenburg, Hans (b. 1932). Born in Bottrop, Westphalia, Koppenburg was educated in Munich and studied conducting with Markevitch in Salzburg. He was first a choral repetiteur and conductor in theatres in FR Germany, became first conductor of the Hessian Symphony Orchestra (1956), founded and conducted the Frankfurt Chamber Orchestra (1959–73) and then founded the Weilburger Schlosskonzerte. His repertoire is extensive, from the early baroque to contemporary compositions. CBS have issued discs of him conducting the Frankfurt Chamber Orchestra in Mozart's Symphony K. 16, J. C. Bach's Symphony Op. 3 No. 4, Mozart's three Piano Concertos K. 107 (with Engel) and pieces by Sammartini and Piccinni.

Kord, Kazimierz (b. 1930). Born at Pogorze, in Silesia, Kord was educated at the Leningrad Academy of Music and at the State Academy of Music at Kraków. He was a choral conductor at the Warsaw Opera in 1959 and made his debut as a conductor there in 1961. He became artistic director of the Kraków Opera (1962–70), and artistic director of the Polish National Radio and Television Orchestra at Katowice (1969–73). He first conducted abroad in Kiev in 1967, and has since conducted at many opera houses in Eastern and Western Europe, the United States and Canada. He first appeared at the New York Metropolitan Opera in 1972 in *The Queen of Spades* and at Covent Garden in 1976 in *Eugene Onegin*. In 1974 he conducted the Toronto Symphony Orchestra on a tour of Europe. He recorded Lalo's *Symphonie espagnole* and Saint-Saëns' *Introduction et rondo capriccioso* (with Kulka and the Polish National Radio and Television Orchestra for Polskie Nagrania), Tchaikovsky's Piano Concerto No. 1 (with Vered and the London Symphony Orchestra for Decca), *Finlandia*, *Valse triste*, *The Swan of Tuonela* and the *Karelia* suite (with the New Philharmonia Orchestra for Decca), and Szymanowski's *Symphonie concertante* (with Blumental and the Polish Radio Symphony Orchestra, issued by Unicorn).

Korn, Richard (b. 1908). Born in New York and educated at Princeton University, Korn studied further at the Juilliard Graduate School, the National Orchestral Association and with Koussevitzky at Tanglewood, and made his debut as a conductor at the New York Stadium Concerts in 1946. He has conducted the Ballet Russe (1947–8), the Baton Rouge Symphony Orchestra (1950–51), was music director of the Orchestra of America in New York (1959–65) with which he presented concerts at Carnegie Hall entirely devoted to American music, and has appeared as a guest conductor in London, Tokyo, Paris and elsewhere. He has recorded Mozart's Serenade K. 375 and Brahms' *Serenade No. 2* (with the National Orchestral Association Alumni, on 78s for Victor), Berlinski's *Symphonic Visions* and Wood's *Poem for Orchestra* (with the Tokyo Asahi Orchestra for Composers Recordings), and a series for Allegro with the Hamburg Philharmonic Orchestra, including Copland's *Quiet City*, Creston's *Rumor*, Chadwick's *Symphonic Sketches No. 3*, an interlude from Harris's Symphony No. 4, McDonald's *Lamie*, Barber's *Essay No. 2*, Stringfield's *Cripple Creek*, Deems Taylor's *Casanova* ballet music, Fry's *Overture to Macbeth*, Gottschalk's Symphony No. 1, Gram's *Death Song of an Indian Chief*, Griffes' *The Vale of Dreams*, Hadley's *Scherzo dia-*

bolique, Paine's *As You Like It* overture, an interlude from Parker's *Mona*, excerpts from Carpenter's ballet *Krazy Kat*, Sullivan's *The Mikado* and his arrangement of Arne's music called *Arniana*.

Korngold, Erich (1897–1957). Born in Brno, Korngold studied with his father, the Viennese music critic Julius Korngold, and with Fuchs, von Zemlinsky and Grädener in Vienna. From his early teens he was writing compositions which were being performed in Vienna and Leipzig, and in 1911 he presented a concert of his own music in Hamburg. After conducting and teaching in Hamburg and Vienna, he went to the United States in 1935 and composed music for films. Many of his compositions have been recorded, including his violin concerto (by Heifetz), *Symphony in F sharp major* (by Kempe and the Munich Philharmonic Orchestra) and his opera *Die tote Stadt* (by Leinsdorf and the Munich Radio Orchestra *et al.*). Korngold himself conducted an orchestra with the tenor Tauber singing arias from his opera *Lied der Liebe*, on 78s for Decca (US).

Kórody, András (b. 1922). Born in Budapest, Kórody studied at the Franz Liszt Academy there under Weiner, Lajtha and Ferencsik, and as a student was engaged as a coach at the Budapest State Opera (1945). He became a conductor, then in 1963 principal conductor at the Opera; at the same time, since 1957, he has taught conducting at the Academy, and since 1967 has been chief conductor of the Budapest Philharmonic Orchestra. His guest appearances have been throughout Eastern and Western Europe; he was the first Hungarian conductor to conduct at the Bolshoi Theatre in Moscow, and led the Tokyo Symphony Orchestra in a four-week tour of Japan. Supraphon issued a 78 r.p.m. set in which he conducted the Budapest Philharmonic Orchestra in the Bartók *Concerto for Orchestra*; Qualiton have issued LP discs of him conducting the Budapest Philharmonic, Hungarian State and Hungarian State Opera Orchestras in the Beethoven Piano Concerto No. 1 (with Szegedi), Triple Concerto (with Szegedi, Kovács and Perényi) and *Prometheus* overture, the overtures to *Rosamunde*, *Dichter und Bauer*, and Mendelssohn's *Die Hochzeit des Camacho*, also Mendelssohn's Symphony No. 3 and music for *A Midsummer Night's Dream*, Liszt's Piano Concerto No. 1 and *Malédiction* (with Gabos), *Le Carnaval des animaux*, *Boléro*, *Ma Mère l'Oye* and *Rapsodie espagnole*, Debussy's First Rhapsody for Clarinet (with Kocsis), Strauss's Concertino (with Kocsis and Fülemile), Prokofiev's Piano Concerto No. 1 (with Berman), the Bartók Viola Concerto (with Németh), and Violin Concertos Nos 1 and 2 (with Kovács), *The Wooden Prince*, Suite No. 2 and *Romanian Folk Dance No. 1*, David's Viola Concerto (with Lukács), Erkel's *Festival Overture*, Szokolay's *The Blood Wedding* and *Samson*, Sárközy's *The Poor One*, Mihály's Violin Concerto (with Kovács), Vincze's *Symphonic Movement*, and discs of excerpts from *Don Giovanni*, *Lucia di Lammermoor*, *Don Carlos*, *Aida* and *La forza del destino*, and arias from Verdi operas (with Déry).

Košler, Zdeněk (b. 1928). Born in Prague where his father was a violist in the National Theatre Orchestra, Košler was a member of the Kühn Children's Choir. He studied piano with Grünfeldová, theory and composition with Jeremiáš and Řídký, and conducting with Dědeček, started his career as a coach with the Czech Choir (1945–8), and then studied conducting with Doležil, Ančerl and Brock at the Prague Academy of Music (1948–52). At the same time he was a repetiteur at the Prague National Theatre (1948–51), and became a conductor there (1951–8). In 1956 he won first prize at the young conductors' competition at Besançon; he was artistic director of the Olomouc Opera (1958–62), chief conductor of the Ostrava Opera (1962–4), again won first prize and the gold medal at the Dmitri Mitropoulos International Conductors' Competition in New York (1963), was assistant conductor to Bernstein with the New York Philharmonic Orchestra (1963–4), was first conductor of the Prague Symphony Orchestra (1964–6), chief conductor of the Berlin Komische Oper (1967–8), permanent conductor of the Czech Philharmonic Orchestra and chief conductor of the Bratislava National Theatre (1971). Since 1968 he has visited Japan every year to conduct Japanese orchestras and to teach at the Geijutsu Daigaku University in Tokyo. He is recognised as one of the most outstanding of younger Czech conductors, although he is little known in the West.

Košler made an impressive first appearance on record in 1966 with Dvořák's Symphony No. 7, with the Czech Philharmonic Orchestra for Supraphon, but only a few of his records have been released in Britain or the United States. Among them are Schubert's *Overture in the Italian Style*, *Overture in E minor*, the overture *Alfonso und Estrella*, and excerpts from *Rosamunde*, Wagner's *Wesendonck Lieder* (with Kniplová) and *Siegfried Idyll*, Bořkovec's Piano Concerto (with Panenka), Martinů's Cello Concerto No. 1 (with Chuchro) and

Violin and Piano Concerto (with Grumlíková and Kolář), Kalabis' Symphony No. 4, cantatas by Smetana, Dvořák and Foerster, and Boháč's *Suita drammatica* (with the Czech Philharmonic Orchestra for Supraphon), Eben's *Apologia Sokratus* and *Ubi caritas et amor*, (with the Prague Symphony Orchestra for Supraphon), Concertos for Two Horns by Vivaldi, Haydn and Telemann (with Zdeněk and Bedřich Tylšar and the Prague Chamber Orchestra for Supraphon), Mozart's Symphony No. 38, some *Slavonic Dances* of Dvořák, and Tchaikovsky's Symphony No. 4 (with the London Symphony Orchestra for Connoisseur), Dvořák's Symphonies Nos 8 and 9, and *Symphonie fantastique* (with the Slovak Philharmonic Orchestra for Supraphon), Pauer's *Initials* and *Intrade* (with the Prague Chamber Soloists for Panton), Válek's Symphony No. 6, Prokofiev's *Scythian Suite*, Bartók's *Dance Suite*, and Bořkovec's Symphony No. 3 and *Symphonic Allegro* (with the Czech Philharmonic Orchestra for Panton), Britten's *Variations on a Theme of Frank Bridge*, *Peter and the Wolf* (with the Tokyo Metropolitan Symphony Orchestra), excerpts from *The Bartered Bride*, Cikker's opera *Coriolanus* and Jeremiáš' *The Brothers Karamazov* (with the Prague National Theatre), and Cikker's *Symphony 1945* (with the Slovak Philharmonic Orchestra). Other contemporary Czech composers he has recorded are Burghauser and Moyzes.

Koslik, Gustav (b. 1902). Born in Vienna where he studied at the Hochschule für Musik and the Vienna University, Koslik was a repetiteur and conductor at Essen (1925–30), first conductor at Saarbrücken (1930–35), general music director at Koblenz (1935–41) and Colmar (1941–4), chief conductor with the South German Radio at Stuttgart (1946) and chief conductor of the Lower Austrian Orchestra (1952–62). Remington (US) recorded him in the early years of LP, with the Austrian Symphony Orchestra, in the Handel/Harty *Water Music*, some overtures of Mozart, the *L'Arlésienne* Suite No. 1, Verdi's *Requiem*, the overture to *Der fliegende Holländer*, *A Night on the Bare Mountain* and the overture and Polovtsian Dances from *Prince Igor*.

Kostelanetz, André (1901–80). Born into a musically sophisticated family at St Petersburg, Kostelanetz studied at the conservatory there, and at the age of 19 obtained a position as assistant conductor at the St Petersburg Opera. He left the USSR to join his family in the United States in 1922, and, after six years as an accompanist and coach to opera singers in New York and Chicago, joined the Atlantic Broadcasting Company, which was the forerunner of the Columbia Broadcasting System. For CBS he arranged and produced innumerable commercial radio shows, commanding a huge audience in the US. He also conducted concerts with many major orchestras, led the New York Philharmonic Orchestra in promenade concerts, toured with his former wife the soprano Lily Pons, directed music for films, and became a household name as a populariser of music.

Viewing Kostelanetz's career as a conductor and recording artist, it is difficult to decide whether to condemn or condone. There is no doubting his material success; by 1973 he had sold 52 million records, and once drew a crowd of 250,000 to a performance he conducted in Chicago. He was a most skilful conductor, and his editing of scores and preparation of orchestras was immensely professional and exact. He is claimed to have made more converts to classical music than anybody else. Among the music he commissioned are some distinguished pieces, such as Copland's *A Lincoln Portrait* and Schuman's *New England Triptych*, and his records have many spirited and well-honed performances, such as Walton's *Capriccio burlesco* (another commissioned work) and a collection of the light music of Shostakovitch. Although he concentrated mostly on music scarcely less familiar than the waltzes of Tchaikovsky or Strauss, he once recorded *On Hearing the First Cuckoo in Spring* of Delius and Hovhaness's *And God Created Whales*, which incorporates in the score the actual noises made by whales under the water. His other records included Prokofiev's *Stone Flower*, Gershwin's Piano Concerto (with Levant), Enesco's *Romanian Rhapsody No. 1*, *Invitation to the Dance* and an arrangement of Tchaikovsky's *The Queen of Spades* (with the New York Philharmonic Orchestra), the *L'Arlésienne* suites, *Peter and the Wolf*, Villa-Lobos' *Little Train of the Caipira*, *Bachianas brasileiras No. 5* and *Magdalena Suite*, the *Romeo and Juliet* fantasy-overture, suites from *Swan Lake*, *The Sleeping Beauty* and *Nutcracker*, Grofé's *Grand Canyon* Suite, *Ma Mère l'Oye*, Gershwin's Piano Concerto and *Rhapsody in Blue* (with Previn), Britten's *Soirées musicales*, Walton's *Johannesburg Festival Overture*, Hovhaness' *Floating World*, the prelude to *Khovanshchina*, Rachmaninov's *Aleko* suite, a disc of Strauss waltzes, collections of music by Bizet, Mendelssohn and Shostakovich, and numerous other arrangements and shorter pieces (with his own orchestra for CBS).

But whatever the music may be, it served Kostelanetz's purpose; he was not music's servant, he was its master. No liberty was beyond him to condense, re-arrange, homogenise great music. Once he combined a movement of a Tchaikovsky symphony with a Tin Pan Alley song; on another occasion he shortened the *Romeo and Juliet* fantasy-overture from 16 to 4¾ minutes. Then he explained that 60 per cent of a symphonic overture is given to the development of themes and that this 'is intended for musicians and confuses a lot of people'. One wonders how he would re-arrange the first movement of Beethoven's Symphony No. 5, using these principles. Some of his best-selling records have been instrumental arrangements of the operas *Carmen*, *Rigoletto*, *Aida* and *La traviata*, without the voices, the music shortened to fit on to one LP, the keys changed here and there, and the music made continuous. Nonetheless, one has to recognise that Kostelanetz was a good conductor, and made many records, whatever his artistic ideals.

Koussevitzky, Serge (1874–1951). Koussevitzky was the first Russian conductor to win an international reputation. He had already become famous in Europe as a virtuoso player of the double bass, as an orchestral conductor and as a music publisher before World War I, but he reached full status as an international celebrity when he was appointed conductor of the Boston Symphony Orchestra in 1924. He was then aged 50, and he remained with the orchestra for 25 years. He elevated it to such a degree of splendour that it was regarded as the finest in the United States, if not in the world. During the decade following 1929 he made a series of superb recordings of music ranging from Bach to Shostakovich, and they were one of the cornerstones of the 78 r.p.m. catalogue.

Koussevitzky's birthplace was at Tver near Moscow. Almost from childhood he was convinced that he should be a conductor. He won a scholarship at the conservatory of the Moscow Philharmonic Society, but only on condition that he should study the double bass, as there was a vacancy for that instrument in the institute's orchestra. It took him five months to complete the course for the instrument, instead of the prescribed five years. While playing in the orchestra of the Imperial Theatre he also won fame in Russia and abroad as a solo performer on the double bass; he attracted the attention of Nikisch and played one of the Saint-Saëns cello concertos on the double bass at a concert at Leipzig. Later, some records were issued of his double-bass performances, and he also wrote several pieces for the instrument, including a concerto which he composed with Glière's assistance. At the same time as he was giving double-bass recitals in London and Paris, he was studying conducting at the Hochschule für Musik in Berlin, and there observed Nikisch conducting. He first conducted himself in Berlin (1907) and London (1908), and in the four years following 1910 he toured Russia with his own orchestra, hiring a boat specially to take them all down the Volga River. The story is that when he married the heiress of a Russian tea millionaire, Natalie Oushkoff, he asked for an 85-man symphony orchestra as a wedding present, and it was with this orchestra that he made these legendary tours. With his wife he also founded a music-publishing house in Moscow, Éditions Russes de Musique, and actively promoted the new music of Stravinsky, Scriabin and Prokofiev.

The Russian Revolution was a watershed in his life. He lost his wealth and property, but was offered the directorship of the State Symphony Orchestra and of the Grand Opera in Moscow. The new regime, however, had no appeal for him, and in 1920 he and his wife left the country. At first he toured with his double bass, and conducted some concerts in London. In 1921 he settled in Paris, assembled a Russian orchestra and established the Concerts Koussevitzky, which became famous for their programmes of new music. His great opportunity came in 1924 when he was invited to become conductor of the Boston Symphony Orchestra. Until 1939 Paris remained his true home, whither he returned each year after the season in the United States; in fact he only slowly assimilated with the American community, and it was only after the outbreak of World War II, when his annual return to Paris became impossible, that he became an American citizen.

His appointment with the Boston Symphony had a hazardous start, since, although he was intuitively a great interpreter, he had an uncertain technique. The orchestra took almost two years to accustom itself to the vagaries of his beat and to his highly personal way of rehearsing. Eventually the players learned to play together by listening carefully to each other and by following their section leaders, and so they developed an excellent ensemble almost in spite of the conductor. (Some say that this happened later with Klemperer.) His relations with the orchestra were worsened by a number of dismissals and replacements. He kept his orchestra to himself and himself to the orchestra, except for his annual tours to Europe, rarely made guest appearances with other American orchestras, hardly ever conducted opera, and the only guest conductors he would permit with the Boston Symphony were from Europe. Because the Boston Symphony was a non-union orchestra he could rehearse them exhaustively and he allowed no one to be present at rehearsals. Few soloists were engaged for his concerts; the fact was that he was a poor accompanist. The outcome was that he took over a good orchestra and made it a great one. It was entirely his own, and it played his repertoire exactly as he conceived it. Stories that he could scarcely read a score were nonsense, and arose from his practice of learning scores by having a pianist (Jesus Maria Sanroma) play the music as he wished it phrased, while he made the motions of conducting the work with the score.

Koussevitzky was one of the great *romantic* conductors. His instinct was to *interpret* music, to create a glowing orchestral colour that stressed its dramatic and lyrical qualities. Ernest Newman once wrote that it was hardly possible for a conductor to raise some works to a higher pitch of nervous incandescence than Koussvitzky did, but the nervousness never got out of hand. 'It is Koussevitzky's servant, not master. The excitement is always perfectly under control; one great plastic line runs through and through the work.' He trained his orchestra to produce the sonorities and expressive nuances of romantic music with extraordinary effect, but when he turned to earlier periods the style was much less suitable. Rhythms tended to become rigid, and string tone not instinctively flexible; expressiveness could not come, as in romantic music, from the orchestral colour or the intensity of the melodic line, but had to emerge from the balance and structure of the movement, as much as from phasing and nuance. This did not mean that all of his performances of Bach, Haydn and Mozart were unsuccessful – his recording of Haydn's Symphony No. 94 was, in its way, very fine. In 1970 RCA re-issued his Beethoven Symphony No. 3 with the Boston Symphony, and it was then fascinating to read of its reception by critics completely attuned to the far more literal readings of the great conductors in the decades after Koussevitzky, especially Karajan, Klemperer and Szell. To these critics Koussevitzky's idiosyncratic approach was almost beyond comprehension; one English reviewer wrote that 'only Koussevitzky devotees are likely to be convinced by this eccentric *Eroica* with its arbitrary changes of tempi and its lack of feeling for structure. The performance is often physically exciting but there is not much depth in it' (*EMG Monthly Letter*, June 1970).

Lasting fame for Koussevitzky and the Boston Symphony, at least for the world at large, came from their recorded performances of many works by a handful of composers – Berlioz, Debussy, Ravel, Tchaikovsky, Prokofiev, Sibelius and Strauss – which were of an incredibly high standard. He thought that some of his readings of these composers were as good as they could possibly be, and although this is an overstatement, his *Daphnis et Chloé* Suite No. 2, *Till Eulenspiegel*, *Classical Symphony* and *Tapiola* come close to it. His Sibelius recordings were as significant as any in widening the popularity of the composer; the recordings of some of the Strauss tone poems were shattering in their day. Russian music was his speciality; he gave the first performance of the Ravel orchestration of *Pictures at an Exhibition* in 1923, and recorded it in 1931. The prelude to Act I of *Khovanshchina*, played at a very slow tempo, was remarkably beautiful; a contrast was the *Classical Symphony*, which was taken at an extremely fast tempo, and has not been surpassed for its wit and sparkle. The first recording of the Boston Symphony made with him, in 1928, was *Petrushka*, and while his concert performances of *Le Sacre du printemps* were much admired, he never recorded the work. Maybe the most famous of his Russian recordings were the last three Tchaikovsky symphonies, the *Romeo and Juliet* fantasy-overture and *Francesca da Rimini*, which exhibited his exceptional dramatic power and the orchestra's superb playing. Debussy and Ravel were also particularly suited to the orchestra's magnificent tonal qualities; his recording of *La Mer* was celebrated, but many of its interpretative ideas raise eyebrows today, and the opening is slower than in most performances. It was re-issued in Britain in 1970 by RCA, coupled with *Pictures at an Exhibition*. His best recordings of American music were *El Salón México* and *Appalachian Spring* of Copland, and Roy Harris's Symphony No. 3. Two major works that have scarcely been eclipsed since they were issued were Berlioz's *Harold in Italy* (with Primrose) and Liszt's *Mephisto Waltz*; *Harold in Italy* displayed all the virtues of both conductor and orchestra – rock-like firmness and an inevitability about the performance, which was powerful and expressive. Curiously, Koussevitzky was less certain with Wagner, and recorded very little of the composer; on the other hand, his Brahms Symphony No. 3 was an exemplary performance.

Except for some records made in London in 1933–4 (Sibelius' Symphony No. 7 with the BBC Symphony Orchestra, and Beethoven's Symphonies Nos 3 and 5, Mozart's Symphony No. 40 and the finale from Haydn's Symphony No. 88, with the London Philharmonic Orchestra), all Koussevitzky's recordings were with the Boston Symphony Orchestra. The first, *Petrushka*, was made in 1928 and the last, Grieg's *Two Elegiac Melodies*, in 1950. They were the Bach *Brandenburg Concertos*, orchestral suites, the sinfonia from Cantata No. 4, an arrangement of the prelude from the Violin Sonata No. 6, and the *St Matthew Passion*, the C. P. E. Bach *Orchestra Suite in D* (arranged by Steinberg), Vivaldi's Concerto Grosso Op. 3 No. 11, the third movement of Handel's Concerto Grosso Op. 6 No. 12, and 'O Sleep, why dost thou leave me?' from *Semele* (with Maynor), Haydn's Symphonies Nos 92, 94, 102 and 104, Mozart's Symphonies Nos 26, 29, 33, 34, 36, 39 and 40, *Eine kleine Nachtmusik*, the overtures to *La clemenza di Tito* and *Der Schauspieldirektor*, five movements from the Serenade K. 361 and an aria from *Die Zauberflöte* (with Maynor), Leopold Mozart's *Toy Symphony*, Beethoven's Symphonies Nos 2, 3, 5, 6, 8 and 9, *Egmont* overture and *Missa Solemnis*, Schubert's Symphonies Nos 5 and 8 (twice, in 1936 and 1945), and the *Ballet in G* from *Rosamunde*, Schumann's Symphony No. 1, Mendelssohn's Symphony No. 4 (twice, in 1935 and 1947), *Harold in Italy* (with Primrose), the overture *Le Carnaval romain* and excerpts from *La Damnation de Faust*, the overtures to *Oberon* and *Der fliegende Holländer*, the prelude to Act I of *Lohengrin*, the prelude to Act I and the Good Friday Music from *Parsifal* and the *Siegfried Idyll*, Brahms' Symphonies Nos 3 and 4, Violin Concerto (with Heifetz) and *Academic Festival Overture*, *Mephisto Waltz*, *Pictures at an Exhibition*, the prelude to Act I of *Khovanshchina*, Rimsky-Korsakov's *Dubinushka* and The Battle of Kershenetz from *The Legend of the Invisible City of Kitezh*, Tchaikovsky's Symphonies Nos 4, 5 and 6, *Serenade in C major*, *Francesca da Rimini* and the *Romeo and Juliet* fantasy-overture, Satie's *Gymnopédies Nos 1* and *3* (the No. 1 twice, in 1930 and 1949), Rachmaninov's *Isle of the Dead* and *Vocalise*, Prokofiev's Symphonies Nos 1 (twice, in 1929 and 1947), and 5, the finale from *Chout*, the Violin Concerto No. 2 (with Heifetz), suites from *Lieutenant Kijé* and *The Love of Three Oranges* (twice, in 1929 and 1936); *Peter and the Wolf* (twice, in 1939 with Hale and in 1950 with Eleanor Roosevelt) and the *Romeo and Juliet* Suite No. 2, Shostakovich's Symphony No. 9, Khachaturian's Piano Concerto (with Kapell), Liadov's *The Enchanted Lake*, Stravinsky's *Capriccio* (with Sanroma), *Petrushka*, Apollon et Terpsichore from *Apollon Musagète* and *Song of the Volga Boatmen*, Sibelius' Symphonies Nos 2 (twice, in 1935 and 1950) and 5, *Tapiola*, *Pohjola's Daughter* and The Maiden with Roses from *Swanwhite*, Debussy's *La Mer*, *Prélude à l'après-midi d'un faune*, and *Danse* and *Sarabande* (orch. Ravel), Ravel's *Boléro* and *Ma Mère l'Oye* (both twice, in 1930 and 1947), *Daphnis et Chloé* Suite No. 2 (twice, in 1928 and 1944), *Pavane pour une infante défunte*, *Rapsodie espagnole* and *La Valse*, Fauré's *Élégie* (with Bedette) and excerpts from *Pelléas et Mélisande*, Grieg's *Two Elegiac Melodies* (twice, in 1940 and 1950), the Strauss waltzes *Frühlingsstimmen* and *Wiener Blut*, *Don Juan*, *Till Eulenspiegel* and *Also sprach Zarathustra*, Copland's *Appalachian Spring*, *A Lincoln Portrait* (with M. Douglas) and *El Salón México*, Foote's *Suite in E*, Hanson's Symphony No. 3 and *Serenade*, Harris's *Symphony 1933* and Symphony No. 3, McDonald's *San Juan Capistrano*, Piston's Symphony No. 3 and *Prelude and Allegro* (with E. Power Biggs), Thompson's *A Testament of Freedom* and the Sousa marches *Semper Fidelis* and *The Stars and Stripes Forever*. As a double-bass player, he recorded, with Pierre Luboschutz, the largo from Eccles' *Sonata in G*, Laska's *Wiegenlied*, and his own *Chanson triste*, *Fair Harvard*, *Valse miniature* and the andante from his Double-Bass Concerto.

Koussevitzky was a commanding figure in his day, and his 25 years with the Boston Symphony Orchestra saw one of the most illustrious partnerships in the history of orchestral music. His records were one of the peaks of the 78 r.p.m. catalogue, and one would give a hundred of the present LPs of his successors to have, say, a four-track LP of his *Daphnis et Chloé* or *Till Eulenspiegel*. The transfers of his performances that have been issued in recent years have not really done him justice, not so much because of their inevitably inferior sound, but because his highly personal readings suffer when judged by today's interpretative conventions. LP transfers have been made of the Beethoven Symphony No. 3, *Till Eulenspiegel*, *Peter and the Wolf*, *La Mer* and *Daphnis et Chloé* Suite No. 2, but the only ones listed in the Schwann catalogue now are the Brahms Violin Concerto and Prokofiev's Violin Concerto No. 2 (with Heifetz), Sibelius' Symphony No. 2, and Harris' *Symphony 1933*; in the Gramophone catalogue, available in Britain (in 1977) there are Prokofiev's Symphony No. 5 and *Romeo and Juliet* Suite No. 2, and the Sibelius Symphony No. 7 (with the BBC Symphony Orchestra). Private 'pirate' records are available of the *Daphnis et Chloé* Suite No. 2, *The Isle of the Dead*, *Poème d'extase* and *Scythian Suite*, as well as the Sibelius Symphonies Nos 1, 5, 6 and 7.

Kout, Jiří (b. 1937). The Czechoslovak conductor Kout has been active in Prague, and has recorded Schulhoff's Piano Concerto No. 2 (with Baloghová and the Prague Chamber Orchestra for Supraphon), and Krejčí's *Ballet Music* and Doubrava's *Pastorale* (with the Studio Orchestra for Panton).

Kovalev, Pavel (b. 1890). Born in Nikolayev, Russia, Kovalev studied at the Odessa Conservatory and in Kraków and Leipzig. He conducted in France and Germany, was a professor at the Odessa Conservatory (1919–22), then took up residence in Moscow. His compositions include an opera *Ariadne and Bluebeard*; he recorded Glazunov's *Slavonic Festival*, excerpts from *Khovanshchina*, Rachmaninov's Symphony No. 3, Balakirev's Symphony No. 2, Rimsky-Korsakov's *Overture on Russian Themes*, Arensky's Symphony No. 2 and Millöcker's *Der Bettelstudent* (with the Moscow Radio Symphony Orchestra *et al.*).

Kovalyov, Aleksei (b. 1914). Kovalyov began his career as assistant to Golovanov at the Bolshoi Theatre, Moscow, and in the opera department of the Stanislavsky Studio. He is director of the Large Opera and Symphony Orchestra of the All-Union Radio, and is musical editor-in-chief of the committee concerned with the production of new operas, ballets and musical comedies. He has recorded, together with the conductor Akulov, *Le Coq d'or*, with the Moscow Radio Orchestra *et al.*

Kox, Hans (b. 1930). Born in Arnhem, the Dutch composer Kox has received a number of awards for his compositions, including the Visser-Neerlandia Prize for his Symphony No. 1 (1959), the Prix Italia for *In those days* (1970), and the Rostrum of Composers' first prize for *L'Allegria* (1967). Many of his compositions, including the opera *Dorian Gray*, have also been recorded by Donemus, and for that company he conducted the Amsterdam Concertgebouw Orchestra in his Symphony No. 2.

Krachmalnick, Samuel (b. 1928). Born at St Louis, Missouri, Krachmalnick studied at the Juilliard School with Morel, was a horn player in the National Symphony Orchestra in Washington D.C., and made his debut as a symphonic conductor with the Boston Pops Orchestra at Des Moines in 1951, and in opera with Menotti's *The Saint of Bleecker Street* in New York in 1954. He was awarded the Koussevitzky Memorial Prize and the Frederic Mann Prize, and has conducted opera companies in Canada, Italy, Mexico and Switzerland, as well as in the United States. In 1958 he recorded for Columbia (US) Blitzstein's opera *Regina* (with the New York City Opera Orchestra *et al.*), and Desto also recorded him with the same orchestra and company in Moore's *Carry Nation*.

Kraft, William (b. 1923). Born in Chicago, Kraft studied composition with Luening and musicology with Lang at Columbia University, and since 1962 has been principal percussionist with the Los Angeles Philharmonic Orchestra. His many compositions often include prominent parts for percussion, and a number have been recorded, including *Concerto Grosso*, *Triangles*, *Momentum*, *Theme and Variations*, *Contextures*, Concerto for Four Percussion Soloists and Orchestra, *Des Imagistes*, *Encounters II* and *IV*, *In Memoriam Igor Stravinsky*, *Collage I* and *Morris Dance*. As a conductor he recorded Harrison's Concerto for Violin and Percussion Orchestra, and Linn's Concertino for Violin and Wind Octet (with Eudice Shapiro and the Los Angeles Percussion Ensemble and Crystal Chamber Orchestra, for Crystal), his *Des Imagistes* (with Geer and Kermoyan and the Los Angeles Percussion Ensemble for Delos) and *Nonet* (with the Los Angeles Brass Quintet for Crystal), Campo's *Madrigals* and Schmidt's Concertino for Piano and Brass Quintet (with Davis and the Los Angeles Brass Quintet for Crystal), and his *Collage I* (with the Los Angeles Horn Club for EMI).

Krannhals, Alexander (1908–1961). Born in Frankfurt am Main of Swiss parents, Krannhals studied with Frey and Lavater in Zürich and with Weingartner in Basel. His appointments were conductor at the Lucerne City Theatre (1929–34), conductor at the Basel City Theatre (1934–53), director of the conducting course at the Basel Conservatory (1948–53), music director of the St Gall Symphony Concerts (1949–54), co-founder and artistic director of the Basel popular music concerts (1941–61), chief conductor of the Netherlands Opera (1953–61), and general music director at Karlsruhe, where he conducted opera and symphony concerts (1955–61). He was also a guest conductor in many European countries and conducted opera in South America (1956–9). He recorded Janáček's *From the House of the Dead* (for Philips, a production of the Holland Festival), and for La Guilde Internationale du Disque Mozart's Symphony No. 41 and the Beethoven Violin Concerto (with Parikian, and the Frankfurt Radio Symphony Orchestra),

Die Zauberflöte, the overture to *Le nozze di Figaro* and an abridged *Il barbiere di Siviglia* (with the Netherlands Philharmonic Orchestra *et al.*), *Don Giovanni*, Mozart's *Exsultate jubilate* (with Dobbs) and a collection of choruses from Verdi operas (with the Baden State Opera Company Orchestra *et al.*), the Chorus of Hebrew Slaves from *Nabucco* (with the Bavarian Radio Symphony Orchestra *et al.*), and Bach's Violin Concertos Nos 1 and 2 (with Parikian and the Baden Chamber Orchestra).

Kraus, Richard (1902–78). Born in Charlottenburg, Berlin, and the son of the heldentenor Ernst Kraus (1863–1941), Kraus studied at the Hochschule für Musik in Berlin and became a repetiteur under Blech and Kleiber at the Berlin Staatsoper (1923–7). He was a conductor at Kassel (1927–8), Stuttgart (1933–7), general music director at Halle (1937–44) and at Cologne (1948–53), was a guest conductor at the Berlin City Opera (1953) and then was chief conductor of the North-West German Philharmonic Orchestra at Herford (1963–9). His recordings include Liszt's *Hungarian Rhapsodies Nos 1* and *2* and incidental music from *Peer Gynt* (with the Bamberg Symphony Orchestra for DGG), the Tchaikovsky Piano Concerto No. 2 (with Cherkassky) and Henze's *Five Neapolitan Songs* (with Fischer-Dieskau and the Berlin Philharmonic Orchestra for DGG), the two *Peer Gynt* Suites, the Homage March from *Sigurd Jorsalfar* and *Wedding Day at Troldhaugen* (with the Hamburg Symphony Orchestra for DGG), excerpts from *Les Contes d'Hoffmann* and a recital with Rita Streich (with the Berlin Radio Symphony Orchestra *et al.* for DGG), and discs of excerpts from *La Bohème*, *Madama Butterfly*, *Cavalleria rusticana*, *Pagliacci* and *Lohengrin* (with orchestras of Berlin opera houses *et al.* for Ariola).

Krauss, Clemens (1893–1954). Born in Vienna into a family with a distinguished musical ancestry, Krauss could read music before he could spell, and was a boy chorister in the Imperial Chapel. He graduated from the Vienna Conservatory in 1912 after studying under Reinhold, Grädener and Heuberger, and his first appointment was as chorus master at the Brno State Theatre where he made his debut as a conductor with *Zar und Zimmermann*, in 1913. He became second conductor at the German Theatre at Riga (1913–14) and at Nuremberg (1915–16), first conductor at Stettin (1916–21), conductor of opera and concerts at Graz (1921–2), conductor of the Vienna State Opera under Schalk, and teacher of conducting at the Vienna Academy of Music (1922–4), conductor of the Vienna Tonkünstlerkonzerte (1923–7), and musical director of the opera and Museum concerts at Frankfurt am Main (1923–7). He first conducted at the Salzburg Festivals in 1926, and was a regular conductor there between 1929 and 1934; his most successful Salzburg performance was *Der Rosenkavalier*.

In 1929 Krauss was appointed first conductor of the Vienna State Opera and conductor of the Vienna Philharmonic Orchestra (1929–34); at the Opera he collaborated with the great designer Alfred Roller. When Kleiber resigned from the Berlin Staatsoper in 1934, Krauss was selected to take his place as first conductor, but his tenure at Berlin was not successful and he moved to Munich to become music director of the Bavarian State Opera (1937–40). He was music director at the Mozarteum at Salzburg (1939–45), and finally from 1945 conductor at the Vienna State Opera and of the Vienna Philharmonic Orchestra. He first visited South America in 1927, and in 1929 made his debut in the United States with the New York Philharmonic and Philadelphia Orchestras. His British debut was at Covent Garden in 1934; after World War II he returned in 1947 with the Vienna State Opera, to lead *Fidelio* and *Salome*, and later conducted *Falstaff*, *Tosca*, *Tristan und Isolde* and *Die Meistersinger* at Covent Garden. He was in fact a staunch Anglophile, spoke English well, and before his death in Mexico in 1954 had planned to undertake more engagements at Covent Garden. At the Bayreuth Festivals of 1953 and 1954 he conducted *The Ring*, and in 1953 *Parsifal* as well. He was married to Viorica Ursuleac, a soprano whom he frequently accompanied on the piano at recitals.

Krauss's relationship with the Nazi party has been a source of controversy. Some evidence suggested that he succeeded Kleiber in Berlin at Hitler's wish, and David Wooldridge states (in *Conductor's World*, p. 227) that he joined the Nazi party in 1938 and 'pursued the Nazi ideology', although Wooldridge also points out that Krauss assisted countless victims of Nazi persecution to escape from Germany and Austria. He was in Vienna when the Russians occupied the city at the end of the war, and conducted the first concert arranged by the Soviet commandant. However one of the four occupying powers prohibited his public appearance as a conductor, one of the reasons being that Krauss had once discussed with Hitler the erection of an opera house. In its obituary for Krauss, *The New York Times* of 17 May 1954 stated that 'he had been cleared by the Austrian Commission in December 1946 and it was proved that he had never belonged to the Nazi party or held any political position. He was declared to have been neither a Nazi nor Nazi sympathiser, but was criticised for having worked as a musician in Nazi Germany.'

Between the wars Krauss was certainly one of the foremost European conductors and was considered among the finest interpreters of the German romantic composers. He was at his best in the opera house in the operas of Mozart, Wagner, Strauss and Verdi; *Die Fledermaus* was also magnificent under his baton, and his Austrian première of *Wozzeck* in Vienna in 1929 was praised. He was a friend and collaborator of Richard Strauss and was identified particularly as perhaps the finest conductor of his operas; he led the première of *Arabella* in Dresden in 1933, of *Friedenstag* at Munich in 1938, and of *Die Liebe der Danae* at Salzburg in 1952, and wrote the libretto of *Capriccio*, in which the character of the theatrical producer La Roche is said to be a self-portrait. In the concert hall, he was effective with large symphonic forms, to which he brought wit and imagination, although some considered him unequal to the grand gesture in the greatest symphonic music. This may have sprung from his sense of humour and his refusal to take himself too seriously. His orchestral texture was clear, with a sensuous refinement, and the music was given a marked rhythmic stamp. On the podium his gestures were economical, and he could command a massive *forte* with the smallest indication. As an opera director he was painstaking in nurturing his singers; in Vienna he aimed at developing an ensemble, and this caused some singers – Elisabeth Schumann and Lotte Lehmann in particular – to leave, but others remained loyal to him.

Before World War II Krauss made a number of records with the Vienna Philharmonic Orchestra for HMV. The major works recorded were Haydn's Symphony No. 88, Beethoven's Symphony No. 2, Brahms' Symphony No. 3 and the scherzo from Bruckner's Symphony No. 4. Others were the overtures to *Le nozze di Figaro*, *Così fan tutte*, *Die Entführung aus dem Serail*, *Zampa*, Weber's *Peter Schmoll und seine Nachbarn* and *Jubel*, and Goldmark's *Im Frühling*, the Ballet Music in G major from *Rosamunde*, Strauss's *Le Bourgeois gentilhomme* and the Love Scene from *Feuersnot*, a number of waltzes and polkas of Johann Strauss, and waltzes of Lanner and Ziehrer. Telefunken also recorded him conducting *Till Eulenspiegel*, part of *The Three-cornered Hat* (with the Vienna Philharmonic Orchestra) and Schubert's Symphony No. 9 (with the Vienna State Opera Orchestra); Supraphon Haydn's Symphony No. 37 (with the Vienna State Opera Orchestra); and Polydor the final scene from *Capriccio*. In the latter, Viorica Ursuleac *et al.* sang with the Bavarian State Opera Orchestra; BASF issued an LP transfer in 1975. Vox also released a *Der Rosenkavalier* on LP, in which Krauss conducted the Bavarian State Opera with Ursuleac as the Marschallin in 1944.

After the war Krauss recorded primarily for Decca and Vox; first on 78s, and later on mono LP. The Decca 78s included *Till Eulenspiegel* (with the La Scala Orchestra), *Tod und Verklärung* (with the London Philharmonic Orchestra), the prelude and Liebestod from *Tristan und Isolde* (with the Vienna Philharmonic Orchestra), Brahms' *Variations on the St Antony Chorale*, *Academic Festival Overture*, *Hungarian Dances* Nos 1 and 3 (with the London Symphony Orchestra) and the *Alto Rhapsody* (with Kathleen Ferrier and the London Philharmonic Choir and Orchestra); the latter performance has been re-issued many times and is one of the treasures of the gramophone. When LP arrived in Britain in 1951, *Also sprach Zarathustra* with Krauss conducting the Vienna Philharmonic was among the first Decca releases; it was followed by a magnificent series of the Strauss tone poems – *Till Eulenspiegel*, *Don Juan*, *Symphonia domestica*, *Ein Heldenleben*, *Don Quixote* and *Aus Italien*, as well as the opera *Salome* and the suite from *Le Bourgeois gentilhomme*. These performances have set a standard rarely equalled by other conductors; Krauss had an instinctive feeling for the Strauss idiom and an unerring comprehension for phrasing and rubato, no doubt arising out of his close association with the composer himself and his performance of the works over many years. The scores are not displayed as orchestral showpieces alone, and the wit, humanity and depth of feeling in the music is revealed as scarcely any other interpreter has done. Fortunately, Decca have in recent years re-issued the performances, and although the sound cannot compare with that of more recent recordings, the discs are invaluable for their interpretations alone. Krauss was equally successful in his recordings of the music of Johann and Josef Strauss, which were one of the highlights of the early Decca LP catalogue. In addition to discs of overtures, waltzes, polkas, etc. there were the two operettas *Der Zigeunerbaron* and *Die Fledermaus*, both with the Vienna Philharmonic Orchestra, Vienna State Opera Chorus and members. Krauss lavished as much care on an operetta of Johann Strauss as on an opera by Mozart, and these performances were superbly accomplished. His *Die Fledermaus* was undoubtedly one of the most felicitious operatic recordings ever made.

Other LP records Krauss made for Decca with the Vienna Philharmonic included the prelude and Liebestod from *Tristan und Isolde*, the prelude and Good Friday Music from *Parsifal*, the three *Leonore* and *Fidelio* overtures, and Beethoven's Piano Concertos Nos 2, 4 and 5 (with Backhaus). Musical Masterpiece Society issued *The Creation* (with the Vienna Philharmonic Orchestra *et al.*); Odeon, *The Seasons* and *Ariadne auf Naxos* (originally recorded with Ursuleac, Berger and the Stuttgart Orchestra in 1935); Amadeo, Strauss's *Metamorphosen*, waltzes from *Der Rosenkavalier*, *Suite from Harpsichord Pieces by Couperin* and *Sinfonische Zwischenspiele aus Intermezzo* (with Ursuleac, and with the Bamberg Symphony Orchestra, some of which were issued in Britain by World Record Club), Haydn's Symphonies Nos 88 and 93 (with the Bavarian Radio Orchestra) and Schubert's Symphony No. 8 (with the Bamberg Symphony Orchestra); Vox, Mozart's Serenade K. 250, the incidental music from *A Midsummer Night's Dream*, Schubert's *Gesang der Geister über den Wassern* and Beethoven's *Choral Fantasia* (with the Vienna Symphony Orchestra, Wührer, *et al.*), Telefunken dances from *The Three-cornered Hat* (with the Vienna Philharmonic Orchestra); Urania, Haydn's Cello Concerto No. 1 (with Hoelscher and the Berlin Philharmonic Orchestra); Turnabout, Beethoven's *Cantata on the Death of Emperor Joseph II* (with the Vienna Symphony Orchestra *et al.*); and BASF *Capriccio*, and excerpts from *Der Rosenkavalier* and *Der fliegende Holländer* (with the Bavarian State Opera Orchestra *et al.*), *Ariadne auf Naxos* and Puccini's *Il tabarro* (with the Stuttgart Reichssenders Orchestra *et al.*, in German).

Kremer, Gidon (b. 1947). Kremer was born in Riga; his mother came from Karlsruhe and a grandfather from Sweden. He studied the violin with Oistrakh in Moscow, won the 1970 Tchaikovsky Competition there, and is now acclaimed as one of the most distinguished of the younger generation of violinists. While he performs the standard repertoire with the greatest authority, his inclination is towards baroque and earlier music, and he has championed Schoenberg, Webern and contemporary composers. In 1977 he toured Austria and FR Germany as soloist with the Vilna Chamber Orchestra from the USSR, and then applied to the Soviet Ministry of Culture for extraordinary permission to reside in the West for two years, but not for political or commercial motivations. 'I believe', he has said, 'it is really very important for every artist, not only for me, to see and experience a lot, not only in his own country but in the whole world. That doesn't mean I want to work more, to drive myself. Perhaps I'll find the peace and quiet which will give me the possibility to assimilate better what I experience and see, so that in my artistic activity I may become more intensive and true' (*Musical America*, March 1978, p. 35). For Ariola/Eurodisc he both played and conducted the Mozart Violin Concerto K. 216 and the *Concertone* (with the Vienna Symphony Orchestra, and with Gridenko in the latter).

Křenek, Ernst (b. 1900). Born in Vienna, Křenek studied first in Vienna and then in Berlin with Schreker, and was a conductor at the Kassel Opera (1925–7) and at Wiesbaden. He returned to Vienna as a correspondent for *Frankfurter Zeitung*, and then migrated to the United States in 1937 and filled academic positions, at Vassar College and Hamline University. He settled in California, became a US citizen in 1954, and was awarded the Grand Prize of Austria in 1963. His numerous compositions are written in many contemporary styles, and include five symphonies; his opera *Jonny spielt auf*, which was first performed in Leipzig in 1927, was the first jazz opera and brought him international fame. He has conducted on records his *Horizon Circled*, *From Three Makes Seven* and *Von Vorn Herein* (with the South-West German Radio Orchestra for Orion), and excerpts from his operas *Der goldene Bock*, *Sardakai* and *Mr Milson, I Presume* (with the Hamburg State Philharmonic Orchestra for EMI, in FR Germany). He has also recorded some of his own instrumental and vocal music, as accompanist.

Krenz, Jan (b. 1926). Born in Wloclawek, Poland, Krenz studied at a secret conservatory in Warsaw during the German occupation, then later continued his studies at the State Academy of Music at Łódź, and was granted a UNESCO scholarship to study in Paris. His debut as a conductor was with the Łódź Philharmonic Orchestra (1946); he was appointed conductor of the Poznań Philharmonic Orchestra (1948), second conductor of the Polish National Radio Symphony Orchestra at Katowice (1950), three years later succeeding Fitelberg as its artistic director and first conductor, and was artistic director of the Great Theatre at Warsaw (1968–73). He is now conductor of the Beethovenhalle Orchestra and at the City Theatre, Bonn, and has been a guest conductor in the USSR, the Far East, India, Australasia and throughout Europe. His compositions include symphonies, choral and chamber works.

Krenz has recorded music by a number of Polish composers with the Polish National Radio Orchestra for Polskie Nagrania. Included are Paderewski's Piano Concerto and Różycki's *Ballade* (with Hesse-Bukowska), Lutosławski's Symphony No. 1, *Poème*, *Deux Poèmes d'Henri Michaux*, *Postludium* and *Livre pour orchestre*, overtures by Malawski and Czalowski, Serocki's *Musica concertante*, Szableski's *Toccata*, Concerto Grosso and Flute Concerto (with Bronkowski), Rudziński's *Gaude Mater Polonia*, Baird's Symphony No. 3, Szeligowski's *Epitaph to Szymanowski's Memory* and *Lublin* suite, two Moniuszko overtures, Dankowski's *Symphony in D major*, Perkowski's *Nocturne*, and Wiechowicz's *Wedding Dance*. Wergo also released some of these performances, in addition to Serocki's *Segmenti*, and *Symphonic frescoes*, Górecki's *Epitaph*, *Scontri*, *Genesis II* and *Refrain*, and Penderecki's *Capriccio*. For Composers Recordings (US) he also led the Polish National Radio Orchestra in music by American composers: Diamond's *Romeo and Juliet*, Donovan's *Epos* and *Passacaglia on Vermont Folk Tunes*, Gerschefski's *Fanfare*, *Fugato and Finale*, Holby's Piano Concerto and R. Smith's Piano Concerto No. 2 (with Stefanski), Porter's Harpsichord Concerto (with Pleasants) and Riegger's *Organ Fantasia and Fugue*.

Krenz's other recordings include Beethoven's Symphony No. 5 and two Weber overtures (with the Polish Radio Orchestra for DGG), Beethoven's Piano Concerto No. 2 and the Grieg Piano Concerto (with Czerny-Stefanska), the Brahms Violin Concerto (with Wronski), the two Liszt Piano Concertos (with Kedra), Gershwin's *Rhapsody in Blue* and Piano Concerto (with Krenz), the overtures to *Die Meistersinger* and *The Merry Wives of Windsor*, *Les Préludes*, *Don Juan* and *Pavane pour une infante défunte* (with the Polish Radio Orchestra, for Polskie Nagrania), Szymanowski's Violin Concerto No. 2 and Wieniawski's Violin Concerto No. 2 (with Szeryng and the Bamberg Symphony Orchestra for Philips), Prokofiev's Violin Concerto No. 1 and Szymanowski's Violin Concerto No. 1 (with Ishikawa and the Czech Philharmonic Orchestra for Supraphon), the two Chopin Piano Concertos (with Varsi and the Monte Carlo National Orchestra for DGG), the Mendelssohn Violin Concertos in D minor and E minor and the Tchaikovsky Violin Concerto (with Grumiaux and the New Philharmonia Orchestra for Philips).

Kreuder, Peter (b. 1905). Born in Aachen, Kreuder studied at the Munich Academy of Music and in Hamburg, conducted at the Reinhardt Theatre in Berlin (1928–30), at the Munich Theatre (1930–33), and became state music director in Munich (1936). He has spent five years in Argentina (1950–55). For Telefunken he recorded on 78s, apparently when he was in Berlin, with the Berlin Philharmonic Orchestra the overtures to Strauss's *Eine Nacht in Venedig* and Suppé's *Flotte Bursche*.

Krips, Henry (b. 1912). Brother of Josef Krips, Henry Krips was born in Vienna and studied at the Vienna University and Conservatory. He became chief conductor of the Innsbruck Municipal Theatre (1932), migrated to Australia (1938) where he first conducted opera and ballet, was appointed resident conductor of the Perth Symphony Orchestra (1946–9) and then the South Australian Symphony Orchestra at Adelaide (1949–72). During overseas visits he has conducted orchestras in London and on the Continent, as well as at the Sadler's Wells Opera; in 1976 he led *Eine Nacht in Venedig* at the English National Opera. His compositions include opera, ballet, scores, songs and piano works. For EMI he recorded collections of waltzes by Strauss and Waldteufel, and overtures by Suppé; the orchestra was the Philharmonia, but was identified on the discs as the Philharmonic Promenade Orchestra. Josef Krips had also recorded Viennese music for EMI, and in the many re-issues of Henry's records, some of Josef's performances became confused. Krips also recorded, in Australia, Hill's Symphony *Australia* and Viola Concerto (with Pikler and the Sydney Symphony Orchestra for RCA), Tahourdin's Symphony No. 2 (with the South Australia Symphony Orchestra for Festival) and Mirrie Hill's *Aboriginal Themes* and *Avinu Molkeinu* (with the South Australia Symphony Orchestra for World Record Club).

Krips, Josef (1902–74). Born in Vienna and son of a doctor, Krips sang as a boy in the choir of the Carmelite Church in Vienna, studied at the Vienna Academy of Music, and with Weingartner and Mandyczewski. He was first violinist with the Volksoper (1918–21), and was engaged by Weingartner in 1921 as coach and choirmaster there. That year he made his debut as a conductor in *Un ballo in maschera*, substituting at short notice and conducting the opera without a score. He also conducted his first symphony concert at the Redoutensaal in Vienna in 1921. He became chief conductor at Aussig an der Elbe (1924–5), conductor at the Dortmund Municipal Theatre (1925–6) and general music director at Karlsruhe, conducting both opera and concerts (1926–33). There he led a Bruckner festival in 1929 and a Handel festival in 1930, and appeared in other European cities. He left Karlsruhe and was appointed permanent conductor at the Vienna State Opera (1933–8), first conducted at Salzburg in 1935, and was made a professor at the Vienna Academy of Music (1935–8). After the annexation of Austria by Germany in 1938 he was dismissed from these positions as his grandparents were Jewish, although Krips himself was a Catholic; he conducted concerts and opera at Belgrade (1938–9), but was forced to leave because of German influence there. During World War II, formal musical activities were denied to him, but he managed to work as a clandestine opera coach while working as a storekeeper in a food-processing factory.

After World War II the Soviet occupation authorities immediately gave Krips the responsibility of reconstructing musical activities in Vienna, and he proceeded to re-establish the Staatsoper virtually singlehanded. He conducted *Fidelio* two weeks after the war in Europe ended, and in May 1945 the Staatsoper opened at the Volksoper building with *Le nozze di Figaro*. From 1945 to 1950 he was at the Staatsoper, conducted the Vienna Symphony Orchestra, was chief conductor of the Hofmusikkapelle, and took part in the first Salzburg Festivals. Between 1947 and 1950 he toured with the Vienna Staatsoper and the Vienna Philharmonic Orchestra in France, Belgium, England, Switzerland and Italy; their performances of *Don Giovanni*, *Le nozze di Figaro* and *Così fan tutte* at Covent Garden in 1947 made an indelible impression. In 1950 he was invited to conduct the Chicago Symphony Orchestra, but when he arrived in New York, he was refused admittance by the immigration authorities, presumably because he had conducted in Soviet Russia in 1947. He was principal conductor of the London Symphony Orchestra (1950–54), and contributed to making it the great orchestra it is today. He eventually made his debut in the United States with the Buffalo Philharmonic Orchestra in 1953, which led to his appointment as conductor of the orchestra (1954–63). He also conducted the Montreal Symphony Orchestra, toured Australia, Mexico *et al.*, appeared at the New York Metropolitan Opera, returned to Covent Garden, led the New York Philharmonic Orchestra for ten weeks in 1964–5, which included a cycle of the Bruckner symphonies, conducted Beethoven cycles in London, Vienna and New York, and was conductor of the San Francisco Symphony Orchestra (1963–70). In 1955 he was awarded the medal of the Bruckner Society, and in 1962 the Ehrenring of the City of Vienna.

Although nurtured on the Viennese classics, Krips had a broad repertoire. At Karlsruhe he conducted German, French and Italian operas; he was a celebrated conductor of Haydn, Mozart, Beethoven, Schubert, Brahms, Bruckner, Mahler, Johann and Richard Strauss, yet he was also impressive with Bartók, Hindemith and Stravinsky, and gave local first performances of much new music, including major works by Janáček, Britten, Blacher and Shostakovich. In his own words, 'I conduct everything. And everything I try to do as if it were by Mozart' (*New York Times*, 17 October 1971). A veneration for Mozart was the cornerstone of his musical life, and he advised students wishing to become opera conductors to start by studying the Mozart operas: 'Every opera is by Mozart; even Wagner, even Richard Strauss, has to sound clear, transparent and spirited, or we have a bad performance.' He once said that Mozart's Symphony No. 40 was one of the most difficult pieces ever written, and that he spent 25 years studying it before he was prepared to conduct it. 'Mozart is, of all composers, the most difficult to conduct. And I can tell you why: two bars and you are suddenly transported to heaven. It is very hard to keep your bearings when you are there.' Like Mahler, he had a high opinion of *Carmen*; he considered it one of the most sophisticated scores in the literature, and thought it essential to stick meticulously to Bizet's instructions. Although he had conducted it scores of times and heard many other performances, he said he had never heard a real *Carmen*, because nobody can realise the dynamic shadings and nuances.

Having experienced this preparation himself, Krips believed that an opera conductor should play the piano, should have studied the voice, should have a period as a coach, and should know the language of the operas he conducts. He warned that young conductors should be patient and not accept assignments for which they are not ready. In the opera house he personally took charge, from the first piano rehearsals to the first night. In conducting the orchestra, he sought to make the instruments sing or breathe, and this lyricism typified all his music-making. While he maintained a firm discipline over the orchestra, he was a genial, cheerful leader, exuding enthusiasm and enjoyment in his task. This was admirably demonstrated when he conducted *Till Eulenspiegel*, when his animation and gestures reflected the fun and mock-tragedy of the story. He cautioned that good conductors take many years to mature: 'Only after 25 years can a conductor teach an orchestra. For the first 25 years a conductor learns from an orchestra.' Krips' seemingly inborn feeling for Mozart and the great Viennese and German symphonic classics was imbued with warmth and lyricism, but a lack of tension sometimes affected the dramatic quality of the music and made it sound facile and lightweight. His *Don Giovanni*, for instance, was perfectly proportioned and phrased, but in the process the dramatic urgency, the demon, was lost.

Krips came to London after World War II and recorded for EMI and Decca on 78s; included were Mozart's Piano Concerto K. 503 (with Fischer), the overtures to *The Merry Wives of Windsor* and *Die Fledermaus*, the *Pizzicato Polka* and *Radetzky March*, some Mozart arias with Berger, Schwarzkopf, Seefried and Cebotari (with the Philharmonia Orchestra), excerpts from *Hänsel und Gretel* (with Schwarzkopf and Seefried) and an aria from *Il re pastore* (with Schwarzkopf, and the Vienna Philharmonic Orchestra, for EMI); Schubert's Symphony No. 6 and the *Rosamunde* overture, Mozart's Symphony No. 41 and overture to *Le nozze di Figaro*, arias from *Don Giovanni*, *Le nozze di Figaro* and *La Bohème* (with Gueden), *Manon* and *Les Pêcheurs de perles* (with Lewis), and Brahms' Symphony No. 4 (with the London Symphony Orchestra), *An der schönen blauen Donau* and some Mozart arias (with Dermota, and the National Symphony Orchestra), *Kaiserwalzer*, *Accelerationen* and *Rosen aus dem Süden* (with the New Symphony Orchestra) and arias from *Boris Godunov* (with Arie and the London Philharmonic Orchestra, for Decca). Many were issued later on LP.

His subsequent recordings on LP for Decca included Haydn's Symphonies Nos 92 and 104, Mozart's Symphonies Nos 31, 39, 40 and 41, Piano Concertos K. 488 and K. 491 (with Curzon) and overtures to *Die Entführung aus dem Serail*, *Der Schauspieldirektor*, *Die Zauberflöte*, *Don Giovanni*, *Così fan tutte* and *Le nozze di Figaro*, the Beethoven Violin Concerto (with Campoli), Schubert's Symphonies Nos 8 and 9, Mendelssohn's Symphony No. 4, Schumann's Symphonies Nos 1 and 4, the Dvořák Cello Concerto (with Nelsova), *Perpetuum mobile*, *Annen-Polka*, *Piefke und Pufke Polka*, *Tritsch-Tratsch Polka*, *Wiener Blut* and *Wein, Weib und Gesang* (with the London Symphony Orchestra); the Mozart *Requiem* (with the Vienna Hofmusikkapelle *et al.*); Beethoven's Symphony No. 4 and Schubert's Symphony No. 9 (with the Amsterdam Concertgebouw Orchestra); Haydn's Symphonies Nos 94 and 99, *Die Entführung aus dem Serail*, *Don Giovanni*, Brahms' Symphony No. 1 and Tchaikovsky's Symphony No. 5 (with the Vienna Philharmonic Orchestra *et al.*); *Elijah* (with the London Philharmonic Orchestra *et al.*); and Mozart's Symphonies Nos 35 and 41 (with the Israel Philharmonic Orchestra). EMI issued on the Seraphim label in the US a later recording of *Die Entführung aus dem Serail* (with the Vienna Philharmonic Orchestra *et al.*).

Everest recorded the nine Beethoven symphonies and the *Egmont* and *Leonore No. 3* overtures (with the London Symphony Orchestra), which received wide circulation in the US. La Guilde Internationale du Disque issued another series, which were also issued on the Concert Hall label, comprising the overtures to *Le nozze di Figaro*, *Don Giovanni*, *Der Schauspieldirektor*, *Die Zauberflöte*, *Die Entführung aus dem Serail*, *La clemenza di Tito*, *Così fan tutte*, *La finta giardiniera* and *Idomeneo*, Brahms' Symphony No. 2 and *Academic Festival Overture*, Dvořák's Symphony No. 9 and Tchaikovsky's Symphony No. 6 (with the Zürich Tonhalle Orchestra), the *Fidelio*, *Leonore No. 3*, *Egmont*, *Coriolan*, *Die Ruinen von Athen* and *Die Weihe des Hauses* overtures, Schubert's Symphonies Nos 6 and 8, the overtures to *Die Fledermaus* and *Waldmeister*, the march from *Der Zigeunerbaron*, *I-Tipferl Polka*, *Kaiserwalzer* and *An der schönen blauen Donau* (with the Vienna Festival Orchestra). In 1959 RCA issued the five Beethoven Piano Concertos, the Schumann Piano Concerto and Brahms' Piano Concerto No. 2 (with Rubinstein and the Symphony of the Air); Reader's Digest Mozart's Symphony No. 35 and Haydn's Symphony No. 104 (with the Royal Philharmonic Orchestra); and EMI *L'Oiseau de feu* and the waltzes from *Der Rosenkavalier* (with the Philharmonia Orchestra). In 1973 Philips embarked on a series of Mozart symphonies, with Krips directing the Concertgebouw Orchestra, but only Symphonies Nos 35, 39, 40 and 41 were completed before his death. Of all his records, Krips is best remembered, paradoxically, not for his Haydn or Mozart, but by the coupling of Schumann's Symphonies Nos 1 and 4, which was first issued by Decca in 1960, and was still available in Britain and the US in 1977, and was still among the finest performances recorded, and by his Tchaikovsky Symphony No. 5, Schubert's Symphony No. 9, and *Elijah*.

Krombholc, Jaroslav (b. 1918). Born in Prague, and educated at the Charles University and Prague Conservatory, Krombholc studied composition with Novák (1937–40) and conducting with Dědeček, Ostrčil and more especially Talich (1940–41). He was a distinguished pianist and composer, and his *Suite for Piano and Orchestra* was awarded first prize in a competition sponsored by the Czech Philharmonic Orchestra in 1939. He became a conductor at the Prague National Theatre (1940–43), was a guest conductor with the Czech Philharmonic Orchestra, was conductor at the Ostrava Opera (1944–5), and again at the Prague National Theatre (1945–62), was appointed chief conductor in 1962 and then head of the Theatre (1968–70). In 1973 he became chief conductor of the Prague Radio Symphony Orchestra, and in 1978 was awarded the Order of the Republic. He has conducted abroad, in Eastern and Western Europe, toured with the Prague National Theatre to Moscow in 1955, to Brussels in 1958, to the Edinburgh Festival in 1964 and to Vienna in 1967, presenting operas by Smetana, Janáček and Dvořák, and has conducted *Don Giovanni* at Covent Garden and *Jenůfa* at the State Opera at Munich. One of the leading Czech conductors, he is an outstanding interpreter of the operas of Smetana, Dvořák, Fibich, Janáček and Martinů, as well as the symphonic works of Dvořák, Novák, Suk, Ostrčil, Janáček, Martinů, Prokofiev and Shostakovich. His recordings, for Supraphon, have been mostly with the Prague National Theatre Company and have included Dvořák's *Rusálka*, Smetana's *The Secret*, *Libuše*, *Dalibor*, and *The Two Widows*, Janáček's *Káťa Kabanová*, Fibich's *The Bride of Messina*, *Sarka* and *The Wooing of Pelops*, and Martinů's *Julietta*. With the Czech Philharmonic Orchestra he also recorded Dvořák's *The Spectre's Bride* and the overtures *Carnival*, *Othello*, *In Nature's Realm* and *Josef Kajetán Tyl* and Novák's *The Storm*. Urania also released a complete *Swan Lake* in which he conducted the Prague National Theatre Orchestra.

Kromer, Oskar (1904–49). Born in Steinschönau, Czechoslovakia, Kromer studied at the Prague Academy of Music, and attended chamber music courses at Salzburg. He was concertmaster of the Pupp Concert Orchestra at Karlsbad (1924–5), joined the Winterthur Symphony as a viola player (1926), became the solo violist with the orchestra (1928), was a member of the Winterthur String Quartet (1928–49), taught at the Winterthur Academy of Music (1930–49), first conducted in 1941, and became conductor of the Musik Collegium of Winterthur in 1941. Concert Hall issued a disc on which he conducted the Winterthur Symphony Orchestra in Bach's Clavier Concerto No. 3 (with Hans Andreae) and Haydn's *Organ Concerto in F major* (with Matthei).

Krueger, Karl (b. 1894). Born at Atchison, Kansas, Krueger studied at the Universities of Vienna, Heidelberg and Kansas, and from 1919 to 1924 was assistant conductor of the Vienna Symphony Orchestra. He then was conductor of the Seattle Symphony Orchestra (1926–32), of the Kansas City Philharmonic Orchestra (1933–42) and of the Detroit Symphony Orchestra (1943–9). The orchestra at Detroit was revived by Henry H. Reichhold in 1944, but it came to an end in 1950, to be re-formed when Paray became its musical director two years later. Krueger was recorded on 78s by RCA Victor, accompanying Arrau in the Schumann Piano Concerto and in the overture *Orphée aux enfers*. Later, New Records (US) issued the Schumann Symphony No. 4 and Pizzetti's *Concerto dell'estate*, in which he conducted the Vienna State Opera Orchestra.

Krukowski, Stanislaw (b. 1924). Born in Kosów, Poland, Krukowski studied chemistry at the Technical University at Wrocław (1946–51), then conducting with Ormicki and Kopyciński at the State High School at Wrocław (1952–7). He has been instructor (since 1950), conductor (since 1958) and artistic manager (1973) of the Polish Radio Choir, Wrocław, and professor at the State Music High School there (since 1970). He has specialised in and published studies in the interpretation of early music, and has presented historical concerts of old Polish choral and instrumental music, ranging from the Middle Ages to the pre-classical period. His honours include the Order of Mary Magdalen. Muza have recorded him conducting the Polish Radio Choir in recitals of medieval vocal music and Renaissance motets, in the Musica Antiqua Polonica series, and Veriton Rachmaninov's *Vesper Mass*.

Kubelík, Rafael (b. 1914). Born in Bychory in Czechoslovakia, Kubelík is the son of the great violin virtuoso Jan Kubelík, who taught him to play the violin so that he could perform the concert repertoire. He attended the Prague Conservatory (1928–33), made his debut as a conductor with the Czech Philharmonic Orchestra in 1934, and was sufficiently accomplished as a pianist to accompany his father on tours in Europe and the United States (1934–6). He also conducted when Jan Kubelík performed 30 violin concertos at a cycle of ten concerts. He became acting conductor of the Czech Philharmonic (1936–9), and in 1937 took the orchestra to Belgium and England. He was conductor at the Brno National Theatre (1939–41) and then artistic director of the Czech Philharmonic (1942–8). During World War II he consistently refused to co-operate with the Nazi occupation authorities in Prague; when the Communists took control of Czechoslovakia in 1948 he was in Britain conducting *Don Giovanni* with the Glyndebourne Festival Opera at the Edinburgh Festival, and he did not return to his native country. He conducted in Britain, Mexico, and South America, and began his association with the Amsterdam Concertgebouw Orchestra.

His first appearance in the United States was with the Chicago Symphony Orchestra in 1949; he made such an impression that he was appointed music director of the orchestra in 1950. In Chicago he was the centre of controversy; one issue was the high proportion of new pieces included in his programmes, another was the black artists he invited to perform with the orchestra. As a final gesture of propitiation following his resignation in 1953 he led a concert performance of *Parsifal*. Sharing the podium with van Beinum he toured the US with the Concertgebouw Orchestra, and in 1957–8 conducted the New York Philharmonic Orchestra. He was appointed music director of the Royal Opera House at Covent Garden in 1955, but resigned three years later when he was deeply offended by a public attack on Covent Garden by Sir Thomas Beecham. In his years at Covent Garden he had scored notable successes with *Otello*, *Les Troyens*, *Jenůfa* and *Die Meistersinger*; he was criticised for giving more rehearsals for new productions than previously, which tended to limit the repertoire. In 1961 he was appointed to the Bavarian Radio Symphony Orchestra, and in 1973 he had a short-lived term of six months as music director of the New York Metropolitan Opera. He resigned under pressure because his commitments in Munich made it impossible for him to give the time expected of him to the New York company. His second wife is Elsie Morison, the Australian soprano; she had sung in his London performance of *The Bartered Bride*, and her last performance as a professional singer was with her husband conducting in the recording of Mahler's Symphony No. 4. He devotes much time to composing, and his output includes operas and other music including three Requiems, the third written on the death of his first wife, the violinist Ludmilla Bertlová. His honours include the Gustav Mahler medal which he was awarded in 1960.

Kubelík is an intense and dynamic conductor, whose performances, of a repertoire from Mozart to Berg, are thoroughly considered, unmannered, straightforward, and devoid of eccentricity. Although they may not be illuminated by arresting strokes of genius or by the highest inspiration, they are exemplary in their musicianship, warmth and sensitivity. If he has a fault it is that his natural expressiveness occasionally tends to produce a rhythmic slackness and a rubato that may be excessive and can rob the music of some of its strength. As a young man he heard Toscanini, Krauss, Weingartner and Walter, and was profoundly impressed by them. He has no open preference for any particular composer or school or composition. He is sufficiently self-critical to admit that he is scarcely able to reach the high artistic aims he sets for himself: 'There was never in my life an evening when I could have said that it was really as I thought it should be. And I have conducted thousands of performances.' He prefers to perform before an audience, and before making a recording he performs the work in public. In the studio he goes straight through the work, listens to the tape to ensure that it sounds exactly as he heard it on the podium, and then the second take is the final recording. He values recordings because they often reveal more of the music than can possibly be heard in the concert hall; Mahler, for instance, can be better heard on record than at a concert.

HMV recorded Kubelík first on 78s with the Czech Philharmonic Orchestra with a three-disc set of *Moldau* and *From Bohemia's Meadows and Forests* from Smetana's *Má Vlast*. After World War II they issued the three Dvořák overtures *Carnival*, *Othello* and *In Nature's Realm*, and the Janáček *Sinfonietta*, which was a revelation when it was released. He also recorded for Supraphon and Ultraphon with the Czech Philharmonic Orchestra Smetana's *Haakon Jarl*, *Wallenstein's Camp* and *Richard III*, Martinů's Symphony No. 4 and Jírovek's *Symphony in E flat*. EMI recorded a series of 78 r.p.m. discs with him in London conducting the Philharmonia Orchestra; included were the Mozart overtures to *Idomeneo*, *Così fan tutte*, *Le nozze di Figaro*, *La clemenza di Tito* and *Der Schauspieldirektor*, Haydn's Cello Concerto No. 1 (with Fournier), the Beethoven Violin Concerto and Bruch's Violin Concerto No. 1 (with Haendel), Mendelssohn's Piano Concerto No. 1 (with Lympany), the overture to Gluck's *Iphigénie en*

Aulide, Brahms' Symphony No. 2 and Piano Concerto No. 1 (with Solomon), Dvořák's Symphony No. 7, Cello Concerto (with Fournier), *Scherzo capriccioso* and *Légende* Op. 59 No. 10, the overture and dances from *The Bartered Bride* and Martinů's *Concerto for Double String Orchestra, Piano and Timpani*. Later, on LP, EMI issued a coupling of excerpts from the incidental music from *A Midsummer Night's Dream* and the overture and dances from *The Bartered Bride*, Dvořák's Symphonies Nos 7 and 8, the Mozart overtures mentioned above (with the Philharmonia Orchestra), Janáček's *Taras Bulba*, Martinů's *Les Fresques de Piero della Francesca* and the Bartók *Concerto for Orchestra* and *Two Portraits* (with the Royal Philharmonic Orchestra).

In 1951 Mercury recorded a series of outstanding LP discs with Kubelík conducting the Chicago Symphony Orchestra, noted for the distinction of the performances as much as for their exceptionally fine technical quality. Some were re-issued in 1973. The music included Mozart's Symphonies Nos 34 and 38, Dvořák's Symphony No. 9, Smetana's *Má Vlast* (the first of his three recordings up to 1977), Tchaikovsky's Symphonies Nos 4 and 6, *Pictures at an Exhibition*, Hindemith's *Symphonic Metamorphosis on Themes by Weber*, Brahms' Symphony No. 1, Schoenberg's *Five Pieces for Orchestra*, Bloch's *Concerto Grosso No. 1*, and Bartók's *Music for Strings, Percussion and Celesta*. Later, in the 1950s, he recorded for Decca with the Vienna Philharmonic Orchestra the four Brahms symphonies (still available in the US in 1977), Mahler's Symphony No. 1, Dvořák's Symphonies Nos 7 and 9, some Slavonic Dances and the Cello Concerto (with Fournier), *Má Vlast*, Janáček's *Sinfonietta*, Mozart's Symphonies Nos 35 and 41, and the *Romeo and Juliet* fantasy-overture. Another disc with the Israel Philharmonic Orchestra was of Dvořák's *Serenade in E major* (for Decca), and EMI also issued the Tchaikovsky Symphony No. 5 and Borodin's Symphony No. 2 and the Polovtsian Dances from *Prince Igor*, with the Vienna Philharmonic Orchestra.

Since his connection with the Bavarian Radio Symphony Orchestra in 1961, Kubelík has recorded exclusively, and extensively, for DGG, both with that orchestra and with the Berlin Philharmonic. Paramount among his recordings are the complete nine symphonies of Mahler, with the Bavarian Radio Orchestra; he did not add the version of the Symphony No. 10 completed by Deryck Cooke, believing that Mahler so often altered his ideas during composition that his final version really cannot be guessed at, and that it is not possible to put oneself in Mahler's mind. Kubelík's series appeared at much the same time as those of Solti, Abravanel, Haitink and Bernstein; the tone is not particularly beautiful; it is not the lyrical and introspective element in Mahler that attracts him, but rather the dramatic quality of Mahler's idiom, and his readings are expressive, sensitive and musically convincing. His command of large forces is demonstrated on some of his other recordings too: Schoenberg's *Gurrelieder*, Haydn's Mass No. 7, Janáček's *Glagolitic Mass*, *Lohengrin* and Pfitzner's *Palestrina*. The latter was the first recording of this remarkable and unusual work, where his warmth and enthusiasm resulted in a highly impressive performance. His other records with the Bavarian Radio Orchestra *et al.* include Mozart's Serenade K. 250, the Masses K. 220 and K. 317 and *Ave verum corpus*, Beethoven's Symphony No. 7, Weber's *Oberon* and the overtures to *Oberon*, *Abu Hassan*, *Der Freischütz*, *Euryanthe*, *Preciosa* and *Jubel*, the incidental music for *A Midsummer Night's Dream*, Schumann's Piano Concerto and *Introduction and Allegro Appassionato* (with Kempff), Dvořák's *The Golden Spinning Wheel*, *Water Goblin*, *The Noon Day Witch*, *The Wood Dove*, *Symphonic Variations*, *My Home*, *Scherzo capriccioso* and *Slavonic Dances* Op. 46, Smetana's *Richard III*, *Wallenstein's Camp*, *Haakon Jarl* and *Carnival in Prague*, Falla's *Nights in the Gardens of Spain* and Martinů *Fantaisie concertante* (with Weber), Tcherepnin's Piano Concertos Nos 2 and 5 (with the composer the soloist), Janáček's *Sinfonietta* and *Taras Bulba*, Schoenberg's Piano Concerto (with Brendel) and Violin Concerto (with Zeitlin), Berg's Violin Concerto and Martinon's Violin Concerto No. 2 (with Szeryng), Hartmann's Symphonies Nos 4 and 8, and Orff's *Oedipus the Tyrant*.

With the Berlin Philharmonic Orchestra (for DGG) he recorded Handel's *Water Music* and *Music for the Royal Fireworks*, the Mozart Clarinet Concerto and Weber's Clarinet Concerto No. 1 (with Leister), Dvořák's Symphonies Nos 6, 7, 8 and 9, the Schumann and Grieg Piano Concertos (with Anda), the preludes to *Lohengrin* and *Die Meistersinger*, the prelude and Liebestod from *Tristan und Isolde* and the *Siegfried Idyll*. He also recorded the Dvořák *Serenade in E major* and his own *Quattro forme per archi* (with the English Chamber Orchestra for DGG), the complete *Má Vlast*, his third (with the Boston Symphony Orchestra for DGG), *Rigoletto* (with the La Scala Orchestra *et al.* for DGG), Hartmann's *Gesangsszene zu Giraudoux's Sodom und Gomorrha* (with Fischer-Dieskau and the

Bavarian Radio Orchestra for Wergo) and Mahler's *Lieder eines fahrenden Gesellen* (with Fischer-Dieskau and the Bavarian Radio Orchestra for DGG); he also played the piano in Janáček's *The Diary of One Who Disappeared* (with Griffel and Haefliger for DGG). DGG departed from the usual practice of recording all the Beethoven symphonies with one conductor and orchestra by having Kubelík record each with a different orchestra; these were the London Symphony (for No. 1), the Concertgebouw Orchestra (No. 2), the Berlin Philharmonic (No. 3), the Israel Philharmonic (No. 4), the Boston Symphony (No. 5), the Paris Orchestra (No. 6), the Vienna Philharmonic Orchestra (No. 7), the Cleveland Orchestra (No. 8) and the Bavarian Radio Symphony Orchestra *et al.* (No. 9). While some critics were disturbed by a certain rhythmic slackness in the interpretations, Richard Osborne in *The Gramophone* hailed the series as 'a notable undertaking – sanely, humanely, at times gloriously realised. In an often troubled and divided world its message, quite literally, crosses frontiers'. But of all Kubelík's recordings those that have received the highest praise have included the music for *A Midsummer Night's Dream*, *Gurrelieder*, Schumann's Symphony No. 2, the Janáček discs, Dvořák's Symphony No. 8, the Handel music and the Bartók *Concerto for Orchestra*. This indicates the true depth of his musicianship.

Kubik, Gail (b. 1914). Born at Coffeyville, Oklahoma, and educated at the Eastman School of Music, Kubik has taught at a number of universities and colleges in the United States and has been a guest conductor in the US and Europe. His compositions include film scores and some with titles such as *Thunderbolt Overture*, *In Praise of Johnny Appleseed* and *Piccolo Boston Baked Beans*. For Composers Recordings he has directed the French Radio Orchestra in his own *Symphony Concertante*, and for Contemporary (US) his Divertimentos Nos 1 and 2.

Kuentz, Paul (b. 1930). Born in Mulhouse, the French musician Kuentz founded and conducted the Paul Kuentz Chamber Orchestra, with which he made numerous recordings for many companies. These included Bach's four Suites (for Trianon), *Ein musikalisches Opfer* (for La Guilde Internationale du Disque) and *Mass in B minor* (for DGG), Vivaldi's Organ Concertos (with Isoir for DGG), *The Four Seasons* (with Frasca-Colombier for DGG), *L'estro armonico* (for DGG), Flute Concertos Op. 10 Nos 2, 3, 5 and 6 (with Lardé for EMI), Oboe Concerto P. 406 (with Maugras for Edici), Two-Trumpet Concerto P. 75 (for Edici), Violin and Organ Concerto P. 311 (with Frasca-Colombier and Alain for Edici) and Two-Cello Concerto P. 411 (with Gamard and Brion for Edici), Delalande's *Symphonies pour les soupers du Roy*, Suite No. 4 (for DGG), D. Gabrieli's *Trumpet Sonata in D major*, Torelli's *Two-Trumpet Concerto in D major*, and Mouret's *Fanfares in D major* and *Symphonies pour violon, hautbois et cors de chasse* (with Scherbaum *et al.* for DGG), Handel's *Water Music* (for Edici) and Organ Concertos Op. 4 (with Boudlet for EMI), Gluck's Minuet, Leclair's Flute Concerto Op. 7 No. 3, Pergolesi's Flute Concerto No. 3, Haydn's Flute Concerto and Blavet's Flute Concerto (with Lardé for EMI and Edici), Haydn's Violin Concerto No. 1 (with Frasca-Colombier for EMI), Mozart's Flute Concerto No. 2 (with Lardé) and Flute and Harp Concerto (with Lardé and Jamet for Club International du Disque), *Requiem* (for DGG), *Bastien und Bastienne* (for Adès), Epistle Sonatas Nos 2, 7 and 17 (with Alain for Edici) and Adagio and Rondo K. 617 (with Zabaleta for DGG), Harp Concertos by Handel, Boieldieu, Eichner, Dittersdorf, Albrechtsberger and Wagenseil, and Debussy's *Danse sacrée et danse profane* (with Jamet for EMI and Zabaleta for DGG), Haydn's Symphony No. 101 and Leopold Mozart's *Toy Symphony* (for Decca), Dubois' Saxophone Concerto, Glazunov's Saxophone Concerto, Ibert's Concerto da camera for Saxophone and Villa-Lobos' *Fantaisie* (with Rousseau for DGG), Ravel's *Introduction et allegro* (with Zabaleta for DGG), Casterède's *Prélude et fugue*, Jacques Charpentier's *Prélude pour la Genèse*, and Lesur's *Sérénade* (for Edici), and Vittoria's Violin Concerto (with Frasca-Colombier for Edici).

Kuentz's other recordings include Boieldieu's Harp Concerto (with Jamet and the Paris Chamber Orchestra for Turnabout), Corelli's Church Sonatas Op. 1 Nos 11 and 12 (with the Collegium Pro Musica de Paris for EMI), and Haydn's Symphonies Nos 85 and 101 (with the Paris Chamber Orchestra for EMI).

Kuljerić, Igor (b. 1938). Born in Šibenik, Yugoslavia, Kuljerić studied at the Zagreb Academy of Music and with Markevitch (1968), was an assistant conductor at the Croatian National Opera, harpsichord player with I Solisti di Zagreb, and Horvat's assistant at the Zagreb Philharmonic Orchestra. He is now permanent conductor of the Zagreb Radio and Television Chorus and an assistant professor at the Zagreb Academy of Music, and has composed numerous works, being awarded the Ljubljana Radio and Television prize (1967), SKOJ Award (1970), the City of Zagreb Award (1972) and other prizes for his compositions. His recordings, for Jugoton, include music by Devčić, Ulrich and Koci, and his own *Figurazioni con tromba*, *Solo solisti*, *Balade Petrice Kerempuha*, *Impulsi II* and *Omaggio a Lukačić* (with the Zagreb Radio and Television Orchestra *et al.*).

Kulka, János (b. 1929). Born in Budapest, Kulka studied composition and conducting at the Franz Liszt Academy, where his teachers were Ferencsik and Somogyi. He was a repetiteur and choirmaster at the Budapest State Opera (from 1950), became a conductor there (1953–7), and also conducted symphony concerts and taught at the Academy. In 1957 he went to Vienna, was engaged by Fricsay and conducted at the Bavarian State Opera at Munich (1957–9), became conductor at the Württemberg State Opera at Stuttgart (1959–61), principal conductor at the Hamburg State Opera (1961–4), music director at the Wuppertal Opera (1964–75), and general music director at the State Opera, Stuttgart, and chief conductor of the North-West German Philharmonic Orchestra at Herford (since 1975). He has conducted in major opera houses in Europe, including Cologne, Geneva, Brussels, Vienna, Barcelona and Copenhagen, as well as in the United States (at Boston, 1969) and South America (at Buenos Aires, 1970–73), with a repertoire including Mozart, Gluck, Verdi, Puccini, Wagner, Strauss, Schoenberg, Berg, Weill, Janáček, Orff, Penderecki and Dallapiccola. He has made a number of records for DGG, Europäische Phonoclub and Intercord. The only one to have been issued widely in Britain and the US is the coupling of Chopin's Piano Concerto No. 2 and *Andante spianato et Grande Polonaise* (with Vásáry and the Berlin Philharmonic Orchestra for DGG); others include recitals by Speiss, Bumbry, Konya, Stratas, Fassbaender, Dominguez, Berry, *et al.*, a disc of excerpts from *Il trovatore* (with the Württemberg State Opera Orchestra *et al.*, for DGG), a collection including the overture *Le Carnaval romain*, *Moldau*, Liszt's *Hungarian Fantasy* (with Havenith) and two *Slavonic Dances of* Dvořák (with the North-West German Philharmonic Orchestra), and a recital with Tipton (with the South German Radio Orchestra for RBM).

Künnecke, Eduard (1885–1953). Born in Emmerich am Rhein, Künnecke studied with Bruch at the Hochschule für Musik in Berlin, and composed operas, operettas, film music and songs; the German catalogue includes excerpts from a number of his operettas, including *Die grosse Sünderin*, *Lady Hamilton*, *Liselott* and *Die lockende Flamme*. For Telefunken he recorded the overture to his operetta *Glückliche Reise*, and his *Biedermeier* suite (with the Graunke Symphony Orchestra), *Lönslieder* suite (with the Berlin German Opera House Orchestra) and *Tänzerische Suite* (with Jazzband and the Berlin Philharmonic Orchestra).

Kunzel, Erich (b. 1935). Born of German parents in New York, Kunzel played percussion instruments in school bands, and at high school conducted performances of operettas, and organised and conducted a popular weekly radio concert. He continued his studies at Dartmouth College, completed postgraduate studies at Harvard and Brown Universities, and studied conducting with Monteux, whose personal assistant he became (1963–4). Previously he had joined the Santa Fe Opera Company as a conductor (1957) and was assistant conductor of the Rhode Island Philharmonic Orchestra (1960–65) and director of choral music at Brown University. He was appointed assistant conductor of the Cincinnati Symphony Orchestra under Rudolf (1965–7), became its associate conductor (1965–7) and then resident conductor (1969–74). He has been a guest conductor in the United States, Europe and the Far East, was an associate professor at the University of Cincinnati (1965–71), and since 1974 has been musical director of the New Haven Symphony Orchestra.

Kunzel has conducted in four discs of the music of the jazz pianist Dave Brubeck: *The Gates of Justice* (with the Dave Brubeck Trio, the Cincinnati Symphony Orchestra *et al.* for Decca, US), *The Light in the Wilderness* (with the Cincinnati Symphony Orchestra *et al.* for Decca), *Truth is Fallen* (with Brubeck, a rock group and the Cincinnati Symphony Orchestra for Atlantic), and a disc of shorter pieces (with the Dave Brubeck Trio and the Cincinnati Symphony Orchestra *et al.* for Decca). Another disc brought together the jazz pianist Duke Ellington and the Cincinnati Symphony in three pieces of Ellington (for Decca). Kunzel has also recorded a disc coupling the overture *Le Carnaval romain* and *Pictures at an Exhibition* (with the Cincinnati Symphony Orchestra for Decca).

Kurtz, Efrem (b. 1900). Born in St Petersburg, Kurtz studied at the conservatory there with Tcherepnin, Glazunov and Vitol, at the University of Riga (1918–20), and at the Stern Academy in Berlin, where he graduated in 1922. His debut as a conductor was in 1921 when he substituted for Nikisch at short notice for a performance of the dancer Isadora Duncan. This led to his being engaged to conduct concerts with the Berlin Philharmonic Orchestra, and after conducting in many German cities he became permanent conductor of the Stuttgart Philharmonic Orchestra (1924–33), and supervisor of radio programmes in southern Germany. In 1927 he toured in England and South America with Anna Pavlova, and appeared at the Salzburg Festivals in 1930 and 1931. Obliged to leave Nazi Germany in 1933 he was musical director of the Ballet Russe de Monte Carlo (1933–42), visiting and conducting in the United States and Australia, as well as Europe. He was conductor of the Kansas City Philharmonic Orchestra (1943–8), became a naturalised US citizen in 1944, was conductor of the Houston Symphony Orchestra (1948–54), and joint-conductor with Pritchard of the Liverpool Philharmonic Orchestra (1955–7). In 1966 he visited the USSR and conducted the Leningrad and Moscow Philharmonic Orchestras. His awards include the Gold Medal of the Bruckner Society of America; he married the flautist Elaine Shaffer in 1955.

Kurtz made his name initially as a conductor for ballet, but he is equally skilled as a symphonic conductor, particularly of Russian composers. He has pointed out the limitations of the ballet conductor and that in classical ballet he must follow the dancer exactly; he once described (in 1941) the problem of the ballet conductor as 'preserving the highest standards of musicianship while, at the same time, maintaining interpretation, synchronizing the accompaniment to the movements of the dancers, and fully expanding the choreographer's ideas'. The Ballet Russe de Monte Carlo presented some ballets to symphonic scores, such as *Les Présages* (to Tchaikovsky's Symphony No. 5), *Choreatium* (to Brahms' Symphony No. 4), *Symphonie fantastique* and *Scheherazade*. Kurtz accepted this, but said that when he conducted them he kept his eyes closed; 'when I am conducting something like Brahms' Fourth I do not want to see a Mickey Mouse come out and cavort'.

Kurtz's first records on 78s for Columbia were almost all ballet scores. With the London Philharmonic Orchestra he conducted selections from *Coppélia*, *Swan Lake* and *The Sleeping Beauty*, *L'Épreuve d'amour*, which was an arrangement of Mozart pieces by Ludwig Seitz, and the Rosenthal arrangement of Offenbach's music *Gaîté parisienne*. The latter was perhaps the best recording made of this perennial favourite, and he recorded it again with the Columbia Symphony Orchestra. With the New York Philharmonic-Symphony for Columbia (US) he made LP discs of *Les Sylphides* (in Gretchaninov's arrangement), the overture *Zampa*, Kabalevsky's *The Comedians*, the ballet suites Nos 1 and 2 from *Gayaneh*, the Grieg Piano Concerto (with Levant), Wieniawski's Violin Concerto No. 2 (with Stern), the first recorded performance of Shostakovich's Symphony No. 9, the *Lieutenant Kijé* suite, Villa-Lobos' *Uirapurú*, and Lecocq's ballet *La Fille de Madame Angot*; with the Houston Symphony Orchestra Satie's *Parade* and Auric's *Matelots*, and with the Columbia Symphony Orchestra Revueltas' *Janitzio*, Shostakovich's *Ballet russe*, Tchaikovsky's *Sérénade mélancolique* and the *Gaîté parisienne*. In fact, Columbia Records awarded him a golden disc after the three millionth sale of his recordings with the New York Philharmonic-Symphony. In London he recorded with the Philharmonia and Royal Philharmonic Orchestras for EMI a number of fine discs, which showed his excellent touch, particularly with Russian music. Included were excerpts from *Swan Lake*, *The Sleeping Beauty* and *The Nutcracker* (with Menuhin the soloist; the set is still available on Seraphim in the US), *La Boutique fantasque*, *Capriccio espagnol*, Prokofiev's Symphonies Nos 1 and 7, the *Lieutenant Kijé* suite, *Peter and the Wolf*, a suite from the ballet *Romeo and Juliet* and the *Overture on Hebrew Themes*, Shostakovich's Symphonies Nos 1 and 10 and *Age of Gold*, *L'Oiseau de feu*, *Petrushka* and *Suites Nos 1* and *2* of Stravinsky, Liadov's *Kikimora*, *The Enchanted Lake*, *Baba Yaga*, and *Musical Snuff Box*, the Mendelssohn Violin Concerto (with Menuhin), *Le Carnaval des animaux*, the two Mozart Flute Concertos and *Andante* K. 315 (with Shaffer), a suite from *Der Rosenkavalier*, Rimsky-Korsakov's *Tsar Saltan* suite, *Dubinushka*, and *Snow Maiden* suite, Khachaturian's *Masquerade* suite, Barber's *Souvenirs* ballet, some symphonic marches, and a collection of ballet pieces under the title *Homage to Pavlova*.

Kurz, Siegfried (b. 1930). Born in Dresden, where he studied at the Academy of Music, Kurz was director of music at the Dresden Theatre (1949–60), became a conductor at the Dresden State Opera (1960), and was appointed general music director there in 1975. In addition to the conventional repertoire, he has successfully presented many operas by contemporary composers. His compositions include symphonic and chamber works; Eterna have recorded him conducting the Dresden Staatskapelle in his own Horn Concerto (with Damm) and Trumpet Concerto (with Sandau). He has also recorded discs of excerpts from *Rigoletto* and *Don Pasquale*, and of music by modern East German composers: Köhler's Symphony No. 3 and Piano Concerto (with Webersinke), Kurzbach's Piano Concerto (with Mitzscherling) and Rosenfeld's Violin Concerto No. 2 (with Schmahl, and the Dresden Staatskapelle), and Zimmermann's *Levins Mühle* (with the Leipzig Radio Symphony Orchestra *et al.*), all for Eterna.

Kuusisto, Ilkka (b. 1933). Born in Helsinki, Kuusisto studied at the Sibelius Academy there, at the School of Sacred Music and the Union Theological Seminary in New York, and in FR Germany and Vienna. He has been choral director for the Finnish National Opera Company, conductor of the Finnish Radio Symphony Choir and musical director of the Helsinki City Theatre. For Aurora he has recorded a disc of choral works of Sibelius, Brahms and Schumann, with the Finnish Radio Symphony Choir.

L

Lagacé, Bernard (b. 1930). Born at St Hyacinthe, Quebec, Lagacé was educated at the University of Montreal and studied the organ with Marchal and Heiller. He has been professor of organ at the Montreal Conservatoire de Musique, has performed in France, Britain, the United States and Canada, and has been a jury member at competitions in Britain and Belgium. Orion have issued a disc in which he conducts the Arts-Quebec Instrumental Ensemble *et al.* in Bach's *Magnificat* S. Anh. 21.

Lambert, Constant (1905–51). Lambert was born in London; his father was the Australian painter George Lambert and his brother the sculptor Maurice Lambert. He was a student at Christ's Hospital, where he composed a short operetta for a school concert, and at the Royal College of Music, where he studied with Vaughan Williams, Sargent, Fryer, Morris and Dyson. One of his fellow students was Leslie Heward, who later became a distinguished conductor and who also died before his time. Lambert moved in a brilliant circle in London, which included the young Walton, the Sitwells, Hyam Greenbaum, Bernard van Dieren and Anthony Powell; he was influenced by jazz, as well as by Russian and French music. When he was scarcely 20 he was commissioned by Diaghilev to write a ballet; *Romeo and Juliet* was his first published composition, but Diaghilev produced it in circumstances which drew Lambert's disapproval.

Lambert was extraordinarily gifted and versatile. In the words of Hubert Foss, 'in his eminence of soul, Constant Lambert stood alone, defying the statistics, and all his life creating new circumstances into which his person might fit' (*The Gramophone*, September 1951). His genius flowered in three directions – as composer, as conductor, and as critic. After *Romeo and Juliet* he wrote much music; his first and probably most successful piece, *The Rio Grande*, appeared in 1927 – a setting of a poem by Sacheverell Sitwell for chorus, piano solo and orchestra which employs jazz rhythms. The work was performed so often that Lambert came to dislike it. At that time he also wrote the *Music for Orchestra* (1927) and the *Piano Sonata* (1928–9); later his commitments as a conductor restricted his composing, but he was to complete a ballet *Pomona* (1931), the Piano Concerto (1934), *Summer's Last Will and Testament* (1936), the ballet *Horoscope* (1938), music for the films *Merchant Seaman* and *Anna Karenina*, and arrangements for the ballet of music by Meyerbeer (*Les Patineurs*), Boyce (*The Prospect Before Us*), Liszt (*Apparitions*) and others. As a critic he wrote for many papers and journals, but mainly the *Sunday Referee* and *New Statesman*. He could be devastating and often witty, as he was in conversation. His best known writing is *Music Ho!*, published in 1934, which became one of the most influential books to appear on the British musical scene in that decade. Its subtitle *A Study of Music in Decline* gave a clue to its theme, the division between the unpopular music of the contemporary highbrow composers and the popular music of the lowbrow composers of musical comedy. His scathing remarks about Stravinsky and Brahms and the English folk-song school, and his praise of Liszt, Balakirev, Glinka, Puccini, Sibelius, Weill and others demonstrated his wit and acute observation, and his readiness to fly in the face of current musical fashion.

In 1930 Lambert was chosen to be conductor of the Comargo Society, formed in London to keep alive the work of Diaghilev, who had died the year before. Out of the Society grew the Vic-Wells Ballet, which became the Sadler's Wells Ballet and finally the Royal Ballet. Lambert was conductor of the Vic-Wells Ballet from 1931 to 1947; he also conducted, from time to time, the Scottish Orchestra in Glasgow, the Royal Opera at Covent Garden, the BBC Symphony, the Hallé and the London Philharmonic Orchestras. He was a brilliant conductor, despite deafness in his right ear, and was a ballet conductor of the first rank. In the concert hall he found the French and Russian repertoire the most congenial; he also performed Haydn, Mozart and the even-numbered Beethoven symphonies, and was especially attracted to composers of lighter music such as Chabrier and Waldteufel. But he avoided the symphonies of Brahms, and the German and Austrian romantics. During World War II he toured Britain with the Sadler's Wells Ballet, usually playing the piano to accompany the dancers. One of his finest achievements was the production of *The Faery Queen* in 1946 at Covent Garden; this took up six months of his time, but was one of the first major events heralding the revival of interest in Purcell's music. His programmes with the BBC

Symphony Orchestra after the war were of great interest for their unusual repertoire. The reason for his resignation from Sadler's Wells in 1947 is somewhat obscure, and it appears that his death in 1951 was as much the result of alcoholism and the hostile reception by some critics to his last ballet *Tiresias*, as of the broncho-pneumonia and diabetes officially recorded.

Lambert recorded extensively for HMV and Columbia, and the largest-scale works were Tchaikovsky's Symphonies Nos 4 and 5 (with the Hallé and London Philharmonic Orchestras respectively) and Borodin's Symphony No. 2 (with the Hallé Orchestra). Writing in 1948 and comparing this Tchaikovsky Symphony No. 5 with others, David Hall commented that 'Constant Lambert and the London Philharmonic Orchestra are the only ones who play the music all the way through in the manner in which the composer intended it to be played. There is no fussy lily-painting here – just clean, brilliant and straightforward music-making.' The others included Stokowski, Mengelberg, Ormandy, Koussevitzky, Kletzki, Rodzinski and Beecham. His other discs included the overtures *Orphée aux enfers* and *Fra Diavolo*, *Le Roi l'a dit*, *Le Cheval de bronze*, *Les Diamants de la couronne*, the Coronation March from *Le Prophète*, Liszt's *Hungarian Fantasy* (with Moiseiwitsch), Weinberger's *Under the Spreading Chestnut Tree*, *On Hearing the First Cuckoo in Spring*, and Chabrier's *Marche joyeuse* (with the London Philharmonic Orchestra), Purcell's *Comus*, Tchaikovsky's *Hamlet* overture, Waldteufel's *Estudiantina*, La Calinda from *Koanga* and the interlude and serenade from *Hassan* of Delius (with the Hallé Orchestra), Bliss' *Miracle in the Gorbals*, excerpts from *Coppélia*, Gordon's ballet *The Rake's Progress*, suites from *The Sleeping Beauty*, and *Giselle* (with the Covent Garden Orchestra), Boyce's *The Prospect before Us*, *Les Patineurs* of Meyerbeer, the ballet music from *William Tell*, a suite from *The Sleeping Beauty* and Liszt's *Dante Sonata* (with Kentner, and the Sadler's Wells Orchestra), Purcell's *Dido and Aeneas* (with the Philharmonia String Orchestra *et al.*), Warlock's *Capriol Suite* and *Serenade for Frederick Delius* (with the Constant Lambert String Orchestra), the Letter Scene from *Eugene Onegin* (with Hammond and the Liverpool Philharmonic Orchestra), the overture to *Ivan the Terrible* (with the Liverpool Philharmonic Orchestra), Bliss's *Phoenix March*, *In the Steppes of Central Asia*, the Delius Piano Concerto (with Moiseiwitsch), Berlioz's *Rêverie et caprice* (with Szigeti), Purcell's *Chaconne*, an excerpt from *Apparitions*, *Mephisto Waltz*, Rawsthorne's *Street Corner* overture and *Symphonic Studies*, Rimsky-Korsakov's *Skazka*, the overture *Morgen, Mittag und Abend in Wien*, Waldteufel's waltzes *The Skaters*, *Pomone*, *Estudiantina* and *Sur la plage*, the two suites from Walton's *Façade* and the polka and fugue from *Schwanda* (with the Philharmonia Orchestra). Of his own compositions he twice recorded *The Rio Grande* (the first time with Hamilton Harty the pianist and the Hallé Orchestra *et al.*, and the second with Greenbaum and the Philharmonia Orchestra *et al.*), and excerpts from *Horoscope* (with the Liverpool Philharmonic Orchestra). There was also another set of records of Tchaikovsky's *Romeo and Juliet* fantasy-overture, with an unidentified orchestra.

Lambrecht, Heinz (b. 1920). Born in Hildesheim, near Hannover, Lambrecht was educated as a musician, studied the piano with Gieseking, and after war service with the German army became a conductor with the Vienna Volksoper in 1946. In 1950 he assumed Austrian citizenship. He has been a ballet conductor at the Vienna State Opera since 1952, has conducted in Europe and in the United States, and has led performances of many American musical comedies at the Vienna Volksoper. Decca released a disc of him conducting Lehár's *Das Land des Lächelns*, with the Vienna Volksoper *et al.*

Lambro, Phillip (b. 1935). Born in Wellesley Hills, Massachusetts, Lambro studied at the Music Academy of the West, California, has composed and conducted music for films, and has written a number of other works which have been widely performed in the United States and Europe. Crystal has recorded him conducting the US International Orchestra in his *Structures* and *Music for Wind, Brass and Percussion*, and Cortes' *Meditation*.

Lanchbery, John (b. 1923). Born in London, Lanchbery served in the Royal Armoured Corps (1943–5) and studied at the Royal Academy of Music (1945–7). He was musical director of the Metropolitan Ballet (1948–50), the Sadler's Wells Theatre Ballet (1951–7) and the Australian Ballet (since 1972) and principal conductor of the Royal Ballet, Covent Garden (1960–72). He has composed and arranged a number of ballets, including *Pleasuredome*, *Eve of St Agnes*, *House of Birds*, *La Fille mal gardée* (after Hérold), *The Dream*, *Don Quixote* (after Minkus), *La Sylphide* and *Tales of Beatrix Potter*, and more recently a ballet from *Die lustige Witwe* ('*The Merry Widow*') for the Australian Ballet. His records include *La Fille mal gardée* (with the Covent Garden Orchestra for Decca), *Tales of Beatrix Potter* (with the Covent Garden Orchestra for EMI), *Pineapple Poll* (with the Covent Garden Orchestra for Decca US), *Swan Lake* (with the Vienna Symphony Orchestra for EMI), Bennett's *Jazz Calendar* (with an ensemble for Philips), *Don Quixote* (with the Elizabethan Trust Melbourne Orchestra for EMI) and the arrangements from *Die lustige Witwe* (with the Adelaide Symphony Orchestra for EMI), *Onegin* and *The Fool on the Hill* (from Beatles themes) (with the Sydney Symphony Orchestra for EMI), and a collection of pieces by Ketèlbey (with the Philharmonia Orchestra for EMI).

Landau, Siegfried (b. 1921). Born in Berlin, Landau studied at the Klindworth-Scharwenka Conservatory there and at the Guildhall School of Music and Trinity College of Music, London, and at the Mannes College and with Monteux in the United States. He has been permanent conductor of the Brooklyn Philharmonia Orchestra and Choral Society (1955–71), has been a guest conductor with the New York Philharmonic Orchestra and the Carnegie Pops Orchestra, has conducted in Norway, FR Germany and Mexico, has been music director of the Chattanooga Opera Association (since 1960), has been head of the orchestra and opera department of the New York College of Music, lectures at various universities, and in 1971 was elected a Fellow of the Jewish Academy of Arts and Sciences. Since its inception he has been conductor and music director of the Music for Westchester Symphony Orchestra and is also conductor of the Westphalian Symphony Orchestra in FR Germany. His compositions include ballet scores, music for films, piano suites, an opera and other pieces.

Landau has recorded for Vox, on the Turnabout and Candide labels. With the Westchester Symphony Orchestra he recorded a suite from Glière's *The Red Poppy*, Ippolitov-Ivanov's *Caucasian Sketches*, Hanson's Symphony No. 6, Nielsen's Symphony No. 6, Weill's *Kleine Dreigroschenmusik*, Kurka's *The Good Soldier Schweik*, Liszt's *Ce qu'on entend sur la montagne* and Still's *From the Black Belt* and *Darker America*; with the Westphalian Symphony Orchestra, Glazunov's Piano Concerto No. 2 (with Ponti), Gounod's *Fantasy on the Russian National Hymn*, Massenet's Piano Concerto and Saint-Saëns' *Africa* (with Dosse), Liszt's *Mephisto Waltz*, *Les Préludes*, *Hexaméron*, *Morceau de concert* (with List), *Hungarian Rhapsody* (with Glenn), *Tasso* and *Von der Wiege bis zum Grabe*, MacDowell's Piano Concerto No. 2 (with List) and *Indian Suite*, Saint-Saëns' Cello Concerto No. 2 (with Varga), Thomson's *Louisiana Story* suite, Weill's *Quodlibet* and Korngold's *Much Ado About Nothing* suite.

Lane, Louis (b. 1923). Born at Eagle Pass, Texas, Lane studied at the University of Texas, the Eastman School of Music and at the Berkshire Music Center at Tanglewood. He was associated with Szell and the Cleveland Orchestra, winning a competition in 1947 to become an apprentice conductor, and later in 1956 he became assistant conductor of the orchestra. He was appointed conductor of the Akron Symphony Orchestra, Ohio (1959), conducted the Cleveland Orchestra at some concerts during its European tour of 1965, and has been a guest conductor with various United States orchestras. From 1955 he has been conductor of the Cleveland Pops, and is co-principal conductor of the Dallas Symphony Orchestra. In 1971 he received the Mahler Medal of Honor from the Bruckner Society of America. He has recorded for CBS and Epic with the Cleveland Orchestra and its offshoots, the Cleveland Pops and the Cleveland Sinfonietta; included have been the Mozart Divertimento K. 334, Beethoven's ballet *Die Geschöpfe des Prometheus*, the Schubert Symphony No. 1 and the Mendelssohn Symphony No. 1 (with the Cleveland Orchestra), Griffes' *Poem*, Foote's *Night Piece*, Honegger's *Concerto da camera* and Hanson's *Serenade* (with flautist Sharp and the Cleveland Sinfonietta), Vaughan Williams' *The Lark Ascending*, Sibelius' *Romance in C*, the Serenade from Delius' *Hassan*, Françaix's *Serenade* and Warlock's *Serenade* (with the Cleveland Sinfonietta), six waltzes by Tchaikovsky, *España*, Alfvén's *Midsummer Vigil*, Enesco's *Romanian Rhapsody No. 1*, Herbert's *Irish Rhapsody, Liszt's Hungarian Rhapsody No. 2*, Piston's *Incredible Flutist*, Riegger's *Dance Rhythms*, excerpts from Gould's *Latin American Symphonette*, Benjamin's *From San Domingo*, *Jamaican Rhumba*, *Andalucia* and *Malaguena*, Guarnieri's *Brazilian Dance*, excerpt from Villa-Lobos' *Bachianas brasileiras No. 2*, Copland's *Outdoor Overture* and *Rodeo* and Elwell's ballet *The Happy Hypocrite* (with the Cleveland Pops Orchestra).

Lange, Hans (1884–1960). Born in Istanbul of German parents, Lange studied at the Prague Conservatory and in 1902 made his debut as a violinist at Frankfurt am Main. He migrated to the United States in 1923, was assistant conductor of the New York Philharmonic Orchestra (1923–33) and then associate conductor of the orchestra (1933–6), associate conductor of the Chicago Symphony Orchestra (1939–46) and conductor of the Albuquerque Civic Symphony Orchestra (1951–8). He accompanied Flagstad in Dich, teure Halle and Elisabeths Gebet from *Tannhäuser*, and the Liebestod from *Tristan und Isolde*, with an unidentified orchestra on 78s for Victor, and on LP conducted the Vienna Symphony Orchestra in Mendelssohn's *Piano Concerto in A minor*, with Kyriakou for Turnabout.

Lankester, Michael (b. 1944). Born in London, Lankester studied at the Royal College of Music, where he was a conducting pupil of Boult. In 1968 he formed and has been musical director of the ensemble Contrapuncti; he was musical director of the National Theatre (1969–75), made his debut at the Promenade Concerts with the London Symphony Orchestra in 1974, joined the staff of the Royal College of Music in 1974 and became the head of music-opera there in 1976. After conducting Crosse's opera *Purgatory* at the official opening of the Royal Northern College of Music, he recorded the work with the College's orchestra *et al.* for Argo, and also recorded Crosse's *Ariadne* for oboe and twelve players, with Francis and the London Symphony Orchestra.

Larsson, Lars-Erik (b. 1908). Born at Åkarp, Sweden, Larsson studied at the Stockholm Conservatory, and later at Leipzig and Vienna, where he was a pupil of Berg. He was a repetiteur with the Royal Swedish Opera (1930–31), a music critic (1933–7), conductor with the Swedish Broadcasting Company (1937–54), professor at the Royal Music High School (1947–59) and director of music at Uppsala (1961–5). His compositions include operas, symphonies, concertos, orchestral and chamber music, and in the 1930s some of his works were performed at ISCM festivals. He directed the Stockholm Radio Orchestra in a recording of his Saxophone Concerto (with Rascher the soloist), and the Stockholm Concert Society Orchestra in the *Ostinato* from his Symphony No. 2.

Lauer, Heribert (b. 1926). Born of Swiss parents in Berlin, Lauer studied at the Hochschule für Musik in Munich and at the Zürich Conservatory, and was a violinist in the Zürich Tonhalle Orchestra, becoming the orchestra's concertmaster in 1958 and the concertmaster of the Lucerne Festival Orchestra in 1961. He has played as a soloist and in chamber groups in many European countries, and in 1958 formed the Zürich Chamber Music Ensemble, with which he recorded Divertimenti by Joseph and Michael Haydn (for Schwann), and Tischhauser's *Octet* (for Ex Libris).

Lawrence, Thomas (1880–1953). Born in Liverpool, Lawrence conducted his school's military band and learned to play all its instruments. He studied at the Liverpool School of Music, and while following a business career until 1934 was a noted choral conductor. In 1929 he formed the Fleet Street Singers and the London Madrigal Group, with whom he toured the United States in 1930. He performed in particular the music of the English Tudor composers, in the new editions of Fellowes and others, and played an important part in the revival of interest in this great musical tradition. Among the first Decca LPs were recordings of Lawrence and the Fleet Street Singers performing Byrd's *Mass for Four Voices*, *Mass for Five Voices* and *Ave verum corpus*, Rubbra's *Missa in honorem Sancti Dominici* and Vaughan Williams' *Mass in G minor*; Sackville-West and Shawe-Taylor in *The Record Guide* were, however, somewhat critical of the style in each of these performances.

Lazarev, Alexander. The Russian conductor Lazarev studied at the conservatories in Leningrad and Moscow, was the winner at the Third All-Union Conductors Competition in 1971, and at the Karajan International Competition in Berlin in 1972. He first conducted at the Bolshoi Theatre, Moscow, in 1973, and has been a resident conductor there. With the USSR State Symphony Orchestra he has recorded Tchaikovsky's *Concert Overture in G minor* and *Coronation March*, and Rachmaninov's Piano Concerto No. 3 (with Gavrilov).

Lazarof, Henri (b. 1932). Born in Sofia, Lazarof emigrated to Israel in 1948 and studied with Ben-Haim in Jerusalem, and with Petrassi in Rome. He went to the United States, studying with Shapero at Brandeis University (1957–9), and became a lecturer at UCLA. His compositions include concertos and chamber music; his Viola Concerto was awarded first prize at the International Competition of Monaco in 1962. Some of his music has been recorded; Lazarof himself has directed his *Tempi Concertante* (with the American Chamber Ensemble for Everest), *Textures* (with Ogdon and the Utah Symphony Orchestra for

Candide), *Espaces* (with the Los Angeles Chamber Ensemble for Composers Recordings) and *Octet* (with the UCLA Wind Ensemble for Composers Recordings).

Le Conte, Pierre-Michel (b. 1921). Born in Rouen, Le Conte studied violin, bassoon and composition at the Paris Conservatoire, where he was also a conducting pupil of Fourestier. He conducted the 'Cadets du Conservatoire' Orchestra, was a conductor for the French Radio and Television (1945), was appointed conductor and music director of Radio Nice (1947–9), and Radio Toulouse (1949–50), was a guest conductor with the Paris Radio Symphony Orchestra, the National Radio Orchestra and Radio Lyric Orchestra (1950–60), was permanent conductor of the Lyric Orchestra of the ORTF (1960–73), and was a guest conductor with the Paris Opéra and Opéra-Comique. In addition, he has been a regular guest conductor in countries in Western and Eastern Europe, Israel, Canada and Turkey.

Le Conte recorded extensively for La Guilde Internationale du Disque, including Tchaikovsky's *Variations on a Rococo Theme* and the Schumann Cello Concerto (with Parisot and the Vienna State Opera Orchestra); the *William Tell* overture (with the Vienna Festival Orchestra); *Symphonie fantastique*, the overture to *Benvenuto Cellini*, *La Mer*, the *Daphnis et Chloé* Suite No. 2 and *Pavane pour une infante défunte* (with the Paris Opéra Orchestra); *Invitation to the Dance*, a complete *Carmen*, excerpts from *Les Contes d'Hoffmann*, Chabrier's *España*, *Suite pastorale*, *Bourrée fantasque*, *Marche joyeuse*, *Fête polonaise* and *Danse slave*, and the overtures to *Si j'étais roi*, *Zampa*, *Fra Diavolo*, *Le Cheval de bronze*, *Le Roi d'Ys*, *Le Calife de Bagdad* and *La Dame blanche* (with the Paris Concerts Orchestra *et al.*); and excerpts from *La Damnation de Faust* and Berlioz's *Romeo et Juliette* symphony, the overture and an aria from *William Tell*, the overtures to *La gazza ladra*, *Der Freischütz*, *Abu Hassan* and *Oberon* (with the Frankfurt Radio Symphony Orchestra *et al.*). For ORTF he also recorded Tansman's *Six Movements for String Orchestra* (with the ORTF Chamber Orchestra).

Lederer, Felix (1877–1957). Born in Prague, Lederer studied at the Prague Conservatory and the Vienna Academy of Music (1896–97), was first a repetiteur at Breslau and then conductor at Nuremberg (1899–1903), Augsburg (1903–5), Barmen (1905–8), Bremen (1908–10), Mannheim (1910–22), and Saarbrücken (1922–45), and was professor at the Hochschule für Musik in Berlin (1945–57). He recorded Beethoven's *Wellington's Victory*, Glazunov's Symphony No. 7 and an arrangement for orchestra of Arensky's *Suite No. 2 for Two Pianos*, with the Berlin Radio Orchestra for Urania.

Ledger, Philip (b. 1937). Born at Bexhill, Ledger was a major scholar at King's College, Cambridge, and was appointed organist at Chelmsford Cathedral (1962–5). He was director of music at the University of East Anglia (1965–73), artistic director of the Aldeburgh Festival (from 1968), and director of music at King's College, Cambridge (from 1974). He performs and has recorded as a harpsichordist, organist and pianist, as well as conductor of the King's College Chapel Choir, and for EMI has recorded with the Choir the Monteverdi *Vespro della beata Vergine* (with the Early Music Consort *et al.*), Bach's *Christmas Oratorio* and *Magnificat*, Handel's *Hercules*, and Vivaldi's *Magnificat* (with the Academy of St Martin-in-the-Fields *et al.*), Elgar's *Coronation Ode* and Parry's *I was Glad* (with the New Philharmonia Orchestra *et al.*), Purcell's *Funeral Music for Queen Mary*, *Hear My Prayer*, *Remember not, Lord*, *Rejoice in the Lord*, *My Beloved Spake*, and *Blessed are they that fear the Lord* (with the Philip Jones Brass Ensemble), Britten's *Festival Te Deum*, *Te Deum in C*, *Rejoice in the Lamb* and *Jubilate Deo*, Bernstein's *Chichester Psalms*, two motets of Brahms, Schubert's *Psalm 23*, *Gott im Ungewitter* and *Christ ist erstanden*, and Delius' *To be Sung of a Summer Night on the Water*. He also recorded Hadley's *The Hills* (with the Cambridge University Musical Society Chorus, the London Philharmonic Orchestra *et al.* for EMI) and a recital of Handel arias by the bass Forbes Robinson (with the Academy of St Martin-in-the-Fields for Decca).

Leduc, Roland (b. 1907). Born in Montreal, Leduc studied at the Conservatoire Royal, Brussels, and with Monteux in the United States, was a cellist in Belgian and Canadian orchestras, taught the cello at the Quebec Conservatoire, became the Conservatoire's director in 1960, conducted the CBC Little Symphonies Orchestra (from 1948) and has been a guest conductor with many Canadian symphony orchestras. CBC issued discs in which he conducted Champagne's *Concerto*, *Images* and *Paysana*, Cusson's *Suite No. 2*, Papineau-Couture's *Prélude*, Morel's *Cassation* and Fiala's *Concertino*; for RCA he conducted the Little Symphonies Orchestra in Pépin's

Symphony No. 2 and Morel's *Le Rituel de l'espace.*

Leeuw, Ton de (b. 1926). Born in Rotterdam, de Leeuw studied under Messiaen, Hartmann and Leibowitz in Paris, became interested in non-Western and electronic music, and toured India and the Far East. His oratorio *Job* was awarded the Italia Prize in 1956; he published *Music of the 20th Century* (1964), was director of the American Conservatory (1972–3), and has been lecturer in contemporary music at the University of Amsterdam. A number of his compositions have been recorded by Donemus; for the same company he conducted Escher's *Sinfonia per dieci strumenti.*

Legrand, Michel (b. 1932). Born in Paris, Legrand started his studies at the Paris Conservatoire at the age of eleven, and while a student embarked on a career as a jazz arranger and composer for radio, television and films, of which his score for the film *Les Parapluies de Cherbourg* was especially successful. Philips issued a disc, released by Mercury in the United States, in which he conducts the Grand Symphony Orchestra for Gershwin's *An American in Paris* and *Rhapsody in Blue*, with himself the pianist in the latter.

Lehár, Franz (1870–1948). Born in Komorn, Hungary, the composer of *Die lustige Witwe* was the son of a military bandmaster, studied the violin at the Prague Conservatory, and composition with Fibich. He was a violinist in the Elberfeld orchestra (1880), played in and assisted his father conducting his military band in Vienna, then led other bands in Italy and Hungary, and conducted at the Theater an der Wien in Vienna. His first success as a composer was the operetta *Kukushka* (1896); *Die lustige Witwe* was first produced in Vienna in 1905, and it thereafter swept the world. Lehár recorded some of his own music; for HMV on 78 r.p.m. discs with the Vienna Philharmonic Orchestra, the overtures to *Die lustige Witwe* and *Eva*, and excerpts from some of the operettas with Reining and Réthy. After World War II he came out of retirement to record for Decca some discs of waltzes and other pieces from some of his operettas, with the Zürich Tonhalle Orchestra.

Lehel, György (b. 1926). Born in Budapest and a graduate of the Franz Liszt Academy there, where he studied with Kadosa and Somogyi, Lehel made his debut as a conductor in 1947. Since 1962 he has been music director and chief conductor of the Budapest Symphony Orchestra, and has appeared as a guest conductor throughout Eastern and Western Europe, the United States and Japan; his repertoire extends from Bach and Vivaldi to Webern and Lutosławski, and he is an admired interpreter of the music of his fellow Hungarians Bartók, Kodály and Dohnányi. In 1955 and 1962 he was awarded the Liszt Prize, in 1968 the title Merited Artist of the Hungarian People's Republic and in 1973 the Kossuth Prize.

Lehel has recorded for Qualiton and Hungaroton, Westminster, Supraphon and DGG with various Hungarian Orchestras. For Westminster the works he has recorded include Dohnányi's *Ruralia Hungarica* and *Variations on a Nursery Theme* (with Zempléni), Bartók's *Music for Strings, Percussion and Celesta* and the *Dante Symphony* of Liszt; for DGG Bartók's *Dance Suite*, *Miraculous Mandarin* and *Cantata Profana*, and Kodály's *Peacock Variations*, and for Supraphon accompaniments to Bach's Harpsichord Concertos Nos 1 and 2 (with Růžičková and the Czech Chamber Orchestra). His records for Qualiton and Hungaroton include Bach's Violin Concerto No. 1 (with Gertler) and the *St John Passion*, Mozart's Piano Concertos K. 491 (with Kiss, and with Kovács) and K. 537 (with Kovács), the Violin Concertos K. 218 and K. 219 (with Kovács) and the Clarinet Concerto (with Kovács), the two Beethoven Romances (with Kovács), Handel's *Music for the Royal Fireworks*, the Schumann Piano Concerto (with Ránki), Liszt's Piano Concerto No. 2 and *Dante Sonata* (with Vlasenko), *Hungarian Fantasy* (with Katona), *Concerto pathétique* (with Antal) and *Spanish Rhapsody* (with Vaszy), Albrechtsberger's Harp Concerto (with Lubik) and Trombone Concerto (with Zilcz), Brahms' Symphony No. 4, *Hungarian Dances Nos 1* to *8* and *No. 10*, and *Sixteen Waltzes* (arranged by Darvas), Stamitz's Viola Concerto (with Lukács), Hindemith's Cello Concerto (with Perényi), *Die Fledermaus*, *La Mer*, *Daphnis et Chloé* Suite No. 2 and *La Valse*, Kodály's *Peacock Variations* and *Adagio* and *Fantasy on a Theme of Paganini* (with Lukács), Bartók's three Piano Concertos (Nos 1 and 2 with Kocsis, and Nos 1, 2 and 3 with Gabos), *Rhapsody No. 1* (with Gabos), *Scherzo for Piano and Orchestra* (with Tusa), *Kossuth*, *The Miraculous Mandarin*, *Dance Suite*, and *Music for Strings, Percussion and Celesta*, Mihály's Symphony No. 3, Mosonyi's Piano Concerto (with Nemes), Farkas' *Prelude and Fugue*, Durkó's *Hungarian Rhapsody*, *Organismi* (with Szücs), and *Hungarian Arabesque*, Kodosa's *Sonata for Orchestra* and

Piano Concerto (with the composer as pianist), Hidas' *Concertino*, Maros' *Two Laments*, *Symphony for Strings*, *Musica da ballo*, *Eufonia 1*, *2* and *3*, and *Five Studies for Orchestra*, Szabó's *Tunes*, Soprini's Cello Concerto (with Mëzo), Szöllösy's *Transfigurazioni per orchestra* and *Musica per orchestra*, Sárközi's *Shepherd's Ballade*, Sárai's Symphony No. 1, Lendvay's *Orogensis*, Symphony No. 3 and *Psalms of Rapture*, Lutosławski's Cello Concerto, Mihály's Cello Concerto, Farkas' *Concerto all'antica* and Martin's *Ballade* (with Perényi), Weiner's Divertimento No. 3, Balassa's *Luperkalia*, *Xenia*, *Tabulae*, *Legend*, *Cantata* and *Requiem for Lajos Kassák*, Mihály's *Apokriphs* and Hasse's *Two Dances*.

Lehmann, Fritz (1904–56). Born in Mannheim, the son of an organist and choirmaster, Lehmann studied at the Mannheim Conservatory and at the Heidelberg and Göttingen Universities. He was first a choral coach at Heidelberg, a conductor at the Göttingen Theatre (1923–7), conductor at Hildesheim (1927–38) and at Hannover (1929–38), music director of the Handel festivals at Göttingen (1934 onwards), general music director at Bad Pyrmont (1935–8), at Wuppertal (1938–47) and at the Göttingen Theatre (1946–50). He was in charge of the conductors' class at the Munich Academy (1953 onwards), and after World War II was a guest conductor in France, Belgium, the Netherlands, Austria, Switzerland and Argentina, and toured Spain with the Bamberg Symphony Orchestra. He died suddenly during an intermission at a performance of the *St Matthew Passion* at Munich. Lehmann was a distinguished and versatile musician, with a wide range of sympathies, his repertoire spanning from Bach to Stravinsky. He had a reputation for seeking to avoid self-publicity, gave special attention to unfamiliar music, and to fostering young soloists whose talent he recognised, and he worked to restore musical life in Germany after the devastation of World War II.

Lehmann recorded extensively. On 78 r.p.m. discs, his records included the *Music for the Royal Fireworks*, Beethoven's Symphony No. 2, Brahms' *Variations on the St Antony Chorale*, *Tod und Verklärung*, Franck's *Rédemption*, Reger's *Romantic Suite* and Kodály's *Galánta Dances* (with the Brussels Radio Orchestra for Odeon); *Eine kleine Nachtmusik* (with the Berlin Philharmonic Orchestra for Odeon); Corelli's Concerto Grosso Op. 6 No. 8, the overtures to *Le nozze di Figaro, Così fan tute* and *La Fille du régiment*, and *Serenata notturna* (with the Berlin State Opera Orchestra for Odeon); Dvořák's *Serenade in E minor*, Sibelius' *Night Ride and Sunrise*, Wolf's *Italian Serenade*, Casella's *Scarlattiana*, the *Háry János* suite, Reger's *Lustspiel* overture, and the overtures *Preciosa* and *Zar und Zimmermann* (with the German Opera House Orchestra for Odeon); a suite from *The Three-cornered Hat* (with the Berlin Radio Orchestra for Odeon); Bach's *St Matthew Passion* (with the Berlin Radio Orchestra *et al.* for Discophiles français); the overtures to *Fra Diavolo* and *Le Domino noir*, the ballet music from *Faust*, and a suite from *Sylvia* (with the Munich Philharmonic Orchestra for DGG); Handel's Concerti Grossi Op. 6 Nos 1, 2 and 3, Dvořák's *Slavonic Rhapsody No. 2*, and the overtures to *Si j'étais Roi*, *La Muette de Portici*, *Le Calife de Bagdad* and *Russlan and Ludmilla* (with the Bamberg Symphony Orchestra for DGG); Bach's Violin Concerto No. 2 (with Varga), Cherubini's *Anacreon* overture, *Water Music*, Haydn's Cello Concerto No. 1 (with Mainardi) and Chopin's Piano Concerto No. 2 (with Askenase, and the Berlin Philharmonic Orchestra for DGG); Bach's Cantatas No. 4 (with the Bach Festival Orchestra *et al.* for DGG) and No. 170 (with the Bavarian State Orchestra *et al.* for DGG), and a Corelli Concerto Grosso (with the Bavarian State Orchestra for DGG). He also recorded, as a pianist, the Adagio from Grazioli's Sonata Op. 5, with the cellist Mainardi.

Lehmann's numerous LP discs included some of the performances on 78s for DGG. All his LPs were for DGG except for Mozart's Symphony No. 35, *Euryanthe* overture, and Poot's *Ouverture joyeuse* (with the Berlin Philharmonic Orchestra for Philips), Beethoven's Symphonies Nos 6 and 8 (with the Cento Soli Orchestra for Club Français du Disque), Barber's Symphony No. 1 (with the Stockholm Symphony Orchestra for Classic), Bach's *Mass in B minor*, and Dvořák's *Wood Dove* and six *Legends* (with the Berlin Radio Orchestra *et al.* for Urania). For DGG he recorded Bach's *St Matthew Passion*, *Christmas Oratorio*, *Mass in B minor*, and Cantatas Nos 1, 19, 21, 39, 53, 79, 105, 189 and 200, Handel's Concerto Grosso Op. 3 No. 3 and *Music for the Royal Fireworks*, Haydn's Symphonies Nos 45 and 94, Mozart's *Eine kleine Nachtmusik*, overtures to *La clemenza di Tito*, *Idomeneo*, *Così fan tutte*, *Don Giovanni*, *Le nozze di Figaro*, *Die Entführung aus dem Serail*, *Der Schauspieldirektor* and *Die Zauberflöte*, Serenade K. 361, Piano Concertos K. 466 (with Foldès), K. 503 and K. 537 (with Seeman) and K. 365 (with Foldès and Seeman), and excerpts from *Don Giovanni*, Beethoven's Symphony No. 2,

Coriolan and *Leonore No. 3* overtures, and *Choral Fantasia* (with Foldès), Schubert's Symphony No. 8, complete *Rosamunde* music, *Psalm 23* and *Serenade*, Brahms' *Tragic Overture*, *Ein deutsches Requiem* and *Schicksalslied*, Mendelssohn's Violin Concerto (with Varga) and overtures *The Hebrides* and *Meeresstille und glückliche Fahrt*, *Don Juan*, *El amor brujo* (with Eustrati), dances from *The Three-cornered Hat*, the overtures to *Alceste*, *Abu Hassan* and *Der Freischütz*, *Prélude à l'après-midi d'un faune*, *España*, *Boléro*, *Les Préludes* and *Finlandia* (with the Berlin Philharmonic Orchestra); Handel's Concerti Grossi Op. 6, Mozart's Symphony No. 32 and Rondos K. 382 and K. 386 (with Seeman) and Flute Concerto K. 314 (with Scheck), Dvořák's Symphony No. 8, *Serenade in E major* and *Slavonic Rhapsodies Nos 2* and *3*, Franck's *Symphony in D minor*, Schumann's *Manfred* overture, the *Romeo and Juliet* fantasy-overture, Grieg's *Symphonic Dances Nos 1* and *2*, *Pulcinella*, Bizet's *Symphony in C major*, suites from *Coppélia*, *The Sleeping Beauty* and *Nutcracker*, Mendelssohn's two Piano Concertos (with Roloff), the overtures to *La Dame blanche*, *Norma*, *Prince Igor* and *Peter Schmoll und seine Nachbarn*, *Danse macabre*, the Coronation March from *Le Prophète*, the waltzes from *Der Rosenkavalier*, and the Bacchanale from *Samson et Dalila* (with the Bamberg Symphony Orchestra); Handel's Concerto Grosso Op. 6 No. 1, and excerpts from *Don Pasquale* (with the Bavarian Radio Symphony Orchestra); and *Hänsel und Gretel*, three songs of Richard Strauss (with Anders), waltzes from *Les Contes d'Hoffmann*, *Eugene Onegin* and *Hänsel und Gretel*, and the ballet music from *William Tell* and *Otello* (with the Munich Philharmonic Orchestra *et al.*).

Leibowitz, René (1913–75). Born in Warsaw, Leibowitz came to Paris with his family in 1926, studied composition in Berlin with Schoenberg, and in Vienna with Webern (1930–33). After returning to France he became an important and influential composer, teacher and interpreter of 12-tone music, and wrote some significant books, *Schoenberg and his School* (1947), *Introduction to 12-tone Music* (1949), and *Thinking for Orchestra* (1958).

After World War II, Leibowitz also became known as a conductor, and made records for a number of French and other companies. Included were Webern's Symphony Op. 21 (on 78s, for Columbia, and on LP for Dial); Berg's *Chamber Concerto* and *Four Songs* (with Joachim for Classic); the *Gayaneh* and *Masquerade* suites (with the Paris Opéra Orchestra for Urania); Mozart's *Requiem* and other sacred music, Beethoven's *Wellington's Victory*, Schubert's Symphony No. 9, *Symphonie fantastique*, *Invitation to the Dance*, *Valse triste*, the waltz from Tchaikovsky's *Serenade in C major*, and some Strauss waltzes (with the Vienna State Opera Orchestra *et al.* for Westminster); Berlioz's *Lélio* (with the Paris Symphony Orchestra *et al.* for Vox); Liszt's two Piano Concertos (with Pennario and the London Symphony Orchestra for RCA); Brahms' *Rinaldo* (with the Pasdeloup Orchestra *et al.* for Vox); Prokofiev's Piano Concerto No. 2 (with Frager and the Paris Conservatoire Orchestra for RCA); *Werther* (with the Rome Opera Orchestra *et al.* for RCA); excerpts from *Manon Lescaut* and *Manon* (with Moffo and the RCA Italiana Orchestra for RCA); *La Boutique fantasque* and *Gaîté parisienne* (with the London Philharmonic Orchestra, issued by Saga); Mozart's Symphony No. 41, Schubert's Symphony No. 9, Grieg's Piano Concerto (with Wild), Mendelssohn's Violin Concerto (with Bress), the Scherzo from Mendelssohn's Octet, and the overtures to *Die Meistersinger*, *Oberon* and *A Midsummer Night's Dream* (with the Royal Philharmonic Orchestra for Reader's Digest); *Le Sacre du printemps* and *Prélude à l'après-midi d'un faune* (with the London Festival Orchestra for Reader's Digest); Schumann's Symphony No. 3 and *Mephisto Waltz* (with the International Symphony Orchestra for Reader's Digest); *España*, *Escales*, *Boléro*, *Rapsodie espagnole* and *Alborada del gracioso* (with the Rome Philharmonic Orchestra for Reader's Digest); Schoenberg's *Gurrelieder* (with the Paris New Symphony Orchestra *et al.*, issued by Haydn Society and Nixa), *Ode to Napoléon Bonaparte* (for Esquire), and *Pierrot Lunaire* (for Argo and Westminster); Beethoven's Piano Concerto No. 2, and *Piano Concerto in E major* (the latter reconstructed by Hess, with Jacobs), *Wellington's Victory*, Leopold Mozart's *Toy Symphony*, *La Valse*, *Rapsodie espagnole*, *Boléro*, *Pavane pour une infante défunte*, *Alborada del gracioso*, *L'Heure espagnole*, Roussel's *Le Festin de l'araignée* and *Le Marchand de sable qui passe*, Schoenberg's Piano Concerto (with Helffner), Mussorgsky's *The Marriage*, Rimsky-Korsakov's *Mozart and Salieri*, and *Un ballo in maschera* (with the French Radio Symphony Orchestra, the French National Radio Orchestra and the Paris Radio Orchestra *et al.*, for various labels); Mozart's *Zaide*, Gluck's *Alceste*, *L'Ivrogne corrigé* and Flute Concerto (with Rampal), *German Dances* of Mozart, Beethoven and Schubert, Fauré's *Requiem*, Satie's *Socrate*,

Auric's *La Fontaine de jouvence* and *Malbrouck s'en va-t-en guerre*, *Aida*, *Les Pêcheurs de perles*, *La Belle Hélène* and *Orphée aux enfers* (with the Paris Philharmonic Orchestra *et al.*, for various labels); and Donizetti's *Rita* (with the Orchestra Societa Arzignajo *et al.* for Cetra).

Leinsdorf, Erich (b. 1912). Born in Vienna, Leinsdorf learned the piano as a boy, studied at the University and the Academy of Music at Vienna, and in 1934 went to Salzburg to assist Walter at the Festival. He worked with Toscanini at the Festivals in 1935–7, also helped to prepare performances at the Florence May Festivals in 1935–7, and conducted concerts and opera in Italy, France and Belgium. In 1937 he migrated to the United States, and on Toscanini's recommendation was engaged to assist Bodanzky at the New York Metropolitan Opera, where he made his debut with *Die Walküre* in 1938, also conducting *Elektra* and *Parsifal* in the same season. In Kolodin's words, he 'performed with vitality and excellent musical taste, demonstrating a control of the unrehearsed ensembles uncommon in so young a man'. After Bodanzky's death in 1939 he became responsible for the German repertoire, and remained there until 1943. He was appointed conductor of the Cleveland Orchestra in 1943, and was then the youngest man to lead a major symphony orchestra in the US. He was conscripted into the US army, was discharged after eight months, found he had lost his position at Cleveland, conducted at the Metropolitan Opera, with the St Louis Symphony and Los Angeles Philharmonic Orchestras, and then was re-appointed to the Cleveland Orchestra in 1945. He was music director of the Rochester Philharmonic Orchestra (1947–56), director of the New York City Opera Company (1956) where he led a season of contemporary operas which was an artistic success but a box-office disaster, and was music consultant and director of the Metropolitan Opera (1957–62). Then he succeeded Münch as music director of the Boston Symphony Orchestra (1962–9), was director of the Berkshire Music Center (1963–9), and since then has been appointed principal conductor of the Berlin Radio Symphony Orchestra (1977).

A man of short stature and always impeccably dressed, Leinsdorf has the reputation of being a good talker and great wit. His professionalism is much admired by his players and he controls singers with unusual sympathy. He is a strong disciplinarian with a passion for thoroughness and precision. As a musical interpreter his intellectual interest in musical structure predominates over lyrical line and emotional expression; in fact his performances are objective and tightly reined, to the point where he is regarded by many as too cold and unfeeling. Certainly he eschews dramatic exaggeration and sentimentality, and his readings err on the side of plainness and severity. As Paul Henry Lang put it, when describing his recordings of the Beethoven symphonies, 'he is not adept at those early imperceptible tempo and dynamic adjustments that give life to music' (*The Recordings of Beethoven*, London, 1971). His musical preferences also reflect this outlook, for while his repertoire is based essentially on the great masterpieces of the 19th century, he dislikes the sentiment and easy-going lyricism of composers such as Glazunov and Saint-Saëns; characteristically he prefers late to early Prokofiev, and early to late Stravinsky. Like Boulez, he believes he has a duty to perform the music of the second Viennese school (Schoenberg, Berg and Webern), which is the bridge from the late romantic composers to modern music. However, in his view it is the disappearance of amateur domestic music-making that has caused the lack of interest in music written since Mahler, and consequently 'composers have come to write for their own satisfaction, not to be listened to or performed' (*The Gramophone*, November 1969, p. 740).

Leinsdorf's career reached its zenith when he became conductor of the Boston Symphony Orchestra in 1962. He took it over from Münch, who had inherited a superb musical institution from Koussevitzky. Münch's relaxed and expressive approach modified the style of the orchestra, but with Leinsdorf its precision was certainly restored; yet most have agreed that in the last years of his tenure the orchestra became something less than it was. His somewhat rigid, unsmiling concept of the standard repertoire eventually affected its former brilliance as an interpretative instrument. He is at his best in opera, where his command of large forces and musical structures is a considerable virtue. To be fair, he was put in a difficult position; he became conductor of the Boston Symphony with a major recording contract which made it mandatory for him to record the great Austrian and German classics which have the largest record sales, but these call for a style more lyrical and sympathetic than he could bring to them.

As a recording artist Leinsdorf has been remarkably active, from some Beethoven symphonies with the Rochester Philharmonic Orchestra to *Le Sacre du printemps* with the London Philharmonic Orchestra in 1975. Included in his discography are the complete symphonies of Mozart, Beethoven, Brahms and Prokofiev, and about 20 complete operas. He first recorded in the United States and in Britain on 78 r.p.m. discs; included were a complete Act III of *Siegfried* (with Farrell, Svanholm and the Rochester Philharmonic Orchestra for RCA), an abridged *Carmen* (with the RCA Victor Symphony Orchestra *et al.* for RCA), Schumann's Symphony No. 1, Dvořák's Symphony No. 6, Rimsky-Korsakov's *Antar*, an orchestral suite from Debussy's *Pelléas et Mélisande*, some Strauss waltzes, polkas and marches, Mozart's Minuet K. 409, the *Rosamunde Ballet Music in G Major* and his own arrangement of a Brahms chorale prelude (with the Cleveland Orchestra for Columbia), Sibelius' Symphony No. 5 and *alla marcia* from the *Karelia* suite, the overture to *Der Freischütz*, the Theme and Variations from Tchaikovsky's Suite No. 3 and Rachmaninov's Piano Concerto No. 2 (with Lympany, and the London Philharmonic Orchestra for Decca), Haydn's Symphony No. 45 (with a commentary by Deems Taylor, for Pilotone) and Mozart's overture *Der Schauspieldirektor* (for Silvertone).

When he was with the Rochester Philharmonic Orchestra, Leinsdorf recorded with them for Columbia Beethoven's Symphonies Nos 3 and 7, Mozart's Symphonies Nos 35, 40 and 41 and *Eine kleine Nachtmusik*, Schubert's Symphony No. 8 and excerpts from the *Rosamunde* music, Mendelssohn's Symphony No. 4 and Rachmaninov's *Symphonic Dances*. His other early LP recordings included Dvořák's Symphony No. 9, Tchaikovsky's Symphony No. 6, *Tod und Verklärung*, *La Mer*, the *Daphnis et Chloé* Suite No. 2, the prelude and Liebestod from *Tristan und Isolde*, the Grieg Piano Concerto, Tchaikovsky's Piano Concerto No. 1, Rachmaninov's Piano Concerto No. 2 and *Rhapsody on a Theme of Paganini* (with Pennario, and the Los Angeles Philharmonic Orchestra for Capitol), *Scheherazade*, *España*, *Moldau*, the *Russian Easter Festival* overture, *L'Apprenti sorcier*, ballet music from operas including *William Tell*, *Aida*, *La Gioconda* and *Samson et Dalila,* the preludes to Acts I and III of *Lohengrin*, the Funeral Music from *Götterdämmerung* and the overtures to *Tannhäuser* and *Die Meistersinger* (with the Concert Arts Symphony Orchestra for Capitol), Brahms' Symphony No. 1, Franck's *Symphony in D minor*, Grieg's Piano Concerto and Mendelssohn's Piano Concerto No. 1 (with Dorfmann and the Robin Hood Dell Orchestra for RCA), Haydn's Symphony No. 45 (with the Metropolitan Opera Orchestra for Grand Award) and Beethoven's Symphony No. 5 (with the American Artists Orchestra for Grand Award). In Europe for EMI he recorded his own arrangement of orchestral music from *Die Frau ohne Schatten*, *Till Eulenspiegel* and the Dance from *Salome*, Brahms' Symphony No. 3 and *Variations on the St Anthony Chorale*, the overtures *Le nozze di Figaro*, *La forza del destino*, *Die Meistersinger*, *L'Italiana in Algeri*, *Oberon* and *Leonore No. 3*, Prokofiev's Piano Concerto No. 3 and Ravel's *Piano Concerto for Left Hand* (with Browning), the Beethoven Violin Concerto (with Milstein and the Philharmonia Orchestra), and Schubert's Mass No. 6 (with the Berlin Philharmonic Orchestra *et al.*). He also recorded the entire symphonies of Mozart with the London Philharmonic Orchestra for Westminster.

With the Boston Symphony Orchestra, the major works Leinsdorf recorded for RCA included Bartók's *Concerto for Orchestra* and Violin Concerto No. 2 (with Silverstein), the Beethoven Symphonies and Piano Concertos (with Rubinstein), the Brahms Symphonies, *Tragic Overture*, Piano Concertos (with Rubinstein, and No. 1 with Cliburn), and *Ein deutsches Requiem*, Bruckner's Symphony No. 4, Dvořák's Symphony No. 6, Mozart's Symphonies Nos 36, 39 and 41 and the *Requiem*, Haydn's Symphonies Nos 93 and 96, Mahler's Symphonies Nos 1, 3, 5 and 6, Kodály's *Háry János* suite and *Peacock Variations*, Mendelssohn's music for *A Midsummer Night's Dream*, Berg's *Der Wein* and excerpts from *Wozzeck*, the seven Prokofiev symphonies, the Piano Concertos (with Browning), a *Romeo and Juliet* suite, the two Violin Concertos (with Friedman and Perlman) and the *Lieutenant Kijé* suite, Strauss's *Ein Heldenleben* and excerpts from *Die Ägyptische Helena* and *Salome*, Verdi's *Requiem*, Tchaikovsky's Piano Concerto No. 1 (twice, with Rubinstein and Dichter), Carter's Piano Concerto (with Lateiner), Colgrass's *As Quiet As*, Dello Joio's *Fantasy and Variations for Piano and Orchestra* and Ravel's *Piano Concerto in G* (with Hollander), the Tchaikovsky Violin Concerto and Dvořák's *Romance* (with Perlman), Fauré's *Élégie* and Prokofiev's *Sinfonia concertante* (with Mayes), Ginastera's Piano Concerto (with Martins) and *Variaciones concertantes*, *Le Coq d'or* suite, *Agon* and *L'Oiseau de feu* suite, Scharwenka's Piano Concerto No. 1 (with Wild), Schuller's *Seven Studies on Themes of Paul Klee* and a disc of marches. The greatest enterprise of all his Boston discs was the complete *Lohengrin*, probably the largest operatic recording made in the United States. Other orchestral LP records he made were of

Brahms' Piano Concerto No. 2 (with Richter and the Chicago Symphony Orchestra for RCA), *Le Sacre du printemps* (with the London Philharmonic Orchestra for Decca), the Franck *Symphonic Variations* and Liszt's *Totentanz* (with Watts and the London Symphony Orchestra for CBS), the overture and Venusberg Music from *Tannhäuser* and a suite from *Der Rosenkavalier* (with the London Symphony Orchestra for Decca). He also accompanied baritone Milnes on the piano in Brahms' *Vier ernste Gesänge*.

From the Act III of *Siegfried* on 78s, Leinsdorf went on to record a profusion of operas, which make him one of the most significant operatic conductors on record. Many were distinguished interpretations. For RCA there was *Don Giovanni* and *Le nozze di Figaro* (with the Vienna State Opera Orchestra *et al.*), *Die Walküre* (with the London Symphony Orchestra *et al.*), the *Lohengrin* mentioned above, *Il barbiere di Siviglia* and *Macbeth* (with the Metropolitan Opera Orchestra *et al.*), *Salome* and *Aida* (with the London Symphony Orchestra *et al.*), *Il tabarro* (with the New Philharmonia Orchestra *et al.*), *La Bohème*, *Madama Butterfly*, *Tosca*, *Turandot* and *Lucia di Lammermoor* (with the Rome Opera Orchestra *et al.*), *Un ballo in maschera* and *Madama Butterfly* (with the RCA Italian Opera Orchestra *et al.*) and Korngold's *Die tote Stadt* (with the Bavarian Radio Symphony Orchestra *et al.*). For EMI he made Cornelius' *Der Barbier von Bagdad* (with the Philharmonia Orchestra *et al.*) and for Decca *Ariadne auf Naxos* (with the Vienna Philharmonic Orchestra *et al.*). Of these, probably *Turandot*, *Die Walküre* and *Ariadne auf Naxos* were the most notable successes; *Die Walküre* was re-issued by Decca in 1973. Finally, for Donemus he recorded the Dutch composer Ketting's *Due canzoni per orchestra* (with the Amsterdam Concertgebouw Orchestra).

Leitner, Ferdinand (b. 1912). Educated at the Hochschule für Musik in his native Berlin, Leitner distinguished himself as a pianist, accompanying artists such as Erna Berger, Peter Anders and Georg Kulenkampff. After World War II Jochum engaged him for the Hamburg Opera (1946); he conducted at the Bavarian State Opera at Munich (1947) and then was at the Württemberg State Opera at Stuttgart (1947), where he was appointed music director (1950). He remained in Stuttgart until 1969, when he was appointed music director at the Zürich Opera and is now conductor of the Residentie Orchestra at the Hague. As a guest conductor he has appeared in many European countries, in North and South America, Australia and the Far East. His repertoire covers the standard operas from Mozart to Strauss, and he has presented many less familiar works by Handel, Donizetti, Verdi and others. In 1951 he led one of the first performances of Stravinsky's *The Rake's Progress*, and has given premières of works by Egk and Orff. He believes that the proven masterpieces of the 20th century should be regularly performed, and is acutely aware of the widening gap between the creative artist and the general public; he considers that this danger appeared first in the middle of the last century, perhaps with *Tristan und Isolde*.

Under contract to DGG since the 1940s, Leitner has made many records of popular overtures and other orchestral pieces with various German orchestras, as well as discs of operatic excerpts and complete operas. He was one of the conductors employed by DGG to build up their catalogue in the early days of LP, but these discs have inevitably been superseded and are now almost entirely deleted. His recorded performances were straightforward and musical, but in the great masterpieces he was not especially distinctive. In the years when he was most actively recording, from the 1940s to the 1960s, his discography ranged from Bach's *Magnificat* to Orff's *Antigonae*; included were Monteverdi's *Lamento d'Arianna* (with Höngen and the Württemberg State Opera Orchestra), Bach's *Brandenburg Concerto No. 3*, and *Magnificat* (with the Ansbach Festival Orchestra *et al.*), Mozart's Symphonies Nos 31 and 36 and Serenade K. 320 (with the Bavarian Radio Symphony Orchestra), Serenade K. 250, Piano Concertos K. 246, K. 488, K. 491 and K. 595 (with Kempff) and overtures *Les petits riens*, *Idomeneo*, *Il re pastore* and *La clemenza di Tito* (with the Bamberg Symphony Orchestra), Piano Concerto K. 488 (with Haas and the Berlin Philharmonic Orchestra), Violin Concerto K. 219 (with Schneiderhan) and excerpts from *Il re pastore* (with the Vienna Symphony Orchestra), Haydn's Symphonies Nos 100 and 102 (with the Bamberg Symphony Orchestra), the five Beethoven Piano Concertos (with Kempff and the Berlin Philharmonic Orchestra), Piano Concertos Nos 1 and 3 (with Foldès, and the Bamberg Symphony and Berlin Philharmonic Orchestras respectively), the two *Romances* (with Koeckert and the Bamberg Symphony Orchestra), the *Egmont* music (with the Württemberg Symphony Orchestra) and the *Fidelio* overture (with the Bamberg Symphony Orchestra), Schumann's Symphony No. 3, *Ruy Blas* overture, Brahms' *Alto Rhapsody* (with

Höngen *et al.*), Dvořák's Symphony No. 7, Strauss's *Le Bourgeois gentilhomme* suite, *Marche slave* and *Capriccio italien* (with the Berlin Philharmonic Orchestra), the Bruch Violin Concerto (with Schneiderhan), Liszt's *Hungaria*, Mendelssohn's Symphony No. 3, *Peer Gynt* Suite No. 1, *L'Arlésienne* Suites Nos 1 and 2, *Invitation to the Dance*, and the overtures *Medea*, *Euryanthe*, *Jubel*, *Preciosa*, *Peter Schmoll und seine Nachbarn*, *La Fille du régiment*, *Martha* and *La forza del destino*, the preludes to Acts I and III of *La traviata*, the storm music from *William Tell* and the intermezzo from *Pagliacci* (with the Bamberg Symphony Orchestra), Brahms' *Variations on the St Antony Chorale*, Grieg's *Symphonic Dances*, intermezzi from *Notre Dame* and *I gioielli della Madonna* and the overtures to *Donna Diana*, *Ariadne auf Naxos*, *Tannhäuser*, and *Die Meistersinger* and the prelude and Liebestod from *Tristan und Isolde* (with the Württemberg State Opera Orchestra), the overtures to *Alessandro Stradella* and *Orphée aux enfers*, and Orff's *Antigonae* and *Die Bernauerin* (with the Bavarian Radio Symphony Orchestra *et al.*), *Carmina Burana*, *Catulli Carmina* and *Trionfi di Afrodite*, and *Prometheus* (with the Cologne Radio Symphony Orchestra *et al.*, now released by BASF), and Pfitzner's *Symphony in C major* and preludes to *Palestrina* (with the Berlin Philharmonic Orchestra), His recordings for other companies than DGG also include the Mozart Clarinet Concerto (with Dörr and the Bamberg Symphony Orchestra for Nonesuch), and Serenade K. 250 (with the Württemberg State Opera Orchestra for Turnabout), the Beethoven Violin Concerto (with Eto and the London Symphony Orchestra for RCA) and Piano Concerto No. 5 (with Gelber and the New Philharmonia Orchestra for EMI, issued in the United States by Seraphim).

Leitner's operatic recordings include a complete *Orphée aux enfers* (with the Munich Philharmonic Orchestra *et al.*), *Zar und Zimmermann*, *La serva padrona* and *Madama Butterfly* (the last in German; with the Württemberg State Opera Orchestra *et al.*) and discs of excerpts from *Der Freischütz*, *Die Entführung aus dem Serail*, *Fidelio*, *Martha*, *Mignon*, *The Merry Wives of Windsor*, *Cavalleria rusticana*, *The Bartered Bride*, *Der Rosenkavalier*, *Die Meistersinger*, *Parsifal*, *Rienzi*, *Tristan und Isolde*, *Tannhäuser*, *Die Walküre* (a complete Act I), *Siegfried*, and *Götterdämmerung* (with the Bamberg Symphony, Württemberg State Opera, Bavarian Radio, Berlin Philharmonic and Munich Philharmonic Orchestras, *et al.*). He also recorded with Borg and Janowitz in recitals of arias. As a pianist, Leitner recorded some songs of Sibelius with Rautawaara, which were issued on 78 r.p.m. discs by Capitol.

Lemaire, Géry (b. 1928). Born in Guignies, Belgium, Lemaire studied at the Tournai Conservatoire, and with Dumortier and Bourguinon at the Brussels Conservatoire, and then studied the organ, religious music and conducting, receiving the diploma at the Tournai diocesan Institute of Gregorian Music (1950). He was organist at La Louvière (1951–5), and then became conductor of the Solistes de Liège, with which he has established a reputation for his sure sense of style, sensitivity and enthusiasm.

With the Solistes de Liège *et al.* he has recorded Bach's *Ein musikalisches Opfer*, Vivaldi's Violin Concertos Op. 6 No. 1, Op. 11 Nos 2 and 6, *et al.*, Albinoni's *Adagio*, Pachelbel's *Canon* and *Gigue*, Chartrain's *Symphonie concertante in A major*, Pasquini's *Arietta*, Corelli's Concerto Grossi Op. 6, Mozart's *Serenata notturna*, Joseph I's *Regina coeli*, J. Stamitz's *Oboe Concerto in C major* (with Antoine) and Symphonies Nos 1, 2 and 3, K. Stamitz's Sinfonia Concertante and *Viola Concerto in D major*, Haydn's Symphonies Nos 58 and 59, Weber's two Piano Concertos (with Dumortier), Brenta's *Airs variés pour les belles écouteuses*, Leduc's Concertino, Michel's *Inframorphoses*, J. C. Bach's Sinfonia Concertante and Symphonies Op. 6 No. 6 and Op. 18 No. 5, W. F. Bach's *Symphony in D minor*, Helmont's *Accensa furore* and *Overture in D major*, Loeillet's Two-Trumpet Concerto (with André *et al.*), van Maldere's Symphony Op. 4 No. 3, Bréhy's *Overture in C*, de Croes' Flute Concertos Nos 2, 4 and 5 (with Rampal), Flute and Violin Concerto No. 6 (with Isselée and Koch) and *Quam terribilia*, Boutmy's *Jubilate Deo*, Willaert's four *Ricercare*, oboe concertos of Hamal, Loeillet, Valentini and Vivaldi, arranged for trumpet (with André), Fiocco's *Missa Solemnis in D major* and *Jubilate Deo*, trumpet concertos of de Fesch, Graupner and Loeillet, and a viola concerto of Telemann transcribed for trumpet (with André), a suite from *Céphale et Pocris*, a symphony and a dance suite by Grétry, Hamal's *Symphony in A major* and *In Exitu Israel*, Pieltan's *Violin Concerto in G major*, Lekeu's *Esquisses*, Devreese's *Mouvement*, Leclerc's *Noir sur blanc*, Ysaÿe's *Harmonies du soir* and Lemaire-Sindorff's Concertino. These recordings were for Erato and Alpha; some were issued in the United States by Musical Heritage Society, and some in Britain by Oryx.

Leonard, Lawrence. Born in London and educated at the Royal Academy of Music and the École Normale in Paris, and privately with Kleiber and Ansermet, Lawrence was associate conductor of the BBC Northern Orchestra (1957–8), conducted the musical *West Side Story* (1959–60), toured South Africa (1960), was professor of conducting at the Guildhall School of Music (1960–65), was associate conductor of the Hallé Orchestra (1964–7), musical director of the Edmonton Symphony Orchestra, Canada (from 1968) and founded the Morley College Symphony Orchestra. With the latter orchestra he took part in 1956 in the legendary satiric Hoffnung Music Festival at the Royal Festival Hall, which was recorded and later issued by EMI. Saga issued mono LPs of the Bach Harpsichord Concertos, in which he conducted the Goldsbrough Orchestra with Wood the soloist, and of Tchaikovsky's *Francesca da Rimini* and excerpts from *The Sleeping Beauty* (with the Hamburg Pro Musica Orchestra), and Enigma released a disc in 1977 in which he conducted the English Chamber Orchestra in Hoffmeister's Flute Concerto and the Telemann *Suite in A minor* (with Dingfelder the soloist).

Leoncavallo, Ruggiero (1858–1919). Of Leoncavallo's many operas, *Pagliacci* was the only one which was successful, and to the present day it is firmly entrenched in the universal operatic repertoire, especially with its twin, Mascagni's *Cavalleria rusticana*. Toscanini led the première of *Pagliacci* in Milan in 1892, and Leoncavallo himself conducted it during a tour of the United States and Canada in 1906. He also conducted during visits to London and the US some years later, but he has been described as an 'inept' conductor. As early as 1903, HMV recorded an almost complete *Pagliacci* in Milan under Leoncavallo; it was advertised that the recording would settle 'any question arising in the future concerning the composer's intentions', but the myriad conductors who have presented it since appear content to rely upon their own judgement.

Leonhardt, Gustav (b. 1928). Born in Amsterdam, Leonhardt and his family were confined to their house during the German occupation of Holland in World War II, when he devoted much of his time to music. In 1946 he went to Basel and attended the Schola Cantorum under Sacher, studying harpsichord and organ with Muller and ensemble playing and instrumentation under Wenzinger, and in 1950 he was in Vienna doing research and studying conducting with Swarowsky. He gave harpsichord recitals in Vienna and Amsterdam; in 1952 he was appointed professor of musicology and harpsichord at the Vienna Academy of Music, and the next year filled a similar position at the Amsterdam Conservatory. In 1955 he settled permanently in Amsterdam and three years later formed the Leonhardt Consort, to perform preclassical music. The group consisted of two violins, two violas, a cello and keyboard, all Dutch players. He has toured the United States many times and in 1962 was a professor at Harvard University. He has performed with his Consort and as a player of the organ, harpsichord, clavichord and fortepiano, his particular interests being Bach, the English keyboard composers of the 17th century, Frescobaldi, Froberger, Louis Couperin and Rameau. His performances are the outcome of his intense study of the styles and practices of the period, and his musicianship has made a profound impression wherever he has played. His dedication as an artist is absolute; he considers it unnecessary or dishonest to make concessions to the public.

Apart from numerous recordings he has made as an instrumentalist for Telefunken, BASF and Philips, of the keyboard music of Bach, Handel, Rameau, Scarlatti, Blow and many others, Leonhardt has led his Consort, for Telefunken, in records of the music of Monteverdi, J. S. Bach and his sons, Purcell, Lawes, Byrd, Tomkins and a number of other 17th-century composers. Also he has joined Nikolaus Harnoncourt in recording the complete edition of the Bach cantatas, of which the first were issued in 1972 by Telefunken. The intention of this vast series is to present the cantatas as Bach envisaged them, with boy treble soloists and a counter-tenor, a small choir and a group of instrumentalists playing original instruments, all performing in a style presumed to be as it was in Bach's day. Leonhardt's performances are noted particularly for his acute sense of rhythm. While fully acknowledging the exceptional care taken in preparing them, there has been some criticism that they have gone too far in eschewing emotional expression.

Leonhardt's other recordings include Campra's *L'Europe galante* and *Le Bourgeois gentilhomme* (with La Petite Bande *et al.* for BASF), Telemann's *Suite in D major* and *Suite in A minor* (with Koch and Linde, and the Collegium Aureum for BASF), Bach's Cantatas Nos 54 and 170 (with the Leonhardt Baroque Ensemble *et al.* for Vanguard), Vivaldi's Concertos Op. 3 No. 10 (with Pfersmann) and Op. 12 No. 1 (with Tomasow, and the Vienna State Opera Orchestra *et al.* for Amadeo, and issued in Britain by Nixa).

Leppard, Raymond (b. 1927). Born in Bath, Leppard was a choral scholar at Trinity College, Cambridge (1948–52), where he conducted the Cambridge Philharmonic Society. In 1952 he formed the Leppard Ensemble in London, became established as a harpsichordist, and made records as such with de Vito and Menuhin, and was the keyboard player with the Philharmonia Orchestra (1953–4). He was engaged as a repetiteur at the Glyndebourne Festival Opera (1954–5), and in 1958 became lecturer in music at Cambridge University, a position he filled for ten years. In the meantime his conducting career proceeded: he formed his own chamber orchestra, which merged with the Goldsbrough Orchestra and became the English Chamber Orchestra, and in the 1960s was permanent conductor of the Essex Youth Orchestra. In 1962 he prepared the complete *L'Incoronazione di Poppea* of Monteverdi for performance at Glyndebourne; the next year he took five months' sabbatical leave to search libraries in Italy for the scores of the operas of Monteverdi and Cavalli, which led to new productions of their operas in Britain. After he left Cambridge in 1968, he toured with the English Chamber Orchestra, conducted at festivals, made his debut in the United States in 1969 with the New York Philharmonic Orchestra, later made his American operatic debut at Sante Fe in 1974, led some Mozart operas at Covent Garden, and also conducted operas at San Francisco, the Scottish Opera, Stockholm and Oslo. In 1970 he premièred Maw's *Rising of the Moon* at Glyndebourne, and in 1973 was appointed permanent conductor of the BBC Northern Orchestra.

Leppard became an authority on the music of the baroque era, particularly of Venetian music of the 17th century. He prepared editions of Monteverdi's operas *L'Incoronazione di Poppea* in 1962, *La favola d'Orfeo* in 1965 and *Il ritorno d'Ulisse in patria* in 1972, and of Cavalli's *L'Ormindo* in 1967 and *La Calisto* in 1969, and these operas were performed at Glyndebourne with much success. *L'Incoronazione di Poppea* was recorded by Pritchard in 1964, with the Glyndebourne production in Leppard's edition; Leppard himself conducted the recordings of *L'Ormindo* and *La Calisto* for Argo in 1969 and 1972 respectively. These operas have come down to us in fragmentary form, existing only in short scores and containing mostly only the voice parts and bass line. Leppard has attempted to make them readily acceptable to present-day audiences, but in doing so he has aroused the hostility of musicologists and musical purists who believe that he has misrepresented the composer's intentions. In the first place, the length of the arias, and indeed the scores, have been cut to fit into the contemporary performing conventions. This has had the effect of seriously altering the roles of some of the major characters and of drastically simplifying the plots. The second objection is that his scoring is far too opulent and that this is historically false. A third is the transposition of arias from other works into the operas, but as this was the custom of the day, the objection can scarcely be sustained. The fact is that Leppard has rescued these works from oblivion and has made them accessible to audiences accustomed mostly to opera of the 18th and 19th centuries.

The other major contribution that Leppard has made to the gramophone catalogues is the orchestral music of Handel (except the organ concertos), recorded with the English Chamber Orchestra and with oboist Holliger, and released by Philips in nine records in 1973. There may be some reservations about these performances, but generally they are elegantly presented. He also directed a number of British singers, the Glyndebourne Chorus, the Ambrosian Singers and the English Chamber Orchestra in Monteverdi's *Madrigali guerrieri et amorosi*, *madrigali e canzonette*, *scherzi musicale*, etc.; this five-disc set, also issued by Philips, is praiseworthy in every respect, and is a significant contribution to the current revival of interest in this composer. His other recordings include excerpts from operas by Monteverdi and Cavalli (with the Bath Festival Orchestra *et al.* for EMI), songs and ayres by Dowland (with a Consort, for Nonesuch), Purcell's *Dido and Aeneas* (with the English Chamber Orchestra *et al.* for Erato), Bach's Brandenburg Concertos, orchestral suites and Violin Concertos Nos 1 and 2 (with Grumiaux), Handel's Concerti Grossi Op. 6, *Concerti a due cori Nos 1*, *2* and *3*, *Water Music*, some overtures, and collections of arias (with Ameling and Souzay, and the English Chamber Orchestra for Philips), Handel's Concerti Grossi Op. 3 and *Alexander's Feast* (with the Leipzig Gewandhaus Bach Orchestra for Eterna), operatic arias of Lully and Rameau (with Souzay and the English Chamber Orchestra for Philips), Rameau's *Le Temple de la Gloire*, a suite of ballet music by Grétry, Leclair's *Scylla et Glaucis* suite and Destouches' *Issé* suite (with the English Chamber Orchestra for L'Oiseau Lyre), Rameau's *Les Fêtes d'Hébé* (with the English Chamber Orchestra for EMI), flute concertos by Devienne and Ibert (with Graf and the English Chamber Orchestra for Claves), some sinfonias by C. P. E. Bach, J. C.

Bach's Oboe Concerto (with Holliger), a sinfonia by J. C. F. Bach, a suite by J. L. Bach, a sinfonia and harpsichord concerto by W. F. Bach (with the English Chamber Orchestra *et al.* for Philips), J. C. Bach's overture to *Catone in Utica* and some sinfonias, Locatelli's *Introduttione teatrale No. 5*, Pergolesi's overture *L'Olimpiade*, Scarlatti's *Sinfonia in B flat*, overtures by Grétry, Rameau, Bononcini, Sacchini and Méhul (with the New Philharmonia Orchestra for Philips), Haydn's Symphonies Nos 22, 23, 26, 34, 39, 47, 48, 70 and 77 (with the English Chamber Orchestra for Philips) and Nos 94 and 103 (with the London Philharmonic Orchestra for Classics for Pleasure), Haydn's Violin Concerto No. 2, Mozart's Adagio K. 261, Rondo K. 373 and Schubert's *Rondo in A major* (with Grumiaux and the New Philharmonia Orchestra for Philips), Boccherini's Cello Concerto and the Haydn *Cello Concerto in C major* (with Gendron and the New Philharmonia Orchestra for Philips), the Schubert *Overture in E minor* and *Overture in B flat* (with the London Philharmonic Orchestra for Philips), the Mendelssohn Symphonies Nos 4 and 5 (with the English Chamber Orchestra for Erato), the Dvořák *Legends* (with the London Philharmonic Orchestra for Philips), the Bax Symphonies Nos 5 and 7 (with the London Philharmonic Orchestra for Lyrita) and Virgil Thomson's *The Mother of Us All* (with the Sante Fe Opera Company for New World Records).

While the Monteverdi and Cavalli operas certainly established Leppard's career, he is now working to cast off the role of a specialist in 17th-century music. His appointment with the BBC Northern Orchestra gave him this opportunity; he has said that there is nothing he does not want to conduct, except new music which he cannot hear when he reads it, and Bruckner, about whom he remarked: 'Bruckner's structure I cannot understand. I listened very carefully to Bruckner's Seventh the other day and thought it was a mess.'

Le Roux, Maurice (b. 1923). Born in Paris, Le Roux studied at the Paris Conservatoire with Messiaen, and was a pupil of Philipp, Nat, de la Bruchollerie and Leibowitz. He was then employed at the electronic studios of Radiodiffusion Française, and in 1952 won first prizè at a conductors' competition, and adopted conducting as a career. He was conductor of the Orchestre National de L'ORTF (1960–68), and has made many tours abroad. His compositions, using serial procedures, include orchestral and film music, including the ballet *Le Petit Prince* and the score for the film *The Red Balloon*, and he has written an *Introduction to Contemporary Music* (1947) and a study of Monteverdi (1951). His recordings include *Eine kleine Nachtmusik* (with the Lamoureux Orchestra for Philips), Monteverdi's *Vespro della beata Vergine* (with the French National Radio Chorus and Orchestra, for La Guilde Internationale du Disque), Messiaen's *Turangalîla Symphony* (with J. Loriod and the ORTF Orchestra, for Vega, and also issued by Decca), *Boléro*, *Pavane pour une infante défunte*, *Valses nobles et sentimentales* and *Alborada del gracioso* (with the ORTF Orchestra for GID), Xenakis' *Metastasis* and *Pithoprakta* (with the French National Radio Orchestra for Le Chant du Monde, issued in the US by Vanguard), and his own compositions *Le Cercle des métamorphoses*, *Un Koan*, *Inventions à deux voix* (with Beroff) and *Au Pays de la magie* (with Benoit, and the ORTF Orchestra, for ORTF).

Leskovic, Bogomir (b. 1909). Born in Vienna, Leskovic studied at the conservatory at Laibach/Ljubljana and at the Vienna Academy of Music, conducted opera in Baden in Lower Austria, and since 1945 has been conductor of the Slovenian Philharmonic Orchestra and the Slovenian National Opera at Ljubljana. For Philips he conducted the Slovenian National Opera company in Prokofiev's *The Love of Three Oranges*, which was issued on mono LP.

Levén, Ake (b. 1930). The Swedish musician Levén studied orchestral and choral conducting at the Salzburg Mozarteum, has been organist at the Stockholm Concert Hall since 1954, and recital organist at the Gustav Vasa Church in Stockholm (1957–67). He has conducted various orchestras, and now lives in England under the name Ralph Davier. For the Swedish company Discophil he has recorded Olsson's *Te Deum*, *Holy Spirit Visit Us* and *Psalm 121* (with the Gustav Vasa Chorus and the Stockholm Philharmonic Orchestra).

Levine, James (b. 1943). Born in Cincinnati into a musical family, Levine studied the piano from the age of three and at ten performed Mendelssohn's Piano Concerto No. 2 with the Cincinnati Symphony Orchestra. He studied with Levin, the first violin of the La Salle Quartet, chamber music, orchestral repertoire, style and interpretation, with Rosina Lhevinne and with Serkin at the Marlboro Festival, and was at the Juilliard School where he studied conducting with Morel. In 1964 he joined the Ford Foundation's American Conductors Project; Szell heard him and invited him to become a member of the conducting staff of the Cleveland Orchestra. First an apprentice conductor, he was assistant conductor (1964–70), attended Szell's rehearsals, concerts and recording sessions and analysed operatic and symphonic scores with him. He filled guest engagements with major orchestras in the United States and Europe, and in 1971 made his debut at the New York Metropolitan Opera with *Tosca*; the next year he was appointed its principal conductor and in 1976 became musical director. He spends seven months of each year at the Met., and in the remaining five months conducts elsewhere and occasionally gives piano recitals. In 1972 he first conducted the New York Philharmonic Orchestra, since 1973 has been musical director of the Ravinia Festival in Chicago where he conducts the Chicago Symphony Orchestra, and in 1974 made his debut at Covent Garden with *Der Rosenkavalier*. He is music director of the Cincinnati May Festival, conducts opera and concerts at the Salzburg Festival and has annual guest engagements with the London Symphony and Berlin Philharmonic Orchestras.

Levine has embarked on recording the cycle of Mahler symphonies, and his interpretative approach finds strong sympathy among the younger generation of listeners. He is enormously attracted to Mahler, the man and composer: 'As a conductor, the more I perform his symphonies, and the more I study them, the more fascinated I become with their potential for self-renewal and capacity to offer fresh discoveries' (*New York Times Supplement*, 26 September 1976). He goes on to say: 'In essence each symphony is simply part of one gigantic piece, and they are all interrelated through the use of direct musical quotes, cross-references or ideas hinted in one symphony only to be fully developed in the next. The ten symphonies are really one big cosmos, a constantly growing organism unified by Mahler's unique musical personality.' At the New York Met. he has specialised in Italian opera, and, outgrowing an early brashness, is now a subtle and finished opera conductor. He has received wide acclaim in European opera houses as well as in New York for his command of the operas he conducts; he believes strongly in thorough preparation and in an intimate knowledge of the score, insisting that a conductor must know the music by memory if he is to lead the orchestra conceptually (*sic*). He also has defined the conductor's task as to produce a performance as faithful to the composer's intention as possible but he is not interested in technical efficiency: 'You can read the words of composers from Bach to Stravinsky, and what you find them screaming into the night about is not the technical execution but the conception, the balance, the spirit, the purpose, what was supposed to be conveyed' (*New York Times*, 2 March 1976). Although his dedication to music is complete, some critics still perceive in his direction of the big romantic symphonic scores a detachment which does not go beyond the precise statement of the composer, somewhat reminiscent of his mentor, Szell. Levine himself wishes to record works about which he feels strongly, or which may have some documentary value, and restricts accompanying to artists with whom he has a long and close working relationship. In recording he insists on complete takes, to maintain momentum.

Levine's first recording was Verdi's *Giovanna d'Arco* (with the London Symphony Orchestra *et al.* for EMI, in 1973). Since then there has been *I vespri siciliani* (with the New Philharmonia Orchestra *et al.* for RCA), *Il barbiere di Siviglia* and *La forza del destino* (with the London Symphony Orchestra *et al.* for EMI), and *Andrea Chénier* (with the National Philharmonic Orchestra *et al.* for RCA). He has also embarked on recording the Brahms and Mahler symphonies; RCA have issued Brahms' Symphony No. 1 (with the Chicago Symphony Orchestra), Mahler's Symphonies No. 1 (with the London Symphony Orchestra) and No. 4 (with Blegen and the Chicago Symphony Orchestra). He recorded with Harrell and the London Symphony Orchestra the Dvořák Cello Concerto, and as a pianist the Beethoven Cello Sonatas, for RCA.

Levine, Joseph (b. 1912). Born in Philadelphia and a graduate of the Curtis Institute, where he was a pupil of Reiner, Rodzinski, Hofmann and Landowska, Levine was a member of the faculty at Curtis (1933–40). He was assistant conductor of the Philadelphia Grand Opera Company (1938–40), founder and conductor of the New Center of Music Orchestra, Philadelphia (1940–43), conductor of the Chamber Opera Society (1946–50), music director of the Co-Opera Company, Philadelphia (1947–50), conductor of the American Ballet Theater, New York (1950–58), conductor of the Omaha Symphony Orchestra (1958–69), music director of the Omaha Civic Opera (1961–9), assistant conductor of the Seattle Symphony Orchestra (1973), and conductor with the Royal Ballet, London (1963–5). He was also pianist with the Philadelphia Orchestra and the Robin Hood Dell Orchestra, and was accompanist to the violinist Josef Szigeti (1946–50). Between 1952 and 1957, Levine recorded for Capitol with the Ballet Theater Orchestra a number of suites from ballets, including *Les Sylphides*, *Swan Lake*, *Sleeping Beauty*, *Les Patineurs*, Dorati's arrangements *Graduation Ball*, *Helen of Troy* and *Barbe Bleue*, Copland's *Rodeo* and *Billy the Kid*, Bernstein's *Fancy Free* and *Facsimile*, Gould's *Fall River Legend*, Banfield's *The Combat*, Schuman's *Undertow* and Antheil's *Capital of the World*. He also recorded two works by Weill: *Down in the Valley* (for Decca, US) and *September Song* and other American songs, with Lotte Lenya (for Columbia, US). Some of the ballet discs were released in Britain by Music for Pleasure.

Lewenthal, Raymond (b. 1926). Born in San Antonio, Texas, Lewenthal studied at the Juilliard School and the Accademia Chigiana at Siena, and with Lydia Cherkassky, Olga Samaroff-Stokowski, Cortot and Agosti. He has published a study of the piano music of Alkan, and presents imaginatively prepared concerts of the neglected virtuoso piano music of the 19th century, dressed in period costume. In addition to his recordings as a pianist, EMI (Angel) recorded him conducting an ensemble of toy instruments and strings in *Kindersymphonien* by Reinecke and Gurlitt, excerpts from Taylor's *Toy Symphony*, Kling's *Kitchen Symphony*, Steibelt's *Three Bacchanales* and Méhul's *Ouverture burlesque*.

Lewis, Sir Anthony (b. 1915). Born in Bermuda, Lewis was an organ scholar at Cambridge University, and in 1935 joined the music staff of the BBC, where he was responsible for the revival of much 16th- to 18th-century music. It was in this repertoire that he was to make a significant impact on British musical life. After service in the British army in World War II he rejoined the BBC in 1946, was Peyton-Barber Professor of Music at the University of Birmingham (1947–68) and dean of the Faculty of Arts there (1961–4), president of the Royal Musical Association (1963–7), chairman of the Music Advisory Panel of the Arts Council of Great Britain (1954–65), member of the Music Advisory Committee of the British Council (1967–73) and principal of the Royal Academy of Music (from 1968). His compositions include several concertos, orchestral and choral music, and he has edited and published music of Purcell, Blow, Arne and Handel, as well as contributing articles to musical periodicals.

Lewis has been an important pioneer in recording the music of the 17th and 18th centuries; his records may not always be the last word in polish, but style and vitality are very evident. His contribution to a wide appreciation of much music that was hitherto unknown is immense. On 78 r.p.m. discs he recorded excerpts from Blow's *Venus and Adonis* for L'Oiseau Lyre; he made many records in the early years of LP for L'Oiseau Lyre and Argo, and a number have since been re-issued by Decca. Included were six overtures by Boyce, Arne's masque *Comus*, two suites for strings by Blow and his opera *Venus and Adonis*, Purcell's operas *The Fairy Queen*, *King Arthur* and *Dido and Aeneas*, the ode *Come Ye Sons of Art*, airs and dances from *The Tempest*, *Dioclesian*, *The Virtuous Wife* and *Timon of Athens*, Monteverdi's *Vespro della beata Vergine*, Mozart's *Litaniae Lauretanae* and *Litaniae de venerabili altaris sacramento*, Rameau's *Hippolyte et Aricie*, Couperin's *Leçons des ténèbres*, Lully's *Miserere*, and Handel's cantata *Apollo e Daphne*, operas *Semele* and *Sosarme*, and excerpts from *Jephtha* and *Theodora*, the oboe concertos and collections from arias and dances from *Alcina*, *Rodrigo* and *Esther*; one of the singers in the last disc was Joan Sutherland, and this was the first recording she ever made. The orchestras were the Boyd Neel, the London Philomusica, the Lamoureux, the English Chamber and Oiseau Lyre.

Lewis, Henry (b. 1932). Born in Los Angeles, Lewis was educated at the University of Southern California, and at the age of sixteen was playing the double-bass in the Los Angeles Philharmonic Orchestra. After military service (1955–9) when he played in and conducted the Seventh Army Symphony Orchestra in Europe, he returned to California and founded the Los Angeles Chamber Orchestra, and toured Europe with it in 1963 under the auspices of the US State Department. He conducted the Los Angeles Philharmonic and American Symphony Orchestras, and in 1968 was appointed music director and conductor of the New Jersey Symphony Orchestra, and was the first Negro to lead a state orchestra in the United States. In 1972 he was engaged to conduct at the Metropolitan Opera, and has appeared as a guest conductor with major orchestras in the US, Britain and Italy. His recordings show him to be a painstaking and straightforward interpreter, whose natural restraint keeps him from imposing himself too much on the music. They include *Also sprach Zarathustra*, *Don Juan*, *Till Eulenspiegel*, Beethoven's Symphony No. 6, Tchaikovsky's Symphony No. 6, Tchaikovsky's Piano Concerto No. 1 and Rachmaninov's Piano Concerto No. 2 (with Wild), excerpts from *Carmen*, Rossini's *Assiedo di Corinto* and *La donna del lago*, and Wagner's *Wesendonck Lieder* and Mahler's *Kindertotenlieder* (with his wife, the soprano

Marilyn Horne); all were with the Royal Philharmonic Orchestra for Decca. He has also recorded a recital of Bach and Handel arias (with Horne and the Vienna Cantata Orchestra for Decca) and another aria recital (with Horne and the Covent Garden Orchestra for Decca), Massenet's *La Navarraise* (with the London Symphony Orchestra *et al.* for RCA) and Meyerbeer's *Le Prophète* (with the Royal Philharmonic Orchestra *et al.* for CBS).

Lewis, Robert Hall (b. 1926). Born in Portland, Oregon, Lewis studied at the University of Rochester, the Paris Conservatoire, the Vienna Academy of Music and the French Institute in London. He has received many awards for his compositions, which have been performed in the United States and Europe. He has been professor of music at Goucher College and the Johns Hopkins University, a teacher of composition at the Peabody Institute and music director of the Chamber Music Society of Baltimore, where he has lived since 1957. Composers Recordings issued a disc in which he conducted the London Symphony Orchestra in his Symphony No. 2.

Lewis, Samuel (b. 1936). Born in London, Lewis studied the viola at the Royal College of Music, and conducting at the Guildhall School of Music, and played the viola in the London Symphony Orchestra (1957–63). He participated in the first Dmitri Mitropoulos International Conductors' Competition in New York, and became musical director for the London theatre impressario HM Tennant Ltd., conducting performances at the Theatre Royal, London *et al.* He formed the Scottish Strings (1965), was a conductor for the BBC and ABC Television, and emigrated to Israel where he was appointed musical director of the Netanya Orchestra (1969). With the Scottish Strings he recorded a disc of Scottish melodies for EMI.

Lhotka, Fran (1883–1962). Born in Užice, Serbia, (modern Yugoslavia), Lhotka studied at the Prague Conservatory and with Dvořák, taught at the conservatory at Ekaterinoslav, Russia, was a conductor of opera and choir in Zagreb, and was rector of the State Music Academy there. His compositions included several operas, a symphony and the ballet *The Devil in the Village*, which he recorded for Decca with the Zagreb National Opera Orchestra.

Lindberg, Nils (b. 1933). The Swedish composer and conductor Lindberg first studied classical music and became a jazz pianist and arranger, and made arrangements for Duke Ellington and his orchestra. He has composed clarinet and trumpet concertos, and an orchestral suite. For Discophil he has recorded his own *Noah's Ark* and *Variations on Folk Tunes*, with the Swedish Radio Symphony Orchestra *et al.*

Lindenberg, Eduard (1908–73). Born in Bucharest, Lindenberg studied at the Universities of Vienna and Berlin, and was a pupil of Scherchen. After conducting the Bucharest Philharmonic Orchestra he went to Japan to conduct the Tokyo Symphony Orchestra, and then settled in Paris. His only recordings to be released in Britain and the United States appear to have been one of Bizet's *Jeux d'enfants* and suite from *La jolie fille de Perth*, and Chabrier's *Suite pastorale*, and songs by Debussy and Ravel (with Souzay, and the Paris Conservatoire Orchestra for Decca), but he also recorded Beethoven's Symphony No. 3 and Tchaikovsky's Symphony No. 6 (with the Vienna Volksoper Orchestra for BSAF), Beethoven's Symphonies Nos 5 and 7, the four Brahms symphonies, Dvořák's Symphony No. 9 and Tchaikovsky's Symphony No. 6 (with the North-West German Philharmonic Orchestra for Erato), *Eine kleine Nachtmusik*, the overture to *Die Entführung aus dem Serail*, Brahms' *Hungarian Dances* 1 to 6, Massenet's *Scènes pittoresques* and *Scènes algériennes* and a dance from *La vida breve* (with the Pasdeloup Orchestra for Odeon), the Hungarian March from *La Damnation de Faust*, Bizet's *Jeux d'enfants* and suites from *Carmen* and *La jolie fille de Perth*, the Ritual Fire Dance from *El amor brujo*, Liszt's *Hungarian Rhapsody No. 2* and *Les Préludes* (with the Paris Conservatoire Orchestra for Odeon), the overtures to *Die Zauberflöte* and *Tannhäuser*, Saint-Saëns' *Havanaise* and *Introduction et rondo capriccioso* (with Szeryng), *Le Carnaval des animaux*, *Danse macabre*, Schubert's Symphony No. 8, and *Rosamunde* music, *Siegfried Idyll*, *Invitation to the Dance* and *In the Steppes of Central Asia* (with the French National Radio Orchestra for Odeon), and Vivaldi's *The Four Seasons* (with the Vienna Chamber Orchestra for Mondio Music).

Lipkin, Arthur Bennett (d. 1974). Lipkin received his early musical training in London, was at the age of eighteen the youngest member of the Philadelphia Orchestra, and was also for 20 years first violinist of the Philadelphia String Quartet. He represented the players on the board of the Philadelphia Orchestra, helped to establish the orchestra's summer outdoor concerts in the Robin Hood Dell, and was elected president of the American Symphony Orchestra League three times. He was originally the conductor of the Main Line and Germantown Orchestras in Pennsylvania, then the Birmingham Symphony Orchestra in Alabama (1950–60) and from 1962 until his death the resident conductor of the Portland Symphony Orchestra in Maine. He was a guest conductor with many orchestras in the US and abroad, toured internationally on behalf of the US Committee to Further American Contemporary Music, and in Portland gave the premières of new works by Kay, Pinkham, Piston, Hovhaness and others. For Composers Recordings he conducted the Oslo Philharmonic Orchestra in Kay's *Fantasy Variations*, Berezowski's *Christmas Festival* overture, and Dello Joio's *New York Profiles*, and the Royal Philharmonic Orchestra in Hovhaness's *The Holy City*.

Lippe, Anton (b. 1905). Born in St Anna am Aigen, Austria, Lippe studied church music in Rome, was choirmaster at the Graz Cathedral (1935–64), conductor of the Hofmusikkapelle in Vienna (1948–64), and choirmaster at St Hedwig's Cathedral in East Berlin and president of the Church Music section of the Berlin bishopric (1964). He has an international reputation as a choral and orchestral conductor and has toured widely. For Amadeo he recorded Franz Schmidt's *Das Buch mit sieben Siegeln*, with the Munich Philharmonic Orchestra *et al.*

Liška, Bohumír (b. 1914). Born in Čejetičké in Czechoslovakia, Liška studied conducting with Doležil and Dědeček at the Prague Conservatory (1936–7); previously he had been a repetiteur and conductor of the Student Philharmonic Orchestra in Prague (1931–8). He was choral conductor at the Prague National Theatre (1937–40) and then became, on Kubelík's recommendation, conductor at the Brno Opera (1940–55). At that time he was also teacher of conducting at the Brno Conservatory (1942–57) and was appointed director of the Opera House at Plzeň (1955). He visited Britain to conduct the London Philharmonic Orchestra (1957–60), and taught at the Prague Conservatory (1959) and at the Prague Academy of Music (1961). Liška recorded Martinů's *Field Mass* (with the Czech Philharmonic Orchestra *et al.* for Supraphon), Pauer's *Le Malade imaginaire* (with the Czech Philharmonic Orchestra *et al.* for Panton), the overtures *Così fan tutte*, *Iphigénie en Aulide* and *Tancredi* (with the Czech Philharmonic Orchestra for Supraphon), and Stich-Punto's Horn Concerto No. 5 and Brixi's Organ Concerto No. 2 (with Štefek and Dobrodinský, respectively, and the Prague Symphony Orchestra for Supraphon), and Jirko's *Requiem* (with the Czech Symphony Orchestra *et al.* for Panton).

List, Kurt (1913–70). Born in Vienna, List studied at the Vienna Academy of Music and University (1936–8), and took private lessons with Berg and Webern (1932–8). In 1938 he migrated to the United States, became a noted musicologist and critic, and produced gramophone records. After World War II he lived in Europe. His compositions include two operas and chamber music. His records included the *Brandenburg Concertos Nos 5* and *6*, Haydn Symphony No. 104, Schubert's *Rosamunde* Ballet No. 9, the Schumann Symphony No. 1, the overture to *Tannhäuser* and preludes to *Lohengrin*, *Die Meistersinger*, *Tristan und Isolde* and *Götterdämmerung*, *Moldau*, the overture to *The Merry Wives of Windsor*, the ballet music from *Les Troyens*, *Also sprach Zarathustra*, suites from *The Nutcracker*, *Swan Lake* and *The Sleeping Beauty*, the *Romeo and Juliet* fantasy-overture, the Dance of the Hours from *La Gioconda*, *L'Oiseau de feu*, *Le Sacre du printemps*, *Boléro* and *Finlandia* (with the Berlin Symphony Orchestra for Royale); Mendelssohn's Symphony No. 4 and the overtures *Athalie* and *The Hebrides* (with the Philharmonic Orchestra for Allegro); *Les Contes d'Hoffmann* (with the Dresden Staatskapelle *et al.* for EMI); Telemann's *Two-Flute Concerto in A minor* (with Riessberger and Kunz) and *Oboe Concerto in F minor* (with Hertel and the Austrian Tonkünstler Orchestra for Musical Heritage Society); Vivaldi's *Violin Concerto in G minor* (with Glenn), Viotti's *Piano and Violin Concerto in B flat* (with Eugene List and Glenn), Haydn's Violin and Piano Concerto (with Glenn and Eugene List) and Mozart's Rondo K. 382 (with List and the Biedermeier Orchestra for Musical Heritage Society); and Strauss's *Burleske* and Violin Concerto (with Eugene List and Glenn, respectively, and the Vienna Volksoper Orchestra, issued in the United States by Odyssey, and the Violin Concerto in Britain by World Record Club). The pianist Eugene List is not a relative of Kurt List; Carroll Glenn, the violinist in some of these recordings, is Eugene List's wife.

Litschauer, Franz (1903–72). Born in Laa, Austria, Litschauer studied at the Vienna Academy of Music under Scherchen (1938–41) and was conductor of the Women's Symphony Orchestra (1940). After military service in World War II he was conductor of the Vienna

Chamber Orchestra (1948–52), the Cairo Symphony Orchestra (1956–60), the Cape Town Symphony Orchestra (1959) and the Athens Radio Orchestra (1960). During his years in Vienna he made a number of records for Vanguard (US), mostly with the Vienna State Opera Orchestra; his direction of music by American composers in this series attracted the comment that it was not idiomatic. The works recorded included pieces by Locatelli and Purcell, concertos by Haydn and Handel, some dances by Mozart and Beethoven, the Bach/Walton suite *The Wise Virgins*, the Scarlatti/Tommasini suite *The Good-humoured Ladies*, Respighi's *Gli uccelli*, *Trittico Botticelliano* and the three suites of *Ancient Airs and Dances*, Bloch's *Israel* Symphony, Copland's *Appalachian Spring* and *El Salón México*, Grieg's *Norwegian Dances*, Sibelius' *Valse triste* and *Rakastava*, Petrassi's *Il ritratto di Don Chisciotte*, Kupferman's *Little Symphony*, Swanson's *Short Symphony* and Weingartner's arrangement of the Schubert *Symphony in E* (called the Symphony No. 7), which was reissued in Britain in 1971. For the Haydn Society (US) he recorded Haydn's Symphonies Nos 1 to 8, Nos 21, 42 and 47, and the *Notturni* Nos 1, 3, 4 and 6 (with the Vienna Chamber Orchestra). Many of these discs were released in Britain by Nixa.

Littaur, David (b. 1925). Born in London, Littaur spent part of his boyhood in Argentina, and served in the Royal Air Force in World War II as a navigator. After the war he studied at the Guildhall School under Lewis and Del Mar, and in 1956 won the Ricordi Prize for Conductors. He conducted chamber concerts at Wigmore Hall, London (1953–4), first conducted the London Symphony Orchestra in 1958, and toured South Africa (1961). In 1972 he became artistic director and principal conductor of the London Philomusica. In 1969 EMI issued discs of Littaur conducting the New Philharmonia Orchestra in the Bach *Brandenburg Concertos*; although he employs more than one player for each part, and has broader tempi than in performances attempting to be historically accurate, these discs are musical in the best sense of the term. On an early LP for Waverley he had recorded the *Brandenburg Concerto No. 4*, two Mozart Divertimenti, K. 247 and K. 287, and a March, with the Festival Players.

Litvin, Karol (b. 1932). Born in Bucharest, Litvin studied at the Tchaikovsky Conservatory at Moscow (1951–8), appeared with orchestras in Moscow, Kiev and Odessa, and conducted at the Stanislavski Musical Theatre at Moscow. He became conductor of the Bucharest Radio-Television Symphony Orchestra and Choir (1958), was director of music for Bucharest Radio-Television (1959–64), has conducted at the Romanian Opera (since 1958), taught at the Ciprian Porumbescu Conservatory at Bucharest (since 1959) and toured FR Germany with the West Berlin Ballet (1974). With the Bucharest Radio-Television and Film Orchestras he has recorded for Electrecord recitals of arias, Liszt's *Faust* Symphony, the operas *Turandot* and *Samson et Dalila*, and works by the Romanian composers Barbu, Kirculescu, Profeta, Golestan, Popovici, Sarchizov, Paşcanu, Zarzor, Caudella, Mureşianu, Flechtenmacher, Ştephănescu, Negrea and Drăgoi.

Lloyd-Jones, David (b. 1934). Born in London, Lloyd-Jones studied at Oxford University, where he conducted choral and orchestral concerts, and in London with Iain Hamilton. He was a repetiteur at Covent Garden Opera, assisted Pritchard in the Liverpool series of Musica Viva concerts, was assistant conductor with the New Opera Company (1950), conductor of the John Lewis Partnership Music Society, conducted premières of Orr's *The Wager* (1962) and Jones' *The Knife* (1963) at Sadler's Wells for the New Opera Company, became associated with the BBC Welsh Orchestra, conducted at the Dartington Summer School of Music (1963–8), and conducted opera at various British festivals and opera companies and on television. He is now a senior member of the music staff at the English National Opera, and has prepared a new edition of *Boris Godunov* which was recently recorded by EMI under Semkow's direction, and a new translation of Tchaikovsky's *The Queen of Spades* for the Welsh National Opera. His only recording has been for Philips with the London Philharmonic Orchestra of Balakirev's *King Lear* overture, Rimsky-Korsakov's *Legend of Sadko*, Borodin's Symphony No. 3 and the original version of Mussorgsky's *A Night on the Bare Mountain*.

Lockhart, James (b. 1930). Born in Edinburgh, Lockhart was educated at the University there and at the Royal College of Music, London; he was an assistant organist and choirmaster at St Giles' Cathedral and St Mary's Episcopal Church at Edinburgh (1946–51), and then organist and choirmaster at two churches in London (1951–4). He became an apprentice conductor with the Yorkshire Symphony Orchestra (1954–5), a repetiteur and assistant conductor at the Münster Opera in FR Germany (1955–6), at the Bavarian State Opera in Munich (1956–7), at the Glyndebourne Festival Opera (1957–9), director of the opera workshop at the University of Texas (1957–9), repetiteur at Covent Garden (1959–60), assistant conductor of the BBC Scottish Orchestra (1960–61), guest conductor at the Sadler's Wells Opera (1960–61), conductor at Sadler's Wells (1961–2), conductor at Covent Garden (1962–8), professor at the Royal College of Music (1962–8), musical director of the Welsh National Opera Company (from 1968) and general music director at Kassel (from 1977). In 1963 he recorded discs of excerpts, in English, from *Rigoletto* and *The Bartered Bride* with the Sadler's Wells Company for EMI; with the soprano Margaret Price he recorded a recital of Mozart arias (with the English Chamber Orchestra for RCA), Hoddinott's *Roman Dream* (with the Cardiff Festival Players for Argo), and accompanied her on the piano in a lieder recital (for Classics for Pleasure). He has also recorded Walton's opera *The Bear* (with the English Chamber Orchestra *et al.* for EMI) and the Mendelssohn Symphony No. 4 and the overture and some of the incidental music to *A Midsummer Night's Dream*, and the overtures to *Tannhäuser*, *Der Freischütz*, *The Merry Wives of Windsor*, *Hänsel und Gretel* and *Ruy Blas* (with the London Philharmonic Orchestra for Classics for Pleasure).

Loehrer, Edwin (b. 1906). Born in St Gallen, Switzerland, Loehrer studied music in Munich, Vienna and Zürich, and took his doctorate in 1936; his thesis was a critical revision of the masses of the 16th-century Swiss composer Ludwig Senfl. He was music director at St Gallen (1930–35), and in 1936 joined the Swiss Italian Radio in Lugano, and became widely known for his productions of Italian vocal and polyphonic music which were broadcast by the European Broadcasting Union, as well as in the United States, Canada, South Africa and Japan. In 1961 he founded the Società Cameristica di Lugano, with which he conducted at many European festivals and made a series of recordings, between 1962 and 1968, for Eurodisc; many were released in the US and elsewhere by Nonesuch. Included in this series were Monteverdi's *Il combattimento di Tancredi e Clorinda*, *Madrigali guerrieri et amorosi*, *Il ballo dell'ingrate*, *Lamento d'Arianna e Sestina* and the complete eighth book of madrigals, Caldara's *Il gioco del Quadriglio* and other pieces, Vivaldi's cantatas *Cessate, omai* and *Piango*, a collection of music by Lotti, Rossini's *Péchés de vieillesse*, and an arrangement by Sgrizzi of *Laudario 91 di Cortona*. His other recordings included Rossini's *Petite Messe solennelle*, Pergolesi's *Stabat Mater* and *Salve Regina*, and A. Scarlatti's *Stabat Mater*, Cantata *Su le sponde del Tibro* and Recitative and Aria *Caldo Sangue* (for Erato, with some being issued in the US by Musical Heritage Society), Barberini's *In honorem Lucani*, Soliva's *Ave Maria* and motets by Senfl (with the Swiss Italian Radio Chorus, for CTS, Switzerland), and Vivaldi's *La ninfa e il pastore* (with the Milan Chamber Orchestra *et al.* for Vox).

Loibner, Wilhelm (1909–71). Born in Vienna, Loibner studied at the Hochschule für Musik there under Schmidt and Krauss, graduated in 1930, and became a repetiteur at the Vienna State Opera (1931). In 1937 he was appointed a resident conductor at the Opera and in 1949 professor at the Vienna Academy of Music. He was a guest conductor in Europe and North America, was principal conductor of the NHK Symphony Orchestra in Japan (1957–9) and was artistic director of the Elizabethan Trust Opera Company in Australia (1963). His recordings include Haydn's Symphonies Nos 12, 23, 29 and 30 (with the Vienna Academy of Music Chamber Orchestra for Lyrichord), Mozart's Symphony No. 39 (with the Berlin Staatskapelle for Eterna) and Piano Concerto K. 491 (with Biro and the Austrian Symphony Orchestra for Remington), the Beethoven and Brahms Violin Concertos (with Spalding and the Austrian Symphony Orchestra for Remington), excerpts from *Fidelio*, *The Bartered Bride*, *Un ballo in maschera*, *The Merry Wives of Windsor* and *Die Meistersinger*, the ballet music from *Undine*, the clog dance from *Zar und Zimmermann*, the overtures to *Hans Heiling*, *Martha*, *La forza del destino* and *I vespri siciliani*, the preludes to Acts I and III of *La traviata*, the ballet music from *Aida* and *Otello*, Liszt's *Hungarian Rhapsody No. 2* and Waldteufel's *Les Patineurs* (with the Vienna Symphony Orchestra *et al.* for Philips), Bruch's Violin Concerto No. 1 and *Kol Nidrei* (with Auclair and the Austrian Symphony Orchestra for Remington), the Dvořák Violin Concerto (with Magyar and the Vienna Symphony Orchestra for Philips), and *La Bohème* and *Madama Butterfly* (with Austrian Symphony Orchestra *et al.* for Remington).

Lolov, Vassil (b. 1913). Born in Yambol, Bulgaria, Lolov studied at the Sofia Academy of Music, and was among the first Bulgarian-trained conductors. He performed as a violinist in Berlin, studied composition there with

Wunsch, founded the Lolov String Quartet in Sofia, was conductor of the State Symphony Orchestra in Burgas, director and artistic manager of the Plovdic National Opera, teacher at the Sofia School of Music, director of the musical department of the Bulgarian Radio, associate professor of chamber music at the Bulgarian State Conservatory, secretary-general of the Union of Bulgarian Composers (1969–72), and founder of the Collegium for Chamber Music (1968). In many of his compositions and in his work both as teacher and conductor he has striven to develop the level of aesthetic taste and to widen his audience, and many of his compositions are based on Bulgarian folklore. For Balkanton he has recorded with the Collegium for Chamber Music nonets by Martinů and Yaroh, Yossifov's *Sinfonietta*, Hindemith's *Kammermusiken Nos 2* and *3*, Raichev's Symphony No. 5 and Pekov's *Music for Chamber Music Ensemble No. 2*.

Lombard, Alain (b. 1940). Born in Paris, Lombard joined Gaston Poulet's class at the Paris Conservatoire at the age of nine, and two years later conducted his first concert. He studied conducting with Fricsay and was appointed second conductor (1960) then principal conductor (1962–4) at the Lyon Opera. He assisted Bernstein and Karajan at the Salzburg Summer Festival in 1966; in the same year he was awarded the Gold Medal at the Dmitri Mitropoulos International Conductors Competition in New York, and conducted a performance of *Hérodiade* at the New York Metropolitan Opera, at Régine Crespin's bidding. In 1967 he became musical director of the Miami Philharmonic Orchestra, returned to France to be musical director of the Strasbourg Philharmonic Orchestra (1972) and artistic director of the Opéra du Rhin (1974), which was founded in 1972 and performs in the three Alsatian cities of Strasbourg, Mulhouse and Colmar. At Strasbourg there is also an orchestra attached to the ORTF, but whereas this orchestra plays an important part in the promotion of contemporary music, the Strasbourg Philharmonic generally is concerned with more conventional repertoire, and also takes part in the productions of the Opéra du Rhin. He has, in addition, been a guest conductor with many European and United States orchestras and opera houses, and has established a considerable reputation for style and brilliance.

Lombard has recorded for EMI and Erato. With the Strasbourg Philharmonic Orchestra his discs for Erato have shown the orchestra to be one of the finest in France; included are *Symphonie fantastique*, *Harold in Italy*, the *Roméo et Juliette* symphony, Bartók's *Concerto for Orchestra* and *The Miraculous Mandarin*, *Also sprach Zarathustra*, excerpts from Prokofiev's *Romeo and Juliet* and *Cinderella* ballets, *La Valse*, *Boléro*, *Daphnis et Chloé* Suite No. 2, *Petrushka*, the two Ravel Piano Concertos (with Anne Queffélec), the two Prokofiev Violin Concertos (with Amoyal), Bizet's *Symphony in C major* and *L'Arlésienne*, the Franck *Symphony in D minor*, *Carmen*, Rachmaninov's Piano Concerto No. 2 (with Bachauer), the Verdi *Requiem*, *Prélude à l'après-midi d'un faune*, Fauré's *Pavane* and *Pelléas et Mélisande* suite, Roussel's *Bacchus et Ariane* Suite No. 2, the overture to *Tannhäuser* and Elisabeth's arias, the prelude and Liebestod from *Tristan und Isolde* (with Caballé), Landowski's Trumpet Concerto (with André) and Jolivet's *Songe à nouveau rêvé* and *Poèmes intimes* (with Herzog). For EMI he has recorded Gounod's *Roméo et Juliette* and selections from *William Tell* (with the Paris Opéra Orchestra *et al.*), *Lakmé* (with the Paris Opéra-Comique Orchestra *et al.*), *Der Zigeunerbaron* (with the Pasdeloup Orchestra *et al.*), and *Eine kleine Nachtmusik*, Schubert's Symphony No. 8 and Albinoni's *Adagio* (with the Paris Conservatoire Orchestra).

Lombard has explained how the Strasbourg Philharmonic has developed, under his direction, into one of the most distinguished orchestras in France. From the beginning he wished to prove that there are excellent orchestras in France outside Paris, and that the musicians themselves had to become aware of this. A record contract was negotiated with Erato and each concert was repeated several times; the orchestra was the first regional one to be successful in Paris; there were two important tours, one in the USSR in 1974 and another in the USA in 1975, and young new players were added to the orchestra. Much 20th-century music, of Bartók, Stravinsky, Ravel, Strauss and Roussel for example, was played, which called for great care and enabled the orchestra to progress. Frequently, on tour, the players themselves asked for additional rehearsals, and always have striven to improve as an ensemble.

London, Edwin (b. 1929). Born in Philadelphia, London was educated at Oberlin College, and the University of Iowa, and studied composition with Dallapiccola and Milhaud. He received a Guggenheim Fellowship in 1969, is professor of music at the University of Illinois, has published a number of compositions, and is conductor of the Contemporary Chamber Players of the University of Illinois. Composers Recordings have issued a disc in which he leads the Players in G. B. Wilson's *Concatenations* and *Exigencies*.

Long, Lancelot (1891–1978). Long was originally chorister at Westminster Cathedral, and subsequently became Master of Music there (1924–39). Between 1927 and 1930 he directed the Westminster Cathedral Choir in a series of records for HMV, which included the first complete recording of Palestrina's *Missa Papae Marcelli*.

López-Cobos, Jesús (b. 1940). Born in Toro, Spain, into a musical family where his father was a prominent member of Madrid's Wagner Society, López-Cobos studied at the Universities of Granada and Madrid, where he took his doctorate in philosophy. He learned some music in Granada, joined and occasionally conducted the university choir in Madrid, took lessons in conducting with Ferrara in Venice, came under the influence of Cristobal Halffter, was assistant conductor at the Madrid Opera (1964–6), and in 1966 went to Vienna to study with Swarowsky, where he graduated from the Hochschule für Musik. He won third prize at the Nicolai Malko Conductors Competition in Copenhagen (1968), and first prize at the International Competition for Young Conductors at Besançon (1969), and in that year made his professional debut as a conductor at the Prague Spring Festival. He studied conducting with Maag at the Accademia Chigiana at Siena and with Morel at the Juilliard School in New York, and became Maag's assistant in Venice, where he conducted his first opera, Donizetti's *Le convenienze ed inconvenienze teatrali*. He appeared at the Teatro Colón in Buenos Aires, and after conducting at the Deutsche Oper in Berlin in 1970 was offered a five-year contract as a resident conductor. Symphony orchestras he has conducted are the Vienna Philharmonic at the Salzburg Festival, the four major London orchestras, and others in FR Germany, Holland, Switzerland, Italy and Scandinavia, as well as the Los Angeles Philharmonic; he toured with the London Symphony and the Royal Philharmonic Orchestras in Spain and with the New Philharmonia Orchestra in Holland, and has conducted in opera houses in San Francisco, Munich, Hamburg, Chicago, Paris and London. He is anxious to dissociate himself from the convention that Latin conductors must only conduct Italian and French works in the opera house: 'In concert, also when I tour in Spain, I play Bruckner, Mahler, all the German masterworks. This is the repertoire I learned and absorbed during the years I studied in Vienna' (*Musical America*, June 1978, p. 5). He has impressed in concert appearances in London with his command of the orchestra, his care with detail, his disinclination to exaggerate and his firm clear beat, but his reading of Beethoven's Symphony No. 9, although vital and authoritative, seemed to many to lack something in spiritual grandeur.

López-Cobos has recorded *Lucia di Lammermoor* (with the New Philharmonic Orchestra *et al.* for Philips), Bruch's *Scottish Fantasy* and Violin Concerto No. 2 (with Perlman and the New Philharmonia Orchestra for EMI), an overture and symphony of Arriaga (with the English Chamber Orchestra for Christophorus) and Mozart's Divertimenti K. 136, K. 137 and K. 138 and Symphony No. 13 (with the English Chamber Orchestra for Ensayo).

Loughran, James (b. 1931). Born in Glasgow, where he received his education, Loughran began his career as an assistant to Maag at the Bonn Opera, and later held similar positions in Amsterdam and Milan. He returned to England in 1961, and won first prize at the Philharmonia Orchestra's Young Conductors' Competition; he was appointed associate conductor to Silvestri with the Bournemouth Symphony Orchestra (1962–5), was principal conductor of the BBC Scottish Symphony Orchestra (1965–71), in 1971 was appointed principal conductor and artistic adviser of the Hallé Orchestra, in succession to Barbirolli, and in 1977 became principal conductor of the Bamberg Symphony Orchestra. He has conducted opera at Covent Garden, Sadler's Wells, the Scottish Opera and with the English Opera Group, made his debut in the United States with the New York Philharmonic Orchestra in 1972, has been a guest conductor with all the major British orchestras, as well as orchestras in the United States and Europe where he regularly conducts the Munich Philharmonic Orchestra, and has taken part in the Henry Wood Promenade Concerts and the Edinburgh Festival. His contract with the Hallé Orchestra permits him to conduct elsewhere for half of the year; in 1975 he toured with the orchestra in Germany and Switzerland.

Loughran is the first British conductor to be appointed to a major German orchestra, no doubt because of his reputation as an interpreter of the German classical repertoire. Under his leadership the Hallé Orchestra has regained much of its former high standards and vitality, and he has brought many imaginative ideas into arranging the concert programmes, so as to move away from the traditional pattern of overture, concerto and symphony. In his engagements abroad, he feels no necessity to conduct a British work for the first time in any place, believing that British conductors should be judged on their performances of the international rather than the national repertoire. He is modest, direct, and shuns flamboyance; he sees his musicians as collaborators, and rather than impose his will he seeks to create mutual understanding and rapport, which can result in sensitive and committed performances. Although he is interested in performing 20th-century music, he is disappointed that, despite the great talent of composers, so little moves beyond the experimental stage, and that so much is unnecessarily difficult to perform. In 1970 the BBC chose him to record for broadcast the nine Beethoven symphonies with the London Symphony Orchestra, which led him to study the original manuscripts in Germany.

In 1974 Classics for Pleasure commenced a series of recordings with the Hallé Orchestra under Loughran, because the north of England was one area where their record sales were poor. Whatever the reason, many fine discs have resulted, which have re-established the Hallé Orchestra as a recording orchestra, and Loughran as an artist capable of straightforward, careful and thoroughly musical readings. The first were Rachmaninov's Symphony No. 2, the four Brahms symphonies, the *Academic Festival* and *Tragic Overtures*, *Variations on the St Antony Chorale*, the Violin Concerto (with Hasson, and the London Philharmonic Orchestra), some *Hungarian Dances* and the *Alto Rhapsody* (with Bernadette Greevy), *Belshazzar's Feast*, *The Planets*, the overtures *Le Carnaval romain*, *Le Corsaire*, *Béatrice et Bénédict*, *Benvenuto Cellini*, *Le Roi Lear*, *Le nozze di Figaro*, *Prometheus*, *Rosamunde*, *Die Fledermaus*, *Dichter und Bauer* and *Der Opernball*, and music by the Strauss family. He has also embarked on a series of the Beethoven symphonies with the Hallé Orchestra, starting with Nos 3 and 7 (for Enigma); his other recordings have been McCabe's *Chagall Windows* and *Variations on a Theme of Hartmann* (with the Hallé Orchestra for EMI), and Brian's Symphony No. 10 (with the Leicestershire Schools Symphony Orchestra for Transatlantic/Unicorn).

Loussier, Jacques (b. 1936). The jazz pianist Loussier was born in Angers, France, educated at the Paris Conservatoire and has become internationally famous for his concerts and records with the Loussier Trio in jazz arrangements of Bach pieces, *inter alia*. Decca recorded him leading the Royal Philharmonic Orchestra and his Trio in a programme of Bach arrangements, including the *Brandenburg Concerto No. 5*.

Löwlein, Hans (b. 1909). Born in Ingolstadt, Germany, Löwlein studied at the Academy of Music at Munich, and became a repetiteur at the Bavarian State Opera there (1933–4). He was conductor at Stettin (1934–42), and Dresden (1946–9), was with Felsenstein at the Berlin Komische Oper (1949–50), was conductor at the Berlin Staatsoper (1950–61), at Frankfurt am Main (1962–4), and in 1964 was appointed chief conductor at Basel. His recordings include discs of excerpts from *Tiefland* (with the Berlin German Opera Orchestra *et al.* for DGG), from *The Merry Wives of Windsor* and *Der fliegende Holländer* (with the Bamberg Symphony Orchestra *et al.* for DGG), a recital of Verdi arias with Grace Bumbry (with the Berlin German Opera Orchestra for DGG) and excerpts from *Il barbiere di Siviglia* (with the Bavarian State Opera Orchestra *et al.* for Ariola).

Lualdi, Adriano (1885–1971). Born in Larino, Campobasso, Italy, Lualdi studied with Falchi and Wolf-Ferrari, and for the first years of his career conducted opera (1908–13). He became music critic of the *Secolo* in Milan (1923–7) and then later of *Giornale d'Italia* in Rome (1936–42), and also published books of his impressions after travelling in Europe, South America and Russia. He directed festivals at Venice and Florence, was principal of the Conservatorio di Musica S. Pietro a Maiella at Naples (1936–43), and director of the Conservatorio di Musica L. Cherubini at Florence (1947–56); he represented the Sindicato Musicisti in the Fascist parliament. His compositions included a number of opera, vocal, orchestral and instrumental music. At the Conservatorio in Naples he formed a chamber orchestra with which he recorded for HMV before and during World War II; the works recorded included Cherubini's *Symphony in D major*, Paisiello's ballet *Proserpina* and Piano Concerto (with Castagnone), Cimarosa's overture *I traci amanti*, Durante's *Concerto in G minor*, Pergolesi's *Concerto in B flat major* and the Recitativo from Bonporti's *Concerto in B flat major* (with Pelliccia), a concerto by Scarlatti, Porpora's *Royal Fanfares*, and the overture to his own opera *La Granceola*. He arranged many of these pieces for performance.

Lubbock, John (b. 1945). Born in Hertfordshire and educated at the Royal Academy of Music, Lubbock was a bass singer in Swingle II, and made his debut as a conductor in 1967 with a student orchestra, the Camden Chamber Orchestra. This ensemble grew into a fully professional group, and was renamed the Orchestra of St John's, Smith Square, London, in 1973. It soon grew in reputation; its first tour was to the United States in 1975, and then later it visited FR Germany, Spain, Norway and the Netherlands, and performed with great success at a Promenade concert at the Royal Albert Hall in 1976. It performs especially the 20th-century string repertoire, and now plays about 60 concerts a year. Lubbock himself has been a guest conductor with the BBC regional orchestras. With the orchestra he has recorded a suite from Stravinsky's *Pulcinella*, *Ma Mère l'oye*, two *Romanian Dances* of Bartók, Elgar's *Introduction and Allegro* and *Serenade in E minor*, Tippett's *Fantasia Concertante* and *Little Music for Strings*, and Mozart's Piano Concertos K. 271 and K. 467 (with Milkina, for Pye), Vogel's Violin Concerto (with Lütschg) and *Abschied* (for Tudor). With the Camden Chamber Orchestra he has also recorded six symphonies of Sammartini (for Christophorus).

Lucier, Alvin (b. 1931). Born in Nashua, New Hampshire, and educated at Yale and Brandeis Universities where he studied with Porter, Berger, Fine and Shapero, and also with Foss at Tanglewood, Lucier was in Rome on a Fulbright Scholarship (1960–62), and returned to the United States to teach at Brandeis University (1962–70) and then at Wesleyan University. His compositions (*sic*) employ many esoteric sounds, such as magnetic disturbances in the ionosphere and electroencephalographic waves. Odyssey issued a disc in which he conducted the Brandeis University Chamber Chorus in works by Ashley, Cage, Oliveros, Feldman, Ichiyanagi and himself.

Ludwig, Leopold (b. 1908). Born in Witkowitz, then in Austria and now in Czechoslovakia, Ludwig was playing the organ at church services at the age of ten, and from 1927 to 1930 studied at the Vienna Academy of Music. He decided to be a conductor after hearing a broadcast performance of Furtwängler's *Tristan und Isolde* from Bayreuth in 1931, obtained engagements at the German opera houses at Gablonz, Teplitz-Schönau and Troppau in Czechoslovakia (1931–5), and was appointed general music director at Oldenburg State Theatre (1936–9). Then he was a conductor at the Vienna State Opera (1939–43), at the Deutsche Oper, Berlin (1943–5), guest conductor at both the Berlin Staatsoper and Berlin Deutsche Oper (1945–51), general music director at Hamburg (1951–70), guest conductor at the Vienna State Opera (1963 onwards), San Francisco (1959 onwards), the New York Metropolitan Opera (1970 and 1972), chief guest conductor at the Hamburg Opera (1970–73) and artistic director of the Basel Music Society (1969 onwards). He also took part in the Edinburgh Festival (1952 and 1956) and the Glyndebourne Opera Festival (1959). His honours include the Mozart Medal (Vienna, 1941), the Brahms Medal (Hamburg, 1958) and the title of Professor awarded by the Senate of the City of Hamburg (1968).

Ludwig is a vastly experienced conductor with a range of musical sympathies extending from Bach to Berg. His performances in the standard repertoire are invariably musical and without mannerism; he is one of a number of fine Austrian and German conductors to emerge between the wars, who, while they may not rank in the very top flight, are nonetheless completely reliable interpreters of the operatic and symphonic music of these two countries. He has made numerous records for many companies; his first were 78 r.p.m. discs for Polydor, HMV and Decca, and were all with Berlin orchestras. The major pieces he recorded at this time were Haydn's Symphony No. 103, Mozart's Symphony No. 39 and the *Leonore No. 3* overture (with the Berlin Philharmonic Orchestra for Polydor); the others were the overtures *Mignon*, *Orphée aux enfers*, *Nabucco* and *The Hebrides*, the waltz and polonaise from *Eugene Onegin*, the intermezzo from *Cavalleria rusticana*, two preludes from *Carmen* and some arias with Schock and Lemnitz (with the Berlin Staatsoper Orchestra for HMV), the overtures *Iphigénie en Aulide* (with the same orchestra for Polydor), *Hans Heiling* (with the Dresden Philharmonic Orchestra for Polydor), *Abu Hassan*, *Così fan tutte*, *Don Giovanni*, *Alessandro Stradella*, *Donna Diana* and *Rienzi* (with the Berlin Staatsoper Orchestra for Polydor), *Oberon* and *Tannhäuser* (with the Berlin Philharmonic Orchestra for Polydor), as well as the intermezzi from *Pagliacci* and *Cavalleria rusticana* (with the Berlin Staatsoper Orchestra for HMV), the march from Beethoven's music to *Die Ruinen von Athen*, the Entrance of the Guests from *Tannhäuser* and Strauss's *Kaiserwalzer* (with the Berlin Philharmonic Orchestra for Polydor) and the prelude to Act III of *Lohengrin*, and excerpts from Act III of *Die Meistersinger* (with the Berlin Staatsoper Orchestra for Polydor).

Ludwig's LP records have included Bach's *Brandenburg Concerto No. 2* and Violin Concerto No. 2 (with Stevens), Handel's Concerti Grossi Op. 3 Nos 1, 3 and 5, Boccherini's Cello Concerto (with Sindler), Beethoven's Symphonies Nos 4 and 8 and overtures *Egmont*, *Fidelio*, *Leonore Nos 1* and *2* and *Namensfeier*,

Harold in Italy and the Berlioz overtures *Benvenuto Cellini*, *Le Roi Lear*, *Béatrice et Bénédict* and *Le Carnaval romain*, the *Romeo and Juliet* fantasy-overture, the *1812* overture, the *Hebrides* overture, two preludes from *Carmen*, the *Tragic* and *Academic Festival Overtures* of Brahms, excerpts from *Swan Lake*, the preludes from *La traviata* and some Strauss waltzes (with the Berlin Symphony Orchestra for Royale), Beethoven's Symphony No. 9 (with the Berlin Symphony Orchestra *et al.*, issued by CBS), Mozart's Symphony No. 40, Schubert's Symphony No. 8, Dvořák's Symphony No. 9, *Ein Heldenleben* and Mahler's Symphony No. 9 (with the London Symphony Orchestra for Everest, some being issued by World Record Club), Tchaikovsky's Symphony No. 6, and some *Hungarian Rhapsodies* of Liszt and *Hungarian Dances* of Brahms (with the Hamburg National Philharmonic Orchestra for Baccarola), Haydn's Symphony No. 94 (with the Hamburg Philharmonic Orchestra for Eurodisc), the two Beethoven *Romances* (with Ferras and the Hamburg Philharmonic Orchestra for DGG), *Les Préludes*, Tchaikovsky's Piano Concerto No. 1 (with Cherkassky), the Grieg Piano Concerto (with Aeschbacher), Mozart's Piano Concertos K. 450 and K. 503, two Liszt Piano Concertos and Rachmaninov's Piano Concerto No. 2 (with Földes, and the Berlin Philharmonic Orchestra for DGG), excerpts from *Mathis der Maler*, *Die Walküre* and *Götterdämmerung* and Mozart's Horn Concerto K. 495 (with Blank, and the Berlin Radio Symphony Orchestra *et al.* for DGG), Mahler's Symphony No. 4 (with Schlemm and the Saxon State Orchestra for DGG), three songs by Strauss (with De Luca and the Bavarian Radio Symphony Orchestra for DGG), the march from *Aida* and overture *Béatrice et Bénédict* (with the Munich Philharmonic Orchestra for DGG), Haydn's Cello Concerto No. 1 (with Navarra and the Hamburg State Philharmonic Orchestra for Ariola), Haydn's Symphony No. 94 and Mozart's Symphony No. 41 (with the North-West German Radio Orchestra for Vox), the *Water Music* and *Music for the Royal Fireworks* (with the Hamburg State Philharmonic Orchestra for Turnabout), Weber's *Abu Hassan* (with the Berlin Staatsoper Orchestra *et al.* for Urania), Berg's *Lulu* (with the Hamburg State Opera Orchestra *et al.* for EMI), *A Night on the Bare Mountain*, the polonaise from *Boris Godunov*, Dance of the Persian Slaves and entr'acte from *Khovanshchina* (with the Berlin Philharmonic Orchestra, issued by Urania, Nixa, and Music Treasures of the World), *Lieder eines fahrenden Gesellen* (with Metternich and the Berlin Radio Orchestra for Urania), excerpts from *Die Meistersinger* (with the Hamburg State Opera Orchestra *et al.* for Ducretet-Thomson), Liszt's *Hungarian Rhapsodies Nos 1, 2, 3* and *4*, *Capriccio italien*, *Marche slave* and the *Nutcracker* suite (with the Bavarian Radio Symphony Orchestra for EMI), Beethoven's Piano Concertos Nos 3, 4 and 5 (with Gilels and the Philharmonia Orchestra for EMI), Kodály's *Galánta Dances* and *Marosszék Dances* (with the Philharmonia Orchestra for EMI), Massenet's *Scènes pittoresques*, and Rimsky-Korsakov's *Sinfonietta on Russian Themes*, *Christmas Eve* suite and ballet music from *The Snow Maiden* (with the Berlin Radio Orchestra for Urania), and Tchaikovsky's *Serenade in C major* (with the Bamberg Symphony Orchestra for Mercury).

Luening, Otto (b. 1900). Born in Milwaukee, Luening studied in Europe at the Munich Academy of Music, at the Zürich Conservatory and University, and privately with Busoni. After some experience as a conductor and as a flautist and percussionist with the Zürich Tonhalle Orchestra he returned to the United States and became co-founder of the American Grand Opera Company at Chicago (1920). He directed the opera department at the Eastman School of Music (1925–8), conducted for radio and musical comedy, then filled professorial positions at the University of Arizona (1932–4), Bennington College (1934–44) and Barnard College (1944–59). Luening is regarded as one of the important composers in the early years of modern American music; his compositions, which embrace many styles, techniques and media, include an opera, orchestral, chamber and instrumental music. Since 1959 he has been co-director with Babbitt and Ussachevsky of the Columbia-Princeton Electronic Music Center, and with Ussachevsky wrote a concerted piece for electronic tape with orchestra, which was the first work to combine tape-recorded sounds with live performers. Composers Recordings (of whose board he has been chairman since 1970) have issued several discs of his music; on one he directs the Royal Danish Radio Orchestra in the piece for tape and orchestra mentioned above.

Lukács, Ervin (b. 1928). Born in Budapest, Lukács studied at the Fodor Conservatory and at the Franz Liszt Academy of Music, graduated in 1956, and at the same time completed a diploma in medicine. He was conductor of the Hungarian Army Orchestra (1954–6), and at Miskolc (1957), was a repetiteur at the Hungarian State Opera (1957) and was appointed conductor there in 1958. He was also professor of conducting at the Academy (1957–9) and in 1962 was awarded first prize at the International Conductors Competition in Rome. He regularly conducts the Budapest Symphony and Hungarian State Symphony Orchestras, has been a guest conductor in both Germanies, Italy, Poland, China and the USSR, and in 1972 toured the United States with the Hungarian State Symphony Orchestra as an associate conductor. His repertoire ranges from Bach, Haydn and Mozart to Britten, Prokofiev and the present-day Hungarian composers.

Lúkacs' recordings, for Qualiton, include Beethoven's Piano Concerto No. 4 (with Kocsis), Schubert's Symphony No. 9, Rachmaninov's Piano Concerto No. 2 and Franck's *Symphonic Variations* (with Gabos), *Cavalleria rusticana*, excerpts from *Lohengrin*, *Turandot* and *Faust*, Kodály's *The Bad Wife*, Bartók's Violin Concerto No. 2 and Violin Concertos of Dávid and Mihály (with Kovács), Mihály's cantata *Fly Poem*, Láng's *Laudate Hominem*, *Chamber Cantata* and *Funeral Music*, Dávid's *Sinfonietta*, Kacsóh's *János Vitéz*, and a recital by Komlóssy. The orchestras are the Budapest Philharmonic, the Budapest Symphony, the Hungarian State Opera and the Hungarian Radio and Television.

Lukáš, Zdeněk (b. 1928). Born in Prague and a graduate of the Educational Institute of Prague, Lukáš studied with Modrý (1943–6) and Řidky (1955), completed his military service and joined the Czech Radio at Plzeň. His compositions include several string quartets. Supraphon have issued a disc in which he conducts the Prague Chamber Harmony and Soloists in a recital of Mozart arias with soprano Jonasova.

Lumsden, David (b. 1928). Born in Newcastle-upon-Tyne, Lumsden studied at Selwyn College, Cambridge, was organist at Southwell Minster, Fellow and organist at New College, Oxford, and founder and conductor of the Nottingham Bach Society. He is a visiting professor at Yale University, has made numerous appearances as organist, harpsichordist and choral conductor, is a past president of the Incorporated Society of Organists, has edited collections of lute music, and has composed sacred settings *et al.* With the New College Choir he has recorded two discs of Britten's sacred music, including *A Ceremony of Carols*, *Missa brevis*, *Te Deum in C*, *Jubilate Deo*, *Antiphon* and *Hymn to St Peter* (for Saga), Purcell's *Magnificat*, *Nunc dimittis*, *O Lord God of Hosts* and *Praise the Lord* (for Saga), Wesley's *Magnificat in E*, *Nunc dimittis in E* and other pieces (for Oryx), Leighton's *Crucifixus pro nobis*, *God's grandeur* (for Abbey), sacred pieces by Gibbons, Holborne, Byrd, Jenkins, Bull, Messaus, Coperario, Munninckx, de Leeuw and Sweelinck (for Abbey), Stanford's *Magnificat* and *Nunc dimittis*, and pieces by Parry, Mendelssohn, Drayton and excerpt from Mozart's Mass K. 317 (for Abbey), Byrd's *Magnificat*, *Nunc dimittis*, Psalms 47, 54, 55 and 119 *et al.* (for Abbey), Victoria's *O quam gloriosum* and Byrd's *Sing joyfully* and other pieces (for Abbey). As an instrumentalist he recorded a disc of Boyce trio sonatas (for Oryx).

Lund, Gustav. No biographical information is available concerning Lund, who conducted the Stuttgart Ton Studio Orchestra *et al.* on early LPs of Mozart's *Il re pastore*, *La clemenza di Tito* and *Les petits riens* (for Classic, France), Violin Concertos K. 207, K. 211 and K. 271a (with Stucki), Horn Concerto K. 412 (with Görmer) and Flute and Harp Concerto (with Mess and Wagner, for Elite), and the overtures *Don Giovanni*, *Die Zauberflöte*, and *Le nozze di Figaro* (for Period).

Lundquist, Torbjörn (b. 1920). Born in Stockholm, Lundquist studied composition with Wirén, piano with Flyckt and choral conducting with Hammerström. His debut as a conductor occurred in Stockholm in 1949, and he has been a conductor at the Drottningholm Theatre (1949–56), conductor of the Torbjörn Lundquist Chamber Orchestra (1949–56), and has conducted various other orchestras in Sweden. He has recorded his own *Berlings Saga Suite* (with the Stockholm Philharmonic Orchestra for Swedish Radio), Judex from Gounod's *Mors et Vita* and the intermezzo from *Cavalleria rusticana* (with the Odense Municipal Orchestra for EMI).

Lupi, Roberto (b. 1908). Born in Milan where he studied at the Conservatorio, Lupi was a professor at the Conservatorio Cherubini at Florence, and edited works of Galuppi, Caldara, Stradella *et al.* He published a book *Armonia di gravitazione* (Rome, 1946), and composed a cantata and other music. With the Naples Scarlatti Orchestra for Colosseum he recorded dances from *I Scolari* of Zanetti, the 18th-century Italian composer.

Lútosławski, Witold (b. 1913). The Polish composer Lutosławski was born in Warsaw; he studied music at the Warsaw Conservatory and mathematics at the University of Warsaw. He appeared as a pianist between 1932 and 1955, and from time to time since 1952 has conducted his own compositions. Of his own works he has recorded his Symphony No. 2 (with the Polish National Philharmonic Orchestra), *Three Poems* (with the Polish Radio Choir), *Preludium and Fugue* (with the Warsaw Philharmonic Chamber Orchestra), *Six Children's Songs* (with the Polish Radio Choir), *Ten Polish Dances* (with the Warsaw Philharmonic Orchestra), *Paroles tissées* (with Pears and the London Sinfonietta for Decca) and Cello Concerto (with Rostropovich and the Orchestre de Paris for EMI).

Lutze, Walter (b. 1891). Born in Wittenberg, Germany, Lutze studied at the Halle Conservatory, was a conductor at Bremen (1911–14), Bremerhaven (1916–20), Schwerin (1920–35) and at the German Opera, Berlin (1935–44), and was music director at Dessau (1951–2). He was also a guest conductor at the Berlin Staatsoper, and composed orchestral and vocal works. He recorded excerpts from *Der Freischütz* and the overture to *Nabucco* (with the Berlin Staatsoper Orchestra *et al.* for Telefunken) and the overture to *Der Waldmeister* (with the German Opera House Orchestra, Berlin, for HMV).

Lylloff, Bent (b. 1930). Born in Copenhagen, Lylloff was educated at the Royal Conservatory there and at the Juilliard School, New York. He was a timpanist in the Tivoli Symphony and Royal Symphony Orchestras, Copenhagen, has led various percussion ensembles, has taught at (*inter alia*) the Det Jydske Conservatory at Arhus, Denmark, and the Malmö Conservatory, Sweden, and has led a children's television music programme. He recorded the percussion pieces Nørgaard's *Waves* and *Rondo*, Varèse's *Ionisation* and his own *Places* (with the Copenhagen Percussion Ensemble, for Cambridge).

Lysy, Alberto (b. 1935). Born in Buenos Aires, Lysy studied the violin in Argentina with Spiller, was a prizewinner at the Queen Elisabeth of Belgium International Contest in Brussels (1955), and became associated with Menuhin, first as a pupil and then at Menuhin's school in Britain. Lysy has toured in many countries, including the United States and the USSR, has conducted chamber orchestras in Europe and America, and is director of the International Academy of Chamber Music in Switzerland. Odyssey have released a disc in which he conducted the Bariloche Camerata in music by Vivaldi, Purcell and Zanetti.

M

Maag, Peter (b. 1919). Maag was born in St Gallen in Switzerland; he was descended from the famous musical family of Steinbach, and his father was Otto Maag, the well-known theologian and musician who was once Swiss consul in Dresden, where Fritz Reiner was a frequent house guest. Maag studied philosophy, theology and literature at the universities at Zürich, Basel and Geneva, and then studied the piano with Marek. In 1943 he became choirmaster at the Opera at Biel-Solothurn, soon becoming second, then first conductor. In 1946 he visited Paris and Rome to learn about the production of French and Italian opera; he conducted concerts with the Suisse Romande Orchestra and with others in Europe and elsewhere, and in Geneva led a Mozart cycle of twelve concerts. He was appointed first conductor at the Düsseldorf Opera (1952–4), and at the same time assisted Ansermet at Geneva. Afterwards he was general music director at the Bonn Opera (1954–9), where he was especially successful with the Mozart operas and seldom-heard works such as Dvořák's *Rusalka*, Cavalieri's *La rappresentazione di anima e di corpo*. At Bonn he also led performances of composers such as Toch, Martin, Hindemith, Martinů and Menotti.

When he had completed his tenure at Bonn, Maag unexpectedly withdrew from musical life. He retired to a Buddhist monastery in Hong Kong, impelled to re-assess himself and his relationship with music. In his own words, he felt he had become too ambitious, and that between him and the music was his own shadow. He remained at the monastery for two and a half years, and the outcome was to increase his ability to communicate 'with patience'. He resumed conducting, appeared as a guest with many orchestras in Europe, Japan and North and South America, and at major opera houses, including La Scala, Covent Garden and the Colón, as well as at international festivals such as Glyndebourne, Aix-en-Provence, Holland, Venice, Florence and Salzburg. He became associated with the Japan Philharmonic Orchestra, Italian Radio and Television, the Teatro San Carlo at Naples and the Chicago Lyric Opera; the Vienna Volksoper appointed him its director (1964–8), he was a professor at the Accademia Chigiana at Siena (from 1968) and artistic director of the Parma Opera (from 1972). In 1972 he first appeared at the New York Metropolitan Opera.

Throughout his career Maag has been identified as a Mozart interpreter of considerable distinction, although this is by no means the only music in which he is adept. His Mozart is elegant, poised and above all stylish; it has elements of both the precise brilliance of Szell and the lyrical warmth of Walter, as well as its own dimension of spontaneity and feeling. His records of Mozart with the London Symphony Orchestra are superlative object lessons of Mozart grace and style. His readings of Mendelssohn have much the same virtues; Robert Layton (writing in 1967) selected Maag's disc coupling *The Hebrides* overture and the Symphony No. 3 as one of the 'great records'.

Maag's first records were made for Decca in the early 1950s with the Suisse Romande Orchestra, and were of Mozart's Symphonies Nos 28, 29 and 34, and the Serenade K. 320 (*Posthorn*). He went on to record for Decca with the London Symphony Orchestra Mozart's Symphonies Nos 32 and 38, the Piano Concertos K. 415 and K. 466 (with Katchen) and K. 491 (with Gulda), the *Notturno* K. 286, *Serenata notturna*, the overture to *Lucio Silla* and the interludes from *Thamos, König von Ägypten*, and Mendelssohn's Symphony No. 3, *The Hebrides* overture and incidental music to *A Midsummer Night's Dream*, Mozart's Serenade K. 203 (with the New Symphony Orchestra), *Les Sylphides* and Delibes' *La Source* (with the Paris Conservatoire Orchestra). His other recordings include Mysliveček's oratorio *Abraham and Isaac* (with the Czech Philharmonic Orchestra *et al.* for Supraphon), scenes from Gluck's operas (with the Prague National Theatre Orchestra *et al.* for Supraphon), Britten's Violin Concerto and Vaughan Williams' *Concerto accademico* (with Grumlíková and the Prague Symphony Orchestra for Supraphon), the Dvořák Violin Concerto and Ravel's *Tzigane* (with Peinemann and the Czech Philharmonic Orchestra for DGG), Mozart's Symphonies Nos 39 and 41 (with the Japan Philharmonic Orchestra for Crossroads), Oboe Concertos by Bellini and Cimarosa, Donizetti's Concertino for Cor Anglais (with Holliger) and Salieri's Concerto for Oboe and Flute (with Holliger and Nicolet, and the

Bamberg Symphony Orchestra for DGG), the Schumann Piano Concerto and Chopin's Piano Concerto No. 2 (with Fou Ts'ong and the London Symphony Orchestra for Westminster), and Verdi's *Luisa Miller* (with the National Philharmonic Orchestra *et al.* for Decca).

Vox, on its Turnabout label, has been responsible for Maag's largest recording enterprises, which comprised the complete Schubert symphonies, overtures and the *Rosamunde* incidental music, and Mozart's Symphonies Nos 35, 36, 38, 39, 40 and 41, and a two-disc album of the Mozart Masonic music. These were potentially major issues, but Maag did not have the advantage of leading an orchestra of the calibre of the London Symphony, however good the Philharmonia Hungarica are in the Schubert and Mozart symphonies, and the Vienna Volksoper Orchestra in the Mozart Masonic music. Except for the Masonic music, these discs do not appear to have been released in Britain; compared to Maag's best, they were disappointing. He also recorded Mozart's Piano Concertos K. 451 and K. 488, with Klien and the Volksoper Orchestra for Turnabout.

Maazel, Lorin (b. 1930). Born at Neuilly, France, of a Slav father and Dutch mother, Maazel was brought to the United States as a child, and studied the violin, piano and conducting with Vladimir Bakaleinikoff in Pittsburgh. Then followed an extraordinary career as a child prodigy; he made his debut as a conductor at the age of seven, with a programme of a Handel overture and Schubert's *Symphony No. 8*; in 1939 he led the New York Philharmonic Orchestra at Lewisohn Stadium, and between 1941 and 1945 he conducted most of the professional symphony orchestras in the US, with a repertoire of about 30 works. In 1941 Toscanini invited him to appear with the NBC Symphony Orchestra; after he had conducted Mozart's Symphony No. 40, Toscanini blessed him. In 1945 he made his debut in Pittsburgh as a violinist, and several years later he joined the Pittsburgh Symphony Orchestra as a violinist and assistant conductor. At the same time, he attended the University of Pittsburgh (1946) and became interested in mathematics and philosophy, but the conductor de Sabata convinced him that music was his true vocation. In 1951 Koussevitzky invited him to take part in the Tanglewood Festival, and in 1952 he was awarded a Fulbright scholarship and went to Rome to study baroque music. He returned to Italy in 1953 to conduct with many orchestras there, and, in his own words, learned the trade. After engagements throughout Europe, the US, Australia, *et al.*, his major appointments were as artistic director of the Deutsche Oper, West Berlin (1965–71), music director of the Berlin Radio Symphony Orchestra (1965–74), associate principal conductor of the New Philharmonia Orchestra (1970–72), music director of the Cleveland Orchestra, in succession to Szell (1971, until 1981), and principal guest conductor of the New Philharmonia Orchestra (1976), and the Orchestre National de France. He has conducted at La Scala, the New York Metropolitan and the Vienna State Operas, and was both the youngest conductor and the first American to conduct at Bayreuth, when he led *Lohengrin* in 1960. His first appearance as a mature conductor was in 1962 when he toured with the Orchestre National de France; since then he has regularly conducted the Philadelphia, Boston Symphony and New York Philharmonic Orchestras, and altogether has conducted almost 3,500 concerts in approximately 20 years, including every major orchestra in the world, has been on countless world tours, and while he was director of the Deutsche Oper in Berlin gave 300 performances of 20 operas.

Maazel is now one of the most distinguished conductors on the international scene. His repertoire extends from Bach to Stravinsky and includes about 40 operas, but his interest in modern music is confined to works which have an immediate impact on the listener. Since childhood he has been noted for his excellent aural memory – he always conducts without a score – and his sense of perfect pitch. Conducting presents no difficulties to him; orchestral players everywhere recognise him as having a superb baton technique, and he takes the greatest pains to achieve what he wants. His performances are polished and imaginative, and he has the ability to rouse the players of the most famous orchestras to high levels, although many may resent his methods and his approach to them. With baroque and classical music he is neat and precise, if not especially perceptive; his strength lies in larger romantic scores which require fine orchestral control and care for detail. In his musical personality there is a coolness and calculation that give his performances a clinical brilliance, but no sense of emotional involvement. He is seldom content to present the symphonies of Beethoven and Brahms, for instance, in a straightforward, literal way; having brought the orchestra to this level, he then imposes his 'interpretation', stressing particular details, introducing an unusual phrasing, colour or balance. Sometimes he would drive the music hard, as if ignorant of its lyricism or nobility. His performances are invariably arresting and novel, but cumulative tension and the inner meaning of the music are not so evident. He does not believe that any performance can be definitive: 'The greater the composer, the more flexible the possibilities.' In this way, he is somewhat reminiscent of the conductors of the pre-war years, especially Mengelberg; in fact, because of his experiences as a child prodigy, he sees himself as one of the few present conductors of his generation who knew the great musicians who were active then, and which were, in his opinion, superior to most of the present day. 'I have the advantage over many other conductors of my generation of having had direct contact with Reiner, de Sabata and Rodzinski. Through a fluke of circumstance, I represent a link between a kind of music-making that has all but vanished today.' More recently, his personality seems to have undergone a transformation, both in relation to orchestral players and in his concept of the music. As one concert-master has put it: 'Players see in him a constant struggle between the genius and the human being.' His performances have become less idiosyncratic exhibitions of orchestral technique and more authentic musical experiences.

The Cleveland Orchestra under Maazel has retained its place amongst American orchestras, but it is no longer the ensemble which excelled all its peers in its execution of the Viennese classics. To be fair, Maazel's strengths are in other directions; he has, for example, done much to persuade audiences in Paris and Vienna to accept Sibelius with his fine performances of the Finnish composer's symphonies, whose greatness became apparent to him through Barbirolli's interpretations with the Berlin Philharmonic Orchestra. Mahler and Bruckner are comparative late-comers to his repertoire, and he still has reservations about Mahler's Symphonies Nos 3 and 8. When he took over the Cleveland Orchestra after Szell, he worked to transform the customary concert programme of overture-concerto-symphony to something new, which brings the orchestra and the audience closer to the creative musician. He has programmed unusual music outside the regular subscription series, and part of the orchestra is allocated for a series of contemporary music. Other media have been introduced into concerts: poetry readings related to the music have been given at the end of concerts, and once dramatised selections from Beethoven's sketch books were presented. At first audiences, accustomed to the standard repertoire performed to perfection by Szell, drastically declined, but Maazel's new approach has created a new public. He also introduced performances of Beethoven's Symphony No. 9 and Mahler's Symphony No. 2 in which schoolchildren sang with the orchestra. He acknowledges the importance of performing contemporary music, for the sake of both the composers and the public, but says that he has not heard a really striking work for some time. Contemporary scores have been interesting, but no more. Records have helped him to come to terms with much modern music: 'I have bought many records of experimental contemporary music and they have made me very tolerant of sonorities at first rather shocking. One gets used to it little by little and is able to differentiate between composers. I listen especially to music I don't know, much baroque, oriental, Indian, and music from the Japanese Imperial Court, which is incredibly interesting.'

Maazel's first records were an impressive trio made with the Berlin Philharmonic Orchestra for DGG in 1958; they were of the *Romeo and Juliet* scores by Berlioz, Prokofiev and Tchaikovsky, or at least parts thereof. Then followed in the next few years, with the same orchestra, some brisk readings of Schubert's Symphonies Nos 2, 3, 4, 5, 6 and 8 and Mendelssohn's Symphonies Nos 4 and 5, Beethoven's Symphonies Nos 5 and 6, the overture *Die Weihe des Hauses* and twelve *Country Dances*, Brahms' Symphony No. 3 and *Tragic Overture*, Tchaikovsky's Symphony No. 4, *Pictures at an Exhibition*, *A Night on the Bare Mountain*, *Pini di Roma* and *Capriccio espagnol*. At this time he also recorded for DGG with the Berlin Radio Symphony Orchestra *L'Oiseau de feu* suite and *Le Chant du rossignol*, dances from *The Three-cornered Hat* and the Franck *Symphony in D minor*; of these the Stravinsky pieces, the Falla dances, *Pini di Roma* and the Franck symphony were especially successful. He also recorded the two Ravel one-act operas, *L'Heure espagnole* and *L'Enfant et les sortilèges*, *Peter and the Wolf* and Britten's *Young Person's Guide to the Orchestra*, with the French National Radio Orchestra *et al.*

In the mid 1960s Philips recorded Maazel with the Berlin Radio Symphony Orchestra *et al.* in a Bach series, which included the *Brandenburg Concertos*, the orchestral suites, the *Mass in B minor* and the *Easter Oratorio*. These performances were too variable to attract very favourable critical attention. Other works recorded by Philips were the *Water Music* and *Music for the Royal Fireworks*, Mozart's Symphonies Nos 40 and 41, Pergolesi's *Stabat Mater* and Dvořák's Symphony No. 9. He also made records with the same orchestra, for La Guilde Internationale du Disque, of Haydn's Symphonies Nos 92 and

103, Mozart's Symphonies Nos 25 and 29, Bruckner's Symphony No. 3, *L'Oiseau de feu*, excerpts from *The Sleeping Beauty* and Mahler's Symphony No. 4 (with Harper); the latter was issued by Turnabout.

For EMI Maazel has recorded *Boléro*, *Alborada del gracioso*, *Pavane pour une infante défunte*, and *La Valse*, the three Tchaikovsky Piano Concertos (with Gilels, and the New Philharmonia Orchestra), *Also sprach Zarathustra*, *Till Eulenspiegel*, *Prélude à l'après-midi d'un faune* and *Pictures at an Exhibition* (with the Philharmonia Orchestra) and Prokofiev's Piano Concerto No. 5 (with Richter and the London Symphony Orchestra). With Decca have been many of his major recording ventures: the complete Sibelius symphonies, with *Tapiola* and the *Karelia* suite, and the complete Tchaikovsky symphonies, with *Manfred* (all with the Vienna Philharmonic Orchestra), as well as the operas *Fidelio* (with the Vienna Philharmonic, *et al.*), *La traviata* (with the Berlin Deutsche Oper *et al.*) and *Tosca* (with the Santa Cecilia Orchestra *et al.*). The Sibelius and Tchaikovsky are both most noteworthy series, despite one or two lapses in some of the symphonies. His other recordings for Decca include Bruckner's Symphony No. 5, the Berlioz *Roméo et Juliette* symphony, *Don Quixote* (with Brabec), the suite *Le Bourgeois gentilhomme*, *Tod und Verklärung*, *Don Juan*, *Hamlet* and *Romeo and Juliet* fantasy-overture (with the Vienna Philharmonic Orchestra), *Pictures at an Exhibition*, Prokofiev's Piano Concerto No. 3 (with Israela Margalit, his wife), *Tod und Verklärung*, Massenet's *Thaïs*, and *Francesca da Rimini* (with the New Philharmonia Orchestra *et al.*), Tchaikovsky's Piano Concerto No. 1 (with Ashkenazy and the London Symphony Orchestra), and Scriabin's Piano Concerto and *Prometheus* (with Ashkenazy and the London Philharmonic Orchestra), the three *Leonore* and *Fidelio* overtures (with the Israel Philharmonic Orchestra). Since he has been at Cleveland, Decca have produced some remarkable recordings of him leading the orchestra: *Daphnis et Chloé*, a disc of ballet music from Verdi operas, the complete *Romeo and Juliet* ballet music of Prokofiev, a disc of Gershwin's orchestral music, Brahms' Symphony No. 1, Franck's *Symphony in D minor* and *Symphonic Variations* (with Roge), and the overtures *Prometheus*, *Le Carnaval romain*, *Academic Festival*, *Russlan and Ludmilla*, *La gazza ladra* and *La forza del destino*, and the first complete recording of *Porgy and Bess*. He has also appeared as a soloist on a disc of two Mozart Violin Concertos (with the English Chamber Orchestra, for Klavier, US); he also recorded excerpts from *Carmen* (with the Berlin Deutsche Oper for Ariola). In 1976 he signed a three-year contract with CBS and to the end of 1977 had recorded *Suor Angelica* and *Gianni Schicchi* (with the New Philharmonia and London Symphony Orchestras *et al.* respectively). Rococo have also issued a disc in which he accompanies Solomon in Brahms' Piano Concerto No. 1 (with the Italian Radio Orchestra).

Macal, Zdenek (b. 1936). Born in Brno, Czechoslovakia, Macal studied at the Conservatory there and later at the Janáček Academy of Musical Arts. Soon afterwards he was appointed principal conductor of the Prague Symphony Orchestra, and won international attention as prizewinner at the Conductors Competition at Besançon in 1965, and at the Dmitri Mitropoulos international Conductors' Competition in New York in 1966. He then toured Germany with the Czech Philharmonic Orchestra, and was invited to appear with the Berlin Philharmonic, BBC Symphony, Suisse Romande and Radio Italiana Rome Orchestras, as well as at many festivals. He became general music director of the Cologne Radio Symphony Orchestra (1970–74), and is now conductor of the Italian Radio and Television Orchestra, Milan; he made his United States debut in 1972, and has conducted many orchestras in Europe and the US. He has recorded for Supraphon with the Czech Philharmonic Orchestra the Dvořák Cello Concerto (with Thauer), Brahms' *Alto Rhapsody* (with Soukupová), Mozart's piano concertos K. 488 and K. 595 (with Štěpán) and the Suk *Fantastic Scherzo* and *Radúz and Mahulena*; for Decca, the original version of the Dvořák Piano Concerto (with Rigutto and the ORTF Orchestra); and for BASF Schoeck's *Penthesilea* (with the Cologne Radio Symphony Orchestra). He was awarded the 1973 Italia Prize for a television recording of works by Blacher, Ravel and Stravinsky with the Cologne Radio Symphony Orchestra, and in 1978 conducted the Philharmonic Orchestra in his own orchestration of *Pictures at an Exhibition*.

McArthur, Edwin (b. 1907). Born in Denver, Colorado, McArthur studied at the Juilliard School and privately with Josef and Rosina Lhevinne. He was an accompanist of some distinction, giving recitals with a number of singers, including Kirsten Flagstad, Elisabeth Rethberg, Ezio Pinza and Maria Jeritza; Flagstad stipulated that he should conduct orchestras with which she was engaged to perform, and as a result he led *Tristan und Isolde* at the

New York Metropolitan Opera with Flagstad in the 1940–41 season, although he failed to attract favourable attention as a conductor. After war service he became musical director of the St Louis Municipal Theatre Association (1945), has been conductor of the Harrisburg Symphony Orchestra, Pennsylvania, since 1950, and is head of the opera department of the Eastman School of Music. On 78 r.p.m. records McArthur conducted the San Francisco Symphony and RCA Victor Symphony Orchestras in excerpts from the Wagner operas with Flagstad and Melchior, and a mono LP was issued in which these two sang excerpts from *Lohengrin* and *Parsifal*; another disc of Wagner excerpts was issued by Orfeo Sonic, with Flagstad and the Symphony of the Air. Columbia also released a five-disc 78 r.p.m. set in which McArthur conducted excerpts from Kern's *Show Boat*.

McCarthy, John (b. 1919). Born in London and educated at St Edmund's College and Oratory School, McCarthy also studied under Seiber, was tenor soloist at Brompton Oratory, as well as a soloist in oratorio, opera and musical comedy. He was choral director for Beecham, Britten, Sargent, Boult, Muti, Giulini, Maazel, Previn *et al.*, has been choral director for numerous films and musicals, musical director at the Carmelite Church, Kensington, director of the Ambrosian Singers, Ambrosian Opera Chorus and St Anthony Singers, and professor at the Royal College of Music, and is a specialist in all early music. As a conductor in his own right he has recorded with the Carmelite Choir sacred music of Palestrina and Victoria, and a disc of Gregorian Chant (for L'Oiseau-Lyre), with the Ambrosian Singers music for Holy Week (for Everest), and with the Vienna Renaissance Players music by Machaut, Isaac, Senfl *et al.* (for Nonesuch).

McCauley, William (b. 1917). Born in Tofield, Alberta, Canada, McCauley started his musical career as a pianist, trombonist and arranger for dance bands; after service in the Royal Canadian Air Force in World War II he studied at the Toronto Conservatory and then graduated Doctor of Musical Arts from the Eastman School of Music. He played the trombone in the Ottawa Philharmonic Orchestra (1947–55), studied conducting with Monteux (1959), was director of music for Crawley Films (1949–60) and for Christopher Chapman Films (1969–70), director of music at York University (1960–69), conductor of North York Symphony Orchestra, and director of music at both Seneca College and the O'Keefe Center, Toronto. He has written and conducted music for over 150 documentary, television and full-length films, for which he has won many awards, and has composed a number of other works often with a specific Canadian theme. His recordings include choral music with his own choir (for Columbia), his *Saskatchewan Suite* (for Canadian Talent Library), his *Concerto Grosso for Brass Quintet and Symphony Orchestra* (for Canadian Broadcasting Corporation), and his *Five Miniatures for Flutes and Strings* (for Composers Recordings).

McCulloch, Derek (b. 1938). Born in Liverpool and educated at Durham University (1957–61), at Tübingen and at the Hochschule für Musik at Stuttgart, McCulloch was appointed to St George's Chapel at Windsor (1970). He translated a biography of Schütz, founded the Collegium Sagittarii (1967), and with the ensemble recorded a disc of cantatas by Schütz, Bernhard, Rosenmüller, Geist and Buxtehude (for Oryx), Monteverdi's *Magnificat* and Carissimi's *Jephte* (for Turnabout), and Schütz's *Christmas Story* and *St Matthew Passion* (for Argo).

McDonald, Harl (1899–1955). Born in Boulair, Colorado, McDonald learned the piano with his mother from the age of four, and at seven wrote his first composition. In his teens he played the horn with the Los Angeles Philharmonic Orchestra, then studied at the Universities of Southern California and Redlands, California, and at the Leipzig Conservatory. He lectured at the Académie Tournefort in Paris (1922), returned to the United States to appear as a pianist and as a conductor in Los Angeles, Philadelphia *et al.*, and also visited Europe as a pianist and conductor. He taught at the Philadelphia Music Academy and from 1927 at the University of Pennsylvania, where he was conductor of the university choral society and was head of the music department from 1931. From 1930 to 1933 he did research work in the measurement of musical and vocal tone, with a Rockefeller grant, which led to the publication of his *New Methods of Measuring Sound* (1935). In 1939 he was appointed business manager of the Philadelphia Orchestra.

McDonald's compositions include four symphonies, symphonic poems, choral and chamber music, and the suite for harp and orchestra, *From Childhood*, which he recorded on 78s with the Philadelphia Orchestra for RCA. His other recordings as a conductor were the *Magnificat* of C. P. E. Bach, and the Mozart *Requiem* (with the University of Pennsylvania Choral Society and the Philadelphia Orchestra *et al.*), a Catalonian *Mass for the Dead*, Palestrina's *O bone Jesu*, Casciolini's *Quaerite primum* and Arcadelt's *Ave Maria* (with the same choir for RCA), and his cantata *The Builders of America* and *Children's Symphony* (with the Columbia Symphony Orchestra *et al.* for Columbia). Stokowski also recorded his *Concerto for Two Pianos* (with Behrend and Kelberine), the Rhumba from the Symphony No. 2 and a dance from *Festival of the Workers* (with the Philadelphia Orchestra for RCA), Ormandy his Symphony No. 1 (*The Santa Fe Trail*) and *Two Hebraic Poems* (with the Philadelphia Orchestra for RCA) and Koussevitzky his *San Juan Capistrano* (with the Boston Symphony Orchestra for RCA), but now McDonald's music has completely disappeared from the catalogues.

Mackenzie, Sir Alexander (1847–1935). Born in London, Mackenzie studied at the Sonderhausen Conservatory (1857–62), studied under Sainton, Jewson and Lucas at the Royal Academy of Music (1862), and was a teacher, conductor and violinist in Edinburgh (1865–79). He conducted Novello's Oratorio Concerts in London (1885–7), was principal of the Royal Academy of Music (1888–1924), conductor of the Philharmonic Society, and was general president of the International Music Society (1908–12). He conducted the London premières of Tchaikovsky's Symphony No. 6 and Borodin's Symphony No. 2, and toured Canada in 1903. He spent some years in Florence to give his time to composing (1879–88), and his numerous works included seven operas, and many orchestral, choral, vocal and instrumental pieces, but all are virtually forgotten today. Of his music he recorded the *Britannia* overture and the overture to *The Little Minister* (with the New Queen's Hall Orchestra for Columbia), Under the Clock from *London Day by Day*, the saltarello from *Colomba* and the overture to *Cricket on the Hearth* (with an orchestra for HMV).

Mackerras, Sir Charles (b. 1925). Although a fifth-generation Australian, Mackerras was born in Schenectady, New York, but was educated at the New South Wales Conservatorium of Music in Sydney. He played the oboe in cinema and theatre orchestras, then was principal oboe with the Sydney Symphony Orchestra (1943–6). In 1947 he won a British Council scholarship and studied under Talich at the Prague Academy of Music; this experience made him one of the finest conductors of Czech music, particularly Janáček's operas, outside Czechoslovakia. He was a conductor at the Sadler's Wells Opera (1948–53), principal conductor of the BBC Concert Orchestra (1954–6), freelance conductor with most British orchestras, as well as a frequent conductor for radio and television (1957–66), first conductor of the Hamburg Opera (1966–9), music director of the English National Opera (formerly the Sadler's Wells Opera; from 1970), and chief guest conductor of the BBC Symphony Orchestra. He has made many tours to conduct concert and opera in Scandinavia, FR Germany, Italy, Czechoslovakia, Romania, Hungary, the United States, the USSR, Belgium, Holland, South Africa, Canada and Australia, where he conducted the opening concert at the Sydney Opera House in 1973. He has arranged music from the Gilbert and Sullivan operas in a successful ballet suite, *Pineapple Poll* (1951), and also music from the Verdi operas, in *The Lady and the Fool*. He was awarded the CBE in 1974 and was knighted in 1979.

Mackerras is a widely experienced and versatile conductor, and although he resists the tendency to mark him off as a specialist, he is nonetheless noted for his performances of baroque music, as well as an operatic conductor. He was a pioneer in the authentic performance of baroque music, particularly of Handel and Bach, and his performance of *Le nozze di Figaro* at Sadler's Wells in 1966 was exceptional in the introduction of ornamentation in the arias. But he finds it disappointing that he has not been able to record the Mozart operas in performances of authentic style, despite the record companies' interest in recording baroque music with authentic instruments: 'Because Mozart was a much greater composer than his contemporaries doesn't mean that he should be treated any differently. I add ornaments and appoggiaturas in the voice parts and slightly crisper rhythms in the orchestra, short notes rather than long ones . . . which are all the features of baroque and early classical style.' His interest in the Janáček operas was fired when he studied *Káťa Kabanová* with Talich in Prague; he introduced the opera to Britain when he returned from Czechoslovakia in 1951, went on to give first performances in Britain of *The Makropoulos Affair* (1964) and *From the House of the Dead* (1965), led *The Cunning Little Vixen* at Sadler's Wells and a broadcast performance of *The Excursions of Mr Brouček* (1970), a new production of *Káťa Kabanová* in his own edition (1973), and then *Jenufa* at Covent Garden (1974). He has also conducted most of Janáček's operas in the composer's home town of Brno, and in 1977 his recording of *Káťa Kabanová* was issued by Decca, with the promise of a complete series of the operas if it proved commercially successful. Because Janáček's instructions for the performance of his music were not absolutely clear, and sometimes contradictory, Mackerras has re-edited *Káťa Kabanová* and *The Makropoulos Affair*, and has attempted to determine as near as possible the composer's intentions. This care in preparing his operatic performances is typical; he visited Shostakovich to discuss *Katerina Ismailova* before conducting the work at Covent Garden, and similarly took great pains with his production of *Billy Budd*. The English National Opera has flourished under his direction, and with that company he has emerged as a major conductor of the Wagner operas. He also confesses a special fondness for Verdi. He has a liking for recording, and has a wide knowledge of recorded performances, going back to the 78 r.p.m. sets with which he became familiar in his years in Australia. Until the end of 1977 he has had virtually no opportunity to record opera except for some excerpts from Wagner.

The first recording Mackerras made was in 1952 for EMI, and was a 78 r.p.m. set of *Pineapple Poll*; it was with the Sadler's Wells Orchestra and was later released on a mono LP; ten years later he recorded the piece on stereo again with the Royal Philharmonic Orchestra. EMI then recorded him with the Philharmonia Orchestra in mono LPs of ballet music and shorter popular works, such as music by Eric Coates, Verdi overtures, and suites by Delibes and Messager. On the 200th anniversary of Handel's death in 1959, he recorded for Pye the *Music for the Royal Fireworks*, with its original wind scoring of 24 oboes, twelve bassoons and contra-bassoons, nine horns, nine trumpets, side drums and three pairs of kettle drums. The recording itself had to be done at midnight when all these instrumentalists were available in London, and the record, which was coupled with a Double Concerto of Handel, became a best seller. For Pye he also recorded Janáček's *Sinfonietta*, which itself is scored for twelve trumpets, the preludes to *From the House of the Dead*, *Jenůfa*, *Káťa Kabanová* and *The Makropoulos Affair*, Mozart's *Les petits riens*, Divertimento, K. 113, Two Minuets K. 604, Two Marches K. 408 and Six German Dances K. 600, the overtures to *The Bartered Bride*, *Don Pasquale* and *La Fille du régiment*, the Polka and Fugue from *Schwanda* and dances from *The Three-cornered Hat* (with the Pro Arte Orchestra). In 1967 he recorded, with great vitality and perception, a revolutionary performance of *Messiah* (with the English Chamber Orchestra *et al.* for EMI), using Basil Lam's edition, which purported to be the kind of performance Handel himself directed, and which added ornamentations and appoggiaturas, authentic bowing and phrasing. A year earlier, L'Oiseau Lyre had issued Purcell's *The Indian Queen* (with the English Chamber Orchestra *et al.*), and later DGG put out Purcell's *Dido and Aeneas*, in a performance he had conducted at Hamburg. DGG also released Purcell's *Ode on St Cecilia's Day*, Handel's *Israel in Egypt* and *Saul*, and Mozart's arrangement of *Messiah*, a curious contrast with the Lam edition recorded earlier. The *Israel in Egypt* and *Saul* were recorded with the English Chamber Orchestra at the Leeds Triennial Festival; the Handel/Mozart *Messiah* was a performance recorded in Vienna with the Austrian Radio Orchestra *et al.* He also recorded an *Orfeo ed Euridice* of Gluck for Vanguard, with the Vienna State Opera Orchestra *et al.*

Mackerras' other recordings include Voříšek's *Symphony in D* and Dvořák's *Czech Suite* (with the English Chamber Orchestra for Philips), a suite from Rameau's *Castor et Pollux*, the ballet music from *Orfeo ed Euridice*, overtures by Strauss, Nicolai, Thomas and Suppé and other popular pieces (with the London Symphony Orchestra for Philips), Brahms' Symphony No. 1, Tchaikovsky's Symphonies Nos 4 and 6 and Dvořák's Symphony No. 8 (with the Hamburg Philharmonic Orchestra, for Checkmate and other labels), two violin concertos of Viotti (with Röhn and the English Chamber Orchestra for DGG), the Mozart Symphonies Nos 36, 38, 40 and 41, *Don Juan* and *Till Eulenspiegel*, and excerpts from *Götterdämmerung* (with the London Philharmonic Orchestra *et al.* for Classics for Pleasure), *Káťa Kabanová* (with the Vienna Philharmonic Orchestra *et al.* for Decca), *Petrushka* (with the London Symphony Orchestra for Vanguard), *Pictures at an Exhibition* and the prelude to *Khovanshchina* (with the New Philharmonia Orchestra for Vanguard), Mozart concert arias (with von Stade and the Bavarian Radio Symphony Orchestra for DGG), the Australian Sitsky's Concerto for Woodwind Quartet and Orchestra (with the New Sydney Woodwind Quartet and the Sydney Symphony Orchestra for World Record Club), a re-run of his earlier success, the *Music for the Royal Fireworks*, coupled with *Concertos in F* and *D*, and *Concerto No. 2 a due Cori* (with the London Symphony Orchestra *et al.* for EMI), the Saint-Saëns Cello Concerto No. 1, Lalo's Cello Concerto and Fauré's *Élégie* (with Schiff and the New Philharmonia Orchestra for DGG), and the ballet suites *Les deux Pigeons* and *La Source* (with the Covent Garden Orchestra for EMI).

McKie, Sir William (b. 1901). Born in Melbourne, Australia, McKie studied at the Royal College of Music, London, and Worcester College, Oxford. He was city organist at Melbourne (1931–8), organist at Magdalen College, Oxford (1938–41), served with the Royal Air Force (1941–5), was organist and Master of the Choristers, Westminster Abbey (1941–63), and director of music at the coronation of Queen Elizabeth II (1953). EMI issued a record of him directing the Abbey Choir in Handel's *Zadok the Priest*, at the coronation service itself; with the Choir he also recorded anthems and sacred music by Gibbons, Purcell, Tye, Humfrey, Walmisley and Kirbye (for Columbia) and Holst's *Lullay, My Liking* and *In the Bleak Mid-Winter* (for HMV).

Maclean, Alick (1872–1936). Born in Eton, where he was educated, Maclean had written several operas before he was 22. He became known as both conductor and composer, and in 1895 won the Moody-Manners prize for his one-act opera *Petruccio*. He was conductor with Sir Charles Wyndham (1899), of the Scarborough Spa Company (1911) and the Queen's Hall Light Orchestra (1915–23). His compositions included altogether six operas. He recorded first in 1918 for HMV with the New Queen's Hall Orchestra Luigini's *Ballet égyptien*, the *Faust* ballet music, the overture to *Orphée aux enfers*, Coates' *Miniature Suite* and pieces by Fletcher, and later with the New Queen's Hall Light Orchestra Coates' *Summer Days* Suite, the Bacchanale from Glazunov's *The Seasons*, Haydn-Wood's *Variations on If You Want to Know the Time*, and Luigini's *Ballet russe*, and with the New Queen's Hall Orchestra two of de Greef's *Four Flemish Songs*. For Columbia he also recorded with the New Queen's Hall Orchestra Coleridge-Taylor's *Petite suite de concert* (in 1920 and again on an electrical recording in 1926) and ballet music from *Hiawatha*, dances from German's *Henry VIII*, *Nell Gwynne* and *Tom Jones*, Quilter's *Children's Overture*, the *Peer Gynt* Suite No. 1, Rosse's suite *The Merchant of Venice*, and discs of orchestral arrangements of some popular operas.

MacMillan, Sir Ernest (1893–1973). A Canadian of Scottish descent, MacMillan was born in Mimico, Ontario, went to Britain and became an Associate of the Royal College of Organists (1913), then a Fellow, and gained a B.Mus. at Oxford University at the age of 17. He studied at the Edinburgh University under Hollens and Niecks, and then read modern history at the Toronto University. He went to Paris in 1914, but while attending the Bayreuth Festival was interned in Ruhleben in Germany for the duration of the war; during his imprisonment he was awarded the degree Doctor of Music *in absentia* from Oxford, for his arrangement of Swinburne's ode, *England*. After returning to Canada after the war, he toured as an organist, and was appointed principal of the Toronto Conservatory of Music (1926–42), later becoming dean of the faculty of music at Toronto University (1927–52). In 1931 he was appointed conductor of the Toronto Symphony Orchestra, and remained there until his retirement in 1956; from 1942 to 1957 he was conductor of the Mendelssohn Choir at Toronto, was guest conductor with a number of major orchestras in the United States, Britain, Brazil and Australia, and was knighted in 1935. He composed choral and chamber music, and edited books of Canadian folk songs. MacMillan was the foremost Canadian conductor and musician of his time, and during his tenure with the Toronto Symphony Orchestra it became one of the finest ensembles in North America.

With the Toronto Symphony Orchestra, MacMillan made some fine 78 r.p.m. sets for HMV-Victor, but they never received wide international circulation. They were *The Planets*, *Pomp and Circumstance Marches Nos 1* to *4*, Jacob's arrangement of pieces from the *Fitzwilliam Virginal Book* of Byrd, and an arrangement for string orchestra of the serenade from Haydn's String Quartet Op. 3 No. 3. Later, in the 1950s, he recorded for several Canadian companies: the *St Matthew Passion*, Handel's *Messiah* and *Chandos Anthem No. 2*, Mozart's *Exsultate jubilate* and Tchaikovsky's Symphony No. 5 (with the Toronto Symphony Orchestra *et al.* for Beaver), Handel's *Coronation Anthem No. 2* and a suite from the *Water Music* (with the CBC Symphony Orchestra *et al.* for Beaver), and Elwell's *Pastorale* (with Lois Marshall, who appeared in some of the recordings above, and the Toronto Symphony Orchestra for Hallmark).

McPhee, George (b. 1937). Born in Glasgow, and educated at the Royal Scottish Academy of Music and Edinburgh University, McPhee has been a lecturer at the Academy, organist and choirmaster at Paisley Abbey (since 1963) and conductor of the Scottish Chamber Choir. His recordings with the Choir include Monteverdi's *Missa in illo tempore* and Schütz's *Deutsches Magnificat* (for Decca).

Maderna, Bruno (1920–73). Born in Venice, Maderna studied at the Milan Conservatory, at the Accademia Chigiana in Siena and at the Accademia di Santa Cecilia in Rome, and was a conducting pupil of Molinari, Guarnieri and Scherchen. He took up residence at Darmstadt in FR Germany in 1951 and became a naturalised German citizen in 1963. At Darmstadt he was active with summer courses and seminars, and in 1961 founded and conducted the Darmstadt International Chamber Ensemble. He was also associated with the electronic music studio of the Milan Radio since its foundation in 1955. He was a highly accomplished conductor, and toured internationally; his compositions were initially influenced by Bartók and Stravinsky, but after his arrival in Germany he turned to twelve-tone techniques and to electronic sounds which were combined with live performances. Of all his compositions, the critic William Mann considers his Oboe Concerto No. 3 as probably Maderna's most substantial claim to be considered a great composer.

Maderna specialised in performing contemporary music, but his fate was described by Maazel, the conductor, who had first met Maderna in Turin in the late 1950s. Maderna then said to him: 'You're a young man confirmed in the bourgeois practice of doing repertoire pieces. It's your duty to perform Luigi Nono.' Maazel then asked him what modern works of significance he thought had been written; Maderna thought and said: 'Schoenberg's *Music for an Imaginary Film*.' In the late 1960s, Maazel came across Maderna again at Cologne, where he was conducting Strauss's *Salome*. 'Why are you performing this dreadful work?' he asked; Maderna replied: 'Because I have to earn a living.' Six months before his death, Maderna confided to Maazel that he had given 1,500 first performances of works by every imaginable composer. 'When I look back', he said, 'it's like a desert. None of it changed me.' He then admitted that there was one thing which would make him happy, 'to conduct *Don Giovanni*'. He apparently achieved his wish, and must have died a happy man.

Maderna made records of contemporary music with his Darmstadt ensemble, including Ligeti's *Adventures* and *More Adventures* (for DGG) and Clementi's *Triplum*, Kotoński's *Canto for Eighteen Instruments* and Schoenberg's *Three Little Orchestral Pieces* (released by Mainstream, US). His other discs include Nono's *Polifonica*, *Monodia* and *Ritmica* and his own Serenade No. 2 (with the English Chamber Orchestra for Time), Schoenberg's Serenade Op. 24 (with John Carol Case and the Melos Ensemble for L'Oiseau Lyre), Brown's *Available Forms 1*, Pousseur's *Rimes pour différentes sources sonores*, Stockhausen's *Kontra-Punkte* and Penderecki's *Threnody for the Victims of Hiroshima*, his own Oboe Concerto (with Faber), Berio's Serenade No. 1, Fukushima's *Hi-Kyo*, Lehmann's *Quanti 1*, and Nono's *Epitaffio per Garcia Lorca*, Part 2 (with Gazzelloni, and the Rome Symphony Orchestra, issued by RCA in the US), Stockhausen's *Gruppen* and *Carré* (with other conductors Gielen, Kagel and Makowski, and the Cologne Radio Symphony Orchestra, for DGG), Bartók's *The Miraculous Mandarin* and *Dance Suite* (with the Monte Carlo National Orchestra for La Guilde Internationale du Disque), the Bartók Piano Concerto No. 3 and the Prokofiev Piano Concerto No. 3 (with Helffer and the Monte Carlo National Orchestra for La Guilde Internationale du Disque), Bakfark's *Fantaisie No. 1* (with Gazzelloni and the South-West German Radio Symphony Orchestra for Wergo), Hermanson's *In nuce* (with the South-West German Radio Symphony Orchestra for Discophil), Barren's Piano Concerto and Vlijmen's Serenata I (with the Amsterdam Concertgebouw Orchestra for Donemus) and Straesser's *22 Pages* and Vlijmen's Serenata II (with the Netherland's Radio Philharmonic Orchestra *et al.* for Donemus). In 1975 a set of two records was issued posthumously by Telefunken, of a concert conducted by Maderna at the 1973 Salzburg Festival, with the Vienna Radio Orchestra; the works were Messiaen's *Et exspecto resurrectionem mortuorum*, Stravinsky's *Canticum sacrum*, Boulez's *e. e. cummings ist der Dichter* and Lutosławski's *Trois Poèmes d'Henri Michaux*.

By way of contrast, Maderna also recorded Torelli's Symphonies G. 11, G. 20, G. 26 and G. 36, and Concerti Grossi Op. 8 Nos 1, 3, 7 and 9, in Santi's edition (with the Angelicum Orchestra for Angelicum).

Maes, Georges (1914–76). Born in Ostend, Maes studied at the University of Ghent, was a violin pupil of Zimmer and Jacobsen in Brussels, and studied conducting with de Sutter. He was a violinist in the Ghent orchestra (1935–7), the Ghent Royal Opera (1935–41), the de Groote String Quartet (1940–45), and in the Belgian National Orchestra (1945–59), founded and was leader of the Haydn String Quartet (1945–58), was a professor at the Royal Conservatory at Brussels (1957–70) and at the Royal Conservatory at Ghent (1970–76), director of the Ostend Conservatory (1960–76), a professor at the Chapelle Royale Reine Élisabeth (1975), and founded and conducted the Belgian Chamber Orchestra (1958–76). With the Belgian Chamber Orchestra in particular he gave many concerts in Western and Eastern Europe, with a repertoire from Bach to Stravinsky and including many Belgian composers. He recorded Loeillet's *Divertimento in B major*, Bréhy's Sonata for Oboe and Strings, Poot's *Muziek voor Snaren*, Chevreuille's *Récréation de midi*, Van Rossum's *Sinfonietta*, Cabus' *Concerto Grosso*, Fontyn's *Mouvements concertants* (with Marcelle and Birguer) and Kersters' *Suite in the form of a French Overture* (with the Belgian Chamber Orchestra for Alpha), four Vivaldi concertos, and pieces by Bach, Haydn, Mozart, Fiocco, Debussy and de Meester (with the Belgian Chamber Orchestra for Decca).

Mága, Othmar (b. 1929). Born in Brno, Mága studied at the Hochschule für Musik at Stuttgart (1948–52) and at Tübingen University (1952–8), and was a pupil of van Kempen at the Accademia Chigiana at Siena (1954–5), and of Celibidache (1960–62). He was conductor of the Göttingen Symphony Orchestra (1963–7), of the Nuremberg Symphony Orchestra (1968–70) and in 1971 was appointed general music director at Bochum. He has been a guest conductor with many major European orchestras, toured Japan with NHK Symphony Orchestra, has taken part in the summer Collegium Musicum at Schloss Weissenstein and teaches conducting at the Folkwangschule at Essen. He has recorded Bach's Suite No. 2 and Harpsichord Concerto No. 1 (with Zartner) and the Beethoven Triple Concerto (with von der Golz, Polacek and Hjort, and the Nuremberg Symphony Orchestra for Audio Fidelity), the Mozart Two-Piano Concerto K. 365, the Poulenc Piano Concerto (with Bung and Bauer), Berg's *Lulu* Suite, Handel's *Music for the Royal Fireworks*, the two Weber symphonies, Glazunov's *The Seasons* and Tcherepnin's *Abyss* (with the Nuremberg Symphony Orchestra for Colosseum), Borodin's Symphony No. 2 and *In the Steppes of Central Asia*, the Nielsen Clarinet and Flute Concertos (with Deak and Pázmandi, respectively), the Piano Concerto No. 4 of Rubinstein and the Piano Concertos of Moscheles and Henselt (with Ponti and the Philharmonia Hungarica, for Turnabout and Candide), J. C. Bach's Sinfonias Op. 6 No. 1 and Op. 9 No. 1 and the Beethoven Violin Concerto (with Klepper, and the South German Philharmonic Orchestra for BASF), the Dvořák Violin Concerto (with Metzger and the Nuremberg Symphony Orchestra for Intercord), Válek's Violin Concerto (with David and the Prague Symphony Orchestra for Supraphon), Glazunov's *Scènes de ballet* (with the Bochum Symphony Orchestra for Vox, coupled with *The Seasons*, above) and Tchaikovsky's *The Tempest* (with the Bochum Symphony Orchestra for Da Camera).

Maghini, Ruggero (b. 1913). Born at Sesto Calende, Varese, Maghini studied at the Parma and Turin Conservatories and at the Salzburg Mozarteum, has conducted the string orchestra and choir of the Italian Radio at Turin, and has given solo concerts as pianist and organist. He has recorded J. C. Bach's *Dies Irae*, Fiorini's *Dies venit exspectata*, Mozart's *Exsultate jubilate* (with Rizzoli), Sarti's *Regina Coeli*, and Stradella's Trumpet Sonata (with Battagliola) and *Cantata per il S. S. Natale* (with the Milan Angelicum Orchestra *et al.* for Angelicum), and Cilea's *L'Arlesiana* (with the Turin Radio Orchestra *et al.* for OLPC).

Mahler, Fritz (1901–73). Born in Vienna, and the nephew of Gustav Mahler, Fritz Mahler was educated at the University of Vienna and at the Vienna Academy of Music, and studied composition with Schoenberg, Berg and Webern, and conducting with Reichwein. He conducted in opera houses in Mannheim, Berlin and Vienna, and was conductor of the Copenhagen Symphony Orchestra (1930–35). After migrating to the United States he became musical director of the Philadelphia La Scala Opera (1937–40), taught at the Juilliard School (1939–50), was conductor of the Erie Philharmonic Orchestra, Pennsylvania (1947–52) and the Hartford Symphony Orchestra (1953–64), also conducting in Poland, Japan, Korea and other countries, specialising in the music of his uncle. He made a number of LP discs with the Hartford Symphony Orchestra *et al.* including the *Hungarian Dances* of Brahms (for Decca, US), *Eine kleine Nachtmusik* and a Vivaldi Concerto (for Spoken Arts), Mahler's *Das klagende Lied*, Berlioz' *Grande Messe des morts*, the ballet suites arranged by Mottl from music by Rameau, Grétry and Gluck, suites from Purcell's *Abdelazer*, *The Married Beau*, *The Gordian Knot Untied* and *The Virtuous Wife*, Orff's *Carmina Burana*, Bloch's *Three Jewish Poems for Orchestra* and Copland's *Orchestral Variations* (for Vanguard).

Mahler, Gustav (1860–1911). 'Toscanini was the greatest conductor of his generation, but Mahler was a hundred times greater,' said Klemperer. Today the popularity of Mahler the composer has obscured the fact that he was one of the most remarkable conductors ever, and that he had a profound impact on artistic standards and on opera production. He composed the symphonies and other works in his summer holidays. His career as a conductor began in Bad Hall in Upper Austria (1880); he went on to Ljubjlana (1881), Olmutz, Vienna, Kassel, Prague, Leipzig and Budapest Opera (1888–90), by when his greatness had come to be recognised. He was then at the Hamburg Opera (1891–7), at the Vienna Court Opera (1897–1907) and finally with the New York Metropolitan Opera and the New York Philharmonic Orchestra (1907–11). He was primarily a conductor of opera; the New York Philharmonic was the first and last orchestra of which he was musical director, although he did conduct symphony concerts throughout his career.

Accounts of Mahler the conductor vary, and some are contradictory: Klemperer said that his tempi were very strict in the classics, but Schoenberg wrote (in *The Great Conductors*), presumably on good authority, that his 'rubatos, speed ups and slow downs would today be received with sheer incredulity'. He most certainly astonished both audiences and critics with his unconventional interpretations, which contrasted with the usual readings of the day in their selection of tempi and their intensity and dramatic expression, and also for the liberties he took in altering the scoring of many works. There was absolutely nothing routine in any of his performances; in each he entered the mind and world of the composer, and his precision and clarity were comparable to Toscanini's. But to him precision was not an end in itself; as Walter pointed out, 'With him, precision was a means toward bringing the soul of the work to life,' and Mahler himself insisted that 'the best in music is not set down in the notes'. It was Klemperer's conviction that Mahler's interpretations were never in dispute: 'When he conducted, you felt it could not be better and it couldn't be otherwise,' but many contemporary critics would not have agreed with him.

Mahler's rehearsals were exacting and exhausting. He terrified orchestral players and singers alike with his demands and his tantrums, stamping his feet and waving his baton when dissatisfied, and upbraiding the weaker players. He lost favour and was disliked by orchestral musicians in both Vienna and New York for his behaviour towards them, even though he was motivated by the highest artistic standards, and strove unceasingly to impose them on his players. His beat was less then perfect, but it was the expressiveness of his eyes and hands that conveyed his meaning, especially his eyes, which had an extraordinary effect on the musicians; some could not play at all under the intensity of his gaze, but with most he could achieve any nuance he required. At the beginning of his career his movements on the podium were very pronounced, but in his last years, when the heart disease that was to cause his death became apparent, his movements grew restrained and simplified. Like Strauss, he always conducted with the score in front of him.

Many of Mahler's readings caused a furore, since they were so different to the conventional ones of the day. The slow tempo of the *andante* of Beethoven's Symphony No. 6 astounded audiences in Hamburg and Vienna. His *Tristan und Isolde* was a revelation and was described as 'feverish and delirious', and generally his tempi in Wagner were novel. Although he demanded complete faithfulness to the score, he did not hesitate to retouch the Beethoven symphonies, doubling the woodwind and having additional kettledrums in No. 6, reducing the strings and doubling the flutes in Mozart's Symphony No. 40, re-orchestrating the Schumann symphonies, adding instruments to *Don Juan*, once shortening Tchaikovsky's *Francesca da Rimini* almost by half, and cutting Bruckner; he once called the Bruckner Symphony No. 4 'musical junk' with the 'worst kind of absurdities', even though 'it had divine ideas and themes'. He arranged the Beethoven String Quartet Op. 95 for full string orchestra, and was tempted to re-score Brahms' Symphony No. 3. His influence on opera production and performance was lasting: he demanded that all soloists, no matter how eminent, attend all rehearsals, allowed no deputies in the orchestras at rehearsals, eliminated spurious top notes and cadenzas inserted into Mozart arias, tried (unsuccessfully) to abolish the claque, dimmed the lights before the curtain rose, shut out latecomers, and himself supervised every detail of the production and performance. He preferred singers able to act, to those with excellent voices but unable to bring dramatic life to their roles. He sought simplified stage scenes, in contrast to the extravagant and romantic realism of the day. In Mozart, he restored the recitatives with the harpsichord. He is usually held responsible for introducing the practice of performing the *Leonore No. 3* overture between the two scenes in Act II of *Fidelio*, but it appears that this was first done by Mottl at Karlsruhe. He performed Wagner without cuts; his *Die Walküre* was played as if it were chamber music.

According to his wife, Alma Mahler, Mahler 'performed a great deal of music merely to hear it himself and to get to know it, without bothering whether it went down with the public'. In New York, his programmes in the seasons

1909–10 and 1910–11 contained much Beethoven and Wagner, symphonies by Mendelssohn, Schumann, Berlioz, Brahms, Bruckner and Tchaikovsky, his own Symphonies Nos 1 and 4 and *Kindertotenlieder*, and symphonic poems of Strauss and Liszt; the modern composers of the day, Busoni, Sibelius, Debussy, Enesco, Pfitzner, Martucci, and Rachmaninov were presented, as were the American composers Chadwick, Hadley and MacDowell, as well as Elgar's *Enigma Variations* and Stanford's *Irish Symphony*.

Mahler made a recording, but not as a conductor: in 1905 he recorded extracts from his Symphony No. 4 in a piano arrangement which was transferred to a piano roll. Telefunken issued them on an LP record in 1962, and it is still available in FR Germany. How he conducted his music can scarcely be judged by the later recorded performances of his works by his young disciples, Klemperer, Walter, Mengelberg and Fried, as they all differ as much as their performances of other music differ. In 1904 at a concert in Amsterdam, Mahler conducted his Symphony No. 4 in the first half of the programme, and Mengelberg led a performance of the same symphony in the second half, but the LP of the symphony by Mengelberg issued by Turnabout from a performance about 40 years later could scarcely reveal anything about the original Mahler interpretation. Walter wrote that the decisive quality of Mahler's conducting and the source of his power 'was the warmth of his heart'; this is evident in all his music, and it seems inevitable that his performances of his own music shone with the same spirit.

Maier, Franzjosef (b. 1925). Born in Menningen, Germany, into a family with a long musical tradition, Maier as a boy learned the piano, violin, viola and later the oboe, and at 13 was a pupil at the Augsburg Conservatory. He went on to study at the Academy of Music at Munich and at the Music Gymnasium at Frankfurt am Main, where he was a violin student of Isselmann and studied composition with Thomas. At 17 he gave his first solo recital, at Munich, and was soloist with the Reichs Symphony Orchestra on a tour in Germany. His string quartet was performed at Frankfurt, and after his graduation he lectured at the Landesmusikschule at Saarbrücken. During war service in the German army he was wounded and taken prisoner-of-war; after the war he studied at the Hochschule für Musik at Cologne, was one of the founders of the Collegium Musicum of the West German Radio at Cologne, and performed with the Schäffer Quartet and the Schubert Trio. He lectured at the Robert Schumann Conservatory at Düsseldorf (1949), became a professor and chairman of the violin master classes at the Hochschule für Musik at Cologne (1959), participated in many first performances of contemporary chamber works, and developed an interest in the performance of baroque and early classical music with original instruments. This led to him being the co-founder of the Collegium Aureum in the early 1960s, which is an independent association of professors of different conservatories in Germany, as well as soloists and leaders from the great German orchestras; Maier is the concertmaster and conductor. The ensemble has many conformations of instruments, according to the work being performed, and the performances are on original instruments in the original style of the respective period: the stringed instruments have narrow scaling and catgut strings, and are played with light bows. Most are instruments of the 17th and 18th centuries. The wind instruments are originals or accurate copies. In 1970 Maier also became the leader of the new quartet of the Collegium Aureum.

The Collegium Aureum, under Maier's leadership, has made a number of superlatively performed and fascinating recordings, and in many he has been the violin soloist. Included are a suite from Campra's *Les Fêtes vénitiennes*, Leclair's Violin Concerto Op. 7 No. 2, a suite from Lully's *Amadis*, a collection of dance music by Moderne, Susato, Gervaise *et al.*, Albinoni's *Sinfonia e concerti a cinque*, Op. 2, Locatelli's *Concerto a quattro in F*, a Vivaldi Violin Concerto, hymns, choruses and songs by Dufay, sacred and secular music of Dunstable, Bach's Suites, *Brandenburg Concertos*, Harpsichord Concerto No. 1 (with Leonhardt) and excerpts from Cantatas Nos 202, 209, 211 and 212 (with Ameling, Peters, Nimsgern and English), Handel's Concerti Grossi Opp. 3 and 6, *Alexander's Feast*, *Water Music*, *Music for the Royal Fireworks*, *Concerto in F major* and Organ Concertos (with Ewerhart), J. C. Bach's Symphonies Op. 6 No. 6 and Op. 18 No. 4, and Sinfonia Concertante, C. P. E. Bach's four *Hamburg Symphonies*, *Harpsichord Concerto in D minor* (with Leonhardt), *Oboe Concerto in E Major* (with Hucke), Cello Concerto No. 2 (with May) and Two-Harpsichord Concerto (with Leonhardt and Curtis), Pergolesi's *La serva padrona*, Haydn's Symphonies Nos 85 and 87, *Piano Concerto in D major* (with Demus), Violin Concerto No. 1, *Horn Concerto in D major* (with Penzel) and Flute Concerto (with Linde), Mozart's Symphonies Nos 33 and 40, Divertimentos K. 205, K. 247, K. 251 and K. 287, Serenades K. 250, K. 320,

K. 375 and K. 388, *Eine kleine Nachtmusik*, Piano Concertos K. 246, K. 414, K. 467, K. 488, K. 537 and K. 595 (with Demus), Horn Concerto K. 447 (with Crüts), Clarinet Concerto (with Deinzer), Rondo K. 373, Mass K. 317, *Requiem* and *Vesperae solennes de confessore*, Beethoven's Symphony No. 3, Piano Concerto No. 4 (with Badura-Skoda) and Triple Concerto (with Maier, Bylsma and Badura-Skoda). These records were issued, variously, by Harmonia Mundi and BASF; some were released in the United States by RCA on the Victrola label.

Mainardi, Enrico (b. 1897). Born in Milan where he studied the cello under Magnini at the conservatory, Mainardi continued his studies with Becker in Berlin, and made his debut as a cellist in Milan in 1909. He performed throughout Europe as a soloist and chamber player, and became a teacher at the Accademia di Santa Cecilia in Rome in 1932, and later at the Salzburg Mozarteum and the Lucerne Conservatory. He has composed orchestral, chamber and vocal music, has made many records as a cellist, and has also appeared as a conductor. Mace issued an LP on which he conducts the Vienna Volksoper Orchestra in Boccherini's *Cello Concerto in B flat* and his arrangement of a *Largo* for cello (himself the soloist), Geminiani's Concerto Grosso Op. 3 No. 2 and Vivaldi's *Concerto in C.*

Maksymiuk, Jerzy (b. 1936). The Polish conductor Maksymiuk studied with Madey at the Warsaw Conservatory; originally a composition student, he took conducting lessons to perform one of his own works, and from then devoted his entire time to conducting. He has been a prize winner in the Fitelberg and Malawski composition competitions and the Paderewski piano competition, received the Polish Prime Minister's award for composition in 1973, and in that year conducted his ballet *Metaphrases* at a festival at Essen. He became conductor of the Polish National Radio Symphony Orchestra in Katowice; in 1972 he formed the Polish Chamber Orchestra, under the auspices of the Warsaw Chamber Opera, and in 1974 he and the orchestra undertook the first of its foreign tours. Until the end of 1977 he remained principal conductor of the Polish National Radio Symphony Orchestra, but then shared the work with a number of other conductors. The Polish Chamber Orchestra under Maksymiuk visited London in 1977 and attracted warm praise; EMI contracted them to make series of records over the next three years. Previously he had recorded Telemann's *Don Quixote*, Purcell's *The Fairy Queen* and Mozart's Symphony No. 28 (with the Polish Chamber Orchestra for Polskie Nagrania), Chopin's Piano Concerto No. 1 (with Zimerman and the Polish Radio Orchestra, issued by Erato) and Piano Concertos Nos 1 and 2 and *Krakowiak* (with Ohlsson and the Polish Radio Orchestra for EMI).

Malcolm, George (b. 1917). Born in London, Malcolm studied at the Royal College of Music and at Balliol College, Oxford, of which he became an Honorary Fellow in 1966. He originally trained as a pianist, but after World War II he changed to the harpsichord and has since become one of the leading players of the instrument. He was Master of the Music at Westminster Cathedral (1947–59), shared the original performances of Britten's *A Midsummer Night's Dream* with the composer (1960), was principal conductor of the Philomusica of London (1962–6), and associate conductor of the BBC Scottish Symphony Orchestra (1965–7). He has conducted most of the London orchestras, the English Opera Group and the Northern Sinfonia, and has been invited as guest conductor to overseas orchestras such as the Israel Chamber Orchestra, the Scarlatti Orchestra in Naples and the Cologne Chamber Orchestra. In 1965 he was awarded the CBE. In addition to many excellent recordings which he has made as a harpsichordist of the music of Bach, Scarlatti, Couperin, Rameau, Handel, *et al.*, Malcolm has recorded as a conductor; his recordings have included Britten's *Missa Brevis* (with the Westminster Cathedral Choir for Decca), Victoria's *Tenebrae Responsories* (with the Westminster Cathedral Choir for Argo), a disc of Gregorian Chant, Anerio's *Missa pro defunctis* and Monteverdi's *Magnificat a 6 voce* and *Magnificat a 4 voce (with the Carmelite Priory Choir for L'Oiseau Lyre),* Britten's *Cantata Academica*, *Hymn to St Cecilia*, *Hymn to the Virgin* and the choral dances from *Gloriana* (with the London Symphony Chorus and Orchestra, *et al.* for L'Oiseau Lyre), the realisation by Leonard Isaacs of Bach's *Die Kunst der Fuge* (for Argo, and re-issued by Decca in 1973), and Bach's *Brandenburg Concertos* and Handel's Concerti Grossi Op. 3 (with the Northern Sinfonia for Enigma).

Malgoire, Jean-Claude (b. 1940). Born in Avignon where he began his musical studies, Malgoire studied the oboe and chamber music at the Paris Conservatoire, played the oboe in provincial symphony orchestras and later in l'Orchestre de Paris, and won the Geneva

International Prize for oboe. He developed a great interest in early music and instruments, searched for lost scores and old manuscripts in many European libraries, and studied the authentic re-creation of the musical instruments of early times, and ornamentation, instrumentation and style in early music. In 1966 he founded two ensembles: La Grande Écurie et la Chambre du Roy, to revive the tradition of Renaissance and later music, which originated with François I. It consists of two groups, those who 'make much noise' with trumpets, drums and percussion, called La Grande Écurie, and those 'gentle to the ear', with oboes and violins, called La Chambre du Roy. Initially, these two ensembles fulfilled quite different purposes, and met together at festival times; the advent of the symphony orchestra in the 18th century brought both together. The other ensemble he created, in 1970, is the Florilegium Musicum de Paris, a more flexible group which performs works written for voices and old instruments from the 13th century to the present day. With these groups he has presented works by Lully, Rameau, Cavalli, Campra, Purcell *et al.*, and has led performances of them at various festivals, as well as performing pieces written for him by contemporary composers. A large number of musicians able to handle different instruments must be available to meet the needs of both ensembles.

Malgoire has been very influential in introducing the French musical public to early music performed on original instruments in the authentic manner. He had copies made of old instruments for his ensembles, and made the first recordings in France with them. He has edited himself all the musical material employed by his ensembles, including Monteverdi's *L'Incoronazione di Poppea*, which he conducted at Drottningholm. His vast range of musical interests, however, prevents him from becoming a specialist; 'I have no ambition', he says, 'to become a great conductor or great oboist playing the same music all the time. . . . I am fighting against conductors and instrumentalists who are prisoners of only a century and a half of music.' After studying the authentic style of performance of music to the beginning of the 18th century, he is now looking at the correct performance of music from Haydn to the romantic period, believing that present-day performances of romantic music, with their rich, big sound, are unlike those heard by audiences of the time, and presumably different from the composers' ideas. He has pointed out, for instance, that Ravel's music is frequently misrepresented, as Ravel wrote for instruments not usually in the symphony orchestra, and no attempt is made to introduce these instruments and perform the music as Ravel intended.

Malgoire's first record with his two groups was in 1966, and was of music by Lully and Campra, with the trumpet player, André (for CBS). Since then he has recorded, all for CBS, Charpentier's *Concert à quatre parties*, *Messe* and other pieces, Handel's Concerti Grossi Opp. 3 and 6, *Water Music* and *Music for the Royal Fireworks*, Rameau's *Les Indes galantes* and excerpts from *Les Paladins*, Lully's *Alceste*, *Ballet des ballets*, *Psyché*, *Le Bourgeois gentilhomme* and *Pastorale comique*, Vivaldi's *Beatus Vir*, *Gloria* and six Flute Concertos (with Veilhan), Handel's *Rinaldo*, Cavalli's *Ercole amante*, a disc of pieces by Albinoni, G. and A. Gabrieli and Vivaldi, and another of Renaissance dance music. With the Florilegium Musicum de Paris he also recorded discs entitled *Music for the Field of the Cloth of Gold*, *Music of the Time of the Crusades*, *Italian Concerti for Oboe* and *Music of the Time of the Popes in Avignon*, and with both ensembles together, there is also a collection of courtly and village dances of the 16th century.

Malko, Nicolai (1888–1961). Born in Brailov, Russia, Malko studied at St Petersburg University and at the Conservatory there under Rimsky-Korsakov, Liadov, Glazunov and Tcherepnin. After training as a conductor with Mottl in Munich, he returned to Russia, taught conducting at the Moscow Conservatory (1922), and in 1926 was appointed conductor of the Leningrad Opera and of the Leningrad Philharmonic Orchestra (1926–9), where he succeeded Glazunov. He became a professor at the Leningrad Conservatory (1925), where Mravinsky was one of his pupils. He toured Europe and the United States, introducing many new Russian compositions, particularly of Prokofiev and Shostakovich, whose Symphony No. 1 he had premièred in Leningrad in 1926. Leaving the USSR in 1928, he was for several years in London, conducted in Europe and South America, was a guest conductor with the Royal Danish Orchestra at Copenhagen (1928–32), and returned to Denmark frequently between 1932 and 1955, where he had a long association with the Danish State Radio Symphony Orchestra. During World War II he was resident in the US, lecturing at the school of music at the de Paul University in Chicago, conducting some of the major orchestras and leading a series of summer concerts at Chicago. He became a US citizen in 1946. From 1954 to 1956 he was conductor of the Yorkshire Symphony Orchestra in England, and his last permanent appointment was musical director of the Sydney Symphony Orchestra in Australia (1956–61), where he succeeded Goossens. He visited the USSR and conducted concerts there in 1959, and toured Japan in 1960. His compositions included a clarinet concerto, and he wrote a book, *The Conductor and his Baton*.

Malko was a distinguished conductor, and while he tended to be regarded as a specialist in Russian music, of which he was undoubtedly an authoritative interpreter, his readings of the Viennese classics, from Haydn to Brahms, were most distinctive and had admirable balance, clarity and style. He was incapable of any touch of the sensational; he was a reticent man, and the complete absence of flamboyance in his personality probably hindered his career as a conductor. Nonetheless the Russian classics such as *Scheherazade* and the later Tchaikovsky symphonies were in his blood and he gave completely convincing and idiomatic performances of them; a major work such as Beethoven's Symphony No. 9 received in his hands a dramatic and superbly balanced reading. His repertoire was too limited to sustain him as a permanent conductor of an orchestra; his Mahler, for instance, was unexpectedly insecure.

After World War II, Malko recorded extensively for EMI, in Britain and in Denmark, and was one of EMI's prime 'plum label' artists. His first records were 78 r.p.m. discs, and he later made some LPs, repeating several works. A good number of the records were fine examples of his musicianship. Included in his discography were Haydn's Symphonies Nos 92 and 100, Grieg's *Elegiac Melodies*, and a suite from *The Love of Three Oranges* (with the Copenhagen Opera Orchestra); *Egmont* overture, Saint-Saëns' Piano Concerto No. 2 (with Schiøler), *Danse macabre*, *Prélude à l'après-midi d'un faune*, Dvořák's Symphony No. 9, Tchaikovsky's *Serenade in C major*, *Andante cantabile*, *Capriccio italien* and waltz from *The Sleeping Beauty*, *Capriccio espagnol*, Stravinsky's Suite No. 2, Svendsen's *Carnival in Paris* and *Festival Polonaise*, and Saeverud's *Galdreslåtten* (with the Danish Radio Symphony Orchestra); the *Coriolan*, *Prometheus* and *Leonore No. 3* overtures, Dvořák's *Slavonic Dances* Op. 46 and Op. 72, and Symphony No. 9, Brahms' *Hungarian Dance No. 1*, Mendelssohn's *The Hebrides* and *Ruy Blas* overtures and *Capriccio brilliant* (with Lympany), Grieg's *Lyric Suite*, *Finlandia*, the overtures *Oberon*, *Zampa* and *Dichter und Bauer*, Glinka's *Valse-fantaisie*, *Jota Aragonesa* and *Russlan and Ludmilla* overture, Delibes' *Naila* waltz, *A Night on the Bare Mountain*, the gopak from *Sorochintsy Fair*, the entr'acte from *Khovanshchina* and Pimen's Monologue from *Boris Godunov* (with Christoff), Tchaikovsky's Symphonies Nos 4 and 6, *1812* overture, Theme and Variations from the Suite No. 3, *Nutcracker* suite, and gopak from *Mazeppa*, the overture to *Der fliegende Holländer*, Liadov's *Eight Russian Folksongs* and *Polka*, Borodin's Symphonies Nos 2 and 3, the overture, march and Polovtsian Dances from *Prince Igor*, Glazunov's *The Seasons* and *Les Vendredis*, Judex from Gounod's *Mors et Vita*, Rachmaninov's Piano Concerto No. 2 (with Lympany), Prokofiev's Symphonies Nos 1 and 7, a suite from *The Love of Three Oranges*, the Sailors' Dance from Glière's *The Red Poppy*, the Cortège and Dance of the Tumblers from *The Snow Maiden*, the Flight of the Bumble Bee from *Tsar Saltan*, an excerpt from *Ivan the Terrible*, and excerpts from *Gayaneh* (with the Philharmonia Orchestra). He also recorded for Decca *Peter and the Wolf* and *The Young Person's Guide to the Orchestra* (with the London Philharmonic Orchestra), and for RCA in Australia Hughes' *Sinfonietta* and English's *Death of a Wombat* (with the Sydney Symphony Orchestra).

Mann, Alfred (b. 1917). Born in Hamburg, Mann emigrated to the United States and studied at the Curtis Institute in Philadelphia and at Columbia University. He was appointed professor of music at Rutgers University in New Jersey, wrote extensively for musical periodicals, published an English edition of Fux's *Gradus ad Parnassum*, and other musical treatises. He directed the Collegium Musicum of Rutgers University which recorded on three LP discs for Vanguard with the Royal Philharmonic Orchestras the complete *Chandos Anthems* of Handel; these were issued in 1964 and were distinguished performances, at the same time scholarly and dramatically performed. Spauda also issued recordings of Handel's Psalms Nos 11, 42, 51, 96, 100 and 145 (with the Rutgers University Collegium Musicum), and Urania released an LP, which appeared in Britain with the Saga label, of a collection of sacred choral music by Buxtehude, in which Mann conducted the New York Cantata Singers and an unidentified string orchestra.

Mann, Robert (b. 1920). Born in Portland, Oregon, Mann studied the violin at the Juilliard Graduate School with Déthier, and also conducting and composition with various teachers in New York. He won the Naumburg Competition (1941), made his debut as a violinist in New

York, served in the US army (1943–6), then taught at the Juilliard School. He founded the Juilliard String Quartet, which has since become internationally famous, has toured widely, and has made numerous recordings. As a conductor he has a special interest in modern music; he has also been associated with the Aspen Festival, Colorado, and became president of the Walter W. Naumburg Foundation (1971). He conducted in a recording of Bartók's Piano Concerto No. 1 (with Hambro and the Zimbler Sinfonietta, for Bartók).

Mann, Tor (1894–1974). The Swedish conductor Mann made his debut in 1919, was chief conductor at Göteborg (1922–39), and then for 20 years conducted the Swedish Radio Symphony Orchestra. His recordings included, on 78s, Söderman's *Maid of Orleans* overture, Alfvén's *Festspel*, Stenhammar's *Sentimental Romance* (with Asti) and Svendsen's *Festival Polonaise* (with the Göteborg Symphony Orchestra for HMV), Sibelius' Symphonies No. 1 (with the Stockholm Radio Orchestra for Tono) and No. 2 (with the Stockholm Concert Society Orchestra for Telefunken), the Intermezzo and Railway Fugue from *Rosenberg's Journey to America* (with the Stockholm Radio Orchestra) Nystroem's *Sinfonia de mare* (with the Stockholm Radio Orchestra) and *Sinfonia espressiva* (with the Stockholm Concert Society Orchestra for HMV). On LP, he recorded Rosenberg's Symphony No. 3 (with the Stockholm Radio Orchestra for Decca), Rangström's Symphony No. 1 (with the Stockholm Concert Society Orchestra for Decca), Stenhammar's Symphony No. 2 (with the Stockholm Philharmonic Orchestra for Discophil) and Nystroem's *Songs at the Seaside* (with Rautawaara and the Stockholm Radio Orchestra for Westminster).

Mannino, Franco (b. 1924). Born in Palermo, the pianist, conductor and composer Mannino studied at the Accademia di Santa Cecilia in Rome, and graduated in 1940. He toured as a pianist, received the Columbus Prize (1950), became a conductor of opera (1952), toured the United States as a pianist and conductor with the Maggio Musicale Fiorentino (1957), and was appointed music director of the Teatro San Carlo in Naples (1969). As a pianist he has given brilliant performances of Liszt, and he has composed orchestral works and operas. He has recorded his opera *Viva* (with the San Remo Philharmonic Orchestra *et al.* for Cetra), as well as Haydn's Horn Concerto No. 2 (with Ceccarossi and the Angelicum Orchestra for Angelicum).

Mansurov, Fuat (b. 1928). Born in Kazakhstan, USSR, Mansurov studied conducting at the Alma Ata Conservatory and was conductor of the Kazakh Folk Instruments Orchestra (1949–52). He then was conductor of the Abaya Theatre in Alma Ata (1953–6), principal conductor of the Kazakh Radio and Television Symphony Orchestra, principal conductor of the Abaya Theatre (1963), and at the Dzhalil Theatre in Kazan (1968). In 1974 EMI released the Melodiya recording in which he conducted the Bolshoi Theatre Orchestra *et al.* in Rimsky-Korsakov's *The Tsar's Bride*; he has also recorded Delibes' *Sylvia* (with the Bolshoi Theatre Orchestra), Haydn's *Piano Concerto in D major* and Weber's *Konzertstück* (with Timofejeiva and the Bolshoi Theatre Orchestra), Beethoven's overture *Die Weihe des Hauses* and Grieg's *Norwegian Dances* (with the Moscow Radio Symphony Orchestra), Tchaikovsky's Piano Concerto No. 1 (with Gavrilov and the Moscow Radio Symphony Orchestra), and Kabalevsky's Violin Concerto (with Pikaizen) and Piano Concerto No. 3 (with Felsman and the Moscow Philharmonic Orchestra).

Mantovani, Annunzio (1905–80). Born in Venice, Mantovani came to England at the age of four, where his father became the leader of the orchestra at Covent Garden. He studied the violin at Trinity College, London, performed the Bruch Violin Concerto in public at the age of 16, gave recitals in London, performed with an orchestra at the Midland Hotel, Birmingham (1923), led the salon orchestra at the Hotel Metropol in London, formed the Tipicia Orchestra (1932), was naturalised as a British subject (1933), was Noel Coward's musical director (1945), and then formed his own orchestra, the Mantovani Orchestra. In 1951, with the help of Ronnie Binge, he introduced into his orchestral arrangements the 'tumbling strings' effect, where the entrances of the much increased string sections of the orchestra overlapped fractionally; then followed a number of best-selling records for Decca, exploiting this technique. The disc of the waltz *Charmaine*, which became his signature tune, soon sold a million copies in the United States; he was the first musician in the world to sell more than one million stereophonic LPs, and at least twelve of his LPs won Golden Discs with sales in the US of over 250,000 each. The total sales of his records exceeded 100 million. With his orchestra he toured Europe, the US and Canada, and was an equally successful radio and television star. Although a popular entertainer rather than a serious interpreter of 'classical' music,

Mantovani recorded with his orchestra a collection of waltzes by Strauss, Gershwin's *Rhapsody in Blue* and *Piano Concerto in F* (with Katchen), and a song recital with tenor Del Monaco.

Margaritov, Atanas (b. 1912). Born in Harmanli, Bulgaria, Margaritov was educated at the Bulgarian State Conservatory and at the Vienna Academy of Music, and was a pupil of Weingartner. He has been conductor at the Sofia State Opera since 1940, conductor of the Bulgarian Chamber Orchestra since 1967, conductor of the Sofia State Philharmonic Orchestra, professor at the State Conservatory (1950–65), music director of the Royal Opera at Ghent, Belgium, since 1974, and has toured as a guest conductor in Eastern and Western Europe. His records include a coupling of Britten's *Simple Symphony* and Respighi's *Ancient Airs and Dances*, Suite No. 3, (with the Bulgarian Chamber Orchestra for La Guilde Internationale du Disque), Mussorgsky's opera *Khovanshchina* (with the Sofia National Opera), Hoistov's *Chamber Suite* and Cello Concerto (with Yordonov and the Bulgarian Chamber Orchestra) and *Chansons bulgares* (with Les Choeurs de Sofia, issued by Harmonia Mundi).

Margittay, Sándor (b. 1927). The Hungarian organist and conductor Margittay graduated from the Franz Liszt Academy at Budapest, where his professors were Schmidthauer and Ferencsik. He is conductor of the Hungarian State Symphony Orchestra, gives organ recitals and has edited Liszt's organ music. He has recorded organ concertos of Handel (Op. 4 Nos 2 and 3) and Haydn (in C major), with Peskó and Sebestyén respectively, and the Hungarian State Symphony Orchestra for Hungaroton.

Margraf, Horst-Tanu (b. 1893). Born in Dresden, Margraf studied at the Hannover Conservatory (1919–22) and at Bonn (1923–5). He conducted at Hannover, Neusse, Bonn, Hildesheim, Darmstadt, Chemnitz, Remscheid-Solingen and Lemberg (1922–40), saw service in World War II, was conductor of the Hamburg Symphony Orchestra (1945–8), the Bavarian Chamber Opera at Munich (1948), at Monaco (1948), at the Landestheater at Coburg (1949–51), and at Halle (from 1952), where he became the music director at the university. He was specially concerned with productions of Handel's works and founded the Handel Festivals at Halle, the composer's birthplace. In 1959 he was awarded the Handel Prize. Philips issued, on mono LPs, discs of Handel's Concerti Grossi Op. 6, in which he conducted the Handel Festival Orchestra.

Mari, Jean-Baptiste (b. 1912). Born in Palestro, Algeria, Mari studied at the Paris Conservatoire, and played the tuba in the Algiers Radio Orchestra (1934–45), the French National Orchestra (1946–9) and in the Paris Opéra Orchestra (1949–77). He occasionally conducted the French National and the Lamoureux Orchestras, and gave a series of concerts with the Paris Conservatoire Orchestra (1961–2). In 1962 he became permanent conductor of the Lamoureux Orchestra, and has since been a guest conductor. He has recorded Pierné's *Cydalise et le chèvre-pied* and *Ramuntcho*, the complete *Coppélia* and Chabrier's *España*, *Habanera*, *Marche joyeuse*, *Suite pastorale*, Danse slave and Fête polonaise from *Le Roi malgré lui* (with the Paris Opéra Orchestra for EMI), Boscha's Harp Concerto No. 1 (with Laskine) and Hummel's Trumpet Concerto (with André, and the Lamoureux Orchestra for Erato, and issued in the United States by Musical Heritage Society), and two Lyra Concertos of Haydn, arranged for guitars (with Pompono and Zarate, and the Lamoureux Chamber Orchestra for RCA).

Mariétan, Pierre (b. 1935). Born in Monthey, Switzerland, Mariétan was educated at the Geneva Conservatory (1959–60), the Basel Academy of Music (1961–3) and the Cologne Hochschule für Musik (1960–62), and participated in the Darmstadt summer courses (1960–61) and Cologne Courses for New Music (1963–6). He has been a conductor since 1961, was co-founder of the Groupe d'Étude et de Réalisation Musicales in Paris (1966), has taught composition at Dartington (1967) and at Sion, Switzerland (1968–70). For ORTF he recorded (with other pieces) Barbaud's *Mu-Joken*, with the Groupe d'Étude et de Réalisation Musicales.

Marinov, Ivan (b. 1928). Born in Sofia, where he studied at the State Conservatory under Goleminov, Stoyanov and Khadjiev, Marinov conducted at Plovdiv and at the Sofia Opera. His compositions include orchestral, vocal and chamber music; for the Bulgarian record company he recorded his Symphony No. 1 (with Gerdjikov, bass) and Pipkov's opera *Momchil* (with the Sofia State Opera Orchestra *et al.*).

Marinuzzi, Giuseppe (1882–1945). Born in Palermo and a graduate of the conservatory there, Marinuzzi made his debut as a conductor in Catania, conducted opera in Italy, Spain and at the Teatro Colón in Buenos Aires, where he led the first performance of *Parsifal* in 1913, before the work was officially permitted to be performed away from Bayreuth. He was director of the Liceo Musicale in Bologna (1915–18), conducted the première of *La Rondine* in Monte Carlo in 1917, was artistic director of the Chicago Opera in succession to Campanini (1920–21), chief conductor at the Rome Opera (1928–34) and chief conductor with de Sabata at La Scala, Milan (1934–45). He was assassinated by partisans in Milan in August 1945. Marinuzzi wrote three operas and recorded *La forza del destino* during World War II in Italy for Soria, with the EIAR Orchestra *et al.*; the set was later issued on LP by Cetra. His other records included the overtures *La gazza ladra* and *Il Signor Bruschino*, the Cena di Pasqua from Giordano's *Siberia*, the Dance of the Hours from *La Gioconda*, and the intermezzi from *Manon Lescaut* and *Cavalleria rusticana*, the ritornello from Act III of Wolf-Ferrari's *Il campiello* and his arrangement of an andante by Geminiani (with the La Scala Orchestra for HMV), the overtures to *Il barbiere di Siviglia* and Pizzetti's *Fedra* (with the La Scala Orchestra for Telefunken), Schumann's *Manfred* overture (with the Florence May Festival Orchestra for Cetra), and a chorus from *I Lombardi* (with the EIAR Chorus and Orchestra for Cetra).

Markevitch, Igor (b. 1912). Born in Kiev into an aristocratic family of landowners, Markevitch left Russia with his parents in 1913 and settled with them in Vevey in Switzerland in 1916. He studied at the Collège de Vevey, and was introduced to music when he heard, as a boy, the Suisse Romande Orchestra under Ansermet. He began to study the piano and composition at Lausanne, and attracted the attention of Cortot, who in 1925 brought him to Paris to enter the École Normale; there he studied the piano under Cortot, composition under Nadia Boulanger, and orchestration under Rieti. At the age of sixteen he met Diaghilev who was so impressed with his talent that he commissioned him to write a piano concerto, which was played a year later at a concert at Covent Garden, with the conductor Desormière. Diaghilev also commissioned a ballet, *Rébus*, but unfortunately died in 1929 before the commission was completed. In 1930 Markevitch studied conducting with Scherchen, who inspired him to take it up as a profession; his debut occurred that year, when he was eighteen, in a programme of his own compositions with the Amsterdam Concertgebouw Orchestra.

During the 1930s Markevitch composed much music, including concertos, ballets, orchestral and vocal works; as a student of Boulanger, his compositions were considerably influenced by Stravinsky, and remained tonal. The best known are the ballet *L'Envoi d'Icare* (1933), an oratorio *Paradise Lost* (1935–6) and a *Psaume* for soprano and orchestra (1934); the latter caused a controversy about its merits when it was performed at the ISCM Festival at Florence. He recorded *L'Envoi d'Icare* and another work, *Le Nouvel Âge*, on 78s with the Belgian National Orchestra for HMV; the ferocity and violent dynamics of this music and its apparent absence of sentiment hinted at its close relationship with *Le Sacre du printemps* and with the *Scythian Suite* of Prokofiev, but his later compositions show an infusion of feeling resulting from his view of the ennobling purpose of music. By the end of the 1930s Markevitch had turned his attention more and more to conducting. In 1940 he went to Italy to gather material for a cantata he was writing about Lorenzo the Magnificent, which was completed and premièred by him in Rome in 1941. The entry of Italy into the war compelled him to remain in Florence, and when the city was liberated in 1944 the Allies appointed him to organise the Florence May Festival. After the war he toured Europe to conduct opera and concerts, and appeared at major music festivals; he also taught conducting at the Salzburg Mozarteum (1947–53), at the Pan-American conducting courses in Mexico (1955–6), and more recently, at the Moscow Conservatory (1963) and at the Jerusalem Academy (1976). His permanent appointments as conductor have been with the Stockholm Concert Society Orchestra (1952–5), the Havana Philharmonic Orchestra (1957–8), the Montreal Symphony Orchestra (1956–60), the Lamoureux Orchestra in Paris (1954–61), the Spanish Radio and Television Orchestra which he founded (1965–7), the USSR State Symphony Orchestra in Moscow (1965), the Monte Carlo Opera (1967–72) and the Santa Cecilia Orchestra, Rome (1973–5). He took part in the 1954–5 season at Covent Garden, London, made his debut in the United States with the Boston Symphony Orchestra in 1955, and in 1968 visited Japan to conduct the Japan Philharmonic Orchestra. He has also toured many other countries and has conducted a great number of the major symphony orchestras. In recent years he has prepared a new edition of the Beethoven symphonies, with new analyses and annotations.

Consistent with his style as a composer, Markevitch brings considerable tension and incisiveness to his conducting, and naturally feels a special affinity with the music of Stravinsky and Bartók. His performances of the Viennese classics are equally firm and well considered, although on occasion the geniality of the music is attenuated. He is particularly successful with ballet scores and highly colourful romantic music. He is a distinguished teacher of conducting, and believes that the special circumstances of today call for a far more intensive training for conductors than before. This training, he states, should begin at the age of 12 or 14, and should go on for about ten years. Conductors today are usually required to give many more concerts than in the past, with much less time to prepare each; they must command a vast repertoire encompassing many different styles, and there are also the demands of recording. The education of the conductor, he explains, should include the training of the body in correct breathing, developing independence of the arms and reflexes and agility, and the preparation of the ear so that errors can be recognised infallibly. The would-be conductor should have a knowledge of all the classical symphonies, the most important operas and oratorios and the standard concertos, as well as a close study of the most important contemporary pieces, of which he gives as examples *Le Sacre du printemps*, Bartók's *Concerto for Orchestra*, Messiaen's *Turangalîla Symphony*, Schoenberg's *Variations for Orchestra* Op. 31, and Boulez's *Le Marteau sans maître*. He adds to this a comprehensive musical and cultural education, including the study of the life and work of each composer, and a command of several languages to facilitate contact with the orchestral players of other countries. Above all, the conductor can only re-create a musical work if he knows how to communicate with his musicians, how to convince them of his approach and to move them to do what he wants them to do.

Markevitch has been a prolific recording artist, and has made records of a vast range of music, from his own arrangement of Bach's *Die Kunst der Fuge* to the Berg Violin Concerto. His performances of *Le Sacre du printemps* were celebrated, and he recorded the work twice, in 1952 and 1960, both times with the Philharmonia Orchestra; his major recording achievement was the six Tchaikovsky symphonies, and *Manfred*, with the London Symphony Orchestra, superb performances but unfortunately remaining in the record catalogues only for a short time. In addition to his *L'Envoi d'Icare* and *Le Nouvel Âge*, he recorded on 78 r.p.m. discs *A Night on the Bare Mountain*, *Invitation to the Dance*, *Mephisto Waltz*, *La Valse* and Chabrier's *Fête polonaise* (with the Florence May Festival Orchestra for Parlophone), Handel's Concerto Grosso Op. 6 No. 5, *Peter and the Wolf*, *Invitation to the Dance* and the Verdi overtures *Giovanna d'Arco*, *La battaglia di Legnano*, *Luisa Miller* and *La forza del destino* (with the Philharmonia Orchestra for EMI).

His LP recordings include Nielsen's Symphony No. 4 and *Saga-Drøm* (with the Royal Orchestra, Copenhagen, for DGG); the *1812* and *Russian Easter Festival* overtures, the Polovtsian Dances from *Prince Igor* and the Berg Violin Concerto (with Grumiaux, and the Amsterdam Concertgebouw Orchestra for Philips); the six Tchaikovsky symphonies and *Manfred*, *Scheherazade*, *Capriccio espagnol* and Stravinsky's Suites Nos 1 and 2, *Four Norwegian Impressions*, *Circus Polka* and *Apollon Musagète* (with the London Symphony Orchestra for Philips); Haydn's Symphonies Nos 103 and 104, Mozart's Piano Concertos K. 466 and K. 491 (with Haskil), Beethoven's Symphonies Nos 1, 5, 6, 8 and 9, and Piano Concerto No. 3 (with Haskil), Chopin's Piano Concerto No. 2, and *Nights in the Gardens of Spain* (with Haskil), a *Carmen* suite and the two *L'Arlésienne* suites (with the Lamoureux Orchestra for Philips); Haydn's *Sinfonia concertante*, the Mozart Bassoon Concerto (with Allard), Gluck's *Symphony in G major*, Beethoven's Symphony No. 6 and the *Coriolan*, *Fidelio*, *Egmont*, *Leonore No. 3* and *Namensfeier* overtures, *Symphonie fantastique* and *La Damnation de Faust*, Brahms' Symphony No. 4, *Francesca da Rimini*, *Le Coq d'or* suite, the *Russian Easter Festival*, *May Night* and *Russlan and Ludmilla* overtures, Liadov's *Fragments from the Apocalypse*, *In the Steppes of Central Asia*, Debussy's *Danse sacrée et danse profane* and *La Mer*, Gounod's Symphony No. 2, Honegger's Symphony No. 5, Milhaud's *Choéphores* and *L'Orestie*, the prelude to Act I of *Lohengrin*, Bizet's *Jeux d'enfants* and Roussel's *Bacchus et Ariane* (with the Lamoureux Orchestra *et al.* for DGG).

Markevitch also recorded *The Creation* of Haydn, Mozart's Symphonies Nos 34 and 38 and Mass K. 317, Schubert's Symphonies Nos 3 and 4, *Pictures at an Exhibition*, Tchaikovsky's Symphony No. 6, *Symphonie fantastique* and *Harold in Italy* (with Kirchner), the *Siegfried Idyll*, Ride of the Valkyries from *Die Walküre* and the overture and Venusberg Music from *Tannhäuser*, and Berwald's Symphonies Nos 2 and 3 (with the Berlin Philharmonic Orchestra *et al.* for DGG); his arrangement of *Die Kunst der Fuge*, Haydn's Symphonies Nos 101 and 102, Schubert's Symphony No. 8, Mendelssohn's Symphony No. 4, the overtures to *La scala di seta*, *Il barbiere di Siviglia*, *William Tell*, *La gazza ladra*, *L'Italiana in Algeri* and *La Cenerentola*, *A Night on the Bare Mountain*, the *Romeo and Juliet* fantasy-overture, the Polovtsian Dances from *Prince Igor*, Shostakovich's Symphony No. 1, *Scythian Suite*, *Pulcinella* and *Le Baiser de la fée* (with the French National Radio Orchestra for EMI); *L'Apprenti sorcier*, dances from *The Three-cornered Hat*, *Le Carnaval des animaux*, *The Young Person's Guide to the Orchestra*, Bartók's *Dance Suite*, Prokofiev's Symphony No. 1, *La Valse*, the *Romeo and Juliet* fantasy-overture and *Nutcracker* suite, *Le Sacre du printemps* (twice), a collection entitled *Homage to Diaghilev* including the *Daphnis et Chloé* Suite No. 2, Satie's *Parade*, *Invitation to the Dance*, Prokofiev's *Le Pas d'acier*, Liadov's *Kikimora* and excerpts from *Swan Lake*, *Les Sylphides*, *The Good-Humoured Ladies* and *Petrushka*, another collection entitled *Portrait of the Waltz* including *Danse macabre*, *Valse triste*, Mozart's *German Dance* K. 605 No. 3, Busoni's *Tanzwalzer*, *Mephisto Waltz*, *Danse des sylphes* from *La Damnation de Faust*, the waltz from Stravinsky's Suite No. 2 and Chabrier's *Fête polonaise* (with the Philharmonia Orchestra for EMI); *Pictures at an Exhibition* and *A Night on the Bare Mountain* (with the Leipzig Gewandhaus Orchestra for Eterna); Gounod's *Messe solennelle à Sainte Cécile* and Cherubini's *Requiem* (with the Czech Philharmonic Orchestra *et al.* for DGG); Bartók's Piano Concerto No. 3 (with Annie Fischer and the London Symphony Orchestra for EMI); Offenbach's *La Périchole* (with the Lamoureux Orchestra *et al.* for Pathé, and issued by the World Record Club in Britain); Mendelssohn's Symphony No. 4 and the Schubert overtures *In the Italian Style*, *Alfonso und Estrella* and *Overture in E minor* (with the Japan Philharmonic Orchestra for La Guilde Internationale du Disque); the *Romeo and Juliet* fantasy-overture, *Marche slave*, *Capriccio italien*, the *L'Arlésienne* Suite No. 1, Poulenc's *Les Biches*, Sauget's *La Chatte*, Milhaud's *Le Train bleu*, Satie's *Jack in the box* and Auric's *Les Fâcheux* (with the Monte Carlo National Orchestra for GID); Mozart's Mass K. 427 (with the Berlin Radio Symphony Orchestra *et al.* for DGG); the Brahms *Tragic Overture* and *Alto Rhapsody* (with Arkhipova), Stravinsky's *Symphony of Psalms*, songs by Mussorgsky (with Vishnevskaya), Tcherepnin's *Tati-Tati* (with Olga Rostropovich), Kodály's *Psalmus Hungaricus* and Bizet's *Jeux d'enfants* (with the USSR State Symphony Orchestra *et al.* for Philips); the Verdi *Requiem* and Leopold Mozart's *Toy Symphony* (with the Moscow Philharmonic Orchestra *et al.* for Philips, and issued on other labels); Dallapiccola's *Canti di prigionia*, Delage's *Quatre poèmes hindous* and *Berceuse* (with the Santa Cecilia Orchestra *et al.* for EMI); Beethoven's Symphony No. 3 and Brahms' Symphony No. 1 (with the Symphony of the Air for DGG); Stravinsky's *L'Histoire du soldat* (with Cocteau and an ensemble for Philips); Glinka's *A Life for the Tsar* (with the Lamoureux Orchestra *et al.* for EMI); Lili Boulanger's *Psaumes Nos 34* and *129*, *Du fond de l'abîme*, *Vieille Prière bouddhique* and *Pie Jesu* (with the Lamoureux Orchestra *et al.*) and *Faust et Hélène* and *Pour les Funérailles d'un soldat* (with the Monte Carlo National Orchestra for GID); *Boléro*, the *Preciosa* overture, *El amor brujo* (with Rivadeneyra) and Falla's *Seven Spanish Popular Songs* (with Chamorro), Granados' *Spanish Dances Nos 4*, *8* and *9*; *Zapateado* and intermezzo from *Goyescas*, and Halffter's *Fanfare (in memoriam Enrique Granados)* (with the Spanish Radio-Television Symphony Orchestra for Philips).

Markis, Lev (b. 1930). After studying at the Moscow Conservatory and the Gnessin Institute under Jankelewitsch, Markis was a violinist and soloist with the Moscow Chamber Orchestra, and in 1964 became artistic director of the Rosconcert Chamber Orchestra and a soloist with the Moscow Philharmonic Orchestra. For Melodiya he recorded as conductor of an unnamed chamber orchestra Bach's *Two-Harpsichord Concertos in C major* and *C minor* (with Lyubimov and Berman), Mozart's Cassation No. 1 and Harpsichord Concertos K. 37, K. 40 and K. 41 (with Lyubimov), Haydn's Feldpartit No. 6 and *Cassation in F major*, and the Mozart, Krommer and two Weber Clarinet Concertos (with Sokolov).

Markowski, Andrzy (b. 1924). Born in Lublin, Markowski studied music secretly during the German occupation of Poland, fought in the Warsaw uprising of 1944, was deported from Poland and finally landed in England where he studied at the Trinity College of Music (1946–7). He returned to Warsaw, graduated from the Academy of Music there, and started his career as a conductor with the Poznań Philharmonic Orchestra (1954). He has been conductor of the Silesian Philharmonic Orchestra at Katowice (1956–9), conductor of the Kraków Philharmonic Orchestra (1960–64), chief conductor of the Wrocław Philharmonic Orchestra (1965–8), and assistant conductor and then permanent conductor of the Warsaw National Philharmonic Orchestra (since 1968).

At Wrocław he organised the Oratorio and Cantata Music Festival; in 1961 he toured the United States with the Kraków Philharmonic Orchestra, in 1969 Britain with the Polish National Radio Orchestra and in 1970–76 made major tours with the Warsaw National Philharmonic Orchestra to the Middle East, Australia, the Federal Republic of Germany and Japan. He has won an international reputation as an interpreter of contemporary music and has appeared as a guest conductor at cities and festivals in Eastern and Western Europe. He has been awarded the annual Orpheus Prize of Polish music critics (1968–71), and in 1974 received the Polish Government Award, First Class. He composes for films and the theatre, and is interested in jazz.

Markowski's major recordings have been of the music of present-day Polish composers, such as Pendrecki's *Utrenia*, *Psalms of David*, *Sonata for Cello and Orchestra*, *Anaklasis*, *Stabat Mater*, *Fluorescences*, *Kosmogonia* and *De natura sonoris* II, Lutosławski's *Five Songs after Poems by K. Iłłakowicz*, Serocki's *Eyes of Air*, Bloch's *Meditations*, Turski's Symphony No. 2, Sikorski's *Concerto breve*, Szabelski's Symphony No. 5 and Górecki's *Old Polish Music* (with the Warsaw Philharmonic Orchestra *et al.* for Polskie Nagrania, and some also issued by Philips and Wergo). He has also recorded Bach's Cantata No. 211, Brahms' *Alto Rhapsody*, *Schicksalslied* and *Academic Festival Overture*, and a recital with Łukomska (with the Warsaw Philharmonic Orchestra *et al.* for Polskie Nagrania), Chopin's Piano Concerto No. 2 (with Magin and the Warsaw Philharmonic Orchestra for Decca) and Milhaud's *Le Boeuf sur le toit* (with the Silesian Philharmonic Orchestra for DGG).

Marriner, Neville (b. 1924). Marriner was born in London and was first taught the violin by his father when he was a small boy. He received lessons from Frederick Mountney, and then went to the Royal College of Music in London at the age of thirteen. During World War II he served in the British army, was wounded in France in 1943, and during his convalescence in a military hospital met Thurston Dart, who was to have a crucial influence on his career. After the war he completed his studies at the RCM, then went to Paris to study the violin with René Benedetti and to attend the Paris Conservatoire. Returning to England he was a member of the teaching staff at Eton College for a year, was a founder-member of some chamber-music groups, and formed a duo with Dart, who played the harpsichord, specialising in 17th- and 18th-century music. From this emerged the Jacobean Ensemble, which made records of the Purcell Trio Sonatas for Argo in 1950. Previously, in 1948, Marriner had been appointed professor at the Royal Academy of Music, and in 1956 he joined the London Symphony Orchestra as principal second violin. He remained with the orchestra until 1969; his association with Dart continued until the latter's death in 1971.

In 1957 Marriner was asked by the director of music at the church of St Martin-in-the-Fields, Trafalgar Square, London, to provide music after evensong. He agreed to arrange six programmes, and formed a chamber orchestra of four first and four second violins, two violas, two cellos and a double-bass, most of whom were principals from the London orchestras. The ensemble was given the name, somewhat lightheartedly, of the Academy of St Martin-in-the-Fields. L'Oiseau Lyre contracted Marriner and the orchestra to record Couperin's *Les Nations*, and an initial favourable review of this disc assured the orchestra's future. At first Marriner conducted the Academy (as he came to call the orchestra) from the first desk, but in 1959 he went to the United States to study with Monteux, who taught him to conduct from the podium. Marriner and the Academy went on to make many more records for Argo and later for Philips and EMI; it is now unquestionably the most successful – maybe the best – chamber orchestra to have made gramophone records. Its players are drawn from a pool; none is under contract, and they are engaged entirely for their quality. Wind players have been added so that the repertoire can be extended to include Haydn, Mozart, early Schubert and Beethoven, and Rossini. The orchestra tours extensively, and in fact gives many more concerts overseas than in Britain.

In 1969 Marriner received an invitation to go to California and direct the newly formed Los Angeles Chamber Orchestra. This group is made up chiefly of young players as well as others drawn from professional freelance musicians in Hollywood. Marriner has spent twelve weeks each year in Los Angeles with the orchestra, and in 1975 toured with them in Europe. His success in Los Angeles has led to invitations to conduct some of the major US orchestras such as the Boston Symphony, New York Philharmonic, Cleveland, Minneapolis Symphony, National Symphony, San Francisco Symphony and Detroit Symphony, but he has found it less easy to be engaged to conduct orchestras in Britain. In 1971 he was appointed conductor of the Northern Sinfonia, based at Newcastle-upon-Tyne, and in 1975 musical adviser to the South Bank Summer Festival in

London. He has also conducted opera, but since he is concerned about becoming stale with the chamber orchestra's repertoire, he is anxious to return to the symphony orchestra and to accept several appointments as musical director, probably in the United States and in Europe simultaneously.

Until his appointment with the Los Angeles Chamber Orchestra, Marriner's name, as a conductor, was inseparable from the Academy of St Martin-in-the-Fields. Since then he has developed a more independent identity and has become respected as a conductor in his own right. Like other conductors of chamber orchestras, records have contributed enormously to his international fame; each of his records now sells sufficient numbers to permit him to select his own repertoire. He is a perfectionist and is meticulous in all matters of scholarship in preparing performances, for which his experience with Dart was invaluable. He will not, however, listen to other conductors' recorded performances before he records himself, for, to him, the outcome could only be a subconscious influence or a conscious reaction. While his musical taste is catholic, he has no time for 'squeaky-wheel' *avant-garde* music which introduces electronics or improvisations, as it generally gives little pleasure to either players or audience. He believes that 'nobody has really advanced string technique satisfactorily since Bartók'. The sound and style of the Academy is frequently characterised as 'athletic' and 'crisp', which tends to indicate a certain slickness and conceals the superb ensemble, sense of style and absolute technical proficiency of the orchestra. Even so, the Academy has a special sound: completely focused, the utmost clarity and a bright tone, which some may feel not entirely right for all the music it plays. Marriner himself believes the Academy to be the best chamber orchestra at the moment, and that its recorded performances have become definitive, although he has great respect for the Warsaw Chamber Orchestra. But, he admits, 'people may still buy our records of baroque music because they like the way we play it and there are other equally interesting ways of performing it now', and that 'our repertoire of baroque music should be taken over by people who play on original instruments; that is the next step'.

Marriner and the Academy have made over 200 recordings, in a repertoire extending from Vivaldi, Telemann and Bach to Bartók, Stravinsky, Tippett, Schoenberg, Shostakovich and Prokofiev. Apart from discs containing collections of smaller pieces, the works recorded included Bach's *Brandenburg Concertos* (for Philips), orchestral Suites (for Argo and Philips), *Die Kunst der Fuge*, Violin Concertos Nos 1 and 2 and Double Violin Concerto (with Szeryng and Hasson, for Philips), Violin and Oboe Concerto (with Kaine and Miller, for Decca), *Flute Concerto in G minor* (with Bennett, for Decca), Three-Violin Concerto (with Kaine, Studt and Thomas), Violin and Flute Concerto (with Kaine and Bennett), Violin, Flute and Oboe Concerto (with Kaine, Bennett and Black), Oboe Concerto BWV 1053 (with Black), Oboe d'amore Concerto BWV 1055 (with Black, for Argo), Sinfonia from the *Christmas Oratorio* (for EMI), Cantatas Nos 56, 82, 159 and 170 (for L'Oiseau Lyre), 147, 202 and 209 (with Ameling), and a recital of Bach arias (with Janet Baker, for EMI), Vivaldi's *L'estro armonico*, *La Stravaganza* (with Kaine and Loveday), *The Four Seasons* (with Loveday) and Two-Trumpet Concerto P. 75 (with Wilbraham and Jones, for Argo), and *Cello Concerto in C major* (with Heath, for L'Oiseau Lyre), Bononcini's Sinfonia (for Philips), Corelli's Concerti Grossi Op. 6, Geminiani's Concerto Grosso Op. 3 No. 3, Locatelli's Concerto Grosso Op. 1 No. 9, Torelli's Concerto Op. 6 No. 10, Albicastro's Concerto No. 6, Gabrieli's *Canzona noni toni* (for L'Oiseau Lyre), *Canzona primi toni No. 1*, *Canzon 1 a 4* and *Canzon a 8*, Vejvanowský's *Sonata natalis*, *Sonata la posta*, *Harmonia roman*, *Sonata tribus quandram* and *Balleti pro tabula* (for Argo), Manfredini's Concerto Op. 3 No. 10 (for L'Oiseau Lyre), Purcell's *Chacony in G* (for EMI), Albinoni's Adagio (for EMI), Concerto Op. 5 No. 5 (for L'Oiseau Lyre) and *Trumpet Concerto in C major* (with Wilbraham, for Argo), Avison's Concerto Op. 9 No. 11 (for L'Oiseau Lyre), Arne's Overture No. 1 and Harpsichord Concerto No. 5 (with Malcolm), Clarke's *Trumpet Voluntary*, the rondeau from Purcell's *Abdelazar*, Pachelbel's *Canon*, Fasch's *Trumpet Concerto in D*, Hertel's *Concerto in D*, Albrechtsberger's *Concerto in E flat* and Hummel's *Trumpet Concerto in E flat* (with Wilbraham), Telemann's *Don Quichotte* Suite, *Overture in D major*, *Overture in C major – Hamburger Ebb und Fluth*, *Ouverture des nations anciennes et modernes*, *Overture in C major*, *Viola Concerto in G major* (with Shingles) and *Trumpet Concerto in D major* (with Wilbraham, for Argo), *Tafelmusik* – Suite No. 2 (for L'Oiseau Lyre), *Suite in A major* (with Munrow) and Horn Concerto (with Tuckwell, for EMI), Handel's Concerti Grossi Op. 3 and Op. 6, *Water Music*, *Music for the Royal Fireworks*, Overture, Ballet Music and Dream music from *Alcina*, Overture, Sinfonia,

Pastorale and Ballet Music from *Ariodante*, Hunting Scene from *Il pastor fido*, Oboe Concertos Nos 1, 2 and 3 (with Lord), *Berenice* overture, Arrival of the Queen of Sheba from *Solomon*, and *Variant in F major* (for Argo), Pastoral Symphony from *Messiah*, Minuet from *Berenice*, and Concerto Op. 4 No. 6 (with Munrow, for EMI), *Messiah* and Organ Concertos (with Malcolm, for Argo), Double Concertos Nos 1, 2 and 3, and *Agrippina* and *Arianna* overtures (for EMI), Grétry's *Flute Concerto in C major*, Leclair's *Flute Concerto in C major*, Loeillet's *Flute Concerto in D major* and Quantz's Flute Concerto No. 17 (with Monteux, for L'Oiseau Lyre), Giuliani's *Guitar Concerto in A major* (with Romero, for Philips), Sammartini's *Recorder Concerto in F major* (with Munrow, for EMI), Boccherini's Quintet Op. 37 No. 7 (for Argo), and excerpt from Quintet Op. 13 No. 5, and Schmelzer's *Sacro-profanus concentus musicus* (for Philips).

Also recorded, were C. P. E. Bach's Symphony No. 2 W. 183, and *Piano Concerto in C major* (with Malcolm, for Argo), J. C. Bach's Symphonies Op. 3 (for Philips) and *Harpsichord Concerto in A major* (with Malcolm), Gluck's *Don Juan* (for Decca), Haydn's Symphonies Nos 43, 52, 53, 59, 100 and 103 (for Philips), Overture to *Acide* (for Argo), Six German Dances (for Argo), *Harpsichord Concerto in D major* (with Malcolm, for Decca), Horn Concertos Nos 1 and 2 (with Tuckwell), Organ Concerto No. 1 (with Preston), Trumpet Concerto (with Stringer, for Argo) and Serenade from Quartet Op. 3 No. 5 (for Philips), Michael Haydn's Divertimento (with Shingles and Heath, for EMI), Viola and Organ Concerto (with Shingles and Preston) and Horn Concerto (with Tuckwell, for Argo), Dittersdorf's Sinfonia Concertante (with Shingles and Slatford, for EMI), Cherubini's Étude No. 2, Weber's Horn Concertino, Förster's *Horn Concerto in E flat*, Leopold Mozart's Horn Concerto and Telemann's *Horn Concerto in D major* (with Tuckwell for EMI), Leopold Mozart's *Toy Symphony* (for EMI), Trumpet Concerto (with Wilbraham) and Eight Minuets (for Argo), Mozart's Symphonies Nos 13, 14, 15, 16, 23, 24, 25, 26, 27, 29 and 32 (for Argo), 35, 36 and 40 (for Philips), Divertimentos K. 136, K. 137, K. 138 and K. 334, Notturno K. 286, *Serenata notturna*, March K. 408 No. 2 (for Argo), March K. 335 No. 1 and Dance K. 605 No. 3 (for EMI), overtures to *Il re pastore*, *Lucio Silla*, *La finta semplice*, *Der Schauspieldirektor* and *Les petits riens* (for EMI), *Eine kleine Nachtmusik* (for Argo and EMI), Piano Concertos K. 414, K. 453, K. 456, K. 459, K. 466 and K. 488 (with Brendel, for Philips), Violin Concerto K. 216 (with Loveday, for Argo), Rondo K. 373 and Adagio K. 261 (with Suk, for EMI), Sinfonia Concertante K. 364 (with Loveday and Shingles), Concertone (with Brown and Kaine, for Argo), Sinfonia Concertante K. 297b (for Philips), Clarinet Concerto (with Brymer, for Philips), Oboe Concerto (with Black), Bassoon Concerto (with Chapman), Flute Concerto No. 1 and Andante K. 315 (with Monteux), Flute and Harp Concerto (with Monteux and Ellis), four Horn Concertos and Rondo K. 371 (with Tuckwell, for EMI, and with Civil), arrangements of early piano works by Erik Smith (for Philips), *Litaniae Lauretanae*, Mass K. 317 and *Requiem* (for Argo) and *Exsultate jubilate* and arias (with Spoorenberg for Decca), Beethoven's Symphonies Nos 1, 2 and 4 and *Grosse Fuge* (for Philips), Twelve Country Dances and two Romances (with Suk, for EMI), Schubert's Rondo D. 438 (with Suk, for EMI) and excerpt from *Rosamunde* (for Philips), Donizetti's *Quartet in D* (for Argo), Rossini's String Sonatas Nos 1 to 6 (for Argo), and *Duetto* (with Heath, for EMI), and overtures to *Il barbiere di Siviglia*, *L'Italiana in Algeri*, *La cambiale di matrimonio*, *La scala di seta*, *Tancredi*, *Il Signor Bruschino*, *Il Turco in Italia* and *L'inganno felice* (for Philips), Dvořák's *Serenade in E major*, Mendelssohn's String Symphonies Nos 9, 10 and 12 (for Argo), two Piano Concertos (with Perahia, for Philips), *Piano Concerto in A minor* and Two-Piano Concerto (with Ogdon and Lucas, for Argo), Octet (for Argo), Scherzo from the Octet (for EMI), and Scherzo from music for *A Midsummer Night's Dream* (for Philips), Bellini's Oboe Concerto (with Lord, for L'Oiseau Lyre), Bizet's *Symphony in C major*, Grieg's *Holberg Suite*, Tchaikovsky's *Serenade in C major* and *Souvenir de Florence*, the Adagio attributed to Wagner (with Brymer), and Wagner's *Siegfried Idyll*, Strauss's *Metamorphosen*, and Mahler's *Lieder eines fahrenden Gesellen* (with Tear, for Argo).

Of 20th-century music, Marriner recorded Elgar's *Elegy*, *Introduction and Allegro*, *Serenade in E minor*, *Sospiri* and *The Spanish Lady* (for Argo), Delius' *Two Aquarelles*, Holst's *St Paul's Suite* (for EMI), Vaughan Williams' *Fantasia on a Theme of Thomas Tallis*, *Fantasia on Greensleeves*, *The Lark Ascending* (with Brown) and *Five Variants of Dives and Lazarus* (for Argo) and *Rhosymedre* (for EMI), Walton's two pieces from *Henry V*, *Façade* (with Fielding and Flanders, for EMI), and *Sonata for Strings* (for Argo), Butterworth's *Banks of Green Willow*, *A Shropshire Lad* and

Two English Idylls (for Argo), Britten's *Simple Symphony* (for EMI), *Variations on a Theme of Frank Bridge*, and *Nocturne* (with Tear), Tippett's Concerto for Double String Orchestra, *Little Music* and *Variations on a Theme of Corelli*, Stravinsky's *Capriccio* (with Ogdon), *Apollo* and *Pulcinella*, Shostakovich's Piano Concerto No. 1 (with Ogdon and Wilbraham), Schoenberg's *Verklärte Nacht*, Webern's Five Movements, Hindemith's *Five Pieces for String Orchestra* (for Argo), Rodrigo's *Concierto madrigal* (with P. and A. Romero, for Philips), Bartók's *Divertimento* and *Music for Strings, Percussion and Celesta*, Prokofiev's Symphony No. 1 and *Visions fugitives* (arranged by Barshai, for Argo), Respighi's *Gli uccelli* and *Trittico botticelliano* (for EMI), Ives' Symphony No. 3, Copland's *Quiet City*, Cowell's *Hymn and Fuguing Tune*, Creston's *A Rumour* and Barber's *Adagio* (for Argo).

With other orchestras, Marriner has recorded the Bach Harpsichord Concertos (with Kipnis and the London Strings for CBS), Britten's *Les Illuminations* and *Serenade for Tenor, Horn and Strings* (with Harper and Tear, and the Northern Sinfonia for EMI), Chihara's Double Bass Concerto and *Ceremony I and III* (with Neidlinger and the London Symphony Orchestra for Turnabout), Janáček's *Suite*, Suk's *Serenade* and the Introduction for String Sextet from Strauss's *Capriccio* (with the Los Angeles Chamber Orchestra for Argo), Stravinsky's *Concerto in D major*, *Danses concertantes* and *Dumbarton Oaks Concerto*, Respighi's *Ancient Airs and Dances* Suites 1 to 3, and Thomson's *Autumn*, *The Plough that broke the Plains* Suite and *The River* Suite (with the Los Angeles Chamber Orchestra for EMI). The discs with the Los Angeles Chamber Orchestra were recorded when the group was in London; Marriner has explained that in the United States musicians' fees, and the union requirement for a 20 minute break each hour in a recording session, make it necessary on grounds of cost to record in two sessions what would normally take up to five in London. He has found that while US musicians may play better because they are taught better, they lack the instinctive ensemble sense of British players.

Marschner, Wolfgang (b. 1926). Grandson of the composer of *Hans Heiling*, Marschner was born in Dresden and studied the violin there and at the Mozarteum in Salzburg, toured as an infant prodigy, and after World War II was concertmaster in orchestras in Hannover and Cologne. He has been a teacher at the Folkwangschule at Essen, and at the Hochschule für Musik at Cologne. As soloist he recorded the Schoenberg Violin Concerto (with the South-West German Radio Orchestra under Gielen, for Turnabout); as conductor he directed his own chamber orchestra in Locatelli's Concerto Grosso Op. 8 No. 5, Corelli's Concerto Grosso Op. 6 No. 8, Manfredini's Concerto Grosso Op. 3 No. 12 and Torelli's Concerto Grosso Op. 8 No. 6 (for Christophorus), C. P. E. Bach's *Flute Concerto in G major* (with Delius, issued in the United States by Musical Heritage Society), and Bach's Harpsichord Concertos Nos 4, 5 and 13, in versions for violins (with himself, Gawriloff and Hori, for RBM).

Martin, Frank (1890–1974). The Swiss composer Martin, who from 1964 lived in Amsterdam, never followed a career as a conductor. In his early years he was pianist and harpsichordist to the Société de Musique de Chambre in Geneva, and the first performances of his compositions have been led by conductors such as Sacher, Baud-Bovy and Ansermet. Nevertheless some records have been issued in which he conducts his own music: in 1964, DGG released a coupling of the *Jedermann* monologues and excerpts from the opera *Der Sturm*, with Fischer-Dieskau and the Berlin Philharmonic Orchestra. The *Jedermann* monologues were re-issued in 1976. Other discs have been the Violin Concerto and Piano Concerto No. 2 (with Schneiderhan and Badura-Skoda respectively, and the Luxembourg Radio Orchestra for Vox), the *Ballade for Piano and Orchestra*, the *Ballade for Trombone and Orchestra* and the *Concerto for Harpsichord and Small Orchestra* (with Benda, Rosin and Jaccottet respectively and the Lausanne Chamber Orchestra for Vox), and *Der Cornet* (with Mayer-Reinach and the Swiss Italian Radio Orchestra for Jecklin).

Martin, Louis (b. 1907). Born in Nantes, Martin studied with Gédalge and Gaubert, was with Radio France (1936–53), and then pursued an international career as a conductor. He has recorded Lully's *Le Bourgeois gentilhomme* (with the Paris Concerts Orchestra for La Guilde Internationale du Disque), the Haydn Symphonies Nos 101 and 104 and Ravel's *Ma Mère l'Oye* (with the Pasdeloup Orchestra for GID), Mozart's Divertimento K. 287 (with the Paris Soloists Orchestra for Nonesuch), *Boléro*, *Rapsodie espagnole*, *Pavane pour une infante défunte* and *Don Quichotte à Dulcinée* (with Mollet, and the Paris Soloists Orchestra for BASF), the intermezzo from *Cavalleria rusticana*, Schubert's *Rondo in A major* and Ravel's *Tzigane* (with

Rohn, and the Hamburg Philharmonic Orchestra for Telefunken).

Martini, Juan (b. 1913). Born in Buenos Aires, the Argentinian conductor and composer Martini studied at the Buenos Aires Conservatory, at Turin (1931–2) and at the Accademia di Santa Cecilia in Rome (1932). He was a conductor at the Teatro Colón, Buenos Aires (1934), was the artistic director of the opera school at the Teatro Colón (1955) and since 1959 has been professor of conducting at the Pontificia Universidad Católica Argentina Sta Maria de los Buenos Aires, and is also music director of the Teatro Colón Orchestra. He has composed orchestral, chamber and vocal music. His recordings include the overtures *Semiramide* and *Il barbiere di Siviglia*, the prelude to Saint-Saëns' *Le Déluge*, the Dance of the Hours from *La Gioconda*, the intermezzos from *L'Amico Fritz* and *Cavalleria rusticana*, and excerpts from Ginastera's *Estancias* (with the Teatro Colón Orchestra for Odeon).

Martini, Louis (b. 1912). Born in Marseille and educated at the Paris Conservatoire where he studied conducting with Gaubert and Bigot, Martini was a violist in the Pasdeloup and Paris Conservatoire Orchestras and in the Loewenguth Quartet (1934–5). He founded the Chorale des Jeunesses Musicales de France (1935), first conducted in 1945, and appeared with major orchestras in Paris. A specialist in choral music and major works for soloists, choir and orchestra, he has been a teacher of choral singing at the Paris Conservatoire since 1966. He led important revivals of music by Charpentier, Delalande, and others, directed radio recitals of motets of the Versailles school, and at the same time performed compositions by contemporary composers such as Honegger, Webern and Stravinsky, whose *Threni* he premièred in France in 1958. With the Chorale des Jeunesses Musicales de France he has made numerous recordings, including Charpentier's *Te Deum*, *Magnificat* and *Messe de minuit*, Giroust's *Messe de sacre de Louis XVI* and *Super Flumina Babylonis*, the *Te Deum* of Gilles and Delalande, and collections entitled *Chansons de Provence* and *Musique de la Révolution française* (for Erato), Fauré's *Requiem* (for Club National du Disque), Charpentier's *Miserere des Jésuites*, *Le Reniement de St Pierre*, *De Profundis*, *Missa Assumpta Est Maria* and *Lamentations*, Gervais' *Exaudite Te* and *Te Deum*, Lully's *Dies Irae*, Bernier's *Confitebor tibi Domine*, Delalande's *De Profundis*, and *Te Deum*, Campra's *Psaume 53* and Victoria's *O vos omnes* (for Pathé), and Villa-Lobos' *Choros No. 10* (for Columbia), Charpentier's *Le Malade imaginaire*, Lully's *Le Bourgeois gentilhomme* and collections of music of that period (for La Guilde Internationale du Disque). Some of these discs have been issued by Bach Guild, Turnabout and Musical Heritage Society. He also recorded de Mondonville's *Cantate Domino* (with the Paillard Orchestra *et al.*, issued by Music Guild).

Martinon, Jean (1910–76). Born into a musical family at Lyon, Martinon studied at the conservatoire there (1924–5) and then at the Paris Conservatoire (1926–9) where he was a pupil of d'Indy and Roussel. He played the violin in the Paris Conservatoire Orchestra, gave solo recitals, composed, took a master's degree in Arts at the Sorbonne (1932), and studied conducting with Munch and Desormière. He first conducted when he was asked to direct one of his own compositions at a concert where he was also appearing as a solo violinist, and soon after had to take over unexpectedly from Munch. In World War II he served in the French army, was taken prisoner in 1940 and spent two years in a German prisoner-of-war camp, from which he escaped and was recaptured three times. In captivity he wrote a symphony, a motet *Absolve Domine*, in memory of French musicians who perished in the war, and a setting of Psalm 136 which became known as the *Chant des Captifs*. Munch gave this work its first performance in Paris in 1942, and the audience, then suffering under the Nazi occupation, gave it an unusually warm reception because of its obvious implications.

After his return to civil life in 1943, Martinon was asked to conduct a concert of the Pasdeloup Orchestra as his own symphony was in the programme. His success led to his appointment as conductor of the Bordeaux Symphony Orchestra (1943–5), after which he became assistant conductor to Munch with the Paris Conservatoire Orchestra (1944–6). He made guest appearances in Britain and South America, and was appointed associate conductor to Boult with the London Philharmonic Orchestra (1949–51), artistic director of the Concerts Lamoureux (1951–8), artistic director of the Israel Philharmonic Orchestra (1958–60), general music director at Düsseldorf (1960–64), artistic director of the Chicago Symphony Orchestra (1963–8), director of the principal orchestra of the French radio and television network, the French National Radio

Orchestra (1968 onwards), and music director of the Hague Philharmonic Orchestra (1974 onwards), which is also known as the Residentie Orchestra. He toured widely in many continents, both as a guest conductor and with the Paris Conservatoire, French National Radio and Hague Philharmonic Orchestras. His list of compositions is extensive and includes five symphonies, concertos and chamber music; two of his symphonies and his Violin Concerto No. 2 have been recorded. In 1948 he was awarded the Prix Béla Bartók for his String Quartet No. 1; his other honours included the Grand Prix de la Ville de Paris (1945), Officier de la Légion d'Honneur and Chevalier des Arts et Lettres.

Martinon was an elegant conductor with an exemplary technique. Although he enjoyed conducting the French repertoire, his real preference was for the German classics, which he attributed to his Alsatian ancestry. In Chicago he gave polished and impressive performances of Haydn, Mozart, Beethoven, Schubert, Schumann, Mendelssohn, Brahms, Wagner and Mahler, and a Beethoven Symphony No. 9 which he led towards the end of his second season there attracted high praise. But he found that he was always called to conduct French music, and his identification with French composers caused him to regret at the end of his life that he had never been asked to record Mahler. His Beethoven and Brahms in particular stood apart from the accepted interpretations of the German school of conductors; his characteristically French style emphasised clarity at the expense of expression and power. He also believed that the public never took him seriously as a composer, but he was not the only conductor to suffer that fate. His mild temperament and his disinclination to confront orchestras or their managements were part of the reason for his unhappy experience with the Chicago orchestra. His appointment was made without the prior knowledge or approval of Reiner, his predecessor, who had controlled the players with something akin to terror. The orchestra, too, was not sympathetic to conductors of the French school, such as Defauw, who had been their conductor from 1943 to 1949. Furthermore, the critic of *The Chicago Tribune*, Claudia Cassidy, held a disproportionately powerful position in forming local musical opinion, and she was antagonistic to Martinon, as indeed to many others. An untenable situation developed with the orchestra and its supporters divided into two warring camps. After he left he still retained his high admiration for the orchestra, but he described Chicago as a provincial town he was not sorry to leave.

His wide experience of conducting in many countries brought home to Martinon the differences between national styles in orchestral playing, and the problem of the guest conductor in imposing his interpretation on a relatively strange orchestra. It is, for example, difficult to ask players with solo passages in standard works to play them differently from their practice for many years. Then, inadvertently correcting a strong player instead of a weak one can destroy the conductor's rapport with the entire orchestra. He found that orchestras do not always appreciate that French music and German music call for different attacks, endings, and rates of crescendo and diminuendo.

Decca was the first company to engage Martinon as a conductor, at the time when he was with the London Philharmonic Orchestra. Among his first discs were 78s of *Le Tombeau de Couperin* and Chabrier's *Suite pastorale* (with the London Philharmonic Orchestra), which attracted warm praise for their precision and nuance. On LP he then recorded (with the London Philharmonic Orchestra) the overtures *Si j'étais Roi*, *Zampa*, *Le Calife de Bagdad*, *La Dame blanche*, *Orphée aux enfers*, *La Grande-Duchesse de Gérolstein*, *Barbe-bleue*, *La Belle Hélène* and *Le Mariage aux lanternes*, *Le Beau Danube* (of Johann Strauss, arranged by Désormière), the ballet music from *William Tell*, the polka and fugue from *Schwanda*, *Les Patineurs* (of Meyerbeer, arranged by Lambert), the ballet music from *Le Cid*, *Namouna* Suites Nos 1 and 2, Ibert's *Divertissement*, Fauré's *Ballade* and Françaix's *Concertino* (with Kathleen Long), Saint-Saëns' Piano Concerto No. 2 (with Lympany), Liszt's *Totentanz* and Mendelssohn's *Capriccio brilliant* and *Rondo brilliant* (with Katin), and an aria from Tchaikovsky's *The Maid of Orleans* (with Zareska). He also recorded for Decca *Giselle*, *Jeux d'enfants*, *Danse macabre*, *Le Rouet d'Omphale*, Prokofiev's Symphonies Nos 5 and 7 and *Russian Overture*, the Hungarian March from *La Damnation de Faust* and the overtures *Le Carnaval romain*, *Benvenuto Cellini*, *Le Corsaire* and *Béatrice et Bénédict* (with the Paris Conservatoire Orchestra) and Tchaikovsky's Symphony No. 6 (with the Vienna Philharmonic Orchestra); the last listed was an admirably dramatic account, made in 1959.

Martinon's other recordings were mostly from the French repertoire. Included were Prokofiev's Symphony No. 1 and suite from *The Love of Three Oranges*, *L'Apprenti sorcier*, *Prélude à l'après-midi d'un faune*, *El amor brujo*, *Nights in the Gardens of Spain* (with del Pueyo), *Bacchus et Ariane*, *Le Festin de l'araignée*, *Pastorale d'été* and Fauré's *Pavane* (with the Lamoureux Orchestra for Philips); Enesco's *Romanian Rhapsody No. 1*, a *Slavonic Dance* of Dvořák, and the Hungarian March from *La Damnation de Faust* (with the London Philharmonic Orchestra for Parlophone and MGM); Franck's *Symphony in D minor* and *Symphonic Variations* (with Entremont), Saint-Saëns' Symphony No. 3, *Danse macabre* and *Le Rouet d'Omphale*, Khachaturian's Flute Concerto (with Rampal), Pierné's *Cydalise et le chèvre-pied*, *Divertissement sur un thème pastoral*, and *Konzertstück pour harpe et orchestre* (with Laskine), Poulenc's Organ Concerto (with Alain) and *Concerto champêtre* (with Veyron-Lacroix), Landowski's Symphony No. 2 and Piano Concerto No. 2 (with d'Arco), and Roussel's Symphony No. 2, *Petite suite*, *Le Festin de l'araignée*, *Bacchus et Ariane*, *Aeneas* and *Pour une fête de printemps* (with the ORTF Orchestra for Erato); Saint-Saëns' Cello Concerto No. 1, Lalo's Cello Concerto and Bruch's *Kol Nidrei* (with Fournier and the Lamoureux Orchestra for DGG); Lalo's *Namouna* Suites Nos 1 and 2, and *Rapsodie norvégienne*, Bizet's *Symphony in C major*, *Jeux d'enfants* and suite from *La jolie fille de Perth* (with the ORTF Orchestra for DGG); Lalo's *Symphonie espagnole* (with David Oistrakh and the Philharmonia Orchestra for EMI); Dutilleux's Symphony No. 1 and his own Symphony No. 2 (with the ORTF Orchestra for ORTF); *Les Patineurs* and the ballet music from *Le Cid* (with the Israel Philharmonic Orchestra for Decca); Dvořák's *Slavonic Dances* Op. 46 and some from Op. 72, Borodin's Symphony No. 2, *Capriccio espagnol*, the March from *Tsar Saltan*, Shostakovich's Symphony No. 1 and suite from *The Age of Gold* (with the London Symphony Orchestra for RCA, later re-issued by Decca); the overtures *Le Carnaval romain*, *Le Corsaire* and *Le Roi Lear* (with the Lamoureux Orchestra for Urania); *The Three-cornered Hat* (complete, with the Paris Opéra-Comique Orchestra for Urania, issued in Britain by Nixa); *L'Enfance du Christ* (with the French National Radio Orchestra *et al.* for La Guilde Internationale du Disque, issued in the US by Nonesuch); Prokofiev's Piano Concerto No. 1 (with Foldès and the Lamoureux Orchestra for Vox); Chausson's *Poème* (with Perlman and l'Orchestre de Paris for EMI), Liszt's *Hungarian Rhapsody No. 2* (with the London Philharmonic Orchestra for Mercury), Piano Concerto No. 1 and *Hungarian Fantasia* (with Bianca and the Lamoureux Orchestra for Plymouth).

When Martinon was with the Chicago Symphony Orchestra, RCA produced a series that approached Reiner's, with the same orchestra, for style and brilliance. The works included Nielsen's Symphony No. 4 and *Helios* overture, Bizet's *Symphony in C major* and two *L'Arlésienne* suites, excerpts from the incidental music for *A Midsummer Night's Dream*, Ravel's *Introduction et allegro*, *Boléro*, *Ma Mère l'Oye*, *Rapsodie espagnole*, *Alborada del gracioso* and *Daphnis et Chloé* Suite No. 2, the overture to *Le Roi d'Ys*, Weber's two Clarinet Concertos (with Benny Goodman), *Bacchus et Ariane*, *The Miraculous Mandarin*, *Nobilissima visione*, Martin's *Concerto for Seven Wind Instruments, Strings and Percussion*, Varèse's *Arcana*, Mennin's Symphony No. 7 and his own Symphony No. 4.

In 1974 Vox released in two of their Vox Boxes, Prokofiev's seven Symphonies, the *Overture on Hebrew Themes* and the *Russian Overture* (with the ORTF Orchestra). Then in the last years of Martinon's life, EMI cast him again in the role of specialist in French music, in two superb sets of Debussy's orchestral music, and of Ravel's orchestral music and works for solo instruments and orchestra. The Debussy collection included *La Mer*, *Danse* (arranged by Ravel), *Nocturnes*, *Berceuse héroïque*, *Jeux*, *Images pour orchestre*, *La Boîte à joujoux*, *Children's Corner* (arranged by Caplet), *Petite suite* (arranged by Büsser), *Fantaisie* (with Ciccolini), *La plus que lente*, *Première rapsodie* (with Dangain), *Rapsodie* (with Londeix), *Danse sacrée et danse profane*, *Prélude à l'après-midi d'un faune*, *Khamma*, *Printemps*, *Musiques pour le Roi Lear* and *Marche écossaise* (with the ORTF Chorus and ORTF National Orchestra). The Ravel series included *Boléro*, the overture *Shéhérazade*, *Rapsodie espagnole*, *La Valse*, *Daphnis et Chloé*, *Tzigane* (with Perlman), *Valses nobles et sentimentales*, *Ma Mère l'Oye*, *Le Tombeau de Couperin*, *Pavane pour une infante défunte*, *Alborada del gracioso*, *Une Barque sur l'océan*, *Menuet antique* and *Piano Concerto in G major* and *Piano Concerto for the Left Hand in D major* (with Ciccolini, and l'Orchestre de Paris). Critics have inevitably found fault with some recordings in the two sets, but they contain some of the finest performances of the pieces recorded; the general level of performance aspires to greatness, and makes the series a major recording achievement and undoubtedly Martinon's finest legacy to us. His remaining recordings are *Symphonie fantastique* and its sequel *Lélio*, Dukas' Symphony No. 1, *La Péri*, *L'Apprenti sorcier* and *Polyeucte* overture, Honegger's *Une Cantate de Noël*, *Pacific 231*, *Rugby* and *Pastorale d'été*, Saint-Saëns' five Symphonies, Ibert's *Escales*, *Ouverture de fête* and *Tropismes pour des amours imaginaires*, Schmitt's *Psaume XLVII* and *La Tragédie de Salomé* (with the French National Radio Orchestra for EMI), and Schumann's Symphony No. 4, Brahms' *Tragic Overture*, and excerpts from *La Damnation de Faust* (with l'Orchestre Mondial des Jeunesses Musicales for EMI).

Martorell, Oriol (b. 1927). Born in Barcelona, Martorell studied music privately, qualified as a music teacher and choral director, and graduated as doctor in the history of art at the University of Barcelona, where he is professor of the history of music. He also lectures at the Universities of Illinois and California, teaches choral conducting at the Manuel de Falla Summer School at Granada, has written books and articles, music criticism and record reviews, and is a member of the organisations concerned with music in Catalonia. In 1949 he founded and is director of the 'Coral Sant Jordi'; he has given numerous concerts with the ensemble throughout Europe, and with them has recorded recitals of Spanish songs of the Renaissance, Catalan songs, and popular Spanish Nativity songs (for Columbia), Spanish polyphonic music of the 15th and 16th centuries (for Studio SM, France), Stravinsky's *Mass* (for Vergara), traditional Catalan songs (for Apollo), Marti's *Magnificat*, Casanovas' *Responsoris de Semana Santa* (for Edigsa) and chorales for Advent and Christmas of Bach (for Concentric).

Marx, Burle (b. 1902). Born in São Paulo, Brazil, Marx toured the country as a pianist when a child, then studied in Berlin. He returned to Brazil in 1930, founded and conducted an orchestra which became the Philharmonic Orchestra of Rio de Janeiro, and taught music at the Rio de Janeiro University. He was a guest conductor in South America, the United States and Germany, and wrote symphonic and choral works. Victor released a 78 r.p.m. disc on which he conducted an ensemble in Villa-Lobos' *Bachianas brasileiras No. 1.*

Märzendorfer, Ernst (b. 1921). A native of Salzburg and a pupil of Krauss, Märzendorfer studied at the Mozarteum Academy, and started his career as a conductor at the Graz Opera (1945–51). He then conducted at the Salzburg Opera, and was chief instructor of the conducting classes at the Mozarteum (1951), was on the staff of the Teatro Colón at Buenos Aires (1952–3), and returned to the Mozarteum to become conductor of the orchestra there (1953–8), which he led on a tour of the United States in 1956, as part of the Mozart bicentennial celebrations. He became a conductor at the Deutsche Oper in West Berlin (1958) and at the Vienna State Opera (1961), made his debut at the New York Metropolitan Opera (1965), and has appeared in many leading European opera houses. Märzendorfer has a wide range of musical sympathies, from Haydn and Mozart to contemporary music, encompassing Wagner, Strauss, Verdi, Mahler and Bruckner; his direction of the operas of Mozart and Strauss has been particularly acclaimed. In 1969 he premièred at Graz his reconstruction of the fourth movement of Bruckner's Symphony No. 9, which is 25 minutes long, and has been described by him as 'quite modern, going towards Schoenberg', and moving 'from a spirit of pessimism to one of near serenity near the end'.

Märzendorfer's immense contribution to the gramophone has been the recording of the complete 106 symphonies of Haydn, which he completed in 1971 after four years. The orchestra is the Vienna Chamber Orchestra, and the enterprise was for Musical Heritage Society in the United States. The set naturally stands beside that of Dorati, which was recorded at much the same time. Märzendorfer is an individualistic conductor, and demonstrates a true sense of style, although he does not impose the tension and drive of Dorati; his direction becomes more effective in the more mature and larger-scale symphonies. Like Dorati, he uses the authentic modern scores by Universal Edition, Vienna, edited by H. C. Robbins Landon, but he ignores the convention of bassoon continuo, and almost entirely omits the harpsichord in the smaller-scale symphonies. Nonetheless, the series is, as a whole, a notable achievement.

Märzendorfer's other records have included Haydn's Symphony No. 85 and some Schubert dances (with the Milan Angelicum Orchestra for Angelicum), Mozart's Symphonies K. 45a, K. 45b, K. 75, K. 76, K. 81, K. 95, K. 96, K. 97, K. 120 and K. 141a, Leopold Mozart's *Symphony in G major*, the overture to Piccinni's *Iphigénie en Tauride*, Salieri's *Symphony in D*, Pergolesi's Concertino No. 1, Bellini's Oboe Concerto (with Hertel), Hasse's *Flute Concerto in D* (with Riessberger), and Gluck's *Symphony in G* and Suite du Divertissement from *Iphigénie en Aulide* (with the Austrian Tonkünstler Orchestra for Erato), Mozart's Bassoon Concerto (with Klepai), a Horn Concerto (with Blank), German Dances K. 586 and Marches K. 335 (with the Salzburg Mozarteum Orchestra for DGG), Divertimentos K. 113 and K. 334, and Minuets K. 463

(with the Salzburg Mozarteum Orchestra for Decca), Boieldieu's Harp Concerto and Rodrigo's *Concerto Serenade* (with Zabaleta and the Berlin Radio Symphony Orchestra for DGG), Mozart's Flute and Harp Concerto (with Zöller and Zabaleta) and Reinecke's Harp Concerto (with Zabaleta, and the Berlin Philharmonic Orchestra for DGG), Mendelssohn's Violin and Piano Concerto (with Glenn, List and the Vienna Chamber Orchestra for Westminster), *L'elisir d'amore* (with the Berlin Symphony Orchestra *et al.* for Ariola), *Eine Nacht in Venedig* (with the MAV Symphony Orchestra *et al.* for Hungaroton), and Hildach's *Der Lenz* (with van Dijk and the Berlin Radio Symphony Orchestra for DGG).

Mascagni, Pietro (1863–1945). The composer of *Cavalleria rusticana* was, at the outset of his career, a conductor of the municipal band in the small Italian town of Cerignola. He became well known as a conductor in Italy, and toured South America and the United States with his own company, conducting *Cavalleria rusticana*, *L'Amico Fritz*, *Zanetto* and *Iris*. He recorded *Cavalleria rusticana* and *L'Amico Fritz* for HMV and Cetra respectively, the first in 1940 to mark the 50th anniversary of its première. The cast included Gigli and Simionato, and Mascagni proclaimed on the first of the 22 sides that the cast was unrivalled and that the performance was exemplary. Despite his recommendation, it was by any standards a crude and boisterous recording. The singers were invariably too loud and the conductor/composer ignored his own markings. It appears that he was no better a conductor in his earlier years; when he conducted *Cavalleria rusticana* in Cologne in 1906, according to a witness, Alfred Sendrey, the performance 'dragged and crept along, without the fire and colour of the Italian verismo'. But with Mascagni's recording of *L'Amico Fritz* it is the opposite; it is unquestionably a more refined piece of music, even if it is not as popular as *Cav.*, and the principals, Tagliavini and Tassinari, sing beautifully. Cetra transferred the thirteen 78 r.p.m. discs to two LPs and these were issued in the US by Everest. Mascagni also recorded the intermezzos from *Cav.*, and *L'Amico Fritz* and the overture to *Le maschere* (for DGG), the overture to *I vespri siciliani* (with the Berlin Staatsoper Orchestra for DGG), *Il barbiere di Siviglia* and *William Tell*, and the dances from *Iris* and *Die Rantzau* (with the Berlin Staatsoper Orchestra for Odeon).

Masini, Gianfranco (b. 1937). Born in Reggio Emilia, Italy, Masini studied at Parma and Bologna Conservatories and with Scherchen, became a repetiteur, assistant conductor and chorus-master at theatres in the province of Emilia, and made his debut with *La Bohème* in 1963. He has since conducted opera companies in Bulgaria, Czechoslovakia, France, Spain, and at the New York Metropolitan. He led a very successful recording of Rossini's *Elisabetta Regina d'Inghilterra* (with the London Symphony Orchestra *et al.* for Philips), as well as aria recitals with Caballé (and the Barcelona Symphony Orchestra for Decca) and Mesplé (with the Paris Opéra Orchestra for EMI).

Massini, Egizzio (1894–1966). Born in Alexandria, where his father was the director of an opera company, Massini studied at the Pesaro Conservatory, first conducted at Istanbul, was a conductor in Romania and then contributed to the foundation of the Bucharest Opera. He conducted at the Opera for 40 years, was its general director (1946–50), and introduced to Romania many operas of the 19th and 20th centuries. For Electrecord he recorded *Il trovatore*, with the Bucharest Opera.

Masson, Diego (b. 1935). Born in Tossa, Spain, Masson studied at the Paris Conservatoire, for composition under Leibowitz and Maderna, and for conducting with Boulez. He worked as a percussionist (1955–66), made his debut in Paris in 1966 as a conductor, and in that year founded the Ensemble Musique Vivante. More recently he has been appointed musical director of the Marseille Opera; he has been a guest conductor in Britain, the Netherlands, Austria, Sweden, Switzerland, *et al.*, with a repertoire ranging from Handel to Berio, but is mostly concerned with operas and modern music. His recordings have included a collection of Renaissance music for brass (for Nonesuch), Berio's *Laborintus 2*, Globokar's *Fluide* and Boulez's *Domaines* (with l'Ensemble Musique Vivante for Harmonia Mundi), Boulez's *Le Marteau sans maître* (with Minton and L'Ensemble Musique Vivante for CBS), Globokar's *Accord* (with l'Ensemble Musique Vivante for Wergo), Stockhausen's *Aus den sieben Tagen*, *Fais voile vers le soleil* and *Liaison* (with l'Ensemble Musique Vivante for EMI), Dresden's *Chorus Tragicus* (with the Hague Philharmonic Orchestra *et al.* for Donemus) and Keuris' Alto Saxophone Concerto (with Bogaard and the Netherlands Radio Philharmonic Orchestra for Donemus).

Masters, John Randolph. No biographical details can be obtained for the conductor John Randolph Masters, whom Oryx have issued conducting *Symphonie fantastique* (with the

Musicians of the Paris Opéra), Brahms' Violin Concerto (with Michaels and the Berlin Pro Musica Symphony Orchestra), Schubert's Symphonies Nos 2 and 8 (with the Vienna Symphony Orchestra), and Brahms' Symphonies Nos. 1, 2 and 3 and the *Academic Festival Overture*, Dvořák's Symphony No. 9, the Grieg Piano Concerto (with Haansen) and the two *Peer Gynt* suites, and Mahler's Symphony No. 1 (with the Symphony Orchestra of the Philadelphia Music Guild).

Masur, Kurt (b. 1927). Born in Brieg, Germany, Masur studied the piano and cello at the national music school at Breslau (1942–4), then after war service attended the Hochschule für Musik at Leipzig (1946–8), where he was a pupil of Bongartz for conducting. He was a repetiteur and occasional conductor at the Halle State Theatre (1948–51), conductor at Erfurt (1951–3), first conductor at the Leipzig Opera and guest conductor with the Leipzig and Dresden Radio Orchestras (1953–5), second conductor of the Dresden Philharmonic Orchestra (1955–8), then became the orchestra's general music director (1958), general music director of the Schwerin Opera (1958–60) and music director at the Berlin Komische Oper (1960–64) where he worked with Walter Felsenstein, the founder of the new realist school of musical theatre. He has been a guest conductor in Eastern and Western Europe, Japan and South America (1964–7), became chief conductor of the Dresden Philharmonic Orchestra (1967–72), was awarded the National Prize of the German Democratic Republic (1969 and 1970), and since 1970 has been chief conductor of the Leipzig Gewandhaus Orchestra. He is also principal guest conductor of the Dallas Symphony Orchestra, Texas, has conducted the New Philharmonia Orchestra in London, led the Gewandhaus Orchestra to the Edinburgh Festival, and has appeared at the Salzburg and Prague Spring Festivals, as well as in the festivals in DR Germany. He is a commanding figure before the orchestra, is vigorous and animated in his gestures, and conducts without a score. His performances of Beethoven, Brahms, Schumann, Bruckner and Wagner in particular are impressive; he is restrained, disciplined and correct, but lacks nothing in virtuosity, sensitivity and majesty. His tempi can be flexible, but nonetheless convincing.

Masur has appeared, as a recording artist, on a number of labels in the West. His major recordings have been with the Leipzig Gewandhaus Orchestra, initially for Eterna; the first released, in 1972, was a set of the complete twelve early string symphonies of Mendelssohn (issued by DGG – Archiv), which were warmly praised for their superb string playing and committed direction. Other Mendelssohn works followed, the five symphonies and the overtures *The Hebrides*, *Meeresstille und glückliche Fahrt*, *Die schöne Melusine*, *Ruy Blas* and *Trumpet Overture*, and *Die erste Walpurgisnacht*. In 1974 RCA issued the Beethoven *Missa Solemnis*, but the performance was only moderately praised by the record critics; it was not until the nine Beethoven symphonies and the overtures were released by Philips in 1975 that it was recognised that Masur was an artist of considerable stature. His direction of the great Leipzig orchestra demonstrated a concentration, sensitivity, subtlety in phrasing and dynamics and a vitality, all transformed by a profound conception of Beethoven's nobility and grandeur. Indeed, this set for many eclipsed those of other conductors in the West much more celebrated and internationally renowned.

His other recordings include the Beethoven Violin Concerto (with Accardo), the four Schumann symphonies and the overtures *Hermann und Dorothea*, *Julius Caesar*, *Genoveva* and *Die Braut von Messina*, and the *Overture, Scherzo and Finale*, the four Brahms symphonies and the Piano Concerto No. 2 (with Ousset), Bruckner's Symphonies Nos 4, 5, 7 and 9, the piano arrangement of the Beethoven Violin Concerto (with Webersinke), the five Prokofiev Piano Concertos (with Béroff) and *Overture on Hebrew Themes*, and Gershwin's *Porgy and Bess* suite, *Cuban Overture*, *An American in Paris*, *Rhapsody in Blue* and *Piano Concerto* (with Stöckigt, and with the Leipzig Gewandhaus Orchestra), Bach's Cantatas Nos 51 and 202 (with Adele Stolte and the Leipzig Gewandhaus Orchestra) Haydn's Symphonies Nos 5 and 61 (with the Berlin Radio Symphony Orchestra) and Nos 96 and 102 (with the Dresden Philharmonic Orchestra), Handel's cantata *Armida abbandonata* (with Woytowicz and the Berlin Chamber Orchestra), a number of the Mozart Piano Concertos (with Annerose Schmidt and the Dresden Philharmonic Orchestra) and the Violin Concertos K. 211 and K. 268 (with Andrade), the Grieg Piano Concerto and Weber's *Konzertstück* (with Schmidt and the Dresden Philharmonic Orchestra), Ravel's *Piano Concerto for the Left Hand* and Nowka's *Piano Concerto for the Left Hand* (with Rapp and the Dresden Philharmonic Orchestra), Shostakovich's Violin Concerto No. 1 (with Schmahl and the Dresden Philharmonic Orchestra), the Beethoven Triple Concerto (with

Suk, Chuchro and Panenka and the Czech Philharmonic Orchestra for Supraphon), a recital with soprano Geszty (with the Dresden Philharmonic Orchestra), Brahms' Piano Concerto No. 1 (with Woodward and the New Philharmonia Orchestra for RCA), Double Concerto (with Ruggiero and G. Ricci) and Schumann's *Violin Fantasia in C* (with Ricci, and the New Philharmonia Orchestra for Turnabout), Prokofiev's Symphony No. 1, Reinhold's *Concert Music for Flute, Brass and Orchestra* and *Triptych for Orchestra* and Griesbach's *African Symphony* (with the Dresden Philharmonic Orchestra), excerpts from Gerster's opera *Enoch Arden* (with the Leipzig Radio Orchestra *et al.*), Görner's *Variations on a Theme of Smetana* (with the Leipzig Radio Orchestra), and Kochan's cantata, *Die Asche von Birkenau*.

Mata, Eduardo (b. 1942). Born in Mexico City into a musical environment, Mata first learned the guitar, then studied at the National Conservatory of Music under Chávez and Halffter, and at the Berkshire Music Center in the United States under Leinsdorf and Schuller, and became the resident conductor there. He made his first impact in Mexico with performances of major *avant-garde* works, was musical director of the Mexican Ballet Company (1963–4), of the Guadalajara Symphony Orchestra (1965–6), of the University Philharmonic Orchestra of the National University of Mexico (1966–76), principal guest conductor, musical adviser then principal conductor of the Phoenix Symphony Orchestra, Arizona (1970–78), artistic director of the Pueblo Ciudad Musical Festival (since 1974) and music director of the Dallas Symphony Orchestra (since 1977). He has been a guest conductor in many countries and has appeared with acclaim in New York, Tokyo, Paris, Stockholm, London, Berlin and Hamburg, as well as conducting major orchestras in the US. In Mexico he has led first performances of music by Boulez, Stockhausen, *et al.*, was director of the Casals Festival (1976), toured Mexico with the New Philharmonia Orchestra (1976), led a Mahler cycle with the National Symphony Orchestra (1975), and has been awarded the Golden Lyre of the Mexican Union of Musicians (1973) and the Elias Sourasky Prize (1976). His compositions include symphonic and chamber works, ballets and vocal music, and pieces composed directly for tape.

Mata is an impressive conductor, with an excellent technique, and has a personality that appeals to orchestral players. Much as he enjoys conducting the major symphony orchestras, he prefers to work with one orchestra and to try to achieve results over a long period, so that his criteria prevail in every aspect of interpretation. In Dallas he plans to programme Messiaen, Schoenberg, Webern, Penderecki, Bruckner and Mahler, who have rarely, if ever, been played there. Also, he aims to give the Dallas orchestra a more European sound, with a mellow dark string tone, a more individual woodwind sound and brass that will blend better with the strings. Dvořák, Brahms and Strauss are other composers in whom he has a special interest.

RCA Victor and Voz Viva de Mexico have both recorded Mata on a number of discs with the University Philharmonic Orchestra, in music by Revueltas, Chávez, Halffter, Galindo, Muench, Moncayo, Cosio, Jimenez, Mabarak, Quintanar, Heras, Kuri-Aldana, Ponce and himself, but none of these records has been released in the US or Europe. In London RCA have more recently recorded him conducting the complete works of Revueltas on two discs (with the New Philharmonia Orchestra), the complete *El amor brujo* and *The Three-cornered Hat* (with the London Symphony Orchestra).

Matačić, Lovro von (b. 1899). Born in Sušak, Habsburg Croatia (now Yugoslavia), Matačić was a member of the Vienna Boys Choir, studied at the Vienna Conservatory, and began his conducting career as a repetiteur at the Cologne Opera. He was then conductor at Osijek (1919–20), Novi Sad (1920–22), Ljubljana (1924–6), Belgrade (1926–32), Zagreb (1932–8) and Belgrade again (1938–41). After World War II he was conductor at Skopje, general music director of the Dresden Staatskapelle and conductor at the Berlin Staatsoper (1956–8), conductor at La Scala, Milan and in Vienna (1958), general music director at Frankfurt am Main (1961–5), regular guest conductor at the Vienna State Opera, and conductor of the Zagreb Philharmonic Orchestra (since 1965). He has appeared with orchestras in Europe and North and South America, and at music festivals in Salzburg, Venice, Florence, Rome, Naples *et al.*

In the years 1955–63 Matačić made a number of recordings for EMI, including *Pagliacci* and *La fanciulla del West* (with the La Scala Orchestra *et al.*), *Die lustige Witwe* and excerpts from *Arabella* (with the Philharmonia Orchestra *et al.*), *Scheherazade*, Bruckner's Symphony No. 4, *Overture in G minor* and Scherzo from the Symphony No. 0, Balakirev's Symphony No. 1, *Russia*, *Islamey*, *Tamara* and *Overture on Three Russian Themes*, the overture, prelude to Act III and Polovtsian Dances from *Prince Igor*, *A Night on the Bare Mountain*, and *Russian Easter Festival* overture (with the Philharmonia Orchestra), Tchaikovsky's Theme and Variations from the *Suite No. 3*, *Capriccio italien* and a dance from *Eugene Onegin* (with the La Scala Orchestra), Paganini's Violin Concerto No. 1 and Glazunov's Violin Concerto (with Rabin and the Philharmonia Orchestra), Bruch's Violin Concerto No. 1 and Prokofiev's Violin Concerto No. 1 (with Oistrakh and the London Symphony Orchestra), and the Grieg and Schumann Piano Concertos (with Richter and the Monte Carlo Opera Orchestra). He has also recorded Beethoven's Symphony No. 3, Tchaikovsky's Symphonies Nos 5 and 6, Bruckner's Symphonies Nos 5 and 7, orchestral excerpts from *Götterdämmerung* and Korte's symphonic poem, *The Story of the Flutes* (with the Czech Philharmonic Orchestra for Supraphon), *Der Freischütz* (with the Berlin Deutsche Oper Orchestra *et al.* for Eurodisc/Ariola, also issued by Cetra), excerpts from *Boris Godunov* (with the Berlin Deutsche Oper Orchestra *et al.*) and from *Fidelio* (with the Frankfurt State Opera Orchestra *et al.*), and Tchaikovsky's Symphony No. 5 (with the Zagreb Philharmonic Orchestra for Jugoton).

Matačić is an interesting conductor for modern listeners, as he has a concept of interpretation typical of an earlier generation, which included Stokowski, Koussevitzky, Mengelberg and Furtwängler. It finds little favour among today's music critics, who have been deeply influenced by conductors such as Toscanini, Szell and Klemperer, whose literal readings avoid tempi variations within movements and exaggerated phrasings. It is instructive to listen to Matačić's recorded performances of the Tchaikovsky and Bruckner symphonies, where the basic tempi are quickened and relaxed according to the lyrical or dramatic nature of the passage; he imposes in many places an unusual degree of expression on the music, disturbing to those who know it exactly as it is written. It can be argued that without this 'interpretation' the music would be lifeless, but the problem is that the degree to which it is tolerable depends on the performing conventions of the time. In Bruckner's Symphony No. 5, Matačić uses the Schalk edition, which is regarded as unacceptable today because of its re-orchestration in certain parts, and he makes cuts in the finale, another practice deplored now. However, the recording of *Die lustige Witwe*, which he made for EMI in 1963, was a triumph, and remains in the catalogue today as one of the finest opera sets produced by Walter Legge. The cast included Schwarzkopf, Gedda and Waechter, and the records were, to quote Edward Greenfield, 'a magical set, guaranteed to send shivers of delight through any listener with its vivid sense of atmosphere and superb musicianship'.

Matchavariani, Alexey (b. 1913). Born in Gory, Caucasus, Matchavariani studied at the Tiflis (Tbilisi) Conservatory, where from 1940 he was a teacher. He has written orchestral music, concertos, an opera, an oratorio, ballets and many popular songs, and conducted the Moscow Radio Orchestra in a recording of his Violin Concerto, with the soloist Vaiman.

Matheson, John (b. 1928). Born in Seacliff, New Zealand, and educated at Otago University, Matheson came to England in 1950, studied at the Royal College of Music, and made his debut as a conductor at Sadler's Wells Opera in 1953. He was on the staff at Covent Garden Opera (1953–60); since then he has been a freelance conductor, and has appeared in Europe, New Zealand, Australia and Canada, particularly in opera, where his repertoire includes, in addition to many standard works, Henze's *Boulevard Solitude*, Poulenc's *Les Dialogues des Carmélites*, and other comparatively lesser-known operas. In 1963–4 he recorded discs of excerpts from *La Belle Hélène* and *La traviata*, with the Sadler's Wells Company for EMI, and later accompanied the bass Rouleau in a disc of arias for Decca.

Mathias, William (b. 1934). Born in Whitland, Wales, Mathias was educated at the University College of Wales, and lectured at the University College of North Wales (1959–68 and since 1970) and at the University of Edinburgh (1968). He has composed orchestral, choral and chamber works, some of which have been recorded by Atherton and the English Chamber and the London Symphony Orchestras, and by Groves and the Royal Philharmonic Orchestra. He himself has recorded for Pye his own *Sinfonietta* with the Leicestershire Schools Symphony Orchestra.

Mathieson, Muir (1911–75). Born in Stirling, Scotland, and educated at the Royal College of Music, London, Mathieson conducted his first concert at the age of 13 and in 1935 was selected by Weill to direct the music in his comic opera *A Kingdom for a Cow* at its première in London. He joined Alexander Korda at London Films (1935–9) and then the J. Arthur Rank organisation, and was intimately connected with British films as an arranger and musical director. Altogether he directed the music for more than 600 films, and worked with composers such as Vaughan Williams, Bliss, Benjamin, Ireland and Toch in arranging their music for films. During World War II he was with the army and RAF film units and with the Central Office of Information, and later was musical director for the J. Arthur Rank film organisation. He directed a number of educational films, including *The Instruments of the Orchestra*, for which Britten wrote his *Variations and Fugue on a Theme of Purcell*, better known as *The Young Person's Guide to the Orchestra*. In addition he conducted most of the leading British orchestras, and for more than 15 years conducted a series of children's concerts at Harrow with the London Symphony Orchestra. Mathieson made some 78 r.p.m. discs of themes and music from various films including *Hamlet* (by Walton), *49th Parallel* and *The Invaders* (by Vaughan Williams), *The Overlanders* (by Ireland), *Malta GC* and *Oliver Twist* (by Bax), *Men of Two Worlds* and *The Shape of Things to Come* (by Bliss) and *The Red Shoes* (by Easdale); these were with the London Symphony, Philharmonia and National Symphony Orchestras, for EMI and Decca. He also recorded Benjamin's *Jamaican Song* and *Jamaican Rhumba* (with the London Symphony Orchestra for Decca) and a Tchaikovsky symphony and the *L'Arlésienne* and *Carmen* suites (with a London orchestra for World Record Club).

Mattes, Willy (b. 1916). Born in Vienna, Mattes studied at the Vienna Academy of Music with Weingartner (1937), conducted at Oldenburg and Leipzig (1937–9), composed for films in Berlin (1939–43), was a conductor for the Swedish Radio at Stockholm (1944–50) and for the South German Radio (from 1951), and has been chief conductor of the South German Radio Orchestra at Stuttgart since 1971. He has composed a violin concerto, orchestral pieces, and music for over 90 films, and has also published with the pseudonym Charles Wildman. He has made a number of records for EMI, including Korngold's Violin Concerto (with Hoelscher), incidental music to *Much Ado About Nothing* and *Theme and Variations* (with the Stuttgart Radio Orchestra), accompaniments for recitals by Gedda and Prey (with the Graunke Symphony Orchestra), and discs of excerpts from the operettas *Wiener Blut*, *Ein Walzertraum*, *Die Csardasfürstin*, *Gräfin Maritza*, *Giuditta*, *Der Graf von Luxemburg*, *Das Land des Lächelns*, *Die lustige Witwe*, *Der Zarewitsch*, *Der Bettelstudent*, *Die ungarische Hochzeit*, *Clivia*, *Der Vetter aus Dingsda* and *Schwarzwaldmädel* (with the Munich Symphony, Graunke Symphony and Stuttgart Philharmonic Orchestras *et al.*) and for Telefunken *Der Vogelhändler* and *The White Horse Inn*.

Matteucci, Juan. After early musical studies, the Italian musician Matteucci became principal cellist with the Symphony Orchestra of Chile at the age of 20, studied conducting with Busch and with Giulini and Votto at Milan, and returned to Chile to become assistant conductor of the Symphony Orchestra of Chile, then principal conductor of the Philharmonic Orchestra of Chile. He was appointed resident conductor of the New Zealand Symphony Orchestra (1964) and of the Auckland Symphonia; he has been a guest conductor in many countries, and toured the USSR in 1975 and 1977. Oryx released a disc on which he conducted the New Zealand Radio Orchestra in Lilburn's Symphony No. 3 and *Aotearoa Overture*.

Matzerath, Otto (1914–63). Born in Düsseldorf, where he studied at the conservatory, Matzerath was a repetiteur at the Mönchen-Gladbach-Rheydt State Theatre (1935), was conductor of opera at Krefeld (1936–8), at Würzburg (1938–40), general music director at Karlsruhe (1940–55), chief conductor of the Hessian Radio Orchestra at Frankfurt (1955–61) and finally conductor of the Turkish State Orchestra at Ankara. He also conducted the Yomiuri-Nippon Symphony Orchestra in Tokyo just before his death. His recordings include Mozart's Symphony No. 36 (with the Berlin Municipal Orchestra for Polydor, on 78s), Beethoven's Symphony No. 2 (with the Hessian Radio Orchestra for Vox), Schumann's Symphony No. 1 (with the RIAS Orchestra for Remington), Tchaikovsky's Piano Concerto No. 1 (with Gimpel and the Berlin Symphony Orchestra, for Maritim), Saint-Saëns' Cello Concerto No. 1 and the Boccherini Cello Concerto (with Hoelscher and the Berlin Philharmonic Orchestra for DGG).

Mauersberger, Erhard (b. 1903). Brother of Rudolf (below), Mauersberger was born in Mauersberg, Germany, was a member of the St Thomas Church Choir at Leipzig, and studied at the Leipzig Conservatory under Straube and Weinrich. He was choirmaster and organist at Aachen (1925–8) and Mainz (1928–30), where he also taught at the Hochschule für Musik, was musical director of churches of Thüringen in Eisenach (1930–61), where he also conducted the Bach Choir and was director of the Thüringen School of Church Music, and professor at the Franz Liszt Academy at Weimar.

In 1961 he was appointed cantor at the St Thomas Church at Leipzig, and with the Choir, the Leipzig Gewandhaus Orchestra and the Thomanenchor, *et al.*, recorded Bach's Cantatas Nos 18, 55, 62, 80, 140 and 189, parts of the *St Matthew Passion* and the *St John Passion*, and accompanied the tenor Schreier in a recital of arias from the Bach passions. Some of the cantatas were re-issued by DGG.

Mauersberger, Rudolf (1889–1971). Born in Mauersberg, Germany, Mauersberger studied at the Leipzig Conservatory and was a choral conductor and organist at Aachen and Eisenach (1919–30), and thereafter was a choral teacher and conductor at Dresden, where he conducted the Dresden Kreuzchor. His compositions included liturgical works for chorus, and a *Dresdner Requiem*, completed in 1948 and commemorating the destruction of Dresden by an Allied air raid in February, 1945. He recorded Schütz's *Kleine geistliche Konzerte*, *Musikalische Exequien*, *Die sieben Worte Jesu Christi am Kreuz*, *Doppelchörige Motetten*, *Deutsches Magnificat*, *St Luke Passion* and *Cantiones Sacrae*, and part of the *St Matthew Passion* and the Dona Nobis Pacem from the *Mass in B minor* of Bach, as well as a collection of his own choral and vocal works, with the Dresden Kreuzchor; some of these performances were released in Europe by DGG-Archiv.

Maxwell Davies, Peter (b. 1934). Born in Manchester, Maxwell Davies studied at the Royal Manchester College of Music, with Petrassi in Rome (1957–8), then after three years' teaching at the Cirencester Grammar School, studied with Sessions at Princeton University (1962–4). In 1965 he was composer-in-residence at Adelaide University in Australia, and in 1967, with Harrison Birtwistle, founded the Pierrot Players, an exceptional group of young musicians, who re-named themselves the Fires of London in 1970. For this ensemble a number of new compositions have been written. Maxwell Davies is perhaps the leading British composer of his generation and has produced a wide range of works, from the sequence of carols and instrumental sonatas *O Magnum Mysterium* to the *Second Fantasia on John Taverner's In Nomine*, which was first performed in 1965 by Pritchard and the London Philharmonic Orchestra, after a year's postponement because of its difficulty for the orchestra. His opera *Taverner* was given its première at Covent Garden in 1972. Among his other compositions is *Revelation and Fall*, which was commissioned by the Koussevitzky Foundation, but was declared unplayable in the United States. Even so, Maxwell Davies himself recorded the work with the Pierrot Players and soprano Mary Thomas for EMI in 1968. He has recorded some others of his compositions: *From Stone to Thorn*, *Hymnos*, *Antechrist*, and *Missa super l'Homme armé* (for L'Oiseau-Lyre), *Songs for a Mad King* (for Unicorn), points and dances from *Taverner* (for Argo) and *Vesalii Icones* (for Unicorn), all with the Fires of London, and *O Magnum Mysterium*, with the Cirencester School Choir and Orchestra (for Argo). In 1974, on the centenary of Schoenberg's birth, Maxwell Davies and the Fires of London recorded *Pierrot Lunaire*, coupled with Webern's arrangement for quintet of Schoenberg's *Chamber Symphony No. 1*.

Mayer, Thomas (b. 1907). Born in Norwawes, Germany, Mayer was a pupil of Busch, Kleiber, Prüwer and Szell at the Berlin Academy of Music, and first conducted in Berlin. He conducted opera and concerts in Leipzig (1931–3), Teplitz, Czechoslovakia (1933–8), Buenos Aires and Montevideo (1938–47), with the New York Metropolitan Opera, at Caracas, Halifax and Ottawa (1947–60). He went to Australia, was conductor of the West Australia Symphony Orchestra and the Elizabethan Trust Opera (1967–73), and then settled in Austria. He has conducted many leading orchestras in Europe and the United States. His records include the Symphony No. 6 and ballet suite *The Beach Inspector and the Mermaid* by the Australian composer Penberthy (with the West Australian Symphony Orchestra for Philips), Williamson's Violin Concerto (with Thomas, and the same orchestra for World Record Club) and Hill's Trumpet Concerto (with Johnson and the same orchestra for World Record Club).

Mayer, Uri. After graduating at the Academy of Music in Tel-Aviv and the Juilliard School in New York, Mayer conducted with the New York Youth Symphony Orchestra and the National Youth Symphony of Israel (from 1964), and in 1970 was invited by Stokowski to be assistant conductor of the American Symphony Orchestra. He was music director of the Canada Symphony at Montreal (1972–4), conducted the University Symphony at Interlochen and several Canadian orchestras (1975) and now teaches conducting at McGill University where he conducts the University Symphony Orchestra. For Orion he recorded Ghezzo's *Thalla*, with the Contemporary Directions Ensemble of the University of Michigan.

Measham, David (b. 1937). Born in Nottingham, Measham studied at the Guildhall School of Music and Drama, where his teacher for conducting was Del Mar. He was a violinist with the BBC Symphony, City of Birmingham Symphony and London Symphony Orchestras, was assistant to Bernstein in preparing for concerts and recordings in London, founded the English Chamber Choir, and in 1974 was appointed principal conductor of the West Australian Symphony Orchestra in Perth. He also has appeared with major British and Australian orchestras, in New Zealand, with the American Symphony Orchestra in New York and at the Bergen Festival in Norway. He has recorded Barber's Symphony No. 1, two *Essays for Orchestra* and *Night Flight* (with the London Symphony Orchestra for Unicorn), *Knoxville: Summer of 1915* (with McGurk) and Violin Concerto (with Thomas) and *Music for a Scene from Shelley* (with the West Australian Symphony Orchestra for Unicorn), Miaskovsky's Symphony No. 21 and Kabalevsky's Symphony No. 2 (with the New Philharmonia Orchestra for Unicorn), and Carmichael's Trumpet Concerto (with Johnston and the West Australian Symphony Orchestra for World Record Club). He also recorded the symphonic rock work *Journey to the Centre of the Earth* by Rick Wakeman, with whom he toured the United States and Japan, and directed other rock records for which he has been awarded nine Gold Discs.

Medveczky, Ádám (b. 1941). Born in Budapest Medveczky studied the piano and percussion at the Béla Bartók Secondary School of Music, and for nine years was a timpanist with the Hungarian State Concert Orchestra. He studied conducting under Kórody at the Franz Liszt Academy of Music (1968–71), and attended Ferrara's courses at Rome and Venice (1971). Since 1969 he has conducted orchestral concerts and at the Hungarian State Opera House, lectured at the Franz Liszt Academy (since 1974), and won second prize at the international conductors' competition arranged by Hungarian Television in 1974. For Hungaroton he has recorded Brahms' Symphony No. 2, Dvořák's Symphony No. 9, *L'Arlésienne* Suite No. 2, *Peer Gynt* Suite No. 2, *Moldau*, Szervánsky's *Serenade for Clarinet and Orchestra* and Clarinet Concerto (with Kovacs) and *Variations for Orchestra*, and a disc of Mozart arias (with tenor Jozsef Réti), all with the Budapest Symphony Orchestra.

Mehta, Zubin (b. 1936). Mehta is a Parsi Indian, born in Bombay, where his father Meli Mehta had founded the Bombay String Quartet and the Bombay Symphony Orchestra, of which he was concertmaster then conductor. Meli Mehta had also played under Barbirolli in the Hallé Orchestra, and later went to Los Angeles, where he teaches and conducts the American Youth Orchestra. Zubin learned the piano and violin as a boy, and at sixteen was conducting his father's orchestra at rehearsals. For two years he studied medicine, but abandoned it and went to Vienna in 1954 to enrol in the Vienna Academy of Music, where he studied conducting with Swarowsky, played the double bass in the Vienna Chamber Orchestra and had the opportunity of observing Furtwängler and Karajan. In 1955 he won first prize in a conducting competition at Liverpool, which enabled him to work with Pritchard and conduct a number of concerts with the Liverpool Philharmonic Orchestra. In the next year he went to the Accademia Chigiana at Siena to study with Zecchi, and after taking part in another competition for conductors at Tanglewood, Massachusetts, he attracted the attention of Munch.

In the following years Mehta was a guest conductor with many orchestras, particularly in Brussels and Belgrade, and substituted for other conductors. In 1961 he became the youngest conductor to lead the Berlin and Vienna Philharmonic Orchestras, and in that year he substituted for Ormandy at a concert with the Montreal Symphony Orchestra, and for Reiner with the Los Angeles Philharmonic Orchestra. These events led to his engagement as musical director of both orchestras; he remained at Montreal until 1967, and his contract in Los Angeles terminated when he took up the appointment of musical director with the New York Philharmonic in 1978, in succession to Boulez. In Los Angeles, when the orchestra originally engaged him for guest appearances, he was asked to conduct further concerts but without the knowledge of Solti, who had just been appointed musical director. This caused Solti to resign abruptly, and Mehta stepped into his shoes. Mehta first conducted the Israel Philharmonic Orchestra in 1962; his association with the orchestra grew, he led them on tour in 1966, and at the outbreak of the Israel-Arab war in 1967 he returned to Israel to conduct special concerts. In 1969 he was appointed musical adviser to the orchestra and in 1977 music director. He first conducted at La Scala, Milan, in 1962, and at the New York Metropolitan in 1965, and has appeared there and in other major opera houses regularly.

Mehta's Viennese training has implanted in him a strong preference for the Austrian and

German classics, for the late romantics such as Bruckner, Mahler, Strauss and Wagner, and for the second Viennese school; composers such as Sibelius, Prokofiev and Vaughan Williams have much less appeal to him, although he is able to direct a score like Ravel's *La Valse* with ravishing effect. The conductor whom he most admires is Furtwängler, and he understands with him that the music must *flow*, from the first to the last: 'Line seems to me the most essential thing in any performance – you must conceive the end at the beginning – too many climaxes won't work.' Sound, too, is important for him; in Los Angeles he strove to create the 'Viennese' sound with a round, sumptuous string tone, and when he took charge of the orchestra he persuaded the management to invest $300,000 to buy new instruments to improve the orchestra's sound. A Mehta performance is marked by this warmth of tone, and the style and approach to the score is relaxed and lyrical; there is little of the surface tension of Solti, the kinetic energy of Bernstein or the clinical precision of Boulez. In fact, New York audiences will find his glowing readings of the 19th-century repertoire a startling and not unwelcome contrast to Boulez. He wins ready favour with both audiences and musicians for his charm and respectful manner, as much as for his authoritative musicianship. His gestures are simple and his beat very clear; he usually conducts without a score. Sometimes his interpretations are criticised for being too flamboyant and theatrical, and his performances of major works superficial, as though he were unable to convey his conception of the music's depth. He occasionally attempts to do too much, and then has to be prepared to lead performances unworthy of him; at the Israel Summer Festival in 1977, for instance, he programmed three Beethoven symphonies in one concert in these circumstances. But, despite the glamorous image with which he was promoted in Los Angeles, he is a musician of complete integrity, whose natural instinct is to put the composer before himself.

Mehta's records are the best evidence of his strengths and weaknesses as a conductor. He professes that he does not like to record too much, and that he must perform works, including opera, often before he commits them to a record. Apart from an early accompaniment for Brendel in the Beethoven Piano Concerto No. 5 (with the Vienna Pro Musica Orchestra for Vox), and some operas for RCA and EMI, he has recorded for Decca only, and almost entirely with the Vienna Philharmonic, Los Angeles Philharmonic and Israel Philharmonic Orchestras. He made his first discs with the Vienna Philharmonic in 1965, Bruckner's Symphony No. 9, an auspicious and unexpectedly fine performance. Then followed a coupling of *Les Préludes* and some Wagner preludes, and the Symphony No. 4 of Franz Schmidt. The extensive series with the Los Angeles Philharmonic has been highly successful commercially, and Decca have taken special care to produce records of a high technical standard. Many of them too are performed with exemplary style and panache, such as the *Enigma Variations*, Ives' Symphony No. 1, Liszt's *Hunnenschlacht*, *Mazeppa* and *Orpheus*, Respighi's *Feste romane*, Schoenberg's Chamber Symphony No. 1, *Variations for Orchestra* Op. 31 and *Verklärte Nacht*, Saint-Saëns' Symphony No. 3, Scriabin's Symphony No. 4 and Varèse's *Arcana*, *Intégrales* and *Ionisation*. Despite his avowed preference for the music of Bruckner and Strauss, his records of their music, judged by the highest standards, are not so impressive; the performances of Bruckner's Symphonies Nos 4 and 8, and *Don Juan*, *Also sprach Zarathustra*, *Don Quixote*, *Ein Heldenleben*, *Alpensinfonie* and *Symphonia domestica* are certainly brilliant and powerful, but in the case of Bruckner there is a certain lack of insight and in Strauss a want of subtlety and refinement. Much the same criticism has been levelled at his Nielsen Symphony No. 4; some performances, such as Beethoven's Symphony No. 7 and *Le Sacre du printemps*, exploit fast tempi very effectively, but in some other records, particularly *Petrushka* and *Scheherazade*, the readings are surprisingly flaccid. A more recent recording, issued in 1975, this time with the Vienna Philharmonic Orchestra *et al.*, of Mahler's Symphony No. 2 showed a refinement and lyricism somewhat different from his Los Angeles performances.

His remaining discs with the Los Angeles Philharmonic, many of which are good in their own way, are the Tchaikovsky Symphony No. 4, *Marche slave* and *Romeo and Juliet* fantasy-overture, *Boléro*, *Daphnis et Chloé* Suite No. 2, *La Valse* and *Ma Mère l'Oye*, preludes from *Carmen*, the Dvořák Symphony No. 9, *Pictures at an Exhibition*, Verdi's *Pezzi sacri*, Copland's *Appalachian Spring* and *A Lincoln Portrait*, *An American in Paris*, Ives' Symphony No. 2, *Decoration Day* and *Variations on America*, Stravinsky's *Circus Polka* and *Miniatures*, Kraft's Percussion Concerto and *Contextures*, Haydn's Trumpet Concerto (with Stevens), a Vivaldi Piccolo Concerto (with Zentner), Weber's Clarinet Concertino (with Zukovsky), Wieniawski's *Polonaise de concert* and *Scherzo-tarantelle* (with Dicterow), and the overtures *Le nozze di Figaro*, *Egmont*,

La gazza ladra, *Der Freischütz*, *La forza del destino*, *Rienzi*, *Carnival*, *1812*, *Die Fledermaus*, *Dichter und Bauer* and *Candide*. With the Israel Philharmonic, Mehta recorded an excellent disc of Beethoven's ballet *Die Geschöpfe des Prometheus*, in addition to Bloch's *Schelomo* and *Voice in the Wilderness* (with Starker), Dvořák's Symphony No. 7 and Tchaikovsky's Symphony No. 5; a new series commenced in 1976 with a superb *Harold in Italy* (with Benyamini), followed by Mahler's Symphony No. 1, the Bartók *Concerto for Orchestra* and *Hungarian Sketches*, Brahms' Piano Concerto No. 1 (with Rubinstein), Mozart's Symphonies Nos 34 and 39, Schubert's Symphonies Nos 3, 5 and 9, and Paganini's Violin Concerto No. 1 (with Belkin). He also accompanied Ashkenazy in Brahms' Piano Concerto No. 2 (with the London Symphony Orchestra for Decca). His opera sets, *Turandot* (with the London Philharmonic Orchestra *et al.* for Decca), *Aida* (with the Rome Opera Orchestra *et al.* for EMI), *Tosca* and *Il trovatore* (with the New Philharmonia Orchestra *et al.* for RCA) suggest that his natural gifts and sense of drama are more at home in opera than with the late German and Austrian romantics. Mehta has also recorded music by Canadian composers: Matton's *Mouvement symphonique No. 2* and Mercure's *Lignes et points* (with the Montreal Symphony Orchestra for RCA).

Meier, Gustav (b. 1929). Born in Wettingen, Switzerland, Meier studied at the Zürich Conservatory, was a choral repetiteur at Lucerne, conducted with the Vienna Chamber Orchestra and at the Zürich Theatre, and studied further with van Kempen at Siena and de Carvalho at Tanglewood, Massachusetts. His subsequent activities in the US include productions of contemporary American and European composers, conducting opera in New Jersey and the New Haven Chorale, teaching at Yale University, and conducting the Greater Bridgeport Symphony Orchestra, Connecticut; he has also returned to Switzerland to conduct at Zürich and Winterthur. He has recorded Cello Concertos by Villa-Lobos and Guarnieri (with Parisot and the Vienna State Opera Orchestra for Westminster) and Carter's Double Concerto (with Kirkpatrick, Rosen and a chamber orchestra for Epic).

Melichar, Alois (b. 1896). Son of the conductor Franz Melichar, Melichar was born in Vienna, studied at the Vienna Academy of Music (1917–20) and the Berlin Academy of Music, and was music director and singing teacher at the German High School at Helenendorf in Soviet Azerbaijan, where he studied Caucasian folk music (1923–6). Then he was music critic for the *Deutsche Allgemeine Zeitung* (1926–7), conductor and music adviser for Deutsche Grammophon Gesellschaft (1927–33), composed film music, and after World War II was in charge of the Studio for Modern Music in Vienna (1946–9) and a freelance conductor. His compositions include lieder, piano, chamber, orchestral and choral music, and the operetta *Der Walzerkrieg*. He also wrote the books *The Indivisible Music* (1952), *Music in Straightjacket* (1958) and *Schoenberg and After* (1960), in which he argues with some force that both the primitivism of Orff and the twelve-tone method of Schoenberg are mistaken paths in the development of modern music.

Melichar has recorded extensively for Polydor (DGG) in the pre-war years, with the Berlin Philharmonic, and the Berlin Staatsoper Orchestras, and in several instances, with the Berlin Charlottenburg Opera Orchestra. Many of the discs were overtures and waltzes of Johann and Josef Strauss, Suppé and Waldteufel; others included Schubert's Symphony No. 8, *Finlandia*, *Invitation to the Dance*, the *Romeo and Juliet* fantasy-overture, *Capriccio italien*, Chabrier's *Fête polonaise*, the *Caucasian Sketches* of Ippolitov-Ivanov, Massenet's *Scènes pittoresques*, *Pictures at an Exhibition*, the *Brandenburg Concertos* (except, it appears, the *No. 3*), an arrangement of the Bach *Toccata and Fugue in D minor*, some marches of Richard Strauss, the waltzes from *Der Rosenkavalier* and the ballet *Schlagobers*, some choruses from the Wagner operas, Glinka's *Kamarinskaya*, the polonaise from *Eugene Onegin*, the gavotte from *Mignon*, the grand march from *Aida*, the overtures to *Mignon*, *Raymond*, *The Bartered Bride*, *La Princesse jaune*, *Die Zwillingsbrüder*, *Der Barbier von Bagdad*, *Die Felsen Mühle von Etalières*, *Flotte Bursche*, *Leichte Kavallerie* and *Die schöne Galatea*, and arias by Patzak and Völker. Later, he recorded on LP Haydn's Symphony No. 45 (with the Munich Philharmonic Orchestra for Mercury), Glazunov's Piano Concertos Nos 1 and 2 (with E. Glazunov, the composer's daughter, and the Hamburg Philharmonic Orchestra for Telefunken), and a filmed version of *Die Fledermaus* (with the Vienna Symphony Orchestra *et al.*, released by Nixa).

Melik-Pashayev, Aleksandr (1905–1964). Born in Tiflis, (now Tbilisi), Melik-Pashayev was educated at the Tbilisi Conservatory and at the Leningrad Conservatory, where he studied under Gauk and graduated in 1930. His career had commenced previously in 1921 as a pianist, and in 1922 he joined the Tbilisi Theatre as a conductor. In 1931 he made his debut at the Bolshoi Theatre in Moscow with *Aida*, and became chief conductor there (1953–62). His repertoire included Italian and Russian operas, and he received two Stalin Prizes (1942 and 1943) and other Soviet awards. A distinguished conductor, he recorded Russian operas in highly idiomatic performances with the Bolshoi Theatre Orchestra and Company, which included artists such as Petrov and Arkhipova. On 78 r.p.m. discs there appeared *Prince Igor*, *Eugene Onegin*, and Tchaikovsky's *The Tempest*; on LP *Aida*, *A Life for the Tsar*, *Russlan and Ludmilla*, *The Queen of Spades*, *Vakula the Smith*, *Boris Godunov*, A. G. Rubinstein's *The Demon*, Shaporin's *The Decembrists* and Prokofiev's *War and Peace*. It appears that two recordings of *Boris Godunov* were issued; the first was with the Russian bass-baritone Ivan Petrov as Boris; in the other version, which was issued by CBS in the United States and Britain, the scenes with Petrov were replaced by a new recording with the Canadian baritone George London, who had sung the part at the Bolshoi Theatre in 1960. Melik-Pashayev also recorded a disc of selections from *Carmen*, Tchaikovsky's Symphony No. 6, Grieg's *Peer Gynt* Suite No. 1 and *Norwegian Dances*, and excerpts from *Undine* and *Dmitri the Impostor* of Tchaikovsky (with the Bolshoi Theatre Orchestra, issued in some cases by Saga and MK in the West), an aria recital by Vishnevskaya (with the Bolshoi Theatre Orchestra), Arensky's *The Fountain of Bakhchisarai* (with the Moscow Symphony Orchestra) and the wedding march from *A Midsummer Night's Dream* (with the USSR State Symphony Orchestra).

Melkus, Eduard (b. 1928). Born in Baden, Melkus studied the violin at the Vienna Academy of Music, and musicology at the Vienna University (1943–53). He continued his violin studies at Paris with Touche (1953), at Zürich with Schaichet (1956), and at Winterthur with Rybar (1958), was principal viola in the Zürich Orchestra (1955–6), in the Winterthur Symphony Orchestra (1957), and then was first violin with the New Zürich String Quartet (1955–8). In 1958 he became professor of violin at the Vienna Academy and then toured in Europe and the United States as a soloist, lecturing about interpretation and style in the performance of string music, and playing in chamber music ensembles. He also founded a seminar in the playing of historical instruments, and in 1965 he established and conducted the Vienna Capella Academica, an orchestra whose players use original instruments. He is a member of the Society for the Publication of Monuments of Music in Austria, whose publications include studies of the interpretation of the music of Mozart and Beethoven.

Melkus has recorded extensively as a violinist, both as a soloist and chamber player, and as a conductor. In the latter capacity, the works recorded include J. C. Bach's Harpsichord Concertos Op. 7 Nos 1 to 6, and Op. 8 Nos 1 to 6 (with Haebler and the Capella Academica for Philips), Fux's *Symphony in B flat*, *Partita in F*, *Sonata a quattro in D*, and arias from *Psiche* and *Il testimento di nostro signor Jesu Christo* (with Hückl and the Melkus Ensemble, for Musical Heritage Society), J. S. Bach's two Violin Concertos (with himself) and Double Violin Concerto (with himself and Rantos), C. P. E. Bach's *Sonatina in D minor* (with I. Küchler), *Sonatina in D major* (with R. and I. Küchler), and Two-Harpsichord Concerto (with R. and I. Küchler), Leopold Mozart's *Sinfonia burlesca in G major*, *Die Bauernhochzeit* and *Eine musikalische Schlittenfahrt*, dances by C. P. E. Bach, Rameau and Strazer, and Viennese dances of Eybler, Haydn, Gluck, Mozart, Wrantizky, Beethoven and Salieri (with the Melkus Ensemble for DGG-Archiv).

Melles, Carl (b. 1926). Born in Budapest and educated at the Budapest Academy of Music, Melles received the Franz Liszt Prize in 1954. He has conducted major European orchestras, including the Berlin and Vienna Philharmonic, and the New Philharmonia, and has taken part in various festivals. He accompanied Haebler in Mozart's Piano Concertos K. 459 and K. 466 (with the Vienna Symphony Orchestra for Vox), and Slenzynska in Liszt's Piano Concerto No. 1 (with a Vienna orchestra for Decca, US).

Mendel, Arthur (b. 1905). Born in Boston and educated at Harvard College and the École Normale in Paris (1925–7), Mendel taught at the Dalcroze and Diller-Quaile Schools of Music in New York (1938–50), was a literary editor with G. Schirmer Inc. (1930–38), music critic and editor of musical journals, and was appointed professor of music at Princeton University (1952), becoming Professor Emeritus (1973). He conducted the Cantata Singers (1936–53), with whom he recorded Schütz's *Musikalische Exequien* and *The Christmas Story* (for R. E. Blake).

Mengelberg, Willem (1871–51). The great Dutch conductor Mengelberg was born at Utrecht of German parents who had come from Cologne; his father was a church architect. He received his training at the School of Music at Utrecht and at the Cologne Conservatory, where he studied the piano with Seiss and became an excellent pianist. His first professional appearance as a conductor was with the Gürzenich Orchestra at Cologne, and in 1891 he was appointed musical director at Lucerne. In 1895 he was offered the position of music director of the Concertgebouw Orchestra in Amsterdam, which had been established just seven years earlier by Willem Kes. He first appeared in Amsterdam as a pianist playing Liszt's Piano Concerto No. 1 at Kes's farewell concert, and at his first concert as conductor Beethoven's Symphony No. 5 was on the programme. He remained with the orchestra for 50 years, although poor health restricted his activities in the last few years. In addition he was director of the Toonkunst Choir in Amsterdam (from 1898), of the Museum Concerts Society at Frankfurt am Main (1907–20), and conductor of the Caecilienverein there (from 1908). He toured Russia, Norway and Italy with the Concertgebouw Orchestra (1898), first visited London in 1903 to conduct at a Strauss festival, and became a regular visitor there between 1913 and World War II, and conducted in Paris; he was appointed professor of music at Utrecht University in 1933.

Mengelberg visited the United States in 1905 to conduct the New York Philharmonic Orchestra briefly, and was invited by Bodanzky in 1920 to be a guest conductor of his National Symphony Orchestra, which was merged with the New York Philharmonic in 1922 at Mengelberg's suggestion, and he was permanent conductor of the orchestra until 1930. He then resigned from the New York Philharmonic and left the US for good; his reaction to Toscanini's rising popularity in New York, where he had also been conducting the New York Philharmonic since 1926, was to exaggerate some of his interpretations: this brought about a deterioration in his musicianship. Also, his repertoire was restricted by painstaking and slow preparation, and when the directors of the orchestra insisted on more frequent changes of programme, the new works were apt to be inadequately performed. Another cause of dissatisfaction was his custom of lecturing the orchestra at length at rehearsals about the composer to be played. Nevertheless his years in the US had a significant effect on standards of orchestral performance there, and conductors who had held sway previously, such as Stransky and Damrosch, were forced to stand aside, a fate which Mengelberg himself suffered at the hands of Toscanini.

Under Mengelberg the Concertgebouw Orchestra became one of the finest virtuoso orchestras in the world, and its greatness today had its origin in those times. In 1897 his performance of Tchaikovsky's Symphony No. 6 was sensationally received; Grieg, who was in the audience, leapt on a chair and addressed the audience, urging them to be proud of the orchestra and its conductor. Strauss dedicated *Ein Heldenleben* to the orchestra and to Mengelberg, as did Mahler his Symphonies Nos 5 and 8; Mengelberg promoted the music of both composers, who on occasion conducted his orchestra. He collaborated closely with Mahler in the performance of his symphonies in Amsterdam, and conducted a festival of his music there in 1920. In 1904 Mahler came to Amsterdam to conduct his Symphony No. 4 with the orchestra, and at the same concert half an hour later Mengelberg conducted the symphony again; for him this was the first time. His reading of *Ein Heldenleben* was legendary, and in 1899 he established the annual Palm Sunday concert of the *St Matthew Passion*, for which he was also much admired. He invited the world's most famous conductors and soloists to appear with his orchestra, led a Beethoven festival each year, and his associate conductors with the orchestra were, in turn, Muck, Monteux and Walter. He championed contemporary composers, especially Ravel, Debussy, Reger, Schoenberg and Stravinsky, and presented festivals of Dutch music in 1902, 1913 and 1935. Except on a few occasions in Lucerne, he did not conduct in the opera house. In his early years he composed a Mass for mixed choir, solo voices and orchestra, some songs, a *Praeludium on the Dutch National Hymn* and *Rembrandt Variations*, and had a reputation for his knowledge of art. During the Nazi occupation of the Netherlands in World War II he collaborated with the invaders and conducted in Germany; after the war the Netherlands Honours Council forbade him from ever participating in the musical life of the country again, and he died in Switzerland in 1951.

Mengelberg achieved his extraordinarily high standards by preparing his scores meticulously and by drilling his orchestra exhaustively. *Till Eulenspiegel* was rehearsed for a full month before it was presented. He believed his role as a conductor was to discover what the composer intended behind the notes, to express it freely, and to improvise as the mood of the work unfolded. Of course, this can be read another way: he discovered what he intended behind the notes, and improvised according to the mood the work invoked in him as it unfolded. This subjective and romantic style of conducting, which would cause an uproar today, was more the rule than the exception at the time, and it took the overwhelming influence of Toscanini to sweep it aside. (More recently, conductors such as Szell, Karajan and Haitink and Abbado amongst the younger generation, who are literalists rather than romantics, have become the most admired. Even Jochum, whose performances today attract frequent criticism for their romantic approach, would be considered literalist in comparison to Mengelberg.) Listening to a Mengelberg performance nowadays, with the hindsight of countless later performances of the same piece, one is astonished at the remarkable skill used to achieve the distortions he imposed on the score. Adjectives such as 'wilful', 'exaggerated', 'egotistical' come to our lips, as they did, after all, to his listeners and critics. But Mengelberg believed that the true meaning of the piece was revealed uniquely to him, and he was at perfect liberty to present this meaning as he found it. To him a literal reading destroyed feeling and life, and limited excitement; it would, in a word, be dull. Many of his performances were intensely interesting and thrilling; in his time the gramophone record was conceived more as a concert performance, when individuality could be admired, rather than as an attempt to present the once-and-for-all exact statement of the score, as it has often become today. A conductor who interposes himself between the music and the listener with his own private inspiration is today, rightly or wrongly, thought to be betraying a trust. Mengelberg followed Strauss's advice to conductors: 'Do whatever you like, but never be dull.'

Mengelberg was a foremost recording artist, from the early 1920s to World War II. His first records were made in the US by Victor in 1922: they were of *Coriolan*, a movement from Beethoven's Symphony No. 5, and *Les Préludes*, of which his performances were very famous; the later recording of it was described by David Hall in 1940 as 'one of the most hair-raising things on record'. He went on to record for Columbia, Brunswick-Cliftophone, Decca, Philips, Polydor, Telefunken and Victor, and many of the performances also appeared on other labels such as Parlophone, Odeon, Pacific, Supraphon, Ultraphone and Capitol. Over 40 composers and 90 pieces were issued commercially, and the Netherlands Broadcasting Company has another 40 or so pieces in its archives. Some scores – the *Egmont* overture, Beethoven's Symphony No. 1 and Tchaikovsky's Symphony No. 5 – were recorded three times. Most of the discs were with the Concertgebouw Orchestra, and some with the New York Philharmonic Orchestra. Included in the discography were all the Beethoven and Brahms symphonies and most of the overtures, the *St Matthew Passion*, Schubert's Symphonies Nos 8 and 9, Dvořák's Symphony No. 9, Tchaikovsky's Symphonies Nos 4, 5 and 6 and the *Romeo and Juliet* fantasy-overture, Mahler's Symphony No. 4 and the *Adagietto* from the Symphony No. 5, *Les Préludes*, *Tod und Verklärung*, *Don Juan* and *Ein Heldenleben*, and some overtures of Gluck, Cherubini, Weber and Wagner. Haydn and Mozart are missing, except for the overture to *Die Zauberflöte* and *Eine kleine Nachtmusik*; the other pieces he recorded included a sinfonia of J. C. Bach, excerpts from *La Damnation de Faust* and *L'Arlésienne*, a few Strauss waltzes, Grieg's *Elegiac Melodies*, his cousin Rudolf Mengelberg's *Salve Regina*, Andriessen's *Magna res est*, Schillings' *A Victory Ball*, Dopper's *Ciaccona gothica*, and Johan Wagenaar's *Cyrano de Bergerac* overture. The Schillings piece was one of Victor's first electrical recordings.

Some of these recordings were transferred to LP by Philips and Telefunken, and with the current revival of interest in conductors of the 1930s, some of his great performances are now appearing on various labels. Tchaikovsky's Symphonies Nos 5 and 6 have been released by Telefunken and Symphony No. 4 by World Record Club, the *St Matthew Passion* by Philips, Brahms' Symphony No. 3 and *Academic Festival Overture* by EMI, *Ein Heldenleben* by RCA and the nine Beethoven symphonies by Philips, taken from broadcasts on the Netherlands Radio in 1940, except for Symphony No. 3, apparently a Telefunken recording of the same year. Turnabout issued Mahler's Symphony No. 4 (with Jo Vincent), and Philips issued in the US a commemorative edition of four LPs to mark the 80th anniversary of the Concertgebouw Orchestra, and it included Mengelberg's Schubert Symphony No. 9. Rococo have also released a number of Mengelberg performances with the Concertgebouw Orchestra, seemingly taken from various sources, and including Beethoven's Symphonies Nos 3, 4 and 7, Tchaikovsky's Symphony No. 4, *Romeo and Juliet* fantasy-overture and *Serenade in C major*, *Les Préludes*, *Boléro*, *Don Juan*, *Psyché et Éros*, *Háry János* suite and the *Peacock Variations*, Bruch's Violin Concerto No. 1 (with Bustabo), Rachmaninov's Piano Concerto No. 2 (with Gieseking), Pfitzner's Cello Concerto (with Cassado), Strauss's *Perpetuum mobile*, Dopper's *Ciaccona gothica*, Röntgen's *Alt-Niederländische Tänze* and the overtures *Alceste*, *Rosamunde*, *Tannhäuser*, *Die Meister-*

singer and *Le Carnaval romain*. These records, however, have had limited appeal except of course to those interested in the history of the performance of symphonic music and in great conductors of the past. Mengelberg once ranked with Nikisch and Mahler, and these discs give some notion of his unique artistry and of the standards of interpretation of a past era.

Menges, Herbert (1903–72). Menges' father was a German violinist and the director of the conservatory at Brighton, England, and his elder sister was Isolde Menges, the violinist. He was born at Hove, and himself made his first public appearance as a violinist at the age of four. Later he studied the piano with Verne and de Greef, and composition at the Royal Academy of Music under Holst and Vaughan Williams. In 1925 he was appointed conductor to the Brighton Philharmonic Society, afterwards conducted the London String Players, and from 1931 to 1950 was director of music to the Old Vic Theatre Company, writing and arranging music for almost all of Shakespeare's plays. From 1940 to 1944 he was an associate conductor of Sadler's Wells Opera Company, and in 1945 he inaugurated and conducted the Southern Philharmonic Orchestra, which was based at Brighton. He was a guest conductor with many of the leading British orchestras, and visited South Africa and the United States in 1946 and 1947. Menges was a widely respected conductor who balanced expression and restraint with some judgement. Apart from conducting Holst's *St Paul's Suite* and Warlock's *Capriol Suite* (with the Philharmonia Orchestra for EMI) and the overture to *The Wasps* of Vaughan Williams (with the London Symphony Orchestra for EMI), he was cast as an accompanist in his career as a recording artist, and in this he acquitted himself admirably. His recordings included Beethoven's Piano Concertos Nos 1 and 3, Mozart's Piano Concertos K. 488 and K. 491 and the Grieg and Schumann Piano Concertos (with Solomon and the Philharmonia Orchestra), Mozart's Piano Concertos K. 414 and K. 467, Mendelssohn's Piano Concerto No. 1 and *Rondo brilliant*, and Rawsthorne's Piano Concerto No. 1 (with Lympany and the Philharmonia Orchestra), the Britten Piano Concerto (with Abram and the Philharmonia Orchestra), Rachmaninov's *Rhapsody on a Theme of Paganini* (with Cherkassky and the London Symphony Orchestra), Prokofiev's Piano Concerto No. 2 (with Cherkassky and the Philharmonia Orchestra), Saint-Saëns' Cello Concerto No. 2 (with Tortelier and the Philharmonia Orchestra), all for EMI; and the Brahms Violin Concerto, Prokofiev's Violin Concerto No. 1 (with Szigeti and the London Symphony Orchestra) and Tchaikovsky's Piano Concerto No. 1 (with Janis and the London Symphony Orchestra), for Mercury.

Menuhin, Yehudi (b. 1916). One of the most celebrated violinists of the century, Menuhin was born in New York of Russian parents who then moved to San Francisco, and there, as a child, he studied the violin with Louis Persinger. At the age of seven he played Lalo's *Symphonie espagnole* with the San Francisco orchestra under Hertz, and shortly afterwards made his debut in Paris, Berlin, New York and London. He later studied with Busch and Enesco; his career as a child prodigy and as a mature artist brought him the greatest distinctions and the highest musical accolades. As a violinist and chamber music player he has great warmth of tone and deep intensity, although in recent years his performances have been variable on occasion. He has recorded almost the entire violin repertoire in both concerto and chamber music forms, and is constantly seeking to perform and record new music; especially successful, at least commercially, have been his recordings with the Indian sitar player Ravi Shankar and the jazz violinist Stephane Grappelli. One of the most famous recordings he has made as a violinist is the Elgar Violin Concerto, which he made with the composer conducting the London Symphony Orchestra in 1932. From 1958 to 1968 he was the artistic director of the Bath Festival, and founded the Bath Festival Orchestra. He was also director of the Festival of Windsor, and for 20 years has been artistic director of the Yehudi Menuhin Festival at Gstaad in Switzerland. In addition he founded a boarding school at Stoke d'Abernon in Surrey, to develop young musical talent, from the age of six.

With the Bath Festival Orchestra, Menuhin made a superb series of recordings for EMI, in which, in many instances, he played the solo violin part besides conducting the orchestra. The works recorded included Bach's Suites and *Brandenburg Concertos*, *Ein musikalisches Opfer*, Violin and Oboe Concerto (with Leon Goossens), Flute, Violin and Harpsichord Concerto (with Bennett and Malcolm) and Cantatas Nos 82 and 169 (with Baker *et al.*), C. P. E. Bach's *Harpsichord Concerto in D* (with Malcolm), Vivaldi's Concerto Op. 3 No. 10, Corelli's Concerto Grosso Op. 6 No. 2, selections from (amongst others) Purcell's *The Fairy Queen*, *The Indian Queen*, *King Arthur*, Handel's Concerti Grossi Op. 6, Oboe Concertos Nos 1 to 3 (with Leon Goossens), Organ

Concertos (with Preston), and *Water Music*, Haydn's Symphonies Nos 26, 44, 45, 48 and 49 and *Violin Concerto in G*, Mozart's Symphony No. 29, Violin Concertos, Concertone, Sinfonia Concertante K. 364 (with Barshai), Piano Concertos K. 499 and K. 459 (with Hephzibah Menuhin) and K. 365 (with Hephzibah Menuhin and Fou Ts'ong), *Eine kleine Nachtmusik*, *Serenata notturna*, Serenades K. 203 and K. 250, Divertimenti K. 136, K. 138 and K. 287 and *Die Entführung aus dem Serail*, Schubert's Symphonies Nos 2 and 6, Bartók's *Divertimento*, Stravinsky's *Concerto in D*, Hindemith's *Five Pieces* and Tippett's *Fantasia Concertante on a Theme of Corelli.* He also recorded the Telemann *Suite in A minor* and the Mozart Flute and Harp Concerto (with Shaffer and Costello, and the Philharmonia Orchestra), and the Mozart Three-Piano Concerto (with Hephzibah, Yaltah and Jeremy Menuhin, and the London Philharmonic Orchestra). He broke with the Bath Festival in 1968 on the issue of retaining opera in the festival: he had performed *Così fan tutte*, the first opera in the festival, in 1966, and later released the Bath performance of *Die Entführung aus dem Serail*, in English. He then became artistic director of the Festival of Windsor, but continued to record with the same orchestra under a new name, the Menuhin Festival Orchestra. His later recordings have included the Bach Harpsichord Concertos (with Malcolm *et al.*), the Boyce symphonies, Handel's *Music for the Royal Fireworks*, *Double Concerto in B flat* and *Violin Concerto in B flat*, Mozart's Violin Concertos K. 271a and K. 294a, Haydn's Symphonies Nos 82 to 87, Beethoven's ballet *Die Geschöpfe des Prometheus* and Schubert's Symphonies Nos 1, 3, 4, 5, 8 and 9. He has toured with the orchestra in the United States, Australia and the Far East.

As a conductor Menuhin displays the same qualities as he does as a violinist: warmth, vitality, a fine sense of rhythm, a splendid ear for balance and style, and great musical insight. Like many other instrumentalists, he has come to conducting through recognising that the orchestra is the complete instrument with a repertoire he is keen to explore. He is anxious to avoid being regarded as a specialist, is prepared to conduct anything, and in his recording schedule he sees to it that a baroque work is followed by a modern piece or a chamber music disc. In 1973 he substituted for Karajan and conducted the Berlin Philharmonic in the four Brahms symphonies, although he was doing Symphonies Nos 1 and 4 for the first time. Of all the great conductors with whom he has played as a soloist, he reserves the highest praise for Toscanini and Furtwängler. He centres his activities in London, and has great respect for British musicians: 'I believe that the British musician has a sense of style – more flexible, more aware of subtleties – that exists nowhere else in the world. . . . Nowhere else in the world can you find, as you can in this country, a natural habitat for the whole range of music from Monteverdi to Stockhausen' (*The Gramophone*, April 1976, p. 1575). He likes recording: 'Some of my happiest hours of music-making have been in the recording studio. It has an atmosphere of almost monastic concentration, of single-minded dedication to the music, from which every extraneous element is excluded, and during which the critical faculty, alternating between performance and play-back, reaches its highest awareness.' At the same time, 'there are moments in concerts when something happens, and one wished that *that* could be recorded for posterity. . . . Like all other artists what I look for in recording is the spark, the fire of a real performance. I know most people believe that records today are pieced together from odd bits of tape, but I do really try to keep as complete a single performance as possible.'

Menuhin wrote amusingly about his recordings of the Bach Suites. 'Those recording sessions, speaking for myself, were feasts. Generations of cooks have left a vast choice of recipes. Sometimes we tried plain, boiled Bach with Aioli sauce – but there was too great a discrepancy between the bare meat and the rich sauce. Then there was Bach à l'orange, served in flaming Cointreau – somehow it seemed overdramatic. (It is left to the reader to guess whose recipes those are). So we settled for good old English roast Bach, with two veg, and three oboes, and finally for pungency, added some ninth overtone – unfortunately we had only spice; fresh herbs were out of season' (Record-sleeve note).

Mermoud, Robert (b. 1912). Born at Eclagnens, Switzerland, Mermoud studied at the Basel Conservatory with Reichel, Haug and Hans Münch, and graduated as a conductor in 1947. He also studied conducting with Weingartner, and orchestration with Geiser. He taught singing and conducted the Petit Choeur at the Collège de Montreux, and with the choir toured France, made records and gave radio performances. He has conducted orchestras and choirs in Switzerland and abroad, has given many first performances of old and new works, and has several times prepared choirs for performances by Ansermet and Schuricht. His recordings include excerpts from *La Fête des* *vignerons*, by Doret, Grast and de Senger, excerpts from Hemmerling's *Invocation au printemps* and Jaques-Dalcroze's *Le Jeu du feuillu* (with the Lausanne Chamber Orchestra *et al.* for CT), an excerpt from Martin's *La Nique à Satan* (with the Lausanne Chamber Orchestra for Ex Libris), and his own *Les très riches Heures* (with an ensemble for Disques VDE).

Mersson, Boris (b. 1921). Mersson was born in Berlin of Swiss parents; his father was of Russian descent and was a violinist in the Blüthner and Berlin Philharmonic Orchestras. He commenced his musical studies at an early age, and in 1935 entered the Lausanne Conservatory. During World War II he was in military service, and afterwards became leader of the Basel Radio Orchestra (1946–51). He studied composition with Scherchen (1950–51), conducting with Karajan (1955), toured Europe as a member of a chamber music ensemble (1957), and since 1959 has been musical adviser, conductor and recording director of Musical Masterpieces Society, with which La Guilde Internationale du Disque (in Paris) and Concert Hall (in Frankfurt am Main) are associated. He has made many records for these companies; as a pianist he recorded, *inter alia*, the Beethoven Cello Sonatas (with Alexander Stein) and his own *Variations*.

As a conductor, Mersson has recorded the Beethoven *Cantata on the Death of Emperor Joseph II* and a two-disc abridgement of *Tristan und Isolde* (with the Monte Carlo National Orchestra *et al.*); Mozart's Piano Concertos K. 246 and K. 503 (with Zadra and the South-West German Philharmonic Orchestra); Chopin's Piano Concerto No. 2 (with Favre and the Rome Festival Orchestra); Mendelssohn's *Song without Words* and Tchaikovsky's *Sérénade mélancolique* (with Ferras and the Collegium Academicum de Genève); Mozart's Horn Concerto K. 495 (with Freund) and Tchaikovsky's *Méditation* (with Varga, and the Vienna Festival Orchestra); *Les Sylphides*, the *Tsar Saltan* suite, the Dance of the Hours from *La Gioconda*, an arrangement from Chopin's *Étude No. 3* and excerpts from *Der Graf von Luxemburg*, *Das Land des Lächelns* and *Die lustige Witwe* (with the Paris Concerts Orchestra *et al.*); *Das Land des Lächelns* (with the Hamburg Symphony Orchestra *et al.*); excerpts from *Dido and Aeneas*, *Don Pasquale*, *Der Freischütz*, *Tannhäuser*, *Tristan und Isolde*, *Die Meistersinger*, *Die Walküre*, *Manon* and *Madama Butterfly* (with the Zürich Opera Orchestra *et al.*); excerpts from *The Mikado* (with the Opera Society Orchestra *et al.*); *Der Zarewitsch*, *Die Dollarprinzessen*, *Die Czardasfürstin*, *Madame de Pompadour*, *Die lustige Witwe*, *Orphée aux enfers*, *Paganini*, *Viktoria und ihr Husar* and *Maske in blau* (with the Vienna Operetta Orchestra *et al.*); and excerpts from *Fiddler on the Roof* (with the Broadway Musical Society). He also recorded collections of popular orchestral pieces and arrangements, including the pastoral symphony from *Messiah* and *See the Conquering Hero Comes*, Torelli's *Christmas Concerto*, Reger's *Mary's Cradle Song*, Schubert's *Ave Maria*, Elgar's *Salut d'amour*, Khachaturian's *Sabre Dance*, Heykens' *Serenade*, the gallop from Kabalevsky's *The Comedians*, Ketèlby's *In a Persian Market*, Liszt's *Liebestraum*, Rubinstein's *Melody in F*, Waldteufel's *España*, and Tchaikovsky's *Andante cantabile*, *Chanson triste* and *None but the Lonely Heart* (with orchestras variously described as the Vienna Concerts Promenade Orchestra and 'Boris Mersson and his orchestra').

Messner, Joseph (1893–1969). Born in Schwaz, Austria, Messner studied at Innsbruck University and the Munich Academy of Music, became the cathedral organist at Salzburg (1922), and then was appointed conductor (1926). He conducted the cathedral concerts at the Salzburg Festivals from 1926, and was director of the church music seminary at the Salzburg Mozarteum. His compositions included operas, motets, symphonies and concerted pieces, and he edited two early masses of Bruckner, and music by Caldara, Michael Haydn *et al.* After reviving the *Festival Mass* of Orazio Benevoli 1602–72), which had been written for the consecration of Salzburg Cathedral, he recorded this work with the cathedral choir, the Vienna Symphony Orchestra and soloists (for Philips). His other records were Mozart's Masses K. 115, K. 317 and *Requiem*, the Bruckner *Te Deum* (with the Salzburg Festival Chorus and Orchestra for Festival), *Messiah*, Rossini's *Stabat Mater* and Haydn's *Die sieben letzte Worte des Erlösers am Kreuz* (with the Mozarteum Orchestra *et al.* for Remington) and Telemann's *Pimpinone* (with the Salzburg String Quartet *et al.* for Oceanic). Victor also released a 78 r.p.m. made in the 1930s, in which Messner accompanies soprano Noréna in an aria from Haydn's *The Creation*.

Mester, Jorge (b. 1935). Born of Hungarian parents in Mexico City, Mester studied conducting with Morel at the Juilliard School in New York, graduated in 1958, took lessons with Bernstein at Tanglewood, joined the staff at Juilliard and directed the Juilliard Theatre

Orchestra (1962–8). He conducted for the New York City Opera, the Washington Opera Society and for dance companies, was music director of the St Louis Philharmonic Orchestra (1959–60), music director of the Greenwich Village Symphony Orchestra (1961–2), conducted orchestras in Japan and Europe (1965–6), appeared with major American symphony orchestras (1967–71), conducted at the Spoleto summer festivals in Italy, was appointed music director of the Aspen Music Festival in Colorado (1969) and music director of the Kansas City Philharmonic Orchestra (1971).

In 1967 Mester succeeded Robert Whitney as music director and conductor of the Louisville Orchestra, which had been founded in 1937 by Whitney; since 1954 an extensive series of LP records has been issued on a subscription basis under the First Edition label, with the Louisville Orchestra conducted until 1967 by Whitney and since then by Mester. Nearly 50 LP records have been made by Mester for First Edition Records, of music hitherto unrecorded, and in addition there have been unfamiliar works by other composers such as Bizet, Strauss, Reger, Hindemith, *et al.* This series has always been one of the most enterprising and rewarding features of the recording scene in the United States, and by any standard Mester's contribution to the catalogue, in widening the horizon of available recorded music, has been inestimable. The works recorded include Adam's Cello Concerto (with Kates), Barber's *Die Natali*, Addison's Trumpet Concerto, Villa-Lobos' *Dansas*, Arnold's Two-Violin Concerto (with Kling and McHugh), Balada's *Guernica*, Dallapiccola's *Piccola musica notturna*, Schuller's *Five Bagatelles*, Balada's *Maria Sabina* (with Dunham), Bamert's *Septuria Lunaris*, Husa's *Two Sonnets from Michelangelo*, Becerra's Symphony No. 1, Gandini's *Fantasie-Impromptu for Piano*, Pinzón's *Study for Orchestra*, Quintanar's *Sideral II*, Becker's Symphony No. 3, Labunski's *Canto di aspirazione*, Schuman's *Prayer in Time of War*, Bernat's *In Memoriam: J. F. Kennedy*, Schuman's Symphony No. 4, Bizet's *Variations chromatiques*, Moszkowski's *Suite No. 3*, Napravnik's *Festive March*, Reger's *Comedy Overture*, Blacher's *Ornaments*, Milhaud's *Cortège funèbre*, Poulenc's *Deux Marches et un intermède*, Blackwood's Violin Concerto (with Kling), Hindemith's *Concert Music for Viola* (with Hillyer), Briccetti's *Fountain of Youth* overture, Rorem's Piano Concerto (with Lowenthal), Turok's *Lyric Variations* for oboe (with McAninch), Bruch's Symphony No. 2, Rietz's *Concert Overture*, Chávez's *Horsepower*, Granados' *Dante*, Cowell's *Hymn and Fuguing Tune*, *2* and *3*, and *Ballad*, Koechlin's *Cinq chorales dans les modes du Moyen-âge*, Starer's *Mutabili*, Cowell's *Sinfonietta*, Surinach's *Melorhythmic Dramas*, Crosse's *Some Marches on a Ground*, Crumb's *Echoes of Time and the River (Echoes II)*, Ellis's *Kaleidoscope for Orchestra, Synthesizer and Soprano* (with Wall), Dennis' *Pennsylvania Station*, Schickele's *Fantastic Garden*, Walden's *Circus*, Floyd's *In Celebration*, Gould's *Soundings* and *Columbia*, Grandjany's *Harp Aria in Classic Style* (with Kling), Seiber's Concertino, Tauriello's *Ilinx* (with Livingston), Guarnieri's *Dança brasileira*, *Dança selvagem* and *Dança negra*, Ibert's *Bacchanale*, Talmi's *Overture on Mexican Themes*, Toch's *Miniature Overture*, Tosar's *Toccata*, Giraud's *The Fantastic Hunt*, Moszkowski's *Violin Concerto in C* (with Treger), Gutché's *Genghis Khan*, Husa's *Music for Prague*, Penderecki's *De natura sonoris*, Hindemith's *Kammermusik 2*, Petrassi's *Noche oscura*, Ibert's *Ballade de la geôle de Reading*, Koechlin's *Partita*, Joachim's Violin Concerto (with Treger), Keyes' *Abysses, Bridges, Chasms*, Laderman's *Magic Prison*, Kirchner's *Toccata*, Shostakovich's *Hamlet* incidental music, Laderman's *Stanzas*, Mennin's Cello Concerto (with Starker), Honegger's *Prélude d'Aglavaine et Sélysette*, Milhaud's *Quatre Chansons de Ronsard* (with Seibel) and Symphony No. 6, Persichetti's Symphony No. 8, Riegger's *Study in Sonority*, Piston's Symphonies Nos 7 and 8, Rayki's *Elegiac Variations*, and *Lamentation*, Riegger's *Dichotomy*, Rhodes' *Lament of Michal* (with Bryn-Julson) and *From Paradise Lost* (with Bryn-Julson, McDonald, Horton *et al.*), Schickele, Dennis and Walden's *Three Views from The Open Window*, Revueltas' *Redes*, Ginastera's *Ollontay*, Strauss's *Six Songs*, Op. 68 (with Shane), Martin's Cello Concerto (with Kates), McKuen's *The City* and *I Hear America Singing*, Widdoes' *Morning Music*, Sculthorpe's *Sun Music III*, and Hovhaness's *Avak, the Healer* (with Farris and Rapier). RCA have released in Britain Bruch's Symphony No. 2, Milhaud's Symphony No. 6 and *Chansons de Ronsard*, the Rietz *Concert Overture* and a disc of pieces by Crosse, Arnold, Addison and Seiber.

Meylan, Jean (b. 1915). Born in Geneva, Meylan studied law and music at the Geneva University and also attended the Conservatoire there. At the age of sixteen he founded and conducted amateur music groups, and a university orchestra, and in 1941 he became a professional conductor with the Geneva Chamber Orchestra and the Collegium Musicum. He was Weingartner's last pupil at Lausanne (1940–42), attended Kletzki's classes at the Lausanne Conservatoire, and also took lessons from Schuricht at Geneva. He was appointed chief conductor of the Cologne Radio Orchestra (1947), conducted at St Gallen (1953–9), Beromünster (1955), and led the Geneva Chamber Orchestra (1953–4). In 1957 he became choirmaster at the Geneva Opera and soon afterwards was appointed the music director. He has been a guest conductor in many countries apart from his native Switzerland, has promoted the music of Swiss composers, and in 1958 was awarded the Arnold Bax Medal. Among the early Supraphon LPs were some discs in which Meylan conducted the Czech Philharmonic Orchestra: a coupling of Beethoven's Symphonies Nos 1 and 8, *El amor brujo* and Schubert's *Rosamunde* music, as well as the *Cinderella* ballet music of Prokofiev, with the Prague Radio Symphony Orchestra. These were competent if not particularly distinguished performances. He has also recorded Beck's Violin Concerto (with Kägi and the Suisse Romande Orchestra for Decca), Gaspard's Symphony Op. 6 No. 3 and Albicastro's Concerto Op. 7 No. 4 (with the Lausanne Chamber Orchestra for CT).

Meyrowitz, Selmar (1875–1941). Born at Bartenstein, East Prussia, Meyrowitz studied at the Leipzig Conservatory with Reinecke and Jadassohn (1892–5) and at the Berlin Akademie der Künste with Bruch (1895–7). He came to the notice of Mottl, who in 1897 engaged him as his assistant at the Karlsruhe Court Theatre, and when Mottl went to the New York Metropolitan Opera in 1900 he took Meyrowitz with him. In the United States he also toured as the accompanist to the German singer Johanna Gadski. On his return to Europe he was conductor at the Prague National Theatre (1905–6), Berlin Komische Oper (1907–10), the Munich Court Theatre (1912–14) and the Hamburg State Theatre (1914–18). He gave concerts with the Berlin Philharmonic Orchestra (1918–23), was conductor of the Blüthner Orchestra (1920), conducted concerts in Hamburg, Vienna and Rome, was musical director of the Berlin Radio, was appointed conductor of the Berlin Staatsoper (1924–33) and toured the United States with the German Grand Opera Company (1929–31). With the advent of the Nazi regime in 1933 he left Germany and lived in Paris, where he remained until his death.

Meyrowitz made records in both Berlin and Paris. With the Berlin Philharmonic Orchestra for Telefunken he recorded Mozart's *Les petits riens*, Wagner's *Kaisermarsch*, the Dance of the Hours from *La Gioconda*, and the overtures to *Zampa*, *Die Meistersinger* and *The Merry Wives of Windsor*, and with the Berlin Staatsoper Orchestra the overture to *Die Zauberflöte*. Ultraphone also recorded him with the soprano Charles-Cahier and the Berlin Staatsoper Orchestra in the fourth movement of Mahler's Symphony No. 2 and a *Rückert* Song. In Paris, he recorded for Columbia very distinguished and significant performances of *Symphonie fantastique* and Liszt's *Faust Symphony*, both with the Paris Philharmonic Orchestra, called on the record labels 'Grand Orchestre Philharmonique'. His other Paris discs included Schubert's Symphony No. 8 (with the Paris Philharmonic for Pathé), the Ballet Music in G major from *Rosamunde* (with the Paris Symphony Orchestra for Pathé), Liszt's *Hungarian Fantasy* (with Kilenyi and the Paris Symphony for Pathé), the *Oberon* overture (with the Paris Philharmonic for Telefunken), and *Les Préludes*, the *Siegfried Idyll*, Chabrier's *Bourrée fantasque*, Grétry's *La Rosière républicaine* (with the Paris Philharmonic for Columbia) and Liszt's *Totentanz* and arrangement of the *Wanderer Fantasy* (with Kilenyi and a symphony orchestra for Columbia).

Michael, Hermann (b. 1937). Born at Schwäbisch Gmünd, Michael studied at the Stuttgart State Academy of Music (1955–60), and at the Berlin Conservatory (1960–62), and attended conducting courses with Swarowsky (1958), Kubelík (1961), and Karajan (1960–62). He was Karajan's assistant at the Vienna State Opera (1962–4), was conductor at the Frankfurt Opera (1965–7), and then general music director at Bremen (since 1970). He has recorded Bach's Harpsichord Concerto No. 3 and Harpsichord and Two-Flute Concerto BWV 1057 (with van den Lyck *et al.* and the Stuttgart Ton Studio Orchestra for Period, and issued in Britain by Nixa), and Wittinger's *OM* (with the Hessian Radio Symphony Orchestra for Wergo).

Miedél, Rainer. Born in Regensburg, FR Germany, Miedél studied at the universities of Detmold and Berlin, and was a pupil of Ferrara in Siena, of Navarra in Paris, and of Kertesz in Salzburg. He won first prize in the Swedish Broadcasting Corporation's Young Conductors' Competition (1965), became a cellist in the Stockholm Philharmonic Orchestra, made his debut as a conductor with the orchestra (1967), was music director of the Gävleborg

Orchestra in Sweden (1969–76), was assistant to Dorati with the Stockholm Philharmonic, became assistant then associate conductor of the Baltimore Symphony Orchestra (1969–73) and music director of the Seattle Symphony Orchestra (since 1976). In addition, he has been a guest conductor with some major orchestras in the United States, FR Germany and Japan. EMI issued a disc in which he conducted the Gävleborg Orchestra in Linde's Violin Concerto (with Mannberg), and Kabalevsky's *The Comedians*.

Mielenz, Hans (b. 1909). Born in Berlin where he studied at the Academy for Church and School Music (1928–32), at the university, and at the Academy of Music (1933–4), Mielenz was a freelance musician, composer and conductor (1927–39). After World War II he was conductor at the 'Neue Scala' Variété in Berlin (1946) and of the Grosse Tanzorchester of East Berlin Radio (1950), was a freelance composer at Aschau (1956), then conductor at the Baden City Theatre in Lower Austria (1968–9). His compositions include works for solo instruments, chamber ensembles and arrangements, and he has also been known by the pseudonym Peter Rambo. He has recorded Bach's *Quodlibet*, with the Berlin Radio Chamber Ensemble *et al.* for Eterna.

Mierzejewski, Mieczysław (b. 1905). Born in Posen (now Poznań), Mierzejewski studied at the conservatories at Poznań and Warsaw (1927–8) and at the Hochschule für Musik in Berlin (1930–32), and first conducted at the Poznań Opera (1926). He conducted the Warsaw Opera and Philharmonic Orchestra (from 1929), the Polish Radio Symphony Orchestra (1935–7), the Polish Army Theatre (1945–6), the Slask Opera in Bytom, and then was conductor again of the Warsaw Philharmonic Orchestra and musical director of the Warsaw Opera (from 1947). Before World War II he conducted in New York, London, Paris, Berlin, Budapest, and Frankfurt am Main, and after the war in Eastern and Western Europe and in the United States. In 1949 he produced Szymanowski's opera *King Roger* at the International Festival at Palermo, and in 1953, 1955 and 1957 led Moniuszko's *Halka* in European opera houses. He has received many awards in his native Poland, and composed symphonic works, lieder, film and stage music, and a folk-opera *Dożynki*. He has recorded *King Roger* and *Halka*, and selections from Moniuszko's *Hrabina*, with the Warsaw State Opera Orchestra *et al.* for Muza, and selections from *Halka*, with the Berlin Radio Symphony Orchestra *et al.* for DGG.

Mihály, András (b. 1917). After studying the cello, composition and chamber music at the Academy in his birthplace, Budapest, Mihály directed workers' choirs (1941–6), was a cellist in the Budapest Opera House Orchestra (1946–8), and was general secretary of the Opera (1948–9). He taught chamber music at the Budapest Academy (from 1950), has been musical adviser to the Budapest Radio (since 1963), and founded and conducted the Budapest Chamber Orchestra (1968). He is also recognised as one of Hungary's leading composers, whose output includes symphonies and a requiem mass. With the Budapest Chamber Orchestra *et al.* he has recorded for Qualiton Schoenberg's *Pierrot Lunaire*, Webern's *Fünf Canons* and *Zwei Lieder* (with Sziklay), Berg's *Chamber Concerto*, Ligeti's *Chamber Concerto*, Boulez's *Improvisation sur Mallarmé I–II*, Székely's *Musica notturna*, Maros' *Lament*, Lendvay's *Concerto da camera*, Láng's *Impulsioni*, Kadosa's *Serenade*, Durkó's *Iconography 2*, Balassa's *Iris* and *Antinomia*, Kocsár's *Lonely Song on Poems of Attila József*, and his own *Three Movements*. He also recorded his own *Apokriphs*, with the Györ Girls' Choir.

Miles, Maurice (b. 1908). Born in Epsom, Miles won a choral scholarship to Wells Cathedral, then studied at the Royal Academy of Music under Curzon for piano, and Reed and Wood for conducting; and later under Krauss at the Salzburg Mozarteum. While still in his teens he conducted a performance of *The Dream of Gerontius* at Uxbridge. He joined the staff of the BBC (1930–36), became conductor of the Buxton and Bath Municipal Orchestras (1936–9), and toured South America (1939); after three years' army service he rejoined the BBC to direct music broadcasts to Latin America. His later appointments were conductor of the Yorkshire Symphony Orchestra (1947–54), professor of conducting at the Royal Academy of Music (from 1953), conductor of the City of Belfast Orchestra (1955–66), of the Ulster Orchestra (1966–7), and of the Belfast Philharmonic Society (1955–67). Miles made some 78 r.p.m. discs for EMI of Butterworth's *The Banks of Green Willow* (with the Philharmonia Orchestra), the overture to *The Merry Wives of Windsor* (with the Liverpool Philharmonic Orchestra) and the overture and Pastoral Symphony from *Messiah* (with the London Symphony Orchestra).

Milhaud, Darius (1892–1974). The French composer Milhaud was extraordinarily prolific in his output, writing altogether more than 400 works. He had no particular reputation as a conductor, but he was nonetheless an effective interpreter of his own music. During the last 25 years of his life he was afflicted with arthritis; although when he appeared as a conductor he had to be brought to the podium either in a wheelchair or supporting himself with canes, once seated before the orchestra his conducting was energetic and convincing. He recorded many of his compositions both on 78s and on LP; on 78s, for Columbia, with various ensembles, there were *La Création du monde*, Piano Concerto (with Marguerite Long), *Suite française* (with the New York Philharmonic-Symphony Orchestra), Symphony No. 1, three *Opéras-minute*, *Les Songes* (with the Paris Symphony Orchestra), *Les Amours de Ronsard*, *L'Abandon d'Ariane*, *La Délivrance de Thésée* and *L'Enlèvement d'Europe*. Other 78s were the *Concertino de printemps* (with Astruc, for Polydor), *Salade – ballet-chanté* (for HMV) and *L'Homme et son désir*.

The LP records which he directed of his own music included *The Four Seasons* (with the Lamoureux Soloists for Philips), the *Aspen Serenade*, *Suite de Quatrains* and *Septet for Strings* (for Adès and released in the United States by Everest), *Saudades* and *Suite provençale*, Violin Concerto No. 2 (with Kaufman), *Concertino de printemps*, *Opus Americanum No. 2* and *Moses* (with the French National Radio Orchestra for EMI), Symphonies Nos 1, 2, 3 and 5 (with the Concert Hall Orchestra for Concert Hall), *L'Homme et son désir* and *Revers de Jacob* suite (with the Ensemble Roger Desormière for Boîte à Musique), *Le Carnaval d'Aix* (with Seeman), *Concerto for Percussion and Small Orchestra* (with Daniel), Viola Concerto (with Koch), Symphonies Nos 1 to 6, and *L'Homme et son désir* (with the Radio Luxembourg Orchestra *et al.* for Vox), *Le Boeuf sur le toit* and *La Création du monde* (with l'Orchestre du Théâtre des Champs-Élysées for Charlin), *Le Château de feu*, *Suite provençale* and *Introduction et marche funèbre* (with the Paris Philharmonic Orchestra for Le Chant du Monde), Symphonies Nos 4 and 8 (with the ORTF Orchestra for Le Chant du Monde), *Les Amours de Ronsard* and *Concertino d'été* (with the Philharmonic Chamber Orchestra for Contemporary Records), Symphony No. 1 and *In Memoriam* (with the CBS Symphony Orchestra for Columbia), Symphony No. 3 and the Two-Piano Concerto (with the Paris Conservatoire Orchestra *et al.* for Westminster) and the *Sacred Service* (with the Paris Opéra Orchestra *et al.* for Westminster). He also conducted the ballet *Les Mariés de la Tour Eiffel*, parts of which were contributed by Auric, Honegger, Poulenc, Tailleferre and himself (with the ORTF Orchestra for Adès).

Millet, Luis (1867–1941). Born near Barcelona, Millet studied there under Vidiella and Pedrell, and founded and conducted the 'Orfeó Català' to perform large choral and orchestral works (1891–1935). He was director of the municipal music school at Barcelona, composed songs and choral music, and wrote a book about popular Catalan songs. For HMV in the late 1920s he recorded Beethoven's *Missa Solemnis* (with the Barcelona Choir and Orchestra), Bach's Cantata No. 4 and excerpts from the Cantata No. 140, Segarra's *Himne nacional de Catelunya*, *Himne patriotic* and *El cant del poble*, Moya's *Els fadrins de Sant Boi*, his own *Els remers del Volga* and (*c.* 1936) Nicolau's *Death of a Novice* (with the Orfeó Català).

Milstein, Nathan (b. 1904). Born in Odessa where he studied at the Conservatory, Milstein was a student of Stoliarsky and Auer at the St Petersburg Conservatory, and of Ysaÿe in Brussels. He gave concerts in Russia with Horowitz, went to Paris in 1925, and eventually to the United States in 1928, where he became a US citizen and pursued a brilliant career as a violin virtuoso. He has recorded many of the major violin concertos, and made appearances as violinist-conductor for EMI discs of Mozart's Violin Concertos K. 218 and K. 219 (with the Philharmonia Orchestra), and in four Violin Concertos of Vivaldi (with an unnamed orchestra).

Mirouze, Marcel (1906–57). Born in Toulouse, and educated at the Paris Conservatoire, Mirouze was conductor of the Paris Radio Orchestra (1935–40) and at Monte Carlo (1940–43). His compositions included ballet and film music, a piano concerto and an opera *Geneviève de Paris*, to commemorate the 2,000th anniversary of the foundation of the city of Paris (1952). For Pathé he recorded the Rossini overtures *La scala di seta*, *Semiramide* and *Il barbiere di Siviglia* (with the French National Radio Orchestra).

Mitchell, Howard (b. 1911). Born in Lyons, Nebraska, Mitchell studied the piano, tuba, trumpet and cello as a boy, and in 1928 won a scholarship to the Peabody Conservatory at Baltimore. There he studied the cello, became a cellist with the National Symphony Orchestra at Washington, DC, under the conductor Hans Kindler, and later was a student at the Curtis Institute at Philadelphia. His debut as a conductor came in 1941 with the National Symphony Orchestra at some 'Pop' concerts; in 1944 he was appointed an assistant conductor, in 1948 associate conductor and finally in 1949 he succeeded Kindler as permanent conductor. From 1955 he was a guest conductor with various European orchestras, and in 1969 he resigned as conductor of the National Symphony. He recorded for RCA with the orchestra Shostakovich's Symphony No. 5, some concerto accompaniments for the violinist Laredo, and a series of popular items entitled *Adventures in Music*, and for Westminster the Brahms Violin Concerto (with Olevsky), Shostakovich's Symphony No. 1 and *The Age of Gold* suite, Copland's *El Salón México*, *Fanfare for the Common Man*, and suites from *Appalachian Spring* and *Billy the Kid*, and Creston's Symphonies Nos 2 and 3. These performances were competent, if not inspired.

Mitropoulos, Dmitri (1896–1960). Born in Athens, Mitropoulos was the grandson of a priest and the nephew of an archbishop, and it was intended that he should become a monk. However, this was not to be; he studied the piano at seven, and showed evidence of an extraordinary musical gift in memorising by the age of 14 many of the most popular operas. Attending the Athens Conservatory and University, he studied the piano and composition and in 1920 his opera *Soeur Béatrice*, based on a play of Maeterlinck, was produced. Saint-Saëns was present in the audience and was sufficiently impressed to arrange a scholarship for Mitropoulos to study with Gilson in Brussels and with Busoni in Berlin. Busoni was to convince him to abandon composition altogether, and to become an interpretative artist. From 1921 to 1925 Mitropoulos was at the Berlin Staatsoper under Kleiber, as a repetiteur, and on Kleiber's recommendation he was appointed conductor of the symphony orchestra at the Hellenic Conservatory in Athens. He transferred to the Athens Concert Society Orchestra in 1925 and then in 1927 became conductor of the State Symphony Orchestra in Greece. He was invited to conduct the Berlin Philharmonic Orchestra in 1930, and created a sensation by playing and conducting from the keyboard Prokofiev's Piano Concerto No. 3, when the soloist, Petri, was indisposed. This feat he repeated in Paris in 1932, in London and in the United States.

Mitropoulos conducted in Italy, England, the USSR and in Monte Carlo, and in 1936 Koussevitzky invited him to some guest appearances with the Boston Symphony Orchestra. In 1937 he was appointed musical director of the Minneapolis Symphony Orchestra, succeeding Ormandy, and in 1940 he was awarded the American Mahler Medal of Honour, for his work in promoting the composer. After twelve years at Minneapolis, during which time he conducted the New York Philharmonic-Symphony Orchestra (1947–9), he was invited to share the principal conductorship of the New York orchestra with Stokowski in 1949, and became the sole conductor that same year when Stokowski resigned. He became a US citizen in 1946 and remained in New York until 1959, in the meantime taking Walter's place as musical director of the Metropolitan Opera in 1954. In 1951 he led the New York Philharmonic Orchestra (as it changed its name) at the Edinburgh Festival, in 1955 in a tour of Europe, and shared the podium with Bernstein in a tour of Latin America in 1958. He died in Milan while rehearsing Mahler's Symphony No. 3 with the La Scala Orchestra.

Mitropoulos was an incredibly gifted musician, but he stood outside the traditional German school of interpretation. As his conducting career developed, he gave up composing; his most important work, *Concerto Grosso*, was premièred in 1929, but he never recorded his own music. There have been several recordings of him as a pianist, Prokofiev's Piano Concerto No. 3 with the Robin Hood Dell Orchestra with (naturally) himself conducting, and a coupling of Loeffler's *Rhapsody for Oboe, Violin and Piano* and the Hindemith Oboe Sonata, both with the oboist Gomberg. His exhaustive and infallible memory was the wonder of his fellow musicians; he rehearsed even the most complicated works, such as *Wozzeck*, without a score. He would demonstrate his photographic memory by taking the New York telephone directory, opening it at random, studying it for a few minutes, then reciting names, addresses and numbers in perfect detail. He was a tall, lean, bald man, reserved and shy, and lived completely without ostentation in an almost monastic fashion. He avoided the social activities usually imposed on conductors, although he was generous to students and to struggling composers. As a conductor he was exaggeratively demonstrative in his manner; he directed the orchestra with jerky movements of his hands, rarely used a baton, and his body appeared to vibrate with the music. His great nervous intensity brought to bear on the music more expressive weight than it could sometimes take. Virgil Thomson, who witnessed many of his concerts in New York, described him as 'oversensitive, overweaning, overbrutal, overintelligent, underconfident and wholly without ease. . . . His personal excitement bordered on hysteria and distorted music with nervous passion' (*Music Reviewed, 1940–54*, New York, pp. 67–8). These qualities scarcely fitted him for the music of Haydn, Mozart, Beethoven and the early 19th century, but his readings of later romantic and modern music were highly expressive, individual and subjective, although short of the grand and dramatic gestures of a Stokowski or Koussevitzky. He performed much modern music, perhaps more than his audiences were prepared to listen to, championed Schoenberg, Webern and Berg; of English composers he admired Vaughan Williams, particularly his Symphony No. 4, and Joseph Holbrook, whose neglect he could not understand.

At the New York Metropolitan Opera, Mitropoulos was a dynamic force; he introduced many new operas, and gave highly dramatic performances of the standard repertoire. His *Wozzeck*, *Boris Godunov*, *Un ballo in maschera*, and *Vanessa* of Barber, with the Metropolitan Company, were recorded by Columbia and Victor (for the last two), and his *Elektra* with the company was released by the Off-the-air Record Club. Of these, *Wozzeck* was outstanding. Many critics have commented that his concert performances were extremely variable and his interpretations were much subject to the mood of the moment; sometimes the concert performances would be quite different from the rehearsal. His control of the New York Philharmonic was unsure, as he was fundamentally too mild a man to assert his authority. This situation finally led to his resignation, and according to some he left New York a broken man. As a recording artist he enjoyed a substantial career with Columbia (US), first with the Minneapolis Symphony Orchestra and then with the New York Philharmonic. He avoided the major Viennese classics, except for Beethoven's Symphony No. 6 and Brahms' *Variations on the St Antony Chorale*, although his recording of Mendelssohn's Symphony No. 3 was admired. The recording that took his name around the world was that of Mahler's Symphony No. 1, made in 1941 with the Minneapolis Symphony; it was the first ever of the work in the US. The last he made was of the same composer's Symphony No. 8, in his final year, in Salzburg. His series with the Minneapolis Symphony included arrangements of the Bach *Fantasia and Fugue in G minor*, *Grosse Fuge* and *Toccata, Adagio and Fugue in C major*, Lully's *Le Temple de la paix*, entr'actes from Mozart's *Thamos, König in Ägypten*, Beethoven's Symphony No. 6 and *Coriolan* and *Leonore No. 3* overtures, Mendelssohn's Symphony No. 3, the *Capriccio brilliant* (with Graudan) and scherzo from the Octet, the Schumann Symphony No. 3, the Liszt *Rhapsodie espagnole* (with Graudan), *Chopiniana* (arranged by Rogel-Levitzky), Weber's *Jubel* overture, Brahms' *Variations on the St Antony Chorale*, the Coronation March from *Le Prophète*, Chopin's Piano Concerto No. 1 (with Kilenyi), Dvořák's *Slavonic Dances Nos 1* and *3*, *Le Coq d'or* suite, the Franck *Symphony in D minor*, *Le Tombeau de Couperin*, the polka and fugue from *Schwanda*, Milhaud's *Le Boeuf sur le toit*, Chausson's *Symphony in B flat major*, Vaughan Williams' *Fantasia on a Theme of Thomas Tallis*, Glazunov's *Overture on Greek Themes*, Grieg's *Elegiac Melodies*, Massenet's *Scènes alsaciennes*, Rachmaninov's Symphony No. 2 and *The Isle of the Dead*, Tchaikovsky's Symphonies Nos 2 and 4, Mahler's Symphony No. 1, Chabrier's *Marche joyeuse*, Walton's overture *Portsmouth Point*, Siegmeister's *Ozark Set* and Prokofiev's Symphony No. 1.

The New York Philharmonic recordings include Bach's Three-Harpsichord Concerto, BWV 1063, (with Robert, Gaby and Jean Casadesus), excerpts from Couperin's *La Sultane*, Beethoven's Piano Concerto No. 5 (with Robert Casadesus), Mendelssohn's Symphonies Nos 3 and 5 and the Violin Concerto (with Francescatti), Tchaikovsky's Symphonies Nos 5 and 6, the Suite No. 1, *Romeo and Juliet* fantasy-overture, *Marche slave*, *Capriccio italien* and Violin Concerto (with Francescatti), *Symphonie fantastique* and the orchestral movements from Berlioz's *Roméo et Juliette* symphony, *Les Préludes*, *La Mer*, Bruch's Violin Concerto No. 1, Saint-Saëns' Violin Concerto No. 3 and *Symphonie espagnole* (with Francescatti), Vaughan Williams' Symphony No. 4 and *Fantasia on a Theme of Thomas Tallis*, the polka and fugue from *Schwanda*, the Borodin Symphony No. 2, *In the Steppes of Central Asia* and Polovtsian Dances from *Prince Igor*, *L'Apprenti sorcier*, *A Night on the Bare Mountain*, *Petrushka*, *Háry János* suite, dances from *The Three-cornered Hat*, and interlude and dance from *La vida breve*, Rubinstein's and Khachaturian's Piano Concertos (with Levant), Schoenberg's *Erwartung*, *Verklärte Nacht* and Violin Concerto (with Krasner), Rabaud's *La Procession nocturne*, Prokofiev's Violin Concerto No. 1 (with Stern) and *Lieutenant Kijé* suite, Scriabin's *Poème d'extase* and *Prometheus* (with Hambro), Shostakovich's Symphonies Nos 5 and 10 and

Violin Concerto (with Oistrakh), the dance from *Salome*, Ippolitov-Ivanov's *Caucasian Sketches*, Skalkottas' *Greek Dances*, Křenek's *Symphonic Elegy*, Bloch's *Schelomo* and Saint-Saëns' Cello Concerto No. 1 (with Rose), Kirchner's Piano Concerto (with Kirchner), Gottschalk's *Cakewalk* ballet, Sessions' Symphony No. 2, Mennin's Symphony No. 3, Milhaud's Symphony No. 1, Gould's *Fall River Legend*, and Travis' *Symphonic Allegro*. Recordings he made with other orchestras included Berlioz's *Nuits d'été* (with Steber and the Columbia Symphony Orchestra for Columbia), Tchaikovsky's Piano Concerto No. 1 (with Rubinstein and the RCA Victor Symphony Orchestra for RCA), Prokofiev's *Overture on Hebrew Themes* and Swanson's *Night Music* (with the New York Philharmonic Scholarship winners, for Brunswick), Malipiero's Symphony No. 7 (with the Turin Radio Orchestra for Cetra), *Elektra* (with the Florence May Festival Orchestra *et al.* for Everest), Schoenberg's Serenade Op. 24 (with the ISCM Concert Group, for Everest), the third movement from Mahler's Symphony No. 3 (with the West German Radio Orchestra for BIEM), Mozart's Two-Piano Concerto K. 365 (with Vronsky and Babin), Poulenc's Two-Piano Concerto (with Whittemore and Lowe), Prokofiev's Piano Concerto No. 3 (with himself as conductor and soloist), Menotti's ballet *Sebastian* and intermezzi from *Manon Lescaut*, *Cavalleria rusticana* and *I gioielli della Madonna* (with the Robin Hood Dell Orchestra for Columbia). Off-the-Air Record Club also released some records in which Mitropoulos conducted the New York Philharmonic Orchestra, including the Mozart Symphony No. 39, the Beethoven Piano Concerto No. 4 (with Rubinstein), *Elektra* and Bax's *Overture to a Picaresque Comedy*. Mahler's Symphony No. 8, with the Vienna Festival Orchestra *et al.* was issued by Everest; recently, recordings have been issued of his New York Met. performances of *Die Walküre*, *Un ballo in maschera* and *Ernani*, and of a Florence performance of *La forza del destino*.

Except perhaps for *Wozzeck*, few of Mitropoulos' records can aspire to the status of 'great recordings of the century'. His style was too personal for his readings of the standard repertoire to gain general acceptance. But he was always an interesting and individual artist who had the power to produce absorbing performances. Some of his recordings have been reissued by Columbia on the Odyssey label and give an excellent impression of his work: *Symphonie fantastique*, Tchaikovsky's Symphony No. 6, *Fantasia on a Theme of Thomas Tallis*, *Verklärte Nacht* and (in Britain) Vaughan Williams' Symphony No. 4. A memorial to the conductor is the Dmitri Mitropoulos International Competition for Conductors, which is held annually in New York, for young conductors between the ages of 20 and 33.

Mitzelfelt, H. Vincent (b. 1934). The American Mitzelfelt graduated in music at Union College, Nebraska, and in medicine from Loma Linda Medical School, California, and has pursued a double career as doctor and musician. He founded and conducted the Mitzelfelt Chorale (1958), and the Los Angeles Camerata Chorale and Orchestra (1973), with which he toured Europe in 1976. He has recorded Bach's Cantata No. 210 (with Stevenson and the Mitzelfelt Orchestra for Crystal), Vivaldi's Chamber Mass (with the Mitzelfelt Orchestra and Chorale for Crystal), Mozart's *Vesperae de Dominica* and concert aria *Ah, se in ciel* (with Stevenson), Beach's *Then Said Isaiah*, Kantor's *Playthings of the Winds*, and Stravinsky's *Ave Maria*, *Anthem* and *Pater Noster* (with the Los Angeles Camerata Orchestra *et al.* for Crystal), Toch's *Geographical Fugue* and *Waltz for Spoken Chorus* (with the Los Angeles Camerata Chorale for Crystal), Schubert's *Mass in C major* and two *Salve Reginas* (with chorus and orchestra for Grand Prix), and the choral movement from Beethoven's Symphony No. 9 (for M and K Realtime Records).

Mizerit, Klaro (b. 1914). Born in Monfalcone, Italy, Mizerit studied conducting and composition at the Academy of Music at Ljubljana, and at the Academy of Music and University in Vienna. He was a member of the radio symphony orchestra and string quartet at Ljubljana, became music director of the Dubrovnik Festival Orchestra (1951) and of the Rheinische Philharmonie Orchestra at Koblenz (1958), conducted throughout Europe and in the United States and Canada, became music director of the Atlantic Symphony Orchestra at Halifax, Canada (1968), and founded and directed the Atlantic Chamber Orchestra and Atlantic Choir. He has also been co-director of the Pierre Monteux Summer School for orchestral training and conducting. He is now a Canadian citizen. Canadian Broadcasting Corporation has issued discs in which he conducts the Atlantic Symphony Orchestra in the Handel/Harty *Water Music* suite, Schumann's Symphony No. 4, two dances from *La vida breve*, Dela's *Scherzo*, Mercure's *Kaleidoscope*, and Coulthard's Overture; Garnet have also issued Haydn's Symphony No. 87 and Trumpet Concerto (with Schmidhausler) and a

Mozart dance (with the Rheinische Philharmonie).

Molajoli, Lorenzo. Biographical details concerning Molajoli are not known; he had apparently no career at all in the opera house as a conductor, although he was a musical coach, and conducted for Columbia a number of opera sets in the early years of electrical 78 r.p.m. recordings. These included *La Gioconda*, *Aida*, *Cavalleria rusticana*, *Il barbiere di Siviglia*, *Andrea Chénier*, *Fedora*, *La Bohème*, *Madama Butterfly*, *Tosca*, *Mefistofele*, *Manon Lescaut*, *Ernani*, *Rigoletto*, *Il trovatore*, *Carmen* (in Italian), *Pagliacci*, *L'elisir d'amore*, *Don Pasquale*, *La favorita*, *Lucia di Lammermoor* and *I due Foscari* (with the La Scala Orchestra *et al.*), in addition to the overtures to *Giovanna d'Arco*, *Medée*, *Il matrimonio segreto*, *Semiramide*, *Mignon* and *Norma*, Gounod's *Judex* and the prelude and waltz from *Faust*, Mascagni's *Danza esotica* and sinfonia from *La maschere*, the Dance of the Hours from *La Gioconda*, a movement from Respighi's *Ancient Airs and Dances* Suite No. 1, *Fontane di Roma*, *Pini di Roma*, Mancinelli's *Ero e Leandro* suite, Cartini's *L'isola del garda*, the bacchanale from *Samson et Dalila*, the preludes to Acts I and III of *La traviata*, and the intermezzi from Acts I and III of *I gioielli della Madonna* (with the Milan Symphony Orchestra), and his arrangement of Vivaldi's *Concerto in A major* (with the Accademia di Santa Cecilia Orchestra for HMV). Some of the operas were abridged; not all were well cast.

Molinari, Bernardino (1880–1952). Born in Rome and a graduate of the Accademia di Santa Cecilia, Molinari became principal conductor of the Augusteo Orchestra in Rome in 1909. He was appointed artistic director of the orchestra (1920–43), toured with it in Italy, Switzerland, Germany and Czechoslovakia, and also was a guest conductor in Europe, South America and the United States, where he made his debut with the New York Philharmonic Orchestra in 1928, and for a time was conductor of the Los Angeles Philharmonic Orchestra and of the St Louis Symphony Orchestra (1929–30). In Rome he won national acclaim for his festivals of the music of Scarlatti, Beethoven and Debussy, and he transcribed for orchestra works by Debussy, Monteverdi and Vivaldi. He was one of the foremost Italian conductors of his generation, and although best known abroad as a conductor of Italian opera, he was equally distinguished in the concert hall; members of the Israel Philharmonic Orchestra have memories of a remarkably moving performance of Brahms' Symphony No. 4 which he led at Tel-Aviv. In his autobiography (*Overture and Beginners*, London, 1951, p. 253), Goossens commented about Molinari in St Louis in 1928: 'The most ridiculously hot-tempered of all *maestri*, was giving the orchestra the "works" with a vengeance. Stories of his stick-breaking, desk-biting and watch-smashing exploits at rehearsal have long since passed into the realm of legend.' Giulini recalls Molinari as a great orchestral trainer, and as a meticulous and exact rehearser, but when the concert came, he could not relax and became too cautious.

Molinari's records, all 78s except for some transferred to LP, were made for Cetra and Columbia. Included were Vivaldi's *The Four Seasons* (with the Santa Cecilia Orchestra for Cetra), Haydn's Symphony No. 88 and *Prélude à l'après-midi d'un faune* (with the Augusteo Orchestra for Cetra), *Pini di Roma* and *Fontane di Roma*, the Dance of the Persian Slaves from *Khovanshchina*, and the overtures to *Semiramide* and *La vestale* (with the Milan Symphony Orchestra for Columbia) and complete *La Gioconda* and *Il trovatore* (with the La Scala Company for Columbia).

Molinari-Pradelli, Francesco (b. 1911). Born in Bologna, Molinari-Pradelli studied in Bologna and in Rome, where he was a pupil in conducting with Molinari. He first appeared as a conductor in 1937 with a performance of *L'elisir d'amore*, conducted orchestras in Brescia and Bergamo (1939), and in 1946 made his debut at La Scala, Milan. In 1950 he became artistic director at the Arena at Verona, and in 1951 at Busseto for the Verdi 50th-anniversary celebrations. Abroad, he has appeared at Covent Garden (1955 and 1960), and has conducted regularly at San Francisco (since 1957), Vienna (since 1959) and New York (since 1966). He is known particularly for his performances of Wagner and Puccini, and his immense competence and reliability as a conductor of opera has brought him to record with a number of companies. Among the mono LPs issued by Decca were *La traviata*, *Tosca*, *Manon Lescaut* and *La forza del destino*, which he conducted (with the Santa Cecilia Orchestra *et al.*), and *L'elisir d'amore* (with the Maggio Musicale Fiorentino *et al*); some of these were later issued on stereo, together with *Pagliacci* (with the Santa Cecilia Orchestra *et al.*). He also recorded *La Bohème*, *Rigoletto*, *Gianni Schicchi* and *Don Pasquale* (with the San Carlo Opera Orchestra, Naples, *et al.* for Philips), *Martha*, *Werther*, *Simon Boccanegra*, *Il tabarro* and *Tosca* (with the Italian Radio Orchestra *et al.* for Cetra), *La rondine* (with the RCA Italian Opera Orchestra *et al.* for RCA), *L'elisir d'amore*, *Rigoletto* and *Turandot* (with the Rome Opera Orchestra *et al.* for EMI), the overtures to *Il barbiere di Siviglia*, *Semiramide*, *La scala di seta*, *La gazza ladra*, *Il viaggio a Reims*, *Il signor Bruschino* and *Tancredi* (with the Vienna Symphony Orchestra for Philips), and excerpts from *Il barbiere di Siviglia*, *L'elisir d'amore* and *Aida* (with the San Carlo Opera Orchestra, Naples, *et al.* for Philips).

Molnár, Imre (1888–1977). Born at Péterréve, Czechoslovakia, Molnár was professor of voice at the Budapest Academy of Music, and was author of a series of books on singing. Fidelity issued an LP disc naming him as the conductor of the Budapest Symphony Orchestra in a performance of Dvořák's Symphony No. 9.

Moltkau, Hans (b. 1911). Born in Magdeburg, Moltkau was educated at the Hochschule für Musik in Berlin, and studied the cello with Mainardi and Feuermann (1929–30), and conducting with Schmalstich (1933–4). He was a conductor at Saarbrücken, Aldenburg, Plauen, and Innsbruck (1941), then conducted the Austrian Radio Orchestra (1945–59) and the Bavarian Radio Orchestra (1960–62). He has written several operettas, chamber music *et al.*, and his recordings include the Brahms Violin Concerto (with Rybar and an orchestra entitled the West Austrian Radio Orchestra for Club International du Disque, and the Musical Masterpieces Symphony Orchestra for Musical Masterpieces Society), Mendelssohn's overtures *Meeresstille und glückliche Fahrt* and *Die schöne Melusine* (with the Vienna Symphony Orchestra for Vox), and Millöcker's *Der Bettelstudent* (with the Bavarian Radio Symphony Orchestra *et al.* for Ariola).

Mommer, Hans Günter (b. 1925). Born in Dortmund, Mommer served in the German army in World War II and was a prisoner-of-war (1943–7), became solo viola in the Dortmund Chamber Orchestra (1948–9) and studied at the North-West German Music Academy at Detmold (1949–52), where his teacher for conducting was Kurt Thomas. He was a member of the Stuttgart Chamber Orchestra (1952–5), worked with the West German Radio at Cologne (1956–9) and studied conducting with van Otterloo at Hilversum (1957–9). He was chief conductor of the National Symphony Orchestra of Peru (1960–63), the Iraqi National Symphony Orchestra (1963–6 and 1971–2) and of the Pro Musica Orchestra, Thailand (1967–71 and 1972–5), and is now musical director and principal conductor of the Hong Kong Philharmonic Orchestra (from 1975). He has achieved much in developing musical standards in these countries. With the Pro Musica Orchestra of Thailand he recorded arrangements of traditional Thai melodies.

Monod, Jacques-Louis (b. 1927). Born in Paris, Monod studied at the Paris Conservatoire, the Juilliard School, the West Berlin Conservatory and at Columbia University, where he taught for some years. He has conducted orchestras in North and Central America, Scandinavia, Eastern and Western Europe, was musical director of the BBC Third Programme for six years, and as a pianist and conductor has presented world premières of works by Schoenberg, Berg, Webern, Stravinsky, Babbitt, Carter, Dallapiccola *et al.*; in Paris and New York in 1951 he gave the first concerts devoted entirely to Webern's music. For his own compositions he has received a citation from the National Institute of Arts and Letters, and other awards, and has been president of the Guild of Composers Inc., and the René Leibowitz Association, and is a director of publications at several musical publishing companies. He has made the first recordings of works by Berg and Webern (for Dial in 1949), and has recorded Carter's ballet *Pocahontas* (with the Zürich Radio Orchestra, for Epic) and works by Mills, Schwartz, Pisk and Gideon (with the Zürich Radio Orchestra for Composers Recordings) and by Shifrin (with the London Sinfonietta for Composers Recordings). For Composers Recordings he also directed his own *Cantus Contra Cantum I*.

Monterosso, Raffaelo (b. 1925). Born in Cremona, Monterosso studied at the University of Pavia in the Paleographic Musical School, where he was engaged on research into the theory and history of musical notation in the medieval and Renaissance periods. He became professor (1952) of musical history at the university, and also a professor at the Parma Conservatory (1959–68), published many studies in musicology, and also has been active as a conductor and harpsichordist. For Vox he conducted members of the Milan Opera and the Milan Chamber Orchestra in an abridgement of Vivaldi's *La fida ninfa*.

Montani, Nicola (1880–1948). Born in Utica, New York, Montani first studied in the United States and then under Perosi and Capocci in Rome, and under Mocquereau and Eudine on the Isle of Wight (1905–6). He was organist and choirmaster at churches in Philadelphia and New York (1906–24), and from 1925 filled academic positions in eastern US. He was an outstanding authority on Gregorian chant, founded in 1914 the Society of St Gregory of America to restore the usage of Gregorian chant, in 1915 founded the Catholic Choral Club which became the Palestrina Choir, edited hymn books and liturgical music for several music publishers, composed masses and other sacred works, and wrote the books *Essentials in Sight Singing* and *The Art of A Capella Singing*. For Victor he recorded Arcadelt's *Ave Maria* and Palestrina's *Adoramus te*, *Improperia* and *Sicut cervus*, with the Palestrina Choir.

Monteux, Claude (b. 1920). Son of Pierre Monteux, Claude Monteux was born at Brookline, Massachusetts, and is known as both flautist and conductor. He was conductor of the Columbus Symphony Orchestra, Ohio, (1951–6) and of the Hudson Valley Philharmonic Orchestra. In 1971 Decca released a disc of Ravel's *Boléro*, *La Valse* and *Pavane pour une infante défunte*, in which he conducted the Royal Philharmonic Orchestra; for Cambridge he also led the Boston Chamber Ensemble in Hummel's Trumpet Concerto, with Ghitalla.

Monteux, Pierre (1875–1964). Born in Paris, Monteux started to learn the violin when he was six, entered the Paris Conservatoire at nine, conducted his first concert at 12, and then toured with an orchestra with Cortot as soloist. In 1894 he was playing at concerts as a member of a string quartet, and in 1896 shared with Thibaud the first prize for violin playing at the Conservatoire. He then became a violist with the Colonne and Opéra-Comique orchestras, and was appointed choirmaster, assistant conductor, then conductor of the Colonne Orchestra. He conducted the orchestra at the Dieppe Casino (1910), organised his own Concerts Berlioz at the Casino de Paris (1911), and came to the notice of Diaghilev who engaged him as principal conductor for his Ballets Russes Company, with which he conducted the premières of *Petrushka* (1911), *Daphnis et Chloé* (1912), *Le Sacre du printemps* (1913), *Jeux* (1913) and *Le Rossignol* (1914). The first night of *Le Sacre du printemps* in Paris caused a sensation with uproar among the audience. In 1913–14 he also conducted at the Paris Opéra, was a guest conductor at Covent Garden and Drury Lane in London, as well as in Berlin, Budapest and Vienna. In 1914 he founded La Société des Concerts Populaires in Paris.

Monteux served with the French army in 1913 and 1914, and saw action at Verdun, Rheims, Soissons and the Argonne. He was then recalled from the army to join the Ballets Russes in the United States, and to make propaganda for the Allied cause there. He conducted the Ballets Russes (1916–17), the Civic Orchestral Society in New York (1917), took over the French repertoire at the New York Metropolitan Opera (1917–19), and then was appointed musical director of the Boston Symphony Orchestra (1919–24) He then faced difficulties in Boston, since the orchestra was on strike, trying unsuccessfully to force its members into a union; as a result 20 players, including the concertmaster left. Monteux resigned, and was succeeded by Koussevitzky; for ten years he was an associate conductor with Mengelberg with the Amsterdam Concertgebouw Orchestra (1924–34), as well as conducting the Amsterdam Wagner Society. In 1928 he returned to the US to conduct the Philadelphia Orchestra during a temporary absence of Stokowski; he then became conductor of the Paris Symphony Orchestra (1929–38), was permanent conductor of the San Francisco Symphony Orchestra (1935–52), and organised and conducted the first concerts of the NBC Symphony Orchestra (1937). During Munch's time with the Boston Symphony (1949–62) he was a regular guest conductor with the orchestra, became a US citizen in 1942, re-appeared at the New York Met. in 1954 and 1958, was chief conductor of the London Symphony Orchestra (1961, until his death in 1964), and from 1941 trained many student conductors at his home in Hancock, Maine.

Monteux was one of the most charming of men and at the same time one of the most important conductors of this century. His personality completely lacked pretension, and he disliked any form of exhibition or histrionics. Maybe for this reason he was never fully appreciated by audiences on the East Coast of the US, although in San Francisco he was venerated. Certainly some New York critics recognised his stature; Virgil Thomson wrote in 1944 that he had transformed the New York Philharmonic-Symphony Orchestra with the exceptional beauty he drew from them. He was a short, thick figure, and his manner before the orchestra was almost without emotion, quite restrained and always even tempered. He rarely needed to use a score, and his conducting seemed effortless. Toscanini remarked that Monteux had the finest baton technique of any conductor he knew. But his eyes and face, particularly his smile, conveyed everything to his players. At rehearsals he spared no effort, but at the concert he directed with unruffled calm. Every piece he conducted was treated as if he were doing it for the first time, although he admitted that some of the scores of Debussy and Ravel which he was called on to conduct often, had lost their appeal. He continued to be interested in new music until the end of his life; at 80 he was studying music by Hindemith, Britten and Bliss, and first conducted Elgar's *Enigma Variations*, from memory, and the British musicians who played under him declared the performance closer to the composer's than any other. He refused to touch up a score, or to change a note, without, in cases where possible, consulting the composer.

Monteux was nurtured in the music of Mozart, Beethoven and Brahms, and frequently pointed out that he had to learn the French repertoire, since much of it had not been written when he was a young man. Unlike many French conductors, he gave superb performances of Beethoven and Brahms, with a lighter orchestral texture than most European conductors. His Wagner, Strauss and Tchaikovsky were equally fine. He had little interest in post-impressionist music, despite his keenness to programme new works. He had an extraordinary sense of orchestral colour and nuance, and an ability to see each musical piece as a whole and not as a series of episodes. One critic pointed out that he could create a sense in the listener's mind that he was simultaneously hearing some sounds from far away, and others from nearby. He never imposed his own personality on the music, saying 'I have no interpretation; I play the music.' However, he did realise that it was not possible to teach his students any more than technique, declaring that 'Music must be second nature. That's something you cannot learn.' He compiled some rules for young conductors, of which some were that the conductor must always conduct with a baton, so that the players far from him can see the beat; that one must never conduct for the audience; not adhere pedantically to the metronome time, but vary the tempo according to the subject or phrase and give each its own character; not to be disrespectful to the players; not to forget individuals' rights as persons; and not to undervalue the members of the orchestra or treat them simply as cogs in the machinery. Orchestral players and soloists all appreciated his humanity, scholarship and understanding, yet his self-effacing personality put him at a disadvantage compared to his charismatic rivals, and brought him many personal disappointments. One tragedy he never mentioned was the slaughter of his relatives by the Nazis in World War II, because of their activities in the Résistance in France, and because they were Jews.

Monteux had a long and distinguished recording career, which ranged from Bach to Stravinsky. He recorded on 78 r.p.m. discs with the Paris Symphony Orchestra for HMV in the 1930s, the works recorded including Bach's Two-Violin Concerto (with Menuhin and Enesco), Mozart's Violin Concerto K. 271a and Paganini's Violin Concerto No. 1 (with Menuhin), *Symphonie fantastique*, the overture to *Benvenuto Cellini*, the prelude to Act III of *Les Troyens*, *La Valse*, and excerpt from *Ma Mère l'Oye*, Chabrier's *Fête polonaise*, *Petrushka*, *Le Sacre du printemps*, and *Interlude dramatique* of Piero Coppola. Then RCA undertook a major series with him leading the San Francisco Orchestra; these 78 r.p.m. and later LP records were technically significant as they were the first to be recorded on magnetic tape. Included were the Bach (arranged by Respighi) *Passacaglia and Fugue in C minor*, and the sinfonia from the *Christmas Oratorio*, Beethoven's Symphonies Nos 2, 4 and 8, and the overture to *Der Ruinen von Athen*, *Symphonie fantastique*, the Hungarian March from *La Damnation de Faust* and the overtures to *Benvenuto Cellini* and *Béatrice et Bénédict*, Schumann's Symphony No. 4, the *Siegfried Idyll*, Brahms' Symphony No. 2 and *Schicksalslied*, Rimsky-Korsakov's Symphony No. 2, *Scheherazade*, *Sadko* and the Cortège from *Le Coq d'or*, the overtures *Ruy Blas* and to *Le Roi d'Ys*, Franck's *Symphony in D minor* and *Pièce héroïque* (arranged by O'Connell), Debussy's *Images*, Chausson's *Symphony in B flat*, Ibert's *Escales*, d'Indy's *Istar*, Symphony No. 2, *Symphonie sur un chant montagnard* (with Shapiro) and introduction to *Fervaal*, the *Daphnis et Chloé* Suite No. 2, *La Valse*, *Valses nobles et sentimentales* and *Alborada del gracioso*, *Tod und Verklärung*, *Le Sacre du printemps*, *Poème d'extase*, *Kindertotenlieder* (with Marion Anderson), Milhaud's *Protée* and Louis Gruenberg's Violin Concerto (with Heifetz).

Monteux's other discs for RCA, on LP, included Haydn's Symphonies Nos 94 and 101, Beethoven's Symphonies Nos 1, 3, 6 and 8, *Symphonie fantastique*, excerpts from the incidental music for *A Midsummer Night's Dream* and *Rosamunde*, and Brahms' Symphony No. 2 (with the Vienna Philharmonic Orchestra); Beethoven's Symphonies Nos 2, 4 and 7, Brahms' Symphony No. 2, *Variations on the St Antony Chorale* and Violin Concerto (with Szeryng), Dvořák's Symphony No. 7, Sibelius' Symphony No. 2, *Scheherazade*, the

Enigma Variations and excerpts from *The Sleeping Beauty* (with the London Symphony Orchestra); Mozart's Piano Concertos K. 414 and K. 456 (with Lili Kraus), excerpts from *Coppélia* and *Sylvia*, *La Source*, *Les Préludes*, Tchaikovsky's Symphonies Nos 4, 5 and 6, *Poème d'extase*, *Petrushka*, *Le Sacre du printemps* and the Khachaturian Violin Concerto (with Kogan, and the Boston Symphony Orchestra), Chausson's *Poème de l'amour et de la mer* (with Swarthout and the RCA Victor Symphony Orchestra); Franck's *Symphony in D minor* (with the Chicago Symphony Orchestra); and *Petrushka*, *Le Sacre du printemps* and *L'Oiseau de feu* (with the Paris Conservatoire Orchestra).

His remaining records included the Schubert Symphony No. 8 and the Brahms Symphony No. 3 (with the Amsterdam Concertgebouw Orchestra for Philips); Brahms' Symphony No. 2 and *Academic Festival Overture*, *Images*, *Boléro*, *Ma Mère l'Oye*, *La Valse*, Symphonic Fragments from *Le Martyre de Saint-Sébastien*, and excerpts from *Swan Lake* (with the London Symphony Orchestra for Philips); Beethoven's Symphony No. 9 and Berlioz's *Roméo et Juliette* symphony (with the London Symphony Orchestra *et al.* for Westminster); Bach's Suite No. 2, Mozart's Flute Concerto K. 314 and Dance of the Blessed Spirits from *Orfeo ed Euridice* (with Claude Monteux), Brahms' Piano Concerto No. 1 (with Katchen), Nuages and Fêtes from *Nocturnes*, *Prélude à l'après-midi d'un faune*, *Rapsodie espagnole* and *Pavane pour une infante défunte* (with the London Symphony Orchestra for Decca); the complete *Daphnis et Chloé* (with the Royal Opera House Orchestra, Covent Garden, for Decca); *Manon* (with the Paris Opéra-Comique Orchestra *et al.* for EMI); *Orfeo ed Euridice* (with the Rome Opera House Orchestra *et al.* for RCA), the Mozart Symphonies Nos 35 and 39, the Beethoven Symphonies Nos 2 and 4, and the overture and *adagio* from *Die Geschöpfe des Prometheus*; *Symphonie fantastique*, Liszt's *Hungarian Fantasy* (with Bianca), Tchaikovsky's Symphony No. 5 and *Romeo and Juliet* fantasy-overture, *A Night on the Bare Mountain*, *Capriccio espagnol*, the Polovtsian Dances from *Prince Igor*, the overture to *Der fliegende Holländer*, the prelude and Liebestod from *Tristan und Isolde*, and the overture and Venusberg Music from *Tannhäuser* (with the North-West German Radio Symphony Orchestra for La Guilde Internationale du Disque).

Many of these recordings have been reissued on cheap labels, and are, by any standards, superb performances. In this outstanding category, and as examples of Monteux's distinctive art, are the suites from *Swan Lake* (Philips) and *The Sleeping Beauty* (Decca), Brahms' Symphony No. 2 (RCA and Decca), *Enigma Variations* and the three Tchaikovsky symphonies (RCA), *Boléro*, *Ma Mère l'Oye* and *La Valse* (Philips), *Daphnis et Chloé* (Decca), *Nuages*, *Fêtes*, *Prélude à l'après-midi d'un faune*, *Pavane pour une infante défunte* and *Rapsodie espagnole* (Decca) and *Scheherazade* (Decca). His *Manon*, unfortunately now withdrawn from the catalogues, was a magnificent and intense performance, and included Victoria de los Angeles in her prime in the cast. RCA still retain in their American Victrola series a coupling of *Tod und Verklärung* and the *Siegfried Idyll*, an interesting reminder of his years with the San Francisco Symphony Orchestra.

Montgomery, Kenneth (b. 1943). Born in Belfast, Montgomery studied at the Royal Belfast Academic Institution, was encouraged in his musical studies by Arthur Martin, and regularly observed Maurice Miles at rehearsals with the City of Belfast Orchestra. He moved to the Royal College of Music in London, where his teachers of conducting were Phillips and Boult, and studied further at the Accademia Chigiana at Siena with Celibidache. In 1964 he joined the musical staff at the Glyndebourne Festival Opera, first appeared there as a conductor in 1967, conducted with the Sadler's Wells Opera Company (1967–70), was assistant conductor of the Bournemouth Symphony Orchestra and Bournemouth Sinfonietta (1970), and then was appointed director of the Sinfonietta (1973). He also was musical director of the Glyndebourne Touring Company (1974), and after some appearances at the Netherlands Opera, was appointed chief conductor of the Netherlands Radio Orchestra (1976). In 1976 EMI released a fine disc in which Montgomery conducts the Bournemouth Sinfonietta in symphonies by Arne and Wesley ; later, with the same orchestra, two discs were released of excerpts from *Messiah*, *Berenice*, *Water Music* and other works of Handel, and Dvořák's *Notturno*, Grieg's *Two Norwegian Melodies*, Nielsen's *Little Suite*, Wirén's *Serenade* and Tchaikovsky's *Elegy*, and with the English Chamber Orchestra and Marco Bakker a recital of Handel arias.

Moores, Michael (b. 1930). Born in Birkenhead, Moores studied classics and music at Liverpool University, was joint-conductor of the Liverpool Mozart Orchestra, solo pianist to the Royal Signals Band for two years, and joined Sadler's Wells Opera Company as a repetiteur in 1954. He studied conducting with

Markevitch at Salzburg, and made his debut at Sadler's Wells in 1957 with *The Moon and Sixpence*. Subsequently, he conducted several West End musicals and light music programmes for the BBC. In EMI's English-language opera series with the Sadler's Wells Company, he conducted a disc of excerpts from *Il trovatore*.

Moralt, Rudolf (1902–58). Born in Munich into a musical family, and a nephew of Richard Strauss, Moralt studied at the Munich Academy of Music and in 1919 became a choral coach at the Bavarian State Opera at Munich, eventually becoming a conductor there in 1923, working with Walter and Knappertsbusch. He then was conductor at the German Opera House at Brno (1928–30), at Kaiserslautern (1932–4), Braunschweig (1934–6), director at the Styrian Opera at Graz (1937–40) and then principal conductor and director at the Vienna State Opera (1940–58). From 1945 he frequently conducted the Vienna Philharmonic and Symphony Orchestras, was a guest conductor with the Berlin and Budapest Philharmonic Orchestras, led concerts at Rome and Naples, conducted opera at La Scala, Milan, and the Teatro Fenice in Venice, at the Cannes International Music Festival in 1948 and at the Wagner Festival at Nice in 1947. At the Vienna State Opera he was acclaimed for new presentations of *The Ring*, *Elektra* and *Arabella*, and he had a reputation for his complete reliability, musicianship and devotion to his task. As well as having a natural gift for the operas of Richard Strauss, he was an affectionate interpreter of the music of the other Strauss, Johann.

Moralt recorded in the early years of LP, mainly for Philips and Vox. His recordings included Mozart's Serenade K. 388, *Eine kleine Nachtmusik*, *Serenata notturna*, the Violin Concertos K. 216 and K. 218 (with Grumiaux), the Masses K. 275, K. 317 and K. 427, *Don Giovanni* and *Così fan tutte*, the Mendelssohn Violin Concerto (with Grumiaux), the Grieg and Schumann Piano Concertos (with Richter-Haaser), the Brahms Violin Concerto (with Senofsky), the *Nutcracker* suite, the Dvořák and Schumann Cello Concertos (with de Malucha), the preludes to *Tristan und Isolde* and *Die Meistersinger*, the overtures to *Der fliegende Holländer* and *Tannhäuser*, Wotan's Farewell from *Die Walküre*, and a Wagner recital (with Brouwenstijn), an abridged *Der Zigeunerbaron*, the overture to *Die Fledermaus* and a collection of Strauss waltzes, *Salome*, *Tiefland*, Schmidt's Symphony No. 4, the Khachaturian Violin Concerto (with Magyar), Kodály's *Galánta Dances* and *Marosszék Dances*, and the overtures to *Dichter und Bauer* and *Boccaccio* (with the Vienna Symphony Orchestra *et al.* for Philips); Mozart's Piano Concertos K. 459, K. 482, K. 488, K. 491, K. 537 and Rondo K. 382 (with Lili Kraus), Beethoven's Piano Concerto No. 3 (with Kraus), and *Mass in C major*, Mendelssohn's Piano Concerto No. 1 (with Frugoni), Piano Concerto No. 2 (with Wührer) and Two-Piano Concerto (with Frugoni and Taddei), Schubert's Symphony No. 5, 17 *German Dances* and Mass No. 6, and the Dvořák Piano Concerto (with Wührer, and the Vienna Symphony Orchestra for Vox); Tchaikovsky's Piano Concerto No. 1 (with de la Bruchollerie and the Vienna State Philharmonic Orchestra for Vox); Lalo's Cello Concerto, Saint-Saëns' Cello Concerto No. 1 and Fauré's *Élégie* (with Cassado and the Vienna Pro Musica Orchestra for Vox); Rubinstein's Piano Concerto No. 4 (with Wührer and the Vienna Philharmonia Orchestra for Vox); the *Leonore No. 3* overture and choruses from *I Lombardi* (with the Hague Philharmonic Orchestra *et al.* for Philips); *Giuditta* (with the Vienna Symphony Orchestra *et al.* for Decca); a recital by Welitsch (with the Vienna State Opera Orchestra for Decca); Wotan's Farewell from *Die Walküre* (with Schoeffler and the Vienna Philharmonic Orchestra for Decca, and with Hermann and the same orchestra for EMI); Gluck's *Don Juan*, Pergolesi's Two-Violin Sonata No. 13, Corelli's Concerto Grosso Op. 6 No. 9, and Giuseppe Sammartini's Concerto Grosso Op. 11 No. 4 (with the Vienna Symphony Orchestra for Westminster), and Marx's *Old Vienna Serenades* and Siegel's Piano Concerto (with Radluker) and *Between Two Worlds* (with the Vienna Symphony Orchestra for Abbey).

Morel, Jean (1903–75). Born in Abbeville, France, Morel studied under Philipp, Gallon, Emmanuel, Hahn and Pierné at the Paris Conservatoire, and first conducted at the Théâtre des Champs-Élysées in 1933, at a performance of Stravinsky's *Les Noces*. He then conducted at the Opéra-Comique, was with the French National Radio Orchestra (1936–9), and succeeded Monteux as conductor of the Paris Symphony Orchestra (1938). He also taught at the American Conservatory at Fontainebleau (1921–36). In 1939 he departed for the United States, taught at the Brooklyn College (1940–43), conducted the New York City Symphony Orchestra (1942–52), conducted opera in Rio de Janeiro, Mexico City (1943–8), with the New York City Opera (1944–52), San Francisco Opera and New York Metropolitan Opera (1956–71), taught conducting at the

Juilliard School (1949–71), and was a guest conductor with the New York Philharmonic, Boston Symphony and some other major US orchestras. In the opera house, Morel was a specialist in the French repertoire, but also at the New York Met. led many performances of *Madama Butterfly*. He recorded the two *L'Arlésienne* suites, Chabrier's *España* and *Marche joyeuse*, and excerpts from *Swan Lake* (with the Royal Opera House Orchestra, Covent Garden, for RCA), Albéniz's *Iberia* and Ravel's *Rapsodie espagnole* (with the Paris Conservatoire Orchestra for RCA), the Offenbach/Rosenthal *Gaîté parisienne*, Berlioz's *Zaïde* (with Steber) and the two Beethoven *Romances* (with Francescatti, and the Columbia Symphony Orchestra for Columbia), the Franck *Symphonic Variations* and Liszt's *Totentanz* (with Brailowsky and the Victor Symphony Orchestra for RCA), Mozart's Piano Concerto K. 467 (with Lhevinne and the Juilliard Orchestra for Columbia), Chabrier's *Habanera* (with the RCA Victor Symphony Orchestra for RCA), Handel's Organ Concerto Op. 4 No. 6, arranged for harp (with Grandjany and a chamber orchestra for RCA), accompaniments to arias by Kirsten, Merrill and Albanèse (with the RCA Victor Symphony Orchestra for RCA), two arias from Monsigny's *Le Déserteur* (with Teyte and an orchestra for Victor, described by David Hall in *Records*, New York, 1950, p. 324 as 'utter perfection'), and excerpts from Offenbach's *La Périchole* (with the New York Metropolitan Opera Orchestra *et al.* for RCA).

Morelli, Giuseppe (b. 1907). Born in Rome where he was a choirboy at St Peter's, Morelli studied at the Accademia di Santa Cecilia and with Molinari; he conducted at opera houses in Rome, Naples, Palermo, Parma, Bologna and Venice, in Belgium, Austria, Spain, Holland *et al.*, and made his debut in the United States with the New York City Opera in 1970. He has recorded *Aida*, arranged for orchestra (with the Rome Symphony Orchestra, for Fiesta and Kingsway), Pergolesi's *La contadina astuta*, Donizetti's *Betly*, and Rossini's *La scala di seta*, *La cambiale di matrimonio*, *Il cambio della valigia* and *Messe solennelle* (with the Rome Quartet Society *et al.* for La Guilde Internationale du Disque, and issued variously by Period, Nixa and Dover), and the choruses from *I Lombardi* (with the Rome Opera Chorus and Orchestra for EMI).

Morgan, Wesley (b. 1918). Born in Barnsdall, Oklahoma, Morgan studied at Occidental College, Los Angeles, Union Theological Seminary, New York City, and at the University of Southern California, and held academic posts at the University of the Pacific, California (1943–51), the University of Southern California (1954–8) and the Southern Illinois University (1958–70), before becoming professor of musicology, chairman of the department of music and director of the school of music at the University of Kentucky (since 1973). He is also musical director of Pleiades Records, Southern Illinois University Press (since 1967) and has directed the Collegium Musicum of the Southern Illinois University (1970–76). For Pleiades Records he has recorded five discs with the Collegia Musica of the Universities of Chicago, Southern Illinois and Kentucky, in collections of music from the late medieval period, the 15th and 16th centuries; these records were issued between 1969 and 1971.

Mori, Tadashi (b. 1921). Born in Osaka and a graduate of the school of music in the Tokyo National University of Fine Arts and Music, Mori is professor of music at Toho University and conductor of the Tokyo Broadcasting Symphony Orchestra and the Fujiwara Opera. He has recorded the two Beethoven *Romances*, Saint-Saëns' *Introduction et rondo capriccioso* and Sarasate's *Zigeunerweisen* (with Unno and the Tokyo CBS Symphony Orchestra for CBS), Akutagawa's *Music for Symphony Orchestra* and *Triptyque for String Orchestra*, and Mayazumi's *Bacchanale* and *Phonologie Symphonique* (with the Tokyo Symphony Orchestra for EMI).

Mörike, Eduard (1877–1929). Born in Stuttgart, Mörike was a great-nephew of the poet Mörike; he was a pupil of Ruthardt, Piutti and Sitt, and was a distinguished pianist and teacher as well as a conductor. He conducted in various German opera houses and was chief of the Dresden Vocal Academy (1925–9). In 1919 Parlophone (in Germany) issued recordings of him conducting the Berlin Staatsoper Orchestra in the overtures to *Rienzi* and *Der fliegende Holländer*, the prelude to Act III of *Der fliegende Holländer*, and the Rhine Journey from *Götterdämmerung*; they were uncut versions, whereas previously record companies had generally abridged works to be accommodated on a 12-inch record. He also recorded Beethoven's Symphony No. 7, Schubert's Symphony No. 8, *Les Préludes*, the overture *The Hebrides*, *Scheherazade*, *Le Rouet d'Omphale*, *Don Juan*, *Tod und Verklärung*, *Till Eulenspiegel*, *Ein Heldenleben*, Tchaikovsky's Symphony No. 6, some excerpts from *Parsifal*, the Crusaders' March from Liszt's *The Legend of Saint*

Elizabeth (with an orchestra named 'Opera House Orchestra', for Parlophone), and *Moldau*, the *Blue Danube* waltz, the *Nutcracker* suite and the grand march from *Aida* (with the Berlin Staatsoper Orchestra for Odeon).

Morris, Andrew (b. 1948). Educated at the Westminster Abbey Choir School, the Royal Academy of Music and the Goldsmiths' College at the University of London, Morris was a professor at the London College of Music (1972–4), conductor of the University of London Choir (1970–72), director of music at Christ's College, Finchley (from 1972), director of music at the Priory Church of St Bartholomew-the-Great, London (from 1971), artistic director of the St Bartholomew's Festivals (1973, 1977 and 1978) and conductor of the New English Singers (from 1974). For Abbey he has recorded with the Choir and Sinfonia of St Bartholomew-the-Great a disc of Mozart's church music, and another of music by Tallis, Byrd, Victoria, Palestrina, Tomkins, Schütz, Purcell, Stravinsky and Brockless.

Morris, Wyn (b. 1929). After studying at the Royal Academy of Music and at the Salzburg Mozarteum, Morris was an apprentice conductor with the Yorkshire Symphony Orchestra (1950–51), musical director of an army band (1951–3), and founded and conducted the Welsh Symphony Orchestra (1954–7). In 1957 he was winner of the Koussevitzky Memorial Prize of the Boston Symphony Orchestra, and then was with Szell at the Cleveland Orchestra as an observer (1957–60), at the same time conducting the Cleveland Orpheus Choir and the Cleveland Chamber Orchestra (1958–60). Returning to Britain, he became conductor of the Choir of the Royal National Eisteddfod of Wales (1960–62), made his debut in London with the Royal Philharmonic Orchestra in 1963, was conductor of the Royal Choral Society (1968–70) leading the Choir on a tour of the United States in 1969, and has been conductor of the Huddersfield Choral Society (since 1969) and of the Bruckner-Mahler Chorale (since 1970).

Morris made his name as a conductor of Mahler, and in 1968 was awarded the Mahler Memorial Medal of the Bruckner and Mahler Society of America. He first appeared on record exclusively as a conductor of Mahler: Symphony No. 1, in its original 1893 version (with the New Philharmonia Orchestra for Virtuoso), Symphony No. 8 (with the Symphonica of London *et al.* for Independent World Releases), the final revised edition of Cooke's reconstruction of the Symphony No. 10 (with the New Philharmonia Orchestra for Philips), *Das klagende Lied* and *Des Knaben Wunderhorn* (with the New Philharmonia and London Philharmonic Orchestras, respectively, *et al.* for Delysé, and later re-issued by Decca in Britain, and for *Das klagende Lied* by Angel in the US), Symphony No. 5 and *Lieder eines fahrenden Gesellen* (with Hermann, and the Symphonica of London, for Symphonica). Morris is a powerful and sensitive interpreter of Mahler; his readings are generally devoid of sentimental expression, possibly the result of his years with Szell. He obtains dramatic playing from his orchestras, perhaps not always with the polish of most of the other conductors who have recorded this music, but this is compensated for by an original and thoroughly convincing understanding of the music. He has also recorded, in two discs with the Symphonica of London for Pye, the *Egmont* overture, Brahms' *Liebeslieder Walzer*, the Schumann Piano Concerto (with Cherkassky), the overture to Méhul's *Les deux aveugles de Tolède*, Saint-Saëns' *Introduction et rondo capriccioso* and *Havanaise* and Ravel's *Tzigane* (with Y. Tortelier), *Pavane pour une infante défunte*, and Debussy's *Danse sacrée et dance profane* (with Manson), and an aria recital with Rita Streich. His other recordings have been of Rachmaninov's *Vesper Mass* and Kastalsky's *Four Motets* (with the Bruckner-Mahler Choir of London for Philips), and Bliss's *A Knot of Riddles* (with Shirley-Quirk) and *Lie Strewn the White Flocks* (with Michelow and the London Chamber Orchestra for Pye).

Moryl, Richard (b. 1929). Born in Newark, New Jersey, Moryl was educated at Columbia and Brandeis Universities and at the Hochschule für Musik in Berlin, receiving a number of scholarships and grants for composition. He has been associated with the Columbia–Princeton and Brandeis University electronic studios, with Ussachevsky, Luening and Babbit, is chairman of the music department at Western Connecticut State College (since 1975) and is conductor and director of the New England Contemporary Ensemble. His compositions have often been performed in the United States, Europe and South America, and he has recorded some for Desto and Serenus, including *Fluorescents* and *Chorales* (with the West Connecticut State College Instrumentalists) and *Illuminations* (with the New England Contemporary Ensemble).

Moyse, Louis (b. 1912). Born in Scheveningen, Holland, Moyse attended the Paris Conservatoire where he studied the flute with Gaubert and his father, Marcel Moyse. He assisted his father at the Conservatoire flute class (1932–48), was flautist with several Paris orchestras and with the Adolf Busch Chamber Players, and was both flautist and pianist with the Moyse Trio. After serving in the French army in World War II, he left France to teach at Marlboro College, Vermont, where he was co-founder of the Marlboro School of Music and Music Festival. He was also associated with the Brattleboro Music Center (1951–75), the Summer Chamber Music School of Saint-Prex, Switzerland (1960), and became professor of flute and chamber music at the University of Toronto. He is first a flautist, pianist and composer, and conducts for a hobby, but has often conducted the Marlboro Festival Players. Columbia recorded him conducting that ensemble in Dvořák's *Serenade in D minor*, and Beethoven's *Octet in E flat*, and Marlboro Recording Society in Mozart's Serenade K. 361. He has also recorded for many other companies as flautist and pianist.

Mravinsky, Yevgeni (b. 1903). Born in St Petersburg, Mravinsky was active in theatrical productions while still at school, and later was an accompanist at the Leningrad Ballet School. He studied at the Leningrad Conservatory (1924–30) under Scherbachov for composition, and Gauk and Malko for conducting. His debut as a conductor was in 1929; he was with the Leningrad Opera and Ballet Theatre (now the Kirov Theatre) from 1932 to 1938. In 1937 he premièred Shostakovich's Symphony No. 5, and since then has been closely associated with Shostakovich, leading the first performances of most of his music. In 1938 he won the first prize in the All-Union Conductors' Competition, and in the same year was appointed chief conductor of the Leningrad Philharmonic Orchestra. With the orchestra he toured the United States in 1946 and 1957, and Western Europe in 1956 and 1961. In 1946 he was awarded the Stalin Prize, and in 1961 the Lenin Prize.

Mravinsky is one of the foremost Soviet conductors, and the Leningrad Philharmonic is one of the most distinguished Soviet orchestras. His interpretations are quite literal in that he performs the music exactly as it was written, and his technique is such that he can make the orchestra play the music precisely as he wishes to hear it. The orchestral texture is exceptionally clear; his readings are not in the least influenced by convention and frequently have an electrifying effect, although a certain restlessness is occasionally present. His selection of tempi is always interesting, and sometimes unusual, as in the relatively slow first movement of Beethoven's Symphony No. 7, and the very fast finale of Tchaikovsky's Symphony No. 4. But there appears to be, in his performances, a concern for orchestral virtuosity for its own sake, as if he were only performing the notes without heed to the feeling or poetic content of the music, so that some music, such as the Symphony No. 6 of Beethoven, gives an impression of chilliness that belies his own love of the score. In the words of his long-time colleague, Kurt Sanderling, to the author 'He has a heart but it does not show.' Nonetheless, it is surprising that such an important artist has appeared so sparsely in the EMI Melodiya series that has been issued in Britain and the United States, and that many of the records released, and indeed available, in the USSR, have been of live concert performances taped years before.

His early 78 r.p.m. discs, made in the USSR, included Tchaikovsky's Symphony No. 6 (with the USSR State Symphony Orchestra), *Francesca da Rimini* (with the Moscow Philharmonic Orchestra), Glazunov's Symphony No. 4 and Shostakovich's Symphony No. 5 (with the Leningrad Philharmonic Orchestra) and Shostakovich's *Song of the Forests* (with the USSR State Symphony Orchestra *et al.*). Recordings of performances of him with the Leningrad Philharmonic Orchestra, on LP, include Haydn's Symphony No. 101, Mozart's Symphony No. 39 and overture to *Le nozze di Figaro*, Beethoven's Symphonies Nos 4, 5, 6 and 7, the overture to *Russlan and Ludmilla*, the prelude to *Khovanshchina*, Brahms' Symphony No. 1, Tchaikovsky's Symphonies Nos 4, 5 and 6 (recorded in London in 1961 and issued by DGG), and Piano Concerto No. 1 (with Richter), Bruckner's Symphony No. 8, Shostakovich's Symphonies Nos 6, 7, 10, 11 and 12 and Violin Concerto No. 1 (with Oistrakh), Prokofiev's Symphony No. 7, the prelude to Act III of *Lohengrin*, *Prélude à l'après-midi d'un faune*, Scriabin's *Poème d'extase*, Liadov's *Baba Yaga*, an excerpt from Glazunov's *Raymonda*, Sibelius' Symphony No. 7 and *The Swan of Tuonela*, Stravinsky's *Apollon Musagète*, Hindemith's symphony *Die Harmonie der Welt*, Bartók's *Music for Strings, Percussion and Celesta* and Honegger's Symphony No. 3.

Muck, Karl (1859–1940). Born at Darmstadt, Muck spent his youth in Switzerland, played the piano at a chamber recital at the age of 11, and as a boy played the violin in a symphony orchestra. He studied philology at Heidelberg and Leipzig Universities, and when at Leipzig attended the conservatory. He appeared as a pianist at the Gewandhaus in 1879, the same year as he gained his Ph.D., and his career as a conductor started as a chorusmaster at Zürich. He went on to appointments in Salzburg, Brno, Graz and at the German Opera at Prague in 1886; by this time he was acclaimed as one of the leading German conductors. In 1892 he became conductor at the Berlin Royal Opera, alongside Strauss and the young Bruno Walter, at the same time conducting the Royal Orchestra. He was active at the Berlin Opera for 20 years, and in this period conducted 1,071 performances of 103 operas. Between 1903 and 1906 he shared the leadership of the Vienna Philharmonic Orchestra and conducted the Wagner operas in Russia, London and other European cities.

Muck visited the United States to conduct the Boston Symphony Orchestra in the years 1906 and 1908, and in 1912 was appointed permanent conductor at Boston. His years there were brilliant, and he made the Boston Symphony the leading orchestra in the US. However, in 1918 he became the centre of a political scandal: he was known to have been a friend of Kaiser Wilhelm II, from his Berlin days; a wave of war hysteria was fed by his alleged pro-German sympathies and his unfortunate refusal to play *The Star-spangled Banner* at the beginning of a concert. He was arrested at his home in 1918 and interned as an enemy alien until the end of the war. He returned to Europe in 1919, was first active as a guest conductor in Munich, Amsterdam and other cities, and in 1922 was appointed conductor of the Hamburg Philharmonic Orchestra. Lucrative offers from the US were spurned. He retired from Hamburg in 1933, and in that year conducted his last concert at Leipzig on the 50th anniversary of Wagner's death. His final public appearance was to receive from Hitler on his last birthday the order of the German Eagle. He died of nicotine poisoning, said to have been caused by smoking 100 cigarettes a day for many years.

Muck was one of the greatest conductors of his day, and contemporaries such as Schnabel, Paderewski and Weingartner had the utmost respect for him. His repertoire was considerable, and he performed much of the new symphonic music of his time: Debussy, Mahler, Sibelius and Schoenberg. He was an intensely dedicated and thorough musician, and took infinite care over arranging his programmes and preparing individual works. Olin Downes wrote in the *New York Times* that he was the 'most industrious and implacable of drill-masters'. In contrast to today's practice, he would never conduct without a score. In an age when the subjectively romantic style of Mahler and Nikisch were the vogue, Muck's tempi were firm, his rhythm certain, and he adhered strictly to the score, and in this respect he anticipated conductors such as Toscanini, Szell and Karajan. He scoffed at the idea of inner meaning in music, saying that 'a dotted eighth note was a dotted eighth note without any secret significance' (*Current Biography*, New York, 1940, p. 606). Writing in 1917, Richard Aldridge, the critic of the *New York Times*, said of Muck's performance of Brahms' Symphony No. 4: 'A reading full of life, of sinuous grace in the first movement, of immense vigor in the third and last movements, of lovely sentiment in the andante; everywhere of beautiful color and subtle adjustment of the instrumental voices, of finely tuned and pregnant phrasing, of subtle nuancing of tempo.' As a man, Muck could be sharp in temper and wit; someone attempted to interest him in a new composer by suggesting that he was a 'self-made man', to which Muck retorted: 'A self-made man? Where I come from, everyone has a father and mother' (H. Schonberg, *The Great Conductors*, New York, 1967, p. 220).

In 1917 the Boston Symphony Orchestra under Muck became the first orchestra in the US to make a gramophone record. The music recorded at the Victor Talking Machine Company at Camden, New Jersey, was the last movement of Tchaikovsky's Symphony No. 4 and the *Marche militaire* from his Suite No. 1, and the prelude to Act III of *Lohengrin*. The last of these was included in an LP disc entitled *Boston Symphony Orchestra: The Sound History of a Great Orchestra on RCA*, which was issued in Britain in 1971. The primitive recording conditions of 1917 required each first-desk violinist to play into a horn of his own, and when the other players had important passages they had to dash to one of the horns and then resume their seats.

Muck was famous as a conductor of Wagner, and was a favourite with Cosima Wagner. He was the celebrated interpreter of *Parsifal*, which he directed at Bayreuth continuously from 1901 to 1930, although in his last years he really lacked the strength to rehearse, and had then become a crotchety old man. In 1928 HMV recorded some substantial excerpts from *Parsifal* with Muck and the Bayreuth Festival Orchestra, and these were re-issued on a fine LP transfer in an Austrian series called *Lebendige Vergangenheit*. This extended example of Muck's musicianship sounds remarkably well for its age, although the pitch of the disc appeared to be slightly faulty. Muck also recorded the *Siegfried Idyll*, the preludes to *Die Meistersinger* and *Parsifal*, and the overture to *Tann-*

häuser (for Columbia), and the overture to *Der fliegende Holländer* and the prelude to *Tristan und Isolde* for HMV, all with the Berlin State Opera Orchestra, although he was disinclined to perform excerpts from the Wagner operas at his symphony concerts.

Mudde, Willem (b. 1909). Born in Amsterdam, Mudde studied at the Organ School of Jan Zwart, Amsterdam, and at the Hochschule für Kirchenmusik, Berlin, and has been the director of music at various Lutheran churches in Holland. He founded the Lutheran Working Group for Church Music (1946), the Utrecht Choral Society (1947) and the publication *Musica Sacra* (1958), has been president of the Mitteleuropäische Kontakte für Evangelische Kirchemusik, has made concert tours in Europe and the United States, and has composed organ, choral and other music. For Cantate he recorded motets by Sweelinck and Lassus with the Utrecht Motetgezelschap.

Mudie, Michael (1914–62). Born in Manchester, Mudie studied at the Royal College of Music, London, conducted the Carl Rosa Opera Company (1935–9) and the Sadler's Wells Opera Company (1946–53), but then retired because of ill-health. He led the first English performance of *Simon Boccanegra*, and was well regarded for his conducting, particularly of Italian operas. EMI issued a 78 r.p.m. recording of him conducting Frederick Austin's version of *The Beggar's Opera* of Pepusch and Gay, with the Glyndebourne Opera Company.

Mühler-Brühl, Helmut (b. 1933). Educated at the Humanistisches Gymnasium in Brühl, Germany, Mühler-Brühl studied theology, philosophy and musicology, and as an undergraduate studied the viola with Nippes, theory with Petzold and conducting with Stefani. He also took part in violin master-classes with Schneiderhan in Lucerne. In 1958 the Brühl Palace concerts under him were established; this led to the formation of the Cologne Ensemble, which was renamed the Cologne Chamber Orchestra in 1964, the players being drawn from the two principal symphony orchestras in Cologne. Together with the orchestra, he soon became widely known, touring Europe, Africa and the United States; he also appeared as guest conductor with other chamber and symphony orchestras, and became director of a chamber-music master-class at the International Academy of Chamber Music in Rome.

With the Cologne Chamber Orchestra, Mühler-Brühl has made many fine recordings for Schwann. Most have been of baroque music, and many of these discs have been issued in the United States and elsewhere by Nonesuch, Monarch and Musical Heritage Society. Included are Bach's Cantatas Nos 199 and 209, and an aria from Cantata No. 208 (with Stader) and the sinfonia from Cantata No. 75, W. F. Bach's Sinfonias F. 64, F. 65 and F. 67, C. P. E. Bach's Sinfonia Wq 183, Sonatina for Two Harpsichords and Orchestra (with Fetz and Scheidegger) and Organ Concerto Wq 34 (with Fetz), J. C. Bach's Sinfonias Nos 1, 2, 3, 4, 6, 10, 12 and 20, *Flute Concerto in D* (with Sebon) and Bassoon Concerto (with Thunemann), Vivaldi's Concerti Grossi Nos 5, 12, 14, 19, 22 and 26, Cello Concerto No. 14 (with Starck), *Flute Concerto in A* (with Nicolet) and Flute Concerto No. 13 (with Möhring), Biber's *Serenade in C major*, Boccherini's *Serenade in C major*, Fasch's *Oboe Concerto in G minor* (with Passin) and *Trumpet Concerto in D major* (with André), Molter's *Clarinet Concerto in A major* (with Stalder), Telemann's *Violin and Trumpet Concerto in D major* (with Meyer-Schierning and Schneidewind), *Oboe d'amore Concerto in A major* (with Aussen and with Koch), *Horn Concerto in D major* (with Penzel), *Suite for Three Oboes in C major* (with Koch, Passin and Theis), *Concerto Grosso in D major*, *Don Quixote* and *Two-Violetta Concerto in G major* (with Christ and Engel), Torelli's *Trumpet Concerto in D major* and Sonata Op. 3 No. 7 (with Schneidewind), Rolla's *Basset-horn Concerto in F major* (with Stalder), C. Stamitz's *Clarinet Concertos in E major* (with Stalder) and *B major* (with Klein), and *Cello Concerto in A major* (with Starck), Danzi's Bassoon Concerto (with Sax), Devienne's Bassoon Concerto (with Sax), Reicha's Trios for Three Horns (with Lexutt, H. Alfing and K. Alfing), Hoffmeister's Piano Concerto Op. 24 (with Neuhaus) and *Flute Concerto in G major* (with Möhring), Albinoni's Oboe Concerto Op. 9 No. 5 (with Hucke), dall'Abaco's Serenata and Violin Concerto Op. 6 No. 2 (with Kussmaul), Tartini's Violin Concerto D. 80 (with Kussmaul), Touchemoulin's *Flute Concerto in A major* (with Meisen), Dittersdorf's *Oboe Concerto in A major* (with Passin), Platti's *Oboe Concerto in G minor* (with Passin), Stölzel's *Oboe Concerto in D major* (with Passin), Fasch's *Oboe Concerto in G minor* (with Passin), Pleyel's Sinfonie Concertanti Nos 5 and 6, Roman's *Drottningholm Suite* and Violin Concerto (with Liljefors), excerpts from Bach's *Christmas Oratorio*, Charpentier's Mass *In Nativitatem Domini*, *Messiah*, Mozart's Mass

K. 427 and Schiassi's *Sinfonia pastorale in D major*; Haydn's Symphonies Nos 6, 7, 8, 31, 53, 55, 63, 64 and 67, overtures to *Acide e Galatea*, *Der Apotheker*, *L'infedeltà delusa*, *La fedeltà premiata*, *L'incontro improviso* and *Orfeo ed Euridice* and the Overture No. 4, Cassation No. 3, Horn Concerto No. 2 (with Penzel), Piano Concerto No. 3 (with Neuhaus), Piano and Violin Concerto (with Trimborn and Kussmaul) and Cello Concertos Nos 1 and 4 (with Nyffenegger), and No. 4 (with Starck), Michael Haydn's *Viola Concerto in C major* (with Christ), Leopold Mozart's *Toy Symphony* and *Sinfonia di caccia in G major*, W. A. Mozart's Symphonies Nos 23, 29 and 30, Sinfonias K. 248c and K. 320g from the Serenades K. 248 and K. 320 respectively, *Serenata notturna*, Clarinet Concerto (with Stalder, basset-horn), Bassoon Concerto (with Sax) and *Rondo for Horn in D major* (with Penzel), Schubert's Rondo D. 438 and Mendelssohn's *Violin Concerto in D minor* (with Soh), and Dvořák's *Notturno*. He has also recorded Beethoven's *Ritterballet* and *Die Geschöpfe des Prometheus* (with the Basel Orchestra Society), Haydn's Violin Concerto No. 4 and Tomasini's *Violin Concerto in A major* (with Melkus and the Capella Academica Wien) and the Dvořák Piano Concerto (with Frantz and the North-West German Philharmonic Orchestra).

Mule, Pol (b. 1926). Born at Beaumont-le-Roger, France, Mule studied at the Paris Conservatoire (1940–45), graduated with first prize for flute and chamber music, studied conducting with Cluytens and Fourestier, and first conducted in 1952. He conducted a number of French orchestras for the ORTF (1952–62), was permanent conductor of l'Orchestre de Nice (1962–74), was with the ORTF (1974), became professor of conducting at the Marseille Conservatoire (1976) and permanent conductor of the Orchestre du Capitole de Toulouse. He has conducted at many French festivals and with various European orchestras, and has given special attention to works by contemporary composers. For Barclay he recorded Françaix's Clarinet Concerto, with Lancelot and the Nice Radio Symphony Orchestra.

Müller-Kray, Hans (1908–69). Born at Essen, where he studied at the Folkwangschule, Müller-Kray joined the Essen State Theatre (1932), then was conductor at Münster (1934–41), with the Frankfurt Radio (1942–5), at Wiesbaden (1945–8) and then with the Stuttgart Radio Symphony Orchestra (1948–68). With the latter orchestra *et al.* he recorded for La Guilde Internationale du Disque abridged versions of *Oberon* and Handel's *Rodelinda* and the two Chopin Piano Concertos (with Musulen). These recordings have been released in the United States by Period and (in the case of *Rodelinda*) by Lyrichord.

Munch, Charles (1891–1968). Munch was born in Strasbourg, then part of Germany, into a musical family; the original spelling of his name was Münch. His father was the founder of the Choeur St Guillaume and a professor at the Strasbourg Conservatory, and Albert Schweitzer was a distant relative. Munch studied the violin at the conservatory whose director was then Pfitzner, and went to Paris to continue his violin studies under Capet. He started on a career as a solo violinist, but at the outbreak of World War I he was enlisted in the German army, was gassed at Péronne and wounded at Verdun. After the war, he became a French citizen with the return of Alsace-Lorraine to France, and came to Berlin to study the violin with Flesch. Returning to France, he was professor of violin at Strasbourg Conservatoire and concertmaster of the municipal orchestra there (1919–26), but went to Leipzig where he taught the violin at the conservatory and played in the Gewandhaus Orchestra under Furtwängler and Walter. When he refused to become a German national, he was forced to resign from the orchestra in 1929, and with the advent of the Nazis he left Germany altogether.

Munch made his debut as a conductor in 1932, at the age of 41, with the Straram Orchestra in Paris, and after conducting the Paris Symphony Orchestra in the next year he was invited to conduct other orchestras in Paris, such as the Lamoureux. A fortunate marriage released him from the necessity of supporting himself as a violinist; he devoted himself entirely to conducting, studying it with Alfred Sendrey in Paris (1933–40). In 1935 he was appointed principal conductor of the Paris Philharmonic Orchestra, which had been founded by Cortot; he became a professor at the École Normale de Musique (1936), principal conductor at the International Society for Contemporary Music (1937), and conductor of the Paris Conservatoire Orchestra, in succession to Gaubert (1938–46). He kept the orchestra alive during World War II, but refused to collaborate with the Nazis in any way, declining the directorship of the Paris Opéra because it meant involving himself with them. He assisted the Résistance, protected his players from religious persecution, and at his country house Allied pilots and refugees were harboured on the escape route. At the end of the war he was awarded the Légion d'Honneur. However, his championship of the music of contemporaries such as Honegger and Milhaud, and his neglect of more familiar music in his programmes, eventually brought his resignation from the Paris Conservatoire Orchestra; he then toured Europe and South America, made his debut in the United States in 1946, and visited the US with the French National Radio Orchestra in 1948. The impression he made brought his appointment as conductor of the Boston Symphony Orchestra, following Koussevitzky (1948–62), and he led the orchestra on a tour of the Soviet Union (1956); it was the first time an American orchestra had played in that country. After some years as a guest conductor he became the first music director of the Orchestre de Paris, which had been founded in 1967 by André Malraux, the Minister of Culture, to create a French orchestra comparable to the leading ones in Europe. Munch died in the US when he was on tour with the orchestra in 1968.

Munch was the antithesis of Koussevitzky, from whom he had inherited possibly the finest orchestra existing at the time. Koussevitzky was authoritarian, ruthless with his players, and exhaustively painstaking at rehearsal; his readings had superlative polish. Munch was a gracious, charming but shy man, considerate to his musicians, and always mindful of his own experience as an orchestral violinist. His lack of pretension is exemplified in his remark to his friends that he was a conductor 'only because I am too stupid to do anything else'. On occasion he also expressed criticism of Koussevitzky's severity with the orchestra and his rigorous rehearsal methods. But like Koussevitzky he performed the French repertoire with great distinction, and when he brought the French National Radio Orchestra to the US the elegance and polish of its style and sound were particularly noted. Munch was never concerned with small details in rehearsal, and his performances had a spontaneity missing from Koussevitzky's readings. The Boston Symphony remained a great orchestra, if not the greatest one; its position was taken by the Cleveland Orchestra, who achieved the same standard of precision under Szell. Observers have written that in successive performances of the same work Munch's tempi were not always the same; spontaneity never left him. Despite his early years in Germany, he was a typically French conductor, naturally concerned with colour, clarity and balance rather than profundity or sentiment. His performances of Haydn, Mozart, Beethoven, Schubert, Brahms *et al.* had an impetuosity and a somewhat superficial brilliance and attracted the criticism that he was too fast and loud with the central repertoire. Even so, David Wooldridge (in his *Conductor's World*, 1970) suggested a different view, writing that Munch's 'performances of the Third, Sixth and Seventh Symphonies of Beethoven, and the First and Fourth of Brahms, were among the ultimate pinnacles of music-making'. Certainly his recordings of Beethoven's Symphony No. 3, Schubert's Symphony No. 9 and Brahms' Symphonies Nos 1 and 4, with the Boston Symphony Orchestra, were revealing examples of his special sound and spirit. On the other hand, Beethoven's Symphony No. 9, also with the Boston Symphony, reduced these qualities to brusqueness and disregard for nuance equal to gross insensitivity. In his book, *I am a Conductor*, Munch wrote that a critic once reproached Richard Strauss for having conducted a Mozart symphony too quickly. Strauss replied: 'These gentlemen of the press seem to have a direct wire to Olympus.'

Munch's recording career started in Paris before World War II. The discs he then recorded included Bach's Cantata No. 189, Mozart's Piano Concerto K. 466 (with Doyen) and Violin Concerto K. 219 (with Thibaud, and an unidentified orchestra for HMV); Haydn's Symphony No. 45, Saint-Saëns' Piano Concerto No. 4 and Ravel's Piano Concerto for Left Hand (with Cortot), *La Valse* and *Pavane pour une infante défunte*, *La Mer*, Honegger's Symphony No. 2 and *La Danse des morts*, Delannoy's *Sérénade concertante* and ballet *La Pantoufle de vair*, Aubert's *Habanera* and the Chopin arrangement *La Nuit ensorcelée*, and Jolivet's *Trois Complaintes du soldat* (with the Paris Conservatoire Orchestra for HMV); Beethoven's Piano Concerto No. 5 and Halffter's *Portuguese Rhapsody* (with Marguerite Long), Tchaikovsky's Piano Concerto No. 1 (with Konstantinov), Ravel's Piano Concerto for the Left Hand (with Février) and Bloch's Violin Concerto (with Szigeti, and the Paris Conservatoire Orchestra for Columbia); excerpts from Honegger's *Le Roi David* (with the Strasbourg Municipal Orchestra *et al.* for Polydor); Vivaldi's Concerto Op. 3 No. 9 and Mozart's Violin Concerto K. 271a (with Soriano), and Liszt's Piano Concerto No. 1 (with Benevenuto, and the Paris Conservatoire Orchestra for Pathé); Haydn's Sinfonia Concertante and Mozart's *Adagio and Fugue in C minor* (with an unidentified orchestra for L'Oiseau Lyre); Widor's Fantasy (with Herrenschmidt and the Paris Philharmonic Orchestra for Polydor); and Ravel's Piano Concerto for the Left Hand (with Blancard and the Paris Conservatoire Orchestra for Polydor).

After World War II, Munch came under contract for Decca, and recorded mostly with the Paris Conservatoire and London Philharmonic Orchestras, using the new full-frequency-range-recording technique. Initially, these performances were on 78 r.p.m. discs, and some were later issued on mono LPs. Apart from Beethoven's Symphony No. 8, Mendelssohn's Symphony No. 5, Tchaikovsky's Symphony No. 6 and Prokofiev's Symphony No. 1 (with the Paris Conservatoire Orchestra), Schumann's Symphony No. 4 (with the London Philharmonic Orchestra), and the Brahms Violin Concerto (with Renardy and the Amsterdam Concertgebouw Orchestra), all the works recorded were of French composers, and demonstrated that while Munch was superlative in the French repertoire, with the others he was less distinguished. Included were the overtures *Le Corsaire* and *Benvenuto Cellini*, Roméo seul, La fête des Capulets and Queen Mab Scherzo from the *Roméo et Juliette* symphony, The Royal Hunt and Storm from *Les Troyens*, the prelude to d'Indy's *Fervaal*, *Boléro*, the *Daphnis et Chloé* Suites Nos 1 and 2, Ravel's *Piano Concerto in G major* (with Henriot), Fauré's *Pavane*, Franck's *Symphony in D minor* and *Symphonic Variations* (with Joyce), Debussy's *Iberia* and *Berceuse héroïque*, and Roussel's *Petite suite* (with the Paris Conservatoire Orchestra), Bizet's *Symphony in C major*, Fauré's incidental music for *Pelléas et Mélisande*, and Roussel's *Le Festin de l'araignée* and *Suite in F major* (with the London Philharmonic Orchestra) and *Danse macabre* (with the Amsterdam Concertgebouw Orchestra). He also recorded *Symphonie fantastique* (with the French National Radio Orchestra for EMI). Much later, in the last years of his life, he again recorded for Decca with the New Philharmonia Orchestra, this time *Pini di Roma* and *Fontane di Roma*, *Gaîté parisienne*, the two *L'Arlésienne* suites, and a *Carmen* suite.

In the United States, Munch first recorded for Columbia (CBS) with the New York Philharmonic-Symphony Orchestra on 78s Mozart's Piano Concertos K. 467 and K. 595 (with Robert Casadesus) and Saint-Saëns' Symphony No. 3. Later, on LP, he recorded for Columbia the Minuet, Dance of the Sylphs and March from *La Damnation de Faust*, with the Philadelphia Orchestra. When he became conductor of the Boston Symphony Orchestra, RCA embarked on a significant series, with a wide-ranging repertoire, but again the most successful performances were those of French music: *Symphonie fantastique*, *Harold in Italy* (with Primrose), *Nuits d'été* (with Los Angeles), *Roméo et Juliette* symphony, *Grande Messe des morts*, *L'Enfance du Christ*, *La Damnation de Faust*, the Royal Hunt and Storm from *Les Troyens*, and the overtures *Le Carnaval romain*, *Le Corsaire*, *Béatrice et Bénédict* and *Benvenuto Cellini*, Franck's *Symphony in D minor* and *Le Chasseur maudit*, *La Mer*, *Nuages*, *Fêtes*, *Images*, *Prélude à l'après-midi d'un faune*, *Le Martyre de Saint-Sébastien*, *Printemps*, *La Damoiselle élue* (with Los Angeles), *Boléro*, *Valses nobles et sentimentales*, *Pavane pour une infante défunte*, *La Valse*, *Rapsodie espagnole*, *Ma Mère l'Oye*, *Daphnis et Chloé*, *Escales*, Fauré's *Pelléas et Mélisande* suite, Chausson's *Symphony in B flat major* and *Poème* (with David Oistrakh), d'Indy's *Symphonie sur un chant montagnard français* (with Henriot-Schweitzer), Milhaud's *La Création du monde* and *Suite provençale*, Poulenc's Organ Concerto (with Zamkochian), Honegger's Symphonies Nos 2 and 5, Saint-Saëns' Symphony No. 3 and *Le Rouet d'Omphale*, *L'Apprenti sorcier*, and Bizet's *Symphony in C major*, *Patrie* and *Jeux d'enfants*.

From the regular repertoire, Munch's records with the Boston Symphony Orchestra included the *Brandenburg Concertos* and Bach's Violin Concerto No. 1 (with Laredo), *Water Music* (in Harty's arrangement), Haydn's Symphony No. 103, Mozart's Clarinet Concerto (with Goodman) and overture to *Le nozze di Figaro*, Beethoven's Symphonies Nos 1, 3, 5, 6, 7 and 9, overtures *Leonore Nos 1* and *3*, *Coriolan*, *Fidelio* and *Prometheus*, Violin Concerto (with Heifetz) and Piano Concerto No. 1 (with Richter), Schubert's Symphonies Nos 2, 8 and 9, Schumann's Symphonies Nos 1 and 4 and overtures *Manfred* and *Genoveva*, Chopin's Piano Concerto No. 1 (with Graffman), Mendelssohn's Symphonies Nos 3, 4 and 5, scherzo from the Octet, Violin Concerto (with Heifetz and Laredo), and *Capriccio brilliant* (with Graffman), the overture and Venusberg music from *Tannhäuser*, prelude and Liebestod from *Tristan und Isolde* (with Farrell), Magic Fire Music from *Die Walküre*, the Rhine Journey and Immolation from *Götterdämmerung* (with Farrell), Brahms' Symphonies Nos 1 and 4, and Piano Concerto No. 1 (with Graffman), Tchaikovsky's Symphonies Nos 4 and 6, *Francesca da Rimini*, *Romeo and Juliet* fantasy-overture and *Serenade in C major*, Dvořák's Symphony No. 8 and Cello Concerto (with Piatigorsky), *Till Eulenspiegel* and *Don Quixote* (with Piatigorsky), *Kindertotenlieder* and *Lieder eines fahrenden Gesellen* (with Forrester), Stravinsky's *Jeu de cartes*, Scriabin's *Poème d'extase*, Prokofiev's *Romeo and Juliet* suite, Piano Concerto No. 2 (with Henriot-Schweitzer) and Violin Concerto No. 2 (with Heifetz), Rachmaninov's Piano Concerto No. 3 (with Janis), Elgar's *Introduction and Allegro* and *Serenade in E minor*, Piston's Symphony No. 6, Haieff's Symphony No. 2, Bloch's *Schelomo* and Walton's Cello Concerto (with Piatigorsky), Menotti's Violin Concerto (with Spivakovsky), Meditation and Dance of Vengeance from Barber's *Medea*, Martinů's Symphony No. 6 and Blackwood's Symphony No. 1.

After he left Boston, Munch recorded another *Grande Messe des morts* (with the Bavarian Radio Symphony Orchestra *et al.* for DGG); *Symphonie fantastique*, Brahms' Symphony No. 1, Honegger's Symphony No. 2, *Boléro*, *Rapsodie espagnole*, *Pavane pour une infante défunte*, and *Daphnis et Chloé* Suite No. 2 (with l'Orchestre de Paris for EMI); Honegger's Symphony No. 2 and *La Danse des morts* (with the Paris Conservatoire Orchestra for EMI); Beethoven's Symphony No. 6 and Franck's *Symphony in D minor* (with the Rotterdam Philharmonic Orchestra for La Guilde Internationale du Disque); *Moldau*, *In the Steppes of Central Asia*, the prelude to *Khovanshchina*, the *Russian Easter Festival* overture, the Introduction and Cortège from *Le Coq d'or*, Bizet's *Symphony in C major*, *Patrie* and *Jeux d'enfants*, *Prélude à l'après-midi d'un faune*, *La Mer*, *Iberia* and *Nocturnes*, and Arbós' arrangement of Albéniz's *Iberia* (with the French National Radio Orchestra for La Guilde Internationale du Disque, some being issued in the United States and in Britain by Nonesuch); Roussel's Symphonies Nos 3 and 4, Lalo's Cello Concerto and Saint-Saëns' Cello Concerto No. 1 (with Navarra, and the Lamoureux Orchestra for Erato); Roussel's *Suite in F* and Dutilleux's Symphony No. 2 (with the Lamoureux Orchestra for Westminster; some of the recordings with the Lamoureux Orchestra were released in Britain by World Record Club and in the US by Musical Heritage Society); and *Francesca da Rimini* (with the Royal Philharmonic Orchestra for Reader's Digest).

A number of Munch's records with the Boston Symphony Orchestra are still available in the US, and some have been re-issued on the Victrola label, including the *Roméo et Juliette* symphony, *Grande Messe des morts*, *L'Enfance du Christ*, discs of overtures by Beethoven and Berlioz, Brahms' Symphony No. 1, *La Mer*, *Rapsodie espagnole*, *La Valse*, *Daphnis et Chloé*, *Romeo and Juliet* fantasy-overture and *Francesca da Rimini*. In Britain, much less is available, except for the EMI series with l'Orchestre de Paris, and the Decca discs with the New Philharmonia Orchestra, all of which, taken together, demonstrate his strengths and weaknesses. Of them, the *Symphonie fantastique* is characteristically impetuous and wilful, but in the Ravel collection he retains his touch.

Münch, Ernst (1859–1928). An Alsatian, and father of Charles Munch, Ernst Münch was a professor at the Strasbourg Conservatory, and founded and conducted the Choeur St Guillaume. With the Choeur and the Strasbourg Municipal Orchestra he recorded the Requiem aeternam, Dies Irae and Lachrymosa from Mozart's *Requiem* (for Parlophone); the performance was noted for its fire and effectiveness.

Münch, Hans (b. 1893). Born in Mulhouse, Münch comes from a musical family; his father, Eugen Münch, was a conductor and Charles Munch was his cousin. He studied with Schweitzer, settled in Basel in 1912 and became a Swiss citizen, studied at the Basel Conservatory, was a cellist in orchestras (1914–26), taught the piano at the conservatory (1918–32), was a repetiteur at the Basel State Theatre, conducted the Basel Bach Chorus (1921–6), and succeeded Weingartner as conductor of the Allgemeine Musikgesellschaft Basel (1935) and as director of the Basel Conservatory (1935–47). He also made guest appearances in other Swiss cities, in FR Germany, Britain, France, Holland, Italy and Austria. For CT (Switzerland) he recorded Suter's *Symphony in D minor* and *Le laudi di San Francesco d'Assisi* (with the Basel Orchestral Society Orchestra *et al.*).

Münchinger, Karl (b. 1915). Born in Stuttgart, Münchinger learned several instruments at an early age, and composed cantatas in the style of Bach, to whose works he was devoted. He studied at the Stuttgart Academy of Music, taking his diploma in composition and choral conducting, was a revolutionary young composer, and also organist and choirmaster at St Martin's Church at Stuttgart. He was a pupil of Abendroth of Leipzig, Krauss at Salzburg and came under the influence of Furtwängler, became first conductor of the Lower Saxony Orchestra at Hannover (1941–3), and after World War II returned to Stuttgart, where he founded the Stuttgart Chamber Orchestra, which was made up of musicians many of whom had been his fellow students. He gave his first concert with the orchestra in September 1945, and in its first ten years, under Münchinger, it became internationally famous, primarily in the music of Bach. Subsequently the orchestra's repertoire extended; he was more frequently engaged as a guest conductor with major symphony orchestras, especially the Vienna Philharmonic and the Paris Conservatoire, and he also founded the Stuttgart Classical Philharmonia Orchestra in 1966. He and the Stuttgart Chamber Orchestra toured five continents, and have played more than 3,000 concerts, appeared at festivals in Edinburgh, Salzburg, Athens and elsewhere, and toured in the USSR, in Eastern Europe and in the Chinese People's Republic.

While the reputation of the Stuttgart Chamber Orchestra arises from its performances of baroque music, especially that of Bach, the orchestra's repertoire includes Mozart and romantics such as Dvořák, and moderns such as Honegger and Martin. In rehearsal Münchinger insists on great accuracy; he never talks about the music, and is extremely demanding about dynamics. His strongly accented rhythms and uncompromising attack could be said to be characteristically German, and contrast with the styles of other celebrated chamber orchestras such as I Musici, the Academy of St Martin-in-the-Fields and the Jean-François Paillard Orchestra, to name only three. Each of these represents a certain national style in its performance of the baroque masters, in particular. In general, the Stuttgart style is straightforward and crisp, and devoid of sentimentality.

Münchinger and the Stuttgart Chamber Orchestra have been under an exclusive recording contract with Decca almost since the orchestra's inception. Several 78 r.p.m. sets were issued, Bach's Suite No. 3 and some *Brandenburg Concertos*, but with the advent of LP started their superb series of discs, which were one of the highlights of the early LP catalogue. The *Brandenburg Concertos*, which were recorded again later for stereo, were first issued in 1951 and quickly became best-sellers. Similarly, their record of Vivaldi's *The Four Seasons* was one of those that aroused almost universal interest in the composer and was the prelude to his enormous popularity and the flood of records of baroque music that followed. The other discs of the Stuttgart Chamber Orchestra that appeared on mono, and later on stereo, included the four Bach suites, *Die Kunst der Fuge*, *Ein musikalisches Opfer*, the Harpsichord Concertos Nos 1 and 2 (with Malcolm), Cantatas Nos 51 and 202 (with Danco), the *St Matthew Passion*, *St John Passion*, *Mass in B minor*, *Magnificat*, *Christmas Oratorio* and *Easter Oratorio*, arrangements of the *Fugues in A minor* and *G minor*, Corelli's Concerto Grosso Op. 3 No. 8, Pachelbel's *Canon*, Gluck's *Chaconne*, Concert Pieces of Couperin (arranged by Bazelaire), Vivaldi's *Cello Concerto in E minor*, Haydn's *Cello Concerto in D major* and Boccherini's Cello Concerto (with Fournier), Haydn's Symphony No. 45, Mozart's Divertimenti K. 136 and K. 251, *Ein musikalischer Spass*, *Eine kleine Nachtmusik*, *Les petits riens*, Piano Concertos K. 271 and K. 450 (with Kempff) and Violin Concertos K. 216 and K. 268 (with Ferras), some minuets and dances of Schubert, the *Grosse Fuge* of Beethoven, Pergolesi's *Concerti armonica* Nos 1 to 6 and Flute Concertos Nos 1 and 2 (with Rampal), Telemann's Viola Concerto (with Kirchner), Grieg's *Holberg Suite*, Barber's *Adagio*, Berkeley's *Serenade*, Wolf's *Italian Serenade*, Hindemith's *Five Pieces*, Martin's *Passacaglia*, Suk's *Serenade* and the Introduction for String Sextet to Strauss's *Capriccio*. Of these the most notable were the Bach choral works; the *St Matthew Passion*, which was released in 1965, remains probably the finest recording made of the work, and with one or two exceptions, the other performances are scarcely less good.

Other recordings by Münchinger for Decca are the overtures *Alceste* and *Manfred*, and the *Siegfried Idyll* (with the Suisse Romande Orchestra), Liszt's *Prometheus*, *Mazeppa*, *Hamlet* and *Mephisto Waltz* (with the Paris Conservatoire Orchestra), Haydn's Symphonies Nos 83, 88, 96, 100 and 104, *The Creation*, Mozart's Symphonies Nos 33 and 40, Flute and Harp Concerto (with Tripp and Jellinek), Clarinet Concerto (with Prinz) and Serenade K. 250, Schubert's Symphonies Nos 2, 3, 4, 5, 6 and 8, and the overtures *Egmont*, *Coriolan*, *Leonore No. 3*, *Anacreon*, *Preciosa*, *Meeresstille und glückliche Fahrt* and *Genoveva* (with the Vienna Philharmonic Orchestra *et al.*), Mozart's Symphonies Nos 31, 32 and 35 and Schubert's Symphony No. 9 (with the Stuttgart Classical Philharmonia Orchestra). Of all of these, *The Creation* was unquestionably the most impressive.

Munclinger, Milan (b. 1923). Born at Košice, into an artistic family, Munclinger learned to play the flute as a boy, and studied at the Prague Conservatory. During World War II he was transferred to Germany as an orchestral player, and after the war resumed his studies at the Conservatory and at the Charles University at Prague, also studying with Talich at the Academy of Musical Arts. Munclinger's name has been associated primarily with a number of distinguished records issued by Supraphon, in which he leads the Ars Rediviva Ensemble in baroque music. Included have been the Bach suites and *Brandenburg Concertos*, *Die*

Kunst der Fuge, *Ein musikalisches Opfer*, trio sonatas and sinfonias from the cantatas, Concerto for Flute and Violin and Concerto for Oboe and Violin, concertos by Telemann, Richter, Benda and Vivaldi, sinfonias by J. C., W. F. and C. P. E. Bach, ten symphonies of Benda, Handel's *Water Music* and *Music for the Royal Fireworks*, Zelenka's *Sinfonia concertante* and *Lamentationes Jeremiae Prophetae* and Couperin's *Le Parnasse ou l'apothéose de Corelli*. He has also recorded Haydn's *Die sieben letzten Worte des Erlösers am Kreuz* (with the Prague Chamber Orchestra), four orchestral trios of Stamitz and the Mozart Oboe Concerto (with Hanták, and the Czech Philharmonic Orchestra), as well as other pieces in which he is the flautist.

Munrow, David (1942–76). Born in Birmingham, Munrow joined a cathedral choir at the age of 11, but when his voice broke he took up the recorder. He studied at Cambridge and Birmingham Universities; at Cambridge he was encouraged by Thurston Dart to play instruments of the past, and became a wind virtuoso specialising in the recorder and in early wind instruments. He played the recorder in the wind band of the Royal Shakespeare Theatre at Stratford-on-Avon (1966–8), founded the Early Music Consort of London (1967), and made his debut as a performer at Wigmore Hall, London, in 1968. He lectured at Leicester University, gave lecture recitals with his wife, Gillian Reid, played the recorder in recitals of baroque and modern music and became a well-known figure with a large regular audience through his BBC radio programme, *Pied Piper*. This was originally intended for children, but soon attracted many older listeners, and covered all kinds of music, from Bach to the present day. Since *Pied Piper* started in 1971, Munrow presented 600 separate programmes. His concerts with his Early Music Consort were also extremely popular, and it was written at his early death that he did more to popularise early music and to enrich Britain's music-making than almost any other musician since World War II.

Munrow was responsible for a number of fine records, including recitals of the music of 16th century Spain, Dufay, Praetorius, the 14th century and 14th century Florence, the music of the Crusades, the 16th century and a compilation of the instruments of the Middle Ages and the Renaissance, which were issued by EMI and Argo. He also played the solo recorder in some other discs. In producing these records, he was concerned about every aspect, from the careful selection of the pieces to be included in the recital discs so that a unifying principle could be followed, to arranging the layout, selecting the cover picture and writing the sleeve notes. His vast enthusiasm, virtuosity as a player and particular attention to detail were some of the causes of his popularity, both personally and for the music in which he specialised. Two reasons can be given for the current popularity of early music: nostalgia for the past in preference to looking towards an uncertain future; and because 'composers today have, in the main, failed to satisfy the demand, the kind of thing the concert-going, record-buying, radio-listening public wants (Bernard Levin, *The Times*).

Mura, Péter (b. 1924). Born in Budapest, Mura was educated at the Conservatory and Academy of Music there, studied conducting with Ferencsik, and first conducted in 1943. He was a répétiteur at the Hungarian State Opera (1945–50), became a conductor (1950–53), was director and chief conductor of the Miskolc National Theatre Opera Company (1953–7), conductor at the Warsaw State Opera (1957–8), at the Silesian Opera, Bytom, Poland, and a professor at the Academy of Music at Katowice (1958–61), and from 1961 has been director and chief conductor of the Miskolc Symphony Orchestra. He has toured in the USSR, DR and FR Germany, Poland, Yugoslavia, Bulgaria and Cuba. For Hungaroton he recorded Mozart's Symphony No. 21 and the ballet music from *Idomeneo*, with the Miskolc Symphony Orchestra.

Musgrave, Thea (b. 1928). The Scottish composer Thea Musgrave was born in Edinburgh, studied at Edinburgh University and with Nadia Boulanger in Paris, and was first a concert pianist. Her compositions include the operas *The Abbot Drimock*, *The Decision* and *The Voice of Ariadne*, orchestral pieces, concertos and works for voice and orchestra. In 1972 she was the pianist in a disc with the Argo label containing, amongst other pieces, her *Monologue* and *Excursions*. In 1975 Decca issued a coupling of her *Concerto for Orchestra*, played by the Scottish National Orchestra under Gibson, and her Horn Concerto, with the same orchestra led by herself and the solo horn superbly played by Tuckwell, for whom it was written. This concerto requires the trumpeters and orchestral horn players to move their places in the orchestra and in the auditorium; this effect is arresting in live performance, but inevitably less striking on record.

Muti, Riccardo (b. 1941). Born in Naples, the son of a doctor, Muti learned the piano and violin as a boy, studied music and philosophy at Naples University, and the piano at Naples Conservatory. He first conducted with a student orchestra there, then studied conducting and composition with Votto at the Milan Conservatory, and was the first Italian to win the Guido Cantelli competition for conducting, in 1967. The next year he made his professional debut, accompanying Richter at the Maggio Musicale Fiorentino, and in 1969 was appointed principal conductor of the Florence orchestra. He has conducted opera in many Italian cities, in Vienna and London, and has appeared with the Berlin Philharmonic, Vienna Philharmonic, Chicago Symphony and the Philadelphia Orchestras regularly, as well as taking part in major musical festivals in Europe. In 1973 he substituted for Klemperer at a concert with the New Philharmonia Orchestra, and as a result became its principal conductor, in 1977, when the orchestra reverted to its original title, the Philharmonia Orchestra. He has retained his position as conductor of the Maggio Musicale Fiorentino, and was appointed principal guest conductor of the Philadelphia Orchestra; his association with the Philadelphia Orchestra started when he impressed Ormandy during the orchestra's visit to Europe in 1970, and he was then engaged for the 1972 season.

Muti is an intensely exciting and dramatic conductor, much in the Toscanini mould; in fact he regards himself as a successor to Toscanini, whom he considers the greatest, and constantly refers to him when rehearsing the orchestra; but he also professes to admire Furtwängler. His performances impress for their precision, intensity and sheer physical exhilaration, but frequently the spiritual content and meaning of the music evades him. He has a somewhat different attitude from an earlier Philadelphian, Stokowski; about rearranging scores he says: 'I cannot admire the desire to change every score on your desk. I think you shouldn't touch a note. If you don't like a score, don't play it. It is like going to a museum to see the paintings. "Oh, very beautiful", I say, "but here, let me just touch up this corner and add paint there." It is unthinkable in painting, but common in music' (*Musical America*, March 1978, p. 7). The extreme polish of his performances is the result, at least partly, of his insistence on perfection of execution; he often takes one section of the orchestra and goes over a particular passage slowly, as the individual players would if they were practising. Despite his interest in opera, he is disinclined to undertake more than three new operatic ventures each year, so that his interpretations can be developed from the outset of each production. He has spent much time studying the Verdi operas and their performance, and believes that it is important to understand the libretto fully before conducting them: 'Verdi was a great man of the theatre; sometimes the dramatic side is even more important than the music. And the recitatives can be even more fantastic than the arias.' Among modern composers, he is attracted to Penderecki, Berio and Ligeti, the last of whom 'has found a way to make the orchestra a contemporary instrument that's both new and very old'. Much as he admires the great orchestras in the United States, he says that 'there's the New Philharmonia and the whole European tradition – a warmth and spontaneity which the more virtuosic American orchestras can't quite manage'.

Since 1975 Muti has recorded for EMI with the Philharmonia Orchestra. The initial recordings (when the orchestra was the New Philharmonia) were of Cherubini's *Requiem in D minor*, and *Aida*, the latter being the first of a series of Verdi operas which have continued, to include *Macbeth*, *Un ballo in maschera* and *Nabucco*. Complete cycles of the symphonies of Mendelssohn, Schumann and Tchaikovsky were also commenced, with Mendelssohn's Symphonies Nos 3 and 4 and *Meeresstille und glückliche Fahrt* overture, Schumann's Symphony No. 4 and Tchaikovsky's Symphony No. 1; his other recordings have been of Mozart's Symphonies Nos 25 and 29, Dvořák's Symphony No. 5 and Verdi's overtures *Nabucco*, *Giovanna d'Arco*, *La battaglia di Legnano*, *Luisa Miller*, *I vespri siciliani* and *La forza del destino*.

N

Naidenov, Assen (b. 1899). Born at Varna, Bulgaria, Naidenov studied at the Vienna Academy of Music under Marx, and at Leipzig under Graener (1920–23), and became a conductor at the Sofia National Opera, where he was eventually appointed chief conductor. He has also conducted opera and symphony concerts abroad, and appeared at Leningrad (1962–3) and at the Bolshoi Theatre, Moscow (1963–4). His recordings include *Don Carlos*, made in 1964 with the Bolshoi Theatre Company, the Rimsky-Korsakov edition of *Boris Godunov*, with the Sofia National Opera in 1974 and issued by BASF, and accompaniments to arias and excerpts from operas with soloists, the choir and orchestra of the Sofia National Opera.

Nash, Royston (b. 1933). Born in Southampton, Nash studied at the Royal Academy of Music, London, and was awarded the certificate of merit for conducting. He was director of music with the Royal Marines (1959–70), was appointed associate conductor with the D'Oyly Carte Opera Company in 1970, became its musical director in 1971, and toured Canada and the United States with the company. In the years 1972–6 he recorded for Decca with the company and the Royal Philharmonic Orchestra the Gilbert and Sullivan operas *The Mikado*, *Iolanthe*, *Trial by Jury*, *Utopia Ltd.*, and *The Grand Duke*, as well as Sullivan's overture to *Macbeth* and *Henry VIII* dances.

Natschinski, Gerd (b. 1928). Born in Chemnitz (now Karl-Marx-Stadt), Natschinski studied in Dresden and Karl-Marx-Stadt (1945-8) and with Eisler in Berlin (1951–2). He led orchestras in Leipzig and Berlin (1952–4), and then composed music for films, radio, television and the theatre. He conducted recordings of excerpts from his operettas *Casanova*, *Mein Freund Bunbury* and *Terzett* (with the Berlin Radio Symphony Orchestra *et al.* for Nova).

Naumann, Siegfried (b. 1919). Born in Malmö, Sweden, Naumann was educated at the Stockholm Music High School, the Accademia di Santa Cecilia, Rome, and at the Salzburg Mozarteum. He is conductor, in Stockholm, of the Musica Nova Group and professor at the Royal Academy of Music, has conducted in Scandinavia, Italy, Britain and FR Germany, and has written a number of compositions, of which *Il cantico del sole* was performed at the ISCM Festival in 1965. With Musica Nova he has recorded for Caprice Britten's *Les Illuminations*, Varèse's *Octandre*, Nilsson's *20 Gruppen*, Sandström's *In the Meantime*, Welin's *Warum nicht?*, and his own *Riposte* and *Cadenze per 9 strumenti*.

Navarro, Garcia (b. 1941). Born in Chiva, Spain, Navarro studied at the conservatories at Valencia and Madrid, and then was a conducting pupil of Oesterreicher in France, Ferrara in Italy and Swarowsky in Austria. In 1963 he founded the National Universities Orchestra in Spain, was a prizewinner at the conductors' competition at Besançon (1967), was director of the Valencia Municipal Orchestra (1968–71), conducted at the Bach Festival (1973), and with the Warsaw Philharmonic Orchestra (1974), toured in Sweden, Holland, France, Portugal, Austria and Britain, was appointed chief conductor of the Portuguese Radio (1976) and also conducts the North Holland Philharmonic Orchestra at Haarlem. He has recorded guitar concertos by Villa-Lobos and Castelnuovo-Tedesco (with Yepès and the London Symphony Orchestra for DGG).

Neary, Martin (b. 1940). Born in London and educated at Caius College, Cambridge, Neary is a Fellow of the Royal College of Organists, and has been organist and master of music at St Margaret's, Westminster (1963–71), professor of organ at the Trinity College of Music (from 1963) and organist and master of music at Winchester Cathedral (from 1972). He has recorded as organist and harpsichordist, and as a conductor with the Winchester Cathedral Choir and the Bournemouth Sinfonietta in coronation music by Walton, Parry, Stanford, Vaughan Williams, S. S. Wesley, Handel and Gibbons, and on another disc Britten's *A Ceremony of Carols*, *The Golden Vanity* and *Missa brevis in D major* (for Pye).

Nebolsin, Vassily (1898–1958). Born in Kharkov, Nebolsin studied the violin and composition at the Moscow Philharmonic College, and started his career as a conductor in 1918. He became choirmaster in 1920 and then conductor in 1922 at the Bolshoi Theatre, and was a professor at the Moscow Conservatory

(1940–45). His repertoire included the operas of Wagner, Bizet and others, in addition to those of Russian composers, and he also conducted symphony concerts. His compositions included orchestral and chamber music, and he was awarded the Stalin Prize in 1950. His recordings for Melodiya included the complete operas *A May Night*, *Mazeppa*, Dargomizhsky's *Russalka* and Nápravník's *Dubrovsky*, and Russian-language versions of *Carmen*, *Faust* and *Roméo et Juliette*, as well as short excerpts from *Sorochintsy Fair*, *Tale of the Tsar Saltan*, *Prince Igor* and *Boris Godunov*, all with the Bolshoi Theatre Company. He also directed the Moscow Radio Orchestra, with Kogan the soloist, in the Tchaikovsky Violin Concerto and *Valse Scherzo* (issued in Britain by Saga), Paganini's Violin Concerto No. 1 and Sarasate's *Carmen Fantasia*.

Neel, Louis Boyd (b. 1905). Born at Blackheath, England, Boyd Neel was educated at Dartmouth and Cambridge University, where he studied medicine. While practising as a doctor in London he was active in amateur musical circles, and in 1932 founded the Boyd Neel Orchestra, bringing together many of the finest string players available in London. The orchestra made its debut at the Aeolian Hall in June 1933, and, to extend its repertoire, Boyd Neel made a special study of the music of the 18th century. At that time public knowledge and appreciation of baroque music was extremely limited, and only one string concerto of Vivaldi was available in print. Boyd Neel and his orchestra were in the vanguard of the baroque revival which flourished so abundantly with the arrival of the LP record. The Boyd Neel orchestra soon won a reputation for its superb, stylish playing, and when Decca offered him a recording contract Boyd Neel put aside medicine to devote all his time to conducting.

Neel and the orchestra toured Europe, and were invited to the Salzburg Festival in 1937, when Britten's *Variations on a Theme of Frank Bridge* was first played. During World War II, Boyd Neel returned to medicine, but was nonetheless active conducting the Sadler's Wells Opera Company in 1944–5. In 1947 the Boyd Neel Orchestra visited Paris and toured Australia and New Zealand under the auspices of the British Council; in 1948–9 the orchestra visited Holland, Germany and Portugal, and gave concerts at the Edinburgh Festival. In 1950–51 they again toured throughout Europe, and in 1952 went to the United States and Canada. Following the visit to Canada, Boyd Neel was appointed Dean of the Royal Conservatory at Toronto (1952), and a year later formed the Hart House Orchestra in Toronto, and toured Europe and the United States with them; in 1958 they represented Canada at the Brussels World Fair. Boyd Neel himself toured Australia as a guest conductor in 1964 and South Africa in 1971; he returned to Britain every year to work with the Boyd Neel Orchestra until 1964, when the orchestra undertook its final tour of Europe. The orchestra still exists, if only on paper, but Boyd Neel does not intend to re-establish it permanently. 'After all', he has said, 'it achieved everything it set out to do. It played everywhere in the world. It recorded nearly all its repertoire and was regarded as the greatest of all chamber orchestras. It has made history. So what else remained? Just to remain at the top. And that can be a very boring and soul-destroying life. So we decided to just let it rest on its laurels' (*Montreal Star*, 5 May 1973). He retired from the Royal Conservatory at Toronto in 1971, to resume his career as a conductor, and has been founder and director of the Mississauga Symphony Orchestra, near Toronto (since 1972). He was awarded the CBE in 1953, and in 1972 received the Order of Canada.

The Boyd Neel Orchestra's first recording was in 1934 and was of the *St Paul's Suite* of Holst. Decca issued this set, and all Boyd Neel's other British discs until 1951. Up to 1939 a number of other sets were released, notably of Handel's Concerti Grossi Op. 6 Nos 1 to 12, which established an impeccable standard of performance in this music. Other works recorded before 1940 included Mozart's Symphony No. 13, Divertimenti K. 136 and K. 138, *Serenata notturna* and Piano Concertos K. 414, K. 449 and K. 491 (with Kathleen Long), Pergolesi's *Concertino in F minor*, the third of Respighi's suites of *Ancient Airs and Dances*, Grieg's *Holberg Suite*, Arensky's *Variations on a Theme of Tchaikovsky*, Lekeu's *Adagio for Strings*, the six-part *Ricercare* of Bach, Abel's *Symphony in E flat*, Avison's *Concerto in E minor*, J. C. Bach's *Symphony in B flat*, Sibelius' *Rakastava* and *Romance in C*, and Stravinsky's *Apollon Musagète*. A significant number of these pre-war releases were of music by British composers; in 1935 appeared the première recording of Vaughan Williams' *Fantasia on a Theme of Thomas Tallis*, which was made under the composer's supervision, later followed by *The Lark Ascending* and *Concerto accademico* (with Grinke the violinist, who was the leader of the orchestra). Other major British works recorded at this time were Elgar's *Introduction and Allegro for Strings*, Bridge's *Suite for Strings*, Howells' *Elegy for*

Viola, String Quartet and String Orchestra, Ireland's *Concertino pastorale*, Leigh's *Piano Concertino* (with Kathleen Long), Britten's *Variations on a Theme of Frank Bridge* and *Simple Symphony*, the last-named being both the first performance and recording. Many of these recordings were the first ever made of the pieces.

Boyd Neel made no records during World War II, but resumed activity in 1946, recording with his own orchestra and with the National Symphony Orchestra first on 78 r.p.m. discs, and later among the first Decca LPs. The 78 r.p.m. discs included the *Brandenburg Concertos*, Barber's *Adagio*, the Dvořák *Serenade in E*, Finzi's *Dies Natalis* (with soprano Joan Cross), Hamerik's Symphony No. 6, Byrd's Six-Part Fantasy No. 1, Geminiani's Concerto Grosso Op. 2 No. 2, several Handel overtures, pieces by Grainger, Delius's *Air and Dance* and *Two Aquarelles*, *Eine kleine Nachtmusik*, Liszt's *Malédiction* (with Osborne), Sistek's *Slavonic Scherzo*, and Suk's *Serenade* and *Meditation on an Old Bohemian Chorale* (all with the Boyd Neel Orchestra); Elgar's *Dream Children*, *Three Bavarian Dances* and the overture *In the South*, Mozart's Violin Concerto K. 219 (with Grinke) and Piano Concertos K. 450 (with Kathleen Long) and K. 488 (with Curzon), the Fauré *Ballade* and Mendelssohn's *Capriccio brilliant* (with Kathleen Long), Saint-Saëns' *Danse macabre*, a number of overtures by Mozart, as well as *Leichte Cavallerie* and *Raymond*, and intermezzi from *I gioielli della Madonna*. A new recording of Handel's Concerti Grossi Op. 6 was among the first Decca LPs, which was followed by the Concerti Grossi Op. 3 and *Water Music* and some Handel overtures, *St Paul's Suite*, *Variations on a Theme of Frank Bridge*, Warlock's *Capriol Suite* and *Serenade for Frederick Delius*, Barber's *Adagio*, Grieg's *Holberg Suite* and *Cowkeeper's Tune and Country Dance*.

In 1956 Boyd Neel and his orchestra made some discs for Unicorn which were issued only in the United States, and included a set of the *Brandenburg Concertos* with Leon Goossens, Dennis Brain, Emmanuel Hurwitz and George Malcolm. La Guilde Internationale du Disque have also issued the ensemble performing the *Brandenburg Concertos*, *Eine kleine Nachtmusik* and the Dvořák Serenade. In Britain, almost all of the discs of the Boyd Neel Orchestra have been discontinued, except for the *Water Music* and the Concerti Grossi Op. 3 of Handel, which Decca re-issued in 1973 and 1969 respectively. Writing in *The Gramophone* in October 1972, Stanley Sadie compared recordings of these Concerti Grossi by Leppard and Marriner with the older ones by Boyd Neel, which were originally made in 1955. He remarked (pp. 692–3) that Neel's 'sturdy rhythms and acute judgment of tempo are a touchstone', and that 'for the truest Handelian style I shall continue to turn to Boyd Neel'. DGG, in its first disc to be made in America, in 1970, recorded Boyd Neel with the Hart House Orchestra playing Elgar's *Serenade in E minor*, the Holst *Fugal Concerto* and three Handel overtures, and Canadian Broadcasting Corporation recorded Boyd Neel with the CBC Winnipeg String Orchestra in Vaughan Williams' *Fantasia on a Theme of Thomas Tallis* and Byrd's *Pavane*.

Negri, Vittorio (b. 1923). Born in Milan, Negri studied composition and conducting at the Conservatory there, but his studies were interrupted by World War II and a serious illness. After the war he was a pupil for two years with Paumgartner at the Salzburg Mozarteum. His career has taken three separate but simultaneous courses: as conductor, musicologist and record producer. When he was with Paumgartner he began an association with Philips, and when the producer of I Musici's recordings became ill in Amsterdam in the mid 1950s, he substituted for him, and has since been a major producer for that company, responsible for recordings by Davis, I Musici, Ozawa, the Quartetto Italiano *et al.* He has said that his experience as a producer has taught him that to be successful, one must know the music at least as well as the musicians, and that one must be an excellent psychologist to enable the artists to feel relaxed. As a musicologist, his interest has centred on the music of Venice, especially of Vivaldi; he was surprised to find, when preparing editions from some of Vivaldi's music for two choirs and orchestra, that the composer himself had made mistakes. Negri believes that the ubiquitous success of recordings of *The Four Seasons* has led to a very biased view of Vivaldi's genius, towards his instrumental music at the expense of his vocal works, both sacred and operatic; in fact, some of Vivaldi's sacred music, he maintains, is fully comparable to Bach's. He learned from Paumgartner to approach the text with great humility: 'What is important is *music*, and one should be at the service of music as a conductor, and not use the music for our own purposes.'

As a conductor, Negri has appeared at major international festivals such as Salzburg, Montreux and Sagra Musicale Umbria. His rediscovery of Cimarosa's *Requiem in G minor* led to its first modern performance under his baton at the Montreux Festival, and to his recording of it, released in 1970, with the Lausanne Chamber Orchestra and Montreux Festival Chorus *et al.* (for Philips). His other recordings have been a disc of oboe concertos by Marcello, Telemann, Leclair and Vivaldi (with Holliger and the Dresden Staatskapelle), Vivaldi's *Juditha triumphans* (with the Berlin Chamber Orchestra *et al.*), *Te Deum*, *Salve Regina*, *Gloria*, *Te Deum in D*, and *Magnificat in G minor* (with the Orchestre Teatro de la Fenice *et al.*), Concerti Op. 8 Nos 1 to 4 (*The Four Seasons*) (with Ayo and the Berlin Chamber Orchestra), four Violin Concertos (with Grumiaux and the Dresden Staatskapelle) and eight Viola d'amore Concertos (with Giuranna and the Dresden Staatskapelle) and Albinoni's Concertos Op. 7 (with the Berlin Chamber Orchestra), all for Philips; Albinoni's *Concerti a Cinque* Op. 9 (with the Italian Baroque Ensemble for Dover), and several discs of music by Gabrieli (with the Greg Smith Singers, the Texas Boys Choir, the Edward Tarr Brass Ensemble and E. Power Biggs, for CBS).

Neidlinger, Günter (b. 1930). Born in Heidelberg, Neidlinger was at the age of 15 a horn player in the Heidelberg Municipal Orchestra; he became a repetiteur and then conductor at Heidelberg and Mannheim, and by the age of 17 had conducted many operas and operettas. He was awarded a prize at the first international meeting of music students at Heidelberg (1949), studied conducting with Müller-Kray in Stuttgart, choral conducting with Thomas, singing with Kretzschmar, and was a pupil of Celibidache at the Accademia Chigiana at Siena. He also studied at Heidelberg University. He was conductor at the Saarbrücken Municipal Theatre (1962), chief conductor and then general music director of the Bodensee Symphony Orchestra (1966) and in 1970 was appointed chief conductor of the Nuremberg Symphony Orchestra. He has recorded Mozart's *Andante* K. 315 (with Thalheimer and the Hamburg Symphony Orchestra for Turnabout), the Beethoven Violin Concerto and two *Romances* (with Marschner and the South-West German Philharmonic Orchestra for Intercord), Schubert's *German Dances* (with the same orchestra for Intercord), Weber's Piano Concerto No. 2 (with Sagara), Concertino for Horn (with Orval), Andante (with Koch) and *Romanza siciliana* (with Thalheimer, and the Hamburg Symphony Orchestra for Turnabout), Reger's *Concerto in the Old Style* and *Suite in the Old Style*, Borodin's Symphony No. 3, Glazunov's *Stenka Razin*, Tcherepnin's *Symphonic Prayer*, Saint-Saëns' Piano Concertos Nos 1, 3 and 5 and the two Ravel Piano Concertos (with Nakajima), Strauss's *Panathenäenzug* (with Leimer) and *Metamorphosen* (with the Nuremberg Symphony Orchestra for Colosseum).

Németh, Gyula (b. 1930). Born in Budapest, Németh received his early training in Hungary, studied at the Leningrad Academy of Music, was assistant to Mravinsky with the Leningrad Philharmonic Orchestra for several years, and then was a pupil of Ferrara at the Accademia di Santa Cecilia in Rome. Since his return to Hungary he has been resident conductor of the Hungarian State Symphony Orchestra, and has also appeared in Bulgaria, the USSR, Czechoslovakia and other countries; he made his debut in London in 1963. His recordings (for Qualiton, sometimes released elsewhere on other labels) with the Hungarian State Symphony and Budapest Symphony Orchestras include Beethoven's Piano Concerto No. 5 (with Antal), Mendelssohn's Symphony No. 4 and Violin Concerto (with Kovács), Liszt's *Mazeppa*, *Mephisto Waltz*, *Les Préludes*, *Spanish Rhapsody* (orchestrated by Darvas) and *Hungarian Rhapsodies Nos 2* and *6*, *Pictures at an Exhibition*, *A Night on the Bare Mountain*, the prelude to *Khovanshchina*, Tchaikovsky's *Serenade in C major* and *Capriccio italien*, Bartók's *Rhapsody for Piano and Orchestra* (with Tusa), Viski's symphonic poem *Enigma*, Vincze's *Movimento Sinfonico* and Szabó's oratorio *In Fury Rose the Ocean*.

Nesbitt, Dennis (b. 1919). Born at Monkseaton and educated at the Royal College of Music, London, Nesbitt is a professor at the Royal Academy of Music, London, performs with the viola da gamba, the treble viola and cello, and has given recitals in Europe and the United States. In addition to his recordings as a soloist, he conducted a selection of the music of Locke (with the Elizabethan Consort of Viols and the Golden Age Singers, for Westminster).

Neuhaus, Rudolf (b. 1914). Born in Cologne where he studied at the Hochschule für Musik under Abendroth, Neuhaus was conductor at Neustrelitz (1934–44), Schwerin (1945–53), at the Dresden State Opera (1953) where he became general music director in 1975, was professor at the Hochschule für Musik at Dresden, and has been a guest conductor with major orchestras and opera houses in DR Germany, the USSR, Czechoslovakia, Poland and Yugoslavia. He has recorded discs of excerpts from *Der Rosenkavalier* (with the Dresden Staatskapelle *et al.*, issued by EMI), and *Die lustige Witwe* (with the Dresden Philharmonic Orchestra *et al.* for Eterna), and Schwaen's *Leonce und Lena* (with the Berlin Staatskapelle Chamber Orchestra *et al.* for Nova).

Neumann, Horst (b. 1934). Born in Leipa, Bohemia, Neumann was educated at the Hochschule für Musik in Berlin, was director of the State Folklore Ensemble of DR Germany (1959–65), leader of the Leipzig Radio Choir (1967), the Leipzig Radio Chamber Orchestra (from 1970), deputy chief conductor (1974–7) and then conductor (from 1977) of the Leipzig Radio Symphony Orchestra. He taught at the Hochschule für Musik at Leipzig (1971–4), received the Art Prize of DR Germany, and has been a guest conductor in Eastern Europe and the USSR, West Berlin, Cuba, Austria, Luxembourg and Central and South America. He has prepared the Leipzig Radio Choir for recordings with Böhm, Karajan, Carlos Kleiber, Sawallisch, *et al.*, and for Eterna recorded choral works by Eisler, Geisler's *Der zerbrochene Krug*, Kunad's *Antiphonic*, Kurzbach's Serenade No. 6, Rosenfeld's *Rifugio d'uccelli notturni*, Wagner-Régeny's *Genesis* and Zimmermann's *Mutazioni* (with the Leipzig Radio Symphony Orchestra and Chorus).

Neumann, Václav (b. 1920). Born in Prague into a musical family, Neumann learned the violin as a boy, and played in chamber music groups at high school. He studied history, Czech philology and musicology, but since universities in Czechoslovakia were closed during World War II he entered the Prague Conservatory and studied the violin and conducting. In 1941 he founded, with Antonín Kohout, the chamber ensemble that was later to become famous as the Smetana Quartet. He was a member of the Quartet for seven years, initially as the first violin and later as the viola player. He then became a member of the Czech Philharmonic Orchestra (1945), and in 1948, when Kubelik, the permanent conductor of the orchestra, fell sick, he deputised for him and launched his career as a conductor. He first conducted at Karlovy Vary (1951) and Brno (1954), was conductor of the Prague Symphony Orchestra (1956–63), the Prague Philharmonic Orchestra (1963–4), and was chief conductor of the Berlin Komische Oper (1957–60), where he came to international attention for his presentation of Janáček's *The Cunning Little Vixen* in Felsenstein's production. He was appointed conductor of the Leipzig Gewandhaus Orchestra and general music director of the Leipzig Opera (1964–7); in 1968 he returned to Czechoslovakia as chief conductor of the Czech Philharmonic, and with the orchestra has now performed more than 250 compositions and has given almost 500 concerts at home and abroad. He also was music director of the Württemberg State Theatre at Stuttgart, in succession to Leitner (1970–71), he toured Europe with the Leipzig Gewandhaus Orchestra in 1964, and later visited the United States with the Czech Philharmonic. In 1966 he received the National Prize of DR Germany, and was named honoured artist in 1967.

Neumann has now emerged as one of the major Czech conductors, and as conductor of the Czech Philharmonic Orchestra is in direct succession to Talich, Kubelík and Ančerl. In addition to being a distinguished interpreter of the music of his native country, his musical sympathies extend to composers such as Gershwin and Elgar. He has recorded for the Czech labels Supraphon and Panton, and for the East German label Eterna, and many of these performances have been released in the West by Philips, Telefunken, Eurodisc, Decca, EMI, Vanguard, Nonesuch, and Turnabout. He first came to notice as a recording artist with the Prague Symphony Orchestra in Dvořák's Symphonies Nos 1, 2 and 4, in the first recordings of these works to be generally available; he subsequently re-recorded all the Dvořák symphonies with the Czech Philharmonic Orchestra. His other recordings include Schubert's Symphonies Nos 3 and 8, two sinfonias of Gluck, the Brahms Violin Concerto (with Suk), the Grieg Piano Concerto (with Panenka), *Norwegian Dances* and *Lyric Suite*, *Kindertotenlieder*, *Lieder eines fahrenden Gesellen* and a song from *Des Knaben Wunderhorn* (with Soukapová), the overtures to *Don Giovanni*, *Carmen*, *Il barbiere di Siviglia*, *Fidelio*, *The Kiss*, *The Devil and Kate*, *Russlan und Ludmilla*, *Der Opernball*, *Der Waldmeister*, *Die schöne Galatea*, *Wiener Frauen* and *Orphée aux enfers*, Dvořák's *Notturno*, *Symphonic Variations*, *Scherzo capriccioso*, *Lord Have Mercy on Us* and an excerpt from *St Ludmilla*, Smetana's *Má Vlast*, *Richard III*, *Haakon Jarl*, *Wallenstein's Camp* and *Shakespearian Festival March*, Martinů's Violin Concertos Nos 1 and 2 (with Suk), marches and other pieces by Fučik, Honegger's Cello Concerto (with Sádlo), Shostakovich's Symphonies Nos 7 and 9, and Cello Concerto No. 1 (with Sádlo), Messiaen's *Réveil des oiseaux*, *Oiseaux exotiques* and *La Bouscarle* (with Loriod), Sommer's *Choral Symphony*, Kalabis' *Symphonic Variations*, Boháč's *Suita drammatica*, Vaňhal's Sinfonia, Hanuš' *Musica concertante* (with Chuchro and Panenka), Mácha's *Variations*, Havelka's *Foam*, Pauer's *Panychide*, Eben's *Vox*

Clamantis, Chaun's *The Trial*, Dvořáček's *Ex Post* and Dobiáš' *Gospodine* and Sonata (with the Czech Philharmonic Orchestra); Dvořák's *Te Deum* (with the Prague FOK Orchestra *et al.*); Tchaikovsky's *The Seasons* (with the Film Studio Orchestra); Smetana's *The Secret*, Janáček's *The Cunning Little Vixen* and *The Excursions of Mr Brouček* (with the Prague National Theatre Orchestra *et al.*); the *Peer Gynt* Suites Nos 1 and 2 and *Lyric Suite* of Grieg, Gershwin's Piano Concerto (with Knor) and *Cuban Overture*, Roussel's *Le Festin de l'araignée*, Milhaud's *La Création du monde*, Stravinsky's *Feux d'artifice*, and Martinů's Violin Concerto No. 1 (with Bělček, and the Prague Symphony Orchestra); the complete Bach Harpsichord Concertos (with Růžičková and the Prague Chamber Soloists); Dobiáš' song-cycle *Prague, My Only One* (with Jindrák and the Czech Radio Symphony Orchestra); Janáček's *Sinfonietta* (with the Leipzig Radio Symphony Orchestra); Brahms' *Volkslieder* (with the Leipzig Radio Chorus); Beethoven's overtures *Fidelio*, *Leonore No. 3*, *Egmont*, *Die Weihe des Hauses*, *Die Ruinen von Athen* and *König Stephan*, Gluck's *Orfeo ed Euridice*, Liszt's *Hungarian Rhapsodies Nos 2* and *6*, *Les Préludes* and *Hungarian Fantasia* (with Stöckigt), some *Hungarian Dances* of Brahms, Bruckner's Symphony No. 1, Mahler's Symphonies Nos 5, 6, 7 and 9, Dvořák's *Slavonic Dances* Opp. 46 and 72, *Czech Suite*, *The Wood Dove*, three *Slavonic Rhapsodies* and excerpts from *The Devil and Kate*, Smetana's *Má Vlast* and excerpts from *The Bartered Bride*, Glinka's *Kamarinskaya*, Grieg's incidental music for *Peer Gynt* (with Stolte) and Janáček's *Lachian Dances* (with the Leipzig Gewandhaus Orchestra), and Roussel's Symphony No. 3 and *Bacchus et Ariane* Suite No. 2 (with the Brno State Philharmonic Orchestra). Critical reception of these records has been varied; the Dvořák, Smetana and Janáček works are recognised as authoritative, but the Schubert Symphony No. 8 was thought uninspired. The recordings of the Mahler, Bruckner and Shostakovich have never gained wide currency in the West.

Neumeyer, Fritz (b. 1900). After studying at the universities of Cologne and Berlin, Neumeyer conducted at the Saarbrücken Municipal Theatre (1924–7), was leader and harpsichordist of the Saarbrücken Association for Early Music (1927), with Scheck and Wenzinger formed a chamber trio for performing early music (1935–62), lectured at the Hochschule für Musik in Berlin (1939–44), was professor of historical keyboard instruments at the Hochschule für Musik at Freiburg/Breisgau (1946–69), and harpsichordist with the Capella Coloniensis and the Wiener Solisten (since 1968). His compositions include vocal and chamber works. He has made numerous records as a harpsichordist, and in addition Turnabout issued an LP disc in which he conducted a Munich instrumental ensemble in a collection entitled *In Praise of Pleasure*.

Newman, Alfred (1901–70). Born in New Haven, Connecticut, Newman studied the piano with Stojowski and composition with Goldmark, and with Schoenberg in Los Angeles. He started his musical career as a pianist in a vaudeville theatre, then in 1930 he came to Hollywood and wrote some hundreds of film scores. Eight of these won Oscars from the Motion Picture Academy, the most successful being for the films *All About Eve*, *The Egyptian* and *Love is a Many-Splendored Thing*. Slonimsky described his style as 'mimicking the most popular works of Tchaikovsky, Rachmaninov, Wagner and Liszt, and amalgamating these elements in an iridescent free fantasia'. Newman conducted the Hollywood Bowl Symphony Orchestra in some discs for Capitol, which included Gershwin's *Cuban Overture*, *I Got Rhythm Variations*, the *Rhapsody No. 2*, *An American in Paris* and excerpts from *Porgy and Bess* (with pianist Pennario), suites from Kabalevsky's *The Comedians* and Khachaturian's *Gayaneh* and *Masquerade*, and an orchestral arrangement of music from the opera *Madama Butterfly*.

Newman, Anthony (b. 1941). The harpsichordist and organist Newman was born in Los Angeles and studied at the Mannes College, New York, and at Harvard and Boston Universities. He has a reputation for originality: in a recording of *Das wohltemperierte Klavier*, for instance, he shares the music between harpsichord, clavichord and organ, sometimes performing a prelude on one instrument and the fugue on another. CBS recorded him with an ensemble directing the *Brandenburg Concertos*.

Newstone, Harry (b. 1921). Born in Winnipeg, Canada, of Russian parents, Newstone came to Britain with his family in 1927, studied with Howells, then was a pupil of conducting under Cundell and Buesst at the Guildhall School of Music (1945), and later studied conducting with Previtali at the Accademia di Santa Cecilia in Rome (1954–6). In 1949 he founded and conducted the Haydn Orchestra in London, and performed for a broadcast series the *London*

Symphonies of Haydn, using his own revised texts. He has conducted in Berlin, Hamburg, Denmark, Israel, Prague and Canada, and in 1965 became musical director of the Sacramento Symphony Orchestra in California.

In the 1950s records were released in which Newstone conducted the Haydn Orchestra in exemplary performances of Haydn's Symphonies Nos 49 and 73 (issued by Nixa), Nos 46 and 52 (by L'Oiseau Lyre) and Mozart's Symphony No. 41 and *Serenata notturna* (by Monarch); Supraphon issued a coupling of the Haydn and Mozart Oboe Concertos (with Hanták and the Prague Symphony Orchestra), Pye (and Vanguard in the US) Bach's Clavier Concertos Nos 1 and 5 (with Katz and the Pro Arte Orchestra), and he also accompanied some Haydn and Mozart arias with the soprano Vyvyan (with the Haydn Orchestra, originally released by L'Oiseau Lyre), and recorded *Una cosa rara* of Soler, arranged by Salter (with the Vancouver Chamber Orchestra *et al.* for CBC). Other recordings distinguished by his imaginative direction were the six *Brandenburg Concertos* (with the Hamburg Chamber Orchestra), a collection of Mozart overtures (with the Hamburg Pro Musica Symphony Orchestra) and Stravinsky's *Dumbarton Oaks* (with the Haydn Orchestra), issued in Britain by Saga.

Nicholson, Sir Sydney (1875–1947). Born in London and educated at New College, Oxford, Nicholson studied at the Royal College of Music in London under Parratt and Stanford, and with Knorr at Frankfurt am Main. He was organist at Carlisle Cathedral (1904), Manchester Cathedral (1908–18), and Westminster Abbey (1918–27), was chairman of the Church Music Society, founded the School of English Church Music (1927), and organised the College of St Nicolas at Chislehurst. He toured overseas in 1934 and 1938, composed a comic opera *The Mermaid*, was knighted in 1938, and published, *inter alia*, *Quires and Places Where They Sing*. HMV recorded him conducting the Westminster Abbey Choir in Pearsall's *In dulce jubilo*, and Columbia Stanford's *O for a Closer Walk with God* (with the Royal School of Church Music Choir).

Nick, Edmund (1891–1974). Born in Reichenberg, Nick studied in Vienna and Dresden, graduated as a doctor of laws, and became a conductor with the Breslau Radio (1924). Later he was a conductor in Berlin (1933–40), musical director of the Munich State Operetta (1947–8), professor of musical history at the Munich Academy of Music (1949) and conductor of the North-West German Radio at Cologne (1952). He wrote music for films and operettas, and has recorded Liszt's *Hungarian Rhapsodies Nos 2* and *12* and waltzes by Lanner (with the Bavarian Radio Orchestra for DGG), Liszt's *Hungarian Fantasia* (with Karolyi) and Waldteufel's *España* Waltz (with the Munich Philharmonic Orchestra for DGG).

Nikisch, Arthur (1855–1922). Born in Lébényi Szant Niklos in Hungary, Nikisch showed remarkable musical talent in childhood, and at the age of 11 entered the Vienna Conservatory to study the violin and piano. In later life he was to say that all conductors should learn the violin, not only for its own sake, but because of the command it gives to the wrist. As a violinist in the Vienna Court Orchestra (1872–4) he played under Brahms, Wagner, Verdi, Rubinstein and Liszt, and his memory was such that he could recall every detail of their performances for the rest of his life. His career as a conductor started in 1878 at Leipzig, and during his lifetime his appointments included the Boston Symphony Orchestra (1889–93), the Budapest Opera (1893–5), the Leipzig Opera (1879–89), the Hamburg Philharmonic Orchestra (1897–1922), and the Leipzig Gewandhaus and Berlin Philharmonic Orchestras simultaneously (1895–1922). He toured often in Europe and Russia, frequently visited Britain where he led several cycles of *The Ring* at Covent Garden (1913–14), conducted at the Leeds Festival and with the London Symphony Orchestra, which he took on a tour of the United States (1912). He often appeared in London as piano accompanist to the great lieder singer Elena Gerhardt.

Nikisch was a unique and incomparable conductor; Boult, who studied with him in Leipzig for two years, regarded him as a perfect technical model; Klemperer had the highest opinion of him, saying that he was 'really a virtuoso', (P. Heyworth, *Conversations with Klemperer*, London, p. 89), and conducted the Schumann symphonies wonderfully; 'His parade pieces were the *Tannhäuser* overture and, above all, Tchaikovsky's *Symphonie Pathétique*, which he did phenomenally – great beauty of sound, controlled and yet very passionate'. His extraordinary power was a combination of a feeling for colour, melodic phrasing, dynamic graduations, rhythmic freedom, rubato, and a constant variation between tension and relaxation, all of which was entirely instinctive. Even so, many critics disapproved of his supposedly erratic tempi, exaggerated rubatos and dynamics, and some remarked that he never played the one piece the same way twice. He had a mesmeric control over every player in the orchestra; he was called *der Magier*, and magical power was attributed to him. Listeners and indeed orchestral players were hypnotised by the movement of his beautiful hands, and by the visible three inches of his sleeve cuffs. He always conducted from memory, and commanded complete obedience effortlessly. His baton technique was so exceptional that it indicated every nuance, his left hand was used sparingly and it never doubled his right. When rehearsing he never stopped, but his left hand and eyes would indicate to the players the need for correction. It is said that he commenced the *Oberon* overture by just raising his eyebrows, and often gave directions with a nod. Boult remembered a remarkable performance of a Brahms symphony in which Nikisch's hand never rose above his face. No matter what orchestra he conducted, his wonderfully warm tone was always evident; Boult said 'we could hear Nikisch at work if we listened blindfolded to the first bar of *Tristan*'. At the same time, when he conducted a strange orchestra, he never imposed his will on every detail, but adapted the orchestra's normal reading as close as possible to his own conception. Tchaikovsky saw Nikisch when he was a young man, and wrote: 'Herr Nikisch is elegantly calm, sparing of superfluous movements, yet at the same time wonderfully strong and self-possessed. He does not seem to conduct, but rather to exercise some mysterious spell; he hardly makes a sign and never tries to call attention to himself, yet we feel that the great orchestra, like an instrument in the hands of a wonderful master, is completely under the control of its chief.' Nikisch displayed his intuitive understanding of his players even when talking to them, and he believed that the personality of the different instrumentalists varied according to the instruments they played, so that he would speak quietly and delicately to an oboist or violinist, but would be much more forcible when addressing, say, a trombone player. There are, however, two sides to the coin; Olin Downes wrote that Nikisch was a poor drillmaster and that the technical standard of the Boston Symphony Orchestra was materially lowered during his regime.

Nikisch apparently wrote nothing about conducting, but said that he himself was not conscious of any technical objectives. 'If one of my colleagues were to ask me after a concert how I had produced this or that particular effect, I should be unable to tell him. People ask me how I convey my feeling to musicians. I just do so, without knowing how. When I conduct a work, it is the thrilling power of the music that sweeps me on; I certainly do not follow any hard and fast rules of interpretation. I don't sit down and think out in advance how I am going to have every note of the composition played. And so it comes about that the details of my interpretations vary almost with every performance, in harmony with the powers of feeling that are aroused in me most strongly. But I must emphasise, only the details. To experience a Beethoven symphony in one way today and in an entirely different manner tomorrow would be as absurd as it would be illogical.' He did not hesitate to acknowledge the supreme importance of the interpreter: 'It is only through the personality of the conductor that all our modern instrumental music comes to life'; but he also recognised that each interpreter, or conductor must of necessity, give his own individual stamp to the same piece of music. To Henry Wood he once said: 'Music is a dead thing without interpretation. We all feel things differently. A metronome can keep a four-square indication, if they like it that way, but never forget that you should make every performance a great improvisation – even though you direct the same work every day of the year.'

DGG recorded Nikisch conducting the Berlin Philharmonic Orchestra in Beethoven's Symphony No. 5 in 1913, and this was the first recording of a complete symphony. Later, in 1920 with the same orchestra, Liszt's *Hungarian Rhapsody No. 1* and the overture *Le Carnaval romain* were issued. In 1914, HMV recorded him with the London Symphony Orchestra performing the overtures *Egmont*, *Le nozze di Figaro*, *Der Freischütz* and *Oberon*, and the *Hungarian Rhapsody No. 1*. G & T and HMV also issued a number of records in which he accompanied Elena Gerhardt in lieder by Schubert, Schumann, Brahms, Wolf *et al.* The Beethoven Symphony No. 5 has been re-issued several times, and more recently in DGG's album *The Early Years*; whether the performance as recorded is truly representative of Nikisch is open to doubt, for Toscanini remarked that he had heard Nikisch conduct the symphony and that the record was not the same. As the records were made in 1913, the technical problems of the primitive recording process as much as Nikisch's variability would be to blame.

Nilius, Rudolf (1883–1962). Born in Vienna, Nilius was a cellist with the Vienna Philharmonic Orchestra (1904–12), conducted the Vienna Tonkünstlerorchester (1912–21), and in 1912 founded the Philharmonic Chamber Orchestra concerts in Vienna. He recorded with the Vienna Radio Orchestra the overtures to *Le nozze di Figaro*, *Die Entführung aus dem Serail*, *Der Schauspieldirektor*, *La Belle Hélène*, *Orphée aux enfers*, *Donna Diana*, *Mignon* and *Abu Hassan*, Schubert's *Marche militaire No. 1*, *Valse triste*, Pierné's *Sérénade*, waltzes and other pieces by Strauss, and an intermezzo from Wolf-Ferrari's *I quattro rusteghi*, which were issued on the Viennola label.

Nobel, Felix de (b. 1907). Born in Haarlem, Nobel studied at the Amsterdam Conservatory, where he later taught piano accompaniment and lieder interpretation, and was also on the staff of the Hague Conservatory. He was accompanist for the Netherlands Radio, was a member of the Concertgebouw Quintet, and conductor of the Netherlands Chamber Choir (1937–73), with which he made many international tours. He has recorded Monteverdi's *Mass* (1651) and Lassus' *Domine, ne in furore* (with the Amsterdam Motet Choir for Concert Hall), Bach's *O Lamm Gottes unschuldig*, the Kyrie and Gloria from Ockeghem's Mass *Sine nomine*, Lotti's *Vere languores nostros*, Lassus' *Matona, mia cara* and *Adoramus te*, and Handel's *Ecco quomodo moritur justus*; also Stravinsky's *Les Noces*, *Mass*, *Pater Noster* and *Ave Maria* (with the Netherlands Chamber Choir *et al.* for Philips), a capella pieces by Sweelinck, Josquin, Klerk, Obrecht, Schuyt, Strategier, Horst, Escher, Flothuis and H. Andriessen (with the Netherlands Chamber Choir for Donemus), and Pijper's *Halewijn* (with the Netherlands Chamber Choir and the Utrecht Symphony Orchestra for Donemus).

Noble, Jeremy (b. 1930). Born in London and music critic for newspapers and record critic for *The Gramophone*, Noble recorded, as a conductor, with the Josquin Choir Josquin des Prés' *Missa – l'homme armé*, *Regina coeli*, *Absalom fili mi* and *Illibata Dei Virgo Nutrix* (for Pye).

Nohejl, Jaromír (b. 1925). Born at Kutná Hora, Czechoslovakia, Nohejl received his first violin lessons from his father, who was a composer of popular music. He studied at the Kutná Hora Music School (1942–4) and at the Prague Conservatory (1945–9), where he was a conducting pupil of Dědeček. He first appeared as a conductor with the Kutná Hora Music School Student Orchestra (1943), led the teachers' choir there, and was conductor and choirmaster of the Army Artists' Group (1950–54), which gave concerts in Hungary, Poland, China and the USSR. In 1956 he won a national competition for conductors, became a conductor with the Moravian Philharmonic Orchestra at Olomouc, and was appointed the orchestra's chief conductor in 1960. He has toured Eastern Europe and the USSR, and has given many first performances of contemporary composers. He has recorded Paganini's Violin Concerto No. 1 and Ravel's *Tzigane* (with Hudeček and the Prague Symphony Orchestra for Panton), Šesták's Symphony No. 3, Chaun's *Five Pictures for Orchestra* and Sternwald's *Symphonic Picture* (with the Moravian Philharmonic Orchestra for Panton), Kučera's *Picture*, Páleníček's *Symphonic Variations* and Vacek's *Poem of Fallen Heroes* (with Soukupová and the Czech Radio Symphony Orchestra for Panton).

Nono, Luigi (b. 1924). The Italian composer Nono studied with Maderna and Scherchen, and has taught at the New Music Summer School at Darmstadt since 1957 and at the Dartington Hall Music Summer School in Devon (1957–60). Of his compositions he has conducted a recording of *A floresta e jovem e chea de vida* (with the Studio di Fonologia, Milan, *et al.*, for Harmonia Mundi); this work is an oratorio to texts from the pronouncements of Angolan guerillas (1966), consistent with Nono's acknowledged membership of the Italian Communist Party.

Nord, Edward (b. 1948). The United States conductor Nord learned the piano as a boy, was the state winner of the National Piano Playing Auditions, continued his studies with Julius Chajes, and gave many public performances. He studied at the University of California at Berkeley and at the University of Southern California, and became assistant conductor of its orchestra. He attended the Berkshire Music Center at Tanglewood, studied under Boulanger at the American Conservatory at Fontainebleau, and under Blomstedt and Markevitch at Monte Carlo, where he also conducted the Monte Carlo National Opera Orchestra. For Orion he recorded concert suites from Monteverdi's *La favola d'Orfeo* and *L'Incoronazione di Poppea* (arranged by Rodriguez), and Robert Rodriguez's *Concerto III* (with Segal), *Canto* and *Lyric Variations* (with the Orion Chamber Orchestra *et al.*).

Norrington, Roger (b. 1934). Born in Oxford and educated at Clare College, Cambridge, and the Royal College of Music, Norrington became director of the Schütz Choir of London and the London String Players in 1962, and was musical director of the Kent Opera from 1966. He has written articles for musical periodicals, and arranged and conducted Monteverdi's *L'Incoronazione di Poppea* in a version considerably more idiomatic than others at present popular. Although primarily a specialist in baroque music, when called upon he has shown admirable skill with music as far removed from that era as Ravel and Falla. His records with the Schütz Choir, and with one exception all for Argo, have included fine and perceptive performances of music by Schütz, foremost the *St Matthew Passion* and *Resurrection of Jesus Christ* (also with the London Cornet Ensemble and Elizabethan Consort, *et al.*), Bruckner's Mass No. 2 (with the Schütz Choir and the Philip Jones Wind Ensemble) and choral music by Monteverdi, Scarlatti, Mendelssohn and Berlioz. He also recorded Liszt's *Totentanz* and *Hungarian Fantasy* (with Clidat and the Hague Philharmonic Orchestra for IPG), and Fauré's *Prométhée* and *Caligula* (with the Monte Carlo National Opera Orchestra *et al.* for IPG).

Nott, David (b. 1934). Born in Milwaukee, Wisconsin, Nott studied at Carroll College, the Union Theological Seminary School of Sacred Music, and the Cincinnati Conservatory. He has been director of choral activities at Monmouth, Hastings, Yankton and Simpson Colleges, and at the Illinois Wesleyan University, and with the latter's School of Music Chorus recorded Bach's Cantatas Nos 131 and 182 for Everest.

Nowak, Lionel (b. 1911). Born in Cleveland, Ohio, Nowak made his debut as a pianist at the age of four, studied with Fischer in Berlin (1929) and at the Cleveland Institute of Music, from which he graduated in 1936. He was musical director of the Humphrey-Weidman Modern Dance Company (1938–42), professor of music at Syracuse University (1946–8), and at Bennington College (since 1948). He has composed concertos, chamber and vocal music, and for Composers Recordings directed the Bennington String Ensemble in his own *Concert Piece for Kettledrums* (with Calabro).

Nussio, Otmar (b. 1902). Born in Grosseto, Nussio studied the piano and flute at the Giuseppe Verdi Conservatory in Milan, and with Respighi at the Accademia di Santa Cecilia in Rome. He has won prizes at the National Musical Competition at Lugano (1938) and with the Bukowna Ballet at Brussels (1956), from 1938 has been conductor of the Swiss Italian Radio Orchestra at Lugano, has conducted at festivals in Austria, Switzerland, Belgium and Spain, and has conducted orchestras in Western and Eastern Europe, Egypt and the United States. His compositions include numerous symphonic poems, overtures, suites, ballets and other works, and of these he has recorded *Folklore d'Engadina* (for EMI), *Trittico toscano*, *Danze friulane* and *Canto di nostalgia* (with the Rome Philharmonic Orchestra for Philips), as well as two pieces of Flury, the intermezzo from *Der schlimmheilige Vitalis* and overture to *Casanova e l'Albertolli* (with the Swiss Radio Orchestra for Fono). As a flautist he recorded a disc of sonatas by Handel, Purcell, Leonardo Vinci and Bach (with Hans Andreae, harpsichord, for Elite).

Nyazi, Tagy-Zade (b. 1912). Born in Tiflis (or Tbilisi), Nyazi was conductor then chief conductor at the Azerbaijan Opera Theatre (1937–51), and chief conductor and artistic director of the Gazibekov Symphony Orchestra at Baku. He has been known professionally simply as Nyazi, dropping his first names. In 1959 he was named People's Artist of the USSR, having already received the State Award of the USSR in 1951 and 1952. He has composed operas, is a specialist in the music of Azerbaijan, and has arranged an edition of the opera *Ker-Ogly* of Uzier Gazibekov, who was the founder of the Azerbaijan National Opera. Nyazi's recordings include the overture to *Ker-Ogly*, Sultan Gazibekov's Symphony No. 1 and symphonic poem *Caravan* (with the Gazibekov Symphony Orchestra), Ippolitov-Ivanov's *Armenian Rhapsody* and Karayev's suite *The Seven Beauties* (with the Moscow Radio Orchestra), Karayev's suite *The Seven Beauties*, Amirov's *Shur*, and his own *Lezginka* (with the USSR State Symphony Orchestra) and *Gaitagy* waltz (with the Gazibekov Symphony Orchestra), and for Supraphon Tchaikovsky's Symphony No. 4 and his own *Rast* (with the Czech Philharmonic Orchestra).

O

Oberfrank, Géza (b. 1936). Born in Budapest, Oberfrank graduated from the Franz Liszt Academy there (1961), where he studied composition and conducting, and then joined the Budapest State Opera as a conductor. He premièred Szokolay's operas *Blood Wedding* and *Hamlet*, has appeared as a guest conductor in FR and DR Germany, Poland and the United States, and was a finalist in the Karajan International Competition for Young Conductors in 1969. He was commissioned by Felsenstein to conduct *Háry János* at the Berlin Komische Oper (1973), and then was appointed its general music director (1974–6); he conducted Felsenstein's last production before his death, *Le nozze di Figaro*. In 1976 he became principal conductor of the Budapest Concert Orchestra. For Hungaroton he has recorded Beethoven's music to *König Stephan* and *Die Ruinen von Athen*, Schubert's Symphonies Nos 4 and 8 (with the Budapest Philharmonic Orchestra), the Sibelius Violin Concerto, Ravel's *Tzigane* and Saint-Saëns' *Introduction et rondo capriccioso* (with Koté and the Hungarian State Orchestra) and Ribari's suite for soprano *Metamorphoses* (with the Hungarian Radio Orchestra).

Ochs, Siegfried (1858–1929). Born in Frankfurt am Main, Ochs at first studied medicine and chemistry, then attended the Hochschule für Musik in Berlin, and was associated with von Bülow. He founded and conducted the Philharmonic Choir, which became famous and presented the first performances of many contemporary choral works, and taught and conducted the choir at the Berlin Hochschule für Musik. He also edited Bach's cantatas and the *St Matthew Passion*, and wrote a comic opera and some operettas; his *Humoristische Variationen über 's kommt ein Vogel geflogen* is listed in the German catalogue in two separate recordings. He recorded Mendelssohn's *Ave Maria* and the *Laudate Dominum* from Mozart's *Vesperae solennes de confessore* (with Van Diemen and the Berlin Philharmonic Choir and Orchestra for HMV); the latter was described by Sackville-West and Shawe-Taylor in *The Record Guide* as 'one of the most serene and beautiful of soprano records'.

O'Connell, Charles (1900–62). Born in Chicopee, Massachusetts, and educated at the College of the Holy Cross, O'Connell studied the organ and conducting with Widor and Marimer in Paris, and from 1930 to 1940 was music director for Victor Red Seal Records, being responsible for all of RCA Victor's classical recordings, and then from 1944 to 1947 filled a similar position for Columbia. He was assistant conductor of the Philadelphia Orchestra (1936–7), conducted the New York Philharmonic's Lewisohn Stadium concerts (1939), was a guest conductor with other North American orchestras, and in 1935 was awarded the Bruckner Medal. His publications included the *Victor Book of the Symphony* (1934), *Victor Book of the Opera* (1937) and *The Other Side of the Record* (1947), a candid account of his experiences recording Koussevitzky, Stokowski, Toscanini, Monteux, Fiedler, Ormandy, Iturbi and other RCA artists. He also arranged some pieces for orchestra. His records included accompaniments for Kreisler, Marian Anderson, Richard Crooks, Helen Traubel, Rose Bampton, Eleanor Steber *et al.*, Albéniz's *Cordoba*, *Valse triste*, the Angélus from Massenet's *Scènes pittoresques*, the prelude to Act III of *Lohengrin*, the Entry of the Gods into Valhalla from *Das Rheingold*, and arrangements of Bach's *Komm, süsser Tod*, Debussy's *Clair de lune* and Mendelssohn's *On Wings of Song* (with the Victor Symphony Orchestra for RCA) and the Bacchanale from *Samson et Dalila* (with the Carnegie Pops Orchestra for Columbia). The Victor Symphony Orchestra in these recordings was suspected of being the Philadelphia Orchestra, which may have accounted for the excellent quality of the playing.

Ohmiya, Makoto. After studying composition, conducting and musical aesthetics at the Kyoto State University, Ohmiya graduated in 1947, and collaborated in the complete edition of the works of Haydn, and became a leading Haydn specialist. He founded the Haydn Ensemble in 1971 to perform the music of the composer and other Viennese classics, and toured Europe with the Ensemble in 1975. With them he recorded the *Notturni* of Haydn for Bärenreiter.

Oistrakh, David (1908–74). Born in Odessa, where his father was an amateur violinist and his mother a singer at the opera, Oistrakh started learning the violin at the age of five, and before he graduated from the Odessa Conservatory in 1926 he gave the first performance of Prokofiev's Violin Concerto No. 1 at his final examination. He played as a soloist with Glazunov conducting in various Russian cities (1926–7) and first appeared in Leningrad in 1928, with Malko and the Leningrad Philharmonic Orchestra, and then came to Moscow in 1929. His career as one of the most distinguished violinists of the era followed, initially in the USSR, then internationally when he took second place (to Ginette Neveu) at the Wieniawski Competition in Warsaw (1935), and first place at the Eugène Ysaÿe Competition in Brussels (1937). He visited Britain in 1954, made his first records as a violinist for EMI in Sweden that year, and toured Japan and the United States in 1955. After 1964 he was obliged to restrict the number of his recitals as his health began to fail.

Although Oistrakh had studied conducting in his early years and always wished to be a conductor, his first opportunity only came in 1959 at a recording session in London when the conductor engaged to accompany him in a Mozart concerto was not available. Afterwards he conducted at a concert when his son Igor was the soloist, and in 1963 he led, in the USSR, his first complete programme – Brahms' Symphony No. 2, a Prokofiev concerto and *Harold in Italy*. Soon he was conducting the Moscow Philharmonic and other orchestras in the Soviet Union and abroad, and first appeared in London as a conductor in 1967. He continued to give concerts as a violin soloist, and occasionally conducted his own accompaniment; just before his death in 1974 he had undertaken a series of concerts, with the Amsterdam Concertgebouw Orchestra, of all the orchestral works of Brahms. His repertoire was mostly from the classical and romantic periods, and included Russian composers who were his contemporaries, such as Prokofiev and Shostakovich. As a personality, Oistrakh was a genial, kindly and reserved man, of immense patience, whose great calmness and self-discipline could be mistaken for a subdued temperament. His technique served his musicianship supremely on the violin, though as a conductor he was less well equipped to attain a comparable level of excellence.

Oistrakh's first record as a conductor, mentioned above, was of Mozart's Violin Concerto K. 216 (with the Philharmonia Orchestra for EMI); later, in 1972, he recorded again as both soloist and conductor all the authentic Mozart violin concertos, the Sinfonia Concertante and Concertone (with the Berlin Philharmonic Orchestra *et al.* for EMI). He accompanied his son Igor in the Beethoven Violin Concerto (with the Vienna Symphony Orchestra for Ariola), Bruch's Violin Concerto No. 1 (with the Royal Philharmonic Orchestra for DGG), the Brahms Violin Concerto and Lalo's *Symphonie espagnole* (with the USSR State Symphony Orchestra) and the Tchaikovsky Violin Concerto (with the Moscow Philharmonic Orchestra), and also recorded concertos by Marcello, Pergolesi and Vivaldi, the Corelli Concerti Grossi Op. 6 Nos 1 to 4, Tchaikovsky's Symphony No. 6, *Harold in Italy* (with Barshai), Prokofiev's Symphony No. 5, Mahler's Symphony No. 4, Bach's Suite No. 2 and the Handel/Harty *Water Music* (with the Moscow Philharmonic Orchestra), the Bach Two-Violin Concerto and a Vivaldi Two-Violin Concerto (with Igor and himself and the Vienna Symphony and Royal Philharmonic Orchestras, respectively, for DGG), as well as accompanying the Russian violinists Kogan, Pikaizen and Fain in concerto recordings. The recordings with Soviet orchestras and the Brahms Violin Concerto were for Melodiya, but many have been released in the West by Eurodisc and on other labels.

Oistrakh, Igor (b. 1931). Born in Odessa, Oistrakh was a violin pupil of his father, David, at the Moscow Conservatory, graduating in 1955. Previously he had won first prize at the International Wieniawski Violin Competition at Poznań in 1952. In addition to his many records as a violin soloist, he has appeared as a conductor for Melodiya with the Moscow Philharmonic Orchestra in *Eine kleine Nachtmusik* and Mozart's Sinfonia Concertante K. 364 (with himself and Pikaizen).

Olof, Victor (1898–1974). Born in London, as Victor Olof Ahlquist, Olof studied the violin, piano and composition, became a professional musician and was founder and leader of the Victor Olof Sextet, which broadcast for many years. In 1942 he assisted Sidney Beer in forming and managing the National Symphony Orchestra, and later in 1948 helped Beecham to organise the Royal Philharmonic Orchestra. When the Decca Record Company began to expand its catalogue after World War II, he was engaged as its musical adviser, and showed his great technical and musical understanding in the production of the records of Kleiber, Böhm, Ansermet, Krauss, Krips, Knappertsbusch *et al.* which distinguished Decca's early catalogue. In 1956 he joined EMI in a similar capacity and worked with Beecham and other great artists recording for that company. He also did some conducting; for Parlophone he recorded Delibes' *La Source*, the incidental music from *The Merchant of Venice* and selections from musical comedies (with the Victor Olof Salon Orchestra and the Parlophone Salon Orchestra), and Decca issued 78s of him directing the London Symphony, the National Symphony and the (so-called) Kingsway Symphony Orchestra in Paganini's Violin Concerto No. 1 (with Campoli), the overtures *The Merry Wives of Windsor*, *William Tell*, *La Muette de Portici*, *Le Cheval de bronze*, and *Morgen, Mittag und Abend in Wien*, and other popular pieces such as *Valse triste* and *España*. Later, on Decca mono LPs, he conducted the New Symphony Orchestra in excerpts from German's operettas *Henry VIII*, *Nell Gwynn* and *Merrie England*, and the Suisse Romande Orchestra in the overtures to *Il barbiere di Siviglia* and *The Merry Wives of Windsor*, Järnefelt's *Praeludium*, and a suite from *La Source* of Delibes.

Ord, Boris (1897–1961). Born in Bristol, Ord studied the organ at the Royal College of Music in London, served in World War I as a pilot in the Royal Flying Corps, and after completing his studies in 1920 became Organ Scholar at Corpus Christi College at Cambridge. He was a Fellow at King's College (1923–61) and organist there (1929–57), performed with the Cambridge University Madrigal Society, was a member of the staff of the Cologne Opera, was appointed lecturer at Cambridge (1936), became conductor of the Cambridge University Musical Society, and directed the King's College Chapel Choir. In 1958 he was awarded the CBE. For Columbia, he recorded with the King's College Chapel Choir anthems and sacred pieces by Byrd, Weelkes, Tallis, Gibbons, Taverner, Batten, Wesley, Johnson, Dering, Mundy, Farrant, Howells and Vaughan Williams, and with the Golden Age Singers and the Cambridge University Madrigal Society, a collection of partsongs by Bliss, Bax, Tippett, Vaughan Williams, Berkeley, Ireland, Howells, Finzi, Rawsthorne and Rubbra, which were commissioned by the Arts Council in 1953 to celebrate the coronation of Queen Elizabeth II.

Orff, Carl (b. 1895). After studying at the Academy of Music at his birthplace, Munich, the composer, educationalist and musicologist Orff was in his early years a repetiteur and conductor in Munich, Mannheim and Darmstadt. He then returned to Munich to devote himself to composition and to develop methods of musical education. Many of his compositions have been recorded, but unquestionably the most successful and widely performed of his works is *Carmina Burana*. He recorded, as conductor, his *Musik für Kinder* Nos 1 and 2 (for EMI), *Die Weinachtsgeschichte*, *Musica Poetica*, *Musikalisches Hausbuch* and *Guten Morgen*, *Spielman* (for BASF).

Orlov, Aleksander (1873–1948). Born in St Petersburg and educated at the conservatory there, Orlov conducted the Kuban Army Symphony Orchestra (1902), studied conducting with Juon in Berlin (1906), conducted opera and concerts in Rostov, Odessa, Kiev, Yalta *et al.* (1907), conducted the Koussevitzky Symphony Orchestra in Moscow (1912–17), was conductor of the Zimin Opera Theatre (1917–25), chief conductor of the Shevchenko Opera and Ballet Theatre (1925–9), professor at the Moscow Conservatory (from 1927) and conductor of the Grand Symphony Orchestra, All-Union Radio, i.e. the Moscow Radio Orchestra (from 1930). His major recordings were the Operas *Eugene Onegin* and *La traviata* (both with the Bolshoi Theatre Company, and the latter in Russian), and Tchaikovsky's *The Oprichnik* (with the Moscow Radio Orchestra *et al.*). He also recorded, variously with the Moscow Radio Orchestra, the Bolshoi Theatre Orchestra and the USSR State Symphony Orchestra, *In the Steppes of Central Asia*, Rubinstein's *Trepak*, Glinka's *Jota Aragonesa* and *A Night in Madrid*, Rimsky-Korsakov's *Fantasia on Serbian Themes* and *May Night* overture, Mussorgsky's *Intermezzo*, Glazunov's Violin Concerto (with Polyakin), Moskowski's *Spanish Dances*, and Balakirev's *Overture on Russian Themes*.

Ormandy, Eugene (b. 1899). Born in Budapest, the son of a dentist who was determined that his son should be a violinist, Ormandy started to learn on an eighth-size instrument when he was two, and is said to have been able to identify popular symphonies at the same age. At five he entered the Budapest Royal Academy of Music, studied with Hubay, Weiner and Kodály, graduated with a master's degree at 14, and won an Artist's diploma for violin at 16. He also took a degree in philosophy at Budapest University. Before 1914 he toured Germany and Austria as a prodigy, and in 1919 was a professor at the Hungarian State Conservatory of Music. In 1920 he went to the United States on the promise of concerts as a violinist, but when this came to nothing he joined the orchestra at the Capitol Theatre in New York, and soon became its concertmaster. Eight months later, in 1921, he was asked to conduct when the conductor fell ill, and this led to his appointment as conductor of the orchestra, where he remained seven years, conducting some works 20 times a week. He then conducted the CBS Radio Orchestra, attended the rehearsals of Mengelberg, Furtwängler and Toscanini, who were then conducting the New York Philharmonic Orchestra, and soon came to regard Toscanini as his exemplar. In 1927 he became a US citizen.

In 1930 Ormandy was asked to conduct the New York Philharmonic Orchestra in some concerts at the Lewisohn Stadium, and the next year he substituted for Toscanini with the Philadelphia Orchestra, and also took Verbrugghen's place with the Minneapolis Symphony Orchestra. As a result, he was appointed conductor of the Minneapolis Symphony in 1931. When Stokowski sought to reduce his commitment with the Philadelphia Orchestra, Ormandy was appointed his co-conductor, and when in 1938 Stokowski finally left, Ormandy became musical director. He has remained in that position until the present day, although he does accept some engagements as guest conductor with other orchestras. In 1936 he conducted at the Bruckner Festival at Linz, in 1944 toured Australia conducting the Australian Broadcasting Commission's orchestras, and in 1949 visited Britain with the Philadelphia Orchestra. He tours the US regularly with the orchestra, and plays each year at the Saratoga Springs Festival in New York. He conducted at the New York Metropolitan Opera, once, in 1950, and in 1973 took the Philadelphia Orchestra on tour to China. In 1936 the Bruckner Society of America awarded him its medal.

A genial, well-mannered and almost unassuming man, Ormandy could be termed a self-made conductor. His most important influence in his formative years was Toscanini; later Klemperer also influenced him. He has an infallible ear and a prodigious memory, is extraordinarily quick in assimilating new scores, and conducts all music except concertos and contemporary works from memory, but believes that conducting with or without a score makes no difference. Technically he is the equal of any living conductor; his stance on the podium is firm, and he does not feel the need to conduct every note, and mistakes by the players do not upset him. He does not shrink from altering a score if he thinks the change will improve it; he even arranged the choruses from Handel's *Messiah* for orchestra. For a time, a physical impairment prevented him from using a baton. At Minneapolis he had a reputation for severity, but at Philadelphia his relations with his players relaxed considerably. Perhaps this was because he was anxious to ingratiate himself with what was then, in the mid 1930s, one of the finest orchestras in the world. His experience in Minneapolis gave him a special insight into making records effectively; a flaw in the musicians' contract gave them no extra income for recording, and as RCA was interested in building up its classical catalogue, it recorded the orchestra under Ormandy, in two separate sessions of two weeks for 42 hours each week, in 100 separate works. In addition, these records gave him a national reputation as a brilliant recording artist. In any event, he readily acceded to the extensive recording programme RCA had for the Philadelphia Orchestra, and which was vital for the orchestra's financial welfare. Concert programmes and recording schedules were closely integrated so that a minimum of rehearsals were needed for recording. In contrast to Stokowski, Ormandy cultivated good relations with the orchestra's management, although the intensity of the orchestra's activities strained harmony with the players. He chose programmes with obvious box-office appeal, and reduced the number of new or novel scores performed; in fact, he has been criticised for having an outlook primarily economic and utilitarian rather than motivated by artistic values. Even so, Ormandy naturally prefers a conservative approach to programming. Although he performs Bartók, Kodály, Hindemith, Martinů, Prokofiev, Shostakovich, Walton, Penderecki and other 20th-century composers, and has made many fine recordings of modern music, he has no predilection for it, and believes little music written today can compare with the best work of Stravinsky, Berg or Schoenberg. He now plays more contemporary music than he did in his early years with the Philadelphia Orchestra, but then the problem was to retain its audience in difficult economic circumstances. The orchestra's management was happy to be relieved of Stokowski's spectacular excursions into the realm of the musically exotic and expensive.

Ormandy's very virtues, as well as those of the Philadelphia Orchestra, have often led him to be underrated as a conductor. His records are frequently dismissed as highly-polished, glossy performances of little depth or insight, a charge once levelled at Koussevitzky and sometimes more lately at Karajan. The observation has been made, however, that the Ormandy of the recording studio is a contrast to the Ormandy of the concert hall, where passion and spontaneity are certainly not missing. He himself has said: 'Every time I walk on the platform I consider that my life depends on that performance. Of course, that doesn't mean that I'm always at my best, or what comes across is everything I should like, but I am always trying.' Stokowski had created an inimitable sound and style with the Philadelphia Orchestra, which Ormandy has largely maintained, if somewhat modified. He soon abandoned Stokowski's innovation of individual bowing with the strings but could retain their sumptuous, seamless legato. Indeed, in all its departments the orchestra has kept its superb quality. Ormandy has claimed that this special sound is his, and not the orchestra's; this is resented by the orchestra, but, to be fair, it does not take long for Ormandy to recreate that same sound when conducting other orchestras, and when Klemperer came to conduct the Philadelphia Orchestra in his latter years, it sounded like the Philharmonia. The effect produced by Toscanini in his recordings with the orchestra is another case in point. Probably, the sound we hear is a fusion of Ormandy and the orchestra, as may be the case with Karajan and the Berlin Philharmonic.

Some styles of music, such as the baroque and classical, do not come easily to the Philadelphia Orchestra, and by inference to Ormandy; his metier is essentially the middle and late romantics, including Prokofiev and Shostakovich, whose symphonies he has recorded with great success. The classical composers, especially Haydn, Mozart and Schubert, call for a flexibility and elegance of style for which the orchestra's opulence is almost grotesquely unsuited; but Ormandy's Beethoven is scrupulous and weighty, if sometimes a shade too sober. In the 1930s his recordings of Mahler's Symphony No. 2 and Bruckner's Symphony No. 7, although not the first of the latter symphony as he believes (Fried recorded it for Polydor in 1924), made these great works familiar to thousands; however his recent recordings of Bruckner's Symphonies Nos 5 and 7, and Mahler's Symphonies Nos 1 and 2, were sadly short of the standards set by today's interpreters of these composers, being too extrovert, obvious in gesture and occasionally unimaginative. Sibelius, too, is another composer who owed much to Ormandy's pioneering; one of his finest mono LPs was a coupling of the Symphonies Nos 4 and 5, and among his best 78s was an extraordinary *The Return of Lemminkäinen*. In 1963 he surprised many with a very fine disc of music by Delius, regarded at least until then as the sole preserve of British interpreters. The Philadelphia Orchestra has commissioned symphonies by the American composers Harris, Sessions, and Piston, and under Ormandy gave the first performances of Rachmaninov's *Symphonic Dances*, Bartók's Piano Concerto No. 3, and Martinů's Symphony No. 4.

Since his first records with the Minneapolis Symphony Orchestra in 1934–5, Ormandy has become one of the most widely known and most prolific conductors in the history of the record. The Minneapolis discs included many spectacular performances of major and sometimes novel works, as well as more familiar repertoire. Included were the Mahler and Bruckner symphonies mentioned above, Rachmaninov's Symphony No. 2, Sibelius' Symphony No. 1, Schoenberg's *Verklärte Nacht*, Schumann's Symphony No. 4, Beethoven's Symphony No. 4, Griffes' *Pleasure Dome of Kubla Khan* and Carpenter's *Adventures in a Perambulator*. After his arrival in Philadelphia he continued to record with RCA until 1943, and then in 1968 the association was renewed; between 1943 and 1968 Columbia recorded the orchestra. In the first phase with RCA, the major works recorded included Telemann's *Suite in A minor* for flute and strings, a suite from Purcell's *Dido and Aeneas*, Beethoven's Symphonies Nos 1, 7 and 9, Mozart's Divertimento K. 247, Brahms' Symphony No. 2, Double Concerto (with Heifetz and Feuermann) and *Alto Rhapsody* (with Marian Anderson), *Les Préludes*, *Pictures at an Exhibition*, *Daphnis et Chloé* Suite No. 2, *Ein Heldenleben*, *Don Quixote* (with Feuermann) and *Symphonia domestica*, Tchaikovsky's Symphonies Nos 5 and 6, Rachmaninov's Piano Concertos Nos 1, 3 and 4 (with Rachmaninov), Barber's *Essay for Orchestra No. 1*, Harl McDonald's Symphony No. 1 and shorter pieces by Sibelius.

The period with Columbia (1943–68) was incredibly productive, so much so that Ormandy's catalogue of records is far too long to detail. It embraced a few years of 78s, then mono LPs and finally stereo, which called for repeat recordings of some of the staple items. In general, the repertoire was concentrated on the later romantic composers, although the nine Beethoven symphonies, five piano concertos and the Violin Concerto, and the four Brahms symphonies, *Variations on the St Antony Chorale* and *Ein deutsches Requiem* and most of the concertos are represented. Among the works listed are Sibelius' Symphonies Nos 1, 2, 4, 5 and 7, Tchaikovsky's Symphonies Nos 4, 5 and 6 and the reconstruction by Bogatirev called the No. 7, the *Serenade in C major*, the *Romeo and Juliet* fantasy-overture, *1812* overture, *Francesca da Rimini* and suites from the ballets, *Scheherazade*, a suite from *Le Coq d'or* and the *Russian Easter Festival* overture, *Pictures at an Exhibition* (in an orchestration by Lucien Caillet, the bass-clarinettist in the Philadelphia Orchestra, who also arranged some Bach transcriptions), the Franck *Symphony in D minor*, Glière's Symphony No. 3, *Daphnis et Chloé* Suite No. 2, *La Valse*, *Rapsodie espagnole*, *Boléro*, *Le Tombeau de Couperin*, and *Alborada del gracioso*, *La Mer*, *Nocturnes*, *Iberia*, *Prélude à l'après-midi d'un faune* and *La Damoiselle élue*, Saint-Saëns' Symphony No. 3, Rachmaninov's three symphonies, *The Isle of the Dead*, *The Bells* and *Symphonic Dances*, *L'Oiseau de feu*, *Petrushka* and *Le Sacre du printemps*, Delius' *Brigg Fair*, *In a Summer Garden*, Mahler's Symphony No. 10 (in the Deryck Cooke reconstruction) and *Das Lied von der Erde* (with Chookasian and Lewis), the Nielsen Symphonies Nos 1 and 6, Elgar's *Cockaigne* overture and *Enigma Variations*, Vaughan Williams' *Fantasia on a Theme of Thomas Tallis*, Kodály's *Háry János* suite, *Concerto for Orchestra*, *Galánta Dances* and *Marosszék Dances*, Bruckner's Symphony No. 5 and *Te Deum*, the Verdi *Requiem*, some preludes and excerpts from the Wagner operas, Reger's Piano Concerto (with Serkin), Respighi's *Pini di Roma*, *Fontane di Roma*, *Feste Romane*, *Gli uccelli* and *Vetrate di chiesa*, *Don Juan*, *Till Eulenspiegel*, *Also sprach Zarathustra*, *Ein Heldenleben*, *Tod und Verklärung*, *Don Quixote* (with Monroe) and suites from *Der Rosenkavalier* and *Die Frau ohne Schatten*, Prokofiev's Symphonies Nos 1, 4, 5, 6 and 7, the *Lieutenant Kijé* suite, *Scythian Suite* and *Alexander Nevsky*, Bartók's *Bluebeard's Castle*, *Concerto for Orchestra* and a suite from *The Miraculous Mandarin*, Shostakovich's Symphonies Nos 1, 4, 5, 10 and 13, Hindemith's *Nobilissima Visione*, *Mathis der Maler* symphony, *Concert Music for Strings and Brass* and *Symphonic Metamorphosis on Themes by Weber*, Walton's *Belshazzar's Feast* and *Façade* suite, Roussel's *Bacchus et Ariane*, Honegger's *Jeanne d'Arc au bûcher*, Casella's *Paganiniana*, Miaskovsky's Symphony No. 21, Orff's *Carmina Burana* and *Catulli Carmina*, Britten's *Young Person's Guide to the Orchestra*, Ibert's *Escales* and Herbert's *Pan Americana*, *American Fantasy* and *Irish Rhapsody*.

Some of the earlier romantic composers are less evident. Of Dvořák there were Symphony No. 9 and the Cello Concerto (with Rose) – Symphony No. 9 he also recorded with the London Symphony Orchestra; of Schubert, Symphonies Nos 8 and 9, of Schumann, Symphony No. 2; of Berlioz, *Symphonie fantastique* and *Grande Messe des morts*; and of Mendelssohn, Symphony No. 4 and the incidental music for *A Midsummer Night's Dream*. The most popular music of Grieg and Bizet was also recorded. Among the baroque composers, a shortened version, on two LP discs, of *Messiah*, was one of his most popular releases, although its style would have horrified scholars concerned with authenticity. Other Handel music included his own arrangements of the *Water Music* and *Music for the Royal Fireworks*; of Bach he recorded the *Mass in B minor* and *Easter Oratorio*, Violin Concertos No. 1 (with Stern) and No. 2 (with D. Oistrakh), and, in the tradition of Stokowski, a number of transcriptions, including the *Passacaglia and Fugue in C minor*, the *Toccata and Fugue in D minor* and the *Toccata, Adagio and Fugue in C major*. He also recorded Corelli's Concerto Grosso Op. 6 No. 8, Vivaldi's Two-Violin Concertos P. 2, P. 189, P. 281, P. 366 and P. 436 (with Stern and D. Oistrakh), C. P. E. Bach's *Concerto in D* (arranged by Steinberg), J. C. Bach's Sinfonias Op. 18 Nos 1 and 3, W. F. Bach's Sinfonia for Two Flutes and Strings, Haydn's Symphonies Nos 7, 45, 88, 96 and 101, Mozart's Symphonies Nos 30, 31, 40 and 41, the Sinfonia Concertante K. 297b and *Eine kleine Nachtmusik*.

Among Ormandy's earlier 78s were some scenes from Berg's *Wozzeck*, and much later on stereo he recorded the suite from *Lulu*. Other music of the second Viennese school was Schoenberg's *Theme and Variations* op. 43b and Webern's *Im Sommerwind* and *Three Pieces* (both first recordings). American composers were not neglected; he recorded Ives' Symphony No. 1, Harris's *Symphony 1933* and Symphony No. 7, Schuman's Symphonies Nos 3, 4 and 6, *New England Triptych* and *Credendum* (released by Composers Recordings), and symphonies by McDonald, Vincent, Piston, Persichetti, and Rochberg, and other pieces by Hanson, Thomson, Barati, Phillips, Gershwin, Copland, Dello Joio, Kirchner, Gesensway, Gottschalk, Herbert, Barber, Grofé and Yardumian. In addition there were many discs of shorter pieces – overtures, dances, ballet suites, waltzes, marches and arrangements, some of which were extremely popular, and accompaniments to concertos played by Serkin, Arrau, Entremont, Francescatti, Istomin *et al.*

Since his return to RCA in 1968, Ormandy's repertoire has included some additions, although he has repeated many of his previous recorded performances, such as *Pictures at an Exhibition*, *Alexander Nevsky*, Rachmaninov's Symphony No. 2 and *The Bells*, *Scheherazade*, Saint-Saëns' Symphony No. 3, Shostakovich's Symphony No. 5, Sibelius' Symphony No. 2, *Also sprach Zarathustra*, *Pini di Roma*, Tchaikovsky's Symphonies Nos 4, 5 and 6 and suites from the ballets. There have also been accompaniments to concertos played by

Cliburn, Rubinstein, *et al.*, among them the *Yellow River Concerto*. The works to be recorded by Ormandy for the first time included Ives' Symphonies Nos 2 and 3 and *Three Places in New England*, Mahler's Symphonies Nos 1 and 2, Mendelssohn's *Elijah*, Scriabin's *Poème d'extase* and *Prometheus*, the Shostakovich's Symphonies Nos 14 and 15, and Penderecki's The Entombment of Christ from *Utrenja*.

Ormicki, Włodzimierz (1905–74). Born in Kraków, Ormicki studied at the Kraków Conservatory and later at the Vienna and Munich Academies of Music. He was conductor at the Solothurn-Biel Theatre in Switzerland (1927–9), was a teacher at the Kraków School of Music, an assistant at the Bayreuth and Salzburg Festivals (1931–4), appeared as a conductor and accompanist in Vienna, and was conductor at the Operetta at Warsaw (1934–7) and with the Kraków Symphony Orchestra (1937–9). From 1939 to 1945 he was a prisoner in a concentration camp; after the war he resumed his career as co-organiser and conductor of the Polish National Radio Orchestra in Katowice. Then he was successively conductor of the Łódź Philharmonic Orchestra (1948–50), of the Wrocław Opera (1950–53), of the State Opera at Bytom, Silesia, director and conductor of the Wrocław Philharmonic Orchestra and leader of the conductors' classes at the Wrocław and Katowice Academies of Music, conductor of the Polish National Radio and Television Orchestra at Katowice (1965–9), and conductor at the Bydogszcz Opera (1969–74). He often appeared as a guest conductor in Czechoslovakia, Bulgaria, DR Germany and Romania, and at the Grieg Music Festival in Bergen, Norway. Composers Recordings (US) recorded him conducting the Polish National Radio Orchestra in Procter's Symphony No. 1, Adolphus' *Elegy* and Pisk's *Three Ceremonial Rites*.

Ornadel, Cyril (b. 1924). Born in London and educated at the Royal College of Music, Ornadel has been musical director for musical comedies, television productions and films, has composed music for films and stage shows, was director of recording and musical supervisor for *The Living Bible* with Sir Laurence Olivier, conducted the Starlight Symphony Orchestra (1960–68), was founder and director of the RCA Stereoaction Orchestra series (1970), and in 1973 was made an honorary member of the Johann Strauss Society of Great Britain. He recorded for Polydor a two-disc set of the music of the Strauss family, with the London Symphony Orchestra, for which he was awarded a Gold Record LP.

Ostrčil, Otakar (1879–1935). Born at Smechov, near Prague, Ostrčil received a university education, and until 1920 was a professor of modern languages. At the same time he studied at the Prague Conservatory (1893–5), was a pupil for composition with Fibich (1895–1900), and conducted an amateur orchestra (1909–22). He became the operatic conductor at the Vinohrady Theatre in Prague (1914–19), and was principal conductor at the Prague National Opera (1920–35), where he enjoyed a distinguished tenure. He composed operas and orchestral music, of which the opera *Poupě* (1911) and the *Calvary Variations* for orchestra (1928) are amongst the best known. HMV issued on 78 r.p.m. discs a complete recording of *The Bartered Bride*, in which he conducted the Czech National Opera Orchestra.

Otten, Kees (b. 1924). Otten studied at the Amsterdam Lyceum of Music, and in the years 1945–60 became the leading authority on the recorder and its music in the Netherlands. He studied the music of the early periods of musical history, and in 1963 formed and directed the Syntagma Musicum, a group dedicated to recreate the music of the Middle Ages and Renaissance, played on original instruments. With the Syntagma Musicum he recorded an outstanding three-disc album, which included a representative selection of music from the 13th to the 17th centuries, and which was issued in the United States by Seraphim.

Otterloo, Willem van (1907–78). Born at Winterswijk, Holland, Otterloo first studied medicine but finally entered the Amsterdam Conservatory where he studied the cello and composition under Dresden (1928–32). In 1932 he won a competition for composition and conducted his winning Suite with the Concertgebouw Orchestra; that year he became an assistant conductor with the Utrecht Municipal Orchestra, in which he had been a cellist, and studied conducting with Schuricht. He was appointed chief conductor of the Utrecht orchestra (1937–47), conducted opera in Amsterdam (1947–9), and was conductor of the Hague Philharmonic Orchestra, which is also known as the Residentie Orchestra (1949–72), and the Radio Philharmonic Orchestra at Hilversum. In 1967 he became chief conductor of the Melbourne Symphony Orchestra in Australia, then was its principal guest conductor (1969–71), and in 1973, until his death, was chief conductor of the Sydney Symphony Orchestra. He was from 1972 also general music director of the Düsseldorf Symphony Orchestra, taught at the international courses for conducting held annually by the Netherlands Radio Union, and was a guest conductor in many European countries, in Japan and in North and South America. In 1963 he toured with the Hague Philharmonic Orchestra in the United States, and took the Melbourne Symphony Orchestra to Expo '67 in Canada, and later to the US in 1970. His compositions were influenced by Stravinsky and included a symphony and other orchestral works. He died in a car accident in Melbourne on the eve of his retirement.

Otterloo was a complete musician and an accurate interpreter of music ranging from Haydn to the 20th century. His performances of Haydn, Mozart, Schubert, Beethoven and Brahms were stylish and distinctive, although cool in temperament. With Franck, Berlioz, Mahler and Bruckner he was authoritative; his three recordings of *Symphonie fantastique* were especially distinguished. He conducted mostly from memory, and his exhaustive knowledge of scores made him unloved among musicians. At rehearsals he was strict and economical, talked sparingly, and corrected only technical mistakes. Before an audience, his undemonstrative manner disguised his involvement with the music he was conducting.

In the 1950s in particular, Otterloo made a prolific number of recordings. Prior to this he had recorded several 78 r.p.m. sets for Decca of Brahms' *Tragic Overture*, *Hungarian Dance No. 1*, and Glazunov Violin Concerto (with Szekely, and the Hague Philharmonic Orchestra). For Philips, on LP, he recorded with a number of orchestras, and included in his discography were many shorter pieces, as well as major symphonic works and many concerto accompaniments. With his own Hague Philharmonic Orchestra he recorded, for Philips, Bach's Double Violin Concerto (with Krebbers and Olof) the Handel/Harty *Water Music* and *Music for the Royal Fireworks*, Haydn's Symphonies Nos 45, 55 and 92, Mozart's Symphonies Nos 29 and 34, Beethoven's Symphonies Nos 8 and 9, the overtures *Coriolan*, *Egmont* and *Leonore No. 2*, Piano Concerto No. 5 (with de Groot), Violin Concerto (with Krebbers) and Romances Nos 1 (with Olof) and 2 (with Krebbers), Schubert's Symphony No. 8, the overture *Die Zauberharfe*, pieces from *Rosamunde* and *Marche militaire No. 1*, Schumann's *Manfred* overture and Piano Concerto (with Haskil), *Les Préludes*, *Mazeppa* and *Hungaria*, and Liszt's Piano Concerto No. 2 (with de Groot), the overture to *Der Freischütz* and *Invitation to the Dance*, Chopin's Piano Concerto No. 1 (with Uninsky) and *Krakowiak* (with Magaloff), *Symphonie fantastique* and the overtures *Béatrice et Bénédict* and *Les Francs-juges*, Siegfried Idyll, Brahms' Symphony No. 1, *Academic Festival* and *Tragic Overtures*, and *Variations on the St Antony Chorale*, Bruckner's Symphony No. 4, Franck's *Symphony in D minor* and *Psyché*, Saint-Saëns' Symphony No. 3 and *Introduction et rondo capriccioso* (with Krebbers), Tchaikovsky's Symphony No. 4, Piano Concerto No. 1 (with Uninsky and Magaloff) and excerpts from *The Sleeping Beauty*, the two *L'Arlésienne* suites, the Glazunov and Sibelius Violin Concertos (with Magyar), the Grieg Piano Concerto (with Simon), the two *Peer Gynt* suites, *Four Norwegian Dances* and *Two Elegiac Melodies*, Alfvén's *Swedish Rhapsody No. 1*, the Lalo Cello Concerto, Bloch's *Schelomo* and Bruch's *Kol Nidrei* (with de Machula), Rachmaninov's Piano Concertos Nos 1 and 2 (with de Groot) and *Rhapsody on a Theme of Paganini* (with Simon), Reger's *Romantic Suite* and *Variations and Fugue on a Theme of Mozart*, Mahler's Symphony No. 4 (with Stich-Randall) and *Kindertotenlieder* (with Schey), Ravel's *Alborada del gracioso*, *Valses nobles et sentimentales*, *Daphnis et Chloé* Suites Nos 1 and 2, and *Pavane pour une infante défunte*, Khachaturian's Piano Concerto (with Boukoff), Prokofiev's Piano Concerto No. 3 (with Uninsky), Vieuxtemps' Violin Concerto No. 4 (with Krebbers), Gould's *Spirituals* and *Interplay* (with de Groot), Falla's *Three-cornered Hat* dances, Orthel's Symphony No. 2, Andriessen's *Kuhnau Variations* and *Ricercare*, Wagenaar's overtures *The Taming of the Shrew* and *Cyrano de Bergerac*, Diepenbrock's *Elektra* suite and Dresden's *Dance Flashes for Orchestra*.

For Philips he also recorded the Franck *Symphony in D minor* and *Les Éolides* (with the Amsterdam Concertgebouw Orchestra), the overtures *Le Carnaval romain* and *Benvenuto Cellini*, the March from *Les Troyens*, and excerpts from the *Roméo et Juliette* symphony and *La Damnation de Faust* (with the Lamoureux Orchestra), *Symphonie fantastique* (with the Berlin Philharmonic Orchestra), Mozart's Symphonies Nos 36 and 38, and Piano Concertos K. 414 and K. 415 (with de Groot), Beethoven's Symphonies Nos 4, 5 and 6, several overtures and Piano Concertos Nos 1, 2, 3 and 4 (with de Groot) and No. 5 (with Magaloff), Paganini's Violin Concerto No. 1 (with Krebbers), the Brahms Violin Concerto (with Auclair), Bruckner's Symphony No. 7 and *Overture in G minor*, the Polovtsian Dances from *Prince Igor*, *A Night on the Bare*

Mountain and excerpts from *The Sleeping Beauty* (with the Vienna Symphony Orchestra). His other recordings included Chopin's Piano Concerto No. 1 and *Krakowiak* (with Askenase and the Hague Philharmonic Orchestra for DGG), Beethoven's Symphonies Nos 8 and 9, Schumann's Symphony No. 4, Brahms' Piano Concerto No. 2, Tchaikovsky's Piano Concerto No. 1 and Chopin's *Krakowiak* (with Magaloff, and the Hague Philharmonic Orchestra *et al.* for La Guilde Internationale du Disque), Beethoven's Symphony No. 7 and *König Stephan* overture, *Scheherazade* and Mahler's Symphony No. 1 (with the Vienna Festival Orchestra for GID), Mozart's Oboe Concerto (with Webb) and Serenade K. 361, Beethoven's Symphony No. 7, *Symphonie fantastique* and the overture *Le Carnaval romain*, *Daphnis et Chloé* Suite No. 2, *Psyché*, *Ein Heldenleben*, Debussy's *Danse sacrée et danse profane*, Ravel's *Introduction et allegro* and Martin's *Petite suite concertante* (with the Sydney Symphony Orchestra for RCA), Brahms' Symphony No. 4 and the prelude to *Die Meistersinger* (with the Sydney Symphony Orchestra for Darrell Fraser), and the Australian composer Hughes' *Sinfonietta* (with the Melbourne Symphony Orchestra for World Record Club). He also conducted a series of discs of music by Dutch composers for Donemus: H. Andriessen's Symphony No. 3, J. Andriessen's Flute Concerto (with Verheul), Badings' Harp Concerto (with Berghout) and Pijper's Piano Concerto (with Bruins and the Netherlands Radio Orchestra), Diepenbrock's *Elektra* Suite (with the Amsterdam Concertgebouw Orchestra), Monnikendam's *Arbeid*, Pijper's Symphony No. 3, Roos' *Suggestioni* and Voormolen's *Chaconne and Fugue* (with the Hague Philharmonic Orchestra), Paap's *Garlands of Music* (with the Netherlands Radio Chamber Orchestra) and his own *Sinfonietta* (with the Utrecht Symphony Orchestra).

Ötvös, Gabor (b. 1935). Born in Budapest, Ötvös commenced his musical studies there, went to Italy in 1956 where he made his debut as a conductor in Trieste, conducted the Santa Cecilia Orchestra and the Italian Radio Orchestra in Rome, and at the operas in Naples and Venice, then conducted in Hamburg, Berlin, Frankfurt am Main, Vienna and Amsterdam. He became chief conductor of the Hamburg Symphony Orchestra (1961), first conductor of the Frankfurt Opera (1967), conducted at the New York City Opera and in Los Angeles (1969) and after a sensational performance of Janáček's *The Makropoulos Affair* in New York, was engaged for the New York Metropolitan Opera (1971–3). Since 1972 he has been general music director at Augsburg, where he has led a repertoire from Mozart to Shostakovich. For Westminster he recorded symphonies by Kraus and Flitz, and a sinfonia concertante by J. C. Bach, with the Vienna Radio Orchestra.

Oubradous, Fernand (b. 1903). Born in Paris, Oubradous was educated at the Paris Conservatoire, was musical director of the Théâtre de l'Atelier (1925–30), solo bassoon player with the French National Radio Orchestra (1934–5) and with the Paris Opéra Orchestra (1935–53), and artistic director and conductor at the Lille Theatre (1947–8). He was also a professor at the Paris Conservatoire (1942–70) and at the Salzburg Mozarteum (1954–8), was president and founder of the International Summer Academy at Nice (from 1958), president of the French Chamber Music Association (1961), and a member of the programme committee of the French Radio-Television Organisation (1964–73). In 1927 he founded his own chamber music ensemble, Le Trio d'Anches, in 1940 was president and founder of the Orchestre Fernand Oubradous, and has appeared at many European festivals. His compositions include orchestral and chamber music, and he has edited works of many baroque composers, which have been published by Éditions Musicales Transatlantiques, along with scores of modern French composers such as Jolivet, Françaix and Sauget. His publications also include the study *The Technique of the Bassoon*. He has been made, *inter alia*, Commandeur de l'Ordre National du Mérite (1973).

Oubradous has recorded as a bassoonist and as a conductor; in the latter capacity he has made 78 r.p.m. recordings for HMV and L'Oiseau Lyre with the Paris Wind Instruments Society, the L'Oiseau Lyre Ensemble and other groups. The works recorded include Bach's *Ein musikalisches Opfer* (in his own arrangement) and *Brandenburg Concerto No. 1*, a number of Mozart cassations, divertimenti, serenades and concertos, in particular the Serenades K. 361 and K. 388 and the Sinfonia Concertante K. 297b and Horn Concerto K. 447 (with Trevet), Beethoven's *Rondino in E flat major*, as well as Gounod's *Petite Symphonie*, Hahn's *Concerto provençal*, and pieces by Pierné, Ibert and Roussel. Pathé issued a number of LP discs in the 1950s in which he directed the Paris Chamber Orchestra and other groups in more Mozart works, such as the Symphony No. 31, *Les petits riens*, the Sinfonia Concertante K. 297b, the *Overture in B flat* K. 311a, the

Clarinet Concerto (with Delécluse), Horn Concertos K. 417 (with Del Vescovo) and K. 447 (with Thenet) and Flute and Harp Concerto (with Brun and Laskine), also music by Couperin, Rameau and Grétry, Ibert's *Symphonie concertante*, Hindemith's *Concerto da camera* for flute and oboe, Stravinsky's Suites Nos 1 and 2, and *L'Histoire du soldat*. Classics Club have also released a record with him conducting an unnamed group in Milhaud's *La Création du monde*, and Vogue eight concertos of Vivaldi (with the Paris Chamber Orchestra), and Rococo Hahn's *Piano Concerto in E major* (with Tagliafero) and *Concerto provençal* (with an unnamed orchestra).

Overhoff, Kurt (b. 1902). Born in Vienna, Overhoff studied there, and in 1925 his opera *Mira* was staged with great success at Essen. He was conductor at Münster for twelve years, was an assistant to Furtwängler and Roller at the Vienna State Opera, and was music director at Koblenz and general music director at Heidelberg. From 1940 until the resumption of the Bayreuth Festivals in 1951 he was entrusted with the musical education of Wieland Wagner, who made his first successful production of *The Ring* at Altenburg, with Overhoff conducting. More recently he has been involved in producing Siegfried Wagner's fairy-tale operas, and has written several important books about the Wagner operas. In 1947 he formed the Bayreuth Symphony Orchestra which was composed of refugee musicians from Eastern Europe; he has also more recently been a visiting professor at the University of Texas. In 1962 Overhoff wrote his *Bayreuth Bilderbogen* suite, which was dedicated to the city of Bayreuth and was widely performed. He recorded the work for Colosseum with the Nuremberg Symphony Orchestra.

Ozawa, Seiji (b. 1935). Born of Japanese parents in Hoten, Manchuria, when it was occupied by the Japanese, Ozawa was introduced to Western music by his Christian mother; his father was a Buddhist. He studied the piano from the age of seven, and before his mid teens he was familiar with all of Bach's keyboard music. The family moved to Tokyo, and in 1951 he entered the Toho School of Music, studying composition and conducting under Saito. Because of an injury to two of his fingers, he was obliged to abandon a career as a pianist, and took up conducting. In 1954 he conducted the NHK and Japanese Philharmonic Orchestras, but scarcity of opportunity in Japan, apart from writing film music, caused him to come to Europe, having persuaded a Japanese motor company to give him a motor scooter to drive around Europe as a form of promotion. In Paris he studied conducting with Bigot, entered and won the International Competition for Young Conductors at Besançon in 1959, and then Munch invited him to study at Tanglewood, Massachusetts. There, after a year, he was awarded the Koussevitzky Memorial Scholarship, and made his debut as a conductor at Carnegie Hall, New York, in 1961. That year he won another scholarship to study in Berlin with Karajan; in Berlin Bernstein met him when he was touring with the New York Philharmonic Orchestra, and took him as assistant conductor on a tour of Japan with the orchestra. Again, in Japan, he found limited opportunities, and went to the United States as assistant to Bernstein. He was musical director of the Chicago Symphony Orchestra's summer concerts at Ravinia Park (1963–4), conducted the Lewisohn Stadium Orchestra in New York (1963–4) and the Toho String Orchestra during its tour to New York (1964). He was then appointed musical director of the Toronto Symphony Orchestra (1965–8) which he led on tours to the United States, Britain and France, and at the same time was musical director of the Nissei Theatre at Tokyo. He was musical director of the San Francisco Symphony Orchestra (1970–75) and retained his connection with it afterwards as musical adviser and guest conductor, is musical adviser to the New Japan Philharmonic Orchestra (since 1968), was joint artistic director of the Boston Symphony Orchestra's summer music festival at Tanglewood, and then was appointed musical director of the Boston Symphony in 1973. In that year he toured Europe with the San Francisco Symphony. Previously he had made his London debut with the London Symphony Orchestra in 1964, appeared at the Salzburg Festival in 1969, and at Covent Garden in 1976.

Ozawa is one of the foremost of the younger generation of conductors, and possesses an indefinable charismatic quality, maybe learned from his mentors Karajan and Bernstein. In his reluctance to discuss himself, he has a reputation for aloofness and arrogance, not to say inscrutability, with journalists and the public, although he has good rapport with his players. His musical tastes are eclectic and he has on occasion attempted to bring together, at concerts, jazz and serious music. His choice of dress eschews the conventional Western manner. He is, nonetheless, an exact, energetic and authoritative musician, with an exemplary baton technique and a most sensitive ear for tone and balance. On the podium his movements are extrovert and graceful. His performances are praised for their transparent texture, well conceived tempi and superlative playing, and under him the Boston Symphony Orchestra has been restored to the magnificence of its days with Koussevitzky and Munch. Some critics in Boston find his interpretations uninteresting and occasionally superficial, despite their polish; perhaps for this reason he is at his best in the music of the impressionists and the 20th century.

RCA, EMI, DGG, CBS and Philips have all recorded Ozawa, with a variety of orchestras. His first discs were of the *Turangalîla Symphony* of Messiaen, and Takemitsu's *November Steps*, *Asterism*, *Requiem* and *Green – The Dorian Horizon* (with the Toronto Symphony Orchestra for RCA), *Symphonie fantastique* (with the Toronto Symphony, for CBS, and re-issued later on Odyssey), and Honegger's *Jeanne d'Arc au bûcher* (with the London Symphony Orchestra *et al.* for CBS). Subsequently with the Chicago Symphony Orchestra he recorded Bartók's *Concerto for Orchestra*, Kodály's *Dances of Galánta*, Janáček's *Sinfonietta*, Lutosławski's *Concerto for Orchestra*, *Scheherazade* and the Polovtsian Dances from *Prince Igor* (for EMI); and Tchaikovsky's Symphony No. 5, Beethoven's Symphony No. 5, Schubert's Symphony No. 8, *A Night on the Bare Mountain*, *Le Sacre du printemps*, *Petrushka*, *L'Oiseau de feu*, *Pictures at an Exhibition* and *The Young Person's Guide to the Orchestra* (for RCA); with the Boston Symphony Orchestra Beethoven's Piano Concerto No. 5 (with Eschenbach), *La Damnation de Faust*, *Symphonie fantastique* and the *Roméo et Juliette* symphony, *The Three-cornered Hat*, the Shostakovich Cello Concerto No. 2 and Glazunov's *Chant du Ménestrel* (with Rostropovich), *Boléro*, *Rapsodie espagnole*, *La Valse*, *Daphnis et Chloé*, *Valses nobles et sentimentales*, *Alborada del gracioso*, *Une Barque sur l'océan*, *Pavane pour une infante défunte*, *Menuet antique*, *Le Tombeau de Couperin* and *Ma Mère l'Oye*, Ives' Symphony No. 4 and *Central Park in the Dark* (for DGG); with the New Philharmonia Orchestra Mozart's Symphonies Nos 28 and 35, the Beethoven Violin Concerto arranged for piano (with Peter Serkin) and *Carmina Burana* (for RCA), Beethoven's Symphony No. 9 (for Philips), Khachaturian's Piano Concerto No. 1 and Liszt's *Hungarian Fantasia* (with Entremont, for CBS); with the San Francisco Symphony Orchestra a suite from *West Side Story* and Russo's *Three Pieces for Blues Band and Orchestra*, the *Romeo and Juliet* fantasy-overture, excerpts from Prokofiev's *Romeo and Juliet* and from Berlioz' *Roméo et Juliette* symphony (for DGG), Beethoven's Symphony No. 3 (for Philips); with the Orchestre de Paris Tchaikovsky's Symphony No. 6, *L'Oiseau de feu*, excerpts from *Nutcracker* and *The Sleeping Beauty* (for Philips) and concerto accompaniments for Weissenberg and Beroff (for EMI); with the Japan Philharmonic Orchestra Takemitsu's *Cassiopeia* (for EMI); oboe concertos by Telemann, Vivaldi and Handel (with Gomberg and the Columbia Chamber Orchestra for CBS); with the London Symphony Orchestra Tchaikovsky's Piano Concerto No. 1 (with Browning), the Mendelssohn and Tchaikovsky Violin Concertos (with Friedman) Strauss's *Burleske* and the Schumann Piano Concerto (with Pennario, for RCA); and MacMillan's *Sketches for Strings on French Canadian Airs*, Freedman's *Images*, Mercure's *Triptyque* and Morel's *L'Étoile noire* (with the Toronto Symphony Orchestra for CBS).

P

Page, Willis (b. 1918). Born in Rochester, NY, Page graduated at the Eastman School of Music and studied conducting with Monteux. He played the double-bass in the Boston Symphony Orchestra (1940–55), was conductor of the New Orchestral Society of Boston (later the Boston Festival Orchestra), was associate conductor of the Buffalo Philharmonic Orchestra (1954–9), conductor of the Nashville Symphony Orchestra (1959–67) and of the Yomiuri Nippon Symphony Orchestra (1962–3), thus being the first American to be a regular conductor of a major Japanese orchestra. He was conductor of the Des Moines Symphony Orchestra (1969–71) and has been conductor and musical director of the Jacksonville Symphony Orchestra, Florida, since 1971. His academic appointments include professor of conducting at the Eastman School (1967–9) and also at the Drake University, Des Moines (1969–71). In 1976 he conducted a special concert at the Kennedy Center, Washington DC, for the US bicentennial celebrations, and was conductor of an orchestra made of graduates, students and faculty members of the Eastman School to commemorate Howard Hanson's 80th birthday.

In the mid 1950s, Page made a series of ten LP discs for Cook Laboratories with the Boston Orchestral Society, which was in reality composed entirely of members of the Boston Symphony Orchestra. These performances were competent enough, but were distinguished more by the exceptional standard of the recording; some were claimed to be the first stereophonic records made in the US. The works recorded included the Brandenburg Concerto No. 3 and a suite for strings arranged by Bachrich from movements of Bach's violin sonatas and partitas, Haydn's Symphony No.100, Mozart's Symphony No. 40, Beethoven's Symphony No. 5, Brahms' Symphony No. 1, Tchaikovsky's *Romeo and Juliet* fantasy-overture and *Serenade in C major*, Dubois' *The Seven Last Words of Christ*, Debussy's *Nuages*, *Fêtes*, *Danse* and *Prélude à l'après-midi d'un faune*, Honegger's *Pacific 231*, Barber's *Adagio*, Stravinsky's *Concerto for String Orchestra*, Villa-Lobos' *Bachianas brasileiras No. 5*, the overtures to *Euryanthe* and *La gazza ladra*, *Danse macabre*, *Kaiserwalzer*, the prelude to Act I of *Carmen*, Brahms' *Hungarian Dance No. 5*, and short pieces by Mendelssohn and Rimsky-Korsakov. Rondo also issued Schubert's Symphony No. 8 (with the Boston Orchestral Society) and Kapp the *Rhapsody in Blue* (with Williams and the Symphony of the Air).

Paillard, Jean-François (b. 1928). Born in Vitry-le-François, Paillard studied at the Paris Conservatoire, with Dufourcq for musicology, and with Markevitch at the Salzburg Mozarteum for conducting. In 1953 he founded the Ensemble Instrumental Jean-Marie Leclair, which was renamed in 1959 the Jean-François Paillard Chamber Orchestra, with which he has toured many countries, including Japan (four times), Korea, North and South America and Australia. He conducted the Osaka Philharmonic Orchestra (1970), teaches at spring and summer conducting courses, has published *La Musique française classique* (1960), since 1962 has been director of 'Archives de la Musique Instrumentale' and of 'Archives de la Musique Religieuse' for the Éditions Costallat, Paris, and has received the order Chevalier de l'Ordre National du Mérite. With his orchestra, Paillard has achieved an international reputation, partly through gramophone records; the orchestra's repertoire is primarily of the French baroque composers, such as Lully and Corrette, whom he was largely instrumental in reviving. The orchestra uses modern instruments, and its style of performance, although polished, straightforward and spirited, is now tending to be recognised as not fully authentic. Nonetheless, as with other great European chamber orchestras of the pre-war and post-war decades, the music of the baroque era was revealed virtually for the first time to a vast audience, particularly through records which have been immensely popular in many countries as well as France. Paillard has been awarded nineteen Grands Prix du Disque of the Académie Charles Cros, Disque Français and Disque Lyrique, the Prix Edison (Holland), the German Record Prize and the Gold Record (Japan).

Paillard and his orchestra have made over 200 discs for Erato, and many of them have been issued in other countries by Westminster, Musical Heritage Society, Epic, RCA, World Record Club, *et al.* Included have been the Bach *Brandenburg Concertos*, Suites, *Ein musikalisches Opfer*, Harpsichord Concertos (with Veyron-Lacroix *et al.*) and excerpts from Cantatas Nos 75 and 140, Handel's *Alexander's Feast*, Concerti Grossi Op. 3 and 6, Flute Concerto (with Rampal), two Harp Concertos (with Laskine), three Oboe Concertos (with Pierlot), Organ Concertos (with Alain), Trumpet Concerto (with André), Violin Concerto (with Jarry), Concerto for Double Orchestra No. 1, *Music for the Royal Fireworks*, *Water Music* and *Dettingen Te Deum*, Albinoni's Concertos Op. 5 No. 5 and Op. 7 No. 3 and Trumpet Concertos (with André), Aldrovandini's Sinfonia for Trumpet and Orchestra No. 2 (with André), Aubert's Four-Violin Concerto (with Fernandez), Sinfonias by Bononcini, Biscogli's Oboe, Trumpet and Bassoon Concerto (with Pierlot, André and Hongne), Corelli's Concerti Grossi Op. 6 Nos 7 to 10, Couperin's *Les Nations* and Sonata No. 1, Delalande's Suite No. 4 from *Symphonies pour les soupers du Roy*, Exaudet's *Minuetto gracioso*, Charpentier's *Messe de minuit*, *Te Deum*, *Magnificat*, and excerpt from *In nativitatem Domini* and Sonate à 8, Fasch's Trumpet and Two-Oboe Concerto (with André, Pierlot and Chambon) and two Sinfonias, Corrette's Concerto Comique No. 4, Gossec's Sinfonia Concertante, Saint-Georges's Sinfonia Concertante, Schobert's Harpsichord Concerto (with Beckensteiner), Morin's *La Chasse du cerf*, Francoeur's Suites Nos 2 and 4 from *Simphonie du festin* (with André), eleven Canzoni and two Sonatas from Gabrieli's *Sacrae symphoniae*, Jacchini's Trumpet Concerto and Sonata for Trumpet and Strings (with André), Flute Concertos by Corrette, Devienne, Leclair and Molter (with Rampal), Trumpet Concertos by Stradella, Telemann, Torelli, Vivaldi, Manfredini, Hertel, Tessarini, Veracini, Leopold Mozart and Haydn (with André), Marais' *Alcyone* suite, Oboe Concertos by Leclair, Cimarosa, and Bellini (with Pierlot), Lully's *Amadis* Suite de Symphonies, minuet from *Le Bourgeois gentilhomme*, scenes from *Isis*, *Armide* and *Hippolyte et Aricie*, *Dies Irae*, *Miserere* and *Te Deum*, Mouret's *Symphonies de chasse* and two suites, Pachelbel's *Canon* and two suites, a sinfonia of Pallavicino, Rameau's *Les Indes galantes* and *Concerts en sextuor No. 2*, Ricciotti's Six Concertinos (formerly attributed to Pergolesi), an overture and sinfonia of Sammartini, concertos and suites by Telemann and Vivaldi, Zipoli's Adagio, three Violin Concertos of Leclair (with Fernandez), two concertos of Locatelli, Michael Haydn's Horn Concerto (with Barboteu), Organ Concerto (with Alain) and Trumpet Concertos Nos 2 and 3 (with André), Haydn's Piano Concerto No. 1 (with Alain), Two-Horn Concertos (with Barboteu and Coursier) and Violin Concertos Nos 1, 2 and 4 (with Jarry), Hummel's Mandolin Concerto (with Saint-Clivier), Introduction, Theme and Variations (with Chambon) and *Rondeau de société* (with Queffélec), Harp Concertos of Krumpholz and Boieldieu (with Laskine), the minuet from Gluck's *Orfeo ed Euridice*, Leopold Mozart's Sinfonia di Caccia, Mozart's Divertimenti K. 187, K. 188 and K. 334, Clarinet Concerto (with Lancelot), Violin Concertos K. 218 and K. 219 (with Jarry), Flute and Harp Concerto (with Rampal and Laskine) and *German Dances*, Schubert's *German Dances*, C. P. E. Bach's *Organ Concerto in E flat* (with Alain), Tchaikovsky's *Serenade in C major*, Dvořák's *Serenade in E minor*, Poulenc's *Aubade* (with Richter), Blavet's Flute Concerto (with Rampal) and *Le Jaloux corrigé*, Debussy's *Danse sacrée et danse profane* (with Laskine), *Épigraphes antiques* and *Petite suite*, Honegger's Symphony No. 2, Roussel's *Sinfonietta*, Schmitt's *Janiana Symphony*, Shostakovich's Piano Concerto No. 1 (with d'Arco and André), Mihalovici's *Esercizio per archi* and Villa-Lobos' Guitar Concerto (with Santos) and *Sextuor mystique*. Also with a brass and woodwind ensemble, Paillard recorded music by Dampierre, Lully, Philidor *et al.*, under the title *La Grande Écurie de Versailles*.

Paita, Carlos (b. 1932). Born in Buenos Aires, Paita first studied law, but abandoned it for a musical career, although continuing to study philosophy at the University of Buenos Aires. He was a pupil of Neuchoff for piano, Fischer for composition and Rodzinski for conducting, and came into contact with Furtwängler when the latter visited Argentina and later in Europe. Paita's first appearances as a conductor were in Buenos Aires with the National Radio Chamber Orchestra, and in 1964 he led a performance of the Verdi *Requiem* at the Teatro Colón, as a tribute to President Kennedy. In that year he was invited by the United States government to make a study tour of the US, and when he returned to Buenos Aires in 1965 he conducted a gala performance of Mahler's Symphony No. 2, which was the work's première in South America. During a visit to Europe he was engaged to conduct the Belgian Radio Orchestra; soon after the Decca Record Company took him under contract. He has since conducted many of the major European orchestras, and since 1969 has lived in Geneva. His first disc for Decca was in 1969 with the New Philharmonia Orchestra, of the prelude to *Die Meistersinger*, the overture to *Der fliegende Holländer* and the prelude and Liebestod to *Tristan und Isolde*; it was immediately acclaimed for its insight and musicality. His later recordings, of the overtures *Le Carnaval romain*, *Leonore No. 3*, *Academic Festival* and *Rienzi* (with the Netherlands Radio Orchestra), and the Verdi *Requiem* (with the Royal Philharmonic Orchestra *et al.*), were noted for their committed and highly dramatic readings.

Pál, Tamás (b. 1937). After studying with Viski and Kórody at the Franz Liszt Academy at Budapest, Pál graduated in 1964, joined the Budapest State Opera as a conductor, and also became acclaimed as a symphonic conductor. He led the Budapest State Opera in performances at the Edinburgh Festival (1973) and the Wiesbaden May Festival (1974), received the Liszt Prize (1974), and was appointed principal conductor of the Szeged Symphony Orchestra and Opera (1975). His recordings, for Hungaroton, include Liszt's Piano Concerto No. 2 (with Kiss and the Hungarian State Orchestra), Kalmar's *Notturno No. 1*, and Brahms' Symphony No. 3 and *Academic Festival Overture* (with the Budapest Symphony Orchestra).

Panizza, Ettore (1875–1967). Born in Buenos Aires of Italian parents, Panizza studied in Milan at the Giuseppe Verdi Conservatory, and started his career as a conductor in Italy in 1899. He appeared at opera houses at Palermo, Naples, Rome, Bologna *et al.*, conducted the Italian repertoire at Covent Garden (1907–14 and in 1924), was co-director with Toscanini at La Scala, Milan (1921–9, returning there in 1930–32 and 1946–8); he was chief conductor at the New York Metropolitan (1934–42), and also conducted opera and symphony concerts in Berlin, Vienna, Chicago, Buenos Aires *et al.* At La Scala he conducted *The Ring* (1926) and the first performances in Italy of *Khovanshchina* and *Tsar Saltan*. His own compositions included symphonic music and operas, of which *Aurora* and *Besanzo* were successfully presented in Buenos Aires; he translated Berlioz's treatise on orchestration into Italian. As a conductor he was comparable in style to Toscanini and de Sabata. He recorded, in Italy well before World War II, Mendelssohn's Symphony No. 4, and the Wedding March, from *A Midsummer Night's Dream* the overtures to *Anacreon* and *Il segreto di Susanna*, Casella's *Il convento veneziano*, excerpts from Mancinelli's *Cleopatra* and *Scene veneziane*, Nápravník's *Song of the Nightingale*, Martucci's *Notturno* and Pick-Mangiagalli's *Notturno – Rondo fantastico* (with the La Scala Orchestra for HMV), Respighi's *Pini di Roma* (with the Milan Symphony Orchestra for Decca), and some accompaniments to operatic arias. Rococo have recently issued *Un ballo in maschera*, which he conducts.

Panufnik, Andrzej (b. 1914). Born in Warsaw where his father was a violin maker and his mother a musician of English origin, Panufnik studied at the Warsaw Conservatory (1932–6), was a pupil of Weingartner at the Vienna Academy of Music (1937–8), and continued his musical studies in Paris and London. He was in Poland throughout World War II, took an active part in the underground and played the piano together with Lutosławski in night-clubs in occupied Warsaw. All his compositions were destroyed in the Warsaw uprising of 1944. He was appointed conductor of the Kraków Philharmonic Orchestra and music director of Polish State Film Productions (1945–6), was director of the Warsaw Philharmonic Orchestra (1946–7), began to achieve recognition as a composer, and was awarded prizes for his *Nocturne* and *Sinfonia rustica*, was elected vice-chairman (with Honegger) of the International Music Council of UNESCO (1950) and travelled throughout China as the head of a Polish cultural delegation (1953). The communist authorities in Poland denounced his music, but nonetheless he went to Helsinki to conduct his *Heroic Overture* at the Olympic Games in 1952; in 1954 he left Poland as a protest against political control over creative artists, settled in Britain with his British-born wife, conducted leading British orchestras and was music director and conductor of the City of Birmingham Symphony Orchestra (1957–9). He then gave up full-time conducting to concentrate mainly on composition; his works have been performed and recorded by Horenstein and Stokowski, he won first prize with his *Sinfonia sacra* in the Prince Rainier Competition in 1963, and was awarded the Sibelius Centenary Medal for composition in 1965. In 1967 he recorded for Unicorn his *Sinfonia sacra* and *Sinfonia rustica* with the Monte Carlo Opera Orchestra, and the disc was re-issued in 1974; some have described this music as pretentious, but Edward Greenfield, in *The Gramophone*, somewhat paradoxically called the *Sinfonia rustica* a 'finely judged Soviet-style symphony full of colourful ideas presented skilfully'. For EMI he also conducted the Menuhin Festival Orchestra in his *Sinfonia concertante* and Violin Concerto, with Menuhin the soloist.

Panula, Jorma (b. 1930). Born in Kauhajoki, Finland, Panula studied at the Church Music College and Sibelius Academy in Helsinki

(1949–53) with Funtek, with Dean Dixon at Lund, with Wolff and Ferrara at Hilversum, and in Austria and France. He conducted at theatres at Lahti (1953–5), Tampere (1955–8) and Helsinki (1958–62), founded the chamber orchestra at the Sibelius Academy, was conductor of the Turku City Orchestra (1963–5), the Helsinki Philharmonic Orchestra (1965–7) and the Aarhus City Orchestra in Denmark (1973), as well as the student orchestra at the Helsinki Institute of Technology (1959–63) and the Choir 'Akateeminen Laulu' at Helsinki (1961–3). He has been a guest conductor in the USSR, the United States and Europe, has a special interest in Mahler, Bruckner, Bartók and Shostakovich, and is recognised in his own country for his sensitivity and rapport with his players, and for his association with contemporary music, particularly of Finnish composers. He has been professor of conducting at the Sibelius Academy (since 1973), and has composed orchestral, choral and vocal works, musicals, and music for films, radio and television. His recordings include Klami's *Kalevala* Suite and *Cheremissian Fantasy* for cello and orchestra (with Noras), Madetoja's Symphony No. 3 and *Comedy Overture* (with the Helsinki Philharmonic Orchestra for Finnlevy), Palmgren's Piano Concerto No. 2 and Englund's Piano Concerto (with Tateno and the Helsinki Philharmonic Orchestra for EMI), and Madetoja's opera *Pohjalaisia* (with the Finnish National Opera Company for Finnlevy).

Paoletti, Alberto (b. 1905). Born in Rome where he studied under Casella, Respighi and Bustini at the Accademia di Santa Cecilia, Paoletti was a repetiteur with the Italian Radio, at the Naples and Genoa Operas, and was a conductor at the Rome Opera (1945–71). With the Rome Opera Orchestra *et al.* he recorded *Lucia di Lammermoor* (for La Guilde Internationale du Disque), *Andrea Chénier* (released by Nixa), *La Bohème* (by Royale), and excerpts from *Aida* (by Capitol) and *Otello* (by Urania and Vox).

Papandopulo, Boris (b. 1906). Born at Honnef am Rhein, Germany, Papandopulo studied at the Zagreb Academy of Music and the Vienna Conservatory, and has been a conductor at Zagreb, Split, Sarajevo and Rijeka. For Jugoton he has recorded his own *Osorski Requiem* (with soloists and Radio Zagreb Chorus), and a recital of operatic arias with the baritone Ruždjak.

Papi, Gennaro (1886–1941). Born in Naples and educated at the conservatory there, Papi was a conductor in Warsaw (1909–10), Turin (1911), Covent Garden, London (1911–12), Milan, Odessa and Buenos Aires, the New York Metropolitan Opera (1913–25), the Chicago Civic Opera (1925–32), at Milan, Mexico City and Buenos Aires, and then again at the New York Met. (from 1935). With the New York Metropolitan Orchestra he made early 78 r.p.m. discs for Vocalion of the overture to *Il barbiere di Siviglia*, the intermezzo from *Goyescas*, and selections from *Aida* and *La Bohème*.

Paray, Paul (b. 1886). Born at Le Tréport, Normandy, where his father was an organist and choirmaster, Paray showed exceptional musical gifts as a child, and at the age of nine was enrolled at the Rouen Choir School. At 12 he could play from memory all Bach's organ works. He studied under Caussade and Le Roux at the Paris Conservatoire, won the Prix de Rome in 1911, and lived for three years in Rome. At the outbreak of World War I he joined the French army, fought in Belgium and on the Marne, and was a prisoner-of-war for four years. After the war, he conducted a small orchestra at the summer resort of Cauteret, became assistant conductor to Chevillard with the Lamoureux Orchestra (1920–23), and was principal conductor of the orchestra from 1923 to 1928. In 1928 he was made music director of the Monte Carlo Municipal Orchestra (1928–33), then succeeded Pierné as conductor of the Colonne Orchestra (1932–40), and for ten years conducted Wagner at the Paris Opéra. In 1940 he left Paris because the Nazis demanded that the orchestra's name be changed since Colonne was a Jew (Paray himself is a Catholic). He went to Limoges, Marseille and finally Monte Carlo, and was a leading figure in the Résistance movement of French artists, for which he was later honoured by the French government. At the conclusion of the war he returned to Paris and was again conductor of the Colonne Orchestra (1945–52).

Paray first conducted in the United States in 1939, with the New York Philharmonic-Symphony Orchestra; he was the first French artist to visit the US after the war, when Koussevitzky invited him to conduct the Boston Symphony Orchestra. He was a guest conductor with the Pittsburgh Symphony Orchestra (1949–52), and then re-formed and was musical director of the Detroit Symphony Orchestra (1952–63). His first visit to Israel was in 1948, and since World War II he has regularly conducted the Israel Philharmonic Orchestra. The French government awarded him the title of Grand Officier de la Légion d'Honneur, and the Grand Cross of the National Order of Merit. His compositions include three symphonies, chamber music, a ballet, and a Mass for the 300th anniversary of the death of Joan of Arc, which he has recorded with the Detroit Symphony Orchestra, *et al.*

Paray has had a long and very distinguished career: on the jury which awarded him the Prix de Rome were Saint-Saëns, Massenet, Fauré and Dubois, and in his 91st year he is still conducting with vitality and distinction, even if his movements are sparing. His repertoire has been conventional, based on the classical and romantic composers of the 19th century, and he is an authoritative interpreter of Berlioz, Franck, Ravel, Debussy and other French composers. His style is typically French: tempi are usually swift, and the orchestral texture is clear and relatively light, but the music is propelled with vigour and firm rhythm. He has an exceptional memory and normally conducts without a score. He believes there is only one correct tempo for a work, which he arrives at through close familiarity with the score. He never listens to other performances, on record or in concerts, and during his entire life has been to only four concerts, of Furtwängler, Toscanini, Schuricht and Mengelberg; on the radio he once heard Toscanini conducting the last movement of the *Pastoral* symphony, which he thought was at the correct tempo. Few contemporary composers appear on his programmes; he is unsympathetic to much modern music, saying that 'Music is a language with its grammar. There must be evolution, not a complete break' (interview with author, 1976).

Paray recorded, on pre-electric 78 r.p.m. discs, Beethoven's Symphony No. 6 (with the Colonne Orchestra); on 78s he also conducted the march from Beethoven's *Die Ruinen von Athen*, d'Indy's *Symphonie sur un chant montagnard français* and Mozart's Piano Concerto K. 488 (with Marguerite Long), and *A Night on the Bare Mountain* (with the Colonne Orchestra for Columbia), the fanfare from Dukas' *La Péri* and the overture to *Benvenuto Cellini* (with the Colonne Orchestra for Polydor), Beethoven's *Piano Concerto in E flat*, 1784 (with Frugoni and the Pro Musica Chamber Orchestra) and some Mozart concertos (with Gaby Casadesus, Thibaud and Long, with the Lamoureux Orchestra, for Vox). Later, with the Detroit Symphony Orchestra he made a series of LP discs for Mercury, recording an extensive repertoire. Included were Haydn's Symphony No. 96, Mozart's Symphony No. 35, Beethoven's Symphonies Nos 1, 2, 6 and 7, Schubert's Symphony No. 8, the four Schumann symphonies and the *Manfred* overture, Mendelssohn's Symphony No. 5 and music from *A Midsummer Night's Dream*, Berlioz' overtures *Le Carnaval romain* and *Le Corsaire*, *Symphonie fantastique* and marches from *Les Troyens* and *La Damnation de Faust*, Brahms' Symphony No. 4, *Les Préludes* and *Mephisto Waltz*, the prelude to *Die Meistersinger*, the overture to *Tannhäuser*, the preludes to Acts I and III of *Lohengrin*, the Good Friday Music from *Parsifal*, Forest Murmurs from *Siegfried*, the Ride of the Valkyries and Magic Fire Music from *Die Walküre*, the overtures to *Rienzi* and *Der fliegende Holländer* and the *Siegfried Idyll*, Dvořák's Symphony No. 9 and *Carnival* overture, *Tod und Verklärung*, *Capriccio espagnol*, *Antar* and the *Russian Easter Festival* overture, Sibelius' Symphony No. 2, Rachmaninov's Symphony No. 2, *Invitation to the Dance*, the dance from *Salome*, excerpts from *Les Contes d'Hoffmann*, a *Carmen* suite, *Patrie* overture and the two *L'Arlésienne* suites, the overtures to *The Bartered Bride*, *Le Roi d'Ys*, *Dichter und Bauer*, *Pique Dame*, *Boccaccio*, *Morgen, Mittag und Abend in Wien*, *Die schöne Galatea*, *Mignon*, *Raymond*, *Si j'étais Roi*, *Zampa*, *Gwendoline*, *Les Diamants de la couronne*, *Le Cheval de bronze*, *La Dame blanche*, *William Tell* and *Orphée aux enfers*, the Franck *Symphony in D minor* and *Psyché*, *L'Apprenti sorcier*, *La Valse*, the *Daphnis et Chloé* Suite No. 2, *Le Tombeau de Couperin*, *Valses nobles et sentimentales*, *Pavane pour une infante défunte*, *Ma Mère l'Oye*, *Boléro* and *Rapsodie espagnole*, *La Mer*, *Iberia*, *Nocturnes*, *Prélude à l'après-midi d'un faune* and *Petite Suite*, Roussel's *Suite in F* and *Le Festin de l'araignée*, Gounod's *Marche funèbre d'une Marionette*, the march from *Le Prophète*, Saint-Saëns' Symphony No. 3, *Marche héroïque*, *Danse macabre* and *Le Carnaval des animaux*, Schmitt's *La Tragédie de Salomé*, the Chausson *Symphony in B flat*, Chabrier's *España*, *Bourrée fantasque* and *Marche joyeuse*, Lalo's *Namouna* suite, Fauré's *Pavane* and *Pelléas et Mélisande* suite, Ibert's *Escales* and his own *Mass* (mentioned above). For other companies he recorded the two Ravel piano concertos (with Monique Haas and the French National Radio Orchestra for DGG), Lalo's *Symphonie espagnole* and *Rhapsodie norvégienne* (with Amoyal and the Monte Carlo National Opera Orchestra for Erato), Schumann's Symphony No. 2 and Mendelssohn's Symphony No. 5 (with the Detroit Symphony Orchestra for La Guilde Internationale du Disque), *Les Préludes*, *Mephisto Waltz*, *Orpheus* and *Mazeppa*, *L'Apprenti sorcier*, *La Valse*, and Chabrier's *España* and *Suite pastorale* (with the Monte Carlo National Opera

Orchestra for La Guilde Internationale du Disque). Bärenreiter have also issued a Mass, arranged from Bach chorales by André Lavagne, and sung in French by the Légion d'Honneur Chorale, with Gazin (organ).

Pařík, Otakar (1901–55). Born in Mistek, Czechoslovakia, Pařík studied at the German Music Academy in Prague, where he was taught by Ansorge, a disciple of Liszt. He played, as a pianist, in the Czech Trio, and accompanied soloists such as Jan Kubelík and Emmy Destinn. He was assistant, then first, conductor with the Prague Radio Symphony Orchestra (1926–45), chief conductor of the FOK Symphony Orchestra (1945–54), and first chief conductor of the Janáček Philharmonic Orchestra at Ostrava (1954–5), and directed the music for 60 long films and about 200 short ones. His recordings, for Supraphon, were Dvořák's *Vanda* overture, Hlobil's *The Folk Gaiety*, Kubín's *Ostrava* and *In Beskydy Mountains*, a suite from Nedbal's *From Fairy Tale into Fairy Tale*, scenes from Offenbach's *La Belle Hélène*, Ostrčil's *The Peasant Feast*, Popy's *Oriental Suite*, suites from Trojan's film scores *The Emperor's Nightingale* and *Prince Bajaja*, and Weis's *Gallopade*. Most were with the FOK Symphony Orchestra, on LP.

Parikian, Manoug (b. 1920). Born in Mersin, Turkey, of Armenian parents, Parikian was educated at the Trinity College of Music, and was concertmaster of the Liverpool Philharmonic Orchestra (1947–8) and the Philharmonia Orchestra (1948–57). He has recorded as a solo violinist, and as a conductor directed the Yorkshire Sinfonia in a recording of Bach's *Ein musikalisches Opfer* (for CRD/Enigma).

Partch, Harry (1901–74). Born in Oakland, California, Partch was a self-taught musician who after much experience and research developed a highly original new musical language that avoided atonality and electronic music, which he regarded as inhibiting creativity. He established a new scale, elaborated in his book *Genesis of Music* (1949), and once described his music as 'based on a monophonic system of acoustic intervals and an expandable source scale of more than 40 notes to the so-called scale'. He used this method of composition in a number of works, including *Oedipus* (1952) and *Water, Water* (1962), and also created a number of exotic musical instruments, two of which are called the kithera and the bloboys. He has received, *inter alia*, the award of the National Institute of Arts and Letters. On his own Gate 5 label he issued a series of recordings of his own music; Composers Recordings have also released a disc of him directing the Gate 5 Ensemble in his *And on the Seventh Day Petals Fell in Petaluma*.

Pasternack, Josef (1881–1940). Born in Czestochowa, Poland, Pasternack studied at the Warsaw Conservatory, migrated to the United States in 1895, and played the viola in the New York Metropolitan Opera Orchestra. He became assistant conductor at the Met. (1909–10), conductor of the Sunday Concerts (1910–13), of the Century Opera Company (1913–14), of the Ravinia Park opera and concerts, Chicago, the Boston Pops concerts (1916), the Philadelphia Philharmonic Orchestra and the Robin Hood Dell opera and concerts. He was music director of the Victor Phonograph Company and the Stanley Company of America (1916–27), and from 1927 was a conductor of radio programmes for the National Broadcasting Company. He made many orchestral arrangements and composed an operetta, *Countess Clou*. He made some records with the Victor Symphony Orchestra for RCA, including the Triumphal March from *Sigurd Jorsalfar* and the overture to *The Merry Wives of Windsor*; of the latter, Kolodin wrote in 1941 that 'it is a curio to remind one of the atrocities that were accepted docilely by record collectors in the long ago'.

Patané, Franco (1908–68). Born in Acireale, Sicily, Patané studied music and conducted at the operas in London, Paris, Lisbon, Monte Carlo, Nice, New York and elsewhere, and was also active in Europe as a symphonic conductor. He was director of the Music Academy at Philadelphia, and in 1967 was appointed director of the Royal Opera at Copenhagen. He recorded for EMI with the Covent Garden Orchestra intermezzi from *Cavalleria rusticana*, *Pagliacci*, *Manon Lescaut* and Zandonai's *Giulietta e Romeo*, as well as accompaniments to arias sung by Tagliabue and Carosio.

Patané, Giuseppe (b. 1932). Son of Franco Patané, Patané was born in Naples, at the age of eight was a repetiteur with Mascagni, and after studying at the Conservatorio de Musica S. Pietro a Magella at Naples, made his debut as a conductor at sixteen at the Mercadante Theatre in Venice, with *La traviata*, in which Gigli was Alfredo. He conducted from memory, and can now write down, note by note, 250 operas from memory. Early in his career he gained experience as an operatic conductor in Britain, Egypt, South Africa, Switzerland and FR Germany; he conducted at Linz

(1951–62), is responsible for the Italian repertoire at the Deutsche Oper in West Berlin (from 1963), and has been active at the Bavarian State Opera, Munich, and at the San Francisco Opera in particular. He recorded *Madama Butterfly* and *Samson et Dalila* (with the Bavarian Radio Symphony Orchestra *et al.* for Ariola, the *Samson et Dalila* being issued in the United States by RCA), Bellini's *I Capuletti ed i Montecchi* (with the New Philharmonia Orchestra *et al.* for EMI), the Verdi *Requiem* (with the Leipzig Radio Symphony Orchestra *et al.* for Eterna), a recital of operatic arias (with Lorengar and the Santa Cecilia Academy Orchestra for Decca), a recital of Mozart arias (with Hallstein for Eterna), and excerpts, in German, from *La traviata*, *Turandot*, *La forza del destino* and *Carmen* (with the Dresden Staatskapelle *et al.* for Eterna).

Patterson, Russell (b. 1928). Born in Greenville, Mississippi, Patterson studied at the Louisiana State University, New England Conservatory of Music, the Hochschule für Musik at Munich and the University of Missouri. He has conducted the New Orleans Symphony Orchestra and the New Orleans Opera Association, has been general director of the Kansas City Lyric Theatre, and has also performed with the Boston Symphony Orchestra, at the Bavarian State Opera and with the Netherlands Radio Orchestra, and is a lecturer in music at the University of Missouri. His recordings include the operas *The Taming of the Shrew* of Giannini (for Composers Recordings) and *The Sweet Bye and Bye* of Beeson (for Desto), both with the company and orchestra of the Kansas City Lyric Theatre.

Patzak, Julius (1898–1974). Born in Vienna, Patzak joined the Civil Service after completing his schooling, and at the same time studied music at the Vienna University, intending to become a conductor. However, he appeared in popular song festivals, in 1926 gave a solo concert, and that year sang Radames in *Aida* in a provincial Czech opera house. He was a leading tenor at the Bavarian State Opera (1928–45) and then at the Vienna State Opera (1945–58), and made many records as a tenor, the most enduring being *Das Lied von der Erde*, with Kathleen Ferrier and the Vienna Philharmonic Orchestra under Walter, issued originally by Decca in 1952. He occasionally appeared as a conductor with the Vienna Symphony and other orchestras, and La Guilde Internationale du Disque issued a record of him conducting the Hamburg Chamber Orchestra in Mozart's Serenade K. 250 (the *Haffner*).

Paul, Tibor (1909–73). The Hungarian-born conductor Paul was educated at the Franz Liszt Academy at Budapest, and studied conducting with Scherchen and Weingartner. He founded and directed the Budapest Concert Orchestra, and in 1950 emigrated to Australia, gaining Australian citizenship in 1955. Until his death, and except for a period when he was director of music for Radio Eireann in Dublin and principal conductor of the Dublin Symphony Orchestra, he was conductor of various orchestras of the Australian Broadcasting Commission in Sydney, Melbourne, Adelaide and Perth, as well as touring Europe and South Africa; he also taught conducting at the New South Wales State Conservatorium of Music. He recorded for Philips with the Vienna Symphony Orchestra a disc of a selection of Brahms *Hungarian Dances* and Dvořák's *Slavonic Dances*, and another of the *Háry János* suite of Kodály, *Les Préludes* and the *Hungarian Rhapsodies Nos 1* and *2* of Liszt, and with the West Australian Symphony Orchestra Alfred Hill's Symphony No. 8 and Carmichael's *Concierto folklorico*, for World Record Club.

Paulik, Anton (1901–75). Born in Pressburg (now Bratislava), Paulik was conductor at the Theater an der Wien and a guest conductor at the Vienna State Opera (1921–38), and conductor at the Volksoper, Vienna (from 1938), where he was first conductor and head of the classical operetta department. He was appointed professor in 1950, decorated with the Golden Badge of Honour for Services to Austria in 1958, and was awarded the Austrian Cross of Honour for Science and the Arts in 1971. A master of the Viennese operetta, Paulik made records of many of them, as well as discs of waltzes and dances of Strauss, Lanner, Waldteufel, *et al.*; these were issued on many labels, and included were Strauss's *Eine Nacht in Venedig* and *Der Zigeunerbaron*, Kálmán's *Die Csardasfürstin*, Lehár's *Der Graf von Luxemburg*, Suppé's *Boccaccio* and *Die schöne Galatea* and Millöcker's *Der Bettelstudent* (with either the Vienna Symphony or Vienna State Opera Orchestras, *et al.*). *Die schöne Galatea* was issued in Britain by Saga, and is an excellent example of his musicianship. Another successful disc was of German university songs with the baritone Kunz and the Vienna Volksoper Orchestra (issued in the United States by Vanguard).

Paulmüller, Alexander (b. 1912). Born in Innsbruck, Paulmüller studied at the Vienna Academy of Music, was a choral conductor at the Vienna State Opera with Walter, and then conducted at Graz, Nuremberg, Vienna, Breslau, Kaiserslautern, Regensburg, Linz and Frankfurt am Main, and was chief conductor at the Württemberg State Opera (1964–72). His recordings include Schubert's Symphony No. 5 (with the Austrian Symphony Orchestra for Remington), the Mendelssohn overture *Meeresstille und glückliche Fahrt* (with the same orchestra for Plymouth), Tchaikovsky's Piano Concerto No. 1 (with Schwertmann and the same orchestra for Remington) and Hummel's *Piano Concerto in A* and Violin and Piano Concerto (with Galling and Lautenbacher and the Stuttgart Philharmonic Orchestra for Turnabout).

Paumgartner, Bernhard (1887–1971). Born in Vienna, where his father, Dr Hans Paumgartner, was a composer and critic, and his mother a singer and teacher, Paumgartner grew up in an intensely musical environment; he knew Bruckner and Wolf, was a pupil of Walter, and studied law and music at the University of Vienna. He became a repetiteur at the Vienna Opera, was conductor of the Vienna Tonkünstler Orchestra (before it became the Vienna Symphony Orchestra), and taught at the Academy of Music. After service in the Austrian army in World War I, he was discharged in 1917 to become director of the Salzburg Mozarteum, where he remained until 1938. During World War II, he lived in Florence, teaching at the German Academy and studying early Florentine music, and later moved to Switzerland. He returned to Salzburg in 1945, resumed his position as director of the Mozarteum, until he finally retired in 1959. There he founded the Salzburg Mozarteum Orchestra and the Camerata Academica (a chamber orchestra), was one of the founders of the Salzburg Festival in 1945, and became its president in 1960; in 1949 he was appointed president of the Academy of Music and Dramatic Art in Salzburg, and was the founder and director of the international summer courses at the Mozarteum. He appeared as a guest conductor in London, Paris, Budapest, Japan and the USSR, and in 1965 visited the United States to conduct Mozart's *Requiem* at Dallas, in a memorial concert for President Kennedy. A leading Mozart scholar, he published a biography of the composer (1927), edited some of his works, as well as Leopold Mozart's *Versuch einer gründlichen Violinschule*. He also wrote biographies of Schubert (1945), Handel (1947) and Bach (1950), collaborated with Ernest Irving in the film about Mozart, *Whom the Gods Love*, and himself composed music, including the operas *Rossini in Neapel* and *Die Höhle von Salamanca*, which he led at the Salzburg Festival in 1928, and incidental music for plays, notably Reinhardt's production of *Faust* in Salzburg (1933), as well as orchestral and choral music. In 1969 his memoirs were published.

For much of his life, Paumgartner had a major influence on musical activities at Salzburg; in Walter's words, he did 'much to preserve and intensify the local musical atmosphere'. Although rarely an incisive or arresting conductor, he made numerous records, and Philips engaged him to be the editor of their Mozart jubilee editions in 1956. He conducted many performances himself in this series, including Symphonies Nos 25, 28, 29, 31 and 33 (with the Mozarteum Orchestra), Divertimentos K. 213, K. 240, K. 252, K. 253, K. 270 and K. 289, Serenades K. 375, K. 388 and *Eine kleine Nachtmusik*, the Violin Concertos K. 207, K. 211, K. 216, K. 218, K. 219 and K. 271a (with Grumiaux), Piano Concertos K. 466 and K. 488, and Rondo K. 386 (with Haskil), K. 238 and K. 449 (with Henkemans), Rondo K. 373, Adagio K. 261 and Rondo concertante K. 269 (with de Klijn), Sinfonia concertante K. 364, Clarinet Concerto (with Schönhofer), Horn Concertos (with Penzel), Oboe Concerto (with de Klerk), *German Dances* K. 600 and K. 605, the overtures to *Don Giovanni*, *Le nozze di Figaro*, *Così fan tutte* and *Die Entführung aus dem Serail* (with the Vienna Symphony Orchestra), *Thamos, König von Ägypten* (with the Vienna Chamber Orchestra *et al.*), the Masonic cantatas *Dir, Seele des Weltalls*, *Die Maurerfreude* and *Eine kleine Freimaurerkantate* and the *Maurerische Trauermusik* (with the Vienna Symphony Orchestra *et al.*). His other records for Philips included Telemann's *Suite in A minor*, flute concertos of Quantz, Haydn and Gluck (with Barwahser and the Vienna Symphony Orchestra), cello concertos by Haydn and Boccherini (with de Machula and the Vienna Symphony Orchestra), Handel's *Acis and Galatea* (with the Camerata Academica *et al.*), oboe concertos by Handel, Telemann, Dittersdorf, Haydn and Mozart (with Tricht and the Vienna Symphony Orchestra) and Haydn's Trumpet Concerto (with Sevenstern).

Paumgartner also recorded, for other companies, Mozart's Divertimento K. 113, Serenade K. 100 and Cassation K. 63 (with the Camerata Academica for EMI), Piano Concerto K. 414 (with Scholz), Flute Concerto K. 313 (with Tassinari), Divertimento K. 136, Recitative and Aria K. 294 (with Streich, and the Camerata Academica for DGG); a cantata by A. Scarlatti and Mozart's Divertimento

K. 251 (with the Salzburg Mozarteum Orchestra *et al.* for DGG); some Mozart dances (with the Camerata Academica for La Guilde Internationale du Disque); Mozart's Oboe Concerto (with Saillet and the Mozarteum Orchestra for Renaissance); Mozart's Symphony No. 40 (with the Camerata Academica for Strand); Haydn's Symphony No. 94 and Mozart's Symphony No. 41 (with the Camerata Academica for Ariola); Mozart's Harpsichord Concerto K. 107 (with Ahlgrimm) and *Galimathias musicum* K. 32 (with the Camerata Academica for Ariola); Mozart's Oboe Concerto (with Briançon), Flute and Harp Concerto, Bassoon Concerto (with Allard), a Horn Concerto (with Bernard), Symphony No. 10 and Divertimento K. 287 (with the Mozarteum Orchestra *et al.* for Le Club français du Disque); Mozart's Symphony No. 40 and *Eine kleine Nachtmusik* (with the Mozarteum Orchestra for BASF); Mozart's Piano Concertos K. 466 and K. 488 (with de la Bruchollerie and the Camerata Academica for Nonesuch); Mozart's Divertimento K. 287 (with the Vienna State Opera Orchestra for Vanguard); Mozart's Piano Concerto K. 488 (with Thyssens-Valentin and the Salzburg Chamber Orchestra for Telefunken), A. Scarlatti's *Su le sponde del Tebro* (with Stich-Randall), Biber's *Fidicinium sacroprofanum*, Leopold Mozart's *Eine musikalische Schlittenfahrt*, Muffat's *Florilegium*, Michael Haydn's Trumpet Concerto (with Scherbaum), *Turkish March*, *Wedding in Alm* and *Divertimento in G* (with the Camerata Academica for Ariola); Telemann's Viola Concerto (with Doktor), Torelli's *Concerto in A minor*, suites for gamba and orchestra by Fesch and Caix d'Hervelois (with Schwamberger), and some concertos by Albinoni (with the Mozarteum Orchestra for Le Club français du Disque); Leopold Mozart's *Divertimento in G* and Trumpet Concerto (with Scherbaum), Michael Haydn's *Turkish March* and Biber's Sonata No. 1 (with the Camerata Academica for Musical Heritage Society).

Pauspertl, Karl (1897–1963). The Austrian composer and conductor Pauspertl's great-uncle was Bruckner's teacher in Linz; he studied under Schmidt and Krauss at the Academy of Music in Vienna, and conducted theatre orchestras in Vienna, Troppau and Berlin. He was also assistant choir conductor at the Vienna State Opera, conducted the Vienna Radio Orchestra, wrote music for films, and composed operettas. Vox released an LP on which he conducted the Vienna Symphony Orchestra *et al.* in *Der lustige Krieg* of Johann Strauss, and Bellaphon excerpts from Berté's *Das Dreimäderlhaus*, with the Vienna Unterhaltungsorchester *et al.*

Pavlik, Justus (b. 1926). Born in Mníchova Lehota, in Slovakia, Pavlik studied the clarinet at the Bratislava Conservatory, and played in the Košice National Theatre Orchestra (1948–9), the Bratislava Radio Symphony Orchestra (1949–70), was in Egypt (1970–72) and then was a member of the Slovak Philharmonic Orchestra (from 1972). Since 1972 he has been leader of the Bratislava Chamber Harmony, and for Opus he recorded with them Hummel's *Military Septet* and *Octet-Partita*, and Družecký's *Partita in E flat*.

Pears, Sir Peter (b. 1910). Born at Farnham, Pears was an Organ Scholar at Hertford College, Oxford, became a schoolmaster and then won a scholarship to the Royal College of Music where he studied with Elena Gerhardt. As a tenor he performed with the BBC Singers (1934–7), the New England Singers (1936–8) and with the Glyndebourne Opera (1938), and became associated with Benjamin Britten as a recitalist (1939). Throughout his subsequent career he was inseparable from Britten and his music, in concert, opera, and recorded performances (as well as in lieder recitals with Britten as accompanist), making a special impression in *Peter Grimes*. He gave the first performances of many of Britten's works, and of others by Tippett and Berkeley, and with Britten published an edition of Purcell's music. As a conductor, Pears has recorded madrigals of Wilbye (with the Wilbye Consort for Decca).

Pedrollo, Arrigo (1878–1964). Born in Montebello near Vicenza, and educated at the Milan Conservatory, the Italian composer and conductor Pedrollo was active as a conductor of opera and radio concerts in Milan, and in 1930 became professor of composition at the Giuseppe Verdi Conservatory there. A symphony written by him as a student was performed in Milan by Toscanini, and he also wrote operas and chamber music which enjoyed some success, including an opera to a libretto based on Dostoyevsky's *Crime and Punishment*. He recorded on 78s Pergolesi's *La serva padrona* (with the Milan Philharmonic Orchestra *et al.* for Columbia), and Casella's arrangement of Vivaldi's *Gloria* (with the Milan Teatro Nuovo *et al.*).

Pedrotti, Antonio (b. 1901). Born at Trento, Pedrotti studied under Respighi at the Accademia di Santa Cecilia, Rome, conducted the Trento Symphony Orchestra (1929), and was a conducting pupil of Molinari at the Augusteo, Rome (1937–8). He was a teacher and conductor at the Accademia di Santa Cecilia (1938–44), conducted throughout Europe, and made his debut in Prague in 1950, where he has frequently returned to conduct the Czech Philharmonic Orchestra. He has been resident conductor of the Haydn Orchestra of Bolzano, which was founded in 1960.

Pedrotti recorded, on 78s, the Schumann Piano Concerto (with Michelangeli and the La Scala Orchestra for Telefunken), and on LP has made a number of discs with the Czech Philharmonic Orchestra for Supraphon and Ultraphon. The works recorded have been excerpts from Monteverdi's *La favola d'Orfeo*, Mendelssohn's Symphony No. 4, Brahms' Symphony No. 4 and *Variations on the St Antony Chorale*, Vivaldi's *Sinfonia in B minor*, *Prélude à l'après-midi d'un faune*, *Daphnis et Chloé* Suite No. 2, *Pavane pour une infante défunte*, *Ma Mère l'Oye*, *Pini di Roma*, *Fontane di Roma*, *Feste romane*, *La Boutique fantasque*, *Pictures at an Exhibition*, Prokofiev's Symphony No. 1, a suite from Khachaturian's *Masquerade*, *Nights in the Gardens of Spain*, the preludes to Acts I and III of *La traviata*, the overture to *I vespri siciliani*, and Mahler's *Lieder eines fahrenden Gesellen* (in Czech, with Krasova). He also recorded Haydn's Symphonies Nos 1, 13 and 28 (with the Bolzano Haydn Orchestra for Turnabout). Generally, his performances have been colourful and energetic.

Pelletier, Wilfred (b. 1896). Born in Montreal, Pelletier was taught the piano and musical theory by his father, and as a boy could play all the instruments of the orchestra. In 1914 he won a scholarship to study in Paris, and after returning to Canada in 1916 he was an assistant conductor first with the Montreal Opera Company, and then with the New York Metropolitan Opera (1917–22). He became a conductor at the Met. (1922–31), conducted with the Ravinia Opera Company, Chicago (1922–31), at the San Francisco Opera (1921–31) and for the National Broadcasting Company (1934–6). In 1935 he formed the Montreal Festival Orchestra, became director of the Institute of Music and Dramatic Art at Quebec (1942), founded and was director of the Montreal Conservatoire (1942–61), founded and conducted the Quebec Symphony Orchestra (1951–7), continued his activities in broadcast music and opera, conducted the Canadian National Youth Orchestra (1960–61), and was appointed Director of Music by the Quebec government in 1961.

Pelletier has enjoyed a reputation as a tireless and painstaking musician, and as a conductor of considerable energy, who was especially skilled in the Italian and French repertoire. He married the soprano Rose Bampton in 1937, and made many records accompanying her, both as pianist and conductor, and also accompanied other great singers then performing at the Met. His recordings, for RCA, included *Faust* and excerpts from *Carmen* and *Otello* (with the New York Met. Orchestra *et al.*), and Fauré's *Requiem* and the Agnus Dei from the Mozart *Mass in C minor* K. 427 (with Les Disciples de Massenet Choir and the Montreal Festival Orchestra *et al.*).

Penderecki, Krzysztof (b. 1933). The Polish composer Penderecki was born at Debica and studied at the Kraków State School of Music, where he later became professor of composition (1958–66). His first composition to become internationally known was the *St Luke Passion*, which was widely acclaimed when it was issued in two recordings conducted by Czyż for Philips and RCA; the full catalogue of Penderecki's complex, athematic musical vocabulary was presented in this score: imaginative sonorities, varying metrical and rhythmic patterns, choral glissandi and other vocal effects, splitting of single words among different voices, serial elements, etc. The ultimate impression of this work, as with some others, is that of a series of effects that proceeds without any logical progression, and that the musical material may be insufficient for the length of the work. In 1973 he visited Britain and was guest conductor of the London Symphony Orchestra; in the next year EMI released a disc on which he conducts the orchestra in his *Symphony* and *Anaklasis*. EMI have also released discs of him conducting a number of his own compositions with the Polish National Radio Orchestra, including the *Capriccio for Violin and Orchestra* (with Wilkomirska), the Cello Concerto (with Palm), *De natura sonoris* Nos 1 and 2, *The Dream of Jacob*, *Emanations for Two String Orchestras*, *Fonogrammi*, *Kanon*, *Partita for Harpsichord and Orchestra*, *Threnody for the Victims of Hiroshima*, *Canticum canticorum Salomonis* and *Magnificat*.

Pensis, Henri (1900–58). Born in Luxembourg, Pensis studied at the Conservatoire there, the Conservatoire Royal at Brussels and at the Hochschule für Musik in Cologne, with Abendroth, Unger and Jarnach. He first appeared publicly as a violinist in 1920, became concertmaster of the West German Radio and Gürzenich Orchestras at Cologne, and was appointed music director and conductor of the Radio Luxembourg Symphony Orchestra (1932), where he played a crucial part in developing musical life in Luxembourg. During World War II he was active in the US, was music consultant to the United Nations, music director of the New Jersey Philharmonic, the Sioux City Symphony and the Lincoln Symphony Orchestras, and a guest conductor in New York and Philadelphia. Virgil Thomson wrote of him (in *The New York Times*, April 1942).that he was 'extraordinarily dependable both technically and musically, an artist of high intelligence and power'. Pensis recorded for Festival (US) in the early days of LP a disc of Verdi overtures and preludes, Donatoni's *Concerto for Timpani, Bass and String Orchestra*, harp concertos by Handel, Boieldieu and Damase and Ravel's *Introduction et allegro* (with Flour), and some documentary music by Thiriet, with the Radio Luxembourg Symphony Orchestra.

Peress, Maurice (b. 1930). Born in New York and educated at the Mannes School of Music and New York Graduate School of Arts and Sciences, Peress studied with Sachs, Reese, Bamberger *et al.*, and was an assistant to Bernstein with the New York Philharmonic Orchestra (1960–61). He was music director of the Corpus Christi Symphony Orchestra (1961–75), the Austin Symphony Orchestra (1963–71) and the Kansas City Philharmonic Orchestra (since 1974), also conducting the Robert Joffrey Ballet (1967), the Washington Opera Society (1968–9) and at the San Francisco Opera (1972). In 1971 he conducted the première of Bernstein's *Mass* at the opening of the Kennedy Center in Washington DC; in the recording, Bernstein is named the conductor and Peress the musical director. He recorded Rheinberger's Organ Concertos Nos 1 and 2 with Biggs and the Columbia Symphony Orchestra for CBS.

Perlea, Jonel (1900–70). Born in Ograda, Romania, of a German mother and a Romanian father, Perlea studied at Munich with Wallbrunn and at the Leipzig Conservatory under Reger and Lohse. He made his debut as a conductor in 1923 in Bucharest, leading one of his own compositions. He was engaged as assistant conductor at the Leipzig Opera, moved to Rostock (1924–5), and in 1926 was conscripted for a year's military service in Romania. In 1930 he joined the Royal Opera at Bucharest as a conductor, became its musical director (1934–44), also being director of the Royal Academy of Music and of the Bucharest Philharmonic Orchestra, and appearing in many European cities as a guest conductor. At the Opera he led the first performances in Romania of *Der Rosenkavalier*, *Falstaff* and *Die Meistersinger*. In 1944 he attempted to travel to France with his wife, but they were taken into custody by the Nazi authorities in Vienna, and interned in concentration camps for a year. After their release in 1945, he went to Italy, first conducted the Santa Cecilia Orchestra in Rome, then at the La Scala Opera. In 1949 he made his first appearance at the New York Metropolitan with *Tristan und Isolde*, as he had at La Scala; he conducted at the San Francisco Opera (1950), the NBC Symphony Orchestra (1950–51), the San Antonio Opera, Texas (1951), returned to Romania to conduct the Bucharest Philharmonic Orchestra (1952 and 1967), taught conducting at the Manhattan School of Music (1955–70), was conductor of the Connecticut Symphony Orchestra (1955), and appeared in festivals in Europe. In 1957 he suffered a heart attack, and then a stroke in 1958, which deprived him of the use of his right arm, but he continued to conduct, employing only his left arm.

When he appeared at the New York Met. with *Tristan und Isolde*, Perlea impressed with his restraint and the eloquence of his chamber-music-like concept of the opera, yet his *Rigoletto*, *Carmen* and *La traviata* were sufficiently dramatic. Generally, his performances of symphonic music, as represented by his records, were characterised by lyricism and clarity, rather than by propulsive excitement; yet, although well-proportioned and highly musical, they lacked the final touch of conviction. His repertoire was reputed to encompass over 80 operas and 650 symphonic works.

Before coming to the United States, Perlea made a 78 r.p.m. disc for Decca with the La Scala Orchestra of the ballet music from *Samson et Dalila*. For RCA he recorded the operas *Aida*, *Rigoletto* and *Manon Lescaut* (with the Rome Opera Orchestra *et al.*) and *Lucrezia Borgia* (with the RCA Italiana Opera Orchestra *et al.*). Although actually made in 1951, the *Rigoletto* was not released by RCA until 1958; the *Aida*, *Rigoletto* and *Manon Lescaut* were available in 1976 on the Victrola label. He also made many LP records for Vox, including the Boccherini Cello Concerto, Haydn's *Cello Concerto in D major* and Vivaldi's *Cello Concerto in E minor* (with Cassado), Mozart's Symphonies Nos 40 and 41, Beethoven's Symphony No. 1 and Piano Concerto No. 5 (with Novaes), Schubert's Symphony No. 9 Chopin's Piano Concerto No. 1 (with Novaes),

Berlioz' *Symphonie fantastique, Scheherazade*, Dvořák's Symphony No. 8, the *Slavonic Dances* Opp. 46 and 72, *Carnival* overture and *Scherzo capriccioso*, some Brahms *Hungarian Dances*, the two *Peer Gynt* suites, *A Night on the Bare Mountain*, Kodály's *Dances from Galánta*, the Rossini overtures *William Tell*, *Il barbiere di Siviglia*, *La gazza ladra*, *La Cenerentola*, *Semiramide* and *La scala di seta*, *Moldau*, the *Nutcracker* suite, Balakirev's *Tamara* and *Islamey*, the Polovtsian Dances from *Prince Igor*, Cui's *Tarantella*, Enesco's *Romanian Rhapsody No. 1*, Glinka's *Jota Aragonesa*, *Valse-fantaisie*, *Kamarinskaya*, *Recuerdos di Castilla*, *Summer Night in Madrid* and the overtures to *Russlan and Ludmilla* and *A Life for the Tsar*, Liadov's *Baba Yaga*, *Kikimora* and *Eight Russian Folksongs* (with the Bamberg Symphony Orchestra), Mozart's Piano Concertos K. 467 and K. 503 (with Tipo), and Symphonies Nos 25, 29 and 33, Beethoven's Symphonies Nos 4, 7 and 8, Dvořák's Cello Concerto (with Cassadó), the *1812* overture, the *Romeo and Juliet* fantasy-overture, *Marche slave* and *Capriccio italien* (with the Vienna Pro Musica Orchestra), the Dance of the Hours from *La Gioconda* (with the South-West German Radio Symphony Orchestra), Rachmaninov's *Rhapsody on a Theme of Paganini* (with de la Bruchollerie and the Colonne Orchestra for Delta); he also recorded for Remington Liszt's Piano Concerto No. 1 and *Totentanz*, and Brahms' Piano Concerto No. 2 (with Kilenyi), excerpts from *Swan Lake*, Glanville-Hicks' *Three Gymnopedies*, Debussy's *La Boîte à joujoux*, Rhudyar's *Sinfonietta* and *Le Carnaval des animaux* (with the RIAS Orchestra, Berlin) and Ulysses Kay's *Concerto for Orchestra* (with the La Fenice Theatre Orchestra, Venice), and for CBS-Realm a suite from *Swan Lake* (with the Berlin Radio Symphony Orchestra).

Perlman, Itzhak (b. 1945). Born in Tel-Aviv of Russian parents, Perlman gave his first violin recital at the age of nine, and after studies at the Juilliard School in New York with Galamian and Delay, first performed at Carnegie Hall in 1963. Since then he has pursued a brilliant international career as one of the finest violin virtuosos of the younger generation, despite being handicapped by poliomyelitis. In addition to his many records as soloist, for EMI he both conducted and was soloist with the London Philharmonic Orchestra in Vivaldi's *The Four Seasons*.

Perras, John (b. 1932). Born in New York City, Perras studied music privately there, and started his career as a saxophone player. He then was a flautist in the Toronto Symphony Orchestra (1956–8), organised the Dorian Quintet in New York (1959), studied at the Berkshire Music Center at Tanglewood, toured for the US State Department in South America, Africa and Europe, and first conducted with the Paul Taylor Dance Company in New York (1965). He studied in Paris (1965–9), was assistant conductor at the New England Conservatory (1970), associate conductor of the National Orchestral Association in New York (1971–2), music director of the Peoria Symphony Orchestra, Illinois (1973), music director of the Contemporary Dance Theatre in London (1974–5), conductor of the Kansas City Philharmonic Orchestra, and has since been a guest conductor in Europe and the US. For Arion he has recorded Rossini's *Tancredi* (with the Orchestre du Centre d'Action Musicale de l'Ouest *et al.*) and for Bärenreiter Schubert's Symphonies Nos 1 and 2 (with the Bamberg Symphony Orchestra).

Persichetti, Vincent (b. 1915). Born in Philadelphia and educated at the Combs Conservatory and the Curtis Institute under Olga Samaroff, Harris and Reiner, Persichetti became head of the composition department at the Juilliard School (1948), taught at the Philadelphia Conservatory (1942–8), and was director of publications at the Elgin-Vogel Company. He published *20th-Century Harmony* (1961), and of his many compositions he has recorded, as conductor, his Symphony No. 6, Serenade No. 11, *Psalm*, *Bagatelles* and *So Pure the Star* (with the Ohio State University Concert Band, for Coronet).

Pešek, Libor (b. 1933). Educated at the Academy of Music at his birthplace, Prague, Pešek was a repetiteur at the Plzeň Theatre and the Prague National Theatre. In 1959 he founded the Prague Chamber Harmony, a woodwind ensemble, and in 1965 the Prague Sebastian Orchestra. He was conductor of the North Bohemian Symphony Orchestra (1963–9), the Czechoslovak State Chamber Orchestra (1969) and is now chief conductor of the East Bohemian State Symphony Orchestra. In addition, he has been conductor of the Frysk Orchestra and the Overýssel Philharmonic Orchestra in Holland, and has appeared as a guest conductor in other European countries. Supraphon have issued a number of records of him as conductor; with the Prague Chamber Harmony he has recorded excerpts from Bach's *Ein musikalisches Opfer* and from the cantatas and instrumental works, Mozart's Serenade K. 361,

Krommer's *Harmony in F*, Mysliveček's Octets Nos 1 and 2, Dvořák's *Serenade in D minor*, Hindemith's *Concert Music for Piano, Two Harps and Brass*, Ibert's *Concerto for Cello and Wind Instruments*, Milhaud's Symphony No. 5, Stravinsky's *L'Histoire du soldat*, *Ebony Concerto*, *Ragtime*, *Octet* and *Symphonies of Wind Instruments*, Berg's *Chamber Concerto*, Blatný's Suite for Wind Instruments, Dušek's *Parthia*, Fiala's *Parthia*, Klusák's *Pictures*, Martinů's *Concertino*, Mysliveček's *Notturnos*, Rössler-Rosetti's *Notturno*, Vejvanovský's Sonatas, *Offertur* and Serenade, and some Mozart concert arias (with Jonašová). His other discs include trumpet concertos by Telemann, Haydn, Leopold Mozart and Richter (with Preis), Handel's Organ Concertos Nos 8, 9 and 10 (with Slechtar, and the Sebastian Orchestra), Serenatas and Sonatas by Vejvanovský (with the Czech Philharmonic Orchestra), Mozart's Flute and Harp Concerto (with Novák and Patras) and Klusák's *Mahler Variations* (with the Prague Symphony Orchestra); for Panton he also recorded Mozart's Symphony No. 35, Shostakovich's *Sinfonietta* and Kovaříček's *Capriccio* (with the East Bohemian State Chamber Orchestra). These records have had limited circulation in the West; the performance of the Berg *Chamber Concerto*, however, attracted particular attention in Britain for its perception and execution.

Peters, Reinhard (b. 1926). Born in Magdeburg, Peters studied the violin and piano at the Hochschule für Musik in Berlin, and after military service in World War II he became a violinist and choirmaster with the Berlin City Opera. He studied further with Enesco, Thibaud and Cortot in Paris, and won first prize at the International Competition for Young Conductors at Besançon in 1951. In 1952 he was appointed conductor with the Berlin City Opera, making his debut with *Rigoletto*, and in the same year conducted the Berlin Philharmonic Orchestra at his first symphony concert. He was conductor at the Düsseldorf Opera (1957–61), general music director at Münster (1961–70), permanent guest conductor at the Berlin Deutsche Oper (formerly the Berlin City Opera, in West Berlin; since 1970) and chief conductor of the Philharmonia Hungarica (since 1974). As a guest conductor he has appeared with many orchestras in Europe, North and South America, and has conducted at the Salzburg, Spoleto, Edinburgh and Glyndebourne festivals. His repertoire is comprehensive and includes operas from Monteverdi to Henze, and he is specially interested in modern operas and concert music. At his own concerts he occasionally acts as a violin or piano soloist.

Peters has recorded for a number of companies. His discs include suites from Rameau's *Dardanus*, Lully's *Amadis de Gaule* and Purcell's *King Arthur* (with the Collegium Aureum, recorded by Harmonia Mundi and issued in the United States by RCA-Victrola); Leclair's Violin Concerto Op. 7 No. 2 (with Maier), Handel's Organ Concertos Op. 4 Nos 1 and 2, Op. 7 No. 12, and Nos 13 and 15, *Praise of Harmony* and *Look Down, Harmonious Saint* (with Altmeyer), and three Italian cantatas (with Ameling), C. P. E. Bach's Harpsichord Concerto Wq 23 (with Leonhardt) and Oboe Concerto Wq 165 (with Hucke), and J. C. Bach's Sinfonia concertante and Symphony Op. 18 No. 1 (with the Collegium Aureum for BASF), arias by Haydn and Mozart (with Fischer-Dieskau and the Vienna Haydn Orchestra, for Decca), Haydn's Symphonies Nos 59 and 96 (with the Hamburg Symphony Orchestra for Intercord), Mozart's Symphonies Nos 40 and 41 (with the Rhineland Philharmonic Orchestra for CBS), viola concertos by Paganini, Stamitz and Hoffmeister (with Arad and the Philharmonia Hungarica for Turnabout), the Glazunov Violin Concerto and *Meditation* (with Ricci and the Philharmonia Hungarica for Turnabout), Adam's *Le Postillon de Longjumeau* (in German, with the Berlin Radio Symphony Orchestra *et al.* for Eurodisc), excerpts from *La traviata* (in German, with the Berlin Deutsche Oper Orchestra *et al.* for Ariola), an aria recital by Streich (with the same orchestra for DGG), Rodrigo's *Concierto de Aranjuez* and Castelnuovo-Tedesco's Guitar Concerto (with Behrend and the Berlin Philharmonic Orchestra for DGG), and Genzmer's *Der Zauberspiegel* (with the Munich Philharmonic Orchestra for Da Camera).

Petit, Jean-Louis (b. 1937). Petit studied conducting with Bigot, Barzin, Sipusch, Auriacombe, Markevitch, Pérrisson, Ferrara and Boulez, and also with Plé-Caussade and Messiaen; he organised musical activities in the region of Champagne (1959), formed several ensembles to perform music, from ancient to contemporary, for television, radio and public performances, toured Europe and the United States, and since 1973 has directed, with the founder Bernard Bonaldi, the Summer Festival of Paris, and has been director of the Conservatoire at Ville d'Avray. He is the founder of the Group 'Musique Plus' which performs contemporary music, and his compositions include transcriptions of ancient music and original works for the groups he conducts. In 1964 he made 30 recordings for Decca of French ancient music, including compositions by Rameau, Boismortier, Lully, Leclair, Marais, Aubert, Guillemain, Mouret, Naudot, Devienne, Blavet, Loeillet, Campra, Balbastre, d'Auvergne, Francoeur, Couperin, Mondoville, Bréval, Caix d'Hervelois and Ozi. For Da Camera he also recorded Roussel's *Sinfonietta* and some marches by Lully. In 1967 Decca issued in Britain his recording of d'Auvergne's *Les Troqueurs*.

Pfitzner, Hans (1869–1949). Pfitzner was born in Moscow, where his father, a native of Saxony, was a violinist at the Opera. He was still a child when the family went back to Germany where his father had obtained an appointment as a conductor at Frankfurt am Main; Pfitzner studied there at Hoch's Conservatory under Kwast and Knorr. He taught the piano at Koblenz Conservatory (1892–3), was a repetiteur at the Mainz Opera (1894–6), and taught at the Stern Conservatory in Berlin (1897–1906). He was appointed first conductor at the Theater des Westens in Berlin (1903–6), was conductor of the Kaim Orchestra at Munich (1907–8), then became director of concerts at Strasbourg, director of the Strasbourg Conservatory and first conductor of the Opera there (1908–16). At the conservatory two of his pupils were Furtwängler and Klemperer; later he was closely associated with Walter. He left Strasbourg in 1916 and settled in Unterschöndorf near Munich, taught at the Munich Academy of Music, conducted the Munich Concert Society (1919–20) and in 1920 was appointed general music director for Bavaria. He taught at the Prussian Academy of Arts and Sciences in Berlin (1920–29), then was professor of composition at the Munich Academy of Music (1930–34), and, after his retirement, resumed conducting.

An ardent German nationalist, Pfitzner refused to conduct at the Salzburg Festival in 1933 because of the antagonism of the Austrian chancellor, Dollfuss, towards Hitler. He welcomed the Nazis in 1933, hoping that they would bring Germany's regeneration, but was soon disillusioned; they eventually banned his music as degenerate. In one of his publications he attacked the destructive effect on music of Jewish composers, apparently referring to Schoenberg, Schreker and Mahler, although the latter often performed his operas; at the same time he stood up against the Nazis for many of his Jewish friends. In World War II Allied bombs destroyed his house and music at Munich, and he lived in severe poverty until, through the intervention of the chairman of the Vienna Philharmonic Orchestra, he was brought to live his final days in Salzburg. For this he gave the manuscript of *Palestrina* to the Vienna Philharmonic, and, in accordance with his wish, he was buried in the same cemetery in Vienna as Mozart, Beethoven and Schubert.

As a composer Pfitzner was one of the German romantics, and first came into prominence when he conducted a concert of his own music in Berlin in 1893. Of his five operas, the first two, *Der arme Heinrich* and *Die Rose vom Liebesgarten*, were once often performed in Germany and Austria, but the third, *Palestrina*, is his masterpiece and his only work to have received any wide measure of recognition outside Germany, and this was greatly accelerated only recently by Kubelík's superb recording with the Bavarian Radio Symphony Orchestra *et al.* Of his other works, the *Symphony No. 2 in C major* and the cantata *Von deutscher Seele* have also been available on LP records, and a number of lieder, piano and chamber works are currently listed in the German catalogues.

Pfitzner was said to have preferred composing to conducting and teaching. He possessed a remarkable memory, and could repeat a number of Shakespeare's plays by heart. Once, when he was conducting *Die Meistersinger* in Strasbourg, the singer playing Beckmesser suddenly fell ill; Pfitzner handed the baton to the assistant conductor, went on to the stage and sang the part for the rest of the performance. He was particularly interested in opera production and was responsible for producing the first performance of *Palestrina* in 1917, which Walter conducted. His wayward artistic temperament and his impatience with careless performances caused him to be misunderstood by many. As a conductor, he had a predilection for Beethoven, Weber and Schumann; some critics have written about the spontaneity and absence of calculation in his conducting, but Klemperer remarked that although Pfitzner was a very fine musician he was not a conductor. Klemperer may have been given to exaggeration; he also said that some passages in the text of *Palestrina*, which Pfitzner wrote himself, could compare with Goethe.

Between 1928 and 1934 Pfitzner made a number of recordings for DGG, which were released in some instances outside Germany by Decca and Brunswick. The works recorded included Haydn's Symphony No. 28 (with the Berlin Staatsoper Orchestra), Beethoven's Symphonies Nos 1 and 3 (with the Berlin Philharmonic Orchestra), No. 4 (twice, with the Berlin Staatsoper Orchestra), No. 6 (two separate recordings, with the New Symphony Orchestra, Berlin, and the Berlin Staatsoper

Orchestra), No. 7 (with the Berlin Symphony Orchestra) and No. 8 (with the Berlin Philharmonic Orchestra), Schumann's Symphonies Nos 1 and 2 (with the Berlin Staatsoper Orchestra) and No. 4 (twice, with the Berlin Philharmonic Orchestra and Berlin Symphony Orchestra), the overtures *Zar und Zimmermann*, *The Hebrides*, *Così fan tutte*, *Der Freischütz*, *Jubel*, *Oberon* and *Preciosa* (with the Berlin Philharmonic Orchestra, Lanner's *Pesther Walzer* (with the Berlin Staatsoper Orchestra) and Bruch's *Die Loreley* (with the Munich Radio Orchestra *et al.*), and of his own works, Symphony No. 2 (with the Berlin Philharmonic Orchestra for DGG), the overture to the opera *Christelflein* (with separate recordings with the Berlin Symphony and Berlin Staatsoper Orchestras for DGG), the preludes to Acts I and III of *Palestrina* (with the Berlin Staatsoper Orchestra, three times, for DGG), the overture and introduction to Act II from the incidental music to Ibsen's *The Feast at Solhoug*, the Liebesmelodie from *Das Herz*, the overture and orchestral excerpts from the incidental music to Kleist's *Käthchen von Heilbronn*, the funeral march from *Die Rose vom Liebesgarten* (with the Berlin Philharmonic Orchestra for DGG), and the overture to *Käthchen von Heilbronn* (with the Vienna Philharmonic Orchestra for Urania), and the Duo for Violin and Cello with Orchestra (with Strub, Hoelscher and the Berlin Staatsoper Orchestra for HMV). He also made records as a pianist, accompanying Gerhard Hüsch in some of his own songs (for HMV). DGG included in its album *The Early Years* (1973) the performance of Schumann's Symphony No. 2.

Pflüger, Gerhard (b. 1907). Born in Dresden, Pflüger studied at the Dresden Staatskapelle Orchestra School under Busch and Striegler (1924–7), and started his career as a choral conductor at Tilsit (1927–30). He was then a conductor at Stralsund (1930–32), Gotha (1932–5), Altenburg (1938–40), Meiningen (1940–44), Rostock (1946–9), with the Leipzig Radio Orchestra (1949–57), was general music director at the German National Theatre and with the Staatskapelle at Weimar (1957–73), taught at the Hochschule für Musik and at the Franz Liszt Academy at Weimar, where he became a professor in 1962.

With the Leipzig Radio and Leipzig Philharmonic Orchestra, Pflüger made a number of records in the 1950s for Eterna, many of which were released in the United States by Urania. A Bruckner Symphony No. 5 and Wagner's *Symphony in C major* were also issued in Britain by Saga. Other recordings in this series included Mozart's *Les petits riens*, the Gluck/Mottl ballet suite, Beethoven's Piano Concerto No. 1 (with Steurer), Hoffman's Mandolin Concerto (with Lindner-Bonelli) Weber's Symphony No. 1 and *Invitation to the Dance*, Liszt's *Hungaria*, *Festklänge* and *Hungarian Rhapsody No. 4*, Smetana's *Wedding Scenes* (arranged for orchestra), Dvořák's Symphonies Nos 8 and 9, Borodin's Symphony No. 2, Glinka's *Waltz Fantasy*, Bartók's *Dance Suite* and suite from *The Wooden Prince*, Shostakovich's Symphony No. 1, Prokofiev's Symphony No. 1, Wisłocki's Piano Concerto (with Kedra), Spies' Symphony No. 2 and Elgar's overtures *In the South* and *Froissart*. These Elgar overtures were apparently the same performances as those issued on a Saga disc by the Metropolitan Symphony Orchestra conducted by one Purser. Vox also issued a disc of excerpts from *Fidelio*, in which Pflüger conducted the Leipzig Radio Orchestra *et al.*

Pierné, Gabriel (1863–1937). The French conductor and composer Pierné was born in Metz, graduated from the Paris Conservatoire, succeeded Franck as organist at Sainte-Clotilde (1890–98), was deputy conductor of the Concerts Colonne and became the conductor at Colonne's death (1910–32). He was a distinguished musician and a devoted performer of French music. Just before World War I he was involved in a strange incident with Casals, who had contracted to play the Dvořák Cello Concerto with Pierné conducting the Colonne Orchestra. Before the performance, Pierné declared the work to be *une cochonnerie* – rubbish – but his reason for saying this has never been revealed. Casals refused to perform the concerto with him, was sued and lost the case for breach of contract.

Pierné made a number of records with the Colonne Orchestra, including Chabrier's *Bourrée fantasque*, the *Peer Gynt* Suite No. 1, Debussy's *Nocturnes* and *Iberia*, Dukas' *La Péri*, Berlioz's overtures *Le Carnaval romain* and *Benvenuto Cellini*, and Romeo's Rêverie and the Fête des Capulets from the *Roméo et Juliette* symphony, Franck's *Psyché* and his arrangement of the Chorale from the *Prélude, Chorale et Fugue*, Ravel's *Pavane pour une infante défunte*, *Ma Mère l'Oye* and *Rapsodie espagnole*, *Till Eulenspiegel*, Stravinsky's *Feux d'artifice*, polka from the Suite No. 2, *Petrushka* and the berceuse from *L'Oiseau de feu*, a suite from his own ballet *Cydalise et le chèvre-pied*, his ballet suites *Giration* and *Impression de music hall* and the incidental music to *Ramuntcho*, *In the Steppes of Central Asia*, the

L'Arlésienne Suite No. 1, the introduction and Cortège from *Le Coq d'or* and *The Flight of the Bumble Bee*, the Bacchanale from *Samson et Dalila*, the preludes to Acts I and III of *Die Meistersinger*, Lalo's *Rapsodie norvégienne* and the overture to *Le Roi d'Ys*, the Scherzo and the Nocturne from *A Midsummer Night's Dream*. These were for Odeon, and some were issued in the US by Decca.

Pikler, Robert (b. 1909). Born in Budapest, Pikler studied at the Franz Liszt Academy and after graduating toured as a violinist. He took his own orchestra to India and the Far East (1934–42), was interned during World War II by the Japanese (1942–5), went to Sydney and there formed and was leader of the Musica Viva Chamber Players. He was principal viola player with the Sydney Symphony Orchestra (1952–66), artistic director and violist of the Sydney String Quartet, conductor of his own chamber orchestra, and head of the string school of the New South Wales State Conservatorium of Music in Sydney. Pikler has been a major source of inspiration in the development of chamber music in Australia, and has achieved much in training string players in New South Wales. He has recorded, as a conductor, Haydn's Symphony No. 55, Mozart's Sinfonia Concertante K. 297b, Bassoon Concerto (with Cran), Oboe Concerto (with Webb) and Clarinet Concerto (with Westlake), Hummel's Trumpet Concerto (with Webb), Goossens' Oboe Concerto (with Webb) and the overture to *Benvenuto Cellini* (with the Sydney Symphony Orchestra for RCA).

Pini, Carl (b. 1934). The son of the cellist Anthony Pini, Pini was born in London, and studied the violin under Lasserson and Benedetti. In 1955 he joined the Boyd Neel Orchestra, whose players later became the Philomusica, and led the orchestra for many concerts, at the same time leading the London String Quartet. He became professor of violin at the New South Wales State Conservatorium of Music in Sydney (1968), founded and conducted his own chamber orchestra, the Sinfonia of Sydney, and led the Carl Pini Quartet, while also appearing as soloist and conductor with orchestras in Australia and New Zealand. He returned to England to become the co-leader of the English Chamber Orchestra, concertmaster of the New Philharmonia Orchestra, and professor at the Royal College of Music. He recorded as a conductor the overture to Méhul's *La Chasse du jeune Henri* and *Five Variants of Dives and Lazarus* of Vaughan Williams, with the Sydney Symphony Orchestra for RCA.

Pinnock, Trevor (b. 1946). Born in Canterbury and educated at the Royal College of Music, London (1964–7), Pinnock was a member of the Galliard Harpischord Trio (1966–72) and then directed the English Concert, a group performing baroque music on original instruments, which has given radio broadcasts and has appeared at many festivals. He has recorded as a harpsichordist, and in 1975 led the English Consort in a recording of Bach's Harpsichord Concerto No. 3 and C. P. E. Bach's *Harpsichord Concerti in E* and *G* (with himself as soloist) and in 1976 Vivaldi's *The Four Seasons* (with Standage), both for CRD.

Pinkas, Jiři (b. 1920). Born in Prague, Pinkas appeared in public as a pianist at the age of six, studied privately with Štěpánová-Kurzová, and gave a concert with the Czech Philharmonic Orchestra at the age of twelve. He was the pianist with the Prague Trio (1943–5), studied conducting with Dědeček and Špidra at the Prague Conservatory, graduated in 1955, and attended Markevitch's conducting course at Salzburg in 1956. He was artistic director of the Czech Radio Choir (1945–55), conductor at the Janáček Opera House, Brno (1955), and conductor of the Brno State Philharmonic Orchestra (1962). His recordings, for Supraphon, include Dvořák's *Legends*, Tchaikovsky's Piano Concerto No. 1, Rachmaninov's Piano Concerto No. 1 and *Rhapsody on a Theme of Paganini* (with Kamenikova), and Martinů's Piano Concerto No. 4 (with Páleníček, and the Brno State Philharmonic Orchestra), Janáček's cantatas *Eternal Gospel*, *Lord Have Mercy*, *Our Father* and *There Upon the Mountain* (with the Prague Symphony Orchestra *et al.*), and a disc of opera choruses.

Pinkham, Daniel (b. 1923). Born at Lynn, Massachusetts, Pinkham was educated at Harvard University and studied with Landowska, Biggs, Boulanger, Honegger and Piston. He has taught at Harvard and Boston Universities, Dartington Hall, Devon, and at the New England Conservatory at Boston. His compositions include orchestral music, concertos, cantatas and chamber music. His recordings include five cantatas of Buxtehude (with the Cambridge Festival Orchestra *et al.* for Westminster), music by Schütz (with the Vienna Symphony Orchestra *et al.* for Westminster), Purcell's *The Fairy Queen* (with the Cambridge Festival Orchestra *et al.* for Allegro), Couperin's *Première leçon des ténèbres* and *Audite omnes et expavescite* (with Cuénod and a chamber ensemble for Allegro), pieces by Rorem, Wuorinen, Kay and Flanagan (wth the Cambridge Festival Strings *et al.* for Cambridge), and Sims' *Cantata on Chinese Poems* (with a chamber ensemble for Composers Recordings). He also recorded as a harpsichordist.

Piradov (1892–1954). Conductor at the Kiev Opera and Ballet Theatre, and a professor at the Kiev Conservatory, Piradov recorded with the Kiev Opera Orchestra *et al.* Rimsky-Korsakov's *The Tsar's Bride*, Act III of Rubinstein's *The Demon* and Dankevich's *Bogdan Khmelnitzky*.

Pitamic, Alexander von (b. 1918). Born in Klagenfurt, Pitamic spent his childhood in Vienna where he studied at the Academy of Music (1938–9) and later with Krauss at the Salzburg Mozarteum (1942). He was a violist in orchestras in Vienna, played under Furtwängler, Böhm, Strauss, Krauss *et al.*, and after World War II became conductor at the Salzburg Landestheater. In 1953 he was appointed professor at the Mozarteum, and assistant to Paumgartner in the Camerata Academica, continued as a solo violist, conducted the Winterthur Municipal Orchestra in Switzerland for a Mozart festival, toured Europe with the Salzburg Mozart Opera, led a conducting course in Lisbon, and conducted in Japan. His recordings include Haydn's Symphonies Nos 83 and 85 (with the South German Philharmonic Orchestra, issued by Pye), Mozart's Symphonies Nos 36 and 38 (with the South German Philharmonic Orchestra for Intercord), and Piano Concertos K. 453 and K. 466 (with Lang and the Nuremberg Symphony Orchestra for Intercord), Chopin's Piano Concerto No. 1 (with Gröschel and the Munich Philharmonic Orchestra for Intercord), Beethoven's Symphony No. 3, Schubert's Symphony No. 8 and *Rosamunde* music, *Don Juan*, the Bruckner's Symphony No. 7, Brahms' Double Concerto and Mendelssohn Violin Concerto (with the NHK Symphony Orchestra *et al.*).

Pitt, Percy (1870–1932). A Londoner, Pitt studied in Paris, in Leipzig under Reinecke and Jadassohn, and in Munich under Rheinberger, and returned to England in 1893. He was chorus-master for concerts given by Mottl (1895), organist at the Queen's Hall orchestral concerts (1896), musical adviser and conductor at Covent Garden (1902–7), musical adviser to the Grand Opera Syndicate (1907), conductor with the Beecham Opera Company (1915–18), artistic director of the British National Opera Company (1920–24), chief music director to the BBC (1922–30) and music director at Covent Garden (1924), where he conducted first performances of, among other works, *Bastien und Bastienne*, *L'Enfant prodigue*, *Ivanhoe*, *L'Heure espagnole*, *Thérèse* and *Khovanshchina*. He composed a symphony and other music. He made records for Columbia and HMV; the first were a coupling of the intermezzi from Acts I and III of Wolf-Ferrari's *I gioielli della Madonna* (*c.* 1916, with the Imperial Symphony Orchestra) and the Rhine Journey from *Götterdämmerung* and Forest Murmurs from *Siegfried* (*c.* 1920, with an unidentified orchestra). His later discs were selections from *Aida*, *Tosca* and other operas (with the New Queen's Hall Light Orchestra for Columbia), *La Boutique fantasque*, and selections from *Lohengrin*, *Samson et Dalila*, *Il trovatore* and some Gilbert and Sullivan operas (with the BBC Wireless Symphony Orchestra for Regal-Zonaphone), and with the BBC Symphony Orchestra the overtures *Ruy Blas*, *Il barbiere di Siviglia* and *Semiramide*, the Glazunov *Concert Waltz No. 1*, Elgar's *Empire March*, the Pilgrims' Chorus from *Tannhäuser* and excerpts from *La Boutique fantasque* (for Columbia), the overture *Dichter und Bauer*, a suite from *Nutcracker* and the *Raymond* overture (for HMV; the last-named was with an unidentified orchestra).

Pittaluga, Gustavo (b. 1906). Born in Madrid, Pittaluga studied at the Madrid University, with Esplá, and in Paris, conducted in Spain and Mexico, and was on the staff of the Spanish Embassy in Washington (1936–9), and then remained in the United States. He composed a ballet, *La Roméria de los Cornudos* (1933), which he recorded with the soprano Estramera and an orchestra for HMV.

Pittman, Richard (b. 1935). Born in Baltimore, Pittman graduated from the Peabody Conservatory in 1957, and then studied conducting with Halasz in New York, Celibidache at the Accademia Chigiana in Siena, with Brückner-Rüggeberg in Hamburg, Boulez in Basel, Lert in Virginia and with Susskind in St Louis. He taught conducting and was conductor of the opera department at the Eastman School of Music and there founded the Eastman Musica Viva (1965–8), was appointed conductor of the Concord Orchestra, Massachusetts (from 1969), founded and is musical director of the Boston Musica Viva, with which he toured Europe in 1973, is conductor of the Repertory Orchestra and teacher of conducting at the New England Conservatory at Boston, and has been a guest conductor in Washington DC, New York, Boston and Hamburg. He has recorded with the Boston Musica Viva music by Seeger, Mekeel, Musgrave, Schwantner, Ives, Berio, Davidovsky and David Harrison (for Delos) and pieces by Heiss and Edwards (for Composers Recordings), and with the New England Conservatory Repertory Orchestra Schwantner's *Modus Caelestis* (for Composers Recordings).

Pitz, Wilhelm (1897–1973). Born at Breinig, near Aachen, Pitz studied the violin and piano, and started his career as a violinist with the Aachen Municipal Orchestra in 1913. In 1933 he became director of the chorus at the Aachen Opera House, and in 1946 the principal conductor. He was director of the Cologne Men's Glee Club (1949–57) and of the Bayreuth Festival Chorus (1951), and was engaged by Legge as chorus-master of the Philharmonia Chorus, which he trained and developed to an extraordinary standard. The Philharmonia Chorus was re-named the New Philharmonia Chorus after 1964, when Legge ceased to control the Philharmonia Orchestra; it returned to its old name in 1977. The Bayreuth chorus appeared in many sets of the Wagner operas recorded at Bayreuth, and the Philharmonia Chorus was associated with the Philharmonia Orchestra in many distinguished recordings under Klemperer, Giulini and others. Pitz made records on his own account; he conducted the Bayreuth Festival Chorus and Orchestra in choruses from the Wagner operas (for DGG) and in excerpts from *Tannhäuser* (for EMI), and the New Philharmonia Chorus and Orchestra in Brahms' *Nänie* and choral pieces by Wolf, Nuffel, Mozart, Bruckner and Beethoven.

Pizzetti, Ildebrando (1880–1968). The distinguished Italian composer Pizzetti was also a teacher and critic, was director of the Milan Conservatory (1924–36), and professor of composition at the Accademia di Santa Cecilia (from 1936). In the latter part of his life he was active as a conductor, particularly of his own operas. He made at least one record, with the La Scala Orchestra, of several numbers from his incidental music to *La Pisanella*.

Plasson, Michel (b. 1933). Born in Paris, into a professionally musical family, Plasson studied the piano as a child, and then was a percussion student at the Paris Conservatoire. He was awarded first prize at the International Competition for Young Conductors at Besançon in 1962, then studied conducting in the United States with Monteux, Leinsdorf and Stokowski. On his return to France he became musical director at Metz, and then general music director of the Toulouse Capitole Orchestra in 1968. He has conducted in Japan, Bulgaria, Italy and DR and FR Germany, toured the United States with the Paris Opéra in 1976, and appeared at the New York Metropolitan Opera. His recordings include Offenbach's *La Vie parisienne* (for EMI), and *La Grande Duchesse de Gérolstein* (for CBS), Chausson's *Symphony in B flat major* and *Soir de fête*, and the five Saint-Saëns piano concertos (with Entremont, for CBS). All have been with the Toulouse Capitole Orchestra *et al.*

Plichta, Jan (b. 1898). Born in Kouřím, Plichta studied for a time at the Prague Conservatory (1912–14), played in a cinema orchestra, served in the army (1916–18), and was concertmaster (1919–24) and then conductor (1927–9) at the South Bohemian Theatre at České Budějovíce. He also led the South Bohemian Quartet, studied theory and composition, was leader of the Ostrava Radio Orchestra, was chief of radio programmes at Ostrava (1929–36), music director at Brno (1936–51), violist with the Dolezalov Quartet (1950–55) and taught at the Brno Conservatory. His compositions include operettas and chamber music. For Supraphon he recorded *Eight Moravian Dances* of Axman with the Brno Radio Orchestra.

Pohl, Rudolf (b. 1924). Born at Aachen, Pohl studied philosophy, theology and musicology, and has been conductor of the cathedral choral school and of the boys' choir at Aachen since 1954, and cathedral kapellmeister since 1964. With the choir *et al.* he has recorded Bach's Cantata No. 106, Telemann's Cantata, *Du aber Daniel*, and Hassler's *Missa octavi toni*, *Sanctus* and *Agnus Dei*, and some motets (for BASF), and Hassler's *Domine Dominus Noster* (for Harmonia Mundi).

Polgar, Tibor (b. 1907). Born in Budapest and educated at the Royal Academy of Music and University there, Polgar was composer-in-residence with the Hungarian Broadcasting Corporation (1925–48), artistic director of the Hungarian Radio (1948–50), associate conductor of the Philharmonia Hungarica (1962–4), and then joined the teaching staff of the opera department at the Toronto University in Canada in 1966. His compositions include operas, a cantata, and numerous film and radio scores. Qualiton issued a disc on which he conducts the Hungarian State Symphony Orchestra in Weiner's *Concertino* (with soloist Hernadi).

Polidori, Ivan (b. 1921). Born in Viareggio, Lucca, Polidori studied the violin and composition at the Boccherini Conservatory at Lucca, and conducted first with Radio Italiana in 1958. He conducted the Orchestra da Camera of Genoa, and the Piccolocoro Polifonico del Teatro Carlo Felice in Genoa; he recorded Boccherini's *Stabat Mater* with the Genoa Chamber Orchestra *et al.* for Disco Vibrafon, which was issued in the United States by Musical Heritage Society.

Pomykalo, Ferdo (1915–73). Born in Banya Luka, Yugoslavia, Pomykalo studied composition and conducting privately, was director of the Zagreb Radio Symphony Orchestra and conductor at the Komedija Theatre in Zagreb. For Jugoton he recorded Tijardović's *Mala Floramye*, with the Zagreb Opera Orchestra *et al.*

Poole, John (b. 1934). Born in Birmingham, Poole was educated at Balliol College, Oxford, and is a Fellow of the Royal College of Organists. Since 1972 he has been director of the BBC Singers, and with them recorded Dallapiccola's *Tempus destruendi*, and Shaw's *Lesson from Ecclesiastes*, *Music When Soft Voices Die*, *To the Bandusian Spring* and *Peter and the Lame Man* (for Argo, the last-named with the BBC Symphony Orchestra *et al.*).

Pope, Stanley (b. 1916). Born in London, Pope studied in London, Vienna and Switzerland, where his teachers included Frank Martin for composition and Kletzki for conducting at the Lausanne Conservatory. Later he was associated with Weingartner and Schuricht, acted as a repetiteur at the Basel Theatre, and taught chamber music at the Geneva Conservatoire. After World War II he conducted orchestras in Britain, Switzerland, FR Germany and in other European countries, in particular specialising in Haydn, Beethoven, Brahms and Richard Strauss. In the mid 1950s he made several LPs for Philips with the Royal Philharmonic Orchestra; they were four of the five *Pomp and Circumstance* marches of Elgar, and a fine performance of Schumann's No. 4, in its original version.

Popesco, Trajan (b. 1921). Born in Florica, Buzău, Romania, Popesco studied at the National Academy of Music at Bucharest, and at the Paris Conservatoire, and made a career as a violinist, conductor, orchestral leader, teacher and composer. He has conducted the French National Orchestra and the Belgian Radio Orchestra, has toured Europe with his own chamber orchestra, and in 1955 was awarded the Prix International des Jeunes Chefs d'Orchestre. His recordings include Charpentier's *Missa Solemnis* (with Orchestre de Chambre de la Radio-Télévision Français *et al.* for Schwann), and a collection *Musique byzantine* (for Harmonia Mundi).

Popescu, Paul. Born in Brasov, Romania, Popescu attended the Ciprian Porumbescu Conservatory in Bucharest, and studied conducting with Georgescu, Silvestri and Rogalski. He was appointed conductor of the Timişoara Philharmonic Orchestra after graduating in 1954, was leader of the Film Symphony Orchestra (1959), and also conducted the George Enesco Philharmonic Orchestra in Bucharest. He taught conducting at the Ciprian Porumbescu Conservatory (1961–5), and conducted the Youth Symphony Orchestra, studied conducting with Swarowsky in Vienna (1962–3), founded and conducted a chamber orchestra formed from the members of the Bucharest Philharmonic Orchestra, became permanent conductor of the Romanian Opera at Bucharest (1966), and has toured extensively in East and West Europe, with a repertoire extending from the baroque composers to Schoenberg and Bartók, and also including many contemporary Romanian composers. He has recorded for Electrecord Gershwin's *Rhapsody in Blue* and *Piano Concerto in F* (with Mizrachy), Andricu's *Serenade* and Dumitrescu's suite *The Retezat Mountain* (with the Romanian Film Orchestra), Toduţa's Four *Intabulations* and Popovici's *Byzantine Poem* and *Codex Caioni* (with the Bucharest Philharmonic Chamber Orchestra).

Popper, Jan (b. 1907). Born at Reichenberg (Liberec), Czechoslovakia, Popper studied at the German Music Academy at Prague, the Vienna Conservatory, the Leipzig Conservatory and with Teichmüller at Leipzig, and made his debut as a conductor at the Reichenberg Theatre in 1930. He was conductor at Reichenberg (1930–35), and at the Prague German Opera (1935–9), then migrated to the United States and became director of the opera schools at Stanford University (1939–49) and the University of California, Los Angeles (1949–75), as well as being a guest conductor in Japan, Belgium, Iran and California. He has conducted the US premières of Bloch's *Macbeth*, and Bennett's *The Mines of Sulphur*, in addition to many first performances on the US West Coast, and received the awards of the National Association of American Composers and Conductors in 1959 and 1964. For Orion he conducted the Royal Philharmonic Orchestra *et al.* in Travis' *The Passion of Oedipus*, *Symphonic Allegro*, Piano Concerto (with Vallecillo) and *Songs and Epilogues* (with Enns).

Porter, Quincy (1897–1966). Born in New Haven, Connecticut, and a student of Horatio Parker, David Stanley Smith, d'Indy and Bloch, Porter was a distinguished teacher at the Cleveland Institute of Music, Vassar College, the New England Conservatory and Yale University. His compositions included orchestral music, concertos and chamber music, and he once recorded his own solo viola suite (for New Music Recording, on 78s). He conducted the Colonne Orchestra in his Symphony No. 1, *Dance in Three-Time* and *Concerto Concertante for Two Pianos* (for Overtone, on LP).

Post, Joseph (1906–72). Born in Sydney where his father was an amateur conductor, Post studied at the State Conservatorium of Music in Sydney, won distinction as an oboist, and became first known as a conductor with an Italian opera company visiting Australia and New Zealand in 1932. He conducted the Melbourne Symphony Orchestra (1936–9), was for five years in the Australian army in World War II, became assistant conductor to Goossens with the Sydney Symphony Orchestra (1947–56), and at the same time was principal conductor of the Australian National Opera. In 1950 he conducted the BBC Northern Orchestra for a season, in 1956 was musical director of the Elizabethan Theatre Opera Company in Australia, and in 1966 became director of the State Conservatorium of Music in Sydney. Post was a competent conductor who made a valuable contribution to the widespread post-war development of music in Australia. He recorded the music of Australian composers, with the Sydney Symphony Orchestra: trumpet concertos by Hanson and Lovelock (with Robertson for RCA), Hughes' Symphony No. 1 (for Festival), Meale's *Very High Kings* (for World Record Club), and Cugley's *Pan the Lake* and *Prelude for Orchestra*, Hill's Violin Concerto (with Elliott) and Hughes' *Xanadu* Suite (for EMI).

Poulet, Gaston (1892–1974). Born in Paris, Poulet graduated from the Paris Conservatoire in 1910 with the first prize for violin, embarked on a career as a soloist and as a duo with Yves Nat, the pianist, and founded the Poulet String Quartet, which gave concerts throughout Europe. Debussy wrote his *Sonata for Violin and Piano* for him, and after the Poulet Quartet had played his String Quartet, Debussy said that it was not at all as he had imagined it, but that henceforth it should be played in that way. Poulet turned to conducting, founded the Concerts Poulet in Paris, and conducted in South America and Europe (1925–30). In the 1930s he was appointed director of the Bordeaux Conservatoire, established the Bordeaux Municipal Orchestra, and was the first conservatory director to start a class for operetta. He became professor of conducting at the Paris Conservatoire (1945–6), founded the International Music Festival at Besançon (1947), was conductor of the Colonne Orchestra in the 1950s, conducted many major European orchestras including the London Symphony, and helped to establish the French National Railwaymen's Orchestra. He recorded chamber music by Debussy, Franck, Fauré, *et al.* His wife was Jane Évrard, the conductor, and his son, Gérard Poulet, the violinist.

As a conductor, Poulet recorded, on 78s, Franck's *Rédemption*, Mendelssohn's Symphony No. 4, Schmitt's *Rondo burlesque* and excerpts from Prokofiev's *Chout* and *The Love of Three Oranges* (with the Poulet Orchestra, released in Britain by Parlophone and Decca), Debussy's *Iberia* (with the Pierné Society Orchestra for Columbia), and Elizalde's Violin Concerto (with Ferras and the London Symphony Orchestra for Decca). His LPs were few, and included Saint-Saëns' Violin Concerto No. 3 (with Menuhin and the Philharmonia Orchestra for EMI), Mozart's Violin Concertos K. 216 and K. 218 (with Gérard Poulet and the Austrian Symphony Orchestra for Remington), the Albéniz/Arbós *Iberia*, Turina's *La Procesión del rocío*, the intermezzo from Granados' *Goyescas*, the interlude and dance from *La vida breve*, Ravel's *Pavane pour une infante défunte*, *Une Barque sur l'océan* and *Alborada del gracioso*, and the *Pelléas et Mélisande* suite of Fauré (with the London Symphony Orchestra for Parlophone).

Pousseur, Henri (b. 1929). Born in Malmédy, Belgium, Pousseur studied in Brussels and with Souris and Boulez, and became a member of *Variation*, a group of *avant-garde* composers at Liège. His compositions include works employing aleatoric elements and electronic sounds, and he published a book *Fragments théoriques sur la musique expérimentale* (Brussels, 1970). BASF recorded him directing the Ensemble Musique Nouvelle Bruxelles in his *Votre Faust*. This opera, written in 1961–7, is a synthesis of many styles of composition and has allusions to the music of the past; Berio said of it that 'the main personage . . . is the history of music, not out of the old Faustian urge to use the past, but out of the desire and the need to deal with realities wherever they may be'.

Prausnitz, Frederik (b. 1920). Born in Cologne, Prausnitz migrated to the United States before World War II, graduated from the Juilliard School and subsequently became a professor and dean at the School. His debut as a conductor was with the Detroit Symphony Orchestra in 1944; he conducted the New England Conservatory Symphony Orchestra (1956–61) and the Syracuse Symphony Orchestra (since 1971), has been a guest conductor with many symphony orchestras in the US and Europe, and was director of the International Society for Contemporary Music (1960–62). Although he seeks to avoid classification as a specialist in modern music, Prausnitz is known to record-collectors for his discs of 20th-century music: Ruggles' *Evocations*, *Lilacs*, and *Portals* (with the Juilliard String Orchestra for CBS), Dallapiccola's *Liriche greche*, Nos 1 and 3, *Goethe Lieder*, *Cinque canti* and *Concerto per la notte di natale dell'anno* (with soloists and an instrumental ensemble, for CBS), Walton's *Façade* (with Dame Edith Sitwell and a chamber orchestra for CBS), Carter's *Double Concerto* and *Variations for Orchestra* (with the New Philharmonia Orchestra *et al.* for CBS), Schoenberg's *Chamber Symphony No. 2* (with the New Philharmonia Orchestra for EMI), Musgrave's *Night Music for Two Horns*, Riegger's *Dichotomy*, and Sessions' Symphony No. 8 and *Rhapsody* (with the London Sinfonietta and New Philharmonia Orchestra for Argo).

Preston, Simon (b. 1938). Born in Bournemouth and educated at the Royal Academy of Music and King's College, Cambridge, Preston was sub-organist at Westminster Abbey (1962–7), and has been organist and lecturer in music at Christ Church, Oxford since 1970. He has composed a Missa Brevis for choir and organ, organ and choral pieces, has made outstanding records as an organist, and conducted the Northern Sinfonia *et al.* in Arne's opera *Thomas and Sally* (for Pye) and the English Chamber Orchestra *et al.* in Handel's *Israel in Egypt* (for Argo).

Prêtre, Georges (b. 1924). Born in Douai, France, Prêtre was educated at the conservatoire there and at the Paris Conservatoire (1939–44), was a trumpet player, and studied conducting with Cluytens and at the Strarum Foundation. As a teenager he had become familiar with the operatic repertoire by sitting through countless performances in the orchestral pits at the Paris Opéra and Opéra-Comique. His first ambition was to become a composer; he wrote a symphony and several operettas, but he found conducting too strong an attraction. He made his debut at the Marseille Opera House with *Samson et Dalila* in 1946; he remained at Marseille (1946–7), then was conductor at Lille (1948), Casablanca (1949–50) and Toulouse (1951–4), then became music director at the Opéra-Comique, Paris (1955–9), a conductor at the Paris Opéra (1959–70), and music director at the Paris Opéra (1970–71). His debut in the United States was at the Chicago Lyric Opera (1959); he conducted at Covent Garden (1961), the New York Metropolitan (1964–5) and La Scala (1965–6), conducted the major French orchestras, was a permanent conductor at the Vienna State Opera, has been a guest conductor with many major symphony orchestras in Europe and the US, and has performed at festivals such as Salzburg (1966). In 1962 he was invited by Beecham to conduct his Royal Philharmonic Orchestra, and after Beecham's death became an associate conductor of the orchestra (1962), and toured the US with them in 1963. He gave the première of Poulenc's *La Voix humaine* in 1959, and has led first performances of others of the composer's works. He has also been associated with the soprano Callas, in concert, opera and on record.

In his native France, Prêtre has always performed a wide repertoire, from Mozart to Wagner and Strauss, and modern French composers such as Poulenc, and is equally committed to operatic and symphonic music. His style is distinctive; in concert performances, especially in French music, he applies more rubato than usual, but on record his performances of Berlioz, in particular, are not notably perceptive. Like many Italian and French conductors, who regularly perform Italian and German operas in their home countries, abroad he is expected primarily to conduct music of his native country; his performances of the rest of the repertoire are regarded as unidiomatic. Perhaps this is another way of saying that French and Italian conductors have traditions of performing the general repertoire different from others.

Prêtre has recorded extensively for EMI and RCA, mainly, again, music of French composers. Of Poulenc he has recorded (all for EMI) the *Suite française*, *Sinfonietta*, *La Baigneuse de Trouville*, *Deux Marches et un intermède* (with the Paris Orchestra), *Les*

Biches, *Aubade*, and Piano Concerto (with Tacchino), *Concert champêtre*, *Two-Piano Concerto* (with Poulenc and Février), *Stabat Mater*, *Les Animaux modèles* and *Babar le petit éléphant* (with the Paris Conservatoire Orchestra *et al.*) and Organ Concerto (with Duruflé) and *Gloria* (with the French National Radio Orchestra *et al.*); for Vox he also recorded *La Voix humaine* (with the Paris Opéra-Comique Orchestra *et al.*). His other records include *La Damnation de Faust*, excerpts from *Les Troyens*, *Carmen*, *Lakmé*, *Werther*, *Samson et Dalila*, *Alceste* and excerpts from *Hérodiade* (with the Paris Opéra Orchestra *et al.* for EMI), *Lucia di Lammermoor* and *La traviata* (with the RCA Italiana Orchestra *et al.* for RCA), *Tosca*, *Iphigénie en Tauride* and excerpts from Bécaud's *Opéra d'Aran* (with the Paris Conservatoire Orchestra *et al.* for EMI), *Louise* (with the New Philharmonia Orchestra *et al.* for CBS), *Symphonie fantastique* (with the Boston Symphony Orchestra for RCA), the Tchaikovsky Symphony No. 5 (with the Philharmonia Orchestra for EMI), *In the Steppes of Central Asia*, *A Night on the Bare Mountain*, *Capriccio espagnol*, and Polovtsian Dances from *Prince Igor* (with the Royal Philharmonic Orchestra for EMI), Rachmaninov's Piano Concerto No. 2 (with Weissenberg and the Chicago Symphony Orchestra for RCA), Saint-Saëns' Symphony No. 3, *Le Carnaval des animaux*, Dutilleux's *Le Loup*, Milhaud's *La Création du monde*, Harsányi's *Story of the Little Tailor*, Berg's *Chamber Concerto* and Violin Concerto (with Ferras) and Gershwin's *Concerto in F* and *Rhapsody in Blue* (with Wayenberg, and with the Paris Conservatoire Orchestra *et al.* for EMI), Franck's *Psyché et Eros*, Debussy's *Nuages* and *Fêtes* and the *Daphnis et Chloé* Suite No. 2 (with the Royal Philharmonic Orchestra for Reader's Digest), and accompaniments for Callas, Crespin and Benoit.

Previn, André (b. 1929). Born in Berlin as Ludwig Andreas Priwin, Previn grew up in an intensely musical background under the influence of his father, Jacob Priwin, who was a successful lawyer and judge. He was taken to his first symphony concert – Furtwängler and the Berlin Philharmonic Orchestra – when he was five, and the next year he was enrolled in the Hochschule für Musik. By the time he was eight he was a fluent pianist and was playing piano duets with his father, but then he was expelled from the Hochschule because he was Jewish. The family fled to Paris, where Previn was for a year at the Paris Conservatoire, studying under Dupré, and then in 1939 the family moved to the United States, to take up residence in Los Angeles, a relative there being the head of the music department at Universal Studios. As a boy, Previn soon became well known as a pianist, and when still at school he was a professional composer of film music for the MGM Studios. There he had the opportunity to conduct his own music with the studio orchestra, to conduct the players after-hours in some of the symphonic repertoire, and to conduct the California Youth Symphony Orchestra. At this time he took lessons in composition from Castelnuovo-Tedesco, Achron and Toch. He became a US citizen in 1943.

Previn's reputation as a jazz pianist soon spread, and in 1945 he made a couple of records for RCA, which sold over 200,000 copies. As the pianist in a jazz trio he recorded discs for Contemporary, and one of these, an arrangement of *My Fair Lady*, sold over 500,000 copies. Altogether, in his Hollywood years he made over 100 records as a jazz pianist or film composer. His first film score, for a Lassie film, was in 1949, and in the 1950s he arranged scores and wrote original music for films. When he was on the staff of MGM he won an Oscar for his arrangement of *Gigi* (1958), and then was awarded three more Oscars for *Porgy and Bess* (1959), *Irma la Douce* (1963) and *My Fair Lady* (1964). At this time his interest was turning more towards serious music; earlier, during a two-year period in the army when he became concertmaster of the Sixth Army Band, he started conducting lessons with Monteux in San Francisco, and continued them for a year after his army discharge. He established a name in Los Angeles as a classical pianist, gave concerts with the Pacific Arts Trio, made records for CBS of music by Barber, Hindemith, Martin *et al.*, and appeared with major orchestras as a soloist. By 1954 he had determined to cast off his Hollywood activities altogether and to become a conductor, but, because he refused to conduct light-music programmes with the major orchestras, for some time he took engagements with provincial and semi-professional orchestras so that he could perform the classical repertoire.

Records were a critical influence in propelling Previn to the forefront as a conductor. He made his first and only record as a conductor for CBS in 1962, Britten's *Sinfonia da Requiem* and Copland's *The Red Pony* with the St Louis Symphony Orchestra, and two years later recorded accompaniments in London for RCA with pianists Hollander and Pennario, with the Royal Philharmonic Orchestra. In 1965 RCA brought him back to London to record Shostakovich's Symphony No. 5 and Tchaikovsky's Symphony No. 2, with *Eight Russian*

Folksongs of Liadov, with the London Symphony Orchestra; the success of these records led to others with the London Symphony, and to a close association with the orchestra in concert engagements. In the meantime, he was appointed music director of the Houston Symphony Orchestra (1967–9), and in 1968 he became principal conductor of the London Symphony in succession to Kertész. In 1976 he was engaged as principal conductor of the Pittsburgh Symphony Orchestra, his contract running to the 1981–2 season; he remained with the London Symphony until 1979, when he was succeeded by Abbado. He has toured the US with the London Symphony five times, as well as visiting the USSR and the Far East, and in 1972–3 was the organiser of the South Bank Summer Music Festival in London. His compositions include two concert overtures, a symphony for strings, concertos for cello and guitar, vocal and piano music.

Previn's years with the London Symphony have brought him and the orchestra immense success, in concert, on record and as television personalities. His period in Hollywood gave him excellent experience in rehearsing and controlling symphony orchestras, even if it was in performing music of quite ephemeral value. Much as he would like to lose his association with film and jazz, he has not entirely been able to do so; his sharp-witted glib volubility, the familiar cosiness of his manner, and his undeniable liking for public exposure on television have scarcely assisted. Nonetheless he cannot be mistaken for anything but a most serious and highly accomplished musician with a superb touch for, in his own words, 'colourful music, with a strong nationalistic flavour'. Since he joined the London Symphony his repertoire has expanded rapidly; he professes the greatest devotion to Mozart, but his genius as a conductor is inevitably with the music of composers such as Tchaikovsky, Rachmaninov, Shostakovich and Prokofiev. Since his early years he has been attracted to British music, particularly Vaughan Williams, Walton and Britten, and he has been one of their most enthusiastic and effective proponents; in fact he is said to have done more for 20th-century British music than any other present-day conductor. His television shows, with the London Symphony, have been extremely popular in Britain, and he has introduced serious music to a vast public. The *New Statesman* (28 December 1973) rather cruelly described his television performances as 'a Strauss-and-Rachmaninov sandwich, perhaps, stuffed with a little Vaughan Williams and garnished with a loose-lipped lowbrow introduction'.

Previn's compliant personality makes his relationship with the orchestra a relaxed, give-and-take one, the opposite of the usual stereotype. His perfect pitch was evident from childhood; he quickly assimilates scores but does not claim a photographic memory. He retains his facility with the piano, and has recorded and appeared as a soloist and chamber player. Like many other American conductors, he has an extroverted predilection for tonal weight, and less concern for the finesse of style and touch necessary for Haydn and Mozart, but then the German and Austrian classics are not the natural focus of his musical culture. In fact, Previn finds himself unsympathetic to Bruckner and Wagner, although not to Mahler; contemporary music is also of limited interest, and he dislikes performing music for which he has no feeling. It is facile to dismiss him for the weaknesses in his repertoire rather than to recognise him for his strengths; he is undoubtedly overexposed as a musician, and anyone who believes a great conductor is judged on how he performs the greatest music must suspend judgement on Previn.

Ignoring his records as a jazz pianist, solo and ensemble pianist, and taking into account only the records which he has made as an orchestral conductor, Previn has a remarkable number of distinguished discs to his credit. His first LP was with the St Louis Symphony Orchestra (mentioned above); in the series for RCA with the London Symphony dating from 1965 there have been Vaughan Williams' nine symphonies, *England of Elizabeth* suite, *Concerto accademico* (with Buswell) Tuba Concerto (with Fletcher) and overture to *The Wasps*, Prokofiev's Symphony No. 1, Tchaikovsky's Symphony No. 2, Liadov's *Eight Russian Folksongs*, Walton's Symphony No. 1, Shostakovich's Symphony No. 5, Rachmaninov's Symphonies Nos 2 and 3 and *The Rock*, Françaix's *L'Horloge de Flore*, Satie's *Gymnopédies* Nos 1 and 3, Ibert's *Symphonie concertante*, Strauss's *Don Juan* and a suite from *Der Rosenkavalier*, Mendelssohn's Symphony No. 4 and *Ruy Blas* overture, *Scheherazade* and the March and Flight of the Bumble Bee from *Tsar Saltan*, the Nielsen Symphony No. 1 and the prelude to Act II of *Saul and David*, Lalo's *Symphonie espagnole* and Ravel's *Tzigane* (with Perlman).

His subsequent records with the London Symphony Orchestra for EMI include Haydn's Symphonies Nos 88 and 96, Beethoven's Symphonies Nos 5 and 7 and *Prometheus overture*, Mendelssohn's incidental music for *A Midsummer Night's Dream*, the Berlioz overtures *Le Carnaval romain*, *Béatrice et Bénédict*, *Le*

Corsaire, *Benvenuto Cellini* and *Les Francs-juges*, the three symphonies of Rachmaninov and *The Rock*, *The Bells*, *Vocalise*, *Symphonic Dances*, *The Isle of the Dead* and excerpts from *Aleko*, Prokofiev's Symphonies Nos 5 and 6, *Alexander Nevsky*, *Lieutenant Kijé* suite, *Peter and the Wolf*, and the complete *Romeo and Juliet*, Tchaikovsky's *Manfred* symphony, the complete *Nutcracker*, *Swan Lake* and *The Sleeping Beauty*, the *Romeo and Juliet* fantasy-overture, *1812* overture and *Marche slave*, Walton's Symphony No. 2, *Scapino* and *Portsmouth Point* overtures, *Belshazzar's Feast*, *Improvisations on an Impromptu of Britten* and *Orb and Sceptre*, *Prélude à l'après-midi d'un faune*, *L'Apprenti sorcier*, *La Valse*, Shostakovich's Symphonies Nos 6 and 8, Britten's *Young Person's Guide to the Orchestra*, *Sinfonia da Requiem*, and interludes from *Peter Grimes*, Holst's *The Planets*, *Egdon Heath*, *The Perfect Fool* and *The Wandering Scholar*, Orff's *Carmina Burana*, Gershwin's *An American in Paris*, Piano Concerto and *Rhapsody in Blue* (with himself as pianist), Vaughan Williams' *Greensleeves*, Enesco's *Romanian Rhapsody No. 1*, Lambert's *Rio Grande* (with Temperley, Ortiz and the London Madrigal Singers), Barber's *Adagio*, Albinoni's *Adagio*, the overtures to *Hänsel und Gretel*, *Russlan and Ludmilla* and Bernstein's *Candide*, excerpts from *The Three-cornered Hat*, Butterworth's *The Banks of Green Willow*, the *Kaiserwalzer* of Strauss, Dvořák's *Slavonic Dance No. 6*, the Mendelssohn Violin Concerto, Bruch's Violin Concerto No. 1 and Bartók's Violin Concerto No. 2 (with Perlman), Tchaikovsky's Piano Concerto No. 1 and Liszt's Piano Concerto No. 1 (with Gutierrez), Rodrigo's *Concierto de Aranjuez* and *Fantasia para un gentilhombre* (with Romero), Mozart's Piano Concerto K. 466 (with himself) and Two-Piano Concerto K. 365 (with himself and Lupu). He also recorded Ponce's *Concierto del Sur* and his own Guitar Concerto (with Williams, for CBS), the Grieg and Schumann Piano Concertos (with Lupu for Decca), the five Prokofiev Piano Concertos, the four Rachmaninov Piano Concertos and the *Rhapsody on a Theme of Paganini* (with Ashkenazy, for Decca), Shankar's Sitar Concerto (with Shankar for EMI), Violin Concertos by Tchaikovsky, Sibelius, Stravinsky and Walton and the two Prokofiev Violin Concertos (with Kyung-Wha Chung for Decca), all again with the London Symphony Orchestra. As a pianist, he has recorded the Gershwin *Concerto in F*, Mozart's Piano Concerto K. 466, the Brahms Piano Quintet and the Ravel and Shostakovich Trios; his first recording with the Pittsburgh Symphony Orchestra, in 1977, was Sibelius' Symphony No. 2.

Previtali, Fernando (b. 1907). Born in Adria and a graduate of the Giuseppe Verdi Conservatory at Turin, where he studied composition with Alfano, Previtali was assistant to Gui when the latter organised the orchestra for the Florence May Festivals (Maggio Musicale Fiorentino), from 1928 to 1936. He then was musical adviser to Italian Radio and conductor of the Rome Radio Orchestra (1936–53), principal conductor at La Scala, Milan (1942–3 and 1946–8), led a cycle of Verdi operas on Italian Radio (1951), was artistic director of the Accademia di Santa Cecilia, where he taught conducting and was permanent conductor of the orchestra (1953–73), was musical director of the Teatro Regio, Turin (1971), and conductor of the Teatro San Carlo, Naples. He first toured the United States in 1955, and has been a guest conductor with many major orchestras and at opera houses in Europe, the US, South America, the USSR, Japan, Israel and Australia. His compositions include orchestral, choral, chamber and instrumental music, and he has written a book about conducting. His musical sympathies are wide, ranging from the baroque to contemporary music, and he has premièred many works by modern Italian composers, such as Dallapiccola and Ghedini. As a conductor, he avoids romantic or expressive exaggerations, following to some extent the example of Toscanini.

Previtali first recorded on 78s for Cetra (and Parlophone) with the EIAR Orchestra (the Italian Radio Orchestra) the *Brandenburg Concerto No. 5* and the overture to *L'Italiana in Algeri*. For Cetra he made many LP recordings of operas with the Italian Radio Orchestra *et al.*, many of which were released in the US by Everest; included were *Le nozze di Figaro*, *Il barbiere di Siviglia*, *Don Carlos*, *Il trovatore*, *Suor Angelica*, *La battaglia di Legnano*, *Ernani*, *Nabucco* and *La vestale*. For RCA he also recorded *La forza del destino* and *La Gioconda* (with the Santa Cecilia Orchestra *et al.*) and *La traviata* (with the Rome Opera Orchestra *et al.*); Everest also released a two-disc set of overtures by Rossini (with the Santa Cecilia Orchestra). His other recordings included some exceptional mono LPs of Petrassi's *Concerto for Orchestra*, Respighi's *Pini di Roma* and Casella's *La Giara* (with the Santa Cecilia Orchestra for Decca); Mendelssohn's Symphony No. 3 and overture *Meeresstille und glückliche Fahrt*, Stravinsky's *Feux d'artifice* and *L'Oiseau de feu*, and Bartok's *The Miraculous Mandarin* (with the Royal Philharmonic Orchestra for EMI); *Ma Mère l'Oye*, a suite from *Carmen*, Grieg's *Three Norwegian Dances*, Kodály's *Marosszék Dances*, the ballet music from *William Tell*, the overture to *Il segreto di Susanna* and an intermezzo from *I quattro rusteghi* (with the London Symphony Orchestra for EMI); *L'Apprenti sorcier* and the overtures to *La forza del destino* and *William Tell* (with the Rome Symphony Orchestra for EMI); the *Oberon* overture (with the Rome Radio Orchestra for RCA); a recital by Labò (with the Santa Cecilia Orchestra for RCA); *Pini di Roma* and *Fontane di Roma* (with the Santa Cecilia Orchestra for Classici Musica Classica); and the Busoni Violin Concerto (with Szigeti and the Italian Radio Orchestra, issued by the Bruno Walter Society, US).

Price, Paul (b. 1921). Born in Fitchburg, Massachusetts, Price studied at the New England Conservatory and the Cincinnati Conservatory, was conductor of the Manhattan Percussion Ensemble, and a member of the American Symphony Orchestra of Stokowski, taught at the Universities of Illinois and Boston, Ithaca College, Newark College and the Manhattan School of Music (from 1957), toured the Near East for the US State Department (1967–8), and has been president and editor of Music for Percussion, Inc. He has recorded with the Manhattan Percussion Ensemble Cage's *Construction in Metal* and *Qr, She is Asleep* (from Avakian), Cage and Harrison's *Double Music for Percussion* (for Time), Chávez's *Toccata*, Hovhaness's *October Mountain* and Lo Presti's *Sketch* (for Urania), Cowell's *Ostinato Pianissimo*, Harrison's *Canticle No. 1*, Roldán's *Ritmicas 5* and *6*, and W. Russell's *Three Dance Movements* (for Mainstream), Harrison's *Suite* and Perry's *Homunculus* (for Composers Recordings), and with the University of Illinois Percussion Ensemble Chávez's *Toccata* and Varèse's *Ionisation* (for the University of Illinois).

Priem-Bergrath, Hans (b. 1925). Born in Aachen, Priem-Bergrath studied the violin with Pfeiffer at the Aachen Conservatory, saw war service (1943–5), was a violinist in the Aachen Theatre Orchestra (1945–8), concertmaster at the Mönchengladbach City Theatre (1948–50), and since 1950 has been assistant viola soloist with the Berlin Philharmonic Orchestra. He studied with Rother (1953–9), Ahlendorf (1960–66), Pitz (1967–70), Barbirolli (1968–70) and with Karajan, and since 1969 has conducted in FR Germany, Asia, Latin and South America. He has particularly impressed with his performances of music by Bartók, Shostakovich, Stravinsky and Mahler. For DGG he recorded Beethoven's marches for military band, with the wind players of the Berlin Philharmonic Orchestra.

Priestman, Brian (b. 1927). Born in Birmingham, Priestman studied at Birmingham University and at the Brussels Conservatoire, and has since followed a career as a conductor that has taken him to the United States, Canada and New Zealand. He was assistant conductor with the Yorkshire Symphony Orchestra (1952–4), conductor for the BBC, musical director of the Halifax Orchestral Society (1952–8), chorus-master of the National Opera Company (1958–61), musical director of the Shakespeare Memorial Theatre, Stratford (1960–63), conductor of the Orchestra da Camera (1957–62), musical director of the Edmonton Symphony Orchestra, Canada (1964–8), conductor of the Handel Opera Society in New York (1966), resident conductor of the Baltimore Symphony Orchestra (1968–9), musical director and conductor of the Denver Symphony Orchestra (since 1970), and principal conductor of the New Zealand Broadcasting Corporation (since 1971). He has also conducted major orchestras in Britain, Canada, the US and Australia.

In the mid 1960s, Priestman conducted a number of discs released by Westminster, including the Handel operas *Serse* and *Rodelinda*, and the secular oratorio *Hercules* (with the Vienna Academy Choir and Vienna Radio Orchestra); among the soloists were Stich-Randall, Young and Forrester, and with them he also directed discs of music by Purcell, Arne and Handel. His other records for Westminster (with the Vienna Radio Orchestra) were Mozart's Serenades K. 203 and K. 204, Piano Concertos K. 271 and K. 414 (with Fou Ts'ong, which was later released by Music for Pleasure in Britain), operatic recitals by Stich-Randall (with the Vienna Volksoper Orchestra) and Anne Ayer (with the West Austrian Tonkünstler Orchestra). He also recorded a two-disc set of arias from Bach's cantatas (with the Bach Aria Group for Desto), Bach's Cantatas Nos 3 and 102 (for Peerless), Ginastera's cantata *Milena* (with Curtin) and Chopin's Piano Concerto No. 2 (with Barrett and the Denver Symphony Orchestra for Desto), and Bliss's *Serenade* (with Shirley-Quirk and the London Symphony Orchestra for RCA).

Prieur, André. Prieur graduated from the Paris Conservatoire and made a reputation in Paris as a brilliant flautist. In 1950 he became principal flautist and soloist with the Radio Telefis Eireann Symphony Orchestra, Dublin, founded and conducted the Prieur Ensemble, a chamber orchestra, and has been a guest conductor with the RTE Orchestra. For the New Irish Recording Company he has conducted the New Irish Chamber Orchestra in recordings of Haydn's Symphonies Nos 65, 73 and 85, Stravinsky's *Dumbarton Oaks*, Victory's *Miroirs*, Berlioz's *Nuits d'été* and Berkeley's *Four Poems of St Teresa of Avila* (with Greevy), and Duff's *Echoes of Georgian Dublin*.

Prin, Yves (b. 1933). Born in Sainte-Savine, France, Prin studied at the Paris Conservatoire, and first conducted in 1959. After conducting orchestras in France, Holland and Switzerland, he was assistant to Bruno Maderna at the Salzburg Mozarteum (1968), and was appointed musical director of the Orchestre Philharmonique des Pays de la Loire (1971). He has composed an oratorio, a concerto for percussion and brass ensemble, and other pieces. Inédits de l'ORTF have released Loucheur's *Concertino pour percussion et orchestre*, in which he conducts the ORTF Philharmonic Orchestra, with Gemignani.

Pritchard, John (b. 1921). The son of a professional violinist, Pritchard was born in London, took lessons from his father on the violin, studied the piano with Petri, and went to Italy in his teens to learn about opera. In the army in World War II he was stationed at Derby, where he began conducting with the Derby String Orchestra (1943–51). On Roy Henderson's recommendation he was accepted on the staff at the Glyndebourne Festival Opera in 1947, became chorus-master in 1949, and made his debut as a conductor there when he took over from a sick Busch in the middle of a performance in 1951. He assisted Busch and was largely influenced by him at Glyndebourne; in 1963 he became principal conductor, and in 1969 musical director and artistic counsellor, until his resignation in 1977. He has also been conductor of the Jacques Orchestra (1950–52), music director and conductor of the Royal Liverpool Philharmonic Orchestra (1957–63), principal conductor of the London Philharmonic Orchestra (1962–6), co-director of the Marseille Opera (1966–8) and musical director of the Huddersfield Choral Society (from 1973). He led the London Philharmonic in tours to the Far East in 1962, 1969 and 1973, and to the United States in 1971; on the 1973 tour he conducted the orchestra in Hong Kong and China, and in 1972 took the English Chamber Orchestra on tour to South America. He first appeared at the Edinburgh Festival in 1951, at the Vienna State Opera in 1951, in the US with the Pittsburgh Symphony Orchestra in 1963, with the San Francisco Opera in 1970 and at the New York Metropolitan in 1971, and has conducted at most of the major opera houses and with many major orchestras throughout the world. He was awarded the CBE in 1962, and in 1978 became chief conductor at the Cologne Opera.

In recent years Pritchard has been a freelance conductor and is in strong demand by opera houses in particular. In his career he has avoided any form of specialisation; he is equally at home in the opera house and with the symphony orchestra, and his repertoire ranges from Monteverdi to Henze. When he premièred the Leppard arrangement of *L'Incoronazione di Poppea* at Glyndebourne in 1962 he was a leader in the great awakening of interest in Monteverdi; musicians regard him as one of the most reliable conductors with modern scores. In Liverpool he introduced the Musica Viva series, in which concerts of modern works were preceded by explanatory talks, and were followed by discussion, an educational method later practised to great effect by others. In many ways he is the complete conductor, but his urbanity, indifference to self-promotion, quiet professionalism, and the utter lack of drama or sensationalism in his background have kept him from the highest rewards in British musical life. At the same time, his recorded performances give many examples of his fine musicianship; they are invariably well executed, but frequently appear to lack strong personal commitment.

Among Pritchard's earliest recordings, on LP, were the Glyndebourne productions of *Idomeneo*, *L'Incoronazione di Poppea* and Busoni's *Arlecchino*, all for EMI; the *Idomeneo* has been re-issued in the US by Seraphim. Another significant release was Tippett's oratorio *A Child of Our Time*, coupled with the Ritual Dances from *The Midsummer Marriage* (with the Royal Liverpool Orchestra and the Covent Garden Orchestra *et al.*); this set was originally issued by Pye but has been re-issued by Argo. Other mono LPs for EMI were the Haydn Symphony No. 80 and the Mozart *Serenata notturna* and *Notturno No. 5* (with the Philharmonia Orchestra), Stravinsky's *L'Histoire du soldat*, Fricker's Symphony No. 2 (with the Royal Liverpool Philharmonic Orchestra), Mozart's Violin Concertos K. 216 and K. 218 (with Menuhin and the Philharmonia Orchestra). His other records included Hindemith's *Der Schwanendreher* and Walton's Viola Concerto (with Primrose and a Chamber Orchestra for CBS), Chopin's Piano Concerto No. 2 and Liszt's Piano Concerto No. 1 (with Rosen and the New Philharmonia

Orchestra for CBS), *Lucia di Lammermoor* and *La traviata* (with Sutherland, the Santa Cecilia Orchestra and the Maggio Musicale Fiorentino Orchestra *et al.*, respectively, for Decca), selections from *Aida* (with Nilsson and the Covent Garden Orchestra for Decca), *L'elisir d'amore* (with the Covent Garden Orchestra *et al.* for CBS), concerti grossi by Handel, Corelli and Manfredini, Mozart's *Bastien und Bastienne*, Beethoven's Symphonies Nos 1 and 8, the Mozart Flute Concertos (with Barwahser) and Piano Concertos K. 451, K. 456, K. 459 and K. 595 (with Henkemans), and an aria recital (by Hollweg and the Vienna Symphony Orchestra for Philips).

More recently Classics for Pleasure released records in which Pritchard has conducted the London Philharmonic Orchestra in Haydn's Symphonies Nos 44 and 45, Schubert's Symphonies Nos 5, 8 and 9, excerpts from the Glyndebourne 1972 performance of *Die Entführung aus dem Serail*, the Bartók *Concerto for Orchestra*, *Pictures at an Exhibition*, the *Romeo and Juliet* fantasy-overture, the Grieg Piano Concerto (with Katin) and some excerpts from *Peer Gynt*, Tchaikovsky's Piano Concerto No. 1 and the Scherzo from Litolff's *Concerto symphonique* (with Katin), the Britten Violin Concerto (with Friend) and *Serenade for Tenor, Horn and Strings* (with Partridge and Busch), *España*, *Rapsodie espagnole* and *Capriccio espagnol*, and Sibelius' Symphony No. 2. He also has recorded Rawsthorne's Symphony No. 1 and *Symphonic Studies* (with the London Philharmonic Orchestra for Lyrita), the *Prélude à l'après-midi d'un faune*, the Royal Hunt and Storm from *Les Troyens* and a suite from *L'Oiseau de feu* (with the London Philharmonic Orchestra for Pye), Handel's anthems *Zadok the Priest*, *My Heart is Inditing*, *Let Thy Hand* and *The King shall Rejoice* (with the Huddersfield Choral Society and the Northern Sinfonia for Enigma), recitals of Mozart arias by Burrows (with the London Philharmonic Orchestra for L'Oiseau Lyre) and Berganza (with the London Symphony Orchestra for Decca) and an operatic recital by Cotrubas (with the New Philharmonic Orchestra for CBS).

Prohaska, Felix (b. 1912). Born in Vienna, the son of Karl Prohaska (1869–1927), the Austrian composer, conductor and teacher, Prohaska studied with his father and graduated from the Vienna University. He was first conductor at the Graz Opera (1937–9), then at the Duisburg Opera (1939–41), the Strasbourg Opera (1941–3), the German Opera, Prague (1943–5), the Vienna State Opera (1945–56 and 1964–7), the Frankfurt am Main Opera (1955–67) and Hannover Opera (1965–74). At the same time he has taught at the Graz Conservatory and Hochschule für Musik (1936–9), Strasbourg Conservatory (1941–3), the Vienna Academy of Music (1945–6), Vienna State Conservatory (1947–50) and the Hochschule für Musik at Hannover (1961–75), and has taken part in the Salzburg Festival (1945–6) and the Copenhagen Festival (1956). He has conducted all the major Austrian orchestras and performing groups, as well as orchestras in many European countries and in South America, where he has toured eight times between 1952 and 1975. A versatile and accomplished musician, Prohaska is typical of his Viennese background, and is a sensitive interpreter most particularly of the music of the baroque and classical periods, and is noted for his performances of Bach and Mozart. His repertoire also includes more recent composers such as Berg, Schoenberg, Britten, Hartmann, Janáček, Martin, Martinů and Skalkottas, and in the opera house he has been praised for his performances of Mozart, Wagner, Egk, Strauss, Pfitzner, and Stravinsky, *inter alia*.

Prohaska recorded mostly in Vienna and his performances appeared on a number of labels, in addition to those he originally recorded for. His records included Bach's four orchestral suites, *Brandenburg Concertos*, Violin Concerto No. 2 (with Tomasow), *Magnificat*, *Easter Oratorio* and Cantatas Nos 4, 31, 50, 70, 78, 79, 80, 106, 137, 140, 146, 161 and 202, C. P. E. Bach's *Magnificat* and Suite (arranged by Steinberg), oboe concertos by Albinoni, Handel, Haydn and Mozart (with Lardrot) and Handel's Concerti Grossi Op. 3 and *Alexander's Feast* (with the Vienna State Opera Orchestra *et al.* issued in the US by Bach Guild and in some cases in Britain by Nixa); *Water Music* and *Music for the Royal Fireworks*, Mozart's Symphonies Nos 40 and 41, the overtures to *Don Giovanni*, *Le nozze di Figaro* and *Die Zauberflöte*, Divertimentos K. 287 and K. 334 and *Eine kleine Nachtmusik*, Beethoven's Symphony No. 5, Schubert's Symphony No. 8 and Joachim's arrangement for orchestra of the *Grand Duo*, Mendelssohn's Symphony No. 5 and *Die schöne Melusine* overture, Widor's *Conte d'avril* and Reinecke's Flute Concerto (with Meylan), excerpts from *Die Walküre* and *Die Meistersinger* (with Schoeffler) and some discs of Mahler songs, including *Des Knaben Wunderhorn* and the *Rückert Songs* (with Felbermayer and Poell, and with the Vienna State Opera Orchestra for Amadeo, issued in the US by Vanguard and in some instances in Britain by Philips); cello concertos of Haydn and Boccherini (with Janigro and the Vienna State Opera Orchestra for Westminster); Mozart's Piano Concertos K. 491 and K. 595 (with Badura-Skoda and the Vienna Symphony Orchestra for Westminster), K. 456 and K. 503 (with Engel and the Bavarian Radio Symphony Orchestra for EMI) and the Sinfonia Concertante K. 364 (with Barylli and Doktor, and the Vienna State Opera Orchestra for Westminster); the Liszt Piano Concertos (with Vásáry and the Bamberg Symphony Orchestra for DGG), Chopin's Piano Concerto No. 1 and Liszt's *Hungarian Fantasy* (with Kilenyi and the Austrian Symphony Orchestra for Remington), Bach's Cantatas Nos 4 and 40 (with the Vienna Chamber Orchestra *et al.* for La Guilde Internationale du Disque), and accompaniments to arias from *Fidelio* (with Weber and the Vienna Philharmonic Orchestra for EMI) and *Don Giovanni* (with Ludwig and the Vienna Symphony Orchestra for EMI).

Prokofiev, Serge (1891–1953). In his days as student at the St Petersburg Conservatory, Prokofiev attended Tcherepnin's classes on conducting, and although he did lead some student orchestras, he did not become an accomplished conductor until later. His appearances in this role seem to have been restricted to performances of his own music. He conducted the world premières of his *Scythian Suite* (at Petrograd 1916), Symphony No. 1 (Petrograd, 1918), *Chout* (Paris, 1921), *The Love of Three Oranges* (Chicago, 1921), Violin Concerto No. 2 (with Oistrakh, Madrid, 1935), *Alexander Nevsky* (Moscow, 1938), Piano Concerto No. 5 (with Richter, Moscow, 1940), and Symphony No. 5 (Moscow, 1944), after which his conducting ceased owing to an injury from a fall. He was to have been a guest conductor in New York in 1940, but could not obtain a visa to leave the USSR.

The only recorded performances we have of Prokofiev as a conductor are some 78 r.p.m. sets which he made in the USSR, several of which were later released in the West on LP. These are of the Violin Concerto No. 1 (with Oistrakh and the USSR National Philharmonic Orchestra), which was issued by Everest in the United States in 1975, and Symphony No. 1 (*Classical*) and Suites Nos 1 and 2 from *Romeo and Juliet* (with the Moscow Philharmonic Orchestra), of which the Suite No. 2 was issued on Turnabout. The performance of the latter was mediocre and lacked fire and conviction, and the record itself adequately reproduced the starved tone of the original. Prokofiev's recordings as a pianist performing his own music were another matter altogether; his recording of the Piano Concerto No. 3 with Coppola and the London Symphony Orchestra was especially brilliant.

Provotorov, Gennadi. The Russian conductor Provotorov was active at the Moscow Opera School, and now is with the Stanislavsky and Nemiovich-Dantchenko Music Theatre in Moscow. With the orchestra of the theatre he recorded Shostakovich's *Katerina Ismailova*, which was released in Britain in 1976. He also recorded Ovchinnikov's overture, *At a Russian Festival* (with the Moscow Radio Symphony Orchestra).

Prüwer, Julius (1874–1943). Born in Vienna, Prüwer studied conducting with Richter and was associated with Brahms. He was conductor at Bielitz, the Cologne Opera (1894–5), Breslau (1896–1923) and Weimar (1923–4), was a professor at the Berlin Hochschule für Musik and conducted popular concerts of the Berlin Philharmonic Orchestra (1924–33). In 1933 he went to Leningrad and conducted opera there, returned to Austria, then migrated to New York, where he died. In 1898 he conducted in St Petersburg the first performance there of *Tristan und Isolde*. He recorded for Polydor with the Berlin Philharmonic Orchestra Schubert's Symphony No. 8, the overtures to *Rienzi*, *Raymond* and *Les Huguenots*, and the Strauss waltzes *Kaiserwalzer*, *Liebeslieder* and *G'schichten aus dem Wiener Wald* (the latter with the Berlin Charlottenburg Opera Orchestra), and Wotan's Farewell from *Die Walküre* (with Rode and the Charlottenburg Opera Orchestra).

Ptáčník, Jiří (b. 1921). Born in Kolin, Czechoslovakia, Ptáčník studied at the Prague Conservatory (1936–43), was a violinist at the Brno Theatre (1943–5), with the Heusler Quartet, the Czech Radio Orchestra and the Hefman Trio, and became leader of the Prague Chamber Orchestra. Supraphon have issued discs in which he conducts the Prague Chamber Orchestra in Haydn's Symphonies Nos 88 and 103, Cherubini's *Symphony in D* and the overture to *Médée*.

Pujol, Francesc (1878–1945). Born in Barcelona where he studied at the Conservatory and with Millet, Pujol was assistant conductor of the Orfeó Catalá at Barcelona, composed orchestral and vocal music, and published collections and studies of Catalan songs. For HMV's History of Music in Sound he conducted the Montserrat Monastery Choir in Victoria's *O Domine Jesu*.

Q

Quadri, Argeo (b. 1911). Born at Como, Quadri graduated from the Milan Conservatory in 1933, after studying composition, piano and choral singing. During his career he has conducted at all the major Italian opera houses, at Covent Garden (1956) and at the Vienna State Opera and Volksoper (from 1957), where he has for many years been conductor of the Italian repertoire in particular. The Italian government appointed him *Commendatore* for his artistic achievements, and the Austrian President made him Professor. He recorded excerpts from *Il trovatore* (with the Milan Symphony Orchestra *et al.* for HMV on 78s), and on LP for Westminster in the 1950s, his discs including a *Don Pasquale* and *Tosca*, as well as *Scheherazade*, and a coupling of *Pini di Roma* and *Fontane di Roma* (with the Vienna State Opera Orchestra *et al.*), Corelli's Concerti Grossi Op. 6 (with the English Baroque Orchestra), Revueltas' *Cuauhnahuac* and *Sensemayá*, Mossolov's *Steel Foundry*, *España* and *Marche joyeuse* of Chabrier, *L'Apprenti sorcier*, *Danse macabre* and the Bacchanale from *Samson et Dalila* (with the London Philharmonic Symphony Orchestra). He also recorded discs of excerpts from *Aida* (with the Vienna Volksoper Orchestra *et al.* for DGG), *Carmen* and *Rigoletto* (with the same orchestra for Ariola), and accompaniments for aria recitals by Lászlő (for Westminster), Corena, Sciutti, Nilsson, and Tatum (for Decca), and Giordano's *Fedora* (with the La Scala Orchestra *et al.*, released in Britain by Nixa). Rosenthal, in his history of Covent Garden, dismissed Quadri as 'no better or worse than many other Italian conductors of the second rank', but Sackville-West and Shawe-Taylor in *The Record Guide* wrote that his account of *Pini di Roma* and *Fontane di Roma* 'yields nothing to Toscanini's'. Quadri's *Scheherazade* was also highly praised.

Queler, Eve (b. 1936). Born in New York, Queler was educated at the Mannes College of Music and the City College of New York, was a horn player, and studied conducting with Rosenstock, Bamberger and Lert. She became a rehearsal accompanist and coach with the New York City Opera and Metropolitan Opera Company, and made her debut as a conductor in New Jersey with *Cavalleria rusticana* in 1966. Seeking the opportunity to conduct opera, she formed the Opera Orchestra of New York in 1967, at first to present standard operas with young American singers in concert performances, and commenced with *Don Giovanni* in 1969. Since then, she has performed, with professional singers, rarely heard operas of the 19th century such as *L'Africaine*, *Dalibor*, *I Lombardi*, *Le Cid*, *William Tell*, and Donizetti's *Parisina d'Este*. She was associate conductor of the Fort Wayne Symphony Orchestra (1970–71), was an assistant conductor with the New York City Opera for five seasons, conducted her first major orchestra, the San Antonio Symphony, in 1975, appeared with the Philadelphia Orchestra in 1976, and is conductor of the Hammar Chamber Ensemble, New York. She has conducted orchestras and opera companies in the United States, Canada, France and Spain, and became the first woman to conduct a recording of a complete opera, and is distinguished for implementing a revival of opera recording in the US. 'I have never felt discriminated against because I was a woman', she has said; 'young American male conductors have just as hard a time getting established'. She conducts from memory, and presents operas in their original language. Her initial operatic recording, in 1977 with the Opera Orchestra of New York *et al.* for CBS, was Massenet's *Le Cid*, and it has been followed by Donizetti's *Gemma di Vergy* and Puccini's *Edgar*.

Querol Gavalda, Miguel (b. 1922). Born in Ulldecona, Spain, and educated at the Benedictine Monastery at Montserrat (1926–36) and at the Universities of Barcelona and Madrid, Querol Gavalda has composed choral and other pieces and has published studies of Spanish music. He recorded, as conductor, a collection entitled *The Pleasures of Cervantes* (with the Barcelona Polyphonic Ensemble, for Nonesuch).

Questa, Angelo (1901–60). Born in Genoa, Questa studied composition with Parodi and conducting with Mancinelli at the Genoa Conservatory, and first appeared as a conductor in Genoa in 1920. He was a deputy at La Scala to Toscanini, Serafin and de Sabata, and his first success as a conductor came in Rome in 1928 when he led *Boris Godunov* with Chaliapin. He toured South America several times, was artistic director of the Carlo Felice Theatre at Genoa (1933–7), and directed the Italian opera season at Barcelona in 1951. He was known particularly as an interpreter of Pizzetti's music. Questa recorded some complete operas for Cetra with the Italian Radio Orchestra and distinguished casts, including *Aida*, *Rigoletto*, *Un ballo in maschera*, *Otello*, *La favorita*, *Mefistofele*, *Madama Butterfly* and *Il segreto di Susanna*; all except the last have been released in the United States by Everest. His other discs include Haydn's Symphony No. 94, the *Egmont*, *Leonore No. 3* and *Die Meistersinger* overtures, Tchaikovsky's Symphonies Nos 5 and 6, Borodin's Symphony No. 2 and the Polovtsian Dances from *Prince Igor*, and Chopin's Piano Concerto No. 1 (with Vidusso, and the Rome Symphony Orchestra for Royale), the *Romeo and Juliet* fantasy-overture and excerpts from *Swan Lake* (with the Rome Opera Orchestra for Varsity), excerpts from *Le nozze di Figaro* and *Carmen* (with the La Scala Orchestra *et al.* for Royale), *Don Giovanni*, *Il barbiere di Siviglia* and *William Tell* (with the Rome Opera Orchestra *et al.* for Royale). Royale and Varsity are US labels.

Quinet, Marcel (b. 1915). Born in Binche, Belgium, and educated at the Conservatoire Royal at Brussels, Quinet taught at the Conservatoire (from 1943) and at the Chapelle Musicale Reine Elisabeth (1956–9 and 1968–71), and became director of the music academy at St Josse-ten-Noode, Schaerbeeck. His compositions include orchestral, chamber and instrumental music and an opera. For Decca he recorded with the Belgian National Orchestra Poot's Symphony No. 2, Jongen's Piano Concerto (with del Pueyo) and *Troisième suite*, Absil's Piano Concerto (with Dumortier) and *Hommage à Lekeu*.

Quitin, José (b. 1915). Born in Liège where he studied at the University and Academy of Music, Quitin has taught at schools (1937–71), has been a professor at the Royal Conservatory (from 1945) and at the Academy of Music (from 1936), all at Liège, and has written monographs about Ysaÿe *et al.* He has recorded Delange's Ouverture No. 6 and *Sinfonia in E flat major*, (with Les Solistes de Liège, for Musique en Wallonie).

R

Raabe, Peter (1872–1945). Born in Frankfurt an der Oder, Raabe studied at the Hochschule für Musik in Berlin. He was conductor at Königsberg, Zwickau, and Elberfeld (1894–9), first conductor of the Dutch Opera, Amsterdam (1899–1903), conductor of the Kaim Orchestra at Munich (1903–6), of the Kaim Orchestra at Mannheim (1906–9), and first conductor at the Hoftheater at Weimar (1909–20). In 1910 he became custodian of the Liszt Museum at Weimar, and was chief editor of the complete edition of Liszt's works, and published an important biography of Liszt. He was conductor and later general music director at Aachen (1920–35), where he was succeeded by Karajan. After Strauss's resignation from the Reichsmusikkammer in 1935, Raabe became its president and was identified with the Nazi regime and its policies towards music. For Polydor he recorded Beethoven's Piano Concerto No. 5 (with Kempff and the Berlin Philharmonic Orchestra).

Rabaud, Henri (1873–1949). Born in Paris, the son of the professor of cello at the Paris Conservatoire, Rabaud studied at the Conservatoire with Gédalge and Massenet, won the Prix de Rome in 1894, and later founded orchestras in Rome and Vienna to give performances of French music. He was conductor at the Paris Opéra and Opéra-Comique (1908), director of the Opéra (1914–18), conductor of the Boston Symphony Orchestra where he succeeded Muck (1918–20), and director of the Paris Conservatoire (1920–41). His compositions include four operas, orchestral music and songs, and his best known works are the opera *Mârouf, savetier du Caire*, the oratorio *Job*, a string quartet and two orchestral pieces *Églogue* and *La Procession nocturne*, which was based on a scene from Lenau's *Faust*, and was recorded by Mitropoulos and the New York Philharmonic-Symphony Orchestra. Rabaud himself recorded *La Procession nocturne* and the ballet music from *Mârouf, savetier du Caire* (with a symphony orchestra for HMV).

Rabenschlag, Friedrich (b. 1902). Born in Herford, Westphalia, Rabenschlag studied at the University of Tübingen, and also at Leipzig and Cologne. He founded the Leipzig Student Madrigal Group (1926), which joined with the Leipzig University Kantorei (in 1938) to become the Leipzig University Choir. With the Choir he gave regular concerts, especially of the works of Bach and Schütz and contemporary composers, and toured in Germany and abroad. He was appointed conductor of the Leipzig Singakademie (1947) and then professor (1954). One of his recordings is of the choral works of Brahms, with the Leipzig University Choir (issued by Nonesuch).

Rabinovich, Nikolai (1908–72). Born in St Petersburg, Rabinovich graduated from the Leningrad Conservatory (1931), and studied conducting with Gauk and Malko. He was musical director at Lenfilm film studio (1931–2), head of the music committee of Radio Leningrad (1933–8), conducted the Leningrad Philharmonic Orchestra (from 1938), was conductor at the Maly Opera House, Leningrad (1944–8), was chief conductor of the second orchestra of the Leningrad Philharmonic Society (1950–57), conducted the Leningrad Chamber Orchestra (from 1967), taught conducting at the Leningrad Conservatory (from 1957), and led seminars in conducting in Weimar (1970). He is said to be the founder of the new Soviet school of conducting, and taught many prominent young conductors. He was one of the first Russian conductors to record for films, conducting the music for *The Boyhood of Maxim* (1935) and *Maxim's Return* (1937), and Shostakovich's music for the film *Hamlet* (1964). He also edited and added notes to Malko's book *The Conductor and His Baton*.

Rabinovich recorded with the Leningrad Philharmonic Orchestra Mozart's Symphony No. 25, the *Leonore No. 3* overture, Berlioz's *Waverley* overture, *Capriccio espagnol*, Dvořák's Symphony No. 8, Alabiev's *The Enchanted Drum*, and Manevich's Clarinet Concerto (with Roginsky).

Rachmaninov, Sergey (1873–1943). Posterity recalls the great Russian musician Rachmaninov first as a composer, then as a pianist. It is often overlooked that in his early years he devoted almost all his time to conducting. After the devastating critical rejection of his Symphony No. 1 at its première in St Petersburg in 1897, when it was damned by Cui and Rimsky-Korsakov, Rachmaninov's confidence as a composer was all but destroyed, and he became an assistant conductor with a small opera company in Moscow, and made his debut with *Samson et Dalila*. His career as an operatic conductor flourished, and in 1905–6 he conducted at the Imperial Opera in Moscow. Previously he appeared in London in 1899, presenting his own music, and later returned to England in 1910 to conduct the première of his Symphony No. 2 at the Leeds Festival. He also toured the United States as both pianist and conductor, and on two occasions (in 1909 and 1918) the Boston Symphony Orchestra invited him to be their permanent conductor; both times he refused. In those days his repertoire included Debussy, Elgar, Berlioz, Strauss, Brahms, Franck and Grieg, in addition to Russian composers from Glinka to Scriabin and himself; his interpretations of Mozart's Symphony No. 40 and Tchaikovsky's Symphony No. 5 were reputed to be extraordinary. After leaving Russia in 1917, Rachmaninov's conducting activities gave way to composition and to his legendary recitals as a virtuoso pianist. In addition to the many records he made as a solo, chamber and concerto pianist, he recorded three works of his own as a conductor: *The Isle of the Dead*, *Vocalise*, and the Symphony No. 3. All were with the Philadelphia Orchestra, which he greatly admired, the first two being made in 1929 and the symphony in 1939. The Philadelphia Orchestra, under Stokowski and Ormandy, also accompanied him in his recordings of the piano concertos and the *Rhapsody on a Theme of Paganini*. All his recordings were re-issued by RCA in 1975, and show him as an admirable conductor of his own music; one can only wonder what his Debussy, Ravel or Elgar would have sounded like with the Philadelphia Orchestra. He had a curious aversion to broadcasting; he could never be persuaded to play for a radio audience, and stipulated that gramophone records be substituted when he performed during a broadcast programme.

Rachmilovich, Jacques (1895–1956). Born in Odessa, Rachmilovich studied at the St Petersburg Conservatory, migrated to the United States in 1925, and made his home in California, where he founded the Santa Monica Symphony Orchestra in 1945. He was recorded conducting this orchestra in Kabalevsky's *Fête populaire*, Tchaikovsky's Symphonies Nos 1 and 2 and Piano Concerto No. 2 (with Cherkassky), Rachmaninov's *The Bells*, Saint-Saëns' Violin Concerto No. 3 (with Kaufman), Prokofiev's *Summer Day* and Khachaturian's *Masquerade* suite (for Concert Hall Society and Disc). Capitol recorded him conducting the Santa Cecilia Orchestra, on early LPs, in Glazunov's Symphony No. 4, Glière's Symphony No. 3, Kabalevsky's Symphony No. 2, Glinka's *Jota aragonesa*, *Valse-Fantaisie*, *Kamarinskaya* and the overture to *Russlan and Ludmilla*; other recordings included Rachmaninov's Symphony No. 1, Tchaikovsky's *Hamlet* and *The Tempest* (with the Stockholm Radio Orchestra for Mercury), Khachaturian's Violin Concerto (with Kaufman and the Santa Cecilia Orchestra for Concert Hall), and Rachmaninov's *The Rock* and *Études-tableaux* (arranged by Respighi, with the Rome Symphony Orchestra and Chorus).

Rachoń, Stefan (b. 1906). Born in Ostrów Lubelski, Poland, Rachoń studied at the Moniuszko Music School in Lublin, where he led a string quartet and was concertmaster of the Lublin Philharmonic Orchestra. He moved to Warsaw, studied first the violin at the Conservatory (1929–34) and then conducting with Fitelberg (1934–6). He was a concert violinist until 1939, conducted in Paris, Prague, Brno and Bratislava, and after World War II was conductor of a light musical orchestra for the Polish Radio. For the Polish record company he recorded with the Polish Radio Orchestra a Haydn symphony, Shostakovich's Ballet Suite No. 3 and music for the film *Piragov*, and the Suppé overtures *Boccaccio*, *Dichter und Bauer*, *Leichte Cavallerie*, *Die schöne Galatea*, *Pique Dame* and *Morgen, Mittag und Abend in Wien*, which was released by DGG on their Helidor label in 1975.

Rajter, Ľudovít (b. 1906). Born in Pezinek, near Bratislava, Rajter studied at the Vienna Academy of Music with Schmidt and Marx for composition, and with Krauss and Wunderer for conducting, and then studied composition with Dohnányi in Budapest. He was assistant to Krauss at the summer master courses at Salzburg (1929–33), was chief conductor with the Budapest Radio (1933–45), a professor at the Franz Liszt Academy at Budapest (1938–45), chief conductor of the Radio Symphony Orchestra at Bratislava (1945–9 and since 1968), chief conductor of the Slovak Philharmonic Orchestra at Bratislava and a professor at the academy of music there (since 1949). In 1966 he was the head of the conducting class at the International Summer School at Salzburg, and has been a guest conductor in many West and East European countries.

Rajter has made records for the Opus company at Bratislava with his Slovak Philharmonic Orchestra, including Mozart's Symphonies Nos 31 and 36, the Liszt tone poems *Die Ideale* and

Prometheus, the four Brahms symphonies, the *Academic Festival* and *Tragic Overtures* and the *Variations on the St Antony Chorale*, Dvořák's *Carnival* overture, Berlioz's overture *Le Carnaval romain*, Svendsen's *Carnival in Paris* and the intermezzo and Carnival from Schmidt's *Notre Dame*, as well as music by Babušek, Cikker, Ferenczy, Jurovský, Moyzes and Suchoň. For Supraphon he recorded Mozart's Symphony No. 39 and *Serenata notturna*, Brahms' *Tragic Overture* and music by Bella, Ferenczy, Hrušovský, Jurovský Kardoš, Moyzes and Zelenka (with the Slovak Philharmonic Orchestra), for RCA Italiana Kodály's *Dances of Galánta*, Sinding's *Rustle of Spring* and the overture to *Il segreto di Susanna* (with the Slovak Philharmonic Orchestra), and for Orion the Grieg Piano Concerto and Liszt's Piano Concerto No. 1 (with Varro and the Moravian Philharmonic Orchestra).

Rakhlin, Nathan (b. 1905). Born in Snovsk, in the Chernigov district, Rakhlin was first a trumpet player, then studied the violin at the Kiev Conservatory (1923–7), and conducting with Bierdiajew, and with Maximilian Steinberg in Leningrad (1931–5). He was conductor of the Kharkov Radio Symphony Orchestra (1932–4), chief conductor at Donetzk (1934–7), conductor of the Ukrainian State Symphony Orchestra (1937–41 and 1946–62), conductor of the USSR State Symphony Orchestra (1941–5), then, since 1966, chief conductor and founder of the Kazan Philharmonic Orchestra and professor at the Kazan Conservatory. He led the première of Shostakovich's Symphony No. 11, and was given the title People's Artist (1948) and the State Award of the USSR (1952). Many Russian musicians hold him in the highest esteem; Ahronovich has described him as one of the century's great conductors and a man of real genius, and Sanderling considers him to be one of the most gifted musicians. However, others regard his interpretations, particularly of Tchaikovsky, as excessively sentimental.

Rakhlin's recordings include the *Symphonie fantastique*, Schubert's Symphonies Nos 5 and 8, Tchaikovsky's Symphony No. 2, *Scheherazade*, the two *L'Arlésienne* suites, *Les Préludes*, *Tasso* and the *Hungarian Rhapsodies Nos 2* and *14*, Glazunov's *Fantasia*, Dvořák's Symphony No. 9, the Schumann and Dvořák Cello Concertos (with Rostropovich) and Glière's Symphony No. 3 (with the Moscow Radio Symphony Orchestra); Mendelssohn's Symphony No. 3, the Tchaikovsky *Manfred* symphony, Kalinnikov's two symphonies, the Shostakovich Symphony No. 11, Peiko's *Moldavian Suite*, Revutsky's Symphony No. 2, Miaskovsky's Symphony No. 21, Babajanian's *Heroic Ballad*, and a collection of Strauss waltzes (with the USSR State Symphony Orchestra); and Kalinnikov's Symphony No. 2 (with the Bolshoi Symphony Orchestra). Some of these records have been issued in the West, such as the Kalinnikov symphonies and the Peiko suite (by Westminster), *Scheherazade* (by Saga), *Manfred* (by MK) and the Schumann and Dvořák Cello Concertos (by Period).

Ramin, Günter (1898–1956). Born in Karlsruhe, Ramin studied at the Thomaskirche and Conservatory at Leipzig (1910–14), and remained associated with Leipzig for the rest of his life. He was an organ pupil of Straube (1914–17), became organist at the Thomaskirche (1918) and then cantor (1940), in succession to Straube. He was also conductor of the Leipzig Teachers' Choral Society (1923–35), organist at the Leipzig Gewandhaus concerts, teacher of organ at the Berlin Hochschule für Musik (1931–3), toured the United States (1933–4), was conductor of the Gewandhaus Chorus (1945–51), was a teacher at the Leipzig Conservatory, was conductor of the Berlin Philharmonic Chorus (1933–43), was leader of the German Bach Festivals at Leipzig (1950, 1953 and 1955), was guest professor at the Salzburg Summer Courses (1951), toured North and South America and the USSR with the Thomaskirche Choir from Leipzig (1952–4), and was known for his exceptional ability as an improvisor on the organ.

During World War II, Ramin recorded the *St Matthew Passion* of Bach with the Thomaskirche Choir, the Gewandhaus Orchestra and soloists Lemnitz, Beckmann, Erb, Hüsch and Schulze; the performance was unusual because of 'some rhythmic slackness and lack of definition in the choral singing' (Sackville-West and Shawe-Taylor, in *The Record Guide*). An LP transfer of the performance was issued in Europe in 1975. He also recorded Bach's *St John Passion* (with the same choral and orchestral forces, *et al.*, for DGG), *Mass in B minor* (with the Thomaskirche Choir, the Gewandhaus Orchestra *et al.* for Spauda, and with the Bavarian State Orchestra *et al.* for La Guilde Internationale du Disque), *Christmas Oratorio* (with the Hamburg Chamber Orchestra *et al.*), Cantatas Nos 11, 12, 24, 36, 41, 42, 43, 51, 57, 65, 67, 72, 73, 78, 79, 92, 95, 103, 106, 111, 117, 119, 128, 131, 137, 138, 144, 177 and 179 (with the Gewandhaus Orchestra *et al.*, issued by Eterna and many by Eurodisc), Christmas music by Bach and Corelli (with the Hamburg Chamber Orchestra for La Guilde Internationale du Disque), Bach's Motets (with the Berlin Motet Choir for DGG), and the *Brandenburg Concerto No. 4* (with the Gewandhaus Orchestra for Eterna), as well as the *Goldberg Variations*, Partita No. 4 and *Chromatic Fantasy and Fugue*, and some organ works of Bach (for La Guilde Internationale du Disque, and Cantate).

Rampal, Jean-Pierre (b. 1922). The eminent flautist Rampal was born in Marseille, and studied with his father, a professor at the Marseille Conservatoire, and then at the Paris Conservatoire. He first played in the orchestras of the Vichy and Paris Operas, but soon established an international reputation as one of the foremost virtuosi of the instrument. He was appointed a professor at the Paris Conservatoire (1968), and founded the Paris Baroque Ensemble and the French Wind Quintet. His numerous recordings, mainly of baroque and contemporary works for the flute, have won him many distinguished prizes. As a conductor and flautist he has recorded Bach's Suite No. 2, Benda's *Flute Concerto in E minor*, and Telemann's *Suite in A minor* (with the Paris Festival Strings, for Harmonia Mundi, and issued in the United States by Orion), and Debussy's *Danse sacrée et danse profane* (with Laskine and the Jean-François Paillard Chamber Orchestra for Erato, and issued in the United States by Musical Heritage Society).

Randolph, David (b. 1914). Born in New York and educated at Columbia University, Randolph has been a lecturer at New York and Fordham Universities and Montclair State College, New Jersey. He formed and conducted the Randolph Singers, and has been a regular broadcaster in New York. His publications include *This is Music* (1964), and he has recorded with the Randolph Singers Morley's *The Triumphs of Oriana* (for Westminster, issued in Britain by Nixa), a selection of madrigals by Monteverdi, and madrigals by Bateson, Weelkes and Wilbye (for Westminster), Satie's *Messe des pauvres* (for Esoteric), Claflin's *Lament for April 15* and madrigals by American composers Canby, Dvorkin, Harman, Kay, List, Mills, Pinkham and Stevens (for Composers Recordings), a collection entitled *Catch Clubs* (for Elektra), and also *Messiah* (with the Masterworks Chorus *et al.* for Design).

Rankl, Karl (1898–1968). Born at Gaaden, the fourteenth son of an Austrian peasant, Rankl studied privately in Vienna with Schoenberg and Webern, and after service in the Austrian army in World War I was a coach and chorus-master at the Vienna Volksoper under Weingartner in 1922. His subsequent appointments were at Reichenberg (1925–7), Königsberg (1927–8), the Kroll Opera in Berlin with Klemperer (1928–31), Wiesbaden (1931–3), Graz (1933–7) and Prague (1937–9), where he was the director of the German Opera House. Here he conducted the première of Křenek's *Karl V*. He escaped to England in 1939, was interned during the early years of the war, but later became a British citizen. After a time as a concert conductor, he was appointed the first post-war musical director at the Royal Opera House, Covent Garden, in 1946; he remained there until 1951. Harold Rosenthal has written that 'his work in building up the new opera company was invaluable, though his conducting of Wagner and Verdi did not meet with general approval' (*Concise Oxford Dictionary of Opera*, 1964); nonetheless Rankl's most notable achievement was the production of the complete *Ring* in 1950. He conducted many leading British orchestras, was conductor of the Scottish National Orchestra (1952–7), and of the Elizabethan Trust Opera Company in Australia (1958–60). He composed eight symphonies, some chamber and vocal music, and an opera, *Deirdre of the Sorrows*, which won a prize at a competition in connection with the Festival of Britain in 1951, but was never performed.

Rankl made a number of recordings for Decca in the last decade of 78s, with the London Symphony, London Philharmonic and National Symphony Orchestras. The major undertakings were Beethoven's Symphony No. 1, Brahms' Symphony No. 4, Dvořák's Symphony No. 9 and Schubert Symphony No. 4. In addition he recorded an excerpt from Bach's Cantata No. 53, Dvořák's *Scherzo capriccioso*, Cello Concerto (with Gendron) and Violin Concerto (with Haendel), the overtures to *Il matrimonio segreto*, *Euryanthe*, *The Bartered Bride*, *William Tell*, *La gazza ladra*, and *Egmont* and *Carnival*, Wotan's Farewell from *Die Walküre* (with Schoeffler) and an aria from Bach's Cantata No. 53 (with Jarred). Rankl was undoubtedly an artist of great sincerity, and the performances he recorded were sound in conception and communicated a nobility of purpose. One in particular, of Schubert's Symphony No. 4, attracted high praise. At times, however, a certain laxity would become evident in the orchestral playing, which reduced the stature of the performance. Although he was still active as a conductor after the arrival of LP, he did not record in that medium. As with his years at Covent Garden, his gramophone records gave only modified rapture.

Ràpalo, Ugo (b. 1914). Born in Naples, Ràpalo studied at the Conservatorio di Musica San Pietro a Maiella, Naples, graduated in 1935, and was an assistant conductor at the Teatro San Carlo at Naples (1934–41). He conducted the Orchestra da Camera (1944–6), was artistic director at San Carlo (1946–7), at the Teatro Comunale at Modena, and has also conducted at Salzburg, Barcelona and Covent Garden, London, as well as in other cities in Italy, Europe and South America. He is now artistic director of the Teatro San Carlo. His compositions include an opera and a mass; his repertoire as a conductor is primarily of the operas of Rossini, Bellini, Donizetti, Verdi and Puccini, and he has edited music by Cimarosa, Jommelli, Hasse, Leo *et al.* He recorded, in the first decade or so of LP, Paisiello's *Il duello* (for Haydn Society), *Cavalleria rusticana* and *Pagliacci* (with the San Carlo Orchestra *et al.* for Philips), Puccini's Mass (with the Scarlatti Orchestra *et al.* for Colosseum, also issued by Bruno with the orchestra named Orchestra di Napoli), *La Bohème* and *Madama Butterfly* (for Fabbri-BASF, Italy).

Rapf, Kurt (b. 1922). Born in Vienna and educated at the Academy of Music there, Rapf was the founder and conductor of the Collegium Musicum Wien (1945–56), assistant conductor to Knappertsbusch at Zürich, professor at the Vienna Academy, music director at Innsbruck (1953–60), leader of the music department of the city of Vienna (1970) and president of the Austrian Composers' Society (1970). He has taken part in radio and television activities and music festivals in Austria, has composed orchestral, choral, chamber and instrumental music, and has made numerous records as a harpsichordist, pianist, organist and conductor. In the latter capacity he recorded Mozart's *Der Schauspieldirektor* and *Oca del Cairo* (with the Vienna Volksoper Orchestra *et al.* for Amadeo), and Pfitzner's Symphony Op. 44 (with the Collegium Musicum, released in the US by Cook).

Ratjen, Hans Georg (b. 1909). Born in Berlin-Charlottenburg, and educated at the Cologne Institute for Music, Ratjen conducted at the Kroll Opera, Berlin (1932), the Staatsoper, Berlin (1933), at the Würzburg Civic Theatre (1935) and at the Innsbruck Civic Theatre (1939), was first conductor at the Munich State Opera (1945) and then general music director at Oldenburg (1950) and Wuppertal (1955). Mercury released an LP on which he conducted the Munich Philharmonic Orchestra in Schumann's Symphony No. 2.

Rattle, Simon (b. 1955). Born in Liverpool, Rattle demonstrated remarkable talent for music as a child, and at the age of fifteen was an occasional percussion player in the Royal Liverpool Philharmonic Orchestra, and in the National Youth Orchestra under Boulez. His first experience as a conductor was with the Merseyside Youth Orchestra; in 1971 he commenced studying conducting and the piano at the Royal Academy of Music, and there in 1973 led performances of Mahler's Symphonies Nos 2 and 6, and *L'Enfant et les sortilèges.* In 1974, the youngest to enter, he won first prize in the Bournemouth John Player International Conductors' Competition, and then became assistant conductor with the Bournemouth Symphony Orchestra and the Bournemouth Sinfonietta (1974–6). In 1975 he conducted the English Chamber Orchestra at Barcelona, appeared with some provincial British orchestras, then in 1976 led the New Philharmonia Orchestra at the Royal Festival Hall, London, in a programme consisting of Berlioz' *King Lear* overture, a Mozart piano concerto and the Shostakovich Symphony No. 10. He conducted *The Rake's Progress* for the Glyndebourne Touring Company, and in 1976 was appointed assistant conductor to the BBC Symphony Orchestra. A modest and self-deprecating man, Rattle has rare gifts as a conductor for his age; his rhythmic sense and capacity to control large forces, evident in Mahler's Symphony No. 2 and in the opera house, have marked him off as a major talent. He recognises Furtwängler as the greatest musical influence of all conductors, and places Giulini as the only conductor who carries on his school today; Haitink, Boulez and Carewe have also been formative influences. He finds an affinity with many composers, such as Haydn, Berlioz, Dvořák, Mahler, Berg, Ravel and Maxwell Davies, and has a name as an interpreter of contemporary music. Some composers, for example Tchaikovsky, he would rather avoid, and some large works, like Beethoven's Symphony No. 9, he believes he could not approach for many years. Mozart, too, he finds at this stage too difficult to conduct. Until the end of 1977, his only recording was, for Argo, an accompaniment with the Nash Ensemble for Felicity Palmer in a recital of songs by Ravel.

Raugel, Felix (b. 1881). Born in Saint-Quentin, France, Raugel studied at the Lille Conservatoire and the Schola Cantorum, Paris, and with

Roussel, d'Indy, Decaux and Libert. He was choirmaster at Saint Eustache (1911–28), Saint Honoré d'Eylau (1928–40) and conductor of the Handel Society (1909–14), the Reims Philharmonic Society (1926–62) and the choirs of Radiodiffusion Française (1934–47). He published many musicological studies, including a book on Palestrina (1930); he recorded with the Anthologie Sonore Choir Mozart's sacred music K. 117, K. 222, K. 273, K. 276, K. 277, K. 342 and K. Anh 21 (for Anthologie Sonore, and issued in the US by Everest).

Ravel, Maurice (1875–1937). Ravel conducted his own music from time to time, but was never considered an accomplished performer in this role. He conducted a performance of an unpublished overture *Shéhérazade* in 1899, in Paris, and in 1928 he toured the United States for four months, playing and conducting his own works. He is reported to have said that he had little interest in a score once he had finished it. As a conductor, he recorded three of his compositions, the *Introduction et allegro* (in 1926), *Boléro* (with the Lamoureux Orchestra, in 1928), and the *Piano Concerto in G major* (with Marguerite Long, in 1932), and the concerto has been included in the Seraphim LP set, *Age of the Great Instrumentalists – Six Concertos*. *Boléro* has been re-issued on an LP transfer by Turnabout, but Ravel's conducting is not particularly distinguished. *Boléro* was a popular success from its first performance, and Ravel was asked to conduct it very frequently; the recording was made by him for Polydor a few months after its première. On that occasion a lady in the audience remarked very loudly: 'He is mad!' Ravel, answered, with a smile, that she understood the piece.

Rawsthorne, Alan (1905–71). The British composer Rawsthorne was born in Haslingden, Lancashire, and attended the Royal Manchester College of Music (1926–9). He taught at Dartington Hall, Colnes (1932–4), but later settled in London to give his full time to composition. Not specially noted as a conductor, he nonetheless recorded some of his own music: the *Madame Chrysanthème* suite, *Street Corner* overture, and music from *Practical Cats* (in 1958, with the Pro Arte Orchestra, for Pye), and the complete *Practical Cats* (to verses by T. S. Eliot, in 1957, with Robert Donat and the Philharmonic Orchestra for EMI).

Raybould, Clarence (1886–1972). Born in Birmingham, Raybould was the first Bachelor of Music to graduate from Birmingham University (1912). He was first a church organist, then taught at the Midlands Institute School of Music in Birmingham, and assisted Rutland Boughton as conductor and pianist at the early Glastonbury festivals (1914). After service in the British army in World War I, he conducted with the Beecham Opera Company (1919–26), toured as a pianist in Britain and abroad, was musical adviser to the Columbia Gramophone Company (1927–31), and taught at the Guildhall School of Music and Drama (1930–36). He toured as a conductor in Europe and the United States, presenting much British music, was chief assistant conductor to Boult with the BBC Symphony Orchestra (1939–45), was director of the senior orchestra of the Royal Academy of Music (1944–61), founded and conducted the National Youth Orchestra (1945–66), and was for a time the Honorary Bard of Wales. He composed an opera, some piano and chamber works and songs, and also composed, arranged and conducted for the first British film to have its own music. Boult considered Raybould a very distinguished musician, who was very popular with the orchestra in his years with the BBC.

For Regal, Raybould recorded in the 1920s with the Classic Symphony Orchestra the overtures *1812*, *William Tell*, *Egmont*, *The Merry Wives of Windsor*, *Zampa*, *Raymond* and *Leichte Cavallerie*, and excerpts from *Coppélia*. Later, he recorded the finale from Holbrooke's Symphony No. 3 (with a symphony orchestra for Decca), *Dido and Aeneas* (with Evans, Henderson, the Boyd Neel Orchestra *et al.* for Decca), Turina's *Rapsodia sinfónica* (with Joyce and an orchestra for Decca), Mozart's Rondo K. 386 (with Joyce and an orchestra for Parlophone), a Mozart aria (with Souez for Columbia), the *Fidelio* overture (included in the Columbia History of Music), the *Cockaigne* overture (with the USSR Symphony Orchestra for Melodiya), and Dvořák's Symphony No. 9 (with the Welsh National Youth Orchestra for Cwaliton).

Raytchev, Russlan. After studying the piano with Sauer in Milan and conducting with Böhm in Vienna, Raytchev was general music director of a number of Bulgarian orchestras, founded the National Operas at Varna and Plovdiv, was conductor at the Sofia Opera (1958–74), and general music director of the National Theatre and Symphony Orchestra of Schleswig-Holstein (1974–8). He has recorded for Balkanton Rachmaninov's *Aleko* (with the Plovdiv Radio Orchestra *et al.*), Shostakovich's Symphony No. 12 (with the Bulgarian Radio and Television Orchestra), an aria recital by Selmisky (with the Sofia National Orchestra), and a disc of popular Bulgarian songs (with the Bulgarian Goussla-Chorus, this last for La Guilde Internationale du Disque).

Redel, Kurt (b. 1918). Born in Breslau (now Wrocław), Redel studied the flute, piano, violin, composition and conducting at the conservatory there, and at the age of 20 was appointed professor at the Salzburg Mozarteum and also at the Detmold Academy of Music. He first conducted with the Beromünster Radio Orchestra, and in 1952 founded the Pro Arte Orchestra at Munich with which he has toured extensively. He has also been music director of the Easter Festival at Lourdes, France, and of the Nuits Musicales at Châteauneuf-du-Pape, and of the Mozart Chamber Orchestra at Salzburg. His repertoire as a conductor embraces baroque, classical, romantic and modern music, but his special interest is the baroque and Mozart.

With the Pro Arte Orchestra Redel has made many recordings, on occasion performing as soloist in flute concertos and concerted pieces. These records have been issued principally by Erato, but also by Decca, Philips, Vox, Telefunken, MG, Ducretet-Thomson and Musical Heritage Society. Included have been Bach's *Brandenburg Concertos*, five Suites, *Ein musikalisches Opfer*, *Die Kunst der Fuge*, the Harpsichord Concertos (with Reinhardt), the Harpsichord, Flute and Violin Concerto (with Priegnitz, Redel and Barchet), the two Violin Concertos (with Erlih) and Double Violin Concerto (with Erlih and Merckel), arrangements of the *Passacaglia and Fugue in C minor*, *Toccata and Fugue in D minor*, *Fantasia and Fugue in A minor*, *Fugues in C minor* and *A minor*, and the Chorales *Nun komm der Heiden Heiland*, *Wachet auf* and *Jesu, Joy of Man's Desiring*, *Magnificat*, Masses BWV 233, BWV 234, BWV 235 and BWV 236, and excerpts from Cantatas Nos 33, 36, 42, 78, 80, 115, 142, 146, 202 and 208, Telemann's 20 Little Fugues, Five Little Fugues dedicated to Marcello, *Flute Concertos in G* and *D*, *Adagio for Flute in G major*, *Introduction and Rondo for Flute in D minor*, *Oboe Concerto in E minor* (with Kalmus), *Trumpet Concerto in D* (with Scherbaum), Viola Concertos Nos 1 and 2 (with Schmidt), Flute and Oboe Concerto (with himself and Clement), *Oboe d'amore Concerto in A major* (with Clement), Two-Flute, Oboe and Violin Concerto (with himself, Walter and Clement), *Minuet in G minor*, *Overture a sette*, *St Mark Passion*, *St Matthew Passion* and two Motets, Vivaldi's *The Four Seasons*, Concertos Op. 3 No. 8 and No. 11 (adagio and fugue), Pastorale from *Nisi Dominus* and Organ Concertos, transcribed by Bach (with Cochereau), *Two-Guitar Concerto in C major* (with Presti and Lagoya), *Mandolin Concerto in G major*, transcribed for two guitars (with Presti and Lagoya), *Lute Concerto in D major*, *Viola d'amore Concerto in D major* and *Cello Sonata in A minor*, transcribed for guitar (with Presti), Handel's Concerto Grosso Op. 3 No. 5 (fugue), Concerti Grossi Op. 6, *Overture in G major*, *Chaconne in A major*, overture, recitative and Largo from *Xerxes*, and a chorus from *Judas Maccabaeus*, Albinoni's *Adagio*, Concerto Op. 8 No. 8 and Sonata Op. 2 No. 6, Pachelbel's *Canon*, *Fugue in C major* and *Fugue on 'Herzlich tut mich verlangen'*, Isaac's *Innsbruck ich muss dich lassen*, Durante's *Harpsichord Concerto in F major* and *Ricercare*, Pergolesi's *Introduction and Fugue on a Canon of Palestrina* and Introduction to *Stabat Mater*, A. Scarlatti's Concerto Grosso No. 3 (fugue), Schmuegel's *Sinfonia di chiesa*, Stölzel's *Concerto Grosso in G major*, *Flute and Oboe Concerto in E minor* and *Oboe and Violin Concerto in F major*, Torelli's Concerto Grosso Op. 3 No. 3 (fugue), Corelli's Concerto Grosso Op. 6 No. 9, Richter's *Sinfonia in G minor* (introduction), F. Couperin's *Motet de Saint Barthélémy* and prelude to *Troisième Leçon de Ténèbres*, Marais' *Sonnerie de Sainte Geneviève du Mont de Paris*, an air from Caldara's *Mirti, faggi, tronchi* (with Wenkel), Carissimi's canzona *No, non si speri* (with Wenkel), Méhul's *Ouverture burlesque*, A. Marcello's *Oboe Concerto in D minor*, transcribed for two guitars (with Presti and Lagoya), Monteverdi's *Lamento d'Arianna* (with Wenkel), Bernhard Romberg's *Symphonie burlesque*, K. Stamitz's Clarinet and Bassoon Concerto (with Schroeder and Popp), *Flute Concerto in D major* and *Quartet for Orchestra in C major*, W. F. Bach's *Harpsichord Concertos in F major* and *A minor* (with Haudebourg), C. P. E. Bach's Sinfonia No. 2, Haydn's Flute Concerto, Oboe Concerto (with Chambon), Two-Lyra Concerto, transcribed for two guitars (with Presti and Lagoya) and Serenade from String Quartet Op. 3 No. 5, excerpts from Leopold Mozart's *Toy Symphony* and *Eine musikalische Schlittenfahrt*, Mozart's Symphonies Nos 39, 40 and 41, Divertimentos K. 136, K. 137, K. 138 and K. 251, *Eine kleine Nachtmusik*, *Les petits riens*, *Adagio and Fugue in C minor*, Flute Concertos, Andante K. 315, Rondo K. 373, Country dances K. 609 and K. 610, German Dances K. 605, Marches K. 335a and K. 335b and Epistle Sonatas Nos 1, 2, 4, 8, 11, 12, 14, 15, 16 and 17 (with Cochereau), dances from Gluck's *Orfeo ed Euridice*, *Armide* and

Don Juan, and arrangements of *Ave Marias* by Brahms, Bruckner, Cherubini, Franck, Gounod, Liszt, Saint-Saëns, Schubert and Verdi.

Redel also recorded the Bach Harpsichord Concertos (with Demus and Badura-Skoda and the Vienna State Opera Orchestra for Westminster); the Bach Three-Harpsichord and Four-Harpsichord Concertos (with the Dresden Staatskapelle *et al.* for Eterna); Vivaldi's *Cello Concertos in A minor*, *G major* and *G minor* (with Walevska and the Netherlands Chamber Orchestra for Erato); K. Stamitz's *Flute Concertos in D* and *G* (with the L'Oiseau Lyre Orchestra for L'Oiseau Lyre); Haydn's Trumpet Concerto (with Jeannoutot), *Divertimentos in D* and *E flat* and Serenade from the Quartet Op. 3 No. 5, Mozart's Sinfonia Concertante K. 364 (with Suk and Skampa), the overtures *Coriolan* and *Prometheus*, and Schubert's Symphony No. 4 (with the Czech Philharmonic Orchestra for Supraphon). He also has performed as flautist in recordings of, *inter alia*, the Mozart flute sonatas, quartets and concertos (for Arion, France).

Reed, H. Owen (b. 1910). Born in Odessa, Missouri, Reed studied at the University of Missouri, Louisiana State University, the Eastman School of Music and the Berkshire Music Center, where he was a pupil of Martinů, Copland, Bernstein and Chappel. He also studied with Harris at Colorado Springs. He taught at Michigan State University (1939–76), where he was awarded the title Professor Emeritus (1976), and has lectured at many other universities. His compositions include operas, orchestral, band, chamber, choral and other works, and his Cello Concerto won the 1949 Composers' Press Symphonic Award; he has written text books for colleges, as well as *Scoring for Percussion* and *The Material of Music Composition*. He was assistant conductor of the Louisiana Kings, a brass ensemble, and played the trumpet in several orchestras. His recordings, as a conductor, include an excerpt from his folk-opera *Peter Homan's Dream* and *The Ox-Driving Song* (with the Michigan State University Symphony Orchestra and Singers, for Michigan State University) and his Cello Concerto (with Potter and the same orchestra for Dorian).

Reesen, Emil (b. 1887). Born in Copenhagen, Reesen studied the piano there (where he made his debut as a pianist in 1911), and in Paris (1925–7). He conducted in theatres in Copenhagen (1919–25), with the Danish Radio Symphony Orchestra, together with Grøndahl (1927–36), was conductor at the Dansk Koncertforening (1937–40), was a guest conductor at the Copenhagen Royal Theatre (1931) and was later conductor there (1950). He also was a guest conductor in Sweden, France and Germany, composed an opera, ballets, a cantata, musical comedies, stage and film music, and received the Danish Cultural Foundation's Prize of Honour (1957). His recordings include his own *Himmerland-Rapsodi* (with the Danish Radio Symphony Orchestra for Decca), the ballet music from Kuhlau's *The Elves' Hill* (with the Danish Radio Symphony Orchestra for Columbia), the overture and Dance of the Cockerels from Nielsen's *Maskarade* (with the Berlin Philharmonic Orchestra for Polydor, on 78s), excerpts from Nielsen's *Aladdin* (with the Copenhagen Royal Opera Orchestra and Danish Radio Symphony Orchestra for Philips), and Sarasate's *Zigeunerweisen* (with Tworek and the Danish Radio Symphony Orchestra for Polydor).

Reeves, Herbert Wynn (b. 1880). Born in London, Reeves studied at the Guildhall School of Music and Drama, founded and conducted the Enfield Subscription Concerts (1911–14), conducted the Hampstead Musical Society (1933–7) and the London Amateur Orchestra (1922–39). He was a violinist in many London orchestras, and was musical director and conductor of the Carl Rosa Opera Company (1937–9) and of the International Ballet (1943–7). With a London orchestra for Fidelity he recorded the *Romeo and Juliet* fantasy-overture, suites from *Swan Lake*, *The Sleeping Beauty* and *Nutcracker*, *Capriccio italien*, *A Night on the Bare Mountain*, and the Polovtsian Dances from *Prince Igor*.

Refice, Licinio (1883–1954). The Italian composer Refice was born at Patrica near Rome, studied at the Liceo Santa Cecilia, Rome, was ordained a priest and became professor of church music at the Scuola Pontifica in Rome in 1910. His compositions included both sacred and secular works; he conducted recordings of his *Ave Maria*, *Umbra di nube* and two arias from his opera *Cecilia* (with Muzio, for Columbia, on 78s), and his *Lilium Crucis* and an interlude from *Trittico Francescano* (with the Naples Scarlatti Orchestra *et al.* for Colosseum, US), in addition to Lassus' *Jubilate Deo*, Palestrina's *Regina coeli* and *Incipit oratio Jeremiae Prophetae – Lamentation*, Victoria's *Gaudent in coelis* and Viadana's *Exsultate justi* (with the Rome Vatican Choir for Seva).

Rehmann, Theodor (1895–1963). Born at Essen, and educated at the Universities of Münster and Bonn and at the Regensburg College of Church Music, Rehmann served in the German army in World War I, and was conductor at the Aachen Cathedral from 1924, as well as acting municipal director of music at Aachen (1945–6). He was also a professor at the Hochschule für Musik at Cologne (from 1946), editor of *Gregoriusblatt* (1926–38), and a member of the German Section of the International Music Council of UNESCO and of the executive board of the International Society for New Church Music at Frankfurt am Main. His compositions included choral, chamber and solo music. In 1955 he was created a Monsignor, and was awarded the Bruckner Medal by the International Bruckner Society in Vienna. On 78s Rehmann recorded an exceptionally good Mass No. 2 of Bruckner (with the Aachen Cathedral Choir *et al.* for HMV), Brahms' *Nänie*, Bruch's *Jubilate* and Handel's *Psalm 112* (with the Aachen Cathedral Choir and the Prussian State Symphony Orchestra, for HMV); later, on LP, he recorded Verdi's *Ave Maria*, *Stabat Mater*, *Laudi alla Vergine Maria* and *Te Deum*, Bruckner's motets, Palestrina's *Missa Papae Marcelli*, *Stabat Mater*, *Improperia* and *Lamentatio* and Ingegneri's *Ecce vidimus sum – Responsorium* (with the Aachen Cathedral Choir *et al.* for DGG-Archiv), and Palestrina's *Surge, illuminare* and *Urbs acquiensis* and Lotti's *Crucifixus* (with the Aachen Cathedral Choir and Symphony Orchestra, released in the United States by Mace).

Reichwein, Leopold (1878–1945). Born in Breslau, Reichwein was a conductor at Breslau, Mannheim and Karlsruhe, at the Vienna Opera (1913–21), was music director of the Gesellschaft der Musikfreunde in Vienna (1921–6) and at Bochum (1926–38), and returned to the Vienna Opera (1938). He committed suicide after the war, following accusations that he had had connections with the Nazis. Parlophone issued a disc on which he conducted the Vienna State Opera Orchestra in the overture to *Der Freischütz*.

Reid, William (b. 1925). The British conductor Reid studied science at the Battersea Polytechnic, and graduated from the Royal College of Music in 1949. He was a repetiteur with the Carl Rosa Opera Company (1954–5), worked with the Welsh National Opera and English Opera Group, and conducted some operas on television; he was an assistant conductor with Sadler's Wells Opera (1958–60), toured Australia with them with *Die lustige Witwe*, and has since conducted for the Australian Opera Company and with the Elizabethan Trust Orchestras in Sydney and Melbourne. EMI recorded the performance of *Die lustige Witwe* with the Sadler's Wells Company.

Reinartz, Hanns (b. 1911). Born in Düsseldorf where he attended the Conservatory, Reinartz studied further at the Rhine Music School and at the Hochschule für Musik at Cologne. He was a conductor at the Düsseldorf Opera (1933), music director at the Bonn Opera (1940–45), music director at Solingen (1946–51), first conductor at the Wuppertal Opera (1951–4), and at the Weimar Opera (1954–6). He taught conducting at the Bergisches Landeskonservatorium (1946–54), became director of the Bavarian State Conservatory at Würzburg (1956), professor of conducting at the Hochschule für Musik at Munich (1963), and president of the Hochschule für Musik at Würzburg (1973). He has recorded Bach's Suite No. 3 and Handel's *Music for the Royal Fireworks* (with the Orchestra of Professors of the Bavarian State Conservatory, for RBM); the *Brandenburg Concertos*, Telemann's *Oboe d'amore Concerto in G* and *Viola Concerto in G*, Vivaldi's *Cello Concerto in D*, Boccherini's *Cello Concerto in B flat*, Haydn's *Cello Concerto in D* (with Metzger), Albinoni's Concerto Op. 9 No. 2, Geminiani's Concerto Grosso Op. 7 No. 1, A. Scarlatti's *Flute Concerto in A*, dell'Abaco's Concerto da chiesa, Marcello's *Oboe Concerto in D minor* (with Hausmann) and Mozart's Symphony No. 10 (with the Würzburg Camerata Accademica, for Sonopresse in France, and issued by Pye in Britain).

Reiner, Fritz (1888–1963). Born in Budapest, the son of a merchant, Reiner began to learn the piano at the age of six under the influence of his mother who was an amateur musician, and then showed evidence of an exceptional memory. At 10 he entered the Budapest Academy of Music, where one of his teachers was Bartók; at 12 he conducted a high school orchestra, at 13 played a Mozart piano concerto in public, and from 15 to 19 he played the kettledrum in the Academy orchestra. Reiner's father wished him to become a lawyer, and for a time he studied law at Budapest University. Previously the composer Weiner had convinced him that he should be a conductor; at 20 he became a choral coach at the Budapest Comic Opera, and conducted a performance of *Carmen* when the conductor fell sick. He then was conductor at Ljubljana Opera (1910–14), where he performed *Parsifal* when, for the first time, the opera could be performed away from Bayreuth. He became Royal Court conductor at Dresden (1914–22); on his arrival there he was asked to conduct the four operas of Wagner's *Ring* without rehearsal. There also he came to know Strauss, and directed an early performance of *Die Frau ohne Schatten*. At Dresden he also conducted concerts with the Saxon State Orchestra, and was a guest conductor in Berlin, Hamburg and Vienna, but he left in 1922 because he was refused permission to conduct at Rome and Barcelona, where he had also been a guest conductor for a year. When he was invited to succeed Ysaÿe with the Cincinnati Symphony Orchestra, he migrated to the United States to become the orchestra's conductor (1922–31), and was granted US citizenship in 1928. He was head of the opera and orchestral departments at the Curtis Institute at Philadelphia (1931–41), where among his pupils were Bernstein, Foss and Hendl. He took part in the opera venture with the Philadelphia Orchestra and the Philadelphia Grand Opera (1934–5), conducted at the Hollywood Bowl, was music director of the Pittsburgh Symphony Orchestra (1938–48), conductor at the New York Metropolitan Opera (1949–53), and finally conductor of the Chicago Symphony Orchestra (1953–62), which he took over at a low ebb of the orchestra's fortunes. He was a frequent visitor to Europe, Mexico and South America, conducted the La Scala Orchestra at Milan (1926–30), led operas of Wagner and Gluck at Covent Garden (1936–7), conducted at the San Francisco Opera (1936–8), and was invited to conduct *Die Meistersinger* at the reopening of the Vienna State Opera (1955). He toured very little with the Chicago Symphony Orchestra, and rejected the opportunity to visit Europe with the orchestra in 1959 because of the excessive demands made by the travelling schedule.

Reiner was one of the most significant conductors of his time, and together with the Chicago Symphony Orchestra he ranked with Toscanini, Koussevitzky, Stokowski, Mengelberg, Beecham and Furtwängler and their respective orchestras. His formative influences were Muck, Mahler, Strauss and more particularly Nikisch, whose methods he studied at Leipzig, and who was a model for his own style and technique. Reiner combined extraordinary precision of execution with flexibility in phrasing and expression; his performances, especially in his last years with the Chicago Symphony, were incredibly brilliant, with unique qualities of rubato and dynamic shading. He reached these superlative standards through an almost inhuman demand for perfection, and the most meticulous preparation and rehearsal. In both opera and orchestral concerts no detail escaped his scrutiny, and he left nothing to chance. His ear was remarkably acute; at rehearsal his most frequent call to the orchestra was: 'It is *not* clean. It must be clean' (*Hi Fidelity*, April 1964). His precision was not for the sole purpose of performing the music exactly as written, but to reveal its inherent dramatic and musical qualities. Stravinsky called the Chicago Symphony Orchestra under Reiner 'the most precise and flexible in the world'. Reiner's musical scholarship was profound, and his repertoire comprehensive. He performed baroque music with exemplary style, and said once that his favourite composer was Mozart; he performed Haydn with more freedom than most. His programmes were built around the Viennese classics, but he was also celebrated for his interpretations of Mendelssohn, Berlioz, Brahms, Strauss, Stravinsky, Bartók and Hindemith. His players noted that the tension rose when he conducted Strauss and Wagner. He took great pleasure in performing lighter music, such as Strauss waltzes, and gave them the same scrupulous attention as to the most serious symphonies; his discs of Strauss waltzes with the Chicago Symphony show a rare degree of finesse. Although he occasionally programmed American composers, he was scarcely a committed advocate for them. He liked Schoenberg, but his interest in Stravinsky did not go later than *Agon*. With soloists he was an excellent collaborator.

Amongst musicians Reiner's baton technique was a legend. He could beat any rhythm, but his baton, usually a large one, moved in very small patterns, apparently to make the players keep their eyes on him. He regarded his eyes as the important contact with every player, who were caught in an almost hypnotic effect, in the manner of Nikisch. To the audience, he appeared motionless and therefore uninteresting, but he said himself that 'the best conducting technique is that which achieves the maximum musical result with the minimum of physical effort' (*Etude*, October 1951): paradoxically, Bernstein was one of his students at the Curtis Institute. At rehearsals he spoke little, and in a familiar piece he was precise in his demands; sometimes he would impassively run through a score with his eyes on the music, as if he were making up his mind how it should sound. At concerts he was even more restrained and gave few cues, but always permitted the principal players freedom to phrase in their own way. He had an acid wit, and was known to be amiable but unapproachable in everyday life; however, before the orchestra at rehearsals he was quite irascible: 'any day he failed to lose his temper was a day when he was too sick to conduct', one player remarked. Musicians respected his knowledge and musical authority, but he was certainly not liked by them. Some even thought that he was trying to fool the orchestra. Later, in 1972, Solti remarked that the Chicago Symphony had 'lost that kind of Reiner fear that the musical director was a natural enemy' (*Stereo Review*, September 1972). In Chicago he was an enigma, divorcing himself completely from all social activities, which estranged him from the orchestra's management and the civic authorities.

Although he was not interested in recording techniques as such, Reiner always carefully planned and rehearsed his recorded performances, which usually took place after concerts where the works were programmed. He is said to have made records in Europe in 1920, but the first existing listing of him as a recording artist is in the series *World's Greatest Music* (for the *New York Post* and RCA Victor), in which he conducted the New York Philharmonic-Symphony Orchestra in records, issued in 1938, of Debussy's *Nuages* and *Fêtes*, and the *Prélude à l'après-midi d'un faune*, and the preludes to *Die Meistersinger* and *Parsifal*. He then recorded with the Pittsburgh Symphony Orchestra, first on 78s and then on LP, from 1941 to 1948, for Columbia, Bach's Suite No. 2 and Caillet's arrangement of the *Fugue in G minor*, Mozart's Symphonies Nos 35 and 40, Beethoven's Symphony No. 2, Brahms' Piano Concerto No. 1 (with Serkin) and some *Hungarian Dances*, *Don Juan*, *Ein Heldenleben*, *Don Quixote* (with Piatigorsky), the *Le Bourgeois gentilhomme* suite, the prelude to Act III and Dance of the Apprentices and March of the Mastersingers from *Die Meistersinger*, the Ride from *Die Walküre*, Forest Murmurs from *Siegfried*, the preludes to Acts I and III of *Lohengrin*, the Bacchanale from *Tannhäuser*, Debussy's *Iberia* and *Danse* (orch. Ravel), Ravel's *La Valse*, Mahler's *Lieder eines fahrenden Gesellen* (with Carol Brice), a symphonic picture (arr. Bennett) from *Porgy and Bess*, Bartók's *Concerto for Orchestra*, *El amor brujo* (with Brice), Shostakovich's Symphony No. 6, the Bacchanale from *Samson et Dalila*, some Viennese waltzes, Glinka's *Kamarinskaya*, *A Night on the Bare Mountain*, and the overtures to *Il Signor Bruschino* and *Colas Breugnon*. For Columbia he also recorded the *Brandenburg Concertos* (with a chamber ensemble in New York), the closing scene from *Salome* and some Mozart arias (with Welitsch and the Metropolitan Opera Orchestra for Columbia), and Honegger's Concerto (with Levant and the Columbia Symphony Orchestra for Columbia).

After 1950, Reiner recorded for RCA Victor, with the NBC Symphony Orchestra, the Robin Hood Dell Orchestra (i.e. the summertime Philadelphia Orchestra), the RCA Victor Symphony Orchestra, his own Symphony Orchestra and the Chicago Symphony Orchestra; it is with the latter that he made his most illustrious recordings. With the RCA Victor Symphony Orchestra he recorded the four Bach suites, Beethoven's Piano Concerto No. 5 and Rachmaninov's Piano Concerto No. 3 (with Horowitz), *Carmen* and an abridged *Die Fledermaus*, the Brahms *Alto Rhapsody* (with Marian Anderson), Liszt's *Totentanz* (with Brailowsky), Saint-Saëns' Cello Concerto No. 1 (with Piatigorsky), *Till Eulenspiegel* and the closing scene from *Der Rosenkavalier* (with Stevens and Berger), the prelude to Act III of *Lohengrin*, the Grand March from *Tannhäuser*, the Dream Pantomime from *Hänsel und Gretel*, the waltzes from Tchaikovsky's Symphony No. 5, *The Sleeping Beauty*, *Swan Lake*, *Nutcracker* and *Eugene Onegin* and arias and excerpts from Gluck's *Orfeo ed Euridice* and *Le nozze di Figaro* (with Stevens); with the NBC Symphony Orchestra Mozart's Divertimento K. 251 and *Ein musikalischer Spass*, Debussy's *Petite Suite* (arr. Busser) and Ravel's *Le Tombeau de Couperin*; and, with the Robin Hood Dell Orchestra, the incidental music from *A Midsummer Night's Dream*, Brahms' Double Concerto (with Milstein and Piatigorsky) and Rachmaninov's *Rhapsody on a Theme of Paganini* (with Kapell).

The recordings with the Chicago Symphony Orchestra encompassed some new music, in addition to his repertoire already recorded. Included were Haydn's Symphony No. 88, Mozart's Symphonies Nos 36, 39, 40 and 41, the Divertimento K. 334, *Eine kleine Nachtmusik*, the *Don Giovanni* overture and the Piano Concerto K. 503 (with Tchaikovsky), Beethoven's Symphonies Nos 1, 3, 5, 6, 7 and 9, *Coriolan* and *Fidelio* overtures, the Piano Concertos Nos 4 and 5 (with Cliburn), Schubert's Symphonies Nos 5 and 8, the Schumann Piano Concerto (with Cliburn), the Rossini overtures *Il barbiere di Siviglia*, *William Tell*, *La scala di seta*, *Il Signor Bruschino*, *La Cenerentola* and *La gazza ladra*, Berlioz's *Nuits d'été* (with Price), Brahms' Symphony No. 3, *Tragic Overture*, Violin Concerto (with Heifetz) and Piano Concertos Nos 1 (with Rubinstein) and 2 (with Cliburn and Gilels), *Invitation to the Dance*,

Dvořák's Symphony No. 9 and *Carnival* overture, two collections of Strauss waltzes, Liszt's *Mephisto Waltz* and *Totentanz* (with Janis), *Scheherazade*, Tchaikovsky's Symphony No. 6, Violin Concerto (with Heifetz), Piano Concerto No. 1 (with Gilels), *Nutcracker* suite, *1812* overture, *Marche slave*, *Pictures at an Exhibition*, the Polovtsian March from *Prince Igor*, *A Night on the Bare Mountain*, Dawn, the Rhine Journey and Funeral Music from *Götterdämmerung*, the preludes to Acts I and III, the Dance of the Apprentices and the Procession of the Mastersingers from *Die Meistersinger*, *La Mer*, *Iberia*, *Rapsodie espagnole*, *Valses nobles et sentimentales*, *Pavane pour une infante défunte*, *Alborada del gracioso*, *Also sprach Zarathustra* (twice), *Don Juan* (twice), *Ein Heldenleben*, *Don Quixote* (with Janigro), *Tod und Verklärung*, *Symphonia domestica*, *Le Bourgeois gentilhomme* suite, *Burleske* (with Janis), excerpts from *Elektra* and *Salome* (with Borkh *et al.*), the waltzes from *Der Rosenkavalier*, *El amor brujo* (with Price), dances from *The Three-cornered Hat*, *Nights in the Gardens of Spain* (with Rubinstein), the intermezzo and dance from *La vida breve*, Albéniz's *Navarra* and pieces from *Iberia*, the intermezzo from Granados' *Goyescas*, *Le Baiser de la fée*, *Le Chant du rossignol*, *Alexander Nevsky*, the *Lieutenant Kijé* suite, *Pini di Roma* and *Fontane di Roma*, Rachmaninov's Piano Concertos No. 1 (with Janis) and 2 (with Rubinstein and Cliburn) and *Rhapsody on a Theme of Paganini* (with Rubinstein), *The Isle of the Dead*, the Bartók *Concerto for Orchestra*, *Hungarian Sketches* and *Music for Strings, Percussion and Celesta*, Hovhaness's *The Mysterious Mountain*, Liebermann's *Concerto for Jazz Band and Orchestra*, the polka and fugue from *Schwanda*, the overtures *The Hebrides*, *Colas Breugnon*, *Russlan and Ludmilla* and *The Bartered Bride*, Mahler's Symphony No. 4 (with Della Casa) and *Das Lied von der Erde* (with Forrester and Lewis).

Reiner also recorded the Verdi *Requiem*, *Till Eulenspiegel*, *Tod und Verklärung*, and selections of *Slavonic Dances* of Dvořák and *Hungarian Dances* of Brahms (with the Vienna Philharmonic Orchestra *et al.* for Decca), Brahms' Symphony No. 4 (with the Royal Philharmonic Orchestra for Reader's Digest, and later re-issued by RCA), and Haydn's Symphonies Nos 95 and 101 (with an ensemble selected from the players in the New York orchestras, for RCA; this was his last record before his death).

The United States Schwann catalogue still lists many of Reiner's most important recordings with the Chicago Symphony, and a number have been re-issued on cheaper labels in the US and Britain, as have others with the Vienna Philharmonic, Royal Philharmonic and his own Orchestras. In 1976 RCA re-issued in the US Haydn's Symphonies Nos 95 and 101, Brahms' Symphony No. 3, the excerpts from *Die Meistersinger* and *Götterdämmerung*, and another containing four waltzes of J. Strauss, the waltzes from *Der Rosenkavalier* and *Invitation to the Dance*, in 1977 in Britain Brahms' Symphony No. 4, and in FR Germany Mozart's Symphonies Nos 36, 39, 40 and 41. Add to them Beethoven's Symphony No. 6 issued in Britain and the Strauss tone poems still available in the US, and the resulting collection at least gives a glimpse of the magnitude of Reiner's stature as a conductor, and the glory of the Chicago Symphony Orchestra as it was then.

In addition to these commercial recordings, some 'pirate' ones have been available, issued by Golden Age of Opera, Rococo, the Bruno Walter Society, Unique Opera Recordings and International Piano Library. These have been of *Don Giovanni*, *Salome*, *Elektra* and *Der fliegende Holländer* (with the Metropolitan Opera Orchestra *et al.*), *Tristan und Isolde* (with Flagstad, Melchior and the Covent Garden Orchestra *et al.*), Act II of *Die Walküre* (with the San Francisco Opera Orchestra *et al.*) part of Act I of *Götterdämmerung* (with the Lewisohn Stadium Orchestra *et al.*) and excerpts from *Parsifal* (with the London Philharmonic Orchestra *et al.*).

Reinhardt, Rolf (b. 1927). Born at Heidelberg, Reinhardt studied the piano with Kwast-Hodapp and composition with Fortner, and first conducted at Heidelberg in 1946. He has since appeared at opera houses at Darmstadt, Stuttgart and Trier, and from 1968 has been a professor at the Hochschule für Musik at Frankfurt am Main. He is a familiar name to older record collectors, and has made many LP discs. These include Vivaldi's Concertos Op. 4 and Op. 8, Geminiani's Concerti Grossi Op. 3, Torelli's Concertos Op. 8, Bach's *Magnificat*, Cantatas Nos 32, 57, 78, 203 and 211, Harpsichord Concertos Nos 1, 2 and 3, the *Two Harpsichord Concerto in C*, *Three Harpsichord Concerto in C* and *Four-Harpsichord Concerto in A* (with Elsner *et al.*), the Flute, Violin and Harpsichord Concerto (with Mess, Lautenbacher and Elsner) and the Violin and Oboe Concerto (with Beh and Milde), Handel's Organ Concertos Op. 4 and Op. 7 (with Kraft), Haydn's Symphony No. 96, Sinfonia Concertante, *Harpsichord Concertos in C, D* and *G* (with Elsner), Trumpet Concerto (with Gleisle), Horn Concerto No. 2 (with Arnold) and Oboe Concerto (with Milde), viola concertos by Stamitz and Telemann (with Wigand), Mozart's violin concertos (with Barchet), *Eine kleine Nachtmusik*, *Ein musikalischer Spass*, Sinfonia Concertante K. 297b, *Les Petits Riens* and *Thamos, König in Ägypten*, Beethoven's Symphony No. 9, Brahms' Piano Concerto No. 2 (with de la Bruchollerie), Bartók's *Music for Strings, Percussion and Celesta*, Schumann's Cello Concerto (with Dorner), Fantasia for Violin and Orchestra (with Stücki), *Introduction and Allegro in D minor* (with Bohle) and *Konzertstück for Four Horns* (with the Stuttgart Pro Musica Orchestra for Vox), Mozart's Flute Concerto No. 1 and Flute and Harp Concerto (with Glass and Stein), Brahms' Piano Concerto No. 2 (with Sandor), Berlioz's *Rêverie et Caprice*, Chausson's *Poème*, Ravel's *Tzigane* and Saint-Saëns' *Havanaise* (with Rosand), the Dvořák and Goldmark Violin Concertos (with Gimpel), Bartók's Piano Concerto No. 1 and Rhapsody (with Sandor) and *The Wooden Prince* and *The Miraculous Mandarin* (with the South-West German Radio Orchestra for Vox); *Bastien und Bastienne* and *La finta giardiniera* (with the Stuttgart Ton Studio Orchestra *et al.*, released by Nixa and Period); the *Brandenburg Concertos*, Haydn's *Salve Regina*, Mozart's *Litaniae Lauretanae*, two church sonatas, Handel's *Silete Venti* and *Joseph* overture, suites by Telemann, five Concertos for Strings by Durante, and K. Stamitz's *Sinfonias concertante in D major* and *A major*, *Symphony in E flat major* and *Viola Concerto in A major* (with Koch and the Collegium Aureum *et al.* for Harmonia Mundi, and many being issued in the US by RCA-Victrola).

Reinhart, Walther (b. 1886). Born in Winterthur, Switzerland, Reinhart studied at the Conservatory at Frankfurt am Main and at the Royal Academy of Music in Berlin under Bruch and Ochs. He became conductor of the Görlitz Philharmonic Orchestra (1911), studied with Reger at Meiningen (1913), conducted the Teachers' Choir at Frankfurt (1914–18), founded the Reinhart Choir in Zürich, and became conductor of the Winterthur Choir (1919). He composed a number of choral works and some violin sonatas. With his Reinhart Choir he recorded a number of sections from Bach's Cantata No. 78 (for Columbia, on 78s), and then recorded the complete Cantata and the *Magnificat*.

Reinshagen, Victor (b. 1908). Born in Riga, Reinshagen grew up in Zürich where he studied at the Academy of Music, and also attended the Hochschule für Musik in Berlin. His first appointment as a conductor was at the theatre at Solothurn-Biel in Switzerland in 1927; he was conductor of the Beromünster Radio Orchestra (1935–8) and at the Zürich City Theatre where he became music director in 1942, was permanent guest conductor at the Bavarian State Opera at Munich (1950), again was with the Beromünster Radio Orchestra, conducted in Vienna, Marseille and Paris, and was appointed artistic director at the Hamburg State Opera (1968–73). For DGG he recorded excerpts from Lortzing's *Undine* (with the Bamberg Symphony Orchestra *et al.*), and for Decca excerpts from the operettas *Der Graf von Luxemburg*, *Die lustige Witwe*, *Gräfin Maritza*, *Der Zarewitsch* and *Der Vetter aus Dingsda* (with the Zürich Tonhalle Orchestra *et al.*).

Remoortel, Edouard van (1926–77). Born in Brussels, Remoortel first studied the cello at the Brussels and Geneva Conservatories before deciding to become a conductor, and made his debut at Geneva at the age of 17. He was a pupil of Guarnieri and Galliera at the Accademia Chigiana at Siena, and later of Josef Krips. On his return to Belgium he became conductor of the Concerts Populaires in Brussels and then chief conductor of the Belgian National Orchestra (1951). Between 1950 and 1960 he also conducted at numerous festivals and with major orchestras in Europe, North and South America, Japan, Australia and New Zealand, and at opera houses in New York, Brussels, Monte Carlo and elsewhere. He was appointed musical director and permanent conductor of the St Louis Symphony Orchestra (1958–62) and musical adviser to the Monte Carlo National Opera Orchestra (1965–70). One of the most significant Belgian conductors, he received awards from both the Belgian and French governments, including the Ordre de Léopold and the Ordre de la Couronne (Belgium). His performances were distinguished by their sure technique, spirit and sense of style, but, in the words of the obituary in *The Musical Times*, 'his early promise was never quite fulfilled'.

Remoortel made a number of records for Vox in the first decade of LP. Included were Haydn's Symphonies Nos 100 and 103, *German Dances* of Mozart and Beethoven, and Mozart's Serenades K. 239 and K. 320 (with the Stuttgart Pro Musica Orchestra), Beethoven's Symphony No. 1 (with the Vienna Musikgesellschaft Orchestra), Symphonies Nos 7 and 8 (with the London Symphony Orchestra) and *Egmont* incidental music (with the

South-West German Radio Symphony Orchestra), Mendelssohn's Symphony No. 3 (with the same orchestra), Symphony No. 4 and incidental music to *A Midsummer Night's Dream* (with the Vienna Volksoper Orchestra), Grieg's *Holberg* and *Lyric Suites*, *Wedding Day at Troldhaugen*, *Norwegian Dances* and *Sigurd Jorsalfar* suite (with the Bamberg Symphony Orchestra), *Symphonic Dances* and *Elegiac Melodies* (with the Vienna Pro Musica Orchestra), Schumann's Symphony No. 3 (with the Vienna Volksoper Orchestra) and Symphony No. 4 (with the South-West German Radio Orchestra), Tchaikovsky's *Capriccio italien* (with the Vienna Musikgesellschaft Orchestra), excerpts from *Swan Lake* and *The Sleeping Beauty* (with the Vienna Symphony Orchestra), the Brahms Violin Concerto (with Schneiderhan and the Bamberg Symphony Orchestra), dances from *The Three-cornered Hat* and *La vida breve* (with Madeira and the Vienna Symphony Orchestra), *L'Apprenti sorcier*, *España*, the *Prélude à l'après-midi d'un faune* and *Boléro* (with the Vienna Symphony Orchestra).

He recorded with the Monte Carlo National Orchestra for Philips excerpts from Khachaturian's *Spartacus*, Kabalevsky's *The Comedians* and excerpts from *Colas Breugnon*, Ravel's *Daphnis et Chloé* and *Tzigane* (with Szeryng), Debussy's *Prélude à l'après-midi d'un faune*, *Children's Corner* (arranged by Caplet) and *La Boîte à joujoux*, Barber's Violin Concerto and Milhaud's Violin Concerto No. 2 (with Bernard), Lalo's *Symphonie espagnole* (with Szeryng), Saint-Saëns' Violin Concertos Nos 1 and 2 and *Caprice pour violon* (with Gitlis), Violin Concerto No. 3, *Havanaise* and *Introduction et rondo capriccioso* (with Szeryng), and a collection commemorating 100 years of the Monte Carlo Ballet. He also recorded Prokofiev's *Scythian Suite* and excerpts from *The Love of Three Oranges* (with the St Louis Symphony Orchestra for CBS, US); the two *L'Arlésienne* suites and *España* (with the Vienna Symphony Orchestra for CBS, France), Stehman's *Symphonie de poche* and *Chant funèbre* (with the Belgian National Orchestra for Decca); Litolff's Concerto symphonique No. 4 and Reinecke's Piano Concertos Nos 1 and 2 (with Robbins); and Goetz's *Symphony in F* and overtures *Frühlings*, *The Taming of the Shrew* and *Francesca da Rimini* (with the Monte Carlo National Orchestra for Genesis).

Rennert, Wolfgang (b. 1922). Born in Cologne and the brother of Günther Rennert, the opera producer and director, Rennert studied with Solti and with Krauss at the Mozarteum in Salzburg, was a repetiteur at the Deutsche Oper am Rhein, Düsseldorf (1947–53), first conducting there in 1948, was conductor at Kiel (1950–53), general music director at Frankfurt am Main (1953–67), chief conductor at the Gartnerplatz Theatre at Munich (1967–71), and then conductor with the Staatsoper in East Berlin (1971). He has also been a guest conductor in Vienna, Paris, Rome and at the Salzburg Festival. He has recorded Weill's *Die Dreigroschenoper* (with the Frankfurt Opera Orchestra *et al.* for Philips), and excerpts from *Rusalka* and *The Tsar's Bride* (with the Berlin Radio Symphony Orchestra *et al.* for DGG).

Rescigno, Nicola. Born in New York, Rescigno studied law in Italy, and made his debut as a conductor at the Brooklyn Academy of Music in New York in 1943. He was co-founder and director of the Chicago Lyric Opera (1954–6) and of the Dallas Civic Opera (1957–75), becoming the latter company's general director and resident conductor. He has also conducted in Canada, Italy, Mexico, Portugal and England, and with other opera companies in the United States. For Decca he recorded excerpts from Zandonai's *Francesca da Rimini* and an aria recital by del Monaco (with the Monte Carlo Opera Orchestra) and another aria recital by Pavarotti (with the Vienna State Opera Orchestra); L'Estro Armonico have also released a performance of Bellini's *Il Pirata*, which he conducted in Carnegie Hall in 1959.

Reuss, Wilhelm (1886–1945). Born in Karlsruhe, Reuss studied under Draeseke and von Schillings, and was a conductor at Berlin (1923–7), Kassel (1927–33) and Königsberg (from 1935), where he eventually died in a Russian prisoner-of-war camp. For Telefunken he recorded the intermezzo from J. Strauss's *Indigo* (with the Berlin Philharmonic Orchestra) and two excerpts from Act III of *Die Meistersinger* (with Reinmar and the Berlin Staatsoper Orchestra and Chorus).

Reustlen, Erich (b. 1926). Born in Stuttgart, Reustlen studied in Ulm and Constance with Keller, David and Marx, in Vienna with Koslik, and in Tübingen with Gerstenberg, and graduated as a conductor from the Hochschule für Musik in Stuttgart (1954). He founded the Reutlingen Youth Orchestra (1949), and founded and was artistic director of the South German Youth Orchestra (1956–76), and with these orchestras toured France, Luxembourg, Spain, Italy and Turkey. He taught at the Pädagogische Hochschule in Reutlingen, and became professor at the Hochschule für Musik in Trossingen (1978). He recorded Boccherini's *Cello Concerto in B flat* and Haydn's *Cello Concerto in D* (with Wolf and the South German Youth Orchestra, for Da Camera, and with the orchestra renamed the Reutlingen Symphony Orchestra, for CMS-Oryx).

Reuter, Rolf (b. 1926). Born in Leipzig, Reuter comes from a musical family; his father, Fritz Reuter, was a composer and teacher, his sister is a violinist, and his son a conductor. He was educated at the Hochschule für Musik at Dresden, was conductor at Eisenach (1951–5), general music director at Meiningen (1955–61) and then at the Leipzig Opera (1961–76), and since 1966 has taught at the Hochschule für Musik at Leipzig. He has been a guest conductor in Yugoslavia, Czechoslovakia, Cuba, France and in FR Germany. Reuter has a comprehensive repertoire; he feels that the conductor's task, apart from establishing and keeping the tempi, is a spiritual one. He admired Furtwängler above all others, and also Markevitch, for his style and finesse. He conducted *The Ring* at the Paris Opéra in 1978, and directed *Tristan und Isolde* at the Berlin Staatsoper at short notice without rehearsal, although he had not conducted the work for 17 years. His recordings, for Eterna, have been the *Egmont* music of Beethoven, a melodrama by Max Butting, and a collection of works by his father, Fritz Reuter, with the Leipzig Gewandhaus Orchestra, *et al.*

Revenaugh, Daniell (b. 1934). Born in Louisville, Kentucky, Revenaugh played Beethoven's Piano Concerto No. 1 at the age of 14 with the Louisville Orchestra under Whitney, studied at the Florida State University, and was closely associated with the pianist Egon Petri until the latter's death in 1962. He studied conducting with Dohnányi, Ganz, Lert, Ondrejka and Boult, and composition with Milhaud, and made his New York debut conducting the American Symphony Orchestra in 1966, and his London debut with the Royal Philharmonic Orchestra in 1967. As a result of his connection with Petri, he developed a keen interest in the music of Busoni, and conducted many performances of his works. In 1965 he founded the Busoni Society, and in 1966 directed the United States première of Busoni's *Concerto for Piano and Male Chorus*. He was appointed music director and conductor of the Jacksonville Symphony Orchestra (1969), conducted the first concerts of the Electric Symphony Orchestra at Berkeley, California (1972), was appointed director-general of the Institute for Advanced Musical Studies in Montreux, Switzerland (1973), accompanied Kempe on many of his major concert tours (1973–6), and was invited by him to conduct the Munich Philharmonic Orchestra (1975). Revenaugh has also given concert performances as a pianist, and has been carrying out research on Ernst von Dohnányi. In 1968 EMI issued a recording of the Busoni concerto, and the *Sarabande* and *Cortège* (two studies for *Doktor Faust*) played by Ogden and with the Royal Philharmonic Orchestra *et al.* conducted by Revenaugh.

Reyentovich, Yuli (b. 1914). Born in Tobow, Russia, Reyentovich studied the violin with his father and at the Tobow Music Insitute, and with Yampolsky in Moscow (1931–5). He was then a violin soloist, became concertmaster of the Bolshoi Theatre Orchestra, Moscow (1952), and founded and conducted the Bolshoi Theatre Violinists' Ensemble (1956), which performs, with great virtuosity, programmes of specially arranged classical and modern pieces, and newly written compositions. The Ensemble has toured abroad, and has recorded some of its repertoire, including arrangements of the Chaconne from Bach's Violin Partita No. 2 and arias by Handel, and Shchedrin's *Chamber Suite*.

Rezler, Arnold (b. 1909). Brother of the conductor Alfons Rezler, Rezler was born in Moszczenic, Poland, studied at the Poznań Conservatory, and was a cellist with the opera and orchestra at Poznań (1931–7). He taught at the Karłowicz Conservatory at Vilna (1937–45), formed and was conductor of the Poznań Symphony Orchestra (1945–56), and the Polish Radio Symphony Orchestra in Bydgoszczy, was conductor of the Warsaw National Philharmonic Orchestra (1956–8) and at the Warsaw Opera (from 1958), and was a professor at the Warsaw Conservatory. His recordings, for Polskie Nagrania, include a Wieniawski violin concerto and other concerted pieces (with Gimpel and the National Philharmonic Orchestra), and songs by Moniuszko, Nowowiejski, Gall, Noskowski, Kamieński and Karłowicz (with the National Philharmonic Orchestra *et al.*).

Rhené-Baton (1879–1940). Born at Courseulles-sur-Mer, Calvados, France, as Rhené Baton, Rhené-Baton studied at the Paris Conservatoire, and was first a music critic for a Paris newspaper. He became chorus director at the Paris Opéra-Comique, then was conductor of orchestral concerts at Angers and Bordeaux, of the Concerts Durand in Paris, and in

1910 directed a festival of French music at Munich. He was a conductor with the Diaghilev Ballets in London, Paris and South America, and then conductor of the Pasdeloup Concerts (1916–23), of the Lamoureux Concerts, and also was a guest conductor abroad. He had a reputation as a fine symphonic conductor, characterised by his 'flexibility, suppleness, bigness of design, more than by precision or inflexible rhythm' (Dominique Sordet). As a composer he wrote piano music and songs; his recordings appear to be Honegger's symphonic poem *Le Chant de Nigamon* and the Franck *Symphony in D minor* (both with the Pasdeloup Orchestra for Decca) and *Symphonie fantastique* (with the same orchestra for HMV).

Ricci, Ruggiero (b. 1918). The violinist Ricci was born in San Francisco, studied with Persinger, Piastro, Stassevich and Kulenkampff, and made his debut in New York in 1929. His career as one of the most outstanding virtuosi on his instrument was temporarily interrupted by service in the United States air force (1942–5). In addition to his many records as violinist, Unicorn issued a disc in 1969 in which he plays and conducts the City of London Chamber Ensemble in the two Bach Violin Concertos and an arrangement of the Harpsichord Concerto No. 1.

Richartz, Willy (b. 1900). Born in Cologne, Richartz studied in Bonn and Cologne, and was a conductor at Cologne and Gelsenkirchen (1923–7), with the Bavarian Radio, Munich (1927–33) and with the Berlin Radio (1934–57). He was a co-founder of the International Society for Copyright and was also vice-president of the Union of German Composers. His works include orchestral music and operas; he recorded his own *Romantic Prelude*, *Little Minuet*, *Galant Gavotte* and *Old German Lullaby* (with the Berlin Philharmonic Orchestra for DGG, on mono LP) and *The Rose Garden* (with the Bamberg Symphony Orchestra for DGG), as well as the overtures to Gomes' opera *Il Guarany* and Strauss's *Waldmeister*, and waltzes by Lanner and Millöcker (with the Bamberg Symphony Orchestra for DGG), Borodin's *Nocturne*, Glinka's *Souvenir d'une mazurka* and Tchaikovsky's *Danse russe* (with the Berlin Philharmonic Orchestra for DGG).

Richter, Hans Werner. A number of enigmatic conductors have appeared on the Oryx label, for whom biographical details are difficult to obtain. One is Hans Werner Richter, who is said to have recorded the nine Beethoven symphonies, the *Egmont*, *Coriolan* and *Leonore No. 3* overtures, Violin Concerto (with Varga) and Piano Concerto No. 5 (with Drescher), Schumann's Symphony No. 4 and Piano Concerto (with da Cardoba), Franck's *Symphony in D minor*, and the preludes to *Die Meistersinger* and *Lohengrin*, the overture to *Tannhäuser*, the prelude and Liebestod from *Tristan und Isolde*, and the Ride from *Die Walküre*. The orchestra named on the discs is the Berlin Pro Musica Symphony Orchestra.

Richter, Karl (b. 1926). Born at Plauen, Saxony, the son of an Evangelical clergyman, Richter grew up in an environment closely associated with church tradition and the music of Bach. As a boy he was a member of the Dresden Kreuzchor, and after World War II studied at Leipzig with Mauersberger, Straube, Ramin and Kobler. He was choirmaster at Christ Church, Leipzig (1946), organist at St Thomas's Church there (1949), then he moved to Munich in 1951 to become cantor (i.e. organist, choirmaster, conductor and improvisor) at the St Mark's Church, where he still plays the organ on Sunday when his schedule permits. He formed the Heinrich Schütz Circle, to perform the music of that composer, but changed the name to the Munich Bach Choir. The choir consists of 70 to 120 voices, is an amateur body and gives usually two concerts each month. He also established the Munich Bach Orchestra, which draws its players from the three major orchestras in the city, and also engages leading wind and brass players. In addition, he is a professor at the Munich Academy of Music.

One of Germany's most distinguished harpsichordists, organists, choral and orchestral conductors, Richter has a special reputation for his performances of baroque music, particularly Bach. His style in this music is distinctive; it is literal with marked rhythmic accents. While it leads to stiffness in the faster movements (a quality called 'Teutonic' by some British commentators), his interpretations of Bach and Handel have great power and vitality. He gives scrupulous attention to the preparation of his performances, to finding the balance between technique, intellect and expression, and the result is performances of the highest technical standard and musicianship.

Richter first recorded in 1952, as the continuo player in Lehmann's recording of Handel's Concerti Grossi Op. 6, with the Bamberg Symphony Orchestra. Since then he has made over 100 records for DGG, mainly on the Archiv label, with his Munich Bach Choir and Orchestra, and in some instances with the

Ansbach Bach Festival Ensemble, and in 1976 he received a special award, the 'Golden Gramophone', from Polydor for his achievement. He has played the harpsichord in recordings of Bach concertos, *Ein musikalisches Opfer* and some Handel pieces, recorded for Decca the Handel Organ Concertos (originally in 1960 and re-issued in 1975), and also made discs of collections of Bach organ works for Decca and DGG, some of which have been superlative in their musicianship. His major recording enterprises have been the great choral masterpieces with the Munich Bach Choir and Orchestra *et al.*: the *St Matthew Passion*, the *St John Passion*, the *Mass in B minor*, the *Christmas Oratorio* and the *Magnificat*, as well as a number of cantatas, including Nos 1, 4, 8, 10, 13, 21, 24, 26, 38, 45, 49, 51, 55, 56, 58, 60, 61, 63, 64, 65, 78, 81, 82, 106, 108, 111, 121, 124, 132, 135, 147, 171, 189 and 202, the *Brandenburg Concertos*, the four orchestral suites, Violin and Oboe Concerto (with Büchner and Shann), Two-Violin Concerto (with Büchner and Guntner), and Two-Harpischord Concerto No. 1 (with himself and Bilgram). His other discs include A. Scarlatti's *Su le sponde* (with Stader), Handel's *Messiah* (in German), *Samson* and *Giulio Cesare*, and the Concerti Grossi Op. 3 and Op. 6 (with the Munich Bach Orchestra and Choir *et al.*), Schütz's *Musikalische Exequien* (with the Munich Schütz Choir *et al.*), the overtures to Handel's *Alcina*, *Belshazzar*, *Agrippina*, *Deidamia*, *Jeptha*, *Radamisto*, *Rinaldo*, *Rodelinda* and *Susanna* (with the London Philharmonic Orchestra), the *Music for the Royal Fireworks* and Double Concertos Nos 2 and 3 (with the English Chamber Orchestra), Gluck's *Orfeo ed Euridice*, Mozart's *Requiem* and Beethoven's *Mass in C major* (with the Munich Bach Choir and Orchestra *et al.*), Haydn's Symphonies Nos 94 and 101 (with the Berlin Philharmonic Orchestra), and Handel's Oboe Concertos Op. 3 Nos 1 to 3, Telemann's *Flute Concertos in B major* and *G major*, and *Oboe Concertos in C minor* and *B minor* (with André and the Munich Bach Orchestra). For Telefunken, he directed the Munich Bach Players in Mozart's Symphony No. 29, J. C. Bach's Sinfonia Op. 18 No. 2, C. P. E. Bach's *Sinfonia in D major*, Mozart's Flute and Harp Concerto (with Nicolet and Stein), two Flute Concertos and Andante K. 315 (with Nicolet), and the Dance of the Blessed Spirits from *Orfeo ed Euridice* (with Nicolet).

Ridout, Alan (b. 1934). Born in Kent and educated at the Royal College of Music, the composer Ridout studied in Holland, and in 1960 was appointed a professor at the RCM. He taught at Birmingham University (1961–2), at London University (1964–5) and at Cambridge University (since 1963). His compositions include five symphonies, seven operas, chamber, vocal and other music; many of these compositions have been recorded by Pye, EMI and Abbey. His publications include *Background to Music* (1962) and *Background to Musical Form* (1964). In 1968 Pye issued a disc containing, *inter alia*, a performance of his *Concertante Music*, in which he conducted the Leicestershire Schools Symphony Orchestra.

Riede, Erich (b. 1903). Born in London, the German conductor and composer Riede studied at the Hochschule für Musik at Frankfurt am Main (1919–23) and in Berlin (1923–5). He was an assistant at Bayreuth (1926–7), at Darmstadt and Stuttgart (1925–9), at the New York Metropolitan Opera (1929–33) and again at Bayreuth (1930–31). He conducted at Cologne (1933–9), Koblenz (1940–43), Reichenberg (1943–5), Mannheim (1949–50) and Dresden (1950–52), and was general music director at Dessau (1952–4), Kaiserslautern (1954–6), Nuremberg (1956–64) and Würzburg (1964–9). His compositions include five operas, orchestral and concerted works and lieder. He made records with the Hamburg Pro Musica Orchestra, which were released in 1961 in Britain by Saga, of Beethoven's Symphony No. 5 and *Egmont* overture, *The Hebrides* overture and excerpts from the incidental music to *A Midsummer Night's Dream*, Liszt's Piano Concerto No. 1 and the Schumann Piano Concerto (with Fiorentino).

Rieger, Fritz (b. 1910). Born in Oberaltstadt in Bohemia, Rieger studied at the Prague Conservatory, where he was a pupil of Szell for conducting. He conducted in Prague (1931–8), Aussig (1939–41), Bremen (1941–5) and Mannheim (1947–9), was general music director and chief conductor of the Munich Philharmonic Orchestra (1949–67), general music director at Monte Carlo and chief conductor of the Melbourne Symphony Orchestra (1968–71), as well as conducting in various opera houses in Europe. His recordings reveal a thoroughly competent and reliable musician, and include Haydn's Symphonies Nos 85, 92 and 98 and the *Sinfonia concertante*, Brahms' *Tragic Overture* and some Strauss waltzes (with the Munich Philharmonic Orchestra for Mercury), the Beethoven Violin Concerto (with Borries), Schubert's Symphony No. 8, and *Moldau* (with the Munich Philharmonic Orchestra for Ariola-Eurodisc), Beethoven's

Piano Concerto No. 5 (with Then-Bergh and the Munich Philharmonic Orchestra for Ariola-Eurodisc, also issued by Baccarola), Mozart's Symphony No. 30 and Sinfonia Concertante K. 297b (with the Winterthur City Orchestra for Pelca), Bach's Suites Nos 2 and 3 (with a chamber ensemble for DGG), and Three-Harpsichord Concerto BWV 1064 (with the Ansbach Festival Orchestra *et al.* for DGG), Beethoven's overtures *Prometheus* and *Die Ruinen von Athen*, Schubert's Symphony No. 5, Mendelssohn's Symphony No. 4, some songs of Grieg (with Kupper), Ravel's *Tzigane* (with Zsigmondy), Lalo's *Symphonie espagnole* (with Gimpel, and the Munich Philharmonic Orchestra for DGG), some *Slavonic Dances* of Dvořák (with the Munich Philharmonic Orchestra for DGG and also issued by Ariola), Schoeck's *Lebendig begraben* (with Fischer-Dieskau and the Berlin Radio Symphony Orchestra for DGG), Brahms' Piano Concerto No. 2 (with Małcużyński and the Philharmonia Orchestra for EMI) and Werder's Violin Concerto (with Dommett and the Melbourne Symphony Orchestra for Festival).

Rieu, André (b. 1917). Born in Haarlem, Rieu studied at Utrecht and at the Amsterdam Conservatory, and was a staff conductor with the Netherlands Radio (1946–9). He became principal conductor of the Limburger Symphony Orchestra at Maastricht, has toured as a conductor in Holland, Belgium, France, FR Germany, Poland, Austria, Britain and Greece, has performed with the Netherlands Opera, and has also been conductor of the Amsterdam Chamber Orchestra, which was founded in 1957, sharing the orchestra's direction with Anthon van der Horst. With this orchestra *et al.* he has recorded Bach's Cantatas Nos 2, 8, 206 and 208, an overture and concertos by Telemann, a sinfonia by C. P. E. Bach, Trumpet Concertos by Telemann, Purcell, Haydn and Leopold Mozart (with Mertens), Haydn's Violin and Piano Concerto (with Schroeder and Leonhardt), Hellendaal's *Concerto Grosso in D minor*, Quantz's *Flute Concerto in D* (with Barwahser), Dittersdorf's *Sinfonia concertante* and Mozart's Symphony No. 23 (for Telefunken), some Handel and Haydn Organ Concertos (with de Klerk), Mozart's Symphony No. 29 (for BASF), and the two Haydn Violin Concertos (with Krebbers, the orchestra's concertmaster). With the Limburger Symphony Orchestra he also recorded (for Donemus) J. Andriessen's *Movimenti*, Frid's *Sinfonietta*, Landré's *Anagrams* and Mul's *Lettre* (with Kruysen).

Rifkin, Joshua (b. 1944). The composer, pianist, conductor and music historian Rifkin was born in New York, graduated from the Juilliard School in New York in 1964, and studied further at the Universities of New York, Princeton and Göttingen, and at the Darmstadt International Music Institute summer course. Since 1970 he has been assistant professor of music at Brandeis University. As a pianist he has recorded (for Nonesuch) three highly successful discs of the rags of Scott Joplin; Nonesuch have also recorded him conducting a disc of fanfares and sonatas by Speer, Loewe, Pezel and Hammerschmidt (with the London Brass Players), 17th-century student music by Krieger and Rosenmüller (with the Little Orchestra of London), sonatas by Biber (with the London Sinfonia String Ensemble), chansons by Busnois and secular music by Josquin (with the Nonesuch Consort), and, by contrast, the *Nude Paper Sermon* of Eric Salzman (b. 1933) (with the Nonesuch Consort).

Rigacci, Bruno (b. 1921). Born in Florence, the pianist, composer and conductor Rigacci studied there and in Rome with Casella. He taught and conducted the orchestra at the Accademia Chigiana at Siena (1958), conducted opera (from 1965), and became the permanent conductor of the Settimane musicale senesi. He has written choral and other works, and has arranged music by Mozart, Paisiello, A. Scarlatti and Donizetti. He conducted a mono LP recording of excerpts from *La Bohème* (with the Berlin Radio Symphony Orchestra and Italian soloists).

Rignold, Hugo (1905–76). Born at Kingston-on-Thames, the son of a conductor and an opera singer, Rignold moved as a boy with his family to Canada, where he was educated and studied the violin at Kelvin College, Winnipeg. He returned to Britain with a scholarship to the Royal Academy of Music (1921), where he studied a number of instruments in addition to the violin. He was principal violinist with Jack Hylton's jazz orchestra (1925–30), led his own orchestra and recorded dance music in the 1930s. He then served in the RAF in World War II, when he conducted the Palestine Symphony Orchestra and was conductor of the Cairo Symphony Orchestra, which he developed from a radio orchestra to one able to perform the classical repertoire. He became a conductor with the Sadler's Wells Ballet (1947), principal conductor of the Liverpool Philharmonic Orchestra (1948–54), directed the music at a performance of *A Midsummer*

Night's Dream at the Edinburgh Festival in 1954, and subsequently toured the United States with the production, was conductor of the Cape Town Symphony Orchestra (1956–7), musical director of the Royal Ballet (1957–60), musical director and principal conductor of the City of Birmingham Symphony Orchestra (1960–68), and afterwards was a guest conductor in Britain and abroad. In 1963 he toured FR Germany and Switzerland, and in 1968 Eastern Europe with the City of Birmingham Symphony Orchestra.

An accomplished conductor, Rignold was especially successful with the Royal Ballet Company, and his years in Birmingham saw the orchestra develop in every way. Through the Feeney Trust he commissioned new works from Bliss, Rawsthorne, Fricker, Musgrave, Panufnik *et al.*, and performed these pieces, with others, in the orchestra's series entitled Masterpieces of Twentieth-Century Music. In the 1940s he made records for EMI with the Covent Garden Orchestra of excerpts from Lecocq's *La Fille de Madame Angot*, Messager's *Les deux Pigeons*, *Swan Lake* and *Sleeping Beauty*, and Ravel's *Shéhérazade* (with Teyte), and later Parlophone released on LP performances with the same orchestra of *Les Patineurs*, *Carnaval*, *La Boutique fantasque*, *Les Sylphides*, *Sylvia* and the ballet music from *Faust*. Columbia issued on 78s some discs of him conducting the Liverpool Philharmonic Orchestra, the Serenade and Entr'acte from Delius's *Hassan*, Haydn's Symphony No. 100 and the Dance of the Blessed Spirits from *Orfeo ed Euridice*. Decca released LP discs of him conducting ballet music: *Sylvia*, *Invitation to the Dance* and the Dance of the Hours from *La Gioconda* (with the Covent Garden Orchestra); RCA issued Prokofiev's *Cinderella*, *Les Patineurs* and *Carnaval* (with the same orchestra) and suites from *Coppélia* and *Sylvia* (with the Paris Conservatoire Orchestra). His other recordings included *L'Apprenti sorcier*, Dvořák's Symphony No. 9, suites from *The Three-cornered Hat* and *El amor brujo*, *A Night on the Bare Mountain*, *Boléro* and suites from *Le Coq d'or* and *Petrushka* (with the London Philharmonic Orchestra, issued in the US by Somerset and some in Britain by Pye), *Improvisations* by Matyas Seiber and John Dankworth (played by Dankworth and his band and the London Philharmonic Orchestra, for Saga), Khachaturian's Piano Concerto (with Katin and the London Symphony Orchestra for Everest), Rachmaninov's Piano Concerto No. 2 and *Rhapsody on a Theme of Paganini* (with Moiseiwitsch and the Philharmonia Orchestra for EMI), Bliss's *Music for Strings* and *Meditation on a Theme of John Blow* (with the City of Birmingham Symphony Orchestra for Lyrita and issued in the US by Musical Heritage Society), and Gershwin's Piano Concerto (with Fiorentino) and suite from *Porgy and Bess* (with the London Philharmonic Orchestra for Saga).

Riley, Terry (b. 1935). Born in Colfax, California, and educated at the University of California, Berkeley, Riley travelled to Europe and India, and is a composer of aleatoric *avant-garde* music. His *Im C*, for orchestra, is 'notated in fragments to be played any number of times at will in the spirit of aleatory latitudinarianism, all within the key of C major, with an occasional F sharp providing a *trompe l'oreille* effect' (M. Slonimsky, in *Baker's Biographical Dictionary of Musicians*, 1971, supp., p. 199). Its first performance was at San Francisco in 1965; Columbia (US) has issued a version of the work conducted by Riley with the New York State University Art Center Orchestra.

Rilling, Helmuth (b. 1933). Born in Stuttgart, the son of a musicologist and a violinist, Rilling studied the organ and composition at the Hochschule für Musik there, and then was a pupil of the organist Germani at the Accademia di Santa Cecilia in Rome (1955–7). Since 1957 he has been cantor and organist at the Memorial Church at Stuttgart, since 1963 has taught choral conducting and the organ at the School of Church Music at Berlin-Spandau, and has been professor of organ music at the Accademia Chigiana at Siena. In 1953 he founded the Gächinger Kantorei Chorus at Gächingen, a small village outside Stuttgart, and the choir retained that name when it moved into the city. The choir usually performs together with the Bach Collegium Stuttgart; its members come from South-western Germany and the German-speaking regions of Switzerland, and are required to have a high standard of musical training. Under Rilling's leadership the choir has won a considerable reputation and has toured in the United States, Mexico, Japan and Israel.

Rilling has been a very active and successful recording artist, particularly with the music of Bach, with the Gächinger Kantorei, the Stuttgart Memorial Church Choir, the Bach Collegium Stuttgart *et al.* Foremost are the complete Bach Cantatas, which have been released since 1970 at the rate of about ten a year, by the Claudius Publishing House in Munich, but which are not being recorded in numerical order. Some of them have been issued by Erato in France and by Musical Heritage Society in the US. Bärenreiter-Musicaphon have also recorded some of the later cantatas (Nos 201, 205, 206, 213, 215 and 249), the Motets, the four Lutheran Masses and the Choral Preludes from the *Orgelbüchlein*, the latter played by Rilling on the organ and with the choral settings; these were issued in the US by Nonesuch. His other recordings include Handel's oratorio *Belshazzar* (for Vox), Carissimi's *Jephte* and *Judicum Salomonis*, *Magnificats* by Schütz, Monteverdi, Bach and Buxtehude, Bach's Cantata No. 208, the Bach Harpsichord Concertos (with Galling and the Bach Collegium), Telemann's cantata *Ino* and opera *Pimpinone*, Haydn's Symphonies Nos 31 and 59, Mozart's Sinfonia Concertante K. 364 and the Concertone (for Vox and issued by Turnabout), Schütz' *Cantiones Sacrae*, *Italienische Madrigale*, *Geistliche Chormusik* and *Symphoniae Sacrae*, the Brahms *Liebeslieder* waltzes and some Schumann choral music (recorded by BASF and Bärenreiter and issued in the US by Nonesuch), Mozart's Mass K. 317 and *Vesperae solennes de confessore* (for Intercord, and issued in the US by Musical Heritage Society), Bruckner's Mass No. 2, Messiaen's *Cinq Rechants*, choral music by Scheidt (for Bärenreiter), Schütz' *St Matthew Passion*, cantatas by Buxtehude and music by Lechner and Distler (for Cantate). He also recorded, as organist, a recital of Spanish organ music and a disc of organ concertos and other pieces (for Vox, on Turnabout).

Ristenpart, Karl (1900–69). Born in Kiel, Ristenpart was taken by his parents to Chile as a boy, where his father, an astronomer, was director of the observatory at Santiago. On the death of his father he returned to Berlin with his mother in 1913, and came into contact with Scherchen who inspired him to become a musician. Scherchen had been his mother's music teacher; she had financed his first concerts in Berlin, and she eventually married him. Ristenpart studied in Vienna, and after returning to Berlin in 1932 formed his own chamber orchestra. However, his refusal to join the Nazi party kept him from appointments conducting the major German orchestras, and eventually forced him to disband his chamber orchestra. At the end of World War II, he was engaged by the Radio-in-American-Sector, Berlin (RIAS) to organise a chamber choir and orchestra, and he conducted the RIAS Orchestra, together with Fricsay, for five years. In 1953 he moved to Saarbrücken and founded and conducted the Saar Chamber Orchestra, with which his name became connected internationally.

Ristenpart was a distinguished musician with a wide range of musical sympathies extending beyond the repertoire of the chamber orchestra, to which circumstances generally restricted him. While Bach and Mozart were to him 'the towering peaks in lonely heights, the cornerstones in (his) musical thoughts', next in his affections came Mahler, who had been revealed to him in an early performance of the Symphony No. 5 by Scherchen. Ristenpart became known to the international musical public through the medium of records; in Richard Freed's words (*The Saturday Review*, November 1966), he 'must be regarded as one of the most consistently satisfying conductors on records. Always enlivening, frequently inspired, and never less than thoroughly musical, he delighted in demonstrating, as every great interpreter does, that "style" has more to do with imaginativeness than with tradition.' His records were mostly with the Saar Chamber Orchestra (sometimes named the Saar Radio Chamber Orchestra by some companies), and have been issued on at least 12 labels in Europe and the United States; a good number were for Erato and Club français du Disque, and were released in the US by Musical Heritage Society and Nonesuch, some of the latter being issued in Britain and elsewhere.

The first record by Ristenpart was made in 1954 by DGG-Archiv, with the Berlin Motet Choir and Chamber Orchestra and Dietrich Fischer-Dieskau, of Bach's Cantatas Nos 56 and 82. He then went on to record with the Saar Chamber Orchestra the Bach *Brandenburg Concertos*, the four Suites, the Harpsichord Concertos (with Neumeyer), the Flute Concertos and Violin Concerto No. 1 arranged for flute (with Rampal), the Three-Violin Concerto (with Hendel, Schlupp and Bünte), the Flute, Violin and Harpsichord Concerto (with Cromm, Hendel and Kind), the Two-Harpsichord Concerto No. 3 (with Neumeyer and Berger), the complete Three-Harpsichord Concertos (with Neumeyer, Berger and Burr), the Four-Harpsichord Concertos (with Neumeyer, Berger, Burr and Urbuteit), *Die Kunst der Fuge*, *Magnificat*, the Mass BWV 233, and Cantatas Nos 32, 51, 56, 57, 79, 82, 140, 159, 169 and 212, C. P. E. Bach's Sinfonia Wg 182 No. 2, *Flute Concerto in B flat* (with Rampal) and Harpsichord and Piano Concerto (with Dreyfus and Veyron-Lacroix), J. C. Bach's *Sinfonias in C* and *D*, Albinoni's *Adagio*, Concerto Op. 7 No. 6, Oboe Concerto Op. 9 No. 2 (with Chambon), *Sinfonia in B flat*, Sonata Op. 2 No. 6 and *Trumpet Concerto in B flat* (with André), A. Scarlatti's Sinfonia No. 1, D. Scarlatti's three sinfonias,

Marcello's Oboe Concerto (with Pierlot), Vivaldi's Guitar and viola d'amore concerto P. 266 (with Probst and Lemmen), Bassoon Concerto P. 137 (with Allard), Oboe and Violin Concerto P. 406 (with Chambon and Hendel), Two-Cello Concerto P. 411 (with Hindrichs and Dommisch), Concerto for Orchestra P. 235, two piccolo concertos (with Bourdin), Violin Concerto Op. 3 No. 6 (with Hendel), *Two-Violin Concerto in D* (with Hendel and Schlupp) and Three-Violin Concerto (with Hendel, Schlupp and Bünte), Concertos Op. 3 Nos 8, 10 and 11, Flute Concertos Op. 10 (with Rampal) and Oboe Concerto (with Schneider), Biber's *Serenade in C*, three flute concertos of Pergolesi (with Rampal), flute concertos of Tartini, Telemann and Giuseppe Sammartini (with Rampal), Telemann's Suite for Cello and Strings (with Hindrichs), *Oboe Concerto in C minor* (with Pierlot), Trumpet and Two-Oboe Concerto (with André, Winschermann and Bolz, and also with André, Pierlot and Chambon), Three-Trumpet and Two-Oboe Concerto (with André, Winschermann, *et al.*), Three-Oboe Concerto (with Winschermann, Bolz and Trenz), Two-Violin Concerto (with Karau and Hendel, and also with Hendel and Bünte), *Overture in C*, two motets, two cantatas and *Sanctus*, Fiorenza's *Concerto in D* and *Siciliana in C*, Sarro's *Sonata in A*, Galuppi's *Flute Concerto in D* (with Rampal), Hasse's Mandolin Concerto (with Thomas), K. Stamitz's *Symphony in F*, Sinfonia Concertante, *Flute Concerto in G* (with Rampal) and *Viola Concerto in D* (with Schmid), Zelter's Viola Concerto (with Schmid), Cimarosa's Two-Flute Concerto (with Rampal and Pierlot) and Oboe Concerto (with Schneider), Paisiello's *Harpsichord Concerto in C* (with Veyron-Lacroix), Locatelli's Concerto Grosso Op. 1 No. 8 and *Sinfonia funebre*, Lechner's Flute Concerto (with Rampal), Winter's Concertino for Clarinet and Cello (with Michaels and Güdel), Vaňhal's *Symphony in A*, trumpet concertos by Stölzel, Tartini and Vivaldi (with André), Handel's *Ode for St Cecilia's Day*, German Cantata *Preis der Tonkunst* and *Agrippina* overture, Haydn's Symphonies Nos 6, 7, 8, 21, 48, 81, 90 and 91, Sinfonia Concertante, Notturnos Nos 2, 6 and 7, *Organ Concerto in D* (with Hölderlin) and *Cello Concerto in D* (with Navarra), Michael Haydn's *Symphony in C*, Mozart's Symphonies Nos 24 to 26, 28, 29, 31, 34 to 36 and 38 to 41, Divertimentos K. 136, K. 137, K. 138 and K. 251, Serenades K. 203, K. 250, *Eine kleine Nachtmusik* and *Serenata notturna*, Dances K. 606, Marches K. 408, Piano Concertos K. 107 and K. 246 (with Veyron-Lacroix) and K. 503 and K. 595 (with Boegner), Violin Concertos K. 216 and K. 218 (with Makanowitzky), K. 216, the Rondo K. 373 and a Violin Concerto arranged from the Serenade K. 250 (with Hendel), the Flute and Harp Concerto (with Rampal and Wagner), Sinfonia Concertante K. 297b, Sinfonia Concertante K. 364 (with Büchner and Schmid), the Mass K. 317, *Vesperae solennes de confessore*, *Exsultate jubilate* and the Laudamus Te from the Mass K. 427 (with Stich-Randall), Schubert's Symphonies Nos 2, 5 and 6, and *Salve Regina* (with Stich-Randall), Mendelssohn's Two-Piano Concerto (with Billard and Azaïs) and overture *Die schöne Melusine*, Schumann's *Konzertstück for 4 Horns* and *Introduction and Allegro appassionato* (with Boutry), and Roussel's *Sinfonietta* and *Concerto for Small Orchestra*. In 1967, towards the end of his life, he made some records for Checkmate, a sister label to Nonesuch, with an *ad hoc* ensemble called the Stuttgart Symphony Orchestra, of Beethoven's Symphonies Nos 3 and 7, Schubert's Symphonies Nos 1 and 2, Brahms' Serenade No. 2 and the *Siegfried Idyll*. The Schubert symphonies were later re-issued by Nonesuch.

Rivoli, Gianfranco (b. 1921). Born in Milan where he studied at the Conservatory, Rivoli won a national competition for the piano (1937), conducted the Milan University Orchestra (1938–40) and the ballet at La Scala (1948–50). He has conducted orchestras and at festivals in Europe and the United States, and has been conductor at the Düsseldorf and Lisbon Operas and artistic director of the Gulbenkian Music Festival in Portugal. His compositions include ballets and symphonic music. Rivoli has recorded extensively for La Guilde Internationale du Disque and its associate labels; the works include Mozart's Piano Concertos K. 459 and K. 537 and Beethoven's Piano Concerto No. 3 and *Fantasy in C minor* (with Kraus and the Amsterdam Philharmonic Orchestra *et al.*), Beethoven's Piano Concertos Nos 2 and 4 (with Magaloff) and ballet music from *William Tell*, *La favorita*, *I vespri siciliani* and *Aida* (with the Zürich Radio Orchestra); the overtures to *La scala di seta*, *Semiramide*, *La Cenerentola*, *Il Signor Bruschino*, *Tancredi*, *Il barbiere di Siviglia* and *L'Italiana in Algeri*, the Mendelssohn Violin Concerto, Paganini's Violin Concerto No. 1 and *Concert Rondo*, Sarasate's *Airs gitanos* and *Zigeunerweisen*, Chausson's *Poème* and Saint-Saëns' *Havanaise* and *Introduction et rondo capriccioso* (with Odnoposoff, and the Geneva Radio Orchestra); the Verdi

Requiem and *Te Deum*, *Rigoletto*, *La traviata* and *Faust*, and excerpts from *L'elisir d'amore*, *Norma* and *William Tell* (with the Vienna State Opera Orchestra *et al.*); *Giselle* and excerpts from *The Sleeping Beauty* (with the Paris Concerts Orchestra); Grieg's *Symphonic Dances*, *Norwegian Dances*, *Lyric Suite* and *Peer Gynt* Suites Nos 1 and 2 (with the Vienna Festival Orchestra); *Nutcracker* Suite (with the Amsterdam Philharmonic Orchestra); *Il barbiere di Siviglia* (with the Monte Carlo Opera Orchestra *et al.*); and Giordano's *Mese Mariano* (with the La Scala Orchestra *et al.*). He also recorded Almeida's *La spinalba* (with the Gulbenkian Chamber Orchestra for Philips).

Roberton, Sir Hugh (1874–1952). Born in Glasgow, Roberton founded the Glasgow Orpheus Choir in 1906, which became legendary for its high musical standards, and for its performances, mainly of arrangements of Scottish folk-songs. With Roberton the Choir toured in the United States and Canada, but he finally disbanded it in 1951. Roberton adjudicated at choral festivals, and himself composed about 300 pieces for solo voice and choral groups. He was knighted in 1931. Although most of the Choir's recordings were of collections of Scottish songs, also included were *Jesu, Joy of Man's Desiring* from Bach's Cantata No. 147, and Haste thee Nymph from Handel's *L'allegro ed il penseroso*.

Robertson, James (b. 1912). Born in Liverpool and educated at Trinity College, Cambridge, the Leipzig Conservatory and the Royal College of Music, London, Robertson was on the music staff of the Glyndebourne Festival (1937–8), and chorus-master of the Carl Rosa Opera Company (1938–9). He was a conductor with the Canadian Broadcasting Corporation (1939–40), was director and conductor at the Sadler's Wells Opera (1946–54), conductor of the New Zealand National Orchestra (1954–7), conductor with the Carl Rosa Opera Company (1958), guest conductor at Sadler's Wells (1958–63), adviser to the Théâtre de la Monnaie, Brussels (1960), artistic director to the New Zealand Opera and conductor of the New Zealand Broadcasting Corporation's Concert Orchestra (1962–3), and director of the London Opera Centre (from 1964). He recorded two arias from *Le nozze di Figaro* (with Gobbi and the Philharmonia Orchestra, on a 78 r.p.m. disc, for HMV).

Robinson, Eric (1908–78). Born in Leeds and educated at the Royal College of Music, London, Robinson started his career as a violinist at Lyons Corner House in London, joined the BBC Theatre Orchestra in 1923 and then the television service. After war service in the army, he rejoined the BBC as a conductor in 1947, and became musical director and a celebrated TV personality. His publications include *Conducted Personally* and *Adventures in Music*. For Reader's Digest he conducted the National Philharmonic Orchestra in a number of popular pieces, such as *España*, *Pomp and Circumstance March No. 1*, some Brahms *Hungarian Dances*, Strauss polkas, and marches by Eric Coates.

Robinson, Stanford (b. 1904). Born in Leeds, Robinson studied at the Royal College of Music and in Europe. From 1924 to 1966 he was with the BBC, first as founder and director of the BBC Singers, the BBC Chorus and the BBC Choral Society (1924–32), then as conductor of the BBC Theatre Orchestra (1932–46), musical director of the BBC Variety Department (1932–6), director of musical productions (1936–49), conductor and organiser of opera (1949–52), and associate conductor of the BBC Symphony Orchestra (1946–9). He has also conducted at Covent Garden, Sadler's Wells, at Promenade concerts, and with many European orchestras, toured Australia and New Zealand (1966–7) and was conductor of the Queensland Symphony Orchestra at Brisbane (1968–9). His compositions include orchestral and vocal music.

Robinson's one significant recording, made before World War II for Columbia, was a substantially complete performance of *Elijah*, with the BBC Chorus and Orchestra, and with Isobel Baillie and Harold Williams among the soloists. He also recorded for Decca on 78s *Sylvia*, extracts from *The Sleeping Beauty*, the Anvil Chorus from *Il trovatore*, Luigini's *Ballet égyptien*, J. Strauss' *Frühlingstimmen* and overture to *Die Fledermaus*, and German's *Henry VIII* dances (with the BBC Theatre Orchestra *et al.*), the waltz from *Eugene Onegin*, the *Nutcracker* suite and the overture to *Orphée aux enfers* (with the National Symphony Orchestra), and a scene from *Boris Godunov* (with the London Symphony Orchestra *et al.*); later for Decca he made LPs of the music of Ketèlby and a selection from the Gilbert and Sullivan operas (with the New Symphony Orchestra), and the Grieg Piano Concerto (with Atwell and the London Philharmonic Orchestra). His other records include Ireland's *Epic March* (with the New Concert Orchestra for Boosey and Hawkes), Coates' *Cinderella* (with the Pro Arte Orchestra for Pye), and accompaniments for Gigli, de los Angeles and Thomas (for EMI).

Rodan, Mendi (b. 1929). Born in Romania with the name of Rosenblum, Rodan studied at the Bucharest Conservatory with Silvestri, and was permanent conductor of the Romanian Radio and Television Orchestra until 1958. He settled in Israel in 1961, conducted the Israel Philharmonic Orchestra the following year, was chief conductor of the Israel Broadcasting Symphony Orchestra (1963–72), founded and conducted the Jerusalem Chamber Orchestra, and was appointed assistant head of the Rubin Academy of Music in Jerusalem. In addition to conducting the Israeli orchestras regularly, he has been a guest conductor with many others in Europe, the Far East, Australia, South Africa and the United States, toured the US with the Oslo Philharmonic Orchestra (1974), and Europe with the Jerusalem Symphony Orchestra (previously the Israel Broadcasting Symphony Orchestra; 1975). He has made a number of recordings for La Guilde Internationale du Disque, including *Messiah*, Tartini's *Symphony in D major*, Boccherini's Symphony Op. 1 No. 3, C. P. E. Bach's *Sinfonia in C major*, J. C. Bach's *Sinfoniettas in A major*, *D major* and *C major*, W. F. Bach's *Sinfonia per due traversi ed archi* and *Harpsichord Concerto in C minor* (with Pelleg), J. S. Bach's *Two-Harpsichord Concerto in C minor*, *Three-Harpsichord Concerto in C major* and *Four-Harpischord Concerto in A minor* (with Pelleg, Jaccottet, Born and Low), Mendelssohn's String Symphonies Nos 9 and 12, Bloch's *Concerto Grosso* and Schoenberg's *Verklärte Nacht* (with the Jerusalem Chamber Orchestra), and Albinoni's *Sonata a cinque* Op. 5 No. 9 and Concerto Op. 7 No. 1, and a suite by Corelli (with the Ramat-Gan Chamber Orchestra).

Rodzinski, Artur (1892–1958). Born in Spalato (modern Split, Yugoslavia), where his father, a Polish army officer, was stationed, Rodzinski studied and graduated in law at the University of Vienna, later attended the Academy of Music, and graduated Doctor of Music. During World War I he served in the Austrian army in Russia, and was wounded in action; he returned to Vienna and studied conducting with Schalk, the piano with Sauer and composition with Schreker. His career began at Lwow (Poland, now in the USSR), where he was first a choral conductor and then conductor at the opera. He was engaged as conductor at the Warsaw Opera, and also conducted the Warsaw Philharmonic Orchestra (1919–24). On a visit to Poland, Stokowski heard him leading a performance of *Die Meistersinger*, and invited him to the United States; as a result he was assistant conductor with the Philadelphia Orchestra under Stokowski (1925–9), at the same time directing the orchestral and opera departments at the Curtis Institute, and conducting the Philadelphia Grand Opera. He was appointed permanent conductor of the Los Angeles Philharmonic Orchestra (1929–33) and of the Cleveland Orchestra (1933–45); he conducted the Vienna Philharmonic Orchestra at the Salzburg Festival (1936 and 1937), was guest conductor with the New York Philharmonic-Symphony Orchestra for eight weeks in 1937, and at Toscanini's request organised and prepared for him the NBC Symphony Orchestra (1937–8). For four years he was musical director at the New York Philharmonic-Symphony Orchestra (1943–7); he commenced his tenure dramatically by dismissing fifteen of the players, including the concertmaster, although he was forced to re-instate five of them later. He resigned on the grounds of incomplete artistic control of the orchestra, and because the orchestra's manager (Arthur Judson), who was also the head of a major concert artists' agency, was promoting the careers of artists under the agency's management through the orchestra. His subsequent appointment as musical director of the Chicago Symphony Orchestra was even shorter (1947), because of a series of disagreements with the management. In the last decade of his life he suffered grave ill-health; he took up residence in Rome, conducted opera and concerts in Italy, Britain and in other European countries and in South America. In 1953 he conducted Prokofiev's *War and Peace* at the Florence May Festival, this being the first performance of the opera outside the USSR, and just before his death at Boston he led a brilliant performance of *Tristan und Isolde* at the Chicago Lyric Opera. The Polish government honoured him in 1937 and 1938 for conducting programmes of Polish music at the Paris International Exhibition.

Rodzinski was one of the outstanding conductors on the American scene during his years there. He was a strong and controversial personality, but was respected for his musicianship. As an interpreter, his strength was essentially with the romantic composers such as Berlioz, Rimsky-Korsakov, Tchaikovsky, Sibelius, Wagner and Strauss, where his flexible beat, emotional intensity and penchant for orchestral brilliance were completely at home. Probably his most celebrated performance was *Ein Heldenleben*. He was less suited to the music of earlier composers such as Haydn, Mozart and Beethoven. As Toscanini had recognised at Salzburg, he was a superb trainer of orchestras, and the great improvement of the New York Philharmonic-Symphony was clear, even after his relatively short tenure there. Virgil Thomas considered that he had done more for the orchestra than any other conductor of the century, and in 1947 commented that the Philharmonic, for the first time in his memory, was the equal of the Boston and Philadelphia orchestras, and probably their superior (*Music Reviewed, 1940–1945*, p. 199). Rodzinski's baton technique was exemplary, although he was undemonstrative and unspectacular to the audience. He always conducted with the score, scorning the notion of conducting from memory, primarily because it brought a sense of apprehension to the players that the conductor would forget. He believed that great music played by great orchestras should reach as wide a public as possible; he was interested in promoting music among school-children, and in Cleveland introduced concert performances of opera. Towards the end of his life he conducted at the San Carlo Opera in Naples, but found the superintendent's love of opera not equalled by his knowledge: when it was suggested that *Tristano ed Isotta* (*Tristan und Isolde*) be given, he declared: 'We can't afford both. We'll do *Tristano* this season, *Isotta* the next!'. Somebody objected to *Lulu* because Countess Geschwitz was a Lesbian. The superintendent saw no difficulty; she could be changed to be an Austrian (H. Rodzinski, *Our Two Lives*, New York, 1976, p. 336).

Rodzinski made a considerable number of records, but rarely strayed from his customary repertoire. His first records were for Columbia with the Cleveland Orchestra, and included the Beethoven Symphony No. 1, *Symphonie fantastique*, *Scheherazade*, excerpts from the music for *A Midsummer Night's Dream*, Tchaikovsky's Symphonies Nos 5 and 6, the *1812* overture, the *Romeo and Juliet* fantasy-overture, the overture to *Der Freischütz*, the prelude to *Khovanshchina*, *La Mer*, the *Daphnis et Chloé* Suite No. 2, *Rapsodie espagnole*, *Alborada del gracioso*, Sibelius' Symphony No. 5, *Finlandia*, *Till Eulenspiegel*, *Ein Heldenleben*, the waltzes from *Der Rosenkavalier*, Shostakovich's Symphonies Nos 1 and 5, Weinberger's *Under the Spreading Chestnut Tree* and the Berg and Schoenberg Violin Concertos (with Krasner). With the New York Philharmonic-Symphony Orchestra, also for Columbia, he recorded another brilliant series, including the *Mephisto Waltz*, Brahms' Symphonies Nos 1 and 2, *Pictures at an Exhibition*, Bizet's *Symphony in C major*, Tchaikovsky's Symphony No. 6, Suite No. 4 (*Mozartiana*), a suite from *Nutcracker*, Act III from *Die Walküre*, the preludes to Acts I and III and other excerpts from *Tristan und Isolde* and *Lohengrin* (with Traubel *et al.*), the *Siegfried Idyll*, Prokofiev's Symphony No. 5, *La Mer*, Sibelius' Symphony No. 4, Ibert's *Escales*, *An American in Paris*, Gould's *Spirituals*, Copland's *A Lincoln Portrait*, Rachmaninov's Symphony No. 2 and Piano Concerto No. 2 (with Sandor), the overture to *Il segreto di Susanna* and Enesco's *Romanian Rhapsody No. 1*. In the short time he was with the Chicago Symphony Orchestra he made records of the Mendelssohn Symphony No. 3, *Also sprach Zarathustra*, the preludes to Acts I and III and the Liebestod from *Tristan und Isolde*, and the *Gayane* ballet. With the Columbia Symphony Orchestra he also recorded the overtures to *William Tell* and *Orphée aux enfers*, and the Liszt *Hungarian Rhapsody No. 2*.

After his departure from the United States, Rodzinski made several discs for EMI, including notable performances of Strauss's *Dance Suite after Couperin*, *Tod und Verklärung*, and the dance from *Salome* (with the Philharmonic Orchestra), the *Russian Easter Festival* overture, the *Romeo and Juliet* fantasy-overture, the overture to *Russlan and Ludmilla*, the prelude to *Khovanshchina*, *The Three-cornered Hat* Suites Nos 1 and 2, the Ritual Fire Dance from *El amor brujo* and Albéniz's *Navarra* (completed by Séverac and orchestrated by Arbós) (with the Royal Philharmonic Orchestra). The discs are still available in the US on the Seraphim label. In another series for Westminster with an orchestra named the Philharmonic Symphony Orchestra of London, recently called the London Philharmonic Orchestra on the record label, but identified by Rodzinski's wife in her biography of him as the Royal Philharmonic Orchestra, he recorded Beethoven's Symphony No. 5, Schubert's Symphony No. 8, the Brahms Violin Concerto (with Morini), Chopin's Piano Concertos Nos 1 and 2 (in truncated versions, with Badura-Skoda), Dvořák's Symphony No. 9 and *Slavonic Dances* Op. 46 and 72, Tchaikovsky's Symphonies Nos 4, 5 and 6, the complete *Nutcracker* and the Violin Concerto (with Morini), the Grieg Piano Concerto (with Boukoff) and the two *Peer Gynt* suites, the Rimsky-Korsakov Piano Concerto and Franck's *Symphonic Variations* (with Badura-Skoda), a collection of Strauss waltzes, *Don Juan*, *Till Eulenspiegel*, an orchestral suite from *Der Rosenkavalier*, the Ride from *Die Walküre*, the Rhine Journey and Funeral Music from *Götterdämmerung*, the overture to *Tannhäuser*, the prelude and Liebestod from *Tristan und Isolde*, the two *L'Arlésienne* suites and a *Carmen* suite, *Pictures at an Exhibition*, *A Night on the Bare*

Mountain, Bloch's *Schelomo* and Bruch's *Kol Nidrei* and *Canzone* (with Janigro), Ippolitov-Ivanov's *Caucasian Sketches*, the Polovtsian Dances from *Prince Igor*, the *Háry János* suite, *Dances from Galánta* and *Dances from Marosszék*, Prokofiev's Symphony No. 1, a suite from *The Love of Three Oranges*, *Peter and the Wolf*, and Shostakovich's Symphony No. 5. Also for Westminster, he recorded with the Vienna State Opera Orchestra the Mozart Clarinet Concerto (with Wlach) and Bassoon Concerto (with Oehlberger), Schumann's Piano Concerto and *Introduction and Allegro in C major* and *in D major* (with Demus), and Franck's *Symphony in D minor* and *Le Chasseur maudit*. By 1977 very few of these discs remained in the US catalogue. Finally, Rococo have issued a disc of the Beethoven Violin Concerto (with Heifetz and the New York Philharmonic Orchestra).

Rogalsky, Theodor (1901–54). Born in Bucharest, Rogalsky studied at the Conservatory there (1919–20), the Leipzig Conservatory (1920–23) and at the Schola Cantorum, Paris (1924–6). He conducted the Romanian Radio Orchestra (1930–51), the Bucharest Philharmonic Orchestra (1951–4), was professor of orchestration at Bucharest Conservatory (1950–54), and composed orchestral, chamber and piano music. He recorded Negrea's *In the Western Mountains* (with the Bucharest Radio Orchestra) and Andricu's Symphony No. 2 (with the Romanian Symphony Orchestra).

Rogers, Eric (b. 1921). Born in Halifax, England, Rogers served in the Royal Air Force in World War II, then composed music for films, radio and television, was band leader of the Trocadero Restaurant, London, musical director of the London Palladium (1954–7) and of the Decca Record Company (1952–64). He has made over 50 records; included are one of Ketèlbey's music (with the Royal Philharmonic Orchestra), another of the music of Stephen Foster (with his own orchestra), and a collection of ceremonial music of Bullock, Bax, Arne, Davies, Vaughan Williams, Handel and Parry (with the London Festival Orchestra). These were for Decca.

Rögner, Heinz (b. 1929). Born in Leipzig, Rögner studied at the Hochschule für Musik there under Steurer, Bölsche and Gutschlicht, and became a repetiteur and conductor at the Weimar National Theatre (1951–4). He taught at the Hochschule für Musik at Leipzig (1954–8), was chief conductor of the Leipzig Radio Symphony Orchestra (1958–62), general music director at the Berlin Staatsoper in East Berlin (1962–73), chief conductor of the Berlin Radio Symphony Orchestra in East Berlin (since 1973), and of the Berlin Radio Choir (from 1974). In addition, he has been a guest conductor in Sweden, France, Austria, Switzerland, Italy, FR Germany, the USSR, Romania, Hungary, Poland and Czechoslovakia, and with orchestras in Leipzig and Dresden, and has also toured as a pianist and chamber player. Eterna has recorded him in the *Academic Festival Overture* and some *Hungarian Dances* of Brahms, the two Strauss Horn Concertos and Mozart's Rondo K. 371 (with Damm), Handel's Harp Concerto Op. 4 No. 6, Dittersdorf's Harp Concerto and Françaix's *Jeu poétique* (with Zoff), Weber's *Abu Hassan* and Strauss's *Eine Nacht in Venedig* (with the Dresden Staatskapelle *et al.*), duets sung by Geszty and Schreier (with the Dresden Philharmonic Orchestra), excerpts from *Der Zigeunerbaron* and Cilenšek's *Konzertstück for Violin and Orchestra* (with Other, and the Leipzig Radio Symphony Orchestra *et al.*), trumpet concertos of Torelli, Grossi, Fasch and Albinoni (with Güttler and the Berlin Chamber Orchestra), the Haydn and Strauss Oboe Concertos (with Wätzig), Beethoven's *Der glorreiche Augenblick* and *Vestas Feuer Hess*, Schubert's Symphony No. 7, being the arrangement by Weingartner of the *Grand Duo in C*, and Symphony No. 9, the two *L'Arlésienne* suites and Gypsy Dance from *La jolie fille de Perth*, Reger's *Romantic Suite* and *Symphonic Prologue*, Strauss's *Duet Concertino* and waltzes from *Der Rosenkavalier*, *L'Apprenti sorcier*, Milhaud's *La Création du monde*, Enesco's *Romanian Rhapsody No. 1*, *Danse macabre*, the Ritual Fire Dance from *El amor brujo*, Mendelssohn's Two-Piano Concerto (with Lyskova and Lesjek), Beethoven's *Cantata on the Accession of Leopold II* and patriotic and festival music, Weill's *Chansons* (with May), Eisler's Suites Op. 24, Op. 26 and Op. 30, and *Kleine Sinfonie*, Wolf-Ferrari's *Serenade*, overture and intermezzo from *Il segreto di Susanna*, the Neapolitan Dance from *I gioielli della Madonna*, the intermezzo from *I quattro rusteghi*, *I campiello* and the overture to *Le donne curiose*, an aria recital (with Adam), the preludes to Acts I and III of *Palestrina*, Rosenfeld's *Kleistbriefe* and Manfred Schubert's *Cantilena e capriccio* (with Scherzer and the Berlin Radio Symphony Orchestra).

Rohan, Jindřich (1919–78). Born in Brno, Moravia, Rohan studied music as a child, and in 1938 left Czechoslovakia for Britain, where he was a music teacher at Dartington Hall, Devon, and also volunteered for the Czech army then recruited on British soil. After World War II, he returned to Prague, attended the Conservatory and Academy of Music (1945–50), and at the same time coached singers at the Prague National Opera and directed several choirs. He became music director of the Czech Army Symphony Orchestra (1950–54), and then was appointed assistant conductor, to Smetáček, with the Prague FOK Symphony Orchestra (1954); he later became its music director and conductor (1976). With the orchestra he toured throughout Europe and in North and South America, and was the first Czech conductor to perform with the Philadelphia Orchestra. He was also music director of the Yomiuri Symphony Orchestra in Tokyo (1964–5), and taught conducting at the Prague Academy of Music (from 1960). His personal style favoured the music of the 20th century, especially contemporary music, and he presented for the first time many important works of Czech composers, although he also covered the standard repertoire in orchestral music and opera.

Rohan's recordings have been of the Dvořák Piano Concerto (with Ponti), Tomášek's Piano Concerto No. 1 (with Toperczer) and Kaliwoda's Symphony No. 1 (all with the Prague Symphony Orchestra, i.e. the Prague FOK Symphony Orchestra, for Vox, issued on Turnabout and Candide), Tausinger's *Musica evolutiva* (for Panton), Havelka's symphony and cantata, *The Praise of Light*, violin concertos by Železný (with Bělčík), Schoenberg, Stravinsky and Bloch, and Bloch's *Suite hébraïque* (with Bress), Rachmaninov's Symphony No. 3, suites from *Nutcracker* and *The Sleeping Beauty*, Bizet's *Roma*, Kálík's *Peace Symphony*, Dvořáček's *Sunrise* monologues, Řezáč's overture *The Right Thing* and Piano Concerto No. 2 (with Baloghová), Železný's Flute Concerto (with Josífko) and Felix's *The Battlefield* (with the Prague Symphony Orchestra for Supraphon), Thorne's Symphony No. 3 and Rieti's *Sinfonietta* (with the Prague Chamber Soloists for Serenus), and concertos for viola d'amore by Stamitz and Vivaldi (with Stumpf and the Prague Chamber Orchestra for Supraphon).

Roller, A. Clyde (b. 1914). Born in Rogersville, Missouri, Roller was educated at the Eastman School of Music, Rochester, at the Oklahoma City University and at the Berkshire Music Center. After being principal oboist with the Tulsa Philharmonic Orchestra (1935), he made his debut as a conductor with the Oklahoma City Symphony Orchestra in 1937. He was conductor of the GI Symphony Orchestra in Paris, of the Eastman Wind Ensemble, musical director of the Amarillo Symphony Orchestra, Texas, for 13 years, conductor of the New Zealand Broadcasting Corporation Symphony Orchestra, of the Lansing Symphony Orchestra, Michigan (since 1967), and resident conductor of the Houston Symphony Orchestra. His academic appointments have been at the University of Houston, South Methodist University, Dallas, University of Michigan and at the Eastman School of Music, and he has conducted orchestras and at festivals in the US and abroad. For Mercury with the Eastman Wind Ensemble he recorded Giannini's Symphony No. 3 and Hovhaness's Symphony No. 4.

Ronald, Sir Landon (1873–1938). A Londoner and son of the composer of songs, Henry Russell, Ronald studied at the Royal College of Music, London, made his first professional appearance as a conductor at the Lyric Theatre, London, at the age of 17, and the next year was engaged as a repetiteur with the Italian Opera Company of Augustus Harris at Covent Garden. He eventually became a conductor of the company, and in 1894 toured the United States as Melba's accompanist; he was then much in demand in this role, and together with Hamilton Harty was the most sought-after accompanist in London. He conducted at the Drury Lane Theatre (1896), directed a symphony orchestra at Blackpool for a season, but as he found it difficult to find a post with a major British orchestra or musical organisation, he often worked in Europe at this time. However, in 1904 he became associated with the newly formed London Symphony Orchestra, and in 1909 was appointed permanent conductor of the New Symphony Orchestra, which later in 1915 became the Royal Albert Hall Orchestra, with Ronald its conductor. It went out of existence at the time of Ronald's death, but had the distinction of being the first British orchestra to have a recording contract, with HMV. From 1910 to 1935 he was principal of the Guildhall School of Music and Drama, in 1922 was knighted for his services in this capacity, and was also conductor of the Scottish National Orchestra (1919–23). He composed orchestral music and songs, some of which were very popular in their day, especially *O, lovely night* and *Down in the Forest*, as was his incidental music to a stage smash-hit, *The Garden of Allah*.

Beecham wrote of Ronald in his autobiography, *A Mingled Chime* (p. 139): 'He had unquestionably a great and natural talent for conducting, and his bearing and movements in action carried an ease and grace that I have never seen rivalled. His sympathies, however, did not equal his endowment, and this limitation of taste, combined with an inborn inertia, placed a check upon the growth of his repertoire which I often deplored. I judged from the answers to my remonstrances that he was not fully aware of his own unusual ability; and this self-deprecation, highly uncommon in an artist, deprived him of that extra ounce of incentive which is the impelling force behind any sustained endeavour or successful accomplishment.' In addition to his skill with symphonic music, Ronald was a particularly sensitive concerto accompanist. Romantic music was his natural preference, and in the years at the turn of the century he was giving exaggerated performances of the Tchaikovksy symphonies in particular. This phase left him, and he became known as a conductor whose interpretations were well disciplined and completely faithful to the score. He was an early champion of Rachmaninov and Elgar, who greatly influenced him, and he was considered to be Elgar's most thoughtful interpreter. At rehearsals he impressed with his quiet purposefulness and economy of effort; his beat was clear, and his gestures without ostentation. In public performance he left the drama to the music. In Ernest Newman's words, 'Like so many other excellent musicians, he began as a romantic, and when the years brought him wisdom and poise, he developed into a classic.' Ronald played a most significant part in the development of the early gramophone from what might have been a toy, to a serious means of musical reproduction. The Gramophone Company (HMV) engaged him as its musical adviser in 1900, and he retained this position until his death; in these early years he persuaded many great artists to make records, and many of the records he himself made as a conductor before World War I and in the decade afterwards were of works not previously recorded. Bearing in mind the standard of public taste at the time, this required considerable courage and judgement, as most of the recordings were made on his recommendation.

Ronald's first disc as a conductor was in 1911, and was of the Grieg Piano Concerto, with Backhaus; the work was condensed to fit on to the two sides of one disc, and many of his other early records were of similarly truncated pieces; *Scheherazade*, for instance, was cut to be accommodated on four sides. Between 1911 and 1914 he also recorded the overtures *Le nozze di Figaro*, *Egmont*, *Leonore No. 3*, *Oberon*, *Ruy Blas*, *William Tell*, *Zampa*, *The Merry Wives of Windsor*, *1812*, *Der fliegende Holländer*, *Tannhäuser* and Auber's *Zanetta*, the prelude to Act I of *Lohengrin*, an intermezzo from *Carmen*, the overture, Dance of the Apprentices and Entry of the Mastersingers from *Die Meistersinger*, Schubert's Symphony No. 8, the Overture, Scherzo, Nocturne and Wedding March from *A Midsummer Night's Dream*, Mendelssohn's *Bees' Wedding* and *Spring Song*, the scherzo from Tchaikovsky's Symphony No. 6, *Capriccio italien*, *Marche slave*, *Nutcracker* suite and Theme and Variations from the Suite No. 3, the *Prélude à l'après-midi d'un faune*, excerpts from *Sylvia* and *Coppélia*, Saint-Saëns' *Marche militaire française*, *Danse macabre*, *Le Rouet d'Omphale* and the Bacchanale from *Samson et Dalila*, excerpts from Massenet's *Scènes pittoresques*, *Finlandia*, the gopak from *Sorochintsy Fair*, Gounod's *Funeral March of a Marionette*, Judex from *Mors et Vita* and prelude from *Philomen et Baucis*, *Invitation to the Dance*, German's *Henry VIII* dances, Liszt's *Hungarian Rhapsody No. 2*, Grieg's *Norwegian Rustic Dance*, *Peer Gynt* Suite No. 1 and Shepherd Boy from the *Lyric Suite*, excerpts from *L'Arlésienne*, the Hungarian March from *La Damnation de Faust*, Schubert's *Marche militaire No. 1* and the traditional *Russian Boatman's Song*. The orchestra with which he conducted in this series is listed in the HMV catalogue as the Royal Albert Hall, but Roland Gelatt, in *The Fabulous Phonograph* (1954), named it as the New Symphony Orchestra, which had been formed originally by Beecham.

After World War I, from 1920 until the advent of electrical recording in 1925, Ronald recorded again, with the Royal Albert Hall Orchestra. These works included Mozart's Violin Concerto K. 218 (with Kreisler), Beethoven's Symphony No. 5, *Coriolan* and *Egmont* overtures and the Violin Concerto (with Isolde Menges), Schubert's Symphony No. 8, Mendelssohn's Piano Concerto No. 1 (with Moiseiwitsch), the Grieg Piano Concerto, Saint-Saëns' Piano Concerto No. 2, Franck's *Symphonic Variations* and Liszt's Piano Concerto No. 1 and *Hungarian Fantasy* (with de Greef), Brahms' Symphony No. 2, Dvořák's Symphony No. 9, the Schumann Piano Concerto (with Cortot), *L'Apprenti sorcier*, the minuet from the Mozart Divertimento K. 334 and the overture to *Le nozze di Figaro*, the prelude and Liebestod, and the prelude to Act III of *Tristan und Isolde*, the Entry of the Gods into Valhalla from *Das Rheingold* and Siegfried's Funeral Music from *Götterdämmerung*, the Dance of the Hours from *La Gioconda*, the Nocturne from the music to *A Midsummer*

Night's Dream, part of Debussy's *Nocturnes*, Delius' *Brigg Fair*, Svendsen's *Carnival in Paris*, and excerpts from his own *The Garden of Allah*. With the Wireless Orchestra (*sic*) there was also the *Rosamunde* overture.

In 1925, with the Royal Albert Hall Orchestra, Ronald recorded Tchaikovsky's Symphony No. 4; this was the first electrical disc released commercially in England. His electrical recordings, made from then until 1930, included re-makes of earlier discs; they included Beethoven's Symphony No. 5, *Leonore No. 3* overture and Piano Concerto No. 5 (with Backhaus), Dvořák's Symphony No. 9 and *Carnival* overture, the prelude to Act I of *Carmen*, the Liszt *Hungarian Fantasy* (with de Greef), *Finlandia*, Tchaikovsky's Piano Concerto No. 1 (with Hambourg), Grieg's *Lyric Suite*, the Scherzo from *A Midsummer Night's Dream* and the *Prélude à l'après-midi d'un faune* (with the Royal Albert Hall Orchestra), Saint-Saëns' Piano Concerto No. 2 (with de Greef) and Tchaikovsky's Symphony No. 5 (with the New Symphony Orchestra), Liszt's Piano Concerto No. 1 (with Levitsky), the Theme and Variations from Tchaikovsky's Suite No. 3, German's *Welsh Rhapsody* and Schumann's *Carnaval*, arr. Glazunov (with the London Symphony Orchestra) and the Schumann Piano Concerto (with Cortot and the London Symphony Orchestra). In his final period of recording, from 1930 to 1937, he made the Boccherini Cello Concerto (with Casals), Bruch's Violin Concerto No. 1 (with Menuhin) and *Kol Nidrei* (with Casals), Liszt's Piano Concerto No. 2 (with de Greef) and Svendsen's *Carnival in Paris* (with the London Symphony Orchestra), and the Schumann Piano Concerto and Franck *Symphonic Variations* (with Cortot), the Mendelssohn Violin Concerto (with Kreisler), Grieg's *Lyric Suite*, Elgar's *Coronation March* and German's *Coronation March and Hymn* (with the London Philharmonic Orchestra). The Mendelssohn Violin Concerto, which was recorded in 1935, was included in the Seraphim album *The Age of the Great Instrumentalists – Six Concertos*.

Ronly-Riklis, Shalom (b. 1922). Born in Tel-Aviv, Ronly-Riklis was educated at the Israel Academy of Music, and studied conducting with Markevitch in Salzburg. He founded and conducted the Gadna Youth Orchestra, with which he toured in North America in 1964 and 1967, was director of the Kol Israel Symphony Orchestra, and guest conductor with the Israel Philharmonic and Chamber Orchestras. He is now artistic co-ordinator of the Israel Philharmonic. For CBS (Israel) he conducted the Kol Israel Symphony Orchestra in Boscovich's *Semitic Suite* and *The Golden Chain* suite.

Ronnefeld, Peter (1935–65). Born in Dresden, Ronnefeld studied with Blacher and Messiaen, was chorus conductor at the Vienna Opera (1957–9), and also conducted at Kiel. His opera *Die Ameise* was given its first performance at Düsseldorf in 1961. He recorded for Telefunken the Haydn *Cello Concertos in C* and *D* (with Borwitzky and the Vienna Symphony Orchestra), Mozart's *Exsultate jubilate* (with Hoff) and *Sub tuum praesidium* (with Giebel and the Vienna Symphony Orchestra), and a disc of scenes and arias from Lortzing's *Zar und Zimmermann* and *Der Waffenschmied*.

Rooley, Anthony (b. 1944). Born in Leeds, Rooley progressed as a youth from winning a national prize with his skiffle group, to Spanish flamenco music, to an absorbing interest in Bach, then studied the classical guitar at the Royal Academy of Music (1964–7), and took lessons with Bream and Williams. He was professor of guitar at the RAM (1968–70), but in 1969 formed the Consort of Musicke, made up of two lutes, two viols and two singers, with *ad hoc* additions, which gave its first public performance under Rooley in 1972 and made its first record for L'Oiseau Lyre. He was a lute tutor and lecturer in Renaissance music at the Guildhall School of Music and Drama, Morley College and other institutions, has also been solo lutenist in Musica Reservata, the English Consort of Viols, the Early Music Consort and the Purcell Consort of Voices and has given radio and television recitals and talks in Britain, France and Germany. In addition he is carrying out research in lute and Renaissance music and its composers, has published many articles on those subjects, and founded and is director of the Early Music Centre in London in 1976.

The first recording of the Consort of Musicke was a collection entitled *The Leaves be Greene*, of music by Bevin, Holborne, Jones, Hume, Johnson and anonymous pieces; the second, in 1973 was a disc of 16th-century Italian popular music, and in 1975 came a four-disc set of secular music called *Musicke of Sundrie Kindes*, which was compiled from 16th-century composers. It was a considerable enterprise; while all the pieces were finely performed, the selection and sequence of the music has attracted some inevitable criticism. There followed in 1976 and 1977 Dowland's *Lachrimae*, *First Booke of Songes* and *Seconde Booke of Songes*, and Gibbons' Madrigals and Motets (for L'Oiseau Lyre).

Rosada, Luciano (b. 1923). Born in Venice, Rosada studied with Guarnieri and Scherchen, was a violinist in the orchestra at the Accademia Chigiana at Siena, which he first conducted in 1947, was a repetiteur at La Scala, Milan (1948–53), and made his operatic debut as a conductor at Bergamo (1954). He has since conducted opera companies in Italy, France, FR Germany, Hungary, Spain, Switzerland and Turkey, in a repertoire ranging from Mozart to Wolf-Ferrari, and led the world premières of Sonzogno's *Boule de suif* (1970) and Cortese's *Notti bianche* (1973). He also conducted operas for video film, has conducted major orchestras in Europe, and teaches at the Bologna Conservatory. For Angelicum he has made records with the Angelicum Orchestra, Milan, including Carissimi's oratorios *Jephte* and *Judicium extremum*, Torelli's Symphonies G. 11, G. 20, G. 26 and G. 36, Handel's Harp Concerto (with Aldrovandi), Boccherini's *Flute Concerto in D major* (with Gazzelloni), Haydn's Oboe Concerto (with Zanfini), Paganini's Violin Concerto No. 5, *I palpiti*, *Capriccio* and *Cantabile* (with Gulli), and Puccini's *Crisantemi* and Minuetti I and II, Mascagni's *La gavotte della bambole*, Giordano's *Largo e fuga*, Martucci's *Momento musicale e minuetto* and Catalini's *A sera* and *Serenatella*. Some of these performances have been issued in the United States by Musical Heritage Society.

Rosa-Parodi, Armando La (1904–77). Born in Genoa, La Rosa-Parodi studied in Genoa and Milan, and commenced a career as a conductor in Italy in 1929. He was conductor of the Rome Symphony Orchestra of Radio Italiana from 1963, and composed orchestral works, and music for theatre and films. He recorded, on 78s, Vivaldi's Concerto Grosso Op. 3 No. 11, and *Concerto in B minor* (arr. Tamburini, with Salerno, piano) and Bach's Clavier Concerto No. 8, arranged from an unknown composer (arr. Tamburini, also with Salerno, and with the EIAR Symphony Orchestra for Cetra). On LP he recorded Pizzini's *Poema delle Dolomiti* (with the Radio Italiana Orchestra for Cetra), the overture to *Idomeneo* and *Le nozze di Figaro* and the preludes to Acts I and III of *La traviata* (with the Radio Italiana Orchestra for Tempo and Orfeo), *La Gioconda*, *La forza del destino* and *Don Pasquale*, which have been issued in whole or in part by Urania, Vox, Nixa and BASF. Rococo have also issued a disc in which he conducts Victor de Sabata's *Mille a una notte – Primo quadro* (with the Radio Italiana Orchestra); the rest of the record is of dubbings of Sabata 78 r.p.m. recordings.

Rosbaud, Hans (1895–1962). Born in Graz, Austria, Rosbaud was given piano lessons by his mother at the age of five, and later learned to play string and wind instruments. After studying at the Hoch Conservatory at Frankfurt am Main, he became director of the Academy of Music and conductor of the Municipal Orchestra at Mainz (1923–30), musical director and chief conductor at the Frankfurt Radio Orchestra and conductor of the Frankfurt Museum Concertos (1929–37), conductor of opera and concerts at Münster (1937–41) and at Strasbourg (1941–4), conductor of the Munich Philharmonic Orchestra (1945–8), principal conductor of the South-West German Radio Orchestra at Baden-Baden (1948–62), and conductor (1950–58) and music director (1958–62) of the Zürich Tonhalle Orchestra. He conducted regularly at the festivals at Donaueschingen and Aix-en-Provence (1947–59), and at various times toured Europe, North and South America, and in the Middle East.

Although he was an admirable and meticulous conductor of Bach, Mozart, Beethoven, Brahms, Bruckner, Mahler and other major classical and romantic composers, Rosbaud's special reputation was as a performer and consistent advocate of contemporary music, including that of Boulez and Stockhausen. He knew well composers such as Hindemith, Schoenberg, Berg, Webern, Stravinsky, Bartók and Křenek, and conducted performances of Bartók's Piano Concerto No. 2 and Stravinsky's *Capriccio* with the composers at the keyboard. He led the world première of Schoenberg's unfinished opera *Moses und Aron* in a radio performance in Hamburg in 1954, and the first stage performance of the work at Zürich in 1957; the radio performance was recorded and issued by Philips. Also, he conducted notable presentations of *Erwartung* and *Von Heute auf Morgen* at the Holland Festival in 1958, and when he performed Schoenberg's *Variations for Orchestra* Op. 31 at Frankfurt, the composer came to the final rehearsal and heard the music for the first time. At Baden-Baden he was associated with Boulez, who had taken up residence there in 1953, and who eventually succeeded him as conductor of the South-West German Radio Orchestra; Rosbaud's performance, after 44 rehearsals, of *Le Marteau sans maître* was a major event in establishing Boulez's status as a composer.

In the 1930s, Rosbaud recorded a selection from *Tiefland* (with the Berlin Symphony Orchestra for Odeon), Mozart's Piano Concerto K. 271, Beethoven's Piano Concerto No. 1 and

Grieg's Piano Concerto (with Gieseking and the Berlin State Opera Orchestra for Columbia); later, he recorded Rachmaninov's Piano Concerto No. 2 (with Karolyi and the Munich Philharmonic Orchestra for DGG). On LP he appeared on many labels. His most famous recording was that of *Moses und Aron* (mentioned above, with the North-West German Radio Chorus and Orchestra *et al.* for Philips); he also recorded Beethoven's Piano Concerto No. 5 (with Robert Casadesus and the Amsterdam Concertgebouw Orchestra for Philips, available in 1977 on the Odyssey label); *Petrushka* (with the Amsterdam Concertgebouw Orchestra for Philips); Gluck's *Orfeo ed Euridice* (with the Lamoureux Orchestra *et al.* for Philips); Haydn's Symphonies Nos 92 and 104, Mozart's Violin Concerto K. 218 (with Schneiderhan), Blacher's *Concertante Music* and Piano Concerto No. 2 (with Herzog), Sibelius' *Tapiola*, *Karelia* suite, *Finlandia*, *The Swan of Tuonela*, *Festivo* and *Valse triste* (with the Berlin Philharmonic Orchestra for DGG); Schoenberg's *Variations for Orchestra* Op. 31 (with the South-West German Radio Symphony Orchestra for DGG); Mahler's Symphony No. 7 (with the Berlin Radio Symphony Orchestra for Urania, issued in Britain by Saga); Mozart's Piano Concertos K. 466 and K. 503 (with Gieseking and the Philharmonia Orchestra for EMI); Haydn's Symphony No. 45 (with the Berlin Philharmonic Orchestra for EMI); Reger's Piano Concerto (with Then-Berg and the South-West German Radio Symphony Orchestra for EMI); Rameau's *Platée* (with the Paris Conservatoire Orchestra *et al.* for EMI); Berg's *Three Pieces for Orchestra* Op. 6, Webern's *Six Pieces for Orchestra* and Stravinsky's *Agon* (with the South-West German Radio Symphony Orchestra for Westminster); *Das Lied von der Erde* and Bruckner's Symphony No. 7 (with the South-West German Radio Symphony Orchestra *et al.* for Vox and Turnabout); excerpts from *Don Giovanni* and *Le nozze di Figaro* (with the Paris Conservatoire Orchestra *et al.* for Vox and Turnabout); Berg's *Three Pieces for Orchestra* Op. 6, Schoenberg's *Variations for Orchestra* Op. 31 and *Variations for Orchestra* Op. 40, and Haubenstock-Ramati's *Credentials* (with the South-West German Radio Symphony Orchestra for Wergo); Liszt's Piano Concerto No. 1 (with Schmid and the Bavarian Radio Symphony Orchestra for Vox); Haydn's Symphony No. 82, Mozart's Symphonies Nos 39 and 41, Weber's *Konzertstück* (with Westermeir), and Brahms' Serenade No. 2 (with the Bavarian Radio Symphony Orchestra for Mercury).

Rosé, Arnold (1863–1946). Born in Jassy (modern Iasi), Romania, Rosé studied at the Vienna Conservatory, made his debut as a violinist at Leipzig at the age of sixteen, and in 1881 became the leader of the Vienna Court Orchestra. From that time to 1938 (well over 50 years) he led the Vienna Opera orchestra and the Vienna Philharmonic concerts. Bruno Walter in his autobiography, *Theme and Variations*, wrote of Rosé's superb artistry and his great gift as a concertmaster, using his unique authority in the orchestra solely in support of the conductor. In 1883 he founded the Rosé Quartet, which consisted of himself, Fischer, Ruzitska and Buxbaum and which toured Europe extensively, and in 1888 he led the Bayreuth Festival Orchestra for the first time. In 1903 he conducted the première of Schoenberg's *Verklärte Nacht* in Vienna; the audience's reaction led to the formation of the Union of Creative Musicians, to educate listeners and critics, with Mahler the honorary president. Rosé married a sister of Mahler. He was a refugee in London during World War II, where his quartet continued to give performances until his death. His only record as a conductor was with the Vienna Philharmonic Orchestra for HMV, of Beethoven's overture *Die Ruinen von Athen*, which made up the fourth side of Walter's *Leonore No. 3*.

Rose, Barry (b. 1934). Rose was born at Chingford, Essex, was educated at the Rcyal Academy of Music, and since 1960 has been organist and choir-master at Guildford Cathedral. In 1957 he founded and conducted the Jacobean Singers; in 1974 he was appointed sub-organist at St Paul's Cathedral, and also director of religious broadcasting for the BBC. In addition to records of organ recitals and a popular collection of carols, he has recorded with the Guildford Cathedral Choir *et al.* Stainer's *Crucifixion*, and Vaughan Williams' *Fantasia on Christmas Carols*, *And All in the Morning* and *Wassail Song*, and Warlock's *Bethlehem Down* and *Adam Lay y-Bounden*, and with the Pro Arte Orchestra Hely-Hutchinson's *Carol Symphony* (for EMI).

Rose, Bernard (b. 1915). Born at Little Hallingbury, Hertfordshire, Rose was educated at the Salisbury Cathedral School (1925–31), at the Royal College of Music (1933–5), and at St Catharine's College, Cambridge, where he was organ scholar (1935–9). At Oxford he gained a D.Phil. in music, held various positions there, and became Fellow, organist and instructor of music at Magdalen College (1957). He has composed church music, and has edited music by Dunstable, Byttering, Tomkins and Palestrina. With the Bodley Choir he recorded examples of French and English polyphony and of English Church music for HMV's History of Music in Sound, and on LP Argo, Decca and Saga released discs of Magdalen College Choir, presumably under Rose, in recitals of sacred music of the British composers Stanford, Wood, Appleby, Davy, Mason, Preston, Nicolson, Rogers *et al.*; on one of these the Elizabethan Consort is included. He also recorded music by A. Gabrieli, Monteverdi and Bassano with the Choir, for Argo.

Rosen, Albert (b. 1924). Born in Vienna and educated at the Prague Conservatory and the Vienna Academy of Music, Rosen conducted at the Plzeň Opera and with the Prague Symphony Orchestra (1965), was director of the Smetana Theatre, Prague (1965), conducted at the Wexford Festival (1965–7), and has been principal conductor of the RTE (Irish Radio and Television) Symphony Orchestra at Dublin since 1969. He recorded for NIRC Records (Ireland) Boydell's *Symphonic Inscapes* and Victory's *Jonathan Swift* (with the Irish Radio and Television Symphony Orchestra).

Rosenberg, Hilding (b. 1892). The Swedish composer Rosenberg was born in Bosjökloster, and after learning the piano and violin, he studied at the Royal Academy of Music in Stockholm (1914–18). After later studies at Dresden, Berlin, Vienna and Paris, and with Stenhammar in Stockholm, he was a coach and assistant conductor at the Royal Theatre, Stockholm (1932–4), finally becoming a conductor at the theatre. Some of his compositions have been recorded by Dorati, Ehrling and Westerberg; he himself conducted the Stockholm Radio Orchestra for a Swedish company on a 78 r.p.m. disc in a dance from one of his most successful compositions, the ballet *Orpheus in Town*.

Rosenstock, Joseph (b. 1895). The Polish conductor Rosenstock was born at Kraków, studied at the Vienna Conservatory and then with Schreker. He became a teacher at the Berlin Academy of Music, where Fritz Busch advised him to take up conducting, and engaged him as his assistant at Stuttgart. From 1920 to 1925 he was principal conductor at the Darmstadt Opera, and after two years at Wiesbaden he was invited to succeed Bodanzky as conductor of the German repertoire at the New York Metropolitan Opera in 1929. After a year in New York he suffered a nervous breakdown, resigned, returned to Germany and was appointed general music director at Mannheim (1930–33); not at first under immediate threat from the Nazis, he was music director of the Jewish Kulturbund in Berlin (1933–6), but then was obliged to flee Germany. He accepted an invitation to become the conductor of the newly formed Nippon Philharmonic Orchestra (the NHK Orchestra) and music director of the Japanese Broadcasting Corporation, and had a significant part to play in establishing the performance and appreciation of Western music in Japan. The war overtook him, he was exiled in Japan and suffered severely in captivity; when peace returned, he reorganised the Nippon Philharmonic at American request. Coming to the United States in 1946, he conducted at Vancouver, at the Aspen Music Festival at Colorado, and at the New York City Opera, where he was appointed artistic director in 1951. In his first season in that capacity he presented the first repertory production in the US of *Wozzeck*. He also visited Europe, as a guest conductor and sometimes performed in the dual role of pianist and conductor. He resigned from the New York City Opera in 1955, conducted the NHK Symphony Orchestra (1956–7), returned to Germany to become the music director of the Cologne Opera (1958–61), reappeared at the New York Met. in 1961 to lead *Elektra* and *Tristan und Isolde*, and in 1963 took Reiner's place to conduct *Götterdämmerung*. He was nominated honorary conductor of the NHK Orchestra and was one of the teachers of the Japanese conductor Akeo Watanabe.

When he was in Germany prior to 1936 Rosenstock made records for Odeon with the Berlin Staatsoper Orchestra, which included Beethoven's Symphony No. 5 and the overtures *Leonore No. 3*, *Benvenuto Cellini*, *Le Carnaval romain* and *The Hebrides*. Much later the World Record Club issued an LP of him conducting Beethoven's Symphony No. 1 and *Leonore No. 3* overture, with the Mannheim National Symphony Orchestra; these readings were thoroughly musical, well shaped and lively, although in New York he had a reputation for being a conservative conductor whose interpretations were occasionally somnolent. A private recording was also issued by Phoenix IX of him leading the New York City Opera Company in Tamkin's music drama *The Dybbuk*.

Rosenthal, Manuel (b. 1904). Born in Paris, Rosenthal studied the violin with Boucherit at the Paris Conservatoire (1920–23), and his first composition, a sonatina for two violins and piano, was performed at the Société Musicale Indépendante in 1923. After military service when he was a member of the military band at Saarbrücken (1924–6), he studied composition for 11 years with Ravel, and made his debut as a conductor in 1928 at the Concerts Pasdeloup, and then at the Théâtre des Champs-Élysées. In that year he was also awarded the Prix Blumenthal and the fellowship of the American Foundation for the French Arts. He was appointed joint chief conductor with Inghelbrecht of the French National Radio Orchestra (1934–9), was mobilised as an infantryman at the outbreak of World War II, was decorated for bravery, and was then a prisoner-of-war (1940–41). After years of activity in the French Résistance he resumed his musical career in 1944, becoming music director and conductor of the French National Orchestra (1944–7), visited the United States in 1946, and then conducted a programme of his own compositions with the New York Philharmonic-Symphony Orchestra. He was for a year composer-in-residence at the College of Puget Sound, Washington State, and then was appointed permanent conductor of the Seattle Symphony Orchestra (1948–51). His departure from Seattle has been variously attributed to the refusal of the US immigration authorities to re-admit him to the country, and to a misunderstanding about his true relationship to a soprano who appeared with the orchestra. Tours followed in Europe, Scandinavia, the Middle East, Central and South America, and he conducted frequently at the Paris Opéra and Opéra-Comique, leading performances in 1974 of *Moses und Aron*, *Le Sacre du printemps*, and *The Prodigal Son*. In 1962 he was appointed professor of conducting at the Paris Conservatoire, was permanent conductor of the Liège Symphony Orchestra (1964–7) and in 1975 he conducted with the New York City Ballet at a Ravel festival. His compositions have been highly praised; although he wrote opera and opéra-bouffe, dramatic works, orchestral, vocal, chamber and instrumental music, his name today is only known for his brilliant and popular arrangement of melodies from Offenbach known as *Gaîté parisienne*. His musical sympathies and training naturally befit him as an interpreter of French music, but he is also a distinguished performer of 20th-century composers, particularly Hindemith, Bartók and Stravinsky.

Rosenthal's first records, on 78s, were a Handel harp concerto (with Laskine and a chamber orchestra, for Decca) and the Fauré *Ballade* (with Gaby Casadesus and the Lamoureux Orchestra, for Polydor, and later released on LP by Vox). In the 1950s Vega, the French company, recorded a significant series of LP discs in which he conducted the Paris Opéra Orchestra in the complete orchestral works of both Debussy and Ravel, each on a set of five discs, and these were the first integral recordings of these composers. Other music recorded at this time by Vega were Falla's *The Three-cornered Hat*, *El Amor brujo* and *Nights in the Gardens of Spain* (with Loriod), the Albéniz/Arbós *Iberia*, *Tosca* (in a complete French-language version), a Mozart aria recital (with Jacqueline Brumaire), and Rosenthal's own arrangement, *Offenbachiana*. Some of these Debussy, Ravel, Falla and Albéniz performances were released in the US by Westminster. His other recordings include *Gaîté parisienne*, *Offenbachiana* and single-disc selections from each of the Offenbach operas *Barbe-bleue*, *La Fille du tambour-major*, *La Grande-Duchesse de Gérolstein*, and *La Vie parisienne* (with the RIAS Symphony Orchestra *et al.* for Remington), Loeffler's *A Pagan Poem*, Scriabin's *Poème d'extase*, Glazunov's *Raymonda*, *The Sleeping Beauty*, the Debussy *Saxophone Rhapsody* and Ibert's Saxophone Concerto (with Mule, and the Paris Philharmonic Orchestra for Capitol), Satie's *Parade*, *Socrate* Part III, *En Habit de cheval* and *Trois petites pièces montées* (with the French National Radio Orchestra for Everest), *Gaîté parisienne* and the overture to *La Fille du tambour-major* (with the Monte-Carlo National Opera Orchestra for EMI), Saint-Saëns' Violin Concerto No. 3, *Havanaise* and *Introduction et rondo capriccioso*, Vieuxtemps' Violin Concertos Nos 4 and 5, Chausson's *Poème*, Ravel's *Tzigane* and Lalo's *Symphonie espagnole* (with Grumiaux and the Lamoureux Orchestra, for Philips), Chopin's Piano Concerto No. 1 (with Cziffra and the Lamoureux Orchestra for Philips), excerpts from *La Belle Hélène* (with the Paris Opéra-Comique Orchestra *et al.* for Philips), Debussy's *La Damoiselle élue* (with the Paris Philharmonic Orchestra *et al.* for Bärenreiter), *Capriccio italien*, *In the Steppes of Central Asia*, *A Night on the Bare Mountain* and the *Russian Easter Festival* overture (with the Paris Opéra Orchestra for Adès), Milhaud's *Saudades do Brasil*, Barraud's *Symphonie concertante* for trumpet and orchestra (with Delmotte), Lesur's *Andrea del Sarto* and Denis' *Cinq fois je t'aime* (with the ORTF Orchestra for Inédits ORTF).

Ros-Marbà, Antoni (b. 1937). Born in Barcelona, Ros-Marbà studied at the Conservatory there, then with Celibidache at the Accademia Chigiana at Siena and with Martinon in Düsseldorf. He made his debut as a conductor in 1962 at Barcelona, conducted orchestras in Western and Eastern Europe, the United States and Mexico, was conductor of the Spanish Radio and Television Symphony Orchestra (1966–8), conductor of the City of Barcelona Orchestra (since 1967), and artistic director and principal guest conductor of the Mexico National Symphony Orchestra, and took part in the Osaka Festival (1975). His recordings include Rossini's String Sonatas Nos 1 to 4, Vivaldi's *Invicti bellate*, *Longe mala umbrae terrores* and Psalm No. 126 (with Berganza) and Pergolesi's *La serva padrona* (with the English Chamber Orchestra *et al.*, for Ensayo, some being issued in Britain by Pye), Haydn's *Die sieben letzte Worte des Erlösers am Kreuz* (with the Catalonian Chamber Orchestra for Schwann), Beethoven's Piano Concerto No. 4 (with Sanchez and the Barcelona Symphony Orchestra for Ensayo), Rodrigo's *Concierto de estio*, *Música para un jardin* and *Zarabanda* (with Ara and the Spanish Symphony Orchestra for Eurodisc), and Mompou's *Combat del Somni*, Rodrigo's *Triptic de Mosen Cinto* and other Spanish songs (with Los Angeles and the Lamoureux Orchestra for EMI).

Ross, Hugh (b. 1898). Born in Langport, Somerset, Ross was educated at New College, Oxford, and the Royal College of Music, distinguished himself as an organist, and was president of the Oxford University Music Club (1920). He migrated to Canada, became conductor of the Winnipeg Male Voice Choir (1921), founded and conducted the Winnipeg Symphony Orchestra (1923–7), was conductor of the Schola Cantorum in New York (1927), founded the National Choral Union in Washington, DC, was choral director of the Berkshire Music Center, Tanglewood (from 1941), and became music director of the National Chorus of America. He prepared the Schola Cantorum for performances with Toscanini and the New York Philharmonic-Symphony and NBC Symphony Orchestras. With the Schola Cantorum he recorded Villa-Lobos' *Nonetto* and *Quatuor*, the former with the Brazilian Festival Orchestra, and also the Bach motet *Komm, Jesu, Komm* (for Columbia).

Rossellini, Renzo (b. 1908). Born in Rome and educated at the Accademia di Santa Cecilia, the composer, critic and conductor Rossellini was director of the Varèse Musical Institute (1933–40), has taught composition at the Rossini Conservatory at Pesaro since 1940, and has been music critic for *Il Messagero*, Rome. His compositions include a number of lyric operas, and he is a member of organisations such as the National Council of UNESCO and the Italian Authors' and Writers' Society. His recordings are a selection from *Manon Lescaut* (with the Rome Festival Orchestra *et al.* for Fiesta, US) and his own *Vangelo Minimo* suite (with the Santa Cecilia Orchestra for Vox, Italy).

Rossi, Mario (b. 1902). Born in Rome and educated at the Accademia di Santa Cecilia, Rossi conducted a working-men's choir in Rome (1923–6), made his debut as an orchestral conductor at the Augusteo, Rome, in 1926, and then was assistant conductor to Molinari there (1926–37), at the same time teaching conducting at the Accademia di Santa Cecilia. Later he was principal conductor at the Maggio Musicale Fiorentino (1937–44); in 1946 Toscanini requested him to accept the position of artistic secretary at La Scala, Milan, but he preferred to become the artistic director of the Italian Radio Symphony Orchestra at Turin (1946–69). A distinguished conductor, known mainly for his performances of Italian opera in his own and in European countries, he nevertheless has a wide range of musical sympathies. He first came to the notice of British record collectors when Decca released the Mendelssohn Symphony No. 4 in the early post-war years, with him conducting the Turin Symphony Orchestra in a performance of rare polish. Also on 78 r.p.m. discs he recorded the *Preciosa* overture and an andante by Vivaldi (with the Turin Symphony Orchestra for Decca), the overtures to Cimarosa's *Le astuzie femminili* and Vivaldi's *Olimpiade* (with the Italian Radio Symphony Orchestra for Cetra), to *Il Matrimonio per raggiro* and *Der Freischütz* (with the Maggio Musicale Fiorentino Orchestra for Cetra). Later he contributed to the Cetra opera series with the complete *Don Pasquale*, *La Fille du régiment*, *William Tell*, *La Cenerentola*, *Fedora*, *Luisa Miller* and *Falstaff* (with the Italian Radio Symphony Orchestra *et al.*). These sets were at one time released in the United States by Everest.

Amadeo recorded Rossi conducting the Vienna State Opera Orchestra *et al.* in a number of records which were released in the US variously by Vanguard and Bach Guild, and some in Britain by Philips. The works recorded included a three-disc set of Vivaldi's *L'estro armonico* (with Tomasow and Boskovsky), Haydn's Mass No. 9, Pergolesi's *Stabat Mater*, Brahms' *Hungarian Dances* and Dvořák's *Slavonic Dances* Op. 46 and Op. 72 Nos 1, 2, 5 and 7, Bizet's *L'Arlésienne* Suite No. 1 and *Carmen* suite, the Rossini overtures *La Cenerentola*, *Il viaggio a Reims*, *Le Siège de Corinthe*, *Tancredi*, *William Tell*, *Semiramide*,

L'Italiana in Algeri and *Il Turco in Italia*, the *1812* overture, *Capriccio italien*, *Scheherazade*, *Capriccio espagnol*, the *Russian Easter Festival* overture, *L'Histoire du soldat*, *Les Noces*, *Alexander Nevsky*, *Peter and the Wolf*, the *Lieutenant Kijé* suite, and a two-disc set entitled *The Art of Embellishment and Ornamentation in the Renaissance and Baroque*. For the Maestro label he also recorded with the Opera Orchestra (so-called) the overtures to *The Merry Wives of Windsor*, *Si j'étais Roi* and *Dichter und Bauer*, the prelude to Act I of *La traviata* and the intermezzo to *Cavalleria rusticana*; Rococo also issued a performance of Mozart's Piano Concertos K. 450 and K. 466, and Schumann's Piano Concerto with Michelangeli, and Rossi conducting the Italian Radio Orchestra.

Rostropovich, Mstislav (b. 1927). Born in Baku, Rostropovich took lessons on the cello from his father, Leopold Rostropovich (1892–1942); both his father and grandfather were cellists. He was also taught the piano by his mother. In 1935 the family moved to Moscow, where he attended the music school at the Conservatory (1939–41), and first appeared in public as a cellist when he was thirteen, playing a cello concerto by Saint-Saëns. During World War II he first lived in the Urals, then entered the Moscow Conservatory proper to continue his studies in the cello and composition. He won prizes in 1944–5 for his performances, graduated in 1946 with the highest honours, soon won great acclaim as a soloist in the USSR, then, after his first appearance in the West at Florence in 1951, in many countries abroad. He is recognised as one of the finest artists of the day, and composers, including Prokofiev, Shostakovich and Britten have written music especially for him. Altogether 58 major works have been dedicated to him; most were composed at his request. Of all his many recordings as cellist, he regards one of his most recent, of the concertos of Dutilleux and Lutosławski, as the most significant. In 1953 he became a teacher at the Moscow Conservatory; he was elected professor in 1959, and in 1961 was appointed professor at the Leningrad Conservatory. He married the soprano Galina Vishnevskaya in 1955, and from time to time accompanies her in solo recitals.

Rostropovich has said that his interest in being a conductor was aroused when as a boy he toured with his father who conducted orchestras at spas in the USSR. His initial appearance as a conductor was in 1961, but his first major engagement was to lead *Eugene Onegin* at the Bolshoi Theatre in 1968. He is essentially self-taught as a conductor, but admits to having learned much by observing the many great conductors with whom he has performed as a soloist. He believes his cello playing has benefited from his experience as a conductor, and that as a string player he has a special advantage as a conductor: 'I know precisely what I can get from a string section. I think string players trust me, too. If I ask them to change the way they bow, they'll agree to it, because they know I am a player myself' (*Current Biography*, 1966, p. 337). He has great respect for orchestral players, and has said that, when he reads a review with little mention of the conductor but praise of the orchestral playing, he considers a compliment has been paid to the conductor.

Rostropovich's commitment to conducting is deep. His performances have been criticised for their pronounced and sometimes unorthodox expression, but he has reacted sharply: 'If you take the vastly different interpretations of, say, Toscanini, Furtwängler, Walter, Klemperer, in the past, they were not criticised for each going their own very different way. A strong musical personality is bound to express himself by how he feels the music. Besides, you can't always rely on the metronome, and it isn't very thoughtful, in my opinion, to criticise someone for simply not following the marked speeds. I believe that if an artist has the feeling for the music, understands the meaning of *ritardando* and *accelerando*, then he will have faith in what he's doing and it will sound right.' For Tchaikovsky he says he has a particular affinity; in his performances of this composer he gives the closest attention to every detail, sometimes maybe at the expense of the movement's structure; tempo and expressive exaggerations are frequent, but nonetheless arresting. His interpretations are in every way original and personal.

In 1974 Rostropovich left the USSR with his wife, with a two-year visa. Although quite unpolitical, he had given sanctuary to Solzhenitsyn when the latter was being harassed by the Soviet authorities before his expulsion from Russia, and this led to intolerable interference to his life as an artist. Recording sessions were stopped without warning, his concert and opera engagements abruptly cancelled, and he was finally barred from performing with orchestras in the major cities. Other bureaucratic impediments offended him, such as the necessity to obtain the approval of a government concern before making records overseas; when he recorded the Dvořák Cello Concerto with Karajan in FR Germany without the relevant authorisation, difficulties followed. In 1976 he was granted another one-year visa, he accepted the appointment for three years as chief conductor of the National Symphony Orchestra at Washington, DC, and in 1977 he was appointed artistic director of the Aldeburgh Festival. Nonetheless he has no wish to desert his country: 'All my life I wanted to devote myself to making music in my own country. All I can do I am doing for my country. I love my country, but I cannot give up my work. I would not be willing to go back if it meant returning to the conditions under which I had to work.' In March 1978 the Praesidium of the Supreme Soviet took away Soviet citizenship from Rostropovich and his wife, debarring them from returning to the Soviet Union because they had engaged in activities 'harming the prestige of the Soviet Union' (*sic*).

Rostropovich has recorded much of the cello repertoire. As a conductor, his records have been of *Eugene Onegin* (with the Bolshoi Theatre Orchestra *et al.* for Melodiya/EMI), Shostakovich's Symphony No. 14 (with the Moscow Philharmonic Orchestra for Melodiya/EMI), *Scheherazade* (with the Paris Orchestra for EMI), Haydn's Cello Concertos (both as soloist and conductor with the Academy of St Martin-in-the-Fields, for EMI), *Tosca* (with the Paris ORTF Orchestra *et al.* for DGG), and the six symphonies and *Manfred* of Tchaikovsky (with the London Philharmonic Orchestra for EMI).

Rota, Nino (b. 1911). Born in Milan, Rota has composed an oratorio at the age of eleven, studied with Pizzetti and Casella at the Accademia di Santa Cecilia in Rome, with Scalero, Reiner and Beck at the Curtis Institute in Philadelphia, and also at the University of Milan. He has been the director of the Bari Conservatory for more than 25 years, and has composed orchestral and chamber music and several operas, as well as a number of famous film scores, including those for *The Glasshouse* and *The Godfather*, and for all Fellini's films. His opera *Il capello di paglia di Firenze* ('The Italian Straw Hat') was first produced in Palermo in 1955; the exuberance and comic invention of the music caused him to be described as a latter-day Rossini. He recorded the work with the Rome Symphony Orchestra *et al.* for RCA, in a set issued in 1977.

Roth, Feri (1899–1969). Born in Zvolen, Czechoslovakia, Roth studied at the Budapest State Academy, and in 1923 organised the Budapest String Quartet (comprising himself, Schiff, Spitz and Franke), with which he toured Europe. In 1926 he left the Quartet and founded the Roth Quartet (with himself, Antal, Molnar and Scholz), which made its debut in the United States in 1928. Roth was professor of music at the University of California, Los Angeles (1946–69); apart from recordings with the Roth Quartet, he conducted the Roth Chamber Players in Duke's *Oboe Variations on an old Russian Chant* (with Gassman, for Contemporary).

Rother, Artur (1885–1972). Born in Stettin, Rother studied in Berlin and at the University of Tübingen, and became a repetiteur at Wiesbaden (1906). He then was an assistant at Bayreuth (1907–14), general music director at Dessau (1927–34) and at the Deutsche Oper, Berlin (1938–58) where he was made an honorary member in 1965, was chief conductor of the Berlin Radio (1946–9) and guest conductor at the Berlin Staatsoper (1960–61). He was a versatile conductor with a wide range of musical sympathies; although he did not achieve any wide international recognition, he was a very active recording artist; most of his records were made by Eterna and were generally released in the United States by Urania, and some in FR Germany by DGG. He also recorded for Telefunken, and made some 78 r.p.m. discs for EMI.

Rother's first recordings were 78s, of Brahms' *Academic Festival Overture* (with the German Opera House Orchestra for DGG), Mozart's Violin Concerto K. 219 and the Tchaikovsky Violin Concerto (with Kulenkampff and the German Opera House Orchestra for Telefunken), the Grieg Piano Concerto (with Johansen and the German Opera House Orchestra for Telefunken), Beethoven's Piano Concerto No. 3 (with Erdmann and the Berlin Philharmonic Orchestra for Telefunken), and arias from *Carmen* (with Schock and Schlemm) and *The Consul* (with Bork, and the Berlin Staatsoper Orchestra for HMV). The series issued by Urania, on mono LPs, were with the Berlin Philharmonic, Berlin Radio Symphony and Berlin Municipal Orchestras, *et al.*, and included Handel's *Ode for St Cecilia's Day*, Beethoven's Symphonies Nos 1 and 8 and *Egmont* music, Schubert's Symphony No. 9, Brahms' Symphony No. 4, Liszt's *Ce qu'on entend sur la montagne*, the overtures to *Don Pasquale*, *La Fille du régiment*, *Euryanthe*, *Oberon*, *William Tell*, *Il barbiere di Siviglia*, *La forza del destino*, *Aida*, *Libuše* and Pfitzner's *Das Christelflein*, Tchaikovsky's Piano Concertos No. 1 (with de Vries) and No. 2 (with Pinter), a selection of extracts from Wagner's operas (with Lemnitz and Voelker), Strauss's *Aus Italien*, *Burleske* (with Ney), Oboe Concerto (with Ertel), *Suite from Harpsichord Pieces by Couperin*, *Taillefer* and Violin Concerto (with Borries), Schilling's *Glockenlieder* (with Krebs), Busoni's Violin Concerto (with Borries), Kodály's *Psalmus Hungaricus*, Britten's *Diversions on a Theme* (with Rapp), Copland's *Appalachian Spring*, Piston's *The Incredible Flutist*. Stravinsky's *Pulcinella*, a suite from *The Love of Three Oranges*, Rachmaninov's *Variations on a Theme of Paganini* (with Karolyi), *Boléro*, Rakov's Violin Concerto (with Gavrilov), Khachaturian's Piano Concerto (with Pinter) and Kabalevsky's *The Comedians*. For Eterna/Urania he also recorded the operas *The Merry Wives of Windsor*, *Orfeo ed Euridice*, *Martha*, *Tiefland*, *Hänsel und Gretel*, *The Queen of Spades* (abridged, and in German) and excerpts from *Madama Butterfly*.

For Telefunken, Rother recorded the overtures to *Iphigénie en Aulide*, *Preciosa*, *The Merry Wives of Windsor*, *Hänsel und Gretel* and *Königskinder* (with the Berlin Staatsoper Orchestra), *Le nozze di Figaro*, *Rienzi* and *Der fliegende Holländer*, the prelude to *Tristan und Isolde*, the preludes to Acts I and III of *La traviata*, the waltz and polonaise from *Eugene Onegin*, a suite from *Carmen*, the incidental music for *Rosamunde* and *A Midsummer Night's Dream*, a collection of Strauss waltzes, excerpts from *Götterdämmerung* (with the Berlin Municipal Orchestra), Liszt's Piano Concerto No. 1 and Weber's *Konzertstück* (with Mildner and the RIAS Symphony Orchestra), the two Beethoven *Romances* and the Dvořák Violin Concerto (with Field and the Berlin Symphony Orchestra), a disc of operatic choruses (with the Berlin Symphony Orchestra *et al.*), and discs of excerpts from *Lohengrin*, *Tannhäuser*, *Tristan und Isolde*, *Die Walküre* and *Der Freischütz* (with the Berlin Staatsoper Orchestra *et al.*). DGG released *Tiefland*, the overtures to *Der Barbier von Bagdad* and *Iphigénie en Aulide*, and dances from *Orfeo ed Euridice* (with the Munich Philharmonic Orchestra *et al.*), Strauss's *Morgen* (with Anders), and *Pagliacci* and *Cavalleria rusticana* (with the Berlin Radio Symphony Orchestra, in German); BASF, DGG and Musical Treasures of the World *Les Contes d'Hoffmann* (with the Berlin Radio Symphony Orchestra *et al.*, abridged and in German), EMI accompaniments to operatic arias with Bork and Schock (with the Berlin Staatsoper Orchestra), and BASF a complete *Tannhäuser* and excerpts from *Il trovatore*, *Aida*, *La forza del destino*, *Un ballo in maschera*, *Don Carlos*, *Faust*, and *Cavalleria rusticana* (with the Berlin Radio Symphony Orchestra *et al.*).

Rotzsch, Hans-Joachim (b. 1929). Born in Leipzig, Rotzsch studied at the Hochschule für Musik there, was a tenor with the choir of St Thomas' Church and a member of the Leipzig Bach Soloists. He has taught singing at the Hochschule für Musik since 1961 and became a professor in 1972, has conducted the Leipzig University Choir since 1965, and succeeded Mauersberger as the organist and choirmaster at St Thomas' in 1972. For Eterna he has conducted the St Thomas' Church Choir and the Leipzig Gewandhaus Orchestra *et al.* in Bach's *St Matthew Passion* and *St John Passion*, and Cantatas Nos 26, 29, 31, 66, 106 and 119. He has also recorded a recital as a tenor.

Roussel, Albert (1869–1937). There is scarcely any evidence that the French composer Roussel was a conductor of any competence, let alone distinction. Deane's biography makes no mention of him in this capacity. Nonetheless, he recorded for Pathé in 1931 with an unidentified orchestra a symphonic suite from his ballet *Le Festin de l'araignée*. This set included a spoken introduction by the composer. In recent years an LP transfer of the discs, with the commentary, has been issued by Perennial Records, coupled with d'Indy and Schmitt also conducting their *Le Camp de Wallenstein* and *La Tragédie de Salomé*, respectively.

Rowicki, Witold (b. 1914). Born at Taganrog, Russia, Rowicki studied at the Kraków Conservatory, showed an early talent for conducting, and as a student was the musical director of the municipal theatre at Kraków. In 1938 he graduated with distinction in violin and musical theory, continued to study conducting with Rudolph Hindemith (the composer's brother), was appointed professor of violin at the Conservatory, and played the violin and viola in the Kraków Philharmonic Orchestra and in chamber groups. During World War II he lived privately in Poland, studying composition and musical history. In 1945 he re-established the Polish Radio Symphony Orchestra, which he conducted together with Fitelberg, and in 1950 was invited by the Warsaw Philharmonic Society to form and train a new orchestra which in 1954 became known as the Symphony Orchestra of the National Philharmonic Warsaw, although abroad it is still called the Warsaw Philharmonic Orchestra. He was for a time also the artistic manager of the Warsaw Great Theatre, was a guest conductor abroad, toured frequently with the Warsaw Philharmonic, and first visited Britain in 1958 and the United States in 1961. In Britain he has been associated more particularly with the London Symphony Orchestra. In Poland, he has continued to be active as a teacher and composer.

Rowicki is the major Polish conductor to emerge in recent decades, and has achieved much in his own country in forming and training two fine orchestras, and in encouraging and performing, at almost every one of his concerts, music by Polish composers. He is not a particulably notable classical stylist, and shows a closer affinity with romantic and modern music. Although he has recorded all the Dvořák symphonies in Britain, in Poland the repertoire is restricted to the Symphony No. 9, and as Bruckner, Mahler, and many other composers are not performed in Poland, his own repertoire is necessarily restricted. His performances, particularly of Dvořák, are clearcut and vital, his tempi are frequently brisk, and by temperament he is inclined to project the orchestral colour and the rhythmic drive of the music. As a result, his interpretations are exciting, but give the impression of emotional detachment.

With the Warsaw Philharmonic Orchestra for the Polish company Musa, and in some instances for Philips, Rowicki has recorded Beethoven's Symphony No. 2, Schubert's Symphonies Nos 5 and 8, the four Brahms symphonies (also issued in the United States by Musical Heritage Society), *Swan Lake*, *Le Carnaval des animaux*, the overture to *Hänsel und Gretel*, Debussy's *Children's Corner*, Chopin's Piano Concerto No. 1 and *Andante spianato and Grande Polonaise* (with Stefanska), *Variations on Là ci darem* and *Fantasy on Polish Airs* (with Kedra), Wieniawski's Violin Concerto No. 2, Khachaturian's Violin Concerto and Szymanowski's Violin Concerto No. 1 (with Wilkomirska), Szymanowski's Symphony No. 3, *Symphonie concertante* (with Ekier), *Stabat Mater*, Roxana's song from *King Roger* and *Litany for Solo Voice* (with Woytowicz), and *Harnasie*, orchestral pieces by Moniuszko, Baird's *Epiphanium*, *Chansons des trouvères*, *Four Essays*, *Erotica*, *Expressions*, *Variations without a Theme*, and songs (with Szostak-Radkova), Lipinski's Violin Concerto No. 2 (with Ivanov), Lessel's Piano Concerto (with Drzewiecki), Karłowicz's *Serenade* and Violin Concerto (with Wilkomirska), Bacewicz's *Musica Sinfonica*, *Pensieri notturni*, *Concerto for Orchestra*, Overture, Oboe Concerto and *Music for Strings, Trumpet and Percussion*, Noskowski's *The Steppe*, *Charcoal Sketches*, *The Lake*, *Eye of the Sea* and *Polonaise élégiaque*, Żeleński's *In the Tatrai Mountains*, Serocki's *Sinfonietta*, Penderecki's *Threnody for the Victims of Hiroshima*, Malawski's *Symphonic Studies* and Lutosławski's *Concerto for Orchestra*, Funeral Music and *Venetian Games*, and pieces by Rudziński, Dobrowolski, Bogusławski and Kotonski.

His other recordings included Karłowicz's *Stanislaw i Anna Oświęcimowie* (with the Polish Radio Orchestra for Muza), Beethoven's Symphony No. 7, *A Night on the Bare Mountain*, Liadov's *The Enchanted Lake*, excerpts from *Swan Lake* and *The Sleeping Beauty* and the polonaise from *Eugene Onegin* and Shostakovich's Symphony No. 5 (with the Polish Radio Symphony Orchestra for DGG), Mozart's Piano Concerto K. 466, the Schumann Piano Concerto and *Introduction and Allegro* Op. 92, and Rachmaninov's Piano Concerto No. 2 (with Richter and the Warsaw Philharmonic Orchestra for DGG), the Wieniawski Violin Concerto No. 2 (with Wilkomirska and the Warsaw Philharmonic Orchestra for DGG), the *Rosamunde* overture (with the Silesian Philharmonic Orchestra for DGG), the nine symphonies of Dvořák and the overtures *Othello*, *My Home* and *Husitská*, Mozart's Piano Concertos K. 271, K. 414, K. 453, K. 459, K. 467, K. 488 and K. 537 (with Haebler), and the Shostakovich's Symphony No. 5 (with the London Symphony Orchestra for Philips), the *Gayane* Ballet Suite No. 1 and suite from *L'Oiseau de feu* (with the Hague Philharmonic Orchestra for Philips), Różycki's *Pan Twardowski* (for Bruno), Prokofiev's Piano Concertos Nos 3 and 5 (with François and the Philharmonia Orchestra for EMI), Rachmaninov's Piano Concerto No. 3 (with Małcużyński and the Warsaw Philharmonic Orchestra for EMI), Chopin's Piano Concerto No. 1 (with Ohlsson and the Warsaw Philharmonic Orchestra for Connoisseur) and the *Scythian Suite* of Prokofiev (with the Berlin Staatskapelle for Eterna).

For Western record collectors, Rowicki's major enterprise has undoubtedly been the Dvořák symphonies, which were issued in the 1960s. Some were still available in the US and Europe in 1977, but by then all had disappeared from the British catalogue. His many recordings of Polish composers have not been widely circulated in the West.

Rozhdestvensky, Gennady (b. 1931). Born in Moscow, the son of Nicolai Anosov, the conductor, and N. P. Rozhdestvenskaya, a leading soprano, Rozhdestvensky was a pupil at the Gnesin School of Music and at the Moscow Conservatory school for children, where he studied under Oborin, and then entered the Conservatory in 1941 where he studied conducting with his father. His talent for conducting became evident in 1951 when he was working at the Bolshoi Theatre and was asked by the conductor Fayer to take over the rehearsal of *The Sleeping Beauty*, which he conducted entirely from memory. After graduating from the Conservatory in 1954 he was engaged to conduct at the Bolshoi Theatre, visited London that year with the Bolshoi Ballet, and in 1955 brilliantly substituted for Samosud in a performance of Shostakovich's Symphony No. 10. He was principal conductor at the Bolshoi Theatre (1965–70), the youngest ever to hold the position; his departure from the Theatre has been attributed by some to the Soviet authorities' disapproval of his efforts to introduce works of modern foreign composers. He led performances of *Le Sacre du printemps* and Britten's *A Midsummer Night's Dream*; from 1960 to 1965 he was chief conductor and director of the Moscow Radio Symphony Orchestra, and in the concert hall he continued to programme music by Poulenc, Hindemith, Orff, Bartók, Ravel and other comparatively modern composers, works which were being heard for the first time in the USSR. He also revived Prokofiev's Symphonies Nos 2, 3 and 4. He has visited countries in Europe, the United States and Japan as a guest conductor, has appeared in Britain many times, especially with the London Symphony Orchestra, in 1970 led memorable performances of *Boris Godunov* at Covent Garden, and in 1971 conducted the Leningrad Philharmonic Orchestra at three Promenade concerts. He was principal conductor of the Stockholm Philharmonic Orchestra (1975–7), is musical director of the Moscow Chamber Opera, and professor of conducting at the Moscow Conservatory. In 1977 he was appointed chief conductor of the BBC Symphony Orchestra, to take effect from September 1978; he professes a keen interest in the music of Britten, and also admires Vaughan Williams, Walton and Elgar.

Before the Melodiya-EMI agreement was made in the 1960s, recordings of Rozhdestvensky originating in Russia appeared on many labels in the West, such as Monitor, MK, Colosseum, Everest, Artia and Bruno. These included Prokofiev's ballets *Romeo and Juliet* and *Cinderella*, and *Nutcracker* (with the Bolshoi Theatre Orchestra), Bartók's Violin Concerto No. 2 (with David Oistrakh), Rachmaninov's *The Miserly Knight* and the *adagio* from Mahler's Symphony No. 10 (with the Moscow Radio Symphony Orchestra), Prokofiev's Symphonies Nos 2, 3, 4, 6 and 7 and *Peter and the Wolf* (with the USSR State Symphony Orchestra).

Since the agreement, many of his recordings have been issued by EMI in Britain and the United States; some others have been released in FR Germany by Ariola, several he recorded for DGG and Philips, and others have been issued in the USSR by Melodiya and in many instances have found their way to the West on the Melodiya label. Generally, the performances have attracted warm praise for their vigorous and incisive execution, especially the Tchaikovsky and Prokofiev symphonies, although some of the Sibelius symphonies have patches of unexpectedly poor brass playing. These records include, with the Moscow Radio Symphony Orchestra (called on some European labels 'Great Radio Symphony Orchestra of the USSR'), *Symphonie fantastique*, *Don Quixote* (with Simon), Bruckner's Symphony No. 9, Brahms' Piano Concerto No. 2 (with Zhukov), the two Liszt Piano Concertos (with Janis), Grieg's *Lyric Suite*, two *Peer Gynt* suites and Piano Concerto (with Yeresko), the Glazunov Violin Concerto and Vieuxtemps' Violin Concerto No. 4 (with Snitkowski), Bartók's Violin Concerto No. 1, the Hindemith Violin Concerto, Chausson's *Poème*, Ravel's *Tzigane* and Saint-Saëns' *Havanaise* and *Introduction et rondo capriccioso* (with Igor Oistrakh), *Duke Bluebeard's Castle*, Hindemith's *Kammermusik No. 4*, the *adagio* from Mahler's Symphony No. 10, Borodin's Symphony No. 1, Rimsky-Korsakov's Piano Concerto (with Zhukov), the six Tchaikovsky symphonies, *Manfred*, the complete *Swan Lake*, Piano Concertos Nos 2 and 3 (with Zhukov), the cantata *Moscow* and *The Maid of Orleans*, Mycielski's arrangements of 13 Chorale Preludes of Bach, Rachmaninov's Symphony No. 2, Piano Concerto No. 4 (with Petrov) and *The Rock*, Glazunov's *Poème lyrique*, *Cortège solennel* and *Scènes de ballet*, Janáček's *Sinfonietta*, Stravinsky's *Symphony in three movements* and Piano Concerto (with Yudina), Shostakovich's Cello Concerto No. 1 (with Khomitsar), Sibelius' Symphony No. 4, *Rakastava* and Violin Concerto (with David Oistrakh), the seven Prokofiev symphonies, Piano Concerto No. 3 (with Petrov), *Chout*, *Pas d'acier*, *Cinderella*, excerpts from *Romeo and Juliet*, the Waltzes Op. 110, a suite from *The Love of Three Oranges*, portraits from *The Gambler*, the choral pieces *Seven, They are Seven* and *On Guard for Peace*, the Violin Concerto No. 1 (with Igor Oistrakh) and Piano Concerto No. 5 (with Nikolayeva), Vlasov's Cello Concerto No. 1 (with Rostropovich), Ibert's Saxophone Concertino (with Mikhailov), Barsukov's Violin Concerto No. 2 (with Kogan), Shchedrin's Piano Concerto No. 2

(with Shchedrin) and Sviridov's *Triptychon* and *The Old Russia*.

He also recorded *Nutcracker* of Tchaikovsky, Prokofiev's *The Stone Flower* and a suite from *Cinderella*, Taneyev's Symphony No. 4, Shchedrin's *Carmen Ballet*, and trumpet concertos by Harutiunian, Krukov and Vainberg (with Dokshizer, and the Bolshoi Theatre Orchestra), Shostakovich's *The Nose* (with the Moscow Musical Theatre Instrumental Ensemble *et al.*), the Dvořák and Schumann Cello Concertos and Tchaikovsky's *Variations on a Rococo Theme* (with Rostropovich), *Francesca da Rimini*, the Bartók *Concerto for Orchestra*, Sibelius' *Belshazzar's Feast*, *Pelléas et Mélisande*, *Valse triste* and *Romance*, and the *Gayane* Suite No. 1 (with the Leningrad Philharmonic Orchestra), the Elgar Cello Concerto (with Rostropovich and the London Symphony Orchestra, issued by Rococo), the Tchaikovsky Violin Concerto (with David Oistrakh), Ippolitov-Ivanov's *Caucasian Sketches*, Shostakovich's *The New Babylon* and Eschpai's *Concerto for Orchestra* and *Hungarian Songs* (with the Moscow Philharmonic Orchestra), Brahms' Piano Concerto No. 2 (with Lill), Bruckner's Symphony No. 3, *Ein Heldenleben*, *Nights in the Gardens of Spain* (with Jocheles), the seven Sibelius symphonies and Schoenberg's *Pelleas und Melisande* (with the USSR State Symphony Orchestra), *Capriccio espagnol*, the *Russian Easter Festival* overture, *A Night on the Bare Mountain* and the Polovtsian Dances from *Prince Igor* (with l'Orchestre de Paris), and Stravinsky's *L'Histoire du soldat* and Prokofiev's Quintet (with an instrumental ensemble).

Rozsa, Miklos (b. 1907). Born in Budapest, Rozsa was educated at the Leipzig University and studied the piano and composition at the Leipzig Conservatory, graduating in 1929. His Violin Concerto was premièred in Leipzig in that year, and was later recorded by Heifetz. He moved to Paris in 1932, was successful with some of his compositions, particularly the *Theme, Variations and Finale* for orchestra, and there Honegger interested him in writing film music. In 1935 he came to London, studied conducting with Fry at the Trinity College of Music and wrote film scores for Alexander Korda, including those for *The Four Feathers* and *The Thief of Baghdad*, finally settled in Hollywood in 1939, and composed for MGM films. The scores for the films *Spellbound*, *The Red House*, *The Lost Weekend*, *Double Indemnity*, *The Jungle Book*, *Ivanhoe*, *Quo Vadis*, *Ben-Hur*, *King of Kings*, *et al.* won him Academy Awards in 1946, 1948 and 1959, and he recorded, as a conductor, many of these scores. He was president of the Screen Composers of the USA, the Young Musicians' Federation and the American Composers' and Conductors' Association, and taught at the University of Southern California (1945–65). His other compositions include orchestral, concerted and choral music, of which his *Concerto for Strings* has been highly rated.

Decca (US) issued two LP discs in the early 1960s in which Rozsa conducted the Frankenland Symphony Orchestra in a suite from *Lust for Life*, *Background to Violence*, *Concert Overture*, *Three Hungarian Sketches*, and *Theme, Variations and Finale*; these latter compositions were also included in a disc released in 1976 by RCA in which he conducted the RCA Italiana Orchestra. Other recordings were of his *Hungarian Serenade* and *The Vintner's Daughter* (with the Nuremberg Symphony Orchestra for Citadel), *Concerto for Strings*, *Kaleidoscope* and *Variations on a Hungarian Peasant Song* (with Zsigmondy and the Vienna State Opera Orchestra for Westminster), music from *The Lost Weekend* and *The Thief of Baghdad* (with the Royal Philharmonic Orchestra for EMI) and from other films (for EMI and DGG); also, music from *Spellbound*, and other pieces including Beethoven's Piano Sonata Op. 27 No. 2 (*Moonlight*), arranged for piano and orchestra (with Pennario and the Hollywood Bowl Symphony for Capitol).

Rozsnyai, Zoltan (also spelt **Rosnay**) (b. 1926). Born in Budapest, Rozsnyai gave piano recitals when he was 10, studied engineering at the Budapest Technical University, but at the same time was organist at the St Emericus Cathedral and attended the Franz Liszt Academy, where he studied piano, composition and conducting. He finally graduated in 1949 with the master diploma in conducting, and also studied musicology at the University of Vienna and music studies at Florence. His first conducting post was with the Miskolc Philharmonic Orchestra in Hungary (1948–50), then he was music director at Debrecen Opera (1950–53), associate conductor of the Hungarian State Concert Orchestra, conductor of the Hungarian National Philharmonic Orchestra, music director of the Pecs Philharmonic Orchestra and of the Györ Philharmonic Orchestra (1953–6). In 1956 he was a prize winner at the International Conductors Competition in Rome, toured Europe, and was a guest conductor with the Minneapolis Symphony Orchestra.

In 1957 Rozsnyai founded the Philharmonia

Hungarica in Vienna, an orchestra composed of exiled Hungarian musicians, and he became its music director (1957–60) and toured Europe and North America with them (1957–8). In 1961 he emigrated to the United States, was assistant conductor under Bernstein with the New York Philharmonic Orchestra (1962–3), music director of the Cleveland Philharmonic Orchestra (1963), the Utica Symphony Orchestra (1964) and the San Diego Symphony Orchestra (1967–71), artistic adviser to the Southern California Philharmonic Society (1971) and music director of the Golden State Opera Company at Los Angeles (1976). He has taught at conservatories and universities in Hungary, and was head of the music division of the US International University at San Diego (1967–72).

In Hungary, Rozsnyai recorded with the pianist Cziffra and the Hungarian State Concert Orchestra the Grieg Piano Concerto and Gershwin's *Rhapsody in Blue*, and later with the Philharmonia Hungarica accompanied tenor Rosvaenge in a recital. For Columbia (US) he conducted the Columbia Symphony Orchestra with E. Power Biggs in the three organ concertos of Haydn, and the 17 Church Sonatas for Organ and Orchestra of Mozart, played by Biggs on the original Haydn organ at Eisenstadt, Austria. Also with Biggs and presumably the same orchestra he recorded two other discs of popular pieces by Bach and others, as well as Helps' Symphony No. 1, Ruggles' *Sun Treader*, Effinger's Little Symphony No. 1 and Imbrie's Violin Concerto (with Glenn). For Vox he has recorded with the San Diego Symphony Orchestra Schubert's Symphony No. 8, the *Coriolan* overture and the prelude to *Die Meistersinger*.

Rüdel, Hugo (1868–1934). Born in Havelberg, Germany and educated at the Hochschule für Musik in Berlin, Rüdel became a horn player in the Berlin Royal Opera, then the director of the chorus (1901). He then was choral conductor at the Bayreuth Festival (1906), conductor of the Berlin Domchor (1909) and conductor of the Berlin Lehrergesangsverein. With the State Opera Chorus he recorded for HMV Lotti's *Crucifixus* and Corsi's *Adoramus te*.

Rudel, Julius (b. 1921). Born in Vienna, Rudel studied at the Vienna Academy of Music, and by the age of 16 had composed two short operas. When the Nazis occupied Austria in 1938 he emigrated to the United States, and eventually became a US citizen in 1944. At first he studied at the Mannes School of Music, and when the New York City Opera was formed in 1943 he joined the company as a repetiteur, making his debut as a conductor in 1944 with *Der Zigeunerbaron*. In 1957 he became musical director of the company, and was primarily responsible for its high standard and progressive policy, particularly in presenting operas by American composers. He was also director of the Third Street Music School (1945–52), musical director of the New York City Light Opera Company, of the Gilbert and Sullivan Company (1960–61), of the Chautauqua Opera Association (1958–9) and of the Cincinnati May Festival (1971–2), and is director of the Caramoor Festival and musical adviser of the Wolf Trap Farm Park for the Performing Arts.

Rudel has demonstrated his immense skill as a conductor of opera in a number of recordings made in the past decade. The first was Handel's *Giulio Cesare* (with the New York City Opera Company, with Sills and Treigle *et al.*, for RCA); his other sets with these artists have been *I puritani* (with the London Philharmonic Orchestra *et al.* for ABC), *Mefistofele*, *Anna Bolena* and *Les Contes d'Hoffmann* (with the London Symphony Orchestra *et al.* for ABC), *Manon* (with the New Philharmonia Orchestra *et al.* for ABC) and *Thaïs* (with the New Philharmonia Orchestra *et al.* for RCA). The ABC recordings were generally released in Britain by EMI. Previously he had made a series of discs for Westminster in the 1950s with the Vienna State Opera Orchestra, of the two *L'Arlésienne* suites and a suite from *Carmen*, the Suppé overtures *Leichte Cavallerie*, *Dichter und Bauer*, *Die schöne Galatea*, *Morgen, Mittag und Abend in Wien*, *Fatinitza* and *Boccaccio*, a collection of Strauss waltzes, and the Bruch and Mendelssohn Violin Concertos, Wieniawski's Violin Concerto No. 2 and Lalo's *Symphonie espagnole* (with Olevsky). He also recorded Janáček's *Capriccio* and *Concertino* (with Somer), *Ryhadly* and *Sextet for Wind Instruments* (with the Caramoor Festival Orchestra for Desto) and Ginastera's *Bomarzo* (with the Washington Opera Society for CBS).

Rudolf, Max (b. 1902). Born in Frankfurt am Main, Rudolf studied at the Hoch Conservatory there, and became a coach at the Freiburg Municipal Opera (1922–3). He was a conductor at Darmstadt (1923–5), in Italy (1926–7), then again at Darmstadt with Böhm (1927–9), at the German Opera, Prague (1929–35), and conductor of the Göteborg Symphony Orchestra (1935–40). He emigrated to the United States in 1940, taught in New York, became a US citizen in 1946, was first an assistant to Szell and then a conductor with the New York Metropolitan Opera (1946–50), and finally artistic administrator of the Opera (1950–58). He was appointed permanent conductor of the Cincinnati Symphony Orchestra (1958–70), led the orchestra on a world tour (1966) and on a visit to Europe (1969), and became head of the opera department at the Curtis Institute in Philadelphia (1970) and adviser to the New Jersey Symphony Orchestra. In 1949 he published *The Grammar of Conducting*.

At the New York Met. Rudolf was especially successful with the operas of Mozart and Wagner. Columbia (US) issued, on early LPs, fine performances of *Madama Butterfly* and *Hänsel und Gretel*, in which he conducted the Metropolitan Orchestra *et al.*, and an abridged *Die lustige Witwe*. Decca (US) made a series with Rudolf and the Cincinnati Symphony Orchestra, including Haydn's Symphonies Nos 57 and 86, Mozart's Symphonies Nos 28 and 29 and Serenade K. 320, Beethoven's Symphony No. 3, Brahms' Symphony No. 4, Mendelssohn's Symphony No. 5, Berwald's *Symphony in C major* (*Singulière*) Bizet's *Symphony in C major*, Nielsen's Symphony No. 4 and *Maskarade* overture, Tchaikovsky's Symphony No. 6, Bruckner's Symphony No. 7, Dallapiccola's *Variations*, d'Indy's *Istar*, Roussel's *Suite in F*, Mennin's *Canto*, Schuman's *New England Triptych* and Webern's *Passacaglia*, a collection of waltzes by the Strausses, Paganini's Violin Concerto No. 2 and Saint-Saëns' Violin Concerto No. 1 (with Ricci). His other recordings have been a complete *Don Giovanni* (for Cetra), Gutché's Symphony No. 5 (with the Cincinnati Symphony Orchestra for Composers Recordings), the *Siegfried Idyll* (with the Columbia Symphony Orchestra for Columbia (US)), Schubert's Symphony No. 8, Tchaikovsky's Symphony No. 5 (with the New York Stadium Symphony Orchestra for Musical Appreciation) and the Ravel *Piano Concerto for the Left Hand* (with Wittgenstein and the Metropolitan Opera Orchestra, for Orion). Rudolf's symphonic recordings showed him to have a somewhat emphatic style, with a thickly-grained orchestral tone; his interpretations are pointed and to some degree mannered, but undoubtedly sensitive.

Ruhlmann, François (1868–1948). Born in Brussels and educated at the Conservatory there, Ruhlmann was for seven years a member of the orchestra at the Théâtre de la Monnaie. His debut as a conductor occurred at Rouen in 1892; he appeared at Liège, Antwerp and Brussels, and in 1905 conducted *Carmen* at the Opéra-Comique in Paris. He became principal conductor at the Opéra-Comique in succession to Luigini (1906–14), and then was conductor at the Paris Opéra from 1914 to his death, except for one year at the Théâtre de la Monnaie (1920–21), and another at the Opéra-Comique (1922–3). He was also a conductor at the Concerts Colonne. A leading interpreter of French opera, he led the premières of Dukas' *Ariane et Barbe-bleue* (1907), *La vida breve* (1913), *L'Heure espagnole* (1911), Ibert's *Les Rencontres* (1925) *et al.* On early 78s he recorded for Pathé the overtures to Boieldieu's *La Dame blanche* (with the Paris Symphony Orchestra) and Thomas' *Le Carnaval de Venise*, and for Columbia excerpts from *Coppélia*, Grétry's *Danses villageoises*, dances from Rameau's *Les Fêtes d'Hébé*, excerpts from Berlioz' *L'Enfance du Christ* (with Planel), Boccherini's Minuet Op. 13 No. 5, Grieg's *Norwegian Dances* 1 to 4, Saint-Saëns' *Marche héroïque* and Vieuxtemps' *Saltarelle* (with the Paris Symphony and an unidentified orchestra).

S

Sabajno, Carlo. Born in Piedmont, Sabajno was at the beginning of his career a deputy conductor for Toscanini when the latter was director of the Turin Opera. He then became associated with HMV as a house conductor, and served the company for 28 years. With the La Scala Orchestra and Italian casts of eminent and less prominent singers, he recorded a number of opera sets in the pre-war years and before; they were of *Don Pasquale*, *Il barbiere di Siviglia*, *Aida*, *Otello*, *Rigoletto*, *Il trovatore*, *La traviata*, *Carmen*, *Pagliacci* and *Cavalleria rusticana*. He also recorded the Verdi *Requiem*, the overtures to *The Merry Wives of Windsor*, *Nabucco*, *Giovanna d'Arco*, Catalani's *Edmea* and Massenet's *Le Roi de Lahore*, Chabrier's *España*, Elgar's *In the South*, Mascagni's *Danza esotica* and choruses from *I Lombardi* and *Nabucco*. For a certain period in the history of the gramophone, these recordings were the mainstay of the operatic catalogue. *Don Pasquale*, which was originally recorded in 1932, was re-issued in the United States on Seraphim in 1978.

Sabata, Victor de (1892–1967). Born in Trieste, de Sabata studied conducting and composition at the Milan Conservatory, and won the gold medal on graduation in 1911. He first became known as a composer, particularly for his opera *Il Macigno*, which was produced at La Scala, Milan, in 1917. When his career as a conductor started it was in the concert hall, but in 1918 he was appointed conductor at the Monte Carlo Opera, where he remained for 12 years, and there conducted the world première of *L'Enfant et les sortilèges* in 1925. In 1929 he joined La Scala as a conductor, and later was appointed musical and artistic director. He retired from La Scala in 1953. He first visited the United States in 1927, conducted in Vienna in 1936–7, and led *Tristan und Isolde* at Bayreuth in 1939. Coming to London in 1947, he presented a cycle of Beethoven symphonies with the London Philharmonic Orchestra of which the performance of No. 9 was especially memorable. He revisited London in 1950 with the La Scala Company, conducting remarkable performances of *Otello* and *Falstaff*, and performed at the same time at the Edinburgh Festival.

Normally an abstemious and placid man, de Sabata was transformed on the podium, where he became a tense and tyrannical personality. He was particularly harsh with singers. Nevertheless it was not unusual for him to be mentioned in the same breath as Toscanini, especially as a conductor of Wagner and Italian opera. Under his baton the orchestra's sound was lighter and lither than with his North European counterparts: he was the archetype Italian conductor. He could coax the most delicate sounds, but his fortissimi were extremely loud. David Bicknell, who was with EMI for over 40 years, has said (in *The Gramophone*) that 'Sabata, like Furtwängler, was a great one for the mood of the moment. And, as with all conductors, he got his own sound from the orchestra. It was a great tragedy that he decided to retire so early – I think his poor reception in New York upset him.' In the United States, de Sabata had a name for the brilliance and eccentricity of his performances, which were, according to some critics, replete with enormous exaggerations of tempi and dynamics to the point where familiar music lost its cohesion. His memory was incredible; when he was in London in 1947 he found mistakes in the London Philharmonic's scores of the most popular pieces. Even to his last years he was a fine pianist and violinist, and every day played *Scarbo* and *Tzigane*, two of the most difficult pieces for these instruments. He is said to have preferred composition to conducting, and wrote two operas and a number of symphonic poems, some of which were performed. Toscanini conducted two of them, *Juventus* and *Gethsemane*, in his early years in the United States; Maazel revived another, *The Night of Plato*, with the Philadelphia Orchestra in 1968. De Sabata recorded *Juventus* with the EIAR Symphony Orchestra for Cetra; although it was reputed to be his best work, it was described by David Hall (writing in *The Record Book* in 1948) as a 'not strikingly original essay in a Richard Strauss-cum-Puccini romantic manner'. Rococo have also issued a disc which includes La Rosa-Parodi conducting de Sabata's *Mille e una notte – Primo quadro*.

De Sabata made records for four European companies – Cetra, Polydor, HMV and Decca. His Cetra recordings, with the EIAR Symphony Orchestra (the radio orchestra in Turin) were *Juventus* (mentioned above), Mossolov's *The Iron Foundry*, the scherzo and Troubadour's Serenade from Glazunov's *From the Middle Ages*, Stravinsky's *Feux d'artifice* and *Serenade* and the Mozart *Requiem*; the *Requiem* was later re-issued on LP by Everest. For Polydor he recorded with the Berlin Philharmonic Orchestra the prelude and Liebestod from *Tristan und Isolde*, the prelude and grand march from *Aida*, Kodály's *Dances from Galánta*, *Tod und Verklärung*, *Feste romane* and Brahms' Symphony No. 4; most have been re-issued on LP. His discs for HMV, with the Santa Cecilia Orchestra, were of Beethoven's Symphony No. 6, Debussy's *Jeux*, *Nuages* and *Fêtes*, the overture to *Il segreto di Susanna* and the intermezzo from *I quattro rusteghi* of Wolf-Ferrari, the overtures to *William Tell* and *I vespri siciliani*, the preludes to Acts I and III of *La traviata*, and *Fontane di Roma*. He also recorded *Tosca* (with Callas, Stefano, Gobbi *et al.* and the La Scala Chorus and Orchestra) and the Verdi *Requiem* (with Schwarzkopf, Dominguez, Stefano and Siepi, and the same La Scala forces). For Decca there were Beethoven's Symphony No. 3, the overture *Le Carnaval romain*, *Valse triste* and *En Saga*, and the Ride of the Valkyries from *Die Walküre*, all with the London Philharmonic Orchestra. Recently Cetra issued *Macbeth* (from a 1952 La Scala performance) which has also been issued by Turnabout, together with *Falstaff* (from La Scala in 1951); Rococo has released a disc containing LP transfers of *Feux d'artifice*, *The Iron Foundry* and *Jeux*, with *Mille e una notta – Primo quadro* (mentioned above), World Record Club the Beethoven Symphony No. 6, and Decca the London Philharmonic recordings, on LP transfers.

Many of these recordings were superb, and captured de Sabata at his most electrifying. Undoubtedly the greatest was *Tosca*, which was recorded in 1953 and still remains at the top of all operatic recordings; it is de Sabata's unique direction that gives the performance its inspiration. *Jeux* was significant, for at that time this music was rarely heard, and de Sabata had a special affection for it. *En Saga*, the Wolf-Ferrari pieces, *Fontane di Roma* and the Mozart *Requiem* were also exceptional. But some of his recordings were disappointingly eccentric: Beethoven's Symphony No. 3 and the Verdi *Requiem* were both marred by excessively slow tempi. The first movement of the *Eroica* was quite lethargic, and in the Verdi *Requiem* the tempi were described as 'positively grotesque' by the authors of *The Record Guide* (Sackville-West and Shawe-Taylor). To be fair to de Sabata, he had suffered a heart attack before the recording, and apparently was not really equal to the undertaking.

Sacher, Paul (b. 1906). One of the most distinguished and influential Swiss musicians, Sacher was born in Basel, studied at the Basel University under Nef and at the Basel Conservatory under Weingartner and Moser, and made his debut as a conductor in 1926. In that year, at the age of 20, he founded the Basel Chamber Orchestra, and in 1928 the Basel Chamber Choir, his purpose being to perform pre-classical and contemporary music, which he believed was not being given sufficient attention. In 1933 he also founded the Schola Cantorum Basiliensis, to create a revival of ancient music and instruments through teaching, research and performances, and in 1941 the Collegium Musicum Zürich, which in 1954 was combined with the Music School and Conservatory to form the Basel Music Academy, of which he became director (1954–69). He was president of the Swiss section of the International Society for Contemporary Music (1935–46), and in 1938 led a notable performance of the Swiss composer Burkhardt's oratorio, *Das Gesicht Jesajas* in London at the ISCM festival. He was also president of the Association of Swiss Musicians (1944–55), then becoming the honorary president, was awarded the Schoenberg Medal (1953) and the Mozart Medal, Salzburg (1956). After World War II he performed at festivals in Edinburgh, Glyndebourne, Aix-en-Provence, Lucerne, Vienna *et al.*, and has been a guest conductor in many European cities. On the evening of his golden jubilee as conductor of the Basel Chamber Orchestra, he led performances of a new cello concerto of Berio, Stravinsky's *Symphony of Psalms* and Bartók's *Cantata profana*.

Sacher gave significant encouragement to many modern European composers in commissioning, encouraging and performing their compositions. Bartók's *Music for Strings, Percussion and Celesta* was dedicated to him, and the *Divertimento* was composed when Bartók was staying as a guest of Sacher in Switzerland in 1939; Hindemith's symphony *Die Harmonie der Welt* was written for Sacher and the Basel Chamber Orchestra in celebration of the orchestra's 25th anniversary. Among the other works associated with the orchestra are Strauss's *Metamorphosen*, Stravinsky's *Concerto in D for String Orchestra* and *A Sermon, a Narrative and a Prayer*, Britten's *Cantata academica*, Honegger's Symphonies Nos 2 and 4 and *Jeanne d'Arc au bûcher*, and Martin's Violin Concerto and *Petite Suite concertante*. In addition, Sacher was interested in performing the unknown and the little known music of Schütz, Monteverdi, Carissimi, Purcell, Handel, Bach, Haydn, Mozart and the composers of the Mannheim School.

Sacher's recordings reflect his lack of interest in the music of the 19th century: except for Schubert's Symphony No. 4 (on LP with the Vienna Symphony Orchestra, issued by Festival and later by Everest) he recorded none. On 78s he recorded Bach's Cantata No. 65, a cantata by Krieger and Praetorius' *Beati omnes qui tenent Dominum* (with the Basel Chamber Orchestra for Anthologie Sonore), C. P. E. Bach's Symphony No. 5, Mozart's *Adagio in E flat* and Haydn's *Violin Concerto in C major* (with Geyer and the Collegium Musicum Zürich for EMI), Mozart's Divertimento K. 136, Beck's *Serenade for Flute, String Orchestra and Piano* and Martin's *Ballade for Flute, String Orchestra and Piano* (with the Basel Chamber Orchestra *et al.* for EMI). He made a number of LPs for Philips, including, with the Basel Chamber Orchestra, the *Brandenburg Concertos* and Bach's Violin and Oboe Concerto (with Felicani and Shann), J. C. Bach's Sinfonias Op. 18 Nos 1 and 4, *Sinfonia concertante* and Clavier Concerto Op. 7 No. 5 (with Leonhardt), Haydn's Symphonies Nos 44, 53, 67 and 85, Mozart's Piano Concertos K. 217 and K. 488 (with Haskil), Santorsola's Guitar Concerto (with Walker, and the Vienna Symphony Orchestra), Roussel's *Concerto for Small Orchestra*, *Petite Suite* and Piano Concerto (with Gousseau and the Lamoureux Orchestra) and Honegger's *Une Cantate de Noël* (with the Lamoureux Orchestra *et al.*) and Mozart's Cassations K. 63 and K. 99 (with the Collegium Musicum Zürich, later reissued by Turnabout). His other discs included Honegger's *Monopartita* (with the French National Radio Orchestra for Pathé), Schibler's *Concerto 1959* and *Music to an Imaginary Ballet* (with the Collegium Musicum Zürich for Amadeo), Müller's Symphony No. 1 and Burkhard's *Toccata* (with the Collegium Musicum Zürich for Decca), concertos and sinfonias by Albinoni, Sammartini and Scarlatti, Bach's *Violin Concerto in A minor* (with Schneiderhan) and Henze's *Double Concerto for Oboe, Harp and Strings* (with Heinz and Ursula Holliger) and *Sonata for Strings* (with the Collegium Musicum Zürich for DGG), Marescotti's *Concert carougeois No. 2* (with the Geneva Studio Orchestra for CTS), Martin's *Petite Suite concertante*, Binet's *Petit Concert pour clarinette* (with Brunner) and Honegger's *Concerto da camera* (with the Collegium Musicum Zürich *et al.* for CTS), Geiser's *Fantasie* (with the Basel Chamber Orchestra for CTS) and Schibler's *Six Studies for String Orchestra* (with the Collegium Musicum Zürich for Da Camera).

Sachs, Curt (1881–1959). Born in Berlin, Sachs studied at the Hochschule für Musik and the University there, was for a time an art critic, and then was appointed professor of musicology at the University. He also taught at the Hochschule für Musik and at the Academy for Church and School Music, and was curator of the state collection of musical instruments (1919–33). In 1933 he departed for Paris, lectured at the Sorbonne, and became director of L'Anthologie Sonore, a record company specialising in pre-classical and ancient music. In 1937 he finally settled in New York, was a professor at New York University and musical consultant to the New York Public Library. He wrote a number of authoritative studies on the history of musical instruments, ancient music and the history of the dance, numerous articles for musical journals, and *A Short History of World Music*. Sachs himself conducted a number of records in the Anthologie Sonore series, including pieces by Couperin, Bononcini, Franck, Melchior, Gabrieli, Rosenmüller, Rossi, Schein and Vivaldi, a disc (78 r.p.m.) of French dances of the 16th century, and Bach's *Two-Clavier Concerto in C major* (with Gerlin and Charbonnier and a string orchestra).

Sachs, Milan (1884–1968). Born in Lišov near Budejovica in Yugoslavia, Sachs studied the violin at the Prague Conservatory, was a member of the Czech Philharmonic Orchestra and concertmaster in theatre orchestras in Belgrade and Zagreb, and began conducting in 1911 at the Zagreb Opera, where he remained until his death. For Jugoton he recorded Zajc's *Nikola Šubić Zrinski* (with the Zagreb HNK Chorus and Orchestra *et al.*), and operatic recitals by Neralić, Gostič and Radev (with the Zagreb Opera Orchestra).

Sádlo, Miloš (b. 1912). Born in Prague, Sádlo learned the cello as a child. His original name was Zatvrzský, but he adopted the name of his teacher, K. P. Sádlo, at the Prague Conservatory (1938–41). He studied also with Casals, was a member of the Prague Quartet (1941–3), the Czech Trio (1944–56) and the Suk Trio (1957–60), became professor of cello at the Prague Academy of Music (1953), first visited Britain in 1959, led classes at the University of Indiana (1959), and gave the world première of the Khachaturian Cello Concerto. In addition to his records as a solo cellist and chamber player, he has recorded as a conductor, for Supraphon, a disc of violin concertos by Benda, Mysliveček and Stamitz (with Prokop and the Prague Chamber Orchestra).

Saidenberg, Daniel (b. 1906). Born in Winnipeg and educated at the Paris Conservatoire and the Juilliard School, Saidenberg was a cellist in the Philadelphia Orchestra (1925–9) and in the Chicago Symphony Orchestra (1930–36), was director of the cello department at the Chicago Music College (1930–36), music director of the Office of War Information for the United States government (1943–5), conductor of the Connecticut Symphony Orchestra (1948–56) and of the Saidenberg Little Symphony Orchestra in New York (1936–60). With his Little Symphony Orchestra and with other chamber ensembles he recorded for the US labels Decca, Columbia, Brunswick, Concert Hall, American Society and Mercury, but few if any of these discs were issued outside the US. The recorded repertoire included Bach's *Brandenburg Concerto No. 5*, the sinfonia from Cantata No. 156, the *Two-Harpsichord Concerto in C* (with Marlowe and Cook), *Three-Harpsichord Concerto in C* (with Marlowe, Conant and T. Saidenberg) and *Four-Harpsichord Concerto in A* (with Marlowe, Conant, T. Saidenberg and himself) Telemann's *Don Quixote*, Boyce's Symphony No. 8, Milán's *Pavana* and *Giga*, Geminiani's Concerto Grosso Op. 6 No. 2, a Vivaldi flute concerto (with Baron), Purcell's *Gordian Knot Untied*, Handel's Oboe Concerto (with Shulman), Largo for Two Horns and Strings (with Dunn and Buffington) and Arias for Winds (with Shulman), oboe concertos of Mozart, Cimarosa and Vaughan Williams (with Miller), Milhaud's *Concertino d'automne* (with Gold and Fizdale), Griffes' *Poem* and Foote's *Night Piece* (with Baron), Barber's *Capricorn Concerto* and Bowles' Concerto for Two Pianos, Wind and Percussion (with Gold and Fizdale).

Šajnović, Jovan (b. 1924). Born in Belgrade, Šajnović studied conducting, composition and piano at the Academy of Music in Zagreb, and became a conductor at the Zagreb Opera. He has recorded for Jugoton Tijardović's *Proljetna* overture, *Ribarske svade*, *Dalmatinka* and *Judita* (with the Zagreb Radio and Philharmonic Orchestra), recitals of operatic arias with Cvejić (and the Zagreb Opera Orchestra), Ruk-Fočić (with the Slovenian Philharmonic Orchestra) and soloists from the Zagreb Opera (with the Zagreb HNK Orchestra).

Salmhofer, Franz (1900–75). Born in Vienna, Salmhofer was distantly related to Schubert, and after a time as a choirboy, studied at the Vienna Academy of Music under Schreker and Schmidt, and at the Vienna University. After teaching music he was appointed conductor at the Vienna Burg Theatre (1929–39), for which he composed incidental music for about 100 plays, as well as operas and ballets which were performed at the Vienna State Opera. He became a conductor at the Vienna State Opera in 1945 and at the Vienna Volksoper in 1955. For Philips he recorded a disc of Strauss polkas and marches and another of excerpts from *Martha*, with the Vienna Symphony Orchestra *et al.*

Saltzman, Herbert (b. 1928). Born at Abilene, Kansas, Saltzman was educated at Goshen College, Northwestern University and the University of Southern California, and has taught at Messiah College (1950–52), Upland College (1955–9), the University of Southern California (1959–62) and Occidental College (1963), has been professor of choral music and associate dean of the school of music at the University of Oregon (from 1964), and has lectured on choral music in Germany and Latin America. For Turnabout he recorded with the Sine Nomine Singers a recital of music by Monteverdi, Schütz, Josquin, Weelkes, Lawes, Morley, Farmer, Ponce, Lassus, Dowland, and Gesualdo.

Salzedo, Leonard (b. 1921). Born in London and a graduate of the Royal College of Music, Salzedo was a violinist with the London Philharmonic Orchestra (1947–50), the Royal Philharmonic Orchestra (1950–66) and the London Soloists Ensemble (1964–6). Turning to conducting, he was musical director of the Ballet Rambert (1966–72), principal conductor of the Scottish Theatre Ballet (1972–4), conducted many of the major British orchestras, the Festival Ballet Orchestra, orchestras at Bratislava and Kassel, and at festivals at Bath, Harrogate, Salzburg, Vienna and Halle. His compositions include ballets, of which *The Witch Boy* was highly successful, concertos, orchestral and chamber music, and a work for jazz quartet and symphony orchestra. His later compositions reflect the growing influence of Spanish-inspired subjects, derived from the partially Spanish origin of his family. As a conductor he first recorded in 1969 his own *Concerto for Percussion* (with the London Percussion Ensemble for Philips); discs followed of Ibert's *Divertissement* and *The Witch Boy* (with the London Philharmonic Orchestra for Classics for Pleasure), his *Divertimento español* and two *Spanish Dances* of Granados (with the Royal Philharmonic Orchestra for CFP), and a collection of marches by J. C. Bach, Haydn, Beethoven, Paisiello, Méhul *et al.* (with the Military Ensemble of London for CFP).

Samazeuilh, Gustave (1877–1967). Born in Bordeaux and a pupil of Chausson, d'Indy and Dukas, Samazeuilh was also a friend of Strauss and a distinguished music critic and writer. He composed orchestral, choral and chamber music, all very much of its period and influences. He conducted the Paris Conservatoire Orchestra for HMV in two 78 r.p.m. discs of his symphonic poem *La Nuit*, and *Le Cercle des heures* (with the mezzo-soprano Eliette Schenneberg).

Samosud, Samuel (1884–1964). Born in Odessa, Samosud studied the cello at the Tiflis Conservatory, was a pupil of Vigan in Prague and Casals in Paris, and in Paris also studied composition with d'Indy and conducting with Colonne. After his return to Russia, he was a cellist in St Petersburg (1910–17), then conducted at the Maryinsky Theatre, Petrograd (1917–19), and was chief conductor and artistic director at the Maly Theatre, Leningrad (1918–36). He moved to Moscow, became chief conductor at the Bolshoi Theatre (1936–43), then at the Stanislavsky and Nemirovich-Danchenko Musical Theatre (1943–50), founded and conducted the USSR Radio Symphony Orchestra (1953–7), and afterwards conducted the Moscow Radio Symphony Orchestra. In Leningrad he was associated with younger Russian composers, encouraging several to write operas. He led the first performances of Shostakovich's *The Nose* (1930) and *Lady Macbeth of Mtsensk* (1934), Dzerzhinsky's *Quietly Flows the Don* (1935), and Prokofiev's *War and Peace* (1947), as well as Shostakovich's Symphony No. 7 (1942), and Prokofiev's *On Guard for Peace* (1950) and Symphony No. 7 (1952). In the 1930s and later he also led remarkable performances of *Le Coq d'or*, *The Snow Maiden*, *Russlan and Ludmilla*, *A Life for the Tsar* and Tchaikovsky's *Yolanta*. He was respected for his breadth of musical taste, his rare intuition as a conductor, his profound knowledge of the works he performed, and for his skill as a teacher; he received the Stalin Award in 1941, 1947 and 1952, and wrote his memoirs entitled *The Past Arises Before Me*. He was paralysed in the last years of his life and was unable to conduct, and although one of the USSR's most distinguished and learned conductors, he virtually disappeared from public life.

Samosud recorded with the Russian recording organisation, and some of his records were released in the West on the labels Monitor, Westminster, Urania, Classic, Colosseum, Bruno, *et al.* He recorded Tchaikovsky's Symphony No. 4 and *The Queen of Spades*, the ballet music and the final scene from Act IV from *A Life for the Tsar*, the ballet music from *Mignon*, the overtures to *Il barbiere di Siviglia*, *Russlan and Ludmilla* and Taneyev's *Oresteia*, and Glazunov's *Lyric Poem* (with the Bolshoi Theatre Orchestra), Mozart's Symphonies Nos 38 and 40, the ballet music from *Faust*, Tchaikovsky's Piano Concerto No. 1 (with Gilels), the Cossack Dance from *Mazeppa*, Serov's *Russian Dance*, Glinka's *Jota aragonesa*, and Prokofiev's *Winter Holiday*, *On Guard for Peace*, *Lyrical Waltzes* and an excerpt from *The Stone Flower* (with the USSR State Symphony Orchestra), the Schumann Cello Concerto (with Rostropovich) and an arrangement for vocal duet of the *Romeo and Juliet* fantasy-overture of Tchaikovsky (with the Moscow Philharmonic Orchestra), *Il barbiere di Siviglia*, *Orfeo ed Euridice* and *Die Fledermaus* (in Russian-language versions), Rimsky-Korsakov's *Kaschev the Deathless* and *Mozart and Salieri*, excerpts from Millöcker's *Der Bettelstudent*, Bizet's *Petite Suite*, the Dance of the Hours from *La Gioconda*, the ballet music from Saint-Saëns' *Henry VIII*, the overtures to *Le Cheval de bronze*, *Le Domino noir* and *Der Zigeunerbaron*, Tchaikovsky's Suite No. 3, Glazunov's *Album Leaf* and Concert Waltzes Nos 1 and 2, Arensky's *Fantasia on Russian Epic Themes*, Khachaturian's *Masquerade*, the Shostakovich Piano Concerto No. 1 (with Shostakovich), and Prokofiev's Symphony No. 7, *Alexander Nevsky* and excerpts from *The Stone Flower* (with the Moscow Radio Symphony Orchestra). He also recorded Chopin's *Andante spianato and Grande Polonaise* (with Beckman-Shcherbina and an orchestra).

Samuel, Gerhard (b. 1924). Born in Bonn, Samuel studied the violin and emigrated with his family to the United States in 1938. He studied at the Eastman School of Music under Hanson (graduating in 1945), then at Yale University under Hindemith (1947), at the Berkshire Music Center at Tanglewood under Koussevitzky and Goldovsky, and at the Accademia Chigiana at Siena under van Kempen. He was a violinist with the Rochester Philharmonic Orchestra (1941–5), associate conductor with the Minneapolis Symphony Orchestra (1949–59), and was at the same time conductor of the Minneapolis Civic Opera, director of the Collegium Musicum and music director of the Minneapolis Art Institute and Walker Art Center. He was music director of the Oakland Symphony Orchestra (1959–70), of the San Francisco Ballet, associate conductor of the Los Angeles Philharmonic Orchestra

(1970–73), music director of the Ojai and Cabrillo Music Festivals, director of opera and conducting at the California Institute of Arts, and is director of orchestral activities and conducting at the University of Cincinnati's Conservatory of Music (since 1974). His compositions, especially *Requiem for Survivors* (1974), have been widely performed, and he has published a short history of Chinese music. His recordings have been of music by contemporary composers: Ben Weber's Piano Concerto (with Masselos) and Lou Harrison's *Symphony in G* (with the Royal Philharmonic Orchestra for Composers Recordings), Chihara's *Wind Song* (with Solow and the American Symphony Orchestra for Everest) and Brant's *Music 1970 for Two Orchestras* (with the Oakland Symphony Orchestra together with the Oakland Youth Orchestra under Hughes, for Desto).

Sandberg, Herbert (1902–66). Born and educated at Breslau (now Wrocław), Sandberg became a repetiteur at the Breslau Opera (1919–22), and in 1923 went to Berlin to become assistant to Blech at the Royal Opera and to Walter at the Charlottenburg Opera. He later became Blech's son-in-law. He moved to Sweden, was conductor at the Royal Opera, Stockholm (1926–64), was named court conductor (1946), became a Swedish citizen (1932) and was finally chief conductor at the Malmö State Theatre (1964). He translated the libretti of German operas into Swedish, and also *Aniara*, an opera by the Swedish composer Blomdahl into German. For DGG he recorded Grieg's *Holberg Suite* with the Berlin Radio Symphony Orchestra.

Sander, Werner (b. 1902). Born in Breslau (now Wrocław) where he studied at the Silesian Conservatory and conducting with Wetzlar, Sander was a member of a synagogue choir, music teacher and conductor of lay choirs, and in 1933 founded and conducted the Jewish Cultural Association Choir. After World War II he was a music teacher at Meiningen (1945–50), cantor of the Jewish communities in Leipzig and Dresden (1950–62) and conductor of the Leipzig Synagogue Choir (since 1962), which later became the Leipzig Oratory Choir. He has made arrangements of Jewish and Hebrew folk songs, and Eterna and Capitol issued an LP disc in which he conducted the Leipzig Synagogue Choir and the Leipzig Radio Orchestra in music of the Jewish people.

Sanderling, Kurt (b. 1912). Born in Arys in East Prussia, Sanderling received a private education and started his career as a repetiteur at the Berlin Staatsoper, and at the age of 19 was an assistant conductor there with Stiedry and Breisach. With the advent of the Nazis, he left Germany for Switzerland and then the Soviet Union, on the invitation of relatives living there, as he was Jewish. He was first a repetiteur and then assistant conductor with the Moscow Radio Orchestra (1936–41), was appointed chief conductor of the Kharkov Philharmonic Orchestra (1939), but after a guest appearance with the Leningrad Philharmonic Orchestra in 1941 he joined the orchestra as conductor at Novosibirsk in Siberia, where it was evacuated. From then until 1960 he shared their concerts with Mravinsky, the musical director; in 1944 the orchestra returned to Leningrad, and Sanderling taught at the Leningrad Conservatory, with the title of professor. In 1960 he returned to Berlin and was invited to be the general music director of the Berlin Symphony Orchestra in East Berlin, which had been formed to give the city a permanent symphony orchestra in addition to the Berlin Staatskapelle (the orchestra of the Berlin Staatsoper and the Berlin Radio Symphony Orchestra (of the GDR Radio). He was also principal conductor of the Dresden Staatskapelle (1964–7), retired from the Berlin Symphony in 1977, but still conducts them from time to time. He visited London in 1972 to substitute for the sick Klemperer at a concert with the New Philharmonia Orchestra; he regards this occasion as immensely important, as he had admired Klemperer above all other conductors in his days in Berlin when Klemperer was at the Kroll Opera. He now travels in both East and West, has conducted in Japan and Australia, but in the United States has performed only with the Dallas Symphony Orchestra.

Sanderling has remained a profoundly *German* conductor: some recognise in his musicianship a kinship with Klemperer, others more with Walter. In Berlin, Furtwängler, Walter, Kleiber and Toscanini also impressed him deeply, in addition to Klemperer. To Furtwängler he attributes the greatest musical experiences of his life: 'He was interested in only what was written between the notes, and precision in playing was not so important.' As for Toscanini, 'maybe he is the greatest conductor when we are thinking about realisation of the music by the orchestra, but I cannot say that he gave me the greatest musical impression. Perhaps it depended on what he conducted. I cannot imagine better performances of Debussy or Wagner than those of Toscanini, but not his Beethoven or Mozart, or even his

Brahms. These days we are now a little more dependent on the written text, probably due to Toscanini's influence, but this can be a bad thing if taken too far. Sometimes perfection can be wrong, if it is the only purpose. In a lot of music it is possible to give excellent performances with precision alone, but a perfectly played *adagio* from the Beethoven Ninth can be nothing, yet an imperfectly played *adagio* can be wonderful.' He learned much from Mravinsky, especially from rehearsals. Of today's conductors, he considers Karajan to be one of the best interpreters of romantic music; his Bruckner, he says, is 'incredible: just right and marvellous' (personal interview with Sanderling).

Sanderling's own musical preferences are, especially, Mozart, Schubert and Brahms, and he has a great regard for the last works of Mahler, particularly Symphony No. 9. He was the first in the GDR to perform the Cooke version of Mahler's Symphony No. 10. Of all composers, he believes Haydn to be the most difficult to perform: 'It is difficult for the orchestra to play, and it is difficult for the conductor to find the right emotions for the music. Most conductors play Haydn like a composer of earlier days, but he has to be played like a modern composer, as he liked to shock the audience. In his music one has to find the element of originality, as in modern music.' Schoenberg, Webern and Berg are not so near to him: 'I can exist without them.' He was the first conductor to perform all three symphonies of Rachmaninov, but prefers not to conduct them too often now; he recorded the Second with the Leningrad Philharmonic, but would not conduct it again, as he feels that performance cannot be repeated. To him, 'Rachmaninov was not great, but a very fine composer.' In Leningrad he had a close relationship with Shostakovich: 'He was the composer of my time and I lived that time with him. If I were a composer I would have done the same and have written about the same things.' But he believes that in the Western world Shostakovich's music is misunderstood, and is often wrongfully dismissed as 'Party Congress music'. It is, in fact, the reverse: it is not public music, but very private music, of the greatest personal conviction. Of all the symphonies, he regards the Eighth as the composer's most personal, and to him Shostakovich admitted that the first movement of Symphony No. 15 was 'terrible' (i.e. full of terror). Sanderling has pointed out that Shostakovich was a very shy man who spoke very little about himself or his feelings, but what he said about his symphonies publicly should be disregarded, and his music is quite definitely unrelated to his ups and downs with the political system in the USSR. 'His music does not speak about his relations with the political system in which he is living, but about the confrontation of the individual and the community, similar to the symphonies of Tchaikovsky.'

Sanderling's musical personality is admirably demonstrated in that completely idiomatic recording of Rachmaninov's Symphony No. 2, with the four Brahms symphonies, which have been released in the West and in which he conducted the Dresden Staatskapelle with the greatest warmth and depth, and with the six *Paris* symphonies of Haydn, with the Berlin Symphony Orchestra, which illustrate exactly his words about the composer. His authority as a conductor is founded on a compelling and profound musical knowledge, and a strong personality; he avoids any sort of confrontation with his musicians, but demands and wins the greatest respect. In rehearsal he thinks it is essential to speak to the orchestra and to explain the feeling of the music: 'Musicians know how to play, I don't have to tell them, but I have to show them how to feel.' His directions and gestures are economical but absolutely clear, never obtrusive or with any element of exhibitionism; he has the capacity to project to both players and audience his complete devotion to the music and spontaneity in its interpretation. While this is apparent in many of his recordings, he confesses that he dislikes actually making records. 'It is a pity that records make us a little too like teachers, because such precision is not important in performance. In making a record, all technical matters are important, but not so artistic matters; in a concert you can forget about all technical matters. There are conductors who are very fine in recording, but whose concerts are boring, and others, like Furtwängler, whose concerts were marvellous but whose records are unsatisfactory.' Furtwängler's records have astonished him, because the impression from them is so very different from what he remembers of concert performances.

Sanderling has recorded throughout his career, in the USSR and DR Germany, and many of his discs have been released in the West on a number of labels. Included have been Bach's Suite No. 1, Mozart's Divertimento K. 334, and Violin Concerto K. 216 (with Kogan), the five Beethoven Piano Concertos (with Gilels), Brahms' Symphony No. 2, Tchaikovsky's Symphony No. 4, Rachmaninov's Symphonies Nos 1 and 2 and Piano Concerto No. 2 (with Richter), Prokofiev's *Sinfonia concertante* (with Rostropovich) and the Khrennikov Violin Concerto (with Kogan, and the Leningrad Philharmonic Orchestra), Haydn's Symphony No. 88 (with the Leningrad Radio Orchestra), Bach's Harpsichord Concerto No. 1, Mozart's Piano Concerto K. 466, Beethoven's Choral Fantasia and Rachmaninov's Piano Concerto No. 1 (with Richter), and Prokofiev's Piano Concerto No. 2 (with Zak, and the USSR State Symphony Orchestra); *Rosamunde* overture (with the Moscow Radio Symphony Orchestra); Beethoven's Piano Concerto No. 5 (with Zechlin and the Leipzig Gewandhaus Orchestra); Haydn's Symphonies Nos 45 and 104, Weber's two Clarinet Concertos (with Michallik), Franck's *Symphony in D minor*, Brahms' four Symphonies and *Tragic Overture*, and Bruckner's Symphony No. 3 (with the Dresden Staatskapelle); Bach's Harpsichord Concertos (with Pischner), Haydn's Symphonies Nos 82 to 87, Tchaikovsky's Symphonies Nos 4, 5 and 6, Rachmaninov's Piano Concerto No. 3 (with Rösel), Mahler's *Lieder eines fahrenden Gesellen* (with Prey), Sibelius' seven symphonies, *Valse triste*, *Finlandia*, *En Saga* and *Night Ride and Sunrise*, Shostakovich's Symphonies Nos 8, 10 and 15, and *From Jewish Folk Poetry* (with Croonen, Burmeister and Schreier), Wagner-Régeny's *Introduction and Ode*, Meyer's *Serenata pensierosa* and *Songs for Soloists, Choir and Orchestra*, and Kochan's Symphony No. 2 (with the Berlin Symphony Orchestra). He also recorded Beethoven's Piano Concerto No. 3 and *Rondo in B flat* (with Richter and the Vienna Symphony Orchestra for DGG), Poulenc's *Concerto champêtre* (with Růžičková and the Czech Philharmonic Orchestra for Supraphon), and Martinů's Harpsichord Concerto (with Růžičková and the Prague Chamber Orchestra for Supraphon).

Sanderling, Thomas (b. 1942). Born in Novosibirsk in the USSR, where his father Kurt Sanderling and his mother had been evacuated with the Leningrad Philharmonic Orchestra, Thomas Sanderling studied at the Leningrad Conservatory and the Hochschule für Musik in Berlin, and made his debut as a conductor in Berlin in 1962. He was conductor at Sondershausen (1963–4), Reichenbach (1964–6), Halle (1966–7) and since then has conducted orchestras in DR Germany and abroad, at the Berlin Staatsoper and the Hamburg State Opera. For Eterna he has recorded Handel's *Alexander's Feast* and *Ode for St Cecilia's Day* (with the Halle Handel Festival Orchestra *et al.*) and Zimmermann's *Ein Zeuge der Liebe* and *Sieh, meine Augen*, and Wolfgang Strauss's Symphony (with the Leipzig Radio Symphony Orchestra).

Sandi, Luis (b. 1905). One of the leading Mexican composers, Sandi was born in Mexico City and studied the violin and composition at the National Conservatory of Music there. He became a choral conductor, director of the school music section of the Mexican Ministry of Education, and head of the Instituto Nacionale de Bellas Artes, and brought about many reforms in the musical development of the country. He has collected and arranged Mexican folk music, and has composed operas, ballets, orchestral and instrumental music, and a work written for native Mexican instruments, in addition to music for films and the theatre. For Victor he recorded his ballet *Bonampek*, with the Mexican National Symphony Orchestra.

Sandig, Hans (b. 1914). Born in Leipzig, Sandig was first a writer and music teacher, then founded and conducted the Youth Choir of the Central German Radio. From 1951 he was leader of the 'Song of Youth' division of the Radio, and later was chief conductor of the Leipzig Radio Children's Choir. He has directed numerous radio programmes and recordings with the choir, with them has toured in DR Germany and abroad, and has composed and arranged songs and choral music of more popular appeal. For Eterna he has recorded Bach's Cantata No. 212 (with the Leipzig Chamber Orchestra *et al.*), Dessau's *Rummelplatz*, *Kinderlieder* and *Jugendlieder*, Thurm's *Vom Pustewind und anderen Sachen*, Weismann's *Die Hochzeit der Tiere*, and his own *In der Buchhandlung* (with the Leipzig Radio Children's Chorus *et al.*).

Sandloff, Peter (b. 1924). Born in New York, Sandloff studied at the Cologne Academy (1941–3), was a theatre conductor in Bamberg, Munich and Freiburg (1947–53), and since then has been a freelance composer in Berlin. His compositions include orchestral, chamber, choral, film and television music, including the score for the film *Viele kamen vorbei*, which received the Federal Film Prize (1956). In 1961 EMI issued a disc in which he conducted excerpts from operas by Weill.

Sándor, Frigyes (b. 1905). Born in Budapest, Sándor was a pupil of Waldbauer and Mambiny, was concertmaster of the Budapest Song and Orchestral Ensemble (1926–33), and professor at the Franz Liszt Academy at Budapest (1946–9), where he conducted the Academy's chamber orchestra. He was director of the Bartók High School (1949–58), and then professor at the Academy (since 1958). He has published a violin tutor in five volumes, and has edited classic violin works. In 1941 he premièred Bartók's *Divertimento*; he performed the music of many modern Hungarian composers, and was awarded the title Artist of Merit of the Hungarian People's Republic. His recordings, with the Franz Liszt Academy Chamber Orchestra for Hungaroton, include Bach's *Brandenburg Concertos*, the four suites, the Violin and Oboe Concerto, *Die Kunst der Fuge* and Cantatas Nos 161 and 169, Handel's *Water Music*, two cantatas (with Kalmár), several Organ Concertos (with Lehotka) and Flute Concertos (with Czidra), Vivaldi's *Stabat Mater*, *Longe mala umbrae terrores*, five bassoon concertos (with Janota) and five recorder concertos (with Czidra), cantatas by Telemann and Buxtehude, pieces by Albrechtsberger, Prince Eszterházy's *Harmonia caelestis*, Haydn's Horn Concertos (with Tarjáni) and opera *L'infedeltà delusa*, Mozart's Divertimenti K. 136, K. 137, K. 138 and K. 247, Szöllösy's *Concertos for Orchestra Nos 3* and *4*, and Farkas' *Trittico concertato* and *Piccola musica di concerto*.

Sándor, János (b. 1933). A native of Budapest, Sándor studied percussion instruments at the Franz Liszt Academy there, and was first timpanist with the Budapest Symphony Orchestra (1951–61). At the same time he studied conducting with Somogyi and Kórody, graduated as a conductor from the Academy in 1959, took third prize at the International Competition for Young Conductors at Besançon, and was a pupil of Celibidache at the Accademia Chigiana at Siena (1960–61). He conducted the Hungarian State Orchestra (1959), was principal conductor of the Pécs National Theatre (1961–4), chief conductor of the Györ Philharmonic Orchestra (1967–75) with which he toured Austria, Italy *et al.*, and then became conductor of the Budapest State Opera (1975). One of the founders of Hungary's Jeunesses Musicales, he has been invited to conduct at youth orchestra festivals in Britain and Canada. As a guest conductor he has appeared in many countries in Eastern and Western Europe, North and Central America and the Middle East, and was awarded the Liszt Prize (1967) and the title Artist of Merit of the Hungarian People's Republic (1973).

Sándor has made over 30 records for Hungaroton, of which the most distinguished and highly praised has been a disc comprising Bartók's *Dance Suite*, *The Miraculous Mandarin* and *Hungarian Peasant Songs* (with the Budapest Philharmonic Orchestra). His other recordings include Flute Concertos of Vivaldi, Boccherini and Szervánsky (with Jeney), Oboe Concertos of Haydn and Hidas (with Pongrácz), Haydn's *Cello Concerto in D major* (with Perényi), Mozart's Bassoon Concerto (with Janota) and Horn Concerto K. 447 (with Tarjáni), Kalmár's *Cycles*, Lendvai's *Concertino* (with Lanni), Sardi's *Spring Concerto* (with Lanni), Sárközy's *Sinfonia concertante* and overture *To the Youth*, Tardos' *Evocatio* and Láng's *Variations and Allegro* (with the Hungarian Radio Orchestra), Bartók's *Concerto for Two Pianos, Percussion and Orchestra*, and Michael Haydn's *Serenata a piu stromenti, tutti obligati* and *Symphony in D major* (with the Budapest Philharmonic Orchestra), Flute Concertos by Michael Haydn and Josef Haydn (with Kovács), Hofmeister, Rössler-Rosetti and Devienne (with Szebenyi), Albrechtsberger's *Harp Partita* (with Lelkes), waltzes and polkas of Strauss, Brahms' *Hungarian Dances*, Jenei's *Soliloquium No. 1* and Alef's *Hommage à Schoenberg* and other pieces (with the Györ Philharmonic Orchestra).

Santi, Nello (b. 1931). Born in Adria, Italy, Santi studied composition at Padua, and graduated in 1956. He then studied the violin and piano, played the cello, trumpet and timpani in orchestras, and started as a conductor in Padua in 1951 with a performance of *Rigoletto*. He was appointed first conductor at the Zürich City Theatre (1958), conducted at Covent Garden (1960), at the Salzburg Festival (1960), was appointed permanent guest conductor at the Vienna State Opera (1960), conducted Italian operas at the Metropolitan Opera New York (1962–4) and for German and Austrian radio and television stations, and has also conducted at Hamburg, Munich and Cologne. His recordings include *Pagliacci* (with the London Symphony Orchestra *et al.* for RCA), orchestral pieces from Wolf-Ferrari's operas *Il campiello*, *I gioielli della Madonna*, *I quattro rusteghi* and *Il segreto di Susanna* (with the Paris Conservatoire Orchestra for Decca), *Rigoletto*, *Il trovatore*, *Madama Butterfly*, excerpts from *Swan Lake*, a disc of choruses from the Verdi operas and the overtures to *Nabucco*, *La forza del destino* and *Un ballo in maschera* (with the Vienna State Opera Orchestra *et al.*, for La Guilde Internationale du Disque), and accompaniments to recitals by Sutherland (with the Paris Conservatoire Orchestra for Decca), Domingo (with the New Philharmonia and London Symphony Orchestras for RCA, and the Berlin Deutsche Oper Orchestra for Decca), Price (with the New Philharmonia Orchestra for RCA) and Bergonzi (with the New Philharmonia Orchestra for Philips).

Santi, Piero (b. 1923). Born in Milan, Santi studied at the university and conservatory there, and at the Accademia di Santa Cecilia in Rome, with Molinari and Previtali. He also attended the classes of van Kempen at the Accademia Chigiana at Siena, and at the Summer Course of the International Music Institute at Darmstadt, and made his debut as a conductor in 1947. He has taught at the Florence Conservatory, Perugia Music High School, and at the Turin Conservatory, was a musical consultant for Italian Television (1952–8), founded the Italian Contemporary Music Society (1960–67), and was artistic director of La Piccola-Scala, Milan (1967–9). He has contributed to many encyclopedias and musical journals, and has conducted opera and concerts throughout Italy. Santi has recorded Vivaldi's *Stabat Mater* (with the Angelicum Chorus and Orchestra *et al.* for Angelicum), *The Four Seasons* (with Biffoli), Bassoon Concertos P. 64, P. 69, P. 70, P. 71 and P. 401 (with Bianchi), Oboe Concertos P. 41, P. 42, P. 44, P. 187 and P. 306 (with Caroldi), Oboe and Bassoon Concerto P. 129 (with Caroldi and Bianchi) and two-Oboe and Two-Clarinet Concerto P. 73 (with Caroldi, Alvarosi, Schiani and Gerbi), and Corelli's Concerti Grossi Op. 5 (with the Accademici di Milano for Vox), and Martini's *L'impresario delle Canarie* (with the Campagno Teatro Villa Olmo *et al.* for Cetra).

Santini, Gabriele (1886–1964). The Italian opera conductor Santini was born in Perugia, studied there and in Bologna, made his debut in 1906, and was assistant to Toscanini at La Scala, Milan (1925–9). He was conductor at the Rome Opera (1929–32), and later was music director there (1944–62), also conducting at Chicago, Buenos Aires and London. He was reputed to have a profound knowledge of Italian opera, and, according to Victor Olof who was the EMI producer who worked with him on many recordings, he was beloved by everybody, and even the most intractable singers regarded him as a father. With the Rome Opera House Orchestra and singers such as Los Angeles, Carosio, Gobbi, Corelli, Björling and Christoff, he made many distinguished opera recordings after World War II for EMI, which were released on the HMV, Electrola and Angel labels. Included were *Don Carlos*, *Simon Boccanegra*, *L'elisir d'amore*, *Andrea Chénier*, *Cavalleria rusticana*, *La Bohème*, *Madama Butterfly* and *Gianni Schicchi*. For Cetra, also issued by Vox, he recorded *La traviata* and *La Bohème* (with the Italian Radio Orchestra *et al.*), and for DGG *Don Carlos* (with the La Scala Orchestra *et al.*). On the fourth side of the *Cavalleria rusticana* set, he conducted the overtures to the Mascagni operas *Iris*, *Le maschere* and *Guglielmo Ratcliffe*.

Sanzogno, Nino (b. 1911). Educated at the Conservatorio Benedetto Marcello at his birthplace, Venice, where he graduated in 1932, Sanzogno later studied composition with Malipiero and conducting with Scherchen. He was a conductor at the Teatro la Fenice in Venice (1937–9) and of the Gruppo Strumentale Italiano (1938–9), and has conducted at La Scala, Milan, since 1941, becoming a permanent conductor there in 1962. He performs regularly in all the major Italian opera houses, as well as those in Europe and North and South America, conducted the opening performance at La Piccola-Scala, Milan, in 1955, and led the company at the Edinburgh Festival in 1957. He is mostly connected with performances of relatively modern operas, and has conducted the first Italian performances of *Lulu*, *Lady Macbeth of Mtsensk*, *The Cunning Little Vixen*, *Mathis der Maler*, *Les Dialogues des Carmélites*, *Troilus and Cressida* and *The Flaming Angel*, although he also has a preference for Cimarosa, Scarlatti, Cherubini, Piccinni, Paisiello and Donizetti. He has composed a symphonic poem, *The Four Horsemen of the Apocalypse*. His recordings have included Monteverdi's *Il combattimento di Tancredi e Clorinda* (with the La Scala Chamber Ensemble *et al.* for Colosseum, US), Vivilliane's *Romance for Harmonica and String Orchestra* (with Adler and a string orchestra for EMI), Cimarosa's *Il matrimonio segreto* (with the La Scala Orchestra *et al.* for EMI), *Lucia di Lammermoor* (with the La Scala Orchestra *et al.* for DGG and Cetra), *Rigoletto* (with the Santa Cecilia Orchestra *et al.* for Decca) and Menotti's *Amelia at the Ball* (with the La Scala Orchestra *et al.* for EMI). L'Estro Armonico have also issued a recording of *Iphigénie en Tauride*, which he conducted at La Scala in 1957.

Sargent, Sir Malcolm (1895–1967). Born in Ashford, Kent, Sargent grew up at Stamford, Lincolnshire, studied the organ at the Royal College of Organists in London, from 1911 to 1914 was articled to the organist at Peterborough Cathedral, and then became the organist at the Melton Mowbray parish church. As a child, he had learned the piano, and his first experience at conducting was directing *The Yeomen of the Guard* at the age of 14. After graduating B.Mus. at Durham University, he went on to win a doctorate at 21, being, at the time, the youngest to receive the degree in England. Eight months' war service interrupted his career in 1918, after which he studied with the pianist Moiseiwitsch and achieved a reputation as a pianist and accompanist. His first appearance with a professional orchestra was in 1921 when he conducted his own composition *Impressions on a Windy Day* with the Hallé Orchestra when it visited Leicester, and this he repeated at a Promenade Concert in London at Sir Henry Wood's request.

In 1922 Sargent organised the Leicester Symphony Orchestra and appeared occasionally with it as a concert pianist, once playing a Rachmaninov concerto with the young Adrian Boult conducting. His programmes were daring for a fledgling conductor with a novice provincial orchestra, and included *The Dream of Gerontius*, Schubert's Symphony No. 9 and Beethoven's Symphony No. 9. He later recalled that he had heard none of the symphonies of Mozart and Beethoven, except the *Pastoral*, until he conducted them himself. Moving to London in 1924, he embarked on a bewildering series of musical assignments: conducting Gilbert and Sullivan operas with the D'Oyly Carte Company, the Diaghilev Ballets Russes, the British National Opera Company, the Robert Mayer Children's Concerts, and the Royal Choral Society in their spectacular annual presentation of *Hiawatha* of Coleridge-Taylor. He also taught at the Royal College of Music, and conducted the first performances of Vaughan Williams' *Hugh the Drover* and Walton's *Belshazzar's Feast*. His greatest success was the Courtauld/Sargent concerts, which were an annual series of six concerts at reduced prices, started in 1928–9 by Mrs Samuel Courtauld, with Sargent the musical director. In the concerts the London Symphony and Philharmonic Orchestras were conducted by himself and by many notables, including Klemperer, Walter, Beecham, Szell, Kleiber and Schuricht. At these concerts Klemperer made his London debut with Bruckner's Symphony No. 8, Walter conducted *Das Lied von der Erde*, and Schnabel played three concertos at the one concert – the Mozart *D minor*, the Beethoven No. 3 and the Brahms No. 1.

Sargent was particularly in demand as a choral conductor, and regularly directed many choral societies in England, not the least being the Huddersfield Choral Society, with which he toured Europe and the United States, performing *Messiah*. Choral music was his first love, and certainly showed him at his best as a conductor; he confessed that his first preferences in music were *Messiah*, Bach's *Mass in B minor*, Beethoven's Symphony No. 9, and *The Dream of Gerontius*; Beecham once remarked that Sargent was 'the greatest choirmaster we have produced'. In 1932 Sargent assisted Beecham when he formed the London Philharmonic Orchestra, and shared the direction of their concerts with him. His first tour abroad was to Australia in 1936, and he returned there later in 1938 and 1939. He was with the Hallé Orchestra from 1939 to 1943 and the London Philharmonic in 1939; in 1942 he commenced a six-year association with the Liverpool Philharmonic Orchestra, which at that time was a group of considerable distinction and had many of the best players taken from the London Philharmonic. With the Liverpool Philharmonic he conducted 720 concerts and 100 recording sessions. He was knighted in 1947, and in 1950 succeeded Boult as chief conductor of the BBC Symphony Orchestra. This began his intimate connection with the London Promenade Concerts, which lasted almost to his death in 1967, although his appointment with the BBC Symphony terminated in 1957. He toured extensively after World War II, to the United States, Canada, Japan and in Europe, as well as to South Africa, Australia and New Zealand.

Sargent was generally a good conductor, but only occasionally a great one. In English music he was a lesser figure than Wood, Beecham or Boult, and was the direct antithesis of a later conductor of the BBC Symphony Orchestra, Pierre Boulez. His strength was in choral, romantic and British music; all these came together in *The Dream of Gerontius* which he conducted with the utmost conviction, as is testified in his 78 r.p.m. set with the Liverpool Philharmonic Orchestra, the Huddersfield Choral Society *et al.*, recorded in 1945 and reissued on LP in 1975. An untiring advocate of British music, he once advised the Viennese that 'Elgar is fine, forgive me, a finer composer than Bruckner' (C. Reid, *Malcolm Sargent*, London, 1968, p. 344). Despite his love for the Viennese classics, he could rarely rise above the routine in interpreting them. He resolutely refused to accede to the present-day practice of performing the oratorios of Handel and the *Mass in B minor* and Passions of Bach with small choirs and 17th-century instrumentation, maintaining that Handel and Bach intended that their music should be performed by large forces. He had no sympathy with contemporary atonal music, which led the BBC to allocate more and more of the Prom concerts to other conductors competent in this repertoire. He always conducted with the score in front of him, was a rapid assimilator of new scores, and claimed he could conduct immediately a thousand pieces. He abandoned composition early in his career, but later arranged Brahms' *Vier ernste Gesänge* for orchestral accompaniment.

With the public Sargent enjoyed a vast popularity, encouraged by his studied eloquence, set off by the carnation in his buttonhole, and a flair for showmanship unusual among British conductors. His ready wit made him a favourite of the Brains Trust, the BBC radio show. To the world he was the very model of a modern Englishman; to many Englishmen he was just 'Flash Harry'. On the other hand, his peremptory demands and his questionable alterations to scores invited animosity among orchestral players, with whom he often had trouble establishing a lasting authority. His occasional contretemps with them appeared to upset him more than the offended musicians; in 1935 he commented publicly that pensions for orchestral musicians would cause them to play less well, and this estranged him from English orchestral players for many years. Edward Heath (in his book *Music: A Joy for Life*, London, 1976) summed up Sargent well: 'In the last 20 years of his life (he) was probably the British conductor and musician best known to the public, particularly to the promenaders, who adored him. In the world of professional music he was rather more controversial and there were always those ready to sneer. Perhaps as a result of his restless nervous energy, he did conduct too many concerts a year; perhaps his repertoire of major works was somewhat limited; perhaps he did lack sympathy with the *avant-garde* products of contemporary music festivals; and perhaps he was snobbish in his approach to the non-musical world. For all that, he did a great deal to encourage British music and British musicians.'

From his first recording in 1924, of parts of *Hugh the Drover* of Vaughan Williams, Sargent's discography is very extensive. In 1925–6 he recorded six choruses from Messiah (with the Royal Choral Society), and in 1928–30 the Gilbert and Sullivan operas *The Yeomen of the Guard*, *The Pirates of Penzance*, *Iolanthe*, *HMS Pinafore* and *Patience*, and resumed the series in 1940 with *Ruddigore* and *Princess Ida*; later, on LP, he was to again record *HMS Pinafore*, *The Mikado*, *The Gondoliers*, *The Yeomen of the Guard*, *Iolanthe*, *The Pirates of Penzance*, *Trial by Jury* and *Patience* (with the Pro Arte Orchestra *et al.*). His other pre-war recordings included Beethoven's Piano Concertos Nos 1 to 4 and the Rondo Op. 51 No. 2 (with Schnabel, and the London Symphony Orchestra in Nos 1 and 4 and the London Philharmonic in Nos 2 and 3), Mozart's Violin Concerto K. 218 (with Kreisler and the London Philharmonic), Haydn's *Cello Concerto in D major* (with Feuermann and an unidentified orchestra), the Mozart Clarinet Concerto (with Kell and the London Philharmonic), *Les Sylphides* (orchestrated by Ainslie Murray and White, with the London Philharmonic), Vieuxtemps' Violin Concerto No. 5 (with Heifetz and the London Symphony), Strauss's *Le Bourgeois gentilhomme*, Mahler's *Ich atmet' einen linden Duft* (with Kullman and an orchestra), Quilter's *Children's Overture* (with the Light Symphony Orchestra), Grainger's *Handel in the Strand* and *Mock Morris* (with the New Light Symphony Orchestra), *The Song of Hiawatha* of Coleridge-Taylor (with the Royal Choral Society and Royal Albert Hall Orchestra) and the same composer's *Petite Suite de concert* (with the London Symphony Orchestra). All were for HMV and Columbia.

During World War II and in the years immediately afterwards he was very active in the recording studios. With the Liverpool Philharmonic Orchestra for EMI there were the overture and Pastoral Symphony from *Messiah*, the sinfonia from the Bach *Easter Oratorio* (arranged by Whittaker), the Harty arrangement of the *Music for the Royal Fireworks*, another Harty arrangement the *John Field Suite*, Gluck's *Alceste* overture (arranged by Weingartner), Cimarosa's Oboe Concerto (arranged by Benjamin, with Goossens), Mendelssohn's Symphony No. 3, the Weber Bassoon Concerto (with Brooke), Brahms' *Academic Festival Overture*, *Le Rouet d'Omphale*, the Theme and Variations from Tchaikovsky's Suite No. 3, the Cossack Dance from *Mazeppa*, *Valse triste*, the overtures to *Patience* and *The Yeomen of the Guard*, Rachmaninov's *Rhapsody on a Theme of Paganini* and Dohnányi's *Variations on a Nursery Tune* (with Smith), Ireland's *London Overture*, Britten's *The Young Person's Guide to the Orchestra*, Elgar's *Wand of Youth* Suite No. 1 and The Serious Doll from the *Nursery Suite*, Gardiner's *Shepherd Fennel's Dance*, Vaughan Williams' *The Lark Ascending* (with Wise) and the Delius Violin Concerto (with Sammons). On 78 r.p.m. discs at this stage he also recorded Haydn's Symphony No. 98, Schubert's Symphony No. 9 and the Scarlatti arrangement by Tommasini *The Good-humoured Ladies* (with the London Symphony Orchestra for Decca), Harty's arrangement of the *Music for the Royal Fireworks* and the Arrival of the Queen of Sheba from *Solomon*, Beethoven's Symphonies Nos 4 and 5 and the Piano Concerto No. 4 (with Lympany), Grieg's *Lyric Suite*, the overtures *Dichter und Bauer*, *Semiramide* and

Béatrice et Bénédict, Tchaikovsky's Symphony No. 4, and the *Enigma Variations* and *Pomp and Circumstance March No. 5* (with the National Symphony Orchestra for Decca), the Handel/Harty *Water Music*, Brahms' *Variations on the St Antony Chorale*, a *Carmen* suite, the Dance of the Hours from *La Gioconda*, the waltz from *The Sleeping Beauty*, the waltz and polonaise from *Eugene Onegin* and the overture to *The Wasps* and the *Fantasia on Greensleeves* of Vaughan Williams (with the Hallé orchestra for EMI), Arne's *Rule Britannia* and Parry's *Jerusalem* (with the Royal Choral Society and Philharmonia Orchestra for EMI), Handel's *Zadok the Priest*, the Hallelujah and Amen choruses from *Messiah* and the Elgar *Pomp and Circumstance March No. 1* (with the Royal Festival Hall Orchestra and Choir for EMI), Beethoven's Piano Concerto No. 3 (with Moiseiwitsch), the prelude to *Das Rheingold*, Borodin's *Nocturne*, Fauré's *Pavane*, the *L'Arlésienne* Suite No. 2, a *Carmen* suite and some arias sung by Isobel Baillie (with the Philharmonia Orchestra for EMI). He also directed a set illustrating the instruments of the orchestra.

On LP, Sargent recorded for Decca, EMI, Everest, Reader's Digest and for Philips. His series with the Huddersfield Choral Society and the Liverpool Philharmonic Orchestra, made between 1954 and 1959, included *Messiah* (twice, in 1954 and in 1959), *The Dream of Gerontius* (for the second time, in 1955), *Israel in Egypt*, *Elijah*, *Belshazzar's Feast*, *Zadok the Priest* and From the Censer Curling Rise from *Solomon*. Despite criticisms about its style, *Messiah* was something of a best-seller. For Decca he recorded *The Planets*, Bartók's Violin Concerto No. 2 (with Rostal), Albert Coates' arrangement of a suite from Purcell's music, Walton's *Orb and Sceptre*, Bax's *Coronation March*, Elgar's *Enigma Variations* and *Pomp and Circumstance Marches Nos 1* and *4*, Rawsthorne's Piano Concerto No. 2 (with Curzon) and a recital with Kathleen Ferrier (with the London Symphony Orchestra), the Tchaikovsky Violin Concerto (with Ricci and the New Symphony Orchestra) and *The Mikado*, *HMS Pinafore*, *The Pirates of Penzance*, *Princess Ida* and *The Yeomen of the Guard* (with the Royal Philharmonic Orchestra *et al.*). For EMI he recorded *The Beggar's Opera*, *The Gondoliers*, *Iolanthe*, *The Mikado*, *The Pirates of Penzance*, *Trial by Jury*, *The Yeomen of the Guard* and the overtures to *HMS Pinafore*, *The Sorcerer*, *Box and Cox*, *Princess Ida* and *Patience*, and the dances from German's *Nell Gwynn* and *Henry VIII* (with the Pro Arte Orchestra *et al.*); the overtures to *Il barbiere di Siviglia*, *William Tell*, *Semiramide* and *Il viaggio a Reims* (with the Vienna Philharmonic Orchestra); the Mendelssohn Violin Concerto (with de Vito), the Elgar Violin Concerto (with Heifetz), Dohnányi's *Suite in F sharp minor* and Vaughan Williams' *Towards the Unknown Region*, *Serenade to Music*, *Fantasia on Greensleeves* and overture to *The Wasps* (with the London Symphony Orchestra *et al.*), Arne's *Rule Britannia*, the Dvořák *Symphonic Variations* and Cello Concerto (with Tortelier), *Enigma Variations* and *Pomp and Circumstance March No. 1*, Parry's *Jerusalem*, Vaughan Williams' *Fantasia on a Theme by Thomas Tallis*, the *Theme and Variations* from Tchaikovsky's Suite No. 3, Miaskovsky's Cello Concerto and Saint-Saëns' Cello Concerto No. 1 (with Rostropovich), Dohnányi's *Variations on a Nursery Tune* (with Smith) and *Hiawatha's Wedding Feast* of Coleridge-Taylor (with the Philharmonia Orchestra *et al.*); Handel's *Water Music* and *Music for the Royal Fireworks* (arranged by Harty), *Overture in D minor* (arranged by Elgar) and overture to *Samson*, Beethoven's Symphony No. 3, *Má Vlast*, the *Romeo and Juliet* fantasy-overture, *1812* overture, *Marche slave* and waltz from *The Sleeping Beauty*, Schubert's Symphony No. 8 and incidental music to *Rosamunde*, Rachmaninov's Piano Concerto No. 2 (with Lympany), a disc of Strauss waltzes, the overtures to *The Bartered Bride*, *Die Meistersinger*, *La scala di seta*, *The Hebrides* and *Le Carnaval romain*, *La Boutique fantasque*, Britten's *Simple Symphony*, the ballet music from Holst's *The Perfect Fool*, a suite from *Façade*, and Delius' *Songs of Farewell*, *A Song before Sunrise* and Cello Concerto (with du Pré, and the Royal Philharmonic Orchestra); the *Water Music* and *Music for the Royal Fireworks* (arranged by Harty), the incidental music for *A Midsummer Night's Dream* (interpolated into the Old Vic production of the play), Tchaikovsky's Symphony No. 5, *Andante cantabile* and *Marche slave*, Rachmaninov's Symphony No. 3, Dvořák's *Slavonic Dance No. 10*, the Fête polonaise from *Le Roi malgré lui*, Sibelius Symphonies Nos 1, 2 and 5, *Finlandia* and *Pohjola's Daughter*, Elgar's Cello Concerto (with Tortelier) and *Wand of Youth* Suite No. 2, Vaughan Williams' *Fantasia on a Theme of Thomas Tallis*, Britten's *The Young Person's Guide to the Orchestra*, Holst's *Beni Mora* and *The Planets*, the Letter Scene from *Eugene Onegin* (with Hammond), the Scherzo from Litolff's *Concerto symphonique No. 4* (with Cherkassky) and the overtures *Ruy Blas*, *Di Ballo* and to *Hänsel und Gretel* (with the BBC Symphony Orchestra), *Les Sylphides* (in his own arrangement) and the ballet music from *William Tell* (with the Royal Opera House Orchestra). For RCA Victor he recorded the Bach Double Concerto (with Heifetz and Friedman), Bruch's Violin Concerto No. 1 and *Scottish Fantasy*, and Vieuxtemps' Violin Concerto No. 5 (with Heifetz, and the New Symphony Orchestra); for Everest Prokofiev's Symphony No. 5, Tchaikovsky's Symphony No. 5, *Fontane di Roma* and *Pini di Roma*, *Pictures at an Exhibition* and *A Night on the Bare Mountain*, Shostakovich's Symphony No. 9 and the *Lieutenant Kijé* suite (with the London Symphony Orchestra); for Philips Walton's Viola Concerto (with Primrose and the Royal Philharmonic Orchestra) and for Reader's Digest Chopin's Piano Concerto No. 1 (with Wild and the Royal Philharmonic Orchestra).

Sargent was the butt of Beecham's wit more than once. Sir Thomas was asked, after he had appointed Sargent as his assistant with the London Philharmonic Orchestra, why he had such a high opinion of him. He answered that 'if you ever appoint a deputy, appoint one whom you can trust technically; but his calibre must be such that the public will always be glad to see *you* back again'. Beecham always called Sargent 'Flash'; he was told that Sargent had gone to Tokyo. 'Good God', he replied, 'Malcolm in Tokyo! What is he doing there?' 'Conducting. He's having an amazing success.' 'I see,' said Beecham, 'a Flash in Ja-pan.' After a tour of the Middle East, Sargent told Beecham he had been detained and released by the Arabs. 'Released,' exclaimed Beecham. 'Had they heard you play?' But Beecham did not always have the last say. Once he arrived at one of his favourite hotels in the provinces unannounced, and asked for his favourite room, to be told that it was already occupied. He suggested that the occupant might be asked to transfer to another room, but the manager of the hotel said that he thought the man had retired. They both went to the room, knocked at the door, and made their request. 'Certainly not. I'll do nothing of the kind,' was the response. 'But', said the manager, 'this is Sir Thomas Beecham.' The man said: 'I don't care if it's Sir Malcolm Sargent.'

Satanowski, Robert (b. 1918). Born in Łódź, Poland, Satanowski studied at the Academy of Music there, graduated in 1951, and was a conducting pupil of Wodiczki at Warsaw. He was musical director of Radio Gdańsk (1949–50), second conductor of the Lublin Philharmonic Orchestra (1951–4), and artistic director of the Pomeranian Philharmonic Orchestra at Bydgoszcz (1954–8). He studied opera production with Felsenstein at the Komische Oper in East Berlin, and conducting with Karajan (1958–60), became general music director at Karl-Marx-Stadt (1960–61), music director of the Poznań Philharmonic Orchestra (1961–9), founded the Poznań Chamber Orchestra (1962), was music director of the Poznań State Opera (1963–70), general music director of the Niederrheinische Symphony Orchestra and Opera at Krefeld (1969–75), music director of the Kraków Opera (since 1975) and of the Wrocław Opera (since 1977), and has also been a guest conductor in FR Germany, Hungary, the USSR, Romania, Switzerland, Austria, Scandinavia *et al.* His recordings, for Polskie Nagrania, include Gotabeck's Symphonies Nos 1, 2 and 3, Wánski's *Symphonies in D* and *G*, and symphonies by Hazzewski, Putrowski and Bohdanowicz (with the Poznań Chamber Orchestra), Wieniawski's Violin Concertos No. 1 (with Krysa and the Warsaw National Philharmonic Orchestra) and No. 2 and Szymanowski's Violin Concerto No. 2 (with Treger and the Polish National Symphony Orchestra), Moniuszko's one-act opera *Verbum Nobile* (with the Polish State Opera Orchestra *et al.*), Różycki's *Symphonic Scherzo* and Symphonic Poems Op. 8 and Op. 22 (with the Poznań Philharmonic Orchestra). The Wieniawski Violin Concerto No. 1 and the symphonies of Gotabeck and Wánski were re-issued in the United States by Musical Heritage Society.

Sauguet, Henri (b. 1901). Born in Bordeaux, Sauguet studied in Paris with Koechlin and Canteloube, and became associated with Desormière, Jacob and Cliquest-Peyel in a group called 'L'École d'Arcueil', with Satie its patron. He made his debut in 1924 as a composer with the opéra-bouffe *Le Plumet du colonel*, following it with the ballets *Les Roses* and *La Chatte* (1927), which was performed under his leadership by the Diaghilev ballet more than 100 times. His subsequent compositions were numerous and included the opera *La Chartreuse de Parme* (1939) and the ballets *Les Forains* (1939) and *La Dame aux Camélias* (1957). He has called himself a traditionalist but anti-academic composer, whose music is to delight, not frighten. Generally, performances of his compositions have been confined to France, and little of his music has been available on disc elsewhere. He has recorded, as a conductor, his *Concertino for Harmonica and Orchestra* (with Garden and the ORTF Orchestra for Bärenreiter), *Les Forains* (with the Lamoureux Orchestra for Philips and Chant du Monde), *Deux Mouvements pour archets à la mémoire de P. Gilson* (with the ORTF

Chamber Orchestra for Bärenreiter), *Mélodie concertante* (with Rostropovich and the Moscow Radio Symphony Orchestra, for Melodiya, issued in France by Chant du Monde and in the United States by EMI), *Une Inconstante*, *Les Animaux et leurs hommes*, *Crépuscule*, *Neiges*, *L'Instant* and *Chamber Divertimento* (with an ensemble for Charlin).

Savini, Ino. The Italian conductor Savini studied at the Accademia di Santa Cecilia in Rome under Respighi, was conductor at the Royal Opera at Stockholm for four years, and has been chief conductor at the Bologna Opera. In 1972 he conducted at Barcelona. He has recorded for Supraphon a complete *Il trovatore* and *L'elisir d'amore* (with the Prague Chamber Orchestra *et al.*), *La forza del destino* (with the Opera Stabile del Viotti Orchestra *et al.*), selections from *Coppélia* (with the Brno Philharmonic Orchestra) and a recital with the tenor Bordin.

Sawallisch, Wolfgang (b. 1923). Born in Munich, Sawallisch showed early evidence of a talent for music, and was learning the piano at the age of five. At 11 he attended a performance of *Hänsel und Gretel*, which profoundly affected him, so that he determined to become a musician and conductor. After private studies with Ruoff, Haas and Sachse in Munich, he served in the German armed forces (1942–6) and was taken prisoner in Italy. He resumed his studies at the Munich Conservatory after the war, and joined the Augsburg Opera in 1947 as a repetiteur, then became first conductor of operetta (1950–51), and remained there until 1953. He was assistant to Markevitch at the conductors' course at Salzburg (1952–3), was appointed general music director at Aachen (1953–8), then at Wiesbaden (1958–60), was music director at the Cologne Opera (1960–63), principal conductor of the Vienna Symphony Orchestra (1960–70), head of the conductors' class at the Cologne Academy of Music, general music director of the Hamburg Philharmonic Orchestra (1960–73), and has been general music director of the Bavarian State Opera (since 1971), artistic director of the Suisse Romande Orchestra (since 1973), honorary conductor of the NHK Symphony Orchestra, Tokyo, and permanent conductor at La Scala, Milan. He first conducted at the Bayreuth Festivals in 1957 with *Tristan und Isolde*, and has also conducted at festivals at Edinburgh, Vienna and Montreux, *inter alia.* His first visit to London was in 1957 as the accompanist to Schwarzkopf in a Wolf lieder recital; he returned to conduct the Philharmonia Orchestra the next year. In 1964 he toured the United States with the Vienna Symphony Orchestra.

Sawallisch is one of the most distinguished German conductors today. Both as a personality and as a conductor he is conservative and restrained; his musical preferences are for the great classical and romantic composers which he performs with the highest regard for the printed score. He is unsympathetic to the second Viennese school, believing dodecaphonic music to be an aberration, but has performed with enthusiasm the music of Bartók, Hindemith, Honegger, Britten, Orff and Stravinsky (up to, but not including, *Agon*). His disdain for the spectacular, for public acclaim and for the imposition of his personality *per se* on audiences separates him from many of his contemporaries; his correctness as a conductor results in performances that are admirable in many ways, but not for their colour or expressiveness. He has not the musical temperament to be cast as the successor to Walter or Furtwängler; a certain straightforwardness in phrasing and feeling rob his interpretations of composers such as Wagner and Strauss of the final touch of inspiration. He is unattracted by the great international opera houses, has refused approaches from Berlin and New York, preferring to remain with the permanent ensembles of provincial opera houses rather than accepting the conditions imposed by the *ad hoc* assemblies of operatic stars. He conducts from memory, believing that a conductor should be 'so conversant with the music he is interpreting that he has the melody, structure, and metre in his head. In this way there can be much deeper and closer contact with the orchestra. It is as though a barrier had been removed. The conductor stands right in the centre of the music, and there is no distraction from having to turn the pages of a score.'

Remington, the US label, issued some early LPs of Sawallisch conducting the RIAS Symphony Orchestra: Bach's *Brandenburg Concerto No. 4*, Handel's Concerto Grosso Op. 6 No. 5, and Tchaikovsky's Piano Concerto No. 1 (with Hansen). DGG also released the overture to *The Merry Wives of Windsor* (with the Bamberg Symphony Orchestra) and discs of excerpts from *Cavalleria rusticana* and *Der Wildschütz* (with the Bavarian State Opera). He made his first records for EMI in 1957: Orff's *Carmina Burana* (with the Cologne Radio Symphony Orchestra *et al.*), *Die Kluge* and *Der Mond* (with the Philharmonia Orchestra *et al.*). Then followed a series of discs with the Philharmonic Orchestra, which included Strauss's *Le Bourgeois gentilhomme* and the waltz scene from *Intermezzo*, *Capriccio* and the two Horn Concertos (with Brain), suites from *Swan Lake* and *Nutcracker*, Weber's overtures *Abu Hassan*, *Euryanthe*, *Der Freischütz*, *Oberon*, *Preciosa*, *Beherrscher der Geister* and *Jubel*, Dvořák's Symphonies Nos 8 and 9, *Carnival* overture and *Scherzo capriccioso*, Mozart's Piano Concertos K. 467 and K. 482 (with Annie Fischer), and the *Tannhäuser* overture, prelude to *Die Meistersinger*, and the Rhine Journey and Funeral Music from *Götterdämmerung*. Also for EMI he recorded *Die Zauberflöte*, *Abu Hassan*, Handel's *Music for the Royal Fireworks*, Haydn's *St Antony Divertimento*, several movements from Mozart's Serenade K. 361 and Schubert's *Der Zwillingsbrüder* (with the Bavarian State Opera Orchestra *et al.*), the four symphonies of Schumann, the *Manfred* overture and the *Overture, Scherzo and Finale* (with the Dresden Staatskapelle).

For Philips Sawallisch has been a dependable and successful recording artist. His Bayreuth performances of *Der fliegende Holländer* and *Tannhäuser* were recorded, and his other major recordings for the company were Beethoven's Symphonies Nos 6 and 7, with the *König Stephan* and *Fidelio* overtures (with the Amsterdam Concertgebouw Orchestra), the complete symphonies of Schubert and the two overtures *In the Italian Style* (with the Dresden Staatskapelle); also Mendelssohn's complete symphonies (with the New Philharmonia Orchestra) and those of Brahms, with the *Tragic* and *Academic Festival Overtures*, *Variations on the St Antony Chorale*, *Schicksalslied*, *Alto Rhapsody* (with Heynis) and *Ein deutsches Requiem* (with the Vienna Symphony Orchestra *et al.*), as well as Haydn's Symphonies Nos 92, 94, 100 and 101 (with the Vienna Symphony Orchestra), *Elijah* (with the Leipzig Gewandhaus Orchestra *et al.*), Schubert's Masses Nos 5 and 6 (with the Dresden Staatskapelle *et al.*), Tchaikovsky's Symphony No. 5, Mendelssohn's Symphony No. 4, Schubert's Symphony No. 8, the *Siegfried Idyll*, the overtures to *Rienzi* and *Der fliegende Holländer*, the Venusberg Music from *Tannhäuser*, the preludes to Acts I and III of *Lohengrin* and *Die Meistersinger* and the prelude and Good Friday Music from *Parsifal*, and two discs of Strauss waltzes (with the Vienna Symphony Orchestra). For Philips he also accompanied Prey in *Winterreise*, and for Eterna, Ariola and RCA accompanied on the piano and directed Rossini's *Petite Messe solennelle* (with Schreier, Fischer-Dieskau *et al.*). Turnabout re-issued the set of Brahms symphonies in the United States. These recordings, particularly of the Schubert, Schumann and Brahms symphonies were highly praised for their faithful interpretations and for the complete absence of personal idiosyncracies, and it was evident that Sawallisch could elicit the finest playing from the great orchestras he conducted. Unfortunately by 1977 most of his records had been deleted from the catalogues in the US and Britain.

Scaglia, Ferruccio (b. 1921). Born in Turin, Scaglia studied at the Verdi Conservatory there and at the Accademia di Santa Cecilia in Rome, and at the Accademia Chigiana in Siena. He performed as a violinist (1937–48), was concertmaster of the Radio Italiana Orchestra at Rome (1948), and became artistic director and permanent conductor of the Teatro Massimo Bellini in Catania. For La Guilde Internationale du Disque he recorded excerpts from *Il pirata*, *Norma*, *La sonnambula* and *I Capuletti e i Montecchi* (with the Rome Philharmonic Orchestra *et al.*) and for CIDM Petrassi's *Coro di morti* (with the Rome Symphony Orchestra and Chorus).

Schaenen, Lee (b. 1925). Born in New York, Schaenen studied at the Juilliard School and at Columbia University, was a repetiteur and assistant conductor with the New York City Opera (1945–53), and first conducted with the company in 1949. He also conducted at the Teatro San Carlo, Naples (1954), at La Scala, Milan (1956), in other European cities, was chief conductor at Berne, Switzerland (1959–65), has been the music director of the Dallas Civic Orchestra, and teaches at the Southern Methodist University at Dallas. Musical Heritage Society has issued discs in which he conducts the Austrian Tonkünstler Orchestra, in Boccherini's Symphonies Op. 21 Nos 1, 3, 5 and 6, Bonporti's Violin Concerto Op. 11 No. 4 (with Glenn), and Mozart's Serenade K. 185 and March K. 189.

Schalk, Franz (1863–1931). The eminent Austrian conductor Schalk was born in Vienna, studied with Hellmesberger, Epstein and Bruckner, and conducted at Reichenberg (1888–9), Prague (1895–8), the New York Metropolitan Opera (1898–9), the Berlin Royal Opera (1899–1900) and finally at the Vienna Court Opera (1900–28), where he shared the directorship with Strauss until 1924. He also conducted the subscription concerts of the Vienna Philharmonic Orchestra, was conductor of the Vienna Gesellschaft der Musikfreunde (1904–21) and director of the school of conducting at the Imperial Academy of Music in Vienna. In 1920 he was one of the founders of the annual Salzburg Festivals at which he conducted, visited Covent Garden, London, in 1898, 1907 and 1911, conducted the Hallé Orchestra at Manchester in 1911, and took the Vienna Opera to Paris in 1927 to perform *Fidelio* at the Beethoven centenary celebrations.

Schalk and his brother Josef were both enthusiastic advocates for Bruckner and Wolf; together with Loewe they made piano-duet arrangements of some of Bruckner's symphonies and performed these versions in public before the orchestral forms were given. Schalk himself gave the first performance of the Symphony No. 5 at Graz in 1894, and was known as a most sensitive interpreter of the composer. With the intention of making the symphonies more accessible to the public, he altered the scores, but these editions are condemned today. Even as recently as 1973 the conductor Matačić recorded Symphony No. 5 in the Schalk edition, with its cuts in the finale and with sections re-composed and re-orchestrated. Schalk was also a devoted interpreter of Beethoven, Schubert and Bach, at a time when Bach was little known in Vienna, but he disliked modern music. He was very tall, and his long arms appeared to make it difficult for him to give a clear beat; nonetheless his interpretations were considered to be absolutely convincing, concentrated and unique. He was also an outstanding conductor of opera and gave sympathetic and unhurried support to his singers. In Vienna, Schalk collaborated with Mahler, and eventually gave the first performance there in 1924 of the two completed movements of Mahler's Symphony No. 10, but Michael Kennedy, in his biography of Mahler (1974), wrote that Mahler had regarded him as pedestrian and incompetent. Despite his visits to London, Paris and New York, Schalk's fame was mostly limited to Vienna, but this did not disconcert him. He recorded Schubert's Symphony No. 8 (with the Berlin Staatsoper Orchestra for Odeon) and Beethoven's Symphonies Nos 5, 6 and 9, and the *Leonore No. 3* overture (with the Vienna Philharmonic Orchestra for HMV in 1928–9).

Schat, Peter (b. 1935). Born in Utrecht, Schat studied at the Conservatory there, with Seiber in London and with Boulez in Basel. He has written: 'The first performance of one of my pieces was in 1954. A critic thought he heard Schoenberg's influence in the piece, and so I decided to listen to something by the composer quickly. My astonished conclusion was that the critic knew something about music.' Also, 'I work in the Schoenbergian tradition, although I think that his method has resulted, in the second half of this century, in administrative rigidity of tone-material, in mannerism and incomprehensibility – as he predicted himself, incidentally' (Donemus' biographical leaflet). A visit to Cuba led to a collectively composed opera, *Reconstructie*, in which he participated and which caused a sensation, and since 1967 the same group who produced the opera established an electro-instrumental studio which became the Amsterdam Electric Circus, and gives performances in parks and public places. For Donemus, Schat conducted the Netherlands Wind Quintet in his *Thema* and *To You*.

Scheide, William (b. 1914). Born in Philadelphia, Scheide studied at Princeton and Columbia Universities and specialised in the music of J. S. Bach. He taught at Cornell University, and in 1946 formed the Bach Aria Group to perform arias and duets from the cantatas of Bach. The group has included Samuel Baron (flute), Robert Bloom (oboe), Lois Marshall (alto) and other distinguished artists. It has toured the United States, Canada, South America and Europe, and has recorded, under Scheide's direction, collections of Bach arias for Decca (US), Vox, MGM and RCA. Also for RCA Scheide recorded Bach's Cantata No. 42 with the Group and the Victor Symphony Orchestra.

Schenkman, Edgar (b. 1908). Born in New Market, New Jersey, Schenkman studied at the Juilliard School where he conducted the Juilliard Orchestra. He was conductor of the Friends of Music Orchestra at Toledo (1943–50), the Norfolk Symphony Orchestra, Virginia (1948) and the Richmond Symphony Orchestra, Virginia (from 1957, concurrent with his post at Norfolk), and was violist in the Kennedy Quartet which was resident in Bangkok, Thailand, where he also taught the instrument (1969–73). For Concert Hall he recorded Schuman's Symphony No. 5 on 78 r.p.m. discs, with the Concert Hall Society Orchestra.

Scherbaum, Adolf (b. 1909). Born at Eger, Habsburg Hungary, Scherbaum studied the trumpet at Prague and Vienna, played the instrument in the orchestra at Brno (1931–40), in the Berlin Philharmonic Orchestra (1941–5), at Bratislava (1945–51), and settled in Hamburg, where he played in the North German Radio Orchestra (1951–67). Since 1967 he has worked as a soloist, and as professor for trumpet at the Hochschule für Musik at Saarbrücken. As a trumpeter he is a specialist in baroque music and has toured internationally, spending several months of the year regularly in the United States. DGG recorded him conducting and playing with the Hamburg Baroque Ensemble trumpet concertos of Telemann, Torelli and Vivaldi.

Scherchen, Hermann (1891–1966). Born in Berlin, Scherchen was largely self-taught, and played the viola in the Blüthner and Berlin Philharmonic Orchestras (1907–10). He conducted his first concert with the Berlin Philharmonic in 1911, and in that year prepared Schoenberg's *Pierrot Lunaire* for performances by the composer. In 1912 he gave some notable concerts with the Berlin Philharmonic of Schoenberg's *Chamber Symphony*, Mahler's Symphony No. 5 and Bruckner's Symphony No. 9. After a season as conductor of the Riga Symphony Orchestra (1914), he was interned in Russia during World War I, and after returning to Berlin founded and was conductor for the New Music Society, formed the Scherchen Quartet, lectured at the Hochschule für Musik, directed the German Working Men's Choral Society, and founded and edited the journal *Melos* (1921–2), which was devoted to modern music. He was conductor of the New Grotrian-Steinweg Orchestra in Leipzig (1920 and 1925), succeeded Furtwängler as conductor of the Museum Concerts at Frankfurt am Main (1922), conducted concerts at the Musikcollegium at Winterthur (1932–8), was general music director at Königsberg (1928–33), and directed an annual conductors' course in Paris (from 1932).

An outspoken anti-fascist, but not Jewish, Scherchen left Germany in 1933, edited the periodical *Musica Viva* in Brussels (1933–6), conducted for the Musica Viva organisation in Vienna (1937), conducted the music festival at Gstaad (1941–2) and was the music director of the Swiss Radio at Zürich and Beromünster (1945–50). In 1955 in Zürich he founded and toured with the Ars Viva Orchestra; he conducted extensively in Europe and South America, and at the annual festivals of the International Society for Contemporary Music. He directed schools for conductors in Switzerland and at Venice and established a studio at Gravesano for experiments in electro-acoustics (1954). He was a guest conductor at La Scala, Milan (1963–4), gave the first performance of Henze's *König Hirsch* in Berlin (1956) and Dallapicolla's *Il Prigioniero* in Florence (1963), and made his first appearance in the United States with the Philadelphia Orchestra in 1964. He composed choral and instrumental music, and wrote two books, *The Nature of Music*, and *A Handbook of Conducting* which was translated into English by M. D. Calvacoressi.

Scherchen was an extraordinarily versatile and active musician and conductor. He was an indefatigable and ardent champion of modern music; in Dent's words, 'to no other conductor do contemporary composers owe as much as to Scherchen'. Among the first performances he led were Bartók's Violin Concerto No. 2, the orchestral pieces from *Wozzeck*, Roussel's *Aeneas* and Shostakovich's Symphony No. 3. He insisted that his students in his conducting classes should 'hear the work of art in (their) imagination as wholly and completely as the composer conceived it', before they attempted to perform it. He was, in addition, a deeply committed interpreter of Bach, Handel, Haydn, Beethoven and others, of whose music he had a profound knowledge, and he gave unconventional but often arresting performances of the baroque, classical and romantic repertoire. Ironically, although he had such a considerable reputation as an advocate of modern music, he became known to a worldwide musical public as a conductor of the standard repertoire, through the many records he made for Westminster. He conducted widely in Europe, but visited the United States only once, two years before his death; by then his name was familiar to all record collectors.

Scherchen's discography is long, as he was one of the most prolific recording conductors in the first decade or so of LP. Before that time he had made a number of 78 r.p.m. records for HMV with the Winterthur Municipal Orchestra, including dances by Rameau and Gluck, the overture to Rousseau's *Le Devin du village*, Tartini's *Violin Concerto in E major* (with Ribaupierre) and Gluck's Flute Concerto (with Urfer), the overture to Purcell's *Dido and Aeneas*, Mozart's *Les petits riens* and Symphony No. 39, Leopold Mozart's *Toy Symphony*, symphonies by C. P. E. Bach and Fritz, the Serenade from Haydn's String Quartet Op. 3 No. 5, Boccherini's Minuet, the overture to *Orphée aux enfers*, *Kaiserwalzer* and Hsiao-Shusien's *Chinese Dream Pictures*. For Decca he also recorded on 78s with the Winterthur Orchestra the overtures to *La belle Hélène* and *La forza del destino*.

The LP records were issued almost entirely by Westminster in the United States, except for some which were released by Ducretet-Thomson, Decca, Supraphon, Telefunken, Amadeo and Wergo; the Westminster recordings were, in many instances, released on other labels, such as Nixa and Vega, in countries other than the US. Some confusion surrounds the identity of some of the orchestras, particularly those with which he recorded in Vienna and London, and the same performances sometimes appeared on different labels with the orchestras named differently. His records included the Bach *Brandenburg Concertos*, four orchestral Suites, the two Violin Concertos (with Barylli), *St Matthew Passion*, *St John Passion*, the *Mass in B minor* and Cantatas Nos 32, 53, 54, 76, 84, 106, 140, 170, 198, 202 and 210, Vivaldi's Concertos Op. 8 (with *The Four Seasons* released separately), Two-Trumpet Concerto (with Delmotte and Haneuse) and *Gloria*, Gabrieli's *Canzoni in primi toni*, Trumpet Concertos of Torelli and Leopold Mozart (with Delmotte), Two-Trumpet Concertos of Corelli and Manfredini (with Delmotte and Haneuse), Stölzel's *Concerto Grosso a quattro chori*, Telemann's Three-Trumpet and Two-Oboe Concerto, Handel's Concerti Grossi Op. 6, *Water Music*, Two-Trumpet Concerto (with Delmotte and Haneuse) and *Messiah*, Haydn's Symphonies Nos 44, 45, 48, 49, 88, 92, 93, 94, 96, 98 and 101, *Die sieben letzten Worte des Erlösers am Kreuz* and Trumpet Concerto (with Delmotte), Mozart's Piano Concertos K. 242 and K. 365 (with Badura-Skoda and Gianoli), *Eine kleine Nachtmusik* and *Requiem*, Beethoven's Symphonies Nos 1, 3, 6, 7 and 9, five Piano Concertos (with Badura-Skoda), overtures *Leonore Nos 1, 2* and *3*, *Fidelio*, *Coriolan*, *König Stephan*, *Namensfeier*, *Prometheus*, *Die Ruinen von Athen* and *Die Weihe des Hauses*, incidental music for *Egmont*, *Wellington's Victory*, *German Dances* Nos 1, 2, 4, 6, 8, 10 and 12 and *Christus am Ölberge*, Schubert's Symphony No. 6, Mendelssohn's Symphony No. 3, Liszt's two Piano Concertos (with Farnadi), *Les Préludes*, *Hunnenschlacht*, *Mephisto Waltz* and *Mazeppa*, *Siegfried Idyll*, Brahms' Symphony No. 1 and Double Concerto (with Fournier and Janigro), Tchaikovsky's Symphony No. 4 and Piano Concertos Nos 1 and 2 (with Farnadi), *Moldau* and overture and dances from *The Bartered Bride*, the Polovtsian Dances from *Prince Igor*, Flight of the Bumble Bee from *Tsar Saltan*, excerpts from *El amor brujo*, the polka and fugue from *Schwanda the Bagpiper*, Mahler's Symphonies Nos 2, 5, 7, 8 (recorded at a public concert in Vienna in 1951), and the *adagio* from No. 10, *Kindertotenlieder* and *Lieder eines fahrenden gesellen* (with Lucretia West), *Le Carnaval des animaux* and *Danse macabre*, the Peer Gynt Suites Nos 1 and 2, Bartók's Piano Concertos Nos 2 and 3, and Rachmaninov's Piano Concerto No. 2 (with Farnadi), Chabrier's *España*, *L'Apprenti sorcier*, *Boléro*, Enesco's *Romanian Rhapsody No. 1*, *A Night on the Bare Mountain*, a suite from *Gayane*, Orff's *Entrata*, and the overtures to *Der Freischütz*, *Zampa*, *Fra Diavolo*, *Donna Diana*, *William Tell*, *La gazza ladra*, *Orphée aux enfers*, *Barbe-bleue*, *La Belle Hélène*, *La Grande-Duchesse de Gérolstein* and *La Vie parisienne* (with the Vienna State Opera Orchestra, *et al.*).

He also recorded the *Brandenburg Concertos* (with the Cento Soli Orchestra); the four Bach Suites, Handel's Concerti Grossi Op. 6 and Geminiani's Concerti Grossi Op. 3 (with the English Baroque Orchestra); Bach's *Ein musikalisches Opfer* (with an ensemble, for Decca); and *Die Kunst der Fuge* (arranged by Vuataz, with the Beromünster Radio Orchestra for Decca); Mozart's Symphonies Nos 40 and 41 and Flute and Harp Concerto (with Bourden and Laskine, and the Champs-Élysées Theatre Orchestra for Ducretet-Thomson); Werner's Pastorale, sinfonias by C. P. E. Bach and Richter, and Cimarosa's Sinfonia Concertante (with the Ars Viva Orchestra for Amadeo); some Beethoven dances and Schubert's Symphony No. 8 (with the Czech Philharmonic Orchestra for Supraphon); Berlioz's *Grande Messe des morts* (with the Paris Opéra Orchestra *et al.*) and *Les Troyens à Carthage* (with the Paris Conservatoire Orchestra *et al.*); the Weber overtures *Abu Hassan*, *Euryanthe*, *Jubel*, *Obéron*, *Peter Schmoll* and *Preciosa* (with the Paris Opéra Orchestra); Schoenberg's *Erwartung* (with Pilarcyzk and the North-West German Philharmonic Orchestra for Wergo); *Messiah*, *Symphonie fantastique*, *Scheherazade*, *Antar*, *Russian Easter Festival* overture, *Capriccio espagnol*, *Capriccio italien*, *Romeo and Juliet* fantasy-overture, *1812* overture and *Marche slave* (with the London Symphony Orchestra); Haydn's *Sinfonia concertante* and Danzi's *Sinfonia concertante* (with the Vienna Radio Orchestra); *Die Kunst der Fuge*, Haydn's Symphonies Nos 55, 80, 95, 97, 99, 100, 102, 103 and 104, Mozart's Symphonies Nos 35 and 36, *Eine kleine Nachtmusik*, and Schubert's Symphonies Nos 5 and 8 (with the Vienna Symphony Orchestra); Beethoven's Symphonies Nos 2, 4, 5 and 8, *Harold in Italy* (with Riddle), Liszt's *Hungarian Rhapsodies Nos 1, 2, 3, 4, 5, 6, 9, 12* and *14*, Mahler's Symphony No. 1, Glière's Symphony No. 3 and a suite from *The Red Poppy*, *Peter and the Wolf*, *Lieutenant Kijé* and *Scythian Suite*, *L'Oiseau de feu* and *Petrushka*, and Honegger's *Chant de joie*, *Pacific 231*, *Rugby*, *Mouvement symphonique No. 3* and the prelude to *The Tempest* (with the London Philharmonic Symphony Orchestra, also named the London Philharmonic Orchestra).

There is little evidence on record of Scherchen's skill as a conductor of 20th-century music, especially of the second Viennese school, except for some pieces by Glière, Prokofiev and other Russian composers, Honegger, Bartók, Stravinsky, Enesco, Orff and one or two others. But his many discs of Bach, Haydn, and Beethoven in particular afford an excellent evaluation of his standing as an interpreter of the standard repertoire. With Bach's *Mass in B minor*, *St Matthew Passion* and *Messiah*, he was extremely variable; many numbers in these works had a vital energy that impressed when they were issued in the 1950s. The choruses of *Messiah* are generally magnificent, but other numbers were remarkably ineffective and dull in conception and execution. He was in the vanguard of conductors in recording and popularising Haydn, but his recorded performances were on occasion heavy-handed. Among the Beethoven symphonies No. 8 became famous for its very fast last movement, but No. 9 was curiously stiff and pedantic. The Mahler symphonies which he recorded were fine, and were occasionally a contrast with the recordings of Walter which were then available. Many of the records of Russian music, such as Glière's Symphony No. 3, were remarkable; other notable discs were the *Egmont* music of Beethoven, Vuataz's arrangement of *Die Kunst der Fuge*, and *Les Troyens à Carthage*.

Scherman, Thomas (b. 1917). Born in New York and the son of the founder of the Book-of-the-Month Club, Scherman graduated in mathematics from Columbia University in 1937, and studied conducting under Bamberger at the Mannes School of Music, as well as at the Juilliard School and Columbia University. He assisted Klemperer when he conducted a chamber orchestra for the New School of Social Research in New York (1939), was in the US Signal Corps in World War II (1942–6), then conducted for radio programmes in New York, and was assistant conductor at the National Opera at Mexico City (1947). In 1947 he organised and conducted the Little Orchestra Society in New York, to present unusual programmes of old and new works; at the opening concert he performed David Diamond's *Romeo and Juliet*, Dello Joio's Harp Concerto and Douglas Moores' *A Farm Journal*. With the Little Orchestra Society he introduced children's concerts, Saturday-morning concerts where composers presented their own works, and concert performances of less well known operas and oratorios, such as *Idomeneo*, *Euryanthe*, *L'Enfant et les sortilèges*, *Mavra*, *Acis and Galatea*, *Juditha triumphans* and *L'Enfance du Christ*. He also invited audiences to his final rehearsals, where he commented about the works being performed. This led to a series of records issued first in 1954 by the Book-of-the-Month Club, called Music Appreciation records, in which the complete performance of a major work was accompanied by an analysis, often given by Scherman himself. In this series were, *inter alia*, the Schumann Piano Concerto (with Flissler), the Brahms Violin Concerto (with Shumsky), Mendelssohn's Symphony No. 3 and Ravel's *Piano Concerto in G major* (with Henriot), in which Scherman conducted the orchestra. Szell, among other conductors, also recorded for the series.

Scherman's commercial records were generally of music it was then unusual to find on disc. For Columbia he recorded, with the Little Orchestral Society, Mozart's Three-Piano Concerto (with Lhevinne, Vronsky and Babin), Chopin's *Andante spianato and Grande Polonaise brilliante* (with Arrau), Dvořák's *Legends*, the Tchaikovsky Suite No. 3, Berlioz's *L'Enfance du Christ*, Arensky's *Variations on a Theme by Tchaikovsky*, Act II of Rachmaninov's *The Miserly Knight*, Busoni's Violin Concerto (with Szigeti), Falla's *Master Peter's Puppet Show*, Diamond's *Romeo and Juliet* music and overture to *The Tempest* and Dello Joio's Harp Concerto (with Vito); for Decca a fantasia by Purcell, a concertino by Pergolesi, the two Beethoven *Romances* (with Fuchs), Brahms' Serenade No. 1, Hindemith's *Kammermusik No. 1*, Stravinsky's Suites Nos 1 and 2, Copland's *Our Town* and *The Red Pony*, and Thomson's *The Plow that Broke the Plains*, Acadian songs and dances from *Louisiana Story*; for Remington the Mendelssohn Violin Concerto (with Schneiderhan and the Vienna Symphony Orchestra; also issued by Festival, the orchestra called the Austrian Symphony Orchestra); for Concert Hall Society Bloch's *Four Episodes* and Gluck's Flute Concerto (with the Radio Zürich Symphony Orchestra *et al.*), and Telemann's *Don Quixote* and *Suite in E minor for Flute and Strings* (with Nicolet and the Concert Hall Chamber Orchestra); for DGG Stravinsky's *Concerto for Piano and Wind Instruments* (with Seemann and the Berlin Philharmonic Orchestra); for Desto *Judas Maccabaeus* (with the Vienna State Opera Orchestra *et al.*); for Elaine Music Shop Beethoven's Octet Op. 103 and *Rondino for Wind Octet*; and for RCA Rodgers and Hammerstein's *Cinderella*, Rodgers, Mary and

Melnick's *Three to Make Music*, Meyer and Otto's *Hello World* (with Eleanor Roosevelt) and *The Greatest Sound Around*. The Brahms Serenade No. 1 was issued in Britain by Brunswick.

Schermerhorn, Kenneth (b. 1929). Born in Schenectady, New York, and a graduate of the New England Conservatory, Schermerhorn was an instrumentalist in the Kansas City and Boston Symphony Orchestras, and first conducted when serving in the United States army in Germany as director of the US Seventh Army Symphony Orchestra. He was acclaimed for performances of *Fidelio* at Passau (1954) and for his direction of the orchestra at the Royal Albert Hall, London. Returning to the US he taught at the New England Conservatory (1956), studied with Bernstein at Tanglewood and at La Scala, Milan, and was appointed assistant conductor of the New York Philharmonic Orchestra under Bernstein (1959). He was music director of the American Ballet Theatre (1957–70), conductor of the New Jersey Symphony Orchestra (1963–8), and conductor and music director of the Milwaukee Symphony Orchestra (from 1968). He has also conducted many major orchestras in North and South America and Europe, and at the San Francisco Opera and Mostly Mozart Festival in New York. His repertoire is extemely wide, he has premièred many new compositions, and amongst the many works dedicated to him is Sessions' Symphony No. 6. He is married to the soprano Carol Neblett. Turnabout have issued a disc of him conducting the Milwaukee Symphony Orchestra in Barber's Symphony No. 1 and Mayer's *Octagon for Piano and Orchestra* (with Masselos); earlier, in 1963, Decca (US) released a disc of trumpet concertos by Vivaldi, Biber, Manfredini, Telemann and Torelli (the latter's *Sinfonia in D major*) (with Voisin and Rhea and the Milwaukee Symphony Orchestra).

Schibler, Armin (b. 1920). Born in Kreuzlingen, Switzerland, Schibler studied at the Zürich Conservatory (1940–43), and while in England in 1946 came into contact with Rubbra, Tippett and Britten. He also studied at the courses for new music at Darmstadt (1949–53). Since 1947 he has been a music teacher at the Realgymnasium at Zürich, and has composed operatic, vocal, choral, orchestral, chamber and instrumental music. He recorded his ballet *Prisonnier* (with the Zürich Tonhalle Orchestra for Amadeo), the prelude and wedding music from *Bed of Destiny*, *Concertino for Clarinet* and *Fantasy for Viola* (with the Beromünster Radio Orchestra *et al.* for Amadeo).

Schick, George (b. 1908). Born in Prague, where he studied at the Conservatory, Schick was an assistant conductor at the Prague Opera (1927–38), migrated to the United States, was conductor of the San Carlo Touring Opera Company (1943), at Chicago, of the Montreal Little Symphony Orchestra (1948–50), and then became associate conductor of the Chicago Symphony Orchestra (1950–56). He has recorded as an accompanist for the singers Elisabeth Schumann and Dorothy Maynor, and for Allegro conducted a chamber orchestra *et al.* in an abridgement of Pergolesi's *Il maestro di musica*.

Schillings, Max von (1868–1933). Born at Düren in the Rhineland, Schillings studied at Bonn under Brambach and Königslow, and at Munich University. At Munich he came under the influence of Strauss, and became director of rehearsals for the Bayreuth Festivals (1892), then choirmaster at Bayreuth (1902), assistant conductor, then conductor and general music director (1908–18). He was assistant conductor, then conductor, at the Stuttgart Opera (1908–18), was president of the Allgemeiner Deutscher Musikverein (1910–20), succeeded Strauss as director of the Berlin Staatsoper (1919–25), was president of the Prussian Akademie der Künste, and was appointed director of the Berlin Municipal Opera by the Nazis just before he died in 1933. He visited the United States as conductor of German operas in 1924 and 1931. His compositions include symphonic, choral and chamber music, concertos and four operas, of which *Mona Lisa* enjoyed a success; his operas showed much Wagnerian influence. Furtwängler was one of his pupils.

Schillings recorded for Odeon and Polydor. With the Berlin Staatsoper Orchestra for Odeon (released in Britain by Parlophone, and in the United States by Decca) he led Beethoven's Symphonies Nos 3 and 6 and the *Egmont* overture, the overtures to *Oberon*, *Euryanthe* and *Abu Hassan*, Schubert's Symphony No. 8, Schumann's *Manfred* overture, and entr'acte-ranz-des-vaches, *Also sprach Zarathustra*, the preludes to *Die Meistersinger*, Act III of *Tannhäuser* and two Acts I and III of *Tristan und Isolde*, as well as the *Liebestod* and other extracts from that opera, and for Polydor excerpts from *Tannhäuser*, *Parsifal*, *Siegfried* and *Götterdämmerung*, including his own arrangement of the final Immolation Scene. Of his own music, he recorded *Das Hexenlied* (with the

Berlin Philharmonic Orchestra and narrator, for Polydor), the prelude to *Der Pfeifertag* and the Harvest Festival from *Moloch* (with an unnamed orchestra for Odeon). BASF have issued on an LP Schillings conducting the Berlin Staatsoper Orchestra in the prelude to his *Mona Lisa*.

Schippers, Thomas (1930–77). Born in Kalamazoo, Michigan, of parents of German and Dutch descent, Schippers began studying the piano at the age of 4, gave a public performance at 6, and played the piano regularly on a local radio station. He studied the organ at the Curtis Institute, Philadelphia (1945–7), with Hindemith at Yale University, then the piano and composition with Olga Samaroff and at the Berkshire Music Center. At 18 he entered a competition for conductors in Philadelphia, and was one of the finalists; he became a church organist in New York (1948), was music director of the Lemonade Opera at the church in Greenwich Village, and became musical superintendent of Menotti's company which was then preparing *The Consul* (1950). He went on to take part in the production of other Menotti operas, *The Medium* and *Amahl and the Night Visitors* (1951) and later recorded *The Medium* for a film made in Europe. After a tour of service with the US army in FR Germany he made guest appearances with the Philadelphia, Boston Symphony and New York Philharmonic Orchestras, conducted regularly at the New York City Opera (1951–4) where he led the première of Copland's *The Tender Land* (1954), toured Europe (1954), conducted at La Scala, Milan, became a regular conductor at the New York Metropolitan Opera (1955) where he made his debut at the age of 25 with *Don Pasquale*, was the first American conductor to be assigned a first night, and conducted more opening nights there than any other conductor for 40 years; he led *Die Meistersinger* at Bayreuth (1963), toured Europe with the Met. Company (1966), and conducted Barber's *Antony and Cleopatra* at the opening night of the Met. at its new quarters in the Lincoln Center (1966). He was co-founder with Menotti and artistic director of the Spoleto Festival (1958–75), and in Italy was also music director of the Orchestra of the Accademia di Santa Cecilia and was director of special projects for Radio Italiana (1970–71). He toured the USSR with the New York Philharmonic Orchestra (1959 and 1976), and in 1970 succeeded Rudolf as conductor of the Cincinnati Symphony Orchestra. He died from lung cancer, and bequeathed the bulk of his estate to the orchestra, stating that 'It seems only right that I should give back to music what it gave to me. (*Musical America*, April 1978, p. 24). In his repertoire were over 80 operas, all of which he conducted from memory.

After Schippers' debut at the Met. in March 1955 Olin Downes wrote in the *New York Times* that he was 'admirably precise in his beat, clear as a bell in his musical conceptions, and of sensitive taste, interprets without exaggeration or overemphasis or any of the tricks of the trade of a modern conductor who intends at any cost to impress, if not startle, his audience. He is economical of gesture and movement as he is in complete control of the orchestra and himself. . . . He seeks balance, beauty and proportion in his readings, and this with a highly becoming seriousness and modesty of demeanor.' Schippers remained much the same for the rest of his career. He recognised the conductor's dependence on the orchestra: 'It's important that a conductor does not always feel that he is pushing a train. No conductor can have that without talented leaders in the orchestra' (*Musical America*, April 1978, p. 25). To him the Berlin Philharmonic under Karajan was the most versatile of orchestras, but the Philadelphia Orchestra was the one with the greatest sound; Toscanini once told him that he could not understand how Stokowski could get his warm, wonderful sound. Schippers explained this contrast between Toscanini and Stokowski by dividing conductors into two kinds, the string conductors, such as Stokowski and Ormandy, and the anti-string conductors, among whom he included Toscanini, observing that Toscanini did not have an orchestral ear, and did not even choose his own players for the NBC Symphony Orchestra.

Schippers' first recording was in 1954, and was of Menotti's *Amahl and the Night Visitors* (with the original cast and orchestra, for RCA); there followed *The Medium* and *The Saint of Bleecker Street* (for RCA) and *The Unicorn, the Gorgon and the Manticore* (for EMI). He has recorded a number of operas: *Macbeth* (with the Santa Cecilia Orchestra *et al.* for Decca), *Lucia di Lammermoor* (with the London Symphony Orchestra *et al.* for ABC), *Le Siège de Corinthe* (in a disputed version, with the London Symphony Orchestra *et al.* for EMI), *Il barbiere di Siviglia* and *Carmen* (with the Suisse Romande Orchestra *et al.* for Decca), *Ernani* and *La forza del destino* (with the RCA Italiana Orchestra *et al.* for RCA), *La Bohème* and *Il trovatore* (with the Rome Opera Orchestra *et al.* for EMI), and selections from Barber's *Antony and Cleopatra* (with Price and the New Philharmonia Orchestra for RCA) and *Boris Godunov* (with the Columbia Symphony Orchestra *et al.* for CBS); Levon have also issued *Aida* (with the Turin Lyric Orchestra *et al.*). His other recordings included Tchaikovsky's Symphony No. 4 and Prokofiev's Symphony No. 5 (with the Philharmonia Orchestra for EMI), a disc of pieces by Salieri, Vivaldi and Durante (with the Scarlatti Orchestra for EMI), *Pictures at an Exhibition*, Sibelius' Symphony No. 2, Rossini's *Stabat Mater*, the Tchaikovky and Bruch Violin Concertos (with Francescatti), Chopin's Piano Concerto No. 2 (with Watts), and Barber's *Andromache's Farewell* (with Arroyo), *Adagio for Strings*, *Essay No. 2*, Meditation and Dance of Vengeance from *Medea* and overture to *The School for Scandal* (with the New York Philharmonic Orchestra for CBS), Barber's *Knoxville – Summer of 1915* (with Price and the New Philharmonia Orchestra for RCA) and the overtures to *Le nozze di Figaro*, *Il barbiere di Siviglia*, *Der Freischütz* and *The Bartered Bride*, and two preludes from *Carmen* (with the Columbia Symphony Orchestra for CBS).

Schlemm, Gustav Adolf (b. 1902). Born at Giessen, Schlemm studied at the Hoch Conservatory at Frankfurt am Main (1918–23), and was a repetiteur at Königsberg (1923–4). He has been a conductor at Münster (1924–9), music director at Herford (1929–31) and Meiningen (1931–3), was a free-lance composer and guest conductor in Berlin (1933–5), conductor with the Hamburg Radio (1935–7), in Berlin (1937–45), directed the Singing Academy he founded at Wetzlar (1945–53), was music director at Hildesheim (1956) and then settled in Bavaria as a freelance composer. His compositions include two symphonies, orchestral, choral, instrumental and chamber music, and he recorded Spohr's Symphony No. 3 with the Frankfurt Radio Orchestra for Urania.

Schmalstich, Clemens (1880–1960). Born at Posen (now Poznań), Schmalstich studied with Humperdinck in Berlin, became an operatic conductor, lectured at the opera school of the Academy of Music in Berlin, and conducted the Siemens Orchestra in Berlin after 1945. HMV issued, on 78s, Schmalstich conducting the *Tannhäuser* overture (with the Berlin Staatsoper Orchestra), *Der fliegende Holländer* overture and short excerpts from *Lohengrin* and *Die Meistersinger* (with an unidentified orchestra, *et al.*).

Schmeidel, Hermann von (1894–1953). Born in Graz, Schmeidel studied at the Conservatory and University there, and at the Academy of Music and University in Vienna. He taught at the Duesberg Music School in Vienna (1912), founded a ladies' choir and was conductor of the Gesellschaft der Musikfreunde (1915), was conductor of the Vienna Schubert Society (1920), at Elberfeld (1921), the Association of Singing Teachers, Düsseldorf (1924), the Frankfurt am Main Conservatory (1924), the Prague German Choral Association (1926), the German Music Academy, Prague (1927), was a choral conductor at Frankfurt am Main and Mainz (1930–33), and conductor of the Steiermarkische Music Association in Graz (1933–8). He then became musical adviser to the Turkish government in Ankara, became a professor and conductor at the Mozarteum in Salzburg (1946), and was a guest professor at Boston University (1951–2). Lyrichord issued an LP in which he conducted the Salzburg Mozarteum Camerata Academica and Chorus in Mozart's *Missa Brevis* K. 192 and *Dixit et Magnificat* K. 193.

Schmid, Erich (b. 1907). Born at Balsthal, Switzerland, Schmid was educated at the Hoch Conservatory at Frankfurt am Main (1927–30) and attended Schoenberg's master classes in Berlin (1930–31). He was conductor at Glarus, Switzerland (1934–49), of the Zürich Tonhalle Orchestra, succeeding Volkmar Andreae (1949–57), chief conductor of the Beromünster Radio Orchestra (1957–72), leader of the Mixed Choir, Zürich (1949–75), and professor of conducting at the Basel Academy of Music (since 1973). In 1970 the Beromünster Radio Orchestra was dissolved and integrated with the Basel Orchestral Society; Schmid then became permanent guest conductor of the Schweizerische Rundspruchgesellschaft. He has an extensive repertoire, including all the orchestral and choral works of Schoenberg, and has given many first performances of pieces by Webern, Berg, Dallapicolla, Petrassi, Hartmann *et al.*, and is also a noted interpreter of Brahms, Mahler, Busoni and Reger as well as modern Swiss composers. His records include Schoeck's cantata *Vom Fischer und syner Fru* (with the Beromünster Radio Orchestra *et al.* for Armida), Goetz's Piano Concerto (with Paul Baumgartner and the same orchestra for CTS), Beck's Symphony *Aeneas Silvius*, the chaconne from Brün's Symphony No. 5, Schnyder von Wartensee's Piano Concerto (with Leuthold) and Two-Clarinet Concerto (with Leuthold and Moor) and Keller's *Passacaglia* (with the Beromünster Radio Orchestra for CTS), Schibler's *Passacaglia* (for Decca), Huber's *Des Engels Anredung* and Kelterborn's *Elegie* (for Elite).

Schmidt, Heinrich (b. 1904). Born in Wollersdorf, Austria, Schmidt studied at the University and Academy of Music in Vienna, and taught at the Academy (1929–38). He was conductor at the Bavarian State Opera, Munich (1938–46), at the Vienna State Opera (1946–72), was associated with the Salzburg Festival (1942–60), and was an assistant to Furtwängler (1948–55). He also accompanied singers such as Hotter and Schwarzkopf, and with the latter conducted the Philharmonia Orchestra for EMI in a collection of operatic arias. Ronette, an American recording company, issued in the early years of LP a number of recordings in which Schmidt (presumably Heinrich Schmidt) conducted the Hamburg Symphony Orchestra; the recorded repertoire included Beethoven's Symphonies Nos 2 and 5, *Scheherazade*, the two *L'Arlésienne* suites, Dvořák's Symphony No. 9, *Peter and the Wolf*, Rachmaninov's Piano Concerto No. 2 (with Silver), *Boléro*, the overtures to *William Tell*, *Leichte Cavallerie*, *Dichter und Bauer* and *A Midsummer Night's Dream*, the Mendelssohn Violin Concerto (with Ruppert), *Marche slave* and *In the Steppes of Central Asia*.

Schmidt, Ole (b. 1928). Born in Copenhagen, Schmidt was interested in jazz music before entering the Royal Academy of Music at Copenhagen in 1948, where he studied composition, the piano and conducting under Felumb. He later continued studying conducting with Wolff, Kubelik and Celibidache. He made his debut as a conductor at the Swedish Royal Academy in 1955, was conductor at the Royal Opera, Copenhagen (1958–65), chief conductor of the Hamburg Symphony Orchestra (1970–71) and of the Danish Radio Symphony Orchestra (since 1971). In 1975 Unicorn issued the seven symphonies of Nielsen, with Schmidt conducting the London Symphony Orchestra; he revealed himself as an accomplished and perceptive conductor of Nielsen's music, 'in the tradition of the great Nielsen interpreters of the early 1950s, Thomas Jensen and Erik Tuxen' (Robert Layton, *The Gramophone*, January 1975). Nonetheless, some commentators had reservations about accepting the set as definitive, because of certain flaws due to the hurried preparation of the performances. Schmidt also recorded Westergaard's Cello Concerto and *Pezzo Concertanto* (with Bengtsson and the Danish Radio Symphony Orchestra for DGG), Bentzon's *Feature on René Descartes* and Colding-Jørgensen's *To Love Music* (with the Danish Radio Symphony Orchestra for BIS). He was awarded the Carl Nielsen Prize in 1975.

Schmidt-Boelcke, Werner (b. 1903). Schmidt-Boelcke was born in Berlin and educated at the Stern Conservatory there; both his parents were concert pianists; he himself gave piano recitals from the age of 15. He was conductor at the Meinhard-Bernauer Theatre, Berlin (1923–6), at the Phoebus-Palast, Munich (1926–8), and then was chief conductor of the Emelka Theatres, with his seat in Berlin (1927–9). He toured in North America (1929), composed and conducted for over 50 musical films in Berlin, Munich, Paris and Prague (1929–33), conducted for the Berlin Radio and was chief conductor at the Metropol and Admirals-Palast Theatres, Berlin, and at the Zentral Theatre, Dresden (1934–44). He was director of light music for Radio Hamburg (1945–6), and then conducted for the Bavarian Radio at Munich. He has since led concerts and radio programmes in many German cities and abroad, and in 1974 was decorated for his services by FR Germany. For Ariola he has recorded discs of excerpts from Abraham's *Die Blume von Hawaii* and *Viktoria und ihr Husar*, Jarno's *Die Försterchristel*, Kattnigg's *Balkanliebe*, Jessel's *Schwarzwaldmädel*, Künneke's *Der Vetter aus Dingsda*, Lehár's *Giuditta*, *Friederike* and *Schön ist die Welt*, Nedbal's *Polenblut*, Raymond's *Maske in Blau* and Strauss's *Eine Nacht in Venedig*; Electrola also issued records of selections from *Don Pasquale* and *Die Zauberflöte* and operettas by Lehár, Strauss, Millöcker, Hellmesberger and others. He recorded, in addition, *Valse triste*, *Finlandia* and some Offenbach overtures for Ariola. All of these recordings were with the Berlin Symphony Orchestra *et al.*

Schmidt-Gaden, Gerhard (b. 1937). Schmidt-Gaden studied with Thomas in Leipzig, Iro in Vienna, Vedal in New York, and Roswaenge in Munich, at the Mozarteum and Orff Institute in Salzburg (1964–8), and founded and is conductor of the Tölz Boys' Choir, which consists of 50 singers between the ages of ten and 30. The choir has performed at many festivals in Europe under leading conductors, and has made many records, both under Schmidt-Gaden and others. With the choir, Schmidt-Gaden has recorded Dufay's *Missa Se la face ay pale*, *Conditor alme siderum* and *Christe redemptor omnium*, Dunstable's *The Agincourt Hymn*, Palestrina's *Missa Tu es Petrus*, *Ave Maria* and motets *Quam pulchri sunt* and *Tu es Petrus*, Bach's *Christmas Oratorio*, *Magnificat*, Cantata No. 110 and excerpts from the *Notebook of Anna Magdalena Bach*, an anonymous *Salve Regina*, Haydn's Mass No. 18, Mozart's Mass K. 317, *Vesperae solennes de confessore*, and some canons and folksongs, Schubert's *Deutsche Messe*, and Orff's *Musica poetica* (together with Orff). These performances were, in most instances with the Collegium Aureum, *et al.*, and were issued by Harmonia Mundi and BASF.

Schmidt-Isserstedt, Hans (1900–73). Born in Berlin, Schmidt-Isserstedt learned the violin as a boy, studied at the Hochschule für Musik there and at the Universities of Berlin, Heidelberg and Münster, and received his doctorate for a thesis about Italian influences on Mozart's early operas. After hearing Nikisch he decided to become a conductor; his first appointment was as a repetiteur at the Wuppertal Opera (1923–8), where he also played the violin in the orchestra. He was principal conductor at Rostock (1928–31), Darmstadt (1931–3), first conductor at the Hamburg State Opera (1935–42) and general music director at the Deutsche Oper in Berlin (1942–5). Having had no connection with the Nazi party, he was asked by the British occupation authorities in 1945 to form the Nordwest Deutsche Rundfunk Symphony Orchestra (i.e. the Hamburg Radio Orchestra), which he conducted for 26 years (1945–71), and then was appointed its honorary conductor. His debut in the United States was with the Philadelphia Orchestra in 1961; he had visited Britain with the NWDRSO in 1951, and toured the US with the orchestra in 1969. He also conducted throughout Europe, the US, visited the USSR and Australia as a guest conductor, was conductor of the Stockholm Philharmonic Orchestra (1955–64), appeared on occasion at the Hamburg Opera, conducted at Glyndebourne (1958), led *Tristan und Isolde* and *Der fliegende Holländer* (1972) at Covent Garden, conducted the Hamburg Opera in *Mathis der Maler* during its visit to New York (1967), and led *Die Entführung aus dem Serail* at the Bavarian Opera at Munich (1970). In Sweden he was honoured with the Cross of the Commander of the Order of Vasa (1964), and was made a member of the Royal Academy of Music in London (1970). Early in his career he composed orchestral, vocal and chamber music, and a comic opera *Hassan gewinnt*, but later abandoned composition, declaring that 'all the best things have been written already'.

After World War II, Schmidt-Isserstedt's career gravitated from the opera house to the concert hall, where he achieved distinction as one of the finest exponents of the German school of conducting. Under his leadership the Nordwest Deutsche Rundfunk Orchestra developed into one of the finest in FR Germany, although he regretted that, for whatever reason, its records could not attract large sales. His taste in music, like his manner as a conductor, was conservative; he enjoyed a distinguished reputation as an interpreter of Mozart, Beethoven, Brahms, Dvořák, Mahler and Bruckner in particular, but he disliked most contemporary music except for Britten, Tippett, Blomdahl and Henze, whom he performed enthusiastically. In the Viennese classics he was above all concerned with keeping the music's architecture in the foreground, and presented performances that were at the one time imaginative, cool-headed and unmannered. In Beethoven he said: 'There must be an ideal balance of head and heart. Paradoxically, this is something that cannot be learnt and yet it can be achieved only when a conductor has the music really in his bones' (*The Gramophone*, May 1968, p. 584). His recordings of the nine Beethoven symphonies, which were made in the last seven years of his life, illustrate his strengths and weaknesses as a conductor; they have attracted critical comments ranging from 'straightforward, unmannered' and 'thoughtful, poetic' to 'unimaginative' and 'beautifully polished but without power'. Probably the last remark best epitomises the series, and Schmidt-Isserstedt's approach in general.

Commencing in 1932, Telefunken issued a number of records in which Schmidt-Isserstedt conducted the Berlin Philharmonic Orchestra, and in several instances the German Opera Orchestra and the Hamburg Philharmonic Orchestra. Foremost were the concertos with the violinist Georg Kulenkampff, which have remained famous to the present day and have been re-issued on LP; they were the violin concertos of Beethoven, Brahms, Schumann, Mendelssohn and Spohr's No. 8. He also recorded Dvořák's Cello Concerto and that of Haydn in D major (with Cassado), the Dvořák Piano Concerto (with Stech) and the Grieg Piano Concerto (with Johnson). His other discs for Telefunken included the *Brandenburg Concerto No. 4*, the W. F. Bach *Symphony in D* and Françaix's *Sérénade* (with the Hamburg Philharmonic Chamber Orchestra), Haydn's Symphony No. 94 and *Eine kleine Nachtmusik* (later released on LP in the US by Capitol), the overtures to *Don Giovanni*, *Die Entführung aus dem Serail*, *Così fan tutte*, *Der Zauberflöte*, *Martha*, *Dichter und Bauer*, *Pique Dame*, *Die schöne Galatea*, *La forza del destino*, *Hänsel und Gretel*, *Phèdre* and *Der Waffenschmied*, the prelude, march and ballet music from *Aida*, the preludes to Acts I and III of *La traviata*, a *Carmen* suite, the intermezzo from *Notre Dame*, Dvořák's *Carnival* overture, Liszt's

Hungarian Rhapsodies Nos 9 and *13*, the *Rosamunde* Ballet Music in G major, excerpts from *Tannhäuser* (with Konetzi and Lorenz), the Dance of the Apprentices and the Entry of the Mastersingers from *Die Meistersinger*, the Entry of the Gods into Valhalla from *Das Rheingold*, the Ride of the Valkyries from *Die Walküre*, Siegfried's Rhine Journey from *Götterdämmerung*, *Valse triste*, *España*, *The Enchanted Lake*, Järnefelt's *Berceuse*, excerpts from *Mignon* and *Der Freischütz*, the *Naila* waltz, Grieg's two *Elegiac Melodies* and excerpts from *Die lustige Witwe* and *Czardasfürstin*. Another 78 r.p.m. set was of Mozart's Symphony No. 40 (with the Covent Garden Orchestra for HMV).

After World War II, Schmidt-Isserstedt recorded for a number of companies with his Nord West Deutsche Rundfunk Orchestra. These discs included Dvořák's Symphony No. 9 and Tchaikovsky's Symphony No. 6 (for Telefunken), Brahms' Symphony No. 4 (for Vox) and *Hungarian Dances* (for Vanguard), Mozart's Symphony No. 38 and Violin Concerto K. 219 (with Schneiderhan), Tchaikovsky's *Serenade in C major* and *Romeo and Juliet* fantasy-overture, Ravel's *Piano Concerto in G* (with Haas), excerpts from *La traviata* and Fortner's *The Creation* (with Fischer-Dieskau) and *Movements for Piano and Orchestra* (with Seeman, for DGG); Schubert's Symphony No. 5 and incidental music from *Rosamunde* and Sibelius' Symphony No. 2 (for Parlophone); Dvořák's Symphony No. 7, Tchaikovsky's Symphony No. 5 and some *Hungarian Dances* of Brahms and *Slavonic Dances* of Dvořák (for Decca). With the Berlin Philharmonic Orchestra he also recorded Mozart's Violin Concerto K. 218 (with Schneiderhan), four Rossini overtures, *Moldau* and *Valse triste* (for DGG). Of these discs, the Dvořák Symphony No. 7 became something of a classic; although originally issued in 1953 it was still in the catalogue in 1977, and Schmidt-Isserstedt himself regarded it as his best recording with the NWDRSO.

Later, for Decca, Schmidt-Isserstedt conducted the Vienna Philharmonic Orchestra in the complete Beethoven symphonies, with the *Egmont*, *Leonore No. 3* and *Die Weihe des Hauses* overtures, and the five piano concertos (with Backhaus). The sequence of symphonies began with the Nos 3 and 9 in 1966, and their commercial success encouraged Decca to record the rest. His other LP records were of Berwald's *Sinfonie 'Singulière'* and *Sinfonie sérieuse* (with the Stockholm Philharmonic Orchestra for a Swedish label and issued in the US by Nonesuch), Mozart's Symphonies Nos 39 and 41 and Schubert's Symphony No. 6 (with the London Symphony Orchestra for Mercury), Mozart's Piano Concertos K. 238 and K. 466 (with Ashkenazy and the London Symphony Orchestra for Decca), Dvořák's *Serenades in E major* and *D minor* (with the NWDRSO for DGG), the Beethoven Violin Concerto (with Szeryng and the London Symphony Orchestra for Philips), Pfitzner's *Symphony in C sharp minor* (with the Deutsche Oper Orchestra for Urania), an arrangement of the *Italian Concerto* and excerpts from *Ein musikalisches Opfer* of Bach (with the Berlin Philharmonic Orchestra, issued by Capitol in the US), *La finta giardiniera* (with the Hamburg Radio Orchestra *et al.* for Philips), Haydn's Symphony No. 92 (with the Sydney Symphony Orchestra for Telefunken and Radiola), Mozart's Symphonies Nos 31 and 35 (with the Bamberg Symphony Orchestra for BASF), *Idomeneo* (with the Dresden Staatskapelle *et al.* for EMI), Françaix's *Sérénade* (with the Hamburg Philharmonic Chamber Orchestra for Capitol) and Brahms' Symphony No. 4 (with the Philadelphia Music Guild Symphony Orchestra for Oryx). His last recording, made just before his death, was of Brahms' Piano Concerto No. 1 (with Brendel and the Amsterdam Concertgebouw Orchestra for Philips).

Schmitt, Florent (1870–1958). The French composer Schmitt appeared as a pianist, playing his own compositions, and in 1932 visited the United States in this capacity. Little is known of his activities as a conductor. Nonetheless, in 1932 he conducted a recorded performance of his music for the ballet *La Tragédie de Salomé*, and this has recently been re-issued on an LP transfer by Perennial Records, coupled with Roussel conducting his *Le Festin de l'araignée*, and d'Indy his *Le Camp de Wallenstein*. This LP includes the short address by the composer that was included in the original recording.

Schmitz, Paul (b. 1898). Born in Hamburg, Schmitz studied at the Hochschule für Musik in Frankfurt am Main and at Mannheim under Furtwängler, Rehberg and Toch, and was a repetiteur at Kiel (1919), and conductor at Weimar (1921), Stuttgart (1923) and at the Munich State Opera (1927). He was general music director at Leipzig (1933–51), at Kassel (1952–63), and then returned to Leipzig (1964–73), where he was appointed honorary general music director in 1968. He was also a guest conductor with the Gewandhaus Orchestra. Since 1966 he has lived in Munich. For

Polydor, on 78s, he recorded with the Leipzig Gewandhaus Orchestra all the *Brandenburg Concertos*, except *No. 2*, Vivaldi's Concerto Grosso Op. 3 No. 8, Haydn's Symphonies Nos 86 and 90 and the Cherubini symphony; also on 78s he recorded the *Leonore No. 3* overture for Imperial. On LP he accompanied Foldès in Mozart's Piano Concerto K. 467 (with the Berlin Philharmonic Orchestra for DGG), and recorded d'Albert's *Tiefland* (with the Dresden Staatskapelle *et al.* for Electrola), excerpts from *Der Wildschütz* (with the Leipzig Gewandhaus Orchestra *et al.* for Eterna) and Spohr's Violin Concerto No. 8 (with Stiehler and the Leipzig Gewandhaus Orchestra for Urania).

Schmolzi, Herbert (b. 1921). Born in Ludwigsthal in the Saar, Schmolzi studied at the Cologne School of Music (1939–47), and was a lecturer in musicology and choral conducting at the Saarbrücken Conservatory (1947). He then became head of the School Music section (1958), a professor (1960) and then rector (1961–74). He has published a number of articles in musical journals. In 1965 Nonesuch issued a disc on which he conducted the Saar Chamber Orchestra *et al.* in the Bach *Magnificat*.

Schnéevoigt, Georg (1872–1947). One of the foremost Finnish conductors, Schnéevoigt was born at Viipuri, the son of a German musician, and studied in Helsinki, Leipzig, Brussels, Dresden and Vienna. For eight years he was a cellist with the Helsinki Philharmonic Orchestra, gave concerts as a soloist in Finland and abroad, and taught the cello at the Helsinki Conservatory. Sibelius composed a fantasia for cello and piano for Schnéevoigt and his wife, Sigrid Sundgren, who was a pianist. His debut as a conductor was in Riga in 1901; then in 1904 he succeeded Weingartner as conductor of the Kaim Orchestra in Munich, remaining there until 1908. In 1912 he founded a new, major symphony orchestra in Helsinki, which was amalgamated with the Helsinki Philharmonic Orchestra in 1914 to form a new municipal orchestra. He conducted this orchestra from 1914 to 1916; in 1914 he was also conductor of the Concerts Association at Stockholm, and in 1918 founded the Oslo Philharmonic Orchestra. He retained both the Stockholm and Oslo appointments until 1927, and at this time was also general music director at Düsseldorf and performed as a guest conductor in major European musical centres. He first appeared in the United States in 1924 as a guest conductor with the Boston Symphony Orchestra, and in 1927–8 was conductor of the Los Angeles Philharmonic Orchestra. He was appointed permanent conductor of the Finnish National Orchestra at Helsinki in 1932, in succession to Kajanus, and later returned to the US to conduct the NBC Symphony Orchestra at the New York World Fair in 1939, in a programme of the music of Sibelius.

Schnéevoigt's international reputation was as an interpreter of Scandinavian music, particularly that of Sibelius, but at the same time he was noted for his technical ability and for the temperament and originality of his performances of the standard repertoire. He brought the Finnish National Orchestra to London in 1934, and then recorded *Luonnotar* (with Liukonnen) and Symphonies Nos 4 and 6 of Sibelius: the Symphony No. 6 was issued in the Sibelius Society albums, and was the first, and for some time the only recording of the work. In 1973 it was re-issued as part of the album *Sibelius – the Great Interpreters*, by the World Record Club. The later recording of this symphony by Beecham in 1947 revealed the work at full stature; although the world became familiar with the score through Schnéevoigt's recording, it now appears somewhat pallid and hurried compared to Beecham's superb 78s. Perhaps for the same reason, the Sibelius Society eventually released Beecham's recordings of Symphony No. 4, instead of Schnéevoigt's. Other recordings by the Finnish conductor were Grieg's two *Peer Gynt* suites (with the New Queen's Hall Light Orchestra, for Columbia), *Sigurd Jorsalfar* suite and the *Norwegian Dances* (with the London Symphony Orchestra for Columbia) and Sibelius' *Belshazzar's Feast* (with the Helsinki Municipal Orchestra for Odeon).

Schneider, Alexander (b. 1908). Born in Vilna in Russia, Schneider studied the violin at the local conservatory, and at the age of 16 went to Germany to study with Rebner at the Frankfurt am Main Conservatory and with Flesch in Berlin. He became concertmaster of the Frankfurt Symphony Orchestra, played in orchestras at Saarbrücken and Hamburg, and toured with his own string quartet. In 1932 he joined the Budapest String Quartet as second violin; his brother Mischa was the cellist. Just before the outbreak of World War II the Quartet emigrated to the United States; Schneider became a US citizen, and continued to play with it until it was finally disbanded in the mid 1960s. Previously, in 1952, he had founded and led the Schneider Quartet, which performed all the Haydn quartets and recorded 50 of them for the Haydn Society. He also founded the Albeneri Trio and gave recitals with Ralph Kirkpatrick, Rudolf Serkin *et al.* In 1950 he joined Casals at his festival at Prades, and later assisted him at Puerto Rico in 1957. He was active with many chamber music enterprises in New York, founded and was music director of the New School Concerts in 1956, founded and took part in the Marlboro Music Festivals and the New York Mozart Festivals (later called the Mostly Mozart Festivals) and assisted with the Israel Festival in 1960. He first conducted with the Dumbarton Oaks Chamber Music Orchestra in 1944, founded and conducted the Brandenburg Ensemble (1970), and has been a guest conductor with major US orchestras.

Apart from his numerous recordings as solo violinist and chamber music player, notably with the Budapest String Quartet, Schneider has recorded as a conductor. With pianist Rudolf Serkin he directed the Columbia Symphony Orchestra and the Marlboro Festival Orchestra in a number of Mozart piano concertos, K. 271, K. 413, K. 414, K. 456, K. 466, K. 467, K. 488 and K. 595 (for Columbia); with Serkin's son, Peter, he directed the English Chamber Orchestra in the six concertos K. 449, K. 450, K. 451, K. 453, K. 456 and K. 459 (for RCA). Also with the Marlboro Festival Orchestra he conducted other concertos by Bach and Mozart, and the Beethoven Triple Concerto (with Laredo, Parnas and Serkin, for Columbia); the latter was acclaimed as an unusually perceptive performance of the work, and Schneider's contribution as conductor as outstanding. It was first released in 1964 and re-issued in 1976. His other recordings include Handel's Concerti Grossi Op. 6 (with the Alexander Schneider Chamber Orchestra for RCA), Mozart's Divertimento K. 251 and Vivaldi's Concerto Grosso Op. 3 No. 11 (with the Dumbarton Oaks Chamber Orchestra for Mercury), Bach's Suite No. 1 (with the Puerto Rico Festival Casals Orchestra for Columbia), the Mendelssohn Octet (with the Marlboro Festival Orchestra for Columbia), Falla's Harpsichord Concerto (with Kirkpatrick and a chamber orchestra for Mercury), Mozart's Piano Concerto K. 453 (with Kirkpatrick) and Violin Concerto K. 216 (with himself playing and conducting the Dumbarton Oaks Chamber Orchestra for Eurodisc and Nixa), the Mass K. 192, *Dixit Dominus* and *Magnificat* K. 193 (with the Salzburg Mozarteum Chorus and Orchestra for Lyrichord and Nixa), and the Dvořák Cello Concerto (with Casals, and the Casals Festival Orchestra for CBS).

Schneider, Urs (b. 1939). Born in St Gallen, Switzerland, Schneider learned the violin as a child, and founded his own 'Pro Musica' orchestra in his home town at the age of 15. After studying at the Zürich Conservatory, in Ireland, London and Madrid, he visited the United States in 1962 to give concerts, studied conducting with Meylan, Schmid and Klemperer, and has conducted in Europe, the US and South America. In 1963 he founded the East Switzerland Chamber Orchestra, and toured with the ensemble in Europe, and has also been appointed conductor at Passau in southern Bavaria. For Colosseum he has recorded Schubert's Symphony No. 2, Brahms' *Academic Festival* and *Tragic Overtures*, Debussy's Saxophone Rhapsody No. 2 and Martin's *Ballade for Saxophone and Orchestra* (with Perrin) and *Le Carnaval des animaux* (with the Nuremberg Symphony Orchestra).

Schneider, Urs Peter (b. 1939). Born in Berne, Schneider studied there and at the Hochschule für Musik at Cologne and the Academy of Music in Vienna. He has won prizes as both pianist and composer, and in 1968 formed and conducted the Ensemble Neue Horizonte Bern, with which he has given many concerts throughout Europe. With the Ensemble he recorded a disc of works by Grimm, Huber, Frey, Scheidegger, Streiff, Moser and himself (for Jecklin).

Schneidt, Hanns-Martin (b. 1930). Born in Bavaria, Schneidt joined the St Thomas Church Choir at Leipzig at the age of 10, at the same time studying piano and theory with Ramin. He moved to Munich where he studied at the Munich University and Conservatory (1949), passed his examinations for conductor with distinction (1952), published and performed his own compositions (1952), and was awarded the Richard Strauss Prize by the City of Munich (1953). He was appointed director of the Berlin School of Church Music, founded and conducted the Berlin Bach Collegium (1955), made his debut as a conductor with the Berlin Philharmonic Orchestra (1960), and became music director of the City of Wuppertal (1971) and also music director of the Wuppertal Opera (1975). His first records were made in 1972, and were the *Psalmen Davids* of Schütz (with the Regensburg Cathedral Boys' Choir, for DGG-Archiv); there followed the bassoon concertos of Mozart, Weber and Koželuh (with Turkovic and the Bamberg Symphony Orchestra for DGG), the Bach Motets (with the Regensburg Cathedral Boys' Choir for DGG-Archiv), Monteverdi's *Vespro della beata Vergine*, *Magnificats 1* and *2* and the Mass, *In illo tempore* (with the Regensburg Cathedral

Boys' Choir, the Hamburg Early Music Ensemble *et al.* for DGG-Archiv), and the Vivaldi *Gloria* and *Kyrie* (with the Capella Academica of Vienna for DGG-Archiv). The Monteverdi collection received the highest praise when it was issued in 1975, for the excellence of the choir and for Schneidt's outstanding direction. The performance differs from other recordings in using original instruments, and in that the solo singers are all British.

Schoenberg, Arnold (1874–1951). The eminent composer Schoenberg was an experienced conductor; early in his life in Austria he supported himself by conducting music-hall songs and operettas at a theatre in Vienna. Later he conducted his own compositions and those of his contemporaries with many European orchestras, most notably with the Amsterdam Concertgebouw Orchestra. He led the premières of many of his works in Vienna; of *Pelleas und Melisande* he later said: 'The first performance, under my direction, provoked great riots among the audience and even the critics. Reviews were unusually violent and one of the music critics even suggested putting me in an insane asylum and keeping music paper out of my reach' (Joan Peyser, *The New Music*, New York, 1971, p. 28). At another concert in Vienna in 1913, he conducted a programme which included his Chamber Symphony Op. 6, Webern's *Five Pieces for Orchestra* Op. 6 and Berg's *Songs with Orchestra* Op. 4. An uproar developed, the police were called, and the concert was abandoned. Schoenberg left Nazi Germany, emigrated to the United States, and made his debut as a conductor in 1934 with the Boston Symphony Orchestra with his symphonic poem *Pelleas und Melisande*. Eventually he settled in Los Angeles and retired from public life in 1944. It may seem remarkable that the US recording companies did not entice him into the recording studios more than once; in 1941 Columbia recorded his performance of *Pierrot Lunaire*, but that was all. The narrator in this performance was Erika Stiedry-Wagner, the wife of the conductor Fritz Stiedry. It was once available on an LP transfer issued by Odyssey. Goddard Lieberson, who was with CBS (Columbia) at the time, has said that Schoenberg was a very difficult man, perhaps embittered because of his complete neglect for so many years. In fairness to the record companies, recordings of his music were a certain commercial risk, despite Stokowski's success with *Gurrelieder*, which, it may be added, Schoenberg disliked. His experience is a stark contrast with Britten's and Stravinsky's, two other peaks of 20th-century music, who in recent times have been recorded, directing almost all their major scores.

Schoener, Eberhard (b. 1936). Born in Stuttgart, Schoener studied at the North-West German Academy of Music at Detmold, and at the Accademia Chigiana at Siena. He was chief conductor of the Munich Youth Symphony Orchestra (from 1962), artistic director of the Munich Chamber Opera (from 1965), musical director of the Bavarian Opera (1964–9) and conductor of the experimental studios for electronic music of the Bavarian Ateliergesellschaft in Munich (from 1970). He has composed music for stage and films, and recorded Mozart's *Bastien und Bastienne* and *Der Schauspieldirektor* (with the Bavarian State Opera Orchestra *et al.* for EMI).

Scholz, Alfred (b. 1920). Born in Braunau, Czechoslovakia, Scholz studied the violin in Prague with Kalliwoda and Schwejda, and gave over 300 recitals in Germany and abroad. He then studied conducting with Swarowsky in Vienna, conducted in Kapstadt and Johannesburg, and at the Mozarteum in Salzburg. In 1960 he founded his own studio in Schloss Klessheim, and since then has been mainly involved in conducting for records, and in the last eight years has produced over 300 discs. These include Haydn's Symphonies Nos 94 and 101, Mozart's Symphonies Nos 35, 38, 40 and 41, Schubert's Symphony No. 8 and *Les Préludes* (with the South German Philharmonic Orchestra for BASF), *Capriccio italien* (with the Munich Symphony Orchestra for Intercord), the ballet music from *Faust* (with the Salzburg Mozarteum Orchestra for Opp), *Le Carnaval des animaux* (with the Munich Symphony Orchestra, issued by Pye), the Schumann Piano Concerto (with Gröschel), the Brahms Violin Concerto (with Schneider) and Piano Concerto No. 2 (with Goldmann, and the Munich Symphony Orchestra for Intercord), Mendelssohn's Symphony No. 4 and overture *Die Heimkehr aus der Fremde* and the *Nutcracker* suite (with the South German Philharmonic Orchestra for Intercord), and Brahms' *Tragic Overture* (with the Nuremberg Symphony Orchestra for Intercord).

Schönherr, Max (b. 1903). Born in Marburg, Schönherr was educated at the Graz Conservatory, and started his career as a double-bass player. He was choirmaster and conductor at the Graz Opera, also conducted at the Theater an der Wien and at the Vienna Volksoper, and from 1931 was permanent conductor of the Vienna Radio Orchestra. He has been especially associated with Viennese operetta and light music, as conductor, orchestrator and scholar, and is a recognised authority in this field. He collaborated with Karl Reinöhl in producing a thematic catalogue of the music of Johann Strauss, has been the author of many learned articles about the Strausses, and received a doctorate for a study of the operetta composer Ziehrer. He himself has composed a ballet, *Hotel Sacher* and an operetta *Deutschmeister Kappelle*, and has arranged a suite of Austrian peasant dances.

As a recording artist, Schönherr has led a performance of 78 r.p.m. discs of *Die Fledermaus* (with the Vienna Radio Orchestra *et al.* for the Austrian label, Imperial), and Saga released LPs of excerpts from *Die Fledermaus* and *Der Zigeunerbaron* (with the Vienna Light Opera Orchestra *et al.*). His other recordings include *Scheherazade*, *Danse macabre*, *Till Eulenspiegel* and *Prélude à l'après-midi d'un faune* (with an unidentified orchestra for Music Treasures of the World), the two *L'Arlésienne* suites and a *Carmen* suite, the two *Peer Gynt* suites, waltzes and other pieces by Strauss and Lehár, waltzes by Waldteufel, the overtures to *La gazza ladra*, *Si j'étais Roi*, *Le Calife de Bagdad*, *Raymond* and *Abu Hassan*, the prelude to Act I of *La traviata*, a dance from *The Bartered Bride*, and the march from Beethoven's *Die Ruinen von Athen* (with the Vienna Radio Orchestra for Viennola), waltzes by Strauss (with the Vienna Volksoper Orchestra for Capitol), excerpts from *Coppélia* and *Sylvia* (with the Vienna Radio Orchestra for Remington) and the *Naila* waltz (with the Lower Austrian Symphony Orchestra for Remington). He also conducted a series of performances of music by American composers for the American Recording Society in the early 1950s; included were Bacon's *Ford's Theater*, Phillips' *Selections from McGuffey's Readers*, Porter's Viola Concerto (with Angerer), Herbert's Cello Concerto (with Greenhouse), Green's *Sunday Sing Symphony*, Chadwick's *Tam O'Shanter*, Tuthill's *Come Seven*, Converse's *Mystic Trumpeter* and Rogers' *Leaves from the Tale of Pinocchio*. These were first issued by the Society on its own label, with Schönherr conducting the Society's orchestra, but the discs were later re-issued by Desto with the orchestra identified as the Vienna Symphony. The American conductor Walter Hendl also contributed to the series.

Schönzeler, Hans-Hubert (b. 1925). Born in Leipzig, the son of amateur musicians, Schönzeler fled with his family from Germany to Belgium in 1936, and then at the outbreak of World War II to Australia, where he was interned in 1942. At Leipzig he had heard Furtwängler, which inspired him to be a conductor; during internment he met Georg Gruber, the conductor of the Vienna Boys' Choir, who taught him the rudiments of conducting. After the war he studied under Goossens at the New South Wales Conservatorium of Music and was naturalised as an Australian in 1948. He went to London in 1949 where he formed and conducted a chamber orchestra (1957–62) and later returned to Australia several times to conduct orchestras for the Australian Broadcasting Commission. He attended conductors' courses under Zecchi and van Kempen, studied with Kubelik and at the Paris Conservatoire under Bigot, and wrote a book about Bruckner which was published in 1970. His tastes are wide; he has a particular enthusiasm for Bruckner, Weber and Dvořák, but he stops short of dodecaphonic music, saying that 'Bach used mathematics to make music, but Schoenberg used music to make mathematics'.

Schönzeler's recordings have been of Beethoven's incidental music for *König Stephan* and *Die Ruinen von Athen*, and the *Prometheus* ballet music (with the Berlin Symphony Orchestra for Turnabout), Bruckner's *Requiem* and *Four Orchestral Pieces* (with the London Philharmonic Orchestra for Unicorn), Haydn's Symphonies Nos 96 and 102 (with the Royal Philharmonic Orchestra for Classics for Pleasure) Martinů's *Concerto for Double String Orchestra* and Janáček's *Idyll* (with the Prague Chamber Orchestra for RCA), Weber's Symphonies Nos 1 and 2 (with the London Symphony Orchestra for RCA), the Australian composer Sitsky's opera, *The Fall of the House of Usher* (with the West Australian Symphony Orchestra *et al.* for Festival), Rubbra's Symphony No. 10, *A Tribute*, and *Improvisations on Virginal Pieces by Giles Farnaby* (with the Bournemouth Sinfonietta for RCA), and Hoddinott's Piano Concerto No. 3 (with Woodward), *Landscapes* and *Sinfonietta No. 2* (with the New Philharmonia Orchestra for RCA).

Schreier, Peter (b. 1935). Born in Meissen near Dresden, the distinguished lyric tenor Schreier was a member of the Dresden Kreuzchor (1945–54), studied singing privately in Leipzig (1954–6) and at the Dresden Academy of Music (1956–9), and has since been a leading member of the companies of the Dresden Opera and the Berlin Staatsoper, where he was named Kammersänger in 1964. He has also performed abroad with great distinction as a lieder recitalist, in opera (especially Mozart) and as the

Evangelist in the Bach Passions, and has recorded in all these capacities. Recently Eterna have recorded him as a conductor, directing Bach's Cantatas Nos 202, 208, 211 and 212 (with the Berlin Chamber Orchestra *et al.*) and Schubert's Symphonies Nos 5 and 8 (with the Dresden Staatskapelle).

Schreker, Franz (1878–1934). Born in Monaco of Austrian parents, Schreker studied at the Vienna Conservatory, founded and conducted the Vienna Philharmonic Choir (1911) and taught composition at the Vienna Academy of Music (1912). He was appointed director of the Hochschule für Musik in Berlin (1920–32), where his pupils included Křenek, Rosenstock, Gmeindl, Salmhofer, Hába and Horenstein. His operas and other compositions were advanced for their day, but reaction against his musical style, and the artistic policies of the Nazis, forced him to resign his position in Berlin. Of his music he recorded for Polydor the ballet *The Birthday of the Infanta* (with the Berlin Staatsoper Orchestra) and the *Little Suite for Chamber Orchestra* (with the Berlin Philharmonic Orchestra).

Schrems, Theobald (1893–1963). Born in Mitterteich, Oberfranken, Schrems studied in Berlin and Freiburg, and became conductor at the Regensburg Cathedral, being appointed a professor in 1936. With the Regensburg Cathedral Boys' Choir he made many tours, and recorded Reger's *Im Himmelreich ein Haus steht* (for HMV on a 78 r.p.m. disc), and on LP for DGG-Archiv masses, motets and other sacred choral works for Lotti and Palestrina, Haydn's Masses Nos 2 and 5, Schubert's *Deutsche Messe*, *Kyrie* and *Salve Regina* and Mozart's *Missa brevis* K. 259. The Bavarian Radio Symphony Orchestra also took part in the Haydn and Mozart masses. He also accompanied the soprano Streich in a recital (for DGG).

Schroeder, Hermann (b. 1904). Born in Bernkastel, Germany, Schroeder studied at the Innsbruck University (1923–6) and at the Hochschule für Musik at Cologne (1926–30), and lectured at the Rhine Music School at Cologne (1930). He became organist at Trier Cathedral (1938), director of the Trier Academy of Music (1940), professor at the Hochschule für Musik at Cologne (1948) and a lecturer at Cologne University (1958). With his *Symphony in D minor* he won the Music Prize of the City of Düsseldorf (1939); his other compositions include a *Missa Coloniensis* (1956), and with his first teacher Lemarcher he wrote a textbook on counterpoint (1950). His other awards include the Robert Schumann Prize at Düsseldorf (1952), the Art Prize at Rhineland-Pfalz (1952) and an honorary doctorate at Bonn University (1974). Mace (US) released an LP of him conducting the Cologne Bach Soloists *et al.* in Pergolesi's *Stabat Mater*.

Schröder, Jaap (b. 1925). Born in Amsterdam and educated at the Conservatory there, Schröder won first prize for the violin at the École Jacques Thibaud at Paris (1948). He was leader of a radio chamber orchestra (1950–63), a member of the Netherlands String Quartet (1952–69) and founder of the chamber music ensembles Quadro Amsterdam (1960–66), Concerto Amsterdam (since 1962) and Quartetto Esterhazy (since 1971). He is also professor of violin at the Amsterdam Conservatory. With the Concerto Amsterdam *et al.* he has made a number of recordings for Telefunken, which have included the Bach Cantatas Nos 27, 51, 59, 89, 90, 118, 158, 161, 198 and 202, Handel's Organ Concertos (with Chorzempa), Telemann's *Suite in F*, Vivaldi's *The Four Seasons*, *Recorder Concerto in F major* (with Brüggen) and Two-Horn Concerto (with Baumann and van Woudenberg), Boccherini's *Cello Concertos in D major* and *G major* (with Bylsma) and two Concertos for Cello and Two Horns (with Bylsma, Baumann and van Woudenberg), Haydn's Violin Concerto No. 3 (with himself), Hummel's *Trumpet Concerto in E major* (with Groot), Danzi's *Horn Concerto in E major*, Haydn's Horn Concerto No. 1 and Rosetti's *Horn Concerto in D minor* (with Baumann), Locatelli's *L'arte del violino* Op. 3 No. 1 (with himself), Torelli's Trumpet Concertos Nos 1 and 2 (with André), and Danzi's Bassoon Concerto (with Hartmann). For BASF he also recorded Danzi's Sinfonia Concertante, and music for their series *Bavaria's Castles and Residences*, and as a soloist sonatas by Mozart (for Philips); in Telefunken's six-disc edition of Telemann's *Tafelmusik*, he led the Concerto Amsterdam, under Brüggen's direction.

Schröder, Kurt (1888–1962). Born in Hagenow in Mecklenburg, Schröder studied musicology in Berlin and Rostock, and was a chorusmaster and conductor at theatres in Chemnitz (1914–17). He was first conductor at Königsberg City Theatre (1918–20), general music director at Coburg (1920–21) and Münster (1921–3), and first conductor at the Cologne Opera (1923–33), then emigrated to London. After World War II he was musical director of the Hessian Radio at Frankfurt am

Main, and was also active as a conductor. DGG recorded him conducting the Hessian Radio Symphony Orchestra in the overtures to *Tannhäuser* and *I vespri siciliani*, and Telefunken Cimarosa's Oboe Concerto (with Winschermann) and the Gopak from Tchaikovsky's *Mazeppa*, with the same orchestra.

Schüchter, Wilhelm (1911–74). Born in Bonn and educated at the Hochschule für Musik at Cologne, under Abendroth and Jarnach, Schüchter was conductor at Würzburg (1937–40), Aachen (1940–42), at the Berlin Staatsoper (1942–3) and with the Nord-West Deutsche Rundfunk Orchestra with Schmidt-Isserstedt (1947–58), was chief conductor of the NHK Symphony Orchestra in Tokyo (1958–61), general music director at Dortmund (1962–5) and artistic director of the Dortmund Theatre (1965–74). He recorded extensively for EMI and some other companies in the first years of LP, and his major enterprise was a complete *Lohengrin*, issued in 1953 by EMI, with the North-West German Philharmonic Orchestra *et al.* For EMI's German label Electrola he made a number of single discs of excerpts from operas and operettas (with the Berlin Staatsoper Orchestra *et al.*), including *Le nozze di Figaro*, *Die Zauberflöte*, *Die Entführung aus dem Serail*, *Il barbiere di Siviglia*, *The Merry Wives of Windsor*, *Carmen*, *Cavalleria rusticana*, *Lucia di Lammermoor*, *Les Contes d'Hoffmann*, *Nachtlager in Granada*, *Aida*, *La traviata*, *Rigoletto*, *Der Trompeter von Sackingen*, *Madama Butterfly*, *La Bohème*, *Der Waffenschmied*, *Zar und Zimmermann*, *Die Czardsasfürstin*, *Gräfin Maritza*, *Der Vogelhandler*, *Der Zarewitsch*, *Ein Walzertraum* and *Das Land des Lächelns*. Most of the Italian operas were in the German language. He also recorded excerpts from *Der Rosenkavalier* (with the Berlin Philharmonic Orchestra *et al.*) and *Die Fledermaus* and *The Bartered Bride* (with the North-West German Philharmonic Orchestra *et al.* for EMI), from *Martha*, *Oberon* and *Undine* (with the Berlin Symphony Orchestra *et al.*) and *Faust* and *La forza del destino* (with the Deutsche Oper Orchestra *et al.* for Ariola).

Schüchter's other recordings include the *Brandenburg Concertos* (with the Hamburg Chamber Orchestra for Pathé), Handel's Organ Concertos Nos 2, 4, 10 and 14 (with Jones), the overtures *Coriolan*, *Academic Festival*, *The Hebrides*, *The Merry Wives of Windsor*, *Le Corsaire* and *Le Carnaval romain*, the march from *Les Troyens*, *Capriccio espagnol*, *Marche slave*, a suite from *Carmen*, the *Háry János* suite, *Ruralia Hungarica*, Ippolitov-Ivanov's *Caucasian Sketches*, four portraits from Prokofiev's *The Gambler*, a suite from Kabalevsky's *Colas Breugnon*, three *Spanish Dances* of Granados, the Dance of the Persian Slaves from *Khovanshchina*, Turina's *Danzas fantásticas*, some Strauss waltzes and intermezzi from *L'Amico Fritz*, *Cavalleria rusticana*, *I gioielli della Madonna* and *I quattro rusteghi* (with the Philharmonia Orchestra for EMI), Tchaikovsky's Symphony No. 5, Dvořák's Symphony No. 9, *Moldau* and the two *Peer Gynt* suites (with the North-West German Philharmonic Orchestra for EMI), Tchaikovsky's Piano Concerto No. 1 (with Hansen and the RIAS Orchestra for Remington, and with Prochorowa and the North-West German Philharmonic Orchestra for EMI), Chopin's Piano Concertos Nos 1 and 2 (with Karolyi and the Berlin Philharmonic Orchestra for Electrola), Corelli's Concerto Grosso Op. 6 No. 8, Mozart's Symphony No. 40 and *Eine kleine Nachtmusik*, the *Leonore No. 3* overture, Schubert's Symphony No. 8 and excerpts from the *Rosamunde* music, Liszt's *Hungarian Rhapsody No. 2* and *Les Préludes*, Brahms' *Variations on the St Antony Chorale* and four *Hungarian Dances*, *Capriccio italien*, *Scheherazade*, Bruch's Violin Concerto No. 1 and Svendsen's *Romance* (with Kayser), the ballet music from *Faust*, the intermezzo from *Notre Dame*, the preludes to *Die Meistersinger* and Act III of *Tannhäuser*, *España* and the waltzes from *Der Rosenkavalier* (with the North-West German Philharmonic Orchestra for Imperial; some of these latter records were issued on other labels, such as *Scheherazade*, which was released by Musical Heritage Society), the intermezzo from *Pagliacci*, Grieg's *Elegiac Melodies* and two *Peer Gynt* suites and the overture to *Der Zigeunerbaron* (with the North-West German Philharmonic Orchestra for Odeon), Mayuzumi's *Nirvana Symphony* (with the NHK Symphony Orchestra for Mainstream), and Beethoven's Symphony No. 9 (with the German Symphony Orchestra *et al.*, issued by Marble Arch).

Schüler, Johannes (1894–1966). Born in Vietz, Neumark, Germany, Schüler studied at the Hochschule für Musik in Berlin (1914 and 1918–20), was a conductor at Gleiwitz (1920–22), Königsberg (1922–4) and Hannover (1924–8), was music director at Oldenburg (1928–32) and Halle (1932–3), general music director at Essen (1933–6), was at the Berlin Staatsoper, and at Hannover (1960). He made a number of 78 r.p.m. records, including Mozart's Symphony No. 35 (with the Vienna Philharmonic Orchestra for Pathé), Symphony

No. 36 (with the Berlin Philharmonic Orchestra for Imperial), Symphony No. 39 and some *German Dances* (with the Berlin Staatsoper Orchestra for Imperial), Haydn's Symphony No. 100, the overture to *Der Freischütz* and *Invitation to the Dance* (with the Vienna Philharmonic Orchestra for Imperial), the overture to *Il barbiere di Siviglia* (with the Deutsche Oper Orchestra for Imperial), Schubert's Symphony No. 8 and the overture to *Tannhäuser* (with the Berlin Philharmonic Orchestra for Imperial), *Capriccio italien* (with the Berlin Staatsoper Orchestra for Imperial), the two Beethoven *Romances* (with Borries and the Berlin Philharmonic Orchestra for HMV), Blacher's *Concertante Musik* (with the Berlin Philharmonic Orchestra for HMV), arias from *La traviata* (with Berger and the Berlin Staatsoper Orchestra for EMI), two *Hungarian Dances* of Brahms (with the Deutsche Oper Orchestra for Imperial), excerpts from *Martha* (with the Berlin Staatsoper Orchestra *et al.*, released on LP by BASF), the Mendelssohn Violin Concerto (with Gimpel and the Bamberg Symphony Orchestra on LP for Ariola and Maritim), Debussy's *Iberia* (with the Prussian State Orchestra, on LP for Urania), Dvořák's Symphony No. 5 (with the Leipzig Philharmonic Orchestra for Urania) and excerpts from *The Merry Wives of Windsor* and *Eine Nacht in Venedig* (with the Deutsche Oper Orchestra *et al.* for Telefunken).

Schuller, Gunther (b. 1925). The son of a violinist in the New York Philharmonic Orchestra, Schuller was born in New York and became interested in music when he was a member of St Thomas' Choir School. As a boy he learned the French horn, and after studying at Manhattan School of Music, played the horn in the Ballet Theatre Orchestra, and was first horn player with the Cincinnati Symphony Orchestra (1943–5). In 1945 he played his own horn concerto with the orchestra under Goossens. After some years with the New York Metropolitan Opera Orchestra (1945–59), he held a Guggenheim Fellowship (1962–4), visited Yugoslavia, Poland and FR Germany, organised and conducted a series of concerts in New York entitled '20th Century Innovations', was associate professor of music at Yale University (1964–6), associate head of the composition department at the Berkshire Music Center (1965–6), and was appointed president of the New England Conservatory of Music at Boston (1966). He has conducted major orchestras in the United States and Europe in programmes of classical, romantic and contemporary music, led Ives' Symphony No. 4 in Berlin and Paris, and often conducts the Mahler symphonies. He has written several books: *Horn Technique* (1962) and *Early Jazz: Its Roots and Development* (1968). His many awards include the Darius Milhaud Award for the best film score (1960) and the ASCAP Deems Taylor Award (1970). His compositions include a symphony and other orchestral music, concertos and an opera *The Visitation*, first performed at Hamburg in 1966, and a children's opera *The Fisherman and His Wife*, premièred in Boston in 1971. He has also composed and promoted so-called Third Stream music, which combines jazz improvisations and rhythms with contemporary techniques of composition; he is himself a jazz player and composer, and was a founder of Modern Jazz Quartet Music Inc., the first publishing house to produce a serious edition in the jazz field.

Schuller's recordings range from *Ein Heldenleben* and *Le Sacre du printemps* (with the New England Conservatory Symphony Orchestra for Golden Crest) to discs of the music of Ellington and Joplin (with the New England Conservatory Jazz Repertory Orchestra and Ragtime Ensemble, respectively, for Golden Crest); also included are Joplin's opera *Treemonisha* (with the Houston Grand Opera Orchestra *et al.* for DGG), Schoenberg's Chamber Symphony No. 1 (with a New York ensemble for Finnada) and Suite Op. 29 (with an ensemble for Period), Ives' *The Pond* (with the Columbia Chamber Ensemble for CBS), Berger's *Chamber Music for Thirteen Players* (for Composers Recordings), William Smith's Jazz Clarinet Concerto (with Smith and the Orchestra USA for Composers Recordings), Sessions' Violin Concerto (with Zukofsky and the French National Radio Orchestra for Composers Recordings), Sollberger's *Chamber Variations for Twelve Players* (with the Columbia University Group for Contemporary Music, for Composers Recordings), Wilder's Nonet and his own *Lines and Contrasts* (with the Los Angeles Horn Club for EMI), Paine's *Mass in D major* (with the St Louis Symphony Orchestra *et al.* for New World) and a disc of marches by Souza, Ives, Joplin *et al.* (with the Columbia All-Star band, for CBS).

Schulz-Dornburg, Rudolf (1891–1949). Born in Würzburg, Schulz-Dornburg studied at the Cologne Conservatory, was first a choral director then was conductor at Cologne (1912), Mannheim (1913), Bochum (1919), Münster (1925) and Essen (1927–32), conducted for the Berlin Radio (1934) and was general music director at Lübeck (1945–8). For Telefunken he conducted the Berlin Philharmonic Orchestra in Mozart's Piano Concerto K. 466, with Mitja Nikisch, who was the son of Artur Nikisch.

Schuricht, Carl (1880–1967). Born in Danzig, of a German father who was an organ builder and a Polish mother who was a fine musician, Schuricht was educated at the Hochschule für Musik in Berlin under Rudorff and Humperdinck, and studied composition with Reger at Leipzig. He first conducted at Zwickau, Dortmund, Kreuznach, Goslar and Weimar, was conductor of the Rühl Choral Union at Frankfurt am Main (1909–11), and was conductor and the general music director at Wiesbaden (1912–44). In 1944 he found disfavour with the Nazis and fled to Switzerland, which was his home until his death. He first visited the United States in 1927, and toured the US with the Vienna Philharmonic Orchestra in 1956, sharing the podium with Cluytens. In 1933–4 he was conductor of the Berlin Philharmonic Choir, and from 1935 was a frequent guest conductor for the Berlin Radio. Before World War II he was a regular visitor to Holland, where he won great acclaim as a conductor; in 1938 Queen Wilhelmina awarded him the Order of Orange-Nassau. After the war he had no permanent post, but took part in many festivals in Europe, and was a guest conductor with the major orchestras. He composed some orchestral and piano music and songs.

Schuricht was a most distinguished conductor of the German school; his performances were noted for their warmth, sonority, close attention to detail and absence of mannerisms. He was not preoccupied with literalness, and with his interpretations one was always conscious that the music was passing through the mind of a musician fully aware of its beauty and meaning. He became recognised for his readings of the classical and romantic repertoire, but it had not always been so. As he once said: 'When I was young, I concentrated on the moderns – Stravinsky, Bartók, Hindemith and others. I still like them. But more and more I'm in demand as an interpreter of classical and romantic music. In France I am considered a Schumann specialist. In Denmark they call me a Brahms specialist. In Holland I am considered a Bruckner specialist. I am essentially an exponent of the old tradition. I have nothing against what music is now, but I feel that it is important to pass a sense of tradition from age to youth' (David Drew, *Living Musicians*, p. 147). He is one of the few Continental conductors who have championed Delius.

Invariably cast as a symphonic conductor, Schuricht recorded extensively in the 1920s and 1930s. He made a pre-electric 78 r.p.m. disc, for Polydor, of the *Coriolan* overture (with the Berlin Municipal Orchestra), and his other recordings of this period included Beethoven's Symphony No. 6 (with the Berlin Staatsoper Orchestra for Polydor), Beethoven's Symphonies Nos 3 and 7, the Mozart's Symphony No. 34, Bruckner's Symphony No. 7, the overtures to *Der Freischütz*, *Oberon* and *Der fliegende Holländer* (with the Berlin Philharmonic Orchestra for Polydor), Beethoven's Symphonies Nos 4 and 9, the *Egmont* overture, Bruckner's Symphony No. 9, *Le Chasseur maudit* and Stephan's *Musik für Orchester* (with the Berlin Municipal Orchestra for Polydor), Bach's Cantata No. 50 and the opening chorus of Cantata No. 104 (with the Berlin Philharmonic Chorus and Orchestra for Telefunken), Strauss's *Symphonia domestica*, the overture to *Donna Diana* and Zandonai's *Serenata medioevale* (with the La Scala Orchestra for HMV), the *Peer Gynt* Suite No. 1 (with the Berlin Staatsoper Orchestra for Clangor), *Tod und Verklärung* (with the Berlin Symphony Orchestra for a German label), and the prelude to Bruch's *Odysseus* (with the EIAR Symphony Orchestra for Cetra).

After 1945, Schuricht recorded for Decca, first on 78s, Beethoven's Symphony No. 2 and the Brahms Double Concerto (both with the Suisse Romande Orchestra, and the latter with Kulenkampff and Mainardi), Bruch's Violin Concerto No. 1 (with Kulenkampff and the Zürich Tonhalle Orchestra) and Beethoven's Symphony No. 5 (with the Paris Conservatoire Orchestra). The LP discs he made for Decca included Beethoven's Symphonies Nos 1 and 2, the *Leonore No. 2* overture, Mozart's Symphony No. 35, Schubert's Symphony No. 8, Brahms' Symphony No. 2, Violin Concerto (with Ferras) and Piano Concerto No. 2 (with Backhaus) and the Mendelssohn overtures *The Hebrides*, *Die schöne Melusine*, *Ruy Blas* and *Meeresstille und glückliche Fahrt* (with the Vienna Philharmonic Orchestra), the Theme and Variations from Tchaikovsky's Suite No. 3, *Capriccio italien*, Schumann's Symphonies Nos 2 and 3, and the *Overture, Scherzo and Finale*, and the prelude and Liebestod from *Tristan und Isolde* and Dawn and Siegfried's Rhine Journey from *Götterdämmerung* (with the Paris Conservatoire Orchestra). For EMI he led the Paris Conservatoire Orchestra in the nine symphonies of Beethoven, and the Vienna Philharmonic Orchestra in Bruckner's Symphonies Nos 3, 8 and 9.

La Guilde Internationale du Disque also

employed Schuricht as a conductor, and issued a number of his performances on various labels in different countries. Included in the series were Bach's Suites Nos 2 and 3 (with the Frankfurt Radio Orchestra) and *Brandenburg Concertos* (with the Zürich Baroque Ensemble), Mozart's Symphonies Nos 36, 38, 40 and 41 (with the Paris Opéra Orchestra), Schubert's Symphony No. 9, Schumann's Symphony No. 3 and *Manfred* overture, Brahms' Symphony No. 3 and *Variations on the St Antony Chorale*, and the overtures *Oberon*, *Euryanthe*, *Ruy Blas*, *The Hebrides*, *Die schöne Melusine* and *The Merry Wives of Windsor* (with the South German Radio Orchestra), Brahms' Symphony No. 4 and *Tragic Overture*, Handel's Concerti Grossi Op. 3 No. 4 and Op. 6 Nos 4 and 10, and *Alexander's Feast*, excerpts from the incidental music to *A Midsummer Night's Dream*, the *Siegfried Idyll*, the overture to *Rienzi*, the prelude to Act I of *Lohengrin*, the preludes to Acts I and III and the Dance of the Apprentices from *Die Meistersinger* (with the Bavarian Radio Symphony Orchestra), Bruckner's Symphony No. 7 (with the Hague Philharmonic Orchestra) and the Strausses' *Künstlerleben*, *Auf der Jagd*, *Annen-Polka*, *Rosen aus dem Süden*, *Tritsch-Tratsch*, *G'schichten aus dem Wiener Wald*, *Champagne*, *Wiener Blut*, *Wein, Weib und Gesang*, *Perpetuum mobile* and the Treasure Waltz from *Der Zigeunerbaron* (with the Vienna State Opera Orchestra).

Among these discs are many distinguished performances, especially the early Beethoven Symphony No. 5 with the Paris Conservatoire Orchestra (for Decca), the coupling of Mozart's Symphony No. 35 and Schubert's Symphony No. 8 with the Vienna Philharmonic Orchestra (for Decca), and Bruckner's Symphonies Nos 3 and 9 with the Vienna Philharmonic Orchestra for EMI. The Beethoven symphonies which he recorded for EMI are still available in France, but only some of the series were issued in Britain; the performances were not hailed in Britain as being especially distinctive, mostly due to the sound of the French horns, which is disturbing for British ears. The Bruckner Symphonies Nos 3 and 9 have been re-issued in the US on Seraphim, and are exceptionally fine readings. Schuricht, in his best discs, emerges as an exemplary conductor, concerned with beauty and expression, as well as accuracy of execution.

Schwarz, Rudolf (b. 1905). Born and educated in Vienna, Schwarz played the viola in the Vienna Philharmonic Orchestra in 1922, and in 1923 was appointed conductor at the Düsseldorf Opera House. From 1927 to 1933 he was joint-conductor with Josef Krips at the Karlsruhe State Theatre, but was dismissed from the post with the advent of the Nazis. He then became conductor of the Jewish Cultural Organisation in Berlin (1936); in 1939 he was arrested, released the following year, but in 1943 was imprisoned in the Belsen concentration camp. He survived, was released in 1945 and was then taken to Sweden for rehabilitation. After conducting in some Scandinavian countries, he went to England, and was appointed conductor of the Bournemouth Municipal Orchestra (1947), which developed considerably under his leadership. Later he was conductor of the City of Birmingham Symphony Orchestra (1951–7), the BBC Symphony Orchestra (1957–62) and the Northern Sinfonia Orchestra (1966–73), and since then has been principal guest conductor of the Northern Sinfonia and the Bournemouth Symphony Orchestras. He was awarded the CBE in 1973.

Schwarz's first records were 78s he made for EMI with the Bournemouth Municipal Orchestra, of the overtures *La Muette de Portici*, *Si j'étais Roi*, *Les deux journées* and *Die Heimkehr aus der Fremde*. In the early years of LP (1952–9) he recorded for EMI with the Philharmonia Orchestra Schubert's Symphony No. 8, the Brahms Violin Concerto (with de Vito) and Double Concerto (with de Vito and Baldovino), the Schumann Piano Concerto (with Hess), *Les Préludes*, the *Hungarian Rhapsodies Nos 2*, *6*, *9* and *14*, Mozart's Piano Concertos K. 414, K. 449, K. 488 and K. 595 (with Matthews), and the overtures *Die schöne Galatea*, *The Merry Wives of Windsor* and *Euryanthe*; for Capitol with the New Symphony Orchestra there were Dvořák's Symphony No. 9 and Cello Concerto (with Navarra), and Tchaikovsky's Piano Concerto No. 1 (with Yankoff), and for EMI with the BBC Symphony Orchestra the Dvořák Slavonic Dances Op. 42 and Op. 76 and the *Serenade in E minor*. His most ambitious enterprise on records was Mahler's Symphony No. 5, with the London Symphony Orchestra for Everest; it was a good performance, but was made before the London Symphony had achieved its later eminence.

Schwieger, Hans (b. 1910). Born in Cologne, Schwieger studied at the Universities of Cologne and Bonn and at the Hochschule für Musik at Cologne, and in 1930 became Kleiber's assistant at the Berlin Staatsoper. He was then general music director at Mainz (1932–6), music director at the Free State of

Danzig (1936) and conductor of the Imperial Orchestra at Tokyo (1937). After engagements as a guest conductor in Asia and in the United States, he took up residence in the US, became conductor of the Fort Wayne Philharmonic Orchestra (1944–8), music director of the Kansas City Philharmonic Orchestra (1948–71) and of the Aspen Music Festival (1955), and conducted at the San Francisco Opera (1956). In recent years he has been a guest conductor in Europe and in 1958 led the world première of Janáček's opera *Osud* ('Fate') in Stuttgart. He recorded Glazunov's Symphony No. 4, Balakirev's *Overture on Russian Themes*, and Prokofiev's *Gypsy Fantasy* and Waltzes Op. 110 (with the Kansas City Philharmonic Orchestra for Urania), Harmonica Concertos of Villa-Lobos and Tcherepnin (with Sebastian and the Stuttgart Symphony Orchestra for DGG) and a recital of Handel arias (with Peerce and the Vienna State Opera Orchestra for Westminster).

Scimone, Claudio (b. 1934). Born in Padua, Scimone studied with Ferrara at Hilversum in Holland, with Zecchi at the Salzburg Mozarteum, and with Mitropoulos. In 1959 he founded and conducted I Solisti Veneti, which is devoted principally to performing the music of the Italian baroque masters. He has made an extensive study of the music of the period, which has resulted in many revisions and new editions. With I Solisti Veneti he has performed in over 50 countries, and has toured the United States eight times, as well as being a guest conductor in countries of Western and Eastern Europe. He became the artistic adviser and resident conductor of the Padua Chamber Orchestra (1966), has taught in the conservatories at Venice and Verona, is general secretary of the Tartiniana Academy and director of the C. Pollini Conservatory at Padua. His awards include the Elizabeth Sprague Coolidge Memorial Medal (1969) and the Golden Medal, received from the President of the Italian Republic. Many contemporary composers have dedicated pieces to him, including Donatoni, Bussotti, Guaccero, Bucchi, Chailly, Malipiero, Halffter and de Pablo.

Scimone has recorded prolifically for Erato with I Solisti Veneti. His first discs were of the Vivaldi Flute Concertos, with Jean-Pierre Rampal; he has gone on to record virtually all of Vivaldi's orchestral and concerted music, which Philips have issued in a series of 23 records. In addition there has been the Vivaldi opera, *Orlando furioso*. His other recordings include Albinoni's Concerti Grossi Opp. 5, 7 and 9 (with Pierlot, Toso *et al.*) and *Symphonies in G major*, *C major* and *G minor*, Tartini's *Violin Concertos in D major* and *A minor* (with Toso), *Flute Concerto in G major* (with Rampal), *Cello Concerto in D major* (with Zannerini) and *Sonata for Strings*, Marcello's *La Cetra* and adagio from the *Flute Concerto in C major* (with Rampal), Gianelli's Flute Concerto (with Rampal), Corelli's Concerto Grosso Op. 8 No. 6 and Fugue, Torelli's *Pastorale pour la Nativité*, Manfredini's Concerto Grosso Op. 13 No. 12, Locatelli's Sonata Op. 5 No. 5, the Pastoral Symphony from Handel's *Messiah*, Mandolin Concertos by Caudioso, Eterardi, Giuliano and Gabbellone (with Bianchi and Pitrelli), Boccherini's *Symphonies in D minor* and *C minor*, the aria from Zipoli's *Suite in F major*, Cimarosa's Sinfonia Concertante for Two Flutes, Mercadante's Flute Concerto, the andante from Haydn's *Flute Concerto in C major*, the Dance of the Blessed Spirits from *Orfeo ed Euridice* and Doppler's *Fantasy on Rigoletto* (with Rampal), Oboe Concertos of Cimarosa, Bellini, Pedrollo and Wolf-Ferrari (with Pierlot), Rossini's six Sonatas for String Orchestra, Mendelssohn's String Symphonies Nos 9 and 11, Geminiani's *La foresta incantata* and Concerti Grossi Op. 7, Verdi's String Quartet, Wolf-Ferrari's *Serenade for Strings*, and pieces by Bussotti. He has also recorded Mozart's Divertimenti K. 136, K. 137 and K. 138 and *Eine kleine Nachtmusik* (with the Padua Chamber Orchestra, for Pye), the overtures to *Semiramide*, *Giovanna d'Arco*, *Norma*, *La vestale*, Mancinelli's *Cleopatra* and Ponchielli's *I promessi sposi* (with the Orchestre Philharmonique de l'ORTF for Erato) and flute concertos by Doppler and Romberg (with Rampal and Adorjan and the Monte Carlo National Opera Orchestra for Erato). A number of these discs have been released in Britain, but only a few in the US on Columbia, RCA; Musical Heritage Society has issued some also, including the Vivaldi Oboe Concertos and the Rossini String Sonatas.

I Solisti Veneti use modern instruments, Scimone has pointed out that the difficulties in performing with original instruments are, first, that the best performers of today seldom use these instruments, which are generally confined to specialists who are often mediocre performers, and secondly, man's ear has become less sensitive. While Scimone has recorded more Vivaldi than any other artist, he recognises that it is not feasible to consider recording all of the composer's output. Of the 94 or more operas of Vivaldi, for instance, he has recorded one, but it would be necessary to record others with great singers who are willing to give the time to learning the style. But, he says, 'the essential thing in the interpretation of music is to give a modern audience the emotion and message that the composer actually wrote into the music. We mustn't formalise performance practices that don't go into the substance of the music but only into appearances'. (*Hi Fi News and Record Review*, April 1978).

Scott, Charles Kennedy (1876–1965). Born in Romsey, Scott studied the organ at the Brussels Conservatory, where he took first prize (1897), then lived in London where he founded and conducted the Oriana Madrigal Society (1904), which became famous for its performances of old and modern music. In 1919 he also founded and conducted the London Philharmonic Choir, which performed together with the Royal Philharmonic Orchestra. He published a text on madrigal singing and edited carols and choral music of the 16th century. Scott was a most distinguished choral conductor, and both the Oriana Madrigal Society and the Philharmonic Choir were regarded in their time as the best in Britain. He recorded, for HMV on 78 r.p.m. discs, Bach's Cantata No. 147, the sinfonia from Cantata No. 156, *O Jerusalem süss* and *Er is vollbracht* (with the London Bach Cantata Club), two choruses from *Messiah*, the Mozart *Requiem* and the Kyrie from the Mass No. 12, excerpts from Schubert's *Mass in G major*, Holst's Psalm 148, *Evening Hymn* and Elgar's *The Banner of St George* (with the Philharmonic Choir), Holst's Psalm 186 (with the Manchester Philharmonic Choir), Grainger's *Brigg Fair* and *Coventry Carol* (with the Oriana Madrigal Society) and the Nightingale Chorus from Handel's *Solomon* (with the Bach Cantata Club for Columbia).

Seaman, Christopher (b. 1942). Born in Faversham, Kent, Seaman studied music at King's College, Cambridge, and at the Guildhall School of Music, was timpanist with the London Philharmonic Orchestra (1964–8), and became a director of the orchestra. He was appointed assistant conductor of the BBC Scottish Orchestra in 1968, became its chief conductor (1971), and was also appointed principal conductor and artistic director of the Northern Sinfonia Orchestra (1974). He has conducted the major British orchestras, at the Scottish Opera, and also in New Zealand, Italy, Czechoslovakia, Holland, Belgium and Norway. His one recording has been a collection of trumpet concertos by Haydn, Hummel and Neruda (with William Lang and the Northern Sinfonia, for Unicorn).

Sebastian, Georges (b. 1903). Born in Budapest, Sebastian was a pupil of Bartók, Kodály and Weiner at the Franz Liszt Academy, graduated in 1921, and studied conducting with Walter at Munich (1922–3). He became a repetiteur at the Munich Opera, was an assistant conductor at the New York Metropolitan Opera (1923–4), conductor at the Hamburg Municipal Opera (1924–5), at the Leipzig Opera (1925–7), at the Berlin Staatsoper (1927–31), with the Moscow Radio Orchestra (1931–7), with the Scranton Philharmonic Orchestra, Pennsylvania (1940–45), at the San Francisco Opera (1944–7) and at the Paris Opéra (since 1947). In Moscow he presented cycles of the complete symphonies of Beethoven, Brahms and Schumann, and the five major operas of Mozart; he has also taken part in numerous festivals throughout Europe. He has recorded for many companies; paramount is a series for Urania which includes Liszt's *Dante* and *Faust* symphonies and *Mazeppa*, Dukas' *La Péri* and *Symphony in C*, d'Indy's *Istar*, *Lalo's Symphony in G minor* and *Rapsodie norvégienne*, Prokofiev's Symphony No. 4 and a suite from *The Prodigal Son*, Fauré's suite *Pelléas et Mélisande*, Franck's *Les Djinns* (with d'Arco), three *Spanish Dances* of Granados, the Albéniz/Arbós *Iberia*, Respighi's *Brazilian Impressions*, *Le Carnaval des animaux*, Schubert's Symphonies Nos 3 and 6 (with the Concerts Colonne Orchestra), Massenet's *Thaïs* (with the Paris Opéra Orchestra *et al.*), and *Werther* (with the Paris Opéra-Comique Orchestra *et al.*), Berlioz's *Marche funèbre* and a suite from *La Damnation de Faust*, a suite by Bizet, Franck's *Rédemption* and Lalo's *Namouna* Suites Nos 1 and 2 (with the Paris Conservatoire Orchestra), and the ballet music from *Faust* (with the Paris Opéra Orchestra).

Sebastian's other recordings include Bondeville's *Les Illuminations* and *Madame Bovary* (with the Belgian National Radio Orchestra for Decca), *Lakmé* (with the Paris Opéra-Comique Orchestra *et al.* for Decca), *Mignon* (with the Belgian National Radio Orchestra *et al.* for Decca), Chausson's *Poème* and Ravel's *Tzigane* (with Ferras and the Belgian National Radio Orchestra for Decca), an abridged *Carmen* (with the New York Metropolitan Opera Orchestra *et al.* for Columbia, US, and first issued on 78s), the Liebestod from *Tristan und Isolde* (with Varnay), some excerpts from *Siegfried* (with Flagstad, Svanholm and the Philharmonia Orchestra for EMI), Schoenberg's *Verklärte Nacht* and the Adagio from Mahler's Symphony No. 10 (with the Leipzig Gewandhaus Orchestra for EMI), a suite from

Coppélia (with the RIAS Symphony Orchestra for Everest), *Cavalleria rusticana* (with the La Fenice Theatre Orchestra *et al.* for Remington), overtures and orchestral excerpts from the Meyerbeer operas *L'Africaine*, *Les Huguenots*, *Le Pardon de Ploërmel* and *Le Prophète* (with the Paris Opéra Orchestra *et al.* for Nixa), *Symphonie fantastique*, the prelude to *Die Meistersinger* and the prelude, Venusberg Music, March and prelude to Act III from *Tannhäuser* (with the RIAS Symphony Orchestra for Remington), Rossellini's *L'annonce faite à Marie* (with the Italian Radio and Television Orchestra and Choir for La Guilde Internationale du Disque), *Tod und Verklärung* and the waltzes from *Der Rosenkavalier*, and the overture to *Die Fledermaus*, *An der schönen blauen Donau*, *G'schichten aus dem Wiener Wald*, *Kaiserwalzer*, *Künstlerleben* and the *Radetzky March* (with the South-West German Radio Orchestra for Musidisc).

Sebestyén, András (b. 1917). Born in Debrecen, Hungary, Sebestyén studied under Kodály at the Franz Liszt Academy in Budapest, was conductor at the Csokonai Theatre, Debrecen (1946), at the State Youth Theatre and National Theatre, Budapest, and at the Gardonyi Theatre, Eger, then joined Hungarian Radio (1959) and became director of the radio music department. He has composed orchestral, chamber and choral works, and incidental music for radio and the theatre; he recorded some Haydn Piano Concertos (with Frager and the RIAS Sinfonietta for Schwann), and a song recital (with Simándy and the Hungarian Radio and Television Orchestra for Hungaroton).

Segal, Uri (b. 1944). Born in Jerusalem where he studied at the Rubin Academy, Segal came to London in 1966, attended the Guildhall School of Music and was awarded the Ricordi Prize and Kapsalis Cup for conducting. In 1968 he won first prize at the Dmitri Mitropoulos International Conductors' Competition in New York, and was assistant conductor with the New York Philharmonic Orchestra with Bernstein. He made his debut in London in 1971 with the English Chamber Orchestra, then conducted the major British Orchestras, the Berlin Philharmonic, and toured several European countries, New Zealand and Israel. The next year he appeared in the United States with the Chicago Symphony Orchestra; in 1975 he was appointed chief guest conductor with both the South German Radio Orchestra at Stuttgart and the West German Radio Orchestra at Cologne, and now regularly conducts the more important European orchestras. His first record, in 1973, was a coupling of Stravinsky's *Symphony in C* and *L'Oiseau de feu* (with the Suisse Romande Orchestra); later he recorded Mozart's Piano Concertos K. 414 and K. 467 (with Lupu and the English Chamber Orchestra) and K. 467 and K. 488 (with Vered and the London Philharmonic Orchestra), and Beethoven's Piano Concerto No. 5 (with Firkusny and the New Philharmonic Orchestra). All were for Decca; for Colosseum he also recorded trombone concertos by Sachse, Reiche and Gräfe (with Rosin and the Nuremberg Symphony Orchestra).

Segarra, Ireneu, OSB (b. 1917). Born at Ivars d'Urgell in Catalonia, Segarra studied at the Escolania Choir School at the Monastery at Montserrat near Barcelona, and in Paris with Nadia Boulanger. He taught at the Escolania, and became its director in 1953. He has composed masses and sacred pieces for the Monastery, is author of a musical method for training boy singers, has edited and published music, and has prepared many recordings for Spanish and foreign publishing houses of compositions by masters of the Escolania during the 17th and 18th centuries. His recordings include Pergolesi's *Missa romana*, old Spanish music of de Oro, de Morales' *Missa queramus cum pastoribus*, motet *Exultata est Sancta Dei Genetrix* and *Ave Maria*, Monteverdi's *Vespro della beata Vergine* and Benevoli's *Missa Salisburgensis* (with the Escolania, the Collegium Aureum, and in the Benevoli, with the Tölz Boys' Choir, for BASF-Harmonia Mundi), Marti's *Christmas Cantata* (with the Escolania, for Charlin and Musica Sacra), Casanovas' *Responsoris de Settimana Santa* (with the Escolania for Musica Sacra), Victoria's Mass and *Responsories* (with the Escolania for Studios SM), López's *Alma redemptoris Mater* and *Salve Regina* (with the Catalan Chamber Orchestra *et al.* for Schwann), Cererols' *Missa pro defunctis* and *Seis villancicos*, and Julia's *Miserere*, *O Sacrum convivium* and *Psalm 6* (with the Escolania for Schwann), Viola's *Missa Redemptoris Mater*, sacred compositions by Rodamilans and Nees, motets by Mendelssohn, and Britten's *A Ceremony of Carols* (with the Escolania for Victoria-Montserrat), and eight choral works by Casals (with the Escolania for Everest).

Segerstam, Leif (b. 1944). Born at Vaasa, Finland, Segerstam studied at the Sibelius Academy under Hannikainen (1952–63), won a competition for pianists (1962) and made his debut as a violinist in Helsinki (1963), studied at the Juilliard School under Morel (1963–5), and was a conducting pupil of Susskind at Aspen, Colorado (1963). Returning to Finland, he became a teacher at the Sibelius Academy (1965–7), a conductor at the Finnish National Opera (1965–8), conducted symphony orchestras in Finland, toured with the Finnish National Ballet and visited the United States with the Helsinki Philharmonic Orchestra (1968). He was then conductor at the Royal Opera, Stockholm (1968), becoming principal conductor (1970) and musical director (1971), first conductor at the Deutsche Oper in West Berlin (1972–3), director of the Finnish National Opera (1973–4), in 1975 was appointed chief conductor of the Vienna Radio Orchestra, and is also conductor of the Helsinki Radio Symphony Orchestra. Since 1974 he has also been a guest conductor at opera houses and with orchestras in London, Milan, New York, Salzburg, and in Sweden, the USSR, Czechoslovakia, FR Germany *et al.* His compositions include orchestral, concerted, choral, chamber and instrumental works; after 1970 he wrote in his so-called 'free-pulsative' style, and he often conducts his own music in his programmes.

Segerstam's recordings include a complete *Swan Lake* (with the Royal Opera Orchestra, Stockholm, for Interdisc), Alfvén's Symphony No. 2 (with the Stockholm Philharmonic Orchestra, for Discofil and Electra), excerpts from *Parsifal* and *Die Walküre* (with Nilsson, Brillioth and the Covent Garden Orchestra for Philips), Sibelius' *Rakastava*, *Canzonetta* and *Mignonne* suite, Rautavaara's *Pelemannit* and his own *Divertimento* (with the Helsinki Chamber Orchestra for BIS). He has also led the Segerstam String Quartet in his own String Quartets Nos 4 and 5 (for Electra) and Nos 6 and 7 (for BIS).

Seiber, Mátyás (1905–60). Born in Budapest, Seiber studied the cello at the Franz Liszt Academy, and was a composition pupil of Kodály (1919–24). He left Hungary in 1925, taught at a private music school and at Hoch's Conservatory at Frankfurt am Main (1926–33), was the cellist in the Lenzewski Quartet, and in 1935 settled in London, where he was co-founder of the Society for the Promotion of New Music. In 1942 he joined the staff of Morley College, and conducted the College orchestra and the Dorian Singers. As a composer Seiber was first influenced by Kodály, and later by twelve-tone technique and jazz. He had taught jazz at Hoch's Conservatory, and lectured widely about jazz and modern music. In 1960 Decca released a recording of his music under his direction, which included Three Fragments from his chamber cantata *Portrait of the Artist as a Young Man* (with Pears, the Dorian Singers and the Melos Ensemble), and *Elegy* (with Aronowitz, viola, and the London Philharmonic Orchestra).

Seidler-Winkler, Bruno (1880–1960). Born in Berlin where he studied with Jedliczka, Seidler-Winkler was a member of the cathedral choir there, and was a child prodigy as a pianist. He was concertmaster of a theatre orchestra, artistic director for Deutsche Grammophon, conducted in Chicago (1923–5), and then was a conductor of the Berlin Radio Orchestra (1925–33). From 1934 he taught at the Hochschule für Musik in Berlin. He was one of the earliest recording conductors, and was recording for DGG at the turn of the century. He can be identified in a photograph taken at this time, with a group of musicians, with wing-collars and handlebar moustaches, crammed together in a tiny studio, with recording horns projected from the walls. Mauricio Kagel, the present-day composer, was commissioned to write his *1898* to commemorate DGG's 75th birthday; he noted from the photograph that Seidler-Winkler's 'resemblance to Groucho Marx is indisputable'. The music recorded then is not known, but in 1908 Seidler-Winkler made a version of *Carmen*, with Emmy Destinn *et al.*, which has been recently issued on an LP transfer by Discophilia. He recorded in 1911 several overtures, and in 1913 Beethoven's Symphonies Nos 5 and 9 (with the New Symphony Orchestra *et al.* for HMV). His later records included excerpts from Act II of *Die Walküre* (with the Berlin Staatsoper Orchestra and Lehmann, Melchior, Fuchs, Klose, Hotter and List), which completed the part of Act II recorded by Walter of the opera in Vienna, the Liebestod from *Tristan und Isolde* (with Fuchs and the Berlin Staatsoper Orchestra), *Danse macabre*, the overtures *La gazza ladra*, *Dichter und Bauer* and *Der Waffenschmied* (with the Berlin Staatsoper Orchestra) and *Der Wildschütz* (with a concert orchestra), Egk's *Olympische Jugend* and Strauss's *Olympic Hymn* (both written for the 1936 Olympic Games in Berlin), Verdi's *Ave Maria* (with Perras and orchestra), and arias from some Weber operas (with Roswaenge and the Berlin Staatsoper Orchestra) and from *Don Carlos* (with Streinz and the Berlin Radio Orchestra). He also accompanied the violinist Neveu, on the piano, in a piece by Suk and in an arrangement of a Chopin Nocturne, and Roswaenge in some songs. All these discs were for HMV; for Telefunken he recorded the ballet music from

Faust (with the Berlin Philharmonic Orchestra).

Seiler, Robert. Seiler studied in Munich and Berlin, where he was a pupil of Scherchen, and was director of the music section of Radio Munich (1945–9). He has performed with the Munich and Dresden Philharmonic Orchestras, and is a noted Beethoven scholar. He has recorded Beethoven's Piano Concerto No. 1 (with Appel and the Nuremberg Symphony Orchestra for Colosseum), using a historic Beethoven piano.

Šejna, Karel (b. 1896). The eminent Czech conductor Šejna was born in Zájezdy near Strakonice in southern Bohemia, and graduated from the Prague Conservatory in 1920. He toured as a double-bass player in Egypt (1920–21), and joined the Czech Philharmonic Orchestra as first double-bass player in 1921. He began on occasion to conduct the orchestra, and became the conductor of the symphony orchestra of the Czechoslovak Railwaymen (1925–36) and of the Prague Choir Hlahol (1930–36). In 1938 he became conductor of the Czech Philharmonic Orchestra, in 1949 artistic director and in 1950 first conductor. He received the Prize of the City of Prague in 1951 and the title Meritorious Artist in 1960. He is specially noted for his idiomatic interpretations of Smetana, Dvořák, Fibich and composers of the end of the 19th century such as Suk, Novák and Mahler, and for his leadership of major choral works. Similar to many other distinguished Czech conductors, his style is characterised by a vitality and straightforwardness that often prefers exuberance to subtlety.

Some 78 r.p.m. discs were issued by Supraphon with Šejna conducting the Czech Symphony Orchestra, viz, the overture to *The Bartered Bride*, and Dvořák's *The Wild Dove* and *Scherzo capriccioso*. Later, on LP, he recorded for Supraphon a number of discs with the Czech Philharmonic Orchestra, including Mozart's Symphonies Nos 38 and 39, *Eine kleine Nachtmusik* and the overtures to *Le nozze di Figaro, Così fan tutte* and *La clemenza di Tito*, Beethoven's Symphony No. 6, Piano Concerto No. 5 (with Rauch) and the two *Romances* (with Plocek), *Capriccio italien*, the complete *Má Vlast* and Smetana's *Festival Symphony*, *Richard III*, *Wallenstein's Camp*, *Haakon Jarl* and *Shakespearian Festival March*, Dvořák's Symphonies Nos 5, 6 and 7, the *Slavonic Dances*, Opp. 46 and 72, the three *Slavonic Rhapsodies*, *Legends*, *Scherzo Capriccioso*, *Suite in A*, *Symphonic Variations* and *Husitská*, Novák's *The Eternal Longing* and *In the Tatras*, Fibich's Symphony No. 2 and cantata *The Romance of Spring*. Seidel's cantata *People, Behold!*, Mahler's Symphony No. 4 (with Tauberová), d'Indy's *Symphonie sur un chant montagnard français* (with Boschi), Martinů's *Concerto for Two String Orchestras, Piano and Timpani*, Kalabis' Piano Concerto (with Růžičková), the overtures *Le Corsaire*, *Tancredi*, *Semiramide*, *La scala di seta*, *Prince Igor* and *Oberon*, and the prelude to *Parsifal*. With the Brno Philharmonic Orchestra he also recorded Novák's *Slovak Suite* and *Maryša* overture. All of these records were made before the advent of stereo; none of them is now listed in Schwann, but some are available in Britain still.

Semenoff, Ivan (b. 1917). Born in Paris, Semenoff studied at the Paris Conservatoire and with Honegger. Decca recorded, on an early LP, his *Double Concerto for Violin, Piano and Orchestra*, with him conducting the Paris Conservatoire Orchestra and with Ferras and Barbizet the soloists.

Semkow, Jerzy (Georg) (b. 1928). Born at Radomsko, Poland, Semkow studied at the Kraków Conservatory and at the Leningrad Conservatory under Mravinsky, and later with Serafin, Kleiber and Walter. He was assistant conductor to Mravinsky with the Leningrad Philharmonic Orchestra and conductor of the Leningrad Opera Studio (1954–6), conductor at the Bolshoi Theatre, Moscow (1956–8), artistic director and principal conductor of the Warsaw National Opera (1959–61), permanent conductor of the Danish Royal Opera and conductor of the Royal Danish Symphony Orchestra (1966–75). He first conducted in the United States at Boston in 1968, conducted the London Philharmonic Orchestra on its Far Eastern tour in 1969, and in 1975 was appointed musical director and principal conductor of the St Louis Symphony Orchestra, and is also director of the Teatro Fenice, Venice. He has conducted the major orchestras in the US and in London, Berlin, Vienna *et al.*, and at the operas at Covent Garden, La Scala and Rome.

Both in the USSR and in the West, Semkow has frequently conducted the music of Scriabin, and in 1969 he recorded a fine performance of the composer's Symphony No. 2 (with the London Philharmonic Orchestra for CBS). In Poland he recorded Mozart's Symphonies Nos 33 and 36, excerpts from *Carmen*, excerpts from *Halka* and other operas of Moniuszko, *España*, *Capriccio espagnol*, *Rapsodie espagnole* and *El amor brujo* (with the Warsaw Philharmonic Orchestra *et al.*). With the Royal Danish Symphony Orchestra he recorded Holmboe's Symphony No. 8, Nielsen's *Helios* overture and Violin Concerto (with Varga), Per Nørgård's *Constellations* and Riisager's ballets *Etudes* and *Qarrtsiluni* (for Turnabout); his other discs include Chopin's Piano Concerto No. 1 (with Vasary and the Berlin Philharmonic Orchestra for DGG), a complete *Prince Igor* (with the Sofia National Opera for EMI), the original version of *Boris Godunov* (with the Polish Radio Orchestra and Chorus *et al.* for EMI), *Scheherazade*, and the four Schumann symphonies and *Manfred* overture (with the St Louis Symphony Orchestra for Vox) and an aria recital (with Ładysz and the Warsaw Opera Orchestra for Muza).

Serafin, Tullio (1878–1968). Born at Rottanova di Cavarzere, near Venice, Serafin studied at the Milan Conservatory and was a violinist in the La Scala Orchestra. He first conducted at the Theatre at Ferrara (1900), then was conductor at Turin (1903), the Augusteo, Rome (1906), at La Scala, Milan (1909, 1919, 1939–40 and 1946–7), at Covent Garden, London (1907, 1931, 1959 and 1960), at the New York Metropolitan Opera (1924–34) and at Chicago (1956–8); he was artistic director and chief conductor at the Rome Opera (1934–43 and in 1962). His contribution to operatic performance was enormous and has scarcely been paralleled; he gave first performances in Italy of *Der Rosenkavalier*, *Wozzeck*, *Peter Grimes*, *Sorochintsy Fair* and *La vida breve*, introduced *La forza del destino* at Covent Garden, and *Turandot* and *Simon Boccanegra* in New York, gave the first performances in New York of, amongst others, *Merry Mount*, *The Emperor Jones* and *Peter Ibbetson*, and was responsible for the early development of Gigli, Ponselle and Callas, and coached Sutherland for the *Lucia di Lammermoor* which first made her famous.

Serafin's recording career has been equally distinguished, and has marked him as one of the most outstanding conductors of recorded opera. In 1939 he recorded the Verdi *Requiem* in Rome, and during World War II *Aida* and *Un ballo in maschera*, and these were issued on 78s in Britain and the United States after the war; because of the presence of Gigli in particular, the performances were later re-issued on LP. His other 78 r.p.m. discs included *La Boutique fantasque*, the overtures to *Il matrimonio segreto*, *Il barbiere di Siviglia*, *La scala di seta* and *L'Italiana in Algeri*, the ballet music to *William Tell*, the Bacchanale from *Samson et Dalila*, *Venetian Scenes, No. 3*, of Mancinella and Mangiagalli's ballet *Il carillon magico* (with the Florence May Festival, the Santa Cecilia and the Rome Symphony Orchestras, for EMI). In 1953 he commenced the celebrated series of La Scala recordings for EMI in which Callas was, with some exceptions, the principal soloist; the operas were *I puritani*, *Norma*, *Medea*, *Lucia di Lammermoor*, *L'elisir d'amore*, *Cavalleria rusticana*, *Pagliacci*, *La forza del destino*, *Aida*, *Rigoletto*, *La traviata*, *Manon Lescaut* and *Turandot*; *Lucia di Lammermoor* and *Norma* (with the Philharmonia Orchestra *et al.*) were re-made in 1960–61. He also recorded *Linda di Chamounix*, *Tosca* and Rossini's *Mosè* (with the San Carlo Opera Orchestra, Naples, *et al.* for Philips), *Mefistofele*, *Cavalleria rusticana*, *La Bohème* and *Madama Butterfly* (with the Santa Cecilia Orchestra *et al.* for Decca), *La traviata*, *Suor Angelica* and *Gianni Schicchi* (with the Rome Opera Orchestra *et al.* for EMI), *Otello* (with the Rome Opera Orchestra *et al.* for RCA, re-issued in 1976), *Il segreto di Susanna* (with the Florence May Festival Orchestra *et al.*), *Il barbiere di Siviglia* (with the Milan Symphony Orchestra *et al.* for EMI), the Verdi *Requiem* (with the Rome Opera Chorus and Orchestra *et al.* for EMI), *Il trovatore* (with the La Scala Orchestra *et al.* for DGG), excerpts from Mascagni's *Isabeau* (for Cetra), choruses from the Verdi operas (with the La Scala Chorus and Orchestra for EMI), and the overtures to *La forza del destino*, *Giovanna d'Arco*, *Nabucco* and *I vespri siciliani*, the prelude to *Aida* and the preludes to Acts I and III of *La traviata* (with the Philharmonia and Royal Philharmonic Orchestras for EMI), overtures to *Norma*, *Linda di Chamounix*, *Don Pasquale*, *La Cenerentola*, *I vespri siciliani* and *Il segreto di Susanna* and the intermezzo from Act III of *L'amico Fritz* (with the Philharmonia Orchestra for EMI), and the overtures to *La gazza ladra*, *La scala di seta*, *William Tell*, *Il barbiere di Siviglia* and the storm music from *Il barbiere di Siviglia* (with the Rome Opera Orchestra for DGG). L'Estro Armonico also issued a performance of *Armida*, which Serafin conducted at Florence in 1952.

Serebrier, José (b. 1938). Born in Montevideo of Russian and Polish parents, Serebrier studied the violin as a boy, and at the age of 11 made his debut as a conductor with the National Youth Orchestra of Uruguay, with which he gave numerous concerts in South America for four years. After attending the Montevideo School of Music, he came to the United States in 1955 to study with Martinů at the Curtis Institute in Philadelphia. He was an apprentice conductor with Dorati at Minneapolis, graduated from the University of Minnesota, and his Symphony No. 1 (1957), *Elegy for Strings* (1962) and *Poema elegiaco* were given their first performances by Stokowski in New York. He studied conducting with Monteux and Szell, and was associate conductor to Stokowski with the American Symphony Orchestra, assisting Stokowski in 1965 at the première of Ives' Symphony No. 4. He has taught at Syracuse and Michigan Universities and at the Dalcroze School of Music in New York, was invited by Szell to be composer-in-residence with the Cleveland Orchestra (1968–70), was musical director and conductor of the Cleveland Philharmonic Orchestra and of the Worcester Music Festival, Massachusetts, and is principal conductor of the Mexican Opera. In 1970 he made his London debut with the London Symphony Orchestra; Elgar, Delius, Vaughan Williams and Britten are included in his repertoire. His recorded performances have been Barber's *Souvenirs*, Menotti's *Sebastian* (with the London Symphony Orchestra for Desto) and the Ives Symphony No. 4 (with the London Philharmonic Orchestra *et al.* for RCA).

Serly, Tibor (1900–78). The son of a Hungarian composer of popular operettas, Serly emigrated to the United States with his family when he was a child, but returned to Hungary to study with Kodály and Bartók. He was a violinist in the Cincinnati and Philadelphia Orchestras, won a reputation as a composer, and was a teacher of musical theory, having Morton Gould and Robert Russell Bennett among his students. For the five years when Bartók was in the US, Serly devoted his time and energies to assisting him and promoting performances of his music; when Bartók died he had left 17 bars of his Piano Concerto No. 3 unfinished, which Serly completed in the composer's own manuscript in the hope that Bartók would get full credit. He also constructed the Viola Concerto from sections and pieces Bartók had written. Records of Serly's own compositions have been issued by Musical Heritage Society, including his Two-Piano Concerto (with Frid and Ponse, and with Serly conducting the Vienna Volksoper Orchestra), and a completion and orchestration of the fragment of Schubert's Scherzo to his Symphony No. 8. He also conducted the Vienna Symphony Orchestra in Bartók's Piano Concerto No. 3, with Ditta Pásztory Bartók, the composer's wife, as soloist (for MHS). His other recordings, for the Bartók Society, were Bartók's Viola Concerto (with Primrose), *Mikrokosmos* (suite for orchestra), *Two Portraits*, the Rhapsodies for Violin and *Deux Images* (with Vardi) and *The Miraculous Mandarin* (all with the New Symphony Orchestra) and the *Divertimento* and Scarlatti's *Cat's Fugue* (with a string orchestra).

Setti, Giulio (1869–1938). Born in Traviglio, Italy, Setti was a chorus-master at opera houses in Italy, at Cairo, Cologne, Buenos Aires and at the New York Metropolitan (1908–35). He directed the Metropolitan Opera Orchestra in aria recitals by artists such as Gigli, Martinelli and Ponselle for Victor.

Sevitzky, Fabian (1891–1967). Born at Vishny-Voloch, near Tver in Russia, Sevitzky was the nephew of Serge Koussevitzky. He moved with his family to St Petersburg, where he studied at the Conservatory under Rimsky-Korsakov, Liadov and Glazunov, won a gold medal as a double-bass player, and played the instrument at the Imperial Opera in Moscow (1911–15), toured Russia as a double-bass virtuoso, and after service in the Russian army returned to Moscow at the outbreak of the Revolution and played in orchestras there. He left Moscow in 1922 for Warsaw, played in the State Opera and Warsaw Philharmonic Orchestras, and in 1923 emigrated to the United States. He first toured Mexico, then became a double-bass player in the Philadelphia Orchestra (1923–30) and founded and conducted the Philadelphia Chamber String Sinfonietta (1925–37), which, as David Ewen suggests, was the first permanent string orchestra in the world. After 1930 he conducted orchestras in the US and Europe, led the People's Symphony Orchestra in Boston (1934–6), and finally was conductor of the Indianapolis Symphony Orchestra (1937–55). Previously he had conducted Russian opera with the Philadelphia Grand Opera (1927), and in the last years of his life was a guest conductor in the US and abroad.

Sevitzky was an affable, gentle-mannered man who enjoyed good relations with all members of the orchestra. As a conductor he was more enthusiastic than especially distinguished; his term with the Indianapolis orchestra raised it to a high standard. He was most active in promoting US composers, and included an American composition in almost every concert. Each year he received about 100 new American works; half of them he rejected, but the other half he ran through at rehearsals to select those he could include in his concert programmes. Not surprisingly he was honoured in 1938 as having done more for American composers than any other conductor.

Sevitzky recorded for Victor and Capitol with the Philadelphia Chamber String Sinfonietta and the Indianapolis Symphony Orchestra. The works included the sinfonia from Bach's Cantata No. 156, Dubensky's *Gossips*, Grainger's *Londonderry Air*, the march from *Denys le Tyran* and the pantomime from *Zémire et Azore* of Grétry, and Bloch's Concerto Grosso No. 1 (with the Philadelphia Chamber String Sinfonietta); and with the Indianapolis Symphony Orchestra Haydn's Symphony No. 73 and overture to *L'isola disabitata*, the *Peer Gynt* Suite No. 2, *Sigurd Jorsalfar* and the *Symphonic Dances* of Grieg, suites from *Sylvia* and *Coppélia*, Tchaikovsky's Symphony No. 1, *Manfred* symphony and the waltz from *Eugene Onegin*, some *Slavonic Dances* of Dvořák, Kalinnikov's Symphony No. 1, Liadov's *Baba Yaga*, Glazunov's *From the Middle Ages*, the overture to *Russlan and Ludmilla*, Rimsky-Korsakov's *Dubinushka*, suites from Khachaturian's *Masquerade* and *Gayane*, a waltz of Weber, Strauss's *Frühlingstimmen*, the two *Romanian Rhapsodies* of Enesco, Kreisler's *Praeludium and Allegro*, a suite from *Porgy and Bess*, and Dubensky's *Fugue for Eighteen Violins* and *Theme, Variations and Finale – Stephen Foster*. The recordings of the Tchaikovsky and Kalinnikov symphonies were novelties for their time, and, given the limitations of Sevitzky and his orchestra, were commendable performances. Angelicum, in Italy, later issued an LP of Haydn's Symphony No. 95, in which Sevitzky conducted the Angelicum Orchestra.

Seyfarth, Lothar (b. 1931). Born in Bernsbach and educated at the Hochschule für Musik at Leipzig, Seyfarth became a repetiteur at Stralsund (1955–62), was chief conductor at Stendal (1962–4) and with the orchestra of the DR Germany film company (1964–7), conducted the Dresden Philharmonic Orchestra and was appointed chief conductor at the Weimar National Theatre (1973). He has toured in Poland, Czechoslovakia, Bulgaria, Romania, Italy and France, and has actively promoted contemporary East German composers, in addition to the customary standard repertoire. For Eterna he recorded a number of the Handel Organ Concertos (with Köhler and the Weimar Staatskapelle Chamber Orchestra).

Shapey, Ralph (b. 1912). Born in Philadelphia, Shapey studied violin with Zetlin and composition with Wolpe, and became associate professor of music at the University of Chicago, where he is also music director of the Contemporary Chamber Players of the University. For his compositions he has received many awards and commissions, including those from the Dmitri Mitropoulos, Koussevitzky and Fromm Foundations. As a conductor he has recorded Erickson's *Chamber Concerto* (with the Hartt Chamber Orchestra, for Composers Recordings), his own *Rituals* (with the London Sinfonietta for Composers Recordings), *Songs of Ecstasy* (with Pilgrim, Cobb and the Contemporary Chamber Players, for Desto) and *Incantations* (with Beardslee and the Contemporary Chamber Players for Composers Recordings), Putsché's *The Cat and the Moon*, Weinberg's *Cantus Commemorabilis I*, Schindler's *String Sextet*, Thorne's *Six Set Pieces for Thirteen Players*, and Yarden's *Divertimento* (with the Contemporary Chamber Players for Composers Recordings).

Shapirra, Elyakum (b. 1926). Born in Tel-Aviv, Shapirra came to the notice of Bernstein when he took part in a conductors' competition in Israel, and he then went to the United States to study with Bernstein and Koussevitzky at Tanglewood, and at the Juilliard School. He then became assistant conductor with the San Francisco Symphony Orchestra and also with the New York Philharmonic Orchestra (1960–61), which he conducted on tours to Canada and Japan. He was associate conductor of the Baltimore Symphony Orchestra (1962–7), conducted major orchestras in Britain (1968), was chief conductor of the Malmö Symphony Orchestra, Sweden (1969–74) and then in 1975 was appointed chief conductor of the South Australian Symphony Orchestra at Adelaide. He has also conducted opera in Sweden and has been a guest conductor with most of the major US orchestras. In 1972 EMI issued a disc by him including Bruckner's early *Symphony in F minor* and *Overture in G minor* (with the London Symphony Orchestra).

Sharples, Robert. After studying orchestration and conducting with Harty, Sharples was a musical director and arranger for the BBC, Granada, CBS and for other radio and television companies, and also for Decca Records. He composed film music, and was musical adviser for Conroy Records. He recorded as a conductor the *Nutcracker* Suite and *1812* overture (with the London Festival Orchestra for Decca), and a collection of pieces by Ketèlby (with the New Symphony Orchestra for Decca).

Shaw, Robert (b. 1916). Born at Red Bluff, California, the son of a minister, Shaw studied at Pomona College, where he conducted the college Glee Club. In 1938, on Fred Waring's invitation, he went to New York to conduct Fred Waring's Glee Club, which performed in association with Fred Waring's orchestra (1938–45); in 1941 he formed the Collegiate Chorale in New York, which was superseded in 1944 by the Robert Shaw Chorale, an entirely professional body. He was head of the choral departments at the Berkshire Music Center (1942–5) and the Juilliard School (1946–50); in 1944 he had also been director of the RCA Victor Chorale. He toured extensively with the Robert Shaw Chorale in the United States and abroad; in 1952–3 he gave 175 performances of the Mozart *Requiem*, and in 1959–60 36 performances of Bach's *Mass in B minor*. With the Chorale he toured Europe and the Middle East for the State Department in 1956, toured the USSR in 1962 and Latin America in 1964. Previously he had turned his attention to orchestral conducting, was conductor of the San Diego Symphony Orchestra (1953–7), associate conductor with Szell of the Cleveland Orchestra and conductor of the Cleveland Orchestra Chorus (1956–67), and in 1966 became co-conductor with Louis Lane of the Atlanta Symphony Orchestra. In 1943 he was named the most outstanding American conductor of the year by the National Association for American Composers and Conductors.

As a choral conductor Shaw has done more than any other American to raise standards of choral singing in the US. He acknowledges that his greatest influences have been Toscanini, Szell and Julius Herford, a refugee German choral conductor whom Shaw had met at the Juilliard School. With Herford he founded the Anchorage Music Festival in Alaska in 1946; the Robert Shaw Chorale, prepared by Shaw, appeared in many of Toscanini's recordings with the NBC Symphony Orchestra, including Beethoven's Symphony No. 9 and *Missa Solemnis*, and the Verdi *Requiem*; Toscanini considered him the finest choral director with whom he had ever collaborated. In addition to the baroque, classical and romantic choral masterpieces, Shaw conducts modern music, and has commissioned first performances of music by Britten, Copeland, Barber, Ives, Milhaud, Bartók *et al.* A member of one of his choirs said that Shaw appears to be a man who lives under a great deal of internal stress, but who has resolved not to relieve these pressures by attacking the performers. At rehearsals he is quiet, tense and gentle, but at the performance he is less businesslike and more expressive, a characteristic common to other leading conductors – 'In rehearsal his job has been to listen and correct, now his job is to inspire' (Don Ray).

Shaw's first records were with the Collegiate Chorale, for RCA, and were Bach's *Mass in B minor*. He also recorded with the RCA Victor Chorale and Symphony Orchestra Bach's Cantata No. 140 and Bridal Chorus from *Lohengrin*, with the Robert Shaw Chorale Bach's motet *Jesu meine Freude*, some choral songs of Schubert, Britten's *Ceremony of Carols* and Poulenc's *Petites Voix*, and with the Robert Shaw Chorale and the RCA Victor Symphony Orchestra Bach's *Magnificat*, Brahms' *Ein deutsches Requiem*, the Anvil Chorus from *Il trovatore*, and several arias from Bach Cantatas (with Marian Anderson). His LP series with his Chorale and the same orchestra included Vivaldi's *Gloria* (ed. Martens) and *Kyrie* (ed. Aslamin), Bach's *Mass in B minor*, *St John Passion*, Cantatas Nos 4, 56, 82 and 131 and several Motets, Mozart's *Requiem* and *Vesperae solennes de confessore*, *Messiah*, the Beethoven *Missa Solemnis*, Schubert's *Mass No. 2*, Brahms' *Ein deutsches Requiem*, *Alto Rhapsody* and *Liebeslieder Waltzes*, Stravinsky's *Symphony of Psalms*, Poulenc's *Gloria*, Britten's *Rejoice in the Lamb* and *Festival Te Deum*, Schoenberg's *Friede auf Erden*, Ives' *Three Harvest Home Chorales* and Ravel's *Trois Chansons*, as well as popular choral collections of carols, hymns, Negro spirituals, Irish folk songs, Broadway choruses, songs of Stephen Foster and Victor Herbert, sea shanties and operatic choruses. He also recorded Hale Smith's *In Memoriam – Beryl Rubinstein* and Whittaker's cantata *Behold He Cometh with Clouds* (with the Kulas Choir *et al.*) and Bach's Cantatas Nos 42 and 60 (with the Bach Aria Group, the Robert Shaw Chorale *et al.* for RCA).

Shereshevsky, Aron (1906–67). The Russian musician Shereshevsky was a professor at the Moscow Conservatory and was chief conductor of the student opera theatre where those studying to be operatic singers give performances. He recorded Liszt's *Spanish Rhapsody* and Rubinstein's Piano Concerto No. 4 (with Ginsburg and the USSR State Symphony Orchestra).

Sherman, Alec (b. 1907). Born in London, Sherman studied music as a boy, was educated at the Davenant Foundation School, and joined the BBC Symphony Orchestra as a violinist when it was formed in 1930. In 1941 he became permanent conductor of the New London Orchestra, and came to public attention in World War II through performances of all the Mozart

Piano Concertos with Dame Myra Hess. He conducted at the Sadler's Wells Ballet (1943–5), with the Portuguese Symphony Orchestra (1945–6), toured Czechoslovakia and Egypt, and was active for many years in London with the New London Orchestra. He married the Greek pianist Gina Bachauer, and with her and the New London Orchestra recorded (for EMI) Bach's Harpsichord Concerto No. 5 and *Two-Harpsichord Concerto in C major* (with Kabos), Mozart's Piano Concertos K. 271, K. 453, K. 491 and K. 537, Liszt's Piano Concerto No. 1 and *Spanish Rhapsody*, Tchaikovsky's Piano Concerto No. 1, Saint-Saëns' Piano Concerto No. 2, the Fauré *Ballade*, and Rachmaninov's Piano Concerto No. 3. He also conducted the orchestra in Castelnuovo-Tedesco's Guitar Concerto (with Segovia, on 78s, for EMI).

Shilkret, Nathaniel (b. 1895). Born in New York, Shilkret was a clarinettist in orchestras in New York, became musical director of the Victor Talking Machine Company, founded the Victor Salon Orchestra, was a conductor and arranger in Hollywood, and conducted a vast number of radio musical programmes. He recorded for Victor on 78 r.p.m. discs Sibelius' *Finlandia*, *Valse triste*, *Caprice* and excerpts from the *Scaramouche* suite, Tchaikovsky's *Chanson triste*, *Humoresque*, *Romance* and the waltz from the *Serenade in C major*, Schubert's *German Dances*, *Marche militaire No. 1* and arrangements of *Die Forelle* and *Gretchen am Spinnrade*, and Johann Strauss' *Schatz Walzer* and *Kaiserwalzer* (with the Victor Salon Orchestra), the Barcarolle from *Les Contes d'Hoffmann* (with the International Concert Orchestra), the overture to *Raymond*, Carpenter's *Skyscrapers* and Kleinsinger's *I Hear America Singing* (with the Victor Symphony Orchestra) and a number from *Porgy and Bess* (with Jepson and an orchestra). Vanguard also issued an LP in which he conducted Robinson's *Ballad for Americans* (with Robeson, the American People's Chorus and the Victor Symphony Orchestra). Kolodin, in his comments about many of these records in *A Guide to Recorded Music* (1941), was scarcely enthusiastic; concerning the Tchaikovsky waltz, he wrote: 'The Shilkret disc might be labelled "Crime and Punishment", if the purchaser is unwary enough to make the investment.'

Shostakovich, Dmitri (1906–76). The great Russian composer was a distinguished pianist, and has recorded his two piano concertos, and his preludes and fugues. He had no particular reputation as a conductor; Malko led the première of his Symphony No. 1 and Mravinsky that of the Symphony No. 5 and most of his other major works. Nonetheless, Colosseum (US) released a performance of his Symphony No. 10 in which he conducted the USSR National Symphony Orchestra.

Shostakovich, Maxim (b. 1938). The son of the composer, Shostakovich was born in Leningrad, studied under Rabinovich at the Leningrad Conservatory (1961–2), and then under Gauk and Rozhdestvensky at the Moscow Conservatory. He was assistant conductor of the Moscow Symphony Orchestra (1964) and assistant conductor to Svetlanov with the USSR State Symphony Orchestra (1966), and won a conductors' competition in the USSR (1966). Since 1971 he has been principal conductor of the Moscow Radio Symphony Orchestra; he made his debut in London with the London Philharmonic Orchestra in 1968, toured Canada with the USSR State Symphony Orchestra and Svetlanov (1969), and since has been a guest conductor in Europe, North America and Australia. He is also a fine pianist; in 1957 his father composed for him his Piano Concerto No. 2, and for some time he hesitated between becoming a pianist or conductor. For Melodiya he has recorded his father's ballets *Bolt*, *The Age of Gold*, the three Suites, music for the films *Zoya* and *Pirogov* (with the Bolshoi Theatre Orchestra), music for the films *Michurin* and *A Year is Worth a Lifetime*, the *Overture on Russian and Kirghiz Folk Themes*, the Symphony No. 15, the Violin Concerto No. 1 (with Igor Oistrakh) and the *Suite on Verses of Michelangelo* (with Nesterenko, and with the Moscow Radio Symphony Orchestra), and the Symphony No. 5 (with the USSR State Symphony Orchestra), Mendelssohn's Symphony No. 1 and Rimsky-Korsakov's *Sinfonietta on Russian Themes*, *Fantasia on Serbian Themes*, *Sadko* and *Overture on Russian Themes* (with the Moscow Radio Symphony Orchestra); and Mozart's Violin Concerto K. 216 and Mendelssohn's *Violin Concerto in E minor* (with Klimov and the USSR State Symphony Orchestra). For EMI he also recorded Shostakovich's Violin Concerto No. 1 (with David Oistrakh and the New Philharmonia Orchestra). Of these discs, the Shostakovich Symphony No. 5 and the *Suite on Verses of Michelangelo*, issued in 1971 and 1977 respectively, were outstanding.

Sibelius, Jean (1865–1957). Sibelius conducted his own music frequently in Europe, and led the first performances of most of his major compositions. During 1909 he conducted many of his works in England, and returned there in 1921, directing his Symphonies Nos 4 and 5 at the Queen's Hall. However, he never made commercial recordings as a conductor. In 1974 World Record Club issued a disc which brought together the famous performances of the Violin Concerto and *En Saga* (with Heifetz in the concerto, and the London Philharmonic Orchestra under Beecham, made in the 1930s), and added *Andante festivo*, in which Sibelius conducted the Finnish Radio Orchestra. This piece was recorded in 1939 by the Finnish Broadcasting Company, who made the tape available to WRC. As Robert Layton pointed out on the sleeve note, 'One gets some idea of the sheer intensity of feeling that Sibelius could draw from the strings.'

Šídlo, Antonin (b. 1925). Born at Klučenice near Milevsko, Šídlo studied at the Conservatory and Academy of Music at Prague, has been conductor of the Czech Singers since 1950, succeeding Veselka and Kühn, and directed the ensemble at the Handel Festival in Halle in 1959. He has been responsible for the preparation of the Czech Philharmonic Choir in performances of the great choral masterpieces by the Czech Philharmonic Orchestra. For Supraphon he recorded Fišer's *Requiem* (with the Czech Philharmonic Choir and the Prague Symphony Orchestra).

Siegmeister, Elie (b. 1909). Born in New York, Siegmeister studied at Columbia University and at the Juilliard School, and with Friedberger, Riegger, Bingham and Nadia Boulanger, and made his debut as a conductor in New York in 1940. In 1966 he became composer-in-residence at Hofstra University at Long Island. His compositions include operas, stage shows, film and television scores, instrumental, chamber and vocal music; his cantata *I Have a Dream* was telecast nationally in the United States in 1968. A number of his works have been recorded; Composers Recordings issued a disc in which he conducts the Oslo Philharmonic Orchestra in his Symphony No. 3.

Silvestri, Constantin (1913–69). Born in Bucharest, Silvestri gave a public concert as a pianist at the age of eleven, then attended the Bucharest Conservatory where he studied with Enesco, Jora and Muzicescu. After touring as a pianist he first conducted in 1930 with the Bucharest Radio Symphony Orchestra, became a conductor with the Bucharest Opera (1935–46), conductor of the Bucharest Philharmonic Orchestra (1945–55) and teacher of conducting at the Bucharest Conservatory (from 1944). He left Romania in 1957, made his debut with the London Philharmonic Orchestra in London that year, and was appointed principal conductor of the Bournemouth Symphony Orchestra (1961–9). He composed several violin sonatas, string quartets and chamber works, and music for string orchestra. His repertoire as a conductor was comprehensive and his authority impressive; he was an unusual and distinctive musician, who frequently aroused controversy for his unorthodox interpretations, and was accused of imposing wilful distortions to heighten the dramatic effect, so much so that he appeared to be drastically editing the scores. He once performed Beethoven's Symphony No. 3 with very fast tempi and reduced dynamics, in the manner of early Haydn, which was an overwhelming contrast to the customary readings of the work. His Tchaikovsky was replete with mannerisms and uninhibited in his departures from the original scores; while both players and listeners were at times astonished at his liberties, none could deny the compellingly dramatic effects and the high standard of execution he achieved, or the intense preparation he gave to his performances. He stood alongside the great orchestral conductors in producing his own orchestral texture, with a refined and flexible string tone, evident especially in his last recordings with the Bournemouth Symphony Orchestra.

Before coming to the West, Silvestri recorded in Romania, Hungary, Czechoslovakia and the USSR. His recordings included Enesco's Suite No. 3 and *Concertante Overture on Romanian Folk Themes*, Shostakovich's Symphony No. 10, Alfred Mendelssohn's *The Downfall of Doftanea* and Constaninescu's opera *A Stormy Night* (with the Romanian Radio Symphony Orchestra *et al.*), Andricu's *Rustic Pictures*, Enesco's *Romanian Rhapsody No. 1* and *Octet for Strings* and Dimitrescu's *Peasant Dance* (with the Romanian Symphony Orchestra), Beethoven's *Missa Solemnis* (with the Bucharest Philharmonic Orchestra *et al.*), Haydn's Symphony No. 27 (with the Prague Symphony Orchestra), Ravel's *Rapsodie espagnole*, the Lalo Cello Concerto (with Navarra) and the two *Romanian Rhapsodies* of Enesco (with the Czech Philharmonic Orchestra), *El amor brujo* (with the Hungarian State Symphony Orchestra) and Shostakovich's Symphony No. 1 (with the USSR State Symphony Orchestra).

During his first visit to London in 1957, he recorded Tchaikovsky's Symphonies Nos 4, 5 and 6 (with the Philharmonia Orchestra for

EMI). His subsequent recordings for EMI were the two Liszt Piano Concertos (with François), the Tchaikovsky and Mendelssohn Violin Concertos (with Ferras), the Franck *Symphony in D minor*, the *Mathis der Maler* symphony, Bartók's *Divertimento*, the overtures to *Hänsel und Gretel*, *Russlan and Ludmilla*, *A Midsummer Night's Dream* and *Prince Igor*, *Les Préludes* and *Tasso*, Stravinsky's *Symphony in Three Movements* and *Le Chant du rossignol* (with the Philharmonia Orchestra), Dvořák's Symphony No. 8 and *Carnival* overture (with the London Philharmonic Orchestra), Dvořak's Symphony No. 9, Tchaikovsky's Piano Concerto No. 1 and Rachmaninov's Piano Concerto No. 2 (with Ciccoloni) and the *Manfred* symphony (with the French National Radio Symphony Orchestra); *Symphonie fantastique*, the Mendelssohn, Tchaikovsky and Beethoven Violin Concertos (with Kogan), *Prélude à l'après-midi d'un faune*, *La Mer* and *Nocturnes*, *Boléro*, *L'Apprenti sorcier* and *Danse macabre* (with the Paris Conservatoire Orchestra), the Beethoven Violin Concerto (with Menuhin), Dvořák's Symphony No. 7, Shostakovich's Symphony No. 5, Liszt's *Hungarian Rhapsody No. 4*, *Capriccio espagnol*, Ravel's *Rapsodie espagnole*, a suite from *The Love of Three Oranges*, a suite from *Gayane* and Enesco's *Romanian Rhapsody No. 1* (with the Vienna Philharmonic Orchestra), and *Capriccio italien*, the *1812* overture, the polonaise from *Eugene Onegin*, *A Night on the Bare Mountain*, *Finlandia*, *In the Steppes of Central Asia*, *L'Apprenti sorcier*, *Danse macabre*, *Pavane pour une infante défunte*, Elgar's *In the South*, and Vaughan Williams' overture to *The Wasps* and *Fantasia on a Theme of Thomas Tallis* (with the Bournemouth Symphony Orchestra).

Simić, Borivoje (b. 1920). Born in Belgrade, where he studied at the Academy of Music, Simić was conductor of the Ivo Lola Ribar Cultural Society (1944–9), and conductor of the Radio Belgrade Choir (from 1948). He has also appeared as a conductor in other Yugoslav cities and abroad, and has published a number of compositions. He has recorded Stravinsky's *Les Noces*, *Mass*, *Pater Noster* and *Ave Maria*, and Orff's *Catulli Carmina* (with the Belgrade Radio and Television Choir and Orchestra for Philips), and music by Lebić, Maksimović, Radica and Komadina (with the same orchestra *et al.* for Jugoton).

Simmons, Calvin (b. 1950). Simmons started his career as a repetiteur with the San Francisco Opera in 1967, and was appointed assistant conductor in 1972. He was also assistant conductor with the Merola Opera Summer Programme (1970), received the Kurt Herbert Adler Award (1972), studied the piano at the Curtis Institute in Philadelphia and was a conducting student with Max Rudolf. Since 1974 he has been with the musical staff at the Glyndebourne Opera, is music director of the Young Musicians' Foundation Debut Orchestra at Los Angeles, conducts the New York Philharmonic Youth Concerts, and was assistant conductor of the Los Angeles Philharmonic Orchestra (1975–7). With the Los Angeles Philharmonic Orchestra he has recorded for New World Carpenter's *Krazy Kat*, Gilbert's *The Dame in Place Congo*, Weiss's *American Life* and Powell's *Rapsodie nègre*.

Simon, Albert (b. 1926). Simon studied at the Franz Liszt Academy at Budapest under Ferencsik and Somogyi, and since 1969 has been a professor at the Academy and conductor of the students' orchestra. In 1969–70 he founded the New Music School to popularise contemporary Hungarian composers and the 20th-century classics. For Hungaroton he has recorded the Bach Harpsichord Concertos (with Kocsis and the Franz Liszt Academy Orchestra).

Simon, Emil (b. 1936). Born in Chişinău, Romania, Simon attended the Gheorghe Dima Conservatory at Cluj, where he studied under Toduţă and Ciolan, first conducted in 1958, and immediately after his graduation in 1960 was appointed permanent conductor of the Cluj State Philharmonic Orchestra. He went to Paris, studied with Rosenthal, Messiaen and Nadia Boulanger (1964), won first place at the International Competition for Young Conductors at Besançon, and later studied with Celibidache in Stockholm (1968). He has toured extensively in Eastern and Western Europe and in North America, and has a wide repertoire from Bach to Stravinsky, including the music of Romanian composers. His records for Electrecord, with Romanian orchestras, include Brahms' Symphonies Nos 2 and 3, *La Mer* and *Daphnis et Chloé* Suite No. 2, the overture to *Tannhäuser*, the prelude to *Die Meistersinger* and the prelude and Liebestod from *Tristan und Isolde*, and of Romanian composers, Aladár's Symphony, Ede's *The Wonderful Bird*, Boldizsár's *Two Pieces for Orchestra*, Feldman's *Symphonic Variations*, Herman's *Cantilations*, Alessandrescu's *Acteon* and *Five Songs* (with Lucaciu), Moldovan's *Stained Glass Windows*, Georgescu's *Maramureshian Folk Tunes*, Stephănescu's *Romanian Sym-*

phony, Toduţă's *Mioriţa*, Glodeanu's Piano Concerto (with Enghiurlai) and *Ulysses*, Lipatti's *Sinfonia concertante* and symphonic suite *Şătrarii* and a piece by Castaldi. The Romanian compositions were performed with the Cluj State Philharmonic Orchestra.

Simon, Stephen (b. 1937). Born in New York and educated at the School of Music at Yale University, Simon studied choral conducting with Hugh Ross and Julius Herford, and orchestral conducting with Krips, Steinberg and Susskind, and made his debut as a conductor in New York in 1963. He has been musical director of the Orchestral Society of Westchester (since 1963) and of the Handel Society of New York (1970–74), and has been a guest conductor with orchestras in the United States, France, Britain and Israel. His recordings include all the Mozart Piano Concertos with Lili Kraus and the Vienna Festival Orchestra (released in the US by Epic, a CBS label), Handel's oratorios *Solomon* and *Judas Maccabaeus*, and operas *Ariodante* and *Orlando* for the Handel Society of New York (with the Vienna Volksoper Orchestra *et al.* for RCA), and Dvořák's *Serenade in D minor*, and Strauss' *Serenade in E flat* and *Sonatina in F* (with the Boston Woodwind Ensemble, for Boston). His performances in the Mozart concertos and Handel works have been described, at best, as 'conscientious'.

Simonov, Yuri (b. 1941). Born in Leningrad in the USSR, and educated at the Leningrad Conservatory, Simonov was laureate at the Second USSR Competition for Conductors at Moscow in 1966, and won first prize at the Fifth International Competition for Conductors at the Accademia di Santa Cecilia at Rome in 1968. He was conductor of the Kislovodsk Philharmonic Society (1967–9), and then was appointed conductor at the Bolshoi Theatre, Moscow (1969), where he became the chief conductor (1970). With the Bolshoi Theatre and also as a guest conductor he has toured in Western and Eastern Europe. For Melodiya he recorded Shchedrin's ballet *Anna Karenina* and Prokofiev's Symphony No. 5 (with the Bolshoi Theatre Orchestra).

Simonovich, Konstantin (b. 1923). Born in Belgrade, Simonovich studied at the High School for Music there, and gave recitals on the violin at the age of twelve. World War II interrupted his musical activities, which were resumed when he attended the Belgrade Upper Academy of Music (1947–54), the Paris Conservatoire, and studied with Markevitch and Matačić at Salzburg (1955–8), and with Scherchen (1958–66). He taught music at Belgrade high schools (1947–9), at Belgrade University (1947–50), played the timpani with the Belgrade Opera Orchestra where he received his first experience as a conductor (1948–56), and was a professor at the Hochschule für Musik at Hilchenbach bei Siegen (1955–7). In 1958 he founded and directed the Ensemble Instrumental de Musique Contemporaine de Paris, which after 1973 was called the Contemporary Orchestra of Paris; he was director of the instrumental research department of the French Radio and Television (1961–5), founded and directed the Théâtre Musical de Paris (1967), and toured and conducted in France, the United States, Britain, Yugoslavia, Spain, Italy, FR Germany and Sweden. He conducted the Illinois State University Symphony Orchestra (1972), was professor of composition at Louisiana State University (1976) and visiting conductor at the California Institute of the Arts (1977). In addition, he was musical director of films about Varèse (1965 and 1975) and Ferrari (1973), and toured North America with the show Freska Viva. He has won wide praise for his dedication and skill in performing contemporary music, and has introduced to France and the world the music of many present-day composers.

Simonovich's recordings with his Contemporary Orchestra of Paris include Xenakis' *Eonta* (for Chant du Monde and Vanguard), *Polla Ta Dhina*, *Akrata*, *Achorripsis*, *Atrées* and *ST 10/1*, *080262* (for EMI), Varèse's *Déserts*, *Hyperprism*, *Intégrales* and *Density 21,5* (for EMI), and compositions by Earl Brown (for Disques BAM), Canton (for Disques BAM), Benguerel (for Edigsa), Barbaud (for Pathe-Marconi), Bayle (for Philips), Ferrari (for EMI and DGG) and Mestres-Quadreny (for Ediga).

Sinclair, James (b. 1947). Born in Washington, DC, Sinclair studied at the Universities of Indiana and Hawaii, and first conducted with the Yale Theater Orchestra at New Haven in 1974. He has been music director and conductor of the Chamber Orchestra of New England, and is a specialist in American music. In the Charles Ives centenary year in 1974, he conducted 25 premières of orchestral and choral works of Ives, and is editor of the orchestral works for the Charles Ives Society Inc. In 1974 Columbia issued a disc in which he conducted the Yale Theater Orchestra in Ives' *Music for Theater Orchestra* and *Old Songs Deranged*.

Singer, Georg (b. 1908). Born in Prague and educated at the Prague Conservatory, under

Zemlinsky and Finke, Singer emigrated to Palestine in 1939 and conducted the Israel Philharmonic and Jerusalem Symphony Orchestras, and the Israel National Opera. He was also active in Europe, with major orchestras and with opera companies in Munich, Hamburg and Stuttgart, and in 1969 was a guest conductor with the New York City Opera. In 1976 he led the Israel Philharmonic Orchestra *et al.* in concert performances of *Boris Godunov*. He has composed orchestral suites, a concertino and other pieces. Saga have released separate mono LP discs of him conducting the Hamburg Radio Orchestra with the bass Rossi-Lemeni *et al.* in highlights from *Boris Godunov* and *Nabucco*, and the complete *La serva padrona*. In the United States records were issued by Remington in which he led the Austrian Symphony Orchestra (in one disc called the Vienna Symphony Orchestra), in Haydn's Symphony No. 93, Mozart's Symphony No. 29, Weber's Symphony No. 2, the overtures *Coriolan*, *Ruy Blas* and *The Hebrides*, Schubert's Symphonies Nos 3 and 4, *Les Préludes*, *Moldau*, *Le Coq d'or* suite, Dvořák's Symphony No. 9 and *Slavonic Dances* 1 to 8, and a suite from *Carmen*. Kolodin, in his *Guide to Long Playing Records* (1955) commented that the Haydn Symphony No. 93 was 'decidedly good in style', but added, not to Singer's discredit, 'what better-known conductor does this pseudonym cover?'. Singer also recorded Edel's *Suite* and Sternberg's *Five Songs* (with Davrath and the Israel Radio Orchestra for CBS).

Sipe, Leopold (b. 1924). Born in Fountain Inn, South Carolina, Sipe graduated from the Eastman School of Music (1952), and studied conducting with Monteux at Maine (1951) and with Otterloo at Hilversum (1959). He was conductor of the Charlotte Opera Company, North Carolina (1952–6), the Tacoma Symphony Orchestra, Washington (1956–9), the St Paul Chamber Orchestra, Minnesota, (1959–71) and professor of music at Kent State University (from 1971). He has recorded Haydn's Symphony No. 73, Gutche's *Bongo Divertimento* and Fetler's cantata *Nothing but Nature* (with the St Paul Chamber Orchestra *et al.* for St Paul).

Skrowaczewski, Stanislaw (b. 1923). Born in Lwow, (then in Poland, now in the USSR), where his father was a brain surgeon, Skrowaczewski composed his first orchestral piece at the age of 5, and the Lwow Philharmonic Orchestra performed an overture written by him when he was eight. At 11 he made his debut as a pianist, studied at the High School for Music at Kraków, but had to abandon a career as a pianist because of an injury he received during a bombing attack in World War II. After studying at the Lwow University and the Kraków Academy of Music, he went to Paris in 1947, studied conducting with Kletzki, and came into contact with Nadia Boulanger. Between 1947 and 1957 he received many prizes for his compositions, which included *Overture 1947*, *Prelude and Fugue for Orchestra*, *Symphony for Strings* and *Music at Night*. He was appointed music director and conductor of the Polish National Radio Orchestra at Katowice (1949–54) and of the Kraków Philharmonic Orchestra (1955–6); after winning first prize at an international competition for conductors at Rome in 1956 he became conductor of the Warsaw National Philharmonic Orchestra (1957–9).

Skrowaczewski made his debut in the United States with the Cleveland Orchestra in 1958, and in 1960 was appointed conductor of the Minneapolis Symphony Orchestra in succession to Dorati; the orchestra was renamed the Minnesota Orchestra in 1968, and in 1966 he and his wife became US citizens. His debut at the Vienna State Opera occurred in 1964, at the Salzburg Festival in 1968, and at the New York Metropolitan Opera in 1970, and he has been a guest conductor with major orchestras in the US and Europe. He toured with the Amsterdam Concertgebouw Orchestra in Europe, with the Philadelphia Orchestra in Latin America, and with the Cleveland Orchestra in Australia. His conducting commitments forced him to give up composition, but nonetheless his Concerto for Cor anglais was premièred in 1970, and was later recorded by Desto. He is a versatile musician; his programmes are sometimes too adventurous for some of his audiences. He is especially good with large-scale works, and is an advocate of contemporary music: he gave the first performances in the US of Penderecki's *St Luke Passion* in 1967 and *The Devils of Loudun* in 1969. Because of his somewhat severe intellectuality and an apparent lack of spontaneity in his performances he has been likened to Szell, with whom he has an affinity in temperament and style; in fact it was Szell who was one of the first to appreciate his talents.

Unlike some of his contemporaries, Skrowaczewski is optimistic about the future of symphonic music and symphony orchestras: 'In the last 20 years there has been an unsurpassed blossoming of the symphony orchestra and symphonic literature, a great increase in concert activity. Millions of lovers of symphonic music come to concert halls and purchase records each year. . . . [But] music and all the arts are endangered by the growing mess and controversy in aesthetic evaluations. For instance, equating the highest values in art with primitive but popular ones, confusing notions like "mass appeal", "social protest" and "relevance to the times" with purely artistic phenomena. Another danger for the musical arts: the soul pollution of organised noise – so-called "background music" – endangering our thinking, our concentration, dulling our awareness of what music could be, imbuing our mind with banality, may be more dangerous than air and water pollution because the future damage is not easily tangible. . . . But, please put my words down: in 10 or 15 years from now the problem will come suddenly as a big psychological discovery, for one generation too late' (*Symphony*, magazine of the Minnesota Orchestra, October 1969).

Mercury recorded the Minneapolis Symphony Orchestra (and, when it was renamed, the Minnesota Orchestra) under Skrowaczewski performing Schubert's Symphonies Nos 5, 8 and 9 and the *Rosamunde* overture and incidental music, Mendelssohn's Symphony No. 4, Dvořák's Symphony No. 9, Shostakovich's Symphony No. 5, and two suites from Prokofiev's *Romeo and Juliet* ballet; his other recordings include Beethoven's Piano Concerto No. 5 and Brahms' Piano Concerto No. 2 (with Bachauer and the London Symphony Orchestra for Mercury), Chopin's Piano Concerto No. 1 (with Rubinstein and the New Symphony Orchestra for RCA), the Lalo and Schumann Cello Concertos (with Starker and the London Symphony Orchestra for Mercury), Chopin's Piano Concertos Nos 1 and 2, *Andante spianato and Grand Polonaise* and *Grand Fantasia on Polish Airs* (with Weissenberg and the Paris Conservatoire Orchestra for EMI), Mayer's *Two Pastels* and *Andante for Strings* (with the Minnesota Orchestra for Desto), his own Concerto for Cor anglais (with Stacy and the Minnesota Orchestra for Desto), the complete orchestral works of Ravel (with the Minnesota Orchestra for Vox) and *Petrushka* and a suite from *The Love of Three Oranges* (with the Minnesota Orchestra for Vox). The Ravel set is undoubtedly his most distinguished recording, and is a considerable example of both the orchestra's and the conductor's musicianship.

Škvor, František (b. 1898). Born at Varaždinské, Toplice, now in Yugoslavia, Škvor spent three years in military service, then studied at the Charles University in Prague. He became a repetiteur at the Prague National Theatre (1923), there conducted the première of his ballet *Doktor Faust*, and was active as both composer and conductor in Czechoslovakia, Bulgaria *et al.* His recordings, for Supraphon, include Respighi's *Trittico botticelliano* (with the Prague Chamber Orchestra), *Swan Lake* (with the Prague National Theatre Orchestra), and the ballet music from Fibich's *Hédy* (with the Prague National Theatre Orchestra).

Slatkin, Felix (1915–63). Born in St Louis, Missouri, Slatkin studied the violin at the Curtis Institute with Efram Zimbalist Sr, and conducting with Reiner. He made his career in Hollywood, where he was leader of the Hollywood String Quartet; among many fine discs which this ensemble made for Capitol in the early years of LP were Schubert's *String Quintet in C major*, and the Franck and Shostakovich Piano Quintets. He recorded as a conductor for many United States companies, and frequently conducted for popular artists without using his name on the records. For Capitol he conducted a number of discs which included Ibert's *Divertissement*, Britten's *The Young Person's Guide to the Orchestra*, Dohnányi's *Variations on a Nursery Tune* (with Aller, who recorded with the Hollywood String Quartet also), Milhaud's Concerto for Percussion, the Khachaturian Piano Concerto (with Pennario), Ravel's *Introduction et allegro* and Debussy's *Danse sacrée et danse profane* (with Stockton), Shostakovich's Piano Concerto No. 1 (with Aller and Klein, trumpet), Villa-Lobos' arrangement of the Bach Prelude and Fugue No. 8 and *Bachianas brasileiras Nos 1* and *5*, MacDonald's *Suite from Childhood*, Caplet's *Le Masque de la mort rouge*, Chávez's *Toccata*, Delius' *On Hearing the First Cuckoo in Spring* and *Summer Night on the River*, and *Le Carnaval des animaux* (with the Concert Arts Orchestra), the Offenbach/Rosenthal *Gaîté parisienne*, Ippolitov-Ivanov's *Caucasian Sketches*, the incidental music to *A Midsummer Night's Dream*, *Valse triste*, some Strauss waltzes, the *Nutcracker* suite, *An American in Paris* and a suite from *Porgy and Bess*, Gould's *Latin American Symphonette*, the two *Peer Gynt* suites, Grofé's *Grand Canyon* and *Mississippi Suites*, and dances and other popular orchestral and choral pieces (with the Hollywood Bowl Symphony Orchestra *et al.*) and *Eine kleine Nachtmusik* (with the Musical Arts Symphony Orchestra).

Slatkin, Leonard (b. 1948). Both Slatkin's parents were members of the Hollywood String Quartet, and he studied with his father, the conductor and violinist Felix Slatkin. He conducted his college orchestra, and studied conducting with Susskind and with Morel at the Juilliard School. His debut occurred with the Youth Symphony Orchestra of New York; he became assistant conductor of the St Louis Symphony Orchestra in 1968, then associate principal conductor in 1974, but when Susskind resigned from the position of principal conductor, Slatkin declined the appointment and was named principal guest conductor in 1976; he has also been appointed musical director of the New Orleans Philharmonic-Symphony Orchestra. His debut with the New York Philharmonic Orchestra occurred in 1974, when he substituted for Muti; since then he has conducted many major US orchestras and others in Mexico, Britain and the USSR. In 1974 he was also appointed principal guest conductor of the Minnesota Orchestra and principal conductor of the Grant Park Concerts in Chicago. With the St Louis Symphony Orchestra, he has formed the practice of introducing unfamiliar and contemporary works with a short talk, illustrating them by himself on the piano; he feels a responsibility to perform as often as possible music by American composers, and to develop young musicians as orchestral players. His compositions include *The Raven*, based on the poem by Poe, *Dialogue for Two Cellos and Orchestra* and *The Nonsense Book*. For Vox he has recorded with the St Louis Symphony Orchestra Rachmaninov's Symphony No. 1, a three-disc album of the orchestral music of Gershwin, including the *Rhapsody in Blue*, *Concerto in F*, *An American in Paris*, *Cuban Overture*, *Variations on I Got Rhythm*, *Second Rhapsody*, *Lullaby*, *Promenade* and a suite from *Porgy and Bess* (with Siegel the pianist). He also recorded Dello Joio's *Homage to Haydn* (with the Louisville Orchestra for Louisville).

Slonimsky, Nicolas (b. 1894). Born in St Petersburg where he first studied under Vengerova, and with Kalafati and Steinberg at the Conservatory (1908–15), Slonimsky left Russia after the Revolution, toured Europe as a pianist (1920–23), was secretary to Koussevitzky in Paris, and emigrated to the United States in 1923, where he became a naturalised citizen in 1931. He was a coach at the Eastman School of Music at Rochester (1923–5), studied conducting with Coates, was Koussevitzky's secretary, again, (1925–7), wrote musical articles and taught in Boston, directed the Boston Chamber Orchestra (1927–34), and conducted programmes of American and modern music in New York, Paris, Berlin, Budapest, Los Angeles, Rio de Janeiro, Havana and Guatemala City (1931–42). In Paris he conducted a Bartók Concerto with the composer as soloist (1931); he has also appeared as a pianist at chamber music recitals, lectured at the University of California, Los Angeles, and at other US colleges and universities, and in 1962–3 travelled in East Europe and the USSR under the auspices of the State Department. He has been an ardent champion of contemporary composers, and gave world premières of orchestral works by Ives, Cowell, Varèse, Chávez *et al.* He also has a distinguished reputation as a musicologist, his published works including *Music Since 1900*, *Thesaurus of Scales and Melodic Patterns*, *The Road to Music*, *Lexicon of Musical Invective*, the 1958 and 1971 editions of *Baker's Biographical Dictionary of Musicians* and the most recent edition of *Oscar Thompson's Cyclopedia of Music and Musicians*, and contributions to *Cobbett's Cyclopedic Survey of Chamber Music* and *Grove's Dictionary of Music and Musicians*. His own compositions reflect his whimsical sense of humour, always evident in his writings; they include *My Toy Balloon* (1942) requiring 100 balloons to be exploded in the final sforzando, a *Fantasy* which exists in a version for three winds, percussion and portable typewriter, and witty settings of tombstone inscriptions in the songs *Gravestones at Hancock, New Hampshire*.

Slonimsky made 78 r.p.m. recordings for Columbia (US) of Varèse's *Ionisation*, which he had previously conducted in New York in 1932–3, and for the New Music label Varèse's *Octandre*, Ruggles' *Men and Mountains* and Ives' *Music for the Theater*, *Washington's Birthday*, *Barn Dance* and *In the Night* (with the Pan American Orchestra).

Slovák, Ladislav (b. 1919). Born in Bratislava, Slovák studied conducting and the organ at the Conservatory there, then at the newly formed Academy of Music at Bratislava where Talich was his teacher, and with Mravinsky at Leningrad. He became musical producer of the Czechoslovak Broadcasting Company in Bratislava (1946–61), first conductor of the Slovak Philharmonic Orchestra (1961–72), chief conductor of the Prague Symphony Orchestra (1972–6), and chief conductor of the South Australian Symphony Orchestra at Adelaide (1966 and 1972). With the Slovak Philharmonic Orchestra he toured Belgium, Italy, FR Germany and Britain, and with the Czech Philharmonic Orchestra the USSR, China, India, Japan and New Zealand (1959), the United States (1967), separately toured Japan (1962 and 1974), and has also conducted orchestras in Eastern and Western Europe. In 1967 he was awarded the Czechoslovak National Prize.

Slovák's recordings include Tchaikovsky's Symphony No. 6, Shostakovich's Symphonies Nos 2 and 9 and Bartók's *Music for Strings, Percussion and Celesta* (with the Slovak Symphony Orchestra for Opus), Tchaikovsky's Symphony No. 4 and Prokofiev's Symphony No. 5 (with the Czech Philharmonic Orchestra for Supraphon), Marenco's *Excelsior*, Dvořák's *Carnival* overture, *Moldau* and the overture to Rezniček's *Donna Diana* (with the Slovak Philharmonic Orchestra for RCA Italiana), Kubík's *Lament of the Warrior's Wife* (with the Czech Philharmonic Orchestra for Panton), Ryba's *Sonata for Twelve Winds* (with an ensemble for Panton), Loudová's *Spleen: Homage to Charles Baudelaire* (with the Prague Symphony Orchestra for Panton), Albrecht's *Sonatina*, Babušek's *Preludium*, Cikker's *The Morning* and *Meditation*, Kardoš' *Concerto for Orchestra* and Symphonies Nos 3, 4 and 5, Moyzes' Symphonies Nos 4 and 7, *Baladic Cantata*, *Dances from Gemer* and overture to *Jánošík*, Suchoň's *The Psalm of the Carpathian Land* and Zimmer's Symphony No. 1 (with the Slovak Philharmonic Orchestra for Supraphon); in Australia he recorded Dreyfus' Symphony No. 1 (with the Melbourne Symphony Orchestra for EMI).

Slowinski, Wladyslaw (b. 1930). Born in Sadlno, Poland, Slowinski studied at the University and High School for Music at Poznań, has been a conductor at the Operas at Poznań and Łódź, and has also performed in other Polish cities, in the USSR and Yugoslavia. For Muza he recorded with the Polish National Orchestra a collection of symphonic dances and marches.

Smallens, Alexander (1889–1972). Born in St Petersburg, Smallens emigrated with his parents to the United States in 1890, and was naturalised in 1919. His parents changed their family names of Ossipovich and Smolensk to Smallens when they arrived in the US. He was educated at the College of the City of New York, the Juilliard School, the Institute of Musical Art (1905–9), and at the Paris Conservatoire (1909–11), and then joined the Boston Opera Company as an assistant conductor (1911–14). His subsequent appointments were with the Century Opera Company, New York (1914), the Boston National Opera Company (1915–17), conductor for Pavlova when she toured Central and South America (1917–19), conductor of the Chicago Opera Company (1919–22), at the Operas of Berlin, Vienna, Madrid and Buenos Aires (1923), with the Philadelphia Civic Opera Company (1923–30), assistant then associate conductor with Stokowski and the Philadelphia Orchestra (1928–35), continuing his association with the Philadelphia Orchestra until 1947, musical director of Radio City Music Hall, New York (1947–59), conductor of the Ballet Theater, New York (1937–40), guest conductor of the National Symphony Orchestra, Washington (1940–46) and of the New York Philharmonic Orchestra at its Lewisohn Stadium Concerts (1934 onwards), and guest conductor of the Netherlands Opera (1957–8). In 1959 he suffered a heart attack which ended his professional career.

Smallens was a highly experienced and versatile musician, who drew warm praise from many critics for resourcefulness and technical skill as a conductor. He is said to have had a repertoire of over 150 operas, drawn from all national schools, was a guest conductor with virtually every major symphony orchestra in the US, and was the American member of the International Society of Contemporary Music. He premièred Thomson's *Four Saints in Three Acts*, was chosen by Prokofiev to conduct the US première of *The Love of Three Oranges*, and was especially associated with the first productions of Gershwin's *Porgy and Bess*, at its original presentation in 1935 and later between 1941 and 1944. Altogether he led over 1,000 performances of the opera, including several in Moscow and Leningrad in 1956. He was reputed to be one of the finest conductors of Gershwin: Thomson wrote that 'No other conductor reads Gershwin with quite the ease that Smallens does, or half the seriousness. The commercial leaders play the music without depth, and the symphonic conductors play it mostly without feeling. Smallens allows its melodic line to speak in the vernacular without vulgarity and without pomposity. He actually gives you real Gershwin and a real symphonic sound at the same time'. (*Music Reviewed, 1940–1954*, pp. 318–19).

Smallens' recordings included an abridged version of *Porgy and Bess* (on 78s, with the Decca Symphony Orchestra *et al.* for Decca (US)), *Peter and the Wolf* and the *Nutcracker* suite (with the same orchestra for Decca), Berlioz's overture to *Béatrice et Bénédict*, the waltzes from *Der Rosenkavalier* and the dance from *Salome*, the *1812* overture, *Marche slave*, the Waltz and Polonaise from *Eugene Onegin* and the *Andante cantabile* of Tchaikovsky (with the Stadium Concerts Orchestra for Decca), Dvořák's *Carnival* overture (with the Stadium

Concerts Orchestra for Festival) and the Mendelssohn Violin Concerto (with Lack and the Stadium Concerts Orchestra for Music Appreciation).

Smetáček, Václav (b. 1906). Born in Brno, Smetáček studied the violin, viola and oboe, as well as composition under Křička and conducting under Dědeček, at the Prague Conservatory, and also musicology and aesthetics at the Charles University at Prague, where he obtained a Ph.D. He founded and was oboist in the Prague Wind Quintet (1928–56), was first oboist with the Czech Philharmonic Orchestra (1930–33), conductor of the Prague Hlahol Choir (1934–46), and was associated with the Czechoslovakia Broadcasting Corporation (1934–46). In 1942 he was appointed chief conductor of the FOK Symphony Orchestra (i.e. the Film, Opera, Concert Orchestra), which in 1945 was re-organised into a co-operative society, and in 1952 was taken over by the Prague Municipality to become the Prague Symphony Orchestra. Smetáček remained with the orchestra until 1972, and was responsible for its development; he toured with it regularly throughout Europe, and also visited Japan, Latin America and the United States. He has toured as a guest conductor in many countries, and altogether has conducted over 100 orchestras; in 1961 he was five months in Japan, conducting the Tokyo Symphony Orchestra, was a professor at the Prague Conservatory (1945–67), and since 1972 has toured as a guest conductor. In 1976 he was named National Artist of the CSSR. His compositions include a ballet *The Eve of a Summer Day*, some marches and several wind quintets.

Although he has never achieved true international status as a conductor, Smetáček is a distinguished musician and one of the leading Czech conductors of the post-war decades. He has made over 300 recordings, from the 78 r.p.m. days, including major choral and symphonic works, concerto accompaniments and popular orchestral pieces. With the Czech Radio Orchestra he made a series of 78s of pieces by Smetana for Ultraphon (a Czech label), including the marches *Shakespeare Festival*, *National Guard* and *Student Legion*, the polkas *The Country Girl* and *To Our Damsels*, and the overtures *Dr Faust* and *Oldřich a Božena* of Škroup. He also recorded on 78s the ten *Legends* of Dvořák and the *Festival March* (with the Czech Philharmonic Orchestra), Linek's *Pastorella – Christ was Born*, Dvořák's *The Wood Dove* (with the Czech Radio Orchestra), Liadov's *The Enchanted Lake* and *Kikimora* (with the FOK Orchestra), and Chopin's Piano Concerto No. 2 (with Slezarieva and the FOK Orchestra). His other discs with the FOK Orchestra for Supraphon included Brixi's *Magnificat*, Ippolitov-Ivanov's *Caucasian Sketches*, Liszt's *Tasso*, *In the Steppes of Central Asia*, *Danse macabre*, Škroup's *Chrudimská* and *Fidlovačka* overtures, Stravinsky's *Feux d'artifice*, Ferenczy's *Hurbanovská* overture, Fibich's *Komenský Festival* and *Night at Karlstein* overtures, Rossini's *Semiramide* overture, Roussel's *Le Festin de l'araignée*, the Polovtsian Dances from *Prince Igor*, Weis' *Bohemian Dance No. 3*, Seidl's music for the film *Anna Proletářka*, Malát's *Slavonic Girls* suite, Sibelius' *Valse triste* and *The Swan of Tuonela*, the overtures to *Martha*, and *Le Calife de Bagdad*, the overture and Turkish March from Beethoven's *Die Ruinen von Athen*, Brahms' *Academic Festival Overture* and some *Hungarian Dances*, Smetana's *Czech Song*, Glazunov's *Concert Waltzes Nos 1* and *2*, Glinka's *Waltz Fantasy* and *Kamarinskaya*, Liadov's *Baba Yaga*, *The Enchanted Lake* and *Kikimora*, the ballet music from *Faust*, and the Dance of the Brides from Rubinstein's *Feramors*. In addition there were concerto accompaniments, including Krumpholz's Harp Concerto, Saint-Saëns' Violin Concerto No. 3 (with Bělčik), the Schumann Cello Concerto (with Heran), Slavík's Violin Concerto No. 2 (with Gutnikov), Glazunov's Saxophone Concerto (with Krautgartner) the Franck *Symphonic Variations* (with Bernáthová), Gershwin's *Rhapsody in Blue* (with Panenka), Haydn's *Cello Concerto in D major* (with Večtomov), Paganini's Violin Concerto No. 1 (with Novák), Míča's *Concertino Notturno* (with Suk), Schulhoff's Concerto for String Quartet and Wind Orchestra, and Lucký's Violin Concerto (with Grumlíková).

With the Prague Symphony Orchestra *et al.* Smetáček continued his series for Supraphon, from the advent of LP to the present day. The works recorded included the three Bach Violin Concertos (with Suk and Jásek), the Mozart Bassoon Concerto (with Bidlo), and Flute and Harp Concerto, the five Beethoven Piano Concertos and Choral Fantasia (with Panenka), Rejcha's *Te Deum*, Koželuh's Bassoon Concerto (with Pivoňka), Mendelssohn's overtures *The Hebrides*, *A Midsummer Night's Dream* and *Meeresstille und glückliche Fahrt*, Berlioz's *King Lear* overture, Liszt's Piano Concerto No. 2 (with Rauch), the Chopin Piano Concerto No. 1 and *Andante spianato and polonaise brilliante* (with Czerny-Stefanska), Chopin's Piano Concerto No. 2 (with Rauch), Tchaikovsky's Symphony No. 1, *Romeo and*

Juliet fantasy-overture, Suite No. 4 (*Mozartiana*), *Variations on a Rococo Theme* (with Apolín) and a suite from *The Sleeping Beauty*, Smetana's *Macbeth and the Witches*, Dvořák's Symphony No. 3, *St Ludmilla*, *Mass in D major*, *Te Deum* and *Psalm 149*, Borodin's Symphony No. 2, suites from Rimsky-Korsakov's *Le Coq d'or* and *The Invisible City of Kitezh*, the *L'Arlésienne* Suites Nos 1 and 2, Chabrier's *España*, Sibelius' *The Tempest*, Glazunov's Violin Concerto and Wieniawski's Violin Concerto No. 2 (with Haendel), violin concertos by Casella, Milhaud, and Malipiero, and Seiber's *Fantasia concertante* (with Gertler), Foerster's Symphony No. 4 and suite from Glazunov's *Raymonda*, Martinů's *Sinfonia giocosa*, Ravel's *Piano Concerto in G major* (with Bernáthová), Ryba's *Christmas Mass*, Hába's *The Path of Life*, Míča's *Symphony in D*, Sommer's *Antigone* overture, Gershwin's *Cuban Overture*, Orff's *Carmina Burana*, *Catulli Carmina* and *Trionfo di Afrodite*, a collection of overtures by Lehár, Offenbach, Suppé, Strauss and Nedbal, Fils' Flute Concerto (with Slavíček) and Blodek's Flute Concerto (with Hanžl).

Other recordings Smetáček has made for Supraphon include a disc of Strauss waltzes (with the Vienna Symphony Orchestra), a suite from *Coppélia* (with the Prague Smetana Theatre Orchestra), Mozart's Sinfonia Concertante K. 297b (with the Czech Philharmonic Orchestra *et al.*), Dvořák's *Stabat Mater* (with the Czech Philharmonic Orchestra *et al.*, also released by DGG); for Schwann Sarti's *Russisches Oratorium* and *Hospodine pomiluj ny*, Otradovic's *Canticum*, *Litanae Beatae Mariae Virginis*, *Te Deum* and *Missa Pastoralis*, an extract from Dvořák's *St Ludmilla*, sacred pieces by Ryba, Vanhura and Diabelli, Caldara's *Missa Sanctificationis Sancti Joannis Nepomuceni*, the Dvořák *Magnificat* and *Svatý Václave*, and Foerster's Mass (with the Prague Symphony Orchestra); for Charlin Vranický's *Grande symphonie pour la paix avec la République française* (with the Czech Radio Symphony Orchestra), Rejcha's *Musique pour les grands hommes et les grands événements de la République française* and Zelenka's *Suite in F major* (with the Prague Symphony Orchestra), and for Panton the Mozart Violin Concerto K. 219 and the Mendelssohn Violin Concerto (with Hudeček and the Czech Radio Symphony Orchestra), Dvořák's Violin Concerto and *Mazurek* (with Hudeček and the Musici de Praga), Rejcha's *Te Deum* (with Musici de Praga), Karel's *Revolutionary Overture*, Burian's *Overture of Socialism*, Nejedlý's *Dramatic Overture* and Pauer's *Symphonic Prologue* (with the Czech Philharmonic Orchestra), and a selection of symphonic marches by Smetana, Dvořák, Jeremiáš, Řídký *et al.* (with Musici de Praga).

Smith, Gregg (b. 1931). Born in Chicago, Smith studied composition under Foss at the University of California, Los Angeles, where he joined the madrigal chorus. He conducted a church choir in West Los Angeles, composed numerous sacred works for the choir, and in 1955 founded the Gregg Smith Singers which quickly became widely known both inside the United States and abroad for their unique ensemble. He moved to New York from California to become the choral director at both the Peabody Conservatory at Baltimore and Columbia University in New York City. His recordings, in which he conducts the Gregg Smith Singers, include a number of choral works by Billings, Beeson, Copland, Barber, Schuman, Fine, Shifrin, Ives, Schoenberg, Kohn, Pimsleur, G. Gabrieli and Schütz, and were released by various companies including Columbia, MGM, Vox, Everest and Composers Recordings.

Smola, Emmerich (b. 1922). Born in Bergreichenstein, Böhmen, Germany, Smola was an organist and choirmaster (1945–6), bassoon player with the South-West Radio Studio Orchestra at Kaiserslautern (1947–8), became director of the orchestra (1948–51), was on the musical staff of the South-West Radio Studio at Mainz (1951–3), leader of the South-West Radio Orchestra (from 1951) and its musical programmes director (from 1974). He has recorded Haydn's Oboe Concerto, Ohguri's *Ballade for Oboe and String Orchestra*, Doering's *Bolero for Oboe and String Orchestra* and Pilotti's *Konzertstück for English Horn and Orchestra* (with Koch and the South-West Radio Orchestra for Thorofon).

Smyth, Dame Ethel (1858–1944). Born at Foots Cray, Kent, Ethel Smyth studied at the Leipzig Conservatory in Berlin, and as a composer first came to public attention with a performance of her *Mass* at the Royal Albert Hall in 1893. She espoused the cause of the suffragettes, for which she was imprisoned in 1911, and wrote *The March of the Women* for them; however, in 1922 she was created a Dame. Although today she is little more than a fascinating historical figure, in her day she was a widely known and much performed composer. Her most successful works were the operas *The Wreckers* and *The Boatswain's Mate*, and *The Prison*, a symphony with chorus and soprano and baritone solos. In her later years she conducted her own music, and recorded the overtures to *The Wreckers* and *The Boatswain's Mate*. According to Eugene Goossens, her skill as a conductor was limited; he had conducted the first rehearsals for *The Boatswain's Mate*, but 'at the last moment she took over the baton, thinking herself the heaven-sent conductor she was not. This necessitated additional last-minute rehearsals, which she directed with a maximum of fuss, pomposity and ineptitude' (*Overture and Beginners*, London, 1951).

Snashall, John (b. 1930). Of German descent, Snashall was born in Eastbourne and began to conduct his school's orchestra at the age of 14. He studied conducting under Buesst at the Guildhall School of Music and Drama, did two years' National Service (1951–3), was employed by the Nixa Record Company, then by Pye, and in the following years produced over 300 recordings for CBS, RCA and many American companies, these including many for Barbirolli and Boult, with whom he studied the Vaughan Williams symphonies. In 1964 he conducted his first disc of Pergolesi and Vivaldi, and went on to record a number of other discs of music relatively unknown. Since 1971 he has been a free-lance conductor, with his real interest in Mozart, the German repertoire from Bach to Henze, and some French and Russian composers. His discs for Pye were of Pergolesi's *Concerti armonici*, *Salve Regina* and *Violin Concerto in B flat* and two Vivaldi concertos (with the Anglian Ensemble *et al.*), Starer's Viola Concerto and Vaughan Williams' Suite for Viola and Strings (with Berger and the English Chamber Orchestra, also issued by Turnabout), a *Salve Regina in A minor* and one in *C minor* by Pergolesi and six arias from Scarlatti's *Tetide in Sciro* (with Taylor and the Northern Sinfonia), Bush's *Variations, Nocturne and Finale on an old English Sea-Song* (with Wilde and the Royal Philharmonic Or chestra), McCabe's Symphony No. 1, Leighton's *Concerto for Strings* and Cruft's *Divertimento for Strings* (with the London Philharmonic Orchestra). For CBS he also recorded wind suites from four Mozart operas (with the London Symphonic Wind Players), Gagnon's *Mes quatre Saisons* (with Gagnon and the London Baroque Orchestra) and *Les Turluteries* (with Gagon and the Hamburg Philharmonic Orchestra).

Söderblom, Ulf (b. 1930). Born in Turku, Finland, Söderblom studied with Swarowsky at the Vienna Academy of Music, and made his debut as a conductor with the Finnish National Opera in 1957; in 1973 he became artistic director and chief conductor of the Opera. He has conducted orchestras in Finland and abroad, and is conductor of the Savonlinna Opera Festival. He conducted the first Finnish opera to be recorded, Merikanto's *Juha* (for Finnlevy), as well as the same composer's Piano Concerto No. 2, *Partita* and Concert Piece for Cello and Orchestra (for EMI), Sallinen's *The Horseman* (for Finnlevy) and Kokkonen's *The Last Temptations* (for DGG).

Sokoloff, Nikolai (1886–1965). Born near Kiev, Sokoloff came to the United States in his childhood, studied the violin, attended the School of Music at Yale University, and was a violinist in the Boston Symphony Orchestra (1904–7). When touring Europe as a violinist (1911–12) he first conducted at a theatre in Manchester, and after returning to the US conducted at San Francisco (1916), where he had formed a string quartet. He became permanent conductor of the newly-formed Cleveland Symphony Orchestra (1918–33), and in his 15 years with the orchestra established it as a significant ensemble. He then was the first director of the Federal Music Project of the Works Progress Administration (1935–8), was conductor of the Seattle Symphony Orchestra (1938–40), and finally was conductor and director of the Musical Arts Society at La Jolla, California. For Brunswick he recorded with the Cleveland Orchestra Schubert's Symphony No. 8, Rachmaninov's Symphony No. 2, and Halvorsen's *Entry of the Boyars*, and for Concert Hall Rozsa's *Serenade for Orchestra* (with the La Jolla California Festival Orchestra).

Sollberger, Harvey (b. 1938). Born in Cedar Rapids, Ohio, Sollberger studied at the University of Iowa, and with Beeson and Luening at Columbia University, graduated at Columbia in 1964, and was on the staff there (1965–71). He has recorded both as flautist and conductor; in the latter capacity he conducted the Columbia Contemporary Music Group in Westergaard's *Mr and Mrs Discobbolos* (for Composers Recordings) and Davidovsky's *Synchronisms 5* and *6* and *Electronic Study 3* (for Turnabout).

Solomon, Izler (b. 1910). Born in St Paul, Minnesota, Solomon learned the violin as a boy, studied in New York and Philadelphia, and played in orchestras. He became a teacher at Michigan State College at East Lansing (1928–31), continued his violin studies with Michael Press, won the Young Artists' Contest

(1931), and founded, was concertmaster, then conductor of an orchestra at East Lansing (1931–5). He was appointed conductor of the Women's Symphony Orchestra at Chicago (1939), was a guest conductor with major American orchestras, was conductor of the Columbus (Ohio) Philharmonic Orchestra (1941–9), with Koussevitzky and Bernstein conducted the Israel Philharmonic Orchestra in its tour of the United States and Canada (1951), was conductor of the New Orleans Summer Symphony (1943–5 and 1950–52), resident conductor of the Buffalo Philharmonic Orchestra (1952–3), was director of the Aspen Festival at Colorado (1956–61), music director and conductor of the Indianapolis Symphony Orchestra (1956–75), and conductor of the Flagstaff Summer Festival Symphony and Chamber Orchestra. He received the award of the National Association of American Conductors and Composers (1947) and the Alice M. Ditson Award (1950), for services to American composers and American music, and has conducted in Canada, Mexico, Israel and FR Germany.

Solomon's recordings include Bach's Cantata No. 170, C. P. E. Bach's Concerto for Orchestra (arr. Solomon), Pergolesi's *Salve Regina* (with Glaz), Haydn's Symphony No. 85, *Piano Concerto in D major* (with Pressler) and *Cello Concerto in D major* (with Greenhouse), Copland's *Music for the Theater* and *Two Pieces for String Orchestra*, Harris' Fantasy for Piano and Orchestra (with Johana Harris), Weill's Violin Concerto (with Agerman) and *Kleine Dreigroschenmusik*, Strauss's Symphony for Wind Instruments and Sonatina No. 2, Honegger's Symphony No. 2, Rivier's Symphony No. 2, Britten's *Simple Symphony* and Sinfonietta, Ireland's *Concerto pastorale*, Saint-Saëns' *Le Carnaval des animaux*, Chávez' Toccata for Percussion and Sinfonia No. 5, Ben-Haim's Concerto for Strings, Revueltas' *Ocho por Radio*, Surinach's *Rítmo Jondo*, Persichetti's *The Hollow Men*, Villa-Lobos' Choros No. 7, Bloch's *Chamber Episodes* and Concerto Grosso No. 2, Hovhaness's *Khaldis* (with Masselos), Richter's *Lament*, Antheil's Serenade for Strings, Pinkham's Concertante, Diamond's *Rounds*, Porter's *Music for Strings*, Goeb's *Three American Dances* and Křenek's Double Concerto (with the MGM String Orchestra, *et al.*, for MGM), Bloch's *Four Episodes* (with Masselos and the Knickerbocker Chamber Players for MGM), Berger's *Serenade concertante* (with the Brandeis Festival Orchestra for MGM), Chausson's *Poème*, Conus' Violin Concerto, Wieniawski's Violin Concerto No. 2, Glazunov's Violin Concerto, Bruch's Violin Concerto No. 1 and Spohr's Violin Concerto No. 8 (with Heifetz and the RCA Victor Symphony Orchestra for RCA), Mozart's Sinfonia Concertante K. 364 and Benjamin's *Romantic Fantasy* (with Heifetz and Primrose and the RCA Victor Symphony Orchestra for RCA), the Gluck/Mottl ballet suite, Bartók's *Romanian Dances* and Dunlop's *Tequila* (for Discovery), the overture to *Le nozze di Figaro* and Schubert's Symphony No. 9 (with the Indianapolis Symphony Orchestra, for Special), and Bazelon's Symphony No. 5 (with the Indianapolis Symphony Orchestra for Composers Recordings).

Solti, Sir Georg (b. 1912). Born in Budapest, Solti started piano lessons at the age of 6, and was giving recitals in Budapest and in the Hungarian provinces at 12. He studied at the Franz Liszt Academy under Székely, Kodály, Bartók, Weiner and Dohnányi, and decided to become a conductor when he heard Kleiber conduct a Beethoven symphony. At 18 he was a repetiteur at the Budapest Opera; he assisted Walter at the Salzburg Festival in 1935 and Toscanini during the following two years, working with Toscanini in preparing *Die Zauberflöte* and Verdi's *Requiem*; in *Die Zauberflöte* he played the glockenspiel. His experience with Toscanini was decisive, and gave him a great devotion for conducting opera. In March 1938 he made his debut as a conductor in Budapest with *Le nozze di Figaro*, but as a Jew his career in Hungary was blocked; he was invited by Toscanini to assist him at Lucerne where Toscanini, Walter and Adolf Busch were organising a festival. He left for Switzerland in August 1939, two weeks before the border was closed. To support himself in Switzerland he returned to the piano, gave lessons and accompanied, and in 1942 won first prize in the Concours International de Piano at Geneva. His only opportunity to conduct during the war was for a few concerts with the Swiss Radio Orchestra in 1944.

At the conclusion of the war, Solti went to Munich on the invitation of the American Military Government to conduct *Fidelio* at the Bavarian State Opera; since conductors implicated with the Nazis were forbidden to appear in public he was invited to become musical director in place of Krauss. In 1952 he moved to the Frankfurt City Opera, and in 1956 conducted *Die Zauberflöte* at the Salzburg Festival, which brought him to international attention. When he was at Munich and Frankfurt, he conducted the local orchestras, and was a guest conductor in London, Vienna, Berlin, Paris, Rome, Florence, Buenos Aires and in other cities. In 1952 he appeared at the Edinburgh Festival, and the next year made his United States debut at the San Francisco Opera, led the Chicago Symphony Orchestra (1954) and the New York Philharmonic Orchestra (1957), conducted at the New York Metropolitan Opera, and led *Der Rosenkavalier* at Covent Garden, London (1959). The Los Angeles Philharmonic Orchestra engaged him as conductor in 1961, but he resigned before his first concert with them, because the orchestra's management had appointed an assistant conductor (Zubin Mehta) without consulting him. He was musical director at Covent Garden (1961–71), accepting the appointment on Walter's advice; in 1972 he was knighted and became a British citizen. The knighthood was conferred as an expression of gratitude from British musicians for his work in raising Covent Garden to the undisputed status of one of the world's leading opera houses. He was appointed conductor of the Chicago Symphony Orchestra in 1971 for a period of five years, which was extended for another five years in 1976. He was also musical director of l'Orchestre de Paris (1971–5), took the orchestra on a tour of China (1974), was musical adviser to the Paris Opéra, was principal guest conductor of the London Philharmonic Orchestra, and became the orchestra's chief conductor in 1977. His home is in London, and he visits Chicago for two series of concerts each year.

Despite his late start at Munich after the war, Solti is one of the great operatic and symphonic conductors on the scene today; it would be an exaggeration to claim, as some do, that he is the greatest. Without belittling his great talent, one can say that he is an excellent example of how gramophone records can accelerate a conductor's career. According to his own account, the great musical influence on him has been Toscanini, whose style his most resembles, but Furtwängler, Kleiber and Walter also played their part in his development. From Toscanini he learnt, above all, that one cannot take music seriously enough and learn enough: 'The essential and desperate seriousness of making music. It is no joke and is not easy, and that old man . . . never stopped looking at the score' (*Hi Fi News and Record Review*, September 1975, p. 84). But from Furtwängler he learnt to moderate Toscanini's rigidities. His musical sympathies are wide, and he has often criticised the tendency in British musical life to categorise musicians as specialists: 'Everyone says you have to be a specialist, and that if you conduct Wagner you cannot conduct Mozart – this is nonsense: all my life I have fought against this. Obviously some works will suit you better than others, but I have always made a point of playing those works that are *not* natural to me. I want to do things that stretch me musically, and fight the tendency to become complacent and do one kind of music – that is the death of a musician.' He has named Beethoven and Schubert among his favourite composers, in addition to Bartók, Stravinsky, Schoenberg, Berg and Hindemith. To the listening public, he is best known as a great conductor of late romantic music; in his first year with the Chicago Symphony Orchestra he conducted a sensational series of concerts in New York, leading in successive concerts Mahler's Symphony No. 5, Bruckner's Symphony No. 8, Mahler's Symphony No. 7 and *Das Rheingold*. He has little interest in music after Schoenberg, and believes that too many of the earlier great composers' works are relatively unknown and are not performed. In the opera house, he is acclaimed for his Wagner, Strauss and Verdi, and in the concert hall especially for his Mahler. In fact, he feels in complete sympathy with the music of Mahler, and says he can approach him classically and not as a super-romantic.

Solti is revered by his musicians, but he can be imperious, impatient and sometimes autocratic; he drives them to the utmost, which has on occasion led to eruptions. He admits this, but believes he has changed over the years: 'In my orchestra I hate slackness, idle talk and lost time. I always hated this and still hate it. But I can achieve much more when I am quiet and not shouting.' As a musical director, he believes he must have complete authority. Rehearsals are tense and exacting, but at performances he is relatively relaxed. He does not stop the orchestra for mistakes, but points out subtle points of interpretation to section leaders and individual players later. His advice to aspiring young conductors is that technique is the least important thing: 'Above all, you need the gift to lead people. You can learn all about music, but this gift to lead, one cannot learn. The next step follows, the really big hurdle. The conductor learns the piece and has a clear picture of it, and then comes the difficult step, to realise the picture.' His own beat is at first hard to follow, and his movements are angular and jerky, sometimes almost grotesque. Nonetheless, he is acknowledged to be one of the most dynamic conductors alive. Players note that he does not beat rhythms, but the bar lines and accented notes. Although his tempi can be unusually fast, he demands absolute precision, and in the opera house he learnt from Kleiber to be vitally concerned with every aspect of the production. The score is always before him at rehearsals and concerts, although he knows it by heart; this, he believes, dispels any nervousness on the part of the soloists.

Tension is the most obvious thing about a Solti performance, with a Toscanini-like concentration, with fast tempi and exact rhythms. It is with composers which can take this treatment that he excels: Bartók, Kodály, Mahler, Tchaikovsky, Wagner and Verdi. The music of Haydn and Mozart and the early romantics such as Schubert, Schumann and Mendelssohn are kept on a very tight rein, and are often driven too hard to reveal their lyrical qualities, and in this respect he comes close to Toscanini. In the concert hall he sometimes conducts Mozart with more tension than the music can stand, but even so, two of his finest recordings are *Die Zauberflöte* and *Così fan tutte*. His Beethoven is another story; it tends to be cautious and correct, even laboured, and in the last analysis sounds too uncommitted to be convincing. He was at first greatly influenced by Toscanini's Beethoven, with one tempo going through the movement from beginning to end, but later acquaintance with Furtwängler broadened his view: 'Now obviously somewhere in the middle is the truth of Beethoven symphonies for me. Between the two men, somewhere, a truth is lying, and this is what I try to find. Somewhere between the two there is the right approach. One must not be too flexible but not too rigid, not afraid to decide about phrasing, but not break the movement up into little pieces' (From the interview in the note accompanying the Decca set of Beethoven symphonies). His Bruckner is inclined to suffer the same way, when the long paragraphs and the profound sense of mystery can sometimes elude him. His many Wagner records have called forth both high praise and carping criticism; he is at the opposite pole to Knappertsbusch, Kempe, Karajan and Goodall, and sacrifices breadth and depth to headlong excitement. He is not at all lyrical in the German mould, but is a dramatic and intense conductor who has his own unique sound and style. Whether the Chicago Symphony Orchestra has completely retained its magnificence since 1971, based on the refinement, precision and tonal qualities developed by Reiner, is another matter about which there is not always general agreement, but it must be true that the orchestra now plays exactly as Solti wants it to play.

Decca contracted Solti for his first records in 1947, as a pianist to accompany the tenor Max Lichtegg and the violinist Georg Kulenkampff in sonatas by Mozart, Beethoven and Brahms. His first orchestral recordings were the *Egmont* and *Leonore No. 3* overtures (with the Zürich Tonhalle Orchestra for Decca), the *Háry János* suite, and an excerpt from *Elektra* (with the Bavarian State Opera Orchestra *et al.* for DGG). With the arrival of LP, he recorded with the London Philharmonic Orchestra for Decca Haydn's Symphonies Nos 100, 102 and 103, Beethoven's Symphony No. 4 and Violin Concerto (with Elman), Bartók's *Dance Suite* and *Music for Strings, Percussion and Celesta*, Kodály's *Psalmus Hungaricus*, *Dances from Galánta*, *Háry János* suite and *Peacock Variations*, and the overtures to *La forza del destino*, *Leichte Cavallerie*, *Dichter und Bauer*, *Morgen, Mittag und Abend in Wien* and *Pique Dame*. Of these, the *Psalmus Hungaricus* became a classic of the gramophone, and the Suppé overtures were Solti's first hit. In John Culshaw's words, this record was 'perhaps the first step towards establishing Solti as a conductor capable of producing an individual sound from an orchestra'; even now, it stands out for its breathtaking playing. Mozart's Symphonies Nos 25 and 38, and Mendelssohn's Symphony No. 3 (with the London Symphony Orchestra) followed. Other records he also made in the 1950s were Brahms' *Ein deutsches Requiem* (with the Frankfurt Opera and Museum Orchestra and Chorus *et al.* for Capitol); the overtures to *Il barbiere di Siviglia* and *L'Italiana in Algeri* (with the London Philharmonic Orchestra for Decca); the overtures to *Prince Igor* and *Russlan and Ludmilla*, the Prelude and Dance of the Persian Slaves from *Khovanshchina*, and *A Night on the Bare Mountain* (with the Berlin Philharmonic Orchestra for Decca); Rachmaninov's Piano Concerto No. 2 (with Katchen and the London Symphony Orchestra for Decca); a disc of operatic excerpts (with Tebaldi, Bastianini and Simionato and the Chicago Lyric Opera Orchestra for Decca); Tchaikovsky's Symphonies Nos 2 and 5 (with the Paris Conservatoire Orchestra for Decca); *Gaîté parisienne*, the ballet music from *Faust*, the prelude to Act I of *Carmen*, the preludes to Acts I and III of *La traviata*, the overtures to *Semiramide* and *L'Italiana in Algeri*, the barcarolle from *Les Contes d'Hoffmann* and the Dance of the Hours from *La Gioconda* (with the Royal Opera House Orchestra, Covent Garden, for Decca); excerpts from *Fidelio*, *Billy Budd*, *A Midsummer Night's Dream*, *Le nozze di Figaro* and *Der Rosenkavalier* (with artists and the orchestra from the Royal Opera House, Covent Garden, for Decca); *Eine kleine Nachtmusik*, Tchaikovsky's *Serenade in C major*, Mendelssohn's Symphony No. 4, Schubert's Symphony No. 5, *L'Apprenti sorcier* and *La Boutique fantasque* (with the Israel Philharmonic Orchestra for Decca); Beethoven's Symphonies Nos 3, 5 and 7, Tchaikovsky's

Piano Concerto No. 1 (with Curzon), and the overtures *Leichte Cavallerie*, *Dichter und Bauer*, *Morgen, Mittag und Abend in Wien* and *Pique Dame* (with the Vienna Philharmonic Orchestra for Decca).

Solti's first complete recorded opera was *Arabella*, made in 1956 (with the Vienna Philharmonic Orchestra *et al.* for Decca), and from this set he has gone on to become one of the most outstanding conductors of opera on record. In 1958, Decca recorded him in Vienna again leading Act III, and Act II Scene II, of *Die Walküre* (with Flagstad, Svanholm and Edelman), and then proceeded to record *Das Rheingold* (with the Vienna Philharmonic Orchestra and a cast including London, Neidlinger, Svanholm and Flagstad). Its commercial success encouraged the company to continue, and by 1965 *Die Walküre*, *Siegfried* and *Götterdämmerung* were completed, making the first integral recording of *The Ring* to be released. Nilsson was the Brünnhilde, Windgassen the Siegfried and Hotter the Wotan. These records have enjoyed immense success, and were given the accolade in the United States of being issued, together with John Culshaw's book *Ring Resounding* by Time/Life, in an elaborate promotion. Other operas recorded with the Vienna Philharmonic Orchestra, all of superlative standard, have been *Tristan und Isolde*, *Tannhäuser*, *Parsifal*, *Die Meistersinger*, *Salome*, *Elektra*, *Der Rosenkavalier*, *Otello* and *Die Zauberflöte*. He has also recorded *Rigoletto* and *Falstaff* (with the RCA Italian Opera Orchestra *et al.* for RCA); *Aida* (with the Rome Opera Orchestra *et al.* for Decca); *Un ballo in maschera* (with the Santa Cecilia Orchestra *et al.* for Decca); *Così fan tutte*, *Orfeo ed Euridice*, *Don Carlos* and *Eugene Onegin* (with the Covent Garden Orchestra *et al.* for Decca); *Carmen* and *La Bohème* (with the London Philharmonic Orchestra *et al.* for Decca), and *Der fliegende Holländer* (with the Chicago Symphony Orchestra *et al.* for Decca). The chance was missed to record his impressive *Moses und Aron*, which was produced at Covent Garden in 1967.

The first Mahler Symphony to be recorded by Solti was No. 4, in 1959 with the Amsterdam Concertgebouw Orchestra (and Stahlman). Although he recorded the remaining eight during the next twelve years, he will not reconsider recording the No. 4, since it stands as a valid performance, even if his interpretation would now be considerably different. It is a fresh and much less intense reading than his later essays at the Mahler symphonies. He felt the London Symphony Orchestra could give him the sound he required for Mahler, compared to the Vienna Philharmonic Orchestra which he preferred for Wagner, and so Symphonies Nos 1, 2, 3 and 9 were recorded with them. But after he had gone to Chicago, he realised that the Chicago Symphony Orchestra could come closer to his ideal Mahler sound, and he completed the series with Nos 5, 6, 7 and 8, adding *Das Lied von der Erde* (with Minton and Kollo), *Lieder eines fahrenden Gesellen* and some songs from *Des Knaben Wunderhorn* (with Minton). In Chicago he has also recorded the nine Beethoven symphonies, *Egmont*, *Coriolan*, and *Leonore No. 3* overtures, and the five Piano Concertos (with Ashkenazy), *Symphonie fantastique*, *Le Sacre du printemps*, Tchaikovsky's Symphony No. 5, *Don Juan*, *Till Eulenspiegel*, *Also sprach Zarathustra*, *Enigma Variations*, *La Mer*, *Prélude à l'après-midi d'un faune*, *Boléro* and the overtures *Oberon*, *Die Meistersinger*, *Il barbiere di Siviglia* and *Les Francs-Juges* (all for Decca). His other recordings have included Bartók's *Concerto for Orchestra*, *Dance Suite*, *The Miraculous Mandarin* and *Music for Strings, Percussion and Celesta* (with the London Symphony Orchestra for Decca); Schumann's four Symphonies, *Overture, Scherzo and Finale*, and *Julius Caesar* overture, the overtures to *Rienzi* and *Der fliegende Holländer*, the overture and bacchanale from *Tannhäuser*, *Siegfried Idyll* and *Kinderkatechismus*, Tchaikovsky's Piano Concerto No. 1 (with Curzon), Bruckner's Symphonies Nos 7 and 8 and Verdi's *Requiem* (with the Vienna Philharmonic Orchestra *et al.* for Decca); Elgar's two Symphonies, *Cockaigne*, five *Pomp and Circumstance* Marches and arrangement of *God Save the King*, and Walton's *Belshazzar's Feast* and *Te Deum* (with the London Philharmonic Orchestra *et al.* for Decca).

Somary, Johannes (b. 1934). The son of American parents, Somary was born in Zürich, Switzerland, and was educated at Yale University. He has pursued a career as an organist, teacher and conductor; he has given organ recitals in Zürich, Washington and New York, has lectured at Brooklyn College, the New School for Social Research and the New England Conservatory, is the head of the music department at the Horace Mann School (since 1961) and organist and choirmaster at the Church of Our Saviour in New York (since 1959). In 1961 he founded and is music director of the Amor Artis Chorale, which was the first permanent and professional chorus in New York City. With the Chorale he has given American premières of several Handel oratorios, and the world premières of

Surinach's *Cantata de San Juan* and Antheil's *Cabeza de vaca*. He is also conductor of the Bronx Arts Ensemble (since 1974) and of the Fairfield County Chorale (since 1976).

Somary has made a number of distinguished recordings for Vanguard with the English Chamber Orchestra. Together with the Amor Artis Chorale and soloists he recorded the Bach *Mass in B minor* and Cantatas Nos 11 and 80, Handel's oratorios *Messiah*, *Judas Maccabaeus*, *Semele*, *Solomon*, *Theodora* and *Jephtha* and Mozart's Mass K. 427 and *Requiem*. Also with the English Chamber Orchestra for Vanguard he recorded the *Brandenburg Concertos*, suites from Handel's *Water Music* and *Music for the Royal Fireworks*, Britten's *Simple Symphony* and *The Young Person's Guide to the Orchestra*, trumpet concertos by Albinoni, Haydn, Hummel and Torelli (with Berinbaum), Arensky's *Variations on a Theme by Tchaikovsky*, Prokofiev's Symphony No. 1 and *Peter and the Wolf*, Tchaikovsky's *Serenade in C major*, Grieg's *Holberg Suite* and two *Elegiac Melodies*, Wirén's *Serenade* and a collection of pieces by Albinoni, Pachelbel, Borodin *et al.* For Decca (US) he recorded, with the Amor Artis Chorale and Orchestra, Bach's Cantata No. 118, Purcell's *Music for the Funeral of Queen Mary*, Scarlatti's *Stabat Mater*, Carissimi's *Jephte* and *Judicum extremum*, and a collection of motets and cantatas for Christmas. Of these recordings, the Bach and Handel works show Somary to be a competent and frequently inspired interpreter.

Somma, Bonaventura (1893–1960). Born in Chianciano, Italy, Somma studied at the Accademia di Santa Cecilia in Rome, was conductor of the Cappella del Santuario di Valle di Pompei in Rome (1922–3), choral conductor at the Accademia di Santa Cecilia (from 1926), lectured at the Rome Conservatory (from 1939), toured Europe and the United States with the Santa Cecilia Choir, and composed orchestral and choral works and stage music, and transcribed and revised ancient polyphonic music. He recorded a *Hymn of the Pilgrims* (with the Santa Cecilia Choir, on a 78 r.p.m. disc for HMV), and Perosi's *Missa Pontificalis* (with the choir and orchestra for Colosseum).

Somogyi, László (b. 1908). Born in Budapest, Somogyi studied under Kodály and Weiner at the Franz Liszt Academy there, and was a violinist in the Budapest Concert Orchestra (1932–6). He studied with Scherchen in Brussels (1935), conducted his first concert at the Academy at Budapest in 1936, and then conducted in the Netherlands, Belgium, Italy and Austria. He was conductor of the Omike Orchestra (1939–42), of the Budapest Symphony Orchestra (1945–50) and was first conductor of the Hungarian Radio Orchestra (1951–6); at the same time he was active in cities in Eastern Europe. He left Hungary in 1956, conducted in many countries in Western Europe and South America and in Israel, and in 1961 toured the United States.

Before he left Hungary, Somogyi recorded for Qualiton Kodály's *Dances from Galánta* and the *Háry János* Suite (with the Budapest Philharmonic Orchestra), the overture to *Der Zigeunerbaron*, Weiner's Divertimento No. 1, Szabó's *Ludas Matyi*, Bartók's *Hungarian Sketches*, Liszt's *Mephisto Waltz* and Orkel's *Hungade László* (with the Hungarian Radio Orchestra). Afterwards he made records for Westminster with the Vienna Symphony, Vienna State Opera and Vienna Radio Orchestras, some of which were issued by EMI and on other labels. Included were Haydn's Symphonies Nos 22, 78, 89 and 90, Mozart's Piano Concerto K. 482 and Beethoven's Piano Concerto No. 3 and Choral Fantasia (with Barenboim), Dvořák's overtures *Amid Nature*, *Carnaval* and *Othello*, a *Slavonic Rhapsody* and the Piano Concerto (with Firkusny), arias by Mozart, and Strauss's *Vier letzte Lieder* and extracts from *Daphne* (with Stich-Randall). Mercury also issued a disc in which he accompanied Boukoff in the two Liszt Piano Concertos (with the Vienna Symphony Orchestra). Somogyi is an accomplished conductor and his recorded performances are invariably alert and stylish.

Sonninen, Ahti (b. 1914). Born in Kuopio, Finland, Sonninen was educated at the Sibelius Academy in Helsinki, and first gave a concert of his own compositions in 1946. He has conducted many Finnish orchestras and choirs, and with the Finnish Radio Orchestra has recorded his *Pessi and Illusia* (for EMI), *The Seven Brothers* and *Under Lapland's Sky* (for Fennica).

Sorkin, Leonard (b. 1916). Born in Chicago, where he studied at the Chicago Musical College, Sorkin was a violinist with the Chicago Symphony Orchestra (1936–43) and the Seidenberg Symphonette, Chicago, and organised the Fine Arts Quartet (1940), which was the quartet-in-residence at Northwestern University (1946–54), toured Europe, the Far East and Australia many times, and made records of which the Bartók Quartets and the

Beethoven Op. 18 Quartets were the most acclaimed. He became professor of music at the School of Fine Arts at the University of Wisconsin (1967). Everest issued discs in which he conducted the Musical Arts Orchestra in *Eine kleine Nachtmusik*, Bach's *Prelude in F* and Vivaldi's Concerto Op. 3 No. 11, the overture to *Die Fledermaus*, Strauss's *Pizzicato Polka*, *An der schönen blauen Donau*, *Kaiserwalzer*, and *G'schichten aus dem Wiener Wald*, and a collection entitled 'Symphony of the Dance'.

Soudant, Hubert (b. 1946). Born in Maastricht, Holland, where he studied at the Conservatory, Soudant played the horn in the Maastricht Orchestra, took part in an international conducting course with Netherlands Radio at Hilversum in 1967, and became an assistant conductor with the Radio orchestras (1967–70). After studying with Fournet at Hilversum and with Ferrara in Siena, he won first prize at the International Competition for Young Conductors at Besançon in 1971, second prize at the Herbert von Karajan International Conducting Competition in Berlin in 1973 and first prize at the Guido Cantelli International Conducting Competition in Milan in 1975. He continues to conduct the Netherlands Radio orchestras, and has been a guest conductor in FR Germany, Belgium, Italy, the UK and Japan. His recordings include Tchaikovsky's Symphonies Nos 4 and 6, *1812* overture and *Romeo and Juliet* fantasy-overture (with the London Philharmonic Orchestra for Pye), the two Liszt Piano Concertos (with Campanella and the London Philharmonic Orchestra for Pye, also issued by Vogue-Counterpoint), and Straesser's *Ramasasiri* (with the Netherlands Ensemble for Donemus).

Soustrot, Marc (b. 1949). The French conductor Soustrot is the son of a professional soprano; he studied the trombone at the Conservatoire de Lyon and at the Paris Conservatoire with Rosenthal, and conducted for the first time in 1972. He won the Rupert Foundation Competition for Young Conductors in 1974, thus winning a scholarship to work with Previn and the London Symphony Orchestra. He continues to play in the Paris Trombone Quartet, and regularly conducts the Paris Conservatoire Orchestra. For Erato he accompanied André in trumpet concertos and other works by Aldrovandini, Franceschini, Jacchini, A. Scarlatti, Tartini, Telemann and Vivaldi (with the Monte Carlo National Opera Orchestra).

Springer, Alois (b. 1935). Born in Gross Olkowitz, Germany, Springer studied at the Academy of Music at Frankfurt am Main (1953–6), and at the Wuppertal Conservatory studied conducting under Stephani (1956). He became the first violinist and assistant conductor of the Zürich Chamber Orchestra (1956), concertmaster of the Trier Symphony Orchestra (1959), assistant to Leinsdorf and Boult at Tanglewood, Massachusetts (1965), soloist and assistant conductor with the Luxembourg Radio Orchestra (1965–9), assistant to Bernstein with the New York Philharmonic Orchestra (1967–8) and chief conductor of the Philharmonia Hungarica (1968). Springer has recorded extensively for Vox and its associate labels Turnabout and Candide; the works include the string serenades of Tchaikovsky and Elgar, Sibelius' *Rakastava*, extracts from *Eugene Onegin*, Mayr's Piano Concerto No. 1, Ravel's *Piano Concerto in G*, Ries' Piano Concerto No. 3 and Roussel's Piano Concerto (with Littauer, and the Hamburg Symphony Orchestra), Schaeuble's Piano Concerto (with Jones) and *Music for Clarinet and Orchestra* (with Michaels and the South-West German Chamber Orchestra), the overtures to Wagner's *Die Feen* and *Das Liebesverbot*, Bartók's Viola Concerto (with Koch), Violin Concerto No. 1 (with Egger) and Violin Rhapsodies (with Lautenbacher), and Penderecki's *Emanationen* and *Stabat Mater* (with the Luxembourg Radio Orchestra).

Spruit, Henk (b. 1906). Born in Utrecht, Spruit studied at the Conservatory there, where his violin teachers were Veerman and Rijnbergen. He was director of the music school at Harderwijk (1928), a violinist in the Utrecht Symphony Orchestra (1933), professor of violin and viola at the Utrecht Conservatory and conductor of the Utrecht Symphony Orchestra (1945), and chief conductor of the Netherlands Radio Orchestra (1948–71). He conducted the Netherlands Philharmonic Orchestra for Concert Hall (also released in Britain by Nixa) in some early LPs of the ballet music from *Le Cid*, a suite from *Tsar Saltan* and Saint-Saëns' *Henry VIII* music, and the Concert Hall Symphony Orchestra in Bruckner's Symphony No. 0; the latter was the first recorded performance of the work.

Stadlmair, Hans (b. 1929). Born at Neuhofen in Austria, Stadlmair studied the violin, composition and conducting at the Vienna Academy of Music (1946–52), and was a pupil of David at Stuttgart (1952–6), where he also conducted symphony and choral concerts. In 1956 he succeeded Stepp as the conductor of the Munich Chamber Orchestra, and has toured with the orchestra in Western and Eastern Europe, the United States, South America, Africa and Asia. His compositions include orchestral, instrumental, chamber and choral music. He has recorded with the Munich Chamber Orchestra a disc of Handel arias (with Fischer-Dieskau), Haydn's Flute Concerto (with Redel) and Oboe Concerto (with Kalma), Mozart's Flute Concerto K. 313 (with Linde) and Oboe Concerto (with Holliger), Scarlatti's *Il giardino di amore* (with Gayer and Fassbender), trumpet concertos by Joseph and Michael Haydn and Richter (with André), Molter's *Clarinet Concerto in G* (with Michaels), a disc of wind concertos by Vivaldi, Strauss's *Metamorphosen* and the adagio from Mahler's Symphony No. 10 (for DGG); J. C. Bach's *Harpsichord Concerto in A* (with Noe), Festing's Concerto Grosso Op. 3 No. 3, Büchtger's Concerto for String Orchestra and Violin Concerto (with Zsigmondy), Stamitz's Quartet No. 4, and his own *Toccata* (for Camerata); Eder's Symphony No. 3 and his own Violin Concerto (with David, for Amadeo); Mozart's Symphonies Nos 21 and 27, Haydn's Symphonies Nos 36 and 45, Kelterborn's *Vier Nachtstücke* and *Music for Clarinet and Strings* (with Brunner, for Bärenreiter), Haydn's Symphony No. 22, Michael Haydn's *Divertimento in D*, flute concertos by Benda, Hoffmeister and Stamitz (with Larrieu), Beethoven's *Grosse Fuge*, David's Concerto for String Orchestra, Viotti's Violin Concerto No. 2 and Mozart's Violin Concerto K. 219 and Adagio K. 261 (with Wallez, for Classic), Telemann's *Suite in A minor* and Vivaldi's *Flute Concerto in C* (with Stangenberg) and Purcell's *The Married Beau* (for Quadriga Ton); songs of Julius Weismann (with Giebel, for Christophorus), Bach's Two-Violin Concerto and Genzmer's *Moosburger Graduale* and Sonatina (for Lorby); Haydn's *Die sieben letzten Worte des Erlösers am Kreuz*, flute concertos of C. P. E. Bach and Stamitz, and Mozart's Rondo K. 373 (with Larrieu), pieces by J. S., J. C. F., W. F. and J. C. Bach, trumpet concertos by Handel (with Bernard), the Mozart Bassoon Concerto (with Laroque), Clarinet Concerto (with Deplus) and Rondo for Horn K. 371 (with Bourgue, for Decca); Mozart's Divertimento K. 136 and Stamitz's *Symphony in A* (for Nonesuch); Killmayer's *Fin al Punto* (for Wergo); and Tcherepnin's *Serenade* (for Da Camera).

Stallaert, Alphonse (b. 1920). Born in Helmond, the Netherlands, Stallaert was educated at the Conservatory and University of Utrecht, founded the Paris String Orchestra (1947–50), and has composed *inter alia*, a symphony, cello concerto and a piano concerto. He conducted a performance of the latter, with Wayenberg the soloist and the Lamoureux Orchestra, for Philips.

Stanford, Sir Charles Villiers (1852–1924). The Irish composer, conductor and teacher Stanford was a contemporary of Elgar and Parry, and was most influential as professor of composition at the Royal College of Music in London. His activities as a conductor included the direction of the London Bach Choir and the Leeds Triennial Festival; he is reported to have said that 'a conductor need never be nervous – he can't play any wrong notes'. He was a prolific composer; his output included a number of operas, symphonies, chamber works and many songs and choral works. His orchestral works rarely appear on concert programmes now, but in his own day he was widely performed; Mahler presented his *Irish Symphony* twice in his 1910–11 season in New York, and his light opera *Shamus O'Brien* ran for a hundred nights in London in 1896. In the early days of 78 r.p.m. records Stanford himself recorded some of his orchestral music for HMV, including his *Irish Rhapsody No. 1*, and excerpt from the *Irish Symphony*, the overtures to *The Critic* and *Shamus O'Brien*, and two numbers from his *Suite of Ancient Dances*. A selection of these was re-issued in England by Gem in 1974.

Stanger, Russell (b. 1924). Born at Arlington, Massachusetts, Stanger studied at the New England Conservatory and at the Berkshire Music Center at Tanglewood. He was musical director of the Harvard-Radcliffe Orchestra, Cambridge, Mass. (1950–53), conductor of the Pioneer Valley Symphony Orchestra (1953–6), guest conductor in the United States and Canada (1955–8), assistant conductor with the New York Philharmonic Orchestra (1960–61) when he substituted for Bernstein and Böhm, assistant conductor with the Minneapolis Symphony Orchestra (1964–6) and musical director of the Norfolk Symphony Orchestra, Virginia (since 1966). For Composers Recordings he conducted the London Philharmonic Orchestra in Mayer's *Overture for an American* and Straight's *Development*.

Stasevich, Abram (1907–71). Born at Simferopol in the Crimea, Stasevich studied the cello under Kozolunov and conducting under Ginzburg at the Moscow Conservatory, and was conductor of the Moscow Philharmonic

Orchestra (1937). Although active as a conductor at Tbilisi (1941), Novosibirsk (1942–4) and Moscow (1944–52), he never received a permanent appointment. He was awarded the title First Artist (1947) and Honoured Artist of the Russian Republic (1957). He composed a cantata *Borodino* (first performed in 1964), some symphonic and instrumental works, and made an orchestral transcription as an oratorio of Prokofiev's music for the film *Ivan the Terrible*, which he recorded (with the USSR State Symphony Orchestra). His other recordings included the Prokofiev Symphony No. 1 and *Romeo and Juliet* Suites Nos 1 and 3, Taktakishvili's *Piano Concerto in C* (with Yokheles), Shostakovich's Ballet Suites Nos 2 and 3 and the incidental music for *Much Ado About Nothing* by Khrennikov (with the USSR State Symphony Orchestra), Dargomyzhsky's *Baba Yaga, Kazachok, Fantasy on Finnish Themes* and excerpts from *Rogdana*, Prokofiev's *Cinderella* Suite No. 2 and *Romeo and Juliet* Suite No. 3 (with the Bolshoi Theatre Orchestra), Miaskovsky's *Little Overture* and *Divertimento*, Moniuszko's *Fairy Tale Overture*, a suite from Kabalevsky's *Colas Breugnon*, and Karłowicz's *Lithuanian Rhapsody* (with the Moscow Radio Orchestra).

Stefanov, Vasil. The Bulgarian conductor Stefanov studied at the Sofia State Academy, and was assistant concertmaster of the Academy symphony orchestra. He was appointed Popov's assistant when the Imperial Bulgarian Military Symphony Orchestra was formed, which later became the Sofia State Philharmonic Orchestra. He became second conductor of this orchestra (1954), founded the Šumen State Symphony orchestra (1954), taught the violin at the Sofia State Academy (1950–53), where he is an honorary professor, and conducted the Sofia Gusla Men's Choir. He has made a number of records with the Bulgarian Radio and Television Orchestra which were issued by Balkanton, and in some cases re-issued on Western labels such as Monarch; these included Tchaikovsky's Piano Concerto No. 1 (with Mollova), Rachmaninov's Piano Concerto No. 4 (with Drenikov), the two Prokofiev Violin Concertos (with Milanova), Stainov's *Thrace, Thracian Dances*, Symphony No. 5, *Fairy Tale* suite, Symphonic Scherzo, and overture *Burning Dawn*, Tzvetanov's Symphony No. 3, Kyurkchüsky's *Diaphonic Study*, Levi's Symphony No. 2, Hoistov's *Overture with Fanfares*, Koutev's cantata, *Ninth of September* and Tekeliev's *Requiem* and *Poem for Viola and Orchestra* (with Zahariev).

Stein, Fritz (1879–1961). Born in Gerlachsheim, Baden, Stein studied theology at Karlsruhe, then music at Heidelberg and Leipzig, where he was a student of conducting with Nikisch and of the organ with Straube. In 1913 he was professor of musicology at the University of Jena, served in the German army in World War I, was a professor at Kiel University (1918–25) and in 1933 became director of the Hochschule für Musik in Berlin and a member of the Nazi-inspired Reichsmusikkammer, remaining there until 1945. Stein wrote a biography of Reger, and compiled a thematic catalogue of Reger's music. He was responsible for the discovery of the parts of a symphony in the library of the University of Jena, which he claimed was by Beethoven; Breitkopf and Härtel published the score in 1911 as the *Jena Symphony* by Beethoven, and it was widely performed and was recorded as such. In 1957, however, H. C. Robbins Landon proved that the symphony had been written by Friedrich Witt (1770–1837). Stein also edited music by J. C. Bach, Handel, Schütz and others.

With a group variously entitled the Berlin College of Instrumentalists, the Berlin Collegium Musicum and the Berlin Academy Orchestra, Stein recorded, for HMV in the 1930s three numbers from the *St John Passion* and chorales from several cantatas of Bach, Mozart's Symphony No. 28, some *German Dances* of Schubert, and Bach's Violin Concerto No. 1, with Strub the soloist; the last record was made in wartime Germany. In his review of the Mozart symphony written in 1941, Kolodin described Stein as a 'competent workman, a little turgid for a work of this spirit'.

Stein, Horst (b. 1928). Born in Wuppertal, Stein studied at the Musik Gymnasium at Frankfurt am Main and at the Hochschule für Musik at Cologne, and received his first appointment at the age of 19 as assistant conductor at the Wuppertal Town Theatre in 1947. He was conductor at the Hamburg State Opera (1950–55) and at the Staatsoper in East Berlin (1956–61), and then returned to Hamburg as substitute general music director. He became general music director at Mannheim (1963–70), chief conductor at the Vienna State Opera (1969–71), and since 1972 has been general music director at the Hamburg State Opera. He has been a guest conductor in opera houses throughout Europe, North and South America, first conducted in the United States at the San Francisco Opera in 1965, and has frequently conducted the Berlin Philharmonic and Vienna Philharmonic Orchestras. In 1968 he led acclaimed performances of *The Ring* at the Vienna Festival, and since 1969 has regularly conducted at the Bayreuth Festival; he is also honorary conductor of the NHK Symphony Orchestra, Japan.

Stein's recordings include the five Beethoven Piano Concertos (with Gulda and the Vienna Philharmonic Orchestra for Decca), Beethoven's Piano Concerto No. 5 (with Hoffman and the London Philharmonic Orchestra for Pye), Sibelius' *Finlandia*, *En Saga*, *Night Ride and Sunrise* and *Pohjola's Daughter* (with the Suisse Romande Orchestra for Decca), Bruckner's Symphonies Nos 2 and 6 (with the Vienna Philharmonic Orchestra for Decca), the Glazunov Violin Concerto and Prokofiev's Violin Concerto No. 1 (with Sivo and the Suisse Romande Orchestra for Decca), a disc of overtures by Suppé, Offenbach and Reznicek (with the London Philharmonic Orchestra for Pye), another of overtures by Mozart and Lortzing (with the Hamburg State Opera Orchestra for Ariola), the preludes from *Lohengrin*, *Die Meistersinger*, *Der fliegende Holländer*, and the prelude and Liebestod from *Tristan und Isolde* (with the Vienna Philharmonic Orchestra for Decca), *Tosca* (in German, with the Berlin Staatskapelle *et al.* for DGG), and discs of excerpts from *Der Waffenschmied* (with the Hamburg State Opera Orchestra *et al.* for Ariola), *Un ballo in maschera*, *Pagliacci* and *Nabucco* (with the Deutsche Oper Orchestra, Berlin, *et al.* for EMI), *Carmen*, *Don Carlos*, and *Orfeo ed Euridice* (with the Berlin Symphony Orchestra *et al.* for EMI), and Kienzl's *Der Evangelimann* (with the Bavarian Radio Symphony Orchestra *et al.* for DGG), and Gerster's *Festival Overture* and *Upper Hessian Peasant Dances* (with the Leipzig Radio Symphony Orchestra for Eterna). Of these records, the Bruckner Symphony No. 2 is especially remarkable for the beauty and sensitivity of the performance.

Steinberg, William (1899–1978). Born in Cologne as Hans Wilhelm Steinberg, Steinberg studied at the Cologne Conservatory under Abendroth, and as a boy learned the violin and piano. At the age of 19 he won the Wullner Prize for conducting at Cologne, and became assistant to Klemperer at the Cologne Opera in 1920. Soon he was appointed a conductor there, and was subsequently first conductor at the German Opera, Prague (1925–9), where he became director in 1927, music director at the Frankfurt am Main Opera and conductor of the Frankfurt Museum Concerts, also conducting at the Berlin Staatsoper. At Frankfurt he led the second production of *Wozzeck*, and the world premières of Weill's *Aufstieg und Fall der Stadt Mahagonny* and Schoenberg's *Von Heute auf Morgen*.

With the advent of the Nazis, Steinberg was dismissed from all his posts in 1933. He then founded a Jewish Cultural League which gave concerts for the Jewish communities in Frankfurt and Berlin, but he left Germany for Palestine in 1936, taking with him many musicians; there he was co-founder with Huberman of the Palestine Symphony Orchestra (now the Israel Philharmonic Orchestra), and trained it for its first concert in December 1936, which was conducted by Toscanini, who had accepted Huberman's invitation without hesitation. Steinberg conducted the orchestra in the first years of its existence, and in 1938 went to the United States on Toscanini's invitation to assist in founding and training the new NBC Symphony Orchestra. He was an assistant conductor to Toscanini with the orchestra, and appeared as a guest conductor with many other American orchestras, eventually becoming a naturalised US citizen in 1944 and changing his name to William Steinberg. He conducted at the San Francisco Opera (1944–8), was musical director of the Pittsburgh Symphony Orchestra (1952–76), of the London Philharmonic Orchestra (1958–60) and of the Boston Symphony Orchestra (1968–72). He conducted at the New York Metropolitan Opera (1964–5), toured Europe and the Middle East with the Pittsburgh Symphony Orchestra in 1964, conducted the Israel Philharmonic Orchestra on its tour of the US in 1967, and was principal guest conductor of the New York Philharmonic Orchestra in 1964. A performance of Beethoven's Symphony No. 9 with the New York Philharmonic Orchestra in 1965 drew an audience of 75,000. In the last years of his life Steinberg suffered a grave illness which forced him to curtail his activities; he was obliged to retire from his position with the Pittsburgh Symphony Orchestra in 1976, and was then appointed conductor emeritus. Under his leadership the orchestra had become one of the finest half dozen in the US.

Steinberg's formative influences were Toscanini and Klemperer, from whom he learnt, above all, a single-minded devotion to his profession and faithfulness to the score. 'Toscanini and Klemperer were the great masters. They served two purposes, the orchestra and the music, and absolutely nothing more. For one wrong tempo at rehearsal, Klemperer would not speak to me for weeks' (*Los Angeles Times*, 20 June 1976). He deprecated personal interpretations at the expense of the composer's intentions. He said that the conductor can only demonstrate the meaning of a piece by allowing the work to speak for itself; to achieve this he must have all the implied spiritual traits and virtues of character, illuminated by intuition and inspiration and sufficient modesty to avoid the attentions of a crowd seeking entertainment or provocation. His interpretations were honest and literal. His fine musicianship ensured that his intentions were generally convincing and eloquent, although sometimes unexciting. He gave his players freedom in their phrasing, in contrast to many of his peers. Steinberg was at his best in Beethoven, Brahms, Wagner, Bruckner and Mahler, but not quite so exemplary with French music. He believed conductors had an obligation to perform at least some contemporary music for the benefit of their audiences; programmes should inform as well as entertain. He pointed out the advantage of the long experience in opera houses enjoyed by European conductors: 'At the opera house one starts at the bottom . . . This is the principal mistake of conductors in America, who start at the top.' He judged American orchestras better than any other: 'The top 20 orchestras in North America are superior to those in Europe, with the exception of the Berlin Philharmonic.'

Steinberg's first recording, which was made in the late 1920s, was the Tchaikovsky Violin Concerto (with Huberman and the Berlin Staatsoper Orchestra, for Columbia). His American discs were at first 78s; the Schumann Piano Concerto (with Rubinstein and the RCA Victor Symphony Orchestra for RCA), Shostakovich's Symphony No. 7 (with the Buffalo Philharmonic Orchestra for Musicraft/ Allegro), the Glazunov Violin Concerto (with Milstein and the RCA Victor Symphony Orchestra for RCA), Chopin's Piano Concerto No. 2 (with Rubinstein and the NBC Symphony Orchestra for RCA), Mozart's Serenade K. 361 (with the Los Angeles Wind Ensemble for Capitol), and the two Beethoven Romances, Lalo's *Symphonie espagnole*, Bruch's *Scottish Fantasy*, Saint-Saëns' *Havanaise* and *Introduction et rondo capriccioso* and Sarasate's *Zigeunerweisen* (with Heifetz and the RCA Victor Symphony Orchestra for RCA).

He then undertook a wide-ranging series of LP discs with the Pittsburgh Symphony Orchestra for Capitol, in which there were many distinguished performances. Included were the Handel/Harty *Water Music*, Haydn's Symphony No. 94, Mozart's Symphonies Nos 35, 40 and 41 and *Eine kleine Nachtmusik*, the nine Beethoven symphonies, Schubert's Symphonies Nos 2, 5, 6 and 8, Mendelssohn's Symphonies Nos 3 and 4, Tchaikovsky's Symphonies Nos 5 and 6, the *Serenade in C major*, *Marche slave* and *Capriccio italien*, *Scheherazade*, a suite from *Le Coq d'or*, Brahms' Symphony No. 1, Bruckner's Symphony No. 4, Mahler's Symphony No. 1, *Till Eulenspiegel* and *Tod und Verklärung*, a collection of Strauss polkas and waltzes, the prelude and Liebestod from *Tristan und Isolde*, the Rhine Journey and Funeral Music from *Götterdämmerung*, the *Siegfried Idyll*, the prelude to *Die Meistersinger* and excerpts from *Parsifal*, *A Night on the Bare Mountain*, Glinka's *Kamarinskaya*, *Boléro* and *Pavane pour une infante défunte*, Prokofiev's Symphony No. 1, a suite from *The Love of Three Oranges*, the Dance of the Polovtsian Maidens from *Prince Igor*, the *Mathis der Maler* symphony, Toch's Symphony No. 3, Rachmaninov's Symphony No. 2, the *Enigma Variations* and Vaughan Williams' *Five Tudor Portraits* and *Fantasia on a Theme of Thomas Tallis*, Bloch's Concerto Grosso No. 1, Schumann's Symphony No. 5, *Le Sacre du printemps* and Wolf's *Italian Serenade*. The concertos recorded were Beethoven's Piano Concerto No. 5 and Brahms' Piano Concerto No. 1 (with Firkusny), the Beethoven, Brahms, Glazunov, Mendelssohn, Tchaikovsky, Dvořák and Bruch (No. 1) Violin Concertos (with Milstein) and Gershwin's *Piano Concerto in F* (with Pennario).

Steinberg also recorded with the Pittsburgh Symphony Orchestra for other companies. For Command, he covered the nine Beethoven symphonies again, the four Brahms symphonies and *Tragic Overture*, Schubert's Symphonies Nos 3 and 8, Rachmaninov's Symphony No. 2, Bruckner's Symphony No. 7 and *Overture in G minor*, Tchaikovsky's Symphony No. 4, Dvořák's *Scherzo capriccioso*, the *Faust*, *Rienzi*, *Die Meistersinger* and *Der fliegende Holländer* overtures and preludes, the prelude to Act III of *Lohengrin*, the Ride of the Valkyries and the Magic Fire Music from *Die Walküre*, the Rhine Journey and Funeral Music from *Götterdämmerung*, *Valses nobles et sentimentales*, *Petrushka*, *An American in Paris* and a suite from *Porgy and Bess*, and suites from *Appalachian Spring* and *Billy the Kid*. For Audio Fidelity there were an orchestral arrangement of Verdi's *String Quartet in E minor*, and a suite from *Nutcracker*. On the label Pittsburgh's Festival of Contemporary Music appeared Harris' Symphony No. 5, Honegger's Symphony No. 5, Stravinsky's *Symphony of Psalms*, Britten's *Serenade for Tenor, Horn and Strings*, Bartók's *Music for Strings, Percussion and Celesta*, the Berg Violin Concerto (with Goldberg), Milhaud's *Protée* Suite No. 2,

Copland's *A Lincoln Portrait* and a *Bachianas brasileiras* of Villa-Lobos. Everest issued Brahms' Symphony No. 4, *An American in Paris* and *Rhapsody in Blue* (with Sanroma), Bennett's *Commemorative Symphony for Stephen Foster* and a symphonic story (*sic*) of Jerome Kern, and RCA Bruckner's Symphony No. 6. With the Philharmonia Orchestra for EMI he also recorded *Don Juan* and a suite from *Der Rosenkavalier*.

Finally, with the Boston Symphony Orchestra, Steinberg recorded *L'Apprenti sorcier*, *Danse macabre* and *Till Eulenspiegel* (for RCA) and Holst's *The Planets*, *Also sprach Zarathustra*, Bruckner's Symphony No. 6, Schubert's Symphony No. 9, and Hindemith's *Mathis der Maler* symphony and *Concert Music for Strings and Brass* (for DGG). Of all these recordings, he himself was most pleased with two made with the Boston Symphony, the Schubert Symphony No. 9 and the Bruckner Symphony No. 6.

Steiner, Heinrich (b. 1903). Born at Oehringen, Württemberg, Steiner studied at the Hochschule für Musik at Frankfurt am Main and at the Hochschule für Musik in Berlin with Petri, Kreutzer, Prüwer and Juon, and from 1924 pursued a career as a pianist and conductor. He was music director at Würzburg (1935–6), conductor with the Berlin Radio (1936–9) and at Oldenburg (1939–46), and has been general musical director of the Nordmark Symphony Orchestra (since 1952), and music director at Flensburg (since 1952). For DGG he recorded with the Nordmark Symphony Orchestra Glazunov's *Ballet Scenes*, Grieg's *Sigurd Jorsalfar* and *Wedding Day at Troldhaugen*, and Suppé's overture *Dichter und Bauer*.

Steinitz, Paul (b. 1909). Born in Chichester and educated at the Royal Academy of Music in London, Steinitz was organist and choirmaster at the Church of St Bartholomew-the-Great (1949–61). He founded and has been conductor of the London Bach Society and the Steinitz Bach Players, and embarked on a cycle of performances of all the Bach cantatas. In these he has employed authentic 18th-century instruments, and was the first person to use the clarino trumpet, cornett and sackbutt in English Bach performances. In 1952 he performed for the first time in England the *St Matthew Passion* in its complete and original German form. His recordings include Bach's Cantatas Nos 10 and 47 (with the London Bach Society Chorus and English Chamber Orchestra *et al.* for Oryx and Lyrichord), *Magnificat* and Cantata No. 118 (with the London Bach Society *et al.* for Unicorn), Cantata No. 131 and the Handel Wedding Anthem *Sing unto God*, Schütz's *Die Sieben Worte unsers lieben Erlösers* (with the London Bach Society Chorus and the Collegium Sagittari for Bärenreiter), and excerpts from Cantatas Nos 10, 38, 78, 93, 95, 140, 143 and 147, *Kyrie Eleison*, *Dir, dir, Jehova*, *Vergiss mein nicht*, *Gott lebet noch*, *Komm süsser Tod* and *Sanctus in D* of Bach (with the London Bach Society for Oryx). He has also recorded Donald Swann's *Festival Matins* (with the London Bach Society for Argo).

Stephani, Martin (b. 1915). Born at Eisleben, Stephani studied in Berlin under Gmeindl, Stein and Thomas, and founded the Marburger Kantorei, a school for new music, in Marburg (1948). He was conductor of the Wuppertal Concert Society (1951–63), became its general music director in 1959, has been director of the Berge Conservatory (1955–63), taught conducting at the North-West German Music Academy at Detmold (since 1957), was conductor of the Frankfurt Caecilia Society (1957–9), became director of the Detmold Academy (1959) and has been conductor of the Bielefeld Musical Society (since 1959). He has also written a study of the music of Hindemith. For Bärenreiter he recorded Handel's Concerto Grosso Op. 6 No. 6, *Water Music* and instrumental movements from *Saul*, and Distler's Harpsichord Concerto (with the German Bach Soloists *et al.*), and Handel's *Music for the Royal Fireworks*, J. C. Bach's Sinfonia Op. 18 No. 5, and Stravinsky's *Apollon Musagète* (with the Frankfurt Bach Orchestra); some of these performances were released in Britain by Oryx. He also has recorded the Verdi *Te Deum* (with the Philharmonia Hungarica *et al.* for Telefunken), Handel's *Johannespassion* (with the Cologne Chamber Orchestra *et al.* for Schwann), Hindemith's *Vorspiel zu einem Requiem* and Lutosławski's *Concerto for Orchestra* (with the North-West Youth Orchestra for Da Camera).

Stepp, Christoph (b. 1927). Born in Breslau (now Wrocław), Stepp studied at the Hochschule für Musik at Munich under Knappe, Eichhorn and Geierhaas, and in 1950 founded the Munich Chamber Orchestra, which he led until 1956. He then became assistant conductor to Fricsay at the Bavarian State Opera at Munich (1956), was first conductor at Augsburg (1957), and was appointed general music director of the Philharmonic Orchestra der Pfalz at Ludwigshafen. His recordings include Mozart's Divertimenti K. 136 and K. 137, *Eine kleine*

Nachtmusik, the *Country Dances* K. 462 and *Bastien und Bastienne*, and Britten's *Simple Symphony* (with the Munich Chamber Orchestra *et al.*); Haydn's Horn Concerto No. 2 (with Lind) and Trumpet Concerto (with Scherbaum), Mozart's *Ein musikalischer Spass* and Divertimento K. 196f (with the Hamburg Radio Orchestra); and excerpts from *Der Waffenschmied* (with the Berlin Radio Symphony Orchestra *et al.*), all for DGG.

Stern, Isaac (b. 1920). The violin virtuoso Stern was born at Kreminiecz, now in the USSR, migrated to the United States as a boy with his family, and studied at the San Francisco Conservatory. His debut as a violinist took place with the San Francisco Symphony Orchestra in 1934, and at Carnegie Hall in New York in 1943, with Mitropoulos and the New York Philharmonic Orchestra. He has appeared as a concert artist in almost every musical centre in the world and at numerous festivals, especially those with Casals at Puerto Rico (1953–67). In addition to his many recordings in the violin repertoire, Stern has appeared on disc as a conductor-violinist in Bach's Violin Concerto No. 1 and Mozart's Sinfonia Concertante K. 364 (with Trampler, both works with the London Symphony Orchestra for CBS). On the dual role of player and conductor he has commented that 'there is something in the genuflexions of the conducting side that keeps that last measure of laser concentration from happening. You can only do it with a group you've lived and played with for a long time. Then it's like chamber music'.

Sternberg, Jonathan (b. 1919). Born in New York, Sternberg was educated at the Juilliard School (1929–31), New York University (1939–40), the Harvard Summer School (1940), the Manhattan School of Music (1946) and L'École Monteux (1946). He first conducted with the Vienna Symphony Orchestra in 1947, was a guest conductor with orchestras and at opera houses in Europe, was musical director of the Royal Flemish Opera at Antwerp (1961), conductor of the Harkness Ballet, New York (1966) and of the Atlanta Opera and Ballet (1968). He has been professor of conducting at the Eastman School of Music (1969), professor of music at the Temple University College of Music, Philadelphia, and conductor of the Main Line Symphony Orchestra and the Symphony Club of Philadelphia (1971).

In the early years of LP Sternberg made a number of records, mostly with Austrian orchestras, which were released on various labels in the United States and Britain; the performances were in most cases praiseworthy if not especially polished. Included were Bach's Cantatas Nos 1, 21, 34, 46, 56 and 104 (with the Vienna Symphony Orchestra *et al.* for Bach Society), Haydn's Symphonies Nos 1, 13, 22, 28, 31, 34, 35, 38, 39, 44, 48, 82 and 85 (with the Vienna Symphony Orchestra for the Haydn Society) and *Cello Concerto in D* (with the Gendron and the Vienna State Opera Orchestra for Oceanic), Mozart's Piano Concertos K. 449 and K. 482 (with Badura-Skoda and the Vienna State Opera Orchestra for Oceanic) and Serenade K. 320 (with the Vienna State Opera Orchestra for Nixa), *Offertorium* K. 72 and *Kyrie* K. 341 (with the Salzburg Mozarteum Orchestra for Dover), Schubert's Symphonies Nos 2 and 5 (with the Salzburg Mozarteum Orchestra for L'Oiseau Lyre), Rossini's *Stabat Mater* (with the Vienna State Opera Orchestra *et al.* for Saga), Tchaikovsky's Symphony No. 5 (with the Vienna State Opera Orchestra for Urania), Saint-Saëns' Cello Concerto No. 1 (with Gendron and the Vienna State Opera Orchestra for Oceanic), Prokofiev's Piano Concerto No. 5 (with Brendel and the Vienna State Opera Orchestra for Vox), Milhaud's *Fantaisie pastorale* (with Anderson and the Vienna State Opera Orchestra for Oceanic) and Bassett's *Variations for Orchestra* (with the Zürich Radio Symphony Orchestra for Composers Recordings).

Stevens, Denis (b. 1922). Born in High Wycombe, Stevens studied at Jesus College, Oxford, with Wellesz and Morris, and in Paris, and was first a violinist in the Philharmonia Orchestra and in string quartets. He developed an interest in early music, and for five years was on the staff of the BBC as producer of medieval, Renaissance and baroque music for the Third Programme (1949–54). He was co-founder of the Accademia Monteverdiana and founder and conductor of the Ambrosian Singers, and with these ensembles performed in Britain, Europe and the United States. He lectured at the University of California, Berkeley (1962), Pennsylvania State University (1963–4), became professor of musicology at Columbia University, New York (1964), and has been visiting professor at the Royal Academy of Music and Cornell University. He is principally concerned with the notation and interpretation of the music of the 17th century and before, and prefers music for which he has to determine the composer's intentions first. While working with early instruments, he believes that authenticity is achieved through understanding the spirit of the music as much as through performing with authentic instruments.

He inaugurated the *Musica Britannica* series of publications with his edition of the *Mulliner Book*, and has written or edited numerous books, including *Tudor Church Music*, *A History of Song*, *Thomas Tomkins* and, with Alec Robertson, the three-volume *Pelican History of Music*.

In his chosen field, Stevens has made a number of recordings for various companies. With the Accademia Monteverdiana he recorded Monteverdi's *Vespro della beata Vergine* and Purcell's Odes and Welcome Songs, *Celestial Music* and *Now Does the Glorious Day* (for Vanguard); Beethoven's Scottish and Irish songs, Monteverdi's Ninth Book of Madrigals, excerpts from Purcell's music for *Abdelazar*, *Amphitryon*, *Distressed Innocence* and *The Fairy Queen*, pieces by Strizzio, de Wert, Gesualdo and Gastoldi, and a collection entitled *Songs of Love from Four Centuries*, which included pieces by Lassus, Philips, Monteverdi, Luzzaschi, Vicentino, Lawes, Haydn, Beethoven, Mozart, Schumann, Brahms and Bishop (for La Guilde Internationale du Disque); music by Gesualdo, Nenna and Grandi (for Nonesuch); collections titled *Amorous Dialogues of the Renaissance* and *Music in honour of St Thomas of Canterbury* (for Nonesuch); music of Vincentino and the Worcester Fragments (for Vanguard); Albicastro's Concertos Op. 7 Nos 6 and 7, Boyce's *Concerti Grossi in B minor* and *B flat*, Monteverdi's *Il ballo dell'ingrate* and *Il combattimento di Tancredi e Clorinda* (for Expériences Anonymes); and music by Gesualdo (for Pye). With the Ambrosian Singers he recorded sacred works of A. and G. Gabrieli (for EMI); *The Cries of London* (for Penn. State); sacred and secular music of Dunstable (for Expériences Anonymes); Fayrfax's *Missa tecum Principium* and *Aeternae laudis lilium* (for Schwann); Morales' *Missus est Gabriel Angelus*, Victoria's *Magnificat*, Byrd's *Domine, praestolamur adventum tuum*, Gabrieli's Madrigals and Dialogues, Flecha's *Que farem del Pobre Joan* and *Teresa hermana*, and Morley's six canzonets (issued by the Musical Heritage Society and Dover). In addition he recorded a Telemann Violin Concerto and *Suite in D major* (with Kaufman and an orchestra for Concert Hall), a two-disc set titled *The Art of Ornamentation and Embellishment in the Renaissance and Baroque* (for Bach Guild), and Vivaldi's *La Cetra* (with the Accademia Monteverdiana for Musical Heritage Society).

Stewart, Reginald (b. 1900). Born in Edinburgh, Stewart was awarded a D.Mus. at St Mary's College, Edinburgh, and studied further with Hambourg, Philipp and Nadia Boulanger. He started his career as a pianist and teacher of piano at the Canadian Academy of Music (1920), conducted the London Symphony Orchestra at the Royal Albert Hall (1925), led a series of concerts over the Canadian radio network (1931), formed and conducted the Bach Society at Toronto (1933–41), formed the Toronto Philharmonic Orchestra (1934), and was active as both pianist and conductor in Canada and the United States, where he conducted the Detroit Symphony Orchestra (1940–41) and the New York Philharmonic and Chicago Symphony Orchestras (1941). He was director of the Peabody Conservatory of Music, Baltimore (1941–58), conductor of the Baltimore Symphony Orchestra (1942–52), became a teacher and artist-in-residence at the Music Academy of the West at Santa Barbara, California (1962), and was a guest conductor with leading symphony orchestras in Central and South America, and in Europe. In addition to his records as a pianist, he recorded Vivaldi's *Cello Concertos in A minor* and *E minor*, and Boccherini's *Cello Concerto in B flat* (with Parisot and the Baltimore Conservatory Orchestra for Esoteric), Ives' Symphony No. 3 and Donovan's *Suite for Oboe and String Orchestra* (with Genovese and the Baltimore Little Symphony Orchestra for Vanguard).

Stiedry, Fritz (1883–1968). Born in Vienna, Stiedry studied law at the Vienna University and music at the Vienna Conservatory under Mandyczewski. On Mahler's recommendation he was appointed assistant conductor under Schuch at Dresden (1907–8), was a conductor at Teplitz, Poznań, Prague, Nuremberg and Kassel, and then became first conductor at the Berlin Royal Opera (1914–23), although the war prevented him from taking up the appointment for two years. He succeeded Weingartner at the Vienna Volksoper (1924–5), was a guest conductor in Germany and in Rome, Madrid, Barcelona and Stockholm (1925–8), and followed Walter as first conductor at the Berlin Municipal Opera (1928–33), where he gave distinguished performances of Verdi operas and led the première of Weill's *Die Bürgschaft*. He was also president of the Berlin branch of the International Society for Contemporary Music (1929–33). He left Germany in 1933, was conductor of the Leningrad Philharmonic Orchestra (1933–7), emigrated to the United States and became a US citizen. In New York he was director of the New Friends of Music orchestra (1938), conducted the New Opera

Company (1941) and at the Metropolitan Opera (1946–51), where he was the principal Wagner conductor. He first conducted at the Glyndebourne Festival in 1947, and led *The Ring* and *Fidelio* at Covent Garden in 1953–4. He had a long association with Schoenberg, and gave the first performance of his *Chamber Symphony No. 2* in 1940. Stiedry was also a composer and writer about music; deafness finally forced his retirement from the New York Met., and his final years were spent in Majorca and Zürich.

Stiedry recorded in Germany for Polydor before his departure in 1933; he made discs of five movements from Mozart's Serenade K. 361, and of Brahms' *Academic Festival Overture* (with the Berlin Staatsoper Orchestra). In the US Victor released 78 r.p.m. sets of him conducting the New Friends of Music in a Bach *Violin Concerto in D minor* (with Szigeti), Mozart's Sinfonia Concertante K. 364 (with Spalding and Primrose) and of Haydn's Symphonies Nos 67 and 80. Decca (US) also recorded him conducting an unidentified orchestra in Wolf's *Italian Serenade*. In 1953 he conducted *Orfeo ed Euridice* at Glyndebourne with the Southern Philharmonic Orchestra and with Kathleen Ferrier in the cast; Decca (UK) recorded and released the set, and later reissued it on LP; excerpts were still in the catalogue in 1977, although Stiedry's conducting was generally considered somewhat stolid. His other recordings were of *Così fan tutte* (with the New York Metropolitan company for Columbia (US)), and Haydn's Symphony No. 102 (with an unidentified orchestra for Music Appreciation).

Stith, Marice (b. 1926). Born in Johnstown, Ohio, Stith studied the trumpet at the Capital University, Ohio State University and at the Eastman School of Music, and played the instrument in the Syracuse Symphony Orchestra. He has been professor of music at Cornell University, founded and conducted the Cornell University Wind Ensemble, appeared and made records as a trumpet soloist, and was a guest conductor with various orchestras. He conducted the Cornell University Wind Ensemble in a series of 17 records for Cornell University Records, which included music by Schoenberg, Copland, Bielawa, Rimsky-Korsakov, Palmer, Ives, Hovhaness, Reinecke, Shostakovich, Erb, Lijnschooten, Lindenfeld, Bennett, Bergsma, Holst, Vaughan Williams, Erickson, Jenkins, Raleigh, Madden, Borden, Bernstein, Grainger, Adler, Hutchins, Herstein, Williams, Schuman, Toensing, Creston, Hanson, George, Morrill, Rollin, Benson, Lee, Hindemith, Stravinsky, Cope, Geissler, Israel, Green, Rouse, Ross, Lockwood and Strauss.

Stobart, James (b. 1938). Born at Hanley, Staffordshire, Stobart was a cornet player in a Salvation Army band, trained as a communications engineer, was a horn player in an army band during his national service, and then studied at the Guildhall School of Music and Drama. He taught there for eight years after graduating, and conducted the New Cantata Orchestra, and then became director of the Locke Brass Consort in 1976. With them he has recorded discs of brass music, the first including music from Buxtehude to Carr (for Unicorn), and the second of English composers from Elgar to Tippett (for RCA).

Stock, Frederick (1872–1942). Born in Jülich, near Cologne, Stock studied at the Cologne Conservatory where one of his fellow students was Mengelberg. For eight years after his graduation he was a violinist in the Cologne Municipal Orchestra, playing under the batons of Brahms, Tchaikovsky, and Strauss, and then in 1895 he was invited by Theodore Thomas, the conductor of the Chicago Symphony Orchestra, to join his orchestra. After four years as first viola, he became assistant conductor to Thomas, and on the latter's death in 1905, succeeded to the position of permanent conductor. He was with the orchestra for 38 years, until his death in 1942, although for one year, 1918, he was temporarily replaced until he received his US citizenship. In his time the Chicago Symphony Orchestra became one of the leading orchestras in the US, and its present magnificence had its foundation then. Stock had an extensive repertoire, from Bach to the moderns; before Stokowski he was conducting Bach arrangements with a full symphony orchestra, and in 1914 he led the first performance of the final four-movement form of Mahler's Symphony No. 1, and also conducted the first Mahler Symphony No. 8 with all thousand performers. He performed music by many US composers, and among the works he commissioned were Stravinsky's *Symphony in C major*, Kodály's *Concerto for Orchestra* and Walton's *Scapino* overture. He was not a flamboyant or sensational figure, and both as a personality and as a conductor he was somewhat overshadowed by his contemporaries Muck, Mengelberg, Koussevitzky, Toscanini and Stokowski. His readings were sound, musical and expressive; Virgil Thomson wrote that 'In my time only Stock of Chicago has been able to envelop the Brahms symphonies with a dreamy lilt that allows the soft passages to float along and the loud passages to sing out as elements of a single continuity'. (*Music Reviewed 1940–1954*, pp. 133–4). His own compositions were many and included symphonic works, concertos and chamber music, and, although many were frequently performed in Chicago, they have since been virtually forgotten.

Stock recorded exclusively with the Chicago Symphony Orchestra; he made his first disc in 1916 for Victor, his arrangements of *America* and *The Star-spangled Banner*, which was the first known recording of an orchestra in the United States. In 1938 he and the orchestra came under contract for the revitalised Columbia (CBS) company. For Victor his recordings were Bach's Suite No. 2 and his arrangements of the *St Anne* prelude, and of 'Ombra mai fù' from Handel's *Xerxes* (the 'largo'), Mozart's Symphony No. 40, Beethoven's Piano Concertos Nos 4 and 5 (with Schnabel), Schumann's Symphony No. 1, Tchaikovsky's Symphony No. 5, Dvořák's overtures *Amid Nature* and *Carnival*, and the *Slavonic Dance* Op. 46 No. 8, the Flight of the Bumble Bee from *Tsar Saltan*, several numbers from Glazunov's *Scènes de ballet* and *Les Ruses d'amour*, Goldmark's overture *Im Frühling* and the ballet music from *Die Königin von Saba*, the third movement from Strauss's *Aus Italien*, the preludes to Act III of *Lohengrin* and to Act I of *Die Meistersinger*, the grand march from *Tannhäuser* and his arrangement of *Träume* from Wagner's *Wesendonck Lieder*, Chausson's *Symphony in B flat*, Dohnányi's *Suite in F sharp minor*, Elgar's *Pomp and Circumstance March No. 1*, Benjamin's *Overture to an Italian Comedy*, the overtures to *Russlan and Ludmilla*, *The Bartered Bride* and *Mignon*, *Valse triste*, Volkmann's *Serenade*, the intermezzo and polka from Suk's *A Fairy Tale* suite, his arrangements of MacDowell's *To a Wild Rose* and *To a Water Lily*, the Strauss waltzes *Du und Du*, *Kaiserwalzer*, *Rosen aus dem Süden* and *Wein, Weib und Gesang*, and his own *Symphonic Waltz*.

For Columbia, Stock recorded Mozart's Symphony No. 38, Schubert's Symphony No. 9, Schumann's Symphony No. 4, Brahms' Symphony No. 3, *Tragic Overture* and the minuet from the Serenade No. 1, the overtures to *Euryanthe* and *Donna Diana*, Enesco's *Romanian Rhapsody No. 1*, *Also sprach Zarathustra*, *The Swan of Tuonela*, *Danse macabre*, the Dance of the Hours from *La Gioconda*, Glazunov's *Carnival* overture and two *Valses de concert*, the Tchaikovsky Violin Concerto (with Milstein) and *Nutcracker* suite, the third movement from Glière's Symphony No. 3, the Procession of the Sardar from Ippolitov-Ivanov's *Caucasian Sketches*, Paganini's *Moto perpetuo*, Saint-Saëns' Cello Concerto No. 1 (with Piatigorsky), Toch's *Pinocchio* overture and Walton's *Scapino* overture. Mozart's Symphony No. 38 and Schumann's Symphony No. 4 were once re-issued on a mono LP, and more recently RCA re-issued LP transfers of the Beethoven Piano Concertos Nos 4 and 5 (with Schnabel), and Columbia (on Odyssey) the Tchaikovsky Violin Concerto (with Milstein).

Stockhausen, Karlheinz (b. 1928). Born at Mödrath, the German composer, conductor and pianist Stockhausen studied composition with Martin in Cologne, and with Milhaud and Messiaen in Paris, where he met Pierre Schaeffer, the composer of experimental synthetic sound. He returned to Cologne to work in the radio studio for electronic sounds, and in 1963 became artistic manager of the studio. Since 1964 he has taught modern music at Cologne, and has toured extensively with various ensembles, as conductor and player. He is one of the most inventive and controversial of the *avant-garde*; other conductors have recorded his music as well as himself, but many of his compositions do not lend themselves satisfactorily to recording, because of their aleatoric and spatial effects. The recordings he has directed of his own music include *Momente II* (with Arroyo and the Cologne Radio Symphony Orchestra for Nonesuch), *Prozession* (for DGG), *Stimmung* (with the Cologne Collegium Vocale for DGG), *Stop*, *Ylem*, *Adieu*, *Kontra-punkte*, *Kreuzspiel* and *Zeitmasse* (with the London Sinfonietta for DGG), *Punkte*, *Chöre für Doris*, *Choral* and *Atmen gibt das Leben* (with the Hamburg North German Radio Choir and Symphony Orchestra for DGG), *Ensemble* (with the Ensemble Hudba Dneska Bratislava for Wergo) and *Mikrophonie I* (for DGG).

Stokowski, Leopold (1882–1977). Stokowski was born in London, the son of a Polish cabinetmaker and a mother of Irish descent. His grandfather had brought the family from Lublin, where farmers were being dispossessed of their lands by the tsarist secret police. As a boy he learned the piano and violin, and it was the violin that remained his favourite instrument throughout his life. In London he studied at the Royal College of Music, graduated from Queen's College, Oxford, with a B.Mus., and also studied at the Paris Conservatoire and at Munich. He became a Fellow of the Royal College of Organists, and his first musical appointment was organist at St James' Church in Piccadilly, London, in 1902. In those early days in England he anglicised his name to Leo Stokes; although his true name became a controversial point later in his life, he was indisputably christened Leopold Antoni Stanisław Bolesławowicz Stokowski. In 1905 he crossed the Atlantic to become organist at St Bartholomew's Church in New York, where his performances of the music of Bach brought him some local celebrity. The summers he spent in Europe studying conducting; he made his debut as a conductor in Paris in 1908, and appeared in London under the sponsorship of Henry Wood, with whom he had been a pupil. In 1909 he was offered the post of conductor of a new orchestra in Cincinnati, Ohio; he established his first reputation there, although there is little evidence from those years to point towards his later highly personal style, except for a certain feeling that he knew exactly what he wanted, and that his musical sympathies were extremely wide. After three years with the Cincinnati Symphony Orchestra he resigned peremptorily before the expiration of his contract, to become conductor of the Philadelphia Orchestra in 1912.

Stokowski remained with the Philadelphia Orchestra until 1936, and in that time he and the orchestra became a legend throughout the United States and the world, on account of the orchestra's superb qualities, Stokowski's spectacular personality, and the exceptional series of gramophone records they made. He became a United States citizen in 1925, although by then he had assumed a European accent, which he appeared to be able to drop at will. In 1931 he was appointed musical director of the orchestra, but with the onset of the Depression the board controlling the orchestra asked him to restrict his activities, such as performing new works for large orchestras which required more rehearsals than the usual repertoire, and which had little appeal to audiences. The inevitable clash with the board led to his resignation in 1934, but he nonetheless agreed to remain, provided he had final authority in artistic matters. The new arrangement was not to last, since Stokowski's interest had turned to other fields, and the 1935–6 season was his last as principal conductor. Eugene Ormandy, who was then with the Minneapolis Orchestra, joined him as co-principal conductor, and in 1938 he was appointed musical director; Stokowski then ended his contract, but continued to conduct some concerts each year until the season of 1940–41; after a performance of the *St Matthew Passion* he walked off the stage without acknowledging the applause, and did not return to conduct the orchestra again for 19 years.

Other conductors were frequently in awe at the magnificence of the Philadelphia Orchestra in Stokowski's years with it. Klemperer, interviewed at the end of his life, (P. Heyworth, *Conversations with Klemperer*, London, 1973, p. 92) recalled that the orchestra 'was really a giant – it was really overwhelming'; Goossens, who conducted it for seven concerts in 1929, considered it the most opulent of orchestras, its sumptuous sound inconceivably lush and brilliant; he wrote in his autobiography (*Overtures and Beginners*, London, 1951, p. 265) that 'this tonal splendour emanated from a group, each player of which was a virtuoso in his own right. . . . But it was a tribute to Stokowski's qualities as a leader that he succeeded in moulding what might have been an unmalleable group of stars into a homogeneously balanced entity.' The orchestra retained this quality for years after Stokowski's departure, and under Ormandy it remains one of the finest orchestras in the United States, if not the world. In 1941 Toscanini undertook a series of recording sessions with the Philadelphia Orchestra; Charles O'Connell, then the music director of RCA records, wrote that 'the conductor was amazed and delighted with the orchestra. Its quickness, agility, musicianship, glorious tone and unique sonority were a revelation to him. . . . At the first rehearsal he went completely through the programme without once interrupting the orchestra. At the end he bowed, smiled, told the men there was nothing he would suggest to improve the performance and walked off the stage in high good humour' (C. O'Connell, *The Other Side of the Record*, New York, 1947, pp. 121–2). These records were finally issued by RCA in 1976, and it is evident that Toscanini was able to stamp the performances with his own special sound, as much as Stokowski was able to create his own sound with his later recordings with the Houston Symphony Orchestra and with the London orchestras with which he recorded at the end of his life.

After terminating his activities in Philadelphia, Stokowski was no doubt intending to reduce his commitments as a conductor, and to devote more of his attention to film making, technological advances in sound reproduction, and other areas of interest. From 1940 onwards his career was inevitably something of an anticlimax, and, despite the musical miracles he was to perform, in the public's mind he was still the great Stokowski associated with the Philadelphia Orchestra. His ventures elsewhere had no lasting effect, and in the end it is still his achievement as a conductor *per se* that has won him lasting fame. He appeared in two films, *The Big Broadcast of 1937* and *A Hundred Men and a Girl* (with Deanna Durbin), and then in 1939 he collaborated with Walt Disney in making the film *Fantasia*. The original idea was for Stokowski and the Philadelphia Orchestra to provide the sound track for a Mickey Mouse cartoon on the legend of the sorcerer's apprentice (to Dukas' music); the project blossomed and developed to include cartoons to other music played by the orchestra. Mickey Mouse as the sorcerer's apprentice was a happy inspiration, and the abstract patterns to the Bach *Toccata and Fugue in D minor* were novel and striking. But there was also a representation of the evolution of life on the planet Earth to the music of *Le Sacre du printemps*, as well as a gentle satire on Greek mythology to Beethoven's Symphony No. 6, which was cut to 22 minutes. Stravinsky objected to this treatment of his score, but was powerless to prevent it. Beethoven's opinion could not be sought, but the cartoons of romping centaurs whose feminine charms were coyly concealed with brassieres of flowers, as required by the Hays Office, the Hollywood censorship authority, have haunted the memory of many ever since.

In 1940 Stokowski founded the All-American Youth Orchestra; he searched the US for the best orchestral talent between 15 and 25 years of age, and in a short time this ensemble reached a standard of performance scarcely distinguishable from the Philadelphia Orchestra itself. Certainly their recorded performance of the Dvořák Symphony No. 9 was, for many critics, comparable to the celebrated one made earlier by the Philadelphia Orchestra. The All-American Youth Orchestra continued until 1942, and toured the US and South America with Stokowski; it was briefly revived with a new group of players six years later. Stokowski appeared with the NBC Symphony Orchestra for a season, but his predilection for modern music, as well as Toscanini's dislike for his conducting methods, caused NBC to terminate the contract. In fact, Schoenberg's Piano Concerto received its première under Stokowski at an NBC radio concert. The US army appointed him adviser on bands and band music in 1941, and in 1944, on the invitation of the mayor of New York, he formed the New York City Symphony Orchestra, to present low-priced concerts at the New York City Center. The next year he was made musical director at the Hollywood Bowl in Los Angeles, from 1946 to 1949 he was a guest conductor with the New York Philharmonic-Symphony Orchestra, and became co-conductor with Mitropoulos in 1949–50. On Beecham's invitation he visited Britain for the first time in 40 years in 1951, and also appeared at the Salzburg Festival. Between 1951 and 1961 he was a guest conductor at the New York City Opera, and conducted *Carmina Burana*, *Orfeo ed Euridice* and Dallapiccola's *Il Prigioniero*. In 1961 he made his one appearance at the New York Metropolitan Opera with *Turandot*. From 1955 to 1961 he was musical director of the Houston Symphony Orchestra, an illustrious phase in its history; he broke his contract in protest over the refusal of the orchestra's management to allow a choir from a Negro college to sing with white choristers in a performance of *Gurrelieder*. In 1962 he founded the American Symphony Orchestra, made up of comparatively young players, which he conducted without fee, and with which he gave an annual series of concerts in New York. With them he gave the world première of Ives' Symphony No. 4 in 1965; he was then 83, and he subsequently recorded the work. In fact, into his nineties he was still active, conducting and recording in London. He was married four times; his first wife was the pianist Olga Samaroff, and his last Gloria Vanderbilt.

Stokowski's eminence as one of the truly great conductors of the 20th century was the product of a number of factors. First, there was the unique sound of his orchestras, best exemplified by the Philadelphia Orchestra when he was its director. Then there was the imaginative quality of his musical interpretations; he was no literalist, and to him music became great when the conductor revealed its beauty and power through the agency of his mind. (Those who knew him best believe that he had a profound comprehension of the essential meaning of music; he himself said that the conductor must have a complete understanding of the music's emotional content. He went to great trouble to understand the instruments of the orchestra by learning to play them, and when he was in Philadelphia he went to Paris every summer to study a new instrument.) There were also the records he made, first with the Philadelphia Orchestra, and later with the many others with which he was associated; his constant exploration of new music; and finally, his own charismatic personality.

The remarkable, inimitable character of Stokowski's sound is its firm, thick, lustrous legato quality, often with a hint of *portamento*. Many commentators have said that this feeling for *legato* originated in Stokowski's early experience as an organist; others have pointed out that when he directed the orchestra he varied and mixed sound textures as an organist changes his stops. He was a supreme master of orchestral texture, and one is tempted to believe that for him every piece of music was simply a vehicle for this interplay of textures. His sound was majestic, sensuous and seamless; Neville Cardus once said that Stokowski 'embalmed music'. The basis of this sound was his much-discussed innovation of free bowing with the strings, as he insisted that every string player should bow independently of the rest; he also introduced individual breathing for wind and brass, and he was as much concerned with the tonal quality of the instruments his musicians played, as with their technical capacities. He had been known to ask an oboist to change his reed because it was too bright for the grey he wanted. Also, he was careful to place the orchestra according to the demands of the score, and placed twelve double basses in a line across the back of the orchestra.

Stokowski was always an unabashed showman, and in him there was a certain narcissistic quality. When he appeared in the opera house he was concerned that the lighting should play on his hands and on his white hair. Despite his birth and education in England, he affected an indeterminate, curious, foreign accent, but he acted this role so much in his life that he slipped into the person of the one he was acting. He astonished a member of the London Symphony Orchestra who was travelling with him in a taxi across Westminster Bridge in London, in his last years, by pointing to Big Ben and asking him what it was, in his best foreign accent. A delightful example of his flair for showmanship was at an opening concert of a summer series with the Philadelphia Orchestra; after the final number on the programme, Stokowski moved down to the audience, the manager pleaded for an encore, suddenly he sprang to the podium, motioned to the orchestra, and directed a superbly poised performance of the *Blue Danube* waltz. The enchanted audience did not know that there was indeed nothing spontaneous in the act; the orchestra had carefully rehearsed the piece a couple of weeks before, but were puzzled because it had not been programmed. When he came to Philadelphia, Stokowski battled with the aberrations of the Friday-afternoon audience, late-coming and early-leaving; he once directed a concert which opened with a piece by Lekeu in which the music permitted the orchestra to take their seats one by one, and concluded with Haydn's *Farewell* Symphony.

During his lifetime Stokowski is said to have conducted 7,000 concerts live, to ten million people. His repertoire covered most orchestral music from Bach to the present day. Haydn and Mozart received fine performances, but unlike some of his contemporaries he did not seek a great revival of their music. His art was best displayed in the romantic music of the 19th century, and the great scores of the French and Russian masters, all of which gave him full scope for his devotion to orchestral sound. When he arrived in Philadelphia, in 1912, he immediately announced that he would include contemporary composers such as Debussy, Elgar, Sibelius and Strauss in his programmes, and every year he visited Europe and brought back new scores to perform. He gave an extraordinary number of first performances; the number has been estimated at 2,000. They included native American composers as well as the first US performances of *Wozzeck* (1931), *Das Lied von der Erde* (1916), Mahler's Symphony No. 8 (1916), *Gurrelieder* (1932), Sibelius' Symphonies Nos 5, 6 and 7 (1921, 1926 and 1926 respectively), Shostakovich's Symphony No. 6 (1940), *Le Sacre du printemps* (1922), *Oedipus Rex* (1931), *Alpensinfonie* (1916) and Varèse's *Amériques*; he also led the world premières of Rachmaninov's Symphony No. 3, *The Bells* and the *Rhapsody on a Theme of Paganini*, with the composer the pianist. As late in his life as 1973, he studied and gave the first performance of Havergal Brian's Symphony No. 28, with the New Philharmonia Orchestra. He said once that he enjoyed conducting the music of Schoenberg and Berg, and also Sibelius' Symphony No. 4, which he described as 'extremely abstract music' (*Musical America*, January 1978, p. 40).

Musicians have derided Stokowski's arrangements of Bach's music for the modern symphony orchestra. But there is a case to be made in their favour, at least as much as for Beecham's arrangements of Handel. Stokowski had a great devotion to Bach, and believed that only the symphony orchestra could truly reveal the music's majesty. If it is possible to forget temporarily all historical and stylistic reservations, then the gravity, dignity, vigour, serenity and expressiveness of the music represented in his arrangements are impressive indeed. He wished to introduce Bach to his audiences at a time when this music was unfamiliar, although it has been said that the arrangements were intended primarily as orchestral exercises. His favourite piece was the *Toccata and Fugue in D minor*, which he recorded five times – in 1927, 1934, 1941, 1947 and 1958. (The first recording was probably the best, as the later ones became too mannered.) Of all the Bach transcriptions the most satisfactory is the *Passacaglia and Fugue in C minor*. With all music, he had little respect for the literal reading of the score; he once said: 'That's a piece of paper with some marking on it. We have to infuse life into it.'

Stokowski thought it unimportant whether a conductor conducted from the score or from memory. He said that the ideal was to conduct with a score and yet know the music from memory, but in practice he rarely used a score. As a result of an injury to his arm, he discarded the baton early in his career, perhaps also to exploit the dramatic effect of the expressive gestures of his hands. His directions were simple and direct, avoiding impulsive actions. His relations with his players were pleasant but impersonal. At rehearsal he was methodical and cold, and preferred sarcasm when moved to reprove a player. Although he left his players little opportunity for spontaneous expression, he did not prepare his performances as meticulously as, say, Toscanini did. When he was preparing the Philadelphia Orchestra for its two weekly concerts – on Friday afternoon and Saturday evening – he was allowed four rehearsals; at the first he would go straight through the music in the order of the programme, giving attention to special passages, the next rehearsal would be taken up with intensive work on the programmed pieces, in the third he played through any new music in which he might be interested at the time, and the final rehearsal was again a straight run through of the programme. He never tired the orchestra at rehearsal, leaving the final element of expression to the concert itself. In fact, he is said to have preferred rehearsals to concerts.

Stokowski's first records were made with the Philadelphia Orchestra for RCA Victor in 1917; they were two *Hungarian Dances* of Brahms. The Schubert No. 8 was the first complete symphony he recorded, in 1924. His series with the Philadelphia Orchestra was the greatest of its time, rivalled only by Beecham's with the London Philharmonic, which commenced in 1932. Stokowski's last records with the Philadelphia Orchestra were made in 1940, but he returned again in 1960, on Ormandy's invitation, to make several LPs, which included some of his beloved Bach transcriptions, a 'symphonic synthesis' from *Tristan und Isolde*, and a magical performance of Falla's *El amor brujo*. His early recordings were relatively straightforward readings, exhibiting the orchestra's sumptuous tone, and were probably the finest performances he recorded during his life. The tendency to mannerisms and distortions of the music came in later years, with the Philadelphia Orchestra and after. Regrettably few of the earlier performances have been reissued on LP transfers, but even if they were available, they would give only a vague glimpse of the orchestra's magnificence. Among the recordings with the Philadelphia Orchestra were the Bach *Brandenburg Concertos Nos 2* and *5*, and his arrangements of the Adagio from the *Toccata, Adagio and Fugue in C minor*, the Chaconne from the Partita No. 2, the *Fugue in C minor*, the *Little Fugue in G minor*, the *Great Fugue in G minor*, the *Passacaglia and Fugue in C minor*, the *Toccata and Fugue in D minor*, the Sarabande from the English Suite No. 3, the Sarabande from the Partita No. 1, the Siciliana from the Sonata No. 4, the *Fantasia and Fugue in G minor*, the *Prelude and Fugue in E minor*, the first movement of the Trio Sonata No. 1, the sinfonias from Cantata No. 156 and the *Christmas Oratorio*, Es ist vollbracht from the *St John Passion*, O Haupt voll Blut und Wunden from the *St Matthew Passion*, *Ein feste Burg ist unser Gott*, *Christ lag in Todesbanden*, *Wir glauben all' an einen Gott*, *Nun komm' der Heiden Heiland* and *Komm süsser Tod*, Handel's *Overture in D*, the pastoral symphony from *Messiah* and his arrangement of *Water Music*, Lully's *Alceste* overture, march from *Thésée* and the ballet *Le Triomphe de l'amour*, his arrangement of the St Ambrose Coronation Service, Mozart's Sinfonia Concertante K. 297b, Beethoven's Symphonies Nos 2, 5, 7 and 9, Liszt's *Hungarian Rhapsody No. 2*, Schubert's Symphony No. 8 and *Rosamunde* Ballet No. 1, the Hungarian March from *La Damnation de Faust*, the four Brahms symphonies, Dvořák's Symphony No. 9, Vivaldi's Concerto Grosso Op. 3 No. 11, Franck's *Symphony in D minor* and O'Connell's arrangement of *Grande pièce symphonique* for organ, Tchaikovsky's Symphonies Nos 4, 5 and 6, *Capriccio italien*, *Nutcracker* suite, *1812* overture, *Romeo and Juliet* fantasy-overture, an arrangement of *Song Without Words* No. 6, *Pictures at an Exhibition*, his arrangement of *A Night on the Bare Mountain*, Dance of the Persian Slaves from *Khovanshchina*, Debussy's *Nocturnes*, *Prélude à l'après-midi d'un faune* and his arrangement of *La Cathédrale engloutie*, Ravel's *Boléro* and *Rapsodie espagnole*, Rimsky-Korsakov's *Scheherazade*, *Russian Easter Festival* overture, Flight of the Bumble Bee from *Tsar Saltan*, and the prelude to Act 3 of *Ivan the Terrible*, *Tod und Verklärung* and the Dance from *Salome*, Spohr's Violin Concerto No. 8 (with Spalding), the gavotte from *Mignon*, *Le Sacre du printemps*, *Petrushka* and *L'Oiseau de feu*, and Stravinsky's *Pastorale*, his own arrangement of *Invitation to the Dance*, the preludes to Acts I and III, Liebestod and an arrangement of the love duet from Act II of *Tristan und Isolde*, the overture and prelude to Act III of *Tannhäuser*, the preludes to Acts I and III of *Lohengrin*, the preludes to Acts I and III of *Die Meistersinger*, the prelude to Act I, a 'symphonic synthesis' and the Good Friday Music from *Parsifal*, the overture to *Rienzi*, a number of orchestral excerpts from *Das Rheingold*, *Die Walküre*, *Siegfried* and *Götterdämmerung* and the *Wesendonck Lieder* (with Traubel), the Polovtsian Dances from *Prince Igor*, Rachmaninov's Piano Concerto No. 2 and *Rhapsody on a Theme of Paganini* (with the composer the pianist), the Dance No. 1 from Falla's *La vida breve*, *El Corpus en Sevilla* of Albéniz, Glière's Symphony No. 3, Yablochko and the Russian Sailor's Dance from *The Red Poppy*, Prokofiev's Symphony No. 6 and *Peter and the Wolf*, Novaček's *Perpetuum mobile*, an arrangement of Frescobaldi's *Gagliarda*, *Le Carnaval des animaux*, *Danse macabre* and the Bacchanale from *Samson et Dalila*, Satie's *Gymnopédies Nos 1* and *3*, Shostakovich's Symphonies Nos 1, 5 and 6, and his arrangement of the Prelude No. 14, Sibelius' Symphony No. 4, *Finlandia*, *The Swan of Tuonela*, *Valse triste* and the berceuse from *The Tempest*, Scriabin's *Poème d'extase* and *Prometheus*, Liadov's *Eight Russian Folksongs*, Ippolitov-Ivanov's *Caucasian Sketches*, Schoenberg's *Gurrelieder*, McDonald's Dance of the Workers from *Festival of the Workers*, Two-Piano Concerto (with Behrend and Kelberine), *Legend of the Arkansas Traveller* and Rhumba from the Symphony No. 2, Eichheim's *Bali* and *Japanese Nocturne*, the Sousa marches *El Capitán* and *The Stars and Stripes for ever*, the Strauss waltzes *An der schönen blauen Donau* and *G'schichten aus dem Wienerwald*, Konoye's arrangement of *Japanese Ceremonial Prelude*, his own arrangement of *Veni Emanuel*, Bloch's *Schelomo* (with Feuermann), a 'symphonic synthesis' of *Boris Godunov* and suites from *Carmen* and *L'Arlésienne*. The *Danse macabre*, when it was issued in 1925, was Victor's first electrical recording; Beethoven's Symphony No. 5 was issued on a 33⅓ r.p.m. LP in 1931, along with some others, but as they were not technically or commercially successful, the LP era of recording had to wait for another 25 years.

The music encompassed by this Philadelphia series was considerable, even in comparison with today's standards. The sound, too, was exceptional for the records of that time, and O'Connell wrote that the main reason for their excellence was the acoustic properties of the Academy of Music in Philadelphia. Even so, Stokowski was always intensely interested in orchestral tone and its reproduction. Afterwards, he recorded with many orchestras and with many companies. Immediately after he left Philadelphia he was active in the studios with the All-American Youth Orchestra (1940–41) and the NBC Symphony Orchestra (1941–2, and later in 1953–4); other American orchestras with which he made records were the Hollywood Bowl Symphony Orchestra, the New York Philharmonic-Symphony Orchestra, the New York Symphony Orchestra, the New York Stadium Orchestra, the Houston Symphony Orchestra, the American Symphony Orchestra, the Symphony of the Air (formerly the NBC Symphony Orchestra), the Chicago Symphony Orchestra, the Los Angeles Philharmonic Orchestra, the RCA Victor Symphony Orchestra and his own Symphony Orchestra. No doubt some of these names were *noms-de-disque* for well-known ensembles. In these years he recorded (*inter alia*) the Tchaikovsky Symphony No. 4, a *Swan Lake* suite, a suite from *The Love of Three Oranges*, *L'Oiseau de feu*, Tchaikovsky's *Humoresque*, and the *Russian Easter Festival* overture (with the NBC Symphony Orchestra for RCA), Beethoven's Symphony No. 5, Schubert's Symphony No. 8, Brahms' Symphony No. 4, Dvořák's Symphony No. 9, Tchaikovsky's Symphony No. 6 and *Again as Before*, the scherzo from *A Midsummer Night's Dream*, *Tod und Verklärung*, his arrangement of the love duet from Act II of *Tristan und Isolde*, *L'Oiseau de feu*, *Boléro*, a 'symphonic synthesis' from *Boris Godunov*, *Pictures at an Exhibition*, *Peter and the Wolf*, Still's *Afro-American Symphony*, the Ritual Fire Dance from *El amor brujo* and his arrangement of Shostakovich's Prelude No. 14 (with the All-American Youth Orchestra for Columbia, on 78s), Tchaikovsky's Symphony No. 6, *Humoresque* and *Again as Before* (re-titled, as in the earlier recordings, *Solitude*), Brahms' Symphony No. 1, Forest Murmurs from Act II of *Siegfried*, *El amor brujo* (with Merriman), Thomson's *The Plow that Broke the Plains*, Barcarolle from *Les Contes d'Hoffmann*, Clarke's *Trumpet Voluntary*, the Serenade from Haydn's String Quartet No. 17 and the Strauss waltz *Du und Du* (with the Hollywood Bowl Symphony Orchestra for RCA), Vaughan Williams' Symphony No. 6, *Francesca da Rimini*, the *Romeo and Juliet* fantasy-overture, Messiaen's *L'Ascension*, Khachaturian's *Masquerade*, Griffes' *The White Peacock* and Gould's *Philharmonic Waltzes* (with the New York Philharmonic-Symphony Orchestra for Columbia, on mono LP), Shostakovich's Symphony No. 5, *Francesca da Rimini*, *Hamlet*, *Don Juan*, *Till Eulenspiegel* and the Dance from *Salome*, Prokofiev's *The Ugly Duckling* (with Resnik) and *Cinderella* suite, and an arrangement of Debussy's *Children's Corner* suite (with the New York Stadium Symphony Orchestra for Everest), Brahms' Symphony No. 3, Shostakovich's Symphony No. 11, Amirov's *Azerbaijan Mugam*, Scriabin's *Poème d'extase*, the Bartók *Concerto for Orchestra*, Glière's Symphony No. 3, Orff's *Carmina Burana*, the Good Friday Music and 'symphonic synthesis' from Act III of *Parsifal*, Wotan's Farewell and the Magic Fire Music from *Die Walküre*, Canning's *Fantasia on a Hymn of Justin Morgan* (Nos 1 and 2) and arrangements of a Chopin waltz, prelude and mazurka (with the Houston Symphony Orchestra for Everest and Capitol), Beethoven's Symphony No. 7, Ben Haim's *From Israel*, Thomson's *The Plow that Broke the Plains* and *The River* suite, Bloch's *America*, Shostakovich's Symphony No. 1 (with the Symphony of the Air for Vanguard), Handel's *Water Music* and *Music for the Royal Fireworks*, the overture to *The Bartered Bride*, *Moldau*, the Liszt *Hungarian Rhapsody No. 2* and Enesco's *Romanian Rhapsody No. 1* (with the RCA Victor Symphony Orchestra for RCA), Beethoven's Piano Concerto No. 5 (with Gould and the American Symphony Orchestra for Columbia), Dawson's *Negro Folk Symphony* (with the American Symphony Orchestra for Decca, US), Ives' Symphony No. 4 and *Browning* overture (with the American Symphony Orchestra *et al.* for Columbia), Mozart's Serenade K. 361, Tchaikovsky's Symphony No. 4 and his arrangement of Scriabin's Etude Op. 2 No. 1 (with the American Symphony Orchestra for Vanguard), some of Canteloube's *Chants d'Auvergne*, Rachmaninov's *Vocalise* and Villa-Lobos' *Bachianas brasileiras No. 5* (with Moffo and the American Symphony Orchestra for RCA), Stravinsky's suite *L'Histoire du soldat* (for Vanguard), Vivaldi's Concerto Grosso Op. 3 No. 11, arrangements of *Jesu, Joy of Man's Desiring* from Cantata No. 147, *Sheep May Safely Graze* from Cantata No. 208 and the sinfonia from the *Christmas Oratorio* of Bach, and Corelli's Concerto Grosso Op. 6 No. 8 (with his Symphony Orchestra for Bach Guild and Vanguard), his arrangements of the *Toccata and Fugue in D minor*, *Passacaglia and Fugue in C minor*, *Mein Jesu, was für Seelenweh*, *Komm, süsser Tod*, the bourrée from the English Suite No. 2, the sarabande from the Partita No. 1, *Ein feste Burg ist unser Gott*, the Shepherd's Song from the *Christmas Oratorio* and the *Fugue in G minor*, the fanfare for *La Péri* by Dukas, *Finlandia* and *The Swan of Tuonela*, the lento from Gluck's *Iphigénie en Aulide* and sicilienne from *Armide*, the hornpipe from Purcell's *King Arthur*, *Prélude à l'après-midi d'un faune*, *Clair de lune*, *An der schönen blauen Donau*, Barber's *Adagio for Strings*, Turina's *L'Oración del torero*, Loeffler's *A Pagan Poem*, Martin's *Petite Symphonie concertante*, Vaughan Williams' *Fantasia on a Theme of Thomas Tallis* and Schoenberg's *Verklärte Nacht* (with his Symphony Orchestra for Capitol), suites from *L'Oiseau de feu* and *Petrushka* (with the Berlin Philharmonic Orchestra for EMI), Leopold Mozart's *Schlittenfahrt*, Schubert's *Tyrolian Dances*, Sibelius' Symphony No. 1, *Valse triste*, *The Swan of Tuonela* and the berceuse from *The Tempest*, Schumann's Symphony No. 2, orchestral pieces by Grainger, the intermezzo from *Goyescas*, Ibert's *Escales*, Tchaikovsky's Symphony No. 5 and suites from *Nutcracker* and *The Sleeping Beauty*, Bizet's *Symphony in C major* and the two *L'Arlésienne* suites, Debussy's *Nocturnes*, *Prélude à l'après-midi d'un faune* and *Clair de lune*, the overture and Venusberg music from *Tannhäuser*, the prelude, Liebesnacht and Liebestod from *Tristan und Isolde* and the *Wesendonck Lieder* (with Farrell), Enesco's two *Romanian Rhapsodies* and Ben Weber's *Symphony on Poems of William Blake* (with his Symphony Orchestra for RCA), Goeb's Symphony No. 3, Harrison's *Suite for Small Orchestra* (with A. and M. Ajemian) and Cowell's *Persian Set* (with his Symphony Orchestra for Composers Recordings, who also released the Ben Weber work), and Josten's *Canzona seria*, *Concerto sacro 1–11* and *Jungle* (with the American Symphony Orchestra for Composers Recordings).

In 1961 Stokowski recorded for Capitol with the London Symphony Orchestra and the Orchestre National de la Radiodiffusion Française; the application of the stereo technique to the scores of Debussy and Ravel on these discs came in for some heavy criticism, on the grounds that Stokowski added a dimension of reality that cancelled out the fantasy of the music, especially in Fêtes, from Debussy's *Nocturnes*. The other pieces in this series were Ravel's *Rapsodie espagnole* and *Alborada del gracioso*, Ibert's *Escales* and Debussy's *Iberia*; these records have been re-issued on the Seraphim label. In more recent years he made a remarkable series for Decca with some London and European orchestras, which show his art at its best, and in some cases, at its worst. Two of the discs record a concert at the Royal Festival Hall to commemorate the sixtieth anniversary of the first concert he conducted in London, with an identical programme: the prelude to *Die Meistersinger*, the *Prélude à l'après-midi d'un faune*, Glazunov's Violin Concerto, Brahms' Symphony No. 1 and *Marche slave*. At the later concert, he was 90 years of age. Another fascinating album has two performances of Dvořák's Symphony No. 9 – the first a dubbing of his original recording with the Philadelphia Orchestra of 1927, and the second one made with the New Philharmonia Orchestra in 1974. In this incredible last flowering of his career, Stokowski recorded Beethoven's Symphony No. 5, Schubert's Symphony No. 8, the *Nutcracker* suite and the waltz and polonaise from *Eugene Onegin* (with the London Philharmonic Orchestra), Beethoven's Symphonies Nos 3 and 9 and *Coriolan* overture, Brahms' Symphony No. 1, excerpts from *La Damnation de Faust*, excerpts from *Messiah*, Tchaikovsky's Symphony No. 6, *Francesca da Rimini*, *Marche slave*, excerpts from *Swan Lake* and *The Sleeping Beauty* and the *Serenade in C major*, *Scheherazade*, the Entrance of the Gods into Valhalla from *Das Rheingold*, the Ride of the Valkyries from *Die Walküre*, Forest Murmurs from *Siegfried* and the Rhine Journey and Funeral Music from *Götterdämmerung*, Mahler's Symphony No. 2, *L'Oiseau de feu*, *La Mer* and *Prélude à l'après-midi d'un faune*, the *Daphnis et Chloé* Suite No. 2, Messiaen's *L'Ascension* and Ives *Orchestral Set No. 2* (with the London Symphony Orchestra), the Polovtsian Dances from *Prince Igor*, *1812* overture and Stravinsky's *Pastorale* (with the Royal Philharmonic Orchestra), suites from *Carmen* and *L'Arlésienne* (with the National Philharmonic Orchestra), Beethoven's Symphony No. 7 and *Egmont* overture, *Symphonie fantastique*, Vivaldi's *The Four Seasons*, Brahms' Symphony No. 4 and *Academic Festival Overture*, Dvořák's Symphony No. 9, *Pictures at an Exhibition*, his arrangement of Debussy's *La Cathédrale engloutie*, *Capriccio espagnol*, and Tchaikovsky's Symphony No. 5 and waltzes from *Swan Lake* and *The Sleeping Beauty* (with the New Philharmonia Orchestra), Franck's *Symphony in D minor* and the fanfare by Ravel for *L'Éventail de Jeanne* (with the Hilversum Radio Philharmonic Orchestra), the *Romeo and Juliet* fantasy-overture and a 'symphonic synthesis' of *Boris Godunov* (with the Suisse Romande Orchestra), Scriabin's *Poème d'extase*, Dvořák's *Slavonic Dance No. 10*, and his arrangements of the Bach *Toccata and Fugue in D minor*, *Prelude in E flat minor*, *Mein Jesu*, *Wir glauben all' an einen Gott*, a chorale from the *Easter Cantata* and the *Passacaglia and Fugue in C minor* (with the Czech Philharmonic Orchestra). He also recorded Rachmaninov's Symphony No. 3 and *Vocalise* (with the National Philharmonic Orchestra for Desmar), Sibelius' Symphony No. 1 and *The Swan of Tuonela* (with the National Philharmonic Orchestra for CBS), and the overtures *Leonore No. 3*, *Le Carnaval romain*, *Don Giovanni*, *William Tell* and *Rosamunde* (with the National Philharmonic Orchestra for Pye), and discs of shorter orchestral pieces and encores (with the National Philharmonic Orchestra for Decca and Pye). Off-the-Air Records also issued Mahler's Symphony No. 8 (with the New York Philharmonic-Symphony Orchestra *et al.*).

Stokowski returned to England for the last years of his life. He said that he spent his days studying the scores of the great masters; 'Except when I am sleeping, I am thinking of the next time I must conduct great music.' He was interviewed on CBS Television a year before he died, and was asked what technique he employed to get the best results. He answered: 'The eyes. I conduct with my eyes. Naturally, I know the work thoroughly and when I am on the podium I am in eye contact with each member of the orchestra. We communicate with each other and when I require a diversity of nuance, I designate my intentions with a glance or gesture.' Despite the immense fortune he made from music, he once said: 'I've never done a real day's work in my life. I simply make music, and people have always been foolish enough to pay me for it. I never told them that I would have done it all for nothing.'

Stoll, Pierre (b. 1924). Born at Mulhouse, Alsace, Stoll studied at the Conservatory there, and privately with Bour. He was second conductor at the Strasbourg Theatre (1948–9), conductor at the Maîtrise de Tour Sainte, Marseille (1950–51), and at the Strasbourg Opera (1954–72), was general secretary of the International Society for Contemporary Music (1959–69), and has been a guest conductor in France and abroad. He has recorded Boieldieu's *La Dame blanche* (for Vega, and issued in Britain by Decca), Arensky's *Fantasy on Russian Themes*, Rimsky-Korsakov's Piano Concerto and Tcherapnin's Piano Concerto No. 5 (with Wang Gi In), and Rimsky-Korsakov's *Fantasy on Russian Themes* (with Mueller, and the Rhine Philharmonic Orchestra for RBM).

Stolyarov, Grigori (1892–1963). Born in Odessa, Stolyarov was chief conductor of the opera and ballet theatre there (1920–29), and director of the Odessa Conservatory (1923–9). He later conducted at opera houses at Moscow and Alma-Ata, the capital of Kazakhstan, and was also a professor at the conservatories in these cities. The only disc in which he appears and which has been issued in the West was Saint-Saëns' Cello Concerto No. 1, with Rostropovich and the Moscow Radio Symphony Orchestra, released in the United States by Monarch and Westminster, and in Britain by Saga. He also recorded the *Fra Diavolo* overture (with the Moscow Radio Symphony Orchestra).

Stolz, Robert (1880–1975). Born in Graz, where his father was an operatic conductor and a pupil of Bruckner, his mother a concert pianist, his grand-aunt Teresa Stolz a famous singer and friend of Verdi, and where Brahms was a family friend, Stolz toured Europe at the age of seven with his father, giving recitals of Mozart's music. At 11 his first composition was published and he became a repetiteur at the Graz Opera, and at 17 he was conductor with Europe's largest circus. He studied under Fuchs at the Vienna Conservatory and with Humperdinck, and was advised by Johann Strauss to make his career in popular music. After conducting at Brno, Prague, Mannheim and other cities, he succeeded Bodanzky as principal conductor at the Theater an der Wien (1905–17), where he led the original performances of the operettas *Die lustige Witwe* (1905), *The Chocolate Soldier* (1908) and *Der Graf von Luxemburg* (1908). A prolific and extraordinarily successful composer, he wrote over 60 operettas, 1500 songs and 100 film scores; his first operetta was produced in 1899, his *Wild Violets* ran for 400 performances in London, he wrote the score for the first European film musical (*Two Hearts in Waltz Time*, 1929) and won two Oscars for film scores (in 1941 and 1955). Although not Jewish, Stolz left Germany in 1936 and Austria in 1938, and moved to the United States in 1940, where he conducted operettas and concerts in New York until his return to Vienna in 1946. He is honoured in Israel for smuggling many Jews from Germany and Austria to France before he left Europe in 1940; when he was in Paris he dismissed pleas from German envoys to return to Nazi Germany. Until his last years, in his nineties, he continued to compose, conduct and record; he carried with him until the 1970s the Viennese tradition of Johann Strauss, whom he had heard as a young man conducting his waltzes. Stolz's own performances of Strauss's music tended to be in faster tempi than those of many contemporary conductors, but these were the tempi in which he heard Strauss himself perform them.

Stolz made his first record for Edison in 1904, accompanying Selma Kurz in an aria from *Die Zauberflöte*. After World War II he recorded many operettas and discs of light music. For Decca, on early mono LPs, he recorded, *inter alia*, *Die lustige Witwe* (with the Vienna Symphony Orchestra *et al.*), and collections of music by Johann Strauss, Kálmán, Tchaikovsky, Offenbach and himself. He later made a number of recordings of operettas by Millöcker, Lehár, Kálmán, Johann Strauss and himself for Eurodisc, and in some instances for other companies, and also directed a set of 20 discs of Viennese music by the Strausses and their contemporaries. He also recorded a disc of his own music with the Graunke Symphony Orchestra *et al.* for EMI.

Stone, Thompson (1883–1972). Born at Attleboro, Massachusetts, Stone studied in Vienna, Paris, London and at Harvard University, and was a piano student with Leschititzky and a conducting pupil of Muck. He taught music and conducted at James Milliken University, Illinois, was professor of music at Tufts College (1945–55), organist and choirmaster at the Church of the Advent, Boston, conductor of the New England College Glee Club, the Boston Apollo Club, the Boston People's Symphony Orchestra, and the Handel and Haydn Society of Boston (1927–59), received an honorary doctorate in music from Boston University (1934), and was a guest conductor in Boston, Salt Lake City and at the Fine Arts Festival of the State University of Iowa. In 1955 he recorded *Messiah* for Unicorn with the Chorus of the Handel and Haydn Society and the Zimbler Sinfonietta *et al.*

Stoschek, Walter (b. 1912). Born in Löbschütz, Germany, Stoschek studied at the Dresden Conservatory, was a repetiteur and conductor at Beuthen (1935–40), conductor at the Dresden Opera (1941), Coburg (1945–9), with the Dresden Philharmonic Orchestra (1949–51), was general music director at Plauen (1951–7), at Karl-Marx-Stadt (1957–60) and at Freiberg (from 1960). He recorded the Honegger Symphony No. 3 with the Dresden Philharmonic Orchestra, issued by Urania.

Stoutz, Edmond de (b. 1920). Born in Zürich, de Stoutz studied law, then graduated from the Zürich Conservatory, and studied conducting at Lausanne, Salzburg and Vienna with Kletzki, Schmeidel, Robert Wagner, Zecchi and others. After a period as a cellist in orchestras in Zürich he founded his own chamber orchestra in 1946, which in 1951 was named the

Zürich Chamber Orchestra. Yehudi Menuhin wrote in his autobiography (*Unfinished Journey*, London, 1977): 'Among the many professional conductors whom I have come to know over fifty years, there is one who has somehow preserved the freshness of the amateur. This is Edmond de Stoutz, conductor of the Zürich Chamber Orchestra. He occupies a niche in the world of music which is quite his own, carved out of the completeness of his dedication to his orchestra. In it there are first-rate musicians and musicians who are less than first-rate, but under his guidance the *whole* becomes first-rate. Hardly a day passes without his rehearsing them, and he conducts a rehearsal with the same zeal and excitement he brings to a concert. He shares the rigours of bus and boarding house with his players and yet retains his authority by virtue of the fact that he carries the burden. I have never known a person with less vanity; which may sound a contradiction in terms, for the conductor without vanity almost does not exist.'

De Stoutz's records with his orchestra include Bach's Two-Harpsichord Concertos BWV 1060 and BWV 1061 (with Robert and Gaby Casadesus for CBS); Bach's Suite No. 2, *Brandenburg Concerto No. 2* and Violin and Oboe Concerto (with Lehmann and Lardrot), Albinoni's *Sonata a cinque* Op. 2 No. 6, Geminiani's Concerto Grosso Op. 3 No. 2, Locatelli's *Introduzione teatrale VI*, Tartini's *Sinfonia in A* and *Violin Concertos in E, F, G* and *D* (with Gertler, for Vanguard); Handel's Concerti Grossi Op. 6 Nos 4 and 5, and *Oboe Concerto in E flat* (with Parolari, for Mace); concertos and concertinos by Pergolesi (for Bach Guild), Boyce's Symphony No. 3 and a suite from Purcell's *The Married Beau* (for Amadeo), Haydn's *Piano Concertos in G* and *D* (with Michelangeli for EMI), Mozart's Violin Concertos K. 211 and K. 219, Paganini's *Variations on Di tanti palpiti*, a Tartini Violin Concerto and Vitali's *Chaconne* (with Francescatti for CBS), Martin's *Polyptique* (with Menuhin) and *Ballade for Flute, Harpsichord and Strings* (with Nicolet and Bartschi for EMI), Bartók's *Divertimento* and Müller's Symphony No. 2 (for Vanguard, Amadeo and Decca), Stravinsky's *Dumbarton Oaks* and *Concerto for String Orchestra*, Schoenberg's *Verklärte Nacht*, Webern's *Five Movements for Strings* Op. 5, three movements from Berg's *Lyric Suite*, Schoeck's Violin Concerto (with Lehmann) and Horn Concerto (with Brejza) (for Vanguard), Müller's Symphony No. 3 (for Decca), Balissat's *Sinfonietta* (for CTS) and Müller-Zürich's Viola Concerto (with Wiesser and Beromünster Radio Orchestra).

Stracke, Hans (b. 1932). After studying at the Hochschule für Musik at Cologne, Stracke became a repetiteur, choral director and conductor at various theatres, and from 1971 has been the classical music manager with Ariola-Eurodisc at Munich. He has recorded Moszkowski's *Piano Concerto in E major* (with Ponti and the Philharmonia Hungarica for Vox).

Strang, Gerald (b. 1908). Born at Claresholm, Canada, Strang studied at Stanford University and the universities of California and Southern California, and was an engineer with the Douglas Aircraft Company during World War II. He was managing editor of New Music Quarterly Edition (1935–40), and was assistant to Schoenberg at UCLA (1936–8). Composers Recordings issued a disc on which he conducted his Cello Concerto, with Rejto and a chamber orchestra.

Straram, Walther (1876–1933). Born in London of French parents, Straram studied the violin in Paris, and became a member of the Lamoureux Orchestra in 1892. He then was a repetiteur at the Lyon Opera (1896), chorus-master at the Paris Opéra-Comique and Opéra (1906), and assistant to Caplet at the Boston Opera Company (1909–13). He founded and conducted the Concerts Straram in Paris (1926), and gave regular concerts until the time of his death. With the Straram Orchestra he recorded for Columbia Ibert's *Escales*, Roussel's *Le Festin de l'araignée*, and Poulenc's *Aubade* (with the composer as soloist).

Straus, Oscar (1870–1954). The Viennese composer of operettas, Straus, studied in Vienna and Berlin, and was a theatre conductor in Brno, Teplitz, Mainz and Berlin. From 1940 he lived in the United States, where he wrote film music with great success, and in 1948 he returned to Europe. His most successful operettas was *Ein Walzertraum* (A Waltz Dream); he recorded a disc of excerpts from this and also from his *Der letzte Walzer* (with the Vienna Operetta Orchestra *et al.* for La Guilde Internationale du Disque. He also recorded some of his music for Colonial, a US label.

Strauss, Eduard (1910–69). Born in Vienna, Strauss was the sixth and last musician in the Strauss dynasty, the grand-nephew of Eduard Strauss, who was the brother of Johann and Josef Strauss. He studied at the Vienna Academy of Music, was a repetiteur at the opera class of the Vienna Conservatory (1946–56), and started his career as a conductor in 1949 with a concert commemorating the 100th anniversary of the death of Johann Strauss (the father) and the 50th anniversary of the death of Johann Strauss (the son). He later conducted at the Vienna Volksoper and with the Vienna Symphony Orchestra, and conducted Strauss operettas in Europe, the US and Japan. He recorded various collections of music of the Strausses (with the Vienna Symphony Orchestra for Philips, and with the Innsbruck Symphony Orchestra and the Philharmonia Hungarica for Vox and Turnabout).

Strauss, Paul (b. 1920). Born in Chicago, Strauss studied at the North Western University and was a conducting pupil of Frederick Stock. He was assistant to Mitropoulos at the Robin Hood Dell concerts at Philadelphia (1946–7), musical director of the Ballet Russe de Monte Carlo, toured Europe with the American National Ballet Theater (1953), conducted major orchestras in the United States, and in Vienna and Zürich, where he was principal conductor of the Radio Orchestra for two years, and conducted opera in Austria and Italy, where he led performances of *Katerina Ismailova* and *Billy Budd* at the Maggio Musicale Fiorentino. In 1967 he became musical director and permanent conductor of the Orchestre de Liège in Belgium. His recordings include Elgar's *Enigma Variations* (with the Berlin Philharmonic Orchestra for Summit), Dvořák's *Carnival* overture, intermezzi from operas by Puccini, Giordano, Cilea, Mascagni and Wolf-Ferrari, the Offenbach/Rosenthal *Gaîté parisienne*, the Strauss/Desormière *Le Beau Danube*, and an operatic recital by the tenor Simoneau (with the Berlin Radio Symphony Orchestra for DGG), Lekeu's *Seconde Étude symphonique sur Hamlet* and *Fantaisie contrapuntique sur un cramignon liégeois* (with the Orchestre de Liège for Musique de Wallonie), Grétry's overtures *L'Epreuve villageoise*, *Les Mariages samnites* and *Richard Coeur de Lion*, *Céphale et Procris* suite and *Danses villageoises* (the latter arranged by Gevaert), Enesco's two *Romanian Rhapsodies*, the *Háry János* suite, Vieuxtemps' Violin Concertos Nos 5 and 7 (with Werthen), Franck's *Psyché*, *Les Éolides*, *Le Chasseur maudit*, *Les Djinns* and *Symphonic Variations* (with Ciccolini), the Brahms *Hungarian Dances* and a disc of marches by a number of composers (with the Orchestre de Liège for Pathé-Marconi, some also being issued by EMI).

Strauss, Richard (1864–1949). Strauss, the composer of the great and familiar tone poems, operas and songs, was one of the leading symphonic and operatic conductors of his day. His career as a conductor began in 1883 when he was assistant conductor at Meiningen with von Bülow, whom he succeeded there in 1885. He went on to fill many of the most important musical positions in Germany and Austria: conductor of the Munich Court Opera (1886–9), first conductor of the Weimar Court Orchestra (1889), successor to von Bülow as conductor of the Berlin Philharmonic Orchestra (1894–5), conductor at the Berlin Opera (1898–1918), co-director with Schalk of the Vienna Opera (1919–24), and conductor of the Leipzig Gewandhaus Orchestra (1933). He led *Tannhäuser* at Bayreuth at the age of 30, and was a frequent conductor at Salzburg and at other major European opera houses. When the Nazis came to power in Germany in 1933, Strauss did not hesitate to take Walter's place with the Leipzig Gewandhaus Orchestra when the latter was expelled from Germany. He also accepted the chairmanship of the Reichsmusikkammer, the organisation set up by the Nazis to control music; like some other prominent German musicians, he was largely indifferent to the fate of his Jewish colleagues. However, in 1935 he came into conflict with the Nazis for his collaboration with Stefan Zweig, a Jew, in preparing the libretto for *Die schweigsame Frau*, and from then on his relations with the Nazis were uneasy. In 1939 he was actually placed under house arrest for voicing opposition to the invasion of Poland, and Nazi displeasure was also provoked when his son married a Jewess. After World War II he faced a special court at Munich investigating collaborators with the Nazis, and was exonerated, but nevertheless his music to this day is proscribed in Israel, along with that of Wagner and Lehár. When he was asked why he did not leave Germany during the Nazi era, he said that in Germany there were 56 opera houses, and in America two; 'That would have reduced my income' (P. Heyworth, *Conversations with Klemperer*, London, 1973, p. 43).

In 1935, Strauss received a State questionnaire to determine whether he was an Aryan, which requested the names of two witnesses to his professional ability. He answered 'Mozart and Richard Wagner'. (M. Kennedy, *Richard Strauss*, London, 1976, p. 100). He was especially celebrated for his performances of the Mozart and Wagner operas; in Mozart, many thought him a conductor of genius, and Klemperer considered that in Mozart his own creative nature was evident, as he himself was apparent in the music. In the Mozart operas, Strauss would accompany the recitatives himself on the harpsichord, and introduce little decorations. Klemperer also remarked that Strauss once told him, to his astonishment, that he could not conduct a Beethoven symphony unless he had some sort of literal meaning in his mind. Strauss's father had been a leading horn player at the Munich Opera, and had detested Wagner, but Strauss himself was held by his contemporaries to be an exceptional conductor of the Wagner operas; Rosé, the leader of the Vienna Philharmonic Orchestra before World War II, said that Strauss's *Tristan und Isolde* was one of the most unforgettable experiences in music, with an intensity equalled only by Furtwängler. The economy of his conducting style, which required extreme concentration in the musicians, led many in the audience to misunderstand the quiet appearance he assumed when conducting a work like *Tristan*; but the musicians who were watching his eyes, the expression on his face, and the small movements of his baton, knew differently. With the slightest gesture he could achieve overwhelming effects. He wrote once: 'You should not perspire when conducting; only the audience should get warm', and in Klemperer's words '*He* didn't throw himself around like a madman, but the orchestra played as though *it* were possessed.'

Opinions vary about Strauss as a conductor of his own music; some say it was wonderful, others, such as Szell and Beecham, thought he could be very dull, and Strauss himself once remarked that it bored him to perform his own works. In the recordings he made of his works, he is intense, lyrical, casual and cold, frequently in the same work, and occasionally there are patches of poor orchestral ensemble. Fritz Busch explained this phenomenon this way: 'The lack of genuinely warm feeling which Strauss's music often shows was recognised by the composer himself. He knew exactly the place where his music became sentimental and trashy. Nothing annoyed him more than when conductors . . . wallowed in his lyrical outpourings, and thus unpleasantly brought his sins before his eyes. He himself, the older he grew, passed over more indifferently and unemphatically such passages when conducting, as if he were ashamed at having composed them. His inconsistency showed itself in his continuing to write such things. . . . The puzzle of Strauss, who in spite of his marvellous talents, is not really penetrated and possessed of them like other great artists but in fact simply wears them like a suit of clothes which can be taken off at will – this puzzle neither I nor anyone else has yet succeeded in solving' (*Music and Musicians*, August 1977, p. 30). Boult (in *Thoughts on Conducting*, London, 1963), wrote of a performance of Mozart's Symphony No. 40 by Strauss in 1910. He lavished the greatest attention on the symphony in rehearsal, working on it for five hours. It was, in the end, 'a wonderful performance, and obviously the result of much thought and preparation and precision in rehearsal'. Boult was struck by the slow tempi for the first and last movements, but because his accentuation was so widely spaced, the music appeared to flow along quickly. But Boult added: 'A thoughtful friend of mine has linked Strauss's precise rehearsal craftsmanship with his love of card games; his care in planning his resources in rehearsal was in parallel with his playing a hand of his favourite skat.'

Strauss recorded for Polydor *Don Juan*, *Till Eulenspiegel*, *Ein Heldenleben*, *Don Quixote*, *Tod und Verklärung*, the *Le Bourgeois gentilhomme* suite, the *Japanische Festmusik*, waltzes from *Der Rosenkavalier* and the Dance from *Salome*, with the Berlin Philharmonic, Berlin State Opera and Bavarian State Orchestras; *Ein Heldenleben* and *Don Juan* were recorded twice. The later performance of *Don Juan*, in 1932 was included in the album of historical transfers *The Early Days* issued by DGG; about the earlier one, Szell said that he was an assistant conductor to Strauss at the time, 1916–17, and had prepared the orchestra, but Strauss did not come to the studio for the recording itself, although his name appeared on the label. DGG released performances of Strauss on EP and LP, and then in 1977 all the Polydor recordings were re-issued by DGG. Other recordings of Strauss conducting his own music have been *Don Juan*, the Dance from *Salome*, and waltzes from *Der Rosenkavalier* (with the London Symphony Orchestra for Columbia in 1920), *Don Quixote* (with Uhl and the Bavarian State Orchestra for Siemens), *Eine Alpensinfonie* (with the Bavarian State Orchestra, issued in the United States on Seraphim by EMI), a suite from *Der Rosenkavalier* (with the Tivoli Orchestra for HMV in 1925), *Also sprach Zarathustra*, *Don Juan*, *Till Eulenspiegel* and *Tod und Verklärung* (with the Berlin Radio Symphony Orchestra, issued by Bellaphon in Germany), and the *Schlagobers* waltz (with the Berlin Radio Symphony Orchestra, issued by Intercord in Germany). In 1944 Strauss led a series of performances of his music with the Vienna Philharmonic Orchestra to mark his 80th birthday, and these were recorded, apparently, on tape in an empty hall, for later broadcast. Some have appeared on LP: *Le Bourgeois gentilhomme* suite in 1952–3 on Regent and Urania, *Symphonia domestica* on Vox and Turnabout; in 1973 the Bruno Walter Society in the United States issued all except *Symphonia domestica*, and in 1974 Turnabout released *Also sprach Zarathustra* and *Schlagobers* waltz. Finally, in 1976, Vanguard came out with a five-disc album including all the performances: *Don Juan*, *Tod und Verklärung*, *Till Eulenspiegel*, *Also sprach Zarathustra*, *Ein Heldenleben*, *Symphonia domestica*, *Le Bourgeois gentilhomme* and the *Schlagobers* waltz.

Of other music, Strauss recorded for Polydor the Mozart Symphonies Nos 39 and 40 and the overture *Die Zauberflöte*, and the Beethoven Symphonies Nos 5 and 7 (with the Berlin State Opera Orchestra), and the overtures to *Euryanthe*, *Iphigénie en Aulide*, *Der Barber von Bagdad* and *Der fliegende Holländer*, and the prelude to Act I of *Tristan und Isolde* (with the Berlin Philharmonic Orchestra). The Mozart symphonies were re-issued on LP, and the Symphony No. 40 was again included in *The Early Days*; the Beethoven Symphony No. 5 was also issued on an LP transfer by Rococo, with the Dance from *Salome* and excerpts from *Le Bourgeois gentilhomme*.

Stravinsky, Igor (1882–1971). Stravinsky was antipathetic to most of the great conductors of the day, and to the very idea of interpretation. 'What most people call interpretation I call bad habits', he said; at best, 'performances are pale memories of creative acts. In music, as in love, pleasure is the waste product of creation'. He admitted that romantic music may require more than strict or correct performance: 'Romantic pieces are presumed to have messages beyond the purely musical messages of the notes'. But he was firm that his own music is simply to be 'read' or 'executed', and not to be 'interpreted', as nothing in it requires interpretation (I. Stravinsky and R. Craft, *Retrospective and Conclusions*, New York, 1969, p. 48). Many recordings of *Le Sacre du printemps*, for instance, received his disapprobation. Although he received very little training as a conductor, he began to conduct and perform his own music in public in the 1920s, and continued to do so throughout his life. Opinions of him as a conductor have not always been flattering; Giulini, who played under him as a violist in the Santa Cecilia Orchestra, has said that he was a poor conductor, and 'if Stravinsky were his own worst enemy, he could not have done better to destroy Stravinsky' (Personal interview with the author, September 1977). Hoffnung, the cartoonist, who was also an orchestral player, amusingly depicted Stravinsky conducting *Petrushka*, with one arm on his hip, and the other holding up a metronome. Stravinsky's fee for conducting half a concert and part of a rehearsal, in 1965, was $10,000; in a letter to a friend his wife wrote: 'I have noticed that few people listen with attention to the music in these concerts and that, in fact, few seem to have come for that purpose. What they want is to be in his numinous presence. And although $10,000 may be a lot of money, so is Igor a lot of numen.'

Stravinsky regarded his recordings as definitive performances of his works, and as 'indispensable supplements to the printed music'. He has defended himself against criticism of his conducting the performances by pointing out that 'reviewers have certainly resisted me in that capacity for 40 years, in spite of my recordings, in spite of my special qualifications for knowing what the composer wants, and my perhaps one thousand times greater experience conducting my music than anyone else'. However, that a composer is always able to give an ideal performance of his own music, if such could exist, is a proposition scarcely supported by the multitude of fine recorded performances by numerous conductors of music by composer-conductors, even including Stravinsky. In the case of Stravinsky's later recordings, there is room for doubt that every one of them was the definitive reading of the composer himself (see Robert Craft).

Stravinsky signed a contract with Columbia Records (US) in 1928, and made a number of records of his music, both as pianist and conductor. As the former, he recorded his *Duo concertante* and *Danse russe* (with Dushkin *et al.*), and the *Capriccio* (with the Walther Straram Orchestra, conducted by Ansermet), and the *Russian Maiden's Song* (with Szigeti). The orchestral works he conducted in this early series were suites from *Petrushka* and *Pulcinella*, and *Le Sacre du printemps* (with an unidentified orchestra), a suite from *L'Oiseau de feu* (with the Paris Symphony Orchestra), the *Symphony of Psalms* (with the Vlassoff Choir and the Walther Straram Orchestra), *L'Histoire du soldat*, *Ragtime*, *Octet*, *Les Noces* and *Pastorale* (with various ensembles). Later, on 78s, Columbia issued the *Ebony Concerto* (with the Woody Herman Orchestra), suites from *L'Oiseau de feu* and *Petrushka*, *Le Sacre du printemps*, *Symphony in Three Movements*, *Four Norwegian Moods*, *Feux d'artifice*, *Circus Polka*, *Scènes de ballet* and *Ode* (with the New York Philharmonic-Symphony Orchestra) and the *Symphony of Psalms* (with the Columbia Broadcasting Symphony Orchestra *et al.*). His other pre-LP recordings were *Le Baiser de la fée*, *Concerto for String Orchestra*, *Danses concertantes*, *Scherzo à la russe*, *Orpheus*, *Apollon musagète* and the Piano Concerto (with Soulimat Stravinsky, and the RCA Victor Symphony Orchestra for RCA), *Le Baiser de la fée* (with the Mexican Symphony Orchestra for RCA), *Ave Maria*, *Pater Noster* and *Mass* (with the Choir of the New York Church of the Blessed Sacrament for RCA), *Jeu de cartes* (with the Berlin Philharmonic Orchestra for Telefunken), *Dumbarton Oaks* (with an ensemble for Keynote) and the Violin Concerto (with Dushkin and the Lamoureux Orchestra for Vox).

With the advent of LP, Columbia commenced a new series of mono recordings, which included *Oedipus Rex* (with the Cologne Radio Symphony Orchestra and Chorus *et al.*), *Scènes de ballet*, the *Symphony in Three Movements*, *Le Sacre du printemps*, the *Symphony in C*, *Ode*, *Perséphone*, *Feux d'artifice*, *Russian Maiden's Song*, *Four Norwegian Moods* and *Circus Polka* (with the New York Philharmonic Orchestra), *Pulcinella* and the *Symphony in C* (with the Cleveland Orchestra), *The Rake's Progress* (with the Metropolitan Opera House Orchestra *et al.*), the *Cantata* (with the New York Philharmonic Chamber Ensemble *et al.*), the *Canticum Sacrum* (with the Los Angeles Festival Symphony Orchestra *et al.*), the Violin Concerto (with Stern and the Columbia Symphony Orchestra), *The Flood* (with the Columbia Symphony Orchestra *et al.*), the *Septet* and *L'Histoire du soldat* (with ensembles), the *Symphonies of Wind Instruments* (with the Northwest German Radio Orchestra) and *Three Shakespeare Songs* and *In Memoriam* (with a choral group).

Finally, Columbia undertook the re-recording of all Stravinsky's major works and many others, with the Columbia Symphony Orchestra *inter alia*. Many of these records were made in Los Angeles, and the orchestra was prepared by Robert Craft; the latter's part in these recordings is discussed in the entry under his name. Included in this presumably definitive series were *L'Oiseau de feu*, *Petrushka*, *Le Sacre du printemps*, *Apollon musagète*, *Le Baiser de la fée*, *Concerto for String Orchestra*, *Feux d'artifice*, a suite from *L'Histoire du soldat*, *Mass*, *Monumentum pro Gesualdo*, *Movements for Piano and Orchestra* (with Rosen), *Epitaphium for Flute, Clarinet and Harp*, *Double Canon for String Orchestra*, *Pulcinella*, *Pribautki*, *Berceuses du chat* and *Russian Songs* (with Berberian), *Scherzo à la russe*, *Symphony in E flat*, *Le Rossignol*, *Greeting Prelude* and *Variations for Orchestra* (with the Columbia Symphony Orchestra *et al.*), *Orpheus* (with the Chicago Symphony Orchestra), *Agon* (with the Los Angeles Festival Symphony Orchestra), *Abraham and Isaac*, *Introitus*, *Requiem Canticles*, *Cantata*, *Concertino*, *Danses concertantes*, *Dumbarton Oaks*, *In Memoriam Dylan Thomas* (with Young), *Octet*, *Pastorale* (with Baker), *Ragtime*, *Renard*, *Septet*, and songs (with Lear, Berberian and Gramm, and the Columbia Chamber Ensemble *et al.*), the *Symphony of Psalms*, *Circus Polka*, *Études for Orchestra*, *Le Faune et la bergère*, *Instrumental Miniatures*, *Four Norwegian Moods*, *Scènes de ballet*, *Scherzo fantastique*, the Suites Nos 1 and 2, the *Symphony in C*, and *A Sermon, a Narrative and a Prayer* (with the Canadian Broadcasting Corporation Orchestra *et al.*), *The Rake's Progress* (with the Royal Philharmonic Orchestra *et al.*), and some choral pieces (with the Toronto Festival Singers *et al.*). The *Oedipus Rex* has been re-issued on the Odyssey label.

Streatfeild, Simon (b. 1929). Educated at the Royal College of Music, Streatfeild was principal viola with the Sadler's Wells Opera Orchestra (1953–5) and with the London Symphony Orchestra (1956–65). He went to Canada to take up the same position with the Vancouver Symphony Orchestra, became the orchestra's assistant conductor (1967–71), was acting music director (1971–2), and then became associate conductor. He helped to found the Vancouver String Quartet and Baroque Strings, established the Courtenay Youth Music Camp (1967), and was founder and conductor of the Vancouver Bach Choir. With the Vancouver Chamber Group he recorded, for CBC, *Six Bergerettes du Bas Canada*, which were arranged by MacMillan.

Strickland, William (b. 1914). Born in Defiance, Ohio, Strickland studied the organ and voice, and succeeded Stokowski as the organist at St Bartholomew's Church in New York. He was music master at St George's School, Newport, RI (1934–6), founded and conducted the National Youth Administration Sinfonietta in New York (1940), organised and was permanent conductor of the Nashville Symphony Orchestra, Tennessee (1946), taught at the Juilliard School (1948–9) and at the Mozarteum at Salzburg (1953–4), and became musical director of the New York Oratorio Society (1955). He was a guest conductor in Austria and Germany, and commissioned, performed and recorded much contemporary music; in fact he has made an extraordinary number of records of the music of American composers with a surprising collection of orchestras. These works were recorded for Composers Recordings and included Barber's Symphony No. 1,

Bergsma's *Music on a Quiet Theme*, Hovhaness's *Meditations on Orpheus*, Keller's Symphony No. 3, Moore's *In Memoriam* and Symphony No. 2, Perry's *Stabat Mater* and Ward's Symphony No. 2 (with the Japan Philharmonic Orchestra), Barber's Violin Concerto (with Stavonhagen), Fine's *Alceste*, Flanagan's *Concert Ode*, Daniels' *Deep Forest*, Gideon's *Lyric Piece for String Orchestra*, Heilner's *Chinese Songs*, Howe's *Spring Pastoral*, Ives' *Washington's Birthday*, Kerr's Violin Concerto (with Stavonhagen), Perry's *Short Piece for Orchestra*, Talma's *Toccata* and Trimble's *Closing Piece* (with the Tokyo Imperial Philharmonic Orchestra), Becker's *Concerto Arabesque* (with Kayser), Cowell's *... if He please*, Flanagan's *The Lady of Tearful Regret*, Ives' *Hallowe'en*, *Central Park in the Dark* and *The Pond*, Jacobi's Cello Concerto (with Vecchi), Riegger's *Canon and Fugue*, Sowerby's *Classic Concerto for Organ and Strings* (with Karsen), Ward's *Hush'd be the Camps Today* and Warren's *Suite for Orchestra* (with the Oslo Philharmonic Orchestra *et al.*), Beeson's Symphony No. 1, Cowell's *Variations* and *Synchrony*, Hoiby's Piano Concerto (with Atkins), Ives' *Robert Browning Overture*, Josten's *Symphony in F*, Piston's *Concerto for Orchestra*, Ruggles' *Men and Mountains*, Thorne's *Rhapsodic Variations* and *Burlesque* overture and Ward's *Sacred Songs for Pantheists* (with the Polish National Radio Orchestra), Carpenter's *Concertino* (with Mitchell), Ives' *Fourth of July*, and Piston's *Concertino* (with Mitchell, and the Göteborg Symphony Orchestra), Claffin's Piano Concerto (with Magnussen), Cowell's Symphony No. 16, Isolfsson's *Passacaglia*, Ives' *Thanksgiving*, Leif's *Iceland Overture*, and Ward's Symphony No. 3 (with the Iceland Symphony Orchestra), Cowell's Symphony No. 7, Ward's *Adagio and Allegro* and *Jubilation* (with the Vienna Symphony Orchestra), Howe's *Castellana*, *Stars and Sand* (with a Vienna orchestra) and Ives' *Decoration Day* (with the Finnish Radio Symphony Orchestra).

Strickland also recorded for other companies, Field's Piano Concertos Nos 1 and 2 (with Mitchell and the Stuttgart Radio Orchestra, issued by Musical Heritage Society), the Berg Violin Concerto (with Gitlis and the Vienna Pro Musica Orchestra for Vox), Parker's *Hora Novissima* (with the Vienna Symphony Orchestra for American Recording Society, and re-issued by Desto), MacDowell's Piano Concerto No. 2 (with Mitchell, and an orchestra, for Vanguard), Barber's *Knoxville: Summer of 1915* (with Steber and the Dumbarton Oaks Chamber Orchestra, for Columbia and re-issued by Odyssey), Piston's *Concertino* (with Jenner and the Vienna State Academy Orchestra for Vox), Busoni's *Indian Fantasy* and Bortkievich's Piano Concerto (with Mitchell and the Vienna State Opera Orchestra for Decca (US)), the Delius and Britten Piano Concertos (with Mitchell and the North German Radio Symphony Orchestra for Decca (US)), the Grieg Piano Concerto and Rachmaninov's Piano Concerto No. 2 (with Mitchell and an orchestra, for Music Treasures of the World).

Striegler, Karl (b. 1886). Born in Dresden, Striegler studied at the Conservatory there, where he became a teacher in 1913 and director in 1933, being placed there by the Nazis after the dismissal of Fritz Busch. He conducted at the Dresden Opera (from 1912), and also the Volks-Singakademie and Männergesangverein in Dresden. His compositions include symphonies, concertos, chamber music and songs. Urania issued an LP in which he conducted the Saxon State Orchestra in Françaix's *Le Roi nu*.

Stross, Wilhelm (1907–66). Born in Eitorf, the German violinist Stross was a pupil of Eldering, Abendroth and Flesch, took master classes at the Munich Academy of Music (1934–51, 1954–66) and at the Hochschule für Musik at Cologne (1951–4). In addition to giving solo recitals, Stross was a prominent chamber player, performing in the Elly Ney Trio (1931–3), with Arrau (1936–8), in the Stross Quartet (from 1934) and then with his own chamber orchestra (from 1942). HMV issued in Germany 78 r.p.m. recordings of the Stross Chamber Orchestra performing Bach's Suite No. 2 and the *Brandenburg Concerto No. 4*.

Stryja, Karol (b. 1915). Born in Cieszyn, Poland, Stryja studied the violin at the Academy of Music at Katowice, and conducting under Fitelberg, and was a member of the Polish National Radio Symphony Orchestra (1948–51). He conducted the Folk Band of the Silesian Radio, directed the orchestra and choir of the Katowice School of Music, was appointed second conductor of the Silesian Philharmonic Orchestra at Katowice (1951), and two years later became first conductor and artistic manager. He has taught conducting at the School of Music at Katowice, became chief conductor of the Byorkester at Odense, Denmark (1968), with the Silesian Philharmonic Orchestra has toured Eastern and Western Europe, and has also conducted in South America, the USSR and in Eastern and Western Europe. His recordings include the overtures *I vespri siciliani* and *Manfred*, the Polovtsian Dances from *Prince Igor* and Różycki's *Mona Lisa Gioconda* (with the Silesian Philharmonic Orchestra for Polskie Nagrania) and the two *L'Arlésienne* suites (with the Polish Radio Orchestra for Muza).

Stupka, František (1879–1965). Born at Tetražice, Czechoslovakia, Stupka studied the violin at Prague Conservatory, graduated in 1901, and from then until 1919 was active in Russia, where he was concertmaster at the Odessa Opera, professor of violin at the Odessa Conservatory, and formed and performed with a string quartet. After returning to Czechoslovakia in 1919 he was Talich's assistant with the Czech Philharmonic Orchestra (1919–39), taught the viola at the Prague Conservatory (1925–31), conducted the Moravian Symphony Orchestra (1946–56), and was appointed artisic adviser to the Czech Philharmonic Orchestra (1956). In 1948 he was awarded the Liberation Prize of the City of Olomouc, in 1954 he was nominated Meritorious Artist, and in 1959 was awarded the Prize of the City of Prague. Certainly one of the most distinguished Czech conductors of his generation, his performances of Smetana, Dvořák and Tchaikovsky in particular were marked by warmth, spontaneity and expressiveness. Supraphon issued 78 r.p.m. discs of him conducting Tchaikovsky's Symphony No. 6 (with the Czech Philharmonic Orchestra), and Slavík's Violin Concerto (with Plocek and the Czech Radio Orchestra); later, an LP appeared in which he led the *1812* overture with the Prague Symphony Orchestra. In 1976 Panton issued two discs in which he conducted Dvořák's Symphonies Nos 8 and 9 (with the Czech Philharmonic Orchestra); both recordings were made at public concerts, the No. 8 in 1959 and the No. 9 at a concert in honour of his 85th birthday in 1964.

Štych, Jan (b. 1935). Born in Trutnov, Czechoslovakia, Štych graduated from the Higher Musical Education College in Prague (1955), and studied conducting at the Prague Academy of Music under Klíma, Brock and Smetáček. He was a conductor at the Ostrava State Theatre (1960–64), with the Janáček Opera Company at Brno (since 1964) and at the Prague National Theatre (since 1974). He has a wide repertoire, has recorded operas for Prague Television, has been a guest conductor in Luxembourg, FR and DR Germany and Spain, and led the first performance in Czechoslovakia of *Porgy and Bess*. For Supraphon he conducted the Prague National Theatre Orchestra in an aria recital by Bardini.

Suderberg, Robert (b. 1936). Born in Spencer, Iowa, Suderberg was educated at the University of Minnesota, the Yale School of Music and the University of Pennsylvania, and became co-director of the Contemporary Group, University of Washington (1966–74) and chancellor of the North Carolina School of Arts (1974). Of his compositions, *Chamber Music II* and the Piano Concerto have been recorded; he conducted the Contemporary Group in Crumb's *Madrigals* (with his wife, Elizabeth Suderberg, the soprano soloist, for Turnabout).

Suitner, Otmar (b. 1922). Born at Innsbruck, the son of a Tyrolean father and an Italian mother, Suitner studied the piano at the Salzburg Mozarteum (1941–3), and was a pupil of Krauss for conducting. He was first a concert pianist, then made his debut as a conductor at the Innsbruck Theatre (1942–5), was conductor at Remscheid (1952–7), general music director of the Palatinate Symphony Orchestra at Ludwigshafen (1957–60), at the Dresden State Opera and conductor of the Dresden Staatskapelle (1960–64), general music director of the Berlin Staatsoper (in East Berlin) and conductor of the Berlin Staatskapelle (1964–71 and again from 1974). He has been a guest conductor throughout Europe, in the USSR, North and South America and in Japan, where he is an honorary conductor of the NHK Symphony Orchestra. He conducts regularly at the San Francisco Opera, has appeared at many international festivals, led *Der fliegende Holländer* in 1965 and *The Ring* in 1966 and 1967 at the Bayreuth Festivals, and was director of the conductors' course at the Salzburg International Summer School (1975–6). In 1973 he was awarded the Gregorian Order by Pope Paul VI. Suitner is one of the leading conductors of DR Germany, and his performances of the Mozart and Wagner operas are particularly authoritative.

Suitner has made many records for the East German label, Eterna, and some of these discs have been issued in the West by other companies. Included are the operas *Die Zauberflöte*, *Così fan tutte*, *Die Entführung aus dem Serail*, *Le nozze di Figaro*, *Hänsel und Gretel*, *Il barbiere di Siviglia*, *The Bartered Bride*, *Salome* and Dessau's *Einstein* (with either the Berlin Staatskapelle or the Dresden Staatskapelle *et al.*), Haydn's Symphony No. 100 and Mozart's Symphony No. 25 (with the Leipzig Gewandhaus Orchestra), Mozart's Symphonies Nos 25, 28, 29, 30, 31, 32, 33, 34, 35, 36, 38, 39, 40 and 41, *Eine kleine Nachtmusik*, *Serenata notturna*, the Serenade K. 101, the Notturno K. 286, *Ein musikalischer Spass*, the Sinfonia Concertante K. 297b, Piano Concertos K. 450 and K. 467 (with Schmidt), and the Flute and Harp Concerto (with Walter and Zoff), Bizet's *Symphony in C major*, Mahler's Symphony No. 1, Reger's *Concerto in the Old Style*, *Ballet Suite* and *Variations and Fugue on a Theme of Beethoven*, Strauss's *Metamorphosen*, Debussy's *Prélude à l'après-midi d'un faune*, Volkmann's Serenade No. 2, Tchaikovsky's *Serenade in C major*, *Le Sacre du printemps*, Weber's Symphony No. 1, Dessau's *Einstein* and arrangement of Mozart's String Quintet K. 614, Meyer's *Symphony in B*, dances by Lanner, the Suppé overtures *Die schöne Galatea*, *Dichter und Bauer*, *Banditenstreiche*, *Leichte Kavallerie*, *Flotte Bursche* and *Pique Dame*, polkas by Strauss, Eisler's *Klingende Documente II* and arias sung by Schreier, and operatic duets by Schreier and Adam (with the Dresden Staatskapelle), arias sung by Vogel, Adam and Kollo (with the Berlin Staatskapelle), three Violin Concertos of Haydn (with Suske), Mozart's overtures to *La clemenza di Tito*, *Le nozze di Figaro*, *Die Zauberflöte*, *Idomeneo*, *Don Giovanni*, *Die Entführung aus dem Serail*, *Der Schauspieldirektor*, *Così fan tutte* and *La finta giardiniera*, the Weber overtures *Oberon*, *Der Freischütz*, *Euryanthe* and others, Grieg's *Holberg Suite*, *Sigurd Jorsalfar*, *Lyric Suite* and *Norwegian Dances*, Hindemith's *Symphony in E flat* and *Symphonic Metamorphoses on a Theme by Weber*, Reger's *Improvisation on the Blue Danube*, Manfred Schubert's *Canzoni amorosi* and Concerto for Baritone (with Leib), and Meyer's Violin Concerto (with David Oistrakh, and with the Berlin Staatskapelle). Also, he has recorded Liszt's *Orpheus* and *Mazeppa*, and the two *Peer Gynt* suites (with the Bamberg Symphony Orchestra for DGG), and Lortzing's *Opernprobe* and Gluck's *Der betrogene Kadi* (*Le Cadi Dupé*) (with the Bavarian State Opera for EMI).

Suk, Josef (b. 1929). The grandson of Josef Suk the composer, and great grandson of Dvořák, Suk was born in Prague, studied at the Prague Conservatory, and founded the Suk Trio, in memory of his grandfather, in 1950. He was deputy first violinist with the Prague National Theatre Orchestra (1950), appeared as a solo violinist with the Czech Philharmonic Orchestra (1961), made his debut in the United States with the Cleveland Orchestra (1964) and was awarded the Czechoslovak State Prize (1964). In 1974 RCA issued a set of LPs of the Mozart Violin Concertos in which he plays and leads the Prague Chamber Orchestra; however Suk himself has remarked that although the record labels name him as the conductor, the concertmaster of the orchestra, Libor Hlaváček, was no less responsible. Suk has also made numerous records as a solo violinist and chamber player.

Sulyok, Tamás (b. 1930). Born in Budapest, Sulyok was educated as a pianist at the Fodor Music School, the Bela Bartók Conservatory and the Franz Liszt Academy of Music, where his teachers were Székely, Dohnányi and Weiner. He made his debut as a conductor in 1954, conducted at the Csokonai Theatre, Debrecen (1954–8), was chief conductor of the West Hungarian Opera at Györ (1958–9), principal conductor of the Miskolc Symphony Orchestra (1959–61), conductor of the Hungarian National Philharmonic Orchestra, Budapest (1961–6), musical director and associate conductor of the same orchestra under the general music director, Ferencsik (1966–71), principal conductor of the South-West German Philharmonic Orchestra at Konstanz (since 1971) and guest conductor of the Hungarian National Philharmonic Orchestra. Sulyok's special interest is the interpretation of Bartók's music, deriving from his personal contact with the composer; the conductors with whom he has worked closely are Klemperer and Ferencsik. He has recorded suites and a concerto of Muffat (with the Budapest Philharmonic Chamber Orchestra for Qualiton), Spohr's Symphony No. 3 and E. T. A. Hoffman's Symphony and a recital with Tipton (with the South-West German Philharmonic Orchestra for RBM, Mannheim).

Surinach, Carlos (b. 1915). Born in Barcelona, Surinach studied at the Conservatory there, at the Robert Schumann Conservatory at Düsseldorf, the Hochschule für Musik at Cologne, and at the Akademie der Künste, Berlin. He was conductor of the Orquesta Filarmonica and at the Gran Teatro del Liceo Opera House in Barcelona (1944), with major orchestras in Paris (1947–51), and then emigrated to the United States where he became well known both as a composer and musical director, particularly of contemporary music. His compositions include a *Sinfonietta flamenca* and the ballets *Rítmo Jondo*, *The Sibyl* and *David and Bathsheba*. He received the Arnold Bax Society's Medal (1966), and is Knight Commander of the Order of Isabella I of Castile. His recordings include excerpts from Glanville-Hick's *Nausicaa* (with the Athens Symphony Orchestra *et al.* for Composers Recordings), Arne's *The Judgement of Paris*, Purcell's

Abdelazer and Byrd's Fantasia No. 1 (with a chamber orchestra for DGG), Hovhaness's *Anahid*, *Alleluia and Fugue*, *Saint Vartan Symphony*, *Armenian Rhapsody*, *Celestial Fantasy*, *Sharagăn and Fugue*, Piano Concerto No. 1 (with Ajemian), Violin Concerto No. 2 (with Ajemian) and Viola Concerto No. 2 (with Vardi), a collection of music by Revueltas, Villa-Lobos' *Bachianas brasileiras No. 9*, Santa-Cruz's Symphony No. 2 and his own *Rítmo Jondo*, *Cantos Berberes* and *Tientos* (with the MGM Orchestra for MGM), *Capriccio español*, *El amor brujo*, *Spanish Dances* of Granados, and his own overture *Feria Magica*, *Sinfonietta flamenca* and *Concierto for Orchestra* (with the Paris Radio Symphony Orchestra for Montilla), Antheil's *Ballet mécanique* (with the New York Percussion Group for Columbia) and McPhee's *Concerto for Piano and Wind Octet* with Johannesen *et al.* for Composers Recordings).

Susskind, Walter (b. 1913). Born in Prague where his father was a Viennese music critic and newspaper correspondent and his Czech mother a music teacher, Susskind studied at the Prague Conservatory under Suk (1928–33) and at the German Music Academy under Szell, and won for himself a considerable local reputation as a pianist, particularly of contemporary music. He was an assistant to Szell at the German Opera in Prague, where he was responsible for the light opera repertoire of Lehár, Kálmán and Fall, conducted at the Prague Opera (1934–7), and at this time many of his compositions were performed in Europe. When the Nazis occupied Czechoslovakia in March 1939, he was abroad conducting the Concertgebouw Orchestra in Amsterdam; he settled in England during the war, formed the Czech Trio with himself as pianist, conducted the Carl Rosa Opera Company (1942–7), conducted wartime concerts for troops and factory workers, and after the war became a British citizen. He conducted the Liverpool Philharmonic Orchestra in 1945, then received engagements with the major British orchestras, toured Australia (1946), was principal conductor of the Scottish National Orchestra (1946–53), was resident conductor of the Victorian Symphony Orchestra at Melbourne (1953–6), conducted in Israel and South America, succeeded MacMillan as musical director and first conductor of the Toronto Symphony Orchestra (1956–68), was musical director of the St Louis Symphony Orchestra (1968–76) and musical director of the Aspen Musical Festival, Colorado (1962–8). He also appeared with the New York City Opera, and with his particular skill with young musicians conducted the National Youth Orchestras in Britain and Canada, and in 1970–71 was principal conductor of the International Festival of Youth Orchestras in Switzerland. On occasion he performs as a piano soloist and chamber player, and has directed Mozart Piano Concertos from the keyboard. His compositions include songs, incidental music for films and plays, and music for piano, violin and orchestra, as well as orchestral arrangements of piano pieces of Debussy and Prokofiev.

Susskind is a fine musician and has been particularly successful with his symphony orchestras as a musical director. He is specially expressive in the music of his countrymen, Dvořák and Suk, and has introduced Suk's music to audiences around the world. His recording career started in England after World War II, with discs for Columbia with the Philharmonic Orchestra of the Weber overtures *Der Freischütz* and *Beherrscher der Geister* and Reger's arrangement of Wolf's *Italian Serenade*. He has recorded *Messiah* (with the London Philharmonic Chorus and Orchestra *et al.*, issued on budget labels in Britain and the United States, including Musical Heritage Society), and some orchestral music, but most of his several hundred recordings have been concerto accompaniments, and for some years he was virtually the house accompanist for EMI. The soloists whom he accompanied in concerto and recital recordings included Fournier, Rubinstein, Lympany, Leon Goossens, Solomon, Dennis Brain, Firkusny, Ferras, Menuhin, Starker, Schwarzkopf, Neveu, Berger, Welitsch, Goldberg, Thalben-Ball, Małcużyński, Milstein, Pennario, Heifetz, Varga, Matthews, Cohen, Grumiaux and Pougnet. These discs spanned the 78 and LP eras; the record of the Bruch and Mendelssohn Violin Concertos with Menuhin was a perennial best-seller; other notable sets, on 78s, were the Sibelius Violin Concerto with the ill-fated, gifted French violinist Ginette Neveu, and the Letter Scene from *Eugene Onegin* with the soprano Ljuba Welitsch. His orchestral recordings for EMI were restricted to the Offenbach/Rosenthal *Gaîté parisienne* (with the Covent Garden Orchestra), a suite from *Prince Igor*, Grieg's *Norwegian Dances* and two *Peer Gynt* suites, *A Night on the Bare Mountain*, the Introduction to Act I and Gopak from *Sorochintsy Fair*, the Introduction to Act III, the Dance of the Persian Slaves and the entr'acte from Act IV of *Khovanshchina*, and the *Intermezzo in B minor*, *Scherzo in B flat*, and the Triumphal March from *The Capture of Kars* of Mussorgsky (with the Philharmonic

Orchestra); the Mussorgsky collection was reissued for a time by Music for Pleasure.

Susskind's other recordings include Mozart's Piano Concerto K. 491 (with Gould and the CBC Symphony Orchestra for Columbia), Bartók's *Cantata Profana*, *The Wooden Prince* and *Duke Bluebeard's Castle* (with the New Symphony Orchestra *et al.* for Bartók), Schubert's Symphony No. 4 (with the London Symphony Orchestra for Mercury), Prokofiev's *Chout*, Copland's *Appalachian Spring* and *Billy the Kid*, and Gould's *Spirituals* (with the London Symphony Orchestra for Everest; *Billy the Kid* was also issued by World Record Club); Matton's Two-Piano Concerto (with Morrisset and Bouchard and the Toronto Symphony Orchestra for Composers Recordings), Shostakovich's Symphony No. 1 (with the National Youth Orchestra for Pye), the overture *Cockaigne* (with the National Youth Orchestra), Dvořák's Symphony No. 8 (with the 1971 International Festival Youth Orchestra for Concert Hall), Dvořák's *Carnival* overture and Rachmaninov's *Rhapsody on a Theme of Paganini* (with Katin and the 1972 International Festival Youth Orchestra for Concert Hall), Pierné's *A Children's Crusade* (with the Toronto Symphony Orchestra *et al.* for Columbia), Somers' *Suite for Harp and Chamber Orchestra* (with Loman), Adaskin's *Sérénade concertante* and Papineau-Couture's *Pièce concertante No. 1* (with Bernardi, and the CBC Symphony Orchestra for Columbia), Fleming's *Ballet Introduction*, Mercure's *Tétrachromie*, Weinzweig's *Barn Dance*, Surdin's Dances from *The Remarkable Rocket* and Applebaum's Revival Meeting and Finale from *Barbara Allen* (with the Toronto Philharmonia Orchestra for Columbia), the Dvořák Cello Concerto (with Nelsova), Violin Concerto (with Ricci) and Piano Concerto (with Firkusny), *Pictures at an Exhibition*, *A Night on the Bare Mountain*, *The Planets*, *Also sprach Zarathustra* and *Má Vlast* and excerpts from *The Bartered Bride* (with the St Louis Symphony Orchestra for Vox), Heininen's *Adagio* and *Concerto per orchestra in forma di variazioni*, and Merilaïnen's Piano Concerto (with Gillespie and the Royal Philharmonic Orchestra for Philips), *Invitation to the Dance*, the Strauss waltzes *Sphärenklänge* and *Frühlingsstimme*, Waldteufel's waltz *The Skaters*, and the waltzes from *Die lustige Witwe*, *Eugene Onegin* and *Masquerade* (with the Bournemouth Symphony Orchestra for EMI).

Sutkowski, Stefan (b. 1932). Born in Warsaw where he was educated at the Conservatory and University, Sutkowski was an oboist with the Warsaw Philharmonic Orchestra (1954–74), as well as being artistic director of the Warsaw Chamber Orchestra. In 1959 he organised the Musicae Antiquae Collegium Varsoviense, an ensemble to perform old music, and in 1961 founded the Warsaw Chamber Opera. He has written music for the theatre, published studies on performing practices, and in 1974 was appointed president of the Polish Musicians' Association. His recordings include concertos by Vivaldi (with the Warsaw Chamber Orchestra for Polskie Nagrania), music of the Royal Castle in Warsaw, and music of Italian composers who lived in Poland: Marenzio, Pacelli, Cocciola, Cato, Merula and Di Capua (with the Musicae Antiquae Collegium Varsoviense for Polskie Nagrania).

Sveshnikov, Alexandr (b. 1890). Educated at the Moscow Conservatory, Sveshnikov was organiser, artistic adviser and conductor of the All-Union Broadcasting Committee Choir (1928–36), artistic adviser and conductor of the USSR State Choir (1936–7), of the Leningrad Academy Choir (1937–41) and the USSR Academy Choir of Russian Songs (1941–6), and was a professor (1946) then rector (1948) at the Moscow Conservatory. With the RSFSR Academy Choir he recorded Rachmaninov's *Vesper Mass* and collections of Russian folk songs, and with the USSR Chorus a recital of choral pieces by Tchaikovsky (issued by EMI).

Svetlanov, Evgeny (b. 1928). Born in Moscow where his father and mother were singers at the Bolshoi Theatre, Svetlanov was educated at the Gnessin Music Education Institute and the Moscow Conservatory, studying under Shaporin, Neuhaus and Gauk. While still a student he won a competition for the post of assistant conductor with the Bolshoi Symphony Orchestra; he appeared also as a pianist at the outset of his career, after graduating from the Conservatory in 1951, but in that year also made his debut as a conductor with the Moscow Regional Philharmonic Orchestra. He joined the music department of Moscow Radio, was repetiteur and then conductor with the Bolshoi Theatre (1954–62), and succeeded Melik-Pashaev as chief conductor there (1962–4). In 1965 he took Ivanov's place as conductor of the USSR State Symphony Orchestra. He first conducted outside the USSR at Bucharest in 1953, then in Warsaw in 1955, has toured Italy, the Netherlands and Britain, where he conducted the London Philharmonic Orchestra in 1970, and visited La Scala, Milan, with the Bolshoi Theatre Company. He is married to the soprano Larissa Avdeyeva, and received the award People's Artist of the Russian Republic in 1964. His compositions include a symphony, the tone poem *Festival Poem*, and *Daugava, Siberian Fantasy*, a *Rhapsody for Orchestra*, a cantata *My Native Fields*, a piano concerto, string quartet and some ballet scores based on music by Bartók and Rachmaninov.

Svetlanov is one of the leading Soviet conductors, and is a committed and highly effective performer of Russian music in particular, having a preference for Rachmaninov, Shostakovich and Prokofiev, and among non-Russians for Mahler, whom he conducts with conviction; in fact, he is reported to have said that he considers 'Mahler the greatest genius of all peoples and all times'. He also chooses to conduct Bach, Mozart, Brahms, Debussy, Ravel, Stravinsky, Bartók and Honegger, but of his Beethoven a Russian critic wrote that while he conducts him well, 'he accepts Beethoven more with his mind than with his heart'. Svetlanov recognises the influence of Golovanov, Mravinsky and Stokowski on his development, and is also interested in Bernstein, Karajan and Maazel. On the podium he is restrained in gesture, and has a firm disciplinary control of the orchestra. Despite his early experience with conducting opera at the Bolshoi Theatre, he prefers to conduct symphonic music: 'Opera is a very complex medium in which the conductor only too rarely is a true interpreter of the music. Too often he is merely a glorified repetiteur or an accompanist. You are so dependent on other people and factors – the producer, designer, artists. If anyone happens to be feeling ill or off-colour, your own performance is bound to suffer. On the concert platform, I hardly need say, the conductor is *really* in charge' (*The Gramophone*, March 1970, p. 1423).

With one or two exceptions, Svetlanov's recordings have been exclusively of Russian composers, and except where indicated, have been with the USSR State Symphony Orchestra. Foremost are the six symphonies of Tchaikovsky, *Manfred*, *Capriccio italien*, the *Serenade in C major, Francesca da Rimini*, the *Romeo and Juliet* fantasy-overture, *The Tempest*, *Hamlet* and *The Seasons* (orchestrated by Gauk), Liadov's *From the Book of Revelations*, *From The Olden Days*, *Baba Yaga*, *The Enchanted Lake*, *Kikimora*, *Eight Russian Folksongs* and *A Musical Snuffbox*, Glinka's *Kamarinskaya*, *Jota aragonesa*, *Summer Night in Madrid*, *Valse-fantaisie*, *Prayer* and the overture, march and two dances from *Russlan and Ludmilla* (with the Bolshoi Theatre Orchestra), Kalinnikov's Symphony No. 1 (with the State Academy Orchestra), and Symphony No. 2, Borodin's Symphony No. 2, *In the Steppes of Central Asia* and the overture and Polovtsian March from *Prince Igor*, Glazunov's *Raymonda* (with the Bolshoi Theatre Orchestra) and *Finnish Rhapsody* (with the Moscow Radio Symphony Orchestra), *Scheherazade* and the overtures to Rimsky-Korsakov's *May Night*, *Sadko*, *The Tsar's Bride* and *The Maid of Pskov*, suites from *The Snow Maiden* and *Pan Voyevoda* (with the Bolshoi Theatre Orchestra) and excerpts from *Mlada* (with the Moscow Radio Symphony Orchestra *et al.*), Dargomizhsky's *Russalka* (with the Bolshoi Theatre Orchestra *et al.*), the three symphonies of Rachmaninov (No. 2 with the Bolshoi Theatre Orchestra), *Symphonic Dances*, *The Isle of the Dead*, *Caprice bohémien*, a suite from *Aleko*, *Prince Ristoslav*, *Three Russian Songs*, *The Rock* and *Vocalise*, the three symphonies and *Poème de l'extase* of Scriabin, Khachaturian's *Concert Rhapsody*, Miaskovsky's Symphony No. 22, Shostakovich's Symphonies Nos 7 and 10, *Alexander Nevsky*, *Le Sacre du printemps*, *Jeu de cartes*, Shaporin's *The Battle for Russia*, Khrennikov's Piano Concerto No. 2, Galynin's Piano Concerto (with Bashkirov and the Moscow Radio Symphony Orchestra) and the cantata *From Homer* (with the Moscow Philharmonic Orchestra *et al.*), Gordelli's Flute Concerto (with Korneyev and the Moscow Radio Symphony Orchestra), Pakmutova's Trumpet Concerto (with Popov and the Moscow Radio Symphony Orchestra), Shchedrin's Piano Concerto No. 1 (with Shchedrin and the Moscow Radio Symphony Orchestra), Sviridov's *Poem in Memory of Sergei Yesenin* (with the State Academy Orchestra *et al.*), Muradely's *October* (with the Moscow Radio Symphony Orchestra), his own *Festival Poem*, the Beethoven Violin Concerto (with Kogan), Debussy's *Nocturnes* and Ravel's *Pavane pour une infante défunte*.

All these performances have the utmost conviction; Svetlanov shows himself to be an uninhibited interpreter of Russian music, gilding the lily. Some recordings are very fine, such as *Scheherazade* and the *Manfred* symphony, giving the works a power and atmosphere not often heard in interpretations by Western orchestras and conductors. Sometimes this approach borders on brashness, as in the Borodin Symphony No. 2, *Hamlet* and *Romeo and Juliet*, and some critics have taken exception to Svetlanov's addition of percussion parts to the scores of some of Scriabin's pieces, uncharacteristic of the composer's orchestral style. In many instances the orchestral playing is not impeccable. Not all the discs listed above are available in both Britain and the United States. Svetlanov has also recorded as a pianist, in Rachmaninov's *Trio No. 2 in D minor*, with Kogan and Luzanov. His composition which he recorded, *Festival Poem*, has been received rather acidly by Western critics; William Mann wrote in *The Times* that it is 'a blameless pastiche of your favourite Russian nationalistic music, with a big tune irresistible to those who love Tchaikovsky or Rachmaninov – definitely Tsarist by affiliation.'

Swarowsky, Hans (1899–1975). Born in Budapest, Swarowsky studied in Vienna with Schoenberg, Webern and Strauss, and then conducted in opera houses in Hamburg (1932), Berlin (1934) and Zürich (1937–40), was director of the Salzburg Festival (1940–44), was conductor of the Polish Philharmonic Orchestra at Kraków (1944–5), at the Graz Opera (1947–50) and of the Scottish Orchestra, Glasgow (1957–9); he was also principal conductor at the Vienna State Opera (from 1959). From 1946 he taught conducting at the Vienna Academy of Music, where Mehta and Abbado were among his pupils. He made numerous records with various Viennese orchestras, some either *ad hoc* or using a *nom d'enregistrement*, and these have been issued on a variety of labels. All of these performances illustrate his exemplary taste, sense of proportion and moderation as an interpreter of the standard repertoire, and the breadth of his musical sympathies.

Polydor issued 78 r.p.m. discs of Swarowsky conducting the Berlin Staatsoper Orchestra in the overture to Pfitzner's *Die Zaubergeige* and in an aria from Moniuszko's *Halka* (with Ladis). His LPs included Handel's *Giulio Cesare*, Mozart's Piano Concertos K. 271 and K. 466 (with Novaes), and K. 450 and K. 456 (with Haebler), and the two Flute Concertos (with Wanausek), Beethoven's Piano Concerto No. 4 (with Novaes), the Schumann Piano Concerto (twice, with Novaes and Blumenthal), Weber's Piano Concertos Nos 1 and 2 (with Wührer), Mendelssohn's Piano Concerto No. 2, *Rondo brilliant* and *Serenade and allegro giocoso* (with Kyriakou) and Two-Piano Concerto (with Frugoni and Mrazek), the Mendelssohn Violin Concerto and Bruch's Violin Concerto No. 1 (with Gitlis), Chopin's *Andante spianato and Grande Polonaise*, *Krakowiak* and *Variations on Mozart's 'Lą ci darem la mano'* (with Frugoni), Liszt's *Totentanz* (with Frugoni), Brahms' Piano Concertos Nos 1 and 2 (with Frugoni), the Grieg Piano Concerto (twice, with Novaes and Blumenthal), Falla's *Nights in the Gardens of Spain* (with Novaes), Scriabin's Piano Concerto (with Wührer), *Peter and the Wolf* and *The Young Person's Guide to the Orchestra* (with the Vienna Pro Musica Orchestra *et al.* for Vox); Chopin's Piano Concerto No. 1 (with Horszowski) and Brahms' Piano Concerto No. 1 (with Wührer, and the Vienna State Philharmonia Orchestra for Vox); Bach's *St Matthew Passion* and *Christmas Oratorio*, Haydn's Mass No. 9, excerpts from *Don Giovanni* and marches from *Fidelio*, *La Damnation de Faust*, *Le Prophète*, *Tannhäuser* and *Götterdämmerung* (with the Vienna State Symphony Orchestra *et al.* for La Guilde Internationale du Disque); Schütz's *Christmas Oratorio*, Haydn's *Orfeo ed Euridice*, Mass No. 8 and *Cello Concerto in D* (with Parisot), Mozart's Piano Concertos K. 467 and K. 595, and Beethoven's Piano Concerto No. 5 (with Gulda), Liszt's *Hungarian Rhapsodies Nos 1, 2, 3* and *6*, Mendelssohn's Piano Concerto No. 1 and the Chopin Piano Concerto No. 2 (with Pressler), Brahms' *Hungarian Dances Nos 1, 2, 3, 5*, and *6*, the Dvořák Cello Concerto (with Greenhouse) and *Legends Nos 4* and *7*, the waltzes *Frühlingsstimme* and *G'schichten aus dem Wiener Wald* and the czardas from *Ritter Pázmán*, the overtures *Le Carnaval romain*, *Orphée aux enfers*, *Anacreon*, *Zar und Zimmermann*, *Der Wildschütz*, *Preciosa* and *Peter Schmoll und seine Nachbarn* and choruses from *Der Freischütz*, *Der Barbier von Bagdad*, *Der Wildschütz*, *The Merry Wives of Windsor*, *Martha*, *Der fliegende Holländer* and *Tannhäuser* (with the Vienna State Opera Orchestra *et al.* for La Guilde Internationale du Disque).

He also recorded Haydn's Symphony No. 97 (with the Vienna State Opera Orchestra for Supraphon); Haydn's Symphonies Nos 1 and 45, the prelude to *Die Meistersinger* and the overtures to *Rienzi*, *The Merry Wives of Windsor* and *La forza del destino* (with the Vienna Symphony Orchestra for Supraphon); Smetana's *Wallenstein's Camp* (with the Vienna Symphony Orchestra for Westminster); some dances and waltzes by Schubert and Johann Strauss, Mahler's Symphony No. 4 (with Lorenz), Schoenberg's *Pelleas und Melisande* and Webern's *Passacaglia* (with the Czech Philharmonic Orchestra for Supraphon); Haydn's Symphonies Nos 30 and 31, Mozart's Piano Concertos K. 466 and K. 491 (with Matthews) and the four Horn Concertos (with Linder, and the Vienna State Opera Orchestra for Vanguard); Schoenberg's *A Survivor from Warsaw* and Bruch's *Kol Nidrei* (with the Vienna Academy Chamber Choir and Orchestra for CBS); Haydn's Symphonies Nos 54 and 70 and Mozart's Overture K. 311a (with the Vienna State Academy Orchestra for Lyrichord and Nixa); Beethoven's Symphonies Nos 2 and 8 (with the Vienna State Opera Orchestra, issued by World Record Club); Mendelssohn's *Capriccio brilliant* (with Kyriakou and the Vienna Symphony Orchestra for Vox); Beethoven's Symphony No. 5 and Piano Concerto No. 5 (with Kamper, and the Vienna State Opera Orchestra for Vega); Schumann's Symphony No. 3, excerpts from the incidental music for *Rosamunde*, the Hungarian March from *La Damnation de Faust*, *Moldau* and Franck's *Symphonic Variations* (with Wollman, and an unnamed orchestra for Classics Record Club); Saint-Saëns' Piano Concertos Nos 2 and 5 (with Fugoni and the Vienna Symphony Orchestra, issued by Saga); Haydn's Symphonies Nos 87 and 89, the overture to *Die Zauberflöte*, Mendelssohn's Symphony No. 4, an orchestral arrangement of Schumann's *Kinderszenen*, excerpts from Berlioz's *Roméo et Juliette* symphony, the prelude to *Die Meistersinger*, the preludes to Acts I and III of *Lohengrin*, the Rhine Journey from *Götterdämmerung*, the overture to *Il barbiere di Siviglia*, excerpts from *Swan Lake*, the grand march from *Aida*, *L'Apprenti sorcier*, the Bacchanale from *Samson et Dalila*, Offenbach's *Bouffes parisiens* (arranged by Mohaupt), and Enesco's *Romanian Rhapsody No. 1* (with an unnamed orchestra for Musical Treasures of the World); the Haydn Trumpet Concerto (with Moller) and *Overture in D major*, Tchaikovsky's Symphonies Nos 1 and 2, and Saint-Saëns' Symphony No. 3 (with the Vienna Philharmonia or Philharmusica Orchestra, for Urania); the *Semiramide* overture, Storm Music from *Il barbiere di Siviglia*, Tchaikovsky's Symphony No. 3 and the waltzes from *Der Rosenkavalier* (with the Vienna State Opera Orchestra for Urania); Beethoven's Symphonies Nos 3 and 6, Schumann's Symphony No. 1 and Piano Concerto (with Kamper), Brahms' Symphony No. 1 and Piano Concerto No. 2 (with Mrazek), three waltzes of Johann Strauss and the overtures *Morgen, Mittag und Abend im Wien*, *Dichter und Bauer* and *Leichte Cavallerie* (with the Vienna State Opera Orchestra for Audio Fidelity); the overtures to *Tannhäuser* and *Rienzi*, the preludes to *Tristan und Isolde* and *Parsifal*, the waltzes from *Der Rosenkavalier* and some waltzes by Johann Strauss (with the Vienna State Opera Orchestra for Parliament, some probably also listed above); the *Egmont* and *Fidelio* overtures (with the Vienna State Opera Orchestra for Le Chant du Monde); the overtures *The Hebrides*, *Tancredi*, *Die Entführung aus dem Serail*, *Euryanthe* and *Der Freischütz* (with the Vienna State Opera Orchestra for Telefunken, some also issued by Supraphon); Brant's Symphony No. 1, Mennin's *Concertato* and Dello Joio's *Epigraph* and *Serenade* (with the Vienna Symphony Orchestra for Desto); Beethoven's Symphonies Nos 5 and 8, and a complete *Má Vlast* (with the South German Philharmonic Orchestra for Intercord); and Beethoven's Symphony No. 6 (with the Munich Symphony Orchestra for Sonopresse).

Swift, James (b. 1915). Born in North St Paul, Minnesota, and educated at the University of Minnesota, Swift was an engineer and manager with several major companies in California, but at the same time was conductor of the San Fernando Valley Symphony Orchestra (1953–68), the Los Angeles Solo Repertory Orchestra (1968–74) and the Sinfonietta Strings (1971–4). He recorded Haubiel's *Miniatures* and Minuet from the *Suite passacaille* (with the Graunke Symphony Orchestra for Orion).

Swoboda, Henry (b. 1897). Born in Prague, Swoboda studied at the Conservatory there under Talich, at the Charles University, and in Vienna with Richard Robert. He was an assistant conductor at the Prague Opera (1921–3), conductor at Düsseldorf and Elberfeld, a conductor and programme organiser with the Prague Radio (1931–8), and appeared with the Berlin Philharmonic, Dresden Philharmonic and Vienna Symphony Orchestras. After World War II he was appointed conductor for the Westminster and Concert Hall record companies, taught at Harvard University and was conductor of the Harvard-Radcliffe Orchestra (1962–4), was visiting professor and conductor of the orchestra at the University of Texas (1964–8), conducted in Athens, Ankara and Teheran under the auspices of the US State Department, and toured extensively in Europe and South America. He edited a book, *The American Symphony Orchestra* (Basic Books, New York). In the first decade of LP and later, he made a number of recordings for Westminster and Concert Hall, and its associates Musical Masterpieces and La Guilde Internationale du Disque, with various European orchestras, and released on these and other labels such as Nixa and Selmer. Many of the works recorded were then rare to the catalogues, and even though most of the performances were little more than adequate, he played an important role in those years in the vast expansion of the recorded repertoire that occurred with the advent of LP.

Swoboda's recordings included Vivaldi's *The*

Four Seasons (with the Musical Masterpieces Chamber Orchestra, released by Musical Masterpieces); Bach's Suite No. 1, Mozart's Piano Concertos K. 459 and K. 466, and Beethoven's Piano Concerto No. 3 (with Haskil), Mozart's Flute Concerto K. 314 (with Nicolet), Schubert's Symphony No. 1, the Hindemith Violin Concerto (with Rybar) and Dvořák's *Czech Suite* (with the Winterthur Symphony Orchestra, issued by Musical Masterpieces); Haydn's Symphonies Nos 94 and 100, and Mozart's Symphonies Nos 35 and 40 (with the Netherlands Philharmonic Orchestra, issued by Musical Masterpieces); Mozart's Piano Concerto K. 415 (with Balsam and an unnamed orchestra, issued by Musical Masterpieces); Mozart's Symphonies Nos 29, 34 and 35, Beethoven's *Christus am Ölberge*, Schubert's *Rondo in A major* and Lalo's Violin Concerto (with Solovieff), Dvořák's Symphony No. 7 and *Carnival* overture, Goldmark's *Rustic Wedding* symphony, Verdi's *Te Deum*, *Ave Maria*, *Stabat Mater* and *Laudate alla Vergine Maria*, MacDowell's Piano Concerto No. 2 (with Jenner), Carpenter's *Adventures in a Perambulator*, MacBride's *Aria and Toccata in Swing*, Still's *Blues* and *Here's One*, and Copland's Ukelele Serenade and Hoe Down from *Rodeo* (with the Vienna State Opera Orchestra for Concert Hall); Mozart's Symphonies Nos 18, 22, 23 and 30, Concertone and Serenade K. 204, Locatelli's Concerto Grosso Op. 1 No. 8 and *Sinfonia funebre*, Brahms' *Nänie* and *Gesang der Parzen*, Bruckner's Symphony No. 6 and Psalms Nos 112 and 150, Piano Concertos of Rimsky-Korsakov and Scriabin (with Badura-Skoda), Strauss's *Macbeth*, *Aus Italien* and *Wanderers Sturmlied*, Kodály's *Te Deum* and *Theatre Overture*, Smetana's *Wallenstein's Camp*, Suk's *Fantasy* (with Rybar), Martinů's Concerto Grosso, Prokofiev's Sinfonietta and *Divertimento in C major*, and Milhaud's *Maximilien* suite, *Études* for Piano and Orchestra (with Badura-Skoda), *Sérénade* and *Three Rag Pieces* (with the Vienna Symphony Orchestra for Westminster); C. P. E. Bach's *Piano Concerto in A minor* (with Holeček), Haydn's Symphonies Nos 64 and 91, the Dvořák overtures *Carnival*, *Amid Nature* and *Otello*, Symphony No. 3, *Notturno*, *Slavonic Rhapsody No. 2* and *Scherzo capriccioso*, Goldmark's Violin Concerto (with Rybar), Rimsky-Korsakov's *Sinfonietta on Russian Themes*, Janáček's *Taras Bulba* and Suite for String Orchestra, and Hindemith's *The Four Temperaments* (with Holeček, and the Vienna Symphony Orchestra issued by Musical Masterpieces); Martinů's *Partita*, *Serenade* and Concerto for String Quartet and Orchestra (with the Winterthur Symphony Orchestra for Westminster); Tchaikovsky's Symphony No. 3 and *Souvenir de Florence* (with the Vienna State Opera Orchestra for Westminster); Mozart's Sinfonia Concertante K. 297b, Michael Haydn's *Symphony in G major* and incidental music to *Zaïre*, and Ibert's *Capriccio*, *Divertissement* and *Suite élisabéthaine* (with the Vienna Symphony and State Opera Orchestras, for La Guilde Internationale du Disque and issued by Selmer); Corelli's Concerto Grosso Op. 6 No. 2, Haydn's Symphonies Nos 77 and 78, Mozart's Piano Concertos K. 413 and K. 415 (with Balsam), Brahms' Serenade No. 1 and Roussel's Concerto for Small Orchestra (with the Concert Hall Symphony Orchestra for Concert Hall); Mozart's Piano Concerto K. 415, also issued on Musical Masterpieces (see above); Saint-Saëns' Piano Concerto No. 2 (with Slenzynska and the Symphony of the Air for Decca (US)); and Mozart's *Adagio and Rondo in C major* for Glass Harmonica, and Andante K. 315 (with Wanausek and the Vienna Pro Musica Orchestra for Vox).

Szabó, Miklós (b. 1931). Born at Szentgotthárd, Hungary, Szabó first studied music with his father, and then attended the Franz Liszt Academy, graduating in 1953. He taught at the Györ Conservatory (from 1953), then became a professor at the Music Teachers' Training College at Györ (1966). He is conductor of the famous Györ Girls' Choir, and has toured with them in Austria (1966 and 1977), France (1968 and 1970), Italy (1976) and Poland (1977). He was visiting professor at the University of Jyväskylä, Finland (1974) and lectures at the Sibelius Academy at Helsinki. He has recorded for Qualiton with the Györ Girls' Choir music by Dufay, Lassus, Monteverdi and Palestrina, as well as Michael Haydn's *Vesperae in Festo SS. Innocentium*, *Missa Sancti Aloysii* and other works (also with the Györ Philharmonic Orchestra), and Bartók's *a capella* choruses; with the Slovak Philharmonic Choir he recorded songs by Bartók, and with the Budapest Choir Liszt's *Via Crucis* and *Inno a Maria Vergine*. The latter disc was widely acclaimed, winning the Grand Prix de l'Académie Charles Cross (1974) and the Grand Prix of the Hungarian Liszt Society (1975).

Szekeres, Ferenc (b. 1927). Born in Murakeresztur, Hungary, Szekeres studied with Kodály and Ferrara, and in 1950 formed his madrigal ensemble and gave concerts in Hungary and Western Europe, mostly of Renaissance and baroque composers. He is director of the Hungarian Academy of Music. For Hungaroton he has recorded Vivaldi's *Juditha triumphans* (with the Hungarian State Symphony Orchestra *et al.*), *Credo*, *Gloria*, *Beatus Vir*, *Kyrie*, *Lauda Jerusalem* and *Invicta Bellati* (with the Franz Liszt Chamber Orchestra, Budapest Madrigal Choir *et al.*), Haydn's oratorio *Il ritorno di Tobia*, madrigal *The Storm* and cantata *Die Erwählung eines Kapellmeisters* and Paisiello's *Il maestro ed i sui due solari* (with the Hungarian State Symphony Orchestra, the Budapest Madrigal Choir *et al.*). *Il ritorno di Tobia* of Haydn has been especially praised for the beauty of the performance.

Szell, Georg (1897–1970). Born in Budapest where his father was a businessman and lawyer, Szell spent most of his childhood in Vienna. He showed a prodigious talent for music at an early age, learned the piano with Richard Robert, a famous teacher of the day, and made his debut as a pianist at the age of ten with the Vienna Symphony Orchestra. A year later he played at the Royal Albert Hall in London, with Landon Ronald in a programme that included a Mendelssohn concerto and an overture that he himself had composed. He studied at the Vienna Academy of Music under Förster and Mandyczewski, and in Leipzig under Reger, at 15 appeared with the Berlin Philharmonic Orchestra as pianist and composer, and at 17 substituted for the regular conductor of the Vienna Symphony Orchestra. Richard Strauss accepted him as an assistant at the Berlin Staatsoper, and encouraged him to make conducting his career; with Strauss's sponsorship he succeeded Klemperer as first conductor at the Strasbourg Municipal Theatre (1917–24), and at the same time was principal conductor at the Darmstadt Court Theatre (1921–4) and at Düsseldorf (1922–4). He returned to Berlin and became chief conductor of the Berlin Staatsoper and of the orchestra of the Berlin Broadcasting Company (1924–9) and professor at the Hochschule für Musik in Berlin (1927). Moving to Prague, he was appointed musical director of the German Opera House there (1927–37), conducted the Czech Philharmonic Orchestra, and was also a professor at the German Music Academy. In Prague he impressed the pianist Schnabel, who arranged for him to conduct at the Courtauld/Sargent concerts in London (1933); he conducted the major British orchestras and then became conductor of the Scottish Orchestra (1937–9) as well as the Residentie Orchestra at The Hague. His first appearance in the United States was at St Louis (1930–31); on his return from his second visit to Australia in 1939 he found himself in New York at the outbreak of World War II, and thereafter made his career in the US. At first he conducted the Los Angeles Philharmonic Orchestra in some concerts at the Hollywood Bowl; in 1941 he made his debut in New York with the NBC Symphony Orchestra, became principal conductor at the New York Metropolitan Opera (1942–6), conducted the New York Philharmonic-Symphony Orchestra (first in 1944), taught composition at the Mannes School, and became a US citizen (1946). Finally, he was appointed conductor of the Cleveland Orchestra (1946), where he remained until his death, and also was for a year joint-conductor of the Amsterdam Concertgebouw Orchestra (1958–9).

Szell was, by common consent, one of the greatest conductors of the 20th century, and some would claim that his only superior was Toscanini. In his early years he was much influenced by Strauss, after whom he modelled his technique; Toscanini and Nikisch he also revered. However, he doubted whether the present day would tolerate Nikisch's spontaneous and improvisational approach, despite the wonderful sound and freedom of the orchestra. From Toscanini he learned his strict artistic earnestness, his close adherence to the score, a distaste for showmanship of any sort, and the unvarying, single-minded insistence on the highest standards of performance. There was absolutely nothing routine about any Szell performance; rehearsals were serious and meticulous, and he always brought with him the complete rehearsal scores of the works to be performed, densely marked with his own bowings and phrasings. He said that every week his orchestra gave seven concerts, two of which were in public. He made no attempt to ingratiate himself with his players or even to be pleasant to them, and he had a reputation as a ruthless autocrat who inspired respect but scarcely affection. Tall and broad-shouldered, he commanded with a chilly severity and was never inhibited in his criticisms of persons or institutions that did not meet his own exacting standards. The San Francisco Symphony Orchestra was the victim on one occasion, after an unsatisfactory guest engagement; after his abrupt departure from the New York Met. in 1954, someone said to Rudolf Bing, the manager, that 'George Szell is his own worst enemy', to which Bing answered, 'Not while I am alive'. In fairness, Bing made it up with Szell later. Szell's memory was phenomenal; when recording he would play each movement through, and then would correct missed notes or faulty balances.

Szell's name is inevitably connected with the Cleveland Orchestra, which he brought to a pinnacle of excellence perhaps not equalled, certainly not bettered, by any other orchestra in the US or Europe. It was essentially a classical orchestra, with a superb style and tone for the music of Haydn, Mozart and Beethoven, although he also produced the same high standard in his recordings with the Columbia Symphony Orchestra. Although he succeeded in blending American virtuosity and tonal purity with a European sense of tradition, the Cleveland Orchestra was ultimately a purely American product. A certain clinical inflexibility and the avoidance of even the slightest degree of sentiment resulted in performances that were breathtaking for the clarity and clean execution, but spontaneity, warmth and expressiveness were usually discounted; one of his players said, 'He even rehearsed the inspiration.' He believed that the music should speak for itself, and all it required was an accurate performance, which very often was of the highest imaginable degree of technical proficiency, with a superb sweep and power frequently reminiscent of Toscanini. Tempi were not always brisk, but elegant phrasing and shortened note values gave his Haydn, Mozart and Beethoven an incomparable crispness and clarity, perhaps not always justified by the score. Paul Meyers, who produced many of Szell's records, said (in *The Gramophone*, September 1970, p. 402) that 'He always paid the listeners the greatest possible compliment by assuming that they shared an equal knowledge of the work and therefore had the good sense to allow the music to speak for itself without overemphasis or unnecessary histrionics.' He insisted that his players perform as in chamber music, listening to each other, so that their ensemble was exceptional.

Szell's repertoire was limited to the music to which he was attracted: 'If I cannot perform something with complete conviction, I cannot make it sound convincing to the listener.' The composers he performed regularly were Haydn, Mozart, Beethoven, Schubert, Schumann, Brahms, Dvořák, Tchaikovsky, Strauss, Mahler and Bruckner; his programmes also included some Sibelius, Bartók, Prokofiev and Walton. American composers received his attention, for which he received the Laurel Leaf Award of the American Composers Alliance, but he performed comparatively little French or Russian music. He was not particularly at home with Schoenberg, Berg or Webern, although he 'found' the Berg Violin Concerto as late as 1968; his scepticism about programming contemporary compositions was real: 'I do not believe in the mass grave of an all-contemporary concert.' In later years he confined his repertoire to what he felt was the most important in the symphonic literature and discarded many works that he had enjoyed and conducted in early times but no longer held great interest for him.

Before World War II Szell made records in Berlin, Vienna, Prague and London; included were the legendary performances of Dvořák's Cello Concerto (with Casals and the Czech Philharmonic Orchestra for HMV), Brahms' Piano Concerto No. 1 (with Schnabel and the London Philharmonic Orchestra for HMV) and the Beethoven Violin Concerto and *Symphonie espagnole* of Lalo (with Huberman and the Vienna Philharmonic Orchestra for Columbia). His earliest records appear to be the overtures to *The Merry Wives of Windsor*, *Zampa* and *Fra Diavolo* (with the Grand Symphony Orchestra for Odeon and Parlophone); other 78s were the overtures *Rosamunde* (with a symphony orchestra for Odeon), *The Merry Wives of Windsor* (with the Berlin Staatsoper Orchestra for Odeon), *Leonore No. 3* and *Der Barbier von Bagdad* (with the Berlin Staatsoper Orchestra for Polydor), *Oberon* and the prelude to *Die Meistersinger* (with the London Philharmonic Orchestra for HMV), Dvořák's Symphony No. 9 (with the Czech Philharmonic Orchestra for HMV), Beethoven's Piano Concerto No. 5 (with Moiseiwitsch and the London Philharmonic Orchestra for HMV) and Strauss's *Pizzicato Polka*, *Tritsch-Tratsch Polka* and *An der schönen blauen Donau* (with the Vienna Philharmonic Orchestra for HMV).

In the United States, he first recorded on 78s with the New York Philharmonic-Symphony Orchestra, the works including Beethoven's Symphony No. 6, the incidental music to *A Midsummer Night's Dream*, the overtures to *Der Freischütz*, *Oberon*, *Rienzi*, *Tannhäuser* and the prelude to *Die Meistersinger*, Moldau and From Bohemia's Meadows and Forests, from *Má Vlast*. These performances were recently re-issued on LP transfers by Odyssey. In London he also recorded on 78s Beethoven's Piano Concerto No. 5 (with Curzon and the London Philharmonic Orchestra) and Tchaikovsky's Piano Concerto No. 1 (with Curzon and the New Symphony Orchestra), both sets for Decca. Then with the Cleveland Orchestra he recorded a series of discs which rank with the finest ever contributed to the gramophone. All were for CBS-Epic. They spread over the mono and stereo eras, and some works were later re-recorded; one, Mahler's Symphony No. 6, was taken from a concert performance at Cleveland in 1967. The music recorded included Haydn's Symphonies Nos 88 and 92 to 104, Mozart's Symphonies Nos 28, 33, 35, 39, 40 and 41, *Eine kleine Nachtmusik*, the Serenade K. 320, the Divertimento K. 131, the overtures to *Le nozze di Figaro* and *Der Schauspieldirektor*, Piano Concertos K. 450, K. 453, K. 467 and K. 491 (with Robert Casadesus) and K. 503 (with Fleischer), Violin Concertos K. 216 and K. 219 (with Stern), Clarinet Concerto (with Marcellus), Sinfonia Concertante K. 364 (with Druian and Skernick) and *Exsultate jubilate* (with Raskin), the Beethoven symphonies, the overtures *Leonore Nos 1, 2* and *3, Fidelio, Coriolan, Egmont*, and *König Stephan* and the five Piano Concertos (separately with Fleischer and Gilels), Schubert's Symphonies Nos 8 and 9 and the incidental music to *Rosamunde*, Mendelssohn's Symphony No. 4, Violin Concerto (with Francescatti), incidental music to *A Midsummer Night's Dream* and the overture *The Hebrides*, the Rossini overtures *La gazza ladra, L'Italiana in Algeri, La scala di seta, Il Turco in Italia* and *Il viaggio a Reims*, Liszt's Piano Concerto No. 2 (with Robert Casadesus), Weber's *Konzertstück* (with Casadesus), the four Schumann symphonies, *Manfred* overture and Piano Concerto (with Fleischer), the four Brahms symphonies, *Academic Festival* and *Tragic Overtures*, *Variations on the St Antony Chorale*, the two Piano Concertos (separately with Serkin and Fleischer), the Violin Concerto (with David Oistrakh) and Double Concerto (with Oistrakh and Rostropovich), Bruckner's Symphonies Nos 3 and 8, Dvořák's Symphonies Nos 7, 8 and 9, *Slavonic Dances* Opp. 46 and 72, *Carnival* overture and Piano Concerto (with Firkusny), Smetana's *Aus meinem Leben*, the overture and dances from *The Bartered Bride*, and *Moldau*, Tchaikovsky's Symphony No. 5, *Capriccio italien* and Piano Concerto No. 1 (with Graffman), the Entry of the Gods into Valhalla from *Das Rheingold*, the Ride of the Valkyries and Magic Fire Music from *Die Walküre*, Forest Murmurs from *Siegfried*, the Rhine Journey and Funeral Music from *Götterdämmerung*, *Eine Faust Ouvertüre*, the preludes to *Lohengrin* and *Die Meistersinger*, the overtures to *Rienzi* and *Tannhäuser* and the prelude and Liebestod from *Tristan und Isolde*, a disc of music by Johann Strauss, *La Mer*, the *Daphnis et Chloé* Suite No. 2 and *Pavane pour une infante défunte*, the *L'Arlésienne* Suite No. 1, the *Peer Gynt* Suite No. 1, *Don Juan*, *Till Eulenspiegel*, *Tod und Verklärung*, *Symphonia domestica* and *Don Quixote* (with Fournier) and Strauss's Horn Concerto No. 1 (with Bloom), Mahler's Symphonies No. 4 (with Raskin) and 6, and the Purgatorio from the Symphony No. 10, *Pictures at an Exhibition*, the prelude to *Khovanshchina*, *Capriccio espagnol*, the Polovtsian Dances from *Prince Igor*, Prokofiev's Symphony No. 5, *Lieutenant Kijé* suite and Piano Concertos Nos 1 and 3 (with Graffman), Bartók's *Concerto for Orchestra*, Janáček's *Sinfonietta*, the *Háry János* suite, Rachmaninov's *Rhapsody on a Theme of Paganini*, the Grieg Piano Concerto, and Franck's *Symphonic Variations* (with Fleischer), Hindemith's *Symphonic Metamorphosis on Themes by Weber*, the prelude from Delius' *Irmelin*, *L'Oiseau de feu*, Walton's Symphony No. 2, *Partita* and *Variations on a Theme of Hindemith*, Barber's Piano Concerto (with Browning) and Schuman's *Song of Orpheus* (with Rose).

Szell also recorded with the Amsterdam Concertgebouw Orchestra; for Decca he led Brahms' Symphony No. 3 and Dvořák's Symphony No. 8, both amongst the first Decca LPs, and both performances still revered by collectors, and for Philips Mozart's Symphony No. 34, Beethoven's Symphony No. 5, the incidental music from *A Midsummer Night's Dream* and Sibelius' Symphony No. 2. For Decca he also recorded the Tchaikovsky Symphony No. 4, suites from the *Water Music* (arranged by Harty and Szell), the *Music for the Royal Fireworks* (arr. Harty), the minuet from *The Faithful Shepherd* (arr. Beecham) and 'Ombra mai fu' from *Xerxes* (the so-called Largo, arr. Reinhard) of Handel (with the London Symphony Orchestra) and the *Egmont* music of Beethoven (with Lorengar and the Vienna Philharmonic Orchestra); for DGG, the Dvořák Cello Concerto (with Fournier and the Berlin Philharmonic Orchestra); for EMI Strauss's *Vier letzte Lieder* and five other songs (with Schwarzkopf and the Berlin Radio Symphony Orchestra), Mahler's *Des Knaben Wunderhorn* (with Schwarzkopf, Fischer-Dieskau and the London Symphony Orchestra) and concert arias by Mozart and some songs by Strauss (with the London Symphony Orchestra); for CBS (Columbia) with the Columbia Symphony Orchestra Bach's *Violin Concerto in E major* and the Mendelssohn Violin Concerto (with Francescatti), Tartini's *Violin Concerto in D minor* (with Szigeti), and Mozart's Piano Concertos K. 453 and K. 503 (with Serkin), K. 414, K. 482, K. 491 and K. 537 (with Robert Casadesus) and the Two-Piano Concerto K. 365 (with Robert and Gaby Casadesus), and for Music Appreciation Bach's Suite No. 3, also *Moldau* and *Till Eulenspiegel*. Szell has also recorded as a pianist; on 78s, he accompanied Bohnen in Loewe's *Der Erlkönig*, and later, on LP, he joined members of the Budapest String Quartet in Mozart's Piano Quartets K. 478 and K. 493, and the concertmaster of the Cleveland Orchestra, Rafael Druian, in Mozart's Violin and Piano Sonatas K. 296, K. 301, K. 304 and K. 376 (for Columbia).

Many of these records remain available in Britain and the United States, sometimes reissued on cheaper labels. The quality of the performances will ensure their constant revival in the future; perhaps Szell is more fortunate than Toscanini and Furtwängler in that the magnificence of his musicianship emerges more clearly on records. Szell has had a significant influence on a number of young conductors, but there is always the danger that the lesson learnt from him is that precision is enough.

Szenkar, Eugen (b. 1891). Born in Budapest, Szenkar studied at the Budapest Academy with his father, Ferdinand Szenkar, who was a prominent organist and composer. He was conductor at the German Opera, Prague (1911–13), the Budapest Popular Opera (1913–15), the Salzburg Mozarteum (1915–16), Altenburg (1916–20), the Frankfurt am Main Opera (1920–23), the Berlin Volksoper (1923–4), and the Cologne Opera (1924–33). He left Germany, was artistic director of the Moscow Philharmonic Orchestra (1934–7), emigrated to Brazil where he took Brazilian nationality (1941), and founded and was conductor of the Brazilian Symphony Orchestra at Rio de Janeiro (1939–49). He returned to Germany in 1950, was general music director at Mannheim (1950–52), Düsseldorf (1952–60), was conductor at the Deutsche Oper am Rhein (from 1959), and conducted in many European cities. He performed mostly Bartók, Kodály, Strauss and Mahler, was made an honorary member of the International Gustav Mahler Association, and composed symphonic, chamber and vocal music. For Ariola/Eurodisc he recorded with the Cologne Radio Symphony Orchestra *Hungarian Rhapsodies* Nos 1 and 2 and *Les Préludes* of Liszt, and Moldau and Vyšehrad from Smetana's *Má Vlast*.

Szeryng, Henryk (b. 1918). Born in Warsaw, the violin virtuoso Szeryng studied with Flesch, Nadia Boulanger and Bouillon, and was a liaison officer in London to General Sikorski in World War II, after which he went to Mexico. There he taught for 12 years at the faculty of music at the National University and became a Mexican citizen. His international career began after meeting Rubinstein in Mexico in 1954. He has made numerous superlative recordings of the violin concerto repertoire; his appearances on record as a conductor have been in Vivaldi's *Four Seasons* (for RCA/Erato) and Violin Concertos Op. 3 Nos 6, 8, 9 and 10 (for Philips), both with the English Chamber Orchestra and with himself as the soloist, and the two Violin Concertos and Double-Concerto of Bach (with himself and Rybar and the Collegium Musicum at Winterthur, for Mercury).

T

Tabachnik, Michel (b. 1942). Born in Geneva where he studied at the Conservatory, Tabachnik was a pupil of Stockhausen, Pousseur and Boulez at Darmstadt, studied conducting with Boulez at Basel, and became his assistant (1967–71). He has conducted many of the major European orchestras, and is permanent conductor of the Gulbenkian Foundation Orchestra, the European Contemporary Music Ensemble and the Lorraine Philharmonic Orchestra. His compositions have been for orchestra and smaller ensembles. Barclay have issued a disc in which he conducts the Paris ORTF Orchestra in Honegger's Symphony No. 1, *Horace victorieux* and *Mouvement symphonique No. 3*.

Talich, Václav (1883–1961). Born in Kroměříž in Moravia, Talich received his first music lessons from his father, who was a music teacher and composer. He studied the violin with Sevčik at the Prague Conservatory (1897–1903), was a violinist in the Berlin Philharmonic Orchestra and concertmaster at the Odessa Opera (1905), and taught the violin at Tiflis (1906–7), where he first conducted. He returned to Prague, conducted choirs and an orchestral society of amateurs (1907–8), then studied briefly with Reger and Nikisch in Leipzig, and with Vigno in Milan. He became conductor of the orchestra at Ljubljana (1908–12) and the Opera at Plzeň, where he also taught the violin and played the viola in the Bohemian String Quartet, and was a teacher and conductor in Prague (1915–18). In 1918 the Czech Philharmonic Orchestra was reconstituted, and Talich was appointed its chief conductor; with the orchestra he toured the major European cities a number of times in the next decade or so. In 1935 he succeeded Ostrčil as conductor of the Prague National Opera, and to devote full time to this position he resigned from the Czech Philharmonic in 1941. He was also conductor of the Scottish National Orchestra at Glasgow (1926–7) and of the Konsertföreningen Orchestra at Stockholm (1931–4).

At the end of World War II, Talich relinquished his position at the Prague Opera; the reason for his departure is variously attributed to disputes within the company, and accusations that he collaborated with the Nazis during the war. He was cleared of these charges, returned to the company in 1947–8, but soon found himself in disagreement with the communist regime and was dismissed from all his appointments in 1948. Subsequently he became conductor of a chamber ensemble in Bratislava (1949), returned to the Czech Philharmonic Orchestra as artistic adviser (1954), and was awarded the title of National Artist (1957). It is generally agreed that Talich was the first Czech conductor to command an international reputation; he built the Czech Philharmonic into one of the finest ensembles in Europe, a distinction it can claim to the present day. His musical personality is described as forceful, spirited and temperamental; although his tastes were catholic, he was especially distinguished for his highly idiomatic performances of Czech music.

Talich made a number of recordings with the Czech Philharmonic Orchestra. He first recorded for HMV in 1934 Dvořák's Symphony No. 8, and afterwards the overtures *Carnival* and *Amid Nature*, the Symphonies Nos 6 and 7, the Slavonic Dances Opp. 46 and 72 and two Waltzes Op. 54 Nos 1 and 4, Smetana's *Libuše* overture and *Má Vlast*, Suk's *Serenade*, *Fairy Tale Suite* and march *Into a New Life*, and Tchaikovsky's Piano Concerto No. 1 (with Wolf). For Columbia he also recorded, on 78s, the Tchaikovsky Violin Concerto (with Schneiderhan). His recordings for Supraphon included the Mozart Violin Concerto K. 218 (with Novák) and Sinfonia Concertante K. 297b, Benda's *Symphony in B flat* and Bach's Harpsichord Concerto No. 1 (with Richter), Dvořák's Symphony No. 9, *Slavonic Dances* Opp. 46 and 72, *The Golden Spinning Wheel*, *The Water Goblin*, *The Noonday Witch*, *The Wood Dove*, the *Othello* overture, *Serenade in E major* (with the Prague Soloists Orchestra), Cello Concerto (with Rostropovich), Piano Concerto (with Maxian) and *Stabat Mater*, Smetana's *Má Vlast*, *The Prague Carnival* and polka *To Our Damsels*, Tchaikovsky's Symphony No. 6, Suk's *Asrael* Symphony, *Serenade* and symphonic poem *Ripening*, and Janáček's *Taras Bulba*. He also recorded, with the Slovak Philharmonic Orchestra for Supraphon, Bach's Suite No. 3, Mozart's Symphony No. 33, Tchaikovsky's Suite No. 4 and Novák's *Slavonic Suite*, and with the Prague Radio Symphony Orchestra the prelude to *Tristan und Isolde*. A number of these performances have been re-issued in recent years.

Tango, Egisto (1873–1951). Born in Rome, Tango first studied engineering, and then attended the Naples Conservatory, and made his debut as a conductor at the Venice Opera in 1893. He conducted at La Scala, Milan (1895), in Berlin (1903–8), at the New York Metropolitan Opera (1909–10), in Italy (1911–12), at Budapest (1913–19), in Germany and Austria (1920–26), and from 1927 was conductor of the Royal Orchestra at Copenhagen. In Budapest he led the premières of Bartók's *The Wooden Prince* (1917) and *Duke Bluebeard's Castle* (1918), which were significant events in establishing the composer in his native country. Tango's performances were invariably distinguished by their clarity and precision. He recorded with the Royal Orchestra, Copenhagen, the overtures to *Semiramide* and *Der Freischütz*, Nielsen's Violin Concerto (with Telmanyi) and the overture and excerpts from *Maskarade* (for Tono), Nielsen's *Saga-drøm* and accompaniments to arias sung by Schiøtz, Islandi and Brenis (for HMV), and with the Danish Radio Symphony Orchestra Mozart's Symphony No. 40 (for Tono).

Tátrai, Vilmos (b. 1912). Born at Kispest, Hungary, Tátrai studied the violin at the Budapest Conservatory, and as a student organised a string quartet that was to become the famous Hungarian String Quartet. He was a violinist with the Budapest Symphony Orchestra (1933), the Hungarian Radio Orchestra (1938), and was concertmaster of the Metropolitan State Concert Orchestra (1940), taught at the Bartók Music High School (1946–53), and in 1946 founded the Tátrai String Quartet, with which he toured in Eastern and Western Europe many times with tremendous success. Then in 1952 he organised the Hungarian Chamber Orchestra, and again toured in many countries and took part in numerous festivals. His awards include the first prize at the Bartók Competition (1948), the Liszt Prize (1952 and 1972), the Kossuth Prize (1958), Eminent Artist of the Hungarian People's Republic and the Labour Order of Merit, golden degree.

In addition to his many recordings with the Tátrai Quartet, Tátrai has conducted the Hungarian Chamber Orchestra in a series of discs, issued by Qualiton and Hungaroton. These included concertos for two harpsichords by J. S. and W. F. Bach (with Sebestyén), Corelli's Concerto Grosso Op. 6 No. 8, Tartini's *Cello Concerto in D major* (with Dénes), Vivaldi's *Symphony in G minor*, Haydn's Symphonies Nos 6, 7, 8, 20, 26, 27, 31, 39, 43, 44, 45, 47, 49, 54, 55, 56, 59, 67, 68 and 73, Michael's Haydn's *Symphony in D major*, Leopold Mozart's *Divertimenti in B flat* and *C major*, Mozart's Symphonies Nos 33 and 40, Divertimento K. 251, Serenade K. 375, *Serenata notturna*, *Eine kleine Nachtmusik*, Sinfonia Concertante K. 297b and Piano Concerto K. 449 (with Rados), a Dittersdorf harpsichord concerto, Werner's Harpsichord Pastorale and *Prelude and Fugue in C*, Albrechtberger's *Harpsichord Concerto in B major* (with Sebestyén), Gassman's *Sinfonia in A*, an overture by Süssmayr, Szervánsky's Serenade, Monn's *Harpsichord Concerto in D major* (with Sebestyén), Volkmann's Serenade No. 2, Wranitzky's *Symphony in C*, Bartók's Divertimento, two Divertimenti by Weiner, Rózsavölgyi's *Elsö magyar társastánc – Serkentö*, and *Souvenir of Nógrád – Halljuk!*, Sárközi's *Sinfonia concertante* and *Concerto Grosso*, and Sárai's *Serenade*.

Tauber, Richard (1892–1948). The celebrated lyric tenor Tauber was born in Linz, studied at Hoch's Conservatory, Frankfurt am Main, and made his debut at Chemnitz, where his father was intendant. He became noted especially for his roles in the Mozart operas at Dresden, Berlin, Salzburg, Vienna, Munich, London and elsewhere; later in his life his interest turned towards operetta and lighter music, and he won an immensely popular following. He also composed *Old Chelsea* and other operettas, and wrote music for films in which he appeared. In 1940 he became a naturalised British subject. In addition to his many operatic, lieder and other vocal records, Columbia (US) issued a 78 r.p.m. disc in which he conducted the London Symphony Orchestra in an orchestral selection from *La Bohème*.

Tausky, Vilem (b. 1910). Born in Prerov in Czechoslovakia, Tausky studied at the University and Conservatory at Brno, and at the Meisterschule at Prague under Janáček and Suk; as a young man he represented Czechoslovakia as goalkeeper in football matches throughout Europe. At 19 he became a conductor at the Brno Opera (1929–39), and at the outbreak of World War II he came to Britain where he joined the Free Czechoslovak army and also conducted the major British orchestras. He is now a naturalised British subject. He was conductor and musical director of the Carl Rosa Opera Company (1946–50), joined the BBC (1949), was musical director of the BBC Northern Orchestra (1951–66), conducted music for radio concerts ranging from light variety programmes to contemporary compositions, appeared with the London opera companies and provincial orchestras, and toured many European countries. His recordings include the overtures to *Fra Diavolo* and *Les Deux Aveugles de Tolède* (with the Royal Philharmonic Orchestra for EMI), accompaniments to arias sung by Joan Hammond (with the Philharmonia Orchestra for EMI) and duets from operas by Joan Hammond and Charles Craig (with the Royal Philharmonic Orchestra for EMI), to arias sung by Brychan Powell (with the Delyse Symphony Orchestra for Delyse), and excerpts from *Das Land des Lächelns* and *Der Zigeunerbaron* (with the Sadler's Wells Opera Company for EMI). His *Concerto for Harmonica and Orchestra* has been recorded by Reilly and the Academy of St Martin-in-the-Fields, conducted by Marriner (for Argo).

Tavener, John (b. 1944). Born in London and educated at the Royal Academy of Music, Tavener has been organist at the St John's Church, Kensington, London, since 1960. His cantata *The Whale* was performed at the inaugural concert of the London Sinfonietta in January 1968, and since then he has become widely known for a number of compositions, including *A Celtic Requiem*, *Coplas* and *Nomine Jesu*, which, with *The Whale*, have been recorded. He himself has conducted his *Requiem for Father Malachy* (with the King's Singers) and *Canciones españolas* (with the Nash Ensemble *et al.*), for RCA.

Telmányi, Emil (b. 1892). Born in Arad, Habsburg Empire (now Romania), Telemányi was a pupil of Hubay at the Budapest Academy, made his first solo appearance at the age of 10, won a number of prizes for the violin, and toured extensively as a violin virtuoso. In 1911 he gave the first performance in Germany of the Elgar Violin Concerto, at a remarkable debut in Berlin. His first wife was the daughter of the composer Nielsen. He settled in Copenhagen in 1919, and in 1929 founded and conducted a chamber orchestra. He also conducted opera at Copenhagen, visited Budapest in 1926 to lead a concert of music by Stravinsky, who was soloist in his Piano Concerto, was awarded the Carl Nielsen Medal (1953), and became professor of violin at the Århus Conservatory. In addition to his recordings as a violinist, which included the Bach solo works performed with the Vega (arched) bow, he conducted the Vivaldi Concerto Grosso Op. 3 No. 11 (on 78s, with the Telmányi Chamber Orchestra, for Tono).

Temianka, Henri (b. 1906). Born in Greenock, Scotland, Temianka studied in Rotterdam, Berlin and Paris, and at the Curtis Institute of Music at Philadelphia under Flesch. He made his debut as a violinist in New York in 1928, toured widely, was a member of the Paganini String Quartet, and formed and conducted the California Chamber Symphony Orchestra in Los Angeles. His publications include articles for many journals and an autobiography, *Facing the Music* (1973). In addition to his records as a violinist and chamber player, he conducted Ginastera's *Cantata para América mágica* and Chávez's *Toccata for Percussion Instruments* (with the Los Angeles Percussion Ensemble, for CBS).

Temirkanov, Yuri (b. 1938). After graduating from the Leningrad Conservatory in viola and conducting, Temirkanov made his debut at the Maly Opera House with *La traviata*, and won first prize at the national conducting competition in 1966. He was conductor of the Leningrad Philharmonic Orchestra (1968), became principal conductor at the Kirov Theatre (1976), conducted orchestras in Sweden, Denmark, Finland, the United States and elsewhere, and is principal guest conductor of the Royal Philharmonic Orchestra in London. His recordings have been of Haydn's Symphonies Nos 6, 7 and 8, and van Swieten's *Symphony in E flat* (with the Leningrad Chamber Orchestra), the Tchaikovsky Violin Concerto (with Kremer and the USSR State Symphony Orchestra), *Petrushka*, Petrov's ballet *The Creation of the World*, and Tsytovich's *The Good Soldier Schweik* (with the Leningrad Orchestra *et al.*), for Melodiya.

Terian, Mikhail. A teacher of conducting and principal conductor of the Moscow Conservatory Chamber Orchestra, Terian founded the Moscow Youth Chamber Orchestra which won first prize at the Karajan Youth Orchestra Competition in Berlin. With the Moscow Conservatory Chamber Orchestra he has recorded for Melodiya Corelli's Concerto Grosso Op. 6 No. 1, Cello Concertos of Boccherini, Tartini and Vivaldi (with Gutman), Bach's *Fugue in A minor* (arranged by Helmesberger), the *Andante cantabile* from Tchaikovsky's String Quartet No. 1, and Arensky's *Variations on a Theme by Tchaikovsky*.

Terry, Sir Richard (1865–1938). Born in Ellington, Northumberland, Terry was organist and choirmaster at St John's Cathedral, Antigua, West Indies (1892), at Downside Abbey, Somerset (1896) and then at Westminster Cathedral (1901–24). He was the first to give liturgical performances in recent years of the masses of Byrd, Tallis, Mundy *et al.* and of other Tudor sacred music. He resigned from his position at Westminster Cathedral because of his insistence on using such music rather than that which was more immediately popular. He composed masses and other sacred music, edited the *Westminster Hymnal*, wrote *Catholic Church Music* (1907), edited *Musical News*, collections of Tudor motets and folksongs and a *Shanty Book*, and published a performing edition of Byrd's 5-part Mass. His recordings included Palestrina's *Missa Papae Marcelli* and *Nunc dimittis* (with the Westminster Cathedral Choir for HMV and Columbia respectively).

Teutsch, Karol (b. 1921). Born in Kraków, into a family of musicians, Teutsch was taught the violin by his father, who was concertmaster at the Lvov Opera and a professor at the Kraków University. He studied at the High School for Music at Kraków, studied conducting with Bierdiajew and commenced a career as a violin soloist, but this was interrupted by World War II. He became concertmaster of the Kraków Philharmonic Orchestra (1945–59), then went to the National Philharmonic Orchestra at Warsaw, formed the Warsaw Chamber Orchestra (1962) which was made up of members of the Philharmonic Orchestra and of instrumentalists lecturing at the State Academy of Music at Warsaw, and with it soon achieved an international reputation, performing a wide repertoire of baroque, classical and modern music. The Polish record company have released over 50 recordings of the orchestra under Teutsch; some have also been issued by Telefunken, Schwann and Bärenreiter, and in the United States by Musical Heritage Society. Included among the works recorded have been Vivaldi's *Four Seasons* and *Stabat Mater*, concertos by Telemann, Bach, Vivaldi, J. C. Bach, Boccherini, Haydn, Corette, Mozart, Pergolesi and Marcello, Pergolesi's *Salve Regina*, the Organ Concertos of Handel (with Bucher), Mozart's Piano Concertos K. 271, K. 414, K. 453, K. 488, K. 491 and K. 595 (with Buchbinder) and Violin Concertos K. 207 and K. 218 (with Danczowska) and K. 216 and K. 219 (with Jakowicz), several symphonies and divertimenti by Haydn and Mozart, Mozart's Sinfonia Concertante K. 364, Jarzębski's *Bentrovata a 3*, *Canzoni*, *Chromatica a 3*, *Nova Casa a 3*, *Sentinella a 3* and *Tamboretta a 3*, Mielczewski's *Canzona a 3*, Baird's *Four Love Sonnets*, Bacewicz's *Divertimento*, works by Górecki and Paciorkiewicz, and a collection in the series Musica Antiqua Polonica.

Thomas, Kurt (1904–73). Born in Tönning in Schleswig-Holstein, Thomas studied at the Leipzig Conservatory with Grabner, took lessons from A. Mendelssohn at Darmstadt, and was assisted by Straube. He taught at the Leipzig Conservatory (1925–34), at the Hochschule für Musik in Berlin (1934–9) and at Frankfurt am Main (1939–45) and at the Detmold Academy (1947–55); he was kantor at the St Thomas Church at Leipzig, where he succeeded Ramin (1956–60), then returned to FR Germany and taught at the Academies of Music at Hamburg (1960–66) and Lübeck (1966–73). His early compositions, especially an *a capella* mass and a *St Mark Passion* (both 1926), made a strong impression, and his other compositions included a piano trio, a piano concerto, instrumental sonatas and sacred music. Thomas's recordings included Bach's Cantatas Nos 4, 7, 11, 51, 54, 56, 59, 68, 71, 82, 111, 140 and 201, the *Magnificat* and *Christmas Oratorio* (with the Leipzig Gewandhaus Orchestra *et al.* for EMI), Cantatas Nos 68 and 70, the *Mass in B minor*, *St John Passion* and *St Matthew Passion* (with the Frankfurt Collegium Musicum *et al.* for L'Oiseau Lyre), the *Christmas Oratorio* (with the Detmold Academy Orchestra *et al.* for L'Oiseau Lyre), the Motets (with the St Thomas' Church Choir, Leipzig, for DGG), Cantatas Nos 23 and 159 (with the German Bach Soloists *et al.*, issued by Musical Heritage Society) and Cantatas Nos 23 and 159 (with the Cantate Orchestra *et al.* for Cantate), C. P. E. Bach's *Magnificat* (with the Collegium Aureum *et al.* for Harmonia Mundi and issued in the US by Victrola), Handel's Organ Concertos Op. 4 (with Kohler and the Leipzig Gewandhaus Orchestra for EMI) and Schütz's *Christmas Story* (with the Frankfurt Dreikönigskirche Kantorei, for L'Oiseau Lyre).

Thomas, Mansel (b. 1909). Born in Tylorstown, Wales, Thomas studied at the Royal Academy of Music, London, and at Durham University, and was employed by the BBC as a musical assistant for BBC Wales (1936–9), as conductor of the BBC Review Orchestra (1941–3) and the BBC Welsh Orchestra (1946–50), and from 1950 as head of music, BBC Wales. He served in the British army (1943–6), mainly in Brussels, where he conducted the Belgian National Orchestra. His compositions include choral, orchestral and chamber works. He recorded, for Decca in 1950, Grace Williams' *Fantasia on Welsh Nursery Tunes* (with the London Symphony Orchestra), Francis Williams' *Christmas Miniature*, Hubert Davies' *Minuet-Hoffder Gwenllian*, and D. Vaughan Williams' *Seven Songs on Welsh Poems* (with the Boyd Neel String Orchestra *et al.*), and for Delyse a recital of oratorio excerpts (with Geraint Evans and the BBC Welsh Orchestra).

Thomas, Michael Tilson (b. 1944). Thomas was born in Hollywood, where his father was a film writer, producer and director; his grandfather was Boris Tomashefsky who had come to the United States from Kiev and had helped to found the Yiddish Theatre in New York, and his uncle the actor Paul Muni. Thomas was playing the piano by ear at the age of five, and later studied the piano and oboe as a boy. At the University of Southern California he first studied science but changed to music, taking piano with John Crown and theory and conducting with Ingolf Dahl. His career as a conductor started with the Young Musicians' Foundation Orchestra and at the Monday Evening Concerts at the Los Angeles Museum, which were noted for presentations of new music. He assisted Boulez at the Ojai Festival in California, then went to Bayreuth in 1966 to study at Friedland Wagner's classes, but stayed to assist Boulez rehearse *Parsifal*, and to play the glockenspiel at the actual performances. He has said he came to Bayreuth to examine the reasons for his antipathy for Wagner, but remained to admire.

In 1968 Thomas was conducting fellow with the Boston Symphony Orchestra at Tanglewood, was awarded the Koussevitzky Prize, and was engaged as assistant conductor with the Boston Symphony. In October 1969 he substituted for the ailing Steinberg in the middle of a concert, was immediately acclaimed as a remarkable conducting talent, and went on to conduct 37 more concerts with the orchestra that season. In 1970 he was appointed associate conductor, and then was offered the position of permanent conductor; he refused it, and instead became musical director of the Buffalo Philharmonic Orchestra. He has appeared as a guest conductor in London, Tokyo, Tel-Aviv and in other musical centres, as well as conducting major orchestras in the United States.

A highly strung, mercurial and very articulate personality, Thomas has explained (in an interview with Stephen Rubin in the *New York Times*, October 1976) why he refused the Boston appointment. 'I was not joyous about the spirit of musicmaking that was going on. I got tired of looking at people whose eyes were totally dead, whose jaws were utterly fixed in some totally defensive grimace telling me, "Oh no! This is not the nobility of Beethoven!" "This is not what Beethoven's ideas are!" "This is not the way you should perform this!" "This is not respectable". . . . I cannot commit my time to situations where, however glamorous, however progressing up the ladder of a career they may be, you know that you are not going to be getting down to the real question. . . . What I feel now about the big orchestras is that they are excellent ensembles. Because of time and money questions, however, there is no more any leisurely approach to anything. . . . So what they need is a continual stream of personal messiahs. . . . It's a very quantified American approach, a technique we've developed we don't know what to do with yet. Mostly it's used for questions like let's have a little less rehearsal time so that we can a little more efficiently produce another of those "certified by Good Housekeeping" performances. For me, such performances are finally, totally uninteresting . . . I want to be astonished, excited, delighted, outraged.' Recording then perplexes him, as the permanency of any one particular performance is to him not realistic. He questions talk about favourite or 'best' performances: 'In symphonic music there is only permissible mean deviation between the Toscanini version and the Furtwängler' (*New York Times*, 28 October 1971).

Boulez was Thomas's major teacher of conducting, and his baton technique is clear and easy to follow, his movements on the podium economical and graceful, and his manner with the orchestra warm and appreciative. He has an exceptional memory, assimilates scores quickly, plans rehearsals carefully, and while he is meticulous in preparing performances, prefers to leave the final touches to the inspiration of the moment at the concert itself. Reflecting the cultural background of his childhood and youth in Los Angeles, his musical interests are extraordinarily wide, and embrace literally every form of music, without any apparent discrimination. He does not believe that one kind of music is intrinsically superior to any other; away from the symphony orchestra he listens to Japanese, Balinese, Indian and other ethnic music, is a connoisseur of rock music and is a warm admirer of James Brown, the soul singer. His own favourite composers are Stravinsky, Mahler, Ravel and Debussy, as well as Renaissance and early baroque music. At Buffalo he gives his audiences the widest musical perspectives, on the principle that they should hear the music of the past eight centuries, not one and a half centuries. His criticism of fellow conductors who only know and perform music from Haydn to the early 20th century almost borders on scorn; he believes that it is scarcely possible to perform even this music without understanding what came before it, back as far as the Middle Ages. In Los Angeles, Thomas was noticed by the composer Stanley Silverman, who wrote his multi-media opera *Elephant Steps* with Thomas's talents in mind, and Thomas premièred the work at Tanglewood in 1968. A two-disc recording of the work, with him conducting, was issued by CBS in 1975; it was an admirable vehicle for Thomas to demonstrate his comprehensive musical eclecticism, employing pop singers, opera singers, orchestra, rock band, electronic tape, raga group, tape recorder, gypsy ensemble and elephants. Many critics were impressed, some were not. Levering Bronston of *The New Records* wrote: '*Elephant Steps* is a pretentious clap-trap, a monstrous put-on, a congeries of unattractive tunes in a mish-mash of hard acid and soft rock styles. Give me the zoo anytime. . .'

Far removed from the controversial *Elephant Steps* are the other records Thomas has made. When DGG signed up the Boston Symphony Orchestra in 1970, Steinberg and Thomas were included in the contract; his recordings with the orchestra have been an attractive Tchaikovsky Symphony No. 1, a brilliant Debussy disc of *Images* and the *Prélude à l'après-midi d'un faune*, an equally good *Le Sacre du printemps* coupled with Stravinsky's cantata *The King of the Stars*, and two discs of American music, which he has done much to champion – Ives' *Three Places in New England*, Ruggles' *Suntreader*, Piston's Symphony No. 2 and Schuman's Violin Concerto (with Zukofsky). Thomas' exceptional abilities as a pianist are shown in a recital of Debussy's chamber music by the Boston Symphony Chamber Players, issued by DGG in 1971. For CBS he also recorded *An American in Paris* (with the New York Philharmonic Orchestra), and Orff's *Carmina Burana* (with the Cleveland Orchestra *et al.*).

Thomas, Patrick (b. 1932). Born in Brisbane Thomas started his career as an organist and choirmaster, was a flautist with the Queensland Symphony Orchestra for five years, and in 1963 was appointed a conductor with the Australian Elizabethan Theatre Trust Opera Company and the Australian Ballet Company. After being assistant then chief conductor of the Adelaide Symphony Orchestra, musical director of the New Zealand National Opera Company and chief conductor of the Tasmanian Symphony Orchestra, in 1973 he became chief conductor of the Queensland Symphony Orchestra. His repertoire extends from Bach to the music of contemporary Australian composers, and he was widely applauded for his direction of Janáček's *The Excursion of Mr Brouček*, at the Adelaide Festival of Arts in 1974. He conducted the Sydney Symphony Orchestra in three of its international tours. Thomas has recorded Mozart's Flute Concerto No. 1 (with Amadeo) and Sinfonia Concertante K. 297b (with the Sydney Symphony Orchestra *et al.* for RCA), a collection of marches for orchestra (with the Queensland Symphony Orchestra for EMI), and music by Australian composers: Banks' Violin Concerto (with Dommett and the Melbourne Symphony Orchestra for World Record Club), Brumby's *Charlie Bubbles Book of Hours*, Hill's Symphony *Joy of Life*, Penberthy's *Cantata on Hiroshima Panels*, Wesley-Smith's *Interval Piece* and Tibbits' *I Thought You Were All Glittering With Noblest of Carriage* (with the South Australian Symphony Orchestra *et al.* for Festival), Dobie's *Dimensions* (with the West Australia Symphony Orchestra for Festival), Hurst's *Swagman's Promenade* and *Traditional Overture* and James' *Australian Christmas Carols* (with the South Australia Symphony Orchestra *et al.* for EMI), Lovelock's *Sinfonia concertante* (with the South Australia Symphony Orchestra for RCA), Meale's *Soon It Will Die* (with the South Australia Symphony Orchestra for WRC) and Sutherland's *The Young Kabbarli* (with the New Opera Orchestra *et al.* for EMI).

Thome, Joel. After receiving his musical education at the Eastman School of Music, the University of Pennsylvania and the École Internationale in Nice, France, Thome studied conducting with Genhart and Boulez. He has led the Group L'Itinéraire in Paris, was an associate to the Electronic Music Sound Research Center of the Hebrew University in Jerusalem, and founded and conducted the First Israel Percussion Ensemble. Since 1965 he has been music director and conductor of the Philadelphia Composers' Forum; he is also director and conductor of the American Symphony Orchestra da Camera and conductor of the Erick Hawkins Dance Company, and music director and conductor of the Orchestra of Our Time, a major group in performing 20th-century music. He has composed music in many modes, and as a percussionist has performed with the Rochester Symphony Orchestra and the Israel Philharmonic Orchestra. For Desto he has recorded Crumb's *Songs, Drones and Refrains of Death* (with Weller and the Philadelphia Composers' Forum Performing Group), and for Candide Boulez's *Improvisation No. 2*, Dallapiccola's *Concerto for Christmas* and *Parole di San Paolo*, and

Pousseur's *Trois Chants sacrés* (with the same ensemble).

Thomson, Virgil (b. 1896). The American composer and critic Thomson was born in Kansas City, graduated from Harvard University, and studied with Nadia Boulanger in Paris (1921–2). He was organist at King's Chapel, Boston (1922–3), won a Juilliard Fellowship (1923), and in Paris, between 1925 and 1939, came into contact with Les Six, the group of modern French composers, and Gertrude Stein, whose texts he used in his operas *Four Saints in Three Acts* (1928) and *The Mother of Us All* (1947). He was chief music critic for the *New York Herald Tribune* (1940–54), and his perceptive writings are an important account of music in New York, and in the United States, in that period. As a conductor, he led the Philadelphia Orchestra in 1942 with a suite from his film score for *The Plow that Broke the Plains*, and later conducted the New York Philharmonic-Symphony Orchestra. He made 78 r.p.m. recordings of his *Five Portraits* and *Three Pictures* (with the Philadelphia Orchestra for Columbia, US), and an abridged version of *Four Saints in Three Acts* (for RCA-Victor); the latter, although issued in 1948, featured a number of the soloists who appeared in the 1934 première. Many of his other compositions are currently listed in Schwann, including *The Mother of Us All*, in a performance by Leppard and the Sante Fe Opera Company (for New World).

Thorne, Gordon (b. 1912). Born at Wimbledon and educated at Christ's College, Cambridge, the Royal College of Music and the Trinity College of Music, Thorne was assistant organist at St Margaret's, Westminster (1929–30), director of music at Bradfield College (1934–7), deputy conductor of the BBC Northern Orchestra (1938–40 and 1946–53), and head of music, BBC Northern Region and conductor of the BBC Northern Singers (1953–9). In 1961 Saga issued discs in which he conducted the BBC Northern Singers in Liszt's *Via Crucis* and *Missa choralis*.

Tichý, Jan (b. 1921). Born in Zamberk, Czechoslovakia, Tichý studied at the Prague Conservatory (1939–43), became a repetiteur at the Prague National Theatre (1945), made his debut there as a conductor with *Les Contes d'Hoffmann* (1946) and was appointed a conductor in 1950. He has directed both opera and ballet, has toured the USSR, and conducted opera at České Budějovice. For Supraphon he has recorded Smetana's *The Brandenburgers in Bohemia* and a disc of arias from Tchaikovsky operas, with the Prague National Theatre Orchestra *et al.*

Tieri, Emidio (1910–58). Born in Rome, Tieri studied with Brugnoli at the Rome Conservatory, with Frazzi in Florence and with Guarnieri in Siena. He conducted in theatres, at concerts and at numerous festivals, and was professor of conducting at the Florence Conservatory. Ace issued discs of excerpts from *Aida* and *Il trovatore*, in which he conducted the Florence Festival Orchestra *et al.*

Tietjen, Heinz (1881–1967). The son of a German diplomat and a mother of English descent, Tietjen was born in Tangier, Morocco, and studied conducting with Nikisch. He first conducted at the Trier Opera in 1904, and became the company's conductor and stage director (1907–22). He was the manager of the Breslau Opera (1922–5), was appointed the general intendant of the Prussian State Theatres (1925), managing the Berlin Charlottenburg Opera (1925–30) and the Berlin Staatsoper (1927–43); he had little difficulty accommodating himself to the Nazi regime, and played a role in the departure from Berlin of Walter, Klemperer and Kleiber in 1933. Both Walter and Klemperer remarked about his impassive, remote personality. Tietjen also shared with Winifred Wagner the management of the Bayreuth Festivals (1931–44), where he himself conducted, in the years 1933–41, performances which included many of *The Ring*. Under the Nazis he was a member of the Reichskulturkammer and a senator of the Berlin Academy of Arts; after World War II he conducted three Wagner operas at Covent Garden (1950–51), was manager of the Hamburg Opera (1956–9), and returned to Bayreuth to conduct *Lohengrin* in 1958. In the mid 1930s he made a number of recordings of excerpts from the Wagner operas with the Bayreuth Festival Orchestra and Chorus *et al.* for Telefunken.

Tijardović, Ivo (1896–1976). Born in Split, Yugoslavia, Tijardović studied in Split, Vienna and Zagreb, and was a conductor of opera and operetta at the Split Theatre. For Jugoton he recorded his own *Splitski Akvarel*, with a chorus, orchestra *et al.*

Tilegant, Friedrich (b. 1910). Born at Anderbeck, Tilegant studied the violin, first with his father and then in Berlin, and was a conducting pupil of Hindemith and Fritz Stein. He founded and conducted the South-West German Chamber Orchestra at Pforzheim (1945), with which he recorded the *Brandenburg Concertos* (for Europa and issued in the United States by Musical Heritage Society), the two Bach Violin Concertos (with Barchet) and the Double Violin Concerto (with Barchet and Mueren, for CBS-Realm), Telemann's *Suite in A minor* (with Bruggen for Telefunken), Vivaldi's *Four Seasons* (with Barchet, issued by Nonesuch), Handel's Concerto Grosso Op. 6 No. 1 (for Maritim), Haydn's Symphony No. 45 (for Eurodisc) and Grieg's *Holberg Suite* and *Two Elegiac Melodies* (for Bärenreiter).

Tintner, Georg (b. 1917). Born in Vienna, Tintner was a member of the Vienna Boys' Choir (1927–31), studied at the Vienna Academy of Music under Weingartner and Marx, and was an assistant conductor at the Vienna Volksoper before the *Anschluss* obliged him to flee the country. He emigrated to New Zealand where he became naturalised, was conductor of the New Zealand Opera and Ballet Company (1964–8), with the Sadler's Wells Opera Company (1968–70), and was musical director of the West Australian Opera Company (1970). He conducted orchestras in Britain (1969–70), won high praise for his performances of Beethoven and Bruckner, and has since conducted the National Youth Orchestra of Canada, the Australian Opera and the Queensland Theatre Orchestra. His broadcast lectures about composers, relayed in North America, Australia and New Zealand, were extremely successful, as was his direction of *Fidelio* for the Australian Opera in 1975. He recorded the Australian composer Alfred Hill's Symphony No. 8 (with the West Australian Symphony Orchestra for World Record Club) and Piano Concerto No. 1 (with Ballard and the same orchestra for Festival).

Tippett, Sir Michael (b. 1905). Tippett was born in London and studied at the Royal College of Music, where he was a composition pupil of Morris and a conducting pupil of Sargent and Boult. He was then a school teacher for several years, and retired to a small village in Surrey to devote himself to composition, where he conducted a local choir and orchestra. Later, he was the musical director at Morley College (1940–52). Now one of the most eminent of British composers, he was knighted in 1966. He has written the libretti for his own operas, and these are noted for their complex symbolism and apparent obscurity. Most of the recorded performances of his major compositions have been conducted by Colin Davis; he himself has conducted several recordings of his music: *The Vision of St Augustine* and *Fantasy on a Theme of Handel* (with the London Symphony Orchestra *et al.* for RCA), and the *Suite in D* (with the Leicestershire Schools Symphony Orchestra for Pye). Much earlier, he recorded Tallis's motet *Spem in alium nunquam habui* (with the Morley College Choir, for HMV, on a 78 r.p.m. disc), and, in 1957, Purcell's *Ode on St Cecilia's Day* (with the Kalmar Orchestra *et al.* for Pye); the last recording was re-issued in 1975.

Tjeknavorian, Loris (b. 1937). Born in Broudjerd, Iran, of Armenian parents, Tjeknavorian graduated from the Vienna Academy of Music, and while a student composed a violin concerto that was received with acclaim. He studied further with Orff, took his doctorate at Michigan University, was composer-in-residence at Concordia College, and taught at Moorehead State College and Central Minnesota Summer Music Academy. He first came to Britain in 1974 to conduct his Piano Concerto with the Hallé Orchestra, led the major orchestras, and later became the musical director of the London Percussion Ensemble. In Iran he was principal conductor of the Tehran Opera, has composed an opera *Paradis and Parisa*, the Piano Concerto mentioned above, and over 30 film scores. He has recorded, for Unicorn, his *Requiem for the Massacred* (with the London Percussion Ensemble), *Armenian Bagatelles* (with the London Symphony Orchestra) and a ballet *Simorgh* (with the Roudaki Hall Soloists); also for RCA he has recorded Tchaikovsky's Symphony No. 6 (with the London Symphony Orchestra), Sibelius' Symphonies Nos 4 and 5 (with the Royal Philharmonic Orchestra), and Shostakovich's Symphony No. 10 and Khachaturian's *Gayane* ballet (with the National Philharmonic Orchestra); these performances were variable, but at best, as in the *Gayane* music, they were played with warmth and persuasion.

Tobin, John (b. 1891). Born in Liverpool, Tobin was a licentiate of the Royal Academy of Music aged 14½, and a Fellow of the Royal College of Organists at 19. He was music master at several schools (1916–26), became chorus master of the Carl Rosa Opera Company (1917), director of the Liverpool Repertory Opera (1924) and conductor with the British National Opera Company (1926–7), director of music at Toynbee Hall in London (1935–9), conductor of the Liverpool Philharmonic Choir (1940–45) and of the London Choral Society (from 1946). In 1950 he gave the first performance, in London, of Handel's *Messiah*, with the exact orchestration for which it was composed, restoring cadenzas to the arias, and in 1965 he prepared a new *urtext* of the work. A recording was released in 1977 by GHF Records Ltd., Putney Hill, London, of a performance in which Tobin conducts the London Choral Society *et al.* in this edition of the work. Tobin has had a distinguished place in British musical life; in addition to being one of the foremost Handel scholars, he has given first performances of works by Stanford and Holst, and the first in England of Stravinsky's *L'Histoire du soldat*.

Toebosch, Louis (b. 1916). Born in Maastricht, the Dutch composer, conductor and organist Toebosch studied at the Maastricht Conservatory and the Royal Conservatory at Liège (1934–9), was conductor of the Tilburg Municipal Orchestra (1946–50) and director of the Brabant Conservatory at Tilburg (1965–74). For Donemus he recorded with the Orlando di Lasso Chamber Choir his *Bome*.

Toldra, Eduardo (1895–1962). Born in Villanueva y Geltru, in Catalonia, Toldra studied the violin and toured Europe as the member of a string quartet. He was professor of violin at the Barcelona Municipal School of Music (1921), conducted the Barcelona Municipal Orchestra (1943), and composed songs, some of which have been recorded by Da Camera and Ensayo. EMI issued a 78 r.p.m. disc in which he conducted the Barcelona Symphony Orchestra in Turina's *La oración del Torero*, and Philips an LP disc in which he conducted the Lamoureux Orchestra in *Iberia* of Albéniz, in Arbós' arrangement, and EMI Falla's *El retablo de Maese Pedro*, with the French National Radio Orchestra *et al.*

Tomasi, Henri (1901–71). Born in Marseille, Tomasi studied at the Paris Conservatoire, won the Prix de Rome (1927), and was musical director of the Paris Radio and in French Indo-China (1930–35). After service in the French army (1939–40), he was conductor of the Monte Carlo Opera (1946–50) and was awarded the Grand Prix de Musique française (1952). His compositions included operas, ballets, orchestral music and concertos, and recordings of his Trombone and Trumpet Concertos and some other works are available in France. As a conductor he recorded Gluck's *Orfeo ed Euridice* in an abridged version (with the Paris Symphony Orchestra *et al.* for Columbia, before World War II), Mozart's Symphony No. 40 and Tchaikovsky's *Nutcracker* Suite (with the French National Symphony Orchestra for Parade), and Massenet's *Scènes pittoresques* (with the Lamoureux Orchestra for Columbia).

Topolski, Zlatko (b. 1914). Born in what is now Yugoslavia, Topolski studied the violin and conducting at the National Music Academy at Zagreb, was concertmaster first at the Zagreb Opera and Philharmonic Orchestra (1932), and then at the Belgrade Opera and Philharmonic Orchestra (1938), also leading the Zagreb and Belgrade String Quartets and conducting the orchestras. He emigrated to South America where he conducted orchestras in Buenos Aires (1948) and Córdoba (1952), founded his own school for conducting and chamber music, and toured the continent. He returned to Europe in 1955 on the invitation of the Vienna Symphony Orchestra, conducted the Vienna Symphony, Chamber and Tonkünstler Orchestras, and became a professor at the Vienna Academy of Music. He once recorded as a violinist for Electrola; as a conductor he has made records with the Vienna Chamber and Austrian Tonkünstler Orchestras, including Telemann's *Suite in A minor* (with Kneihs), Handel's *Violin Concerto in B flat* (with Totenberg), Torelli's *Sonatas a cinq in D* and *D* (with Spindler), Haydn's *Piano Concerto in C* (with Abram), Mozart's Piano Concertos K. 175 (with Abram), K. 414 and K. 456 (with List), Graun's Oboe d'amore Concerto (with Hertel), Graupner's Bassoon Concerto (with Stiedl), Heinichen's *Violin Concerto in D* (with Totenberg), Pez's *Concerto pastorale in F*, Pisendel's *Violin Concerto in G minor* (with Totenberg), Viotti's *Piano Concerto in G minor* (with List), D. V. M. Puccini's *Piano Concerto in B flat* (with List), Dittersdorf's *Piano Concerto in A* (with Abram), Fasch's *Violin Concerto in D* (with Totenberg), Brahms' Violin Concerto (with Ruben Varga) and Hertel's *Oboe Concerto in G* (with Hertel). These discs were issued in the United States by Musical Heritage Society. Turnabout have also released Liszt's *Hungarian Fantasia* (with List and the Vienna Tonkünstler Orchestra).

Torkanowsky, Werner (b. 1926). Born in Berlin, Torkanowsky was taken by his parents to Palestine as a child, where he studied the violin. He continued his studies in New York with Bronstein (1948), and also was a conducting pupil of Monteux (1954–9), playing meantime in the Pittsburgh Symphony Orchestra. He made his debut as a conductor in New York in 1960, won the Naumberg Award (1961), and was appointed conductor of the New Orleans Symphony Orchestra in 1963. He has appeared with major orchestras in the United States, has taken part in international festivals, toured South Africa with the Israel Philharmonic Orchestra (1974), led the Royal Philharmonic Orchestra at the Santander Festival (1975) and the London Symphony Orchestra at the Casals Festival in Mexico (1976). His repertoire ranges from the baroque to the *avant-garde*. His recordings have been Rochberg's Symphony No. 2 (with the New York Philharmonic Orchestra for CBS), Floyd's *Three Sacred Songs* (with Treigle), Hovhaness's *Fra Angelico* and Rorem's *Lions* (with the New Orleans Symphony Orchestra for Orion), Wyner's *Serenado* and Shapey's *Evocation* (for Composers Recordings) and Colgrass's *Earth's a Baked Apple* (with the Xavier University Chorus and the New Orleans Symphony Orchestra for Orion).

Tortelier, Paul (b. 1914). Born in Paris, Tortelier began playing the cello as a child, studied at the Paris Conservatoire, and led the cello section of the Paris Conservatoire Orchestra (1946–7). His international career as a cellist started in 1934, and in 1937 he performed *Don Quixote* for the first time, with Strauss conducting. Since then he has performed in all European countries, the USSR, Latin America and Japan. He was appointed professor of cello at the Paris Conservatoire (1956) and at the Folkwang Hochschule für Musik at Essen, and has made many distinguished recordings as a cellist, including the six Bach suites. In addition, he has conducted orchestras in Europe, Israel and South America, and has given many lessons in interpretation in France, Canada and on BBC television. His compositions include concertos for cello and for two cellos; his wife, Maud, and daughter Pomone are also cellists, his son Yan Pascal a violinist and his daughter Maria de la Pau a pianist. Tortelier's recordings as a conductor are of Vivaldi's Concerto Op. 3 No. 9, and Paganini's *Variations on a Theme by Rossini* (with Maud Martin-Tortelier and the English Chamber Orchestra for EMI), Couperin's *Les Goûts-réunis* (with Wilbraham) and *Pièces en concert* (with P. Tortelier) and the Bach Suite No. 3 (with the Scottish Chamber Orchestra for EMI), Grieg's *Holberg Suite* and *Two Elegiac Melodies*, and Tchaikovsky's *Variations on a Rococo Theme* and *Pezzo capriccioso* (with the Northern Sinfonia for EMI), C. P. E. Bach's Cello Concerto No. 3 and Haydn's *Cello Concerto in D*, Martin's *Petite Symphonie concertante*, Roussel's *Sinfonietta* and his own *Offrande* (with the London Chamber Orchestra for Unicorn, with himself as soloist in the cello works, as in the Tchaikovsky, above).

Toscanini, Arturo (1867–1957). Toscanini is, by general consent, the greatest conductor of this century, with the possible exception of Mahler. Certainly he has been the most acclaimed. At the time of his death the number of his records sold was over 20 million. Most of his fellow conductors, the musicians who played for him, the soloists and singers he accompanied, and the public who heard him, conceded his precedence over all others: in the words of Boult (*Thoughts on Conducting*, p. 52), he 'controlled a higher candlepower of concentration than any human being except perhaps a few great orators'. Stokowski (*Current Biography*, 1942, p. 840) called him 'the supreme master of all conductors', and Puccini, for whose *La Bohème*, *La fanciulla del West* and *Turandot* Toscanini led the premières, said of him that he 'conducts a work not just as the written score directs, but as the composer imagined it in his head, even though he failed to write it down on paper'. It was real, not false modesty that caused Toscanini to remark: 'I am no genius. I have created nothing. I play the music of other men. I am just a musician.' As a conductor, he was entirely convinced that he was solely to serve the composer, to divine his meaning, and to perform it as faithfully and as best he could. He imposed his own inexorable and uncompromising standards on all the musicians he commanded, great and less great, and in his rigorous demand for absolute accuracy and the highest musicianship he brought about a great leap forward in the level of orchestral execution. There have been and are many other great conductors, but Toscanini's impact on the art of conducting and on orchestral performance has been paramount.

Toscanini was born in Parma in 1867, the son of a tailor, Claudio Toscanini, who was a fervent follower of Garibaldi. Neither of his parents was a musician, but the household nonetheless resounded with the popular operatic arias and choruses of the day. At the age of nine he entered the Parma Conservatory, graduated at nineteen as a cellist (1885), and the next year joined the orchestra of an Italian opera company about to tour South America. Thus, at the age of 20, a sequence of events brought him, literally at a moment's notice, to conduct a performance of *Aida* at Rio de Janeiro; he strode to the conductor's desk, closed the score, and conducted the opera from memory. The performance was a triumph and in that season in South America he conducted another eighteen operas, all from memory. *Aida* was to remain significant for him: he conducted it at his debut at the New York

Metropolitan Opera in 1908 and his last opera performance, a studio recording, was of *Aida* in 1954.

On returning to Italy, he conducted at many opera houses there (1887–95), was a cellist in the La Scala Orchestra at the première of Verdi's *Otello* (1887) and led the first performance of *Pagliacci* (1892). He became conductor at the Turin Regio Opera house (1896), led the first Italian performance of *Götterdämmerung* and the première of *La Bohème* (1896), as well as leading *Tristan und Isolde* and *Die Walküre*. In 1898 he conducted the Turin orchestra in a series of symphony concerts, the programme of the first being Brahms' *Tragic Overture*, the Entry of the Gods into Valhalla from *Das Rheingold*, the *Nutcracker* suite, and Schubert's Symphony No. 9. These concerts were an overwhelming success; after one, Saint-Saëns congratulated Toscanini, saying that it was the first time the symphony had been played with the correct tempi throughout. He then was appointed principal conductor at La Scala, Milan (1899–1908); here he opened his first season with *Die Meistersinger*, gave the first performances in Italy of *Siegfried, Eugene Onegin, Salome, Pelléas et Mélisande* and *Louise*, and also performed many operas unknown today, such as Leoncavallo's *Zaza*, Mascagni's *Le maschere*, Isidore de Lara's *Messaline*, Galletti's *Anton*, Franchetti's *Germania* and *Asrael*, Ponchielli's *I Lituani* and Sinareglia's *Oceana*. In these years he also conducted at Bologna, Turin, Rome and in South America; in 1920, at the age of 35, he led his first performance of the complete Beethoven Symphony No. 9, and during 1905–6 conducted the orchestra at the Accademia di Santa Cecilia, and the Turin Municipal Orchestra, with which he toured northern Italy.

Toscanini first appeared at the New York Metropolitan in 1908; in the same year he became the principal conductor and remained there until 1915. At his first encounter with the Met. orchestra he attempted to rehearse *Aida*, but the players were suspicious of the music and the man. He then asked them to put the Verdi away, and rehearsed the entire *Götterdämmerung* without once consulting the score. After this the orchestra's co-operation in performing Verdi was unreserved. He gave the première of *La fanciulla del West* (1910), and made his New York debut as a symphonic conductor with Beethoven's Symphony No. 9 (1913). In 1915 he returned to Italy and until the end of the war gave performances for soldiers and war sufferers, without fee. Recalled to La Scala in 1919, he re-formed the orchestra and took it on a triumphant tour of Italy and the United States, conducting 32 concerts in as many days in Italy, 68 in 77 days in the US and then 36 in 58 days in Italy. When in the US he and the orchestra made records for the Victor Talking Machine Company at Camden, New Jersey. He remained at La Scala until 1929, in that period leading the première of *Turandot* (1926), but in 1926–7 was a guest conductor with the New York Philharmonic Orchestra, and subsequently became the orchestra's regular conductor in 1928, sharing the season with Mengelberg. In 1928 the New York Philharmonic and New York Symphony Orchestras were merged to form the New York Philharmonic-Symphony Orchestra, and Toscanini became its principal conductor (1929–36). In fact after his departure from La Scala in 1929 he transferred his main activity from the opera house to the concert hall; except for appearances at Bayreuth (1930–31) and Salzburg (1935–7) and studio performances of operas with the NBC Symphony Orchestra, he did not conduct opera again. Thus it was not until he was 60 years of age that he became a full-time conductor of a major symphony orchestra. He toured Europe with the New York Philharmonic-Symphony (1930), first conducted the Philadelphia Orchestra (1930), the Vienna Philharmonic Orchestra (1933) and the BBC Symphony Orchestra (1935); he conducted in Sweden and Denmark (1933) and led the newly-formed Palestine Symphony Orchestra, predecessor to the present Israel Philharmonic Orchestra and made up of Jewish musicians, refugees from Hitler's Germany, in its inaugural concert in 1936, coming back to conduct the orchestra again the next year. In 1931 he had been assaulted by Fascists in Bologna for refusing to play the *Giovinezza*, a Fascist anthem, before a concert in memory of the composer Martucci, and consequently he left Italy and did not conduct there until after World War II. He was the first foreign conductor to appear at Bayreuth (1931), but refused to return in 1933 because of the treatment of Jewish musicians in Nazi Germany. After triumphant appearances at the Salzburg Festival, he finally refused to conduct there in 1937 because Walter's performances at the festival would not be broadcast in Germany. In 1938–9 he conducted at a festival in Lucerne, where the orchestra, led by Adolph Busch, was composed of musicians who had fled from Germany. His opposition to Nazism and Fascism was implacable.

In 1937, David Sarnoff, the president of the Radio Corporation of America which controlled NBC, approached Toscanini who was living in semi-retirement in Italy, through

Samuel Chotzinoff. He offered to engage him to conduct broadcast concerts in the US and to create a new symphony orchestra expressly for this purpose. Toscanini accepted, and suggested that Rodzinski be invited to select and train the orchestra; it was made up of 31 players from the already existing NBC house orchestra, and principal players recruited from other American orchestras. Rodzinski rehearsed the orchestra, Monteux led it in its first concert in November 1937, and after five more concerts under Monteux and Rodzinski, Toscanini conducted it for the first time on Christmas Day 1937, in a programme including Mozart's Symphony No. 40 and Brahms' Symphony No. 1; the broadcast was heard by an audience of 20 million people. He toured with the orchestra to South America (1940) and in a transcontinental tour of the US (1950), continued to conduct the BBC Symphony Orchestra (1939), the Philadelphia Orchestra (1941–2 to 1944) and the New York Philharmonic-Symphony Orchestra on occasions (1944–5), and travelled to London to conduct the Philharmonia Orchestra in two Brahms concerts at the Royal Festival Hall (1952). Except for the 1941–2 season, when the NBC Symphony Orchestra was conducted by Stokowski, Toscanini remained with the orchestra until 1954; at his last concert, which was his last public appearance, he had a memory lapse during the bacchanale from *Tannhäuser*. After his retirement he was embittered at his abrupt departure from the NBC Symphony Orchestra and expressed the feeling that he would have liked to have been invited to conduct the BBC Symphony Orchestra. He died in New York in 1957 at his home in Riverdale, and his body was flown to Milan for burial.

Toscanini had a strong attachment to the NBC Symphony Orchestra, but it is debatable whether he achieved with them his best results. It was not Toscanini's sole possession, as the Boston Symphony was of Koussevitzky or the Philadelphia Orchestra of Stokowski and Ormandy; the players were contracted for 30 hours a week, of which fifteen were for Toscanini's rehearsals and one hour-long concert. Also, he conducted the orchestra for only part of its season. Nonetheless, Ansermet said that it was the finest ensemble he had encountered. It was undoubtedly a virtuoso instrument, which played with the intonation, style and character that Toscanini demanded; its deficiencies, if any, would have to have been Toscanini's deficiencies also. If we judge from the recordings, its sound had not the fullness, nor the bloom, of the New York Philharmonic-Symphony or the BBC Symphony Orchestras. Comparing recorded performances of the same pieces, the New York Philharmonic-Symphony was the better orchestra, and Toscanini himself expressed the opinion once that the best orchestra he had conducted was the BBC Symphony. Before World War II the BBC Symphony had among its principal wind players Thurston, MacDonaugh, Camden and Aubrey Brain, which suited Toscanini's inclination to bring the woodwinds forward. The general inferiority of the NBC Symphony recordings compared to those with the BBC Symphony, however, makes a final judgement difficult. No records exist of Toscanini conducting the pre-war Vienna Philharmonic, except the Salzburg *Die Zauberflöte*, issued by the Arturo Toscanini Society, but it is too poor to consider seriously. In 1977 RCA released a five-disc collection of performances which he recorded with the Philadelphia Orchestra in 1941–2, and these make a fascinating study. After his London concerts in 1952 he said to Walter Legge, the impresario who had formed and managed the Philharmonia Orchestra: 'If I were ten years younger I would devote the rest of my life to recording my whole repertoire with the Philharmonia' (*The Gramophone*, May 1976). We must remember that the Toscanini we hear in his records with the NBC Symphony Orchestra is a musician over 70 years old, virtually at the end of his career, and according to many who knew him well, the peak of his interpretative powers probably occurred in the 1920s and 1930s, when he recorded with the New York Philharmonic-Symphony and BBC Symphony Orchestras.

Toscanini was a small man, slightly bent at the knees, with a high receding forehead, a sharp nose, a short moustache and bushy eyebrows. His head and hands dominated his body, and his small eyes were in absolute control of his orchestra. Every player believed he was watching him all the time. In private life he was a most frugal person and fundamentally a kind and generous man; he was in no way religious. However he was completely, utterly possessed by music, and except for watching boxing on television, music was his entire life. His concentration when conducting has been compared with that of a mystic in contemplation. He had a single-minded conviction of what the composer intended and an unswerving urge to reproduce his mental image of this intention which he derived from an exhaustive study of the score. He was a perfectionist whose ideals were rarely, if ever, realised, and so conducting was an experience which appeared to bring him suffering rather than joy. He was often dissatisfied with his own performances and although his tantrums, baton-throwing and smashing, abuse of players and abrupt departures, were often directed at failures among his musicians to measure up to his own standards of musicianship, his anger was more towards himself. He was unsparing with both; in the opera house or with the orchestra the atmosphere was invariably tense and occasionally unbearable, as everyone was stretched uncompromisingly to the limit of his abilities. Menuhin (*Unfinished Journey*, London, 1978, p. 170) has told the story of the time when he was rehearsing the slow movement of the Beethoven Violin Concerto at Toscanini's home in Riverdale, with Toscanini playing the piano. The telephone rang; Toscanini stopped playing, strode to the wall, ripped out the telephone with wire and plaster flying, then calmly resumed without a word. Because of his scenes with the orchestra, rehearsals were usually in secret. Although he was patient with players' technical mistakes, any lapse in musical taste or disrespect for the great masters would cause uproar. He disliked applause, first because he regarded it as an unmusical sound, but in addition he truly feared that the audience might be applauding him and not the composer.

It cannot be claimed that Toscanini had an exemplary technique, if such exists. He held the baton with three or four fingers and thumb and it moved mostly with the movement of his arm. It created circles so that the bars were transformed into long phrases; he said himself that it was impossible to teach baton technique, and his own was undoubtedly intuitive. His left hand was especially expressive, yet sparingly used; it would indicate pianissimos and he would clutch it over his heart in a passage of feeling. But it was mainly with his eyes that he controlled the orchestra; with them he registered the smallest flaw in intonation. He frequently sang with the orchestra; at Salzburg he was once rehearsing the orchestra, and his own voice soared over the instruments. He stopped the players and demanded: 'Silence, who is singing here?' When no-one owned up, he added: 'Well, whoever it was will now kindly shut up'. Much has been made of his incredible memory, and many conductors have since attempted to emulate his feat of conducting all his concerts and operatic performances from memory. The truth is that he was obliged to memorise his scores from the very beginning because his short-sightedness prevented him from reading a score on the podium. It is estimated that at the end of his career he had in his memory 250 symphonic works, 100 operas and numerous chamber, piano, cello and violin pieces and songs. Some of the stories about his memory are almost beyond belief: in 1942 he saw a score of Tchaikovsky's opera *Yolanta* which he had last come across in 1885; nonetheless he was able to recall the introduction. The NBC had programmed the Prologue to Boito's *Mefistofele*, which required a backstage band, but the night before the rehearsal the librarian of the orchestra, James Dolan, found that the parts for the band had been mislaid; that evening Toscanini wrote out the parts from memory. In Vienna once he was challenged to write out the second bassoon part in Act II of *Die Meistersinger*, which he succeeded in doing. The same instrument features in perhaps the most popular story, when at St Louis an agitated second bassoonist came to him before a concert lamenting that the key for the lowest note in his instrument was broken. Toscanini reflected for a moment and said: 'It is all right – that note does not occur this evening'. His knowledge of the scores was absolutely complete, and the exact way the sound should occur from the visual score in his mind was also clear to him. He would sit in an armchair with his eyes shut for some time, going through scores. Nonetheless, before every concert he would study the score again, no matter how familiar.

The characteristics of Toscanini's interpretations were apparent from the beginning of his career, although he would dispute that he was *interpreting* the composer. Understanding and producing an impeccable performance of a work was not, to him, interpreting it. He said: 'Often I have heard people speaking of the *Eroica* of conductor X, the *Siegfried* of conductor Y, or the *Aida* of conductor Z. And I have always wondered what Beethoven, Wagner and Verdi would have said about the interpretations of those gentlemen, if through them, their works assumed a new paternity. I think that confronted by the *Eroica, Siegfried, Aida*, an interpreter, entering as deeply as possible into the spirit of the composer, should only be willing to render the *Eroica* of Beethoven, the *Siegfried* of Wagner, and the *Aida* of Verdi'. So from the first he claimed absolute fidelity to the score and the clearest and most accurate performance of it as his only tolerated objective, but this has been shown by many writers to be, in practice, somewhat wide of the mark. He did alter scores as freely as most other conductors; additions and amendments were made to the Beethoven symphonies and overtures, especially in the wind and timpani parts. But these were done so discretely that they largely remained unnoticed. Other pieces he altered were the *Manfred* symphony of Tchaikovsky, *Pictures at an Exhibition, Moldau*, and Schumann's Symphony No. 3. At the time of Toscanini's arrival on the scene, many performances had degenerated through romantic excesses and mannerisms; he brushed aside these slovenly conventions and fought an unrelenting battle against poor performing standards, and against singers, impresarios, publishers and audiences who could not appreciate the finest standards. In the orchestra he sacrificed tonal beauty to clarity, with the lines separated rather than blending. String tone was necessarily transparent, a quality that distinguished the NBC Symphony Orchestra, perhaps to its detriment compared to, say, the Vienna Philharmonic or Philadelphia Orchestras; the difference in the string sound in his Philadelphia recordings compared with those of Stokowski and Ormandy is remarkable. Rhythm had to be exactly right; at La Scala he was criticised for the dryness of his rhythm, but it resulted from his demand for accurate playing.

With the New York Philharmonic-Symphony Orchestra, he was superior to Mengelberg, Furtwängler and others who conducted the orchestra at the time because of his precision and clarity. Above all, he showed that it was possible to perform a piece of music of metrical pattern with one tempo throughout, although this ran the risk of the music losing spontaneity and of producing an enveloping tension which stimulated excitement but harmed the music's lyrical qualities. It follows that Toscanini was troubled by music in which rhythms were intricate and where metres constantly changed, such as in Stravinsky and indeed in most modern scores. Even *Daphnis et Chloé* could confuse him. Until he was 60, the keystones of his musical culture were Verdi and Wagner; he had first performed the German symphonic repertoire, particularly Beethoven and Brahms, as he had heard German conductors perform it, but later the leanness of his orchestral tone and the usually faster tempi he adopted produced, by contrast, an electric effect. He could not master the *adagio* style of the German symphonists, because, as has been suggested by Peter J. Pirie, there is no *adagio* in Verdi. His fast tempi were sometimes deceptive, arising from the accuracy and clarity of the playing, as well as the taut rhythm. The critic W. J. Turner once used the analogy that a Toscanini performance was a poem printed clearly and correctly on good paper, compared to a poem printed in smudged ink on blotting paper with the punctuation all wrong. There is another quality of a Toscanini performance that communicates itself to the listener, as indeed his conducting did to the players: his remarkable ability to build tension in the music to lead to what is coming; when conducting he could indicate simultaneously to the players the music of the moment and that of the bar ahead. One of the finest examples of his art has been the recording of Beethoven's Symphony No. 9, of which Desmond Shawe-Taylor and Edward Sackville-West wrote in *The Record Guide* (p. 84): 'He sweeps irresistibly forward, as though in a single fierce creative impulse. At the climax of the first movement, where the main theme returns in the major key, the listener has a strange sensation of being in the heart of a whirlwind: he feels impelled to leave his chair and pace the room . . . In the *Finale* . . . the power of this exalted, exultant movement emerges with all the splendour that has made Toscanini the foremost conductor of our age'. Writing about a performance of Sibelius' Symphony No. 2 many years earlier in New York, Lawrence Gilman commented: 'I cannot remember that he ever surpassed the exhibition of sustained intensity and cumulative power with which he evolved that long crescendo of exultation which Sibelius spread over the entire symphony. It was another Toscanini miracle'.

Toscanini came to every rehearsal completely prepared; with the orchestra he was painstaking and thorough, and never rehearsed them once the work was played to his satisfaction. Frequently final rehearsals were more perfect performances than the concerts, as the tension of the concert could cause the players to make mistakes. At rehearsals his gestures were more pronounced than at concerts. When rehearsing an opera, he would conduct the orchestra without the singers, singing all the roles himself, but would rehearse the singers individually and in ensemble for weeks beforehand. At La Scala and the New York Met. he created the interpretations he required, and many of the greatest singers of the day submitted to his discipline, Stabile, Carosio, Stignani, Supervia, Toti del Monte and Pertile among them. In the opera house he was the complete dictator: all the singers had to adhere to the score and fit within the framework of the ensemble, and he watched every detail of the costumes and staging. Audiences were expected to be punctual, the auditorium was to be in darkness, and encores were not permitted. Eventually, however, his objective of repertory opera, at La Scala, proved economically impossible and he abandoned his struggle to realise perfection in the opera house, and turned to symphonic music.

In his early years Toscanini was regarded as a most versatile conductor; a glance at the list of operas he conducted shows him to be an energetic proponent of the young Italian realist school of composers. He turned 40 in 1907, and so a considerable fraction of today's orchestral repertoire was written by his contemporaries, and he performed a good deal of it. But like many conductors, as he grew older he became less inclined to perform the music of the day: 'I am the man who did Wagner when Wagner was new; who performed all the moderns from Strauss and Debussy to Malipiero and Sibelius. Now let the other men do what I did when I was young . . . I want, I crave the time in these, my last years, to come a little nearer to the secrets of Beethoven and a few other eternal masters.' So, while with the New York Philharmonic-Symphony Orchestra, the standard works of Beethoven, Brahms and Wagner comprised 40 per cent of his programmes. In the US from 1925 to 1954, the works most frequently performed by him were the prelude to *Die Meistersinger* (54 times), *La Mer* of Debussy (53), Beethoven's Symphony No. 3 (52), the prelude and Liebestod from *Tristan und Isolde* (45), Brahms' *Variations on the St Antony Chorale* (40), Beethoven's Symphony No. 6 (38), Beethoven's Symphony No. 7 (35), the *scherzo* from *A Midsummer Night's Dream* (35), Brahms' Symphony No. 2 (34) and Debussy's *Iberia* (31). Bach was omitted, except for the Respighi arrangement of the *Passacaglia and Fugue in C minor*; French music, apart from some Debussy and Ravel, and the Russians, even Tchaikovsky, were largely neglected. He was often criticised for performing the Rossini overtures, which he loved; someone said to him about the *William Tell* overture, 'Isn't it cheap music?', to which he replied, 'You try and compose something as good' (G. Marek, *Toscanini*, New York, 1975, p. 236). American and British music was virtually absent from his programmes: he performed only five pieces by Americans in eleven seasons with the New York Philharmonic-Symphony Orchestra, yet Elgar's *Enigma Variations*, which he first performed in Turin in 1905, received an exemplary performance, and he gave a searing account of the *Fantasia on a Theme of Thomas Tallis* of Vaughan Williams in an NBC broadcast.

He first made records with the La Scala Orchestra, for Victor in the US in 1920–21. Included were the third and fourth movements of Mozart's Symphony No. 39, the finales of Beethoven's Symphonies Nos 1 and 5, extracts from Respighi's *Ancient Airs and Dances* Suite No. 1, Pizzetti's *La Pisanella*, Massenet's *Scènes pittoresques*, *L'Arlésienne* Suite No. 2 and Mendelssohn's incidental music to *A Midsummer Night's Dream*, the overtures to *Don Pasquale* and *Il segreto di Susanna*, the prelude to Act IV of *Carmen* and the Hungarian March from *La Damnation de Faust*. He repeated the *scherzo* from *A Midsummer Night's Dream* with the New York Philharmonic Orchestra for Brunswick in 1926. Then appeared his great series with the New York Philharmonic-Symphony Orchestra: Haydn's Symphony No. 101, Mozart's Symphony No. 35, the Dance of the Blessed Spirits from *Orfeo*, the Mendelssohn *scherzo* again, *L'Apprenti sorcier*, the preludes to Acts I and III of *La traviata* and the overture to *Il barbiere di Siviglia* (1929), Beethoven's Symphony No. 7, Brahms' *Variations on the St Antony Chorale*, the overtures to *Semiramide* and *L'Italiana in Algeri*, the preludes to Acts I and III of *Lohengrin*, Dawn and Siegfried's Rhine Journey from *Götterdämmerung*, and the *Siegfried Idyll* (1936). As we have discussed, these performances are probably more truly representative of the mature Toscanini, together with the ones made in London with the BBC Symphony Orchestra: the overture to *Die Zauberflöte*, Beethoven's Symphonies Nos 1, 4 and 6 and the *Leonore No. 1* overture, the *Tragic Overture* of Brahms, the overture to *La scala di seta* and *Invitation to the Dance* (orchestrated by Berlioz). The Beethoven symphonies have been re-issued constantly and No. 7 in particular has scarcely been eclipsed in its concentration and power. Five of these performances, at least – Beethoven's Symphonies Nos 1 and 7, the *Tragic Overture*, the overture to *Die Zauberflöte* and the *Leonore No. 1* overture – could be counted among the most brilliant performances ever recorded and as the best examples of Toscanini's style.

Apart from the recently released performances recorded with the Philadelphia Orchestra, all of Toscanini's many remaining discs were with the NBC Symphony Orchestra for RCA, starting from 1938. The first were of Haydn's Symphony No. 88, Mozart's Symphony No. 40 and the *lento* and *vivace* from Beethoven's String Quartet Op. 135; the last were issued after his death. The Philadelphia recordings issued in 1977 were of the incidental music to *A Midsummer Night's Dream*, the Queen Mab Scherzo from Berlioz' *Roméo et Juliette* symphony, Tchaikovsky's Symphony No. 6, *La Mer* and *Iberia*, Respighi's *Feste romane*, Strauss's *Tod und Verklärung* and Schubert's Symphony No. 9; the last-named had also been issued earlier, in 1963. The NBC Symphony recordings were not entirely satisfactory, to put it as kindly as possible to the engineers responsible, but their poor technical standard stemmed from the fact that many were made in the notorious Studio 8H at Radio City, which pleased Toscanini acoustically but was disastrous for recording. Toscanini himself was bored by recording and apparently took little interest in the tonal quality of his recordings, although the technical perfection of the performances always concerned him. A vast improvement occurred later, when recording was transferred to Carnegie Hall.

The discography with the NBC Symphony Orchestra is considerable, and includes Haydn's Symphonies Nos 88, 94, 98, 99 and 101, and Sinfonia Concertante, Mozart's Symphonies Nos 35, 39, 40 and 41, Beethoven's symphonies and some overtures, *Fidelio* and the *Missa Solemnis*, the four Brahms symphonies, the *Variations on the St Antony Chorale*, and overtures, Berlioz' *Roméo et Juliette* symphony and *Harold in Italy* (with Cooley), Cherubini's *Requiem Mass* and *Symphony in D major*, Mendelssohn's Symphonies Nos 4 and 5, a number of Rossini overtures, Schubert's Symphonies Nos 5, 8 and 9, Schumann's Symphony No. 3 and *Manfred* overture, Dvořák's Symphony No. 9, Sibelius' Symphony No. 2 and *Pohjola's Daughter*, Tchaikovsky's Piano Concerto No. 1 and Brahms' Piano Concerto No. 2 (with Horowitz), the Beethoven Violin Concerto (with Heifetz), and Piano Concertos Nos 1 (with Dorfman), 3 (with Rubinstein) and 4 (with Serkin), Gershwin's *An American in Paris*, Shostakovich's Symphonies Nos 1 and 7, Puccini's *La Bohème*, Tchaikovsky's Symphony No. 6, *Manfred* symphony and the *Romeo and Juliet* fantasy-overture, Verdi's *La traviata, Un ballo in maschera, Aida, Otello, Falstaff,* Act IV of *Rigoletto, Requiem* and *Te Deum, La Mer, Iberia, Daphnis et Chloé* Suite No. 2, *Rapsodie espagnole, Pini di Roma, Fontane di Roma, Feste romane, L'Apprenti sorcier, Moldau, Don Juan, Till Eulenspiegel, Tod und Verklärung*, Prokofiev's Symphony No. 1, *Enigma Variations*, Franck's *Psyché et Eros, Pictures at an Exhibition*, Dvořák's Symphony No. 9, Saint-Saëns' Symphony No. 3, Act II of Gluck's *Orfeo ed Euridice*, the prologue to *Mefistofele*, a number of preludes, overtures and excerpts from the Wagner operas, as well as the Immolation scene from *Götterdämmerung* (with Traubel) and excerpts from *Die Walküre* (with Melchior and Traubel), and many overtures and shorter pieces by various composers. The Arturo Toscanini Society in the US issued a number of recordings of Toscanini obtained from different sources, including the *Die Zauberflöte* at the pre-war Salzburg Festival, and a Verdi *Requiem* with the BBC Symphony Orchestra *et al.* In more recent years, RCA have re-issued many of the best Toscanini recordings; one of particular note is an outstanding Beethoven Symphony No. 3, from a performance in Carnegie Hall in 1953. Hearing this vital and incandescent reading, one can scarcely believe the conductor to be 86 years of age.

In contrast to his contemporaries, many of today's conductors are repelled by some of the hard-driven performances that were recorded by Toscanini in his later years; Colin Davis, for example, could see no merit in the Beethoven overture, *Die Weihe des Hauses.* His style certainly changed towards the end of his life so that the former electric urgency sometimes became a somewhat relentless rush, such as the recording of *La traviata*, which was greeted rather coldly because of its uneasy tension. Some close to Toscanini at the time have said that he felt that he must not bore his radio audience, others believe he was reacting to the slower tempi of Furtwängler, for whom he had a special dislike. Altogether, however, there are many imperishable performances among these NBC Symphony discs: the Beethoven and Brahms symphonies, the Brahms Piano Concerto No. 2, *Harold in Italy*, the Dvořák and Tchaikovsky symphonies, *Don Juan, Enigma Variations, Otello* and *Falstaff*, at least, should be added to the recordings with the New York Philharmonic-Symphony, Philadelphia and BBC Symphony Orchestras for a representative view of this unique musical interpreter.

Toyama, Yuzo (b. 1931). The Japanese composer Toyama was born in Tokyo, and studied at the Tokyo Academy of Music and in Vienna. For Folkways he recorded with the Juilliard Orchestra his *Japanese Suite* and *Voice of Yamato*.

Toye, Geoffrey (1889–1942). Brother of Francis Toye, the music critic and biographer of Verdi and Rossini, Toye was born at Winchester, studied at the Royal College of Music, and, at the same time as he followed his career as a marine underwriter, was active as a conductor, composer and musical administrator. He conducted at theatres in London, led the first performance of Vaughan Williams' *London Symphony* (1914), served in the Royal Flying Corps in World War I, conducted for the Beecham Opera Company, the Royal Philharmonic Society and the D'Oyly Carte Opera Company, was musical manager and a governor of the Sadler's Wells Theatre (1931) when he wrote and produced a ballet entitled *The Haunted Ballroom* (of which a waltz tune became famous), was managing director of the Covent Garden Opera (1934–6), and produced a film of *The Mikado* (1938). In 1927–9 he recorded for HMV Delius's *On Hearing the First Cuckoo in Spring, In a Summer Garden* and *Brigg Fair* (with the London Symphony Orchestra), and The Walk to the Paradise Garden from *A Village Romeo and Juliet*, and *Summer Night on the River* (with the New Symphony Orchestra), and so was one of the composer's significant early protagonists.

Travis, Francis (b. 1921). Born in Detroit, Travis studied at the music schools of the Michigan State University and the University of Michigan, then went to Switzerland in 1948 to study the piano. He was a conducting pupil of Scherchen, completed his doctorate at the University of Zürich, and started his career as a conductor in 1956, appearing in Switzerland, FR Germany, the Netherlands and Italy, and conducted regularly for Radio Lugano and at the Basel Theatre. His repertoire includes contemporary works as well as the classical and romantic works. He has recorded Holliger's *Siebengesänge* (with Holliger, the Basel Symphony Orchestra *et al.* for DGG), Huber's Violin Concerto (with Schneeberger and the Winterthur State Orchestra for CTS), Bron's *Ephitaphium*, Dresden's Oboe Concerto (with Slogteren) and Kruyf's *Einst dem Grau* (with Melita, and the Netherlands Radio Orchestra for Donemus).

Treiber, Friedrich (b. 1909). Born in Heidelberg, Treiber was a conductor at Heilbronn, Liegnitz, Kiel and Stettin (1934–44), and has been a professor at the Hochschulen für Musik in Vienna and Heidelberg. He has composed orchestral, chamber and choral music, and has written a study of Thuringian and Saxonian church cantatas at the time of Bach's youth. He has recorded Bach's Harpsichord Concerto No. 4 (with Schnauffer and the Munich Bach Orchestra for Mercury).

Trhlík, Otakar (b. 1922). Born in Brno, Czechoslovakia, Trhlík attended the Brno Conservatory (1941–3), then studied conducting with Dědeček and Talich at the Prague Conservatory, graduated in 1947, and later read philosophy and musicology at the Brno University and obtained his doctorate of music (1953). He was assistant conductor to Talich with the Czech Chamber Orchestra (1947–8), conductor of the Ostrava Opera (1948–52), conductor of the Brno Radio Symphony Orchestra (1952–6) and the Brno State Philharmonic Orchestra (1956–62), and was appointed musical director of the Bratislava Radio Symphony Orchestra (1962–8) and then of the Janáček Philharmonic Orchestra at Ostrava. He teaches conducting at the Brno Academy of Music, has conducted throughout Europe, in the United States, Japan and Australia, toured the USSR in 1963, and received the award Artist of Merit in 1973. On the podium he is energetic and authoritative, and his interpretations are vigorous and expressive, and less given to lyrical sentiment.

Trhlík's recordings include Dvořák's *The Golden Spinning Wheel*, Janáček's *Taras Bulba* and *Amarus*, Nedbal's *From Tale to Tale* and *The Tale of Simple Johnny*, Válek's Symphony No. 8, Suk's *Under the Apple Tree* and Strauss' *Aus Italien* (with the Ostrava Janáček Philharmonic Orchestra for Supraphon), Bárta's Symphony No. 3 and Válek's Symphony No. 7 (with the same orchestra for Panton), Bárta's Violin Concerto No. 2, Matěj's Violin Concerto and Fišer's *Crux*, for violin, kettledrum and bells (with Štraus and the Czech Philharmonic Orchestra for Panton).

Tschupp, Räto (b. 1929). Born in Thusis, Switzerland, Tschupp was educated at the Zürich Academy of Music, and was a double-bass play in the Zürich Chamber Orchestra (1952–4) and the Zürich Tonhalle Orchestra (1954–8). He studied conducting with Erich Schmid in Zürich (1954–7), with Kurt Thomas at Detmold (1955) and with van Otterloo at Hilversum (1957–8), founded and conducted the Camerata Zürich (1951), and conducted orchestras in Switzerland, Italy, FR Germany and Britain. He was conductor of the South-West German Chamber Orchestra at Pforzheim (1969–71), is deputy conductor of the Zürich Mixed Choir, conductor of the Collegium Musicum at Basel, and president of the Pro Musica, Zürich, for which he presents regular concerts of contemporary music. In addition, he has been active as a teacher, author and adjudicator.

Tschupp's recordings include A. Scarlatti's Symphonies Nos 1 to 12 (with the South-West German Chamber Orchestra for Thorofon), Boccherini's Cello Concerto No. 1 (with Nyffenegger) and *Flute Concerto in D* (with Graf and the Zürich Chamber Orchestra for Fono, and issued in the United States by Musical Heritage Society); Beethoven's Piano Concertos Nos 1 and 2 (with Nakajima and the Nuremberg Symphony Orchestra for Windmill) and No. 5 (with the same artists for Intercord); Borodin's Symphony No. 2, Tcherepnin's Symphony No. 4, trumpet concertos by Genzmar, Kaminski and Telemann (with Tarr, and the Nuremberg Symphony Orchestra for Colosseum); Liszt's Piano Concerto No. 2 (with Nakajima and the Nuremberg Symphony Orchestra for Audio Fidelity); Schibler's *Curriculum Vitae* and *Music for an Imaginary*

Ballet (with the Camerata Zürich for Amadeo) and *Concerto for Percussion and Piano* (with Benzinger and Weber and the Camerata Zürich for Ex Libris); Pfister's *Ägäisches Tagebuch* and *Sonata*, and Haller's Piano Concerto No. 2 (with Thew and the Camerata Zürich for Disco); Schnyder von Wartensee's Symphony No. 2 (with the Frankfurt Radio Orchestra for Ex Libris); Tischhauser's *Cassation* (with an ensemble for CT) and *Punctus contra punctum* (with the Beromünster Radio Orchestra *et al.* for CT); Furer's Oboe Concerto (with Fuchs and the Swiss Italian Radio Orchestra for CT); and Eichenwald's *Aspekte* (with the Camerata Zürich for CT).

Tučapský, Antonín (b. 1928). Born at Opatovice, Czechoslovakia, Tučapský studied at Brno University and at the Janáček Academy of Music in Brno. He conducted junior choirs (1954–65), the Children's Choir at Ostrava Radio (1960–62), and became chief conductor of the Moravian Teachers' Choir (1964). His compositions include choral and instrumental pieces; he has recorded with the Moravian Teachers' Choir Janáček's music for male chorus (issued by Nonesuch).

Turner, Bruno (b. 1931). Born in England, Turner is a self-taught musician who became interested in Renaissance music, and was choirmaster of St Edward's Church, London (1951–71). He has also been secretary and member of the Renaissance Singers (1950–57), founder and conductor of the Pro Musica Sacra (1958–64), has broadcast talks for the BBC (1964–8), and has been conductor and musical adviser of Pro Cantione Antiqua (since 1968).

Turner's recordings with Pro Cantione Antiqua include Ockeghem's Mass *Ecce ancilla Domini* and motet *Intemerata Dei mater*, Lassus' *Missa pro defunctis*, motets *O bone Jesu*, *Alma redemptoris mater* and *Ave Maria*, and *Magnificat*, Dunstable's *Gloria* and *Credo*, G. Gabrieli's *Sonata pian' e forte* and motets *Quis est iste* and *Maria Virgo*, Taverner's *Missa sine nomine* and motets, motets of Josquin, Dunstable, Power, Cooke and Damett, songs of Purcell, Ravenscroft and Lawes, and collections entitled *Christmas Music of the 15th Century*, *Music of Tudor Times* and *Old English Songs* (with, variously, the Collegium Aureum, the Early Music Consort of London, and Hamburg Old Music Wind Ensemble, for BASF), Josquin's *Déploration sur la mort de Johannes Ockeghem*, Ockeghem's *Missa pro defunctis*, Lassus' *Penitential Psalms*, Byrd's *Mass in Three Parts*, Tallis' *Lamentations of Jeremiah the Prophet*, and motets by Lassus, Dufay, Dunstable, Obrecht and de la Rue (for DGG-Archiv), and Taverner's *Missa Gloria tibi Trinitas* and motet *In pace* (with the Pro Musica Sacra for Schwann).

Turner, Laurence (b. 1901). Born in Huddersfield, and educated at Leeds University, Turner was leader of the Yorkshire String Quartet (1921–9), a member of the Catterall Quartet (1926–31), founder and leader of the Turner String Quartet (1930), sub-leader of the BBC Symphony Orchestra (1930–40), and leader of the Hallé Orchestra (1940–58). He was senior professor of violin at the Huddersfield College of Technology (from 1958), musical director of the Manchester Tuesday Midday Concerts (from 1953) and conductor of the Turner Orchestral Players. He recorded the third movement of Mozart's Divertimento K. 251 with the Hallé Orchestra on a Columbia 78 r.p.m. disc.

Turnovský, Martin (b. 1928). Born in Prague, Turnovský learned the violin as a boy, but his studies were interrupted by the German occupation, and he was sent to a labour camp in 1944. After the war, he studied conducting privately with Dědeček, attended the Prague Conservatory (1948–52), and later studied conducting with Szell at Salzburg (1956). He made his debut with the Prague Symphony Orchestra in 1952, was a choirmaster in the Czech army (1952–5), and conducted the Czech Army Symphony Orchestra (1955–60); in 1958 he won first prize at the International Competition for Young Conductors at Besançon, France. He was appointed conductor of the Brno State Philharmonic Orchestra (1959–63) and the Plzeň Radio Symphony Orchestra (1963–6) and was musical director of the Dresden Opera and Staatskapelle (1967–8). In 1968 he moved to Austria, has been a guest conductor with major orchestras in FR Germany, Britain, the United States, Canada, Australia and New Zealand, and in 1975 became music director of the Norwegian Opera at Oslo.

Turnovský's first record, issued in 1964, was a coupling of Mozart's Symphonies Nos 29 and 40 (with the Czech Philharmonic and Brno State Philharmonic Orchestras, respectively, for Supraphon), and it was warmly welcomed for its sensitivity and style. A subsequent recording, in 1967, of Martinů's Symphony No. 4 and *Tre Ricercari* (with the Czech Philharmonic) was also highly regarded. His other discs have included Bach's Cantata No. 60 (with Musica Pragensis *et al.*), Haydn's Symphonies Nos 94 and 101 (with the Prague Symphony Orchestra), Dvořák's *Serenade in E minor* (with the

Czech Chamber Orchestra) and *Serenade in D minor* (with the Prague Chamber Harmony), Mysliveček's *Symphony in D* (with the Prague Chamber Orchestra), Bartók's Piano Concerto No. 1 (with Baloghová and the Prague Radio Symphony Orchestra), Martinů's Oboe Concerto (with Hanták and the Brno State Philharmonic Orchestra), Prokofiev's and Szymanowski's Violin Concertos No. 2 (with Jásek and the Prague Symphony Orchestra), Ravel's *Shéhérazade* and Chausson's *Poème de l'amour et de la mer* (with Casei and the Prague Chamber Orchestra and Prague Symphony Orchestra respectively), Ibert's Cello Concerto and Martinů's Cello Concertino (with Navarra and the Prague Chamber Harmony), *Le Carnaval des animaux* (with the Prague Symphony Orchestra) and Kalabis' Symphony No. 2 (with the Prague Radio Symphony Orchestra). All were for Supraphon; for Connoisseur he also recorded Beethoven's Piano Concerto No. 4 (with Moravec and the Vienna Symphony Orchestra).

Tuxen, Erik (1902–57). Born in Mannheim of Danish parents, Tuxen first studied architecture, medicine and philosophy, then music at Copenhagen and in Paris, Vienna and Berlin. He was conductor at the Lübeck Opera (1927–9), organised and led for some years a popular dance orchestra, conducted at the Royal Theatre, Copenhagen, and was permanent conductor of the Danish Radio Symphony Orchestra from 1936 until his death, interrupted only for the wartime years, which he spent in Sweden. He toured the United States (1950–51) and South America (1954), and in 1950 conducted the Danish State Radio Symphony Orchestra at the Edinburgh Festival. Here he gave a sensational performance of Nielsen's Symphony No. 5, which made known the Danish composer to the general musical public in Britain. He then recorded this symphony and the Symphony No. 3 with the orchestra for Decca, first on 78s and later released on LP, and this, together with Grøndahl's recording of the Symphony No. 4 (for EMI) caused Nielsen's place as a great composer to be widely recognised.

Tuxen made other recordings, but in these his performances were less convincing. Almost all were with the Danish State Radio Symphony Orchestra. On 78s there were Hartmann's *The Golden Horns*, Gershwin's *Rhapsody in Blue* (with Schiøler), Lange-Müller's *Renaissance* overture, Gram's *Poème lyrique*, Hornemann's *Aladdin* overture and Gurre's *Orchestral Suite* (for Polydor), Nielsen's *Little Suite for Strings* (with the Royal Orchestra, Copenhagen) and prelude to Act III of *Maskarade* (for EMI), Saeverud's incidental music to *Peer Gynt*, Kuhlau's overture *The Brigand's Castle* and Nielsen's overture to *Maskarade*, prelude to Act II of *Saul and David* (for Decca), and Bruch's Violin Concerto No. 1 (with Wolf) and the Grieg Piano Concerto (with Schiøler, and the Danish State Radio Symphony Orchestra for Tono). For Decca he recorded a series of LPs: Liszt's *Hungarian Rhapsody No. 4, Marche slave*, Grieg's *Lyric Suite* and *Two Elegiac Melodies*, Sibelius' Symphony No. 5 and *Finlandia*, Nielsen's *Helios* overture, Prokofiev's Symphony No. 5, Schultz's *Serenade for Strings* and Svendsen's *Festival Polonaise* and *Norwegian Artists' Carnival*. The Sibelius Symphony No. 5 was still in the British catalogue in 1977; Ivan March (in *A Guide to the Bargain Classics*, 1962), observed that Tuxen sets his performance of this symphony at a low temperature throughout and rises to climaxes, but the Prokofiev Symphony No. 5 was not regarded as outstanding.

Tzipine, Georges (b. 1907). Born in Paris, Tzipine studied at the Paris Conservatoire, graduated in 1926 and embarked on a career as a concert violinist. He decided to be a conductor in 1931, and in 1945 was appointed music director at the municipal casino at Cannes. From 1948 he conducted the major French orchestras, toured in Europe, North and South America, and was principal conductor of the Melbourne Symphony Orchestra (1960–65). He is now director of the orchestra and professor of conducting at the Paris Conservatoire, is a Chevalier de la Légion d'Honneur and an Officier de l'Ordre du Mérite National. His musical tastes are eclectic, but with a natural sympathy towards French composers, although his interest in most contemporary music is limited. He has a reputation as an accompanist.

Tzipine has made many records, especially of French composers of the 20th century, pre-Boulez. In 1955 Columbia (of EMI) issued a set of two LP discs with a representative selection of music from *Les Six*: Milhaud's Symphony No. 2, Auric's *Phèdre*, Poulenc's *Sécheresses*, Honegger's *Prélude, Fugue et Postlude*, an overture by Tailleferre, and Durey's *Le Printemps au fond de la mer* (with the Paris Conservatoire Orchestra). His other records include Honegger's Symphony No. 3, *Pacific 231, Rugby, Nicolas de Flue, Cantate de Noël, Cris du monde*, Piano Concerto and Concerto da Camera, Schmitt's *Psaume 47*, Ibert's *Le Chevalier errant*, Ravel's *Piano Concerto for the Left Hand* and Debussy's *Fantasy* (with

Février), Rivier's Symphonies Nos 3 and 5, Roussel's *Psaume 53, Le Bardit des Francs* and Sinfonietta, Ravel's *Piano Concerto in G major* (with M. Long), Challan's *Concerto pastoral*, François' Piano Concerto, Chopin's Piano Concerto No. 1 and Liszt's Piano Concerto No. 1 (with François), Bizet's opera *Ivan le Terrible*, Lesueur's *Marche du sacre de Napoléon 1er*, Barraud's *Numance* symphony, Aubert's *Le Tombeau de Chateaubriand*, Vogel's *Démophon*, Françaix's *Six Imperial Marches* and overtures by Paisiello, Boieldieu and Cimarosa (with the Paris Conservatoire Orchestra), Honegger's Symphony No. 4, and *Mouvement symphonique No. 3*, and Loucheur's *Hop Frog* and *Rapsodie malgache* (with the French National Radio Orchestra), *La Bohème* (in French), Fauré's suites *Dolly*, *Masques et bergamasques* and *Pelléas et Mélisande* (with the Paris Opéra-Comique Orchestra *et al.*), Milhaud's *Le Carnaval d'Aix* and Saint-Saëns' Piano Concerto No. 4 (with Johannesen and the Philharmonia Orchestra), Mussorgsky's *Songs and Dances of Death* (with Christoff and the French National Radio Orchestra) and songs by Balakirev and Borodin (with Christoff and the Lamoureux Orchestra). All these discs were for Columbia (EMI). He also recorded Roussel's Symphony No. 4 and *Suite in F major* (with the Lamoureux Orchestra for Capitol), Vierne's *Symphony in A minor* and Jolivet's Symphony No. 1 (with the ORTF Orchestra for Barclay), Baudrier's *Les Musiciens de la cité* and Delannoy's Piano Concerto (with Gobet, and with the Strasbourg Radio Symphony Orchestra for Barclay).

U

Ulsamer, Josef. After studies in Nuremberg and Erlangen, Ulsamer became a programme planner with the Bavarian Radio in Nuremberg, a teacher at the Nuremberg Conservatory, and at the Instituut voor Huismuziek in Holland, and teacher of instrumental history at the Bavarian State Conservatory in Würzburg. He founded and directed the Nuremberg Chamber Music Circle and the Ulsamer Collegium, which is a group incorporating a consort of viols, dedicated to performing early music on original instruments, and includes his wife, the Belgian harpsichordist Elza van der Veen. With the Ulsamer Collegium he has recorded for DGG Telemann's *Der getreue Musik-Meister*, and collections of dances of the Early Baroque, High Baroque and Renaissance (with guitarist Ragossnig), and as a viola da gamba player he has also recorded music by Bach, Bononcini and Couperin (for DGG).

Ungar, Thomas (b. 1931). Born in Budapest where he was educated at the Academy of Music, Ungar continued his studies at the Giuseppe Verdi Conservatory in Milan and at the Academy of Music in Vienna. He was conductor of the Hungarian Trade Union Symphony Orchestra (1953–6), of the Philharmonia Hungarica in Vienna (1957–9), the Siegerland Orchestra (1959–61), the Remscheid City Orchestra (1961–6), chief conductor of the Regensburg City Orchestra (1966–9) and at the Freiburg City Theatre (1969–73), professor of conducting at the Stuttgart Academy of Music (from 1970), and guest conductor with many major European orchestras. He has recorded Bartók's *Music for Strings, Percussion and Celesta* (with the Philharmonia Hungarica for Turnabout).

Unger, Heinz (1895–1965). Born in Berlin, Unger studied at the universities of Berlin and Munich, and at the Berlin Conservatory. From 1919 to 1933 he conducted the Berlin Philharmonic Orchestra in concerts organised by the Society of Friends of Music, formed the Cecilia Choir in Berlin and conducted it in major choral works, conducted in Magdeburg, Frankfurt am Main, Stuttgart and some European cities. He left Germany in 1933 for England, conducted the major British orchestras as well as others in Spain and other countries, and was conductor of the Leningrad Radio Orchestra (1934–6). His book, *Hammer, Sickle and Baton* (London, 1939) recounted his experiences in the USSR. He became a naturalised British subject in 1946, but moved to Canada in 1948 where he became the musical director of the Toronto Symphony Orchestra. A fine interpreter of Mahler, he was awarded the Gustav Mahler Medal and was made an honorary member of the Bruckner Society of America (both in 1958). During World War II Unger was one of the British conductors brought under contract by Decca to build up its classical catalogue. With the National Symphony Orchestra he recorded Beethoven's Symphony No. 3, Schubert's overture *In the Italian Style*, Mendelssohn's Symphony No. 4 and the overtures *The Hebrides*, *Ruy Blas* and *Athalie*.

Urbanner, Erich (b. 1936). Born in Innsbruck, Urbanner studied at the Vienna Academy of Music where he became professor of composition, and led seminars on dodecaphonic music. He has won prizes for his compositions, including the Förderungspreis of the City of Vienna. Telefunken recorded him conducting the Innsbruck Chamber Orchestra in his Double Bass Concerto, with soloist Streicher; the Alban Berg Quartet has also recorded his String Quartet No. 3 (for Telefunken).

Urbini, Pierluigi (b. 1929). Born in Rome, Urbini studied at the Accademia di Santa Cecilia, was a violin soloist, and made his debut as a conductor at the Teatro Massimo in Palermo. He has since conducted both opera and concerts in many European countries. For Angelicum he recorded Viotti's Violin and Piano Concerto No. 3 and Mendelssohn's Violin and Piano Concerto (with Gulli and Cavallo and the Angelicum Orchestra), which was issued in the United States by Musical Heritage Society.

V

Vajnar, Frantisek (b. 1930). Born in Stracice u Rokycany, Czechoslovakia, Vajnar studied the violin and conducting at the Prague Conservatory, was a member of the Prague National Theatre Orchestra (1950–53), became conductor of the Armed Forces' Opera (1953–5) in Prague, at the Karlina State Theatre (1955–60), and at the Ostrava Opera (1960–62); from 1962 he was chief conductor of the Nejedly Theatre at Usti-on-Labe. He recorded a symphony, octet and cassation by Mysliveček, Zelenka's overture *Ipocondria* and an orchestral quartet of Stamitz (with the Collegium Musicum Pragensis and the Musici de Praga for Panton), Jirásek's *Stabat Mater* (with the Czech Philharmonic Wind Ensemble *et al.* for Supraphon), and Hlobil's Double Bass Concerto (with Fuka and Musici de Praga for Panton).

Válek, Vladimir (b. 1935). Born at Novy Jičin, Czechoslovakia, and a graduate of the Prague Academy of Music, Válek first conducted with the Prague Radio Symphony Orchestra, appeared with orchestras in Czechoslovakia, toured in the USSR, USA, Italy, Germany and Poland, and in 1974 received the Prize of the Czech Music Fund. He has recorded for Supraphon Flosman's Flute Concerto (with Hecl and the Dvořák Chamber Orchestra) and Violin Concerto No. 2 (with Konvalinka and the Prague Radio Symphony Orchestra) and Jiri Válek's Symphony No. 10 (with the Prague Radio Symphony Orchestra), and for Panton Martinů's Double Concerto, Schulhoff's Double Concerto, Hlobil's *The Path of the Living*, Jonák's Trumpet Concerto, Ceremuga's Concerto da Camera (with the Dvořák Chamber Orchestra *et al.*), Matěj's Triple Concerto (with the Czech Philharmonic Wind Ensemble), Hlaváč's suite from the opera *Inultus* and Ostrčil's ballet *Antithesis* (with the Czech Army Symphony Orchestra).

Van den Berg, Maurits (1898–1971). Born in Groningen in the Netherlands, and educated at the Cologne Conservatory, Van den Berg graduated with the soloists' diploma for violin in 1917, was a violinist in the Strasbourg City Orchestra, the Cologne Opera Orchestra, the Berlin Philharmonic and the Vienna Philharmonic Orchestras, and was also a member of the Buxbaum Quartet. He was a conductor in the Netherlands at Arnhem, with the Amsterdam Concertgebouw Orchestra, and with the Dutch Broadcasting Organisation, where he conducted the Netherlands Radio Philharmonic Orchestra, and was permanent conductor of the Netherlands Radio Chamber Orchestra (1949–63). He was also a guest conductor in Switzerland, Belgium, FR Germany, *et al.*, and was active at many important music festivals in the Netherlands. He made records for La Guilde Internationale du Disque (issued by Concert Hall and other labels) of works including Torelli's *Concerto a quattro* ('Christmas'), Marcello's Concerto Grosso Op. 1 No. 4, Durante's Concerto Grosso No. 5, and Grieg's *Holberg Suite* (with the Netherlands Chamber Orchestra), Vivaldi's Viola d'amore Concerto P. 288 (with Sabatini), a suite from Couperin's harpsichord pieces, Saint-Saëns' Violin Concerto No. 3 and *Havanaise* (with Kaufman and the Netherlands Philharmonic Orchestra), J. C. Bach's Sinfonias Op. 18 Nos 2 and 3, W. F. Bach's *Symphony in D minor* and C. P. E. Bach's Symphony No. 2 (with a chamber orchestra). For Donemus he recorded Felderhof's Flute Concerto (with Barwahser and the Netherlands Radio Chamber Orchestra).

Vandernoot, André (b. 1927). Born in Brussels, Vandernoot studied at the Conservatoire there, was among the prizewinners at the International Competition for Young Conductors at Besançon in 1951, and as a result was given a grant to study at the Vienna Academy of Music for two years. After graduating in conducting, he toured Switzerland with the Academy's orchestra, and in the following years conducted major orchestras in Vienna, Brussels, Paris, London, Buenos Aires *et al.*, as well as regularly conducting the Belgian National Orchestra, of which he became the musical director in 1954. He was appointed musical director of the Royal Opera at Brussels in 1960, where he conducted a varied repertoire, and also appeared in the United States and Canada with marked success.

Vandernoot made a number of records for EMI in 1957–9, including Mozart's Symphonies Nos 33, 34, 35, 36, 38, 39, 40 and 41, and Piano Concertos K. 466 and K. 488 (with Heidsieck), Beethoven's Piano Concertos Nos 1 and 2 (with Gilels), Brahms' Serenade No. 1 and the Tchaikovsky Violin Concerto (with Kogan, and the Paris Conservatoire Orchestra), Beethoven's overtures *Egmont*, *Coriolan*, *Fidelio*, *Prometheus* and *Leonore No. 3* (with the Berlin Philharmonic Orchestra), Tchaikovsky's Piano Concerto No. 1, Liszt's Piano Concerto No. 2 and the Grieg Piano Concerto (with Cziffra), Mahler's *Kindertotenlieder* (with Christa Ludwig, and the Philharmonia Orchestra). His other records include *Symphonie fantastique* (with the Orchestre National de la Radiodiffusion Française, for Command), *Pictures at an Exhibition* and *Capriccio espagnol* (with the Paris Conservatoire Orchestra for Command), and Bach's Cantatas Nos 80 and 104 and the *St John Passion* (with the Amsterdam Philharmonic Orchestra *et al.*, for La Guilde Internationale du Disque, and released in the United States by Vanguard and Nonesuch, respectively).

Van Vactor, David (b. 1906). Born at Plymouth, Indiana, the American flautist, composer and conductor Van Vactor was educated at Northwestern University, the Vienna Academy of Music, l'École Normale and the Paris Conservatoire. He was flautist with the Chicago Symphony Orchestra (1931–43), taught music at Northwestern University (1935–47), was assistant conductor of the Kansas Philharmonic Orchestra (1943–7), the Knoxville Symphony Orchestra (1947–72) and head of the department of fine arts at the University of Tennessee (1947–52). He has toured South America with the North American Woodwind Quintet, and has been a guest conductor with orchestras in the United States and Europe. On record, he has conducted much of his own music, including his Symphonies Nos 1 and 2 (with the Frankfurt Radio Orchestra for Composers Recordings), *Overture to a Comedy No. 2, Bagatelles for Strings, Octet for Brass, Variazioni solenne* (with the Hessian Radio Symphony Orchestra for Everest), *Ode, Sarabanda con variazioni, Passacaglia, Chorale and Allegro, Prelude and March, Four Etudes for Winds and Percussion, Pastoral and Dance, Suite on Chilean Folk Tunes, Recitative and Saltarello, Introduction and Presto for Strings, Sinfonia breve*, Viola Concerto and Concerto for Three Flutes and Harp (on three LP discs, with the Hessian Radio Symphony Orchestra for Orion). He has also conducted for Composers Recordings music of the American composers Boda, Sanders and Trythall (with the Knoxville Symphony Orchestra) and Luening and McPhee (with the Hessian Radio Symphony Orchestra).

Varendonck, Dirk (b. 1923). Born in Ghent, Varendonck studied at the Brussels Conservatoire Royal under Defossez, and was founder and principal conductor of the West Flemish Orchestra, which began in 1951 as the Bruges Chamber Orchestra. At the same time he is a civil engineer and general manager of the Société Belgo-Anglaise des Ferry-Boats. With the West Flemish Orchestra he has performed in Holland and Luxembourg, and has conducted the English Chamber Orchestra in concerts in London. For Harmonia Mundi he recorded Martin's Concerto for Seven Wind Instruments, Timpani, Percussion and Strings.

Varga, Tibor (b. 1921). The violinist Varga was born at Györ, Hungary, was educated at the University and the Franz Liszt Academy at Budapest, and has performed throughout Europe. He has made many distinguished recordings as a soloist, including Bartók's Violin Concerto No. 2 and the Nielsen Violin Concerto, and with his own chamber orchestra recorded, as a conductor, Mozart's Divertimento K. 136 (for Nonesuch) and Piano Concerto K. 271 (with Studer, for Claves).

Varviso, Silvio (b. 1924). Born in Zürich where he studied piano and conducting at the Conservatory, Varviso was engaged as assistant conductor at the St Gallen City Theatre (1946–50), and made his first public appearance there with *Die Zauberflöte*. He became principal conductor at the Basel Opera (1950–62), being appointed its artistic director in 1956, conducted at the Berlin Staatsoper (1958–61) and in Paris (from 1958), at the San Francisco Opera (1959), at the Glyndebourne Festival (1962) and at Covent Garden, and from 1969 has conducted each year at the Bayreuth Festivals. He was a conductor at the New York Metropolitan Opera (1962–6), was appointed chief conductor at the Royal Opera, Stockholm (1965–72), where in 1970 the king of Sweden conferred on him the highest musical post in the country, and became general music director at the Württemberg State Theatre, Stuttgart (1971).

Varviso has recorded for Decca Borodin's Symphony No. 2, Tchaikovsky's *Francesca da Rimini* and Prokofiev's *The Stone Flower* (with the Suisse Romande Orchestra), *L'Italiana in Algeri* (with the Maggio Musicale Fiorentino *et al.*), *Cavalleria rusticana* and excerpts from *Mefistofele* (with the Rome Opera Orchestra *et al.*), *Norma* (with the Santa Cecilia Orchestra *et al.*), *Il barbiere di Siviglia* (with the Rossini Orchestra of Naples *et al.*), excerpts from *Der Rosenkavalier* (with the Vienna Philharmonic Orchestra *et al.*) and *Anna Bolena* (with the Vienna State Opera Orchestra *et al.*). Philips recorded the 1974 Bayreuth performance of *Die Meistersinger*, directed by Varviso; of him the authors of the *Penguin Stereo Record Guide* (1977) wrote that he 'proves the most persuasive Wagnerian, one who inspires the authentic ebb and flow of tension, who builds up Wagner's scenes concentratedly over the longest span, and who revels in the lyricism and textural beauty of the score'.

Vasadi-Balogh, Lajos (b. 1921). Born in Budapest, Vasadi-Balogh studied at the Conservatory there, and abroad with Furtwängler, Dobrowen and Krauss, at the same time as he was studying law, philosophy and art at the Budapest and Pécs Universities. He was a teacher at the Budapest Academy (1942), conductor at the Budapest Opera House (1956), and since 1960 of the Postás Symphony Orchestra. His compositions include *Mary Stuart*, an opera after Schiller, symphonies, chamber music, *et al.* With the Postás Symphony Orchestra he recorded for Qualiton the *Symphonie fantastique*.

Vásárhelyi, Zoltán (1900–77). Born in Kecskemét, Hungary, Vásárhelyi taught at the Music School there (1926–42), and then was professor of choral teaching at the Academy of Music at Budapest (1942–77). He composed several choral works, and conducted choruses in Budapest. For Hungaroton he recorded Schubert's Three Choruses, Op. 112 and *Miriams Siegesgesang*, Schumann's *Spanisches Liederspiel*, and a collection of mixed choruses by Kodály (with the Hungarian Radio and Television Choir).

Vašata, Rudolf (b. 1911). Born in Prague, Vasata conducted at Kladno (1932–7), studied with Talich (1934–7), and became a repetiteur and then a conductor at the Prague National Theatre (1937–49). He was director of the Ostrava Opera (1949–56), founded the Ostrava Chamber Orchestra (1953), and in 1960 was appointed chief conductor at the Liberec Opera, and directed an ensemble dedicated to performing contemporary music. His recordings include 78 r.p.m. discs for Ultraphon of an abridged *The Bartered Bride* (with the Prague National Theatre Orchestra *et al.*), and arias from *Jenůfa* and an LP of the overtures to *Euryanthe, I vespri siciliani* and *The Secret* (with the Czech Philharmonic Orchestra), and a collection of extracts from Wagner operas (with Dvořáková and the Prague National Theatre Orchestra).

Vassilenko, Sergey (1872–1956). The Russian composer, teacher and conductor Vassilenko was born and educated at Moscow, and during his lifetime wrote numerous orchestral works, a Violin Concerto, a cantata and some chamber music. From his early compositions, which were derived from traditional Russian church music, his style developed under the influence of the French impressionist composers and the folk music of Russia and other countries. The Russian record company issued 78 r.p.m. discs of him conducting the USSR State Symphony Orchestra in his own Ballet Suite Op. 122 and *The Gypsies*, another ballet suite.

Vaszy, Viktor (b. 1903). Born in Budapest, Vaszy studied composition at the Budapest Academy of Music, graduated in 1927, conducted several orchestras in Budapest, lectured at the Academy of Music, and was music director and conductor of the Szeged Opera Company until he retired. For Qualiton he recorded Liszt's Piano Concerto No. 2 and *Concerto pathétique* (with Antal and the Hungarian State Concert Orchestra) and excerpts from *Madama Butterfly* (with the Hungarian State Opera Orchestra *et al.*).

Vaughan, Denis (b. 1926). Born in Melbourne, Australia, Vaughan studied at the Melbourne University, where he was the university organist (1944–6), and occasionally played the double-bass in the Melbourne Symphony Orchestra. He came to England to study at the Royal College of Music and under André Marchal, joined the Royal Philharmonic Orchestra under Beecham as a double-bass player (1950–54), became the orchestra's organist, pianist and harpsichordist, and was assistant conductor and chorusmaster to Beecham (1954–7), making his debut as a conductor in London. At the same time, he gave organ, harpsichord and piano recitals in England, Europe and in the United States (1948–56), and founded the Beecham Choral Society. Beecham was his greatest teacher: 'His knowledge of style and phrasing has never been surpassed; he marked up his scores quite closely and I was able to study them in the time I was with him' (*Hi Fi News and Record Review*, January 1977, p. 85). In 1976 he was elected as honorary president of the Sir Thomas Beecham Society.

Vaughan went to Milan on a Gulbenkian scholarship to study Italian opera; the result was a long controversy with the publishers of Verdi and Puccini about the considerable number of erroneous markings on virtually every page of the scores. He wrote a book about these mistakes in the Verdi operas (1958) and another on Puccini's orchestration (1960). Similarly he studied the manuscripts and copies of the Schubert symphonies in Vienna, and was surprised to again discover the errors that had occurred in publication. He gained experience at the Operas at Glyndebourne, Hamburg, Munich and La Scala, and is now solo repetiteur and conductor under Sawallisch at the Bavarian State Opera at Munich, as well as being active with the Scarlatti Orchestra at Naples, and has been musical director of opera companies in Australia. He is consultant to UNESCO and the Berne Union for the Protection of Musical Works against Unauthentic Alterations.

Vaughan's recordings include Mozart's *Il re pastore*, and the eleven symphonies K. 128 to K. 196, Haydn's Symphonies Nos 82 to 92 and Sinfonia Concertante, the complete Schubert symphonies, the completed third movement of the *Unfinished, Rosamunde, Zauberharfe* overtures, and two *Overtures in the Italian Style*. These were all recorded by RCA with the Orchestra of Naples, which largely comprises the Orchestra Alessandro Scarlatti. Critical comment about the Haydn and Schubert series agreed on the crisp musical interpretation and the alert playing, although Stanley Sadie added the reservation, in the Haydn, that though the detail is excellent, the necessary breadth is rarely there.

Vaughan Williams, Ralph (1872–1959). The great British composer Vaughan Williams was reputed to be an amateur at conducting; he said that 'If a composer cannot play in an orchestra or sing in a choir, the next best thing he can do in self-education is to try his hand at conducting and really find out what the performers are up against.' He was conductor of the Bach Choir in London for six years and for almost 50 years led the choirs taking part in the Leith Hill musical festival in Surrey. When he took over the Bach Choir, he gave no concerts for the first season, but rehearsed the choir in the *St Matthew Passion*, and gave a number of performances of it the following Easter. Boult has recorded that when he first heard the work under Vaughan Williams 'it was not a fine piece of conducting as such, at all. It was that a very great musician indeed had worked for six months with a large number of intelligent people, and at the end of it he had impressed the whole society with his own view of the Bach *St Matthew Passion* so that the production of it was not conducting in the customary sense. The performance could not proceed except as it had been rehearsed and rehearsed: Bach through the spectacles of Ralph Vaughan Williams. It was a spiritual matter.' Boult also has written that Vaughan Williams gave a most memorable performance of his *London Symphony*; although he rushed through it without lingering to make the most of some expressive passages, 'somehow it sounded absolutely splendid'.

Vaughan Williams did however record his Symphony No. 4 in 1937 with the BBC Symphony Orchestra in an interpretation that is one of the classics of the gramophone. This symphony is held by some people to be a prophetic work presaging World War II, and although it has been recorded by others, such as Mitropoulos, Boult, Bernstein and Previn, none has equalled the ferocious intensity of the composer's own performance. In 1970 an LP transfer appeared of it on the World Record Club label. In 1926 he also recorded with the Aeolian Players his overture to *The Wasps* and ballet *Old King Cole*, which were re-issued on an LP transfer by Pearl.

Venhoda, Miroslav (b. 1915). Born at Moravské, Budějovice, Czechoslovakia, Venhoda studied at the Charles University at Prague (1934–8), travelled in Italy (1938–9), and during World War II was organist and choirmaster of the Dominican Friars at the Strahov Monastery in Prague. In 1946 he published his *Method of Studying Gregorian Chant*. He founded and conducted the Prague Madrigal Singers (1956), with whom he has performed in festivals in Europe and North America. With this choir he has made numerous recordings for Supraphon, including choral works of Lassus, Josquin, Ockeghem, Bořkovec, Dufay, A. and G. Gabrieli, Michna, Monteverdi, Obrecht, Palestrina, English masters such as Tallis, Gibbons and Dowland, and Slavický, Suchoň, Tůma, Zach and Martinů.

Verbrugghen, Henri (1873–1934). Born in Brussels, Verbrugghen first appeared in public as a violinist at the age of ten, and then studied at the Brussels Conservatory under Hubay and Ysaÿe. In 1893 he was appointed concertmaster of the Scottish Orchestra, which had been formed by Henschel, and in 1894 he became leader and deputy conductor of the Lamoureux Orchestra in Paris; later he was concertmaster of the Queen's Hall Orchestra in London. As a violinist, with his string quartet, and as a conductor, he became famous for his performances of Beethoven, and was the first to give performances of the complete Beethoven Violin and Piano Sonatas in England. In 1915 he settled in Australia to become the director of the New South Wales State Conservatorium and conductor of the newly formed State Symphony Orchestra, where he had an important and lasting influence on standards of performance and appreciation. He first appeared in the United States in 1918, conducting the Russian Symphony Orchestra (sic) at Carnegie Hall in a Beethoven programme; Richard Aldrich wrote in *The New York Times* that for Verbrugghen 'the music of Beethoven is . . . a treasure store of subtleties so precious in the extreme that the baton of the conductor cannot overlook or slight a single one of them without destroying the charm and purpose of the entire work. He searches out all the hidden beauties of the work and reveals them so clearly and so gracefully and so completely to the ear of the audience as the mechanical and musical efficiency of his orchestra permits'. In 1923 he left Australia altogether for the US, and was appointed conductor of the Minneapolis Symphony Orchestra, where he remained until 1931 when illness forced his resignation. Until his death he was director of the music department at Carleton College, Northfield, Minnesota. Verbrugghen made some discs for Brunswick with the Minneapolis Symphony Orchestra: the prelude to *Khovanshchina*, *Valse triste* and the overture to *Der Freischütz*.

Veselka, Josef (b. 1910). Born at Nové Město in Moravia, and a student at Palacký University at Olomouc, Czechoslovakia, Veselka founded the Moravian Academic Association (1931), taught voice training and choral singing at the Brno Conservatory and the Janáček Academy, and at the Prague Academy of Music, and became conductor of the Prague Philharmonic Choir (1959). He was active as a music critic, and developed an interest in the performance of early music. As conductor of the Prague Philharmonic Choir he recorded (for Supraphon) Bach's Motets, recitals of old Czech choral music, Palestrina's *Missa Papae Marcelli*, *Hodie Christus natus est*, *Stabat Mater* and *Improperia*, and took part in numerous recordings with the Czech Philharmonic Orchestra in choral works and symphonic music under other conductors. He also recorded Fils' *Missa solemnis* and Brixi's *Missa pastoralis* (with the Prague Symphony Orchestra *et al.* for Supraphon), choruses of Janáček (for Panton), and *L'elisir d'amore* (with the Prague Philharmonic Orchestra *et al.* for La Guilde Internationale du Disque).

Vetö, Tamás (b. 1935). Born in Budapest, and educated at the Budapest Conservatory, Vetö won a piano competition at the age of 13, and studied under Nadia Boulanger in France. He came to Denmark in 1956, and was engaged by the Royal Theatre in Copenhagen in 1957, where he was choirmaster before becoming conductor. He has also led the Prisma Ensemble in performances of contemporary music, and visited Poland to give concerts at the Warsaw Festival with the Group. In addition, he conducts the University Students' Choral Society, and has given piano recitals in Scandinavia and in other European countries. He has recorded Nørgård's *Voyage into the Golden Screen* (with the Danish Radio Symphony Orchestra for Caprice) and Barraque's *Chant après chant* and *Séquence* (with the Prism Ensemble, released in the United States by Musical Heritage Society).

Veyron-Lacroix, Robert (b. 1922). Born in Paris and educated at the Paris Conservatoire, the pianist, harpsichordist and conductor Veyron-Lacroix was a professor at the Schola Cantorum (1955–7) and at the Nice International Academy (from 1959). Vox (Turnabout) released a disc in 1966 in which he led the Froment Chamber Ensemble in the Vivaldi Concerti Op. 10, in which Rampal was the flautist and himself the harpsichordist. He has also made numerous records as a harpsichordist.

Vigner, -. (b. 1906). The Latvian musician Vigner has been conductor of the Latvian Radio Orchestra and Opera Theatre. With the orchestra he recorded Ivanov's Symphony No. 6, for Melodiya.

Villa-Lobos, Heitor (1887–1959). An incredibly prolific composer, the Brazilian Villa-Lobos wrote more than 1300 works, ranging from folk-song arrangements to large-scale orchestral and choral pieces describing the history and folk-lore of his native land. From the 1920s he was active as a conductor, in Brazil and in New York, Paris and London, primarily directing his own music, but he introduced to Brazilian audiences major masterpieces such as Bach's *Mass in B minor* and Beethoven's *Missa solemnis*. He had a penchant for leading concerts with huge musical forces; at one in Brazil in 1935 there were 1,000 musicians and 30,000 choristers. It is said that he was once engaged to conduct a concert of his music with the Los Angeles Philharmonic Orchestra, and that before his arrival the orchestra had been fully rehearsed. However, he demanded two full rehearsals; the manager pointed out that the orchestra did not need much rehearsing as they already played the pieces perfectly. Villa-Lobos was adamant: 'But *I* have to rehearse so I can learn how to conduct my pieces.'

Villa-Lobos recorded of his own music, on 78s, *Bachianas brasileiras Nos 2* and *5* and *Chôros Nos 1* and *7* (with the New York World Fair Orchestra for Victor), *Bachianas bra-*

sileiras No. 5 (with Sayao and an orchestra for Columbia), and five *Serestas* and a *Miniaturas* (with Tourel and an orchestra for Columbia). Later, between 1954 and 1958, he recorded a number of his works in Paris with the Orchestre National de la Radiodiffusion Française and a number of artists and choruses, including Victoria de los Angeles, Felicia Blumental and Magda Tagliaferro; the pieces were *Bachianas brasileiras Nos 1 to 9, Deux Chôros, Chôros Nos 2, 5, 10* and *11*, *Invocation pour la défense de la patrie, La découverte du Brésil*, Symphony No. 4, *Mômo precóce*, Piano Concerto No. 5 and *A prole do Bébé*. A disc of *Bachianas brasileiras Nos 2, 5, 6* and *9* (with Los Angeles in *No. 5*) was later re-issued. His other recordings were of *Chôros No. 6* (with the RIAS Orchestra for Remington), *The Forest of the Amazon* (with Sayao and the Symphony of the Air, for United Artists), and the *Fantasia concertante* and arrangements for a cello ensemble of some of the preludes and fugues of Bach (for Everest).

Vis, Lucas (b. 1947). Born in Bergen, Vis studied at the Amsterdam Music High School (1962–9), and with Maderna at Salzburg (1967), and was a cellist and assistant conductor of the Amsterdam Philharmonic Orchestra (1968–9). He assisted Maderna and Horvat at Salzburg (1969–70), studied with Boulez, Fournet, Constant, Dixon and Hupperts, and won the Koussevitzky Composition Prize at Tanglewood (1971). He has been a guest conductor with orchestras in FR Germany, France and the Netherlands, and since 1976 has been conductor and artistic manager of the Netherlands Ballet Orchestra. For Donemus he has recorded L. Andriessen's *De Staat* (with the Netherlands Vocal Ensemble *et al.*) and Escher's *Nostalgies* (with Langridge and the Netherlands Radio Chamber Orchestra).

Vitalini, Alberico (b. 1921). Born in Rome, Vitalini taught himself the piano and violin as a boy, attended the Accademia di Santa Cecilia (1930–36), where he studied under Molinari, and at the age of twelve was organist at San Carlo di Catinari in Rome. As a student, in 1937, he conducted an ensemble for radio programmes, and started to compose for films; altogether he has written over 250 film scores. He conducted in theatres and concerts, and became associated with the Vatican Radio (1948), and was appointed its director of music (1950). For the Vatican Radio he has composed incidental and occasional music, and among his successful presentations have been Roncalli's *Suite Bergomense* (1959), his own *Missa Virgo Praedicanda* (1962), Tonetti's *Passio San Petri Apostoli* (1971) and Puccini's Mass (1974), which became a successful commercial recording. His more recent compositions include an opera *King David*, and he arranged Mascagni's Mass and Perosi's *The Seven Words of Christ*.

Vitalini's recordings have included, with the Vatican Radio Orchestra *et al.*, Perosi's *Il Natale del Redentore* (for Ricordi) and *In Patris memoriam* (for Cetra), Tonetti's *Passio San Petri Apostoli* (for Hit), Puccini's Mass (for Angelicum), Refice's *Missa in honorem Sanctae Theresiae* (for Cetra), and his own *Impressioni* (for Hit), *Concerto spirituale* (for Cetra), *Fantastica romantica* and *Scherzo* (for Orion), *Meditations on the first Mistero Doloroso* (for Colosseum) and *Sound Expression* (for Hit), and collections of pieces by Roncalli, Handel, Bach, Couperin, Schubert *et al.* (for RCA). He also recorded Rossini's *Petite Messe solennelle* (with the Rome Quartet Society *et al.* for Period), Martucci's *Notturno* and his own *Renascita* (with the Rome Quartet Society for Colosseum) and excerpts from *Don Pasquale* (with the Rome Lyric Opera for Vox).

Vlach, Josef (b. 1923). Born in Ratměřice, Czechoslovakia, Vlach studied the violin at the Prague Conservatory under Novák, Micka and Slajs (1938–43 and 1945–7), and at the Prague Academy of Music under Feld and Pekelský (1947–51). He first appeared as a solo violinist in 1940, and at the Conservatory played in chamber music ensembles. He was leader and soloist in Talich's Czech Chamber Orchestra (1947–8), then was at the Prague National Theatre (1949–56), founded and was first violin of the Vlach String Quartet (1950) and took over the leadership of the Czech Chamber Orchestra (1959). In addition to his many records for Supraphon with the Vlach Quartet, he recorded with the Czech Chamber Orchestra Mozart's *Eine kleine Nachtmusik*, Divertimento K. 136 and *Adagio and Fugue in C minor*, and Piano Concertos K. 449, K. 488 and K. 503 (with Moravec), Zach's *Motetto in D minor*, Dvořák's *Serenade in E major*, Tchaikovsky's *Serenade in C major, Andante cantabile* and *Chant sans paroles* Op. 2 No. 3, Stravinsky's *Apollon Musagète*, Britten's *Variations on a Theme of Frank Bridge*, and Hurník's *Song Without Words*. For Panton he also recorded with the Prague Chamber Orchestra symphonies by Rejcha and Voříšek, Cherubini's Symphony and overture to *Medea*, and Respighi's *Gli uccelli*.

Vladigerov, Alexander (b. 1933). Born in Sofia, the son of the Bulgarian composer Pantcho

Vladigerov, Vladigerov studied with his father and at the Sofia Academy of Music. He was assistant conductor to Rachlin at Kiev, conducted orchestras and gave piano recitals in the USSR and in Eastern Europe, and became conductor of the Symphony Orchestra of the Bulgarian Committee of Television and Radio (1969). He has won international prizes for his compositions, including several musicals. For Balkanton he has recorded, with the orchestra above, *et al.*, Gershwin's *Cuban Overture, Rhapsody in Blue, Piano Concerto in F* and *Variations on I Got Rhythm* (with Mousev) and excerpts from *Porgy and Bess*, Pipkov's Cello Concerto (with Nikolov), Tekeliev's *Requiem*, Christoskov's *Concerto for Orchestra*, Kostov's *Youth Overture* and *Three Diaphonic Dances* and his own musicals *The Wolf and the Seven Kids, Gay Town Musicians* and *Little Red Riding Hood*, and a number of compositions of his father: the Piano Concertos Nos 1 and 2 (with Mousev), No. 4 (with Drennikov) and No. 5 (with the composer), the Violin Concertos No. 1 (with Badev) and No. 2 (with Schneidermann), *Bulgarian Suite, Bulgarian Rhapsody, Improvisation and Toccata*, two suites from *The Legend of the Lake, Four Romanian Symphonic Dances, Two Romanian Symphonic Sketches, Seven Bulgarian Symphonic Dances, Heroic Overture, Concerto Overture, Three Impressions for Orchestra,* Ratchenitza from the opera *Tsar Kaloyan, Ljulin Impressions, Hebrew Poem* and *Jewish Poem*. He also recorded his father's *May Symphony No. 2* (with the Rousse Philharmonic Orchestra) and *Vadar* (with the Moscow Radio Symphony Orchestra).

Vocht, Lodewijk de (1887–1977). Born in Antwerp, de Vocht studied at the Conservatory there, and at the age of 16 played the viola in a local orchestra. He had the opportunity of observing great conductors such as Mahler, Strauss and Nikisch, and in 1910 himself conducted a series of three orchestral concerts. He became choirmaster at the Antwerp Cathedral (1912), founded and conducted the Chorale Caecilia (1916), led a Beethoven festival at Antwerp (1921), became conductor of the New Concert Society there (1923–34), was appointed professor at the Royal Flemish Conservatory (1921) and became its director (1941–52), and between 1931 and 1954 conducted many concerts for the Brussels Philharmonic Society. He made a profound impression with his choir in Paris in 1928 and 1937, and in 1940 gave memorable performances of Honegger's *Jeanne d'Arc au Bûcher*. He recorded the work on 78s (with the Chorale Caecilia, the Belgian National Radio Orchestra, *et al.* for HMV), also Honegger's *Judith*, Milhaud's *L'Orestie d'Éschyle* and Debussy's *Trois Chansons de Charles d'Orléans* (with the Chorale Caecilia *et al.* for Columbia, and, on an LP, his own Violin Concerto (with van Neste and the Belgian National Radio Orchestra for Decca).

Vöchting, Christian (b. 1928). Born in Basel, where he was a pupil at the Conservatory, Vöchting studied with Kägi, Vogt, Güldenstein, von Kulm and Münch, and became a choral repetiteur at Freiburg (1948). He conducted at Biel and Solothurn (1952), Wuppertal (1957), at the Berlin Opera (1959–62) and at Zürich (since 1962). He led the première of Martin's opera *Der Sturm* (Zürich, 1959), and has conducted orchestras throughout Europe. He has recorded Beethoven's Piano Concerto No. 5 (with Perlemuter) and overture *Die Ruinen von Athen*, and Sibelius' Symphony No. 2 (with the Vienna Festival Orchestra for La Guilde Internationale du Disque, the concerto also being released in the United States by Audio Fidelity), and Volkmar Andreae's *Music for Orchestra* (with the Geneva Studio Orchestra for CT).

Vogel, Jaroslav (1894–1970). Born in Plzeň, Czechoslovakia, Vogel studied under Novák at the Prague Conservatory, at the Munich Academy of Music, and under d'Indy at the Schola Cantorum in Paris. He was first a repetiteur at the Prague National Theatre, then was conductor at Ostrava (1919–23) and Plzeň (1926–7), music director at Ostrava (1927–41) and Brno (1941–5). Immediately after World War II he was dismissed from his post at Brno, and after several years as a guest conductor he was appointed conductor at the Prague National Theatre (1949–58), and then chief conductor of the Brno State Philharmonic Orchestra (1959–62). His compositions included three operas, one after Longfellow's *Hiawatha*, orchestral, chamber and vocal music, and he also published a monograph about Janáček. His recordings, all for Supraphon, included the complete *The Bartered Bride* and *Jenůfa*, and excerpts from Dvořák's *Rusalka*, and *The Jacobin*, and Janáček's *From the House of the Dead* and *The Makropoulos Affair*, and the overtures to Dvořák's *Dimitrij* and *Armida* and Fibich's *The Fall of Arcona* (with the Prague National Theatre Orchestra *et al.*) the Good Friday Music from *Parsifal* (with the Czech Philharmonic Orchestra), Novák's *De profundis*, Hindemith's *Symphonic Metamorphosis on Themes by Weber* (with the Brno State Philharmonic Orchestra) and Strauss's Oboe Concerto (with Hanták and the Brno State Philharmonic Orchestra). Heritage recently re-issued, in 1977, the recording of *The Bartered Bride*.

Vogt, Hans (b. 1909). Born in Basel where he studied at the Conservatory (1929–32), Vogt was a conducting pupil with Weingartner (1932–3), studied composition with Dukas and the piano with Cortot in Paris. He worked as a pianist and composer, taught the piano at the Basel Conservatory (1946), and became a conductor for Basel Radio, for which he wrote music for many radio plays. His other compositions include incidental music for the stage, vocal, instrumental and chamber music, and arrangements of Swiss folk songs, and he has written books about piano playing technique and other musical subjects. He recorded overtures by Hiebner and Stuntz, with the Basel Orchestral Society Orchestra, for CT.

Vonk, Hans (b. 1942). Born in Amsterdam where his father was a violinist in the Concertgebouw Orchestra, Vonk learned the violin as a boy, first studied law at the University, and also attended the Amsterdam Conservatory. There he studied the piano and conducting, was a pupil at Scherchen's summer course at Salzburg, and graduated from the Conservatory in 1964. After taking part in the Netherland Radio's conductors' course at Hilversum, he was appointed conductor of the Netherlands National Ballet (1966–70), became assistant conductor of the Amsterdam Concertgebouw Orchestra with Haitink (1973–5), where he observed Kondrashin and Krips, was chief conductor of the Netherlands Radio Philharmonic Orchestra (1973–5), and has been music director of the Netherlands Opera (since 1975) and associate conductor of the Royal Philharmonic Orchestra, London (since 1976). He has been a guest conductor in many countries around the world, has a large repertoire, and his interest in *avant-garde* music stems from his early experience as a composer.

He first recorded for Decca in 1973 Rachmaninov's Piano Concerto No. 2 and *Rhapsody on a Theme of Paganini* (with Vered and the London Symphony Orchestra), and then went on to do Schubert's Symphony No. 9, Mendelssohn's Symphony No. 4 and incidental music to *A Midsummer Night's Dream*, the *Romeo and Juliet* fantasy-overture, *Capriccio italien* and the waltz from *Eugene Onegin* (with the Royal Philharmonic Orchestra), for Composer's Voice Schat's opera *Houdini* (with the Concertgebouw Orchestra *et al.*), and for Donemus Henkemans' *Élégies* (with the Concertgebouw Orchestra), Andriessen's *Respiration*, Vlijmen's *Omaggio a Gesualdo* and Vriend's *Huantan* (with the Netherlands Radio Wind Ensemble).

Voorberg, Marinus (b. 1920). Born at the Hook of Holland, Voorberg learned the clarinet as a boy, studied at the Conservatory and the Royal Academy of Music at The Hague, and was originally a pianist and organist. He studied conducting at the Accademia Chigiana at Siena, became a choral conductor, and was appointed director of the Netherlands Radio Chamber Choir at Hilversum (1950), later becoming the conductor of the Amsterdam Chamber Orchestra and of the South German Radio Choir (1975). He has toured extensively and has conducted a number of European orchestras. His recordings include the twelve Mendelssohn String Symphonies (with the Amsterdam Chamber Orchestra for Telefunken), a concertino by Genzmer and Mendelssohn's String Symphony No. 10 and Lieder Op. 4 Nos 4 and 6 (with the Netherlands Radio Chamber Choir and the Amsterdam Chamber Orchestra for Colosseum), horn concertos and pieces by Cherubini, Reger, Kalliwoda, Schumann and Weismann (with Baumann and the Munich Philharmonic Orchestra for Bärenreiter), and with the Netherlands Radio Vocal Ensemble music by Gesualdo and Handel's *Dixit Dominus* (for Philips), Sweelinck's Psalms 6, 116 and 123, and anthems and motets by Dowland, Purcell and Blow (for Cantate), discs of Renaissance Christmas and other music, and Demantius' *St John Passion* and *Prophecy of the Suffering and Death of Jesus Christ* (for Nonesuch), Křenek's *Lamentatio Jeremiae Prophetae* and Bialas' *Im Anfang* (for Bärenreiter), Benary's *Chormusik zur Passion* (for Camerata), Psalms and *Cantiones sacrae* by Sweelinck and sacred songs of Reger (for J. Stauda Verlag), Heppener's *Canti carnascialeschi*, Ruyneman's *L'Appel* and *Sonata for Chamber Choir*, and Straesser's *Herfst der Muziek* (for Donemus). He has also recorded scenes from the Mozart operas (with the Vienna Symphony Orchestra *et al.* for BASF).

Vorwerk, Paul (b. 1939). Educated at Occidental College and California Institute of Arts, Vorwerk completed postgraduate studies at Occidental College, the University of Southern California and Stanford University, all in California, and at the Musica Electronica Viva at Rome. He was a member and assistant conductor of the Roger Wagner Chorale (1963–6), a singer and conductor with Los Angeles Television and recording studios (1964–8), conductor of the Pacifica Singers, Los Angeles (since 1967), director of Musica Pacifica, a professional ensemble of players and singers of early music (since 1972), teacher of performing practices and analysis at the California Institute of Arts (1974–6), and professor of choral music and teacher of conducting and performance practices, California State University (1975–6). His recordings, as a conductor, have been of da Gagliano's *La Dafne* (with the Musica Pacifica for Command), Monteverdi's *Vespro della Beata Vergine* and a recital of early music (with the Musica Pacifica for Limited Edition recordings).

Vostřák, Zbyněk (b. 1920). Born in Prague, Vostřák studied at the Prague Conservatory under Dědeček and Karl (1939–43), was a member of the Prague Radio Symphony Orchestra (1943–5), professor of the opera class at the Prague Conservatory (1945–8), and also choral repetiteur at the Prague National Opera (1945–8). He gained experience as a conductor with regular guest engagements at the National Theatre and the Prague Radio, and in 1963 founded and directed the Musica Viva Pragensis. His compositions, since 1960, have been twelve-tone and have been influenced especially by the work of Webern. The last of his four operas, *The Broken Jug*, was awarded the 1962 UNESCO Prize in Paris; his *Three Sonnets from Shakespeare* won first prize in the 1964 SIMC Competition in Rome, and was a post-Webern serial work.

Vostřák has recorded a number of his own compositions for Supraphon: the *Three Sonnets from Shakespeare, Cantata, The Birth of the Moon* (with Musica Viva Pragensis), *Meta-Music* and *Mystery of Ellipsis* (with the Prague Radio Symphony Orchestra), *The Broken Jug* (with the Prague Radio Chamber Orchestra *et al.*) two dances from the ballet *Philosopher Story* (with the FISIO Orchestra, Prague), *Viktorka* and a scene from the opera *The King's Mint-Master* (with the Smetana Theatre Orchestra, Prague, *et al*), and two electronic works, *Scales of Light* and *Telepathy*. Of other composers, he has recorded Foerster's *The Luminous Morning*, scenes from Karel's *Three Hairs of Know-All Grandfather*, Wolf's *Integrals*, Bláha's Violin Concerto and Hanousek's *A Passion – Improvisation* (with the Prague Radio Symphony Orchestra), Kopelent's *Meditation, Snehah* and *Still Life*, Schoenberg's Suite Op. 29, Webern's Quartet Op. 22 and Gubajdulina's *Concordanza* (with the Musica Viva Pragensis), Milhaud's *Trois Rag-Caprices* and Martinů's *Le Jazz* and *Shimmy Foxtrot* (with the FOK Symphony Orchestra).

Votto, Antonino (b. 1896). Born in Piacenza, Votto studied at the Conservatorio San Pietro a Majella in Naples, and after serving in the Italian army in World War I, commenced his career in 1919 giving piano recitals in Naples and Rome. He taught the piano at Trieste and made his debut as a conductor there in 1919, and came under the notice of Panizza who recommended him for a position as conductor at the Teatro Colón at Buenos Aires (1921). Toscanini brought him back to La Scala, Milan, where he made his debut with *Manon Lescaut* (1923), and was Toscanini's assistant (1925–9). He conducted at Covent Garden (1924–5) and at other major European opera houses, gave occasional piano recitals in Italy, was appointed professor of conducting at the Conservatorio Giuseppe Verdi at Milan (1941), and has been a regular conductor at La Scala since 1948. His recordings with the La Scala Company, made in the late 1950s, were *La Gioconda, La Bohème, Un ballo in maschera* and *La sonnambula* (for EMI), *La Bohème* (with the Maggio Musicale Fiorentino *et al.* for DGG) and *La traviata* (with the La Scala Company for DGG). He also recorded *La Gioconda* (with the Italian Radio Orchestra *et al.* for Cetra), and a recital of arias with Konya (with the Maggio Musicale Fiorentino for DGG); L'Estro Armonico have also issued performances of *Norma, La Vestale, Il trovatore* and Donizetti's *Poliuto* (with the La Scala Company).

Vriend, Jan (b. 1938). Born at Sijbekarspel in North Holland, Vriend studied at the Amsterdam Conservatory and with Xenakis in Paris and Koenig at Utrecht University. He was first a choral conductor, then founded and conducted the Amsterdam Student Chamber Orchestra, performs as an organist and pianist, taught at Utrecht Conservatory (1968–9), and there conducted ensembles in contemporary music. For Donemus he recorded Kunst's *No Time*.

Vuataz, Roger (b. 1898). Born in Geneva, Vuataz studied there at the Conservatory under Barblan and Jaques-Dalcroze, was a church organist (1917–73), music critic (1940–60), teacher at the Conservatory (1962–9), choral conductor, and director of music programmes for Geneva Radio (1961–71). He composed many orchestral, concerted, chamber, instrumental and choral works, and arranged Bach's *Die Kunst der Fuge* for chamber orchestra; Scherchen recorded this version (with the Beromünster Radio Orchestra for Decca), as Vuataz himself did (with the Solistes de Bruxelles for Alpha).

W

Waart, Edo de (b. 1941). Born in Amsterdam, de Waart's interest in being a conductor was aroused as a boy when he heard Josef Krips conducting *Till Eulenspiegel*. He studied the oboe with Stotijn at the Music Lyceum at Amsterdam, then studied conducting with Spaanderman, and in 1963 was appointed first oboe of the Concertgebouw Orchestra. The next year he took the conducting course at Netherlands Radio at Hilversum, made his first appearance as a conductor with the Netherlands Radio Philharmonic Orchestra, and won a prize at the Dmitri Mitropoulos Competition for Conductors in New York, which entitled him to a year as assistant conductor with the New York Philharmonic Orchestra. He has said that he did not regard this as a useful experience, as in the whole year he conducted only 3½ hours of music, the rest of the time being spent sitting and watching. In 1966 he was appointed artistic director and conductor of the Netherlands Wind Ensemble, became assistant conductor to Haitink with the Concertgebouw Orchestra, in charge of 35 concerts, toured the United States with the orchestra in 1967, and was appointed permanent conductor with Fournet of the Rotterdam Philharmonic Orchestra, becoming the orchestra's artistic director in 1973. In 1972 he toured Japan with the Netherlands Wind Ensemble, and appeared as a guest conductor in many cities in Europe and the United States, and conducted opera in the Netherlands, Britain and the United States. In 1974 he was appointed permanent guest conductor of the San Francisco Symphony Orchestra, and in 1976 became permanent conductor of the orchestra, at the same time continuing to lead the Rotterdam Philharmonic.

De Waart's repertoire includes both the standard works and contemporary scores, although he professes a preference for Mozart, Brahms, Stravinsky and Mahler, and of modern composers Messiaen, Berio, Ligeti and Kagel. He echoes Boulez when he says that audiences cannot be expected to understand music of our time without having first become familiar with Schoenberg, Berg, Webern and (he adds) Ives. He has also suggested that the symphony orchestra should consist of 150 players, who can interchange between separate groups playing pre-classical music, the classical and romantic repertoire, and modern works. Discussing his love of Mozart, he compares him to Charlie Chaplin, who also had the unique capacity to arouse both tears and laughter. De Waart is aware of the impossible task before the conductor: unless he is a tyrant or a quite incredible person, he cannot really communicate to the orchestra what he wants in just three rehearsals. Secure technique and an accurate preparation of the score may ensure an adequate and safe reading, but the conductor has no chance to fashion the material into a personal statement (*The Gramophone*, August 1976, p. 295).

When de Waart was conductor of the Netherlands Wind Ensemble, from 1966 to 1971, he achieved a considerable success with recordings for Philips of the complete Mozart wind divertimenti and serenades, which were issued in 1970. He has also recorded the Serenades K. 203, K. 204, K. 250 and K. 320 and some marches of Mozart (with the Dresden Staatskapelle), and Dvořák's *Serenade in D minor*, Gounod's *Petite Symphonie*, Schubert's *Minuet and Finale* D. 72, Strauss's Serenade, Sonatina, *Suite for 13 Wind Instruments* and *Symphony for Wind Instruments*, Stravinsky's Piano Concerto, Octet, *Ebony Concerto* and *Symphonies of Wind Instruments* (with the Netherlands Wind Ensemble). His other recordings include arias by Mozart (with Ameling and the English Chamber Orchestra) and by Mozart and Rossini (with von Stade and the Rotterdam Philharmonic Orchestra), marches, dances and the *Masonic Funeral Music* of Mozart, *Boléro*, *Pictures at an Exhibition*, Saint-Saëns' Symphony No. 3 and *Wedding Cake* (with Chorzempa) and a suite from Prokofiev's *Romeo and Juliet* (with the Rotterdam Philharmonic Orchestra), *Der Rosenkavalier* (with the Rotterdam Philharmonic Orchestra *et al.*), Gershwin's *Rhapsody in Blue*, Piano Concerto and *Variations on I Got Rhythm* (with Haas and the Monte Carlo National Opera Orchestra), the Mozart and Strauss Oboe Concertos (with Holliger and the New Philharmonia Orchestra), Rachmaninov's *Symphonic Dances* and *Caprice bohémien* (with the London Philharmonic Orchestra), four Piano Concertos and *Rhapsody on a Theme of Paganini* (with Orozco and the Royal Philharmonic Orchestra), Weill's Symphonies Nos 1 and 2 (with the Leipzig Gewandhaus Orchestra), the Tchaikovsky and Bruch Violin Concertos (with Fujikawa and the Rotterdam Philharmonic

Orchestra), Michael Haydn's *Violin Concerto in A major* and Viotti's Violin Concerto No. 22 (with Grumiaux and the Amsterdam Concertgebouw Orchestra), Mozart's *Masonic Funeral Music* (with the New Philharmonia Orchestra), Bach's Two-Violin Concerto (with Grumiaux and Toyoda and the New Philharmonia Orchestra), the Vivaldi Violin Concerto Op. 3 No. 8, the two Beethoven Romances, Berlioz's *Rêverie et Caprice*, Tchaikovsky's *Sérénade mélancolique*, Svendsen's *Romance in G*, and Wieniawski's *Légende* and *Romance* from the Violin Concerto No. 2 (with Grumiaux and the New Philharmonia Orchestra). All these were Philips; for Decca he recorded Brahms' Piano Concerto No. 1 (with Lupu and the London Philharmonic Orchestra), and for Donemus Keuris' *Sinfonia*, Leeuw's *Abschiedsymphonie*, Pijper's *Six Symphonic Epigrams* and Vermeulen's Symphony No. 2 (with the Rotterdam Philharmonic Orchestra). In these records de Waart shows himself to be an imaginative and painstaking musician; his direction of *Der Rosenkavalier* is sensitively phrased and obviously well prepared and considered.

Waddington, Geoffrey (1904–66). Born in Leicester, Waddington went to Canada as a child, studied the violin, became first violinist in the Toronto Symphony Orchestra, organised and directed the Toronto Chamber Music Society, taught at the Royal Conservatory of Music at Toronto, and was the music director of the Canadian Radio Broadcasting Commission (1933–5). He was co-founder of the CBC Opera Company (1949), director of music of the CBC Symphony Orchestra (1952), conducted the Winnipeg Summer Symphony Orchestra (1939–40) and was music director of the All-Canada Radio Facilities (1944). With the Canadian Opera Company he recorded *Così fan tutte*, for OTA.

Wagner, Robert (b. 1915). Born in Vienna and educated at the Vienna Academy of Music and Vienna University, where he received his doctorate for musicology, Wagner first conducted in Vienna. He then was conductor at Graz (1938–45), at the Salzburg Mozarteum (1945–51), was general music director at Münster (1951–61), music director at Innsbruck (1960–66), president of the Academy of Music at the Salzburg Mozarteum (1965–70), and general music director of the Turkish State Opera at Istanbul (since 1970). His compositions include orchestral music, concertos, chamber and stage music; he has been a guest conductor in many countries with major orchestras. His sound, though unremarkable, musicianship has been demonstrated in a number of records; these include excerpts from *Rigoletto* and *Aida* (in French), *Aida, La traviata*, and *Les Contes d'Hoffmann* (in German), and *L'Africaine*, recitals of arias by van Mill, Kozub and Poncet, a disc of operatic choruses and another of Strauss waltzes, and the Mendelssohn and Tchaikovsky Violin Concertos (with Auclair and the Innsbruck Symphony Orchestra, all for Philips), Mozart's Piano Concertos K. 466 and K. 537 and Paderewski's *Polish Fantasy* (with Blumenthal), Piano Concertos by Hummel and Boieldieu (with Galling), the Brahms Violin Concerto (with Lautenbacher), clarinet concertos and other concerted pieces by Stamitz, Weber and Rossini (with Glazer), the two Chopin Piano Concertos and other concerted pieces, and Liszt's *Hungarian Fantasy* (with Frankl), Brahms' *Alto Rhapsody*, Schumann's *Requiem for Mignon*, Mahler's *Rückert Lieder* and Wagner's *Wesendonck Lieder* (with Moreira, Mathis *et al.*), collections of dances by Mozart, Haydn and Beethoven, a three-disc abridgement of *Tristan und Isolde* (with the Innsbruck Symphony Orchestra *et al.* for Vox/Turnabout), and the five Beethoven Piano Concertos (with Blumenthal and the Innsbruck Symphony Orchestra for Orion).

Wagner, Roger (b. 1914). Born in Le Puy, France, the son of an organist at Dijon Cathedral, Wagner came to the United States with his family at the age of seven, and when still young was the organist and choirmaster at a church in Los Angeles. He returned to France to study for five years with Dupré, at the Collège de Montmorency, and at Dijon and Lyon. He took part in the 1936 Olympic Games in Berlin as a competitor in the decathlon; after returning to Los Angeles in 1937 he studied philosophy at the University of Southern California, and was a student of Klemperer and Walter for conducting and of Stravinsky, Schoenberg and Caillet for orchestration. He became music director of St Joseph's Church, was appointed supervisor of youth choruses for the City of Los Angeles Bureau of Music (1945), founded a chorus that became the Roger Wagner Chorale (1947) and with it toured the US, Canada, Latin America, Japan, the USSR and the Middle East, conducted the Los Angeles Master Chorale and Sinfonia Orchestra (1965), and became the director of choral music at the University of California, Los Angeles, and head of the choral department at Marymount College in Los Angeles. He is a most accomplished choral conductor with, to quote the Los Angeles critic Don Ray, 'an astounding combination of vitality, dedication, poetic and intellectual depth, and *chutzpah*'. The University of Montreal awarded him a doctorate for a thesis on the masses of Josquin des Prés, and he was made a Commander Knight of St Gregory by Pope Paul VI.

Wagner has recorded over 60 discs with his Chorale for Allegro, SPA, Lyrichord, Capitol, EMI and Decca, many of popular music ranging from sea shanties to hymns. He has also recorded, *inter alia*, Monteverdi's Madrigals, Book I, Bach's Cantatas Nos 4, 65 and 106 and Vaughan Williams' *Mass in G minor* (with the Concert Arts Orchestra and the Chorale, for Capitol), the Fauré Requiem, Vivaldi's *Gloria* and Peeters' *Entrata Festiva* (with the Paris Conservatoire Orchestra *et al.* for Capitol), Cherubini's *Requiem in C minor* and Walton's *Belshazzar's Feast* (with the Royal Philharmonic Orchestra *et al.* for Capitol); Antheil's *Eight Fragments from Shelley* (for SPA); Foss's *Psalms* and *Behold! I Build a House*, and Warren's *Suite for Orchestra* and *Abram in Egypt* (with the London Philharmonic Orchestra for Composers Recordings); the *Magnificats* of Monteverdi, Morales and Vivaldi, Orff's *Catulli Carmina*, Palestrina's *Missa Papae Marcelli* and three motets of Victoria (for EMI).

Wagner, Siegfried (1869–1930). Born in Triebschen, near Lucerne, the only son of Richard Wagner and (then) Cosima von Bülow, Siegfried Wagner was first educated to become an architect, but after his father's death adopted music as his vocation. After studying with Richter, Humperdinck and Kniese, he conducted concerts in Germany, Austria, Italy and England (1893), was an assistant conductor at Bayreuth (1894), conducted the *Ring* in 1896 and continued to conduct regularly at Bayreuth until 1914. After Cosima's death in 1909 he succeeded her as supervisor, remaining in charge at Bayreuth until his death. He married Winifred Williams, the adopted daughter of Karl Klindworth, and she led the festivals from 1930 to 1944. Siegfried visited the United States in 1923–4 to conduct some concerts of his father's music and to raise funds for the re-opening of the Bayreuth Theatre after World War I. He wrote 15 operas, to his own libretti, not in the heroic style of his father, but mostly on fairy-tale subjects. Mahler presented *Der Bärenhäuter*, probably the most successful, in Vienna in 1899; at that time he was surprised to find that Cosima rated her son's operas as high as her husband's. Another, the tenth opera, *Der Friedensengel*, was revived in London in 1976. Siegfried was a particularly good, if conservative, opera producer and was especially skilled with crowd scenes. He was not a great conductor, by all accounts; he conducted with his left hand and without a score. The conductor Alfred Sendrey once wrote that Siegfried was a guest conductor with his Leipzig Symphony Orchestra in 1929 in a programme of music by Liszt, his father and himself. 'As the closing number, he selected his father's *Tannhäuser* overture. After everything was properly rehearsed and before continuing with *Tannhäuser*, Siegfried felt induced to make a little speech: "Gentlemen, this overture of my father's is generally conducted much too slowly. You must bear in mind, however, that the opening choral theme represents the joyful chant of the pilgrims returning from Rome, expiated (*sic*) from their sins. So – it must be done with joyful spirit, in a lively tempo. Now then, gentlemen!" And then came the dirge of all times – belying that pretty little speech – it dragged – it sounded like a funeral procession. The famous string slurs came out like Czerny exercises' (Letter in the *Los Angeles Times* by A. Sendrey, 17 September 1970).

In 1927 he recorded the prelude to Act I of *Lohengrin*, the *Siegfried Idyll* and *Homage March* (with the London Symphony Orchestra, for HMV) and the prelude to Act III and Good Friday Music from Parsifal (with Kipnis, Wolf and the Bayreuth Festival Orchestra, for Columbia). He also recorded the prelude to Act I and Liebestod from *Tristan und Isolde* (with the Berlin Staatsoper Orchestra, for Odeon).

Wagner-Régeny, Rudolf (1903–69). Born in Szászrégen in Romania, Wagner-Régeny studied in Leipzig and Berlin, was a repetiteur at the Berlin Volksoper (1923–5), travelled in Switzerland, the Netherlands and Austria (1926–9) as composer and conductor with the von Labans Ballet Company, became a free-lance composer (1930–45), was rector at the Hochschule für Musik at Rostock (1947–50), and then taught at the Hochschule für Musik and Deutsche Akademie der Künste in East Berlin (from 1951). Of his own compositions he recorded *Music for Drums and Trumpets* (with the Berlin Symphony Orchestra *et al.* for Nova).

Wahl, Bernard (b. 1922). Born and educated in Paris, Wahl first conducted in 1951, and has been conductor of the Versailles Chamber Orchestra, with which he has given concerts in many countries with a repertoire ranging from Bach to Bartók. He has recorded, with the Versailles Chamber Orchestra *et al.* Rameau's opera *La Guirlande* and pieces by Monteclair,

Corelli, Boismortier, Leclair, Stölzel and Telemann (for Nonesuch) and by Delalande, Lully, Mouret and Clérambault (for Vogue, France).

Wakasugi, Hiroshi (b. 1935). Born in Tokyo, Wakasugi studied conducting with Saito and Hatanaka at the Tokyo University of Arts and was engaged by the NHK Symphony Orchestra as an assistant conductor. His debut occurred in 1958 at the Niki-Kai Opera Company; since then he has become celebrated in Japan as an opera conductor and under the sponsorship of the Japanese Government has studied opera in Vienna, Berlin and Munich. On his return to Japan he founded and became musical director of the Tokyo Chamber Opera (1967). At the same time he was appointed chief conductor of the Yomiuri Nippon Symphony Orchestra (1965), and toured Europe with the orchestra (1971), winning acclaim especially in Paris for a performance of the music of Takemitsu. He is now the music director of the West German Radio Symphony Orchestra; he has a reputation as a conductor of modern music as well as of the repertoire extending back to Monteverdi, has been a member of the Tokyo Contemporary Music Festival, and has performed present-day composers both in Japan and abroad. His records have been of Takemitsu's music: *Coral Island* (with the Yomiuri Nippon Symphony Orchestra for RCA), and *Stanza, Sacrifice, Ring* and *Varelia* (with various Japanese performers, for DGG).

Waldhans, Jiri (b. 1923). After graduating from the conservatory at his birthplace, Brno, Czechoslovakia, Waldhans studied conducting with Markevitch at Salzburg, and was a repetiteur and chorusmaster at the Ostrava Opera (1949–51). He was conductor of the Brno State Philharmonic Orchestra (1951–4), of the Ostrava Symphony Orchestra (1955–62), has been a guest conductor with other Czech orchestras and abroad, and is now, again, the conductor of the Brno State Philharmonic Orchestra. His recordings have included Beethoven's piano arrangement of his Violin Concerto, *Concerto for harpsichord or Fortepiano in E flat, Tempo di Concerto in D*, and *Rondo in B flat* (with Blumenthal and the Brno State Philharmonic Orchestra for Orion), the Dvořák Cello Concerto (with Chuchro and the Czech Philharmonic Orchestra for Supraphon), Fišer's *Fifteen Pages after Dürer's Apocalypse*, Janáček's *Lachian Dances, Jealousy* overture, *The Fiddler's Child* and *The Ballad of Blaník Hill*, suites from Martinů's ballets *Istar* and *Špalíček*, Rachmaninov's Piano Concerto No. 2 (with Pokorná) and *Symphonic Dance No. 1*, and Milhaud's Cello Concertos Nos 1 and 2 (with Apolín, and the Brno State Philharmonic Orchestra, for Supraphon), Schaefer's Symphony, Horký's Symphony No. 4 and Feld's *Frescoes* (with the Brno State Philharmonic Orchestra for Panton).

Waldman, Frederic (b. 1903). Born in Vienna, Waldman studied conducting with Szell, conducted in Danzig, Gera and Berlin, toured Europe, South and North America, settled in New York (1941), was director of the Juilliard Opera Theater, and founded the Musica Aeterna Orchestra and Chorus (1961). With these ensembles he has made a number of recordings for Decca (US), including Bach's Violin Concerto No. 2 and Mozart's Violin Concerto K. 219 (with Morini), Handel's *L'Allegro ed il penseroso, Israel in Egypt* and Harp Concerto (with Grandjany), Monteverdi's *Madrigali guerrieri et amorosi*, Haydn's *The Creation*, Mozart's Serenade K. 361, Sinfonia Concertante K. 364 (with J. and L. Fuchs), *Adagio in E* K. 261 and *Rondo in C* K. 373 (with J. Fuchs) and Flute and Harp Concerto (with Grandjany *et al.*), Beethoven's *Mass in C*, Schubert's Mass No. 6, Mendelssohn's *Die erste Walpurgisnacht* and the overture *Die Heimkehr aus der Fremde*, Dvořák's *Czech Suite* and *Serenade in D minor*, Verdi's *Quatro Pezzi sacri*, Fauré's *Requiem*, Britten's *Serenade for Tenor, Horn and Strings* (with Bressler) and Barber's Cello Concerto (with Garbousova). He also recorded Beeson's *Hello Out There* (with the Columbia Chamber Orchestra *et al.*, for Desto), excerpts from Bergsma's *The Wife of Martin Guerre* (with the original Broadway stars for Composers Recordings), and Varèse's *Intégrales, Density 21.5, Ionisation* and *Octandre* (with the New York Wind Ensemble for EMS).

Walker, James (b. 1929). Born in Rotherham, Yorkshire, Walker is a self-taught musician and the pianist in the Archduke Piano Trio, at the University of Leicester. He was on the music staff of the Royal Shakespeare Theatre, Stratford (1957–64), and has composed instrumental and vocal music, and Shakespeare settings. His recordings include *Scheherazade* (with the Royal Philharmonic Orchestra for Reader's Digest), *H.M.S. Pinafore* (with the D'Oyly Carte Opera Company and Royal Philharmonic Orchestra for Decca), and some arias with Corena (with the Suisse Romande Orchestra for Decca).

Wallberg, Heinz (b. 1923). Born in Herringen, Westphalia, Wallberg studied at the Dortmund

Conservatory and the Hochschule für Musik at Cologne, and was originally a trumpeter, then a violinist. He conducted, successively, at Münster, Trier, Flensburg, Hagen and Wuppertal (1946–54), was music director at Augsburg and general music director at Bremen (1955–60), was conductor at Wiesbaden (1960), artistic director of the Vienna Tonkünstler Orchestra (1963) and is now conductor at Essen and with the Bavarian Radio Symphony Orchestra. He has been a guest conductor with the opera houses at Hamburg, as well as at other major European cities and with the Teatro Colón in Buenos Aires, where he led the German season in 1961–2, toured with the Bamberg Symphony Orchestra, has been permanent guest conductor of the Vienna Musikverein (since 1956) and has performed at the Salzburg and other festivals.

Wallberg has recorded Mendelssohn's Symphony No. 4 and the overture, scherzo and nocturne from *A Midsummer Night's Dream*, the two *L'Arlésienne* suites and a *Carmen* suite (with the Philharmonia Orchestra for EMI); Beethoven's Piano Concertos Nos 3 and 4 (with Brendel and the Vienna Pro Musica Orchestra for Vox) and Piano Concerto No. 2 and *Rondo in B flat* (with Brendel and the Vienna Volksoper Orchestra for Vox); Haydn's Symphony No. 101 and Mozart's Symphony No. 40 (with the Bamberg Symphony Orchestra for CBS-Realm); Bruch's Violin Concerto No. 1 and *Scottish Fantasy* (with Grumiaux and the New Philharmonia Orchestra for Philips); a recital by Nilsson (with the Philharmonia Orchestra for EMI); excerpts from *Le nozze di Figaro* (with the Vienna State Opera Orchestra *et al.* for La Guilde Internationale du Disque); Beethoven's Triple Concerto (with Helffer, Ozim and Natola), *Missa solemnis* and incidental music for *Egmont*, Bruckner's Symphonies Nos 4, 8 and 9 and *Te Deum*, Mahler's *Kindertotenlieder* (with Rössl-Majdan), Bruch's *Kol Nidrei* (with Natola), and J. Strauss's *Frühlingsstimmen, Frisch ins Feld, Lagunen-Walzer, Neue Pizzicato-Polka, Seid umschlungen Millionen, Vergnügungszug-Polka* and *Wo die Zitronen blüh'n* (with the Vienna State Symphony Orchestra for GID); the prelude to *Parsifal*, the Ride of the Valkyries from *Die Walküre*, Forest Murmurs from *Siegfried*, and the Rhine Journey and Funeral Music from *Götterdämmerung* (the Austrian Symphony Orchestra for GID); *Eine kleine Nachtmusik, Serenata notturna* and the overtures to *Le nozze di Figaro, Don Giovanni and Die Zauberflöte* (with the Deutsche Oper Orchestra, Berlin, for Ariola); Liszt's Piano Concerto No. 1 (with Cherkassky and the Bamberg Symphony Orchestra for Ariola); Schubert's *Der vierjährige Posten* and Humperdinck's *Die Königskinder* (with the Bavarian Radio Symphony Orchestra *et al.* for EMI); *Hänsel und Gretel* (with the Gürzenich Orchestra, Cologne, *et al.* for EMI), and *Zar und Zimmermann* (with the Bavarian Radio Symphony Orchestra for BASF).

Wallenstein, Alfred (b. 1898). Son of an Austrian father and a German mother, and a descendant of the General Wallenstein of the Thirty Years' War, Wallenstein was born in Chicago, but came to Los Angeles with his family when he was a boy. He studied the cello, toured the United States playing the instrument when he was 15, and was a member of the San Francisco Symphony Orchestra (1916). He toured South America with the Pavlova Ballet (1917), joined the Los Angeles Philharmonic Orchestra (1919), went to Europe and studied with Klengel at Leipzig (1920), also attended lectures on medicine for a time, and returned to the US to become first cellist with the Chicago Symphony Orchestra under Stock (1922–9) and with the New York Philharmonic-Symphony Orchestra under Toscanini (1929–36). He made his debut as a conductor at the Hollywood Bowl (1931), founded and conducted the Wallenstein Sinfonietta (1933), and for ten years was a radio conductor for Station WOR in New York, the Mutual Broadcasting Company and NBC. In his broadcast programmes he presented a series of Bach cantatas, Haydn symphonies and Mozart piano concertos, and for this major contribution to musical activities he received the Peabody Award in 1942. He was a guest conductor with major symphony orchestras, and then was appointed musical director and conductor of the Los Angeles Philharmonic Orchestra (1943–56), restoring the ensemble to its high position among American orchestras, and was the first American-born and trained musician to lead a major orchestra in the US. In Los Angeles, his programmes included much music by American composers, and there his conducting was remarkable for its precision and emotional involvement.

Wallenstein's first recordings were 78 r.p.m. sets of Mozart's Symphony No. 25 and the Overture K. 311a (with the Wallenstein Sinfonietta for Columbia), Rachmaninov's Piano Concerto No. 2 (with List), Benjamin's *Jamaican Rhumba* and the Dohnányi *Suite in F sharp minor* (with the Los Angeles Symphony Orchestra for Decca, US). Then followed a series for Brunswick with the Los Angeles Philharmonic Orchestra, including Beethoven's Symphony No. 8, Schubert's Symphonies Nos 4 and 5, Liszt's *Dante Symphony*, Brahms' Symphony No. 1, Mendelssohn's Symphony No. 5, orchestral excerpts from *La Damnation de Faust* and *The Bartered Bride*, *Moldau*, the Polovtsian Dances from *Prince Igor*, Enesco's *Romanian Rhapsody No. 1*, Ippolitov-Ivanov's *Caucasian Sketches*, Chabrier's *Marche joyeuse*, *España* and *Habanera*, some Tchaikovsky waltzes, and several Offenbach overtures. Also with the Los Angeles Philharmonic he recorded Rachmaninov's Symphony No. 2 (for Capitol, later released by Seraphim), Szymanowski's *Symphonie concertante* (with Rubinstein for RCA), the Magnificat from Monteverdi's *Vespro della Beata Vergine* and Respighi's *Laud to the Nativity* (with the Roger Wagner Chorale *et al.* for Capitol), Korngold's Violin Concerto, Ravel's *Tzigane*, Sinding's *Suite in A minor*, the two Bach Violin Concertos, Castelnuovo-Tedesco's Violin Concerto No. 2 and Tchaikovsky's *Sérénade mélancolique* (with Heifetz, for RCA). His other recordings include Mozart's Piano Concertos K. 453, K. 466, K. 467 and K. 488 and Liszt's Piano Concerto No. 1 (with Rubinstein and the RCA Victor Symphony Orchestra for RCA), the Brahms Double Concerto (with Heifetz and Piatigorsky and the same orchestra for RCA), Chopin's Piano Concerto No. 2, Franck's *Symphonic Variations* and Saint-Saëns' Piano Concerto No. 2 (with Rubinstein and the Symphony of the Air for RCA), Prokofiev's Symphony No. 1 and Britten's *Young Person's Guide to the Orchestra* (with a symphony orchestra for Music Appreciation), *Symphonie fantastique*, Brahms' Symphony No. 4, Tchaikovsky's Symphony No. 6, *Romeo and Juliet* fantasy-overture and *Nutcracker* suite, *Pictures at an Exhibition*, *Boléro* and a suite from *Carmen* (with the Virtuoso Symphony of London for Audio-Fidelity), the Elgar Cello Concerto (with Fournier and the Berlin Philharmonic Orchestra for DGG) and the Tchaikovsky Violin Concerto (with Perlman and the London Symphony Orchestra for Reader's Digest).

Wallez, Jean Pierre. The French violinist Wallez has been a member of l'Orchestre de Paris, is founder and director of l'Ensemble Instrumental de France, director of the Festival d'Albi, and in 1977 became director of l'Ensemble Orchestral de Paris. He has also been associated with Bruno Rigutto in a violin-and-piano duo. He has recorded as a solo violinist, and as leader of l'Ensemble Instrumental de Paris recorded Bach's *Brandenburg Concerto No. 5*, Flute, Violin and Harpsichord Concerto (with Larrieu and Puyana), Three-Violin Concertos of Bach, Telemann and Vivaldi (with Estournet, Bride, Crenne and Risler), Vivaldi's *Four Seasons, La stravaganza, L'estro armonico*, four Bassoon Concertos (with Laroque) and four Flute Concertos (with Larrieu), Horn Concertos of Telemann (with Bourgue and Fournier), flute concertos by Devienne, Blavet and Touchemoulin (with Larrieu), trumpet concertos by Fasch, Telemann, Stoelzel, Molter, Torelli and Purcell (with Bernard), Rameau's *Zéphyre*, Locatelli's Violin Concertos Op. 4 Nos 4, 8, 10 and 11, Leclair's Violin concertos Op. 7 Nos 3 and 4, Mozart's *Adagio and Fugue in C minor*, Piano Concertos K. 465 and K. 595 (with Puyana), and two Flute Concertos and Andante K. 315 (with Larrieu), Debussy's *Danse sacrée et danse profane* and Ravel's *Introduction et allegro* (with Mildonian), Schoenberg's *Verklärte Nacht*, Stravinsky's *Concerto for Strings* and Webern's *Five Movements for Strings*.

Walter, Bruno (1876–1962). Walter was born in Berlin in what he described as a 'modest Jewish family'; his father was a bookkeeper and the family name was Schlesinger, a common German surname, which he later, at the outset of his career, changed to Walter, inspired by the artistic ideals of Walter von Stolzing of *Die Meistersinger*. When it was discovered that he had extraordinary musical talent, his mother taught him the piano as a young child, and at the age of nine he entered the Stern Conservatory in Berlin. At 13 he made his first public appearance as a pianist with the Berlin Philharmonic Orchestra, playing Moscheles' *Piano Concerto in E flat*. He remained a fine pianist throughout his life, apparently with the ability to retain his technique without constant practice. Also at 13 he heard Hans von Bülow conduct and decided to become a conductor himself. His first engagement as such was at the Cologne Opera, at the age of 17 with *Der Waffenschmied*, where he had been engaged as an assistant conductor. He moved to Hamburg again as assistant conductor in 1894, and there first met Mahler, who had a profound influence on the young man, with his artistic ideals, literary culture and powerful music. From Hamburg Walter had successive appointments, as his career moved rapidly upwards, at Breslau (1896), Pressburg (1897), Temesvár in Hungary, Riga (1898) and then at the Berlin Staatsoper (1900), where he succeeded Schalk and came into contact with Muck and Strauss. In Berlin he conducted his first symphony concert which included the *Symphonie fantastique* of Berlioz, and at the Kroll Opera House one of the first operas he conducted was *The Mikado* of Gilbert and Sullivan. At this time he also conducted his first *Ring*.

In 1901 Mahler invited Walter to Vienna to become his assistant, and director of the Vienna Court Opera; he remained in Vienna until 1913, working with Schalk, but his close connection with Mahler attracted criticism from the press, who saw it as their way of attacking Mahler indirectly. He was undoubtedly Mahler's closest associate and collaborator. To him Mahler played his Symphony No. 3 on the piano, and Walter prepared the soloists for the first performance of the Symphony No. 8 in 1910. After Mahler's death, he gave the first performance of *Das Lied von der Erde* in Munich in 1911 and of the Symphony No. 9 in Vienna in 1912. Mahler entrusted him with the authority to modify the orchestration of his symphonies to suit the acoustics of the halls in which they were to be performed. In Vienna Walter also was a frequent performer in chamber-music ensembles, giving recitals with artists such as Casals and Arnold Rosé; indeed, Casals thought Walter would have become a very great pianist if he had not chosen to conduct instead. Walter became seriously ill, and only recovered after a course of treatment with Sigmund Freud. In 1909 he first visited London to conduct for the Royal Philharmonic Society, and in the next year led *Tristan und Isolde* in the Beecham season at Covent Garden.

In 1913 Walter left Vienna to become Mottl's successor at the Bavarian Court Opera at Munich, where he stayed for ten years. In Munich he reached full maturity as a conductor, achieving international recognition for his performances of the Mozart and Wagner operas; his Verdi was highly regarded too. The Mozart operas under Walter at Munich were celebrated for their unique perfection, the result of his own meticulous preparation. His reason for leaving Munich is not clear; he himself wrote in his autobiography that he had finished his work there, but others say that it was anti-semitism and envy that drove him away. In 1923 he made his home in Vienna again, having previously become an Austrian citizen in 1911. He had made his American debut with Damrosch's New York Symphony Orchestra, but these concerts in New York were not entirely successful, apparently because he could not overcome the orchestra's antagonism to Germans. He returned later to the United States for concert tours in 1924 (New York and Minneapolis), 1925, 1927 (Cleveland and Los Angeles) and 1932–5 (New York). His concert at the Augusteo, Rome, in 1923 was the scene of a disturbance when he performed Schoenberg's *Verklärte Nacht*, and it caused his absence from musical life there, although he conducted at La Scala in 1926. Threats against him caused him to leave Vienna. He was appointed general music director at the Berlin Staatsoper in 1925 and in these years conducted in many European centres, including Moscow where he led Mahler's Symphony No. 4 (1923), Leningrad (1926), Paris (1927) and at the Salzburg Festivals (1925–38), where his Mozart performances reached new pinnacles of glory, and where Toscanini was one of his collaborators. Toscanini was one of the few other great conductors for whom he declared admiration; others were Furtwängler and Beecham. At Covent Garden he was in charge of the German repertoire in 1924–31, and his appearances were distinguished by superb performances of *The Ring*, *Der Rosenkavalier* and the great Mozart operas. The historic cast of Lotte Lehmann, Elisabeth Schumann and Richard Mayr in *Der Rosenkavalier* under Walter first came together in London in 1924, and these artists recorded extensive scenes from the opera in Vienna in 1933, but as Walter was not then available, Heger substituted as conductor for the recording. The records have often been re-issued on LP transfers and are an imperishable reminder of the operatic standards of the time. Walter also conducted the London Symphony Orchestra in 1924 in Elgar's Symphony No. 2. His cycle of Mozart operas at Covent Garden in 1927 was later repeated in Paris with equal acclaim, he conducted at the Sargent-Courtauld Concerts, and during his visit to Leningrad in 1926 he met the young Shostakovich and took his Symphony No. 1 to present it in Berlin.

In 1925 Charlottenburg was incorporated into Greater Berlin and the German Opera House there was re-opened as the Municipal Opera, with Tietjen as intendant (administrator) and Walter as conductor. He was in Berlin until 1929, and in that time the Municipal Opera flourished as one of the finest opera houses in Europe. Furtwängler was then with the Berlin Philharmonic Orchestra, Klemperer with the Kroll Opera and Kleiber with the State Opera. But in 1929 disagreements with the municipal authorities about programmes and production caused Walter's resignation, and after a tour to the United States to conduct at the Hollywood Bowl, he succeeded Furtwängler as the conductor of the Leipzig Gewandhaus Orchestra. The advent of the Nazis into power brought his expulsion from Germany, when his concerts in Leipzig were banned on the grounds that they threatened 'public order and security', and his place at Leipzig was taken over first by Richard Strauss and then by Abendroth. He went to London and to Vienna, was guest conductor with the Vienna State Opera, and in 1935 was appointed its artistic adviser and permanent conductor, and also conducted the Vienna Philharmonic Orchestra. Again with the *Anschluss* he had to flee from the Nazis when they occupied Austria, took up residence in France at the invitation of the French government, became a French citizen only to have his citizenship abrogated in 1940. He conducted the Concertgebouw Orchestra in Amsterdam and shared an international festival in Switzerland with Toscanini, who invited him to conduct the NBC Symphony Orchestra in New York in 1939.

Walter finally migrated to the United States, where he conducted the Los Angeles Philharmonic Orchestra when Klemperer was ill (1939) and led the NBC Symphony, New York Philharmonic-Symphony and Minneapolis Symphony Orchestras (1939–41), first conducted at the New York Metropolitan Opera in 1941 with *Fidelio* and then *Don Giovanni* and *The Bartered Bride* in memorable performances, and continued to appear with the New York Philharmonic-Symphony Orchestra as its conductor and musical adviser (1947–9). He returned to Vienna after World War II to lead *Fidelio* at the State Opera, and was re-united temporarily with the Vienna Philharmonic Orchestra at the first Edinburgh Festival in 1947 in *Das Lied von der Erde* with the great British contralto, Kathleen Ferrier. This performance was later recorded (also with Patzak, the tenor) and Walter considered it, with Ferrier's *Kindertotenlieder*, the recording in which he took special pride. In 1960 he also came to Vienna to conduct the Vienna Philharmonic in Mahler's Symphony No. 4 on the 100th anniversary of the composer's birthday. He had received the Gold Medal of the Royal Philharmonic Society in London in 1957, but in that year suffered a heart attack and had to restrict his conducting, living in Los Angeles where he died in 1962. He published an autobiography, *Theme and Variations*, in 1947, its sequel *Of Music and Music Making* appeared in 1957, and a monograph *Gustav Mahler* in 1958. Early in his career he composed two symphonies and some chamber music, but then abandoned composition altogether.

It is ironic that one of the greatest German musicians of the 20th century was expelled from his own country; anti-semitism made his life uncomfortable no matter where he went in Germany and Austria even before the Nazi era. Some of his fellow German-Jewish conductors have criticised him for his allegedly equivocal attitude to these provocations, accusing him of seeking to ingratiate himself with the authorities. Be that as it may, he followed a distinguished career and enhanced many of the greatest opera houses and orchestras in Europe and the United States, where his performances of Mozart, Beethoven, Schubert, Schumann, Brahms, Mahler, Bruckner, Wagner and Strauss in particular were acclaimed. His performances were idiosyncratic–warm, lyrical, and romantic in the best sense. Precision was not a preoccupation, and this may have prevented him from giving Beethoven especially its ultimate dramatic stature. Technique took second place to expression; he himself said: 'By concentrating on precision one arrives at technique; but by concentrating on technique one does not arrive at precision.' He was always conscious of the spiritual dimension of the great central European masters and ever sought to express it. His humility in the face of these classics may have been exaggerated when he said that he did not conduct Mozart's Symphony No. 40 until he was 50 because he 'felt the responsibility of such a task'. His interpretations were markedly different from Toscanini's, lacking the latter's fire and intensity, and they did not have the improvisatory character of Furtwängler's, but enveloped the listener with their lyrical beauty. Yet his tempi were not exaggerated, and vigour was certainly not absent, as is evident in, say, his recordings of Beethoven's Symphony No. 7.

Walter had a reputation for gentleness and courtly persuasiveness, and his person radiated with the love of music. At rehearsals his temper was under firm control, he had a ready wit, but although tension between him and the players was low, concentration was uppermost. With his players he was very articulate and talked a lot, regarding them as sympathetic collaborators. He scorned the dictatorial methods of many other conductors, but his own personality failed to impress many players, particularly in the United States, where Toscanini's old orchestra, the New York Philharmonic-Symphony, called for a much stronger hand. Gaisberg, who recorded the Vienna Philharmonic for HMV in the 1930s, wrote (in *Music on Record*, New York, 1948, p. 119) that they were 'a cynical lot, snobbish and blasé', who could only be tamed by Toscanini, but nonetheless out of respect for Walter gave him their best. To some musicians this image of Walter as the quiet imperturbable man is misleading, and they would claim that he was in reality as demanding and ruthless as any other.

Certainly he was extremely meticulous in achieving the results he sought. There has always been criticism of his interpretations of symphonic music, as opposed to his magnificence in the opera house; for instance, Virgil Thomson wrote in 1942 (*Music Reviewed*, p. 68) that he was undependable technically and that 'sloppiness of beat and general indifference to ship-shapeness of execution' were evident even in the best of his concerts in New York at the time. Burghauser of the Vienna Philharmonic in the 1930s said that the rhapsodic nature of Mahler's music, with which Walter had had life-long familiarity, was transferred to the music of other composers, and that his weakness in rhythm brought him to include the Bruckner symphonies in his repertoire, because the public accepted a rhapsodic style as appropriate for Bruckner, although professional musicians were aware that it dissolved the music's rhythmic anatomy. But Burghauser concurred that Walter's operatic performances in the decades between the wars were incomparable, as opera did not call for a rigidly rhythmic framework and that his flexibility as an accompanist suited the singers. In fact, a predominant characteristic of Walter's style was that the music had to breathe naturally as if it were being sung, which impaired a strict rhythmic pattern. Walter's decision to perform Bruckner had nothing to do with Burghauser's explanation. Walter related that originally he felt a stranger to the composer's extremes of expression, but after a long illness and the opportunity for re-assessment he came to understand Bruckner's 'solemnity and religious greatness'. With Mahler, Walter naturally emphasised the lyrical and softer side of the music, which made him such a moving interpreter of the Symphony No. 4 and *Das Lied von der Erde*; but, in contrast, he rarely performed the Symphony No. 6. Cardus once asked Klemperer about Walter as a conductor of Mahler. 'Quite good, but not altogether satisfactory', was the answer. 'Why?' Cardus asked; to which Klemperer grunted, 'Too Jewish' (*Recorded Sound*, October 1970, p. 668).

Although a man of deep musical and literary culture, Walter had little concern for historical correctness and performed classical music with large orchestras, corrupt texts and an ignorance of the performance conventions of the times. But he was not alone in this regard among the great conductors of his generation, and even of the present day. He disregarded repeats in Haydn, Mozart, Beethoven and others, his acute sense of structure impelling him to move on with the musical argument. In rehearsal he did not always correct poor ensemble, believing that he could manage it at the performance. Orchestras of less than the first rank were not belaboured to produce standards impossible to them. He conducted from the score until his eyesight grew weaker later in his life, and when he memorised the music he found that without the score he was in much closer contact with the players. His actual baton technique was, according to Boult, not so expressive as that of Nikisch, but 'he was so immersed in the music he was doing that he managed somehow to convey it just as telepathically I think as by putting it into the stick'. He was one of the first to conduct from the piano when he performed a Mozart concerto, although he could not always resolve the ensuing problems of ensemble. The restricted repertoire of his later years concealed the fact that earlier he performed a wide range of music, and was noted for his interpretations of Verdi and Tchaikovsky. All his life he was however antipathetic to twelve-tone music.

Walter's first gramophone recordings were made in Berlin in 1900, some entr'actes from *Carmen*, and his last records were prepared just prior to his death in Los Angeles. This remarkable career stretched from the days of the most primitive recordings to the era of stereophonic sound. In his early years he recorded with the Berlin Philharmonic, the Berlin Staatsoper, the BBC Symphony, the London Symphony, the Royal Philharmonic and the British Symphony Orchestras. His Master's Voice chose to record him with the Vienna Philharmonic when he was in Vienna in the 1930s, and when he left Vienna another series followed with the Paris Conservatoire Orchestra, an ensemble considerably younger on an average than the Vienna Philharmonic, but very sensitive in its response to Walter. After his arrival in the US he recorded with the New York Philharmonic-Symphony, which became the New York Philharmonic, the Philadelphia Orchestra and the Columbia Symphony Orchestra. The latter was assembled from Californian musicians from the Hollywood film studios and the Los Angeles Philharmonic, to record his final valedictory series after he had retired from active concert life to Beverly Hills in Los Angeles.

The repertoire Walter recorded rarely ranged beyond the central European classics and romantics. A Corelli concerto grosso and another by Handel appeared on 78s (with the Paris Conservatoire and London Symphony Orchestras respectively) and were the only pre-classical works he recorded; despite his devotion to the *St Matthew Passion* of Bach, he never recorded it commercially, although the Bruno Walter Society has issued discs of the first part of the work taken from a concert performance in New York in 1943. He was one of the most famous interpreters of Haydn and Mozart and recorded early 78s of Haydn's Symphonies No. 86 (with the London Symphony), No. 92 (with the Paris Conservatoire) and Nos 96 and 100 (with the Vienna Philharmonic), all models of grace, vigour and style. Later came Nos 92 and 102 (with the New York Philharmonic; No. 102 a quite exceptional performance in its drama and power), and the Nos 88 and 100 (with the Columbia Symphony).

Walter's early Mozart style is illustrated by the LP transfer by the Bruno Walter Society of Symphony No. 40 (with the Berlin Staatsoper Orchestra for Polydor); sensitivity of feeling alternates with firmness and vigour. With the Vienna Philharmonic, he recorded (for HMV) Symphonies Nos 38 and 41, *Eine kleine Nachtmusik*, the overtures to *La finta giardiniera* and *La clemenza di Tito*, several German Dances K. 605, and the Piano Concerto K. 466 in which he was both soloist and conductor. No recordings of the Mozart operas, or even parts of them, were made in this period. The Symphony No. 39 (with the BBC Symphony) and *Eine kleine Nachtmusik* and the overture to *Le nozze de Figaro* (with the British Symphony Orchestra) were also issued on 78s. Later in the US he recorded Symphony No. 41, *Exsultate jubilate* (with Lily Pons) and the overture to *Così fan tutte* (with the New York Philharmonic-Symphony), Symphonies Nos 35, 39, 40 and 41 and the *Requiem* (with the New York Philharmonic *et al.*), with an East-Coast Columbia Symphony Orchestra Symphonies Nos 25, 28, 29 and a disc of overtures, *Eine kleine Nachtmusik*, the *Masonic Funeral Music* and some dances, and with the West-Coast Columbia Symphony Orchestra the last six symphonies and the Violin Concertos K. 216 and K. 218 (with Francescatti). These were recorded by CBS, as were all his American recordings. The Vienna Philharmonic performances were inimitable in the langorous and silky sheen of the strings; the style was natural to the orchestra, and probably it was not Walter's direction that produced it. He strove to create this quintessential European sound with his American orchestras, achieved it up to a point with some of his New York recordings, but with the Columbia Symphony in Los Angeles it evaded him, despite their splendid playing. The phrasing and tone became almost too romantically self-indulgent.

The Symphony No. 6, which he recorded with the Vienna Philharmonic, was the only Beethoven symphony which Walter recorded in Europe before the war. He also led the *Leonore No. 3* overture (with the Vienna Philharmonic), the *Coriolan* and *Fidelio* overtures (with the London Symphony), the Violin Concerto (with Szigeti and the British Symphony) and the Piano Concerto No. 5 (with Gieseking and the Vienna Philharmonic); all of these were originally recorded by HMV (except the Piano Concerto No. 5, which was by Columbia), and have been re-issued on various LP transfers. The *Pastoral* is another example of how Walter took advantage of the unique tonal quality of the Vienna Philharmonic to produce a performance of melting and evanescent beauty, where he found the perfect balance between expressiveness and energy. It is a contrast to the later recording of the symphony with the Philadelphia Orchestra in 1946, which has quicker tempi, with the music rushed along and whisked away as if Walter was overawed by a Toscanini hovering in the back of the studio. In the US he recorded the complete Beethoven symphonies twice, first with the New York Philharmonic-Symphony and New York Philharmonic between 1942 and 1953 (except for the Symphony No. 6 with the Philadelphia Orchestra, see above); and secondly with the Columbia Symphony in Los Angeles. Symphonies Nos 3, 5 and 9 were recorded twice with the New York Philharmonic in 1941–2 and 1949–50; the first three movements of No. 9 were recorded in 1949 and the *finale* not until 1953. The second set of the symphonies, with the Columbia Symphony, was generally more successful; this time the *Pastoral* emerged as sunny and relaxed as ever, and No.7 is still considered by some critics to be among the best. Walter's tendency to romanticise, especially in No. 5, reveals the musical aesthetic of a past generation, although he achieved magic in the transition to the *finale*. He avoids all repeats in these performances of the Beethoven symphonies. He also recorded the violin Concerto (with Francescatti) and the Piano Concerto No. 5 (with Serkin), with the Columbia and New York Philharmonic-Symphony Orchestras respectively.

Walter's other recordings made in Europe before World War II were the overture to *Die Zauberflöte* (with an unidentified orchestra), the *Fidelio* overture (with the BBC Symphony), the *Prometheus* overture (with an unidentified orchestra), Schubert's Symphonies Nos 8 (with the Vienna Philharmonic) and No. 9, and the *Rosamunde* ballet music Nos 1 and 2 (with the London Symphony), Schumann's Symphony No. 4 (with the London Symphony and earlier with the Mozart Festival Orchestra, Paris), the *Symphonie fantastique* (with the Paris Conservatoire) and Dance of the Sylphs from *The Damnation of Faust* (with the Royal Philharmonic), Brahms' Symphonies Nos 1 and 3 and the *Academic Festival Overture* (with the Vienna Philharmonic) and Symphony No. 4 (with the BBC Symphony), as well as an early disc of the third movement of Symphony No. 1 (with the Berlin Philharmonic), the Nocturne from *A Midsummer Night's Dream* (with the Royal Philharmonic), the *Siegfried Idyll* (with an unidentified orchestra, and later with the Vienna Philharmonic), the prelude to Act III of *Die Meistersinger*, the Liebestod from *Tristan und Isolde*, the *Siegfried Idyll*, the Venusberg music from *Tannhäuser*, scenes from *Parsifal*, the *Rienzi* overture, the overture and prelude to Act III of *Der fliegende Holländer* and the Rhine Journey from *Götterdämmerung* (with the Royal Philharmonic), the prelude to Act III, Dance of the Apprentices and Entry of the Mastersingers from *Die Meistersinger* (with the British Symphony), Act I and parts of Act II of *Die Walküre* (with the Vienna Philharmonic *et al.*), the overture to *The Bartered Bride* (with the London Symphony), *Don Juan* and *Tod und Verklärung* (with the Royal Philharmonic), the dance from *Salome* and waltzes from *Der Rosenkavalier* (with the Berlin Philharmonic), the overture to *Die Fledermaus* (with the Berlin Staatsoper and Paris Conservatoire), the *Kaiserwalzer* (with the Vienna Philharmonic), the overture to *Der Zigeunerbaron* (with an unidentified orchestra and the London Symphony), the waltzes *Rosen aus dem Süden* (with the Berlin Philharmonic) and *Wiener Blut* (with the Berlin Staatsoper), Mahler's Symphony No. 9, the *adagietto* from the Symphony No. 5, *Das Lied von der Erde* (with Kullman and Thorborg) and the song *Ich bin der Welt abhanden gekommen* (with Thorborg, and the Vienna Philharmonic). Of all of these discs, pride of place must be taken by the Act I of *Die Walküre*, which, with the three soloists Lotte Lehmann, Lauritz Melchior and Emanuel List, must be one of the very finest recordings ever made of a Wagner opera (or part thereof), and by the Mahler recordings made in Vienna. The Symphony No. 9 had a special poignancy as it was made three months before the *Anschluss* at an actual concert in the Musikverein at which Chancellor Schuschnigg and most of the Austrian Cabinet were present. Schuschnigg was later held prisoner by the Nazis, and Walter, Rosé, and many other members of the Vienna Philharmonic were soon to leave Vienna. The performance, recently re-issued on an LP dubbing by Turnabout, is, despite its faults, arresting in its commitment and intensity.

In the US Walter recorded his only performance of a contemporary composer; Barber's Symphony No. 1. His other discs with the New York Philharmonic-Symphony were of Schubert's Symphony No. 9, Schumann's Symphony No. 3, Dvořák's Symphony No. 8, Schumann's Symphonies Nos 1 and 3, the Mendelssohn Violin Concerto (with Milstein) and the *scherzo* from *A Midsummer Night's Dream*, *Kaiserwalzer*, and Mahler's Symphonies Nos 1, 4 and 5. Of these Mahler's Symphony No. 4 was an object-lesson in string playing and was one of the significant recordings which brought the composer to a wider public. Decca recorded *Das Lied von der Erde* and some *Rückert Lieder* of Mahler (with the Vienna Philharmonic, Ferrier and Patzak), and Columbia *Kindertotenlieder* (with the Vienna Philharmonic and Ferrier). The series with the New York Philharmonic, in addition to the Haydn, Mozart and Beethoven works mentioned earlier, included the *Leonore No. 3* overture, the Beethoven Violin Concerto (with Szigeti), the Piano Concerto No. 5 (with Serkin), the Triple Concerto (with Corigliano, Rosé and Hendl) and the *Egmont* overture, Schubert's Symphonies Nos 8 (which was also recorded with the Philadelphia Orchestra) and 9, the four Brahms symphonies, the Double Concerto (with Stern and Rosé), *Ein deutsches Requiem* (which was issued after Walter's death), the *Academic Festival* and *Tragic Overtures, Variations on the St Antony Chorale, Schicksalslied* and some Hungarian Dances, the *Siegfried Idyll, Tod und Verklärung* and *Don Juan*, Mahler's Symphonies Nos 1 and 2, *Das Lied von der Erde* (with Miller and Haefliger) and *Lieder eines fahrenden Gesellen* (with Miller) and the Bruckner *Te Deum*. In the final series with the Columbia Symphony there were also Schubert's Symphonies Nos 5 and 9, the overtures *Coriolan* and *Leonore No. 3*, pieces from the incidental music to *Rosamunde*, the Schumann Piano Concerto (with Istomin), the four Brahms symphonies, the Double Concerto (with Francescatti and Fournier), the *Variations on the St Antony Chorale*, the *Academic Festival* and *Tragic Overtures*, *Alto Rhapsody* (with Miller) and *Schicksalslied*, Bruckner's Symphonies Nos 4, 7 and 9, the prelude to *Die Meistersinger*, the overture to *Der fliegende Holländer*, the prelude and Good Friday Music from *Parsifal*, the prelude to Act III of *Lohengrin*, the *Siegfried Idyll* and the *Tannhäuser* overture and Venusberg music, and a disc of overtures and waltzes of Strauss. In 1947 CBS issued a record of Mahler songs in which he accompanied Desi Halban, the soprano with whom he recorded Mahler's

Symphony No. 4; CBS also issued Schumann's *Frauenliebe und -leben* and *Dichterliebe* with Lotte Lehmann, and IGI a disc coupling him accompanying Kirsten Flagstad, on the piano, in the *Wesendonck Lieder*, and the Immolation Scene from *Götterdämmerung* (with an unnamed orchestra).

The Bruno Walter Society in the US has released a number of discs of performances by Walter, some of which are transfers from earlier 78s. The performances appearing for the first time are *Le nozze di Figaro* and *Don Giovanni* (Salzburg, 1937), another *Don Giovanni* (1942), Part I of Bach's *St Matthew Passion* (1943), Mozart's Piano Concertos K. 449 and K. 466 (with Myra Hess, 1954 and 1956 respectively), and Violin Concertos K. 218 (with Huberman, 1945) and K. 216 (with Szigeti, 1951), Schubert's Symphony No. 8, Mahler's Symphony No. 4 and some Mahler songs (with Schwarzkopf and the Vienna Philharmonic Orchestra, 1960), the *Egmont* overture (1950), Mozart's Symphony No. 40 and *Don Juan* (with the Berlin Philharmonic Orchestra, 1950), *Don Juan, Till Eulenspiegel* and *Tod und Verklärung* (1950 and 1951), Beethoven's Symphony No. 3 (with the Symphony of the Air, 1957), Busoni's Violin Concerto (with Busch and the Amsterdam Concertgebouw Orchestra, 1936), *Fidelio* (with Kirsten Flagstad as Leonore, 1941), and a lieder recital accompanying Kathleen Ferrier, in which the singer gives some brief reminiscences of Walter. The transfers include Haydn's Symphonies No. 86 (with the London Symphony Orchestra), No. 92 (with the Paris Conservatoire Orchestra) and Nos 96 and 100 (with the Vienna Philharmonic Orchestra), Mozart's Symphony No. 40 and the *Die Fledermaus* overture and *Wiener Blut* (with the Berlin Staatsoper Orchestra), Schubert's Symphony No. 9 (with the London Symphony Orchestra), Schumann's Symphonies Nos 1 and 3 (with the New York Philharmonic-Symphony Orchestra) and No. 4 (with the London Symphony Orchestra), Brahms' Symphonies Nos 1 and 3 (with the Vienna Philharmonic Orchestra), No. 2 (with the Paris Radio Orchestra) and No. 4 (with the BBC Symphony Orchestra).

Ariola, in FR Germany, has released Schubert's Symphony No. 9 (with the Stockholm Philharmonic Orchestra), and Rococo, Mozart's Violin Concerto K. 218 (with Huberman and an unnamed orchestra), and a transfer of *Symphonie fantastique* (with the Paris Conservatoire Orchestra). Turnabout, in its historical series, has included transfers of the recordings with the Vienna Philharmonic Orchestra of Mozart's Symphony No. 38, Piano Concerto K. 466, the three overtures and three *German Dances*, Beethoven's Symphony No. 6, *Leonore No. 3* overture, and Piano Concerto No. 5 (with Gieseking) and Brahms' Symphony No. 1, as well as Mozart's Symphony No. 39 (with the BBC Symphony Orchestra); Electrola, in FR Germany, has re-issued all of these transfers, and in addition Beethoven's Violin Concerto (with Szigeti and the British Symphony Orchestra). In Britain, CBS has re-issued Schubert's Symphonies Nos 5 and 8, and Mahler's Symphonies Nos 2, 5 and 9 (with the New York Philharmonic Orchestra), and EMI the *Siegfried Idyll*, Mahler's Symphony No. 9, and the Adagietto from Mahler's Symphony No. 5 (with the Vienna Philharmonic Orchestra). *Das Lied von der Erde* (with Thorborg and Kullman, and the Vienna Philharmonic Orchestra), was also re-issued on LP by Seraphim in the US.

CBS made available recordings of Walter's rehearsals of parts of Brahms' Symphonies Nos 2 and 3, and Beethoven's Symphony No. 5. In 1955, Walter recorded Mozart's Symphony No. 36 with the Columbia Symphony Orchestra, at this time a group of freelance musicians who had played with the NBC Symphony Orchestra and similar ensembles. As he had not performed the work before with these musicians, he carefully rehearsed it from his own marked parts. But unbeknown to him, the entire rehearsal was recorded, and when he was told about it, he exclaimed: 'I have been ambushed, and I am not sure that I approve of this look into the workshop.' He was persuaded, however, to agree to the commercial release of the rehearsals, which became the best-selling set, *The Birth of a Performance*. As Peter Munves, who was present at the rehearsals, has said: 'It was a document of a truly great artist at work, teaching a by now lost central European tradition to gifted instrumentalists.'

Walter, Paul (b. 1906). Born in Vienna and a graduate of the Academy of Music there, where he studied theory with Marx and conducting with Reichwein, Walter was conductor at Mönchengladbach, Erfurt, Trier and Giessen (1931–40), at the Vienna State Opera (1940–45), was chief conductor at the Landestheater at Salzburg and permanent conductor of the Mozarteum Orchestra (1945–54), and the conductor at the Vienna Volksoper (1954–74). He also taught at the Mozarteum for several years. He made records with the Mozarteum Orchestra and the Salzburg Festival Orchestra in the early years of LP, which were released on various labels, such as Remington, Dover,

Pirouette, Contrepoint, Classic, Period, Merit and Festival. The works recorded included Haydn's Symphonies Nos 86, 88 and 95, Mozart's Symphonies Nos 25 and 40, Cassations Nos 1 and 2, some marches, the Sonatas for Organ and Strings (with Messner) and the Divertimento K. 205, Weber's two Clarinet Concertos (with Heine) and an orchestral selection from *Cavalleria rusticana*. His other records were Mozart's Piano Concertos K. 175, K. 414, K. 415, K. 488 and K. 491 (with Haebler), and K. 413 and K. 449 (with Gilberg), all with the Vienna Pro Musica Orchestra for Vox, two Suppé overtures and a collection of Strauss waltzes (with the Vienna Symphony Orchestra for Philips) and Mozart's Piano Concerto K. 488 (with Kilenyi and an orchestra for Remington).

Walther, Hans-Jürgen (b. 1919). Born in Schwerin, Mecklenburg (now in DR Germany), Walther studied music privately and at the Hochschule für Musik in Hamburg (1945–50), was conductor of the Hamburg Chamber Orchestra (1950–57), and became chief conductor of the Swabian Symphony Orchestra at Reutlingen. He recorded, in the early days of LP, a considerable range of music with the Hamburg Philharmonic Orchestra for MGM and Music Sound Books (USA). The works included the Bach Suite No. 3, a suite for strings by Corelli, the *Water Music* and *Music for the Royal Fireworks* suites, *Eine kleine Nachtmusik* and *Les petits riens*, Leopold Mozart's *Toy Symphony*, dances from *Orfeo ed Euridice*, Schubert's *Marche militaire* No. 1 and Ballet Music No. 9 from *Rosamunde*, the March of the Priests from Mendelssohn's *Athalie* and excerpts from the incidental music for *A Midsummer Night's Dream, Invitation to the Dance*, the overtures to *William Tell*, *Oberon*, *The Merry Wives of Windsor*, *Hänsel und Gretel* and Toch's *Pinocchio*, the *Egmont* overture, the Brahms Violin Concerto (with Hamby) and two movements from the Serenade No. 1, the preludes to *Die Meistersinger* and to Act III of *Lohengrin*, the Ride of the Valkyries and the Magic Fire Music from *Die Walküre*, Forest Murmurs from *Siegfried*, *España*, *Sylvia*, *Valse triste*, Tchaikovsky's Piano Concerto No. 1 (with Bianca) and *Nutcracker* suite, the march from *Aida*, Dvořák's *Slavonic Dance No. 1*, Grieg's Piano Concerto (with Bianca), *Two Elegiac Melodies*, two *Peer Gynt* suites and March of the Dwarfs from *Lyric Suite*, Gounod's *Funeral March of a Marionette*, the Cortège from *The Queen of Sheba*, excerpts from *Faust*, Halvorsen's *The Entry of the Boyars*, Pierné's The Entry of the Little Fawns from *Cydalise et le chèvre-pied*, Prokofiev's Symphony No. 1, Quilter's *Children's Overture, Pini di Roma*, Saint-Saëns' Symphony No. 2, *Le Carnaval des animaux*, *Danse macabre*, *Le Rouet d'Omphale* and *Phaëton*, *The Enchanted Lake*, Massenet's Piano Concerto (with Bianca), *Pacific 231*, the *Wand of Youth* Suite No. 2, the overture to *Il segreto di Susanna* and the intermezzo from *I gioielli della Madonna*, *The Age of Gold*, the *Fantasia on Greensleeves*, German's *Nell Gwynn* dances, *An American in Paris*, *Rhapsody in Blue* and Gershwin's *Piano Concerto in F* (with Bianca), Barber's *Adagio for Strings*, Dett's *Juba Dance*, Siegmeister's *Ozark Suite*, Skilton's *Two Indian Dances*, pieces by Grainger, Guion's *Turkey in the Straw*, Haieff's Piano Concerto (with Bianca), Hanson's Symphony No. 1 and Powell's *In Old Virginia* overture. He also recorded discs of excerpts from *Lucia di Lammermoor*, *Pagliacci* and *Otello* (for Royale), Haydn's Sinfonia Concertante (with the Hamburg Chamber Orchestra for La Guilde Internationale du Disque) and Haubiel's *Portraits*, *Solari* and *Pioneers* (with the Hamburg Philharmonic Orchestra for Orion).

Walton, Sir William (b. 1902). Born in Oldham, Lancashire, the son of a music teacher, the eminent British composer Walton has devoted his entire time to composition, and has no interest in lecturing or writing. He is a competent conductor but restricts himself to performing his own music. His first experience on the podium was directing his *Portsmouth Point* overture in 1926; in 1929 the Decca company engaged him to conduct his *Façade*, with Constant Lambert and Edith Sitwell as the narrators. The length of the recording was limited to four 78 r.p.m. sides, and only 11 out of the 21 numbers were recorded. Walton has said that when composing he has since been conscious of the 4½ minute length of a record side. Later for Decca he conducted his Viola Suite, with Frederick Riddle and the London Symphony Orchestra.

In 1937 HMV took Walton under contract, and he recorded the two orchestral suites from *Façade*, and *Siesta* (with the London Philharmonic Orchestra), and the suite of Bach arrangements, *The Wise Virgins* (with the Sadler's Wells Orchestra). During World War II, under the auspices of the British Council, he directed his *Belshazzar's Feast* (with Noble, the Huddersfield Choral Society and the Liverpool Philharmonic Orchestra); this is a recording classic, and was a great technical feat for its time. Much later, in 1960, he recorded the work again with the Philharmonia Orchestra *et al.*; it was with this orchestra, which was formed in

1946, that he recorded many of his compositions, first on 78s and then on LP. Included were numbers from his film music for Olivier's *Henry V*, *Hamlet* and *Richard III*, the Symphony No. 1, *Partita*, a *Façade* suite, the *Scapino*, *Johannesburg Festival* and *Portsmouth Point* overtures, the marches *Crown Imperial* and *Orb and Sceptre*, the Violin Concerto (with Heifetz), the Viola Concerto (with Primrose), and excerpts from *Troilus and Cressida* (with Lewis, Schwarzkopf *et al.*). With the Hallé Orchestra he also conducted the *Spitfire Prelude and Fugue*. More recently he has again recorded some of his own music: the *Capriccio burlesco* and *Siesta* (with the London Philharmonic Orchestra for Lyrita), the *Scapino* and *Portsmouth Point* overtures and *The Quest* ballet (with the London Symphony Orchestra for Lyrita), the Violin and Viola Concertos (with Menuhin and the New Philharmonia and London Symphony Orchestras, respectively, for EMI), and *Façade* (with the London Sinfonietta, and with Peggy Ashcroft and Paul Scofield as narrators, for Argo).

Wand, Günter (b. 1912). Born at Elberfeld, Wand studied philosophy and musicology at the University of Cologne, at the Cologne Academy of Music, where his teacher for conducting was von Hoesslin, and at the Munich Academy of Music. He became conductor at the Cologne Opera (1939–44), but after the destruction of the opera house by Allied bombing, he moved to Salzburg where he was conductor at the Mozarteum (1944–6). He returned to Cologne at the end of the war, and was appointed general music director, conducting both opera and concerts. In 1947 he became chief conductor of the symphony orchestra at the Gürzenich concert hall, one of the oldest orchestras in Germany, and in the next year was appointed professor of conducting at the Cologne Conservatory. He also was a guest conductor in Europe, Japan and the USSR, which he visited in 1959. Previously the Gürzenich Symphony Orchestra had been under the somewhat conservative direction of Abendroth, and Wand transformed the orchestra's repertoire by including modern and contemporary music, including at least one modern work in each programme. Bartók, Hindemith, Stravinsky and other 20th-century composers, who had not been performed in Germany during the war, appeared frequently. He relinquished this position at Cologne in 1974, was at Berne, and often conducts the West German Radio Symphony Orchestra. His compositions include several ballet scores and a concertino.

Wand is a distinguished conductor with a wide range of sympathies, who is not sufficiently well known outside of his native Germany. Nonetheless he has made a number of recordings with the Gürzenich Symphony Orchestra, some of which have been issued on labels such as Nonesuch, Counterpoint and Vanguard. Included have been Haydn's Symphonies Nos 82, 92 and 103 and *The Creation*, Mozart's Symphonies Nos 33, 35, 36, 38, 39, 40 and 41, the Serenades K. 250, K. 320 and *Eine kleine Nachtmusik*, and movements from the Serenade K. 250, the nine Beethoven Symphonies (except apparently No. 8), three overtures and the *Missa solemnis*, Schubert's Symphonies Nos 6 and 8, Schumann's Symphonies Nos 3 and 4, Brahms' Symphonies Nos 2, 3 and 4 and the Serenade No. 1, the Bartók *Divertimento* and *Music for Strings, Percussion and Celesta*, Stravinsky's *Pulcinella* and *Dumbarton Oaks*, Schoenberg's *Five Pieces for Orchestra* Op. 16 and Webern's Cantata No. 1. For Decca, he also conducted the Vienna Philharmonic Orchestra in the Schumann Piano Concerto (with Backhaus), for Urania Shostakovich's Piano Concerto No. 1 (with the Berlin Radio Symphony Orchestra and Pinter), for EMI—Harmonia Mundi Bruckner's Symphonies Nos 5 and 6 (with the West German Radio Symphony Orchestra), and for BASF Bruckner's Symphony No. 8 (with the Gürzenich Symphony Orchestra).

Wangenheim, Volker (b. 1928). Born in Berlin and educated at the Hochschule für Music there, Wangenheim became principal conductor of the Berlin Mozart Orchestra (1950–59), was conductor at Schwerin, Mecklenburg (1951–2), and in 1957 was appointed music director at Bonn and principal conductor of the Beethovenhalle Orchestra and Municipal Choir, becoming general music director in 1963. He has also been musical adviser and principal conductor of the National Youth Orchestra of West Germany (since 1969), conductor of the orchestra of the Academy of Music at Cologne (since 1971), and professor of conducting there (since 1972). He has been a guest conductor abroad, and in 1977 was appointed principal conductor of the Bournemouth Sinfonietta. His compositions include a symphony, other symphonic music and sacred choral music. For EMI he recorded Beethoven's *Christus am Ölberge* (with the Beethovenhalle Orchestra *et al.*), but this disc has not been released in Britain.

Warchal, Bohdan (b. 1930). Born in Orlová, Czechoslovakia, Warchal studied the violin, graduated from the Bratislava Conservatory and from the Janáček Academy of Music Arts at Brno, and became concertmaster of the Slovak Philharmonic Orchestra at Bratislava (1957). He founded and conducted the Slovak Chamber Orchestra (1960), which was made up from members of the Slovak Philharmonic, and in 1966 the orchestra became fully independent in its membership, Warchal giving up his career as a concertmaster to develop it. The orchestra gives more concerts in countries outside Czechoslovakia, and has toured in Eastern and Western Eruope, North America and Cuba. In 1969 Warchal was awarded the distinction of Merited Artist, and in 1972 the orchestra received an award from the President of Czechoslovakia.

Under Warchal the Slovak Chamber Orchestra has recorded Corelli's Concerti Grossi Op. 6, Vivaldi's *The Four Seasons*, three symphonies and an orchestral trio by Stamitz, Vivaldi's Sinfonias Nos 2 and 3, and Concerto P. 143, Manfredini's Sinfonia No. 10 and Albinoni's Sinfonia No. 5 (for Supraphon, and issued in some cases by RCA in Japan and Spain, and by Parliament, Pickwick *et al.*), *Eine kleine Nachtmusik*, a suite from Purcell's *Abdelazer*, the Corelli/Arbós *Sarabande, gigue and badinerie*, Locatelli's Concerto Grosso Op. 8 No. 1, Manfredini's Concerto Grosso Op. 3 No. 12 and Torelli's Concerto Grosso Op. 8 No. 6, Handel's Concerti Grossi Op. 6, flute concertos by Benda and Richter (with Brunner), suites and concertos by Telemann, Galuppi, Corelli, Haydn and Vañhal, Britten's *Simple Symphony*, Suchoň's *Serenade* and Janáček's *Suite for Strings* (for Opus and Victor-Japan), pieces by Telemann, Galuppi, Scarlatti and Vivaldi (on three discs for Panton), guitar concertos by Carulli, Haydn and Vivaldi (with M. Zelenka), Vivaldi's Concerto Op. 3 Nos 6 and 8, Cello Concerto P. 282 (with Alexander) and Two-Violin Concerto P. 436 (with Holbingová and Holbing), Elgar's *Serenade in E minor*, Grieg's *Holberg Suite* and Respighi's *Ancient Airs and Dances*, Suite No. 3 (for Royale).

Washburn, Jon (b. 1942). Born in Rochelle, Illinois, Washburn studied at universities in Illinois and Vancouver, where he performed in choirs, gave recitals and played in orchestras. He moved to Vancouver from Illinois in 1967, formed and conducted the Jon Washburn Singers (1969–71), the Vancouver Bach Choir (1970), the Vancouver Society for Early Music (1970) and the Vancouver Chamber Choir (1971), and teaches in Vancouver. His recordings with the Vancouver Chamber Choir and with various local orchestras include Haydn's *Missa brevis St Joannis de Deo*, Handel's *Utrecht Jubilate*, Brahms' *Deutsche Volkslieder* and *Vier Lieder* Op. 62, the choral dances from Britten's *Gloriana* and other pieces by Debussy, Barber, Willcocks, d'Indy and Kodály, as well as Schafer's *Miniwanka*.

Washington, Henry (b. 1904). Born in King's Heath, Birmingham, Washington was educated at the Birmingham and Midland Institute of Music, and was director of music at Brompton Oratory, London, organist and choirmaster at St Anne's Catholic Church (1920) and at St Chad's Cathedral, Birmingham (1930). He founded and was director of the Schola Polyphonica, and edited masses by Palestrina, Byrd and Victoria. Conducting his Schola Polyphonica and the Brompton Oratory Choir, he made a number of discs for HMV's History of Music in Sound, including motets and sacred music by Dufay, Josquin, Handl, Lassus, Obrecht, Machaut, Ciconia, Dunstable, De la Rue, Taverner, de Monte, Palestrina and Gallus, and other pieces of Byzantine and Ambrosian music, Pre-Gregorian and Gregorian music, early polyphony, French and English polyphony and English Part Songs of the Renaissance.

Watanabe, Akeo (b. 1919). The son of a Japanese clergyman and a Finnish singer, Watanabe was born in Tokyo and was playing the piano sufficiently well at the age of six to perform Beethoven's Piano Concerto Nc. 2. Two years later he started to learn the violin. At the Tokyo Academy of Music he studied conducting with Joseph Rosenstock, the Polish-born conductor of the Nippon Philharmonic Orchestra before World War II, and made his debut as conductor after the war with the Tokyo City Symphony Orchestra (1945). He was appointed permanent conductor of the Tokyo Philharmonic Symphony Orchestra (1948–54), and came to the United States to study conducting with Morel at the Juilliard School. On returning to Japan, he became professor of conducting at the Tokyo University of Arts (1962–7), and in association with Shigeo Mizuno, director of the Nippon Broadcasting System, founded the Japan Philharmonic Orchestra in 1956, and was its permanent conductor until 1968. In 1963 he made his debut in New York, and the following year took the Japan Philharmonic on an extensive tour of the US and Canada. In later years he toured Israel, Sweden, Romania, Britain, the USSR and Finland, where he was honoured by the Finnish government for introducing the music of Sibelius to Japanese audiences. In 1970 he became music director of the Kyoto Symphony Orchestra.

With the Japan Philharmonic Orchestra, Watanabe has made a number of fine recordings for Composers Recordings Inc., a New York based recording company. Most of the music recorded has been by contemporary American composers: Copland's *Dance Symphony*, Cowell's *Music 1957*, Goeb's Symphony no. 4, Ruggles' *Organum*, Sessions' Symphony No. 1, Russell Smith's *Tetrameron*, Halsey Stevens' Symphony No. 1, Tanenbaum's *Variations for Orchestra*, Trimble's *Symphony in Two Movements* and *Five Episodes*, Wuorinen's Symphony No. 3 and Fine's *Concertante for Piano and Orchestra*. These discs form a significant contribution to the body of American music of the 20th century available on record. In addition, Watanabe recorded for CBS-Epic in 1966 the seven symphonies of Sibelius with the Japan Philharmonic Orchestra, but these had only a brief currency in the US, and were not issued in Britain. They were unmannered, incisive and sympathetic performances, not of course the first or only complete series of Sibelius symphonies by the one conductor, but certainly one of the most successful. He also recorded the Bartók Viola Concerto and Hindemith's *Der Schwanendreher* (with Hillyer and the Japan Philharmonic Orchestra for Nonesuch) and Kupferman's *Lyric Symphony*, *Variations for Orchestra* and *Burlesco ostinato* (with the same orchestra for Serenus).

Waxman, Franz (1906–62). Born in Königschüte, Germany, Waxman studied in Dresden and Berlin, migrated to the United States in 1934, and wrote music for films in Hollywood. Most successful was the score for *Sunset Boulevard*, for which he won an Academy Award in 1950. In Los Angeles he also took lessons from Schoenberg, and his other compositions included a *Sinfonietta*, and a fantasy for violin and orchestra on tunes from *Carmen*, which was written for a film and recorded by Stern. As a conductor, he recorded Bach's *Two-Violin Concerto in D minor* (in which Heifetz played both parts, for Victor on 78s), Foss's Piano Concerto No. 2 (with the composer) and his *Sinfonietta* (with the Los Angeles Festival Orchestra for Decca, US, and re-issued by Varèse-Sarabande), Sarasate's *Zigeunerweisen* (with Stern and an orchestra for Columbia), the Cello Concertos of J. C. Bach and of Schumann, and Bruch's *Kol Nidrei* (with Schuster and the Los Angeles Orchestral Society for Capitol), a vocal duet arranged by Tchaikovsky and completed by Taneyev from the *Romeo and Juliet* fantasy-overture (with soloists and the same orchestra for Capitol), and his *Three Sketches, Theme, Variations and Fugato* and a suite from the music for the film *Crime on the Streets* (with the Los Angeles Festival Orchestra for Entr'acte), and *The Spirit of St Louis* (for Entr'acte).

Weber, Henry (1900–70). Born in Berlin of American parents, Weber was brought to the United States as a child, but returned to Europe to study at the Academy of Music and University at Vienna (1911–23). He also attended the University of Chicago. He made his debut as a conductor at the Bremen Opera in 1919, was conductor with the Chicago Civic Opera Company (1924–9), was the musical director of a radio station, was commentator for the Chicago Symphony Orchestra broadcasts, and became artistic director of the Chicago City Opera Company (1940). Classic Records (France) issued performances of him conducting the Chicago Philharmonic Orchestra in the *Nutcracker* suite, *Marche slave*, the overture *Dichter und Bauer* and some orchestral excerpts from the Wagner operas.

Weder, Ulrich (b. 1934). Born in Bremen, Weder studied under Thomas at the North-West German Academy of Music (1951–5), under Paumgartner at the Mozarteum Academy at Salzburg (1958–9), at the Salzburg Opera Studio, with Markevitch and Ferrara at Hilversum, and with Previtali at the Accademia di Santa Cecilia in Rome. He was a repetiteur at the Salzburg Opera Studio (1957–9), music director at Bonn (1962–5), assistant to Maazel at the Berlin Deutsche Oper (1965–8), conductor at the Gärtnerplatz Theatre in Munich (1968–71), becoming its chief conductor (1971–3), and since 1975 has been general music director at Bremerhaven. Turnabout issued a disc of him conducting the Salzburg Mozarteum Camerata Academica *et al.* in an abridged version of Dittersdorf's *Doktor und Apotheker*.

Weemaels, Louis (b. 1909). Born in Brussels, Weemaels was educated at the Brussels Conservatoire under Joseph and Léon Jongen, Quinet, Defauw and Closson, and studied conducting with Kleiber, who had a strong influence on him. He was first conductor of the Jeunesses Musicales de Belgique (1940), of the Brussels Philharmonic Society (1942), founded the Jeunesses Musicales Choir (1944), conducted a Beethoven festival in Brussels (1944–5), founded Les Petits Chanteurs Choir in Brussels (1947), was director of the Tirlemont Academy of Music (1950), founded the Choir and Philharmonic Concerts of the Jeunesses Musicales in Brussels (1950), was professor of conducting at Louvain Conservatoire, of which he was director (1953–69), and became conductor of the Louvain University Orchestra (1970). He toured as a conductor in Belgium and abroad, and was awarded the honours Chevalier de l'Ordre de Léopold and Chevalier de l'Order de la Couronne. He recorded with the Belgian National Orchestra Alpaerts' *James Ensor Suite*, Boeck's *Symphony in G minor*, and Bourguignon's Violin Concerto (with van Neste) and *Recuerdos* (for Decca), and Gilson's *La Mer* (for Telefunken).

Weight, Newell (b. 1916). Born at Springfield, Utah, Weight studied at the University of Southern California, where he eventually received the degree of Doctor of Musical Arts (1961), taught at public schools, was professor of music at Brigham Young University in Provo, Utah, and then professor of music and head of choral music at the University of Utah, Salt Lake City. He first conducted in 1949, and is now musical director of the Utah Chorale, which is the official chorus of the Utah Symphony Orchestra, and has performed in many of the orchestra's recordings under Abravanel, such as the Berlioz *Grande Messe des morts*, the Mahler symphonies and works of Walton and Vaughan Williams. He is also director of the University of Utah A Capella Choir, has been a guest conductor in many cities of the United States, and conducted the Choir during three tours in Europe. For Composers Recordings he conducted the Choir with soprano Otley and the Utah Symphony Orchestra in Ussachevsky's *Missa brevis*, and three scenes from *The Creation*.

Weingartner, Felix (1863–1942). Weingartner was born at Zara (modern Zadar, Yugoslavia), of a German mother and an Austrian father, and after his father's death when he was a child, the family moved to Graz, where he studied the piano and composition with Remy. He started composing as a boy, and on Brahms' recommendation received a stipend from the state and went to study philosophy at Leipzig University in 1881. He soon transferred to the Conservatory there, and became known to Liszt, who convinced him that he should be a conductor. Liszt produced Weingartner's first opera *Sakuntala* at Weimar in 1884, and in that year Weingartner began his career as a conductor at Königsberg. From there, he proceeded to the pinnacles of his profession in Europe, although the restless and irascible side of his nature always kept him on the move. He was at Danzig (1885–7), then became von Bülow's assistant at Hamburg (1887–9); Mannheim followed (1889–91), then the Royal Opera and Royal Orchestra in Berlin (1891–8), the Kaim Orchestra at Munich (1898–1903), the Vienna Opera, where he succeeded Mahler (1908–11), Hamburg (1912–14), Darmstadt (1914–19), the Vienna Volksoper (1919–24) and the Vienna Philharmonic Orchestra (1919–27), the director of the Conservatory and of the Symphony Orchestra at Basel (1927), and finally the Vienna State Opera again (1935–6). He toured Europe, visited London for the first time in 1898 and the United States in 1905; he was also a considerable pianist and chamber player.

A prolific composer, Weingartner shared with some other great conductors a profound disappointment that his compositions were never more than an ephemeral success. But he had assimilated so much of other composers' music that his own was too eclectic to have any strong individuality. His output included eight operas, six symphonies, two concertos, chamber music and songs. The operas included a trilogy from Aeschylus, but many considered him temperamentally unsuited to operatic composition. His third symphony was entitled *Le Sermon d'amour* and its finale consisted of variations on a theme from *Die Fledermaus*. Together with Charles Malherbe he edited the complete works of Berlioz, and in fact was one of the first great conductors to pioneer the modern revival of Berlioz. He also edited *Oberon, Der fliegende Holländer* and Méhul's *Joseph*. He made a number of orchestral arrangements including Weber's *Invitation to the Dance*, which he recorded himself four times, two ballads of Loewe and songs by Beethoven, Haydn and Schubert, Beethoven's *Hammerklavier* Piano Sonata (Op. 106), and Schubert's *Symphony in E major*. Schubert had sketched this symphony and it was completed in a pianoforte arrangement by the English composer John Francis Barnett in 1882, and Weingartner reconstructed the score in 1934. A makeshift recording of it, conducted by Litschauer, was issued by Vanguard in 1958, and was re-issued in 1971. Weingartner himself recorded his arrangement of the *Hammerklavier* sonata with the Royal Philharmonic Orchestra, and Nixa issued an LP of a performance of it by the Bavarian Symphony Orchestra under Graunke.

When Weingartner was in Hamburg in 1887–9, there occurred his momentous clash with von Bülow, which led to Weingartner publishing his *On Conducting* in 1895. He objected to von Bülow's romantic exaggerations and excessive rubato, and himself led a performance of *Carmen* that was scrupulous in its observation of all the composer's directions, a great contrast to von Bülow's own performance of the opera. In his book, Weingartner made an explicit attack on von Bülow's freedom of interpretation, and, at one point, after discussing his tempo variations and instrumental amendments in his performances of the Beethoven symphonies, wrote: 'The impression given by performances of this kind was that not the work but the conductor was the chief thing, and that he wanted to divert the attention of the audience from the music to himself.' Along with Muck, Weingartner was one of the first great conductors to insist on strict adherence to the composer's markings, and on consistent and moderate tempi. His own interpretations were always models of sobriety and elegance, and avoided any romantic exaggeration or distortion. His influence as an interpreter, particularly of Beethoven, was crucial, and the overwhelming majority of European conductors since his day have accepted his principles as sacred writ, as do, one might add, today's record critics.

Weingartner himself was a remote, cold personality, the opposite of the popular stereotype of the egocentric, demonstrative conductor. His baton technique was simple, the wrist doing most of the work, and his manner before the orchestra was restrained, erect and unostentatious; nonetheless his psychological command of the players was complete. Cardus wrote of him in 1939: 'Weingartner does not use the familiar gestures of the modern "dictator" conductors; he retains the old-fashioned belief that an instrumentalist understands how to play his notes correctly and does not need illumination in the form of arts which scarcely belong to that of a conductor—the arts of Terpsichore and of declamation. (His) gestures are quiet: he is always dignified, He is seldom disturbed from a calm physical balance; his laundry-bill probably disappoints those who attend to the weekly linen of most other conductors. He belongs to the cultured epoch of music, the epoch of good manners and taste – and sound scholarship. It is difficult to describe how he obtains his effects; probably the work is done, as every conductor's work should be done, at rehearsal . . . Weingartner respects the composer's own notes and instructions; he never allows a phrase to carry more expression than consistent with the general flow of the rhythm; in other words, he does not take a phrase out of its context. Yet he is seldom a rigid conductor.' Burghauser, bassoonist of the Vienna Philharmonic Orchestra and the orchestra's chairman from 1933 to 1938, said that Weingartner employed only the subtlest modifications of tempo, and achieved the utmost clarity of rhythm. His performances of works such as Schubert's Symphony No. 8 and *Tristan und Isolde* had an almost unparalleled intensity of expression and dramatic power, although Walter wrote (in his autobiography, *Theme and Variations*) that Weingartner had not a dramatic nature, and for that reason was found wanting as an operatic conductor and director, despite his fiery temperament on the platform. Weingartner never hesitated to cut Wagner, and defended his cuts on artistic grounds. In his first period at the Vienna State Opera (1908–10) he introduced new operas, and had a predilection for comic operas, but in his second period (1935–6) he was apparently too old and resigned to be an effective director.

Weingartner made his first records in 1910, which were of some songs of his own, with the American soprano Lucille Marcel, who became the third of his five wives. All of his records were for Columbia; before the advent of electrical recording he had made *Invitation to the Dance*, the Liebestod from *Tristan und Isolde*, and the overture and intermezzo from Act IV of *Carmen* (with the Grand Symphony Orchestra), the Magic Fire Music from *Die Walküre*, the first movement of Tchaikovsky's Symphony No. 6, and the prelude and adagietto from *L'Arlésienne* (with the Columbia Symphony Orchestra), Mozart's Symphony No. 39, Beethoven's Symphonies Nos 5, 7 and 8, Brahms' Symphony No. 1, and the Dance of the Spirits and the entr'acte from his own music for *The Tempest*, *Ferdinand and Miranda* (with the London Symphony Orchestra). The *Symphonie fantastique* (with the London Symphony Orchestra) was recorded in March 1926, and was one of the first electrical recordings to be made in England. His subsequent recordings were of the Handel Concerto Grosso Op. 6 No. 5, Beethoven's Symphonies Nos 2 and 9 and the *Leonore No. 2* overture, Brahms' Symphonies Nos 1, 2 and 4 and *Academic Festival Overture* (with the London Symphony Orchestra), *Eine kleine Nachtmusik*, Beethoven's Symphonies Nos 5, 6, 7 and 8, his orchestration of the Piano Sonata Op. 106, Brahms' Symphony No. 1, *Les Préludes* and the Strauss waltzes *An der schönen blauen Donau* and *Sphärenklänge* (with the Royal Philharmonic Orchestra, all early electrical recordings), Mozart's Symphony No. 39, Beethoven's Symphony No. 4, the overtures *Fidelio*, *Prometheus*, *Die Ruinen von Athen* and *Die Weihe des Hauses*, *Eleven Viennese Dances*, and the larghetto and Death of Klärchen from the *Egmont* music, Handel's Concerto Grosso Op. 6 No. 6, Mendelssohn's Symphony No. 3, Brahms' Symphony No. 3 and *Variations on the St Antony Chorale*, *Mephisto Waltz*, *Invitation to the Dance* and the *Siegfried Idyll* (with the London Philharmonic Orchestra), Leopold Mozart's *Toy Symphony*, and the Strauss waltzes *Tausend und eine Nacht* and *Frühlingsstimmen* (with the British Symphony Orchestra), Beethoven's Symphonies Nos 1, 3, 7, 8 and 9, the overtures *Prometheus* and *Egmont*, and the Triple Concerto (with Odnoposoff, Auber and Morales, and with the Vienna Philharmonic Orchestra), Bach's Suite No. 3, a suite from Handel's *Alcina*, the minuet from Boccherini's Quartet Op. 13, Beethoven's Piano Concerto No. 3 (with M. Long), the two Liszt Piano Concertos (with Sauer), the March from *Les Troyens*, the overture to *Rienzi*, the prelude to Act III of *Tannhäuser*, the prelude to Act III and Liebestod from *Tristan und Isolde*, the Rhine Journey and Funeral Music from *Götterdämmerung*, the Strauss waltz *Wein, Weib und Gesang* (with the Paris Conservatoire Orchestra), and Strauss's *Pizzicato Polka, Invitation to the Dance*, the overture to *Der Freischütz*, and an entr'acte from *Rosamunde* (with the Basel Symphony Orchestra). In some cases, the published discographies differ as to the identity of the orchestras.

Artistically, Weingartner's outlook did not go beyond Brahms and Wagner, as his records reflect, and these composers were performed in a typically straightforward and carefully balanced style, perhaps too coolly for many accustomed to the virtuoso readings of Mengelberg, Stokowski *et al*. His place in the history of musical performance is in his interpretation of Beethoven. His book *On the Performance of Beethoven's Symphonies* had a profound influence and has served as a text book for countless conductors since; in the book he recommended that in many places the symphonies should be rescored, but later in his life he altered his opinion and acknowledged that Beethoven had known better. He recorded all the Beethoven symphonies, some more than once, the most famous being the series he made with the Vienna Philharmonic in the mid-1930s – Symphonies Nos 1, 3, 7, 8 and 9. Of these, the *Eroica* and *Choral* would have to be included in any short list of the greatest recordings ever made. In Japan alone, the *Choral* sold over 100,000 copies. His Beethoven was firm, with an exact balance between precision and expression; to compare, say, his Beethoven Symphony No. 1 with the Vienna Philharmonic, with the other great recorded performance of the 1930s, Toscanini's with the BBC Symphony Orchestra, is to compare two peaks of excellence – Viennese elegance and style with Italian fire and drama. And yet, Weingartner made these recordings in Vienna under odd circumstances. According to Fred Gaisberg of the Gramophone Company, who supervised them, Weingartner treated his orchestra 'with frigid detachment and they responded with grudging correctness' (*Music on Record*, New York, 1948, p. 120).

In 1976 EMI issued a three-disc set of LP transfers of many of Weingartner's recordings, including Beethoven's Symphony No. 3, the *Leonore No. 2* and *Die Ruinen von Athen* overtures, Brahms' Symphony No. 2, the *Rienzi* overture and preludes to Acts III of *Tristan und Isolde* and *Tannhäuser*, *Les Préludes*, *Mephisto Waltz*, part of the *Alcina* music, *Frühlingsstimmen*, *Wein, Weib und Gesang* and the March from *Les Troyens*. In Japan, the nine Beethoven symphonies have been issued, and in FR Germany Beethoven's Symphony No. 3 and the two Liszt Piano Concertos have been released by Electrola, and his song *Liebesfeier* is available in three separate versions.

Weisbach, Hans (1885–1961). Born in Glogau, Germany, Weisbach studied at the Hochschule für Musik and University in Berlin, and began his career as a choral conductor at the Munich Opera under Mottl. He was conductor at Frankfurt am Main, Worms, Wiesbaden, Hagen and Barmen, was general music director at Düsseldorf (1926), chief conductor of the Leipzig Radio Orchestra (from 1933), general music director of the Vienna Konzertverein (from 1939), and then was at Wuppertal (from 1947). He first conducted in Britain in 1930, and during the next six years came regularly to conduct the London Symphony Orchestra. At the first concert of the orchestra's 1932–33 international season, Weisbach conducted Graeser's arrangement of Bach's *Die Kunst der Fuge*. He was an active protagonist for Bruckner, led cycles of the nine symphonies on three separate occasions, and was awarded the medal of the International Bruckner Society. In the early 1930s he recorded, for HMV, Haydn's Symphonies Nos 92 and 97 (with the London Symphony Orchestra) and No. 104 (with the Vienna Philharmonic Orchestra), and, probably earlier, two movements from the Tchaikovsky *Serenade in C major* (with the Berlin Philharmonic Orchestra), and the *Toy Symphony* of Leopold Mozart and the Gingerbread Waltz from *Hänsel und Gretel* (with unidentified orchestras). Much later, there appeared on LP Haydn's Symphonies Nos 6, 13 and 19 (with the Bamberg Symphony Orchestra for

Mercury), Bach's *St Matthew Passion* (with the Leipzig Symphony Orchestra *et al.* for Acanta) and excerpts in German from *Falstaff* (with the Leipzig Radio Orchestra by BASF). Rococo issued a *St Matthew Passion* of Bach, said to have been originally recorded by Weisbach in 1935.

Weisberg, Arthur (b. 1931). Born in New York, Weisberg studied the bassoon with Kovar and conducting with Morel at the Juilliard School, and began his career as a member of the Symphony of the Air, the Houston, Baltimore and Cleveland Orchestras, and of the New York Woodwind Quintet (1956–72), with which he has toured the United States and Europe. He founded and conducted the New Chamber Orchestra of Westchester, conducted the Goddard-Riverside Community Orchestra, was conductor and director of Musica Viva of New York, and teaches at the State University of New York, Yale University, and at the Juilliard School, where his major course is devoted to performing problems of contemporary music. In 1960 he formed and led the Contemporary Chamber Ensemble, which has won a reputation for brilliant performances of advanced contemporary music, and since 1965 has been ensemble-in-residence to Rutgers University.

With the Contemporary Chamber Ensemble, Weisberg has recorded Blackwood's Chamber Symphony, Mayer's *Two News Items*, Pleskow's *Movement for Nine Players*, Blank's *Thirteen Ways of Looking at a Blackbird* (with Lamoree), Cortés' Chamber Concerto, Hamilton's Sextet, Martino's Concerto for Wind Quintet, Moevs' *Musica da Camera*, Sydeman's Chamber Concerto for Cello and Winds, Music for Flute, Guitar and Percussion, and Concerto da Camera No. 2, and MacDougall's *Anacoluthon* (for Composers Recordings), Sydeman's Concerto for Piano Four-Hands (with J. and K. Wentworth) and Moryl's *Multiples* (for Desto), Rieti's *Sonata à Cinq* (for Serenus), Schoenberg's *Pierrot Lunaire* (with De Gaetani), Shifrin's *Satires of Circumstance*, Anderson's *Variations on a Theme by Tolson*, Babbitt's *All Set*, Wernick's *Kaddish Requiem* (with De Gaetani and Gilbert), Myrow's *Songs from the Japanese* (with Bryn-Julson), Reynolds' *Quick are the Mouths of Earth*, Blackwood's Chamber Symphony No. 2, Carter's Harpsichord and Piano Double Concerto (with Jacobs and Kalish), Varèse's *Ecuatorial*, *Octandre*, *Offrandes* (with De Gaetani) and *Intégrales* (with Paul), Crumb's *Ancient Voices of Children* (with De Gaetani and Dash), Druckman's *Incentives*, Harbison's *Confinement*, Schwantner's *Diaphonia Intervallum*, Jones' *Ambiance* (with Bryn-Julson), Rochberg's *Blake Songs* (with De Gaetani) and *Serenata d'estate*, Wolpe's Quartet and Chamber Piece No. 1, Weill's *Kleine Dreigroschenmusik* and Milhaud's *La Création du monde* (for Nonesuch).

Weisgall, Hugo (b. 1912). Born at Ivancící, today in Yugoslavia, Weisgall studied at Johns Hopkins University and the Curtis Institute, and studied composition with Sessions. He was director of the Baltimore String Symphony Orchestra (1937–9), the Baltimore Institute of Musical Arts (1949–50), the Hilltop Opera Company (1951–4), and the Baltimore Chamber Music Society (1951–60), was professor at the Pennsylvania State University (1959–60), chairman of faculty, Cantors Institute, New York College (since 1951), instructor at the Juilliard School (since 1956) and professor at Queens College (since 1960). His compositions include seven operas, cantatas, ballet and vocal pieces, and music for radio and television. Composers Recordings recorded him conducting the Aeolian Chamber Players in his own *Fancies and Inventions* and *The Stronger*.

Weissenborn, Gunther (b. 1911). Born in Coburg, Weissenborn studied in Berlin, became a choirmaster and organist at Halle, Hannover and Göttingen, and a professor at Detmold (1947). He has also been director of the Handel Society of Göttingen, and since 1972 has participated in the annual summer music festival at Hitzacker. He is also a noted lieder accompanist, and has recorded with Hermann Prey and Rita Streich. As a conductor, he recorded Handel's *Deborah* (with the North German Radio Orchestra *et al.*, for Bärenreiter), *Samson* (with the same orchestra *et al.*, released by Everest), and *Apollo e Dafne* (with the Berlin Philharmonic Orchestra *et al.* for DCG) and Telemann's *Der geduldige Sokrates* (with the South-West German Chamber Orchestra *et al.*, released, as with *Deborah*, in the United States by the Musical Heritage Society).

Weissmann, Frieder (b. 1898). Born in Langen, Germany, Weissmann graduated in law and music from Munich University, was conductor at the Berlin Staatsoper (1920–25), at Münster and Königsberg (1925–8), with the Dresden Philharmonic Orchestra (1927–31), with the Berlin Symphony Orchestra, and was a guest conductor with the Berlin Philharmonic and Amsterdam Concertgebouw Orchestras

(1931–3). He appears then to have left Germany, conducted at the Teatro Colón in Buenos Aires (1934–7), at Cincinnati and New York (1937–9), was conductor of the Scranton Philharmonic Orchestra in Pennsylvania (1943–50) and the Havana Philharmonic Orchestra (from 1950). From the 1920s in Germany he made many records for Parlophone, some of which were released by Odeon and in the United States on the Decca label. In the US the orchestra was not identified, but in many of the European releases it was stated to be the Berlin Staatsoper Orchestra. In 1923 he made one of the very first recordings of Beethoven's Symphony No. 9 (with the Blüthner Symphony Orchestra *et al.* for Parlophone), in which cuts were made in the last movement, and tubas were substituted for double-basses. In addition to very many short popular pieces such as the *Naïla* waltz, *1812* overture, *Invitation to the Dance* and the Witch's Ride from *Hänsel und Gretel*, he recorded Beethoven's Symphonies Nos 1, 2, 3, 4, 5, 6 and 8, Haydn's Symphony No. 94, Mozart's Symphonies Nos 39, 40 and 41, some Mozart overtures, *Eine kleine Nachtmusik* and the Violin Concerto K. 219 (with Wolfsthal), Corelli's Concerto Grosso Op. 6 No. 8, Beethoven's *Wellington's Victory* and *Leonore No. 3* overture, overtures by Gluck, Weber, Rossini and Suppé, the *Peer Gynt* Suite No. 1, Leopold Mozart's *Toy Symphony*, *Finlandia*, *Fontane di Roma*, *Danse macabre*, Liszt's Piano Concerto No. 2 (with Pembauer), *Tod und Verklärung*, the overture to *Rienzi*, and a number of vocal excerpts from the Wagner operas and others. There were also some arias recorded in the US with the Victor Symphony Orchestra, as well as Handel's Viola Concerto (with Primrose, for RCA Victor), and excerpts from *Madama Butterfly* (with the Victor Symphony Orchestra for RCA Victor).

Weldon, George (1908–63). Born in Chichester, Weldon played the piano at a very early age, studied at the Royal College of Music under Sargent and Buesst, and gained experience conducting amateur choral and orchestral societies at Tunbridge Wells and Newbury. He was assistant to Harrison with the Municipal Orchestra (1937–9), toured with the London Symphony Orchestra (1940), conducted the London Philharmonic and National Symphony Orchestras and the Royal College of Music orchestra, directed a season of ballet, then was appointed, in succession to Heward, conductor of the City of Birmingham Symphony Orchestra (1944–51), after an open competition. He was second conductor of the Hallé Orchestra (from 1952), conductor of the Sadler's Wells Ballet (1955–6), and a guest conductor in North Africa, Turkey and Yugoslavia. He died in South Africa in 1963. Weldon had a strong preference for Russian and British music, especially that of Elgar and Walton, and was one of the few to include Sullivan in symphony concerts.

Weldon made a considerable number of records, on both 78s and LPs; the performances were competent, if seldom inspired. Included were the overtures *Russlan and Ludmilla*, *Raymond*, *Ruy Blas*, *Carnival* and *di Ballo*, Wachet auf from Bach's Cantata No. 140 (arranged by Granville Bantock), Handel's Organ Concertos Nos 2 and 4 (with Cunningham), Dvořák's Symphony No. 3, the ballet music from *Faust*, Rachmaninov's Piano Concerto No. 3 (with Smith), the Wedding Waltz from Dohnányi's *Pierette's Veil*, Grieg's *Norwegian Dances* and *Peer Gynt* Suite No. 2, Järnefelt's *Berceuse* and *Praeludium*, Moszkowski's *Spanish Dances Nos 1* to *5*, the Élégie and Musette from Sibelius' *King Christian II* suite, and German's *Welsh Rhapsody* (with the City of Birmingham Orchestra for EMI); *Les Sylphides*, *La Péri*, excerpts from *Tsar Saltan*, the overture to *Prince Igor*, *In the Steppes of Central Asia*, *A Night on the Bare Mountain*, *Gayane*, the Grieg Piano Concerto and Liszt's Piano Concerto No. 1 (with Farrell, and with the Hallé Orchestra, for Mercury); the Harty arrangements of *Water Music* and *Music for the Royal Fireworks*, the Grieg Piano Concerto (with Bachauer), *Lyric Suite* and *Norwegian Dances*, *Capriccio italien*, Tatiana's Letter Scene (with Shuard) and the polonaise and waltz from *Eugene Onegin*, suites from *Swan Lake* and *Nutcracker*, the Sullivan overtures *The Sorcerer*, *Cox and Box*, *Princess Ida*, *Ruddigore* and *Patience*, and German's *Nell Gwynn* and *Henry VIII* dances (with the Royal Philharmonic Orchestra for EMI); Handel's *Overture in D minor* (arranged by Elgar), the march from the *Occasional Oratorio* and the Arrival of the Queen of Sheba from *Solomon*, Haydn's Trumpet Concerto and Clarke's *Trumpet Voluntary* (with Mortimer), an arrangement of the Gavotte from Bach's Partita No. 3, Tchaikovsky's *Andante cantabile*, the two *Peer Gynt* suites, Franck's *Symphonic Variations* (with Jean Casadesus), Elgar's *Sea Pictures* (with Gladys Ripley) and *In the South*, the dances from German's *Nell Gwynn*, *Henry VIII*, *Tom Jones* and *Merrie England*, Holst's *The Perfect Fool*, *Somerset Rhapsody* and *Marching Song*, Quilter's *Children's Overture*, the Procession of the Nobles from *Mlada*, Bax's *Tintagel* and Vaughan Williams' music for *The*

Wasps (with the London Symphony Orchestra for EMI); the Air from Bach's Suite No. 3, the minuet from Handel's *Berenice* and the Largo from *Serse*, the overtures *Le nozze di Figaro*, *Carnival, The Hebrides, Russlan and Ludmilla, Leichte Cavallerie, di Ballo, Solomon* and *Orphée aux enfers*, the scherzo from *A Midsummer Night's Dream*, the prelude to Act I of *La traviata*, the polka from *The Bartered Bride*, Tchaikovsky's Piano Concerto No. 1 (with Moiseiwitsch), excerpts from *The Sleeping Beauty*, *1812* overture, *Marche slave* and the waltz from the *Serenade in C major*, the Hungarian March from *La Damnation de Faust*, Leopold Mozart's *Toy Symphony*, Rachmaninov's Piano Concerto No. 2 (with Moiseiwitsch), excerpts from Coates' *London Suite*, A Fair Day from Harty's *Irish Symphony*, excerpts from Vaughan Williams' *English Folksong Suite* and *Fantasia on Greensleeves*, Elgar's *Enigma Variations*, *Cockaigne*, *Chanson de matin* and *Chanson de nuit*, Walton's *Orb and Sceptre* and Bach arrangement *The Wise Virgins*, Holst's *St Paul's Suite* and Jupiter from *The Planets*, Davies' *Solemn Melody* (with Jones), La Calinda from *Koanga*, Grainger's *Mock Morris* and *Londonderry Air*, the Dance of the Hours from *La Gioconda*, *Finlandia*, *Danse macabre*, Liszt's *Hungarian Rhapsody No. 2*, the bacchanale from *Samson et Dalila*, the Procession of the Sardar from Ippolitov-Ivanov's *Caucasian Sketches*, the intermezzo from Granados' *Goyescas*, a dance from *El amor brujo*, the Dream Pantomime from *Hänsel und Gretel*, Medtner's Piano Concerto No. 1 (with Medtner), Boccherini's Minuet, the pizzicato movement from *Sylvia*, the intermezzo from *Cavalleria rusticana*, Grieg's *Holberg Suite*, *Norwegian Melody No. 2, Sigurd Jorsalfar* and *Two Elegiac Melodies*, and the march from *The Love of Three Oranges* (with the Philharmonia Orchestra for EMI); Mozart's Piano Concerto K. 488 (with Matthews) and Rachmaninov's Piano Concerto No. 2 (with Moiseiwitsch, and the Liverpool Philharmonic Orchestra for EMI).

Weller, Walter (b. 1939). Born in Vienna where his father was a violinist in the Vienna Philharmonic Orchestra, Weller studied at the Vienna Academy of Music under Moravec and Samohyl, and in 1956 joined the violins of the Vienna Philharmonic. In 1958 he founded the Weller String Quartet, with which he toured internationally and made a number of successful records for Decca. In 1961 he became concertmaster of the orchestra (at the age of 21), and retained that position until 1969. His debut as a conductor occurred in 1966 when he substituted for Böhm at short notice; for this concert he memorised the scores of Beethoven's Symphony No. 6 and Schubert's Symphony No. 9 in a day. Two months later he substituted for Krips in a concert with the Vienna Symphony Orchestra, performing a similar feat with Beethoven's Symphony No. 3 and Brahms' Symphony No. 1. These successes led to contracts with the Vienna Volksoper and Vienna State Opera, where he first conducted *Abu Hassan* and *Die Entführung aus dem Serail*, respectively. In 1971–2 he was musical director at Duisburg, and is now the musical director of the Niederösterreichisches Tonkünstler Orchestra, the third Viennese orchestra, which in its subscription series under his leadership has come to rival the Vienna Philharmonic and Vienna Symphony Orchestras. He has the opportunity for many rehearsals for each concert, and his programmes contain much music unfamiliar to Vienna. He has been a guest conductor in many European countries, both Western and Eastern, and appears in Britain with the London Philharmonic and London Symphony Orchestras, the Scottish National Orchestra and the Royal Liverpool Philharmonic Orchestra, of which he was appointed principal conductor and artistic adviser in 1976. In the opera house he prefers the German repertoire: Mozart, Beethoven, Weber, Strauss and Wagner, adding some operas of Rossini, Verdi and Puccini.

In his long experience with the Vienna Philharmonic Orchestra, Weller has most admired Knappertsbusch, particularly for his Strauss, Brahms, Wagner and Bruckner, and Schuricht for his Schubert, Schumann, Mozart and Bruckner. Weller's repertoire is essentially the classical and romantic composers, but he does not perform any work until he believes he is ready for it. Modern music since Schoenberg does not attract him; in his own words, the meaning of the music, which the conductor communicates to the orchestra and then to the audience, lies 'between the notes', whereas in dodecaphonic music, the performance may give a correct presentation of all the notes (often demanding great effort and time) but be empty of inner meaning. He feels that modern music can never attract a wide audience, and is essentially written by musicians for other musicians, and that Prokofiev and Britten are probably the last great composers. Weller customarily conducts without a score, except for concertos and opera. He enjoys listening to the records of other conductors' performances, particularly the interpretations of his great predecessors. (Personal interview, March 1976.)

Weller recorded Beethoven's *Contredanses* and *Mödlinger Dances* (with the Vienna Chamber Orchestra, issued in the United States by Musical Heritage Society). He now records for Decca; his first disc as a conductor, of Shostakovich's Symphonies Nos 1 and 9 (with the Suisse Romande Orchestra), appeared in 1973. In that year he also recorded Rachmaninov's Symphonies Nos 1 and 2 (with the Suisse Romande and London Philharmonic Orchestras respectively) and in 1975 he completed the series with Symphony No. 3 and *The Rock* (with the London Philharmonic). They were fine and convincing performances, without exaggeration or affectation. He has embarked on a series of the Prokofiev symphonies, and so far has recorded Nos 1, 5 and 7 (with the London Symphony Orchestra) and No. 6 (with the London Philharmonic Orchestra); his other discs have been of Dukas' *Symphony in C* and *L'Apprenti sorcier* (with the London Philharmonic), Bartók's Piano Concertos Nos 2 and 3 (with Pascal Rogé and the London Symphony Orchestra) and a recital by Lorengar (with the Vienna Opera Orchestra).

Wenzel, Eberhard (b. 1896). Born in Pollnow, Pomerania, Wenzel studied at the Stern Conservatory, the University and the Institute of Church Music in Berlin, and has been an organist and choirmaster there (1921–50). He became director of the Church Music School at Halle (1951–65), and in 1962 received the degree Doctor Honoris Causa at Heidelberg. He has composed oratorios, cantatas, motets and instrumental works; the oratorios were written in a simple and popular style. He recorded his own sacred music and also works by David, Distler and Handel; the latter's *Dixit Dominus* (with the Halle Music School Orchestra *et al.*) was for Cantate and released in Britain by Oryx.

Wenzinger, August (b. 1905). Born in Basel, Wenzinger studied philology at Basel University and the cello at the Basel Conservatory, and continued his studies at the Hochschule für Musik at Cologne with Jarnach and Grümmer (1927–9), and with Feuermann in Berlin. He was first cellist with the Bremen Municipal Orchestra (1929–34), and at the same time became known for his recitals of baroque music on the viola da gamba. He conducted the Scheck-Wenzinger Chamber Group, which was the first baroque music ensemble to use instruments of the period, and the Kabeler Chamber Music Group in Hagen, Westphalia. He returned to Basel in 1934, became a teacher and conductor at the Schola Cantorum Basiliensis, and leader of its viola da gamba consort, remaining with the body until 1970. His two-volume *Gamba Exercises* were published in 1935 and 1938; he also wrote about the art of gamba playing, and edited the Bach Cello Suites and Haydn's *Cello Concerto in D major*. In 1936 he joined the Basel String Quartet and became a teacher of the cello at the Basel Academy of Music. He visited the United States in 1953 and 1954, as the guest of Harvard and Brandeis Universities to give recitals and to lecture on the performance of baroque music, conducted the Capella Coloniensis of the West German Radio at Cologne (1954–6), conducted baroque operas at Hannover-Herrenhausen (since 1958), became a non-resident member of the Royal Swedish Academy of Music (1965), and is now conductor of the Hamburg Chamber Orchestra.

In the first years of LP records, Wenzinger made many discs of baroque and earlier music, which were among the first significant recorded performances of music of these periods to pay attention to the conventions and instruments of the time. Previously he had recorded with the viols of Schola Cantorum Basiliensis pieces by Willaert, Peuerl, Gibbons and Coperario, for the HMV History of Music in Sound. The major works he recorded were Monteverdi's *Orfeo* (with the Hitzacker Festival Orchestra of 1955, *et al.*), Bach's *Brandenburg Concertos* and Cantatas Nos 53, 65, 189 and 200, Handel's *Water Music*, Organ Concertos (with Müller), Concerti Grossi Op. 6, the Brockes (St John) Passion, and several Double Concertos, Telemann's complete *Tafelmusik* and other pieces, Purcell's Fantasias, music by Gibbons, Stradella, Gabrieli *et al.*, and concertos by Boccherini, C. P. E. Bach, Fasch, Quantz, Leclair, Naudot and Müthel (with the Schola Cantorum Basiliensis), Handel's Concerti Grossi Op. 3 and *Alexander's Feast* (with the Capella Coloniensis) and Handel's *Music for the Royal Fireworks* (with the Archiv Orchestra of Ancient Wind Instruments). Other recordings in which he appeared as conductor included two discs of music of Shakespeare's time (issued by EMI and Nonesuch), Haydn's *Flute Concerto in D* (with the Scheck-Wenzinger Chamber Group *et al.* for Urania), Senfl's *Deutsche Lieder* (for CT), and Monteverdi's *Tempro la cetra*, *Tirsi e Clori* and an excerpt from *Il ritorno d'Ulisse* (with Meili and the Schola Cantorum Basiliensis Ensemble, issued by Nixa).

Werner, Fritz (b. 1898). Born in Berlin, the son of a piano maker, Werner studied at the Berlin

Academy of Church Music, and became organist at St Nicholas Church, Potsdam, where he succeeded the father of the pianist Wilhelm Kempff (1923). He studied composition at the Prussian Academy (1932–5), won the Mendelssohn Prize for composition (1935), became director of church music in Potsdam (1938), and during World War II gave concerts in France with a German cultural group. After the war, he settled in Heilbronn, was organist at the St Kilian Church, founded the Heinrich Schütz Choir, and inaugurated and directed the Heilbronn 'Days of Church Music'. He was appointed professor by the State of Baden-Württemberg (1954), and the French Ministry of Culture made him Chevalier de l'Ordre des Arts et Lettres (1974). His compositions include a symphony, instrumental and choral works. His first record, made with the Heinrich Schütz Choir *et al.* for Erato in 1956 was the Schütz *Requiem*; there followed over 25 discs of Bach Cantatas, the *Christmas Oratorio*, the *St John Passion*, the *Easter Oratorio* and Motets; the Cantatas included Nos 1, 4, 6, 8, 10, 11, 21, 30, 32, 34, 43, 51, 53, 57, 65, 67, 68, 70, 76, 78, 80, 85, 87, 90, 92, 98, 102, 104, 110, 131, 137, 140, 147, 149, 180 and 182. These were for Erato, and many were issued in the United States by Musical Heritage Society. He also recorded the Bach *St Matthew Passion* (for Westminster), Zuchau's *Lobe den Herrn* and *Ich will mich mit der verloben* (for Westminster), as well as his own Suite for Trumpet and Orchestra (with André, for Erato). These discs were all with the Heinrich Schütz Choir and the Pforzheim Chamber Orchestra and soloists, with two exceptions, Cantatas Nos 23 and 72, in which he conducted the Württemberg Chamber Orchestra, and his own Suite. These recorded performances were of a uniformly high standard, and have been a major contribution to the Bach discography.

Werner, Jean-Jacques (b. 1935). Born in Strasbourg, Werner was enrolled at the local Conservatoire at an early age, then studied at the Schola Cantorum in Paris under Daniel-Lesur, Wissmer and Barzin, won prizes for composition and conducting, and in 1960 conducted the orchestras of the French Radio and Television. He founded the Ars Musica Group, which later became named the Fontainebleau Chamber Orchestra, with which he has given many concerts in France and abroad. His records with the orchestra include Leclair's Violin Concertos Op. 7 Nos 3, 4 and 6 (with Jodry, for Arion), motets by Bernier (for Arion), Vaughan Williams' *Concerto accademico* (with Jodry) and pieces by Tchaikovsky, Sibelius and Grieg (for Erato).

Wernick, Richard (b. 1934). Born in Boston, Wernick studied at Brandeis University and Mills College and at Tanglewood, under Toch, Blacher and Copland. He was music director at the Royal Winnipeg Ballet (1957–8), composed music for films, television and the theatre (1958–64), and taught at the Universities of Buffalo (1964–5), Chicago (1965–8) and Pennsylvania (since 1968). Turnabout issued a disc in which he conducted the Penn Contemporary Players in Rochberg's *Tableaux*.

Westerberg, Stig (b. 1918). The Swedish conductor Westerberg made his debut with the Stockholm Philharmonic Orchestra (1945), conducted at the Royal Opera House in Stockholm (1958), became chief conductor of the Swedish Radio Symphony Orchestra, and is principal conductor of the Malmö Symphony Orchestra. He has recorded both as pianist and conductor; he led the Stockholm Radio Symphony Orchestra in a popular disc issued in 1960 by Decca of Wirén's *Serenade for Strings*, and Decca also released Larsson's *Pastoral Suite*, performed by the same artists. His subsequent records have been almost all of Swedish composers, and have included Roman's *Sinfonias in D major* and *E minor*, and *Drottningholm Music* Suite, and Bellman's *Bellmaniana* (with the Drottningholm Chamber Orchestra for Discofil), Alfvén's *Swedish Rhapsodies Nos 1* and *3*, Wirén's *Serenade for Strings*, Larsson's *Pastoral Suite* and *Little March*, von Koch's *Oxberg Variations* and Stenhammar's *Serenade* (with the Stockholm Philharmonic Orchestra for Discofil), Larsson's *The Disguised God* and *Variations for Orchestra*, Grieg's *The Sighting of Land* (with Söderström, Saeden *et al.*), Karkoff's Symphony No. 4, Atterberg's Symphony No. 2 and Suite No. 3, de Frumerie's *Pastoral Suite*, Wirén's *Sinfonietta*, Alfvén's Symphony No. 1, Symphony No. 5 (first movement), *Gustav Adolf II* suite and *Legend of the Skerries*, Pettersson's Symphony No. 2 and *Mesto*, Sibelius' incidental music for *The Tempest*, Nystroem's *Sinfonia del mare* (with Söderström) and *Sinfonia concertante* (with Bengtsson), Hermanson's *Appel I–IV* and von Koch's *Nordic Capriccio* (with the Swedish Radio Symphony Orchestra for Discofil), Lidholm's *Nausikaa Lone*, Stenhammar's two *Sentimental Romances*, Rosenberg's ballet suite *Orpheus in Town*, Hambraeus' *Meetings*, Larsson's *Due Auguri*, Berwald's Piano Concerto (with Greta Erikson) and Bucht's Symphony No. 7 (with the Swedish

Radio Symphony Orchestra *et al.* for Caprice-RIKS), Rangstrom's *Divertimento Elegiaco* and *Suite for String Orchestra* (with the Kungl Hovkapellet for Telstar), Alfvén's *En bat med blommer* (with the Swedish Radio Symphony Orchestra for Telstar), Peterson-Berger's Violin Concerto and Romance (with Pierrou and the Swedish Radio Symphony Orchestra for EMI), and Stenhammar's Piano Concerto No. 2 and Liszt's *Totentanz* (with Solyon and the Munich Philharmonic Orchestra for EMI).

Westrup, Sir Jack (1904–75). Born in London and educated at Balliol College, Oxford, Westrup was there a member of the Oxford University Opera Club and prepared Monteverdi's *La favola d'Orfeo* and *L'Incoronazione di Poppea* for performances in 1925 and 1927 respectively, conducting himself the latter production. He was editor of the *Monthly Musical Record* (1933–45), music critic for the *Daily Telegraph* (1934–45) and was a distinguished contributor and writer about music; his studies of Purcell and Handel were especially notable. He was lecturer in music at King's College at Newcastle-upon-Tyne (1941), professor of music at Birmingham University (1944–6) and at Oxford University (1947–71); he enjoyed a reputation as a conductor, and at Oxford was conductor of the O.U. Opera Club, the University Orchestra, the Oxford Bach Choir and the Oxford University Orchestral Society, of which he remained conductor until 1971. With the O.U. Opera Club he led performances of a number of rarely performed works, two at least of which were later issued by Isis, a private label, viz. Wellesz's *Incognita* and Marschner's *Hans Heiling* (the latter in an abridged form). The Wellesz opera had the distinction of being on 31 78 r.p.m. sides. Westrup also contributed to the EMI History of Music in Sound, with excerpts from Monteverdi's *La favola d'Orfeo* and Bach's *St Matthew Passion*, a motet by J. C. Bach, Gibbon's *Behold, Thou hast made my days* and an excerpt from Schütz's *Die sieben letzten Worte* (with various choirs).

Whear, Paul (b. 1925). Born at Auburn, Indiana, Whear studied at Marquette, de Pauw and Western Reserve Universities, and has taught at Baker University, Mount Union College and Doane College, Marshall University, and is conductor of the Huntington Chamber Orchestra. His compositions include many orchestral and other pieces, and he has contributed to musical journals. Advent recorded him conducting the London Concert Orchestra in his *Decade Overture*, *Catharsis Suite*, and *Psalms of Celebration*.

White, John (b. 1924). Born in Houston, White studied at the Cincinnati Conservatory (1941–3), at the Paris Conservatoire (1945) and Colorado College (1952). He has taught at various colleges and universities, and from 1966 to 1970 conducted the New York Pro Musica, after the death of its founder, Noah Greenberg. MCA issued a disc of him conducting the Pro Musica in music by Petrucci and Josquin, as well as another of music of medieval France.

Whiteman, Paul (1890–1967). The great jazz band leader Whiteman was born in Denver, played the viola in the Denver Symphony Orchestra, and in the San Francisco People's Symphony Orchestra, before he formed an orchestra of his own and introduced a musical style called 'symphonic jazz'. He toured the United States and Europe, and became famous in his field. In February 1924 he premièred Gershwin's *Rhapsody in Blue* in New York; the composer recorded the work with Whiteman's orchestra, which also recorded *An American in Paris*, the Rhapsody No. 2 and *Rhumba*, a rearrangement of the *Cuban Overture*. All these were for Decca, but critical appraisal at the time was somewhat cool towards the quality of the performances, in both technical and artistic aspects. Whiteman later recorded the *Rhapsody in Blue* with Pennario for Capitol, and the *Piano Concerto in F major* and Rhapsody No. 2, with Bargy for Brunswick. He also recorded the first disc to sell a million copies, with his Ambassador Orchestra, playing *The Japanese Sandman* and *Whispering*; it was issued in 1920 by Victor.

Whitney, Robert (b. 1904). Born in Newcastle-upon-Tyne of American parents, Whitney was educated at the Chicago Conservatory (1922–8), and studied conducting under Stock and De Lamarter with the Chicago Civic Orchestra, and with Koussevitzky at the Berkshire Music Center (1940–41). He was a radio announcer (1922–5) and pianist with the Whitney Trio (1924–30) at the WMAQ broadcasting station in Chicago, made concert appearances and radio performances (1934–7), and became supervisor of the Chicago Federal Music Programme of the Works Progress Administration (1936–7). He founded, conducted, and was music director of the Louisville Orchestra (1937–67), did research and taught composition (1938–44), was dean of the school of music at the University of Louisville (1956–71), and taught conducting at the University of Cincinnati (1967–70). He also was conductor and lectured at other United States universities, was a guest conductor in Scandinavia,

Chile and in the US, and received the Ditson Award (1954) and many other honours for services to American music.

When Whitney became conductor of the Louisville Orchestra in 1937, on the recommendation of Stock and De Lamarter, the orchestra consisted of 80 players. After World War II, at the suggestion of the president of the Louisville Philharmonic Society, Charles P. Farnsley, the orchestra was reduced to 50 players and a plan was brought into effect whereby every programme included the first performance anywhere of a new work especially commissioned by the orchestra. Each work could be scored for no more than 50 players. In 1955 the Rockefeller Foundation made a grant to the orchestra to establish a project by which the orchestra could both commission and record each year sufficient new works to fill twelve LP records. These records were to be sold, by mail-order, to subscribers. The project got under way, but later the annual releases were reduced to six in number. By 1971, the orchestra had issued 100 discs in its First Editions series; all the works on these discs were newly commissioned by the orchestra except for some previously unrecorded pieces from the 19th century. Until his retirement in 1967, Whitney was responsible for the selection of the commissions, and thereafter this was continued by the orchestra's new conductor, Jorge Mester; Whitney's preference was generally for conservative and academic compositions, which reflected his personal taste as well as the limitations of the orchestra's capacity and available rehearsal time.

The music recorded by Whitney in the Louisville series was Almand's *John Gilbert: A Steamboat Overture*, Antheil's opera *The Wish*, Bacon's *The Enchanted Island*, Badings' *Louisville Symphony*, Bazelon's *Short Symphony*, Ben-Haim's *To the Chief Musician* and *Pastorale variée* (with Livingston, clarinet), Bentzon's *Pezzi Sinfonici*, Berger's *Polyphony*, Bergsma's *A Carol on Twelfth Night*, Berkeley's *Four Ronsard Sonnets* (with Whitesides), Blacher's *Orchestral Fantasy* and *Studie im pianissimo*, Bliss's *Discourse*, Bloch's *Proclamation* (with Rapier, trumpet), Borowski's *The Mirror*, Britten's Violin Concerto (with Kling), Caamano's *Magnificat*, Carter's Symphony No. 1 and *Variations for Orchestra*, Castelnuovo-Tedesco's *Overture to Much Ado About Nothing*, Chou Wen-Chung's *Soliloquy of a Bhiksuni* (with Rapier, trumpet), *And the Fallen Petals* and *All in the Spring Wind*, Copland's *Orchestral Variations*, Cowell's Symphonies Nos 11 and 15, and *Ongaku*, Creston's *Corinthians XIII* and *Invocation and Dance*, Dahl's *The Tower of St Barbara*, Dallapiccola's *Variazioni per orchestra* and *Due pezzi*, Dello Joio's *Triumph of St Joan Symphony*, Diamond's overture *Timon of Athens*, Egge's Symphony No. 2, Egk's Suite from *Abraxas*, Etler's *Triptych* and Concerto for Wind Quintet and Orchestra, Elwell's Concert Suite for Violin and Orchestra (with Harth), Fine's *Diversions* and *Serious Song*, Finney's Symphonies Nos 1 and 2, Fischer's *Overture on an Exuberant Tone Row*, Floyd's *The Mystery* (with Curtin), Foss's *Parable of Death* (with Zorina), Fricker's Symphony No. 1, Garcia-Morillo's *Variaciones Olimpicas*, Gerhard's *Alegrias*, Giannini's Divertimento No. 2, Ginastera's *Pampeana No. 3*, Glanville-Hicks' opera *The Transposed Heads*, Goeb's *Concertino II*, Guarnieri's *Suite IV Centenario*, Haieff's Divertimento and *Ballet in E*, Halffter's *La Madrugada del Panedero*, Hamilton's *Scottish Dances*, Harris's Symphony No. 5, *Kentucky Spring* and *Epilogue to Profiles in Courage – JFK*, Harrison's *Four Strict Songs* and *Suite for Symphonic Strings*, Helm's Piano Concerto No. 2 (with Owen), Henze's Wedding Music from *Undine*, Herder's Movements for Orchestra, Hindemith's *Sinfonietta in E*, Hoiby's opera *Beatrice*, Honegger's *Suite archaïque*, Hovhaness's Symphony No. 15, Concerto No. 7 for Orchestra and *Magnificat*, Ibert's *Louisville Concerto*, Ives' *Decoration Day* and (with Schuman) *Variations on America*, Jolivet's *Suite transocéane*, Ulysses Kay's *Umbrian Scene* and Serenade, Keyes' *Music for Monday Evenings*, Klein's *Musique A Go-Go*, Kodály's *Symphony (1961)*, Korn's *Variations on a Tune from The Beggar's Opera*, Kraft's Concerto Grosso, Křenek's *Eleven Transparencies*, Kubik's Symphony No. 2, Kupferman's Symphony No. 4, Kurka's Symphony No. 2, Serenade and Suite from *The Good Soldier Schweik*, Lees' Symphony No. 2, and Concerto for Orchestra, Letelier's *Aculeo*, Liebermann's opera *School for Wives*, Lopatnikoff's *Music for Orchestra* and *Variazioni concertanti*, Luening and Ussachevsky's *Rhapsodic Variations for Tape Recorder and Orchestra*, Luke's Symphony No. 2, Malipiero's Piano Concerto No. 3 (with Owen), *Notturno de canti e balli* and *Fantasie di ogni giorni*, Martin's Violin Concerto (with Kling), Martinů's Symphony No. 5, *Intermezzo* and *Estampes*, Mayuzumi's *Samsara* and *Pieces for Prepared Piano and Strings* (with Owen), McPhee's Symphony No. 2, Mennin's Symphonies Nos 5 and 6, Milhaud's *Ouverture méditerranéenne* and *Kentuckiana*, Mohaupt's *Town Piper Music* and opera *Double Trouble*, Moncayo's *Cumbres*, Morel's *Antiphonie*,

Morris's *Passacaglia, Adagio and Finale*, Muczynski's Piano Concerto No. 1 (with the composer), Müller-Zürich's Cello Concerto (with Grace Whitney), Nabokov's *Symboli Chrestiani* (with Pickett) and opera *The Holy Devil*, Nono's *Due Expressioni*, Part 1, Nordoff's *Winter Symphony*, Orrego-Salas' Symphony No. 2 and *Serenata concertante*, Overton's Symphony No. 2, Panufnik's *Sinfonia elegiaca*, *Rhapsody* and *Nocturne*, Perle's *Rhapsody*, Persichetti's Symphony for Strings and Serenade No. 5, Petrassi's Concerto No. 5, Pinkham's Symphony No. 2 and *Signs of the Zodiac*, Piston's Symphony No. 5, Viola Concerto (with Doktor) and *Serenata*, Porter's Symphony No. 2, Rathaus' *Prelude*, Read's *Night Flight* and *Toccata giocosa*, Reichel's *Suite symphonique*, Revueltas' *Ventanas*, Riegger's Symphony No. 4, Rieti's *Introduzione e gioco delle ore*, Rochberg's *Night Music*, Rodrigo's *Cuatro madrigales amatorios* (with Nossaman) and *Concerto galante* (with Grace Whitney), Bernard Rogers' *Dance Scenes*, Rohe's *Mainescape*, Rorem's *Eleven Studies for Eleven Players*, and *Design*, Rosenberg's *Louisville Concerto*, Riegger's *Variations for Piano and Orchestra* (with Owen) and *Variations for Violin and Orchestra* (with Harth), Rubbra's *Improvisation for Violin and Orchestra* (with Harth), Saeverud's *Peer Gynt* Suite No. 1, Sanders' *Little Symphony in C* and *Little Syphony No. 2*, Sauguet's *Les Trois Lys*, Schuller's *Dramatic Overture*, Schuman's *Judith* and *Undertow*, Serebrier's *Partita*, Sessions' *Idyll of Theocritus* (with Nossaman), Shapero's *Partita in C* (with Owen), and *Credo*, Hale Smith's *Contours*, Somers' *Passacaglia and Fugue*, Sowerby's *All on a Summer's Day*, Stevens' *Sinfonia breve* and *Triskelion*, Surinach's Symphonic Variations, *Sinfonietta flamenca* and *Feria magica Overture*, Sydeman's *Orchestral Abstractions*, Tansman's *Capriccio*, Tcherepnin's Symphony No. 2, Piano Concerto No. 2 (with the composer) and Suite Op. 87, Thomson's Flute Concerto (with Fuge), Toch's *Notturno*, *Peter Pan*, and *Jephtha*, Van Vactor's *Fantasia, Chaconne and Allegro*, Villa-Lobos' *Erosion*, *Origin of the Amazon River*, and *Dawn in a Tropical Forest*, Vincent's *Symphony in D*, Von Einem's *Meditations*, Wagenaar's *Concert Overture*, Ward's *Euphony*, Weber's *Prelude and Passacaglia* and *Dolmen* and Whitney's own Concertino.

The Louisville First Editions has been the most impressive attempt systematically to record new music. By any measure, its success has been only moderate; the number of subscribers never rose above about 3,000, and even in Louisville itself audiences at the orchestra's concerts developed an indifference to new compositions. Only a handful of the commissioned and recorded works became part of the repertoires of other orchestras: Schuman's *Judith*, Carter's *Variations for Orchestra*, Mennin's Symphonies Nos 4 and 5, and Piston's Symphony No. 5. It must be admitted that the act of commissioning does not ensure that a memorable composition will result, more than any other motivation to compose, and that from the great bulk of music written in any particular era, very little is sufficiently inspired or outstanding to survive its original performance. So the Louisville First Editions are interesting documents of the state of composition in mid-20th century United States (with some additions from other countries), even despite its bias towards a conservative musical vocabulary.

Wich, Günther (b. 1928). Born in Bamberg, Wich studied in Freiburg, where he was a choral repetiteur and conductor. He became chief conductor in Graz (1959), general music director in Hannover (1961), in Düsseldorf, and is principal conductor of the Deutsche Oper am Rhein. He recorded Handel's Concerti Grossi Op. 3 Nos 1, 3, 4 and 6, and *Alexander's Feast*, Haydn's Symphonies Nos 82 to 85, Mozart's Serenade K. 203 and Divertimentos K. 247 and K. 287, Dvořák's *Serenade in E minor*, and Tchaikovsky's *Serenade in C major* (with the South German Chamber Orchestra for Intercord), Mozart's Serenade K. 361 (with the Mozart Ensemble, Stuttgart, for Intercord, and issued in the United States by Musical Heritage Society), Mozart's Piano Concertos K. 37, K. 39, K. 40 and K. 41 (with Galling and the Stuttgart Soloists for Turnabout) and Pfitzner's Violin Concerto (with Lautenbacher and the Philharmonia Hungarica for Candide).

Wicherek, Antoni (b. 1929). Born in Żory, Silesia, Wicherek first studied law at Wrocław University (1949–52), then was a conducting pupil of Wilkomirski at Wrocław, of Bierdiajew at the National School of Music in Warsaw (1951–5), and also of Capuano in Venice. He made his debut as a conductor of both opera and symphonic music at Wrocław (1954), was an assistant conductor and taught music at Wrocław (1954–60), was assistant conductor to Gorzyński at the Moniuszko National Opera at Poznań (1957–62), then became a conductor at the Warsaw National Opera (1962), and was appointed artistic director and resident conductor in 1973. Here he has prepared productions of, *inter alia*, Menotti's *The Consul* and a première performance of *Tannhäuser*. He teaches at the High School of Music in Warsaw, has been a guest conductor of opera in East and West Germany, and has been awarded the Gold Cross of Merit and the Order of the Polish People's Republic. Wicherek's recordings have included Rudziński's operas *The Roof of the World* and *The Dismissal of the Greek Envoys* (with the Warsaw National Opera Company) and Ostromęçki's symphonic poem *Pictures from the Holy Cross Mountains*.

Wiesenhütter, Gerhart (b. 1912). Born in Dresden, Wiesenhütter was educated at the Orchestra School of the Dresden Staatskapelle. He has been music director at Glauchau (1934), deputy conductor of the Berlin Radio Orchestra (1939), first conductor at Saarbrücken (1941–3), chief conductor of the Westmark Ludwigshafen Radio Orchestra (1943–5), chief conductor of the Dresden Philharmonic Orchestra (1945), artistic director of the Leipzig Radio Symphony Orchestra (1946), chief conductor at the Sachsen-Anhalt Landestheater, Halle (1948–9), at the Metropole Theatre, Berlin (1951–3), at the Volkstheater, Rostock (1953–5), at Sondershausen (1959–70), of the Cairo Symphony Orchestra, Egypt (1968–70) and of the Gotha Symphony Orchestra (1970–75). He has toured in the USSR, Poland, Hungary and Czechoslovakia. In DR Germany he recorded with the Berlin Radio Symphony Orchestra, the Leipzig Radio Orchestra *et al.*, *Capriccio italien*, *1812* overture, Grieg's *Norwegian Dances*, Dvořák's *Noonday Witch*, the overtures *The Merry Wives of Windsor* and *Le Carnaval romain*, excerpts from *La Damnation de Faust*, Liszt's *Hungarian Rhapsody No. 2*, Strauss's Horn Concerto No. 1 (with Lohan) and Martinů's and Prokofiev's Piano Concertos for Left Hand. He also recorded Schwaen's *Concerto piccolo for Jazz Orchestra* (with a studio orchestra).

Wilding-White, Raymond (b. 1922). Born at Caterham, Surrey, Wilding-White studied at the Juilliard School, the New England Conservatory and at Boston University; he occupied the Kulas Chair of Music at the Case Institute of Technology, and has been associate professor of music at De Paul University. He founded the Case Electronic Music Studio, the Case Experimental Music Presentations, the Cleveland Portfolio Concert Series, the De Paul Electronic Music Studio and the Loop Group. He has written a number of compositions, and has received the F. S. Crofts Award (twice) and the Cleveland Fine Arts Award. For Composers Recordings, he conducted his *Paraphernalia* (with the Kulas Vocal Ensemble and a chamber orchestra).

Wilhelm, Gerhard (b. 1918). The German choral conductor Wilhelm studied the piano as a boy with Kempff, and was a treble in Kempff's boys' choir at the Stuttgart Academy. He studied at the Prussian Academy of Arts in Berlin under Fischer and Keussler, and after World War II performed as a pianist. He re-established the Stuttgart Hymnus Choir in 1946, and has since been its conductor. With the Choir and others he recorded Haydn's *Missa Sanctae Caeciliae in C major* and Hummel's *Mass in E major* (for EMI), and choral pieces by Lassus, Schütz, Praetorius, Bach, Mendelssohn, Brahms and Bruckner (for Intercord).

Willcocks, Sir David (b. 1919). Born at Newquay, Cornwall, Willcocks was a chorister at Westminster Abbey (1929–33), studied at Clifton College (1934–8) and was an organ scholar at King's College, Cambridge (1939–40 and 1945–7). During World War II he served in the British Infantry, and was awarded the Military Cross (1944). He was a Fellow of King's College, Cambridge (1947–51) and conductor of the Cambridge Philharmonic Society (1947), organist at Salisbury Cathedral and conductor of the Salisbury Musical Society (1947–50), organist at Worcester Cathedral (1950), conductor of the Worcester Festival Choral Society and also the City of Birmingham Choir (1950–57), conductor of the Bradford Festival Choral Society (1956–74), Fellow and director of music at King's College, Cambridge, organist of Cambridge University and conductor of the Cambridge University Music Society (1957–74), musical director of the Bach Choir (since 1960), president of the Royal College of Organists (1966–8), and director of the Royal College of Music (since 1974). He has conducted in most European countries, the United States, Canada, Africa, Japan, and Australia, has composed church and organ music, has been the general editor of *Oxford Church Music, Carols for Choirs* and *Anthems for Men's Voices*, and was awarded the KBE in 1977.

As a recording artist, Willcocks is best known as the conductor of King's College Chapel Choir. The College was founded in 1441 by Henry VI, who directed that there should also be a choir; in 1453 King Henry determined that the number of choristers should be 16, which it has remained since, but is supplemented by choral scholars drawn from the student body of the University. Willcocks has made over 70 records with the Choir and with the Bach Choir, and also with the English Chamber, the Academy of St Martin-in-the-Fields, Jacques, New Philharmonia, Philomusica and London Symphony Orchestras; he is mostly attracted to the music of the Tudor masters, particularly Byrd, Gibbons and Tallis, of which he has made many records. He has said that his favourite recording is Taverner's Mass, *The Western Wind* (*The Gramophone*, September 1966, p. 148). His recordings with the King's College Chapel Choir, and almost all for Argo, include the Bach Motets and *St John Passion*, Vivaldi's *Gloria*, Pergolesi's *Magnificat*, Handel's *Dixit Dominus*, *Messiah*, *Ode for St Cecilia's Day* and the *Chandos Anthems*, Palestrina's *Missa brevis* and *Missa Papae Marcelli*, Charpentier's *Messe de minuit*, Haydn's *The Creation* and Mass No. 9 (*The Nelson*), Elgar's *The Dream of Gerontius*, Fauré's *Requiem*, Howell's *Hymnus paradisi*, Britten's *St Nicolas*, *Ceremony of Carols*, *Hymn to St Cecilia* and *Missa brevis*, and Vaughan Williams' *Mass in G minor*, *Hodie*, *Sancta Civitas* and *Benedicite*. In later years he and the Choir have recorded for EMI. The Haydn Mass No. 9 was first issued in 1962, and was the first recording that brought the glories of Haydn's late masses before the record-buying public. Willcocks also participated, with the Bach Choir, in the first and definitive recording of Britten's *War Requiem*, which was made in 1963 under the composer's direction.

Williams, John (b. 1920). Born at Swansea, Williams was a choral scholar at St John's College, Cambridge and studied under Ord and Darke. After service in the navy in World War II, he became organist and choirmaster at All Saints' Church, Margaret Street, London, and then organist and master of music at the Chapel Royal at the Tower of London, and professor at the Royal College of Music. He conducted the Tower of London Chapel Choir, the Philip Jones Brass Ensemble and the Hurwitz Chamber Ensemble in a recording of music by Gibbons, Blow, Weelkes, Purcell, Locke, Tallis, Henry VIII, Byrd, Albert the Prince Consort, S. S. Wesley and Langford (for Rediffusion).

Williams, Verdon. The Australian conductor, pianist, lecturer, arranger and composer Williams studied at the University of Melbourne Conservatorium of Music, was a piano pupil of Sidel and Percy Grainger, and toured as a pianist. He conducted at Melbourne's National Theatre, was conductor of the West Australian Symphony Orchestra at Perth (1960), the Perth Sinfonietta and the Tasmanian Symphony Orchestra at Hobart. He composed two successful ballets, *The Outlaw* and *Conflict*. For Festival he recorded Pentherby's Saxophone Concerto (with Clinch and the West Australian Symphony Orchestra).

Williamson, John (1887–1964). Born in Canton, Ohio, and educated at the Westerville Conservatory, Ohio, Williamson studied the organ with Straube at Leipzig, in 1921 founded the Westminster Choir at Dayton, Ohio, and in 1926 the Westminster Choir School at Princeton, New Jersey. With the choir he toured in the United States and abroad, and recorded, on 78s for Victor, Palestrina's *Exsultate Deo* and *Hodie Christus natus est*, Alcock's *Celestial Voices*, Kolsolyoff's *Alleluia Christ is Risen*, Lotti's *Crucifixus* and Dvořák's *Goin' Home*.

Winograd, Arthur (b. 1920). Born in New York, Winograd studied at the New England Conservatory (1937–40) and at the Curtis Institute (1940–41). He was a cellist with the Boston Symphony Orchestra (1942–3) and the NBC Symphony Orchestra (1942–3), and then with the Juilliard String Quartet. He taught at the Juilliard School (1946–55), took to conducting, and has been conductor of the Birmingham Symphony Orchestra, Alabama (1960–64), the Hartford Symphony Orchestra, Connecticut (1964–72), and the Worcester Symphony Orchestra, Massachusetts (since 1972). He was also conductor of the MGM Studio Orchestra and recorded extensively for MGM in the series of LPs which this company issued in the 1950s or thereabouts; included were Bach's *Die Kunst der Fuge*, Beethoven's *Grosse Fuge*, Mozart's Serenades K. 203, K. 239, K. 375 and K. 388, the Mendelssohn *Octet* and String Symphony No. 9, the *adagietto* from Mahler's Symphony No. 5, Wolf's *Italian Serenade*, Tchaikovsky's *Souvenir de Florence*, Dvořák's *Notturno*, Grieg's *Holberg Suite* and other pieces, Schoenberg's *Pierrot Lunaire*, Copland's *Music for Radio*, Nielsen's *Little Suite for Strings*, Bernstein's opera *Trouble in Tahiti*, Shapero's *Serenade*, Weber's *Rapsodie concertante*, Glanville-Hicks' *Concerto romantico* and Richter's *Aria and Toccata* (with the MGM Chamber Orchestra, the Winograd String Orchestra, and other ensembles), and Organ Concertos of Poulenc and Hanson (with the Philharmonia Orchestra of Hamburg). *Trouble in Tahiti* was re-issued by Helidor. In another series for Audio Fidelity in which Winograd conducted an orchestra named the Virtuoso Symphony Orchestra of London, six discs of popular marches, overtures and other pieces were included, among them the overtures *Egmont, Academic Festival, Die Meistersinger, Mignon, Oberon* and *La forza del destino*, and suites from *Swan Lake* and *The Sleeping Beauty*. Parliament also issued mono LPs in which he conducted the Pro Musica Symphony Orchestra of Hamburg in Beethoven's Symphonies Nos 5 and 8, the Tchaikovsky Symphony No. 2, and *A Night on the Bare Mountain*.

Winschermann, Helmut. The German oboist and leader of the German Bach Soloists has toured widely with his ensemble, and has made a number of records, both as conductor and oboist. Among other works he has recorded Bach's Cantatas Nos 210 (for Cantate), 32, 51, 56, 57, 82 and 199, the *Missae Breves* BWV 235 and 236 and the sinfonias from a number of Cantatas, two chorales from Cantata No. 147 and two Cantatas of Telemann (for Philips), the *Brandenburg Concerto No. 1, Oboe Concerto in F major*, and sinfonias from the Cantatas (released by Oryx), Telemann's *Sinfonia in F, Overture in C, Concerto in B flat* and *Concerto in B* (for Cantate), an oboe concerto by Albinoni, trumpet concerto by Fasch (with André), horn concerto by Telemann, and flute concerto by Vivaldi (with Nicolet, for Nonesuch), the Mozart Organ Sonatas (with Chorzempa for Philips), organ concertos by Haydn and Albrechtsberger, and Michael Haydn's Concerto for Viola and Organ (with Giuranna and Chorzempa for Philips).

Wirén, Dag (b. 1905). The composer Wirén was born at Striberg, Sweden, was educated at the Royal High School for Music in Stockholm, and was a music critic from 1938 to 1944. Of his symphonies, ballets, concertos and other compositions, he recorded his *Sinfonietta*, with the Stockholm Radio Orchestra, on 78 r.p.m. discs.

Wisłocki, Stanislaw (b. 1921). Born in Rzeszów, Poland, Wisłocki studied at the Lvov Conservatory with Barbag; when World War II broke out he was visiting Romania, and stayed there (1938–45) to study composition with Simonis and Michil at Timişoara Academy of Music. He also came into contact with Enesco, made his first appearance as a conductor in 1940, and became known as a conductor, pianist and composer. When he returned to Poland in 1945 he founded and conducted the Warsaw Chamber Orchestra (1945–7) and then founded and was first conductor of the Poznań State Philharmonic Orchestra (1947–58). Moving to Warsaw, he became second conductor and a close associate to Rowicki with the Warsaw National Philharmonic Orchestra (1961–6); since then he has not been connected permanently with an orchestra. He toured many times with the National Philharmonic Orchestra and appeared as a guest conductor in East and West Europe and Mexico, and has lectured at the Warsaw Academy of Music since 1955. He has composed symphonies, chamber music and music for theatre and films; his Piano Concerto was first recorded by Kedra and the Leipzig Radio Orchestra under Pflüger in 1945. His awards include the Gold Cross of Merit and Chevalier Polonia Restituta.

Wisłocki has recorded for the Polish record company with the Poznań Philharmonic, Warsaw National Philharmonic and the Polish National Philharmonic Orchestras. With the Poznań Philharmonic his performances were of the Beethoven Violin Concerto (with Totenberg, released by DGG and Westminster), Mozart's *Country Dances* K. 609 and some *Hungarian Dances* of Brahms. With the Warsaw National Philharmonic his discs have included Bach's Concertos for Two, Three and Four Harpsichords and the Harpsichord Concerto K. 218 (with Janowski), Beethoven's Symphonies Nos 3 and 6 and Piano Concerto No. 3 (with Bakst), Mendelssohn's Symphony No. 4 and *Overture in C major*, Schumann's *Introduction and Allegro appassionato* and Rachmaninov's Piano Concerto No. 2 (with Richter, released by DGG), Chopin's Piano Concerto No. 2 and Brahms' Piano Concerto No. 1 (with Małcużyński, the latter released by EMI), Paganini's Violin Concerto No. 2 (with Richter, released by DGG), Chopin's Piano Concerto No. 2 and Brahms' Piano Concerto No. 1 (with Małcużyński, the latter released by EMI), Paganini's Violin Concertos Nos 1 and 2 (with Gitlis, issued by Turnabout), the Dvořák Cello Concerto, Saint-Saëns' Cello Concerto No. 1 and Tchaikovsky's *Rococo Variations* (with Catell), Franck's *Symphonic Variations*, Paderewski's *Polish Fantasy* and Szeligowski's Piano Concerto (with Smendzianka), Szymanowski's Violin Concerto No. 1 (with Janowski), the Berg Violin Concerto (with Wronski), two symphonic poems of Karłowicz, Bacewicz's *Music for Strings, Trumpets and Percussion*, Viola Concerto and Two-Piano Concerto, Spisak's *Concerto giocoso* and *Symphonie concertante*, and overtures by Kurpinski and Elsner. With the Polish National Philharmonic Orchestra he also recorded the two Bach Violin Concertos (with Totenberg, and issued by DGG). Probably the most famous of these discs has been Rachmaninov's Piano Concerto No. 2, with Richter, which was first issued in

1960 and was still available in Britain and the United States in 1977.

Witkowski, Georges (1867–1943). Born in Mostaganem, Algeria, Witkowski was first an army officer, composed an opera *Le Maître à chanter* which was produced in Nantes in 1891, then studied with d'Indy in Paris (1894–7). He lived in Lyon, and there founded and conducted a choral society and the Société des Grands Concerts. He composed symphonies, songs, another opera *La Princesse lontaine*, a large choral and orchestral work *Poème de la maison*, and *Mon Lac*, for piano and orchestra, which he recorded for Columbia with Robert Casadesus and the Paris Symphony Orchestra.

Witold, Jean (b. 1913). Born in Paris, Witold studied with St Renesson, Butzoff, Ramin and Fourestier, and has been with the French Radio since 1947. He founded and directed the ORTF (French Radio) Symphony Orchestra (1948), was artistic director of the record company Contrepoint (1954–6), directed the collection Les Grands Musiciens, and has published books about Bach and Mozart. He has recorded the *Brandenburg Concertos* (with an instrumental ensemble for Vega), Vivaldi's Two-Violin and Two-Cello Concerto P. 135, Albinoni's Concertos Op. 5 Nos 7, 11 and 12, Torelli's *Concerto Grosso in G major*, Geminiani's Concerto Grosso Op. 3 No. 2, W. F. Bach's *Symphony in D major*, and C. P. E. Bach's Symphony No. 15, *Piano Concerto in A minor* (with Boschi) and *Two-Piano Concerto in F major* (with Boschi and Castérède, and the Paris Sinfonia Ensemble for Allegro), Vivaldi's *The Four Seasons*, *Eine kleine Nachtmusik*, and Tcherepnin's *Suite for Two Oboes* (with the Paris Sinfonia Ensemble for Contrepoint); Vivaldi's Oboe Concertos P. 259 and Op. 8 No. 9 (with Pierlot) and Bassoon Concerto Op. 8 No. 6 (with Hongne and the Paris Sinfonia Ensemble for Period and London International); Two-Violin Concerto P. 391 (with Lamacque and Oguse) and Two-Violin and Two-Cello Concerto (with the Paris Sinfonia Ensemble for London International); and Mozart's Flute and Harp Concerto (with Challan and Bourdin) and Boieldieu's Harp Concerto (with Challan, and an instrumental ensemble for EMI).

Wodiczko, Bohdan (b. 1911). Born in Warsaw, Wodiczko studied the violin, and attended the Warsaw and Prague Conservatories, and then studied conducting at the Warsaw Conservatory with Bierdiajew. He was conductor of the Baltic Philharmonic Orchestra at Gdańsk and a music director for Polish Radio (1946–50), first conductor of the Łódź Philharmonic Orchestra and a professor at the Academy of Music there (1950–51), first conductor and artistic director of the Kraków State Philharmonic Orchestra (1951–5), first conductor and artistic director of the Warsaw National Philharmonic Orchestra (1955–8), and professor at the Warsaw Academy of Music. He returned to Łódź (1959–60), was conductor of the Reykjavik Orchestra in Iceland (1960–61), director of the Warsaw National Opera (1961–4), again conductor of the Reykjavik Orchestra (1964–8), and finally artistic director of the Polish Radio Symphony Orchestra at Katowice (1968). He toured FR Germany, Belgium and Britain with the Warsaw National Philharmonic Orchestra in 1958, the first post-war overseas tour of a Polish orchestra. He has introduced to Polish orchestras many 20th-century compositions, including Liebermann's *Concerto for Jazz Band and Symphony Orchestra*, and in his popular regular television concerts has included a vast range of music, from classical works to jazz and pop music. His recordings include *Le Sacre du printemps*, *The Miraculous Mandarin* of Bartók and Kodály's *Háry János* suite (with the Polish Radio Symphony Orchestra), symphonies by Paderewski and Karłowicz (with the Pomeranian Symphony Orchestra) and Szymanowski's ballet *Harnasie* (with the Warsaw National Opera House Orchestra), all for Muza. With the Polish Radio Symphony Orchestra he has recorded music by American composers: Porter's *New England Episodes* (for Desto), Piston's *Concerto for Orchestra*, Ruggles' *Men and Mountains* and Hively's *Icarus* (for Composers Recordings).

Wöldike, Mogens (b. 1897). Born in Copenhagen, Wöldike studied Musicology at the University and with Nielsen and Laub, the reformer of Danish church music. He became conductor of the Palestrina Choir (1922), a mixed choir of professional singers founded to perform the *a capella* music of the 16th and 17th centuries; under his baton the Choir won first prize at an international choral competition in Milan in 1928. The Copenhagen Boys' Choir was then founded by him (1924); in its first years it gave several concerts a year, but in 1929 its training and rehearsals were intensified. In that year, at the suggestion of Wöldike and Dr Schepelern, the Copenhagen Municipal Choir School was established, and the Boys' Choir was attached to the Chapel of the Christiansborg Palace in Copenhagen, when Wöldike was appointed organist and choirmaster at the Chapel (1931). The Choir gave its first major concert in 1933, and after World War II it performed in the Scandinavian countries, Austria, Italy, Israel and in Britain, taking part in the festivals at Edinburgh (1958) and Aldeburgh. Wöldike was appointed organist and choirmaster at Copenhagen Cathedral (1959), and took the Choir with him; later (in 1972) the Choir moved to its present school at the St Annae Gymnasium at Frederiksholm. Wöldike has also conducted in many European countries independently of the Choir, is a member of the Swedish Royal Academy of Music, and has received the Nielsen and Buxtehude Prizes.

After World War II Wöldike recorded for EMI on 78 r.p.m. discs Gabrieli's *Jubilate Deo* (with the Danish Radio Madrigal Choir), the Corelli Concerto Grosso Op. 6 No. 7 and Bach's Concerto for Violin and Oboe (with the Copenhagen Chapel Orchestra), the *Brandenburg Concertos* and Cantata No. 82, Roman's Symphonies Nos 16 and 20, Haydn's *German Dances*, and an oboe concerto by Telemann (with the Danish State Radio Chamber Orchestra), Cantatas by Tunder and Weckmann (with a chamber orchestra *et al.*), and for Decca Haydn's Symphony No. 91 and a cantata by Gade (with the Danish State Radio Chamber Orchestra). He also recorded arias and choral pieces by Bach, Buxtehude, Mozart, Goudimel, Praetorius and Pedersen, and cantatas by Schütz and Lübeck.

Wöldike's subsequent LP recordings included Haydn's Symphonies Nos 100 to 104, *The Creation* and Mass No. 7 (with the Vienna State Opera Orchestra *et al.*, for Vanguard, and issued by Philips in Europe); these performances were distinguished by their vigour and sense of style. He also recorded Bach's *St Matthew Passion* (with the Vienna State Opera Orchestra *et al.* for Vanguard); Cantatas Nos 12, 29, 33 and 105 (with the Vienna State Opera Orchestra *et al.* for Bach Guild); Nos 33 and 105 (with the Danish Radio Chamber Orchestra for EMI); Haydn's Symphonies Nos 48, 50 and 61, and Mass No. 8, Handel's *Utrecht Te Deum*, *Let Thy Hand be Strengthened*, and excerpts from *Rinaldo*, an overture by Lully, Mozart's Symphonies Nos 25 and 29, Piano Concertos K. 414 and K. 467 (with Jensen) and Clarinet Concerto (with Cahuzac, and the Danish Radio Symphony Orchestra for the Haydn Society); a four-record anthology entitled *A Treasury of Early Music of the Middle Ages, Renaissance and Baroque* (for the Haydn Society); Haydn's Symphonies Nos 14, 44 and 48, and *Divertimento in G*, J. C. Bach's *Sinfonia in B flat*, Dittersdorf's *Symphony in C*, and Mozart's Symphony No. 14 (with the Danish Radio Symphony Orchestra for Decca); Vivaldi's Cello Concerto P. 434 and Haydn's *Cello Concerto in D major* (with Bengtsson and the Danish Radio Symphony Orchestra for EMI); Marenzio's *S'io parto, i' moro* and Gabrieli's *Jubilate Deo* (with the Danish Radio Madrigal Choir for the Haydn Society and EMI respectively); Haydn's Symphonies Nos 25, 29 and 60 (with the Danish State Radio Symphony Orchestra for Erato): Haydn's Masses Nos 5 and 8 (with the Copenhagen Palace Chamber Orchestra *et al.* for Bach Guild); Nielsen's Violin Concerto (with Menuhin and the Danish Radio Symphony Orchestra for EMI), Clarinet Concerto (with Erikson and the Danish Radio Symphony Orchestra for Decca), the incidental music for *Aladdin*, the cantata *Hymnus amoris*, and *Sleep* (with the Danish Radio Symphony Orchestra *et al.* for EMI) and *Hymn to Denmark* and *Fynsk Foraar* (with the Danish Radio Symphony Orchestra for Philips), and Three Motets (with the Danish Radio Madrigal Choir for Decca).

Wolf, Hans (b. 1912). Born in Hamburg and educated at the New Vienna Conservatory of Music and the Vienna University, where he was awarded a doctorate in 1937, Wolf first conducted, in 1945, with the Innsbruck Symphony Orchestra in Austria when he was a US army soldier. After World War II he conducted orchestras in Austria and Germany, then was music director in Europe for Remington Records (1950–60), the first low-priced label, and Livingstone Audio Products, which produced the first stereophonic tapes. He was conductor for the Riverside Opera Company in California (1961–9), also appearing as a guest conductor with the El Paso Symphony Orchestra, Texas, and since 1969 has been associate conductor and chorus-master with the Seattle Opera Association and conductor of a community symphony orchestra. For Remington he conducted the Vienna Tonkünstler Orchestra in Beethoven's Symphony No. 5 and *Egmont* and *Coriolan* overtures, Mozart's Symphony No. 35, Haydn's *Cello Concerto in D major* (with Cassado), Brahms' Symphony No. 2, and the Franck *Symphony in D minor*.

Wolf-Ferrari, Ermanno (1876–1948). The Italian composer Wolf-Ferrari was born in Venice; his father was a German painter who first wished his son to follow in his footsteps, but Ermanno's musical talents soon became evident, and he was put to study with Rheinberger at Munich. He wrote charming one-act operas, of which *Il Segreto di Susanna* and *I quattro rusteghi* (known in Britain as *The School for Fathers*) are the best known, as well as the veristic melodrama *I gioielli della Madonna* (*The Jewels of the Madonna*). For Decca, he made delightful recordings of the overture to *Il segreto di Susanna*, the intermezzo from *I quattro rusteghi*, the minuet and furlana from *Le Donne curiose* and the intermezzo from Act III of *I gioielli della Madonna*, with the Zürich Tonhalle Orchestra.

Wolf-Ferrari, Ermanno (b. 1911). Son of the composer, Wolf-Ferrari was also born in Venice, where his father was, at the time, director of the Liceo Benedetto Marcello. He studied at the Venice Conservatory and with Guarnieri at the Accademia Chigiana at Siena, and has conducted ballet and opera in Italy and abroad. For Cetra he recorded *Il matrimonio segreto* and *I lombardi* (with the Radio Italiana Orchestra *et al.*), and choruses from *Nabucco* (with the Radio Italiana Chorus).

Wolff, Albert (1884–1970). Born in Paris of Dutch parents, Wolff studied at the Paris Conservatoire, and graduated as a piano accompanist. He taught music in Paris (1904–7), was organist at the St Thomas Aquinas Church (1906–10), became chorus-master at the Paris Opéra-Comique (1908), and made his debut there as a conductor (1911). During World War I he served with distinction in the French army; afterwards he went to the United States and conducted the French repertory at the New York Metropolitan Opera (1919–21), including the première of his own opera *The Blue Bird*. Returning to France, he succeeded Messager as chief conductor of the Opéra-Comique (1922–4), founded the Concerts Modernes in order to perform music by young composers, was musical director of the Champs-Élysées Theatre (1924–8), conducted at the Teatro Colón at Buenos Aires, was conductor of the Concerts Lamoureux (1928–34) and of the Concerts Pasdeloup (1934–40). In 1937 he visited Covent Garden to conduct *Pelléas et Mélisande*; during World War II he toured in South America and then returned to Paris.

Wolff made gramophone records both before and after World War II; at their best these performances were lively and stylish, but on some occasions they were scarcely more than routine. For Polydor he made a series of 78 r.p.m. discs with the Lamoureux Orchestra which included the dances from Rameau's *Castor et Pollux*, Mozart's Piano Concerto K. 41 (with Roesgen-Champion), Méhul's *Le Jeune Henri* overture, *Mephisto Waltz*, *L'Apprenti sorcier*, *Baba Yaga* of Liadov, *A Night on the Bare Mountain*, *Capriccio espagnol*, Flight of the Bumble Bee and the introduction to Act II of *The Tale of Tsar Saltan*, Ravel's *La Valse*, and *Rapsodie espagnole*, Franck's *Symphony in D minor*, *Rédemption*, *Le Chasseur maudit* and *Psyché*, Gounod's *Funeral March of a Marionette*, Chabrier's *España*, *Bourrée fantasque*, *Marche joyeuse*, *Habanera* and *Gwendoline* overture, D'Indy's *Symphonie sur un chant montagnard français* (with Darré) and the prelude to *Fervaal*, Lalo's *Namouna*, *Rapsodie norvégienne* and overture *Le roi d'Ys*, Saint-Saëns' *Romance in F for Horn* (with Deveney), *Le Rouet d'Omphale*, prelude to *Le Déluge* and Bacchanale from *Samson et Dalila*, Schmitt's *Rapsodie viennoise*, Roussel's Symphony No. 3, the gopak from *Khovanshchina*, Rabaud's *La Procession nocturne*, Dupont's overture *La Farce du cuvier* and Prokofiev's *Chout*; also for Polydor with the Berlin Philharmonic Orchestra there was Ravel's *Pavane pour une infante défunte*, for Vox *Ma Mère l'Oye* (with the Lamoureux Orchestra), and for HMV Bach's Clavier Concerto No. 7 (with Roesgen-Champion and the Lamoureux Orchestra).

Decca recorded Wolff in a number of their early LPs. Included were the operas *Carmen* and *Manon*, excerpts from Bondeville's *L'École des maris*, and *Madama Butterfly* (in French) and Daudet's *L'Arlésienne* with Bizet's incidental music (with the Paris Opéra-Comique Orchestra *et al.*), *Boléro*, *Alborada del gracioso*, dances from *The Three-cornered Hat*, Glazunov's *The Seasons*, *Introduction to the Dance*, Balakirev's *Tamara*, Charpentier's *Impressions d'Italie*, Massenet's *Scènes pittoresques* and *Scènes alsaciennes*, and the overtures *Donna Diana*, *Zampa*, *Si j'étais Roi*, *Le Domino noir*, *Pique Dame*, *The Merry Wives of Windsor*, *Masaniello*, *Le Cheval de bronze*, *Fra Diavolo* and *Les Diamants de la couronne* and Liszt's *Hungarian Rhapsody No. 2* (with the Paris Conservatoire Orchestra) and the overtures *Benvenuto Cellini*, *Le Roi d'Ys*, *Phèdre*, *Werther*, *La Nuit de Noël* and *La Princesse jaune* (with the Paris Opéra-Comique Orchestra). Also, Telefunken issued a disc of excerpts from *Les Contes d'Hoffmann* and Pathé a *Madama Butterfly* (both with the Paris Opéra-Comique Orchestra *et al.*), and Vox Prokofiev's *Chout* (with the Lamoureux Orchestra).

Wolters, Gottfried (b. 1910). Born in Emmerich, Wolters studied in Cologne and Berlin, and has achieved distinction as a choral conductor, particularly with the Nordwestdeutsche Singkreis. He has also edited choral and vocal collections. With the Singkreis he has recorded cantatas and other sacred choral music by Buxtehude, motets and *The Resurrec-*

tion of Jesus Christ of Schütz, Carissimi's *Jephte*, and pieces by Zachau, Knüpfer, Hickmann and Kuhnau (for DGG-Archiv), some Bach motets (for Nonesuch) and Distler's *Die Weihnachtgeschichte* (for Bärenreiter), and with the Spandauer Kantorei motets by Distler (for Spauda).

Wood, Sir Henry (1869–1944). Wood was born in London; his father was a prominent singer and his mother gave him his first musical training. At the age of 13 he gave organ recitals, and was appointed organist at the church of Aldermanbury. After studies at the Royal Academy of Music under Prout and Garcia, his first appearance as a conductor was in 1888 when he led a performance of a cantata by McFarren at Clapton; in 1889 he received his first appointment as a conductor with the Arthur Rousbey Opera Company; in 1890 he assisted at rehearsals of Sullivan's opera *Ivanhoe* with the d'Oyly Carte Company, and then conducted with several touring opera companies. At this time he also taught singing. In 1895 the impressario Robert Newman engaged Wood to conduct a series of promenade concerts at the newly-built Queen's Hall in Langham Place, London; Wood led this famous series of concerts for 50 consecutive seasons, until a year before his death. In addition, he conducted numerous other concerts throughout the year with the Queen's Hall Orchestra, and was active in the provinces at many music festivals and with local orchestras. His tours abroad took him as far as the Hollywood Bowl; in 1921 he shared with Nikisch and Pierné the conductorship of the Zürich Music Festival. His commitment to the London Prom concerts brought him to decline overseas engagements and appointments, including the conductorship of the Boston Symphony Orchestra. In 1911 he was knighted, and in 1938 celebrated his fiftieth jubilee as a conductor; for this occasion Vaughan Williams wrote his *Serenade to Music*. Wood's first wife was the soprano and Russian princess Ourousoff, whom he accompanied at many recitals; she died in 1909.

From 1923 Wood taught conducting at the Royal Academy of Music, and many generations of musicians came under his influence. Through the Prom concerts and his many other musical activities he was the first great positive influence in orchestral performance and popular musical appreciation in England; in Boult's words, 'Sir Henry was the greatest popular conductor (in the finest sense of the adjective) that the world has ever seen'. Starting with programmes of unsophisticated appeal, he gradually introduced the music of Beethoven, Wagner, Brahms and Tchaikovsky, so that his audience came more and more to appreciate the standard repertoire. He performed, often for the first time in England, a prodigious amount of new music: the Russian nationalists, Strauss and Schoenberg became familiar to concertgoers, and in the years 1895 to 1919 he presented over 200 works by British composers. Contemporary composers including Strauss, Debussy, Elgar, Delius, Sibelius, Rachmaninov, Bloch, Reger and Scriabin were prominent in his programmes, and many were invited to conduct their own works. Composers were anxious for him to give first performances of their music because his readings were invariably faithful and absolutely clear and accurate. While his orchestra could play virtually any standard repertory work without rehearsal, he took great trouble over new pieces; before Strauss came to conduct *Ein Heldenleben*, Wood had 17 rehearsals to prepare the work. He prepared all his scores very meticulously before rehearsals, and his rehearsals were organised so as not to waste a minute. His baton technique was compared to that of Nikisch in its perfection; he used a very long baton to save arm movement, and to be clearly visible to orchestra and choir. At rehearsals he very often played straight through the work, shouting comments rather than stopping. He was able to have adequate rehearsal time for his normal Queen's Hall concerts, established sectional rehearsals, took immense trouble to have every player accurately tuned, and insisted on unanimity in bowing. He adopted the Continental low pitch (A:435), and introduced women into the orchestra. An extreme case of his care in rehearsal was the preparation of Bach's *Mass in B minor* in Liverpool for which he had 50 rehearsals. For a performance of the *St Matthew Passion* at Sheffield he personally copied breath and expression marks into 400 vocal scores. In fact he was sometimes criticised for being too careful and laborious; Ernest Newman wrote: 'Whatever else might be said against him, it could never be said that he was anything but thorough. In the preparation of some great work, especially, there were no limits to the trouble he was prepared to take.'

An early battle was fought over the prevailing system of deputies in the Queen's Hall Orchestra, which Wood refused to tolerate. Players would send substitutes to attend rehearsals, themselves coming only to the concert performance itself. As a result those players who would not accept his insistence that they attend both rehearsals and concerts left the Queen's Hall Orchestra and in 1904 formed the

London Symphony Orchestra. The Queen's Hall Orchestra under Wood performed in the Proms Season continuously for ten weeks with six concerts a week; their repertoire became enormous, and their skill at sight-reading the wonder of visiting conductors. Wood acknowledged that the orchestral playing at the Prom concerts was not the most polished, but countered that this was not his aim. Even so, he achieved a considerable improvement in the standard of orchestral playing in London. He earned the warmest respect from his fellow musicians; Goossens wrote of him that he had 'never encountered a sincerer artist or a more resourceful, experienced and versatile conductor'. He was the first to make orchestral conducting a full-time occupation for a British-born musician. An amusing sidelight of his career was his arrangements of Bach's *Toccata and Fugue in D minor*, which he published under the pseudonym of Paul Klenovsky; he did not reveal his identity as the arranger until years later.

Wood was one of the first major conductors to make gramophone records, and in 1915 and 1916 he recorded a number of works for Columbia. Many were in abbreviated versions; for instance, the *Coriolan* overture was abridged to one side of a 12-inch disc, *Till Eulenspiegel* to two sides, and the Elgar Violin Concerto to four sides. This practice continued until 1923, when a Beethoven Symphony No. 3 conducted by Wood was issued on three discs, but criticism was so severe about this and other abbreviated works that the record companies discontinued issuing condensed versions of standard works. Wood's first records, in 1915, were of the prelude to Act III of *Lohengrin*, his arrangement of Rachmaninov's *Prelude in C sharp minor*, Grainger's *Shepherd's Hey*, *Irish Tune*, *Clog Dance* and *Handel in the Strand*, the scherzo from Tchaikovsky's Symphony No. 4, the prelude and Liebestod from *Tristan und Isolde*, the march from *Tannhäuser*, his arrangement of the Rhinemaidens' Song from *Götterdämmerung*, the prelude to Act III from *Die Walküre*, the Dance of the Apprentices from *Die Meistersinger* and *Träume* of Wagner, the *Coriolan* overture, *España* of Chabrier, Gardiner's *Shepherd Fennel's Dance*, Brahms' *Hungarian Dances Nos 5* and *6*, the ballet music from *Faust*, Corder's *Prospero* overture, *Till Eulenspiegel*, the Elgar *Violin Concerto* (abridged, with Sammons) and his arrangement *Fantasia on English Sea Songs*, which has become a traditional item played on the final night of the Prom Concerts each year. In 1916 he recorded Holbrooke's *Variations on Three Blind Mice*, and *Capriccio espagnol*, *Capriccio italien*, *L'Apprenti sorcier* and the overture to *Der fliegende Holländer* (both on one disc), a suite from *Carmen*, *Granados' Spanish Dances*, Albéniz's *Catalonia Suite* and the overtures to *Zampa*, *Rienzi* and *Tannhäuser*. Then from 1919 to the advent of electrical recording in 1926, he recorded Beethoven's Symphony No. 3, Schubert's Symphony No. 8, Tchaikovsky's Symphony No. 6, Liszt's *Hungarian Rhapsodies Nos 1* and *2*, *A Night on the Bare Mountain*, *Le Chasseur maudit*, the overtures *Leonore No. 3*, *Semiramide*, *William Tell*, *Fra Diavolo*, *The Hebrides*, *A Midsummer Night's Dream* and Bantock's *The Pierrot of the Minute*, the minuet from Beethoven's Septet, a selection from *Cavalleria rusticana*, Lalo's *Symphonie espagnole* (abridged, on one disc, with Sammons), Tchaikovsky's *The Battle of Poltava*, a movement from Carr's *Three Heroes Suite*, the Venusberg Music from *Tannhäuser*, the Entry of the Gods into Valhalla from *Das Rheingold*, Gounod's *Funeral March of a Marionette* and Mors et Vita from *Judex*, Arcadelt's *Ave Maria*, some *Slavonic Dances* of Dvořák, the Coronation March from *Le Prophète*, the 'Largo' from *Serse* and Turina's *Danzas fantásticas*.

These recordings were with the New Queen's Hall Orchestra, the name the orchestra assumed in 1915, but after the death of its founder, Newman, in 1926, it went out of existence. In the period 1919–26, Wood recorded with the orchestra, again for Columbia, a suite arranged by Wood from Bach's music, a gavotte by Bach, Bach's Harpsichord Concerto No. 1 (with Harriet Cohen), Haydn's Symphony No. 94, Beethoven's Symphony No. 3 (this time on six discs), *Leonore No. 3* overture, a rondino by Beethoven, Schubert's Symphony No. 8, the overtures *Oberon*, *The Merry Wives of Windsor* and *1812*, the Franck *Symphony in D minor*, Delius' *Dance Rhapsody No. 1*, Lalo's *Aubades in D minor* and *G minor*, Elgar's Violin Concerto (with Sammons; reissued in 1972 by EMI), and *Enigma Variations*, Järnefelt's *Praeludium*, *Danse macabre*, Tchaikovsky's *Chant sans paroles* Op. 2 No. 3, a *Slavonic Dance* of Dvořák, and the prelude to Act III of *Die Walküre* and the Rhinemaiden's Song from *Götterdämmerung*. In 1925–6 he also recorded some choruses from *Messiah* (with the Handel Festival Choir and Orchestra, for Columbia).

In the late 1920s and the 1930s Wood continued to record for Columbia, his recordings including the *Brandenburg Concertos Nos 3* (with the British Symphony Orchestra) and *6* (with an unnamed orchestra), Haydn's Symphony No. 45 and the overture to *Don*

Giovanni (with the London Symphony Orchestra), the Liszt Piano Concerto No. 1 and Franck's *Symphonic Variations* (with Gieseking and the London Philharmonic Orchestra), Quilter's *Children's Overture*, Gounod's *Funeral March of a Marionette* and Elgar's *Pomp and Circumstance Marches Nos 1* and *4* (with the London Philharmonic Orchestra), and Grainger's *Molly on the Shore* and *Mock Morris* (with the British Symphony Orchestra). In 1935 he commenced to record for Decca, and for this the Queen's Hall Orchestra was revived; the works recorded were the Handel overtures *Berenice* and *Solomon*, Beethoven's Symphony No. 5, Bach's *Toccata and Fugue in D minor* (arranged by 'Klenovsky'), Brahms' *Variations in the St Antony Chorale*, Bruckner's *Overture in G minor*, Dohnányi's *Symphonic Minutes*, Dvořák's *Humoresque*, *Enigma Variations*, the overture to *Russlan and Ludmilla*, Granados' *Spanish Dances Nos 5* and *6*, Järnefelt's *Praeludium*, Rachmaninov's *Prelude in C sharp minor*, *Valse triste*, and Vaughan Williams' Symphony No. 2, overture to *The Wasps* and *Fantasia on Greensleeves*; the three Vaughan Williams works were reissued on an LP by Decca in 1965. Finally, in 1938 he recorded Vaughan Williams' *Serenade to Music*, with the BBC Symphony Orchestra and the soloists who performed it at his jubilee concert that year.

Except possibly for the Vaughan Williams works, none of Wood's recordings established itself as an imperishable classic of the gramophone. He certainly had not the recording opportunities of Coates or Beecham, although Decca did attempt to promote him and the New Queen's Hall Orchestra in some sort of competition with Beecham and Boult at home, and with Stokowski, Mengelberg *et al.* abroad. Wood's critics may have been right when they described him as a master of the grand gesture but less impressive in the meticulous expression of nuances and mood, essential for successful records. So his records give us short measure on Wood the musician, who did more than anyone to pave the way for the later excellence of London as an international music centre.

Woodgate, Leslie (1902–61). Born in London and a self-taught organist, Woodgate was private secretary to the composer Roger Quilter, and studied at the Royal College of Music (1914–24). He joined the BBC in 1924; from 1934 he was conductor of the BBC Chorus, and from 1940 of the Leicester Philharmonic Society. He composed orchestral, choral, vocal and chamber music, wrote *The Chorus Master* and *The Choral Conductor*, and edited *The Penguin Song Book*. He recorded, on 78s, Bax's *Mater ora filium*, a chorus each from *Messiah* and Mendelssohn's *St Paul*, Warlock's *Corpus Christi* and *Cornish Christmas Carol*, Mendelssohn's *Hymn of Praise* and Holst's *Wassail Song* and *This have I done for my true love* (with the BBC Chorus for HMV), Hughes' *Gweddi* (with the BBC Chorus and the Boyd Neel String Orchestra for Decca), Michael Haydn's *Prope est* and the Agnus Dei from Mozart's *Litaniae Lauretanae* (with a chorus and the London Symphony Orchestra *et al.* in HMV's History of Music in Sound).

Woodworth, G. Wallace (b. 1902). Born in Boston and educated at Harvard University (1922–6) and the Royal College of Music, London (1927–8), Woodworth joined the staff of the music department at Harvard (1925) and became a professor in 1928. He was conductor of the Radcliffe Choral Society (1925) and the Harvard Glee Club (1934), was organist and choirmaster of the Harvard University Chapel (1940), toured Europe with the Harvard Glee Club (1956), and in the 1940s and 1950s conducted the Harvard Glee Club with the Boston Symphony Orchestra in concerts. With the Harvard Glee Club he recorded for Victor, on 78s, Mendelssohn's *Jagdlied* and Piston's *Carnival Song* (also with the Boston Symphony Brass Ensemble), and with the Harvard Glee Club and Radcliffe Choral Society for Technichord Byrd's *Justorum animae, Non vos relinquam orphanos* and *Sacerdotes Domini*; later on LP with the two choirs Thompson's *Alleluia* and *Mass of the Holy Spirit*, and a collection of sacred polyphonic music (for Cambridge), and with the Massed Choruses two LP discs of choral music recorded at the First International University Choral Festival (for RCA).

Wöss, Kurt (b. 1914). Born in Linz, Wöss studied at the Vienna Academy of Music, and first conducted at the age of 22. He has been permanent conductor of the Vienna Tonkünstler Orchestra (1949–51), chief conductor of the NHK Symphony Orchestra in Japan (1951–4), conductor of the Victorian Symphony Orchestra in Melbourne, Australia (1956–60), musical director of the Linz Opera (since 1961) and chief conductor of the Linz Bruckner Orchestra (since 1966). In addition, he has been a guest conductor with orchestras and in opera houses in Europe, Japan and North and South America, has led the Vienna Symphony Orchestra on a tour of Czechoslovakia, the Salzburg Mozarteum Orchestra to the USSR, and the Linz Bruckner Orchestra to Poland, FR Germany and Italy. He has written a study on the performance of Bruckner's symphonies, and has received the highest Austrian award made to artists.

Between 1948 and 1951, Wöss conducted the so-called Austrian Symphony Orchestra in a series of 28 LP records for Remington, New York. Included were Mozart's Symphony No. 41 and Sinfonia Concertante K. 297b, Beethoven's Symphonies Nos 6 and 7 and Piano Concerto No. 5 (with Karrer), Schubert's Symphonies Nos 4, 6 and 9, Brahms' Symphony No. 4, the Dvořák Cello Concerto (with Cassado), the Grieg Piano Concerto and Rachmaninov's Piano Concerto No. 2 (with Karrer), *Don Juan*, *Finlandia*, and Tchaikovsky's Symphony No. 5, Violin Concerto (with Auclair), *1812* overture and the *Romeo and Juliet* fantasy-overture. He also recorded Rachmaninov's Piano Concerto No. 2 (with Kreutzer for CBS-Japan), and several discs of popular orchestral pieces (with the Bamberg Symphony Orchestra for Teldec).

Wührer, Friedrich (b. 1900). The pianist Wührer was born in Vienna and educated at the University and Academy of Music there, and became professor for piano at the Academy (1922–32), at the Hochschule für Musik at Mannheim (1934–6 and 1953–5), director of music at Kiel (1936–9), again at the Vienna Academy (1939–45), at the Mozarteum, Salzburg (1948–51), and at the Hochschule für Musik at Munich (from 1955). He made many distinguished recordings as a pianist for Vox, including the complete Schubert sonatas; Marble Arch issued an LP in 1965 on which he conducted a chamber orchestra in Bach's Suite No. 2, Telemann's *Suite in G* and Vivaldi's Concerto Op. 3 No. 8.

Wulstan, David (b. 1937). Born in Birmingham and educated at Magdalen College, Oxford, Wulstan has been on the staff of the BBC, and has published anthologies of carols and English church music, a study of Gibbons' verse anthems and articles in musical journals. He is conductor of the Clerkes of Oxenford, whom he has conducted in recordings of the music of Tallis and John Sheppard (for EMI), and a disc of carols.

Wunderlich, Heinz (b. 1919). Born in Leipzig, Wunderlich studied the organ and composition at the Church Music Institute there, and was church music director of the Moritz Church at Leipzig (1943–58), where he also taught the organ and harpsichord. He then became director of music at the St Jacobi Church in Hamburg (1958) and professor of organ at the Hochschule für Musik there. He has performed in Germany and abroad as an organist, and has made records as such. Conducting the St Jacobi Choir and the Hamburg Chamber Orchestra he recorded Bach's Cantatas Nos 100 and 175 (for Johannes Stauda Verlag, released in the United States by Vanguard).

Wuorinén, Charles (b. 1938). Born in New York, Wuorinén studied at Columbia University, and has taught at Columbia and Princeton Universities, the New England Conservatory, the University of Iowa, the Manhattan School of Music and the University of South Florida. He has also worked as an accompanist and as a recording engineer, and has sung as a countertenor. As a composer, he received, at the age of 16, the New York Philharmonic Young Composers' Award, and later the Lili Boulanger Memorial Award (1960); among his numerous other awards is the Pulitzer Prize for Music for his electronic work *Time's Encomium* in 1970. Of his own music he has recorded, as conductor, his *Chamber Concerto for Flute and Ten Players* (with Sollberger and the Group for Contemporary Music, for Composers Recordings), *Ringing Changes* (with the New Jersey Percussion Ensemble for Nonesuch), and *Chamber Concerto for Cello and Ten Players* (with the Group for Contemporary Music, for Nonesuch), and as a pianist, his Piano Concerto (with James Dixon and the Royal Philharmonic Orchestra, for Composers Recordings). He also recorded, as conductor, Diamond's *Nonet*, and Varèse's *Déserts* (with the Group for Contemporary Music for Composers Recordings) and two works by Pleskow (with a chamber ensemble for Composers Recordings).

Wyttenbach, Jürg (b. 1935). Born in Berne, Wyttenbach studied at the Berne Conservatory, at the Paris Conservatoire (1955–7), and at the Nierdersächsiche Hochschule für Musik with Engel (1958–9). He has been a teacher at the Biel Academy of Music (from 1959) and at the Berne Conservatory (since 1962), has received awards as a pianist and as a composer, including the Béla Bartók Competition prize at Indiana University (1958), and at a competition for young composers at Stuttgart (1959). For CT (Switzerland) he conducted his own *Divisions for Piano and Solo Strings* (with Brun and an ensemble).

Y

Yamada, Kôsçak (1886–1965). Born in Tokyo, Yamada studied at the Imperial Academy of Music, and with Wolf in Berlin (1909–12). He returned to Japan and founded and conducted the Tokyo Philharmonic Orchestra, with which he performed Western music. He composed symphonic, choral, instrumental and vocal pieces, and recorded, on pre-electric 78s, Beethoven's Symphony No. 5 (with the New Symphony Orchestra for Columbia-Japan), and in 1962 Mahler's *Lieder eines fahrenden Gesellen* and three songs from *Des Knaben Wunderhorn* (with Nayakama and the Tokyo Symphony Orchestra for Toshiba).

Yeltsin, Sergei (1897–1968). Born in St Petersburg, where he studied at the Conservatory, Yeltsin was concertmaster at the Leningrad Kirov Theatre (1918–28), became a conductor there (1928), then artistic manager and principal conductor (1953–6 and 1960–61). He also taught conducting at the Leningrad Conservatory and received the title National Artist of Russia (1944). His repertoire as an opera conductor included Mozart, Rossini and Verdi as well as Russian composers; for Melodiya he accompanied aria recitals with the Kirov orchestra.

Yurlov, Alexander (1927–73). Yurlov studied at the Moscow Conservatory and was a pupil of Sveshnikov, and in 1958 succeeded Lebedev as musical director of the USSR Russian Chorus. The Chorus was originally formed in 1919, and under Yurlov revived the choral music of Russian composers before Glinka, notably at the Festival of Old Music at Bydgoszcz in Poland, and in performances in West Berlin. The Chorus's recordings under Yurlov (for Melodiya) included music of the 17th- and 18th-century Russian composers Diletzky, Krestyanin, Kalashnikov, Berezowsky, Bortniansky and Vedel, choral music of Taneyev and Khrennikov, and Shostakovich's *The Song of the Forests* (the latter also with the USSR Boys' Chorus and the Moscow Philharmonic Orchestra).

Z

Zaliouk, Yuval (b. 1939). Born in Haifa, Zaliouk studied at the Academy of Music there, graduated in law at the Hebrew University in Jerusalem, and at the same time attended the Jerusalem Academy of Music. He then studied conducting at the Guildhall School of Music and Drama in London (1965), won first prize at the International Competition for Young Conductors at Besançon, France (1966), was a conductor with the Royal Ballet, Covent Garden (1966–70) and was one of the winners at the Dmitri Mitropoulos International Conductors' Competition in New York (1970). He worked with Klemperer, conducted orchestras in Europe, the United States and Australia, and was appointed musical adviser of the Haifa Symphony Orchestra (1975). He has recorded Ravel's *Le Tombeau de Couperin* and Stravinsky's *Pulcinella* (with the London Mozart Players for Unicorn), and Williamson's *Epitaphs for Edith Sitwell*, Concerto for Piano and Strings No. 2, and Concerto for Two Pianos and Strings (with Pryor and Williamson, and the English Chamber Orchestra for EMI).

Zallinger, Meinhard von (b. 1897). Born in Vienna, Zallinger studied at Innsbruck and at the Salzburg Mozarteum. He was conductor of the Mozarteum Opera (1920–22), at Munich (1926), Cologne (1929–35), with Krauss at the Munich Opera (1935–44), director of the Landestheater and conductor of the Mozarteum Orchestra at Salzburg (1947), general music director at Graz (1949), conductor at Vienna (1950), general music director at the Berlin Komische Oper (1953) and conductor at the Bavarian State Opera at Munich (1956). He has composed vocal and choral music, and edited a revision of *Die Zauberflöte*. Recordings in which he was the conductor were issued in the first years of LP, and included Haydn's opera *Philemon und Baucis* (with the Vienna Symphony Orchestra *et al.* for Vox), a recital of Haydn's music for soprano and orchestra (with Hopf and the Vienna Symphony Orchestra for Haydn Society and Nixa), Mozart's Mass K. 427, a complete *Idomeneo* and *Les petits riens* (with the Vienna Symphony Orchestra *et al.* issued by Nixa) and Divertimenti K. 187 and K. 188 (with the Salzburg Brass Ensemble, issued by Nixa), highlights from *Eugene Onegin* and *The Queen of Spades* (with the Bavarian State Opera Orchestra *et al.* for EMI) and Carpenter's ballet *Skyscrapers* (with the ARS Symphony Orchestra for ARS).

Zani, Giacomo (b. 1934). Born at Casalmaggiore, Italy, Zani studied at the Milan Conservatory and under Barzin, Blot and Fourestier at the Paris Conservatoire, and first conducted in Milan in 1964. Later he made his operatic debut in Milan in 1967, was general director of the Teatro Massimo at Palermo (1971–3) and has since conducted opera and concerts in many European countries, also appearing at the Edinburgh Festival. For Supraphon he conducted a recording of *Il barbiere di Siviglia* (with the Prague Chamber Orchestra *et al.*).

Zanotelli, Hans (b. 1927). Born in Wuppertal, and largely self-taught apart from some short studies in Cologne, Zanotelli was first a choirmaster at Solingen (1945). He was then conductor at Wuppertal (1950), Düsseldorf (1951–4), Bonn (1954–5) and at the Hamburg State Opera (1955–7), was general music director at Darmstadt (1957–63) and Augsburg (1963–72) and chief conductor of the Stuttgart Philharmonic Orchestra (since 1971), and has been a guest conductor with the Dresden Staatskapelle (1964–7), the Bavarian State Opera (1968–71) and with the Württemberg State Opera. He has also toured in many European countries, led a performance of *Der Rosenkavalier* at Dresden for the State Opera's 300th anniversary and also of the Verdi *Requiem* at Dresden on the anniversary of the destruction of the city in World War II. His operatic and concert repertoire is vast, and includes 125 operas. At Augsburg he became known for his Mozart and Wagner cycles, and for his performances of Gluck, Mahler, Bruckner and Pfitzner; of the latter's *Palestrina* he published a shortened orchestral version. His recordings include Schumann's Symphony No. 3 and some overtures (with the North German Philharmonic Orchestra for Intercord-Ton), *Don Juan* and *Till Eulenspiegel* (with the South German Philharmonic Orchestra for Sonopresse), Tchaikovsky's Piano Concerto No. 1 (with Lang and the North German Philharmonic Orchestra for Sonopresse) and discs of excerpts from *Don Giovanni* and *Il trovatore* (with the Berlin Symphony Orchestra *et al.* for EMI) and

Tiefland (with the Berlin Symphony Orchestra *et al.* for Ariola).

Zaun, Fritz (1893–1966). Born in Cologne, Zaun was conductor in Zürich (1927), general music director at Cologne (1929), chief conductor of the Berlin Staatskapelle, was active in Zagreb, was chief conductor at the Cologne Opera (1951) and conductor at Düsseldorf. His recordings, mostly 78 r.p.m. discs made before World War II, included Mozart's Piano Concerto K. 537 (with Backhaus and the Berlin Staatskapelle for HMV), Beethoven's Piano Concerto No. 2 (with Ney and the Landesorchester for HMV) Schubert's Symphony No. 5 (with the Berlin Municipal Orchestra for Columbia), the Schumann Cello Concerto (with Hoelscher and the Berlin Staatskapelle for HMV), Liszt's *Tasso* (with the Berlin Philharmonic Orchestra for Urania), Bruch's Violin Concerto No. 1 (with Borries and the Prussian State Orchestra for HMV), excerpts from Reger's *Ballet Suite* (with the Reichs Symphony Orchestra for Polydor), Bruckner's Symphony No. 2 and the Scherzos from the Symphonies Nos 0 and 1 (with the Berlin Staatskapelle for HMV), Paganini's Violin Concerto No. 1 and the Sibelius Violin Concerto (with Bustabo and the Berlin Municipal Orchestra for HMV), some orchestral excerpts from Strauss's *Arabella* (with the Berlin Staatskapelle *et al.* for HMV) and excerpts from *Don Giovanni* (with the German Opera on the Rhine Orchestra *et al.* for Ariola).

Zdravković, Živojin (b. 1914). Born in Belgrade, Zdravković studied at the Belgrade and Prague Music Academies, and was a conducting pupil of Talich at Prague. He first conducted with the Belgrade Chamber Orchestra (1948), has been conductor of the Belgrade Radio Symphony Orchestra (1948–51), resident conductor of the Belgrade Philharmonic Orchestra (1951) and then artistic director of the orchestra (since 1960). He is also professor of conducting at the Belgrade Academy, conductor of the Cairo Opera, has written many articles and essays on musical subjects, has toured widely with the Belgrade Philharmonic Orchestra, and has been a guest conductor in Eastern and Western Europe, the USSR and in North and South America.

Zdravković has made a number of significant gramophone records which show his sensibility and vitality as an enterpreter, but few of these have been released in the West. Included are *Le Sacre du printemps* and Bruči's *Sinfonia lesta* (with the Belgrade Philharmonic for Philips), Slavenski's *Sinfonia orienta* (with the Belgrade Philharmonic *et al.* for Decca), *Moldau*, Kodály's *Psalmus Hungaricus* and Tchaikovsky's Piano Concerto No.1 (with Karolyi, and with the Bavarian Radio Symphony Orchestra for EMI), *Scheherazade* and *La Valse* (with the North German Radio Orchestra for EMI), the nine Beethoven and four Brahms symphonies, Schubert's Symphonies Nos 3, 5 and 9, Schumann's Symphony No. 4, Dvořák's Symphonies Nos 8 and 9, *Don Juan* and *Till Eulenspiegel*, the Franck symphony, Tchaikovsky's Symphonies Nos 4, 5 and 6, the *Romeo and Juliet* fantasy-overture, *Francesca da Rimini* and *Capriccio italien* and Messiaen's *Turangalîla Symphony* (with the Belgrade Philharmonic for Radio-Television Belgrade), works by Stevan, Petar and Abou-Bakr, including the latter's Symphonies Nos 2 and 3 and Piano Concerto (with the Belgrade Philharmonic *et al.* for Jugoton), Dvořák's three *Slavonic Rhapsodies*, and the *Slavonic Dances* Opp. 46 and 72, Enesco's *Romanian Rhapsody* No. 1, *In the Steppes of Central Asia*, *A Night on the Bare Mountain*, the *Gayane* ballet suite and Gotovac's *Sinfonischer Kolo* (with the Belgrade Philharmonic for EMI), and Hristić's *Ohridska Legenda* (with the Belgrade Opera Orchestra *et al.* for Jugoton).

Zecchi, Carlo (b. 1903). Born in Rome, Zecchi studied the piano with Bajardi and composition with Refice and Bustin at the Accademia di Santa Cecilia in Rome, and then with Busoni and Schnabel in Berlin. He first appeared as a concert pianist in 1920, toured the United States in 1921, and gave concerts throughout Europe, North and South America. He was also celebrated as a chamber music player, particularly in association with the cellist Mainardi. He studied conducting under Guarnieri and Hans Münch, and first conducted at Basel in 1941, later touring in many countries as a conductor. He has taught the piano at the Accademia di Santa Cecilia and conducting at Salzburg and Hilversum (1973); his advice to pupils is: 'Conduct any way you like; it's the sound that counts.' His special interest as a piano teacher were the Bach and Mozart keyboard works.

Zecchi has recorded, *inter alia*, Schumann's *Kinderszenen* (for Cetra) as a pianist; as a conductor his recordings include Corelli's Concerto Grosso Op. 6 No. 1, Geminiani's Concerto Grosso Op. 3 No. 2, Mozart's *Serenata notturna*, an arrangement by Lauterbach of Boccherini's *Quintet in C major*, and three movements from Brahms' Serenade No. 2 (with the EIAR Symphony Orchestra for Cetra, and issued in Britain by Parlophone on

78s); the Beethoven Piano Concerto No. 4 (with Haskil), Pizzetti's *La Pisanella* and Rossini's overture *La scala di seta* (with the London Philharmonic Orchestra for Decca on 78s); Schumann's Symphony No. 3 and Brahms' Serenade No. 2 (with the Amsterdam Concertgebouw Orchestra for Philips); *Symphonie fantastique* (with the Czech Philharmonic Orchestra for Supraphon); Mozart's Piano Concertos K. 453 and K. 488 (with Zadra and the Romanian Radio Orchestra for Electrecord); Haydn's *Piano Concerto in F* (with Mayerhofer-Langer), *Violin Concerto in A* (with Hitzker) and overture *L'infedeltà delusa*, Michael Haydn's *Symphony in D major*, Dittersdorf's *Oboe Concerto in G major* (with Kautzky), and Mozart's Symphonies K. 16, K. 17 and No. 27 (with the Vienna Chamber Orchestra, issued in the United States by Musical Heritage Society); and Haydn's Symphonies Nos 44 and 49 (with the Slovak Philharmonic Orchestra for Supraphon). Of these recordings, the *La scala di seta* overture was one of Decca's first spectacular ffrr discs, and the two Haydn symphonies, released in 1972, were remarkable for the grave beauty of the slow movements.

Zedda, Alberto (b. 1928). Born in Milan, Zedda studied at the university and conservatory there, and at the University of Parma. He won the 'Primavera' Italian Radio and Television competition for young conductors (1957), was conductor at the Cincinnati University Conservatory (1957–59), appeared in opera houses and with orchestras in Italy and abroad, and was permanent conductor of the New York City Opera (1967–8). A scholar as well as a conductor, he has been co-editor of the Rossini edition for Ricordi, and has edited works of Monteverdi and Vivaldi; in 1976 his revision of *Otello* was staged at La Scala, Milan.

Zedda has made a number of recordings of less familiar music, many of which have been released on various labels in Britain and the United States. Included are Bach's *Four-Harpsichord Concerto in A major* (with Tagliavini, Canino, Ballista and Abbado), Vivaldi's oratorio *Juditha triumphans*, motet *Super flumina Babylonis*, Violin Concertos Op. 3 Nos 3 and 8 (with Salvi) and No. 10 (with Salvi, Stefanato and Ferraresi), Op. 7 No. 11 (with Salvi) and *Two-Violin Concerto in A minor* (with Ferraresi and Stefanato), Carissimi's *Missa a cinque et a novem*, Clementi's *Symphonies in B flat* and *D major*, and *Piano Concerto in C major* (with Gorini), Handel's *Trumpet Suite in D major*, Purcell's *Trumpet Sonata in D major*, Rosier's *Sonata in C major*, Porino's *Concertino* and Lortzing's *Theme and Variations* (with Hunger, and the Angelicum Orchestra and Chorus *et al.*, Milan, for Angelicum, some of which were issued in the United States by Musical Heritage Society); Albéniz's Piano Concerto No. 1, Paisiello's *Piano Concerto in F major* and Viotti's *Piano Concerto in G major* (with Blumental and the Turin Symphony Orchestra for Turnabout); Clementi's *Piano Concerto in C major* and Koželuh's *Piano Concerto in D major* (with Blumental and the New Prague Chamber Orchestra for Turnabout); Hoffmeister's *Piano Concerto in D major* and Vogler's *Variations on 'Marlborough'* (with Blumental and the Prague Chamber Orchestra for Turnabout); the Beethoven *Romance in E* (with Blumental and the Prague Chamber Orchestra for Orion); Leoncavallo's *La Bohème* (with the San Remo Philharmonic Orchestra *et al.* for Cetra); and Verdi's *Otello* (with the Turin Symphony Orchestra *et al.* for Fonit).

Zemlinsky, Alexander von (1871–1942). Born in Vienna of Polish parents, Zemlinsky studied at the Vienna Conservatory and first conducted at various theatres and opera houses in Vienna (1900–1908). He was then conductor at the Mannheim Opera (1909–11), at the German Opera, Prague (1911–27) and director of the German Music Academy in Prague (from 1920), conductor at the Berlin Staatsoper and of the Philharmonic Choir (1927–32), was active in Vienna (1933–8) and then migrated to the United States (1938). He was the teacher of Schoenberg, Bodanzky and Korngold, and married Schoenberg's sister. He wrote six operas which were successfully produced in Germany and Austria. His only records appear to have been the overture to *Die Entführung aus dem Serail* (with the Charlottenburg Opera Orchestra for Polydor) and the *Moldau* (with the Berlin Philharmonic Orchestra for Telefunken).

Zender, Hans (b. 1936). Born in Wiesbaden, Zender studied at the Hochschule für Musik at Frankfurt and at Freiburg, and at the German Academy at Villa Massimo, Rome (1963 and 1968). He has been conductor at Freiburg (1959–63), principal conductor at Bonn (1964–6) and at Düsseldorf (1967–8), general music director at Kiel (1969–72), conductor at the International Youth Festival, Bayreuth (1971), and principal conductor of the Radio Symphony and Chamber Orchestras at Saarbrücken (since 1972). He has also been a guest conductor in opera houses and with orchestras in Germany and abroad, including the Hamburg and Bavarian State Operas, toured Japan and Australia, conducted *Parsifal* at Bayreuth (1975) and the première of Zimmermann's *Die Soldaten* at Hamburg (1977). His compositions include vocal music, works for various instrumental groups and an electronic piece; one of these, *Canto III* (*Der Mann von La Mancha*) he recorded for DGG. His other recordings include Zimmermann's *Photoptosis* (with the Bavarian Radio Symphony Orchestra for Wergo), Stockhausen's *Trans* (with the Saarbrücken Radio Orchestra, also with the South-West German Radio Orchestra under Bour, for DGG), Yun's *Loyang* (with the West German Radio Orchestra for Wergo), and Holliger's *Der magische Tanzer* (with the Basel Symphony Orchestra *et al.* for DGG).

Zhuraytis, Algis (b. 1928). Born in Kaunas in Lithuania, Zhuraytis graduated from the Vilnius Conservatory, and became a repetiteur then a conductor at the Lithuanian State Theatre (1952–4). He studied conducting with Anosov and Gauk at the Moscow Conservatory (1954–8), was conductor with the Moscow Radio Symphony Orchestra (1958–61) and at the Bolshoi Theatre, Moscow (since 1961), won second prize at the conductors' competition at the Accademia di Santa Cecilia in Rome in 1968, has toured in East and West Europe, the USA and South America, and has conducted ballet and opera in Paris. His recordings, for Melodiya, include the ballets *Giselle*, *Chopiniana* (Chopin, arranged by Glazunov), Glière's *The Bronze Knight* Suites Nos 1 and 2, Khachaturian's *Spartacus*, and trumpet concertos by Kryukov and Vainberg (with Dokshizer and the Bolshoi Theatre Orchestra), Glazunov's Piano Concerto No. 1 (with Nassedkin), Shchedrin's *The Humpback Horse* Suite No. 2, and Ovchinnikov's Suites Nos 1, 2 and 3 (with the Moscow Radio Symphony Orchestra).

Ziegler, Klaus Martin (b. 1929). Born in Freiburg, Ziegler studied at the Hochschule für Musik at Karlsruhe (1948–50) and at the Evangelical Church Music Institute in Heidelberg (1950–52). He was cantor at Karlsruhe (1952–60), director of the church music section at the Hochschule für Musik there (1957–60), and director of the Church Music School at Schlüchtern (1968–70), as well as being cantor at St Martin's Church in Kassel. Since 1970 he has been choral director of the Church Music School in Herford and conductor of the Kassel Vocal Ensemble and of the Westphalian Kantorei, introduced the 'international Weeks of Spiritual Music', and has contributed many articles on church music. With the German Bach Soloists and the Kassel Vocal Ensemble *et al.* he recorded Bach's Cantatas Nos 68 and 172 (for Johannes Stauda Verlag, and issued in the United States by Nonesuch), Kelterborn's *Tres cantiones sacrae* (with the Kassel State Theatre Orchestra *et al.* for Cantate), Barbe's *Canticum Simeonis* and Zimmermann's *Psalm Concerto* (with the South-West German Chamber Orchestra *et al.* for Johannes Stauda Verlag), Buxtehude's *Laudate Dominum* and other pieces by Kelterborn, Klebe and Penderecki (with an ensemble for Johannes Stauda Verlag).

Ziino, Ottavio (b. 1902). Born in Palermo, Sicily, Ziino studied there and under Molinari and Pizzetti at the Accademia di Santa Cecilia at Rome. He made his debut as a conductor at Palermo, conducted in Italy and abroad, was conductor at the Spoleto Experimental Theatre (1947) and with the Sicilian Symphony Orchestra (1959); he was appointed director of the Palermo Conservatory (1969) and musical director of the Sicilian Symphony Orchestra (1973). For Supraphon he recorded in recent years *Lucia di Lammermoor* (with the Prague Chamber Orchestra *et al.*).

Zilch, Josef (b. 1928). After studying with Eichhorn and Rieger at the Hochschule für Musik at Munich, Zilch first conducted at Bayreuth (1955), was appointed a professor in 1962, the youngest in Bavaria, and appeared as a guest conductor with many orchestras. He conducted concerts at Aschaffenburg and was awarded the Culture Prize by the Bavarian government (1970). For Colosseum he recorded Haydn's Symphony No. 73 and his own *Hubertus Mass* (with the Nuremberg Symphony Orchestra *et al.*).

Zilcher, Heinz. Zilcher was presumably a relative of the German pianist and composer Hermann Zilcher (1881–1948), who toured as a pianist in Europe and the United States, and taught at Frankfurt am Main, Munich and Würzburg, where he also conducted concerts. Heinz Zilcher conducted the Prussian State Orchestra in Mozart's Piano Concerto K. 595, on 78 r.p.m. discs for HMV, with Hermann Zilcher as soloist.

Zillig, Winfried (1901–63). Born at Würzburg, Zillig studied law, then music at the Würzburg Conservatory, and completed his studies with Schoenberg in Vienna and Berlin (1926–8) and at the Prussian Academy of Art. He was

Kleiber's assistant at the Berlin Staatsoper (1927–8), then was conductor at Oldenburg (1928–32), Essen (1946–7), and musical director of Frankfurt Radio (1947–51) and of Hamburg Radio (1959). His compositions included lieder, which have been recorded by Prey *inter alios*, and music for films. He recorded, on LP, Mahler's *Lieder eines fahrenden Gesellen* and three songs of Strauss (with Schlusnus, the Frankfurt Radio Orchestra and the Berlin Staatskapelle for DGG), Schoenberg's *Pelleas und Melisande* (with the Frankfurt Radio Orchestra for Capitol) and Phillips' *Konzertstück* for Flute and Orchestra (with Jury and the Frankfurt Radio Orchestra for DGG).

Zinman, David (b. 1936). Born in New York, Zinman is a graduate of Oberlin Conservatory and the University of Minnesota. He studied conducting at the Berkshire Music Center and later with Monteux, who took him to Europe in 1961 as his assistant with the London Symphony Orchestra. In 1963 he appeared with the Netherlands Chamber Orchestra at the Holland Festival, substituting for Paul Sacher, and his reception was such that he was at once appointed music director of the orchestra. With them he has appeared at many European festivals; he toured Australia and the Far East in 1974. His debut in the United States occurred in 1967 with the Philadelphia Orchestra, and after conducting many other major orchestras there he was appointed music director of the Rochester Philharmonic Orchestra in 1974. He now divides his time between Rochester and Amsterdam. He has recorded Bach's *Harpsichord Concerto in D minor* and Chopin's Piano Concerto No. 2 (with Ashkenazy and the London Symphony Orchestra for Decca), Schumann's Piano Concerto and Ravel's *Piano Concerto in G major* (with Dechenne and the Hague Philharmonic Orchestra for Musical Heritage Society), Mozart's Symphony No. 29 and Sinfonia Concertante K. 364 (with the Netherlands Chamber Orchestra *et al.* for Iramac), the ballet music from *Idomeneo*, *Les petits riens* and Violin Concertos K. 211 and K. 218 (with Krebbers), J. C. Bach's Symphonies Op. 18, Grieg's *Holberg Suite* and Tchaikovsky's *Serenade in C major* (with the Netherlands Chamber Orchestra for Philips), Badings' Symphony No. 9 and Hellendaal's Concerto Grosso Op. 3 No. 2 (with the Netherlands Chamber Orchestra for Donemus). Many of these discs have been warmly acclaimed; EMI issued in Britain the coupling of Mozart's Symphony No. 29 and the Sinfonia Concertante.

Zipper, Herbert (b. 1904). Born in Vienna where he studied at the Academy of Music, Zipper was assistant conductor at the Burgtheater, Vienna (1923–5), conductor of the Vienna Madrigal Association (1927–9), conductor at Ingolstadt, Bavaria (1929–30), professor at the Düsseldorf Conservatory (1931–3), a guest conductor in Europe (1933–7), and founded the Vienna Concert Orchestra, whose membership consisted of émigré musicians from Germany (1934). He was musical director of the Manila Symphony Orchestra, and director of the Academy of Music at Manila (1939–42); after imprisonment by the Japanese he re-formed the orchestra in 1945 and gave numerous concerts. He went to the United States in 1946 where he conducted in Brooklyn and Chicago, taught at the New School for Social Research (since 1948), has been executive director of the National Guild Community Music Schools (since 1967) and projects director for the University of Southern California School of Performing Arts. Saga (in Britain) issued a Concert-Disc recording in which he led an instrumental ensemble in Schoenberg's *Pierrot Lunaire* (with soprano Howland).

Zlatić, Slavko (b. 1910). Born in Sovinjak in Istra, today in Yugoslavia, Zlatić studied at the Tartini Conservatory in Trieste, became professor of conducting at the Zagreb Academy of Music, director of the music school at Pula, and president of the executive committee of the Yugoslav Composers' Organisation. For Jugoton he recorded Brkanović's *Triptihon* (with the Zagreb Radio Orchestra *et al.*) and choral pieces by Matetić-Ronjgov (with the Zagreb Radio Chorus).

Zukerman, Pinchas (b. 1948). Born in Israel, Zukerman first studied the violin with his father and then with Feher at the Tel-Aviv Academy of Music. Because of his extraordinary talent, he won a number of scholarships from the Sharett Fund for Young Artists, entered the Juilliard School in New York on Isaac Stern's recommendation, won the Leventritt Award in 1967, and made his New York debut with the New York Philharmonic Orchestra in 1969. He is acclaimed as one of the finest violinists of his generation; he is also a distinguished violist and chamber player, and has made numerous recordings as a violinist. He has also conducted the Los Angeles Chamber Orchestra, the English Chamber Orchestra and the Israel Chamber Orchestra; writing of his direction of the six *Brandenburg Concertos* with the English Chamber Orchestra in London in

May 1976, Thomas Walker (of *The Times*) found the performances 'well turned and energetic'. He has recorded, as both conductor and violinist, Vivaldi's Concerti Op. 8, Mozart's Serenades K. 203 and K. 204 and Marches K. 215 and K. 237 (with the English Chamber Orchestra for CBS), the Serenade K. 250 (with the same orchestra for EMI) and the two Flute Concertos (with Eugénie Zukerman and the same orchestra for CBS); as conductor and violist, *Harold in Italy* (with L'Orchestre de Paris for CBS), and as a violinist and conductor Bach's *Brandenburg Concertos*, and the Haydn *Violin Concerto in C major* and Sinfonia Concertante Op. 84 (with the Los Angeles Philharmonic Orchestra for DGG).

Zweig, Fritz (1893–?). Born in Olomouc, formerly Habsburg Empire, now Czechoslovakia, Zweig studied with Schoenberg in Vienna, was conductor at Mannheim (1913–14 and 1919–21), Barmen-Elberfeld (1921–3), the Berlin Grosse Volksoper (1923–5), the Berlin Municipal Opera and Berlin Staatsoper (1927–33), and at the Prague German Opera (1934–38). He was also a guest conductor in Moscow, Leningrad, Paris and New York (1940), and was noted especially for his performances of Mozart and Janáček. From 1947 he taught music privately in Hollywood. For EMI he accompanied the soprano Rethberg with the Berlin Staatsoper Orchestra in extracts from *Lohengrin* and *Tannhäuser*.

SELECT BIBLIOGRAPHY

Carl Bamberger (ed.), *The Conductor's Art*, New York, 1965

Eric Blom (ed.), *Grove's Dictionary of Music and Musicians*, London, 5th edn, 1954

Donald Brook, *Conductors' Gallery*, London, 1945

Robert Chesterman (ed.), *Conversations with Conductors*, London, 1976

David Ewen, *The Man with the Baton*, New York, 1936

——, Dictators of the Baton, New York, 1943

Edward Greenfield, Robert Layton and Ivan March, *Penguin Stereo Record Guide*, London, 2nd edn, 1977

David Hall, *The Record Guide*, New York, 1940 and 1948

——, *Records: 1950 Edition*, New York, 1950

Ernest Kay (ed.), *International Who's Who in Music*, Cambridge, 1975

Irving Kolodin, *A Guide to Recorded Music*, New York, 1941

Hugo Riemann, *Musik Lexikon*, Mainz, 1959–67

Harold Rosenthal and John Warrack, *Concise Oxford Dictionary of Opera*, London, 1964

Edward Sackville-West and Desmond Shawe-Taylor, *The Record Guide*, London, 1951, rev. edn 1955

Harold C. Schonberg, *The Great Conductors*, New York, 1967

Willi Schuh, Hans Ehinger, Pierre Meylan and Hans Peter Schanzlin, *Schweizer Musiker-Lexicon*, Zürich, 1964

Horst Seeger, *Musik Lexikon*, Leipzig, 1966

Bernard Shore, *The Orchestra Speaks*, London, 1938

Nicolas Slonimsky (ed.), *Baker's Biographical Dictionary of Musicians*, New York, 5th edn 1958, supp. 1971, 6th edn 1978

Virgil Thomson, *Music Reviewed, 1940–1954*, New York, 1966

David Woodridge, *Conductor's World*, London, 1970

John Holmes was born in Sydney in 1925; after serving in the Royal Australian Air Force in World War II, he graduated in Economics at the University of Sydney, joined the Australian Public Service and in 1961 went abroad in the Australian Trade Commissioner Service. He has lived in London, Los Angeles, Tel-Aviv and Berlin, as well as in countries in South-East Asia and Africa. He experienced the great development in musical life in Sydney after the war, influenced by Goossens, Cardus, and others, and has been interested in music and in records all his adult life, from the time of 78 r.p.m. discs. His life overseas has brought him into contact with many musicians, orchestras and opera houses; in the Far East he was a newspaper critic, and arranged concerts for visiting artists. He is married, with two children; his Belgian-born wife, Elise, he first met at a performance of *Siegfried* at Covent Garden.